KU-350-285

The NKJV Greek English Interlinear New Testament

The NKJV
Greek-English
Interlinear
New Testament

Features Word Studies & New King James Parallel Text

Translators:
Arthur L. Farstad
Zane C. Hodges
C. Michael Moss
Robert E. Picirilli
Wilbur N. Pickering

THOMAS NELSON PUBLISHERS
NASHVILLE

ACKNOWLEDGEMENTS
The Greek New Testament According to the Majority Text
Editors: Zane C. Hodges, Arthur L. Farstad
Assistant Editor: William C. Dunkin
Consulting Editors: Jakob Van Bruggen, Alfred Martin, Wilbur N. Pickering, Harry A. Sturz

Printed in the United States of America
1 2 3 4 5 6 7 8 9 10 – 98 97 96 95 94

Contents

Abbreviations

cf.	compare	NU	the most prominent modern Critical Text of the Greek New Testament, published in the twenty-sixth edition of the Nestle-Aland Greek New Testament and in the fourth edition of the United Bible Societies' Greek New Testament (see Introduction, "The New Testament Text")
DSS	Dead Sea Scrolls		
etc.	and so forth		
f, ff	following verse, following verses		
i.e.	that is		
lit.	literally		
LXX	Septuagint—an ancient translation of the Old Testament into Greek	OT	Old Testament
M	Majority Text (see Introduction, "The New Testament Text")	TR	Textus Receptus or Received Text (see Introduction, "The New Testament Text")
ms., mss.	manuscript, manuscripts		
NT	New Testament	v., vv.	verse, verses

Bibliography

(A brief listing of sources for Greek study)

Lexicons:

Gingrich, F. Wilbur, and Danker, Frederick W. *A Greek-English Lexicon of the New Testament and Other Early Christian Literature*, 2nd edition. Chicago: University of Chicago Press, 1979.

(BGD) The first edition of 1957, edited by F. Wilbur Gingrich and William F. Arndt, was a translation and adaptation of the German work by Walter Bauer. It is the primary lexicon for students of the Greek New Testament.

Liddell, H. G., and Scott, R. *A Greek-English Lexicon.* 9th edition, edited by H. Stuart Jones and R. McKenzie. Oxford: the University Press, 1968.

This is the standard lexicon for students of Greek of the classical period.

Dictionaries:

Brown, Colin, gen. ed. *The New International Dictionary of New Testament Theology.* 3 vols. Grand Rapids: Zondervan Publishing House, 1975-1978.

(DNTT) A translation, with additions and revisions, of the German work edited by Lothar Coenen, Erich Beyreuther and Hans Bietenhard. The dictionary elucidates Greek vocabulary within a theological focus.

Kittel, Gerhard, and Friedrich, G. eds. *The Theological Dictionary of the New Testament.* 10 vols. Grand Rapids: Eerdmans, 1964-1977.

(TDNT) This dictionary treats theologically significant Greek terms and focuses on the theological usage of those terms.

Balz, Horst, and Schneider, Gerhard, eds. *Exegetical Dictionary of the New Testament.* 3 vols. Grand Rapids: Eerdmans, 1990-1993.

Grammars:

Blass, F., and DeBrunner, A. *A Greek Grammar of the New Testament and Other Early Christian Literature.* Translated and revised by Robert W. Funk. Chicago: University of Chicago Press, 1961.

Dana, H. E., and Mantey, Julius R. *A Manual Grammar of the Greek New Testament.* Toronto: The Macmillan Company, 1927.

Smyth, Herbert Weir. *Greek Grammar.* Revised by Gordon M. Messing. Cambridge: Harvard University Press, 1956.

Introduction
to Greek-English Interlinear Reading

Unfamiliar languages are learned by comparing them to familiar languages—comparing the unknown with the known. *The NKJV Greek-English Interlinear New Testament* offers tools that make comparing Greek with English easier:

Parallel Columns—Each page presents a column of the New King James Version side by side with a parallel column of the Greek New Testament according to the Majority Text. It is easy to compare NKJV English with Majority Text Greek.

Three Texts—The Greek column itself consists of three lines of interlinear texts: (1) Greek, (2) word-for-word English translation, and (3) idiomatic English translation.

Study Notes—Two sets of notes provide information on particular aspects of the Greek text. *Textual notes* indicate differences between the Majority Text, Textus Receptus, and the United Bible Societies/Nestle-Aland Greek texts. *Word studies* offer insights into the meanings of significant Greek words.

INTERLINEAR TRANSLATIONS

Learning an unknown language through a known one is not a modern process. In 1799 Napoleon's troops unearthed a black basalt slab near Rosetta in Lower (Northern) Egypt. It contained a decree from 196 B.C. inscribed in three scripts: hieroglyphic, demotic, Greek. Scholars were able to use the Hellenistic Greek script, which they knew, to decipher the other two scripts, which were of the ancient Egyptian language. Unlike the Rosetta Stone, which simply placed the Egyptian and Greek scripts one after another, an *interlinear* inserts the English translations *between the lines* of Greek, making comparison of Greek to English easier.

Word-For-Word English Translation

The word-for-word interlinear English is the first translation of the Majority Text. However, an interlinear translation is not a final translation. Rather, it presents a literal English equivalent for each Greek word. Because there are many differences of syntax, grammar, and idiomatic expression between Greek and English, an interlinear translation can be confusing to follow. To make the English translation understandable *The NKJV Greek-English Interlinear New Testament* expands the format of previous interlinears.

When the difference between Greek and English word order is simply transposition, the tilde (˜) indicates that two consecutive words of the English are to be transposed (Mark 1:6):

ζώνην δερματίνην
a belt ˜ leather

In more complicated Greek-English differences, word order numbers indicate the correct arrangement of the English line (Mark 1:31):

καὶ ἀφῆκεν αὐτὴν ὁ πυρετὸς εὐθέως,
and [4]left [5]her [2]the [3]fever [1]immediately,

The numbering system is more detailed than that of previous interlinears which numbered only Greek groupings. Here each individual word is numbered, allowing the exact order of the English to be indicated (Mark 8:4):

τούτους	δυνήσεταί	τις	ὧδε	χορτάσαι	ἄρτων
[7]these [8]*people*	[1]will [3]be [4]able	[2]anyone	[11]here	[5]to [6]satisfy	[9]of [10]bread
					with

Word order numbers have been omitted in long phrases for which an idiomatic English equivalent has been provided (Matt. 1:18):

Μνηστευθείσης	γὰρ	τῆς	μητρὸς	αὐτοῦ	Μαρίας
being betrothed	For	-	mother ˜	His	Mary
For after His	mother	Mary	had	been	betrothed

Idiomatic English Translation

Extensive use of a third line of idiomatic English represents a new step for interlinears. When the word-for-word English does not read smoothly, the difficult portion is underlined and accompanied by an idiomatic English translation for easier reading (1 Thess. 2:6):

δυνάμενοι	ἐν	βάρει	εἶναι
being able	in	weight	to be
even though we	were able	to carry	weight

In the course of reading the English translation, the reader will be able to substitute the idiomatic English for the underlined portions of word-for-word English. The following would read idiomatically, "And when Jesus came into the house . . ." (Matt. 8:14):

Καὶ	ἐλθὼν	ὁ	Ἰησοῦς	εἰς	τὴν	οἰκίαν
And	coming	-	Jesus	into	the	house
	when	Jesus	came			

The limitations of typesetting did not always allow for the idiomatic English to be placed *directly* below the corresponding word-for-word English. However, continuous reading of the two translations is still possible, as in Matt. 4:16, "And to those who sat in the land . . ." (Matt. 4:16):

Καὶ	τοῖς	καθημένοις	ἐν	χώρᾳ
And	to the *ones*	sitting	in	*the* land
	those	who sat		

By using the tilde, word order numbers, and idiomatic English translation, even those with no knowledge of Greek will be able to read this interlinear translation of the Majority Text without getting lost in the "awkwardness" of word-for-word interlinear English.

The Benefits of Interlinear Translations

Many different types of readers will benefit from the Interlinear New Testament. Those who have had no (or few) Greek studies will be introduced to the Greek New Testament through the very literal, word-for-word English translation, providing them English equivalents for each Greek word. Others who have had some Greek training, but have not used Greek lately, will be able to follow the Greek text with less effort through the help of the English translations.

All readers will benefit from the accuracy of the translation work. The interlinear English translations were provided by Greek scholars Arthur L. Farstad, Zane C.

Hodges, C. Michael Moss, Robert E. Picirilli and Wilbur N. Pickering, and reflect their years of studying and teaching the Greek New Testament. The translators incorporated insights from many standard Greek sources (see "Bibliography," p. vi) into their renderings of Greek words and idioms. In addition, Dr. Farstad extensively edited the translations of the four Gospels to ensure that the English represents the similarities of the Greek in parallel passages.

MAJORITY TEXT GREEK

The Greek text of the Interlinear New Testament is the text printed in *The Greek New Testament According to the Majority Text.* It is the form of the Greek text found in the majority of the surviving manuscripts.

The New Testament Text

There is more manuscript support for the New Testament than for any other body of ancient literature. Over five thousand Greek, eight thousand Latin, and many more manuscripts in other languages attest the integrity of the New Testament. Minor variations in hand copying have appeared through the centuries, before mechanical printing began about A.D. 1450. Some variations exist in the spelling of Greek words, in word order, and in similar details. These ordinarily do not show up in translation and do not affect the sense of the text.

Other manuscript differences, such as omission or inclusion of a word or a clause, and two paragraphs in the Gospels (Mark 16:9–20; John 7:53—8:11), should not overshadow the overwhelming degree of *agreement* which exists among the ancient records. Bible readers may be assured that the most important differences in English New Testaments of today are due, not to manuscript divergence, but to the way in which translators view the task of translation: How literally should the text be rendered? How does the translator view the matter of biblical inspiration? Does the translator adopt a paraphrase when a literal rendering would be quite clear and more to the point?

Textus Receptus. The King James New Testament was based on the traditional text of the Greek-speaking churches, first published in 1516, and later called the Textus Receptus (Latin for "Received Text"). Although based on the relatively few Greek manuscripts available, these were representative of many more which existed at the time but only became known later. In the late nineteenth century, B. F. Wescott and F. J. A. Hort taught that this text had been officially edited by the fourth-century church, but a total lack of historical evidence for such an event has forced a revision of the theory. It is now widely admitted that the Byzantine Text that largely supports the Textus Receptus has as much right as the Alexandrian or any other tradition to be weighed in determining the text of the New Testament. Those readings in the Textus Receptus which have weak support are indicated in the textual notes as being opposed by both Critical and Majority Texts (see "Textual Notes").

Alexandrian Text. Since the 1880s most contemporary translations of the New Testament have relied upon a relatively few manuscripts discovered chiefly in the late nineteenth and early twentieth centuries. Such translations depend especially on two manuscripts, Codex Vaticanus and Codex Sinaiticus, because of their great age (fourth century). The Greek text obtained by using these sources and the related papyri (our most ancient manuscripts) is known as the Alexandrian Text. However, some scholars have grounds for doubting the faithfulness of Vaticanus and Sinaiticus, since they often disagree with one another, and Sinaiticus exhibits excessive omission.

Majority Text. A third viewpoint of New Testament scholarship favors a text based on the consensus of the majority of existing Greek manuscripts. This text is called the Majority Text. Most of these manuscripts are in substantial agreement. Even though many are late, and none is earlier than the fifth century, usually their readings are verified by some papyri, ancient versions, quotations from the early church fathers, or a combination of these. The Majority Text is similar to the Textus Receptus, but it corrects those readings which have little or (occasionally) no support in the Greek manuscript tradition.

New Testament Textual Study. Today, scholars agree that the science of New Testament textual criticism is in a state of flux. Very few scholars still favor the Textus Receptus as such, and then often only for its historical prestige as the text of Erasmus, Luther, Calvin, Tyndale, and the King James Version. For about a century most have followed a Critical Text (so called because it is edited according to specific principles of textual criticism) which depends heavily upon the Alexandrian type of text. More recently many have abandoned this Critical Text (which is quite similar to the one edited by Westcott and Hort) for one that is more eclectic (selecting readings from various sources). Finally, a small but growing number of scholars prefer the Majority Text, which is close to the traditional text except in the Revelation.

How should scholars reconstruct the original wording of the Greek New Testament? Should they assume that the manuscripts of an earlier date, which are fewer in number, more likely represent the original text precisely *because they are earlier?* Or should they assume that the majority of manuscripts, which are larger in number but of a later date, more likely represent the original text precisely *because they are in the majority?*

The current state of New Testament textual criticism has not produced a "final" Greek text. This interlinear translation offers the Majority Text as a resource for continued study of the Greek text. It may be possible that the Majority Text readings appear in the majority of surviving manuscripts because those same readings were predominant in the ancient world, as well. If the "majority" is the result of a normal process of copying the New Testament manuscripts, the Majority Text is a Greek text worth considering.

THE NEW KING JAMES VERSION

Complete Equivalence in Translation

The translation methodology followed by the New King James Version makes it an ideal English translation to accompany a Greek-English Interlinear. The most complete representation of the original has been rendered by considering the history of usage and etymology of words in their contexts. This principle of complete equivalence seeks to preserve virtually *all* of the information in the text, while presenting it in good literary form. Dynamic equivalence, a recent procedure in Bible translation, commonly results in paraphrasing idioms where a more literal rendering better reflects a specific and vital sense. For example, complete equivalence truly renders the original text in expressions such as "lifted her voice and wept" (Gen. 21:16); "I gave you cleanness of teeth" (Amos 4:6); and "Jesus met them, saying, 'Rejoice!'" (Matt. 28:9). Complete equivalence translates fully, in order to provide an English text that is both accurate and readable.

In keeping with the principle of complete equivalence, it is the policy of the New King James Version to translate interjections which are commonly omitted in modern language renderings of the Bible. As an example, the interjection *behold,* in the older King James editions, continues to have a place in English usage, especially in dramatically calling attention to a spectacular scene, or an event of profound importance such as the Immanuel prophecy of Isaiah 7:14. Consequently, *behold* is retained for these occasions in the New King James Version. However, the Hebrew and Greek originals for this word can be translated variously, depending on the circumstances in the passage. Therefore, in addition to *behold,* words such as *indeed, look, see,* and *surely* are also used to convey the appropriate sense suggested by the context in each case.

Because the New King James Version is the fifth revision of a historic document translated from specific Greek texts, the editors decided to retain the traditional text (see "Textus Receptus") in the body of the New Testament and to indicate major Critical and Majority Text variant readings in the textual notes. Although these variations are duly indicated in the textual notes of the Interlinear New Testament, it is most important to emphasize that fully eighty-five percent of the New Testament text is the same in the Textus Receptus, the Critical Text, and the Majority Text.

The Format

The format of the New King James Version is designed to enhance the vividness and devotional quality of the Holy Scriptures:

- Words or phrases in *italics* indicate expressions in the original language which require clarification by additional English words, as also was done throughout the history of the King James Bible.
- *Oblique type* in the New Testament indicates a quotation from the Old Testament.
- Verse numbers in **bold type** indicate the beginning of a paragraph.
- Poetry is structured as contemporary verse to reflect the poetic form and beauty of the passage in the original language.
- In the Old Testament the covenant name of God is translated from the Hebrew as "LORD" or "GOD" (using capital letters as shown). In addition, the name is so capitalized whenever the covenant name is quoted in the New Testament from a passage in the Old Testament.

STUDY NOTES

Two types of notes appear at the foot of the parallel column offering resources for additional study: textual notes and word studies. Included among the textual notes are cross references to Old Testament passages cited in the New Testament.

Textual Notes

The textual notes in the Interlinear New Testament make no evaluation of readings, but do clearly indicate the manuscript sources of readings. They objectively present the facts without such tendentious remarks as "the best manuscripts omit" or "the most reliable manuscripts read." Such notes are value judgments that differ according to varying viewpoints on the text. By giving a clearly defined set of variants the Interlinear New Testament benefits readers of all textual persuasions.

Where significant variations occur in the New Testament Greek manuscripts, textual notes are classified as follows:

1. NU-Text
   These variations from the traditional text generally represent the Alexandrian or Egyptian type of text described previously in "The New Testament Text." They are found in the Critical Text published in the twenty-sixth edition of the Nestle-Aland Greek New Testament (N) and in the United Bible Societies' fourth edition (U), hence the acronym, "NU-Text" (NU).

2. M-Text

   This symbol indicates points of variation in the Majority Text from the traditional text, as also previously discussed in "The New Testament Text." It should be noted that M stands for whatever reading is printed in the published *Greek New Testament According to the Majority Text,* whether supported by overwhelming, strong, or only a divided majority textual tradition.

The textual notes reflect the scholarship of the past 150 years and will assist the reader to observe the variations between the different manuscript traditions of the New Testament. A *superior letter* in the Greek text indicates words or phrases which are discussed in the textual notes (Matt. 5:11):

πᾶν	πονηρὸν	ῥῆμα[a]	καθ'	ὑμῶν
every	evil	word / thing	against	you

Word Studies

Words are the conveyers of thoughts from the people who write. However, a word will not communicate the proper thought to the reader who does not know the meaning which that particular word had for the writer. This is especially true of the Scriptures. It is fitting for a Greek-English Interlinear to include studies of many significant Greek words, helping readers to understand the meanings attached to those words by the writers of the New Testament.

Word studies are a step towards appreciating and understanding the thoughts of the biblical writers. The symbol of the Greek manuscript marks 342 word studies (see "Index to Word Studies," p. 903), which discuss not only the differences in meaning that words carry from one context to another, but also the changes in meaning that those words underwent during ancient Greek times. An *asterisk* in the Greek text indicates Greek words appearing in the word studies (John 1:1):

'Εν	ἀρχῇ	ἦν	ὁ	Λόγος,*
In	*the* beginning	was	the	Word,

STYLE CONSIDERATIONS

The format, typography, and punctuation of *The NKJV Greek-English Interlinear New Testament* were chosen to present the Greek text and English translations in a clear and readable manner.

Subject Headings. The topics of major sections of Scripture are indicated by subject headings appearing throughout the Greek text. Cross references to parallel passages are located underneath the subject headings, especially in the Gospels.

Punctuation. The most ancient New Testament manuscripts had virtually no punctuation, and only gradually were various breaks indicated. The period (.) and the comma (,) are used in Greek as in English, while the little raised dot (˙) is used in Greek for both the English colon (:) and semicolon (;). Since the Greek question mark (;) is so widely used for a major break in most languages, it has been replaced with the almost universally used question mark (?). Finally, some sentences, especially in the apostle Paul, seemed exciting enough to the editors to end with an exclamation mark (!).

Since interlinear English is not a final translation, but a representation of the Greek, punctuation of the word-for-word English translation represents the Greek punctuation. The idiomatic English translation, however, follows the standard rules of English punctuation.

Quotation Marks. Experience has shown that Greek and Latin classics are easier for students to read when quoted material and conversations are indicated by some sort of quotation marks. While English quotation marks are used for ordinary quotations, French quotation marks (« » , called *guillemets*) are used to distinguish Old Testament quotations in the New Testament Greek text.

Capitalization. The most ancient manuscripts of the New Testament were written in all-large letters (uncials), and these later were replaced by the so-called minuscule script in which everything was written in small letters. Some Greek editions capitalize only the first words of paragraphs. In this edition all Greek sentences begin with a capital letter. In addition, the Christian tradition of capitalizing the names of the persons of the Trinity is followed. Also capitalized are most of the titles of the Lord, such as "Alpha and Omega," "Son of Man," and several more. The ancient manuscripts indicated so-called holy names (*nomina sacra*) in a special way, and it was considered that honorific capitalization was a suitable counterpart to this ancient tradition.

In the English translations, the first word of an English sentence has been capitalized, even though, due to the Greek word order, it may not occur first in the English word order (Matt. 3:1):

Ἐν δὲ ταῖς ἡμέραις ἐκείναις
in ˜ And - days ˜ those

Subscript. The iota subscript that is written below the line with lower case letters (ᾳ, ῃ, ῳ) is written on the line with capital letters (Ὧι; for this convention, see *Greek Grammar* by Herbert Weir Smyth, section 5).

Transliteration. Some words of the Greek New Testament are either derived or transliterated from Hebrew or Aramaic. In the Interlinear New Testament these words have been transliterated into English, rather than translated. See the word studies on ῥακά (Matt. 5:22); Ἀββᾶ (Rom. 8:15); Μαρὰνα θά (1 Cor. 16:22); and ἀμήν (Rev. 22:20). Transliteration has also been used in the rare case, such as χαλκολίβανον (Rev. 1:15), in which English translation is uncertain.

SYMBOLS IN THE WORD-FOR-WORD ENGLISH TRANSLATION

The hyphen (-) in the English line represents a Greek word for which no English translation is required. This is especially common with the Greek definite article (Mark 1:16):

καὶ Ἀνδρέαν τὸν ἀδελφὸν αὐτοῦ
and Andrew - brother ˜ his

The hyphen also occurs with the recitative ὅτι which in Greek introduces direct quotations or discourse. This use of ὅτι may be left untranslated in English, being somewhat equivalent to the English quotation marks (Luke 1:61):

εἶπον πρὸς αὐτὴν ὅτι "Οὐδείς ἐστιν
they said to her - "[3]no [4]one [1]There [2]is

Words or phrases in *italics* indicate additional words which are required in English by the context, but not present in the Greek text (Mark 8:6):

εὐχαριστήσας ἔκλασε καὶ ἐδίδου
having given thanks He broke *them* and was giving *them*

GREEK SYNTAX AND GRAMMAR

It is impossible to cover the grammar of the Greek New Testament in a brief introduction. The following serves only to review some of the primary aspects of New Testament Greek. In addition, it illustrates the procedures the translators followed in order to bring out the significance of many Greek syntactical and grammatical constructions.

The Definite Article

Greek has no indefinite article. The English indefinite articles *a, an* have been used where the context requires (Mark 8:11):

ζητοῦντες παρ' αὐτοῦ σημεῖον
seeking from Him a sign

The Greek article often is used as a possessive pronoun (Matt. 8:3):

Καὶ ἐκτείνας τὴν χεῖρα
And reaching out the hand
His

Having originated from the demonstrative pronoun, the article is sometimes used as a pronoun (Mark 10:20):

Ὁ δὲ ἀποκριθεὶς εἶπεν
[3]the [4]*one* [1]And [2]answering said
he

The Participle

As in English, the Greek participle is a verbal adjective in form. This means that it is formed from a verb but is often used just like an adjective. Greek participles have usually been translated by an English participle ending in *-ing*. Idiomatic English indicates several important participial constructions.

Genitive absolutes (Mark 1:42):

Καὶ εἰπόντος αὐτοῦ,
And saying ~ Him,
when He said this,

Circumstantial participles (Matt. 2:23):

ἐλθὼν κατῴκησεν εἰς πόλιν
coming he settled down in a city
when he arrived

Participle with the article (1 Thess. 2:12):

τοῦ Θεοῦ τοῦ καλοῦντος ὑμᾶς
- of God the *One* calling you
who calls

Periphrastic constructions. The participle is often combined with a finite verb (frequently εἰμί) in a single formation. In these cases the English translates the finite verb/participle construction as a unit, not attempting to render the participle separately with an *-ing* ending (2 Cor. 4:3):

στὶ κεκαλυμμένον,
[8]it [9]is [10]hidden,

The Infinitive

Greek infinitives are more detailed than the English verbal form with the preposition *to.* Not only are there present, aorist, and perfect infinitives (tense differences), but also active, passive, and middle infinitives (voice differences).

The articular infinitive governed by the article in the genitive case can express purpose or result (Acts 18:10):

οὐδεὶς ἐπιθήσεταί σοι τοῦ κακῶσαί σε,
no one will attack you - to harm you,

The accusative case represents the subject of many infinitives (Acts 9:3):

γένετο αὐτὸν ἐγγίζειν
it came about *for* him to draw near
that he drew

The temporal infinitive (Matt. 13:4):

Καὶ ἐν τῷ σπείρειν αὐτόν,
And in - to sow him,
as he sowed,

The infinitive functions as the main verb (Matt. 26:32):

Μετὰ δὲ τὸ ἐγερθῆναί με
after ~ But - to be raised Me
I am raised

The infinitive functions as an imperative (Phil. 3:16):

τῷ αὐτῷ στοιχεῖν κανόνι, [c]
[5]with [6]the [7]same [1]to [2]be [3]in [4]line rule,
keep

Verbs

The Greek verb system is more complex than the English. Whereas English forms tenses largely by using "helping" verbs, such as *will, have, had* (except in the past tense, where either *-ed* or *-t* is added, or the internal vowel changed), Greek makes changes in the verb itself with prefixes and suffixes, plus some other internal changes.

Voice. Like English, Greek has an active voice and a passive voice. In the active voice the subject *does* the action; in the passive the subject *receives* the action. But Greek has a third voice, the "middle." In the present tense it is spelled just like the passive, but it sometimes has a separate form. The easiest middle for English speakers to understand resembles the English reflexive: "I loose myself." The middle voice, however, usually suggests some more subtle interest or involvement of the subject with the action of the verb.

Active: λύω, *I loose*
Passive: λύομαι, *I am loosed*
Middle: λύομαι, *I loose myself* (or *for myself*)

Deponent Verbs. Some verbs are called *deponent* (from the Latin for *put aside*) because they lay aside one form for another. Deponent verbs do not have an active form, but instead a middle or passive form with an active meaning. For example, ἔρχομαι,

I come, has the -ομαι ending of the present middle or passive voice, but it simply means (in an active sense) that the subject does the action of "coming," not (in a middle sense) that the subject "comes for himself or herself."

Person and Number. *Person* in verbs has to do with who is referred to: *first person* is the speaker or actor; *second person* is the person addressed; *third person* is the person spoken about. *Number* has to do with whether there is one (singular) or more (plural) persons involved.

In most cases, the person and number of Greek verbs have been reflected in the English translation. One exception involves Greek neuter plural subjects which generally take a singular verb. The singular Greek verb has been translated with the plural verb that English grammar requires (Luke 12:27):

"Κατανοήσατε	τὰ	κρίνα	πῶς	αὐξάνει·
"Consider	the	lilies	how	they grow;

Tense. In English the tense of a verb (past, present, or future) generally stresses the *time* of the action. In Greek the stress is more on the *kind of action* or aspect. The question is: Is the action specified by the verb viewed as (1) an activity in progress, repeated, or of a certain kind (present, imperfect); (2) a simple attainment or realization (aorist); or (3) a completed act resulting in the current state of affairs (perfect, pluperfect).

The Present Tense. The present tense often, but by no means always, has a linear, that is, a continuous idea. Overemphasis on the linear idea, such as translating "I am believing" instead of "I believe," has been avoided, unless the context demanded a continuous sense. In another usage the present tense denotes a repeated action or the kind of activity that has a certain tendency. A special use of the present tense, the historical present, describes a past event vividly as a present occurrence. In such cases the past event is represented in the idiomatic translation (Matt. 8:4):

Καὶ	λέγει	αὐτῷ	ὁ	Ἰησοῦς,
And	[2]says said	[3]to [4]him	-	[1]Jesus,

The Imperfect Tense. The imperfect, which is built on the present stem of the verb plus the augment (to indicate past time), plus the personal endings, denotes the same kind of action as the present tense, but in past time. Thus the present λύω ("I loose") in the imperfect ἔλυον means "I was loosing," "I used to loose," or "I would loose." The specific nuance of the imperfect is often indicated in the idiomatic translation, such as the inceptive imperfect (Luke 5:3):

Καὶ	καθίσας	ἐδίδασκεν
And	sitting down	He taught began to teach

The Aorist Tense. The Greek scholar A. T. Robertson called Greek "an aorist-loving language." By this he meant that if there was no special reason to stress a completed, progressive, repeated, or linear aspect, the aorist would be used. The common, but incorrect, definition of the aorist as the "once-for-all tense" is misleading. It *is* true that in the indicative mood the aorist commonly represents a simple past tense, as in English *I went, I saw, I gave,* and that some contexts using an aorist *are* about once-for-all events. However, the basic significance of the aorist is to denote the fact of action occurring without reference to its progress or duration.

The aorist also has special uses of importance. In the subjunctive, imperative, and infinitive, the difference between an aorist and a present can be that the present often suggests *linear* or *repeated* action, while the aorist stresses the event as a point in time, thus *punctiliar* action.

The Perfect Tense. The perfect expresses the present state of affairs resulting from a past action. It is similar but not identical in use to the English perfect.

Perfect: λέλυκα, *I have loosed*

The Pluperfect Tense. As with the English past perfect, the pluperfect denotes a past state of affairs resulting from an action yet further in the past. It is usually translated with the helping verb *had.* The pluperfect is not common in the Greek New Testament.

Pluperfect: ἐλελύκειν, *I had loosed*

The Future Tense. The future tense expresses *future time,* rather than aspect. The context determines the aspect. Future tenses in Greek do not have augments or reduplications, but will often have an "s" sound right before the personal ending:

λύσω, *I shall loose* or *I shall be loosing*

Mood. As in English, Greek verbs can occur in various moods: indicative, subjunctive, and imperative. Greek has an additional mood, the optative, which only appears in a few expressions in the New Testament, such as Μὴ γένοιτο, *May it not be!* The infinitive and participle are sometimes classed with the moods.

The Indicative. As in English, the indicative makes a statement or asks a question. Of the moods, it is the most frequently used since it concerns simple facts, either declaring or asking about them. The future indicative is used sometimes for commands (Matt. 19:18):

«Οὐ φονεύσεις,
"«[3]not [1]You [2]shall murder,

The Subjunctive. The subjunctive is much more important and complex in Greek than in English. Unlike the indicative, which makes a statement, the subjunctive expresses possibility, intention, or wish. Usually the subjunctive is found in dependent clauses. It is also used for strong denials, exhortations, negative commands, and deliberative questions. It is not possible to represent in English all occurrences of the subjunctive mood. However, often the English auxiliary verbs "may" or "might" signal the subjunctive (Heb. 4:16):

ἵνα λάβωμεν ἔλεον καὶ χάριν εὕρωμεν
in order that we may receive mercy and [4]grace [1]we [2]may [3]find

The Imperative. An imperative is a *command,* either positive or negative. Greek imperatives differentiate between second person *singular* and second person *plural,* so the form of the imperative indicates whether one or more persons are addressed. Greek also has a third person imperative, meaning basically "Let him (her, them) do something."

Prepositions

Translations of prepositions in the Interlinear New Testament vary according to the different contexts. Some of the meanings of ἐν include *with, in* (1 Cor. 4:21) and *by* (Col. 1:21). It should be noted that there is often room for debate on what many prepositions mean in particular passages, and translators differ.

The reader should always note the case of the noun with which the preposition is allied. Some prepositions have completely different meanings when used with different cases. For example, διά with the genitive case means *through,* but with the accusative case, *because of;* μετά with the genitive case means *with,* but with the accusative case, *after;* ὑπό with the genitive case means *by,* but with the accusative case, *under.*

Miscellaneous Greek Constructions

Dative of possession. The dative case (here of the pronoun) indicates ownership (John 3:1):

Νικόδημος ὄνομα αὐτῷ,
[5]*was* [6]Nicodemus [1]a [2]name [3]to [4]him,
whose name,

Nouns in apposition. A noun is in apposition when added to another noun of the same case to explain or define it (Matt. 20:1):

ἀνθρώπῳ οἰκοδεσπότῃ
a man a master of the house
a certain landowner

Postpositive particles. Some particles, such as γάρ and δέ, cannot occur first in a sentence, but only after one or more other words. The tilde shows that these particles, called "postpositive," must be read first in English (Matt. 9:34):

Οἱ δὲ Φαρισαῖοι ἔλεγον,
the ˜ But Pharisees said,

Double negatives. Negatives are doubled in Greek in order to express an emphatic denial. The combination οὐ μή is quite common (1 Cor. 8:13):

οὐ μὴ φάγω κρέα
not not will I eat meat
by no means

Negative with a question. When the negative particles μή and μήτι introduce questions, the expected answer is "no." Supplied words in the English translation indicate such (John 18:35):

"Μήτι ἐγὼ Ἰουδαῖός εἰμι?
"[3]not [1]I [4]a [5]Jew [2]am, *am I?*

COMPARING ENGLISH AND GREEK

The goal of *The NKJV Greek-English Interlinear New Testament* project has been to provide a resource for reading and studying the New Testament. The resource was planned to combine various features: (1) the accurate and readable New King James Version alongside the Greek according to the Majority Text; (2) new translations, both word-for-word and idiomatic, of the Greek text; (3) textual notes and word studies concerning significant aspects of the Greek manuscripts and language. The translators hope that use of these features will enable all Bible readers to grow in their knowledge of the New Testament.

The Gospel According to

MATTHEW

ΚΑΤΑ ΜΑΤΘΑΙΟΝ
ACCORDING TO MATTHEW

1 1 Βίβλος* γενέσεως Ἰησοῦ Χριστοῦ, υἱοῦ Δαβίδ, υἱοῦ
A book of *the* generation of Jesus Christ, Son of David, Son
The genealogy

Ἀβραάμ.
of Abraham.

The Genealogy of Jesus Christ

(Cf. Luke 3:23–38)

2 Ἀβραὰμ ἐγέννησε τὸν Ἰσαάκ,
Abraham begot - Isaac,

Ἰσαὰκ δὲ ἐγέννησε τὸν Ἰακώβ,
Isaac ˜ and begot - Jacob,

Ἰακὼβ δὲ ἐγέννησε τὸν Ἰούδαν καὶ τοὺς ἀδελφοὺς αὐτοῦ,
Jacob ˜ and begot - Judah and - brothers ˜ his,

3 Ἰούδας δὲ ἐγέννησε τὸν Φάρες καὶ τὸν Ζάρα ἐκ τῆς
Judah ˜ and begot - Perez and - Zerah by -

Θαμάρ,
Tamar,

Φάρες δὲ ἐγέννησε τὸν Ἑσρώμ,
Perez ˜ and begot - Hezron,

Ἑσρὼμ δὲ ἐγέννησε τὸν Ἀράμ,
Hezron ˜ and begot - Aram,

4 Ἀρὰμ δὲ ἐγέννησε τὸν Ἀμιναδάβ,
Aram ˜ and begot - Amminadab,

Ἀμιναδὰβ δὲ ἐγέννησε τὸν Ναασσών,
Amminadab ˜ and begot - Nahshon,

Ναασσὼν δὲ ἐγέννησε τὸν Σαλμών,
Nahshon ˜ and begot - Salmon,

5 Σαλμὼν δὲ ἐγέννησε τὸν Βόοζ ἐκ τῆς Ῥαχάβ,
Salmon ˜ and begot - Boaz by - Rahab,

Βόοζ δὲ ἐγέννησε τὸν Ὠβὴδ ἐκ τῆς Ῥούθ,
Boaz ˜ and begot - Obed by - Ruth,

Ὠβὴδ δὲ ἐγέννησε τὸν Ἰεσσαί,
Obed ˜ and begot - Jesse,

6 Ἰεσσαὶ δὲ ἐγέννησε τὸν Δαβὶδ τὸν βασιλέα.
Jesse ˜ and begot - David the king.

Δαβὶδ δὲ ὁ βασιλεὺς[a] ἐγέννησε τὸν Σολομῶνα ἐκ τῆς
David ˜ And the king begot - Solomon by the *wife*

τοῦ Οὐρίου,
- of Uriah,

7 Σολομὼν δὲ ἐγέννησε τὸν Ῥοβοάμ,
Solomon ˜ and begot - Rehoboam,

Ῥοβοὰμ δὲ ἐγέννησε τὸν Ἀβιά,
Rehoboam ˜ and begot - Abijah,

Ἀβιὰ δὲ ἐγέννησε τὸν Ἀσά,[b]
Abijah ˜ and begot - Asa,

8 Ἀσὰ[c] δὲ ἐγέννησε τὸν Ἰωσαφάτ,
Asa ˜ and begot - Jehoshaphat,

1 The book of the genealogy of Jesus Christ, the
Son of David, the Son of Abraham:
2 Abraham begot Isaac,
Isaac begot Jacob, and Jacob
begot Judah and his brothers.
3 Judah begot Perez and Zerah by Tamar, Perez begot
Hezron, and Hezron begot
Ram.
4 Ram begot Amminadab,
Amminadab begot Nahshon,
and Nahshon begot Salmon.
5 Salmon begot Boaz by Rahab, Boaz begot Obed by Ruth,
Obed begot Jesse,
6 and Jesse begot David the
king.
David the king begot Sol-
omon by her *who had been the*
wife of Uriah.
7 Solomon begot Rehoboam,
Rehoboam begot Abijah, and
Abijah begot Asa.
8 Asa begot Jehoshaphat,

---

[a]**(1:6)** NU omits ο βασιλευς, *the king.* [b]**(1:7)** NU reads Ασαφ, *Asaph.*
[c]**(1:8)** NU reads Ασαφ, *Asaph.*

***(1:1)** *βίβλος (biblos).* Noun, originally the cellular substance in papyrus stems that the Egyptians turned into a kind of "paper" by fixing narrow strips vertically and then sticking horizontal ones on top. The word came to be used for a sheet or a scroll of such paper, hence *book.* It is used of sacred books in the NT and of occult books in Acts 19:19. Here in Matt. 1:1 it is a "scroll of generation," that is, a genealogy. The diminutive form *βιβλίον* had largely lost its diminutive force, which was expressed by *βιβλιδάριον* (Rev. 10:8f; NU *βιβλαρίδιον*). The English word *Bible* is derived from the plural of *βιβλίον*, that is, *τὰ βιβλία, the books.*

Jehoshaphat begot Joram, and Joram begot Uzziah.
9 Uzziah begot Jotham, Jotham begot Ahaz, and Ahaz begot Hezekiah.
10 Hezekiah begot Manasseh, Manasseh begot Amon, and Amon begot Josiah.
11 Josiah begot Jeconiah and his brothers about the time they were carried away to Babylon.
12 And after they were brought to Babylon, Jeconiah begot Shealtiel, and Shealtiel begot Zerubbabel.
13 Zerubbabel begot Abiud, Abiud begot Eliakim, and Eliakim begot Azor.
14 Azor begot Zadok, Zadok begot Achim, and Achim begot Eliud.
15 Eliud begot Eleazar, Eleazar begot Matthan, and Matthan begot Jacob.
16 And Jacob begot Joseph the husband of Mary, of whom was born Jesus who is called Christ.
17 So all the generations from Abraham to David *are* fourteen generations, from David until

Ἰωσαφὰτ δὲ ἐγέννησε τὸν Ἰωράμ,
Jehoshaphat ˜ and begot - Joram,

Ἰωρὰμ δὲ ἐγέννησε τὸν Ὀζίαν,
Joram ˜ and begot - Uzziah,

9 Ὀζίας δὲ ἐγέννησε τὸν Ἰωαθάμ,
Uzziah ˜ and begot - Jotham,

Ἰωαθὰμ δὲ ἐγέννησε τὸν Ἀχάζ,
Jotham ˜ and begot - Ahaz,

Ἀχὰζ δὲ ἐγέννησε τὸν Ἑζεκίαν,
Ahaz ˜ and begot - Hezekiah,

10 Ἑζεκίας δὲ ἐγέννησε τὸν Μανασσῆ,
Hezekiah ˜ and begot - Manasseh,

Μανασσῆς δὲ ἐγέννησε τὸν Ἀμών,[d]
Manasseh ˜ and begot - Amon,

Ἀμὼν[d] δὲ ἐγέννησε τὸν Ἰωσίαν,
Amon ˜ and begot - Josiah,

11 Ἰωσίας δὲ ἐγέννησε τὸν Ἰεχονίαν καὶ τοὺς ἀδελφοὺς
Josiah ˜ and begot - Jeconiah and - brothers ˜

αὐτοῦ ἐπὶ τῆς μετοικεσίας Βαβυλῶνος.
his at the time of the deportation of Babylon.
captivity in

12 Μετὰ δὲ τὴν μετοικεσίαν Βαβυλῶνος
after ˜ And the deportation of Babylon
captivity in

Ἰεχονίας ἐγέννησε τὸν Σαλαθιήλ,
Jeconiah begot - Shealtiel,

Σαλαθιὴλ δὲ ἐγέννησε τὸν Ζοροβαβέλ,
Shealtiel ˜ and begot - Zerubbabel,

13 Ζοροβαβὲλ δὲ ἐγέννησε τὸν Ἀβιούδ,
Zerubbabel ˜ and begot - Abiud,

Ἀβιοὺδ δὲ ἐγέννησε τὸν Ἐλιακείμ,
Abiud ˜ and begot - Eliakim,

Ἐλιακεὶμ δὲ ἐγέννησε τὸν Ἀζώρ,
Eliakim ˜ and begot - Azor,

14 Ἀζὼρ δὲ ἐγέννησε τὸν Σαδώκ,
Azor ˜ and begot - Zadok,

Σαδὼκ δὲ ἐγέννησε τὸν Ἀχείμ,
Zadok ˜ and begot - Achim,

Ἀχεὶμ δὲ ἐγέννησε τὸν Ἐλιούδ,
Achim ˜ and begot - Eliud,

15 Ἐλιοὺδ δὲ ἐγέννησε τὸν Ἐλεάζαρ,
Eliud ˜ and begot - Eleazar,

Ἐλεάζαρ δὲ ἐγέννησε τὸν Ματθάν,
Eleazar ˜ and begot - Matthan,

Ματθὰν δὲ ἐγέννησε τὸν Ἰακώβ,
Matthan ˜ and begot - Jacob,

16 Ἰακὼβ δὲ ἐγέννησε τὸν Ἰωσὴφ τὸν ἄνδρα Μαρίας, ἐξ
Jacob ˜ and begot - Joseph the husband of Mary, of

ἧς ἐγεννήθη Ἰησοῦς ὁ λεγόμενος
whom was born Jesus the *One* being called
who is

Χριστός.
Christ.

17 Πᾶσαι οὖν αἱ γενεαὶ ἀπὸ Ἀβραὰμ ἕως Δαβὶδ
all ˜ So the generations from Abraham till David

γενεαὶ δεκατέσσαρες, καὶ ἀπὸ Δαβὶδ ἕως τῆς
were generations ˜ fourteen, and from David till the

---

[d](1:10) NU reads Αμως, *Amos.*

μετοικεσίας Βαβυλῶνος γενεαὶ δεκατέσσαρες, καὶ ἀπὸ
deportation of Babylon *were* generations ˜ fourteen, and from
captivity in

τῆς μετοικεσίας Βαβυλῶνος ἕως τοῦ Χριστοῦ γενεαὶ
the deportation of Babylon till the Christ *were* generations ˜
captivity in

δεκατέσσαρες.
fourteen.

Jesus Christ Is Born of Mary
(Luke 2:1–7)

18 Τοῦ δὲ Ἰησοῦ Χριστοῦ ἡ γέννησις οὕτως ἦν.
- Now [3]of [4]Jesus [5]Christ [1]the [2]birth [7]thus [6]was.
like this

Μνηστευθείσης γὰρ τῆς μητρὸς αὐτοῦ Μαρίας τῷ Ἰωσήφ,
being betrothed For - mother ˜ His Mary - to Joseph,
For after His mother Mary had been betrothed

πρὶν ἢ συνελθεῖν αὐτούς, εὑρέθη ἐν γαστρὶ ἔχουσα
before - to come together them, she was found in *the* womb having
they came together, pregnant

ἐκ Πνεύματος Ἁγίου. 19 Ἰωσὴφ δὲ ὁ ἀνὴρ αὐτῆς,
by *the* Spirit ˜ Holy. Joseph ˜ Then - husband ˜ her,

δίκαιος ὢν καὶ μὴ θέλων αὐτὴν παραδειγματίσαι,
righteous ˜ being and not wanting [6]*of* [7]her [1]to [2]make [3]a [4]public [5]example,

ἐβουλήθη λάθρᾳ ἀπολῦσαι αὐτήν.
resolved [5]secretly [1]to [2]put [4]away [3]her.
divorce

20 Ταῦτα δὲ αὐτοῦ ἐνθυμηθέντος, ἰδού, ἄγγελος
[5]these [6]*things* [1]But [2]he [3]thinking [4]about, behold, an angel
while he was thinking about,

Κυρίου κατ' ὄναρ ἐφάνη αὐτῷ, λέγων, "Ἰωσὴφ υἱὸς
of *the* Lord in a dream appeared to him, saying, "Joseph son

Δαβίδ, μὴ φοβηθῇς παραλαβεῖν Μαριὰμ τὴν γυναῖκά σου,
of David, not ˜ do be afraid to take along Mary - wife ˜ your,

τὸ γὰρ ἐν αὐτῇ γεννηθὲν ἐκ Πνεύματός ἐστιν Ἁγίου.
[2]the [3]*baby* [1]for [5]in [6]her [4]begotten [8]of [9]*the* [11]Spirit [7]is [10]Holy.

21 Τέξεται δὲ υἱὸν καὶ καλέσεις τὸ ὄνομα αὐτοῦ
[2]she [3]will [4]bear [1]And a Son and you shall call - name ˜ His

Ἰησοῦν, αὐτὸς γὰρ σώσει τὸν λαὸν αὐτοῦ ἀπὸ τῶν ἁμαρτιῶν
Jesus, He ˜ for will save - people ˜ His from - sins ˜

αὐτῶν." 22 Τοῦτο δὲ ὅλον γέγονεν ἵνα
their." this ˜ Now whole *thing* has happened so that

πληρωθῇ τὸ ῥηθὲν ὑπὸ τοῦ Κυρίου διὰ τοῦ
[10]might [11]be [12]fulfilled [1]the [2]*thing* [3]spoken [4]by [5]the [6]Lord [7]through [8]the

προφήτου, λέγοντος,
[9]prophet, saying,

23 «Ἰδού, ἡ παρθένος* ἐν γαστρὶ ἕξει καὶ τέξεται
«Behold, the virgin in *the* womb shall have and shall bear
shall be pregnant

υἱόν,
a Son,

Καὶ καλέσουσι τὸ ὄνομα αὐτοῦ Ἐμμανουήλ,»
And they shall call - name ˜ His Immanuel,»

ὅ ἐστι μεθερμηνευόμενον, «Μεθ' ἡμῶν ὁ Θεός.»[e]
which is being translated, «[2]with [3]us - [1]God.»
means,

24 Διεγερθεὶς δὲ ὁ Ἰωσὴφ ἀπὸ τοῦ ὕπνου ἐποίησεν ὡς
[3]being [4]raised [1]Then - [2]Joseph from - sleep did as

the captivity in Babylon *are*
fourteen generations, and from
the captivity in Babylon until
the Christ *are* fourteen generations.
18 Now the birth of Jesus
Christ was as follows: After His
mother Mary was betrothed to
Joseph, before they came together, she was found with
child of the Holy Spirit.
19 Then Joseph her husband,
being a just *man,* and not wanting to make her a public example, was minded to put her
away secretly.
20 But while he thought about
these things, behold, an angel
of the Lord appeared to him in a
dream, saying, "Joseph, son of
David, do not be afraid to take
to you Mary your wife, for that
which is conceived in her is of
the Holy Spirit.
21 "And she will bring forth a
Son, and you shall call His name
JESUS, for He will save His people from their sins."
22 So all this was done that it
might be fulfilled which was
spoken by the Lord through the
prophet, saying:
23 *"Behold, the virgin shall be
with child, and bear a Son, and
they shall call His name Immanuel,"* which is translated, "God
with us."
24 Then Joseph, being
aroused from sleep, did as the

---

[e](**1:23**) Is. 7:14

***(1:23)** *παρθένος (parthenos).* Noun. In this quotation from the LXX παρθένος translates Hebrew *'almāh,* a *young woman* of marriageable age (in Jewish culture a virgin at marriage). The Greek word itself means a *chaste, pure woman.* It is used in the NT of the Virgin Mary, the ten "bridesmaids" (Matt. 25:1–13), Philip's virgin daughters (Acts 21:9), and chaste singles or virgin daughters (1 Cor. 7:25ff). In 2 Cor. 11:2 it is used figuratively for a church, and in Rev. 14:4 as a masculine noun for chaste or celibate men.

angel of the Lord commanded
him and took to him his wife,
25 and did not know her till
she had brought forth her firstborn Son. And he called His
name JESUS.
2 Now after Jesus was born
in Bethlehem of Judea in
the days of Herod the king, behold, wise men from the East
came to Jerusalem,
2 saying, "Where is He who
has been born King of the
Jews? For we have seen His
star in the East and have come
to worship Him."
3 When Herod the king
heard *this,* he was troubled,
and all Jerusalem with him.
4 And when he had gathered
all the chief priests and scribes
of the people together, he inquired of them where the
Christ was to be born.
5 So they said to him, "In
Bethlehem of Judea, for thus it
is written by the prophet:

6 *'But you, Bethlehem, in*
the land of Judah,
Are not the least among
the rulers of Judah;
For out of you shall come
a Ruler
Who will shepherd My
people Israel.'"

7 Then Herod, when he had
secretly called the wise men,

προσέταξεν αὐτῷ ὁ ἄγγελος Κυρίου καὶ παρέλαβε τὴν
[6]ordered [7]him [1]the [2]angel [3]of [4]*the* [5]Lord and he took along -

γυναῖκα αὐτοῦ, 25 καὶ οὐκ ἐγίνωσκεν αὐτὴν ἕως οὗ ἔτεκε τὸν
wife ˜ his, and not ˜ did know her till - she bore -
but

υἱὸν αὐτῆς τὸν πρωτότοκον.[f] Καὶ ἐκάλεσε τὸ ὄνομα αὐτοῦ
[3]Son [1]her - [2]firstborn. And he called - name ˜ His

ἸΗΣΟΥΝ.
JESUS.

Wise Men Come to Worship the King

2 1 Τοῦ δὲ Ἰησοῦ γεννηθέντος ἐν Βηθλέεμ τῆς Ἰουδαίας
- And Jesus having been born in Bethlehem - of Judea
Now after Jesus was born

ἐν ἡμέραις Ἡρῴδου τοῦ βασιλέως, ἰδού, μάγοι ἀπὸ
in *the* days of Herod the king, behold, Magi from
wise men

ἀνατολῶν παρεγένοντο εἰς Ἱεροσόλυμα, 2 λέγοντες, "Ποῦ
the East arrived in Jerusalem, saying, "Where

ἐστιν ὁ τεχθεὶς Βασιλεὺς τῶν Ἰουδαίων? Εἴδομεν
is the *One* having been born King of the Jews? [2]we [3]saw
have seen

γὰρ αὐτοῦ τὸν ἀστέρα ἐν τῇ ἀνατολῇ καὶ ἤλθομεν
[1]For His - star in the East and we came
have come

προσκυνῆσαι αὐτῷ."
to worship Him."

3 Ἀκούσας δὲ Ἡρῴδης ὁ βασιλεὺς ἐταράχθη καὶ
hearing But Herod the king he was troubled and
But when King Herod heard,

πᾶσα Ἱεροσόλυμα μετ' αὐτοῦ. 4 Καὶ συναγαγὼν
all Jerusalem with him. And having gathered together

πάντας τοὺς ἀρχιερεῖς καὶ γραμματεῖς τοῦ λαοῦ, ἐπυνθάνετο
all the chief priests and scribes of the people, he inquired

παρ' αὐτῶν ποῦ ὁ Χριστὸς γεννᾶται.
from them where the Christ is being born.
Messiah would be

5 Οἱ δὲ εἶπον αὐτῷ, "Ἐν Βηθλέεμ τῆς Ἰουδαίας·
[2]the [3]*ones* [1]And said to him, "In Bethlehem - of Judea;
they

οὕτω γὰρ γέγραπται διὰ τοῦ προφήτου,
thus ˜ for it is written through the prophet,

6 «Καὶ σύ, Βηθλέεμ, γῆ Ἰούδα,
«And you, Bethlehem, *in the* land of Judah,

Οὐδαμῶς ἐλαχίστη εἶ ἐν τοῖς ἡγεμόσιν
[3]by [4]no [5]means [6]least [1]You [2]are among the governors
rulers

Ἰούδα·
of Judah;

Ἐκ σοῦ γὰρ ἐξελεύσεται ἡγούμενος,
[2]out [3]of [4]you [1]For shall come forth a governing *One,*
Ruler,

Ὅστις ποιμανεῖ τὸν λαόν μου τὸν Ἰσραήλ.»"[a]
Who will shepherd - people ˜ My - Israel.»"

7 Τότε Ἡρῴδης, λάθρᾳ καλέσας τοὺς μάγους, ἠκρίβωσε
Then Herod, secretly having called the Magi, ascertained
wise men,

---

[f](1:25) For *τον υιον αυτης τον πρωτοτοκον, her firstborn Son,* NU reads *υιον, a Son.*
[a](2:6) Mic. 5:2

παρ' αὐτῶν τὸν χρόνον τοῦ φαινομένου ἀστέρος. 8 Καὶ
from them the time of the appearing star. And
that the star appeared.

πέμψας αὐτοὺς εἰς Βηθλέεμ εἶπε, "Πορευθέντες ἀκριβῶς
sending them to Bethlehem he said, "Going carefully
"Go and

ἐξετάσατε περὶ τοῦ Παιδίου· ἐπὰν δὲ εὕρητε,
search concerning the young Child; [2]as [3]soon [4]as [1]and you find *Him,*

ἀπαγγείλατέ μοι, ὅπως κἀγὼ ἐλθὼν προσκυνήσω αὐτῷ."
report back to me, so that I also coming may worship Him."
may come and

9 Οἱ δὲ ἀκούσαντες τοῦ βασιλέως ἐπορεύθησαν,
[2]the [3]*ones* [1]And having heard the king journeyed,
when they heard they departed,

καὶ ἰδού, ὁ ἀστὴρ ὃν εἶδον ἐν τῇ ἀνατολῇ προῆγεν
and behold, the star which they saw in the East went before
had seen

αὐτοὺς ἕως ἐλθὼν ἔστη ἐπάνω οὗ ἦν τὸ Παιδίον.
them till coming it stood over where [4]was [1]the [2]young [3]Child.
it came and stood

10 Ἰδόντες δὲ τὸν ἀστέρα, ἐχάρησαν χαρὰν μεγάλην
seeing ˜ And the star, they rejoiced [2]*with* [4]joy [3]great
when they saw

σφόδρα. 11 Καὶ ἐλθόντες εἰς τὴν οἰκίαν εἶδον[b] τὸ
[1]exceedingly. And having come into the house they saw the

Παιδίον μετὰ Μαρίας τῆς μητρὸς αὐτοῦ, καὶ πεσόντες
young Child with Mary - mother ˜ His, and falling down

προσεκύνησαν αὐτῷ, καὶ ἀνοίξαντες τοὺς θησαυροὺς
they worshiped Him, and opening - treasures ˜
when they had opened

αὐτῶν προσήνεγκαν αὐτῷ δῶρα, χρυσὸν καὶ λίβανον καὶ
their they presented to Him gifts, gold and frankincense and

σμύρναν. 12 Καὶ χρηματισθέντες κατ' ὄναρ μὴ
myrrh. And having been divinely warned by a dream not

ἀνακάμψαι πρὸς Ἡρῴδην, δι' ἄλλης ὁδοῦ ἀνεχώρησαν εἰς
to return to Herod, [3]through [4]another [5]way [1]they [2]departed for
by

τὴν χώραν αὐτῶν.
- country ˜ their.

Joseph, Mary, and Jesus Flee to Egypt

13 Ἀναχωρησάντων δὲ αὐτῶν, ἰδού, ἄγγελος Κυρίου
departing And them, behold, an angel of *the* Lord
Now when they had departed,

φαίνεται κατ' ὄναρ τῷ Ἰωσήφ, λέγων, "Ἐγερθεὶς παράλαβε
appears in a dream - to Joseph, saying, "Rising take along
appeared "Arise and

τὸ Παιδίον καὶ τὴν μητέρα αὐτοῦ καὶ φεῦγε εἰς Αἴγυπτον
the young Child and - mother ˜ His and flee to Egypt

καὶ ἴσθι ἐκεῖ ἕως ἂν εἴπω σοι· μέλλει γὰρ Ἡρῴδης ζητεῖν τὸ
and be there until - I tell you; [3]is [4]about [1]for [2]Herod to seek the
stay

Παιδίον τοῦ ἀπολέσαι αὐτό." 14 Ὁ δὲ ἐγερθεὶς
young Child - to destroy it." [2]the [3]*one* [1]And rising
Him." So he arose and

παρέλαβε τὸ Παιδίον καὶ τὴν μητέρα αὐτοῦ νυκτὸς καὶ
took along the young Child and - mother ˜ His at night and

ἀνεχώρησεν εἰς Αἴγυπτον, 15 καὶ ἦν ἐκεῖ ἕως τῆς τελευτῆς
departed for Egypt, and was there until the death

determined from them what time the star appeared.

8 And he sent them to Bethlehem and said, "Go and search carefully for the young Child, and when you have found *Him,* bring back word to me, that I may come and worship Him also."

9 When they heard the king, they departed; and behold, the star which they had seen in the East went before them, till it came and stood over where the young Child was.

10 When they saw the star, they rejoiced with exceedingly great joy.

11 And when they had come into the house, they saw the young Child with Mary His mother, and fell down and worshiped Him. And when they had opened their treasures, they presented gifts to Him: gold, frankincense, and myrrh.

12 Then, being divinely warned in a dream that they should not return to Herod, they departed for their own country another way.

13 Now when they had departed, behold, an angel of the Lord appeared to Joseph in a dream, saying, "Arise, take the young Child and His mother, flee to Egypt, and stay there until I bring you word; for Herod will seek the young Child to destroy Him."

14 When he arose, he took the young Child and His mother by night and departed for Egypt,

15 and was there until the

[b](2:11) TR reads *ευρον, they found.*

death of Herod, that it might be
fulfilled which was spoken by
the Lord through the prophet,
saying, *"Out of Egypt I called
My Son."*
16 Then Herod, when he saw
that he was deceived by the
wise men, was exceedingly angry; and he sent forth and put
to death all the male children
who were in Bethlehem and in
all its districts, from two years
old and under, according to the
time which he had determined
from the wise men.
17 Then was fulfilled what
was spoken by Jeremiah the
prophet, saying:

18 *"A voice was heard in*
Ramah,
Lamentation, weeping,
and great mourning,
Rachel weeping for her
children,
Refusing to be comforted,
Because they are no
more."

19 Now when Herod was
dead, behold, an angel of the
Lord appeared in a dream to Joseph in Egypt,
20 saying, "Arise, take the
young Child and His mother,
and go to the land of Israel, for
those who sought the young
Child's life are dead."
21 Then he arose, took the
young Child and His mother,
and came into the land of Israel.
22 But when he heard that Archelaus was reigning over Judea
instead of his father Herod, he
was afraid to go there. And being warned by God in a dream,

Ἡρῴδου· ἵνα πληρωθῇ τὸ ῥηθὲν ὑπὸ τοῦ
of Herod; so that [10]might [11]be [12]fulfilled [1]the [2]*thing* [3]spoken [4]by [5]the

Κυρίου διὰ τοῦ προφήτου, λέγοντος, «Ἐξ Αἰγύπτου
[6]Lord [7]through [8]the [9]prophet, saying, «Out of Egypt

ἐκάλεσα τὸν Υἱόν μου.»[c]
I called - Son ˜ My.»

Herod Massacres the Babies of Bethlehem

16 Τότε Ἡρῴδης, ἰδὼν ὅτι ἐνεπαίχθη ὑπὸ τῶν μάγων,
Then Herod, seeing that he was deceived by the Magi,
had been wise men,

ἐθυμώθη λίαν, καὶ ἀποστείλας ἀνεῖλε πάντας τοὺς
became angry ˜ exceedingly, and sending he killed all the
he sent and executed

παῖδας τοὺς ἐν Βηθλέεμ καὶ ἐν πᾶσι τοῖς ὁρίοις αὐτῆς ἀπὸ
boys - in Bethlehem and in all - districts ˜ its from

διετοῦς καὶ κατωτέρω, κατὰ τὸν χρόνον ὃν
two years old and lower, according to the time which
under,

ἠκρίβωσε παρὰ τῶν μάγων. **17** Τότε ἐπληρώθη τὸ
he ascertained from the Magi. Then [8]was [9]fulfilled [1]the [2]*thing*
wise men.

ῥηθὲν ὑπὸ[d] Ἰερεμίου τοῦ προφήτου, λέγοντος,
[3]spoken [4]by [5]Jeremiah [6]the [7]prophet, saying,

18 «Φωνὴ ἐν Ῥαμὰ ἠκούσθη,
«A voice in Ramah was heard,

Θρῆνος καὶ[e] κλαυθμὸς καὶ ὀδυρμὸς πολύς,
Lamentation and weeping and mourning ˜ much,

Ῥαχὴλ κλαίουσα τὰ τέκνα αὐτῆς,
Rachel weeping *for* - children ˜ her,

Καὶ οὐκ ἤθελε παρακληθῆναι, ὅτι οὐκ εἰσί.»[f]
And [3]not [1]she [2]did want to be comforted, because [3]not [1]they [2]are.»
she would not were.»

Joseph, Mary, and Jesus Settle in Nazareth

19 Τελευτήσαντος δὲ τοῦ Ἡρῴδου, ἰδού, ἄγγελος
[3]having [4]died [1]And - [2]Herod, behold, an angel
Now after Herod died,

Κυρίου κατ' ὄναρ φαίνεται τῷ Ἰωσὴφ ἐν Αἰγύπτῳ,
of *the* Lord [2]by [3]a [4]dream [1]appears - to Joseph in Egypt,
appeared

20 λέγων, "Ἐγερθεὶς παράλαβε τὸ Παιδίον καὶ τὴν μητέρα
saying, "Rising take along the young Child and - mother ˜
"Arise and

αὐτοῦ καὶ πορεύου εἰς γῆν Ἰσραήλ, τεθνήκασι γὰρ οἱ
His and journey to *the* land of Israel, [11]have [12]died [1]for [2]the [3]*ones*

ζητοῦντες τὴν ψυχὴν τοῦ Παιδίου." **21** Ὁ δὲ
[4]seeking [5]the [6]life [7]of [8]the [9]young [10]Child." [2]the [3]*one* [1]Then
he

ἐγερθεὶς παρέλαβε τὸ Παιδίον καὶ τὴν μητέρα αὐτοῦ καὶ
rising took along the young Child and - mother ˜ His and
rose and

ἦλθεν εἰς γῆν Ἰσραήλ. **22** Ἀκούσας δὲ ὅτι Ἀρχέλαος
came into *the* land of Israel. hearing ˜ But that Archelaus

βασιλεύει ἐπὶ τῆς Ἰουδαίας ἀντὶ Ἡρῴδου τοῦ πατρὸς
is reigning over - Judea instead of Herod - father ˜
was

αὐτοῦ, ἐφοβήθη ἐκεῖ ἀπελθεῖν. Χρηματισθεὶς δὲ κατ'
his, he was afraid [3]there [1]to [2]go. [5]being [6]divinely [7]warned [4]And by

[c](**2:15**) Hos. 11:1
[d](**2:17**) NU reads δια, *through.* [e](**2:18**) NU omits θρηνος και, *lamentation and.* [f](**2:18**) Jer. 31:15

ὄναρ, ἀνεχώρησεν εἰς τὰ μέρη τῆς Γαλιλαίας, **23** καὶ
a dream, he departed for the parts - of Galilee, and
region

ἐλθὼν κατῴκησεν εἰς πόλιν λεγομένην Ναζαρέτ, ὅπως
coming he settled down in a city being called Nazareth, so that
when he arrived called

πληρωθῇ τὸ ῥηθὲν διὰ τῶν προφητῶν ὅτι
[7]might [8]be [9]fulfilled [1]the [2]*thing* [3]spoken [4]through [5]the [6]prophets that

Ναζωραῖος κληθήσεται.
[5]a [6]Nazarene [1]He [2]will [3]be [4]called.
would

John the Baptist Prepares the Way
(Mark 1:1–8; Luke 3:1–7; John 1:19–28)

3 **1** Ἐν δὲ ταῖς ἡμέραις ἐκείναις παραγίνεται Ἰωάννης ὁ
in ˜ And - days ˜ those [4]arrives [1]John [2]the
arrived

Βαπτιστὴς κηρύσσων ἐν τῇ ἐρήμῳ τῆς Ἰουδαίας **2** καὶ
[3]Baptist preaching in the wilderness - of Judea and
Baptizer

λέγων, "Μετανοεῖτε, ἤγγικε γὰρ ἡ βασιλεία τῶν
saying, "Repent, [7]has [8]drawn [9]near [1]for [2]the [3]kingdom [4]of [5]the

οὐρανῶν!" **3** Οὗτος γάρ ἐστιν ὁ ῥηθεὶς ὑπὸ[a] Ἠσαΐου τοῦ
[6]heavens!" this ˜ For is the *thing* spoken by Isaiah the

προφήτου, λέγοντος,
prophet, saying,

«Φωνὴ βοῶντος·
«A voice of *one* crying:

Ἐν τῇ ἐρήμῳ ἑτοιμάσατε τὴν ὁδὸν Κυρίου,
'In the wilderness prepare the way of *the* Lord,

Εὐθείας ποιεῖτε τὰς τρίβους αὐτοῦ.'»[b]
straight ˜ Make - paths ˜ His.'»

4 Αὐτὸς δὲ ὁ Ἰωάννης εἶχε τὸ ἔνδυμα αὐτοῦ ἀπὸ
[3]himself [1]Now - [2]John had - clothing ˜ his *made* from

τριχῶν καμήλου καὶ ζώνην δερματίνην περὶ τὴν ὀσφὺν αὐτοῦ,
hairs of camel and a belt ˜ leather around - loins ˜ his,
camel skin waist

ἡ δὲ τροφὴ αὐτοῦ ἦν ἀκρίδες καὶ μέλι ἄγριον. **5** Τότε
- and food ˜ his was locusts and honey ˜ wild. Then

ἐξεπορεύετο πρὸς αὐτὸν Ἱεροσόλυμα καὶ πᾶσα ἡ Ἰουδαία καὶ
were going out to him Jerusalem and all - Judea and

πᾶσα ἡ περίχωρος τοῦ Ἰορδάνου **6** καὶ
all the surrounding region of the Jordan and

ἐβαπτίζοντο ἐν τῷ Ἰορδάνῃ[c] ὑπ' αὐτοῦ
they were being baptized in the Jordan by him

ἐξομολογούμενοι τὰς ἁμαρτίας αὐτῶν.
confessing - sins ˜ their.

7 Ἰδὼν δὲ πολλοὺς τῶν Φαρισαίων καὶ Σαδδουκαίων
seeing ˜ But many of the Pharisees and Sadducees

ἐρχομένους ἐπὶ τὸ βάπτισμα αὐτοῦ, εἶπεν αὐτοῖς, "Γεννήματα
coming to - baptism ˜ his, he said to them, "Offspring of
"Brood

ἐχιδνῶν! Τίς ὑπέδειξεν ὑμῖν φυγεῖν ἀπὸ τῆς μελλούσης ὀργῆς?
vipers! Who showed you to flee from the coming wrath?
warned

8 Ποιήσατε οὖν καρπὸν ἄξιον[d] τῆς μετανοίας,
produce ˜ Therefore fruit worthy - of repentance,
befitting repentance,

he turned aside into the region of Galilee.
23 And he came and dwelt in a city called Nazareth, that it might be fulfilled which was spoken by the prophets, "He shall be called a Nazarene."
3 In those days John the Baptist came preaching in the wilderness of Judea,
2 and saying, "Repent, for the kingdom of heaven is at hand!"
3 For this is he who was spoken of by the prophet Isaiah, saying:

"The voice of one crying in the wilderness:
'Prepare the way of the LORD;*
Make His paths straight.' "

4 Now John himself was clothed in camel's hair, with a leather belt around his waist; and his food was locusts and wild honey.
5 Then Jerusalem, all Judea, and all the region around the Jordan went out to him
6 and were baptized by him in the Jordan, confessing their sins.
7 But when he saw many of the Pharisees and Sadducees coming to his baptism, he said to them, "Brood of vipers! Who warned you to flee from the wrath to come?
8 "Therefore bear fruits worthy of repentance,

---

[a](**3:3**) NU reads δια, *through.* [b](**3:3**) Is. 40:3 [c](**3:6**) NU adds ποταμω, *River.* [d](**3:8**) For καρπον αξιον, *fruit worthy,* TR reads καρπους αξιους, *fruits worthy.*

9 "and do not think to say to yourselves, 'We have Abraham as *our* father.' For I say to you that God is able to raise up children to Abraham from these stones.

10 "And even now the ax is laid to the root of the trees. Therefore every tree which does not bear good fruit is cut down and thrown into the fire.

11 "I indeed baptize you with water unto repentance, but He who is coming after me is mightier than I, whose sandals I am not worthy to carry. He will baptize you with the Holy Spirit and fire.

12 "His winnowing fan *is* in His hand, and He will thoroughly clean out His threshing floor, and gather His wheat into the barn; but He will burn up the chaff with unquenchable fire."

13 Then Jesus came from Galilee to John at the Jordan to be baptized by him.

14 And John *tried to* prevent Him, saying, "I need to be baptized by You, and are You coming to me?"

15 But Jesus answered and said to him, "Permit *it to be so* now, for thus it is fitting for us to fulfill all righteousness." Then he allowed Him.

16 When He had been baptized, Jesus came up immediately from the water; and behold, the heavens were opened to Him, and He saw the Spirit of God descending like a dove and alighting upon Him.

17 And suddenly a voice *came* from heaven, saying, "This is

9 *καὶ μὴ δόξητε λέγειν ἐν ἑαυτοῖς, 'Πατέρα ἔχομεν τὸν*
and not ˜ do think to say among yourselves, '[4]*as* [5]father [1]We [2]have -

'Αβραάμ.' Λέγω γὰρ ὑμῖν ὅτι δύναται ὁ Θεὸς ἐκ τῶν λίθων
[3]Abraham.' [7]I [8]say [6]For to you that [2]is [3]able - [1]God out of - stones ˜

τούτων ἐγεῖραι τέκνα τῷ 'Αβραάμ. **10** *Ἤδη δὲ καὶ*[e] *ἡ*
these to raise up children - to Abraham. [3]already [1]But [2]also the

ἀξίνη πρὸς τὴν ῥίζαν τῶν δένδρων κεῖται. Πᾶν
ax [4]to [5]the [6]root [7]of [8]the [9]trees [1]is [2]being [3]laid. every ˜

οὖν δένδρον μὴ ποιοῦν καρπὸν καλὸν ἐκκόπτεται καὶ εἰς
Therefore tree not producing fruit ˜ good is cut down and [3]into

πῦρ βάλλεται.
[4]*the* [5]fire [1]is [2]thrown.

11 "*Ἐγὼ μὲν βαπτίζω ὑμᾶς ἐν ὕδατι εἰς μετάνοιαν·*
"I indeed baptize you in water unto repentance;
with

ὁ δὲ ὀπίσω μου ἐρχόμενος ἰσχυρότερός μού ἐστιν,
[2]the [3]*One* [1]but [5]after [6]me [4]coming [8]stronger [9]*than* [10]me [7]is,
I

οὗ οὐκ εἰμὶ ἱκανὸς τὰ ὑποδήματα βαστάσαι. Αὐτὸς ὑμᾶς
whose [4]not [2]I [3]am [5]worthy - [1]sandals to carry. He [3]you

βαπτίσει ἐν Πνεύματι Ἁγίῳ.[f] **12** *οὗ τὸ πτύον*
[1]will [2]baptize in *the* Spirit ˜ Holy, whose - winnowing shovel
with

ἐν τῇ χειρὶ αὐτοῦ, καὶ διακαθαριεῖ τὴν
is in - hand ˜ His, and He will thoroughly clean out -

ἅλωνα αὐτοῦ, καὶ συνάξει τὸν σῖτον αὐτοῦ εἰς τὴν
[2]threshing [3]floor [1]His, and He will gather - wheat ˜ His into the
His

ἀποθήκην, τὸ δὲ ἄχυρον κατακαύσει πυρὶ ἀσβέστῳ."
barn, the ˜ but chaff He will burn up with fire ˜ unquenchable."

John Baptizes Jesus

(Mark 1:9–11; Luke 3:21, 22)

13 *Τότε παραγίνεται ὁ Ἰησοῦς ἀπὸ τῆς Γαλιλαίας ἐπὶ τὸν*
Then arrives ˜ - Jesus from - Galilee at the
arrived

Ἰορδάνην πρὸς τὸν Ἰωάννην τοῦ βαπτισθῆναι ὑπ' αὐτοῦ. **14** *Ὁ*
Jordan to - John - to be baptized by him. -

δὲ Ἰωάννης διεκώλυεν αὐτόν, λέγων, "Ἐγὼ χρείαν ἔχω ὑπὸ
But John would prevent Him, saying, "I need ˜ have by
tried to

σοῦ βαπτισθῆναι, καὶ σὺ ἔρχῃ πρός με?"
You to be baptized, and You are coming to me?"

15 *Ἀποκριθεὶς δὲ ὁ Ἰησοῦς εἶπε πρὸς αὐτόν, "Ἄφες*
answering ˜ But - Jesus said to him, "Permit *it*

ἄρτι, οὕτω γὰρ πρέπον ἐστὶν ἡμῖν πληρῶσαι πᾶσαν
now, thus ˜ for [3]fitting [1]it [2]is for us to fulfill all

δικαιοσύνην." Τότε ἀφίησιν αὐτόν. **16** *Καὶ βαπτισθεὶς*
righteousness." Then he permitted Him. And having been baptized

ὁ Ἰησοῦς ἀνέβη εὐθὺς ἀπὸ τοῦ ὕδατος· καὶ ἰδού,
- Jesus came up immediately from the water; and behold,

ἀνεῴχθησαν αὐτῷ οἱ οὐρανοί, καὶ εἶδε τὸ Πνεῦμα τοῦ
[3]were [4]opened [5]to [6]Him [1]the [2]heavens, and He saw the Spirit -

Θεοῦ καταβαῖνον ὡσεὶ περιστερὰν καὶ ἐρχόμενον ἐπ' αὐτόν.
of God coming down like a dove and coming upon Him.

17 *Καὶ ἰδού, φωνὴ ἐκ τῶν οὐρανῶν, λέγουσα,*
And behold, a voice *came* out of the heavens, saying,

[e](3:10) NU omits *και, also.*
[f](3:11) TR, NU add *και πυρι, and with fire.*

"Οὗτός ἐστιν ὁ Υἱός μου ὁ ἀγαπητός, ἐν ᾧ
"This is - [3]Son [1]My - [2]beloved, in whom

εὐδόκησα."
I have found delight."

Satan Tempts Jesus
(Mark 1:12, 13; Luke 4:1–13)

4 1 Τότε ὁ Ἰησοῦς ἀνήχθη εἰς τὴν ἔρημον ὑπὸ τοῦ
Then - Jesus was led up into the wilderness by the

Πνεύματος πειρασθῆναι ὑπὸ τοῦ διαβόλου. 2 Καὶ νηστεύσας
Spirit to be tempted by the devil. And having fasted

ἡμέρας τεσσαράκοντα καὶ νύκτας τεσσαράκοντα, ὕστερον
days ˜ forty and nights ˜ forty, afterward

ἐπείνασε. 3 Καὶ προσελθὼν αὐτῷ ὁ πειράζων εἶπεν, "Εἰ
He was hungry. And approaching Him the tempting *one* said, "If
tempter

Υἱὸς εἶ τοῦ Θεοῦ, εἰπὲ ἵνα οἱ λίθοι οὗτοι
[3]*the* [4]Son [1]You [2]are - of God, say that - stones ˜ these
speak so that

ἄρτοι γένωνται."
[3]loaves [4]of [5]bread [1]may [2]become."

4 Ὁ δὲ ἀποκριθεὶς εἶπε, "Γέγραπται,
[2]the [3]*One* ˜ [1]But answering said, "It is written,
He

«Οὐκ ἐπ' ἄρτῳ μόνῳ ζήσεται ἄνθρωπος,
«Not on bread alone shall live ˜ man,
by

Ἀλλ' ἐπὶ παντὶ ῥήματι ἐκπορευομένῳ διὰ στόματος
But on every saying coming out through *the* mouth
by

Θεοῦ.»"[a]
of God.»"

5 Τότε παραλαμβάνει αὐτὸν ὁ διάβολος εἰς τὴν ἁγίαν
Then [3]takes [5]along [4]Him [1]the [2]devil to the holy
took

πόλιν, καὶ ἵστησιν[b] αὐτὸν ἐπὶ τὸ πτερύγιον τοῦ ἱεροῦ,
city, and sets Him upon the extremity of the temple,
set pinnacle

6 καὶ λέγει αὐτῷ, "Εἰ Υἱὸς εἶ τοῦ Θεοῦ, βάλε σεαυτὸν
and says to Him, "If [3]*the* [4]Son [1]You [2]are of God, throw Yourself
said

κάτω. Γέγραπται γὰρ ὅτι
down. [2]it [3]is [4]written [1]For -

«Τοῖς ἀγγέλοις αὐτοῦ ἐντελεῖται περὶ σοῦ,
- «To angels ˜ His He will give orders concerning you,

Καὶ ἐπὶ χειρῶν ἀροῦσί σε,
And on *their* hands they will lift up ˜ you,
in

Μήποτε προσκόψῃς πρὸς λίθον τὸν πόδα σου.»"[c]
Lest you strike [3]against [4]a [5]stone - [2]foot [1]your.»"

7 Ἔφη αὐτῷ ὁ Ἰησοῦς, "Πάλιν γέγραπται,
[2]said [3]to [4]Him - [1]Jesus, "Again it is written,

«Οὐκ ἐκπειράσεις Κύριον τὸν Θεόν σου.»"[d]
«[3]not [1]You [2]shall tempt *the* Lord - God ˜ your.»"

8 Πάλιν παραλαμβάνει αὐτὸν ὁ διάβολος εἰς ὄρος
Again [3]takes [5]along [4]Him [1]the [2]devil to a [3]mountain
took

My beloved Son, in whom I am
well pleased."
4 Then Jesus was led up by
the Spirit into the wilderness to be tempted by the
devil.
2 And when He had fasted
forty days and forty nights, afterward He was hungry.
3 Now when the tempter
came to Him, he said, "If You
are the Son of God, command
that these stones become
bread."
4 But He answered and said,
"It is written, *'Man shall not
live by bread alone, but by every word that proceeds from
the mouth of God.'*"
5 Then the devil took Him up
into the holy city, set Him on
the pinnacle of the temple,
6 and said to Him, "If You
are the Son of God, throw
Yourself down. For it is written:

*'He shall give His angels
charge over you,'*

and,

*'In their hands they shall
bear you up,
Lest you dash your foot
against a stone.'*"

7 Jesus said to him, "It is
written again, *'You shall not
tempt the* LORD *your God.'*"
8 Again, the devil took Him
up on an exceedingly high

---

[a](4:4) Deut. 8:3
[b](4:5) NU reads εστησεν, *set.* [c](4:6) Ps. 91:11, 12
[d](4:7) Deut. 6:16

mountain, and showed Him all
the kingdoms of the world and
their glory.
9 And he said to Him, "All
these things I will give You if
You will fall down and worship
me."
10 Then Jesus said to him,
"Away with you, Satan! For it
is written, *'You shall worship
the* LORD *your God, and Him
only you shall serve.'*"
11 Then the devil left Him,
and behold, angels came and
ministered to Him.
12 Now when Jesus heard that
John had been put in prison, He
departed to Galilee.
13 And leaving Nazareth, He
came and dwelt in Capernaum,
which is by the sea, in the regions of Zebulun and Naphtali,
14 that it might be fulfilled
which was spoken by Isaiah the
prophet, saying:

15 *"The land of Zebulun and
the land of Naphtali,
By the way of the sea,
beyond the Jordan,
Galilee of the Gentiles:*
16 *The people who sat in
darkness have seen a
great light,
And upon those who sat
in the region and
shadow of death
Light has dawned."*

17 From that time Jesus began to preach and to say, "Re-

ὑψηλὸν λίαν καὶ δείκνυσιν αὐτῷ πάσας τὰς βασιλείας τοῦ
[2]high [1]very and shows Him all the kingdoms of the
showed

κόσμου καὶ τὴν δόξαν αὐτῶν. **9** Καὶ λέγει[e] αὐτῷ, "Ταῦτα
world and - glory ˜ their. And he says to Him, "[2]these [3]*things*
said

πάντα σοι δώσω ἐὰν πεσὼν προσκυνήσῃς μοι."
[1]All [7]to [8]You [4]I [5]will [6]give if falling down You will worship me."
You will fall down and worship

10 Τότε λέγει αὐτῷ ὁ Ἰησοῦς, "Ὕπαγε ὀπίσω μου,[f]
Then [2]says [3]to [4]him - [1]Jesus, "Go away behind Me,
said

Σατανᾶ! Γέγραπται γάρ,
Satan! [2]it [3]is [4]written [1]For,

«Κύριον τὸν Θεόν σου προσκυνήσεις
«*The* Lord - God ˜ your you shall worship

Καὶ αὐτῷ μόνῳ λατρεύσεις.»"[g]
And Him alone you shall serve.»"

11 Τότε ἀφίησιν αὐτὸν ὁ διάβολος, καὶ ἰδού, ἄγγελοι
Then [3]leaves [4]Him [1]the [2]devil, and behold, angels
left

προσῆλθον καὶ διηκόνουν αὐτῷ.
approached and were serving Him.
began to serve

Jesus Begins His Galilean Ministry
(Mark 1:14, 15; Luke 4:14, 15)

12 Ἀκούσας δὲ ὁ Ἰησοῦς[h] ὅτι Ἰωάννης
[3]hearing [1]Now - [2]Jesus that John
Now when Jesus heard

παρεδόθη, ἀνεχώρησεν εἰς τὴν Γαλιλαίαν. **13** Καὶ
was given over, He departed into - Galilee. And
had been imprisoned,

καταλιπὼν τὴν Ναζαρέτ, ἐλθὼν κατῴκησεν εἰς
leaving behind ˜ - Nazareth, coming He settled down in
He came and

Καπερναοὺμ[i] τὴν παραθαλασσίαν ἐν ὁρίοις Ζαβουλὼν καὶ
Capernaum - by the sea in *the* regions of Zebulun and

Νεφθαλείμ· **14** ἵνα πληρωθῇ τὸ ῥηθὲν διὰ
Naphtali: so that [8]might [9]be [10]fulfilled [1]the [2]*thing* [3]spoken [4]through

Ἠσαΐου τοῦ προφήτου, λέγοντος,
[5]Isaiah [6]the [7]prophet, saying,

15 «Γῆ Ζαβουλὼν καὶ γῆ Νεφθαλείμ,
«Land of Zebulun and land of Naphtali,

Ὁδὸν θαλάσσης, πέραν τοῦ Ἰορδάνου,
The way of *the* sea, beyond the Jordan,

Γαλιλαία τῶν ἐθνῶν,
Galilee of the Gentiles,

16 Ὁ λαὸς ὁ καθήμενος ἐν σκότει
The people - sitting in darkness

Εἶδεν φῶς μέγα,
Saw a light ˜ great,

Καὶ τοῖς καθημένοις ἐν χώρᾳ καὶ σκιᾷ θανάτου
And to the *ones* sitting in *the* land and *the* shadow of death
those who sat

Φῶς ἀνέτειλεν αὐτοῖς.»[j]
Light sprang up on them.»

17 Ἀπὸ τότε ἤρξατο ὁ Ἰησοῦς κηρύσσειν καὶ λέγειν,
From then began ˜ - Jesus to preach and to say,

---

[e](**4:9**) NU reads ειπεν, *he said.* [f](**4:10**) TR, NU omit οπισω μου, *behind Me.*
[g](**4:10**) Deut. 6:13
[h](**4:12**) NU omits ο Ιησους, *Jesus.* [i](**4:13**) NU reads Καφαρναουμ, *Capharnaum.*
[j](**4:15, 16**) Is. 9:1, 2

"Μετανοεῖτε, ἤγγικε γὰρ ἡ βασιλεία τῶν οὐρανῶν."
"Repent, [7]has [8]drawn [9]near [1]for [2]the [3]kingdom [4]of [5]the [6]heavens."

Jesus Calls Four Fishermen
(Mark 1:16–20; Luke 5:1–11)

18 Περιπατῶν δὲ[k] παρὰ τὴν θάλασσαν τῆς Γαλιλαίας
walking ˜ Now alongside the Sea - of Galilee
as He was walking

εἶδε δύο ἀδελφούς, Σίμωνα τὸν λεγόμενον Πέτρον καὶ
He saw two brothers, Simon the *one* being called Peter and
called

Ἀνδρέαν τὸν ἀδελφὸν αὐτοῦ, βάλλοντας ἀμφίβληστρον εἰς τὴν
Andrew - brother ˜ his, casting a circular net into the

θάλασσαν, ἦσαν γὰρ ἁλιεῖς.
sea, [2]they [3]were [1]for fishermen.
19 Καὶ λέγει αὐτοῖς,
And He says to them,
said

"Δεῦτε ὀπίσω μου, καὶ ποιήσω ὑμᾶς ἁλιεῖς ἀνθρώπων."
"Come after Me, and I will make you fishers of men."
for

20 Οἱ δὲ εὐθέως ἀφέντες τὰ δίκτυα ἠκολούθησαν
[2]the [3]*ones* [1]And immediately leaving the nets followed
they left their and followed

αὐτῷ.
Him.
21 Καὶ προβὰς ἐκεῖθεν, εἶδεν ἄλλους δύο
And having gone forth from there, He saw other ˜ two

ἀδελφούς, Ἰάκωβον τὸν τοῦ Ζεβεδαίου καὶ Ἰωάννην τὸν
brothers, James the *son* - of Zebedee and John -

ἀδελφὸν αὐτοῦ, ἐν τῷ πλοίῳ μετὰ Ζεβεδαίου τοῦ πατρὸς αὐτῶν
brother ˜ his, in the boat with Zebedee - father ˜ their

καταρτίζοντας τὰ δίκτυα αὐτῶν. Καὶ ἐκάλεσεν αὐτούς.
mending - nets ˜ their. And He called them.

22 Οἱ δὲ εὐθέως ἀφέντες τὸ πλοῖον καὶ τὸν πατέρα
[2]the [3]*ones* [1]And immediately leaving the boat and - father ˜
they left

αὐτῶν ἠκολούθησαν αὐτῷ.
their followed Him.
and followed

Jesus Heals a Great Multitude
(Luke 6:17–19)

23 Καὶ περιῆγεν ὅλην τὴν Γαλιλαίαν ὁ Ἰησοῦς διδάσκων
And [2]went [3]about [5]whole [4]the [6]Galilee - [1]Jesus teaching
all of

ἐν ταῖς συναγωγαῖς αὐτῶν καὶ κηρύσσων τὸ εὐαγγέλιον τῆς
in - synagogues ˜ their and preaching the gospel of the

βασιλείας καὶ θεραπεύων πᾶσαν νόσον καὶ πᾶσαν μαλακίαν
kingdom and healing every disease and every illness

ἐν τῷ λαῷ.
among the people.
24 Καὶ ἀπῆλθεν ἡ ἀκοὴ αὐτοῦ εἰς ὅλην
And [5]went [6]forth [1]the [2]report [3]of [4]Him into whole ˜
all

τὴν Συρίαν. Καὶ προσήνεγκαν αὐτῷ πάντας τοὺς κακῶς
the Syria. And they brought to Him all the *ones* [3]badly
of those who

ἔχοντας, ποικίλαις νόσοις καὶ βασάνοις συνεχομένους,
[1]having [2]*it*, [5]*with* [6]various [7]diseases [8]and [9]torments [4]suffering,
were ill,

καὶ δαιμονιζομένους καὶ σεληνιαζομένους καὶ
and *who were* being demon-possessed and being moonstruck and
demon-possessed epileptics

pent, for the kingdom of heaven is at hand."
18 And Jesus, walking by the Sea of Galilee, saw two brothers, Simon called Peter, and Andrew his brother, casting a net into the sea; for they were fishermen.
19 Then He said to them, "Follow Me, and I will make you fishers of men."
20 They immediately left *their* nets and followed Him.
21 Going on from there, He saw two other brothers, James *the son* of Zebedee, and John his brother, in the boat with Zebedee their father, mending their nets. He called them,
22 and immediately they left the boat and their father, and followed Him.
23 And Jesus went about all Galilee, teaching in their synagogues, preaching the gospel of the kingdom, and healing all kinds of sickness and all kinds of disease among the people.
24 Then His fame went throughout all Syria; and they brought to Him all sick people who were afflicted with various diseases and torments, and those who were demon-

---

[k]**(4:18)** TR adds ο Ιησους, *Jesus*.

possessed, epileptics, and paralytics; and He healed them.
25 Great multitudes followed Him—from Galilee, and *from* Decapolis, Jerusalem, Judea, and beyond the Jordan.

5 And seeing the multitudes, He went up on a mountain, and when He was seated His disciples came to Him.
2 Then He opened His mouth and taught them, saying:

3 "Blessed *are* the poor in spirit,
For theirs is the kingdom of heaven.
4 Blessed *are* those who mourn,
For they shall be comforted.
5 Blessed *are* the meek,
For they shall inherit the earth.
6 Blessed *are* those who hunger and thirst for righteousness,
For they shall be filled.
7 Blessed *are* the merciful,
For they shall obtain mercy.
8 Blessed *are* the pure in heart,
For they shall see God.
9 Blessed *are* the peacemakers,
For they shall be called sons of God.
10 Blessed are those who are persecuted for righteousness' sake,
For theirs is the kingdom of heaven.

παραλυτικούς. Καὶ ἐθεράπευσεν αὐτούς. **25** Καὶ ἠκολούθησαν
paralytics. And He healed them. And [3]followed

αὐτῷ ὄχλοι πολλοὶ ἀπὸ τῆς Γαλιλαίας καὶ Δεκαπόλεως καὶ
[4]Him [2]crowds [1]large from - Galilee and Decapolis and

Ἱεροσολύμων καὶ Ἰουδαίας καὶ πέραν τοῦ Ἰορδάνου.
Jerusalem and Judea and beyond the Jordan.

The Beatitudes
(Luke 6:20–23)

5 **1** Ἰδὼν δὲ τοὺς ὄχλους ἀνέβη εἰς τὸ ὄρος καί,
seeing ˜ And the crowds He went up into the mountain and,

καθίσαντος αὐτοῦ, προσῆλθον αὐτῷ οἱ μαθηταὶ αὐτοῦ. **2** Καὶ
[2]sitting [3]down [1]Him, [6]approached [7]Him - [5]disciples [4]His. And
after He had sat down,

ἀνοίξας τὸ στόμα αὐτοῦ ἐδίδασκεν αὐτούς, λέγων,
opening - mouth ˜ His He was teaching them, saying,
began to teach

3 "Μακάριοι οἱ πτωχοὶ τῷ πνεύματι,
"Blessed *are* the poor - in spirit,

Ὅτι αὐτῶν ἐστιν ἡ βασιλεία τῶν οὐρανῶν.
Because theirs is the kingdom of the heavens.

4 Μακάριοι οἱ πενθοῦντες,
Blessed *are* the *ones* mourning,
those who mourn,

Ὅτι αὐτοὶ παρακληθήσονται.
Because they will be comforted.

5 Μακάριοι οἱ πραεῖς,
Blessed *are* the meek,
gentle,

Ὅτι αὐτοὶ κληρονομήσουσι τὴν γῆν.
Because they will inherit the earth.

6 Μακάριοι οἱ πεινῶντες καὶ διψῶντες τὴν
Blessed *are* the *ones* hungering and thirsting for -
those who hunger thirst

δικαιοσύνην,
righteousness,

Ὅτι αὐτοὶ χορτασθήσονται.
Because they will be filled.

7 Μακάριοι οἱ ἐλεήμονες,
Blessed *are* the merciful,

Ὅτι αὐτοὶ ἐλεηθήσονται.
Because they will be shown mercy.

8 Μακάριοι οἱ καθαροὶ τῇ καρδίᾳ,
Blessed *are* the pure - in heart,

Ὅτι αὐτοὶ τὸν Θεὸν ὄψονται.
Because they - [3]God [1]will [2]see.

9 Μακάριοι οἱ εἰρηνοποιοί,
Blessed *are* the peacemakers,

Ὅτι αὐτοὶ υἱοὶ Θεοῦ κληθήσονται.
Because they [4]sons [5]of [6]God [1]will [2]be [3]called.

10 Μακάριοι οἱ δεδιωγμένοι ἕνεκεν
Blessed *are* the *ones* having been persecuted for the sake of
those who have

δικαιοσύνης,
righteousness,

Ὅτι αὐτῶν ἐστιν ἡ βασιλεία τῶν οὐρανῶν.
Because theirs is the kingdom of the heavens.

11 "Μακάριοί ἐστε ὅταν ὀνειδίσωσιν ὑμᾶς καὶ
"Blessed are you whenever they revile you and
insult

διώξωσι καὶ εἴπωσι πᾶν πονηρὸν ῥῆμα[a] καθ' ὑμῶν
they persecute and they say every evil word against you
thing

ψευδόμενοι ἕνεκεν ἐμοῦ. 12 Χαίρετε καὶ ἀγαλλιᾶσθε,
lying because of Me. Rejoice and exult,
falsely for My sake.

ὅτι ὁ μισθὸς ὑμῶν πολὺς ἐν τοῖς οὐρανοῖς· οὕτω γὰρ
because - reward ˜ your *is* great in the heavens; thus ˜ for

ἐδίωξαν τοὺς προφήτας τοὺς πρὸ ὑμῶν.
they persecuted the prophets the *ones* before you.
who were

Believers Are Salt and Light
(Mark 9:50; Luke 14:34, 35)

13 "Ὑμεῖς ἐστε τὸ ἅλας τῆς γῆς· ἐὰν δὲ τὸ ἅλας
"You are the salt of the earth; if ˜ but the salt

μωρανθῇ, ἐν τίνι ἁλισθήσεται? Εἰς οὐδὲν ἰσχύει
becomes tasteless, with what shall it be salted? [4]for [5]nothing [1]It [2]is [3]valid
good

ἔτι εἰ μὴ βληθῆναι ἔξω καὶ καταπατεῖσθαι ὑπὸ τῶν
anymore if not to be thrown out and to be trampled down by -
except

ἀνθρώπων.
men.

14 "Ὑμεῖς ἐστε τὸ φῶς τοῦ κόσμου. Οὐ δύναται πόλις
"You are the light of the world. [8]not [7]is [9]able [1]A [2]city

κρυβῆναι ἐπάνω ὄρους κειμένη. 15 Οὐδὲ καίουσι
[10]to [11]be [12]hidden [4]upon [5]a [6]hill [3]set. Nor do they light
located.

λύχνον καὶ τιθέασιν αὐτὸν ὑπὸ τὸν μόδιον, ἀλλ' ἐπὶ
a lamp and put it under the measuring basket, but on
a

τὴν λυχνίαν, καὶ λάμπει πᾶσι τοῖς ἐν τῇ οἰκίᾳ. 16 Οὕτω
the lampstand, and it shines on all *things* - in the house. Thus
a everything

λαμψάτω τὸ φῶς ὑμῶν ἔμπροσθεν τῶν ἀνθρώπων, ὅπως
[1]let [4]shine - [3]light [2]your before - men, so that

ἴδωσιν ὑμῶν τὰ καλὰ ἔργα καὶ δοξάσωσι τὸν Πατέρα
they may see your - good works and they may glorify - Father ˜
noble

ὑμῶν τὸν ἐν τοῖς οὐρανοῖς.
your - in the heavens.

Christ Fulfills the Law

17 "Μὴ νομίσητε ὅτι ἦλθον καταλῦσαι τὸν Νόμον ἢ τοὺς
"not ˜ Do think that I came to destroy the Law or the
suppose

Προφήτας· οὐκ ἦλθον καταλῦσαι ἀλλὰ πληρῶσαι. 18 Ἀμὴν
Prophets; [3]not [1]I [2]came to destroy but to fulfill. amen ˜
assuredly

γὰρ λέγω ὑμῖν, ἕως ἂν παρέλθῃ ὁ οὐρανὸς καὶ ἡ γῆ,
For I say to you, until - [4]may [5]pass [6]away - [1]heaven [2]and - [3]earth,

ἰῶτα* ἓν ἢ μία κεραία οὐ μὴ παρέλθῃ ἀπὸ τοῦ
iota ˜ one or one tittle [2]not [3]not [1]shall [4]pass [5]away from the
serif by no means

11 "Blessed are you when they revile and persecute you, and say all kinds of evil against you falsely for My sake.
12 "Rejoice and be exceedingly glad, for great *is* your reward in heaven, for so they persecuted the prophets who were before you.
13 "You are the salt of the earth; but if the salt loses its flavor, how shall it be seasoned? It is then good for nothing but to be thrown out and trampled underfoot by men.
14 "You are the light of the world. A city that is set on a hill cannot be hidden.
15 "Nor do they light a lamp and put it under a basket, but on a lampstand, and it gives light to all *who are* in the house.
16 "Let your light so shine before men, that they may see your good works and glorify your Father in heaven.
17 "Do not think that I came to destroy the Law or the Prophets. I did not come to destroy but to fulfill.
18 "For assuredly, I say to you, till heaven and earth pass away, one jot or one tittle will by no means pass from the law

---

[a](5:11) NU omits *ρημα, word.*

***(5:18)** *ἰῶτα (iōta).* Noun taken into English as *iota* or as *jot,* referring to the smallest letter of the Greek alphabet (corresponding to the English "i"). It is used only here in the NT. In what was probably the original form of the saying in Matt. 5:18, *ἰῶτα* apparently represented the *yod,* likewise the smallest letter of the Hebrew/Aramaic alphabet.

till all is fulfilled.
19 "Whoever therefore
breaks one of the least of these
commandments, and teaches
men so, shall be called least in
the kingdom of heaven; but
whoever does and teaches
them, he shall be called great in
the kingdom of heaven.
20 "For I say to you, that unless your righteousness exceeds *the righteousness* of the
scribes and Pharisees, you will
by no means enter the kingdom
of heaven.
21 "You have heard that it was
said to those of old, *'You shall*
not murder, and whoever murders will be in danger of the
judgment.'
22 "But I say to you that whoever is angry with his brother
without a cause shall be in danger of the judgment. And whoever says to his brother,
'Raca!' shall be in danger of the
council. But whoever says,
'You fool!' shall be in danger of
hell fire.
23 "Therefore if you bring
your gift to the altar, and there
remember that your brother
has something against you,
24 "leave your gift there before the altar, and go your way.
First be reconciled to your
brother, and then come and offer your gift.
25 "Agree with your adversary quickly, while you are on
the way with him, lest your adversary deliver you to the
judge, the judge hand you over
to the officer, and you be
thrown into prison.
26 "Assuredly, I say to you,

νόμου ἕως ἂν πάντα γένηται. **19** Ὃς ἐὰν οὖν λύσῃ
law until - all *things* come to be. Who ever therefore shall break
happen.

μίαν τῶν ἐντολῶν τούτων τῶν ἐλαχίστων καὶ διδάξῃ
one - of [3]commandments [1]these - [2]least and shall teach

οὕτω τοὺς ἀνθρώπους, ἐλάχιστος κληθήσεται ἐν τῇ βασιλείᾳ
thus ˜ - men, [4]least [1]will [2]be [3]called in the kingdom

τῶν οὐρανῶν· ὃς δ' ἂν ποιήσῃ καὶ διδάξῃ, οὗτος
of the heavens; who ˜ but ever does *them* and teaches *them,* this *one*

μέγας κληθήσεται ἐν τῇ βασιλείᾳ τῶν οὐρανῶν. **20** Λέγω
[4]great [1]will [2]be [3]called in the kingdom of the heavens. [2]I [3]say

γὰρ ὑμῖν ὅτι ἐὰν μὴ περισσεύσῃ ἡ δικαιοσύνη ὑμῶν
[1]For to you that if not [3]is [4]in [5]abundance - [2]righteousness [1]your
unless

πλεῖον τῶν γραμματέων καὶ Φαρισαίων, οὐ μὴ
more *than that* of the scribes and Pharisees, [3]not [4]not
by no means

εἰσέλθητε εἰς τὴν βασιλείαν τῶν οὐρανῶν.
[1]you [2]shall [5]enter into the kingdom of the heavens.

Jesus Warns Against Anger

21 "Ἠκούσατε ὅτι ἐρρέθη τοῖς ἀρχαίοις, «Οὐ
"You heard that it was said to the ancients, «[3]not
have heard

φονεύσεις,»[b] ὃς δ' ἂν φονεύσῃ, ἔνοχος ἔσται τῇ
[1]You [2]shall [4]kill,» who ˜ but ever kills, [3]liable [1]will [2]be to the

κρίσει. **22** Ἐγὼ δὲ λέγω ὑμῖν ὅτι πᾶς ὁ ὀργιζόμενος
judgment. I ˜ But say to you that every - *one* getting angry
everyone who gets

τῷ ἀδελφῷ αὐτοῦ εἰκῇ[c] ἔνοχος ἔσται τῇ κρίσει.
with brother ˜ his without cause [3]liable [1]will [2]be to the judgment.

Ὃς δ' ἂν εἴπῃ τῷ ἀδελφῷ αὐτοῦ, 'Ῥακά,'* ἔνοχος
who ˜ But ever says - to brother ˜ his, 'Raca,' [3]liable
'Empty-head,'

ἔσται τῷ συνεδρίῳ. Ὃς δ' ἂν εἴπῃ, 'Μωρέ,' ἔνοχος
[1]will [2]be to the council. who ˜ But ever says, 'Fool,' [3]liable

ἔσται εἰς τὴν Γέενναν τοῦ πυρός. **23** Ἐὰν οὖν προσφέρῃς
[1]will [2]be to the Gehenna - of fire. If therefore you offer
fiery hell.

τὸ δῶρόν σου ἐπὶ τὸ θυσιαστήριον καὶ ἐκεῖ μνησθῇς ὅτι ὁ
- gift ˜ your on the altar and there you remember that -

ἀδελφός σου ἔχει τι κατὰ σοῦ, **24** ἄφες ἐκεῖ τὸ δῶρόν
brother ˜ your has something against you, leave there - gift ˜

σου ἔμπροσθεν τοῦ θυσιαστηρίου, καὶ ὕπαγε, πρῶτον
your before the altar, and go, first

διαλλάγηθι τῷ ἀδελφῷ σου, καὶ τότε ἐλθὼν πρόσφερε τὸ
be reconciled with - brother ˜ your, and then coming offer the
come and

δῶρόν σου. **25** Ἴσθι εὐνοῶν τῷ ἀντιδίκῳ σου ταχὺ
gift ˜ your. Be well-disposed - with adversary ˜ your quickly
Make friends

ἕως ὅτου εἶ ἐν τῇ ὁδῷ μετ' αὐτοῦ, μήποτέ σε παραδῷ
while - you are on the road with him, lest [4]you [3]hand [5]over

ὁ ἀντίδικος τῷ κριτῇ, καὶ ὁ κριτής σε παραδῷ[d] τῷ
[1]the [2]adversary to the judge, and the judge you ˜ hand over to the

ὑπηρέτῃ, καὶ εἰς φυλακὴν βληθήσῃ. **26** Ἀμὴν λέγω
court attendant, and [4]into [5]prison [1]you [2]be [3]cast. Amen I say
Assuredly

---

[b](**5:21**) Ex. 20:13; Deut. 5:17 [c](**5:22**) NU omits *εικη, without cause.* [d](**5:25**) NU omits *σε παραδω, hands you over.*

*(**5:22**) ῥακά *(rhaka).* Aramaic term of contempt, probably from *rêqā, empty.* It expressed intellectual emptiness, thus meaning *empty-headed,* similar to the English *numbskull* or the slang insult *airhead.*

σοι, οὐ μὴ ἐξέλθῃς ἐκεῖθεν ἕως ἂν ἀποδῷς τὸν
to you, not not will you get out of there until - you pay the
by no means

ἔσχατον κοδράντην!
last quadrans!
penny!

Jesus Condemns Adultery

27 "Ἠκούσατε ὅτι ἐρρέθη,[e] «Οὐ μοιχεύσεις.»[f]
"You heard that it was said, «[3]not [1]You [2]shall commit adultery.»
have heard

28 Ἐγὼ δὲ λέγω ὑμῖν ὅτι πᾶς ὁ βλέπων γυναῖκα
I ~ But say to you that every - *one* looking a woman
everyone who looks at

πρὸς τὸ ἐπιθυμῆσαι αὐτὴν ἤδη ἐμοίχευσεν αὐτὴν ἐν
in order - to lust after her already committed adultery *with* her in
has committed

τῇ καρδίᾳ αὐτοῦ. 29 Εἰ δὲ ὁ ὀφθαλμός σου ὁ δεξιὸς
- heart ~ his. if ~ But - [3]eye [1]your - [2]right

σκανδαλίζει σε, ἔξελε αὐτὸν καὶ βάλε ἀπὸ σοῦ·
[4]causes [6]to [7]stumble [5]you, [8]tear [10]out [9]it and throw *it* from you;

συμφέρει γάρ σοι ἵνα ἀπόληται ἓν τῶν μελῶν
[2]it [3]is [4]advantageous [1]for for you that [5]be [6]lost [1]one - [2]of [4]members
better

σου καὶ μὴ ὅλον τὸ σῶμά σου βληθῇ εἰς Γέενναν. 30 Καὶ εἰ
[3]your and not [2]whole - [3]body [1]your be cast into Gehenna. And if
hell.

ἡ δεξιά σου χεὶρ σκανδαλίζει σε, ἔκκοψον αὐτὴν καὶ
- right ~ your hand causes [2]to [3]stumble [1]you, cut off ~ it and

βάλε ἀπὸ σοῦ· συμφέρει γάρ σοι ἵνα ἀπόληται ἓν
throw *it* from you; [2]it [3]is [4]advantageous [1]for for you that [5]be [6]lost [1]one
better

τῶν μελῶν σου καὶ μὴ ὅλον τὸ σῶμά σου βληθῇ εἰς
[2]of [4]members [3]your and not [2]whole - [3]body [1]your be cast into

Γέενναν.[g]
Gehenna.
hell.

Jesus Censures Divorce
(Matt. 19:9; Mark 10:11, 12; Luke 16:18)

31 "Ἐρρέθη δὲ ὅτι Ὃς ἂν ἀπολύσῃ τὴν γυναῖκα
"[2]it [3]was [4]said [1]And - Who ever divorces - wife ~

αὐτοῦ, δότω αὐτῇ ἀποστάσιον.[h] 32 Ἐγὼ δὲ λέγω ὑμῖν
his, let him give her a divorce certificate. I ~ But say to you

ὅτι ὃς ἂν ἀπολύσῃ[i] τὴν γυναῖκα αὐτοῦ, παρεκτὸς λόγου
that who ever divorces - wife ~ his, except for a matter

πορνείας, ποιεῖ αὐτὴν μοιχᾶσθαι, καὶ ὃς ἐὰν
of fornication, makes her to commit adultery, and who ever
sexual immorality, commit

ἀπολελυμένην γαμήσῃ μοιχᾶται.
[2]*a* [3]*woman* [4]having [5]been [6]divorced [1]marries commits adultery.
a divorcee

Jesus Condemns Oaths

33 "Πάλιν ἠκούσατε ὅτι ἐρρέθη τοῖς ἀρχαίοις, «Οὐκ
"Again you heard that it was said to the ancients, «[3]not
have heard

ἐπιορκήσεις, ἀποδώσεις δὲ τῷ Κυρίῳ τοὺς ὅρκους
[1]You [2]shall [4]swear [5]falsely, [7]you [8]shall [9]pay [6]but to the Lord - oaths ~

you will by no means get out of there till you have paid the last penny.
27 "You have heard that it was said to those of old, *'You shall not commit adultery.'*
28 "But I say to you that whoever looks at a woman to lust for her has already committed adultery with her in his heart.
29 "If your right eye causes you to sin, pluck it out and cast *it* from you; for it is more profitable for you that one of your members perish, than for your whole body to be cast into hell.
30 "And if your right hand causes you to sin, cut it off and cast *it* from you; for it is more profitable for you that one of your members perish, than for your whole body to be cast into hell.
31 "Furthermore it has been said, 'Whoever divorces his wife, let him give her a certificate of divorce.'
32 "But I say to you that whoever divorces his wife for any reason except sexual immorality causes her to commit adultery; and whoever marries a woman who is divorced commits adultery.
33 "Again you have heard that it was said to those of old, 'You shall not swear falsely, but shall perform your oaths to the Lord.'

---

e(**5:27**) TR adds *αρχαιοις, to the ancients.*
f(**5:27**) Ex. 20:14; Deut. 5:18
g(**5:30**) For *βληθη εις Γεενναν, be cast into hell,* NU reads *εις Γεενναν απελθη, go to hell.*
h(**5:31**) Deut. 24:1
i(**5:32**) For *ος αν απολυση, whoever divorces,* NU reads *πας ο απολυων, everyone divorcing.*

34 "But I say to you, do not swear at all: neither by heaven, for it is God's throne;
35 "nor by the earth, for it is His footstool; nor by Jerusalem, for it is the city of the great King.
36 "Nor shall you swear by your head, because you cannot make one hair white or black.
37 "But let your 'Yes' be 'Yes,' and your 'No,' 'No.' For whatever is more than these is from the evil one.
38 "You have heard that it was said, *'An eye for an eye and a tooth for a tooth.'*
39 "But I tell you not to resist an evil person. But whoever slaps you on your right cheek, turn the other to him also.
40 "If anyone wants to sue you and take away your tunic, let him have *your* cloak also.
41 "And whoever compels you to go one mile, go with him two.
42 "Give to him who asks you, and from him who wants to borrow from you do not turn away.
43 "You have heard that it was said, *'You shall love your neighbor* and hate your enemy.'
44 "But I say to you, love your enemies, bless those who curse you, do good to those who hate you, and pray for

---

[j](**5:33**) Lev. 19:12; Num. 30:2; Deut. 23:21
[k](**5:38**) Ex. 21:24; Lev. 24:20; Deut. 19:21
[l](**5:39**) NU reads ραπιζει, *slaps.* [m](**5:43**) Lev. 19:18
[n](**5:44**) NU omits ευλογειτε . . . μισουσιν υμας, *bless . . . hating you.*

***(5:40)** *ἱμάτιον (himation).* Noun, meaning *garment, cloak, mantle,* used often in the NT. The singular form used here (cf. Luke 6:29) usually means the outer cloak or mantle, with openings for the arms, that was thrown over the *χιτών, tunic,* and easily laid aside for some activities (as John 13:4, 12; Acts 7:58; cf. Mark 11:7, 8). In the plural *ἱμάτιον* can refer more generally to any garment. Cf. the cognate verb *ἱματίζω, clothe* (Mark 5:15), and noun *ἱματισμός, clothing, apparel* (Luke 7:25).

σου.»[j] **34** Ἐγὼ δὲ λέγω ὑμῖν μὴ ὀμόσαι ὅλως· μήτε ἐν τῷ
your.» I ˜ But say to you not to swear at all: neither by -

οὐρανῷ, ὅτι θρόνος ἐστὶ τοῦ Θεοῦ· **35** μήτε ἐν τῇ γῇ,
heaven, because [3]*the* [4]throne [1]it [2]is - of God; nor by the earth,

ὅτι ὑποπόδιόν ἐστι τῶν ποδῶν αὐτοῦ· μήτε εἰς
because [3]*the* [4]footstool [1]it [2]is - of feet ˜ His; nor by
for

Ἱεροσόλυμα, ὅτι πόλις ἐστὶ τοῦ μεγάλου βασιλέως·
Jerusalem, because [3]*the* [4]city [1]it [2]is of the great King;

36 μήτε ἐν τῇ κεφαλῇ σου ὀμόσῃς, ὅτι οὐ
nor [4]by - [6]head [5]your [1]shall [2]you [3]swear, because [3]not

δύνασαι μίαν τρίχα λευκὴν ἢ μέλαιναν ποιῆσαι.
[1]you [2]are [4]able [7]one [8]hair [9]white [10]or [11]black [5]to [6]make.

37 Ἔστω δὲ ὁ λόγος ὑμῶν ναὶ ναί, οὒ οὔ· τὸ δὲ περισσὸν
[2]let [5]be [1]But - [4]word [3]your yes yes, no no; - but more *than*

τούτων ἐκ τοῦ πονηροῦ ἐστιν.
these [2]from [3]the [4]evil [5]*one* [1]is.

Going the Second Mile
(Luke 6:29, 30)

38 "Ἠκούσατε ὅτι ἐρρέθη, «Ὀφθαλμὸν ἀντὶ
"You heard that it was said, «An eye in place of
have heard for

ὀφθαλμοῦ» καὶ «ὀδόντα ἀντὶ ὀδόντος.»[k] **39** Ἐγὼ δὲ λέγω
an eye» and «a tooth in place of a tooth.» I ˜ But say
for

ὑμῖν μὴ ἀντιστῆναι τῷ πονηρῷ. Ἀλλ' ὅστις σε ῥαπίσει[l]
to you not to withstand - evil. But whoever [3]you [1]shall [2]slap

ἐπὶ τὴν δεξιάν σου σιαγόνα, στρέψον αὐτῷ καὶ τὴν ἄλλην.
on - right ˜ your cheek, turn to him also the other.

40 Καὶ τῷ θέλοντί σοι κριθῆναι καὶ τὸν
And to the *one* desiring [5]on [6]you [1]to [2]have [3]a [4]judgment and -
to sue you

χιτῶνά σου λαβεῖν, ἄφες αὐτῷ καὶ τὸ ἱμάτιον.* **41** Καὶ
[4]tunic [3]your [1]to [2]take, [5]let [8]have [6]him [7]also the cloak. And
your

ὅστις σε ἀγγαρεύσει μίλιον ἕν, ὕπαγε μετ' αὐτοῦ δύο.
whoever [3]you [1]shall [2]compel *to go* mile ˜ one, go with him two.

42 Τῷ αἰτοῦντί σε δίδου, καὶ τὸν θέλοντα ἀπὸ σοῦ
[2]to [3]the [4]*one* [5]asking [6]you [1]Give, and the *one* desiring [3]from [4]you

δανείσασθαι μὴ ἀποστραφῇς.
[1]to [2]borrow not ˜ do turn away.

Love Your Enemies
(Luke 6:27, 28, 32–36)

43 "Ἠκούσατε ὅτι ἐρρέθη, «Ἀγαπήσεις τὸν πλησίον
"You heard that it was said, «You shall love - neighbor ˜
have heard

σου»[m] καὶ μισήσεις τὸν ἐχθρόν σου. **44** Ἐγὼ δὲ λέγω
your» and you shall hate - enemy ˜ your. I ˜ But say

ὑμῖν, ἀγαπᾶτε τοὺς ἐχθροὺς ὑμῶν, εὐλογεῖτε τοὺς
to you, love - enemies ˜ your, bless the *ones*
those

καταρωμένους ὑμᾶς, καλῶς ποιεῖτε τοῖς μισοῦσιν ὑμᾶς,[n]
cursing you, well ˜ do to the *ones* hating you,
who curse those who hate

καὶ προσεύχεσθε ὑπὲρ τῶν ἐπηρεαζόντων ὑμᾶς καὶ[o]
and pray for the *ones* mistreating you and
those who mistreat

διωκόντων ὑμᾶς, **45** ὅπως γένησθε υἱοὶ τοῦ Πατρὸς
persecuting you, so that you may become sons - of Father ˜
persecute prove to be

ὑμῶν τοῦ ἐν τοῖς οὐρανοῖς, ὅτι τὸν ἥλιον αὐτοῦ
your - in the heavens, because - [4]sun [3]His

ἀνατέλλει ἐπὶ πονηροὺς καὶ ἀγαθούς, καὶ βρέχει
[1]He [2]makes [5]to [6]rise on evil *people* and good *people,* and He makes it rain

ἐπὶ δικαίους καὶ ἀδίκους. **46** Ἐὰν γὰρ ἀγαπήσητε
on righteous *people* and unrighteous *people.* if ˜ For you love

τοὺς ἀγαπῶντας ὑμᾶς, τίνα μισθὸν ἔχετε? Οὐχὶ καὶ οἱ
the *ones* loving you, what reward have you? [2]not [3]even -
those who love

τελῶναι τὸ αὐτὸ ποιοῦσι? **47** Καὶ ἐὰν ἀσπάσησθε τοὺς
[4]tax [5]collectors [7]the [8]same [1]Do [6]do? And if you greet -

φίλους[p] ὑμῶν μόνον, τί περισσὸν ποιεῖτε? Οὐχὶ
friends ˜ your only, what more are you doing *than others?* [2]not

καὶ οἱ τελῶναι[q] οὕτω ποιοῦσιν? **48** Ἔσεσθε οὖν ὑμεῖς
[3]even - [4]tax [5]collectors [7]so [1]Do [6]do? [3]be [2]therefore [1]You

τέλειοι ὥσπερ ὁ Πατὴρ ὑμῶν ὁ ἐν τοῖς οὐρανοῖς[r] τέλειός
perfect just as - Father ˜ your - in the heavens perfect ˜
complete complete

ἐστι.
is.

Give with Sincerity

6 **1** "Προσέχετε τὴν ἐλεημοσύνην[a] ὑμῶν μὴ ποιεῖν
"Take care - [6]charitable [7]giving [5]your [1]not [2]to [3]be [4]doing

ἔμπροσθεν τῶν ἀνθρώπων πρὸς τὸ θεαθῆναι αὐτοῖς. Εἰ
before - men so as - to be seen by them. if ˜
Otherwise,

δὲ μή γε, μισθὸν οὐκ ἔχετε παρὰ τῷ Πατρὶ ὑμῶν τῷ
But not indeed, [4]a [5]reward [3]not [1]you [2]have from - Father ˜ your -

ἐν τοῖς οὐρανοῖς. **2** Ὅταν οὖν ποιῇς ἐλεημοσύνην, μὴ
in the heavens. Whenever therefore you do charitable giving, not ˜

σαλπίσῃς ἔμπροσθέν σου, ὥσπερ οἱ ὑποκριταὶ ποιοῦσιν
do sound a trumpet before you, just like the hypocrites do

ἐν ταῖς συναγωγαῖς καὶ ἐν ταῖς ῥύμαις, ὅπως δοξασθῶσιν
in the synagogues and in the streets, so that they may be glorified
praised

ὑπὸ τῶν ἀνθρώπων. Ἀμὴν λέγω ὑμῖν, ἀπέχουσι τὸν
by - men. Amen I say to you, they receive [3]in [4]full -
Assuredly

μισθὸν αὐτῶν. **3** Σοῦ δὲ ποιοῦντος ἐλεημοσύνην, μὴ
[2]reward [1]their. you ˜ But doing charitable giving, not ˜
But when you do

γνώτω ἡ ἀριστερά σου τί ποιεῖ ἡ δεξιά σου,
do let [4]know - [2]left [3]*hand* [1]your what [4]is [5]doing - [2]right [3]*hand* [1]your,

4 ὅπως ᾖ σου ἡ ἐλεημοσύνη ἐν τῷ κρυπτῷ. Καὶ ὁ
so that [4]may [5]be [1]your - [2]charitable [3]giving in - secret. And -

Πατήρ σου ὁ βλέπων ἐν τῷ κρυπτῷ αὐτὸς ἀποδώσει σοι
Father ˜ your the *One* seeing in - secret Himself ˜ will repay you
who sees

ἐν τῷ φανερῷ.[b]
in the open.
openly.

those who spitefully use you
and persecute you,
45 "that you may be sons of
your Father in heaven; for He
makes His sun rise on the evil
and on the good, and sends rain
on the just and on the unjust.
46 "For if you love those who
love you, what reward have
you? Do not even the tax collectors do the same?
47 "And if you greet your
brethren only, what do you do
more *than others?* Do not even
the tax collectors do so?
48 "Therefore you shall be
perfect, just as your Father in
heaven is perfect.

6 "Take heed that you do
not do your charitable
deeds before men, to be seen
by them. Otherwise you have
no reward from your Father in
heaven.
2 "Therefore, when you do a
charitable deed, do not sound a
trumpet before you as the hypocrites do in the synagogues
and in the streets, that they
may have glory from men. Assuredly, I say to you, they have
their reward.
3 "But when you do a charitable deed, do not let your left
hand know what your right
hand is doing,
4 "that your charitable deed
may be in secret; and your Father who sees in secret will
Himself reward you openly.

---

[o]**(5:44)** NU omits *επηρεαζοντων υμας και, mistreating you and.*
[p]**(5:47)** NU reads *αδελφους, brothers.* [q]**(5:47)** NU reads *εθνικοι, Gentiles* or *heathen.* [r]**(5:48)** NU reads *ουρανιος, heavenly.*
[a]**(6:1)** NU reads *δικαιοσυνην, righteousness.*
[b]**(6:4)** NU omits *εν τω φανερω, openly.*

5 "And when you pray, you
shall not be like the hypocrites.
For they love to pray standing
in the synagogues and on the
corners of the streets, that
they may be seen by men. Assuredly, I say to you, they have
their reward.
6 "But you, when you pray,
go into your room, and when
you have shut your door, pray
to your Father who *is* in the secret *place;* and your Father who
sees in secret will reward you
openly.
7 "And when you pray, do
not use vain repetitions as the
heathen *do.* For they think that
they will be heard for their
many words.
8 "Therefore do not be like
them. For your Father knows
the things you have need of before you ask Him.
9 "In this manner, therefore,
pray:

Our Father in heaven,
Hallowed be Your name.
10 Your kingdom come.
Your will be done
On earth as *it is* in
heaven.
11 Give us this day our daily
bread.
12 And forgive us our debts,
As we forgive our
debtors.
13 And do not lead us into
temptation,
But deliver us from the
evil one.

[c](6:6) NU omits *εν τω φανερω, openly.*
[d](6:12) NU reads *αφηκαμεν, we have forgiven.*

***(6:13)** *πονηρός (ponēros).* Adjective, meaning *evil, wicked, bad,* occasionally referring to a physical condition (Matt. 7:17; Luke 11:34), but most often to moral or ethical evil. Its synonym *κακός, bad, evil,* is often described as broader and more likely to emphasize character, while *πονηρός* is stronger and more likely to emphasize effect, but the two are frequently indistinguishable. *πονηρός* certainly implies malignity. It is often used substantivally, as here where "the evil" may be neuter ("the evil thing," cf. Rom. 12:9) but is more likely masculine ("the evil one," that

Pray with Sincerity

5 "Καὶ ὅταν προσεύχῃ, οὐκ ἔσῃ ὥσπερ οἱ ὑποκριταί,
"And whenever you pray, not ˜ do be just like the hypocrites,

ὅτι φιλοῦσιν ἐν ταῖς συναγωγαῖς καὶ ἐν ταῖς γωνίαις
because they love [4]in [5]the [6]synagogues [7]and [8]in [9]the [10]corners

τῶν πλατειῶν ἑστῶτες προσεύχεσθαι, ὅπως ἂν
[11]of [12]the [13]streets [3]standing [1]to [2]pray, so that -

φανῶσι τοῖς ἀνθρώποις. Ἀμὴν λέγω ὑμῖν ὅτι
they may appear - to men. Amen I say to you that
be seen by Assuredly

ἀπέχουσι τὸν μισθὸν αὐτῶν. 6 Σὺ δέ, ὅταν
they receive [3]in [4]full - [2]reward [1]their. you ˜ But, whenever

προσεύχῃ, εἴσελθε εἰς τὸ ταμιεῖόν σου, καὶ κλείσας τὴν
you pray, enter into - room ˜ your, and having shut -

θύραν σου, πρόσευξαι τῷ Πατρί σου τῷ ἐν τῷ κρυπτῷ.
door ˜ your, pray - to Father ˜ your the *One* in - secret.
who is

Καὶ ὁ Πατήρ σου ὁ βλέπων ἐν τῷ κρυπτῷ ἀποδώσει σοι
And - Father ˜ your the *One* seeing in - secret will repay you
who sees

ἐν τῷ φανερῷ.[c] 7 Προσευχόμενοι δὲ μὴ βαττολογήσητε
in the open. praying ˜ But not ˜ do babble
openly. But when you pray

ὥσπερ οἱ ἐθνικοί, δοκοῦσι γὰρ ὅτι ἐν τῇ πολυλογίᾳ αὐτῶν
just like the heathen, [2]they [3]think [1]for that by - [2]many [3]words [1]their

εἰσακουσθήσονται. 8 Μὴ οὖν ὁμοιωθῆτε αὐτοῖς, οἶδε
they will be heard. [3]not [1]Therefore [2]do [4]be like them, [4]knows

γὰρ ὁ Πατὴρ ὑμῶν ὧν χρείαν ἔχετε πρὸ τοῦ ὑμᾶς
[1]for - [3]Father ˜ [2]your what *things* [3]need [4]of [1]you [2]have before - you

αἰτῆσαι αὐτόν.
to ask Him.
ask

Jesus Teaches the Model Prayer
(Luke 11:2–4)

9 "Οὕτως οὖν προσεύχεσθε ὑμεῖς·
"[4]like [5]this [2]therefore [3]pray [1]You:

Πάτερ ἡμῶν ὁ ἐν τοῖς οὐρανοῖς,
Father ˜ Our - in the heavens,

Ἁγιασθήτω τὸ ὄνομά σου,
Let [3]be [4]hallowed - [2]name [1]Your,

10 Ἐλθέτω ἡ βασιλεία σου,
Let [3]come - [2]kingdom [1]Your,

Γενηθήτω τὸ θέλημά σου,
Let [3]be [4]done - [2]will [1]Your,

Ὡς ἐν οὐρανῷ καὶ ἐπὶ τῆς γῆς.
As in heaven *so* also on the earth.

11 Τὸν ἄρτον ἡμῶν τὸν ἐπιούσιον δὸς ἡμῖν σήμερον.
- [6]bread [4]our - [5]daily [1]Give [2]us [3]today.

12 Καὶ ἄφες ἡμῖν τὰ ὀφειλήματα ἡμῶν,
And forgive us - debts ˜ our,

Ὡς καὶ ἡμεῖς ἀφίεμεν[d] τοῖς ὀφειλέταις ἡμῶν.
As also ˜ we forgive - debtors ˜ our.

13 Καὶ μὴ εἰσενέγκῃς ἡμᾶς εἰς πειρασμόν,
And not ˜ do bring us into temptation,

Ἀλλὰ ῥῦσαι ἡμᾶς ἀπὸ τοῦ πονηροῦ·*
But rescue us from the evil *one;*

Ὅτι σοῦ ἐστιν ἡ βασιλεία καὶ ἡ δύναμις καὶ ἡ
Because of You is the kingdom and the power and the
Yours

δόξα εἰς τοὺς αἰῶνας. Ἀμήν.[e]
glory into the ages. Amen.
forever. So be it.

14 "Ἐὰν γὰρ ἀφῆτε τοῖς ἀνθρώποις τὰ παραπτώματα
"if ˜ For you forgive - men - trespasses ˜

αὐτῶν, ἀφήσει καὶ ὑμῖν ὁ Πατὴρ ὑμῶν ὁ οὐράνιος. 15 Ἐὰν
their, ^{4}will ^{6}forgive ^{5}also ^{7}you - ^{3}Father ^{1}your - ^{2}heavenly. if ˜

δὲ μὴ ἀφῆτε τοῖς ἀνθρώποις τὰ παραπτώματα αὐτῶν,[f]
But ^{3}not ^{1}you ^{2}do forgive - men - trespasses ˜ their,

οὐδὲ ὁ Πατὴρ ὑμῶν ἀφήσει τὰ παραπτώματα ὑμῶν.
neither - ^{3}Father ^{2}your ^{1}will ^{4}forgive - trespasses ˜ your.

For Yours is the kingdom and the power and the glory forever. Amen.

14 "For if you forgive men their trespasses, your heavenly Father will also forgive you.
15 "But if you do not forgive men their trespasses, neither will your Father forgive your trespasses.

Jesus Teaches How to Fast

16 "Ὅταν δὲ νηστεύητε, μὴ γίνεσθε ὥσπερ οἱ
"whenever ˜ But you fast, not ˜ do become ^{2}just ^{3}like ^{4}the

ὑποκριταὶ σκυθρωποί, ἀφανίζουσι γὰρ τὰ πρόσωπα αὐτῶν
^{5}hypocrites ^{1}gloomy, ^{7}they ^{8}disfigure ^{6}for - ^{10}faces ^{9}their

ὅπως φανῶσι τοῖς ἀνθρώποις νηστεύοντες. Ἀμὴν λέγω
so that they may appear to men *to be* fasting. Amen I say
be seen by Assuredly

ὑμῖν ὅτι ἀπέχουσι τὸν μισθὸν αὐτῶν. 17 Σὺ δὲ
to you that they receive ^{3}in ^{4}full - ^{2}reward ^{1}their. you ˜ But
But when

νηστεύων ἄλειψαί σου τὴν κεφαλήν, καὶ τὸ πρόσωπόν σου
fasting anoint your - head, and - ^{3}face ^{2}your
you fast,

νίψαι, 18 ὅπως μὴ φανῇς τοῖς ἀνθρώποις νηστεύων
^{1}wash, so that ^{3}not ^{1}you ^{2}may appear - to men *to be* fasting

ἀλλὰ τῷ Πατρί σου τῷ ἐν τῷ κρυπτῷ. Καὶ ὁ Πατήρ σου
but - to Father ˜ your - in - secret. And - Father ˜ your

ὁ βλέπων ἐν τῷ κρυπτρῷ ἀποδώσει σοι.[g]
the *One* seeing in - secret will repay you.
who sees

16 "Moreover, when you fast, do not be like the hypocrites, with a sad countenance. For they disfigure their faces that they may appear to men to be fasting. Assuredly, I say to you, they have their reward.
17 "But you, when you fast, anoint your head and wash your face,
18 "so that you do not appear to men to be fasting, but to your Father who *is* in the secret *place;* and your Father who sees in secret will reward you openly.

Lay Up Treasures in Heaven
(Luke 12:33, 34)

19 "Μὴ θησαυρίζετε ὑμῖν θησαυροὺς ἐπὶ τῆς γῆς, ὅπου
"not ˜ Do treasure up for you treasures on the earth, where
yourselves

σὴς καὶ βρῶσις ἀφανίζει καὶ ὅπου κλέπται διορύσσουσι καὶ
moth and rust ruin and where thieves dig through and
break in

κλέπτουσι· 20 θησαυρίζετε δὲ ὑμῖν θησαυροὺς ἐν οὐρανῷ,
steal; ^{2}treasure ^{3}up ^{1}but for you treasures in heaven,
yourselves

ὅπου οὔτε σὴς οὔτε βρῶσις ἀφανίζει καὶ ὅπου κλέπται οὐ
where neither moth nor rust ruins and where thieves not ˜

διορύσσουσιν οὐδὲ κλέπτουσιν· 21 ὅπου γάρ ἐστιν ὁ
do dig through nor steal; where ˜ For ^{3}is -
break in

θησαυρὸς ὑμῶν, ἐκεῖ ἔσται καὶ ἡ καρδία ὑμῶν.
^{2}treasure ^{1}your, there ^{3}will ^{4}be ^{5}also - ^{2}heart ^{1}your.

19 "Do not lay up for yourselves treasures on earth, where moth and rust destroy and where thieves break in and steal;
20 "but lay up for yourselves treasures in heaven, where neither moth nor rust destroys and where thieves do not break in and steal.
21 "For where your treasure is, there your heart will be also.

---

e(6:13) NU omits Οτι . . . Αμην, *Because . . . Amen.* f(6:15) NU omits τα παραπτωματα αυτων, *their trespasses.* g(6:18) TR adds εν τω φανερω, *openly.*

is, Satan). The same applies to Matt. 13:19 (cf. Mark 4:15); Eph. 6:12; John 17:15. Cf. the cognate noun πονηρία, *wickedness, maliciousness* (Matt. 22:18; Rom. 1:29).

22 "The lamp of the body is the eye. If therefore your eye is good, your whole body will be full of light.
23 "But if your eye is bad, your whole body will be full of darkness. If therefore the light that is in you is darkness, how great *is* that darkness!
24 "No one can serve two masters; for either he will hate the one and love the other, or else he will be loyal to the one and despise the other. You cannot serve God and mammon.
25 "Therefore I say to you, do not worry about your life, what you will eat or what you will drink; nor about your body, what you will put on. Is not life more than food and the body more than clothing?
26 "Look at the birds of the air, for they neither sow nor reap nor gather into barns; yet your heavenly Father feeds them. Are you not of more value than they?
27 "Which of you by worrying can add one cubit to his stature?
28 "So why do you worry about clothing? Consider the lilies of the field, how they grow: they neither toil nor spin;
29 "and yet I say to you that even Solomon in all his glory was not arrayed like one of these.

The Lamp of the Body

22 "Ὁ λύχνος τοῦ σώματός ἐστιν ὁ ὀφθαλμός. Ἐὰν
"The lamp of the body is the eye. If
οὖν ὁ ὀφθαλμός σου ἁπλοῦς ᾖ, ὅλον τὸ σῶμά σου
therefore - eye ˜ your single ˜ is, [2]whole - [3]body [1]your
sound
φωτεινὸν ἔσται. **23** Ἐὰν δὲ ὁ ὀφθαλμός σου πονηρὸς ᾖ,
[6]shining [4]will [5]be. if ˜ But - eye ˜ your evil ˜ is,
full of light
ὅλον τὸ σῶμά σου σκοτεινὸν ἔσται. Εἰ οὖν τὸ φῶς τὸ ἐν
[2]whole - [3]body [1]your [6]dark [4]will [5]be. If therefore the light - in
σοὶ σκότος ἐστί, τὸ σκότος πόσον!
you darkness ˜ is, [3]the [4]darkness [1]how [2]great!

You Cannot Serve God and Mammon
(Luke 16:13)

24 "Οὐδεὶς δύναται δυσὶ κυρίοις δουλεύειν· ἢ γὰρ τὸν
"No one is able [3]two [4]masters [1]to [2]serve; either ˜ for the
ἕνα μισήσει καὶ τὸν ἕτερον ἀγαπήσει, ἢ ἑνὸς
one he will hate and the other he will love, or [6]one
ἀνθέξεται καὶ τοῦ ἑτέρου καταφρονήσει. Οὐ
[1]he [2]will [3]be [4]devoted [5]to and the other he will despise. [3]not
δύνασθε Θεῷ δουλεύειν καὶ μαμωνᾷ.
[1]You [2]are [4]able [7]God [5]to [6]serve and mammon.
money.

Do Not Worry
(Luke 12:22–34)

25 "Διὰ τοῦτο λέγω ὑμῖν, μὴ μεριμνᾶτε τῇ ψυχῇ
"Because of this I say to you, not ˜ do worry *about* - life ˜
"Therefore
ὑμῶν, τί φάγητε καὶ τί πίητε, μηδὲ τῷ σώματι
your, what you shall eat and what you shall drink, nor *about* - body ˜
ὑμῶν, τί ἐνδύσησθε. Οὐχὶ ἡ ψυχὴ πλεῖόν ἐστι τῆς
your, what you shall put on. [2]not - [3]life [4]more [5]*than* [1]Is -
τροφῆς καὶ τὸ σῶμα τοῦ ἐνδύματος? **26** Ἐμβλέψατε εἰς
food and the body *more than* - clothing? Look at
τὰ πετεινὰ τοῦ οὐρανοῦ, ὅτι οὐ σπείρουσιν οὐδὲ θερίζουσιν
the birds of the heaven, that [3]not [1]they [2]do sow nor do they reap
sky,
οὐδὲ συνάγουσιν εἰς ἀποθήκας, καὶ ὁ Πατὴρ ὑμῶν ὁ οὐράνιος
nor do they gather into barns, yet - [3]Father [1]your - [2]heavenly
τρέφει αὐτά. Οὐχ ὑμεῖς μᾶλλον διαφέρετε αὐτῶν? **27** Τίς
feeds them. [3]not [2]you [5]more [1]Do [4]differ from them? which ˜
Are you not worth more than they?
δὲ ἐξ ὑμῶν μεριμνῶν δύναται προσθεῖναι ἐπὶ τὴν ἡλικίαν
But of you *by* worrying is able to add on - stature ˜
αὐτοῦ πῆχυν ἕνα? **28** Καὶ περὶ ἐνδύματος τί μεριμνᾶτε?
his cubit ˜ one? And [5]about [6]clothes [1]why [2]do [3]you [4]worry?
Καταμάθετε τὰ κρίνα τοῦ ἀγροῦ, πῶς αὐξάνει· οὐ
Notice the lilies of the field, how they grow; [3]not
κοπιᾷ οὐδὲ νήθει. **29** Λέγω δὲ ὑμῖν ὅτι οὐδὲ
[1]they [2]do labor nor do they spin. [2]I [3]say [1]Yet to you that not even
Σολομὼν ἐν πάσῃ τῇ δόξῃ αὐτοῦ περιεβάλετο ὡς ἓν τούτων.
Solomon in all - glory ˜ his was clothed like one of these.
splendor arrayed

30 Εἰ δὲ τὸν χόρτον τοῦ ἀγροῦ, σήμερον ὄντα καὶ
if ˜ But [4]the [5]grass [6]of [7]the [8]field, [10]today [9]being [11]and
which exists

αὔριον εἰς κλίβανον βαλλόμενον, ὁ Θεὸς οὕτως
[12]tomorrow [15]into [16]*the* [17]oven [13]being [14]thrown - [1]God [2]thus
is

ἀμφιέννυσιν, οὐ πολλῷ μᾶλλον ὑμᾶς, ὀλιγόπιστοι?
[3]clothes, *will He* not much more *clothe* you, *O you* of little faith?

31 Μὴ οὖν μεριμνήσητε λέγοντες, 'Τί φάγωμεν?' ἤ
[3]not [1]Therefore [2]do [4]worry saying, 'What shall we eat?' or

'Τί πίωμεν?' ἤ 'Τί περιβαλώμεθα?' **32** Πάντα γὰρ
'What shall we drink?' or 'What shall we put on?' all ˜ For

ταῦτα τὰ ἔθνη ἐπιζητεῖ. Οἶδε γὰρ ὁ Πατὴρ ὑμῶν ὁ
these *things* the Gentiles seek. [5]knows [1]For - [4]Father [2]your -

οὐράνιος ὅτι χρῄζετε τούτων ἁπάντων. **33** Ζητεῖτε δὲ
[3]heavenly that you need [2]these [3]*things* [1]all. seek ˜ But

πρῶτον τὴν βασιλείαν τοῦ Θεοῦ καὶ τὴν δικαιοσύνην αὐτοῦ,
first the kingdom - of God and - righteousness ˜ His,

καὶ ταῦτα πάντα προστεθήσεται ὑμῖν. **34** Μὴ οὖν
and [2]these [3]*things* [1]all will be added to you. [3]not [1]Therefore

μεριμνήσητε εἰς τὴν αὔριον, ἡ γὰρ αὔριον μεριμνήσει
[2]do [4]worry for - tomorrow, - for tomorrow will worry
about

τὰ[h] ἑαυτῆς. Ἀρκετὸν τῇ ἡμέρᾳ ἡ κακία
for the *things* of itself. Sufficient for the day - *is* badness ˜
about its own affairs. Each day has enough trouble of its

αὐτῆς.
its.
own.

Do Not Judge
(Luke 6:37, 38, 41, 42)

7 **1** "Μὴ κρίνετε,* ἵνα μὴ κριθῆτε. **2** Ἐν ᾧ
"not ˜ Do judge, in order that not ˜ you be judged. [2]with [3]what
lest

γὰρ κρίματι κρίνετε, κριθήσεσθε, καὶ ἐν ᾧ μέτρῳ
[1]For judgment you judge, you will be judged, and with what measure

μετρεῖτε,[a] μετρηθήσεται ὑμῖν. **3** Τί δὲ βλέπεις τὸ
you measure, it will be measured to you. why ˜ But do you see the
look at

κάρφος τὸ ἐν τῷ ὀφθαλμῷ τοῦ ἀδελφοῦ σου, τὴν δὲ ἐν τῷ
speck the *one* in the eye - of brother ˜ your, the ˜ but [2]in -
which is

σῷ ὀφθαλμῷ δοκὸν οὐ κατανοεῖς? **4** Ἢ πῶς ἐρεῖς
[3]your [4]eye [1]plank [7]not [5]you [6]do [8]consider? Or how will you say
notice?

τῷ ἀδελφῷ σου, 'Ἄφες ἐκβάλω τὸ κάρφος ἀπὸ τοῦ
- to brother ˜ your, 'Permit *that* I should cast out the speck from -
'Permit me to remove

ὀφθαλμοῦ σου,' καὶ ἰδού, ἡ δοκὸς ἐν τῷ ὀφθαλμῷ σοῦ?
eye ˜ your,' and look, *there is* the plank in - eye ˜ your?
a

5 Ὑποκριτά! Ἔκβαλε πρῶτον τὴν δοκὸν ἐκ τοῦ ὀφθαλμοῦ
Hypocrite! Cast out first the plank out of - eye ˜
Remove

σου, καὶ τότε διαβλέψεις ἐκβαλεῖν τὸ κάρφος ἐκ τοῦ
your, and then you will see clearly to cast out the speck out of the
remove

30 "Now if God so clothes the grass of the field, which today is, and tomorrow is thrown into the oven, *will He* not much more *clothe* you, O you of little faith?
31 "Therefore do not worry, saying, 'What shall we eat?' or 'What shall we drink?' or 'What shall we wear?'
32 "For after all these things the Gentiles seek. For your heavenly Father knows that you need all these things.
33 "But seek first the kingdom of God and His righteousness, and all these things shall be added to you.
34 "Therefore do not worry about tomorrow, for tomorrow will worry about its own things. Sufficient for the day *is* its own trouble.

7 "Judge not, that you be not judged.
2 "For with what judgment you judge, you will be judged; and with the measure you use, it will be measured back to you.
3 "And why do you look at the speck in your brother's eye, but do not consider the plank in your own eye?
4 "Or how can you say to your brother, 'Let me remove the speck from your eye'; and look, a plank *is* in your own eye?
5 "Hypocrite! First remove the plank from your own eye, and then you will see clearly to remove the speck from your

---

[h](6:34) NU omits *τα, the (things)*. [a](7:2) TR reads *αντιμετρηθησεται, it will be measured back.*

---

*(7:1) *κρίνω (krinō)*. Verb, a general legal term meaning *to judge*. It can refer to being brought before a court (Acts 26:6), to rendering legal decisions (John 18:31), and to condemning and punishing defendants on the basis of such decisions (John 7:51; cf. the related verb *κατακρίνω* and its cognates). Frequently in the NT it is used in each of these ways to describe God's actions in "judging" humanity, particularly on the "Day of Judgment" at the end of time (see *κρίσις* at John 3:19). The verb is also used outside formal legal contexts to describe judgments people customarily pass on others, particularly in a negative sense (as here in Matt. 7:1f).

brother's eye.
6 "Do not give what is holy
to the dogs; nor cast your
pearls before swine, lest they
trample them under their feet,
and turn and tear you in pieces.
7 "Ask, and it will be given to
you; seek, and you will find;
knock, and it will be opened to
you.
8 "For everyone who asks
receives, and he who seeks
finds, and to him who knocks it
will be opened.
9 "Or what man is there
among you who, if his son asks
for bread, will give him a stone?
10 "Or if he asks for a fish,
will he give him a serpent?
11 "If you then, being evil,
know how to give good gifts to
your children, how much more
will your Father who is in
heaven give good things to
those who ask Him!
12 "Therefore, whatever you
want men to do to you, do also
to them, for this is the Law and
the Prophets.
13 "Enter by the narrow gate;
for wide *is* the gate and broad *is*
the way that leads to destruction,
and there are many who
go in by it.

κρίνω also designates several mental processes including *to evaluate* (1 Cor. 10:15), *decide* (1 Cor. 2:2; cf. ἐπικρίνω), *prefer* (Rom. 14:5; cf. διακρίνω), or *hold an opinion* (Acts 15:19).

***(7:13)** ἀπώλεια *(apōleia).* Noun that can mean *waste* (Matt. 26:8), but in the NT is nearly always personal, meaning *destruction, ruin, perdition.* Once (Acts 25:16, NU omits) it means physical death, but elsewhere spiritual death, eternal destruction. Derived from ἀπόλλυμι, *perish, be ruined, be destroyed, be lost,* the noun ἀπώλεια appears to focus on utter loss or ruin as a "final destiny" for the wicked (as here in Matt. 7:13; also Rev. 17:8). A "son of perdition" (John 17:12; 2 Thess. 2:3) is one so destined. ἀπώλεια differs little from the synonym ὄλεθρος, *destruction, death, ruin,* and occurs with it in 1 Tim. 6:9.

ὀφθαλμοῦ τοῦ ἀδελφοῦ σου.
eye - of brother ~ your.

6 "Μὴ δῶτε τὸ ἅγιον τοῖς κυσί, μηδὲ βάλητε τοὺς
"not ~ Do give the holy *thing* - to dogs, nor cast -
what is holy

μαργαρίτας ὑμῶν ἔμπροσθεν τῶν χοίρων, μήποτε
pearls ~ your before - pigs, lest

καταπατήσωσιν αὐτοὺς ἐν τοῖς ποσὶν αὐτῶν καὶ
they trample them with - feet ~ their and

στραφέντες ῥήξωσιν ὑμᾶς.
turning they [1]tear [3]to [4]pieces [2]you.
when they turn around

Keep Asking, Seeking, Knocking
(Luke 11:9–13)

7 "Αἰτεῖτε, καὶ δοθήσεται ὑμῖν· ζητεῖτε, καὶ
"Ask, and it will be given to you; seek, and
"Keep asking, keep seeking,

εὑρήσετε· κρούετε, καὶ ἀνοιγήσεται ὑμῖν. **8** Πᾶς γὰρ
you will find; knock, and it will be opened to you. every ~ For
keep knocking, everyone

ὁ αἰτῶν λαμβάνει καὶ ὁ ζητῶν εὑρίσκει καὶ τῷ
- *one* asking receives and the *one* seeking finds and to the *one*
who asks he who seeks him who

κρούοντι ἀνοιγήσεται. **9** Ἢ τίς ἐστιν ἐξ ὑμῶν ἄνθρωπος,
knocking it will be opened. Or what [2]is [3]*there* [4]of [5]you [1]man,
knocks

ὃν ἐὰν αἰτήσῃ ὁ υἱὸς αὐτοῦ ἄρτον, μὴ λίθον
whom if [3]should [4]ask [5]for - [2]son [1]his bread, [3]not [5]a [6]stone

ἐπιδώσει αὐτῷ? **10** Καὶ ἐὰν ἰχθὺν αἰτήσῃ,
[1]he [2]will [4]give to him, *will he?* And if [5]a [6]fish [1]he [2]should [3]ask [4]for,

μὴ ὄφιν ἐπιδώσει αὐτῷ? **11** Εἰ οὖν ὑμεῖς,
[9]not [11]a [12]snake [7]he [8]will [10]give to him, *will he?* If then ~ you,

πονηροὶ ὄντες, οἴδατε δόματα ἀγαθὰ διδόναι τοῖς τέκνοις
evil ~ being, know *how* [4]gifts [3]good [1]to [2]give - to children ~

ὑμῶν, πόσῳ μᾶλλον ὁ Πατὴρ ὑμῶν ὁ ἐν τοῖς
your, by how much more - Father ~ your the *One* in the
who is

οὐρανοῖς δώσει ἀγαθὰ τοῖς αἰτοῦσιν αὐτόν? **12** Πάντα
heavens will give good *things* to the *ones* asking Him? All *things*
those who ask

οὖν ὅσα ἂν θέλητε ἵνα ποιῶσιν ὑμῖν οἱ
therefore as many soever as you may want that [2]should [3]do [4]to [5]you -

ἄνθρωποι, οὕτω καὶ ὑμεῖς ποιεῖτε αὐτοῖς· οὗτος γάρ ἐστιν ὁ
[1]men, thus also you do to them; this ~ for is the

Νόμος καὶ οἱ Προφῆται.
Law and the Prophets.

The Narrow Way
(Luke 13:24)

13 "Εἰσέλθετε διὰ τῆς στενῆς πύλης· ὅτι πλατεῖα ἡ
"Enter in through the narrow gate; because wide *is* the

πύλη καὶ εὐρύχωρος ἡ ὁδὸς ἡ ἀπάγουσα εἰς τὴν
gate and spacious *is* the way the *one* leading away to -
which leads

ἀπώλειαν,* καὶ πολλοί εἰσιν οἱ εἰσερχόμενοι δι'
perdition, and many are the *ones* entering in through
those who enter

αὐτῆς. 14 Τί[b] στενὴ ἡ πύλη καὶ τεθλιμμένη ἡ ὁδὸς ἡ
it. How narrow the gate and confined the way the *one*
which

ἀπάγουσα εἰς τὴν ζωήν, καὶ ὀλίγοι εἰσὶν οἱ εὑρίσκοντες
leading away to - life, and few are the *ones* finding
leads those who find

αὐτήν!
it!

By Their Fruits You Shall Know Them
(Luke 6:43, 44)

15 "Προσέχετε δὲ ἀπὸ τῶν ψευδοπροφητῶν, οἵτινες
"beware ˜ But from - false prophets, who
of

ἔρχονται πρὸς ὑμᾶς ἐν ἐνδύμασι προβάτων, ἔσωθεν δέ εἰσι
come to you in clothing of sheep, inwardly ˜ but they are

λύκοι ἅρπαγες. 16 Ἀπὸ τῶν καρπῶν αὐτῶν ἐπιγνώσεσθε
wolves ˜ ravenous. From - fruits ˜ their you will know

αὐτούς. Μήτι συλλέγουσιν ἀπὸ ἀκανθῶν σταφυλὴν ἢ
them. [3]not [1]They [2]do [4]gather [8]from [9]thorns [5]a [6]grape [7]cluster or

ἀπὸ τριβόλων σῦκα? 17 Οὕτω πᾶν δένδρον ἀγαθὸν
[2]from [3]thistles [1]figs, *do they?* Thus every tree ˜ good

καρποὺς καλοὺς ποιεῖ, τὸ δὲ σαπρὸν δένδρον καρποὺς
[3]fruits [2]good [1]produces, the ˜ but rotten tree [3]fruits
a bad

πονηροὺς ποιεῖ. 18 Οὐ δύναται δένδρον ἀγαθὸν καρποὺς
[2]evil [1]produces. [5]not [4]is [6]able [1]A [3]tree [2]good [10]fruits

πονηροὺς ποιεῖν, οὐδὲ δένδρον σαπρὸν καρποὺς καλοὺς
[9]evil [7]to [8]produce, nor a tree ˜ rotten [4]fruits [3]good
bad

ποιεῖν. 19 Πᾶν δένδρον μὴ ποιοῦν καρπὸν καλὸν
[1]to [2]produce. Every tree not producing fruit ˜ good

ἐκκόπτεται καὶ εἰς πῦρ βάλλεται. 20 Ἄρα γε ἀπὸ τῶν
is cut down and [2]into [3]*the* [4]fire [1]thrown. Consequently from -

καρπῶν αὐτῶν ἐπιγνώσεσθε αὐτούς.
fruits ˜ their you will know them.

I Never Knew You
(Luke 13:25–27)

21 "Οὐ πᾶς ὁ λέγων μοι, 'Κύριε, Κύριε,'
"Not every - *one* saying to Me, 'Lord, Lord,'
everyone who says

εἰσελεύσεται εἰς τὴν βασιλείαν τῶν οὐρανῶν, ἀλλ' ὁ
will enter into the kingdom of the heavens, but the *one*
he who

ποιῶν τὸ θέλημα τοῦ Πατρός μου τοῦ ἐν οὐρανοῖς.
doing the will - of Father ˜ My the *One* in *the* heavens.
does who is

22 Πολλοὶ ἐροῦσί μοι ἐν ἐκείνῃ τῇ ἡμέρᾳ, 'Κύριε, Κύριε,
Many will say to Me in that - day, 'Lord, Lord,

οὐ τῷ σῷ ὀνόματι προεφητεύσαμεν, καὶ τῷ σῷ ὀνόματι
[3]not - [5]in [6]Your [7]name [1]did [2]we [4]prophesy, and - in Your name

δαιμόνια ἐξεβάλομεν, καὶ τῷ σῷ ὀνόματι δυνάμεις
[4]demons [1]we [2]cast [3]out, and - in Your name [4]mighty [5]works

πολλὰς ἐποιήσαμεν?' 23 Καὶ τότε ὁμολογήσω αὐτοῖς ὅτι
[3]many [1]we [2]did?' And then I will confess to them -

14 "Because narrow *is* the gate and difficult *is* the way which leads to life, and there are few who find it.
15 "Beware of false prophets, who come to you in sheep's clothing, but inwardly they are ravenous wolves.
16 "You will know them by their fruits. Do men gather grapes from thornbushes or figs from thistles?
17 "Even so, every good tree bears good fruit, but a bad tree bears bad fruit.
18 "A good tree cannot bear bad fruit, nor *can* a bad tree bear good fruit.
19 "Every tree that does not bear good fruit is cut down and thrown into the fire.
20 "Therefore by their fruits you will know them.
21 "Not everyone who says to Me, 'Lord, Lord,' shall enter the kingdom of heaven, but he who does the will of My Father in heaven.
22 "Many will say to Me in that day, 'Lord, Lord, have we not prophesied in Your name, cast out demons in Your name, and done many wonders in Your name?'
23 "And then I will declare to

[b](7:14) TR reads Ὅτι, *Because.*

them, 'I never knew you; depart from Me, you who practice
lawlessness!'
24 "Therefore whoever hears
these sayings of Mine, and
does them, I will liken him to a
wise man who built his house
on the rock:
25 "and the rain descended,
the floods came, and the winds
blew and beat on that house;
and it did not fall, for it was
founded on the rock.
26 "But everyone who hears
these sayings of Mine, and
does not do them, will be like a
foolish man who built his house
on the sand:
27 "and the rain descended,
the floods came, and the winds
blew and beat on that house;
and it fell. And great was its
fall."
28 And so it was, when Jesus
had ended these sayings, that
the people were astonished at
His teaching,
29 for He taught them as one
having authority, and not as the
scribes.
8 When He had come down
from the mountain, great
multitudes followed Him.
2 And behold, a leper came
and worshiped Him, saying,
"Lord, if You are willing, You
can make me clean."

'Οὐδέποτε ἔγνων ὑμᾶς! 'Αποχωρεῖτε ἀπ' ἐμοῦ οἱ
'never ~ I knew you! Depart from Me the *ones*
you who

ἐργαζόμενοι τὴν ἀνομίαν.'
working - lawlessness.'
practice

Build on the Rock
(Luke 6:47–49)

24 "Πᾶς οὖν ὅστις ἀκούει μου τοὺς λόγους
"every*one* ~ Therefore who hears [3]of [4]Me - [2]words
Mine

τούτους καὶ ποιεῖ αὐτούς, ὁμοιώσω[c] αὐτὸν ἀνδρὶ φρονίμῳ,
[1]these and does them, I will compare him to a man ~ prudent,

ὅστις ᾠκοδόμησε τὴν οἰκίαν αὐτοῦ ἐπὶ τὴν πέτραν. **25** Καὶ
who built - house ~ his on the *bed*rock. And

κατέβη ἡ βροχὴ καὶ ἦλθον οἱ ποταμοὶ καὶ ἔπνευσαν οἱ
[3]came [4]down [1]the [2]rain and [3]came [1]the [2]streams and [3]blew [1]the
floods

ἄνεμοι καὶ προσέπεσον τῇ οἰκίᾳ ἐκείνῃ, καὶ οὐκ ἔπεσε,
[2]winds and fell against - house ~ that, and [3]not [1]it [2]did [4]fall,

τεθεμελίωτο γὰρ ἐπὶ τὴν πέτραν. **26** Καὶ πᾶς ὁ
[6]it [7]had [8]been [9]founded [5]for on the *bed*rock. And every - *one*
everyone who

ἀκούων μου τοὺς λόγους τούτους καὶ μὴ ποιῶν αὐτοὺς
hearing [3]of [4]Me - [2]words [1]these and not doing them
hears of Mine does not do

ὁμοιωθήσεται ἀνδρὶ μωρῷ, ὅστις ᾠκοδόμησε τὴν οἰκίαν
will be compared to a man ~ foolish, who built - house ~

αὐτοῦ ἐπὶ τὴν ἄμμον. **27** Καὶ κατέβη ἡ βροχὴ καὶ ἦλθον
his on the sand. And [3]came [4]down [1]the [2]rain and [3]came

οἱ ποταμοὶ καὶ ἔπνευσαν οἱ ἄνεμοι καὶ προσέκοψαν τῇ
[1]the [2]streams and [3]blew [1]the [2]winds and beat on -
floods

οἰκίᾳ ἐκείνῃ, καὶ ἔπεσε. Καὶ ἦν ἡ πτῶσις αὐτῆς μεγάλη."
house ~ that, and it fell. And [3]was - [2]fall [1]its [4]great."

28 Καὶ ἐγένετο ὅτε συνετέλεσεν ὁ 'Ιησοῦς τοὺς λόγους
And it happened when finished ~ - Jesus - words ~

τούτους, ἐξεπλήσσοντο οἱ ὄχλοι ἐπὶ τῇ διδαχῇ αὐτοῦ,
these, [3]were [4]astonished [1]the [2]crowds at - teaching ~ His,

29 ἦν γὰρ διδάσκων αὐτοὺς ὡς ἐξουσίαν ἔχων καὶ οὐχ ὡς
[2]He [3]was [1]for teaching them as authority ~ having and not like

οἱ γραμματεῖς.[d]
the scribes.

Jesus Cleanses a Leper
(Mark 1:40–45; Luke 5:12–16)

8 **1** Καταβάντι δὲ αὐτῷ ἀπὸ τοῦ ὄρους, ἠκολούθησαν
coming down And Him from the mountain, [3]followed
And when He had come down

αὐτῷ ὄχλοι πολλοί. **2** Καὶ ἰδού, λεπρὸς ἐλθὼν[a] προσεκύνει
[4]Him [2]crowds [1]large. And behold, a leper coming worshiped

αὐτῷ, λέγων, "Κύριε, ἐὰν θέλῃς, δύνασαί με
Him, saying, "Lord, if You are willing, You are able [3]me

καθαρίσαι."
[1]to [2]cleanse."

[c](**7:24**) NU reads ομοιωθησεται, *he shall be compared,* and omits the following αυτον, *him.* [d](**7:29**) NU adds αυτων, *their.* [a](**8:2**) NU reads προσελθων, *approaching.*

3 Καὶ ἐκτείνας τὴν χεῖρα ἥψατο αὐτοῦ ὁ Ἰησοῦς,[b]
And reaching out the hand [2]touched [3]him - [1]Jesus,
His
λέγων, "Θέλω, καθαρίσθητι." Καὶ εὐθέως ἐκαθαρίσθη
saying, "I am willing, be cleansed." And immediately [3]was [4]cleansed
αὐτοῦ ἡ λέπρα. 4 Καὶ λέγει αὐτῷ ὁ Ἰησοῦς, "Ὅρα μηδενὶ
[1]his - [2]leprosy. And [2]says [3]to [4]him - [1]Jesus, "See *that* [3]no [4]one
said
εἴπῃς, ἀλλ' ὕπαγε, σεαυτὸν δεῖξον τῷ ἱερεῖ, καὶ
[1]you [2]tell, but go, yourself ~ show to the priest, and
προσένεγκε τὸ δῶρον ὃ προσέταξε Μωσῆς, εἰς μαρτύριον*
offer the gift which commanded ~ Moses, for a testimony
as
αὐτοῖς."
to them."

Jesus Heals a Centurion's Servant
(Luke 7:1–10)

5 Εἰσελθόντι δὲ αὐτῷ[c] εἰς Καπερναούμ, προσῆλθεν αὐτῷ
entering And Him into Capernaum, [3]approached [4]Him
Now when He entered
ἑκατόνταρχος παρακαλῶν αὐτὸν 6 καὶ λέγων, "Κύριε, ὁ παῖς
[1]a [2]centurion begging Him and saying, "Lord, - servant ~
μου βέβληται ἐν τῇ οἰκίᾳ παραλυτικός, δεινῶς
my has been laid up in the house a paralytic, [3]terribly
βασανιζόμενος."
[1]being [2]tormented."

7 Καὶ λέγει αὐτῷ ὁ Ἰησοῦς,[d] "Ἐγὼ ἐλθὼν θεραπεύσω
And [2]says [3]to [4]him - [1]Jesus, "I coming will heal
said will come and
αὐτόν."
him."

8 Καὶ ἀποκριθεὶς ὁ ἑκατόνταρχος ἔφη, "Κύριε, οὐκ εἰμὶ
And answering the centurion said, "Lord, [3]not [1]I [2]am
ἱκανὸς ἵνα μου ὑπὸ τὴν στέγην εἰσέλθῃς, ἀλλὰ
worthy that [6]my [5]under - [7]roof [1]You [2]should [3]come [4]in, but
μόνον εἰπὲ λόγῳ,[e] καὶ ἰαθήσεται ὁ παῖς μου. 9 Καὶ
only speak in a word, and [3]will [4]be [5]healed - [2]servant [1]my. also ~
In
γὰρ ἐγὼ ἄνθρωπός εἰμι ὑπὸ ἐξουσίαν, ἔχων ὑπ' ἐμαυτὸν
For I [2]a [3]man [1]am under authority, having [2]under [3]myself
fact me
στρατιώτας. Καὶ λέγω τούτῳ, 'Πορεύθητι,' καὶ πορεύεται·
[1]soldiers. And I say to this *one,* 'Go,' and he goes;
καὶ ἄλλῳ, 'Ἔρχου,' καὶ ἔρχεται· καὶ τῷ δούλῳ μου,
and to another, 'Come,' and he comes; and - to slave ~ my,
'Ποίησον τοῦτο,' καὶ ποιεῖ."
'Do this,' and he does *it.*"

10 Ἀκούσας δὲ ὁ Ἰησοῦς ἐθαύμασε καὶ εἶπε τοῖς
hearing And - Jesus He marveled and said to the *ones*
And when Jesus heard, those who
ἀκολουθοῦσιν, "Ἀμὴν λέγω ὑμῖν, οὐδὲ[f] ἐν τῷ Ἰσραὴλ
following, "Amen I say to you, not even in - Israel
were following, "Assuredly
τοσαύτην πίστιν εὗρον! 11 Λέγω δὲ ὑμῖν ὅτι πολλοὶ
so great faith I found! [2]I [3]say [1]And to you that many
have I found!
ἀπὸ ἀνατολῶν καὶ δυσμῶν ἥξουσι καὶ ἀνακλιθήσονται μετὰ
from east and west will come and recline *to eat* with

3 Then Jesus put out *His* hand and touched him, saying, "I am willing; be cleansed." Immediately his leprosy was cleansed.

4 And Jesus said to him, "See that you tell no one; but go your way, show yourself to the priest, and offer the gift that Moses commanded, as a testimony to them."

5 Now when Jesus had entered Capernaum, a centurion came to Him, pleading with Him,

6 saying, "Lord, my servant is lying at home paralyzed, dreadfully tormented."

7 And Jesus said to him, "I will come and heal him."

8 The centurion answered and said, "Lord, I am not worthy that You should come under my roof. But only speak a word, and my servant will be healed.

9 "For I also am a man under authority, having soldiers under me. And I say to this *one,* 'Go,' and he goes; and to another, 'Come,' and he comes; and to my servant, 'Do this,' and he does *it.*"

10 When Jesus heard *it,* He marveled, and said to those who followed, "Assuredly, I say to you, I have not found such great faith, not even in Israel!

11 "And I say to you that many will come from east and west, and sit down with Abra-

---

[b](**8:3**) NU omits ο Ιησους, *Jesus.* [c](**8:5**) TR reads τω Ιησου, *Jesus.*
[d](**8:7**) NU omits Ιησους, *Jesus.* [e](**8:8**) TR reads λογον, *a word.*
[f](**8:10**) NU reads παρ ουδενι, *with no one (in Israel).*

***(8:4)** *μαρτύριον (martyrion).* Noun meaning *testimony* or *proof.* It does not refer only to spoken testimony, but can be used of an action (or a circumstance) which furnishes corroboration or evidence for something or someone (BGD). The word is not confined to courtroom settings, though it may be so used (Matt. 10:18; Mark 13:9). In a number of texts, however, it refers to God's message as proclaimed by men like the apostles, who are portrayed as giving "testimony" or "witness" to divine truth

ham, Isaac, and Jacob in the kingdom of heaven.
12 "But the sons of the kingdom will be cast out into outer darkness. There will be weeping and gnashing of teeth."
13 Then Jesus said to the centurion, "Go your way; and as you have believed, *so* let it be done for you." And his servant was healed that same hour.
14 Now when Jesus had come into Peter's house, He saw his wife's mother lying sick with a fever.
15 So He touched her hand, and the fever left her. And she arose and served them.
16 When evening had come, they brought to Him many who were demon-possessed. And He cast out the spirits with a word, and healed all who were sick,
17 that it might be fulfilled which was spoken by Isaiah the prophet, saying:

"He Himself took our
infirmities
And bore our sicknesses."

18 And when Jesus saw great multitudes about Him, He gave a command to depart to the other side.
19 Then a certain scribe came

Ἀβραὰμ καὶ Ἰσαὰκ καὶ Ἰακὼβ ἐν τῇ βασιλείᾳ τῶν οὐρανῶν·
Abraham and Isaac and Jacob in the kingdom of the heavens;

12 *οἱ δὲ υἱοὶ τῆς βασιλείας ἐκβληθήσονται εἰς τὸ σκότος*
the ˜ but sons of the kingdom will be thrown into the darkness

τὸ ἐξώτερον. Ἐκεῖ ἔσται ὁ κλαυθμὸς καὶ ὁ βρυγμὸς τῶν
- farthest out. There *there* will be - weeping and - gnashing -

ὀδόντων." **13** *Καὶ εἶπεν ὁ Ἰησοῦς τῷ ἑκατοντάρχῃ, "Ὕπαγε,*
of teeth." And said ˜ - Jesus to the centurion, "Go,

καὶ ὡς ἐπίστευσας γενηθήτω σοι." Καὶ ἰάθη ὁ παῖς
and as you believed let it happen to you." And [3]was [4]healed - [2]servant

αὐτοῦ ἐν τῇ ὥρᾳ ἐκείνῃ.
[1]his in - hour ˜ that.

Jesus Heals Peter's Mother-in-Law
(Mark 1:29–31; Luke 4:38, 39)

14 *Καὶ ἐλθὼν ὁ Ἰησοῦς εἰς τὴν οἰκίαν Πέτρου εἶδε τὴν*
And coming - Jesus into the house of Peter He saw -
when Jesus came

πενθερὰν αὐτοῦ βεβλημένην καὶ πυρέσσουσαν. **15** *Καὶ*
mother-in-law ˜ his having been laid up and burning with fever. And

ἥψατο τῆς χειρὸς αὐτῆς, καὶ ἀφῆκεν αὐτὴν ὁ πυρετός· καὶ
He touched - hand ˜ her, and [3]left [4]her [1]the [2]fever; and

ἠγέρθη καὶ διηκόνει αὐτῷ.[g]
she got up and was serving Him.
began to serve

Jesus Heals Many People
(Mark 1:32–34; Luke 4:40, 41)

16 *Ὀψίας δὲ γενομένης, προσήνεγκαν αὐτῷ*
evening ˜ And becoming, they brought to Him
And when evening came,

δαιμονιζομένους πολλούς. Καὶ ἐξέβαλε τὰ πνεύματα
[2]being [3]demon-possessed [1]many. And He cast out the spirits

λόγῳ, καὶ πάντας τοὺς κακῶς ἔχοντας ἐθεράπευσεν,
with a word, and all the *ones* badly having *it* He healed,
who were ill

17 *ὅπως πληρωθῇ τὸ ῥηθὲν διὰ Ἡσαΐου τοῦ*
so that [8]was [9]fulfilled [1]the [2]*thing* [3]spoken [4]through [5]Isaiah [6]the
that which was

προφήτου, λέγοντος,
[7]prophet, saying,

«*Αὐτὸς τὰς ἀσθενείας ἡμῶν ἔλαβε*
«[2]Himself - [5]infirmities [4]our [1]He [3]took

Καὶ τὰς νόσους ἐβάστασεν.»[h]
And [2]the [3]diseases [1]bore.»
our

The Cost of Discipleship
(Luke 9:57–62)

18 *Ἰδὼν δὲ ὁ Ἰησοῦς πολλοὺς ὄχλους*[i] *περὶ αὐτὸν*
seeing And - Jesus large crowds around Him
And when Jesus saw

ἐκέλευσεν ἀπελθεῖν εἰς τὸ πέραν. **19** *Καὶ προσελθὼν εἷς*
He commanded to go off to the other side. And approaching one
gave orders a certain scribe

---

[g]**(8:15)** TR reads *αυτοις, them.* [h]**(8:17)** Is. 53:4 [i]**(8:18)** NU omits *πολλους, large* (many), and reads *οχλον, a crowd.*

(Acts 4:33; 1 Cor. 1:6; 2:1). The one NT reference to the OT tabernacle of "witness" (Acts 7:44) reflects a frequent usage of the word in the LXX.

γραμματεὺς εἶπεν αὐτῷ, "Διδάσκαλε, ἀκολουθήσω σοι ὅπου
scribe said to Him, "Teacher, I will follow You where
approached and

ἐὰν ἀπέρχῃ."
ever You may go."

20 Καὶ λέγει αὐτῷ ὁ Ἰησοῦς, "Αἱ ἀλώπεκες φωλεοὺς
And [2]says [3]to [4]him - [1]Jesus, - "Foxes dens ˜
said

ἔχουσι καὶ τὰ πετεινὰ τοῦ οὐρανοῦ κατασκηνώσεις, ὁ δὲ
have and - birds of the heaven *have* nests, the ˜ but

Υἱὸς τοῦ Ἀνθρώπου οὐκ ἔχει ποῦ τὴν κεφαλὴν
Son - of Man not ˜ does have where [4]the [5]head
has nowhere His

κλίνῃ."
[1]He [2]may [3]lay."

21 Ἕτερος δὲ τῶν μαθητῶν αὐτοῦ εἶπεν αὐτῷ, "Κύριε,
another ˜ And - of disciples ˜ His said to Him, "Lord,

ἐπίτρεψόν μοι πρῶτον ἀπελθεῖν καὶ θάψαι τὸν πατέρα μου."
permit me first to go and to bury - father ˜ my."

22 Ὁ δὲ Ἰησοῦς εἶπεν αὐτῷ, "Ἀκολούθει μοι, καὶ ἄφες
- But Jesus said to him, "Follow Me, and leave

τοὺς νεκροὺς θάψαι τοὺς ἑαυτῶν νεκρούς."
the dead to bury the [2]of [3]themselves [1]dead."
their own

Wind and Wave Obey Jesus
(Mark 4:35–41; Luke 8:22–25)

23 Καὶ ἐμβάντι αὐτῷ εἰς τὸ πλοῖον, ἠκολούθησαν αὐτῷ οἱ
And stepping in Him into the boat, [3]followed [4]Him -
when He got

μαθηταὶ αὐτοῦ. 24 Καὶ ἰδού, σεισμὸς μέγας ἐγένετο ἐν τῇ
[2]disciples [1]His. And behold, [3]a [5]tempest [4]great [1]*there* [2]was in the

θαλάσσῃ, ὥστε τὸ πλοῖον καλύπτεσθαι ὑπὸ τῶν κυμάτων.
sea, so that the boat to be covered by the waves.
was

Αὐτὸς δὲ ἐκάθευδε. 25 Καὶ προσελθόντες οἱ μαθηταὶ
He ˜ But was sleeping. And approaching the disciples
the disciples approached and

ἤγειραν αὐτὸν λέγοντες, "Κύριε, σῶσον ἡμᾶς![j]
awakened Him saying, "Lord, save us!

Ἀπολλύμεθα!"
We are perishing!"

26 Καὶ λέγει αὐτοῖς, "Τί δειλοί ἐστε,
And He says to them, "Why [3]cowardly [1]are [2]you,
said

ὀλιγόπιστοι?" Τότε ἐγερθεὶς ἐπετίμησε τοῖς ἀνέμοις καὶ τῇ
O you of little faith?" Then rising He rebuked the winds and the

θαλάσσῃ, καὶ ἐγένετο γαλήνη μεγάλη.
sea, and *there* was a calm ˜ great.

27 Οἱ δὲ ἄνθρωποι ἐθαύμασαν, λέγοντες, "Ποταπός
the ˜ And men marveled, saying, "Of what sort

ἐστιν οὗτος ὅτι καὶ οἱ ἄνεμοι καὶ ἡ θάλασσα ὑπακούουσιν
is this *man* that even the winds and the sea obey

αὐτῷ?"
Him?"

and said to Him, "Teacher, I will follow You wherever You go."
20 And Jesus said to him, "Foxes have holes and birds of the air *have* nests, but the Son of Man has nowhere to lay *His* head."
21 Then another of His disciples said to Him, "Lord, let me first go and bury my father."
22 But Jesus said to him, "Follow Me, and let the dead bury their own dead."
23 Now when He got into a boat, His disciples followed Him.
24 And suddenly a great tempest arose on the sea, so that the boat was covered with the waves. But He was asleep.
25 Then His disciples came to *Him* and awoke Him, saying, "Lord, save us! We are perishing!"
26 But He said to them, "Why are you fearful, O you of little faith?" Then He arose and rebuked the winds and the sea, and there was a great calm.
27 So the men marveled, saying, "Who can this be, that even the winds and the sea obey Him?"

---

j(8:25) NU omits ημας, *us*.

28 When He had come to the other side, to the country of the Gergesenes, there met Him two demon-possessed *men,* coming out of the tombs, exceedingly fierce, so that no one could pass that way.
29 And suddenly they cried out, saying, "What have we to do with You, Jesus, You Son of God? Have You come here to torment us before the time?"
30 Now a good way off from them there was a herd of many swine feeding.
31 So the demons begged Him, saying, "If You cast us out, permit us to go away into the herd of swine."
32 And He said to them, "Go." So when they had come out, they went into the herd of swine. And suddenly the whole herd of swine ran violently down the steep place into the sea, and perished in the water.
33 Then those who kept *them* fled; and they went away into the city and told everything, including what *had happened* to the demon-possessed *men.*
34 And behold, the whole city came out to meet Jesus. And when they saw Him, they begged *Him* to depart from their region.
9 So He got into a boat, crossed over, and came to His own city.
2 Then behold, they brought

Jesus Heals Two Demon-Possessed Men
(Mark 5:1–20; Luke 8:26–39)

28 Καὶ ἐλθόντι αὐτῷ εἰς τὸ πέραν εἰς τὴν χώραν τῶν
And coming ˜ Him to the other side to the region of the
when He came

Γεργεσηνῶν,[k] ὑπήντησαν αὐτῷ δύο δαιμονιζόμενοι
Gergesenes, *there* met Him two *men* being demon-possessed

ἐκ τῶν μνημείων ἐξερχόμενοι, χαλεποὶ λίαν, ὥστε μὴ
[3]from [4]the [5]tombs [1]coming [2]out, dangerous ˜ very, so that not
it

ἰσχύειν τινὰ παρελθεῖν διὰ τῆς ὁδοῦ ἐκείνης.
to be able anyone to go along through - way ˜ that.
was impossible for anyone

29 Καὶ ἰδού, ἔκραξαν λέγοντες, "Τί ἡμῖν καὶ
And behold, they cried out saying, "What to us and
do we have to do

σοί, Ἰησοῦ,[l] Υἱὲ τοῦ Θεοῦ? Ἦλθες ὧδε πρὸ καιροῦ
to You, Jesus, Son - of God? Did You come here before *the* time
with You,

βασανίσαι ἡμᾶς?" **30** Ἦν δὲ μακρὰν ἀπ' αὐτῶν ἀγέλη
to torment us?" [2]*there* [3]was [1]Now far off from them a herd

χοίρων πολλῶν βοσκομένη. **31** Οἱ δὲ δαίμονες παρεκάλουν
of pigs ˜ many feeding. the ˜ And demons were imploring
kept

αὐτόν, λέγοντες, "Εἰ ἐκβάλλεις ἡμᾶς, ἐπίτρεψον ἡμῖν
Him, saying, "If You cast out ˜ us, permit us

ἀπελθεῖν[m] εἰς τὴν ἀγέλην τῶν χοίρων."
to go off into the herd - of pigs."

32 Καὶ εἶπεν αὐτοῖς, "Ὑπάγετε." Οἱ δὲ ἐξελθόντες
And He said to them, "Go." [2]the [3]*ones* [1]And coming out
So they came out and

ἀπῆλθον εἰς τὴν ἀγέλην τῶν χοίρων.[n] Καὶ ἰδού, ὥρμησε
went off into the herd - of pigs. And behold, [6]rushed

πᾶσα ἡ ἀγέλη τῶν χοίρων[o] κατὰ τοῦ κρημνοῦ εἰς τὴν
[1]all [2]the [3]herd - [4]of [5]pigs down the steep bank into the

θάλασσαν καὶ ἀπέθανον ἐν τοῖς ὕδασιν. **33** Οἱ δὲ
sea and died in the waters. [2]the [3]*ones* [1]But
those

βόσκοντες ἔφυγον, καὶ ἀπελθόντες εἰς τὴν πόλιν ἀπήγγειλαν
feeding *them* fled, and going off into the city they reported
who tended

πάντα καὶ τὰ τῶν δαιμονιζομένων. **34** Καὶ ἰδού,
all *things* and the *news* of the *men* being demon-possessed. And behold,

πᾶσα ἡ πόλις ἐξῆλθεν εἰς συνάντησιν τῷ Ἰησοῦ. Καὶ
all the city came out to a meeting - with Jesus. And
meet

ἰδόντες αὐτὸν παρεκάλεσαν ὅπως μεταβῇ ἀπὸ τῶν
seeing Him they implored *Him* that He might go away from -

ὁρίων αὐτῶν.
borders ˜ their.
region

Jesus Forgives and Heals a Paralytic
(Mark 2:1–12; Luke 5:17–26)

9 **1** Καὶ ἐμβὰς εἰς τὸ πλοῖον διεπέρασε καὶ ἦλθεν εἰς
And stepping in into the boat He crossed over and went into
getting

τὴν ἰδίαν πόλιν. **2** Καὶ ἰδού, προσέφερον αὐτῷ
- His own city. And behold, they were carrying to Him

[k](8:28) NU reads Γαδαρηνων, *Gadarenes.*
[l](8:29) NU omits Ιησου, *Jesus.*
[m](8:31) For επιτρεψον ημιν απελθειν, *permit us to go off,* NU reads αποστειλον ημας, *send us.*
[n](8:32) For την αγελην των χοιρων, *the herd of pigs,* NU reads εις τους χοιρους, *into the pigs.*
[o](8:32) NU omits των χοιρων, *of pigs.*

παραλυτικὸν ἐπὶ κλίνης βεβλημένον. Καὶ ἰδὼν ὁ
a paralytic [5]on [6]a [7]bed [1]having [2]been [3]laid [4]out. And seeing ~ -
lying. when Jesus

Ἰησοῦς τὴν πίστιν αὐτῶν εἶπε τῷ παραλυτικῷ,
Jesus - faith ~ their He said to the paralytic,
saw

"Θάρσει, τέκνον· ἀφέωνταί σοι αἱ ἁμαρτίαι σου."
"Have courage, child; [3]have [4]been [5]forgiven [6]you - [2]sins [1]your."

3 Καὶ ἰδού, τινὲς τῶν γραμματέων εἶπον ἐν ἑαυτοῖς,
And behold, some of the scribes said among themselves,

"Οὗτος βλασφημεῖ!"*
"This *man* blasphemes!"

4 Καὶ ἰδὼν ὁ Ἰησοῦς τὰς ἐνθυμήσεις αὐτῶν εἶπεν,
And seeing ~ - Jesus - thoughts ~ their He said,
when Jesus saw

"Ἱνατί ὑμεῖς ἐνθυμεῖσθε πονηρὰ ἐν ταῖς καρδίαις ὑμῶν?
"Why you ~ do think evil *things* in - hearts ~ your?

5 Τί γάρ ἐστιν εὐκοπώτερον, εἰπεῖν, 'Ἀφέωνταί
which ~ For is easier, to say, '[3]have [4]been [5]forgiven

σου αἱ ἁμαρτίαι,' ἢ εἰπεῖν, 'Ἔγειραι καὶ περιπάτει'?
[1]Your - [2]sins,' or to say, 'Arise and walk'?

6 Ἵνα δὲ εἰδῆτε ὅτι ἐξουσίαν ἔχει ὁ Υἱὸς τοῦ
[2]in [3]order [4]that [1]But you may know that [6]authority [5]has [1]the [2]Son -

Ἀνθρώπου ἐπὶ τῆς γῆς ἀφιέναι ἁμαρτίας" — τότε λέγει
[3]of [4]Man on the earth to forgive sins" — then He says
said

τῷ παραλυτικῷ, "Ἐγερθεὶς ἆρόν σου τὴν κλίνην καὶ
to the paralytic, "Having arisen take up your - bed and
"Arise,

ὕπαγε εἰς τὸν οἶκόν σου." 7 Καὶ ἐγερθεὶς ἀπῆλθεν εἰς τὸν
go to - house ~ your." And having arisen he went off to -

οἶκον αὐτοῦ. 8 Ἰδόντες δὲ οἱ ὄχλοι ἐθαύμασαν[a] καὶ
house ~ his. [4]seeing [1]And [2]the [3]crowds they marveled and
And when the crowds saw

ἐδόξασαν τὸν Θεόν, τὸν δόντα ἐξουσίαν τοιαύτην τοῖς
glorified - God, the *One* giving authority ~ such -
He who had given

ἀνθρώποις.
to men.

Jesus Calls Matthew the Publican
(Mark 2:13–17; Luke 5:27–32)

9 Καὶ παράγων ὁ Ἰησοῦς ἐκεῖθεν εἶδεν ἄνθρωπον
And passing by - Jesus from there He saw a man
as Jesus passed on

καθήμενον ἐπὶ τὸ τελώνιον, Ματθαῖον λεγόμενον, καὶ λέγει
sitting at the tax office, [3]Matthew [1]being [2]called, and He says
called, said

αὐτῷ, "Ἀκολούθει μοι." Καὶ ἀναστὰς ἠκολούθησεν αὐτῷ.
to him, "Follow Me." And arising he followed Him.

10 Καὶ ἐγένετο αὐτοῦ ἀνακειμένου ἐν τῇ οἰκίᾳ, καὶ ἰδού,
And it happened Him reclining *to eat* in the house, and behold,
as He reclined that

πολλοὶ τελῶναι καὶ ἁμαρτωλοὶ ἐλθόντες συνανέκειντο
many tax collectors and sinners having come were reclining *to eat*

τῷ Ἰησοῦ καὶ τοῖς μαθηταῖς αὐτοῦ. 11 Καὶ ἰδόντες
- with Jesus and - with disciples ~ His. And seeing *this*
when the

to Him a paralytic lying on a
bed. When Jesus saw their
faith, He said to the paralytic,
"Son, be of good cheer; your
sins are forgiven you."
3 And at once some of the
scribes said within themselves,
"This Man blasphemes!"
4 But Jesus, knowing their
thoughts, said, "Why do you
think evil in your hearts?
5 "For which is easier, to
say, '*Your* sins are forgiven
you,' or to say, 'Arise and
walk'?
6 "But that you may know
that the Son of Man has power
on earth to forgive sins"—then
He said to the paralytic, "Arise,
take up your bed, and go to
your house."
7 And he arose and departed
to his house.
8 Now when the multitudes
saw *it,* they marveled and glorified God, who had given such
power to men.
9 As Jesus passed on from
there, He saw a man named
Matthew sitting at the tax office. And He said to him, "Follow Me." So he arose and
followed Him.
10 Now it happened, as Jesus
sat at the table in the house,
that behold, many tax collectors
and sinners came and sat down
with Him and His disciples.
11 And when the Pharisees

---

[a](9:8) NU reads *εφοβηθησαν, they were afraid.*

***(9:3)** *βλασφημέω (blasphēmeō).* Verb meaning *blaspheme.* Modern English uses *blasphemy* primarily to mean speaking harshly against God or sacred persons or things. In Greek it was used more widely, including slander of other people. Most NT usages refer to defaming sacred things. The adjective *βλάσφημος* is used by Paul substantivally to describe his preconversion days as a blasphemer and a persecutor (1 Tim. 1:13). The Pharisees accused Christ of blaspheming (here in Matt. 9:3; cf. 26:65), and similar charges were made against the early Christians (cf. the "blasphemous words" in Acts 6:11, 13). Actually, it was they who were guilty of blasphemy against the Holy Spirit in attributing Christ's healings to Satan (cf. Mark 3:28–30).

saw *it,* they said to His disciples, "Why does your Teacher
eat with tax collectors and sinners?"
12 When Jesus heard *that,* He
said to them, "Those who are
well have no need of a physician, but those who are sick.
13 "But go and learn what *this*
means: *'I desire mercy and not
sacrifice.'* For I did not come to
call the righteous, but sinners,
to repentance."
14 Then the disciples of John
came to Him, saying, "Why do
we and the Pharisees fast often, but Your disciples do not
fast?"
15 And Jesus said to them,
"Can the friends of the bridegroom mourn as long as the
bridegroom is with them? But
the days will come when the
bridegroom will be taken away
from them, and then they will
fast.
16 "No one puts a piece of unshrunk cloth on an old garment;
for the patch pulls away from
the garment, and the tear is
made worse.
17 "Nor do they put new wine
into old wineskins, or else the
wineskins break, the wine is
spilled, and the wineskins are
ruined. But they put new wine
into new wineskins, and both
are preserved."

οἱ Φαρισαῖοι εἶπον τοῖς μαθηταῖς αὐτοῦ, "Διὰ
the Pharisees they said - to disciples ˜ His, "On account of
Pharisees saw this, "Why

τί μετὰ τῶν τελωνῶν καὶ ἁμαρτωλῶν ἐσθίει ὁ
what [5]with - [6]tax [7]collectors [8]and [9]sinners [1]does [4]eat -

διδάσκαλος ὑμῶν?"
[3]Teacher [2]your?"

12 Ὁ δὲ Ἰησοῦς ἀκούσας εἶπεν αὐτοῖς,[b] "Οὐ χρείαν
- But Jesus hearing He said to them, "[6]not [8]need
when Jesus heard,

ἔχουσιν οἱ ἰσχύοντες ἰατροῦ ἀλλ' οἱ κακῶς
[5]do [7]have [1]The [2]*ones* [3]being [4]strong of a physician but the *ones* badly
Those who are those who are

ἔχοντες. 13 Πορευθέντες δὲ μάθετε τί ἐστιν, «Ἔλεον
having *it.* going ˜ But learn what it is, «[3]Mercy
ill. go and this means,

θέλω καὶ οὐ θυσίαν.»[c] Οὐ γὰρ ἦλθον καλέσαι
[1]I [2]desire and not sacrifice.» not For I came to call
For I did not come

δικαίους ἀλλὰ ἁμαρτωλοὺς εἰς μετάνοιαν."[d]
righteous *people* but sinners to repentance."

Jesus Is Questioned About Fasting
(Mark 2:18–22; Luke 5:33–39)

14 Τότε προσέρχονται αὐτῷ οἱ μαθηταὶ Ἰωάννου,
Then [5]approach [6]Him [1]the [2]disciples [3]of [4]John,
approached

λέγοντες, "Διὰ τί ἡμεῖς καὶ οἱ Φαρισαῖοι
saying, "On account of what *is it that* we and the Pharisees
"Why

νηστεύομεν πολλά, οἱ δὲ μαθηταί σου οὐ νηστεύουσι?"
fast many *things,* - but disciples ˜ Your not ˜ do fast?"
much,

15 Καὶ εἶπεν αὐτοῖς ὁ Ἰησοῦς, "Μὴ δύνανται οἱ
And [2]said [3]to [4]them - [1]Jesus, "[12]not [11]are [13]able [5]The

υἱοὶ τοῦ νυμφῶνος πενθεῖν ἐφ' ὅσον μετ' αὐτῶν
[6]sons [7]of [8]the [9]bridal [10]chamber to mourn in so far as [4]with [5]them
groomsmen as long as

ἐστιν ὁ νυμφίος? Ἐλεύσονται δὲ ἡμέραι ὅταν
[3]is [1]the [2]bridegroom, [6]*are* [7]*they?* [10]will [11]come [8]But [9]days when

ἀπαρθῇ ἀπ' αὐτῶν ὁ νυμφίος, καὶ τότε
[3]is [4]taken [5]away [6]from [7]them [1]the [2]bridegroom, and then

νηστεύσουσιν. 16 Οὐδεὶς δὲ ἐπιβάλλει ἐπίβλημα
they will fast. [2]no [3]one [1]And puts on a patch

ῥάκους ἀγνάφου ἐπὶ ἱματίῳ παλαιῷ· αἴρει
of a piece of cloth ˜ unshrunk on a(n) garment ˜ old; [2]it [3]takes [4]away

γὰρ τὸ πλήρωμα αὐτοῦ ἀπὸ τοῦ ἱματίου, καὶ χεῖρον σχίσμα
[1]for - [6]completeness [5]its from the garment, and [4]worse [1]*the* [2]tear

γίνεται. 17 Οὐδὲ βάλλουσιν οἶνον νέον εἰς ἀσκοὺς παλαιούς·
[3]becomes. Nor do they put wine ˜ new into wineskins ˜ old;

εἰ δὲ μή γε, ῥήγνυνται οἱ ἀσκοί, καὶ ὁ οἶνος
if ˜ but not, - [3]burst [1]the [2]wineskins, and the wine
otherwise,

ἐκχεῖται καὶ οἱ ἀσκοὶ ἀπολοῦνται. Ἀλλὰ βάλλουσιν οἶνον
spills out and the wineskins will be ruined. But they put wine ˜

νέον εἰς ἀσκοὺς καινούς, καὶ ἀμφότεροι συντηροῦνται."
new into wineskins ˜ new, and both are preserved."

[b](9:12) NU omits *αυτοις, to them.* [c](9:13) Hos. 6:6
[d](9:13) NU omits *εις μετανοιαν, to repentance.*

Jesus Restores a Girl and Heals a Woman

(Mark 5:21–43; Luke 8:40–56)

18 Ταῦτα αὐτοῦ λαλοῦντος αὐτοῖς, ἰδού, ἄρχων εἷς
These *things* Him speaking to them, behold, leader ˜ one
As He spoke these things a certain

ἐλθὼν προσεκύνει* αὐτῷ, λέγων ὅτι "Ἡ θυγάτηρ μου ἄρτι
coming was worshiping Him, saying - - "daughter ˜ My just now

ἐτελεύτησεν· ἀλλὰ ἐλθὼν ἐπίθες τὴν χεῖρά σου ἐπ' αὐτὴν
died; but coming lay - hand ˜ Your on her
come and

καὶ ζήσεται." 19 Καὶ ἐγερθεὶς ὁ Ἰησοῦς ἠκολούθησεν
and she will live." And having arisen - Jesus followed
Jesus rose and

αὐτῷ καὶ οἱ μαθηταὶ αὐτοῦ.
him likewise - disciples ˜ His.

20 Καὶ ἰδού, γυνὴ αἱμορροοῦσα δώδεκα ἔτη
And behold, a woman hemorrhaging *for* twelve years

προσελθοῦσα ὄπισθεν ἥψατο τοῦ κρασπέδου τοῦ ἱματίου
approaching from behind touched the border - of garment ˜

αὐτοῦ. 21 Ἔλεγε γὰρ ἐν ἑαυτῇ, "Ἐὰν μόνον ἅψωμαι τοῦ
His. [2]she [3]said [1]For in herself, "If only I may touch -

ἱματίου αὐτοῦ σωθήσομαι."
garment ˜ His I will be saved."
healed."

22 Ὁ δὲ Ἰησοῦς ἐπιστραφεὶς καὶ ἰδὼν αὐτὴν εἶπε,
- But Jesus turning around and seeing her said,

"Θάρσει, θύγατερ· ἡ πίστις σου σέσωκέ σε." Καὶ ἐσώθη
"Take courage, daughter; - faith ˜ your has saved you." And [3]was [4]saved
healed healed

ἡ γυνὴ ἀπὸ τῆς ὥρας ἐκείνης.
[1]the [2]woman from - hour ˜ that.

23 Καὶ ἐλθὼν ὁ Ἰησοῦς εἰς τὴν οἰκίαν τοῦ ἄρχοντος
And coming ˜ - Jesus into the house of the leader
when Jesus came

καὶ ἰδὼν τοὺς αὐλητὰς καὶ τὸν ὄχλον θορυβούμενον,
and seeing the flutists and the crowd being aroused,
saw making a commotion,

24 λέγει αὐτοῖς, "Ἀναχωρεῖτε, οὐ γὰρ ἀπέθανε τὸ κοράσιον
He says to them, "Go away, not for died the little girl
He said "Make room, for the little girl has not died

ἀλλὰ καθεύδει." Καὶ κατεγέλων αὐτοῦ. 25 Ὅτε δὲ
but she is sleeping." And they were ridiculing Him. when ˜ But

ἐξεβλήθη ὁ ὄχλος, εἰσελθὼν ἐκράτησε τῆς χειρὸς αὐτῆς,
[3]was [4]sent [5]out [1]the [2]crowd, entering He grasped - hand ˜ her,

καὶ ἠγέρθη τὸ κοράσιον. 26 Καὶ ἐξῆλθεν ἡ φήμη αὕτη εἰς
and [4]rose [1]the [2]little [3]girl. And [3]went [4]out - [2]report [1]this into

ὅλην τὴν γῆν ἐκείνην.
[2]whole - [3]land [1]that.

Jesus Heals Two Blind Men

27 Καὶ παράγοντι ἐκεῖθεν τῷ Ἰησοῦ, ἠκολούθησαν αὐτῷ
And passing by from there - Jesus, [4]followed [5]Him
as Jesus passed by from there,

δύο τυφλοί, κράζοντες καὶ λέγοντες, "Ἐλέησον ἡμᾶς,
[1]two [2]blind [3]*men,* crying out and saying, "Have mercy on us,

Υἱὸς Δαβίδ!"
Son of David!"

18 While He spoke these things to them, behold, a ruler came and worshiped Him, saying, "My daughter has just died, but come and lay Your hand on her and she will live."
19 So Jesus arose and followed him, and so *did* His disciples.
20 And suddenly, a woman who had a flow of blood for twelve years came from behind and touched the hem of His garment.
21 For she said to herself, "If only I may touch His garment, I shall be made well."
22 But Jesus turned around, and when He saw her He said, "Be of good cheer, daughter; your faith has made you well." And the woman was made well from that hour.
23 When Jesus came into the ruler's house, and saw the flute players and the noisy crowd wailing,
24 He said to them, "Make room, for the girl is not dead, but sleeping." And they ridiculed Him.
25 But when the crowd was put outside, He went in and took her by the hand, and the girl arose.
26 And the report of this went out into all that land.
27 When Jesus departed from there, two blind men followed Him, crying out and saying, "Son of David, have mercy on us!"

***(9:18)** *προσκυνέω (proskyneō).* Verb meaning *(fall down and) worship, do obeisance to.* The word is derived from *πρός, to, toward,* and *κυνέω, kiss,* designating the act of homage in falling before another (especially a deity, a king, or one's master) and kissing the ground or his feet or garment's hem. It might indicate reverence/worship (of the true God, Matt. 4:10; of an idol, Acts 7:43), supplication (Matt. 18:26), or submission (Rev. 3:9). Used without an object, the word refers to public worship and prayers (Acts 8:27). That people offered such obeisance to Jesus (here in Matt. 9:18; also 8:2) indicates recognition that He at least wielded the power of God and may imply His kingship (cf. Matt. 2:2). Cf. the cognate noun *προσκυνητής, worshiper,* used only in John 4:23.

28 And when He had come
into the house, the blind men
came to Him. And Jesus said to
them, "Do you believe that I
am able to do this?" They said
to Him, "Yes, Lord."
29 Then He touched their
eyes, saying, "According to
your faith let it be to you."
30 And their eyes were
opened. And Jesus sternly
warned them, saying, "See *that*
no one knows *it*."
31 But when they had de-
parted, they spread the news
about Him in all that country.
32 As they went out, behold,
they brought to Him a man,
mute and demon-possessed.
33 And when the demon was
cast out, the mute spoke. And
the multitudes marveled, saying, "It was never seen like this
in Israel!"
34 But the Pharisees said,
"He casts out demons by the
ruler of the demons."
35 Then Jesus went about all
the cities and villages, teaching
in their synagogues, preaching
the gospel of the kingdom, and
healing every sickness and every disease among the people.
36 But when He saw the multitudes, He was moved with
compassion for them, because
they were weary and scattered,
like sheep having no shepherd.
37 Then He said to His disci-

28 Ἐλθόντι δὲ εἰς τὴν οἰκίαν, προσῆλθον αὐτῷ οἱ
coming ˜ And into the house, [4]approached [5]Him [1]the
And when He came

τυφλοί, καὶ λέγει αὐτοῖς ὁ Ἰησοῦς, "Πιστεύετε ὅτι
[2]blind [3]*men*, and [2]says [3]to [4]them - [1]Jesus, "Do you believe that
said

δύναμαι τοῦτο ποιῆσαι?"
I am able [3]this [1]to [2]do?"

Λέγουσιν αὐτῷ, "Ναί, Κύριε."
They say to Him, "Yes, Lord."
said

29 Τότε ἥψατο τῶν ὀφθαλμῶν αὐτῶν, λέγων, "Κατὰ
Then He touched - eyes ˜ their, saying, "According to

τὴν πίστιν ὑμῶν γενηθήτω ὑμῖν." **30** Καὶ ἀνεῴχθησαν αὐτῶν
- faith ˜ your let it happen to you." And [3]were [4]opened [1]their

οἱ ὀφθαλμοί. Καὶ ἐνεβριμήσατο αὐτοῖς ὁ Ἰησοῦς, λέγων,
- [2]eyes. And [2]sternly [3]warned [4]them - [1]Jesus, saying,

"Ὁρᾶτε μηδεὶς γινωσκέτω." **31** Οἱ δὲ ἐξελθόντες
"See *that you* [2]no [3]one [1]let [4]know." [2]the [3]*ones* [1]But going out
they

διεφήμισαν αὐτὸν ἐν ὅλῃ τῇ γῇ ἐκείνῃ.
spread the news about Him in [2]whole - [3]land [1]that.

Jesus Casts Out a Demon

32 Αὐτῶν δὲ ἐξερχομένων, ἰδού, προσήνεγκαν αὐτῷ
they And going out, behold, they brought to Him
And as they were going out,

ἄνθρωπον κωφὸν δαιμονιζόμενον. **33** Καὶ ἐκβληθέντος τοῦ
a man ˜ mute being demon-possessed. And being cast out the
when the demon was

δαιμονίου, ἐλάλησεν ὁ κωφός.
demon, [3]spoke [1]the [2]mute.
cast out,

Καὶ ἐθαύμασαν οἱ ὄχλοι, λέγοντες, "Οὐδέποτε ἐφάνη
And [3]marveled [1]the [2]crowds, saying, "[3]never [1]It [2]was [4]seen

οὕτως ἐν τῷ Ἰσραήλ!"
thus in - Israel!"
like this

34 Οἱ δὲ Φαρισαῖοι ἔλεγον, "Ἐν τῷ ἄρχοντι τῶν
the ˜ But Pharisees said, "By the ruler of the

δαιμονίων ἐκβάλλει τὰ δαιμόνια."
demons He casts out - demons."

Jesus and the Great Harvest

35 Καὶ περιῆγεν ὁ Ἰησοῦς τὰς πόλεις πάσας καὶ τὰς
And [2]was [3]going [4]about - [1]Jesus [6]the [7]cities [5]all and the

κώμας διδάσκων ἐν ταῖς συναγωγαῖς αὐτῶν καὶ κηρύσσων τὸ
villages teaching in - synagogues ˜ their and preaching the

εὐαγγέλιον τῆς βασιλείας καὶ θεραπεύων πᾶσαν νόσον καὶ
good news of the kingdom and healing every disease and

πᾶσαν μαλακίαν ἐν τῷ λαῷ.[e] **36** Ἰδὼν δὲ τοὺς ὄχλους
every illness among the people. seeing ˜ But the crowds

ἐσπλαγχνίσθη περὶ αὐτῶν ὅτι ἦσαν ἐσκυλμένοι[f]
He had compassion concerning them because they were harassed

καὶ ἐρριμμένοι ὡσεὶ πρόβατα μὴ ἔχοντα ποιμένα. **37** Τότε
and prostrated like sheep not having a shepherd. Then

---

e(9:35) NU omits εν τω λαω, *among the people.*
f(9:36) TR reads εκλελυμενοι, *wearied.*

λέγει τοῖς μαθηταῖς αὐτοῦ, "Ὁ μὲν θερισμὸς πολύς, οἱ
He says - to disciples ˜ His, "the ˜ Indeed harvest *is* much, the ˜
said plentiful,

δὲ ἐργάται ὀλίγοι. **38** Δεήθητε οὖν τοῦ Κυρίου τοῦ
but workers *are* few. ask ˜ Therefore the Lord of the
pray to

θερισμοῦ ὅπως ἐκβάλῃ ἐργάτας εἰς τὸν θερισμὸν
harvest that He may put forth workers into - harvest ˜

αὐτοῦ."
His."

The Twelve Receive Authority
(Mark 3:13–19; Luke 9:1–6)

10 **1** Καὶ προσκαλεσάμενος τοὺς δώδεκα μαθητὰς αὐτοῦ
And summoning - [2]twelve [3]disciples [1]His

ἔδωκεν αὐτοῖς ἐξουσίαν πνευμάτων ἀκαθάρτων ὥστε ἐκβάλλειν
He gave them authority of spirits ˜ unclean so as to cast out ˜
over

αὐτὰ καὶ θεραπεύειν πᾶσαν νόσον καὶ πᾶσαν μαλακίαν.
them and to heal every disease and every illness.

2 Τῶν δὲ δώδεκα ἀποστόλων τὰ ὀνόματά ἐστι ταῦτα·
[4]of [5]the [1]Now [6]twelve [7]apostles [2]the [3]names are these:

πρῶτος Σίμων ὁ λεγόμενος Πέτρος καὶ Ἀνδρέας ὁ
first Simon the *one* being called Peter and Andrew -
who was called

ἀδελφὸς αὐτοῦ, Ἰάκωβος ὁ τοῦ Ζεβεδαίου καὶ Ἰωάννης ὁ
brother ˜ his, James the *son* - of Zebedee and John -

ἀδελφὸς αὐτοῦ, **3** Φίλιππος καὶ Βαρθολομαῖος, Θωμᾶς καὶ
brother ˜ his, Philip and Bartholomew, Thomas and

Ματθαῖος ὁ τελώνης, Ἰάκωβος ὁ τοῦ Ἀλφαίου καὶ
Matthew the tax collector, James the *son* - of Alphaeus and

Λεββαῖος ὁ ἐπικληθεὶς[a] Θαδδαῖος, **4** Σίμων ὁ
Lebbaeus the *one* having been named Thaddaeus, Simon the
who was surnamed

Κανανίτης[b] καὶ Ἰούδας Ἰσκαριώτης ὁ καὶ παραδοὺς
Cananite and Judas Iscariot the *one* also handing over ˜
who betrayed

αὐτόν.
Him.

Jesus Commissions the Twelve
(Mark 6:7–13; Luke 9:1–6)

5 Τούτους τοὺς δώδεκα ἀπέστειλεν ὁ Ἰησοῦς, παραγγείλας
These - twelve [2]sent [3]forth - [1]Jesus, commanding

αὐτοῖς, λέγων, "Εἰς ὁδὸν ἐθνῶν μὴ ἀπέλθητε, καὶ εἰς
them, saying, "Into *the* way of *the* Gentiles not ˜ do go off, and into

πόλιν Σαμαρειτῶν μὴ εἰσέλθητε. **6** Πορεύεσθε δὲ μᾶλλον
a city of *the* Samaritans not ˜ do enter. journey ˜ But rather

πρὸς τὰ πρόβατα τὰ ἀπολωλότα οἴκου Ἰσραήλ.
to the sheep ˜ - lost of *the* house of Israel.

7 Πορευόμενοι δὲ κηρύσσετε, λέγοντες ὅτι 'Ἤγγικεν ἡ
journeying ˜ And preach, saying - '[6]has [7]drawn [8]near [1]The
as you go,

βασιλεία τῶν οὐρανῶν.' **8** Ἀσθενοῦντας θεραπεύετε, λεπροὺς
[2]kingdom [3]of [4]the [5]heavens.' [2]ailing [3]*people* [1]Heal, lepers ˜
sick

ples, "The harvest truly *is* plentiful, but the laborers *are* few.
38 "Therefore pray the Lord
of the harvest to send out laborers into His harvest."
10 And when He had
called His twelve disci-
ples to *Him,* He gave them
power *over* unclean spirits, to
cast them out, and to heal all
kinds of sickness and all kinds
of disease.
2 Now the names of the
twelve apostles are these: first,
Simon, who is called Peter, and
Andrew his brother; James the
son of Zebedee, and John his
brother;
3 Philip and Bartholomew;
Thomas and Matthew the tax
collector; James the *son* of Alphaeus, and Lebbaeus, whose
surname was Thaddaeus;
4 Simon the Cananite, and
Judas Iscariot, who also betrayed Him.
5 These twelve Jesus sent
out and commanded them, saying: "Do not go into the way of
the Gentiles, and do not enter a
city of the Samaritans.
6 "But go rather to the lost
sheep of the house of Israel.
7 "And as you go, preach,
saying, 'The kingdom of heaven
is at hand.'
8 "Heal the sick, cleanse the

---

[a](**10:3**) NU omits Λεββαιος ο επικληθεις, *Lebbaeus who was surnamed.*
[b](**10:4**) NU reads Καναναιος, *Cananean.*

lepers, raise the dead, cast out demons. Freely you have received, freely give.
9 “Provide neither gold nor silver nor copper in your money belts,
10 “nor bag for *your* journey, nor two tunics, nor sandals, nor staffs; for a worker is worthy of his food.
11 “Now whatever city or town you enter, inquire who in it is worthy, and stay there till you go out.
12 “And when you go into a household, greet it.
13 “If the household is worthy, let your peace come upon it. But if it is not worthy, let your peace return to you.
14 “And whoever will not receive you nor hear your words, when you depart from that house or city, shake off the dust from your feet.
15 “Assuredly, I say to you, it will be more tolerable for the land of Sodom and Gomorrah in the day of judgment than for that city!
16 “Behold, I send you out as sheep in the midst of wolves. Therefore be wise as serpents and harmless as doves.
17 “But beware of men, for they will deliver you up to councils and scourge you in their synagogues.
18 “You will be brought before governors and kings for My sake, as a testimony to them and to the Gentiles.
19 “But when they deliver you

καθαρίζετε,[c] δαιμόνια ἐκβάλλετε. Δωρεὰν ἐλάβετε, δωρεὰν
cleanse, [3]demons [1]cast [2]out. As a gift you received, as a gift
Freely freely

δότε. 9 Μὴ κτήσησθε χρυσὸν μηδὲ ἄργυρον μηδὲ χαλκὸν εἰς
give. not ˜ Do acquire gold nor silver nor copper for

τὰς ζώνας ὑμῶν, 10 μὴ πήραν εἰς ὁδὸν μηδὲ δύο
- [2]money [3]belts [1]your, not a knapsack for *the* road nor two

χιτῶνας μηδὲ ὑποδήματα μηδὲ ῥάβδους·[d] ἄξιος γὰρ ὁ
tunics nor sandals nor staffs; [5]worthy [1]for [2]the
a

ἐργάτης τῆς τροφῆς αὐτοῦ ἐστιν.
[3]worker - [6]of [8]food [7]his [4]is.

11 “Εἰς ἣν δ' ἂν πόλιν ἢ κώμην εἰσέλθητε,
“[2]into [3]what [1]And ever city or village you may enter,

ἐξετάσατε τίς ἐν αὐτῇ ἄξιός ἐστι· κἀκεῖ μείνατε ἕως ἂν
inquire who in it worthy ˜ is; and there ˜ stay until -

ἐξέλθητε. 12 Εἰσερχόμενοι δὲ εἰς τὴν οἰκίαν, ἀσπάσασθε
you go out. entering ˜ And into the house, greet
as you enter

αὐτήν. 13 Καὶ ἐὰν μὲν ᾖ ἡ οἰκία ἀξία, ἐλθέτω ἡ
it. And if indeed [3]should [4]be [1]the [2]house worthy, [1]let [4]come -

εἰρήνη ὑμῶν ἐπ' αὐτήν· ἐὰν δὲ μὴ ᾖ ἀξία, ἡ
[3]peace [2]your upon it; if ˜ but [3]not [1]it [2]should be worthy, -

εἰρήνη ὑμῶν πρὸς ὑμᾶς ἐπιστραφήτω. 14 Καὶ ὃς ἐὰν μὴ
[3]peace [2]your [5]to [6]you [1]let [4]return. And who ever not ˜

δέξηται ὑμᾶς μηδὲ ἀκούσῃ τοὺς λόγους ὑμῶν, ἐξερχόμενοι
will receive you nor hear - words ˜ your, going out
as you go out

τῆς οἰκίας ἢ τῆς πόλεως ἐκείνης, ἐκτινάξατε τὸν κονιορτὸν
of the house or - of city ˜ that, shake off the dust
from from

τῶν ποδῶν ὑμῶν. 15 Ἀμὴν λέγω ὑμῖν, ἀνεκτότερον
- of feet ˜ your. Amen I say to you, [4]more [5]tolerable
from Assuredly

ἔσται γῇ Σοδόμων καὶ Γομόρρων ἐν ἡμέρᾳ κρίσεως
[1]it [2]will [3]be for *the* land of Sodom and of Gomorrah in *the* day of judgment

ἢ τῇ πόλει ἐκείνῃ!
than - for city ˜ that!

Persecutions Are Coming
(Mark 13:9–13; Luke 21:12–17)

16 “Ἰδού, ἐγὼ ἀποστέλλω ὑμᾶς ὡς πρόβατα ἐν μέσῳ
“Behold, I am sending forth ˜ you like sheep in *the* midst

λύκων. Γίνεσθε οὖν φρόνιμοι ὡς οἱ ὄφεις καὶ ἀκέραιοι
of wolves. be ˜ Therefore wise as - serpents and innocent

ὡς αἱ περιστεραί. 17 Προσέχετε δὲ ἀπὸ τῶν ἀνθρώπων·
as - doves. beware ˜ But from - men;
of

παραδώσουσι γὰρ ὑμᾶς εἰς συνέδρια, καὶ ἐν ταῖς
[2]they [3]will [4]hand [6]over [1]for [5]you to councils, and in -

συναγωγαῖς αὐτῶν μαστιγώσουσιν ὑμᾶς. 18 Καὶ ἐπὶ
synagogues ˜ their they will flog you. And before

ἡγεμόνας δὲ καὶ βασιλεῖς ἀχθήσεσθε ἕνεκεν ἐμοῦ εἰς
governors and also kings you will be brought because of Me as
for My sake

μαρτύριον αὐτοῖς καὶ τοῖς ἔθνεσιν. 19 Ὅταν δὲ
a testimony to them and to the nations. whenever ˜ But

[c]**(10:8)** TR adds *νεκρους εγειρετε, raise the dead;* NU adds *νεκρους εγειρετε* after *θεραπευετε, Heal (sick people).*

[d]**(10:10)** NU reads *ραβδον, a staff.*

παραδιδῶσιν ὑμᾶς, μὴ μεριμνήσητε πῶς ἢ τί
they hand over ˜ you, not ˜ do worry how or what

λαλήσητε. Δοθήσεται γὰρ ὑμῖν ἐν ἐκείνῃ τῇ ὥρᾳ τί
you should speak. [2]it [3]will [4]be [5]given [1]For to you in that - hour what

λαλήσετε· 20 οὐ γὰρ ὑμεῖς ἐστε οἱ λαλοῦντες ἀλλὰ
you should speak; [4]not [1]for [2]you [3]are the *ones* speaking but

τὸ Πνεῦμα τοῦ Πατρὸς ὑμῶν τὸ λαλοῦν ἐν ὑμῖν.
the Spirit - of Father ˜ your the *One* speaking in you.
who is

21 "Παραδώσει δὲ ἀδελφὸς ἀδελφὸν εἰς θάνατον καὶ
"[3]will [4]hand [5]over [1]And [2]brother [6]brother to death and

πατὴρ τέκνον, καὶ ἐπαναστήσονται τέκνα ἐπὶ γονεῖς καὶ
a father a child, and [2]will [3]rise [4]up [1]children against parents and

θανατώσουσιν αὐτούς. 22 Καὶ ἔσεσθε μισούμενοι ὑπὸ πάντων
[1]put [3]to [4]death [2]them. And you will be hated by all *people*

διὰ τὸ ὄνομά μου. Ὁ δὲ ὑπομείνας εἰς τέλος,
because of - name ˜ My. [2]the [3]*one* [1]But enduring to *the* end,
for My name's sake.

οὗτος σωθήσεται.* 23 Ὅταν δὲ διώκωσιν ὑμᾶς ἐν τῇ
this *one* will be saved. whenever ˜ But they persecute you in -
delivered.

πόλει ταύτῃ, φεύγετε εἰς τὴν ἄλλην. Ἀμὴν γὰρ λέγω ὑμῖν,
city ˜ this, flee to the other. amen ˜ For I say to you,
assuredly

οὐ μὴ τελέσητε τὰς πόλεις τοῦ Ἰσραὴλ ἕως ἂν ἔλθῃ
not not will you complete the cities - of Israel until - [5]comes
by no means

ὁ Υἱὸς τοῦ Ἀνθρώπου. 24 Οὐκ ἔστι μαθητὴς ὑπὲρ τὸν
[1]the [2]Son - [3]of [4]Man. [4]not [3]is [1]A [2]disciple above the
his

διδάσκαλον οὐδὲ δοῦλος ὑπὲρ τὸν κύριον αὐτοῦ. 25 Ἀρκετὸν
teacher nor a slave above - master ˜ his. Enough
servant

τῷ μαθητῇ ἵνα γένηται ὡς ὁ διδάσκαλος αὐτοῦ, καὶ ὁ
for the disciple that he become like - teacher ˜ his, and the

δοῦλος ὡς ὁ κύριος αὐτοῦ. Εἰ τὸν οἰκοδεσπότην
slave like - master ˜ his. If [4]the [5]master [6]of [7]the [8]house
servant

Βεελζεβοὺλ ἐπεκάλεσαν, πόσῳ μᾶλλον τοὺς
[9]Beelzebul [2]they [3]called, how much more -

οἰκειακοὺς αὐτοῦ!
[2]household [3]members [1]his!

Fear God, Not Men
(Luke 12:2–7)

26 "Μὴ οὖν φοβηθῆτε αὐτούς. Οὐδὲν γάρ ἐστι
"[3]not [1]Therefore [2]do [4]fear them. nothing ˜ For is

κεκαλυμμένον ὃ οὐκ ἀποκαλυφθήσεται, καὶ κρυπτὸν ὃ
concealed which not ˜ will be revealed, and secret which

οὐ γνωσθήσεται. 27 Ὃ λέγω ὑμῖν ἐν τῇ σκοτίᾳ, εἴπατε ἐν
not ˜ will be known. What I say to you in the dark, say in

τῷ φωτί· καὶ ὃ εἰς τὸ οὖς ἀκούετε, κηρύξατε ἐπὶ τῶν
the light; and what [3]in [4]the [5]ear [1]you [2]hear, proclaim on the

δωμάτων. 28 Καὶ μὴ φοβεῖσθε ἀπὸ τῶν ἀποκτενόντων τὸ
housetops. And not ˜ do be afraid from the ones killing the
of those who kill

σῶμα, τὴν δὲ ψυχὴν μὴ δυναμένων ἀποκτεῖναι. Φοβήθητε δὲ
body, [7]the [1]but [8]soul [2]not [3]being [4]able [5]to [6]kill. fear ˜ But
who are not able

up, do not worry about how or what you should speak. For it will be given to you in that hour what you should speak;
20 "for it is not you who speak, but the Spirit of your Father who speaks in you.
21 "Now brother will deliver up brother to death, and a father *his* child; and children will rise up against parents and cause them to be put to death.
22 "And you will be hated by all for My name's sake. But he who endures to the end will be saved.
23 "When they persecute you in this city, flee to another. For assuredly, I say to you, you will not have gone through the cities of Israel before the Son of Man comes.
24 "A disciple is not above *his* teacher, nor a servant above his master.
25 "It is enough for a disciple that he be like his teacher, and a servant like his master. If they have called the master of the house Beelzebub, how much more *will they call* those of his household!
26 "Therefore do not fear them. For there is nothing covered that will not be revealed, and hidden that will not be known.
27 "Whatever I tell you in the dark, speak in the light; and what you hear in the ear, preach on the housetops.
28 "And do not fear those who kill the body but cannot kill the

---

***(10:22)** σώζω *(sōzō)*. Verb basically meaning *save,* but widely used in the NT with many meanings. It can mean *to deliver* from danger or death, as here from persecution, or elsewhere (Matt. 14:30; Acts 27:31) from drowning. When it is used of saving from disease, it means *to heal* (Mark 5:34), though some cases of physical healing may also involve spiritual salvation. Often σώζω conveys the important NT message of salvation from eternal death (Matt. 1:21; John 3:17; Acts 16:31). However, eternal salvation may not always be in view. The parallel passages of Mark 8:35 and Luke 9:24 possibly speak of saving one's life from being wasted.

soul. But rather fear Him who
is able to destroy both soul and
body in hell.
29 "Are not two sparrows
sold for a copper coin? And not
one of them falls to the ground
apart from your Father's will.
30 "But the very hairs of your
head are all numbered.
31 "Do not fear therefore; you
are of more value than many
sparrows.
32 "Therefore whoever confesses Me before men, him I
will also confess before My Father who is in heaven.
33 "But whoever denies Me
before men, him I will also deny
before My Father who is in
heaven.
34 "Do not think that I came
to bring peace on earth. I did
not come to bring peace but a
sword.
35 "For I have come to *'set a
man against his father, a daughter against her mother, and a
daughter-in-law against her
mother-in-law'*;
36 "and *'a man's enemies will
be those of his own household.'*
37 "He who loves father or
mother more than Me is not
worthy of Me. And he who
loves son or daughter more
than Me is not worthy of Me.
38 "And he who does not take

μᾶλλον τὸν δυνάμενον καὶ τὴν ψυχὴν καὶ τὸ σῶμα
rather the *One* being able [3]both [4]the [5]soul [6]and [7]the [8]body
Him who is able

ἀπολέσαι ἐν Γεέννῃ. **29** *Οὐχὶ δύο στρουθία ἀσσαρίου*
[1]to [2]destroy in Gehenna. [2]not [3]two [4]sparrows [6]for [7]an [8]assarion
hell. a copper coin

πωλεῖται; Καὶ ἓν ἐξ αὐτῶν οὐ πεσεῖται ἐπὶ τὴν γῆν ἄνευ
[1]Are [5]sold? And one of them not ˜ shall fall on the ground without

τοῦ Πατρὸς ὑμῶν. **30** *Ὑμῶν δὲ καὶ αἱ τρίχες τῆς*
- *the will* of Father ˜ your. [6]your [1]But [2]even [3]the [4]hairs -

κεφαλῆς πᾶσαι ἠριθμημέναι εἰσί. **31** *Μὴ οὖν*
[5]of [7]head [9]all [10]numbered [8]are. [3]not [1]Therefore

φοβηθῆτε· πολλῶν στρουθίων διαφέρετε ὑμεῖς.
[2]do [4]be [5]afraid; [11]many [12]sparrows [7]are [8]worth [9]more [10]than [6]you.

Confess Christ Before Men
(Luke 12:8, 9)

32 "*Πᾶς οὖν ὅστις ὁμολογήσει ἐν ἐμοὶ ἔμπροσθεν*
"everyone ˜ Therefore who will confess - Me before

τῶν ἀνθρώπων, ὁμολογήσω κἀγὼ ἐν αὐτῷ ἔμπροσθεν τοῦ
- men, [3]will [4]confess [1]I [2]also - him before -

Πατρός μου τοῦ ἐν οὐρανοῖς. **33** *Ὅστις δ' ἂν ἀρνήσηταί*
Father ˜ My the *One* in *the* heavens. who ˜ But ever denies
who is

με ἔμπροσθεν τῶν ἀνθρώπων, ἀρνήσομαι αὐτὸν κἀγὼ
Me before - men, [3]will [4]deny [5]him [1]I [2]also

ἔμπροσθεν τοῦ Πατρός μου τοῦ ἐν οὐρανοῖς.
before - Father ˜ My the *One* in *the* heavens.
who is

Christ Brings a Sword
(Luke 12:51–53; 14:26, 27)

34 "*Μὴ νομίσητε ὅτι ἦλθον βαλεῖν εἰρήνην ἐπὶ τὴν γῆν.*
"not ˜ Do suppose that I came to bring peace on the earth.

Οὐκ ἦλθον βαλεῖν εἰρήνην ἀλλὰ μάχαιραν. **35** *Ἦλθον γὰρ*
[3]not [1]I [2]came to bring peace but a sword. [2]I [3]came [1]For

διχάσαι ἄνθρωπον
to divide a man
turn

36 «*Κατὰ τοῦ πατρὸς αὐτοῦ*
«Against - father ˜ his

Καὶ θυγατέρα κατὰ τῆς μητρὸς αὐτῆς
And a daughter against - mother ˜ her

Καὶ νύμφην κατὰ τῆς πενθερᾶς αὐτῆς,»
And a daughter-in-law against - mother-in-law ˜ her,»

Καὶ «ἐχθροὶ τοῦ ἀνθρώπου οἱ οἰκειακοὶ
And «*the* enemies of the man - *will be* [2]household [3]members
a

αὐτοῦ.» [e]
[1]his.»

37 "*Ὁ φιλῶν πατέρα ἢ μητέρα ὑπὲρ ἐμὲ οὐκ ἔστι*
"The *one* loving father or mother above Me not ˜ is
"He who loves more than

μου ἄξιος· καὶ ὁ φιλῶν υἱὸν ἢ θυγατέρα ὑπὲρ ἐμὲ
[2]of [3]Me [1]worthy; and the *one* loving son or daughter above Me
he who loves more than

οὐκ ἔστι μου ἄξιος· **38** *καὶ ὃς οὐ λαμβάνει τὸν*
not ˜ is [2]of [3]Me [1]worthy; and *he* who not ˜ does take -

[e](10:36) Mic. 7:6

σταυρὸν αὐτοῦ καὶ ἀκολουθεῖ ὀπίσω μου οὐκ ἔστι μου
cross ˜ his and follow after Me not ˜ is [2]of [3]Me

ἄξιος. 39 Ὁ εὑρὼν τὴν ψυχὴν αὐτοῦ ἀπολέσει αὐτήν, καὶ
[1]worthy. The *one* finding - life ˜ his will lose it, and
He who finds

ὁ ἀπολέσας τὴν ψυχὴν αὐτοῦ ἕνεκεν ἐμοῦ εὑρήσει
the *one* losing - life ˜ his because of Me will find
he who loses for My sake

αὐτήν.
it.

A Cup of Cold Water
(Mark 9:41)

40 "Ὁ δεχόμενος ὑμᾶς ἐμὲ δέχεται, καὶ ὁ ἐμὲ
"The *one* receiving you Me ˜ receives, and the *one* Me ˜
"He who receives he who receives

δεχόμενος δέχεται τὸν ἀποστείλαντά με. 41 Ὁ
receiving receives the *One* having sent Me. The *one*
Me receives Him who sent He who

δεχόμενος προφήτην εἰς ὄνομα προφήτου μισθὸν*
receiving a prophet in *the* name of a prophet [3]*the* [4]reward
receives

προφήτου λήψεται, καὶ ὁ δεχόμενος δίκαιον εἰς
[5]of [6]a [7]prophet [1]will [2]receive, and the *one* receiving a righteous *person* in
he who receives

ὄνομα δικαίου μισθὸν δικαίου
the name of a righteous *person* [3]*the* [4]reward [5]of [6]a [7]righteous [8]*person*

λήψεται. 42 Καὶ ὃς ἐὰν ποτίσῃ ἕνα τῶν μικρῶν
[1]will [2]receive. And who ever gives [11]to [12]drink [1]one - [2]of [4]little [5]*ones*

τούτων ποτήριον ψυχροῦ μόνον εἰς ὄνομα μαθητοῦ,
[3]these [6]a [7]cup [8]of [9]cold [10]*water* only in *the* name of a disciple,

ἀμὴν λέγω ὑμῖν, οὐ μὴ ἀπολέσῃ τὸν μισθὸν αὐτοῦ."
amen I say to you, not not will he lose - reward ˜ his."
assuredly by no means

11 1 Καὶ ἐγένετο ὅτε ἐτέλεσεν ὁ Ἰησοῦς διατάσσων
And it happened when finished ˜ - Jesus directing

τοῖς δώδεκα μαθηταῖς αὐτοῦ, μετέβη ἐκεῖθεν τοῦ
- [2]twelve [3]disciples [1]His, He moved on from there -

διδάσκειν καὶ κηρύσσειν ἐν ταῖς πόλεσιν αὐτῶν.
to teach and to preach in - cities ˜ their.

John the Baptist Sends Messengers to Jesus
(Luke 7:18–35)

2 Ὁ δὲ Ἰωάννης ἀκούσας ἐν τῷ δεσμωτηρίῳ τὰ ἔργα
- But John hearing in - prison the works
when John heard

τοῦ Χριστοῦ, πέμψας δύο[a] τῶν μαθητῶν αὐτοῦ 3 εἶπεν
of the Christ, sending two - of disciples ˜ his he said
Messiah,

αὐτῷ, "Σὺ εἶ ὁ ἐρχόμενος ἢ ἕτερον
to Him, "You ˜ Are the Coming *One* or [5]a [6]different [7]*one*
One who is coming

προσδοκῶμεν?"
[1]do [2]we [3]look [4]for?"

4 Καὶ ἀποκριθεὶς ὁ Ἰησοῦς εἶπεν αὐτοῖς, "Πορευθέντες
And answering - Jesus said to them, "Having gone
"Go and

his cross and follow after Me is not worthy of Me.
39 "He who finds his life will lose it, and he who loses his life for My sake will find it.
40 "He who receives you receives Me, and he who receives Me receives Him who sent Me.
41 "He who receives a prophet in the name of a prophet shall receive a prophet's reward. And he who receives a righteous man in the name of a righteous man shall receive a righteous man's reward.
42 "And whoever gives one of these little ones only a cup of cold *water* in the name of a disciple, assuredly, I say to you, he shall by no means lose his reward."

11 Now it came to pass, when Jesus finished commanding His twelve disciples, that He departed from there to teach and to preach in their cities.
2 And when John had heard in prison about the works of Christ, he sent two of his disciples
3 and said to Him, "Are You the Coming One, or do we look for another?"
4 Jesus answered and said to

---

[a](11:2) NU reads δια, *by (His disciples).*

***(10:41)** μισθός *(misthos).* Noun meaning *pay, wages,* or *reward.* In the NT the word can refer equally well to the literal "pay" of day laborers (James 5:4) or to the spiritual compensation granted for righteous deeds (as here in Matt. 10:41, 42). The sense of reward for righteous living is important also for eschatology (cf. Matt. 5:12; Luke 6:23; 1 Cor. 3:8, 14; Rev. 11:18). As the Judge of the works of both saved and unsaved people alike, Christ will come with everyone's "pay" (Rev. 22:12). But as Paul makes clear (Rom. 4:4), this "pay" does not apply to a person's justification before God, which is by grace through faith alone. μισθός, therefore, is what one has "earned," not what he has been freely given by grace.

them, "Go and tell John the
things which you hear and see:
5 "*The* blind see and *the* lame
walk; *the* lepers are cleansed
and *the* deaf hear; *the* dead are
raised up and *the* poor have the
gospel preached to them.
6 "And blessed is he who is
not offended because of Me."
7 As they departed, Jesus
began to say to the multitudes
concerning John: "What did you
go out into the wilderness to
see? A reed shaken by the
wind?
8 "But what did you go out to
see? A man clothed in soft garments? Indeed, those who
wear soft *clothing* are in kings'
houses.
9 "But what did you go out to
see? A prophet? Yes, I say to
you, and more than a prophet.
10 "For this is *he* of whom it is
written:

'Behold, I send My
messenger before Your
face,
Who will prepare Your
way before You.'

11 "Assuredly, I say to you,
among those born of women
there has not risen one greater
than John the Baptist; but he
who is least in the kingdom of
heaven is greater than he.
12 "And from the days of John
the Baptist until now the kingdom of heaven suffers violence,
and the violent take it by force.
13 "For all the prophets and
the law prophesied until John.
14 "And if you are willing to
receive *it,* he is Elijah who is to
come.
15 "He who has ears to hear,
let him hear!

ἀπαγγείλατε Ἰωάννῃ ἃ ἀκούετε καὶ βλέπετε·
report to John the things which you hear and see:
what

5 τυφλοὶ ἀναβλέπουσι καὶ χωλοὶ περιπατοῦσι, λεπροὶ
blind *people* regain sight and lame *people* walk, lepers

καθαρίζονται καὶ κωφοὶ ἀκούουσι, νεκροὶ ἐγείρονται καὶ
are cleansed and deaf *people* hear, dead *people* are raised and

πτωχοὶ εὐαγγελίζονται. 6 Καὶ μακάριός ἐστιν ὃς
poor *people* are evangelized. And blessed is who
have the Gospel preached to them.

ἐὰν μὴ σκανδαλισθῇ ἐν ἐμοί." 7 Τούτων δὲ
ever not ˜ is offended in Me." these *men* And
because of Now as these

πορευομένων, ἤρξατο ὁ Ἰησοῦς λέγειν τοῖς ὄχλοις περὶ
going, began ˜ - Jesus to say to the crowds concerning
men were going,

Ἰωάννου, "Τί ἐξήλθετε εἰς τὴν ἔρημον θεάσασθαι?
John, "What did you go out into the wilderness to see?

Κάλαμον ὑπὸ ἀνέμου σαλευόμενον? 8 Ἀλλὰ τί ἐξήλθετε
A reed [3]by [4]wind [1]being [2]shaken? But what did you go out

ἰδεῖν? Ἄνθρωπον ἐν μαλακοῖς ἱματίοις[b] ἠμφιεσμένον?
to see? A man [4]in [5]soft [6]garments [1]having [2]been [3]clothed?

Ἰδού, οἱ τὰ μαλακὰ φοροῦντες ἐν τοῖς οἴκοις τῶν
Behold, the *ones* - [2]soft [3]*things* [1]wearing [5]in [6]the [7]houses -
those who wear soft material

βασιλείων[c] εἰσίν. 9 Ἀλλὰ τί ἐξήλθετε ἰδεῖν? Προφήτην?
[8]of [9]kingdoms [4]are. But what did you go out to see? A prophet?

Ναί, λέγω ὑμῖν, καὶ περισσότερον προφήτου. 10 Οὗτος γάρ
Yes, I say to you, and far more *than* a prophet. this ˜ For

ἐστι περὶ οὗ γέγραπται,
is *he* about whom it is written,

«Ἰδού, ἐγὼ ἀποστέλλω τὸν ἄγγελόν μου πρὸ
«Behold, I send - messenger ˜ My before

προσώπου σου,
face ˜ Your,

Ὃς κατασκευάσει τὴν ὁδόν σου ἔμπροσθέν σου.»[d]
Who will prepare - way ˜ Your before You.»

11 Ἀμὴν λέγω ὑμῖν, οὐκ ἐγήγερται ἐν γεννητοῖς
Amen I say to you, [3]not [1]*there* [2]has [4]arisen among *those* born
Assuredly

γυναικῶν μείζων Ἰωάννου τοῦ Βαπτιστοῦ· ὁ δὲ
of women a greater *than* John the Baptist; the ˜ but
but he

μικρότερος ἐν τῇ βασιλείᾳ τῶν οὐρανῶν μείζων αὐτοῦ
least in the kingdom of the heavens [2]greater [3]*than* [4]him
who is least he

ἐστιν. 12 Ἀπὸ δὲ τῶν ἡμερῶν Ἰωάννου τοῦ Βαπτιστοῦ ἕως
[1]is. from ˜ But the days of John the Baptist until

ἄρτι ἡ βασιλεία τῶν οὐρανῶν βιάζεται, καὶ βιασταὶ
now the kingdom of the heavens suffers violence, and violent men

ἁρπάζουσιν αὐτήν. 13 Πάντες γὰρ οἱ προφῆται καὶ ὁ νόμος
seize it. all ˜ For the prophets and the law

ἕως Ἰωάννου προεφήτευσαν. 14 Καὶ εἰ θέλετε δέξασθαι,
[2]until [3]John [1]prophesied. And if you are willing to receive *it,*

αὐτός ἐστιν Ἠλίας ὁ μέλλων ἔρχεσθαι. 15 Ὁ ἔχων
he is Elijah the *one* being about to come. The *one* having
who is He who has

ὦτα ἀκούειν[e] ἀκουέτω.
ears to hear let him hear.

---

[b](11:8) NU omits ιματιοις, *robes.* [c](11:8) NU reads βασιλεων, *of kings.*
[d](11:10) Mal. 3:1
[e](11:15) NU omits ακουειν, *to hear.*

16 “Τίνι δὲ ὁμοιώσω τὴν γενεὰν ταύτην? Ὁμοία
“[2]to [3]what [1]But shall I compare - generation ˜ this? [3]similar

ἐστὶ παιδίοις ἐν ἀγοραῖς καθημένοις, καὶ προσφωνοῦσι
[1]It [2]is to children [2]in [3]*the* [4]marketplaces [1]sitting, and calling
who sit, call

τοῖς ἑτέροις[f] αὐτῶν 17 καὶ λέγουσιν,
- to others ˜ their and saying,
playmates say,

‘Ηὐλήσαμεν ὑμῖν καὶ οὐκ ὠρχήσασθε,
‘We played the flute for you and [3]not [1]you [2]did dance,

Ἐθρηνήσαμεν ὑμῖν[g] καὶ οὐκ ἐκόψασθε.’
We mourned for you and [3]not [1]you [2]did lament.’

18 Ἦλθε γὰρ Ἰωάννης μήτε ἐσθίων μήτε πίνων, καὶ
[3]came [1]For [2]John neither eating nor drinking, and

λέγουσι, ‘Δαιμόνιον ἔχει.’ 19 Ἦλθεν ὁ Υἱὸς τοῦ
they say, ‘[3]a [4]demon [1]He [2]has.’ [5]came [1]The [2]Son -

Ἀνθρώπου ἐσθίων καὶ πίνων, καὶ λέγουσιν, “Ἰδού, ἄνθρωπος
[3]of [4]Man eating and drinking, and they say, ‘Look, a man
a

φάγος καὶ οἰνοπότης, τελωνῶν φίλος καὶ
a glutton and a wine drinker, [3]of [4]tax [5]collectors [1]a [2]friend and
glutton drunkard,

ἁμαρτωλῶν!’ Καὶ ἐδικαιώθη ἡ σοφία ἀπὸ τῶν τέκνων[h]
sinners!’ And [2]was [3]justified - [1]wisdom by - children ˜
And so wisdom is declared right

αὐτῆς.”
her.”

Jesus Pronounces Woes on Unrepentant Cities
(Luke 10:13–15)

20 Τότε ἤρξατο ὀνειδίζειν τὰς πόλεις ἐν αἷς ἐγένοντο αἱ
Then He began to reproach the cities in which were done -
had been

πλεῖσται δυνάμεις αὐτοῦ, ὅτι οὐ μετενόησαν. 21 “Οὐαί
[2]very [3]many [4]miracles [1]His, because [3]not [1]they [2]did repent. “Woe

σοι, Χοραζίν, οὐαί σοι, Βηθσαϊδά, ὅτι εἰ ἐν Τύρῳ καὶ
to you, Chorazin, woe to you, Bethsaida, because if [10]in [11]Tyre [12]and

Σιδῶνι ἐγένοντο αἱ δυνάμεις αἱ γενόμεναι ἐν ὑμῖν,
[13]Sidon [8]were [9]done [1]the [2]miracles [3]the [4]*ones* [5]done [6]in [7]you,
had been which have been done

πάλαι ἂν ἐν σάκκῳ καὶ σποδῷ μετενόησαν.
[18]long [19]ago [20]in [21]sackcloth [22]and [23]ashes [14]they [15]would [16]have [17]repented.

22 Πλὴν λέγω ὑμῖν, Τύρῳ καὶ Σιδῶνι ἀνεκτότερον
Nevertheless I say to you, [6]for [7]Tyre [8]and [9]for [10]Sidon [4]more [5]tolerable

ἔσται ἐν ἡμέρᾳ κρίσεως ἢ ὑμῖν. 23 Καὶ σύ,
[1]it [2]will [3]be in *the* day of judgment than for you. And you,

Καπερναούμ, ἡ ἕως τοῦ οὐρανοῦ ὑψωθεῖσα,[i] ἕως
Capernaum, the *one* [4]to - [5]heaven [1]having [2]been [3]exalted, [11]to
who have

Ἅιδου καταβιβασθήσῃ· ὅτι εἰ ἐν Σοδόμοις
[12]Hades [6]you [7]will [8]be [9]brought [10]down; because if in Sodom

ἐγένοντο αἱ δυνάμεις αἱ γενόμεναι ἐν σοί,
[3]were [4]done [1]the [2]miracles the *ones* done in you,
had been which have been done

ἔμειναν ἂν μέχρι τῆς σήμερον. 24 Πλὴν λέγω
it would have remained - to - today. Nevertheless I say

ὑμῖν ὅτι γῇ Σοδόμων ἀνεκτότερον ἔσται ἐν
to you that [6]for [7]*the* [8]land [9]of [10]Sodom [4]more [5]tolerable [1]it [2]will [3]be in

16 “But to what shall I liken this generation? It is like children sitting in the marketplaces and calling to their companions,
17 “and saying:

‘We played the flute for you,
And you did not dance;
We mourned to you,
And you did not lament.’

18 “For John came neither eating nor drinking, and they say, ‘He has a demon.’
19 “The Son of Man came eating and drinking, and they say, ‘Look, a glutton and a winebibber, a friend of tax collectors and sinners!’ But wisdom is justified by her children.”
20 Then He began to rebuke the cities in which most of His mighty works had been done, because they did not repent:
21 “Woe to you, Chorazin! Woe to you, Bethsaida! For if the mighty works which were done in you had been done in Tyre and Sidon, they would have repented long ago in sackcloth and ashes.
22 “But I say to you, it will be more tolerable for Tyre and Sidon in the day of judgment than for you.
23 “And you, Capernaum, who are exalted to heaven, will be brought down to Hades; for if the mighty works which were done in you had been done in Sodom, it would have remained until this day.
24 “But I say to you that it shall be more tolerable for the land of Sodom in the day of

---

[f](**11:16**) TR reads εταιροις, *friends.* [g](**11:17**) NU omits *υμιν, to you.*
[h](**11:19**) NU reads εργων, *works.* [i](**11:23**) For η . . . . *υψωθεισα, the one . . . having been exalted,* NU reads *μη . . . υψωθηση, Will you be exalted (to heaven)? No, . . .*

judgment than for you."
25 At that time Jesus answered and said, "I thank You, Father, Lord of heaven and earth, that You have hidden these things from *the* wise and prudent and have revealed them to babes.
26 "Even so, Father, for so it seemed good in Your sight.
27 "All things have been delivered to Me by My Father, and no one knows the Son except the Father. Nor does anyone know the Father except the Son, and *the one* to whom the Son wills to reveal *Him.*
28 "Come to Me, all *you* who labor and are heavy laden, and I will give you rest.
29 "Take My yoke upon you and learn from Me, for I am gentle and lowly in heart, and you will find rest for your souls.
30 "For My yoke *is* easy and My burden is light."
12 At that time Jesus went through the grainfields on the Sabbath. And His disciples were hungry, and began to pluck heads of grain and to eat.
2 And when the Pharisees saw *it,* they said to Him, "Look, Your disciples are doing what is not lawful to do on the Sabbath!"
3 But He said to them, "Have you not read what David

ἡμέρᾳ κρίσεως ἢ σοί."
the day of judgment than for you."

Jesus Offers Rest
(Luke 10:21, 22)

25 *Ἐν ἐκείνῳ τῷ καιρῷ ἀποκριθεὶς ὁ Ἰησοῦς εἶπεν,*
In that - time answering ˜ - Jesus said,
At Jesus answered and

"Ἐξομολογοῦμαί σοι, Πάτερ, Κύριε τοῦ οὐρανοῦ καὶ τῆς γῆς,
"I praise You, Father, Lord - of heaven and - earth,

ὅτι ἀπέκρυψας ταῦτα ἀπὸ σοφῶν καὶ συνετῶν καὶ
that You hid these *things* from wise and intelligent *people* and
have hidden

ἀπεκάλυψας αὐτὰ νηπίοις. **26** *Ναί, ὁ Πατήρ, ὅτι οὕτως*
You revealed them to babes. Yes, - Father, because so
have revealed

ἐγένετο εὐδοκία ἔμπροσθέν σου. **27** *Πάντα μοι*
it was good pleasure before You. All *things* [4]to [5]Me
seemed good in Your sight.

παρεδόθη ὑπὸ τοῦ Πατρός μου, καὶ οὐδεὶς ἐπιγινώσκει
[1]were [2]given [3]over by - Father ˜ My, and no one fully knows
have been

τὸν Υἱὸν εἰ μὴ ὁ Πατήρ, οὐδὲ τὸν Πατέρα τις
the Son if not the Father, nor [5]the [6]Father [2]anyone
except

ἐπιγινώσκει εἰ μὴ ὁ Υἱὸς καὶ ᾧ ἐὰν
[1]does [3]fully [4]know if not the Son and *the one* to whom -
except

βούληται ὁ Υἱὸς ἀποκαλύψαι. **28** *Δεῦτε πρός με πάντες*
[3]wills [1]the [2]Son to reveal *Him.* Come to Me all

*οἱ κοπιῶντες καὶ πεφορτισμένοι, κἀγὼ ἀναπαύσω**
the *ones* laboring and having been loaded down, and I will give rest ˜
you who labor are

ὑμᾶς. **29** *Ἄρατε τὸν ζυγόν μου ἐφ' ὑμᾶς καὶ μάθετε ἀπ'*
you. Take - yoke ˜ My upon you and learn from

ἐμοῦ, ὅτι πρᾶός εἰμι καὶ ταπεινὸς τῇ καρδίᾳ, καὶ
Me, because [3]gentle [1]I [2]am and lowly - in heart, and

εὑρήσετε ἀνάπαυσιν ταῖς ψυχαῖς ὑμῶν. **30** *Ὁ γὰρ ζυγός μου*
you will find rest - for souls ˜ your. - For yoke ˜ My

χρηστὸς καὶ τὸ φορτίον μου ἐλαφρόν ἐστιν."
[2]easy [3]and - [5]burden [4]My [6]light [1]is."

Jesus Is Lord of the Sabbath
(Mark 2:23–28; Luke 6:1–5)

12 **1** *Ἐν ἐκείνῳ τῷ καιρῷ ἐπορεύθη ὁ Ἰησοῦς τοῖς*
In that - time went ˜ - Jesus on the
At

σάββασι διὰ τῶν σπορίμων. Οἱ δὲ μαθηταὶ αὐτοῦ
Sabbath through the grainfields. - But disciples ˜ His

ἐπείνασαν, καὶ ἤρξαντο τίλλειν στάχυας καὶ ἐσθίειν.
became hungry, and they began to pick heads of grain and to eat.

2 *Οἱ δὲ Φαρισαῖοι ἰδόντες εἶπον αὐτῷ, "Ἰδού, οἱ μαθηταί*
the ˜ But Pharisees seeing *it* said to Him, "Look, - disciples ˜
But when the Pharisees saw it, they said

σου ποιοῦσιν ὃ οὐκ ἔξεστι ποιεῖν ἐν σαββάτῳ."
Your are doing what not ˜ is lawful to do on a Sabbath."

3 *Ὁ δὲ εἶπεν αὐτοῖς, "Οὐκ ἀνέγνωτε τί*
[2]the [3]*One* [1]But said to them, "[3]not [1]Did [2]you [4]read what
He

(11:28) *ἀναπαύω (anapauō).* Verb meaning in the active voice *to cause to rest, give (someone) rest* and in the passive *to rest.* The sense *refresh* is appropriate in passages like 1 Cor. 16:18; 2 Cor. 7:13; Philem. 7, 20 where there is no real thought of ceasing from labor or toil. But that idea *is* prominent here in Matt. 11:28 (also Rev. 14:13). The thought is that of giving up futile labors (like those engaged in under the law) in order to find Christ's gift of rest, or peace, which is granted without works (cf. Rom. 5:1). In Rev. 14:13, however, the idea is the rest the departed believer finds in the presence of God when all earthly toil is behind him.

ἐποίησε Δαβὶδ ὅτε ἐπείνασεν αὐτὸς καὶ οἱ μετ'
did ˜ David when he became hungry he and the *ones* with
those who were

αὐτοῦ, 4 πῶς εἰσῆλθεν εἰς τὸν οἶκον τοῦ Θεοῦ καὶ τοὺς
him, how they entered into the house - of God and [2]the

ἄρτους τῆς προθέσεως ἔφαγεν, οὓς οὐκ ἐξὸν ἦν αὐτῷ
[3]loaves [4]of [5]the [6]presentation [1]ate, which [2]not [3]lawful [1]was for him
showbread

φαγεῖν οὐδὲ τοῖς μετ' αὐτοῦ, εἰ μὴ τοῖς ἱερεῦσι
to eat nor for the *ones* with him, if not for the priests
those who were except

μόνοις? 5 Ἢ οὐκ ἀνέγνωτε ἐν τῷ νόμῳ ὅτι τοῖς σάββασιν
only? Or [3]not [1]did [2]you [4]read in the law that on the Sabbath

οἱ ἱερεῖς ἐν τῷ ἱερῷ τὸ σάββατον βεβηλοῦσι καὶ ἀναίτιοί
the priests in the temple [2]the [3]Sabbath [1]profane and innocent ˜

εἰσι? 6 Λέγω δὲ ὑμῖν ὅτι τοῦ ἱεροῦ μεῖζόν
are? [2]I [3]say [1]But to you that [4]*than* [5]the [6]temple [1]a [2]greater [3]*thing*

ἐστιν ὧδε. 7 Εἰ δὲ ἐγνώκειτε τί ἐστιν, «Ἔλεον θέλω
is here. if ˜ But you had known what it is, «[3]Mercy [1]I [2]desire
this means,

καὶ οὐ θυσίαν,»[a] οὐκ ἂν κατεδικάσατε τοὺς
and not sacrifice,» [3]not - [1]you [2]would [4]have [5]condemned the

ἀναιτίους. 8 Κύριος γάρ ἐστι[b] τοῦ σαββάτου ὁ Υἱὸς τοῦ
innocent *ones*. [7]Lord [1]For [6]is [8]of [9]the [10]Sabbath [2]the [3]Son -

Ἀνθρώπου."
[4]of [5]Man."

Jesus Heals a Man with a Withered Hand on the Sabbath
(Mark 3:1–6; Luke 6:6–11)

9 Καὶ μεταβὰς ἐκεῖθεν ἦλθεν εἰς τὴν συναγωγὴν αὐτῶν.
And moving on from there He went into - synagogue ˜ their.

10 Καὶ ἰδού, ἄνθρωπος ἦν τὴν χεῖρα ἔχων ξηράν.
And behold, [3]a [4]man [1]*there* [2]was the hand having withered.
who had a withered hand.

Καὶ ἐπηρώτησαν αὐτόν, λέγοντες, "Εἰ ἔξεστι τοῖς σάββασι
And they asked Him, saying, - "Is it lawful on the Sabbath

θεραπεύειν?" — ἵνα κατηγορήσωσιν αὐτοῦ.
to heal?" — so that they might accuse Him.

11 Ὁ δὲ εἶπεν αὐτοῖς, "Τίς ἔσται ἐξ ὑμῶν
[2]the [3]*One* [1]Then said to them, "What [4]will [5]*there* [6]be [2]of [3]you
He

ἄνθρωπος ὃς ἕξει πρόβατον ἕν, καὶ ἐὰν ἐμπέσῃ τοῦτο
[1]man who shall have sheep ˜ one, and if [3]should [4]fall [1]this [2]*one*

τοῖς σάββασιν εἰς βόθυνον, οὐχὶ κρατήσει αὐτὸ καὶ ἐγερεῖ?
on the Sabbath into a ditch, not ˜ will lay hold of it and lift *it* out?

12 Πόσῳ οὖν διαφέρει ἄνθρωπος προβάτου!
By how much then is [3]worth [4]more [5]than [1]a [2]man a sheep!

Ὥστε ἔξεστι τοῖς σάββασι καλῶς ποιεῖν." 13 Τότε λέγει
So then it is lawful on the Sabbath [3]well [1]to [2]do." Then He says
said

τῷ ἀνθρώπῳ, "Ἔκτεινον τὴν χεῖρά σου." Καὶ ἐξέτεινε,
to the man, "Stretch out - hand ˜ your." And he stretched *it* out,

καὶ ἀποκατεστάθη ὑγιὴς ὡς ἡ ἄλλη. 14 Οἱ δε Φαρισαῖοι
and it was restored whole like the other. the ˜ But Pharisees

did when he was hungry, he and those who were with him:

4 "how he entered the house of God and ate the showbread which was not lawful for him to eat, nor for those who were with him, but only for the priests?

5 "Or have you not read in the law that on the Sabbath the priests in the temple profane the Sabbath, and are blameless?

6 "Yet I say to you that in this place there is *One* greater than the temple.

7 "But if you had known what *this* means, *'I desire mercy and not sacrifice,'* you would not have condemned the guiltless.

8 "For the Son of Man is Lord even of the Sabbath."

9 Now when He had departed from there, He went into their synagogue.

10 And behold, there was a man who had a withered hand. And they asked Him, saying, "Is it lawful to heal on the Sabbath?"—that they might accuse Him.

11 Then He said to them, "What man is there among you who has one sheep, and if it falls into a pit on the Sabbath, will not lay hold of it and lift *it* out?

12 "Of how much more value then is a man than a sheep? Therefore it is lawful to do good on the Sabbath."

13 Then He said to the man, "Stretch out your hand." And he stretched *it* out, and it was restored as whole as the other.

14 Then the Pharisees went

---

[a](**12:7**) Hos. 6:6
[b](**12:8**) TR adds *και, even.*

out and plotted against Him, how they might destroy Him.
15 But when Jesus knew *it,* He withdrew from there. And great multitudes followed Him, and He healed them all.
16 Yet He warned them not to make Him known,
17 that it might be fulfilled which was spoken by Isaiah the prophet, saying:

18 *"Behold! My Servant*
whom I have chosen,
My Beloved in whom My
soul is well pleased!
I will put My Spirit upon
Him,
And He will declare
justice to the Gentiles.
19 *He will not quarrel nor*
cry out,
Nor will anyone hear His
voice in the streets.
20 *A bruised reed He will not*
break,
And smoking flax He will
not quench,
Till He sends forth justice
to victory;
21 *And in His name Gentiles*
will trust."

22 Then one was brought to Him who was demon-possessed, blind and mute; and He healed him, so that the blind and mute man both spoke and saw.
23 And all the multitudes were amazed and said, "Could this be the Son of David?"

συμβούλιον ἔλαβον κατ' αὐτοῦ ἐξελθόντες, ὅπως αὐτὸν
counsel ~ took against Him going out, so that [4]Him
plotted as they went out,

ἀπολέσωσιν.
[1]they [2]might [3]destroy.

Behold My Servant

15 *Ὁ δὲ Ἰησοῦς γνοὺς ἀνεχώρησεν ἐκεῖθεν. Καὶ*
- But Jesus knowing He withdrew from there. And
when Jesus knew it

ἠκολούθησαν αὐτῷ ὄχλοι πολλοί, καὶ ἐθεράπευσεν αὐτοὺς
[3]followed [4]Him [2]crowds [1]large, and He healed them

πάντας. **16** *Καὶ ἐπετίμησεν αὐτοῖς ἵνα μὴ φανερὸν αὐτὸν*
all. And He warned them that [3]not [6]manifest [5]Him
known

ποιήσωσιν, **17** *ὅπως πληρωθῇ τὸ ῥηθὲν*
[1]they [2]should [4]make, so that [8]might [9]be [10]fulfilled [1]the [2]*thing* [3]spoken
that which was

διὰ Ἡσαΐου τοῦ προφήτου, λέγοντος,
[4]through [5]Isaiah [6]the [7]prophet, saying,

18 *«Ἰδού, ὁ παῖς μου ὃν ᾑρέτισα,*
«Behold, - Servant ~ My whom I chose,

Ὁ ἀγαπητός μου εἰς ὃν εὐδόκησεν ἡ ψυχή μου·
- Beloved ~ My in whom [3]is [4]well [5]pleased - [2]soul [1]My;

Θήσω τὸ Πνεῦμά μου ἐπ' αὐτόν,
I will put - Spirit ~ My upon Him,

Καὶ κρίσιν τοῖς ἔθνεσιν ἀπαγγελεῖ.
And [4]judgment [5]to [6]the [7]Gentiles [1]He [2]will [3]announce.
justice

19 *Οὐκ ἐρίσει οὐδὲ κραυγάσει,*
[3]not [1]He [2]will quarrel nor will cry out,

Οὐδὲ ἀκούσει τις ἐν ταῖς πλατείαις τὴν φωνὴν αὐτοῦ.
Nor will hear ~ anyone [3]in [4]the [5]streets - [2]voice [1]His.

20 *Κάλαμον συντετριμμένον οὐ κατεάξει,*
A reed having been bruised [3]not [1]He [2]will break,
A bruised reed

Καὶ λίνον τυφόμενον οὐ σβέσει,
And a wick ~ smoldering [3]not [1]He [2]will quench,

Ἕως ἂν ἐκβάλῃ εἰς νῖκος τὴν κρίσιν.
Till - He sends forth [2]to [3]victory - [1]judgment.
justice.

21 *Καὶ τῷ ὀνόματι αὐτοῦ ἔθνη ἐλπιοῦσι.»*[c]
And - in name ~ His Gentiles will hope.»

A House Divided Cannot Stand
(Mark 3:20–27; Luke 11:14–23)

22 *Τότε προσηνέχθη αὐτῷ δαιμονιζόμενος τυφλὸς*
Then was brought to Him *one* being demon-possessed blind
a demon-possessed man

καὶ κωφός· καὶ ἐθεράπευσεν αὐτόν, ὥστε τὸν τυφλὸν καὶ[d]
and mute; and He healed him, so that the blind and

κωφὸν καὶ λαλεῖν καὶ βλέπειν. **23** *Καὶ ἐξίσταντο πάντες*
mute *man* both to speak and to see. And [4]were [5]amazed [1]all
spoke saw.

οἱ ὄχλοι καὶ ἔλεγον, "Μήτι οὗτός ἐστιν ὁ Υἱὸς
[2]the [3]crowds and they said, "[3]not [1]This [2]is the Son

Δαβίδ?"
of David, *is it?"*

---

[c](**12:18–21**) Is. 42:1–4
[d](**12:22**) NU omits *τυφλον και, blind and.*

24 Οἱ δὲ Φαρισαῖοι ἀκούσαντες εἶπον, "Οὗτος οὐκ
the ˜ But Pharisees hearing said, "This *man* not ˜

ἐκβάλλει τὰ δαιμόνια εἰ μὴ ἐν τῷ Βεελζεβοὺλ ἄρχοντι
does cast out - demons if not by - Beelzebul ruler
except

τῶν δαιμονίων."
of the demons."

25 Εἰδὼς δὲ ὁ Ἰησοῦς τὰς ἐνθυμήσεις αὐτῶν εἶπεν
knowing But - Jesus - thoughts ˜ their He said
But when Jesus knew

αὐτοῖς, "Πᾶσα βασιλεία μερισθεῖσα καθ' ἑαυτῆς
to them, "Every kingdom being divided against itself

ἐρημοῦται, καὶ πᾶσα πόλις ἢ οἰκία μερισθεῖσα καθ'
is made desolate, and every city or house being divided against

ἑαυτῆς οὐ σταθήσεται. 26 Καὶ εἰ ὁ Σατανᾶς τὸν Σατανᾶν
itself not ˜ shall stand. And if - Satan - [3]Satan

ἐκβάλλει, ἐφ' ἑαυτὸν ἐμερίσθη. Πῶς οὖν σταθήσεται ἡ
[1]casts [2]out, [7]against [8]himself [4]he [5]was [6]divided. How then will [3]stand -
is

βασιλεία αὐτοῦ? 27 Καὶ εἰ ἐγὼ ἐν Βεελζεβοὺλ ἐκβάλλω τὰ
[2]kingdom [1]his? And if I by Beelzebul cast out -

δαιμόνια, οἱ υἱοὶ ὑμῶν ἐν τίνι ἐκβάλλουσι? Διὰ
demons, - [5]sons [4]your [1]by [2]whom [3]do [6]cast [7]*them* [8]out? On account of
Therefore

τοῦτο αὐτοὶ ὑμῶν ἔσονται κριταί. 28 Εἰ δὲ ἐν Πνεύματι Θεοῦ
this they [3]your [1]will [2]be judges. if ˜ But by *the* Spirit of God

ἐγὼ ἐκβάλλω τὰ δαιμόνια, ἄρα ἔφθασεν ἐφ' ὑμᾶς ἡ
I cast out - demons, then [5]came [6]upon [7]you [1]the
has come

βασιλεία τοῦ Θεοῦ. 29 Ἢ πῶς δύναταί τις εἰσελθεῖν εἰς τὴν
[2]kingdom - [3]of [4]God. Or how is able ˜ one to enter into the

οἰκίαν τοῦ ἰσχυροῦ καὶ τὰ σκεύη αὐτοῦ διαρπάσαι, ἐὰν μὴ
house of the strong *man* and - [4]vessels [3]his [1]to [2]plunder, if not
goods unless

πρῶτον δήσῃ τὸν ἰσχυρόν? Καὶ τότε τὴν οἰκίαν αὐτοῦ
first ˜ he binds the strong *man?* And then - [5]household [4]his

διαρπάσει. 30 Ὁ μὴ ὢν μετ' ἐμοῦ κατ' ἐμοῦ ἐστι,
[1]he [2]will [3]plunder. The *one* not being with Me [2]against [3]Me [1]is,
He who is not

καὶ ὁ μὴ συνάγων μετ' ἐμοῦ σκορπίζει.
and the *one* not gathering with Me scatters.
he who does not gather

Jesus Warns of the Unpardonable Sin
(Mark 3:28–30; Luke 12:10)

31 "Διὰ τοῦτο λέγω ὑμῖν, πᾶσα ἁμαρτία καὶ
"On account of this I say to you, every sin and
"Therefore

βλασφημία ἀφεθήσεται τοῖς ἀνθρώποις, ἡ δὲ τοῦ
blasphemy will be forgiven - to men, the ˜ but [2]of [3]the
against

Πνεύματος βλασφημία οὐκ ἀφεθήσεται τοῖς ἀνθρώποις.
[4]Spirit [1]blasphemy not ˜ will be forgiven - to men.

32 Καὶ ὃς ἐὰν εἴπῃ λόγον κατὰ τοῦ Υἱοῦ τοῦ Ἀνθρώπου,
And who ever says a word against the Son - of Man,

ἀφεθήσεται αὐτῷ· ὃς δ' ἂν εἴπῃ κατὰ τοῦ Πνεύματος
it will be forgiven to him; who ˜ but ever speaks against the Spirit ˜
he will be forgiven;

24 Now when the Pharisees heard *it* they said, "This *fellow* does not cast out demons except by Beelzebub, the ruler of the demons."
25 But Jesus knew their thoughts, and said to them: "Every kingdom divided against itself is brought to desolation, and every city or house divided against itself will not stand.
26 "If Satan casts out Satan, he is divided against himself. How then will his kingdom stand?
27 "And if I cast out demons by Beelzebub, by whom do your sons cast *them* out? Therefore they shall be your judges.
28 "But if I cast out demons by the Spirit of God, surely the kingdom of God has come upon you.
29 "Or how can one enter a strong man's house and plunder his goods, unless he first binds the strong man? And then he will plunder his house.
30 "He who is not with Me is against Me, and he who does not gather with Me scatters abroad.
31 "Therefore I say to you, every sin and blasphemy will be forgiven men, but the blasphemy *against* the Spirit will not be forgiven men.
32 "Anyone who speaks a word against the Son of Man, it will be forgiven him; but whoever speaks against the Holy

Spirit, it will not be forgiven
him, either in this age or in the
age to come.
33 "Either make the tree good
and its fruit good, or else make
the tree bad and its fruit bad;
for a tree is known by *its* fruit.
34 "Brood of vipers! How can
you, being evil, speak good
things? For out of the abundance of the heart the mouth
speaks.
35 "A good man out of the
good treasure of his heart
brings forth good things, and an
evil man out of the evil treasure
brings forth evil things.
36 "But I say to you that for
every idle word men may
speak, they will give account of
it in the day of judgment.
37 "For by your words you
will be justified, and by your
words you will be condemned."
38 Then some of the scribes
and Pharisees answered, saying, "Teacher, we want to see
a sign from You."
39 But He answered and said
to them, "An evil and adulterous generation seeks after a
sign, and no sign will be given
to it except the sign of the
prophet Jonah.
40 "For as Jonah was three
days and three nights in the

[e](12:35) TR adds της καρδιας, *of the (his) heart.*

*(12:33) σαπρός *(sapros).* Adjective applied to things which are *decayed, rotten,* or *spoiled.* Here (also Matt. 7:17, 18; Luke 6:43), "the bad tree" is one that suffers from rot or decay and cannot produce good fruit, while in Matt. 13:48 σαπρός is used of fish that are spoiled or diseased. In the only use of the word outside of Matthew and Luke, Paul warns Christians not to allow any "corrupt word" to go out of their mouths (Eph. 4:29). The worthlessness of such words is stressed by σαπρός, which points to their "decayed," hence morally offensive, character. An allusion back to Jesus' image of the "rotten" tree in Matt. 12:33–37 is likely in Paul's words.

τοῦ Ἁγίου, οὐκ ἀφεθήσεται αὐτῷ οὔτε ἐν τῷ νῦν αἰῶνι
- Holy, [3]not [1]it [2]will be forgiven to him either in the now (present) age

οὔτε ἐν τῷ μέλλοντι.
or in the coming *one.*

A Tree Is Known by Its Fruit
(Luke 6:43–45)

33 *"Ἢ ποιήσατε τὸ δένδρον καλὸν καὶ τὸν καρπὸν αὐτοῦ*
"Either make the tree good and - fruit ˜ its

καλόν, ἢ ποιήσατε τὸ δένδρον σαπρὸν καὶ τὸν καρπὸν αὐτοῦ*
good, or make the tree rotten (bad) and - fruit ˜ its

σαπρόν· ἐκ γὰρ τοῦ καρποῦ τὸ δένδρον γινώσκεται.
rotten; (bad;) by ˜ for the (its) fruit the (a) tree is known.

34 *Γεννήματα ἐχιδνῶν! Πῶς δύνασθε ἀγαθὰ λαλεῖν,*
Offspring of vipers! How are you able [3]good [4]*things* [1]to [2]speak,

πονηροὶ ὄντες? Ἐκ γὰρ τοῦ περισσεύματος τῆς καρδίας τὸ
evil ˜ being? [2]out [3]of [1]For the abundance of the heart the

στόμα λαλεῖ. **35** *Ὁ ἀγαθὸς ἄνθρωπος ἐκ τοῦ ἀγαθοῦ*
mouth speaks. The (A) good man out of the (his) good

θησαυροῦ ἐκβάλλει ἀγαθά, καὶ ὁ πονηρὸς ἄνθρωπος ἐκ
treasure brings forth good *things,* and the (an) evil man out of

τοῦ πονηροῦ θησαυροῦ[e] *ἐκβάλλει πονηρά.* **36** *Λέγω δὲ*
the (his) evil treasure brings forth evil *things.* [2]I [3]say [1]But

ὑμῖν ὅτι πᾶν ῥῆμα ἀργὸν ὃ ἐὰν λαλήσωσιν οἱ ἄνθρωποι,
to you that every saying ˜ idle what ever [2]may [3]speak - [1]men,

ἀποδώσουσι περὶ αὐτοῦ λόγον ἐν ἡμέρᾳ κρίσεως. **37** *Ἐκ*
they will render [3]for [4]it [1]an [2]account in *the* day of judgment. by ˜

γὰρ τῶν λόγων σου δικαιωθήσῃ, καὶ ἐκ τῶν λόγων σου
For - words ˜ your you will be justified, (declared righteous,) and by - words ˜ your

καταδικασθήσῃ."
you will be condemned."

The Sign of Jonah
(Mark 8:11, 12; Luke 11:29–32)

38 *Τότε ἀπεκρίθησάν τινες τῶν γραμματέων καὶ*
Then [7]answered [1]some [2]of [3]the [4]scribes [5]and

Φαρισαίων, λέγοντες, "Διδάσκαλε, θέλομεν ἀπὸ σοῦ σημεῖον
[6]Pharisees, saying, "Teacher, we want [5]from [6]You [3]a [4]sign

ἰδεῖν."
[1]to [2]see."

39 *Ὁ δὲ ἀποκριθεὶς εἶπεν αὐτοῖς, "Γενεὰ*
[2]the [3]*One* (He) [1]But answering (answered and) said to them, "An [4]generation

πονηρὰ καὶ μοιχαλὶς σημεῖον ἐπιζητεῖ, καὶ σημεῖον οὐ
[1]evil [2]and [3]adulterous [6]a [7]sign [5]seeks, and a sign not ˜

δοθήσεται αὐτῇ εἰ μὴ τὸ σημεῖον Ἰωνᾶ τοῦ προφήτου.
will be given to it if not (except) the sign of Jonah the prophet.

40 *Ὥσπερ γὰρ ἦν Ἰωνᾶς ἐν τῇ κοιλίᾳ τοῦ κήτους τρεῖς*
[2]just [3]as [1]For was ˜ Jonah in the belly of the sea monster (great fish) three

ἡμέρας καὶ τρεῖς νύκτας, οὕτως ἔσται ὁ Υἱὸς τοῦ Ἀνθρώπου
days and three nights, so will [5]be [1]the [2]Son - [3]of [4]Man

ἐν τῇ καρδίᾳ τῆς γῆς τρεῖς ἡμέρας καὶ τρεῖς νύκτας.
in the heart of the earth three days and three nights.

41 Ἄνδρες Νινευῖται ἀναστήσονται ἐν τῇ κρίσει μετὰ τῆς
Men Ninevites will rise up in the judgment with -
The men of Nineveh

γενεᾶς ταύτης καὶ κατακρινοῦσιν αὐτήν, ὅτι μετενόησαν
generation ˜ this and will condemn it, because they repented

εἰς τὸ κήρυγμα Ἰωνᾶ, καὶ ἰδού, πλεῖον Ἰωνᾶ ὧδε.
at the preaching of Jonah, and behold, *something* more *than* Jonah *is* here.
message

42 Βασίλισσα νότου ἐγερθήσεται ἐν τῇ κρίσει μετὰ τῆς
The queen of *the* South will be raised in the judgment with -

γενεᾶς ταύτης καὶ κατακρινεῖ αὐτήν, ὅτι ἦλθεν ἐκ
generation ˜ this and she will condemn it, because she came from

τῶν περάτων τῆς γῆς ἀκοῦσαι τὴν σοφίαν Σολομῶνος, καὶ
the ends of the earth to hear the wisdom of Solomon, and

ἰδού, πλεῖον Σολομῶνος ὧδε.
behold, *something* more *than* Solomon *is* here.

An Unclean Spirit Returns
(Luke 11:24–26)

43 "Ὅταν δὲ τὸ ἀκάθαρτον πνεῦμα ἐξέλθῃ ἀπὸ τοῦ
"when ˜ And the unclean spirit goes out from the
an a

ἀνθρώπου, διέρχεται δι' ἀνύδρων τόπων ζητοῦν ἀνάπαυσιν,
man, he goes through waterless places seeking rest,

καὶ οὐχ εὑρίσκει. 44 Τότε λέγει, 'Ἐπιστρέψω εἰς τὸν οἶκόν
and not ˜ does find *any*. Then he says, 'I will return to - house ˜

μου ὅθεν ἐξῆλθον.' Καὶ ἐλθὸν εὑρίσκει σχολάζοντα,
my from where I came out.' And coming he finds *it* standing empty,
he comes and

σεσαρωμένον, καὶ κεκοσμημένον. 45 Τότε πορεύεται καὶ
swept, and put in order. Then he goes and

παραλαμβάνει μεθ' ἑαυτοῦ ἑπτὰ ἕτερα πνεύματα πονηρότερα
takes along with himself seven other spirits more evil

ἑαυτοῦ, καὶ εἰσελθόντα κατοικεῖ ἐκεῖ· καὶ γίνεται τὰ
than himself, and going in he dwells there; and [7]become [1]the

ἔσχατα τοῦ ἀνθρώπου ἐκείνου χείρονα τῶν πρώτων. Οὕτως
[2]last [3]*things* - [4]of [6]man [5]that [8]worse *than* the first *things*. Thus
last state first state.

ἔσται καὶ τῇ γενεᾷ ταύτῃ τῇ πονηρᾷ."
it will be also - for [3]generation [1]this - [2]evil."

The Mother and Brethren of Jesus
(Mark 3:31–35; Luke 8:19–21)

46 Ἔτι δὲ αὐτοῦ λαλοῦντος τοῖς ὄχλοις, ἰδού, ἡ μήτηρ
yet ˜ And Him speaking to the crowds, behold, - [2]mother
And while He was still speaking

καὶ οἱ ἀδελφοὶ αὐτοῦ εἱστήκεισαν ἔξω ζητοῦντες αὐτῷ
[3]and - [4]brothers [1]His stood outside seeking [3]to [4]Him

λαλῆσαι. 47 Εἶπε δέ τις αὐτῷ, "Ἰδού, ἡ μήτηρ σου
[1]to [2]speak. [3]said [1]And [2]someone to Him, "Look, - mother ˜ Your

καὶ οἱ ἀδελφοί σου ἔξω ἑστήκασι ζητοῦντές σοι
and - brothers ˜ Your [3]outside [1]are [2]standing seeking [3]to [4]You

λαλῆσαι."
[1]to [2]speak."

belly of the great fish, so will the Son of Man be three days and three nights in the heart of the earth.

41 "The men of Nineveh will rise up in the judgment with this generation and condemn it, because they repented at the preaching of Jonah; and indeed a greater than Jonah *is* here.

42 "The queen of the South will rise up in the judgment with this generation and condemn it, for she came from the ends of the earth to hear the wisdom of Solomon; and indeed a greater than Solomon *is* here.

43 "When an unclean spirit goes out of a man, he goes through dry places, seeking rest, and finds none.

44 "Then he says, 'I will return to my house from which I came.' And when he comes, he finds *it* empty, swept, and put in order.

45 "Then he goes and takes with him seven other spirits more wicked than himself, and they enter and dwell there; and the last *state* of that man is worse than the first. So shall it also be with this wicked generation."

46 While He was still talking to the multitudes, behold, His mother and brothers stood outside, seeking to speak with Him.

47 Then one said to Him, "Look, Your mother and Your brothers are standing outside, seeking to speak with You."

48 But He answered and said
to the one who told Him, "Who
is My mother and who are My
brothers?"
49 And He stretched out His
hand toward His disciples and
said, "Here are My mother and
My brothers!
50 "For whoever does the will
of My Father in heaven is My
brother and sister and mother."
13 On the same day Jesus
went out of the house
and sat by the sea.
2 And great multitudes were
gathered together to Him, so
that He got into a boat and sat;
and the whole multitude stood
on the shore.
3 Then He spoke many
things to them in parables, saying: "Behold, a sower went out
to sow.
4 "And as he sowed, some
seed fell by the wayside; and the
birds came and devoured them.
5 "Some fell on stony places,
where they did not have much
earth; and they immediately
sprang up because they had no
depth of earth.
6 "But when the sun was up
they were scorched, and because they had no root they
withered away.
7 "And some fell among
thorns, and the thorns sprang
up and choked them.
8 "But others fell on good
ground and yielded a crop:
some a hundredfold, some
sixty, some thirty.

48 Ὁ δὲ ἀποκριθεὶς εἶπε τῷ εἰπόντι αὐτῷ,
[2]the [3]*One* [1]But answering said to the *one* having said *it* to Him,
He answered and who spoke

"Τίς ἐστιν ἡ μήτηρ μου? Καὶ τίνες εἰσὶν οἱ ἀδελφοί μου?"
"Who is - mother ~ My? And who are - brothers ~ My?"

49 Καὶ ἐκτείνας τὴν χεῖρα αὐτοῦ ἐπὶ τοὺς μαθητὰς αὐτοῦ
And stretching out - hand ~ His over - disciples ~ His

εἶπεν, "Ἰδού, ἡ μήτηρ μου καὶ οἱ ἀδελφοί μου! **50** Ὅστις
He said, "Look, - mother ~ My and - brothers ~ My! who ~
"Here are

γὰρ ἂν ποιήσῃ τὸ θέλημα τοῦ Πατρός μου τοῦ ἐν οὐρανοῖς,
For ever does the will - of Father ~ My - in *the* heavens,

αὐτός μου ἀδελφὸς καὶ ἀδελφὴ καὶ μήτηρ ἐστίν."
he [2]My [3]brother [4]and [5]sister [6]and [7]mother [1]is."

The Parable of the Sower

(Mark 4:1–9; Luke 8:4–8)

13 **1** Ἐν δὲ τῇ ἡμέρᾳ ἐκείνῃ ἐξελθὼν ὁ Ἰησοῦς ἀπὸ
on ~ And - day ~ that going out - Jesus from
Jesus went out of the

τῆς οἰκίας ἐκάθητο παρὰ τὴν θάλασσαν. **2** Καὶ
the house sat beside the sea. And
house and

συνήχθησαν πρὸς αὐτὸν ὄχλοι πολλοί, ὥστε αὐτὸν
[3]were [4]gathered [5]together [6]to [7]Him [2]crowds [1]large, so that Him
He

εἰς τὸ πλοῖον ἐμβάντα καθῆσθαι, καὶ πᾶς ὁ ὄχλος ἐπὶ τὸν
[3]into [4]the [5]boat [1]stepping [2]in to sit down, and all the crowd [2]on [3]the
got

αἰγιαλὸν εἱστήκει. **3** Καὶ ἐλάλησεν αὐτοῖς πολλὰ ἐν
[4]shore [1]stood. And He spoke to them many *things* in

παραβολαῖς,* λέγων, "Ἰδού, ἐξῆλθεν ὁ σπείρων τοῦ
parables, saying, "See, [4]went [5]out [1]the [2]sowing [3]*one* -
a sower

σπείρειν. **4** Καὶ ἐν τῷ σπείρειν αὐτόν, ἃ μὲν ἔπεσε παρὰ
to sow. And in - to sow him, some *part* fell alongside
as he sowed,

τὴν ὁδόν· καὶ ἦλθε τὰ πετεινὰ καὶ κατέφαγεν αὐτά. **5** Ἄλλα
the road; and [3]came [1]the [2]birds and devoured them. others ~

δὲ ἔπεσεν ἐπὶ τὰ πετρώδη, ὅπου οὐκ εἶχε γῆν
But fell on the stony ground, where [3]not [1]it [2]did [4]have earth ~

πολλήν· καὶ εὐθέως ἐξανέτειλε διὰ τὸ μὴ ἔχειν βάθος
much; and immediately it sprang up because - not to have depth
it had no

γῆς. **6** Ἡλίου δὲ ἀνατείλαντος, ἐκαυματίσθη, καὶ διὰ τὸ
of earth. *the* sun But rising, it was scorched, and because -
But when the sun rose, it

μὴ ἔχειν ῥίζαν, ἐξηράνθη. **7** Ἄλλα δὲ ἔπεσεν ἐπὶ τὰς
not to have root, it was withered up. others ~ But fell on the
had no

ἀκάνθας, καὶ ἀνέβησαν αἱ ἄκανθαι καὶ ἀπέπνιξαν αὐτά.
thorns, and [3]came [4]up [1]the [2]thorns and choked out ~ them.

8 Ἄλλα δὲ ἔπεσεν ἐπὶ τὴν γῆν τὴν καλὴν καὶ ἐδίδου
others ~ But fell on the ground ~ - good and it was giving
yielding

καρπόν, ὃ μὲν ἑκατόν, ὃ δὲ ἑξήκοντα, ὃ δὲ
fruit, the one a hundred*fold*, the other sixty*fold*, the other
some some some

*(13:3) παραβολή (*parabolē*). Noun (only in the Synoptic Gospels and Hebrews) from παρά, *beside*, and βολή, *a placing*, originally a *comparison* and thus a *parable* or *illustration*. Other kinds of comparisons indicated by the word include a *type* or *figure* (Heb. 9:9; 11:19), or even a *riddle* or *enigmatic saying* (in the LXX). Jesus' parables were usually stories presenting teachings by comparison rather than directly, similar to an analogy. Consequently, while they could clarify truth for some, they might obscure the truth for others (Matt. 13:10–16).

τριάκοντα. 9 Ὁ ἔχων ὦτα ἀκούειν[a] ἀκουέτω."
thirty*fold*. The *one* having ears to hear let him hear."

Jesus Explains the Purpose of Parables
(Mark 4:10–12; Luke 8:9, 10)

10 Καὶ προσελθόντες οἱ μαθηταὶ εἶπον αὐτῷ, "Διὰ
And [3]approaching [1]the [2]disciples said to Him, "On account of
approached and "Why

τί ἐν παραβολαῖς λαλεῖς αὐτοῖς?"
what [6]in [7]parables [1]do [2]You [3]speak [4]to [5]them?"

11 Ὁ δὲ ἀποκριθεὶς εἶπεν αὐτοῖς ὅτι "Ὑμῖν
[2]the [3]*One* [1]And answering said to them - "To you
He

δέδοται γνῶναι τὰ μυστήρια τῆς βασιλείας τῶν
it has been given to know the mysteries of the kingdom of the

οὐρανῶν, ἐκείνοις δὲ οὐ δέδοται. 12 Ὅστις γὰρ
heavens, [2]to [3]those [1]but [6]not [4]it [5]has [7]been [8]given. whoever ˜ For

ἔχει, δοθήσεται αὐτῷ καὶ περισσευθήσεται· ὅστις δὲ οὐκ
has, it will be given to him and he will have abundance; whoever ˜ but not ˜

ἔχει, καὶ ὃ ἔχει ἀρθήσεται ἀπ' αὐτοῦ.
does have, even what he has will be taken away from him.

13 Διὰ τοῦτο ἐν παραβολαῖς αὐτοῖς λαλῶ, ὅτι
On account of this [5]in [6]parables [3]to [4]them [1]I [2]speak, that
Therefore

βλέποντες οὐ βλέπουσι καὶ ἀκούοντες οὐκ ἀκούουσιν οὐδὲ
seeing [3]not [1]they [2]do see and hearing [3]not [1]they [2]do hear nor

συνιοῦσι. 14 Καὶ ἀναπληροῦται αὐτοῖς ἡ προφητεία
do they understand. And [3]is [4]fulfilled [1]in [2]them the prophecy

Ἠσαΐου ἡ λέγουσα,
of Isaiah the *one* saying,
which says,

«'Ακοῇ ἀκούσετε καὶ οὐ μὴ συνῆτε,
«In hearing you shall hear and not not understand,
by no means

Καὶ βλέποντες βλέψετε καὶ οὐ μὴ ἴδητε.
And seeing you shall see and not not perceive.
by no means

15 Ἐπαχύνθη γὰρ ἡ καρδία τοῦ λαοῦ τούτου,
[7]became [8]dull [1]For [2]the [3]heart - [4]of [6]people [5]this,
has become

Καὶ τοῖς ὠσὶ βαρέως ἤκουσαν,
And with the ears heavily they heard,
their ears are hard of hearing,

Καὶ τοὺς ὀφθαλμοὺς αὐτῶν ἐκάμμυσαν,
And - eyes ˜ their they closed,
have closed,

Μήποτε ἴδωσι τοῖς ὀφθαλμοῖς
Lest they should see with the eyes
their

Καὶ τοῖς ὠσὶν ἀκούσωσι
And with the ears they should hear
their

Καὶ τῇ καρδίᾳ συνῶσι, καὶ ἐπιστρέψωσι,
And with the heart they should understand, and turn back,
their

Καὶ ἰάσομαι[b] αὐτούς.»[c]
And I shall heal them.»
should

9 "He who has ears to hear, let him hear!"
10 And the disciples came and said to Him, "Why do You speak to them in parables?"
11 He answered and said to them, "Because it has been given to you to know the mysteries of the kingdom of heaven, but to them it has not been given.
12 "For whoever has, to him more will be given, and he will have abundance; but whoever does not have, even what he has will be taken away from him.
13 "Therefore I speak to them in parables, because seeing they do not see, and hearing they do not hear, nor do they understand.
14 "And in them the prophecy of Isaiah is fulfilled, which says:

'Hearing you will hear and
shall not understand,
And seeing you will see
and not perceive;
15 *For the hearts of this*
people have grown dull.
Their ears are hard of
hearing,
And their eyes they have
closed,
Lest they should see with
their eyes and hear with
their ears,
Lest they should
understand with their
hearts and turn,
So that I should heal
them.'

---

[a](**13:9**) NU omits ακουειν, *to hear*. [b](**13:15**) TR reads ιασωμαι, *I would heal.* [c](**13:14, 15**) Is. 6:9, 10

16 "But blessed *are* your eyes
for they see, and your ears for
they hear;
17 "for assuredly, I say to you
that many prophets and righteous *men* desired to see what
you see, and did not see *it,* and
to hear what you hear, and did
not hear *it.*
18 "Therefore hear the parable of the sower:
19 "When anyone hears the
word of the kingdom, and does
not understand *it,* then the
wicked *one* comes and snatches
away what was sown in his
heart. This is he who received
seed by the wayside.
20 "But he who received the
seed on stony places, this is he
who hears the word and immediately receives it with joy;
21 "yet he has no root in himself, but endures only for a
while. For when tribulation or
persecution arises because of
the word, immediately he stumbles.
22 "Now he who received
seed among the thorns is he
who hears the word, and the
cares of this world and the deceitfulness of riches choke the
word, and he becomes unfruitful.
23 "But he who received seed
on the good ground is he who
hears the word and under-
stands *it,* who indeed bears
fruit and produces: some a
hundredfold, some sixty, some
thirty."

16 Ὑμῶν δὲ μακάριοι οἱ ὀφθαλμοὶ ὅτι βλέπουσι, καὶ τὰ
[4]your [1]But [2]blessed [3]*are* - eyes because they see, and -

ὦτα ὑμῶν ὅτι ἀκούει. **17** Ἀμὴν γὰρ λέγω ὑμῖν ὅτι
ears ˜ your because they hear. amen ˜ For I say to you that
assuredly

πολλοὶ προφῆται καὶ δίκαιοι ἐπεθύμησαν ἰδεῖν
many prophets and righteous *people* desired to see

ἃ βλέπετε καὶ οὐκ εἶδον, καὶ ἀκοῦσαι
the things which you see and [3]not [1]they [2]did see *them,* and to hear

ἃ ἀκούετε καὶ οὐκ ἤκουσαν.
the things which you hear and [3]not [1]they [2]did hear *them.*

Jesus Explains the Parable of the Sower
(Mark 4:13–20; Luke 8:11–15)

18 "Ὑμεῖς οὖν ἀκούσατε τὴν παραβολὴν τοῦ
"You therefore hear the parable of the

σπείροντος. **19** Παντὸς ἀκούοντος τὸν λόγον τῆς
sowing *one.* Every*one* hearing the word of the
sower. When anyone hears message about

βασιλείας καὶ μὴ συνιέντος, ἔρχεται ὁ πονηρὸς καὶ
kingdom and not understanding, [4]comes [1]the [2]evil [3]*one* and
does not understand,

ἁρπάζει τὸ ἐσπαρμένον ἐν τῇ καρδίᾳ αὐτοῦ. Οὗτός
snatches away the *thing* sown in - heart ˜ his. This

ἐστιν ὁ παρὰ τὴν ὁδὸν σπαρείς. **20** Ὁ δὲ ἐπὶ
is the *seed* [3]beside [4]the [5]road [1]being [2]sown. [2]the [3]*seed* [1]But [5]on

τὰ πετρώδη σπαρείς, οὗτός ἐστιν ὁ τὸν λόγον ἀκούων
[6]the [7]stony [8]ground [4]sown, this is the *one* [2]the [3]word [1]hearing
who hears

καὶ εὐθὺς μετὰ χαρᾶς λαμβάνων αὐτόν· **21** οὐκ
and immediately with joy receiving it; [4]not
receives

ἔχει δὲ ῥίζαν ἐν ἑαυτῷ ἀλλὰ πρόσκαιρός ἐστι.
[2]he [3]does [5]have [1]but [6]a [7]root in himself but short-lived ˜ is.

Γενομένης δὲ θλίψεως ἢ διωγμοῦ διὰ τὸν λόγον,
coming But trial or persecution because of the word,
But when trial or persecution comes

εὐθὺς σκανδαλίζεται. **22** Ὁ δὲ εἰς τὰς ἀκάνθας
immediately he is offended. [2]the [3]*seed* [1]But [5]in [6]the [7]thorns

σπαρείς, οὗτός ἐστιν ὁ τὸν λόγον ἀκούων, καὶ ἡ
[4]sown, this is the *one* [2]the [3]word [1]hearing, and the
who hears,

μέριμνα τοῦ αἰῶνος τούτου[d] καὶ ἡ ἀπάτη τοῦ πλούτου
anxiety - of age ˜ this and the deceitfulness - of riches

συμπνίγει τὸν λόγον, καὶ ἄκαρπος γίνεται. **23** Ὁ δὲ
chokes out the word, and [3]fruitless [1]it [2]becomes. [2]the [3]*seed* [1]But

ἐπὶ τὴν γῆν τὴν καλὴν σπαρείς, οὗτός ἐστιν ὁ τὸν
[5]on [6]the [8]ground - [7]good [4]sown, this is the *one* [2]the

λόγον ἀκούων καὶ συνιών, ὃς δὴ καρποφορεῖ καὶ
[3]word [1]hearing and understanding *it,* who indeed bears fruit and
who hears understands

ποιεῖ ὁ μὲν ἑκατόν, ὁ δὲ ἑξήκοντα, ὁ δὲ
produces the one a hundred*fold,* the other sixty*fold,* the other
some some some

τριάκοντα."
thirty*fold.*"

[d](13:22) NU omits τουτου, *this.*

The Parable of the Wheat and the Tares

24 Ἄλλην παραβολὴν παρέθηκεν αὐτοῖς, λέγων,
Another parable He set before them, saying,

"Ὡμοιώθη ἡ βασιλεία τῶν οὐρανῶν ἀνθρώπῳ
"[6]was [7]compared [1]The [2]kingdom [3]of [4]the [5]heavens to a man
"is

σπείροντι καλὸν σπέρμα ἐν τῷ ἀγρῷ αὐτοῦ. 25 Ἐν δὲ τῷ
sowing good seed in - field ˜ his. in ˜ But -
But while the

καθεύδειν τοὺς ἀνθρώπους, ἦλθεν αὐτοῦ ὁ ἐχθρὸς καὶ ἔσπειρε
to sleep the men, [3]came [1]his - [2]enemy and sowed
men were sleeping,

ζιζάνια ἀνὰ μέσον τοῦ σίτου καὶ ἀπῆλθεν. 26 Ὅτε δὲ
tares in the midst of the wheat and went away. when ˜ But

ἐβλάστησεν ὁ χόρτος καὶ καρπὸν ἐποίησε, τότε ἐφάνη καὶ
[3]sprouted [1]the [2]stalk and fruit ˜ produced, then appeared also

τὰ ζιζάνια. 27 Προσελθόντες δὲ οἱ δοῦλοι τοῦ
the tares. [10]approaching [1]So [2]the [3]slaves [4]of [5]the
approached and servants

οἰκοδεσπότου εἶπον αὐτῷ, 'Κύριε, οὐχὶ καλὸν σπέρμα
[6]master [7]of [8]the [9]house said to him, 'Lord, *was it* not good seed
'Sir,

ἔσπειρας ἐν τῷ σῷ ἀγρῷ? Πόθεν οὖν ἔχει ζιζάνια?'
you sowed in - your field? From where then does it have tares?'

28 Ὁ δὲ ἔφη αὐτοῖς, 'Ἐχθρὸς ἄνθρωπος τοῦτο
[2]the [3]*one* [1]But said to them, 'A hostile man this ˜
he 'An enemy

ἐποίησεν.' Οἱ δὲ δοῦλοι εἶπον αὐτῷ, 'Θέλεις οὖν
did.' the ˜ So slaves said to him, 'Do you wish then
servants

ἀπελθόντες συλλέξομεν[e] αὐτά?' 29 Ὁ δέ ἔφη, 'Οὔ,
going off we shall gather up ˜ them?' [2]the [3]*one* [1]But said, 'No,
that we should go and he

μήποτε συλλέγοντες τὰ ζιζάνια, ἐκριζώσητε ἅμα αὐτοῖς τὸν
lest gathering up the tares, you may uproot [3]with [4]them [1]the

σῖτον. 30 Ἄφετε συναυξάνεσθαι ἀμφότερα μέχρι τοῦ
[2]wheat. Leave [2]to [3]grow [4]together [1]both until the

θερισμοῦ· καὶ ἐν καιρῷ τοῦ θερισμοῦ ἐρῶ τοῖς
harvest; and at the time of the harvest I will say to the

θερισταῖς, "Συλλέξατε πρῶτον τὰ ζιζάνια καὶ δήσατε αὐτὰ εἰς
reapers, "Gather up [3]first [1]the [2]tares and bind them into

δέσμας πρὸς τὸ κατακαῦσαι αὐτά, τὸν δὲ σῖτον συναγάγετε
bundles - - to burn them, [4]the [1]but [5]wheat [2]gather [3]together

εἰς τὴν ἀποθήκην μου." ' "
into - barn ˜ my." ' "

The Parable of the Mustard Seed

(Mark 4:30–32; Luke 13:18, 19)

31 Ἄλλην παραβολὴν παρέθηκεν αὐτοῖς, λέγων, "Ὁμοία
Another parable He set before them, saying, "[7]like

ἐστὶν ἡ βασιλεία τῶν οὐρανῶν κόκκῳ σινάπεως, ὃν
[6]is [1]The [2]kingdom [3]of [4]the [5]heavens a grain of mustard, which
a mustard seed,

λαβὼν ἄνθρωπος ἔσπειρεν ἐν τῷ ἀγρῷ αὐτοῦ· 32 ὃ
[3]taking [1]a [2]man sowed in - field ˜ his; which
took and

μικρότερον μέν ἐστι πάντων τῶν σπερμάτων, ὅταν δὲ
[3]smaller [1]indeed [2]is *than* all the seeds, whenever ˜ but

24 Another parable He put forth to them, saying: "The kingdom of heaven is like a man who sowed good seed in his field;
25 "but while men slept, his enemy came and sowed tares among the wheat and went his way.
26 "But when the grain had sprouted and produced a crop, then the tares also appeared.
27 "So the servants of the owner came and said to him, 'Sir, did you not sow good seed in your field? How then does it have tares?'
28 "He said to them, 'An enemy has done this.' The servants said to him, 'Do you want us then to go and gather them up?'
29 "But he said, 'No, lest while you gather up the tares you also uproot the wheat with them.
30 'Let both grow together until the harvest, and at the time of harvest I will say to the reapers, "First gather together the tares and bind them in bundles to burn them, but gather the wheat into my barn." ' "
31 Another parable He put forth to them, saying: "The kingdom of heaven is like a mustard seed, which a man took and sowed in his field,
32 "which indeed is the least of all the seeds; but when it is

---

[e] **(13:28)** TR, NU read *συλλεξωμεν, we should collect.*

grown it is greater than the herbs and becomes a tree, so that the birds of the air come and nest in its branches."
33 Another parable He spoke to them: "The kingdom of heaven is like leaven, which a woman took and hid in three measures of meal till it was all leavened."
34 All these things Jesus spoke to the multitude in parables; and without a parable He did not speak to them,
35 that it might be fulfilled which was spoken by the prophet, saying:

"I will open My mouth in parables;
I will utter things kept secret from the foundation of the world."

36 Then Jesus sent the multitude away and went into the house. And His disciples came to Him, saying, "Explain to us the parable of the tares of the field."
37 He answered and said to them: "He who sows the good seed is the Son of Man.
38 "The field is the world, the good seeds are the sons of the kingdom, but the tares are the sons of the wicked *one.*
39 "The enemy who sowed

αὐξηθῇ, μεῖζον τῶν λαχάνων ἐστὶ καὶ γίνεται
it is grown, [3]greater [4]*than* [5]the [6]garden [7]vegetables [1]it [2]is and becomes

δένδρον, ὥστε ἐλθεῖν τὰ πετεινὰ τοῦ οὐρανοῦ καὶ
a tree, so that [5]to [6]come [1]the [2]birds - [3]of [4]heaven and
come — the air

κατασκηνοῦν ἐν τοῖς κλάδοις αὐτοῦ."
to nest in - branches ˜ its."
nest

The Parable of the Leaven
(Luke 13:20, 21)

33 Ἄλλην παραβολὴν ἐλάλησεν αὐτοῖς· "Ὁμοία ἐστὶν ἡ
Another parable He spoke to them: "[7]like [6]is [1]The

βασιλεία τῶν οὐρανῶν ζύμῃ, ἣν λαβοῦσα γυνὴ ἔκρυψεν
[2]kingdom [3]of [4]the [5]heavens yeast, which [3]taking [1]a [2]woman hid
leaven, — took and — mixed in

εἰς ἀλεύρου σάτα τρία ἕως οὗ ἐζυμώθη ὅλον."
in [3]of [4]meal [2]sata [1]three until - [3]was [4]leavened [1]*the* [2]whole."
with — measures

The Use of Parables Fulfills Prophecy
(Mark 4:33, 34)

34 Ταῦτα πάντα ἐλάλησεν ὁ Ἰησοῦς ἐν παραβολαῖς
[4]these [5]*things* [3]all [2]spoke - [1]Jesus in parables

τοῖς ὄχλοις, καὶ χωρὶς παραβολῆς οὐκ[f] ἐλάλει
to the crowds, and without a parable [3]not [1]He [2]would speak

αὐτοῖς, **35** ὅπως πληρωθῇ τὸ ῥηθὲν διὰ τοῦ
to them, so that [7]might [8]be [9]fulfilled [1]the [2]*thing* [3]spoken [4]through [5]the

προφήτου, λέγοντος,
[6]prophet, saying,

«Ἀνοίξω ἐν παραβολαῖς τὸ στόμα μου,
«I will open [3]in [4]parables - [2]mouth [1]My,

Ἐρεύξομαι κεκρυμμένα ἀπὸ καταβολῆς
I will utter *things* having been hidden from *the* foundation

κόσμου.»[g]
of *the* world.»

Jesus Explains the Parable of the Tares

36 Τότε ἀφεὶς τοὺς ὄχλους ἦλθεν εἰς τὴν οἰκίαν ὁ
Then having dismissed the crowds [2]went [3]into [4]the [5]house -

Ἰησοῦς.[h] Καὶ προσῆλθον αὐτῷ οἱ μαθηταὶ αὐτοῦ, λέγοντες,
[1]Jesus. And [3]approached [4]Him - [2]disciples [1]His, saying,

"Φράσον ἡμῖν τὴν παραβολὴν τῶν ζιζανίων τοῦ ἀγροῦ."
"Explain to us the parable of the tares of the field."

37 Ὁ δὲ ἀποκριθεὶς εἶπεν αὐτοῖς,[i] "Ὁ σπείρων
[2]the [3]*One* [1]And answering said to them, "The *one* sowing
He — answered and

τὸ καλὸν σπέρμα ἐστὶν ὁ Υἱὸς τοῦ Ἀνθρώπου. **38** Ὁ δὲ
the good seed is the Son - of Man. the ˜ And

ἀγρός ἐστιν ὁ κόσμος, τὸ δὲ καλὸν σπέρμα, οὗτοί εἰσιν οἱ
field is the world, the ˜ and good seed, these are the

υἱοὶ τῆς βασιλείας· τὰ δὲ ζιζάνιά εἰσιν οἱ υἱοὶ τοῦ
sons of the kingdom; the ˜ and tares are the sons of the

πονηροῦ, **39** ὁ δὲ ἐχθρὸς ὁ σπείρας αὐτά ἐστιν ὁ
evil *one,* the ˜ and enemy the *one* sowing them is the
who — sowed

---

f(**13:34**) NU reads ουδεν, *nothing.* g(**13:35**) Ps. 78:2; NU brackets κοσμου, *of (the) world.*
h(**13:36**) NU omits ο Ιησους, *Jesus.* i(**13:37**) NU omits αυτοις, *to them.*

διάβολος· ὁ δὲ θερισμὸς συντέλεια τοῦ αἰῶνός ἐστιν,
devil; the ~ and harvest [2]*the* [3]completion [4]of [5]the [6]age [1]is,
end

οἱ δὲ θερισταὶ ἄγγελοί εἰσιν. **40** Ὥσπερ οὖν
the ~ and reapers angels ~ are. [2]just [3]as [1]Therefore

συλλέγεται τὰ ζιζάνια καὶ πυρὶ καίεται, οὕτως ἔσται
[6]are [7]collected [4]the [5]tares and [3]with [4]fire [1]are [2]burned, thus it will be

ἐν τῇ συντελείᾳ τοῦ αἰῶνος τούτου.[j] **41** Ἀποστελεῖ ὁ
in the completion - of age ~ this. [5]will [6]send [7]forth [1]The
end

Υἱὸς τοῦ Ἀνθρώπου τοὺς ἀγγέλους αὐτοῦ, καὶ συλλέξουσιν
[2]Son - [3]of [4]Man - angels ~ His, and they will collect

ἐκ τῆς βασιλείας αὐτοῦ πάντα τὰ σκάνδαλα καὶ τοὺς
out of - kingdom ~ His all the offensive things and the *ones*
everything that is offensive those

ποιοῦντας τὴν ἀνομίαν, **42** καὶ βαλοῦσιν αὐτοὺς εἰς τὴν
doing - lawlessness, and they will throw them into the
who practice

κάμινον τοῦ πυρός. Ἐκεῖ ἔσται ὁ κλαυθμὸς καὶ ὁ βρυγμὸς
furnace - of fire. There *there* will be - weeping and - gnashing

τῶν ὀδόντων. **43** Τότε οἱ δίκαιοι ἐκλάμψουσιν ὡς ὁ ἥλιος ἐν
- of teeth. Then the righteous will shine forth like the sun in

τῇ βασιλείᾳ τοῦ Πατρὸς αὐτῶν. Ὁ ἔχων ὦτα ἀκούειν[k]
the kingdom - of Father ~ their. The *one* having ears to hear
He who has

ἀκουέτω.
let him hear.

The Parable of the Hidden Treasure

44 "Πάλιν ὁμοία ἐστὶν ἡ βασιλεία τῶν οὐρανῶν
"Again [7]like [6]is [1]the [2]kingdom [3]of [4]the [5]heavens

θησαυρῷ κεκρυμμένῳ ἐν τῷ ἀγρῷ, ὃν εὑρὼν ἄνθρωπος
a treasure having been hidden in the field, which [3]finding [1]a [2]man
a found and

ἔκρυψε, καὶ ἀπὸ τῆς χαρᾶς αὐτοῦ ὑπάγει καὶ πάντα ὅσα
hid, and from - joy ~ his he goes and all *things* as many as
for went sold everything

ἔχει πωλεῖ καὶ ἀγοράζει τὸν ἀγρὸν ἐκεῖνον.
he has he sells and buys - field ~ that.
he had bought

The Parable of the Pearl of Great Price

45 "Πάλιν ὁμοία ἐστὶν ἡ βασιλεία τῶν οὐρανῶν
"Again [7]like [6]is [1]the [2]kingdom [3]of [4]the [5]heavens

ἀνθρώπῳ ἐμπόρῳ ζητοῦντι καλοὺς μαργαρίτας, **46** ὃς
a man a merchant seeking beautiful pearls, who
a merchant

εὑρὼν ἕνα πολύτιμον μαργαρίτην, ἀπελθὼν πέπρακε
finding one very valuable pearl, going he has sold
when he found went and sold

πάντα ὅσα εἶχε καὶ ἠγόρασεν αὐτόν.
all *things* as many as he had and bought it.
everything

The Parable of the Dragnet

47 "Πάλιν ὁμοία ἐστὶν ἡ βασιλεία τῶν οὐρανῶν
"Again [7]like [6]is [1]the [2]kingdom [3]of [4]the [5]heavens

σαγήνῃ* βληθείσῃ εἰς τὴν θάλασσαν, καὶ ἐκ παντὸς
a dragnet having been cast into the sea, and [2]of [3]every

them is the devil, the harvest is the end of the age, and the reapers are the angels.
40 "Therefore as the tares are gathered and burned in the fire, so it will be at the end of this age.
41 "The Son of Man will send out His angels, and they will gather out of His kingdom all things that offend, and those who practice lawlessness,
42 "and will cast them into the furnace of fire. There will be wailing and gnashing of teeth.
43 "Then the righteous will shine forth as the sun in the kingdom of their Father. He who has ears to hear, let him hear!
44 "Again, the kingdom of heaven is like treasure hidden in a field, which a man found and hid; and for joy over it he goes and sells all that he has and buys that field.
45 "Again, the kingdom of heaven is like a merchant seeking beautiful pearls,
46 "who, when he had found one pearl of great price, went and sold all that he had and bought it.
47 "Again, the kingdom of heaven is like a dragnet that was cast into the sea and gath-

[j](13:40) NU omits *τουτου, this.* [k](13:43) NU omits *ακουειν, to hear.*

*(13:47) *σαγήνη (sagēnē).* Noun, a *dragnet* or *seine.* Such a net was used by lowering it down into the water, drawing it together in a narrowing circle and then pulling it into the boat. Another fishing method was to drag a semicircular net to shore stretched in the water between two boats.

ered some of every kind,
48 "which, when it was full, they drew to shore; and they sat down and gathered the good into vessels, but threw the bad away.
49 "So it will be at the end of the age. The angels will come forth, separate the wicked from among the just,
50 "and cast them into the furnace of fire. There will be wailing and gnashing of teeth."
51 Jesus said to them, "Have you understood all these things?" They said to Him, "Yes, Lord."
52 Then He said to them, "Therefore every scribe instructed concerning the kingdom of heaven is like a householder who brings out of his treasure *things* new and old."
53 Now it came to pass, when Jesus had finished these parables, that He departed from there.
54 When He had come to His own country, He taught them in their synagogue, so that they were astonished and said, "Where did this *Man* get this wisdom and *these* mighty works?
55 "Is this not the carpenter's son? Is not His mother called Mary? And His brothers James, Joses, Simon, and Judas?
56 "And His sisters, are they

γένους συναγαγούσῃ, **48** ἣν ὅτε ἐπληρώθη, ἀναβιβάσαντες
[4]kind [1]gathering, which when it was filled, pulling *it* up (they pulled up)

ἐπὶ τὸν αἰγιαλὸν καὶ καθίσαντες, συνέλεξαν τὰ καλὰ εἰς
on the shore and sitting down, they collected the good into

ἀγγεῖα, τὰ δὲ σαπρὰ ἔξω ἔβαλον. **49** Οὕτως ἔσται ἐν
vessels, the ˜ but rotten (worthless) [3]out [1]they [2]threw. Thus it will be in

τῇ συντελείᾳ τοῦ αἰῶνος. Ἐξελεύσονται οἱ ἄγγελοι καὶ
the completion (end) of the age. [3]will [4]come [5]forth [1]The [2]angels and

ἀφοριοῦσι τοὺς πονηροὺς ἐκ μέσου τῶν δικαίων
will separate the evil *people* out of *the* midst of the righteous *people*

50 καὶ βαλοῦσιν αὐτοὺς εἰς τὴν κάμινον τοῦ πυρός. Ἐκεῖ
and they will throw them into the furnace - of fire. There

ἔσται ὁ κλαυθμὸς καὶ ὁ βρυγμὸς τῶν ὀδόντων."
there will be - weeping and - gnashing - of teeth."

The Treasury of Truth

51 Λέγει αὐτοῖς ὁ Ἰησοῦς,[l] "Συνήκατε ταῦτα
[2]says (said) [3]to [4]them - [1]Jesus, "Did you understand [2]these [3]*things*

πάντα?"
[1]all?"

Λέγουσιν αὐτῷ, "Ναί, Κύριε."[m]
They say (said) to Him, "Yes, Lord."

52 Ὁ δὲ εἶπεν αὐτοῖς, "Διὰ τοῦτο πᾶς
[2]the [3]*One* (He) [1]Then said to them, "On account of this ("Therefore) every

γραμματεὺς μαθητευθεὶς εἰς τὴν βασιλείαν τῶν
scribe having become a disciple in the kingdom of the

οὐρανῶν ὅμοιός ἐστιν ἀνθρώπῳ οἰκοδεσπότῃ ὅστις ἐκβάλλει
heavens like ˜ is a man (a) a master of a house (householder) who brings

ἐκ τοῦ θησαυροῦ αὐτοῦ καινὰ καὶ παλαιά."
out of - treasury ˜ his new and old *things*."

53 Καὶ ἐγένετο ὅτε ἐτέλεσεν ὁ Ἰησοῦς τὰς παραβολὰς
And it happened when finished ˜ - Jesus - parables ˜

ταύτας, μετῆρεν ἐκεῖθεν.
these, He went away from there.

Jesus Is Rejected at Nazareth
(Mark 6:1–6)

54 Καὶ ἐλθὼν εἰς τὴν πατρίδα αὐτοῦ ἐδίδασκεν αὐτοὺς
And coming into - hometown ˜ His He was teaching (began to teach) them

ἐν τῇ συναγωγῇ αὐτῶν, ὥστε ἐκπλήττεσθαι αὐτοὺς καὶ
in - synagogue their, so that to be astonished (they were astonished) them and

λέγειν, "Πόθεν τούτῳ ἡ σοφία αὕτη καὶ αἱ
to say, (said,) "From where come to this man ("Where did this man get) - wisdom ˜ this and the

δυνάμεις? **55** Οὐχ οὗτός ἐστιν ὁ τοῦ τέκτονος υἱός? Οὐχὶ ἡ
miracles? [3]not [2]this [1]Is the [2]of [3]the [4]carpenter [1]son? [6]not -

μήτηρ αὐτοῦ λέγεται Μαριὰμ καὶ οἱ ἀδελφοὶ αὐτοῦ Ἰάκωβος
[8]mother [7]His [5]Is [9]called Mary and - brothers ˜ His James

καὶ Ἰωσῆς[n] καὶ Σίμων καὶ Ἰούδας? **56** Καὶ αἱ ἀδελφαὶ αὐτοῦ
and Joses and Simon and Jude? And - sisters ˜ His

---

[l](13:51) NU omits Λεγει αυτοις ο Ιησους, *Jesus said to them.*
[m](13:51) NU omits Κυριε, *Lord.* [n](13:55) NU reads Ιωσηφ, *Joseph.*

οὐχὶ πᾶσαι πρὸς ἡμᾶς εἰσι? Πόθεν οὖν τούτῳ
[3]not [4]all [5]with [6]us [1]are [2]they? From where then to this *man are*
Where then did this man get

ταῦτα πάντα?" **57** *Καὶ ἐσκανδαλίζοντο ἐν αὐτῷ.*
[2]these [3]*things* [1]all?" And they were offended at Him.

Ὁ δὲ Ἰησοῦς εἶπεν αὐτοῖς, "Οὐκ ἔστι προφήτης
- But Jesus said to them, "[4]not [3]is [1]A [2]prophet

ἄτιμος εἰ μὴ ἐν τῇ πατρίδι αὐτοῦ καὶ ἐν τῇ οἰκίᾳ
without honor if not in - hometown his and in - house
except

αὐτοῦ." **58** *Καὶ οὐκ ἐποίησεν ἐκεῖ δυνάμεις πολλὰς διὰ*
his." And [3]not [1]He [2]did [4]do [7]there [6]miracles [5]many because of

τὴν ἀπιστίαν αὐτῶν.
- unbelief their.

John the Baptist Is Beheaded
(Mark 6:14–29; Luke 9:7–9)

14 **1** *Ἐν ἐκείνῳ τῷ καιρῷ ἤκουσεν Ἡρῴδης ὁ τετράρχης*
In that - time [4]heard [1]Herod [2]the [3]tetrarch

τὴν ἀκοὴν Ἰησοῦ, **2** *καὶ εἶπε τοῖς παισὶν αὐτοῦ, "Οὗτός*
the report *about* Jesus, and he said - to servants his, "This

ἐστιν Ἰωάννης ὁ Βαπτιστής· αὐτὸς ἠγέρθη ἀπὸ τῶν νεκρῶν,
is John the Baptist; he was raised from the dead,
has been

καὶ διὰ τοῦτο αἱ δυνάμεις ἐνεργοῦσιν ἐν αὐτῷ." **3** *Ὁ γὰρ*
and because of this the powers are at work in him." - For

Ἡρῴδης κρατήσας τὸν Ἰωάννην ἔδησεν αὐτὸν καὶ ἔθετο ἐν
Herod laying hold of - John bound him and put *him* in
had laid hold of John and

φυλακῇ διὰ Ἡρωδιάδα τὴν γυναῖκα Φιλίππου τοῦ
prison on account of Herodias the wife of Philip -

ἀδελφοῦ αὐτοῦ.
brother his.

4 *Ἔλεγε γὰρ αὐτῷ ὁ Ἰωάννης, "Οὐκ ἔξεστί σοι*
[3]would [4]say [1]For [5]to [6]him - [2]John, "[9]not [7]It [8]is [10]lawful for you

ἔχειν αὐτήν." **5** *Καὶ θέλων αὐτὸν ἀποκτεῖναι, ἐφοβήθη τὸν*
to have her." And desiring [3]him [1]to [2]kill, he feared the
Though

ὄχλον, ὅτι ὡς προφήτην αὐτὸν εἶχον. **6** *Γενεσίων*
crowd, because [4]as [5]a [6]prophet [3]him [1]they [2]had. birthday festivities
counted. Now while

δὲ ἀγομένων τοῦ Ἡρῴδου, ὠρχήσατο ἡ θυγάτηρ τῆς
And going on - of Herod, [5]danced [1]the [2]daughter -
Herod's birthday was being celebrated,

Ἡρωδιάδος ἐν τῷ μέσῳ καὶ ἤρεσε τῷ Ἡρῴδῃ. **7** *Ὅθεν*
[3]of [4]Herodias in the midst and she pleased - Herod. From which
Therefore

μεθ' ὅρκου ὡμολόγησεν αὐτῇ δοῦναι ὃ ἐὰν αἰτήσηται.
with an oath he promised [3]her [1]to [2]give what ever she might ask.

8 *Ἡ δέ, προβιβασθεῖσα ὑπὸ τῆς μητρὸς*
[2]the [3]*one* [1]So, having been brought forward by - mother
she prompted

αὐτῆς, "Δός μοι," φησίν, "ὧδε ἐπὶ πίνακι τὴν κεφαλὴν
her, "Give me," she says, "here on a platter the head
said,

Ἰωάννου τοῦ Βαπτιστοῦ." **9** *Καὶ ἐλυπήθη ὁ βασιλεύς,*
of John the Baptist." And [3]was [4]sorry [1]the [2]king,

διὰ δὲ τοὺς ὅρκους καὶ τοὺς συνανακειμένους
[6]because [7]of [5]but the oaths and the *ones* reclining *to eat* with *him*

not all with us? Where then did
this *Man* get all these things?"
57 So they were offended at
Him. But Jesus said to them,
"A prophet is not without honor
except in his own country and
in his own house."
58 Now He did not do many
mighty works there because of
their unbelief.
14 At that time Herod the
tetrarch heard the re-
port about Jesus
2 and said to his servants,
"This is John the Baptist; he is
risen from the dead, and therefore these powers are at work
in him."
3 For Herod had laid hold of
John and bound him, and put
him in prison for the sake of
Herodias, his brother Philip's
wife.
4 Because John had said to
him, "It is not lawful for you to
have her."
5 And although he wanted to
put him to death, he feared
the multitude, because they
counted him as a prophet.
6 But when Herod's birthday
was celebrated, the daughter of
Herodias danced before them
and pleased Herod.
7 Therefore he promised
with an oath to give her whatever she might ask.
8 So she, having been
prompted by her mother, said,
"Give me John the Baptist's
head here on a platter."
9 And the king was sorry;
nevertheless, because of the
oaths and because of those who
sat with him, he commanded *it*

to be given to *her.*
10 So he sent and had John beheaded in prison.
11 And his head was brought on a platter and given to the girl, and she brought *it* to her mother.
12 Then his disciples came and took away the body and buried it, and went and told Jesus.
13 When Jesus heard *it,* He departed from there by boat to a deserted place by Himself. But when the multitudes heard it, they followed Him on foot from the cities.
14 And when Jesus went out He saw a great multitude; and He was moved with compassion for them, and healed their sick.
15 When it was evening, His disciples came to Him, saying, "This is a deserted place, and the hour is already late. Send the multitudes away, that they may go into the villages and buy themselves food."
16 But Jesus said to them, "They do not need to go away. You give them something to eat."
17 And they said to Him, "We have here only five loaves and two fish."
18 He said, "Bring them here to Me."
19 Then He commanded the multitudes to sit down on the grass. And He took the five loaves and the two fish, and looking up to heaven, He

ἐκέλευσε δοθῆναι. 10 Καὶ πέμψας ἀπεκεφάλισε τὸν
he commanded *it* to be given. And having sent he beheaded -

Ἰωάννην ἐν τῇ φυλακῇ. 11 Καὶ ἠνέχθη ἡ κεφαλὴ αὐτοῦ
John in the prison. And [3]was [4]brought - [2]head [1]his

ἐπὶ πίνακι καὶ ἐδόθη τῷ κορασίῳ, καὶ ἤνεγκε τῇ
on a platter and it was given to the girl, and she brought *it* -

μητρὶ αὐτῆς. 12 Καὶ προσελθόντες οἱ μαθηταὶ αὐτοῦ
to mother ˜ her. And [3]approaching - [2]disciples [1]his
came forward

ἦραν τὸ σῶμα[a] καὶ ἔθαψαν αὐτό, καὶ ἐλθόντες ἀπήγγειλαν
they took the body and buried it, and coming they reported
and they came and

τῷ Ἰησοῦ.
- to Jesus.

Jesus Feeds the Five Thousand

(Mark 6:30–44; Luke 9:10–17; John 6:1–14)

13 Καὶ ἀκούσας ὁ Ἰησοῦς ἀνεχώρησεν ἐκεῖθεν ἐν
And hearing ˜ - Jesus He withdrew from there in
when Jesus heard

πλοίῳ εἰς ἔρημον τόπον κατ' ἰδίαν. Καὶ ἀκούσαντες οἱ
a boat for a deserted place privately. And hearing the
when the crowds

ὄχλοι ἠκολούθησαν αὐτῷ πεζῇ ἀπὸ τῶν πόλεων. 14 Καὶ
crowds they followed Him on foot from the cities. And
heard

ἐξελθὼν ὁ Ἰησοῦς[b] εἶδε πολὺν ὄχλον καὶ ἐσπλαγχνίσθη ἐπ'
coming out - Jesus saw a large crowd and He had compassion on

αὐτοῖς καὶ ἐθεράπευσε τοὺς ἀρρώστους αὐτῶν.
them and healed - [2]sick [3]*people* [1]their.

15 Ὀψίας δὲ γενομένης, προσῆλθον αὐτῷ οἱ μαθηταὶ
evening ˜ Now coming on, [3]approached [4]Him - [2]disciples
Now when evening came,

αὐτοῦ, λέγοντες, "Ἔρημός ἐστιν ὁ τόπος καὶ ἡ ὥρα ἤδη
[1]His, saying, "[4]deserted [3]is [1]The [2]place and the hour already
time

παρῆλθεν. Ἀπόλυσον τοὺς ὄχλους, ἵνα ἀπελθόντες εἰς τὰς
went by. Dismiss the crowds, so that going off to the
is late. they may go

κώμας ἀγοράσωσιν ἑαυτοῖς βρώματα."
villages they may buy for themselves foods."
and food."

16 Ὁ δὲ Ἰησοῦς εἶπεν αὐτοῖς, "Οὐ χρείαν ἔχουσιν
- But Jesus said to them, "[3]not [5]need [1]They [2]do [4]have

ἀπελθεῖν. Δότε αὐτοῖς ὑμεῖς φαγεῖν."
to go away. [2]give [3]them [1]You *food* to eat."

17 Οἱ δὲ λέγουσιν αὐτῷ, "Οὐκ ἔχομεν
[2]the [3]*ones* [1]But say to Him, "[3]not [1]We [2]do have *anything*
they said

ὧδε εἰ μὴ πέντε ἄρτους καὶ δύο ἰχθύας."
here if not five loaves of bread and two fish."
except

18 Ὁ δὲ εἶπε, "Φέρετέ μοι αὐτοὺς ὧδε." 19 Καὶ
[2]the [3]*One* [1]But said, "Bring [3]to [4]Me [1]them [2]here." And
He

κελεύσας τοὺς ὄχλους ἀνακλιθῆναι ἐπὶ τοὺς χόρτους, λαβὼν
commanding the crowds to recline on the grass, taking

τοὺς πέντε ἄρτους καὶ τοὺς δύο ἰχθύας, ἀναβλέψας εἰς τὸν
the five loaves of bread and the two fish, looking up to -

[a](**14:12**) NU reads πτωμα, *corpse.* [b](**14:14**) NU omits ο Ιησους, *Jesus.*

οὐρανὸν εὐλόγησε, καὶ κλάσας ἔδωκε τοῖς μαθηταῖς
heaven He blessed, and breaking *them* He gave [3]to [4]the [5]disciples

τοὺς ἄρτους, οἱ δὲ μαθηταὶ τοῖς ὄχλοις. **20** Καὶ ἔφαγον
[1]the [2]loaves, the ˜ and disciples *gave* to the crowds. And they ate ˜

πάντες καὶ ἐχορτάσθησαν, καὶ ἦραν τὸ περισσεῦον
all and were filled, and they took up the *amount* remaining
what they had left

τῶν κλασμάτων, δώδεκα κοφίνους πλήρεις. **21** Οἱ δὲ
of the fragments, twelve baskets full. [2]the [3]*ones* [1]And
Now those

ἐσθίοντες ἦσαν ἄνδρες* ὡσεὶ πεντακισχίλιοι, χωρὶς
eating were [4]men [1]about [2]five [3]thousand, apart from
who ate

γυναικῶν καὶ παιδίων.
women and children.

Jesus Walks on the Sea
(Mark 6:45–52; John 6:15–21)

22 Καὶ εὐθέως ἠνάγκασεν ὁ Ἰησοῦς[c] τοὺς μαθητὰς
And immediately compelled ˜ - Jesus the disciples

ἐμβῆναι εἰς τὸ πλοῖον καὶ προάγειν αὐτὸν εἰς τὸ πέραν,
to step in into the boat and to go ahead of Him to the other side,

ἕως οὗ ἀπολύσῃ τοὺς ὄχλους. **23** Καὶ ἀπολύσας τοὺς
until - He could dismiss the crowds. And having dismissed the

ὄχλους ἀνέβη εἰς τὸ ὄρος κατ' ἰδίαν προσεύξασθαι.
crowds He went up into the mountain privately to pray.

Ὀψίας δὲ γενομένης, μόνος ἦν ἐκεῖ. **24** Τὸ δὲ
evening ˜ And coming on, [4]alone [1]He [2]was [3]there. the ˜ But
Now when evening came,

πλοῖον ἤδη μέσον τῆς θαλάσσης ἦν,[d]
boat already [2]in [3]the [4]middle [5]of [6]the [7]sea [1]was,

βασανιζόμενον ὑπὸ τῶν κυμάτων, ἦν γὰρ ἐναντίος ὁ
being harassed by the waves, [4]was [1]for [5]against *them* [2]the

ἄνεμος.
[3]wind.

25 Τετάρτῃ δὲ φυλακῇ τῆς νυκτὸς ἀπῆλθε πρὸς
[2]in [3]*the* [4]fourth [1]And watch of the night [2]went [3]to

αὐτοὺς ὁ Ἰησοῦς,[e] περιπατῶν ἐπὶ τῆς θαλάσσης. **26** Καὶ
[4]them - [1]Jesus, walking on the sea. And

ἰδόντες αὐτὸν οἱ μαθηταὶ ἐπὶ τὴν θάλασσαν περιπατοῦντα
seeing Him the disciples [2]on [3]the [4]sea [1]walking
when the disciples saw Him

ἐταράχθησαν, λέγοντες ὅτι "Φάντασμά ἐστι!" Καὶ ἀπὸ τοῦ
they were troubled, saying - "[3]a [4]ghost [1]It [2]is!" And from -

φόβου ἔκραξαν.
fear they cried out.

27 Εὐθέως δὲ ἐλάλησεν αὐτοῖς ὁ Ἰησοῦς, λέγων,
immediately ˜ But [2]spoke [3]to [4]them - [1]Jesus, saying,

"Θαρσεῖτε! Ἐγώ εἰμι, μὴ φοβεῖσθε."
"Have courage! I am, not ˜ do be afraid."
It is I,

28 Ἀποκριθεὶς δὲ αὐτῷ ὁ Πέτρος εἶπε, "Κύριε, εἰ σὺ
answering ˜ But Him - Peter said, "Lord, if [3]You

εἶ, κέλευσόν με πρός σε ἐλθεῖν ἐπὶ τὰ ὕδατα."
[1]it [2]is, command me [3]toward [4]You [1]to [2]come on the waters."

29 Ὁ δὲ εἶπεν, "Ἐλθέ." Καὶ καταβὰς ἀπὸ τοῦ
[2]the [3]*One* [1]And said, "Come." And stepping down from the
He

blessed and broke and gave the loaves to the disciples; and the disciples gave to the multitudes.
20 So they all ate and were filled, and they took up twelve baskets full of the fragments that remained.
21 Now those who had eaten were about five thousand men, besides women and children.
22 Immediately Jesus made His disciples get into the boat and go before Him to the other side, while He sent the multitudes away.
23 And when He had sent the multitudes away, He went up on the mountain by Himself to pray. Now when evening came, He was alone there.
24 But the boat was now in the middle of the sea, tossed by the waves, for the wind was contrary.
25 Now in the fourth watch of the night Jesus went to them, walking on the sea.
26 And when the disciples saw Him walking on the sea, they were troubled, saying, "It is a ghost!" And they cried out for fear.
27 But immediately Jesus spoke to them, saying, "Be of good cheer! It is I; do not be afraid."
28 And Peter answered Him and said, "Lord, if it is You, command me to come to You on the water."
29 So He said, "Come." And when Peter had come down out

---

[c]**(14:22)** NU omits ο Ιησους, *Jesus.* [d]**(14:24)** For μεσον της θαλασσης ην, *was in the middle of the sea,* NU reads σταδιους πολλους απο της γης απειχεν, *was many furlongs away from the land.*
[e]**(14:25)** NU omits ο Ιησους, *Jesus.*

***(14:21)** ἀνήρ *(anēr).* Noun meaning *man, husband.* Whereas ἄνθρωπος refers to man in the sense of a human being, this word means man as having masculine traits, in distinction from woman (and from a boy), as here. John the Baptist used ἀνήρ when he identified Jesus as the Christ (John 1:30). It is frequently used, specifically, with the sense *husband* (1 Cor. 7:2; perhaps several times in 1 Cor. 11). The Greeks also had a word to describe a male (ἄρσην) in distinction from a female, placing emphasis on the sexual aspect of nature.

of the boat, he walked on the
water to go to Jesus.
30 But when he saw that the
wind *was* boisterous, he was
afraid; and beginning to sink he
cried out, saying, "Lord, save
me!"
31 And immediately Jesus
stretched out *His* hand and
caught him, and said to him,
"O you of little faith, why did
you doubt?"
32 And when they got into the
boat, the wind ceased.
33 Then those who were in
the boat came and worshiped
Him, saying, "Truly You are
the Son of God."
34 When they had crossed
over, they came to the land of
Gennesaret.
35 And when the men of that
place recognized Him, they
sent out into all that surrounding
region, brought to Him all
who were sick,
36 and begged Him that they
might only touch the hem of His
garment. And as many as
touched *it* were made perfectly
well.
15 Then the scribes and
Pharisees who were
from Jerusalem came to Jesus,
saying,
2 "Why do Your disciples
transgress the tradition of the

πλοίου ὁ Πέτρος περιεπάτησεν ἐπὶ τὰ ὕδατα ἐλθεῖν[f] πρὸς
boat - Peter walked on the waters to go toward

τὸν Ἰησοῦν.
- Jesus.

30 Βλέπων δὲ τὸν ἄνεμον ἰσχυρὸν ἐφοβήθη, καὶ
seeing ˜ But the wind ˜ strong he was afraid, and

ἀρξάμενος καταποντίζεσθαι ἔκραξε, λέγων, "Κύριε, σῶσόν
beginning to sink he cried out, saying, "Lord, save

με!"
me!"

31 Εὐθέως δὲ ὁ Ἰησοῦς ἐκτείνας τὴν χεῖρα ἐπελάβετο
immediately ˜ And - Jesus reaching out the hand laid hold of
His

αὐτοῦ καὶ λέγει αὐτῷ, "Ὀλιγόπιστε, εἰς τί ἐδίστασας?"
him and says to him, "*You* of little faith, - why did you doubt?"
said

32 Καὶ ἐμβάντων αὐτῶν εἰς τὸ πλοῖον, ἐκόπασεν ὁ
And stepping in them into the boat, [3]stopped [1]the
when they had gotten ceased

ἄνεμος. **33** Οἱ δὲ ἐν τῷ πλοίῳ ἐλθόντες[g]
[2]wind. [2]the [3]*ones* [1]And in the boat coming
And those who were came and

προσεκύνησαν αὐτῷ, λέγοντες, "Ἀληθῶς Θεοῦ Υἱὸς
worshiped Him, saying, "Truly [5]of [6]God [3]*the* [4]Son

εἶ!"
[1]You [2]are!"

Many Touch Jesus and Are Made Whole
(Mark 6:53–56)

34 Καὶ διαπεράσαντες ἦλθον εἰς τὴν γῆν Γεννησαρέτ.
And having crossed over they came to the land of Gennesaret.

35 Καὶ ἐπιγνόντες αὐτὸν οἱ ἄνδρες τοῦ τόπου
And having recognized Him the men - of place ˜
when the men of that place recognized

ἐκείνου ἀπέστειλαν εἰς ὅλην τὴν περίχωρον ἐκείνην,
that they sent into [2]whole - [3]surrounding [4]region [1]that,
Him,

καὶ προσήνεγκαν αὐτῷ πάντας τοὺς κακῶς ἔχοντας, **36** καὶ
and they brought to Him all the *ones* [3]badly [1]having [2]*it,* and
those who were ill,

παρεκάλουν αὐτὸν ἵνα μόνον ἅψωνται τοῦ κρασπέδου
they would beg Him that [3]only [1]they [2]might touch the border

τοῦ ἱματίου αὐτοῦ. Καὶ ὅσοι ἥψαντο
- of clothing ˜ His. And as many as touched *Him*

διεσώθησαν.
were completely delivered.
healed.

Defilement Comes from Within
(Mark 7:1–23)

15 **1** Τότε προσέρχονται τῷ Ἰησοῦ οἱ ἀπὸ Ἱεροσολύμων
Then [7]come [8]to - [9]Jesus [1]the [5]from [6]Jerusalem
approached

γραμματεῖς καὶ Φαρισαῖοι, λέγοντες, **2** "Διὰ τί οἱ
[2]scribes [3]and [4]Pharisees, saying, "On account of what -
"Why

μαθηταί σου παραβαίνουσι τὴν παράδοσιν τῶν
[3]disciples [2]Your [1]do [4]transgress the tradition of the

[f](14:29) NU reads και ηλθεν, *and went.*
[g](14:33) NU omits ελθοντες, *coming.*

πρεσβυτέρων? Οὐ γὰρ νίπτονται τὰς χεῖρας αὐτῶν ὅταν
elders? [4]not [1]For [2]they [3]do [5]wash - hands ˜ their whenever

ἄρτον ἐσθίωσιν."
[3]bread [1]they [2]eat."

3 Ὁ δὲ ἀποκριθεὶς εἶπεν αὐτοῖς, "Διὰ τί
[2]the [3]*One* [1]But answering said to them, "On account of what
He "Why

καὶ ὑμεῖς παραβαίνετε τὴν ἐντολὴν τοῦ Θεοῦ διὰ
[3]also [2]you [1]do [4]transgress the commandment - of God on account of

τὴν παράδοσιν ὑμῶν? 4 Ὁ γὰρ Θεὸς ἐνετείλατο, λέλων,[a]
- tradition ˜ your? - For God commanded, saying,

«Τίμα τὸν πατέρα καὶ τὴν μητέρα,»[b] καί, «Ὁ
«Honor the father and the mother,» and «The *one*
your your

κακολογῶν πατέρα ἢ μητέρα θανάτῳ τελευτάτω.»[c]
speaking evil of father or mother with death let him end.»
die.»

5 Ὑμεῖς δὲ λέγετε, 'Ὃς ἂν εἴπῃ τῷ πατρὶ ἢ τῇ μητρί,
you ˜ But say, 'Who ever says to the father or to the mother,
his his

"Δῶρον, ὃ ἐὰν ἐξ ἐμοῦ ὠφεληθῇς," 6 καὶ οὐ
"*It is* a gift, what ever [5]of [6]me [1]you [2]might [3]be [4]profited," and not
by then by no

μὴ τιμήσῃ τὸν πατέρα αὐτοῦ ἢ τὴν μητέρα αὐτοῦ.'[d]
not should he honor - father ˜ his or - mother ˜ his.'
means

Καὶ ἠκυρώσατε τὴν ἐντολὴν[e] τοῦ Θεοῦ διὰ τὴν
And you *thus* nullified the commandment - of God on account of -
have nullified

παράδοσιν ὑμῶν. 7 Ὑποκριταί! Καλῶς προεφήτευσε περὶ
tradition ˜ your. Hypocrites! Well did [2]prophesy [3]about

ὑμῶν Ἠσαΐας, λέγων,
[4]you [1]Isaiah, saying,

8 «Ἐγγίζει μοι ὁ λαὸς οὗτος τῷ στόματι αὐτῶν,
«[3]draws [4]near [5]to [6]Me - [2]people [1]This - with mouth ˜ their,

Καὶ[f] τοῖς χείλεσί με τιμᾷ,
And with the lips [3]Me [1]they [2]honor,
their

Ἡ δὲ καρδία αὐτῶν πόρρω ἀπέχει ἀπ' ἐμοῦ.
- But heart ˜ their far ˜ is away from Me.

9 Μάτην δὲ σέβονταί με,
[2]in [3]vain [1]And they worship Me,

Διδάσκοντες διδασκαλίας ἐντάλματα ἀνθρώπων.»"[g]
Teaching *as* teachings *the* commandments of men.»"

10 Καὶ προσκαλεσάμενος τὸν ὄχλον εἶπεν αὐτοῖς,
And having summoned the crowd He said to them,

"'Ακούετε καὶ συνίετε. 11 Οὐ τὸ εἰσερχόμενον εἰς τὸ
"Hear and understand. Not the *thing* entering into the
what goes

στόμα κοινοῖ τὸν ἄνθρωπον, ἀλλὰ τὸ
mouth makes [3]common [1]the [2]man, but the *thing*
defiles a

ἐκπορευόμενον ἐκ τοῦ στόματος, τοῦτο κοινοῖ τὸν
coming forth out of the mouth, this makes [3]common [1]the
defiles a

ἄνθρωπον."
[2]man."

elders? For they do not wash their hands when they eat bread."
3 He answered and said to them, "Why do you also transgress the commandment of God because of your tradition?
4 "For God commanded, saying, *'Honor your father and your mother'*; and, *'He who curses father or mother, let him be put to death.'*
5 "But you say, 'Whoever says to his father or mother, "Whatever profit you might have received from me *is* a gift *to God*"—
6 'then he need not honor his father or mother.' Thus you have made the commandment of God of no effect by your tradition.
7 "Hypocrites! Well did Isaiah prophesy about you, saying:

8 *'These people draw near to Me with their mouth,*
And honor Me with their lips,
But their heart is far from Me.
9 *And in vain they worship Me,*
Teaching as doctrines the commandments of men.'"

10 When He had called the multitude to *Himself*, He said to them, "Hear and understand:
11 "Not what goes into the mouth defiles a man; but what comes out of the mouth, this defiles a man."

---

[a](**15:4**) For ενετειλατο, λελων, *commanded, saying,* NU reads ειπεν, *said.* [b](**15:4**) Ex. 20:12; Deut. 5:16
[c](**15:4**) Ex. 21:17
[d](**15:6**) NU omits η την μητερα αυτου, *or his mother.* [e](**15:6**) NU reads λογον, *word.*
[f](**15:8**) NU omits Εγγιζει μοι, *draws near to Me,* and τω στοματι αυτων και, *with their mouth and,* thus *This people honors Me . . . .*
[g](**15:8, 9**) Is. 29:13 LXX

12 Then His disciples came and said to Him, "Do You know that the Pharisees were offended when they heard this saying?"
13 But He answered and said, "Every plant which My heavenly Father has not planted will be uprooted.
14 "Let them alone. They are blind leaders of the blind. And if the blind leads the blind, both will fall into a ditch."
15 Then Peter answered and said to Him, "Explain this parable to us."
16 So Jesus said, "Are you also still without understanding?
17 "Do you not yet understand that whatever enters the mouth goes into the stomach and is eliminated?
18 "But those things which proceed out of the mouth come from the heart, and they defile a man.
19 "For out of the heart proceed evil thoughts, murders, adulteries, fornications, thefts, false witness, blasphemies.
20 "These are *the things* which defile a man, but to eat with unwashed hands does not defile a man."
21 Then Jesus went out from there and departed to the region of Tyre and Sidon.
22 And behold, a woman of

12 Τότε προσελθόντες οἱ μαθηταὶ αὐτοῦ εἶπον αὐτῷ,
Then [3]approaching - [2]disciples [1]His said to Him,
approached and

"Οἶδας ὅτι οἱ Φαρισαῖοι ἀκούσαντες τὸν λόγον
"You know that the Pharisees hearing the word
when the Pharisees heard this message

ἐσκανδαλίσθησαν?"
they were offended?"

13 Ὁ δὲ ἀποκριθεὶς εἶπε, "Πᾶσα φυτεία ἣν οὐκ
[2]the [3]*One* [1]But answering said, "Every plant which [5]not
He

ἐφύτευσεν ὁ Πατήρ μου ὁ οὐράνιος ἐκριζωθήσεται. **14** Ἄφετε
[4]did [6]plant - [3]Father [1]My - [2]heavenly will be uprooted. Leave

αὐτούς. Ὁδηγοί εἰσι τυφλοὶ τυφλῶν. Τυφλὸς
them *alone.* [4]guides [1]They [2]are [3]blind of blind *people.* [3]a [4]blind [5]*person*

δὲ τυφλὸν ἐὰν ὁδηγῇ, ἀμφότεροι εἰς βόθυνον
[1]But [7]a [8]blind [9]*person* [2]if [6]guides, both [3]into [4]a [5]ditch

πεσοῦνται."
[1]will [2]fall."

15 Ἀποκριθεὶς δὲ ὁ Πέτρος εἶπεν αὐτῷ, "Φράσον
answering ˜ And - Peter said to Him, "Explain
Then Peter answered and

ἡμῖν τὴν παραβολὴν ταύτην."
to us - parable ˜ this."

16 Ὁ δὲ Ἰησοῦς[h] εἶπεν, "Ἀκμὴν καὶ ὑμεῖς
- And Jesus said, "[4]still [3]also [2]you

ἀσύνετοί ἐστε? **17** Οὔπω[i] νοεῖτε ὅτι
[5]without [6]understanding [1]Are? [3]not [4]yet [1]Do [2]you understand that

πᾶν τὸ εἰσπορευόμενον εἰς τὸ στόμα εἰς τὴν κοιλίαν
every*thing* - entering into the mouth [2]into [3]the [4]belly

χωρεῖ καὶ εἰς ἀφεδρῶνα ἐκβάλλεται? **18** Τὰ δὲ
[1]goes and [4]into [5]a [6]latrine [1]is [2]cast [3]out? [2]the [3]*things* [1]But

ἐκπορευόμενα ἐκ τοῦ στόματος ἐκ τῆς καρδίας
coming forth out of the mouth [3]out [4]of [5]the [6]heart

ἐξέρχεται, κἀκεῖνα κοινοῖ τὸν ἄνθρωπον. **19** Ἐκ
[1]come [2]forth, and those *things* make [3]common [1]the [2]man. [2]out [3]of
defile a

γὰρ τῆς καρδίας ἐξέρχονται διαλογισμοὶ πονηροί, φόνοι,
[1]For the heart come forth thoughts ˜ evil, murders,
designs

μοιχεῖαι, πορνεῖαι, κλοπαί, ψευδομαρτυρίαι, βλασφημίαι.
adulteries, fornications, thefts, false testimonies, blasphemies.

20 Ταῦτά ἐστι τὰ κοινοῦντα τὸν ἄνθρωπον, τὸ δὲ
These are the *things* making [3]common [1]the [2]man, - but
defiling a

ἀνίπτοις χερσὶ φαγεῖν οὐ κοινοῖ τὸν
[3]with [4]unwashed [5]hands [1]to [2]eat [7]not [6]does [8]make [11]common [9]the
defile a

ἄνθρωπον."
[10]man."

A Gentile Is Blessed for Her Faith
(Mark 7:24–30)

21 Καὶ ἐξελθὼν ἐκεῖθεν ὁ Ἰησοῦς ἀνεχώρησεν εἰς τὰ
And going out from there - Jesus withdrew into the

μέρη Τύρου καὶ Σιδῶνος. **22** Καὶ ἰδού, γυνὴ Χαναναία
parts of Tyre and of Sidon. And behold, a woman ˜ Canaanite
region

[h](15:16) NU omits Ιησους, *Jesus.* [i](15:17) NU reads ου, *not.*

ἀπὸ τῶν ὁρίων ἐκείνων ἐξελθοῦσα ἐκραύγασεν αὐτῷ,[j]
[3]from - [5]borders ~ [4]those [1]coming [2]forth cried out to Him,
that region

λέγουσα, "Ἐλέησόν με, Κύριε, Υἱὲ Δαβίδ! Ἡ θυγάτηρ μου
saying, "Have mercy on me, Lord, Son of David! - daughter ~ My

κακῶς δαιμονίζεται."* 23 Ὁ δὲ οὐκ ἀπεκρίθη αὐτῇ
badly ~ is demon-possessed." [2]the [3]*One* [1]But not ~ did answer her
He

λόγον.
a word.

Καὶ προσελθόντες οἱ μαθηταὶ αὐτοῦ ἠρώτων αὐτόν,
And [3]approaching - [2]disciples [1]His urged Him,
approached and

λέγοντες, "Ἀπόλυσον αὐτήν, ὅτι κράζει ὄπισθεν
saying, "Send away ~ her, because she is crying out after

ἡμῶν."
us."

24 Ὁ δὲ ἀποκριθεὶς εἶπεν, "Οὐκ ἀπεστάλην εἰ
[2]the [3]*One* [1]But answering said, "[3]not [1]I [2]was sent if
He except

μὴ εἰς τὰ πρόβατα τὰ ἀπολωλότα οἴκου Ἰσραήλ."
not to the sheep ~ - lost of *the* house of Israel."

25 Ἡ δὲ ἐλθοῦσα προσεκύνησεν αὐτῷ λέγουσα,
[2]the [3]*one* [1]But coming worshiped Him saying,
she came and

"Κύριε, βοήθει μοι!"
"Lord, help me!"

26 Ὁ δὲ ἀποκριθεὶς εἶπεν, "Οὐκ ἔστι καλὸν λαβεῖν
[2]the [3]*One* [1]But answering said, "[3]not [1]It [2]is good to take
He

τὸν ἄρτον τῶν τέκνων καὶ βαλεῖν τοῖς κυναρίοις."
the bread of the children and to throw *it* to the little dogs."

27 Ἡ δὲ εἶπε, "Ναί, Κύριε, καὶ γὰρ τὰ κυνάρια
[2]the [3]*one* [1]But said, "Yes, Lord, even ~ for the little dogs
she

ἐσθίει ἀπὸ τῶν ψιχίων τῶν πιπτόντων ἀπὸ τῆς τραπέζης τῶν
eat from the crumbs - falling from the table -

κυρίων αὐτῶν."
of masters ~ their."

28 Τότε ἀποκριθεὶς ὁ Ἰησοῦς εἶπεν αὐτῇ, "Ὦ γύναι,
Then answering - Jesus said to her, "O woman,

μεγάλη σου ἡ πίστις! Γενηθήτω σοι ὡς θέλεις." Καὶ
great *is* your - faith! Let it be to you as you desire." And

ἰάθη ἡ θυγάτηρ αὐτῆς ἀπὸ τῆς ὥρας ἐκείνης.
[3]was [4]healed - [2]daughter [1]her from - hour ~ that.

Jesus Heals Great Multitudes

29 Καὶ μεταβὰς ἐκεῖθεν ὁ Ἰησοῦς ἦλθε παρὰ τὴν
And moving on from there - Jesus came alongside the

θάλασσαν τῆς Γαλιλαίας, καὶ ἀναβὰς εἰς τὸ ὄρος
Sea - of Galilee, and going up into the mountain
a

ἐκάθητο ἐκεῖ. 30 Καὶ προσῆλθον αὐτῷ ὄχλοι πολλοί,
He sat down there. And [3]approached [4]Him [2]crowds [1]large,

ἔχοντες μεθ' ἑαυτῶν χωλούς, τυφλούς, κωφούς, κυλλούς, καὶ
having with themselves lame *people,* blind, mute, maimed, and
them

ἑτέρους πολλούς, καὶ ἔρριψαν αὐτοὺς παρὰ τοὺς πόδας τοῦ
others ~ many, and they put down ~ them at the feet -

Canaan came from that region and cried out to Him, saying, "Have mercy on me, O Lord, Son of David! My daughter is severely demon-possessed."
23 But He answered her not a word. And His disciples came and urged Him, saying, "Send her away, for she cries out after us."
24 But He answered and said, "I was not sent except to the lost sheep of the house of Israel."
25 Then she came and worshiped Him, saying, "Lord, help me!"
26 But He answered and said, "It is not good to take the children's bread and throw *it* to the little dogs."
27 And she said, "Yes, Lord, yet even the little dogs eat the crumbs which fall from their masters' table."
28 Then Jesus answered and said to her, "O woman, great *is* your faith! Let it be to you as you desire." And her daughter was healed from that very hour.
29 Jesus departed from there, skirted the Sea of Galilee, and went up on the mountain and sat down there.
30 Then great multitudes came to Him, having with them *the* lame, blind, mute, maimed, and many others; and they laid

---

j(**15:22**) NU omits *αυτω, to Him.*

***(15:22)** δαιμονίζομαι *(daimonizomai).* Verb formed on the root δαιμόνιον, *deity* (Acts 17:18), *demon,* thus literally meaning *to demonize.* It is generally translated *be demon-possessed* (as here). The word describes the state of being under demonic influence/control or demonically tormented. It is synonymous with the expression "to have (or 'be with') an unclean spirit" (πνεύμα ἀκαθάτον, Mark 5:2, 15). Cf. the cognate adjective δαιμονιώδης, *demonic,* used only in James 3:15; and noun δαίμων, *demon, evil spirit* (Matt. 8:31).

them down at Jesus' feet, and He healed them.
31 So the multitude marveled when they saw *the* mute speaking, *the* maimed made whole, *the* lame walking, and *the* blind seeing; and they glorified the God of Israel.
32 Now Jesus called His disciples to *Himself* and said, "I have compassion on the multitude, because they have now continued with Me three days and have nothing to eat. And I do not want to send them away hungry, lest they faint on the way."
33 Then His disciples said to Him, "Where could we get enough bread in the wilderness to fill such a great multitude?"
34 Jesus said to them, "How many loaves do you have?" And they said, "Seven, and a few little fish."
35 So He commanded the multitude to sit down on the ground.
36 And He took the seven loaves and the fish and gave thanks, broke *them* and gave *them* to His disciples; and the disciples *gave* to the multitude.
37 So they all ate and were filled, and they took up seven large baskets full of the fragments that were left.
38 Now those who ate were four thousand men, besides women and children.
39 And He sent away the multitude, got into the boat, and came to the region of Magdala.

Ἰησοῦ,[k] καὶ ἐθεράπευσεν αὐτούς· **31** ὥστε τοὺς ὄχλους
of Jesus, and He healed them; so that the crowds

θαυμάσαι βλέποντας κωφοὺς λαλοῦντας, κυλλοὺς ὑγιεῖς,
to marvel seeing mutes speaking, maimed *people* whole,
marveled when they saw

χωλοὺς περιπατοῦντας, καὶ τυφλοὺς βλέποντας· καὶ
lame *people* walking, and blind *people* seeing; and

ἐδόξασαν τὸν Θεὸν Ἰσραήλ.
they glorified the God of Israel.

Jesus Feeds the Four Thousand
(Mark 8:1–10)

32 Ὁ δὲ Ἰησοῦς προσκαλεσάμενος τοὺς μαθητὰς αὐτοῦ
- And Jesus having summoned - disciples ˜ His

εἶπε, "Σπλαγχνίζομαι ἐπὶ τὸν ὄχλον, ὅτι ἤδη ἡμέραι
said, "I have compassion on the crowd, because already days ˜

τρεῖς προσμένουσί μοι καὶ οὐκ ἔχουσι τί
three they remain with Me and [3]not [1]they [2]do have anything
have been remaining

φάγωσι. Καὶ ἀπολῦσαι αὐτοὺς νήστεις οὐ θέλω,
they can eat. And to dismiss them hungry [3]not [1]I [2]do desire,

μήποτε ἐκλυθῶσιν ἐν τῇ ὁδῷ."
lest they faint on the way."

33 Καὶ λέγουσιν αὐτῷ οἱ μαθηταὶ αὐτοῦ, "Πόθεν ἡμῖν
And [3]say [4]to [5]Him - [2]disciples [1]His, "From where to us
said "Where could we get

ἐν ἐρημίᾳ ἄρτοι τοσοῦτοι, ὥστε χορτάσαι
in *this* deserted place [3]loaves [4]of [5]bread [1]so [2]many, so as to satisfy

ὄχλον τοσοῦτον?"
[3]a [4]crowd [1]so [2]great?"

34 Καὶ λέγει αὐτοῖς ὁ Ἰησοῦς, "Πόσους ἄρτους ἔχετε?"
And [2]says [3]to [4]them - [1]Jesus, "How many loaves have you?"
said

Οἱ δὲ εἶπον, "Ἑπτά, καὶ ὀλίγα ἰχθύδια."
[2]the [3]*ones* [1]And said, "Seven, and a few small fish."
they

35 Καὶ ἐκέλευσε[l] τοῖς ὄχλοις ἀναπεσεῖν ἐπὶ τὴν γῆν.
And He commanded the crowds to recline on the ground.

36 Καὶ λαβὼν[m] τοὺς ἑπτὰ ἄρτους καὶ τοὺς ἰχθύας,
And taking the seven loaves and the fish,
He took

εὐχαριστήσας ἔκλασε, καὶ ἔδωκε τοῖς μαθηταῖς
having given thanks He broke *them,* and gave *them* - to disciples ˜

αὐτοῦ, οἱ δὲ μαθηταὶ τῷ ὄχλῳ. **37** Καὶ ἔφαγον πάντες καὶ
His, the ˜ and disciples to the crowd. And they ate ˜ all and

ἐχορτάσθησαν. Καὶ ἦραν τὸ περισσεῦον τῶν
were filled. And they took up the *amount* remaining -
what they had left

κλασμάτων, ἑπτὰ σπυρίδας πλήρεις. **38** Οἱ δὲ ἐσθίοντες
of fragments, seven hampers full. [2]the [3]*ones* [1]And eating
And those who ate

ἦσαν τετρακισχίλιοι ἄνδρες, χωρὶς γυναικῶν καὶ παιδίων.
were four thousand men, apart from women and children.

39 Καὶ ἀπολύσας τοὺς ὄχλους ἀνέβη εἰς τὸ πλοῖον καὶ
And having dismissed the crowds He went up into the boat and
embarked

ἦλθεν εἰς τὰ ὅρια Μαγδαλά.[n]
came to the borders of Magdala.
region

---

[k](**15:30**) NU reads *αυτου, His.* [l](**15:35**) NU reads *παραγγειλας, directing.* [m](**15:36**) For *Και λαβων, And taking,* NU reads *ελαβεν, He took.* [n](**15:39**) NU reads *Μαγαδαν, Magadan.*

Discerning the Signs of the Times
(Mark 8:11–13; Luke 12:54–56)

16 **1** Καὶ προσελθόντες οἱ Φαρισαῖοι καὶ Σαδδουκαῖοι
And [5]approaching [1]the [2]Pharisees [3]and [4]Sadducees
came up and

πειράζοντες ἐπηρώτησαν αὐτὸν σημεῖον ἐκ τοῦ οὐρανοῦ
testing *Him* they asked Him [4]a [5]sign [6]out [7]of - [8]heaven

ἐπιδεῖξαι αὐτοῖς. **2** Ὁ δὲ ἀποκριθεὶς εἶπεν αὐτοῖς,
[1]to [2]show [3]them. [2]the [3]*One* [1]But answering said to them,
He

"Ὀψίας γενομένης λέγετε, 'Εὐδία, πυρράζει γὰρ
"Evening coming you say, '*It will be* fair weather, [4]is [5]red [1]for
"When evening comes

ὁ οὐρανός.' **3** Καὶ πρωΐ, 'Σήμερον χειμών,
[2]the [3]sky.' And in the morning, 'Today *will be* stormy,

πυρράζει γὰρ στυγνάζων ὁ οὐρανός.' Ὑποκριταί![a] Τὸ μὲν
[4]is [5]red [1]for [6]being [7]dark [2]the [3]sky.' Hypocrites! [7]the [1]Indeed
and overcast

πρόσωπον τοῦ οὐρανοῦ γινώσκετε διακρίνειν, τὰ δὲ
[8]face [9]of [10]the [11]sky [2]you [3]know [4]*how* [5]to [6]discern, the ~ but

σημεῖα τῶν καιρῶν οὐ δύνασθε. **4** Γενεὰ
signs of the times [3]not [1]you [2]are [4]able *to discern*. [1]An [5]generation

πονηρὰ καὶ μοιχαλὶς σημεῖον ἐπιζητεῖ, καὶ σημεῖον οὐ
[2]evil [3]and [4]adulterous [7]a [8]sign [6]seeks, and a sign not ~
but

δοθήσεται αὐτῇ εἰ μὴ τὸ σημεῖον Ἰωνᾶ τοῦ προφήτου."[b]
will be given to it if not the sign of Jonah the prophet."
except

Καὶ καταλιπὼν αὐτοὺς ἀπῆλθε.
And leaving behind ~ them He went away.

Beware of the Leaven of the Pharisees and Sadducees
(Mark 8:14–21)

5 Καὶ ἐλθόντες οἱ μαθηταὶ αὐτοῦ εἰς τὸ πέραν
And [3]coming - [2]disciples [1]His to the other side
when His disciples came

ἐπελάθοντο ἄρτους λαβεῖν. **6** Ὁ δὲ Ἰησοῦς εἶπεν αὐτοῖς,
they forgot [3]bread [1]to [2]take. - But Jesus said to them,

"Ὁρᾶτε καὶ προσέχετε ἀπὸ τῆς ζύμης τῶν Φαρισαίων καὶ
"Look out and beware of the leaven of the Pharisees and

Σαδδουκαίων."
Sadducees."

7 Οἱ δὲ διελογίζοντο ἐν ἑαυτοῖς, λέγοντες ὅτι
[2]the [3]*ones* [1]But were reasoning among themselves, saying -
they

"Ἄρτους οὐκ ἐλάβομεν."
"[5]bread [3]not [1]We [2]did [4]take."

8 Γνοὺς δὲ ὁ Ἰησοῦς εἶπεν αὐτοῖς,[c] "Τί
[2]knowing [3]*about* [4]*it* [1]But - Jesus said to them, "Why

διαλογίζεσθε ἐν ἑαυτοῖς, ὀλιγόπιστοι, ὅτι ἄρτους οὐκ
are you reasoning among yourselves, *you* of little faith, because [5]bread [3]not

ἐλάβετε?[d] **9** Οὔπω νοεῖτε, οὐδὲ μνημονεύετε τοὺς
[1]you [2]did [4]take? [3]not [4]yet [1]Do [2]you [5]perceive, nor remember the

πέντε ἄρτους τῶν πεντακισχιλίων καὶ πόσους κοφίνους
five loaves of the five thousand and how many baskets

ἐλάβετε? **10** Οὐδὲ τοὺς ἑπτὰ ἄρτους τῶν τετρακισχιλίων καὶ
you took? Nor the seven loaves of the four thousand and

16 Then the Pharisees
and Sadducees came,
and testing Him asked that He
would show them a sign from
heaven.
2 He answered and said to
them, "When it is evening you
say, '*It will be* fair weather, for
the sky is red';
3 "and in the morning, '*It will
be* foul weather today, for the
sky is red and threatening.'
Hypocrites! You know how to
discern the face of the sky, but
you cannot *discern* the signs of
the times.
4 "A wicked and adulterous
generation seeks after a sign,
and no sign shall be given to it
except the sign of the prophet
Jonah." And He left them and
departed.
5 Now when His disciples
had come to the other side,
they had forgotten to take
bread.
6 Then Jesus said to them,
"Take heed and beware of the
leaven of the Pharisees and the
Sadducees."
7 And they reasoned among
themselves, saying, "*It is* because we have taken no bread."
8 But Jesus, being aware of
it, said to them, "O you of little
faith, why do you reason among
yourselves because you have
brought no bread?
9 "Do you not yet under-
stand, or remember the five
loaves of the five thousand and
how many baskets you took up?
10 "Nor the seven loaves of
the four thousand and how

---

[a](16:3) NU omits υποκριται, *hypocrites.*
[b](16:4) NU omits του προφητου, *the prophet.*
[c](16:8) NU omits αυτοις, *to them.* [d](16:8) NU reads εχετε, *do (not) have.*

many large baskets you took up?
11 "How is it you do not understand that I did not speak to you concerning bread? — *but* to beware of the leaven of the Pharisees and Sadducees."
12 Then they understood that He did not tell *them* to beware of the leaven of bread, but of the doctrine of the Pharisees and Sadducees.
13 When Jesus came into the region of Caesarea Philippi, He asked His disciples, saying, "Who do men say that I, the Son of Man, am?"
14 So they said, "Some *say* John the Baptist, some Elijah, and others Jeremiah or one of the prophets."
15 He said to them, "But who do you say that I am?"
16 Simon Peter answered and said, "You are the Christ, the Son of the living God."
17 Jesus answered and said to him, "Blessed are you, Simon Bar-Jonah, for flesh and blood has not revealed *this* to you, but My Father who is in heaven.
18 "And I also say to you that you are Peter, and on this rock I will build My church, and the gates of Hades shall not prevail against it.
19 "And I will give you the keys of the kingdom of heaven, and whatever you bind on earth will be bound in heaven, and whatever you loose on earth will be loosed in heaven."
20 Then He commanded His

---

*(16:18) πέτρα (petra). Noun meaning *rock*. Generally, but not always, this word indicates a rock mass or bedrock in distinction from πέτρος, a specific *rock* or *stone*. Thus Jesus' tomb was hewn in a rock mass (Matt. 27:60), a house may be built on bedrock (Matt. 7:24), and plants from seed sown on "rocky ground" (Luke 8:6, probably thin soil on a rock base) did not survive. Here in Matt. 16:18 Jesus makes a wordplay on the name He had given Peter (Πέτρος), but the "rock" (πέτρα) that serves as foundation for the church may be the truth indicated in Peter's confession. Cf. also the cognate adjective πετρώδης, used substantivally for *stony ground*, only in Mark 4:5, 16; Matt. 13:5, 20.

πόσας σπυρίδας ἐλάβετε? 11 Πῶς οὐ νοεῖτε ὅτι
how many hampers you took? How *is it* [3]not [1]you [2]do perceive that

οὐ περὶ ἄρτου εἶπον ὑμῖν προσέχειν ἀπὸ τῆς ζύμης τῶν
it was not about bread I told you to beware of the leaven of the

Φαρισαίων καὶ Σαδδουκαίων?" 12 Τότε συνῆκαν ὅτι οὐκ
Pharisees and Sadducees?" Then they understood that [3]not

εἶπε προσέχειν ἀπὸ τῆς ζύμης τοῦ ἄρτου, ἀλλὰ ἀπὸ τῆς
[1]He [2]did say to beware of the leaven - of bread, but from the
of

διδαχῆς τῶν Φαρισαίων καὶ Σαδδουκαίων.
teaching of the Pharisees and Sadducees.

Peter Confesses Jesus as the Christ
(Mark 8:27–30; Luke 9:18–20)

13 Ἐλθὼν δὲ ὁ Ἰησοῦς εἰς τὰ μέρη Καισαρείας τῆς
coming And - Jesus into the parts of Caesarea -
When Jesus came region

Φιλίππου ἠρώτα τοὺς μαθητὰς αὐτοῦ, λέγων, "Τίνα
of Philippi He was questioning - disciples ˜ His, saying, "Whom
"Who

με λέγουσιν οἱ ἄνθρωποι εἶναι, τὸν Υἱὸν τοῦ Ἀνθρώπου?"
[4]Me [1]do [3]say - [2]men [9]to [10]be, [5]the [6]Son - [7]of [8]Man?"
do men say that I, the Son of Man, am?"

14 Οἱ δὲ εἶπον, "Οἱ μὲν Ἰωάννην τὸν
[2]the [3]*ones* [1]And said, "The *ones* on the one hand John the
they "Some

βαπτιστήν, ἄλλοι δὲ Ἠλίαν, ἕτεροι δὲ Ἰερεμίαν ἢ ἕνα
Baptist, others ˜ but Elijah, [2]different [3]*ones* [1]yet Jeremiah or one

τῶν προφητῶν."
of the prophets."

15 Λέγει αὐτοῖς, "Ὑμεῖς δὲ τίνα με λέγετε εἶναι?"
He says to them, "you ˜ But whom [4]Me [1]do [2]you [3]say to be?"
said who do you say that I am?"

16 Ἀποκριθεὶς δὲ Σίμων Πέτρος εἶπε, "Σὺ εἶ ὁ Χριστός,
answering ˜ And Simon Peter said, "You are the Christ,
Messiah,

ὁ Υἱὸς τοῦ Θεοῦ τοῦ ζῶντος."
the Son of the God ˜ - living."

17 Καὶ ἀποκριθεὶς ὁ Ἰησοῦς εἶπεν αὐτῷ, "Μακάριος εἶ,
And answering - Jesus said to him, "Blessed are you,

Σίμων Βαριωνᾶ, ὅτι σὰρξ καὶ αἷμα οὐκ ἀπεκάλυψέ σοι,
Simon Bar-Jonah, because flesh and blood not ˜ did reveal *this* to you,

ἀλλ' ὁ Πατήρ μου ὁ ἐν τοῖς οὐρανοῖς. 18 Κἀγὼ δέ σοι
but - Father ˜ My - in the heavens. [2]I [3]also [1]And [5]to [6]you

λέγω ὅτι σὺ εἶ Πέτρος, καὶ ἐπὶ ταύτῃ τῇ πέτρᾳ* οἰκοδομήσω
[4]say that you are Peter, and on this - rock I will build

μου τὴν ἐκκλησίαν, καὶ πύλαι Ἅιδου οὐ κατισχύσουσιν
My - church, and *the* gates of Hades not ˜ will have power over
prevail

αὐτῆς. 19 Καὶ δώσω σοι τὰς κλεῖς τῆς βασιλείας τῶν
it. And I will give you the keys of the kingdom of the

οὐρανῶν, καὶ ὃ ἐὰν δήσῃς ἐπὶ τῆς γῆς ἔσται δεδεμένον ἐν
heavens, and what ever you bind on the earth will be bound in

τοῖς οὐρανοῖς, καὶ ὃ ἐὰν λύσῃς ἐπὶ τῆς γῆς ἔσται
the heavens, and what ever you loose on the earth will be

λελυμένον ἐν τοῖς οὐρανοῖς." 20 Τότε διεστείλατο τοῖς
loosed in the heavens." Then He ordered -

μαθηταῖς αὐτοῦ ἵνα μηδενὶ εἴπωσιν ὅτι αὐτός ἐστιν
disciples ˜ His that [4]no [5]one [1]they [2]should [3]tell that He is
was

Ἰησοῦς ὁ Χριστός.
Jesus the Christ.
Messiah.

Jesus Predicts His Death and Resurrection
(Mark 8:31–33; Luke 9:21, 22)

21 Ἀπὸ τότε ἤρξατο ὁ Ἰησοῦς δεικνύειν τοῖς μαθηταῖς
From then began ˜ - Jesus to show - to disciples ˜
that time

αὐτοῦ ὅτι δεῖ αὐτὸν ἀπελθεῖν εἰς Ἱεροσόλυμα καὶ
His that it is necessary *for* Him to go off to Jerusalem and
was

πολλὰ παθεῖν ἀπὸ τῶν πρεσβυτέρων καὶ ἀρχιερέων καὶ
[3]many [4]*things* [1]to [2]suffer from the elders and chief priests and

γραμματέων καὶ ἀποκτανθῆναι καὶ τῇ τρίτῃ ἡμέρᾳ
scribes and to be killed and on the third day

ἐγερθῆναι.
to be raised.

22 Καὶ προσλαβόμενος αὐτὸν ὁ Πέτρος ἤρξατο ἐπιτιμᾶν
And taking aside ˜ Him - Peter began to rebuke

αὐτῷ, λέγων, "Ἵλεώς σοι, Κύριε! Οὐ μὴ ἔσται
Him, saying, "*God be* gracious to You, Lord! [3]not [4]not [2]shall [5]be
"God forbid, shall by no means happen

σοι τοῦτο."
[6]to [7]You [1]This."

23 Ὁ δὲ στραφεὶς εἶπε τῷ Πέτρῳ, "Ὕπαγε ὀπίσω
[2]the [3]*One* [1]But turning said - to Peter, "Go away behind
He

μου, Σατανᾶ! Σκάνδαλόν μου εἶ, ὅτι οὐ
Me, Satan! [3]an [4]offensive [5]thing [6]of [7]Me [1]You [2]are, because [3]not
offense to

φρονεῖς τὰ τοῦ Θεοῦ, ἀλλὰ τὰ τῶν
[1]you [2]are mindful of the *things* - of God, but the *things* -

ἀνθρώπων."
of men."

Taking Up the Cross
(Mark 8:34–9:1; Luke 9:23–27)

24 Τότε ὁ Ἰησοῦς εἶπε τοῖς μαθηταῖς αὐτοῦ, "Εἴ τις
Then - Jesus said - to disciples ˜ His, "If anyone

θέλει ὀπίσω μου ἐλθεῖν, ἀπαρνησάσθω ἑαυτὸν καὶ
desires [3]after [4]Me [1]to [2]come, let him deny himself and

ἀράτω τὸν σταυρὸν αὐτοῦ καὶ ἀκολουθείτω μοι. **25** Ὃς
let him take up - cross ˜ his and let him follow Me. who ˜

γὰρ ἂν θέλῃ τὴν ψυχὴν αὐτοῦ σῶσαι ἀπολέσει αὐτήν, ὃς
For ever desires - [4]life [3]his [1]to [2]save will lose it, who ˜
preserve

δ' ἂν ἀπολέσῃ τὴν ψυχὴν αὐτοῦ ἕνεκεν ἐμοῦ εὑρήσει
but ever loses - life ˜ his on account of Me will find

αὐτήν. **26** Τί γὰρ ὠφελεῖται[e] ἄνθρωπος ἐὰν τὸν κόσμον
it. what ˜ For is [3]profited [1]a [2]man if [3]the [5]world

ὅλον κερδήσῃ, τὴν δὲ ψυχὴν αὐτοῦ ζημιωθῇ? Ἢ τί δώσει
[4]whole [1]he [2]gains, - but [3]soul [2]his [1]forfeits? Or what will [3]give

ἄνθρωπος ἀντάλλαγμα τῆς ψυχῆς αὐτοῦ? **27** Μέλλει γὰρ
[1]a [2]man *as* an exchange for - soul ˜ his? [6]is [7]going [1]For

disciples that they should tell no
one that He was Jesus the
Christ.
21 From that time Jesus began to show to His disciples
that He must go to Jerusalem,
and suffer many things from the
elders and chief priests and
scribes, and be killed, and be
raised the third day.
22 Then Peter took Him aside
and began to rebuke Him, saying, "Far be it from You, Lord;
this shall not happen to You!"
23 But He turned and said to
Peter, "Get behind Me, Satan!
You are an offense to Me, for
you are not mindful of the
things of God, but the things of
men."
24 Then Jesus said to His disciples, "If anyone desires to
come after Me, let him deny
himself, and take up his cross,
and follow Me.
25 "For whoever desires to
save his life will lose it, but
whoever loses his life for My
sake will find it.
26 "For what profit is it to a
man if he gains the whole
world, and loses his own soul?
Or what will a man give in exchange for his soul?
27 "For the Son of Man will

---

[e] **(16:26)** NU reads *ωφεληθησεται, will be profited.*

come in the glory of His Father
with His angels, and then He
will reward each according to
his works.
28 "Assuredly, I say to you,
there are some standing here
who shall not taste death till
they see the Son of Man coming in His kingdom."

17 Now after six days Je-
sus took Peter, James,
and John his brother, led them
up on a high mountain by themselves;
2 and He was transfigured
before them. His face shone
like the sun, and His clothes became as white as the light.
3 And behold, Moses and
Elijah appeared to them, talking
with Him.
4 Then Peter answered and
said to Jesus, "Lord, it is good
for us to be here; if You wish,
let us make here three tabernacles: one for You, one for Moses, and one for Elijah."
5 While he was still speaking,
behold, a bright cloud overshadowed them; and suddenly a
voice came out of the cloud,
saying, "This is My beloved
Son, in whom I am well
pleased. Hear Him!"
6 And when the disciples
heard *it,* they fell on their faces
and were greatly afraid.
7 But Jesus came and
touched them and said, "Arise,

ὁ Υἱὸς τοῦ Ἀνθρώπου ἔρχεσθαι ἐν τῇ δόξῃ τοῦ Πατρὸς
[2]the [3]Son - [4]of [5]Man to come in the glory - of Father ˜

αὐτοῦ μετὰ τῶν ἀγγέλων αὐτοῦ, καὶ τότε ἀποδώσει ἑκάστῳ
His with - angels ˜ His, and then He will pay back each
reward

κατὰ τὴν πρᾶξιν αὐτοῦ. 28 Ἀμὴν λέγω ὑμῖν, εἰσί
according to - activity ˜ his. Amen I say to you, *there* are
Assuredly

τινες ὧδε ἑστῶτες οἵτινες οὐ μὴ γεύσωνται θανάτου
some here ˜ standing who not not will taste of death
by no means

ἕως ἂν ἴδωσι τὸν Υἱὸν τοῦ Ἀνθρώπου ἐρχόμενον ἐν τῇ
till they see the Son - of Man coming in -

βασιλείᾳ αὐτοῦ."
kingdom ˜ His."

Jesus Is Transfigured on the Mount

(Mark 9:2–13; Luke 9:28–36)

17 1 Καὶ μεθ' ἡμέρας ἓξ παραλαμβάνει ὁ Ἰησοῦς τὸν
And after days ˜ six [2]takes [3]along - [1]Jesus -
took

Πέτρον καὶ Ἰάκωβον καὶ Ἰωάννην τὸν ἀδελφὸν αὐτοῦ, καὶ
Peter and James and John - brother ˜ his, and

ἀναφέρει αὐτοὺς εἰς ὄρος ὑψηλὸν κατ' ἰδίαν. 2 Καὶ
leads up ˜ them into a mountain ˜ high in private. And
led

μετεμορφώθη ἔμπροσθεν αὐτῶν, καὶ ἔλαμψε τὸ πρόσωπον
He was transformed before them, and [3]shone - [2]face

αὐτοῦ ὡς ὁ ἥλιος, τὰ δὲ ἱμάτια αὐτοῦ ἐγένοντο λευκὰ ὡς τὸ
[1]His like the sun, - and clothes ˜ His became *as* white as the

φῶς. 3 Καὶ ἰδού, ὤφθησαν αὐτοῖς Μωσῆς καὶ Ἠλίας μετ'
light. And behold, [4]appeared [5]to [6]them [1]Moses [2]and [3]Elijah [9]with

αὐτοῦ συλλαλοῦντες.
[10]Him [7]talking [8]together.
conversing.

4 Ἀποκριθεὶς δὲ ὁ Πέτρος εἶπε τῷ Ἰησοῦ, "Κύριε, καλόν
answering ˜ And - Peter said - to Jesus, "Lord, [3]good

ἐστιν ἡμᾶς ὧδε εἶναι· εἰ θέλεις, ποιήσωμεν[a] ὧδε τρεῖς
[1]it [2]is *for* us [3]here [1]to [2]be; if You desire, let us make here three

σκηνάς, σοὶ μίαν καὶ Μωσῇ μίαν καὶ μίαν Ἠλίᾳ."
tents, [2]for [3]You [1]one and [2]for [3]Moses [1]one and one for Elijah."

5 Ἔτι αὐτοῦ λαλοῦντος, ἰδού, νεφέλη φωτεινὴ
Still him speaking, behold, a cloud ˜ bright
While he was still speaking, radiant

ἐπεσκίασεν αὐτούς· καὶ ἰδού, φωνὴ ἐκ τῆς νεφέλης,
overshadowed them; and behold, a voice *came* out of the cloud,

λέγουσα, "Οὗτός ἐστιν ὁ Υἱός μου ὁ ἀγαπητός, ἐν ᾧ
saying, "This is - [3]Son [1]My - [2]beloved, in whom

εὐδόκησα. Αὐτοῦ ἀκούετε!"
I am well pleased. Him ˜ Hear!"

6 Καὶ ἀκούσαντες οἱ μαθηταὶ ἔπεσον ἐπὶ πρόσωπον
And hearing the disciples they fell on face ˜
when the disciples heard this, faces

αὐτῶν καὶ ἐφοβήθησαν σφόδρα. 7 Καὶ προσελθὼν ὁ
their and they were afraid ˜ greatly. And approaching ˜ -
Jesus approached

Ἰησοῦς ἥψατο αὐτῶν καὶ εἶπεν, "Ἐγέρθητε καὶ μὴ
Jesus touched them and said, "Rise and not ˜
and

[a](17:4) NU reads ποιησω, *I will make.*

φοβεῖσθε." 8 Ἐπάραντες δὲ τοὺς ὀφθαλμοὺς αὐτῶν, οὐδένα
do be afraid." [2]lifting [3]up [1]And - eyes ˜ their, [3]no [4]one

εἶδον εἰ μὴ τὸν[b] Ἰησοῦν μόνον.
[1]they [2]saw if not - Jesus only.
except

9 Καὶ καταβαινόντων αὐτῶν ἐκ τοῦ ὄρους, ἐνετείλατο
And coming down them out of the mountain, [2]commanded
as they were coming down from

αὐτοῖς ὁ Ἰησοῦς, λέγων, "Μηδενὶ εἴπητε τὸ ὅραμα ἕως οὗ ὁ
[3]them - [1]Jesus, saying, "[2]no [3]one [1]Tell the vision until - the

Υἱὸς τοῦ Ἀνθρώπου ἐκ νεκρῶν ἀναστῇ."
Son - of Man [3]from [4]*the* [5]dead [1]is [2]risen."

10 Καὶ ἐπηρώτησαν αὐτὸν οἱ μαθηταὶ αὐτοῦ, λέγοντες,
And [3]asked [4]Him - [2]disciples [1]His, saying,

"Τί οὖν οἱ γραμματεῖς λέγουσιν ὅτι Ἠλίαν δεῖ
"Why then [2]the [3]scribes [1]do [4]say that [5]Elijah [1]it [2]is [3]necessary [4]*for*

ἐλθεῖν πρῶτον?"
to come first?"

11 Ὁ δὲ Ἰησοῦς[c] ἀποκριθεὶς εἶπεν αὐτοῖς, "Ἠλίας μὲν
- But Jesus answering said to them, "Elijah indeed

ἔρχεται πρῶτον[d] καὶ ἀποκαταστήσει πάντα. 12 Λέγω δὲ
is coming first and he will restore all *things.* [2]I [3]say [1]But

ὑμῖν ὅτι Ἠλίας ἤδη ἦλθε, καὶ οὐκ ἐπέγνωσαν αὐτόν,
to you that Elijah already came, and [3]not [1]they [2]did recognize him,
has come,

ἀλλὰ ἐποίησαν ἐν αὐτῷ ὅσα ἠθέλησαν. Οὕτω καὶ
but they did with him as many *things* as they wished. Thus also
everything which

ὁ Υἱὸς τοῦ Ἀνθρώπου μέλλει πάσχειν ὑπ' αὐτῶν." 13 Τότε
the Son - of Man is about to suffer by them." Then

συνῆκαν οἱ μαθηταὶ ὅτι περὶ Ἰωάννου τοῦ Βαπτιστοῦ
[3]understood [1]the [2]disciples that [5]about [6]John [7]the [8]Baptist

εἶπεν αὐτοῖς.
[1]He [2]spoke [3]to [4]them.

Jesus Heals a Boy with an Unclean Spirit
(Mark 9:14–29; Luke 9:37–43a)

14 Καὶ ἐλθόντων αὐτῶν πρὸς τὸν ὄχλον, προσῆλθεν αὐτῷ
And coming ˜ them to the crowd, [3]approached [4]Him
when they came

ἄνθρωπος γονυπετῶν αὐτὸν καὶ λέγων, 15 "Κύριε, ἐλέησόν
[1]a [2]man kneeling to Him and saying, "Lord, have mercy on

μου τὸν υἱόν, ὅτι σεληνιάζεται* καὶ κακῶς πάσχει·
my - son, because he is moonstruck and badly ˜ suffers;
has fits

πολλάκις γὰρ πίπτει εἰς τὸ πῦρ καὶ πολλάκις εἰς τὸ ὕδωρ.
often ˜ for he falls into the fire and often into the water.

16 Καὶ προσήνεγκα αὐτὸν τοῖς μαθηταῖς σου, καὶ οὐκ
And I brought him - to disciples ˜ Your, and [3]not

ἠδυνήθησαν αὐτὸν θεραπεῦσαι."
[1]they [2]were [4]able [7]him [5]to [6]heal."

17 Ἀποκριθεὶς δὲ ὁ Ἰησοῦς εἶπεν, "Ὦ γενεὰ ἄπιστος
answering ˜ And - Jesus said, "O [4]generation [1]unbelieving
unfaithful

καὶ διεστραμμένη, ἕως πότε ἔσομαι μεθ' ὑμῶν? Ἕως πότε
[2]and [3]perverted, until when shall I be with you? Until when
how long How long

and do not be afraid."
8 When they had lifted up their eyes, they saw no one but Jesus only.
9 Now as they came down from the mountain, Jesus commanded them, saying, "Tell the vision to no one until the Son of Man is risen from the dead."
10 And His disciples asked Him, saying, "Why then do the scribes say that Elijah must come first?"
11 Jesus answered and said to them, "Indeed, Elijah is coming first and will restore all things.
12 "But I say to you that Elijah has come already, and they did not know him but did to him whatever they wished. Likewise the Son of Man is also about to suffer at their hands."
13 Then the disciples understood that He spoke to them of John the Baptist.
14 And when they had come to the multitude, a man came to Him, kneeling down to Him and saying,
15 "Lord, have mercy on my son, for he is an epileptic and suffers severely; for he often falls into the fire and often into the water.
16 "So I brought him to Your disciples, but they could not cure him."
17 Then Jesus answered and said, "O faithless and perverse generation, how long shall I be with you? How long shall I bear

[b](17:8) NU reads αυτον, *(Jesus) Himself.*
[c](17:11) NU omits Ιησους, *Jesus.* [d](17:11) NU omits πρωτον, *first.*

***(17:15)** σεληνιάζομαι *(selēniazomai).* Verb, from σελήνη, *moon* (cf. English *lunatic* from the Latin *luna,* meaning *moon*). The word literally means *moonstruck,* and probably refers to a form of epilepsy which was thought to be influenced by the moon.

with you? Bring him here to Me."
18 And Jesus rebuked the demon, and it came out of him; and the child was cured from that very hour.
19 Then the disciples came to Jesus privately and said, "Why could we not cast it out?"
20 So Jesus said to them, "Because of your unbelief; for assuredly, I say to you, if you have faith as a mustard seed, you will say to this mountain, 'Move from here to there,' and it will move; and nothing will be impossible for you.
21 "However, this kind does not go out except by prayer and fasting."
22 Now while they were staying in Galilee, Jesus said to them, "The Son of Man is about to be betrayed into the hands of men,
23 "and they will kill Him, and the third day He will be raised up." And they were exceedingly sorrowful.
24 When they had come to Capernaum, those who received the *temple* tax came to Peter and said, "Does your Teacher not pay the *temple* tax?"
25 He said, "Yes." And when he had come into the house, Jesus anticipated him, saying,

ἀνέξομαι ὑμῶν? Φέρετέ μοι αὐτὸν ὧδε." **18** Καὶ
shall I put up with you? Bring [3]to [4]Me [1]him [2]here." And

ἐπετίμησεν αὐτῷ ὁ Ἰησοῦς, καὶ ἐξῆλθεν ἀπ' αὐτοῦ τὸ
[2]rebuked [3]it - [1]Jesus, and [3]came [4]out [5]from [6]him [1]the

δαιμόνιον· καὶ ἐθεραπεύθη ὁ παῖς ἀπὸ τῆς ὥρας ἐκείνης.
[2]demon; and [3]was [4]healed [1]the [2]boy from - hour ˜ that.

19 Τότε προσελθόντες οἱ μαθηταὶ τῷ Ἰησοῦ κατ' ἰδίαν
Then [3]approaching [1]the [2]disciples - Jesus privately
approached

εἶπον, "Διὰ τί ἡμεῖς οὐκ ἠδυνήθημεν ἐκβαλεῖν αὐτό?"
they said, "Because of what [2]we [3]not [1]were [4]able to cast out ˜ it?"
and said, "Why

20 Ὁ δὲ Ἰησοῦς εἶπεν[e] αὐτοῖς, "Διὰ τὴν απιστίαν[f]
- And Jesus said to them, "Because of - unbelief ˜

ὑμῶν. Ἀμὴν γὰρ λέγω ὑμῖν, ἐὰν ἔχητε πίστιν ὡς κόκκον
your. amen ˜ For I say to you, if you have faith like a grain
assuredly mustard

σινάπεως, ἐρεῖτε τῷ ὄρει τούτῳ, 'Μετάβηθι ἐντεῦθεν
of mustard, you will say - to mountain ˜ this, 'Be moved from here
seed,

ἐκεῖ,' καὶ μεταβήσεται· καὶ οὐδὲν ἀδυνατήσει ὑμῖν.
to there,' and it will move; and nothing will be impossible for you.

21 Τοῦτο δὲ τὸ γένος οὐκ ἐκπορεύεται εἰ μὴ ἐν προσευχῇ
this ˜ But - kind not ˜ does go out if not by prayer
except

καὶ νηστείᾳ."[g]
and fasting."

Jesus Again Predicts His Death and Resurrection
(Mark 9:30–32; Luke 9:43b–45)

22 Ἀναστρεφομένων[h] δὲ αὐτῶν ἐν τῇ Γαλιλαίᾳ, εἶπεν
staying And them in - Galilee, [2]said
And while they were staying

αὐτοῖς ὁ Ἰησοῦς, "Μέλλει ὁ Υἱὸς τοῦ Ἀνθρώπου
[3]to [4]them - [1]Jesus, "[9]is [10]about [5]The [6]Son - [7]of [8]Man

παραδίδοσθαι εἰς χεῖρας ἀνθρώπων, **23** καὶ ἀποκτενοῦσιν
to be handed over into *the* hands of men, and they will kill
betrayed

αὐτόν, καὶ τῇ τρίτῃ ἡμέρᾳ ἐγερθήσεται." Καὶ
Him, and on the third day He will be raised." And

ἐλυπήθησαν σφόδρα.
they were grieved ˜ greatly.

Peter and His Master Pay Their Taxes

24 Ἐλθόντων δὲ αὐτῶν εἰς Καπερναούμ, προσῆλθον
coming And them to Capernaum, [7]approached
And when they came

οἱ τὰ δίδραχμα λαμβάνοντες τῷ Πέτρῳ καὶ εἶπον,
[1]the [2]*ones* [4]the [5]double [6]drachma [3]receiving - Peter and said,
those who collected the temple tax

"Ὁ διδάσκαλος ὑμῶν οὐ τελεῖ τὰ δίδραχμα?"
- "Teacher ˜ Your not ˜ does pay the double drachma?"
temple tax?"

25 Λέγει, "Ναί."
He says, "Yes."
said,

Καὶ ὅτε εἰσῆλθεν εἰς τὴν οἰκίαν, προέφθασεν αὐτὸν ὁ
And when he entered into the house, [2]anticipated [3]him -

[e](**17:20**) NU omits Ιησους, *Jesus,* and reads λεγει, *He says.* [f](**17:20**) NU reads ολιγοπιστιαν, *little faith.* [g](**17:21**) NU omits v. 21. [h](**17:22**) NU reads συστρεφομενων, *(while they were) gathering together.*

Ἰησοῦς, λέγων, "Τί σοι δοκεῖ, Σίμων? Οἱ βασιλεῖς
[1]Jesus, saying, "What to you does it seem, Simon? [4]the [5]kings
do you think,

τῆς γῆς ἀπὸ τίνων λαμβάνουσι τέλη ἢ κῆνσον? Ἀπὸ
[6]of [7]the [8]earth [1]From [2]whom [3]do [9]take customs or poll tax? From

τῶν υἱῶν αὐτῶν ἢ ἀπὸ τῶν ἀλλοτρίων?"
- sons ˜ their or from - strangers?"

26 Λέγει αὐτῷ ὁ Πέτρος, "Ἀπὸ τῶν ἀλλοτρίων."
[2]says [3]to [4]Him - [1]Peter, "From - strangers."
said

Ἔφη αὐτῷ ὁ Ἰησοῦς, "Ἄρα γε ἐλεύθεροί εἰσιν οἱ υἱοί.
[2]said [3]to [4]him - [1]Jesus, "So then [4]free [3]are [1]the [2]sons.

27 Ἵνα δὲ μὴ σκανδαλίσωμεν αὐτούς, πορευθεὶς εἰς τὴν
[2]so [3]that [1]But not ˜ we offend them, going to the
But lest go

θάλασσαν βάλε ἄγκιστρον, καὶ τὸν ἀναβαίνοντα πρῶτον
sea cast *in* a hook, and [3]the [6]coming [7]up [4]first
and cast in

ἰχθὺν ἆρον. Καὶ ἀνοίξας τὸ στόμα αὐτοῦ εὑρήσεις
[5]fish [1]take [2]up. And opening - mouth ˜ its you will find
when you have opened

στατῆρα· ἐκεῖνον λαβὼν δὸς αὐτοῖς ἀντὶ ἐμοῦ καὶ σοῦ."
a stater; that ˜ taking give *it* to them for Me and you."
coin;

Greatness in the Kingdom
(Mark 9:33–37; Luke 9:46–48)

18 1 Ἐν ἐκείνῃ τῇ ὥρᾳ προσῆλθον οἱ μαθηταὶ τῷ Ἰησοῦ,
In that - hour [3]approached [1]the [2]disciples - Jesus,
At time

λέγοντες, "Τίς ἄρα μείζων ἐστὶν ἐν τῇ βασιλείᾳ τῶν
saying, "Who really greater ˜ is in the kingdom of the
greatest

οὐρανῶν?"
heavens?"

2 Καὶ προσκαλεσάμενος ὁ Ἰησοῦς[a] παιδίον ἔστησεν
And [2]calling [3]forward - [1]Jesus a little child He set
called and

αὐτὸ ἐν μέσῳ αὐτῶν, 3 καὶ εἶπεν, "Ἀμὴν λέγω ὑμῖν, ἐὰν
it in midst ˜ their, and He said, "Amen I say to you, if
"Assuredly unless

μὴ στραφῆτε καὶ γένησθε ὡς τὰ παιδία, οὐ μὴ
not you are converted and become as - little children, not not
by no means

εἰσέλθητε εἰς τὴν βασιλείαν τῶν οὐρανῶν. 4 Ὅστις
will you enter into the kingdom of the heavens. whoever ˜

οὖν ταπεινώσει ἑαυτὸν ὡς τὸ παιδίον τοῦτο, οὗτός ἐστιν
Therefore will humble himself like - [2]little [3]child [1]this, this *one* is

ὁ μείζων ἐν τῇ βασιλείᾳ τῶν οὐρανῶν. 5 Καὶ ὃς ἐὰν
the greater in the kingdom of the heavens. And who ever
greatest

δέξηται παιδίον τοιοῦτον ἓν ἐπὶ τῷ ὀνόματί μου, ἐμὲ
receives [3]little [4]child [2]such [1]one in - name ˜ My, Me ˜

δέχεται.
receives.

"What do you think, Simon? From whom do the kings of the earth take customs or taxes, from their sons or from strangers?"
26 Peter said to Him, "From strangers." Jesus said to him, "Then the sons are free.
27 "Nevertheless, lest we offend them, go to the sea, cast in a hook, and take the fish that comes up first. And when you have opened its mouth, you will find a piece of money; take that and give it to them for Me and you."

18 At that time the disciples came to Jesus, saying, "Who then is greatest in the kingdom of heaven?"
2 Then Jesus called a little child to Him, set him in the midst of them,
3 and said, "Assuredly, I say to you, unless you are converted and become as little children, you will by no means enter the kingdom of heaven.
4 "Therefore whoever humbles himself as this little child is the greatest in the kingdom of heaven.
5 "Whoever receives one little child like this in My name receives Me.

[a](**18:2**) NU omits ο Ιησους, *Jesus.*

6 "But whoever causes one
of these little ones who believe
in Me to sin, it would be better
for him if a millstone were hung
around his neck, and he were
drowned in the depth of the
sea.
7 "Woe to the world because
of offenses! For offenses must
come, but woe to that man by
whom the offense comes!
8 "If your hand or foot
causes you to sin, cut it off and
cast *it* from you. It is better for
you to enter into life lame or
maimed, rather than having two
hands or two feet, to be cast
into the everlasting fire.
9 "And if your eye causes
you to sin, pluck it out and cast
it from you. It is better for you
to enter into life with one eye,
rather than having two eyes, to
be cast into hell fire.
10 "Take heed that you do not
despise one of these little ones,
for I say to you that in heaven
their angels always see the face
of My Father who is in heaven.
11 "For the Son of Man has
come to save that which was
lost.
12 "What do you think? If a
man has a hundred sheep, and
one of them goes astray, does
he not leave the ninety-nine and
go to the mountains to seek the

Jesus Warns of Offenses
(Mark 9:42–48; Luke 17:1, 2)

6 "Ὃς δ' ἂν σκανδαλίσῃ ἕνα τῶν μικρῶν τούτων
"who ˜ But ever causes to stumble one - of [2]little [3]*ones* [1]these

τῶν πιστευόντων εἰς ἐμέ, συμφέρει αὐτῷ ἵνα
the *ones* believing in Me, it is advantageous for him that
who believe would be better

κρεμασθῇ μύλος ὀνικὸς εἰς[b] τὸν τράχηλον αὐτοῦ καὶ
[6]be [7]hanged [1]a [2]millstone [3]of [4]a [5]donkey on - neck ˜ his and
huge millstone

καταποντισθῇ ἐν τῷ πελάγει τῆς θαλάσσης. **7** Οὐαὶ τῷ
he be drowned in the depth of the sea. Woe to the

κόσμῳ ἀπὸ τῶν σκανδάλων! Ἀνάγκη γὰρ ἐστιν ἐλθεῖν
world from - offenses! necessity For *there* is to come
because of For offenses must come,

τὰ σκάνδαλα, πλὴν οὐαὶ τῷ ἀνθρώπῳ ἐκείνῳ[c] δι' οὗ τὸ
- offenses, but woe - to man ˜ that through whom the

σκάνδαλον ἔρχεται! **8** Εἰ δὲ ἡ χείρ σου ἢ ὁ πούς σου
offense comes! if ˜ And - hand ˜ your or - foot ˜ your

σκανδαλίζει σε, ἔκκοψον αὐτὰ[d] καὶ βάλε ἀπὸ σοῦ.
[1]causes [3]to [4]stumble [2]you, cut off ˜ them and cast *them* from you.

Καλόν σοί ἐστιν εἰσελθεῖν εἰς τὴν ζωὴν χωλὸν ἢ κυλλόν,
[3]good [4]for [5]you [1]It [2]is to enter into - life lame or maimed,
better

ἢ δύο χεῖρας ἢ δύο πόδας ἔχοντα βληθῆναι εἰς τὸ πῦρ τὸ
than [2]two [3]hands [4]or [5]two [6]feet [1]having to be thrown into the fire ˜ -

αἰώνιον. **9** Καὶ εἰ ὁ ὀφθαλμός σου σκανδαλίζει σε,
eternal. And if - eye ˜ your [1]causes [3]to [4]stumble [2]you,

ἔξελε αὐτὸν καὶ βάλε ἀπὸ σοῦ. Καλόν σοί ἐστι
[5]tear [7]out [6]it and cast *it* from you. [3]good [4]for [5]you [1]It [2]is
better

μονόφθαλμον εἰς τὴν ζωὴν εἰσελθεῖν, ἢ δύο ὀφθαλμοὺς
with one eye [3]into - [4]life [1]to [2]enter, than [2]two [3]eyes

ἔχοντα βληθῆναι εἰς τὴν Γέενναν τοῦ πυρός.
[1]having to be thrown into the Gehenna - of fire.
fiery hell.

The Parable of the Lost Sheep
(Luke 15:3–7)

10 "Ὁρᾶτε μὴ καταφρονήσητε ἑνὸς τῶν μικρῶν
"See *that* [3]not [1]you [2]do look down on one - of [2]little [3]*ones*
despise

τούτων, λέγω γὰρ ὑμῖν ὅτι οἱ ἄγγελοι αὐτῶν ἐν οὐρανοῖς
[1]these, [5]I [6]say [4]for to you that - angels ˜ their in *the* heavens

διὰ παντὸς βλέπουσι τὸ πρόσωπον τοῦ Πατρός μου τοῦ ἐν
through all *times* see the face - of Father ˜ My - in
always

οὐρανοῖς. **11** Ἦλθε γὰρ ὁ Υἱὸς τοῦ Ἀνθρώπου σῶσαι τὸ
the heavens. [6]came [1]For [2]the [3]Son - [4]of [5]Man to save the
what

ἀπολωλός.[e] **12** Τί ὑμῖν δοκεῖ? Ἐὰν γένηταί τινι
lost *thing*. What to you does it seem? If *there* is to a certain
was lost. What do you think? a certain man

ἀνθρώπῳ ἑκατὸν πρόβατα, καὶ πλανηθῇ ἓν ἐξ αὐτῶν, οὐχὶ
man a hundred sheep, and [4]goes [5]astray [1]one [2]of [3]them, not
has will he

ἀφεὶς τὰ ἐνενήκοντα ἐννέα ἐπὶ τὰ ὄρη πορευθεὶς
leaving the ninety- nine on the mountains going
not leave and go

---

[b](18:6) NU reads περι, *around;* TR reads επι, *on.* [c](18:7) NU omits εκεινω, *that.* [d](18:8) NU reads αυτο, *it.* [e](18:11) NU omits v. 11.

ζητεῖ τὸ πλανώμενον? 13 Καὶ ἐὰν γένηται εὑρεῖν αὐτό,
he seeks the straying *one?* And if he happens to find it,
and search for

ἀμὴν λέγω ὑμῖν ὅτι χαίρει ἐπ' αὐτῷ μᾶλλον ἢ ἐπὶ τοῖς
amen I say to you that he rejoices over it more than over the
assuredly

ἐνενήκοντα ἐννέα τοῖς μὴ πεπλανημένοις. 14 Οὕτως οὐκ
ninety- nine the *ones* not having gone astray. Thus [3]not
which did not go astray.

ἔστι θέλημα ἔμπροσθεν τοῦ Πατρὸς ὑμῶν τοῦ ἐν οὐρανοῖς ἵνα
[1]it [2]is *the* will before - Father ˜ your - in *the* heavens that

ἀπόληται εἷς τῶν μικρῶν τούτων.
[6]should [7]perish [1]one - [2]of [4]little [5]*ones* [3]these.

Restoration of a Brother
(Luke 17:3, 4)

15 "Ἐὰν δὲ ἁμαρτήσῃ εἰς σὲ ὁ ἀδελφός σου, ὕπαγε
"if ˜ And [3]sins [4]against [5]you - [2]brother [1]your, go

καὶ ἔλεγξον αὐτὸν μεταξὺ σοῦ καὶ αὐτοῦ μόνου. Ἐάν σου
and reprove him between you and him alone. If [3]you
show him his fault

ἀκούσῃ, ἐκέρδησας τὸν ἀδελφόν σου. 16 Ἐὰν δὲ μὴ
[1]he [2]hears, you won - brother ˜ your. if ˜ But [3]not
have won

ἀκούσῃ, παράλαβε μετὰ σοῦ ἔτι ἕνα ἢ δύο, ἵνα
[1]he [2]does hear, take along with you yet one or two, so that

«ἐπὶ στόματος δύο μαρτύρων ἢ τριῶν
«by *the* mouth of two [4]witnesses [1]or [2]of [3]three
«on the basis of the testimony

σταθῇ πᾶν ῥῆμα.»[f] 17 Ἐὰν δὲ παρακούσῃ
[7]may [8]be [9]established [5]every [6]word.» if ˜ But he refuses to hear

αὐτῶν, εἰπὲ τῇ ἐκκλησίᾳ. Ἐὰν δὲ καὶ τῆς ἐκκλησίας
them, tell *it* to the assembly. if ˜ But [3]even [6]the [7]assembly
church. church

παρακούσῃ, ἔστω σοι ὥσπερ ὁ ἐθνικὸς καὶ ὁ
[1]he [2]refuses [4]to [5]hear, let him be to you just like the Gentile and the
a heathen a

τελώνης. 18 Ἀμὴν λέγω ὑμῖν, ὅσα ἐὰν δήσητε ἐπὶ
tax collector. Amen I say to you, as many *things* as you bind on
Assuredly

τῆς γῆς ἔσται δεδεμένα ἐν τῷ οὐρανῷ, καὶ ὅσα ἐὰν
- earth will be bound in - heaven, and as many *things* as

λύσητε ἐπὶ τῆς γῆς ἔσται λελυμένα ἐν τῷ οὐρανῷ. 19 Πάλιν
you loose on - earth will be loosed in - heaven. Again

ἀμὴν[g] λέγω ὑμῖν ὅτι ἐὰν δύο ὑμῶν συμφωνήσωσιν ἐπὶ τῆς
amen I say to you that if two of you agree on -
assuredly

γῆς περὶ παντὸς πράγματος οὗ ἐὰν αἰτήσωνται, γενήσεται
earth about every thing which ever they may ask, it will be done
any

αὐτοῖς παρὰ τοῦ Πατρός μου τοῦ ἐν οὐρανοῖς. 20 Οὗ γάρ
for them by - Father ˜ My - in *the* heavens. where ˜ For

εἰσι δύο ἢ τρεῖς συνηγμένοι εἰς τὸ ἐμὸν ὄνομα, ἐκεῖ
there are two or three gathered together in - My name, there

εἰμι ἐν μέσῳ αὐτῶν."
I am in midst ˜ their."

one that is straying?
13 "And if he should find it,
assuredly, I say to you, he rejoices more over that *sheep* than
over the ninety-nine that did
not go astray.
14 "Even so it is not the will of
your Father who is in heaven
that one of these little ones
should perish.
15 "Moreover if your brother
sins against you, go and tell him
his fault between you and him
alone. If he hears you, you have
gained your brother.
16 "But if he will not hear,
take with you one or two more,
that *'by the mouth of two or
three witnesses every word
may be established.'*
17 "And if he refuses to hear
them, tell *it* to the church. But
if he refuses even to hear the
church, let him be to you like a
heathen and a tax collector.
18 "Assuredly, I say to you,
whatever you bind on earth will
be bound in heaven, and whatever you loose on earth will be
loosed in heaven.
19 "Again I say to you that if
two of you agree on earth concerning anything that they ask,
it will be done for them by My
Father in heaven.
20 "For where two or three
are gathered together in My
name, I am there in the midst of
them."

---

f**(18:16)** Deut. 19:15
g**(18:19)** NU brackets and TR omits *αμην, amen.*

21 Then Peter came to Him and said, "Lord, how often shall my brother sin against me, and I forgive him? Up to seven times?"
22 Jesus said to him, "I do not say to you, up to seven times, but up to seventy times seven.
23 "Therefore the kingdom of heaven is like a certain king who wanted to settle accounts with his servants.
24 "And when he had begun to settle accounts, one was brought to him who owed him ten thousand talents.
25 "But as he was not able to pay, his master commanded that he be sold, with his wife and children and all that he had, and that payment be made.
26 "The servant therefore fell down before him, saying, 'Master, have patience with me, and I will pay you all.'
27 "Then the master of that servant was moved with compassion, released him, and forgave him the debt.
28 "But that servant went out and found one of his fellow servants who owed him a hundred denarii; and he laid hands on him and took *him* by the throat, saying, 'Pay me what you owe!'
29 "So his fellow servant fell down at his feet and begged

The Parable of the Unforgiving Servant

21 Τότε προσελθὼν αὐτῷ ὁ Πέτρος εἶπε, "Κύριε, ποσάκις
Then approaching Him - Peter said, "Lord, how often

ἁμαρτήσει εἰς ἐμὲ ὁ ἀδελφός μου, καὶ ἀφήσω αὐτῷ?
shall [3]sin [4]against [5]me - [2]brother [1]my, and I shall forgive him?

Ἕως ἑπτάκις?"
Up to seven times?"

22 Λέγει αὐτῷ ὁ Ἰησοῦς, "Οὐ λέγω σοι ἕως
[2]says [3]to [4]him - [1]Jesus, "[7]not [5]I [6]do [8]say to you up to
said

ἑπτάκις, ἀλλ' ἕως ἑβδομηκοντάκις ἑπτά. 23 Διὰ
seven times, but up to seventy- seven *times*. On account of
Therefore

τοῦτο ὡμοιώθη ἡ βασιλεία τῶν οὐρανῶν ἀνθρώπῳ
this [6]was [7]compared [1]the [2]kingdom [3]of [4]the [5]heavens to a man
has been certain

βασιλεῖ ὃς ἠθέλησε συνᾶραι λόγον μετὰ τῶν δούλων
a king who wanted to settle *the* account with - slaves ˜
king accounts servants

αὐτοῦ. 24 Ἀρξαμένου δὲ αὐτοῦ συναίρειν, προσηνέχθη αὐτῷ
his. beginning And him to settle up, [3]was [4]brought [5]to [6]him
And when he began

εἷς ὀφειλέτης μυρίων ταλάντων. 25 Μὴ ἔχοντος
[1]one [2]debtor *owing* ten thousand talents. [3]not [4]having
But since he had

δὲ αὐτοῦ ἀποδοῦναι, ἐκέλευσεν αὐτὸν ὁ κύριος αὐτοῦ
[1]But [2]him to repay, [3]commanded [4]him - [2]master [1]his
nothing with which

πραθῆναι, καὶ τὴν γυναῖκα αὐτοῦ καὶ τὰ τέκνα καὶ πάντα
to be sold, and - wife ˜ his and the children and all *things*
everything

ὅσα εἶχε, καὶ ἀποδοθῆναι. 26 Πεσὼν οὖν ὁ
as many as he had, and to be repaid. [2]falling [3]down [1]Therefore the

δοῦλος προσεκύνει αὐτῷ, λέγων 'Κύριε,[h] μακροθύμησον ἐπ'
slave did obeisance to him, saying 'Master, be patient with
servant

ἐμοί, καὶ πάντα σοι ἀποδώσω.' 27 Σπλαγχνισθεὶς δὲ
me, and [4]all [5]*things* [6]to [7]you [1]I [2]will [3]repay.' [2]having [3]compassion [1]And
everything

ὁ κύριος τοῦ δούλου ἐκείνου ἀπέλυσεν αὐτόν, καὶ τὸ δάνειον
the master - of slave ˜ that released him, and [3]the [4]loan
servant

ἀφῆκεν αὐτῷ.
[1]forgave [2]him.

28 "Ἐξελθὼν δὲ ὁ δοῦλος ἐκεῖνος εὗρεν ἕνα τῶν
"having gone out But - slave ˜ that he found one -
"But when that servant went out

συνδούλων αὐτοῦ ὃς ὤφειλεν αὐτῷ ἑκατὸν δηνάρια. Καὶ
of [2]fellow [3]slaves [1]his who owed him a hundred denarii. And
servants

κρατήσας αὐτὸν ἔπνιγε, λέγων, "Ἀπόδος μοι[i] εἴ
taking hold *of him* [4]him [1]he [2]was [3]choking saying, 'Pay back ˜ me if
what

τι ὀφείλεις!' 29 Πεσὼν οὖν ὁ σύνδουλος αὐτοῦ
anything you owe!' [2]falling [3]down [1]Therefore - [8]fellow [9]slave [7]his
servant

εἰς τοὺς πόδας αὐτοῦ[j] παρεκάλει αὐτὸν, λέγων,
[4]at - [6]feet [5]his was begging him, saying,
kept

h(18:26) NU omits Κυριε, *Master*. i(18:28) NU omits μοι, *to me*. j(18:29) NU omits εις τους ποδας αυτου, *at his feet*.

'Μακροθύμησον ἐπ' ἐμοί, καὶ[k] ἀποδώσω σοι.' 30 Ὁ
'Be patient with me, and I will pay back ˜ you.' [2]the [3]*one*
he

δὲ οὐκ ἤθελεν, ἀλλὰ ἀπελθὼν ἔβαλεν αὐτὸν εἰς φυλακὴν
[1]But not ˜ was willing, but going off he threw him into prison

ἕως οὗ ἀποδῷ τὸ ὀφειλόμενον. 31 Ἰδόντες δὲ οἱ
till - he should pay back the *thing* being owed. seeing But -
what was But when his

σύνδουλοι αὐτοῦ τὰ γενόμενα ἐλυπήθησαν
fellow slaves his the *things* having happened they were grieved ˜
fellow servants saw what had

σφόδρα, καὶ ἐλθόντες διεσάφησαν τῷ κυρίῳ ἑαυτῶν
greatly, and coming they reported to the master of themselves
they came and reported to their own master

πάντα τὰ γενόμενα.
all *things* - having happened.
everything that had

32 "Τότε προσκαλεσάμενος αὐτὸν ὁ κύριος αὐτοῦ λέγει
"Then summoning him - master ˜ his says
said

αὐτῷ, 'Δοῦλε πονηρέ, πᾶσαν τὴν ὀφειλὴν ἐκείνην ἀφῆκά σοι,
to him, 'slave ˜ Evil, all - debt ˜ that I forgave you,
'servant

ἐπεὶ παρεκάλεσάς με. 33 Οὐκ ἔδει καὶ σὲ
because you begged me. [3]not [1]Was [2]it [4]necessary [5]*for* [7]also [6]you

ἐλεῆσαι τὸν σύνδουλόν σου, ὡς καὶ ἐγώ σε
to have mercy on - [2]fellow [3]slave [1]your, as also ˜ I [4]you
servant

ἠλέησα?' 34 Καὶ ὀργισθεὶς ὁ κύριος αὐτοῦ παρέδωκεν
[1]had [2]mercy [3]on?' And being angered - master ˜ his handed over ˜

αὐτὸν τοῖς βασανισταῖς* ἕως οὗ ἀποδῷ πᾶν τὸ
him to the tormenters until - he should repay all the *thing*
jailers that was

ὀφειλόμενον αὐτῷ.[l] 35 Οὕτω καὶ ὁ Πατήρ μου ὁ ἐπουράνιος
being owed to him. Thus also - [3]Father [1]My - [2]heavenly

ποιήσει ὑμῖν ἐὰν μὴ ἀφῆτε ἕκαστος τῷ ἀδελφῷ αὐτοῦ
will do to you if [3]not [1]you [2]do forgive each *one* - brother ˜ his
your

ἀπὸ τῶν καρδιῶν ὑμῶν τὰ παραπτώματα αὐτῶν."[m]
[3]from - [5]hearts [4]your - [2]trespasses [1]their."

19 1 Καὶ ἐγένετο ὅτε ἐτέλεσεν ὁ Ἰησοῦς τοὺς λόγους
And it happened when finished ˜ - Jesus - words ˜

τούτους, μετῆρεν ἀπὸ τῆς Γαλιλαίας καὶ ἦλθεν εἰς τὰ
these, He went away from - Galilee and went to the

ὅρια τῆς Ἰουδαίας πέραν τοῦ Ἰορδάνου. 2 Καὶ ἠκολούθησαν
borders - of Judea beyond the Jordan. And [3]followed
region

αὐτῷ ὄχλοι πολλοί, καὶ ἐθεράπευσεν αὐτοὺς ἐκεῖ.
[4]Him [2]crowds [1]large, and He healed them there.

Jesus Teaches on Divorce
(Mark 10:1–12)

3 Καὶ προσῆλθον αὐτῷ οἱ Φαρισαῖοι πειράζοντες αὐτόν,
And [3]approached [4]Him [1]the [2]Pharisees testing Him,

καὶ λέγοντες αὐτῷ,[a] "Εἰ ἔξεστιν ἀνθρώπῳ ἀπολῦσαι τὴν
and saying to Him, - "Is it lawful for a man to divorce -

γυναῖκα αὐτοῦ κατὰ πᾶσαν αἰτίαν?"
wife ˜ his for every reason?"
just any

him, saying, 'Have patience with me, and I will pay you all.'
30 "And he would not, but went and threw him into prison till he should pay the debt.
31 "So when his fellow servants saw what had been done, they were very grieved, and came and told their master all that had been done.
32 "Then his master, after he had called him, said to him, 'You wicked servant! I forgave you all that debt because you begged me.
33 'Should you not also have had compassion on your fellow servant, just as I had pity on you?'
34 "And his master was angry, and delivered him to the torturers until he should pay all that was due to him.
35 "So My heavenly Father also will do to you if each of you, from his heart, does not forgive his brother his trespasses."

19 Now it came to pass, when Jesus had finished these sayings, *that* He departed from Galilee and came to the region of Judea beyond the Jordan.
2 And great multitudes followed Him, and He healed them there.
3 The Pharisees also came to Him, testing Him, and saying to Him, "Is it lawful for a man to divorce his wife for *just* any reason?"

---

[k](18:29) TR adds παντα, *all.* [l](18:34) NU omits αυτω, *to him.* [m](18:35) NU omits τα παραπτωματα αυτων, *their trespasses.*
[a](19:3) NU omits αυτω, *to Him.*

***(18:34)** βασανιστής *(basanistēs).* Noun meaning *torturer* used only here in the NT. Originally it referred to a person who derived information by torture, perhaps softened in meaning here to simply *jailer.* Cf. the cognate verb βασανίζω, *torture, torment* (Matt. 8:6; Rev. 14:10); noun βάσανος, *torment* (Matt. 4:24; Luke 16:23, 28); and noun βασανισμός, *torture* (Rev. 9:5; 14:11).

4 And He answered and said to them, "Have you not read that He who made *them* at the beginning *'made them male and female,'*
5 "and said, *'For this reason a man shall leave his father and mother and be joined to his wife, and the two shall become one flesh'*?
6 "So then, they are no longer two but one flesh. Therefore what God has joined together, let not man separate."
7 They said to Him, "Why then did Moses command to give a certificate of divorce, and to put her away?"
8 He said to them, "Moses, because of the hardness of your hearts, permitted you to divorce your wives, but from the beginning it was not so.
9 "And I say to you, whoever divorces his wife, except for sexual immorality, and marries another, commits adultery; and whoever marries her who is divorced commits adultery."
10 His disciples said to Him, "If such is the case of the man with *his* wife, it is better not to marry."
11 But He said to them, "All cannot accept this saying, but only *those* to whom it has been given:
12 "For there are eunuchs

4 Ὁ δὲ ἀποκριθεὶς εἶπεν αὐτοῖς,[b] "Οὐκ ἀνέγνωτε ὅτι
\- And answering He said to them, "[3]not [1]Did [2]you read that
"never

ὁ ποιήσας[c] ἀπ' ἀρχῆς «ἄρσεν καὶ θῆλυ ἐποίησεν
the *One* making from *the* beginning «[3]male [4]and [5]female [1]made
He who made them

αὐτούς»?[d] **5** Καὶ εἶπεν,
[2]them»? And He said,

«Ἕνεκεν τούτου καταλείψει ἄνθρωπος τὸν πατέρα καὶ
«On account of this [3]shall [4]leave [1]a [2]man the father and
his

τὴν μητέρα
the mother
his

Καὶ προσκολληθήσεται τῇ γυναικὶ αὐτοῦ,
And he shall be joined - to wife ˜ his,

Καὶ ἔσονται οἱ δύο εἰς σάρκα μίαν.»[e]
And [3]shall [4]be [1]the [2]two - flesh ˜ one.»
become

6 Ὥστε οὐκέτι εἰσὶ δύο, ἀλλὰ σὰρξ μία. Ὃ οὖν ὁ
So then no longer are they two, but flesh ˜ one. what ˜ Therefore -

Θεὸς συνέζευξεν, ἄνθρωπος μὴ χωριζέτω."
God joined together, [3]man [2]not [1]let separate."

7 Λέγουσιν αὐτῷ, "Τί οὖν Μωσῆς ἐνετείλατο δοῦναι
They say to Him, "Why then Moses ˜ did command to give
said

βιβλίον ἀποστασίου καὶ ἀπολῦσαι αὐτήν?"
a certificate of divorce and to divorce her?"

8 Λέγει αὐτοῖς ὅτι "Μωσῆς πρὸς τὴν
He says to them - "Moses with reference to -
said because of

σκληροκαρδίαν ὑμῶν ἐπέτρεψεν ὑμῖν ἀπολῦσαι τὰς γυναῖκας
hard-heartedness ˜ your permitted you to divorce - wives ˜

ὑμῶν, ἀπ' ἀρχῆς δὲ οὐ γέγονεν οὕτω. **9** Λέγω δὲ
your, [2]from [3]*the* [4]beginning [1]but [7]not [5]it [6]has been thus. [2]I [3]say [1]But

ὑμῖν ὅτι ὃς ἂν ἀπολύσῃ τὴν γυναῖκα αὐτοῦ μὴ ἐπὶ
to you that who ever divorces - wife ˜ his not for

πορνείᾳ καὶ γαμήσῃ ἄλλην μοιχᾶται·[f] καὶ ὁ
fornication and marries another commits adultery; and the *man*
sexual immorality

ἀπολελυμένην γαμήσας μοιχᾶται."
[2]*a* [3]*woman* [4]having [5]been [6]divorced [1]marrying commits adultery."
a divorcee

10 Λέγουσιν αὐτῷ οἱ μαθηταὶ αὐτοῦ, "Εἰ οὕτως ἐστὶν ἡ
[3]say [4]to [5]Him - [2]disciples [1]His, "If thus it is the
said

αἰτία τοῦ ἀνθρώπου μετὰ τῆς γυναικός, οὐ
occasion of the man with the wife, [3]not
relationship of a a

συμφέρει γαμῆσαι."
[1]it [2]is advantageous to marry."

Jesus Teaches on Celibacy

11 Ὁ δὲ εἶπεν αὐτοῖς, "Οὐ πάντες χωροῦσι τὸν λόγον
\- And He said to them, "[3]not [1]All [2]do [4]accept - word ˜
message

τοῦτον, ἀλλ' οἷς δέδοται. **12** Εἰσὶ γὰρ
this, but *it is for those* to whom it has been given. [2]*there* [3]are [1]For

---

[b](19:4) NU omits αυτοις, *to them.* [c](19:4) NU reads κτισας, *creating.*
[d](19:4) Gen. 1:27; 5:2
[e](19:5) Gen. 2:24
[f](19:9) NU omits the rest of v. 19.

εὐνοῦχοι οἵτινες ἐκ κοιλίας μητρὸς ἐγεννήθησαν οὕτω,
eunuchs who from the womb of the mother were born thus,
their mother's womb

καὶ εἰσὶν εὐνοῦχοι οἵτινες εὐνουχίσθησαν ὑπὸ τῶν
and *there* are eunuchs who were made eunuchs by -

ἀνθρώπων, καὶ εἰσὶν εὐνοῦχοι οἵτινες εὐνούχισαν ἑαυτοὺς
men, and *there* are eunuchs who made eunuchs ˜ themselves

διὰ τὴν βασιλείαν τῶν οὐρανῶν. Ὁ δυνάμενος
because of the kingdom of the heavens. The *one* being able
for the sake He who is able

χωρεῖν χωρείτω."
to accept *this* let him accept *it.*"

Jesus Blesses Little Children

(Mark 10:13–16; Luke 18:15–17)

13 Τότε προσηνέχθη αὐτῷ παιδία, ἵνα τὰς χεῖρας
Then were brought to Him little children, that [4]the [5]hands
His

ἐπιθῇ αὐτοῖς καὶ προσεύξηται· οἱ δὲ μαθηταὶ
[1]He [2]might [3]put [6]on them and pray; the ˜ but disciples

ἐπετίμησαν αὐτοῖς. **14** Ὁ δὲ Ἰησοῦς εἶπεν, "Ἄφετε τὰ
rebuked them. - But Jesus said, "Allow the

παιδία, καὶ μὴ κωλύετε αὐτὰ ἐλθεῖν πρός με· τῶν γὰρ
little children, and not ˜ do forbid them to come to Me; - for

τοιούτων ἐστὶν ἡ βασιλεία τῶν οὐρανῶν." **15** Καὶ
of such *ones* is the kingdom of the heavens." And

ἐπιθεὶς αὐτοῖς τὰς χεῖρας ἐπορεύθη ἐκεῖθεν.
having put [3]on [4]them [1]the [2]hands He went from there.
His

The Rich Young Ruler

(Mark 10:17–22; Luke 18:18–23)

16 Καὶ ἰδού, εἷς προσελθὼν εἶπεν αὐτῷ, "Διδάσκαλε
And behold, one approaching said to Him, "Teacher ˜

ἀγαθέ,[g] τί ἀγαθὸν ποιήσω ἵνα ἔχω ζωὴν αἰώνιον?"
Good, what good *thing* shall I do so that I may have life ˜ eternal?"

17 Ὁ δὲ εἶπεν αὐτῷ, "Τί με λέγεις ἀγαθόν?[h]
- And He said to him, "Why [4]Me [1]do [2]you [3]call good?

Οὐδεὶς ἀγαθὸς* εἰ μὴ εἷς, ὁ Θεός.[i] Εἰ δὲ θέλεις
No one *is* good if not One, - God. if ˜ But you want
except

εἰσελθεῖν εἰς τὴν ζωήν, τήρησον τὰς ἐντολάς."
to enter into - life, keep the commandments."

18 Λέγει αὐτῷ, "Ποίας?"
He says to Him, "Which *ones?*"
said

Ὁ δὲ Ἰησοῦς εἶπε, "Τὸ «Οὐ φονεύσεις, Οὐ
- And Jesus said, - "«[3]not [1]You [2]shall murder, [3]not

μοιχεύσεις, Οὐ κλέψεις, Οὐ
[1]You [2]shall commit adultery, [3]not [1]You [2]shall steal, [3]not

ψευδομαρτυρήσεις, **19** Τίμα τὸν πατέρα καὶ τὴν
[1]You [2]shall bear false witness, Honor the father and the
your your

μητέρα,»[j] καὶ «Ἀγαπήσεις τὸν πλησίον σου ὡς σεαυτόν.»"[k]
mother,» and «You shall love - neighbor ˜ your as yourself.»"

20 Λέγει αὐτῷ ὁ νεανίσκος, "Πάντα ταῦτα
[4]says [5]to [6]Him [1]The [2]young [3]man, "All these *things*
said

who were born thus from *their* mother's womb, and there are eunuchs who were made eunuchs by men, and there are eunuchs who have made themselves eunuchs for the kingdom of heaven's sake. He who is able to accept *it,* let him accept *it.*"

13 Then little children were brought to Him that He might put *His* hands on them and pray, but the disciples rebuked them.

14 But Jesus said, "Let the little children come to Me, and do not forbid them; for of such is the kingdom of heaven."

15 And He laid *His* hands on them and departed from there.

16 Now behold, one came and said to Him, "Good Teacher, what good thing shall I do that I may have eternal life?"

17 So He said to him, "Why do you call Me good? No one *is* good but One, *that is,* God. But if you want to enter into life, keep the commandments."

18 He said to Him, "Which ones?" Jesus said, "'*You shall not murder,' 'You shall not commit adultery,' 'You shall not steal,' 'You shall not bear false witness,'*

19 *'Honor your father and your mother,'* and, *'You shall love your neighbor as yourself.'*"

20 The young man said to

---

[g]**(19:16)** NU omits αγαθε, *good.* [h]**(19:17)** For λεγεις αγαθον, *do you call (Me) good?),* NU reads ερωτας περι του αγαθου, *(Why) do you ask (Me) about what is good?* [i]**(19:17)** For Ουδεις . . . Θεος, *No one . . . God,* NU reads εις εστιν ο αγαθος, *there is One who is good.* [j]**(19:18, 19)** Ex. 20:12–16; Deut. 5:16–20 [k]**(19:19)** Lev. 19:18

***(19:17)** ἀγαθός *(agathos).* A frequent adjective for *good* used synonymously with καλός, also meaning *good.* Yet ἀγαθός is probably the more natural word when referring to something "fit" or "useful" or to inward moral "goodness." καλός, on the other hand, is more natural when the goodness in question is external or has an external aspect, and thus καλός can mean *beautiful* or *free from defect.* The distinction appears in Jesus' words of Matt. 7:17 about "the good tree" (ἀγαθός = inher-

Him, "All these things I have
kept from my youth. What do I
still lack?"
21 Jesus said to him, "If you
want to be perfect, go, sell
what you have and give to the
poor, and you will have treasure in heaven; and come, follow Me."
22 But when the young man
heard that saying, he went
away sorrowful, for he had
great possessions.
23 Then Jesus said to His disciples, "Assuredly, I say to you
that it is hard for a rich man to
enter the kingdom of heaven.
24 "And again I say to you, it
is easier for a camel to go
through the eye of a needle
than for a rich man to enter the
kingdom of God."
25 When His disciples heard
it, they were greatly astonished, saying, "Who then can
be saved?"
26 But Jesus looked at *them*
and said to them, "With men
this is impossible, but with God
all things are possible."
27 Then Peter answered and
said to Him, "See, we have left
all and followed You. Therefore
what shall we have?"
28 So Jesus said to them, "Assuredly I say to you, that in the
regeneration, when the Son of

ἐφυλαξάμην ἐκ νεότητός μου.[l] Τί ἔτι ὑστερῶ?"
I kept from youth ˜ my. What [3]still [1]do [2]I lack?"
have observed

21 Ἔφη αὐτῷ ὁ Ἰησοῦς, "Εἰ θέλεις τέλειος εἶναι, ὕπαγε
[2]said [3]to [4]him - [1]Jesus, "If you want [3]perfect [1]to [2]be, go

πώλησόν σου τὰ ὑπάρχοντα καὶ δὸς πτωχοῖς, καὶ
sell of you the *things* belonging and give to *the* poor, and
your possessions

ἕξεις θησαυρὸν ἐν οὐρανῷ, καὶ δεῦρο ἀκολούθει μοι."
you will have treasure in heaven, and come follow Me."

22 Ἀκούσας δὲ ὁ νεανίσκος τὸν λόγον ἀπῆλθε
hearing But the young man the word he went away
But when the young man heard this message,

λυπούμενος, ἦν γὰρ ἔχων κτήματα πολλά.
sorrowing, [2]he [3]was [1]for having possessions ˜ many.
for he had

Possessions and the Kingdom of God
(Mark 10:23–31; Luke 18:24–30)

23 Ὁ δὲ Ἰησοῦς εἶπε τοῖς μαθηταῖς αὐτοῦ, "Ἀμὴν λέγω
- And Jesus said - to disciples ˜ His, "Amen I say
"Assuredly

ὑμῖν ὅτι δυσκόλως πλούσιος εἰσελεύσεται εἰς τὴν
to you that with difficulty a rich *person* will enter into the

βασιλείαν τῶν οὐρανῶν. **24** Πάλιν δὲ λέγω ὑμῖν,
kingdom of the heavens. again ˜ And I say to you,

εὐκοπώτερόν ἐστι κάμηλον διὰ τρυπήματος ῥαφίδος
[3]easier [1]it [2]is *for* a camel [3]through [4]*the* [5]eye [6]of [7]a [8]needle

διελθεῖν ἢ πλούσιον εἰς τὴν βασιλείαν τοῦ Θεοῦ
[1]to [2]go than *for* a rich *person* [3]into [4]the [5]kingdom - [6]of [7]God

εἰσελθεῖν."
[1]to [2]enter."

25 Ἀκούσαντες δὲ οἱ μαθηταὶ αὐτοῦ
hearing And - disciples ˜ His
And when His disciples heard,

ἐξεπλήσσοντο σφόδρα, λέγοντες, "Τίς ἄρα δύναται
they were astonished ˜ greatly, saying, "Who then is able

σωθῆναι?"
to be saved?"

26 Ἐμβλέψας δὲ ὁ Ἰησοῦς εἶπεν αὐτοῖς, "Παρὰ
[2]looking [3]on [4]*them* [1]And - Jesus said to them, "With

ἀνθρώποις τοῦτο ἀδύνατόν ἐστιν, παρὰ δὲ Θεῷ πάντα
men this impossible ˜ is, with ˜ but God all *things*

δυνατά."
are possible."

27 Τότε ἀποκριθεὶς ὁ Πέτρος εἶπεν αὐτῷ, "Ἰδού, ἡμεῖς
Then answering ˜ - Peter said to Him, "See, we

ἀφήκαμεν πάντα καὶ ἠκολουθήσαμέν σοι. Τί ἄρα ἔσται
left all *things* and followed You. What then shall be
have left shall

ἡμῖν?"
to us?"
we have?"

28 Ὁ δὲ Ἰησοῦς εἶπεν αὐτοῖς, "Ἀμὴν λέγω ὑμῖν ὅτι
- And Jesus said to them, "Amen I say to you that
"Assuredly

ὑμεῖς οἱ ἀκολουθήσαντές μοι, ἐν τῇ Παλιγγενεσίᾳ ὅταν
you the *ones* having followed Me, in the Regeneration when
who have

[l](19:20) NU omits εκ νεοτητος μου, *from my youth.*

ently good) which brings forth "good fruit" (καλός = free of defects). Here, in Matt. 19:17, ἀγαθός describes the perfect moral goodness which God alone possesses in the ultimate sense.

καθίσῃ ὁ Υἱὸς τοῦ Ἀνθρώπου ἐπὶ θρόνου δόξης αὐτοῦ,
[5]shall [6]sit [1]the [2]Son - [3]of [4]Man on *the* throne of glory ˜ His,
His glorious throne,

καθίσεσθε καὶ ὑμεῖς ἐπὶ δώδεκα θρόνους, κρίνοντες τὰς
[3]will [4]sit [2]also [1]you on twelve thrones, judging the

δώδεκα φυλὰς τοῦ Ἰσραήλ. **29** Καὶ πᾶς ὃς ἀφῆκεν οἰκίας
twelve tribes - of Israel. And every*one* who left houses
has left

ἢ ἀδελφοὺς ἢ ἀδελφὰς ἢ πατέρα ἢ μητέρα ἢ γυναῖκα[m] ἢ
or brothers or sisters or father or mother or wife or

τέκνα ἢ ἀγροὺς ἕνεκεν τοῦ ὀνόματός μου
children or fields for the sake of - name ˜ My

ἑκατονταπλασίονα λήψεται καὶ ζωὴν αἰώνιον κληρονομήσει.
[3]a [4]hundredfold [1]shall [2]receive and [4]life [3]eternal [1]shall [2]inherit.

30 Πολλοὶ δὲ ἔσονται πρῶτοι ἔσχατοι, καὶ ἔσχατοι πρῶτοι.
many ˜ But [2]will [3]be [1]first last, and last first.

The Parable of the Workers in the Vineyard

20 **1** "Ὁμοία γάρ ἐστιν ἡ βασιλεία τῶν οὐρανῶν
"[8]like [1]For [7]is [2]the [3]kingdom [4]of [5]the [6]heavens

ἀνθρώπῳ οἰκοδεσπότῃ ὅστις ἐξῆλθεν ἅμα
a man a master of the house who went out at the same time
a certain landowner early

πρωῒ μισθώσασθαι ἐργάτας εἰς τὸν ἀμπελῶνα αὐτοῦ.
in the morning to hire workers for - vineyard ˜ his.

2 Καὶ συμφωνήσας μετὰ τῶν ἐργατῶν ἐκ δηναρίου τὴν
And having agreed with the workers for a denarius the
a

ἡμέραν, ἀπέστειλεν αὐτοὺς εἰς τὸν ἀμπελῶνα αὐτοῦ. **3** Καὶ
day, he sent them into - vineyard ˜ his. And

ἐξελθὼν περὶ τρίτην ὥραν εἶδεν ἄλλους ἑστῶτας ἐν τῇ
going out about *the* third hour he saw others standing in the

ἀγορᾷ ἀργούς. **4** Καὶ ἐκείνοις εἶπεν, 'Ὑπάγετε καὶ ὑμεῖς
marketplace idle. And to those he said, 'Go also ˜ you

εἰς τὸν ἀμπελῶνα, καὶ ὃ ἐὰν ᾖ δίκαιον δώσω ὑμῖν.'
into the vineyard, and what ever may be just I will give you.'

Οἱ δὲ ἀπῆλθον. **5** Πάλιν ἐξελθὼν περὶ ἕκτην καὶ
[2]the [3]*ones* [1]And went off. Again going out about *the* sixth and
they

ἐνάτην ὥραν ἐποίησεν ὡσαύτως. **6** Περὶ δὲ τὴν ἑνδεκάτην
the ninth hour he did likewise. about ˜ And the eleventh

ὥραν[a] ἐξελθὼν εὗρεν ἄλλους ἑστῶτας ἀργούς,[b] καὶ λέγει
hour going out he found others standing idle, and he says
said

αὐτοῖς, 'Τί ὧδε ἑστήκατε ὅλην τὴν ἡμέραν ἀργοί?'
to them, 'Why [4]here [1]do [2]you [3]stand [6]whole [5]the day idle?'

7 Λέγουσιν αὐτῷ, 'Ὅτι οὐδεὶς ἡμᾶς ἐμισθώσατο.' Λέγει
They say to him, 'Because no one us ˜ hired.' He says
said said

αὐτοῖς, 'Ὑπάγετε καὶ ὑμεῖς εἰς τὸν ἀμπελῶνα,[c] καὶ ὃ ἐὰν
to them, 'Go also ˜ you into the vineyard, and what ever

ᾖ δίκαιον λήψεσθε.' **8** Ὀψίας δὲ γενομένης, λέγει
may be just you will receive.' evening ˜ And having come, [6]says
And when evening came, said

ὁ κύριος τοῦ ἀμπελῶνος τῷ ἐπιτρόπῳ αὐτοῦ, 'Κάλεσον
[1]the [2]owner [3]of [4]the [5]vineyard - to foreman ˜ his, 'Call

τοὺς ἐργάτας καὶ ἀπόδος αὐτοῖς τὸν μισθόν, ἀρξάμενος ἀπὸ
the workers and pay them the wage, beginning from
their at

Man sits on the throne of His glory, you who have followed Me will also sit on twelve thrones, judging the twelve tribes of Israel.

29 "And everyone who has left houses or brothers or sisters or father or mother or wife or children or lands, for My name's sake, shall receive a hundredfold, and inherit eternal life.

30 "But many *who are* first will be last, and the last first.

20 "For the kingdom of heaven is like a landowner who went out early in the morning to hire laborers for his vineyard.

2 "Now when he had agreed with the laborers for a denarius a day, he sent them into his vineyard.

3 "And he went out about the third hour and saw others standing idle in the marketplace,

4 "and said to them, 'You also go into the vineyard, and whatever is right I will give you.' So they went.

5 "Again he went out about the sixth and the ninth hour, and did likewise.

6 "And about the eleventh hour he went out and found others standing idle, and said to them, 'Why have you been standing here idle all day?'

7 "They said to him, 'Because no one hired us.' He said to them, 'You also go into the vineyard, and whatever is right you will receive.'

8 "So when evening had come, the owner of the vineyard said to his steward, 'Call the laborers and give them *their*

---

[m](**19:29**) NU omits η γυναικα, *or wife.*
[a](**20:6**) NU omits ωραν, *hour.* [b](**20:6**) NU omits αργους, *idle.*
[c](**20:7**) NU omits the rest of v. 7.

wages, beginning with the last
to the first.'
9 "And when those came
who *were hired* about the eleventh hour, they each received a
denarius.
10 "But when the first came,
they supposed that they would
receive more; and they likewise
received each a denarius.
11 "And when they had re-
ceived *it,* they complained
against the landowner,
12 "saying, 'These last *men*
have worked *only* one hour, and
you made them equal to us who
have borne the burden and the
heat of the day.'
13 "But he answered one of
them and said, 'Friend, I am doing you no wrong. Did you not
agree with me for a denarius?
14 'Take *what is* yours and go
your way. I wish to give to this
last man *the same* as to you.
15 'Is it not lawful for me to do
what I wish with my own
things? Or is your eye evil because I am good?'
16 "So the last will be first,
and the first last. For many are
called, but few chosen."
17 Now Jesus, going up to Jerusalem, took the twelve disciples aside on the road and said
to them,
18 "Behold, we are going up
to Jerusalem, and the Son of
Man will be betrayed to the
chief priests and to the scribes;
and they will condemn Him to
death,
19 "and deliver Him to the
Gentiles to mock and to
scourge and to crucify. And the
third day He will rise again."

τῶν ἐσχάτων ἕως τῶν πρώτων.'
the last *ones* to the first *ones.*'

9 "Καὶ ἐλθόντες οἱ περὶ τὴν ἑνδεκάτην ὥραν ἔλαβον
"And coming the *ones* about the eleventh hour received
those who came

ἀνὰ δηνάριον. 10 Ἐλθόντες δὲ οἱ πρῶτοι ἐνόμισαν ὅτι
each a denarius. coming And the first *ones* they supposed that
And when the first came,

πλεῖονα λήψονται· καὶ ἔλαβον καὶ αὐτοὶ ἀνὰ δηνάριον.
[4]more [1]they [2]will [3]receive; and [3]received [2]also [1]they each a denarius.
would

11 Λαβόντες δὲ ἐγόγγυζον κατὰ τοῦ
[2]receiving [3]*it* [1]And they were grumbling against the
when they received began

οἰκοδεσπότου, 12 λέγοντες ὅτι 'Οὗτοι οἱ ἔσχατοι μίαν ὥραν
master of the house, saying - 'These - last *ones* [2]one [3]hour
landowner,

ἐποίησαν, καὶ ἴσους ἡμῖν αὐτοὺς ἐποίησας τοῖς βαστάσασι
[1]did, and [4]equal [5]to [6]us [3]them [1]you [2]made the *ones* having borne
who bore

τὸ βάρος τῆς ἡμέρας καὶ τὸν καύσωνα.' 13 Ὁ δὲ
the burden of the day and the heat.' [2]the [3]*one* [1]But
he

ἀποκριθεὶς εἶπεν ἑνὶ αὐτῶν, 'Ἑταῖρε, οὐκ ἀδικῶ σε.
answering said to one of them, 'Friend, [3]not [1]I [2]am wronging you.
answered and

Οὐχὶ δηναρίου συνεφώνησάς μοι? 14 *Ἆρον τὸ
[3]not [7]*for* [8]a [9]denarius [1]Did [2]you [4]agree [5]with [6]me? Take the *thing*
what is

σὸν καὶ ὕπαγε. Θέλω δὲ τούτῳ τῷ ἐσχάτῳ δοῦναι ὡς καὶ
yours and go. [2]I [3]want [1]But [6]to [7]this - [8]last [9]*one* [4]to [5]give as also

σοί. 15 Ἢ οὐκ ἔξεστί μοι ποιῆσαι ὃ θέλω ἐν τοῖς
to you. Or [3]not [1]is [2]it lawful for me to do what I want in -
with

ἐμοῖς? Εἰ ὁ ὀφθαλμός σου πονηρός ἐστιν ὅτι ἐγὼ ἀγαθός
my *things*? - - [3]eye [2]your [4]evil [1]Is because I good ~

εἰμι?' 16 Οὕτως ἔσονται οἱ ἔσχατοι πρῶτοι, καὶ οἱ πρῶτοι
am?' Thus [3]shall [4]be [1]the [2]last first, and the first

ἔσχατοι. Πολλοὶ γάρ εἰσι κλητοί, ὀλίγοι δὲ ἐκλεκτοί."[d]
last. many ~ For are called, few ~ but *are* chosen."

Jesus a Third Time Predicts His Death and Resurrection
(Mark 10:32–34; Luke 18:31–34)

17 Καὶ ἀναβαίνων ὁ Ἰησοῦς εἰς Ἱεροσόλυμα παρέλαβε
And going up - Jesus to Jerusalem He took aside
as Jesus was going up

τοὺς δώδεκα μαθητὰς κατ' ἰδίαν ἐν τῇ ὁδῷ καὶ εἶπεν αὐτοῖς,
the twelve disciples privately on the road and He said to them,

18 "Ἰδού, ἀναβαίνομεν εἰς Ἱεροσόλυμα, καὶ ὁ Υἱὸς τοῦ
"Behold, we are going up to Jerusalem, and the Son -

Ἀνθρώπου παραδοθήσεται τοῖς ἀρχιερεῦσι καὶ γραμματεῦσι,
of Man will be handed over to the chief priests and scribes,
betrayed

καὶ κατακρινοῦσιν αὐτὸν θανάτῳ, 19 καὶ παραδώσουσιν
and they will condemn Him to death, and they will hand over ~

αὐτὸν τοῖς ἔθνεσιν εἰς τὸ ἐμπαῖξαι καὶ μαστιγῶσαι* καὶ
Him to the Gentiles - - to mock and to scourge and

σταυρῶσαι. Καὶ τῇ τρίτῃ ἡμέρᾳ ἀναστήσεται."[e]
to crucify. And on the third day He will rise."

---

[d](**20:16**) NU omits πολλοι . . . εκλεκτοι, *For many . . . chosen.* [e](**20:19**) NU reads εγερθησεται, *He will be raised.*

***(20:19)** μαστιγόω *(mastigoō).* Verb meaning *whip, scourge, flog.* It is used both for the whipping administered as part of synagogue discipline (Matt. 10:17; cf. 2 Cor. 11:24) and for that given to those condemned to death (as here). Once figuratively it means *punish, discipline,* referring to punishment administered by God (see Heb. 12:6, where it is parallel to "chastise"). The cognate noun μάστιξ, *a whip, lash,* is also used for a scourging (Acts 22:24) and figuratively for *affliction, scourge (of sickness),* as

Greatness Through Suffering and Service
(Mark 10:35–45)

20 Τότε προσῆλθεν αὐτῷ ἡ μήτηρ τῶν υἱῶν Ζεβεδαίου
Then [8]approached [9]Him [1]the [2]mother [3]of [4]the [5]sons [6]of [7]Zebedee

μετὰ τῶν υἱῶν αὐτῆς, προσκυνοῦσα καὶ αἰτοῦσά τι παρ'
with - sons ~ her, doing obeisance and asking something from

αὐτοῦ. **21** Ὁ δὲ εἶπεν αὐτῇ, "Τί θέλεις?"
Him. [2]the [3]*One* [1]And said to her, "What do you desire?"
He

Λέγει αὐτῷ, "Εἰπὲ ἵνα καθίσωσιν οὗτοι οἱ δύο υἱοί μου
She says to Him, "Say that [5]may [6]sit [1]these - [3]two [4]sons [2]my
said "Grant

εἷς ἐκ δεξιῶν σου καὶ εἷς ἐξ εὐωνύμων σου ἐν τῇ βασιλείᾳ
one at [2]right [3]*parts* [1]Your and one at [2]left [3]*parts* [1]Your in - kingdom ~
on right side on left side

σου."
Your."

22 Ἀποκριθεὶς δὲ ὁ Ἰησοῦς εἶπεν, "Οὐκ οἴδατε τί
answering ~ But - Jesus said, "[3]not [1]You [2]do know what

αἰτεῖσθε. Δύνασθε πιεῖν τὸ ποτήριον ὃ ἐγὼ μέλλω
you are asking. Are you able to drink the cup which I am about

πίνειν ἢ τὸ βάπτισμα ὃ ἐγὼ βαπτίζομαι
to drink or [4]*with* [5]the [6]baptism [7]*with* [8]which [9]I [10]am [11]being [12]baptized

βαπτισθῆναι?"[f]
[1]to [2]be [3]baptized?"

Λέγουσιν αὐτῷ, "Δυνάμεθα."
They say to Him, "We are able."
said

23 Καὶ λέγει αὐτοῖς, "Τὸ μὲν ποτήριόν μου πίεσθε
And He says to them, - "Indeed cup ~ My you will drink
said

καὶ τὸ βάπτισμα ὃ ἐγὼ βαπτίζομαι
and *with* the baptism *with* which I am being baptized

βαπτισθήσεσθε·[g] τὸ δὲ καθίσαι ἐκ δεξιῶν μου καὶ ἐξ
you will be baptized; - but to sit at [2]right [3]*parts* [1]My and at
on right side on

εὐωνύμων μου οὐκ ἔστιν ἐμὸν[h] δοῦναι, ἀλλ' οἷς
[2]left [3]*parts* [1]My not ~ is Mine to give, but *to those* for whom
left side

ἡτοίμασται ὑπὸ τοῦ Πατρός μου."
it has been prepared by - Father ~ My."

24 Καὶ ἀκούσαντες οἱ δέκα ἠγανάκτησαν περὶ τῶν δύο
And hearing the ten they were indignant about the two
when the ten heard,

ἀδελφῶν. **25** Ὁ δὲ Ἰησοῦς προσκαλεσάμενος αὐτοὺς εἶπεν,
brothers. - But Jesus having summoned them said,

"Οἴδατε ὅτι οἱ ἄρχοντες τῶν ἐθνῶν κατακυριεύουσιν αὐτῶν,
"You know that the rulers of the Gentiles lord it over them,

καὶ οἱ μεγάλοι κατεξουσιάζουσιν αὐτῶν. **26** Οὐχ οὕτως δὲ
and the great ones exercise authority over them. [4]not [6]so [1]But
their

ἔσται ἐν ὑμῖν· ἀλλ' ὃς ἐὰν θέλῃ ἐν ὑμῖν μέγας
[2]it [3]shall [5]be among you; but who ever desires among you [3]great

γενέσθαι ἔσται[i] ὑμῶν διάκονος. **27** Καὶ ὃς ἐὰν θέλῃ ἐν
[1]to [2]become shall be your servant. And who ever desires among

ὑμῖν εἶναι πρῶτος ἔστω[j] ὑμῶν δοῦλος· **28** ὥσπερ ὁ Υἱὸς
you to be first let him be your slave; just as the Son

τοῦ Ἀνθρώπου οὐκ ἦλθε διακονηθῆναι, ἀλλὰ διακονῆσαι,
- of Man not ~ did come to be served, but to serve,

20 Then the mother of Zebedee's sons came to Him with her sons, kneeling down and asking something from Him.
21 And He said to her, "What do you wish?" She said to Him, "Grant that these two sons of mine may sit, one on Your right hand and the other on the left, in Your kingdom."
22 But Jesus answered and said, "You do not know what you ask. Are you able to drink the cup that I am about to drink, and be baptized with the baptism that I am baptized with?" They said to Him, "We are able."
23 So He said to them, "You will indeed drink My cup, and be baptized with the baptism that I am baptized with; but to sit on My right hand and on My left is not Mine to give, but *it is for those* for whom it is prepared by My Father."
24 And when the ten heard *it*, they were greatly displeased with the two brothers.
25 But Jesus called them to *Himself* and said, "You know that the rulers of the Gentiles lord it over them, and those who are great exercise authority over them.
26 "Yet it shall not be so among you; but whoever desires to become great among you, let him be your servant.
27 "And whoever desires to be first among you, let him be your slave—
28 "just as the Son of Man did not come to be served, but to

---

f(**20:22**) NU omits η το βαπτισμα ο εγω βαπτιζομαι βαπτισθηναι, *or with the baptism with which I am baptized to be baptized.*
g(**20:23**) NU omits και το βαπτισμα ο εγω βαπτιζομαι βαπτισθησεσθε, *and with the baptism with which I am baptized you will be baptized.*
h(**20:23**) NU adds in brackets τουτο, *this.*
i(**20:26**) TR reads εστω, *let him be.* j(**20:27**) NU reads εσται, *he shall be.*

Mark 3:10. The cognate verb μαστίζω, *to strike with a whip,* occurs only in Acts 22:25.

serve, and to give His life a ransom for many."
29 Now as they went out of
Jericho, a great multitude followed Him.
30 And behold, two blind men
sitting by the road, when they
heard that Jesus was passing
by, cried out, saying, "Have
mercy on us, O Lord, Son of
David!"
31 Then the multitude warned
them that they should be quiet;
but they cried out all the more,
saying, "Have mercy on us,
O Lord, Son of David!"
32 So Jesus stood still and
called them, and said, "What do
you want Me to do for you?"
33 They said to Him, "Lord,
that our eyes may be opened."
34 So Jesus had compassion
and touched their eyes. And
immediately their eyes received sight, and they followed
Him.
21 Now when they drew
near Jerusalem, and
came to Bethphage, at the
Mount of Olives, then Jesus
sent two disciples,
2 saying to them, "Go into
the village opposite you, and
immediately you will find a donkey tied, and a colt with her.
Loose *them* and bring *them* to
Me.
3 "And if anyone says anything to you, you shall say, 'The
Lord has need of them,' and immediately he will send them."
4 All this was done that it

καὶ δοῦναι τὴν ψυχὴν αὐτοῦ λύτρον ἀντὶ πολλῶν."
and to give - life ˜ His *as* a ransom in the place of many."

Two Blind Men Receive Their Sight
(Mark 10:46–52; Luke 18:35–43)

29 Καὶ ἐκπορευομένων αὐτῶν ἀπὸ Ἰεριχώ, ἠκολούθησεν
And going out them from Jericho, [4]followed
as they went out

αὐτῷ ὄχλος πολύς. **30** Καὶ ἰδού, δύο τυφλοὶ καθήμενοι
[5]Him [1]a [3]crowd [2]large. And behold, two blind *men* sitting

παρὰ τὴν ὁδόν, ἀκούσαντες ὅτι Ἰησοῦς παράγει,
alongside the road, hearing that Jesus is passing by,
when they heard was

ἔκραξαν, λέγοντες, "Ἐλέησον ἡμᾶς, Κύριε, Υἱὸς Δαβίδ!"
cried out, saying, "Have mercy on us, Lord, Son of David!"

31 Ὁ δὲ ὄχλος ἐπετίμησεν αὐτοῖς ἵνα σιωπήσωσιν.
the ˜ But crowd warned them that they should be silent.

Οἱ δὲ μεῖζον ἔκραξον, λέγοντες, "Ἐλέησον
[2]the [3]*ones* [1]But [6]all [7]the [8]more [4]cried [5]out, saying, "Have mercy on
they

ἡμᾶς, Κύριε, Υἱὸς Δαβίδ!"
us, Lord, Son of David!"

32 Καὶ στὰς ὁ Ἰησοῦς ἐφώνησεν αὐτοὺς καὶ εἶπε,
And having stood still - Jesus called them and said,

"Τί θέλετε ποιήσω ὑμῖν?"
"What do you desire *that* I should do for you?"

33 Λέγουσιν αὐτῷ, "Κύριε, ἵνα ἀνοιχθῶσιν ἡμῶν οἱ
They say to Him, "Lord, that [3]may [4]be [5]opened [1]our -
said

ὀφθαλμοί." **34** Σπλαγχνισθεὶς δὲ ὁ Ἰησοῦς ἥψατο τῶν
[2]eyes." [2]having [3]compassion [1]And - Jesus touched -

ὀφθαλμῶν αὐτῶν, καὶ εὐθέως ἀνέβλεψαν αὐτῶν οἱ
eyes ˜ their, and immediately [3]received [4]sight [1]their -

ὀφθαλμοί,[k] καὶ ἠκολούθησαν αὐτῷ.
[2]eyes, and they followed Him.

The Triumphal Entry
(Mark 11:1–11; Luke 19:28–40; John 12:12–19)

21 **1** Καὶ ὅτε ἤγγισαν εἰς Ἱεροσόλυμα καὶ ἦλθον εἰς
And when they drew near to Jerusalem and came to

Βηθσφαγὴ[a] πρὸς τὸ Ὄρος τῶν Ἐλαιῶν, τότε ὁ Ἰησοῦς
Bethsphage towards the Mount - of Olives, then - Jesus

ἀπέστειλε δύο μαθητάς, **2** λέγων αὐτοῖς, "Πορεύθητε εἰς τὴν
sent two disciples, saying to them, "Go into the

κώμην τὴν ἀπέναντι ὑμῶν, καὶ εὐθέως εὑρήσετε ὄνον
village - opposite you, and immediately you will find a donkey

δεδεμένην καὶ πῶλον μετ' αὐτῆς. Λύσαντες
tied up and a young donkey with her. Loosing
When you have untied them,

ἀγάγετέ μοι. **3** Καὶ ἐάν τις ὑμῖν εἴπῃ τι, ἐρεῖτε
bring *them* to Me. And if anyone you ˜ asks anything, you shall say

ὅτι "Ὁ Κύριος αὐτῶν χρείαν ἔχει.' Εὐθέως δὲ
- 'The Lord [3]of [4]them [2]need [1]has.' immediately ˜ And

ἀποστέλλει[b] αὐτούς." **4** Τοῦτο δὲ ὅλον[c] γέγονεν ἵνα
he sends them." this Now whole has happened so that
will send Now all this took place

[k](**20:34**) NU omits *αυτων οι οφθαλμοι, their eyes.*
[a](**21:1**) NU, TR read *Βηθφαγη, Bethphage.*
[b](**21:3**) NU, TR read *αποστελει, he will send.*
[c](**21:4**) NU omits *ολον, all.*

πληρωθῇ τὸ ῥηθὲν διὰ τοῦ προφήτου,
[7]might [8]be [9]fulfilled [1]the [2]*thing* [3]spoken [4]through [5]the [6]prophet,

λέγοντος,
saying,

5 «Εἴπατε τῇ θυγατρὶ Σιών,»[d]
«Say to the daughter of Zion,»

«"Ἰδού, ὁ βασιλεύς σου ἔρχεταί σοι
«'Behold, - King ˜ your is coming to you

Πραῢς καὶ ἐπιβεβηκὼς ἐπὶ ὄνον
Humble and mounted on a donkey

Καὶ πῶλον υἱὸν ὑποζυγίου.'»[e]
And a young donkey *the* son of a beast of burden.'»
foal donkey.'»

6 Πορευθέντες δὲ οἱ μαθηταὶ καὶ ποιήσαντες καθὼς
going And the disciples and doing just as
And the disciples having gone and done

προσέταξεν αὐτοῖς ὁ Ἰησοῦς 7 ἤγαγον τὴν ὄνον καὶ τὸν
[2]ordered [3]them - [1]Jesus they brought the donkey and the

πῶλον. Καὶ ἐπέθηκαν ἐπάνω αὐτῶν τὰ ἱμάτια αὐτῶν, καὶ
young donkey. And they laid on them - clothes ˜ their, and

ἐπεκάθισεν ἐπάνω αὐτῶν. 8 Ὁ δὲ πλεῖστος ὄχλος ἔστρωσαν
they set *Him* on them. the ˜ And very large crowd spread

ἑαυτῶν τὰ ἱμάτια ἐν τῇ ὁδῷ, ἄλλοι δὲ ἔκοπτον
[3]of [4]themselves [1]the [2]clothes on the road, others ˜ but were cutting
their own

κλάδους ἀπὸ τῶν δένδρων καὶ ἐστρώννυον ἐν τῇ ὁδῷ.
branches from the trees and were spreading *them* in the road.

9 Οἱ δὲ ὄχλοι οἱ προάγοντες[f] καὶ οἱ ἀκολουθοῦντες
the ˜ And crowds - going in front and the *ones* following

ἔκραζον, λέγοντες,
were crying out, saying,

"«Ὡσαννὰ» τῷ Υἱῷ Δαβίδ!
"«Hosanna» to the Son of David!

«Εὐλογημένος ὁ ἐρχόμενος ἐν ὀνόματι Κυρίου!»[g]
«Blessed *is* the *One* coming in *the* name of *the* Lord!»

«Ὡσαννὰ» ἐν τοῖς ὑψίστοις!"
«Hosanna» in the highest *heights*!"
heaven!"

10 Καὶ εἰσελθόντος αὐτοῦ εἰς Ἱεροσόλυμα, ἐσείσθη πᾶσα
And entering ˜ Him into Jerusalem, [4]was [5]shaken [1]all
when He entered stirred up

ἡ πόλις, λέγουσα, "Τίς ἐστιν οὗτος?"
[2]the [3]city, saying, "Who is this?"

11 Οἱ δὲ ὄχλοι ἔλεγον, "Οὗτός ἐστιν Ἰησοῦς ὁ
the ˜ And crowds were saying, "This is Jesus the

προφήτης ὁ ἀπὸ Ναζαρὲτ τῆς Γαλιλαίας."
prophet - from Nazareth - of Galilee."

Jesus Cleanses the Temple
(Mark 11:15–19; Luke 19:45–48)

12 Καὶ εἰσῆλθεν ὁ Ἰησοῦς εἰς τὸ ἱερὸν τοῦ Θεοῦ[h] καὶ
And entered ˜ - Jesus into the temple - of God and

ἐξέβαλε πάντας τοὺς πωλοῦντας καὶ ἀγοράζοντας ἐν τῷ
He threw out all the *ones* selling and buying in the

ἱερῷ, καὶ τὰς τραπέζας τῶν κολλυβιστῶν κατέστρεψε καὶ
temple, and the tables of the money changers He overturned and

τὰς καθέδρας τῶν πωλούντων τὰς περιστεράς. 13 Καὶ
the seats of the *ones* selling - doves. And

might be fulfilled which was spoken by the prophet, saying:

5 *"Tell the daughter of Zion,*
'Behold, your King is
coming to you,
Lowly, and sitting on a
donkey,
A colt, the foal of a
donkey.' "

6 So the disciples went and did as Jesus commanded them.
7 They brought the donkey and the colt, laid their clothes on them, and set *Him* on them.
8 And a very great multitude spread their clothes on the road; others cut down branches from the trees and spread *them* on the road.
9 Then the multitudes who went before and those who followed cried out, saying:

"Hosanna to the Son of
David!
'Blessed is He who comes
in the name of the
LORD!'
Hosanna in the highest!"

10 And when He had come into Jerusalem, all the city was moved, saying, "Who is this?"
11 So the multitudes said, "This is Jesus, the prophet from Nazareth of Galilee."
12 Then Jesus went into the temple of God and drove out all those who bought and sold in the temple, and overturned the tables of the money changers and the seats of those who sold doves.
13 And He said to them, "It is

---

[d](**21:5**) Is. 62:11
[e](**21:5**) Zech. 9:9
[f](**21:9**) NU adds *αυτον, Him.*
[g](**21:9**) Ps. 118:25, 26
[h](**21:12**) NU omits *του Θεου, of God.*

written, *'My house shall be called a house of prayer,'* but you have made it a *'den of thieves.'* "
14 Then *the* blind and *the* lame came to Him in the temple, and He healed them.
15 But when the chief priests and scribes saw the wonderful things that He did, and the children crying out in the temple and saying, "Hosanna to the Son of David!" they were indignant
16 and said to Him, "Do You hear what these are saying?" And Jesus said to them, "Yes. Have you never read,

'Out of the mouth of babes
and nursing infants
You have perfected
praise'?"

17 Then He left them and went out of the city to Bethany, and He lodged there.
18 Now in the morning, as He returned to the city, He was hungry.
19 And seeing a fig tree by the road, He came to it and found nothing on it but leaves, and said to it, "Let no fruit grow on you ever again." Immediately the fig tree withered away.
20 And when the disciples saw *it,* they marveled, saying, "How did the fig tree wither away so soon?"
21 So Jesus answered and said to them, "Assuredly, I say to you, if you have faith and do not doubt, you will not only do what was done to the fig tree, but also if you say to this mountain,

λέγει αὐτοῖς, "Γέγραπται,
He says to them, "It is written,
said

«Ὁ οἶκός μου οἶκος προσευχῆς κληθήσεται.»[i]
- «house ~ My [4]a [5]house [6]of [7]prayer [1]shall [2]be [3]called.»

Ὑμεῖς δὲ αὐτὸν ἐποιήσατε[j] «σπήλαιον λῃστῶν.»"[k]*
you ~ But it ~ made «a cave of bandits.»"

14 Καὶ προσῆλθον αὐτῷ χωλοὶ καὶ τυφλοὶ ἐν τῷ ἱερῷ,
And [5]approached [6]Him [1]lame [2]and [3]blind [4]*people* in the temple,

καὶ ἐθεράπευσεν αὐτούς. 15 Ἰδόντες δὲ οἱ ἀρχιερεῖς καὶ
and He healed them. seeing But the high priests and
But when the high priests and the

οἱ γραμματεῖς τὰ θαυμάσια ἃ ἐποίησε καὶ τοὺς παῖδας
the scribes the wonders which He did and the children
scribes saw

κράζοντας ἐν τῷ ἱερῷ καὶ λέγοντας, "Ὡσαννὰ τῷ Υἱῷ
crying out in the temple and saying, "Hosanna to the Son

Δαβίδ," ἠγανάκτησαν 16 καὶ εἶπον αὐτῷ, "Ἀκούεις
of David," they became indignant and said to Him, "Do You hear

τί οὗτοι λέγουσιν?"
what these *children* are saying?"

Ὁ δὲ Ἰησοῦς λέγει αὐτοῖς, "Ναί. Οὐδέποτε ἀνέγνωτε ὅτι
- And Jesus says to them, "Yes. [3]never [1]Did [2]you read -
said

«Ἐκ στόματος νηπίων καὶ θηλαζόντων κατηρτίσω
«Out of *the* mouth of babies and sucklings You prepared [2]*for* [3]*Yourself*
nursing infants

αἶνον»?"[l] 17 Καὶ καταλιπὼν αὐτοὺς ἐξῆλθεν ἔξω τῆς
[1]praise»?" And leaving behind ~ them He went forth outside the

πόλεως εἰς Βηθανίαν καὶ ηὐλίσθη ἐκεῖ.
city to Bethany and lodged there.

The Barren Fig Tree
(Mark 11:12–14, 20–24)

18 Πρωΐας δὲ ἐπανάγων εἰς τὴν πόλιν,
[2]in [3]the [4]early [5]morning [1]Now returning to the city,

ἐπείνασε. 19 Καὶ ἰδὼν συκῆν μίαν ἐπὶ τῆς ὁδοῦ,
He became hungry. And seeing [2]fig [3]tree [1]one by the road,
a

ἦλθεν ἐπ' αὐτὴν καὶ οὐδὲν εὗρεν ἐν αὐτῇ εἰ μὴ φύλλα
He went upon it and nothing ~ found on it if not leaves ~
up to except

μόνον. Καὶ λέγει αὐτῇ, "Μηκέτι ἐκ σοῦ καρπὸς γένηται
only. And He says to it, "[3]no [4]longer [6]from [7]you [2]fruit [1]May [5]come
said

εἰς τὸν αἰῶνα." Καὶ ἐξηράνθη παραχρῆμα ἡ συκῆ.
into the age." And [4]was [5]withered [6]immediately [1]the [2]fig [3]tree.
forever."

20 Καὶ ἰδόντες οἱ μαθηταὶ ἐθαύμασαν, λέγοντες, "Πῶς
And seeing *it* the disciples marveled, saying, "How

παραχρῆμα ἐξηράνθη ἡ συκῆ!"
immediately [4]dried [5]up [1]the [2]fig [3]tree!"

21 Ἀποκριθεὶς δὲ ὁ Ἰησοῦς εἶπεν αὐτοῖς, "Ἀμὴν λέγω
answering ~ But - Jesus said to them, "Amen I say
"Assuredly

ὑμῖν, ἐὰν ἔχητε πίστιν καὶ μὴ διακριθῆτε, οὐ μόνον
to you, if you have faith and not ~ do doubt, [3]not [4]only

τὸ τῆς συκῆς ποιήσετε, ἀλλὰ κἂν τῷ ὄρει
[6]the [7]*sign* [8]of [9]the [10]fig [11]tree [1]you [2]will [5]do, but even if - [4]to [6]mountain

---

[i](21:13) Is. 56:7
[j](21:13) NU reads ποιειτε, *you are making.*
[k](21:13) Jer. 7:11
[l](21:16) Ps. 8:3 LXX

*(21:13) λῃστής (*lēstēs*). Noun meaning *robber, bandit,* suggesting more boldness and forcefulness than the near synonym κλέπτης, *thief.* While the latter may be a "sneak thief" or "burglar," (cf. the "thief in the night," in 1 Thess. 5:2), the word λῃστής used here suggests one who may do his work in open daylight, possibly with violence—as of the "highwaymen" in Luke 10:30; cf. John 18:40; 2 Cor. 11:26.

τούτῳ εἴπητε, "Ἄρθητι καὶ βλήθητι εἰς τὴν
[5]this [1]you [2]should [3]say, 'Be taken up and cast into the

θάλασσαν,' γενήσεται. 22 Καὶ πάντα ὅσα ἐὰν
sea,' it will happen. And all *things* as many as -

αἰτήσητε ἐν τῇ προσευχῇ πιστεύοντες λήψεσθε."
you may ask in - prayer believing you will receive."

Jesus' Authority Is Questioned

(Mark 11:27–33; Luke 20:1–8)

23 Καὶ ἐλθόντι αὐτῷ εἰς τὸ ἱερόν, προσῆλθον αὐτῷ
And coming ~ Him into the temple, [10]approached [11]Him
as He came

διδάσκοντι οἱ ἀρχιερεῖς καὶ οἱ πρεσβύτεροι τοῦ λαοῦ,
[12]teaching [1]the [2]chief [3]priests [4]and [5]the [6]elders [7]of [8]the [9]people,
as He taught

λέγοντες, "Ἐν ποίᾳ ἐξουσίᾳ ταῦτα ποιεῖς?
saying, "By what kind of authority [4]these [5]*things* [1]are [2]You [3]doing?

Καὶ τίς σοι ἔδωκε τὴν ἐξουσίαν ταύτην?"
And who You ~ gave - authority ~ this?"

24 Ἀποκριθεὶς δὲ ὁ Ἰησοῦς εἶπεν αὐτοῖς, "Ἐρωτήσω ὑμᾶς
answering ~ And - Jesus said to them, "[3]will [4]ask [5]you

κἀγὼ λόγον ἕνα, ὃν ἐὰν εἴπητέ μοι, κἀγὼ ὑμῖν ἐρῶ ἐν
[1]I [2]also word ~ one, which if you tell Me, I also [3]you [1]will [2]tell by
thing

ποίᾳ ἐξουσίᾳ ταῦτα ποιῶ. 25 Τὸ βάπτισμα
what kind of authority [3]these [4]*things* [1]I [2]do. The baptism

Ἰωάννου πόθεν ἦν? Ἐξ οὐρανοῦ ἢ ἐξ ἀνθρώπων?"
of John from where was it? From heaven or from men?"
—where was it from?

Οἱ δὲ διελογίζοντο παρ' ἑαυτοῖς, λέγοντες, "Ἐὰν
[2]the [3]*ones* [1]And were arguing among themselves, saying, "If
they

εἴπωμεν, 'Ἐξ οὐρανοῦ,' ἐρεῖ ἡμῖν, 'Διὰ τί οὖν
we say, 'From heaven,' He will say to us, 'On account of what then
'Why

οὐκ ἐπιστεύσατε αὐτῷ?' 26 Ἐὰν δὲ εἴπωμεν, 'Ἐξ
[3]not [1]did [2]you believe him?' if ~ But we say, 'From

ἀνθρώπων,' φοβούμεθα τὸν ὄχλον, πάντες γὰρ ἔχουσι τὸν
men,' we fear the crowd, all ~ for have -
consider

Ἰωάννην ὡς προφήτην."
John as a prophet."

27 Καὶ ἀποκριθέντες τῷ Ἰησοῦ εἶπον, "Οὐκ οἴδαμεν."
And answering - Jesus they said, "[3]not [1]We [2]do know."

Ἔφη αὐτοῖς καὶ αὐτός, "Οὐδὲ ἐγὼ λέγω ὑμῖν ἐν
[3]said [4]to [5]them [2]also [1]He, "Neither I ~ do tell you by

ποίᾳ ἐξουσίᾳ ταῦτα ποιῶ.
what kind of authority [3]these [4]*things* [1]I [2]do.

Parable of the Two Sons

28 "Τί δὲ ὑμῖν δοκεῖ? Ἄνθρωπος εἶχε τέκνα δύο.
"what ~ But to you does it seem? A man had children ~ two.
do you think?

Καὶ προσελθὼν τῷ πρώτῳ εἶπε, 'Τέκνον, ὕπαγε σήμερον
And approaching the first he said, 'Child, go today

ἐργάζου ἐν τῷ ἀμπελῶνί μου.' 29 Ὁ δὲ ἀποκριθεὶς
work in - vineyard ~ my.' [2]the [3]*one* [1]But answering
he

'Be removed and be cast into
the sea,' it will be done.
22 "And whatever things you
ask in prayer, believing, you
will receive."
23 Now when He came into
the temple, the chief priests
and the elders of the people
confronted Him as He was
teaching, and said, "By what
authority are You doing these
things? And who gave You this
authority?"
24 But Jesus answered and
said to them, "I also will ask
you one thing, which if you tell
Me, I likewise will tell you by
what authority I do these
things:
25 "The baptism of John—
where was it from? From
heaven or from men?" And
they reasoned among them-
selves, saying, "If we say,
'From heaven,' He will say to
us, 'Why then did you not believe him?'
26 "But if we say, 'From
men,' we fear the multitude, for
all count John as a prophet."
27 So they answered Jesus
and said, "We do not know."
And He said to them, "Neither
will I tell you by what authority
I do these things.
28 "But what do you think? A
man had two sons, and he came
to the first and said, 'Son, go,
work today in my vineyard.'
29 "He answered and said, 'I

will not,' but afterward he regretted it and went.
30 "Then he came to the second and said likewise. And he answered and said, 'I *go,* sir,' but he did not go.
31 "Which of the two did the will of *his* father?" They said to Him, "The first." Jesus said to them, "Assuredly, I say to you that tax collectors and harlots enter the kingdom of God before you.
32 "For John came to you in the way of righteousness, and you did not believe him; but tax collectors and harlots believed him; and when you saw *it,* you did not afterward relent and believe him.
33 "Hear another parable: There was a certain landowner who planted a vineyard and set a hedge around it, dug a winepress in it and built a tower. And he leased it to vinedressers and went into a far country.
34 "Now when vintage-time drew near, he sent his servants to the vinedressers, that they might receive its fruit.
35 "And the vinedressers took his servants, beat one, killed one, and stoned another.
36 "Again he sent other servants, more than the first, and they did likewise to them.
37 "Then last of all he sent his

εἶπεν, 'Οὐ θέλω.' Ὕστερον δὲ μεταμεληθεὶς ἀπῆλθε.
said, '[3]not [1]I [2]do want *to.*' later ˜ But regretting *it* he went.

30 Καὶ προσελθὼν τῷ ἑτέρῳ[m] εἶπεν ὡσαύτως. Ὁ δὲ
And approaching the other *one* he said likewise. [2]the [3]*one* [1]But
he

ἀποκριθεὶς εἶπεν, "Ἐγώ, κύριε·' καὶ οὐκ ἀπῆλθε. **31** Τίς
answering said, 'I *am going,* lord;' yet [3]not [1]he [2]did go. Which
sir;'

ἐκ τῶν δύο ἐποίησε τὸ θέλημα τοῦ πατρός?"
of the two did the will of the father?"

Λέγουσιν αὐτῷ, "Ὁ πρῶτος."
They say to Him, "The first."
said

Λέγει αὐτοῖς ὁ Ἰησοῦς, "Ἀμὴν λέγω ὑμῖν ὅτι οἱ
[2]says [3]to [4]them - [1]Jesus, "Amen I say to you that -
said "Assuredly

τελῶναι καὶ αἱ πόρναι προάγουσιν ὑμᾶς εἰς τὴν βασιλείαν
tax collectors and - harlots go before you into the kingdom

τοῦ Θεοῦ. **32** Ἦλθε γὰρ πρὸς ὑμᾶς Ἰωάννης ἐν ὁδῷ
- of God. [3]came [1]For [4]to [5]you [2]John in *the* way

δικαιοσύνης, καὶ οὐκ ἐπιστεύσατε αὐτῷ· οἱ δὲ τελῶναι
of righteousness, and [3]not [1]you [2]did believe him; - but tax collectors

καὶ αἱ πόρναι ἐπίστευσαν αὐτῷ· ὑμεῖς δὲ ἰδόντες οὐ[n]
and - harlots believed him; you ˜ but seeing *it* [3]not
but when you saw it,

μετεμελήθητε ὕστερον τοῦ πιστεῦσαι αὐτῷ.
[1]you [2]did regret *it* later - *so as* to believe him.

The Parable of the Wicked Vinedressers
(Mark 12:1–12; Luke 20:9–19)

33 "Ἄλλην παραβολὴν ἀκούσατε. Ἄνθρωπός τις[o]
"[2]another [3]parable [1]Hear. [3]a [5]man [4]certain

ἦν οἰκοδεσπότης ὅστις ἐφύτευσεν ἀμπελῶνα καὶ
[1]*There* [2]was a master of the house who planted a vineyard and
landowner

φραγμὸν αὐτῷ περιέθηκε καὶ ὤρυξεν ἐν αὐτῷ ληνὸν καὶ
[2]a [3]hedge [5]it [1]set [4]around and dug in it a winepress and

ᾠκοδόμησε πύργον. Καὶ ἐξέδοτο αὐτὸν γεωργοῖς καὶ
built a tower. And he gave out ˜ it to farmers and
leased

ἀπεδήμησεν. **34** Ὅτε δὲ ἤγγισεν ὁ καιρὸς τῶν
went on a journey. when ˜ And [6]drew [7]near [1]the [2]*harvest* [3]time -

καρπῶν, ἀπέστειλε τοὺς δούλους αὐτοῦ πρὸς τοὺς γεωργοὺς
[4]of [5]fruits, he sent - slaves ˜ his to the farmers
servants

λαβεῖν τοὺς καρποὺς αὐτοῦ. **35** Καὶ λαβόντες οἱ γεωργοὶ
to receive - fruits ˜ his. And [3]taking [1]the [2]farmers
collect took

τοὺς δούλους αὐτοῦ, ὃν μὲν ἔδειραν, ὃν δὲ ἀπέκτειναν, ὃν
- [5]slaves [4]his, one - they beat, one ˜ and they killed, one ˜
servants

δὲ ἐλιθοβόλησαν. **36** Πάλιν ἀπέστειλεν ἄλλους δούλους
and they stoned. Again he sent other slaves
servants

πλείονας τῶν πρώτων, καὶ ἐποίησαν αὐτοῖς ὡσαύτως.
more than the first *ones,* and they did to them likewise.

37 Ὕστερον δὲ ἀπέστειλε πρὸς αὐτοὺς τὸν υἱὸν αὐτοῦ,
later ˜ And he sent to them - son ˜ his,

---

m(**21:30**) TR reads δευτερω, *second.* *n*(**21:32**) NU reads ουδε, *not even.*
o(**21:33**) NU omits τις, *certain.*

λέγων, "Εντραπήσονται τὸν υἱόν μου.' **38** Οἱ δὲ γεωργοὶ
saying, 'They will respect - son ~ my.' the ~ But farmers
But when the farmers

ἰδόντες τὸν υἱὸν εἶπον ἐν ἑαυτοῖς, 'Οὗτός ἐστιν ὁ
seeing the son said among themselves, 'This is the
saw they said

κληρονόμος. Δεῦτε, ἀποκτείνωμεν αὐτὸν καὶ κατάσχωμεν[p]
heir. Come, let us kill him and let us take possession

τὴν κληρονομίαν αὐτοῦ.' **39** Καὶ λαβόντες αὐτὸν ἐξέβαλον
- of inheritance ~ his.' And taking him they threw *him*

ἔξω τοῦ ἀμπελῶνος καὶ ἀπέκτειναν. **40** "Οταν οὖν ἔλθῃ
out of the vineyard and killed *him.* when ~ Therefore [6]comes

ὁ κύριος τοῦ ἀμπελῶνος, τί ποιήσει τοῖς γεωργοῖς
[1]the [2]owner [3]of [4]the [5]vineyard, what will he do - to farmers ~

ἐκείνοις?"
those?"

41 Λέγουσιν αὐτῷ, "Κακοὺς κακῶς ἀπολέσει
They say to him, "*Those* bad *men* [3]badly [1]He [2]will [4]destroy
said miserably

αὐτούς, καὶ τὸν ἀμπελῶνα ἐκδώσεται ἄλλοις γεωργοῖς,
them, and the vineyard he will give out to other farmers,
lease

οἵτινες ἀποδώσουσιν αὐτῷ τοὺς καρποὺς ἐν τοῖς καιροῖς
who will render to him the fruits in - seasons ~

αὐτῶν."
their."

42 Λέγει αὐτοῖς ὁ Ἰησοῦς, "Οὐδέποτε ἀνέγνωτε ἐν ταῖς
[2]says [3]to [4]them - [1]Jesus, "[7]never [5]Did [6]you [8]read in the
said

Γραφαῖς,
Scriptures,

«Λίθον ὃν ἀπεδοκίμασαν οἱ οἰκοδομοῦντες,
«A stone which [4]rejected [1]the [2]*ones* [3]building,
the builders,

Οὗτος ἐγενήθη εἰς κεφαλὴν γωνίας·
This *stone* became - head of a corner;
the cornerstone;

Παρὰ Κυρίου ἐγένετο αὕτη
From *the* Lord [2]came [3]to [4]be [1]this
By

Καὶ ἔστι θαυμαστὴ ἐν ὀφθαλμοῖς ἡμῶν»?[q]
And it is marvelous in eyes ~ our»?

43 Διὰ τοῦτο λέγω ὑμῖν ὅτι ἀρθήσεται ἀφ'
On account of this I say to you that [5]will [6]be [7]taken [8]away [9]from
Therefore

ὑμῶν ἡ βασιλεία τοῦ Θεοῦ καὶ δοθήσεται ἔθνει
[10]you [1]the [2]kingdom - [3]of [4]God and it will be given to a nation
people

ποιοῦντι τοὺς καρποὺς αὐτῆς. **44** Καὶ ὁ πεσὼν ἐπὶ τὸν
producing the fruits of it. And the *one* falling on -

λίθον τοῦτον συνθλασθήσεται· ἐφ' ὃν δ' ἂν πέσῃ,
stone ~ this will be broken to pieces; [2]upon [3]whom [1]but ever it falls,

λικμήσει αὐτόν."[r]
it will crush him."

45 Καὶ ἀκούσαντες οἱ ἀρχιερεῖς καὶ οἱ Φαρισαῖοι τὰς
And hearing the high priests and the Pharisees -
when the high priests and the Pharisees heard

son to them, saying, 'They will respect my son.'
38 "But when the vinedressers saw the son, they said among themselves, 'This is the heir. Come, let us kill him and seize his inheritance.'
39 "So they took him and cast *him* out of the vineyard and killed *him.*
40 "Therefore, when the owner of the vineyard comes, what will he do to those vinedressers?"
41 They said to Him, "He will destroy those wicked men miserably, and lease *his* vineyard to other vinedressers who will render to him the fruits in their seasons."
42 Jesus said to them, "Have you never read in the Scriptures:

'The stone which the
builders rejected
Has become the chief
cornerstone.
This was the LORD'S
doing,
And it is marvelous in our
eyes'?

43 "Therefore I say to you, the kingdom of God will be taken from you and given to a nation bearing the fruits of it.
44 "And whoever falls on this stone will be broken; but on whomever it falls, it will grind him to powder."
45 Now when the chief priests and Pharisees heard His para-

p(21:38) NU reads σχωμεν, *let us have.*
q(21:42) Ps. 118:22, 23
r(21:44) NU brackets v. 44.

bles, they perceived that He was speaking of them.
46 But when they sought to lay hands on Him, they feared the multitudes, because they took Him for a prophet.
22 And Jesus answered and spoke to them again by parables and said:
2 "The kingdom of heaven is like a certain king who arranged a marriage for his son,
3 "and sent out his servants to call those who were invited to the wedding; and they were not willing to come.
4 "Again, he sent out other servants, saying, 'Tell those who are invited, "See, I have prepared my dinner; my oxen and fatted cattle *are* killed, and all things *are* ready. Come to the wedding." '
5 "But they made light of it and went their ways, one to his own farm, another to his business.
6 "And the rest seized his servants, treated *them* spitefully, and killed *them*.
7 "But when the king heard *about it,* he was furious. And he sent out his armies, destroyed those murderers, and burned up their city.
8 "Then he said to his servants, 'The wedding is ready, but those who were invited were not worthy.
9 'Therefore go into the

---

[a](22:4) NU reads ητοιμακα, *I have prepared.*
[b](22:7) For Και ακουσας ο βασιλευς εκεινος, *And when that king heard,* NU reads ο δε βασιλευς, *But the king (was angry);* TR reads ακουσας ο δε βασιλευς, *But when the king heard.*

---

*(22:6) ὑβρίζω *(hybrizō).* Verb, meaning *treat spitefully.* The word indicates arrogant, insulting mistreatment, involving personal animosity, as here. It implies abuse that acts wantonly and with affront. Both Jesus (Luke 18:32) and Paul (Acts 14:5; 1 Thess. 2:2) received such ignominious mistreatment. Cf. the cognate nouns *ὕβρις, spiteful mistreatment, insult* (adopted in English as *hubris,* 2 Cor. 12:10); and *ὑβριστής, a spiteful, injurious person,* as in Rom. 1:30 where Paul classifies himself before his conversion with Gentiles who insolently mistreat God and others.

παραβολὰς αὐτοῦ ἔγνωσαν ὅτι περὶ αὐτῶν λέγει. **46** *Καὶ*
parables ˜ His they knew that about them He is speaking. And
was

ζητοῦντες αὐτὸν κρατῆσαι, ἐφοβήθησαν τοὺς ὄχλους, ἐπειδὴ
seeking [3]Him [1]to [2]seize, they were afraid of the crowds, since

ὡς προφήτην αὐτὸν εἶχον.
[4]as [5]a [6]prophet [3]Him [1]they [2]had.
considered.

The Parable of the Marriage Supper
(Luke 14:15–24)

22 **1** *Καὶ ἀποκριθεὶς ὁ Ἰησοῦς πάλιν εἶπεν αὐτοῖς ἐν*
And answering - Jesus again spoke to them in

παραβολαῖς, λέγων, **2** *"Ὡμοιώθη ἡ βασιλεία τῶν*
parables, saying, "[6]was [7]compared [1]The [2]kingdom [3]of [4]the
"is

οὐρανῶν ἀνθρώπῳ βασιλεῖ ὅστις ἐποίησε γάμους τῷ
[5]heavens to a man a king who made a marriage feast -
a king arranged a wedding

υἱῷ αὐτοῦ. **3** *Καὶ ἀπέστειλε τοὺς δούλους αὐτοῦ καλέσαι*
for son ˜ his. And he sent - slaves ˜ his to call
servants

τοὺς κεκλημένους εἰς τοὺς γάμους, καὶ οὐκ
the *ones* having been invited to the marriage feast, and [3]not
those who were wedding,

ἤθελον ἐλθεῖν. **4** *Πάλιν ἀπέστειλεν ἄλλους δούλους,*
[1]they [2]did want to come. Again he sent other slaves,
servants,

λέγων, 'Εἴπατε τοῖς κεκλημένοις, "Ἰδού, τὸ ἄριστόν
saying, 'Say to the *ones* having been invited, "See, - meal ˜
those who were

μου ἡτοίμασα,[a] *οἱ ταῦροί μου καὶ τὰ σιτιστὰ*
my I prepared, - oxen ˜ my and the fatted cattle

τεθυμένα, καὶ πάντα ἕτοιμα. Δεῦτε εἰς τοὺς
having been killed, and all *things are* ready. Come to the
are butchered,

γάμους."' **5** *Οἱ δὲ ἀμελήσαντες ἀπῆλθον, ὁ μὲν*
marriage feast."' [2]the [3]*ones* [1]But not caring went away, one indeed
wedding."' they

εἰς τὸν ἴδιον ἀγρόν, ὁ δὲ εἰς τὴν ἐμπορίαν αὐτοῦ. **6** *Οἱ*
to - his own field, one ˜ and to - business ˜ his. the ˜

δὲ λοιποὶ κρατήσαντες τοὺς δούλους αὐτοῦ ὕβρισαν καὶ*
But rest seizing - slaves ˜ his mistreated and
servants

ἀπέκτειναν. **7** *Καὶ ἀκούσας ὁ βασιλεὺς ἐκεῖνος*[b] *ὠργίσθη,*
killed *them.* And hearing - king ˜ that he was angry,
when that king heard

καὶ πέμψας τὰ στρατεύματα αὐτοῦ ἀπώλεσε τοὺς φονεῖς
and sending - troops ˜ his he destroyed - murderers ˜

ἐκείνους καὶ τὴν πόλιν αὐτῶν ἐνέπρησε.
those and - [5]city [4]their [1]he [2]burned [3]up.

8 *"Τότε λέγει τοῖς δούλοις αὐτοῦ, 'Ὁ μὲν γάμος*
"Then he says - to slaves ˜ his, 'The indeed ˜ wedding
said servants

ἕτοιμός ἐστιν, οἱ δὲ κεκλημένοι οὐκ ἦσαν ἄξιοι.
ready ˜ is, [2]the [3]*ones* [1]but having been invited not ˜ were worthy.
those who were

9 *Πορεύεσθε οὖν ἐπὶ τὰς διεξόδους τῶν ὁδῶν, καὶ*
go ˜ Therefore on the outlets of the roads, and

ὅσους ἂν εὕρητε καλέσατε εἰς τοὺς γάμους.' **10** Καὶ
as many as - you may find invite to the marriage feast.' And
wedding.'

ἐξελθόντες οἱ δοῦλοι ἐκεῖνοι εἰς τὰς ὁδοὺς
going out - slaves ˜ those into the roads
when those servants had gone out

συνήγαγον πάντας ὅσους[c] εὗρον, πονηρούς τε
they gathered together all as many as they found, [2]evil [3]*people* [1]both
everyone

καὶ ἀγαθούς. Καὶ ἐπλήσθη ὁ γάμος
and good *people*. And [4]was [5]filled [1]the [2]wedding [3]*hall*

ἀνακειμένων. **11** Εἰσελθὼν δὲ ὁ βασιλεὺς θεάσασθαι
with *ones* reclining *to eat*. coming in But the king to see
guests. But when the king came in

τοὺς ἀνακειμένους εἶδεν ἐκεῖ ἄνθρωπον οὐκ ἐνδεδυμένον
the *ones* reclining *to eat* he saw there a man not having been clothed
the guests dressed

ἔνδυμα γάμου. **12** Καὶ λέγει αὐτῷ, 'Ἑταῖρε, πῶς
with clothing for a wedding. And he says to him, 'Friend, how
said

εἰσῆλθες ὧδε μὴ ἔχων ἔνδυμα γάμου?' Ὁ δὲ
did you come here not having clothing for a wedding?' [2]the [3]*one* [1]And
he

ἐφιμώθη.
was silent.
speechless.

13 "Τότε εἶπεν ὁ βασιλεὺς τοῖς διακόνοις, 'Δήσαντες
"Then [3]said [1]the [2]king to the servants, 'Binding
'Tie him

αὐτοῦ πόδας καὶ χεῖρας, ἄρατε αὐτὸν καὶ[d] ἐκβάλετε εἰς
him feet and hands, take away ˜ him and throw *him* out into
up

τὸ σκότος τὸ ἐξώτερον. Ἐκεῖ ἔσται ὁ κλαυθμὸς καὶ ὁ
the darkness - outside. There *there* will be - weeping and -

βρυγμὸς τῶν ὀδόντων.' **14** Πολλοὶ γάρ εἰσι κλητοί, ὀλίγοι δὲ
gnashing - of teeth.' many ˜ For are called, few ˜ but
invited,

ἐκλεκτοί."
are chosen."

Render unto Caesar
(Mark 12:13–17; Luke 20:20–26)

15 Τότε πορευθέντες οἱ Φαρισαῖοι συμβούλιον ἔλαβον
Then going the Pharisees counsel ˜ took
the Pharisees went and plotted

ὅπως αὐτὸν παγιδεύσωσιν ἐν λόγῳ. **16** Καὶ ἀποστέλλουσιν
how [4]Him [1]they [2]might [3]trap in *some* word. And they send
His speech. sent

αὐτῷ τοὺς μαθητὰς αὐτῶν μετὰ τῶν Ἡρῳδιανῶν, λέγοντες,
to Him - disciples ˜ their with the Herodians, saying,

"Διδάσκαλε, οἴδαμεν ὅτι ἀληθὴς εἶ καὶ τὴν ὁδὸν τοῦ
"Teacher, we know that [3]truthful [1]You [2]are and the way -

Θεοῦ ἐν ἀληθείᾳ διδάσκεις, καὶ οὐ μέλει
of God in truth You teach, and [3]not [1]it [2]does make a difference

σοι περὶ οὐδενός, οὐ γὰρ βλέπεις εἰς πρόσωπον
to You about no one, [4]not [1]for [2]You [3]do [5]look at *the* face
anyone, show favoritism

highways, and as many as you find, invite to the wedding.'
10 "So those servants went out into the highways and gathered together all whom they found, both bad and good. And the wedding *hall* was filled with guests.
11 "But when the king came in to see the guests, he saw a man there who did not have on a wedding garment.
12 "So he said to him, 'Friend, how did you come in here without a wedding garment?' And he was speechless.
13 "Then the king said to the servants, 'Bind him hand and foot, take him away, and cast *him* into outer darkness; there will be weeping and gnashing of teeth.'
14 "For many are called, but few *are* chosen."
15 Then the Pharisees went and plotted how they might entangle Him in *His* talk.
16 And they sent to Him their disciples with the Herodians, saying, "Teacher, we know that You are true, and teach the way of God in truth; nor do You care about anyone, for You do not regard the person of men.

---

[c](22:10) NU reads *ους, whom.* [d](22:13) NU omits *αρατε αυτον και, take him away and.*

17 "Tell us, therefore, what do You think? Is it lawful to pay taxes to Caesar, or not?"
18 But Jesus perceived their wickedness, and said, "Why do you test Me, *you* hypocrites?
19 "Show Me the tax money." So they brought Him a denarius.
20 And He said to them, "Whose image and inscription *is* this?"
21 They said to Him, "Caesar's." And He said to them, "Render therefore to Caesar the things that are Caesar's, and to God the things that are God's."
22 When they had heard *these words*, they marveled, and left Him and went their way.
23 The same day the Sadducees, who say there is no resurrection, came to Him and asked Him,
24 saying: "Teacher, Moses said that if a man dies, having no children, his brother shall marry his wife and raise up offspring for his brother.
25 "Now there were with us seven brothers. The first died after he had married, and having no offspring, left his wife to his brother.
26 "Likewise the second also, and the third, even to the seventh.
27 "Last of all the woman died also.
28 "Therefore, in the resurrection, whose wife of the seven will she be? For they all had her."
29 Jesus answered and said to them, "You are mistaken, not

---

e(22:24) Deut. 25:5; Gen. 38:8

ἀνθρώπων. 17 Εἰπὲ οὖν ἡμῖν τί σοι δοκεῖ?
of men. Say therefore to us what to You does it seem?
to persons. do You think?

Ἔξεστι δοῦναι κῆνσον Καίσαρι ἢ οὔ?"
Is it lawful to give a tax to Caesar or not?"
pay taxes

18 Γνοὺς δὲ ὁ Ἰησοῦς τὴν πονηρίαν αὐτῶν εἶπε, "Τί
[3]knowing [1]But - [2]Jesus - wickedness ˜ their said, "Why

με πειράζετε, ὑποκριταί? 19 Ἐπιδείξατέ μοι τὸ νόμισμα τοῦ
[4]Me [1]do [2]you [3]test, hypocrites? Show Me the coin -
tax

κήνσου." Οἱ δὲ προσήνεγκαν αὐτῷ δηνάριον. 20 Καὶ
of tax." [2]the [3]*ones* [1]So brought to Him a denarius. And
money." So they

λέγει αὐτοῖς, "Τίνος ἡ εἰκὼν αὕτη καὶ ἡ ἐπιγραφή?"
He says to them, "Whose *is* - image ˜ this and - inscription?"
said

21 Λέγουσιν αὐτῷ, "Καίσαρος."
They say to Him, "Caesar's."
said

Τότε λέγει αὐτοῖς, "Ἀπόδοτε οὖν τὰ Καίσαρος
Then He says to them, "Give back therefore the *things* of Caesar
said "Render

Καίσαρι καὶ τὰ τοῦ Θεοῦ τῷ Θεῷ." 22 Καὶ ἀκούσαντες
to Caesar and the *things* - of God - to God." And hearing

ἐθαύμασαν, καὶ ἀφέντες αὐτὸν ἀπῆλθον.
they marveled, and leaving Him they went away.

The Sadducees Question the Resurrection
(Mark 12:18–27; Luke 20:27–40)

23 Ἐν ἐκείνῃ τῇ ἡμέρᾳ προσῆλθον αὐτῷ Σαδδουκαῖοι,
On that - day [2]approached [3]Him [1]Sadducees,

οἱ λέγοντες μὴ εἶναι ἀνάστασιν, καὶ ἐπηρώτησαν αὐτόν,
the *ones* saying not to be a resurrection, and they asked Him,
there is no resurrection,

24 λέγοντες, "Διδάσκαλε, Μωσῆς εἶπεν, ἐάν τις ἀποθάνῃ
saying, "Teacher, Moses said, if someone dies

μὴ ἔχων τέκνα, ἐπιγαμβρεύσει ὁ ἀδελφὸς αὐτοῦ τὴν
not having children, [3]shall [4]marry [7]as [8]next [9]of [10]kin - [2]brother [1]his -

γυναῖκα αὐτοῦ καὶ ἀναστήσει σπέρμα τῷ ἀδελφῷ αὐτοῦ.[e]
[6]wife [5]his and shall raise up seed - for brother ˜ his.
offspring

25 Ἦσαν δὲ παρ' ἡμῖν ἑπτὰ ἀδελφοί. Καὶ ὁ πρῶτος
[2]*there* [3]were [1]Now with us seven brothers. And the first

γαμήσας ἐτελεύτησε, καὶ μὴ ἔχων σπέρμα ἀφῆκε τὴν
having married died, and not having seed he left -
offspring

γυναῖκα αὐτοῦ τῷ ἀδελφῷ αὐτοῦ. 26 Ὁμοίως καὶ ὁ δεύτερος
wife ˜ his - to brother ˜ his. Likewise also the second

καὶ ὁ τρίτος, ἕως τῶν ἑπτά. 27 Ὕστερον δὲ πάντων
and the third, up to the seven. last ˜ And of all
all

ἀπέθανε καὶ ἡ γυνή. 28 Ἐν τῇ οὖν ἀναστάσει τίνος
[3]died [4]also [1]the [2]woman. [2]in [3]the [1]Therefore resurrection whose

τῶν ἑπτὰ ἔσται γυνή? Πάντες γὰρ ἔσχον αὐτήν."
[2]of [3]the [4]seven [5]will [6]she [7]be [1]wife? all ˜ For had her."

29 Ἀποκριθεὶς δὲ ὁ Ἰησοῦς εἶπεν αὐτοῖς, "Πλανᾶσθε,
answering ˜ And - Jesus said to them, "You are mistaken,

μὴ εἰδότες τὰς Γραφὰς μηδὲ τὴν δύναμιν τοῦ Θεοῦ. 30 Ἐν
not knowing the Scriptures nor the power - of God. in ˜

γὰρ τῇ ἀναστάσει οὔτε γαμοῦσιν οὔτε
For the resurrection neither do they marry nor

ἐκγαμίζονται, ἀλλ' ὡς ἄγγελοι τοῦ Θεοῦ[f] ἐν οὐρανῷ
are they given in marriage, but [3]like [4]angels - [5]of [6]God [7]in [8]heaven

εἰσι. 31 Περὶ δὲ τῆς ἀναστάσεως τῶν νεκρῶν, οὐκ
[1]they [2]are. concerning ˜ But the resurrection of the dead, [3]not

ἀνέγνωτε τὸ ῥηθὲν ὑμῖν ὑπὸ τοῦ Θεοῦ, λέγοντος,
[1]did [2]you read the *thing* spoken to you by - God, saying,

32 «Ἐγώ εἰμι ὁ Θεὸς Ἀβραὰμ καὶ ὁ Θεὸς Ἰσαὰκ καὶ ὁ
«I am the God of Abraham and the God of Isaac and the

Θεὸς Ἰακώβ»?[g] Οὐκ ἔστιν ὁ Θεὸς Θεὸς νεκρῶν ἀλλὰ
God of Jacob»? [3]not [2]is - [1]God a God of dead *people* but

ζώντων." 33 Καὶ ἀκούσαντες οἱ ὄχλοι ἐξεπλήσσοντο
of living *people*." And hearing the crowds they were astonished
when the crowds heard

ἐπὶ τῇ διδαχῇ αὐτοῦ.
at - teaching ˜ His.

The Two Greatest Commandments
(Mark 12:28–34)

34 Οἱ δὲ Φαρισαῖοι, ἀκούσαντες ὅτι ἐφίμωσε τοὺς
the ˜ But Pharisees, hearing that He silenced the

Σαδδουκαίους, συνήχθησαν ἐπὶ τὸ αὐτό. 35 Καὶ
Sadducees, gathered upon the same. And
together.

ἐπηρώτησεν εἷς ἐξ αὐτῶν νομικός, πειράζων αὐτόν, καὶ
[6]asked [1]one [2]of [3]them [4]a [5]lawyer, testing Him, and

λέγων,[h] 36 "Διδάσκαλε, ποία ἐντολὴ μεγάλη ἐν τῷ
saying, "Teacher, which *is the* commandment ˜ great in the

νόμῳ?"
law?"

37 Ὁ δὲ Ἰησοῦς[i] ἔφη αὐτῷ, "«Ἀγαπήσεις Κύριον τὸν
- And Jesus said to him, "«You shall love *the* Lord -

Θεόν σου ἐν ὅλῃ καρδίᾳ σου καὶ ἐν ὅλῃ ψυχῇ σου»[j]
God ˜ your with [2]whole [3]heart [1]your and with [2]whole [3]soul [1]your»

καὶ ἐν ὅλῃ τῇ διανοίᾳ σου. 38 Αὕτη ἐστὶ πρώτη καὶ
and with [2]whole - [3]mind [1]your. This is *the* first and

μεγάλη ἐντολή. 39 Δευτέρα δὲ ὁμοία αὐτῇ,
great commandment. [2]*the* [3]second [1]And is like it,

«Ἀγαπήσεις τὸν πλησίον σου ὡς σεαυτόν.»[k] 40 Ἐν ταύταις
«You shall love - neighbor ˜ your as yourself.» On these

ταῖς δυσὶν ἐντολαῖς ὅλος ὁ Νόμος καὶ οἱ Προφῆται
- two commandments [3]whole [2]the [4]Law [5]and [6]the [7]Prophets

κρέμανται."
[1]hang."

What Do You Think of Christ?
(Mark 12:35–37; Luke 20:41–44)

41 Συνηγμένων δὲ τῶν Φαρισαίων, ἐπηρώτησεν
having gathered together And the Pharisees, [2]asked
And when the Pharisees had assembled,

αὐτοὺς ὁ Ἰησοῦς, 42 λέγων, "Τί ὑμῖν δοκεῖ περὶ τοῦ
[3]them - [1]Jesus, saying, "What to you does it seem about the
do you think

knowing the Scriptures nor the power of God.
30 "For in the resurrection they neither marry nor are given in marriage, but are like angels of God in heaven.
31 "But concerning the resurrection of the dead, have you not read what was spoken to you by God, saying,
32 *'I am the God of Abraham, the God of Isaac, and the God of Jacob'*? God is not the God of the dead, but of the living."
33 And when the multitudes heard *this,* they were astonished at His teaching.
34 But when the Pharisees heard that He had silenced the Sadducees, they gathered together.
35 Then one of them, a lawyer, asked *Him a question,* testing Him, and saying,
36 "Teacher, which *is* the great commandment in the law?"
37 Jesus said to him, "*'You shall love the* LORD *your God with all your heart, with all your soul, and with all your mind.'*
38 "This is *the* first and great commandment.
39 "And *the* second *is* like it: *'You shall love your neighbor as yourself.'*
40 "On these two commandments hang all the Law and the Prophets."
41 While the Pharisees were gathered together, Jesus asked them,
42 saying, "What do you think about the Christ? Whose Son is

[f](22:30) NU omits Θεου, *of God.* [g](22:32) Ex. 3:6, 15, 16 [h](22:35) NU omits *και λεγων, and saying.* [i](22:37) NU omits Ιησους, *Jesus.* [j](22:37) Deut. 6:5 [k](22:39) Lev. 19:18

He?" They said to Him, *"The
Son* of David."
43 He said to them, "How
then does David in the Spirit
call Him *'Lord,'* saying:

44 *'The LORD said to my
Lord,
"Sit at My right hand,
Till I make Your enemies
Your footstool"'?*

45 "If David then calls Him
'Lord,' how is He his Son?"
46 And no one was able to answer Him a word, nor from that
day on did anyone dare question Him anymore.
23 Then Jesus spoke to
the multitudes and to
His disciples,
2 saying: "The scribes and
the Pharisees sit in Moses'
seat.
3 "Therefore whatever they
tell you to observe, *that* observe and do, but do not do according to their works; for they
say, and do not do.
4 "For they bind heavy burdens, hard to bear, and lay *them*
on men's shoulders; but they
themselves will not move them
with one of their fingers.
5 "But all their works they
do to be seen by men. They
make their phylacteries broad
and enlarge the borders of their
garments.
6 "They love the best places
at feasts, the best seats in the

Χριστοῦ?* Τίνος υἱός ἐστι?"
Christ? (Messiah?) Whose Son is He?"

Λέγουσιν αὐτῷ, "Τοῦ Δαβίδ."
They say (said) to Him, - "David's."

43 Λέγει αὐτοῖς, "Πῶς οὖν Δαβὶδ ἐν Πνεύματι 'Κύριον'
He says (said) to them, "How then [2]David [3]in [4]*the* [5]Spirit [8]'Lord'

αὐτὸν καλεῖ, λέγων,
[7]Him [1]does [6]call, saying,

44 «Εἶπεν ὁ Κύριος τῷ Κυρίῳ μου,
«[3]said [1]The [2]Lord - to Lord ˜ my,

'Κάθου ἐκ δεξιῶν μου
'Sit at [2]right [3]*parts* (hand) [1]My

Ἕως ἂν θῶ τοὺς ἐχθρούς σου ὑποπόδιον[l] τῶν ποδῶν
Till - I put - enemies ˜ Your *as* a footstool - of (for) feet ˜

σου'»?[m]
Your'»?

45 Εἰ οὖν Δαβὶδ καλεῖ αὐτὸν 'Κύριον,' πῶς υἱὸς αὐτοῦ
If therefore David calls Him 'Lord,' how [4]Son [3]his

ἐστι?" **46** Καὶ οὐδεὶς ἐδύνατο αὐτῷ ἀποκριθῆναι λόγον, οὐδὲ
[1]is [2]He?" And no one was able [3]Him [1]to [2]answer a word, nor

ἐτόλμησέ τις ἀπ' ἐκείνης τῆς ἡμέρας ἐπερωτῆσαι αὐτὸν
dared anyone from that - day to question Him

οὐκέτι.
no (any) longer.

Religious Hypocrites Are Denounced
(Mark 12:38–40; Luke 11:37–52, 20:45–47)

23 **1** Τότε ὁ Ἰησοῦς ἐλάλησε τοῖς ὄχλοις καὶ τοῖς
Then - Jesus spoke to the crowds and -

μαθηταῖς αὐτοῦ, **2** λέγων, "Ἐπὶ τῆς Μωσέως καθέδρας
to disciples ˜ His, saying, "On the [2]of [3]Moses [1]seat

ἐκάθισαν οἱ γραμματεῖς καὶ οἱ Φαρισαῖοι. **3** Πάντα οὖν
sat the scribes and the Pharisees. All *things* therefore

ὅσα ἐὰν εἴπωσιν ὑμῖν τηρεῖν,[a] τηρεῖτε καὶ ποιεῖτε,
what ever they may say to you to observe, observe and do,

κατὰ δὲ τὰ ἔργα αὐτῶν μὴ ποιεῖτε· λέγουσι γὰρ καὶ
[2]according [3]to [1]but - works ˜ their not ˜ do do; [2]they [3]say [1]for and

οὐ ποιοῦσι. **4** Δεσμεύουσι γὰρ φορτία βαρέα καὶ
not ˜ do do. [2]they [3]bind [1]For loads heavy and

δυσβάστακτα καὶ ἐπιτιθέασιν ἐπὶ τοὺς ὤμους τῶν ἀνθρώπων,
hard to bear and they lay *them* on the shoulders - of men,

τῷ δὲ δακτύλῳ αὐτῶν οὐ θέλουσι κινῆσαι αὐτά.
- but with finger ˜ their [3]not [1]they [2]do want to move them.

5 "Πάντα δὲ τὰ ἔργα αὐτῶν ποιοῦσι πρὸς τὸ θεαθῆναι
"all ˜ But - works ˜ their they do in order - to be seen

τοῖς ἀνθρώποις. Πλατύνουσι δὲ τὰ φυλακτήρια αὐτῶν καὶ
- by men. [2]they [3]make [4]broad [1]And - phylacteries ˜ their and

μεγαλύνουσι τὰ κράσπεδα τῶν ἱματίων αὐτῶν,[b]
they make large the tassels - of garments ˜ their,

6 φιλοῦσί τε τὴν πρωτοκλισίαν ἐν τοῖς δείπνοις καὶ τὰς
[2]they [3]love [1]and the first couch (place of honor) at the dinners and the

---

[l](22:44) NU reads *υποκατω, underneath.*
[m](22:44) Ps. 110:1
[a](23:3) NU omits *τηρειν, to observe.* [b](23:5) NU omits *των ιματιων αυτων, of their clothes.*

*(22:42) Χριστός *(Christos).* Verbal adjective, used as a noun, derived from *χρίω, anoint,* hence *Anointed One, Messiah.* We begin to feel the impact of the title *Christ* on the original audiences if we sometimes substitute *Messiah* for *Christ* in passages with Jewish connotations. Saying "Jesus Christ" is the same as saying, "Yeshua of Nazareth is the Messiah," anointed by God to be the Savior of the world. Jesus refers to Himself as "Jesus Christ" in John 17:3.

πρωτοκαθεδρίας ἐν ταῖς συναγωγαῖς 7 καὶ τοὺς ἀσπασμοὺς ἐν
first seats in the synagogues and - greetings in
best

ταῖς ἀγοραῖς καὶ καλεῖσθαι ὑπὸ τῶν ἀνθρώπων, 'Ῥαββί,
the marketplaces and to be called by - men, 'Rabbi,

Ῥαββί.'[c]
Rabbi.'

8 "Ὑμεῖς δὲ μὴ κληθῆτε 'Ῥαββί'· εἷς γάρ ἐστιν ὑμῶν
"you ˜ But not ˜ do be called 'Rabbi'; one ˜ for is your

ὁ καθηγητής, ὁ Χριστός,[d] πάντες δὲ ὑμεῖς ἀδελφοί ἐστε.
- teacher, the Christ, [4]all [1]and [2]you [5]brothers [3]are.
Messiah,

9 Καὶ 'πατέρα' μὴ καλέσητε ὑμῶν ἐπὶ τῆς γῆς· εἷς γάρ
And [6]'father' [2]not [1]do [3]call [4]*anyone* [5]your on the earth; one ˜ for

ἐστιν ὁ Πατὴρ ὑμῶν, ὁ ἐν τοῖς οὐρανοῖς.[e] 10 Μηδὲ
is - Father ˜ your, the *One* in the heavens. Neither

κληθῆτε καθηγηταί· εἷς γὰρ ὑμῶν ἐστιν ὁ καθηγητής, ὁ
be called teachers; one ˜ for your ˜ is - teacher, the

Χριστός. 11 Ὁ δὲ μείζων ὑμῶν ἔσται ὑμῶν διάκονος.
Christ. the ˜ But greater of you shall be your servant.
Messiah. greatest

12 Ὅστις δὲ ὑψώσει ἑαυτὸν ταπεινωθήσεται, καὶ ὅστις
whoever ˜ And shall exalt himself will be humbled, and whoever

ταπεινώσει ἑαυτὸν ὑψωθήσεται.
shall humble himself will be exalted.

13 "Οὐαὶ δὲ ὑμῖν, γραμματεῖς καὶ Φαρισαῖοι, ὑποκριταί!
"woe ˜ But to you, scribes and Pharisees, hypocrites!

Ὅτι κατεσθίετε τὰς οἰκίας τῶν χηρῶν καὶ προφάσει
Because you eat up the houses - of widows and [3]in [4]pretense
devour

μακρὰ προσευχόμενοι. Διὰ τοῦτο λήψεσθε
[2]long [1]praying. On account of this you will receive
pray at length. Therefore

περισσότερον κρίμα.[f]
a worse judgment.
condemnation.

14 "Οὐαὶ ὑμῖν, γραμματεῖς καὶ Φαρισαῖοι, ὑποκριταί!
"Woe to you, scribes and Pharisees, hypocrites!

Ὅτι κλείετε τὴν βασιλείαν τῶν οὐρανῶν ἔμπροσθεν τῶν
Because you shut up the kingdom of the heavens before -

ἀνθρώπων· ὑμεῖς γὰρ οὐκ εἰσέρχεσθε, οὐδὲ τοὺς
men; you ˜ for not ˜ do enter, nor the *ones*
those

εἰσερχομένους ἀφίετε εἰσελθεῖν.
entering do you allow to go in.
who are entering

15 "Οὐαὶ ὑμῖν, γραμματεῖς καὶ Φαρισαῖοι, ὑποκριταί!
"Woe to you, scribes and Pharisees, hypocrites!

Ὅτι περιάγετε τὴν θάλασσαν καὶ τὴν ξηρὰν ποιῆσαι
Because you travel around - sea and - dry *land* to make

ἕνα προσήλυτον, καὶ ὅταν γένηται, ποιεῖτε αὐτὸν
one proselyte, and whenever he becomes *one*, you make him
convert,

υἱὸν Γεέννης διπλότερον ὑμῶν.
[4]a [5]son [6]of [7]Gehenna [1]twice [2]as [3]much *as* you.
hell

16 "Οὐαὶ ὑμῖν, ὁδηγοὶ τυφλοί, οἱ λέγοντες, 'Ὃς ἂν
"Woe to you, guides ˜ blind, the *ones* saying, 'Who ever
who say,

synagogues,
7 "greetings in the marketplaces, and to be called by men,
'Rabbi, Rabbi.'
8 "But you, do not be called
'Rabbi'; for One is your
Teacher, the Christ, and you
are all brethren.
9 "Do not call anyone on
earth your father; for One is
your Father, He who is in
heaven.
10 "And do not be called
teachers; for One is your
Teacher, the Christ.
11 "But he who is greatest
among you shall be your servant.
12 "And whoever exalts himself will be humbled, and he
who humbles himself will be exalted.
13 "But woe to you, scribes
and Pharisees, hypocrites! For
you shut up the kingdom of
heaven against men; for you
neither go in *yourselves,* nor do
you allow those who are entering to go in.
14 "Woe to you, scribes and
Pharisees, hypocrites! For you
devour widows' houses, and for
a pretense make long prayers.
Therefore you will receive
greater condemnation.
15 "Woe to you, scribes and
Pharisees, hypocrites! For you
travel land and sea to win one
proselyte, and when he is won,
you make him twice as much a
son of hell as yourselves.
16 "Woe to you, blind guides,
who say, 'Whoever swears by

---

[c](**23:7**) NU omits second *ραββι, Rabbi.*
[d](**23:8**) NU omits ο Χριστος, *the Christ.* [e](**23:9**) For εν τοις ουρανοις, *in the heavens,* NU reads ουρανιος, *heavenly.*
[f](**23:13**) NU omits v. 13 and numbers v. 14 as v. 13.

the temple, it is nothing; but whoever swears by the gold of the temple, he is obliged *to perform it.'*
17 "Fools and blind! For which is greater, the gold or the temple that sanctifies the gold?
18 "And, 'Whoever swears by the altar, it is nothing; but whoever swears by the gift that is on it, he is obliged *to perform it.'*
19 "Fools and blind! For which is greater, the gift or the altar that sanctifies the gift?
20 "Therefore he who swears by the altar, swears by it and by all things on it.
21 "He who swears by the temple, swears by it and by Him who dwells in it.
22 "And he who swears by heaven, swears by the throne of God and by Him who sits on it.
23 "Woe to you, scribes and Pharisees, hypocrites! For you pay tithe of mint and anise and cummin, and have neglected the weightier *matters* of the law: justice and mercy and faith. These you ought to have done, without leaving the others undone.
24 "Blind guides, who strain out a gnat and swallow a camel!
25 "Woe to you, scribes and Pharisees, hypocrites! For you cleanse the outside of the cup and dish, but inside they are full of extortion and self-indulgence.
26 "Blind Pharisee, first cleanse the inside of the cup and dish, that the outside of them may be clean also.
27 "Woe to you, scribes and Pharisees, hypocrites! For you

ὀμόσῃ ἐν τῷ ναῷ, οὐδέν ἐστιν· ὃς δ' ἂν ὀμόσῃ ἐν τῷ
swears by the shrine, [3]nothing [1]it [2]is; [5]who [4]but ever swears by the
temple,

χρυσῷ τοῦ ναοῦ ὀφείλει.' **17** Μωροὶ* καὶ τυφλοί! Τίς γὰρ
gold of the shrine is obligated.' Fools and blind! which ˜ For
temple

μείζων ἐστίν, ὁ χρυσὸς ἢ ὁ ναὸς ὁ ἁγιάζων[g] τὸν χρυσόν?
greater ˜ is, the gold or the shrine - sanctifying the gold?
temple

18 Καί, "Ὃς ἐὰν ὀμόσῃ ἐν τῷ θυσιαστηρίῳ, οὐδέν ἐστιν· ὃς
And, 'Who ever swears by the altar, [3]nothing [1]it [2]is; [5]who

δ' ἂν ὀμόσῃ ἐν τῷ δώρῳ τῷ ἐπάνω αὐτοῦ ὀφείλει.'
[4]but ever swears by the gift - upon it is obligated.'

19 Μωροὶ καὶ[h] τυφλοί! Τί γὰρ μεῖζον, τὸ δῶρον ἢ τὸ
Fools and blind! which ˜ For *is* greater, the gift or the

θυσιαστήριον τὸ ἁγιάζον τὸ δῶρον? **20** Ὁ οὖν
altar - sanctifying the gift? [2]the [3]*one* [1]Therefore

ὀμόσας ἐν τῷ θυσιαστηρίῳ ὀμνύει ἐν αὐτῷ καὶ ἐν πᾶσι
swearing by the altar swears by it and by all

τοῖς ἐπάνω αὐτοῦ. **21** Καὶ ὁ ὀμόσας ἐν τῷ ναῷ
the *things* upon it. And the *one* swearing by the shrine
temple

ὀμνύει ἐν αὐτῷ καὶ ἐν τῷ κατοικήσαντι[i] αὐτόν. **22** Καὶ
swears by it and by the *One* having dwelt in it. And
Him who dwelt in

ὁ ὀμόσας ἐν τῷ οὐρανῷ ὀμνύει ἐν τῷ θρόνῳ τοῦ Θεοῦ καὶ
the *one* swearing by - heaven swears by the throne - of God and

ἐν τῷ καθημένῳ ἐπάνω αὐτοῦ.
by the *One* sitting upon it.

23 "Οὐαὶ ὑμῖν, γραμματεῖς καὶ Φαρισαῖοι, ὑποκριταί!
"Woe to you, scribes and Pharisees, hypocrites!

Ὅτι ἀποδεκατοῦτε τὸ ἡδύοσμον καὶ τὸ ἄνηθον καὶ τὸ
Because you pay a tithe of - mint and - dill and -

κύμινον, καὶ ἀφήκατε τὰ βαρύτερα τοῦ νόμου, τὴν
cummin, and you left the weightier *things* of the law, -
have neglected more important

κρίσιν καὶ τὸν ἔλεον καὶ τὴν πίστιν. Ταῦτα ἔδει
judgment and - mercy and - faith. These *things* it was necessary
justice

ποιῆσαι κἀκεῖνα μὴ ἀφιέναι. **24** Ὁδηγοὶ τυφλοί, οἱ
to do and [4]those [1]not [2]to [3]leave. guides ˜ Blind, the *ones*
neglect. you who

διϋλίζοντες τὸν κώνωπα, τὴν δὲ κάμηλον καταπίνοντες!
straining out the gnat, [4]the [1]but [5]camel [2]drinking [3]down!
strain out a a swallow!

25 "Οὐαὶ ὑμῖν, γραμματεῖς καὶ Φαρισαῖοι, ὑποκριταί!
"Woe to you, scribes and Pharisees, hypocrites!

Ὅτι καθαρίζετε τὸ ἔξωθεν τοῦ ποτηρίου καὶ τῆς
Because you clean the outside of the cup and of the

παροψίδος, ἔσωθεν δὲ γέμουσιν ἐξ ἁρπαγῆς καὶ ἀδικίας.[j]
dish, inside ˜ but they are full of greed and unrighteousness.

26 Φαρισαῖε τυφλέ! Καθάρισον πρῶτον τὸ ἐντὸς τοῦ
Pharisee ˜ Blind! Clean first the inside of the

ποτηρίου καὶ τῆς παροψίδος,[k] ἵνα γένηται καὶ τὸ ἐκτὸς
cup and of the dish, so that [5]may [6]be [8]also [1]the [2]outside

αὐτῶν καθαρόν.
[3]of [4]them [7]clean.

27 "Οὐαὶ ὑμῖν, γραμματεῖς καὶ Φαρισαῖοι, ὑποκριταί!
"Woe to you, scribes and Pharisees, hypocrites!

---

[g](**23:17**) NU reads αγιασας, *having sanctified.*
[h](**23:19**) NU omits μωροι και, *fools and.*
[i](**23:21**) NU, TR read κατοικουντι, *dwelling;* the aorist participle of the M-text may suggest He no longer made the temple His special home.
[j](**23:25**) NU, TR read ακρασιας, *self-indulgence.*
[k](**23:26**) NU omits και της παροψιδος, *and of the dish.*

---

*(**23:17**) μωρός (*mōros*). Adjective (source of English *moron*) meaning *stupid, foolish,* often used (as here and v. 19) substantivally as *foolish (one), fool* or *foolish (thing), foolishness* (1 Cor. 1:27). While the near synonym ἄφρων, *foolish,* (sub-

῞Οτι παρομοιάζετε τάφοις κεκονιαμένοις, οἵτινες
Because you resemble tombs having been whitewashed, which

ἔξωθεν μὲν φαίνονται ὡραῖοι, ἔσωθεν δὲ γέμουσιν ὀστέων
outwardly indeed appear beautiful, inside ˜ but they are full of bones

νεκρῶν καὶ πάσης ἀκαθαρσίας. 28 Οὕτω καὶ ὑμεῖς
of dead *people* and of all uncleanness. Thus also you

ἔξωθεν μὲν φαίνεσθε τοῖς ἀνθρώποις δίκαιοι, ἔσωθεν δὲ
outwardly indeed appear - [2]to [3]men [1]righteous, inside ˜ but

μεστοί ἐστε ὑποκρίσεως καὶ ἀνομίας.
[3]full [1]you [2]are of hypocrisy and of lawlessness.

29 "Οὐαὶ ὑμῖν, γραμματεῖς καὶ Φαρισαῖοι, ὑποκριταί!
"Woe to you, scribes and Pharisees, hypocrites!

῞Οτι οἰκοδομεῖτε τοὺς τάφους τῶν προφητῶν καὶ κοσμεῖτε
Because you build the tombs of the prophets and you adorn

τὰ μνημεῖα τῶν δικαίων, 30 καὶ λέγετε, 'Εἰ ἦμεν ἐν ταῖς
the monuments of the righteous, and you say, 'If we were in the
had lived

ἡμέραις τῶν πατέρων ἡμῶν, οὐκ ἂν ἦμεν κοινωνοὶ
days - of fathers ˜ our, [3]not - [1]we [2]would be partakers
have been

αὐτῶν ἐν τῷ αἵματι τῶν προφητῶν.' 31 ῞Ωστε μαρτυρεῖτε
with them in the blood of the prophets.' So that you testify

ἑαυτοῖς ὅτι υἱοί ἐστε τῶν φονευσάντων τοὺς
against yourselves that [3]sons [1]you [2]are of the *ones* having killed the
those who

προφήτας. 32 Καὶ ὑμεῖς πληρώσατε τὸ μέτρον τῶν πατέρων
prophets. And you, fill up the measure - of fathers ˜

ὑμῶν.
your.

33 "῎Οφεις! Γεννήματα ἐχιδνῶν! Πῶς φύγητε ἀπὸ τῆς
"Serpents! Offspring of vipers! How shall you escape from the

κρίσεως τῆς Γεέννης? 34 Διὰ τοῦτο, ἰδού, ἐγὼ
judgment - of Gehenna? On account of this, behold, I
condemnation to hell? Therefore,

ἀποστέλλω πρὸς ὑμᾶς προφήτας καὶ σοφοὺς καὶ γραμματεῖς·
send to you prophets and wise *men* and scribes;

καὶ ἐξ αὐτῶν ἀποκτενεῖτε καὶ σταυρώσετε, καὶ ἐξ
and *some* of them you will kill and you will crucify, and *some* of

αὐτῶν μαστιγώσετε ἐν ταῖς συναγωγαῖς ὑμῶν καὶ
them you will flog in - synagogues ˜ your and

διώξετε ἀπὸ πόλεως εἰς πόλιν, 35 ὅπως ἔλθῃ ἐφ'
you will persecute from city to city, so that [3]may [4]come [1]on

ὑμᾶς πᾶν αἷμα δίκαιον ἐκχυνόμενον ἐπὶ τῆς γῆς ἀπὸ τοῦ
[2]you all *the* blood ˜ righteous being shed on the earth from the

αἵματος ῞Αβελ τοῦ δικαίου ἕως τοῦ αἵματος Ζαχαρίου υἱοῦ
blood of Abel the righteous up to the blood of Zechariah son of

Βαραχίου, ὃν ἐφονεύσατε μεταξὺ τοῦ ναοῦ καὶ τοῦ
Berechiah, whom you murdered between the shrine and the
temple

θυσιαστηρίου. 36 'Αμὴν λέγω ὑμῖν ὅτι ἥξει πάντα
altar. Amen I say to you that [4]will [5]come [1]all
Assuredly

ταῦτα ἐπὶ τὴν γενεὰν ταύτην.
[2]these [3]*things* on - generation ˜ this.

are like whitewashed tombs which indeed appear beautiful outwardly, but inside are full of dead *men's* bones and all uncleanness.
28 "Even so you also outwardly appear righteous to men, but inside you are full of hypocrisy and lawlessness.
29 "Woe to you, scribes and Pharisees, hypocrites! Because you build the tombs of the prophets and adorn the monuments of the righteous,
30 "and say, 'If we had lived in the days of our fathers, we would not have been partakers with them in the blood of the prophets.'
31 "Therefore you are witnesses against yourselves that you are sons of those who murdered the prophets.
32 "Fill up, then, the measure of your fathers' *guilt*.
33 "Serpents, brood of vipers! How can you escape the condemnation of hell?
34 "Therefore, indeed, I send you prophets, wise men, and scribes: *some* of them you will kill and crucify, and *some* of them you will scourge in your synagogues and persecute from city to city,
35 "that on you may come all the righteous blood shed on the earth, from the blood of righteous Abel to the blood of Zechariah, son of Berechiah, whom you murdered between the temple and the altar.
36 "Assuredly, I say to you, all these things will come upon this generation.

---

stantive) *fool,* tends to suggest being mindless or senseless, the word μωρός suggests dullness or deficiency. Used only by Paul and Matthew, the implication is usually a spiritual deficiency resulting from not knowing God. Cf. the cognate noun *μωρία, foolishness,* and verb *μωραίνω, make foolish,* (passive) *become flavorless* (of salt in Matt. 5:13, parallel Luke 14:34).

37 "O Jerusalem, Jerusalem, the one who kills the prophets and stones those who are sent to her! How often I wanted to gather your children together, as a hen gathers her chicks under *her* wings, but you were not willing!
38 "See! Your house is left to you desolate;
39 "for I say to you, you shall see Me no more till you say, *'Blessed is He who comes in the name of the* LORD!'"
24 Then Jesus went out and departed from the temple, and His disciples came up to show Him the buildings of the temple.
2 And Jesus said to them, "Do you not see all these things? Assuredly, I say to you, not *one* stone shall be left here upon another, that shall not be thrown down."
3 Now as He sat on the Mount of Olives, the disciples came to Him privately, saying, "Tell us, when will these things be? And what *will be* the sign of Your coming, and of the end of the age?"
4 And Jesus answered and said to them: "Take heed that no one deceives you.
5 "For many will come in My

Jesus Laments over Jerusalem
(Luke 13:34, 35)

37 "'Ιερουσαλήμ, 'Ιερουσαλήμ, ἡ ἀποκτένουσα τοὺς
"Jerusalem, Jerusalem! the *one* killing the
who kills

προφήτας καὶ λιθοβολοῦσα τοὺς ἀπεσταλμένους πρὸς
prophets and stoning the *ones* having been sent to
stones those who are

αὐτήν! Ποσάκις ἠθέλησα ἐπισυναγαγεῖν τὰ τέκνα σου,
her! How often I wanted to gather - children ˜ your,

ὃν τρόπον ἐπισυνάγει ὄρνις τὰ νοσσία ἑαυτῆς[l] ὑπὸ
by which manner [3]gathers [1]a [2]hen the chickens of herself under
just like her own

τὰς πτέρυγας, καὶ οὐκ ἠθελήσατε! **38** 'Ιδού, ἀφίεται ὑμῖν
the wings, and [3]not [1]you [2]did want to! See, [3]is [4]left [5]to [6]you
her

ὁ οἶκος ὑμῶν ἔρημος. **39** Λέγω γὰρ ὑμῖν, οὐ μή με
- [2]house [1]your desolate. [2]I [3]say [1]For to you, [3]not [4]not [6]Me
surely not

ἴδητε ἀπ' ἄρτι ἕως ἂν εἴπητε, «Εὐλογημένος ὁ
[1]you [2]will [5]see from now until - you say, «Blessed *is* the *One*
He who

ἐρχόμενος ἐν ὀνόματι Κυρίου.»"[m]
coming in *the* name of *the* Lord.»"
comes

Jesus Predicts the Destruction of the Temple
(Mark 13:1, 2; Luke 21:5, 6)

24 **1** Καὶ ἐξελθὼν ὁ 'Ιησοῦς ἐπορεύετο ἀπὸ τοῦ ἱεροῦ, καὶ
And going out - Jesus was departing from the temple, and

προσῆλθον οἱ μαθηταὶ αὐτοῦ ἐπιδεῖξαι αὐτῷ τὰς οἰκοδομὰς
[3]approached - [2]disciples [1]His to show Him the buildings

τοῦ ἱεροῦ. **2** 'Ο δὲ 'Ιησοῦς[a] εἶπεν αὐτοῖς, "Οὐ βλέπετε
of the temple. - But Jesus said to them, "[3]not [1]Do [2]you see

πάντα ταῦτα? 'Αμὴν λέγω ὑμῖν, οὐ μὴ ἀφεθῇ
all these *things?* Amen I say to you, not not [1]will [4]be [5]left
Assuredly by no means

ὧδε λίθος ἐπὶ λίθον ὃς οὐ καταλυθήσεται."
[6]here [2]a [3]stone upon a stone which not ˜ will be thrown down."

Jesus Describes the End of the Age
(Mark 13:3–13; Luke 21:7–19)

3 Καθημένου δὲ αὐτοῦ ἐπὶ τοῦ Ὄρους τῶν 'Ελαιῶν,
sitting And Him on the Mount - of Olives,
And as He was sitting

προσῆλθον αὐτῷ οἱ μαθηταὶ κατ' ἰδίαν, λέγοντες, "Εἰπὲ ἡμῖν,
[3]approached [4]Him [1]the [2]disciples privately, saying, "Tell us,

πότε ταῦτα ἔσται, καὶ τί τὸ σημεῖον τῆς σῆς
when these *things* will be, and what *will be* the sign - of Your

παρουσίας καὶ τῆς συντελείας τοῦ αἰῶνος?"
coming and of the completion of the age?"
end

4 Καὶ ἀποκριθεὶς ὁ 'Ιησοῦς εἶπεν αὐτοῖς, "Βλέπετε μή
And answering - Jesus said to them, "Watch out lest
"Take care that

τις ὑμᾶς πλανήσῃ. **5** Πολλοὶ γὰρ ἐλεύσονται ἐπὶ τῷ
anyone you ˜ deceive. many ˜ For will come in -
no one

[l](23:37) NU reads αυτης, *her.* [m](23:39) Ps. 118:26
[a](24:2) NU reads αποκριθεις, *answering.*

ὀνόματί μου, λέγοντες, "Ἐγώ εἰμι ὁ Χριστός,' καὶ πολλοὺς
name ˜ My, saying, 'I am the Christ,' and [4]many
Messiah,'

πλανήσουσι. 6 Μελλήσετε δὲ ἀκούειν πολέμους καὶ
[1]they [2]will [3]deceive. [2]you [3]will [4]be [5]about [1]And to hear of wars and
will hear

ἀκοὰς πολέμων. Ὁρᾶτε, μὴ θροεῖσθε· δεῖ
rumors of wars. See *that* not ˜ you be disturbed; [2]it [3]is [4]necessary [5]*for*

γὰρ πάντα[b] γενέσθαι, ἀλλ' οὔπω ἐστὶ τὸ τέλος.
[1]for all *things* to happen, but [4]not [5]yet [3]is [1]the [2]end.

7 Ἐγερθήσεται γὰρ ἔθνος ἐπὶ ἔθνος καὶ βασιλεία ἐπὶ
[3]will [4]be [5]raised [6]up [1]For [2]nation against nation and kingdom against

βασιλείαν, καὶ ἔσονται λιμοὶ καὶ λοιμοὶ[c] καὶ σεισμοὶ
kingdom, and *there* will be famines and pestilences and earthquakes

κατὰ τόπους. 8 Πάντα δὲ ταῦτα ἀρχὴ
according to places. all ˜ But these *things* *are the* beginning
in various

ὠδίνων.
of birth pangs.

9 "Τότε παραδώσουσιν ὑμᾶς εἰς θλῖψιν καὶ
"Then they will hand over ˜ you to affliction and

ἀποκτενοῦσιν ὑμᾶς, καὶ ἔσεσθε μισούμενοι ὑπὸ πάντων τῶν
they will kill you, and you will be hated by all the

ἐθνῶν διὰ τὸ ὄνομά μου. 10 Καὶ τότε
nations on account of - name ˜ My. And then

σκανδαλισθήσονται πολλοὶ καὶ ἀλλήλους παραδώσουσι
[2]will [3]be [4]offended [1]many and [5]one [6]another [1]they [2]will [3]hand [4]over
betray

καὶ μισήσουσιν ἀλλήλους. 11 Καὶ πολλοὶ ψευδοπροφῆται
and they will hate one another. And many false prophets

ἐγερθήσονται καὶ πλανήσουσι πολλούς. 12 Καὶ διὰ τὸ
will be raised up and they will deceive many. And because -

πληθυνθῆναι τὴν ἀνομίαν, ψυγήσεται ἡ ἀγάπη τῶν
to be increased the lawlessness, [6]will [7]grow [8]cold [1]the [2]love [3]of [4]the
lawlessness will increase,

πολλῶν. 13 Ὁ δὲ ὑπομείνας εἰς τέλος, οὗτος
[5]many. [2]the [3]*one* [1]But enduring to *the* end, this *one*
majority.

σωθήσεται. 14 Καὶ κηρυχθήσεται τοῦτο τὸ εὐαγγέλιον τῆς
will be saved. And [6]will [7]be [8]proclaimed [1]this - [2]gospel [3]of [4]the
delivered. good news

βασιλείας ἐν ὅλῃ τῇ οἰκουμένῃ εἰς μαρτύριον πᾶσι τοῖς
[5]kingdom in whole ˜ the inhabited earth for a testimony to all the

ἔθνεσι, καὶ τότε ἥξει τὸ τέλος.
nations, and then will come the end.

The Great Tribulation

(Mark 13:14–23; Luke 21:20–24)

15 "Ὅταν οὖν ἴδητε τὸ βδέλυγμα τῆς ἐρημώσεως τὸ
"when ˜ Therefore you see the abomination - of desolation -

ῥηθὲν διὰ Δανιὴλ τοῦ προφήτου ἑστὼς ἐν τόπῳ ἁγίῳ"
spoken of through Daniel the prophet standing in *the* place ˜ holy"

(ὁ ἀναγινώσκων νοείτω), 16 "τότε οἱ ἐν τῇ
([2]the [3]*one* [4]reading [1]let understand), "then [2]the [3]*ones* [4]in -

Ἰουδαίᾳ φευγέτωσαν ἐπὶ τὰ ὄρη, 17 ὁ ἐπὶ τοῦ
[5]Judea [1]let [6]flee upon the mountains, [2]the [3]*one* [4]on [5]the

δώματος μὴ καταβαινέτω ἆραι τὰ ἐκ τῆς οἰκίας
[6]housetop [7]not [1]let go down to take the *things* out of - house ˜

name, saying, 'I am the Christ,' and will deceive many.

6 "And you will hear of wars and rumors of wars. See that you are not troubled; for all *these things* must come to pass, but the end is not yet.

7 "For nation will rise against nation, and kingdom against kingdom. And there will be famines, pestilences, and earthquakes in various places.

8 "All these *are* the beginning of sorrows.

9 "Then they will deliver you up to tribulation and kill you, and you will be hated by all nations for My name's sake.

10 "And then many will be offended, will betray one another, and will hate one another.

11 "Then many false prophets will rise up and deceive many.

12 "And because lawlessness will abound, the love of many will grow cold.

13 "But he who endures to the end shall be saved.

14 "And this gospel of the kingdom will be preached in all the world as a witness to all the nations, and then the end will come.

15 "Therefore when you see the *'abomination of desolation,'* spoken of by Daniel the prophet, standing in the holy place" (whoever reads, let him understand),

16 "then let those who are in Judea flee to the mountains.

17 "Let him who is on the housetop not go down to take anything out of his house.

---

[b](24:6) NU omits *παντα, all.*
[c](24:7) NU omits *και λοιμοι, and pestilences.*

18 "And let him who is in the
field not go back to get his
clothes.
19 "But woe to those who are
pregnant and to those who are
nursing babies in those days!
20 "And pray that your flight
may not be in winter or on the
Sabbath.
21 "For then there will be
great tribulation, such as has
not been since the beginning of
the world until this time, no,
nor ever shall be.
22 "And unless those days
were shortened, no flesh would
be saved; but for the elect's
sake those days will be shortened.
23 "Then if anyone says to
you, 'Look, here *is* the Christ!'
or 'There!' do not believe *it*.
24 "For false christs and false
prophets will rise and show
great signs and wonders to deceive, if possible, even the
elect.
25 "See, I have told you beforehand.
26 "Therefore if they say to
you, 'Look, He is in the desert!'
do not go out; *or* 'Look, *He is* in
the inner rooms!' do not believe
it.
27 "For as the lightning comes
from the east and flashes to the
west, so also will the coming of
the Son of Man be.
28 "For wherever the carcass
is, there the eagles will be gathered together.
29 "Immediately after the
tribulation of those days the sun
will be darkened, and the moon
will not give its light; the stars

αὐτοῦ, **18** καὶ ὁ ἐν τῷ ἀγρῷ μὴ ἐπιστρεψάτω ὀπίσω
his, and [2]the [3]*one* [4]in [5]the [6]field [7]not [1]let [8]turn back

ἆραι τὰ ἱμάτια αὐτοῦ. **19** Οὐαὶ δὲ ταῖς ἐν γαστρὶ
to take - clothes ˜ his. woe ˜ But to the *women* in *the* womb
those who are

ἐχούσαις καὶ ταῖς θηλαζούσαις ἐν ἐκείναις ταῖς ἡμέραις!
having and to the *women* giving suck in those - days!
pregnant nursing a baby

20 Προσεύχεσθε δὲ ἵνα μὴ γένηται ἡ φυγὴ ὑμῶν
pray ˜ But that [4]not [3]may [5]take [6]place - [2]flight [1]your

χειμῶνος μηδὲ σαββάτῳ. **21** Ἔσται γὰρ τότε θλῖψις
of winter nor on a Sabbath. [3]*there* [4]will [5]be [1]For [2]then tribulation ˜
in

μεγάλη οἵα οὐ γέγονεν ἀπ' ἀρχῆς κόσμου ἕως τοῦ
great such as not ˜ has been from *the* beginning of *the* world until -

νῦν, οὐδ' οὐ μὴ γένηται. **22** Καὶ εἰ μὴ ἐκολοβώθησαν
now, nor not not shall be. And if [4]not [3]were [5]cut [6]short
by any means unless

αἱ ἡμέραι ἐκεῖναι, οὐκ ἂν ἐσώθη πᾶσα σάρξ·
- [2]days [1]those, not - would be saved all flesh;
no flesh would be saved;

διὰ δὲ τοὺς ἐκλεκτοὺς κολοβωθήσονται αἱ ἡμέραι
[2]for [3]the [4]sake [5]of [1]but the elect [3]will [4]be [5]cut [6]short - [2]days
chosen ones

ἐκεῖναι. **23** Τότε ἐάν τις ὑμῖν εἴπῃ, 'Ἰδού, ὧδε ὁ
[1]those. Then if someone [2]to [3]you [1]says, 'Look, here *is* the

Χριστός!' ἤ 'Ὧδε!' μὴ πιστεύσητε. **24** Ἐγερθήσονται γὰρ
Christ!' or 'Here!' not ˜ do believe *him*. [7]will [8]be [9]raised [10]up [1]For
Messiah!'

ψευδόχριστοι* καὶ ψευδοπροφῆται, καὶ δώσουσι σημεῖα
[2]false [3]christs [4]and [5]false [6]prophets, and they will give signs ˜

μεγάλα καὶ τέρατα ὥστε πλανῆσαι, εἰ δυνατόν, καὶ τοὺς
great and wonders so as to deceive, if possible, even the

ἐκλεκτούς. **25** Ἰδού, προείρηκα ὑμῖν. **26** Ἐὰν οὖν
elect. See, I have told [2]in [3]advance [1]you. If therefore
chosen ones.

εἴπωσιν ὑμῖν, 'Ἰδού, ἐν τῇ ἐρήμῳ ἐστί!' μὴ ἐξέλθητε·
they should say to you, 'Look, [3]in [4]the [5]desert [1]He [2]is!' not ˜ do go out;

'Ἰδού, ἐν τοῖς ταμείοις!' μὴ πιστεύσητε. **27** Ὥσπερ γὰρ
'See, in the secret rooms!' not ˜ do believe *them*. as ˜ For

ἡ ἀστραπὴ ἐξέρχεται ἀπὸ ἀνατολῶν καὶ φαίνεται ἕως
the lightning comes out from *the* east and shines to

δυσμῶν, οὕτως ἔσται[d] ἡ παρουσία τοῦ Υἱοῦ τοῦ Ἀνθρώπου.
the west, thus will be the coming of the Son - of Man.

28 Ὅπου γὰρ ἐὰν ᾖ τὸ πτῶμα, ἐκεῖ
where ˜ For ever [3]may [4]be [1]the [2]carcass, there

συναχθήσονται οἱ ἀετοί.
will [3]be [4]gathered [5]together [1]the [2]eagles.
vultures.

The Coming of the Son of Man
(Mark 13:24–27; Luke 21:25–28)

29 "Εὐθέως δὲ μετὰ τὴν θλῖψιν τῶν ἡμερῶν ἐκείνων,
"immediately ˜ And after the tribulation - of days ˜ those,

Ὁ ἥλιος σκοτισθήσεται,
The sun will be darkened,

Καὶ ἡ σελήνη οὐ δώσει τὸ φέγγος αὐτῆς,
And the moon not ˜ will give - radiance ˜ its,

---

[d](24:27) TR adds *καὶ, also*.

*(24:24) ψευδόχριστος (*pseudochristos*). Noun, used only here and in the parallel in Mark 13:22. The compound is derived from ψευδο-, *false, lying* (especially concerning spiritual truth), and Χριστός, *Anointed One, Christ*. Thus, a ψευδόχριστος was a false claimant to be the Messiah.

Καὶ οἱ ἀστέρες πεσοῦνται ἀπὸ τοῦ οὐρανοῦ,
And the stars will fall from - heaven,
(the sky,)

Καὶ αἱ δυνάμεις τῶν οὐρανῶν σαλευθήσονται.
And the powers of the heavens will be shaken.

30 Καὶ τότε φανήσεται τὸ σημεῖον τοῦ Υἱοῦ τοῦ Ἀνθρώπου
And then will appear the sign of the Son - of Man

ἐν τῷ οὐρανῷ, καὶ τότε κόψονται πᾶσαι αἱ φυλαὶ τῆς γῆς
in - heaven, (the sky,) and then [7]will [8]mourn [1]all [2]the [3]tribes [4]of [5]the [6]earth

καὶ ὄψονται τὸν Υἱὸν τοῦ Ἀνθρώπου ἐρχόμενον ἐπὶ τῶν
and they will see the Son - of Man coming on the

νεφελῶν τοῦ οὐρανοῦ μετὰ δυνάμεως καὶ δόξης πολλῆς.
clouds - of heaven (the sky) with power and glory ˜ much.

31 Καὶ ἀποστελεῖ τοὺς ἀγγέλους αὐτοῦ μετὰ σάλπιγγος
And He will send - angels ˜ His with [4]of [5]a [6]trumpet

φωνῆς[e] μεγάλης, καὶ ἐπισυνάξουσι τοὺς ἐκλεκτοὺς
[1]*the* [3]sound [2]great, (loud,) and they will gather together - elect ˜ (chosen ones)

αὐτοῦ ἐκ τῶν τεσσάρων ἀνέμων, ἀπ᾽ ἄκρων
His from the four winds, from *the* farthest parts

οὐρανῶν ἕως ἄκρων αὐτῶν.
of *the* heavens as far as *the* farthest parts of them.

The Parable of the Fig Tree
(Mark 13:28–31; Luke 21:29–33)

32 "Ἀπὸ δὲ τῆς συκῆς μάθετε τὴν παραβολήν· ὅταν
"from ˜ Now the fig tree learn the (this) parable: whenever

ἤδη ὁ κλάδος αὐτῆς γένηται ἁπαλὸς καὶ τὰ φύλλα
[3]already - [2]branch [1]its becomes tender and [4]the [5]leaves

ἐκφύῃ, γινώσκετε ὅτι ἐγγὺς τὸ θέρος. 33 Οὕτω καὶ
[1]it [2]puts [3]forth, you know that [2]*is* [3]near - [1]summer. Thus (In this way) also

ὑμεῖς, ὅταν ἴδητε ταῦτα πάντα, γινώσκετε ὅτι ἐγγύς
you, whenever you see [2]these [3]*things* [1]all, know that [3]near

ἐστιν ἐπὶ θύραις. 34 Ἀμὴν λέγω ὑμῖν, οὐ μὴ
[1]it [2]is at *the* doors. Amen (Assuredly) I say to you, [4]not [5]not (by no means)

παρέλθῃ ἡ γενεὰ αὕτη ἕως ἂν πάντα ταῦτα
[3]will [6]pass [7]away - [2]generation [1]this till - all these *things*

γένηται. 35 Ὁ οὐρανὸς καὶ ἡ γῆ παρελεύσονται, οἱ δὲ
happen. - Heaven and - earth will pass away, - but

λόγοι μου οὐ μὴ παρέλθωσι.
words ˜ My [2]not [3]not (by no means) [1]will [4]pass [5]away.

No One Knows the Day or Hour
(Mark 13:32–37; Luke 17:26–30, 34–36)

36 "Περὶ δὲ τῆς ἡμέρας ἐκείνης καὶ ὥρας οὐδεὶς
"concerning ˜ But - day ˜ that and hour no one

οἶδεν, οὐδὲ οἱ ἄγγελοι τῶν οὐρανῶν,[f] εἰ μὴ ὁ Πατήρ
knows, not even the angels of the heavens, if not (but only) - Father ˜

μου[g] μόνος. 37 Ὥσπερ δὲ αἱ ἡμέραι τοῦ Νῶε, οὕτως
My alone. [2]just [3]as [1]But *were* the days - of Noah, so

will fall from heaven, and the powers of the heavens will be shaken.
30 "Then the sign of the Son of Man will appear in heaven, and then all the tribes of the earth will mourn, and they will see the Son of Man coming on the clouds of heaven with power and great glory.
31 "And He will send His angels with a great sound of a trumpet, and they will gather together His elect from the four winds, from one end of heaven to the other.
32 "Now learn this parable from the fig tree: When its branch has already become tender and puts forth leaves, you know that summer *is* near.
33 "So you also, when you see all these things, know that it is near—at the doors!
34 "Assuredly, I say to you, this generation will by no means pass away till all these things take place.
35 "Heaven and earth will pass away, but My words will by no means pass away.
36 "But of that day and hour no one knows, not even the angels of heaven, but My Father only.
37 "But as the days of Noah

---

[e] **(24:31)** NU omits *φωνης, (the) sound.*
[f] **(24:36)** NU adds *ουδε ο Υιος, nor the Son.*
[g] **(24:36)** NU omits *μου, my.*

were, so also will the coming of the Son of Man be.
38 "For as in the days before the flood, they were eating and drinking, marrying and giving in marriage, until the day that Noah entered the ark,
39 "and did not know until the flood came and took them all away, so also will the coming of the Son of Man be.
40 "Then two *men* will be in the field: one will be taken and the other left.
41 "Two *women will be* grinding at the mill: one will be taken and the other left.
42 "Watch therefore, for you do not know what hour your Lord is coming.
43 "But know this, that if the master of the house had known what hour the thief would come, he would have watched and not allowed his house to be broken into.
44 "Therefore you also be ready, for the Son of Man is coming at an hour you do not expect.
45 "Who then is a faithful and wise servant, whom his master made ruler over his household, to give them food in due season?
46 "Blessed *is* that servant whom his master, when he comes, will find so doing.

ἔσται καὶ[h] ἡ παρουσία τοῦ Υἱοῦ τοῦ Ἀνθρώπου.
will be also the coming of the Son - of Man.

38 Ὥσπερ γὰρ ἦσαν ἐν ταῖς ἡμέραις[i] ταῖς πρὸ τοῦ
[2]just [3]as [1]For they were in the days - before the

κατακλυσμοῦ τρώγοντες καὶ πίνοντες, γαμοῦντες καὶ
flood eating and drinking, marrying and

ἐκγαμίζοντες, ἄχρι ἧς ἡμέρας εἰσῆλθε Νῶε εἰς τὴν
giving in marriage, until which day entered ˜ Noah into the
the

κιβωτόν, 39 καὶ οὐκ ἔγνωσαν ἕως ἦλθεν ὁ
ark, and [3]not [1]they [2]did know *a thing* until [3]came [1]the

κατακλυσμὸς καὶ ἦρεν ἅπαντας, οὕτως ἔσται καὶ ἡ
[2]flood and took away *them* all, so will be also the

παρουσία τοῦ Υἱοῦ τοῦ Ἀνθρώπου. 40 Τότε δύο ἔσονται
coming of the Son - of Man. Then two *men* will be

ἐν τῷ ἀγρῷ· ὁ εἷς παραλαμβάνεται καὶ ὁ εἷς ἀφίεται.
in the field; - one is taken and - one is left.
will be will be

41 Δύο ἀλήθουσαι ἐν τῷ μύλωνι· μία παραλαμβάνεται
Two *women will be* grinding at the mill; one is taken
will be

καὶ μία ἀφίεται. 42 Γρηγορεῖτε* οὖν, ὅτι οὐκ
and one is left. Be watchful therefore, because [3]not
will be

οἴδατε ποίᾳ ὥρᾳ[j] ὁ Κύριος ὑμῶν ἔρχεται. 43 Ἐκεῖνο
[1]you [2]do know in what hour - Lord ˜ your is coming. [3]that
this

δὲ γινώσκετε, ὅτι εἰ ᾔδει ὁ οἰκοδεσπότης ποίᾳ
[1]But [2]know, that if [6]knew [1]the [2]master [3]of [4]the [5]house in what
had known

φυλακῇ ὁ κλέπτης ἔρχεται, ἐγρηγόρησεν ἂν καὶ οὐκ
watch the thief is coming, he would have kept watch - and [3]not
was

ἂν εἴασε διορυγῆναι τὴν οἰκίαν αὐτοῦ.
- [1]he [2]would [4]have [5]allowed [8]to [9]be [10]dug [11]through [7]house [6]his.
broken into

44 Διὰ τοῦτο καὶ ὑμεῖς γίνεσθε ἕτοιμοι, ὅτι ᾗ
On account of this also ˜ you be ready, because in which
Therefore at an

ὥρᾳ οὐ δοκεῖτε ὁ Υἱὸς τοῦ Ἀνθρώπου ἔρχεται.
hour [3]not [1]you [2]do suppose the Son - of Man is coming.
hour which

The Challenge to Faithful Service
(Luke 12:41–48)

45 "Τίς ἄρα ἐστὶν ὁ πιστὸς δοῦλος καὶ φρόνιμος ὃν
"Who then is the faithful [3]slave [1]and [2]prudent whom
servant

κατέστησεν ὁ κύριος αὐτοῦ ἐπὶ τῆς θεραπείας[k] αὐτοῦ τοῦ
[3]appointed - [2]master [1]his over - service ˜ his -
corps of servants

διδόναι αὐτοῖς τὴν τροφὴν ἐν καιρῷ? 46 Μακάριος ὁ δοῦλος
to give them - food in season? Blessed *is* - slave ˜
at the right time? servant

ἐκεῖνος ὃν ἐλθὼν ὁ κύριος αὐτοῦ εὑρήσει ποιοῦντα
that whom coming - master ˜ his will find doing
when he comes

[h](24:37) NU omits και, *also.* [i](24:38) NU adds in brackets εκειναις, *those.* [j](24:42) NU reads ημερα, *day.* [k](24:45) NU reads οικετειας, *household slaves.*

*(24:42) γρηγορέω (*grēgoreō*). Verb meaning either literally *be* or *keep awake* (as possibly in v. 43 and parallels) or figuratively *be watchful* or *be alert, watch* (as here in v. 42). No NT usage appears to be entirely without some sense of being watchful, on guard, vigilant. The word came to be used more or less absolutely as a Christian virtue (1 Cor. 16:13) and to designate watchful preparedness for the Lord's return (Rev. 16:15; see also Col. 4:2). In 1 Thess. 5:10 it takes on the metaphorical meaning of being alive.

οὕτως. 47 Ἀμὴν λέγω ὑμῖν ὅτι ἐπὶ πᾶσι τοῖς
so. Amen I say to you that [5]over [6]all [7]the [8]*things*
Assuredly his

ὑπάρχουσιν αὐτοῦ καταστήσει αὐτόν. 48 Ἐὰν δὲ
[9]belonging [10]of [11]him [1]he [2]will [3]appoint [4]him. if ˜ But
possessions

εἴπῃ ὁ κακὸς δοῦλος ἐκεῖνος ἐν τῇ καρδίᾳ αὐτοῦ,
[4]should [5]say - [2]bad [3]slave [1]that in - heart ˜ his,
servant

'Χρονίζει ὁ κύριός μου ἐλθεῖν,'[l] 49 καὶ ἄρξηται τύπτειν
'[3]is [4]delaying - [2]master [1]My to come,' and should begin to beat

τοὺς συνδούλους, ἐσθίειν δὲ καὶ πίνειν μετὰ τῶν
the fellow slaves, [2]to [3]eat [1]and and to drink with the *ones*
his fellow servants, drunkards,

μεθυόντων, 50 ἥξει ὁ κύριος τοῦ δούλου ἐκείνου ἐν
being drunk, [6]will [7]come [1]the [2]master - [3]of [5]slave [4]that on
servant

ἡμέρᾳ ᾗ οὐ προσδοκᾷ καὶ ἐν ὥρᾳ ᾗ οὐ
a day which [3]not [1]he [2]does expect and in an hour which [3]not

γινώσκει, 51 καὶ διχοτομήσει αὐτόν, καὶ τὸ μέρος αὐτοῦ
[1]he [2]does know, and he will cut [2]in [3]two [1]him, and - [4]share [3]his

μετὰ τῶν ὑποκριτῶν θήσει. Ἐκεῖ ἔσται ὁ κλαυθμὸς
[5]with [6]the [7]hypocrites [1]will [2]appoint. There *there* will be - weeping

καὶ ὁ βρυγμὸς τῶν ὀδόντων.
and - gnashing - of teeth.

The Parable of the Wise and Foolish Virgins

25 1 "Τότε ὁμοιωθήσεται ἡ βασιλεία τῶν οὐρανῶν
"Then [6]will [7]be [8]compared [1]the [2]kingdom [3]of [4]the [5]heavens

δέκα παρθένοις, αἵτινες λαβοῦσαι τὰς λαμπάδας αὐτῶν
to ten virgins, who taking - lamps ˜ their
bridesmaids,

ἐξῆλθον εἰς ἀπάντησιν τοῦ νυμφίου. 2 Πέντε δὲ ἦσαν ἐξ
went out to *the* meeting of the bridegroom. five ˜ Now [3]were [1]of
to meet

αὐτῶν φρόνιμοι καὶ αἱ πέντε μωραί. 3 Αἵτινες[a] μωραί,
[2]them prudent and - five foolish. Those who *were* foolish,

λαβοῦσαι τὰς λαμπάδας αὐτῶν, οὐκ ἔλαβον μεθ' ἑαυτῶν
taking - lamps ˜ their, not ˜ did take [2]with [3]them

ἔλαιον· 4 αἱ δὲ φρόνιμοι ἔλαβον ἔλαιον ἐν τοῖς ἀγγείοις
[1]oil; the ˜ but prudent *ones* took oil in - vessels ˜

αὐτῶν μετὰ τῶν λαμπάδων αὐτῶν. 5 Χρονίζοντος δὲ τοῦ
their with - lamps ˜ their. delaying But the
But while the bridegroom

νυμφίου, ἐνύσταξαν πᾶσαι καὶ ἐκάθευδον.
bridegroom, they dozed ˜ all and slept.
delayed,

6 "Μέσης δὲ νυκτὸς κραυγὴ γέγονεν,
"[2]*in* [3]*the* [4]middle [1]And of *the* night [4]a [5]cry [1]there [2]has [3]been,
was,

'Ἰδού, ὁ νυμφίος ἔρχεται![b] Ἐξέρχεσθε εἰς ἀπάντησιν
'Behold, the bridegroom is coming! Go out to *the* meeting
to meet

αὐτοῦ.' 7 Τότε ἠγέρθησαν πᾶσαι αἱ παρθένοι ἐκεῖναι καὶ
of him.' Then [4]were [5]raised [1]all - [3]virgins [2]those and
him.' arose bridesmaids

ἐκόσμησαν τὰς λαμπάδας αὐτῶν. 8 Αἱ δὲ μωραὶ ταῖς
they trimmed - lamps ˜ their. the ˜ And foolish *ones* [2]to [3]the

47 "Assuredly, I say to you that he will make him ruler over all his goods.
48 "But if that evil servant says in his heart, 'My master is delaying his coming,'
49 "and begins to beat *his* fellow servants, and to eat and drink with the drunkards,
50 "the master of that servant will come on a day when he is not looking for *him* and at an hour that he is not aware of,
51 "and will cut him in two and appoint *him* his portion with the hypocrites. There shall be weeping and gnashing of teeth.

25 "Then the kingdom of heaven shall be likened to ten virgins who took their lamps and went out to meet the bridegroom.
2 "Now five of them were wise, and five *were* foolish.
3 "Those who *were* foolish took their lamps and took no oil with them,
4 "but the wise took oil in their vessels with their lamps.
5 "But while the bridegroom was delayed, they all slumbered and slept.
6 "And at midnight a cry was *heard*: 'Behold, the bridegroom is coming; go out to meet him!'
7 "Then all those virgins arose and trimmed their lamps.
8 "And the foolish said to the

[l](24:48) NU omits ελθειν, *to come.* [a](25:3) NU reads αι γαρ, *for the.*
[b](25:6) NU omits ερχεται, *is coming.*

wise, 'Give us *some* of your oil,
for our lamps are going out.'
9 "But the wise answered,
saying, '*No,* lest there should
not be enough for us and you;
but go rather to those who sell,
and buy for yourselves.'
10 "And while they went to
buy, the bridegroom came, and
those who were ready went in
with him to the wedding; and
the door was shut.
11 "Afterward the other virgins came also, saying, 'Lord,
lord, open to us!'
12 "But he answered and said,
'Assuredly, I say to you, I do
not know you.'
13 "Watch therefore, for you
know neither the day nor the
hour in which the Son of Man is
coming.
14 "For *the kingdom of heaven*
is like a man traveling to a far
country, *who* called his own
servants and delivered his
goods to them.
15 "And to one he gave five
talents, to another two, and to
another one, to each according
to his own ability; and immediately he went on a journey.
16 "Then he who had received
the five talents went and traded
with them, and made another
five talents.
17 "And likewise he who *had*
received two gained two more
also.
18 "But he who had received
one went and dug in the

φρονίμοις εἶπον, 'Δότε ἡμῖν ἐκ τοῦ ἐλαίου ὑμῶν, ὅτι
[4]prudent [5]*ones* [1]said, 'Give us *some* of - oil ˜ your, because

αἱ λαμπάδες ἡμῶν σβέννυνται.' 9 Ἀπεκρίθησαν δὲ αἱ
- lamps ˜ our are being extinguished.' [5]answered [1]But [2]the
going out.'

φρόνιμοι, λέγουσαι, 'Μήποτε οὐκ ἀρκέσῃ ἡμῖν καὶ
[3]prudent [4]*ones,* saying, '*No,* lest not ˜ *there* be enough for you and

ὑμῖν· πορεύεσθε δὲ μᾶλλον πρὸς τοὺς πωλοῦντας καὶ
for us; go ˜ but rather to the *ones* selling and
those who sell

ἀγοράσατε ἑαυταῖς.' 10 Ἀπερχομένων δὲ αὐτῶν
buy for yourselves.' going away But them
But as they were going away

ἀγοράσαι, ἦλθεν ὁ νυμφίος, καὶ αἱ ἕτοιμοι εἰσῆλθον
to buy, [3]came [1]the [2]bridegroom, and the ready *ones* went in
those who were ready

μετ' αὐτοῦ εἰς τοὺς γάμους, καὶ ἐκλείσθη ἡ θύρα.
with him to the marriage feast, and [3]was [4]shut [1]the [2]door.
wedding,

11 "Ὕστερον δὲ ἔρχονται καὶ αἱ λοιπαὶ παρθένοι,
"later ˜ But come also the remaining virgins,
came bridesmaids,

λέγουσαι, 'Κύριε, κύριε, ἄνοιξον ἡμῖν.' 12 Ὁ δὲ
saying, 'Lord, lord, open for us.' [2]the [3]*one* [1]But
he

ἀποκριθεὶς εἶπεν, 'Ἀμὴν λέγω ὑμῖν, οὐκ οἶδα ὑμᾶς.'
answering said, 'Amen I say to you, [3]not [1]I [2]do know you.'
'Assuredly

13 Γρηγορεῖτε οὖν, ὅτι οὐκ οἴδατε τὴν ἡμέραν
Be watchful therefore, because [3]not [1]you [2]do know the day

οὐδὲ τὴν ὥραν[c] ἐν ᾗ ὁ Υἱὸς τοῦ Ἀνθρώπου ἔρχεται.
nor the hour in which the Son - of Man is coming.

The Parable of the Talents
(Luke 19:11–27)

14 "Ὥσπερ γὰρ ἄνθρωπος ἀποδημῶν
"[2]*the* [3]*kingdom* [4]*is* [5]just [6]like [1]For a man going on a journey

ἐκάλεσε τοὺς ἰδίους δούλους καὶ παρέδωκεν αὐτοῖς τὰ
who called - his own slaves and handed over to them the *things*
servants his

ὑπάρχοντα αὐτοῦ. 15 Καὶ ᾧ μὲν ἔδωκε πέντε τάλαντα,*
belonging of him. And to the one - he gave five talents,
possessions.

ᾧ δὲ δύο, ᾧ δὲ ἕν, ἑκάστῳ κατὰ
[2]to [3]the [4]other [1]and two, [2]to [3]the [4]other [1]and one, to each according to

τὴν ἰδίαν δύναμιν, καὶ ἀπεδήμησεν εὐθέως.
- his own power, and he went on a journey immediately.
ability,

16 Πορευθεὶς δὲ ὁ τὰ πέντε τάλαντα λαβὼν
[8]going [1]Then [2]the [3]*one* [5]the [6]five [7]talents [4]receiving
went and

εἰργάσατο ἐν αὐτοῖς καὶ ἐποίησεν[d] ἄλλα πέντε τάλαντα.[e]
worked with them and made other ˜ five talents.
traded

17 Ὡσαύτως καὶ ὁ τὰ δύο ἐκέρδησε καὶ αὐτὸς[f]
Likewise also the *one receiving* the two gained also ˜ he

ἄλλα δύο. 18 Ὁ δὲ τὸ ἓν λαβὼν ἀπελθὼν ὤρυξεν
others ˜ two. [2]the [3]*one* [1]But - [5]one [4]receiving going off dug
went away and

---

[c](**25:13**) NU omits the rest of v. 13.
[d](**25:16**) NU reads εκερδησεν, *gained.*
[e](**25:16**) NU omits ταλαντα, *talents.* [f](**25:17**) NU omits και αυτος, *he also.*

***(25:15)** τάλαντον *(talanton).* Noun meaning *talent,* a unit of weight or coinage occurring in the NT only in this parable and in Matt. 18:24. The weight of the talent varied from 58 to 80 pounds, and the monetary value depended on whether the corresponding weight was in gold or silver. Its value was great. One denarius (δραχμή) was a typical day's wage for laborers, and some sources suggest that the Roman-Attic talent equaled 6,000 denarii in NT times. Cf. the cognate adjective ταλαντιαῖος, *weighing a talent,* occurring only in Rev. 16:21.

ἐν τῇ γῇ καὶ ἀπέκρυψε τὸ ἀργύριον τοῦ κυρίου αὐτοῦ.
in the ground and hid the silver - of master ˜ his.
money

19 "Μετὰ δὲ χρόνον πολὺν ἔρχεται ὁ κύριος τῶν
"after ˜ Then time ˜ much [6]comes [1]the [2]master -
came

δούλων ἐκείνων καὶ συναίρει μετ' αὐτῶν λόγον. 20 Καὶ
[3]of [5]slaves [4]those and settles with them *the* account. And
servants settled accounts with them.

προσελθὼν ὁ τὰ πέντε τάλαντα λαβὼν
[7]approaching [1]the [2]*one* [4]the [5]five [6]talents [3]receiving
approached and who received

προσήνεγκεν ἄλλα πέντε τάλαντα, λέγων, 'Κύριε, πέντε
brought other ˜ five talents, saying, 'Master, [4]five
more

τάλαντά μοι παρέδωκας· ἴδε, ἄλλα πέντε τάλαντα
[5]talents [6]to [7]me [1]you [2]handed [3]over; look, other ˜ five talents
more

ἐκέρδησα ἐπ' αὐτοῖς.'[g] 21 Ἔφη δὲ αὐτῷ ὁ κύριος αὐτοῦ,
I gained besides them.' [4]said [1]And [5]to [6]him - [3]master [2]his,

'Εὖ, δοῦλε ἀγαθὲ καὶ πιστέ, ἐπὶ ὀλίγα ἦς
'Well *done,* [4]slave [1]good [2]and [3]faithful, over a few *things* you were
servant

πιστός, ἐπὶ πολλῶν σε καταστήσω. Εἴσελθε εἰς τὴν χαρὰν
faithful, over many *things* [4]you [1]I [2]will [3]appoint. Enter into the joy

τοῦ κυρίου σου.'
- of master ˜ your.'

22 "Προσελθὼν δὲ καὶ ὁ τὰ δύο τάλαντα λαβὼν[h]
"[9]approaching [1]And [2]also [3]the [4]*one* [6]the [7]two [8]talents [5]receiving
"approached and

εἶπε, 'Κύριε, δύο τάλαντά μοι παρέδωκας· ἴδε, ἄλλα
said, 'Master, two talents [4]to [5]me [1]you [2]handed [3]over; look, other ˜
more

δύο τάλαντα ἐκέρδησα ἐπ' αὐτοῖς.'[i] 23 Ἔφη αὐτῷ ὁ
two talents I gained besides them.' [3]said [4]to [5]him -

κύριος αὐτοῦ, 'Εὖ, δοῦλε ἀγαθὲ καὶ πιστέ, ἐπὶ ὀλίγα
[2]master ˜ [1]His, 'Well *done,* [4]slave ˜ [1]good [2]and [3]faithful, over a few *things*
servant

ἦς πιστός, ἐπὶ πολλῶν σε καταστήσω. Εἴσελθε εἰς
you were faithful, over many *things* [4]you [1]I [2]will [3]appoint. Enter into

τὴν χαρὰν τοῦ κυρίου σου.'
the joy - of master ˜ your.'

24 "Προσελθὼν δὲ καὶ ὁ τὸ ἓν τάλαντον
"[10]approaching [1]And [2]also [3]the [4]*one* [7]the [8]one [9]talent
"approached and

εἰληφὼς εἶπε, 'Κύριε, ἔγνων σε ὅτι σκληρὸς εἶ
[5]having [6]received said, 'Master, I knew you that [4]hard [1]you [2]are

ἄνθρωπος, θερίζων ὅπου οὐκ ἔσπειρας καὶ συνάγων ὅθεν οὐ
[3]a [5]man, reaping where [3]not [1]you [2]did sow and gathering where [3]not

διεσκόρπισας. 25 Καὶ φοβηθεὶς ἀπελθὼν ἔκρυψα τὸ
[1]you [2]did scatter. And being afraid going off I hid -
I went off and

τάλαντόν σου ἐν τῇ γῇ· ἴδε, ἔχεις τὸ σόν.'
talent ˜ your in the ground; look, you have the *thing* *of* yours.'
what is yours.'

26 Ἀποκριθεὶς δὲ ὁ κύριος αὐτοῦ εἶπεν αὐτῷ, 'Πονηρὲ δοῦλε
answering ˜ But - master ˜ his said to him, 'Evil [3]slave
servant

καὶ ὀκνηρέ, ᾔδεις ὅτι θερίζω ὅπου οὐκ ἔσπειρα καὶ συνάγω
[1]and [2]lazy, you knew that I reap where [3]not [1]I [2]did sow and I gather

ground, and hid his lord's money.
19 "After a long time the lord of those servants came and settled accounts with them.
20 "So he who had received five talents came and brought five other talents, saying, 'Lord, you delivered to me five talents; look, I have gained five more talents besides them.'
21 "His lord said to him, 'Well *done,* good and faithful servant; you were faithful over a few things, I will make you ruler over many things. Enter into the joy of your lord.'
22 "He also who had received two talents came and said, 'Lord, you delivered to me two talents; look, I have gained two more talents besides them.'
23 "His lord said to him, 'Well *done,* good and faithful servant; you have been faithful over a few things, I will make you ruler over many things. Enter into the joy of your lord.'
24 "Then he who had received the one talent came and said, 'Lord, I knew you to be a hard man, reaping where you have not sown, and gathering where you have not scattered seed.
25 'And I was afraid, and went and hid your talent in the ground. Look, *there* you have *what is* yours.'
26 "But his lord answered and said to him, 'You wicked and lazy servant, you knew that I reap where I have not sown, and gather where I have not

---

[g](25:20) NU omits *επ αυτοις, besides them.*
[h](25:22) NU omits *λαβων, receiving.*
[i](25:22) NU omits *επ αυτοις, besides them.*

scattered seed.
27 'So you ought to have deposited my money with the bankers, and at my coming I would have received back my own with interest.
28 'Therefore take the talent from him, and give *it* to him who has ten talents.
29 'For to everyone who has, more will be given, and he will have abundance; but from him who does not have, even what he has will be taken away.
30 'And cast the unprofitable servant into the outer darkness. There will be weeping and gnashing of teeth.'
31 "When the Son of Man comes in His glory, and all the holy angels with Him, then He will sit on the throne of His glory.
32 "All the nations will be gathered before Him, and He will separate them one from another, as a shepherd divides *his* sheep from the goats.
33 "And He will set the sheep on His right hand, but the goats on the left.
34 "Then the King will say to those on His right hand, 'Come, you blessed of My Father, inherit the kingdom prepared for you from the foundation of the world:
35 'for I was hungry and you gave Me food; I was thirsty and you gave Me drink; I was a stranger and you took Me in;
36 'I *was* naked and you clothed Me; I was sick and you

ὅθεν οὐ διεσκόρπισα. **27** *Ἔδει οὖν σε*
where [3]not [1]I [2]did scatter. it was necessary *for* Therefore you
Therefore you should

βαλεῖν τὸ ἀργύριόν μου τοῖς τραπεζίταις, καὶ ἐλθὼν
to put - silver ˜ my with the bankers, and coming
have put my money at my coming

ἐγὼ ἐκομισάμην ἂν τὸ ἐμὸν σὺν τόκῳ. **28** *Ἄρατε*
I would have received - the *thing of* mine with interest. take ˜
what is mine

οὖν ἀπ' αὐτοῦ τὸ τάλαντον καὶ δότε τῷ ἔχοντι τὰ
Therefore from him the talent and give *it* to the *one* having the

δέκα τάλαντα. **29** *Τῷ γὰρ ἔχοντι παντὶ δοθήσεται καὶ*
ten talents. - For to having ˜ every*one more* will be given and

περισσευθήσεται· ἀπὸ δὲ τοῦ μὴ ἔχοντος, καὶ ὃ ἔχει
he will have abundance; from ˜ but the *one* not having, even what he has

ἀρθήσεται ἀπ' αὐτοῦ. **30** *Καὶ τὸν ἀχρεῖον δοῦλον*
will be taken away from him. And [3]the [4]useless [5]slave
servant

ἐκβάλετε εἰς τὸ σκότος τὸ ἐξώτερον. Ἐκεῖ ἔσται ὁ
[1]throw [2]out into the darkness - outside. There *there* will be -

κλαυθμὸς καὶ ὁ βρυγμὸς τῶν ὀδόντων.'
weeping and - gnashing - of teeth.'

The Son of Man Will Judge the Nations

31 *"Ὅταν δὲ ἔλθῃ ὁ Υἱὸς τοῦ Ἀνθρώπου ἐν τῇ δόξῃ*
"when ˜ And [5]comes [1]the [2]Son - [3]of [4]Man in - glory ˜

αὐτοῦ καὶ πάντες οἱ ἅγιοι[j] *ἄγγελοι μετ' αὐτοῦ, τότε καθίσει*
His and all the holy angels with Him, then He will sit

ἐπὶ θρόνου δόξης αὐτοῦ. **32** *Καὶ συναχθήσεται ἔμπροσθεν*
on *the* throne of glory ˜ His. And [4]will [5]be [6]gathered [7]before
His glorious throne.

αὐτοῦ πάντα τὰ ἔθνη, καὶ ἀφοριεῖ αὐτοὺς ἀπ'
[8]Him [1]all [2]the [3]nations, and He will separate them from
Gentiles,

ἀλλήλων, ὥσπερ ὁ ποιμὴν ἀφορίζει τὰ πρόβατα ἀπὸ τῶν
one another, just as the shepherd separates the sheep from the
a

ἐρίφων. **33** *Καὶ στήσει τὰ μὲν πρόβατα ἐκ δεξιῶν αὐτοῦ,*
goats. And He will set the - sheep at [2]right [3]*parts* [1]His,
on right side

τὰ δὲ ἐρίφια ἐξ εὐωνύμων.
the ˜ but goats at *the* left *parts.*
on His left side.

34 *"Τότε ἐρεῖ ὁ βασιλεὺς τοῖς ἐκ δεξιῶν αὐτοῦ,*
"Then [3]will [4]say [1]the [2]King to the *ones* at [2]right [3]*parts* [1]His,
those on right side

'Δεῦτε, οἱ εὐλογημένοι τοῦ Πατρός μου, κληρονομήσατε τὴν
'Come, the blessed - of Father ˜ My, inherit the
you

ἡτοιμασμένην ὑμῖν βασιλείαν ἀπὸ καταβολῆς
[2]having [3]been [4]prepared [5]for [6]you [1]kingdom from *the* foundation
prepared

κόσμου. **35** *Ἐπείνασα γὰρ καὶ ἐδώκατέ μοι φαγεῖν,*
of *the* world. [2]I [3]was [4]hungry [1]For and you gave Me to eat,

ἐδίψησα καὶ ἐποτίσατέ με, ξένος ἤμην καὶ
I was thirsty and you gave drink ˜ Me, [3]a [4]stranger [1]I [2]was and

συνηγάγετέ με, **36** *γυμνὸς καὶ περιεβάλετέ με, ἠσθένησα καὶ*
you took in ˜ Me, naked and you clothed Me, I was ill and

[j](25:31) NU omits *αγιοι*, *holy*.

ἐπεσκέψασθέ με, ἐν φυλακῇ ἤμην καὶ ἤλθετε πρός με.'
you visited Me, [3]in [4]prison [1]I [2]was and you came to Me.'

37 Τότε ἀποκριθήσονται αὐτῷ οἱ δίκαιοι, λέγοντες, 'Κύριε,
Then [3]will [4]answer [5]Him [1]the [2]righteous, saying, 'Lord,

πότε σε εἴδομεν πεινῶντα καὶ ἐθρέψαμεν, ἢ διψῶντα καὶ
when [4]You [1]did [2]we [3]see hungering and we fed *You,* or thirsting and

ἐποτίσαμεν? 38 Πότε δέ σε εἴδομεν ξένον καὶ
we gave *You* drink? when ˜ And [4]You [1]did [2]we [3]see a stranger and

συνηγάγομεν, ἢ γυμνὸν καὶ περιεβάλομεν? 39 Πότε δέ σε
we took *You* in, or naked and we clothed *You?* when ˜ And [4]You

εἴδομεν ἀσθενῆ[k] ἢ ἐν φυλακῇ καὶ ἤλθομεν πρός σε?'
[1]did [2]we [3]see ill or in prison and we came to You?'

40 Καὶ ἀποκριθεὶς ὁ βασιλεὺς ἐρεῖ αὐτοῖς, ''Ἀμὴν λέγω
And answering the King will say to them, 'Amen I say
'Assuredly

ὑμῖν, ἐφ' ὅσον ἐποιήσατε ἑνὶ τούτων τῶν ἀδελφῶν μου
to you, inasmuch as you did *it* to one [4]of [5]these - [7]brothers [6]My

τῶν ἐλαχίστων, ἐμοὶ ἐποιήσατε.'
[1]of [2]the [3]least, [11]to [12]Me [8]you [9]did [10]*it.*'

41 "Τότε ἐρεῖ καὶ τοῖς ἐξ εὐωνύμων, 'Πορεύεσθε
"Then He will say also to the ones at the left parts, 'Go
those on His left side,

ἀπ' ἐμοῦ, οἱ κατηραμένοι, εἰς τὸ πῦρ τὸ αἰώνιον τὸ
from Me, the *ones* having been cursed, into the fire ˜ - eternal the one
you cursed, which

ἡτοιμασμένον τῷ διαβόλῳ καὶ τοῖς ἀγγέλοις αὐτοῦ.
having been prepared for the devil and - for angels ˜ his.
was

42 Ἐπείνασα γὰρ καὶ οὐκ ἐδώκατέ μοι φαγεῖν,
[2]I [3]was [4]hungry [1]For and [3]not [1]you [2]did give Me to eat,

ἐδίψησα καὶ οὐκ ἐποτίσατέ με, 43 ξένος
I was thirsty and [3]not [1]you [2]did [4]give [6]to [7]drink [5]Me, [3]a [4]stranger

ἤμην καὶ οὐ συνηγάγετέ με, γυμνὸς καὶ οὐ περιεβάλετέ
[1]I [2]was and [3]not [1]you [2]did [4]take [6]in [5]Me, naked and [3]not [1]you [2]did clothe

με, ἀσθενὴς καὶ ἐν φυλακῇ καὶ οὐκ ἐπεσκέψασθέ με.'
Me, ill and in prison and [3]not [1]you [2]did visit Me.'

44 Τότε ἀποκριθήσονται[l] καὶ αὐτοί, λέγοντες, 'Κύριε, πότε
Then [3]will [4]answer [2]also [1]they, saying, 'Lord, when

σε εἴδομεν πεινῶντα ἢ διψῶντα ἢ ξένον ἢ γυμνὸν ἢ
[4]You [1]did [2]we [3]see hungering or thirsting or a stranger or naked or

ἀσθενῆ ἢ ἐν φυλακῇ καὶ οὐ διηκονήσαμέν σοι?' 45 Τότε
ill or in prison and [3]not [1]we [2]did minister to You?' Then

ἀποκριθήσεται αὐτοῖς, λέγων, ''Ἀμὴν λέγω ὑμῖν, ἐφ' ὅσον
He will answer them, saying, 'Amen I say to you, inasmuch as
'Assuredly

οὐκ ἐποιήσατε ἑνὶ τούτων τῶν ἐλαχίστων, οὐδὲ ἐμοὶ
[3]not [1]you [2]did do *it* to one [4]of [5]these [1]of [2]the [3]least, neither [5]to [6]Me

ἐποιήσατε.' 46 Καὶ ἀπελεύσονται οὗτοι εἰς κόλασιν
[1]did [2]you [3]do [4]*it.*' And [2]will [3]go [4]away [1]these into punishment ˜

αἰώνιον,* οἱ δὲ δίκαιοι εἰς ζωὴν αἰώνιον."
eternal, the ˜ but righteous into life ˜ eternal."

26

1 Καὶ ἐγένετο ὅτε ἐτέλεσεν ὁ Ἰησοῦς πάντας τοὺς
And it happened when finished ˜ - Jesus all -

λόγους τούτους, εἶπε τοῖς μαθηταῖς αὐτοῦ, 2 "Οἴδατε ὅτι
words ˜ these, He said - to disciples ˜ His, "You know that
sayings

μετὰ δύο ἡμέρας τὸ Πάσχα γίνεται, καὶ ὁ Υἱὸς τοῦ
after two days the Passover takes place, and the Son -

visited Me; I was in prison and
you came to Me.'
37 "Then the righteous will
answer Him, saying, 'Lord,
when did we see You hungry
and feed *You,* or thirsty and
give *You* drink?
38 'When did we see You a
stranger and take *You* in, or naked and clothe *You?*
39 'Or when did we see You
sick, or in prison, and come to
You?'
40 "And the King will answer
and say to them, 'Assuredly, I
say to you, inasmuch as you did
it to one of the least of these
My brethren, you did *it* to Me.'
41 "Then He will also say to
those on the left hand, 'Depart
from Me, you cursed, into the
everlasting fire prepared for the
devil and his angels:
42 'for I was hungry and you
gave Me no food; I was thirsty
and you gave Me no drink;
43 'I was a stranger and you
did not take Me in, naked and
you did not clothe Me, sick and
in prison and you did not visit
Me.'
44 "Then they also will answer Him, saying, 'Lord, when
did we see You hungry or
thirsty or a stranger or naked
or sick or in prison, and did not
minister to You?'
45 "Then He will answer
them, saying, 'Assuredly, I say
to you, inasmuch as you did not
do *it* to one of the least of
these, you did not do *it* to Me.'
46 "And these will go away
into everlasting punishment,
but the righteous into eternal
life."

26 Now it came to pass,
when Jesus had fin-
ished all these sayings, *that* He
said to His disciples,
2 "You know that after two
days is the Passover, and the

[k]**(25:39)** NU reads *ασθενουντα, ailing.*
[l]**(25:44)** TR adds *αυτω, Him.*

***(25:46)** *αἰώνιος (aiōnios).* Adjective meaning *eternal, everlasting,* used often in the NT. It may mean *without end* when applied to the redemptive life (or death) experienced by man (as here, where the NKJV "everlasting" and "eternal" both translate the word; cf. John 3:16). However, when applied to God it means *without beginning or end* (Rom. 14:25 in M; 16:26 in NU, TR). In a few instances, modifying "times," it looks to the

Son of Man will be delivered up
to be crucified."
3 Then the chief priests, the
scribes, and the elders of the
people assembled at the palace
of the high priest, who was
called Caiaphas,
4 and plotted to take Jesus
by trickery and kill *Him.*
5 But they said, "Not during
the feast, lest there be an uproar among the people."
6 And when Jesus was in
Bethany at the house of Simon
the leper,
7 a woman came to Him having an alabaster flask of very
costly fragrant oil, and she
poured *it* on His head as He sat
at the table.
8 But when His disciples saw
it, they were indignant, saying,
"Why this waste?
9 "For this fragrant oil might
have been sold for much and
given to *the* poor."
10 But when Jesus was aware
of *it,* He said to them, "Why do
you trouble the woman? For
she has done a good work for
Me.
11 "For you have the poor
with you always, but Me you do
not have always.
12 "For in pouring this fragrant oil on My body, she did *it*

Ἀνθρώπου παραδίδοται εἰς τὸ σταυρωθῆναι."
of Man is handed over - - to be crucified."
will be

The Chief Priests and Elders Plot to Kill Jesus

(Mark 14:1, 2; Luke 22:1, 2; John 11:45–53)

3 Τότε συνήχθησαν οἱ ἀρχιερεῖς καὶ οἱ γραμματεῖς[a]
Then were assembled the high priests and the scribes

καὶ οἱ πρεσβύτεροι τοῦ λαοῦ εἰς τὴν αὐλὴν τοῦ ἀρχιερέως
and the elders of the people into the court of the high priest

τοῦ λεγομένου Καϊάφα **4** καὶ συνεβουλεύσαντο ἵνα τὸν
the *one* being called Caiaphas and they plotted so that -
who was called

Ἰησοῦν δόλῳ κρατήσωσι καὶ ἀποκτείνωσιν.
[4]Jesus [5]by [6]deceit [1]they [2]might [3]seize and they might kill *Him.*
trickery

5 Ἔλεγον δέ, "Μὴ ἐν τῇ ἑορτῇ, ἵνα μὴ θόρυβος
[2]they [3]said [1]But, "Not in the feast, in order that not a disturbance
during lest

γένηται ἐν τῷ λαῷ."
take place among the people."

Jesus Is Anointed at Bethany

(Mark 14:3–9; John 12:1–8)

6 Τοῦ δὲ Ἰησοῦ γενομένου ἐν Βηθανίᾳ ἐν οἰκίᾳ
- And Jesus being in Bethany in *the* house
while Jesus was

Σίμωνος τοῦ λεπροῦ, **7** προσῆλθεν αὐτῷ γυνὴ
of Simon the leper, [3]approached [4]Him [1]a [2]woman

ἀλάβαστρον μύρου ἔχουσα βαρυτίμου καὶ
[6]an [7]alabaster [8]*flask* [9]of [12]perfume [5]having [10]very [11]expensive and

κατέχεεν ἐπὶ τὴν κεφαλὴν αὐτοῦ ἀνακειμένου.
she was pouring *it* on - head ~ His reclining *to eat.*
began to pour as He reclined to eat.

8 Ἰδόντες δὲ οἱ μαθηταὶ αὐτοῦ ἠγανάκτησαν,
seeing But - disciples ~ His they were indignant,
But when His disciples saw it,

λέγοντες, "Εἰς τί ἡ ἀπώλεια αὕτη? **9** Ἠδύνατο γὰρ
saying, "To what *purpose* - *is* waste ~ this? [4]was [5]able [1]For
could have

τοῦτο τὸ μύρον[b] πραθῆναι πολλοῦ καὶ δοθῆναι πτωχοῖς."
[2]this - [3]perfume to be sold for much and to be given to *the* poor."
been have been

10 Γνοὺς δὲ ὁ Ἰησοῦς εἶπεν αὐτοῖς, "Τί
knowing *it* But - Jesus He said to them, "Why
But when Jesus became aware of it,

κόπους παρέχετε τῇ γυναικί? Ἔργον γὰρ καλὸν
[4]troubles [1]are [2]you [3]causing to the woman? a work For good
For she has worked a

εἰργάσατο εἰς ἐμέ. **11** Τοὺς πτωχοὺς γὰρ πάντοτε ἔχετε
she worked for Me. [5]the [6]poor [1]For [3]always [2]you [4]have
beautiful work

μεθ' ἑαυτῶν, ἐμὲ δὲ οὐ πάντοτε ἔχετε. **12** Βαλοῦσα
with yourselves, [7]Me [1]but [4]not [5]always [2]you [3]do [6]have. [4]having [5]put
you,

γὰρ αὕτη τὸ μύρον τοῦτο ἐπὶ τοῦ σώματός μου πρὸς τὸ
[1]For [2]this [3]*woman* - perfume ~ this on - body ~ My - -

---

a(**26:3**) NU omits *και οι γραμματεις, and the scribes.* *b*(**26:9**) NU omits *το μυρον, the perfume.*

past "before time began," as 2 Tim. 1:9. Cf. the cognate noun *αἰών, age, time,* which may refer to the present age or the age to come.

ἐνταφιάσαι με ἐποίησεν. 13 Ἀμὴν λέγω ὑμῖν, ὅπου ἐὰν
[4]to [5]bury [6]Me [1]she [2]did [3]*it*. Amen I say to you, where ever
for My burial Assuredly

κηρυχθῇ τὸ εὐαγγέλιον τοῦτο ἐν ὅλῳ τῷ κόσμῳ,
[3]is [4]proclaimed - [2]gospel [1]this in whole ~ the world,

λαληθήσεται καὶ ὃ ἐποίησεν αὕτη εἰς μνημόσυνον
[5]will [7]be [8]spoken [6]also [1]what [4]did [2]this [3]*woman* for a memory

αὐτῆς."
of her."

Judas Agrees to Betray Jesus for Money
(Mark 14:10, 11; Luke 22:3–6)

14 Τότε πορευθεὶς εἷς τῶν δώδεκα, ὁ λεγόμενος
Then going one of the twelve, the *one* being called
went called

Ἰούδας Ἰσκαριώτης, πρὸς τοὺς ἀρχιερεῖς, 15 εἶπε, "Τί
Judas Iscariot, to the high priests, he said, "What
and

θέλετέ μοι δοῦναι κἀγὼ ὑμῖν παραδώσω αὐτόν?"
are you willing [3]me [1]to [2]give and I [5]to [6]you [1]will [2]hand [4]over [3]Him?"
so that

Οἱ δὲ ἔστησαν αὐτῷ τριάκοντα ἀργύρια. 16 Καὶ ἀπὸ
[8]the [9]*ones* [7]And set for Him thirty silver *coins*. And from
they weighed out

τότε ἐζήτει εὐκαιρίαν ἵνα αὐτὸν παραδῷ.
then *on* he was seeking an opportunity so that [4]Him [1]he [2]might [3]hand [5]over.
betray.

Jesus Celebrates Passover with His Disciples
(Mark 14:12–21; Luke 22:7–13, 21–23; John 13:21–30)

17 Τῇ δὲ πρώτῃ τῶν ἀζύμων προσῆλθον οἱ
[2]on [3]the [1]Now first *day* - of Unleavened Bread [3]approached [1]the

μαθηταὶ τῷ Ἰησοῦ, λέγοντες αὐτῷ,[c] "Ποῦ θέλεις
[2]disciples - [4]Jesus, saying to Him, "Where do You desire

ἑτοιμάσομέν σοι φαγεῖν τὸ Πάσχα?"
that we shall prepare for You to eat the Passover?"

18 Ὁ δὲ εἶπεν, "Ὑπάγετε εἰς τὴν πόλιν πρὸς τὸν
[2]the [3]*One* [1]And said, "Go into the city to -
He

δεῖνα καὶ εἴπατε αὐτῷ, 'Ὁ διδάσκαλος λέγει, "Ὁ καιρός
such a one and say to him, 'The Teacher says, - "time ~

μου ἐγγύς ἐστι· πρὸς σὲ ποιῶ τὸ Πάσχα μετὰ τῶν
My near ~ is; with you I am doing the Passover with -
at your house I will keep

μαθητῶν μου." ' " 19 Καὶ ἐποίησαν οἱ μαθηταὶ ὡς συνέταξεν
disciples ~ My." ' " And [3]did [1]the [2]disciples as [2]directed

αὐτοῖς ὁ Ἰησοῦς, καὶ ἡτοίμασαν τὸ Πάσχα.
[3]them - [1]Jesus, and they prepared the Passover.

20 Ὀψίας δὲ γενομένης, ἀνέκειτο μετὰ τῶν
evening ~ And becoming, He was reclining *to eat* with the
And when it was evening,

δώδεκα. 21 Καὶ ἐσθιόντων αὐτῶν, εἶπεν, "Ἀμὴν λέγω
twelve. And eating ~ them, He said, "Amen I say
while they were eating, "Assuredly

ὑμῖν ὅτι εἷς ἐξ ὑμῶν παραδώσει με."
to you that one of you will hand over ~ Me."
betray

22 Καὶ λυπούμενοι σφόδρα ἤρξαντο λέγειν αὐτῷ
And becoming sorrowful ~ exceedingly they [4]began [5]to [6]say [7]to [8]Him

for My burial.
13 "Assuredly, I say to you,
wherever this gospel is
preached in the whole world,
what this woman has done will
also be told as a memorial to
her."
14 Then one of the twelve,
called Judas Iscariot, went to
the chief priests
15 and said, "What are you
willing to give me if I deliver
Him to you?" And they counted
out to him thirty pieces of silver.
16 So from that time he
sought opportunity to betray
Him.
17 Now on the first *day of the*
Feast of Unleavened Bread the
disciples came to Jesus, saying
to Him, "Where do You want us
to prepare for You to eat the
Passover?"
18 And He said, "Go into the
city to a certain man, and say to
him, 'The Teacher says, "My
time is at hand; I will keep the
Passover at your house with
My disciples." ' "
19 So the disciples did as Jesus had directed them; and
they prepared the Passover.
20 When evening had come,
He sat down with the twelve.
21 Now as they were eating,
He said, "Assuredly, I say to
you, one of you will betray
Me."
22 And they were exceedingly
sorrowful, and each of them be-

[c](26:17) NU omits *αυτω*, *to him*.

gan to say to Him, "Lord, is it I?"
23 He answered and said, "He who dipped *his* hand with Me in the dish will betray Me.
24 "The Son of Man indeed goes just as it is written of Him, but woe to that man by whom the Son of Man is betrayed! It would have been good for that man if he had not been born."
25 Then Judas, who was betraying Him, answered and said, "Rabbi, is it I?" He said to him, "You have said it."
26 And as they were eating, Jesus took bread, blessed and broke *it*, and gave *it* to the disciples and said, "Take, eat; this is My body."
27 Then He took the cup, and gave thanks, and gave *it* to them, saying, "Drink from it, all of you.
28 "For this is My blood of the new covenant, which is shed for many for the remission of sins.
29 "But I say to you, I will not drink of this fruit of the vine from now on until that day when I drink it new with you in My Father's kingdom."
30 And when they had sung a hymn, they went out to the Mount of Olives.

ἕκαστος αὐτῶν,[d] "Μήτι ἐγώ εἰμι, Κύριε?"
[1]each [2]of [3]them, "*Surely* [3]not [1]I [2]am *the one,* Lord?"

23 Ὁ δὲ ἀποκριθεὶς εἶπεν, "Ὁ ἐμβάψας μετ'
[2]the [3]One [1]And answering said, "The *one* having dipped [3]with
He answered and

ἐμοῦ ἐν τῷ τρυβλίῳ τὴν χεῖρα, οὗτός με παραδώσει.
[4]Me [5]in [6]the [7]bowl [1]the [2]hand, this *one* [3]Me [1]will [2]hand over.
his betray.

24 Ὁ μὲν Υἱὸς τοῦ Ἀνθρώπου ὑπάγει καθὼς γέγραπται
the ˜ Indeed Son - of Man goes just as it is written

περὶ αὐτοῦ, οὐαὶ δὲ τῷ ἀνθρώπῳ ἐκείνῳ δι' οὗ ὁ Υἱὸς
about Him, woe ˜ but - to man ˜ that through whom the Son

τοῦ Ἀνθρώπου παραδίδοται! Καλὸν ἦν αὐτῷ εἰ οὐκ
- of Man is handed over! good It was for him if not
betrayed! It would have been better

ἐγεννήθη ὁ ἄνθρωπος ἐκεῖνος."
was born - man that."
for that man not to have been born."

25 Ἀποκριθεὶς δὲ Ἰούδας ὁ παραδιδοὺς αὐτὸν εἶπε,
answering ˜ And Judas the *one* handing over ˜ Him said,
betraying

"Μήτι ἐγώ εἰμι, Ῥαββί?" Λέγει αὐτῷ, "Σὺ εἶπας."
"*Surely* [3]not [1]I [2]am *the one,* Rabbi?" He says to him, "You said *it.*"
said

Jesus Institutes the Lord's Supper

(Mark 14:22–26; Luke 22:14–20; 1 Cor. 11:23–25)

26 Ἐσθιόντων δὲ αὐτῶν, λαβὼν ὁ Ἰησοῦς τὸν ἄρτον καὶ
eating And them, taking ˜ - Jesus the bread and
And as they were eating, Jesus took

εὐχαριστήσας,[e] ἔκλασε καὶ ἐδίδου τοῖς μαθηταῖς καὶ εἶπε,
giving thanks, He broke *it* and gave *it* to the disciples and said,

"Λάβετε, φάγετε, τοῦτό ἐστι τὸ σῶμά μου."
"Take, eat, this is - body ˜ My."

27 Καὶ λαβὼν τὸ[f] ποτήριον καὶ εὐχαριστήσας, ἔδωκεν
And taking the cup and giving thanks, He gave *it*
He took gave thanks, and

αὐτοῖς, λέγων, "Πίετε ἐξ αὐτοῦ πάντες, **28** τοῦτο γάρ ἐστι τὸ
to them, saying, "Drink of it all *of you,* this ˜ for is -

αἷμά μου τὸ τῆς καινῆς[g] διαθήκης τὸ περὶ πολλῶν
blood ˜ My the *blood* of the new covenant the *blood* [3]for [4]many
which

ἐκχυνόμενον εἰς ἄφεσιν ἁμαρτιῶν. **29** Λέγω δὲ ὑμῖν ὅτι
[1]being [2]shed for forgiveness of sins. [2]I [3]say [1]But to you that
is shed

οὐ μὴ πίω ἀπ' ἄρτι ἐκ τούτου τοῦ γεννήματος τῆς
not not will I drink from now *on* of this - fruit of the
by no means

ἀμπέλου ἕως τῆς ἡμέρας ἐκείνης ὅταν αὐτὸ πίνω μεθ' ὑμῶν
vine until - day ˜ that when [3]it [1]I [2]drink with you

καινὸν ἐν τῇ βασιλείᾳ τοῦ Πατρός μου."
new in the kingdom - of Father ˜ My."

30 Καὶ ὑμνήσαντες ἐξῆλθον εἰς τὸ Ὄρος τῶν
And having sung hymns they went out to the Mount -

Ἐλαιῶν.
of Olives.

---

[d](**26:22**) NU reads *εις εκαστος, each one.*
[e](**26:26**) TR, NU read *ευλογησας, blessing.*
[f](**26:27**) NU omits *το, the.*
[g](**26:28**) NU omits *καινης, new.*

Jesus Predicts Peter's Denial
(Mark 14:27–31; Luke 22:31–34; John 13:36–38)

31 Τότε λέγει αὐτοῖς ὁ Ἰησοῦς, "Πάντες ὑμεῖς
Then [2]says [3]to [4]them - [1]Jesus, "all ~ You
said

σκανδαλισθήσεσθε ἐν ἐμοὶ ἐν τῇ νυκτὶ ταύτῃ,
will be made to stumble in Me on - night ~ this,
because of

γέγραπται γάρ,
[2]it [3]is [4]written [1]for,

«Πατάξω τὸν Ποιμένα,
«I will strike the Shepherd,

Καὶ διασκορπισθήσεται τὰ πρόβατα τῆς ποίμνης.»[h]
And [6]will [7]be [8]scattered [1]the [2]sheep [3]of [4]the [5]flock.»

32 Μετὰ δὲ τὸ ἐγερθῆναί με προάξω ὑμᾶς εἰς τὴν
after ~ But - to be raised Me I will go before you to -
I am raised

Γαλιλαίαν."
Galilee."

33 Ἀποκριθεὶς δὲ ὁ Πέτρος εἶπεν αὐτῷ, "Εἰ[i] πάντες
answering ~ But - Peter said to Him, "If all

σκανδαλισθήσονται ἐν σοί, ἐγὼ δὲ[j] οὐδέποτε
will be made to stumble in You, I ~ yet never ~
because of

σκανδαλισθήσομαι."
will be made to stumble."

34 Ἔφη αὐτῷ ὁ Ἰησοῦς, "Ἀμὴν λέγω σοι ὅτι ἐν ταύτῃ
[2]said [3]to [4]him - [1]Jesus, "Amen I say to you that on this
"Assuredly

τῇ νυκτί, πρὶν ἀλέκτορα φωνῆσαι, τρὶς ἀπαρνήσῃ με."
- night, before a rooster to sound, three times you will deny Me."
crows,

35 Λέγει αὐτῷ ὁ Πέτρος, "Κἂν δέῃ με σὺν
[2]says [3]to [4]Him - [1]Peter, "Even if it is necessary *for* me [3]with
said

σοὶ ἀποθανεῖν, οὐ μή σε ἀπαρνήσωμαι." Ὁμοίως δὲ
[4]You [1]to [2]die, not not [4]You [1]will [2]I [3]deny." likewise ~ And
by no means

καὶ πάντες οἱ μαθηταὶ εἶπον.
also all the disciples said.

Jesus Prays in the Garden of Gethsemane
(Mark 14:32–42; Luke 22:39–46)

36 Τότε ἔρχεται μετ' αὐτῶν ὁ Ἰησοῦς εἰς χωρίον λεγόμενον
Then [2]comes [3]with [4]them - [1]Jesus to a place being called
came called

Γεθσημανῆ, καὶ λέγει τοῖς μαθηταῖς, "Καθίσατε αὐτοῦ ἕως
Gethsemane, and He says to the disciples, "Sit here while
said

οὗ ἀπελθὼν προσεύξωμαι ἐκεῖ." **37** Καὶ παραλαβὼν τὸν
- going away I pray there." And taking along -
I go off and pray

Πέτρον καὶ τοὺς δύο υἱοὺς Ζεβεδαίου ἤρξατο λυπεῖσθαι καὶ
Peter and the two sons of Zebedee He began to be sorrowful and

ἀδημονεῖν. **38** Τότε λέγει αὐτοῖς ὁ Ἰησοῦς,[k]
to be distressed. Then [2]says [3]to [4]them - [1]Jesus,
said

31 Then Jesus said to them, "All of you will be made to stumble because of Me this night, for it is written:

'I will strike the Shepherd,
And the sheep of the
flock will be scattered.'

32 "But after I have been raised, I will go before you to Galilee."
33 Peter answered and said to Him, "Even if all are made to stumble because of You, I will never be made to stumble."
34 Jesus said to him, "Assuredly, I say to you that this night, before the rooster crows, you will deny Me three times."
35 Peter said to Him, "Even if I have to die with You, I will not deny You!" And so said all the disciples.
36 Then Jesus came with them to a place called Gethsemane, and said to the disciples, "Sit here while I go and pray over there."
37 And He took with Him Peter and the two sons of Zebedee, and He began to be sorrowful and deeply distressed.
38 Then He said to them, "My

[h]**(26:31)** Zech. 13:7
[i]**(26:33)** TR adds και, *even.*
[j]**(26:33)** TR, NU omit δε, *yet.* [k]**(26:38)** TR, NU omit ο Ιησους, *Jesus.*

soul is exceedingly sorrowful,
even to death. Stay here and
watch with Me."
39 He went a little farther and
fell on His face, and prayed,
saying, "O My Father, if it is
possible, let this cup pass from
Me; nevertheless, not as I will,
but as You *will.*"
40 Then He came to the disciples and found them sleeping,
and said to Peter, "What?
Could you not watch with Me
one hour?
41 "Watch and pray, lest you
enter into temptation. The
spirit indeed *is* willing, but the
flesh *is* weak."
42 Again, a second time, He
went away and prayed, saying,
"O My Father, if this cup cannot pass away from Me unless I
drink it, Your will be done."
43 And He came and found
them asleep again, for their
eyes were heavy.
44 So He left them, went
away again, and prayed the
third time, saying the same
words.
45 Then He came to His disciples and said to them, "Are *you*
still sleeping and resting? Behold, the hour is at hand, and
the Son of Man is being betrayed into the hands of sinners.
46 "Rise, let us be going. See,
My betrayer is at hand."

"Περίλυπός ἐστιν ἡ ψυχή μου ἕως θανάτου. Μείνατε
"[8]deeply [9]grieved [7]is - [6]soul [5]My unto death. Stay
to the point of

ὧδε καὶ γρηγορεῖτε μετ' ἐμοῦ." **39** Καὶ προσελθὼν μικρὸν
here and watch with Me." And approaching *God* a little *way*

ἔπεσεν ἐπὶ πρόσωπον αὐτοῦ προσευχόμενος καὶ λέγων,
He fell on face ˜ His praying and saying,

"Πάτερ μου, εἰ δυνατόν ἐστι, παρελθέτω ἀπ' ἐμοῦ τὸ
"Father ˜ My, if [3]possible [1]it [2]is, [4]let [7]pass [8]from [9]Me -

ποτήριον τοῦτο· πλὴν οὐχ ὡς ἐγὼ θέλω ἀλλ' ὡς σύ."
[6]cup [5]this; nevertheless not as I will but as You *will.*"

40 Καὶ ἔρχεται πρὸς τοὺς μαθητὰς καὶ εὑρίσκει αὐτοὺς
And He comes to the disciples and finds them
came found

καθεύδοντας, καὶ λέγει τῷ Πέτρῳ, "Οὕτως οὐκ
sleeping, and He says - to Peter, "So [3]not
said

ἰσχύσατε μίαν ὥραν γρηγορῆσαι μετ' ἐμοῦ?
[1]were [2]you [4]strong [5]*enough* [8]one [9]hour [6]to [7]watch with Me?

41 Γρηγορεῖτε καὶ προσεύχεσθε, ἵνα μὴ εἰσέλθητε εἰς
Watch and pray, that not you enter into
lest

πειρασμόν. Τὸ μὲν πνεῦμα πρόθυμον, ἡ δὲ σὰρξ
temptation. the ˜ Indeed spirit *is* eager, the ˜ but flesh

ἀσθενής."
is weak."

42 Πάλιν ἐκ δευτέρου ἀπελθὼν προσηύξατο, λέγων,
Again out of a second going away He prayed, saying,
a second time

"Πάτερ μου, εἰ οὐ δύναται τοῦτο τὸ ποτήριον[l] παρελθεῖν ἀπ'
"Father ˜ My, if [4]not [3]is [5]able [1]this - [2]cup to pass from

ἐμοῦ[m] ἐὰν μὴ αὐτὸ πίω, γενηθήτω τὸ θέλημά σου."
Me if not [3]it [1]I [2]drink, [4]let [7]be [8]done - [6]will [5]Your."
unless

43 Καὶ ἐλθὼν εὑρίσκει αὐτοὺς πάλιν καθεύδοντας, ἦσαν γὰρ
And coming He finds them again sleeping, [4]were [1]for
found

αὐτῶν οἱ ὀφθαλμοὶ βεβαρημένοι. **44** Καὶ ἀφεὶς αὐτοὺς
[2]their - [3]eyes weighed down. And leaving them

ἀπελθὼν πάλιν προσηύξατο ἐκ τρίτου, τὸν αὐτὸν λόγον
going away again He prayed out of a third, [2]the [3]same [4]word
He went and prayed a third time, thing

εἰπών. **45** Τότε ἔρχεται πρὸς τοὺς μαθητὰς αὐτοῦ καὶ λέγει
[1]saying. Then He comes to - disciples ˜ His and says
came said

αὐτοῖς, "Καθεύδετε τὸ λοιπὸν καὶ ἀναπαύεσθε. Ἰδού,
to them, "Sleep *for* the remainder and rest. See,
now

ἤγγικεν ἡ ὥρα καὶ ὁ Υἱὸς τοῦ Ἀνθρώπου
[3]has [4]come [5]near [1]the [2]hour and the Son - of Man

παραδίδοται εἰς χεῖρας ἁμαρτωλῶν. **46** Ἐγείρεσθε,
is being handed over into *the* hands of sinners. Rise up,
betrayed

ἄγωμεν. Ἰδού, ἤγγικεν ὁ παραδιδούς με."
let us be going. See, [6]has [7]come [8]near [1]the [2]*one* [3]handing [5]over [4]Me."
who betrays

[l](26:42) NU omits το ποτηριον, *cup.*
[m](26:42) NU omits απ εμου, *from me.*

Jesus Is Betrayed and Arrested in Gethsemane
(Mark 14:43–50; Luke 22:47–53; John 18:3–12)

47 Καὶ ἔτι αὐτοῦ λαλοῦντος, ἰδού,* Ἰούδας εἷς τῶν
And still Him speaking, behold, Judas one of the
while He was still speaking,

δώδεκα ἦλθε, καὶ μετ' αὐτοῦ ὄχλος πολὺς μετὰ μαχαιρῶν καὶ
twelve came, and with him a crowd ˜ large with swords and

ξύλων ἀπὸ τῶν ἀρχιερέων καὶ πρεσβυτέρων τοῦ λαοῦ.
clubs *sent* from the high priests and elders of the people.

48 Ὁ δὲ παραδιδοὺς αὐτὸν ἔδωκεν αὐτοῖς σημεῖον,
[2]the [3]*one* [1]Now handing over ˜ Him gave them a sign,
betraying had given

λέγων, "Ὃν ἂν φιλήσω, αὐτός ἐστι· κρατήσατε αὐτόν."
saying, "Whom ever I shall kiss, He is *the One;* seize Him."

49 Καὶ εὐθέως προσελθὼν τῷ Ἰησοῦ εἶπε, "Χαῖρε,
And immediately coming to - Jesus he said, "Rejoice,
approaching "Greetings,

Ῥαββί!" Καὶ κατεφίλησεν αὐτόν.
Rabbi!" And he affectionately kissed Him.

50 Ὁ δὲ Ἰησοῦς εἶπεν αὐτῷ, "Ἑταῖρε, ἐφ' ᾧ
- But Jesus said to him, "Friend, upon what
why

πάρει?" Τότε προσελθόντες ἐπέβαλον τὰς χεῖρας ἐπὶ τὸν
are you here?" Then approaching they laid - hands on -

Ἰησοῦν καὶ ἐκράτησαν αὐτόν. **51** Καὶ ἰδού, εἷς τῶν μετὰ
Jesus and seized Him. And behold, one of the ones with
those

Ἰησοῦ, ἐκτείνας τὴν χεῖρα, ἀπέσπασε τὴν μάχαιραν αὐτοῦ,
Jesus, stretching out the hand, drew - sword ˜ his,
his

καὶ πατάξας τὸν δοῦλον τοῦ ἀρχιερέως ἀφεῖλεν αὐτοῦ τὸ
and striking the slave of the high priest he cut off his -
servant

ὠτίον. **52** Τότε λέγει αὐτῷ ὁ Ἰησοῦς, "Ἀπόστρεψόν σου τὴν
ear. Then [2]says [3]to [4]him - [1]Jesus, "Put back your -
said

μάχαιραν εἰς τὸν τόπον αὐτῆς, πάντες γὰρ οἱ λαβόντες
sword into - place ˜ its, all ˜ for the ones taking
those who take

μάχαιραν ἐν μαχαίρᾳ ἀποθανοῦνται.[n] **53** Ἢ δοκεῖς ὅτι
a sword [3]by [4]a [5]sword [1]will [2]die. Or do you think that
the the

οὐ δύναμαι ἄρτι παρακαλέσαι τὸν Πατέρα μου, καὶ
[3]not [1]I [2]am [5]able [4]now to call upon - Father ˜ My, and

παραστήσει μοι πλείους ἢ δώδεκα λεγεῶνας ἀγγέλων?
He will place beside Me more than twelve legions of angels?
provide

54 Πῶς οὖν πληρωθῶσιν αἱ Γραφαὶ ὅτι οὕτω δεῖ
How then would [3]be [4]fulfilled [1]the [2]Scriptures that thus it is necessary

γενέσθαι?" **55** Ἐν ἐκείνῃ τῇ ὥρᾳ εἶπεν ὁ Ἰησοῦς τοῖς ὄχλοις,
to happen?" In that - hour said ˜ - Jesus to the crowds,
At time

"Ὡς ἐπὶ λῃστὴν ἐξήλθετε μετὰ μαχαιρῶν καὶ ξύλων
"As against a bandit did you come out with swords and clubs
have

συλλαβεῖν με? Καθ' ἡμέραν πρὸς ὑμᾶς[o] ἐκαθεζόμην
to arrest Me? According to a day with you I was sitting
Daily used to sit

47 And while He was still speaking, behold, Judas, one of the twelve, with a great multitude with swords and clubs, came from the chief priests and elders of the people.
48 Now His betrayer had given them a sign, saying, "Whomever I kiss, He is the One; seize Him."
49 Immediately he went up to Jesus and said, "Greetings, Rabbi!" and kissed Him.
50 But Jesus said to him, "Friend, why have you come?" Then they came and laid hands on Jesus and took Him.
51 And suddenly, one of those *who were* with Jesus stretched out *his* hand and drew his sword, struck the servant of the high priest, and cut off his ear.
52 But Jesus said to him, "Put your sword in its place, for all who take the sword will perish by the sword.
53 "Or do you think that I cannot now pray to My Father, and He will provide Me with more than twelve legions of angels?
54 "How then could the Scriptures be fulfilled, that it must happen thus?"
55 In that hour Jesus said to the multitudes, "Have you come out, as against a robber, with swords and clubs to take Me? I sat daily with you, teach-

---

n(26:52) TR, NU read *απολουνται, will perish.*
o(26:55) NU omits *προς υμας, with you.*

---

*(26:47) *ἰδού (idou).* A very frequent word in the NT, usually translated *behold* or *look.* In Greek grammar it is classed as a demonstrative particle, but in English grammar it could be called an interjection. *ἰδού* is used to direct attention to some person, object, or idea. Its force is normally emphatic, like the English exclamation "Look!" It can also at times approximate the street expressions "Check it out!" or "See for yourself!" Consequently *ἰδού* can be used not only in ordinary situations (Luke 14:2, "And behold, there was a certain man . . ."), but also for weighty declarations (1 Cor. 15:51, "Behold, I show you a mystery . . ."). The frequency of *ἰδού* in the NT suggests that it was a feature of every-

ing in the temple, and you did
not seize Me.
56 "But all this was done that
the Scriptures of the prophets
might be fulfilled." Then all the
disciples forsook Him and fled.
57 And those who had laid
hold of Jesus led *Him* away to
Caiaphas the high priest, where
the scribes and the elders were
assembled.
58 But Peter followed Him at
a distance to the high priest's
courtyard. And he went in and
sat with the servants to see the
end.
59 Now the chief priests, the
elders, and all the council
sought false testimony against
Jesus to put Him to death,
60 but found none. Even
though many false witnesses
came forward, they found none.
But at last two false witnesses
came forward
61 and said, "This *fellow* said,
'I am able to destroy the temple
of God and to build it in three
days.'"
62 And the high priest arose
and said to Him, "Do You answer nothing? What *is it* these
men testify against You?"
63 But Jesus kept silent. And
the high priest answered and
said to Him, "I put You under
oath by the living God: Tell us if
You are the Christ, the Son of
God!"
64 Jesus said to him, "*It is* as
you said. Nevertheless, I say to
you, hereafter you will see the
Son of Man sitting at the right

διδάσκων ἐν τῷ ἱερῷ καὶ οὐκ ἐκρατήσατέ με. **56** Τοῦτο δὲ
teaching in the temple and [3]not [1]you [2]did [4]seize [5]Me. this ~ But

ὅλον γέγονεν ἵνα πληρωθῶσιν αἱ Γραφαὶ τῶν
whole *thing* has happened so that [6]may [7]be [8]fulfilled [1]the [2]Scriptures [3]of [4]the

προφητῶν." Τότε οἱ μαθηταὶ πάντες ἀφέντες αὐτὸν ἔφυγον.
[5]prophets." Then [2]the [3]disciples [1]all leaving Him fled.
forsook Him and

Jesus Before the Sanhedrin

(Mark 14:53–65; Luke 22:54, 55, 63–71; John 18:13, 14, 19–24)

57 Οἱ δὲ κρατήσαντες τὸν Ἰησοῦν ἀπήγαγον πρὸς
[2]the [3]*ones* [1]And having seized - Jesus led *Him* away to

Καϊάφαν τὸν ἀρχιερέα, ὅπου οἱ γραμματεῖς καὶ οἱ
Caiaphas the high priest, where the scribes and the

πρεσβύτεροι συνήχθησαν. **58** Ὁ δὲ Πέτρος ἠκολούθει αὐτῷ
elders were assembled. - But Peter was following Him

ἀπὸ μακρόθεν ἕως τῆς αὐλῆς τοῦ ἀρχιερέως. Καὶ εἰσελθὼν
from a distance up to the courtyard of the high priest. And entering

ἔσω ἐκάθητο μετὰ τῶν ὑπηρετῶν ἰδεῖν τὸ τέλος. **59** Οἱ δὲ
inside he sat down with the attendants to see the end. the ~ And

ἀρχιερεῖς καὶ οἱ πρεσβύτεροι[p] καὶ τὸ συνέδριον ὅλον
high priests and the elders and the council ~ whole

ἐζήτουν ψευδομαρτυρίαν κατὰ τοῦ Ἰησοῦ ὅπως
were seeking false witnesses against - Jesus so that

θανατώσωσιν αὐτόν, **60** καὶ οὐχ εὗρον. Καὶ[q]
they might put [2]to [3]death [1]Him, and [3]not [1]they [2]did find *any*. And

πολλῶν ψευδομαρτύρων προσελθόντων, οὐχ εὗρον.[r]
many false witnesses coming forward, [3]not [1]they [2]did find *any*.
though many came

Ὕστερον δὲ προσελθόντες δύο ψευδομάρτυρες[s] **61** εἶπον,
later ~ But [4]coming [5]forward [1]two [2]false [3]witnesses said,
came and said,

"Οὗτος ἔφη, 'Δύναμαι καταλῦσαι τὸν ναὸν τοῦ Θεοῦ καὶ
"This *man* said, 'I am able to destroy the temple - of God and

διὰ τριῶν ἡμερῶν οἰκοδομῆσαι αὐτόν.'"
after three days to build it.'"
rebuild

62 Καὶ ἀναστὰς ὁ ἀρχιερεὺς εἶπεν αὐτῷ, "Οὐδὲν
And standing up the high priest said to Him, "[4]nothing

ἀποκρίνῃ? Τί οὗτοί σου καταμαρτυροῦσιν?"
[1]Do [2]You [3]answer? What [2]these [3]*men* [6]You [1]are [4]testifying [5]against?"

63 Ὁ δὲ Ἰησοῦς ἐσιώπα.
- But Jesus kept silent.

Καὶ ἀποκριθεὶς[t] ὁ ἀρχιερεὺς εἶπεν αὐτῷ, "Ἐξορκίζω
And answering the high priest said to Him, "I put [2]under [3]oath

σε κατὰ τοῦ Θεοῦ τοῦ ζῶντος ἵνα ἡμῖν εἴπῃς εἰ σὺ εἶ ὁ
[1]You by the God ~ - living that [3]us [1]You [2]tell if You are the

Χριστὸς ὁ Υἱὸς τοῦ Θεοῦ."
Christ the Son - of God."
Messiah

64 Λέγει αὐτῷ ὁ Ἰησοῦς, "Σὺ εἶπας. Πλὴν λέγω ὑμῖν,
[2]says [3]to [4]him - [1]Jesus, "You said *it*. But I say to you,
said

ἀπ' ἄρτι ὄψεσθε τὸν Υἱὸν τοῦ Ἀνθρώπου καθήμενον ἐκ
from now *on* you will see the Son - of Man sitting at

---

[p](**26:59**) NU omits *και οι πρεσβυτεροι, and the elders.* [q](**26:60**) NU omits *Και, And.*
[r](**26:60**) NU omits *ουχ ευρον, they did not find (any).* [s](**26:60**) NU omits *ψευδομαρτυρων, false witnesses.*
[t](**26:63**) NU omits *αποκριθεις, answering.*

---

day speech among Greek-speaking Palestinians.

δεξιῶν τῆς Δυνάμεως καὶ ἐρχόμενον ἐπὶ τῶν νεφελῶν τοῦ
the right parts of the Power and coming on the clouds -
hand

οὐρανοῦ."
of heaven."

65 Τότε ὁ ἀρχιερεὺς διέρρηξε τὰ ἱμάτια αὐτοῦ, λέγων ὅτι
Then the high priest tore - clothes ~ his, saying -

"Ἐβλασφήμησεν! Τί ἔτι χρείαν ἔχομεν μαρτύρων? Ἴδε,
"He blasphemed! What [4]still [1]need [2]do [3]we [5]have of witnesses? Look,
has blasphemed!

νῦν ἠκούσατε τὴν βλασφημίαν αὐτοῦ! 66 Τί ὑμῖν
now you heard - blasphemy ~ His! What to you
do

δοκεῖ?"
does it seem?"
you think?"

Οἱ δὲ ἀποκριθέντες εἶπον, "Ἔνοχος θανάτου ἐστί."
[2]the [3]*ones* [1]And answering said, "[3]deserving [4]of [5]death [1]He [2]is."
they

67 Τότε ἐνέπτυσαν εἰς τὸ πρόσωπον αὐτοῦ καὶ
Then they spat in - face ~ His and

ἐκολάφισαν αὐτόν· οἱ δὲ ἐρράπισαν, 68 λέγοντες,
beat [2]with [3]*their* [4]fists [1]Him; [6]the [7]*ones* [5]and slapped *Him,* saying,
they

"Προφήτευσον ἡμῖν, Χριστέ! Τίς ἐστιν ὁ παίσας σε?"
"Prophesy to us, Christ! Who is the *one* having struck You?"
Messiah! who

Peter Denies Jesus—and Weeps Bitterly
(Mark 14:66–72; Luke 22:54–62; John 18:15–18, 25–27)

69 Ὁ δὲ Πέτρος ἔξω ἐκάθητο ἐν τῇ αὐλῇ. Καὶ
- But Peter outside ~ sat in the courtyard. And

προσῆλθεν αὐτῷ μία παιδίσκη, λέγουσα, "Καὶ σὺ ἦσθα μετὰ
[4]approached [5]him [1]one [2]servant [3]girl, saying, "also ~ You were with
a

Ἰησοῦ τοῦ Γαλιλαίου."
Jesus the Galilean."

70 Ὁ δὲ ἠρνήσατο ἔμπροσθεν αὐτῶν[u] πάντων,
[2]the [3]*one* [1]But denied *it* before them all,
he

λέγων, "Οὐκ οἶδα τί λέγεις."
saying, "[3]not [1]I [2]do know what you are saying."

71 Ἐξελθόντα δὲ αὐτὸν εἰς τὸν πυλῶνα, εἶδεν αὐτὸν
going out And him to the gateway, [3]saw [4]him
And when he had gone out

ἄλλη καὶ λέγει αὐτοῖς ἐκεῖ, "Καὶ οὗτος ἦν μετὰ
[1]another [2]*girl* and says to them there, "[3]also [1]This [2]*man* was with
said

Ἰησοῦ τοῦ Ναζωραίου."
Jesus the Nazarene."

72 Καὶ πάλιν ἠρνήσατο μεθ' ὅρκου ὅτι "Οὐκ οἶδα τὸν
And again he denied *it* with an oath - "[3]not [1]I [2]do know the

ἄνθρωπον!"
man!"

73 Μετὰ μικρὸν δὲ προσελθόντες οἱ ἑστῶτες
[2]after [3]a [4]little [5]*while* [1]And [10]approaching [6]the [7]*ones* [8]standing [9]by
came up and

εἶπον τῷ Πέτρῳ, "Ἀληθῶς καὶ σὺ ἐξ αὐτῶν εἶ, καὶ γὰρ ἡ
said - to Peter, "Truly also ~ you [2]of [3]them [1]are, indeed ~ for -

hand of the Power, and coming on the clouds of heaven."
65 Then the high priest tore his clothes, saying, "He has spoken blasphemy! What further need do we have of witnesses? Look, now you have heard His blasphemy!
66 "What do you think?" They answered and said, "He is deserving of death."
67 Then they spat in His face and beat Him; and others struck *Him* with the palms of their hands,
68 saying, "Prophesy to us, Christ! Who is the one who struck You?"
69 Now Peter sat outside in the courtyard. And a servant girl came to him, saying, "You also were with Jesus of Galilee."
70 But he denied it before *them* all, saying, "I do not know what you are saying."
71 And when he had gone out to the gateway, another *girl* saw him and said to those *who were* there, "This *fellow* also was with Jesus of Nazareth."
72 But again he denied with an oath, "I do not know the Man!"
73 And a little later those who stood by came up and said to Peter, "Surely you also are *one*

u(**26:70**) TR, NU omit *αυτων, them.*

of them, for your speech betrays you."
74 Then he began to curse
and swear, *saying,* "I do not
know the Man!" Immediately a
rooster crowed.
75 And Peter remembered
the word of Jesus who had said
to him, "Before the rooster
crows, you will deny Me three
times." So he went out and
wept bitterly.
27 When morning came,
all the chief priests and
elders of the people plotted
against Jesus to put Him to
death.
2 And when they had bound
Him, they led Him away and
delivered Him to Pontius Pilate
the governor.
3 Then Judas, His betrayer,
seeing that He had been condemned, was remorseful and
brought back the thirty pieces
of silver to the chief priests and
elders,
4 saying, "I have sinned by
betraying innocent blood." And
they said, "What *is that* to us?
You see *to it!*"
5 Then he threw down the
pieces of silver in the temple
and departed, and went and
hanged himself.
6 But the chief priests took
the silver pieces and said, "It is
not lawful to put them into the
treasury, because they are the
price of blood."
7 And they consulted to-
gether and bought with them

λαλιά σου δῆλόν σε ποιεῖ."
speech ˜ your [3]evident [2]you [1]makes."
accent gives you away."

74 Τότε ἤρξατο καταθεματίζειν καὶ ὀμνύειν ὅτι "Οὐκ
Then he began to curse and to swear - "[3]not
οἶδα τὸν ἄνθρωπον!" Καὶ εὐθέως ἀλέκτωρ ἐφώνησε.
[1]I [2]do know the man!" And immediately a rooster sounded.
crowed.

75 Καὶ ἐμνήσθη ὁ Πέτρος τοῦ ῥήματος τοῦ Ἰησοῦ εἰρηκότος
And remembered ˜ - Peter the saying - of Jesus having said
which He
αὐτῷ[v] ὅτι "Πρὶν ἀλέκτορα φωνῆσαι, τρὶς ἀπαρνήσῃ
to him - "Before a rooster to sound, three times you will deny
crows,
με." Καὶ ἐξελθὼν ἔξω ἔκλαυσε πικρῶς.
Me." And going out he wept bitterly.

Jesus Is Delivered to Pontius Pilate
(Mark 15:1; Luke 23:1, 2; John 18:28–32)

27 1 Πρωΐας δὲ γενομένης, συμβούλιον ἔλαβον
early morning And coming, [12]counsel [11]took
And when early morning came, plotted
πάντες οἱ ἀρχιερεῖς καὶ οἱ πρεσβύτεροι τοῦ λαοῦ
[1]all [2]the [3]high [4]priests [5]and [6]the [7]elders [8]of [9]the [10]people
κατὰ τοῦ Ἰησοῦ, ὥστε θανατῶσαι αὐτόν. 2 Καὶ δήσαντες
against - Jesus, so as to put [2]to [3]death [1]Him. And having bound
αὐτὸν ἀπήγαγον καὶ παρέδωκαν αὐτὸν Ποντίῳ[a] Πιλάτῳ
Him they led *Him* away and handed over ˜ Him to Pontius Pilate
delivered
τῷ ἡγεμόνι.
the governor.

Judas Hangs Himself
(Acts 1:18, 19)

3 Τότε ἰδὼν Ἰούδας ὁ παραδιδοὺς αὐτὸν ὅτι
Then [7]seeing [1]Judas [2]the [3]*one* [4]handing [6]over [5]Him that
betraying
κατεκρίθη, μεταμεληθεὶς ἀπέστρεψε τὰ τριάκοντα
He was condemned, feeling regret returned the thirty
ἀργύρια τοῖς ἀρχιερεῦσι καὶ τοῖς πρεσβυτέροις, 4 λέγων,
silver *coins* to the high priests and to the elders, saying,
"Ἥμαρτον παραδοὺς αἷμα ἀθῷον."
"I sinned *by* handing over blood ˜ innocent."
have sinned by betraying
Οἱ δὲ εἶπον, "Τί πρὸς ἡμᾶς? Σὺ ὄψει!"
[2]the [3]*ones* [1]But said, "What *is that* to us? You shall see *to it!*"
they

5 Καὶ ῥίψας τὰ ἀργύρια ἐν τῷ ναῷ, ἀνεχώρησε· καὶ
And throwing the silver *coins* in the sanctuary, he departed; and
ἀπελθὼν ἀπήγξατο.
going away he hanged himself.

6 Οἱ δὲ ἀρχιερεῖς λαβόντες τὰ ἀργύρια εἶπον, "Οὐκ
the ˜ But chief priests taking the silver *coins* said, "[3]not
ἔξεστι βαλεῖν αὐτὰ εἰς τὸν κορβανᾶν, ἐπεὶ τιμὴ
[1]It [2]is lawful to put them into the temple treasury, since [3]*the* [4]price
αἵματός ἐστι." 7 Συμβούλιον δὲ λαβόντες ἠγόρασαν ἐξ
[5]of [6]blood [1]they [2]are." [3]counsel [1]And [2]taking they bought with

---

v(**26:75**) NU omits αυτω, *to him.* *a*(**27:2**) NU omits αυτον Ποντιω, *Him (to) Pontius.*

αὐτῶν τὸν ἀγρὸν τοῦ κεραμέως, εἰς ταφὴν τοῖς ξένοις.
them the field of the potter, for a burial - for strangers.

8 Διὸ ἐκλήθη ὁ ἀγρὸς ἐκεῖνος Ἀγρὸς Αἵματος ἕως τῆς
Therefore [3]was [4]called - [2]field [1]that Field of Blood until -

σήμερον. 9 Τότε ἐπληρώθη τὸ ῥηθὲν διὰ Ἱερεμίου
today. Then [8]was [9]fulfilled [1]the [2]*thing* [3]spoken [4]through [5]Jeremiah

τοῦ προφήτου, λέγοντος,
[6]the [7]prophet, saying,

«Καὶ ἔλαβον τὰ τριάκοντα ἀργύρια, τὴν τιμὴν τοῦ
«And they took the thirty silver *coins,* the price of the

τετιμημένου, ὃν ἐτιμήσαντο ἀπὸ υἱῶν
one having been priced, whom they priced from the sons

Ἰσραήλ, 10 καὶ ἔδωκαν αὐτὰ εἰς τὸν ἀγρὸν τοῦ
of Israel, and they gave them for the field of the

κεραμέως, καθὰ συνέταξέ μοι Κύριος.» [b]
potter, just as [3]directed [4]me [1]*the* [2]Lord.»

Jesus Before Pilate

(Mark 15:2–5; Luke 23:3–5; John 18:33–38)

11 Ὁ δὲ Ἰησοῦς ἔστη ἔμπροσθεν τοῦ ἡγεμόνος. Καὶ
- But Jesus stood before the governor. And

ἐπηρώτησεν αὐτὸν ὁ ἡγεμών, λέγων, "Σὺ εἶ ὁ Βασιλεὺς
[3]asked [4]Him [1]the [2]governor, saying, "You ˜ Are the King

τῶν Ἰουδαίων?"
of the Jews?"

Ὁ δὲ Ἰησοῦς ἔφη αὐτῷ, [c] "Σὺ λέγεις." 12 Καὶ
- And Jesus said to him, "You are saying *what is so.*" And

ἐν τῷ κατηγορεῖσθαι αὐτὸν ὑπὸ τῶν ἀρχιερέων καὶ τῶν
in - [2]to [3]be [4]accused [1]Him by the high priests and the
while He was being accused

πρεσβυτέρων οὐδὲν ἀπεκρίνατο.
elders [3]nothing [1]He [2]answered.

13 Τότε λέγει αὐτῷ ὁ Πιλᾶτος, "Οὐκ ἀκούεις
Then [2]says [3]to [4]Him - [1]Pilate, "[7]not [5]Do [6]You [8]hear
said

πόσα σου καταμαρτυροῦσι?" 14 Καὶ οὐκ ἀπεκρίθη
how many *things* [4]You [1]they [2]testify [3]against?" And [3]not [1]He [2]did answer

αὐτῷ πρὸς οὐδὲ ἓν ῥῆμα, ὥστε θαυμάζειν τὸν ἡγεμόνα
him [3]to [1]not [2]even one word, so that to marvel the governor
charge, the governor was amazed

λίαν.
very much.

Give Us Barabbas

(Mark 15:6–15; Luke 23:13–25; John 18:39–19:16)

15 Κατὰ δὲ ἑορτὴν εἰώθει ὁ ἡγεμὼν ἀπολύειν
at ˜ Now a feast [3]was [4]accustomed [1]the [2]governor to release
the

ἕνα τῷ ὄχλῳ δέσμιον ὃν ἤθελον. 16 Εἶχον
one [2]to [3]the [4]crowd [1]prisoner whom they were wishing. [2]they [3]had
would wish.

δὲ τότε δέσμιον ἐπίσημον λεγόμενον [d] Βαραββᾶν.
[1]And then a prisoner ˜ notorious being called Barabbas.
called

17 Συνηγμένων οὖν αὐτῶν, εἶπεν αὐτοῖς ὁ Πιλᾶτος,
gathering together Therefore them, [2]said [3]to [4]them - [1]Pilate,
Therefore when they had assembled,

the potter's field, to bury strangers in.
8 Therefore that field has been called the Field of Blood to this day.
9 Then was fulfilled what was spoken by Jeremiah the prophet, saying, *"And they took the thirty pieces of silver, the value of Him who was priced,* whom they of the children of Israel priced,
10 *"and gave them for the potter's field, as the LORD directed me."*
11 Now Jesus stood before the governor. And the governor asked Him, saying, "Are You the King of the Jews?" Jesus said to him, *"It is as* you say."
12 And while He was being accused by the chief priests and elders, He answered nothing.
13 Then Pilate said to Him, "Do You not hear how many things they testify against You?"
14 But He answered him not one word, so that the governor marveled greatly.
15 Now at the feast the governor was accustomed to releasing to the multitude one prisoner whom they wished.
16 And at that time they had a notorious prisoner called Barabbas.
17 Therefore, when they had gathered together, Pilate said

[b](**27:10**) Jer. 32:6–9; cf. Zech. 11:12, 13
[c](**27:11**) NU omits αυτω, *to him.* [d](**27:16**) NU adds in brackets Ιησουν, *Jesus (Barabbas).*

to them, "Whom do you want me to release to you? Barabbas, or Jesus who is called Christ?"
18 For he knew that they had handed Him over because of envy.
19 While he was sitting on the judgment seat, his wife sent to him, saying, "Have nothing to do with that just Man, for I have suffered many things today in a dream because of Him."
20 But the chief priests and elders persuaded the multitudes that they should ask for Barabbas and destroy Jesus.
21 The governor answered and said to them, "Which of the two do you want me to release to you?" They said, "Barabbas!"
22 Pilate said to them, "What then shall I do with Jesus who is called Christ?" *They* all said to him, "Let Him be crucified!"
23 Then the governor said, "Why, what evil has He done?" But they cried out all the more, saying, "Let Him be crucified!"
24 When Pilate saw that he could not prevail at all, but rather *that* a tumult was rising, he took water and washed *his* hands before the multitude, saying, "I am innocent of the blood of this just Person. You see *to it*."
25 And all the people answered and said, "His blood *be*

"Τίνα θέλετε ἀπολύσω ὑμῖν,[e] Βαραββᾶν ἢ
"Whom do you wish *that* I should release to you, Barabbas or
Ἰησοῦν* τὸν λεγόμενον Χριστόν?" 18 Ἤιδει γὰρ ὅτι
Jesus the *One* being called Christ?" [2]he [3]knew [1]For that
who is called Messiah?"
διὰ φθόνον παρέδωκαν αὐτόν.
because of envy they handed over ~ Him.
had delivered

19 Καθημένου δὲ αὐτοῦ ἐπὶ τοῦ βήματος, ἀπέστειλε
sitting And him on the judgment seat, [3]sent
Now as he was sitting
πρὸς αὐτὸν ἡ γυνὴ αὐτοῦ, λέγουσα, "Μηδὲν σοὶ καὶ τῷ
[4]to [5]him - [2]wife [1]his, saying, "Nothing to you and -
"Have nothing to do with
δικαίῳ ἐκείνῳ, πολλὰ γὰρ ἔπαθον σήμερον κατ'
to righteous *man* that, [4]many [5]*things* [1]for [2]I [3]suffered today in
that righteous man, have suffered
ὄναρ δι' αὐτόν." 20 Οἱ δὲ ἀρχιερεῖς καὶ οἱ
a dream because of Him." the ~ But chief priests and the
πρεσβύτεροι ἔπεισαν τοὺς ὄχλους ἵνα αἰτήσωνται τὸν
elders persuaded the crowds that they should ask for -
Βαραββᾶν, τὸν δὲ Ἰησοῦν ἀπολέσωσιν.
Barabbas, - but Jesus they should destroy.

21 Ἀποκριθεὶς δὲ ὁ ἡγεμὼν εἶπεν αὐτοῖς, "Τίνα
[4]answering [1]And [2]the [3]governor said to them, "Which
θέλετε ἀπὸ τῶν δύο ἀπολύσω ὑμῖν?"
[4]do [5]you [6]wish [1]of [2]the [3]two [7]*that* I should release to you?"
Οἱ δὲ εἶπον, "Βαραββᾶν."
[2]the [3]*ones* [1]And said, "Barabbas."
they

22 Λέγει αὐτοῖς ὁ Πιλᾶτος, "Τί οὖν ποιήσω Ἰησοῦν
[2]says [3]to [4]them - [1]Pilate, "What then shall I do with Jesus
said
τὸν λεγόμενον Χριστόν?"
the *One* being called Christ?"
who is called Messiah?"
Λέγουσιν αὐτῷ[f] πάντες, "Σταυρωθήτω!"
[1]They [3]say [4]to [5]him [2]all, "Let Him be crucified!"
said

23 Ὁ δὲ ἡγεμὼν[g] ἔφη, "Τί γὰρ κακὸν ἐποίησεν?"
the ~ Then governor said, "what ~ For evil did He do?"
But
Οἱ δὲ περισσῶς ἔκραζον, λέγοντες,
[2]the [3]*ones* [1]But [7]even [8]more [4]were [5]crying [6]out, saying,
they kept
"Σταυρωθήτω!"
"Let Him be crucified!"

24 Ἰδὼν δὲ ὁ Πιλᾶτος ὅτι οὐδὲν ὠφελεῖ ἀλλὰ
[3]seeing [1]And - [2]Pilate that nothing is being gained but
was
μᾶλλον θόρυβος γίνεται, λαβὼν ὕδωρ ἀπενίψατο τὰς
rather a disturbance is becoming, taking water he washed [3]clean [1]the
riot was starting, his
χεῖρας ἀπέναντι τοῦ ὄχλου, λέγων, "Ἀθῷός εἰμι ἀπὸ τοῦ
[2]hands in front of the crowd, saying, "[3]innocent [1]I [2]am from the
of
αἵματος τοῦ δικαίου[h] τούτου. Ὑμεῖς ὄψεσθε."
blood - [1]of [3]righteous [4]*man* [2]this. You shall see *to it*."

25 Καὶ ἀποκριθεὶς πᾶς ὁ λαὸς εἶπε, "Τὸ αἷμα αὐτοῦ
And answering all the people said, - "blood ~ His

---

[e](27:17) NU adds in brackets Ιησουν τον, *Jesus (Barabbas)*.
[f](27:22) NU omits αυτω, *to him*. [g](27:23) NU omits ηγεμων, *governor*.
[h](27:24) NU omits του δικαιου, *righteous*.

*(27:17) Ἰησοῦς (*Iēsous*). Proper noun, *Jesus*, a Greek form of Hebrew *Yēshua'*, that is, *Joshua*. Since Greek has no "sh" sound, as in Hebrew, the Greek sigma had to suffice in transliteration. The final sigma was added to approximate the Greek nominative case inflection (cf. the genitive case Ἰησοῦ). The name *Jesus* means "Jehovah is salvation" and was a popular name among Jews. In addition to Jesus of Nazareth, the name is used in the NT of Joshua, son of Nun (Acts 7:45; Heb. 4:8), of Paul's coworker "Jesus who is called Justus" (Col. 4:11), in the compound name of a

ἐφ' ἡμᾶς καὶ ἐπὶ τὰ τέκνα ἡμῶν." **26** Τότε ἀπέλυσεν
be on us and on - children ˜ our." Then he released

αὐτοῖς τὸν Βαραββᾶν, τὸν δὲ Ἰησοῦν φραγελλώσας
to them - Barabbas, - but [3]Jesus [1]having [2]flogged

παρέδωκεν ἵνα σταυρωθῇ.
he handed *Him* over so that He might be crucified.
delivered Him

The Soldiers Mock Jesus
(Mark 15:16–20; John 19:2, 3)

27 Τότε οἱ στρατιῶται τοῦ ἡγεμόνος, παραλαβόντες τὸν
Then the soldiers of the governor, having taken -

Ἰησοῦν εἰς τὸ πραιτώριον, συνήγαγον ἐπ' αὐτὸν ὅλην
Jesus to the Praetorium, gathered together against Him whole ˜

τὴν σπεῖραν. **28** Καὶ ἐκδύσαντες αὐτὸν περιέθηκαν αὐτῷ
the cohort. And having stripped Him they put around Him
garrison.

χλαμύδα κοκκίνην. **29** Καὶ πλέξαντες στέφανον ἐξ ἀκανθῶν
a cloak ˜ scarlet. And having plaited a crown out of thorns

ἐπέθηκαν ἐπὶ τὴν κεφαλὴν αὐτοῦ καὶ κάλαμον ἐπὶ τὴν
they put *it* on - head ˜ His and a reed in -

δεξιὰν αὐτοῦ, καὶ γονυπετήσαντες ἔμπροσθεν αὐτοῦ
[2]right [3]*hand* [1]His, and kneeling before Him

ἐνέπαιζον αὐτῷ, λέγοντες, "Χαῖρε, ὁ Βασιλεὺς τῶν
they were mocking Him, saying, "Rejoice, - King of the
would mock "Hail,

Ἰουδαίων!" **30** Καὶ ἐμπτύσαντες εἰς αὐτὸν ἔλαβον τὸν
Jews!" And spitting at Him they took the

κάλαμον καὶ ἔτυπτον εἰς τὴν κεφαλὴν αὐτοῦ. **31** Καὶ
reed and were striking *Him* on - head ˜ His. And

ὅτε ἐνέπαιξαν αὐτῷ, ἐξέδυσαν αὐτὸν τὴν χλαμύδα καὶ
when they mocked Him, they stripped Him *of* the cloak and
had mocked

ἐνέδυσαν αὐτὸν τὰ ἱμάτια αὐτοῦ, καὶ ἀπήγαγον αὐτὸν εἰς
dressed in ˜ Him - clothes ˜ His, and they led away ˜ Him for
in order

τὸ σταυρῶσαι.
- to crucify *Him*.

Jesus Is Crucified
(Mark 15:21–32; Luke 23:26–43; John 19:17–27)

32 Ἐξερχόμενοι δὲ εὗρον ἄνθρωπον Κυρηναῖον ὀνόματι
[2]going [3]out [1]And they found a man a Cyrenian [2]by [3]name
of Cyrene

Σίμωνα. Τοῦτον ἠγγάρευσαν ἵνα ἄρῃ τὸν
[1]Simon. [6]this [7]*man* [4]They [5]pressed [8]into [9]service that he might carry -

σταυρὸν αὐτοῦ. **33** Καὶ ἐλθόντες εἰς τόπον λεγόμενον Γολγοθᾶ,
cross ˜ His. And coming to a place being called Golgotha,
called

ὅ ἐστι λεγόμενος Κρανίου Τόπος, **34** ἔδωκαν αὐτῷ
which is being called [2]of [3]a [4]Skull [1]Place, they gave Him
means

πιεῖν ὄξος[i] μετὰ χολῆς μεμιγμένον. Καὶ
[3]to [4]drink [1]sour [2]wine [8]with [9]gall [5]having [6]been [7]mixed. And

γευσάμενος οὐκ ἤθελε πιεῖν. **35** Σταυρώσαντες δὲ
having tasted *it* [3]not [1]He [2]was wanting to drink. [2]having [3]crucified [1]And

αὐτὸν διεμερίσαντο τὰ ἱμάτια αὐτοῦ βάλλοντες
Him they divided among themselves - clothes ˜ His *by* casting

on us and on our children."
26 Then he released Barabbas
to them; and when he had
scourged Jesus, he delivered
Him to be crucified.
27 Then the soldiers of the
governor took Jesus into the
Praetorium and gathered the
whole garrison around Him.
28 And they stripped Him and
put a scarlet robe on Him.
29 When they had twisted a
crown of thorns, they put *it* on
His head, and a reed in His
right hand. And they bowed the
knee before Him and mocked
Him, saying, "Hail, King of the
Jews!"
30 Then they spat on Him,
and took the reed and struck
Him on the head.
31 And when they had
mocked Him, they took the
robe off Him, put His *own*
clothes on Him, and led Him
away to be crucified.
32 Now as they came out,
they found a man of Cyrene, Simon by name. Him they compelled to bear His cross.
33 And when they had come
to a place called Golgotha, that
is to say, Place of a Skull,
34 they gave Him sour wine
mingled with gall to drink. But
when He had tasted *it,* He
would not drink.
35 Then they crucified Him,
and divided His garments, casting lots, that it might be fulfilled
which was spoken by the
prophet:

"They divided My
garments among them,
And for My clothing they
cast lots."

---

[i](**27:34**) NU reads οινον, *wine.*

sorcerer, Bar-Jesus (Βαριησοῦν, *Son of Jesus,* Acts 13:6), and in some manuscripts as the given name of Barabbas (Matt. 27:16, 17).

36 Sitting down, they kept watch over Him there.
37 And they put up over His head the accusation written against Him:

THIS IS JESUS THE KING OF THE JEWS.

38 Then two robbers were crucified with Him, one on the right and another on the left.
39 And those who passed by blasphemed Him, wagging their heads
40 and saying, "You who destroy the temple and build *it* in three days, save Yourself! If You are the Son of God, come down from the cross."
41 Likewise the chief priests also, mocking with the scribes and elders, said,
42 "He saved others; Himself He cannot save. If He is the King of Israel, let Him now come down from the cross, and we will believe Him.
43 "He trusted in God; let Him deliver Him now if He will have Him; for He said, 'I am the Son of God.' "
44 Even the robbers who were crucified with Him reviled Him with the same thing.
45 Now from the sixth hour until the ninth hour there was darkness over all the land.
46 And about the ninth hour Jesus cried out with a loud voice, saying, "Eli, Eli, lama sabachthani?" that is, *"My God, My God, why have You forsaken Me?"*

κλῆρον.[j] **36** Καὶ καθήμενοι ἐτήρουν αὐτὸν ἐκεῖ. **37** Καὶ
the lot. And sitting down they guarded Him there. And

ἐπέθηκαν ἐπάνω τῆς κεφαλῆς αὐτοῦ τὴν αἰτίαν αὐτοῦ
they put over - head ˜ His the charge [4]*against* [5]Him
crime

γεγραμμένην·
[1]having [2]been [3]written:

ΟΥΤΟΣ ΕΣΤΙΝ ΙΗΣΟΥΣ Ο ΒΑΣΙΛΕΥΣ ΤΩΝ
THIS IS JESUS THE KING OF THE

ΙΟΥΔΑΙΩΝ
JEWS

38 Τότε σταυροῦνται σὺν αὐτῷ δύο λησταί, εἷς ἐκ δεξιῶν
Then they crucify with Him two bandits, one at *the* right *parts*
crucified on His right side

καὶ εἷς ἐξ εὐωνύμων. **39** Οἱ δὲ παραπορευόμενοι
and one at *the* left *parts.* [2]the [3]*ones* [1]And passing by
on His left side.

ἐβλασφήμουν αὐτόν, κινοῦντες τὰς κεφαλὰς αὐτῶν **40** καὶ
were blaspheming Him, shaking - heads ˜ their and

λέγοντες, "Ὁ καταλύων τὸν ναὸν καὶ ἐν τρισὶν
saying, "*You are* the *One* destroying the temple and in three

ἡμέραις οἰκοδομῶν, σῶσον σεαυτόν! Εἰ Υἱὸς εἶ τοῦ
days building *it,* save Yourself! If [3]*the* [4]Son [1]You [2]are -
rebuilding

Θεοῦ, κατάβηθι ἀπὸ τοῦ σταυροῦ."
of God, come down from the cross."

41 Ὁμοίως δὲ καὶ οἱ ἀρχιερεῖς ἐμπαίζοντες μετὰ τῶν
likewise ˜ And also the chief priests mocking *Him* with the

γραμματέων καὶ πρεσβυτέρων καὶ Φαρισαίων[k] ἔλεγον,
scribes and elders and Pharisees said,

42 "Ἄλλους ἔσωσεν, ἑαυτὸν οὐ δύναται σῶσαι. Εἰ[l]
"Others He saved, Himself [3]not [1]He [2]is able to save. If

βασιλεὺς Ἰσραὴλ ἐστι, καταβάτω νῦν ἀπὸ τοῦ σταυροῦ
[3]*the* [4]King [5]of [6]Israel [1]He [2]is, let Him come down now from the cross

καὶ πιστεύσομεν ἐπ' αὐτῷ. **43** Πέποιθεν ἐπὶ τὸν Θεόν,
and we will believe on Him. He has trusted in - God,

ῥυσάσθω νῦν αὐτὸν εἰ θέλει αὐτόν. Εἶπε γὰρ ὅτι
let Him rescue now ˜ Him if He wants Him. [2]He [3]said [1]For -

'Θεοῦ εἰμι Υἱός.' " **44** Τὸ δ' αὐτὸ καὶ οἱ
'[5]of [6]God [1]I [2]am [3]*the* [4]Son.' " [2]*with* [3]the [1]And same *insult* even the

λησταὶ οἱ συσταυρωθέντες αὐτῷ ὠνείδιζον αὐτόν.
bandits the *ones* having been crucified with Him were reviling Him.
who were

[j](27:35) TR adds *ινα πληρωθη το ρηθεν υπο του προφητου διεμερισαντο τα ιματια μου εαυτοις και επι τον ιματισμον μου εβαλον κληρον, that it might be fulfilled which was spoken by the prophet: They divided My garments among them, and for My clothing they cast lots;* see Ps. 22:18 and cf. John 19:24. [k](27:41) TR, NU omit *και Φαρισαιων, and Pharisees.*
[l](27:42) NU omits *ει, if.*
[m](27:46) TR reads *λαμα, lama;* NU reads *λεμα, lema.* [n](27:46) Ps. 22:1

Jesus Dies on the Cross
(Mark 15:33–41; Luke 23:44–49; John 19:28–30)

45 Ἀπὸ δὲ ἕκτης ὥρας σκότος ἐγένετο ἐπὶ πᾶσαν τὴν
from ˜ Now *the* sixth hour darkness came upon all the

γῆν ἕως ὥρας ἐνάτης. **46** Περὶ δὲ τὴν ἐνάτην ὥραν
land until *the* hour ˜ ninth. about ˜ And the ninth hour

ἀνεβόησεν ὁ Ἰησοῦς φωνῇ μεγάλῃ, λέγων, "«Ἠλί, Ἠλί,
[2]cried [3]out - [1]Jesus with a voice ˜ great, saying, "«Eli, Eli,
loud,

λιμὰ[m] σαβαχθάνι?»" τοῦτ' ἔστι, «Θεέ μου, Θεέ μου, ἱνατί με
lima sabachthani?»" this is, «God ˜ My, God ˜ My, why [4]Me
that

ἐγκατέλιπες?»[n]
[1]did [2]You [3]forsake?»

47 Τινὲς δὲ τῶν ἐκεῖ ἑστώτων ἀκούσαντες
some ˜ And of the *ones* there ˜ standing hearing
those when they heard this

ἔλεγον ὅτι "Ἠλίαν φωνεῖ οὗτος."
said - "[5]Elijah [3]is [4]calling [1]This [2]*man.*"

48 Καὶ εὐθέως δραμὼν εἷς ἐξ αὐτῶν καὶ λαβὼν
And immediately [4]running [1]one [2]of [3]them and taking
ran took

σπόγγον, πλήσας τε ὄξους καὶ περιθεὶς
a sponge, [2]having [3]filled [1]and *it with* sour wine and having put *it* around
filled

καλάμῳ, ἐπότιζεν αὐτόν. 49 Οἱ δὲ λοιποὶ ἔλεγον,
a reed, was giving a drink *to* Him. the ˜ But rest said,

"Ἄφες, ἴδωμεν εἰ ἔρχεται Ἠλίας σώσων αὐτόν."
"Leave *Him* alone, let us see if [2]is [3]coming [1]Elijah saving Him."
to save

50 Ὁ δὲ Ἰησοῦς πάλιν κράξας φωνῇ μεγάλῃ ἀφῆκε
- But Jesus again crying out with a voice ˜ great [1]let [4]go
loud released

τὸ πνεῦμα. 51 Καὶ ἰδού, τὸ καταπέτασμα τοῦ ναοῦ
[2]the [3]spirit. And behold, the veil of the temple
His

ἐσχίσθη εἰς δύο ἀπὸ ἄνωθεν ἕως κάτω, καὶ ἡ γῆ ἐσείσθη,
was split in two from above to bottom, and the earth was shaken,
top

καὶ αἱ πέτραι ἐσχίσθησαν, 52 καὶ τὰ μνημεῖα ἀνεῴχθησαν
and the rocks were split, and the tombs were opened

καὶ πολλὰ σώματα τῶν κεκοιμημένων ἁγίων ἠγέρθη,
and many bodies of the [2]having [3]fallen [4]asleep [1]saints were raised,
who had passed away

53 καὶ ἐξελθόντες ἐκ τῶν μνημείων μετὰ τὴν ἔγερσιν
and coming forth out of the tombs after - resurrection ˜

αὐτοῦ εἰσῆλθον εἰς τὴν ἁγίαν πόλιν καὶ ἐνεφανίσθησαν
His they entered into the holy city and appeared

πολλοῖς.
to many.

54 Ὁ δὲ ἑκατόνταρχος καὶ οἱ μετ' αὐτοῦ τηροῦντες
the ˜ And centurion and the *ones* with him guarding

τὸν Ἰησοῦν, ἰδόντες τὸν σεισμὸν καὶ τὰ
- Jesus, seeing the earthquake and the *things*
when they saw

γενόμενα, ἐφοβήθησαν σφόδρα, λέγοντες, "Ἀληθῶς
having happened, they were afraid ˜ exceedingly, saying, "Truly
that had

Θεοῦ Υἱὸς ἦν οὗτος!"
[5]of [6]God [3]*the* [4]Son [2]was [1]this!"

55 Ἦσαν δὲ ἐκεῖ γυναῖκες πολλαὶ ἀπὸ μακρόθεν
[2]*there* [3]were [1]And [6]there [5]women [4]many [8]from [9]a [10]distance

θεωροῦσαι, αἵτινες ἠκολούθησαν τῷ Ἰησοῦ ἀπὸ τῆς Γαλιλαίας
[7]observing, who followed - Jesus from - Galilee

διακονοῦσαι αὐτῷ· 56 ἐν αἷς ἦν Μαρία ἡ Μαγδαληνὴ
ministering to Him; among whom was Mary - Magdalene

καὶ Μαρία ἡ τοῦ Ἰακώβου καὶ Ἰωσῆ[o] μήτηρ καὶ ἡ μήτηρ
and Mary the - [2]of [3]James [4]and [5]Joses [1]mother and the mother

τῶν υἱῶν Ζεβεδαίου.
of the sons of Zebedee.

47 Some of those who stood there, when they heard *that,* said, "This Man is calling for Elijah!"
48 Immediately one of them ran and took a sponge, filled *it* with sour wine and put *it* on a reed, and offered it to Him to drink.
49 The rest said, "Let Him alone; let us see if Elijah will come to save Him."
50 And Jesus cried out again with a loud voice, and yielded up His spirit.
51 Then, behold, the veil of the temple was torn in two from top to bottom; and the earth quaked, and the rocks were split,
52 and the graves were opened; and many bodies of the saints who had fallen asleep were raised;
53 and coming out of the graves after His resurrection, they went into the holy city and appeared to many.
54 So when the centurion and those with him, who were guarding Jesus, saw the earthquake and the things that had happened, they feared greatly, saying, "Truly this was the Son of God!"
55 And many women who followed Jesus from Galilee, ministering to Him, were there looking on from afar,
56 among whom were Mary Magdalene, Mary the mother of James and Joses, and the mother of Zebedee's sons.

---

[o](27:56) NU reads Ιωσηφ, *Joseph.*

57 Now when evening had come, there came a rich man from Arimathea, named Joseph, who himself had also become a disciple of Jesus.
58 This man went to Pilate and asked for the body of Jesus. Then Pilate commanded the body to be given to him.
59 When Joseph had taken the body, he wrapped it in a clean linen cloth,
60 and laid it in his new tomb which he had hewn out of the rock; and he rolled a large stone against the door of the tomb, and departed.
61 And Mary Magdalene was there, and the other Mary, sitting opposite the tomb.
62 On the next day, which followed the Day of Preparation, the chief priests and Pharisees gathered together to Pilate,
63 saying, "Sir, we remember, while He was still alive, how that deceiver said, 'After three days I will rise.'
64 "Therefore command that the tomb be made secure until the third day, lest His disciples come by night and steal Him *away,* and say to the people, 'He has risen from the dead.' So the last deception will be worse than the first."
65 Pilate said to them, "You have a guard; go your way, make *it* as secure as you know how."
66 So they went and made the

Jesus Is Buried in Joseph's Tomb
(Mark 15:42–47; Luke 23:50–56; John 19:38–42)

57 Ὀψίας δὲ γενομένης, ἦλθεν ἄνθρωπος πλούσιος
evening ˜ Now having come, *there* came a man ˜ rich

ἀπὸ Ἀριμαθαίας, τοὔνομα Ἰωσήφ, ὃς καὶ αὐτὸς
from Arimathea, the name Joseph, who also himself
named

ἐμαθήτευσε* τῷ Ἰησοῦ. **58** Οὗτος προσελθὼν τῷ Πιλάτῳ
became a disciple - of Jesus. This *man* approaching - Pilate
had become

ᾐτήσατο τὸ σῶμα τοῦ Ἰησοῦ. Τότε ὁ Πιλᾶτος ἐκέλευσεν
asked for the body - of Jesus. Then - Pilate commanded

ἀποδοθῆναι τὸ σῶμα.[p] **59** Καὶ λαβὼν τὸ σῶμα ὁ Ἰωσὴφ
[3]to [4]be [5]given [1]the [2]body. And taking the body - Joseph

ἐνετύλιξεν αὐτὸ σινδόνι καθαρᾷ **60** καὶ ἔθηκεν αὐτὸ ἐν
wrapped up ˜ it in [1]a [3]linen [4]cloth [2]clean and placed it in

τῷ καινῷ αὐτοῦ μνημείῳ ὃ ἐλατόμησεν ἐν τῇ πέτρᾳ. Καὶ
- new ˜ his tomb which he cut in the rock. And
had cut

προσκυλίσας λίθον μέγαν τῇ θύρᾳ τοῦ μνημείου
having rolled a stone ˜ great *against* the door of the tomb
large

ἀπῆλθεν. **61** Ἦν δὲ ἐκεῖ Μαρία ἡ Μαγδαληνὴ καὶ
he went away. [2]*there* [3]was [1]And there Mary - Magdalene and

ἡ ἄλλη Μαρία καθήμεναι ἀπέναντι τοῦ τάφου.
the other Mary sitting opposite the grave.

Pilate Sets a Guard by the Tomb

62 Τῇ δὲ ἐπαύριον, ἥτις ἐστὶ μετὰ τὴν Παρασκευήν,
[2]on [3]the [1]And morrow, which is after the Preparation *Day,*
next day,

συνήχθησαν οἱ ἀρχιερεῖς καὶ οἱ Φαρισαῖοι πρὸς
[7]were [8]gathered [9]together [1]the [2]high [3]priests [4]and [5]the [6]Pharisees to

Πιλᾶτον, **63** λέγοντες, "Κύριε, ἐμνήσθημεν ὅτι ἐκεῖνος ὁ
Pilate, saying, "Sir, we remember that that -

πλάνος εἶπεν ἔτι ζῶν, 'Μετὰ τρεῖς ἡμέρας ἐγείρομαι.'
deceiver said *while* still living, 'After three days I am rising.'
will rise.'

64 Κέλευσον οὖν ἀσφαλισθῆναι τὸν τάφον ἕως τῆς τρίτης
command ˜ Therefore to be secured the grave until the third
that the grave be made secure

ἡμέρας, μήποτε ἐλθόντες οἱ μαθηταὶ αὐτοῦ νυκτὸς[q]
day, lest [3]coming - [2]disciples [1]His by night
come

κλέψωσιν αὐτὸν καὶ εἴπωσι τῷ λαῷ, 'Ἠγέρθη ἀπὸ
they may steal Him and they may say to the people, 'He was raised from
and say

τῶν νεκρῶν,' καὶ ἔσται ἡ ἐσχάτη πλάνη χείρων τῆς
the dead,' and [4]will [5]be [1]the [2]last [3]deception worse *than* the

πρώτης."
first."

65 Ἔφη δὲ αὐτοῖς ὁ Πιλᾶτος, "Ἔχετε κουστωδίαν·
[3]said [1]And [4]to [5]them - [2]Pilate, "You have a guard;

ὑπάγετε ἀσφαλίσασθε ὡς οἴδατε." **66** Οἱ δὲ
go secure *it* as you know *how.*" [2]the [3]*ones* [1]So
make it as secure they

---

[p](27:58) NU omits το σωμα, *the body.*
[q](27:64) NU omits νυκτος, *by night.*

---

*(27:57) μαθητεύω (*mathēteuō*). Verb meaning *teach, disciple.* The cognate noun μαθητής, *disciple, learner,* is derived from μανθάνω, *learn.* When μαθητεύω is used as an intransitive verb, it means *to be a learner, pupil,* or *disciple,* as here in Matt. 27:57. With an object the verb means *to make disciples,* as Jesus commanded in the Great Commission (Matt. 28:19; cf. Acts 14:21). Cf. the feminine noun μαθήτρια, *a female disciple* (Acts 9:36), and the use of μαθητής in Acts for Christians generally (Acts 6:1, 2).

πορευθέντες ἠσφαλίσαντο τὸν τάφον, σφραγίσαντες τὸν λίθον,
going secured the grave, sealing the stone,
went and

μετὰ τῆς κουστωδίας.
with the guard.

He Is Not Here for He Is Risen
(Mark 16:1–8; Luke 24:1–12; John 20:1–10)

28 1 Ὀψὲ δὲ σαββάτων, τῇ ἐπιφωσκούσῃ εἰς
after ˜ But *the* Sabbath, at the dawning toward

μίαν σαββάτων, ἦλθε Μαρία ἡ Μαγδαληνὴ καὶ ἡ ἄλλη
the first *day* of *the* week, [7]came [1]Mary - [2]Magdalene [3]and [4]the [5]other

Μαρία θεωρῆσαι τὸν τάφον. 2 Καὶ ἰδού, σεισμὸς ἐγένετο
[6]Mary to see the tomb. And behold, [1]a [3]earthquake [4]occurred

μέγας· ἄγγελος γὰρ Κυρίου καταβὰς ἐξ οὐρανοῦ,
[2]great; [6]an [7]angel [5]for of *the* Lord having come down out of heaven,

προσελθὼν ἀπεκύλισε τὸν λίθον ἀπὸ τῆς θύρας[a] καὶ
having approached rolled back the stone from the door and

ἐκάθητο ἐπάνω αὐτοῦ. 3 Ἦν δὲ ἡ ἰδέα αὐτοῦ ὡς
sat on it. [4]was [1]And - [3]appearance [2]his like

ἀστραπὴ καὶ τὸ ἔνδυμα αὐτοῦ λευκὸν ὡσεὶ χιών. 4 Ἀπὸ δὲ
lightning and - clothing ˜ his white like snow. from ˜ And
for

τοῦ φόβου αὐτοῦ ἐσείσθησαν οἱ τηροῦντες καὶ ἐγένοντο
- fear of him [4]were [5]shaken [1]the [2]*ones* [3]guarding and they became
guards

ὡσεὶ νεκροί.
like dead *men*.

5 Ἀποκριθεὶς δὲ ὁ ἄγγελος εἶπε ταῖς γυναιξί, "Μὴ
answering ˜ But the angel said to the woman, "[2]not

φοβεῖσθε ὑμεῖς, οἶδα γὰρ ὅτι Ἰησοῦν τὸν
[1]Do [4]fear [3]you, [6]I [7]know [5]for that [3]Jesus [4]the [5]*One*
who

ἐσταυρωμένον ζητεῖτε. 6 Οὐκ ἔστιν ὧδε! Ἠγέρθη
[6]having [7]been [8]crucified [1]you [2]seek. [3]not [1]He [2]is here! [2]He [3]was [4]raised
was is risen

γάρ, καθὼς εἶπε. Δεῦτε ἴδετε τὸν τόπον ὅπου ἔκειτο ὁ
[1]For, just as He said. Go see the place where [3]was [4]lying [1]the

Κύριος.[b] 7 Καὶ ταχὺ πορευθεῖσαι εἴπατε τοῖς μαθηταῖς
[2]Lord. And swiftly ˜ going tell - disciples ˜

αὐτοῦ ὅτι 'Ἠγέρθη ἀπὸ τῶν νεκρῶν,' καὶ ἰδού,
His - 'He was raised from the dead,' and behold,
is risen

προάγει ὑμᾶς εἰς τὴν Γαλιλαίαν, ἐκεῖ αὐτὸν
He is going before you into - Galilee, there [4]Him

ὄψεσθε. Ἰδού, εἶπον ὑμῖν." 8 Καὶ ἐξελθοῦσαι[c] ταχὺ ἀπὸ
[1]you [2]will [3]see. Behold, I told you." And going out swiftly from

τοῦ μνημείου μετὰ φόβου καὶ χαρᾶς μεγάλης ἔδραμον
the tomb with fear and joy ˜ great they ran

ἀπαγγεῖλαι τοῖς μαθηταῖς αὐτοῦ.
to report - to disciples ˜ His.

The Women Worship the Risen Lord

9 Ὡς δὲ επορεύοντο ἀπαγγεῖλαι τοῖς μαθηταῖς
as ˜ And they were going to report - to disciples ˜

αὐτοῦ,[d] καὶ ἰδού, Ἰησοῦς ἀπήντησεν αὐταῖς, λέγων,
His, and behold, Jesus met them, saying,
that

tomb secure, sealing the stone
and setting the guard.

28 Now after the Sabbath,
as the first *day* of the
week began to dawn, Mary
Magdalene and the other Mary
came to see the tomb.
2 And behold, there was a
great earthquake; for an angel
of the Lord descended from
heaven, and came and rolled
back the stone from the door,
and sat on it.
3 His countenance was like
lightning, and his clothing as
white as snow.
4 And the guards shook for
fear of him, and became like
dead *men*.
5 But the angel answered
and said to the women, "Do not
be afraid, for I know that you
seek Jesus who was crucified.
6 "He is not here; for He is
risen, as He said. Come, see
the place where the Lord lay.
7 "And go quickly and tell His
disciples that He is risen from
the dead, and indeed He is going before you into Galilee;
there you will see Him. Behold,
I have told you."
8 So they went out quickly
from the tomb with fear and
great joy, and ran to bring His
disciples word.
9 And as they went to tell
His disciples, behold, Jesus met
them, saying, "Rejoice!" So

[a](28:2) NU omits *απο της θυρας, from the door.*
[b](28:6) NU omits *ο Κυριος, the Lord.* [c](28:8) NU reads *απελθουσαι, going away.*
[d](28:9) NU omits *ως δε . . . μαθηταις αυτου, And as . . . His disciples.*

they came and held Him by the
feet and worshiped Him.
10 Then Jesus said to them,
"Do not be afraid. Go *and* tell
My brethren to go to Galilee,
and there they will see Me."
11 Now while they were going, behold, some of the guard
came into the city and reported
to the chief priests all the things
that had happened.
12 When they had assembled
with the elders and consulted
together, they gave a large sum
of money to the soldiers,
13 saying, "Tell them, 'His
disciples came at night and
stole Him *away* while we slept.'
14 "And if this comes to the
governor's ears, we will appease him and make you secure."
15 So they took the money
and did as they were in-
structed; and this saying is
commonly reported among the
Jews until this day.
16 Then the eleven disciples
went away into Galilee, to the
mountain which Jesus had appointed for them.
17 When they saw Him, they
worshiped Him; but some
doubted.
18 And Jesus came and spoke

"Χαίρετε!" Αἱ δὲ προσελθοῦσαι ἐκράτησαν αὐτοῦ τοὺς
"Rejoice!" [2]the [3]*ones* [1]And approaching held His -
"Greetings!" And they approached and

πόδας καὶ προσεκύνησαν αὐτῷ. 10 Τότε λέγει αὐταῖς ὁ
feet and worshiped Him. Then [2]says [3]to [4]them -
said

Ἰησοῦς· "Μὴ φοβεῖσθε. Ὑπάγετε ἀπαγγείλατε τοῖς ἀδελφοῖς
[1]Jesus; "not ˜ Do be afraid. Go report - to brothers ˜

μου ἵνα ἀπέλθωσιν εἰς τὴν Γαλιλαίαν, καὶ ἐκεῖ με
My that they should go away to - Galilee, and there [4]Me

ὄψονται."
[1]they [2]will [3]see."

The Soldiers Are Bribed to Lie

11 Πορευομένων δὲ αὐτῶν, ἰδού, τινὲς τῆς κουστωδίας
going And them, behold, some of the guard
Now while they were going,

ἐλθόντες εἰς τὴν πόλιν ἀπήγγειλαν τοῖς ἀρχιερεῦσιν ἅπαντα
coming into the city reported to the chief priests all *things*
everything

τὰ γενόμενα. 12 Καὶ συναχθέντες μετὰ τῶν
- having happened. And being assembled with the
that had

πρεσβυτέρων, συμβούλιόν τε λαβόντες, ἀργύρια ἱκανὰ
elders, [3]counsel [1]and [2]taking, [7]silver [8]*coins* [6]sufficient

ἔδωκαν τοῖς στρατιώταις, 13 λέγοντες, "Εἴπατε ὅτι 'Οἱ
[4]they [5]gave to the soldiers, saying, "Say - -

μαθηταὶ αὐτοῦ νυκτὸς ἐλθόντες ἔκλεψαν αὐτὸν ἡμῶν
'disciples ˜ His [2]by [3]night [1]coming stole Him us
while we

κοιμωμένων.' 14 Καὶ ἐὰν ἀκουσθῇ τοῦτο ἐπὶ τοῦ
sleeping.' And if [2]is [3]heard [1]this before the
were sleeping.' this reaches the governor's

ἡγεμόνος, ἡμεῖς πείσομεν αὐτὸν καὶ ὑμᾶς ἀμερίμνους
governor, we will persuade him and [4]you [5]worry [6]free
ears, influence secure

ποιήσομεν." 15 Οἱ δὲ λαβόντες τὰ ἀργύρια ἐποίησαν
[1]we [2]will [3]make." [2]the [3]*ones* [1]And taking the silver *coins* did
they

ὡς ἐδιδάχθησαν. Καὶ διεφημίσθη ὁ λόγος οὗτος παρὰ
as they were instructed. And [3]was [4]spread [5]widely - [2]word [1]this among
has been tale

Ἰουδαίοις μέχρι τῆς σήμερον.
Jews until - today.

The Great Commission
(Mark 16:14–18; Luke 24:36–49; John 20:19–23; Acts 1:6–8)

16 Οἱ δὲ ἕνδεκα μαθηταὶ ἐπορεύθησαν εἰς τὴν Γαλιλαίαν
the ˜ And eleven disciples went to - Galilee

εἰς τὸ ὄρος οὗ ἐτάξατο αὐτοῖς ὁ Ἰησοῦς. 17 Καὶ
to the mountain which [2]appointed [3]for [4]them - [1]Jesus. And
had appointed

ἰδόντες αὐτὸν προσεκύνησαν αὐτῷ,[e] οἱ δὲ
seeing Him they worshiped Him, [2]the [3]*ones* [1]but
when they saw some

ἐδίστασαν. 18 Καὶ προσελθὼν ὁ Ἰησοῦς ἐλάλησεν αὐτοῖς,
doubted. And approaching - Jesus spoke to them,
Jesus came up and

[e](28:17) NU omits αυτω, *Him.*

λέγων, "Ἐδόθη μοι πᾶσα ἐξουσία ἐν οὐρανῷ καὶ
saying, "[8]was [9]given [10]to [11]Me [1]All [2]authority [3]in [4]heaven [5]and
"has been granted

ἐπὶ γῆς. **19** Πορευθέντες μαθητεύσατε πάντα τὰ ἔθνη,
[6]on [7]earth. Going make disciples of all the nations,
When you go,

βαπτίζοντες* αὐτοὺς εἰς τὸ ὄνομα τοῦ Πατρὸς καὶ τοῦ Υἱοῦ
baptizing them in the name of the Father and of the Son

καὶ τοῦ Ἁγίου Πνεύματος, **20** διδάσκοντες αὐτοὺς τηρεῖν
and of the Holy Spirit, teaching them to keep
observe

πάντα ὅσα ἐνετειλάμην ὑμῖν· καὶ ἰδού, ἐγὼ μεθ'
all *things* as many as I commanded you; and behold, I [2]with
everything that I have commanded

ὑμῶν εἰμι πάσας τὰς ἡμέρας ἕως τῆς συντελείας τοῦ αἰῶνος.
[3]you [1]am all the days until the completion of the age.
end

Ἀμήν."[f]
Amen."
So be it."

to them, saying, "All authority has been given to Me in heaven and on earth.
19 "Go therefore and make disciples of all the nations, baptizing them in the name of the Father and of the Son and of the Holy Spirit,
20 "teaching them to observe all things that I have commanded you; and lo, I am with you always, *even* to the end of the age." Amen.

---

f**(28:20)** NU omits Αμην, *Amen.*

***(28:19)** βαπτίζω *(baptizō).* Verb used often in the NT, usually translated by its English derivative, *baptize.* It is used in reference to baptism by John (Mark 1:4), Jesus (John 4:1, but cf. 4:2), the apostles (here in Matt. 28:19), other Christians (Acts 8:38), and even the Corinthians in their controversial practice (1 Cor. 15:29). The Jews baptized persons or things (Mark 7:4, the cognate noun βαπτισμός, *washing*). It may be used figuratively also (Mark 10:39; 1 Cor. 10:2). Cf. the cognate verb βάπτω, *dip, immerse,* and the noun βάπτισμα, *baptism.*

The Gospel According to

MARK

1 The beginning of the gospel of Jesus Christ, the Son of God.
2 As it is written in the Prophets:

> *"Behold, I send My messenger before Your face,*
> *Who will prepare Your way before You."*

3 *"The voice of one crying in the wilderness:*
'Prepare the way of the LORD*;*
Make His paths straight.'"

4 John came baptizing in the wilderness and preaching a baptism of repentance for the remission of sins.
5 Then all the land of Judea, and those from Jerusalem, went out to him and were all baptized by him in the Jordan River, confessing their sins.
6 Now John was clothed with camel's hair and with a leather belt around his waist, and he ate locusts and wild honey.
7 And he preached, saying, "There comes One after me who is mightier than I, whose sandal strap I am not worthy to stoop down and loose.

ΚΑΤΑ ΜΑΡΚΟΝ
ACCORDING TO MARK

1 **1** ΑΡΧΗ ΤΟΥ ΕΥΑΓΓΕΛΙΟΥ ΙΗΣΟΥ
THE BEGINNING OF THE GOSPEL OF JESUS

ΧΡΙΣΤΟΥ, ΥΙΟΥ ΤΟΥ ΘΕΟΥ.[a]
CHRIST, *THE* SON - OF GOD.

John the Baptist Prepares the Way
(Matt. 3:1–12; Luke 3:1–17; John 1:19–28)

2 Ὡς γέγραπται ἐν τοῖς προφήταις,[b]
As it is written in the prophets,

«Ἰδού, ἐγὼ ἀποστέλλω τὸν ἄγγελόν μου πρὸ
«Behold, I send - messenger ˜ My before

προσώπου σου,
face ˜ Your,

Ὃς κατασκευάσει τὴν ὁδόν σου ἔμπροσθέν σου.»[c]
Who will prepare - way ˜ Your before You.»

3 «Φωνὴ βοῶντος·
«A voice of *one* crying:

'Ἐν τῇ ἐρήμῳ ἑτοιμάσατε τὴν ὁδὸν Κυρίου,
'In the wilderness prepare the way of *the* Lord,

Εὐθείας ποιεῖτε τὰς τρίβους αὐτοῦ.'»[d]
straight ˜ Make - paths ˜ His.'»

4 Ἐγένετο Ἰωάννης βαπτίζων ἐν τῇ ἐρήμῳ καὶ κηρύσσων
came ˜ John baptizing in the wilderness and preaching
appeared

βάπτισμα μετανοίας εἰς ἄφεσιν ἁμαρτιῶν. **5** Καὶ
a baptism of repentance for *the* forgiveness of sins. And

ἐξεπορεύετο πρὸς αὐτὸν πᾶσα ἡ Ἰουδαία χώρα καὶ οἱ
[5]was [6]going [7]out [8]to [9]him [1]all [2]the [3]Judean [4]country and the

Ἱεροσολυμῖται, καὶ ἐβαπτίζοντο πάντες ἐν τῷ
Jerusalemites, and they were [2]being [3]baptized [1]all in the
inhabitants of Jerusalem,

Ἰορδάνῃ ποταμῷ ὑπ' αὐτοῦ, ἐξομολογούμενοι τὰς ἁμαρτίας
Jordan River by him, confessing - sins ˜

αὐτῶν. **6** Ἦν δὲ ὁ Ἰωάννης ἐνδεδυμένος τρίχας καμήλου καὶ
their. [3]was [1]Now - [2]John clothed with hairs of a camel and
camel skin

ζώνην δερματίνην περὶ τὴν ὀσφὺν αὐτοῦ, καὶ ἐσθίων
a belt ˜ leather around - loins ˜ his, and *was* eating
waist

ἀκρίδας καὶ μέλι ἄγριον. **7** Καὶ ἐκήρυσσε, λέγων,
locusts and honey ˜ wild. And he was preaching, saying,

"Ἔρχεται ὁ ἰσχυρότερός μου ὀπίσω μου, οὗ οὐκ
"[6]is [7]coming [1]The [2]*One* [3]stronger [4]*than* [5]me after me, of whom [3]not
I

εἰμὶ ἱκανὸς κύψας λῦσαι τὸν ἱμάντα τῶν ὑποδημάτων
[1]I [2]am worthy stooping down to loose the strap - of sandals ˜
to stoop down and

---

[a](1:1) NU brackets ΥΙΟΥ ΘΕΟΥ, SON OF GOD. [b](1:2) NU reads *τω Ησαια τω προφητη, in Isaiah the prophet.* [c](1:2) Mal. 3:1 [d](1:3) Is. 40:3

αὐτοῦ. 8 Ἐγὼ μὲν ἐβάπτισα ὑμᾶς ἐν ὕδατι, αὐτὸς δὲ
His. I - baptized you in water, He ˜ but
with

βαπτίσει ὑμᾶς ἐν Πνεύματι Ἁγίῳ."
will baptize you in *the* Spirit ˜ Holy."
with

John Baptizes Jesus
(Matt. 3:13–17; Luke 3:21, 22)

9 Καὶ ἐγένετο ἐν ἐκείναις ταῖς ἡμέραις, ἦλθεν
And it happened in those - days, *that* came ˜

Ἰησοῦς ἀπὸ Ναζαρὲτ τῆς Γαλιλαίας καὶ ἐβαπτίσθη ὑπὸ
Jesus from Nazareth - of Galilee and was baptized by

Ἰωάννου εἰς τὸν Ἰορδάνην. 10 Καὶ εὐθέως ἀναβαίνων ἀπὸ[e]
John in the Jordan. And immediately coming up from

τοῦ ὕδατος, εἶδε σχιζομένους τοὺς οὐρανοὺς καὶ τὸ Πνεῦμα
the water, He saw ^{3}splitting ^{1}the ^{2}heavens and the Spirit
parting

ὡσεὶ περιστερὰν καταβαῖνον ἐπ' αὐτόν. 11 Καὶ φωνὴ ἐγένετο
like a dove coming down upon Him. And a voice came

ἐκ τῶν οὐρανῶν, "Σὺ εἶ ὁ Υἱός μου ὁ ἀγαπητός, ἐν ᾧ
from the heavens, "You are - ^{3}Son ^{1}My - ^{2}beloved, in whom

εὐδόκησα."
I have found delight."

Jesus Is Tempted by Satan
(Matt. 4:1–11; Luke 4:1–13)

12 Καὶ εὐθὺς τὸ Πνεῦμα αὐτὸν ἐκβάλλει εἰς τὴν
And immediately the Spirit Him ˜ impels into the
impelled

ἔρημον. 13 Καὶ ἦν ἐκεῖ ἐν τῇ ἐρήμῳ ἡμέρας
wilderness. And He was there in the wilderness days ˜

τεσσεράκοντα πειραζόμενος ὑπὸ τοῦ Σατανᾶ καὶ ἦν μετὰ
forty being tempted by - Satan and He was with

τῶν θηρίων, καὶ οἱ ἄγγελοι διηκόνουν αὐτῷ.
the wild animals, and the angels were ministering to Him.

Jesus Begins His Galilean Ministry
(Matt. 4:12–17; Luke 4:14, 15)

14 Μετὰ δὲ τὸ παραδοθῆναι τὸν Ἰωάννην ἦλθεν ὁ
after ˜ Now the to be handed over - John came ˜ -
John was imprisoned,

Ἰησοῦς εἰς τὴν Γαλιλαίαν κηρύσσων τὸ εὐαγγέλιον τῆς
Jesus into - Galilee preaching the gospel of the

βασιλείας[f] τοῦ Θεοῦ 15 καὶ λέγων ὅτι "Πεπλήρωται ὁ
kingdom - of God and saying - "^{3}has ^{4}been ^{5}fulfilled ^{1}The

καιρὸς καὶ ἤγγικεν ἡ βασιλεία τοῦ Θεοῦ. Μετανοεῖτε
^{2}time and ^{5}has ^{6}drawn ^{7}near ^{1}the ^{2}kingdom - ^{3}of ^{4}God. Repent
is at hand

καὶ πιστεύετε ἐν τῷ εὐαγγελίῳ."
and believe in the gospel."

Jesus Calls Four Fishermen
(Matt. 4:18–22; Luke 5:1–11)

16 Περιπατῶν δὲ παρὰ τὴν θάλασσαν τῆς Γαλιλαίας
walking ˜ Now alongside the Sea - of Galilee
as He was walking

8 "I indeed baptized you with water, but He will baptize you with the Holy Spirit."
9 It came to pass in those days *that* Jesus came from Nazareth of Galilee, and was baptized by John in the Jordan.
10 And immediately, coming up from the water, He saw the heavens parting and the Spirit descending upon Him like a dove.
11 Then a voice came from heaven, "You are My beloved Son, in whom I am well pleased."
12 Immediately the Spirit drove Him into the wilderness.
13 And He was there in the wilderness forty days, tempted by Satan, and was with the wild beasts; and the angels ministered to Him.
14 Now after John was put in prison, Jesus came to Galilee, preaching the gospel of the kingdom of God,
15 and saying, "The time is fulfilled, and the kingdom of God is at hand. Repent, and believe in the gospel."
16 And as He walked by the Sea of Galilee, He saw Simon

[e](1:10) NU reads εκ, *out of.*
[f](1:14) NU omits της βασιλειας, *of the kingdom.*

and Andrew his brother casting
a net into the sea; for they
were fishermen.
17 Then Jesus said to them,
"Follow Me, and I will make
you become fishers of men."
18 They immediately left their
nets and followed Him.
19 When He had gone a little
farther from there, He saw
James the *son* of Zebedee, and
John his brother, who also *were*
in the boat mending their nets.
20 And immediately He called
them, and they left their father
Zebedee in the boat with the
hired servants, and went after
Him.
21 Then they went into Capernaum, and immediately on
the Sabbath He entered the
synagogue and taught.
22 And they were astonished
at His teaching, for He taught
them as one having authority,
and not as the scribes.
23 Now there was a man in
their synagogue with an unclean
spirit. And he cried out,
24 saying, "Let *us* alone!
What have we to do with You,
Jesus of Nazareth? Did You
come to destroy us? I know
who You are — the Holy One of
God!"
25 But Jesus rebuked him,
saying, "Be quiet, and come
out of him!"
26 And when the unclean
spirit had convulsed him and
cried out with a loud voice, he
came out of him.

εἶδε Σίμωνα καὶ Ἀνδρέαν τὸν ἀδελφὸν αὐτοῦ τοῦ
He saw Simon and Andrew - brother ~ his -

Σίμωνος βάλλοντας ἀμφίβληστρον ἐν τῇ θαλάσσῃ·
that is Simon's casting a circular net in the sea;

ἦσαν γὰρ ἁλιεῖς. **17** *Καὶ εἶπεν αὐτοῖς ὁ Ἰησοῦς,*
[2]they [3]were [1]for fishermen. And [2]said [3]to [4]them - [1]Jesus,

"Δεῦτε ὀπίσω μου, καὶ ποιήσω ὑμᾶς γενέσθαι ἁλιεῖς
"Come after Me, and I will make you to become fishers

ἀνθρώπων." **18** *Καὶ εὐθέως ἀφέντες τὰ δίκτυα αὐτῶν*
of men." And immediately leaving - nets ~ their
for

ἠκολούθησαν αὐτῷ. **19** *Καὶ προβὰς ἐκεῖθεν ὀλίγον*
they followed Him. And having gone forth from there a little

εἶδεν Ἰάκωβον τὸν τοῦ Ζεβεδαίου καὶ Ἰωάννην τὸν ἀδελφὸν
He saw James the *son* - of Zebedee and John - brother ~

αὐτοῦ, καὶ αὐτοὺς ἐν τῷ πλοίῳ καταρτίζοντας τὰ δίκτυα.
his, and them in the boat mending the nets.
who also were

20 *Καὶ εὐθέως ἐκάλεσεν αὐτούς. Καὶ ἀφέντες τὸν πατέρα*
And immediately He called them. And leaving - father ~
after they left

αὐτῶν Ζεβεδαῖον ἐν τῷ πλοίῳ μετὰ τῶν μισθωτῶν
their Zebedee in the boat with the hired workers

ἀπῆλθον ὀπίσω αὐτοῦ.
they went away after Him.

Jesus Casts Out an Unclean Spirit
(Luke 4:31–37)

21 *Καὶ εἰσπορεύονται εἰς Καπερναούμ. Καὶ εὐθέως τοῖς*
And they are going into Capernaum. And immediately on the
were

σάββασιν εἰσελθὼν εἰς τὴν συναγωγὴν ἐδίδασκε.
Sabbath entering into the synagogue He was teaching.
He entered the synagogue and began teaching.

22 *Καὶ ἐξεπλήσσοντο ἐπὶ τῇ διδαχῇ αὐτοῦ, ἦν γὰρ*
And they were astonished at - teaching ~ His, [2]He [3]was [1]for

διδάσκων αὐτοὺς ὡς ἐξουσίαν ἔχων καὶ οὐχ ὡς οἱ
teaching them like authority ~ having and not like the
one who had authority

γραμματεῖς. **23** *Καὶ ἦν ἐν τῇ συναγωγῇ αὐτῶν ἄνθρωπος*
scribes. And *there* was in - synagogue ~ their a man

ἐν πνεύματι ἀκαθάρτῳ, καὶ ἀνέκραξε, **24** *λέγων, "Ἔα,*
with a(n) spirit ~ unclean, and he cried out, saying, "Let *us* alone,
"Ah!

τί ἡμῖν καὶ σοί, Ἰησοῦ Ναζαρηνέ? Ἦλθες
what to us and to You, Jesus Nazarene? Did You come
What have we to do with You,

ἀπολέσαι ἡμᾶς? Οἶδά σε τίς εἶ, ὁ ἅγιος τοῦ Θεοῦ!"
to destroy us? I know You who You are, the Holy *One* - of God!"

25 *Καὶ ἐπετίμησεν αὐτῷ ὁ Ἰησοῦς, λέγων, "Φιμώθητι καὶ*
And [2]rebuked [3]him - [1]Jesus, saying, "Be muzzled and
silenced

ἔξελθε ἐξ αὐτοῦ!" **26** *Καὶ σπαράξαν αὐτὸν τὸ πνεῦμα τὸ*
come out from him!" And convulsing him the spirit ~ -
the unclean spirit threw him into

ἀκάθαρτον καὶ κράξαν φωνῇ μεγάλῃ ἐξῆλθεν ἐξ αὐτοῦ.
unclean and crying out with a voice ~ great came out from him.
a convulsion loud

27 Καὶ ἐθαμβήθησαν πάντες, ὥστε συζητεῖν πρὸς
And they were amazed ~ all, so as to be questioning to
so that they were disputing among

ἑαυτούς, λέγοντας, "Τί ἐστι τοῦτο? Τίς ἡ διδαχὴ ἡ καινὴ
themselves, saying, "What is this? What - [2]teaching - [1]new *is*

αὕτη, ὅτι κατ' ἐξουσίαν[g] καὶ τοῖς πνεύμασι τοῖς
this, that according to authority even the spirits ~ -
with

ἀκαθάρτοις ἐπιτάσσει, καὶ ὑπακούουσιν αὐτῷ?" **28** Ἐξῆλθε
unclean He commands, and they obey Him?" [7]went [8]out

δὲ ἡ ἀκοὴ αὐτοῦ εὐθὺς εἰς ὅλην τὴν περίχωρον
[1]And [3]the [4]report [5]of [6]Him [2]immediately into whole ~ the surrounding region

τῆς Γαλιλαίας.
- of Galilee.

Jesus Heals Peter's Mother-in-Law
(Matt. 8:14, 15; Luke 4:38, 39)

29 Καὶ εὐθέως ἐκ τῆς συναγωγῆς ἐξελθόντες
And immediately out of the synagogue going forth
when they went out from the synagogue,

ἦλθον εἰς τὴν οἰκίαν Σίμωνος καὶ Ἀνδρέου μετὰ Ἰακώβου
they came to the house of Simon and Andrew with James

καὶ Ἰωάννου. **30** Ἡ δὲ πενθερὰ Σίμωνος κατέκειτο
and John. the ~ And mother-in-law of Simon was lying down

πυρέσσουσα, καὶ εὐθέως λέγουσιν αὐτῷ περὶ αὐτῆς.
burning with fever, and immediately they say to Him about her.
spoke

31 Καὶ προσελθὼν ἤγειρεν αὐτήν, κρατήσας τῆς χειρὸς
And approaching He raised up ~ her, grasping - hand ~
He came and

αὐτῆς· καὶ ἀφῆκεν αὐτὴν ὁ πυρετὸς εὐθέως, καὶ
her; and [4]left [5]her [2]the [3]fever [1]immediately, and

διηκόνει αὐτοῖς.
she was serving them.
began to serve

Jesus Heals Many People
(Matt. 8:16, 17; Luke 8:40, 41)

32 Ὀψίας δὲ γενομένης, ὅτε ἔδυ ὁ ἥλιος,
evening ~ And becoming, when [3]set [1]the [2]sun,
And when evening came,

ἔφερον πρὸς αὐτὸν πάντας τοὺς κακῶς ἔχοντας καὶ
they were bringing to Him all the *ones* [3]badly [1]having [2]*it* and
those who were ill

τοὺς δαιμονιζομένους. **33** Καὶ ἡ πόλις ὅλη
the *ones* being demon-possessed. And the city ~ whole

ἐπισυνηγμένη ἦν πρὸς τὴν θύραν. **34** Καὶ ἐθεράπευσε
gathered ~ was at the door. And He healed

πολλοὺς κακῶς ἔχοντας ποικίλαις νόσοις, καὶ δαιμόνια
many [3]badly [1]having [2]*it* with various diseases, and [5]demons
who were ill

πολλὰ ἐξέβαλε, καὶ οὐκ ἤφιε λαλεῖν τὰ
[4]many [1]He [2]cast [3]out, and [3]not [1]He [2]was [4]permitting [7]to [8]speak [5]the
He would not permit

δαιμόνια, ὅτι ᾔδεισαν αὐτόν.
[6]demons, because they knew Him.

27 Then they were all amazed, so that they questioned among themselves, saying, "What is this? What new doctrine *is* this? For with authority He commands even the unclean spirits, and they obey Him."
28 And immediately His fame spread throughout all the region around Galilee.
29 Now as soon as they had come out of the synagogue, they entered the house of Simon and Andrew, with James and John.
30 But Simon's wife's mother lay sick with a fever, and they told Him about her at once.
31 So He came and took her by the hand and lifted her up, and immediately the fever left her. And she served them.
32 At evening, when the sun had set, they brought to Him all who were sick and those who were demon-possessed.
33 And the whole city was gathered together at the door.
34 Then He healed many who were sick with various diseases, and cast out many demons; and He did not allow the demons to speak, because they knew Him.

---

g(**1:27**) NU reads *Τι εστιν τουτο? διδαχη καινη κατ εξουσιαν, What is this? A new doctrine with authority.*

35 Now in the morning, having risen a long while before daylight, He went out and departed to a solitary place; and there He prayed.
36 And Simon and those *who were* with Him searched for Him.
37 When they found Him, they said to Him, "Everyone is looking for You."
38 But He said to them, "Let us go into the next towns, that I may preach there also, because for this purpose I have come forth."
39 And He was preaching in their synagogues throughout all Galilee, and casting out demons.
40 Now a leper came to Him, imploring Him, kneeling down to Him and saying to Him, "If You are willing, You can make me clean."
41 Then Jesus, moved with compassion, stretched out *His* hand and touched him, and said to him, "I am willing; be cleansed."
42 As soon as He had spoken, immediately the leprosy left him, and he was cleansed.
43 And He strictly warned him and sent him away at once,
44 and said to him, "See that you say nothing to anyone; but go your way, show yourself to the priest, and offer for your cleansing those things which Moses commanded, as a testimony to them."
45 However, he went out and began to proclaim *it* freely, and

Jesus Preaches Throughout Galilee
(Luke 4:42–44)

35 Καὶ πρωῒ ἔννυχον λίαν ἀναστὰς ἐξῆλθε
And early in *the* night very arising He went out
in the very early morning before dawn He arose and

καὶ ἀπῆλθεν εἰς ἔρημον τόπον κἀκεῖ προσηύχετο. 36 Καὶ
and went away to a deserted place and there He was praying. And

κατεδίωξαν αὐτὸν ὁ Σίμων καὶ οἱ μετ' αὐτοῦ, 37 καὶ
[7]sought [9]out [8]Him - [1]Simon [2]and [3]the [4]*ones* [5]with [6]him, and

εὑρόντες αὐτὸν λέγουσιν αὐτῷ ὅτι "Πάντες σε
finding Him they say to Him - "All [4]You
when they found said

ζητοῦσίν."
[1]are [2]looking [3]for."

38 Καὶ λέγει αὐτοῖς, "Ἄγωμεν εἰς τὰς ἐχομένας
And He says to them, "Let us go to the neighboring
said

κωμοπόλεις, ἵνα καὶ ἐκεῖ κηρύξω· εἰς τοῦτο γὰρ
market towns, that also ˜ there I may preach: [2]for [3]this [4]*reason* [1]for

ἐξελήλυθα." 39 Καὶ ἦν κηρύσσων ἐν ταῖς συναγωγαῖς
I have come forth." And He was preaching in - synagogues ˜

αὐτῶν εἰς ὅλην τὴν Γαλιλαίαν καὶ τὰ δαιμόνια ἐκβάλλων.
their in whole ˜ the Galilee and - [3]demons [1]casting [2]out.
all of

Jesus Cleanses a Leper
(Matt. 8:1–4; Luke 5:12–16)

40 Καὶ ἔρχεται πρὸς αὐτὸν λεπρὸς παρακαλῶν αὐτὸν καὶ
And [3]comes [4]to [5]Him [1]a [2]leper imploring Him and
came

γονυπετῶν αὐτὸν καὶ λέγων αὐτῷ ὅτι "Ἐὰν θέλῃς,
kneeling before Him and saying to Him - "If You are willing,

δύνασαί με καθαρίσαι."
You are able [3]me [1]to [2]cleanse."

41 Ὁ δὲ Ἰησοῦς σπλαγχνισθείς, ἐκτείνας
- And Jesus being moved with compassion, *and* reaching out

τὴν χεῖρα ἥψατο αὐτοῦ καὶ λέγει αὐτῷ, "Θέλω,
the hand touched him and says to him, "I am willing,
His said

καθαρίσθητι." 42 Καὶ εἰπόντος αὐτοῦ, εὐθέως ἀπῆλθεν
be cleansed." And saying ˜ Him, immediately [3]went [4]away
when He said this, left

ἀπ' αὐτοῦ ἡ λέπρα,* καὶ ἐκαθαρίσθη. 43 Καὶ
[5]from [6]him [1]the [2]leprosy, and he was cleansed. And

ἐμβριμησάμενος αὐτῷ, εὐθέως ἐξέβαλεν αὐτόν, 44 καὶ
after sternly warning him, immediately He thrust forth ˜ him, and
sent him away,

λέγει αὐτῷ, "Ὅρα μηδενὶ μηδὲν εἴπῃς, ἀλλ' ὕπαγε,
says to him, "See *that* [4]to [5]no [6]one [3]nothing [1]you [2]say, but go,
said anyone

σεαυτὸν δεῖξον τῷ ἱερεῖ καὶ προσένεγκε περὶ τοῦ
yourself ˜ show to the priest and bring *as* an offering concerning -

καθαρισμοῦ σου ἃ προσέταξε Μωσῆς, εἰς
cleansing ˜ your *the things* which prescribed ˜ Moses, as

μαρτύριον αὐτοῖς." 45 Ὁ δὲ ἐξελθὼν ἤρξατο κηρύσσειν
a testimony to them." [2]the [3]*one* [1]But going out began to proclaim
he went out and began

***(1:42)** λέπρα *(lepra)*. Noun meaning *leprosy* (cf. Matt. 8:3; Luke 5:12, 13). In biblical times any eruptive skin disease was called leprosy. Thus, λέπρα could refer to what is called leprosy today, the degenerative illness caused by Hansen's bacillus, but also to other skin diseases, such as "psoriasis, lupus, ringworm, and favus" (BGD). According to the Mosaic law, leprosy was regarded as an affliction that rendered one ritually unclean. Cf. the cognate adjective λεπρός, *leprous*, sometimes used as a substantive for *leprous one, leper.*

πολλὰ καὶ διαφημίζειν τὸν λόγον, ὥστε μηκέτι αὐτὸν
many things and to spread widely the word, so that no longer Him
freely report, He was no longer

δύνασθαι φανερῶς εἰς πόλιν εἰσελθεῖν, ἀλλ' ἔξω ἐν
to be able openly [3]into [4]a [5]city [1]to [2]enter, but [3]outside [4]in
able

ἐρήμοις τόποις ἦν· καὶ ἤρχοντο πρὸς αὐτὸν
[5]uninhabited [6]places [1]He [2]was; and they were coming to Him

πανταχόθεν.
from everywhere.

Jesus Forgives and Heals a Paralytic
(Matt. 9:1–8; Luke 5:17–26)

2 1 Καὶ εἰσῆλθεν πάλιν εἰς Καφαρναοὺμ δι' ἡμερῶν καὶ
And He entered again into Capernaum after *some* days and

ἠκούσθη ὅτι εἰς οἶκόν ἐστι. 2 Καὶ εὐθέως [a]
it was heard that [3]in [4]a [5]*certain* [6]house [1]He [2]is. And immediately
was.

συνήχθησαν πολλοὶ ὥστε μηκέτι χωρεῖν
[2]were [3]gathered [4]together [1]many so that no longer to be room
there was no longer any room

μηδὲ τὰ πρὸς τὴν θύραν, καὶ ἐλάλει αὐτοῖς τὸν
not even the *places* at the door, and He was speaking to them the

λόγον. 3 Καὶ ἔρχονται πρὸς αὐτὸν παραλυτικὸν φέροντες,
word. And they come to Him [2]a [3]paralytic [1]bringing,
came

αἰρόμενον ὑπὸ τεσσάρων. 4 Καὶ μὴ δυνάμενοι προσεγγίσαι
being carried by four *men*. And not being able to get near

αὐτῷ διὰ τὸν ὄχλον, ἀπεστέγασαν τὴν στέγην ὅπου
Him because of the crowd, they unroofed the roof where
removed the tiles from

ἦν, καὶ ἐξορύξαντες χαλῶσι τὸν κράβαττον ἐφ' ᾧ
He was, and having dug through they let down the pallet on which

ὁ παραλυτικὸς κατέκειτο. 5 Ἰδὼν δὲ ὁ Ἰησοῦς τὴν
the paralytic was lying. [3]seeing [1]And - [2]Jesus -
And when Jesus saw their

πίστιν αὐτῶν λέγει τῷ παραλυτικῷ, "Τέκνον,*
faith ~ their He says to the paralytic, "Child,
faith, He said

ἀφέωνταί σοι αἱ ἁμαρτίαι σου."
[3]have [4]been [5]forgiven [6]you - [2]sins [1]your."

6 Ἦσαν δέ τινες τῶν γραμματέων ἐκεῖ καθήμενοι
[6]were [1]And [2]some [3]of [4]the [5]scribes there ~ sitting

καὶ διαλογιζόμενοι ἐν ταῖς καρδίαις αὐτῶν, 7 "Τί οὗτος
and reasoning in - hearts ~ their, "Why [2]this [3]*man*

οὕτω λαλεῖ βλασφημίας? Τίς δύναται ἀφιέναι
[6]in [7]this [8]way [1]does [4]speak [5]blasphemies? Who is able to forgive

ἁμαρτίας εἰ μὴ εἷς, ὁ Θεός?"
sins if not One, - God?"
except

8 Καὶ εὐθέως ἐπιγνοὺς ὁ Ἰησοῦς τῷ πνεύματι αὐτοῦ
And immediately knowing ~ - Jesus - in spirit ~ His
when Jesus recognized

ὅτι οὕτως αὐτοὶ διαλογίζονται ἐν ἑαυτοῖς εἶπεν αὐτοῖς,
that thus they were reasoning among themselves He said to them,

"Τί ταῦτα διαλογίζεσθε ἐν ταῖς καρδίαις ὑμῶν?
"Why [4]these [5]*things* [1]are [2]you [3]reasoning in - hearts ~ your?

9 Τί ἐστιν εὐκοπώτερον, εἰπεῖν τῷ παραλυτικῷ,
Which is easier, to say to the paralytic,

to spread the matter, so that Jesus could no longer openly enter the city, but was outside in deserted places; and they came to Him from every direction

2 And again He entered Capernaum after *some* days, and it was heard that He was in the house.
2 Immediately many gathered together, so that there was no longer room to receive *them,* not even near the door. And He preached the word to them.
3 Then they came to Him, bringing a paralytic who was carried by four *men.*
4 And when they could not come near Him because of the crowd, they uncovered the roof where He was. So when they had broken through, they let down the bed on which the paralytic was lying.
5 When Jesus saw their faith, He said to the paralytic, "Son, your sins are forgiven you."
6 And some of the scribes were sitting there and reasoning in their hearts,
7 "Why does this *Man* speak blasphemies like this? Who can forgive sins but God alone?"
8 But immediately, when Jesus perceived in His spirit that they reasoned thus within themselves, He said to them, "Why do you reason about these things in your hearts?
9 "Which is easier, to say to the paralytic, '*Your* sins are for-

[a](2:2) NU omits ευθεως, *immediately.*

***(2:5)** τέκνον *(teknon);* τεκνίον *(teknion).* τέκνον, *child,* is used about a hundred times in the NT, while the diminutive form, *teknion, little child,* occurs rarely. In the plural, τέκνον can refer to someone's posterity or descendants. It is the word almost always used by John to describe a Christian's relationship to God, while υἱος, *son,* is his word to describe Jesus as God's Son (except Rev. 21:7). τέκνον is used in a metaphorical sense in 2 Pet. 2:14 where the expression "accursed children" (lit. "children of a curse") probably stigmatizes the ungodly teachers as the "progeny of a curse." Like similar Oriental expressions (cf. "wisdom's children," Matt. 11:19), it highlights the moral character which their behavior expresses.

given you,' or to say, 'Arise,
take up your bed and walk'?
10 "But that you may know
that the Son of Man has power
on earth to forgive sins"—He
said to the paralytic,
11 "I say to you, arise, take
up your bed, and go to your
house."
12 Immediately he arose, took
up the bed, and went out in the
presence of them all, so that all
were amazed and glorified God,
saying, "We never saw *any-*
thing like this!"
13 Then He went out again by
the sea; and all the multitude
came to Him, and He taught
them.
14 As He passed by, He saw
Levi the *son* of Alphaeus sitting
at the tax office. And He said to
him, "Follow Me." So he arose
and followed Him.
15 Now it happened, as He
was dining in *Levi's* house, that
many tax collectors and sinners
also sat together with Jesus and
His disciples; for there were
many, and they followed Him.
16 And when the scribes and
Pharisees saw Him eating with
the tax collectors and sinners,
they said to His disciples, "How
is it that He eats and drinks
with tax collectors and sinners?"
17 When Jesus heard *it,* He
said to them, "Those who are
well have no need of a physi-

"Ἀφέωνταί σου αἱ ἁμαρτίαι,' ἢ εἰπεῖν, 'Ἔγειραι καὶ
'[3]have [4]been [5]forgiven [6]you [1]the [2]sins,' or to say, 'Arise and
your

ἆρόν σου τὸν κράββατον καὶ περιπάτει'? 10 Ἵνα δὲ
take up your - pallet and walk'? [2]in [3]order [4]that [1]But

εἰδῆτε ὅτι ἐξουσίαν ἔχει ὁ Υἱὸς τοῦ Ἀνθρώπου ἀφιέναι
you may know that [6]authority [5]has [1]the [2]Son - [3]of [4]Man to forgive

ἐπὶ τῆς γῆς ἁμαρτίας" — λέγει τῷ παραλυτικῷ,
[2]on [3]the [4]earth [1]sins" — He says to the paralytic,
said

11 "Σοὶ λέγω, ἔγειραι καὶ ἆρον τὸν κράββατόν σου καὶ
"[3]to [4]you [1]I [2]say, arise and take up - pallet ˜ your and

ὕπαγε εἰς τὸν οἶκόν σου." 12 Καὶ ἠγέρθη εὐθέως καὶ ἄρας
go to - house ˜ your." And he arose immediately and taking

τὸν κράββατον ἐξῆλθεν ἐναντίον πάντων, ὥστε ἐξίστασθαι
the pallet he went out before all, so that [2]to [3]be [4]amazed
his were

πάντας καὶ δοξάζειν τὸν Θεόν, λέγοντας ὅτι "Οὐδέποτε οὕτως
[1]all and to glorify - God, saying - "[2]never [5]like [6]this
glorified

εἴδομεν!"
[1]We [3]saw [4]*it!*"

Jesus Calls Sinners to Repentance
(Matt. 9:9–13; Luke 5:27–32)

13 Καὶ ἐξῆλθε πάλιν παρὰ τὴν θάλασσαν· καὶ πᾶς ὁ
And He went out again alongside the sea; and all the

ὄχλος ἤρχετο πρὸς αὐτόν, καὶ ἐδίδασκεν αὐτούς. 14 Καὶ
crowd was coming to Him, and He was teaching them. And

παράγων εἶδε Λευὶν τὸν τοῦ Ἀλφαίου καθήμενον ἐπὶ τὸ
passing by He saw Levi the *son* - of Alphaeus sitting at the

τελώνιον, καὶ λέγει αὐτῷ, "Ἀκολούθει μοι." Καὶ ἀναστὰς
tax office, and He says to him, "Follow Me." And arising
said

ἠκολούθησεν αὐτῷ.
he followed Him.

15 Καὶ ἐγένετο ἐν τῷ κατακεῖσθαι αὐτὸν ἐν τῇ οἰκίᾳ
And it happened in the to recline *to eat* Him in - house ˜
while He was dining

αὐτοῦ, καὶ πολλοὶ τελῶναι καὶ ἁμαρτωλοὶ συνανέκειντο
his, and many tax collectors and sinners were reclining *to eat*
Levi's, that dining

τῷ Ἰησοῦ καὶ τοῖς μαθηταῖς αὐτοῦ· ἦσαν γὰρ πολλοὶ καὶ
- with Jesus and - disciples ˜ His; [2]*there* [3]were [1]for many and

ἠκολούθησαν αὐτῷ. 16 Καὶ οἱ γραμματεῖς καὶ οἱ
they followed Him. And the scribes and the

Φαρισαῖοι,[b] ἰδόντες αὐτὸν ἐσθίοντο μετὰ τῶν τελωνῶν
Pharisees, seeing Him eating with the tax collectors
when they saw

καὶ ἁμαρτωλῶν, ἔλεγον τοῖς μαθηταῖς αὐτοῦ, "Τί ὅτι μετὰ τῶν
and sinners, said - to disciples ˜ His, "Why with the

τελωνῶν καὶ ἁμαρτωλῶν ἐσθίει καὶ πίνει?"[c]
tax collectors and sinners does He eat and drink?"

17 Καὶ ἀκούσας ὁ Ἰησοῦς λέγει αὐτοῖς, "Οὐ χρείαν
And hearing - Jesus says to them, "[6]not [8]need
when He heard, said

ἔχουσιν οἱ ἰσχύοντες ἰατροῦ ἀλλ' οἱ κακῶς
[5]do [7]have [1]The [2]*ones* [3]being [4]strong of a physician but the *ones* [3]badly
Those who are well those who are

[b](2:16) NU reads *οι γραμματεις των Φαρισαιων, the scribes of the Pharisees.*
[c](2:16) NU omits *και πινει, and drink.*

ἔχοντες. Οὐκ ἦλθον καλέσαι δικαίους ἀλλὰ
[1]having [2]*it*. [6]not [4]I [5]did come to call righteous *people* but
ill.

ἁμαρτωλοὺς εἰς μετάνοιαν."[d]
sinners to repentance."

Jesus Is Questioned About Fasting
(Matt. 9:14–17; Luke 5:33–39)

18 Καὶ ἦσαν οἱ μαθηταὶ Ἰωάννου καὶ οἱ τῶν
And [11]were [1]the [2]disciples [3]of [4]John [5]and [6]the [7]*disciples* [8]of [9]the

Φαρισαίων νηστεύοντες. Καὶ ἔρχονται καὶ λέγουσιν αὐτῷ,
[10]Pharisees fasting. And they come and say to Him,
came said

"Διὰ τί οἱ μαθηταὶ Ἰωάννου καὶ οἱ τῶν
"Why [2]the [3]disciples [4]of [5]John [6]and [7]the [8]*disciples* [9]of [10]the

Φαρισαίων νηστεύουσιν, οἱ δὲ σοὶ μαθηταὶ οὐ νηστεύουσι?"
[11]Pharisees [1]do fast, - but Your disciples not ˜ do fast?"

19 Καὶ εἶπεν αὐτοῖς ὁ Ἰησοῦς, "Μὴ δύνανται οἱ
And [2]said [3]to [4]them - [1]Jesus, "[12]not [11]are [13]able [5]The

υἱοὶ τοῦ νυμφῶνος, ἐν ᾧ ὁ νυμφίος
[6]sons [7]of [8]the [9]bridal [10]chamber, [16]in [17]which [18]*time* [19]the [20]bridegroom
groomsmen, while

μετ' αὐτῶν ἐστι, νηστεύειν? Ὅσον χρόνον μεθ'
[22]with [23]them [21]is, [14]to [15]fast, *are they?* As much time [5]with
As long as

ἑαυτῶν ἔχουσι τὸν νυμφίον οὐ δύνανται νηστεύειν.
[6]themselves [1]they [2]have [3]the [4]bridegroom [9]not [7]they [8]are [10]able to fast.
them

20 Ἐλεύσονται δὲ ἡμέραι ὅταν ἀπαρθῇ ἀπ' αὐτῶν
[3]will [4]come [1]But [2]days when [3]will [4]be [5]taken [6]away [7]from [8]them

ὁ νυμφίος, καὶ τότε νηστεύσουσιν ἐν ἐκείναις ταῖς
[1]the [2]bridegroom, and then they will fast in those -

ἡμέραις.
days.

21 "Καὶ οὐδεὶς ἐπίβλημα ῥάκους ἀγνάφου
"And no one [2]a [3]patch [4]of [5]a [6]piece [7]of [9]cloth [8]unshrunk

ἐπιρράπτει ἐπὶ ἱματίῳ παλαιῷ· εἰ δὲ μή, αἴρει τὸ
[1]sews on a(n) garment ˜ old; if ˜ but not, it takes away -
or else,

πλήρωμα αὐτοῦ τὸ καινὸν τοῦ παλαιοῦ, καὶ χεῖρον
completeness ˜ its the new *piece* from the old *garment*, and [4]worse

σχίσμα γίνεται. 22 Καὶ οὐδεὶς βάλλει οἶνον νέον εἰς ἀσκοὺς
[1]*the* [2]tear [3]becomes. And no one puts wine ˜ new into wineskins ˜

παλαιούς· εἰ δὲ μή, ῥήσσει ὁ οἶνος ὁ νέος τοὺς
old; if ˜ but not, [4]bursts [1]the [3]wine - [2]new the
otherwise,

ἀσκούς, καὶ ὁ οἶνος ἐκχεῖται καὶ οἱ ἀσκοὶ ἀπολοῦνται.
wineskins, and the wine spills out and the wineskins will be ruined.

Ἀλλὰ οἶνον νέον εἰς ἀσκοὺς καινοὺς βλητέον."
But [2]wine [1]new [6]into [8]wineskins [7]new [3]must [4]be [5]put."

Jesus Is Lord of the Sabbath
(Matt. 12:1–8; Luke 6:1–5)

23 Καὶ ἐγένετο παραπορεύεσθαι αὐτὸν ἐν τοῖς σάββασι
And it happened to be going along Him on the Sabbath
as He was going along

cian, but those who are sick. I
did not come to call *the* righteous, but sinners, to repentance."
18 The disciples of John and of
the Pharisees were fasting.
Then they came and said to
Him, "Why do the disciples of
John and of the Pharisees fast,
but Your disciples do not fast?"
19 And Jesus said to them,
"Can the friends of the bridegroom fast while the bridegroom is with them? As long as
they have the bridegroom with
them they cannot fast.
20 "But the days will come
when the bridegroom will be
taken away from them, and
then they will fast in those
days.
21 "No one sews a piece of
unshrunk cloth on an old garment; or else the new piece
pulls away from the old, and the
tear is made worse.
22 "And no one puts new wine
into old wineskins; or else the
new wine bursts the wineskins,
the wine is spilled, and the
wineskins are ruined. But new
wine must be put into new
wineskins."
23 Now it happened that He
went through the grainfields on
the Sabbath; and as they went

[d](2:17) NU omits *εις μετανοιαν, to repentance.*

His disciples began to pluck the
heads of grain.
24 And the Pharisees said to
Him, "Look, why do they do
what is not lawful on the Sabbath?"
25 But He said to them,
"Have you never read what David did when he was in need and
hungry, he and those with him:
26 "how he went into the
house of God *in the days* of Abiathar the high priest, and ate
the showbread, which is not
lawful to eat except for the
priests, and also gave some to
those who were with him?"
27 And He said to them, "The
Sabbath was made for man, and
not man for the Sabbath.
28 "Therefore the Son of Man
is also Lord of the Sabbath."
3 And He entered the synagogue again, and a man
was there who had a withered
hand.
2 So they watched Him
closely, whether He would heal
him on the Sabbath, so that
they might accuse Him.
3 And He said to the man
who had the withered hand,
"Step forward."
4 Then He said to them, "Is
it lawful on the Sabbath to do
good or to do evil, to save life
or to kill?" But they kept silent.
5 And when He had looked
around at them with anger, being grieved by the hardness of
their hearts, He said to the

διὰ τῶν σπορίμων, καὶ ἤρξαντο οἱ μαθηταὶ αὐτοῦ ὁδὸν
through the grainfields, and [3]began - [2]disciples [1]His [6]*their* [7]way
that

ποιεῖν τίλλοντες τοὺς στάχυας. **24** Καὶ οἱ Φαρισαῖοι
[4]to [5]make picking the heads of grain. And the Pharisees

ἔλεγον αὐτῷ, "Ἴδε τί ποιοῦσιν ἐν τοῖς σάββασιν ὃ οὐκ
said to Him, "Look why do they do on the Sabbath what not ~

ἔξεστι?"
is lawful?"

25 Καὶ αὐτὸς ἔλεγεν αὐτοῖς, "Οὐδέποτε ἀνέγνωτε τί
And He said to them, "[3]never [1]Did [2]you read what

ἐποίησε Δαβίδ, ὅτε χρείαν ἔσχε καὶ ἐπείνασεν, αὐτὸς καὶ
did ~ David, when [3]need [1]he [2]had and became hungry, he and

οἱ μετ' αὐτοῦ? **26** Πῶς εἰσῆλθεν εἰς τὸν οἶκον τοῦ Θεοῦ
the *ones* with him? How he entered into the house - of God

ἐπὶ Ἀβιάθαρ ἀρχιερέως, καὶ τοὺς ἄρτους τῆς
at the time of Abiathar *the* high priest, and [2]the [3]loaves [4]of [5]the
showbread

προθέσεως ἔφαγεν, οὓς οὐκ ἔξεστι φαγεῖν εἰ μὴ τοῖς
[6]presentation [1]ate, which [3]not [1]it [2]is [4]lawful to eat if not for the
except

ἱερεῦσι, καὶ ἔδωκε καὶ τοῖς σὺν αὐτῷ οὖσι?" **27** Καὶ
priests, and he gave ~ also to the *ones* [2]with [3]him [1]being?" And
who were?"

ἔλεγεν αὐτοῖς, "Τὸ σάββατον διὰ τὸν ἄνθρωπον
He said to them, "The Sabbath [4]for [5]the [6]sake [7]of - [8]man

ἐγένετο, οὐχ ὁ ἄνθρωπος διὰ τὸ σάββατον.
[1]came [2]into [3]existence, not - man for the sake of the Sabbath.

28 Ὥστε Κύριός ἐστιν ὁ Υἱὸς τοῦ Ἀνθρώπου καὶ τοῦ
So then [6]Lord [5]is [1]the [2]Son - [3]of [4]Man even of the

σαββάτου."
Sabbath."

Jesus Heals a Man with a Withered Hand on the Sabbath

(Matt. 12:9–14; Luke 6:6–11)

3 **1** Καὶ εἰσῆλθε πάλιν εἰς τὴν συναγωγήν. Καὶ ἦν ἐκεῖ
And He entered again into the synagogue. And [3]was [4]there

ἄνθρωπος ἐξηραμμένην ἔχων τὴν χεῖρα. **2** Καὶ
[1]a [2]man [7]withered [5]having [6]the [8]hand. And
with a

παρετήρουν αὐτὸν εἰ τοῖς σάββασι θεραπεύσει
they were observing Him if on the Sabbath He will heal
whether would

αὐτόν, ἵνα κατηγορήσωσιν αὐτοῦ. **3** Καὶ λέγει τῷ
him, so that they might accuse Him. And He says to the
said

ἀνθρώπῳ τῷ ἐξηραμμένην ἔχοντι τὴν χεῖρα, "Ἔγειραι εἰς
man the *one* [3]withered [1]having [2]the [4]hand, "Arise to
who had his hand withered,

τὸ μέσον." **4** Καὶ λέγει αὐτοῖς, "Ἔξεστι τοῖς σάββασιν
the midst." And He says to them, "Is it lawful on the Sabbath
"Step forward." said

ἀγαθοποιῆσαι ἢ κακοποιῆσαι, ψυχὴν σῶσαι ἢ ἀποκτεῖναι?"
to do good or to do evil, [3]life [1]to [2]save or to kill?"

Οἱ δὲ ἐσιώπων. **5** Καὶ περιβλεψάμενος αὐτοὺς μετ'
[2]the [3]*ones* [1]But kept silent. And looking around at them with
they when He had looked

ὀργῆς, συλλυπούμενος ἐπὶ τῇ πωρώσει τῆς καρδίας αὐτῶν,
anger, being grieved at the hardness - of heart ~ their,

λέγει τῷ ἀνθρώπῳ, "Ἔκτεινον τὴν χεῖρα σου." Καὶ
He says to the man, "Stretch out - hand ~ your." And
said

ἐξέτεινε, καὶ ἀποκατεστάθη ἡ χεὶρ αὐτοῦ ὑγιὴς ὡς ἡ
he stretched *it* out, and [3]was [4]restored - [2]hand [1]his whole like the

ἄλλη.[a] 6 Καὶ ἐξελθόντες οἱ Φαρισαῖοι εὐθέως μετὰ
other. And going out the Pharisees immediately with
the Pharisees went out with

τῶν Ἡρῳδιανῶν συμβούλιον ἐποίουν κατ' αὐτοῦ ὅπως αὐτὸν
the Herodians a council were making against Him how [4]Him
the Herodians and immediately conspired

ἀπολέσωσι.
[1]they [2]might [3]destroy.

A Great Multitude Follows Jesus

7 Καὶ ὁ Ἰησοῦς ἀνεχώρησε μετὰ τῶν μαθητῶν αὐτοῦ πρὸς
And - Jesus withdrew with - disciples ~ His to

τὴν θάλασσαν· καὶ πολὺ πλῆθος ἀπὸ τῆς Γαλιλαίας
the sea; and a large multitude from - Galilee

ἠκολούθησαν αὐτῷ καὶ ἀπὸ τῆς Ἰουδαίας 8 καὶ ἀπὸ
followed Him and from - Judea and from

Ἱεροσολύμων καὶ ἀπὸ τῆς Ἰδουμαίας καὶ πέραν τοῦ Ἰορδάνου
Jerusalem and from - Idumea and beyond the Jordan

καὶ οἱ περὶ Τύρον καὶ Σιδῶνα, πλῆθος πολύ,
and the *ones* around Tyre and Sidon, a multitude ~ large,

ἀκούσαντες ὅσα ἐποίει ἦλθον πρὸς αὐτόν. 9 Καὶ
hearing as many *things* as He was doing came to Him. And
when they heard everything

εἶπε τοῖς μαθηταῖς αὐτοῦ ἵνα πλοιάριον προσκαρτερῇ
He said - to disciples ~ His that a little boat should be kept ready

αὐτῷ διὰ τὸν ὄχλον ἵνα μὴ θλίβωσιν αὐτόν.
for Him because of the crowd so that [3]not [1]they [2]might crowd Him.

10 Πολλοὺς γὰρ ἐθεράπευσεν, ὥστε ἐπιπίπτειν αὐτῷ
[4]many [1]For [2]He [3]healed, so that to be falling upon Him
had healed, all who had afflictions were

ἵνα αὐτοῦ ἅψωνται, ὅσοι εἶχον μάστιγας.
so that Him they might touch, as many as had torments.
crowding upon Him so that they might touch Him.

11 Καὶ τὰ πνεύματα τὰ ἀκάθαρτα, ὅταν αὐτὸν
And the spirits ~ - unclean, whenever [4]Him

ἐθεώρει, προσέπιπτεν αὐτῷ καὶ ἔκραζε, λέγοντα
[1]they [2]would [3]notice, would fall before Him and would cry out, saying

ὅτι "Σὺ εἶ ὁ Υἱὸς τοῦ Θεοῦ." 12 Καὶ πολλὰ
- "You are the Son - of God." And [5]many [6]*things*
very much

ἐπετίμα αὐτοῖς ἵνα μὴ φανερὸν αὐτὸν ποιήσωσι.
[1]He [2]would [3]warn [4]them that [3]not [6]known [5]Him [1]they [2]should [4]make.

Jesus Chooses the Twelve
(Matt. 10:1–4; Luke 6:12–16)

13 Καὶ ἀναβαίνει εἰς τὸ ὄρος καὶ προσκαλεῖται
And He goes up into the mountain and summons
went summoned

οὓς ἤθελεν αὐτός, καὶ ἀπῆλθον πρὸς αὐτόν. 14 Καὶ
those whom wanted ~ He, and they came away to Him. And

ἐποίησε δώδεκα[b] ἵνα ὦσι μετ' αὐτοῦ καὶ ἵνα
He made twelve so that they might be with Him and so that
appointed

man, "Stretch out your hand." And he stretched *it* out, and his hand was restored as whole as the other.
6 Then the Pharisees went out and immediately plotted with the Herodians against Him, how they might destroy Him.
7 But Jesus withdrew with His disciples to the sea. And a great multitude from Galilee followed Him, and from Judea
8 and Jerusalem and Idumea and beyond the Jordan; and those from Tyre and Sidon, a great multitude, when they heard how many things He was doing, came to Him.
9 So He told His disciples that a small boat should be kept ready for Him because of the multitude, lest they should crush Him.
10 For He healed many, so that as many as had afflictions pressed about Him to touch Him.
11 And the unclean spirits, whenever they saw Him, fell down before Him and cried out, saying, "You are the Son of God."
12 But He sternly warned them that they should not make Him known.
13 And He went up on the mountain and called to *Him* those He Himself wanted. And they came to Him.
14 Then He appointed twelve, that they might be with Him

[a](3:5) NU omits υγιης ως η αλλη, *whole like the other.*
[b](3:14) NU adds ους και αποστολους ωνομασιν, *whom He also named apostles.*

and that He might send them
out to preach,
15 and to have power to heal
sicknesses and to cast out demons:
16 Simon, to whom He gave
the name Peter;
17 James the *son* of Zebedee
and John the brother of James,
to whom He gave the name Boanerges, that is, "Sons of
Thunder";
18 Andrew, Philip, Bartholomew, Matthew, Thomas,
James the *son* of Alphaeus,
Thaddaeus, Simon the Cananite;
19 and Judas Iscariot, who
also betrayed Him. And they
went into a house.
20 Then the multitude came
together again, so that they
could not so much as eat bread.
21 But when His own people
heard *about this,* they went out
to lay hold of Him, for they
said, "He is out of His mind."
22 And the scribes who came
down from Jerusalem said, "He
has Beelzebub," and, "By the
ruler of the demons He casts
out demons."
23 So He called them to *Him-*
self and said to them in parables: "How can Satan cast out
Satan?
24 "If a kingdom is divided
against itself, that kingdom cannot stand.
25 "And if a house is divided
against itself, that house cannot
stand.
26 "And if Satan has risen up
against himself, and is divided,

ἀποστέλλῃ αὐτοὺς κηρύσσειν **15** καὶ ἔχειν ἐξουσίαν
He might send them to preach and to have authority

θεραπεύειν τὰς νόσους καὶ[c] ἐκβάλλειν τὰ δαιμόνια. **16** Καὶ[d]
to heal - diseases and to cast out - demons. And

ἐπέθηκε τῷ Σίμωνι ὄνομα Πέτρον, **17** καὶ Ἰάκωβον τὸν
He put upon - Simon *the* name Peter, and James the *son*
gave

τοῦ Ζεβεδαίου καὶ Ἰωάννην τὸν ἀδελφὸν τοῦ Ἰακώβου, καὶ
- of Zebedee and John the brother - of James, and

ἐπέθηκεν αὐτοῖς ὀνόματα "Βοανεργές," ὅ ἐστιν "Υἱοὶ
He put upon them *the* names "Boanerges," which is "Sons
gave means

βροντῆς"· **18** καὶ Ἀνδρέαν καὶ Φίλιππον καὶ Βαρθολομαῖον
of Thunder"; and Andrew and Philip and Bartholomew

καὶ Ματθαῖον καὶ Θωμᾶν καὶ Ἰάκωβον τὸν τοῦ Ἀλφαίου
and Matthew and Thomas and James the *son* - of Alphaeus

καὶ Θαδδαῖον καὶ Σίμωνα τὸν Κανανίτην* **19** καὶ Ἰούδαν
and Thaddaeus and Simon the Cananite and Judas

Ἰσκαριώτην, ὅς καὶ παρέδωκεν αὐτόν.
Iscariot, who also gave over˜ Him.
betrayed

A House Divided Cannot Stand

(Matt. 12:22–30; Luke 11:14–23)

20 Καὶ ἔρχονται εἰς οἶκον. Καὶ συνέρχεται πάλιν
And they come into a house. And [4]comes [5]together [1]again
came assembled

ὄχλος, ὥστε μὴ δύνασθαι αὐτοὺς μήτε ἄρτον φαγεῖν.
[2]a [3]crowd, so that not to be able them not even [3]bread [1]to [2]eat.
they were not even able to eat food.

21 Καὶ ἀκούσαντες οἱ παρ' αὐτοῦ ἐξῆλθον
And hearing the *ones* from the side of Him they came out
when His relatives heard,

κρατῆσαι αὐτόν, ἔλεγον γὰρ ὅτι "Ἐξέστη."
to seize Him, [2]they [3]were [4]saying [1]for - "He has lost his mind."

22 Καὶ οἱ γραμματεῖς οἱ ἀπὸ Ἱεροσολύμων
And the scribes the *ones* from Jerusalem
who were

καταβάντες ἔλεγον ὅτι "Βεελζεβοὺλ ἔχει," καὶ ὅτι "Ἐν
coming down were saying - "[3]Beelzebul [1]He [2]has," and - "By
came down and

τῷ ἄρχοντι τῶν δαιμονίων ἐκβάλλει τὰ δαιμόνια."
the ruler of the demons He casts out - demons."

23 Καὶ προσκαλεσάμενος αὐτοὺς ἐν παραβολαῖς ἔλεγεν
And having summoned them in parables He said
He began to say to them

αὐτοῖς, "Πῶς δύναται Σατανᾶς Σατανᾶν ἐκβάλλειν? **24** Καὶ
to them, "How [1]is [3]able [2]Satan [7]Satan [4]to [5]cast [6]out? And
in parables,

ἐὰν βασιλεία ἐφ' ἑαυτὴν μερισθῇ, οὐ δύναται σταθῆναι ἡ
if a kingdom [3]against [4]itself [1]is [2]divided, [8]not [7]is [9]able [10]to [11]stand -

βασιλεία ἐκείνη. **25** Καὶ ἐὰν οἰκία ἐφ' ἑαυτὴν
[6]kingdom [5]that. And if a household [3]against [4]itself

μερισθῇ, οὐ δύναται σταθῆναι ἡ οἰκία ἐκείνη. **26** Καὶ εἰ
[1]is [2]divided, [8]not [7]is [9]able [10]to [11]stand - [6]household [5]that. And if

ὁ Σατανᾶς ἀνέστη ἐφ' ἑαυτὸν καὶ μεμέρισται, οὐ
- Satan rose up against himself and has become divided, [3]not

---

[c](3:15) NU omits θεραπευειν τας νοσους και, *to heal diseases and.*
[d](3:16) NU adds και εποιησεν τους δωδεκα, *And He appointed the twelve.*

*(3:18) Κανανίτης *(Kananitēs).* Noun used here and in Matt. 10:4 (NU reads Καναναῖος in both verses) of the lesser-known Simon among the apostles, apparently meaning *Cananite* (one from Cana). This disciple is called "Simon the Zealot" in Luke 6:15 and Acts 1:13, and a few scholars have suggested that Κανανίτης may really be a transliteration of an Aramaic word meaning *zealot.*

δύναται σταθῆναι ἀλλὰ τέλος ἔχει. 27 Οὐδεὶς δύναται τὰ
[1]he [2]is able to stand but an end has. No one is able the
is finished. to

σκεύη τοῦ ἰσχυροῦ, εἰσελθὼν εἰς τὴν οἰκίαν αὐτοῦ,
things of the strong *man,* entering into - household ˜ his,
enter the strong man's house and plunder his

διαρπάσαι ἐὰν μὴ πρῶτον τὸν ἰσχυρὸν δήσῃ, καὶ τότε
to plunder if not [2]first [4]the [5]strong [6]*man* [1]he [3]binds, and then
possessions unless

τὴν οἰκίαν αὐτοῦ διαρπάσῃ.
- [5]household [4]his [1]he [2]may [3]plunder.

Jesus Warns of the Unpardonable Sin
(Matt. 12:31, 32; Luke 12:10)

28 "Ἀμὴν λέγω ὑμῖν ὅτι πάντα ἀφεθήσεται τὰ
"Amen I say to you that all [2]will [3]be [4]forgiven -
"Assuredly

ἁμαρτήματα* τοῖς υἱοῖς τῶν ἀνθρώπων, καὶ βλασφημίαι
[1]sins the sons - of men, also blasphemies

ὅσας ἂν βλασφημήσωσιν· 29 ὃς δ' ἂν βλασφημήσῃ
as many as - they may blaspheme; who ˜ but ever blasphemes

εἰς τὸ Πνεῦμα τὸ Ἅγιον οὐκ ἔχει ἄφεσιν εἰς
against the Spirit ˜ - Holy [3]not [1]he [2]does have forgiveness into
he never has forgiveness,

τὸν αἰῶνα, ἀλλ' ἔνοχός ἐστιν αἰωνίου κρίσεως" —
the age, but [2]under [3]sentence [4]of [1]is eternal judgment" —
condemnation" —

30 ὅτι ἔλεγον, "Πνεῦμα ἀκάθαρτον ἔχει."
because they were saying, "[3]a(n) [5]spirit [4]unclean [1]He [2]has."

The Mother and Brothers of Jesus
(Matt. 12:46–50; Luke 8:19–21)

31 Ἔρχονται οὖν οἱ ἀδελφοὶ καὶ ἡ μήτηρ αὐτοῦ καὶ
[6]come [1]Then - [3]brothers [4]and - [5]mother [2]His and
came

ἔξω ἑστῶτες ἀπέστειλαν πρὸς αὐτόν, φωνοῦντες
outside standing they sent *someone* to Him, calling for
as they stood outside

αὐτόν. 32 Καὶ ἐκάθητο ὄχλος περὶ αὐτόν· εἶπον δὲ
Him. And [3]was [4]sitting [1]a [2]crowd around Him; [2]they [3]said [1]and

αὐτῷ, "Ἰδού, ἡ μήτηρ σου καὶ οἱ ἀδελφοί σου καὶ αἱ
to Him, "Look, - mother ˜ Your and - brothers ˜ Your and -

ἀδελφαί σου[e] ἔξω ζητοῦσί σε."
sisters ˜ Your [4]outside [1]are [2]seeking [3]You."

33 Καὶ ἀπεκρίθη αὐτοῖς λέγων, "Τίς ἐστιν ἡ μήτηρ μου
And He answered them saying, "Who is - mother ˜ My

ἢ οἱ ἀδελφοί μου?" 34 Καὶ περιβλεψάμενος κύκλῳ τοὺς
or - brothers ˜ My?" And looking around [4]at [1]in [2]a [3]circle the *ones*
when He had looked

περὶ αὐτὸν καθημένους λέγει, "Ἴδε ἡ μήτηρ μου καὶ οἱ
[2]around [3]Him [1]sitting He says, "See - mother ˜ My and -
said, "Here are

ἀδελφοί μου! 35 Ὃς γὰρ ἂν ποιήσῃ τὸ θέλημα τοῦ Θεοῦ,
brothers ˜ My! who ˜ For ever does the will - of God,

οὗτος ἀδελφός μου καὶ ἀδελφή μου καὶ μήτηρ ἐστί."
this *one* [3]brother [2]My [4]and [6]sister [5]My [7]and [8]mother [1]is."

he cannot stand, but has an end.
27 "No one can enter a strong man's house and plunder his goods, unless he first binds the strong man. And then he will plunder his house.
28 "Assuredly, I say to you, all sins will be forgiven the sons of men, and whatever blasphemies they may utter;
29 "but he who blasphemes against the Holy Spirit never has forgiveness, but is subject to eternal condemnation"—
30 because they said, "He has an unclean spirit."
31 Then His brothers and His mother came, and standing outside they sent to Him, calling Him.
32 And a multitude was sitting around Him; and they said to Him, "Look, Your mother and Your brothers are outside seeking You."
33 But He answered them, saying, "Who is My mother, or My brothers?"
34 And He looked around in a circle at those who sat about Him, and said, "Here are My mother and My brothers!
35 "For whoever does the will of God is My brother and My sister and mother."

---

[e](3:32) TR omits *και αι αδελφαι σου, and Your sisters.*

---

*(3:28) *ἁμάρτημα (hamartēma).* Noun usually translated *sin,* meaning "an individual act of sin." Whereas the synonymous noun *ἁμαρτία* (see *ἁμαρτία* at John 9:41) stresses the action of or committing of sin, *ἁμάρτημα* emphasizes that a particular action is a violation of God's will, and thus a sin. Here "blasphemy" is specified as one of many kinds of sinful acts. Cf. also the cognate verb *ἁμαρτάνω, to sin;* and the adjective *ἁμαρτωλός, sinful, sinner.*

4 And again He began to
teach by the sea. And a
great multitude was gathered to
Him, so that He got into a boat
and sat *in it* on the sea; and the
whole multitude was on the
land facing the sea.
2 Then He taught them many
things by parables, and said to
them in His teaching:
3 "Listen! Behold, a sower
went out to sow.
4 "And it happened, as he
sowed, *that* some *seed* fell by
the wayside; and the birds of
the air came and devoured it.
5 "Some fell on stony
ground, where it did not have
much earth; and immediately it
sprang up because it had no
depth of earth.
6 "But when the sun was up
it was scorched, and because it
had no root it withered away.
7 "And some *seed* fell among
thorns; and the thorns grew up
and choked it, and it yielded no
crop.
8 "But other *seed* fell on good
ground and yielded a crop that
sprang up, increased and produced: some thirtyfold, some
sixty, and some a hundred."
9 And He said to them, "He
who has ears to hear, let him
hear!"
10 But when He was alone,
those around Him with the
twelve asked Him about the
parable.
11 And He said to them, "To
you it has been given to know

The Parable of the Sower
(Matt. 13:1–9; Luke 8:4–8)

4 1 Καὶ πάλιν ἤρξατο διδάσκειν παρὰ τὴν θάλασσαν. Καὶ
And again He began to teach beside the sea. And

συνήχθη πρὸς αὐτὸν ὄχλος πολύς, ὥστε αὐτὸν ἐμβάντα
[4]was [5]gathered [6]to [7]Him [1]a [3]crowd [2]large, so that Him stepping in
He got aboard

εἰς τὸ πλοῖον καθῆσθαι ἐν τῇ θαλάσσῃ, καὶ πᾶς ὁ ὄχλος
into the boat to sit in the sea, and all the crowd
on the sea and sat,

πρὸς τὴν θάλασσαν ἐπὶ τῆς γῆς ἦν. 2 Καὶ ἐδίδασκεν
[5]by [6]the [7]sea [2]upon [3]the [4]land [1]was. And He was teaching

αὐτοὺς ἐν παραβολαῖς πολλά, καὶ ἔλεγεν αὐτοῖς ἐν τῇ
them [3]in [4]parables [1]many [2]*things,* and He said to them in -

διδαχῇ αὐτοῦ, 3 "'Ακούετε. 'Ιδού, ἐξῆλθεν ὁ σπείρων τοῦ
teaching ˜ His, "Listen. See, [4]went [5]out [1]the [2]sowing [3]*one* -
a sower

σπεῖραι. 4 Καὶ ἐγένετο ἐν τῷ σπείρειν ὃ μὲν ἔπεσε
to sow. And it happened in the to sow some *part* fell
as he sowed

παρὰ τὴν ὁδόν, καὶ ἦλθε τὰ πετεινὰ[a] καὶ κατέφαγεν αὐτό.
alongside the road, and [3]came [1]the [2]birds and devoured it.

5 Ἄλλο δὲ ἔπεσεν ἐπὶ τὸ πετρῶδες ὅπου οὐκ
[2]another [3]*part* [1]And fell on the stony ground where [3]not

εἶχε γῆν πολλήν, καὶ εὐθέως ἐξανέτειλε διὰ τὸ μὴ
[1]it [2]did have earth ˜ much, and immediately it sprang up because - not
it had

ἔχειν βάθος γῆς. 6 Ἡλίου δὲ ἀνατείλαντος, ἐκαυματίσθη,
to have depth of earth. *the* sun But rising, it was scorched,
no But when the sun rose,

καὶ διὰ τὸ μὴ ἔχειν ῥίζαν ἐξηράνθη. 7 Καὶ ἄλλο
and because - not to have root it was withered up. And another *part*
it had no

ἔπεσεν εἰς τὰς ἀκάνθας, καὶ ἀνέβησαν αἱ ἄκανθαι καὶ
fell into the thorns, and [3]came [4]up [1]the [2]thorns and

συνέπνιξαν αὐτό, καὶ καρπὸν οὐκ ἔδωκε. 8 Καὶ ἄλλο
choked out ˜ it, and [5]fruit [3]not [1]it [2]did [4]give. And another *part*
yield.

ἔπεσεν εἰς τὴν γῆν τὴν καλήν, καὶ ἐδίδου καρπὸν
fell into the earth ˜ - good, and it was giving fruit
yielding

ἀναβαίνοντα καὶ αὐξάνοντα, καὶ ἔφερεν ἓν τριάκοντα
coming up and growing, and it was bearing one *part* thirty*fold*

καὶ ἓν ἑξήκοντα καὶ ἓν ἑκατόν." 9 Καὶ ἔλεγεν,[b]
and one *part* sixty*fold* and one *part* a hundred*fold."* And He said,

"Ὁ ἔχων ὦτα ἀκούειν ἀκουέτω."
"The *one* having ears to hear let him hear."

Jesus Explains the Purpose of Parables
(Matt. 13:10–17; Luke 8:9, 10)

10 Ὅτε δὲ ἐγένετο κατὰ μόνας, ἠρώτησαν αὐτὸν
when ˜ But He was in the manner of alone, [9]asked [11]about [10]Him
by Himself,

οἱ περὶ αὐτὸν σὺν τοῖς δώδεκα τὴν παραβολήν.
[1]the [2]*ones* [3]around [4]Him [5]together [6]with [7]the [8]twelve the parable.
those

11 Καὶ ἔλεγεν αὐτοῖς, "Ὑμῖν δέδοται γνῶναι τὸ
And He said to them, "To you it has been given to know the

---

[a](4:4) TR adds *του ουρανου, of the air.* [b](4:9) TR adds *αυτοις, to them.*

μυστήριον τῆς βασιλείας τοῦ Θεοῦ· ἐκείνοις δὲ τοῖς
mystery of the kingdom - of God; [2]to [3]those [1]but the *ones* (who are)

ἔξω ἐν παραβολαῖς τὰ πάντα γίνεται, 12 ἵνα
outside [4]in [5]parables - [1]all [2]*things* [3]are, that

«Βλέποντες βλέπωσι καὶ μὴ ἴδωσι,
«Seeing they may see and not perceive,

Καὶ ἀκούοντες ἀκούωσι καὶ μὴ συνιῶσι,
And hearing they may hear and not understand,

Μήποτε ἐπιστρέψωσι καὶ ἀφεθῇ αὐτοῖς τὰ
Lest they turn and [3]be [4]forgiven [5]them [1]the (their)

ἁμαρτήματα.»[c]
[2]sins.»

Jesus Explains the Parable of the Sower
(Matt. 13:18–23; Luke 8:11–15)

13 Καὶ λέγει αὐτοῖς, "Οὐκ οἴδατε τὴν παραβολὴν
And He says (said) to them, "[3]not [1]Do [2]you know - parable ˜

ταύτην? Καὶ πῶς πάσας τὰς παραβολὰς γνώσεσθε?
this? And how [4]all [5]the [6]parables [1]will [2]you [3]know?

14 Ὁ σπείρων τὸν λόγον σπείρει. 15 Οὗτοι δέ εἰσιν
The *one* sowing [2]the [3]word [1]sows. these ˜ And are

οἱ παρὰ τὴν ὁδὸν ὅπου σπείρεται ὁ λόγος, καὶ ὅταν
the *seeds* beside the road where [3]is [4]sown [1]the [2]word, and whenever

ἀκούσωσιν εὐθέως ἔρχεται ὁ Σατανᾶς καὶ αἴρει τὸν
they hear immediately comes ˜ - Satan and takes away the

λόγον τὸν ἐσπαρμένον ἐν ταῖς καρδίαις αὐτῶν. 16 Καὶ
word the *one* (which was) sown in - hearts ˜ their. And

οὗτοί εἰσιν ὁμοίως οἱ ἐπὶ τὰ πετρώδη σπειρόμενοι,
these are similarly the *seeds* [3]on [4]the [5]stony [6]ground [1]being [2]sown,

οἵ, ὅταν ἀκούσωσι τὸν λόγον εὐθέως μετὰ χαρᾶς
which, whenever they hear the word immediately with joy

λαμβάνουσιν αὐτόν, 17 καὶ οὐκ ἔχουσι ῥίζαν ἐν ἑαυτοῖς
they receive it, and [3]not [1]they [2]do have root in themselves

ἀλλὰ πρόσκαιροί εἰσιν. Εἶτα γενομένης θλίψεως ἢ
but short-lived ˜ are. Afterward coming (when) a trial (trials) or (or)

διωγμοῦ διὰ τὸν λόγον, εὐθέως σκανδαλίζονται.
persecution (persecution come) because of the word, immediately they are offended.

18 Καὶ οὗτοί εἰσιν οἱ εἰς τὰς ἀκάνθας σπειρόμενοι,
And these are the *seeds* [3]in [4]the [5]thorns [1]being [2]sown,

οἱ τὸν λόγον ἀκούοντες, 19 καὶ αἱ μέριμναι τοῦ αἰῶνος
the *ones* (who are) [2]the [3]word [1]hearing, and the anxieties - of age ˜

τούτου καὶ ἡ ἀπάτη τοῦ πλούτου καὶ αἱ περὶ τὰ
this and the deceitfulness - of riches and the [2]about (for) -

λοιπὰ ἐπιθυμίαι εἰσπορευόμεναι συμπνίγουσι τὸν
[3]remaining (other) [4]*things* [1]desires coming in choke out the

λόγον, καὶ ἄκαρπος γίνεται. 20 Καὶ οὗτοί εἰσιν οἱ ἐπὶ
word, and [3]fruitless [1]it [2]becomes. And these are the *seeds* [2]on

τὴν γῆν τὴν καλὴν σπαρέντες, οἵτινες ἀκούουσι τὸν λόγον
[3]the [5]ground - [4]good [1]sown, such who hear the word

---

the mystery of the kingdom of God; but to those who are outside, all things come in parables,
12 "so that

'Seeing they may see and not perceive,
And hearing they may hear and not understand;
Lest they should turn,
And their sins be forgiven them.'"

13 And He said to them, "Do you not understand this parable? How then will you understand all the parables?
14 "The sower sows the word.
15 "And these are the ones by the wayside where the word is sown. When they hear, Satan comes immediately and takes away the word that was sown in their hearts.
16 "These likewise are the ones sown on stony ground who, when they hear the word, immediately receive it with gladness;
17 "and they have no root in themselves, and so endure only for a time. Afterward, when tribulation or persecution arises for the word's sake, immediately they stumble.
18 "Now these are the ones sown among thorns; *they are* the ones who hear the word,
19 "and the cares of this world, the deceitfulness of riches, and the desires for other things entering in choke the word, and it becomes unfruitful.
20 "But these are the ones sown on good ground, those who hear the word, accept *it,*

---

[c](**4:12**) Is. 6:9, 10

and bear fruit: some thirtyfold, some sixty, and some a hundred."

21 Also He said to them, "Is a lamp brought to be put under a basket or under a bed? Is it not to be set on a lampstand?

22 "For there is nothing hidden which will not be revealed, nor has anything been kept secret but that it should come to light.

23 "If anyone has ears to hear, let him hear."

24 Then He said to them, "Take heed what you hear. With the same measure you use, it will be measured to you; and to you who hear, more will be given.

25 "For whoever has, to him more will be given; but whoever does not have, even what he has will be taken away from him."

26 And He said, "The kingdom of God is as if a man should scatter seed on the ground,

27 "and should sleep by night and rise by day, and the seed should sprout and grow, he himself does not know how.

28 "For the earth yields crops by itself: first the blade, then the head, after that the full grain in the head.

29 "But when the grain ripens, immediately he puts in the sickle, because the harvest has come."

30 Then He said, "To what shall we liken the kingdom of

---

*(4:22) φανερόω (phaneroō). Verb meaning *to reveal, make known, make manifest, show.* It is used nearly 50 times in the NT, of which most appear in the writings of Paul and the apostle John. In the passive voice it can indicate the idea of "being revealed" or of "becoming visible," and in both active and passive voices it often contains overtones of revelation or of supernatural manifestation. So Paul can say that "the righteousness of God apart from the law *is revealed*" (Rom. 3:21), i.e., it is a divine revelation just as much as was the OT law (see Rom. 3:19, 20). On the other hand, the Christian himself will "appear," meaning to be manifested, fully disclosed and examined, "before the judgment seat of Christ" (2 Cor. 5:10). But this, too, will be a work of divine, supernatural disclosure.

καὶ παραδέχονται καὶ καρποφοροῦσιν, ἓν τριάκοντα καὶ
and welcome *it* and bear fruit, one *part* thirty*fold* and

ἓν ἑξήκοντα καὶ ἓν ἑκατόν."
one *part* sixty*fold* and one *part* a hundred*fold.*"

Light Under a Bushel
(Luke 8:16–18)

21 *Καὶ ἔλεγεν αὐτοῖς, "Μήτι ὁ λύχνος ἔρχεται ἵνα*
And He said to them, "[4]not [1]The [2]lamp [3]does come so that
(A)

ὑπὸ τὸν μόδιον τεθῇ ἢ ὑπὸ τὴν κλίνην?
[5]under [6]the [7]measuring [8]basket [1]it [2]may [3]be [4]put or under the bed, *does it?*
(a) (a)

Οὐχ ἵνα ἐπὶ τὴν λυχνίαν ἐπιτεθῇ? **22** *Οὐ*
Does it not *come* so that [5]on [6]the [7]lampstand [1]it [2]may [3]be [4]put? [11]not
(a)

*γάρ ἐστί τι κρυπτὸν ὃ ἐὰν μὴ φανερωθῇ,**
[8]For [9]*there* [10]is [12]anything hidden which - not ˜ will be made manifest,

οὐδὲ ἐγένετο ἀπόκρυφον ἀλλ' ἵνα εἰς φανερὸν ἔλθῃ.
nor was it hidden but that [4]to [5]manifestation [1]it [2]may [3]come.

23 *Εἴ τις ἔχει ὦτα ἀκούειν ἀκουέτω."*
If anyone has ears to hear let him hear."

24 *Καὶ ἔλεγεν αὐτοῖς, "Βλέπετε τί ἀκούετε. Ἐν ᾧ*
And He said to them, "Watch what you hear. By what

μέτρῳ μετρεῖτε μετρηθήσεται ὑμῖν καὶ
measure you measure out it will be measured out to you and

προστεθήσεται ὑμῖν τοῖς ἀκούουσιν. **25** *Ὃς γὰρ ἂν ἔχῃ,*
more will be added to you the *ones* hearing. who ˜ For ever has,
(who) (hear.)

δοθήσεται αὐτῷ, καὶ ὃς οὐκ ἔχει, καὶ ὃ
more will be given to him, and *the one* who not ˜ does have, even what

ἔχει ἀρθήσεται ἀπ' αὐτοῦ."
he has will be taken away from him."

The Parable of the Growing Seed

26 *Καὶ ἔλεγεν, "Οὕτως ἐστὶν ἡ βασιλεία τοῦ Θεοῦ ὡς ἐὰν*
And He said, "Thus is the kingdom - of God as -

ἄνθρωπος βάλῃ τὸν σπόρον ἐπὶ τῆς γῆς **27** *καὶ*
a man should cast the seed on the ground and

καθεύδῃ καὶ ἐγείρηται νύκτα καὶ ἡμέραν, καὶ ὁ σπόρος
should sleep and should arise night and day, and the seed

βλαστάνῃ καὶ μηκύνηται ὡς οὐκ οἶδεν αὐτός.
should sprout and should grow how [4]not [1]he [3]does [5]know [2]himself.

28 *Αὐτομάτη γὰρ ἡ γῆ καρποφορεῖ, πρῶτον χόρτον, εἶτα*
[6]of [7]itself [1]For [2]the [3]earth [4]produces [5]fruit, first a shoot, then

στάχυν, εἶτα πλήρη σῖτον ἐν τῷ στάχυϊ. **29** *Ὅταν*
a head of grain, then full wheat in the head of grain. whenever ˜

δὲ παραδῷ ὁ καρπός, εὐθέως ἀποστέλλει τὸ δρέπανον,
But [3]permits [1]the [2]fruit, immediately he sends forth the sickle,
(is ready)

ὅτι παρέστηκεν ὁ θερισμός."
because [3]has [4]come [1]the [2]harvest."

The Parable of the Mustard Seed
(Matt. 13:31, 32; Luke 13:18, 19)

30 *Καὶ ἔλεγε, "Τίνι ὁμοιώσομεν τὴν βασιλείαν τοῦ*
And He said, "To what shall we compare the kingdom -

Θεοῦ, ἢ ἐν ποίᾳ παραβολῇ παραβάλωμεν αὐτήν?
of God, or by what sort of parable shall we illustrate it?

31 Ὡς κόκκον σινάπεως, ὃς ὅταν σπαρῇ ἐπὶ τῆς
It is like a seed of mustard, which whenever it is sown on the
mustard seed,

γῆς, μικρότερος πάντων τῶν σπερμάτων ἐστὶ τῶν ἐπὶ τῆς
ground, ^{2}smaller ^{3}than ^{4}all ^{5}of ^{6}the ^{7}seeds ^{1}is - on the

γῆς, 32 καὶ ὅταν σπαρῇ, ἀναβαίνει καὶ γίνεται πάντων
earth, and whenever it is sown, it comes up and becomes ^{2}*than* ^{3}all

τῶν λαχάνων μείζων καὶ ποιεῖ κλάδους μεγάλους,
^{4}of ^{5}the ^{6}garden ^{7}vegetables ^{1}greater and produces branches ~ great,

ὥστε δύνασθαι ὑπὸ τὴν σκιὰν αὐτοῦ τὰ πετεινὰ τοῦ
so that ^{5}to ^{6}be ^{7}able ^{10}under - ^{12}shade ^{11}its ^{1}the ^{2}birds -
are

οὐρανοῦ κατασκηνοῦν."
^{3}of ^{4}heaven ^{8}to ^{9}nest."

Jesus Tells Many Parables
(Matt. 13:34, 35)

33 Καὶ τοιαύταις παραβολαῖς πολλαῖς ἐλάλει αὐτοῖς
And by ^{2}such ^{3}parables ^{1}many He would speak to them

τὸν λόγον, καθὼς ἐδύναντο ἀκούειν. 34 Χωρὶς δὲ
the word, just as they were able to hear *it*. ^{2}apart ^{3}from ^{1}And

παραβολῆς οὐκ ἐλάλει αὐτοῖς, κατ' ἰδίαν δὲ
a parable ^{3}not ^{1}He ^{2}did ^{4}speak to them, privately ~ however

τοῖς μαθηταῖς αὐτοῦ ἐπέλυε πάντα.
to disciples ~ His He would explain all *things*.

Wind and Wave Obey Jesus
(Matt. 8:23–27; Luke 8:22–25)

35 Καὶ λέγει αὐτοῖς ἐν ἐκείνῃ τῇ ἡμέρᾳ, ὀψίας
And He says to them on that - day, evening
said when evening

γενομένης, "Διέλθωμεν εἰς τὸ πέραν." 36 Καὶ ἀφέντες
having become, "Let us go across to the other side." And leaving
had come,

τὸν ὄχλον παραλαμβάνουσιν αὐτὸν ὡς ἦν ἐν τῷ πλοίῳ. Καὶ
the crowd they take along ~ Him as He was in the boat. ^{6}also
took

ἄλλα δὲ πλοιάρια ἦν μετ' αὐτοῦ. 37 Καὶ γίνεται
^{2}other ^{1}But ^{3}little ^{4}boats ^{5}were with Him. And *there* becomes
there was

λαῖλαψ ἀνέμου μεγάλη, τὰ δὲ κύματα ἐπέβαλεν εἰς τὸ
^{1}a ^{3}storm ^{4}of ^{5}wind ^{2}great, the ~ and waves dashed up into the
a severe wind storm,

πλοῖον, ὥστε αὐτὸ ἤδη γεμίζεσθαι. 38 Καὶ ἦν αὐτὸς ἐπὶ
boat, so that it *was* already to be filling up. And was ~ He in
filling up.

τῇ πρύμνῃ ἐπὶ τὸ προσκεφάλαιον καθεύδων· καὶ
the stern ^{2}upon ^{3}the ^{4}cushion ^{1}sleeping; and

διεγείρουσιν αὐτὸν καὶ λέγουσιν αὐτῷ, "Διδάσκαλε! Οὐ
they awakened Him and say to Him, "Teacher! ^{3}not
said

μέλει σοι ὅτι ἀπολλύμεθα?"
^{1}Does ^{2}it matter to You that we are perishing?"

39 Καὶ διεγερθεὶς ἐπετίμησε τῷ ἀνέμῳ καὶ εἶπε τῇ
And having awakened He rebuked the wind and He said to the

God? Or with what parable shall we picture it?
31 "*It is* like a mustard seed which, when it is sown on the ground, is smaller than all the seeds on earth;
32 "but when it is sown, it grows up and becomes greater than all herbs, and shoots out large branches, so that the birds of the air may nest under its shade."
33 And with many such parables He spoke the word to them as they were able to hear *it*.
34 But without a parable He did not speak to them. And when they were alone, He explained all things to His disciples.
35 On the same day, when evening had come, He said to them, "Let us cross over to the other side."
36 Now when they had left the multitude, they took Him along in the boat as He was. And other little boats were also with Him.
37 And a great windstorm arose, and the waves beat into the boat, so that it was already filling.
38 But He was in the stern, asleep on a pillow. And they awoke Him and said to Him, "Teacher, do You not care that we are perishing?"
39 Then He arose and rebuked the wind, and said to the

sea, "Peace, be still!" And the
wind ceased and there was a
great calm.
40 But He said to them, "Why
are you so fearful? How *is it*
that you have no faith?"
41 And they feared exceedingly, and said to one another,
"Who can this be, that even the
wind and the sea obey Him!"
5 Then they came to the
other side of the sea, to
the country of the Gadarenes.
2 And when He had come out
of the boat, immediately there
met Him out of the tombs a
man with an unclean spirit,
3 who had *his* dwelling
among the tombs; and no one
could bind him, not even with
chains,
4 because he had often been
bound with shackles and chains.
And the chains had been pulled
apart by him, and the shackles
broken in pieces; neither could
anyone tame him.
5 And always, night and day,
he was in the mountains and in
the tombs, crying out and cutting himself with stones.
6 When he saw Jesus from
afar, he ran and worshiped
Him.
7 And he cried out with a
loud voice and said, "What have
I to do with You, Jesus, Son of
the Most High God? I implore
You by God that You do not torment me."
8 For He said to him, "Come
out of the man, unclean spirit!"

θαλάσσῃ, "Σιώπα, πεφίμωσο!" Καὶ ἐκόπασεν ὁ ἄνεμος, καὶ
sea, "Be quiet, be muzzled!" And [3]abated [1]the [2]wind, and
silenced!"

ἐγένετο γαλήνη μεγάλη. 40 Καὶ εἶπεν αὐτοῖς, "Τί δειλοί
there was [3]calm [1]a [2]great. And He said to them, "Why [4]fearful

ἐστε οὕτως? Πῶς οὐκ ἔχετε[d] πίστιν?"
[1]are [2]you [3]thus? How *is it that* [3]not [1]you [2]do have faith?"
so?

41 Καὶ ἐφοβήθησαν φόβον μέγαν, καὶ ἔλεγον πρὸς
And they feared a fear ˜ great, and were saying to

ἀλλήλους, "Τίς ἄρα οὗτός ἐστιν ὅτι καὶ ὁ ἄνεμος καὶ ἡ
one another, "Who then this ˜ is that even the wind and the

θάλασσα ὑπακούουσιν αὐτῷ?"
sea obey Him?"

Jesus Heals a Demon-Possessed Man

(Matt. 8:28–34; Luke 8:26–39)

5 1 Καὶ ἦλθον εἰς τὸ πέραν τῆς θαλάσσης εἰς τὴν
And they came to the other side of the sea to the

χώραν τῶν Γαδαρηνῶν.[a] 2 Καὶ ἐξελθόντι αὐτῷ ἐκ τοῦ
region of the Gadarenes. And coming out Him out of the
when He got

πλοίου, εὐθέως ἀπήντησεν αὐτῷ ἐκ τῶν μνημείων
boat, immediately *there* met Him from the tombs

ἄνθρωπος ἐν πνεύματι ἀκαθάρτῳ, 3 ὃς τὴν κατοίκησιν εἶχεν
a man with a(n) spirit ˜ unclean, who [2]the [3]dwelling [1]had
his

ἐν τοῖς μνήμασιν. Καὶ οὔτε ἁλύσεσιν[b] οὐδεὶς ἐδύνατο
among the tombs. And not even with chains no one was able
was anyone able

αὐτὸν δῆσαι, 4 διὰ τὸ αὐτὸν πολλάκις πέδαις καὶ
[3]him [1]to [2]bind, because - him often [5]with [6]shackles [7]and
he

ἁλύσεσι δεδέσθαι καὶ διεσπάσθαι ὑπ᾽
[8]chains [1]to [2]have [3]been [4]bound and [3]to [4]have [5]been [6]torn [7]apart [8]by
had been had been

αὐτοῦ τὰς ἁλύσεις, καὶ τὰς πέδας συντετρίφθαι, καὶ οὐδεὶς
[9]him [1]the [2]chains, and the shackles to have been broken, and no one
had been

αὐτὸν ἴσχυε δαμάσαι. 5 Καὶ διὰ παντός, νυκτὸς καὶ
[5]him [1]was [2]able [3]to [4]subdue. And through everything, of night and
always, by

ἡμέρας, ἐν τοῖς ὄρεσι καὶ ἐν τοῖς μνήμασιν ἦν κράζων
day, in the mountains and in the tombs he was crying out

καὶ κατακόπτων ἑαυτὸν λίθοις. 6 Ἰδὼν δὲ τὸν Ἰησοῦν
and cutting himself with stones. seeing ˜ And - Jesus
bruising

ἀπὸ μακρόθεν ἔδραμε καὶ προσεκύνησεν αὐτῷ 7 καὶ κράξας
from a distance he ran and worshiped Him and crying out

φωνῇ μεγάλῃ εἶπε, "Τί ἐμοὶ καὶ σοί, Ἰησοῦ,
with a voice ˜ great he said, "What to me and to You, Jesus,
loud "What have I to do with You,

Υἱὲ τοῦ Θεοῦ τοῦ ὑψίστου? Ὁρκίζω σε τὸν Θεόν, μή με
Son - of [4]God [1]the [2]Most [3]High? I adjure by ˜ You - God, [2]not [4]me

βασανίσῃς!"
[1]do [3]torment!"

8 Ἔλεγε γὰρ αὐτῷ, "Ἔξελθε, τὸ πνεῦμα τὸ
[2]He [3]was [4]saying [1]For to him, "Come out, - spirit ˜ -

[d](4:40) NU reads ουπω εχετε, *Do you not yet have.* [a](5:1) NU reads Γερασηνων, *Gerasenes.* [b](5:3) NU adds ουκετι, *no longer.*

ἀκάθαρτον, ἐκ τοῦ ἀνθρώπου." 9 Καὶ ἐπηρώτα αὐτόν,
unclean, from the man." And He was asking him,

"Τί σοι ὄνομα?"
"What *is* your name?"

Καὶ ἀπεκρίθη, λέγων, "Λεγεὼν ὄνομά μοι, ὅτι πολλοί
And he answered, saying, "Legion *is* name ˜ my, because [3]many

ἐσμεν." 10 Καὶ παρεκάλει αὐτὸν πολλὰ ἵνα μὴ αὐτοὺς
[1]we [2]are." And he was imploring Him many *times* that [2]not [4]them

ἀποστείλῃ ἔξω τῆς χώρας.
[1]He [3]send out of the region.

11 Ἦν δὲ ἐκεῖ πρὸς τῷ ὄρει ἀγέλη χοίρων
[2]*there* [3]was [1]Now there near the mountain a [2]herd [3]of [4]pigs

μεγάλη βοσκομένη. 12 Καὶ παρεκάλεσαν αὐτὸν πάντες οἱ
[1]large feeding. And [4]implored [5]Him [1]all [2]the

δαίμονες, λέγοντες, "Πέμψον ἡμᾶς εἰς τοὺς χοίρους, ἵνα εἰς
[3]demons, saying, "Send us into the pigs, so that [4]into

αὐτοὺς εἰσέλθωμεν." 13 Καὶ ἐπέτρεψεν αὐτοῖς εὐθέως
[5]them [1]we [2]may [3]enter." And [3]gave [5]permission [4]them [1]immediately

ὁ Ἰησοῦς.[c] Καὶ ἐξελθόντα τὰ πνεύματα τὰ ἀκάθαρτα
- [2]Jesus. And coming out the spirits ˜ - unclean
when the unclean spirits came out,

εἰσῆλθον εἰς τοὺς χοίρους, καὶ ὥρμησεν ἡ ἀγέλη κατὰ τοῦ
they entered into the pigs, and [3]rushed [1]the [2]herd down the

κρημνοῦ εἰς τὴν θάλασσαν (ἦσαν δὲ ὡς δισχίλιοι)
steep bank into the sea ([2]they [3]were [1]now about two thousand)

καὶ ἐπνίγοντο ἐν τῇ θαλάσσῃ. 14 Οἱ δὲ βόσκοντες τοὺς
and they choked in the sea. the ˜ But *ones* feeding the
drowned

χοίρους ἔφυγον, καὶ ἀνήγγειλαν εἰς τὴν πόλιν καὶ εἰς τοὺς
pigs fled, and they reported *it* in the city and in the

ἀγρούς. Καὶ ἐξῆλθον ἰδεῖν τί ἐστι τὸ γεγονός.
fields. And they came out to see what is the *thing* having happened.
country. what it was that had happened.

15 Καὶ ἔρχονται πρὸς τὸν Ἰησοῦν καὶ θεωροῦσι τὸν
And they come to - Jesus and they observe the *one*
came observed him who

δαιμονιζόμενον καθήμενον καὶ ἱματισμένον καὶ
being demon-possessed sitting and having been clothed and
had been

σωφρονοῦντα, τὸν ἐσχηκότα τὸν λεγεῶνα, καὶ
being of sound mind, the *one* having had the legion, and
who had

ἐφοβήθησαν. 16 Διηγήσαντο δὲ αὐτοῖς οἱ ἰδόντες πῶς
they were afraid. [5]related [1]And [6]to [7]them [2]the [3]*ones* [4]seeing how
who saw

ἐγένετο τῷ δαιμονιζομένῳ καὶ περὶ τῶν χοίρων.
it happened to the *one* being demon-possessed and about the pigs.
him who had been

17 Καὶ ἤρξαντο παρακαλεῖν αὐτὸν ἀπελθεῖν ἀπὸ τῶν ὁρίων
And they began to implore Him to go away from - borders ˜
region

αὐτῶν.
their.

18 Καὶ ἐμβάντος αὐτοῦ εἰς τὸ πλοῖον, παρεκάλει αὐτὸν
And stepping in Him into the boat, [6]was [7]imploring [8]Him
when He got

ὁ δαιμονισθεὶς ἵνα ᾖ μετ' αὐτοῦ.
[1]the [2]*one* [3]having [4]been [5]demon-possessed that he might be with Him.
who had been

9 Then He asked him, "What
is your name?" And he answered, saying, "My name *is*
Legion; for we are many."
10 Also he begged Him earnestly that He would not send
them out of the country.
11 Now a large herd of swine
was feeding there near the
mountains.
12 So all the demons begged
Him, saying, "Send us to the
swine, that we may enter
them."
13 And at once Jesus gave
them permission. Then the unclean spirits went out and entered the swine (there were
about two thousand); and the
herd ran violently down the
steep place into the sea, and
drowned in the sea.
14 So those who fed the swine
fled, and they told *it* in the city
and in the country. And they
went out to see what it was that
had happened.
15 Then they came to Jesus,
and saw the one *who had been*
demon-possessed and had the
legion, sitting and clothed and
in his right mind. And they
were afraid.
16 And those who saw it
told them how it happened to
him *who had been* demon-
possessed, and about the
swine.
17 Then they began to plead
with Him to depart from their
region.
18 And when He got into the
boat, he who had been demon-
possessed begged Him that he
might be with Him.

---

[c](5:13) NU omits ευθεως ο Ιησους, *immediately Jesus*, and reads *He gave*.

19 However, Jesus did not permit him, but said to him, "Go home to your friends, and tell them what great things the Lord has done for you, and how He has had compassion on you."
20 And he departed and began to proclaim in Decapolis all that Jesus had done for him; and all marveled.
21 Now when Jesus had crossed over again by boat to the other side, a great multitude gathered to Him; and He was by the sea.
22 And behold, one of the rulers of the synagogue came, Jairus by name. And when he saw Him, he fell at His feet
23 and begged Him earnestly, saying, "My little daughter lies at the point of death. Come and lay Your hands on her, that she may be healed, and she will live."
24 So *Jesus* went with him, and a great multitude followed Him and thronged Him.
25 Now a certain woman had a flow of blood for twelve years,
26 and had suffered many things from many physicians. She had spent all that she had and was no better, but rather grew worse.
27 When she heard about Jesus, she came behind *Him* in the crowd and touched His garment.
28 For she said, "If only I may

19 Ὁ δὲ Ἰησοῦς οὐκ ἀφῆκεν αὐτόν, ἀλλὰ λέγει αὐτῷ,
- But Jesus not ˜ did permit him, but says (said) to him,

"Ὕπαγε εἰς τὸν οἶκόν σου πρὸς τοὺς σούς, καὶ
"Go to (home) - house ˜ your to the *ones* (your) of yours (own family), and

ἀνάγγειλον αὐτοῖς ὅσα σοι ὁ Κύριός πεποίηκε
report to them as many *things* as (all the things that) [5]for [6]you [1]the [2]Lord [3]has [4]done

καὶ ἠλέησέ σε." **20** Καὶ ἀπῆλθε καὶ ἤρξατο
and *how* He showed mercy ˜ you." And he departed and began

κηρύσσειν ἐν τῇ Δεκαπόλει ὅσα ἐποίησεν αὐτῷ ὁ
to proclaim in the Decapolis as many *things* as (all the things that) [2]did [3]for [4]him -

Ἰησοῦς, καὶ πάντες ἐθαύμαζον.
[1]Jesus, and all were marveling.

Jesus Restores a Girl and Heals a Woman
(Matt. 9:18–26; Luke 8:40–56)

21 Καὶ διαπεράσαντος τοῦ Ἰησοῦ ἐν τῷ πλοίῳ[d] πάλιν
And crossing ˜ (when Jesus) - Jesus (had crossed) in the boat again

εἰς τὸ πέραν, συνήχθη ὄχλος πολὺς ἐπ' αὐτόν, καὶ
to the other side, [4]was [5]gathered [1]a [3]crowd [2]large to Him, and

ἦν παρὰ τὴν θάλασσαν. **22** Καὶ ἰδού, ἔρχεται εἷς τῶν
He was beside the sea. And behold, *there* comes (came) one of the

ἀρχισυναγώγων, ὀνόματι Ἰάειρος, καὶ ἰδὼν αὐτὸν πίπτει
synagogue leaders, [2]by [3]name [1]Jairus, and seeing (when he saw) Him he falls (fell)

πρὸς τοὺς πόδας αὐτοῦ **23** καὶ παρεκάλει αὐτὸν πολλά,
at - feet ˜ His and was imploring Him many *times*,

λέγων ὅτι "Τὸ θυγάτριόν μου ἐσχάτως ἔχει, ἵνα ἐλθὼν
saying - - "[2]little [3]daughter [1]My at end (is near) has, (death,) *oh,* that (please) coming (come)

ἐπιθῇς αὐτῇ τὰς χεῖρας ὅπως σωθῇ καὶ
You may lay (and lay) [3]on [4]her [1]the (Your) [2]hands so that she may be saved (healed) and

ζήσεται." **24** Καὶ ἀπῆλθε μετ' αὐτοῦ. Καὶ ἠκολούθει
live." And He went away with him. And [4]was [5]following

αὐτῷ ὄχλος πολύς, καὶ συνέθλιβον αὐτόν.
[6]Him [1]a [3]crowd [2]large, and they were pressing against Him.

25 Καὶ γυνή τις οὖσα ἐν ῥύσει αἵματος ἔτη
And a woman ˜ certain being (suffering) with (from) a flow of blood *for* years ˜

δώδεκα **26** καὶ πολλὰ παθοῦσα ὑπὸ πολλῶν ἰατρῶν καὶ
twelve and many *things* (who had) suffering (suffered much) under many physicians and

δαπανήσασα τὰ παρ' αὐτῆς πάντα καὶ μηδὲν
spending (who had spent) the *things* (everything) with (at) her (her) all (disposal) and [3]nothing (who had benefited)

ὠφεληθεῖσα ἀλλὰ μᾶλλον εἰς τὸ χεῖρον ἐλθοῦσα,
[1]having [2]benefited (not at all) but rather - - worse ˜ (having) coming, (become worse,)

27 ἀκούσασα περὶ τοῦ Ἰησοῦ, ἐλθοῦσα ἐν τῷ ὄχλῳ
hearing (when she heard) about - Jesus, coming (she came) in the crowd

ὄπισθεν ἥψατο τοῦ ἱματίου αὐτοῦ. **28** Ἔλεγε γὰρ
from behind *and* touched - clothing ˜ His. [2]she [3]was [4]saying [1]For

[d](5:21) NU brackets εν τω πλοιω, *in the boat.*

ὅτι "Κἂν τῶν ἱματίων αὐτοῦ ἅψωμαι, σωθήσομαι." 29 Καὶ
- "If only - [4]clothes [3]His [1]I [2]touch, I will be saved." And
healed."

εὐθέως ἐξηράνθη ἡ πηγὴ τοῦ αἵματος αὐτῆς, καὶ
immediately [6]was [7]dried [8]up [1]the [2]fountain - [3]of [5]blood [4]her, and
flow

ἔγνω τῷ σώματι ὅτι ἴαται ἀπὸ τῆς μάστιγος.
she knew in the body that she had been healed from the affliction.
her

30 Καὶ εὐθέως ὁ Ἰησοῦς ἐπιγνοὺς ἐν ἑαυτῷ τὴν ἐξ
And immediately - Jesus knowing in Himself the [5]of
when Jesus perceived

αὐτοῦ δύναμιν ἐξελθοῦσαν ἐπιστραφεὶς ἐν τῷ ὄχλῳ
[6]Him [1]power [2]having [3]gone [4]out turning in the crowd *and*
He turned

ἔλεγε, "Τίς μου ἥψατο τῶν ἱματίων?"
said, "Who [2]My [1]touched - [3]clothes?"

31 Καὶ ἔλεγον αὐτῷ οἱ μαθηταὶ αὐτοῦ, "Βλέπεις τὸν
And [3]said [4]to [5]Him - [2]disciples [1]His, "You see the

ὄχλον συνθλίβοντά σε, καὶ λέγεις, 'Τίς μου ἥψατο?' "
crowd pressing against You, and You say, 'Who Me ˜ touched?' "

32 Καὶ περιεβλέπετο ἰδεῖν τὴν τοῦτο ποιήσασαν.
And He was looking around to see the *one* [3]this [1]having [2]done

33 Ἡ δὲ γυνὴ φοβηθεῖσα καὶ τρέμουσα, εἰδυῖα ὃ
the ˜ And woman fearing and trembling, knowing what

γέγονεν ἐπ' αὐτῇ, ἦλθε καὶ προσέπεσεν αὐτῷ καὶ εἶπεν
had happened to her, came and fell down before Him and told

αὐτῷ πᾶσαν τὴν ἀλήθειαν. 34 Ὁ δὲ εἶπεν αὐτῇ,
Him all the truth. [2]the [3]*One* [1]And said to her,
He

"Θυγάτερ, ἡ πίστις σου σέσωκέ σε. Ὕπαγε εἰς εἰρήνην καὶ
"Daughter, - faith ˜ your has saved you. Go in peace and
healed

ἴσθι ὑγιὴς ἀπὸ τῆς μάστιγός σου."
be well from - affliction ˜ your."

35 Ἔτι αὐτοῦ λαλοῦντος, ἔρχονται ἀπὸ τοῦ
still Him speaking, they come from the
While He was still speaking, they came

ἀρχισυναγώγου, λέγοντες ὅτι "Ἡ θυγάτηρ σου ἀπέθανε. Τί
synagogue leader, saying - - "daughter ˜ your died. Why

ἔτι σκύλλεις τὸν διδάσκαλον?"
[3]still [1]do [2]you [4]trouble the Teacher?"

36 Ὁ δὲ Ἰησοῦς εὐθέως ἀκούσας[e] τὸν λόγον
- But Jesus immediately hearing the word
when He heard message

λαλούμενον λέγει τῷ ἀρχισυναγώγῳ, "Μὴ φοβοῦ, μόνον
being spoken says to the synagogue leader, "not ˜ Do be afraid, only
said

πίστευε." 37 Καὶ οὐκ ἀφῆκεν οὐδένα αὐτῷ
believe." And [3]not [1]He [2]did permit no one [4]with [5]Him
anyone

συνακολουθῆσαι εἰ μὴ Πέτρον καὶ Ἰάκωβον καὶ Ἰωάννην
[1]to [2]follow [3]along if not Peter and James and John
except for

τὸν ἀδελφὸν Ἰακώβου. 38 Καὶ ἔρχεται εἰς τὸν οἶκον τοῦ
the brother of James. And He comes to the house of the
went

ἀρχισυναγώγου καὶ θεωρεῖ θόρυβον, κλαίοντας καὶ
synagogue leader and observes a commotion, *people* weeping and
observed

touch His clothes, I shall be made well."
29 Immediately the fountain of her blood was dried up, and she felt in *her* body that she was healed of the affliction.
30 And Jesus, immediately knowing in Himself that power had gone out of Him, turned around in the crowd and said, "Who touched My clothes?"
31 But His disciples said to Him, "You see the multitude thronging You, and You say, 'Who touched Me?' "
32 And He looked around to see her who had done this thing.
33 But the woman, fearing and trembling, knowing what had happened to her, came and fell down before Him and told Him the whole truth.
34 And He said to her, "Daughter, your faith has made you well. Go in peace, and be healed of your affliction."
35 While He was still speaking, *some* came from the ruler of the synagogue's *house* who said, "Your daughter is dead. Why trouble the Teacher any further?"
36 As soon as Jesus heard the word that was spoken, He said to the ruler of the synagogue, "Do not be afraid; only believe."
37 And He permitted no one to follow Him except Peter, James, and John the brother of James.
38 Then He came to the house of the ruler of the synagogue, and saw a tumult and those who wept and wailed loudly.

---

[e](**5:36**) NU reads *παρακουσας, overhearing* or *ignoring.*

39 When He came in, He said
to them, "Why make this commotion and weep? The child is
not dead, but sleeping."
40 And they ridiculed Him.
But when He had put them all
outside, He took the father and
the mother of the child, and
those *who were* with Him, and
entered where the child was lying.
41 Then He took the child by
the hand, and said to her, "Talitha, cumi," which is translated,
"Little girl, I say to you, arise."
42 Immediately the girl arose
and walked, for she was twelve
years *of age.* And they were
overcome with great amazement.
43 But He commanded them
strictly that no one should know
it, and said that *something*
should be given her to eat.
6 Then He went out from
there and came to His
own country, and His disciples
followed Him.
2 And when the Sabbath had
come, He began to teach in the
synagogue. And many hearing
Him were astonished, saying,
"Where *did* this Man *get* these
things? And what wisdom *is*
this which is given to Him, that
such mighty works are performed by His hands!
3 "Is this not the carpenter,
the Son of Mary, and brother of

*(6:1) πατρίς *(patris).* Originally an adjective but used only as a noun in the NT, meaning *fatherland, native country, hometown.* The word is related to πατήρ, *father* (cf. English *patriotism*). Here and in the parallel at Matt. 13:54 it refers to Jesus' hometown of Nazareth. Most often in the NT, however, it has the more general meaning *homeland* as in the proverb found in Mark 6:4 (parallel Matt. 13:57; also Luke 4:24; John 4:44; cf. Heb. 11:14). Cf. the cognate noun πατριά, *nation, people* (descended from a common "father").

ἀλαλάζοντας πολλά. 39 Καὶ εἰσελθὼν λέγει αὐτοῖς,
wailing many *things.* And entering He says to them,
much. when He went in, He said

"Τί θορυβεῖσθε καὶ κλαίετε? Τὸ παιδίον οὐκ
"Why are you making *such* commotion and weeping? The child not ˜
is

ἀπέθανεν ἀλλὰ καθεύδει." 40 Καὶ κατεγέλων αὐτοῦ. Ὁ
did die but she is asleep." And they were ridiculing Him. -
not dead

δὲ ἐκβαλὼν πάντας παραλαμβάνει τὸν πατέρα τοῦ
But sending out all *present* He takes along the father of the
after He sent out took

παιδίου καὶ τὴν μητέρα καὶ τοὺς μετ' αὐτοῦ, καὶ
child and the mother and the *ones* with Him, and
those

εἰσπορεύεται ὅπου ἦν τὸ παιδίον ἀνακείμενον. 41 Καὶ
He goes in where [3]was [1]the [2]child lying. And
went

κρατήσας τῆς χειρὸς τοῦ παιδίου λέγει αὐτῇ, "Ταλιθά,
having grasped the hand of the child He says to her, "Talitha,
said

κοῦμι," ὅ ἐστι μεθερμηνευόμενον, "Τὸ κοράσιον, σοὶ
koumi," which is being translated, - "Little girl, to you
means,

λέγω, ἔγειραι." 42 Καὶ εὐθέως ἀνέστη τὸ κοράσιον καὶ
I say, arise." And immediately [4]arose [1]the [2]little [3]girl and

περιεπάτει, ἦν γὰρ ἐτῶν δώδεκα. Καὶ
was walking about, [2]she [3]was [1]for of years twelve. And
twelve years old.

ἐξέστησαν ἐκστάσει μεγάλῃ. 43 Καὶ διεστείλατο
they were amazed with amazement ˜ great. And He ordered

αὐτοῖς πολλὰ ἵνα μηδεὶς γνῷ τοῦτο, καὶ
them many *things* that no one should know this, and
strictly

εἶπε δοθῆναι αὐτῇ φαγεῖν.
He said *for something* to be given to her to eat.

Jesus Is Rejected at Nazareth
(Matt. 13:54–58)

6 1 Καὶ ἐξῆλθεν ἐκεῖθεν καὶ ἦλθεν εἰς τὴν πατρίδα*
And He went out from there and came to - hometown ˜

αὐτοῦ, καὶ ἀκολουθοῦσιν αὐτῷ οἱ μαθηταὶ αὐτοῦ. 2 Καὶ
His, and [3]follow [4]Him - [2]disciples [1]His. And
followed

γενομένου σαββάτου, ἤρξατο ἐν τῇ συναγωγῇ διδάσκειν.
[3]coming [1]*the* [2]Sabbath, He began [3]in [4]the [5]synagogue [1]to [2]teach.
when the Sabbath had come,

Καὶ πολλοὶ ἀκούοντες ἐξεπλήσσοντο, λέγοντες, "Πόθεν
And many hearing were astonished, saying, "From where
when they heard "Where did

τούτῳ ταῦτα? Καὶ τίς ἡ σοφία ἡ δοθεῖσα
to this *man are* these *things?* And what *is* the wisdom the *one* given
this man get which is

αὐτῳ, καὶ δυνάμεις τοιαῦται διὰ τῶν χειρῶν αὐτοῦ
to Him, and [2]miracles [1]such [6]by - [8]hands [7]His
that

γίνονται? 3 Οὐχ οὗτός ἐστιν ὁ τέκτων, ὁ υἱὸς
[3]are [4]coming [5]about? [3]not [2]this [1]Is the carpenter, the son

Μαρίας, ἀδελφὸς δὲ Ἰακώβου καὶ Ἰωσῆ καὶ Ἰούδα καὶ
of Mary, brother ˜ and of James and Joses and Jude and

Σίμωνος? Καὶ οὐκ εἰσὶν αἱ ἀδελφαὶ αὐτοῦ ὧδε πρὸς ἡμᾶς?"
Simon? And not ˜ are - sisters ˜ His here with us?"

Καὶ ἐσκανδαλίζοντο ἐν αὐτῷ.
And they were offended at Him.

4 Ἔλεγε δὲ αὐτοῖς ὁ Ἰησοῦς ὅτι "Οὐκ ἔστι προφήτης
[3]said [1]But [4]to [5]them - [2]Jesus - "[9]not [8]is [6]A [7]prophet

ἄτιμος εἰ μὴ ἐν τῇ πατρίδι αὐτοῦ καὶ ἐν τοῖς
without honor if not in - hometown ˜ his and among the
except his

συγγενέσι καὶ ἐν τῇ οἰκίᾳ αὐτοῦ." 5 Καὶ οὐκ ἠδύνατο
relatives and in - house ˜ his." And [3]not [1]He [2]was [4]able

ἐκεῖ οὐδεμίαν δύναμιν ποιῆσαι, εἰ μὴ ὀλίγοις ἀρρώστοις
[9]there [7]no [8]miracle [5]to [6]do, if not [5]on [6]a [7]few [8]sick [9]*people*
any except that

ἐπιθεὶς τὰς χεῖρας ἐθεράπευσε. 6 Καὶ ἐθαύμαζε διὰ
[1]*by* [2]laying [3]the [4]hands He healed *them.* And He marveled because of
His

τὴν ἀπιστίαν αὐτῶν. Καὶ περιῆγε τὰς κώμας κύκλῳ
- unbelief ˜ their. And He was going about the villages in a circuit

διδάσκων.
teaching.

Jesus Commissions the Twelve
(Matt. 10:1, 5–15; Luke 9:1–6)

7 Καὶ προσκαλεῖται τοὺς δώδεκα καὶ ἤρξατο αὐτοὺς
And He summons the twelve and began [3]them
called to Himself

ἀποστέλλειν δύο δύο, καὶ ἐδίδου αὐτοῖς ἐξουσίαν τῶν
[1]to [2]send [4]out two *by* two, and He was giving to them authority of the
over

πνευμάτων τῶν ἀκαθάρτων. 8 Καὶ παρήγγειλεν αὐτοῖς ἵνα
spirits ˜ - unclean. And He commanded them that

μηδὲν αἴρωσιν εἰς ὁδὸν εἰ μὴ ῥάβδον μόνον, μὴ
[4]nothing [1]they [2]should [3]take for *the* road if not a staff only, not
journey except

πήραν, μὴ ἄρτον, μὴ εἰς τὴν ζώνην χαλκόν,
a knapsack, not bread, not [4]for [5]the [6]money [7]belt [1]a [2]copper [3]*coin,*
their

9 ἀλλ' ὑποδεδεμένους σανδάλια καὶ μὴ ἐνδύσησθε δύο
but *to go* having put on sandals and not ˜ do put on two
to

χιτῶνας. 10 Καὶ ἔλεγεν αὐτοῖς, "Ὅπου ἐὰν εἰσέλθητε εἰς
tunics. And He said to them, "Where ever you may enter into

οἰκίαν, ἐκεῖ μένετε ἕως ἂν ἐξέλθητε ἐκεῖθεν. 11 Καὶ
a house, there ˜ stay until - you go out from there. And

ὅσοι[a] ἂν μὴ δέξωνται ὑμᾶς μηδὲ ἀκούσωσιν ὑμῶν,
as many as - not ˜ do receive you nor hear you,

ἐκπορευόμενοι ἐκεῖθεν ἐκτινάξατε τὸν χοῦν τὸν ὑποκάτω τῶν
going out from there shake off the dust - underneath -
as you leave

ποδῶν ὑμῶν εἰς μαρτύριον αὐτοῖς. Ἀμὴν[b] λέγω ὑμῖν,
feet ˜ your as a testimony to them. Amen I say to you,
against Assuredly

ἀνεκτότερον ἔσται Σοδόμοις ἢ Γομόρροις ἐν ἡμέρᾳ
[4]more [5]tolerable [1]it [2]will [3]be for Sodom or for Gomorrah in *the* day

κρίσεως ἢ τῇ πόλει ἐκείνῃ."
of judgment than - [3]city [1]for [2]that."

James, Joses, Judas, and Simon? And are not His sisters here with us?" So they were offended at Him.

4 But Jesus said to them, "A prophet is not without honor except in his own country, among his own relatives, and in his own house."

5 Now He could do no mighty work there, except that He laid His hands on a few sick people and healed *them.*

6 And He marveled because of their unbelief. Then He went about the villages in a circuit, teaching.

7 And He called the twelve to *Himself,* and began to send them out two *by* two, and gave them power over unclean spirits.

8 He commanded them to take nothing for the journey except a staff—no bag, no bread, no copper in *their* money belts—

9 but to wear sandals, and not to put on two tunics.

10 Also He said to them, "In whatever place you enter a house, stay there till you depart from that place.

11 "And whoever will not receive you nor hear you, when you depart from there, shake off the dust under your feet as a testimony against them. Assuredly, I say to you, it will be more tolerable for Sodom and Gomorrah in the day of judgment than for that city!"

---

[a](**6:11**) For οσοι αν, *as many as,* NU reads ος αν τοπος, *whatever place.*
[b](**6:11**) NU omits the last sentence of v. 11.

12 So they went out and preached that *people* should repent.
13 And they cast out many demons, and anointed with oil many who were sick, and healed *them.*
14 Now King Herod heard *of Him,* for His name had become well known. And he said, "John the Baptist is risen from the dead, and therefore these powers are at work in him."
15 Others said, "It is Elijah." And others said, "It is the Prophet, or like one of the prophets."
16 But when Herod heard, he said, "This is John, whom I beheaded; he has been raised from the dead!"
17 For Herod himself had sent and laid hold of John, and bound him in prison for the sake of Herodias, his brother Philip's wife; for he had married her.
18 Because John had said to Herod, "It is not lawful for you to have your brother's wife."
19 Therefore Herodias held it against him and wanted to kill him, but she could not;
20 for Herod feared John, knowing that he *was* a just and holy man, and he protected him. And when he heard him, he did many things, and heard

12 Καὶ ἐξελθόντες ἐκήρυσσον ἵνα
And going out they were preaching that
when they went out,

μετανοήσωσι, **13** καὶ δαιμόνια πολλὰ ἐξέβαλλον,
people should repent, and [6]demons [5]many [1]they [2]were [3]casting [4]out,

καὶ ἤλειφον ἐλαίῳ πολλοὺς ἀρρώστους καὶ
and they were anointing with oil many sick *people* and

ἐθεράπευον.
were healing *them.*

John the Baptist Is Beheaded
(Matt. 14:1–12; Luke 9:7–9)

14 Καὶ ἤκουσεν ὁ βασιλεὺς Ἡρῴδης, φανερὸν γὰρ
And [3]heard - [1]King [2]Herod, [8]well [9]known [4]for

ἐγένετο τὸ ὄνομα αὐτοῦ, καὶ ἔλεγεν[c] ὅτι "Ἰωάννης ὁ
[7]became - [6]name [5]His, and he said - "John the

βαπτίζων ἐκ νεκρῶν ἠγέρθη, καὶ διὰ τοῦτο
baptizing *one* [3]from [4]*the* [5]dead [1]was [2]raised, and because of this
Baptizer has been for this reason

ἐνεργοῦσιν αἱ δυνάμεις ἐν αὐτῷ."
[3]are [4]at [5]work [1]the [2]miracles in him."

15 Ἄλλοι ἔλεγον ὅτι "Ἠλίας ἐστίν."
Others said - "[3]Elijah [1]He [2]is."

Ἄλλοι δὲ ἔλεγον ὅτι "Προφήτης ἐστὶν[d] ὡς εἷς τῶν
others ~ But said - "[3]a [4]prophet [1]He [2]is like one of the

προφητῶν."
prophets."

16 Ἀκούσας δὲ ὁ Ἡρῴδης εἶπεν ὅτι "Ὃν ἐγὼ
[3]hearing [1]But - [2]Herod said - "*The one* whom I
when he heard

ἀπεκεφάλισα Ἰωάννην, οὗτός ἐστιν· αὐτὸς ἠγέρθη ἐκ
beheaded John, this *man* is he; he was raised from
has been

νεκρῶν!"
the dead!"

17 Αὐτὸς γὰρ ὁ Ἡρῴδης ἀποστείλας ἐκράτησε τὸν
[3]himself [1]For - [2]Herod sending laid hold of -
had sent and

Ἰωάννην καὶ ἔδησεν αὐτὸν ἐν φυλακῇ διὰ Ἡρῳδιάδα
John and bound him in prison on account of Herodias

τὴν γυναῖκα Φιλίππου τοῦ ἀδελφοῦ αὐτοῦ, ὅτι αὐτὴν
the wife of Philip - brother ~ his, because [3]her

ἐγάμησεν.
[1]he [2]married.
had married.

18 Ἔλεγε γὰρ ὁ Ἰωάννης τῷ Ἡρῴδῃ ὅτι "Οὐκ ἔξεστί
[3]would [4]say [1]For - [2]John - to Herod - "[3]not [1]It [2]is lawful

σοι ἔχειν τὴν γυναῖκα τοῦ ἀδελφοῦ σου." **19** Ἡ δὲ
for you to have the wife - of brother ~ your." - And

Ἡρῳδιὰς ἐνεῖχεν αὐτῷ καὶ ἤθελεν αὐτὸν
Herodias held a grudge against him and was desiring [3]him

ἀποκτεῖναι, καὶ οὐκ ἠδύνατο· **20** ὁ γὰρ Ἡρῴδης ἐφοβεῖτο
[1]to [2]kill, and [3]not [1]she [2]was able; - for Herod was afraid of

τὸν Ἰωάννην, εἰδὼς αὐτὸν ἄνδρα δίκαιον καὶ ἅγιον, καὶ
- John, knowing him *to be* a [4]man [1]righteous [2]and [3]holy, and

συνετήρει αὐτόν. Καὶ ἀκούσας αὐτοῦ πολλὰ
he was protecting him. And hearing him [3]many [4]*things*
when he heard

---

[c](6:14) NU reads ελεγον, *they were saying.*
[d](6:15) NU omits εστιν, *He is.*

ἐποίει,[e] καὶ ἡδέως αὐτοῦ ἤκουε.
[1]he [2]did, and [5]gladly [4]him [1]he [2]would [3]hear.
but

21 Καὶ γενομένης ἡμέρας εὐκαίρου, ὅτε Ἡρῴδης τοῖς
And coming about a day well-timed, when Herod -
when an opportune day arrived,

γενεσίοις αὐτοῦ δεῖπνον ἐποίει τοῖς
[1]for [3]birthday [4]festivities [2]his [8]a [9]supper [5]was [6]putting [7]on -

μεγιστᾶσιν αὐτοῦ καὶ τοῖς χιλιάρχοις καὶ τοῖς πρώτοις τῆς
for courtiers ˜ his and the chiliarchs and the chief men -

Γαλιλαίας, 22 καὶ εἰσελθούσης τῆς θυγατρὸς αὐτῆς τῆς[f]
of Galilee, and entering the daughter herself -
when of Herodias herself

Ἡρῳδιάδος καὶ ὀρχησαμένης καὶ ἀρεσάσης τῷ Ἡρῴδῃ καὶ
of Herodias and dancing and pleasing - Herod and
came in danced pleased

τοῖς συνανακειμένοις, εἶπεν ὁ βασιλεὺς τῷ κορασίῳ,
the *ones* reclining *to eat* with *him*, [3]said [1]the [2]king to the girl,
his dinner guests,

"Αἴτησόν με ὃ ἐὰν θέλῃς, καὶ δώσω σοί."
"Ask me what ever you may want, and I will give *it* to you."

23 Καὶ ὤμοσεν αὐτῇ ὅτι "Ὃ ἐάν με αἰτήσῃς δώσω
And he swore to her - "What ever [4]me [1]you [2]may [3]ask I will give

σοι ἕως ἡμίσους τῆς βασιλείας μου."
you up to half - of kingdom ˜ my."

24 Ἡ δὲ ἐξελθοῦσα εἶπε τῇ μητρὶ αὐτῆς,
- And going out she said - to mother ˜ her,
when she had gone out,

"Τί αἰτήσομαι?"
"What shall I ask?"

Ἡ δὲ εἶπε, "Τὴν κεφαλὴν Ἰωάννου τοῦ Βαπτιστοῦ!"
- And she said, "The head of John the Baptist!"

25 Καὶ εἰσελθοῦσα εὐθέως μετὰ σπουδῆς πρὸς τὸν
And entering immediately with haste to the
she came in

βασιλέα ᾐτήσατο, λέγουσα, "Θέλω ἵνα μοι δῷς
king *and* she requested, saying, "I desire that [3]me [1]you [2]give

ἐξαυτῆς ἐπὶ πίνακι τὴν κεφαλὴν Ἰωάννου τοῦ Βαπτιστοῦ."
at once on a platter the head of John the Baptist."

26 Καὶ περίλυπος γενόμενος ὁ βασιλεύς, διὰ
And [4]exceedingly [5]sorry [3]becoming [1]the [2]king, because of
became

τοὺς ὅρκους καὶ τοὺς συνανακειμένους οὐκ ἠθέλησεν
the oaths and the *ones* reclining *to eat* with *him* [3]not [1]he [2]did [4]want
his

αὐτὴν ἀθετῆσαι. 27 Καὶ εὐθέως ἀποστείλας ὁ βασιλεὺς
[7]her [5]to [6]refuse. And immediately [3]having [4]sent [1]the [2]king

σπεκουλάτορα ἐπέταξεν ἐνεχθῆναι τὴν κεφαλὴν αὐτοῦ. Ὁ
an executioner commanded [3]to [4]be [5]brought - [2]head [1]his. -

δὲ ἀπελθὼν ἀπεκεφάλισεν αὐτὸν ἐν τῇ φυλακῇ 28 καὶ
And having departed he beheaded him in the prison and

ἤνεγκε τὴν κεφαλὴν αὐτοῦ ἐπὶ πίνακι καὶ ἔδωκεν αὐτὴν τῷ
brought - head ˜ his on a platter and gave it to the

κορασίῳ, καὶ τὸ κοράσιον ἔδωκεν αὐτὴν τῇ μητρὶ αὐτῆς.
girl, and the girl gave it - to mother ˜ her.

29 Καὶ ἀκούσαντες οἱ μαθηταὶ αὐτοῦ ἦλθον καὶ ἦραν τὸ
And [3]having [4]heard - [2]disciples [1]his they came and took -
when his disciples heard,

him gladly.
21 Then an opportune day came when Herod on his birthday gave a feast for his nobles, the high officers, and the chief *men* of Galilee.
22 And when Herodias' daughter herself came in and danced, and pleased Herod and those who sat with him, the king said to the girl, "Ask me whatever you want, and I will give *it* to you."
23 He also swore to her, "Whatever you ask me, I will give you, up to half my kingdom."
24 So she went out and said to her mother, "What shall I ask?" And she said, "The head of John the Baptist!"
25 Immediately she came in with haste to the king and asked, saying, "I want you to give me at once the head of John the Baptist on a platter."
26 And the king was exceedingly sorry; *yet*, because of the oaths and because of those who sat with him, he did not want to refuse her.
27 Immediately the king sent an executioner and commanded his head to be brought. And he went and beheaded him in prison,
28 brought his head on a platter, and gave it to the girl; and the girl gave it to her mother.
29 When his disciples heard *of it*, they came and took away his

[e](6:20) NU reads ηπορει, *he was (very) disturbed.*
[f](6:22) For αυτης της, *herself,* NU reads αυτου, *his (daughter Herodias).*

corpse and laid it in a tomb.
30 Then the apostles gathered
to Jesus and told Him all things,
both what they had done and
what they had taught.
31 And He said to them,
"Come aside by yourselves to a
deserted place and rest a
while." For there were many
coming and going, and they did
not even have time to eat.
32 So they departed to a deserted place in the boat by
themselves.
33 But the multitudes saw
them departing, and many
knew Him and ran there on foot
from all the cities. They arrived
before them and came together
to Him.
34 And Jesus, when He came
out, saw a great multitude and
was moved with compassion for
them, because they were like
sheep not having a shepherd.
So He began to teach them
many things.
35 When the day was now far
spent, His disciples came to
Him and said, "This is a deserted place, and already the
hour *is* late.
36 "Send them away, that
they may go into the surrounding country and villages and buy
themselves bread; for they
have nothing to eat."
37 But He answered and said
to them, "You give them something to eat." And they said to
Him, "Shall we go and buy two

---

[g](6:33) TR adds οι οχλοι, *the multitudes (saw).* [h](6:33) NU omits the rest of v. 33. [i](6:36) NU ends v. 36 here, reading τι φαγωσιν, *something they may eat.*

---

*(6:35) ἔρημος (erēmos). Used in the NT both as an adjective (*abandoned, desolate*) and as a noun (*desert, wilderness, grassland*). In these substantive senses it stands "in contrast to cultivated and inhabited country" (BGD). We should not think of this word as though it indicated a desert of the sort we envisage for the African Sahara, though the stony, barren Judean wilderness in the area of the Dead Sea has some resemblances to that kind of desert. But the word equally can indicate a sparsely settled area where grassland is available to sheep, as it apparently

πτῶμα αὐτοῦ καὶ ἔθηκαν αὐτὸ ἐν μνημείῳ.
corpse ~ his and placed it in a tomb.

Jesus Feeds the Five Thousand
(Matt. 14:13–21; Luke 9:10–17; John 6:1–14)

30 Καὶ συνάγονται οἱ ἀπόστολοι πρὸς τὸν Ἰησοῦν, καὶ
And [3]gather [1]the [2]apostles to - Jesus, and
gathered

ἀπήγγειλαν αὐτῷ πάντα, καὶ ὅσα ἐποίησαν καὶ
they reported to Him all *things*, both as many *things* as they did and
everything they had done

ὅσα ἐδίδαξαν. **31** Καὶ εἶπεν αὐτοῖς, "Δεῦτε ὑμεῖς
as many *things* as they taught. And He said to them, "Come you
everything they had taught.

αὐτοὶ κατ' ἰδίαν εἰς ἔρημον τόπον καὶ ἀναπαύεσθε
yourselves privately to a deserted place and rest

ὀλίγον." Ἦσαν γὰρ οἱ ἐρχόμενοι καὶ οἱ ὑπάγοντες
a little." [9]were [1]For [2]the [3]*ones* [4]coming [5]and [6]the [7]*ones* [8]going

πολλοί, καὶ οὐδὲ φαγεῖν εὐκαίρουν. **32** Καὶ
[10]many, and [3]not [4]even [7]to [8]eat [1]they [2]were [5]finding [6]opportunity. And

ἀπῆλθον εἰς ἔρημον τόπον τῷ πλοίῳ κατ' ἰδίαν. **33** Καὶ
they went away to a deserted place in the boat privately. And

εἶδον αὐτοὺς ὑπάγοντας,[g] καὶ ἐπέγνωσαν αὐτὸν πολλοί, καὶ
they saw them going, and [2]recognized [3]Him [1]many, and

πεζῇ ἀπὸ πασῶν τῶν πόλεων συνέδραμον ἐκεῖ καὶ
on foot from all the cities they ran together there and

προῆλθον αὐτοὺς καὶ[h] συνῆλθον πρὸς αὐτόν. **34** Καὶ
preceded them and they came together to Him. And

ἐξελθὼν εἶδεν ὁ Ἰησοῦς πολὺν ὄχλον, καὶ
coming out saw ~ - Jesus a large crowd, and
when He had disembarked,

ἐσπλαγχνίσθη ἐπ' αὐτοῖς ὅτι ἦσαν ὡς πρόβατα μὴ
He had compassion on them because they were like sheep not

ἔχοντα ποιμένα, καὶ ἤρξατο διδάσκειν αὐτοὺς πολλά.
having a shepherd, and He began to teach them many *things*.

35 Καὶ ἤδη ὥρας πολλῆς γενομένης, προσελθόντες
And already an hour much having come, [3]approaching
when it grew late, came

αὐτῷ οἱ μαθηταὶ αὐτοῦ λέγουσιν ὅτι "Ἔρημός* ἐστιν ὁ
[4]to [5]Him - [2]disciples [1]His *and* say - "[4]deserted [3]is [1]the
said

τόπος καὶ ἤδη ὥρα πολλή. **36** Ἀπόλυσον αὐτούς, ἵνα
[2]place and already *the* hour *is* much. Dismiss them, so that
late.

ἀπελθόντες εἰς τοὺς κύκλῳ ἀγροὺς καὶ κώμας ἀγοράσωσιν
going away into the surrounding farms and villages they may buy
they may go and

ἑαυτοῖς ἄρτους.[i] Τί γὰρ φάγωσιν οὐκ
for themselves food. something ~ For they may eat [3]not

ἔχουσιν."
[1]they [2]do [4]have."

37 Ὁ δὲ ἀποκριθεὶς εἶπεν αὐτοῖς, "Δότε αὐτοῖς ὑμεῖς
- But answering He said to them, "[2]give [3]them [1]You

φαγεῖν."
something to eat."

Καὶ λέγουσιν αὐτῷ, "Ἀπελθόντες ἀγοράσωμεν δηναρίων
And they say to Him, "Having left shall we buy [3]denarii
said

διακοσίων ἄρτους καὶ δῶμεν αὐτοῖς φαγεῖν?"
[1]two [2]hundred *worth of* loaves of bread and give them to eat?"

38 Ὁ δὲ λέγει αὐτοῖς, "Πόσους ἄρτους ἔχετε?
- But He says to them, "How many loaves of bread do you have?
said

Ὑπάγετε καὶ ἴδετε."
Go and see."

Καὶ γνόντες λέγουσι, "Πέντε, καὶ δύο ἰχθύας."
And having known they say, "Five, and two fish."
when they found out, they said,

39 Καὶ ἐπέταξεν αὐτοῖς ἀνακλῖναι πάντας συμπόσια
And He gave orders for them [2]to [3]recline [1]all group
in

συμπόσια ἐπὶ τῷ χλωρῷ χόρτῳ. 40 Καὶ ἀνέπεσον πρασιαὶ
group on the green grass. And they reclined party
groups in

πρασιαὶ ἀνὰ ἑκατὸν καὶ ἀνὰ πεντήκοντα. 41 Καὶ λαβὼν τοὺς
party each hundred and each fifty. And taking the
parties of hundreds of fifties.

πέντε ἄρτους καὶ τοὺς δύο ἰχθύας, ἀναβλέψας εἰς τὸν οὐρανὸν
five loaves and the two fish, looking up to - heaven

εὐλόγησε καὶ κατέκλασε τοὺς ἄρτους καὶ ἐδίδου τοῖς
He blessed and broke the loaves and was giving *them* -

μαθηταῖς αὐτοῦ ἵνα παραθῶσιν αὐτοῖς, καὶ τοὺς
to disciples ˜ His so that they might set *them* before them, and the

δύο ἰχθύας ἐμέρισε πᾶσι. 42 Καὶ ἔφαγον πάντες καὶ
two fish He divided to all. And they ate ˜ all and

ἐχορτάσθησαν. 43 Καὶ ἦραν κλασμάτων δώδεκα κοφίνους
were filled. And they took up [4]of [5]fragments [1]twelve [2]baskets

πλήρεις καὶ ἀπὸ τῶν ἰχθύων. 44 Καὶ ἦσαν οἱ
[3]full and from the fish. And [7]were [1]the [2]*ones*

φαγόντες τοὺς ἄρτους[j] πεντακισχίλιοι ἄνδρες.
[3]having [4]eaten [5]the [6]loaves five thousand men.

Jesus Walks on the Sea
(Matt. 14:22–33; John 6:15–21)

45 Καὶ εὐθέως ἠνάγκασε τοὺς μαθητὰς αὐτοῦ ἐμβῆναι
And immediately He compelled - disciples ˜ His to step in

εἰς τὸ πλοῖον καὶ προάγειν εἰς τὸ πέραν πρὸς
into the boat and to go on ahead to the other side to

Βηθσαϊδάν, ἕως αὐτὸς ἀπολύσῃ τὸν ὄχλον. 46 Καὶ
Bethsaida, until He could dismiss the crowd. And

ἀποταξάμενος αὐτοῖς ἀπῆλθεν εἰς τὸ ὄρος
having taken leave of them He departed to the mountain

προσεύξασθαι. 47 Καὶ ὀψίας γενομένης, ἦν τὸ πλοῖον ἐν
to pray. And evening having come, [3]was [1]the [2]boat in
when it was evening,

μέσῳ τῆς θαλάσσης, καὶ αὐτὸς μόνος ἐπὶ τῆς γῆς. 48 Καὶ
the middle of the sea, and He *was* alone on the land. And

εἶδεν αὐτοὺς βασανιζομένους ἐν τῷ ἐλαύνειν, ἦν γὰρ ὁ
He saw them straining in - to row, [4]was [1]for [2]the
at rowing,

ἄνεμος ἐναντίος αὐτοῖς. Καὶ περὶ τετάρτην φυλακὴν τῆς
[3]wind against them. And about *the* fourth watch of the

νυκτὸς ἔρχεται πρὸς αὐτοὺς περιπατῶν ἐπὶ τῆς θαλάσσης, καὶ
night He comes to them walking on the sea, and
came

hundred denarii worth of bread and give them *something* to eat?"
38 But He said to them, "How many loaves do you have? Go and see." And when they found out they said, "Five, and two fish."
39 Then He commanded them to make them all sit down in groups on the green grass.
40 So they sat down in ranks, in hundreds and in fifties.
41 And when He had taken the five loaves and the two fish, He looked up to heaven, blessed and broke the loaves, and gave *them* to His disciples to set before them; and the two fish He divided among *them* all.
42 So they all ate and were filled.
43 And they took up twelve baskets full of fragments and of the fish.
44 Now those who had eaten the loaves were about five thousand men.
45 Immediately He made His disciples get into the boat and go before Him to the other side, to Bethsaida, while He sent the multitude away.
46 And when He had sent them away, He departed to the mountain to pray.
47 Now when evening came, the boat was in the middle of the sea; and He *was* alone on the land.
48 Then He saw them straining at rowing, for the wind was against them. Now about the fourth watch of the night He came to them, walking on the

---

j(6:44) TR adds ωσει, *about,* before the number; NU brackets τους αρτους, *the loaves.*

---

does in Luke 15:4. It seems that the ἔρημος of Mark 6:35, 36 in which Jesus was teaching had cultivated fields and inhabited towns surrounding it.

sea, and would have passed them by.
49 And when they saw Him walking on the sea, they supposed it was a ghost, and cried out;
50 for they all saw Him and were troubled. But immediately He talked with them and said to them, "Be of good cheer! It is I; do not be afraid."
51 Then He went up into the boat to them, and the wind ceased. And they were greatly amazed in themselves beyond measure, and marveled.
52 For they had not understood about the loaves, because their heart was hardened.
53 When they had crossed over, they came to the land of Gennesaret and anchored there.
54 And when they came out of the boat, immediately the people recognized Him,
55 ran through that whole surrounding region, and began to carry about on beds those who were sick to wherever they heard He was.
56 Wherever He entered, into villages, cities, or the country, they laid the sick in the marketplaces, and begged Him that they might just touch the hem of His garment. And as many as touched Him were made well.

ἤθελε παρελθεῖν αὐτούς. **49** Οἱ δέ, ἰδόντες αὐτὸν
He wanted to pass by them. [2]the [3]*ones* [1]But, seeing Him
they

περιπατοῦντα ἐπὶ τῆς θαλάσσης, ἔδοξαν φάντασμα
walking on the sea, supposed [4]a [5]ghost

εἶναι, καὶ ἀνέκραξαν· **50** πάντες γὰρ αὐτὸν εἶδον καὶ
[1]*Him* [2]to [3]be, and they cried out; [3]all [1]for [5]Him [2]they [4]saw and

ἐταράχθησαν. Καὶ εὐθέως ἐλάλησε μετ' αὐτῶν, καὶ λέγει
were troubled. And immediately He spoke with them, and says
said

αὐτοῖς, "Θαρσεῖτε! Ἐγώ εἰμι· μὴ φοβεῖσθε." **51** Καὶ
to them, "Have courage! I am; [2]not [1]do [3]be afraid." And
It is I;

ἀνέβη πρὸς αὐτοὺς εἰς τὸ πλοῖον, καὶ ἐκόπασεν ὁ
He went up with them into the boat, and [3]ceased [1]the

ἄνεμος. Καὶ λίαν ἐκ περισσοῦ ἐν ἑαυτοῖς
[2]wind. And very much out of measure among themselves
beyond

ἐξίσταντο καὶ ἐθαύμαζον. **52** Οὐ γὰρ
they were astounded and were marveling. [4]not [1]For
For they

συνῆκαν ἐπὶ τοῖς ἄρτοις, ἦν γὰρ αὐτῶν ἡ
[2]they [3]did understand on the loaves, [4]was [1]for [2]their -
had not understood concerning were

καρδία πεπωρωμένη.
[3]heart hardened.
hearts

Many Touch Jesus and Are Made Whole
(Matt. 14:34–36)

53 Καὶ διαπεράσαντες ἦλθον ἐπὶ τὴν γῆν Γεννησαρὲτ
And having crossed over they came onto the land Gennesaret

καὶ προσωρμίσθησαν. **54** Καὶ ἐξελθόντων αὐτῶν ἐκ τοῦ
and anchored *there*. And coming out them of the
when they came out

πλοίου, εὐθέως ἐπιγνόντες αὐτόν, **55** περιδραμόντες
boat, immediately having recognized Him, running about

ὅλην τὴν περίχωρον ἐκείνην ἤρξαντο ἐπὶ τοῖς
[2]whole - [3]surrounding [4]region [1]that they began [8]on [9]the
their

κραββάτοις τοὺς κακῶς ἔχοντας περιφέρειν ὅπου
[10]pallets [3]the [4]*ones* [7]badly [5]having [6]*it* [1]to [2]bring wherever
those who were ill

ἤκουον ὅτι ἐκεῖ ἐστι. **56** Καὶ ὅπου ἂν εἰσεπορεύετο
they would hear that [3]there [1]He [2]is. And where ever He would enter
was.

εἰς κώμας ἢ πόλεις ἢ ἀγρούς, ἐν ταῖς ἀγοραῖς
into villages or towns or country areas, [7]in [8]the [9]marketplaces

ἐτίθουν τοὺς ἀσθενοῦντας, καὶ παρεκάλουν αὐτὸν ἵνα
[1]they [2]would [3]lay [4]the [5]*ones* [6]ailing, and they would beg Him that

κἂν τοῦ κρασπέδου τοῦ ἱματίου αὐτοῦ ἅψωνται. Καὶ
at least [4]the [5]border - [6]of [8]clothing [7]His [1]they [2]might [3]touch. And

ὅσοι ἂν ἥπτοντο αὐτοῦ ἐσῴζοντο.
as many as - would touch Him would be delivered.
healed.

Defilement Comes from Within
(Matt. 15:1–20)

7 1 Καὶ συνάγονται πρὸς αὐτὸν οἱ Φαρισαῖοι καί τινες
And [8]gather [9]together [10]to [11]Him [1]the [2]Pharisees [3]and [4]some
gathered

τῶν γραμματέων, ἐλθόντες ἀπὸ Ἱεροσολύμων. 2 Καὶ
[5]of [6]the [7]scribes, coming from Jerusalem. And
after they came

ἰδόντες τινὰς τῶν μαθητῶν αὐτοῦ κοιναῖς χερσί,
seeing some - of disciples ˜ His with common hands,
when they saw ceremonially unclean

τοῦτ' ἔστιν ἀνίπτοις, ἐσθίοντας ἄρτους ἐμέμψαντο.[a]
this is with unwashed *hands*, eating bread they found fault.
that

3 Οἱ γὰρ Φαρισαῖοι καὶ πάντες οἱ Ἰουδαῖοι, ἐὰν μὴ
the ˜ For Pharisees and all the Jews, if not
unless

πυγμῇ νίψωνται τὰς χεῖρας, οὐκ ἐσθίουσι, κρατοῦντες τὴν
with *their* fist they wash the hands, not ˜ do eat, holding to the
their

παράδοσιν τῶν πρεσβυτέρων. 4 Καὶ ἀπὸ ἀγορᾶς,
tradition of the elders. And *coming* from *the* marketplace,

ἐὰν μὴ βαπτίσωνται, οὐκ ἐσθίουσι. Καὶ ἄλλα πολλά
if not they bathe, [3]not [1]they [2]do eat. And [4]other [5]*things* [3]many
unless

ἐστιν ἃ παρέλαβον κρατεῖν, βαπτισμοὺς
[1]*there* [2]are which they received *by tradition* to hold to, ablutions
washings

ποτηρίων καὶ ξεστῶν καὶ χαλκίων καὶ κλινῶν.[b] 5 Ἔπειτα
of cups and pitchers and copper vessels and couches. Then

ἐπερωτῶσιν αὐτὸν οἱ Φαρισαῖοι καὶ οἱ γραμματεῖς,
[6]asked [7]Him [1]the [2]Pharisees [3]and [4]the [5]scribes,

"Διὰ τί οἱ μαθηταί σου οὐ περιπατοῦσι κατὰ τὴν
"Because of what - [3]disciples [2]Your [4]not [1]do walk according to the
"Why

παράδοσιν τῶν πρεσβυτέρων, ἀλλὰ ἀνίπτοις χερσὶν
tradition of the elders, but with unwashed hands

ἐσθίουσι τὸν ἄρτον?"
they eat the bread?"
their

6 Ὁ δὲ ἀποκριθεὶς εἶπεν αὐτοῖς ὅτι "Καλῶς
[2]the [3]*One* [1]And answering said to them - "Well
He

προεφήτευσεν Ἠσαΐας περὶ ὑμῶν τῶν ὑποκριτῶν,* ὡς
did prophesy ˜ Isaiah about you - hypocrites, as

γέγραπται,
it is written,

«Οὗτος ὁ λαὸς τοῖς χείλεσί με τιμᾷ,
«This - people with the lips Me ˜ honors,
their

Ἡ δὲ καρδία αὐτῶν πόρρω ἀπέχει ἀπ' ἐμοῦ.
- But heart ˜ their far ˜ is away from Me.

7 Μάτην δὲ σέβονταί με,
[2]in [3]vain [1]And they worship Me,

Διδάσκοντες διδασκαλίας ἐντάλματα ἀνθρώπων.»[c]
Teaching *as* teachings *the* commandments of men.»

8 Ἀφέντες γὰρ τὴν ἐντολὴν τοῦ Θεοῦ κρατεῖτε τὴν
[2]having [3]left [1]For the commandment - of God you hold to the

7 Then the Pharisees and
some of the scribes came
together to Him, having come
from Jerusalem.
2 Now when they saw some
of His disciples eat bread with
defiled, that is, with unwashed
hands, they found fault.
3 For the Pharisees and all
the Jews do not eat unless they
wash *their* hands in a special
way, holding the tradition of the
elders.
4 *When they come* from the
marketplace, they do not eat
unless they wash. And there
are many other things which
they have received and hold,
like the washing of cups,
pitchers, copper vessels, and
couches.
5 Then the Pharisees and
scribes asked Him, "Why do
Your disciples not walk according to the tradition of the
elders, but eat bread with unwashed hands?"
6 He answered and said to
them, "Well did Isaiah prophesy
of you hypocrites, as it is written:

'This people honors Me
with their lips,
But their heart is far from
Me.
7 *And in vain they worship*
Me,
Teaching as doctrines the
commandments of
men.'

8 "For laying aside the commandment of God, you hold the

---

[a](7:2) NU omits εμεμψαντο, *they found fault.*
[b](7:4) NU brackets και κλινων, *and couches.*
[c](7:7) Is. 29:13 LXX

***(7:6)** ὑποκριτής *(hypokritēs).* Noun, *hypocrite,* used always by Christ, and nearly always of the Pharisees. The word originated in the Greek theater where actors used large masks. Literally, it means *answer* (κρίνομαι) *from under* (ὑπό) *a mask.* Hypocrisy occurs in the person who recognizes a certain good category, such as that of a Christian, and pretends to be one, knowing all the while that he or she is playacting. Here Jesus accused the Pharisees of being just such hypocrites as Isaiah predicted (Is. 29:13): they tradition of men—the washing of pitchers and cups, and many other such things you do."

9 He said to them, "*All too* well you reject the commandment of God, that you may keep your tradition.

10 "For Moses said, *'Honor your father and your mother'*; and, *'He who curses father or mother, let him be put to death.'*

11 "But you say, 'If a man says to his father or mother, "Whatever profit you might have received from me *is* Corban"—' (that is, a gift *to God*),

12 "then you no longer let him do anything for his father or his mother,

13 "making the word of God of no effect through your tradition which you have handed down. And many such things you do."

14 When He had called all the multitude to *Himself,* He said to them, "Hear Me, everyone, and understand:

15 "There is nothing that enters a man from outside which can defile him; but the things which come out of him, those are the things that defile a man.

16 "If anyone has ears to hear, let him hear!"

17 When He had entered a house away from the crowd, His disciples asked Him concerning the parable.

18 So He said to them, "Are you thus without understanding also? Do you not perceive that whatever enters a man from outside cannot defile him,

19 "because it does not enter his heart but his stomach, and

[d](7:8) NU omits the rest of the verse. [e](7:9) NU reads στησητε, *you may confirm.* [f](7:10) Ex. 20:12; Deut. 5:16 [g](7:10) Ex. 21:17 [h](7:16) NU omits v. 16.

pretended to be righteous by keeping punctilious traditions of hand washings and tithing mint, meanwhile they cheated widows and violently opposed the only completely righteous Person who ever lived!

παράδοσιν τῶν ἀνθρώπων,[d] βαπτισμοὺς ξεστῶν καὶ
tradition - of men, *the* ablutions of pitchers and
washing

ποτηρίων, καὶ ἄλλα παρόμοια τοιαῦτα πολλὰ ποιεῖτε."
of cups, and [3]other [5]*things* [4]similar [2]such [1]many you do."

9 Καὶ ἔλεγεν αὐτοῖς, "Καλῶς ἀθετεῖτε τὴν ἐντολὴν τοῦ
And He said to them, "Well do you set aside the commandment -

Θεοῦ, ἵνα τὴν παράδοσιν ὑμῶν τηρήσητε.[e] 10 Μωσῆς
of God, so that - [5]tradition [4]your [1]you [2]may [3]keep. Moses ˜

γὰρ εἶπε, «Τίμα τὸν πατέρα σου καὶ τὴν μητέρα σου,»[f] καί,
For said, «Honor - father ˜ your and - mother ˜ your,» and,

«Ὁ κακολογῶν πατέρα ἢ μητέρα θανάτῳ τελευτάτω.»[g]
«The *one* speaking evil of father or mother with death let him end.»
die.»

11 Ὑμεῖς δὲ λέγετε, 'Ἐὰν εἴπῃ ἄνθρωπος τῷ πατρὶ ἢ τῇ
you ˜ But say, 'If [3]says [1]a [2]man - to *his* father or -

μητρί, "Κορβᾶν" (ὅ ἐστι, δῶρον) "ὃ ἐὰν ἐξ ἐμοῦ
to *his* mother, "Corban" (which is, gift) "what ever [5]of [6]me
by

ὠφεληθῇς" '· 12 καὶ οὐκέτι ἀφίετε αὐτὸν οὐδὲν
[1]you [2]might [3]be [4]profited" '; and [2]no [3]longer [1]you allow him [3]nothing
anything

ποιῆσαι τῷ πατρὶ αὐτοῦ ἢ τῇ μητρὶ αὐτοῦ,
[1]to [2]do - for father ˜ his or - for mother ˜ his,

13 ἀκυροῦντες τὸν λόγον τοῦ Θεοῦ τῇ παραδόσει ὑμῶν ᾗ
thus nullifying the word - of God - by tradition ˜ your which

παρεδώκατε. Καὶ παρόμοια τοιαῦτα πολλὰ ποιεῖτε."
you have handed down. And [3]similar [2]such [4]*things* [1]many you do."

14 Καὶ προσκαλεσάμενος πάντα τὸν ὄχλον ἔλεγεν αὐτοῖς,
And having summoned all the crowd He said to them,

"Ἀκούετέ μου πάντες καὶ συνίετε. 15 Οὐδέν ἐστιν
"Hear Me all *of you* and understand. [3]nothing [1]*There* [2]is

ἔξωθεν τοῦ ἀνθρώπου εἰσπορευόμενον εἰς αὐτὸν ὃ
from outside the man entering into him which
a

δύναται αὐτὸν κοινῶσαι· ἀλλὰ τὰ ἐκπορευόμενά
is able [3]him [1]to [2]make common; but the *things* coming out
defile;

ἀπ' αὐτοῦ, ἐκεῖνά ἐστι τὰ κοινοῦντα τὸν ἄνθρωπον.
from him, those are the *things* making common the man.
defiling a

16 Εἴ[h] τις ἔχει ὦτα ἀκούειν ἀκουέτω." 17 Καὶ ὅτε
If anyone has ears to hear let him hear." And when

εἰσῆλθεν εἰς οἶκον ἀπὸ τοῦ ὄχλου, ἐπηρώτων αὐτὸν οἱ
He entered into a house from the crowd, [3]were [4]asking [5]Him -

μαθηταὶ αὐτοῦ περὶ τῆς παραβολῆς. 18 Καὶ λέγει αὐτοῖς,
[2]disciples [1]His about the parable. And He says to them,
said

"Οὕτω καὶ ὑμεῖς ἀσύνετοί ἐστε? Οὐ
"[4]thus [3]also [2]you [5]without [6]understanding [1]Are? [9]not

νοεῖτε ὅτι πᾶν τὸ ἔξωθεν εἰσπορευόμενον εἰς
[7]Do [8]you understand that every*thing* - from outside entering into
nothing

τὸν ἄνθρωπον οὐ δύναται αὐτὸν κοινῶσαι, 19 ὅτι οὐκ
the man not ˜ is able [3]him [1]to [2]make common, because [3]not
a can defile him,

εἰσπορεύεται αὐτοῦ εἰς τὴν καρδίαν ἀλλ' εἰς τὴν κοιλίαν, καὶ
[1]it [2]does enter his ˜ into - heart but into the stomach, and

εἰς τὸν ἀφεδρῶνα ἐκπορεύεται, καθαρίζον[i] πάντα τὰ
[2]into [3]the [4]latrine [1]passes, *thus* purifying all -
βρώματα?" 20 Ἔλεγε δὲ ὅτι "Τὸ ἐκ τοῦ ἀνθρώπου
foods?" [2]He [3]said [1]And - "The *thing* [3]out [4]of [5]the [6]man
"That which is a
ἐκπορευόμενον, ἐκεῖνο κοινοῖ τὸν ἄνθρωπον.
[1]coming [2]forth, that makes [3]common [1]the [2]man.
defiles a

21 Ἔσωθεν γάρ, ἐκ τῆς καρδίας τῶν ἀνθρώπων, οἱ
[2]from [3]within [1]For, out of the heart - of men, -
διαλογισμοὶ οἱ κακοὶ ἐκπορεύονται, μοιχεῖαι,* πορνεῖαι,
[4]thoughts - [3]evil [1]come [2]forth, adulteries, fornications,
designs
φόνοι, 22 κλοπαί, πλεονεξίαι, πονηρίαι, δόλος,
murders, thefts, covetous desires, wickednesses, deceit,
ἀσέλγεια, ὀφθαλμὸς πονηρός, βλασφημία, ὑπερηφανία,
debauchery, an eye ˜ evil, blasphemy, arrogance,
ἀφροσύνη. 23 Πάντα ταῦτα τὰ πονηρὰ ἔσωθεν ἐκπορεύεται
foolishness. All these - evil *things* from within come forth
καὶ κοινοῖ τὸν ἄνθρωπον."
and make common the man."
defile a

A Gentile Is Blessed for Her Faith
(Matt. 15:21–28)

24 Καὶ ἐκεῖθεν ἀναστὰς ἀπῆλθεν εἰς τὰ μεθόρια
And from there rising up He went away into the boundaries
He rose up and region
Τύρου καὶ Σιδῶνος.[j] Καὶ εἰσελθὼν εἰς οἰκίαν οὐδένα
of Tyre and of Sidon. And entering into a house [3]no [4]one
having entered
ἤθελε γνῶναι, καὶ οὐκ ἠδυνήθη λαθεῖν.
[1]He [2]wanted [5]to [6]know, and [3]not [1]He [2]was able to escape notice.
25 Ἀκούσασα γὰρ γυνὴ περὶ αὐτοῦ, ἧς εἶχε τὸ
[4]hearing [1]For [2]a [3]woman about Him, of whom [4]had -
For when a woman heard whose young
θυγάτριον αὐτῆς πνεῦμα ἀκάθαρτον, ἐλθοῦσα
[2]young [3]daughter [1]her a(n) spirit ˜ unclean, coming
daughter had she came and
προσέπεσε πρὸς τοὺς πόδας αὐτοῦ. 26 Ἦν δὲ ἡ γυνὴ
fell at - feet ˜ His. [4]was [1]Now [2]the [3]woman
Ἑλληνίς, Συροφοινίκισσα τῷ γένει, καὶ ἠρώτα αὐτὸν ἵνα
a Greek, a Syro-Phoenician - by race, and she was asking Him that
τὸ δαιμόνιον ἐκβάλῃ ἐκ τῆς θυγατρὸς αὐτῆς.
[5]the [6]demon [1]He [2]would [3]cast [4]out from - daughter ˜ her.
27 Ὁ δὲ Ἰησοῦς εἶπεν αὐτῇ, "Ἄφες πρῶτον χορτασθῆναι
- But Jesus said to her, "Allow [6]first [3]to [4]be [5]filled
τὰ τέκνα, οὐ γάρ καλόν ἐστι λαβεῖν τὸν ἄρτον τῶν τέκνων
[1]the [2]children, [10]not [7]for [11]good [8]it [9]is to take the bread of the children
καὶ βαλεῖν τοῖς κυναρίοις."*
and to throw *it* to the little dogs."
28 Ἡ δὲ ἀπεκρίθη καὶ λέγει αὐτῷ, "Ναί,[k] Κύριε,
[2]the [3]*one* [1]But answered and says to Him, "Yes, Lord,
she said
καὶ γὰρ τὰ κυνάρια ὑποκάτω τῆς τραπέζης ἐσθίει ἀπὸ τῶν
even ˜ for the little dogs underneath the table eat from the
yet
ψιχίων τῶν παιδίων."
crumbs of the children."

is eliminated, *thus* purifying all foods?"
20 And He said, "What comes out of a man, that defiles a man.
21 "For from within, out of the heart of men, proceed evil thoughts, adulteries, fornications, murders,
22 "thefts, covetousness, wickedness, deceit, lewdness, an evil eye, blasphemy, pride, foolishness.
23 "All these evil things come from within and defile a man."
24 From there He arose and went to the region of Tyre and Sidon. And He entered a house and wanted no one to know *it*, but He could not be hidden.
25 For a woman whose young daughter had an unclean spirit heard about Him, and she came and fell at His feet.
26 The woman was a Greek, a Syro-Phoenician by birth, and she kept asking Him to cast the demon out of her daughter.
27 But Jesus said to her, "Let the children be filled first, for it is not good to take the children's bread and throw *it* to the little dogs."
28 And she answered and said to Him, "Yes, Lord, yet even the little dogs under the table eat from the children's crumbs."

---

[i](**7:19**) NU reads καθαριζων, *(He was) purifying*, thus ending the quotation after εκπορευεται and setting off the last phrase as Mark's explanation.
[j](**7:24**) NU omits και Σιδωνος, *and Sidon*.
[k](**7:28**) NU omits Ναι, *Yes*.

***(7:21)** μοιχεία *(moicheia)*. Noun meaning *adultery*. Whereas πορνεία, *sexual immorality*, was a general term describing any form of sexual misconduct, μοιχεία was strictly limited in its use within Hellenistic Greek. It referred to sexual relations of a married woman with a man other than her husband, both of whom thereby committed *adultery*. However, sexual relations between a married man and any unmarried woman were not considered μοιχεία, but rather πορνεία. Thus, the marital status of the woman determined whether a particular act of sexual misconduct was called μοιχεία. Cf. the cognate verb μοιχεύω, *commit adultery;* the nouns μοιχαλίς, *adulteress,* and

29 Then He said to her, "For
this saying go your way; the demon has gone out of your
daughter."
30 And when she had come to
her house, she found the demon gone out, and her daughter lying on the bed.
31 Again, departing from the
region of Tyre and Sidon, He
came through the midst of the
region of Decapolis to the Sea
of Galilee.
32 Then they brought to Him
one who was deaf and had an
impediment in his speech, and
they begged Him to put His
hand on him.
33 And He took him aside
from the multitude, and put His
fingers in his ears, and He spat
and touched his tongue.
34 Then, looking up to
heaven, He sighed, and said to
him, "Ephphatha," that is, "Be
opened."
35 Immediately his ears were
opened, and the impediment of
his tongue was loosed, and he
spoke plainly.
36 Then He commanded them
that they should tell no one; but
the more He commanded them,
the more widely they pro-
claimed *it*.
37 And they were astonished
beyond measure, saying, "He
has done all things well. He
makes both the deaf to hear and
the mute to speak."
8 In those days, the multitude being very great and
having nothing to eat, Jesus

29 Καὶ εἶπεν αὐτῇ, "Διὰ τοῦτον τὸν λόγον ὕπαγε,
And He said to her, "Because of this - word go,
saying

ἐξελήλυθε τὸ δαιμόνιον ἐκ τῆς θυγατρός σου." **30** Καὶ
[3]has [4]gone [5]out [1]the [2]demon of - daughter ˜ your." And

ἀπελθοῦσα εἰς τὸν οἶκον αὐτῆς εὗρε τὸ δαιμόνιον
going away to - house ˜ her she found the demon

ἐξεληλυθὸς καὶ τὴν θυγατέρα βεβλημένον ἐπὶ τῆς κλίνης.
having gone out and the daughter having been placed on the bed.
her

Jesus Heals a Deaf-mute

31 Καὶ πάλιν ἐξελθὼν ἐκ τῶν ὁρίων Τύρου καὶ Σιδῶνος
And again coming out from the borders of Tyre and Sidon
region

ἦλθε πρὸς τὴν θάλασσαν τῆς Γαλιλαίας ἀνὰ μέσον τῶν
He went to the sea - of Galilee in the midst of the

ὁρίων Δεκαπόλεως. **32** Καὶ φέρουσιν αὐτῷ κωφὸν
borders of Decapolis. And they bring to Him a deaf *man*
region brought

μογγιλάλον καὶ παρακαλοῦσιν αὐτὸν ἵνα ἐπιθῇ
impeded in speech and they beg Him that He would lay upon
begged

αὐτῷ τὴν χεῖρα. **33** Καὶ ἀπολαβόμενος αὐτὸν ἀπὸ τοῦ
him the hand. And [1]taking [3]aside [2]him from the
His when He had taken him aside

ὄχλου κατ' ἰδίαν ἔβαλε τοὺς δακτύλους αὐτοῦ εἰς τὰ ὦτα αὐτοῦ
crowd privately He put - fingers ˜ His in - ears ˜ his

καὶ πτύσας ἥψατο τῆς γλώσσης αὐτοῦ. **34** Καὶ ἀναβλέψας
and having spit He touched - tongue ˜ his. And looking up

εἰς τὸν οὐρανὸν ἐστέναξε, καὶ λέγει αὐτῷ, "Ἐφφαθά," ὅ
into - heaven He sighed, and says to him, "Ephphatha," which
said that

ἐστι, "Διανοίχθητι." **35** Καὶ εὐθέως διηνοίχθησαν αὐτοῦ αἱ
is, "Be opened." And immediately [3]were [4]opened [1]his -

ἀκοαί, καὶ ἐλύθη ὁ δεσμὸς τῆς γλώσσης αὐτοῦ, καὶ
[2]ears, and [6]was [7]loosed [1]the [2]bond - [3]of [5]tongue [4]his, and

ἐλάλει ὀρθῶς. **36** Καὶ διεστείλατο αὐτοῖς ἵνα μηδενὶ
he was speaking correctly. And He ordered them that [4]no [5]one

εἴπωσιν· ὅσον δὲ αὐτὸς αὐτοῖς διεστέλλετο,
[1]they [2]should [3]tell; [7]as [8]much [9]as [6]but [10]He [12]them [11]ordered,
the more

μᾶλλον περισσότερον ἐκήρυσσον.
the more exceedingly they would proclaim *it*.

37 Καὶ ὑπερπερισσῶς ἐξεπλήσσοντο, λέγοντες,
And [4]beyond [5]measure [1]they [2]were [3]astonished, saying,

"Καλῶς πάντα πεποίηκε. Καὶ τοὺς κωφοὺς ποιεῖ
"[6]well [4]all [5]*things* [1]He [2]has [3]done. [9]both [10]the [11]deaf [7]He [8]makes

ἀκούειν καὶ τοὺς ἀλάλους λαλεῖν."
to hear and the mutes to speak."

Jesus Feeds the Four Thousand
(Matt. 15:32–39)

8 **1** Ἐν ἐκείναις ταῖς ἡμέραις παμπόλλου ὄχλου
In those - days [2]very [3]great [1]a [4]crowd
when a great crowd

ὄντος καὶ μὴ ἐχόντων τί φάγωσι,
being and not having anything they could eat,
had gathered

μοιχός, adulterer; and the verb *μοιχάω, cause to commit adultery.* As in the OT, the word family may refer to spiritual adultery (as James 4:4).

***(7:27)** *κυνάριον (kynarion).* Noun used here and in the parallel at Matt. 15:26, 27. It is the diminutive of *κύων, dog,* used both for the animal and metaphorically for one who is unclean (cf. Phil. 3:2; Rev. 22:15). Jews used the word for Gentiles who were considered to be ceremonially impure. Here the word means *little dog* (a house pet) or *puppy,* such as would beg food from children.

προσκαλεσάμενος ὁ Ἰησοῦς τοὺς μαθητὰς αὐτοῦ λέγει αὐτοῖς,
[2]having [3]summoned - [1]Jesus - [5]disciples [4]His says to them,
said

2 "Σπλαγχνίζομαι ἐπὶ τὸν ὄχλον ὅτι ἤδη ἡμέραι τρεῖς
"I have compassion on the crowd because already days ~ three

προσμένουσί μοι καὶ οὐκ ἔχουσι τί φάγωσι.
they remain with Me and [3]not [1]they [2]do have anything they can eat.
have been remaining to eat.

3 Καὶ ἐὰν ἀπολύσω αὐτοὺς νήστεις εἰς οἶκον αὐτῶν
And if I dismiss them hungry to house ~ their

ἐκλυθήσονται ἐν τῇ ὁδῷ, τινὲς γὰρ αὐτῶν μακρόθεν
they will faint on the way, some ~ for of them [3]from [4]a [5]distance

ἥκουσι."
[1]have [2]come."

4 Καὶ ἀπεκρίθησαν αὐτῷ οἱ μαθηταὶ αὐτοῦ, "Πόθεν
And [3]answered [4]Him - [2]disciples [1]His, "From where

τούτους δυνήσεταί τις ὧδε χορτάσαι ἄρτων ἐπ'
[7]these [8]*people* [1]will [3]be [4]able [2]anyone [11]here [5]to [6]satisfy [9]of [10]bread in
with

ἐρημίας?"
this deserted place?"

5 Καὶ ἐπηρώτα αὐτούς, "Πόσους ἔχετε ἄρτους?"
And He asked them, "How many [2]do [3]you [4]have [1]loaves?"

Οἱ δὲ εἶπον, "Ἑπτά." **6** Καὶ παρήγγειλλε τῷ ὄχλῳ
[2]the [3]*ones* [1]And said, "Seven." And He commanded the crowd
they

ἀναπεσεῖν ἐπὶ τῆς γῆς. Καὶ λαβὼν τοὺς ἑπτὰ ἄρτους
to recline on the ground. And taking the seven loaves
He took

εὐχαριστήσας ἔκλασε καὶ ἐδίδου τοῖς μαθηταῖς
having given thanks He broke *them* and was giving *them* - to disciples ~

αὐτοῦ ἵνα παραθῶσι, καὶ
His so that they might set *them* before *the people,* and

παρέθηκαν τῷ ὄχλῳ. **7** Καὶ εἶχον ἰχθύδια ὀλίγα· καὶ
they set *them* before the crowd. And they had [3]small [4]fish [1]a [2]few; and

εὐλογήσας εἶπε παραθεῖναι καὶ αὐτά.
having blessed *them* He said to set [3]before [4]*the* [5]*people* [2]also [1]them.

8 Ἔφαγον δὲ καὶ ἐχορτάσθησαν, καὶ ἦραν
[2]they [3]ate [1]And and were filled, and they took up

περισσεύματα κλασμάτων ἑπτὰ σπυρίδας. **9** Ἦσαν δὲ
an abundance of fragments seven hampers *full.* [6]were [1]And

οἱ φαγόντες ὡς τετρακισχίλιοι. Καὶ ἀπέλυσεν
[2]the [3]*ones* [4]having [5]eaten about four thousand. And He dismissed

αὐτούς. **10** Καὶ εὐθέως ἐμβὰς εἰς τὸ πλοῖον μετὰ τῶν
them. And immediately stepping in into the boat with -

μαθητῶν αὐτοῦ ἦλθεν εἰς τὰ μέρη Δαλμανουθά.
disciples ~ His He came to the parts of Dalmanutha.
region

The Pharisees Seek a Sign
(Matt. 16:1–4)

11 Καὶ ἐξῆλθον οἱ Φαρισαῖοι καὶ ἤρξαντο συζητεῖν αὐτῷ,
And [3]came [4]out [1]the [2]Pharisees and began to question Him,

ζητοῦντες παρ' αὐτοῦ σημεῖον ἀπὸ τοῦ οὐρανοῦ, πειράζοντες
seeking from Him a sign from - heaven, testing

αὐτόν. **12** Καὶ ἀναστενάξας τῷ πνεύματι αὐτοῦ λέγει, "Τί ἡ
Him. And sighing deeply - in spirit ~ His He says, "Why -
said,

called His disciples *to Him* and said to them,
2 "I have compassion on the multitude, because they have now continued with Me three days and have nothing to eat.
3 "And if I send them away hungry to their own houses, they will faint on the way; for some of them have come from afar."
4 Then His disciples answered Him, "How can one satisfy these people with bread here in the wilderness?"
5 He asked them, "How many loaves do you have?" And they said, "Seven."
6 So He commanded the multitude to sit down on the ground. And He took the seven loaves and gave thanks, broke *them* and gave *them* to His disciples to set before *them;* and they set *them* before the multitude.
7 They also had a few small fish; and having blessed them, He said to set them also before *them.*
8 So they ate and were filled, and they took up seven large baskets of leftover fragments.
9 Now those who had eaten were about four thousand. And He sent them away,
10 immediately got into the boat with His disciples, and came to the region of Dalmanutha.
11 Then the Pharisees came out and began to dispute with Him, seeking from Him a sign from heaven, testing Him.
12 But He sighed deeply in His spirit, and said, "Why does

this generation seek a sign? Assuredly, I say to you, no sign shall be given to this generation."
13 And He left them, and getting into the boat again, departed to the other side.
14 Now the disciples had forgotten to take bread, and they did not have more than one loaf with them in the boat.
15 Then He charged them, saying, "Take heed, beware of the leaven of the Pharisees and the leaven of Herod."
16 And they reasoned among themselves, saying, *"It is* because we have no bread."
17 But Jesus, being aware of *it,* said to them, "Why do you reason because you have no bread? Do you not yet perceive nor understand? Is your heart still hardened?
18 "Having eyes, do you not see? And having ears, do you not hear? And do you not remember?
19 "When I broke the five loaves for the five thousand, how many baskets full of fragments did you take up?" They said to Him, "Twelve."
20 "Also, when I broke the seven for the four thousand, how many large baskets full of fragments did you take up?" And they said, "Seven."
21 So He said to them, "How *is it* you do not understand?"

γενεὰ αὕτη σημεῖον ἐπιζητεῖ? Ἀμὴν λέγω ὑμῖν, εἰ
[3]generation [2]this [5]a [6]sign [1]does [4]seek? Amen (Assuredly) I say to you, [1]if (no)

δοθήσεται τῇ γενεᾷ ταύτῃ σημεῖον!"
[4]shall [5]be [6]given - [7]to [9]generation [8]this [2]a [3]sign!" (, sign!")

Beware of the Leaven of the Pharisees and Herod
(Matt. 16:5–12)

13 *Καὶ ἀφεὶς αὐτούς, ἐμβὰς πάλιν εἰς πλοῖον*
And having dismissed them, stepping in again into a boat

ἀπῆλθεν εἰς τὸ πέραν. **14** *Καὶ ἐπελάθοντο λαβεῖν ἄρτους,*
He went away to the other side. And they forgot to take bread,

καὶ εἰ μὴ ἕνα ἄρτον οὐκ εἶχον μεθ' ἑαυτῶν
and if (except) not *for* one loaf [3]not [1]they [2]did have *any* with themselves

ἐν τῷ πλοίῳ. **15** *Καὶ διεστέλλετο αὐτοῖς, λέγων, "Ὁρᾶτε,*
in the boat. And He charged them, saying, "Look out,

βλέπετε ἀπὸ τῆς ζύμης τῶν Φαρισαίων καὶ τῆς ζύμης
beware from (of) the leaven of the Pharisees and the leaven

Ἡρῴδου."
of Herod."

16 *Καὶ διελογίζοντο πρὸς ἀλλήλους, λέγοντες ὅτι*
And they were reasoning with one another, saying -

"Ἄρτους οὐκ ἔχομεν."
"[5]bread [3]not [1]We [2]do [4]have."

17 *Καὶ γνοὺς ὁ Ἰησοῦς λέγει αὐτοῖς, "Τί*
And knowing *about it* - Jesus says (said) to them, "Why

διαλογίζεσθε ὅτι ἄρτους οὐκ ἔχετε? Οὔπω
are you reasoning because [5]bread [3]not [1]you [2]do [4]have? [8]not [9]yet

νοεῖτε οὐδὲ συνίετε? Ἔτι[a] *πεπωρωμένην**
[6]Do [7]you perceive nor (or) understand? [3]still [7]hardened

ἔχετε τὴν καρδίαν ὑμῶν? **18** *Ὀφθαλμοὺς ἔχοντες οὐ*
[1]Do [2]you [4]have - [6]heart [5]your? eyes ˜ Having [3]not

βλέπετε καὶ ὦτα ἔχοντες οὐκ ἀκούετε? Καὶ οὐ
[1]do [2]you see and ears ˜ having [3]not [1]do [2]you hear? And [3]not

μνημονεύετε? **19** *Ὅτε τοὺς πέντε ἄρτους ἔκλασα εἰς τοὺς*
[1]do [2]you remember? When [3]the [4]five [5]loaves [1]I [2]broke for the

πεντακισχιλίους, πόσους κοφίνους πλήρεις κλασμάτων
five thousand, how many baskets full of fragments

ἤρατε?"
did you take up?"

Λέγουσιν αὐτῷ, "Δώδεκα."
They say (said) to Him, "Twelve."

20 *"Ὅτε δὲ τοὺς ἑπτὰ εἰς τοὺς τετρακισχιλίους,*
"when ˜ And the seven for the four thousand,

πόσων σπυρίδων πληρώματα κλασμάτων ἤρατε?"
of (in) how many [2]of [3]hampers [1]fullnesses of fragments did you take up?"

Οἱ δὲ εἶπον, "Ἑπτά."
[2]the [3]*ones* (they) [1]And said, "Seven."

21 *Καὶ ἔλεγεν αὐτοῖς, "Πῶς οὐ συνίετε?"*
And He said to them, "How *is it* [3]not [1]you [2]do understand?"

---

[a](8:17) NU omits Ετι, *still.*

*(8:17) *πωρόω (pōroō).* Verb meaning *to harden, petrify.* In the NT it is only used metaphorically of the hardening (of the "heart," as here) or blinding (of "minds," 2 Cor. 3:14) of human beings to some aspect of divine truth. The two instances in Mark (cf. also 6:52) both refer to the inability of Jesus' disciples to properly perceive truth. In John 12:40 it occurs in a quotation from Is. 6:10 explaining the reason why so many of the Jewish rulers failed to believe in Jesus even when confronted by His miracles (see John 12:37).

Jesus Heals a Blind Man at Bethsaida

22 Καὶ ἔρχεται εἰς Βηθσαϊδάν. Καὶ φέρουσιν αὐτῷ
And He comes to Bethsaida. And they bring to Him
came brought

τυφλὸν καὶ παρακαλοῦσιν αὐτὸν ἵνα αὐτοῦ ἅψηται.
a blind *man* and beg Him that [4]him [1]He [2]might [3]touch.
begged

23 Καὶ ἐπιλαβόμενος τῆς χειρὸς τοῦ τυφλοῦ ἐξήγαγεν αὐτὸν
And having taken the hand of the blind *man* He led him

ἔξω τῆς κώμης, καὶ πτύσας εἰς τὰ ὄμματα αὐτοῦ, ἐπιθεὶς
outside the village, and having spit into - eyes ˜ his, having laid

τὰς χεῖρας αὐτῷ, ἐπηρώτα αὐτὸν εἴ τι βλέπει.
the hands on him, He asked him if [3]anything [1]he [2]sees.
His saw.

24 Καὶ ἀναβλέψας ἔλεγε, "Βλέπω τοὺς ἀνθρώπους ὅτι ὡς
And looking up he said, "I see - men that like
when he looked

δένδρα ὁρῶ περιπατοῦντας."
trees I see *them* walking."

25 Εἶτα πάλιν ἐπέθηκε τὰς χεῖρας ἐπὶ τοὺς ὀφθαλμοὺς
Then again He put the hands on - eyes ˜
His

αὐτοῦ καὶ ἐποίησεν αὐτὸν ἀναβλέψαι. Καὶ ἀποκατεστάθη καὶ
his and made him to look up. And he was restored and

ἀνέβλεψε τηλαυγῶς ἅπαντας. 26 Καὶ ἀπέστειλεν αὐτὸν εἰς τὸν
saw [3]again [2]clearly [1]everyone. And He sent him to -

οἶκον αὐτοῦ, λέγων, "Μηδὲ εἰς τὴν κώμην εἰσέλθῃς[b] μηδὲ
house ˜ his, saying, "Neither [2]into [3]the [4]village [1]enter nor

εἴπῃς τινὶ ἐν τῇ κώμῃ."
say anything in the village."

Peter Confesses Jesus as the Christ

(Matt. 16:13–20; Luke 9:18–20)

27 Καὶ ἐξῆλθεν ὁ Ἰησοῦς καὶ οἱ μαθηταὶ αὐτοῦ εἰς τὰς
And [5]went [6]out - [1]Jesus [2]and - [4]disciples [3]His into the

κώμας Καισαρείας τῆς Φιλίππου· καὶ ἐν τῇ ὁδῷ
villages of Caesarea - of Philip; and on the road
Philippi;

ἐπηρώτα τοὺς μαθητὰς αὐτοῦ, λέγων αὐτοῖς, "Τίνα με
He was questioning - disciples ˜ His, saying to them, "[1]Whom [5]Me
"Who do

λέγουσιν οἱ ἄνθρωποι εἶναι?"
[2]do [4]say - [3]men [6]to be?"
people say that I am?"

28 Οἱ δὲ ἀπεκρίθησαν, "Ἰωάννην τὸν Βαπτιστήν,
[2]the [3]*ones* [1]And answered, "John the Baptist,
they

καὶ ἄλλοι Ἠλίαν, ἄλλοι δὲ ἕνα τῶν προφητῶν."
and others Elijah, others ˜ and one of the prophets."

29 Καὶ αὐτὸς λέγει αὐτοῖς, "Ὑμεῖς δὲ τίνα με
And He says to them, "you ˜ But whom [4]Me
said who do you

λέγετε εἶναι?"
[1]do [2]you [3]say to be?"
say that I am?"

Ἀποκριθεὶς δὲ ὁ Πέτρος λέγει αὐτῷ, "Σὺ εἶ ὁ Χριστός."
answering ˜ And - Peter says to Him, "You are the Christ."
said

22 Then He came to Bethsaida; and they brought a blind man to Him, and begged Him to touch him.
23 So He took the blind man by the hand and led him out of the town. And when He had spit on his eyes and put His hands on him, He asked him if he saw anything.
24 And he looked up and said, "I see men like trees, walking."
25 Then He put *His* hands on his eyes again and made him look up. And he was restored and saw everyone clearly.
26 Then He sent him away to his house, saying, "Neither go into the town, nor tell anyone in the town."
27 Now Jesus and His disciples went out to the towns of Caesarea Philippi; and on the road He asked His disciples, saying to them, "Who do men say that I am?"
28 So they answered, "John the Baptist; but some *say,* Elijah; and others, one of the prophets."
29 He said to them, "But who do you say that I am?" Peter answered and said to Him, "You are the Christ."

---

[b]**(8:26)** NU omits the rest of the verse, thus reading *Do not even enter into the village.*

30 Then He strictly warned them that they should tell no one about Him.
31 And He began to teach them that the Son of Man must suffer many things, and be rejected by the elders and chief priests and scribes, and be killed, and after three days rise again.
32 He spoke this word openly. Then Peter took Him aside and began to rebuke Him.
33 But when He had turned around and looked at His disciples, He rebuked Peter, saying, "Get behind Me, Satan! For you are not mindful of the things of God, but the things of men."
34 When He had called the people to *Himself,* with His disciples also, He said to them, "Whoever desires to come after Me, let him deny himself, and take up his cross, and follow Me.
35 "For whoever desires to save his life will lose it, but whoever loses his life for My sake and the gospel's will save it.
36 "For what will it profit a man if he gains the whole world, and loses his own soul?
37 "Or what will a man give in exchange for his soul?
38 "For whoever is ashamed of Me and My words in this

30 Καὶ ἐπετίμησεν αὐτοῖς ἵνα μηδενὶ λέγωσι περὶ
And He warned them that [4]no [5]one [1]they [2]should [3]tell about

αὐτοῦ.
Him.

Jesus Predicts His Death and Resurrection
(Matt. 16:21–23; Luke 9:21, 22)

31 Καὶ ἤρξατο διδάσκειν αὐτοὺς ὅτι δεῖ τὸν
And He began to teach them that it is necessary *for* the
was

Υἱὸν τοῦ Ἀνθρώπου πολλὰ παθεῖν καὶ ἀποδοκιμασθῆναι
Son - of Man [3]many [4]*things* [1]to [2]suffer and to be rejected

ἀπὸ τῶν πρεσβυτέρων καὶ τῶν ἀρχιερέων καὶ τῶν γραμματέων
by the elders and the chief priests and the scribes

καὶ ἀποκτανθῆναι καὶ μετὰ τρεῖς ἡμέρας ἀναστῆναι. **32** Καὶ
and to be killed and after three days to rise. And

παρρησίᾳ τὸν λόγον ἐλάλει. Καὶ προσλαβόμενος
[6]with [7]boldness [4]the [5]word [1]He [2]was [3]speaking. And taking aside ˜
this saying

αὐτὸν ὁ Πέτρος ἤρξατο ἐπιτιμᾶν αὐτῷ.
Him - Peter began to rebuke Him.

33 Ὁ δὲ ἐπιστραφεὶς καὶ ἰδὼν τοὺς μαθητὰς αὐτοῦ
- But turning and seeing - disciples ˜ His
when He had turned seen

ἐπετίμησε τῷ Πέτρῳ, λέγων, "Ὕπαγε ὀπίσω μου, Σατανᾶ,
He rebuked - Peter, saying, "Go away behind Me, Satan,

ὅτι οὐ φρονεῖς τὰ τοῦ Θεοῦ ἀλλὰ τὰ
because [3]not [1]you [2]are mindful of the *things* - of God but the *things*

τῶν ἀνθρώπων."
- of men."

Taking Up the Cross
(Matt. 16:24–28; Luke 9:23–27)

34 Καὶ προσκαλεσάμενος τὸν ὄχλον σὺν τοῖς
And having summoned the crowd together with -

μαθηταῖς αὐτοῦ εἶπεν αὐτοῖς, "Ὅστις θέλει ὀπίσω μου
disciples ˜ His He said to them, "Whoever desires [3]after [4]Me

ἀκολουθεῖν, ἀπαρνησάσθω ἑαυτὸν καὶ ἀράτω τὸν
[1]to [2]follow, let him deny himself and let him take up -

σταυρὸν* αὐτοῦ καὶ ἀκολουθείτω μοι. **35** Ὃς γὰρ ἂν θέλῃ
cross ˜ his and let him follow Me. who ˜ For ever desires

τὴν ψυχὴν αὐτοῦ σῶσαι ἀπολέσει αὐτήν· ὃς δ' ἂν
- [4]life [3]his [1]to [2]save will lose it; who ˜ but ever
preserve

ἀπολέσῃ τὴν ἑαυτοῦ ψυχὴν ἕνεκεν ἐμοῦ καὶ τοῦ
loses the of himself life on account of Me and the
his own

εὐαγγελίου, οὗτος σώσει αὐτήν. **36** Τί γὰρ ὠφελήσει
gospel, this *one* will save it. what ˜ For will it profit
preserve

ἄνθρωπον ἐὰν κερδήσῃ τὸν κόσμον ὅλον καὶ ζημιωθῇ τὴν
a man if he gains the world ˜ whole and forfeits -

ψυχὴν αὐτοῦ? **37** Ἢ τί δώσει ἄνθρωπος ἀντάλλαγμα τῆς
soul ˜ his? Or what will [3]give [1]a [2]man *as* an exchange for -

ψυχῆς αὐτοῦ? **38** Ὃς γὰρ ἐὰν ἐπαισχυνθῇ με καὶ τοὺς ἐμοὺς
soul ˜ his? who ˜ For ever is ashamed of Me and - My

***(8:34)** σταυρός *(stauros).* Noun meaning *cross,* originally a *stake* or *upright pole.* It always designates an instrument of execution (one regarded as particularly insulting and shameful, as Phil. 2:8). It is used with a variety of verbs for "to take up" or "to carry," figuratively meaning "to endure suffering or even death" (as here in Mark 8:34; also Matt. 10:38; Luke 14:27). Whether the σταυρός included a horizontal crosspiece (either at the top or slightly lower) by the time of Jesus is debated. It was most probably this crosspiece that was carried by the condemned person to the execution site where the σταυρός proper would have previously been erected (cf. the story about Simon Cyrene, Matt. 27:32; Mark 15:21; Luke 23:26). Cf.

λόγους ἐν τῇ γενεᾷ ταύτῃ τῇ μοιχαλίδι καὶ ἁμαρτωλῷ,
words in - [5]generation [1]this - [2]adulterous [3]and [4]sinful,
among

καὶ ὁ Υἱὸς τοῦ Ἀνθρώπου ἐπαισχυνθήσεται αὐτὸν ὅταν
[10]also [6]the [7]Son - [8]of [9]Man will be ashamed of him whenever

ἔλθῃ ἐν τῇ δόξῃ τοῦ Πατρὸς αὐτοῦ μετὰ τῶν ἀγγέλων τῶν
He comes in the glory - of Father ~ His with the angels ~ -

ἁγίων."
holy."

9 1 Καὶ ἔλεγεν αὐτοῖς, "Ἀμὴν λέγω ὑμῖν ὅτι εἰσί τινες
And He said to them, "Amen I say to you that *there* are some
"Assuredly

τῶν ὧδε ἑστηκότων οἵτινες οὐ μὴ γεύσωνται θανάτου
of the *ones* here ~ standing who not not will taste of death
by no means

ἕως ἂν ἴδωσι τὴν βασιλείαν τοῦ Θεοῦ ἐληλυθυῖαν ἐν
until - they see the kingdom - of God having come in

δυνάμει."
power."

Jesus Is Transfigured on the Mount
(Matt. 17:1–13; Luke 9:28–36)

2 Καὶ μεθ' ἡμέρας ἓξ παραλαμβάνει ὁ Ἰησοῦς τὸν Πέτρον
And after days ~ six [2]takes [3]along - [1]Jesus - Peter
took

καὶ τὸν Ἰάκωβον καὶ Ἰωάννην, καὶ ἀναφέρει αὐτοὺς εἰς
and - James and John, and leads up ~ them into
led

ὄρος ὑψηλὸν κατ' ἰδίαν μόνους. Καὶ μετεμορφώθη
a mountain ~ high in private alone. And He was transformed

ἔμπροσθεν αὐτῶν, 3 καὶ τὰ ἱμάτια αὐτοῦ ἐγένοντο στίλβοντα,
before them, and - clothes ~ His became shining,

λευκὰ λίαν ὡς χιών, οἷα γναφεὺς ἐπὶ τῆς γῆς οὐ δύναται
white ~ very like snow, such as a bleacher on - earth not ~ is able
launderer

λευκᾶναι. 4 Καὶ ὤφθη αὐτοῖς Ἠλίας σὺν Μωσῇ,
to whiten. And [2]appeared [3]to [4]them [1]Elijah together with Moses,

καὶ ἦσαν συλλαλοῦντες τῷ Ἰησοῦ.
and they were talking - with Jesus.
conversing

5 Καὶ ἀποκριθεὶς ὁ Πέτρος λέγει τῷ Ἰησοῦ, "Ῥαββί,
And answering - Peter says - to Jesus, "Rabbi,
said

καλόν ἐστιν ἡμᾶς ὧδε εἶναι, καὶ ποιήσωμεν σκηνὰς τρεῖς,
[3]good [1]it [2]is *for* us [3]here [1]to [2]be, and let us make tents ~ three,

σοὶ μίαν καὶ Μωσῇ μίαν καὶ Ἠλίᾳ μίαν." 6 Οὐ γὰρ
[2]for [3]You [1]one and [2]for [3]Moses [1]one and [2]for [3]Elijah [1]one." [4]not [1]For

ᾔδει τί λαλήσει, ἦσαν γὰρ ἔκφοβοι.
[2]he [3]did know what he shall say, [2]they [3]were [1]for terrified.
should

7 Καὶ ἐγένετο νεφέλη ἐπισκιάζουσα αὐτοῖς, καὶ ἦλθε
And [3]became [1]a [2]cloud overshadowing them, and [3]came
appeared

φωνὴ ἐκ τῆς νεφέλης, "Οὗτός ἐστιν ὁ Υἱός μου ὁ
[1]a [2]voice out of the cloud, "This is - [3]Son [1]My -

ἀγαπητός. Αὐτοῦ ἀκούετε!" 8 Καὶ ἐξάπινα περιβλεψάμενοι,
[2]beloved. Him ~ Hear!" And suddenly looking around,

adulterous and sinful generation, of him the Son of Man also
will be ashamed when He
comes in the glory of His Father with the holy angels."
9 And He said to them,
"Assuredly, I say to you
that there are some standing
here who will not taste death till
they see the kingdom of God
present with power."
2 Now after six days Jesus
took Peter, James, and John,
and led them up on a high
mountain apart by themselves;
and He was transfigured before
them.
3 His clothes became shining, exceedingly white, like
snow, such as no launderer on
earth can whiten them.
4 And Elijah appeared to
them with Moses, and they
were talking with Jesus.
5 Then Peter answered and
said to Jesus, "Rabbi, it is good
for us to be here; and let us
make three tabernacles: one for
You, one for Moses, and one
for Elijah"—
6 because he did not know
what to say, for they were
greatly afraid.
7 And a cloud came and overshadowed them; and a voice
came out of the cloud, saying,
"This is My beloved Son. Hear
Him!"
8 Suddenly, when they had
looked around, they saw no one

the cognate verb σταυρόω, *crucify.*

anymore, but only Jesus with
themselves.
9 Now as they came down
from the mountain, He commanded them that they should
tell no one the things they had
seen, till the Son of Man had
risen from the dead.
10 So they kept this word to
themselves, questioning what
the rising from the dead meant.
11 And they asked Him, saying, "Why do the scribes say
that Elijah must come first?"
12 Then He answered and
told them, "Indeed, Elijah is
coming first and restores all
things. And how is it written
concerning the Son of Man,
that He must suffer many
things and be treated with contempt?
13 "But I say to you that Elijah has also come, and they did
to him whatever they wished,
as it is written of him."
14 And when He came to the
disciples, He saw a great multitude around them, and scribes
disputing with them.
15 Immediately, when they
saw Him, all the people were
greatly amazed, and running to
Him, greeted Him.
16 And He asked the scribes,
"What are you discussing with
them?"
17 Then one of the crowd answered and said, "Teacher, I
brought You my son, who has a
mute spirit.

οὐκέτι οὐδένα εἶδον ἀλλὰ τὸν Ἰησοῦν μόνον μεθ'
[2]no [3]longer [5]no [6]one [1]they [4]saw but - Jesus ˜ only with
any

ἑαυτῶν.
themselves.

9 Καταβαινόντων δὲ αὐτῶν ἀπὸ τοῦ ὄρους,
[3]coming [4]down [1]And [2]them from the mountain,
And as they were coming down

διεστείλατο αὐτοῖς ἵνα μηδενὶ διηγήσωνται ἃ
He ordered them that [3]to [4]no [5]one [1]they [2]recount *the things* which

εἶδον, εἰ μὴ ὅταν ὁ Υἱὸς τοῦ Ἀνθρώπου ἐκ νεκρῶν
they saw, if not whenever the Son - of Man [3]from [4]*the* [5]dead
except

ἀναστῇ. 10 Καὶ τὸν λόγον ἐκράτησαν πρὸς ἑαυτούς,
[1]should [2]rise. And the word they kept to themselves,
this saying

συζητοῦντες τί ἐστι τὸ ἐκ νεκρῶν ἀναστῆναι.
questioning what it is - [3]from [4]*the* [5]dead [1]to [2]rise.
meant

11 Καὶ ἐπηρώτων αὐτόν, λέγοντες, "Ὅτι λέγουσιν οἱ
And they asked Him, saying, "Why [1]do [4]say [2]the

γραμματεῖς ὅτι Ἠλίαν δεῖ ἐλθεῖν πρῶτον?"
[3]scribes that [5]Elijah [1]it [2]is [3]necessary [4]*for* to come first?"

12 Ὁ δὲ ἀποκριθεὶς εἶπεν αὐτοῖς, "Ἠλίας μὲν ἐλθὼν
- And answering He said to them, "Elijah indeed coming

πρῶτον ἀποκαθιστᾷ πάντα· καὶ πῶς γέγραπται ἐπὶ τὸν
first restores all *things*; and how is it written concerning the

Υἱὸν τοῦ Ἀνθρώπου ἵνα πολλὰ πάθῃ καὶ
Son - of Man that [4]many [5]*things* [1]He [2]should [3]suffer and

ἐξουδενωθῇ? 13 Ἀλλὰ λέγω ὑμῖν ὅτι καὶ Ἠλίας
be treated with contempt? But I say to you that indeed Elijah

ἐλήλυθε, καὶ ἐποίησαν αὐτῷ ὅσα ἠθέλησαν, καθὼς
has come, and they did to him as many things as they wished, just as
everything which

γέγραπται ἐπ' αὐτόν."
it is written concerning him."

Jesus Heals a Boy with an Unclean Spirit
(Matt. 17:14–21; Luke 9:37–43a)

14 Καὶ ἐλθὼν πρὸς τοὺς μαθητὰς εἶδεν ὄχλον
And coming to the disciples He saw a crowd ˜
when He came

πολὺν περὶ αὐτοὺς καὶ γραμματεῖς συζητοῦντας αὐτοῖς.
large around them and scribes disputing with them.

15 Καὶ εὐθέως πᾶς ὁ ὄχλος ἰδὼν αὐτὸν
And immediately all the crowd seeing Him
when they saw

ἐξεθαμβήθη, καὶ προστρέχοντες ἠσπάζοντο αὐτόν. 16 Καὶ
were greatly amazed, and running to *Him* they greeted Him. And

ἐπηρώτησε τοὺς γραμματεῖς, "Τί συζητεῖτε πρὸς
He asked the scribes, "What are you disputing about with

αὐτούς?"
them?"

17 Καὶ ἀπεκριθεὶς εἷς ἐκ τοῦ ὄχλου εἶπε, "Διδάσκαλε,
And [5]answering [1]one [2]from [3]the [4]crowd said, "Teacher,

ἤνεγκα τὸν υἱόν μου πρὸς σέ, ἔχοντα πνεῦμα ἄλαλον.
I brought - son ˜ my to You, having a spirit ˜ mute.
because he has

18 Καὶ ὅπου ἂν αὐτὸν καταλάβῃ ῥήσσει αὐτόν, καὶ
And where ever [3]him [1]it [2]seizes it throws down ˜ him, and

ἀφρίζει καὶ τρίζει τοὺς ὀδόντας αὐτοῦ καὶ
he foams at the mouth and gnashes - teeth ˜ his and

ξηραίνεται. Καὶ εἶπον τοῖς μαθηταῖς σου ἵνα αὐτὸ
he becomes rigid. And I spoke - to disciples ˜ Your that [4]it

ἐκβάλωσι, καὶ οὐκ ἴσχυσαν."
[1]they [2]might [3]cast [5]out, and [3]not [1]they [2]were able."

19 Ὁ δὲ ἀποκριθεὶς αὐτῷ λέγει, "Ὦ γενεὰ
[2]the [3]*One* [1]And answering him says, "O generation ˜
He said,

ἄπιστος,* ἕως πότε πρὸς ὑμᾶς ἔσομαι? Ἕως πότε
unbelieving, until when [4]with [5]you [1]shall [2]I [3]be? Until when
how long How long

ἀνέξομαι ὑμῶν? Φέρετε αὐτὸν πρός με." 20 Καὶ
shall I put up with you? Bring him to Me." And

ἤνεγκαν αὐτὸν πρὸς αὐτόν. Καὶ ἰδὼν αὐτόν, εὐθέως
they brought him to Him. And seeing Him, immediately
when he saw

τὸ πνεῦμα ἐσπάραξεν αὐτόν, καὶ πεσὼν ἐπὶ τῆς γῆς
the spirit convulsed him, and having fallen on the ground

ἐκυλίετο ἀφρίζων. 21 Καὶ ἐπηρώτησε τὸν
he was rolling about foaming at the mouth. And He asked -

πατέρα αὐτοῦ, "Πόσος χρόνος ἐστὶν ὡς τοῦτο
father ˜ his, "How long a time is it *that* [4]like [5]this
has it been

γέγονεν αὐτῷ?"
[1]it [2]has [3]happened to him?"

Ὁ δὲ εἶπε, "Παιδιόθεν. 22 Καὶ πολλάκις αὐτὸν
[2]the [3]*one* [1]And said, "From childhood. And often [3]him
he

καὶ εἰς τὸ πῦρ ἔβαλε καὶ εἰς ὕδατα ἵνα ἀπολέσῃ
[4]both [5]into [6]the [7]fire [1]it [2]threw and into *the* waters so that it may destroy

αὐτόν. Ἀλλ' εἴ τι δύνασαι, βοήθησον ἡμῖν
him. But if [6]anything [1]You [2]are [3]able [4]*to* [5]*do,* help us

σπλαγχνισθεὶς ἐφ' ἡμᾶς."
having compassion on us."
and have compassion

23 Ὁ δὲ Ἰησοῦς εἶπεν αὐτῷ, "Τὸ εἰ δύνασαι
- And Jesus said to him, - "If you are able

πιστεῦσαι·[a] πάντα δυνατὰ τῷ πιστεύοντι."
to believe: all *things are* possible to the *one* believing."
who believes."

24 Καὶ εὐθέως κράξας ὁ πατὴρ τοῦ παιδίου μετὰ
And immediately crying out the father of the child with

δακρύων[b] ἔλεγε, "Πιστεύω, Κύριε, βοήθει μου τῇ ἀπιστίᾳ!"
tears said, "I believe, Lord, help my - unbelief!"

25 Ἰδὼν δὲ ὁ Ἰησοῦς ὅτι ἐπισυντρέχει ὄχλος,
seeing And - Jesus that [3]is [4]running [5]together [1]a [2]crowd,
And when Jesus saw was

ἐπετίμησε τῷ πνεύματι τῷ ἀκαθάρτῳ, λέγων αὐτῷ, "Τὸ
He rebuked the spirit ˜ - unclean, saying to him, -

πνεῦμα τὸ ἄλαλον καὶ κωφόν, ἐγώ σοι ἐπιτάσσω, ἔξελθε ἐξ
"[4]spirit - [1]Mute [2]and [3]deaf, I you ˜ command, come out of

αὐτοῦ καὶ μηκέτι εἰσέλθῃς εἰς αὐτόν." 26 Καὶ κράξαν
him and no longer enter into him." And having cried out

καὶ πολλὰ σπαράξαν αὐτὸν ἐξῆλθε. Καὶ ἐγένετο ὡσεὶ
and many *things* having convulsed him it came out. And he became like
greatly

18 "And wherever it seizes him, it throws him down; he foams at the mouth, gnashes his teeth, and becomes rigid. So I spoke to Your disciples, that they should cast it out, but they could not."
19 He answered him and said, "O faithless generation, how long shall I be with you? How long shall I bear with you? Bring him to Me."
20 Then they brought him to Him. And when he saw Him, immediately the spirit convulsed him, and he fell on the ground and wallowed, foaming at the mouth.
21 So He asked his father, "How long has this been happening to him?" And he said, "From childhood.
22 "And often he has thrown him both into the fire and into the water to destroy him. But if You can do anything, have compassion on us and help us."
23 Jesus said to him, "If you can believe, all things *are* possible to him who believes."
24 Immediately the father of the child cried out and said with tears, "Lord, I believe; help my unbelief!"
25 When Jesus saw that the people came running together, He rebuked the unclean spirit, saying to it: "Deaf and dumb spirit, I command you, come out of him and enter him no more!"
26 Then *the spirit* cried out, convulsed him greatly, and came out of him. And he be-

---

[a](9:23) NU omits πιστευσαι, thus: *"'If You are able!' All things . . . ."*
[b](9:24) NU omits μετα δακρυων, *with tears.*

***(9:19)** ἄπιστος *(apistos).* Adjective usually meaning *unbelieving, faithless,* formed from the root πίστις, *faith,* and the prefixed α- negative (see πιστεύω at Acts 16:31). The word may refer to a specific manifestation of disbelief (as here; see John 20:27) or (used substantivally) to non-Christian unbelievers in general. ἄπιστος sometimes implies active wickedness (Rev. 21:8). Once (Acts 26:8) it means *unbelievable, incredible.* The adjective does not share the meaning *unfaithful* found with the cognate noun ἀπιστία, *unbelief, un-*

came as one dead, so that many
said, "He is dead."
27 But Jesus took him by the
hand and lifted him up, and he
arose.
28 And when He had come
into the house, His disciples
asked Him privately, "Why
could we not cast it out?"
29 So He said to them, "This
kind can come out by nothing
but prayer and fasting."
30 Then they departed from
there and passed through Galilee, and He did not want anyone to know *it.*
31 For He taught His disciples
and said to them, "The Son of
Man is being betrayed into the
hands of men, and they will kill
Him. And after He is killed, He
will rise the third day."
32 But they did not understand this saying, and were
afraid to ask Him.
33 Then He came to Caper-
naum. And when He was in the
house He asked them, "What
was it you disputed among
yourselves on the road?"
34 But they kept silent, for on
the road they had disputed
among themselves who *would
be the* greatest.
35 And He sat down, called
the twelve, and said to them,
"If anyone desires to be first,
he shall be last of all and ser-

νεκρός, ὥστε πολλοὺς λέγειν ὅτι ἀπέθανεν. 27 Ὁ δὲ
a dead *person,* so that many to be saying that he died. - But
were was dead.

Ἰησοῦς κρατήσας αὐτὸν τῆς χειρὸς ἤγειρεν αὐτόν, καὶ
Jesus having grasped him by the hand lifted him, and

ἀνέστη.
he stood up.

28 Καὶ εἰσελθόντα αὐτὸν εἰς οἶκον, οἱ μαθηταὶ αὐτοῦ
And entering ˜ Him into a house, - disciples ˜ His
after He entered

ἐπηρώτων αὐτὸν κατ' ἰδίαν, "Ὅτι ἡμεῖς οὐκ ἠδυνήθημεν
were asking Him privately, "Why [2]we [3]not [1]were [4]able

ἐκβαλεῖν αὐτό?"
to cast out ˜ it?"

29 Καὶ εἶπεν αὐτοῖς, "Τοῦτο τὸ γένος ἐν οὐδενὶ δύναται
And He said to them, "This - kind [6]by [7]nothing [1]is [2]able

ἐξελθεῖν εἰ μὴ ἐν προσευχῇ καὶ νηστείᾳ."[c]
[3]to [4]come [5]out if not by prayer and fasting."
except

Jesus Again Predicts His Death and Resurrection
(Matt. 17:22, 23; Luke 9:43b–45)

30 Καὶ ἐκεῖθεν ἐξελθόντες παρεπορεύοντο διὰ τῆς
And from there having gone out they were passing through -

Γαλιλαίας, καὶ οὐκ ἤθελεν ἵνα τις γνῷ.
Galilee, and [3]not [1]He [2]did wish that anyone should know.

31 Ἐδίδασκε γὰρ τοὺς μαθητὰς αὐτοῦ καὶ ἔλεγεν αὐτοῖς
[2]He [3]was [4]teaching [1]For - disciples ˜ His and He said to them

ὅτι "Ὁ Υἱὸς τοῦ Ἀνθρώπου παραδίδοται εἰς χεῖρας
- "The Son - of Man is being handed over into hands
betrayed

ἀνθρώπων, καὶ ἀποκτενοῦσιν αὐτόν, καὶ ἀποκτανθεὶς τῇ
of men, and they will kill Him, and *after* being killed on the

τρίτῃ ἡμέρας ἀναστήσεται." 32 Οἱ δὲ ἠγνόουν
third day He will rise." [2]the [3]*ones* [1]But did not understand
they

τὸ ῥῆμα, καὶ ἐφοβοῦντο αὐτὸν ἐπερωτῆσαι.
the saying, and they were afraid [3]Him [1]to [2]ask.
this

Greatness in the Kingdom
(Matt. 18:1–5; Luke 9:46–48)

33 Καὶ ἦλθεν εἰς Καπερναούμ. Καὶ ἐν τῇ οἰκίᾳ
And He came to Capernaum. And [2]in [3]the [4]house

γενόμενος ἐπηρώτα αὐτούς, "Τί ἐν τῇ ὁδῷ πρὸς ἑαυτοὺς
[1]being He asked them, "What [8]on [9]the [10]road [5]with [6]one [7]another

διελογίζεσθε?" 34 Οἱ δὲ ἐσιώπων, πρὸς
[1]were [2]you [3]disputing [4]about?" [2]the [3]*ones* [1]But were silent, [4]with
they

ἀλλήλους γὰρ διελέχθησαν ἐν τῇ ὁδῷ τίς μείζων.
[5]one [6]another [1]for [2]they [3]discussed on the road who *was the* greatest.
had discussed

35 Καὶ καθίσας ἐφώνησε τοὺς δώδεκα καὶ λέγει αὐτοῖς,
And having sat down He called the twelve and says to them,
said

"Εἴ τις θέλει πρῶτος εἶναι, ἔσται πάντων ἔσχατος καὶ
"If anyone desires [3]first [1]to [2]be, he shall be [2]of [3]all [1]last and

---

[c](9:29) NU omits *και νηστεια, and fasting.*

faithfulness, and verb ἀπιστέω, disbelieve, be unfaithful.

πάντων διάκονος."* 36 Καὶ λαβὼν παιδίον ἔστησεν αὐτὸ ἐν
[2]of [3]all [1]servant." And taking a child He stood it in

μέσῳ αὐτῶν καὶ ἐναγκαλισάμενος αὐτὸ εἶπεν αὐτοῖς, 37 ""Ὃς
midst ˜ their and taking [2]in [3]His [4]arms [1]it He said to them, "Who

ἐὰν ἓν τῶν τοιούτων παιδίων δέξηται ἐπὶ τῷ
ever [2]one - [3]of [4]such [7]as [8]these [5]little [6]children [1]receives in -

ὀνόματί μου, ἐμὲ δέχεται· καὶ ὃς ἐὰν ἐμὲ δέξηται, οὐκ ἐμὲ
name ˜ My, Me ˜ receives; and who ever Me ˜ receives, [2]not [3]Me

δέχεται ἀλλὰ τὸν ἀποστείλαντά με."
[1]receives but the *One* sending Me."
who sent

Jesus Forbids Sectarianism
(Luke 9:49, 50)

38 Ἀπεκρίθη δὲ αὐτῷ Ἰωάννης, λέγων, "Διδάσκαλε,
[3]answered ˜ [1]And [4]Him [2]John, saying, "Teacher,

εἴδομεν τινα τῷ ὀνόματί σου ἐκβάλλοντα δαιμόνια, ὃς
we saw someone - in name ˜ Your casting out demons, *one* who

οὐκ ἀκολουθεῖ ἡμῖν·[d] καὶ ἐκωλύσαμεν αὐτόν, ὅτι οὐκ
not ˜ does follow with us; and we forbade him, because [3]not

ἀκολουθεῖ ἡμῖν."
[1]he [2]is following with us."

39 Ὁ δὲ Ἰησοῦς εἶπε, "Μὴ κωλύετε αὐτόν, οὐδεὶς γάρ
- But Jesus said, "not ˜ Do forbid him, [4]no [5]one [1]for

ἐστιν ὃς ποιήσει δύναμιν ἐπὶ τῷ ὀνόματί μου καὶ δυνήσεται
[2]*there* [3]is who will do a miracle in - name ˜ My and will be able
perform that

ταχὺ κακολογῆσαί με. 40 Ὃς γὰρ οὐκ ἔστι καθ' ὑμῶν,[e]
soon to speak evil of Me. [2]*he* [3]who [1]For not ˜ is against you,

ὑπὲρ ὑμῶν[f] ἐστιν.
[2]for [3]you [1]is.

A Cup of Cold Water
(Matt. 10:40–42)

41 ""Ὃς γὰρ ἂν ποτίσῃ ὑμᾶς ποτήριον ὕδατος ἐν
"who ˜ For ever gives [2]to [3]drink [1]you a cup of water in

ὀνόματί μου, ὅτι Χριστοῦ ἐστε, ἀμὴν λέγω ὑμῖν, οὐ
name ˜ My, because [3]Christ's [1]you [2]are, amen I say to you, not
assuredly by no

μὴ ἀπολέσῃ τὸν μισθὸν αὐτοῦ.
not will he lose - reward ˜ his.
means

Jesus Warns of Offenses
(Matt. 18:6–9; Luke 17:1, 2)

42 "Καὶ ὃς ἐὰν σκανδαλίσῃ ἕνα τῶν μικρῶν τῶν
"And who ever causes to stumble one of the little *ones* the *ones*
who

πιστευόντων εἰς ἐμέ, καλόν ἐστιν αὐτῷ μᾶλλον εἰ
believing in Me, [4]good [1]it [2]is [5]for [6]him [3]rather if
believe it would be better for him

περίκειται λίθος μυλικὸς περὶ τὸν τράχηλον αὐτοῦ καὶ
[6]is [7]put [1]a [2]stone [3]of [4]a [5]mill around - neck ˜ his and
were a millstone

βέβληται εἰς τὴν θάλασσαν. 43 Καὶ ἐὰν σκανδαλίζῃ σε
he is thrown into the sea. And if [3]causes [5]to [6]stumble [4]you
be

vant of all."
36 Then He took a little child and set him in the midst of them. And when He had taken him in His arms, He said to them,
37 "Whoever receives one of these little children in My name receives Me; and whoever receives Me, receives not Me but Him who sent Me."
38 Now John answered Him, saying, "Teacher, we saw someone who does not follow us casting out demons in Your name, and we forbade him because he does not follow us."
39 But Jesus said, "Do not forbid him, for no one who works a miracle in My name can soon afterward speak evil of Me.
40 "For he who is not against us is on our side.
41 "For whoever gives you a cup of water to drink in My name, because you belong to Christ, assuredly, I say to you, he will by no means lose his reward.
42 "But whoever causes one of these little ones who believe in Me to stumble, it would be better for him if a millstone were hung around his neck, and he were thrown into the sea.
43 "If your hand causes you to

[d](9:38) NU omits ος ουκ ακολουθει ημιν, *who does not follow with us.*
[e](9:40) NU reads ημων, *us.*
[f](9:40) NU reads ημων, *us.*

***(9:35)** διάκονος *(diakonos).* Noun meaning *servant.* While δοῦλος refers to a *bondslave,* the διάκονος was probably originally a waiter of tables (Matt. 22:13), with the meaning extended to fit various kinds of service or help in general, as here. The διάκονος might have something of an "official" capacity as an attendant, a nuance lying behind the use of the word for the office of church deacon (1Tim. 3:8; Phil. 1:1). Whether the feminine use in Rom. 16:1 (of Phoebe) refers to a deaconess is debated. Cf. the cognate abstract noun διακονία for the *service* rendered or *office of deacon;* and the verb διακονέω, *wait on, serve, serve as deacon.*

sin, cut it off. It is better for you to enter into life maimed, rather than having two hands, to go to hell, into the fire that shall never be quenched—
44 "where

'Their worm does not die,
And the fire is not
quenched.'

45 "And if your foot causes you to sin, cut it off. It is better for you to enter life lame, rather than having two feet, to be cast into hell, into the fire that shall never be quenched—
46 "where

'Their worm does not die,
And the fire is not
quenched.'

47 "And if your eye causes you to sin, pluck it out. It is better for you to enter the kingdom of God with one eye, rather than having two eyes, to be cast into hell fire—
48 "where

'Their worm does not die,
And the fire is not
quenched.'

49 "For everyone will be seasoned with fire, and every sacrifice will be seasoned with salt.
50 "Salt *is* good, but if the salt loses its flavor, how will you season it? Have salt in yourselves, and have peace with one another."

10 Then He arose from there and came to the

---

[g](9:44) NU omits v. 44.
[h](9:44) Is. 66:24 (also in Mark 9:46, 48)
[i](9:45) NU omits the final phrase, *into the inextinguishable fire.*
[j](9:46) NU omits v. 46.
[k](9:49) NU omits the second clause of v. 49.

*(9:44) *σκώληξ (skōlēx).* Noun meaning *worm,* appearing only in this passage in the NT (NU only Mark 9:48; M also vv. 44, 46). The quotation of Is. 66:24 reflects the Hebrew idea of worms being part of the grave and feeding on dead bodies. Here in Mark the use of *σκώληξ* suggests that a never-dying worm (as well as fire) torments the damned eternally.

ἡ χείρ σου, ἀπόκοψον αὐτήν. Καλόν σοί ἐστι κυλλὸν εἰς
- [2]hand [1]your, cut off ˜ it. [3]good [4]for [5]you [1]It [2]is [10]maimed [8]into
It would be better for you

τὴν ζωὴν εἰσελθεῖν ἢ τὰς δύο χεῖρας ἔχοντα ἀπελθεῖν εἰς
- [9]life [6]to [7]enter [11]than - [13]two [14]hands [12]having to go away into

τὴν Γέενναν, εἰς τὸ πῦρ τὸ ἄσβεστον, **44** ὅπου[g]
- Gehenna, into the fire ˜ - inextinguishable, where
hell,

«Ὁ σκώληξ* αὐτῶν οὐ τελευτᾷ
- «worm ˜ Their not ˜ does die

Καὶ τὸ πῦρ οὐ σβέννυται.»[h]
And the fire not ˜ is extinguished.»

45 Καὶ ἐὰν ὁ πούς σου σκανδαλίζῃ σε, ἀπόκοψον αὐτόν.
And if - foot ˜ your causes [2]to [3]stumble [1]you, cut off ˜ it.

Καλόν ἐστί σοι εἰσελθεῖν εἰς τὴν ζωὴν χωλὸν ἢ τοὺς
[3]good [1]It [2]is for you to enter into - life lame than -
It would be better

δύο πόδας ἔχοντα βληθῆναι εἰς τὴν Γέενναν, εἰς[i] τὸ πῦρ τὸ
[2]two [3]feet [1]having to be thrown into - Gehenna, into the fire ˜ -
hell,

ἄσβεστον, **46** ὅπου[j]
inextinguishable, where

«Ὁ σκώληξ αὐτῶν οὐ τελευτᾷ
- «worm ˜ Their not ˜ does die

Καὶ τὸ πῦρ οὐ σβέννυται.»
And the fire not ˜ is extinguished.»

47 Καὶ ἐὰν ὁ ὀφθαλμός σου σκανδαλίζῃ σε, ἔκβαλε
And if - eye ˜ your causes [2]to [3]stumble [1]you, tear out ˜

αὐτόν. Καλόν σοί ἐστι μονόφθαλμον εἰσελθεῖν εἰς τὴν
it. [3]good [4]for [5]you [1]It [2]is with one eye to enter into the
It would be better for you

βασιλείαν τοῦ Θεοῦ ἢ δύο ὀφθαλμοὺς ἔχοντα βληθῆναι εἰς
kingdom - of God than [2]two [3]eyes [1]having to be thrown into

τὴν Γέενναν τοῦ πυρός, **48** ὅπου
the Gehenna - of fire, where
fiery hell,

«Ὁ σκώληξ αὐτῶν οὐ τελευτᾷ
- «worm ˜ Their not ˜ does die

Καὶ τὸ πῦρ οὐ σβέννυται.»
And the fire not ˜ is extinguished.»

Believers Are to Have Salt
(Matt. 5:13–16; Luke 14:34, 35)

49 "Πᾶς γὰρ πυρὶ ἁλισθήσεται καὶ[k] πᾶσα θυσία
"[2]every [3]*one* [1]For with fire will be salted and every sacrifice

ἁλὶ ἁλισθήσεται. **50** Καλὸν τὸ ἅλας· ἐὰν δὲ τὸ ἅλας
with salt will be salted. [2]*is* [3]good - [1]Salt; if ˜ but the salt

ἄναλον γένηται, ἐν τίνι αὐτὸ ἀρτύσετε? Ἔχετε ἐν
unsalty ˜ becomes, by what [4]it [1]will [2]you [3]season? Have [2]in

ἑαυτοῖς ἅλας, καὶ εἰρηνεύετε ἐν ἀλλήλοις."
[3]yourselves [1]salt, and be at peace with one another."

Jesus Censures Divorce
(Matt. 5:31, 32; 19:1–10; Luke 16:18)

10 **1** Κἀκεῖθεν ἀναστὰς ἔρχεται εἰς τὰ ὅρια τῆς
And from there having risen up He comes to the borders -
came region

Ἰουδαίας διὰ τοῦ πέραν τοῦ Ἰορδάνου, καὶ συμπορεύονται
of Judea by the other side of the Jordan, and [2]come [3]together
came

πάλιν ὄχλοι πρὸς αὐτόν, καὶ ὡς εἰώθει πάλιν
[4]again [1]crowds to Him, and as He was accustomed again

ἐδίδασκεν αὐτούς. 2 Καὶ προσελθόντες Φαρισαῖοι
He was teaching them. And [3]approaching [1]*some* [2]Pharisees
approached and

ἐπηρώτησαν αὐτὸν εἰ ἔξεστιν ἀνδρὶ γυναῖκα ἀπολῦσαι,
asked Him if it is lawful for a man [3]*his* [4]wife [1]to [2]divorce,

πειράζοντες αὐτόν.
testing Him.

3 Ὁ δὲ ἀποκριθεὶς εἶπεν αὐτοῖς, "Τί ὑμῖν
[3]the [4]*One* [1]But [2]answering said to them, "What [4]you
He

ἐνετείλατο Μωσῆς?"
[1]did [3]command [2]Moses?"

4 Οἱ δὲ εἶπον, "Μωσῆς ἐπέτρεψε «βιβλίον
[2]the [3]*ones* [1]And said, "Moses permitted *a man* «[3]a [4]certificate
they

ἀποστασίου γράψαι καὶ ἀπολῦσαι.»" [a]
[5]of [6]divorce [1]to [2]write and to divorce *her.*»"

5 Καὶ ἀποκριθεὶς ὁ Ἰησοῦς εἶπεν αὐτοῖς, "Πρὸς
And answering - Jesus said to them, "With reference to
"Because of

τὴν σκληροκαρδίαν ὑμῶν ἔγραψεν ὑμῖν τὴν ἐντολὴν
- hard-heartedness ˜ your he wrote to you - commandment ˜

ταύτην. 6 Ἀπὸ δὲ ἀρχῆς κτίσεως, «ἄρσεν καὶ θῆλυ
this. from ˜ But *the* beginning of creation, «[4]male [5]and [6]female

ἐποίησεν αὐτοὺς» [b] ὁ Θεός.
[2]made [3]them» - [1]God.

7 «Ἕνεκεν τούτου καταλείψει ἄνθρωπος τὸν πατέρα
«On account of this [3]shall [4]leave [1]a [2]man - father ˜

αὐτοῦ καὶ τὴν μητέρα
his and - mother

Καὶ [c] προσκολληθήσεται* πρὸς τὴν γυναῖκα αὐτοῦ,
And he shall be joined to - wife ˜ his,

8 Καὶ ἔσονται οἱ δύο εἰς σάρκα μίαν.» [d]
And [3]shall [4]be [1]the [2]two - flesh ˜ one.»
become

Ὥστε οὐκέτι εἰσὶ δύο ἀλλὰ μία σάρξ. 9 Ὃ οὖν ὁ
So then no longer are they two but one flesh. what ˜ Therefore -

Θεὸς συνέζευξεν, ἄνθρωπος μὴ χωριζέτω."
God joined together, [3]man [2]not [1]let separate."

10 Καὶ ἐν τῇ οἰκίᾳ πάλιν οἱ μαθηταὶ αὐτοῦ περὶ τοῦ
And in the house [5]again - [2]disciples [1]His [6]about [7]the

αὐτοῦ ἐπηρώτησαν αὐτόν. 11 Καὶ λέγει αὐτοῖς, "Ὃς
[8]same [9]*matter* [3]asked [4]Him. And He says to them, "Who
said

ἐὰν ἀπολύσῃ τὴν γυναῖκα αὐτοῦ καὶ γαμήσῃ ἄλλην
ever divorces - wife ˜ his and marries another

μοιχᾶται ἐπ' αὐτήν, 12 καὶ ἐὰν γυνὴ ἀπολύσῃ τὸν
commits adultery against her, and if a wife divorces -

ἄνδρα αὐτῆς καὶ γαμηθῇ ἄλλῳ μοιχᾶται."
husband ˜ her and gets married to another she commits adultery."

region of Judea by the other side of the Jordan. And multitudes gathered to Him again, and as He was accustomed, He taught them again.
2 The Pharisees came and asked Him, "Is it lawful for a man to divorce *his* wife?" testing Him.
3 And He answered and said to them, "What did Moses command you?"
4 They said, "Moses permitted *a man* to write a certificate of divorce, and to dismiss *her.*"
5 And Jesus answered and said to them, "Because of the hardness of your heart he wrote you this precept.
6 "But from the beginning of the creation, God *'made them male and female.'*
7 *'For this reason a man shall leave his father and mother and be joined to his wife,*
8 *'and the two shall become one flesh'*; so then they are no longer two, but one flesh.
9 "Therefore what God has joined together, let not man separate."
10 In the house His disciples also asked Him again about the same *matter.*
11 So He said to them, "Whoever divorces his wife and marries another commits adultery against her.
12 "And if a woman divorces her husband and marries another, she commits adultery."

---

[a](10:4) Deut. 24:1, 3
[b](10:6) Gen. 1:27; 5:2
[c](10:7) NU brackets the last phrase of v. 7.
[d](10:8) Gen. 2:24

*(10:7) προσκολλάω *(proskollaō).* Verb meaning *to stick to, adhere closely to, to join (someone).* The simple verb κολλάω, from which προσκολλάω is derived, meant "to glue in contrast to nailing, to join together tightly" (DNTT, 2:348). In the NT, where προσκολλάω occurs only in the passive voice, it is used 3 times of the marriage relationship (here and Matt. 19:5; Eph. 5:31), and in each case appears within a quotation from Gen. 2:24. The word is also used once of the adherents of Theudas who joined him in his futile insurrection (Acts 5:36).

13 Then they brought little children to Him, that He might touch them; but the disciples rebuked those who brought *them.*
14 But when Jesus saw *it,* He was greatly displeased and said to them, "Let the little children come to Me, and do not forbid them; for of such is the kingdom of God.
15 "Assuredly, I say to you, whoever does not receive the kingdom of God as a little child will by no means enter it."
16 And He took them up in His arms, laid *His* hands on them, and blessed them.
17 Now as He was going out on the road, one came running, knelt before Him, and asked Him, "Good Teacher, what shall I do that I may inherit eternal life?"
18 So Jesus said to him, "Why do you call Me good? No one *is* good but One, *that is,* God.
19 "You know the commandments: *'Do not commit adultery,' 'Do not murder,' 'Do not steal,' 'Do not bear false witness,'* 'Do not defraud,' *'Honor your father and your mother.'* "
20 And he answered and said to Him, "Teacher, all these things I have kept from my youth."
21 Then Jesus, looking at him, loved him, and said to him, "One thing you lack: Go your

Jesus Blesses Little Children
(Matt. 19:13–15; Luke 18:15–17)

13 Καὶ προσέφερον αὐτῷ παιδία ἵνα ἅψηται
And they were bringing to Him little children that He might touch

αὐτῶν· οἱ δὲ μαθηταὶ ἐπετίμων τοῖς προσφέρουσιν.
them; the ˜ but disciples were rebuking the *ones* bringing *them* to *Him.*

14 Ἰδὼν δὲ ὁ Ἰησοῦς ἠγανάκτησε καὶ εἶπεν αὐτοῖς,
seeing But - *this* Jesus He was indignant and said to them,
But when Jesus saw this,

" Ἄφετε τὰ παιδία ἔρχεσθαι πρός με, μὴ κωλύετε αὐτά,
"Allow the little children to come to Me, not ˜ do forbid them,

τῶν γὰρ τοιούτων ἐστὶν ἡ βασιλεία τοῦ Θεοῦ. **15** Ἀμὴν
- for of such *ones* is the kingdom - of God. Amen
Assuredly

λέγω ὑμῖν, ὃς ἐὰν μὴ δέξηται τὴν βασιλείαν τοῦ Θεοῦ
I say to you, who ever not ˜ does receive the kingdom - of God

ὡς παιδίον, οὐ μὴ εἰσέλθῃ εἰς αὐτήν." **16** Καὶ
as a little child, not not will enter into it." And
by no means

ἐναγκαλισάμενος αὐτά, τιθεὶς τὰς χεῖρας ἐπ' αὐτά, εὐλόγει
[1]taking [3]in [4]His [5]arms [2]them, laying the hands on them, He blesses
His blessed

αὐτά.
them.

The Rich Young Ruler
(Matt. 19:16–22; Luke 18:18–23)

17 Καὶ ἐκπορευομένου αὐτοῦ εἰς ὁδόν, προσδραμὼν
And going out Him into *the* road, [3]running [4]up
as He went out

εἷς καὶ γονυπετήσας αὐτὸν ἐπηρώτα αὐτόν,
[1]one [2]*came* and having knelt before Him he asked Him,

"Διδάσκαλε ἀγαθέ, τί ποιήσω ἵνα ζωὴν αἰώνιον
"Teacher ˜ Good, what shall I do so that [5]life [4]eternal

κληρονομήσω?"
[1]I [2]may [3]inherit?"

18 Ὁ δὲ Ἰησοῦς εἶπεν αὐτῷ, "Τί με λέγεις ἀγαθόν?
- But Jesus said to him, "Why [4]Me [1]do [2]you [3]call good?

Οὐδεὶς ἀγαθὸς εἰ μὴ εἷς, ὁ Θεός. **19** Τὰς ἐντολὰς
No one *is* good if not One, - God. The commandments
except

οἶδας, «Μὴ μοιχεύσῃς, Μὴ φονεύσῃς, Μὴ
you know, «not ˜ Do commit adultery, not ˜ Do commit murder, not ˜

κλέψῃς, Μὴ ψευδομαρτυρήσῃς, Μὴ ἀποστερήσῃς, Τίμα τὸν
Do steal, not ˜ Do bear false witness, not ˜ Do defraud, Honor -

πατέρα σου καὶ τὴν μητέρα.»"[e]
father ˜ your and - mother.»"

20 Ὁ δὲ ἀποκριθεὶς εἶπεν αὐτῷ, "Διδάσκαλε, ταῦτα
[3]the [4]*one* [1]And [2]answering said to Him, "Teacher, these ˜
he

πάντα ἐφυλαξάμην ἐκ νεότητός μου."
all I kept from youth ˜ my."
have observed

21 Ὁ δὲ Ἰησοῦς ἐμβλέψας αὐτῷ ἠγάπησεν αὐτόν, καὶ
- And Jesus looking at him loved him, and

εἶπεν αὐτῷ, "Ἕν σοι ὑστερεῖ· ὕπαγε, ὅσα
said to him, "One *thing* for you is lacking: go, as many *things* as
you lack: all that

---
[e](**10:19**) Ex. 20:12–16; Deut. 5:16–20

ἔχεις πώλησον καὶ δὸς πτωχοῖς, καὶ ἕξεις θησαυρὸν
you have sell and give to *the* poor, and you will have treasure

ἐν οὐρανῷ, καὶ δεῦρο ἀκολούθει μοι, ἄρας τὸν
in heaven, and come follow Me, having taken up the

σταυρόν." **22** Ὁ δὲ στυγνάσας ἐπὶ τῷ λόγῳ
cross." - But having become gloomy at the word
saying

ἀπῆλθε λυπούμενος, ἦν γὰρ ἔχων κτήματα
he went away grieving, [2]he [3]was [1]for [4]*one* [5]having [7]possessions

πολλά.
[6]many.

Possessions and the Kingdom of God

(Matt. 19:23–30; Luke 18:24–30)

23 Καὶ περιβλεψάμενος ὁ Ἰησοῦς λέγει τοῖς μαθηταῖς
And having looked around - Jesus says - to disciples ˜
said

αὐτοῦ, "Πῶς δυσκόλως οἱ τὰ χρήματα ἔχοντες εἰς τὴν
His, "How with difficulty [2]the [3]*ones* - [5]possessions [4]having [7]into [8]the

βασιλείαν τοῦ Θεοῦ εἰσελεύσονται!" **24** Οἱ δὲ μαθηταὶ
[9]kingdom - [10]of [11]God [1]will [6]enter!" the ˜ And disciples

ἐθαμβοῦντο ἐπὶ τοῖς λόγοις αὐτοῦ. Ὁ δὲ Ἰησοῦς πάλιν
were amazed at - words ˜ His. - And Jesus again

ἀποκριθεὶς λέγει αὐτοῖς, "Τέκνα, πῶς δύσκολόν ἐστι τοὺς
answering says to them, "Children, how difficult it is *for* the ones
said those who

πεποιθότας ἐπὶ χρήμασιν[f] εἰς τὴν βασιλείαν τοῦ
having put confidence in possessions [3]into [4]the [5]kingdom -
have

Θεοῦ εἰσελθεῖν. **25** Εὐκοπώτερόν ἐστι κάμηλον διὰ
[6]of [7]God [1]to [2]enter. [3]easier [1]It [2]is *for* a camel [3]through

τῆς τρυμαλιᾶς τῆς ῥαφίδος εἰσελθεῖν ἢ πλούσιον εἰς
[4]the [5]eye [6]of [7]the [8]needle [1]to [2]enter than *for* a rich person [3]into
a

τὴν βασιλείαν τοῦ Θεοῦ εἰσελθεῖν."
[4]the [5]kingdom - [6]of [7]God [1]to [2]enter."

26 Οἱ δὲ περισσῶς ἐξεπλήσσοντο, λέγοντες πρὸς
[2]the [3]*ones* [1]And [5]exceedingly [4]were [6]astonished, saying to
they among

ἑαυτούς, "Καὶ τίς δύναται σωθῆναι?"
themselves, "And then ˜ who is able to be saved?"

27 Ἐμβλέψας δὲ αὐτοῖς ὁ Ἰησοῦς λέγει, "Παρὰ ἀνθρώποις
[2]looking [3]at [1]But them - Jesus says, "With men
said,

ἀδύνατον ἀλλ' οὐ παρὰ Θεῷ, πάντα γὰρ δυνατά ἐστι
it is impossible, but not with God, [2]all [3]*things* [1]for [5]possible [4]are

παρὰ τῷ Θεῷ."
with - God."

28 Ἤρξατο ὁ Πέτρος λέγειν αὐτῷ, "Ἰδού, ἡμεῖς ἀφήκαμεν
began ˜ - Peter to say to Him, "See, we left
have left

πάντα καὶ ἠκολουθήσαμέν σοι."
all *things* and followed You."
have followed

29 Ἀποκριθεὶς δὲ ὁ Ἰησοῦς εἶπεν, "Ἀμὴν λέγω ὑμῖν,
answering ˜ And - Jesus said, "Amen I say to you,
"Assuredly

way, sell whatever you have
and give to the poor, and you
will have treasure in heaven;
and come, take up the cross,
and follow Me."
22 But he was sad at this
word, and went away sorrowful,
for he had great possessions.
23 Then Jesus looked around
and said to His disciples, "How
hard it is for those who have
riches to enter the kingdom of
God!"
24 And the disciples were astonished
at His words. But Jesus
answered again and said to
them, "Children, how hard it is
for those who trust in riches to
enter the kingdom of God!
25 "It is easier for a camel to
go through the eye of a needle
than for a rich man to enter the
kingdom of God."
26 And they were greatly astonished,
saying among themselves,
"Who then can be
saved?"
27 But Jesus looked at them
and said, "With men *it is* impossible,
but not with God; for with
God all things are possible."
28 Then Peter began to say to
Him, "See, we have left all and
followed You."
29 So Jesus answered and
said, "Assuredly, I say to you,

[f](**10:24**) NU omits τους πεποιθοτας επι χρημασιν, *(for) those who have put confidence in possessions.*

there is no one who has left house or brothers or sisters or father or mother or wife or children or lands, for My sake and the gospel's,
30 "who shall not receive a hundredfold now in this time—houses and brothers and sisters and mothers and children and lands, with persecutions—and in the age to come, eternal life.
31 "But many *who are* first will be last, and the last first."
32 Now they were on the road, going up to Jerusalem, and Jesus was going before them; and they were amazed. And as they followed they were afraid. Then He took the twelve aside again and began to tell them the things that would happen to Him:
33 "Behold, we are going up to Jerusalem, and the Son of Man will be betrayed to the chief priests and to the scribes; and they will condemn Him to death and deliver Him to the Gentiles;
34 "and they will mock Him, and scourge Him, and spit on Him, and kill Him. And the third day He will rise again."
35 Then James and John, the sons of Zebedee, came to Him, saying, "Teacher, we want You to do for us whatever we ask."
36 And He said to them, "What do you want Me to do for you?"

οὐδείς ἐστιν ὅς ἀφῆκεν οἰκίαν ἢ ἀδελφοὺς* ἢ ἀδελφὰς* ἢ
[3]no [4]one [1]*there* [2]is who left (has left) house or brothers or sisters or

πατέρα ἢ μητέρα ἢ γυναῖκα[g] ἢ τέκνα ἢ ἀγροὺς ἕνεκεν
father or mother or wife or children or fields for the sake of

ἐμοῦ καὶ ἕνεκεν τοῦ εὐαγγελίου, **30** ἐὰν μὴ λάβῃ
Me and for the sake of the gospel, if not he receives (who shall not receive)

ἑκατονταπλασίονα νῦν ἐν τῷ καιρῷ τούτῳ οἰκίας καὶ ἀδελφοὺς
a hundredfold now in - time ˜ this houses and brothers

καὶ ἀδελφὰς καὶ μητέρας καὶ τέκνα καὶ ἀγρούς, μετὰ
and sisters and mothers and children and fields, along with

διωγμῶν, καὶ ἐν τῷ αἰῶνι τῷ ἐρχομένῳ ζωὴν αἰώνιον.
persecutions, and in the age ˜ - coming life ˜ eternal.

31 Πολλοὶ δὲ ἔσονται πρῶτοι ἔσχατοι καὶ ἔσχατοι πρῶτοι."
[2]many [1]But [4]shall [5]be [3]first last and last first."

Jesus a Third Time Predicts His Death and Resurrection
(Matt. 20:17–19; Luke 18:31–34)

32 Ἦσαν δὲ ἐν τῇ ὁδῷ ἀναβαίνοντες εἰς Ἱεροσόλυμα,
[2]they [3]were [1]Now on the road going up to Jerusalem,

καὶ ἦν προάγων αὐτοὺς ὁ Ἰησοῦς, καὶ ἐθαμβοῦντο,
and [2]was [3]going [4]ahead [5]of [6]them - [1]Jesus, and they were amazed,

καὶ ἀκολουθοῦντες ἐφοβοῦντο. Καὶ παραλαβὼν πάλιν τοὺς
and *as they were* following they were afraid. And taking aside [3]again [1]the

δώδεκα ἤρξατο αὐτοῖς λέγειν τὰ μέλλοντα αὐτῷ
[2]twelve He began [3]them [1]to [2]tell the *things* being about (which were) [3]to [4]Him

συμβαίνειν, **33** ὅτι "Ἰδού, ἀναβαίνομεν εἰς Ἱεροσόλυμα, καὶ
[1]to [2]happen, - "See, we are going up to Jerusalem, and

ὁ Υἱὸς τοῦ Ἀνθρώπου παραδοθήσεται τοῖς ἀρχιερεῦσι καὶ
the Son - of Man will be handed over (betrayed) to the chief priests and

γραμματεῦσι, καὶ κατακρινοῦσιν αὐτὸν θανάτῳ καὶ
scribes, and they will condemn Him to death and

παραδώσουσιν αὐτὸν τοῖς ἔθνεσι **34** καὶ ἐμπαίξουσιν αὐτῷ
will hand over ˜ Him to the Gentiles and they will mock Him

καὶ μαστιγώσουσιν αὐτὸν καὶ ἐμπτύσουσιν αὐτῷ καὶ
and scourge Him and spit on Him and

ἀποκτενοῦσιν αὐτόν, καὶ τῇ τρίτῃ ἡμέρᾳ ἀναστήσεται."
kill Him, and on the third day He will rise."

Greatness Through Suffering and Service
(Matt. 20:20–28)

35 Καὶ προσπορεύονται αὐτῷ Ἰάκωβος καὶ Ἰωάννης οἱ
And [8]come [9]up (came) [10]to [11]Him [1]James [2]and [3]John [4]the

υἱοὶ Ζεβεδαίου, λέγοντες, "Διδάσκαλε, θέλομεν ἵνα ὃ ἐὰν
[5]sons [6]of [7]Zebedee, saying, "Teacher, we desire that [5]what [6]ever

αἰτήσωμέν ποιήσῃς ἡμῖν."
[7]we [8]may [9]ask [1]You [2]do [3]for [4]us."

36 Ὁ δὲ εἶπεν αὐτοῖς, "Τί θέλετε ποιῆσαί με
[2]the [3]*One* (He) [1]And said to them, "What do you desire [2]to [3]do [1]Me

ὑμῖν?"
for you?"

---

[g](10:29) NU omits η γυναικα, *or wife.*

***(10:29)** ἀδελφός (*adelphos*); ἀδελφή (*adelphē*). Nouns meaning *brother* and *sister,* respectively. These words literally refer to siblings by birth, as here, but are commonly extended figuratively to describe a spiritual relationship or communion (Phil. 1:14, Rom. 16:1). The plural ἀδελφοί, *brothers,* often including men and women, thus "brothers and sisters," is the most commonly used word for Christians in the NT. The words may also be used figuratively of anyone sharing a close bond with the speaker, such as a *countryman* (Acts 2:29) or a *neighbor* (Matt. 5:22).

37 Οἱ δὲ εἶπον αὐτῷ, "Δὸς ἡμῖν ἵνα εἷς ἐκ
[2]the [3]ones [1]And said to Him, "Grant to us that one at
they on

δεξιῶν σου καὶ εἷς ἐξ εὐωνύμων σου καθίσωμεν ἐν τῇ
[2]right [3]*parts* [1]Your and one at [2]left [3]*parts* [1]Your we may sit in -
right side on left side

δόξῃ σου."
glory ~ Your."

38 Ὁ δὲ Ἰησοῦς εἶπεν αὐτοῖς, "Οὐκ οἴδατε τί
- But Jesus said to them, "[3]not [1]You [2]do know what

αἰτεῖσθε. Δύνασθε πιεῖν τὸ ποτήριον ὃ ἐγὼ πίνω καὶ
you are asking. Are you able to drink the cup which I drink and

τὸ βάπτισμα ὃ ἐγὼ βαπτίζομαι βαπτισθῆναι?"
[4]*with* [5]the [6]baptism [7]*with* [8]which [9]I [10]am [11]baptized [1]to [2]be [3]baptized?"

39 Οἱ δὲ εἶπον αὐτῷ, "Δυνάμεθα."
[2]the [3]ones [1]And said to Him, "We are able."
they

Ὁ δὲ Ἰησοῦς εἶπεν αὐτοῖς, "Τὸ μὲν ποτήριον ὃ ἐγὼ
- But Jesus said to them, "the ~ Indeed cup which I

πίνω πίεσθε καὶ τὸ βάπτισμα ὃ ἐγὼ βαπτίζομαι
drink you will drink and the baptism *with* which I am baptized

βαπτισθήσεσθε, **40** τὸ δὲ καθίσαι ἐκ δεξιῶν μου καὶ ἐξ
you will be baptized *with*, - but to sit at [2]right [3]*parts* [1]My and at
on right side on

εὐωνύμων οὐκ ἔστιν ἐμὸν δοῦναι, ἀλλ' οἷς
My left *parts* not ~ is Mine to give, but *to those* for whom
My left side

ἡτοίμασται." **41** Καὶ ἀκούσαντες οἱ δέκα ἤρξαντο
it has been prepared." And having heard *this* the twelve began

ἀγανακτεῖν περὶ Ἰακώβου καὶ Ἰωάννου. **42** Ὁ δὲ Ἰησοῦς
to be indignant about James and John. - But Jesus

προσκαλεσάμενος αὐτοὺς λέγει αὐτοῖς, "Οἴδατε ὅτι οἱ
having summoned them says to them, "You know that the *ones*
said

δοκοῦντες ἄρχειν τῶν ἐθνῶν κατακυριεύουσιν αὐτῶν καὶ οἱ
being reputed to be ruling the Gentiles lord it over them and -

μεγάλοι αὐτῶν κατεξουσιάζουσιν αὐτῶν. **43** Οὐχ οὕτω δέ
[2]great [3]ones [1]their exercise authority over them. [4]not [6]so [1]But

ἔσται ἐν ὑμῖν· ἀλλ' ὃς ἐὰν θέλῃ γενέσθαι μέγας ἐν
[2]it [3]will [5]be among you; but who ever desires to become great among

ὑμῖν, ἔσται ὑμῶν διάκονος, **44** καὶ ὃς ἐὰν θέλῃ ὑμῶν
you, shall be your servant, and who ever [3]desires [1]of [2]you

γενέσθαι πρῶτος, ἔσται πάντων δοῦλος. **45** Καὶ γὰρ ὁ Υἱὸς
to become first, shall be [2]of [3]all [1]slave. even ~ For the Son

τοῦ Ἀνθρώπου οὐκ ἦλθε διακονηθῆναι ἀλλὰ διακονῆσαι καὶ
- of Man not ~ did come to be served but to serve and

δοῦναι τὴν ψυχὴν αὐτοῦ λύτρον* ἀντὶ πολλῶν."
to give - life ~ His *as* a ransom in the place of many."

Jesus Heals Blind Bartimaeus
(Matt. 20:29–34; Luke 18:35–43)

46 Καὶ ἔρχονται εἰς Ἰεριχώ. Καὶ ἐκπορευομένου αὐτοῦ ἀπὸ
And they come to Jericho. And going out Him from
came as He was going out

Ἰεριχὼ καὶ τῶν μαθητῶν αὐτοῦ καὶ ὄχλου ἱκανοῦ, υἱὸς
Jericho and - disciples ~ His and a crowd ~ large, a son
along with

37 They said to Him, "Grant
us that we may sit, one on Your
right hand and the other on
Your left, in Your glory."
38 But Jesus said to them,
"You do not know what you
ask. Are you able to drink the
cup that I drink, and be baptized with the baptism that I am
baptized with?"
39 They said to Him, "We are
able." So Jesus said to them,
"You will indeed drink the cup
that I drink, and with the baptism I am baptized with you will
be baptized;
40 "but to sit on My right
hand and on My left is not Mine
to give, but *it is for those* for
whom it is prepared."
41 And when the ten heard *it,*
they began to be greatly displeased with James and John.
42 But Jesus called them to
Himself and said to them, "You
know that those who are considered rulers over the Gentiles
lord it over them, and their
great ones exercise authority
over them.
43 "Yet it shall not be so
among you; but whoever desires to become great among
you shall be your servant.
44 "And whoever of you desires to be first shall be slave of
all.
45 "For even the Son of Man
did not come to be served, but
to serve, and to give His life a
ransom for many."
46 Now they came to Jericho.
As He went out of Jericho with
His disciples and a great multitude, blind Bartimaeus, the son

---

***(10:45)** λύτρον *(lytron).* Noun, used here and in the parallel (Matt. 20:28), from λύω, *loose,* hence *a means of release* or *ransom.* In the LXX it refers to the price paid for the freedom of a prisoner of war, a slave, or a debtor. In the NT it speaks of Christ's substitutionary (used with ἀντί, *in place of*) death for sinners. Cf. the strengthened form ἀντίλυτρον (1Tim. 2:6) which is used with ὑπέρ, meaning that Christ paid the ransom vicariously *"on behalf of all."*

of Timaeus, sat by the road begging.
47 And when he heard that it was Jesus of Nazareth, he began to cry out and say, "Jesus, Son of David, have mercy on me!"
48 Then many warned him to be quiet; but he cried out all the more, "Son of David, have mercy on me!"
49 So Jesus stood still and commanded him to be called. Then they called the blind man, saying to him, "Be of good cheer. Rise, He is calling you."
50 And throwing aside his garment, he rose and came to Jesus.
51 So Jesus answered and said to him, "What do you want Me to do for you?" The blind man said to Him, "Rabboni, that I may receive my sight."
52 Then Jesus said to him, "Go your way; your faith has made you well." And immediately he received his sight and followed Jesus on the road.
11 Now when they drew near Jerusalem, to Bethphage and Bethany, at the Mount of Olives, He sent two of His disciples;
2 and He said to them, "Go into the village opposite you; and as soon as you have entered it you will find a colt tied, on which no one has sat. Loose it and bring *it*.

Τιμαίου, Βαρτιμαῖος ὁ τυφλός, ἐκάθητο παρὰ τὴν ὁδὸν
of Timaeus, Bartimaeus the blind *man*, was sitting alongside the road

προσαιτῶν. 47 Καὶ ἀκούσας ὅτι Ἰησοῦς ὁ Ναζωραῖός
begging. And hearing that [3]Jesus [4]the [5]Nazarene
when he heard

ἐστιν ἤρξατο κράζειν καὶ λέγειν, "Ὁ υἱὸς Δαβίδ, Ἰησοῦ,
[1]it [2]is he began to cry out and to say, - "Son of David, Jesus,
was

ἐλέησόν με." 48 Καὶ ἐπετίμων αὐτῷ πολλοὶ ἵνα
have mercy on me." And [2]were [3]warning [4]him [1]many that

σιωπήσῃ· ὁ δὲ πολλῷ μᾶλλον ἔκραζεν, "Υἱὲ
he should be silent; - but by much more he would cry out, "Son
all the more

Δαβίδ, ἐλέησόν με!"
of David, have mercy on me!"

49 Καὶ στὰς ὁ Ἰησοῦς εἶπεν αὐτόν φωνηθῆναι.
And having stood still - Jesus said *for* him to be called.

Καὶ φωνοῦσι τὸν τυφλόν, λέγοντες αὐτῷ, "Θάρσει,
And they call the blind *man*, saying to him, "Have courage,
called

ἔγειραι, φωνεῖ σε." 50 Ὁ δὲ ἀποβαλὼν τὸ
rise, He is calling you." [2]the [3]*one* [1]And having thrown off -
he

ἱμάτιον αὐτοῦ ἀναστὰς ἦλθε πρὸς τὸν Ἰησοῦν.
garment ˜ his *and* having risen came to - Jesus.

51 Καὶ ἀποκριθεὶς λέγει αὐτῷ ὁ Ἰησοῦς, "Τί
And answering [2]says [3]to [4]him - [1]Jesus, "What
said

θέλεις ποιήσω σοί?"
do you desire *that* I should do for you?"

Ὁ δὲ τυφλὸς εἶπεν αὐτῷ, "Ῥαββουνί, ἵνα
the ˜ And blind *man* said to Him, "Rabboni, that

ἀναβλέψω."
I may recover *my* sight."

52 Ὁ δὲ Ἰησοῦς εἶπεν αὐτῷ, "Ὕπαγε, ἡ πίστις σου
- And Jesus said to him, "Go, - faith ˜ your

σέσωκέ σε." Καὶ εὐθέως ἀνέβλεψε, καὶ
has saved you." And immediately he recovered *his* sight, and
made you well."

ἠκολούθει τῷ Ἰησοῦ ἐν τῇ ὁδῷ.
he was following - Jesus on the road.

Jesus Enters Jerusalem in Triumph
(Matt. 21:1–11; Luke 19:28–40; John 12:12–19)

11 1 Καὶ ὅτε ἐγγίζουσιν εἰς Ἱερουσαλήμ, εἰς
And when they are drawing near to Jerusalem, to
were

Βηθσφαγὴ[a] καὶ Βηθανίαν, πρὸς τὸ Ὄρος τῶν Ἐλαιῶν,
Bethsphage and Bethany, towards the Mount - of Olives,

ἀποστέλλει δύο τῶν μαθητῶν αὐτοῦ 2 καὶ λέγει αὐτοῖς,
He sends two - of disciples ˜ His and says to them,
sent said

"Ὑπάγετε εἰς τὴν κώμην τὴν κατέναντι ὑμῶν, καὶ εὐθέως
"Go into the village - opposite you, and immediately

εἰσπορευόμενοι εἰς αὐτὴν εὑρήσετε πῶλον δεδεμένον
entering into it you will find a young donkey tied up

ἐφ᾽ ὃν οὐδεὶς ἀνθρώπων κεκάθικε. Λύσαντες αὐτὸν
on which no one of men has sat. Loosing him
When you have untied

[a](11:1) NU, TR read Βηθφαγη, *Bethphage.*

ἀγάγετε. 3 Καὶ ἐάν τις ὑμῖν εἴπῃ, ‘Τί ποιεῖτε τοῦτο?’
bring *him*. And if anyone [2]to [3]you [1]says, ‘Why are you doing this?’

εἴπατε ὅτι ‘Ὁ Κύριος αὐτοῦ χρείαν ἔχει,’ καὶ εὐθέως αὐτὸν
say - ‘The Lord [3]of [4]him [2]need [1]has,’ and immediately [3]him

ἀποστέλλει ὧδε.”
[1]he [2]sends here.”
will send

4 Ἀπῆλθον δὲ καὶ εὗρον πῶλον[b] δεδεμένον
[2]they [3]went [4]away [1]And and found a young donkey tied up

πρὸς τὴν θύραν ἔξω ἐπὶ τοῦ ἀμφόδου, καὶ λύουσιν αὐτόν.
by the door outside in the street, and they loose him.
untied

5 Καί τινες τῶν ἐκεῖ ἑστηκότων ἔλεγον αὐτοῖς, “Τί
And some of the *ones* there ˜ standing said to them, “What

ποιεῖτε λύοντες τὸν πῶλον?” 6 Οἱ δὲ εἶπον
are you doing loosing the young donkey?” [2]the [3]*ones* [1]And told
untying they

αὐτοῖς καθὼς ἐνετείλατο ὁ Ἰησοῦς· καὶ ἀφῆκαν
them just as commanded ˜ - Jesus; and they gave permission ˜

αὐτούς. 7 Καὶ ἤγαγον τὸν πῶλον πρὸς τὸν Ἰησοῦν, καὶ
them. And they brought the young donkey to - Jesus, and

ἐπέβαλον αὐτῷ τὰ ἱμάτια αὐτῶν, καὶ ἐκάθισεν ἐπ’ αὐτῷ.
placed on him - clothes ˜ their, and He sat on him.

8 Πολλοὶ δὲ τὰ ἱμάτια αὐτῶν ἔστρωσαν εἰς τὴν ὁδόν, ἄλλοι
many ˜ And - [3]clothes [2]their [1]spread in the road, others ˜

δὲ στοιβάδας ἔκοπτον ἐκ τῶν δένδρων καὶ
and [3]leafy [4]branches [1]were [2]cutting from the trees and

ἐστρώννυον εἰς τὴν ὁδόν. 9 Καὶ οἱ προάγοντες καὶ
were spreading *them* in the road. And the *ones* going in front and

οἱ ἀκολουθοῦντες ἔκραζον, λέγοντες,
the *ones* following were crying out, saying,

“«Ὡσαννά!*
“«Hosanna!

Εὐλογημένος ὁ ἐρχόμενος ἐν ὀνόματι Κυρίου!»[c]
Blessed *is* the *One* coming in *the* name of *the* Lord!»

10 Εὐλογημένη ἡ ἐρχομένη βασιλεία ἐν ὀνόματι Κυρίου[d]
Blessed *is* the coming kingdom in *the* name of *the* Lord

τοῦ πατρὸς ἡμῶν Δαβίδ·
- of father ˜ our David;

«Ὡσαννὰ» ἐν τοῖς ὑψίστοις!”
«Hosanna» in the highest *heights*!”
heaven!”

11 Καὶ εἰσῆλθεν εἰς Ἱεροσόλυμα ὁ Ἰησοῦς, καὶ εἰς τὸ
And [2]entered [3]into [4]Jerusalem - [1]Jesus, and into the

ἱερόν. Καὶ περιβλεψάμενος πάντα, ὀψίας ἤδη οὔσης τῆς
temple. And having looked around at all *things*, [5]late [3]already [4]being [1]the

ὥρας, ἐξῆλθεν εἰς Βηθανίαν μετὰ τῶν δώδεκα.
[2]hour, He went out to Bethany with the twelve.

The Barren Fig Tree
(Matt. 21:18, 19)

12 Καὶ τῇ ἐπαύριον ἐξελθόντων αὐτῶν ἀπὸ Βηθανίας
And on the next day coming out them from Bethany
after they had come out

ἐπείνασε. 13 Καὶ ἰδὼν συκῆν μακρόθεν ἔχουσαν
He became hungry. And seeing a fig tree from a distance having

3 “And if anyone says to you, ‘Why are you doing this?’ say, ‘The Lord has need of it,’ and immediately he will send it here.”
4 So they went their way, and found the colt tied by the door outside on the street, and they loosed it.
5 But some of those who stood there said to them, “What are you doing, loosing the colt?”
6 And they spoke to them just as Jesus had commanded. So they let them go.
7 Then they brought the colt to Jesus and threw their clothes on it, and He sat on it.
8 And many spread their clothes on the road, and others cut down leafy branches from the trees and spread *them* on the road.
9 Then those who went before and those who followed cried out, saying:

“Hosanna!
‘Blessed is He who comes in the name of the LORD!*’*
10 Blessed *is* the kingdom of our father David
That comes in the name of the Lord!
Hosanna in the highest!”

11 And Jesus went into Jerusalem and into the temple. So when He had looked around at all things, as the hour was already late, He went out to Bethany with the twelve.
12 Now the next day, when they had come out from Bethany, He was hungry.
13 And seeing from afar a fig

---

[b](**11:4**) TR reads τον πωλον, *the young donkey.*
[c](**11:9**) Ps. 118:26
[d](**11:10**) NU omits εν ονοματι Κυριου, *in (the) name of (the) Lord,* thus *the coming kingdom of our father David.*

***(11:9)** ὡσαννά *(hōsanna).* Aramaic form of the Hebrew for “Save now, I pray” in Ps. 118:25. It occurs in the NT only in the accounts of Jesus’ Triumphal Entry into Jerusalem. By Jesus’ time it had become an acclamation of praise (as used today in En-

tree having leaves, He went to see if perhaps He would find something on it. When He came to it, He found nothing but leaves, for it was not the season for figs.
14 In response Jesus said to it, "Let no one eat fruit from you ever again." And His disciples heard *it.*
15 So they came to Jerusalem. Then Jesus went into the temple and began to drive out those who bought and sold in the temple, and overturned the tables of the money changers and the seats of those who sold doves.
16 And He would not allow anyone to carry wares through the temple.
17 Then He taught, saying to them, "Is it not written, *'My house shall be called a house of prayer for all nations'*? But you have made it a *'den of thieves.'"*
18 And the scribes and chief priests heard it and sought how they might destroy Him; for they feared Him, because all the people were astonished at His teaching.
19 When evening had come, He went out of the city.
20 Now in the morning, as they passed by, they saw the fig tree dried up from the roots.
21 And Peter, remembering, said to Him, "Rabbi, look! The fig tree which You cursed has withered away."

[e](11:17) Is. 56:7
[f](11:17) Jer. 7:11
[g](11:19) NU reads *εξεπορευοντο, they were going forth.*

glish), but the fact that the messianic psalm from which it is taken was read at Passover may have reminded some of its earlier meaning. Although shouts of "hosanna" were part of the liturgical observance of both the feasts of Passover and Tabernacles, the specific practice of waving branches is only documented for the latter. The last day of the Feast of Tabernacles was called "the Day of Hosanna," and the branches were also called "hosannas."

φύλλα ἦλθεν εἰ ἄρα εὑρήσει τι ἐν αὐτῇ. Καὶ
leaves He went *to see* if perhaps He would find something on it. And

ἐλθὼν ἐπ' αὐτὴν οὐδὲν εὗρεν εἰ μὴ φύλλα, οὐ γὰρ
coming upon it [3]nothing [1]He [2]found if not leaves, [4]not [1]for
having reached except for

ἦν καιρὸς σύκων. 14 Καὶ ἀποκριθεὶς ὁ Ἰησοῦς εἶπεν αὐτῇ,
[2]it [3]was *the* time of figs. And answering - Jesus said to it,

"Μηκέτι ἐκ σου εἰς τὸν αἰῶνα μηδεὶς καρπὸν φάγοι."
"[8]no [9]longer [6]from [7]you [10]into [11]the [12]age [2]no [3]one [5]fruit [1]May [4]eat."
"any forever

Καὶ ἤκουον οἱ μαθηταὶ αὐτοῦ.
And [3]were [4]listening - [2]disciples [1]His.

Jesus Cleanses the Temple
(Matt. 21:12–17; Luke 19:45–48)

15 Καὶ ἔρχονται εἰς Ἱεροσόλυμα. Καὶ εἰσελθὼν ὁ Ἰησοῦς
And they come to Jerusalem. And entering ˜ - Jesus
came when Jesus entered

εἰς τὸ ἱερὸν ἤρξατο ἐκβάλλειν τοὺς πωλοῦντας καὶ
into the temple He began to throw out the *ones* selling and

ἀγοράζοντας ἐν τῷ ἱερῷ, καὶ τὰς τραπέζας τῶν κολλυβιστῶν
buying in the temple, and the tables of the money changers

καὶ τὰς καθέδρας τῶν πωλούντων τὰς περιστερὰς
and the seats of the *ones* selling the doves

κατέστρεψε. 16 Καὶ οὐκ ἤφιεν ἵνα τις διενέγκῃ
He overturned. And [3]not [1]He [2]would [4]permit that anyone should bring

σκεῦος διὰ τοῦ ἱεροῦ. 17 Καὶ ἐδίδασκε, λέγων αὐτοῖς,
a vessel through the temple. And He was teaching, saying to them,

"Οὐ γέγραπται ὅτι «Ὁ οἶκός μου οἶκος προσευχῆς
"[3]not [1]Is [2]it written - - «house ˜ My [4]a [5]house [6]of [7]prayer

κληθήσεται πᾶσι τοῖς ἔθνεσιν»?[e] Ὑμεῖς δὲ ἐποιήσατε
[1]shall [2]be [3]called for all the nations»? you ˜ But made

αὐτὸν «σπήλαιον λῃστῶν.»"[f]
it «a cave of bandits.»"

18 Καὶ ἤκουσαν οἱ γραμματεῖς καὶ οἱ ἀρχιερεῖς, καὶ
And [7]heard [1]the [2]scribes [3]and [4]the [5]chief [6]priests, and

ἐζήτουν πῶς αὐτὸν ἀπολέσωσιν· ἐφοβοῦντο
they were seeking how [4]Him [1]they [2]might [3]destroy; [6]they [7]were [8]afraid [9]of

γὰρ αὐτὸν ὅτι πᾶς ὁ ὄχλος ἐξεπλήσσετο ἐπὶ τῇ διδαχῇ
[5]for Him because all the crowd were astonished at - teaching ˜

αὐτοῦ. 19 Καὶ ὅτε ὀψὲ ἐγένετο, ἐξεπορεύετο[g] ἔξω τῆς
His. And when [3]late [1]it [2]became, He was going forth outside the
evening

πόλεως.
city.

The Lesson from the Withered Fig Tree
(Matt. 21:20–22)

20 Καὶ πρωῒ παραπορευόμενοι εἶδον τὴν συκῆν
And in the morning *while* passing by they saw the fig tree

ἐξηραμμένην ἐκ ῥιζῶν. 21 Καὶ ἀναμνησθεὶς ὁ Πέτρος
dried up from *its* roots. And remembering - Peter
when he remembered,

λέγει αὐτῷ, "Ῥαββί, ἴδε! Ἡ συκῆ ἣν κατηράσω
says to Him, "Rabbi, look! The fig tree which You cursed
said

ἐξήρανται."
has dried up."

22 Καὶ ἀποκριθεὶς ὁ Ἰησοῦς λέγει αὐτοῖς, "Ἔχετε πίστιν
And answering - Jesus says to them, "Have faith
said

Θεοῦ. **23** Ἀμὴν γὰρ λέγω ὑμῖν ὅτι ὃς ἂν εἴπῃ τῷ
of God. amen ˜ For I say to you that who ever says -
in assuredly

ὄρει τούτῳ, 'Ἄρθητι καὶ βλήθητι εἰς τὴν θάλασσαν,'
to mountain ˜ this, 'Be taken up and cast into the sea,'

καὶ μὴ διακριθῇ ἐν τῇ καρδίᾳ αὐτοῦ ἀλλὰ πιστεύσῃ ὅτι
and not ˜ does doubt in - heart ˜ his but believes that

ἃ λέγει γίνεται, ἔσται αὐτῷ ὃ ἐὰν
the things which he says are coming to pass, [5]shall [6]be [7]to [8]him [1]what [2]ever
his

εἴπῃ. **24** Διὰ τοῦτο λέγω ὑμῖν, πάντα ὅσα ἂν
[3]he [4]says. Because of this I say to you, all *things* as many as -
Therefore

προσευχόμενοι αἰτῆσθε, πιστεύετε ὅτι λαμβάνετε,[h]
praying you may ask for, believe that you *will* receive *them,*
in prayer

καὶ ἔσται ὑμῖν.
and they will be to you.
yours.

Prayer Requires a Forgiving Spirit

25 "Καὶ ὅταν στήκετε προσευχόμενοι, ἀφίετε εἴ τι
"And whenever you stand praying, forgive if [3]anything

ἔχετε κατά τινος, ἵνα καὶ ὁ Πατὴρ ὑμῶν ὁ ἐν τοῖς
[1]you [2]have against anyone, so that also - Father ˜ your the *One* in the
who is

οὐρανοῖς ἀφῇ ὑμῖν τὰ παραπτώματα ὑμῶν. **26** Εἰ[i] δὲ
heavens may forgive you - trespasses ˜ your. if ˜ But
heaven

ὑμεῖς οὐκ ἀφίετε, οὐδὲ ὁ Πατὴρ ὑμῶν ὁ ἐν τοῖς
you not ˜ do forgive, neither - [3]Father [2]your [4]the [5]*One* [6]in [7]the
who is

οὐρανοῖς ἀφήσει τὰ παραπτώματα ὑμῶν."
[8]heavens [1]will [9]forgive - trespasses ˜ your."
heaven

The Authority of Jesus Is Questioned
(Matt. 21:23–27; Luke 20:1–8)

27 Καὶ ἔρχονται πάλιν εἰς Ἱεροσόλυμα. Καὶ ἐν τῷ ἱερῷ
And they come again to Jerusalem. And in the temple
came

περιπατοῦντος αὐτοῦ, ἔρχονται πρὸς αὐτὸν οἱ ἀρχιερεῖς καὶ
walking about Him, *there* comes to Him the chief priests and
as He was walking about, there came

οἱ γραμματεῖς καὶ οἱ πρεσβύτεροι. **28** Καὶ λέγουσιν αὐτῷ,
the scribes and the elders. And they say to Him,
said

"Ἐν ποίᾳ ἐξουσίᾳ ταῦτα ποιεῖς? Καὶ τίς σοι
"By what kind of authority [4]these [5]*things* [1]are [2]You [3]doing? And who [2]You

τὴν ἐξουσίαν ταύτην ἔδωκεν ἵνα ταῦτα ποιῇς?"
- [4]authority [3]this [1]gave that [3]these [4]*things* [1]You [2]do?"

29 Ὁ δὲ Ἰησοῦς ἀποκριθεὶς εἶπεν αὐτοῖς, "Ἐπερτήσω
- But Jesus answering said to them, "[3]will [4]ask

ὑμᾶς καὶ ἐγὼ ἕνα λόγον, καὶ ἀποκρίθητέ μοι, καὶ ἐρῶ ὑμῖν
[5]you [2]also [1]I one word, and you answer Me, and I will tell you
thing,

22 So Jesus answered and said to them, "Have faith in God.
23 "For assuredly, I say to you, whoever says to this mountain, 'Be removed and be cast into the sea,' and does not doubt in his heart, but believes that those things he says will be done, he will have whatever he says.
24 "Therefore I say to you, whatever things you ask when you pray, believe that you receive *them,* and you will have *them.*
25 "And whenever you stand praying, if you have anything against anyone, forgive him, that your Father in heaven may also forgive you your trespasses.
26 "But if you do not forgive, neither will your Father in heaven forgive your trespasses."
27 Then they came again to Jerusalem. And as He was walking in the temple, the chief priests, the scribes, and the elders came to Him.
28 And they said to Him, "By what authority are You doing these things? And who gave You this authority to do these things?"
29 But Jesus answered and said to them, "I also will ask you one question; then answer Me, and I will tell you by what

---

[h]**(11:24)** NU reads ελαβετε, *you received (them).*
[i]**(11:26)** NU omits v. 26.

authority I do these things:
30 "The baptism of John—
was it from heaven or from
men? Answer Me."
31 And they reasoned among
themselves, saying, "If we say,
'From heaven,' He will say,
'Why then did you not believe
him?'
32 "But if we say, 'From
men'"—they feared the people, for all counted John to have
been a prophet indeed.
33 So they answered and said
to Jesus, "We do not know."
And Jesus answered and said to
them, "Neither will I tell you by
what authority I do these
things."
12 Then He began to
speak to them in para-
bles: "A man planted a vineyard
and set a hedge around *it,* dug *a
place for* the wine vat and built a
tower. And he leased it to vinedressers and went into a far
country.
2 "Now at vintage-time he
sent a servant to the vinedressers, that he might receive
some of the fruit of the vineyard from the vinedressers.
3 "And they took *him* and
beat him and sent *him* away
empty-handed.
4 "Again he sent them an-
other servant, and at him they
threw stones, wounded *him* in
the head, and sent *him* away
shamefully treated.
5 "And again he sent an-
other, and him they killed; and
many others, beating some and
killing some.

---

[a](12:4) NU omits λιθοβολησαντες, *stoning.*

***(12:1)** ἀποδημέω (*apodēmeō*). Verb meaning *leave home on a journey.* It is derived from the adjective ἀπόδημος (Mark 13:34), a compound of the preposition ἀπό (*from*) and the noun δῆμος (*home district* or *people*), meaning *away from home, away on a journey.* The verb ἀποδημέω emphasizes the idea of "journeying" (as here in Mark 12:1) in distinction from the verb ἐκδημέω which stresses the state of being away from one's rightful place (*be absent;* cf. 2 Cor. 5:6). The words could be used interchangeably, however.

ἐν ποίᾳ ἐξουσίᾳ ταῦτα ποιῶ. **30** Τὸ βάπτισμα
by what kind of authority [3]these [4]*things* [1]I [2]do. [2]the [3]baptism

Ἰωάννου ἐξ οὐρανοῦ ἦν ἢ ἐξ ἀνθρώπων? Ἀποκρίθητέ
[4]of [5]John [6]from [7]heaven [1]Was or from men? Answer

μοι."
Me."

31 Καὶ ἐλογίζοντο πρὸς ἑαυτούς, λέγοντες, "Ἐὰν
And they were debating with themselves, saying, "If

εἴπωμεν, 'Ἐξ οὐρανοῦ,' ἐρεῖ, 'Διὰ τί οὖν οὐκ
we say, 'From heaven,' He will say, 'Because of what then [3]not
'Why

ἐπιστεύσατε αὐτῷ?' **32** Ἀλλ' εἴπωμεν, "Ἐξ
[1]did [2]you believe him?' But should we say, 'From

ἀνθρώπων'?" — ἐφοβοῦντο τὸν λαόν, ἅπαντες γὰρ εἶχον τὸν
men'?" — they feared the people, all ˜ for had -
considered

Ἰωάννην ὅτι ὄντως προφήτης ἦν. **33** Καὶ ἀποκριθέντες
John that [2]truly [4]a [5]prophet [1]he [3]was. And answering

λέγουσι τῷ Ἰησοῦ, "Οὐκ οἴδαμεν."
they say to Jesus, "[3]not [1]We [2]do know."
said

Καὶ ὁ Ἰησοῦς ἀποκριθεὶς λέγει αὐτοῖς, "Οὐδὲ ἐγὼ λέγω
And - Jesus answering says to them, "Neither I ˜ do tell
said

ὑμῖν ἐν ποίᾳ ἐξουσίᾳ ταῦτα ποιῶ."
you by what kind of authority [3]these [4]*things* [1]I [2]do."

The Parable of the Wicked Vinedressers

(Matt. 21:33–45; Luke 20:9–19)

12 **1** Καὶ ἤρξατο αὐτοῖς ἐν παραβολαῖς λέγειν,
And He began [3]to [4]them [5]with [6]parables [1]to [2]speak,

"Ἀμπελῶνα ἐφύτευσεν ἄνθρωπος, καὶ περιέθηκε φραγμὸν
"[10]a [11]vineyard [9]planted [7]A [8]man, and [1]set [4]around [5]*it* [2]a [3]hedge

καὶ ὤρυξεν ὑπολήνιον καὶ ᾠκοδόμησε πύργον καὶ ἐξέδετο
and dug a wine vat and built a tower and gave out ˜
leased

αὐτὸν γεωργοῖς, καὶ ἀπεδήμησε.* **2** Καὶ ἀπέστειλε πρὸς
it to farmers, and went on a journey. And he sent to

τοὺς γεωργοὺς τῷ καιρῷ δοῦλον, ἵνα παρὰ τῶν
the farmers in the *harvest* time a slave, in order that from the

γεωργῶν λάβῃ ἀπὸ τοῦ καρποῦ τοῦ
farmers he might receive *his part* from the fruit of the

ἀμπελῶνος. **3** Οἱ δὲ λαβόντες αὐτὸν ἔδειραν καὶ
vineyard. the *ones* But taking him beat *him* and
But they took him and

ἀπέστειλαν κενόν. **4** Καὶ πάλιν ἀπέστειλε πρὸς αὐτοὺς
sent *him* away empty-*handed.* And again he sent to them

ἄλλον δοῦλον, κἀκεῖνον λιθοβολήσαντες[a]
another slave, and that *one* stoning
servant, they wounded

ἐκεφαλαίωσαν καὶ ἀπέστειλαν ἠτιμωμένον.
they wounded in the head and they sent *him* away shamefully treated.
in the head with stones

5 Καὶ πάλιν ἄλλον ἀπέστειλε, κἀκεῖνον ἀπέκτειναν,
And again [3]another [1]he [2]sent, and that *one* they killed,

καὶ πολλοὺς ἄλλους, τοὺς μὲν δέροντες, τοὺς δὲ
and *so with* many others, some ˜ beating, others ˜

ἀποκτένοντες. **6** Ἔτι οὖν ἕνα υἱὸν ἔχων ἀγαπητὸν αὐτοῦ,
killing. [2]still [1]Therefore [4]one [5]son [3]having beloved ˜ his,

ἀπέστειλε καὶ αὐτὸν πρὸς αὐτοὺς ἔσχατον, λέγων ὅτι
he sent even him to them last, saying -

‘Ἐντραπήσονται τὸν υἱόν μου.’ **7** Ἐκεῖνοι δὲ οἱ γεωργοὶ εἶπον
‘They will respect - son ˜ my.’ those ˜ But - farmers said

πρὸς ἑαυτοὺς ὅτι ‘Οὗτός ἐστιν ὁ κληρονόμος. Δεῦτε,
to themselves - ‘This is the heir. Come,
one another

ἀποκτείνωμεν αὐτόν, καὶ ἡμῶν ἔσται ἡ κληρονομία.’ **8** Καὶ
let us kill him, and [5]ours [3]will [4]be [1]the [2]inheritance.’ And

λαβόντες αὐτὸν ἀπέκτειναν, καὶ ἐξέβαλον ἔξω τοῦ
taking him they killed *him*, and threw *him* out of the

ἀμπελῶνος.
vineyard.

9 “Τί οὖν ποιήσει ὁ κύριος τοῦ ἀμπελῶνος?
“what ˜ Therefore will [6]do [1]the [2]owner [3]of [4]the [5]vineyard?

Ἐλεύσεται καὶ ἀπολέσει τοὺς γεωργοὺς καὶ δώσει τὸν
He will come and will destroy the farmers and will give the

ἀμπελῶνα ἄλλοις. **10** Οὐδὲ τὴν Γραφὴν ταύτην
vineyard to others. [3]not [4]even - [7]Scripture [6]this

ἀνέγνωτε,
[1]Have [2]you [5]read,

«Λίθον ὃν ἀπεδοκίμασαν οἱ οἰκοδομοῦντες,
«A stone which [4]rejected [1]the [2]*ones* [3]building,
the builders,

Οὗτος ἐγενήθη εἰς κεφαλὴν γωνίας.
This *stone* became - head of a corner.
the cornerstone.

11 Παρὰ Κυρίου ἐγένετο αὕτη,
From *the* Lord [2]came [3]to [4]be [1]this,
By

Καὶ ἔστι θαυμαστὴ ἐν ὀφθαλμοῖς ἡμῶν»?”[b]
And it is marvelous in eyes ˜ our»?”

12 Καὶ ἐζήτουν αὐτὸν κρατῆσαι, καὶ ἐφοβήθησαν
And they were seeking [3]Him [1]to [2]seize, and they were afraid of
arrest,

τὸν ὄχλον, ἔγνωσαν γὰρ ὅτι πρὸς αὐτοὺς τὴν παραβολὴν
the crowd, [2]they [3]knew [1]for that against them [3]the [4]parable

εἶπε. Καὶ ἀφέντες αὐτὸν ἀπῆλθον.
[1]He [2]told. And leaving Him they went away.

Render unto Caesar
(Matt. 22:15–22; Luke 20:20–26)

13 Καὶ ἀποστέλλουσι πρὸς αὐτόν τινας τῶν Φαρισαίων καὶ
And they send to Him some of the Pharisees and
sent

τῶν Ἡρῳδιανῶν ἵνα αὐτὸν ἀγρεύσωσι λόγῳ.
of the Herodians in order that [4]Him [1]they [2]might [3]catch in *some* word.
His speech.

14 Οἱ δὲ ἐλθόντες λέγουσιν αὐτῷ, “Διδάσκαλε, οἴδαμεν
the *ones* And coming say to Him, “Teacher, we know
And they came and said

ὅτι ἀληθὴς εἶ καὶ οὐ μέλει σοι περὶ
that [3]truthful [1]You [2]are and [3]not [1]it [2]does make a difference to You about

οὐδενός, οὐ γὰρ βλέπεις εἰς πρόσωπον ἀνθρώπων, ἀλλ’
no one, [4]not [1]for [2]You [3]do look on *the* face of men, but
anyone, for You do not show favoritism to persons,

6 “Therefore still having one son, his beloved, he also sent him to them last, saying, ‘They will respect my son.’
7 “But those vinedressers said among themselves, ‘This is the heir. Come, let us kill him, and the inheritance will be ours.’
8 “So they took him and killed *him* and cast *him* out of the vineyard.
9 “Therefore what will the owner of the vineyard do? He will come and destroy the vinedressers, and give the vineyard to others.
10 “Have you not even read this Scripture:

‘The stone which the
builders rejected
Has become the chief
cornerstone.
11 *This was the* LORD’S
doing,
And it is marvelous in our
eyes’?”

12 And they sought to lay hands on Him, but feared the multitude, for they knew He had spoken the parable against them. So they left Him and went away.
13 Then they sent to Him some of the Pharisees and the Herodians, to catch Him in *His* words.
14 When they had come, they said to Him, “Teacher, we know that You are true, and care about no one; for You do not regard the person of men,

[b](12:11) Ps. 118:22, 23

but teach the way of God in
truth. Is it lawful to pay taxes to
Caesar, or not?
15 "Shall we pay, or shall we
not pay?" But He, knowing
their hypocrisy, said to them,
"Why do you test Me? Bring
Me a denarius that I may see
it."
16 So they brought *it.* And He
said to them, "Whose image
and inscription *is* this?" They
said to Him, "Caesar's."
17 And Jesus answered and
said to them, "Render to Caesar the things that are Caesar's, and to God the things
that are God's." And they marveled at Him.
18 Then *some* Sadducees,
who say there is no resurrection, came to Him; and they
asked Him, saying:
19 "Teacher, Moses wrote to
us that if a man's brother dies,
and leaves *his* wife behind, and
leaves no children, his brother
should take his wife and raise
up offspring for his brother.
20 "Now there were seven
brothers. The first took a wife;
and dying, he left no offspring.
21 "And the second took her,
and he died; nor did he leave
any offspring. And the third
likewise.
22 "So the seven had her and
left no offspring. Last of all the
woman died also.
23 "Therefore, in the resurrection, when they rise, whose

ἐπ' ἀληθείας τὴν ὁδὸν τοῦ Θεοῦ διδάσκεις. Ἔξεστι κῆνσον
in truth [3]the [4]way - [5]of [6]God [1]you [2]teach. Is it lawful [3]a [4]tax

Καίσαρι δοῦναι ἢ οὔ? 15 Δῶμεν ἢ μὴ δῶμεν?"
[5]to [6]Caesar [1]to [2]give (pay) or not? Should we give (pay) or [3]not [1]should [2]we give? (pay?")

Ὁ δὲ εἰδὼς αὐτῶν τὴν ὑπόκρισιν εἶπεν αὐτοῖς, "Τί
- But knowing their - hypocrisy He said to them, "Why
(because He knew their)

με πειράζετε? Φέρετέ μοι δηνάριον ἵνα ἴδω."
[4]Me [1]do [2]you [3]test? Bring Me a denarius so that I may see *it.*"

16 Οἱ δὲ ἤνεγκαν. Καὶ λέγει αὐτοῖς, "Τίνος ἡ εἰκὼν
[2]the [3]*ones* (they) [1]And brought *one.* And He says (said) to them, "Whose - image

αὕτη καὶ ἡ ἐπιγραφή?"
[3]*is* [4]this [1]and - [2]inscription?"

Οἱ δὲ εἶπον αὐτῷ, "Καίσαρος."
[2]the [3]*ones* (they) [1]And said to Him, "Caesar's."

17 Καὶ ἀποκριθεὶς ὁ Ἰησοῦς εἶπεν αὐτοῖς, "Ἀπόδοτε
And answering - Jesus said to them, "Give back ("Render)

τὰ Καίσαρος Καίσαρι καὶ τὰ τοῦ Θεοῦ τῷ Θεῷ."
the *things* of Caesar to Caesar and the *things* - of God - to God."

Καὶ ἐθαύμασαν ἐπ' αὐτῷ.
And they marveled at Him.

The Sadducees Question the Resurrection

(Matt. 22:23–33; Luke 20:27–40)

18 Καὶ ἔρχονται Σαδδουκαῖοι πρὸς αὐτόν, οἵτινες λέγουσιν
And come ˜ (came) Sadducees to Him, those who say

ἀνάστασιν μὴ εἶναι, καὶ ἐπηρώτησαν αὐτόν, λέγοντες,
resurrection not to be, (that there is no resurrection,) and they asked Him, saying,

19 "Διδάσκαλε, Μωσῆς ἔγραψεν ἡμῖν ὅτι «ἐάν τινος
"Teacher, Moses wrote to us that «if someone's

ἀδελφὸς ἀποθάνῃ» καὶ καταλίπῃ γυναῖκα «καὶ τέκνα μὴ
brother dies» and leaves behind a wife «and [4]children [2]not

ἀφῇ,» ἵνα «λάβῃ ὁ ἀδελφὸς αὐτοῦ τὴν γυναῖκα αὐτοῦ
[1]does [3]leave,» that «[3]should [4]take - [2]brother [1]his - wife ˜ his

καὶ ἐξαναστήσῃ σπέρμα τῷ ἀδελφῷ αὐτοῦ.»[c] 20 Ἑπτὰ
and raise up seed (offspring) - for brother ˜ his.» [3]seven

ἀδελφοὶ ἦσαν. Καὶ ὁ πρῶτος ἔλαβε γυναῖκα, καὶ
[4]brothers [1]*There* [2]were. And the first took a wife, and

ἀποθνῄσκων οὐκ ἀφῆκε σπέρμα. 21 Καὶ ὁ δεύτερος
dying (he died) [3]not [1]he [2]did leave (and left no) seed (offspring). And the second

ἔλαβεν αὐτήν, καὶ ἀπέθανε· καὶ οὐδὲ αὐτὸς ἀφῆκε σπέρμα.
took her, and died; and neither he ˜ did leave seed (offspring).

Καὶ ὁ τρίτος ὡσαύτως. 22 Καὶ ἔλαβον αὐτὴν οἱ ἑπτὰ καὶ
And the third likewise. And [3]took [4]her [1]the [2]seven and

οὐκ ἀφῆκαν σπέρμα. Ἐσχάτη πάντων ἀπέθανε καὶ ἡ
not ˜ did leave seed (offspring). Last of all [4]died [3]also [1]the

γυνή. 23 Ἐν τῇ ἀναστάσει, ὅταν ἀναστῶσι,[d] τίνος
[2]woman. In the resurrection, whenever they rise, whose

---

[c](12:19) Gen. 38:8; Deut. 25:5 [d](12:23) NU brackets *οταν αναστωσι, whenever they rise.*

αὐτῶν ἔσται γυνή? Οἱ γὰρ ἑπτὰ ἔσχον αὐτὴν γυναῖκα."
²of ³them ⁴will ⁵she ⁶be ¹wife? the ˜ For seven had her *as* wife."

24 Καὶ ἀποκριθεὶς ὁ Ἰησοῦς εἶπεν αὐτοῖς, "Οὐ διὰ
And answering - Jesus said to them, "³not ⁵because ⁶of

τοῦτο πλανᾶσθε, μὴ εἰδότες τὰς Γραφὰς μηδὲ
⁷this ¹Are ²you ⁴mistaken, not knowing the Scriptures nor
because you know neither

τὴν δύναμιν τοῦ Θεοῦ? 25 Ὅταν γὰρ ἐκ νεκρῶν
the power - of God? whenever ˜ For ³from ⁴*the* ⁵dead

ἀναστῶσιν, οὔτε γαμοῦσιν οὔτε γαμίσκονται, ἀλλ'
¹they ²rise, neither do they marry nor are they given in marriage, but

εἰσὶν ὡς ἄγγελοι οἱ ἐν τοῖς οὐρανοῖς. 26 Περὶ δὲ τῶν
they are like angels - in the heavens. concerning ˜ But the
heaven.

νεκρῶν, ὅτι ἐγείρονται, οὐκ ἀνέγνωτε ἐν τῇ βίβλῳ Μωσέως,
dead, that they rise, ³not ¹did ²you read in the book of Moses,

ἐπὶ τοῦ βάτου, ὡς εἶπεν αὐτῷ ὁ
in connection with *the passage about* the *burning* bush, how ²spoke ³to ⁴him -

Θεός, λέγων, «Ἐγὼ ὁ Θεὸς Ἀβραὰμ καὶ ὁ Θεὸς Ἰσαὰκ καὶ
¹God, saying, «I *am* the God of Abraham and the God of Isaac and

ὁ Θεὸς Ἰακώβ»?[e] 27 Οὐκ ἔστιν ὁ Θεὸς νεκρῶν ἀλλὰ
the God of Jacob»? ³not ¹He ²is the God of dead *people* but

Θεὸς ζώντων. Ὑμεῖς οὖν πολὺ πλανᾶσθε."
God of living *people*. you ˜ Therefore greatly ˜ are mistaken."

The Two Greatest Commandments
(Matt. 22:34–40)

28 Καὶ προσελθὼν εἷς τῶν γραμματέων ἀκούσας
And approaching one of the scribes hearing
one of the scribes, after he heard them

αὐτῶν συζητούντων, εἰδὼς[f] ὅτι καλῶς αὐτοῖς
them debating, knowing that ⁴well ³them
disputing and realized that He had answered them well,

ἀπεκρίθη, ἐπηρώτησεν αὐτόν, "Ποία ἐστὶ πρώτη πάντων
¹He ²answered, asked Him, "Which is *the* first ²of ³all
approached and asked

ἐντολή?"
¹commandment?"

29 Ὁ δὲ Ἰησοῦς ἀπεκρίθη αὐτῷ ὅτι "Πρώτη πάντων τῶν
- And Jesus answered him - "*The* first of all the

ἐντολῶν, «Ἄκουε, Ἰσραήλ, Κύριος ὁ Θεὸς ἡμῶν, Κύριος
commandments *is*, «Hear, Israel, *the* Lord - God ˜ our, ³Lord

εἷς ἐστι, 30 καὶ ἀγαπήσεις Κύριον τὸν Θεόν σου ἐξ ὅλης
²one ¹is, and you shall love *the* Lord - God ˜ your out of ²whole
with

τῆς καρδίας σου καὶ ἐξ ὅλης τῆς ψυχῆς σου καὶ ἐξ
- ³heart ¹your and out of ²whole - ³soul ¹your and out of
with self with

ὅλης τῆς διανοίας σου καὶ ἐξ ὅλης τῆς ἰσχύος σου.»[g]
²whole - ³mind ¹your and out of ²whole - ³strength ¹your.»
with

Αὕτη[h] πρώτη ἐντολή. 31 Καὶ δευτέρα ὁμοία αὐτῇ,
This *is* *the* first commandment. And *the* second *is* like it,

«Ἀγαπήσεις τὸν πλησίον σου ὡς σεαυτόν.»[i] Μείζων
«You shall love - neighbor ˜ your as yourself.» ⁵greater

τούτων ἄλλη ἐντολὴ οὐκ ἔστι."
⁶*than* ⁷these ²other ³commandment ¹No ⁴is."

wife will she be? For all seven had her as wife."
24 Jesus answered and said to them, "Are you not therefore mistaken, because you do not know the Scriptures nor the power of God?
25 "For when they rise from the dead, they neither marry nor are given in marriage, but are like angels in heaven.
26 "But concerning the dead, that they rise, have you not read in the book of Moses, in the *burning* bush *passage*, how God spoke to him, saying, *'I am the God of Abraham, the God of Isaac, and the God of Jacob'*?
27 "He is not the God of the dead, but the God of the living. You are therefore greatly mistaken."
28 Then one of the scribes came, and having heard them reasoning together, perceiving that He had answered them well, asked Him, "Which is the first commandment of all?"
29 Jesus answered him, "The first of all the commandments *is*: *'Hear, O Israel, the* LORD *our God, the* LORD *is one.*
30 *'And you shall love the* LORD *your God with all your heart, with all your soul, with all your mind, and with all your strength.'* This *is* the first commandment.
31 "And the second, like *it, is* this: *'You shall love your neighbor as yourself.'* There is no other commandment greater than these."

[e] **(12:26)** Ex. 3:6, 15
[f] **(12:28)** NU reads ιδων, *seeing*. [g] **(12:30)** Deut. 6:4, 5 [h] **(12:30)** NU omits this final sentence.
[i] **(12:31)** Lev. 19:18

32 So the scribe said to Him, "Well *said*, Teacher. You have spoken the truth, for there is one God, and there is no other but He.
33 "And to love Him with all the heart, with all the understanding, with all the soul, and with all the strength, and to love one's neighbor as oneself, is more than all the whole burnt offerings and sacrifices."
34 Now when Jesus saw that he answered wisely, He said to him, "You are not far from the kingdom of God." But after that no one dared question Him.
35 Then Jesus answered and said, while He taught in the temple, "How *is it* that the scribes say that the Christ is the Son of David?
36 "For David himself said by the Holy Spirit:

'The LORD said to my
Lord,
"Sit at My right hand,
Till I make Your enemies
Your footstool."'

37 "Therefore David himself calls Him *'Lord'*; how is He *then* his Son?" And the common people heard Him gladly.
38 Then He said to them in His teaching, "Beware of the

32 Καὶ εἶπεν αὐτῷ ὁ γραμματεύς, "Καλῶς, διδάσκαλε,
And [3]said [4]to [5]Him [1]the [2]scribe, "Well, Teacher,

ἐπ' ἀληθείας εἶπας ὅτι «εἷς ἐστι καὶ οὐκ ἔστιν ἄλλος
in truth You said that «[3]one [1]He [2]is and [3]not [1]*there* [2]is another

πλὴν αὐτοῦ.»[j] **33** Καὶ τὸ «ἀγαπᾶν αὐτὸν ἐξ ὅλης τῆς
except Him.» And - «to love Him out of whole ˜ the
with

καρδίας καὶ ἐξ ὅλης τῆς συνέσεως* καὶ[k] ἐξ ὅλης τῆς
heart and out of whole ˜ the understanding and out of whole ˜ the
with with

ψυχῆς καὶ ἐξ ὅλης τῆς ἰσχύος» καὶ τὸ «ἀγαπᾶν τὸν
soul and out of whole ˜ the strength» and - «to love the
self with one's

πλησίον ὡς ἑαυτόν» πλεῖόν ἐστι πάντων τῶν ὁλοκαυτωμάτων
neighbor as oneself» more ˜ is *than* all the whole burnt offerings

καὶ θυσιῶν."
and sacrifices."

34 Καὶ ὁ Ἰησοῦς ἰδὼν αὐτὸν ὅτι νουνεχῶς
And - Jesus seeing him that thoughtfully
when He saw that he had answered

ἀπεκρίθη, εἶπεν αὐτῷ, "Οὐ μακρὰν εἶ ἀπὸ τῆς
he answered, said to him, "[3]not [4]far [1]You [2]are from the
wisely,

βασιλείας τοῦ Θεοῦ." Καὶ οὐδεὶς οὐκέτι ἐτόλμα αὐτὸν
kingdom - of God." And no one no longer dared [3]Him
any

ἐπερωτῆσαι.
[1]to [2]question.

What Do You Think of Christ?
(Matt. 22:41–46; Luke 20:41–44)

35 Καὶ ἀποκριθεὶς ὁ Ἰησοῦς ἔλεγε διδάσκων ἐν τῷ
And answering - Jesus said *as He was* teaching in the

ἱερῷ, "Πῶς λέγουσιν οἱ γραμματεῖς ὅτι ὁ Χριστὸς υἱός ἐστι
temple, "How do [3]say [1]the [2]scribes that the Christ [3]Son [1]is
Messiah

Δαβίδ? **36** Αὐτὸς γὰρ Δαβὶδ εἶπεν ἐν Πνεύματι Ἁγίῳ,
[2]David's? [3]himself [1]For [2]David said by *the* Spirit ˜ Holy,

«Λέγει ὁ Κύριος τῷ Κυρίῳ μου,
«[3]says [1]The [2]Lord - to Lord ˜ my,
«said

'Κάθου ἐκ δεξιῶν μου
'Sit at [2]right [3]*parts* [1]My
hand

Ἕως ἂν θῶ τοὺς ἐχθρούς σου ὑποπόδιον τῶν ποδῶν
Till - I put - enemies ˜ Your *as* a footstool - of feet ˜
for

σου.'»[l]
Your.'»

37 Αὐτὸς οὖν Δαβὶδ λέγει αὐτὸν 'Κύριον,' καὶ πόθεν υἱός
[3]himself [1]Therefore [2]David calls Him 'Lord,' and how [4]Son

αὐτοῦ ἐστι?" Καὶ ὁ πολὺς ὄχλος ἤκουεν αὐτοῦ ἡδέως.
[3]his [1]is [2]He?" And the large crowd was hearing Him gladly.

Religious Hypocrites Are Denounced
(Matt. 23:1–36; Luke 11:37–52; 20:45–47)

38 Καὶ ἔλεγεν αὐτοῖς ἐν τῇ διδαχῇ αὐτοῦ, "Βλέπετε ἀπὸ
And He said to them in - teaching ˜ His, "Be watchful from
"Beware of

[j] **(12:32)** Deut. 4:35, 39 [k] **(12:33)** NU omits *και εξ ολης της ψυχης*, *with all the soul.* [l] **(12:36)** Ps. 110:1

***(12:33)** *συνεσις* (*synesis*). Noun meaning the *faculty of comprehension, intelligence, insight, understanding* (cf. Luke 2:47; 1 Cor. 1:19). To love God with all one's "understanding" would apparently cover the entirety of one's inner, conscious life. In Paul's epistles, the word appears to emphasize spiritual insight as given by God, for example, Col. 1:9 (where it is defined as "spiritual"); 2:2; Eph. 3:4; 2 Tim. 2:7. Cf. the cognate verb *συνιημι*, *understand, comprehend, gain insight (into).*

τῶν γραμματέων τῶν θελόντων ἐν στολαῖς περιπατεῖν
the scribes the *ones* desiring ^{4}in ^{5}long ^{6}robes ^{1}to ^{2}walk ^{3}about
who desire

καὶ ἀσπασμοὺς ἐν ταῖς ἀγοραῖς **39** καὶ πρωτοκαθεδρίας
and *desire* greetings in the marketplaces and first seats
the best

ἐν ταῖς συναγωγαῖς καὶ πρωτοκλισίας ἐν τοῖς δείπνοις·
in the synagogues and first couches at the dinners;
the places of honor

40 οἱ κατεσθίοντες τὰς οἰκίας τῶν χηρῶν καὶ προφάσει
the *ones* eating up the houses of the widows and ^{3}in ^{4}pretense
who devour

μακρὰ προσευχόμενοι. Οὗτοι λήψονται περισσότερον
^{2}long ^{1}praying. These will receive greater
pray at length. more severe

κρίμα."
judgment."
condemnation."

The Widow's Two Mites
(Luke 21:1–4)

41 Καὶ καθίσας ὁ Ἰησοῦς κατέναντι τοῦ γαζοφυλακίου
And sitting - Jesus opposite the treasury
Jesus sat down

ἐθεώρει πῶς ὁ ὄχλος βάλλει χαλκὸν εἰς τὸ
He was observing how the crowd is putting copper *coins* into the
and was money

γαζοφυλάκιον. Καὶ πολλοὶ πλούσιοι ἔβαλλον πολλά.
treasury. And many rich *people* were putting *in* many.
much.

42 Καὶ ἐλθοῦσα μία χήρα πτωχὴ ἔβαλε λεπτὰ* δύο, ὅ
And coming one widow ~ poor put *in* lepta ~ two, which
when she came mites

ἐστι κοδράντης. **43** Καὶ προσκαλεσάμενος τοὺς μαθητὰς
is a quadrans. And having summoned - disciples ~
equals

αὐτοῦ λέγει αὐτοῖς, "Ἀμὴν λέγω ὑμῖν ὅτι ἡ χήρα αὕτη ἡ
His He says to them, "Amen I say to you that - ^{3}widow ^{1}this -
said "Assuredly

πτωχὴ πλεῖον πάντων βέβληκε τῶν βαλλόντων εἰς τὸ
^{2}poor ^{7}more ^{8}*than* ^{9}all ^{4}has ^{5}put ^{6}*in* the *ones* putting into the
those who are

γαζοφυλάκιον. **44** Πάντες γὰρ ἐκ τοῦ περισσεύοντος
treasury. ^{3}all ^{1}For ^{6}out ^{7}of ^{8}the ^{9}*amount* ^{10}abounding
their

αὐτοῖς ἔβαλον, αὕτη δὲ ἐκ τῆς ὑστερήσεως
^{11}to ^{12}them ^{2}they ^{4}put ^{5}*in*, ^{14}this ^{15}*woman* ^{13}but out of - lack ~
excess poverty

αὐτῆς πάντα ὅσα εἶχεν ἔβαλεν, ὅλον τὸν βίον
her all as much as she had put *in*, ^{2}whole - ^{3}livelihood
put in everything she had,

αὐτῆς."
^{1}her."

Jesus Predicts the Destruction of the Temple
(Matt. 24:1, 2; Luke 21:5, 6)

13 **1** Καὶ ἐκπορευομένου αὐτοῦ ἐκ τοῦ ἱεροῦ, λέγει
And going out Him from the temple, ^{5}says
as He was going out said

scribes, who desire to go
around in long robes, *love*
greetings in the marketplaces,
39 "the best seats in the synagogues, and the best places at
feasts,
40 "who devour widows'
houses, and for a pretense
make long prayers. These will
receive greater condemnation."
41 Now Jesus sat opposite the
treasury and saw how the people put money into the treasury. And many *who were* rich
put in much.
42 Then one poor widow
came and threw in two mites,
which make a quadrans.
43 So He called His disciples
to *Himself* and said to them,
"Assuredly, I say to you that
this poor widow has put in more
than all those who have given to
the treasury;
44 "for they all put in out of
their abundance, but she out of
her poverty put in all that she
had, her whole livelihood."
13 Then as He went out
of the temple, one of
His disciples said to Him,

***(12:42)** λεπτόν *(lepton)*. Noun identifying the smallest Greek copper coin, often translated as a "mite." In NT times, apparently 128 of these were required to equal the Roman denarius, which was the standard day's wage of a laborer. According to this passage, two λεπτὰ equaled one κοδράντης, the Greek name for the smallest Roman copper coin, the quadrans (Matt. 5:26). It seems that the λεπτόν represented a very small amount. λεπτόν occurs elsewhere only in Luke 12:59; 21:2.

"Teacher, see what manner of
stones and what buildings *are*
here!"
2 And Jesus answered and
said to him, "Do you see these
great buildings? Not *one* stone
shall be left upon another, that
shall not be thrown down."
3 Now as He sat on the
Mount of Olives opposite the
temple, Peter, James, John,
and Andrew asked Him pri-
vately,
4 "Tell us, when will these
things be? And what *will be* the
sign when all these things will
be fulfilled?"
5 And Jesus, answering
them, began to say: "Take
heed that no one deceives you.
6 "For many will come in My
name, saying, 'I am *He,*' and
will deceive many.
7 "But when you hear of
wars and rumors of wars, do
not be troubled; for *such things*
must happen, but the end *is* not
yet.
8 "For nation will rise against
nation, and kingdom against
kingdom. And there will be
earthquakes in various places,
and there will be famines and
troubles. These *are* the begin-
nings of sorrows.
9 "But watch out for yourselves, for they will deliver you
up to councils, and you will be
beaten in the synagogues. You
will be brought before rulers
and kings for My sake, for a
testimony to them.
10 "And the gospel must first
be preached to all the nations.

αὐτῷ εἷς τῶν μαθητῶν αὐτοῦ, "Διδάσκαλε, ἴδε, ποταποὶ
[6]to [7]Him [1]one - [2]of [4]disciples [3]His, "Teacher, see, what sort of

λίθοι καὶ ποταπαὶ οἰκοδομαί!"
stones and what sort of buildings!"

2 Καὶ ὁ Ἰησοῦς ἀποκριθεὶς εἶπεν αὐτῷ, "Βλέπεις ταύτας
And - Jesus ˜ answering said to him, "Do you see these

τὰς μεγάλας οἰκοδομάς? Οὐ μὴ ἀφεθῇ λίθος ἐπὶ
- great buildings? Not not [1]will [4]be [5]left [2]a [3]stone upon
By no means

λίθῳ ὃς οὐ μὴ καταλυθῇ."
a stone which not not will be thrown down."
will in any way escape destruction."

Jesus Describes the End of the Age
(Matt. 24:3–14; Luke 21:7–19)

3 Καὶ καθημένου αὐτοῦ εἰς τὸ Ὄρος τῶν Ἐλαιῶν
And sitting Him on the Mount - of Olives
as He was sitting

κατέναντι τοῦ ἱεροῦ, ἐπηρώτων αὐτὸν κατ' ἰδίαν Πέτρος καὶ
opposite the temple, [8]were [9]asking [10]Him [11]privately [1]Peter [2]and
began

Ἰάκωβος καὶ Ἰωάννης καὶ Ἀνδρέας, **4** "Εἰπὲ ἡμῖν πότε
[3]James [4]and [5]John [6]and [7]Andrew, "Tell us when

ταῦτα ἔσται? Καὶ τί τὸ σημεῖον ὅταν μέλλῃ
these *things* will be? And what *will be* the sign whenever [4]are [5]about

πάντα ταῦτα συντελεῖσθαι?"
[1]all [2]these [3]*things* to be fulfilled?"

5 Ὁ δὲ Ἰησοῦς ἀποκριθεὶς αὐτοῖς ἤρξατο λέγειν,
- But Jesus answering them began to say,

"Βλέπετε μή τις ὑμᾶς πλανήσῃ. **6** Πολλοὶ γὰρ ἐλεύσονται
"Watch out lest anyone you ˜ deceive. many ˜ For will come
"Take care that no one

ἐπὶ τῷ ὀνόματί μου, λέγοντες ὅτι 'Ἐγώ εἰμι,' καὶ πολλοὺς
in - name ˜ My, saying - 'I am *He,*' and [4]many

πλανήσουσιν. **7** Ὅταν δὲ ἀκούσητε πολέμους καὶ ἀκοὰς
[1]they [2]will [3]deceive. whenever ˜ But you hear of wars and rumors

πολέμων, μὴ θροεῖσθε· δεῖ γὰρ
of wars, not ˜ do be disturbed; [2]it [3]is [4]necessary [5]*for* [1]for
for these things

γενέσθαι, ἀλλ' οὔπω τὸ τέλος. **8** Ἐγερθήσεται
these things to happen, but [4]not [5]yet [1]the [2]end [3]*is.* [3]will [4]be [5]raised [6]up
must occur,

γὰρ ἔθνος ἐπὶ ἔθνος καὶ βασιλεία ἐπὶ βασιλείαν, καὶ
[1]For [2]nation against nation and kingdom against kingdom, and

ἔσονται σεισμοὶ κατὰ τόπους, καὶ ἔσονται λιμοὶ
there will be earthquakes according to places, and *there* will be famines
in various

καὶ[a] ταραχαί. Ἀρχαὶ ὠδίνων ταῦτα.
and disturbances. [3]*the* [4]beginnings [5]of [6]birth [7]pangs [1]These [2]*are.*
uprisings.

9 "Βλέπετε δὲ ὑμεῖς ἑαυτούς· παραδώσουσι γὰρ
"[3]watch [4]out [1]But [2]you *for* yourselves; [2]they [3]will [4]hand [6]over [1]for

ὑμᾶς εἰς συνέδρια καὶ εἰς συναγωγὰς δαρήσεσθε καὶ ἐπὶ
[5]you to councils and in synagogues you will be flogged and before

ἡγεμόνων καὶ βασιλέων σταθήσεσθε ἕνεκεν ἐμοῦ εἰς
rulers and kings you will stand because of Me as
for My sake

μαρτύριον αὐτοῖς. **10** Καὶ εἰς πάντα τὰ ἔθνη δεῖ
a testimony to them. And to all the nations it is necessary *for*

---

[a](13:8) NU omits *και ταραχαι, and disturbances.*

πρῶτον κηρυχθῆναι τὸ εὐαγγέλιον. 11 Ὅταν δὲ
6first 3to 4be 5proclaimed 1the 2gospel. whenever ~ But

ἀγάγωσιν ὑμᾶς παραδιδόντες, μὴ προμεριμνᾶτε
they lead *you* forth you ~ handing over, not ~ do worry beforehand *as to*
to deliver you over,

τί λαλήσητε μηδὲ[b] μελετᾶτε. Ἀλλ' ὃ ἐὰν δοθῇ
what you should say nor rack your brains. But what ever is given

ὑμῖν ἐν ἐκείνῃ τῇ ὥρᾳ, τοῦτο λαλεῖτε, οὐ γάρ ἐστε ὑμεῖς
to you in that - hour, this ~ speak, 4not 1for 3are 2you

οἱ λαλοῦντες ἀλλὰ τὸ Πνεῦμα τὸ Ἅγιον. 12 Παραδώσει
the *ones* speaking but the Spirit ~ - Holy. 4will 5hand 6over

δὲ ἀδελφὸς ἀδελφὸν εἰς θάνατον καὶ πατὴρ τέκνον, καὶ
1And 2a 3brother a brother to death and a father a child, and

ἐπαναστήσονται τέκνα ἐπὶ γονεῖς καὶ θανατώσουσιν
2will 3rise 4up 1children against parents and will put 2to 3death
cause them to be

αὐτούς. 13 Καὶ ἔσεσθε μισούμενοι ὑπὸ πάντων διὰ
1them. And you will be hated by all *people* because of
put to death.

τὸ ὄνομά μου. Ὁ δὲ ὑπομείνας εἰς τέλος, οὗτος
- name ~ My. 2the 3*one* 1But enduring to *the* end, this *one*

σωθήσεται.
will be saved.
delivered.

The Great Tribulation

(Matt. 24:15–28; Luke 21:20–24)

14 "Ὅταν δὲ ἴδητε τὸ βδέλυγμα τῆς ἐρημώσεως
"whenever ~ Now you see the abomination - of desolation

τὸ[c] ῥηθὲν ὑπὸ Δανιὴλ τοῦ προφήτου ἑστὼς ὅπου οὐ
the *one was* spoken of by Daniel the prophet standing where not
which he

δεῖ" — ὁ ἀναγινώσκων νοείτω — "τότε
it is needful" — 2the 3*one* 4reading 1let understand — "then
must not" —

οἱ ἐν τῇ Ἰουδαίᾳ φευγέτωσαν εἰς τὰ ὄρη. 15 Ὁ
2the 3*ones* 4in - 5Judea 1let flee to the mountains. 3the 4*one*

δὲ ἐπὶ τοῦ δώματος μὴ καταβάτω εἰς τὴν οἰκίαν μηδὲ
1And 5on 6the 7housetop 8not 2let go down into the house nor

εἰσελθέτω ἆραί τι ἐκ τῆς οἰκίας αὐτοῦ. 16 Καὶ ὁ
let him go in to take anything out of - house ~ his. And 2the 3*one*

εἰς τὸν ἀγρὸν ὢν μὴ ἐπιστρεψάτω εἰς τὰ ὀπίσω
5in 6the 7field 4being 8not 1let return to the *things* behind *him*

ἆραι τὸ ἱμάτιον αὐτοῦ. 17 Οὐαὶ δὲ ταῖς ἐν γαστρὶ
to take - garment ~ his. woe ~ And to the *women* in *the* womb
those who are pregnant

ἐχούσαις καὶ ταῖς θηλαζούσαις ἐν ἐκείναις ταῖς ἡμέραις!
having and to the *women* giving suck in those - days!
nursing a baby

18 Προσεύχεσθε δὲ ἵνα μὴ γένηται ἡ φυγὴ ὑμῶν
pray ~ But that 4not 3does 5take 6place - 2flight 1your

χειμῶνος. 19 Ἔσονται γὰρ αἱ ἡμέραι ἐκεῖναι θλῖψις οἵα
of winter. 4will 5be 1For - 3days 2those a tribulation such as
in

οὐ γέγονε τοιαύτη ἀπ' ἀρχῆς κτίσεως ἧς ἔκτισεν
3not 1*there* 2has been the like from *the* beginning of creation which created ~

ὁ Θεὸς ἕως τοῦ νῦν, καὶ οὐ μὴ γένηται. 20 Καὶ εἰ μὴ
- God until - now, and not not shall be. And if not
never again unless

11 "But when they arrest *you* and deliver you up, do not worry beforehand, or premeditate what you will speak. But whatever is given you in that hour, speak that; for it is not you who speak, but the Holy Spirit.
12 "Now brother will betray brother to death, and a father *his* child; and children will rise up against parents and cause them to be put to death.
13 "And you will be hated by all for My name's sake. But he who endures to the end shall be saved.
14 "So when you see the *'abomination of desolation,'* spoken of by Daniel the prophet, standing where it ought not" (let the reader understand), "then let those who are in Judea flee to the mountains.
15 "Let him who is on the housetop not go down into the house, nor enter to take anything out of his house.
16 "And let him who is in the field not go back to get his clothes.
17 "But woe to those who are pregnant and to those who are nursing babies in those days!
18 "And pray that your flight may not be in winter.
19 "For *in* those days there will be tribulation, such as has not been since the beginning of the creation which God created until this time, nor ever shall be.
20 "And unless the Lord had

b(13:11) NU omits *μηδε μελετατε, nor rack your brains.* *c*(13:14) NU omits *το ρηθεν υπο Δανιηλ του προφητου, which was spoken of by Daniel the prophet.*

shortened those days, no flesh
would be saved; but for the
elect's sake, whom He chose,
He shortened the days.
21 "Then if anyone says to
you, 'Look, here *is* the Christ!'
or, 'Look, *He is* there!' do not
believe it.
22 "For false christs and false
prophets will rise and show
signs and wonders to deceive,
if possible, even the elect.
23 "But take heed; see, I have
told you all things beforehand.
24 "But in those days, after
that tribulation, the sun will be
darkened, and the moon will
not give its light;
25 "the stars of heaven will
fall, and the powers in the heavens will be shaken.
26 "Then they will see the
Son of Man coming in the
clouds with great power and
glory.
27 "And then He will send His
angels, and gather together His
elect from the four winds, from
the farthest part of earth to the
farthest part of heaven.
28 "Now learn this parable
from the fig tree: When its
branch has already become tender, and puts forth leaves, you

Κύριος ἐκολόβωσε τὰς ἡμέρας, οὐκ ἂν ἐσώθη πᾶσα
the Lord cut short the days, not ˜ - would be saved all
no flesh would be

σάρξ. Ἀλλὰ διὰ τοὺς ἐκλεκτοὺς οὓς ἐξελέξατο
flesh. But for the sake of the elect whom He chose
saved. chosen ones

ἐκολόβωσε τὰς ἡμέρας. 21 Καὶ τότε ἐάν τις ὑμῖν εἴπῃ,
He cut short the days. And then if anyone [2]to [3]you [1]says,

"Ἰδού, ὧδε ὁ Χριστός!' ἤ "Ἰδού, ἐκεῖ!' μὴ πιστεύετε.
'Look, here *is* the Christ!' or 'Look, there *He is*!' not ˜ do believe *him*.
Messiah!'

22 Ἐγερθήσονται γὰρ ψευδόχριστοι καὶ ψευδοπροφῆται καὶ
[7]will [8]be [9]raised [10]up [1]For [2]false [3]christs [4]and [5]false [6]prophets and

δώσουσι σημεῖα καὶ τέρατα πρὸς τὸ ἀποπλανᾶν, εἰ
they will give signs and wonders for - to lead astray, if
in order

δυνατόν, καὶ τοὺς ἐκλεκτούς. 23 Ὑμεῖς δὲ βλέπετε· ἰδού,
possible, even the elect. you ˜ But watch out; see,
chosen ones.

προείρηκα ὑμῖν πάντα.
I have told [4]in [5]advance [1]you [2]all [3]*things*.

The Coming of the Son of Man
(Matt. 24:29–31; Luke 21:25–28)

24 "Ἀλλ' ἐν ἐκείναις ταῖς ἡμέραις, μετὰ τὴν θλῖψιν
"But in those - days, after - tribulation ˜

ἐκείνην,
that,

Ὁ ἥλιος σκοτισθήσεται,
The sun will be darkened,

Καὶ ἡ σελήνη οὐ δώσει τὸ φέγγος αὐτῆς,
And the moon not ˜ will give - radiance ˜ its,

25 Καὶ οἱ ἀστέρες τοῦ οὐρανοῦ ἔσονται ἐκπίπτοντες,
And the stars - of heaven will be falling,

Καὶ αἱ δυνάμεις αἱ ἐν τοῖς οὐρανοῖς σαλευθήσονται.
And the powers - in the heavens will be shaken.

26 Καὶ τότε ὄψονται τὸν Υἱὸν τοῦ Ἀνθρώπου ἐρχόμενον ἐν
And then they will see the Son - of Man coming in

νεφέλαις μετὰ δυνάμεως πολλῆς καὶ δόξης. 27 Καὶ τότε
the clouds with power ˜ great and glory. And then

ἀποστελεῖ τοὺς ἀγγέλους αὐτοῦ καὶ ἐπισυνάξει τοὺς
He will send - angels ˜ His and they will gather together -

ἐκλεκτοὺς αὐτοῦ ἐκ τῶν τεσσάρων ἀνέμων ἀπ' ἄκρου
elect ˜ His from the four winds from *the* farthest part
chosen ones

γῆς ἕως ἄκρου οὐρανοῦ.
of earth to *the* farthest part of heaven.

The Parable of the Fig Tree
(Matt. 24:32–35; Luke 21:29–33)

28 "Ἀπὸ δὲ τῆς συκῆς μάθετε τὴν παραβολήν· ὅταν
"from ˜ Now the fig tree learn the parable: whenever
this

αὐτῆς ἤδη ὁ κλάδος ἁπαλὸς γένηται καὶ ἐκφύῃ τὰ
its already ˜ - branch tender ˜ becomes and it puts forth the
its

φύλλα, γινώσκετε ὅτι ἐγγὺς τὸ θέρος ἐστίν. **29** Οὕτω καὶ
leaves, you know that [3]near - [1]summer [2]is. Thus also
In this way

ὑμεῖς, ὅταν ταῦτα ἴδητε γινόμενα, γινώσκετε ὅτι
you, whenever [3]these [4]*things* [1]you [2]see happening, know that

ἐγγύς ἐστιν ἐπὶ θύραις. **30** Ἀμὴν λέγω ὑμῖν ὅτι οὐ μὴ
[3]near [1]it [2]is at *the* doors. Amen I say to you that [4]not [5]not
Assuredly by no means

παρέλθῃ ἡ γενεὰ αὕτη μέχρις οὗ πάντα ταῦτα
[3]will [6]pass [7]away - [2]generation [1]this till all these *things*

γένηται. **31** Ὁ οὐρανὸς καὶ ἡ γῆ παρελεύσεται, οἱ δὲ λόγοι
happen. - Heaven and - earth will pass away, - but words ~

μου οὐ μὴ παρέλθωσι.
My [2]not [3]not [1]will [4]pass [5]away.
by no means

No One Knows the Day or Hour
(Matt. 24:36–44)

32 "Περὶ δὲ τῆς ἡμέρας ἐκείνης ἢ ὥρας οὐδεὶς οἶδεν,
"concerning ~ But - day ~ that or hour no one knows,

οὐδὲ οἱ ἄγγελοι οἱ ἐν οὐρανῷ οὐδὲ ὁ Υἱός, εἰ μὴ ὁ
not even the angels - in heaven nor the Son, if not the
but only

Πατήρ. **33** Βλέπετε, ἀγρυπνεῖτε* καὶ προσεύχεσθε·[d] οὐκ
Father. Be watchful, stay awake and pray; [4]not

οἴδατε γὰρ πότε ὁ καιρός ἐστιν. **34** Ὡς ἄνθρωπος
[2]you [3]do [5]know [1]for when the time is. *It is* like a man

ἀπόδημος ἀφεὶς τὴν οἰκίαν αὐτοῦ καὶ δοὺς τοῖς
away on a journey having left - house ~ his and having given -
who left gave

δούλοις αὐτοῦ τὴν ἐξουσίαν καὶ ἑκάστῳ τὸ ἔργον αὐτοῦ, καὶ
to slaves ~ his - authority and to each - work ~ his, and

τῷ θυρωρῷ ἐνετείλατο ἵνα γρηγορῇ. **35** Γρηγορεῖτε
the doorkeeper he commanded that he should be watchful. Be watchful

οὖν, οὐκ οἴδατε γὰρ πότε ὁ κύριος τῆς οἰκίας
therefore, [4]not [2]you [3]do [5]know [1]for when the master of the house

ἔρχεται, ὀψὲ ἢ μεσονυκτίου ἢ ἀλεκτοροφωνίας ἢ
is coming, late in the day or *at* midnight or *at* cockcrow or
at evening dawn

πρωΐ, **36** μὴ ἐλθὼν ἐξαίφνης εὕρῃ ὑμᾶς
early in the morning, lest having come suddenly he find you

καθεύδοντας. **37** Ἃ δὲ ὑμῖν λέγω, πᾶσι
sleeping. [2]*the* [3]*things* [4]which [1]And [7]to [8]you [5]I [6]say, [11]to [12]all

λέγω· Γρηγορεῖτε!"
[9]I [10]say: Be watchful!"

The Chief Priests and Scribes Plot to Kill Jesus
(Matt. 26:1–5; Luke 22:1, 2; John 11:45–53)

14 **1** Ἦν δὲ τὸ Πάσχα καὶ τὰ Ἄζυμα
[2]it [3]was [1]Now the Passover and the *Feast of* Unleavened Bread

μετὰ δύο ἡμέρας. Καὶ ἐζήτουν οἱ ἀρχιερεῖς καὶ οἱ
after two days. And [7]were [8]seeking [1]the [2]chief [3]priests [4]and [5]the

γραμματεῖς πῶς αὐτὸν ἐν δόλῳ κρατήσαντες
[6]scribes how Him with deceit seizing
they might seize Him by trickery and

ἀποκτείνωσιν. **2** Ἔλεγον δέ, "Μὴ ἐν τῇ ἑορτῇ,
they might kill *Him*. [2]they [3]said [1]But, "Not at the feast,
during

know that summer is near.
29 "So you also, when you see
these things happening, know
that it is near—at the doors!
30 "Assuredly, I say to you,
this generation will by no
means pass away till all these
things take place.
31 "Heaven and earth will
pass away, but My words will
by no means pass away.
32 "But of that day and hour
no one knows, not even the angels in heaven, nor the Son, but
only the Father.
33 "Take heed, watch and
pray; for you do not know when
the time is.
34 "*It is* like a man going to a
far country, who left his house
and gave authority to his servants, and to each his work,
and commanded the door-
keeper to watch.
35 "Watch therefore, for you
do not know when the master
of the house is coming—in the
evening, at midnight, at the
crowing of the rooster, or in
the morning—
36 "lest, coming suddenly, he
find you sleeping.
37 "And what I say to you, I
say to all: Watch!"
14 After two days it was
the Passover and *the*
Feast of Unleavened Bread.
And the chief priests and the
scribes sought how they might
take Him by trickery and put
Him to death.
2 But they said, "Not during

---

[d](13:33) NU omits *και προσευχεσθε, and pray.*

*(13:33) ἀγρυπνέω *(agrypneō)*. Verb, literally meaning *stay awake*. The word always occurs in the NT with figurative meanings. Here it means *be alert* for signs of some future threat (cf. Luke 21:36 and Eph. 6:18). This figurative meaning is extended in Heb. 13:17 to mean *take care of, look after.* ἀγρυπνέω is roughly synonymous in its base and figurative meanings with γρηγορέω, *watch*. Cf. the noun ἀγρυπνία, *sleeplessness,* in 2 Cor. 6:5.

the feast, lest there be an uproar of the people."
3 And being in Bethany at
the house of Simon the leper,
as He sat at the table, a woman
came having an alabaster flask
of very costly oil of spikenard.
Then she broke the flask and
poured *it* on His head.
4 But there were some who
were indignant among themselves, and said, "Why was this
fragrant oil wasted?
5 "For it might have been
sold for more than three hundred denarii and given to the
poor." And they criticized her
sharply.
6 But Jesus said, "Let her
alone. Why do you trouble her?
She has done a good work for
Me.
7 "For you have the poor
with you always, and whenever
you wish you may do them
good; but Me you do not have
always.
8 "She has done what she
could. She has come beforehand to anoint My body for
burial.
9 "Assuredly, I say to you,
wherever this gospel is
preached in the whole world,
what this woman has done will
also be told as a memorial to
her."
10 Then Judas Iscariot, one of
the twelve, went to the chief

μήποτε θόρυβος ἔσται τοῦ λαοῦ."
lest perhaps [4]a [5]disturbance [1]*there* [2]will [3]be of the people."

Jesus Is Anointed at Bethany
(Matt. 26:6–13; John 12:1–8)

3 Καὶ ὄντος αὐτοῦ ἐν Βηθανίᾳ ἐν τῇ οἰκίᾳ Σίμωνος τοῦ
And being Him in Bethany in the house of Simon the
while He was

λεπροῦ, κατακειμένου αὐτοῦ, ἦλθε γυνὴ ἔχουσα
leper, reclining Him, [3]came [1]a [2]woman having
as He was reclining for a meal,

ἀλάβαστρον μύρου νάρδου πιστικῆς πολυτελοῦς. Καὶ
an alabaster *flask* of perfume of [4]nard [3]pure [1]very [2]costly. And

συντρίψασα τὸ ἀλάβαστρον, κατέχεεν αὐτοῦ κατὰ τῆς
having broken the alabaster *flask*, she was pouring it down on the
began to pour out over His

κεφαλῆς.
head.

4 Ἦσαν δέ τινες ἀγανακτοῦντες πρὸς ἑαυτοὺς καὶ
[3]were [1]But [2]some expressing indignation to themselves and
one another

λέγοντες, "Εἰς τί ἡ ἀπώλεια αὕτη τοῦ μύρου
saying, "To what *purpose* - [3]waste [2]this [4]of [5]the [6]perfume

γέγονεν? 5 Ἠδύνατο γὰρ τοῦτο πραθῆναι ἐπάνω
[1]has [7]occurred? [2]it [3]was [4]possible [1]For *for* this to be sold for more than

τριακοσίων δηναρίων καὶ δοθῆναι τοῖς πτωχοῖς." Καὶ
three hundred denarii and to be given to the poor." And

ἐνεβριμῶντο αὐτῇ.
they were scolding her.

6 Ὁ δὲ Ἰησοῦς εἶπεν, "Ἄφετε αὐτήν. Τί αὐτῇ
- But Jesus said, "Leave alone ˜ her. Why [4]her

κόπους παρέχετε? Καλὸν ἔργον εἰργάσατο ἐν ἐμοί.
[5]troubles [1]are [2]you [3]causing? [8]a [9]good [10]work [6]She [7]worked in Me.
beautiful has worked for

7 Πάντοτε γὰρ τοὺς πτωχοὺς ἔχετε μεθ' ἑαυτῶν, καὶ
[3]always [1]For [5]the [6]poor [2]you [4]have with yourselves, and
you,

ὅταν θέλητε δύνασθε αὐτοὺς εὖ ποιῆσαι, ἐμὲ δὲ οὐ
whenever you wish you are able [3]them [4]good [1]to [2]do, [11]Me [5]but [8]not

πάντοτε ἔχετε. 8 Ὃ ἔσχεν αὕτη ἐποίησε.
[9]always [6]you [7]do [10]have. What she had this *woman* did.
could

Προέλαβε μυρίσαι μου τὸ σῶμα εἰς τὸν
She undertook beforehand to anoint My - body for -

ἐνταφιασμόν. 9 Ἀμὴν δὲ λέγω ὑμῖν, ὅπου ἐὰν κηρυχθῇ
burial. amen ˜ And I say to you, where ever [3]is [4]proclaimed
assuredly

τὸ εὐαγγέλιον τοῦτο εἰς ὅλον τὸν κόσμον, καὶ ὃ ἐποίησεν
- [2]gospel [1]this to whole ˜ the world, [6]also [1]what [4]did
in

αὕτη λαληθήσεται εἰς μνημόσυνον αὐτῆς."
[2]this [3]*woman* [5]will be spoken of as a memorial of her."

Judas Agrees to Betray Jesus for Money
(Matt. 26:14–16; Luke 22:3–6)

10 Καὶ ὁ Ἰούδας ὁ Ἰσκαριώτης, εἷς τῶν δώδεκα, ἀπῆλθε
And - Judas - Iscariot, one of the twelve, went off

πρὸς τοὺς ἀρχιερεῖς ἵνα παραδῷ αὐτὸν αὐτοῖς.
to the chief priests so that he might hand over ˜ Him to them.
betray

11 Οἱ δὲ ἀκούσαντες ἐχάρησαν καὶ ἐπηγγείλαντο
[2]the [3]*ones* [1]And hearing they were glad and promised
And when they heard,

αὐτῷ ἀργύριον δοῦναι. Καὶ ἐζήτει πῶς
[3]him [4]money [1]to [2]give. And he was seeking how

εὐκαίρως αὐτὸν παραδῷ.
[6]conveniently [4]Him [1]he [2]might [3]hand [5]over.
at some convenient time betray.

Jesus Celebrates Passover with His Disciples
(Matt. 26:17–25; Luke 22:7–12, 21–23; John 13:21–30)

12 Καὶ τῇ πρώτῃ ἡμέρᾳ τῶν ἀζύμων, ὅτε τὸ
And on the first day - of Unleavened Bread, when the

Πάσχα ἔθυον, λέγουσιν αὐτῷ οἱ μαθηταὶ αὐτοῦ,
Passover was sacrificed, [3]say [4]to [5]Him - [2]disciples [1]His,
Paschal Lamb said

"Ποῦ θέλεις ἀπελθόντες ἑτοιμάσομεν ἵνα φάγῃς τὸ
"Where do You desire going away we shall prepare that You may eat the
that we go and prepare

Πάσχα?"
Passover?"

13 Καὶ ἀποστέλλει δύο τῶν μαθητῶν αὐτοῦ καὶ λέγει
And He sends two - of disciple ˜ His and says
sent said

αὐτοῖς, "Ὑπάγετε εἰς τὴν πόλιν, καὶ ἀπαντήσει ὑμῖν
to them, "Go into the city, and [3]will [4]meet [5]you

ἄνθρωπος κεράμιον ὕδατος βαστάζων· ἀκολουθήσατε αὐτῷ.
[1]a [2]man [7]a [8]jar [9]of [10]water [6]carrying; follow him.

14 Καὶ ὅπου ἐὰν εἰσέλθῃ εἴπατε τῷ οἰκοδεσπότῃ ὅτι
And where ever he goes in say to the master of the house -

'Ὁ διδάσκαλος λέγει, "Ποῦ ἐστι τὸ κατάλυμα ὅπου τὸ
'The teacher says, "Where is the guest room where [4]the

Πάσχα μετὰ τῶν μαθητῶν μου φάγω?"' 15 Καὶ αὐτὸς
[5]Passover [6]with - [8]disciples [7]My [1]I [2]may [3]eat?"' And he

ὑμῖν δείξει ἀνώγεον μέγα ἐστρωμένον ἕτοιμον· ἐκεῖ
[3]you [1]will [2]show [4]a(n) [6]upper [7]room [5]large spread *and* ready; there
furnished

ἑτοιμάσατε ἡμῖν." 16 Καὶ ἐξῆλθον οἱ μαθηταὶ αὐτοῦ καὶ
prepare for us." And [3]went [4]out - [2]disciples [1]His and

ἦλθον εἰς τὴν πόλιν καὶ εὗρον καθὼς εἶπεν αὐτοῖς, καὶ
came into the city and found *it* just as He said to them, and

ἡτοίμασαν τὸ Πάσχα.
they prepared the Passover.

17 Καὶ ὀψίας γενομένης ἔρχεται μετὰ τῶν δώδεκα. 18 Καὶ
And evening becoming He comes with the twelve. And
when it was evening, He came

ἀνακειμένων αὐτῶν καὶ ἐσθιόντων, εἶπεν ὁ Ἰησοῦς,
reclining them and eating, said ˜ - Jesus,
while they were reclining

"Ἀμὴν λέγω ὑμῖν ὅτι εἷς ἐξ ὑμῶν παραδώσει με, ὁ
"Amen I say to you that one of you will hand over ˜ Me, the *one*
"Assuredly betray

ἐσθίων μετ' ἐμοῦ."
eating with Me."

priests to betray Him to them.
11 And when they heard *it,*
they were glad, and promised
to give him money. So he
sought how he might conve-
niently betray Him.
12 Now on the first day of Unleavened Bread, when they
killed the Passover *lamb,* His
disciples said to Him, "Where
do You want us to go and prepare, that You may eat the
Passover?"
13 And He sent out two of His
disciples and said to them, "Go
into the city, and a man will
meet you carrying a pitcher of
water; follow him.
14 "Wherever he goes in, say
to the master of the house,
'The Teacher says, "Where is
the guest room in which I may
eat the Passover with My disciples?"'
15 "Then he will show you a
large upper room, furnished
and prepared; there make
ready for us."
16 So His disciples went out,
and came into the city, and
found it just as He had said to
them; and they prepared the
Passover.
17 In the evening He came
with the twelve.
18 Now as they sat and ate,
Jesus said, "Assuredly, I say to
you, one of you who eats with
Me will betray Me."

19 And they began to be sorrowful, and to say to Him one by one, "*Is* it I?" And another *said,* "*Is* it I?"
20 He answered and said to them, "*It is* one of the twelve, who dips with Me in the dish.
21 "The Son of Man indeed goes just as it is written of Him, but woe to that man by whom the Son of Man is betrayed! It would have been good for that man if he had never been born."
22 And as they were eating, Jesus took bread, blessed and broke *it,* and gave *it* to them and said, "Take, eat; this is My body."
23 Then He took the cup, and when He had given thanks He gave *it* to them, and they all drank from it.
24 And He said to them, "This is My blood of the new covenant, which is shed for many.
25 "Assuredly, I say to you, I will no longer drink of the fruit of the vine until that day when I drink it new in the kingdom of God."
26 And when they had sung a hymn, they went out to the Mount of Olives.
27 Then Jesus said to them,

---

[a](14:19) NU omits this last sentence.
[b](14:22) NU omits φαγετε, *eat.* [c](14:24) NU omits καινης, *new.*

---

*(14:24) διαθήκη (*diathēkē*). Noun meaning *last will and testament* (as apparently in Heb. 9:16, 17; Gal. 3:15), but in the NT usually a *covenant.* The usage in the NT has been influenced by the LXX, although there is disagreement among some NT interpreters whether to translate the word as "testament" or "covenant." Such a covenant is not a compact made by equal parties but a declaration of God's will; He alone prescribes the conditions. A covenant relationship between God and His people includes defined structure and observances (as in Acts 7:8). Both OT and NT refer to the "new" covenant established by Jesus, spoken of here in Mark 14:24 (cf. Heb. 8:8–13) as

19 Οἱ δὲ ἤρξαντο λυπεῖσθαι καὶ λέγειν αὐτῷ εἷς
[2]the [3]*ones* [1]And began to be sorrowful and to say to Him one
they

καθ' εἷς, "Μήτι ἐγώ?"
by one, "*Surely* not I?"

Καὶ[a] ἄλλος, "Μήτι ἐγώ?"
And another, "*Surely* not I?"

20 Ὁ δὲ ἀποκριθεὶς εἶπεν αὐτοῖς, "Εἷς ἐκ τῶν δώδεκα,
- But answering He said to them, "One of the twelve,

ὁ ἐμβαπτόμενος μετ' ἐμοῦ εἰς τὸ τρύβλιον. 21 Ὁ μὲν
the *one* dipping with Me in the bowl. the ~ Indeed

Υἱὸς τοῦ Ἀνθρώπου ὑπάγει καθὼς γέγραπται περὶ αὐτοῦ,
Son - of Man is going away just as it is written about Him,

οὐαὶ δὲ τῷ ἀνθρώπῳ ἐκείνῳ δι' οὗ ὁ Υἱὸς τοῦ
woe ~ but - to man ~ that through whom the Son -

Ἀνθρώπου παραδίδοται! Καλὸν ἦν αὐτῷ εἰ οὐκ ἐγεννήθη
of Man is handed over! good It was for him if not was born
betrayed! It would have been better for that man

ὁ ἄνθρωπος ἐκεῖνος."
- man that."
not to have been born."

Jesus Institutes the Lord's Supper

(Matt. 26:26–30; Luke 22:15–20; 1 Cor. 11:23–25)

22 Καὶ ἐσθιόντων αὐτῶν, λαβὼν ὁ Ἰησοῦς ἄρτον,
And eating them, taking - Jesus bread,
as they were eating, Jesus took bread, blessed

εὐλογήσας ἔκλασε καὶ ἔδωκεν αὐτοῖς καὶ εἶπε, "Λάβετε,
blessing *it* broke *it* and gave to them and said, "Take,
it and

φάγετε,[b] τοῦτό ἐστι τὸ σῶμά μου." 23 Καὶ λαβὼν τὸ
eat, this is - body ~ My." And taking the
He took

ποτήριον εὐχαριστήσας ἔδωκεν αὐτοῖς, καὶ ἔπιον ἐξ
cup giving thanks He gave *it* to them, and they [2]drank [3]from
gave thanks and

αὐτοῦ πάντες. 24 Καὶ εἶπεν αὐτοῖς, "Τοῦτό ἐστι τὸ αἷμά μου,
[4]it [1]all. And He said to them, "This is - blood ~ My,

τὸ τῆς καινῆς[c] διαθήκης,* τὸ περὶ πολλῶν
the *blood* of the new covenant, the *blood* [3]for [4]many
which

ἐκχυνόμενον. 25 Ἀμὴν λέγω ὑμῖν ὅτι οὐκέτι οὐ μὴ
[1]being [2]shed. Amen I say to you that no longer not not
is shed. Assuredly by any means

πίω ἐκ τοῦ γενήματος τῆς ἀμπέλου ἕως τῆς ἡμέρας
will I drink from the fruit of the vine until - day ~

ἐκείνης ὅταν αὐτὸ πίνω καινὸν ἐν τῇ βασιλείᾳ τοῦ Θεοῦ."
that when [3]it [1]I [2]drink new in the kingdom - of God."

26 Καὶ ὑμνήσαντες ἐξῆλθον εἰς τὸ Ὄρος τῶν
And having sung hymns they went out to the Mount -

Ἐλαιῶν.
of Olives.

Jesus Predicts Peter's Denial

(Matt. 26:31–35; Luke 22:31–34; John 13:36–38)

27 Καὶ λέγει αὐτοῖς ὁ Ἰησοῦς ὅτι "Πάντες
And [2]says [3]to [4]them - [1]Jesus - "all ~
said

σκανδαλισθήσεσθε ἐν[d] ἐμοὶ ἐν τῇ νυκτὶ ταύτῃ, ὅτι
You will be made to stumble in Me on - night ˜ this, because
because of

γέγραπται,
it is written,

«Πατάξω τὸν Ποιμένα,
«I will strike the Shepherd,

Καὶ διασκορπισθήσεται τὰ πρόβατα.»[e]
And [3]will [4]be [5]scattered [1]the [2]sheep.»

28 Ἀλλὰ μετὰ τὸ ἐγερθῆναί με προάξω ὑμᾶς εἰς τὴν
But after the to be raised Me I will go before you to -
I am raised,

Γαλιλαίαν."
Galilee."

29 Ὁ δὲ Πέτρος ἔφη αὐτῷ, "Καὶ εἰ πάντες
- But Peter said to Him, "Even if all

σκανδαλισθήσονται, ἀλλ' οὐκ ἐγώ."
will be made to stumble, yet not I."

30 Καὶ λέγει αὐτῷ ὁ Ἰησοῦς, "Ἀμὴν λέγω σοι, ὅτι σύ,
And [2]says [3]to [4]him - [1]Jesus, "Amen I say to you, that you,
said "Assuredly

σήμερον ἐν τῇ νυκτὶ ταύτῃ πρὶν ἢ δὶς ἀλέκτορα φωνῆσαι
today on - night ˜ this before [5]twice [1]a [2]rooster [3]to [4]sound
crows

τρίς ἀπαρνήσῃ με."
three times you will deny Me."

31 Ὁ δὲ ἐκ περισσοῦ ἔλεγε μᾶλλον, "Ἐάν
- But [4]of [5]excess [1]he [2]was [3]saying rather, "If
profusely all the more,

με δέῃ συναποθανεῖν σοι, οὐ μή σε
[5]me [1]it [2]is [3]necessary [4]*for* to die with You, not not [4]You
by no means

ἀπαρνήσωμαι." Ὡσαύτως δὲ καὶ πάντες ἔλεγον.
[1]will [2]I [3]deny." likewise ˜ And also all ˜ they said.

"All of you will be made to stumble because of Me this night, for it is written:

'I will strike the Shepherd,
And the sheep will be
scattered.'

28 "But after I have been raised, I will go before you to Galilee."
29 Peter said to Him, "Even if all are made to stumble, yet I *will* not *be.*"
30 Jesus said to him, "Assuredly, I say to you that today, *even* this night, before the rooster crows twice, you will deny Me three times."
31 But he spoke more vehemently, "If I have to die with You, I will not deny You!" And they all said likewise.
32 Then they came to a place which was named Gethsemane; and He said to His disciples, "Sit here while I pray."
33 And He took Peter, James, and John with Him, and He began to be troubled and deeply distressed.
34 Then He said to them, "My soul is exceedingly sorrowful, *even* to death. Stay here and watch."
35 He went a little farther, and fell on the ground, and

Jesus Prays in the Garden of Gethsemane
(Matt. 26:36–46; Luke 22:39–46)

32 Καὶ ἔρχονται εἰς χωρίον οὗ τὸ ὄνομα Γεθσημανῆ,
And they come to a place of which the name Gethsemane,
came which was named

καὶ λέγει τοῖς μαθηταῖς αὐτοῦ, "Καθίσατε ὧδε ἕως
and He says - to disciples ˜ His, "Sit here while
said

προσεύξωμαι." 33 Καὶ παραλαμβάνει τὸν Πέτρον καὶ Ἰάκωβον
I pray." And He takes along - Peter and James
took

καὶ Ἰωάννην μεθ' ἑαυτοῦ, καὶ ἤρξατο ἐκθαμβεῖσθαι* καὶ
and John with Himself, and He began to be alarmed and
Him,

ἀδημονεῖν. 34 Καὶ λέγει αὐτοῖς, "Περίλυπός ἐστιν ἡ
to be distressed. And He says to them, "[4]deeply [5]grieved [3]is -
said

ψυχή μου ἕως θανάτου. Μείνατε ὧδε καὶ γρηγορεῖτε."
[2]soul [1]My unto death. Stay here and watch."
to the point of

35 Καὶ προσελθὼν μικρὸν ἔπεσεν ἐπὶ τῆς γῆς, καὶ
And approaching *God* a little *way* He fell on the ground, and

---

[d](14:27) NU omits *εν εμοι εν τη νυκτι ταυτη, because of me on this night.*
[e](14:27) Zech. 13:7

put in force by the shedding of Jesus' blood, thus replacing the "old" (Mosaic) covenant.

***(14:33)** *ἐκθαμβέω (ekthambeō).* Verb occurring only in the passive in the NT, meaning *astound greatly.* It is more emphatic than simple *θαμβέω* (*astound;* cf. the relationship of meanings between the more common synonyms *θαυμάζω, marvel; ἐκθαυμάζω, marvel greatly*). The word may imply either positive (*be astounded,* Mark 9:15) or negative results (*be alarmed,* here in 14:33; 16:5f). Cf. the cognate adjective *ἔκθαμβος* (*utterly astonished,* Acts 3:11).

prayed that if it were possible,
the hour might pass from Him.
36 And He said, "Abba, Father, all things *are* possible for
You. Take this cup away from
Me; nevertheless, not what I
will, but what You *will.*"
37 Then He came and found
them sleeping, and said to Peter, "Simon, are you sleeping?
Could you not watch one hour?
38 "Watch and pray, lest you
enter into temptation. The
spirit indeed *is* willing, but the
flesh *is* weak."
39 Again He went away and
prayed, and spoke the same
words.
40 And when He returned, He
found them asleep again, for
their eyes were heavy; and
they did not know what to answer Him.
41 Then He came the third
time and said to them, "Are you
still sleeping and resting? It is
enough! The hour has come;
behold, the Son of Man is being
betrayed into the hands of sinners.
42 "Rise, let us be going. See,
My betrayer is at hand."
43 And immediately, while He
was still speaking, Judas, one of
the twelve, with a great multitude with swords and clubs,
came from the chief priests and
the scribes and the elders.
44 Now His betrayer had
given them a signal, saying,

προσηύχετο ἵνα, εἰ δυνατόν ἐστι, παρέλθῃ ἀπ' αὐτοῦ ἡ
He was praying that, if [3]possible [1]it [2]is, [6]might [7]pass [8]from [9]Him [4]the
were,

ὥρα. **36** *Καὶ ἔλεγεν, "Ἀββὰ ὁ Πατήρ, πάντα δυνατά*
[5]hour. And He said, "Abba - Father, all *things are* possible

σοι. Παρένεγκε τὸ ποτήριον ἀπ' ἐμοῦ τοῦτο· ἀλλ' οὐ τί
for You. Take away - [2]cup [3]from [4]Me [1]this; but not what

ἐγὼ θέλω ἀλλὰ τί σύ." **37** *Καὶ ἔρχεται καὶ εὑρίσκει*
I will but what You *will.*" And He comes and finds
came found

αὐτοὺς καθεύδοντας, καὶ λέγει τῷ Πέτρῳ, "Σίμων,
them sleeping, and He says - to Peter, "Simon,
said

καθεύδεις; Οὐκ ἴσχυσας μίαν ὥραν
are you sleeping? [3]not [1]Were [2]you strong *enough* [3]one [4]hour

γρηγορῆσαι; **38** *Γρηγορεῖτε καὶ προσεύχεσθε, ἵνα μὴ*
[1]to [2]watch? Watch and pray, that not
lest

εἰσέλθητε εἰς πειρασμόν. Τὸ μὲν πνεῦμα πρόθυμον, ἡ δὲ
you enter into temptation. the ~ Indeed spirit *is* eager, the ~ but

σὰρξ ἀσθενής." **39** *Καὶ πάλιν ἀπελθὼν προσηύξατο, τὸν*
flesh *is* weak." And again going away He prayed, [2]the
He went away again and

αὐτὸν λόγον εἰπών. **40** *Καὶ ὑποστρέψας εὗρεν αὐτοὺς*
[3]same [4]word [1]saying. And returning He found them
thing when He returned,

πάλιν καθεύδοντας, ἦσαν γὰρ οἱ ὀφθαλμοὶ αὐτῶν βεβαρημένοι,
again sleeping, [4]were [1]for - [3]eyes [2]their weighed down,

καὶ οὐκ ᾔδεισαν τί αὐτῷ ἀποκριθῶσι. **41** *Καὶ*
and [3]not [1]they [2]did know what [4]Him [1]they [2]should [3]answer. And

ἔρχεται τὸ τρίτον καὶ λέγει αὐτοῖς, "Καθεύδετε
He comes the third *time* and says to them, "Sleep on
came said

λοιπὸν καὶ ἀναπαύεσθε. Ἀπέχει· ἦλθεν ἡ
for the remainder and rest. It is enough: [3]came [1]the
now has come

ὥρα· ἰδού, παραδίδοται ὁ Υἱὸς τοῦ Ἀνθρώπου εἰς τὰς
[2]hour; behold, [5]is [6]being [7]handed [8]over [1]the [2]Son - [3]of [4]Man into the
betrayed

χεῖρας τῶν ἁμαρτωλῶν. **42** *Ἐγείρεσθε, ἄγωμεν. Ἰδού,*
hands - of sinners. Rise up, let us be going. See,

ὁ παραδιδούς με ἤγγικε."
the *one* handing over ~ Me has come near."
who betrays

Jesus Is Betrayed and Arrested in Gethsemane
(Matt. 26:47–56; Luke 22:47–53; John 18:2–12)

43 *Καὶ εὐθέως, ἔτι αὐτοῦ λαλοῦντος, παραγίνεται*
And immediately, still Him speaking, arrives ~
while He was still arrived

Ἰούδας, εἷς ὢν τῶν δώδεκα, καὶ μετ' αὐτοῦ ὄχλος πολὺς
Judas, one ~ being of the twelve, and with him a crowd ~ large

μετὰ μαχαιρῶν καὶ ξύλων παρὰ τῶν ἀρχιερέων καὶ τῶν
with swords and clubs *sent* from the chief priests and the

γραμματέων καὶ τῶν πρεσβυτέρων.
scribes and the elders.

44 *Δεδώκει δὲ ὁ παραδιδοὺς αὐτὸν σύσσημον*
[7]had [8]given [1]Now [2]the [3]*one* [4]handing [6]over [5]Him a signal
betraying

αὐτοῖς, λέγων, "Ὃν ἂν φιλήσω, αὐτός ἐστι· κρατήσατε
to them, saying, "Whom ever I shall kiss, He is *the One*; seize

αὐτὸν καὶ ἀπαγάγετε ἀσφαλῶς." 45 Καὶ ἐλθών, εὐθέως
Him and lead *Him* away safely." And coming, immediately
when he arrived,

προσελθὼν αὐτῷ, λέγει αὐτῷ, "Ῥαββί, ῥαββί!" καὶ
coming to Him, he says to Him, "Rabbi, Rabbi!" and
immediately he approached Him and said

κατεφίλησεν αὐτόν. 46 Οἱ δὲ ἐπέβαλον ἐπ' αὐτὸν
he affectionately kissed Him. [2]the [3]*ones* [1]And laid [3]on [4]Him
they

τὰς χεῖρας αὐτῶν καὶ ἐκράτησαν αὐτόν. 47 Εἷς δέ τις
- [2]hands [1]their and seized Him. [4]one [1]But [2]a [3]certain

τῶν παρεστηκότων σπασάμενος τὴν μάχαιραν ἔπαισε
of the *ones* standing by drawing the sword struck
drew his sword and struck

τὸν δοῦλον τοῦ ἀρχιερέως καὶ ἀφεῖλεν αὐτοῦ τὸ ὠτίον.
the slave of the high priest and cut off his - ear.

48 Καὶ ἀποκριθεὶς ὁ Ἰησοῦς εἶπεν αὐτοῖς, "Ὡς ἐπὶ
And answering - Jesus said to them, "As against

λῃστὴν ἐξήλθετε μετὰ μαχαιρῶν καὶ ξύλων συλλαβεῖν
a bandit did you come out with swords and clubs to arrest

με? 49 Καθ' ἡμέραν ἤμην πρὸς ὑμᾶς ἐν τῷ ἱερῷ
Me? According to a day I was with you in the temple
Daily

διδάσκων καὶ οὐκ ἐκρατήσατέ με· ἀλλ' ἵνα πληρωθῶσιν αἱ
teaching and [3]not [1]you [2]did seize Me; but that [3]may [4]be [5]fulfilled [1]the

Γραφαί." 50 Καὶ ἀφέντες αὐτὸν πάντες ἔφυγον.
[2]Scriptures." And leaving Him all ~ they fled.
they all forsook Him and fled.

A Young Man Flees

51 Καὶ εἷς τις νεανίσκος ἠκολούθησεν αὐτῷ
And one certain young man followed Him
had followed

περιβεβλημένος σινδόνα ἐπὶ γυμνοῦ. Καὶ
with [4]having [5]been [6]thrown [7]around [1]a [2]linen [3]cloth on *his* naked *body*. And
wrapped

κρατοῦσιν αὐτὸν οἱ νεανίσκοι, 52 ὁ δὲ καταλιπὼν τὴν
[4]seize [5]him [1]the [2]young [3]men, - but leaving behind the
seized

σινδόνα γυμνὸς ἔφυγεν ἀπ' αὐτῶν.
linen cloth [3]naked [1]he [2]fled from them.

Jesus Before the Sanhedrin

(Matt. 26:57–68; Luke 22:54, 55, 63–71; John 18:19–24)

53 Καὶ ἀπήγαγον τὸν Ἰησοῦν πρὸς τὸν ἀρχιερέα, καὶ
And they led away ~ - Jesus to the high priest, and

συνέρχονται αὐτῷ πάντες οἱ ἀρχιερεῖς καὶ οἱ
there come together with him all the chief priests and the
assembled

πρεσβύτεροι* καὶ οἱ γραμματεῖς. 54 Καὶ ὁ Πέτρος ἀπὸ
elders and the scribes. And - Peter from

μακρόθεν ἠκολούθησεν αὐτῷ ἕως ἔσω εἰς τὴν αὐλὴν
a distance followed Him to *a point* within in the courtyard
right into

τοῦ ἀρχιερέως, καὶ ἦν συγκαθήμενος μετὰ τῶν ὑπηρετῶν
of the high priest, and he was sitting together with the attendants

"Whomever I kiss, He is the One; seize Him and lead *Him* away safely."
45 As soon as He had come, immediately he went up to Him and said to Him, "Rabbi, Rabbi!" and kissed Him.
46 Then they laid their hands on Him and took Him.
47 And one of those who stood by drew his sword and struck the servant of the high priest, and cut off his ear.
48 Then Jesus answered and said to them, "Have you come out, as against a robber, with swords and clubs to take Me?
49 "I was daily with you in the temple teaching, and you did not seize Me. But the Scriptures must be fulfilled."
50 Then they all forsook Him and fled.
51 Now a certain young man followed Him, having a linen cloth thrown around *his* naked *body*. And the young men laid hold of him,
52 and he left the linen cloth and fled from them naked.
53 And they led Jesus away to the high priest; and with him were assembled all the chief priests, the elders, and the scribes.
54 But Peter followed Him at a distance, right into the courtyard of the high priest. And he sat with the servants and

***(14:53)** πρεσβύτερος *(presbyteros)*. Adjective meaning *older, elder,* which may be used merely of age (as Luke 15:25 for the "older" brother) or substantivally of the office of *elder*. In the NT elders had leadership responsibility in local Jewish synagogues and in the Sanhedrin (as here), as well as in the early Christian congregations (as Acts 14:23; 20:17)—perhaps modeled after the synagogues. How closely this πρεσβύτερος equated to the church's ἐπίσκοπος, *bishop* (cf. Titus 1:5, 7), or ποιμήν, *pastor,* is debated, as is the precise import of the 24 "elders" in Rev. 4:4, etc. The title obviously carries great dignity in 2 John 1; 3 John 1. Cf. the cognate nouns πρεσβυτέριον, *council of elders* (Acts 22:5; 1 Tim. 4:14) and πρεσβύτης, *old man* (Philem. 9).

warmed himself at the fire.
55 Now the chief priests and all the council sought testimony against Jesus to put Him to death, but found none.
56 For many bore false witness against Him, but their testimonies did not agree.
57 Then some rose up and bore false witness against Him, saying,
58 "We heard Him say, 'I will destroy this temple made with hands, and within three days I will build another made without hands.'"
59 But not even then did their testimony agree.
60 And the high priest stood up in the midst and asked Jesus, saying, "Do You answer nothing? What *is it* these men testify against You?"
61 But He kept silent and answered nothing. Again the high priest asked Him, saying to Him, "Are You the Christ, the Son of the Blessed?"
62 Jesus said, "I am. And you will see the Son of Man sitting at the right hand of the Power, and coming with the clouds of heaven."
63 Then the high priest tore his clothes and said, "What further need do we have of witnesses?
64 "You have heard the blasphemy! What do you think?" And they all condemned Him to be deserving of death.
65 Then some began to spit on Him, and to blindfold Him,

καὶ θερμαινόμενος πρὸς τὸ φῶς. **55** Οἱ δὲ ἀρχιερεῖς καὶ
and warming himself at the light. the ˜ And chief priests and
fire.

ὅλον τὸ συνέδριον ἐζήτουν κατὰ τοῦ Ἰησοῦ μαρτυρίαν εἰς
whole ˜ the council were seeking against - Jesus testimony for
in

τὸ θανατῶσαι αὐτόν, καὶ οὐχ εὕρισκον.
- [1]to [2]put [4]to [5]death [3]Him, and [3]not [1]they [2]were finding *it*.
order

56 Πολλοὶ γὰρ ἐψευδομαρτύρουν κατ' αὐτοῦ, καὶ ἴσαι
many ˜ For were testifying falsely against Him, and [5]the [6]same

αἱ μαρτυρίαι οὐκ ἦσαν.
[1]the [2]testimonies [4]not [3]were.

57 Καί τινες ἀναστάντες ἐψευδομαρτύρουν κατ' αὐτοῦ,
And some standing up were testifying falsely against Him,
stood up and

λέγοντες **58** ὅτι "Ἡμεῖς ἠκούσαμεν αὐτοῦ λέγοντος ὅτι 'Ἐγὼ
saying - "We heard Him saying - 'I

καταλύσω τὸν ναὸν τοῦτον τὸν χειροποίητον καὶ διὰ τριῶν
will destroy - temple ˜ this - made with hands and after three

ἡμερῶν ἄλλον ἀχειροποίητον οἰκοδομήσω.'" **59** Καὶ
days another *one* not made with hands I will build.'" And

οὐδὲ οὕτως ἴση ἦν ἡ μαρτυρία αὐτῶν.
not even thus [4]the [5]same [1]was - [3]testimony [2]their.
in this way

60 Καὶ ἀναστὰς ὁ ἀρχιερεὺς εἰς μέσον ἐπηρώτησε
And standing up the high priest in *the* midst questioned
the high priest stood up and came forward and

τὸν Ἰησοῦν, λέγων, "Οὐκ ἀποκρίνῃ οὐδέν? Τί οὗτοί
- Jesus, saying, "[3]not [1]Do [2]You answer nothing? What [2]these [3]*men*
anything?

σου καταμαρτυροῦσιν?" **61** Ὁ δὲ ἐσιώπα καὶ οὐδὲν
[6]You [1]are [4]testifying [5]against?" - But He kept silent and nothing ˜

ἀπεκρίνατο. Πάλιν ὁ ἀρχιερεὺς ἐπηρώτα αὐτὸν καὶ λέγει
answered. Again the high priest was questioning Him and says
said

αὐτῷ, "Σὺ εἶ ὁ Χριστός, ὁ Υἱὸς τοῦ Εὐλογητοῦ?"
to Him, "You ˜ Are the Christ, the Son of the Blessed *One*?"
Messiah,

62 Ὁ δὲ Ἰησοῦς εἶπεν, "Ἐγώ εἰμι, καὶ ὄψεσθε τὸν Υἱὸν
- And Jesus said, "I am, and you will see the Son

τοῦ Ἀνθρώπου ἐκ δεξιῶν καθήμενον τῆς Δυνάμεως καὶ
- of Man [2]at [3]*the* [4]right [5]*parts* [1]sitting of the Power and
hand

ἐρχόμενον μετὰ τῶν νεφελῶν τοῦ οὐρανοῦ."
coming with the clouds - of heaven."

63 Ὁ δὲ ἀρχιερεὺς διαρρήξας τοὺς χιτῶνας αὐτοῦ λέγει,
the ˜ And high priest tearing - clothes ˜ his says,
said,

"Τί ἔτι χρείαν ἔχομεν μαρτύρων? **64** Ἠκούσατε τῆς
"What [4]still [1]need [2]do [3]we have of witnesses? You heard the

βλασφημίας! Τί ὑμῖν φαίνεται?"
blasphemy! What [4]to [5]you [1]does [2]it [3]appear?"
How

Οἱ δὲ πάντες κατέκριναν αὐτὸν εἶναι ἔνοχον
[2]the [3]*ones* [1]And all condemned Him to be deserving
they

θανάτου. **65** Καὶ ἤρξαντό τινες ἐμπτύειν αὐτῷ καὶ
of death. And began ˜ some to spit on Him and

περικαλύπτειν τὸ πρόσωπον αὐτοῦ καὶ κολαφίζειν
to cover - face ˜ His and to beat [2]with [3]*their* [4]fists

αὐτὸν καὶ λέγειν αὐτῷ, "Προφήτευσον!" Καὶ οἱ ὑπηρέται
[1]Him and to say to Him, "Prophesy!" And the attendants

ῥαπίσμασιν αὐτὸν ἔβαλλον.[f]
[5]with [6]slaps [7]*to* [8]*the* [9]*face* [4]Him [1]were [2]hurling [3]at.
striking.

Peter Denies Jesus and Weeps Bitterly
(Matt. 26:69–75; Luke 22:54–62; John 18:15–18, 25–27)

66 Καὶ ὄντος τοῦ Πέτρου ἐν τῇ αὐλῇ κάτω, ἔρχεται
And being - Peter in the courtyard below, *there* comes
while Peter was came

μία τῶν παιδισκῶν τοῦ ἀρχιερέως. **67** Καὶ ἰδοῦσα τὸν
one of the servant girls of the high priest. And seeing -
when she saw

Πέτρον θερμαινόμενον, ἐμβλέψασα αὐτῷ λέγει, "Καὶ σὺ
Peter warming himself, looking at him she says, "also ˜ You
she looked at and said,

μετὰ τοῦ Ναζαρηνοῦ Ἰησοῦ ἦσθα."
[2]with [4]the [5]Nazarene [3]Jesus [1]were."

68 Ὁ δὲ ἠρνήσατο, λέγων, "Οὐκ οἶδα οὔτε
[2]the [3]*one* [1]But denied *it*, saying, "[3]not [1]I [2]do know nor
he

ἐπίσταμαι τί σὺ λέγεις." Καὶ ἐξῆλθεν ἔξω εἰς τὸ
do I understand what you are saying." And he went out outside into the

προαύλιον, καὶ[g] ἀλέκτωρ ἐφώνησε.
forecourt, and a rooster sounded.
crowed.

69 Καὶ ἡ παιδίσκη ἰδοῦσα αὐτὸν πάλιν ἤρξατο λέγειν
And the servant girl seeing him again began to say
when she saw

τοῖς παρεστηκόσιν ὅτι "Οὗτος ἐξ αὐτῶν ἐστιν."
to the *ones* standing by - "This *man* [2]*one* [3]of [4]them [1]is."
those who were

70 Ὁ δὲ πάλιν ἠρνεῖτο.
- But again he was denying *it*.

Καὶ μετὰ μικρὸν πάλιν οἱ παρεστῶτες ἔλεγον τῷ
And after a little again the *ones* standing by said -
those who were

Πέτρῳ, "Ἀληθῶς ἐξ αὐτῶν εἶ, καὶ γὰρ Γαλιλαῖος
to Peter, "Truly [3]*one* [4]of [5]them [1]you [2]are, [9]also [6]for [10]a [11]Galilean

εἶ, καὶ[h] ἡ λαλιά σου ὁμοιάζει."
[7]you [8]are, and - speech ˜ your is like *theirs*."
accent

71 Ὁ δὲ ἤρξατο ἀναθεματίζειν καὶ ὀμνύναι ὅτι "Οὐκ
[2]the [3]*one* [1]But began to curse and to swear - "[3]not
he

οἶδα τὸν ἄνθρωπον τοῦτον ὃν λέγετε." **72** Καὶ
[1]I [2]do know - man ˜ this whom you are speaking of." And

ἐκ δευτέρου ἀλέκτωρ ἐφώνησε. Καὶ ἀνεμνήσθη ὁ Πέτρος τὸ
of a second *time* a rooster sounded. And remembered ˜ - Peter the
for the crowed.

ῥῆμα ὃ εἶπεν αὐτῷ ὁ Ἰησοῦς ὅτι "Πρὶν ἀλέκτορα
saying which [2]said [3]to [4]him - [1]Jesus - "Before a rooster
had said

φωνῆσαι δίς, ἀπαρνήσῃ με τρίς." Καὶ
to sound twice, you will deny Me three times." And
crows

and to beat Him, and to say to
Him, "Prophesy!" And the officers struck Him with the palms
of their hands.
66 Now as Peter was below in
the courtyard, one of the servant girls of the high priest
came.
67 And when she saw Peter
warming himself, she looked at
him and said, "You also were
with Jesus of Nazareth."
68 But he denied it, saying, "I
neither know nor understand
what you are saying." And he
went out on the porch, and a
rooster crowed.
69 And the servant girl saw
him again, and began to say to
those who stood by, "This is
one of them."
70 But he denied it again. And
a little later those who stood by
said to Peter again, "Surely you
are *one* of them; for you are a
Galilean, and your speech
shows *it*."
71 Then he began to curse
and swear, "I do not know this
Man of whom you speak!"
72 A second time *the* rooster
crowed. Then Peter called to
mind the word that Jesus had
said to him, "Before the
rooster crows twice, you will
deny Me three times." And

[f]**(14:65)** NU reads ελαβον, *received.*
[g]**(14:68)** NU brackets και αλεκτωρ εφωνησε, *and a rooster crowed.*
[h]**(14:70)** NU omits this last clause.

when he thought about it, he wept.

15 Immediately, in the morning, the chief priests held a consultation with the elders and scribes and the whole council; and they bound Jesus, led *Him* away, and delivered *Him* to Pilate.
2 Then Pilate asked Him, "Are You the King of the Jews?" He answered and said to him, *"It is as* you say."
3 And the chief priests accused Him of many things, but He answered nothing.
4 Then Pilate asked Him again, saying, "Do You answer nothing? See how many things they testify against You!"
5 But Jesus still answered nothing, so that Pilate marveled.
6 Now at the feast he was accustomed to releasing one prisoner to them, whomever they requested.
7 And there was one named Barabbas, *who was* chained with his fellow rebels; they had committed murder in the rebellion.
8 Then the multitude, crying aloud, began to ask *him to do* just as he had always done for them.
9 But Pilate answered them, saying, "Do you want me to release to you the King of the Jews?"
10 For he knew that the chief priests had handed Him over because of envy.

ἐπιβαλὼν ἔκλαιε.
casting upon he was weeping.
when he thought about it, he began to weep.

Jesus Before Pilate
(Matt. 27:1, 2, 11–14; Luke 23:1–5; John 18:28–38)

15 1 Καὶ εὐθέως ἐπὶ τὸ πρωΐ συμβούλιον ποιήσαντες
And immediately in the morning a consultation making
the chief priests, along

οἱ ἀρχιερεῖς μετὰ τῶν πρεσβυτέρων καὶ γραμματέων
the chief priests with the elders and scribes
with the elders and scribes and the whole

καὶ ὅλον τὸ συνέδριον δήσαντες τὸν Ἰησοῦν
and whole ˜ the council having bound - Jesus
Sanhedrin held a consultation,

ἀπήνεγκαν καὶ παρέδωκαν τῷ Πιλάτῳ. 2 Καὶ
they led *Him* away and handed *Him* over - to Pilate. And

ἐπηρώτησεν αὐτὸν ὁ Πιλᾶτος, "Σὺ εἶ ὁ βασιλεὺς τῶν
[2]asked [3]Him - [1]Pilate, "You ˜ Are the king of the

Ἰουδαίων?"
Jews?"

Ὁ δὲ ἀποκριθεὶς εἶπεν αὐτῷ, "Σὺ λέγεις."
[3]the [4]*One* [1]And [2]answering said to him, "You are saying *what is so.*"
He

3 Καὶ κατηγόρουν αὐτοῦ οἱ ἀρχιερεῖς πολλά.
And [4]were [5]accusing [6]Him [1]the [2]chief [3]priests *of* many *things.*

4 Ὁ δὲ Πιλᾶτος πάλιν ἐπηρώτησεν αὐτόν, λέγων, "Οὐκ
- And Pilate again questioned Him, saying, "[3]not

ἀποκρίνῃ οὐδέν? Ἴδε πόσα σου
[1]Do [2]you answer nothing? See how many *things* [4]You
anything?

καταμαρτυροῦσιν."[a] 5 Ὁ δὲ Ἰησοῦς οὐκέτι οὐδὲν
[1]they [2]testify [3]against." - But Jesus no longer nothing ˜
anything ˜

ἀπεκρίθη, ὥστε θαυμάζειν τὸν Πιλᾶτον.
answered, so that to marvel - Pilate.
Pilate was amazed.

Give Us Barabbas
(Matt. 27:15–26; Luke 23:13–25; John 18:39–19:16)

6 Κατὰ δὲ ἑορτὴν ἀπέλυεν αὐτοῖς ἕνα δέσμιον
at ˜ Now a feast he would release to them one prisoner
the

ὅνπερ ᾐτοῦντο. 7 Ἦν δὲ ὁ λεγόμενος
whomever they would request. [2]*there* [3]was [1]And [4]the [5]*one* [6]called

Βαραββᾶς μετὰ τῶν συστασιαστῶν δεδεμένος
[7]Barabbas [11]with [12]the [13]fellow [14]insurrectionists [8]having [9]been [10]bound
his

οἵτινες ἐν τῇ στάσει φόνον πεποιήκεισαν. 8 Καὶ
who in the insurrection [3]murder [1]had [2]committed. And

ἀναβοήσας[b] ὁ ὄχλος ἤρξατο αἰτεῖσθαι καθὼς ἀεὶ
crying out the crowd began to request *that* just as always
the crowd cried out and began

ἐποίει αὐτοῖς. 9 Ὁ δὲ Πιλᾶτος ἀπεκρίθη αὐτοῖς,
he would do *this* for them. - But Pilate answered them,

λέγων, "Θέλετε ἀπολύσω ὑμῖν τὸν βασιλέα τῶν
saying, "Do you desire *that* I release to you the king of the

Ἰουδαίων?" 10 Ἐγίνωσκε γὰρ ὅτι διὰ φθόνον
Jews?" [2]he [3]knew [1]For that because of envy

---

[a](15:4) NU reads κατηγορουσιν, *they accuse (you) of.* [b](15:8) NU reads αναβας, *going up.*

παραδεδώκεισαν αὐτὸν οἱ ἀρχιερεῖς. 11 Οἱ δὲ ἀρχιερεῖς
4had 5handed 7over 6Him 1the 2chief 3priests. the ~ But chief priests

ἀνέσεισαν τὸν ὄχλον ἵνα μᾶλλον τὸν Βαραββᾶν
stirred up the crowd so that 3rather - 5Barabbas

ἀπολύσῃ αὐτοῖς. 12 Ὁ δὲ Πιλᾶτος ἀποκριθεὶς πάλιν
1he 2should 4release to them. - But Pilate answering again
answered and

εἶπεν αὐτοῖς, "Τί οὖν θέλετε ποιήσω
said to them, "What then do you desire *that* I should do

ὃν[c] λέγετε βασιλέα τῶν Ἰουδαίων?"
with the One whom you call king of the Jews?"

13 Οἱ δὲ πάλιν ἔκραξαν, "Σταύρωσον αὐτόν!"
3the 4*ones* 1And 2again cried, "Crucify Him!"
they

14 Ὁ δὲ Πιλᾶτος ἔλεγεν αὐτοῖς, "Τί γὰρ κακὸν
- But Pilate said to them, "what ~ For evil
But

ἐποίησεν?"
did He do?"

Οἱ δὲ περισσοτέρως ἔκραξαν, "Σταύρωσον αὐτόν!"
2the 3*ones* 1And more abundantly cried out, "Crucify Him!"
they

15 Ὁ δὲ Πιλᾶτος βουλόμενος τῷ ὄχλῳ τὸ
- And Pilate willing 6for 7the 8crowd 3the 5*thing*
because he willed to do what

ἱκανὸν ποιῆσαι ἀπέλυσεν αὐτοῖς τὸν Βαραββᾶν, καὶ
4satisfactory 1to 2do released to them - Barabbas, and
would gratify the crowd

παρέδωκε τὸν Ἰησοῦν, φραγελλώσας, ἵνα
handed over - Jesus, flogging, so that
after he had Him flogged,

σταυρωθῇ.
He might be crucified.

The Soldiers Mock Jesus
(Matt. 27:27–31; John 19:2, 3)

16 Οἱ δὲ στρατιῶται ἀπήγαγον αὐτὸν ἔσω τῆς αὐλῆς,
the ~ And soldiers led away ~ Him into the courtyard,

ὅ ἐστι Πραιτώριον, καὶ συγκαλοῦσιν ὅλην τὴν σπεῖραν.
which is *the* Praetorium, and call together whole ~ the cohort.
assembled garrison.

17 Καὶ ἐνδύουσιν αὐτὸν πορφύραν καὶ περιτιθέασιν
And they clothe with ~ Him purple and 6they 7put 8*it* 9around
clothed

αὐτῷ πλέξαντες ἀκάνθινον στέφανον,* 18 καὶ ἤρξαντο
10Him 1having 2plaited 3a 4thorny 5crown, and they began
His head

ἀσπάζεσθαι αὐτόν, "Χαῖρε, ὁ βασιλεὺς τῶν Ἰουδαίων!"
to salute Him, "Rejoice, - king of the Jews!"
"Hail,

19 Καὶ ἔτυπτον αὐτοῦ τὴν κεφαλὴν καλάμῳ καὶ
And they were striking His - head with a reed and

ἐνέπτυον αὐτῷ, καὶ τιθέντες τὰ γόνατα προσεκύνουν
were spitting on Him, and placing the knees they would worship
kneeling down

αὐτῷ. 20 Καὶ ὅτε ἐνέπαιξαν αὐτῷ, ἐξέδυσαν αὐτὸν τὴν
Him. And when they mocked Him, they stripped Him *of* the
had mocked

11 But the chief priests stirred up the crowd, so that he should rather release Barabbas to them.
12 Pilate answered and said to them again, "What then do you want me to do *with Him* whom you call the King of the Jews?"
13 So they cried out again, "Crucify Him!"
14 Then Pilate said to them, "Why, what evil has He done?" But they cried out all the more, "Crucify Him!"
15 So Pilate, wanting to gratify the crowd, released Barabbas to them; and he delivered Jesus, after he had scourged *Him,* to be crucified.
16 Then the soldiers led Him away into the hall called Praetorium, and they called together the whole garrison.
17 And they clothed Him with purple; and they twisted a crown of thorns, put it on His *head,*
18 and began to salute Him, "Hail, King of the Jews!"
19 Then they struck Him on the head with a reed and spat on Him; and bowing the knee, they worshiped Him.
20 And when they had mocked Him, they took the

[c](15:12) NU brackets ον λεγετε, *(Him) whom you call.*

***(15:17)** στέφανος *(stephanos).* Noun meaning *garland, crown, wreath,* generally distinguished from the διάδημα, the *diadem* or *royal crown* (as Rev. 19:12). The στέφανος is usually identified with the victor's festal crown, which might be worn by a triumphant athlete or general, by someone honored, or even by royalty at a festive celebration (cf. Rev. 14:14). It was typically woven from any of various kinds of plants, which may explain its use here in Mark 15:17, even though the soldiers meant it as mockery of Jesus' kingship. See the cognate verb στεφανόω, *to crown,* Heb. 2:9.

purple off Him, put His own
clothes on Him, and led Him
out to crucify Him.
21 Then they compelled a certain man, Simon a Cyrenian,
the father of Alexander and Rufus, as he was coming out of the
country and passing by, to bear
His cross.
22 And they brought Him to
the place Golgotha, which is
translated, Place of a Skull.
23 Then they gave Him wine
mingled with myrrh to drink,
but He did not take *it.*
24 And when they crucified
Him, they divided His garments, casting lots for them to
determine what every man
should take.
25 Now it was the third hour,
and they crucified Him.
26 And the inscription of His
accusation was written above:

THE KING OF THE JEWS.

27 With Him they also crucified two robbers, one on His
right and the other on His left.
28 So the Scripture was fulfilled which says, *"And He was
numbered with the transgressors."*
29 And those who passed by
blasphemed Him, wagging their
heads and saying, "Aha! *You*
who destroy the temple and
build *it* in three days,
30 "save Yourself, and come
down from the cross!"
31 Likewise the chief priests
also, mocking among them-

πορφύραν καὶ ἐνέδυσαν αὐτὸν τὰ ἱμάτια τὰ ἴδια. Καὶ
purple and dressed in ˜ Him - [3]clothing - [1]His [2]own. And

ἐξάγουσιν αὐτὸν ἵνα σταυρώσωσιν αὐτόν.
they lead out ˜ Him so that they might crucify Him.
led

Jesus Is Crucified

(Matt. 27:32–44; Luke 23:26–43; John 19:17–27)

21 Καὶ ἀγγαρεύουσι παράγοντά τινα Σίμωνα
And they press into service [4]passing [5]by [1]a [2]certain [3]*man* Simon
pressed

Κυρηναῖον ἐρχόμενον ἀπ' ἀγροῦ, τὸν πατέρα
a Cyrenian *as he was* coming from *the* country, the father

Ἀλεξάνδρου καὶ Ῥούφου, ἵνα ἄρῃ τὸν σταυρὸν αὐτοῦ.
of Alexander and of Rufus, that he might carry - cross ˜ His.

22 Καὶ φέρουσιν αὐτὸν ἐπὶ Γολγοθᾶ τόπον, ὅ ἐστι
And they bring Him to [3]Golgotha [1]*the* [2]place, which is
brought

μεθερμηνευόμενον, "Κρανίου Τόπος." 23 Καὶ ἐδίδουν
being translated, "[2]of [3]a [4]Skull [1]Place." And they were giving
means,

αὐτῷ πιεῖν ἐσμυρνισμένον οἶνον, ὁ δὲ οὐκ ἔλαβε.
Him [5]to [6]drink [2]mixed [3]with [4]myrrh [1]wine, - but [3]not [1]He [2]did take *it.*

24 Καὶ σταυρώσαντες αὐτὸν διαμερίζονται τὰ ἱμάτια αὐτοῦ
And having crucified Him they divide - clothes ˜ His
divided

βάλλοντες κλῆρον ἐπ' αὐτὰ τίς τί ἄρῃ.
by casting *the* lot over them *to determine* who [3]what [1]would [2]take.

25 Ἦν δὲ ὥρα τρίτη καὶ ἐσταύρωσαν αὐτόν. 26 Καὶ
[2]it [3]was [1]Now [6]hour [4]*the* [5]third and they crucified Him. And
when

ἦν ἡ ἐπιγραφὴ τῆς αἰτίας αὐτοῦ ἐπιγεγραμμένη·
there was the inscription - of charge ˜ His having been inscribed:
crime which had

Ο ΒΑΣΙΛΕΥΣ ΤΩΝ ΙΟΥΔΑΙΩΝ
THE KING OF THE JEWS

27 Καὶ σὺν αὐτῷ σταυροῦσι δύο λῃστάς, ἕνα ἐκ
And together with Him they crucify two bandits, one at
crucified on

δεξιῶν καὶ ἕνα ἐξ εὐωνύμων αὐτοῦ. 28 Καὶ[d] ἐπληρώθη
the right *parts* and one at [2]left [3]*parts* [1]His. And [3]was [4]fulfilled
the right side on left side

ἡ Γραφὴ ἡ λέγουσα, «Καὶ μετὰ ἀνόμων
[1]the [2]Scripture the *one* saying, «And with lawless *ones*
which says, outlaws

ἐλογίσθη.»[e]
He was classed.»

29 Καὶ οἱ παραπορευόμενοι ἐβλασφήμουν αὐτὸν
And the *ones* passing by were blaspheming Him

κινοῦντες τὰς κεφαλὰς αὐτῶν καὶ λέγοντες, "Οὐά,
shaking - heads ˜ their and saying, "Aha,

ὁ καταλύων τὸν ναὸν καὶ ἐν τρισὶν ἡμέραις
You are the *One* destroying the temple and in three days

οἰκοδομῶν, 30 σῶσον σεαυτὸν καὶ κατάβα ἀπὸ τοῦ σταυροῦ!"
building *it,* save Yourself and come down from the cross!"
rebuilding

31 Ὁμοίως καὶ οἱ ἀρχιερεῖς ἐμπαίζοντες πρὸς ἀλλήλους
Likewise also the chief priests mocking *Him* to each other

---

[d](**15:28**) NU omits this verse. [e](**15:28**) Is. 53:12

μετὰ τῶν γραμματέων ἔλεγον, "Ἄλλους ἔσωσεν, ἑαυτὸν
along with the scribes said, "Others He saved, Himself

οὐ δύναται σῶσαι. 32 Ὁ Χριστὸς ὁ βασιλεὺς τοῦ
[3]not [1]He [2]is able to save. [2]the [3]Christ [4]the [5]king -
Messiah

Ἰσραὴλ καταβάτω νῦν ἀπὸ τοῦ σταυροῦ, ἵνα ἴδωμεν
[6]of [7]Israel [1]Let come down now from the cross, so that we may see

καὶ πιστεύσωμεν αὐτῷ."[f] Καὶ οἱ συνεσταυρωμένοι
and may believe Him." And the *ones* having been crucified with
those who were

αὐτῷ ὠνείδιζον αὐτόν.
Him were reviling Him.

Jesus Dies on the Cross
(Matt. 27:45–56; Luke 23:44–49; John 19:28–30)

33 Γενομένης δὲ ὥρας ἕκτης, σκότος ἐγένετο ἐφ'
becoming Now hour *the* sixth, darkness came upon
Now when the sixth hour had come,

ὅλην τὴν γῆν ἕως ὥρας ἐνάτης. 34 Καὶ τῇ ὥρᾳ τῇ ἐνάτῃ
whole ~ the land until [3]hour [1]*the* [2]ninth. And - at [3]hour [1]the [2]ninth

ἐβόησεν ὁ Ἰησοῦς φωνῇ μεγάλῃ, λέγων, "«Ἐλωΐ, Ἐλωΐ,
[5]cried [6]out - [4]Jesus with a voice ~ great, saying, "«Eloi, Eloi,
loud,

λιμᾶ σαβαχθανί?»"* ὅ ἐστι μεθερμηνευόμενον, «Ὁ Θεός
lima sabachthani?»" which is being translated, - «God ~
means,

μου, ὁ Θεός μου, εἰς τί με ἐγκατέλιπες?»[g]
My, - God ~ My, for what [4]Me [1]did [2]You [3]forsake?»
why

35 Καί τινες τῶν παρεστηκότων ἀκούσαντες ἔλεγον,
And some of the *ones* standing by hearing *this* said,
when they heard

"Ἰδού, Ἠλίαν φωνεῖ."
"Look, [4]Elijah [1]He [2]is [3]calling."

36 Δραμὼν δέ εἷς καὶ γεμίσας σπόγγον ὄξους,
[3]running [1]And [2]one and having filled a sponge *with* vinegar,
ran filled

περιθεὶς τε καλάμῳ, ἐπότιζεν αὐτόν, λέγων,
[2]having [3]put [4]*it* [5]around [1]and a reed, was giving a drink *to* Him, saying,

"Ἄφετε, ἴδωμεν εἰ ἔρχεται Ἠλίας καθελεῖν αὐτόν."
"Leave *Him* alone, let us see if [2]is [3]coming [1]Elijah to take down ~ Him."

37 Ὁ δὲ Ἰησοῦς ἀφεὶς φωνὴν μεγάλην ἐξέπνευσε. 38 Καὶ
- But Jesus releasing a voice ~ great expired. And
uttering a loud cry

τὸ καταπέτασμα τοῦ ναοῦ ἐσχίσθη εἰς δύο ἀπὸ ἄνωθεν
the veil of the sanctuary was split in two from above
top

ἕως κάτω.
to bottom.

39 Ἰδὼν δὲ ὁ κεντυρίων ὁ παρεστηκὼς ἐξ
[11]seeing [1]Now [2]the [3]centurion [4]the [5]*one* [6]standing [7]by [8]from
Now when the centurion who stood across from

ἐναντίας αὐτοῦ ὅτι οὕτω κράξας[h] ἐξέπνευσεν, εἶπεν,
[9]opposite [10]Him that thus crying out He expired, said,
Him saw He cried out and breathed His last in this way, he said,

"Ἀληθῶς ὁ ἄνθρωπος οὗτος Υἱὸς ἦν Θεοῦ."
"Truly - man ~ this [2]*the* [3]Son [1]was of God."

40 Ἦσαν δὲ καὶ γυναῖκες ἀπὸ μακρόθεν θεωροῦσαι,
[2]*there* [3]were [1]Now also women [2]from [3]a [4]distance [1]observing,

selves with the scribes, said,
"He saved others; Himself He
cannot save.
32 "Let the Christ, the King
of Israel, descend now from the
cross, that we may see and believe." Even those who were
crucified with Him reviled Him.
33 Now when the sixth hour
had come, there was darkness
over the whole land until the
ninth hour.
34 And at the ninth hour Jesus
cried out with a loud voice, saying, "Eloi, Eloi, lama sabachthani?" which is translated,
*"My God, My God, why have
You forsaken Me?"*
35 Some of those who stood
by, when they heard *that,* said,
"Look, He is calling for Elijah!"
36 Then someone ran and
filled a sponge full of sour wine,
put *it* on a reed, and offered *it*
to Him to drink, saying, "Let
Him alone; let us see if Elijah
will come to take Him down."
37 And Jesus cried out with a
loud voice, and breathed His
last.
38 Then the veil of the temple
was torn in two from top to bottom.
39 So when the centurion,
who stood opposite Him, saw
that He cried out like this and
breathed His last, he said,
"Truly this Man was the Son of
God!"
40 There were also women
looking on from afar, among

[f](15:32) NU,TR omit *αυτω, Him.* [g](15:34) Ps. 22:1
[h](15:39) NU omits *κραξας, crying out.*

*(15:34) *σαβαχθανί (sabachthani).* Aramaic verb, occuring only here and in the parallel at Matt. 27:46 (accented *σαβαχθάνι*). *σαβαχθανί* transliterates into Greek letters the Aramaic equivalent of the Hebrew *'azabtani, You have forsaken Me* (Ps. 22:1).

whom were Mary Magdalene,
Mary the mother of James the
Less and of Joses, and Salome,
41 who also followed Him and
ministered to Him when He
was in Galilee, and many other
women who came up with Him
to Jerusalem.
42 Now when evening had
come, because it was the Preparation Day, that is, the day before the Sabbath,
43 Joseph of Arimathea, a
prominent council member,
who was himself waiting for the
kingdom of God, coming and
taking courage, went in to Pilate and asked for the body of
Jesus.
44 Pilate marveled that He
was already dead; and summoning the centurion, he asked him
if He had been dead for some
time.
45 So when he found out from
the centurion, he granted the
body to Joseph.
46 Then he bought fine linen,
took Him down, and wrapped
Him in the linen. And he laid
Him in a tomb which had been
hewn out of the rock, and rolled
a stone against the door of the
tomb.
47 And Mary Magdalene and
Mary *the mother* of Joses observed where He was laid.
16 Now when the Sabbath
was past, Mary Mag-
dalene, Mary *the mother* of
James, and Salome bought

ἐν αἷς ἦν καὶ Μαρία ἡ Μαγδαληνὴ καὶ Μαρία ἡ τοῦ
among whom were both Mary - Magdalene and Mary the -

Ἰακώβου τοῦ μικροῦ καὶ Ἰωσῆ μήτηρ καὶ Σαλώμη, 41 αἳ
[2]of [3]James [4]the [5]little [6]and [7]of [8]Joses [1]mother and Salome, who
younger

καὶ ὅτε ἦν ἐν τῇ Γαλιλαίᾳ ἠκολούθουν αὐτῷ καὶ
also when He was in - Galilee would follow Him and

διηκόνουν αὐτῷ, καὶ ἄλλαι πολλαὶ αἱ
would minister to Him, and [2]other [3]*women* [1]many the *ones*
who had

συναναβᾶσαι αὐτῷ εἰς Ἱεροσόλυμα.
coming up together with Him to Jerusalem.
come

Jesus Is Buried in Joseph's Tomb

(Matt. 27:57–61; Luke 23:50–56; John 19:38–42)

42 Καὶ ἤδη ὀψίας γενομένης, ἐπεὶ ἦν Παρασκευή,
And now evening having come, since it was Preparation *Day,*

ὅ ἐστι προσάββατον, 43 ἦλθεν Ἰωσὴφ ὁ ἀπὸ
which is *the day* before the Sabbath, *there* came Joseph - from

Ἀριμαθαίας, εὐσχήμων βουλευτής, ὃς καὶ αὐτὸς ἦν
Arimathea, a prominent council member, who also himself was

προσδεχόμενος τὴν βασιλείαν τοῦ Θεοῦ, τολμήσας εἰσῆλθε
waiting for the kingdom - of God, taking courage he went in

πρὸς Πιλᾶτον καὶ ᾐτήσατο τὸ σῶμα τοῦ Ἰησοῦ. 44 Ὁ δὲ
to Pilate and asked for the body - of Jesus. - And

Πιλᾶτος ἐθαύμασεν εἰ ἤδη τέθνηκε· καὶ
Pilate marveled if [3]already [1]He [2]has died; and
that had

προσκαλεσάμενος τὸν κεντυρίωνα ἐπηρώτησεν αὐτὸν εἰ πάλαι
having summoned the centurion he asked him if [4]long

ἀπέθανε. 45 Καὶ γνοὺς ἀπὸ τοῦ κεντυρίωνος
[1]He [2]was [3]dead. And knowing from the centurion
had been when he found out

ἐδωρήσατο τὸ σῶμα τῷ Ἰωσήφ. 46 Καὶ ἀγοράσας σινδόνα
he granted the body - to Joseph. And having bought a linen cloth

καὶ καθελὼν αὐτὸν ἐνείλησε τῇ σινδόνι καὶ
and [1]having [2]taken [4]down [3]Him he wrapped *Him* in the linen cloth and

κατέθηκεν αὐτὸν ἐν μνημείῳ ὃ ἦν λελατομημένον ἐκ
set down ~ Him in a tomb which was having been cut out of
had been cut

πέτρας, καὶ προσεκύλισε λίθον ἐπὶ τὴν θύραν τοῦ μνημείου.
rock, and rolled a stone upon the door of the tomb.

47 Ἡ δὲ Μαρία ἡ Μαγδαληνὴ καὶ Μαρία Ἰωσῆ
- And Mary - Magdalene and Mary *the mother* of Joses

ἐθεώρουν ποῦ τίθεται.
were observing where He is placed.
was

He Is Not Here for He Is Risen

(Matt. 28:1–8; Luke 24:1–12; John 20:1–10)

16 1 Καὶ διαγενομένου τοῦ σαββάτου, Μαρία ἡ
And having passed the Sabbath, Mary -
when the Sabbath was past,

Μαγδαληνὴ καὶ Μαρία Ἰακώβου καὶ Σαλώμη ἠγόρασαν
Magdalene and Mary *the mother* of James and Salome bought

ἀρώματα ἵνα ἐλθοῦσαι ἀλείψωσιν αὐτόν. **2** Καὶ λίαν
spices so that coming they might anoint Him. And very
they might come and anoint

πρωΐ τῆς μιᾶς σαββάτων ἔρχονται ἐπὶ τὸ μνημεῖον,
early of the first *day* of *the* week they come to the tomb,
on came

ἀνατείλαντος τοῦ ἡλίου. **3** Καὶ ἔλεγον πρὸς ἑαυτάς, "Τίς
having risen the sun. And they said to themselves, "Who
when the sun had risen. one another,

ἀποκυλίσει ἡμῖν τὸν λίθον ἐκ τῆς θύρας τοῦ μνημείου?"
will roll away for us the stone from the door of the tomb?"

4 Καὶ ἀναβλέψασαι θεωροῦσιν ὅτι ἀποκεκύλισται ὁ
And looking up they see that [3]had [4]been [5]rolled [6]away [1]the
when they looked up, they saw

λίθος — ἦν γὰρ μέγας σφόδρα. **5** Καὶ εἰσελθοῦσαι
[2]stone — [8]it [9]was [7]for [11]great [10]exceedingly. And entering
large when they entered

εἰς τὸ μνημεῖον εἶδον νεανίσκον καθήμενον ἐν τοῖς δεξιοῖς
into the tomb they saw a young man sitting on the right *parts*
side

περιβεβλημένον στολὴν λευκήν, καὶ ἐξεθαμβήθησαν.
clothed with a robe ˜ white, and they were alarmed.

6 Ὁ δὲ λέγει αὐταῖς, "Μὴ ἐκθαμβεῖσθε. Ἰησοῦν
[2]the [3]*one* [1]But says to them, "not ˜ Do be alarmed. [4]Jesus
he said

ζητεῖτε τὸν Ναζαρηνὸν τὸν ἐσταυρωμένον.
[1]You [2]are [3]seeking the Nazarene the *One* having been crucified.
who was crucified.

Ἠγέρθη! Οὐκ ἔστιν ὧδε! Ἴδε, ὁ τόπος ὅπου ἔθηκαν
He was raised! [3]not [1]He [2]is here! See, the place where they put
He has arisen!

αὐτόν. **7** Ἀλλ' ὑπάγετε εἴπατε τοῖς μαθηταῖς αὐτοῦ καὶ τῷ
Him. But go tell - disciples ˜ His and -

Πέτρῳ ὅτι 'Προάγει ὑμᾶς εἰς τὴν Γαλιλαίαν· ἐκεῖ αὐτὸν
Peter - 'He is going before you into - Galilee; there [4]Him

ὄψεσθε, καθὼς εἶπεν ὑμῖν.' " **8** Καὶ ἐξελθοῦσαι[a] ἔφυγον
[1]you [2]will [3]see, just as He said to you.'" And going out they fled

ἀπὸ τοῦ μνημείου, εἶχε δὲ αὐτὰς τρόμος καὶ ἔκστασις· καὶ
from the tomb, [5]held [1]but [6]them [2]trembling [3]and [4]amazement; and

οὐδενὶ οὐδὲν εἶπον, ἐφοβοῦντο γάρ.
[4]to [5]no [6]one [3]nothing [1]they [2]said, [8]they [9]were [10]afraid [7]for.
anyone

Jesus Appears to Mary Magdalene
(Matt. 28:9, 10; John 20:11–18)

9 Ἀναστὰς[b] δὲ πρωῒ πρώτῃ σαββάτου ἐφάνη
[2]having [3]arisen [1]Now early on *the* first *day* of *the* week He appeared

πρῶτον Μαρίᾳ τῇ Μαγδαληνῇ, ἀφ' ἧς ἐκβεβλήκει ἑπτὰ
first to Mary - Magdalene, from whom He had cast out seven

δαιμόνια. **10** Ἐκείνη πορευθεῖσα ἀπήγγειλε τοῖς μετ'
demons. That *one* going reported to the *ones* [3]with
She went and those who

αὐτοῦ γενομένοις, πενθοῦσι καὶ κλαίουσι. **11** Κἀκεῖνοι
[4]Him [1]having [2]been, mourning and weeping. And those
had been, as they were mourning

ἀκούσαντες ὅτι ζῇ καὶ ἐθεάθη ὑπ' αὐτῆς ἠπίστησαν.
hearing that He lives and was seen by her disbelieved.
when they heard was alive had been

spices, that they might come
and anoint Him.
2 Very early in the morning,
on the first *day* of the week,
they came to the tomb when
the sun had risen.
3 And they said among themselves, "Who will roll away the
stone from the door of the tomb
for us?"
4 But when they looked up,
they saw that the stone had
been rolled away—for it was
very large.
5 And entering the tomb,
they saw a young man clothed
in a long white robe sitting on
the right side; and they were
alarmed.
6 But he said to them, "Do
not be alarmed. You seek Jesus
of Nazareth, who was crucified.
He is risen! He is not here. See
the place where they laid Him.
7 "But go, tell His disciples
—and Peter—that He is going
before you into Galilee; there
you will see Him, as He said to
you."
8 So they went out quickly
and fled from the tomb, for they
trembled and were amazed.
And they said nothing to anyone, for they were afraid.
9 Now when *He* rose early
on the first *day* of the week, He
appeared first to Mary Magdalene, out of whom He had cast
seven demons.
10 She went and told those
who had been with Him, as
they mourned and wept.
11 And when they heard that
He was alive and had been seen
by her, they did not believe.

[a](**16:8**) TR adds *ταχυ, quickly.*
[b](**16:9–20**) NU brackets vv. 9–20 as not original.

12 After that, He appeared in
another form to two of them as
they walked and went into the
country.
13 And they went and told *it*
to the rest, *but* they did not believe them either.
14 Later He appeared to the
eleven as they sat at the table;
and He rebuked their unbelief
and hardness of heart, because
they did not believe those who
had seen Him after He had
risen.
15 And He said to them, "Go
into all the world and preach the
gospel to every creature.
16 "He who believes and is
baptized will be saved; but he
who does not believe will be
condemned.
17 "And these signs will follow
those who believe: In My name
they will cast out demons; they
will speak with new tongues;
18 "they will take up serpents; and if they drink anything deadly, it will by no means
hurt them; they will lay hands
on the sick, and they will recover."
19 So then, after the Lord had
spoken to them, He was received up into heaven, and sat

Jesus Appears to Two Disciples
(Luke 24:13–35)

12 Μετὰ δὲ ταῦτα δυσὶν ἐξ αὐτῶν περιπατοῦσιν
after ˜ Now these *things* to two of them walking
as they were walking

ἐφανερώθη ἐν ἑτέρᾳ μορφῇ, πορευομένοις εἰς ἀγρόν.
He appeared in a different form, going into *the* country.
as they were going

13 Κἀκεῖνοι ἀπελθόντες ἀπήγγειλαν τοῖς λοιποῖς· οὐδὲ
And those going back reported to the rest; neither
returned and

ἐκείνοις ἐπίστευσαν.
[4]those [1]did [2]they [3]believe.
them

The Great Commission
(Matt. 28:16–20; Luke 24:36–49; John 20:19–23; Acts 1:6–8)

14 Ὕστερον ἀνακειμένοις αὐτοῖς τοῖς ἕνδεκα
Later reclining *to eat* them [3]to [4]the [5]eleven
as they were reclining at the table

ἐφανερώθη· καὶ ὠνείδισε τὴν ἀπιστίαν αὐτῶν καὶ
[1]He [2]appeared; and He reproved - disbelief ˜ their and

σκληροκαρδίαν ὅτι τοῖς θεασαμένοις αὐτὸν
hard-heartedness because the *ones* seeing Him
those who saw Him after

ἐγηγερμένον οὐκ ἐπίστευσαν. **15** Καὶ εἶπεν αὐτοῖς,
having been raised not ˜ did believe. And He said to them,
He had been raised

"Πορευθέντες εἰς τὸν κόσμον ἅπαντα κηρύξατε τὸ εὐαγγέλιον
"Going into [2]the [3]world [1]all proclaim the gospel
"When you go

πάσῃ τῇ κτίσει. **16** Ὁ πιστεύσας καὶ βαπτισθεὶς
to all - creation. The *one* believing and being baptized
He who believes is

σωθήσεται, ὁ δὲ ἀπιστήσας κατακριθήσεται.
will be saved, [2]the [3]*one* [1]but disbelieving will be condemned.
he who disbelieves

17 Σημεῖα δὲ τοῖς πιστεύσασι ταῦτα παρακολουθήσει· ἐν
[3]signs [1]And [6]the [7]*ones* [8]believing [2]these [4]will [5]accompany; in
those who have believed

τῷ ὀνόματί μου δαιμόνια ἐκβαλοῦσι, γλώσσαις
- name ˜ My [5]demons [1]they [2]will [3]cast [4]out, [9]with [11]tongues

λαλήσουσι καιναῖς, **18** ὄφεις[c] ἀροῦσι, κἂν
[6]they [7]will [8]speak [10]new, [5]serpents [1]they [2]will [3]pick [4]up, and if

θανάσιμόν τι πίωσιν οὐ μὴ αὐτοὺς βλάψῃ, ἐπὶ
[4]deadly [5]*thing* [3]any [1]they [2]drink not not [4]them [1]will [2]it [3]hurt, [9]on
by no means

ἀρρώστους χεῖρας ἐπιθήσουσι καὶ καλῶς ἕξουσιν."
[10]sick [11]*people* [8]hands [5]they [6]will [7]lay and well they shall have."
they will be well."

The Lord Ascends to God's Right Hand
(Luke 24:50–53; Acts 1:9–11)

19 Ὁ μὲν οὖν Κύριος, μετὰ τὸ λαλῆσαι αὐτοῖς,
[3]the [1]So [2]then Lord, after - to speak to them,
He had spoken

ἀνελήφθη εἰς τὸν οὐρανὸν καὶ ἐκάθισεν ἐκ δεξιῶν τοῦ
was taken up into - heaven and sat down at *the* right *parts* -
hand

---

[c](16:18) NU adds *και εν ταις χερσιν, and in their hands.*

Θεοῦ. 20 Ἐκεῖνοι δὲ ἐξελθόντες ἐκήρυξαν πανταχοῦ, τοῦ
of God. those ˜ But going out preached everywhere, the
they went out and

Κυρίου συνεργοῦντος καὶ τὸν λόγον βεβαιοῦντος* διὰ τῶν
Lord working with *them* and [2]the [3]word [1]confirming through the
message by

ἐπακολουθούντων σημείων. Ἀμήν.
following upon signs. Amen.
accompanying So be it.

down at the right hand of God.
20 And they went out and preached everywhere, the Lord working with *them* and confirming the word through the accompanying signs. Amen.

*(16:20) βεβαιόω *(bebaioō).* Verb, literally meaning *make firm, establish.* In the NT this word and its cognates are always used in relationship to the Christian message. The verb is used to speak about both *verifying* the gospel message (Rom. 15:8; 1 Cor. 1:6) and *establishing* or *strengthening* faith in that message (2 Cor 1:21). Thus, here in Mark 16:20 the word may indicate that the "accompanying signs" *confirmed* the validity of the word which the disciples preached, or that the signs caused people *to believe* or *strengthened* their faith. Cf. the cognate noun βέβαιωσις (*verification,* Heb. 6:16, reflecting the legal background of the words) and adjective βέβαιος (*certain, trustworthy,* 2 Pet. 1:10).

The Gospel According to

LUKE

ΚΑΤΑ ΛΟΥΚΑΝ
ACCORDING TO LUKE

1 Inasmuch as many have
taken in hand to set in order a narrative of those things
which have been fulfilled among
us,
2 just as those who from the
beginning were eyewitnesses
and ministers of the word delivered them to us,
3 it seemed good to me also,
having had perfect understanding of all things from the very
first, to write to you an orderly
account, most excellent Theophilus,
4 that you may know the cer-
tainty of those things in which
you were instructed.
5 There was in the days of
Herod, the king of Judea, a certain priest named Zacharias, of
the division of Abijah. His wife
was of the daughters of Aaron,
and her name *was* Elizabeth.
6 And they were both righteous before God, walking in all
the commandments and ordinances of the Lord blameless.
7 But they had no child, because Elizabeth was barren,
and they were both well advanced in years.

Dedication to Theophilus by Luke

1 **1** Ἐπειδήπερ πολλοὶ ἐπεχείρησαν ἀνατάξασθαι διήγησιν
Inasmuch as many took in hand to set in order a narrative
Since have attempted to arrange

περὶ τῶν πεπληροφορημένων ἐν ἡμῖν πραγμάτων, **2** καθὼς
about the [2]having [3]been [4]fulfilled [5]among [6]us [1]things, just as
which have taken place matters,

παρέδοσαν ἡμῖν οἱ ἀπ᾽ ἀρχῆς
[14]delivered [15]*them* [16]to [17]us [1]the [2]*ones* [3]*who* [4]from [5]*the* [6]beginning
those who

αὐτόπται καὶ ὑπηρέται γενόμενοι τοῦ λόγου,
[8]eyewitnesses [9]and [10]servants [7]becoming [11]of [12]the [13]word,
attendants became

3 ἔδοξε κἀμοί, παρηκολουθηκότι ἄνωθεν πᾶσιν
it seemed good also to me, having followed from the first all *things*
investigated

ἀκριβῶς, καθεξῆς σοι γράψαι, κράτιστε Θεόφιλε,
accurately, in orderly fashion [3]to [4]you [1]to [2]write, most excellent Theophilus,
carefully, distinguished

4 ἵνα ἐπιγνῷς περὶ ὧν κατηχήθης λόγων
so that you may know [6]about [7]which [8]you [9]were [10]instructed [3]of [4]*the* [5]words
things

τὴν ἀσφάλειαν.
[1]the [2]certainty.

Gabriel Announces John's Birth to Zacharias

5 Ἐγένετο ἐν ταῖς ἡμέραις Ἡρῴδου τοῦ βασιλέως τῆς
There was in the days of Herod the king -

Ἰουδαίας ἱερεύς τις ὀνόματι Ζαχαρίας, ἐξ ἐφημερίας
of Judea a priest ˜ certain by name Zacharias, of *the* division
named

Ἀβιά. Καὶ ἡ γυνὴ αὐτοῦ ἐκ τῶν θυγατέρων Ἀαρών, καὶ τὸ
of Abijah. And - wife ˜ his *was* of the daughters of Aaron, and -

ὄνομα αὐτῆς Ἐλισάβετ. **6** Ἦσαν δὲ δίκαιοι ἀμφότεροι
name ˜ her *was* Elizabeth. [2]they [3]were [1]And [5]righteous [4]both

ἐνώπιον τοῦ Θεοῦ, πορευόμενοι ἐν πάσαις ταῖς ἐντολαῖς
before - God, going in all the commandments
walking

καὶ δικαιώμασι τοῦ Κυρίου ἄμεμπτοι. **7** Καὶ οὐκ ἦν
and righteous deeds of the Lord blameless. And [3]not [1]*there* [2]was
requirements they had no

αὐτοῖς τέκνον, καθότι ἡ Ἐλισάβετ ἦν στεῖρα, καὶ ἀμφότεροι
to them a child, because - Elizabeth was barren, and both
children,

προβεβηκότες ἐν ταῖς ἡμέραις αὐτῶν ἦσαν.
[2]advanced [3]in - [5]days [4]their [1]were.
years

8 Ἐγένετο δὲ ἐν τῷ ἱερατεύειν αὐτὸν ἐν τῇ τάξει
[2]it [3]happened [1]Now in - to serve as priest him in the order
while he was serving as priest

τῆς ἐφημερίας αὐτοῦ ἔναντι τοῦ Θεοῦ, 9 κατὰ τὸ ἔθος
- of division ˜ his before - God, according to the custom

τῆς ἱερατείας, ἔλαχε τοῦ θυμιάσαι εἰσελθὼν
of the priesthood, he obtained by lot - to burn incense entering
he was selected when he entered

εἰς τὸν ναὸν τοῦ Κυρίου. 10 Καὶ πᾶν τὸ πλῆθος ἦν
into the sanctuary of the Lord. And all the multitude [4]was

τοῦ λαοῦ προσευχόμενον ἔξω τῇ ὥρᾳ τοῦ θυμιάματος.
[1]of [2]the [3]people praying outside at the hour - of incense.

11 Ὤφθη δὲ αὐτῷ ἄγγελος Κυρίου, ἑστὼς ἐκ
[7]appeared [1]And [8]to [9]him [2]an [3]angel [4]of [5]*the* [6]Lord, standing on
Then

δεξιῶν τοῦ θυσιαστηρίου τοῦ θυμιάματος. 12 Καὶ
the right parts of the altar - of incense. And
side

ἐταράχθη Ζαχαρίας ἰδών, καὶ φόβος ἐπέπεσεν ἐπ'
[2]was [3]troubled [1]Zacharias seeing, and fear fell upon
when he saw him,

αὐτόν.
him.

13 Εἶπε δὲ πρὸς αὐτὸν ὁ ἄγγελος, "Μὴ φοβοῦ,
[4]said [1]But [5]to [6]him [2]the [3]angel, "not ˜ Do be afraid,

Ζαχαρία, διότι εἰσηκούσθη ἡ δέησίς σου, καὶ ἡ γυνή σου
Zacharias, because [3]was [4]heard - [2]prayer [1]your, and - wife ˜ your
has been

Ἐλισάβετ γεννήσει υἱόν σοι, καὶ καλέσεις τὸ ὄνομα αὐτοῦ
Elizabeth will bear a son to you, and you shall call - name ˜ his

Ἰωάννην. 14 Καὶ ἔσται χαρά σοι καὶ ἀγαλλίασις, καὶ
John. And there will be joy to you and exultation, and
you will have joy gladness,

πολλοὶ ἐπὶ τῇ γεννήσει αὐτοῦ χαρήσονται. 15 Ἔσται
many at - birth ˜ his will rejoice. [2]he [3]will [4]be
because of

γὰρ μέγας ἐνώπιον τοῦ Κυρίου, καὶ οἶνον καὶ σίκερα* οὐ
[1]For great before the Lord, and wine and strong drink [3]not
by no

μὴ πίῃ, καὶ Πνεύματος Ἁγίου πλησθήσεται ἔτι
[4]not [1]he [2]shall [5]drink, and [5]of [6]*the* [8]Spirit [7]Holy [1]he [2]will [3]be [4]filled still
means with while

ἐκ κοιλίας μητρὸς αὐτοῦ. 16 Καὶ πολλοὺς τῶν υἱῶν
from *the* womb of mother ˜ his. And many of the sons
still in children

Ἰσραὴλ ἐπιστρέψει ἐπὶ Κύριον τὸν Θεὸν αὐτῶν. 17 Καὶ
of Israel he will turn to *the* Lord - God ˜ their. And

αὐτὸς προελεύσεται ἐνώπιον αὐτοῦ ἐν πνεύματι καὶ δυνάμει
himself ˜ he will go before Him in *the* spirit and power

Ἠλίου, ἐπιστρέψαι καρδίας πατέρων ἐπὶ τέκνα, καὶ
of Elijah, to turn *the* hearts of fathers to children, and

ἀπειθεῖς ἐν φρονήσει δικαίων, ἑτοιμάσαι Κυρίῳ
disobedient *ones* in *the* prudence of righteous *ones*, to prepare for *the* Lord
to

λαὸν κατεσκευασμένον."
a people having been fully prepared."
well equipped."

18 Καὶ εἶπε Ζαχαρίας πρὸς τὸν ἄγγελον, "Κατὰ τί
And said ˜ Zacharias to the angel, "According to what
"How

8 So it was, that while he was serving as priest before God in the order of his division,
9 according to the custom of the priesthood, his lot fell to burn incense when he went into the temple of the Lord.
10 And the whole multitude of the people was praying outside at the hour of incense.
11 Then an angel of the Lord appeared to him, standing on the right side of the altar of incense.
12 And when Zacharias saw *him,* he was troubled, and fear fell upon him.
13 But the angel said to him, "Do not be afraid, Zacharias, for your prayer is heard; and your wife Elizabeth will bear you a son, and you shall call his name John.
14 "And you will have joy and gladness, and many will rejoice at his birth.
15 "For he will be great in the sight of the Lord, and shall drink neither wine nor strong drink. He will also be filled with the Holy Spirit, even from his mother's womb.
16 "And he will turn many of the children of Israel to the Lord their God.
17 "He will also go before Him in the spirit and power of Elijah, *'to turn the hearts of the fathers to the children,'* and the disobedient to the wisdom of the just, to make ready a people prepared for the Lord."
18 And Zacharias said to the angel, "How shall I know this?

***(1:15)** *σίκερα (sikera).* Aramaic noun transliterated into Greek letters and used only here in the NT. The word, meaning *strong drink,* was probably broad enough to refer to almost any alcoholic drink, including wine. However, *σίκερα* is usually distinguished from *οἶνος, wine,* in the LXX, where the two are often mentioned together. Perhaps this word was especially appropriate for those drinks that were more quickly intoxicating.

For I am an old man, and my
wife is well advanced in years."
19 And the angel answered
and said to him, "I am Gabriel,
who stands in the presence of
God, and was sent to speak to
you and bring you these glad
tidings.
20 "But behold, you will be
mute and not able to speak until
the day these things take place,
because you did not believe my
words which will be fulfilled in
their own time."
21 And the people waited for
Zacharias, and marveled that he
lingered so long in the temple.
22 But when he came out, he
could not speak to them; and
they perceived that he had seen
a vision in the temple, for he
beckoned to them and remained
speechless.
23 So it was, as soon as the
days of his service were completed, that he departed to his
own house.
24 Now after those days his
wife Elizabeth conceived; and
she hid herself five months,
saying,
25 "Thus the Lord has dealt
with me, in the days when He
looked on *me,* to take away my
reproach among people."
26 Now in the sixth month the
angel Gabriel was sent by God
to a city of Galilee named Nazareth,
27 to a virgin betrothed to a

γνώσομαι τοῦτο? Ἐγὼ γάρ εἰμι πρεσβύτης καὶ ἡ γυνή μου
shall I know this? I ~ For am an old man and - wife ~ my

προβεβηκυῖα ἐν ταῖς ἡμέραις αὐτῆς."
is advanced in - days ~ her."
years

19 *Καὶ ἀποκριθεὶς ὁ ἄγγελος εἶπεν αὐτῷ, "Ἐγώ εἰμι*
And answering the angel said to him, "I am

Γαβριὴλ ὁ παρεστηκὼς ἐνώπιον τοῦ Θεοῦ, καὶ ἀπεστάλην
Gabriel the *one* standing before - God, and I was sent
who stands

λαλῆσαι πρὸς σὲ, καὶ εὐαγγελίσασθαί σοι ταῦτα.
to speak to you, and to proclaim the good news to you *of* these *things.*

20 *Καὶ ἰδού, ἔσῃ σιωπῶν καὶ μὴ δυνάμενος*
And behold, you will be keeping silent and not being able
mute unable

λαλῆσαι ἄχρι ἧς ἡμέρας γένηται ταῦτα, ἀνθ'
to speak until which day *when* [3]happen [1]these [2]*things,* on account of
the because

ὧν οὐκ ἐπίστευσας τοῖς λόγοις μου, οἵτινες πληρωθήσονται
which [3]not [1]you [2]did believe - words ~ my, which will be fulfilled

εἰς τὸν καιρὸν αὐτῶν."
in - season ~ their."
own time

21 *Καὶ ἦν ὁ λαὸς προσδοκῶν τὸν Ζαχαρίαν, καὶ*
And [3]was [1]the [2]people waiting for - Zacharias, and
were

ἐθαύμαζον ἐν τῷ χρονίζειν αὐτόν ἐν τῷ ναῷ.
they marveled in - to delay him in the sanctuary.
while he was delaying

22 *Ἐξελθὼν δὲ οὐκ ἠδύνατο λαλῆσαι αὐτοῖς· καὶ*
[2]coming [3]out [1]But [6]not [4]he [5]was able to speak to them; and
when he came out

ἐπέγνωσαν ὅτι ὀπτασίαν ἑώρακεν ἐν τῷ ναῷ· καὶ
they perceived that [4]a [5]vision [1]he [2]had [3]seen in the sanctuary; and

αὐτὸς ἦν διανεύων αὐτοῖς, καὶ διέμενε κωφός. **23** *Καὶ*
he was motioning to them, and remained mute. And

ἐγένετο, ὡς ἐπλήσθησαν αἱ ἡμέραι τῆς λειτουργίας αὐτοῦ,
it happened, when [6]were [7]fulfilled [1]the [2]days - [3]of [5]service [4]his,

ἀπῆλθεν εἰς τὸν οἶκον αὐτοῦ.
that he went away to - house ~ his.

24 *Μετὰ δὲ ταύτας τὰς ἡμέρας συνέλαβεν Ἐλισάβετ ἡ*
after ~ Now these - days [4]conceived [1]Elizabeth -

γυνὴ αὐτοῦ καὶ περιέκρυβεν ἑαυτὴν μῆνας πέντε, λέγουσα
[3]wife [2]his and hid herself months ~ five, saying
stayed in seclusion

25 *ὅτι "Οὕτω μοι πεποίηκεν ὁ Κύριος ἐν ἡμέραις αἷς*
- "Thus [5]to [6]me [3]has [4]done [1]the [2]Lord in *the* days in which

ἐπεῖδεν ἀφελεῖν τὸ ὄνειδός μου ἐν ἀνθρώποις."
He looked on *me* to take away - reproach ~ my among men."
people."

Gabriel Announces Christ's Birth to Mary

26 *Ἐν δὲ τῷ μηνὶ τῷ ἕκτῳ ἀπεστάλη ὁ ἄγγελος*
in ~ Now the month ~ - sixth [4]was [5]sent [1]the [2]angel

Γαβριὴλ ὑπὸ τοῦ Θεοῦ εἰς πόλιν τῆς Γαλιλαίας ᾗ
[3]Gabriel by - God to a city - of Galilee to which
named

ὄνομα Ναζαρέτ, **27** *πρὸς παρθένον μεμνηστευμένην*
was a name Nazareth, to a virgin having been betrothed
-

ἀνδρὶ ᾧ ὄνομα Ἰωσήφ, ἐξ οἴκου Δαβίδ. Καὶ τὸ
to a man to whom *was* a name Joseph, of *the* house of David. And the
named

ὄνομα τῆς παρθένου Μαριάμ. 28 Καὶ εἰσελθὼν ὁ
name of the virgin *was* Mary. And having come in the

ἄγγελος πρὸς αὐτὴν εἶπε, "Χαῖρε, κεχαριτωμένη,* ὁ Κύριος
angel [2]to [3]her [1]said, "Rejoice, favored *woman,* the Lord
"Greetings,

μετὰ σου, εὐλογημένη σὺ ἐν γυναιξίν!"[a] 29 Ἡ δὲ
is with you, blessed *are* you among women!" [2]the [3]*one* [1]But
when she

ἰδοῦσα[b] διεταράχθη ἐπὶ τῷ λόγῳ αὐτοῦ, καὶ
seeing she was greatly perplexed at - word ~ his, and
saw him, by message

διελογίζετο ποταπὸς εἴη ὁ ἀσπασμὸς οὗτος. 30 Καὶ
she considered what sort of [3]might [4]be - [1]greeting [2]this. And
wondered was

εἶπεν ὁ ἄγγελος αὐτῇ, "Μὴ φοβοῦ, Μαριάμ, εὗρες
[3]said [1]the [2]angel to her, "not ~ Do be afraid, Mary, [2]you [3]found
have found

γὰρ χάριν παρὰ τῷ Θεῷ. 31 Καὶ ἰδού, συλλήμψῃ ἐν
[1]for favor with - God. And behold, you will conceive in
grace

γαστρὶ καὶ τέξῃ Υἱόν, καὶ καλέσεις τὸ ὄνομα αὐτοῦ
your womb and will bear a Son, and you shall call - name ~ His

Ἰησοῦν. 32 Οὗτος ἔσται μέγας καὶ Υἱὸς Ὑψίστου
Jesus. This *One* will be great and [5]*the* [6]Son [7]of [8]*the* [9]Most [10]High
He

κληθήσεται· καὶ δώσει αὐτῷ Κύριος ὁ Θεὸς τὸν
[1]He [2]will [3]be [4]called; and [4]will [5]give [6]to [7]Him [1]*the* [2]Lord - [3]God the

θρόνον Δαβὶδ τοῦ πατρὸς αὐτοῦ. 33 Καὶ βασιλεύσει ἐπὶ τὸν
throne of David - father ~ His. And He will reign over the

οἶκον Ἰακὼβ εἰς τοὺς αἰῶνας, καὶ τῆς βασιλείας αὐτοῦ οὐκ
house of Jacob to the ages, and - of kingdom ~ His [3]not
forever,

ἔσται τέλος."
[1]*there* [2]will be an end."

34 Εἶπε δὲ Μαριὰμ πρὸς τὸν ἄγγελον, "Πῶς ἔσται
[3]said [1]And [2]Mary to the angel, "How shall be ~
can

τοῦτο, ἐπεὶ ἄνδρα οὐ γινώσκω?"
this, since [5]a [6]man [3]not [1]I [2]do [4]know?"

35 Καὶ ἀποκριθεὶς ὁ ἄγγελος εἶπεν αὐτῇ, "Πνεῦμα
And answering the angel said to her, "*The* Spirit ~

Ἅγιον ἐπελεύσεται ἐπὶ σέ, καὶ δύναμις Ὑψίστου
Holy will come upon you, and power of *the* Most High
from

ἐπισκιάσει σοι· διὸ καὶ τὸ γεννώμενον Ἅγιον
will overshadow you; therefore also the [3]being [4]born [1]Holy [2]*thing*
Holy Baby which is to be born

κληθήσεται Υἱὸς Θεοῦ. 36 Καὶ ἰδού, Ἐλισάβετ ἡ συγγενής
will be called *the* Son of God. And behold, Elizabeth - relative ~

σου, καὶ αὐτὴ συνειληφυῖα[c] υἱὸν ἐν γήρει αὐτῆς, καὶ οὗτος
your, also ~ she having conceived a son in [2]old [3]age [1]her, and this
has

μὴν ἕκτος ἐστὶν αὐτῇ τῇ καλουμένῃ στείρᾳ.
[2]*the* [4]month [3]sixth [1]is for her the *one* being called barren.
she who was

man whose name was Joseph, of the house of David. The virgin's name *was* Mary.
28 And having come in, the angel said to her, "Rejoice, highly favored *one,* the Lord *is* with you; blessed *are* you among women!"
29 But when she saw *him,* she was troubled at his saying, and considered what manner of greeting this was.
30 Then the angel said to her, "Do not be afraid, Mary, for you have found favor with God.
31 "And behold, you will conceive in your womb and bring forth a Son, and shall call His name JESUS.
32 "He will be great, and will be called the Son of the Highest; and the Lord God will give Him the throne of His father David.
33 "And He will reign over the house of Jacob forever, and of His kingdom there will be no end."
34 Then Mary said to the angel, "How can this be, since I do not know a man?"
35 And the angel answered and said to her, "*The* Holy Spirit will come upon you, and the power of the Highest will overshadow you; therefore, also, that Holy One who is to be born will be called the Son of God.
36 "Now indeed, Elizabeth your relative has also conceived a son in her old age; and this is now the sixth month for her who was called barren.

---

[a]**(1:28)** NU omits *ευλογημενη συ εν γυναιξιν, blessed are you among women.* [b]**(1:29)** NU omits *ιδουσα, seeing.* [c]**(1:36)** NU reads *συνειληφεν, conceived.*

***(1:28)** *χαριτόω (charitoō).* Verb meaning *favor, bestow favor or grace on,* from *χάρις, grace.* The form here is passive: Mary has been favored, literally "graced," made the recipient (not the fountain) of grace (cf. v. 30). The only other NT use is in Eph. 1:6: "to the praise of the glory of His grace by which He *graced* (bestowed favor upon) us."

37 "For with God nothing will be impossible."
38 Then Mary said, "Behold the maidservant of the Lord! Let it be to me according to your word." And the angel departed from her.
39 Now Mary arose in those days and went into the hill country with haste, to a city of Judah,
40 and entered the house of Zacharias and greeted Elizabeth.
41 And it happened, when Elizabeth heard the greeting of Mary, that the babe leaped in her womb; and Elizabeth was filled with the Holy Spirit.
42 Then she spoke out with a loud voice and said, "Blessed *are* you among women, and blessed *is* the fruit of your womb!
43 "But why *is* this *granted* to me, that the mother of my Lord should come to me?
44 "For indeed, as soon as the voice of your greeting sounded in my ears, the babe leaped in my womb for joy.
45 "Blessed *is* she who believed, for there will be a fulfillment of those things which were told her from the Lord."
46 And Mary said:

"My soul magnifies the Lord,

37 Ὅτι οὐκ ἀδυνατήσει παρὰ τῷ Θεῷ πᾶν
Because [4]not [3]will [5]be [6]impossible [7]with - [8]God [1]every
nothing will be impossible with God."

ῥῆμα."
[2]word."

38 Εἶπε δὲ Μαριάμ, "Ἰδού, ἡ δούλη Κυρίου·
[3]said [1]And [2]Mary, "Behold, the slave girl of *the* Lord;
maidservant

γένοιτό μοι κατὰ τὸ ῥῆμά σου." Καὶ ἀπῆλθεν ἀπ'
may it be to me according to - word ˜ your." And [3]departed [4]from

αὐτῆς ὁ ἄγγελος.
[5]her [1]the [2]angel.

Mary Visits Elizabeth

39 Ἀναστᾶσα δὲ Μαριὰμ ἐν ταῖς ἡμέραις ταύταις
[3]rising [4]up [1]And [2]Mary in - days ˜ these
Now when Mary rose up

ἐπορεύθη εἰς τὴν ὀρεινὴν μετὰ σπουδῆς, εἰς πόλιν
she traveled into the mountainous *country* with haste, to a city

Ἰούδα, **40** καὶ εἰσῆλθεν εἰς τὸν οἶκον Ζαχαρίου καὶ
of Judah, and she entered into the house of Zacharias and

ἠσπάσατο τὴν Ἐλισάβετ. **41** Καὶ ἐγένετο ὡς ἤκουσεν ἡ
greeted - Elizabeth. And it happened when heard ˜ -

Ἐλισάβετ τὸν ἀσπασμὸν τῆς Μαρίας, ἐσκίρτησε τὸ βρέφος
Elizabeth the greeting - of Mary, [3]skipped [1]the [2]baby
leaped

ἐν τῇ κοιλίᾳ αὐτῆς, καὶ ἐπλήσθη Πνεύματος Ἁγίου ἡ
in - womb ˜ her, and [2]was [3]filled [4]with [5]*the* [7]Spirit [6]Holy -

Ἐλισάβετ.
[1]Elizabeth.

42 Καὶ ἀνεφώνησε φωνῇ μεγάλῃ καὶ εἶπεν,
And she called out with a voice ˜ great and said,
loud

"Εὐλογημένη σὺ ἐν γυναιξί, καὶ εὐλογημένος ὁ Καρπὸς
"Blessed *are* you among women, and blessed *is* the Fruit

τῆς κοιλίας σου! **43** Καὶ πόθεν μοι τοῦτο, ἵνα
- of womb ˜ your! And from where to me *is* this, that
why am I favored thus,

ἔλθῃ ἡ μήτηρ τοῦ Κυρίου μου πρὸς με? **44** Ἰδοὺ
[6]should [7]come [1]the [2]mother - [3]of [5]Lord [4]my to me? behold ˜

γάρ, ὡς ἐγένετο ἡ φωνὴ τοῦ ἀσπασμοῦ σου εἰς τὰ ὦτά
For, when [6]came [1]the [2]voice - [3]of [5]greeting [4]your in - ears ˜
sounded

μου, ἐσκίρτησε τὸ βρέφος ἐν ἀγαλλιάσει ἐν τῇ κοιλίᾳ μου.
my, [3]skipped [1]the [2]baby with exultation in - womb ˜ my.
leaped for joy

45 Καὶ μακαρία ἡ πιστεύσασα, ὅτι ἔσται
And blessed *is* the *woman* believing, because *there* will be
happy she who has believed,

τελείωσις τοῖς λελαλημένοις αὐτῇ παρὰ Κυρίου."
a fulfillment to the *things* having been spoken to her from *the* Lord."

Mary's *Magnificat*

46 Καὶ εἶπεν Μαριάμ,
And said ˜ Mary,

47 "Μεγαλύνει ἡ ψυχή μου τὸν Κύριον,
"[3]magnifies - [2]soul [1]My the Lord,

Καὶ ἠγαλλίασε τὸ πνεῦμά μου ἐπὶ τῷ Θεῷ τῷ
and [3]exulted - [2]spirit [1]my over - God -
has rejoiced because of

Σωτῆρί μου.
Savior ˜ my.

48 Ὅτι ἐπέβλεψεν ἐπὶ τὴν ταπείνωσιν τῆς δούλης
Because He looked upon the lowly state - of [2]slave [3]girl
maidservant

αὐτοῦ·
[1]His;

Ἰδοὺ γάρ, ἀπὸ τοῦ νῦν μακαριοῦσί με πᾶσαι
behold ˜ For, from - now *on* [3]will [4]call [6]blessed [5]me [1]all

αἱ γενεαί.
- [2]generations.

49 Ὅτι ἐποίησέ μοι μεγαλεῖα[d] ὁ Δυνατός,
Because [4]did [7]for [8]me [5]marvelous [6]*things* [1]the [2]Mighty [3]*One,*
has done

Καὶ ἅγιον τὸ ὄνομα αὐτοῦ.
And holy *is* - name ˜ His.

50 Καὶ τὸ ἔλεος αὐτοῦ εἰς γενεὰς γενεῶν
And - mercy ˜ His *is* to generations of generations
for generation after generation

Τοῖς φοβουμένοις αὐτόν.
To the *ones* fearing Him.
those who fear

51 Ἐποίησε κράτος ἐν βραχίονι αὐτοῦ·
He did might with arm ˜ His;
has performed mightily

Διεσκόρπισεν ὑπερηφάνους* διανοίᾳ
He scattered haughty *people* in *the* understanding
opinion

καρδίας αὐτῶν.
of hearts ˜ their.

52 Καθεῖλε δυνάστας ἀπὸ θρόνων,
He brought down rulers from thrones,
has overthrown

Καὶ ὕψωσε ταπεινούς.
And He exalted humble *people.*

53 Πεινῶντας ἐνέπλησεν ἀγαθῶν,
Hungering *people* He filled with good *things,*

Καὶ πλουτοῦντας ἐξαπέστειλε κενούς.
And *ones* being rich He sent out empty.
those who are

54 Ἀντελάβετο Ἰσραὴλ παιδὸς αὐτοῦ,
He helped [3]Israel [2]servant [1]His,

Μνησθῆναι ἐλέους,
In order to remember *His* mercy,

55 Καθὼς ἐλάλησε πρὸς τοὺς πατέρας ἡμῶν,
Just as He spoke to - fathers ˜ our,

Τῷ Ἀβραὰμ καὶ τῷ σπέρματι αὐτοῦ εἰς τὸν
- To Abraham and - to seed ˜ his into the
descendants forever."

αἰῶνα."
age."

56 Ἔμεινε δὲ Μαριὰμ σὺν αὐτῇ ὡσεὶ μῆνας τρεῖς, καὶ
[3]remained [1]And [2]Mary with her about months ˜ three, and

ὑπέστρεψεν εἰς τὸν οἶκον αὐτῆς.
she returned to - house ˜ her.

47 And my spirit has rejoiced
in God my Savior.
48 For He has regarded the
lowly state of His
maidservant;
For behold, henceforth all
generations will call me
blessed.
49 For He who is mighty has
done great things for
me,
And holy *is* His name.
50 And His mercy *is* on
those who fear Him
From generation to
generation.
51 He has shown strength
with His arm;
He has scattered *the*
proud in the imagination
of their hearts.
52 He has put down the
mighty from *their*
thrones,
And exalted *the* lowly.
53 He has filled *the* hungry
with good things,
And *the* rich He has sent
away empty.
54 He has helped His servant
Israel,
In remembrance of *His*
mercy,
55 As He spoke to our
fathers,
To Abraham and to his
seed forever."

56 And Mary remained with
her about three months, and
returned to her house.

---

[d](1:49) NU reads μεγαλα, *great things.*

***(1:51)** *ὑπερήφανος (hyperēphania).* Adjective used in the NT only with the unfavorable meanings *arrogant, haughty, proud.* It is included in the NT vice lists along with related words, such as *ὑβριστής, insolent man,* and *ἀλαζών, boaster, braggart* (cf. Rom. 1:30; 2 Tim. 3:2). Those described by *ὑπερήφανος* are contrasted with those who are humble (James 4:6; 1 Pet. 5:5). The cognate noun *ὑπερηφανία, arrogance,* occurs only at Mark 7:22, where it denotes an arrogant resistance to God as well as disdain for others.

57 Now Elizabeth's full time came for her to be delivered, and she brought forth a son.
58 When her neighbors and relatives heard how the Lord had shown great mercy to her, they rejoiced with her.
59 So it was, on the eighth day, that they came to circumcise the child; and they would have called him by the name of his father, Zacharias.
60 His mother answered and said, "No; he shall be called John."
61 But they said to her, "There is no one among your relatives who is called by this name."
62 So they made signs to his father—what he would have him called.
63 And he asked for a writing tablet, and wrote, saying, "His name is John." So they all marveled.
64 Immediately his mouth was opened and his tongue *loosed,* and he spoke, praising God.
65 Then fear came on all who dwelt around them; and all these sayings were discussed throughout all the hill country of Judea.
66 And all those who heard *them* kept *them* in their hearts, saying, "What kind of child will this be?" And the hand of the Lord was with him.

The Birth of John the Baptist

57 Τῇ δὲ Ἐλισάβετ ἐπλήσθη ὁ χρόνος τοῦ τεκεῖν
- And for Elizabeth [3]was [4]fulfilled [1]the [2]time - *for* [2]to [3]bear

αὐτήν, καὶ ἐγέννησεν υἱόν. **58** Καὶ ἤκουσαν οἱ περίοικοι καὶ
[1]her, and she bore a son. And [5]heard - [2]neighbors [3]and

οἱ συγγενεῖς αὐτῆς ὅτι ἐμεγάλυνε Κύριος τὸ ἔλεος αὐτοῦ
- [4]relatives [1]her that [3]magnified [1]*the* [2]Lord - mercy ˜ His
had magnified

μετ᾽ αὐτῆς, καὶ συνέχαιρον αὐτῇ.
with her, and they rejoiced with her.

The Circumcision of John the Baptist

59 Καὶ ἐγένετο ἐν τῇ ὀγδόῃ ἡμέρᾳ ἦλθον περιτεμεῖν
And it happened on the eighth day *that* they came to circumcise

τὸ παιδίον, καὶ ἐκάλουν αὐτὸ ἐπὶ τῷ ὀνόματι τοῦ πατρὸς
the child, and they were calling him by the name - of father ˜
started to call

αὐτοῦ Ζαχαρίαν.
his Zacharias.

60 Καὶ ἀποκριθεῖσα ἡ μήτηρ αὐτοῦ εἶπεν, "Οὐχί, ἀλλὰ
And answering - mother ˜ his said, "No indeed, but

κληθήσεται Ἰωάννης."
he shall be called John."

61 Καὶ εἶπον πρὸς αὐτὴν ὅτι "Οὐδείς ἐστιν ἐν τῇ
And they said to her - "[3]no [4]one [1]There [2]is among -

συγγενείᾳ[e] σου ὃς καλεῖται τῷ ὀνόματι τούτῳ."
relationship ˜ your who is called by name ˜ this."
relatives

62 Ἐνένευον δὲ τῷ πατρὶ αὐτοῦ τὸ τί ἂν
[2]they [3]made [4]signs [1]And - to father ˜ his - as to what -
So about

θέλοι καλεῖσθαι αὐτόν.
he might wish [2]to [3]be [4]called [1]him.
wished

63 Καὶ αἰτήσας πινακίδιον ἔγραψε λέγων, "Ἰωάννης ἐστὶ
And asking for a writing tablet he wrote saying, "John is

τὸ ὄνομα αὐτοῦ." Καὶ ἐθαύμασαν πάντες. **64** Ἀνεῴχθη δὲ
- name ˜ his." And they marveled ˜ all. [4]was [5]opened [1]And

τὸ στόμα αὐτοῦ παραχρῆμα καὶ ἡ γλῶσσα αὐτοῦ, καὶ
- [3]mouth [2]his immediately and - tongue ˜ his, and

ἐλάλει εὐλογῶν τὸν Θεόν. **65** Καὶ ἐγένετο ἐπὶ πάντας
he was speaking blessing - God. And [2]came [3]upon [4]all
started to speak praising

φόβος τοὺς περιοικοῦντας αὐτούς· καὶ ἐν ὅλῃ τῇ
[1]fear the *ones* dwelling around them; and in whole ˜ the
those who lived

ὀρεινῇ τῆς Ἰουδαίας διελαλεῖτο πάντα τὰ
mountainous *country* - of Judea [4]were [5]being [6]discussed [1]all -

ῥήματα ταῦτα.
[3]sayings [2]these.
things

66 Καὶ ἔθεντο πάντες οἱ ἀκούσαντες ἐν τῇ καρδίᾳ
And [6]put [7]*them* [1]all [2]the [3]*ones* [4]hearing [5]*them* in - heart ˜
kept those who heard

αὐτῶν, λέγοντες, "Τί ἄρα τὸ παιδίον τοῦτο ἔσται?" Καὶ
their, saying, "What then - [3]child [2]this [1]will [4]be?" And

χεὶρ Κυρίου ἦν μετ᾽ αὐτοῦ.
the hand of *the* Lord was with him.

---

[e](1:61) NU reads *εκ της συγγενειας σου*, *of your relatives.*

Zacharias' *Benedictus*

67 Καὶ Ζαχαρίας ὁ πατὴρ αὐτοῦ ἐπλήσθη Πνεύματος
And Zacharias - father ˜ his was filled with *the* Spirit ˜

῾Αγίου καὶ προεφήτευσε λέγων,
Holy and he prophesied saying,

68 "Εὐλογητὸς Κύριος ὁ Θεὸς τοῦ ᾿Ισραήλ,
"Blessed *is* *the* Lord the God - of Israel,

῞Οτι ἐπεσκέψατο καὶ ἐποίησε λύτρωσιν τῷ
Because He visited and made redemption -
brought about a deliverance

λαῷ αὐτοῦ,
for people ˜ His,

69 Καὶ ἤγειρε κέρας σωτηρίας* ἡμῖν
And He raised up a horn of salvation for us

᾿Εν τῷ οἴκῳ Δαβὶδ τοῦ παιδὸς αὐτοῦ.
In the house of David - servant ˜ His.

70 Καθὼς ἐλάλησε διὰ στόματος τῶν ἁγίων τῶν ἀπ᾿
Just as He spoke through *the* mouth - [3]holy - [5]from

αἰῶνος προφητῶν αὐτοῦ,
[6]*the* [7]age [4]prophets [1]of [2]His,
antiquity

71 Σωτηρίαν ἐξ ἐχθρῶν ἡμῶν καὶ ἐκ χειρὸς
Announcing salvation from enemies ˜ our and from *the* hand

πάντων τῶν μισούντων ἡμᾶς,
of all the *ones* hating us,
those who hate

72 Ποιῆσαι ἔλεος μετὰ τῶν πατέρων ἡμῶν
In order to do mercy with - fathers ˜ our
show to

Καὶ μνησθῆναι διαθήκης ἁγίας αὐτοῦ,
And *in order* to remember [3]covenant [2]holy [1]His,

73 ῞Ορκον ὃν ὤμοσεν πρὸς ᾿Αβραὰμ τὸν πατέρα
Performing the oath which He swore to Abraham - father ˜

ἡμῶν·
our;

Τοῦ δοῦναι ἡμῖν **74** ἀφόβως ἐκ χειρὸς
- To give to us *that* [13]without [14]fear [4]from [5]*the* [6]hand
grant

τῶν ἐχθρῶν ἡμῶν ῥυσθέντας,
- [7]of [9]enemies [8]our [1]having [2]been [3]rescued,

Λατρεύειν αὐτῷ **75** ἐν ὁσιότητι καὶ δικαιοσύνῃ
[10]To [11]serve [12]Him in holiness and righteousness
We might

᾿Ενώπιον αὐτοῦ πάσας τὰς ἡμέρας τῆς ζωῆς ἡμῶν.
Before Him all the days - of life ˜ our.

76 Καὶ σύ, παιδίον, προφήτης ῾Υψίστου κληθήσῃ,
And you, child, [4]a [5]prophet [6]of [7]*the* [8]Most [9]High [1]will [2]be [3]called,

Προπορεύσῃ γὰρ πρὸ προσώπου Κυρίου[f]
[11]you [12]will [13]go [10]For before *the* face of *the* Lord

῾ετοιμάσαι ὁδοὺς αὐτοῦ,
to prepare ways ˜ His,

77 Τοῦ δοῦναι γνῶσιν σωτηρίας τῷ λαῷ αὐτοῦ
- To give knowledge of salvation - to people ˜ His

᾿Εν ἀφέσει ἁμαρτιῶν αὐτῶν,
By *the* forgiveness of sins ˜ their,

78 Διὰ σπλάγχνα ἐλέους Θεοῦ ἡμῶν,
Because of *the* compassions of *the* mercy of God ˜ our,
the merciful compassions

---

67 Now his father Zacharias was filled with the Holy Spirit, and prophesied, saying:

68 "Blessed *is* the Lord God
of Israel,
For He has visited and
redeemed His people,
69 And has raised up a horn
of salvation for us
In the house of His
servant David,
70 As He spoke by the
mouth of His holy
prophets,
Who *have been* since the
world began,
71 That we should be saved
from our enemies
And from the hand of all
who hate us,
72 To perform the mercy
promised to our fathers
And to remember His
holy covenant,
73 The oath which He swore
to our father Abraham:
74 To grant us that we,
Being delivered from the
hand of our enemies,
Might serve Him without
fear,
75 In holiness and
righteousness before
Him all the days of our
life.

76 "And you, child, will be
called the prophet of
the Highest;
For you will go before the
face of the Lord to
prepare His ways,
77 To give knowledge of
salvation to His people
By the remission of their
sins,
78 Through the tender mercy
of our God,

---

f(**1:76**) NU reads *ενωπιον Κυριου, before the Lord.*

***(1:69, 77)** *σωτηρία (sōtēria).* Noun used frequently in the NT, almost always referring to *salvation* in the sense of deliverance from sin and its damning effects through the redemptive work of Christ. The basic meaning is *deliverance, preservation,* as from death or danger (see Acts 27:34; NKJV "survival"). In the more common NT usage, it may refer to salvation in its initiation (as Luke 19:9; probably 2 Cor. 6:2) or to its consummation ("final salva-

With which the Dayspring
from on high has visited
us;
79 To give light to those who
sit in darkness and the
shadow of death,
To guide our feet into the
way of peace."

80 So the child grew and became strong in spirit, and was
in the deserts till the day of his
manifestation to Israel.
2 And it came to pass in
those days *that* a decree
went out from Caesar Augustus
that all the world should be registered.
2 This census first took place
while Quirinius was governing
Syria.
3 So all went to be registered, everyone to his own
city.
4 Joseph also went up from
Galilee, out of the city of Nazareth, into Judea, to the city of
David, which is called Bethlehem, because he was of the
house and lineage of David,
5 to be registered with
Mary, his betrothed wife, who
was with child.
6 So it was, that while they
were there, the days were
completed for her to be delivered.
7 And she brought forth her
firstborn Son, and wrapped Him
in swaddling cloths, and laid

Ἐν οἷς ἐπεσκέψατο[g] ἡμᾶς ἀνατολὴ ἐξ ὕψους·
With which [3]visited [4]us [1]*the* [2]dawn from *the* height;
rising sun on high;

79 Ἐπιφᾶναι τοῖς ἐν σκότει καὶ σκιᾷ
To appear to the *ones* [2]in [3]darkness [4]and [5]*the* [6]shadow
shine on those who are

θανάτου καθημένοις,
[7]of [8]death [1]sitting,
living,

Τοῦ κατευθῦναι τοὺς πόδας ἡμῶν εἰς ὁδὸν
- To guide - feet ˜ our into *the* way

εἰρήνης."
of peace."

80 Τὸ δὲ παιδίον ηὔξανε καὶ ἐκραταιοῦτο
the ˜ And child was growing and was becoming strong
So

πνεύματι, καὶ ἦν ἐν ταῖς ἐρήμοις ἕως ἡμέρας
in spirit, and he was in the deserts till *the* day
wilderness places

ἀναδείξεως αὐτοῦ πρὸς τὸν Ἰσραήλ.
of manifestation ˜ his to - Israel.
for

Christ Is Born of Mary
(Matt. 1:18–25)

2 1 Ἐγένετο δὲ ἐν ταῖς ἡμέραις ἐκείναις ἐξῆλθε
[2]it [3]happened [1]Now in - days ˜ those *that* [3]went [4]out

δόγμα παρὰ Καίσαρος Αὐγούστου ἀπογράφεσθαι πᾶσαν
[1]a [2]decree from Caesar Augustus *that* to be registered all
the Emperor a census be taken of

τὴν οἰκουμένην. 2 Αὕτη ἡ ἀπογραφὴ πρώτη ἐγένετο
the *Roman* world. This - registration [2]*the* [3]first [4]*one* [1]was
empire. census

ἡγεμονεύοντος τῆς Συρίας Κυρηνίου. 3 Καὶ ἐπορεύοντο
[6]governing - [7]Syria [5]Quirinius. And [2]were [3]traveling
while Quirinius was governing Syria.

πάντες ἀπογράφεσθαι, ἕκαστος εἰς τὴν ἰδίαν πόλιν.
[1]all to be registered, each to - his own city.

4 Ἀνέβη δὲ καὶ Ἰωσὴφ ἀπὸ τῆς Γαλιλαίας ἐκ
[4]went [5]up [1]And [3]also [2]Joseph from - Galilee out of

πόλεως Ναζαρέτ, εἰς τὴν Ἰουδαίαν, εἰς πόλιν Δαβίδ, ἥτις
the city of Nazareth, to - Judea, to *the* city of David, which

καλεῖται Βηθλέεμ, διὰ τὸ εἶναι αὐτὸν ἐξ οἴκου καὶ
is called Bethlehem, on account of - [2]to [3]be [1]him of *the* house and
because he was

πατριᾶς Δαβίδ, 5 ἀπογράψασθαι σὺν Μαριὰμ τῇ
family of David, to be registered with Mary the

μεμνηστευμένῃ αὐτῷ γυναικί,[a] οὔσῃ ἐγκύῳ.
[2]having [3]been [4]betrothed [5]to [6]him [1]woman, being pregnant.
who was

6 Ἐγένετο δὲ ἐν τῷ εἶναι αὐτοὺς ἐκεῖ, ἐπλήσθησαν
[2]it [3]happened [1]Now in - [2]to [3]be [1]them there, [3]were [4]completed
while they were

αἱ ἡμέραι τοῦ τεκεῖν αὐτήν. 7 Καὶ ἔτεκε τὸν Υἱὸν αὐτῆς
[1]the [2]days - *for* [2]to [3]bear [1]her. And she bore - [3]Son [1]her

τὸν πρωτότοκον, καὶ ἐσπαργάνωσεν αὐτόν, καὶ ἀνέκλινεν
- [2]firstborn, and swaddled Him, and laid
wrapped Him in strips of cloth,

---

g(**1:78**) NU reads ἐπισκέψεται, *will visit.*
a(**2:5**) NU omits γυναικι, *woman.*

tion," as in Rom. 13:11), or more broadly to all phases of redemption (as here in Luke). Cf. the cognate noun σωτήρ, *savior;* and the root verb σῴζω, *save.*

αὐτὸν ἐν τῇ φάτνῃ, διότι οὐκ ἦν αὐτοῖς τόπος ἐν
Him in the manger, because [3]not [1]*there* [2]was [6]for [7]them [4]a [5]place in
a feed trough,

τῷ καταλύματι.
the inn.

Gloria in Excelsis Deo

8 Καὶ ποιμένες ἦσαν ἐν τῇ χώρᾳ τῇ αὐτῇ ἀγραυλοῦντες
And shepherds were in the region ˜ - same living in the fields
country

καὶ φυλάσσοντες φυλακὰς τῆς νυκτὸς ἐπὶ τὴν ποίμνην
and keeping watch *in the* watches of the night over - flock ˜
nightly watches

αὐτῶν. 9 Καὶ ἰδού, ἄγγελος Κυρίου ἐπέστη αὐτοῖς, καὶ
their. And behold, an angel of *the* Lord stood before them, and

δόξα Κυρίου περιέλαμψεν αὐτούς, καὶ ἐφοβήθησαν φόβον
the glory of *the* Lord shone around them, and they feared a fear ˜
greatly.

μέγαν.
great.

10 Καὶ εἶπεν αὐτοῖς ὁ ἄγγελος, "Μὴ φοβεῖσθε, ἰδοὺ
And [3]said [4]to [5]them [1]the [2]angel, "not ˜ Do be afraid, behold ˜

γάρ, εὐαγγελίζομαι ὑμῖν χαρὰν μεγάλην ἥτις ἔσται
for, I am announcing good news to you *of* joy ˜ great which will be

παντὶ τῷ λαῷ. 11 Ὅτι ἐτέχθη ὑμῖν σήμερον Σωτήρ,
to all - people. Because [3]was [4]born [5]to [6]you [7]today [1]a [2]Savior,

ὅς ἐστι Χριστὸς Κύριος, ἐν πόλει Δαβίδ. 12 Καὶ τοῦτο
who is Christ *the* Lord, in *the* city of David. And this

ὑμῖν τὸ σημεῖον· εὑρήσετε Βρέφος
[5]to [6]you [1]*will* [2]*be* [3]the [4]sign: you will find a Baby

ἐσπαργανωμένον, κείμενον ἐν φάτνῃ."
having been swaddled, lying in a manger."
wrapped in strips of cloth, feed trough."

13 Καὶ ἐξαίφνης ἐγένετο σὺν τῷ ἀγγέλῳ πλῆθος
And suddenly *there* was with the angel a multitude

στρατιᾶς οὐρανίου αἰνούντων τὸν Θεὸν καὶ λεγόντων,
of *the* army ˜ heavenly praising - God and saying,
host

14 "Δόξα ἐν ὑψίστοις Θεῷ,
"Glory in *the* heights to God,

Καὶ ἐπὶ γῆς εἰρήνη,*
And on earth peace,

Ἐν ἀνθρώποις εὐδοκία!"[b]
[3]among [4]men [1]Good [2]will!"
God's good pleasure!"

15 Καὶ ἐγένετο ὡς ἀπῆλθον ἀπ' αὐτῶν εἰς τὸν
And it happened when [3]went [4]away [5]from [6]them [7]into -
had departed

οὐρανὸν οἱ ἄγγελοι, καὶ οἱ ἄνθρωποι[c] οἱ ποιμένες
[8]heaven [1]the [2]angels, and the men the shepherds
that who were

εἶπον πρὸς ἀλλήλους, "Διέλθωμεν δὴ ἕως Βηθλέεμ καὶ
said to one another, "Let us go then to Bethlehem and

ἴδωμεν τὸ ῥῆμα τοῦτο τὸ γεγονὸς ὃ ὁ Κύριος
let us see - word ˜ this the *thing* having happened which the Lord
matter which has taken place

ἐγνώρισεν ἡμῖν." 16 Καὶ ἦλθον σπεύσαντες καὶ ἀνεῦραν
made known to us." And they came having hurried and found
has made with haste located

Him in a manger, because there was no room for them in the inn.

8 Now there were in the same country shepherds living out in the fields, keeping watch over their flock by night.

9 And behold, an angel of the Lord stood before them, and the glory of the Lord shone around them, and they were greatly afraid.

10 Then the angel said to them, "Do not be afraid, for behold, I bring you good tidings of great joy which will be to all people.

11 "For there is born to you this day in the city of David a Savior, who is Christ the Lord.

12 "And this *will be* the sign to you: You will find a Babe wrapped in swaddling cloths, lying in a manger."

13 And suddenly there was with the angel a multitude of the heavenly host praising God and saying:

14 "Glory to God in the highest,
And on earth peace, goodwill toward men!"

15 So it was, when the angels had gone away from them into heaven, that the shepherds said to one another, "Let us now go to Bethlehem and see this thing that has come to pass, which the Lord has made known to us."

16 And they came with haste

---

[b](**2:14**) NU reads ευδοκιας, *(toward men) of goodwill.*
[c](**2:15**) NU omits και οι ανθρωποι, *and the men.*

---

*(**2:14**) *εἰρήνη (eirēnē).* Noun occurring frequently in the NT (and the LXX) meaning *peace.* The frequent usage results partly from its Hebrew equivalent, *shālôm,* which was a standard greeting among the Jews. The NT meaning often shows the influence of the Hebrew concept that equated it to *well-being* or *wholeness* in a broad variety of ways. εἰρήνη especially indicates the spiritual well-being that flows from a right relationship with God (as in Rom. 5:1). Here in Luke it may be even broader, implying the peace associated with the messianic kingdom of the Christ. Cf. the cognate verb εἰρηνεύω, *be at peace, keep peace* (2 Cor.13:11); and the adjective εἰρηνικός,

and found Mary and Joseph,
and the Babe lying in a manger.
17 Now when they had seen
Him, they made widely known
the saying which was told them
concerning this Child.
18 And all those who heard *it*
marveled at those things which
were told them by the shepherds.
19 But Mary kept all these
things and pondered *them* in her
heart.
20 Then the shepherds re-
turned, glorifying and praising
God for all the things that they
had heard and seen, as it was
told them.
21 And when eight days were
completed for the circumcision
of the Child, His name was
called JESUS, the name given by
the angel before He was conceived in the womb.
22 Now when the days of her
purification according to the law
of Moses were completed, they
brought Him to Jerusalem to
present *Him* to the Lord
23 (as it is written in the law
of the Lord, *"Every male who
opens the womb shall be called
holy to the LORD"*),
24 and to offer a sacrifice according to what is said in the
law of the Lord, *"A pair of
turtledoves or two young pigeons."*
25 And behold, there was a
man in Jerusalem whose name

τήν τε Μαριὰμ καὶ τὸν Ἰωσήφ, καὶ τὸ Βρέφος κείμενον ἐν
\- both Mary and - Joseph, and the Baby lying in

τῇ φάτνῃ. **17** Ἰδόντες δὲ διεγνώρισαν[d]
the manger. seeing ˜ And they made widely known
feed trough. when they had seen Him, spread the news

περὶ τοῦ ῥήματος τοῦ λαληθέντος αὐτοῖς περὶ τοῦ
about the word the *one* having been spoken to them about -
matter which had been told

Παιδίου τούτου. **18** Καὶ πάντες οἱ ἀκούσαντες ἐθαύμασαν
Child ˜ this. And all the *ones* hearing marveled
those who heard

περὶ τῶν λαληθέντων ὑπὸ τῶν ποιμένων πρὸς αὐτούς.
about the *things* spoken by the shepherds to them.

19 Ἡ δὲ Μαριὰμ πάντα συνετήρει τὰ ῥήματα ταῦτα,
\- But Mary all ˜ kept - words ˜ these,
treasured things

συμβάλλουσα ἐν τῇ καρδίᾳ αὐτῆς. **20** Καὶ ὑπέστρεψαν οἱ
considering *them* in - heart ˜ her. And [3]returned [1]the

ποιμένες, δοξάζοντες καὶ αἰνοῦντες τὸν Θεὸν ἐπὶ πᾶσιν οἷς
[2]shepherds, glorifying and praising - God over all *things* which
for

ἤκουσαν καὶ εἶδον, καθὼς ἐλαλήθη πρὸς αὐτούς.
they heard and saw, just as it was spoken to them.
had heard had seen,

The Circumcision of Jesus

21 Καὶ ὅτε ἐπλήσθησαν ἡμέραι ὀκτὼ τοῦ περιτεμεῖν
And when [3]were [4]completed [2]days [1]eight - to circumcise
so they could

αὐτόν,[e] καὶ ἐκλήθη τὸ ὄνομα αὐτοῦ Ἰησοῦς, τὸ κληθὲν
Him, - [3]was [4]called - [2]name [1]His Jesus, the *name* called
given

ὑπὸ τοῦ ἀγγέλου πρὸ τοῦ συλλημφθῆναι αὐτὸν ἐν τῇ κοιλίᾳ.
by the angel before - [2]to [3]be [4]conceived [1]Him in the womb.
He was conceived

Jesus Is Presented in the Temple

22 Καὶ ὅτε ἐπλήσθησαν αἱ ἡμέραι τοῦ καθαρισμοῦ
And when [6]were [7]completed [1]the [2]days - [3]of [5]purification

αὐτῶν κατὰ τὸν νόμον Μωσέως, ἀνήγαγον αὐτὸν εἰς
[4]their according to the law of Moses, they brought up ˜ Him to

Ἱεροσόλυμα παραστῆσαι τῷ Κυρίῳ **23** (καθὼς γέγραπται ἐν
Jerusalem to present *Him* to the Lord (just as it is written in

νόμῳ Κυρίου ὅτι «Πᾶν ἄρσεν διανοῖγον μήτραν ἅγιον τῷ
the law of *the* Lord - «Every male opening a womb [4]holy [5]to [6]the
who opens

Κυρίῳ κληθήσεται»),[f] **24** καὶ τοῦ δοῦναι θυσίαν κατὰ
[7]Lord [1]shall [2]be [3]called»), and - to give a sacrifice according to

τὸ εἰρημένον ἐν νόμῳ Κυρίου, «Ζεῦγος τρυγόνων
the *thing* having been spoken in *the* law of *the* Lord, «A pair of doves
what had been said

ἢ δύο νεοσσοὺς περιστερῶν.»[g]
or two young *ones* of pigeons.»

Simeon's *Nunc Dimittis*

25 Καὶ ἰδού, ἦν ἄνθρωπος ἐν Ἱερουσαλὴμ ᾧ
And behold, *there* was a man in Jerusalem to whom
whose

---

[d](2:17) NU reads *εγνωρισαν, they made known.* [e](2:21) Many mss., TR read *το Παιδιον, the Child.* [f](2:23) Ex. 13:2, 12, 15 [g](2:24) Lev. 12:8

peaceable, peaceful (James 3:17).

ὄνομα Συμεών, καὶ ὁ ἄνθρωπος οὗτος δίκαιος καὶ
was a name Simeon, and - man ˜ this *was* righteous and
name was

εὐλαβής, προσδεχόμενος παράκλησιν τοῦ Ἰσραήλ, καὶ
devout, waiting for *the* consolation - of Israel, and
expecting comforting help for

Πνεῦμα ἦν Ἅγιον ἐπ' αὐτόν. **26** Καὶ ἦν αὐτῷ
[1]*the* [3]Spirit [4]was [2]Holy upon him. And it was to him
it had been

κεχρηματισμένον ὑπὸ τοῦ Πνεύματος τοῦ Ἁγίου μὴ
having been revealed by the Spirit ˜ - Holy not
revealed to him that he would

ἰδεῖν θάνατον πρὶν ἢ ἴδῃ τὸν Χριστὸν Κυρίου.
to see death before - he should see the Christ of *the* Lord.
not see Lord's Messiah.

27 Καὶ ἦλθεν ἐν τῷ Πνεύματι εἰς τὸ ἱερόν. Καὶ ἐν τῷ
And he came in the Spirit into the temple. And in -
by when

εἰσαγαγεῖν τοὺς γονεῖς τὸ Παιδίον Ἰησοῦν τοῦ ποιῆσαι αὐτοὺς
[3]to [4]bring [5]in [1]the [2]parents the Child Jesus - [2]to [3]do [1]them
brought that they might do

κατὰ τὸ εἰθισμένον τοῦ νόμου περὶ
according to the *thing* having become customary of the law concerning
the custom in

αὐτοῦ, **28** καὶ αὐτὸς ἐδέξατο αὐτὸ εἰς τὰς ἀγκάλας αὐτοῦ καὶ
Him, and he received Him into - arms ˜ his and
took

εὐλόγησε τὸν Θεὸν καὶ εἶπε,
blessed - God and said,

29 "Νῦν ἀπολύεις τὸν δοῦλόν σου, Δέσποτα,
"Now You are releasing - slave ˜ Your, Master,
servant

Κατὰ τὸ ῥῆμά σου, ἐν εἰρήνῃ·
According to - word ˜ Your, in peace;

30 Ὅτι εἶδον οἱ ὀφθαλμοί μου τὸ σωτήριόν σου
Because [3]saw - [2]eyes [1]my - salvation ˜ Your
have seen

31 Ὃ ἡτοίμασας κατὰ πρόσωπον πάντων τῶν λαῶν,
Which You prepared before *the* face of all the peoples,

32 Φῶς εἰς ἀποκάλυψιν ἐθνῶν,*
A light for a revelation of Gentiles,
to

Καὶ δόξαν λαοῦ σου Ἰσραήλ."
And a glory of people ˜ Your Israel."
to

33 Καὶ ἦν Ἰωσὴφ[h] καὶ ἡ μήτηρ αὐτοῦ θαυμάζοντες ἐπὶ
And [5]were [1]Joseph [2]and - [4]mother [3]His marveling at

τοῖς λαλουμένοις περὶ αὐτοῦ. **34** Καὶ εὐλόγησεν αὐτοὺς
the *things* being spoken about Him. And [2]blessed [3]them

Συμεών, καὶ εἶπε πρὸς Μαριὰμ τὴν μητέρα αὐτοῦ, "Ἰδού,
[1]Simeon, and said to Mary - mother ˜ His, "Behold,

οὗτος κεῖται εἰς πτῶσιν καὶ ἀνάστασιν πολλῶν ἐν τῷ
this *One* is set for *the* fall and rise of many in -
appointed

Ἰσραήλ, καὶ εἰς σημεῖον ἀντιλεγόμενον **35** (καὶ σοῦ δὲ
Israel, and for a sign being spoken against ([2]also [10]of [11]you [1]but
which will be

αὐτῆς τὴν ψυχὴν διελεύσεται ῥομφαία), ὅπως ἂν
[12]yourself [8]the [9]soul [5]will [6]go [7]through [3]a [4]sword), so that -

was Simeon, and this man was
just and devout, waiting for the
Consolation of Israel, and the
Holy Spirit was upon him.
26 And it had been revealed to
him by the Holy Spirit that he
would not see death before he
had seen the Lord's Christ.
27 So he came by the Spirit
into the temple. And when the
parents brought in the Child Jesus, to do for Him according to
the custom of the law,
28 he took Him up in his arms
and blessed God and said:

29 "Lord, now You are letting
Your servant depart in
peace,
According to Your word;
30 For my eyes have seen
Your salvation
31 Which You have prepared
before the face of all
peoples,
32 A light to *bring* revelation
to the Gentiles,
And the glory of Your
people Israel."

33 And Joseph and His mother
marveled at those things which
were spoken of Him.
34 Then Simeon blessed
them, and said to Mary His
mother, "Behold, this *Child* is
destined for the fall and rising of
many in Israel, and for a sign
which will be spoken against
35 "(yes, a sword will pierce
through your own soul also),

---

[h](**2:33**) NU reads ο πατηρ αυτου, *His father.*

***(2:32)** ἔθνος *(ethnos).* Noun, common in the NT, meaning *people, nation.* The singular can refer to any nation or people, including the Jewish nation (as Acts 26:4). The plural can mean *nations* in general (Gal. 3:8), but often indicates Gentile peoples in particular distinction from Jews (as here in Luke 2:32; cf. 1 Thess. 4:5). The notion of the church as the "true Israel" led to the extension of the meaning *Gentiles* to include reference to non-Christians (as 1 Pet. 2:12; 4:3). Cf. the cognate adjective ἐθνικός, *Gentile, pagan,* used only substantivally in the NT for *(the) Gentiles, heathens, pagans* (Matt. 6:7; 18:17); and the adverb ἐθνικῶς, *like Gentiles* (only Gal. 2:14).

that the thoughts of many
hearts may be revealed."
36 Now there was one, Anna,
a prophetess, the daughter of
Phanuel, of the tribe of Asher.
She was of a great age, and had
lived with a husband seven
years from her virginity;
37 and this woman *was* a
widow of about eighty-four
years, who did not depart from
the temple, but served *God*
with fastings and prayers night
and day.
38 And coming in that instant
she gave thanks to the Lord,
and spoke of Him to all those
who looked for redemption in
Jerusalem.
39 So when they had per-
formed all things according to
the law of the Lord, they returned to Galilee, to their *own*
city, Nazareth.
40 And the Child grew and became strong in spirit, filled with
wisdom; and the grace of God
was upon Him.
41 His parents went to Jerusalem every year at the Feast of
the Passover.
42 And when He was twelve
years old, they went up to Jerusalem according to the custom
of the feast.
43 When they had finished the
days, as they returned, the Boy

ἀποκαλυφθῶσιν ἐκ πολλῶν καρδιῶν διαλογισμοί."
[6]may [7]be [8]revealed [3]of [4]many [5]hearts [1]*the* [2]reasonings."
thoughts."

Anna Witnesses About the Redeemer

36 Καὶ ἦν Ἄννα προφῆτις, θυγάτηρ Φανουήλ, ἐκ
And *there* was Anna a prophetess, a daughter of Phanuel, of

φυλῆς Ἀσήρ. Αὕτη προβεβηκυῖα ἐν ἡμέραις πολλαῖς,
the tribe of Asher. This *woman* having advanced in days ˜ many,
was

ζήσασα ἔτη μετὰ ἀνδρὸς ἑπτὰ ἀπὸ τῆς παρθενίας
having lived [5]years [6]with [7]a [8]husband [4]seven [1]from - [3]virginity

αὐτῆς· 37 καὶ αὐτὴ χήρα ὡς ἐτῶν ὀγδοήκοντα
[2]her; and she *was* a widow *of* about [3]years [1]eighty

τεσσάρων, ἣ οὐκ ἀφίστατο ἀπὸ τοῦ ἱεροῦ, νηστείαις καὶ
[2]four, who not ˜ did depart from the temple, with fastings and

δεήσεσι λατρεύουσα νύκτα καὶ ἡμέραν. 38 Καὶ αὐτὴ αὐτῇ
supplications serving night and day. And she at very ˜
at that

τῇ ὥρᾳ ἐπιστᾶσα ἀνθωμολογεῖτο τῷ Κυρίῳ[i] καὶ ἐλάλει
the hour coming up was giving thanks to the Lord and was speaking
very time

περὶ αὐτοῦ πᾶσι τοῖς προσδεχομένοις λύτρωσιν ἐν
about Him to all the *ones* waiting for redemption in
those who waited

Ἱερουσαλήμ.
Jerusalem.

The Family Returns to Nazareth

39 Καὶ ὡς ἐτέλεσαν ἅπαντα τὰ κατὰ τὸν νόμον
And when they finished all *things* the *ones* according to the law
everything

Κυρίου, ὑπέστρεψαν εἰς τὴν Γαλιλαίαν, εἰς τὴν πόλιν
of *the* Lord, they returned to - Galilee, to the city
their own

ἑαυτῶν Ναζαρέτ. 40 Τὸ δὲ Παιδίον ηὔξανε καὶ
of themselves Nazareth. the ˜ And Child was growing and
city

ἐκραταιοῦτο πνεύματι,[j] πληρούμενον σοφίας· καὶ
was becoming strong in spirit, being filled with wisdom; and

χάρις Θεοῦ ἦν ἐπ' αὐτό.
the grace of God was upon Him.

The Boy Jesus Amazes the Doctors of the Law

41 Καὶ ἐπορεύοντο οἱ γονεῖς αὐτοῦ κατ' ἔτος εἰς
And [3]traveled - [2]parents [1]His by year to
yearly

Ἱερουσαλὴμ τῇ ἑορτῇ τοῦ Πάσχα. 42 Καὶ ὅτε ἐγένετο
Jerusalem to the feast of the Passover. And when He became

ἐτῶν δώδεκα, ἀναβάντων αὐτῶν εἰς Ἱεροσόλυμα[k]
[2]of [3]years [1]twelve, going up them to Jerusalem
years old when they went up

κατὰ τὸ ἔθος τῆς ἑορτῆς 43 καὶ τελειωσάντων τὰς
according to the custom of the feast and completing the
when they completed

ἡμέρας, ἐν τῷ ὑποστρέφειν αὐτούς, ὑπέμεινεν Ἰησοῦς ὁ
days, in - [2]to [3]return [1]them, [7]remained [6]Jesus [4]the
while they were returning,

[i](**2:38**) NU reads τῳ Θεῳ, *to God.* [j](**2:40**) NU omits πνευματι, *in spirit.* [k](**2:42**) NU omits εις Ιεροσολυμα, *to Jerusalem.*

Παῖς ἐν Ἰερουσαλήμ· καὶ οὐκ ἔγνω Ἰωσὴφ καὶ ἡ μήτηρ
[5]Child in Jerusalem; and [6]not [5]did [7]know [1]Joseph [2]and - [4]mother

αὐτοῦ.[l] 44 Νομίσαντες δὲ αὐτὸν ἐν τῇ συνοδίᾳ εἶναι,
[3]His. supposing ˜ But Him [3]in [4]the [5]caravan [1]to [2]be,

ἦλθον ἡμέρας ὁδόν, καὶ ἀνεζήτουν αὐτὸν ἐν
they went [3]of [4]a [5]day [1]*the* [2]road, and they were looking for Him among
a day's journey,

τοῖς συγγενέσι καὶ ἐν τοῖς γνωστοῖς. 45 Καὶ μὴ
the relatives and among the acquaintances. And not
their their when they

εὑρόντες αὐτόν, ὑπέστρεψαν εἰς Ἰερουσαλήμ, ζητοῦντες αὐτόν.
finding Him, they returned to Jerusalem, seeking Him.
did not find

46 Καὶ ἐγένετο μεθ' ἡμέρας τρεῖς εὗρον αὐτὸν ἐν τῷ
And it happened after days ˜ three they found Him in the

ἱερῷ καθεζόμενον ἐν μέσῳ τῶν διδασκάλων, καὶ ἀκούοντα
temple sitting in *the* midst of the teachers, both hearing

αὐτῶν καὶ ἐπερωτῶντα αὐτούς. 47 Ἐξίσταντο δὲ πάντες
them and questioning them. [7]were [8]astonished [1]And [2]all

οἱ ἀκούοντες αὐτοῦ ἐπὶ τῇ συνέσει καὶ ταῖς
[3]the [4]*ones* [5]hearing [6]Him at - [2]understanding [3]and -
those who heard

ἀποκρίσεσιν αὐτοῦ. 48 Καὶ ἰδόντες αὐτὸν ἐξεπλάγησαν·
[4]answers [1]His. And seeing Him they were amazed;
when they saw

καὶ πρὸς αὐτὸν ἡ μήτηρ αὐτοῦ εἶπε, "Τέκνον, τί ἐποίησας
and [4]to [5]Him - [2]mother [1]His [3]said, "Child, why did You do
have You

ἡμῖν οὕτως? Ἰδού, ὁ πατήρ σου κἀγὼ ὀδυνώμενοι
to us thus? Look, - father ˜ Your and I grieving
treated us this way? anxiously

ἐζητοῦμέν σε."
were seeking You."

49 Καὶ εἶπε πρὸς αὐτούς, "Τί ὅτι ἐζητεῖτέ με?
And He said to them, "Why *is it* that you were seeking Me?

Οὐκ ᾔδειτε ὅτι ἐν τοῖς τοῦ Πατρός μου
[3]not [1]Did [2]you know that in the *things* - of Father ˜ My
I must be about My

δεῖ εἶναί με?" 50 Καὶ αὐτοὶ οὐ συνῆκαν τὸ
it is necessary *for* [2]to [3]be [1]Me?" And they not ˜ did understand the
Father's business?"

ῥῆμα ὃ ἐλάλησεν αὐτοῖς.
saying which He spoke to them.
statement

Jesus Advances in Wisdom and Favor

51 Καὶ κατέβη μετ' αὐτῶν καὶ ἦλθεν εἰς Ναζαρέτ, καὶ
And He went down with them and came to Nazareth, and

ἦν ὑποτασσόμενος αὐτοῖς. Καὶ ἡ μήτηρ αὐτοῦ διετήρει πάντα
was submitting to them. And - mother ˜ His kept all
subject

τὰ ῥήματα ταῦτα ἐν τῇ καρδίᾳ αὐτῆς. 52 Καὶ Ἰησοῦς
- sayings ˜ these in - heart ˜ her. And Jesus
things

προέκοπτε σοφίᾳ καὶ ἡλικίᾳ, καὶ χάριτι παρὰ Θεῷ καὶ
was advancing in wisdom and stature, and in favor with God and
increased

ἀνθρώποις.
men.

Jesus lingered behind in Jerusalem. And Joseph and His mother did not know *it;*
44 but supposing Him to have been in the company, they went a day's journey, and sought Him among *their* relatives and acquaintances.
45 So when they did not find Him, they returned to Jerusalem, seeking Him.
46 Now so it was *that* after three days they found Him in the temple, sitting in the midst of the teachers, both listening to them and asking them questions.
47 And all who heard Him were astonished at His understanding and answers.
48 So when they saw Him, they were amazed; and His mother said to Him, "Son, why have You done this to us? Look, Your father and I have sought You anxiously."
49 And He said to them, "Why did you seek Me? Did you not know that I must be about My Father's business?"
50 But they did not understand the statement which He spoke to them.
51 Then He went down with them and came to Nazareth, and was subject to them, but His mother kept all these things in her heart.
52 And Jesus increased in wisdom and stature, and in favor with God and men.

---

l(2:43) For ουκ εγνω Ιωσηφ και η μητηρ αυτου, *Joseph and His mother did not know,* NU reads ουκ εγνωσαν οι γονεις αυτου, *His parents did not know.*

3 Now in the fifteenth year
of the reign of Tiberius
Caesar, Pontius Pilate being
governor of Judea, Herod being
tetrarch of Galilee, his brother
Philip tetrarch of Iturea and the
region of Trachonitis, and Lysanias tetrarch of Abilene,
2 while Annas and Caiaphas
were high priests, the word of
God came to John the son of
Zacharias in the wilderness.
3 And he went into all the region around the Jordan, preaching a baptism of repentance for
the remission of sins,
4 as it is written in the book
of the words of Isaiah the
prophet, saying:

"The voice of one crying in
the wilderness:
'Prepare the way of the
LORD;
Make His paths straight.
5 *Every valley shall be filled*
And every mountain and
hill brought low;
The crooked places shall
be made straight
And the rough ways
smooth;
6 *And all flesh shall see the*
salvation of God.' "

7 Then he said to the multitudes that came out to be baptized by him, "Brood of vipers!
Who warned you to flee from

---

[a](3:2) TR reads *αρχιερεων, of the high priests.*
[b](3:6) Is. 40:3–5

*(3:3) *κηρύσσω (kēryssō).* Verb meaning *proclaim,* often with the underlying idea of acting on behalf of an official (cf. Rom. 10:15). It originally indicated the proclamation or announcement of a herald. The word was also used of prophets and preachers and may therefore mean *preach* (though not with our modern idea of sermonic delivery). *κηρύσσω* usually takes an object indicating what is proclaimed/preached, such as: baptism (here in Luke 3:3), Moses (Acts 15:21), circumcision (Gal. 5:11), Christ (Acts 8:5), the word (2 Tim. 4:2), and especially the gospel (Mark 16:15). Cf. the cognate nouns *κῆρυξ, herald, preacher;* and *κήρυγμα, proclamation;* and the verb *εὐαγγελίζω, preach the gospel,* which contains within it the idea of announcing good news and needs no object.

John the Baptist Prepares the Way
(Matt. 3:1–6; Mark 1:1–6)

3 1 Ἐν ἔτει δὲ πεντεκαιδεκάτῳ τῆς ἡγεμονίας
[2]in [3]*the* [5]year [1]Now [4]fifteenth of the rule
reign

Τιβερίου Καίσαρος, ἡγεμονεύοντος Ποντίου Πιλάτου τῆς
of Tiberius Caesar, [3]governing [1]Pontius [2]Pilate -
while Pontius Pilate was governing

Ἰουδαίας, καὶ τετραρχοῦντος τῆς Γαλιλαίας Ἡρῴδου,
Judea, and [2]being [3]tetrarch - [4]of [5]Galilee [1]Herod,
while Herod governed as tetrarch of Galilee,

Φιλίππου δὲ τοῦ ἀδελφοῦ αὐτοῦ τετραρχοῦντος τῆς
Philip ˜ and - brother ˜ his being tetrarch -
and while Philip governed as tetrarch

Ἰτουραίας καὶ Τραχωνίτιδος χώρας, καὶ Λυσανίου τῆς
of Iturea and [3]of [4]Trachonitis [1]*the* [2]region, and Lysanias -
while Lysanias

Ἀβιληνῆς τετραρχοῦντος, 2 ἐπὶ ἀρχιερέως[a] Ἄννα
[3]of [4]Abilene [1]being [2]tetrarch, in the time of *the* high priest Annas
governed as tetrarch over Abilene,

καὶ Καϊάφα, ἐγένετο ῥῆμα Θεοῦ ἐπὶ Ἰωάννην
and *the high priest* Caiaphas, [5]came [1]*the* [2]word [3]of [4]God to John

τὸν Ζαχαρίου υἱὸν ἐν τῇ ἐρήμῳ. 3 Καὶ ἦλθεν εἰς πᾶσαν
the [2]of [3]Zacharias [1]son in the wilderness. And he went into all

τὴν περίχωρον τοῦ Ἰορδάνου, κηρύσσων* βάπτισμα
the surrounding region of the Jordan, preaching a baptism

μετανοίας εἰς ἄφεσιν ἁμαρτιῶν, 4 ὡς γέγραπται ἐν
of repentance for *the* forgiveness of sins, as it is written in

βίβλῳ λόγων Ἠσαΐου τοῦ προφήτου, λέγοντος,
the book of *the* words of Isaiah the prophet, saying,

«Φωνὴ βοῶντος·
«A voice of *one* crying:

"Ἐν τῇ ἐρήμῳ ἑτοιμάσατε τὴν ὁδὸν Κυρίου,
'In the wilderness prepare the way of *the* Lord,

Εὐθείας ποιεῖτε τὰς τρίβους αὐτοῦ.
straight ˜ Make - paths ˜ His.

5 Πᾶσα φάραγξ πληρωθήσεται
Every ravine shall be filled

Καὶ πᾶν ὄρος καὶ βουνὸς ταπεινωθήσεται·
And every mountain and hill shall be brought low;
humbled;

Καὶ ἔσται τὰ σκολιὰ εἰς εὐθεῖαν
And [4]shall [5]be [1]the [2]crooked [3]*things* into a straight *road*
the crooked roads shall become straight

Καὶ αἱ τραχεῖαι εἰς ὁδοὺς λείας·
And the rough *roads* into roads ˜ smooth;
shall become smooth;

6 Καὶ ὄψεται πᾶσα σὰρξ τὸ σωτήριον τοῦ Θεοῦ.'»[b]
And [3]shall [4]see [1]all [2]flesh the salvation - of God.'»
humanity

John Exhorts and Preaches to the People
(Matt. 3:7–12; Mark 1:7, 8; John 1:19–28)

7 Ἔλεγεν οὖν τοῖς ἐκπορευομένοις ὄχλοις βαπτισθῆναι
[2]he [3]said [1]Then to the [2]coming [3]out [1]crowds to be baptized
which came out

ὑπ' αὐτοῦ, "Γεννήματα ἐχιδνῶν! Τίς ὑπέδειξεν ὑμῖν φυγεῖν
by him, "Offspring of vipers! Who showed you to flee
"Brood warned

ἀπὸ τῆς μελλούσης ὀργῆς? **8** Ποιήσατε οὖν καρποὺς
from the coming wrath? produce ˜ Therefore fruits

ἀξίους τῆς μετανοίας, καὶ μὴ ἄρξησθε λέγειν ἐν
worthy - of repentance, and not ˜ do begin to say within
befitting repentance, among

ἑαυτοῖς, ‘Πατέρα ἔχομεν τὸν Ἀβραάμ.’ Λέγω γὰρ ὑμῖν ὅτι
yourselves, ‘[4]*as* [5]father [1]We [2]have - [3]Abraham.’ [2]I [3]say [1]For to you that

δύναται ὁ Θεὸς ἐκ τῶν λίθων τούτων ἐγεῖραι τέκνα τῷ
[2]is [3]able - [1]God out of - stones ˜ these to raise up children -

Ἀβραάμ. **9** Ἤδη δὲ καὶ ἡ ἀξίνη πρὸς τὴν ῥίζαν τῶν
to Abraham. [3]already [1]But [2]also the ax [4]to [5]the [6]root [7]of [8]the

δένδρων κεῖται. Πᾶν οὖν δένδρον μὴ ποιοῦν
[9]trees [1]is [2]being [3]laid. every ˜ Therefore tree not producing

καρπὸν καλὸν ἐκκόπτεται καὶ εἰς πῦρ βάλλεται.”
fruit ˜ good is cut down and [3]into [4]*the* [5]fire [1]is [2]thrown.”

10 Καὶ ἐπηρώτων αὐτὸν οἱ ὄχλοι λέγοντες, “Τί οὖν
And [3]were [4]asking [5]him [1]the [2]crowds saying, “What then

ποιήσωμεν?”
shall we do?”

11 Ἀποκριθεὶς δὲ λέγει αὐτοῖς, “Ὁ ἔχων δύο
answering ˜ And he says to them, “[2]the [3]*one* [4]having [5]two
said him who has

χιτῶνας μεταδότω τῷ μὴ ἔχοντι, καὶ ὁ ἔχων
[6]tunics [1]Let [7]give to the *one* not having *any*, and [2]the [3]*one* [4]having
shirts him who has none, him who has

βρώματα ὁμοίως ποιείτω.”
[5]foods [7]likewise [1]let [6]do.”
food

12 Ἦλθον δὲ καὶ τελῶναι βαπτισθῆναι, καὶ εἶπον
[5]came [1]And [2]also [3]tax [4]collectors to be baptized, and they said

πρὸς αὐτόν, “Διδάσκαλε, τί ποιήσωμεν?”
to him, “Teacher, what shall we do?”

13 Ὁ δὲ εἶπε πρὸς αὐτούς, “Μηδὲν πλέον παρὰ
he ˜ And said to them, “[2]nothing [3]more [4]than

τὸ διατεταγμένον ὑμῖν πράσσετε.”
[5]the [6]*amount* [7]having [8]been [9]commanded [10]to [11]you [1]Practice.”
which has Collect.”

14 Ἐπηρώτων δὲ αὐτὸν καὶ στρατευόμενοι,
[7]were [8]asking [1]And [9]him [6]also [2]*ones* [3]serving [4]as [5]soldiers,
soldiers,

λέγοντες, “Καὶ ἡμεῖς τί ποιήσωμεν?”
saying, “And [3]we [1]what [2]shall [4]do?”

Καὶ εἶπε πρὸς αὐτούς, “Μηδένα διασείσητε
And he said to them, “[4]*from* [5]no [6]one [1]Violently [2]extort [3]money

μηδὲ συκοφαντήσητε,* καὶ ἀρκεῖσθε τοῖς ὀψωνίοις ὑμῶν.”
nor accuse *anyone* falsely, and be content - with wages ˜ your.”

15 Προσδοκῶντος δὲ τοῦ λαοῦ καὶ διαλογιζομένων
[4]waiting [1]Now [2]the [3]people and considering ˜
Now while the people waited while all

πάντων ἐν ταῖς καρδίαις αὐτῶν περὶ τοῦ Ἰωάννου, μήποτε
all in - hearts ˜ their about - John, whether
considered

αὐτὸς εἴη ὁ Χριστός, **16** ἀπεκρίνατο ὁ Ἰωάννης ἅπασι
he might be the Christ, answered ˜ - John [2]to [3]all
Messiah,

λέγων, “Ἐγὼ μὲν ὕδατι βαπτίζω ὑμᾶς· ἔρχεται δὲ
[1]saying, “I indeed [3]with [4]water [1]baptize [2]you; [10]is [11]coming [5]but

the wrath to come?
8 “Therefore bear fruits
worthy of repentance, and do
not begin to say to yourselves,
‘We have Abraham as *our* father.’ For I say to you that God
is able to raise up children to
Abraham from these stones.
9 “And even now the ax is
laid to the root of the trees.
Therefore every tree which
does not bear good fruit is cut
down and thrown into the fire.”
10 So the people asked him,
saying, “What shall we do
then?”
11 He answered and said to
them, “He who has two tunics,
let him give to him who has
none; and he who has food, let
him do likewise.”
12 Then tax collectors also
came to be baptized, and said to
him, “Teacher, what shall we
do?”
13 And he said to them, “Collect no more than what is appointed for you.”
14 Likewise the soldiers
asked him, saying, “And what
shall we do?” So he said to
them, “Do not intimidate anyone or accuse falsely, and be
content with your wages.”
15 Now as the people were in
expectation, and all reasoned in
their hearts about John,
whether he was the Christ *or*
not,
16 John answered, saying to
all, “I indeed baptize you with

***(3:14)** συκοφαντέω *(sykophanteō)*. Verb used only twice in the NT, *accuse falsely, slander* (as here), or *take by false accusation, extort* (Luke 19:8). Both instances may carry the idea of oppression, given that the word generally designated a malignant informer, one who accused others for the sake of personal gain. The English *sycophant* comes from the same Greek root but has a derived meaning of a *self-seeking flatterer*.

water; but One mightier than I
is coming, whose sandal strap I
am not worthy to loose. He will
baptize you with the Holy Spirit
and fire.
17 "His winnowing fan *is* in
His hand, and He will thoroughly clean out His threshing
floor, and gather the wheat into
His barn; but the chaff He will
burn with unquenchable fire."
18 And with many other exhortations he preached to the
people.
19 But Herod the tetrarch,
being rebuked by him concerning Herodias, his brother
Philip's wife, and for all the
evils which Herod had done,
20 also added this, above all,
that he shut John up in prison.
21 When all the people were
baptized, it came to pass that
Jesus also was baptized; and
while He prayed, the heaven
was opened.
22 And the Holy Spirit descended in bodily form like a
dove upon Him, and a voice
came from heaven which said,
"You are My beloved Son; in
You I am well pleased."
23 Now Jesus Himself began
His ministry at about thirty
years of age, being (as was supposed) *the* son of Joseph, *the*
son of Heli,

ὁ ἰσχυρότερός μου, οὗ οὐκ εἰμὶ ἱκανὸς λῦσαι τὸν
- [6]*One* [7]mightier [8]*than* [9]Me, of whom [3]not [1]I [2]am worthy to loose the
I,

ἱμάντα τῶν ὑποδημάτων αὐτοῦ. Αὐτὸς ὑμᾶς βαπτίσει ἐν
strap - of sandals ~ His. He [3]you [1]will [2]baptize in
with

Πνεύματι Ἁγίῳ καὶ πυρί· 17 οὗ τὸ πτύον ἐν τῇ
the Spirit ~ Holy and fire; whose - winnowing shovel *is* in -

χειρὶ αὐτοῦ καὶ διακαθαριεῖ[c] τὴν ἅλωνα αὐτοῦ
hand ~ His and He will thoroughly clean out - [2]threshing [3]floor [1]His

καὶ συνάξει[d] τὸν σῖτον εἰς τὴν ἀποθήκην αὐτοῦ, τὸ δὲ
and will gather the wheat into - barn ~ His, the ~ but

ἄχυρον κατακαύσει πυρὶ ἀσβέστῳ."
chaff He will burn up with fire ~ unquenchable."

18 Πολλὰ μὲν οὖν καὶ ἕτερα παρακαλῶν
[4]many [1]So [2]then [7]also [5]other [6]*things* [3]exhorting

εὐηγγελίζετο τὸν λαόν. 19 Ὁ δὲ Ἡρῴδης ὁ
he proclaimed good news to the people. - But Herod the

τετράρχης, ἐλεγχόμενος ὑπ' αὐτοῦ περὶ Ἡρῳδιάδος τῆς
tetrarch, being rebuked by him about Herodias the
because he was

γυναικὸς[e] τοῦ ἀδελφοῦ αὐτοῦ, καὶ περὶ πάντων ὧν ἐποίησε
wife - of brother ~ His, and about all [4]which [6]did
had done

πονηρῶν ὁ Ἡρῴδης, 20 προσέθηκε καὶ τοῦτο ἐπὶ
[1]*the* [2]wicked [3]*things* - [5]Herod, he added also this to

πᾶσι καὶ κατέκλεισε τὸν Ἰωάννην ἐν τῇ φυλακῇ.
all *things* and locked up - John in the prison.
his other sins his

Jesus Is Baptized by John
(Matt. 3:13–17; Mark 1:19–11)

21 Ἐγένετο δὲ ἐν τῷ βαπτισθῆναι ἅπαντα τὸν λαόν,
[2]it [3]happened [1]Now in - [4]to [5]be [6]baptized [1]all [2]the [3]people,
when were

καὶ Ἰησοῦ βαπτισθέντος καὶ προσευχομένου,
also ~ Jesus having been baptized and *was* praying,
was

ἀνεῳχθῆναι τὸν οὐρανὸν 22 καὶ καταβῆναι τὸ Πνεῦμα
that [3]to [4]be [5]opened [1]the [2]heaven and [4]to [5]come [6]down [1]the [3]Spirit ~
was sky came

τὸ Ἅγιον σωματικῷ εἴδει ὡσεὶ περιστερὰν ἐπ' αὐτόν, καὶ
- [2]Holy in bodily form like a dove upon Him, and

φωνὴν ἐξ οὐρανοῦ γενέσθαι λέγουσαν, "Σὺ εἶ ὁ Υἱός μου
a voice [3]out [4]of [5]heaven [1]to [2]be saying, "You are - [3]Son [1]My
from came

ὁ ἀγαπητός, ἐν σοὶ εὐδόκησα."
- [2]beloved, in You I have found delight."

The Genealogy of Jesus Christ
(Cf. Matt. 1:1–17)

23 Καὶ αὐτὸς ἦν ὁ Ἰησοῦς ὡσεὶ ἐτῶν τριάκοντα
And [2]Himself [3]was - [1]Jesus about [2]of [3]years [1]thirty
years old

ἀρχόμενος, ὢν ὡς ἐνομίζετο υἱὸς Ἰωσήφ,
beginning, being as it was supposed *the* son of Joseph,
when He began,

τοῦ Ἡλί,
- *the son* of Heli,

---

[c](3:17) For *και διακαθαριει, and He will thoroughly clean out,* NU reads *διακαθαραι, to thoroughly clean out.*
[d](3:17) NU reads *συναγαγειν, to gather.*
[e](3:19) TR adds Φιλιππου, *of Philip.*

24 τοῦ Ματθάτ, τοῦ Λευί, τοῦ Μελχί,
- *the son* of Matthat, - *the son* of Levi, - *the son* of Melchi,
τοῦ Ἰαννά, τοῦ Ἰωσήφ,
- *the son* of Janna, - *the son* of Joseph,
25 τοῦ Ματταθίου, τοῦ Ἀμώς, τοῦ Ναούμ,
- *the son* of Mattathiah, - *the son* of Amos, - *the son* of Nahum,
τοῦ Ἐσλί, τοῦ Ναγγαί,
- *the son* of Esli, - *the son* of Naggai,
26 τοῦ Μάαθ, τοῦ Ματταθίου, τοῦ Σεμεεί,
- *the son* of Maath, - *the son* of Mattathiah, - *the son* of Semei,
τοῦ Ἰωσήφ,[f] τοῦ Ἰούδα,[g]
- *the son* of Joseph, - *the son* of Judah,
27 τοῦ Ἰωανάν, τοῦ Ῥησά, τοῦ Ζοροβάβελ,
- *the son* of Joanan, - *the son* of Rhesa, - *the son* of Zerubbabel,
τοῦ Σαλαθιήλ, τοῦ Νηρί,
- *the son* of Shealtiel, - *the son* of Neri,
28 τοῦ Μελχί, τοῦ Ἀδδί, τοῦ Κωσάμ,
- *the son* of Melchi, - *the son* of Addi, - *the son* of Cosam,
τοῦ Ἐλμωδάμ, τοῦ Ἤρ,
- *the son* of Elmodam, - *the son* of Er,
29 τοῦ Ἰωσή,[h] τοῦ Ἐλιέζερ, τοῦ Ἰωρείμ,
- *the son* of Jose, - *the son* of Eliezer, - *the son* of Jorim,
τοῦ Ματθάτ, τοῦ Λευί,
- *the son* of Matthat, - *the son* of Levi,
30 τοῦ Συμεών, τοῦ Ἰούδα, τοῦ Ἰωσήφ,
- *the son* of Simeon, - *the son* of Judah, - *the son* of Joseph,
τοῦ Ἰωνάν, τοῦ Ἐλιακείμ,
- *the son* of Jonan, - *the son* of Eliakim,
31 τοῦ Μελεᾶ, τοῦ Μαϊνάν, τοῦ Ματταθά,
- *the son* of Melea, - *the son* of Menan, - *the son* of Mattathah,
τοῦ Ναθάν, τοῦ Δαβίδ,
- *the son* of Nathan, - *the son* of David,
32 τοῦ Ἰεσσαί, τοῦ Ὠβήδ, τοῦ Βόοζ,
- *the son* of Jesse, - *the son* of Obed, - *the son* of Boaz,
τοῦ Σαλμών, τοῦ Ναασσών,
- *the son* of Salmon, - *the son* of Nahshon,
33 τοῦ Ἀμιναδάβ, τοῦ Ἀράμ,[i] τοῦ Ἰωράμ,[j]
- *the son* of Amminadab, - *the son* of Aram, - *the son* of Joram,
τοῦ Ἑσρώμ,
- *the son* of Hezron,
τοῦ Φάρες, τοῦ Ἰούδα,
- *the son* of Perez, - *the son* of Judah,
34 τοῦ Ἰακώβ, τοῦ Ἰσαάκ, τοῦ Ἀβραάμ,
- *the son* of Jacob, - *the son* of Isaac, - *the son* of Abraham,
τοῦ Θάρρα, τοῦ Ναχώρ,
- *the son* of Terah, - *the son* of Nahor,
35 τοῦ Σερούχ, τοῦ Ῥαγαῦ, τοῦ Φάλεγ,
- *the son* of Serug, - *the son* of Reu, - *the son* of Peleg,
τοῦ Ἔβερ, τοῦ Σαλά,
- *the son* of Eber, - *the son* of Shelah,
36 τοῦ Καϊνάν, τοῦ Ἀρφαξάδ, τοῦ Σήμ,
- *the son* of Cainan, - *the son* of Arphaxad, - *the son* of Shem,
τοῦ Νῶε, τοῦ Λάμεχ,
- *the son* of Noah, - *the son* of Lamech,
37 τοῦ Μαθουσαλά, τοῦ Ἑνώχ, τοῦ Ἰάρεδ,
- *the son* of Methuselah, - *the son* of Enoch, - *the son* of Jared,

24 *the son* of Matthat, *the son*
of Levi, *the son* of Melchi, *the*
son of Janna, *the son* of Joseph,
25 *the son* of Mattathiah, *the*
son of Amos, *the son* of Nahum,
the son of Esli, *the son* of Naggai,
26 *the son* of Maath, *the son* of
Mattathiah, *the son* of Semei,
the son of Joseph, *the son* of Judah,
27 *the son* of Joannas, *the son*
of Rhesa, *the son* of Zerubbabel, *the son* of Shealtiel, *the son*
of Neri,
28 *the son* of Melchi, *the son* of
Addi, *the son* of Cosam, *the son*
of Elmodam, *the son* of Er,
29 *the son* of Jose, *the son* of
Eliezer, *the son* of Jorim, *the*
son of Matthat, *the son* of Levi,
30 *the son* of Simeon, *the son*
of Judah, *the son* of Joseph, *the*
son of Jonan, *the son* of Eliakim,
31 *the son* of Melea, *the son* of
Menan, *the son* of Mattathah,
the son of Nathan, *the son* of David,
32 *the son* of Jesse, *the son* of
Obed, *the son* of Boaz, *the son*
of Salmon, *the son* of Nahshon,
33 *the son* of Amminadab, *the*
son of Ram, *the son* of Hezron,
the son of Perez, *the son* of Judah,
34 *the son* of Jacob, *the son* of
Isaac, *the son* of Abraham, *the*
son of Terah, *the son* of Nahor,
35 *the son* of Serug, *the son* of
Reu, *the son* of Peleg, *the son* of
Eber, *the son* of Shelah,
36 *the son* of Cainan, *the son* of
Arphaxad, *the son* of Shem, *the*
son of Noah, *the son* of Lamech,
37 *the son* of Methuselah, *the*
son of Enoch, *the son* of Jared,

---

[f]**(3:26)** NU reads Ιωσηχ, *Josech.* [g]**(3:26)** NU reads Ιωδα, *Joda.*
[h]**(3:29)** NU reads Ιησου, *Jesus* (= Joshua).
[i]**(3:33)** NU reads Αδμιν, *Admin.* [j]**(3:33)** NU reads Αρνι, *Arni;* TR omits του Ιωραμ, *of Joram.*

the son of Mahalalel, *the son* of Cainan,
38 *the son* of Enosh, *the son* of Seth, *the son* of Adam, *the son* of God.

4 Then Jesus, being filled with the Holy Spirit, returned from the Jordan and was led by the Spirit into the wilderness,
2 being tempted for forty days by the devil. And in those days He ate nothing, and afterward, when they had ended, He was hungry.
3 And the devil said to Him, "If You are the Son of God, command this stone to become bread."
4 But Jesus answered him, saying, "It is written, *'Man shall not live by bread alone, but by every word of God.'*"
5 Then the devil, taking Him up on a high mountain, showed Him all the kingdoms of the world in a moment of time.
6 And the devil said to Him, "All this authority I will give You, and their glory; for *this* has been delivered to me, and I give it to whomever I wish.
7 "Therefore, if You will worship before me, all will be Yours."
8 And Jesus answered and said to him, "Get behind Me, Satan! For it is written, *'You shall worship the* LORD *your God, and Him only you shall serve.'*"

τοῦ Μαλελεήλ, τοῦ Καϊνάν,
- *the son* of Mahalalel, - *the son* of Cainan,
38 τοῦ Ἐνώς, τοῦ Σήθ, τοῦ Ἀδάμ,
- *the son* of Enos, - *the son* of Seth, - *the son* of Adam,
τοῦ Θεοῦ.
- *the son* of God.

Satan Tempts Jesus
(Matt. 4:1–11; Mark 1:12, 13)

4 1 Ἰησοῦς δὲ Πνεύματος Ἁγίου πλήρης ὑπέστρεψεν ἀπὸ
Jesus ˜ Then [2]of [3]*the* [5]Spirit [4]Holy [1]full returned from
τοῦ Ἰορδάνου καὶ ἤγετο ἐν τῷ Πνεύματι εἰς τὴν ἔρημον
the Jordan and was led in (by) the Spirit into the wilderness
2 ἡμέρας τεσσαράκοντα πειραζόμενος ὑπὸ τοῦ διαβόλου. Καὶ
[4]days [3]forty [1]being [2]tempted by the devil. And
οὐκ ἔφαγεν οὐδὲν ἐν ταῖς ἡμέραις ἐκείναις, καὶ
[3]not [1]He [2]did eat nothing (anything) in - days ˜ those, and
συντελεσθεισῶν αὐτῶν, ὕστερον[a] ἐπείνασε. 3 Καὶ εἶπεν
[2]being [3]completed (when they were) [1]them, (completed,) afterward He was hungry. And [3]said
αὐτῷ ὁ διάβολος, "Εἰ Υἱὸς εἶ τοῦ Θεοῦ εἰπὲ τῷ
[4]to [5]Him [1]the [2]devil, "If [3]*the* [4]Son [1]You [2]are - of God say (speak) -
λίθῳ τούτῳ ἵνα γένηται ἄρτος."
to stone ˜ this that it may become bread."
4 Καὶ ἀπεκρίθη Ἰησοῦς πρὸς αὐτόν, λέγων, "Γέγραπται
And answered ˜ Jesus to him, saying, "It is written
ὅτι
-

«Οὐκ ἐπ' ἄρτῳ μόνῳ ζήσεται ἄνθρωπος
«Not on (by) bread alone shall live ˜ man
Ἀλλ' ἐπὶ παντὶ ῥήματι Θεοῦ.»"[b]
But by every word of God.»"

5 Καὶ ἀναγαγὼν αὐτὸν ὁ διάβολος εἰς ὄρος
And [3]leading [5]up [4]Him [1]the [2]devil into a mountain ˜
ὑψηλὸν[c] ἔδειξεν αὐτῷ πάσας τὰς βασιλείας τῆς οἰκουμένης
high showed to Him all the kingdoms of the world
ἐν στιγμῇ χρόνου. 6 Καὶ εἶπεν αὐτῷ ὁ διάβολος, "Σοὶ
in a moment of time. And [3]said [4]to [5]Him [1]the [2]devil, "To You
δώσω τὴν ἐξουσίαν ταύτην ἅπασαν καὶ τὴν δόξαν αὐτῶν·
I will give - [3]authority [2]this [1]all and - glory ˜ their;
ὅτι ἐμοὶ παραδέδοται, καὶ ᾧ ἐὰν θέλω δίδωμι αὐτήν.
because to me it has been given, and to whom ever I wish I give it.
7 Σὺ οὖν ἐὰν προσκυνήσῃς ἐνώπιον ἐμοῦ, ἔσται σου
[3]You [1]Therefore [2]if worship before me, [2]will [3]be [4]Yours
πᾶσα."
[1]all."
8 Καὶ ἀποκριθεὶς αὐτῷ εἶπεν ὁ Ἰησοῦς, "Ὕπαγε ὀπίσω
And [2]answering [3]him [4]said - [1]Jesus, "Go away behind
μου, Σατανᾶ![d] Γέγραπται,
Me, Satan! It is written,

«Προσκυνήσεις Κύριον τὸν Θεόν σου,
«You shall worship *the* Lord - God ˜ your,
Καὶ αὐτῷ μόνῳ λατρεύσεις.»"[e]
And Him alone you shall serve.»"

---

[a](**4:2**) NU omits υστερον, *afterward*.
[b](**4:4**) Deut. 8:3; NU omits αλλ επι παντι ρηματι Θεου, *but by every word of God*.
[c](**4:5**) NU omits ο διαβολος εις ορος υψηλον, *the devil into a high mountain*.
[d](**4:8**) NU omits Υπαγε οπισω μου Σατανα, *go away behind Me, Satan*.
[e](**4:8**) Deut. 6:13

9 Καὶ ἤγαγεν αὐτὸν εἰς Ἰερουσαλὴμ καὶ ἔστησεν αὐτὸν
And he brought Him to Jerusalem and set Him

ἐπὶ τὸ πτερύγιον τοῦ ἱεροῦ καὶ εἶπεν αὐτῷ, "Εἰ Υἱὸς
on the extremity of the temple and said to Him, "If [3]*the* [4]Son
pinnacle

εἶ τοῦ Θεοῦ, βάλε σεαυτὸν ἐντεῦθεν κάτω.
[1]You [2]are - of God, throw Yourself [2]from [3]here [1]down.

10 Γέγραπται γὰρ ὅτι
[2]it [3]is [4]written [1]For -

«Τοῖς ἀγγέλοις αὐτοῦ ἐντελεῖται περὶ σοῦ,
- «To angels ˜ His He will give orders concerning You,

Τοῦ διαφυλάξαι σε,»
- To guard You,»

11 καὶ
and

«Ἐπὶ χειρῶν ἀροῦσί σε,
«On *their* hands they will lift up ˜ You,
«In

Μήποτε προσκόψῃς πρὸς λίθον τὸν πόδα σου.»"[f]
Lest you strike [3]against [4]a [5]stone - [2]foot [1]Your.»"

12 Καὶ ἀποκριθεὶς εἶπεν αὐτῷ ὁ Ἰησοῦς ὅτι "Εἴρηται,
And answering [2]said [3]to [4]him - [1]Jesus - "It has been said,

«Οὐκ ἐκπειράσεις Κύριον τὸν Θεόν σου.»"[g] 13 Καὶ
«[3]not [1]You [2]shall tempt *the* Lord - God ˜ your.»" And

συντελέσας πάντα πειρασμὸν ὁ διάβολος ἀπέστη ἀπ'
having completed every temptation the devil departed from

αὐτοῦ ἄχρι καιροῦ.
Him until a season.
an opportune time.

Jesus Begins His Galilean Ministry
(Matt. 4:12–17; Mark 1:14, 15)

14 Καὶ ὑπέστρεψεν ὁ Ἰησοῦς ἐν τῇ δυνάμει τοῦ
And returned ˜ - Jesus in the power of the

Πνεύματος εἰς τὴν Γαλιλαίαν, καὶ φήμη ἐξῆλθε καθ'
Spirit to - Galilee, and a report went out throughout
news

ὅλης τῆς περιχώρου περὶ αὐτοῦ. 15 Καὶ αὐτὸς ἐδίδασκεν
whole ˜ the surrounding region about Him. And He taught
would teach

ἐν ταῖς συναγωγαῖς αὐτῶν, δοξαζόμενος ὑπὸ πάντων.
in - synagogues ˜ their, being glorified by all.

Jesus Is Rejected at Nazareth

16 Καὶ ἦλθεν εἰς τὴν Ναζαρέτ, οὗ ἦν τεθραμμένος.
And He came to - Nazareth, where He was brought up.
had been

Καὶ εἰσῆλθε, κατὰ τὸ εἰωθὸς αὐτῷ, ἐν τῇ ἡμέρᾳ τῶν
And He entered, according to the custom with Him, in *the* day of the
on the Sabbath day

σαββάτων εἰς τὴν συναγωγήν, καὶ ἀνέστη ἀναγνῶναι.
Sabbath into the synagogue, and He stood up to read.

17 Καὶ ἐπεδόθη αὐτῷ βιβλίον Ἠσαΐου τοῦ προφήτου. Καὶ
And [7]was [8]given [9]to [10]Him [1]*the* [2]book [3]of [4]Isaiah [5]the [6]prophet. And

9 Then he brought Him to Jerusalem, set Him on the pinnacle of the temple, and said to Him, "If You are the Son of God, throw Yourself down from here.
10 "For it is written:

'He shall give His angels
charge over you,
To keep you,'

11 "and,

'In their hands they shall
bear you up,
Lest you dash your foot
against a stone.'"

12 And Jesus answered and said to him, "It has been said, *'You shall not tempt the* LORD *your God.'"*
13 Now when the devil had ended every temptation, he departed from Him until an opportune time.
14 Then Jesus returned in the power of the Spirit to Galilee, and news of Him went out through all the surrounding region.
15 And He taught in their synagogues, being glorified by all.
16 So He came to Nazareth, where He had been brought up. And as His custom was, He went into the synagogue on the Sabbath day, and stood up to read.
17 And He was handed the book of the prophet Isaiah. And

[f](**4:11**) Ps. 91:11, 12
[g](**4:12**) Deut. 6:16

when He had opened the book, He found the place where it was written:

18 *"The Spirit of the* LORD *is upon Me,*
Because He has anointed Me
To preach the gospel to the poor;
He has sent Me to heal the brokenhearted,
To proclaim liberty to the captives
And recovery of sight to the blind,
To set at liberty those who are oppressed;
19 *To proclaim the acceptable year of the* LORD*."*

20 Then He closed the book, and gave *it* back to the attendant and sat down. And the eyes of all who were in the synagogue were fixed on Him.
21 And He began to say to them, "Today this Scripture is fulfilled in your hearing."
22 So all bore witness to Him, and marveled at the gracious words which proceeded out of His mouth. And they said, "Is this not Joseph's son?"
23 He said to them, "You will surely say this proverb to Me, 'Physician, heal yourself! Whatever we have heard done in Capernaum, do also here in Your country.'"
24 Then He said, "Assuredly, I say to you, no prophet is accepted in his own country.
25 "But I tell you truly, many

ἀναπτύξας τὸ βιβλίον, εὗρε τὸν τόπον οὗ ἦν
having unrolled the scroll, He found the place where it was
had been

γεγραμμένον,
written,

18 «Πνεῦμα Κυρίου ἐπ' ἐμέ,
«*The* Spirit of *the* Lord *is* upon Me,

Οὗ εἵνεκεν ἔχρισέ με
[4]which [1]On [2]account [3]of He anointed Me

Εὐαγγελίσασθαι πτωχοῖς.
To proclaim good news to poor *people*.

᾿Απέσταλκέ με ἰάσασθαι τοὺς συντετριμμένους τὴν
He has sent Me to heal the *ones* having been broken - *in*
the brokenhearted,

καρδίαν,[h]
heart,

Κηρύξαι αἰχμαλώτοις ἄφεσιν
To preach [2]to [3]captives [1]release

Καὶ τυφλοῖς ἀνάβλεψιν,
And [4]to [5]blind [6]*people* [1]recovery [2]of [3]sight,

᾿Αποστεῖλαι τεθραυσμένους ἐν ἀφέσει,
To send forth oppressed *ones* in release,
those who are oppressed to freedom,

19 Κηρύξαι ἐνιαυτὸν Κυρίου δεκτόν.»[i]
To preach [1]*the* [3]year [4]of [5]*the* [6]Lord [2]acceptable.»

20 Καὶ πτύξας τὸ βιβλίον, ἀποδοὺς τῷ
And having rolled up the scroll, giving *it* to the
when He had given

ὑπηρέτῃ, ἐκάθισε. Καὶ πάντων ἐν τῇ συναγωγῇ οἱ
attendant, He sat down. And [3]of [4]all [5]in [6]the [7]synagogue [1]the

ὀφθαλμοὶ ἦσαν ἀτενίζοντες αὐτῷ. 21 Ἤρξατο δὲ λέγειν
[2]eyes were looking intently at Him. [2]He [3]began [1]And to say

πρὸς αὐτοὺς ὅτι "Σήμερον πεπλήρωται ἡ γραφὴ αὕτη ἐν
to them - "Today [3]has [4]been [5]fulfilled - [2]Scripture [1]this in

τοῖς ὠσὶν ὑμῶν."
- ears ˜ your."

22 Καὶ πάντες ἐμαρτύρουν αὐτῷ καὶ ἐθαύμαζον ἐπὶ
And all were bearing witness to Him and were marveling at

τοῖς λόγοις τῆς χάριτος τοῖς ἐκπορευομένοις ἐκ τοῦ στόματος
the words - of grace the *ones* going out of - mouth ˜
which came out

αὐτοῦ. Καὶ ἔλεγον, "Οὐχ οὗτος ἐστιν ὁ υἱός Ἰωσήφ?"
His. And they said, "[2]not [3]this [1]Is the son of Joseph?"

23 Καὶ εἶπε πρὸς αὐτούς, "Πάντως ἐρεῖτέ μοι τὴν
And He said to them, "By all means you will tell Me -
"Surely

παραβολὴν ταύτην, 'Ἰατρέ, θεράπευσον σεαυτόν.
parable ˜ this, 'Physician, heal yourself.

Ὅσα ἠκούσαμεν γενόμενα ἐν τῇ Καπερναοὺμ
As many *things* as we heard having been done in - Capernaum
Whatever was

ποίησον καὶ ὧδε ἐν τῇ πατρίδι σου.'"
do also here in - hometown ˜ Your.'"

24 Εἶπε δέ, "'Ἀμὴν λέγω ὑμῖν ὅτι οὐδεὶς προφήτης
[2]He [3]said [1]Then, "Amen I tell you that no prophet
"Assuredly

δεκτός ἐστιν ἐν τῇ πατρίδι αὐτοῦ. 25 Ἐπ' ἀληθείας δὲ
acceptable ˜ is in - hometown ˜ his. [2]in [3]truth [1]But

---

[h](**4:18**) NU omits *ιασασθαι τους συντετριμμενους την καρδιαν, to heal the brokenhearted.*
[i](**4:19**) Is. 61:1, 2

λέγω ὑμῖν, πολλαὶ χῆραι ἦσαν ἐν ταῖς ἡμέραις Ἠλίου ἐν
I tell you, [3]many [4]widows [1]*there* [2]were in the days of Elijah in

τῷ Ἰσραήλ, ὅτε ἐκλείσθη ὁ οὐρανὸς ἐπὶ ἔτη τρία καὶ
- Israel, when [3]was [4]shut [1]the [2]heaven for years ~ three and
sky

μῆνας ἕξ, ὡς ἐγένετο λιμὸς μέγας ἐπὶ πᾶσαν τὴν γῆν·
months ~ six, when *there* was a famine ~ great over all the land;

26 καὶ πρὸς οὐδεμίαν αὐτῶν ἐπέμφθη Ἠλίας εἰ μὴ εἰς
and to not one of them was sent ~ Elijah if not to
except

Σάρεπτα τῆς Σιδῶνος πρὸς γυναῖκα χήραν. 27 Καὶ πολλοὶ
Zarephath - of Sidon to a woman ~ widow. And [3]many
near

λεπροὶ ἦσαν ἐπὶ Ἐλισσαίου τοῦ προφήτου ἐν τῷ
[4]lepers [1]*there* [2]were in the time of Elisha the prophet in -

Ἰσραήλ· καὶ οὐδεὶς αὐτῶν ἐκαθαρίσθη εἰ μὴ Νεεμὰν ὁ
Israel; and not one of them was cleansed if not Naaman the
except

Σύρος." 28 Καὶ ἐπλήσθησαν πάντες θυμοῦ ἐν τῇ
Syrian." And [5]were [6]filled [1]all [7]with [8]wrath [2]in [3]the

συναγωγῇ ἀκούοντες ταῦτα, 29 καὶ ἀναστάντες ἐξέβαλον
[4]synagogue hearing these *things,* and rising up they threw
as they heard

αὐτὸν ἔξω τῆς πόλεως καὶ ἤγαγον αὐτὸν ἕως ὀφρύος τοῦ
Him out of the city and brought Him to *the* brow of the

ὄρους ἐφ' οὗ ἡ πόλις αὐτῶν ᾠκοδόμητο, εἰς τὸ
hill on which - city ~ their was built, for -
in order

κατακρημνίσαι αὐτόν. 30 Αὐτὸς δὲ διελθὼν διὰ μέσου
to throw down ~ Him. He ~ But having passed through *the* midst

αὐτῶν ἐπορεύετο.
of them went on.

Jesus Casts Out an Unclean Spirit
(Mark 1:21–28)

31 Καὶ κατῆλθεν εἰς Καπερναοὺμ, πόλιν τῆς Γαλιλαίας,
And He went down to Capernaum, a city - of Galilee,

καὶ ἦν διδάσκων αὐτοὺς ἐν τοῖς σάββασι. 32 Καὶ
and He was teaching them on the Sabbath. And

ἐξεπλήσσοντο ἐπὶ τῇ διδαχῇ αὐτοῦ, ὅτι ἐν ἐξουσίᾳ
they were astonished at - teaching ~ His, because [4]with [5]authority

ἦν ὁ λόγος αὐτοῦ.
[3]was - [2]word [1]His.

33 Καὶ ἐν τῇ συναγωγῇ ἦν ἄνθρωπος ἔχων πνεῦμα
And in the synagogue *there* was a man having a spirit

δαιμονίου ἀκαθάρτου. Καὶ ἀνέκραξε φωνῇ μεγάλῃ,
of a(n) demon ~ unclean. And he cried out with a voice ~ great,
loud,

34 λέγων, "Ἔα! Τί ἡμῖν καὶ σοί, Ἰησοῦ
saying, "Let *us* alone! What to us and to You, Jesus
"Ah! What have we to do with You,

Ναζαρηνέ? Ἦλθες ἀπολέσαι ἡμᾶς? Οἶδά σε τίς εἶ,
Nazarene? Did You come to destroy us? I know You who You are,

ὁ Ἅγιος τοῦ Θεοῦ!"
the Holy *One* - of God!"

35 Καὶ ἐπετίμησεν αὐτῷ ὁ Ἰησοῦς, λέγων, "Φιμώθητι, καὶ
And [2]rebuked [3]him - [1]Jesus, saying, "Be muzzled, and
silenced,

widows were in Israel in the days of Elijah, when the heaven was shut up three years and six months, and there was a great famine throughout all the land;
26 "but to none of them was Elijah sent except to Zarephath, *in the region* of Sidon, to a woman *who was* a widow.
27 "And many lepers were in Israel in the time of Elisha the prophet, and none of them was cleansed except Naaman the Syrian."
28 So all those in the synagogue, when they heard these things, were filled with wrath,
29 and rose up and thrust Him out of the city; and they led Him to the brow of the hill on which their city was built, that they might throw Him down over the cliff.
30 Then passing through the midst of them, He went His way.
31 Then He went down to Capernaum, a city of Galilee, and was teaching them on the Sabbaths.
32 And they were astonished at His teaching, for His word was with authority.
33 Now in the synagogue there was a man who had a spirit of an unclean demon. And he cried out with a loud voice,
34 saying, "Let *us* alone! What have we to do with You, Jesus of Nazareth? Did You come to destroy us? I know who You are—the Holy One of God!"
35 But Jesus rebuked him, saying, "Be quiet, and come

out of him!" And when the demon had thrown him in *their* midst, it came out of him and did not hurt him.
36 Then they were all amazed and spoke among themselves, saying, "What a word this *is!* For with authority and power He commands the unclean spirits, and they come out."
37 And the report about Him went out into every place in the surrounding region.
38 Now He arose from the synagogue and entered Simon's house. But Simon's wife's mother was sick with a high fever, and they made request of Him concerning her.
39 So He stood over her and rebuked the fever, and it left her. And immediately she arose and served them.
40 When the sun was setting, all those who had any that were sick with various diseases brought them to Him; and He laid His hands on every one of them and healed them.
41 And demons also came out of many, crying out and saying, "You are the Christ, the Son of God!" And He, rebuking *them,* did not allow them to speak, for they knew that He was the Christ.

ἔξελθε ἐξ αὐτοῦ!" Καὶ ῥίψαν αὐτὸν τὸ δαιμόνιον
come out from him!" And [3]throwing [5]down [4]him [1]the [2]demon
when the demon had thrown him down

εἰς μέσον ἐξῆλθεν ἀπ' αὐτοῦ, μηδὲν βλάψαν αὐτόν.
in *the* midst it came out from him, [3]nothing [1]hurting [2]him.
in no way

36 Καὶ ἐγένετο θάμβος ἐπὶ πάντας, καὶ συνελάλουν
And came ˜ amazement upon all, and they spoke together

πρὸς ἀλλήλους, λέγοντες, "Τίς ὁ λόγος οὗτος, ὅτι ἐν
with one another, saying, "What - *is* word ˜ this, because with

ἐξουσίᾳ καὶ δυνάμει ἐπιτάσσει τοῖς ἀκαθάρτοις πνεύμασι,
authority and power He commands the unclean spirits,

καὶ ἐξέρχονται?" 37 Καὶ ἐξεπορεύετο ἦχος περὶ αὐτοῦ εἰς
and they come out?" And [3]went [4]out [1]a [2]report about Him into

πάντα τόπον τῆς περιχώρου.
every place of the surrounding region.

Jesus Heals Peter's Mother-in-Law
(Matt. 8:14, 15; Mark 1:29–31)

38 Ἀναστὰς δὲ ἐκ τῆς συναγωγῆς εἰσῆλθεν εἰς τὴν
[2]rising [3]up [1]And from the synagogue He entered into the
when He rose

οἰκίαν Σίμωνος. Πενθερὰ δὲ τοῦ Σίμωνος ἦν
house of Simon. [2]*the* [3]mother-in-law [1]But - of Simon was

συνεχομένη πυρετῷ μεγάλῳ, καὶ ἠρώτησαν αὐτὸν περὶ
suffering from a fever ˜ great, and they requested of Him about
high,

αὐτῆς. 39 Καὶ ἐπιστὰς ἐπάνω αὐτῆς ἐπετίμησε τῷ
her. And standing by over her He rebuked the
when He stood

πυρετῷ, καὶ ἀφῆκεν αὐτήν. Παραχρῆμα δὲ ἀναστᾶσα
fever, and it left her. immediately ˜ And rising up

διηκόνει αὐτοῖς.
she was serving them.
began to serve

Jesus Heals Many After Sabbath Sunset
(Matt. 8:16, 17; Mark 1:32–34)

40 Δύνοντος δὲ τοῦ ἡλίου, πάντες ὅσοι εἶχον
[4]setting [1]Now [2]the [3]sun, all as many as had
Now when the sun was setting, who

ἀσθενοῦντας νόσοις ποικίλαις ἤγαγον αὐτοὺς πρὸς αὐτόν·
ones being sick with diseases ˜ various brought them to Him;
those who were

ὁ δὲ ἑνὶ ἑκάστῳ αὐτῶν τὰς χεῖρας ἐπιθεὶς
[10]the [11]*One* [1]and [7]one [5]on [6]each [8]of [9]them - [4]hands [2]having [3]put
He

ἐθεράπευσεν αὐτούς. 41 Ἐξήρχετο δὲ καὶ δαιμόνια
healed them. [4]were [5]coming [6]out [1]And [2]also [3]demons

ἀπὸ πολλῶν, κράζοντα καὶ λέγοντα ὅτι "Σὺ εἶ ὁ Χριστὸς[j]
from many, crying and saying - "You are the Christ

ὁ Υἱὸς τοῦ Θεοῦ!" Καὶ ἐπιτιμῶν οὐκ εἴα αὐτὰ
the Son - of God!" And rebuking *them* [3]not [1]He [2]did allow them

λαλεῖν, ὅτι ᾔδεισαν τὸν Χριστὸν αὐτὸν εἶναι.
to speak, because they knew [4]the [5]Christ [1]Him [2]to [3]be.
that He was the Messiah.

[j](**4:41**) NU omits ο Χριστος, *the Christ.*

Jesus Preaches in Galilee
(Mark 1:35–39)

42 Γενομένης δὲ ἡμέρας, ἐξελθὼν ἐπορεύθη εἰς
[3]becoming [1]Now [2]day, going out He went to
Now when day came,

ἔρημον τόπον, καὶ οἱ ὄχλοι ἐπεζήτουν αὐτόν, καὶ
an uninhabited place, and the crowds were searching for Him, and

ἦλθον ἕως αὐτοῦ, καὶ κατεῖχον αὐτὸν τοῦ μὴ πορεύεσθαι
they came to Him and held back ~ Him - not to go
tried to restrain that He might not go

ἀπ᾽ αὐτῶν. 43 Ὁ δὲ εἶπε πρὸς αὐτοὺς ὅτι "Καὶ ταῖς
from them. [2]the [3]*One* [1]But said to them - "Also to the
He

ἑτέραις πόλεσιν εὐαγγελίσασθαί με δεῖ
other cities [6]to [7]proclaim [8]good [9]news [5]Me [1]it [2]is [3]necessary [4]*for*
I must proclaim the good news

τὴν βασιλείαν τοῦ Θεοῦ, ὅτι εἰς τοῦτο
about the kingdom - of God because for this *purpose*

ἀπέσταλμαι." 44 Καὶ ἦν κηρύσσων ἐν ταῖς συναγωγαῖς
I have been sent." And He was preaching in the synagogues

τῆς Γαλιλαίας.[k]
- of Galilee.

Jesus Calls Four Fishermen
(Matt. 4:18–22; Mark 1:16–20)

5 1 Ἐγένετο δὲ ἐν τῷ τὸν ὄχλον ἐπικεῖσθαι αὐτῷ τοῦ
[2]it [3]happened [1]Now in - the crowd to press upon Him -
while pressed

ἀκούειν τὸν λόγον τοῦ Θεοῦ καὶ αὐτὸς ἦν ἑστὼς παρὰ τὴν
to hear the word - of God and He was standing alongside the

λίμνην Γεννησαρέτ, 2 καὶ εἶδε δύο πλοῖα ἑστῶτα παρὰ τὴν
Lake of Gennesaret, and He saw two boats standing by the
that

λίμνην· οἱ δὲ ἁλιεῖς ἀποβάντες ἀπ᾽ αὐτῶν ἀπέπλυναν
lake; the ~ but fishermen *after* getting out of them washed
were washing

τὰ δίκτυα. 3 Ἐμβὰς δὲ εἰς ἓν τῶν πλοίων, ὃ ἦν τοῦ
the nets. [2]stepping [3]in [1]But into one of the boats, which was -
their

Σίμωνος, ἠρώτησεν αὐτὸν ἀπὸ τῆς γῆς ἐπαναγαγεῖν ὀλίγον.
Simon's, He asked him [6]from [7]the [8]land [1]to [2]put [3]out [4]a [5]little.

Καὶ καθίσας ἐδίδασκεν ἐκ τοῦ πλοίου τοὺς ὄχλους.
And sitting down He taught [3]from [4]the [5]boat [1]the [2]crowds.
began to teach

4 Ὡς δὲ ἐπαύσατο λαλῶν, εἶπε πρὸς τὸν Σίμωνα,
when ~ Now He stopped speaking, He said to - Simon,

"Ἐπανάγαγε εἰς τὸ βάθος καὶ χαλάσατε τὰ δίκτυα ὑμῶν εἰς
"Put out into the deep and lower - nets ~ your for

ἄγραν."
a catch."

5 Καὶ ἀποκριθεὶς ὁ Σίμων εἶπεν αὐτῷ, "Ἐπιστάτα,
And answering - Simon said to Him, "Master,

δι᾽ ὅλης τῆς νυκτὸς κοπιάσαντες οὐδὲν ἐλάβομεν,
through whole ~ the night toiling [3]nothing [1]we [2]took,
although we toiled throughout the night, caught,

ἐπὶ δὲ τῷ ῥήματί σου χαλάσω τὸ δίκτυον."[a] 6 Καὶ τοῦτο
on ~ but - word ~ Your I will lower the net." And [3]this
when they

42 Now when it was day, He
departed and went into a deserted place. And the crowd
sought Him and came to Him,
and tried to keep Him from
leaving them;
43 but He said to them, "I
must preach the kingdom of
God to the other cities also, because for this purpose I have
been sent."
44 And He was preaching in
the synagogues of Galilee.
5 So it was, as the multitude pressed about Him
to hear the word of God, that
He stood by the Lake of Gennesaret,
2 and saw two boats standing
by the lake; but the fishermen
had gone from them and were
washing *their* nets.
3 Then He got into one of
the boats, which was Simon's,
and asked him to put out a little
from the land. And He sat down
and taught the multitudes from
the boat.
4 When He had stopped
speaking, He said to Simon,
"Launch out into the deep and
let down your nets for a catch."
5 But Simon answered and
said to Him, "Master, we have
toiled all night and caught nothing; nevertheless at Your word
I will let down the net."
6 And when they had done

[k](4:44) NU reads Ιουδαιας, *of Judea.* [a](5:5) NU reads τα δικτυα, *the nets.*

this, they caught a great number of fish, and their net was
breaking.
7 So they signaled to *their*
partners in the other boat to
come and help them. And they
came and filled both the boats,
so that they began to sink.
8 When Simon Peter saw *it,*
he fell down at Jesus' knees,
saying, "Depart from me, for I
am a sinful man, O Lord!"
9 For he and all who were
with him were astonished at the
catch of fish which they had
taken;
10 and so also *were* James and
John, the sons of Zebedee, who
were partners with Simon. And
Jesus said to Simon, "Do not be
afraid. From now on you will
catch men."
11 So when they had brought
their boats to land, they forsook all and followed Him.
12 And it happened when He
was in a certain city, that behold, a man who was full of leprosy saw Jesus; and he fell on
his face and implored Him, saying, "Lord, if You are willing,
You can make me clean."
13 Then He put out *His* hand
and touched him, saying, "I am
willing; be cleansed." Immediately the leprosy left him.
14 And He charged him to tell
no one, "But go and show yourself to the priest, and make an
offering for your cleansing, as a
testimony to them, just as Mo-

ποιήσαντες συνέκλεισαν πλῆθος ἰχθύων πολύ, διερρήγνυτο
[1]having [2]done they enclosed [1]a [3]multitude [4]of [5]fish [2]much, [9]was [10]tearing
had done this, they caught great,

δὲ τὸ δίκτυον αὐτῶν. **7** Καὶ κατένευσαν τοῖς μετόχοις
[6]and - [8]net [7]their. And they signaled to the partners
their

τοῖς ἐν τῷ ἑτέρῳ πλοίῳ τοῦ ἐλθόντας συλλαβέσθαι αὐτοῖς.
the *ones* in the other boat - having come to help them.
who were to come and help

Καὶ ἦλθον καὶ ἔπλησαν ἀμφότερα τὰ πλοῖα ὥστε
And they came and filled both the boats so that

βυθίζεσθαι αὐτά. **8** Ἰδὼν δὲ Σίμων Πέτρος προσέπεσε
[2]to [3]sink [1]they. seeing ˜ And Simon Peter fell down at
were sinking when he saw it,

τοῖς γόνασιν Ἰησοῦ, λέγων, "Ἔξελθε ἀπ' ἐμοῦ, ὅτι ἀνὴρ
the knees of Jesus, saying, "Go away from me, because [3]a [5]man

ἁμαρτωλός εἰμι, Κύριε." **9** Θάμβος γὰρ περιέσχεν αὐτὸν
[4]sinful [1]I [2]am, Lord." astonishment ˜ For gripped him

καὶ πάντας τοὺς σὺν αὐτῷ ἐπὶ τῇ ἄγρᾳ τῶν ἰχθύων ᾗ
and all the *ones* with him at the catch of the fishes which
those

συνέλαβον, **10** ὁμοίως δὲ καὶ Ἰάκωβον καὶ Ἰωάννην,
they enclosed, likewise ˜ and also *it gripped* James and John,
had caught,

υἱοὺς Ζεβεδαίου, οἳ ἦσαν κοινωνοὶ* τῷ Σίμωνι.
the sons of Zebedee, who were partners - with Simon.

Καὶ εἶπε πρὸς τὸν Σίμωνα ὁ Ἰησοῦς, "Μὴ φοβοῦ. Ἀπὸ τοῦ
And [2]said [3]to - [4]Simon - [1]Jesus, "not ˜ Do fear. From -

νῦν ἀνθρώπους ἔσῃ ζωγρῶν." **11** Καὶ καταγαγόντες
now *on* [5]men [1]you [2]will [3]be [4]catching." And [1]bringing [4]down
putting in

τὰ πλοῖα ἐπὶ τὴν γῆν, ἀφέντες ἅπαντα ἠκολούθησαν αὐτῷ.
[2]the [3]boats to - land, leaving all *things* they followed Him.
they left everything and

Jesus Cleanses a Leper

(Matt. 8:1–4; Mark 1:40–45)

12 Καὶ ἐγένετο ἐν τῷ εἶναι αὐτὸν ἐν μιᾷ τῶν πόλεων,
And it happened in - [2]to [3]be [1]Him in one of the cities,
while He was

καὶ ἰδού, ἀνὴρ πλήρης λέπρας. Καὶ ἰδὼν τὸν Ἰησοῦν,
and behold, a man full of leprosy. And seeing - Jesus,
that there was when he saw

πεσὼν ἐπὶ πρόσωπον ἐδεήθη αὐτοῦ, λέγων, "Κύριε, ἐὰν
falling on *his* face he begged Him, saying, "Lord, if

θέλῃς, δύνασαί με καθαρίσαι."
You are willing, You are able [3]me [1]to [2]cleanse."

13 Καὶ ἐκτείνας τὴν χεῖρα ἥψατο αὐτοῦ εἰπών,
And reaching out the hand He touched him saying,
His

"Θέλω, καθαρίσθητι." Καὶ εὐθέως ἡ λέπρα ἀπῆλθεν
"I am willing, be cleansed." And immediately the leprosy departed

ἀπ' αὐτοῦ. **14** Καὶ αὐτὸς παρήγγειλεν αὐτῷ μηδενὶ εἰπεῖν,
from him. And He ordered him [3]no [4]one [1]to [2]tell,

"Ἀλλὰ ἀπελθὼν δεῖξον σεαυτὸν τῷ ἱερεῖ καὶ προσένεγκε
"But departing show yourself to the priest and bring an offering
depart and show

περὶ τοῦ καθαρισμοῦ σου καθὼς προσέταξε Μωσῆς, εἰς
for - cleansing ˜ your just as prescribed ˜ Moses, for

---

*(5:10) κοινωνός *(koinōnos).* Noun derived from the adjective κοινός, *common,* meaning *partaker* or *partner.* Here it is used in the sense of "business partners" in the fishing trade. The scribes and Pharisees denied that they would have been "partakers" with their ancestors in murdering the prophets (Matt. 23:30). Paul used κοινωνός once in referring to Titus (2 Cor. 8:23) and once of himself as Philemon's partner (Philem. 17). The first recipients of the Book of Hebrews were *companions* of those who suffered for Christ (Heb. 10:33). Peter called himself "a *partaker* of the glory that will be revealed" (1 Pet. 5:1) and prayed that his readers "may be *partakers* of the divine nature" (2 Pet. 1:4).

μαρτύριον αὐτοῖς." 15 Διήρχετο δὲ μᾶλλον ὁ λόγος περὶ
a testimony to them." [6]spread [1]But [7]more [2]the [3]word [4]about
all the more report

αὐτοῦ· καὶ συνήρχοντο ὄχλοι πολλοὶ ἀκούειν καὶ
[5]Him; and [3]were [4]coming [5]together [2]crowds [1]many to hear and
great

θεραπεύεσθαι ὑπ' αὐτοῦ[b] ἀπὸ τῶν ἀσθενειῶν αὐτῶν.
to be healed by Him from - sicknesses ˜ their.

16 Αὐτὸς δὲ ἦν ὑποχωρῶν ἐν ταῖς ἐρήμοις καὶ
[3]Himself [1]But [2]He [4]was withdrawing in the uninhabited *places* and
would withdraw

προσευχόμενος.
praying.
would pray.

Jesus Forgives and Heals a Paralytic

(Matt. 9:1–8; Mark 2:1–12)

17 Καὶ ἐγένετο ἐν μιᾷ τῶν ἡμερῶν καὶ αὐτὸς ἦν
And it happened in one of the days and He was
on those that

διδάσκων, καὶ ἦσαν καθήμενοι Φαρισαῖοι καὶ
teaching, and [7]were [8]sitting [9]*there* [1]Pharisees [2]and

νομοδιδάσκαλοι, οἳ ἦσαν ἐληλυθότες ἐκ πάσης κώμης
[3]teachers [4]of [5]the [6]law, who were having come out of every village
had come

τῆς Γαλιλαίας καὶ Ἰουδαίας καὶ Ἱερουσαλήμ. Καὶ δύναμις
- of Galilee and Judea and Jerusalem. And *the* power

Κυρίου ἦν εἰς τὸ ἰᾶσθαι αὐτούς.[c] 18 Καὶ ἰδού,
of *the* Lord was *present* for - to heal them. And behold,
to heal them.

ἄνδρες φέροντες ἐπὶ κλίνης ἄνθρωπον ὃς ἦν
men *were* carrying [3]on [4]a [5]bed [1]a [2]man who was

παραλελυμένος, καὶ ἐζήτουν αὐτὸν εἰσενεγκεῖν καὶ
paralyzed, and they were seeking [3]him [1]to [2]bring in and

θεῖναι ἐνώπιον αὐτοῦ. 19 Καὶ μὴ εὑρόντες ποίας
to lay *him* before Him. And not finding by what *way*
when they did not find

εἰσενέγκωσιν αὐτὸν διὰ τὸν ὄχλον, ἀναβάντες ἐπὶ τὸ
they might bring in ˜ him because of the crowd, going up on the

δῶμα, διὰ τῶν κεράμων καθῆκαν αὐτὸν σὺν τῷ κλινιδίῳ
roof, through the tiles they lowered him with the bed
his

εἰς τὸ μέσον ἔμπροσθεν τοῦ Ἰησοῦ.
into the midst in front of - Jesus.

20 Καὶ ἰδὼν τὴν πίστιν αὐτῶν εἶπεν αὐτῷ, "Ἄνθρωπε,
And seeing - faith ˜ their He said to him, "Man,

ἀφέωνταί σοι αἱ ἁμαρτίαι σου."
[3]have [4]been [5]forgiven [6]you - [2]sins [1]your."

21 Καὶ ἤρξαντο διαλογίζεσθαι οἱ γραμματεῖς καὶ οἱ
And [6]began [7]to [8]reason [1]the [2]scribes [3]and [4]the

Φαρισαῖοι, λέγοντες, "Τίς ἐστιν οὗτος ὃς λαλεῖ
[5]Pharisees, saying, "Who is this *Man* who speaks

βλασφημίας? Τίς δύναται ἀφιέναι ἁμαρτίας εἰ μὴ μόνος ὁ
blasphemies? Who is able to forgive sins if not alone ˜ -
except

Θεός?"
God?"

ses commanded."
15 However, the report went around concerning Him all the more; and great multitudes came together to hear, and to be healed by Him of their infirmities.
16 So He Himself *often* withdrew into the wilderness and prayed.
17 Now it happened on a certain day, as He was teaching, that there were Pharisees and teachers of the law sitting by, who had come out of every town of Galilee, Judea, and Jerusalem. And the power of the Lord was *present* to heal them.
18 Then behold, men brought on a bed a man who was paralyzed, whom they sought to bring in and lay before Him.
19 And when they could not find how they might bring him in, because of the crowd, they went up on the housetop and let him down with *his* bed through the tiling into the midst before Jesus.
20 When He saw their faith, He said to him, "Man, your sins are forgiven you."
21 And the scribes and the Pharisees began to reason, saying, "Who is this who speaks blasphemies? Who can forgive sins but God alone?"

---

[b](5:15) NU omits *υπ αυτου, by him.* [c](5:17) NU reads *αυτον, (was there for) Him (to heal).*

22 But when Jesus perceived their thoughts, He answered and said to them, "Why are you reasoning in your hearts?
23 "Which is easier, to say, 'Your sins are forgiven you,' or to say, 'Rise up and walk'?
24 "But that you may know that the Son of Man has power on earth to forgive sins"—He said to the man who was paralyzed, "I say to you, arise, take up your bed, and go to your house."
25 Immediately he rose up before them, took up what he had been lying on, and departed to his own house, glorifying God.
26 And they were all amazed, and they glorified God and were filled with fear, saying, "We have seen strange things today!"
27 After these things He went out and saw a tax collector named Levi, sitting at the tax office. And He said to him, "Follow Me."
28 So he left all, rose up, and followed Him.
29 Then Levi gave Him a great feast in his own house. And there were a great number of tax collectors and others who sat down with them.
30 And their scribes and the Pharisees complained against His disciples, saying, "Why do You eat and drink with tax collectors and sinners?"
31 Jesus answered and said to them, "Those who are well

22 Ἐπιγνοὺς δὲ ὁ Ἰησοῦς τοὺς διαλογισμοὺς αὐτῶν
[3]knowing [1]But - [2]Jesus - [5]reasonings [4]their
But when Jesus perceived

ἀποκριθεὶς εἶπε πρὸς αὐτούς, "Τί διαλογίζεσθε ἐν ταῖς
answering He said to them, "Why are you reasoning in -

καρδίαις ὑμῶν? **23** Τί ἐστιν εὐκοπώτερον εἰπεῖν,
hearts ˜ your? Which is easier to say,

'Ἀφέωνταί σοι αἱ ἁμαρτίαι σου,' ἢ εἰπεῖν, 'Ἔγειραι
'[3]have [4]been [5]forgiven [6]you - [2]sins [1]your,' or to say, 'Arise

καὶ περιπάτει'? **24** Ἵνα δὲ εἰδῆτε ὅτι ἐξουσίαν
and walk'? [2]in [3]order [4]that [1]But you may know that [6]authority

ἔχει ὁ Υἱὸς τοῦ Ἀνθρώπου ἐπὶ τῆς γῆς ἀφιέναι
[5]has [1]the [2]Son - [3]of [4]Man on the earth to forgive

ἁμαρτίας" — εἶπε τῷ παραλελυμένῳ, "Σοὶ λέγω,
sins" — He said to the *one* having been paralyzed, "[3]to [4]you [1]I [2]say,
to the paralytic,

ἔγειραι, καὶ ἄρας τὸ κλινίδιόν σου πορεύου εἰς τὸν
arise, and having taken up - bed ˜ your go to -

οἶκόν σου." **25** Καὶ παραχρῆμα ἀναστὰς ἐνώπιον αὐτῶν,
house ˜ your." And immediately arising before them,

ἄρας ἐφ' ὃ κατέκειτο, ἀπῆλθεν εἰς τὸν οἶκον
taking up *the bed* on which he was lying, he went off to - house ˜
had been

αὐτοῦ, δοξάζων τὸν Θεόν. **26** Καὶ ἔκστασις ἔλαβεν ἅπαντας,
his, glorifying - God. And amazement gripped *them* all,

καὶ ἐδόξαζον τὸν Θεόν, καὶ ἐπλήσθησαν φόβου,
and they were glorifying - God, and they were filled with fear,

λέγοντες ὅτι "Εἴδομεν παράδοξα* σήμερον!"
saying - "We saw wonderful *things* today!"

Jesus Calls Matthew the Publican
(Matt. 9:9–13; Mark 2:13–17)

27 Καὶ μετὰ ταῦτα ἐξῆλθε καὶ ἐθεάσατο τελώνην
And after these *things* He went out and saw a tax collector

ὀνόματι Λευὶν καθήμενον ἐπὶ τὸ τελώνιον, καὶ εἶπεν αὐτῷ,
[2]by [3]name [1]Levi sitting at the tax office, and He said to him,

"Ἀκολούθει μοι." **28** Καὶ καταλιπὼν ἅπαντα ἀναστὰς
"Follow Me." And leaving all *things* arising
he rose

ἠκολούθησεν αὐτῷ. **29** Καὶ ἐποίησε δοχὴν μεγάλην Λευὶς
he followed Him. And [2]made [3]a [5]banquet [4]great [1]Levi
and followed

αὐτῷ ἐν τῇ οἰκίᾳ αὐτοῦ. Καὶ ἦν ὄχλος τελωνῶν
for Him in - house ˜ his. And *there* was [1]a [3]crowd [4]of [5]tax [6]collectors

πολὺς καὶ ἄλλων οἳ ἦσαν μετ' αὐτῶν κατακείμενοι.
[2]great and of others who were with them reclining *to eat.*

30 Καὶ ἐγόγγυζον οἱ γραμματεῖς αὐτῶν καὶ οἱ
And [6]were [7]complaining - [2]scribes [1]their [3]and [4]the

Φαρισαῖοι[d] πρὸς τοὺς μαθητὰς αὐτοῦ, λέγοντες, "Διὰ
[5]Pharisees against - disciples ˜ His, saying, "Because of
"Why

τί μετὰ τῶν τελωνῶν καὶ ἁμαρτωλῶν ἐσθίετε καὶ
what [6]with [7]the [8]tax [9]collectors [10]and [11]sinners [1]do [2]you [3]eat [4]and

πίνετε?"
[5]drink?"

31 Καὶ ἀποκριθεὶς ὁ Ἰησοῦς εἶπε πρὸς αὐτούς, "Οὐ χρείαν
And answering - Jesus said to them, "[6]not [8]need

---

d(5:30) NU reads οι Φαρισαιοι και οι γραμματεις αυτων, *the Pharisees and their scribes.*

***(5:26)** παράδοξος *(paradoxos).* Adjective occurring only here in the NT. It is a compound form from παρά, *contrary to,* and δόξα, *opinion,* and thus refers to things that are *strange, unexpected, remarkable,* or *wonderful* in nature. παράδοξος is the source of the English *paradox.*

ἔχουσιν οἱ ὑγιαίνοντες ἰατροῦ, ἀλλ' οἱ κακῶς
[5]do [7]have [1]The [2]*ones* [3]being [4]well of a physician, but the *ones* [3]badly
Those who are well those who are

ἔχοντες. 32 Οὐκ ἐλήλυθα καλέσαι δικαίους, ἀλλὰ
[1]having [2]*it*. [3]not [1]I [2]have come to call righteous *people,* but
ill.

ἁμαρτωλοὺς εἰς μετάνοιαν."
sinners to repentance."

Jesus Is Questioned About Fasting
(Matt. 9:14–17; Mark 2:18–22)

33 Οἱ δὲ εἶπον πρὸς αὐτόν, "Διὰ τί[e] οἱ μαθηταὶ
they ~ But said to Him, "Because of what [2]the [3]disciples
"Why

Ἰωάννου νηστεύουσι πυκνὰ καὶ δεήσεις ποιοῦνται, ὁμοίως καὶ
[4]of [5]John [1]do [6]fast often and prayers ~ make, likewise also
say,

οἱ τῶν Φαρισαίων, οἱ δὲ σοὶ ἐσθίουσι καὶ
the *disciples* of the Pharisees, - but Yours eat and

πίνουσιν?"
drink?"

34 Ὁ δέ[f] εἶπε πρὸς αὐτούς, "Μὴ δύνασθε τοὺς
[2]the [3]*One* [1]But said to them, "[3]not [1]You [2]are [4]able [7]the
He

υἱοὺς τοῦ νυμφῶνος ἐν ᾧ ὁ
[8]sons [9]of [10]the [11]bridal [12]chamber [15]in [16]which [17]*time* [18]the
groomsmen while

νυμφίος μετ' αὐτῶν ἐστι ποιῆσαι νηστεύειν?
[19]bridegroom [21]with [22]them [20]is [5]to [6]make [13]to [14]fast *are you?*

35 Ἐλεύσονται δὲ ἡμέραι, καὶ ὅταν ἀπαρθῇ ἀπ'
[3]will [4]come [1]But [2]days, also ~ when [3]will [4]be [5]taken [6]away [7]from

αὐτῶν ὁ νυμφίος, τότε νηστεύσουσιν ἐν ἐκείναις ταῖς
[8]them [1]the [2]bridegroom, then they will fast in those -

ἡμέραις."
days."

36 Ἔλεγε δὲ καὶ παραβολὴν πρὸς αὐτοὺς ὅτι "Οὐδεὶς
[2]He [4]told [1]And [3]also a parable to them, - "No one

ἐπίβλημα[g] ἱματίου καινοῦ[h] ἐπιβάλλει ἐπὶ ἱμάτιον
[2]a [3]patch [4]of [5]a [7]garment [6]new [1]puts on a(n) garment ~

παλαιόν· εἰ δὲ μή γε, καὶ τὸ καινὸν σχίζει[i] καὶ
old; if ~ but not, - both the new *garment* tears and
or else,

τῷ παλαιῷ οὐ συμφωνεῖ[j] τὸ ἀπὸ τοῦ
[10]with [11]the [12]old [13]*garment* [8]not [7]does [9]agree [1]the [2]*patch* [3]from [4]the

καινοῦ. 37 Καὶ οὐδεὶς βάλλει οἶνον νέον εἰς ἀσκοὺς
[5]new [6]*garment*. And no one puts wine ~ new into wineskins ~

παλαιούς· εἰ δὲ μή γε, ῥήξει ὁ νέος οἶνος τοὺς
old; if ~ but not, - [4]will [5]burst [1]the [2]new [3]wine the
otherwise,

ἀσκούς, καὶ αὐτὸς ἐκχυθήσεται καὶ οἱ ἀσκοὶ ἀπολοῦνται.
wineskins, and it will be spilled and the wineskins will be ruined.

38 Ἀλλὰ οἶνον νέον εἰς ἀσκοὺς καινοὺς βλητέον καὶ
But [5]wine [4]new [6]into [8]wineskins [7]new [1]*one* [2]must [3]put and

ἀμφότεροι συντηροῦνται.[k] 39 Καὶ οὐδεὶς πιὼν
both are preserved together. And no one having drunk

have no need of a physician, but those who are sick.
32 "I have not come to call *the* righteous, but sinners, to repentance."
33 Then they said to Him, "Why do the disciples of John fast often and make prayers, and likewise those of the Pharisees, but Yours eat and drink?"
34 And He said to them, "Can you make the friends of the bridegroom fast while the bridegroom is with them?
35 "But the days will come when the bridegroom will be taken away from them; then they will fast in those days."
36 Then He spoke a parable to them: "No one puts a piece from a new garment on an old one; otherwise the new makes a tear, and also the piece that was *taken* out of the new does not match the old.
37 "And no one puts new wine into old wineskins; or else the new wine will burst the wineskins and be spilled, and the wineskins will be ruined.
38 "But new wine must be put into new wineskins, and both are preserved.
39 "And no one, having drunk

e(**5:33**) NU omits *Δια τι, Why.* *f*(**5:34**) NU adds *Ιησους, Jesus.*
g(**5:36**) NU adds *απο, from.*
h(**5:36**) NU adds *σχισας, tearing; thus tears a patch from a new garment and puts.* *i*(**5:36**) NU reads *σχισει, will tear.*
j(**5:36**) NU adds *το επιβλημα, the patch;* TR adds *επιβλημα, patch.*
k(**5:38**) NU omits *και αμφοτεροι συντηρουνται, and both are preserved together.*

old *wine,* immediately desires
new; for he says, 'The old is
better.' "
6 Now it happened on the
second Sabbath after the
first that He went through the
grainfields. And His disciples
plucked the heads of grain and
ate *them,* rubbing *them* in *their*
hands.
2 And some of the Pharisees
said to them, "Why are you doing what is not lawful to do on
the Sabbath?"
3 But Jesus answering them
said, "Have you not even read
this, what David did when he
was hungry, he and those who
were with him:
4 "how he went into the
house of God, took and ate the
showbread, and also gave some
to those with him, which is not
lawful for any but the priests to
eat?"
5 And He said to them, "The
Son of Man is also Lord of the
Sabbath."
6 Now it happened on an-
other Sabbath, also, that He
entered the synagogue and
taught. And a man was there
whose right hand was withered.
7 So the scribes and Pharisees watched Him closely,
whether He would heal on the
Sabbath, that they might find an
accusation against Him.
8 But He knew their

παλαιὸν εὐθέως[l] θέλει νέον· λέγει γάρ, 'Ὁ παλαιὸς
old *wine* immediately desires new; [2]he [3]says [1]For, 'The old

χρηστότερός ἐστιν.' "
better ~ is.' "

The Disciples Pluck Grain on the Sabbath
(Matt. 12:1–8; Mark 2:23–28)

6 1 Ἐγένετο δὲ ἐν σαββάτῳ δευτεροπρώτῳ[a]
[2]it [3]happened [1]Now on *the* Sabbath second-first
the first Sabbath of the second month

διαπορεύεσθαι αὐτὸν διὰ τῶν σπορίμων. Καὶ ἔτιλλον οἱ
to go through Him through the grainfields. And [3]were [4]picking -
that He was going

μαθηταὶ αὐτοῦ τοὺς στάχυας καὶ ἤσθιον[b] ψώχοντες
[2]disciples [1]His the heads of grain and were eating *them* rubbing *them*
as they rubbed

ταῖς χερσί. 2 Τινὲς δὲ τῶν Φαρισαίων εἶπον αὐτοῖς, "Τί
in the hands. certain ~ But of the Pharisees said to them, "Why
their

ποιεῖτε ὃ οὐκ ἔξεστι ποιεῖν ἐν[c] τοῖς σάββασι?"
do you do what not ~ is lawful to do on the Sabbath?"

3 Καὶ ἀποκριθεὶς πρὸς αὐτοὺς εἶπεν ὁ Ἰησοῦς, "Οὐδὲ
And replying to them said ~ - Jesus, "[3]not [4]even

τοῦτο ἀνέγνωτε ὃ ἐποίησε Δαβὶδ ὁπότε ἐπείνασεν
[6]this [1]Did [2]you [5]read which did ~ David when he became hungry

αὐτὸς καὶ οἱ μετ' αὐτοῦ ὄντες? 4 Ὡς εἰσῆλθεν εἰς τὸν
he and the *ones* [2]with [3]him [1]being? How he entered into the
those who were?

οἶκον τοῦ Θεοῦ καὶ τοὺς ἄρτους τῆς προθέσεως ἔλαβε καὶ
house - of God and [2]the [3]loaves [4]of [5]the [6]presentation [1]took and
the showbread

ἔφαγε καὶ ἔδωκε καὶ τοῖς μετ' αὐτοῦ, οὓς οὐκ
ate and gave also to the *ones* with him, which [3]not
those who were

ἔξεστι φαγεῖν εἰ μὴ μόνους τοὺς ἱερεῖς?" 5 Καὶ ἔλεγεν
[1]it [2]is lawful to eat if not [3]alone [1]the [2]priests?" And He said
except for

αὐτοῖς ὅτι "Κύριός ἐστιν ὁ Υἱὸς τοῦ Ἀνθρώπου καὶ τοῦ
to them - "[6]Lord [5]is [1]The [2]Son [3]of [4]Man even of the

Σαββάτου."
Sabbath."

Jesus Heals a Man with a Withered Hand on the Sabbath
(Matt. 12:9–14; Mark 3:1–6)

6 Ἐγένετο δὲ καὶ ἐν ἑτέρῳ σαββάτῳ εἰσελθεῖν αὐτὸν
[2]it [3]happened [1]Now also on another Sabbath to enter Him
that He entered

εἰς τὴν συναγωγὴν καὶ διδάσκειν. Καὶ ἦν ἐκεῖ ἄνθρωπος,
into the synagogue and to teach. And [3]was [4]there [1]a [2]man
was teaching.

καὶ ἡ χεὶρ αὐτοῦ ἡ δεξιὰ ἦν ξηρά. 7 Παρετήρουν δὲ[d] οἱ
and - [3]hand [1]his - [2]right was withered. [7]were [8]observing [1]And [2]the

γραμματεῖς καὶ οἱ Φαρισαῖοι εἰ ἐν τῷ σαββάτῳ θεραπεύσει,
[3]scribes [4]and [5]the [6]Pharisees if on the Sabbath He will heal,
would

ἵνα εὕρωσι κατηγορίαν αὐτοῦ. 8 Αὐτὸς δὲ ᾔδει τοὺς
so that they might find an accusation of Him. He ~ But knew -
against

---

[l](5:39) NU omits ευθεως, *immediately.*
[a](6:1) NU omits δευτεροπρωτω, *second-first.*
[b](6:1) NU changes word order to και ησθιον τους σταχυας, *and they were eating the heads of grain.*
[c](6:2) NU omits ποιειν εν, *to do on.* [d](6:7) NU, TR add αυτον, *him.*

διαλογισμοὺς* αὐτῶν καὶ εἶπε τῷ ἀνθρώπῳ τῷ ξηρὰν
reasonings ˜ their and said to the man the *one* [3]withered
who

ἔχοντι τὴν χεῖρα, "Ἔγειραι καὶ στῆθι εἰς τὸ μέσον." Ὁ δὲ
[1]having [2]the hand, "Arise and stand in the midst." he ˜ And
had

ἀναστὰς ἔστη. 9 Εἶπεν οὖν ὁ Ἰησοῦς πρὸς αὐτούς,
rising stood. [3]said [1]Then - [2]Jesus to them,
rose up and

"Ἐπερωτήσω ὑμᾶς τι·[e] Ἔξεστι τοῖς σάββασιν
"I will ask you something: Is it lawful on the Sabbath

ἀγαθοποιῆσαι ἢ κακοποιῆσαι, ψυχὴν σῶσαι ἢ ἀποκτεῖναι?"[f]
to do good or to do evil, [3]life [1]to [2]save or to kill?"

10 Καὶ περιβλεψάμενος πάντας αὐτοὺς εἶπεν αὐτῷ,[g]
And looking around at all *of* them He said to him,
when He had looked

"Ἔκτεινον τὴν χεῖρά σου." Ὁ δὲ ἐποίησε καὶ ἀποκατεστάθη
"Stretch out - hand ˜ your." he ˜ And did *so* and [3]was [4]restored

ἡ χεὶρ αὐτοῦ ὑγιὴς ὡς ἡ ἄλλη.[h] 11 Αὐτοὶ δὲ ἐπλήσθησαν
- [2]hand [1]his whole like the other. they ˜ But were filled

ἀνοίας, καὶ διελάλουν πρὸς ἀλλήλους τί ἂν
with fury, and they were discussing with one another what -

ποιήσειαν τῷ Ἰησοῦ.
they might do - to Jesus.

Jesus Chooses the Twelve

(Matt. 10:1–4; Mark 3:13–19)

12 Ἐγένετο δὲ ἐν ταῖς ἡμέραις ταύταις ἐξῆλθεν εἰς
[2]it [3]happened [1]Now in - days ˜ these *that* He went out into

τὸ ὄρος προσεύξασθαι, καὶ ἦν διανυκτερεύων ἐν τῇ
the mountain to pray, and He was spending the night in -

προσευχῇ τοῦ Θεοῦ. 13 Καὶ ὅτε ἐγένετο ἡμέρα,
prayer - of God. And when it became day,
to

προσεφώνησε τοὺς μαθητὰς αὐτοῦ, καὶ ἐκλεξάμενος ἀπ'
He summoned - disciples ˜ His, and having chosen [2]from

αὐτῶν δώδεκα, οὓς καὶ ἀποστόλους ὠνόμασε,
[3]them [1]twelve, whom [2]also [4]apostles [1]He [3]named,

14 Σίμωνα ὃν καὶ ὠνόμασε Πέτρον, καὶ Ἀνδρέαν τὸν
He chose Simon whom also ˜ He named Peter, and Andrew -

ἀδελφὸν αὐτοῦ, Ἰάκωβον καὶ Ἰωάννην, Φίλιππον καὶ
brother ˜ his, James and John, Philip and

Βαρθολομαῖον, 15 Ματθαῖον καὶ Θωμᾶν, Ἰάκωβον τὸν τοῦ
Bartholomew, Matthew and Thomas, James the *son* -

Ἀλφαίου καὶ Σίμωνα τὸν καλούμενον Ζηλωτήν, 16 Ἰούδαν
of Alphaeus and Simon the *one* being called *the* Zealot, Judas

Ἰακώβου καὶ Ἰούδαν Ἰσκαριώτην, ὃς καὶ ἐγένετο
the son of James and Judas Iscariot, who also became

προδότης.
a traitor.

Jesus Heals a Great Multitude

(Matt. 4:23–25)

17 Καὶ καταβὰς μετ' αὐτῶν ἔστη ἐπὶ τόπου
And having come down with them He stood on a place ˜

πεδινοῦ, καὶ ὄχλος[i] μαθητῶν αὐτοῦ, καὶ πλῆθος πολὺ
level, and a crowd of disciples ˜ His, and a multitude ˜ large
with

thoughts, and said to the man who had the withered hand, "Arise and stand here." And he arose and stood.
9 Then Jesus said to them, "I will ask you one thing: Is it lawful on the Sabbath to do good or to do evil, to save life or to destroy?"
10 And when He had looked around at them all, He said to the man, "Stretch out your hand." And he did so, and his hand was restored as whole as the other.
11 But they were filled with rage, and discussed with one another what they might do to Jesus.
12 Now it came to pass in those days that He went out to the mountain to pray, and continued all night in prayer to God.
13 And when it was day, He called His disciples to *Himself;* and from them He chose twelve whom He also named apostles:
14 Simon, whom He also named Peter, and Andrew his brother; James and John; Philip and Bartholomew;
15 Matthew and Thomas; James the *son* of Alphaeus, and Simon called the Zealot;
16 Judas *the son* of James, and Judas Iscariot who also became a traitor.
17 And He came down with them and stood on a level place with a crowd of His disciples and a great multitude of people

---

[e]**(6:9)** NU reads επερωτω υμας ει, *I ask you whether (it is lawful).* [f]**(6:9)** NU, TR read απολεσαι, *to destroy.* [g]**(6:10)** TR reads τω ανθρωπω, *to the man.* [h]**(6:10)** NU omits υγιης ως η αλλη, *whole like the other.* [i]**(6:17)** NU adds πολυς, *great.*

***(6:8)** διαλογισμός *(dialogismos).* Noun used several times in the NT with a wide range of meanings. Here it refers to *thought, opinion, design* (cf. Luke 2:35), but elsewhere it means *evil designs* (Matt. 15:19); the *decisions* of judges (James 2:4); or even *doubt* (Luke 24:38) and *dispute, argument* (Luke 9:46; Phil. 2:14). Cf. the cognate verb διαλογίζομαι, *consider, ponder, reason* (Matt. 16:7; Luke 1:29), *discuss, argue* (Mark 8:16; Luke 20:14). The prefix διά in these compound words means, at

from all Judea and Jerusalem,
and from the seacoast of Tyre
and Sidon, who came to hear
Him and be healed of their diseases,
18 as well as those who were
tormented with unclean spirits.
And they were healed.
19 And the whole multitude
sought to touch Him, for power
went out from Him and healed
them all.
20 Then He lifted up His eyes
toward His disciples, and said:

"Blessed *are you* poor,
For yours is the kingdom of God.
21 Blessed *are you* who hunger now,
For you shall be filled.
Blessed *are you* who weep now,
For you shall laugh.
22 Blessed are you when men hate you,
And when they exclude you,
And revile *you*, and cast out your name as evil,
For the Son of Man's sake.
23 Rejoice in that day and leap for joy!
For indeed your reward *is* great in heaven,
For in like manner their fathers did to the prophets.

24 "But woe to you who are rich,
For you have received your consolation.

---

root, *two,* and so these words often suggest debate with others or within oneself (at least a "thinking through").

***(6:24)** ἀπέχω *(apechō).* Verb having divergent meanings depending on syntactical relationships. When it occurs in the active voice with a stated object, as here, it means to *receive* something or even someone (Philem. 15) as payment in full. When it occurs without an object, it means *be away from* and is usually accompanied by a prepositional phrase with ἀπό, *from,* giving the place from which one is separated (Luke 24:13). The verb means *keep away from, abstain from* when it occurs in the middle voice with its object in the genitive case (Acts 15:29; 1 Thess. 5:22).

τοῦ λαοῦ ἀπὸ πάσης τῆς Ἰουδαίας καὶ Ἱερουσαλήμ, καὶ τῆς
of the people from all - Judea and Jerusalem, and the

παραλίου Τύρου καὶ Σιδῶνος, οἳ ἦλθον ἀκοῦσαι αὐτοῦ καὶ
seacoast of Tyre and Sidon, who came to hear Him and

ἰαθῆναι ἀπὸ τῶν νόσων αὐτῶν· **18** καὶ οἱ ὀχλούμενοι
to be healed from - diseases ˜ their; and the *ones* being troubled
as well as those who were

ὑπὸ πνευμάτων ἀκαθάρτων, καὶ ἐθεραπεύοντο. **19** Καὶ
by spirits ˜ unclean, and they were being healed. And

πᾶς ὁ ὄχλος ἐζήτει ἅπτεσθαι αὐτοῦ, ὅτι δύναμις παρ'
all the crowd was seeking to touch Him, because power [4]from
trying

αὐτοῦ ἐξήρχετο καὶ ἰᾶτο πάντας.
[5]Him [1]was [2]going [3]out and was healing *them* all.

The Beatitudes
(Matt. 5:1–12)

20 Καὶ αὐτὸς ἐπάρας τοὺς ὀφθαλμοὺς αὐτοῦ εἰς τοὺς
And [8]He [1]lifting [2]up - [4]eyes [3]His [5]to -

μαθητὰς αὐτοῦ ἔλεγε,
[7]disciples [6]His said,

"Μακάριοι οἱ πτωχοί,
"Blessed *are* the poor *ones*,
you who are poor,

Ὅτι ὑμετέρα ἐστὶν ἡ βασιλεία τοῦ Θεοῦ.
Because [6]yours [5]is [1]the [2]kingdom - [3]of [4]God.

21 Μακάριοι οἱ πεινῶντες νῦν,
Blessed *are* the *ones* hungering now,
you who hunger

Ὅτι χορτασθήσεσθε.
Because you shall be filled.

Μακάριοι οἱ κλαίοντες νῦν,
Blessed *are* the *ones* weeping now,
you who weep

Ὅτι γελάσετε.
Because you shall laugh.

22 Μακάριοί ἐστε ὅταν μισήσωσιν ὑμᾶς οἱ ἄνθρωποι, καὶ
Blessed are you when [2]shall [3]hate [4]you - [1]men, and

ὅταν ἀφορίσωσιν ὑμᾶς καὶ ὀνειδίσωσι καὶ ἐκβάλωσι τὸ
when they shall exclude you and shall revile *you* and cast out -

ὄνομα ὑμῶν ὡς πονηρόν, ἕνεκα τοῦ Υἱοῦ τοῦ Ἀνθρώπου.
name ˜ your as evil, because of the Son - of Man.

23 Χάρητε ἐν ἐκείνῃ τῇ ἡμέρᾳ καὶ σκιρτήσατε, ἰδοὺ γάρ, ὁ
Rejoice in that - day and leap *for joy*, behold ˜ for, -

μισθὸς ὑμῶν πολὺς ἐν τῷ οὐρανῷ· κατὰ ταῦτα γὰρ
reward ˜ your *is* great in - heaven; [2]according [3]to [4]these [5]*things* [1]for
in like manner

ἐποίουν τοῖς προφήταις οἱ πατέρες αὐτῶν.
[8]were [9]doing [10]to [11]the [12]prophets - [7]fathers [6]their.

Jesus Pronounces Woes

24 "Πλὴν οὐαὶ ὑμῖν τοῖς πλουσίοις!
"But woe to you the rich *ones*!
who are rich!

Ὅτι ἀπέχετε* τὴν παράκλησιν ὑμῶν.
Because you have in full - consolation ˜ your.

25 Οὐαὶ ὑμῖν, οἱ ἐμπεπλησμένοι![j]
Woe to you, the *ones* having been filled!
who have

Ὅτι πεινάσετε.
Because you will be hungry.

Οὐαὶ ὑμῖν,[k] οἱ γελῶντες νῦν!
Woe to you, the *ones* laughing now!
who laugh

Ὅτι πενθήσετε καὶ κλαύσετε.
Because you will mourn and weep.

26 Οὐαὶ[l] ὅταν καλῶς ὑμᾶς εἴπωσι[m] οἱ ἄνθρωποι!
Woe *to you* when [4]well [6]you [2]shall [3]speak [5]of - [1]men!

Κατὰ ταῦτα γὰρ ἐποίουν τοῖς ψευδοπροφήταις
[8]according [9]to [10]these [11]*things* [7]For [14]would [15]do [16]to [17]the [18]false [19]prophets
in like manner

οἱ πατέρες αὐτῶν.
- [13]fathers [12]their.

Love Your Enemies
(Matt. 5:43–48)

27 "Ἀλλ' ὑμῖν λέγω τοῖς ἀκούουσιν· Ἀγαπᾶτε τοὺς
"But [3]to [4]you [1]I [2]say the *ones* hearing: Love -
who hear:

ἐχθροὺς ὑμῶν, καλῶς ποιεῖτε τοῖς μισοῦσιν ὑμᾶς,
enemies ˜ your, well ˜ do to the *ones* hating you,
those who hate

28 εὐλογεῖτε τοὺς καταρωμένους ὑμῖν, προσεύχεσθε ὑπὲρ
bless the *ones* cursing you, pray for
who curse

τῶν ἐπηρεαζόντων ὑμᾶς. **29** Τῷ τύπτοντί σε ἐπὶ τὴν
the *ones* mistreating you. To the *one* striking you on the
those who mistreat him who strikes

σιαγόνα, πάρεχε καὶ τὴν ἄλλην. Καὶ ἀπὸ τοῦ αἴροντός
cheek, offer also the other. And from the *one* taking away
him who takes

σου τὸ ἱμάτιον, καὶ τὸν χιτῶνα μὴ κωλύσῃς. **30** Παντὶ
your - *outer* garment, [6]also [4]the [5]tunic [2]not [1]do [3]forbid. [2]to [3]every
And to

δὲ τῷ αἰτοῦντί σε δίδου. Καὶ ἀπὸ τοῦ αἴροντος τὰ
[1]And the *one* asking you give. And from the *one* taking away the
everyone who asks him who takes away your

σὰ μὴ ἀπαίτει. **31** Καὶ καθὼς θέλετε ἵνα
your *things* not ˜ do ask for *them* back. And just as you want that
belongings

ποιῶσιν ὑμῖν οἱ ἄνθρωποι, καὶ ὑμεῖς[n] ποιεῖτε αὐτοῖς
[2]should [3]do [4]to [5]you - [1]men, also ˜ you do to them

ὁμοίως. **32** Καὶ εἰ ἀγαπᾶτε τοὺς ἀγαπῶντας ὑμᾶς, ποία
likewise. And if you love the *ones* loving you, what
those who love

ὑμῖν χάρις ἐστί? Καὶ γὰρ οἱ ἁμαρτωλοὶ τοὺς ἀγαπῶντας
[4]to [5]you [1]credit [2]is [3]*it?* also ˜ For - sinners [2]the [3]*ones* [4]loving
In fact those who love

αὐτοὺς ἀγαπῶσι. **33** Καὶ ἐὰν ἀγαθοποιῆτε τοὺς
[5]them [1]love. And if you do good to the *ones*
those who

ἀγαθοποιοῦντας ὑμᾶς, ποία ὑμῖν χάρις ἐστί? Καὶ γὰρ οἱ
doing good to you, what [4]to [5]you [1]credit [2]is [3]*it?* also ˜ For -
do In fact

25 Woe to you who are full,
For you shall hunger.
Woe to you who laugh now,
For you shall mourn and weep.
26 Woe to you when all men speak well of you,
For so did their fathers to the false prophets.

27 "But I say to you who
hear: Love your enemies, do
good to those who hate you,
28 "bless those who curse
you, and pray for those who
spitefully use you.
29 "To him who strikes you
on the *one* cheek, offer the
other also. And from him who
takes away your cloak, do not
withhold *your* tunic either.
30 "Give to everyone who
asks of you. And from him who
takes away your goods do not
ask *them* back.
31 "And just as you want men
to do to you, you also do to
them likewise.
32 "But if you love those who
love you, what credit is that to
you? For even sinners love
those who love them.
33 "And if you do good to
those who do good to you, what
credit is that to you? For even

---

[j](6:25) NU adds *νυν, now.* [k](6:25) NU omits *υμιν, to you.* [l](6:26) TR adds *υμιν, to you.* [m](6:26) NU, TR, some mss. add *παντες, all.* [n](6:31) NU omits *και υμεις, also you.*

sinners do the same.
34 "And if you lend *to those*
from whom you hope to receive
back, what credit is that to you?
For even sinners lend to sinners to receive as much back.
35 "But love your enemies, do
good, and lend, hoping for nothing in return; and your reward
will be great, and you will be
sons of the Most High. For He
is kind to the unthankful and
evil.
36 "Therefore be merciful,
just as your Father also is merciful.
37 "Judge not, and you shall
not be judged. Condemn not,
and you shall not be con-
demned. Forgive, and you will
be forgiven.
38 "Give, and it will be given
to you: good measure, pressed
down, shaken together, and
running over will be put into
your bosom. For with the same
measure that you use, it will be
measured back to you."
39 And He spoke a parable to
them: "Can the blind lead the
blind? Will they not both fall into
the ditch?
40 "A disciple is not above his
teacher, but everyone who is
perfectly trained will be like his
teacher.
41 "And why do you look at
the speck in your brother's
eye, but do not perceive the
plank in your own eye?
42 "Or how can you say to

ἁμαρτωλοὶ τὸ αὐτὸ ποιοῦσι. **34** Καὶ ἐὰν δανείζητε
sinners [2]the [3]same [4]*thing* [1]do. And if you lend *to those*

παρ' ὧν ἐλπίζετε ἀπολαβεῖν, ποία ὑμῖν χάρις ἐστί?
from whom you hope to receive *it* back, what [4]to [5]you [1]credit [2]is [3]*it?*

Καὶ γὰρ ἁμαρτωλοὶ ἁμαρτωλοῖς δανείζουσιν ἵνα
also ˜ For sinners [2]to [3]sinners [1]lend so that
In fact

ἀπολάβωσι τὰ ἴσα. **35** Πλὴν ἀγαπᾶτε τοὺς
they may receive [4]back [1]the [2]equal [3]*things*. But love -
same amount.

ἐχθροὺς ὑμῶν καὶ ἀγαθοποιεῖτε καὶ δανείζετε, μηδὲν
enemies ˜ your and do good and lend, [4]nothing

ἀπελπίζοντες· καὶ ἔσται ὁ μισθὸς ὑμῶν πολύς, καὶ
[1]hoping [2]to [3]receive [5]back; and [3]will [4]be - [2]reward [1]your great, and

ἔσεσθε υἱοὶ Ὑψίστου· ὅτι αὐτὸς χρηστός* ἐστιν ἐπὶ
you will be sons of *the* Most High; because He kind ˜ is to

τοὺς ἀχαρίστους καὶ πονηρούς. **36** Γίνεσθε οὖν
the unthankful and evil. be ˜ Therefore

οἰκτίρμονες, καθὼς καὶ ὁ Πατὴρ ὑμῶν οἰκτίρμων ἐστί.
compassionate, just as also - Father ˜ your compassionate ˜ is.

Do Not Judge
(Matt. 7:1–6)

37 "Καὶ μὴ κρίνετε, καὶ οὐ μὴ κριθῆτε. Μὴ
"And not ˜ do judge, and [3]not [4]not [1]you [2]will [5]be [6]judged. not ˜
certainly

καταδικάζετε, καὶ οὐ μὴ καταδικασθῆτε. Ἀπολύετε,
Do condemn, and [3]not [4]not [1]you [2]will [5]be [6]condemned. Forgive,
certainly

καὶ ἀπολυθήσεσθε. **38** Δίδοτε, καὶ δοθήσεται ὑμῖν·
and you will be forgiven. Give, and it will be given to you;
something

μέτρον καλόν, πεπιεσμένον καὶ σεσαλευμένον καὶ
a measure ˜ good, pressed down and shaken and

ὑπερεκχυνόμενον δώσουσιν εἰς τὸν κόλπον ὑμῶν. Τῷ
running over they will give into - bosom ˜ your. [2]with [3]the

γὰρ αὐτῷ μέτρῳ ᾧ [o] μετρεῖτε ἀντιμετρηθήσεται
[1]For same measure with which you measure it will be measured back

ὑμῖν."
to you."

39 Εἶπε δὲ παραβολὴν αὐτοῖς· "Μήτι δύναται
[2]He [3]told [1]And a parable to them; "[5]not [4]is [6]able

τυφλὸς τυφλὸν ὁδηγεῖν? Οὐχὶ ἀμφότεροι εἰς
[1]A [2]blind [3]*man* [9]a [10]blind [11]*man* [7]to [8]guide [12]*is* [13]*he?* [15]not [16]both [18]into

βόθυνον πεσοῦνται? **40** Οὐκ ἔστι μαθητὴς ὑπὲρ τὸν
[19]a [20]ditch [14]Will [17]fall? [4]not [3]is [1]A [2]disciple above -

διδάσκαλον αὐτοῦ, [p] κατηρτισμένος δὲ πᾶς ἔσται
teacher ˜ his, [3]having [4]been [5]fully [6]trained [1]but [2]every*one* will be

ὡς ὁ διδάσκαλος αὐτοῦ. **41** Τί δὲ βλέπεις τὸ κάρφος
like - teacher ˜ his. why ˜ But do you see the speck
look at

τὸ ἐν τῷ ὀφθαλμῷ τοῦ ἀδελφοῦ σου, τὴν δὲ δοκὸν τὴν
the *one* in the eye - of brother ˜ your, the ˜ but plank the *one*
which is which is

ἐν τῷ ἰδίῳ ὀφθαλμῷ οὐ κατανοεῖς? **42** Ἢ πῶς
in - your own eye [3]not [1]you [2]do [4]consider? Or how
notice?

---

o(6:38) For *τω γαρ αυτω μετρω ω, For with the same measure with which,* NU reads *ω γαρ μετρω, for with the measure.*
p(6:40) NU omits *αυτου, his.*

*(6:35) *χρηστός (chrēstos).* Adjective meaning *good, kind, easy.* Its base meaning describes something as being appropriate or superior for a particular use: thus it figuratively defines Jesus' yoke as "easy" (Matt. 11:30), and the comparative form *χρηστότερος* defines old wine as "better" than new wine (Luke 5:39). *χρηστός* may also describe the moral quality of things ("*good* habits," 1 Cor. 15:33), or define the actions of people (Eph.

δύνασαι λέγειν τῷ ἀδελφῷ σου, "Ἀδελφέ, ἄφες
can you say - to brother ˜ your, 'Brother, permit *that*
permit me

ἐκβάλω τὸ κάρφος τὸ ἐν τῷ ὀφθαλμῷ σου,'
I should cast out the speck the *one* in - eye ˜ your,'
to remove which is

αὐτὸς τὴν ἐν τῷ ὀφθαλμῷ σου δοκὸν οὐ βλέπων?
yourself [3]the [5]in - [7]eye [6]your [4]plank [1]not [2]seeing?
when you yourself do not see?

Ὑποκριτά! Ἔκβαλε πρῶτον τὴν δοκὸν ἐκ τοῦ ὀφθαλμοῦ σου,
Hypocrite! Cast out first the plank out of - eye ˜ your,
Remove

καὶ τότε διαβλέψεις ἐκβαλεῖν τὸ κάρφος τὸ ἐν τῷ
and then you will see clearly to cast out the speck the *one* in the
remove which is

ὀφθαλμῷ τοῦ ἀδελφοῦ σου.
eye - of brother ˜ your.

By Their Fruits You Shall Know Them
(Matt. 7:15–20; Matt. 12:33–37)

43 "Οὐ γάρ ἐστι δένδρον καλὸν ποιοῦν καρπὸν
"[4]no [1]For [2]*there* [3]is [6]tree [5]good producing fruit ˜
which produces

σαπρόν, οὐδὲ[q] δένδρον σαπρὸν ποιοῦν καρπὸν
rotten, neither *is there* a tree ˜ rotten producing fruit ˜
bad, bad which produces

καλόν. 44 Ἕκαστον γὰρ δένδρον ἐκ τοῦ ἰδίου καρποῦ
good. each ˜ For tree [3]from - [4]its [5]own [6]fruit

γινώσκεται. Οὐ γὰρ ἐξ ἀκανθῶν συλλέγουσι σῦκα, οὐδὲ
[1]is [2]known. [10]not [7]For [13]from [14]thorns [8]they [9]do [11]gather [12]figs, nor

ἐκ βάτου τρυγῶσι σταφυλήν. 45 Ὁ ἀγαθὸς
[7]from [8]a [9]thornbush [1]do [2]they [3]pick [4]a [5]grape [6]cluster. The good
A

ἄνθρωπος ἐκ τοῦ ἀγαθοῦ θησαυροῦ τῆς καρδίας αὐτοῦ[r]
man out of the good treasure - of heart ˜ his

προφέρει τὸ ἀγαθόν, καὶ ὁ πονηρὸς ἄνθρωπος[s] ἐκ τοῦ
produces the good *thing*, and the evil man out of the
what is good,

πονηροῦ θησαυροῦ τῆς καρδίας αὐτοῦ[t] προφέρει τὸ πονηρόν.
evil treasure - of heart ˜ his produces the evil *thing*.
what is evil.

Ἐκ γὰρ τοῦ περισσεύματος τῆς καρδίας λαλεῖ τὸ στόμα
[2]out [3]of [1]For the abundance of the heart [3]speaks - [2]mouth

αὐτοῦ.
[1]his.

Build on the Rock
(Matt. 7:24–29)

46 "Τί δέ με καλεῖτε, 'Κύριε, Κύριε,' καὶ οὐ
"why ˜ But [4]Me [1]do [2]you [3]call, 'Lord, Lord,' yet [3]not

ποιεῖτε ἃ λέγω? 47 Πᾶς ὁ ἐρχόμενος πρός
[1]you [2]do [4]do *the things* which I say? Every - *one* coming to
Everyone who comes

με καὶ ἀκούων μου τῶν λόγων καὶ ποιῶν αὐτούς, ὑποδείξω ὑμῖν
Me and hearing My - words and doing them, I will show you
hears does

τίνι ἐστὶν ὅμοιος· 48 ὅμοιός ἐστιν ἀνθρώπῳ οἰκοδομοῦντι
to whom he is like; [3]like [1]he [2]is a man building

your brother, 'Brother, let me remove the speck that *is* in your eye,' when you yourself do not see the plank that *is* in your own eye? Hypocrite! First remove the plank from your own eye, and then you will see clearly to remove the speck that is in your brother's eye.
43 "For a good tree does not bear bad fruit, nor does a bad tree bear good fruit.
44 "For every tree is known by its own fruit. For *men* do not gather figs from thorns, nor do they gather grapes from a bramble bush.
45 "A good man out of the good treasure of his heart brings forth good; and an evil man out of the evil treasure of his heart brings forth evil. For out of the abundance of the heart his mouth speaks.
46 "But why do you call Me 'Lord, Lord,' and not do the things which I say?
47 "Whoever comes to Me, and hears My sayings and does them, I will show you whom he is like:
48 "He is like a man building a

[q](**6:43**) NU adds παλιν, *again.* [r](**6:45**) NU omits αυτου, *his.*
[s](**6:45**) NU omits ανθρωπος, *man.* [t](**6:45**) NU omits θησαυρου της καρδιας αυτου, *treasure of his heart.*

4:32) or God (as here in Luke 6:35) as being *kind.* Cf. the cognate noun χρηστότης (*kindness,* Col. 3:12); and the verb χρηστεύομαι (*act kindly,* 1 Cor. 13:4).

house, who dug deep and laid the foundation on the rock. And when the flood arose, the stream beat vehemently against that house, and could not shake it, for it was founded on the rock.
49 "But he who heard and did nothing is like a man who built a house on the earth without a foundation, against which the stream beat vehemently; and immediately it fell. And the ruin of that house was great."
7 Now when He concluded all His sayings in the hearing of the people, He entered Capernaum.
2 And a certain centurion's servant, who was dear to him, was sick and ready to die.
3 So when he heard about Jesus, he sent elders of the Jews to Him, pleading with Him to come and heal his servant.
4 And when they came to Jesus, they begged Him earnestly, saying that the one for whom He should do this was deserving,
5 "for he loves our nation, and has built us a synagogue."
6 Then Jesus went with them. And when He was already not far from the house, the centurion sent friends to Him, saying to Him, "Lord, do not trouble Yourself, for I am

οἰκίαν, ὃς ἔσκαψε καὶ ἐβάθυνε καὶ ἔθηκε θεμέλιον ἐπὶ τὴν
a house, who dug and went deep and laid a foundation on the

πέτραν. Πλημμύρας δὲ γενομένης, προσέρρηξεν ὁ ποταμὸς
*bed*rock. [2]a [3]flood [1]And occurring, [3]burst [4]upon [1]the [2]stream
And when a flood occurred,

τῇ οἰκίᾳ ἐκείνῃ, καὶ οὐκ ἴσχυσε σαλεῦσαι αὐτήν,
- house ˜ that, and [3]not [1]it [2]was able to shake it,

τεθεμελίωτο γὰρ ἐπὶ την πέτραν.[u] 49 Ὁ δὲ
[2]it [3]had [4]been [5]founded [1]for on the *bed*rock. [2]the [3]*one* [1]But
he who

ἀκούσας καὶ μὴ ποιήσας ὅμοιός ἐστιν ἀνθρώπῳ
hearing and not doing like ˜ is a man
hears does not do

οἰκοδομήσαντι οἰκίαν ἐπὶ τὴν γῆν χωρὶς θεμελίου,
building a house on the ground without a foundation,

ᾗ προσέρρηξεν ὁ ποταμός, καὶ εὐθέως ἔπεσε.[v]
against which [3]burst [4]upon [1]the [2]stream, and immediately it fell.

Καὶ ἐγένετο τὸ ῥῆγμα τῆς οἰκίας ἐκείνης μέγα."
And [6]was [1]the [2]breaking - [3]of [5]house [4]that great."
wreck

Jesus Heals a Centurion's Servant
(Matt. 8:5–13)

7 1 Ἐπεὶ δὲ ἐπλήρωσε πάντα τὰ ῥήματα αὐτοῦ εἰς τὰς
when ˜ Now He finished all - words ˜ His in the
sayings

ἀκοὰς τοῦ λαοῦ, εἰσῆλθεν εἰς Καπερναούμ. 2 Ἑκατοντάρχου
ears of the people, He entered into Capernaum. [5]of [6]a [7]centurion
hearing

δέ τινος δοῦλος κακῶς ἔχων ἔμελλε τελευτᾶν, ὃς ἦν
[1]And [2]a [3]certain [4]slave [10]badly [8]having [9]*it* was about to die, who was
being ill

αὐτῷ ἔντιμος. 3 Ἀκούσας δὲ περὶ τοῦ Ἰησοῦ
[3]by [4]him [1]highly [2]valued. hearing ˜ And about - Jesus
when he heard

ἀπέστειλε πρὸς αὐτὸν πρεσβυτέρους τῶν Ἰουδαίων, ἐρωτῶν
he sent to Him elders of the Jews, asking

αὐτὸν ὅπως ἐλθὼν διασώσῃ τὸν δοῦλον αὐτοῦ. 4 Οἱ
Him that coming He might save - slave ˜ his. [2]the [3]*ones*
He might come and heal And when

δὲ παραγενόμενοι πρὸς τὸν Ἰησοῦν, παρεκάλουν αὐτὸν
[1]And coming to - Jesus they begged Him
they came

σπουδαίως, λέγοντες ὅτι "Ἄξιός ἐστιν ᾧ παρέξει
earnestly, saying - [3]"worthy [1]He [2]is for whom He should grant
was

τοῦτο, 5 ἀγαπᾷ γὰρ τὸ ἔθνος ἡμῶν καὶ τὴν συναγωγὴν
this, [2]he [3]loves [1]for - nation ˜ our and [4]the [5]synagogue

αὐτὸς ᾠκοδόμησεν ἡμῖν." 6 Ὁ δὲ Ἰησοῦς ἐπορεύετο σὺν
[2]himself [1]he [3]built for us." - And Jesus went with

αὐτοῖς.
them.

Ἤδη δὲ αὐτοῦ οὐ μακρὰν ἀπέχοντος ἀπὸ τῆς οἰκίας,
already ˜ And He not far ˜ being away from the house,
And when He was already not far away

ἔπεμψε πρὸς αὐτὸν[a] ὁ ἑκατόνταρχος φίλους, λέγων αὐτῷ,
[3]sent [5]to [6]Him [1]the [2]centurion [4]friends, saying to Him,

"Κύριε, μὴ σκύλλου, οὐ γὰρ εἰμι ἱκανὸς ἵνα μου
"Lord, not ˜ do trouble Yourself, [4]not [1]for [2]I [3]am worthy that [5]my

---

[u]**(6:48)** For τεθεμελιωτο γαρ επι την πετραν, *for it had been founded on the rock,* NU reads δια το καλως οικοδομησθαι αυτην, *because it was built well.*
[v]**(6:49)** NU reads συνεπεσεν, *fell together* (or, *collapsed*).
[a]**(7:6)** NU omits προς αυτον, *to him.*

ὑπὸ τὴν στέγην εἰσέλθῃς. 7 Διὸ οὐδὲ ἐμαυτὸν
[4]under - [6]roof [1]You [2]should [3]enter. Therefore [3]not [4]even [6]myself

ἠξίωσα πρός σε ἐλθεῖν. Ἀλλ' εἰπὲ λόγῳ,
[1]I [2]did [5]consider [7]worthy [10]to [11]You [8]to [9]come. But speak in a word,

καὶ ἰαθήσεται ὁ παῖς μου. 8 Καὶ γὰρ ἐγὼ ἄνθρωπός εἰμι
and [3]will [4]be [5]healed - [2]servant [1]my. also ~ For I [2]a [3]man [1]am
In fact

ὑπὸ ἐξουσίαν τασσόμενος, ἔχων ὑπ' ἐμαυτὸν στρατιώτας.
[6]under [7]authority [4]being [5]placed, having [2]under [3]myself [1]soldiers.
who has been me

Καὶ λέγω τούτῳ 'Πορεύθητι,' καὶ πορεύεται· καὶ ἄλλῳ,
And I say to this *one* 'Go,' and he goes; and to another,

'Ἔρχου,' καὶ ἔρχεται· καὶ τῷ δούλῳ μου, 'Ποίησον τοῦτο,' καὶ
'Come,' and he comes; and - to slave ~ my, 'Do this,' and

ποιεῖ."
he does *it*."

9 Ἀκούσας δὲ ταῦτα ὁ Ἰησοῦς ἐθαύμασεν αὐτόν,
hearing ~ And these *things* - Jesus marveled at him,
when He heard

καὶ στραφεὶς τῷ ἀκολουθοῦντι αὐτῷ ὄχλῳ εἶπε, "Λέγω
and turning to the [2]following [3]Him [1]crowd He said, "I say

ὑμῖν οὔτε ἐν τῷ Ἰσραὴλ τοσαύτην πίστιν εὗρον!"
to you, not even in - Israel [3]so [4]great [5]faith [1]I [2]found!"
have I found!"

10 Καὶ ὑποστρέψαντες οἱ πεμφθέντες εἰς τὸν οἶκον
And [6]returning [1]the [2]*ones* [3]having [4]been [5]sent to the house
when those who were sent returned

εὗρον τὸν ἀσθενοῦντα[b] δοῦλον ὑγιαίνοντα.
they found the [2]being [3]sick [1]slave being well.
slave well who had been sick.

Jesus Raises the Son of the Widow of Nain

11 Καὶ ἐγένετο ἐν τῷ ἑξῆς, ἐπορεύετο εἰς πόλιν
And it happened on the next *day*, He went to a city

καλουμένην Ναΐν, καὶ συνεπορεύοντο αὐτῷ οἱ μαθηταὶ αὐτοῦ
being called Nain, and [4]went [5]with [6]Him - [3]disciples [1]His
called

ἱκανοί,[c] καὶ ὄχλος πολύς. 12 Ὡς δὲ ἤγγισε τῇ
[2]many, and a crowd ~ large. as ~ And He came near to the
when

πύλῃ τῆς πόλεως, καὶ ἰδού, ἐξεκομίζετο
gate of the city, and behold, [4]was [5]being [6]carried [7]out
that

τεθνηκώς, υἱὸς μονογενὴς τῇ μητρὶ αὐτοῦ, καὶ
[1]*one* [2]having [3]died, a(n) son ~ only - to mother ~ his, and
a dead men, of

αὐτὴ χήρα, καὶ ὄχλος τῆς πόλεως ἱκανὸς σὺν αὐτῇ.
she *was* a widow, and a [2]crowd [3]of [4]the [5]city [1]large *was* with her.
from

13 Καὶ ἰδὼν αὐτὴν ὁ Κύριος ἐσπλαγχνίσθη ἐπ' αὐτῇ
And seeing her the Lord had compassion on her
when He saw

καὶ εἶπεν αὐτῇ, "Μὴ κλαῖε." 14 Καὶ προσελθὼν ἥψατο
and said to her, "not ~ Do weep." And approaching He touched

τῆς σοροῦ, οἱ δὲ βαστάζοντες ἔστησαν. Καὶ εἶπε,
the coffin, [2]the [3]*ones* [1]and carrying *it* stood still. And He said,
those who carried

"Νεανίσκε, σοὶ λέγω, ἐγέρθητι." 15 Καὶ ἀνεκάθισεν ὁ
"Young man, to you I say, arise." And [4]sat [5]up [1]the

not worthy that You should enter under my roof.
7 "Therefore I did not even
think myself worthy to come to
You. But say the word, and my
servant will be healed.
8 "For I also am a man
placed under authority, having
soldiers under me. And I say to
one, 'Go,' and he goes; and to
another, 'Come,' and he comes;
and to my servant, 'Do this,'
and he does *it*."
9 When Jesus heard these
things, He marveled at him,
and turned around and said to
the crowd that followed Him, "I
say to you, I have not found
such great faith, not even in Israel!"
10 And those who were sent,
returning to the house, found
the servant well who had been
sick.
11 Now it happened, the day
after, *that* He went into a city
called Nain; and many of His
disciples went with Him, and a
large crowd.
12 And when He came near
the gate of the city, behold, a
dead man was being carried
out, the only son of his mother;
and she was a widow. And a
large crowd from the city was
with her.
13 When the Lord saw her,
He had compassion on her and
said to her, "Do not weep."
14 Then He came and touched
the open coffin, and those who
carried *him* stood still. And He
said, "Young man, I say to you,
arise."
15 So he who was dead sat up

---

[b](7:10) NU omits ασθενουντα, *being sick*.
[c](7:11) NU omits ικανοι, *many*.

and began to speak. And He
presented him to his mother.
16 Then fear came upon all,
and they glorified God, saying,
"A great prophet has risen up
among us"; and, "God has visited His people."
17 And this report about Him
went throughout all Judea and
all the surrounding region.
18 Then the disciples of John
reported to him concerning all
these things.
19 And John, calling two of his
disciples to *him,* sent *them* to
Jesus, saying, "Are You the
Coming One, or do we look for
another?"
20 When the men had come to
Him, they said, "John the Baptist has sent us to You, saying,
'Are You the Coming One, or
do we look for another?' "
21 And that very hour He
cured many of infirmities, afflictions, and evil spirits; and to
many blind He gave sight.
22 Jesus answered and said to
them, "Go and tell John the
things you have seen and
heard: that *the* blind see, *the*
lame walk, *the* lepers are
cleansed, *the* deaf hear, *the*
dead are raised, *the* poor have
the gospel preached to them.
23 "And blessed is *he* who is

νεκρὸς καὶ ἤρξατο λαλεῖν. Καὶ ἔδωκεν αὐτὸν τῇ μητρὶ
[2]dead [3]*man* and began to speak. And He gave him - to mother ˜

αὐτοῦ.
his.

16 Ἔλαβε δὲ φόβος πάντας, καὶ ἐδόξαζον τὸν
[3]took [4]hold [5]of [1]And [2]fear all, and they were glorifying -

Θεόν, λέγοντες ὅτι "Προφήτης μέγας ἐγήγερται ἐν ἡμῖν,"
God, saying - "A prophet ˜ great has arisen among us,"

καὶ ὅτι "Ἐπεσκέψατο ὁ Θεὸς τὸν λαὸν αὐτοῦ." 17 Καὶ
and - "visited ˜ - God - people ˜ His." And
has visited

ἐξῆλθεν ὁ λόγος οὗτος ἐν ὅλῃ τῇ Ἰουδαίᾳ περὶ αὐτοῦ καὶ ἐν
[3]went [4]out - [2]word [1]this in all - Judea about Him and in
report

πάσῃ τῇ περιχώρῳ.
all the surrounding region.

John the Baptist Sends Messengers to Jesus
(Matt. 11:2–19)

18 Καὶ ἀπήγγειλαν Ἰωάννῃ οἱ μαθηταὶ αὐτοῦ περὶ πάντων
And [3]reported [4]to [5]John - [2]disciples [1]his about all

τούτων. 19 Καὶ προσκαλεσάμενος δύο τινὰς τῶν
these *things.* And summoning [3]two [1]a [2]certain -
when he summoned

μαθητῶν αὐτοῦ ὁ Ἰωάννης ἔπεμψε πρὸς τὸν Ἰησοῦν,[d]
[4]of [6]disciples [5]his - John sent *them* to - Jesus,

λέγων, "Σὺ εἶ ὁ Ἐρχόμενος, ἢ ἄλλον προσδοκῶμεν?"
saying, "You ˜ Are the Coming *One,* or [5]another [1]do [2]we [3]look [4]for?"
One who is coming,

20 Παραγενόμενοι δὲ πρὸς αὐτὸν οἱ ἄνδρες εἶπον,
coming ˜ And to Him the men said,
when they came

"'Ιωάννης ὁ Βαπτιστὴς ἀπέσταλκεν ἡμᾶς πρὸς σε, λέγων,
"John the Baptist has sent us to You, saying,

'Σὺ εἶ ὁ Ἐρχόμενος, ἢ ἄλλον προσδοκῶμεν?' " 21 Ἐν
'You ˜ Are the Coming *One,* or [5]another [1]do [2]we [3]look [4]for?' " [2]in
One who is coming,

αὐτῇ δὲ τῇ ὥρᾳ ἐθεράπευσε πολλοὺς ἀπὸ νόσων καὶ
[3]that [4]very [1]And - hour He healed many from diseases and

μαστίγων καὶ πνευμάτων πονηρῶν, καὶ τυφλοῖς πολλοῖς
torments and spirits ˜ evil, and to [2]blind [3]*people* [1]many

ἐχαρίσατο τὸ βλέπειν.
He granted the *ability* to see.
sight.

22 Καὶ ἀποκριθεὶς ὁ Ἰησοῦς[e] εἶπεν αὐτοῖς, "Πορευθέντες
And answering - Jesus said to them, "Having gone
"Go and

ἀπαγγείλατε Ἰωάννῃ ἃ εἴδετε καὶ ἠκούσατε· ὅτι
report to John *the things* which you saw and heard; that
what you have seen

τυφλοὶ ἀναβλέπουσι, χωλοὶ περιπατοῦσι, λεπροὶ
blind *people* regain sight, lame *people* walk, lepers

καθαρίζονται, κωφοὶ ἀκούουσι, νεκροὶ ἐγείρονται,
are cleansed, deaf *people* hear, dead *people* are raised,

πτωχοὶ εὐαγγελίζονται. 23 Καὶ μακάριός ἐστιν
poor *people* are evangelized. And blessed is
have the gospel preached to them.

---

[d](**7:19**) NU reads Κυριον, *(the) Lord.*
[e](**7:22**) NU omits ο Ιησους, *Jesus.*

ὃς ἐὰν μὴ σκανδαλισθῇ ἐν ἐμοί."
who ever not ˜ is offended in Me."
because of

24 Ἀπελθόντων δὲ τῶν ἀγγέλων Ἰωάννου, ἤρξατο
[6]departing [1]Now [2]the [3]messengers [4]of [5]John, He began
Now when John's messengers had departed,

λέγειν τοῖς ὄχλοις περὶ Ἰωάννου, "Τί ἐξεληλύθατε εἰς
to say to the crowds concerning John, "What have you gone out into

τὴν ἔρημον θεάσασθαι? Κάλαμον ὑπὸ ἀνέμου σαλευόμενον?
the wilderness to see? A reed [3]by [4]wind [1]being [2]shaken?

25 Ἀλλὰ τί ἐξεληλύθατε ἰδεῖν? Ἄνθρωπον ἐν μαλακοῖς
But what have you gone out to see? A man [2]in [3]soft

ἱματίοις ἠμφιεσμένον? Ἰδού, οἱ ἐν ἱματισμῷ ἐνδόξῳ καὶ
[4]garments [1]clothed? Behold, the *ones* [2]in [4]clothing [3]glorious [5]and
those who

τρυφῇ* ὑπάρχοντες ἐν τοῖς βασιλείοις εἰσίν. **26** Ἀλλὰ τί
[6]in [7]luxury [1]being [9]in - [10]royal [11]*palaces* [8]are. But what
are

ἐξεληλύθατε ἰδεῖν? Προφήτην? Ναί, λέγω ὑμῖν, καὶ
have you gone out to see? A prophet? Yes, I say to you, and

περισσότερον προφήτου. **27** Οὗτός ἐστι περὶ οὗ γέγραπται,
far more *than* a prophet. This is *he* about whom it is written,

«Ἰδού, ἐγὼ ἀποστέλλω τὸν ἄγγελόν μου πρὸ
«Behold, I send - messenger ˜ My before

προσώπου σου,
face ˜ Your,

Ὃς κατασκευάσει τὴν ὁδόν σου ἔμπροσθέν σου.»[f]
Who will prepare - way ˜ Your before You.»

28 Λέγω γὰρ ὑμῖν, μείζων ἐν γεννητοῖς γυναικῶν
[2]I [3]say [1]For to you, [5]greater [7]among [8]*those* [9]born [10]of [11]women

προφήτης Ἰωάννου τοῦ Βαπτιστοῦ[g] οὐδείς ἐστιν· ὁ δὲ
[4]a [6]prophet [12]*than* [13]John [14]the [15]Baptist [1]no [2]one [3]is; [17]the [16]but
but he who

μικρότερος ἐν τῇ βασιλείᾳ τοῦ Θεοῦ μείζων αὐτοῦ ἐστι."
least *one* in the kingdom - of God [2]greater [3]*than* [4]he [1]is."
is least

29 Καὶ πᾶς ὁ λαὸς ἀκούσας καὶ οἱ τελῶναι
And all the people [5]hearing [1]and [2]the [3]tax [4]collectors
And when heard

ἐδικαίωσαν τὸν Θεόν, βαπτισθέντες τὸ βάπτισμα
they justified - God, having been baptized *with* the baptism
declared God just, because they had

Ἰωάννου. **30** Οἱ δὲ Φαρισαῖοι καὶ οἱ νομικοὶ τὴν βουλὴν τοῦ
of John. the ˜ But Pharisees and the lawyers [2]the [3]counsel -

Θεοῦ ἠθέτησαν εἰς ἑαυτούς, μὴ βαπτισθέντες ὑπ'
[4]of [5]God [1]rejected for themselves, not having been baptized by
because they had not

αὐτοῦ.
him.

31 "Τίνι[h] οὖν ὁμοιώσω τοὺς ἀνθρώπους τῆς
"[2]to [3]what [1]Therefore shall I compare the men -

γενεᾶς ταύτης, καὶ τίνι εἰσὶν ὅμοιοι? **32** Ὅμοιοί
of generation ˜ this, and to what are they similar? [3]similar

εἰσι παιδίοις τοῖς ἐν ἀγορᾷ καθημένοις καὶ
[1]They [2]are to children the *ones* [2]in [3]*the* [4]marketplace [1]sitting and
who sit

προσφωνοῦσιν ἀλλήλοις καὶ λέγουσιν,
calling to one another and saying,
call say,

not offended because of Me."
24 When the messengers of John had departed, He began to speak to the multitudes concerning John: "What did you go out into the wilderness to see? A reed shaken by the wind?
25 "But what did you go out to see? A man clothed in soft garments? Indeed those who are gorgeously appareled and live in luxury are in kings' courts.
26 "But what did you go out to see? A prophet? Yes, I say to you, and more than a prophet.
27 "This is *he* of whom it is written:

'Behold, I send My messenger before Your face,
Who will prepare Your way before You.'

28 "For I say to you, among those born of women there is not a greater prophet than John the Baptist; but he who is least in the kingdom of God is greater than he."
29 And when all the people heard *Him,* even the tax collectors justified God, having been baptized with the baptism of John.
30 But the Pharisees and lawyers rejected the will of God for themselves, not having been baptized by him.
31 And the Lord said, "To what then shall I liken the men of this generation, and what are they like?
32 "They are like children sitting in the marketplace and calling to one another, saying:

f(**7:27**) Mal. 3:1
g(**7:28**) NU omits *του Βαπτιστου, the Baptist.*
h(**7:31**) TR reads *ειπεν δε ο Κυριος τινι, but the Lord said, to whom.*

*(**7:25**) *τρυφή (tryphē).* Noun meaning *luxury, splendor* (as here), or *reveling, carousing* (2 Pet. 2:13), the only two occurrences in the NT. In both, the underlying idea is that of self-indulgence. Many scholars find here in Luke also the idea of softness or "delicate" living. Cf. the cognate verb *τρυφάω, live in luxury or self-indulgence, revel, carouse* (only in James 5:5); also the

'We played the flute for
you,
And you did not dance;
We mourned to you,
And you did not weep.'

33 "For John the Baptist came neither eating bread nor drinking wine, and you say, 'He has a demon.'
34 "The Son of Man has come eating and drinking, and you say, 'Look, a glutton and a winebibber, a friend of tax collectors and sinners!'
35 "But wisdom is justified by all her children."
36 Then one of the Pharisees asked Him to eat with him. And He went to the Pharisee's house, and sat down to eat.
37 And behold, a woman in the city who was a sinner, when she knew that *Jesus* sat at the table in the Pharisee's house, brought an alabaster flask of fragrant oil,
38 and stood at His feet behind *Him* weeping; and she began to wash His feet with her tears, and wiped *them* with the hair of her head; and she kissed His feet and anointed *them* with the fragrant oil.
39 Now when the Pharisee who had invited Him saw *this,* he spoke to himself, saying, "This Man, if He were a prophet, would know who and what manner of woman *this is* who is touching Him, for she is a sinner."
40 And Jesus answered and said to him, "Simon, I have something to say to you." So he

'Ηὐλήσαμεν ὑμῖν, καὶ οὐκ ὠρχήσασθε·
'We played the flute for you, and [3]not [1]you [2]did dance;
'Εθρηνήσαμεν ὑμῖν,[i] καὶ οὐκ ἐκλαύσατε.'
We mourned for you, and [3]not [1]you [2]did weep.'

33 'Ελήλυθε γὰρ 'Ιωάννης ὁ Βαπτιστὴς μήτε ἄρτον ἐσθίων
[5]has [6]come [1]For [2]John [3]the [4]Baptist neither bread ˜ eating
μήτε οἶνον πίνων, καὶ λέγετε, 'Δαιμόνιον ἔχει.'
nor wine ˜ drinking, and you say, '[3]a [4]demon [1]He [2]has.'

34 'Ελήλυθεν ὁ Υἱὸς τοῦ 'Ανθρώπου ἐσθίων καὶ πίνων, καὶ
[5]has [6]come [1]The [2]Son - [3]of [4]Man eating and drinking, and
λέγετε, "Ἰδού, ἄνθρωπος φάγος καὶ οἰνοπότης, φίλος
you say, 'Look, a man a glutton and a wine drinker, a friend
a glutton drunkard,
τελωνῶν καὶ ἁμαρτωλῶν!' 35 Καὶ ἐδικαιώθη ἡ
of tax collectors and sinners!' And [2]was [3]justified -
And so wisdom is declared
σοφία ἀπὸ τῶν τέκνων αὐτῆς πάντων."
[1]wisdom by - [3]children [2]her [1]all."
right

Jesus Forgives a Sinful Woman

36 Ἠρώτα δέ τις αὐτὸν τῶν Φαρισαίων ἵνα
[8]asked [1]Now [2]a [3]certain [4]*one* [9]Him [5]of [6]the [7]Pharisees that
to
φάγῃ μετ' αὐτοῦ. Καὶ εἰσελθὼν εἰς τὴν οἰκίαν τοῦ
He might eat with him. And entering into the house of the
eat
Φαρισαίου ανεκλίθη. 37 Καὶ ἰδού, γυνὴ ἐν τῇ πόλει
Pharisee He reclined *to eat.* And behold, a woman in the city
ἥτις ἦν ἁμαρτωλός, ἐπιγνοῦσα ὅτι ἀνάκειται ἐν τῇ
who was a sinner, knowing that He is reclining in the
when she found out was
οἰκίᾳ τοῦ Φαρισαίου, κομίσασα ἀλάβαστρον μύρου,
house of the Pharisee, bringing an alabaster flask of perfume,
brought

38 καὶ στᾶσα παρὰ τοὺς πόδας αὐτοῦ ὀπίσω κλαίουσα,
and standing [2]by - [4]feet [3]His [1]behind weeping,
ἤρξατο βρέχειν τοὺς πόδας αὐτοῦ τοῖς δάκρυσι καὶ ταῖς
she began to wet - feet ˜ His with the tears and with the
her
θριξὶ τῆς κεφαλῆς αὐτῆς ἐξέμασσε, καὶ κατεφίλει
hairs - of head ˜ her she was wiping *them* off, and was kissing
τοὺς πόδας αὐτοῦ καὶ ἤλειφε τῷ μύρῳ. 39 Ἰδὼν δὲ
- feet ˜ His and anointing *them* with the perfume. [9]seeing [1]And
And when
ὁ Φαρισαῖος ὁ καλέσας αὐτόν, εἶπεν ἐν ἑαυτῷ
[2]the [3]Pharisee [4]the [5]*one* [6]having [7]invited [8]Him, he spoke within himself
the Pharisee who had invited Him saw it,
λέγων, "Οὗτος, εἰ ἦν προφήτης, ἐγίνωσκεν ἂν τίς καὶ
saying, "This *Man,* if He were a prophet, would know - who and
ποταπὴ ἡ γυνὴ ἥτις ἅπτεται αὐτοῦ, ὅτι ἁμαρτωλός
what sort of - woman *it is* who touches Him, because [3]a [4]sinner
ἐστι."
[1]she [2]is."

40 Καὶ ἀποκριθεὶς ὁ Ἰησοῦς εἶπε πρὸς αὐτόν, "Σίμων,
And answering ˜ - Jesus said to him, "Simon,
ἔχω σοί τι εἰπεῖν."
I have [4]to [5]you [1]something [2]to [3]say."

[i](7:32) NU omits υμιν, *for you.*

synonym ἐντρυφάω (only in 2 Pet. 2:13).

Ὁ δέ φησι, "Διδάσκαλε, εἰπέ."
[2]the [3]*one* [1]And says, "Teacher, speak."
he said,

41 "Δύο χρεωφειλέται ἦσαν δανιστῇ τινί. Ὁ εἷς
"Two debtors were to a creditor ˜ certain. The one
"A certain creditor had two debtors.

ὤφειλε δηνάρια πεντακόσια, ὁ δὲ ἕτερος πεντήκοντα.
owed [3]denarii [1]five [2]hundred, the ˜ but other *owed* fifty.

42 Μὴ ἐχόντων δὲ αὐτῶν ἀποδοῦναι, ἀμφοτέροις
[3]not [4]having [1]And [2]them *anything* to pay back, [4]both
And when they did not have

ἐχαρίσατο. Τίς οὖν αὐτῶν, εἰπέ, πλεῖον αὐτὸν
[1]he [2]freely [3]forgave. which ˜ Therefore of them, tell *Me,* [4]more [3]him

ἀγαπήσει?"
[1]will [2]love?"

43 Ἀποκριθεὶς δὲ ὁ Σίμων εἶπεν, "Ὑπολαμβάνω
answering ˜ And - Simon said, "I suppose

ὅτι ᾧ τὸ πλεῖον ἐχαρίσατο."
that *it is the one* to whom - [4]more [1]he [2]freely [3]forgave."

Ὁ δέ εἶπεν αὐτῷ, "Ὀρθῶς ἔκρινας." 44 Καὶ
[2]the [3]*One* [1]And said to him, "[3]correctly [1]You [2]judged." And
He

στραφεὶς πρὸς τὴν γυναῖκα, τῷ Σίμωνι ἔφη, "Βλέπεις
turning to the woman, [3]to [4]Simon [1]He [2]said, "Do you see

ταύτην τὴν γυναῖκα? Εἰσῆλθόν σου εἰς τὴν οἰκίαν· ὕδωρ ἐπὶ
this - woman? I entered your ˜ into - house; [5]water [6]for

τοὺς πόδας μου οὐκ ἔδωκας, αὕτη δὲ τοῖς
- [8]feet [7]My [3]not [1]you [2]did [4]give, [10]this [11]*woman* [9]but with the
her

δάκρυσιν ἔβρεξέ μου τοὺς πόδας καὶ ταῖς θριξὶ τῆς
tears wet My - feet and with the hairs -

κεφαλῆς[j] αὐτῆς ἐξέμαξε. 45 Φίλημά μοι οὐκ
of head ˜ her wiped *them* off. [5]a [6]kiss [7]to [8]Me [3]not

ἔδωκας, αὕτη δὲ ἀφ' ἧς εἰσῆλθον οὐ
[1]You [2]did [4]give, [10]this [11]*woman* [9]but from which *hour* I entered not ˜
since

διέλιπε καταφιλοῦσά μου τοὺς πόδας. 46 Ἐλαίῳ τὴν κεφαλήν
did stop kissing My - feet. [7]with [8]oil - [6]head

μου οὐκ ἤλειψας, αὕτη δὲ μύρῳ ἤλειψέ μου
[5]My [3]not [1]You [2]did [4]anoint, [10]this [11]*woman* [9]but with perfume anointed My

τοὺς πόδας. 47 Οὗ χάριν, λέγω σοι, ἀφέωνται αἱ
- feet. Of which reason, I say to you, [4]have [5]been [6]forgiven -
For

ἁμαρτίαι αὐτῆς αἱ πολλαί, ὅτι ἠγάπησε πολύ.
[3]sins [1]her - [2]many, because she loved much.

Ὧ δὲ ὀλίγον ἀφίεται, ὀλίγον ἀγαπᾷ."
[2]*the* [3]*one* [4]to [5]whom [1]But little is forgiven, little ˜ loves."

48 Εἶπεν δὲ αὐτῇ, "Ἀφέωνταί σου αἱ ἁμαρτίαι."
[2]He [3]said [1]And to her, "[3]have [4]been [5]forgiven [1]Your - [2]sins."
Then

49 Καὶ ἤρξαντο οἱ συνανακείμενοι λέγειν
And [8]began [1]the [2]*ones* [3]reclining [4]*to* [5]*eat* [6]with [7]*Him* to say
those who were

ἐν ἑαυτοῖς, "Τίς οὗτός ἐστιν ὃς καὶ ἁμαρτίας ἀφίησιν?"
within themselves, "Who this ˜ is who even sins ˜ forgives?"

50 Εἶπε δὲ πρὸς τὴν γυναῖκα, "Ἡ πίστις σου σέσωκέ
[2]He [3]said [1]And to the woman, - "faith ˜ Your has saved

σε. Πορεύου εἰς εἰρήνην."
you. Go in peace."

said, "Teacher, say it."
41 "There was a certain creditor who had two debtors. One owed five hundred denarii, and the other fifty.
42 "And when they had nothing with which to repay, he freely forgave them both. Tell Me, therefore, which of them will love him more?"
43 Simon answered and said, "I suppose the *one* whom he forgave more." And He said to him, "You have rightly judged."
44 Then He turned to the woman and said to Simon, "Do you see this woman? I entered your house; you gave Me no water for My feet, but she has washed My feet with her tears and wiped *them* with the hair of her head.
45 "You gave Me no kiss, but this woman has not ceased to kiss My feet since the time I came in.
46 "You did not anoint My head with oil, but this woman has anointed My feet with fragrant oil.
47 "Therefore I say to you, her sins, *which are* many, are forgiven, for she loved much. But to whom little is forgiven, *the same* loves little."
48 Then He said to her, "Your sins are forgiven."
49 And those who sat at the table with Him began to say to themselves, "Who is this who even forgives sins?"
50 Then He said to the woman, "Your faith has saved you. Go in peace."

j(7:44) NU omits της κεφαλης, *of (the) head.*

8 Now it came to pass, afterward, that He went through every city and village, preaching and bringing the glad tidings of the kingdom of God. And the twelve *were* with Him,
2 and certain women who had been healed of evil spirits and infirmities—Mary called Magdalene, out of whom had come seven demons,
3 and Joanna the wife of Chuza, Herod's steward, and Susanna, and many others who provided for Him from their substance.
4 And when a great multitude had gathered, and they had come to Him from every city, He spoke by a parable:
5 "A sower went out to sow his seed. And as he sowed, some fell by the wayside; and it was trampled down, and the birds of the air devoured it.
6 "Some fell on rock; and as soon as it sprang up, it withered away because it lacked moisture.
7 "And some fell among thorns, and the thorns sprang up with it and choked it.
8 "But others fell on good ground, sprang up, and yielded a crop a hundredfold." When He had said these things He

Many Women Minister to Jesus

8 1 Καὶ ἐγένετο ἐν τῷ καθεξῆς καὶ αὐτὸς
And it happened in - what follows and He
afterward that

διώδευε κατὰ πόλιν καὶ κώμην κηρύσσων καὶ
was traveling through every city and village preaching and

εὐαγγελιζόμενος τὴν βασιλείαν τοῦ Θεοῦ, καὶ οἱ δώδεκα
proclaiming the gospel *of* the kingdom - of God, and the twelve

σὺν αὐτῷ, 2 καὶ γυναῖκές τινες αἳ ἦσαν
were with Him, and women ˜ certain who were
had been

τεθεραπευμέναι ἀπὸ πνευμάτων πονηρῶν καὶ ἀσθενειῶν,
healed from spirits ˜ evil and infirmities,

Μαρία ἡ καλουμένη Μαγδαληνή, ἀφ' ἧς δαιμόνια
Mary the *woman* being called Magdalene, from whom demons ˜
who was

ἑπτὰ ἐξεληλύθει, 3 καὶ Ἰωάννα γυνὴ Χουζᾶ ἐπιτρόπου
seven had gone out, and Joanna *the* wife of Chuza a steward
supervisor

Ἡρῴδου, καὶ Σωσάννα, καὶ ἕτεραι πολλαί, αἵτινες
of Herod, and Susanna, and [2]other [3]*women* [1]many, who

διηκόνουν αὐτοῖς[a] ἀπὸ τῶν ὑπαρχόντων αὐταῖς.
were ministering to them from the *things* belonging to them.
their possessions.

The Parable of the Sower
(Matt. 13:1–9; Mark 4:1–9)

4 Συνιόντος δὲ ὄχλου πολλοῦ καὶ τῶν κατὰ
[5]gathering [1]And [2]a [4]crowd [3]large and the *people* according to
And when a large crowd gathered from every

πόλιν ἐπιπορευομένων πρὸς αὐτόν, εἶπε διὰ παραβολῆς,
city coming to Him, He spoke by a parable,
came

5 "Ἐξῆλθεν ὁ σπείρων τοῦ σπεῖραι τὸν σπόρον αὐτοῦ. Καὶ
"[4]went [5]out [1]The [2]sowing [3]*one* - to sow - seed ˜ his. And
A sower

ἐν τῷ σπείρειν αὐτόν, ὃ μὲν ἔπεσε παρὰ τὴν ὁδόν, καὶ
in - [2]to [3]sow [1]him, some *seed* fell alongside the road, and
as he sowed,

κατεπατήθη, καὶ τὰ πετεινὰ τοῦ οὐρανοῦ κατέφαγεν αὐτό.
it was trampled down, and the birds - of heaven devoured it.

6 Καὶ ἕτερον ἔπεσεν ἐπὶ τὴν πέτραν, καὶ φυὲν
And other *seed* fell on the rock, and growing up
when it grew up

ἐξηράνθη διὰ τὸ μὴ ἔχειν ἰκμάδα. 7 Καὶ ἕτερον
it withered on account of - not to have moisture. And other *seed*
because it had no

ἔπεσεν ἐν μέσῳ τῶν ἀκανθῶν, καὶ συμφυεῖσαι αἱ
fell in *the* midst of the thorns, and growing up with *it* the
when the thorns grew up

ἄκανθαι ἀπέπνιξαν αὐτό. 8 Καὶ ἕτερον ἔπεσεν εἰς τὴν
thorns choked it. And other *seed* fell into -
with it, they

γῆν τὴν ἀγαθήν, καὶ φυὲν ἐποίησε καρπὸν
ground ˜ - good, and growing up it produced fruit
when it grew up

ἑκατονταπλασίονα." Ταῦτα λέγων ἐφώνει, "Ὁ
a hundredfold." [2]these [3]*things* [1]Saying He was calling out, "The *one*
"He

[a](8:3) Many mss., TR read αυτω, *to him*.

ἔχων ὦτα ἀκούειν ἀκουέτω."
having ears to hear let him hear."
who has

Jesus Explains the Purpose of Parables
(Matt. 13:10–17; Mark 4:10–12)

9 Ἐπηρώτων δὲ αὐτὸν οἱ μαθηταὶ αὐτοῦ, λέγοντες, "Τίς
[4]were [5]asking [1]And [6]Him - [3]disciples [2]His, saying, "What
Then

εἴη ἡ παραβολὴ αὕτη?"
[1]might [4]be - [3]parable [2]this?"
does this parable mean?"

10 Ὁ δὲ εἶπεν, "Ὑμῖν δέδοται γνῶναι τὰ
[2]the [3]*One* [1]And said, "To you it has been given to know the
He

μυστήρια* τῆς βασιλείας τοῦ Θεοῦ, τοῖς δὲ λοιποῖς ἐν
mysteries of the kingdom - of God, [2]to [3]the [1]but rest *they are* in

παραβολαῖς, ἵνα
parables, that

«Βλέποντες μὴ βλέπωσι
«Seeing [3]not [1]they [2]may see

Καὶ ἀκούοντες μὴ συνιῶσιν.»[b]
And hearing [3]not [1]they [2]may understand.»

Jesus Explains the Parable of the Sower
(Matt. 13:18–23; Mark 4:13–20)

11 "Ἔστι δὲ αὕτη ἡ παραβολή· Ὁ σπόρος ἐστὶν ὁ
"[3]is [1]Now [2]this the parable: The seed is the

λόγος τοῦ Θεοῦ. 12 Οἱ δὲ παρὰ τὴν ὁδόν εἰσιν οἱ
word - of God. [2]the [3]*ones* [1]And beside the road are the *ones*
those

ἀκούοντες, εἶτα ἔρχεται ὁ διάβολος καὶ αἴρει τὸν λόγον
hearing, then [3]comes [1]the [2]devil and takes away the word
who hear,

ἀπὸ τῆς καρδίας αὐτῶν, ἵνα μὴ πιστεύσαντες
from - heart ˜ their, so that [3]not [6]*by* [7]believing
lest they believe

σωθῶσιν. 13 Οἱ δὲ ἐπὶ τῆς πέτρας
[1]they [2]should [4]be [5]saved. [2]the [3]*ones* [1]And on the rock
and be saved.

οἵ, ὅταν ἀκούσωσι, μετὰ χαρᾶς δέχονται τὸν
are those who, whenever they hear, with joy receive the

λόγον, καὶ οὗτοι ῥίζαν οὐκ ἔχουσιν, οἳ πρὸς καιρὸν
word, and these [4]root [2]not [1]do [3]have, who for a time

πιστεύουσι καὶ ἐν καιρῷ πειρασμοῦ ἀφίστανται. 14 Τὸ
believe and in time of testing withdraw. [2]the [3]*seed*
fall away.

δὲ εἰς τὰς ἀκάνθας πεσόν, οὗτοί εἰσιν οἱ ἀκούσαντες,
[1]But [5]into [6]the [7]thorns [4]falling, these are the *ones* hearing,
which fell, those who heard,

καὶ ὑπὸ μεριμνῶν καὶ πλούτου καὶ ἡδονῶν τοῦ βίου
and by *the* anxieties and riches and pleasures - of life

πορευόμενοι συμπνίγονται, καὶ οὐ τελεσφοροῦσι.
going they are choked, and [3]not [1]they [2]do bear fruit to maturity.
as they go

15 Τὸ δὲ ἐν τῇ καλῇ γῇ, οὗτοί εἰσιν οἵτινες ἐν
[2]the [3]*seed* [1]And in the good ground, these are such who with

cried, "He who has ears to hear, let him hear!"
9 Then His disciples asked Him, saying, "What does this parable mean?"
10 And He said, "To you it has been given to know the mysteries of the kingdom of God, but to the rest *it is given* in parables, that

'Seeing they may not see,
And hearing they may not understand.'

11 "Now the parable is this: The seed is the word of God.
12 "Those by the wayside are the ones who hear; then the devil comes and takes away the word out of their hearts, lest they should believe and be saved.
13 "But the ones on the rock *are those* who, when they hear, receive the word with joy; and these have no root, who believe for a while and in time of temptation fall away.
14 "Now the ones *that* fell among thorns are those who, when they have heard, go out and are choked with cares, riches, and pleasures of life, and bring no fruit to maturity.
15 "But the ones *that* fell on the good ground are those who,

---

[b](8:10) Is. 6:9

***(8:10)** μυστήριον *(mystērion).* Noun meaning *secret, mystery.* Unlike its English derivative *mystery* that refers to something people try to reason out, μυστήριον in the NT refers to God's secret plans and thoughts that are completely hidden from human understanding. As a result, the "mysteries of God" must be revealed to humanity. Here (and in the synoptic parallels) it refers to the coming of the kingdom of God into the world, recognized only by believers. The word is most often found in Paul's letters, where it refers to the whole saving activity of God revealed by the proclamation of Christ (Col. 1:27). Its incomprehensibility to human understanding is seen in the ecstatic utterances of *mysteries* (1 Cor. 14:2). The word is also applied to the *secret* or unperceived evil activity of the Antichrist (the "mystery of lawlessness," 2 Thess. 2:7).

having heard the word with a noble and good heart, keep *it* and bear fruit with patience.

16 "No one, when he has lit a lamp, covers it with a vessel or puts *it* under a bed, but sets *it* on a lampstand, that those who enter may see the light.

17 "For nothing is secret that will not be revealed, nor *anything* hidden that will not be known and come to light.

18 "Therefore take heed how you hear. For whoever has, to him *more* will be given; and whoever does not have, even what he seems to have will be taken from him."

19 Then His mother and brothers came to Him, and could not approach Him because of the crowd.

20 And it was told Him *by some,* who said, "Your mother and Your brothers are standing outside, desiring to see You."

21 But He answered and said to them, "My mother and My brothers are these who hear the word of God and do it."

22 Now it happened, on a certain day, that He got into a boat

καρδίᾳ καλῇ καὶ ἀγαθῇ, ἀκούσαντες τὸν λόγον κατέχουσι καὶ
[1]a [5]heart [2]noble [3]and [4]good, hearing (when they heard) the word hold on to *it* and

καρποφοροῦσιν ἐν ὑπομονῇ.
bear fruit with endurance.

Light Under a Vessel
(Mark 4:21–25)

16 "Οὐδεὶς δὲ λύχνον ἅψας καλύπτει αὐτὸν σκεύει ἢ
"[2]no [3]one [1]And [5]a [6]lamp [4]lighting covers it with a vessel or

ὑποκάτω κλίνης τίθησιν, ἀλλ᾽ ἐπὶ λυχνίας ἐπιτίθησιν, ἵνα
[3]under [4]a [5]bed [1]puts [2]*it,* but [3]on [4]a [5]lampstand [1]puts [2]*it,* so that

οἱ εἰσπορευόμενοι βλέπωσι τὸ φῶς. **17** Οὐ γάρ ἐστι
the *ones* entering (those who enter) may see the light. [4]not [1]For [2]*there* [3]is (nothing)

κρυπτὸν ὃ οὐ φανερὸν γενήσεται, οὐδὲ ἀπόκρυφον
a hidden *thing* (hidden) which [2]not [4]manifest [1]will [3]become, nor a concealed *thing* (anything concealed)

ὃ οὐ γνωσθήσεται καὶ εἰς φανερὸν ἔλθῃ. **18** Βλέπετε
which not ˜ will be known and [2]into [3]manifestation [1]come. watch ˜

οὖν πῶς ἀκούετε. Ὃς γὰρ ἐὰν ἔχῃ, δοθήσεται αὐτῷ,
Therefore how you hear. who ˜ For ever has, *more* will be given to him,

καὶ ὃς ἐὰν μὴ ἔχῃ, καὶ ὃ δοκεῖ ἔχειν
and who ever not ˜ does have, even what he seems (thinks) to have (he has)

ἀρθήσεται ἀπ᾽ αὐτοῦ."
will be taken away from him."

Jesus' Mother and Brothers Send for Him
(Matt. 12:46–50; Mark 3:31–35)

19 Παρεγένοντο δὲ πρὸς αὐτὸν ἡ μήτηρ καὶ οἱ ἀδελφοὶ
[6]came [1]And [7]to [8]Him - [3]mother [4]and - [5]brothers

αὐτοῦ, καὶ οὐκ ἠδύναντο συντυχεῖν αὐτῷ διὰ τὸν
[2]His, and [3]not [1]they [2]were able to get together with Him because of the

ὄχλον. **20** Καὶ ἀπηγγέλη αὐτῷ λεγόντων, "Ἡ μήτηρ
crowd. And it was reported to Him of *ones* saying, (by some who said,) - "mother ˜

σου καὶ οἱ ἀδελφοί σου ἑστήκασιν ἔξω ἰδεῖν σε
Your and - brothers ˜ Your are standing outside [2]to [3]see [4]You

θέλοντες."
[1]desiring."

21 Ὁ δὲ ἀποκριθεὶς εἶπε πρὸς αὐτούς, "Μήτηρ μου
[2]the [3]*One* (He) [1]But answering said to them, "mother ˜ My

καὶ ἀδελφοί μου οὗτοί εἰσιν, οἱ τὸν λόγον τοῦ Θεοῦ
and brothers ˜ My these ˜ are, the *ones* (those who) [2]the [3]word - [4]of [5]God

ἀκούοντες καὶ ποιοῦντες αὐτόν."[c]
[1]hearing (hear) and doing (do) it."

Wind and Wave Obey Jesus
(Matt. 8:23–27; Mark 4:35–41)

22 Καὶ ἐγένετο ἐν μιᾷ τῶν ἡμερῶν καὶ αὐτὸς ἐνέβη
And it happened on one of the (those) days and (that) He stepped in (got)

---

[c](**8:21**) NU omits *αυτον, it.*

εἰς πλοῖον καὶ οἱ μαθηταὶ αὐτοῦ, καὶ εἶπε πρὸς αὐτούς,
into a boat and - disciples ˜ His, and He said to them,
in with

"Διέλθωμεν εἰς τὸ πέραν τῆς λίμνης." Καὶ
"Let us go across to the other side of the lake." And

ἀνήχθησαν. 23 Πλεόντων δὲ αὐτῶν ἀφύπνωσε. Καὶ
they put out to sea. [3]sailing [1]But [2]them He fell asleep. And
But as they sailed,

κατέβη λαῖλαψ ἀνέμου εἰς τὴν λίμνην, καὶ
[5]came [6]down [1]a [2]storm [3]of [4]wind onto the lake, and
a windstorm

συνεπληροῦντο, καὶ ἐκινδύνευον.
they were being filled *with water,* and were in danger.

24 Προσελθόντες δὲ διήγειραν αὐτόν, λέγοντες,
approaching ˜ And they awakened Him, saying,

"Ἐπιστάτα, ἐπιστάτα, ἀπολλύμεθα!"
"Master, Master, we are perishing!"

Ὁ δὲ ἐγερθεὶς ἐπετίμησε τῷ ἀνέμῳ καὶ τῷ κλύδωνι
[2]the [3]*One* [1]And rising rebuked the wind and the waves
Then He arose and

τοῦ ὕδατος. Καὶ ἐπαύσαντο, καὶ ἐγένετο γαλήνη. 25 Εἶπε
- of water. And they ceased, and *there* was a calm. [2]He [3]said

δὲ αὐτοῖς, "Ποῦ ἐστιν ἡ πίστις ὑμῶν?"
[1]But to them, "Where is - faith ˜ your?"

Φοβηθέντες δὲ ἐθαύμασαν, λέγοντες πρὸς ἀλλήλους,
[2]becoming [3]afraid [1]But they marveled, saying to one another,

"Τίς ἄρα οὗτός ἐστιν ὅτι καὶ τοῖς ἀνέμοις ἐπιτάσσει καὶ
"Who then this ˜ is that [3]both [4]the [5]winds [1]He [2]commands and

τῷ ὕδατι, καὶ ὑπακούουσιν αὐτῷ?"
the water, and they obey Him?"

Jesus Heals a Demon-Possessed Man

(Matt. 8:28–34; Mark 5:1–20)

26 Καὶ κατέπλευσαν εἰς τὴν χώραν τῶν Γαδαρηνῶν,[d]
And they sailed to the region of the Gadarenes,

ἥτις ἐστὶν ἀντιπέραν τῆς Γαλιλαίας. 27 Ἐξελθόντι δὲ αὐτῷ
which is opposite - Galilee. coming out And Him
And when He got out

ἐπὶ τὴν γῆν, ὑπήντησεν αὐτῷ ἀνήρ τις ἐκ τῆς πόλεως ὃς
on the land, *there* met Him a man ˜ certain of the city who

εἶχε δαιμόνια ἐκ χρόνων ἱκανῶν. Καὶ[e] ἱμάτιον οὐκ
had demons from times long. And [5]a [6]garment [3]not
had had a long time.

ἐνεδιδύσκετο καὶ ἐν οἰκίᾳ οὐκ ἔμενεν ἀλλ' ἐν τοῖς
[1]he [2]did [4]wear and [5]in [6]a [7]house [3]not [1]he [2]did [4]stay but among the

μνήμασιν. 28 Ἰδὼν δὲ τὸν Ἰησοῦν, καὶ ἀνακράξας,
tombs. seeing ˜ And - Jesus, and crying out,

προσέπεσεν αὐτῷ, καὶ φωνῇ μεγάλῃ εἶπε, "Τί ἐμοὶ
he fell down before Him, and with a voice ˜ great he said, "What to me
loud "What have I

καὶ σοί, Ἰησοῦ, Υἱὲ τοῦ Θεοῦ τοῦ Ὑψίστου? Δέομαί
and to You, Jesus, Son - [5]God [1]of [2]the [3]Most [4]High? I beg
to do with You,

σου, μή με βασανίσῃς!" 29 Παρήγγειλε γὰρ τῷ πνεύματι
You, [2]not [4]me [1]do [3]torment!" [2]He [3]commanded [1]For the spirit ˜
had commanded

τῷ ἀκαθάρτῳ ἐξελθεῖν ἀπὸ τοῦ ἀνθρώπου. Πολλοῖς γὰρ
- unclean to come out from the man. many ˜ For

with His disciples. And He said
to them, "Let us cross over to
the other side of the lake." And
they launched out.
23 But as they sailed He fell
asleep. And a windstorm came
down on the lake, and they
were filling *with water,* and
were in jeopardy.
24 And they came to Him and
awoke Him, saying, "Master,
Master, we are perishing!"
Then He arose and rebuked the
wind and the raging of the water. And they ceased, and there
was a calm.
25 But He said to them,
"Where is your faith?" And
they were afraid, and marveled,
saying to one another, "Who
can this be? For He commands
even the winds and water, and
they obey Him!"
26 Then they sailed to the
country of the Gadarenes,
which is opposite Galilee.
27 And when He stepped out
on the land, there met Him a
certain man from the city who
had demons for a long time.
And he wore no clothes, nor did
he live in a house but in the
tombs.
28 When he saw Jesus, he
cried out, fell down before Him,
and with a loud voice said,
"What have I to do with You,
Jesus, Son of the Most High
God? I beg You, do not torment
me!"
29 For He had commanded
the unclean spirit to come out
of the man. For it had often

---

[d](8:26) NU reads Γερασηνων, *Gerasenes.*

[e](8:27) NU reads και, *and,* after δαιμονια, *demons,* thus *having demons and for a long time he wore no garment.*

seized him, and he was kept under guard, bound with chains and shackles; and he broke the bonds and was driven by the demon into the wilderness.
30 Jesus asked him, saying, "What is your name?" And he said, "Legion," because many demons had entered him.
31 And they begged Him that He would not command them to go out into the abyss.
32 Now a herd of many swine was feeding there on the mountain. So they begged Him that He would permit them to enter them. And He permitted them.
33 Then the demons went out of the man and entered the swine, and the herd ran violently down the steep place into the lake and drowned.
34 When those who fed *them* saw what had happened, they fled and told *it* in the city and in the country.
35 Then they went out to see what had happened, and came to Jesus, and found the man from whom the demons had departed, sitting at the feet of Jesus, clothed and in his right mind. And they were afraid.
36 They also who had seen *it* told them by what means he who had been demon-possessed was healed.
37 Then the whole multitude

---

f(8:31) NU reads *παρεκαλουν, they were imploring.* *g*(8:34) TR adds *απελθοντες, departing.*

χρόνοις συνηρπάκει αὐτόν, καὶ ἐδεσμεῖτο ἁλύσεσι καὶ
times it had seized him, and he was bound with chains and
would be bound, kept under guard

πέδαις φυλασσόμενος, καὶ διαρρήσσων τὰ δεσμὰ ἠλαύνετο
shackles being guarded, and breaking the bonds he was driven
with chains and shackles, he would break and would be

ὑπὸ τοῦ δαίμονος εἰς τὰς ἐρήμους.
by the demon into the uninhabited *areas.*

30 *Ἐπηρώτησε δὲ αὐτὸν ὁ Ἰησοῦς, λεγων, "Τί σοι*
[3]asked [1]And [4]him - [2]Jesus, saying, "What to you
is

ἐστὶν ὄνομα?"
is a name?"
your name?"

Ὁ δὲ εἶπε, "Λεγεών," ὅτι δαιμόνια πολλὰ
[2]the [3]*one* [1]And said, "Legion," because demons ˜ many
he

εἰσῆλθεν εἰς αὐτόν. **31** *Καὶ παρεκάλει*[f] *αὐτὸν ἵνα μὴ*
entered into him. And he was imploring Him that [3]not
had entered kept

ἐπιτάξῃ αὐτοῖς εἰς τὴν ἄβυσσον ἀπελθεῖν.
[1]He [2]would command them [4]into [5]the [6]abyss [1]to [2]go [3]away.

32 *Ἦν δὲ ἐκεῖ ἀγέλη χοίρων ἱκανῶν βοσκομένων ἐν*
[2]*there* [3]was [1]Now there a herd of pigs ˜ many feeding on

τῷ ὄρει. Καὶ παρεκάλουν αὐτὸν ἵνα ἐπιτρέψῃ αὐτοῖς
the mountain. And they were imploring Him that He would permit them
kept

εἰς ἐκείνους εἰσελθεῖν. Καὶ ἐπέτρεψεν αὐτοῖς. **33** *Ἐξελθόντα*
[3]into [4]those [1]to [2]enter. And He permitted them. coming out
Then when

δὲ τὰ δαιμόνια ἀπὸ τοῦ ἀνθρώπου εἰσῆλθον εἰς τοὺς
Then the demons from the man they entered into the
the demons came out

χοίρους, καὶ ὥρμησεν ἡ ἀγέλη κατὰ τοῦ κρημνοῦ εἰς τὴν
pigs, and [3]rushed [1]the [2]herd down the steep bank into the

λίμνην καὶ ἀπεπνίγη. **34** *Ἰδόντες δὲ οἱ*
lake and choked. [7]seeing [1]And [2]the [3]*ones*
drowned. And when those who tended

βόσκοντες τὸ γεγενημένον ἔφυγον καὶ[g] *ἀπήγγειλαν*
[4]feeding [5]*the* [6]*pigs* the *thing* having happened they fled and reported *it*
the pigs saw what had happened,

εἰς τὴν πόλιν καὶ εἰς τοὺς ἀγρούς. **35** *Ἐξῆλθον δὲ ἰδεῖν*
in the city and in the fields. [2]they [3]came [4]out [1]And to see
country.

τὸ γεγονός, καὶ ἦλθον πρὸς τὸν Ἰησοῦν, καὶ εὗρον
the *thing* having happened, and they came to - Jesus, and found
what had

καθήμενον τὸν ἄνθρωπον ἀφ' οὗ τὰ δαιμόνια
[10]sitting [1]the [2]man [3]from [4]whom [5]the [6]demons

ἐξεληλύθει, ἱματισμένον καὶ σωφρονοῦντα παρὰ τοὺς
[7]had [8]come [9]out, having been clothed and being of sound mind at the

πόδας τοῦ Ἰησοῦ. Καὶ ἐφοβήθησαν. **36** *Ἀπήγγειλαν δὲ*
feet - of Jesus. And they were afraid. [6]reported [1]And

αὐτοῖς καὶ οἱ ἰδόντες πῶς ἐσώθη ὁ
[8]to [9]them [7]also [2]the [3]*ones* [4]having [5]seen how [6]was [7]saved [1]the [2]*one*
those who saw the demon-possessed

δαιμονισθείς. **37** *Καὶ ἠρώτησαν αὐτὸν ἅπαν τὸ*
[3]having [4]been [5]demon-possessed. And [11]asked [12]Him [1]all [2]the
man was healed.

πλῆθος τῆς περιχώρου τῶν Γαδαρηνῶν[h] ἀπελθεῖν
[3]multitude [4]of [5]the [6]surrounding [7]region [8]of [9]the [10]Gadarenes to go away
from

ἀπ' αὐτῶν, ὅτι φόβῳ μεγάλῳ συνείχοντο. Αὐτὸς
from them, because [4]with [6]fear [5]great [1]they [2]were [3]gripped. He ˜

δὲ ἐμβὰς εἰς τὸ πλοῖον ὑπέστρεψεν.
And stepping into the boat returned.
got and returned.

38 Ἐδέετο δὲ αὐτοῦ ὁ ἀνὴρ ἀφ' οὗ
[11]was [12]begging [1]Now [13]Him [2]the [3]man [4]from [5]whom
kept

ἐξεληλύθει τὰ δαιμόνια εἶναι σὺν αὐτῷ. Ἀπέλυσε
[8]had [9]come [10]out [6]the [7]demons to be with Him. [3]sent [5]away
that he might be

δὲ αὐτὸν ὁ Ἰησοῦς[i] λέγων, **39** "Ὑπόστρεφε εἰς τὸν οἶκόν
[1]But [4]him - [2]Jesus saying, "Return to - house ˜

σου, καὶ διηγοῦ ὅσα ἐποίησέ σοι ὁ Θεός." Καὶ
your, and tell how many *things* [2]did [3]for [4]you - [1]God." And
has done

ἀπῆλθε καθ' ὅλην τὴν πόλιν κηρύσσων ὅσα
he departed [2]throughout [4]whole [3]the [5]city [1]proclaiming as many *things* as
all the things that

ἐποίησεν αὐτῷ ὁ Ἰησοῦς.
[2]did [3]for [4]him - [1]Jesus.

Jesus Restores a Girl and Heals a Woman
(Matt. 9:18–26; Mark 5:21–43)

40 Ἐγένετο δὲ ἐν[j] τῷ ὑποστρέψαι τὸν Ἰησοῦν,
[2]it [3]happened [1]And in - to return - Jesus,
when Jesus returned,

ἀπεδέξατο αὐτὸν ὁ ὄχλος, ἦσαν γὰρ πάντες
[3]welcomed [4]Him [1]the [2]crowd, [6]they [7]were [5]for all

προσδοκῶντες αὐτόν. **41** Καὶ ἰδού, ἦλθεν ἀνὴρ ᾧ
waiting for Him. And behold, *there* came a man to whom
whose

ὄνομα Ἰάειρος, καὶ αὐτὸς ἄρχων τῆς συναγωγῆς
a name *was* Jairus, and he [2]a [3]leader [4]of [5]the [6]synagogue
name

ὑπῆρχε. Καὶ πεσὼν παρὰ τοὺς πόδας τοῦ Ἰησοῦ παρεκάλει
[1]was. And falling at the feet - of Jesus he was imploring

αὐτὸν εἰσελθεῖν εἰς τὸν οἶκον αὐτοῦ, **42** ὅτι θυγάτηρ
Him to enter into - house ˜ his, because a(n) daughter ˜
he had

μονογενὴς ἦν αὐτῷ ὡς ἐτῶν δώδεκα, καὶ αὕτη
only was to him about [2]of [3]years [1]twelve, and this *one*
an only daughter years old she

ἀπέθνῃσκεν. Ἐν δὲ τῷ ὑπάγειν αὐτὸν οἱ ὄχλοι
was dying. in ˜ But - to go Him the crowds
But as He was going,

συνέπνιγον αὐτόν.
were pressing against Him.

43 Καὶ γυνὴ οὖσα ἐν ῥύσει αἵματος ἀπὸ ἐτῶν
And a woman being in a flow of blood from years ˜
suffering from for

δώδεκα, ἥτις ἰατροῖς προσαναλώσασα ὅλον τὸν
twelve, who [5]on [6]physicians [1]spending [2]*her* [3]whole -
though she had spent

of the surrounding region of the
Gadarenes asked Him to depart
from them, for they were
seized with great fear. And He
got into the boat and returned.
38 Now the man from whom
the demons had departed
begged Him that he might be
with Him. But Jesus sent him
away, saying,
39 "Return to your own
house, and tell what great
things God has done for you."
And he went his way and proclaimed throughout the whole
city what great things Jesus had
done for him.
40 So it was, when Jesus returned, that the multitude welcomed Him, for they were all
waiting for Him.
41 And behold, there came a
man named Jairus, and he was a
ruler of the synagogue. And he
fell down at Jesus' feet and
begged Him to come to his
house,
42 for he had an only daughter
about twelve years of age, and
she was dying. But as He went,
the multitudes thronged Him.
43 Now a woman, having a
flow of blood for twelve years,
who had spent all her livelihood

[h]**(8:37)** NU reads Γερασηνων, *Gerasenes.*
[i]**(8:38)** NU omits ο Ιησους, *Jesus.* [j]**(8:40)** For εγενετο δε εν, *and it happened in,* NU reads εν δε, *and in* (or *when*).

on physicians and could not be
healed by any,
44 came from behind and
touched the border of His garment. And immediately her
flow of blood stopped.
45 And Jesus said, "Who
touched Me?" When all denied
it, Peter and those with him
said, "Master, the multitudes
throng and press You, and You
say, 'Who touched Me?' "
46 But Jesus said, "Somebody
touched Me, for I perceived
power going out from Me."
47 Now when the woman saw
that she was not hidden, she
came trembling; and falling
down before Him, she declared
to Him in the presence of all the
people the reason she had
touched Him and how she was
healed immediately.
48 And He said to her,
"Daughter, be of good cheer;
your faith has made you well.
Go in peace."
49 While He was still speaking, someone came from the
ruler of the synagogue's *house,*
saying to him, "Your daughter
is dead. Do not trouble the
Teacher."
50 But when Jesus heard *it,*
He answered him, saying, "Do
not be afraid; only believe, and
she will be made well."
51 When He came into the
house, He permitted no one to
go in except Peter, James, and
John, and the father and

βίον οὐκ ἴσχυσεν ὑπ᾽ οὐδενὸς θεραπευθῆναι,
[4]livelihood not ˜ was able by no one to be healed,
anyone

44 προσελθοῦσα ὄπισθεν ἥψατο τοῦ κρασπέδου* τοῦ
approaching from behind touched the border -

ἱματίου αὐτοῦ. Καὶ παραχρῆμα ἔστη ἡ ῥύσις τοῦ αἵματος
of garment ˜ His. And immediately [6]stood [1]the [2]flow - [3]of [5]blood
stopped

αὐτῆς.
[4]her.

45 Καὶ εἶπεν ὁ Ἰησοῦς, "Τίς ὁ ἁψάμενός μου?"
And said ˜ - Jesus, "Who is the *one* having touched Me?"
the person who

Ἀρνουμένων δὲ πάντων, εἶπεν ὁ Πέτρος καὶ οἱ μετ᾽
denying And all, [7]said - [1]Peter [2]and [3]the [4]*ones* [5]with
And when all denied it, those

αὐτοῦ,[k] "'Επιστάτα, οἱ ὄχλοι συνέχουσί σε καὶ
[6]him, "Master, the crowds are pressing hard ˜ You and

ἀποθλίβουσι, καὶ λέγεις, 'Τίς ὁ ἁψάμενός μου?' "[l]
crowding *You,* and You say, 'Who is the *one* having touched Me?' "
the person who

46 Ὁ δὲ Ἰησοῦς εἶπεν, "Ἥψατό μού τις, ἐγὼ γὰρ
- But Jesus said, "[2]touched [3]Me [1]Someone, I ˜ for

ἔγνων δύναμιν ἐξελθοῦσαν ἀπ᾽ ἐμοῦ." 47 Ἰδοῦσα δὲ
knew power going out from Me." seeing And
perceived that has gone And when the

ἡ γυνὴ ὅτι οὐκ ἔλαθε, τρέμουσα ἦλθε καὶ
the woman that [3]not [1]she [2]was hidden, trembling she came and
woman saw

προσπεσοῦσα αὐτῷ, δι᾽ ἣν αἰτίαν ἥψατο αὐτοῦ
falling down before Him, [9]for [10]which [11]reason [12]she [13]touched [14]Him
the reason why she had touched

ἀπήγγειλεν αὐτῷ ἐνώπιον παντὸς τοῦ λαοῦ καὶ ὡς
[1]she [2]recounted [3]to [4]Him [5]before [6]all [7]the [8]people and how

ἰάθη παραχρῆμα. 48 Ὁ δὲ εἶπεν αὐτῇ
she was healed immediately. [2]the [3]*One* [1]And said to her
He

"Θάρσει,[m] θύγατερ, ἡ πίστις σου σέσωκέ σε. Πορεύου εἰς
"Take courage, daughter, - faith ˜ your has saved you. Go in
healed

εἰρήνην."
peace."

49 Ἔτι αὐτοῦ λαλοῦντος, ἔρχεταί τις παρὰ τοῦ
Still ˜ Him speaking, comes ˜ someone from the
While He was still came

ἀρχισυναγώγου, λέγων αὐτῷ ὅτι "Τέθνηκεν ἡ θυγάτηρ σου.
synagogue leader, saying to him - "[3]has [4]died - [2]daughter [1]your.

Μὴ σκύλλε τὸν διδάσκαλον."
not ˜ Do trouble the Teacher."

50 Ὁ δὲ Ἰησοῦς ἀκούσας ἀπεκρίθη αὐτῷ, λέγων, "Μὴ
- But Jesus hearing He answered him, saying, "not ˜
when Jesus heard,

φοβοῦ, μόνον πίστευε καὶ σωθήσεται." 51 Ἐλθὼν
Do be afraid, only believe and she will be saved." coming ˜
healed." when He came

δὲ εἰς τὴν οἰκίαν οὐκ ἀφῆκεν εἰσελθεῖν οὐδένα[n] εἰ
And into the house [3]not [1]He [2]did [4]permit [7]to [8]enter [5]no [6]one if
anyone except

μὴ Πέτρον καὶ Ἰωάννην καὶ Ἰάκωβον[o] καὶ τὸν πατέρα τῆς
not Peter and John and James and the father of the

---

[k](8:45) NU omits *και οι μετ αυτου, and the ones with Him.* [l](8:45) NU omits *και λεγεις τις ο αψαμενος μου, and You say, 'Who is the one having touched Me?'* [m](8:48) NU omits *θαρσει, Take courage.* [n](8:51) NU reads *τινα συν αυτω, anyone with Him.* [o](8:51) TR reads *Πετρον και Ιακωβον και Ιωαννην, Peter and James and John.*

---

*(8:44) *κράσπεδον (kraspedon).* Noun used 5 times in the NT, meaning *hem, border.* Four times (here and the parallel Matt. 9:20; Matt. 14:36 and the parallel Mark 6:56) it refers to the hem/border of Jesus' garment touched by persons seeking healing. In Matt 23:5 it is used of the *tassels* or *fringe* on the hems of the Pharisees' garments, worn as a sign of their religious zeal for the law.

παιδὸς καὶ τὴν μητέρα. **52** Ἔκλαιον δὲ πάντες καὶ
child and the mother. [3]were [4]weeping [1]Now [2]all and

ἐκόπτοντο αὐτήν. Ὁ δὲ εἶπε, "Μὴ κλαίετε· οὐκ
were mourning *for* her. [2]the [3]*One* [1]But said, "not ˜ Do weep; [3]not
He she is

ἀπέθανεν ἀλλὰ καθεύδει." **53** Καὶ κατεγέλων αὐτοῦ,
[1]she [2]did die but she is asleep." And they were ridiculing Him,
not dead

εἰδότες ὅτι ἀπέθανεν. **54** Αὐτὸς δὲ ἐκβαλὼν ἔξω πάντας,
knowing that she did die. He ˜ But sending out all *of them*,
had died. sent them all out

καὶ[p] κρατήσας τῆς χειρὸς αὐτῆς, ἐφώνησε λέγων, "Ἡ
and having grasped - hand ˜ her, He called saying, -

παῖς, ἐγείρου." **55** Καὶ ἐπέστρεψε τὸ πνεῦμα αὐτῆς, καὶ
"Child, arise." And [3]returned - [2]spirit [1]her, and

ἀνέστη παραχρῆμα. Καὶ διέταξεν αὐτῇ
she arose immediately. And He commanded *something* [4]to [5]her

δοθῆναι φαγεῖν. **56** Καὶ ἐξέστησαν οἱ γονεῖς αὐτῆς·
[1]to [2]be [3]given to eat. And [3]were [4]amazed - [2]parents [1]her;

ὁ δὲ παρήγγειλεν αὐτοῖς μηδενὶ εἰπεῖν τὸ
[2]the [3]*One* [1]but charged them [7]to [8]no [9]one [1]to [2]tell [3]the [4]*thing*
He what

γεγονός.
[5]having [6]happened.
had happened.

Jesus Sends Out the Twelve
(Matt. 10:5–15; Mark 6:7–13)

9 **1** Συγκαλεσάμενος δὲ τοὺς δώδεκα[a] ἔδωκεν αὐτοῖς
[2]having [3]called [4]together [1]And the twelve He gave them

δύναμιν καὶ ἐξουσίαν ἐπὶ πάντα τὰ δαιμόνια, καὶ νόσους
power and authority over all the demons, and [3]diseases

θεραπεύειν. **2** Καὶ ἀπέστειλεν αὐτοὺς κηρύσσειν τὴν
[1]to [2]heal. And He sent them to preach the

βασιλείαν τοῦ Θεοῦ καὶ ἰᾶσθαι τοὺς ἀσθενοῦντας. **3** Καὶ
kingdom - of God and to cure the *ones* being sick. And
the sick.

εἶπε πρὸς αὐτούς, "Μηδὲν αἴρετε εἰς τὴν ὁδόν, μήτε
He said to them, "nothing ˜ Take for the road, neither
journey,

ῥάβδους μήτε πήραν μήτε ἄρτον μήτε ἀργύριον, μήτε ἀνὰ
staffs nor knapsack nor bread nor silver, neither [5]apiece
money,

δύο χιτῶνας ἔχειν. **4** Καὶ εἰς ἣν ἂν οἰκίαν εἰσέλθητε,
[3]two [4]tunics [1]to [2]have. And into which ever house you may enter,
have.

ἐκεῖ μένετε, καὶ ἐκεῖθεν ἐξέρχεσθε. **5** Καὶ ὅσοι ἐὰν
there ˜ stay, and from there go out. And as many as -

μὴ δέξωνται ὑμᾶς, ἐξερχόμενοι ἀπὸ τῆς πόλεως ἐκείνης καὶ
not ˜ do receive you, going out from - city ˜ that [3]even
as you leave

τὸν κονιορτὸν ἀπὸ τῶν ποδῶν ὑμῶν ἀποτινάξατε εἰς μαρτύριον
[4]the [5]dust [6]from - [8]feet [7]your [1]shake [2]off as a testimony

ἐπ' αὐτούς." **6** Ἐξερχόμενοι δὲ διήρχοντο
against them." [2]going [3]out [1]And they were going about
As they went out,

mother of the girl.
52 Now all wept and mourned for her; but He said, "Do not weep; she is not dead, but sleeping."
53 And they ridiculed Him, knowing that she was dead.
54 But He put them all outside, took her by the hand and called, saying, "Little girl, arise."
55 Then her spirit returned, and she arose immediately. And He commanded that she be given *something* to eat.
56 And her parents were astonished, but He charged them to tell no one what had happened.

9 Then He called His twelve disciples together and gave them power and authority over all demons, and to cure diseases.
2 He sent them to preach the kingdom of God and to heal the sick.
3 And He said to them, "Take nothing for the journey, neither staffs nor bag nor bread nor money; and do not have two tunics apiece.
4 "Whatever house you enter, stay there, and from there depart.
5 "And whoever will not receive you, when you go out of that city, shake off the very dust from your feet as a testimony against them."
6 So they departed and went

---

p(**8:54**) NU omits *εκβαλων εξω παντας, και, sending out all (of them), and.*
a(**9:1**) TR adds *μαθητας αυτου, His (twelve) disciples.*

through the towns, preaching
the gospel and healing everywhere.
7 Now Herod the tetrarch
heard of all that was done by
Him; and he was perplexed, because it was said by some that
John had risen from the dead,
8 and by some that Elijah had
appeared, and by others that
one of the old prophets had
risen again.
9 Herod said, "John I have
beheaded, but who is this of
whom I hear such things?" So
he sought to see Him.
10 And the apostles, when
they had returned, told Him all
that they had done. Then He
took them and went aside privately into a deserted place belonging to the city called
Bethsaida.
11 But when the multitudes
knew *it,* they followed Him; and
He received them and spoke to
them about the kingdom of
God, and healed those who had
need of healing.
12 When the day began to
wear away, the twelve came
and said to Him, "Send the multitude away, that they may go
into the surrounding towns and
country, and lodge and get provisions; for we are in a deserted place here."

κατὰ τὰς κώμας, εὐαγγελιζόμενοι καὶ θεραπεύοντες
according to the villages, evangelizing and healing
village by village, preaching the gospel

πανταχοῦ.
everywhere.

John the Baptist Is Beheaded
(Matt. 14:1–12; Mark 6:14–29)

7 *Ἤκουσε δὲ Ἡρῴδης ὁ τετράρχης τὰ*
[5]heard [1]Now [2]Herod [3]the [4]tetrarch [7]the [8]*things*

γινόμενα ὑπ' αὐτοῦ[b] *πάντα· καὶ διηπόρει διὰ τὸ*
[9]being [10]done [11]by [12]Him [6]all; and he was perplexed because of the
because it was

λέγεσθαι ὑπό τινων ὅτι Ἰωάννης ἐγήγερται ἐκ νεκρῶν, **8** *ὑπό*
to be said by some that John had risen from *the* dead, [2]by
said

τινων δὲ ὅτι Ἠλίας ἐφάνη, ἄλλων δὲ ὅτι προφήτης
[3]others [1]but that Elijah has appeared, [2]of [3]others [1]and that a prophet
had appeared, by one of

εἷς τῶν ἀρχαίων ἀνέστη. **9** *Καὶ εἶπεν Ἡρῴδης, "Ἰωάννην*
one of the ancient *ones* arose. And said ˜ Herod, "John
the ancient prophets had arisen.

ἐγὼ ἀπεκεφάλισα· τίς δέ ἐστιν οὗτος περὶ οὗ ἐγὼ ἀκούω
I beheaded; who ˜ but is this *man* about whom I hear

τοιαῦτα?" Καὶ ἐζήτει ἰδεῖν αὐτόν.
such *things?"* And he was seeking to see Him.
trying

Jesus Feeds About Five Thousand Men
(Matt. 14:13–21; Mark 6:30–44; John 6:1–14)

10 *Καὶ ὑποστρέψαντες οἱ ἀπόστολοι διηγήσαντο αὐτῷ*
And returning the apostles recounted to Him
when they returned,

ὅσα ἐποίησαν. Καὶ παραλαβὼν αὐτοὺς ὑπεχώρησε
as many *things* as they did. And taking along ˜ them He withdrew
had done.

κατ' ἰδίαν εἰς τόπον ἔρημον πόλεως καλουμένης[c]
privately into a place ˜ deserted of a city being called
belonging to called

Βηθσαϊδάν. **11** *Οἱ δὲ ὄχλοι γνόντες ἠκολούθησαν αὐτῷ.*
Bethsaida. the ˜ But crowds knowing they followed Him.
But when the crowds found out,

Καὶ δεξάμενος αὐτοὺς ἐλάλει αὐτοῖς περὶ τῆς βασιλείας
And receiving them He was speaking to them about the kingdom
He welcomed and

τοῦ Θεοῦ, καὶ τοὺς χρείαν ἔχοντας θεραπείας ἰᾶτο.
\- of God, and the *ones* need ˜ having of healing He cured.
those who needed healing

12 *Ἡ δὲ ἡμέρα ἤρξατο κλίνειν· προσελθόντες δὲ οἱ*
\- Now day began to decline; [4]having [5]approached [1]and [2]the

δώδεκα εἶπον αὐτῷ, "Ἀπόλυσον τὸν ὄχλον, ἵνα
[3]twelve said to Him, "Dismiss the crowd, so that

ἀπελθόντες[d] *εἰς τὰς κύκλῳ κώμας καὶ τοὺς ἀγροὺς*
going away into the surrounding villages and the farms

καταλύσωσι καὶ εὕρωσιν ἐπισιτισμόν· ὅτι ὧδε ἐν
they may find lodging and find provisions; because here [3]in

ἐρήμῳ τόπῳ ἐσμέν."
[4]a [5]deserted [6]place [1]we [2]are."

---

b(9:7) NU omits *υπ αυτου, by Him.* c(9:10) For *τοπον ερημον πολεως καλουμενης, a deserted place of a city called,* NU reads *πολιν καλουμενην, a city called.*
d(9:12) NU reads *πορευθεντες, going.*

13 Εἶπε δὲ πρὸς αὐτούς, "Δότε αὐτοῖς ὑμεῖς
[2]He [3]said [1]But to them, "[2]give [3]them [1]You

φαγεῖν."
something to eat."

Οἱ δὲ εἶπον, "Οὐκ εἰσὶν ἡμῖν πλεῖον ἢ πέντε
[2]the [3]*ones* [1]And said, "[5]not [1]*There* [2]are [3]to [4]us more than five
they We do not have

ἄρτοι καὶ ἰχθύες δύο, εἰ μήτι πορευθέντες ἡμεῖς
loaves of bread and fish ˜ two, if not going we
unless we go and

ἀγοράσωμεν εἰς πάντα τὸν λαὸν τοῦτον βρώματα."
may buy [2]for [3]all - [5]people [4]this [1]foods."
buy food.

14 Ἦσαν γὰρ ὡσεὶ ἄνδρες πεντακισχίλιοι.
[2]*there* [3]were [1]For about [3]men [1]five [2]thousand.

Εἶπε δὲ πρὸς τοὺς μαθητὰς αὐτοῦ, "Κατακλίνατε αὐτοὺς
[2]He [3]said [1]And to - disciples ˜ His, "Make recline ˜ them

κλισίας ἀνὰ πεντήκοντα." 15 Καὶ ἐποίησαν οὕτω, καὶ
in groups each fifty." And they did so, and
of fifties."

ἀνέκλιναν ἅπαντας. 16 Λαβὼν δὲ τοὺς πέντε ἄρτους καὶ τοὺς
made [3]recline [1]*them* [2]all. taking ˜ And the five loaves and the

δύο ἰχθύας, ἀναβλέψας εἰς τὸν οὐρανόν, εὐλόγησεν αὐτοὺς καὶ
two fish, looking up to - heaven, He blessed them and

κατέκλασε καὶ ἐδίδου τοῖς μαθηταῖς παρατιθέναι τῷ
broke *them* and was giving *them* to the disciples to set before the

ὄχλῳ. 17 Καὶ ἔφαγον καὶ ἐχορτάσθησαν πάντες, καὶ
crowd. And they ate and were filled ˜ all, and

ἤρθη τὸ περισσεῦσαν αὐτοῖς κλασμάτων
[6]was [7]taken [8]up [1]the [2]*amount* [3]remaining [4]to [5]them [11]of [12]fragments
what they had left

κόφινοι δώδεκα.
[10]baskets [9]twelve.

Peter Confesses Jesus as the Christ
(Matt. 16:13–20; Mark 8:27–30)

18 Καὶ ἐγένετο ἐν τῷ εἶναι αὐτὸν προσευχόμενον
And it happened in - [2]to [3]be [1]Him praying
while He was

κατὰ μόνας, συνῆσαν αὐτῷ οἱ μαθηταί, καὶ
in the manner of alone, *that* [3]were [4]with [5]Him [1]the [2]disciples, and
by Himself,

ἐπηρώτησεν αὐτούς, λέγων, "Τίνα με λέγουσιν οἱ ὄχλοι
He questioned them, saying, "Whom [5]Me [1]do [4]say [2]the [3]crowds
"Who do the crowds say that

εἶναι?"
to be?"
I am?"

19 Οἱ δὲ ἀποκριθέντες εἶπον, "Ἰωάννην τὸν
[2]the [3]*ones* [1]And answering said, "John the
they

Βαπτιστήν, ἄλλοι δὲ Ἠλίαν, ἄλλοι δὲ ὅτι προφήτης τις
Baptist, others ˜ and Elijah, others ˜ and that a prophet ˜ certain
one of the

τῶν ἀρχαίων ἀνέστη."
of the ancient *ones* arose."
ancient prophets has arisen."

13 But He said to them, "You
give them something to eat."
And they said, "We have no
more than five loaves and two
fish, unless we go and buy food
for all these people."
14 For there were about five
thousand men. Then He said to
His disciples, "Make them sit
down in groups of fifty."
15 And they did so, and made
them all sit down.
16 Then He took the five
loaves and the two fish, and
looking up to heaven, He
blessed and broke *them,* and
gave *them* to the disciples to set
before the multitude.
17 So they all ate and were
filled, and twelve baskets of the
leftover fragments were taken
up by them.
18 And it happened, as He
was alone praying, *that* His disciples joined Him, and He asked
them, saying, "Who do the
crowds say that I am?"
19 So they answered and said,
"John the Baptist, but some *say*
Elijah; and others *say* that one
of the old prophets has risen
again."

20 He said to them, "But who do you say that I am?" Peter answered and said, "The Christ of God."
21 And He strictly warned and commanded them to tell this to no one,
22 saying, "The Son of Man must suffer many things, and be rejected by the elders and chief priests and scribes, and be killed, and be raised the third day."
23 Then He said to *them* all, "If anyone desires to come after Me, let him deny himself, and take up his cross daily, and follow Me.
24 "For whoever desires to save his life will lose it, but whoever loses his life for My sake will save it.
25 "For what profit is it to a man if he gains the whole world, and is himself destroyed or lost?
26 "For whoever is ashamed of Me and My words, of him the Son of Man will be ashamed when He comes in His *own* glory, and *in His* Father's, and of the holy angels.
27 "But I tell you truly, there are some standing here who shall not taste death till they see the kingdom of God."

20 Εἶπε δὲ αὐτοῖς, "Ὑμεῖς δὲ τίνα με λέγετε
[2]He [3]said [1]And to them, "you ˜ But whom [4]Me [1]do [2]you [3]say
But who do you say that

εἶναι?"
to be?"
I am?"

Ἀποκριθεὶς δὲ ὁ Πέτρος εἶπε, "Τὸν Χριστὸν τοῦ Θεοῦ."
answering ˜ And - Peter said, "The Christ - of God."

Jesus Predicts His Death and Resurrection
(Matt. 16:21–23; Mark 8:31–33)

21 Ὁ δὲ ἐπιτιμήσας αὐτοῖς παρήγγειλε μηδενὶ
[2]the [3]*One* [1]And warning them commanded *them* [4]to [5]no [6]one
He

εἰπεῖν τοῦτο, **22** εἰπὼν ὅτι "Δεῖ τὸν Υἱὸν τοῦ
[1]to [2]tell [3]this, saying - "It is necessary *for* the Son -

Ἀνθρώπου πολλὰ παθεῖν καὶ ἀποδοκιμασθῆναι ἀπὸ τῶν
of Man [3]many [4]*things* [1]to [2]suffer and to be rejected by the

πρεσβυτέρων καὶ ἀρχιερέων καὶ γραμματέων, καὶ
elders and chief priests and scribes, and

ἀποκτανθῆναι, καὶ τῇ τρίτῃ ἡμέρᾳ ἐγερθῆναι."
to be killed, and [4]on [5]the [6]third [7]day [1]to [2]be [3]raised."

Take Up the Cross and Follow Him
(Matt. 16:24–28; Mark 8:34–9:1)

23 Ἔλεγε δὲ πρὸς πάντας, "Εἴ τις θέλει ὀπίσω μου
[2]He [3]said [1]And to all, "If anyone desires [3]after [4]Me

ἐλθεῖν, ἀπαρνησάσθω ἑαυτὸν καὶ ἀράτω τὸν σταυρὸν[e]
[1]to [2]come, let him deny himself and let him take up - cross ˜

αὐτοῦ, καὶ ἀκολουθείτω μοι. **24** Ὃς γὰρ ἐὰν θέλῃ τὴν ψυχὴν
his, and let him follow Me. who ˜ For ever desires - [4]life

αὐτοῦ σῶσαι, ἀπολέσει αὐτήν· ὃς δ' ἂν ἀπολέσῃ τὴν
[3]his [1]to [2]save, will lose it; who ˜ but ever loses -

ψυχὴν αὐτοῦ ἕνεκεν ἐμοῦ, οὗτος σώσει αὐτήν. **25** Τί
life ˜ his on account of Me, this *one* will save it. what ˜
preserve

γὰρ ὠφελεῖται ἄνθρωπος κερδήσας τὸν κόσμον ὅλον, ἑαυτὸν
For [1]is [4]profited [2]a [3]man gaining the world ˜ whole, [5]himself
if he gains

δὲ ἀπολέσας ἢ ζημιωθείς? **26** Ὃς γὰρ ἂν ἐπαισχυνθῇ με
[1]but [2]losing [3]or [4]forfeiting? who ˜ For ever is ashamed of Me
loses forfeits?

καὶ τοὺς ἐμοὺς λόγους, τοῦτον ὁ Υἱὸς τοῦ Ἀνθρώπου
and - My words, [9]this [10]*person* [1]the [2]Son - [3]of [4]Man

ἐπαισχυνθήσεται, ὅταν ἔλθῃ ἐν τῇ δόξῃ αὐτοῦ
[5]will [6]be [7]ashamed [8]of, whenever He comes in - glory ˜ His

καὶ τοῦ Πατρὸς καὶ τῶν ἁγίων ἀγγέλων. **27** Λέγω δὲ
and *the glory* of the Father and of the holy angels. [2]I [3]say [1]But

ὑμῖν ἀληθῶς, εἰσὶ τινες τῶν ὧδε ἑστώτων οἳ
to you truly, *there* are certain *ones* of the *ones* here ˜ standing who
certain of those

οὐ μὴ γεύσωνται θανάτου ἕως ἂν ἴδωσι τὴν βασιλείαν
not not will taste of death until - they see the kingdom
by no means

τοῦ Θεοῦ."
- of God."

---

[e](9:23) TR, NU add καθ ημεραν, daily.

Jesus Is Transfigured on the Mount
(Matt. 17:1–13; Mark 9:2–13)

28 Ἐγένετο δὲ μετὰ τοὺς λόγους τούτους ὡσεὶ ἡμέραι
[2]it [3]happened [1]Now [7]after - [9]words [8]these [4]about [6]days

ὀκτώ, καὶ παραλαβὼν Πέτρον καὶ Ἰωάννην καὶ Ἰάκωβον,
[5]eight, and taking along Peter and John and James,
that

ἀνέβη εἰς τὸ ὄρος προσεύξασθαι. **29** Καὶ ἐγένετο ἐν
He went up into the mountain to pray. And it happened in
while

τῷ προσεύχεσθαι αὐτόν, τὸ εἶδος τοῦ προσώπου αὐτοῦ
- [2]to [3]pray Him, *that* the appearance - of face ˜ His
He was praying,

ἕτερον καὶ ὁ ἱματισμὸς αὐτοῦ λευκὸς ἐξαστράπτων.
became different and - clothing ˜ His *became* white *and* gleaming.
glistening.

30 Καὶ ἰδού, ἄνδρες δύο συνελάλουν αὐτῷ, οἵτινες ἦσαν
And behold, men ˜ two were talking with Him, who were

Μωσῆς καὶ Ἠλίας, **31** οἳ ὀφθέντες ἐν δόξῃ ἔλεγον
Moses and Elijah, who appearing in glory were talking about

τὴν ἔξοδον* αὐτοῦ ἣν ἔμελλε πληροῦν ἐν Ἱερουσαλήμ.
- departure ˜ His which He was about to fulfill in Jerusalem.
decease accomplish

32 Ὁ δὲ Πέτρος καὶ οἱ σὺν αὐτῷ ἦσαν βεβαρημένοι
- But Peter and the *ones* with him were weighed down

ὕπνῳ· διαγρηγορήσαντες δὲ εἶδον τὴν δόξαν αὐτοῦ καὶ
with sleep; [2]becoming [3]fully [4]awake [1]but they saw - glory ˜ His and

τοὺς δύο ἄνδρας τοὺς συνεστῶτας αὐτῷ. **33** Καὶ ἐγένετο ἐν
the two men the *ones* standing with Him. And it happened in
who stood as

τῷ διαχωρίζεσθαι αὐτοὺς ἀπ' αὐτοῦ, εἶπεν Πέτρος πρὸς τὸν
- [2]to [3]part [1]them from Him, *that* said ˜ Peter to -
they parted

Ἰησοῦν, "Ἐπιστάτα, καλόν ἐστιν ἡμᾶς ὧδε εἶναι· καὶ
Jesus, "Master, [3]good [1]it [2]is *for* us [3]here [1]to [2]be; and
so

ποιήσωμεν σκηνὰς τρεῖς, μίαν σοὶ καὶ μίαν Μωσῇ καὶ
let us make tents ˜ three, one for You and one for Moses and

μίαν Ἠλίᾳ," μὴ εἰδὼς ὃ λέγει.
one for Elijah," not knowing what he says.
was saying.

34 Ταῦτα δὲ αὐτοῦ λέγοντος, ἐγένετο νεφέλη καὶ
these *things* Now him saying, [3]became [1]a [2]cloud and
Now as he said these things, appeared

ἐπεσκίασεν αὐτούς· ἐφοβήθησαν δὲ ἐν τῷ ἐκείνους
overshadowed them; [2]they [3]were [4]afraid [1]and in - those
as they entered

εἰσελθεῖν εἰς τὴν νεφέλην. **35** Καὶ φωνὴ ἐγένετο ἐκ τῆς
to enter into the cloud. And a voice came out of the

νεφέλης λέγουσα, "Οὗτός ἐστιν ὁ Υἱός μου ὁ ἀγαπητός.[f]
cloud saying, "This is - [3]Son [1]My - [2]beloved.

Αὐτοῦ ἀκούετε!" **36** Καὶ ἐν τῷ γενέσθαι τὴν φωνὴν εὑρέθη
Him ˜ Hear!" And in - [3]to [4]come [1]the [2]voice [6]was [7]found
after the voice came,

ὁ Ἰησοῦς μόνος. Καὶ αὐτοὶ ἐσίγησαν καὶ οὐδενὶ
- [5]Jesus alone. And they kept silent and [3]to [4]no [5]one

28 Now it came to pass, about eight days after these sayings, that He took Peter, John, and James and went up on the mountain to pray.
29 As He prayed, the appearance of His face was altered, and His robe *became* white *and* glistening.
30 And behold, two men talked with Him, who were Moses and Elijah,
31 who appeared in glory and spoke of His decease which He was about to accomplish at Jerusalem.
32 But Peter and those with him were heavy with sleep; and when they were fully awake, they saw His glory and the two men who stood with Him.
33 Then it happened, as they were parting from Him, *that* Peter said to Jesus, "Master, it is good for us to be here; and let us make three tabernacles: one for You, one for Moses, and one for Elijah"—not knowing what he said.
34 While he was saying this, a cloud came and overshadowed them; and they were fearful as they entered the cloud.
35 And a voice came out of the cloud, saying, "This is My beloved Son. Hear Him!"
36 When the voice had ceased, Jesus was found alone. But they kept quiet, and told no

---

f(**9:35**) NU reads εκλελεγμενος, *chosen.*

***(9:31)** ἔξοδος *(exodos).* Noun, meaning *going out,* from ἐκ, *out,* and ὁδός, *way, road.* The word is used of the Exodus from Egypt (Heb. 11:22) and as a euphemism for *death* as a *departure* from this life (here in Luke 9:31 and 2 Pet. 1:15).

one in those days any of the
things they had seen.
37 Now it happened on the
next day, when they had come
down from the mountain, that a
great multitude met Him.
38 Suddenly a man from the
multitude cried out, saying,
"Teacher, I implore You, look
on my son, for he is my only
child.
39 "And behold, a spirit seizes
him, and he suddenly cries out;
it convulses him so that he
foams *at the mouth;* and it departs from him with great difficulty, bruising him.
40 "So I implored Your disciples to cast it out, but they
could not."
41 Then Jesus answered and
said, "O faithless and perverse
generation, how long shall I be
with you and bear with you?
Bring your son here."
42 And as he was still coming,
the demon threw him down and
convulsed *him.* Then Jesus rebuked the unclean spirit, healed
the child, and gave him back to
his father.
43 And they were all amazed
at the majesty of God. But
while everyone marveled at all
the things which Jesus did, He
said to His disciples,
44 "Let these words sink
down into your ears, for the

ἀπήγγειλαν ἐν ἐκείναις ταῖς ἡμέραις οὐδὲν ὧν
[1]they [2]reported in those - days none of which *things*
any of the things

ἑωράκασιν.
they have seen.
they had

Jesus Heals a Boy with an Unclean Spirit
(Matt. 17:14–21; Mark 9:14–29)

37 Ἐγένετο δὲ ἐν τῇ ἑξῆς ἡμέρᾳ, κατελθόντων αὐτῶν
[2]it [3]happened [1]Now on the next day, [2]coming [3]down [1]them
when they came down

ἀπὸ τοῦ ὄρους, συνήντησεν αὐτῷ ὄχλος πολύς. **38** Καὶ
from the mountain, [4]met [5]Him [1]a [3]crowd [2]large. And

ἰδού, ἀνὴρ ἀπὸ τοῦ ὄχλου ἀνεβόησε, λέγων, "Διδάσκαλε,
behold, a man from the crowd cried out, saying, "Teacher,

δέομαί σου ἐπιβλέψαι ἐπὶ τὸν υἱόν μου, ὅτι μονογενής ἐστί
I beg You to look upon - son ˜ my, because an only *son* he is
he is my only

μοι. **39** Καὶ ἰδού, πνεῦμα λαμβάνει αὐτόν, καὶ ἐξαίφνης
to me. And behold, a spirit seizes him, and suddenly
son.

κράζει, καὶ σπαράσσει αὐτὸν μετὰ ἀφροῦ, καὶ μόγις
he cries out, and it convulses him with foam, and [5]with [6]difficulty
foaming,

ἀποχωρεῖ ἀπ' αὐτοῦ, συντρῖβον αὐτόν. **40** Καὶ ἐδεήθην τῶν
[1]it [2]departs [3]from [4]him, bruising him. And I begged -

μαθητῶν σου ἵνα ἐκβάλωσιν αὐτό, καὶ οὐκ ἠδυνήθησαν."
disciples ˜ Your that they would cast out ˜ it, and [3]not [1]they [2]could."

41 Ἀποκριθεὶς δὲ ὁ Ἰησοῦς εἶπεν, "Ὦ γενεὰ ἄπιστος
answering ˜ And - Jesus said, "O [4]generation [1]unbelieving
unfaithful

καὶ διεστραμμένη, ἕως πότε ἔσομαι πρὸς ὑμᾶς καὶ ἀνέξομαι
[2]and [3]perverted, until when shall I be with you and put up with
how long

ὑμῶν? Προσάγαγε τὸν υἱόν σου ὧδε." **42** Ἔτι δὲ
you? Bring - son ˜ your here." still But
But as

προσερχομένου αὐτοῦ, ἔρρηξεν αὐτὸν τὸ δαιμόνιον καὶ
coming him, [3]threw [5]down [4]him [1]the [2]demon and
he was still coming,

συνεσπάραξεν. Ἐπετίμησε δὲ ὁ Ἰησοῦς τῷ πνεύματι τῷ
convulsed *him.* [3]rebuked [1]Then - [2]Jesus the spirit ˜ -

ἀκαθάρτῳ, καὶ ἰάσατο τὸν παῖδα καὶ ἀπέδωκεν αὐτὸν τῷ
unclean, and cured the child and gave back ˜ him -

πατρὶ αὐτοῦ. **43** Ἐξεπλήσσοντο δὲ πάντες ἐπὶ τῇ
to father ˜ his. [3]were [4]amazed [1]And [2]all at the

μεγαλειότητι* τοῦ Θεοῦ.
greatness - of God.

Jesus Again Predicts His Death
(Matt. 17:22, 23; Mark 9:30–32)

Πάντων δὲ θαυμαζόντων ἐπὶ πᾶσιν οἷς ἐποίησεν ὁ
all ˜ And marveling at all *things* which did ˜ -
And as all marveled

Ἰησοῦς,[g] εἶπε πρὸς τοὺς μαθητὰς αὐτοῦ, **44** "Θέσθε ὑμεῖς
Jesus, He said to - disciples ˜ His, "put ˜ You

εἰς τὰ ὦτα ὑμῶν τοὺς λόγους τούτους, ὁ γὰρ Υἱὸς τοῦ
[3]into - [5]ears [4]your - [2]words [1]these, the ˜ for Son -

---

[g](9:43) NU omits ο Ιησους, *Jesus.*

---

*(9:43) μεγαλειότης (*megaleiotēs*). Noun meaning *majesty, magnificence,* used especially in connection with a deity. Here it refers to the majesty of God; in Acts 19:27 it refers to that of the Ephesian goddess Artemis. In 2 Pet. 1:16 μεγαλειότης describes the majesty of the transfigured Christ, and comes close to being a reverent way of referring to Him personally, as when someone refers to a judge as "your honor." See also the cognate adjective μεγαλεῖος, *magnificent, mighty,* at Acts 2:11.

Ἀνθρώπου μέλλει παραδίδοσθαι εἰς χεῖρας ἀνθρώπων.”
of Man is about to be handed over into *the* hands ˜ men's.”
betrayed

45 Οἱ δὲ ἠγνόουν τὸ ῥῆμα τοῦτο, καὶ ἦν
[2]the [3]*ones* [1]But did not understand - saying ˜ this, and it was
they

παρακεκαλυμμένον ἀπ' αὐτῶν ἵνα μὴ αἴσθωνται αὐτό·
concealed from them so that [3]not [1]they [2]did perceive it;

καὶ ἐφοβοῦντο ἐρωτῆσαι αὐτὸν περὶ τοῦ ῥήματος τούτου.
and they were afraid to ask Him about - saying ˜ this.

Who Is the Greatest?
(Matt. 18:1–5; Mark 9:33–37)

46 Εἰσῆλθε δὲ διαλογισμὸς ἐν αὐτοῖς, τὸ τίς ἂν
[4]came [5]in [1]Now [2]a [3]dispute among them, the which -
up as to

εἴη μείζων αὐτῶν. 47 Ὁ δὲ Ἰησοῦς ἰδὼν[h] τὸν
[3]might [4]be [5]greatest [1]of [2]them. - But Jesus perceiving the

διαλογισμὸν τῆς καρδίας αὐτῶν, ἐπιλαβόμενος παιδίου,
reasoning - of heart ˜ their, taking a little child,

ἔστησεν αὐτὸ παρ' ἑαυτῷ, 48 καὶ εἶπεν αὐτοῖς, “Ὃς ἐὰν
He stood it beside Himself, and said to them, “Who ever

δέξηται τοῦτο τὸ παιδίον ἐπὶ τῷ ὀνόματί μου ἐμὲ δέχεται· καὶ
receives this - little child in - name ˜ My Me ˜ receives; and

ὃς ἐὰν ἐμὲ δέξηται δέχεται τὸν ἀποστείλαντά με. Ὁ
who ever Me ˜ receives receives the *One* sending Me. [2]the [3]*one*
Him who sent he who

γὰρ μικρότερος ἐν πᾶσιν ὑμῖν ὑπάρχων οὗτος ἔσται[i]
[1]For [5]least [6]among [8]all [7]you [4]being this *one* will be
is

μέγας.”
great.”

Jesus Forbids Sectarianism
(Mark 9:38–40)

49 Ἀποκριθεὶς δὲ ὁ Ἰωάννης εἶπεν, “Ἐπιστάτα, εἴδομέν
[3]answering [1]And - [2]John said, “Master, we saw

τινα ἐπὶ τῷ ὀνόματί σου ἐκβάλλοντα δαιμόνια, καὶ
someone in - name ˜ Your casting out demons, and

ἐκωλύσαμεν αὐτόν, ὅτι οὐκ ἀκολουθεῖ μεθ' ἡμῶν.”
we forbade him, because [3]not [1]he [2]is following with us.”

50 Καὶ εἶπε πρὸς αὐτὸν ὁ Ἰησοῦς, “Μὴ κωλύετε, ὃς
And [2]said [3]to [4]him - [1]Jesus, “not ˜ Do forbid *him*, [2]*he* [3]who

γὰρ οὐκ ἔστι καθ' ἡμῶν ὑπὲρ ἡμῶν[j] ἐστιν.”
[1]for [5]not [4]is against us [2]for [3]us [1]is.”

A Samaritan Village Rejects the Savior

51 Ἐγένετο δὲ ἐν τῷ συμπληροῦσθαι τὰς ἡμέρας τῆς
[2]it [3]happened [1]And in - to approach the days -
as the days approached for Him to

ἀναλήψεως αὐτοῦ, καὶ αὐτὸς τὸ πρόσωπον αὐτοῦ ἐστήριξε τοῦ
of receiving up His, and He - [3]face [2]His [1]set -
be received up, that

πορεύεσθαι εἰς Ἱερουσαλήμ, 52 καὶ ἀπέστειλεν ἀγγέλους
to go to Jerusalem, and He sent messengers

πρὸ προσώπου αὐτοῦ. Καὶ πορευθέντες εἰσῆλθον εἰς κώμην
before face ˜ His. And going they entered into a village
as they went,

Son of Man is about to be betrayed into the hands of men.”
45 But they did not understand this saying, and it was hidden from them so that they did not perceive it; and they were afraid to ask Him about this saying.
46 Then a dispute arose among them as to which of them would be greatest.
47 And Jesus, perceiving the thought of their heart, took a little child and set him by Him,
48 and said to them, “Whoever receives this little child in My name receives Me; and whoever receives Me receives Him who sent Me. For he who is least among you all will be great.”
49 Now John answered and said, “Master, we saw someone casting out demons in Your name, and we forbade him because he does not follow with us.”
50 But Jesus said to him, “Do not forbid *him*, for he who is not against us is on our side.”
51 Now it came to pass, when the time had come for Him to be received up, that He steadfastly set His face to go to Jerusalem,
52 and sent messengers before His face. And as they went, they entered a village of

---

[h](9:47) NU reads ειδως, *knowing.* [i](9:48) NU reads εστιν, *is.* [j](9:50) For καθ ημων υπερ ημων, *against us for us,* NU reads καθ υμων υπερ υμων, *against you for you.*

the Samaritans, to prepare for
Him.
53 But they did not receive
Him, because His face was *set*
for the journey to Jerusalem.
54 And when His disciples
James and John saw *this,* they
said, "Lord, do You want us to
command fire to come down
from heaven and consume
them, just as Elijah did?"
55 But He turned and rebuked
them, and said, "You do not
know what manner of spirit you
are of.
56 "For the Son of Man did
not come to destroy men's lives
but to save *them.*" And they
went to another village.
57 Now it happened as they
journeyed on the road, *that*
someone said to Him, "Lord, I
will follow You wherever You go."
58 And Jesus said to him,
"Foxes have holes and birds of
the air *have* nests, but the Son
of Man has nowhere to lay *His*
head."
59 Then He said to another,
"Follow Me." But he said,
"Lord, let me first go and bury
my father."
60 Jesus said to him, "Let the
dead bury their own dead, but
you go and preach the kingdom
of God."
61 And another also said,
"Lord, I will follow You, but let

Σαμαρειτῶν, ὥστε ἑτοιμάσαι αὐτῷ. **53** Καὶ οὐκ
of Samaritans, so as to prepare for Him. And [3]not
so they might prepare

ἐδέξαντο αὐτόν, ὅτι τὸ πρόσωπον αὐτοῦ ἦν
[1]they [2]did receive Him, because - face ˜ His was
He was determined to

πορευόμενον εἰς Ἰερουσαλήμ. **54** Ἰδόντες δὲ οἱ
going to Jerusalem. seeing ˜ And -
go And when they saw this,

μαθηταὶ αὐτοῦ Ἰάκωβος καὶ Ἰωάννης εἶπον, "Κύριε,
disciples ˜ His James and John said, "Lord,

θέλεις εἴπωμεν πῦρ καταβῆναι ἀπὸ τοῦ οὐρανοῦ καὶ
do You wish *that* we should tell fire to come down from - heaven and
command

ἀναλῶσαι αὐτοὺς ὡς καὶ Ἠλίας ἐποίησε?"[k]
to consume them as also Elijah did?"

55 Στραφεὶς δὲ ἐπετίμησεν αὐτοῖς[l] καὶ εἶπεν, "Οὐκ
turning ˜ But He rebuked them and said, "[3]not

οἴδατε οἵου πνεύματός ἐστε ὑμεῖς. **56** Ὁ γὰρ Υἱὸς
[1]You [2]do know of what sort of spirit are ˜ you. the ˜ For Son

τοῦ Ἀνθρώπου οὐκ ἦλθε ψυχὰς ἀνθρώπων ἀπολέσαι* ἀλλὰ
- of Man not ˜ did come [3]*the* [4]lives [5]of [6]men [1]to [2]destroy but

σῶσαι."[m] Καὶ ἐπορεύθησαν εἰς ἑτέραν κώμην.
to save *them.*" And they went to another village.

Follow Him
(Matt. 8:18–22)

57 Ἐγένετο δὲ πορευομένων αὐτῶν ἐν τῇ ὁδῷ, εἶπέ
[2]it [3]happened [1]And going them on the road, *that* said ˜
as they went

τις πρὸς αὐτόν, "Ἀκολουθήσω σοι ὅπου ἂν ἀπέρχῃ,
someone to Him, "I will follow You where ever You go,

Κύριε."[n]
Lord."

58 Καὶ εἶπε αὐτῷ ὁ Ἰησοῦς, "Αἱ ἀλώπεκες φωλεοὺς
And [2]said [3]to [4]him - [1]Jesus, - "Foxes dens ˜

ἔχουσι καὶ τὰ πετεινὰ τοῦ οὐρανοῦ κατασκηνώσεις, ὁ δὲ
have and - birds of the heaven *have* nests, the ˜ but

Υἱὸς τοῦ Ἀνθρώπου οὐκ ἔχει ποῦ τὴν κεφαλὴν
Son - of Man not ˜ does have where [4]the [5]head
has nowhere His

κλίνῃ." **59** Εἶπε δὲ πρὸς ἕτερον, "Ἀκολούθει μοι."
[1]He [2]may [3]lay." [2]He [3]said [1]And to another, "Follow Me."

Ὁ δὲ εἶπε, "Κύριε,[o] ἐπίτρεψόν μοι ἀπελθόντι πρῶτον
[2]the [3]*one* [1]But said, "Lord, permit me having gone first
he to go first

θάψαι τὸν πατέρα μου."
to bury - father ˜ my."
and

60 Εἶπε δὲ αὐτῷ ὁ Ἰησοῦς,[p] "Ἄφες τοὺς νεκροὺς θάψαι
[3]said [1]And [4]to [5]him - [2]Jesus, "Leave the dead to bury

τοὺς ἑαυτῶν νεκρούς, σὺ δὲ ἀπελθὼν διάγγελλε τὴν
the [2]of [3]themselves [1]dead, you ˜ but having gone proclaim the
their own go and

βασιλείαν τοῦ Θεοῦ."
kingdom - of God."

61 Εἶπε δὲ καὶ ἕτερος, "Ἀκολουθήσω σοι, Κύριε, πρῶτον
[4]said [1]And [3]also [2]another, "I will follow You, Lord, first ˜

---

[k](9:54) NU omits ως και Ηλιας εποιησε, *as also Elijah did.*
[l](9:55) NU, many mss. omit the rest of v. 55.
[m](9:56) NU, many mss. omit the first sentence of v. 56.
[n](9:57) NU omits Κυριε, *Lord.*
[o](9:59) NU omits Κυριε, *Lord.*
[p](9:60) NU omits ο Ιησους, *Jesus.*

***(9:56)** ἀπόλλυμι *(apollymi).* Verb, the common and general term for *destroy.* It describes the destruction of both objects (wineskins, Luke 5:37) and persons (here in 9:56). In the latter case, it can mean either the destruction of one's physical life (thus *die;* Matt. 26:52) or of one's spiritual life (Matt. 10:28). The word also has the less severe meaning *lose,* either in the sense of "to misplace" (Luke 15:4, 8) or of the permanent loss of something one already owns (2 John 8) or hopes to gain (Mark 10:41). This meaning of loss can have a spiritual nuance, *the*

δὲ ἐπίτρεψόν μοι ἀποτάξασθαι τοῖς εἰς τὸν οἶκόν μου."
but permit me to say farewell to the *ones* in - house ˜ my."
to those at home."

62 Εἶπε δὲ ὁ Ἰησοῦς πρὸς αὐτόν, "Οὐδεὶς ἐπιβαλὼν τὴν
[3]said [1]And - [2]Jesus to him, "No one having put -

χεῖρα αὐτου ἐπ' ἄροτρον, καὶ βλέπων εἰς τὰ ὀπίσω,
hand ˜ his on a plow, and looking to the *things* behind,
back,

εὔθετός ἐστιν εἰς τὴν βασιλείαν τοῦ Θεοῦ."
usable ˜ is for the kingdom - of God."

Jesus Sends Out the Seventy

10 1 Μετὰ δὲ ταῦτα ἀνέδειξεν ὁ Κύριος καὶ ἑτέρους
after ˜ Now these *things* [3]appointed [1]the [2]Lord also others ˜

ἑβδομήκοντα,[a] καὶ ἀπέστειλεν αὐτοὺς ἀνὰ δύο πρὸ
seventy, and He sent them each ˜ two before
two by two

προσώπου αὐτοῦ εἰς πᾶσαν πόλιν καὶ τόπον οὗ ἔμελλεν
face ˜ His into every city and place where [2]was [3]about

αὐτὸς ἔρχεσθαι. 2 Ἔλεγεν οὖν πρὸς αὐτούς, "Ὁ μὲν
[1]He to come. [2]He [3]said [1]Then to them, "The indeed ˜

θερισμὸς πολύς, οἱ δὲ ἐργάται ὀλίγοι· δεήθητε οὖν
harvest *is* great, the ˜ but workers *are* few; pray ˜ therefore

τοῦ Κυρίου τοῦ θερισμοῦ ὅπως ἐκβάλῃ ἐργάτας εἰς
to the Lord of the harvest that He may put forth workers into

τὸν θερισμὸν αὐτοῦ. 3 Ὑπάγετε· ἰδού, ἐγὼ ἀποστέλλω ὑμᾶς
- harvest ˜ His. Go; behold, I send you

ὡς ἄρνας ἐν μέσῳ λύκων. 4 Μὴ βαστάζετε βαλάντιον, μὴ
as lambs in *the* midst of wolves. not ˜ Do carry a money bag, nor

πήραν, μηδὲ ὑποδήματα, καὶ μηδένα κατὰ τὴν ὁδὸν
a knapsack, nor sandals, and [2]no [3]one [4]along [5]the [6]road

ἀσπάσησθε. 5 Εἰς ἣν δ' ἂν οἰκίαν εἰσέρχησθε, πρῶτον
[1]greet. [2]into [3]which [1]And ever house you enter, first

λέγετε, 'Εἰρήνη τῷ οἴκῳ τούτῳ.' 6 Καὶ ἐὰν ᾖ ἐκεῖ υἱὸς[b]
say, 'Peace - [3]house [1]to [2]this.' And if *there* is there a son

εἰρήνης, ἐπαναπαύσεται ἐπ' αὐτὸν ἡ εἰρήνη ὑμῶν· εἰ δὲ μή
of peace, [3]will [4]rest [5]upon [6]it - [2]peace [1]your; if ˜ but not,

γε, ἐφ' ὑμᾶς ἀνακάμψει. 7 Ἐν αὐτῇ δὲ τῇ οἰκίᾳ μένετε,
- [4]upon [5]you [1]it [2]will [3]return. [2]in [4]very [1]And [3]the house remain,
that

ἐσθίοντες καὶ πίνοντες τὰ παρ' αὐτῶν, ἄξιος γὰρ ὁ
eating and drinking the *things* with them, [5]worthy [1]for [2]the
what they have,

ἐργάτης τοῦ μισθοῦ αὐτοῦ ἐστι. Μὴ μεταβαίνετε ἐξ οἰκίας
[3]worker - [6]of [8]reward [7]his [4]is. not ˜ Do move from house
pay

εἰς οἰκίαν. 8 Καὶ εἰς ἣν ἂν πόλιν εἰσέρχησθε, καὶ
to house. And into which ever city you enter, and

δέχωνται ὑμᾶς, ἐσθίετε τὰ παρατιθέμενα ὑμῖν. 9 Καὶ
they receive you, eat the *things* being set before you. And
what is

θεραπεύετε τοὺς ἐν αὐτῇ ἀσθενεῖς, καὶ λέγετε αὐτοῖς,
heal the [3]in [4]it [1]sick [2]*ones*, and say to them,
sick who are,

'Ἤγγικεν ἐφ' ὑμᾶς ἡ βασιλεία τοῦ Θεοῦ.' 10 Εἰς
'[5]has [6]drawn [7]near [8]to [9]you [1]The [2]kingdom - [3]of [4]God.' [2]into

ἣν δ' ἂν πόλιν εἰσέρχησθε, καὶ μὴ δέχωνται ὑμᾶς,
[3]which [1]But ever city you enter, and [3]not [1]they [2]do receive you,

me first go *and* bid them farewell who are at my house."

62 But Jesus said to him, "No one, having put his hand to the plow, and looking back, is fit for the kingdom of God."

10 After these things the Lord appointed seventy others also, and sent them two by two before His face into every city and place where He Himself was about to go.

2 Then He said to them, "The harvest truly *is* great, but the laborers *are* few; therefore pray the Lord of the harvest to send out laborers into His harvest.

3 "Go your way; behold, I send you out as lambs among wolves.

4 "Carry neither money bag, knapsack, nor sandals; and greet no one along the road.

5 "But whatever house you enter, first say, 'Peace to this house.'

6 "And if a son of peace is there, your peace will rest on it; if not, it will return to you.

7 "And remain in the same house, eating and drinking such things as they give, for the laborer is worthy of his wages. Do not go from house to house.

8 "Whatever city you enter, and they receive you, eat such things as are set before you.

9 "And heal the sick there, and say to them, 'The kingdom of God has come near to you.'

10 "But whatever city you enter, and they do not receive

---

[a](10:1) NU adds in brackets δυο, *two*. [b](10:6) TR reads ο υιος, *the son*.

---

lost (Luke 19:10). Cf. the compound verb συναπόλλυμι, *perish with* (Heb. 11:31); the noun ἀπώλεια, *destruction* (Rom. 9:22); and the name of the underworld angel Ἀπολλύων, *Apollyon, the Destroyer* (Rev. 9:11).

you, go out into its streets and say,
11 'The very dust of your city which clings to us we wipe off against you. Nevertheless know this, that the kingdom of God has come near you.'
12 "But I say to you that it will be more tolerable in that Day for Sodom than for that city.
13 "Woe to you, Chorazin! Woe to you, Bethsaida! For if the mighty works which were done in you had been done in Tyre and Sidon, they would have repented long ago, sitting in sackcloth and ashes.
14 "But it will be more tolerable for Tyre and Sidon at the judgment than for you.
15 "And you, Capernaum, who are exalted to heaven, will be brought down to Hades.
16 "He who hears you hears Me, he who rejects you rejects Me, and he who rejects Me rejects Him who sent Me."
17 Then the seventy returned with joy, saying, "Lord, even the demons are subject to us in Your name."
18 And He said to them, "I saw Satan fall like lightning from heaven.
19 "Behold, I give you the authority to trample on serpents and scorpions, and over all the power of the enemy, and noth-

ἐξελθόντες εἰς τὰς πλατείας αὐτῆς εἴπατε, **11** *'Καὶ τὸν*
going out into - streets ˜ its say, 'Even the

κονιορτὸν τὸν κολληθέντα ἡμῖν ἐκ τῆς πόλεως ὑμῶν[c]
dust - clinging to us from - city ˜ your

ἀπομασσόμεθα ὑμῖν. Πλὴν τοῦτο γινώσκετε, ὅτι
we wipe off to you. Nevertheless this ˜ know, that
against

ἤγγικεν ἐφ' ὑμᾶς[d] *ἡ βασιλεία τοῦ Θεοῦ.'* **12** *Λέγω*
[5]has [6]drawn [7]near [8]to [9]you [1]the [2]kingdom - [3]of [4]God.' I say

ὑμῖν ὅτι Σοδόμοις ἐν τῇ ἡμέρᾳ ἐκείνῃ ἀνεκτότερον ἔσται
to you that [6]for [7]Sodom [8]in - [10]day [9]that [4]more [5]tolerable [1]it [2]will [3]be

ἢ τῇ πόλει ἐκείνῃ.
than - for city ˜ that.

Woe to the Impenitent Cities
(Matt. 11:20–24)

13 *"Οὐαί σοι, Χοραζίν! Οὐαί σοι, Βηθσαϊδά! Ὅτι εἰ*
"Woe to you, Chorazin! Woe to you, Bethsaida! Because if

ἐν Τύρῳ καὶ Σιδῶνι ἐγένοντο αἱ δυνάμεις αἱ
[10]in [11]Tyre [12]and [13]Sidon [8]were [9]done [1]the [2]miracles [3]the [4]*ones*
had been which have

γενόμεναι ἐν ὑμῖν, πάλαι ἂν ἐν σάκκῳ καὶ σποδῷ
[5]done [6]in [7]you, [18]long [19]ago - [21]in [22]sackcloth [23]and [24]ashes
been done

καθήμεναι μετενόησαν. **14** *Πλὴν Τύρῳ*
[20]sitting [14]they [15]would [16]have [17]repented. Nevertheless [6]for [7]Tyre

καὶ Σιδῶνι ἀνεκτότερον ἔσται ἐν τῇ κρίσει ἢ ὑμῖν.
[8]and [9]Sidon [4]more [5]tolerable [1]it [2]will [3]be in the judgment than for you.

15 *Καὶ σύ, Καπερναούμ, ἡ ἕως τοῦ οὐρανοῦ*
And you, Capernaum, the *one* to - heaven
who are exalted to heaven,

ὑψωθεῖσα,[e] *ἕως Ἅιδου καταβιβασθήσῃ.* **16** *Ὁ*
having been exalted, [5]to [6]Hades [1]will [2]be [3]brought [4]down. The *one*
He who

ἀκούων ὑμῶν ἐμοῦ ἀκούει, καὶ ὁ ἀθετῶν ὑμᾶς ἐμὲ ἀθετεῖ,
hearing you Me ˜ hears, and the *one* rejecting you Me ˜ rejects,
hears he who rejects

ὁ δὲ ἐμὲ ἀθετῶν ἀθετεῖ τὸν ἀποστείλαντά με."
[2]the [3]*one* [1]and Me ˜ rejecting rejects the *One* having sent Me."
he who rejects Him who sent

The Seventy Return with Joy

17 *Ὑπέστρεψαν δὲ οἱ ἑβδομήκοντα*[f] *μετὰ χαρᾶς,*
[4]returned [1]And [2]the [3]seventy with joy,
Then

λέγοντες, "Κύριε, καὶ τὰ δαιμόνια ὑποτάσσεται ἡμῖν ἐν τῷ
saying, "Lord, even the demons are subject to us in -

ὀνόματί σου."
name ˜ Your."

18 *Εἶπε δὲ αὐτοῖς, "Ἐθεώρουν τὸν Σαταναν ὡς*
[2]He [3]said [1]And to them, "I saw - Satan [3]like

ἀστραπὴν ἐκ τοῦ οὐρανοῦ πεσόντα. **19** *Ἰδού, δίδωμι*[g]
[4]lightning [5]out [6]of - [7]heaven [1]having [2]fallen. Behold, I give

ὑμῖν τὴν ἐξουσίαν τοῦ πατεῖν ἐπάνω ὄφεων καὶ σκορπίων,
you the authority - to trample on serpents and scorpions,

καὶ ἐπὶ πᾶσαν τὴν δύναμιν τοῦ ἐχθροῦ, καὶ οὐδὲν ὑμᾶς οὐ
and over all the power of the enemy, and nothing you not
will by

[c]**(10:11)** NU adds *εις τους ποδας, to our feet.*
[d]**(10:11)** NU omits *εφ υμας, to you.*
[e]**(10:15)** For *η εως του ουρανου υψωθεισα, the one having been exalted to heaven,* NU reads *μη εως ουρανου υψωθηση, you will not be exalted to heaven, will you?*
[f]**(10:17)** NU adds in brackets *δυο, two.*
[g]**(10:19)** NU reads *δεδωκα, I have given.*

μὴ ἀδικήσῃ. **20** Πλὴν ἐν τούτῳ μὴ χαίρετε ὅτι τὰ
not will hurt. Nevertheless [4]in [5]this [2]not [1]do [3]rejoice that the
any means hurt you.

πνεύματα ὑμῖν ὑποτάσσεται, χαίρετε δὲ ὅτι τὰ ὀνόματα
spirits [3]to [4]you [1]are [2]subject, rejoice ˜ but that - names ˜

ὑμῶν ἐγράφη ἐν τοῖς οὐρανοῖς."
your were written in the heavens."
have been

Jesus Rejoices in the Spirit
(Matt. 11:25–27; 13:16, 17)

21 Ἐν αὐτῇ τῇ ὥρᾳ ἠγαλλιάσατο τῷ Πνεύματι[h] ὁ
In very ˜ the hour [2]exulted [3]in [4]the [5]Spirit -
that

Ἰησοῦς καὶ εἶπεν, "Ἐξομολογοῦμαί* σοι, Πάτερ, Κύριε τοῦ
[1]Jesus and said, "I praise You, Father, Lord -

οὐρανοῦ καὶ τῆς γῆς, ὅτι ἀπέκρυψας ταῦτα ἀπὸ σοφῶν
of heaven and - of earth, that You hid these *things* from wise
have hidden

καὶ συνετῶν, καὶ ἀπεκάλυψας αὐτὰ νηπίοις. Ναί, ὁ
and intelligent *people,* and You revealed them to babes. Yes, -
have revealed

Πατήρ, ὅτι οὕτως ἐγένετο εὐδοκία ἔμπροσθέν σου."
Father, because so it was good pleasure before You."
seemed good in Your sight."

22 Καὶ στραφεὶς πρὸς τοὺς μαθητὰς εἶπε,[i] "Πάντα μοι
And turning to the disciples He said, "All *things* [4]to [5]Me

παρεδόθη ὑπὸ τοῦ Πατρός μου, καὶ οὐδεὶς γινώσκει τίς
[1]were [2]given [3]over by - Father ˜ My, and no one knows who
have been

ἐστιν ὁ Υἱὸς εἰ μὴ ὁ Πατήρ, καὶ τίς ἐστιν ὁ Πατὴρ
[3]is [1]the [2]Son if not the Father, and who [3]is [1]the [2]Father
except

εἰ μὴ ὁ Υἱὸς καὶ ᾧ ἐὰν βούληται ὁ Υἱὸς
if not the Son and *the one* to whom - [3]wills [1]the [2]Son
except

ἀποκαλύψαι." **23** Καὶ στραφεὶς πρὸς τοὺς μαθητὰς κατ' ἰδίαν
to reveal *Him.*" And turning to the disciples privately

εἶπε, "Μακάριοι οἱ ὀφθαλμοὶ οἱ βλέποντες ἃ
He said, "Blessed *are* the eyes the *ones* seeing *the things* which
which see

βλέπετε. **24** Λέγω γὰρ ὑμῖν ὅτι πολλοὶ προφῆται καὶ
you see. [2]I [3]say [1]For to you that many prophets and

βασιλεῖς ἠθέλησαν ἰδεῖν ἃ ὑμεῖς βλέπετε, καὶ οὐκ
kings desired to see *the things* which you see, and [3]not
have desired

εἶδον, καὶ ἀκοῦσαι ἃ ἀκούετε, καὶ οὐκ
[1]they [2]did see *them,* and to hear *the things* which you hear, and [3]not

ἤκουσαν."
[1]they [2]did hear *them.*"

The Parable of the Good Samaritan

25 Καὶ ἰδού, νομικός τις ἀνέστη, ἐκπειράζων αὐτὸν καὶ
And behold, a lawyer ˜ certain stood up, testing Him and

λέγων, "Διδάσκαλε, τί ποιήσας ζωὴν αἰώνιον
saying, "Teacher, [3]what [1]*by* [2]doing [8]life [7]eternal

κληρονομήσω?"
[4]shall [5]I [6]inherit?"

ing shall by any means hurt you.

20 "Nevertheless do not rejoice in this, that the spirits are subject to you, but rather rejoice because your names are written in heaven."

21 In that hour Jesus rejoiced in the Spirit and said, "I thank You, Father, Lord of heaven and earth, that You have hidden these things from *the* wise and prudent and revealed them to babes. Even so, Father, for so it seemed good in Your sight.

22 "All things have been delivered to Me by My Father, and no one knows who the Son is except the Father, and who the Father is except the Son, and *the one* to whom the Son wills to reveal *Him.*"

23 Then He turned to *His* disciples and said privately, "Blessed *are* the eyes which see the things you see;

24 "for I tell you that many prophets and kings have desired to see what you see, and have not seen *it,* and to hear what you hear, and have not heard *it.*"

25 And behold, a certain lawyer stood up and tested Him, saying, "Teacher, what shall I do to inherit eternal life?"

---

[h](**10:21**) NU adds τω Αγιω, *the Holy,* and omits the following ο Ιησους, *Jesus.*
[i](**10:22**) NU omits the first part of v. 22.

***(10:21)** ἐξομολογέω *(exomologeō).* Verb originally meaning *promise, consent* (as Luke 22:6). Like the simple ὁμολογέω, it can mean *confess, admit, acknowledge* (as Matt. 3:6; Mark 1:5; James 5:16; Phil. 2:11), but with some added emphasis on *public* or *open* confession. Here in Luke 10:21, growing out of the idea of confession, it refers to *praise,* especially praise of God, as also in the rest of the NT (Matt. 11:25; Rom. 14:11; 15:9).

26 He said to him, "What is
written in the law? What is your
reading *of it?*"
27 So he answered and said,
"'*You shall love the* LORD *your*
God with all your heart, with all
your soul, with all your
strength, and with all your
mind,' and *'your neighbor as*
yourself.' "
28 And He said to him, "You
have answered rightly; do this
and you will live."
29 But he, wanting to justify
himself, said to Jesus, "And
who is my neighbor?"
30 Then Jesus answered and
said: "A certain *man* went
down from Jerusalem to Jericho, and fell among thieves,
who stripped him of his clothing, wounded *him,* and departed, leaving *him* half dead.
31 "Now by chance a certain
priest came down that road.
And when he saw him, he
passed by on the other side.
32 "Likewise a Levite, when
he arrived at the place, came
and looked, and passed by on
the other side.
33 "But a certain Samaritan,
as he journeyed, came where
he was. And when he saw him,
he had compassion.
34 "So he went to *him* and
bandaged his wounds, pouring
on oil and wine; and he set him
on his own animal, brought him
to an inn, and took care of him.
35 "On the next day, when he

26 Ὁ δὲ εἶπε πρὸς αὐτόν, "Ἐν τῷ νόμῳ τί
[2]the [3]*One* [1]And said to him, "In the law what
He

γέγραπται? Πῶς ἀναγινώσκεις?"
is written? How do you read *it?*"

27 Ὁ δὲ ἀποκριθεὶς εἶπεν, "«Ἀγαπήσεις Κύριον τὸν
[2]the [3]*one* [1]And answering said, "«You shall love *the* Lord -
he

Θεόν σου ἐξ ὅλης τῆς καρδίας σου καὶ ἐξ ὅλης τῆς
God ˜ your out of [2]whole - [3]heart [1]your and out of [2]whole -
with with

ψυχῆς σου καὶ ἐξ ὅλης τὴν ἰσχύος σου καὶ ἐξ ὅλης τῆς
[3]soul [1]your and out of [2]whole - [3]strength [1]your and out of [2]whole -
self with with

διανοίας σου,»[j] καὶ «τὸν πλησίον σου ὡς σεαυτόν.»"[k]
[3]mind [1]your,» and - «neighbor ˜ your as yourself.»"

28 Εἶπε δὲ αὐτῷ, "Ὀρθῶς ἀπεκρίθης· τοῦτο ποίει
[2]He [3]said [1]And to him, "[3]correctly [1]You [2]answered; this ˜ do
have answered;

καὶ ζήσῃ."
and you will live."

29 Ὁ δὲ θέλων δικαιοῦν ἑαυτὸν εἶπε πρὸς τὸν
[6]the [7]*one* [1]But [2]wishing [3]to [4]justify [5]himself said to -
he

Ἰησοῦν, "Καὶ τίς ἐστί μου πλησίον?"
Jesus, "And who is my neighbor?"

30 Ὑπολαβὼν δὲ ὁ Ἰησοῦς εἶπεν, "Ἄνθρωπός τις
replying ˜ And - Jesus said, "A man ˜ certain

κατέβαινεν ἀπὸ Ἱερουσαλὴμ εἰς Ἱεριχώ, καὶ λῃσταῖς
was going down from Jerusalem to Jericho, and [3]bandits

περιέπεσεν, οἳ καὶ ἐκδύσαντες αὐτὸν καὶ πληγὰς
[1]fell [2]among, who both having stripped him and [3]wounds
encountered, after

ἐπιθέντες ἀπῆλθον, ἀφέντες ἡμιθανῆ τυγχάνοντα.[l]
[1]having [2]inflicted departed, leaving *him* half dead turning out.
as it turned out half dead.

31 Κατὰ συγκυρίαν δὲ ἱερεύς τις κατέβαινεν ἐν
[2]according [3]to [4]coincidence [1]And a priest ˜ certain was coming down on
by chance

τῇ ὁδῷ ἐκείνῃ. Καὶ ἰδὼν αὐτὸν
- road ˜ that. And seeing him
when he saw

ἀντιπαρῆλθεν. **32** Ὁμοίως δὲ καὶ Λευίτης
he passed by on the opposite side. likewise ˜ And also a Levite

γενόμενος κατὰ τὸν τόπον ἐλθὼν καὶ ἰδὼν
arriving at the place coming and seeing
came saw and

ἀντιπαρῆλθε. **33** Σαμαρείτης δέ τις ὁδεύων
passed by on the opposite side. [2]a [4]Samaritan [1]But [3]certain traveling
as he traveled

ἦλθε κατ' αὐτὸν καὶ ἰδὼν αὐτὸν[m] ἐσπλαγχνίσθη, **34** καὶ
came by him and seeing him felt compassion, and
when he saw

προσελθὼν κατέδησε τὰ τραύματα αὐτοῦ, ἐπιχέων ἔλαιον καὶ
coming to *him* he bound up - wounds ˜ his, pouring on oil and

οἶνον· ἐπιβιβάσας δὲ αὐτὸν ἐπὶ τὸ ἴδιον κτῆνος, ἤγαγεν
wine; putting ˜ and him on - his own animal, he brought
mount,

αὐτὸν εἰς πανδοχεῖον, καὶ ἐπεμελήθη αὐτοῦ. **35** Καὶ ἐπὶ τὴν
him to an inn, and he took care of him. And on the

---

[j](**10:27**) Deut. 6:5
[k](**10:27**) Lev. 19:18
[l](**10:30**) NU omits *τυγχανοντα, turning out.*
[m](**10:33**) NU omits αυτον, *him.*

αὔριον ἐξελθών,[n] ἐκβαλὼν δύο δηνάρια ἔδωκε τῷ
next day going away, taking out two denarii he gave *them* to the
when he departed, he took out and

πανδοχεῖ, καὶ εἶπεν αὐτῷ, "Ἐπιμελήθητι αὐτοῦ· καὶ ὅ τι ἂν
innkeeper, and said to him, 'Take care of him; and - what ever

προσδαπανήσῃς, ἐγὼ ἐν τῷ ἐπανέρχεσθαί με ἀποδώσω σοι.'
you spend in addition, I in - to come back me will repay you.'
when I come back, I

36 Τίς οὖν τούτων τῶν τριῶν πλησίον δοκεῖ σοι
Which then of these - three [9]a [10]neighbor [1]does [2]it [3]seem [4]to [5]you

γεγονέναι τοῦ ἐμπεσόντος εἰς τοὺς λῃστάς?"
[6]to [7]have [8]become of the *one* falling among the bandits?"
proved to be to the man who fell

37 Ὁ δὲ εἶπεν, "Ὁ ποιήσας τὸ ἔλεος μετ'
[2]the [3]*one* [1]And said, "The *one* doing the mercy with
he who showed to

αὐτοῦ."
him."

Εἶπεν οὖν αὐτῷ ὁ Ἰησοῦς, "Πορεύου καὶ σὺ ποίει
[3]said [1]Therefore [4]to [5]him - [2]Jesus, "Go and you do

ὁμοίως."
likewise."

Mary and Martha Worship and Serve

38 Ἐγένετο δὲ ἐν τῷ πορεύεσθαι αὐτούς, καὶ αὐτὸς
[2]it [3]happened [1]Now in - [2]to [3]travel [1]them, and He
as they traveled that

εἰσῆλθεν εἰς κώμην τινά. Γυνὴ δέ τις ὀνόματι
entered into a village ˜ certain. [2]a [4]woman [1]And [3]certain [6]by [7]name

Μάρθα ὑπεδέξατο αὐτὸν εἰς τὸν οἶκον αὐτῆς.[o] **39** Καὶ
[5]Martha received Him into - house ˜ her. And
welcomed

τῇδε ἦν ἀδελφὴ καλουμένη Μαρία ἣ καὶ
to this *woman* was a sister being called Mary who also
the woman had called

παρακαθίσασα παρὰ τοὺς πόδας τοῦ Ἰησοῦ[p] ἤκουε τὸν
having sat down at the feet - of Jesus was listening to -

λόγον αὐτοῦ. **40** Ἡ δὲ Μάρθα περιεσπᾶτο περὶ πολλὴν
word ˜ His. - But Martha was distracted about much

διακονίαν· ἐπιστᾶσα δὲ εἶπε, "Κύριε, οὐ μέλει σοι
service; [2]coming [3]up [1]and she said, "Lord, [3]not [1]is [2]it a care to You
don't You care

ὅτι ἡ ἀδελφή μου μόνην με κατέλειπε διακονεῖν? Εἰπὲ
that - sister ˜ my [5]alone [2]me [1]left [3]to [4]serve? tell ˜
has left

οὖν αὐτῇ ἵνα μοι συναντιλάβηται!"
Therefore her that [4]me [1]she [2]should [3]help!"

41 Ἀποκριθεὶς δὲ εἶπεν αὐτῇ ὁ Ἰησοῦς,[q] "Μάρθα,
answering ˜ And [2]said [3]to [4]her - [1]Jesus, "Martha,

Μάρθα, μεριμνᾷς καὶ τυρβάζῃ περὶ πολλά.
Martha, you are worried and are troubled about many *things*.

42 Ἑνὸς δέ ἐστι χρεία, Μαρία δὲ τὴν ἀγαθὴν μερίδα
[2]of [3]one [4]*thing* [1]But *there* is a need, Mary ˜ and [2]the [3]good [4]part

ἐξελέξατο, ἥτις οὐκ ἀφαιρεθήσεται ἀπ' αὐτῆς."
[1]chose, which not ˜ will be taken away from her."
has chosen,

departed, he took out two denarii, gave *them* to the innkeeper, and said to him, 'Take care of him; and whatever more you spend, when I come again, I will repay you.'
36 "So which of these three do you think was neighbor to him who fell among the thieves?"
37 And he said, "He who showed mercy on him." Then Jesus said to him, "Go and do likewise."
38 Now it happened as they went that He entered a certain village; and a certain woman named Martha welcomed Him into her house.
39 And she had a sister called Mary, who also sat at Jesus' feet and heard His word.
40 But Martha was distracted with much serving, and she approached Him and said, "Lord, do You not care that my sister has left me to serve alone? Therefore tell her to help me."
41 And Jesus answered and said to her, "Martha, Martha, you are worried and troubled about many things.
42 "But one thing is needed, and Mary has chosen that good part, which will not be taken away from her."

---

[n](**10:35**) NU omits εξελθων, *going away.*
[o](**10:38**) NU omits εις τον οικον αυτης, *into her house.* [p](**10:39**) NU reads Κυριου, *of (the) Lord.*
[q](**10:41**) NU reads ο Κυριου, *the Lord.*

11 Now it came to pass, as He was praying in a certain place, when He ceased, *that* one of His disciples said to Him, "Lord, teach us to pray, as John also taught his disciples."
2 So He said to them, "When you pray, say:

Our Father in heaven,
Hallowed be Your name.
Your kingdom come.
Your will be done
On earth as *it is* in heaven.
3 Give us day by day our daily bread.
4 And forgive us our sins,
For we also forgive everyone who is indebted to us.
And do not lead us into temptation,
But deliver us from the evil one."

5 And He said to them, "Which of you shall have a friend, and go to him at midnight and say to him, 'Friend, lend me three loaves;
6 'for a friend of mine has come to me on his journey, and I have nothing to set before him';
7 "and he will answer from within and say, 'Do not trouble me; the door is now shut, and my children are with me in bed;

Jesus Teaches the Model Prayer
(Matt. 6:5–15)

11 1 Καὶ ἐγένετο ἐν τῷ εἶναι αὐτὸν ἐν τόπῳ τινὶ
And it happened in - [2]to [3]be [1]Him in a place ˜ certain
while He was

προσευχόμενον, ὡς ἐπαύσατο, εἶπέ τις τῶν
praying, when He ceased, [7]said [1]a [2]certain [3]*one* -

μαθητῶν αὐτοῦ πρὸς αὐτόν, "Κύριε, δίδαξον ἡμᾶς
[4]of [6]disciples [5]His to Him, "Lord, teach us

προσεύχεσθαι, καθὼς καὶ Ἰωάννης ἐδίδαξε τοὺς μαθητὰς
to pray, just as also ˜ John taught - disciples ˜

αὐτοῦ."
his."

2 Εἶπε δὲ αὐτοῖς, "Ὅταν προσεύχησθε, λέγετε,
[2]He [3]said [1]And to them, "Whenever you pray, say,

Πάτερ ἡμῶν ὁ ἐν τοῖς οὐρανοῖς,[a]
Father ˜ Our - in the heavens,

Ἁγιασθήτω τὸ ὄνομά σου.
Let [3]be [4]hallowed - [2]name [1]Your.

Ἐλθέτω ἡ βασιλεία σου.[b]
Let [3]come - [2]kingdom [1]Your.

Γενηθήτω τὸ θέλημά σου,
Let [3]be [4]done - [2]will [1]Your,

Ὡς ἐν οὐρανῷ, καὶ ἐπὶ τῆς γῆς.
As in heaven, also upon the earth.

3 Τὸν ἄρτον ἡμῶν τὸν ἐπιούσιον δίδου ἡμῖν τὸ καθ'
- [4]bread [3]our - [5]for [6]the [7]day [1]Give [2]us - according to
day by

ἡμέραν.
a day.
day.

4 Καὶ ἄφες ἡμῖν τὰς ἁμαρτίας ἡμῶν,
And forgive us - sins ˜ our,

Καὶ γὰρ αὐτοὶ ἀφίεμεν παντὶ ὀφείλοντι ἡμῖν.
also ˜ For ourselves ˜ we forgive everyone owing to us.
who is indebted

Καὶ μὴ εἰσενέγκῃς ἡμᾶς εἰς πειρασμόν,[c]
And not ˜ do lead us into temptation,

Ἀλλὰ ῥῦσαι ἡμᾶς ἀπὸ τοῦ πονηροῦ."
But rescue us from the evil *one*."

A Friend Comes at Midnight

5 Καὶ εἶπε πρὸς αὐτούς, "Τίς ἐξ ὑμῶν ἕξει φίλον,
And He said to them, "Which of you shall have a friend,

καὶ πορεύσεται πρὸς αὐτὸν μεσονυκτίου καὶ εἴπῃ αὐτῷ, 'Φίλε,
and shall go to him at midnight and say to him, 'Friend,

χρῆσόν μοι τρεῖς ἄρτους, 6 ἐπειδὴ φίλος[d] παρεγένετο ἐξ
lend me three loaves, for a friend came [3]from
has come

ὁδοῦ πρός με, καὶ οὐκ ἔχω ὃ παραθήσω
[4]a [5]journey [1]to [2]me, and [3]not [1]I [2]do have what I could set before
anything to

αὐτῷ'· 7 κἀκεῖνος ἔσωθεν ἀποκριθεὶς εἴπῃ, 'Μή μοι κόπους
him'; and that one from within answering will say, '[2]not [4]me [5]troubles
he will answer from within and

πάρεχε· ἤδη ἡ θύρα κέκλεισται, καὶ τὰ παιδία μου μετ'
[1]Do [3]cause; already the door has been shut, and - children ˜ my [2]with

---

[a](**11:2**) NU omits *ημων ο εν τοις ουρανοις*, *our (Father) the One in the heavens.*
[b](**11:2**) NU omits the rest of v. 2. [c](**11:4**) NU omits the rest of v. 4.
[d](**11:6**) TR, NU add *μου*, *my.*

ἐμοῦ εἰς τὴν κοίτην εἰσίν· οὐ δύναμαι ἀναστὰς δοῦναί σοι'?
[3]me [4]in - [5]bed [1]are; [8]not [6]I [7]am able rising to give to you'?
to get up and

8 Λέγω ὑμῖν, εἰ καὶ οὐ δώσει αὐτῷ ἀναστάς, διὰ
I say to you, if ˜ even [3]not [1]he [2]will give to him rising, because of
he will not get up and give to him, because

τὸ εἶναι αὐτοῦ φίλον, διά γε τὴν ἀναίδειαν αὐτοῦ
- to be his friend, [2]on [3]account [4]of [1]yet - shamelessness ˜ his
he is persistence

ἐγερθεὶς δώσει αὐτῷ ὅσον χρῄζει.
arising he will give to him as many as he needs.
he will get up and

Keep Asking, Seeking, and Knocking
(Matt. 7:7–11)

9 "Κἀγὼ ὑμῖν λέγω, αἰτεῖτε, καὶ δοθήσεται ὑμῖν·
"And I [2]to [3]you [1]say, ask, and it will be given to you;

ζητεῖτε, καὶ εὑρήσετε· κρούετε, καὶ ἀνοιγήσεται ὑμῖν.
seek, and you will find; knock, and it will be opened to you.

10 Πᾶς γὰρ ὁ αἰτῶν λαμβάνει, καὶ ὁ ζητῶν
every ˜ For - *one* asking receives, and the *one* seeking
For everyone who asks he who seeks

εὑρίσκει, καὶ τῷ κρούοντι ἀνοιγήσεται. 11 Τίνα δὲ
finds, and to the *one* knocking it will be opened. which ˜ And
to him who knocks

ὑμῶν τὸν πατέρα αἰτήσει ὁ υἱὸς ἄρτον, μὴ λίθον
[2]of [3]you - [1]father [4]will [7]ask [8]for [5]the [6]son bread, [3]not [6]a [7]stone
among his

ἐπιδώσει αὐτῷ? Ἢ καὶ[e] ἰχθύν, μὴ[f] ἀντὶ
[1]he [2]will [4]give [5]him, *will he?* Or also *if he asks for* a fish, [3]not [8]instead

ἰχθύος ὄφιν ἐπιδώσει αὐτῷ? 12 Ἢ καὶ ἐὰν
[9]of [10]a [11]fish [6]a [7]serpent [1]he [2]will [4]give [5]him *will he?* Or also if

αἰτήσῃ ᾠόν, μὴ[g] ἐπιδώσει αὐτῷ σκορπίον? 13 Εἰ
he asks for an egg, [3]not [1]he [2]will give him a scorpion *will he?* If

οὖν ὑμεῖς πονηροὶ ὑπάρχοντες οἴδατε δόματα ἀγαθὰ διδόναι
then ˜ you evil ˜ being know *how* [4]gifts [3]good [1]to [2]give

τοῖς τέκνοις ὑμῶν, πόσῳ μᾶλλον ὁ Πατὴρ ὁ ἐξ
- to children ˜ your, by how much more [2]the [3]Father - [4]of
heavenly

οὐρανοῦ δώσει Πνεῦμα Ἅγιον τοῖς αἰτοῦσιν αὐτόν?"
[5]heaven [1]will [6]give *the* Spirit ˜ Holy to the *ones* asking Him?"
Father those who ask

A House Divided Cannot Stand
(Matt. 12:22–30; Mark 3:20–27)

14 Καὶ ἦν ἐκβάλλων δαιμόνιον, καὶ αὐτὸ ἦν κωφόν.
And He was casting out a demon, and it was mute.

Ἐγένετο δέ, τοῦ δαιμονίου ἐξελθόντος, ἐλάλησεν ὁ
[2]it [3]happened [1]But, the demon having come out, [3]spoke [1]the
when the demon came

κωφός. Καὶ ἐθαύμασαν οἱ ὄχλοι. 15 Τινὲς δὲ ἐξ αὐτῶν
[2]mute. And [3]marveled [1]the [2]crowds. some ˜ But of them

εἶπον, "Ἐν Βεελζεβοὺλ ἄρχοντι τῶν δαιμονίων ἐκβάλλει τὰ
said, "By Beelzebul *the* ruler of the demons He casts out -

δαιμόνια." 16 Ἕτεροι δὲ πειράζοντες σημεῖον παρ' αὐτοῦ
demons." others ˜ But testing *Him* [5]a [6]sign [3]from [4]Him

ἐζήτουν ἐξ οὐρανοῦ.
[1]were [2]seeking from heaven.

I cannot rise and give to you'?
8 "I say to you, though he will not rise and give to him because he is his friend, yet because of his persistence he will rise and give him as many as he needs.
9 "So I say to you, ask, and it will be given to you; seek, and you will find; knock, and it will be opened to you.
10 "For everyone who asks receives, and he who seeks finds, and to him who knocks it will be opened.
11 "If a son asks for bread from any father among you, will he give him a stone? Or if *he asks* for a fish, will he give him a serpent instead of a fish?
12 "Or if he asks for an egg, will he offer him a scorpion?
13 "If you then, being evil, know how to give good gifts to your children, how much more will *your* heavenly Father give the Holy Spirit to those who ask Him!"
14 And He was casting out a demon, and it was mute. So it was, when the demon had gone out, that the mute spoke; and the multitudes marveled.
15 But some of them said, "He casts out demons by Beelzebub, the ruler of the demons."
16 Others, testing *Him,* sought from Him a sign from heaven.

---

[e] **(11:11)** NU omits αρτον μη λιθον επιδωσει αυτω η και, *bread not a stone he will give him? Or also.*
[f] **(11:11)** NU reads και, *and.*
[g] **(11:12)** NU omits μη, *not.*

17 But He, knowing their thoughts, said to them: "Every kingdom divided against itself is brought to desolation, and a house *divided* against a house falls.

18 "If Satan also is divided against himself, how will his kingdom stand? Because you say I cast out demons by Beelzebub.

19 "And if I cast out demons by Beelzebub, by whom do your sons cast *them* out? Therefore they will be your judges.

20 "But if I cast out demons with the finger of God, surely the kingdom of God has come upon you.

21 "When a strong man, fully armed, guards his own palace, his goods are in peace.

22 "But when a stronger than he comes upon him and overcomes him, he takes from him all his armor in which he trusted, and divides his spoils.

23 "He who is not with Me is against Me, and he who does not gather with Me scatters.

24 "When an unclean spirit goes out of a man, he goes through dry places, seeking rest; and finding none, he says, 'I will return to my house from which I came.'

25 "And when he comes, he finds *it* swept and put in order.

26 "Then he goes and takes with *him* seven other spirits more wicked than himself, and they enter and dwell there; and

17 Αὐτὸς δὲ εἰδὼς αὐτῶν τὰ διανοήματα εἶπεν αὐτοῖς,
He ˜ But knowing their - thoughts said to them,

"Πᾶσα βασιλεία ἐφ' ἑαυτὴν διαμερισθεῖσα ἐρημοῦται,
"Every kingdom [2]against [3]itself [1]divided is made desolate,

καὶ οἶκος ἐπὶ οἶκον πίπτει. **18** Εἰ δὲ καὶ ὁ Σατανᾶς
and a house *divided* against a house falls. if ˜ And also - Satan

ἐφ' ἑαυτὸν διεμερίσθη, πῶς σταθήσεται ἡ βασιλεία αὐτοῦ?
[3]against [4]himself [1]is [2]divided, how [1]will [4]stand - [3]kingdom [2]his?

Ὅτι λέγετε ἐν Βεελζεβοὺλ ἐκβάλλειν με τὰ δαιμόνια.
Because you say *that* by Beelzebul to cast out Me - demons.
I cast out

19 Εἰ δὲ ἐγὼ ἐν Βεελζεβοὺλ ἐκβάλλω τὰ δαιμόνια, οἱ υἱοὶ
if ˜ But I by Beelzebul cast out - demons, - [5]sons

ὑμῶν ἐν τίνι ἐκβάλλουσι? Διὰ τοῦτο κριταὶ ὑμῶν
[4]your [1]by [2]whom [3]do [6]cast [7]*them* [8]out? On account of this [5]judges [4]your
Therefore

αὐτοὶ ἔσονται. **20** Εἰ δὲ ἐν δακτύλῳ Θεοῦ ἐκβάλλω τὰ
[1]they [2]will [3]be. if ˜ But by *the* finger of God I cast out -

δαιμόνια, ἄρα ἔφθασεν ἐφ' ὑμᾶς ἡ βασιλεία τοῦ Θεοῦ.
demons, then [5]came [6]upon [7]you [1]the [2]kingdom - [3]of [4]God.
has come

21 Ὅταν ὁ ἰσχυρὸς καθωπλισμένος φυλάσσῃ τὴν ἑαυτοῦ
When the strong *man* being fully armed guards the [2]of [3]himself
a his own

αὐλήν, ἐν εἰρήνῃ ἐστὶ τὰ ὑπάρχοντα αὐτοῦ. **22** Ἐπὰν
[1]palace, [9]in [10]peace [8]are [4]the [5]*things* [6]being [7]his. when ˜
his possessions.

δὲ ὁ ἰσχυρότερος αὐτοῦ ἐπελθὼν νικήσῃ αὐτόν,
But the *one* stronger *than* him comes upon *him* he overcomes him,
a stronger one he

τὴν πανοπλίαν αὐτοῦ αἴρει ἐφ' ᾗ ἐπεποίθει, καὶ
- [5]full [6]armor [4]his [1]he [2]takes [3]away in which he had trusted, and

τὰ σκῦλα αὐτοῦ διαδίδωσιν. **23** Ὁ μὴ ὢν μετ' ἐμοῦ
- [4]spoils [3]his [1]he [2]distributes. The *one* not being with Me
He who is not

κατ' ἐμοῦ ἐστι, καὶ ὁ μὴ συνάγων μετ' ἐμοῦ σκορπίζει.
[2]against [3]Me [1]is, and the *one* not gathering with Me scatters.
he who does not gather

An Unclean Spirit Returns
(Matt. 12:43–45)

24 "Ὅταν τὸ ἀκάθαρτον πνεῦμα ἐξέλθῃ ἀπὸ τοῦ ἀνθρώπου,
"When the unclean spirit goes out from the man,
an a

διέρχεται δι' ἀνύδρων τόπων, ζητοῦν ἀνάπαυσιν· καὶ μὴ
he goes through waterless places, seeking rest; and not

εὑρίσκον λέγει, 'Ὑποστρέψω εἰς τὸν οἶκόν μου ὅθεν
finding *any* he says, 'I will return to - house ˜ my from where

ἐξῆλθον.' **25** Καὶ ἐλθὸν εὑρίσκει σεσαρωμένον καὶ
I came out.' And coming he finds *it* swept and
he comes and

κεκοσμημένον. **26** Τότε πορεύεται καὶ παραλαμβάνει ἑπτὰ
put in order. Then he goes and takes along seven

ἕτερα πνεύματα πονηρότερα ἑαυτοῦ, καὶ ἐλθόντα κατοικεῖ
other spirits more evil *than* himself, and coming they dwell
they come and

ἐκεῖ· καὶ γίνεται τὰ ἔσχατα τοῦ ἀνθρώπου ἐκείνου χείρονα
there; and [7]become [1]the [2]last [3]*things* - [4]of [6]man [5]that worse *than*
last state

τῶν πρώτων."
the first *things*."
first state."

Jesus Blesses the Doers of the Word

27 Ἐγένετο δὲ ἐν τῷ λέγειν αὐτὸν ταῦτα,
[2]it [3]happened [1]Now in - [2]to [3]speak [1]Him these *things*,
while He spoke

ἐπάρασά τις γυνὴ φωνὴν ἐκ τοῦ ὄχλου εἶπεν αὐτῷ,
[7]raising [1]a [2]certain [3]woman [8]*her* [9]voice [4]from [5]the [6]crowd said to Him,

"Μακαρία ἡ κοιλία ἡ βαστάσασά σε καὶ μαστοὶ οὓς
"Blessed *is* the womb the *one* having borne You and *the* breasts which
which bore

ἐθήλασας!"
You sucked!"

28 Αὐτὸς δὲ εἶπε, "Μενοῦν γε μακάριοι οἱ ἀκούοντες
He ˜ But said, "rather ˜ Blessed *are* the *ones* hearing
those who hear

τὸν λόγον τοῦ Θεοῦ καὶ φυλάσσοντες αὐτόν!"
the word - of God and guarding it!"
who obey

The Pharisees Seek a Sign

(Matt. 12:38–42; Mark 8:11, 12)

29 Τῶν δὲ ὄχλων ἐπαθροιζομένων, ἤρξατο λέγειν, "Ἡ
the ˜ Now crowds gathering even more, He began to say, -
Now as the crowds gathered

γενεὰ αὕτη[h] πονηρά ἐστι. Σημεῖον ἐπιζητεῖ, καὶ σημεῖον
"generation ˜ This evil ˜ is. [3]a [4]sign [1]It [2]seeks, and a sign

οὐ δοθήσεται αὐτῇ εἰ μὴ τὸ σημεῖον Ἰωνᾶ τοῦ
not ˜ will be given to it if not the sign of Jonah the
except

προφήτου.[i] **30** Καθὼς γὰρ ἐγένετο Ἰωνᾶς σημεῖον τοῖς
prophet. [2]just [3]as [1]For [5]became [4]Jonah a sign to the

Νινευίταις, οὕτως ἔσται καὶ ὁ Υἱὸς τοῦ Ἀνθρώπου τῇ
Ninevites, so [2]will [7]be [1]also [3]the [4]Son - [5]of [6]Man -

γενεᾷ ταύτῃ. **31** Βασίλισσα νότου ἐγερθήσεται ἐν
to generation ˜ this. *The* queen of *the* South will be raised in

τῇ κρίσει μετὰ τῶν ἀνδρῶν τῆς γενεᾶς ταύτης καὶ
the judgment with the men - of generation ˜ this and

κατακρινεῖ αὐτούς, ὅτι ἦλθεν ἐκ τῶν περάτων τῆς
she will condemn them, because she came from the ends of the

γῆς ἀκοῦσαι τὴν σοφίαν Σολομῶνος· καὶ ἰδού, πλεῖον
earth to hear the wisdom of Solomon; and see, more *than*

Σολομῶνος ὧδε. **32** Ἄνδρες Νινευὴ ἀναστήσονται ἐν τῇ
Solomon *is* here. *The* men of Nineveh will rise up in the

κρίσει μετὰ τῆς γενεᾶς ταύτης καὶ κατακρινοῦσιν αὐτήν,
judgment with - generation ˜ this and they will condemn it,

ὅτι μετενόησαν εἰς τὸ κήρυγμα Ἰωνᾶ· καὶ ἰδού, πλεῖον
because they repented at the proclamation of Jonah; and see, more *than*
preaching

Ἰωνᾶ ὧδε.
Jonah *is* here.

the last *state* of that man is worse than the first."
27 And it happened, as He spoke these things, that a certain woman from the crowd raised her voice and said to Him, "Blessed *is* the womb that bore You, and *the* breasts which nursed You!"
28 But He said, "More than that, blessed *are* those who hear the word of God and keep it!"
29 And while the crowds were thickly gathered together, He began to say, "This is an evil generation. It seeks a sign, and no sign will be given to it except the sign of Jonah the prophet.
30 "For as Jonah became a sign to the Ninevites, so also the Son of Man will be to this generation.
31 "The queen of the South will rise up in the judgment with the men of this generation and condemn them, for she came from the ends of the earth to hear the wisdom of Solomon; and indeed a greater than Solomon *is* here.
32 "The men of Nineveh will rise up in the judgment with this generation and condemn it, for they repented at the preaching of Jonah; and indeed a greater than Jonah *is* here.

---

[h](**11:29**) NU adds γενεα, *generation.*
[i](**11:29**) NU omits του προφητου, *the prophet.*

33 "No one, when he has lit a lamp, puts *it* in a secret place or under a basket, but on a lampstand, that those who come in may see the light.
34 "The lamp of the body is the eye. Therefore, when your eye is good, your whole body also is full of light. But when *your eye* is bad, your body also *is* full of darkness.
35 "Therefore take heed that the light which is in you is not darkness.
36 "If then your whole body *is* full of light, having no part dark, *the* whole *body* will be full of light, as when the bright shining of a lamp gives you light."
37 And as He spoke, a certain Pharisee asked Him to dine with him. So He went in and sat down to eat.
38 When the Pharisee saw *it,* he marveled that He had not first washed before dinner.
39 Then the Lord said to him, "Now you Pharisees make the outside of the cup and dish clean, but your inward part is full of greed and wickedness.
40 "Foolish ones! Did not He who made the outside make the inside also?
41 "But rather give alms of such things as you have; then indeed all things are clean to you.
42 "But woe to you Pharisees! For you tithe mint and

The Lamp of the Body
(Matt. 5:15; 6:22, 23)

33 "Οὐδεὶς δὲ λύχνον ἅψας εἰς κρύπτην
"[2]no [3]one [1]And [6]a [7]lamp [4]having [5]lit [10]into [11]a [12]secret [13]place

τίθησιν οὐδὲ ὑπὸ τὸν μόδιον, ἀλλ' ἐπὶ τὴν λυχνίαν, ἵνα
[8]puts [9]*it* or under the (a) peck-measure (bushel basket), but on the lampstand, so that

οἱ εἰσπορευόμενοι τὸ φέγγος βλέπωσιν. **34** Ὁ λύχνος
the *ones* (those) entering (who come in) [3]the [4]light [1]may [2]see. The lamp

τοῦ σώματός ἐστιν ὁ ὀφθαλμός.[j] Ὅταν οὖν ὁ
of the body is the eye. when ˜ Therefore -

ὀφθαλμός σου ἁπλοῦς* ᾖ καὶ ὅλον τὸ σῶμά σου φωτεινόν
eye ˜ your clear ˜ (sound) is [4]also [2]whole - [3]body [1]your [6]full [7]of [8]light

ἐστιν. Ἐπὰν δὲ πονηρὸς ᾖ, καὶ τὸ σῶμά σου σκοτεινόν.
[5]is. when ˜ But [3]evil (unsound) [1]it [2]is, [6]also - [5]body [4]your *is* dark.

35 Σκόπει οὖν μὴ τὸ φῶς τὸ ἐν σοὶ σκότος ἐστίν.
[2]take [3]heed [1]Therefore lest the light the *one* (which is) in you darkness ˜ is (be).

36 Εἰ οὖν τὸ σῶμά σου ὅλον φωτεινόν, μὴ ἔχον τι
if ˜ Therefore - [3]body [1]your [2]whole *is* full of light, not having any

μέρος σκοτεινόν, ἔσται φωτεινὸν ὅλον, ὡς ὅταν ὁ
part dark, [3]will [4]be [5]full [6]of [7]light [1]*the* [2]whole, as when the (a)

λύχνος τῇ ἀστραπῇ φωτίζῃ σε."
lamp by the (its) shining gives light to you."

Jesus Pronounces Woes on the Pharisees and Lawyers
(Matt. 23:1–36; Mark 12:38–40; Luke 20:45–47)

37 Ἐν δὲ τῷ λαλῆσαι, ἠρώτα αὐτὸν Φαρισαῖός τις[k] ὅπως
in ˜ And - to speak (And as He spoke), [4]asked [5]Him [1]a [3]Pharisee [2]certain that

ἀριστήσῃ παρ' αὐτῷ. Εἰσελθὼν δὲ ἀνέπεσεν.
He would eat with him. [2]having [3]entered [1]And He reclined *to eat.*

38 Ὁ δὲ Φαρισαῖος ἰδὼν ἐθαύμασεν ὅτι οὐ πρῶτον
the ˜ But Pharisee seeing marveled because [3]not [4]first (He did not)

ἐβαπτίσθη πρὸ τοῦ ἀρίστου.
[1]He [2]was [5]washed (first wash) before the meal.

39 Εἶπε δὲ ὁ Κύριος πρὸς αὐτόν, "Νῦν ὑμεῖς οἱ
[4]said [1]And [2]the [3]Lord to him, "Now you -

Φαρισαῖοι τὸ ἔξωθεν τοῦ ποτηρίου καὶ τοῦ πίνακος
Pharisees [2]the [3]outside [4]of [5]the [6]cup [7]and [8]of [9]the [10]dish

καθαρίζετε, τὸ δὲ ἔσωθεν ὑμῶν γέμει ἁρπαγῆς καὶ πονηρίας.
[1]clean, the ˜ but inside of you is full of greed and evil.

40 Ἄφρονες! Οὐχ ὁ ποιήσας τὸ ἔξωθεν καὶ τὸ
Fools! [2]not [3]the [4]*One* (He who) [5]making (made) [6]the [7]outside [8]also [10]the

ἔσωθεν ἐποίησε? **41** Πλὴν τὰ ἐνόντα δότε
[11]inside [1]Did [9]make? Nevertheless [2]the [3]*things* (what is) [4]being [5]inside (inside) [1]give

ἐλεημοσύνην· καὶ ἰδού, πάντα καθαρὰ ὑμῖν ἐστιν.
as alms; and see, all *things* [2]clean [3]to [4]you [1]are.

42 "Ἀλλ' οὐαὶ ὑμῖν τοῖς Φαρισαίοις! Ὅτι ἀποδεκατοῦτε
"But woe to you - Pharisees! Because you pay a tithe of

---

j(11:34) NU adds σου, *your.*
k(11:37) NU omits τις, *certain.*

*(11:34) ἁπλοῦς *(haplous).* Adjective, used only here and in the parallel Matt. 6:22, meaning *simple, single,* also *pure* or *sincere.* When modifying the word *eye,* as here, it apparently means *clear, sound, healthy,* resulting from the idea of openness implicit in the root meaning. Some think it indicates a "singleness of purpose" that keeps one from having double-mindedness and a divided heart. Cf. the cognate noun ἁπλότης, which can mean either *simplicity, sincerity* (as 2 Cor. 11:3; Eph. 6:5) or *generosity, liberality* (as 2 Cor. 8:2; 9:11)—apparently from the idea of openhandedness. Cf. also the adverb ἁπλῶς,

τὸ ἡδύοσμον καὶ τὸ πήγανον καὶ πᾶν λάχανον, καὶ
\- mint and - rue and every vegetable, and

παρέρχεσθε τὴν κρίσιν καὶ τὴν ἀγάπην τοῦ Θεοῦ. Ταῦτα
you pass by - judgment and the love - of God. These *things*
justice

ἔδει ποιῆσαι κακεῖνα μὴ ἀφιέναι.
it was necessary *for you* to do and [4]those [5]*things* [1]not [2]to [3]leave [6]*undone.*

43 "Οὐαὶ ὑμῖν τοῖς Φαρισαίοις! Ὅτι ἀγαπᾶτε τὴν
"Woe to you - Pharisees! Because you love the

πρωτοκαθεδρίαν ἐν ταῖς συναγωγαῖς καὶ τοὺς ἀσπασμοὺς ἐν
first seat in the synagogues and - greetings in
best

ταῖς ἀγοραῖς.
the marketplaces.

44 "Οὐαὶ ὑμῖν, γραμματεῖς καὶ Φαρισαῖοι, ὑποκριταί![l]
"Woe to you, scribes and Pharisees, hypocrites!

Ὅτι ἐστὲ ὡς τὰ μνημεῖα τὰ ἄδηλα, καὶ οἱ ἄνθρωποι
Because you are like - graves ˜ - unseen, and the men
unmarked,

περιπατοῦντες ἐπάνω οὐκ οἴδασιν."
walking over *them* not ˜ do know *it.*"

45 Ἀποκριθεὶς δέ τις τῶν νομικῶν* λέγει αὐτῷ,
[6]answering [1]And [2]one [3]of [4]the [5]lawyers [7]says to Him,
said

"Διδάσκαλε, ταῦτα λέγων καὶ ἡμᾶς ὑβρίζεις."
"Teacher, [2]these [3]*things* [1]saying [5]also [7]us [4]You [6]insult."
by saying

46 Ὁ δὲ εἶπε, "Καὶ ὑμῖν τοῖς νομικοῖς οὐαί! Ὅτι
[2]the [3]*One* [1]But said, "And to you - lawyers woe! Because
He

φορτίζετε τοὺς ἀνθρώπους φορτία δυσβάστακτα, καὶ αὐτοὶ
you load - men *with* burdens hard to bear, and [2]yourselves

ἑνὶ τῶν δακτύλων ὑμῶν οὐ προσψαύετε τοῖς φορτίοις.
[8]with [9]one - [10]of [12]fingers [11]your [4]not [1]you [3]do [5]touch [6]the [7]burdens.

47 "Οὐαὶ ὑμῖν! Ὅτι οἰκοδομεῖτε τὰ μνημεῖα τῶν
"Woe to you! Because you build the tombs of the

προφητῶν, οἱ δὲ πατέρες ὑμῶν ἀπέκτειναν αὐτούς.
prophets, - and fathers ˜ your killed them.

48 Ἄρα μάρτυρεῖτε[m] καὶ συνευδοκεῖτε τοῖς ἔργοις
Consequently you bear witness to and approve of the deeds

τῶν πατέρων ὑμῶν· ὅτι αὐτοὶ μὲν ἀπέκτειναν αὐτούς,
\- of fathers ˜ your; because they indeed killed them,
to be sure

ὑμεῖς δὲ οἰκοδομεῖτε αὐτῶν τὰ μνημεῖα.[n] 49 Διὰ τοῦτο
you ˜ but build their - tombs. Because of this
Therefore

καὶ ἡ σοφία τοῦ Θεοῦ εἶπεν, 'Ἀποστελῶ εἰς αὐτοὺς
also the wisdom - of God said, 'I will send to them

προφήτας καὶ ἀποστόλους, καὶ ἐξ αὐτῶν ἀποκτενοῦσι καὶ
prophets and apostles, and *some* of them they will kill and

ἐκδιώξουσιν,' 50 ἵνα ἐκζητηθῇ τὸ αἷμα πάντων
they will persecute,' so that [17]may [18]be [19]required [1]the [2]blood [3]of [4]all

τῶν προφητῶν τὸ ἐκχυνόμενον ἀπὸ καταβολῆς
[5]the [6]prophets [7]the [8]*blood* [9]being [10]shed [11]from [12]*the* [13]foundation
which was

κόσμου ἀπὸ τῆς γενεᾶς ταύτης, 51 ἀπὸ τοῦ αἵματος
[14]of [15]*the* [16]world from - generation ˜ this, from the blood

rue and all manner of herbs, and pass by justice and the love of God. These you ought to have done, without leaving the others undone.
43 "Woe to you Pharisees! For you love the best seats in the synagogues and greetings in the marketplaces.
44 "Woe to you, scribes and Pharisees, hypocrites! For you are like graves which are not seen, and the men who walk over *them* are not aware *of them.*"
45 Then one of the lawyers answered and said to Him, "Teacher, by saying these things You reproach us also."
46 And He said, "Woe to you also, lawyers! For you load men with burdens hard to bear, and you yourselves do not touch the burdens with one of your fingers.
47 "Woe to you! For you build the tombs of the prophets, and your fathers killed them.
48 "In fact, you bear witness that you approve the deeds of your fathers; for they indeed killed them, and you build their tombs.
49 "Therefore the wisdom of God also said, 'I will send them prophets and apostles, and *some* of them they will kill and persecute,'
50 "that the blood of all the prophets which was shed from the foundation of the world may be required of this generation,
51 "from the blood of Abel to

---

[l]**(11:44)** NU omits *γραμματεις και Φαρισαιοι, υποκριται, scribes and Pharisees, hypocrites.*
[m]**(11:48)** NU reads *μαρτυρες εστε, you are witnesses.*
[n]**(11:48)** NU omits *αυτων τα μνηεια, their tombs.*

used only in James 1:5 with the meaning *generously, liberally.*

***(11:45)** *νομικός (nomikos).* Adjective meaning *pertaining to the law,* but used this way only in Titus 3:9. Elsewhere it is used substantivally to mean *one learned in the law, lawyer.* In this sense it identifies Zenas (Titus 3:13) who might have been an expert in Jewish or Roman law, but mostly refers to the Jewish *lawyers* (Matt. 22:35), mentioned together with the Pharisees (Luke 7:30; 14:3). These were scholars devoted to the

the blood of Zechariah who perished between the altar and the temple. Yes, I say to you, it shall be required of this generation.

52 "Woe to you lawyers! For you have taken away the key of knowledge. You did not enter in yourselves, and those who were entering in you hindered."

53 And as He said these things to them, the scribes and the Pharisees began to assail *Him* vehemently, and to cross-examine Him about many things,

54 lying in wait for Him, and seeking to catch Him in something He might say, that they might accuse Him.

12 In the meantime, when an innumerable multitude of people had gathered together, so that they trampled one another, He began to say to His disciples first *of all,* "Beware of the leaven of the Pharisees, which is hypocrisy.

2 "For there is nothing covered that will not be revealed, nor hidden that will not be known.

3 "Therefore whatever you have spoken in the dark will be heard in the light, and what you have spoken in the ear in inner rooms will be proclaimed on the housetops.

῎Αβελ ἕως τοῦ αἵματος Ζαχαρίου τοῦ ἀπολομένου μεταξὺ
of Abel to the blood of Zechariah the *one* perishing between
who perished

τοῦ θυσιαστηρίου καὶ τοῦ οἴκου. Ναί, λέγω ὑμῖν,
the altar and the house. Yes, I say to you,
temple.

ἐκζητηθήσεται ἀπὸ τῆς γενεᾶς ταύτης.
it will be required from - generation ˜ this.

52 "Οὐαὶ ὑμῖν τοῖς νομικοῖς, ὅτι ἤρατε τὴν κλεῖδα
"Woe to you - lawyers, because you took away the key
have taken

τῆς γνώσεως. Αὐτοὶ οὐκ εἰσήλθετε, καὶ τοὺς
- of knowledge. [2]yourselves [4]not [1]You [3]did [5]enter [6]in, and the *ones*
those who

εἰσερχομένους ἐκωλύσατε."
entering in you hindered."
were entering in

53 Λέγοντος δὲ αὐτοῦ ταῦτα πρὸς αὐτούς,[o] ἤρξαντο
saying And Him these *things* to them, [6]began
And as He said

οἱ γραμματεῖς καὶ οἱ Φαρισαῖοι δεινῶς ἐνέχειν καὶ
[1]the [2]scribes [3]and [4]the [5]Pharisees [9]dreadfully [7]to [8]be [10]hostile and

ἀποστοματίζειν αὐτὸν περὶ πλειόνων, 54 ἐνεδρεύοντες αὐτόν,
to cross-examine Him about many *things,* lying in wait for Him,

ζητοῦντες[p] θηρεῦσαί τι ἐκ τοῦ στόματος αὐτοῦ
seeking to catch something out of - mouth ˜ His
Him in something He might say

ἵνα κατηγορήσωσιν αὐτοῦ.[q]
so that they might accuse Him.

Beware of Pharisaical Hypocrisy
(Matt. 10:26, 27)

12 1 Ἐν οἷς ἐπισυναχθεισῶν τῶν μυριάδων
In which *things* being gathered together the myriads
When the crowd's uncounted thousands had gathered

τοῦ ὄχλου, ὥστε καταπατεῖν ἀλλήλους, ἤρξατο
of the crowd, so that to tread one another, He began
together, they were stepping on

λέγειν πρὸς τοὺς μαθητὰς αὐτοῦ πρῶτον, "Προσέχετε
to say to - disciples ˜ His first, "Take heed

ἑαυτοῖς ἀπὸ τῆς ζύμης τῶν Φαρισαίων, ἥτις ἐστὶν
to yourselves from the leaven of the Pharisees, which is
because of

ὑπόκρισις. 2 Οὐδὲν δὲ συγκεκαλυμμένον ἐστὶν ὃ οὐκ
hypocrisy. [4]nothing [1]But [5]concealed [2]*there* [3]is which not ˜

ἀποκαλυφθήσεται, καὶ κρυπτὸν ὃ οὐ γνωσθήσεται.
will be revealed, and *nothing* secret which not ˜ will be known.

3 Ἀνθ' ὧν ὅσα ἐν τῇ σκοτίᾳ εἴπατε
In return for which *things* as many *things* as [3]in [4]the [5]dark [1]you [2]said
Therefore have spoken

ἐν τῷ φωτὶ ἀκουσθήσεται, καὶ ὃ πρὸς τὸ οὖς ἐλαλήσατε
[9]in [10]the [11]light [6]will [7]be [8]heard, and what [3]in [4]the [5]ear [1]you [2]spoke
have spoken

ἐν τοῖς ταμείοις* κηρυχθήσεται ἐπὶ τῶν δωμάτων.
in - secret rooms will be proclaimed on the housetops.
behind closed doors

---

[o](11:53) For Λεγοντος δε αυτου ταυτα προς αυτους, *And as He said these things to them,* NU reads Κακειθεν εξελθοντος αυτου, *And when He left there.*
[p](11:54) NU omits ζητουντες, *seeking.*
[q](11:54) NU omits ινα κατηγορησωσιν αυτου, *so that they might accuse Him.*

mastery of Mosaic and rabbinic law, especially its ethical application. The NT associates them with the scribes and Pharisees.

***(12:3)** *ταμεῖον (tameion).* Noun originally meaning a *storeroom* (as Luke 12:24), then an *inner room* or *secret room* (as here; cf. Matt. 24:26). As a room into which someone typically goes to pray in private (Matt. 6:6), it reflects the idea of an inside room (but not a modern "closet") that could be closed off and thus escape notice. The ταμεῖον implies a contrast with the public, open place.

Jesus Teaches the Fear of God
(Matt. 10:28–31)

4 “Λέγω δὲ ὑμῖν τοῖς φίλοις μου, μὴ φοβηθῆτε ἀπὸ
“[2]I [3]say [1]And to you - friends ~ My, not ~ do be afraid of

τῶν ἀποκτενόντων τὸ σῶμα καὶ μετὰ ταῦτα μὴ ἐχόντων
the *ones* killing the body and after these *things* not having
those who kill do not have

περισσότερόν τι ποιῆσαι. 5 Ὑποδείξω δὲ ὑμῖν τίνα
further ~ anything to do. [2]I [3]will [4]show [1]But you whom

φοβηθῆτε· φοβήθητε τὸν μετὰ τὸ ἀποκτεῖναι ἐξουσίαν
you should fear; fear the *One* after - to kill authority ~
Him who after He kills has

ἔχοντα ἐμβαλεῖν εἰς τὴν Γέενναν· ναί, λέγω ὑμῖν, τοῦτον
having to cast into - Gehenna; yes, I say to you, [2]this [3]*One*
authority hell;

φοβήθητε! 6 Οὐχὶ πέντε στρουθία πωλεῖται ἀσσαρίων δύο?
[1]fear! [2]not [3]five [4]sparrows [1]Are sold *for* assaria ~ two?
two copper coins?

Καὶ ἓν ἐξ αὐτῶν οὐκ ἔστιν ἐπιλελησμένον ἐνώπιον τοῦ Θεοῦ.
And one of them not ~ is forgotten before - God.

7 Ἀλλὰ καὶ αἱ τρίχες τῆς κεφαλῆς ὑμῶν πᾶσαι ἠρίθμηνται.
But even [2]the [3]hairs - [4]of [6]head [5]your [1]all are numbered.

Μὴ οὖν φοβεῖσθε· πολλῶν στρουθίων
[3]not [1]Therefore [2]do [4]fear; [10]many [11]sparrows

διαφέρετε.
[5]you [6]are [7]worth [8]more [9]than.

Confess Christ Before Men
(Matt. 10:32, 33)

8 “Λέγω δὲ ὑμῖν, πᾶς ὃς ἂν ὁμολογήσῃ ἐν ἐμοὶ
“[2]I [3]say [1]And to you, every*one* who - confesses - Me

ἔμπροσθεν τῶν ἀνθρώπων, καὶ ὁ Υἱὸς τοῦ Ἀνθρώπου
before - men, [5]also [1]the [2]Son [3]of [4]Man

ὁμολογήσει ἐν αὐτῷ ἔμπροσθεν τῶν ἀγγέλων τοῦ Θεοῦ.
will confess - him before the angels - of God.

9 Ὁ δὲ ἀρνησάμενός με ἐνώπιον τῶν ἀνθρώπων
[2]the [3]*one* [1]But denying Me before - men
he who denies

ἀπαρνηθήσεται ἐνώπιον τῶν ἀγγέλων τοῦ Θεοῦ. 10 Καὶ
will be denied before the angels - of God. And

πᾶς ὃς ἐρεῖ λόγον εἰς τὸν Υἱὸν τοῦ Ἀνθρώπου,
every*one* who shall speak a word against the Son - of Man,

ἀφεθήσεται αὐτῷ· τῷ δὲ εἰς τὸ Ἅγιον Πνεῦμα
it will be forgiven him; [2]to [3]the [4]*one* [1]but [6]against [7]the [8]Holy [9]Spirit
to him who

βλασφημήσαντι οὐκ ἀφεθήσεται. 11 Ὅταν δὲ
[5]blaspheming [12]not [10]it [11]will be forgiven. whenever ~ And
blasphemes

προσφέρωσιν ὑμᾶς ἐπὶ τὰς συναγωγὰς καὶ τὰς ἀρχὰς καὶ
they bring you before - synagogues and - rulers and

τὰς ἐξουσίας, μὴ μεριμνᾶτε πῶς ἢ τί ἀπολογήσησθε, ἢ
- authorities, not ~ do worry how or what you should answer, or

τί εἴπητε. 12 Τὸ γὰρ Ἅγιον Πνεῦμα διδάξει ὑμᾶς ἐν
what you should say. the ~ For Holy Spirit will teach you in

αὐτῇ τῇ ὥρᾳ ἃ δεῖ εἰπεῖν.”
very ~ the hour the *things* which it is necessary to say.”
that what you must say.”

4 “And I say to you, My friends, do not be afraid of those who kill the body, and after that have no more that they can do.
5 “But I will show you whom you should fear: Fear Him who, after He has killed, has power to cast into hell; yes, I say to you, fear Him!
6 “Are not five sparrows sold for two copper coins? And not one of them is forgotten before God.
7 “But the very hairs of your head are all numbered. Do not fear therefore; you are of more value than many sparrows.
8 “Also I say to you, whoever confesses Me before men, him the Son of Man also will confess before the angels of God.
9 “But he who denies Me before men will be denied before the angels of God.
10 “And anyone who speaks a word against the Son of Man, it will be forgiven him; but to him who blasphemes against the Holy Spirit, it will not be forgiven.
11 “Now when they bring you to the synagogues and magistrates and authorities, do not worry about how or what you should answer, or what you should say.
12 “For the Holy Spirit will teach you in that very hour what you ought to say.”

13 Then one from the crowd
said to Him, "Teacher, tell my
brother to divide the inheritance with me."
14 But He said to him, "Man,
who made Me a judge or an arbitrator over you?"
15 And He said to them,
"Take heed and beware of covetousness, for one's life does
not consist in the abundance of
the things he possesses."
16 Then He spoke a parable to
them, saying: "The ground of a
certain rich man yielded plenti-
fully.
17 "And he thought within
himself, saying, 'What shall I
do, since I have no room to
store my crops?'
18 "So he said, 'I will do this:
I will pull down my barns and
build greater, and there I will
store all my crops and my
goods.
19 'And I will say to my soul,
"Soul, you have many goods
laid up for many years; take
your ease; eat, drink, *and* be
merry." '
20 "But God said to him,
'Fool! This night your soul will
be required of you; then whose
will those things be which you
have provided?'
21 "So *is* he who lays up treasure for himself, and is not rich
toward God."
22 Then He said to His disciples, "Therefore I say to you,
do not worry about your life,
what you will eat; nor about the

The Parable of the Rich Fool

13 Εἶπε δέ τις αὐτῷ ἐκ τοῦ ὄχλου, "Διδάσκαλε,
[6]said [1]And [2]someone [7]to [8]Him [3]from [4]the [5]crowd, "Teacher,

εἰπὲ τῷ ἀδελφῷ μου μερίσασθαι μετ' ἐμοῦ τὴν κληρονομίαν."
tell - brother ~ my to divide with me the inheritance."

14 Ὁ δὲ εἶπεν αὐτῷ, "Ἄνθρωπε, τίς με κατέστησε
[2]the [3]*One* [1]But said to him, "Man, who Me ~ appointed
He

δικαστὴν ἢ μεριστὴν ἐφ' ὑμᾶς?" **15** Εἶπε δὲ πρὸς αὐτούς,
a judge or a divider over you?" [2]He [3]said [1]And to them,
an arbitrator

"Ὁρᾶτε καὶ φυλάσσεσθε ἀπὸ τῆς[a] πλεονεξίας ὅτι οὐκ
"Take heed and be on guard from - covetousness because not
against no

ἐν τῷ περισσεύειν τινὶ ἡ ζωὴ αὐτῷ ἐστιν
in - to abound to anyone - life to him is
one's life consists of the abundance of his possessions."

ἐκ τῶν ὑπαρχόντων αὐτοῦ."
out of the *things* belonging of him."

16 Εἶπε δὲ παραβολὴν πρὸς αὐτούς, λέγων, "Ἀνθρώπου
[2]He [3]told [1]And a parable to them, saying, "[3]of [4]a [7]man

τινὸς πλουσίου εὐφόρησεν ἡ χώρα. **17** Καὶ διελογίζετο
[5]certain [6]rich [8]produced [9]well [1]The [2]field. And he reasoned

ἐν ἑαυτῷ λέγων, 'Τί ποιήσω, ὅτι οὐκ ἔχω ποῦ
within himself saying, 'What shall I do, because [3]not [1]I [2]do have anywhere

συνάξω τοὺς καρπούς μου?' **18** Καὶ εἶπε, 'Τοῦτο ποιήσω·
I may gather - fruits ~ my?' And he said, 'This I will do;
crops

καθελῶ μου τὰς ἀποθήκας καὶ μείζονας οἰκοδομήσω,
I will tear down my - barns and [4]greater [5]*ones* [1]I [2]will [3]build,
bigger

καὶ συνάξω ἐκεῖ πάντα τὰ γενήματά μου[b] καὶ τὰ
and I will gather there all - crops ~ my and -

ἀγαθά μου. **19** Καὶ ἐρῶ τῇ ψυχῇ μου, "Ψυχή, ἔχεις
[2]good [3]*things* [1]my. And I will say - to soul ~ my, "Soul, you have

πολλὰ ἀγαθὰ κείμενα εἰς ἔτη πολλά· ἀναπαύου, φάγε,
many good *things* laid away for years ~ many; relax, eat,

πίε, εὐφραίνου." ' **20** Εἶπε δὲ αὐτῷ ὁ Θεός, 'Ἄφρον, ταύτῃ
drink, enjoy yourself." ' [3]said [1]But [4]to [5]him - [2]God, 'Fool, this

τῇ νυκτὶ τὴν ψυχήν σου ἀπαιτοῦσιν ἀπὸ σοῦ·
- night - [5]life [4]your [1]they [2]will [3]demand from you;
your life will be demanded

ἃ δὲ ἡτοίμασας, τίνι ἔσται?' **21** Οὕτως
[6]*the* [7]*things* [8]which [1]and [9]you [10]prepared, [2]to [3]whom [4]will [5]be?' So *is*
who will have?'

ὁ θησαυρίζων ἑαυτῷ καὶ μὴ εἰς Θεὸν
the *one* treasuring up for himself and [2]not [4]toward [5]God
he who accumulates treasure

πλουτῶν."
[1]being [3]rich."
is

Do Not Worry
(Matt. 6:19–21, 25–34)

22 Εἶπε δὲ πρὸς τοὺς μαθητὰς αὐτοῦ, "Διὰ τοῦτο
[2]He [3]said [1]And to - disciples ~ His, "Because of this
"Therefore

ὑμῖν λέγω, μὴ μεριμνᾶτε τῇ ψυχῇ ὑμῶν, τί φάγητε·
[3]to [4]you [1]I [2]say, not ~ do worry about - life ~ your, what you will eat;

---

[a](12:15) NU reads *πασης*, *all*. [b](12:18) For *τα γενηματα μου*, *my crops*, NU reads *τον σιτον*, *the grain*.

μηδὲ τῷ σώματι, τί ἐνδύσησθε. 23 Ἡ ψυχὴ πλεῖόν ἐστι
nor about the body, what you will wear. - Life more ˜ is
your
τῆς τροφῆς, καὶ τὸ σῶμα τοῦ ἐνδύματος.
- *than* food, and the body *is more* - *than* clothing.
24 Κατανοήσατε τοὺς κόρακας, ὅτι οὐ σπείρουσιν οὐδὲ
Consider the ravens, because [3]not [1]they [2]do sow nor
θερίζουσιν, οἷς οὐκ ἔστι ταμεῖον οὐδὲ ἀποθήκη, καὶ ὁ
reap, to which not ˜ is storeroom nor barn, and -
which do not have
Θεὸς τρέφει αὐτούς. Πόσῳ μᾶλλον ὑμεῖς διαφέρετε τῶν
God feeds them. By how much rather you differ -
How much more are worth
πετεινῶν? 25 Τίς δὲ ἐξ ὑμῶν μεριμνῶν δύναται προσθεῖναι
than birds? which ˜ And of you *by* worrying is able to add
ἐπὶ τὴν ἡλικίαν αὐτοῦ πῆχυν ἕνα? [c] 26 Εἰ οὖν οὔτε
to - stature ˜ his cubit ˜ one? if ˜ Therefore not
you
ἐλάχιστον δύνασθε, τί περὶ τῶν λοιπῶν
the least *thing* you can *do*, why [4]about [5]the [6]remaining [7]*things*
cannot do a very little thing, rest
μεριμνᾶτε?
[1]do [2]you [3]worry?

27 "Κατανοήσατε τὰ κρίνα πῶς αὐξάνει· οὐ κοπιᾷ
"Consider the lilies how they grow; [3]not [1]they [2]do toil
οὐδὲ νήθει· λέγω δὲ ὑμῖν, οὐδὲ Σολομὼν ἐν πάσῃ τῇ δόξῃ
nor spin; [2]I [3]say [1]but to you, not even Solomon in all - glory ˜
αὐτοῦ περιεβάλετο ὡς ἓν τούτων. 28 Εἰ δὲ τὸν χόρτον ἐν τῷ
his was clothed like one of these. if ˜ But [4]the [5]grass [7]in [8]the
arrayed
ἀγρῷ σήμερον ὄντα, καὶ αὔριον εἰς κλίβανον
[9]field [10]today [6]being, [11]and [12]tomorrow [15]into [16]an [17]oven
although it is,
βαλλόμενον ὁ Θεὸς οὕτως ἀμφιέννυσι, πόσῳ μᾶλλον
[13]being [14]thrown - [1]God [2]so [3]clothes, by how much rather
is
ὑμᾶς, ὀλιγόπιστοι? 29 Καὶ ὑμεῖς μὴ ζητεῖτε τί
will He clothe you, *O you* of little faith? And you not ˜ do seek what
φάγητε ἢ τί πίητε, καὶ μὴ μετεωρίζεσθε.
you may eat or what you may drink, and not ˜ do be anxious.
30 Ταῦτα γὰρ πάντα τὰ ἔθνη τοῦ κόσμου ἐπιζητεῖ,
[3]these [4]*things* [1]For [2]all the nations of the world seek,
ὑμῶν δὲ ὁ Πατὴρ οἶδεν ὅτι χρῄζετε τούτων. 31 Πλὴν
your ˜ but - Father knows that you need these *things*. But
ζητεῖτε τὴν βασιλείαν τοῦ Θεοῦ, [d] καὶ ταῦτα πάντα [e]
seek the kingdom - of God, and [2]these [3]*things* [1]all
προστεθήσεται ὑμῖν.
will be added to you.

32 "Μὴ φοβοῦ, τὸ μικρὸν ποίμνιον, ὅτι εὐδόκησεν*
"not ˜ Do fear, - little flock, because [3]was [4]well [5]pleased
is
ὁ Πατὴρ ὑμῶν δοῦναι ὑμῖν τὴν βασιλείαν. 33 Πωλήσατε
- [2]Father [1]your to give to you the kingdom. Sell
τὰ ὑπάρχοντα ὑμῶν καὶ δότε ἐλεημοσύνην. Ποιήσατε
the *things* belonging of you and give alms. Make
your possessions
ἑαυτοῖς βαλάντια μὴ παλαιούμενα, θησαυρὸν
for yourselves money bags not becoming old, a(n) treasure ˜
which do not grow old,

body, what you will put on.
23 "Life is more than food, and the body *is more* than clothing.
24 "Consider the ravens, for they neither sow nor reap, which have neither storehouse nor barn; and God feeds them. Of how much more value are you than the birds?
25 "And which of you by worrying can add one cubit to his stature?
26 "If you then are not able to do *the* least, why are you anxious for the rest?
27 "Consider the lilies, how they grow: they neither toil nor spin; and yet I say to you, even Solomon in all his glory was not arrayed like one of these.
28 "If then God so clothes the grass, which today is in the field and tomorrow is thrown into the oven, how much more *will He clothe* you, O *you* of little faith?
29 "And do not seek what you should eat or what you should drink, nor have an anxious mind.
30 "For all these things the nations of the world seek after, and your Father knows that you need these things.
31 "But seek the kingdom of God, and all these things shall be added to you.
32 "Do not fear, little flock, for it is your Father's good pleasure to give you the kingdom.
33 "Sell what you have and give alms; provide yourselves money bags which do not grow

---

[c](**12:25**) NU omits *ενα, one.*
[d](**12:31**) For *του Θεου, of God,* NU reads *αυτου, His.*
[e](**12:31**) NU omits *παντα, all.*

***(12:32)** *εὐδοκέω (eudokeō).* Verb derived from *εὐ, good, well,* and *δοκέω, consider, think,* and meaning *to be well pleased.* The basic meaning is used in two ways: (1) *to think* or *consider it good* to do something; or (2) *to take pleasure* or *delight* in something or someone. The first usage is common in the papyri in legal documents, where it stresses the willingness of one's intentions concerning the good. Here in Luke 12:32 it shows the Father's willing resolve to grant the king-old, a treasure in the heavens that does not fail, where no thief approaches nor moth destroys.

34 "For where your treasure is, there your heart will be also.

35 "Let your waist be girded and *your* lamps burning;

36 "and you yourselves be like men who wait for their master, when he will return from the wedding, that when he comes and knocks they may open to him immediately.

37 "Blessed *are* those servants whom the master, when he comes, will find watching. Assuredly, I say to you that he will gird himself and have them sit down *to eat,* and will come and serve them.

38 "And if he should come in the second watch, or come in the third watch, and find *them* so, blessed are those servants.

39 "But know this, that if the master of the house had known what hour the thief would come, he would have watched and not allowed his house to be broken into.

40 "Therefore you also be ready, for the Son of Man is coming at an hour you do not expect."

41 Then Peter said to Him, "Lord, do You speak this parable *only* to us, or to all *people?*"

42 And the Lord said, "Who then is that faithful and wise

ἀνέκλειπτον ἐν τοῖς οὐρανοῖς, ὅπου κλέπτης οὐκ ἐγγίζει
unfailing in the heavens, where a thief not ~ does come near

οὐδὲ σὴς διαφθείρει. **34** Ὅπου γάρ ἐστιν ὁ θησαυρὸς
nor [2]a [3]moth [1]does destroy. where ~ For [3]is - [2]treasure

ὑμῶν, ἐκεῖ καὶ ἡ καρδία ὑμῶν ἔσται.
[1]your, there also - [4]heart [3]your [1]will [2]be.

The Faithful Servant and the Bad Servant
(Matt. 24:45–51)

35 "Ἔστωσαν ὑμῶν αἱ ὀσφύες περιεζωσμέναι καὶ οἱ
"[1]Let [4]be [2]your - [3]loins (waist) girded and the (your)

λύχνοι καιόμενοι, **36** καὶ ὑμεῖς ὅμοιοι ἀνθρώποις
lamps burning, and you *be* like men

προσδεχομένοις τὸν κύριον ἑαυτῶν, πότε ἀναλύσει ἐκ
waiting for the master ~ of themselves (their master), when he will return from

τῶν γάμων, ἵνα ἐλθόντος καὶ κρούσαντος,
the wedding celebration, so that coming (when he comes) and knocking (and knocks),

εὐθέως ἀνοίξωσιν αὐτῷ. **37** Μακάριοι οἱ δοῦλοι ἐκεῖνοι,
immediately they may open to him. Blessed *are* - slaves ~ (servants) those,

οὓς ἐλθὼν ὁ κύριος εὑρήσει γρηγοροῦντας. Ἀμὴν
whom coming (when he comes) the master will find watching. Amen (Assuredly)

λέγω ὑμῖν ὅτι περιζώσεται καὶ ἀνακλινεῖ αὐτούς,
I say to you that he will gird himself and [1]have [3]recline [4]*to* [5]*eat* [2]them,

καὶ παρελθὼν διακονήσει αὐτοῖς. **38** Καὶ ἐὰν ἔλθη[f] ἐν
and coming alongside (he will come) he will (and) serve them. And if he comes in

τῇ δευτέρᾳ φυλακῇ,[g] καὶ ἐν τῇ τρίτῃ φυλακῇ ἔλθη, καὶ
the second watch, and (or) [2]in [3]the [4]third [5]watch [1]comes, and

εὕρῃ οὕτω, μακάριοί εἰσιν οἱ δοῦλοι[h] ἐκεῖνοι. **39** Τοῦτο δὲ
finds *them* so, blessed are - slaves ~ (servants) those. [3]this [1]But

γινώσκετε, ὅτι εἰ ᾔδει ὁ οἰκοδεσπότης ποίᾳ ὥρᾳ
[2]know, that if [6]knew (had known) [1]the [2]master [3]of [4]the [5]house in what hour

ὁ κλέπτης ἔρχεται, ἐγρηγόρησεν ἄν, καὶ[i] οὐκ ἂν
the thief is (was) coming, he would have kept watch, - and [3]not -

ἀφῆκε διορυγῆναι τὸν οἶκον αὐτοῦ.
[1]he [2]would [4]have [5]allowed [8]to [9]be [10]dug [11]through (broken into) - [7]house [6]his.

40 Καὶ ὑμεῖς οὖν γίνεσθε ἕτοιμοι, ὅτι ᾗ ὥρᾳ
[3]also [2]you [1]Therefore be ready, because in which (at an) hour (hour which)

οὐ δοκεῖτε ὁ Υἱὸς τοῦ Ἀνθρώπου ἔρχεται."
[3]not [1]you [2]do suppose the Son - of Man is coming."

41 Εἶπε δὲ αὐτῷ ὁ Πέτρος, "Κύριε, πρὸς ἡμᾶς τὴν
[3]said [1]And [4]to [5]Him - [2]Peter, "Lord, [6]to [7]us -

παραβολὴν ταύτην λέγεις, ἢ καὶ πρὸς πάντας?"
[5]parable [4]this [1]do [2]You [3]tell, or also to all?"

42 Εἶπε δὲ ὁ Κύριος, "Τίς ἄρα ἐστὶν ὁ πιστὸς
[4]said [1]And [2]the [3]Lord, "Who then is the (a) faithful

[f](12:38) For και εαν ελθη, *and if He comes,* NU reads καν, *and if.*
[g](12:38) NU omits φυλακη, *watch.* [h](12:38) NU omits οι δουλοι, *(the) slaves.*
[i](12:39) NU omits εγρηγορησεν αν, και, *he would have kept watch, and.*

dom. The second usage is found in Matt. 3:17 to express the Father's delight and pleasure in His Son's perfect life of obedience at His baptism. Cf. the noun εὐδοκία (Eph. 1:5, 9; Phil. 2:13; 2 Thess. 1:11) which is not a begrudging willingness but an active *goodwill* or *good pleasure.*

οἰκονόμος καὶ φρόνιμος, ὃν καταστήσει ὁ κύριος ἐπὶ τῆς
[3]steward [1]and [2]prudent, whom [3]will [4]appoint [1]the [2]master over -
his

θεραπείας αὐτοῦ, τοῦ διδόναι ἐν καιρῷ τὸ
service ~ his, - to give [4]in [5]season [1]the
corps of servants at the right time

σιτομέτριον?* 43 Μακάριος ὁ δοῦλος ἐκεῖνος, ὃν
[2]food [3]allowance? Blessed *is* - slave ~ that, whom
servant

ἐλθὼν ὁ κύριος αὐτοῦ εὑρήσει ποιοῦντα οὕτως.
coming - master ~ his will find doing so.
when he comes

44 Ἀληθῶς λέγω ὑμῖν ὅτι ἐπὶ πᾶσι τοῖς ὑπάρχουσιν
Truly I say to you that [5]over [6]all [7]the [8]*things* [9]belonging
his possessions

αὐτοῦ καταστήσει αὐτόν. 45 Ἐὰν δὲ εἴπῃ ὁ δοῦλος
[10]of [11]him [1]he [2]will [3]appoint [4]him. if ~ But [3]should [4]say - [2]slave
servant

ἐκεῖνος ἐν τῇ καρδίᾳ αὐτοῦ, 'Χρονίζει ὁ κύριός μου ἔρχεσθαι,'
[1]that in - heart ~ his, '[3]is [4]delaying - [2]master [1]My to come,'

καὶ ἄρξηται τύπτειν τοὺς παῖδας καὶ τὰς παιδίσκας,
and should begin to beat the male servants and the female servants,

ἐσθίειν τε καὶ πίνειν καὶ μεθύσκεσθαι, 46 ἥξει ὁ
[2]to [3]eat [1]and and to drink and to be drunk, [6]will [7]come [1]the

κύριος τοῦ δούλου ἐκείνου ἐν ἡμέρᾳ ᾗ οὐ προσδοκᾷ,
[2]master - [3]of [5]slave [4]that on a day which [3]not [1]he [2]does expect,
servant

καὶ ἐν ὥρᾳ ᾗ οὐ γινώσκει· καὶ διχοτομήσει αὐτὸν
and in an hour which [3]not [1]he [2]does know; and he will cut [2]in [3]two [1]him

καὶ τὸ μέρος αὐτοῦ μετὰ τῶν ἀπίστων θήσει.
and - [4]share [3]his [5]with [6]the [7]unfaithful [8]*ones* [1]will [2]appoint.
unbelieving

47 Ἐκεῖνος δὲ ὁ δοῦλος ὁ γνοὺς τὸ θέλημα τοῦ κυρίου
that ~ But - slave the *one* knowing the will - of master ~
servant who knew

ἑαυτοῦ καὶ μὴ ἑτοιμάσας μηδὲ ποιήσας πρὸς τὸ θέλημα
his and not getting ready nor doing according to - will ~
did not get do

αὐτοῦ, δαρήσεται πολλάς. 48 Ὁ δὲ μὴ γνούς,
his, will be beaten *with* many *blows.* [2]the [3]*one* [1]But not knowing,
he who did not know,

ποιήσας δὲ ἄξια πληγῶν, δαρήσεται ὀλίγας.
doing ~ but *things* worthy of blows, will be beaten *with* few *blows.*
but did

Παντὶ δὲ ᾧ ἐδόθη πολύ, πολὺ ζητηθήσεται
[2]to [3]every*one* [1]And to whom [2]was [3]given [1]much, much will be demanded
has been

παρ' αὐτοῦ· καὶ ᾧ παρέθεντο πολύ, περισσότερον
from him; and to whom [2]was [3]entrusted [1]much, [7]more

αἰτήσουσιν αὐτόν.
[4]they [5]will [6]ask [8]from him.

Christ Brings Division
(Matt. 10:34–36)

49 "Πῦρ ἦλθον βαλεῖν εἰς τὴν γῆν, καὶ τί θέλω εἰ ἤδη
"[5]fire [1]I [2]came [3]to [4]cast to the earth, and how I wish - [3]already

ἀνήφθη! 50 Βάπτισμα δὲ ἔχω βαπτισθῆναι, καὶ
[1]it [2]was [4]kindled! [8]a [9]baptism [5]But [6]I [7]have to be baptized *with,* and

steward, whom *his* master will make ruler over his household, to give *them their* portion of food in due season?
43 "Blessed *is* that servant whom his master will find so doing when he comes.
44 "Truly, I say to you that he will make him ruler over all that he has.
45 "But if that servant says in his heart, 'My master is delaying his coming,' and begins to beat the male and female servants, and to eat and drink and be drunk,
46 "the master of that servant will come on a day when he is not looking for *him,* and at an hour when he is not aware, and will cut him in two and appoint *him* his portion with the unbelievers.
47 "And that servant who knew his master's will, and did not prepare *himself* or do according to his will, shall be beaten with many *stripes.*
48 "But he who did not know, yet committed things deserving of stripes, shall be beaten with few. For everyone to whom much is given, from him much will be required; and to whom much has been committed, of him they will ask the more.
49 "I came to send fire on the earth, and how I wish it were already kindled!
50 "But I have a baptism to be baptized with, and how dis-

***(12:42)** *σιτομέτριον (sitometrion).* Noun compounded from *σῖτος, wheat, grain,* and *μέτρον, measure,* thus literally meaning a *measured allowance of grain* or *food.* It appears only here in the NT, referring to the steward's assigned responsibility of apportioning the appropriate food allotments to the rest of the servants during the master's absence.

tressed I am till it is accomplished!
51 "Do *you* suppose that I
came to give peace on earth? I
tell you, not at all, but rather
division.
52 "For from now on five in
one house will be divided: three
against two, and two against
three.
53 "Father will be divided
against son and son against father, mother against daughter
and daughter against mother,
mother-in-law against her
daughter-in-law and daughter-
in-law against her mother-in-
law."
54 Then He also said to the
multitudes, "Whenever you see
a cloud rising out of the west,
immediately you say, 'A shower
is coming'; and so it is.
55 "And when you see the
south wind blow, you say,
'There will be hot weather'; and
there is.
56 "Hypocrites! You can discern the face of the sky and of
the earth, but how *is it* you do
not discern this time?
57 "Yes, and why, even of
yourselves, do you not judge
what is right?
58 "When you go with your
adversary to the magistrate,
make every effort along the
way to settle with him, lest he
drag you to the judge, the judge
deliver you to the officer, and
the officer throw you into

πῶς συνέχομαι ἕως οὗ τελεσθῇ! **51** Δοκεῖτε ὅτι
how pressed I am till - it has been completed! Do you think that
distressed

εἰρήνην παρεγενόμην δοῦναι ἐν τῇ γῇ? Οὐχί, λέγω ὑμῖν,
[5]peace [1]I [2]came [3]to [4]give on the earth? Not at all, I tell you,

ἀλλ' ἤ διαμερισμόν. **52** Ἔσονται γὰρ ἀπὸ τοῦ νῦν
but rather division. [9]will [10]be [1]For [2]from - [3]now [4]*on*

πέντε ἐν οἴκῳ ἑνὶ διαμεμερισμένοι, τρεῖς ἐπὶ δυσὶ καὶ δύο
[5]five [6]in [8]house [7]one divided, three against two and two

ἐπὶ τρισί.
against three.

53 Διαμερισθήσεται πατὴρ ἐπὶ υἱῷ
[3]will [4]be [5]divided [1]A [2]father against a son

Καὶ υἱὸς ἐπὶ πατρί,
And a son against a father,

Μήτηρ ἐπὶ θυγατρὶ
A mother against a daughter

Καὶ θυγάτηρ ἐπὶ μητρί,
And a daughter against a mother,

Πενθερὰ ἐπὶ τὴν νύμφην αὐτῆς
A mother-in-law against - daughter-in-law ˜ her

Καὶ νύμφη ἐπὶ τὴν πενθερὰν αὐτῆς."
And a daughter-in-law against - mother-in-law ˜ her."

Discern the Time

(Matt. 16:2, 3)

54 Ἔλεγε δὲ καὶ τοῖς ὄχλοις, "Ὅταν ἴδητε τὴν
[2]He [4]said [1]And [3]also to the crowds, "Whenever you see the
a

νεφέλην ἀνατέλλουσαν ἀπὸ[j] δυσμῶν, εὐθέως λέγετε,
cloud rising from *the* west, immediately you say,

'Ὄμβρος ἔρχεται,' καὶ γίνεται οὕτω. **55** Καὶ ὅταν
'A rainstorm is coming,' and it happens thus. And whenever *you see*

νότον πνέοντα, λέγετε ὅτι 'Καύσων ἔσται,' καὶ
a south wind blowing, you say - '[4]heat [1]*There* [2]will [3]be,' and
a hot day

γίνεται. **56** Ὑποκριταί! Τὸ πρόσωπον τῆς γῆς καὶ τοῦ
it happens. Hypocrites! [6]the [7]face [8]of [9]the [10]earth [11]and [12]the

οὐρανοῦ οἴδατε δοκιμάζειν, τὸν δὲ καιρὸν τοῦτον
[13]sky [1]You [2]know [3]*how* [4]to [5]discern, - but [9]time [8]this

πῶς οὐ δοκιμάζετε?[k]
[1]how [2]*is* [3]*it* [6]not [4]you [5]do [7]discern?

Be Reconciled with Your Adversary

57 "Τί δὲ καὶ ἀφ' ἑαυτῶν οὐ κρίνετε τὸ
"why ˜ But also [7]of [8]yourselves [6]not [4]do [5]you [9]judge the
what

δίκαιον? **58** Ὡς γὰρ ὑπάγεις μετὰ τοῦ ἀντιδίκου σου ἐπ'
righteous *thing*? as ˜ For you go forth with - adversary ˜ your to
is right?

ἄρχοντα, ἐν τῇ ὁδῷ δὸς ἐργασίαν ἀπηλλάχθαι ἀπ' αὐτοῦ,
a ruler, on the road give work to be released from him,
make an effort to make a settlement with

μήποτε κατασύρῃ σε πρὸς τὸν κριτήν, καὶ ὁ κριτής σε
lest he drag you to the judge, and the judge you ˜

παραδῷ τῷ πράκτορι, καὶ ὁ πράκτωρ σε βάλῃ εἰς
give over to the bailiff, and the bailiff you ˜ throw into

[j](12:54) NU reads επι, *in.*
[k](12:56) For ου δοκιμαζετε, *do you not discern,* NU reads ουκ οιδατε δοκιμαζειν, *do you not know (how) to discern.*

φυλακήν. 59 Λέγω σοι, οὐ μὴ ἐξέλθῃς ἐκεῖθεν ἕως
prison. I say to you, not not will you go out from there till
by no means

οὗ καὶ τὸν ἔσχατον λεπτὸν ἀποδῷς."
- [3]even [4]the [5]last [6]lepton [1]you [2]pay."
mite

Repent or Perish

13 1 Παρῆσαν δέ τινες ἐν αὐτῷ τῷ καιρῷ
[4]were [5]present [1]And [2]some [3]*people* at very ~ the time
that

ἀπαγγέλλοντες αὐτῷ περὶ τῶν Γαλιλαίων ὧν τὸ αἷμα
reporting to Him about the Galileans whose - blood

Πιλᾶτος ἔμιξε μετὰ τῶν θυσιῶν αὐτῶν. 2 Καὶ ἀποκριθεὶς ὁ
Pilate mixed with - sacrifices ~ their. And answering -
had mixed

Ἰησοῦς[a] εἶπεν αὐτοῖς "Δοκεῖτε ὅτι οἱ Γαλιλαῖοι οὗτοι
Jesus said to them, "Do you think that - Galileans ~ these

ἁμαρτωλοὶ παρὰ πάντας τοὺς Γαλιλαίους ἐγένοντο,
[2]sinners [3]more [4]than [5]all [6]the [7]*other* [8]Galileans [1]were,

ὅτι τοιαῦτα[b] πεπόνθασιν? 3 Οὐχί, λέγω ὑμῖν· ἀλλ'
because [4]such [5]*things* [1]they [2]have [3]suffered? Not at all, I tell you; but

ἐὰν μὴ μετανοῆτε πάντες ὡσαύτως ἀπολεῖσθε! 4 Ἢ
if not you repent [3]all [4]likewise [1]you [2]will [5]perish! Or
unless

ἐκεῖνοι οἱ δέκα καὶ ὀκτὼ ἐφ' οὓς ἔπεσεν ὁ πύργος ἐν τῷ
those - ten and eight on whom [5]fell [1]the [2]tower [3]in -
eighteen

Σιλωὰμ καὶ ἀπέκτεινεν αὐτούς, δοκεῖτε ὅτι οὗτοι[c]
[4]Siloam and killed them, do you think that these

ὀφειλέται* ἐγένοντο παρὰ πάντας ἀνθρώπους τοὺς
debtors ~ were more than all *the* men the *ones*
offenders who

κατοικοῦντας ἐν Ἱερουσαλήμ? 5 Οὐχί, λέγω ὑμῖν· ἀλλ' ἐὰν
dwelling in Jerusalem? Not at all, I tell you; but if
dwell unless

μὴ μετανοῆτε πάντες ὁμοίως ἀπολεῖσθε!"
not you repent [3]all [4]likewise [1]you [2]will [5]perish!"

The Parable of the Barren Fig Tree

6 Ἔλεγε δὲ ταύτην τὴν παραβολήν· "Συκῆν εἶχέ
[2]He [3]told [1]And this - parable: "[5]a [6]fig [7]tree [4]had

τις ἐν τῷ ἀμπελῶνι αὐτοῦ πεφυτευμένην, καὶ ἦλθε
[1]A [2]certain [3]*man* [9]in - [11]vineyard [10]his [8]planted, and he came

ζητῶν καρπὸν ἐν αὐτῇ καὶ οὐχ εὗρεν. 7 Εἶπε δὲ
looking for fruit on it and [3]not [1]he [2]did find *any*. [2]he [3]said [1]And

πρὸς τὸν ἀμπελουργόν, 'Ἰδού, τρία ἔτη[d] ἔρχομαι ζητῶν
to the vinedresser, 'Look, three years I come looking for
have come

καρπὸν ἐν τῇ συκῇ ταύτῃ καὶ οὐχ εὑρίσκω. Ἔκκοψον
fruit on - [2]fig [3]tree [1]this and [3]not [1]I [2]do find *any*. Cut down ~
I have not found

αὐτήν· ἱνατί καὶ τὴν γῆν καταργεῖ?' 8 Ὁ δὲ
it; why [3]even [5]the [6]ground [1]does [2]it [4]waste?' [2]the [3]*one* [1]But
he

ἀποκριθεὶς λέγει αὐτῷ, 'Κύριε, ἄφες αὐτὴν καὶ τοῦτο τὸ
answering says to him, 'Sir, let alone ~ it also this -
said

prison.
59 "I tell you, you shall not depart from there till you have paid the very last mite."

13 There were present at that season some who told Him about the Galileans whose blood Pilate had mingled with their sacrifices.
2 And Jesus answered and said to them, "Do you suppose that these Galileans were worse sinners than all *other* Galileans, because they suffered such things?
3 "I tell you, no; but unless you repent you will all likewise perish.
4 "Or those eighteen on whom the tower in Siloam fell and killed them, do you think that they were worse sinners than all *other* men who dwelt in Jerusalem?
5 "I tell you, no; but unless you repent you will all likewise perish."
6 He also spoke this parable: "A certain *man* had a fig tree planted in his vineyard, and he came seeking fruit on it and found none.
7 "Then he said to the keeper of his vineyard, 'Look, for three years I have come seeking fruit on this fig tree and find none. Cut it down; why does it use up the ground?'
8 "But he answered and said to him, 'Sir, let it alone this

[a](**13:2**) NU omits ο Ιησους, *Jesus*. [b](**13:2**) NU reads ταυτα, *these things*. [c](**13:4**) NU reads αυτοι, *they*. [d](**13:7**) NU adds αφ ου, *from which* (= *since*).

*(**13:4**) ὀφειλέτης *(opheiletēs)*. Noun meaning *debtor* (Matt. 18:24), *one obligated*, even in a good sense (as Rom. 1:14; 15:27). Out of this meaning developed the nuance of *one liable (for wrongdoing)*, as in Matt. 6:12, and thus a *sinner*, as here in Luke 13:4. Cf. the cognate nouns ὀφείλημα and ὀφειλή, *debt*, and the verb ὀφείλω, *owe, ought*, which can also be used of ordinary debt, of ethical obligation, or of sinful guilt and liability.

year also, until I dig around it
and fertilize *it.*
9 'And if it bears fruit, *well.*
But if not, after that you can cut
it down.' "
10 Now He was teaching in
one of the synagogues on the
Sabbath.
11 And behold, there was a
woman who had a spirit of infirmity eighteen years, and was
bent over and could in no way
raise *herself* up.
12 But when Jesus saw her,
He called *her* to *Him* and said to
her, "Woman, you are loosed
from your infirmity."
13 And He laid *His* hands on
her, and immediately she was
made straight, and glorified
God.
14 But the ruler of the synagogue answered with indignation, because Jesus had healed
on the Sabbath; and he said to
the crowd, "There are six days
on which men ought to work;
therefore come and be healed
on them, and not on the Sabbath day."
15 The Lord then answered
him and said, "Hypocrite! Does
not each one of you on the Sabbath loose his ox or donkey
from the stall, and lead *it* away
to water it?
16 "So ought not this woman,
being a daughter of Abraham,
whom Satan has bound—think
of it—for eighteen years, be
loosed from this bond on the

[e](13:15) TR reads υποκριτα, *hypocrite.*

ἔτος, ἕως ὅτου σκάψω περὶ αὐτὴν καὶ βάλω κόπρια·
year, until - I dig around it and [1]put [3]on [4]*it* [2]manure;

9 κἂν μὲν ποιήσῃ καρπόν· εἰ δὲ μή γε, εἰς τὸ μέλλον
And if - it produces fruit *fine;* if ˜ but not, - in the coming *year*

ἐκκόψεις αὐτήν.' "
you will cut down ˜ it.' "

Jesus Heals a Crippled Woman on the Sabbath

10 Ἦν δὲ διδάσκων ἐν μιᾷ τῶν συναγωγῶν ἐν τοῖς
[2]He [3]was [1]Now teaching in one of the synagogues on the

σάββασι. 11 Καὶ ἰδού, γυνὴ ἦν πνεῦμα ἔχουσα
Sabbath. And behold, a woman *there* was [2]a [3]spirit [1]having
had a spirit

ἀσθενείας ἔτη δέκα καὶ ὀκτώ, καὶ ἦν συγκύπτουσα καὶ
of infirmity years ten and eight, and she was bending over and
eighteen years, bent double

μὴ δυναμένη ἀνακύψαι εἰς τὸ παντελές. 12 Ἰδὼν δὲ
not being able to straighten up to the complete *thing.* seeing ˜ And
able at all.

αὐτὴν ὁ Ἰησοῦς προσεφώνησε καὶ εἶπεν αὐτῇ, "Γύναι,
her - Jesus called *her* to *Him* and said to her, "Woman,

ἀπολέλυσαι τῆς ἀσθενείας σοῦ." 13 Καὶ ἐπέθηκεν
you have been loosed - from infirmity ˜ your." And He laid
are

αὐτῇ τὰς χεῖρας, καὶ παραχρῆμα ἀνωρθώθη, καὶ
on her the hands, and immediately she was made erect, and
His

ἐδόξαζε τὸν Θεόν.
she was glorifying - God.
began to praise

14 Ἀποκριθεὶς δὲ ὁ ἀρχισυνάγωγος, ἀγανακτῶν ὅτι
[5]answering [1]And [2]the [3]synagogue [4]leader, being indignant that
because he was

τῷ σαββάτῳ ἐθεράπευσεν ὁ Ἰησοῦς, ἔλεγε τῷ ὄχλῳ,
[3]on [4]the [5]Sabbath [2]healed - [1]Jesus, said to the crowd,

"Ἓξ ἡμέραι εἰσὶν ἐν αἷς δεῖ ἐργάζεσθαι· ἐν
"[3]six [4]days [1]*There* [2]are in which it is necessary to work; [2]on
one should work;

ταύταις οὖν ἐρχόμενοι θεραπεύεσθε καὶ μὴ τῇ ἡμέρᾳ
[3]these [4]*days* [1]therefore coming be healed and not on the day
come and Sabbath

τοῦ σαββάτου."
of the Sabbath."
day."

15 Ἀπεκρίθη οὖν αὐτῷ ὁ Κύριος καὶ εἶπεν,
[4]answered [1]Therefore [5]him [2]the [3]Lord and said,

"Ὑποκριταί![e] Ἕκαστος ὑμῶν τῷ σαββάτῳ οὐ λύει
"Hypocrites! [3]each [4]of [5]you [6]on [7]the [8]Sabbath [2]not [1]Does [9]loose

τὸν βοῦν αὐτοῦ ἢ τὸν ὄνον ἀπὸ τῆς φάτνης, καὶ ἀπαγαγὼν
- [11]ox [10]his or - donkey from the stall, and leading *it* away

ποτίζει? 16 Ταύτην δέ, θυγατέρα Ἀβραὰμ οὖσαν,
let *it* drink? [2]this [3]*woman* [1]And, [5]a [6]daughter [7]of [8]Abraham [4]being,
since she is,

ἣν ἔδησεν ὁ Σατανᾶς, ἰδού, δέκα καὶ ὀκτὼ ἔτη, οὐκ
whom bound ˜ - Satan, lo, ten and eight years, [3]not
has bound eighteen years, should

ἔδει λυθῆναι ἀπὸ τοῦ δεσμοῦ τούτου τῇ ἡμέρᾳ
[1]was [2]it necessary to be loosed from - bond ˜ this on the day
she not be loosed Sabbath

τοῦ σαββάτου?" **17** Καὶ ταῦτα λέγοντος αὐτοῦ,
of the Sabbath?" And [3]these [4]*things* [2]saying [1]Him,
day?" as He said,

κατῃσχύνοντο πάντες οἱ ἀντικείμενοι αὐτῷ· καὶ πᾶς
[6]were [7]put [8]to [9]shame [1]all [2]the [3]*ones* [4]opposing [5]Him; and all
His opponents;

ὁ ὄχλος ἔχαιρεν ἐπὶ πᾶσι τοῖς ἐνδόξοις τοῖς
the crowd was rejoicing over all the glorious *things* the *ones*
which

γινομένοις ὑπ' αὐτοῦ.
being done by Him.
were

The Parable of the Mustard Seed
(Matt. 13:31, 32; Mark 4:30–32)

18 Ἔλεγε δέ, "Τίνι ὁμοία ἐστὶν ἡ βασιλεία τοῦ Θεοῦ,
[2]He [3]said [1]And, "What [6]like [1]is [2]the [3]kingdom - [4]of [5]God,

καὶ τίνι ὁμοιώσω αὐτήν? **19** Ὁμοία ἐστὶ κόκκῳ
and to what shall I compare it? [3]like [1]It [2]is a seed
a mustard

σινάπεως, ὃν λαβὼν ἄνθρωπος ἔβαλεν εἰς κῆπον ἑαυτοῦ,
of mustard, which [3]taking [1]a [2]man put into a garden of himself,
seed, took and his garden,

καὶ ηὔξησε καὶ ἐγένετο εἰς δένδρον μέγα,[f] καὶ τὰ πετεινὰ
and it grew and became - a tree ˜ great, and the birds
large

τοῦ οὐρανοῦ κατεσκήνωσεν ἐν τοῖς κλάδοις αὐτοῦ."
- of heaven nested in - branches ˜ its."

The Parable of the Leaven
(Matt. 13:33)

20 Πάλιν εἶπε, "Τίνι ὁμοιώσω τὴν βασιλείαν τοῦ
Again He said, "To what shall I compare the kingdom -

Θεοῦ? **21** Ὁμοία ἐστὶ ζύμῃ, ἣν λαβοῦσα γυνὴ
of God? [3]like [1]It [2]is yeast, which [3]taking [1]a [2]woman
leaven, took and

ἐνέκρυψεν εἰς ἀλεύρου σάτα τρία ἕως οὗ ἐζυμώθη
hid in [3]of [4]meal [2]sata [1]three until - [3]was [4]leavened
mixed in with measures

ὅλον."
[1]*the* [2]whole."

The Narrow Way
(Matt. 7:13, 14; 21–23)

22 Καὶ διεπορεύετο κατὰ πόλεις καὶ κώμας
And He was traveling through according to cities and villages
various

διδάσκων, καὶ πορείαν ποιούμενος εἰς Ἱερουσαλήμ.
teaching, and [2]a [3]journey [1]making to Jerusalem.

23 Εἶπε δέ τις αὐτῷ, "Κύριε, εἰ ὀλίγοι οἱ
[3]said [1]And [2]someone to Him, "Lord, are *there* few the *ones*
who

σῳζόμενοι?"
being saved?"
are saved?"

Ὁ δὲ εἶπε πρὸς αὐτούς, **24** "Ἀγωνίζεσθε εἰσελθεῖν
[2]the [3]*One* [1]And said to them, "Strive to enter in
He

Sabbath?"
17 And when He said these
things, all His adversaries were
put to shame; and all the multitude rejoiced for all the glorious
things that were done by Him.
18 Then He said, "What is the
kingdom of God like? And to
what shall I compare it?
19 "It is like a mustard seed,
which a man took and put in his
garden; and it grew and became
a large tree, and the birds of
the air nested in its branches."
20 And again He said, "To
what shall I liken the kingdom
of God?
21 "It is like leaven, which a
woman took and hid in three
measures of meal till it was all
leavened."
22 And He went through the
cities and villages, teaching,
and journeying toward Jerusalem.
23 Then one said to Him,
"Lord, are there few who are
saved?" And He said to them,
24 "Strive to enter through

---

f(**13:19**) NU omits μεγα, *great.*

the narrow gate, for many, I
say to you, will seek to enter
and will not be able.
25 "When once the Master of
the house has risen up and shut
the door, and you begin to
stand outside and knock at the
door, saying, 'Lord, Lord, open
for us,' and He will answer and
say to you, 'I do not know you,
where you are from,'
26 "then you will begin to say,
'We ate and drank in Your presence, and You taught in our
streets.'
27 "But He will say, 'I tell you
I do not know you, where you
are from. Depart from Me, all
you workers of iniquity.'
28 "There will be weeping and
gnashing of teeth, when you
see Abraham and Isaac and Jacob and all the prophets in the
kingdom of God, and your-
selves thrust out.
29 "They will come from the
east and the west, from the
north and the south, and sit
down in the kingdom of God.
30 "And indeed there are last
who will be first, and there are
first who will be last."
31 On that very day some
Pharisees came, saying to Him,
"Get out and depart from here,
for Herod wants to kill You."
32 And He said to them, "Go,
tell that fox, 'Behold, I cast out
demons and perform cures today and tomorrow, and the
third *day* I shall be perfected.'
33 "Nevertheless I must journey today, tomorrow, and the
day following; for it cannot be

διὰ τῆς στενῆς πύλης,[g] ὅτι πολλοί, λέγω ὑμῖν,
through the narrow gate, because many, I say to you,

ζητήσουσιν εἰσελθεῖν καὶ οὐκ ἰσχύσουσιν. **25** Ἀφ' οὗ
will seek to enter and [3]not [1]they [2]will be able. From what

ἂν ἐγερθῇ ὁ οἰκοδεσπότης καὶ ἀποκλείσῃ τὴν
ever *time* [6]rises [1]the [2]Master [3]of [4]the [5]house and shuts the

θύραν, καὶ ἄρξησθε ἔξω ἑστάναι καὶ κρούειν τὴν
door, [3]also [1]you [2]will [4]begin [7]outside [5]to [6]stand and to knock on the

θύραν, λέγοντες, 'Κύριε,[h] Κύριε, ἄνοιξον ἡμῖν!' Καὶ
door, saying, 'Lord, Lord, open to us!' And

ἀποκριθεὶς ἐρεῖ ὑμῖν, 'Οὐκ οἶδα ὑμᾶς πόθεν
answering He will say to you, '[3]not [1]I [2]do know you [4]from [1]where

ἐστέ.' **26** Τότε ἄρξεσθε λέγειν, 'Ἐφάγομεν ἐνώπιόν
[2]you [3]are.' Then you will begin to say, 'We ate before
in Your

σου καὶ ἐπίομεν, καὶ ἐν ταῖς πλατείαις ἡμῶν ἐδίδαξας.'
You and drank, and in - streets ~ our You taught.'
presence

27 Καὶ ἐρεῖ, 'Λέγω ὑμῖν, οὐκ οἶδα ὑμᾶς πόθεν
And He will say, 'I say to you, [3]not [1]I [2]do know you [4]from [1]where

ἐστέ. Ἀπόστητε ἀπ' ἐμοῦ, πάντες οἱ ἐργάται τῆς
[2]you [3]are. Depart from Me, all *you* - workers -

ἀδικίας.' **28** Ἐκεῖ ἔσται ὁ κλαυθμὸς καὶ ὁ βρυγμὸς
of unrighteousness.' There *there* will be - weeping and - gnashing

τῶν ὀδόντων, ὅταν ὄψησθε Ἀβραὰμ καὶ Ἰσαὰκ καὶ Ἰακὼβ καὶ
- of teeth, when you see Abraham and Isaac and Jacob and

πάντας τοὺς προφήτας ἐν τῇ βασιλείᾳ τοῦ Θεοῦ, ὑμᾶς δὲ
all the prophets in the kingdom - of God, you ~ but
yourselves

ἐκβαλλομένους ἔξω. **29** Καὶ ἥξουσιν ἀπὸ ἀνατολῶν καὶ
being thrown outside. And they will come from east and
thrown

δυσμῶν καὶ[i] βορρᾶ καὶ νότου, καὶ ἀνακλιθήσονται* ἐν τῇ
west and north and south, and will recline *to eat* in the

βασιλείᾳ τοῦ Θεοῦ. **30** Καὶ ἰδού, εἰσὶν ἔσχατοι οἳ ἔσονται
kingdom - of God. And behold, *there* are last *ones* who will be

πρῶτοι, καὶ εἰσὶ πρῶτοι οἳ ἔσονται ἔσχατοι."
first, and *there* are first *ones* who will be last."

Jesus and Herod

31 Ἐν αὐτῇ τῇ ἡμέρᾳ[j] προσῆλθόν τινες Φαρισαῖοι,
On very ~ the day [3]approached [1]some [2]Pharisees,
that

λέγοντες αὐτῷ, "Ἔξελθε καὶ πορεύου ἐντεῦθεν, ὅτι
saying to Him, "Get out and go from here, because

Ἡρῴδης θέλει σε ἀποκτεῖναι."
Herod wants [3]You [1]to [2]kill."

32 Καὶ εἶπεν αὐτοῖς, "Πορευθέντες εἴπατε τῇ ἀλώπεκι
And He said to them, "Going tell - fox ~
"Go and

ταύτῃ, 'Ἰδού, ἐκβάλλω δαιμόνια καὶ ἰάσεις ἐπιτελῶ σήμερον
this, 'Behold, I cast out demons and [3]cures [1]I [2]perform today

καὶ αὔριον, καὶ τῇ τρίτῃ τελειοῦμαι.' **33** Πλὴν
and tomorrow, and the third *day* I will be finished.' Nevertheless
finish My goal.'

δεῖ με σήμερον καὶ αὔριον καὶ τῇ ἐχομένῃ
it is necessary *for* Me [3]today [4]and [5]tomorrow [6]and [7]the [8]following [9]*day*
I must

---

g(13:24) NU reads *θυρας, door.* h(13:25) NU omits Κυριε, *Lord.*
i(13:29) TR, NU add *απο, from.* j(13:31) NU reads *ωρα, hour.*

*(13:29) *ἀνακλίνω (anaklinō).* Verb originally meaning *to cause to lie down, lay down* (as Luke 2:7). Since in first-century culture formal meals were eaten while reclining on couches, the word usually has that context in the NT. It came to mean, simply, *to recline (for a meal),* as in Luke 12:37 (cf. Jesus' feeding of the crowds in Matt. 14:19). Here in Luke 13:29 (and in the parallel Matt. 8:11) the reference is to the messianic banquet. The similar compound verb κατακλίνω has essentially the same range of meanings.

πορεύεσθαι· ὅτι οὐκ ἐνδέχεται προφήτην ἀπολέσθαι
[1]to [2]travel; because [3]not [1]it [2]is possible *for* a prophet to perish
journey;

ἔξω Ἱερουσαλήμ!
outside Jerusalem!

Jesus Laments over Jerusalem
(Matt. 23:37–39)

34 "Ἱερουσαλήμ, Ἱερουσαλήμ, ἡ ἀποκτένουσα τοὺς
"Jerusalem, Jerusalem, the *one* killing the
who kills

προφήτας καὶ λιθοβολοῦσα τοὺς ἀπεσταλμένους πρὸς
prophets and stoning the *ones* having been sent to
stones those who are sent

αὐτήν! Ποσάκις ἠθέλησα ἐπισυνάξαι τὰ τέκνα σου ὃν
her! How often I wanted to gather - children ˜ your by which
just

τρόπον ὄρνις τὴν ἑαυτῆς νοσσιὰν ὑπὸ τὰς πτέρυγας,
manner a hen *gathers* the [2]of [3]herself [1]brood under the wings,
like her own her

καὶ οὐκ ἠθελήσατε. **35** Ἰδού, ἀφίεται ὑμῖν ὁ οἶκος ὑμῶν
and [3]not [1]you [2]did want to. See, [3]is [4]left [5]to [6]you - [2]house [1]your

ἔρημος.[k] Λέγω δὲ[l] ὑμῖν ὅτι οὐ μή με ἴδητε ἕως ἂν
desolate. [2]I [3]say [1]And to you that [3]not [4]not [6]Me [1]you [2]will [5]see until -
surely not

ἥξῃ ὅτε εἴπητε, «Εὐλογημένος ὁ ἐρχόμενος ἐν
the time comes when you say, «Blessed *is* the *One* coming in
He who comes

ὀνόματι Κυρίου.»"[m]
the name of *the* Lord.»"

Jesus Heals a Man with Dropsy on the Sabbath

14 **1** Καὶ ἐγένετο ἐν τῷ ἐλθεῖν αὐτὸν εἰς οἶκόν τινος
And it happened in - [2]to [3]come [1]Him into *the* house of one
when He came

τῶν ἀρχόντων τῶν Φαρισαίων σαββάτῳ φαγεῖν ἄρτον, καὶ
of the rulers of the Pharisees on a Sabbath to eat bread, and
that

αὐτοὶ ἦσαν παρατηρούμενοι αὐτόν. **2** Καὶ ἰδού, ἄνθρωπός
they were watching closely ˜ Him. And behold, a man ˜

τις ἦν ὑδρωπικὸς ἔμπροσθεν αὐτοῦ. **3** Καὶ ἀποκριθεὶς ὁ
certain [3]was [4]dropsical [1]before [2]Him. And answering -
had dropsy

Ἰησοῦς εἶπε πρὸς τοὺς νομικοὺς καὶ Φαρισαίους, λέγων, "Εἰ
Jesus spoke to the lawyers and Pharisees, saying, -

ἔξεστι τῷ σαββάτῳ θεραπεύειν?"[a] **4** Οἱ δὲ
"Is it lawful [3]on [4]the [5]Sabbath [1]to [2]heal?" [2]the [3]*ones* [1]But
they

ἡσύχασαν. Καὶ ἐπιλαβόμενος ἰάσατο αὐτὸν καὶ ἀπέλυσε.
were silent. And taking hold of *him* He cured him and let *him* go.

5 Καὶ ἀποκριθεὶς[b] πρὸς αὐτοὺς εἶπε, "Τίνος ὑμῶν
And replying to them He said, "[5]of [6]which [7]of [8]you

υἱὸς[c] ἢ βοῦς εἰς φρέαρ ἐμπεσεῖται, καὶ οὐκ εὐθέως
[1]*The* [2]son [3]or [4]ox [11]into [12]a [13]pit [9]will [10]fall, and [3]not [4]immediately

ἀνασπάσει αὐτὸν ἐν τῇ ἡμέρᾳ τοῦ σαββάτου?" **6** Καὶ οὐκ
[1]he [2]will [5]pull [7]up [6]him on the day of the Sabbath?" And [3]not
Sabbath day?"

ἴσχυσαν ἀνταποκριθῆναι αὐτῷ πρὸς ταῦτα.
[1]they [2]were able to answer back ˜ Him regarding these *things*.

that a prophet should perish outside of Jerusalem.
34 "O Jerusalem, Jerusalem, the one who kills the prophets and stones those who are sent to her! How often I wanted to gather your children together, as a hen *gathers* her brood under *her* wings, but you were not willing!
35 "See! Your house is left to you desolate; and assuredly, I say to you, you shall not see Me until *the time* comes when you say, *'Blessed is He who comes in the name of the* LORD!'"

14 Now it happened, as He went into the house of one of the rulers of the Pharisees to eat bread on the Sabbath, that they watched Him closely.
2 And behold, there was a certain man before Him who had dropsy.
3 And Jesus, answering, spoke to the lawyers and Pharisees, saying, "Is it lawful to heal on the Sabbath?"
4 But they kept silent. And He took *him* and healed him, and let him go.
5 Then He answered them, saying, "Which of you, having a donkey or an ox that has fallen into a pit, will not immediately pull him out on the Sabbath day?"
6 And they could not answer Him regarding these things.

---

[k] **(13:35)** Many mss., NU omit ερημος, *desolate.*
[l] **(13:35)** TR reads αμην δε λεγω, *and assuredly I say.*
[m] **(13:35)** Ps. 118:26
[a] **(14:3)** NU adds η ου, *or not.* [b] **(14:5)** NU omits αποκριθεις, *answering.*
[c] **(14:5)** TR reads ονος, *donkey.*

7 So He told a parable to those who were invited, when He noted how they chose the best places, saying to them:
8 "When you are invited by anyone to a wedding feast, do not sit down in the best place, lest one more honorable than you be invited by him;
9 "and he who invited you and him come and say to you, 'Give place to this man,' and then you begin with shame to take the lowest place.
10 "But when you are invited, go and sit down in the lowest place, so that when he who invited you comes he may say to you, 'Friend, go up higher.' Then you will have glory in the presence of those who sit at the table with you.
11 "For whoever exalts himself will be humbled, and he who humbles himself will be exalted."
12 Then He also said to him who invited Him, "When you give a dinner or a supper, do not ask your friends, your brothers, your relatives, nor rich neighbors, lest they also invite you back, and you be repaid.
13 "But when you give a feast, invite *the* poor, *the* maimed, *the* lame, *the* blind.
14 "And you will be blessed, because they cannot repay you; for you shall be repaid at the resurrection of the just."

Take the Lowly Place

7 Ἔλεγε δὲ πρὸς τοὺς κεκλημένους
[2]He [3]told [1]And [6]to [7]the [8]*ones* [9]having [10]been [11]invited
those who were

παραβολήν, ἐπέχων πῶς τὰς πρωτοκλισίας ἐξελέγοντο,
[4]a [5]parable, noting how [3]the [4]first [5]couches [1]they [2]chose,
when He noted places of honor

λέγων πρὸς αὐτούς, **8** "Ὅταν κληθῇς ὑπό τινος εἰς
saying to them, "Whenever you are invited by someone to

γάμους, μὴ κατακλιθῇς εἰς τὴν πρωτοκλισίαν,
a wedding celebration, not ˜ do recline *to eat* in the first couch,
place of honor,

μήποτε ἐντιμότερός σου ᾖ κεκλημένος ὑπ'
lest a more honorable *person than* you was invited by
has been

αὐτοῦ, **9** καὶ ἐλθὼν ὁ σὲ καὶ αὐτὸν καλέσας ἐρεῖ σοι,
him, and coming the *one* [2]you [3]and [4]him [1]inviting will say to you,
he who invited you and him shall come and say

'Δὸς τούτῳ τόπον,' καὶ τότε ἄρξῃ μετ' αἰσχύνης τὸν
'Give [2]to [3]this [4]*man* [1]place,' and then you begin with shame [3]the

ἔσχατον τόπον κατέχειν. **10** Ἀλλ' ὅταν κληθῇς,
[4]last [5]place [1]to [2]take. But whenever you are invited,

πορευθεὶς ἀνάπεσε εἰς τὸν ἔσχατον τόπον, ἵνα ὅταν ἔλθῃ
going recline in the last place, so that when [6]comes
go and

ὁ κεκληκώς σε, εἴπῃ σοι, 'Φίλε, προσανάβηθι
[1]the [2]*one* [3]having [4]invited [5]you, he shall say to you, 'Friend, go up
he who invited

ἀνώτερον.' Τότε ἔσται σοι δόξα ἐνώπιον[d] τῶν
higher.' Then *there* will be [2]for [3]you [1]glory before the *ones*
in the presence of those who

συνανακειμένων σοι. **11** Ὅτι πᾶς ὁ ὑψῶν ἑαυτὸν
reclining with you. Because every - *one* exalting himself
recline everyone who exalts

ταπεινωθήσεται, καὶ ὁ ταπεινῶν* ἑαυτὸν ὑψωθήσεται."
will be humbled, and the *one* humbling himself will be exalted."
he who humbles

12 Ἔλεγε δὲ καὶ τῷ κεκληκότι αὐτόν, "Ὅταν
[2]He [3]said [1]And also to the *one* having invited Him, "Whenever

ποιῇς ἄριστον ἢ δεῖπνον, μὴ φώνει τοὺς φίλους σου, μηδὲ
you make a luncheon or a dinner, not ˜ do call - friends ˜ your, nor
give invite

τοὺς ἀδελφούς σου, μηδὲ τοὺς συγγενεῖς σου, μηδὲ γείτονας
- brothers ˜ your, nor - relatives ˜ your, nor neighbors ˜

πλουσίους, μήποτε καὶ αὐτοί σε ἀντικαλέσωσι, καὶ γένηταί
rich, lest also they you ˜ invite back, and it will be
you will

σοι ἀνταπόδομα. **13** Ἀλλ' ὅταν ποιῇς δοχήν, κάλει
to you a repayment. But whenever you make a banquet, invite
have give

πτωχούς, ἀναπήρους, χωλούς, τυφλούς· **14** καὶ μακάριος
poor *people,* crippled *people,* lame *people,* blind *people;* and [4]blessed

ἔσῃ, ὅτι οὐκ ἔχουσιν ἀνταποδοῦναί σοι,
[1]you [2]will [3]be, because [3]not [1]they [2]do have *anything* to repay you,

ἀνταποδοθήσεται γάρ σοι ἐν τῇ ἀναστάσει τῶν δικαίων."
[2]it [3]will [4]be [5]repaid [1]for to you in the resurrection of the righteous."

---

d(**14:10**) NU adds παντων, *all.*

***(14:11)** ταπεινόω *(tapeinoō).* Verb with the root meaning *make low, make small* or *little.* In Luke 3:5 it refers to *leveling* a mountain. Sometimes it has the negative connotation *to humiliate, humble* people by assigning them to a lower place or exposing them to shame (as 2 Cor. 12:21). But it often indicates the positive virtue of *humbling* oneself like a child in contrast to manifesting pride (Matt. 18:4; here in Luke 14:11; James 4:10; 1 Pet. 5:6). Jesus sets the example (Phil. 2:8). Cf. the cognate adjective ταπεινός, *lowly, humble* (James 1:9; 4:6); and the cognate noun ταπείνωσις, *humiliation, humility* (Luke 1:48; Phil. 3:21). See also ταπεινοφροσύνη at Acts 20:19.

The Parable of the Marriage Supper
(Matt. 22:1–14)

15 Ἀκούσας δέ τις τῶν συνανακειμένων
[9]hearing [1]And [2]one [3]of [4]the [5]*ones* [6]reclining [7]*to* [8]*eat*
heard And when

ταῦτα εἶπεν αὐτῷ, "Μακάριος ὅς φάγεται ἄριστον[e] ἐν
these *things* he said to Him, "Blessed *is he* who shall eat lunch in

τῇ βασιλείᾳ τοῦ Θεοῦ!"
the kingdom - of God!"

16 Ὁ δὲ εἶπεν αὐτῷ, "Ἄνθρωπός τις ἐποίησε
[2]the [3]One [1]And said to him, "A man ˜ certain made
He gave

δεῖπνον μέγα, καὶ ἐκάλεσε πολλούς, **17** καὶ ἀπέστειλε τὸν
a dinner ˜ great, and he invited many, and he sent -

δοῦλον αὐτοῦ τῇ ὥρᾳ τοῦ δείπνου εἰπεῖν τοῖς
slave ˜ his at the hour of the dinner to say to the *ones*
servant those who

κεκλημένοις, 'Ἔρχεσθε, ὅτι ἤδη ἕτοιμά ἐστι πάντα.'[f]
having been invited, 'Come, because [4]now [5]ready [3]are [1]all [2]*things*.'
were

18 Καὶ ἤρξαντο ἀπὸ μιᾶς παραιτεῖσθαι πάντες.
And they [2]began [3]with [4]one [5]*accord* [6]to [7]excuse [8]themselves [1]all.

Ὁ πρῶτος εἶπεν αὐτῷ, 'Ἀγρὸν ἠγόρασα, καὶ ἔχω ἀνάγκην
The first said to him, '[3]a [4]field [1]I [2]bought, and I have a need

ἐξελθεῖν καὶ ἰδεῖν αὐτόν. Ἐρωτῶ σε, ἔχε με παρῃτημένον.'
to go out and to see it. I ask you, have me excused.'

19 Καὶ ἕτερος εἶπε, 'Ζεύγη βοῶν ἠγόρασα πέντε, καὶ
And another said, '[4]yoke [5]of [6]oxen [1]I [2]bought [3]five, and

πορεύομαι δοκιμάσαι αὐτά. Ἐρωτῶ σε, ἔχε με παρῃτημένον.'
I am going to test them. I ask you, have me excused.'

20 Καὶ ἕτερος εἶπε, 'Γυναῖκα ἔγημα, καὶ διὰ τοῦτο
And another said, '[3]a [4]wife [1]I [2]married, and on account of this
have married therefore

οὐ δύναμαι ἐλθεῖν.' **21** Καὶ παραγενόμενος ὁ δοῦλος
[3]not [1]I [2]am able to come.' And [3]coming [4]up - [2]slave
came and servant

ἐκεῖνος[g] ἀπήγγειλε τῷ κυρίῳ αὐτοῦ ταῦτα. Τότε
[1]that reported - [3]to [5]master [4]his [1]these [2]*things*. Then

ὀργισθεὶς ὁ οἰκοδεσπότης εἶπε τῷ δούλῳ αὐτοῦ,
being angry the master of the house said - to slave ˜ his,
because he was servant

'Ἔξελθε ταχέως εἰς τὰς πλατείας καὶ ῥύμας τῆς πόλεως, καὶ
'Go out quickly into the streets and lanes of the city, and

τοὺς πτωχοὺς καὶ ἀναπήρους καὶ χωλοὺς καὶ τυφλοὺς
[4]the [5]poor [6]and [7]crippled [8]and [9]lame [10]and [11]blind

εἰσάγαγε ὧδε.' **22** Καὶ εἶπεν ὁ δοῦλος, 'Κύριε, γέγονεν ὡς
[1]bring [2]in [3]here.' And [3]said [1]the [2]slave, 'Master, it is done as
servant,

ἐπέταξας, καὶ ἔτι τόπος ἐστί.' **23** Καὶ εἶπεν ὁ κύριος
you commanded, and still [3]place [1]*there* [2]is.' And [3]said [1]the [2]master
room

πρὸς τὸν δοῦλον, 'Ἔξελθε εἰς τὰς ὁδοὺς καὶ φραγμούς, καὶ
to the slave, 'Go out into the roads and hedges, and
servant,

ἀνάγκασον εἰσελθεῖν, ἵνα γεμισθῇ ὁ οἶκός μου.
compel *them* to come in, so that [3]may [4]be [5]filled - [2]house [1]my.

24 Λέγω γὰρ ὑμῖν ὅτι οὐδεὶς τῶν ἀνδρῶν ἐκείνων τῶν
[2]I [3]say [1]For to you that none - of men ˜ those the *ones*
who

15 Now when one of those who sat at the table with Him heard these things, he said to Him, "Blessed *is* he who shall eat bread in the kingdom of God!"
16 Then He said to him, "A certain man gave a great supper and invited many,
17 "and sent his servant at supper time to say to those who were invited, 'Come, for all things are now ready.'
18 "But they all with one *accord* began to make excuses. The first said to him, 'I have bought a piece of ground, and I must go and see it. I ask you to have me excused.'
19 "And another said, 'I have bought five yoke of oxen, and I am going to test them. I ask you to have me excused.'
20 "Still another said, 'I have married a wife, and therefore I cannot come.'
21 "So that servant came and reported these things to his master. Then the master of the house, being angry, said to his servant, 'Go out quickly into the streets and lanes of the city, and bring in here *the* poor and *the* maimed and *the* lame and *the* blind.'
22 "And the servant said, 'Master, it is done as you commanded, and still there is room.'
23 "Then the master said to the servant, 'Go out into the highways and hedges, and compel *them* to come in, that my house may be filled.
24 'For I say to you that none

---

[e] **(14:15)** TR, NU read αρτον, *bread.* [f] **(14:17)** NU omits παντα, *all (things).*
[g] **(14:21)** NU omits εκεινος, *that.*

of those men who were invited
shall taste my supper.' "
25 Now great multitudes went
with Him. And He turned and
said to them,
26 "If anyone comes to Me
and does not hate his father and
mother, wife and children,
brothers and sisters, yes, and
his own life also, he cannot be
My disciple.
27 "And whoever does not
bear his cross and come after
Me cannot be My disciple.
28 "For which of you, intending to build a tower, does not
sit down first and count the
cost, whether he has *enough* to
finish *it*—
29 "lest, after he has laid the
foundation, and is not able to
finish, all who see *it* begin to
mock him,
30 "saying, 'This man began
to build and was not able to finish.'
31 "Or what king, going to
make war against another king,
does not sit down first and consider whether he is able with
ten thousand to meet him who
comes against him with twenty
thousand?
32 "Or else, while the other is
still a great way off, he sends a
delegation and asks conditions
of peace.
33 "So likewise, whoever of
you does not forsake all that he

κεκλημένων γεύσεταί μου τοῦ δείπνου.' "
having been invited shall taste my - dinner.' "
were

It Costs to Follow Christ
(Matt. 10:37–39)

25 Συνεπορεύοντο δὲ αὐτῷ ὄχλοι πολλοί. Καὶ
[4]were [5]traveling [6]with [1]And [7]Him [3]crowds [2]large. And

στραφεὶς εἶπε πρὸς αὐτούς, **26** "Εἴ τις ἔρχεται πρός με
turning He said to them, "If anyone comes to Me

καὶ οὐ μισεῖ τὸν πατέρα αὐτοῦ καὶ τὴν μητέρα, καὶ τὴν
and not ˜ does hate - father ˜ his and - mother, and -

γυναῖκα καὶ τὰ τέκνα, καὶ τοὺς ἀδελφοὺς καὶ τὰς ἀδελφάς,
wife and - children, and - brothers and - sisters,

ἔτι δὲ καὶ τὴν ἑαυτοῦ ψυχήν, οὐ δύναταί μου
[2]in [3]addition [1]and even the [2]of [3]himself [1]life, [6]not [4]he [5]is [7]able [10]My
his own

μαθητὴς εἶναι. **27** Καὶ ὅστις οὐ βαστάζει τὸν σταυρὸν
[11]disciple [8]to [9]be. And whoever not ˜ does bear - cross ˜

αὐτοῦ καὶ ἔρχεται ὀπίσω μου οὐ δύναται εἶναί μου μαθητής.
his and come after Me not ˜ is able to be My disciple.

28 "Τίς γὰρ ἐξ ὑμῶν ὁ θέλων πύργον οἰκοδομῆσαι,
"which ˜ For of you the *one* wanting [3]a [4]tower [1]to [2]build,
who wants

οὐχὶ πρῶτον καθίσας ψηφίζει τὴν δαπάνην, εἰ ἔχει
does not first sitting down count up the cost, whether he has
sit down and

τὰ [h] εἰς ἀπαρτισμόν? **29** Ἵνα μήποτε θέντος αὐτοῦ
the *things* for completion? Lest perhaps [2]having [3]laid [1]him
resources to complete it? after he has laid

θεμέλιον καὶ μὴ ἰσχύοντος ἐκτελέσαι, πάντες οἱ
a foundation and not ˜ being able to finish, all the *ones*
is those who

θεωροῦντες ἄρξωνται ἐμπαίζειν αὐτῷ, **30** λέγοντες ὅτι 'Οὗτος ὁ
viewing *it* begin to mock him, saying - 'This -
view

ἄνθρωπος ἤρξατο οἰκοδομεῖν καὶ οὐκ ἴσχυσεν ἐκτελέσαι.'
man began to build and not ˜ was able to finish.'

31 "Ἢ τίς βασιλεὺς πορευόμενος συμβαλεῖν ἑτέρῳ
"Or what king going to engage another

βασιλεῖ εἰς πόλεμον οὐχὶ καθίσας πρῶτον βουλεύεται
king in battle *does* not sitting down first consider
sit down first and

εἰ δυνατός ἐστιν ἐν δέκα χιλιάσιν ἀπαντῆσαι τῷ
whether [3]able [1]he [2]is with ten thousand to meet the *one*
him who

μετὰ εἴκοσι χιλιάδων ἐρχομένῳ ἐπ' αὐτόν? **32** Εἰ δὲ μή
[4]with [5]twenty [6]thousand [1]coming [2]against [3]him? if ˜ And not
comes

γε ἔτι πόρρω αὐτοῦ ὄντος, πρεσβείαν ἀποστείλας
- [3]still [4]far [5]away [1]him [2]being, [7]a [8]delegation [6]sending
Otherwise while he is, he sends

ἐρωτᾷ τὰ πρὸς εἰρήνην. **33** Οὕτως οὖν πᾶς ἐξ
he asks the *terms* for peace. likewise ˜ Therefore every*one* of
and

ὑμῶν ὃς οὐκ ἀποτάσσεται πᾶσι τοῖς ἑαυτοῦ
you who not ˜ does renounce all the *things* of himself
say farewell to his own possessions,

---

h(14:28) NU omits τα, *the (things)*.

ὑπάρχουσιν, οὐ δύναταί μου εἶναι μαθητής.
belonging, not˜ is able [3]My [1]to [2]be disciple.

Tasteless Salt Is Worthless
(Matt. 5:13; Mark 9:50)

34 "Καλὸν τὸ ἅλας·* ἐὰν δὲ τὸ ἅλας μωρανθῇ ἐν
"[2]*is* [3]good - [1]Salt; if˜ but the salt becomes tasteless, with
τίνι ἀρτυθήσεται? 35 Οὔτε εἰς γῆν οὔτε εἰς κοπρίαν
what shall it be seasoned? Neither for *the* ground nor for a dunghill
εὔθετόν ἐστιν· ἔξω βάλλουσιν αὐτό. Ὁ ἔχων ὦτα ἀκούειν
[3]fit [1]is [2]it; [7]out [4]they [5]throw [6]it. The *one* having ears to hear
He who has
ἀκουέτω!"
let him hear!"

The Parable of the Lost Sheep
(Matt. 18:10–14)

15 1 Ἦσαν δὲ ἐγγίζοντες αὐτῷ πάντες οἱ
[8]were [1]Now [9]drawing [10]near [11]to [12]Him [2]all [3]the
τελῶναι καὶ οἱ ἁμαρτωλοὶ ἀκούειν αὐτοῦ. 2 Καὶ
[4]tax [5]collectors [6]and - [7]sinners to hear Him. And
διεγόγγυζον οἱ[a] Φαρισαῖοι καὶ οἱ γραμματεῖς λέγοντες ὅτι
[6]were [7]grumbling [1]the [2]Pharisees [3]and [4]the [5]scribes saying -
"Οὗτος ἁμαρτωλοὺς προσδέχεται καὶ συνεσθίει αὐτοῖς."
"This *man* sinners˜ welcomes and eats with them."
3 Εἶπε δὲ πρὸς αὐτοὺς τὴν παραβολὴν ταύτην, λέγων,
[2]He [3]told [1]And [6]to [7]them - [5]parable [4]this, saying,
4 "Τίς ἄνθρωπος ἐξ ὑμῶν ἔχων ἑκατὸν πρόβατα, καὶ
"What man of you having a hundred sheep, and
ἀπολέσας ἓν ἐξ αὐτῶν, οὐ καταλείπει τὰ ἐνενήκοντα
losing one of them, not˜ does leave behind the ninety-
ἐννέα ἐν τῇ ἐρήμῳ καὶ πορεύεται ἐπὶ τὸ ἀπολωλὸς
nine in the wilderness and goes after the *one* having been lost
the lost one
ἕως εὕρῃ αὐτό? 5 Καὶ εὑρὼν ἐπιτίθησιν ἐπὶ τοὺς
until he finds it? And having found *it* he puts *it* on the
his own
ὤμους ἑαυτοῦ χαίρων. 6 Καὶ ἐλθὼν εἰς τὸν οἶκον,
shoulders of himself rejoicing. And coming into the house,
συγκαλεῖ τοὺς φίλους καὶ τοὺς γείτονας, λέγων αὐτοῖς,
he calls together the friends and the neighbors, saying to them,
his his
'Συγχάρητέ μοι, ὅτι εὗρον τὸ πρόβατόν μου τὸ
'Rejoice with me, because I found - sheep˜ my the *one*
which
ἀπολωλός.' 7 Λέγω ὑμῖν ὅτι οὕτω χαρὰ ἔσται ἐν τῷ
having been lost.' I say to you that likewise [4]joy [1]*there* [2]will [3]be in -
was lost.'
οὐρανῷ ἐπὶ ἑνὶ ἁμαρτωλῷ μετανοοῦντι ἢ ἐπὶ
heaven over one sinner repenting more than over
ἐνενήκοντα ἐννέα δικαίοις οἵτινες οὐ χρείαν ἔχουσι
ninety- nine righteous *people* who [2]not [4]need [1]do [3]have
μετανοίας.
of repentance.

The Parable of the Lost Coin

8 "Ἢ τίς γυνὴ δραχμὰς ἔχουσα δέκα, ἐὰν ἀπολέσῃ
"Or what woman [3]drachmas [1]having [2]ten, if she loses

has cannot be My disciple.
34 "Salt *is* good; but if the salt has lost its flavor, how shall it be seasoned?
35 "It is neither fit for the land nor for the dunghill, *but* men throw it out. He who has ears to hear, let him hear!"
15 Then all the tax collectors and the sinners drew near to Him to hear Him.
2 And the Pharisees and scribes complained, saying, "This Man receives sinners and eats with them."
3 So He spoke this parable to them, saying:
4 "What man of you, having a hundred sheep, if he loses one of them, does not leave the ninety-nine in the wilderness, and go after the one which is lost until he finds it?
5 "And when he has found *it,* he lays *it* on his shoulders, rejoicing.
6 "And when he comes home, he calls together *his* friends and neighbors, saying to them, 'Rejoice with me, for I have found my sheep which was lost!'
7 "I say to you that likewise there will be more joy in heaven over one sinner who repents than over ninety-nine just persons who need no repentance.
8 "Or what woman, having ten silver coins, if she loses one

[a](15:2) NU adds τε, *both.*

***(14:34)** ἅλας *(halas).* Noun meaning *salt.* Here (and in the parallels Matt. 5:13; Mark 9:49, 50) Jesus may have been thinking about one or more of the properties of salt. Interpreters debate whether it is the seasoning, preserving, or fertilizing of salt that is paralleled by the spiritual qualities of disciples. In Col. 4:6, a similar quality is figuratively applied to a Christian's speech.

coin, does not light a lamp,
sweep the house, and search
carefully until she finds *it?*
9 "And when she has found
it, she calls *her* friends and
neighbors together, saying,
'Rejoice with me, for I have
found the piece which I lost!'
10 "Likewise, I say to you,
there is joy in the presence of
the angels of God over one sinner who repents."
11 Then He said: "A certain
man had two sons.
12 "And the younger of them
said to *his* father, 'Father, give
me the portion of goods that
falls *to me.*' So he divided to
them *his* livelihood.
13 "And not many days after,
the younger son gathered all together, journeyed to a far country, and there wasted his
possessions with prodigal living.
14 "But when he had spent all,
there arose a severe famine in
that land, and he began to be in
want.
15 "Then he went and joined
himself to a citizen of that country, and he sent him into his
fields to feed swine.
16 "And he would gladly have
filled his stomach with the pods
that the swine ate, and no one
gave him *anything.*
17 "But when he came to himself, he said, 'How many of my
father's hired servants have
bread enough and to spare, and
I perish with hunger!
18 'I will arise and go to my

δραχμὴν μίαν, οὐχὶ ἅπτει λύχνον καὶ σαροῖ τὴν οἰκίαν καὶ
drachma ˜ one, not ˜ does light a lamp and sweep the house and

ζητεῖ ἐπιμελῶς ἕως ὅτου εὕρῃ? 9 Καὶ εὑροῦσα
search carefully until - she finds *it?* And finding *it*
when she finds it,

συγκαλεῖται τὰς φίλας καὶ τὰς γείτονας, λέγουσα,
she calls together the *women* friends and the *women* neighbors, saying,
her her

'Συγχάρητέ μοι, ὅτι εὗρον τὴν δραχμὴν ἣν ἀπώλεσα.'
'Rejoice with me, because I found the drachma which I lost.'

10 Οὕτω, λέγω ὑμῖν, χαρὰ γίνεται ἐνώπιον τῶν ἀγγέλων τοῦ
Thus, I say to you, [3]joy [1]*there* [2]is before the angels -
Just so,

Θεοῦ ἐπὶ ἑνὶ ἁμαρτωλῷ μετανοοῦντι."
of God over one sinner repenting."

The Parable of the Lost Son

11 Εἶπε δέ, "Ἄνθρωπός τις εἶχε δύο υἱούς. 12 Καὶ
[2]He [3]said [1]And "A man ˜ certain had two sons. And

εἶπεν ὁ νεώτερος αὐτῶν τῷ πατρί, 'Πάτερ, δός μοι τὸ
[5]said [1]the [2]younger [3]of [4]them to the father, 'Father, give to me the
his

ἐπιβάλλον μέρος τῆς οὐσίας.' Καὶ διεῖλεν αὐτοῖς τὸν
[5]falling [6]to [7]*me* [1]share [2]of [3]the [4]wealth.' And he divided to them the
which falls between them his

βίον. 13 Καὶ μετ' οὐ πολλὰς ἡμέρας
means of subsistence. And [4]after [1]not [2]many [3]days

συναγαγὼν ἅπαντα ὁ νεώτερος υἱὸς ἀπεδήμησεν
having gathered together all *things* the younger son went on a journey

εἰς χώραν μακράν, καὶ ἐκεῖ διεσκόρπισε τὴν οὐσίαν αὐτοῦ
to a country ˜ distant, and there he squandered - wealth ˜ his

ζῶν ἀσώτως. 14 Δαπανήσαντος δὲ αὐτοῦ πάντα, ἐγένετο
by living dissolutely. having spent But him all *things,* [4]came
But when he had spent everything,

λιμὸς ἰσχυρὸς κατὰ τὴν χώραν ἐκείνην, καὶ αὐτὸς
[1]a [3]famine [2]strong throughout - country ˜ that, and he
severe

ἤρξατο ὑστερεῖσθαι. 15 Καὶ πορευθεὶς ἐκολλήθη ἑνὶ
began to be in need. And going he was joined to one
he went and joined himself

τῶν πολιτῶν τῆς χώρας ἐκείνης, καὶ ἔπεμψεν αὐτὸν εἰς
of the citizens - of country ˜ that, and he sent him into

τοὺς ἀγροὺς αὐτοῦ βόσκειν χοίρους. 16 Καὶ ἐπεθύμει
- fields ˜ his to feed swine. And he was longing

γεμίσαι τὴν κοιλίαν αὐτοῦ ἀπὸ[b] τῶν κερατίων ὧν
to fill - belly ˜ his with the carob pods which
stomach

ἤσθιον οἱ χοῖροι, καὶ οὐδεὶς ἐδίδου αὐτῷ. 17 Εἰς
[3]were [4]eating [1]the [2]swine, and no one was giving *any* to him. [4]to
would give

ἑαυτὸν δὲ ἐλθὼν εἶπε, 'Πόσοι μίσθιοι τοῦ
[5]himself [1]But [2]having [3]come he said, 'How many hired servants -

πατρός μου περισσεύουσιν ἄρτων, ἐγὼ δὲ λιμῷ
of father ˜ my have an abundance of bread, I ˜ but [3]with [4]hunger

ἀπόλλυμαι! 18 'Ἀναστὰς πορεύσομαι πρὸς τὸν πατέρα μου
[1]am [2]perishing! Rising I will go to - father ˜ my
I will arise and go

[b](15:16) For γεμισαι την κοιλιαν αυτου απο, *to fill his belly from,* NU reads χορτασθηναι εκ, *to be satisfied from.*

καὶ ἐρῶ αὐτῷ, "Πάτερ, ἥμαρτον εἰς τὸν οὐρανὸν καὶ
and I will say to him, "Father, I sinned (have sinned) against - heaven and

ἐνώπιόν σου, 19 καὶ οὐκέτι εἰμὶ ἄξιος κληθῆναι υἱός σου.
before you, and no longer am I worthy to be called son ˜ your.

Ποίησόν με ὡς ἕνα τῶν μισθίων σου."' 20 Καὶ
Make me like one - of [2]hired [3]servants [1]your."' And

ἀναστὰς ἦλθε πρὸς τὸν πατέρα αὐτοῦ. Ἔτι δὲ αὐτοῦ
rising (he arose) he went (and went) to - father ˜ his. still (But) But (while) him (he)

μακρὰν ἀπέχοντος, εἶδεν αὐτὸν ὁ πατὴρ αὐτοῦ καὶ
far (was) being away (still far off), [3]saw [4]him - [2]father [1]his and

ἐσπλαγχνίσθη καὶ δραμὼν ἐπέπεσεν ἐπὶ τὸν τράχηλον αὐτοῦ
felt compassion and running (he ran) he fell (and) on (gave him) - (a) neck ˜ his (hug)

καὶ κατεφίλησεν αὐτόν. 21 Εἶπε δὲ αὐτῷ ὁ υἱός,
and kissed affectionately ˜ him. [4]said [1]And [5]to [6]him [2]the [3]son,

'Πάτερ, ἥμαρτον εἰς τὸν οὐρανὸν καὶ ἐνώπιόν σου, καὶ
'Father, I sinned (have sinned) against - heaven and before you, and

οὐκέτι εἰμὶ ἄξιος κληθῆναι υἱός σου.' 22 Εἶπε δὲ ὁ πατὴρ
no longer am I worthy to be called son ˜ your.' [4]said [1]But [2]the [3]father

πρὸς τοὺς δούλους αὐτοῦ,[c] "Ἐξενέγκατε τὴν στολὴν τὴν
to - slaves (servants) ˜ his, 'Bring out the robe ˜ -

πρώτην καὶ ἐνδύσατε αὐτόν, καὶ δότε δακτύλιον εἰς τὴν χεῖρα
first (best) and put *it* on him, and give (put) a ring to (on) - hand ˜

αὐτοῦ καὶ ὑποδήματα εἰς τοὺς πόδας. 23 Καὶ ἐνέγκαντες τὸν
his and sandals to (on) the (his) feet. And bringing in the

μόσχον τὸν σιτευτὸν θύσατε, καὶ φαγόντες εὐφρανθῶμεν,
calf ˜ - fatted slaughter *it*, and eating (let us eat) let us be merry (and be joyful),

24 ὅτι οὗτος ὁ υἱός μου νεκρὸς ἦν καὶ ἀνέζησε, καὶ
because this - son of mine dead ˜ was and came to life, and

ἀπολωλὼς ἦν καὶ εὑρέθη.' Καὶ ἤρξαντο εὐφραίνεσθαι.
[3]lost [1]he [2]was and was found.' And they began to be merry.

25 "Ἦν δὲ ὁ υἱὸς αὐτοῦ ὁ πρεσβύτερος ἐν ἀγρῷ. Καὶ
"[5]was [1]Now - [4]son [2]his - [3]older in *the* field. And

ὡς ἐρχόμενος ἤγγισε τῇ οἰκίᾳ, ἤκουσε συμφωνίας καὶ
while coming he drew near to the house, he heard music and

χορῶν. 26 Καὶ προσκαλεσάμενος ἕνα τῶν παίδων,[d]
dancing. And having summoned one of the servants,

ἐπυνθάνετο τί εἴη ταῦτα. 27 Ὁ δὲ εἶπεν
he was inquiring what [3]might (were) [4]be [1]these [2]*things*. [2]the (he) [3]one [1]And said

αὐτῷ ὅτι 'Ὁ ἀδελφός σου ἥκει, καὶ ἔθυσεν ὁ πατήρ
to him - - 'brother ˜ Your has come, and [3]slaughtered (has slaughtered) - [2]father

σου τὸν μόσχον τὸν σιτευτόν, ὅτι ὑγιαίνοντα αὐτὸν
[1]your the calf ˜ - fatted, because [5]being [6]in [7]health (in good health) [3]him

ἀπέλαβεν.' 28 Ὠργίσθη δὲ καὶ οὐκ ἤθελεν
[1]he [2]received [4]back.' [2]he [3]was [4]angry [1]But and [3]not [1]he [2]did want

εἰσελθεῖν. Ὁ οὖν πατὴρ αὐτοῦ ἐξελθὼν παρεκάλει αὐτόν.
to go in. - Then father ˜ his coming out (came out) was pleading (and began to plead) with him.

father, and will say to him, "Father, I have sinned against heaven and before you,
19 "and I am no longer worthy to be called your son. Make me like one of your hired servants."'
20 "And he arose and came to his father. But when he was still a great way off, his father saw him and had compassion, and ran and fell on his neck and kissed him.
21 "And the son said to him, 'Father, I have sinned against heaven and in your sight, and am no longer worthy to be called your son.'
22 "But the father said to his servants, 'Bring out the best robe and put *it* on him, and put a ring on his hand and sandals on *his* feet.
23 'And bring the fatted calf here and kill *it*, and let us eat and be merry;
24 'for this my son was dead and is alive again; he was lost and is found.' And they began to be merry.
25 "Now his older son was in the field. And as he came and drew near to the house, he heard music and dancing.
26 "So he called one of the servants and asked what these things meant.
27 "And he said to him, 'Your brother has come, and because he has received him safe and sound, your father has killed the fatted calf.'
28 "But he was angry and would not go in. Therefore his father came out and pleaded with him.

---

[c](15:22) NU adds *ταχυ*, *quickly*. [d](15:26) TR adds *αυτου*, *his*.

29 "So he answered and said to *his* father, 'Lo, these many years I have been serving you; I never transgressed your commandment at any time; and yet you never gave me a young goat, that I might make merry with my friends.
30 'But as soon as this son of yours came, who has devoured your livelihood with harlots, you killed the fatted calf for him.'
31 "And he said to him, 'Son, you are always with me, and all that I have is yours.
32 'It was right that we should make merry and be glad, for your brother was dead and is alive again, and was lost and is found.' "

16 He also said to His disciples: "There was a certain rich man who had a steward, and an accusation was brought to him that this man was wasting his goods.
2 "So he called him and said to him, 'What is this I hear about you? Give an account of your stewardship, for you can no longer be steward.'
3 "Then the steward said within himself, 'What shall I do? For my master is taking the stewardship away from me. I cannot dig; I am ashamed to beg.
4 'I have resolved what to do, that when I am put out of the stewardship, they may receive me into their houses.'
5 "So he called every one of

29 Ὁ δὲ ἀποκριθεὶς εἶπε τῷ πατρί, "Ἰδού, τοσαῦτα
[2]the [3]*one* [1]But answering said to the father, 'Lo, so many
he his

ἔτη δουλεύω σοι καὶ οὐδέποτε ἐντολήν σου παρῆλθον, καὶ
years I am serving you and never [3]command [2]your [1]transgressed, and
have been

ἐμοὶ οὐδέποτε ἔδωκας ἔριφον ἵνα μετὰ τῶν φίλων
[7]to [8]me [2]never [1]you [3]gave [4]a [5]young [6]goat so that with - friends ˜

μου εὐφρανθῶ. **30** Ὅτε δὲ ὁ υἱός σου οὗτος ὁ
my I might be merry. when ˜ But - [2]son [3]of [4]you [1]this the *one*
yours who

καταφαγών σου τὸν βίον μετὰ πορνῶν ἦλθεν,
having eaten up your - means of subsistence with prostitutes came,
has devoured

ἔθυσας αὐτῷ τὸν μόσχον τὸν σιτευτόν.' **31** Ὁ δὲ
you slaughtered [4]for [5]him [1]the [3]calf - [2]fatted.' [2]the [3]*one* [1]And
he

εἶπεν αὐτῷ, 'Τέκνον, σὺ πάντοτε μετ' ἐμοῦ εἶ, καὶ πάντα
said to him, 'Child, you [2]always [3]with [4]me [1]are, and all *things* ˜
'Son,

τὰ ἐμὰ σά ἐστιν. **32** Εὐφρανθῆναι δὲ καὶ χαρῆναι
- my yours ˜ are. [5]to [6]be [7]merry [1]But [8]and [9]to [10]rejoice

ἔδει, ὅτι ὁ ἀδελφός σου οὗτος νεκρὸς ἦν καὶ
[2]it [3]was [4]necessary, because - [2]brother [3]of [4]you [1]this [6]dead [5]was and
yours

ἀνέζησε[e] καὶ ἀπολωλὼς ἦν καὶ εὑρέθη.' "
came to life and lost ˜ was and was found.' "
has come back

The Parable of the Crafty Steward

16 **1** Ἔλεγε δὲ καὶ πρὸς τοὺς μαθητὰς αὐτοῦ,
[2]He [3]said [1]And also to - disciples ˜ His,

"Ἄνθρωπός τις ἦν πλούσιος ὃς εἶχεν οἰκονόμον, καὶ
"A man ˜ certain was rich who had a steward, and
manager,

οὗτος διεβλήθη αὐτῷ ὡς διασκορπίζων τὰ ὑπάρχοντα
this *man* was accused to him as wasting the *things* belonging
his possessions.

αὐτοῦ. **2** Καὶ φωνήσας αὐτὸν εἶπεν αὐτῷ, 'Τί τοῦτο ἀκούω
of him. And calling him he said to him, 'What *is* this I hear

περὶ σοῦ? Ἀπόδος τὸν λόγον τῆς οἰκονομίας σου, οὐ γὰρ
about you? Give over the account - of stewardship ˜ your, [4]not [1]for
Render an management

δυνήσῃ ἔτι οἰκονομεῖν.' **3** Εἶπε δὲ ἐν ἑαυτῷ ὁ
[2]you [3]will be able still ˜ to be steward.' [4]said [1]And [5]within [6]himself [2]the
manager.'

οἰκονόμος, 'Τί ποιήσω, ὅτι ὁ κύριός μου ἀφαιρεῖται τὴν
[3]steward, 'What shall I do, because - master ˜ my is taking away the
manager,

οἰκονομίαν ἀπ' ἐμοῦ? Σκάπτειν οὐκ ἰσχύω, ἐπαιτεῖν
stewardship from me? [5]to [6]dig [3]not [1]I [2]am [4]able, [10]to [11]beg
management

αἰσχύνομαι. **4** Ἔγνων τί ποιήσω, ἵνα ὅταν
[7]I [8]am [9]ashamed. I knew what I will do, so that whenever
know

μετασταθῶ τῆς οἰκονομίας, δέξωνταί με εἰς τοὺς
I am removed from the stewardship, they will receive me into -
management, welcome

οἴκους αὐτῶν.' **5** Καὶ προσκαλεσάμενος ἕνα ἕκαστον τῶν
houses ˜ their.' And having summoned one ˜ each of the

[e](15:32) NU reads εζησεν, *lived.*

χρεωφειλετῶν τοῦ κυρίου ἑαυτοῦ ἔλεγε τῷ πρώτῳ,
debtors of the master of himself he said to the first,
of his master

'Πόσον ὀφείλεις τῷ κυρίῳ μου?' **6** Ὁ δὲ εἶπεν,
'How much do you owe - to master ˜ my?' [2]the [3]*one* [1]And said,
he

''Ἑκατὸν βάτους ἐλαίου.' Καὶ εἶπεν αὐτῷ, 'Δέξαι σου τὸ
'A hundred baths of olive oil.' And he said to him, 'Take your -

γράμμα[a] καὶ καθίσας ταχέως γράψον πεντήκοντα.'
writing and sitting down quickly write fifty.'
bill sit down and

7 Ἔπειτα ἑτέρῳ εἶπε, 'Σὺ δὲ πόσον ὀφείλεις?'
Then to another he said, '[5]you [1]And [2]how [3]much [4]do [6]owe?'

Ὁ δὲ εἶπεν, 'Ἑκατὸν κόρους σίτου.' Καὶ λέγει αὐτῷ,
[8]the [9]*one* [7]And said, 'A hundred kors of wheat.' And he says to him,
measures said

'Δέξαι σου τὸ γράμμα[b] καὶ γράψον ὀγδοήκοντα.' **8** Καὶ
'Take your - writing and write eighty.' And
bill

ἐπῄνεσεν ὁ κύριος τὸν οἰκονόμον τῆς ἀδικίας ὅτι
[3]praised [1]the [2]master the steward - of unrighteousness because
dishonest steward

φρονίμως ἐποίησεν. Ὅτι οἱ υἱοὶ τοῦ αἰῶνος τούτου
[3]prudently [1]he [2]did. Because the sons - of age ˜ this
he has dealt shrewdly.

φρονιμώτεροι ὑπὲρ τοὺς υἱοὺς τοῦ φωτὸς εἰς τὴν
[2]more [3]prudent [9]than [10]the [11]sons - [12]of [13]light [4]in [5]the
shrewder their own

γενεὰν τὴν ἑαυτῶν εἰσι. **9** Κἀγὼ ὑμῖν λέγω,
[6]generation - [7]of [8]themselves [1]are. And I [2]to [3]you [1]say,

ποιήσατε ἑαυτοῖς φίλους ἐκ τοῦ μαμωνᾶ* τῆς
make [2]for [3]yourselves [1]friends from the mammon -
by

ἀδικίας, ἵνα ὅταν ἐκλείπητε,[c] δέξωνται
of unrighteousness, so that whenever you fail, they may receive
welcome

ὑμᾶς εἰς τὰς αἰωνίους σκηνάς. **10** Ὁ πιστὸς ἐν
you into the eternal tents. The *one who is* faithful in *the*
dwellings. He what

ἐλαχίστῳ καὶ ἐν πολλῷ πιστός ἐστι, καὶ ὁ ἐν
least *thing* [2]also [4]in [5]*the* [6]much [7]*thing* [3]faithful [1]is, and the *one who is* [2]in
is least what is much he

ἐλαχίστῳ ἄδικος καὶ ἐν πολλῷ ἄδικός
[3]*the* [4]least [5]*thing* [1]unrighteous [7]also [9]in [10]*the* [11]much [12]*thing* [8]unrighteous
what is least what is much

ἐστιν. **11** Εἰ οὖν ἐν τῷ ἀδίκῳ μαμωνᾷ πιστοὶ οὐκ
[6]is. if ˜ Therefore [5]in [6]the [7]unrighteous [8]mammon [4]faithful [3]not
with

ἐγένεσθε, τὸ ἀληθινὸν τίς ὑμῖν πιστεύσει? **12** Καὶ
[1]you [2]were, [14]the [15]genuine [16]*thing* [9]who [12]to [13]you [10]will [11]entrust? And
what is genuine

εἰ ἐν τῷ ἀλλοτρίῳ πιστοὶ οὐκ ἐγένεσθε, τὸ
if in the *thing* belonging to another [4]faithful [3]not [1]you [2]were, [10]the
what belongs what

ὑμέτερον τίς ὑμῖν δώσει? **13** Οὐδεὶς οἰκέτης
[11]your [12]*thing* [5]who [8]to [9]you [6]will [7]give? No household servant
is yours

δύναται δυσὶ κυρίοις δουλεύειν· ἢ γὰρ τὸν ἕνα μισήσει
is able [3]two [4]masters [1]to [2]serve; either ˜ for [4]the [5]one [1]he [2]will [3]hate

his master's debtors to *him,*
and said to the first, 'How much
do you owe my master?'
6 "And he said, 'A hundred
measures of oil.' So he said to
him, 'Take your bill, and sit
down quickly and write fifty.'
7 "Then he said to another,
'And how much do you owe?'
So he said, 'A hundred measures of wheat.' And he said to
him, 'Take your bill, and write
eighty.'
8 "So the master com-
mended the unjust steward because he had dealt shrewdly.
For the sons of this world are
more shrewd in their generation than the sons of light.
9 "And I say to you, make
friends for yourselves by unrighteous mammon, that when
you fail, they may receive you
into an everlasting home.
10 "He who *is* faithful in *what*
is least is faithful also in much;
and he who is unjust in *what is*
least is unjust also in much.
11 "Therefore if you have not
been faithful in the unrighteous
mammon, who will commit to
your trust the true *riches?*
12 "And if you have not been
faithful in what is another
man's, who will give you what
is your own?
13 "No servant can serve two
masters; for either he will hate

---

[a](**16:6**) NU reads τα γραμματα, *documents.*
[b](**16:7**) NU reads τα γραμματα, *documents.*
[c](**16:9**) NU reads εκλιπη, *it fails.*

---

*(**16:9**) *μαμωνᾶς (mamōnas).* Greek translation of an Aramaic noun meaning *riches, wealth, property* (cf. English *mammon).* Here and in v. 11 it is used somewhat disparagingly of material possessions in contrast to "true," spiritual riches. In v. 13 and the parallel Matt. 6:24 it is personified as a rival god of affluence.

the one and love the other, or
else he will be loyal to the one
and despise the other. You cannot serve God and mammon."
14 Now the Pharisees, who
were lovers of money, also
heard all these things, and they
derided Him.
15 And He said to them, "You
are those who justify yourselves before men, but God
knows your hearts. For what is
highly esteemed among men is
an abomination in the sight of
God.
16 "The law and the prophets
were until John. Since that time
the kingdom of God has been
preached, and everyone is
pressing into it.
17 "And it is easier for heaven
and earth to pass away than for
one tittle of the law to fail.
18 "Whoever divorces his
wife and marries another commits adultery; and whoever
marries her who is divorced
from *her* husband commits adultery.
19 "There was a certain rich
man who was clothed in purple
and fine linen and fared sumptu-
ously every day.
20 "But there was a certain
beggar named Lazarus, full of
sores, who was laid at his gate,
21 "desiring to be fed with the
crumbs which fell from the rich

καὶ τὸν ἕτερον ἀγαπήσει, ἢ ἑνὸς ἀνθέξεται καὶ τοῦ
and [2]the [3]other [1]love, or [6]one [1]he [2]will [3]be [4]devoted [5]to and [2]the

ἑτέρου καταφρονήσει. Οὐ δύνασθε Θεῷ δουλεύειν καὶ
[3]other [1]despise. [6]not [4]You [5]are [7]able [10]God [8]to [9]serve and

μαμωνᾷ."
mammon."

The Kingdom and the Law

(Matt. 5:31, 32; 11:12, 13; Mark 10:11, 12)

14 Ἤκουον δὲ ταῦτα πάντα καὶ οἱ Φαρισαῖοι
[9]were [10]hearing [1]Now [12]these [13]*things* [11]all [4]also [2]the [3]Pharisees

φιλάργυροι ὑπάρχοντες, καὶ ἐξεμυκτήριζον αὐτόν. **15** Καὶ
[6]lovers [7]of [8]money [5]being, and they were mocking Him. And
who were,

εἶπεν αὐτοῖς, "Ὑμεῖς ἐστε οἱ δικαιοῦντες ἑαυτοὺς
He said to them, "You are the *ones* justifying yourselves
those who justify

ἐνώπιον τῶν ἀνθρώπων, ὁ δὲ Θεὸς γινώσκει τὰς καρδίας ὑμῶν.
before - men, - but God knows - hearts ~ your.

Ὅτι τὸ ἐν ἀνθρώποις ὑψηλὸν βδέλυγμα
Because the [3]among [4]men [1]exalted [2]*thing* *is* an abomination
that which is exalted

ἐνώπιον τοῦ Θεοῦ. **16** Ὁ νόμος καὶ οἱ προφῆται ἕως
before - God. The law and the prophets *were* until

Ἰωάννου. Ἀπὸ τότε ἡ βασιλεία τοῦ Θεοῦ εὐαγγελίζεται καὶ
John. From then the kingdom - of God is being preached and
Since has been

πᾶς εἰς αὐτὴν βιάζεται. **17** Εὐκοπώτερον δέ ἐστι τὸν
every*one* [3]into [4]it [1]enters [2]forcibly. [4]easier [1]And [2]it [3]is - *for*

οὐρανὸν καὶ τὴν γῆν παρελθεῖν ἢ τοῦ νόμου μίαν
heaven and - earth to pass away than *for* [3]of [4]the [5]law [1]one

κεραίαν πεσεῖν.
[2]tittle to fall.
serif fail.

18 "Πᾶς ὁ ἀπολύων τὴν γυναῖκα αὐτοῦ καὶ γαμῶν
"Every - *one* divorcing - wife ~ his and marrying
"Everyone who divorces marries

ἑτέραν μοιχεύει· καὶ πᾶς[d] ὁ ἀπολελυμένην
another commits adultery; and every - *one a woman* having been divorced
everyone who marries a woman

ἀπὸ ἀνδρὸς γαμῶν μοιχεύει.
from a husband marrying commits adultery.
divorced from a husband

The Rich Man and Lazarus

19 "Ἄνθρωπος δέ τις ἦν πλούσιος, καὶ ἐνεδιδύσκετο
"[2]a [4]man [1]Now [3]certain was rich, and was dressed in

πορφύραν καὶ βύσσον, εὐφραινόμενος καθ' ἡμέραν λαμπρῶς.
purple and fine linen, making merry [2]every [3]day [1]splendidly.
enjoying himself

20 Πτωχὸς δέ τις ἦν[e] ὀνόματι Λάζαρος ὅς[f]
[6]poor [7]*man* [1]But [4]a [5]certain [2]*there* [3]was by name Lazarus who
named

ἐβέβλητο πρὸς τὸν πυλῶνα αὐτοῦ ἡλκωμένος **21** καὶ
had been placed at - gate ~ his covered with sores and

ἐπιθυμῶν χορτασθῆναι ἀπὸ τῶν ψιχίων[g] τῶν πιπτόντων ἀπὸ
longing to be satisfied from the crumbs - falling from
with

[d](**16:18**) NU omits πας, *every*. [e](**16:20**) NU omits ην, *(there) was*.
[f](**16:20**) NU omits ος, *who*.
[g](**16:21**) NU omits των ψιχιων, *the crumbs*.

τῆς τραπέζης τοῦ πλουσίου. Ἀλλὰ καὶ οἱ κύνες ἐρχόμενοι
the table of the rich *man.* But even the dogs coming
came and

ἀπέλειχον τὰ ἕλκη αὐτοῦ. **22** Ἐγένετο δὲ ἀποθανεῖν
were licking - sores ~ his. [2]it [3]came [4]to [5]pass [1]And to die
would lick that the

τὸν πτωχὸν καὶ ἀπενεχθῆναι αὐτὸν ὑπὸ τῶν ἀγγέλων εἰς τὸν
the poor *man* and to be carried away him by the angels to the
poor man died he was carried away

κόλπον Ἀβραάμ. Ἀπέθανε δὲ καὶ ὁ πλούσιος καὶ
bosom of Abraham. [5]died [1]And [6]also [2]the [3]rich [4]*man* and

ἐτάφη. **23** Καὶ ἐν τῷ Ἅιδῃ* ἐπάρας τοὺς ὀφθαλμοὺς αὐτοῦ,
was buried. And in - Hades lifting up - eyes ~ his,

ὑπάρχων ἐν βασάνοις, ὁρᾷ τὸν Ἀβραὰμ ἀπὸ μακρόθεν, καὶ
being in torments, he sees - Abraham from afar, and
saw

Λάζαρον ἐν τοῖς κόλποις αὐτοῦ. **24** Καὶ αὐτὸς φωνήσας εἶπε,
Lazarus in - bosoms ~ his. And he calling said,
bosom called and

'Πάτερ Ἀβραάμ, ἐλέησόν με καὶ πέμψον Λάζαρον ἵνα
'Father Abraham, have mercy on me and send Lazarus so that

βάψῃ τὸ ἄκρον τοῦ δακτύλου αὐτοῦ ὕδατος καὶ καταψύξῃ
he may dip the tip - of finger ~ his in water and cool

τὴν γλῶσσάν μου· ὅτι ὀδυνῶμαι ἐν τῇ φλογὶ ταύτῃ.'
- tongue ~ my; because I am tormented in - flame ~ this.'

25 Εἶπε δὲ Ἀβραάμ, 'Τέκνον, μνήσθητι ὅτι ἀπέλαβες σὺ τὰ
[3]said [1]But [2]Abraham, 'Child, remember that received ~ you -

ἀγαθά σου ἐν τῇ ζωῇ σου, καὶ Λάζαρος ὁμοίως τὰ
[2]good [3]*things* [1]your in - life ~ your, and Lazarus likewise -

κακά· νῦν δὲ ὧδε[h] παρακαλεῖται, σὺ δὲ ὀδυνᾶσαι.
bad things; now ~ but here he is comforted, you ~ but are tormented.

26 Καὶ ἐπὶ πᾶσι τούτοις, μεταξὺ ἡμῶν καὶ ὑμῶν
And in addition to all these *things,* between us and you

χάσμα μέγα ἐστήρικται, ὅπως οἱ θέλοντες διαβῆναι
a chasm ~ great has been fixed, so that the *ones* wanting to cross
gulf those who want

ἔνθεν πρὸς ὑμᾶς μὴ δύνωνται, μηδὲ οἱ ἐκεῖθεν
from here to you not ~ are able, neither [2]the [3]*ones* [4]from [5]here
those

πρὸς ἡμᾶς διαπερῶσιν.' **27** Εἶπε δέ, 'Ἐρωτῶ οὖν
[8]to [9]you [1]may [6]pass [7]over.' [2]he [3]said [1]But, 'I ask therefore ~

σε, πάτερ, ἵνα πέμψῃς αὐτὸν εἰς τὸν οἶκον τοῦ πατρός
you, father, that you would send him to the house - of father ~

μου, **28** ἔχω γὰρ πέντε ἀδελφούς, ὅπως διαμαρτύρηται
my, [2]I [3]have [1]for five brothers, so that he may testify

αὐτοῖς, ἵνα μὴ καὶ αὐτοὶ ἔλθωσιν εἰς τὸν τόπον τοῦτον τῆς
to them, that [4]not [2]also [1]they [3]may [5]come to - place ~ this -
lest

βασάνου.' **29** Λέγει αὐτῷ Ἀβραάμ, 'Ἔχουσι Μωσέα καὶ τοὺς
of torture.' [2]says [3]to [4]him [1]Abraham, 'They have Moses and the
said

προφήτας· ἀκουσάτωσαν αὐτῶν.' **30** Ὁ δὲ εἶπεν, 'Οὐχί,
prophets; let them hear them.' [2]the [3]*one* [1]But said, 'No,
he

πάτερ Ἀβραάμ· ἀλλ' ἐάν τις ἀπὸ νεκρῶν πορευθῇ πρὸς
father Abraham; but if someone from *the* dead should go to

αὐτούς, μετανοήσουσιν.' **31** Εἶπε δὲ αὐτῷ, 'Εἰ Μωσέως καὶ
them, they will repent.' [2]he [3]said [1]But to him, 'If [5]Moses [6]and

man's table. Moreover the dogs came and licked his sores.
22 "So it was that the beggar died, and was carried by the angels to Abraham's bosom. The rich man also died and was buried.
23 "And being in torments in Hades, he lifted up his eyes and saw Abraham afar off, and Lazarus in his bosom.
24 "Then he cried and said, 'Father Abraham, have mercy on me, and send Lazarus that he may dip the tip of his finger in water and cool my tongue; for I am tormented in this flame.'
25 "But Abraham said, 'Son, remember that in your lifetime you received your good things, and likewise Lazarus evil things; but now he is comforted and you are tormented.
26 'And besides all this, between us and you there is a great gulf fixed, so that those who want to pass from here to you cannot, nor can those from there pass to us.'
27 "Then he said, 'I beg you therefore, father, that you would send him to my father's house,
28 'for I have five brothers, that he may testify to them, lest they also come to this place of torment.'
29 "Abraham said to him, 'They have Moses and the prophets; let them hear them.'
30 "And he said, 'No, father Abraham; but if one goes to them from the dead, they will repent.'
31 "But he said to him, 'If they do not hear Moses and the

---

[h]**(16:25)** TR reads οδε, *this (one).*

***(16:23)** ᾅδης *(hadēs).* Noun referring to *Hades, the realm of the dead.* In Matt. 11:23 (parallel Luke 10:15) and Acts 2:27, 31 it translates Hebrew *she'ōl,* likewise a broad word for the realm of the dead. It is used in close association with death in Rev. 1:18; 6:8; 20:13, 14. Here in Luke 16:23 it is specifically the realm of the wicked dead in torment and thus essentially synonymous with Gehenna (see γέεννα at James 3:6).

prophets, neither will they be
persuaded though one rise from
the dead.' "
17 Then He said to the
disciples, "It is impos-
sible that no offenses should
come, but woe *to him* through
whom they do come!
2 "It would be better for him
if a millstone were hung around
his neck, and he were thrown
into the sea, than that he should
offend one of these little ones.
3 "Take heed to yourselves.
If your brother sins against
you, rebuke him; and if he repents, forgive him.
4 "And if he sins against you
seven times in a day, and seven
times in a day returns to you,
saying, 'I repent,' you shall forgive him."
5 And the apostles said to
the Lord, "Increase our faith."
6 So the Lord said, "If you
have faith as a mustard seed,
you can say to this mulberry
tree, 'Be pulled up by the roots
and be planted in the sea,' and it
would obey you.
7 "And which of you, having
a servant plowing or tending
sheep, will say to him when he
has come in from the field,
'Come at once and sit down to
eat'?
8 "But will he not rather say
to him, 'Prepare something for

τῶν προφητῶν οὐκ ἀκούουσιν, οὐδὲ ἐάν τις ἐκ
[7]the [8]prophets [3]not [1]they [2]do [4]hear, neither [5]if [6]someone [9]from

νεκρῶν ἀναστῇ πεισθήσονται.' "
[10]*the* [11]dead [7]should [8]rise [1]will [2]they [3]be [4]persuaded.' "

Jesus Warns of Offenses
(Matt. 18:6, 7, 21, 22; Mark 9:42)

17 1 Εἶπε δὲ πρὸς τοὺς μαθητάς,[a] "Ἀνένδεκτόν ἐστι
[2]He [3]said [1]Then to the disciples, "[3]impossible [1]It [2]is

τοῦ μὴ ἐλθεῖν τὰ σκάνδαλα, οὐαὶ δὲ[b] δι' οὗ
- *for* [2]not [3]to [4]come - [1]offenses, woe ~ but *to the one* through whom

ἔρχεται! 2 Λυσιτελεῖ αὐτῷ εἰ μύλος ὀνικὸς[c] περίκειται
they come! It is better for him if a millstone of a donkey is put
would be huge millstone were

περὶ τὸν τράχηλον αὐτοῦ, καὶ ἔρριπται εἰς τὴν
around - neck ~ his, and he had been thrown into the
be

θάλασσαν, ἢ ἵνα σκανδαλίσῃ ἕνα τῶν μικρῶν τούτων.
sea, than that he should offend one - of [2]little [3]*ones* [1]these.

3 Προσέχετε ἑαυτοῖς. Ἐὰν δὲ ἁμάρτῃ εἰς σὲ[d] ὁ
Take heed to yourselves. if ~ And [3]sins [4]against [5]you -

ἀδελφός σου ἐπιτίμησον αὐτῷ· καὶ ἐὰν μετανοήσῃ, ἄφες
[2]brother [1]your rebuke him; and if he repents, forgive

αὐτῷ. 4 Καὶ ἐὰν ἑπτάκις τῆς ἡμέρας ἁμάρτῃ εἰς σέ, καὶ
him. And if seven times in the day he sins against you, and
a

ἑπτάκις τῆς ἡμέρας[e] ἐπιστρέψῃ,[f] λέγων, 'Μετανοῶ,'
seven times in the day he returns, saying, 'I repent,'
a

ἀφήσεις αὐτῷ."
you shall forgive him."

Faith and Duty

5 Καὶ εἶπον οἱ ἀπόστολοι τῷ Κυρίῳ, "Πρόσθες ἡμῖν
And [3]said [1]the [2]apostles to the Lord, "Add to us
"Increase our

πίστιν."
faith."

6 Εἶπε δὲ ὁ Κύριος, "Εἰ ἔχετε[g] πίστιν ὡς κόκκον
[4]said [1]And [2]the [3]Lord, "If you have faith as a grain
mustard

σινάπεως, ἐλέγετε ἂν τῇ συκαμίνῳ ταύτῃ, 'Ἐκριζώθητι
of mustard, you could say - - to [2]mulberry [3]tree [1]this, 'Be uprooted
seed,

καὶ φυτεύθητι ἐν τῇ θαλάσσῃ,' καὶ ὑπήκουσεν ἂν ὑμῖν.
and be planted in the sea,' and it would obey - you.

7 "Τίς δὲ ἐξ ὑμῶν δοῦλον ἔχων ἀροτριῶντα ἢ
"which ~ And of you [2]a [3]slave [1]having plowing or
servant

ποιμαίνοντα, ὃς εἰσελθόντι ἐκ τοῦ ἀγροῦ ἐρεῖ
tending sheep, who [4]*to* [5]*him* [6]coming [7]in [8]from [9]the [10]field [1]will [3]say
when he comes in

εὐθέως, 'Παρελθὼν ἀνάπεσε'? 8 Ἀλλ' οὐχὶ ἐρεῖ
[2]immediately, 'Having come along recline *to eat*'? But [3]not [1]will [2]he say
'Come and

αὐτῷ, ' Ἑτοίμασον τί δειπνήσω, καὶ
to him, 'Prepare something *that* I may dine, and

---

[a](17:1) NU adds αυτου, *His*.
[b](17:1) NU reads πλην, *nevertheless*.
[c](17:2) NU reads λιθος μυλικος, *a stone of a mill*.
[d](17:3) NU omits εις σε, *against you*.
[e](17:4) NU omits της ημερας, *in the day*.
[f](17:4) TR adds επι σε, *to you*; NU adds προς σε, *to you*.
[g](17:6) Many mss., TR read ειχετε, *you had*.

περιζωσάμενος διακόνει μοι ἕως φάγω καὶ πίω, καὶ μετὰ
having girded yourself serve me until I eat and drink, and after
gird yourself and

ταῦτα φάγεσαι καὶ πίεσαι σύ'? 9 Μὴ χάριν ἔχει
these *things* [2]will [3]eat [4]and [5]drink [1]you'? [3]not [5]thanks [1]He [2]does [4]have

τῷ δούλῳ ἐκείνῳ[h] ὅτι ἐποίησε τὰ
- for slave ~ that, *does he* because he did the *things*
servant

διαταχθέντα?[i] Οὐ δοκῶ.[j] 10 Οὕτω καὶ ὑμεῖς, ὅταν
having been commanded? [3]not [1]I [2]think. So also you, whenever

ποιήσητε πάντα τὰ διαταχθέντα ὑμῖν, λέγετε ὅτι
you do all the *things* having been commanded to you, say -

'Δοῦλοι ἀχρεῖοί ἐσμεν. Ὅτι[k] ὃ ὠφείλομεν ποιῆσαι
'[4]slaves [3]useless [1]We [2]are. Because [4]what [5]we [6]ought [7]to [8]do
servants

πεποιήκαμεν.' "
[1]we [2]have [3]done.' "

Jesus Cleanses Ten Lepers

11 Καὶ ἐγένετο ἐν τῷ πορεύεσθαι αὐτὸν εἰς
And it happened in - [2]to [3]travel [1]Him to
while He was traveling

Ἰερουσαλήμ, καὶ αὐτὸς διήρχετο διὰ μέσου Σαμαρείας καὶ
Jerusalem, and He was going through *the* midst of Samaria and
that

Γαλιλαίας. 12 Καὶ εἰσερχομένου αὐτοῦ εἴς τινα κώμην,
Galilee. And entering ~ Him into a certain village,
as He entered

ἀπήντησαν αὐτῷ δέκα λεπροὶ ἄνδρες, οἳ ἔστησαν πόρρωθεν.
[4]met [5]Him [1]ten [2]leprous [3]men, who stood at a distance.

13 Καὶ αὐτοὶ ἦραν φωνήν, λέγοντες, "Ἰησοῦ, ἐπιστάτα,
And they lifted *their* voice, saying, "Jesus, Master,

ἐλέησον ἡμᾶς!"
have mercy on us!"

14 Καὶ ἰδὼν εἶπεν αὐτοῖς, "Πορευθέντες ἐπιδείξατε
And seeing *them* He said to them, "Going show
"Go and

ἑαυτοὺς τοῖς ἱερεῦσι." Καὶ ἐγένετο ἐν τῷ ὑπάγειν
yourselves to the priests." And it happened in - [2]to [3]go [4]away
as they went away,

αὐτούς, ἐκαθαρίσθησαν. 15 Εἷς δὲ ἐξ αὐτῶν, ἰδὼν ὅτι
[1]them, they were cleansed. one ~ And of them, seeing that

ἰάθη, ὑπέστρεψε, μετὰ φωνῆς μεγάλης δοξάζων τὸν
he was cured, returned, [3]with [4]a [6]voice [5]great [1]glorifying -
loud

Θεόν· 16 καὶ ἔπεσεν ἐπὶ πρόσωπον παρὰ τοὺς πόδας αὐτοῦ,
[2]God; and he fell on *his* face at - feet ~ His,

εὐχαριστῶν* αὐτῷ. Καὶ αὐτὸς ἦν Σαμαρείτης. 17 Ἀποκριθεὶς
thanking Him. And he was a Samaritan. answering ~

δὲ ὁ Ἰησοῦς εἶπεν, "Οὐχὶ οἱ δέκα ἐκαθαρίσθησαν? Οἱ δὲ
And - Jesus said, "[2]not [3]the [4]ten [1]Were [5]cleansed? [9]the [6]But

ἐννέα ποῦ? 18 Οὐχ εὑρέθησαν ὑποστρέψαντες δοῦναι
[10]nine [7]where [8]*are?* [2]not [3]*any* [1]Were found returning to give

δόξαν τῷ Θεῷ εἰ μὴ ὁ ἀλλογενὴς οὗτος?" 19 Καὶ εἶπεν
glory - to God if not - foreigner ~ this?" And He said
except

αὐτῷ, "Ἀναστὰς πορεύου. Ἡ πίστις σου σέσωκέ σε."
to him, "Arising go. - faith ~ Your has saved you."
"Arise and made you well."

my supper, and gird yourself and serve me till I have eaten and drunk, and afterward you will eat and drink'?
9 "Does he thank that servant because he did the things that were commanded him? I think not.
10 "So likewise you, when you have done all those things which you are commanded, say, 'We are unprofitable servants. We have done what was our duty to do.' "
11 Now it happened as He went to Jerusalem that He passed through the midst of Samaria and Galilee.
12 Then as He entered a certain village, there met Him ten men who were lepers, who stood afar off.
13 And they lifted up *their* voices and said, "Jesus, Master, have mercy on us!"
14 So when He saw *them,* He said to them, "Go, show yourselves to the priests." And so it was that as they went, they were cleansed.
15 And one of them, when he saw that he was healed, returned, and with a loud voice glorified God,
16 and fell down on *his* face at His feet, giving Him thanks. And he was a Samaritan.
17 So Jesus answered and said, "Were there not ten cleansed? But where *are* the nine?
18 "Were there not any found who returned to give glory to God except this foreigner?"
19 And He said to him, "Arise, go your way. Your faith has made you well."

---

[h](17:9) NU omits *εκεινω, that.* [i](17:9) TR adds *αυτω, to him.* [j](17:9) NU omits *ου δοκω, I think not.* [k](17:10) NU omits *οτι, because.*

***(17:16)** *εὐχαριστέω (eucharisteō).* Verb meaning *give thanks.* The word may emphasize either the act of communicating thanks or the attitude of *being thankful, feeling obligated to thank.* Its use here illustrates the difficulty of determining which nuance is more central in a particular occurrence. In the NT it always describes the giving of thanks to God, except Rom. 16:4 where Paul expresses thanks to Priscilla and Aquila. εὐχαριστέω is also used

20 Now when He was asked by the Pharisees when the kingdom of God would come, He answered them and said, "The kingdom of God does not come with observation;
21 "nor will they say, 'See here!' or 'See there!' For indeed, the kingdom of God is within you."
22 Then He said to the disciples, "The days will come when you will desire to see one of the days of the Son of Man, and you will not see *it*.
23 "And they will say to you, 'Look here!' or 'Look there!' Do not go after *them* or follow *them*.
24 "For as the lightning that flashes out of one *part* under heaven shines to the other *part* under heaven, so also the Son of Man will be in His day.
25 "But first He must suffer many things and be rejected by this generation.
26 "And as it was in the days of Noah, so it will be also in the days of the Son of Man:
27 "They ate, they drank, they married wives, they were given in marriage, until the day that Noah entered the ark, and the flood came and destroyed them all.
28 "Likewise as it was also in the days of Lot: They ate, they drank, they bought, they sold, they planted, they built;
29 "but on the day that Lot went out of Sodom it rained fire and brimstone from heaven and destroyed *them* all.
30 "Even so will it be in the day when the Son of Man is

[l](17:21) NU omits Ιδου, *Look.* [m](17:30) NU reads *τα αυτα, the same (things).*

with the meaning *offer the table benediction, say grace* (Mark 14:23; Rom. 14:6), a technical use it shares with *εὐλογέω* (cf. Mark 8:6, 7 where both words appear). Cf. the cognate noun *εὐχαριστία, thanksgiving, gratitude* (2 Cor. 9:11; Acts 24:3); and the adjective *εὐχάριστος, thankful* (Col. 3:15).

How the Kingdom Will Come
(Matt. 24:23–28, 37–41; Mark 13:21–23)

20 Ἐπερωτηθεὶς δὲ ὑπὸ τῶν Φαρισαίων πότε ἔρχεται
[2]being [3]asked [1]Now by the Pharisees when [5]is [6]coming
when He was asked was

ἡ βασιλεία τοῦ Θεοῦ, ἀπεκρίθη αὐτοῖς καὶ εἶπεν, "Οὐκ
[1]the [2]kingdom - [3]of [4]God, He answered them and said, "[6]not

ἔρχεται ἡ βασιλεία τοῦ Θεοῦ μετὰ παρατηρήσεως·
[5]does [7]come [1]The [2]kingdom - [3]of [4]God with observation;

21 οὐδὲ ἐροῦσιν, 'Ἰδοὺ ὧδε,' ἤ, 'Ἰδοὺ[l] ἐκεῖ.' Ἰδοὺ
neither will they say, 'Look here,' or, 'Look there *it is*.' behold ˜

γάρ, ἡ βασιλεία τοῦ Θεοῦ ἐντὸς ὑμῶν ἐστιν."
For, the kingdom - of God [2]among [3]you [1]is."

22 Εἶπε δὲ πρὸς τοὺς μαθητάς, "Ἐλεύσονται ἡμέραι
[2]He [3]said [1]And to the disciples, "[2]will [3]come [1]Days

ὅτε ἐπιθυμήσετε μίαν τῶν ἡμερῶν τοῦ Υἱοῦ τοῦ
when you will desire [3]one [4]of [5]the [6]days [7]of [8]the [9]Son -

Ἀνθρώπου ἰδεῖν, καὶ οὐκ ὄψεσθε. **23** Καὶ ἐροῦσιν
[10]of [11]Man [1]to [2]see, and [3]not [1]you [2]will see *it*. And they will say

ὑμῖν, 'Ἰδοὺ ὧδε,' ἤ, 'Ἰδοὺ ἐκεῖ.' Μὴ ἀπέλθητε μηδὲ διώξητε.
to you, 'Look here,' or, 'Look there.' not ˜ Do go forth nor follow *them*.

24 Ὥσπερ γὰρ ἡ ἀστραπὴ ἡ ἀστράπτουσα ἐκ
[2]just [3]as [1]For the lightning the *kind* flashing out of
which flashes

τῆς ὑπ' οὐρανὸν εἰς τὴν ὑπ' οὐρανὸν
the *one part* under heaven [2]to [3]the [4]*other* [5]*part* [6]under [7]heaven

λάμπει, οὕτως ἔσται ὁ Υἱὸς τοῦ Ἀνθρώπου ἐν τῇ ἡμέρᾳ
[1]shines, so [5]will [6]be [1]the [2]Son - [3]of [4]Man in - day ˜

αὐτοῦ. **25** Πρῶτον δὲ δεῖ αὐτὸν πολλὰ παθεῖν
His. first ˜ But it is necessary *for* Him [3]many [4]*things* [1]to [2]suffer
He must suffer

καὶ ἀποδοκιμασθῆναι ἀπὸ τῆς γενεᾶς ταύτης. **26** Καὶ καθὼς
and to be rejected by - generation ˜ this. And just as
be rejected

ἐγένετο ἐν ταῖς ἡμέραις Νῶε, οὕτως ἔσται καὶ ἐν ταῖς
it happened in the days of Noah, so it will be also in the

ἡμέραις τοῦ Υἱοῦ τοῦ Ἀνθρώπου. **27** Ἤσθιον,
days of the Son - of Man. They were eating,

ἔπινον, ἐγάμουν, ἐξεγαμίζοντο,
they were drinking, they were marrying, they were being given in marriage,

ἄχρι ἧς ἡμέρας εἰσῆλθε Νῶε εἰς τὴν κιβωτόν, καὶ ἦλθεν ὁ
until which day entered ˜ Noah into the ark, and [3]came [1]the
the

κατακλυσμὸς καὶ ἀπώλεσεν ἅπαντας. **28** Ὁμοίως καὶ ὡς
[2]flood and destroyed *them* all. Likewise also as

ἐγένετο ἐν ταῖς ἡμέραις Λώτ· ἤσθιον, ἔπινον,
it happened in the days of Lot; they were eating, they were drinking,

ἠγόραζον, ἐπώλουν, ἐφύτευον, ᾠκοδόμουν·
they were buying, they were selling, they were planting, they were building;

29 ᾗ δὲ ἡμέρᾳ ἐξῆλθε Λὼτ ἀπὸ Σοδόμων, ἔβρεξε πῦρ
[2]in [3]which [1]but day [2]went [3]out [1]Lot from Sodom, it rained fire
the

καὶ θεῖον ἀπ' οὐρανοῦ καὶ ἀπώλεσεν ἅπαντας.
and brimstone from heaven and destroyed *them* all.
sulfur the sky

30 Κατὰ ταῦτα[m] ἔσται ᾗ ἡμέρᾳ ὁ Υἱὸς τοῦ
According to these *things* it will be in which day the Son -
In the same way the

Ἀνθρώπου ἀποκαλύπτεται. **31** Ἐν ἐκείνῃ τῇ ἡμέρᾳ, ὃς
of Man is revealed. In that - day, *he* who

ἔσται ἐπὶ τοῦ δώματος, καὶ τὰ σκεύη αὐτοῦ ἐν τῇ οἰκίᾳ, μὴ
shall be on the housetop, and - goods ˜ his in the house, [3]not

καταβάτω ἆραι αὐτά. Καὶ ὁ ἐν τῷ ἀγρῷ
[1]let [2]him come down to take away ˜ them. And the *one* in the field

ὁμοίως μὴ ἐπιστρεψάτω εἰς τὰ ὀπίσω.
likewise [3]not [1]let [2]him turn back for the *things left* behind.

32 Μνημονεύετε τῆς γυναικὸς Λώτ. **33** Ὃς ἐὰν ζητήσῃ τὴν
Remember the wife of Lot. Who ever seeks -

ψυχὴν αὐτοῦ σῶσαι[n] ἀπολέσει αὐτήν, καὶ ὃς ἐὰν ἀπολέσῃ
[4]life [3]his [1]to [2]save will lose it, and who ever loses

αὐτὴν[o] ζῳογονήσει αὐτήν. **34** Λέγω ὑμῖν, ταύτῃ τῇ νυκτὶ
it will preserve it. I say to you, in that - night

ἔσονται δύο ἐπὶ κλίνης μιᾶς· εἷς[p] παραληφθήσεται καὶ
[3]will [4]be [1]two [2]*men* on bed ˜ one; one will be taken and

ὁ ἕτερος ἀφεθήσεται. **35** Δύο ἔσονται ἀλήθουσαι
the other will be left. Two *women* will be grinding

ἐπὶ τὸ αὐτό· μία παραληφθήσεται καὶ ἡ ἑτέρα
at the same *thing*; one will be taken and the other
together;

ἀφεθήσεται."[q]
will be left."

37 Καὶ ἀποκριθέντες λέγουσιν αὐτῷ, "Ποῦ, Κύριε?"
And answering they say to Him, "Where, Lord?"
said

Ὁ δὲ εἶπεν αὐτοῖς, "Ὅπου τὸ σῶμα, ἐκεῖ
[2]the [3]*One* [1]And said to them, "Where the body *is*, there
He

συναχθήσονται οἱ ἀετοί."
[3]will [4]be [5]gathered [6]together [1]the [2]eagles."

The Parable of the Persistent Widow

18 **1** Ἔλεγε δὲ καὶ παραβολὴν αὐτοῖς πρὸς τὸ
[2]He [3]told [1]And also a parable to them to the
that

δεῖν πάντοτε προσεύχεσθαι[a] καὶ μὴ ἐκκακεῖν,
to be necessary always to be praying and not ˜ to lose heart,
one must always pray not lose

2 λέγων, "Κριτής τις ἦν ἔν τινι πόλει τὸν Θεὸν μὴ
saying, "A judge ˜ certain was in a certain city - [3]God [1]not
who did not

φοβούμενος καὶ ἄνθρωπον μὴ ἐντρεπόμενος. **3** Χήρα δὲ
[2]fearing and [3]man [1]not [2]regarding. [2]a [3]widow [1]And
fear God nor have regard for men.

ἦν ἐν τῇ πόλει ἐκείνῃ, καὶ ἤρχετο πρὸς αὐτόν, λέγουσα,
was in - city ˜ that, and she would come to him, saying,
kept coming

'Ἐκδίκησόν με ἀπὸ τοῦ ἀντιδίκου μου.' **4** Καὶ οὐκ
'Give justice to me against - adversary ˜ my.' And [3]not

ἠθέλησεν ἐπὶ χρόνον· μετὰ δὲ ταῦτα εἶπεν ἐν ἑαυτῷ,
[1]he [2]did want to for a time; after ˜ but these *things* he said in himself,

'Εἰ καὶ τὸν Θεὸν οὐ φοβοῦμαι καὶ ἄνθρωπον οὐκ
'Since indeed - [5]God [3]not [1]I [2]do [4]fear and [5]man [3]not
'Although

ἐντρέπομαι, **5** διά γε τὸ παρέχειν μοι κόπον τὴν χήραν
[1]I [2]do [4]regard, because ˜ yet - [3]to [4]cause [5]me [6]trouble - [2]widow
have regard for, bothers me

---

revealed.
31 "In that day, he who is on the housetop, and his goods *are* in the house, let him not come down to take them away. And likewise the one who is in the field, let him not turn back.
32 "Remember Lot's wife.
33 "Whoever seeks to save his life will lose it, and whoever loses his life will preserve it.
34 "I tell you, in that night there will be two *men* in one bed: the one will be taken and the other will be left.
35 "Two *women* will be grinding together: the one will be taken and the other left.
36 "Two *men* will be in the field: the one will be taken and the other left."
37 And they answered and said to Him, "Where, Lord?" So He said to them, "Wherever the body is, there the eagles will be gathered together."

18 Then He spoke a parable to them, that men always ought to pray and not lose heart,
2 saying: "There was in a certain city a judge who did not fear God nor regard man.
3 "Now there was a widow in that city; and she came to him, saying, 'Get justice for me from my adversary.'
4 "And he would not for a while; but afterward he said within himself, 'Though I do not fear God nor regard man,
5 'yet because this widow

---

[n]**(17:33)** NU reads *περιποιησασθαι, to preserve.*
[o]**(17:33)** NU omits *αυτην, it.*
[p]**(17:34)** TR, NU read *ο εις, the one.*
[q]**(17:35)** Some mss. add *δυο εσονται εν τω αγρω ο εις παραληφθησεται και ο ετερος αφεθησεται, two shall be in the field the one will be taken and the other will be left.*
[a]**(18:1)** Many mss., NU add *αυτους, (for) them.*

troubles me I will avenge her,
lest by her continual coming
she weary me.' "
6 Then the Lord said, "Hear
what the unjust judge said.
7 "And shall God not avenge
His own elect who cry out day
and night to Him, though He
bears long with them?
8 "I tell you that He will
avenge them speedily. Nevertheless, when the Son of Man
comes, will He really find faith
on the earth?"
9 Also He spoke this parable
to some who trusted in themselves that they were righteous, and despised others:
10 "Two men went up to the
temple to pray, one a Pharisee
and the other a tax collector.
11 "The Pharisee stood and
prayed thus with himself, 'God,
I thank You that I am not like
other men—extortioners, unjust, adulterers, or even as this
tax collector.
12 'I fast twice a week; I give
tithes of all that I possess.'
13 "And the tax collector,
standing afar off, would not so
much as raise *his* eyes to
heaven, but beat his breast,
saying, 'God, be merciful to me
a sinner!'
14 "I tell you, this man went
down to his house justified

ταύτην ἐκδικήσω αὐτήν, ἵνα μὴ εἰς τέλος ἐρχομένη
[1]this I will give justice to her, so that not to *the* end coming
lest she wear me out by forever

ὑποπιάζῃ με.' " **6** Εἶπε δὲ ὁ Κύριος, "Ἀκούσατε τί ὁ
she wear out ˜ me.' " [4]said [1]And [2]the [3]Lord, "Hear what the
coming to me.' "

κριτὴς τῆς ἀδικίας λέγει. **7** Ὁ δὲ Θεὸς οὐ μὴ ποιήσῃ τὴν
judge - of injustice says. - And [2]God [3]not [4]not [1]will [5]do -
unjust judge said. surely not

ἐκδίκησιν τῶν ἐκλεκτῶν αὐτοῦ τῶν βοώντων πρὸς αὐτὸν
justice - [1]for [3]elect [4]*ones* [2]His the *ones* crying to Him
chosen who cry

ἡμέρας καὶ νυκτός, καὶ μακροθυμῶν ἐπ' αὐτοῖς? **8** Λέγω
day and night, and *He is* bearing long over them? I say
and yet He is patient with

ὑμῖν ὅτι ποιήσει τὴν ἐκδίκησιν αὐτῶν ἐν τάχει.
to you that He will do - justice for them with speed.
speedily.

Πλὴν ὁ Υἱὸς τοῦ Ἀνθρώπου ἐλθὼν ἆρα εὑρήσει
Nevertheless [2]the [3]Son - [4]of [5]Man [6]coming [7]really [1]will [8]find
when He comes

τὴν πίστιν ἐπὶ τῆς γῆς?"
- faith on the earth?"

The Parable of the Pharisee and the Publican

9 Εἶπε δὲ πρός τινας τοὺς πεποιθότας ἐφ'
[2]He [3]told [1]And to some the *ones* having put confidence in
who trusted

ἑαυτοῖς ὅτι εἰσὶ δίκαιοι, καὶ ἐξουθενοῦντας τοὺς λοιπούς,
themselves that they are righteous, and despising the rest,
were despised

τὴν παραβολὴν ταύτην· **10** "Ἄνθρωποι δύο ἀνέβησαν εἰς τὸ
- parable ˜ this: "men ˜ Two went up to the

ἱερὸν προσεύξασθαι, ὁ εἷς Φαρισαῖος καὶ ὁ ἕτερος
temple to pray, the one a Pharisee and the other

τελώνης. **11** Ὁ Φαρισαῖος σταθεὶς πρὸς ἑαυτὸν ταῦτα
a tax collector. The Pharisee standing to himself [3]these [4]*things*
by thus

προσηύχετο, 'Ὁ Θεός, εὐχαριστῶ σοι ὅτι οὐκ εἰμὶ ὥσπερ οἱ
[1]was [2]praying, - 'God, I thank You that [3]not [1]I [2]am just like the

λοιποὶ τῶν ἀνθρώπων, ἅρπαγες, ἄδικοι, μοιχοί, ἢ καὶ ὡς
rest - of men, swindlers, unjust, adulterers, or even like

οὗτος ὁ τελώνης. **12** Νηστεύω δὶς τοῦ σαββάτου,
this - tax collector. I fast twice in the week,

ἀποδεκατῶ πάντα ὅσα κτῶμαι.' **13** Καὶ ὁ τελώνης
I tithe all *things* as many as I acquire.' And the tax collector

μακρόθεν ἑστὼς οὐκ ἤθελεν οὐδὲ τοὺς ὀφθαλμοὺς εἰς τὸν
[2]far [3]away [1]standing not ˜ did wish ˜ even [3]the [4]eyes [5]to -
his

οὐρανὸν ἐπᾶραι, ἀλλ' ἔτυπτεν εἰς τὸ στῆθος αὐτοῦ, λέγων,
[6]heaven [1]to [2]raise, but he was beating on - chest ˜ his, saying,

'Ὁ Θεός, ἱλάσθητί* μοι τῷ ἁμαρτωλῷ!' **14** Λέγω ὑμῖν,
- 'God, be propitiated to me the sinner!' I say to you,
merciful a

κατέβη οὗτος δεδικαιωμένος εἰς τὸν οἶκον αὐτοῦ
[3]went [4]down [1]this [2]*man* [8]having [9]been [10]justified [5]to - [7]house [6]his
justified

***(18:13)** ἱλάσκομαι *(hilaskomai)*. Verb meaning *propitiate, expiate*. Here its meaning is more closely related to the root adjective ἵλεως, *gracious, merciful*, thus, "God *be merciful* to me, the sinner!" *To propitiate* means "to satisfy the demands of, appease" in this case, an offended Deity. Sacrifice for sins is the method God chose to make satisfaction for sins. In Heb. 2:17 Jesus propitiated, or made satisfaction for, the sins of His people; His sacrificial death paid the penalty of sin, satisfying the righteous wrath of God. Cf. the cognate nouns ἱλασμός, *propitiation, expiation* (1 John 2:2; 4:10); and ἱλαστήριον, *means of propitiation, expiation.*

ἤ γὰρ ἐκεῖνος· ὅτι πᾶς ὁ ὑψῶν ἑαυτὸν
rather than in fact that *other one;* because every - *one* exalting himself
everyone who exalts

ταπεινωθήσεται, ὁ δὲ ταπεινῶν ἑαυτὸν ὑψωθήσεται."
will be humbled, [2]the [3]*one* [1]but humbling himself will be exalted."
he who humbles

Jesus Blesses Little Children
(Matt. 19:13–15; Mark 10:13–16)

15 Προσέφερον δὲ αὐτῷ καὶ τὰ βρέφη ἵνα αὐτῶν
[2]they [3]were [4]bringing [1]And to Him also - infants that [4]them

ἅπτηται· ἰδόντες δὲ οἱ μαθηταὶ ἐπετίμησαν αὐτοῖς.
[1]He [2]might [3]touch; [8]seeing [5]but [6]the [7]disciples they rebuked them.
but when the disciples saw it,

16 Ὁ δὲ Ἰησοῦς προσκαλεσάμενος αὐτὰ εἶπεν, "Ἄφετε τὰ
- But Jesus summoning them said, "Allow the

παιδία ἔρχεσθαι πρός με καὶ μὴ κωλύετε αὐτά· τῶν γὰρ
little children to come to Me and not ~ do forbid them; - for

τοιούτων ἐστὶν ἡ βασιλεία τοῦ Θεοῦ. 17 Ἀμὴν λέγω
of such *ones* is the kingdom - of God. Amen I say
Assuredly

ὑμῖν, ὃς ἐὰν μὴ δέξηται τὴν βασιλείαν τοῦ Θεοῦ ὡς
to you, who ever not ~ does receive the kingdom - of God as

παιδίον, οὐ μὴ εἰσέλθῃ εἰς αὐτήν."
a little child, [2]not [3]not [1]will enter into it."
by no means

The Rich Young Ruler
(Matt. 19:16–22; Mark 10:17–22)

18 Καὶ ἐπηρώτησέ τις αὐτὸν ἄρχων, λέγων,
And [4]asked [1]a [2]certain [5]Him [3]ruler, saying,

"Διδάσκαλε ἀγαθέ, τί ποιήσας ζωὴν αἰώνιον
"Teacher ~ Good, what ~ doing [5]life [4]eternal
by doing

κληρονομήσω?"
[1]shall [2]I [3]inherit?"

19 Εἶπε δὲ αὐτῷ ὁ Ἰησοῦς, "Τί με λέγεις ἀγαθόν?
[3]said [1]But [4]to [5]him - [2]Jesus, "Why [4]Me [1]do [2]you [3]call good?

Οὐδεὶς ἀγαθὸς εἰ μὴ εἷς, ὁ Θεός. 20 Τὰς ἐντολὰς
No one *is* good if not One, - God. The commandments
except

οἶδας· «Μὴ μοιχεύσῃς, Μὴ φονεύσῃς, Μὴ κλέψῃς,
you know: «not ~ Do commit adultery, not ~ Do murder, not ~ Do steal,

Μὴ ψευδομαρτυρήσῃς, Τίμα τὸν πατέρα σου καὶ τὴν μητέρα
not ~ Do bear false witness, Honor - father ~ your and - mother ~

σου.»"
your.»"

21 Ὁ δὲ εἶπε, "Ταῦτα πάντα ἐφυλαξάμην ἐκ
[2]the [3]*one* [1]And said, "these ~ All I kept from
he have observed

νεότητός μου."
youth ~ my."

22 Ἀκούσας δὲ ταῦτα[b] ὁ Ἰησοῦς εἶπεν αὐτῷ, "Ἔτι
hearing ~ And these *things* - Jesus said to him, "Still
when He heard

ἕν σοι λείπει. Πάντα ὅσα ἔχεις πώλησον καὶ
one *thing* for you is lacking. All *things* as many as you have sell and
you lack.

rather than the other; for everyone who exalts himself will be humbled, and he who humbles himself will be exalted."
15 Then they also brought infants to Him that He might touch them; but when the disciples saw *it,* they rebuked them.
16 But Jesus called them to *Him* and said, "Let the little children come to Me, and do not forbid them; for of such is the kingdom of God.
17 "Assuredly, I say to you, whoever does not receive the kingdom of God as a little child will by no means enter it."
18 Now a certain ruler asked Him, saying, "Good Teacher, what shall I do to inherit eternal life?"
19 So Jesus said to him, "Why do you call Me good? No one *is* good but One, *that is,* God.
20 "You know the commandments: *'Do not commit adultery,' 'Do not murder,' 'Do not steal,' 'Do not bear false witness,' 'Honor your father and your mother.'* "
21 And he said, "All these things I have kept from my youth."
22 So when Jesus heard these things, He said to him, "You still lack one thing. Sell all that

[b](18:22) NU omits ταυτα, *these (things).*

you have and distribute to the
poor, and you will have treasure in heaven; and come, follow Me."
23 But when he heard this, he
became very sorrowful, for he
was very rich.
24 And when Jesus saw that
he became very sorrowful, He
said, "How hard it is for those
who have riches to enter the
kingdom of God!
25 "For it is easier for a camel
to go through the eye of a needle than for a rich man to enter
the kingdom of God."
26 And those who heard it
said, "Who then can be saved?"
27 But He said, "The things
which are impossible with men
are possible with God."
28 Then Peter said, "See, we
have left all and followed You."
29 So He said to them, "Assuredly, I say to you, there is
no one who has left house or
parents or brothers or wife or
children, for the sake of the
kingdom of God,
30 "who shall not receive
many times more in this present time, and in the age to
come eternal life."
31 Then He took the twelve
aside and said to them, "Behold, we are going up to Jerusa-

διάδος πτωχοῖς, καὶ ἕξεις θησαυρὸν ἐν οὐρανῷ· καὶ
distribute to *the* poor, and you will have treasure in heaven; and

δεῦρο, ἀκολούθει μοι." **23** Ὁ δὲ ἀκούσας ταῦτα
come, follow Me." [2]the [3]*one* [1]But hearing these *things*
when he heard

περίλυπος ἐγένετο, ἦν γὰρ πλούσιος σφόδρα.
[3]very [4]sad [1]he [2]became, [6]he [7]was [5]for [9]rich [8]extremely.

God Can Save Even the Rich
(Matt. 19:23–30; Mark 10:23–31)

24 Ἰδὼν δὲ αὐτὸν ὁ Ἰησοῦς περίλυπον γενόμενον
[3]seeing [1]And [4]him - [2]Jesus [6]very [7]sad [5]becoming
And when Jesus saw that he became

εἶπε, "Πῶς δυσκόλως οἱ τὰ χρήματα ἔχοντες
He said, "How with difficulty [2]the [3]*ones* - [5]possessions [4]having

εἰσελεύσονται εἰς τὴν βασιλείαν τοῦ Θεοῦ! **25** Εὐκοπώτερον
[1]will [6]enter into the kingdom - of God! [4]easier

γάρ ἐστι κάμηλον διὰ τρυμαλιᾶς ῥαφίδος εἰσελθεῖν ἢ
[1]For [2]it [3]is *for* a camel [4]through [5]*the* [6]hole [7]of [8]a [9]needle [1]to [2]go [3]in than

πλούσιον εἰς τὴν βασιλείαν τοῦ Θεοῦ εἰσελθεῖν."
for a rich *person* [3]into [4]the [5]kingdom - [6]of [7]God [1]to [2]enter."

26 Εἶπον δὲ οἱ ἀκούσαντες, "Καὶ τίς δύναται
[5]said [1]And [2]the [3]*ones* [4]hearing, "then ˜ Who is able
those who heard,

σωθῆναι?"
to be saved?"

27 Ὁ δὲ εἶπε, "Τὰ ἀδύνατα παρὰ
[2]the [3]*One* [1]But said, "The *things* impossible with
He "These things which are

ἀνθρώποις δυνατά ἐστι παρὰ τῷ Θεῷ."
men possible ˜ are with - God."

28 Εἶπε δὲ Πέτρος, "Ἰδού, ἡμεῖς ἀφήκαμεν πάντα καὶ[c]
[3]said [1]And [2]Peter, "See, we left all *things* and
have left

ἠκολουθήσαμέν σοι."
followed You."

29 Ὁ δὲ εἶπεν αὐτοῖς, "Ἀμὴν λέγω ὑμῖν ὅτι
[2]the [3]*One* [1]And said to them, "Amen I say to you that
He "Assuredly

οὐδείς ἐστιν ὃς ἀφῆκεν οἰκίαν ἢ γονεῖς ἢ ἀδελφοὺς ἢ
[3]no [4]one [1]*there* [2]is who left house or parents or brothers or
has left

γυναῖκα ἢ τέκνα ἕνεκεν τῆς βασιλείας τοῦ Θεοῦ, **30** ὃς
wife or children for the sake of the kingdom - of God, who

οὐ μὴ ἀπολάβῃ πολλαπλασίονα ἐν τῷ καιρῷ τούτῳ, καὶ
[2]not [3]not [1]shall [4]receive many times more in - time ˜ this, and
certainly

ἐν τῷ αἰῶνι τῷ ἐρχομένῳ ζωὴν αἰώνιον."
in the age the *one* coming life ˜ eternal."
to come

Jesus a Third Time Predicts His Death and Resurrection
(Matt. 20:17–19; Mark 10:32–34)

31 Παραλαβὼν δὲ τοὺς δώδεκα, εἶπε πρὸς αὐτούς,
[2]taking [3]aside [1]Now the twelve, He said to them,

"Ἰδού, ἀναβαίνομεν εἰς Ἱεροσόλυμα, καὶ τελεσθήσεται
"Behold, we are going up to Jerusalem, and [13]will [14]be [15]accomplished

---

[c](18:28) For *αφηκαμεν παντα και, have left all (things) and,* NU reads *αφεντες τα ιδια, leaving our own (things).*

πάντα τὰ γεγραμμένα διὰ τῶν προφητῶν τῷ
[1]all [2]the [3]*things* [4]written [5]through [6]the [7]prophets [8]about [9]the
by

Υἱῷ τοῦ Ἀνθρώπου. 32 Παραδοθήσεται γὰρ τοῖς
[10]Son - [11]of [12]Man. [2]He [3]will [4]be [5]handed [6]over [1]For to the
betrayed

ἔθνεσι, καὶ ἐμπαιχθήσεται καὶ ὑβρισθήσεται καὶ
Gentiles, and will be mocked and will be insulted and

ἐμπτυσθήσεται, 33 καὶ μαστιγώσαντες ἀποκτενοῦσιν αὐτόν.
will be spit upon, and having scourged *Him* they will kill Him.

Καὶ τῇ ἡμέρᾳ τῇ τρίτῃ ἀναστήσεται." 34 Καὶ αὐτοὶ οὐδὲν
And on the day ˜ - third He will rise again." And they [2]none

τούτων συνῆκαν, καὶ ἦν τὸ ῥῆμα τοῦτο κεκρυμμένον
[3]of [4]these [5]*things* [1]understood, and [3]was - [2]saying [1]this hidden
what He said

ἀπ' αὐτῶν, καὶ οὐκ ἐγίνωσκον τὰ λεγόμενα.
from them, and [3]not [1]they [2]did know the *things* being said.
what was

A Blind Man Receives His Sight
(Matt. 20:29–34; Mark 10:46–52)

35 Ἐγένετο δὲ ἐν τῷ ἐγγίζειν αὐτὸν εἰς Ἰεριχώ,
[2]it [3]happened [1]Now in - [2]to [3]draw [4]near [1]Him to Jericho,
as He was drawing near

τυφλός τις ἐκάθητο παρὰ τὴν ὁδὸν προσαιτῶν.
[1]a [3]blind [4]*man* [2]certain was sitting alongside the road begging.

36 Ἀκούσας δὲ ὄχλου διαπορευομένου, ἐπυνθάνετο
hearing ˜ And a crowd traveling through *the city,* he asked
when he heard

τί εἴη τοῦτο. 37 Ἀπήγγειλαν δὲ αὐτῷ ὅτι Ἰησοῦς ὁ
what was ˜ this. [2]they [3]reported [1]And to him that Jesus the

Ναζωραῖος παρέρχεται. 38 Καὶ ἐβόησε, λέγων, "Ἰησοῦ, Υἱὲ
Nazarene is going by. And he shouted, saying, "Jesus, Son
was

Δαβίδ, ἐλέησόν με!" 39 Καὶ οἱ προάγοντες
of David, have mercy on me!" And the *ones* going before
those who preceded Him

ἐπετίμων αὐτῷ ἵνα σιωπήσῃ· αὐτὸς δὲ πολλῷ μᾶλλον
were warning him that he should be quiet; he ˜ but [4]much [5]more

ἔκραζεν, "Υἱὲ Δαβίδ, ἐλέησόν με!"
[1]was [2]crying [3]out, "Son of David, have mercy on me!"

40 Σταθεὶς δὲ ὁ Ἰησοῦς ἐκέλευσεν αὐτὸν ἀχθῆναι
[2]standing [3]still [1]And - Jesus commanded him to be brought

πρὸς αὐτόν. Ἐγγίσαντος δὲ αὐτοῦ ἐπηρώτησεν αὐτόν, λέγων,
to Him. drawing near And him He asked him, saying,
And when he drew near

41 "Τί σοι θέλεις ποιήσω?"
"What [8]for [9]you [1]do [2]you [3]desire [4]*that* [5]I [6]should [7]do?"

Ὁ δὲ εἶπε, "Κύριε, ἵνα ἀναβλέψω."
[2]the [3]*one* [1]And said, "Lord, that I may recover *my* sight."
he

42 Καὶ ὁ Ἰησοῦς εἶπεν αὐτῷ "Ἀνάβλεψον. Ἡ πίστις
And - Jesus said to him "Recover *your* sight. - faith ˜

σου σέσωκέ σε." 43 Καὶ παραχρῆμα ἀνέβλεψε, καὶ
Your has saved you." And immediately he recovered *his* sight, and
made you well."

ἠκολούθει αὐτῷ δοξάζων τὸν Θεόν. Καὶ πᾶς ὁ λαὸς
was following Him glorifying - God. And all the people

lem, and all things that are
written by the prophets concerning the Son of Man will be
accomplished.
32 "For He will be delivered
to the Gentiles and will be
mocked and insulted and spit
upon.
33 "They will scourge *Him*
and kill Him. And the third day
He will rise again."
34 But they understood none
of these things; this saying was
hidden from them, and they did
not know the things which were
spoken.
35 Then it happened, as He
was coming near Jericho, that a
certain blind man sat by the
road begging.
36 And hearing a multitude
passing by, he asked what it
meant.
37 So they told him that Jesus
of Nazareth was passing by.
38 And he cried out, saying,
"Jesus, Son of David, have
mercy on me!"
39 Then those who went before warned him that he should
be quiet; but he cried out all the
more, "Son of David, have
mercy on me!"
40 So Jesus stood still and
commanded him to be brought
to Him. And when he had come
near, He asked him,
41 saying, "What do you want
Me to do for you?" He said,
"Lord, that I may receive my
sight."
42 Then Jesus said to him,
"Receive your sight; your faith
has made you well."
43 And immediately he re-
ceived his sight, and followed
Him, glorifying God. And all the

people, when they saw *it,* gave
praise to God.
19 Then *Jesus* entered
and passed through
Jericho.
2 Now behold, *there was* a
man named Zacchaeus who was
a chief tax collector, and he was
rich.
3 And he sought to see who
Jesus was, but could not because of the crowd, for he was
of short stature.
4 So he ran ahead and
climbed up into a sycamore tree
to see Him, for He was going to
pass that *way.*
5 And when Jesus came to
the place, He looked up and
saw him, and said to him, "Zacchaeus, make haste and come
down, for today I must stay at
your house."
6 So he made haste and came
down, and received Him joyfully.
7 But when they saw *it,* they
all complained, saying, "He has
gone to be a guest with a man
who is a sinner."
8 Then Zacchaeus stood and
said to the Lord, "Look, Lord, I
give half of my goods to the
poor; and if I have taken anything from anyone by false accusation, I restore fourfold."
9 And Jesus said to him, "Today salvation has come to this
house, because he also is a son
of Abraham;
10 "for the Son of Man has
come to seek and to save that

ἰδὼν ἔδωκεν αἶνον τῷ Θεῷ.
seeing *this* gave praise - to God.
when they saw

Jesus Comes to Zacchaeus' House

19 1 Καὶ εἰσελθὼν διήρχετο τὴν Ἰεριχώ. 2 Καὶ
And entering He was going through - Jericho. And
He entered and went through

ἰδού, ἀνὴρ ὀνόματι καλούμενος Ζακχαῖος, καὶ αὐτὸς
behold, *there was* a man by name being called Zacchaeus, and he
named

ἦν ἀρχιτελώνης, καὶ οὗτος ἦν πλούσιος. 3 Καὶ
was a chief tax collector, and this *man* was rich. And

ἐζήτει ἰδεῖν τὸν Ἰησοῦν τίς ἐστι, καὶ οὐκ ἠδύνατο ἀπὸ
he was trying to see - Jesus who He is, and not ~ could because
who Jesus was,

τοῦ ὄχλου, ὅτι τῇ ἡλικίᾳ* μικρὸς ἦν. 4 Καὶ
of the crowd, because - [4]in [5]stature [3]small [1]he [2]was. And
short

προδραμὼν ἔμπροσθεν ἀνέβη ἐπὶ συκομωραίαν ἵνα
running ahead in front he went up on a sycamore tree so that
into

ἴδῃ αὐτόν, ὅτι ἐκείνης ἔμελλε διέρχεσθαι.
he might see Him, because [7]that [8]*way* [1]He [2]was [3]about [4]to [5]go [6]through.

5 Καὶ ὡς ἦλθεν ἐπὶ τὸν τόπον, ἀναβλέψας ὁ Ἰησοῦς εἶδεν
And when He came upon the place, looking up - Jesus saw
that

αὐτόν, καὶ[a] εἶπε πρὸς αὐτόν, "Ζακχαῖε, σπεύσας κατάβηθι,
him, and He said to him, "Zacchaeus, hastening come down,
hurry and

σήμερον γὰρ ἐν τῷ οἴκῳ σου δεῖ με μεῖναι."
today ~ for [8]in - [10]house [9]your [1]it [2]is [3]necessary [4]*for* [5]Me [6]to [7]stay."
I must stay."

6 Καὶ σπεύσας κατέβη, καὶ ὑπεδέξατο αὐτὸν χαίρων.
And hastening he came down, and he welcomed Him rejoicing.
he hurried and

7 Καὶ ἰδόντες, πάντες διεγόγγυζον, λέγοντες ὅτι
And seeing, all *the people* were complaining, saying -
when they saw it,

"Παρὰ ἁμαρτωλῷ ἀνδρὶ εἰσῆλθε καταλῦσαι."
"[6]with [7]a [8]sinful [9]man [1]He [2]went [3]in [4]to [5]lodge."
be a guest."

8 Σταθεὶς δὲ Ζακχαῖος εἶπε πρὸς τὸν Κύριον, "Ἰδού, τὰ
standing ~ And Zacchaeus said to the Lord, "Look, -

ἡμίση τῶν ὑπαρχόντων μου, Κύριε, δίδωμι τοῖς
half of the *things* belonging of me, Lord, I give to the
of my possessions,

πτωχοῖς καὶ εἴ τινός τι ἐσυκοφάντησα, ἀποδίδωμι
poor and if [4]from [5]anyone [3]anything [1]I [2]extorted, I give back
restore

τετραπλοῦν."
fourfold."

9 Εἶπε δὲ πρὸς αὐτὸν ὁ Ἰησοῦς ὅτι "Σήμερον σωτηρία
[3]said [1]And [4]to [5]him - [2]Jesus - "Today salvation

τῷ οἴκῳ τούτῳ ἐγένετο, καθότι καὶ αὐτὸς υἱὸς Ἀβραάμ
- [2]to [4]house [3]this [1]came, because also ~ he [2]a [3]son [4]of [5]Abraham
has come,

ἐστιν. 10 Ἦλθε γὰρ ὁ Υἱὸς τοῦ Ἀνθρώπου ζητῆσαι καὶ
[1]is. [6]came [1]For [2]the [3]Son - [4]of [5]Man to seek and

---

[a](19:5) NU omits ειδεν αυτον και, saw him and.

*(19:3) ἡλικία *(hēlikia).* Noun meaning either *physical/bodily stature* (as here, referring to Zacchaeus' *height*) or *age, life span,* including the *age of (legal) maturity* (John 9:21, 23). Consequently there are different opinions among interpreters whether the word means age or physical stature in Luke 2:52; Eph. 4:13 (in both, *stature* seems more likely, but *mature age* is possible). The problem is more difficult in Matt. 6:27 (parallel Luke 12:25). The addition of one cubit (πῆχυς) seems to favor the meaning *height,* but a growth of 18 inches would hardly be trivial as implied by the saying. Most scholars now believe "cubit" is used metaphorically for a measure of time; thus, "add one hour to his life span."

σῶσαι τὸ ἀπολωλός."
to save the *thing* having been lost."
that which was lost."

The Parable of the Minas
(Matt. 25:14–30)

11 Ἀκουόντων δὲ αὐτῶν ταῦτα, προσθεὶς εἶπε
hearing And them these *things,* adding He told
Now as they heard again

παραβολήν, διὰ τὸ ἐγγὺς αὐτὸν εἶναι Ἱερουσαλὴμ καὶ
a parable, because - [4]near [1]Him [2]to [3]be Jerusalem and
He was

δοκεῖν αὐτοὺς ὅτι παραχρῆμα μέλλει ἡ βασιλεία τοῦ
[2]to [3]think [1]them that [9]immediately [5]is [6]about [1]the [2]kingdom -
they thought was

Θεοῦ ἀναφαίνεσθαι. **12** Εἶπεν οὖν, "Ἄνθρωπός
[3]of [4]God [7]to [8]appear. [2]He [3]said [1]Therefore, "[7]man

τις εὐγενὴς ἐπορεύθη εἰς χώραν μακρὰν λαβεῖν
[4]A [5]certain [6]wellborn traveled to a country ˜ far to receive

ἑαυτῷ βασιλείαν καὶ ὑποστρέψαι. **13** Καλέσας δὲ δέκα
[3]for [4]himself [1]a [2]kingdom and to return. [2]having [3]called [1]And ten

δούλους ἑαυτοῦ, ἔδωκεν αὐτοῖς δέκα μνᾶς, καὶ εἶπε πρὸς
slaves of himself, he gave them ten minas, and said to
of his servants,

αὐτούς, 'Πραγματεύσασθε ἕως ἔρχομαι.' **14** Οἱ δὲ πολῖται
them, 'Do business till I come.' - But citizens ˜

αὐτοῦ ἐμίσουν αὐτόν, καὶ ἀπέστειλαν πρεσβείαν ὀπίσω αὐτοῦ,
his hated him, and sent a delegation after him,

λέγοντες, 'Οὐ θέλομεν τοῦτον βασιλεῦσαι ἐφ' ἡμᾶς.'
saying, '[3]not [1]We [2]do [4]want this *man* to reign over us.'

15 Καὶ ἐγένετο ἐν τῷ ἐπανελθεῖν αὐτὸν λαβόντα τὴν
And it happened in - [2]to [3]return [1]him having received the
when he returned

βασιλείαν, καὶ εἶπε φωνηθῆναι αὐτῷ τοὺς δούλους
kingdom, and he said *for* [3]to [4]be [5]called [6]to [7]him - [2]slaves
that he commanded

τούτους οἷς ἔδωκε τὸ ἀργύριον, ἵνα γνῷ τίς
[1]those to whom he gave the silver, so that he might know who
had given money,

τί διεπραγματεύσατο.[b] **16** Παρεγένετο δὲ ὁ πρῶτος,
what ˜ gained by trading. [5]came [1]And [2]the [3]first [4]*one,*

λέγων, 'Κύριε, ἡ μνᾶ σου προσειργάσατο δέκα μνᾶς.' **17** Καὶ
saying, 'Master, - mina ˜ your earned ten minas.' And

εἶπεν αὐτῷ, 'Εὖ, ἀγαθὲ δοῦλε· ὅτι ἐν ἐλαχίστῳ
he said to him, 'Well *done,* good slave; because [4]in [5]a [6]least [7]*thing*
servant; very little

πιστὸς ἐγένου, ἴσθι ἐξουσίαν ἔχων ἐπάνω δέκα πόλεων.'
[3]faithful [1]you [2]were, be authority ˜ having over ten cities.'
have authority

18 Καὶ ἦλθεν ὁ δεύτερος, λέγων, 'Κύριε, ἡ μνᾶ σου
And [4]came [1]the [2]second [3]*one,* saying, 'Master, - mina ˜ your

ἐποίησε πέντε μνᾶς.' **19** Εἶπε δὲ καὶ τούτῳ, 'Καὶ σὺ
made five minas.' [2]he [3]said [1]And also to this *one,* 'And you

γίνου ἐπάνω πέντε πόλεων.' **20** Καὶ ἕτερος ἦλθε, λέγων,
be over five cities.' And another *one* came, saying,

'Κύριε, ἰδού, ἡ μνᾶ σου ἣν εἶχον ἀποκειμένην ἐν
'Master, look, - mina ˜ your which I had laid away in
here is

which was lost."
11 Now as they heard these
things, He spoke another parable, because He was near Jerusalem and because they thought
the kingdom of God would appear immediately.
12 Therefore He said: "A certain nobleman went into a far country to receive for himself a kingdom and to return.
13 "So he called ten of his servants, delivered to them ten minas, and said to them, 'Do business till I come.'
14 "But his citizens hated him, and sent a delegation after him, saying, 'We will not have this *man* to reign over us.'
15 "And so it was that when he returned, having received the kingdom, he then commanded these servants, to whom he had given the money, to be called to him, that he might know how much every man had gained by trading.
16 "Then came the first, saying, 'Master, your mina has earned ten minas.'
17 "And he said to him, 'Well *done,* good servant; because you were faithful in a very little, have authority over ten cities.'
18 "And the second came, saying, 'Master, your mina has earned five minas.'
19 "Likewise he said to him, 'You also be over five cities.'
20 "Then another came, saying, 'Master, here is your mina, which I have kept put away in a

[b](19:15) NU reads τι διεπραγματευσαντο, *what they had gained by trading.*

handkerchief.
21 'For I feared you, because
you are an austere man. You
collect what you did not deposit, and reap what you did not
sow.'
22 "And he said to him, 'Out
of your own mouth I will judge
you, *you* wicked servant. You
knew that I was an austere
man, collecting what I did not
deposit and reaping what I did
not sow.
23 'Why then did you not put
my money in the bank, that at
my coming I might have collected it with interest?'
24 "And he said to those who
stood by, 'Take the mina from
him, and give *it* to him who has
ten minas.'
25 ("But they said to him,
'Master, he has ten minas.')
26 'For I say to you, that to
everyone who has will be
given; and from him who does
not have, even what he has will
be taken away from him.
27 'But bring here those enemies of mine, who did not want
me to reign over them, and slay
them before me.'"
28 When He had said this, He
went on ahead, going up to Jerusalem.
29 And it came to pass, when
He drew near to Bethphage and
Bethany, at the mountain called
Olivet, *that* He sent two of His
disciples,
30 saying, "Go into the village

σουδαρίῳ. **21** Ἐφοβούμην γάρ σε, ὅτι ἄνθρωπος αὐστηρὸς
a facecloth. [2]I [3]feared [1]For you, because [3]a(n) [5]man [4]austere
exacting

εἶ. Αἴρεις ὃ οὐκ ἔθηκας καὶ θερίζεις ὃ
[1]you [2]are. You take up what [3]not [1]you [2]did put down and you reap what
deposit

οὐκ ἔσπειρας.' **22** Λέγει δὲ αὐτῷ, "Ἐκ τοῦ στόματός σου
[3]not [1]you [2]did sow.' [2]he [3]says [1]But to him, 'Out of - mouth ˜ your

κρινῶ σε, πονηρὲ δοῦλε. Ἤδεις ὅτι ἐγὼ ἄνθρωπος
I will judge you, evil slave. You knew that I [2]a(n) [4]man
servant.

αὐστηρός εἰμι, αἴρων ὃ οὐκ ἔθηκα καὶ θερίζων ὃ
[3]austere [1]am, taking up what [3]not [1]I [2]did put down and reaping what
exacting deposit

οὐκ ἔσπειρα. **23** Καὶ διὰ τί οὐκ ἔδωκας τὸ
[3]not [1]I [2]did sow. And on account of what [3]not [1]did [2]you give -
So why

ἀργύριόν μου ἐπὶ τράπεζαν,* καὶ ἐγὼ ἐλθὼν σὺν
silver ˜ my to a *money changer's* table, and I ˜ coming [5]with
money the bank, when I came, I

τόκῳ ἂν ἔπραξα αὐτό?' **24** Καὶ τοῖς
[6]interest - [1]would [2]have [3]collected [4]it?' And to the *ones*

παρεστῶσιν εἶπεν, "Ἄρατε ἀπ' αὐτοῦ τὴν μνᾶν καὶ δότε
standing by he said, 'Take [3]away [4]from [5]him [1]the [2]mina and give
bystanders

τῷ τὰς δέκα μνᾶς ἔχοντι.' **25** Καὶ εἶπον αὐτῷ, 'Κύριε,
to the *one* [2]the [3]ten [4]minas [1]having.' And they said to him, 'Master,
him who has.'

ἔχει δέκα μνᾶς.' **26** 'Λέγω γὰρ ὑμῖν ὅτι παντὶ τῷ ἔχοντι
he has ten minas.' '[2]I [3]say [1]For to you that to every - *one* having
So everyone who has

δοθήσεται· ἀπὸ δὲ τοῦ μὴ ἔχοντος, καὶ ὃ ἔχει
more will be given; from ˜ but the *one* not having, even what he has
him who does not have,

ἀρθήσεται ἀπ' αὐτοῦ.[c] **27** Πλὴν τοὺς ἐχθρούς μου
will be taken from him. Nevertheless - [2]enemies [3]of [4]me
mine

ἐκείνους,[d] τοὺς μὴ θελήσαντάς με βασιλεῦσαι ἐπ' αὐτούς,
[1]those, the *ones* not wanting me to reign over them,
who did not want

ἀγάγετε ὧδε καὶ κατασφάξατε[e] ἔμπροσθέν μου.'"
bring here and slay *them* before me.'"

Jesus Enters Jerusalem in Triumph
(Matt. 21:1–11; Mark 11:1–11; John 12:12–19)

28 Καὶ εἰπὼν ταυτα, ἐπορεύετο ἔμπροσθεν,
And having said these *things,* He went in front,

ἀναβαίνων εἰς Ἱεροσόλυμα. **29** Καὶ ἐγένετο ὡς ἤγγισεν
going up to Jerusalem. And it happened as He drew near

εἰς Βηθσφαγὴ[f] καὶ Βηθανίαν, πρὸς τὸ ὄρος τὸ
to Bethsphage and Bethany, to the mountain the *one*
which

καλούμενον Ἐλαιῶν, ἀπέστειλε δύο τῶν μαθητῶν αὐτοῦ,
being called Of Olives, He sent two - of disciples ˜ His,
is called Olivet,

30 εἰπών, "Ὑπάγετε εἰς τὴν κατέναντι κώμην, ἐν ᾗ
saying, "Go into the [2]opposite [3]*you* [1]village, in which

---

c(**19:26**) NU omits απ αυτου, *from him.*
d(**19:27**) NU reads τουτους, *these.* e(**19:27**) NU adds αυτους, *them.*
f(**19:29**) Many mss., TR, NU read Βηθφαγη, *Bethphage.*

***(19:23)** *τράπεζα (trapeza).* Noun meaning *table,* especially for a meal (Luke 16:21) and so also the *meal* itself (as Acts 16:34) or even a sacred meal (cf. 1 Cor. 10:21). In Heb. 9:2 it is the tabernacle table for the showbread. Here in Luke 19:23 it refers to a money changer's table and so in effect a *bank.* Cf. the cognate noun *τραπεζίτης, money changer* (working at such a "table") or *banker,* used only in the parallel Matt. 25:27.

εἰσπορευόμενοι εὑρήσετε πῶλον δεδεμένον, ἐφ' ὃν
entering you will find a young donkey tied up, on which
when you enter

οὐδεὶς πώποτε ἀνθρώπων ἐκάθισε. Λύσαντες αὐτὸν
no one [3]ever [1]of [2]men sat. Loosing him
When you have untied

ἀγάγετε. 31 Καὶ ἐάν τις ὑμᾶς ἐρωτᾷ, 'Διὰ τί
bring *him.* And if anyone you ˜ asks, 'On account of what
'Why

λύετε?' οὕτως ἐρεῖτε αὐτῷ ὅτι ''Ὁ Κύριος αὐτοῦ
are you loosing *him?*' thus you shall say to him - 'The Lord [3]of [4]him

χρείαν ἔχει.' "
[2]need [1]has.' "

32 'Απελθόντες δὲ οἱ ἀπεσταλμένοι εὗρον καθὼς
having gone away And the *ones* having been sent found *it* just as
And those who had been sent departed and

εἶπεν αὐτοῖς.
He told them.

33 Λυόντων δὲ αὐτῶν τὸν πῶλον, εἶπον οἱ κύριοι
[3]loosing [1]And [2]them the young donkey, [3]said - [2]owners
And as they loosed

αὐτοῦ πρὸς αὐτούς, "Τί λύετε τὸν πῶλον?"
[1]his to them, "Why are you loosing the young donkey?"

34 Οἱ δὲ εἶπον, "Ὁ Κύριος αὐτοῦ χρείαν ἔχει."
[2]the [3]*ones* [1]And said, "The Lord [3]of [4]him [2]need [1]has."
they

35 Καὶ ἤγαγον αὐτὸν πρὸς τὸν 'Ιησοῦν. Καὶ ἐπιρρίψαντες
And they brought him to - Jesus. And throwing
when they threw

ἑαυτῶν τὰ ἱμάτια ἐπὶ τὸν πῶλον, ἐπεβίβασαν
[3]of [4]themselves [1]the [2]clothes on the young donkey, they caused [2]to [3]mount
their

τὸν 'Ιησοῦν. 36 Πορευομένου δὲ αὐτοῦ,
- [1]Jesus. [3]going [1]And [2]Him,
And as He went,

ὑπεστρώννυον τὰ ἱμάτια αὐτῶν ἐν τῇ ὁδῷ.
they were spreading [3]under [4]*Him* - [2]clothes [1]their in the road.

37 'Εγγίζοντος δὲ αὐτοῦ ἤδη πρὸς τῇ καταβάσει τοῦ
[4]drawing [5]near [1]And [2]Him [3]now to the descent of the
as He was

Ὄρους τῶν 'Ελαιῶν, ἤρξαντο ἅπαν τὸ πλῆθος τῶν
Mount - of Olives, [7]began [1]all [2]the [3]multitude [4]of [5]the

μαθητῶν χαίροντες αἰνεῖν τὸν Θεὸν φωνῇ μεγάλῃ περὶ
[6]disciples rejoicing to praise - God with a voice ˜ great for
to rejoice and loud

πασῶν ὧν εἶδον δυνάμεων, 38 λέγοντες,
all [3]which [4]they [5]saw [1]*the* [2]miracles, saying,
had seen

"«Εὐλογημένος ὁ ἐρχόμενος Βασιλεὺς ἐν ὀνόματι
"«Blessed *is* the *One* coming as King in *the* name
the King who comes

Κυρίου!»
of *the* Lord!»

Εἰρήνη ἐν οὐρανῷ
Peace in heaven

Καὶ δόξα ἐν ὑψίστοις!"
And glory in *the* highest heights!"
heaven!"

39 Καί τινες τῶν Φαρισαίων ἀπὸ τοῦ ὄχλου εἶπον πρὸς
And some of the Pharisees from the crowd said to

opposite *you,* where as you enter you will find a colt tied, on which no one has ever sat. Loose it and bring *it here.*
31 "And if anyone asks you, 'Why are you loosing *it?*' thus you shall say to him, 'Because the Lord has need of it.' "
32 So those who were sent went their way and found *it* just as He had said to them.
33 But as they were loosing the colt, the owners of it said to them, "Why are you loosing the colt?"
34 And they said, "The Lord has need of him."
35 Then they brought him to Jesus. And they threw their own clothes on the colt, and they set Jesus on him.
36 And as He went, *many* spread their clothes on the road.
37 Then, as He was now drawing near the descent of the Mount of Olives, the whole multitude of the disciples began to rejoice and praise God with a loud voice for all the mighty works they had seen,
38 saying:

" 'Blessed is the King who comes in the name of the LORD!'
Peace in heaven and glory in the highest!"

39 And some of the Pharisees called to Him from the crowd,

"Teacher, rebuke Your disciples."
40 But He answered and said to them, "I tell you that if these should keep silent, the stones would immediately cry out."
41 Now as He drew near, He saw the city and wept over it,
42 saying, "If you had known, even you, especially in this your day, the things *that make* for your peace! But now they are hidden from your eyes.
43 "For days will come upon you when your enemies will build an embankment around you, surround you and close you in on every side,
44 "and level you, and your children within you, to the ground; and they will not leave in you one stone upon another, because you did not know the time of your visitation."
45 Then He went into the temple and began to drive out those who bought and sold in it,
46 saying to them, "It is written, *'My house is a house of prayer,'* but you have made it a *'den of thieves.'* "
47 And He was teaching daily in the temple. But the chief priests, the scribes, and the leaders of the people sought to destroy Him,
48 and were unable to do anything; for all the people were

αὐτόν, "Διδάσκαλε, ἐπιτίμησον τοῖς μαθηταῖς σου."
Him, "Teacher, rebuke - disciples ˜ Your."

40 Καὶ ἀποκριθεὶς εἶπεν αὐτοῖς, "Λέγω ὑμῖν ὅτι, ἐὰν
And answering He said to them, "I say to you that, if

οὗτοι σιωπήσωσιν, οἱ λίθοι κεκράξονται!"
these should keep silent, the stones will cry out!"

Jesus Weeps over Jerusalem

41 Καὶ ὡς ἤγγισεν, ἰδὼν τὴν πόλιν ἔκλαυσεν* ἐπ'
And as He drew near, seeing the city He wept over

αὐτῇ, 42 λέγων ὅτι "Εἰ ἔγνως καὶ σύ, καί γε[g] ἐν τῇ
it, saying - "If you knew (had known), even you, at least in -

ἡμέρᾳ σου ταύτῃ, τὰ πρὸς εἰρήνην σου! Νῦν δὲ
[3]day [2]your [1]this, the *things* pertaining to peace ˜ your! now ˜ But

ἐκρύβη ἀπὸ ὀφθαλμῶν σου. 43 Ὅτι ἥξουσιν ἡμέραι
they were (have been) hidden from eyes ˜ your. Because [2]will [3]come [1]days

ἐπὶ σὲ καὶ περιβαλοῦσιν οἱ ἐχθροί σου χάρακά
upon you and (when) [3]will [4]throw [5]up [8]around - [2]enemies [1]your [6]an [7]embankment

σοι καὶ περικυκλώσουσί σε καὶ συνέξουσί σε πάντοθεν,
you and will surround you and press hard (hem you) ˜ you (in) from every side,

44 καὶ ἐδαφιοῦσί σε καὶ τὰ τέκνα σου ἐν
and [1]they [2]will [3]raze [5]to [6]the [7]ground [4]you and (with) - children ˜ your in

σοί· καὶ οὐκ ἀφήσουσιν ἐν σοὶ λίθον ἐπὶ λίθῳ, ἀνθ'
you; and [3]not [1]they [2]will leave in you a stone upon a stone, because (because)

ὧν οὐκ ἔγνως τὸν καιρὸν τῆς ἐπισκοπῆς σου."
of which *things* [3]not [1]you [2]did know the season (time) - of visitation ˜ your."

Jesus Cleanses the Temple
(Matt. 21:12–17; Mark 11:15–19)

45 Καὶ εἰσελθὼν εἰς τὸ ἱερὸν ἤρξατο ἐκβάλλειν
And entering (when He entered) into the temple He began to throw out

τοὺς πωλοῦντας ἐν αὐτῷ καὶ ἀγοράζοντας,[h] 46 λέγων
the *ones* selling [3]in [4]it [1]and [2]buying, saying

αὐτοῖς, "Γέγραπται,
to them, "It is written,

«Ὁ οἶκός μου οἶκος προσευχῆς ἐστιν,»[i]
- «house ˜ My [2]a [3]house [4]of [5]prayer [1]is,»

Ὑμεῖς δὲ αὐτὸν ἐποιήσατε «σπήλαιον λῃστῶν.»"
you ˜ But it ˜ made «a cave of bandits.»"

47 Καὶ ἦν διδάσκων τὸ καθ' ἡμέραν ἐν τῷ ἱερῷ.
And He was teaching - according to a day (day by day) in the temple.

Οἱ δὲ ἀρχιερεῖς καὶ οἱ γραμματεῖς ἐζήτουν αὐτὸν
the ˜ But chief priests and the scribes [8]were [9]seeking [12]Him

ἀπολέσαι, καὶ οἱ πρῶτοι τοῦ λαοῦ, 48 καὶ οὐχ
[10]to [11]destroy, [1]and [2]the [3]first [4]*men* (leaders) [5]of [6]the [7]people, and [3]not (they)

εὕρισκον τὸ τί ποιήσωσιν, ὁ λαὸς γὰρ ἅπας
[1]they [2]were [4]finding (could not find out) - what they might do, [3]the [4]people [1]for [2]all

---

[g](19:42) NU omits και γε, *at least.* [h](19:45) NU omits εν αυτω και αγοραζοντας, *in it and buying.*
[i](19:46) NU reads και εσται ο οικος μου οικος προσευχης, *and My house will be a house of prayer.*

***(19:41)** κλαίω *(klaiō).* Common verb in the NT, meaning *weep, cry, mourn.* Both κλαίω and the synonym ἀλαλάζω (Mark 5:38) emphasize the noise which accompanies the weeping, whereas δρακύω (John 11:35) stresses the shedding of tears. When κλαίω occurs with an object, that object gives the reason for the weeping: "Rachel *weeping for* her children" (Matt. 2:18; cf. the use of the ἐπί prepositional phrase here in Luke 19:41). Cf. the cognate noun κλαυθμός, *crying.*

ἐξεκρέματο αὐτοῦ ἀκούων.
were hanging on Him hearing.
gave rapt attention as they heard Him.

The Authority of Jesus Is Questioned
(Matt. 21:23–27; Mark 11:27–33)

20 1 Καὶ ἐγένετο ἐν μιᾷ τῶν ἡμερῶν ἐκείνων,[a]
And it happened on one - of days ˜ those,

διδάσκοντος αὐτοῦ τὸν λαὸν ἐν τῷ ἱερῷ καὶ εὐαγγελιζομένου,
teaching ˜ Him the people in the temple and preaching the gospel,
as He taught preached

ἐπέστησαν οἱ ἱερεῖς[b] καὶ οἱ γραμματεῖς σὺν τοῖς
[9]approached [1]the [2]priests [3]and [4]the [5]scribes [6]with [7]the

πρεσβυτέροις 2 καὶ εἶπον πρὸς αὐτόν, λέγοντες, "Εἰπὲ
[8]elders and they spoke to Him, saying, "Tell

ἡμῖν ἐν ποίᾳ ἐξουσίᾳ ταῦτα ποιεῖς? Ἢ τίς
us by what kind of authority [4]these [5]*things* [1]are [2]You [3]doing? Or who

ἐστιν ὁ δούς σοι τὴν ἐξουσίαν ταύτην?"
is the *one* having given to You - authority ˜ this?"
he who gave

3 Ἀποκριθεὶς δὲ εἶπε πρὸς αὐτούς, "Ἐρωτήσω ὑμᾶς
answering ˜ And He said to them, "I will ask you
"I also will ask

κἀγὼ ἕνα[c] λόγον, καὶ εἴπατέ μοι· 4 Τὸ βάπτισμα Ἰωάννου
also I one word, and tell Me: The baptism of John
you thing, and so

ἐξ οὐρανοῦ ἦν ἢ ἐξ ἀνθρώπων?"
[3]from [4]heaven [1]was [2]it or from men?"

5 Οἱ δὲ συνελογίσαντο πρὸς ἑαυτούς, λέγοντες
[2]the [3]*ones* [1]And debated among themselves, saying
they

ὅτι "Ἐὰν εἴπωμεν, 'Ἐξ οὐρανοῦ,' ἐρεῖ, 'Διὰ τί οὐκ
- "If we say, 'From heaven,' He will say, 'Because of what [3]not
'Why

ἐπιστεύσατε αὐτῷ?' 6 Ἐὰν δὲ εἴπωμεν, 'Ἐξ ἀνθρώπων,' πᾶς
[1]did [2]you believe him?' if ˜ But we say, 'From men,' all

ὁ λαὸς καταλιθάσει ἡμᾶς, πεπεισμένος γάρ ἐστιν
the people will stone us, [4]persuaded [5]*that* [1]for [2]they [3]are

Ἰωάννην προφήτην εἶναι." 7 Καὶ ἀπεκρίθησαν μὴ
John [3]a [4]prophet [1]to [2]be." And they answered not
is." that they

εἰδέναι πόθεν.
to know from where.
did not know where it was from.

8 Καὶ ὁ Ἰησοῦς εἶπεν αὐτοῖς, "Οὐδὲ ἐγὼ λέγω ὑμῖν ἐν
And - Jesus said to them, "Neither I ˜ do tell you by

ποίᾳ ἐξουσίᾳ ταῦτα ποιῶ."
what kind of authority [3]these [4]*things* [1]I [2]do."

The Parable of the Wicked Vinedressers
(Matt. 21:33–46; Mark 12:1–12)

9 Ἤρξατο δὲ πρὸς τὸν λαὸν λέγειν τὴν παραβολὴν
[2]He [3]began [1]And [8]to [9]the [10]people [4]to [5]tell - [7]parable

ταύτην· "Ἄνθρωπος[d] ἐφύτευσεν ἀμπελῶνα, καὶ ἐξέδοτο αὐτὸν
[6]this: "A man planted a vineyard, and gave out ˜ it
leased

γεωργοῖς, καὶ ἀπεδήμησε χρόνους ἱκανούς. 10 Καὶ ἐν
to farmers, and went on a journey times sufficient. And in
for some time.

very attentive to hear Him.
20 Now it happened on
one of those days, as
He taught the people in the
temple and preached the gospel, *that* the chief priests and
the scribes, together with the
elders, confronted *Him*
2 and spoke to Him, saying,
"Tell us, by what authority are
You doing these things? Or who
is he who gave You this authority?"
3 But He answered and said
to them, "I also will ask you one
thing, and answer Me:
4 "The baptism of John—
was it from heaven or from
men?"
5 And they reasoned among
themselves, saying, "If we say,
'From heaven,' He will say,
'Why then did you not believe
him?'
6 "But if we say, 'From
men,' all the people will stone
us, for they are persuaded that
John was a prophet."
7 So they answered that they
did not know where *it was*
from.
8 And Jesus said to them,
"Neither will I tell you by what
authority I do these things."
9 Then He began to tell the
people this parable: "A certain
man planted a vineyard, leased
it to vinedressers, and went
into a far country for a long
time.
10 "Now at vintage-time he

---
[a](20:1) NU omits *εκεινων*, *those*. [b](20:1) TR, NU read *αρχιερεις*, *chief priests*. [c](20:3) NU omits *ενα*, *one*. [d](20:9) NU (in brackets), TR add *τις*, *certain*.

sent a servant to the vinedressers, that they might give him some of the fruit of the vineyard. But the vinedressers beat him and sent *him* away empty-handed.
11 "Again he sent another servant; and they beat him also, treated *him* shamefully, and sent *him* away empty-handed.
12 "And again he sent a third; and they wounded him also and cast *him* out.
13 "Then the owner of the vineyard said, 'What shall I do? I will send my beloved son. Probably they will respect *him* when they see him.'
14 "But when the vinedressers saw him, they reasoned among themselves, saying, 'This is the heir. Come, let us kill him, that the inheritance may be ours.'
15 "So they cast him out of the vineyard and killed *him*. Therefore what will the owner of the vineyard do to them?
16 "He will come and destroy those vinedressers and give the vineyard to others." And when they heard *it* they said, "Certainly not!"
17 Then He looked at them and said, "What then is this that is written:

'The stone which the builders rejected
Has become the chief cornerstone'?

18 "Whoever falls on that stone will be broken; but on whomever it falls, it will grind him to powder."

καιρῷ ἀπέστειλε πρὸς τοὺς γεωργοὺς δοῦλον, ἵνα ἀπὸ
harvest time he sent [3]to [4]the [5]farmers [1]a [2]slave, that [5]*some* [6]from
servant, of

τοῦ καρποῦ τοῦ ἀμπελῶνος δῶσιν αὐτῷ. Οἱ δὲ
[7]the [8]fruit [9]of [10]the [11]vineyard [1]they [2]might [3]give [4]him. the ˜ But

γεωργοὶ δείραντες αὐτὸν ἐξαπέστειλαν κενόν. 11 Καὶ
farmers having flogged him sent *him* away empty-*handed.* And

προσέθετο πέμψαι ἕτερον δοῦλον· οἱ δὲ κἀκεῖνον
he added to send another slave; [2]the [3]*ones* [1]and [6]also [7]that [8]*one*
again he sent servant; and they flogged him

δείραντες καὶ ἀτιμάσαντες ἐξαπέστειλαν
[4]having [5]flogged and having treated *him* shamefully sent *him* away
also treated him shamefully and

κενόν. 12 Καὶ προσέθετο πέμψαι τρίτον· οἱ δὲ
empty-*handed.* And he added to send a third *slave;* [2]the [3]*ones* [1]but
again he sent but they

καὶ τοῦτον τραυματίσαντες ἐξέβαλον. 13 Εἶπε δὲ ὁ
also this *one* having wounded threw *him* out. [7]said [1]And [2]the
wounded him also and

κύριος τοῦ ἀμπελῶνος, 'Τί ποιήσω? Πέμψω τὸν υἱόν μου
[3]owner [4]of [5]the [6]vineyard, 'What shall I do? I will send - [3]son [1]my

τὸν ἀγαπητόν. Ἴσως τοῦτον ἰδόντες[e] ἐντραπήσονται.'
- [2]beloved. Perhaps this *one* seeing they will respect *him.*'
when they see him,

14 Ἰδόντες δὲ αὐτὸν οἱ γεωργοὶ διελογίζοντο πρὸς ἑαυτούς,
seeing ˜ But him the farmers reasoned among themselves,

λέγοντες, 'Οὗτός ἐστιν ὁ κληρονόμος. Δεῦτε,[f] ἀποκτείνωμεν
saying, 'This is the heir. Come, let us kill

αὐτόν, ἵνα ἡμῶν γένηται ἡ κληρονομία.' 15 Καὶ
him, so that [5]ours [3]may [4]be [1]the [2]inheritance.' And

ἐκβαλόντες αὐτὸν ἔξω τοῦ ἀμπελῶνος, ἀπέκτειναν. Τί οὖν
throwing him out of the vineyard, they killed *him.* What then

ποιήσει αὐτοῖς ὁ κύριος τοῦ ἀμπελῶνος? 16 Ἐλεύσεται
will [6]do [7]to [8]them [1]the [2]owner [3]of [4]the [5]vineyard? He will come

καὶ ἀπολέσει τοὺς γεωργοὺς τούτους καὶ δώσει τὸν ἀμπελῶνα
and will destroy - farmers ˜ these and will give the vineyard

ἄλλοις."
to others."

Ἀκούσαντες δὲ εἶπον, "Μὴ γένοιτο!"
hearing ˜ And they said, "[3]not [1]May [2]it happen!"
And when they heard this,

17 Ὁ δὲ ἐμβλέψας αὐτοῖς εἶπε, "Τί οὖν ἐστι
[2]the [3]*One* [1]But looking at them said, "What then is
He looked and said,

τὸ γεγραμμένον τοῦτο,
the *thing* having been written this,
this which is written,

«Λίθον ὃν ἀπεδοκίμασαν οἱ οἰκοδομοῦντες,
«A stone which [4]rejected [1]the [2]*ones* [3]building,
the builders,

Οὗτος ἐγενήθη εἰς κεφαλὴν γωνίας»?
This *stone* became - head of a corner»?
the cornerstone»?

18 "Πᾶς ὁ πεσὼν ἐπ' ἐκεῖνον τὸν λίθον
"Every - *one* falling on that - stone
"Everyone who falls

συνθλασθήσεται· ἐφ' ὃν δ' ἂν πέσῃ, λικμήσει αὐτόν."
will be broken to pieces; [2]on [3]whom [1]but ever it falls, it will crush him."

---

[e](20:13) NU omits ιδοντες, *seeing.* [f](20:14) NU omits δευτε, *come.*

19 Καὶ ἐζήτησαν οἱ ἀρχιερεῖς καὶ οἱ γραμματεῖς
And [7]sought [1]the [2]chief [3]priests [4]and [5]the [6]scribes

ἐπιβαλεῖν ἐπ᾽ αὐτὸν τὰς χεῖρας ἐν αὐτῇ τῇ ὥρᾳ, καὶ
to lay [3]on [4]Him [1]the [2]hands in very ˜ the hour, and
their that

ἐφοβήθησαν,[g] ἔγνωσαν γὰρ ὅτι πρὸς αὐτοὺς τὴν
were afraid, [2]they [3]knew [1]for that [5]against [6]them -

παραβολὴν ταύτην εἶπε.
[4]parable [3]this [1]He [2]told.

Render unto Caesar
(Matt. 22:15–22; Mark 12:13–17)

20 Καὶ παρατηρήσαντες ἀπέστειλαν ἐγκαθέτους,
And having watched *Him* closely they sent spies,

ὑποκρινομένους ἑαυτοὺς δικαίους εἶναι, ἵνα
pretending themselves [3]righteous [1]to [2]be, so that
who pretended that they were righteous,

ἐπιλάβωνται αὐτοῦ λόγου, εἰς τὸ παραδοῦναι αὐτὸν τῇ
they might seize on His word, for - to give over ˜ Him to the
speech, in order deliver

ἀρχῇ καὶ τῇ ἐξουσίᾳ τοῦ ἡγεμόνος. **21** Καὶ ἐπηρώτησαν
rule and the authority of the governor. And they asked

αὐτόν, λέγοντες, "Διδάσκαλε, οἴδαμεν ὅτι ὀρθῶς λέγεις καὶ
Him, saying, "Teacher, we know that [5]rightly [1]you [2]speak [3]and

διδάσκεις, καὶ οὐ λαμβάνεις πρόσωπον, ἀλλ᾽ ἐπ᾽ ἀληθείας
[4]teach, and [3]not [1]You [2]do receive a face, but [7]in [8]truth
show favoritism,

τὴν ὁδὸν τοῦ Θεοῦ διδάσκεις. **22** Ἔξεστιν ἡμῖν Καίσαρι
[3]the [4]way - [5]of [6]God [1]You [2]teach. Is it lawful for us [4]to [5]Caesar

φόρον δοῦναι ἢ οὔ?"
[3]tribute [1]to [2]give or not?"
to pay taxes

23 Κατανοήσας δὲ αὐτῶν τὴν πανουργίαν, εἶπε πρὸς
observing ˜ But their - craftiness, He said to

αὐτούς, "Τί με πειράζετε?[h] **24** Ἐπιδείξατέ μοι δηνάριον.
them, "Why [4]Me [1]do [2]you [3]test? Show Me a denarius.

Τίνος ἔχει εἰκόνα καὶ ἐπιγραφήν?"
Whose [4]does [5]it [6]have [1]image [2]and [3]inscription?"

Ἀποκριθέντες δὲ εἶπον, "Καίσαρος."
answering ˜ And they said, "Caesar's."

25 Ὁ δὲ εἶπεν αὐτοῖς, "Ἀπόδοτε τοίνυν τὰ
[2]the [3]*One* [1]And said to them, "Give back therefore the *things*
He "Render Caesar's

Καίσαρος Καίσαρι, καὶ τὰ τοῦ Θεοῦ τῷ Θεῷ." **26** Καὶ
of Caesar to Caesar, and the *things* - of God - to God." And
things God's things

οὐκ ἴσχυσαν ἐπιλαβέσθαι αὐτοῦ ῥήματος ἐναντίον τοῦ
[3]not [1]they [2]were able to lay hold of His word in front of the
to catch Him in

λαοῦ. Καὶ θαυμάσαντες ἐπὶ τῇ ἀποκρίσει αὐτοῦ, ἐσίγησαν.
people. And marveling at - answer ˜ His, they kept silent.

The Sadducees Question the Resurrection
(Matt. 22:23–33; Mark 12:18–27)

27 Προσελθόντες δέ τινες τῶν Σαδδουκαίων, οἱ
[13]coming [14]to [15]*Him* [1]And [2]some [3]of [4]the [5]Sadducees, [6]the [7]*ones*
those

19 And the chief priests and the scribes that very hour sought to lay hands on Him, but they feared the people—for they knew He had spoken this parable against them.
20 So they watched *Him,* and sent spies who pretended to be righteous, that they might seize on His words, in order to deliver Him to the power and the authority of the governor.
21 Then they asked Him, saying, "Teacher, we know that You say and teach rightly, and You do not show personal favoritism, but teach the way of God in truth:
22 "Is it lawful for us to pay taxes to Caesar or not?"
23 But He perceived their craftiness, and said to them, "Why do you test Me?
24 "Show Me a denarius. Whose image and inscription does it have?" They answered and said, "Caesar's."
25 And He said to them, "Render therefore to Caesar the things that are Caesar's, and to God the things that are God's."
26 But they could not catch Him in His words in the presence of the people. And they marveled at His answer and kept silent.
27 Then some of the Saddu-

[g](20:19) NU adds *τον λαον, of the people.*
[h](20:23) NU omits *Τι με πειραζετε, Why do you test Me?*

cees, who deny that there is a
resurrection, came to *Him* and
asked Him,
28 saying: "Teacher, Moses
wrote to us *that* if a man's
brother dies, having a wife, and
he dies without children, his
brother should take his wife and
raise up offspring for his
brother.
29 "Now there were seven
brothers. And the first took a
wife, and died without children.
30 "And the second took her
as wife, and he died childless.
31 "Then the third took her,
and in like manner the seven
also; and they left no children,
and died.
32 "Last of all the woman died
also.
33 "Therefore, in the resurrection, whose wife does she
become? For all seven had her
as wife."
34 Jesus answered and said to
them, "The sons of this age
marry and are given in marriage.
35 "But those who are
counted worthy to attain that
age, and the resurrection from
the dead, neither marry nor are
given in marriage;
36 "nor can they die anymore,
for they are equal to the angels
and are sons of God, being sons
of the resurrection.
37 "But even Moses showed
in the *burning* bush *passage* that
the dead are raised, when he
called the Lord *'the God of
Abraham, the God of Isaac, and
the God of Jacob.'*
38 "For He is not the God of
the dead but of the living, for all
live to Him."
39 Then some of the scribes
answered and said, "Teacher,
You have spoken well."
40 But after that they dared
not question Him anymore.

ἀντιλέγοντες ἀνάστασιν μὴ εἶναι, ἐπηρώτησαν αὐτόν,
[8]denying [9]resurrection [10]not [11]to [12]be, asked Him,
who deny that there is a resurrection,

28 λέγοντες, "Διδάσκαλε, Μωσῆς ἔγραψεν ἡμῖν, ἐάν τινος
saying, "Teacher, Moses wrote to us, if [3]of [4]anyone

ἀδελφὸς ἀποθάνῃ ἔχων γυναῖκα, καὶ οὗτος ἄτεκνος
[1]a [2]brother dies having a wife, and this *man* childless ~

ἀποθάνῃ,[i] ἵνα λάβῃ ὁ ἀδελφὸς αὐτοῦ τὴν γυναῖκα καὶ
dies, that [3]should [4]take - [2]brother [1]his the wife and
his

ἐξαναστήσῃ σπέρμα τῷ ἀδελφῷ αὐτοῦ. 29 Ἑπτὰ οὖν
raise up seed - for brother ~ his. [4]seven [1]Now
offspring

ἀδελφοὶ ἦσαν. Καὶ ὁ πρῶτος λαβὼν γυναῖκα
[5]brothers [2]*there* [3]were. And the first having taken a wife

ἀπέθανεν ἄτεκνος. 30 Καὶ ἔλαβεν[j] ὁ δεύτερος[k] τὴν
died childless. And [3]took [1]the [2]second the

γυναῖκα, καὶ οὗτος ἀπέθανεν ἄτεκνος. 31 Καὶ ὁ τρίτος
woman, and this *man* died childless. And the third

ἔλαβεν αὐτήν. Ὡσαύτως δὲ καὶ οἱ ἑπτὰ οὐ κατέλιπον
took her. likewise ~ And [3]also [1]the [2]seven [5]not [4]did leave

τέκνα, καὶ ἀπέθανον. 32 Ὕστερον δὲ πάντων ἀπέθανε καὶ
children, and they died. last ~ And of all [3]died [4]also

ἡ γυνή. 33 Ἐν τῇ οὖν[l] ἀναστάσει, τίνος αὐτῶν
[1]the [2]woman. [2]in [3]the [1]Therefore resurrection, whose [2]of [3]them

γίνεται γυνή? Οἱ γὰρ ἑπτὰ ἔσχον αὐτὴν γυναῖκα."
[4]does [5]she [6]become [1]wife? the ~ For seven had her *as* wife."

34 Καὶ ἀποκριθεὶς[m] εἶπεν αὐτοῖς ὁ Ἰησοῦς, "Οἱ υἱοὶ τοῦ
And answering [2]said [3]to [4]them - [1]Jesus, "The sons -

αἰῶνος τούτου γαμοῦσι καὶ ἐκγαμίσκονται. 35 Οἱ δὲ
of age ~ this marry and are given in marriage. [2]the [3]*ones* [1]But
those who

καταξιωθέντες τοῦ αἰῶνος ἐκείνου τυχεῖν καὶ τῆς
being counted worthy - [4]age [3]that [1]to [2]attain and the
have been

ἀναστάσεως τῆς ἐκ νεκρῶν οὔτε γαμοῦσιν οὔτε
resurrection - from *the* dead neither marry nor

ἐκγαμίζονται. 36 Οὔτε γὰρ ἀποθανεῖν ἔτι δύνανται,
are given in marriage. neither ~ For [5]to [6]die [3]still [1]are [2]they [4]able,

ἰσάγγελοι γάρ εἰσι, καὶ υἱοί εἰσι τοῦ Θεοῦ,
[10]equal [11]to [12]angels [7]for [8]they [9]are, and [3]sons [1]they [2]are - of God,

τῆς ἀναστάσεως υἱοὶ ὄντες. 37 Ὅτι δὲ ἐγείρονται οἱ
[3]of [4]the [5]resurrection [2]sons [1]being. that ~ But [3]are [4]raised [1]the

νεκροί, καὶ Μωσῆς ἐμήνυσεν ἐπὶ τῆς βάτου,
[2]dead, even Moses revealed in *the passage about* the *burning* bush,

ὡς λέγει «Κύριον τὸν Θεὸν Ἀβραὰμ καὶ τὸν Θεὸν Ἰσαὰκ
when he says «*the* Lord - God of Abraham and the God of Isaac

καὶ τὸν Θεὸν Ἰακώβ.» 38 Θεὸς δὲ οὐκ ἔστι νεκρῶν,
and the God of Jacob.» [5]*the* [6]God [1]Now [4]not [2]He [3]is of dead *people,*

ἀλλὰ ζώντων, πάντες γὰρ αὐτῷ ζῶσιν."
but of living *people,* all ~ for [3]to [4]Him [1]are [2]alive."

39 Ἀποκριθέντες δέ τινες τῶν γραμματέων εἶπον,
answering ~ And some of the scribes said,

"Διδάσκαλε, καλῶς εἶπας." 40 Οὐκέτι δὲ ἐτόλμων
"Teacher, [3]well [1]You [2]spoke." [3]no [4]longer [1]And [2]they [5]dared

ἐπερωτᾶν αὐτὸν οὐδέν.
to ask Him no thing.
anything.

[i](**20:28**) NU reads η, *is.*
[j](**20:30**) NU omits ελαβεν, *took.* [k](**20:30**) NU omits the rest of v. 30.
[l](**20:33**) NU adds η γυνη, *the woman.*
[m](**20:34**) NU omits αποκριθεις, *answering.*

What Do You Think of Christ?
(Matt. 22:41–46; Mark 12:35–37)

41 Εἶπε δὲ πρὸς αὐτούς, "Πῶς λέγουσι τὸν Χριστὸν
[2]He [3]said [1]And to them, "How do they say the Christ
that the Messiah

Υἱὸν Δαβὶδ εἶναι? 42 Καὶ αὐτὸς Δαβὶδ λέγει ἐν Βίβλῳ
[3]*the* [4]Son [5]of [6]David [1]to [2]be? Even himself ~ David says in *the* Book
is?

Ψαλμῶν,
of Psalms,

«Εἶπεν ὁ Κύριος τῷ Κυρίῳ μου·
«[3]said [1]The [2]Lord - to Lord ~ my:

'Κάθου ἐκ δεξιῶν μου,
'Sit at [2]right [3]*parts* [1]My,
hand

43 Ἕως ἂν θῶ τοὺς ἐχθρούς σου ὑποπόδιον τῶν ποδῶν
Till - I put - enemies ~ Your *as* a footstool - of feet ~
for

σου.'»
Your.'»

44 Δαβὶδ οὖν 'Κύριον' αὐτὸν καλεῖ, καὶ πῶς Υἱός αὐτοῦ
David ~ Therefore [3]'Lord' [2]Him [1]calls, and how [4]Son [3]his

ἐστιν?"
[1]is [2]He?"

Jesus Pronounces Woes on the Scribes
(Matt. 23:1–36; Mark 12:38–40; Luke 11:37–52)

45 Ἀκούοντος δὲ παντὸς τοῦ λαοῦ, εἶπε τοῖς
hearing And all the people, He said -
And as all the people listened,

μαθηταῖς αὐτοῦ, 46 "Προσέχετε ἀπὸ τῶν γραμματέων τῶν
to disciples ~ His, "Beware from the scribes the *ones*
of who

θελόντων περιπατεῖν ἐν στολαῖς καὶ φιλούντων ἀσπασμοὺς ἐν
desiring to walk about in long robes and loving greetings in
desire love

ταῖς ἀγοραῖς καὶ πρωτοκαθεδρίας ἐν ταῖς συναγωγαῖς καὶ
the marketplaces and first seats in the synagogues and
the best

πρωτοκλισίας ἐν τοῖς δείπνοις, 47 οἳ κατεσθίουσι τὰς οἰκίας
first couches at - dinners, who eat up the houses
the places of honor devour

τῶν χηρῶν, καὶ προφάσει μακρὰ προσεύχονται. Οὗτοι
of the widows, and in pretense [3]long [1]they [2]pray. These
at length

λήψονται περισσότερον κρίμα."
will receive greater judgment."
more severe condemnation."

The Widow's Two Mites
(Mark 12:41–44)

21 1 Ἀναβλέψας δὲ εἶδε τοὺς βάλλοντας τὰ δῶρα
[2]looking [3]up [1]And He saw the [3]putting - [5]gifts

αὐτῶν εἰς τὸ γαζοφυλάκιον πλουσίους. 2 Εἶδε δὲ
[4]their [6]into [7]the [8]treasury [1]rich [2]*people.* [2]He [3]saw [1]And

τινα καὶ χήραν πενιχρὰν βάλλουσαν ἐκεῖ δύο λεπτά.
[5]a [6]certain [4]also [8]widow [7]poor putting *in* there two lepta.
mites.

41 And He said to them, "How can they say that the Christ is the Son of David?
42 "Now David himself said in the Book of Psalms:

'The LORD said to my
Lord,
"Sit at My right hand,
43 *Till I make Your enemies*
Your footstool."'

44 "Therefore David calls Him *'Lord'*; how is He then his Son?"
45 Then, in the hearing of all the people, He said to His disciples,
46 "Beware of the scribes, who desire to go around in long robes, love greetings in the marketplaces, the best seats in the synagogues, and the best places at feasts,
47 "who devour widows' houses, and for a pretense make long prayers. These will receive greater condemnation."
21 And He looked up and saw the rich putting their gifts into the treasury,
2 and He saw also a certain poor widow putting in two mites.

3 So He said, "Truly I say to you that this poor widow has put in more than all;
4 "for all these out of their abundance have put in offerings for God, but she out of her poverty put in all the livelihood that she had."
5 Then, as some spoke of the temple, how it was adorned with beautiful stones and donations, He said,
6 "These things which you see—the days will come in which not *one* stone shall be left upon another that shall not be thrown down."
7 So they asked Him, saying, "Teacher, but when will these things be? And what sign *will there be* when these things are about to take place?"
8 And He said: "Take heed that you not be deceived. For many will come in My name, saying, 'I am *He,*' and, 'The time has drawn near.' Therefore do not go after them.
9 "But when you hear of wars and commotions, do not be terrified; for these things must come to pass first, but the end *will not come* immediately."
10 Then He said to them, "Nation will rise against nation, and kingdom against kingdom.
11 "And there will be great earthquakes in various places, and famines and pestilences;

3 Καὶ εἶπεν, "Ἀληθῶς λέγω ὑμῖν ὅτι ἡ χήρα ἡ πτωχὴ αὕτη
And He said, "Truly I say to you that - [3]widow - [2]poor [1]this

πλεῖον πάντων ἔβαλεν. **4** Ἅπαντες γὰρ οὗτοι ἐκ τοῦ
[6]more [7]*than* [8]all [4]put [5]*in.* all ˜ For these out of the *amount* (their)

περισσεύοντος αὐτοῖς ἔβαλον εἰς τὰ δῶρα τοῦ Θεοῦ,[a]
abounding (abundance) to them put into the gifts - of God, (for)

αὕτη δὲ ἐκ τοῦ ὑστερήματος αὐτῆς ἅπαντα τὸν
[2]this [3]*woman* [1]but out of - lack ˜ (poverty) her [3]all [4]the (her)

βίον ὃν εἶχεν ἔβαλε."
[5]livelihood [6]which [7]she [8]had [1]put [2]*in.*"

Jesus Predicts the Destruction of the Temple
(Matt. 24:1, 2; Mark 13:1, 2)

5 Καί τινων λεγόντων περὶ τοῦ ἱεροῦ, ὅτι λίθοις
And some saying (as some spoke) about the temple, that [5]with [7]stones

καλοῖς καὶ ἀναθήμασι κεκόσμηται, εἶπε,
[6]beautiful [8]and [9]with [10]votive [11]offerings (donations) [1]it [2]has (had) [3]been [4]adorned, He said,

6 "Ταῦτα ἃ θεωρεῖτε ἐλεύσονται ἡμέραι ἐν αἷς οὐκ
"These *things* which you see [2]will [3]come [1]days in which [4]not

ἀφεθήσεται λίθος ἐπὶ λίθῳ ὃς οὐ καταλυθήσεται."
[3]will [5]be [6]left [1]a [2]stone upon a stone which not ˜ will be thrown down."

Jesus Gives the Signs of the Times
(Matt. 24:3–14; Mark 13:3–13)

7 Ἐπηρώτησαν δὲ αὐτόν, λέγοντες, "Διδάσκαλε, πότε
[2]they [3]asked [1]And Him, saying, "Teacher, when ˜

οὖν ταῦτα ἔσται? Καὶ τί τὸ σημεῖον ὅταν
so [2]these [3]*things* [1]will [4]be? And what *will be* the sign when

μέλλῃ ταῦτα γίνεσθαι?"
[3]are [4]about [1]these [2]*things* to happen?"

8 Ὁ δὲ εἶπε, "Βλέπετε μὴ πλανηθῆτε.
[2]the [3]*One* (He) [1]And said, "Watch out *that* not ˜ you be deceived.

Πολλοὶ γὰρ ἐλεύσονται ἐπὶ τῷ ὀνόματί μου, λέγοντες ὅτι 'Ἐγώ
many ˜ For will come in - name ˜ My, saying - 'I

εἰμι,' καί, 'Ὁ καιρὸς ἤγγικε.' Μὴ οὖν πορευθῆτε
am *He,*' and, 'The time has drawn near.' [3]not [1]Therefore [2]do go

ὀπίσω αὐτῶν. **9** Ὅταν δὲ ἀκούσητε πολέμους καὶ
after them. whenever ˜ But you hear of wars and

ἀκαταστασίας, μὴ πτοηθῆτε· δεῖ γὰρ
insurrections, not ˜ do be terrified; [2]it [3]is [4]necessary [5]*for* (for these) [1]for (things)

ταῦτα γενέσθαι πρῶτον, ἀλλ' οὐκ εὐθέως τὸ τέλος."
these *things* to happen (must) first, but [3]*is* [4]not [5]immediately [1]the [2]end."

10 Τότε ἔλεγεν αὐτοῖς, "Ἐγερθήσεται ἔθνος ἐπὶ ἔθνος,
Then He said to them, "[2]will [3]be [4]raised [5]up [1]Nation against nation,

καὶ βασιλεία ἐπὶ βασιλείαν. **11** Σεισμοί τε μεγάλοι
and kingdom against kingdom. [6]earthquakes [1]And [5]great

κατὰ τόπους καὶ λιμοὶ καὶ λοιμοὶ ἔσονται,
[7]according [8]to (in various) [9]places [10]and [11]famines [12]and [13]pestilences [2]*there* [3]will [4]be,

[a](21:4) NU omits του Θεου, *of God.*

φόβητρά τε καὶ σημεῖα ἀπ᾽ οὐρανοῦ μεγάλα
[18]fearful [19]events [14]and [20]and [22]signs [23]from [24]heaven [21]great

ἔσται. 12 Πρὸ δὲ τούτων πάντων ἐπιβαλοῦσιν
[15]*there* [16]will [17]be. before ˜ But [2]these [3]*things* [1]all they will lay

ἐφ᾽ ὑμᾶς τὰς χεῖρας αὐτῶν καὶ διώξουσι,
[3]on [4]you - [2]hands [1]their and they will persecute *you,*

παραδιδόντες εἰς συναγωγὰς καὶ φυλακάς, ἀγομένους ἐπὶ
handing *you* over to synagogues and prisons, being led away before
delivering when you are

βασιλεῖς καὶ ἡγεμόνας ἕνεκεν τοῦ ὀνόματός μου.
kings and rulers on account of - name ˜ My.

13 Ἀποβήσεται δὲ ὑμῖν εἰς μαρτύριον. 14 Θέσθε οὖν εἰς
[2]it [3]will [4]turn [5]out [1]And for you for a testimony. Put *it* then in
Settle

τὰς καρδίαις ὑμῶν μὴ προμελετᾶν ἀπολογηθῆναι·
- hearts ˜ your not to practice beforehand to give a defense;
giving your

15 ἐγὼ γὰρ δώσω ὑμῖν στόμα καὶ σοφίαν ᾗ οὐ
I ˜ for will give you a mouth and wisdom which [7]not

δυνήσονται ἀντειπεῖν οὐδὲ ἀντιστῆναι πάντες οἱ
[6]will [8]be [9]able [10]to [11]contradict [12]nor [13]to [14]withstand [1]all [2]the [3]*ones*
your

ἀντικείμενοι ὑμῖν. 16 Παραδοθήσεσθε δὲ καὶ ὑπὸ
[4]opposing [5]you. [2]you [3]will [5]be [6]handed [7]over [1]And [4]also by
opponents. betrayed

γονέων καὶ συγγενῶν καὶ φίλων καὶ ἀδελφῶν, καὶ
parents and relatives and friends and brothers, and

θανατώσουσιν ἐξ ὑμῶν. 17 Καὶ ἔσεσθε μισούμενοι
they will put *some* [3]to [4]death [1]of [2]you. And you will be being hated
hated

ὑπὸ πάντων διὰ τὸ ὄνομά μου. 18 Καὶ θρὶξ ἐκ
by all *people* on account of - name ˜ My. And a hair from
for My name's sake. not a hair

τῆς κεφαλῆς ὑμῶν οὐ μὴ ἀπόληται. 19 Ἐν τῇ ὑπομονῇ
- head ˜ your [2]not [3]not [1]will [4]perish. In - endurance ˜
will by any means perish.

ὑμῶν κτήσασθε τὰς ψυχὰς* ὑμῶν.
your possess - souls ˜ your.

Jesus Warns of Jerusalem's Fall
(Matt. 24:15–28; Mark 13:14–23)

20 "Ὅταν δὲ ἴδητε κυκλουμένην ὑπὸ στρατοπέδων τὴν
"when ˜ But you see [2]being [3]surrounded [4]by [5]troops -

Ἰερουσαλήμ, τότε γνῶτε ὅτι ἤγγικεν ἡ ἐρήμωσις αὐτῆς.
[1]Jerusalem, then know that [3]has [4]drawn [5]near - [2]desolation [1]its.

21 Τότε οἱ ἐν τῇ Ἰουδαίᾳ φευγέτωσαν εἰς τὰ
Then [2]the [3]*ones* [4]in - [5]Judea [1]let [6]flee to the
those who are

ὄρη, καὶ οἱ ἐν μέσῳ αὐτῆς ἐκχωρείτωσαν, καὶ
mountains, and [2]the [3]*ones* [4]in [6]midst [5]her [1]let [7]depart, and
those who are

οἱ ἐν ταῖς χώραις μὴ εἰσερχέσθωσαν εἰς αὐτήν.
[2]the [3]*ones* [4]in [5]the [6]fields [7]not [1]let [8]enter into her.
those who are

22 Ὅτι ἡμέραι ἐκδικήσεως αὗταί εἰσι, τοῦ πλησθῆναι
Because [3]days [4]of [5]vengeance [1]these [2]are, - to fulfill

πάντα τὰ γεγραμμένα. 23 Οὐαὶ δὲ ταῖς ἐν
all the *things* having been written. woe ˜ But to the *women* in
that has been those who are

and there will be fearful sights
and great signs from heaven.
12 "But before all these
things, they will lay their hands
on you and persecute *you,* delivering *you* up to the synagogues and prisons. You will be
brought before kings and rulers
for My name's sake.
13 "But it will turn out for you
as an occasion for testimony.
14 "Therefore settle *it* in your
hearts not to meditate beforehand on what you will answer;
15 "for I will give you a mouth
and wisdom which all your adversaries will not be able to
contradict or resist.
16 "You will be betrayed even
by parents and brothers, relatives and friends; and they will
put *some* of you to death.
17 "And you will be hated by
all for My name's sake.
18 "But not a hair of your
head shall be lost.
19 "By your patience possess
your souls.
20 "But when you see Jerusalem surrounded by armies, then
know that its desolation is near.
21 "Then let those who are in
Judea flee to the mountains, let
those who are in the midst of
her depart, and let not those
who are in the country enter
her.
22 "For these are the days of
vengeance, that all things which
are written may be fulfilled.
23 "But woe to those who are

***(21:19)** ψυχή *(psychē).* Noun often translated *soul,* but occurring frequently in the NT with a variety of meanings. The most basic meaning relates to the life principle—earthly, animating life—correctly translated into English as *life* (Matt. 2:20; cf. 1 Thess. 2:8). This life principle may be individualized, and so mean the *person* or *self* that is physically alive (perhaps reflecting LXX usage, as Ezek. 18:4; cf. Acts 2:41). The word can also be used for the inner self (especially as a being with emotions and feelings, as Luke 2:35). ψυχή also designates the self that survives physical death (James 1:21; cf. Luke 12:20; Matt. 10:28), although in such uses it is still not so much a "part" as the "whole" self. The difficulty of isolating one of these vari-

pregnant and to those who are
nursing babies in those days!
For there will be great distress
in the land and wrath upon this
people.
24 "And they will fall by the
edge of the sword, and be led
away captive into all nations.
And Jerusalem will be trampled
by Gentiles until the times of
the Gentiles are fulfilled.
25 "And there will be signs in
the sun, in the moon, and in the
stars; and on the earth distress
of nations, with perplexity, the
sea and the waves roaring;
26 "men's hearts failing them
from fear and the expectation of
those things which are coming
on the earth, for the powers of
the heavens will be shaken.
27 "Then they will see the
Son of Man coming in a cloud
with power and great glory.
28 "Now when these things
begin to happen, look up and lift
up your heads, because your
redemption draws near."
29 Then He spoke to them a
parable: "Look at the fig tree,
and all the trees.
30 "When they are already
budding, you see and know for
yourselves that summer is now
near.
31 "So you also, when you see
these things happening, know
that the kingdom of God is
near.
32 "Assuredly, I say to you,
this generation will by no

γαστρὶ ἐχούσαις καὶ ταῖς θηλαζούσαις ἐν ἐκείναις ταῖς
the womb having and to the *women* giving suck in those -
pregnant those who are nursing a baby

ἡμέραις! Ἔσται γὰρ ἀνάγκη μεγάλη ἐπὶ τῆς γῆς καὶ ὀργὴ
days! [4]will [5]be [1]For [3]distress [2]great in the land and wrath

ἐν[b] τῷ λαῷ τούτῳ. 24 Καὶ πεσοῦνται στόματι
among - people ˜ this. And they will fall by *the* mouth
edge

μαχαίρας, καὶ αἰχμαλωτισθήσονται εἰς πάντα τὰ ἔθνη. Καὶ
of *the* sword, and they will be led captive into all - nations. And

Ἱερουσαλὴμ ἔσται πατουμένη ὑπὸ ἐθνῶν, ἄχρι πληρωθῶσι
Jerusalem will be trampled by *the* Gentiles, until [6]are [7]fulfilled

καιροὶ ἐθνῶν.
[1]*the* [2]times [3]of [4]*the* [5]Gentiles.

The Coming of the Son of Man
(Matt. 24:29–31; Mark 13:24–27)

25 "Καὶ ἔσται σημεῖα ἐν ἡλίῳ καὶ σελήνῃ καὶ
"And *there* will be signs in *the* sun and *the* moon and

ἄστροις, καὶ ἐπὶ τῆς γῆς συνοχὴ ἐθνῶν ἐν ἀπορίᾳ,
the stars, and on the earth distress of nations with perplexity,

ἠχούσης[c] θαλάσσης καὶ σάλου, 26 ἀποψυχόντων
sounding sea and surge, [2]ceasing [3]to [4]breathe
as the sea and the waves roar, while people stop

ἀνθρώπων ἀπὸ φόβου καὶ προσδοκίας τῶν ἐπερχομένων τῇ
[1]men from fear and expectation of the *things* coming upon the
breathing about what is

οἰκουμένῃ, αἱ γὰρ δυνάμεις τῶν οὐρανῶν σαλευθήσονται.
inhabited earth, the ˜ for powers of the heavens will be shaken.

27 Καὶ τότε ὄψονται τὸν Υἱὸν τοῦ Ἀνθρώπου ἐρχόμενον ἐν
And then they will see the Son - of Man coming in

νεφέλῃ μετὰ δυνάμεως καὶ δόξης πολλῆς. 28 Ἀρχομένων δὲ
a cloud with power and glory ˜ much. beginning And
And when these

τούτων γίνεσθαι, ἀνακύψατε καὶ ἐπάρατε τὰς κεφαλὰς
these *things* to happen, straighten up and lift up - heads ˜
things begin look

ὑμῶν, διότι ἐγγίζει ἡ ἀπολύτρωσις ὑμῶν."
your, because [3]is [4]drawing [5]near - [2]redemption [1]your."

The Parable of the Fig Tree
(Matt. 24:32–35; Mark 13:28–31)

29 Καὶ εἶπε παραβολὴν αὐτοῖς· "Ἴδετε τὴν συκῆν καὶ
And He told a parable to them: "Look at the fig tree and

πάντα τὰ δένδρα. 30 Ὅταν προβάλωσιν ἤδη,
all the trees. When they are [2]putting [3]out [1]already,
budding

βλέποντες ἀφ' ἑαυτῶν γινώσκετε ὅτι ἤδη ἐγγὺς τὸ θέρος
seeing from yourselves you know that [3]already [4]near - [1]summer
when you see it you know of yourselves

ἐστίν. 31 Οὕτω καὶ ὑμεῖς ὅταν ἴδητε ταῦτα γινόμενα,
[2]is. Thus also you when you see these *things* happening,
In this way

γινώσκετε ὅτι ἐγγύς ἐστιν ἡ βασιλεία τοῦ Θεοῦ.
know that [6]near [5]is [1]the [2]kingdom - [3]of [4]God.

32 Ἀμὴν λέγω ὑμῖν ὅτι οὐ μὴ παρέλθῃ ἡ γενεὰ
Amen I say to you that [4]not [5]not [3]will [6]pass [7]away - [2]generation
Assuredly by no means

---

[b](21:23) NU omits εν, *among.* [c](21:25) NU reads ηχους, *at (the) sound (of the sea).*

ous meanings for a particular occurrence is obvious here in Luke 21:19, since it can imply either the course of natural life or the continuing aspect of one's existence. Cf. the cognate adjective ψυχικός, *natural, physical* (see ψυχικός at 1 Cor. 15:46).

αὕτη ἕως ἂν πάντα γένηται. 33 Ὁ οὐρανὸς καὶ ἡ γῆ
[1]this until - all *things* happen. - Heaven and - earth

παρελεύσονται, οἱ δὲ λόγοι μου οὐ μὴ παρέλθωσι.
will pass away, - but words ~ My [2]not [3]not [1]will [4]pass [5]away.
by no means

Jesus Teaches Watchfulness

34 "Προσέχετε δὲ ἑαυτοῖς μήποτε βαρηθῶσιν
"[2]take [3]heed [1]But to yourselves lest [3]be [4]weighed [5]down

ὑμῶν αἱ καρδίαι ἐν κραιπάλῃ καὶ μέθῃ καὶ μερίμναις
[1]your - [2]hearts with carousing and drunkenness and *the* worries

βιωτικαῖς, καὶ αἰφνίδιος ἐφ' ὑμᾶς ἐπιστῇ ἡ ἡμέρα ἐκείνη.
of life, and [6]suddenly [4]upon [5]you [3]come - [2]day [1]that.

35 Ὡς παγὶς γὰρ ἐπελεύσεται ἐπὶ πάντας τοὺς
[5]as [6]a [7]snare [1]For [2]it [3]will [4]come on all the *ones*
those

καθημένους ἐπὶ πρόσωπον πάσης τῆς γῆς. 36 Ἀγρυπνεῖτε
sitting on *the* face of all the earth. Watch
who live

οὖν ἐν παντὶ καιρῷ δεόμενοι ἵνα καταξιωθῆτε[d]
therefore in every time praying that you may be counted worthy
praying always

ἐκφυγεῖν πάντα[e] τὰ μέλλοντα γίνεσθαι, καὶ σταθῆναι
to escape all the *things* being about to happen, and to stand
everything that is

ἔμπροσθεν τοῦ Υἱοῦ τοῦ Ἀνθρώπου."
before the Son - of Man."

37 Ἦν δὲ τὰς ἡμέρας ἐν τῷ ἱερῷ διδάσκων, τὰς δὲ
[2]He [3]was [1]And [5]the [6]days [7]in [8]the [9]temple [4]teaching, the ~ but
by day but at

νύκτας ἐξερχόμενος ηὐλίζετο εἰς τὸ ὄρος τὸ
nights going out He was lodging on the mountain the *one*
night He went out and would lodge which

καλούμενον Ἐλαιῶν. 38 Καὶ πᾶς ὁ λαὸς ὤρθριζε
being called Of Olives. And all the people were rising very early
is called Olivet. used to come early in

πρὸς αὐτὸν ἐν τῷ ἱερῷ ἀκούειν αὐτοῦ.
to come to Him in the temple to hear Him.
the morning to

The Chief Priests and Elders Plot to Kill Jesus
(Matt. 26:1–5; Mark 14:1, 2; John 11:45–53)

22 1 Ἤγγιζε δὲ ἡ ἑορτὴ τῶν ἀζύμων,
[7]drew [8]near [1]Now [2]the [3]Feast - [4]of [5]Unleavened [6]Bread,

ἡ λεγομένη Πάσχα. 2 Καὶ ἐζήτουν οἱ ἀρχιερεῖς καὶ
the *one* being called Passover. And [7]were [8]seeking [1]the [2]chief [3]priests [4]and
which is

οἱ γραμματεῖς τὸ πῶς ἀνέλωσιν αὐτόν, ἐφοβοῦντο γὰρ τὸν
[5]the [6]scribes - how they might kill Him, [2]they [3]feared [1]for the

λαόν.
people.

Judas Agrees to Betray Jesus for Money
(Matt. 26:14–16; Mark 14:10, 11)

3 Εἰσῆλθε δὲ Σατανᾶς εἰς Ἰούδαν τὸν
[3]entered [1]And [2]Satan into Judas the *one*
who was

means pass away till all things take place.
33 "Heaven and earth will pass away, but My words will by no means pass away.
34 "But take heed to yourselves, lest your hearts be weighed down with carousing, drunkenness, and cares of this life, and that Day come on you unexpectedly.
35 "For it will come as a snare on all those who dwell on the face of the whole earth.
36 "Watch therefore, and pray always that you may be counted worthy to escape all these things that will come to pass, and to stand before the Son of Man."
37 And in the daytime He was teaching in the temple, but at night He went out and stayed on the mountain called Olivet.
38 Then early in the morning all the people came to Him in the temple to hear Him.

22 Now the Feast of Unleavened Bread drew near, which is called Passover.
2 And the chief priests and the scribes sought how they might kill Him, for they feared the people.
3 Then Satan entered Judas,

---

[d](21:36) NU reads *κατισχυσητε, you may be able.* [e](21:36) NU adds *ταυτα, these.*

surnamed Iscariot, who was
numbered among the twelve.
4 So he went his way and
conferred with the chief priests
and captains, how he might betray Him to them.
5 And they were glad, and
agreed to give him money.
6 So he promised and sought
opportunity to betray Him to
them in the absence of the multitude.
7 Then came the Day of Unleavened Bread, when the
Passover must be killed.
8 And He sent Peter and
John, saying, "Go and prepare
the Passover for us, that we
may eat."
9 So they said to Him,
"Where do You want us to prepare?"
10 And He said to them, "Behold, when you have entered
the city, a man will meet you
carrying a pitcher of water; follow him into the house which he
enters.
11 "Then you shall say to the
master of the house, 'The
Teacher says to you, "Where is
the guest room where I may
eat the Passover with My disciples?"'
12 "Then he will show you a
large, furnished upper room;
there make ready."
13 So they went and found it
just as He had said to them, and
they prepared the Passover.

ἐπικαλούμενον[a] Ἰσκαριώτην, ὄντα ἐκ τοῦ ἀριθμοῦ τῶν
being surnamed Iscariot, being of the number of the
surnamed who was

δώδεκα. 4 Καὶ ἀπελθὼν συνελάλησε τοῖς ἀρχιερεῦσι καὶ
twelve. And going off he spoke with the chief priests and
he went off and

στρατηγοῖς τὸ πῶς αὐτὸν παραδῷ αὐτοῖς. 5 Καὶ
captains - *about* how [4]Him [1]he [2]might [3]hand [5]over to them. And
betray

ἐχάρησαν, καὶ συνέθεντο αὐτῷ ἀργύριον δοῦναι. 6 Καὶ
they were glad, and agreed [4]to [5]him [3]money [1]to [2]give. And

ἐξωμολόγησε, καὶ ἐζήτει εὐκαιρίαν τοῦ παραδοῦναι αὐτὸν
he promised, and was seeking an opportunity - to hand over ~ Him
betray

αὐτοῖς ἄτερ ὄχλου.
to them without a crowd.
in the absence of

Jesus and His Disciples Prepare the Passover
(Matt. 26:17–19; Mark 14:12–16)

7 Ἦλθε δὲ ἡ ἡμέρα τῶν ἀζύμων, ἐν ᾗ
[7]came [1]Now [2]the [3]Day - [4]of [5]Unleavened [6]Bread, in which

ἔδει θύεσθαι τὸ Πάσχα. 8 Καὶ ἀπέστειλε
it was necessary *that* [3]to [4]be [5]killed [1]the [2]Passover. And He sent
be Paschal Lamb.

Πέτρον καὶ Ἰωάννην, εἰπών, "Πορευθέντες ἑτοιμάσατε ἡμῖν
Peter and John, saying, "Going prepare [3]for [4]us
"Go and

τὸ Πάσχα, ἵνα φάγωμεν."
[1]the [2]Passover, so that we may eat *it*."

9 Οἱ δὲ εἶπον αὐτῷ, "Ποῦ θέλεις
[2]the [3]*ones* [1]And said to Him, "Where do You desire *that*
they

ἑτοιμάσομεν?"
we shall prepare *it*?"

10 Ὁ δὲ εἶπεν αὐτοῖς, "Ἰδού, εἰσελθόντων ὑμῶν
[2]the [3]*One* [1]And said to them, "Behold, entering you
He when you have entered

εἰς τὴν πόλιν, συναντήσει ὑμῖν ἄνθρωπος κεράμιον ὕδατος
into the city, [3]will [4]meet [5]you [1]a [2]man [7]a [8]jar [9]of [10]water

βαστάζων· ἀκολουθήσατε αὐτῷ εἰς τὴν οἰκίαν οὗ
[6]carrying; follow him into the house where

εἰσπορεύεται. 11 Καὶ ἐρεῖτε τῷ οἰκοδεσπότῃ τῆς
he goes in. And you will say to the master of the

οἰκίας, 'Λέγει σοι ὁ Διδάσκαλος, "Ποῦ ἐστι τὸ
house, '[3]says [4]to [5]you [1]The [2]Teacher, "Where is the

κατάλυμα ὅπου τὸ Πάσχα μετὰ τῶν μαθητῶν μου
guest room where [4]the [5]Passover [6]with - [8]disciples [7]My

φάγω?"' 12 Κἀκεῖνος ὑμῖν δείξει ἀνώγεον μέγα
[1]I [2]may [3]eat?"' And that *man* [3]you [1]will [2]show [4]a(n) [7]upper [8]room [5]large

ἐστρωμένον· ἐκεῖ ἑτοιμάσατε." 13 Ἀπελθόντες δὲ εὗρον
[6]spread; there prepare *it*." [2]going [3]off [1]And they found *it*
furnished; they went and

καθὼς εἴρηκεν αὐτοῖς, καὶ ἡτοίμασαν τὸ Πάσχα.
just as He had said to them, and they prepared the Passover.

[a](22:3) NU reads καλουμενον, *called*.

Jesus Institutes the Lord's Supper
(Matt. 26:26–30; Mark 14:22–26; 1 Cor. 11:23–25)

14 Καὶ ὅτε ἐγένετο ἡ ὥρα, ἀνέπεσε, καὶ οἱ
And when [3]came [1]the [2]hour, He reclined *to eat,* and the
had come

δώδεκα[b] ἀπόστολοι σὺν αὐτῷ. 15 Καὶ εἶπε πρὸς αὐτούς,
twelve apostles with Him. And He said to them,

"Ἐπιθυμίᾳ ἐπεθύμησα τοῦτο τὸ Πάσχα φαγεῖν μεθ' ὑμῶν
"With desire I desired [3]this - [4]Passover [1]to [2]eat with you
"I have fervently desired

πρὸ τοῦ με παθεῖν. 16 Λέγω γὰρ ὑμῖν ὅτι οὐκέτι[c] οὐ
before - Me to suffer. [2]I [3]say [1]For to you that no longer not
I suffer. by any

μὴ φάγω ἐξ αὐτοῦ ἕως ὅτου πληρωθῇ ἐν τῇ βασιλείᾳ τοῦ
not will I eat of it until - it is fulfilled in the kingdom -
means

Θεοῦ." 17 Καὶ δεξάμενος ποτήριον, εὐχαριστήσας εἶπε,
of God." And taking a cup, giving thanks He said,
He took gave thanks and

"Λάβετε τοῦτο καὶ διαμερίσατε ἑαυτοῖς. 18 Λέγω γὰρ
"Take this and divide *it* among yourselves. [2]I [3]say [1]For

ὑμῖν ὅτι οὐ μὴ πίω[d] ἀπὸ τοῦ γενήματος τῆς ἀμπέλου
to you that not not will I drink from the fruit of the vine
at all

ἕως ὅτου ἡ βασιλεία τοῦ Θεοῦ ἔλθῃ."
until - the kingdom - of God comes."

19 Καὶ λαβὼν ἄρτον, εὐχαριστήσας ἔκλασε καὶ ἔδωκεν
And taking bread, giving thanks He broke *it* and gave
He took gave thanks and

αὐτοῖς, λέγων, "Τοῦτό ἐστι τὸ σῶμά μου, τὸ ὑπὲρ ὑμῶν
to them, saying, "This is - body ~ My, the *one* [3]for [4]you
which

διδόμενον· τοῦτο ποιεῖτε εἰς τὴν ἐμὴν ἀνάμνησιν."
[1]being [2]given; this ~ do in - My remembrance."
is remembrance of Me."

20 Ὡσαύτως καὶ τὸ ποτήριον μετὰ τὸ δειπνῆσαι,
Likewise also *He took* the cup after - to eat supper,
they ate

λέγων, "Τοῦτο τὸ ποτήριον ἡ καινὴ διαθήκη ἐν τῷ αἵματί
saying, "This - cup *is* the new covenant in - blood ~

μου, τὸ ὑπὲρ ὑμῶν ἐκχυνόμενον. 21 Πλὴν ἰδού, ἡ
My, the *blood* [3]for [4]you [1]being [2]shed. Nevertheless behold, the
which is

χεὶρ τοῦ παραδιδόντος με μετ' ἐμοῦ ἐπὶ τῆς τραπέζης.
hand of the *one* handing over ~ Me *is* with Me on the table.
who betrays

22 Καὶ ὁ μὲν Υἱὸς τοῦ Ἀνθρώπου πορεύεται κατὰ
And the ~ indeed Son - of Man goes according to

τὸ ὡρισμένον, πλὴν οὐαὶ τῷ ἀνθρώπῳ ἐκείνῳ
the *thing* having been determined, nevertheless woe - to man ~ that
what is determined,

δι' οὗ παραδίδοται!" 23 Καὶ αὐτοὶ ἤρξαντο συζητεῖν
through whom He is handed over!" And they began to discuss
by betrayed!"

πρὸς ἑαυτοὺς τὸ τίς ἄρα εἴη ἐξ αὐτῶν ὁ τοῦτο
with themselves - who [3]then [4]might [5]be [1]of [2]them the *one* [5]this
one another

μέλλων πράσσειν.
[1]being [2]about [3]to [4]do.
who was

14 When the hour had come, He sat down, and the twelve apostles with Him.
15 Then He said to them, "With *fervent* desire I have desired to eat this Passover with you before I suffer;
16 "for I say to you, I will no longer eat of it until it is fulfilled in the kingdom of God."
17 Then He took the cup, and gave thanks, and said, "Take this and divide *it* among yourselves;
18 "for I say to you, I will not drink of the fruit of the vine until the kingdom of God comes."
19 And He took bread, gave thanks and broke *it,* and gave *it* to them, saying, "This is My body which is given for you; do this in remembrance of Me."
20 Likewise He also *took* the cup after supper, saying, "This cup *is* the new covenant in My blood, which is shed for you.
21 "But behold, the hand of My betrayer *is* with Me on the table.
22 "And truly the Son of Man goes as it has been determined, but woe to that man by whom He is betrayed!"
23 Then they began to question among themselves, which of them it was who would do this thing.

---

[b]**(22:14)** NU omits δωδεκα, *twelve.* [c]**(22:16)** NU omits ουκετι, *no longer.*
[d]**(22:18)** NU adds απο του νυν, *from now on.*

24 Now there was also a dispute among them, as to which
of them should be considered
the greatest.
25 And He said to them, "The
kings of the Gentiles exercise
lordship over them, and those
who exercise authority over
them are called 'benefactors.'
26 "But not so *among* you; on
the contrary, he who is greatest among you, let him be as
the younger, and he who gov-
erns as he who serves.
27 "For who *is* greater, he
who sits at the table, or he who
serves? *Is* it not he who sits at
the table? Yet I am among you
as the One who serves.
28 "But you are those who
have continued with Me in My
trials.
29 "And I bestow upon you a
kingdom, just as My Father bestowed *one* upon Me,
30 "that you may eat and drink
at My table in My kingdom, and
sit on thrones judging the
twelve tribes of Israel."
31 And the Lord said, "Simon,
Simon! Indeed, Satan has asked
for you, that he may sift *you* as
wheat.
32 "But I have prayed for you,
that your faith should not fail;
and when you have returned to
Me, strengthen your brethren."
33 But he said to Him, "Lord,
I am ready to go with You, both
to prison and to death."
34 Then He said, "I tell you,
Peter, the rooster shall not

The Disciples Argue About Greatness

24 Ἐγένετο δὲ καὶ φιλονεικία ἐν αὐτοῖς τὸ τίς
[2]*there* [3]became [1]And also a dispute among them - *as to* which
arose

αὐτῶν δοκεῖ εἶναι μείζων. **25** Ὁ δὲ εἶπεν αὐτοῖς,
of them seems to be greater. [2]the [3]*One* [1]But said to them,
seemed the greatest. He

"Οἱ βασιλεῖς τῶν ἐθνῶν κυριεύουσιν αὐτῶν, καὶ οἱ
"The kings of the Gentiles lord it over them, and the *ones*
those who

ἐξουσιάζοντες αὐτῶν εὐεργέται καλοῦνται. **26** Ὑμεῖς
exercising authority over them [3]benefactors [1]are [2]called. you ˜
exercise

δὲ οὐχ οὕτως· ἀλλ' ὁ μείζων ἐν ὑμῖν γενέσθω
But *shall* not *be* thus; but [2]the [3]greater [4]*one* [5]among [6]you [1]let [7]become
greatest

ὡς ὁ νεώτερος, καὶ ὁ ἡγούμενος ὡς ὁ διακονῶν.
as the younger *one,* and the *one* leading as the *one* serving.
youngest, he who leads he who serves.

27 Τίς γὰρ μείζων, ὁ ἀνακείμενος ἢ ὁ διακονῶν?
who ˜ For *is* greater, the *one* reclining *to eat* or the *one* serving?

Οὐχὶ ὁ ἀνακείμενος? Ἐγὼ δὲ εἰμι ἐν μέσῳ ὑμῶν ὡς
Is it not the *one* reclining? I ˜ But am in midst ˜ your as

ὁ διακονῶν. **28** Ὑμεῖς δέ ἐστε οἱ διαμεμενηκότες
the *One* serving. you ˜ Now are the *ones* having remained
those who have remained

μετ' ἐμοῦ ἐν τοῖς πειρασμοῖς μου. **29** Κἀγὼ διατίθεμαι ὑμῖν,
with Me in - trials ˜ My. And I confer on you,

καθὼς διέθετό μοι ὁ Πατήρ μου, βασιλείαν, **30** ἵνα
just as [3]conferred [4]on [5]Me - [2]Father [1]My, a kingdom, so that

ἐσθίητε καὶ πίνητε ἐπὶ τῆς τραπέζης μου, ἐν τῇ βασιλείᾳ
you may eat and drink at - table ˜ My, in - kingdom ˜

μου, καὶ καθίσεσθε ἐπὶ θρόνων κρίνοντες τὰς δώδεκα φυλὰς
My, and you will sit on thrones judging the twelve tribes

τοῦ Ἰσραήλ."
- of Israel."

Jesus Predicts Peter's Denial
(Matt. 26:31–35; Mark 14:27–31; John 13:36–38)

31 Εἶπε δὲ ὁ Κύριος,[e] "Σίμων, Σίμων, ἰδού, ὁ
[4]said [1]And [2]the [3]Lord, "Simon, Simon, behold, -

Σατανᾶς ἐξῃτήσατο ὑμᾶς τοῦ σινιάσαι ὡς τὸν σῖτον. **32** Ἐγὼ
Satan asked for you - to sift *you* like - wheat. I ˜

δὲ ἐδεήθην περὶ σοῦ ἵνα μὴ ἐκλίπῃ ἡ πίστις σου· καὶ σύ
But prayed for you that [4]not [3]should [5]fail - [2]faith [1]your; and you
have prayed so

ποτε ἐπιστρέψας* στήριξον τοὺς ἀδελφούς σου."
when turning back strengthen - brothers ˜ your."
you have turned

33 Ὁ δὲ εἶπεν αὐτῷ, "Κύριε, μετὰ σοῦ ἕτοιμός εἰμι
[2]the [3]*one* [1]And said to Him, "Lord, [6]with [7]You [3]ready [1]I [2]am
he

καὶ εἰς φυλακὴν καὶ εἰς θάνατον πορεύεσθαι."
[8]both [9]to [10]prison [11]and [12]to [13]death [4]to [5]go."

34 Ὁ δὲ εἶπε, "Λέγω σοι, Πέτρε, οὐ μὴ
[2]the [3]*One* [1]And said, "I say to you, Peter, [4]not [5]not
He by no means

---

e(22:31) NU omits *ειπε δε ο Κυριος, and the Lord said.*

***(22:32)** *ἐπιστρέφω (epistrephō).* Verb meaning *turn, turn around, turn back, return,* transitive only in Luke 1:16, 17; James 5:19, 20; elsewhere intransitive. The base meaning *return, turn around* may be seen in Matt. 12:44 and John 21:20. Often however the "turning" is a spiritual or moral action and may mean *be converted,* or perhaps even *repent* (see Acts 3:19; 1 Thess. 1:9). Whether Jesus uses the word here in Luke 22:32 in the sense of *repented* or *returned* is debated among interpreters. In Gal. 4:9 it indicates the opposite of repentance, namely *turning back* to one's former way of life and away from God (cf. the powerful image in 2 Pet.

φωνήση σήμερον ἀλέκτωρ[f] πρὶν ἢ τρὶς ἀπαρνήση
3will 6call 7today 1a 2rooster before - 4three 5times 1you 2will 3deny
crow

μὴ εἰδέναι με."
not to know Me."
that you know

Wallet, Bag, and Sword

35 Καὶ εἶπεν αὐτοῖς, "Ὅτε ἀπέστειλα ὑμᾶς ἄτερ
And He said to them, "When I sent forth ~ you without

βαλαντίου καὶ πήρας καὶ ὑποδημάτων, μή τινος
a money bag and a knapsack and sandals, 3not 5anything

ὑστερήσατε?"
1you 2did 4lack, *did you?*"

Οἱ δὲ εἶπον, "Οὐθενός."
2the 3*ones* 1And said, "Nothing."
they

36 Εἶπεν οὖν αὐτοῖς, "Ἀλλὰ νῦν ὁ ἔχων βαλάντιον
2He 3said 1Then to them, "But now the *one* having a money bag
he who has

ἀράτω, ὁμοίως καὶ πήραν· καὶ ὁ μὴ ἔχων
let him take *it* up, likewise also a knapsack; and the *one* not having *one*
he who does not have

πωλησει[g] τὸ ἱμάτιον αὐτοῦ καὶ ἀγοράσει[h] μάχαιραν.
shall sell - garment ~ his and shall buy a sword.

37 Λέγω γὰρ ὑμῖν ὅτι ἔτι τοῦτο τὸ γεγραμμένον
2I 3say 1For to you that 11still 5this 6the 7*thing* 8having 9been 10written
this which has been written

δεῖ τελεσθῆναι ἐν ἐμοί, τὸ «Καὶ μετὰ
1it 2is 3necessary 4*for* to be accomplished in Me, the *saying* «And with
must still be

ἀνόμων ἐλογίσθη.» Καὶ γὰρ τὰ[i] περὶ ἐμοῦ
lawless *ones* He was classed.» also ~ For the *things* concerning Me
outlaws In fact

τέλος ἔχει."
2an 3end 1have."
a fulfillment

38 Οἱ δὲ εἶπον, "Κύριε, ἰδού, μάχαιραι ὧδε
2the 3*ones* 1And said, "Lord, look, 4swords 1here 2*are*
they

δύο."
3two."

Ὁ δὲ εἶπεν αὐτοῖς, "Ἱκανόν ἐστι."
2the 3*One* 1And said to them, "3enough 1It 2is."
He

Jesus Prays in the Garden of Gethsemane
(Matt. 26:36–46; Mark 14:32–42)

39 Καὶ ἐξελθὼν ἐπορεύθη κατὰ τὸ ἔθος εἰς τὸ Ὄρος
And going out He went according to the custom to the Mount
His

τῶν Ἐλαιῶν· ἠκολούθησαν δὲ αὐτῷ καὶ οἱ μαθηταὶ αὐτοῦ.
- of Olives; 5followed 1and 6Him 4also - 3disciples 2His.

40 Γενόμενος δὲ ἐπὶ τοῦ τόπου, εἶπεν αὐτοῖς,
2having 3come 1And to the place, He said to them,

"Προσεύχεσθε μὴ εἰσελθεῖν εἰς πειρασμόν." 41 Καὶ αὐτὸς
"Pray not to enter into temptation." And He

crow this day before you will
deny three times that you know
Me."
35 And He said to them,
"When I sent you without
money bag, knapsack, and sandals, did you lack anything?" So
they said, "Nothing."
36 Then He said to them,
"But now, he who has a money
bag, let him take *it,* and likewise a knapsack; and he who
has no sword, let him sell his
garment and buy one.
37 "For I say to you that this
which is written must still be
accomplished in Me: *'And He
was numbered with the transgressors.'* For the things concerning Me have an end."
38 So they said, "Lord, look,
here *are* two swords." And He
said to them, "It is enough."
39 Coming out, He went to
the Mount of Olives, as He was
accustomed, and His disciples
also followed Him.
40 When He came to the
place, He said to them, "Pray
that you may not enter into
temptation."
41 And He was withdrawn

[f](22:34) NU reads εως, *until* for πριν η, *before.*
[g](22:36) TR, NU read πωλησατω, *let him sell.*
[h](22:36) TR, NU read αγορασατω, *let him buy.*
[i](22:37) NU reads το, *the (thing).*

2:22). Cf. the cognate noun ἐπιστροφή, *conversion,* used only in Acts 15:3.

from them about a stone's
throw, and He knelt down and
prayed,
42 saying, "Father, if it is
Your will, take this cup away
from Me; nevertheless not My
will, but Yours, be done."
43 Then an angel appeared to
Him from heaven, strengthening Him.
44 And being in agony, He
prayed more earnestly. Then
His sweat became like great
drops of blood falling down to
the ground.
45 When He rose up from
prayer, and had come to His
disciples, He found them sleeping from sorrow.
46 Then He said to them,
"Why do you sleep? Rise and
pray, lest you enter into temptation."
47 And while He was still
speaking, behold, a multitude;
and he who was called Judas,
one of the twelve, went before
them and drew near to Jesus to
kiss Him.
48 But Jesus said to him, "Judas, are you betraying the Son
of Man with a kiss?"
49 When those around Him
saw what was going to happen,
they said to Him, "Lord, shall
we strike with the sword?"
50 And one of them struck the
servant of the high priest and
cut off his right ear.
51 But Jesus answered and
said, "Permit even this." And
He touched his ear and healed
him.

ἀπεσπάσθη ἀπ' αὐτῶν ὡσεὶ λίθου βολήν, καὶ θεὶς
was withdrawn from them about [3]of [4]a [5]stone [1]a [2]throw, and placing
kneeling

τὰ γόνατα προσηύχετο, 42 λέγων, "Πάτερ, εἰ βούλει
the knees He prayed, saying, "Father, if You will
down

παρενεγκεῖν[j] τὸ ποτήριον τοῦτο ἀπ' ἐμοῦ — πλὴν μὴ
to remove - cup ~ this from Me — nevertheless [2]not
remove

τὸ θέλημά μου, ἀλλὰ τὸ σὸν γενέσθω." 43 Ὤφθη δὲ
- [4]will [3]My, [5]but - [6]Yours [1]let [7]be [8]done." [6]appeared [1]And

αὐτῷ ἄγγελος ἀπ' οὐρανοῦ ἐνισχύων αὐτόν. 44 Καὶ
[7]to [8]Him [2]an [3]angel [4]from [5]heaven strengthening Him. And

γενόμενος ἐν ἀγωνίᾳ, ἐκτενέστερον προσηύχετο. Ἐγένετο δὲ
being in agony, [3]more [4]fervently [1]He [2]prayed. [8]became [5]And
very

ὁ ἱδρὼς αὐτοῦ ὡσεὶ θρόμβοι αἵματος καταβαίνοντες ἐπὶ τὴν
- [7]sweat [6]His like clots of blood falling down onto the
great drops

γῆν.[k] 45 Καὶ ἀναστὰς ἀπὸ τῆς προσευχῆς, ἐλθὼν πρὸς τοὺς
ground. And rising up from - prayer, coming to the

μαθητάς,[l] εὗρεν αὐτοὺς κοιμωμένους ἀπὸ τῆς λύπης.
disciples, He found them sleeping from - sorrow.

46 Καὶ εἶπεν αὐτοῖς, "Τί καθεύδετε? Ἀναστάντες
And He said to them, "Why do you sleep? Arising
Arise and

προσεύχεσθε, ἵνα μὴ εἰσέλθητε εἰς πειρασμόν."
pray, that [3]not [1]you [2]may [4]enter into temptation."

Jesus Is Betrayed and Arrested in Gethsemane

(Matt. 26:47–56; Mark 14:43–50; John 18:2–12)

47 Ἔτι δὲ αὐτοῦ λαλοῦντος, ἰδού, ὄχλος, καὶ ὁ
still ~ And Him speaking, behold, a crowd, and the *one*
And while He was still speaking, he who

λεγόμενος Ἰούδας, εἷς τῶν δώδεκα, προήρχετο αὐτοὺς καὶ
being called Judas, one of the twelve, was going before them and
was

ἤγγισε τῷ Ἰησοῦ φιλῆσαι αὐτόν. 48 Ὁ δὲ Ἰησοῦς εἶπεν
drew near - Jesus to kiss Him. - And Jesus said

αὐτῷ, "Ἰούδα, φιλήματι τὸν Υἱὸν τοῦ Ἀνθρώπου
to him, "Judas, with a kiss [5]the [6]Son - [7]of [8]Man

παραδίδως?"
[1]do [2]you [3]hand [4]over?"
betray?"

49 Ἰδόντες δὲ οἱ περὶ αὐτὸν τὸ ἐσόμενον
[6]seeing [1]And [2]the [3]*ones* [4]around [5]Him the *thing* going to be,
those what was about to happen,

εἶπον αὐτῷ, "Κύριε, εἰ πατάξομεν ἐν μαχαίρᾳ?" 50 Καὶ
said to Him, "Lord, - shall we strike with a sword?" And

ἐπάταξεν εἷς τις ἐξ αὐτῶν τὸν δοῦλον τοῦ ἀρχιερέως
[6]struck [1]*a* [3]one [2]certain [4]of [5]them the slave of the high priest
servant

καὶ ἀφεῖλεν αὐτοῦ τὸ οὖς τὸ δεξιόν.
and cut off his - ear ~ - right.

51 Ἀποκριθεὶς δὲ ὁ Ἰησοῦς εἶπεν, "Ἐᾶτε ἕως
answering ~ And - Jesus said, "Leave alone as far as
"Stop right there."

τούτου." Καὶ ἁψάμενος τοῦ ὠτίου αὐτοῦ, ἰάσατο αὐτόν.
this." And touching - ear ~ his, He healed him.

---

[j](22:42) NU reads the command *παρενεγκε*, *remove*. [k](22:43, 44) NU brackets vv. 43 and 44 as doubtful. [l](22:45) TR adds *αυτου*, *His*.

52 Εἶπε δὲ ὁ Ἰησοῦς πρὸς τοὺς παραγενομένους ἐπ᾽ αὐτὸν
[3]said [1]And - [2]Jesus to the [10]coming [11]upon [12]Him
who came

ἀρχιερεῖς καὶ στρατηγοὺς τοῦ ἱεροῦ καὶ πρεσβυτέρους,
[1]chief [2]priests [3]and [4]captains [5]of [6]the [7]temple [8]and [9]elders,

"Ὡς ἐπὶ λῃστὴν ἐξεληλύθατε μετὰ μαχαιρῶν καὶ ξύλων?
"As against a bandit have you come out with swords and clubs?

53 Καθ᾽ ἡμέραν ὄντος μου μεθ᾽ ὑμῶν ἐν τῷ ἱερῷ, οὐκ
According to a day being ~ Me with you in the temple, [3]not
When I was daily

ἐξετείνατε τὰς χεῖρας ἐπ᾽ ἐμέ. Ἀλλ᾽ αὕτη ὑμῶν ἐστιν
[1]you [2]did stretch out the hands against Me. But this your ~ is
your

ἡ ὥρα,* καὶ ἡ ἐξουσία τοῦ σκότους."
- hour, and the power - of darkness."

Peter Denies Jesus and Weeps Bitterly
(Matt. 26:58, 69–75; Mark 14:54, 66–72; John 18:15–18, 25–27)

54 Συλλαβόντες δὲ αὐτὸν ἤγαγον καὶ εἰσήγαγον
[2]having [3]arrested [1]And Him they led *Him* and brought

αὐτὸν[m] εἰς τὸν οἶκον τοῦ ἀρχιερέως. Ὁ δὲ Πέτρος
Him into the house of the high priest. - But Peter

ἠκολούθει μακρόθεν. 55 Ἁψάντων δὲ πῦρ ἐν μέσῳ
was following from a distance. [3]lighting [1]And [4]a [5]fire [6]in [7]*the* [8]midst
had lit

τῆς αὐλῆς καὶ συγκαθισάντων αὐτῶν, ἐκάθητο ὁ
[9]of [10]the [11]courtyard [12]and [13]sitting [14]down [15]together [2]they, [17]sat -
sat when they,

Πέτρος ἐν μέσῳ αὐτῶν.
[16]Peter in midst ~ their.

56 Ἰδοῦσα δὲ αὐτὸν παιδίσκη τις καθήμενον πρὸς
[6]seeing [1]And [7]him [2]a [4]servant [5]girl [3]certain sitting at

τὸ φῶς καὶ ἀτενίσασα αὐτῷ, εἶπε, "Καὶ οὗτος σὺν αὐτῷ
the fire and gazing at him, said, "[3]also [1]This [2]*man* [5]with [6]Him

ἦν."
[4]was."

57 Ὁ δὲ ἠρνήσατο αὐτόν,[n] λέγων, "Γύναι, οὐκ
[2]the [3]*one* [1]But denied Him, saying, "Woman, [3]not
he

οἶδα αὐτόν."
[1]I [2]do know Him."

58 Καὶ μετὰ βραχὺ ἕτερος ἰδὼν αὐτὸν ἔφη, "Καὶ
And after a little *while* another *person* seeing Him said, "also ~

σὺ ἐξ αὐτῶν εἶ."
You [2]*one* [3]of [4]them [1]are."

Ὁ δὲ Πέτρος εἶπεν, "Ἄνθρωπε, οὐκ εἰμί!"
- But Peter said, "Man, [3]not [1]I [2]am!"

59 Καὶ διαστάσης ὡσεὶ ὥρας μιᾶς, ἄλλος τις
And passing about hour ~ one, a(n) other ~ certain *man*
after about one hour had passed,

διϊσχυρίζετο, λέγων, "Ἐπ᾽ ἀληθείας καὶ οὗτος μετ᾽
was firmly insisting, saying, "On truth [3]also [1]this [2]*man* [5]with
kept "Surely

αὐτοῦ ἦν, καὶ γὰρ Γαλιλαῖός ἐστιν."
[6]Him [4]was, [9]also [7]for [11]a [12]Galilean [8]he [10]is."

60 Εἶπε δὲ ὁ Πέτρος, "Ἄνθρωπε, οὐκ οἶδα ὃ
[3]said [1]And - [2]Peter, "Man, [3]not [1]I [2]do know what

52 Then Jesus said to the chief priests, captains of the temple, and the elders who had come to Him, "Have you come out, as against a robber, with swords and clubs?
53 "When I was with you daily in the temple, you did not try to seize Me. But this is your hour, and the power of darkness."
54 Having arrested Him, they led *Him* and brought Him into the high priest's house. But Peter followed at a distance.
55 Now when they had kindled a fire in the midst of the courtyard and sat down together, Peter sat among them.
56 And a certain servant girl, seeing him as he sat by the fire, looked intently at him and said, "This man was also with Him."
57 But he denied Him, saying, "Woman, I do not know Him."
58 And after a little while another saw him and said, "You also are of them." But Peter said, "Man, I am not!"
59 Then after about an hour had passed, another confidently affirmed, saying, "Surely this *fellow* also was with Him, for he is a Galilean."
60 But Peter said, "Man, I do

[m](22:54) Many mss., NU omit *αυτον*, *Him*.
[n](22:57) NU omits *αυτον*, *Him*.

***(22:53)** *ὥρα (hōra).* Noun used to designate various measures of time. It may refer to a specific hour or *time* of the day (Mark 11:11), a period of time measured as an *hour* (Rev. 9:15; John 11:9), or a less specific period of time, especially a short or defined period (John 5:35). It often carries the idea seen here in Luke 22:53, as an opportune time or a time when some specific event (or series of events) has taken place or is "appointed" to take place (Matt. 8:13; John 16:21). In 1 John 2:18 the phrase "the last hour" apparently signifies the present age as building toward its climax.

not know what you are saying!"
Immediately, while he was still
speaking, the rooster crowed.
61 And the Lord turned and
looked at Peter. Then Peter remembered the word of the
Lord, how He had said to him,
"Before the rooster crows, you
will deny Me three times."
62 So Peter went out and
wept bitterly.
63 Now the men who held Jesus mocked Him and beat Him.
64 And having blindfolded
Him, they struck Him on the
face and asked Him, saying,
"Prophesy! Who is the one who
struck You?"
65 And many other things
they blasphemously spoke
against Him.
66 As soon as it was day, the
elders of the people, both chief
priests and scribes, came together and led Him into their
council, saying,
67 "If You are the Christ, tell
us." But He said to them, "If I
tell you, you will by no means
believe.
68 "And if I also ask *you,* you
will by no means answer Me or
let *Me* go.
69 "Hereafter the Son of Man

λέγεις!" Καὶ παραχρῆμα, ἔτι λαλοῦντος αὐτοῦ,
you are saying!" And immediately, still speaking him,
while he was still speaking,

ἐφώνησεν ἀλέκτωρ.[o] 61 Καὶ στραφεὶς ὁ Κύριος ἐνέβλεψε
[3]sounded [1]a [2]rooster. And [3]turning [1]the [2]Lord looked at
crowed turned and

τῷ Πέτρῳ. Καὶ ὑπεμνήσθη ὁ Πέτρος τοῦ λόγου[p] τοῦ Κυρίου,
- Peter. And remembered ˜ - Peter the word of the Lord,

ὡς εἶπεν αὐτῷ ὅτι "Πρὶν ἀλέκτορα φωνῆσαι,[q] ἀπαρνήσῃ
how He said to him - "Before a rooster to sound, you will deny
had said crows,

με τρίς." 62 Καὶ ἐξελθὼν ἔξω ὁ Πέτρος[r] ἔκλαυσε
Me three times." And going outside - Peter wept

πικρῶς.
bitterly.

Jesus Is Mocked and Beaten
(Matt. 26:67, 68; Mark 14:65)

63 Καὶ οἱ ἄνδρες οἱ συνέχοντες τὸν Ἰησοῦν[s]
And the men the *ones* holding - Jesus
who were

ἐνέπαιζον αὐτῷ, δέροντες. 64 Καὶ περικαλύψαντες αὐτόν,
were mocking Him, *and* beating *Him.* And covering Him,
having blindfolded

ἔτυπτον αὐτοῦ τὸ πρόσωπον καὶ[t] ἐπηρώτων αὐτόν,
they were striking His - face and were asking Him,
would strike would ask

λέγοντες, "Προφήτευσον! Τίς ἐστιν ὁ παίσας σε?"
saying, "Prophesy! Who is the *one* having struck You?"
who

65 Καὶ ἕτερα πολλὰ βλασφημοῦντες ἔλεγον εἰς
And other ˜ many *things* blaspheming they were saying to
they would say to Him as they

αὐτόν.
Him.
blasphemed.

Jesus Faces the Sanhedrin
(Matt. 26:59–66; Mark 14:55–64; John 18:19–24)

66 Καὶ ὡς ἐγένετο ἡμέρα, συνήχθη τὸ
And when it became day, [9]was [10]assembled [1]the

πρεσβυτέριον τοῦ λαοῦ, ἀρχιερεῖς[u] καὶ γραμματεῖς,
[2]council [3]of [4]the [5]elders [6]of [7]the [8]people, *the* chief priests and scribes,

καὶ ἀνήγαγον αὐτὸν εἰς τὸ συνέδριον αὐτῶν, λέγοντες, 67 "Εἰ
and they led Him into - council ˜ their, saying, "If

σὺ εἶ ὁ Χριστός, εἰπὲ ἡμῖν."
You are the Christ, tell us."
Messiah,

Εἶπε δὲ αὐτοῖς, "Ἐὰν ὑμῖν εἴπω, οὐ μὴ
[2]He [3]said [1]And to them, "If [3]you [1]I [2]tell, [6]not [7]not
by no means

πιστεύσητε. 68 Ἐὰν δὲ καὶ ἐρωτήσω, οὐ μὴ
[4]you [5]will [8]believe. if ˜ But also ˜ I question *you,* [3]not [4]not
by no means

ἀποκριθῆτέ μοι ἢ ἀπολύσητε.[v] 69 Ἀπὸ τοῦ νῦν ἔσται
[1]you [2]will [5]answer Me or release *Me.* From the now [5]will [6]be
Hereafter

[o](22:60) TR reads ο αλεκτωρ, *the rooster.*
[p](22:61) NU reads ρηματος, *saying.* [q](22:61) NU adds σημερον, *today.*
[r](22:62) NU omits ο Πετρος, *Peter.* [s](22:63) NU reads αυτον, *Him.*
[t](22:64) NU omits ετυπτον αυτου το προσωπον και, *they were striking His face and.* [u](22:66) Many mss., TR, NU add τε, *both.*
[v](22:68) NU omits μοι η απολυσητε, *Me or release (Me).*

ὁ Υἱὸς τοῦ Ἀνθρώπου καθήμενος ἐκ δεξιῶν τῆς
[1]the [2]Son - [3]of [4]Man sitting at *the* right parts of the
hand

δυνάμεως τοῦ Θεοῦ."
power - of God."

70 Εἶπον δὲ πάντες, "Σὺ οὖν εἶ ὁ Υἱὸς τοῦ Θεοῦ?"
[2]they [4]said [1]And [3]all, "[6]You [7]then [5]Are the Son - of God?"

Ὁ δὲ πρὸς αὐτοὺς ἔφη, "Ὑμεῖς λέγετε ὅτι ἐγώ
[2]the [3]*One* [1]And [5]to [6]them [4]said, "You *rightly* say that I
He

εἰμι."
am."

71 Οἱ δὲ εἶπον, "Τί ἔτι χρείαν ἔχομεν
[2]the [3]*ones* [1]And said, "What [4]still [1]need [2]do [3]we [5]have
they

μαρτυρίας? Αὐτοὶ γὰρ ἠκούσαμεν ἀπὸ τοῦ στόματος αὐτοῦ!"
of testimony? [3]ourselves [1]For [2]we heard *it* from - mouth ˜ His!"
for have heard

Jesus Is Delivered to Pontius Pilate
(Matt. 27:1, 2; Mark 15:1; John 18:28–32)

23 **1** Καὶ ἀναστὰν ἅπαν τὸ πλῆθος αὐτῶν, ἤγαγον
And [6]rising [7]up [1]all [2]the [3]multitude [4]of [5]them, led

αὐτὸν ἐπὶ τὸν Πιλᾶτον. **2** Ἤρξαντο δὲ κατηγορεῖν αὐτοῦ,
Him to - Pilate. [2]they [3]began [1]And to accuse Him,

λέγοντες, "Τοῦτον εὕρομεν διαστρέφοντα τὸ ἔθνος,[a] καὶ
saying, "[3]this [4]*Man* [1]We [2]found perverting the nation, and

κωλύοντα Καίσαρι φόρους διδόναι, λέγοντα ἑαυτὸν Χριστὸν
forbidding [4]to [5]Caesar [3]tribute [1]to [2]give, saying *that* Himself [3]Christ
to pay taxes He Himself

Βασιλέα εἶναι."
[4]a [5]King [1]to [2]be."
is."

Jesus Faces Pilate
(Matt. 27:11–14; Mark 15:2–5; John 18:33–38)

3 Ὁ δὲ Πιλᾶτος ἐπηρώτησεν αὐτόν, λέγων, "Σὺ εἶ ὁ
- And Pilate questioned Him, saying, "You ˜ Are the

Βασιλεὺς τῶν Ἰουδαίων?"
King of the Jews?"

Ὁ δὲ ἀποκριθεὶς αὐτῷ ἔφη, "Σὺ λέγεις."
[2]the [3]*One* [1]But answering him said, "You are saying *what is so.*"
He answered him and

4 Ὁ δὲ Πιλᾶτος εἶπε πρὸς τοὺς ἀρχιερεῖς καὶ τοὺς
- But Pilate said to the chief priests and the

ὄχλους, "Οὐδὲν εὑρίσκω αἴτιον ἐν τῷ ἀνθρώπῳ τούτῳ."
crowds, "[3]no [1]I [2]find guilt in - man ˜ this."

5 Οἱ δὲ ἐπίσχυον, λέγοντες ὅτι "Ἀνασείει τὸν
[2]the [3]*ones* [1]But insisted, saying - "He stirs up the
they

λαόν, διδάσκων καθ' ὅλης τῆς Ἰουδαίας, ἀρξάμενος
people, teaching throughout *the* whole - of Judea, beginning
all

ἀπὸ τῆς Γαλιλαίας ἕως ὧδε."
from - Galilee to here."

will sit on the right hand of the
power of God."
70 Then they all said, "Are
You then the Son of God?" So
He said to them, "You *rightly*
say that I am."
71 And they said, "What further testimony do we need?
For we have heard it ourselves
from His own mouth."
23 Then the whole multi-
tude of them arose and
led Him to Pilate.
2 And they began to accuse
Him, saying, "We found this *fellow* perverting the nation, and
forbidding to pay taxes to Caesar, saying that He Himself is
Christ, a King."
3 Then Pilate asked Him,
saying, "Are You the King of
the Jews?" He answered him
and said, "*It is as* you say."
4 So Pilate said to the chief
priests and the crowd, "I find
no fault in this Man."
5 But they were the more
fierce, saying, "He stirs up the
people, teaching throughout all
Judea, beginning from Galilee to
this place."

[a](23:2) NU adds ἡμων, *our.*

6 When Pilate heard of Galilee, he asked if the Man were a Galilean.
7 And as soon as he knew that He belonged to Herod's jurisdiction, he sent Him to Herod, who was also in Jerusalem at that time.
8 Now when Herod saw Jesus, he was exceedingly glad; for he had desired for a long *time* to see Him, because he had heard many things about Him, and he hoped to see some miracle done by Him.
9 Then he questioned Him with many words, but He answered him nothing.
10 And the chief priests and scribes stood and vehemently accused Him.
11 Then Herod, with his men of war, treated Him with contempt and mocked *Him,* arrayed Him in a gorgeous robe, and sent Him back to Pilate.
12 That very day Pilate and Herod became friends with each other, for previously they had been at enmity with each other.
13 Then Pilate, when he had called together the chief priests, the rulers, and the people,
14 said to them, "You have brought this Man to me, as one who misleads the people. And indeed, having examined *Him* in your presence, I have found no fault in this Man concerning

Jesus Faces Herod

6 Πιλᾶτος δὲ ἀκούσας Γαλιλαίαν[b] ἐπηρώτησεν εἰ ὁ
Pilate ~ And hearing about Galilee he asked if the
And when Pilate heard

ἄνθρωπος Γαλιλαῖός ἐστι. 7 Καὶ ἐπιγνοὺς ὅτι ἐκ τῆς
man [2]a [3]Galilean [1]is. And finding out that [3]from [4]the
were. when he found

ἐξουσίας Ἡρῴδου ἐστίν, ἀνέπεμψεν αὐτὸν πρὸς Ἡρῴδην, ὄντα
[5]jurisdiction [6]of [7]Herod [1]He [2]is, he sent Him to Herod, being
was, since

καὶ αὐτὸν ἐν Ἱεροσολύμοις ἐν ταύταις ταῖς ἡμέραις. 8 Ὁ
also him in Jerusalem in these - days. -
he also was those

δὲ Ἡρῴδης ἰδὼν τὸν Ἰησοῦν ἐχάρη λίαν· ἦν
And Herod seeing - Jesus he was glad ~ exceedingly; [2]he [3]was
when Herod saw had been

γὰρ θέλων ἐξ ἱκανοῦ ἰδεῖν αὐτόν, διὰ τὸ ἀκούειν
[1]for desiring from sufficient *time* to see Him, because of - to hear
for a long time because he had heard

πολλὰ[c] περὶ αὐτοῦ, καὶ ἤλπιζέ τι σημεῖον ἰδεῖν ὑπ'
many *things* about Him, and he was hoping [3]some [4]sign [1]to [2]see [7]by

αὐτοῦ γινόμενον. 9 Ἐπηρώτα δὲ αὐτὸν ἐν λόγοις ἱκανοῖς·
[8]Him [5]being [6]done. [2]he [3]questioned [1]And Him with words ~ sufficient;
many;

αὐτὸς δὲ οὐδὲν ἀπεκρίνατο αὐτῷ. 10 Εἱστήκεισαν δὲ οἱ
He ~ but [3]nothing [1]answered [2]Him. [8]stood [1]And [2]the

ἀρχιερεῖς καὶ οἱ γραμματεῖς, εὐτόνως κατηγοροῦντες
[3]chief [4]priests [5]and [6]the [7]scribes, vehemently accusing

αὐτοῦ. 11 Ἐξουθενήσας δὲ αὐτὸν ὁ Ἡρῴδης
Him. [6]having [7]treated [9]with [10]contempt [1]And [8]Him - [2]Herod

σὺν τοῖς στρατεύμασιν αὐτοῦ, καὶ ἐμπαίξας,
[3]with - [5]troops [4]his, and having mocked *Him,*

περιβαλὼν αὐτὸν[d] ἐσθῆτα λαμπράν, ἀνέπεμψεν αὐτὸν τῷ
having put [3]on [4]Him [2]clothing [1]bright, sent back ~ Him -
elegant,

Πιλάτῳ. 12 Ἐγένοντο δὲ φίλοι ὅ τε Πιλᾶτος καὶ ὁ
to Pilate. [6]became [1]And [7]friends - [2]both [3]Pilate [4]and -

Ἡρῴδης ἐν αὐτῇ τῇ ἡμέρᾳ μετ' ἀλλήλων·
[5]Herod [11]on [13]very [12]the [14]day [8]with [9]each [10]other;
that

προϋπῆρχον γὰρ ἐν ἔχθρᾳ ὄντες πρὸς ἑαυτούς.
[16]previously [17]they [18]were [15]for [20]at [21]enmity [19]being with each other.
had been living

Jesus Dies in Place of Barabbas

(Matt. 27:15–26; Mark 15:6–15; John 18:39—19:16)

13 Πιλᾶτος δὲ συγκαλεσάμενος τοὺς ἀρχιερεῖς καὶ τοὺς
Pilate ~ And having called together the chief priests and the

ἄρχοντας καὶ τὸν λαόν, 14 εἶπε πρὸς αὐτούς,
rulers and the people, said to them,

"Προσηνέγκατέ μοι τὸν ἄνθρωπον τοῦτον, ὡς
"You have brought to me - man ~ this, as *one*
on the

ἀποστρέφοντα τὸν λαόν. Καὶ ἰδού, ἐγὼ ἐνώπιον ὑμῶν
misleading the people. And behold, I before you
charge of misleading when I examined Him in

ἀνακρίνας οὐδὲν εὗρον ἐν τῷ ἀνθρώπῳ τούτῳ αἴτιον
examining *Him* no ~ found [2]in - [4]man [3]this [1]guilt
your presence, I

---

[b](23:6) NU omits Γαλιλαιαν, *Galilee.*
[c](23:8) NU omits πολλα, *many (things).*
[d](23:11) NU omits αυτον, *Him.*

ὧν κατηγορεῖτε κατ' αὐτοῦ. 15 Ἀλλ'
of which *things* you bring charges against Him. But
in the matters which you bring as charges

οὐδὲ Ἡρῴδης· ἀνέπεμψα γὰρ ὑμᾶς πρὸς αὐτόν,[e] καὶ
not even *did* Herod; [2]I [3]sent [1]for you to him, and

ἰδού, οὐδὲν ἄξιον θανάτου ἐστὶ πεπραγμένον αὐτῷ.
behold, nothing worthy of death is done by Him.
consistent with death has been

16 Παιδεύσας οὖν αὐτὸν ἀπολύσω."
flogging ˜ Therefore Him I will release *Him.*"
Therefore when I have flogged Him

17 Ἀνάγκην[f] δὲ εἶχεν ἀπολύειν αὐτοῖς κατὰ ἑορτὴν
[4]a [5]necessity [1]Now [2]he [3]had to release [2]to [3]them [4]at [5]*the* [6]feast

ἕνα.
[1]one.

18 Ἀνέκραξαν δὲ παμπληθεί, λέγοντες, "Αἶρε
[2]they [3]cried [4]out [1]But all together, saying, "Take away

τοῦτον, ἀπόλυσον δὲ ἡμῖν Βαραββᾶν" — 19 ὅστις ἦν
this *man,* release ˜ and to us Barabbas" — who [15]was
had been

διὰ στάσιν τινὰ γενομένην ἐν τῇ πόλει
[1]because [2]of [3]a(n) [5]insurrection [4]certain [6]having [7]occurred [8]in [9]the [10]city

καὶ φόνον βεβλημένος εἰς φυλακήν. 20 Πάλιν
[11]and [12]*because* [13]*of* [14]murder [16]cast into prison. again ˜

οὖν ὁ Πιλᾶτος προσεφώνησε, θέλων ἀπολῦσαι τὸν
Therefore - Pilate called out *to them,* wishing to release -
because he wished

Ἰησοῦν.
Jesus.

21 Οἱ δὲ ἐπεφώνουν, λέγοντες, "Σταύρωσον,
[2]the [3]*ones* [1]But cried out, saying, "Crucify,
they

σταύρωσον αὐτόν!"
crucify Him!"

22 Ὁ δὲ τρίτον εἶπε πρὸς αὐτούς, "Τί γὰρ
[2]the [3]*one* [1]But [5]a [6]third [7]*time* [4]said to them, "what ˜ For
he But

κακὸν ἐποίησεν οὗτος? Οὐδὲν αἴτιον θανάτου εὗρον ἐν
evil did [3]do [1]this [2]*man?* [6]no [7]guilt [8]of [9]death [4]I [5]found in
He? deserving

αὐτῷ. Παιδεύσας οὖν αὐτὸν ἀπολύσω."
Him. flogging ˜ Therefore Him I will release *Him.*"
Therefore when I have flogged

23 Οἱ δὲ ἐπέκειντο φωναῖς μεγάλαις, αἰτούμενοι
[2]the [3]*ones* [1]But were urgent with voices ˜ great, demanding
they loud,

αὐτὸν σταυρωθῆναι. Καὶ κατίσχυον αἱ φωναὶ αὐτῶν καὶ
Him to be crucified. And [9]prevailed - [2]voices [1]their [3]and [4]*those*
that He be

τῶν ἀρχιερέων.[g] 24 Ὁ δὲ Πιλᾶτος ἐπέκρινε
[5]of [6]the [7]chief [8]priests. - And Pilate decided *that*

γενέσθαι τὸ αἴτημα αὐτῶν. 25 Ἀπέλυσε δὲ[h] τὸν
[3]to [4]be [5]done - [2]request [1]their. [2]he [3]released [1]And the *one*
should be carried out. him who

διὰ στάσιν καὶ φόνον βεβλημένον εἰς τὴν
[6]because [7]of [8]insurrection [9]and [10]murder [1]having [2]been [3]thrown [4]into -
for had

those things of which you accuse Him;
15 "no, neither did Herod, for
I sent you back to him; and indeed nothing deserving of death
has been done by Him.
16 "I will therefore chastise
Him and release *Him*"
17 (for it was necessary for
him to release one to them at
the feast).
18 And they all cried out at
once, saying, "Away with this
Man, and release to us
Barabbas"—
19 who had been thrown into
prison for a certain rebellion
made in the city, and for murder.
20 Pilate, therefore, wishing
to release Jesus, again called
out to them.
21 But they shouted, saying,
"Crucify *Him,* crucify Him!"
22 Then he said to them the
third time, "Why, what evil has
He done? I have found no reason for death in Him. I will
therefore chastise Him and let
Him go."
23 But they were insistent,
demanding with loud voices that
He be crucified. And the voices
of these men and of the chief
priests prevailed.
24 So Pilate gave sentence
that it should be as they requested.
25 And he released to them
the one they requested, who
for rebellion and murder had
been thrown into prison; but he

[e](23:15) For *ανεπεμψα γαρ υμας προς αυτον, for I sent you to him,* NU reads *ανεπεμψεν γαρ αυτον προς ημας, for he sent Him back to us.* [f](23:17) NU omits v. 17. [g](23:23) NU omits *και των αρχιερεων, and (those) of the chief priests.* [h](23:25) TR adds *αυτοις, to them.*

delivered Jesus to their will.

26 Now as they led Him away, they laid hold of a certain man, Simon a Cyrenian, who was coming from the country, and on him they laid the cross that he might bear *it* after Jesus.

27 And a great multitude of the people followed Him, and women who also mourned and lamented Him.

28 But Jesus, turning to them, said, "Daughters of Jerusalem, do not weep for Me, but weep for yourselves and for your children.

29 "For indeed the days are coming in which they will say, 'Blessed *are* the barren, wombs that never bore, and breasts which never nursed!'

30 "Then they will begin *'to say to the mountains, "Fall on us!" and to the hills, "Cover us!"'*

31 "For if they do these things in the green wood, what will be done in the dry?"

32 There were also two others, criminals, led with Him to be put to death.

33 And when they had come to the place called Calvary, there they crucified Him, and the criminals, one on the right hand and the other on the left.

34 Then Jesus said, "Father, forgive them, for they do not

φυλακήν, ὃν ἠτοῦντο· τὸν δὲ Ἰησοῦν παρέδωκε
[5]prison, whom they were requesting; - but [3]Jesus [1]he [2]gave over
delivered

τῷ θελήματι αὐτῶν.
- to will ˜ their.

Jesus Is Crucified
(Matt. 27:32–34; Mark 15:21–32; John 19:17–27)

26 Καὶ ὡς ἀπήγαγον αὐτόν, ἐπιλαβόμενοι Σίμωνός
And as they led away ˜ Him, laying hold of [3]Simon

τινος Κυρηναίου ἐρχομένου ἀπ' ἀγροῦ ἐπέθηκαν
[1]a [2]certain a Cyrenian *as he was* coming from *the* country they laid on

αὐτῷ τὸν σταυρὸν φέρειν ὄπισθεν τοῦ Ἰησοῦ.
Him the cross to carry behind - Jesus.

27 Ἠκολούθει δὲ αὐτῷ πολὺ πλῆθος τοῦ λαοῦ καὶ
[8]followed [1]And [9]Him [2]a [3]great [4]multitude [5]of [6]the [7]people and

γυναικῶν αἳ καὶ ἐκόπτοντο καὶ ἐθρήνουν αὐτόν.
women who also were mourning and were lamenting Him.

28 Στραφεὶς δὲ πρὸς αὐτὰς ὁ Ἰησοῦς εἶπε, "Θυγατέρες
turning ˜ But to them - Jesus said, "Daughters

Ἰερουσαλήμ, μὴ κλαίετε ἐπ' ἐμέ, πλὴν ἐφ ἑαυτὰς κλαίετε
of Jerusalem, not ˜ do weep for Me, but [2]for [3]yourselves [1]weep

καὶ ἐπὶ τὰ τέκνα ὑμῶν. **29** Ὅτι ἰδού, ἔρχονται ἡμέραι
and for - children ˜ your. Because behold, [2]are [3]coming [1]days

ἐν αἷς ἐροῦσι, 'Μακάριαι αἱ στεῖραι, καὶ κοιλίαι αἳ
in which they will say, 'Blessed *are* the barren, and *the* wombs which

οὐκ ἐγέννησαν, καὶ μαστοὶ οἳ οὐκ ἐθήλασαν.'[i]
not ˜ did give birth, and *the* breasts which not ˜ did give suck.'
nurse.'

30 "Τότε ἄρξονται «λέγειν τοῖς ὄρεσι·
"Then they will begin «to say to the mountains:

'Πέσετε ἐφ' ἡμᾶς!'
'Fall on us!'

Καὶ τοῖς βουνοῖς·
And to the hills:

'Καλύψατε ἡμᾶς!'»
'Cover us.!'»

31 Ὅτι εἰ ἐν τῷ ὑγρῷ ξύλῳ ταῦτα ποιοῦσιν, ἐν τῷ
Because if [5]in [6]the [7]green [8]tree [3]these [4]*things* [1]they [2]do, [12]in [13]the
a

ξηρῷ τί γένηται?"
[14]dry [15]*tree* [9]what [10]will [11]happen?"

32 Ἤγοντο δὲ καὶ ἕτεροι δύο κακοῦργοι σὺν
[2]they [4]were [5]leading [1]And [3]also [7]other [6]two evildoers with
criminals

αὐτῷ ἀναιρεθῆναι.
Him to be put to death.

33 Καὶ ὅτε ἀπῆλθον ἐπὶ τὸν τόπον τὸν καλούμενον
And when they came to the place the *one* being called
which is

Κρανίον, ἐκεῖ ἐσταύρωσαν αὐτόν, καὶ τοὺς κακούργους, ὃν μὲν
Skull, there they crucified Him, and the evildoers, one -
Calvary, criminals,

ἐκ δεξιῶν, ὃν δὲ ἐξ ἀριστερῶν.
at *the* right *parts,* one ˜ and at *the* left *parts.*
on the right side, on the left side.

34 Ὁ δὲ Ἰησοῦς ἔλεγε, "Πάτερ, ἄφες αὐτοῖς, οὐ γὰρ
- And Jesus said, "Father, forgive them, [4]not [1]for

---

[i](23:29) NU reads εθρεψαν, did (not) nurse.

οἴδασι τί ποιοῦσι."[j] Διαμεριζόμενοι δὲ τὰ ἱμάτια
[2]they [3]do [5]know what they are doing." dividing ˜ And - garments ˜

αὐτοῦ, ἔβαλον κλῆρον. **35** Καὶ εἱστήκει ὁ λαὸς θεωρῶν.
His, they cast a lot. And [3]stood [1]the [2]people observing.

Ἐξεμυκτήριζον* δὲ καὶ οἱ ἄρχοντες σὺν αὐτοῖς,[k]
[7]were [8]sneering [1]And [6]also [2]the [3]rulers [4]with [5]them,

λέγοντες, "Ἄλλους ἔσωσε, σωσάτω ἑαυτόν, εἰ οὗτός
saying, "[3]others [1]He [2]saved, let Him save Himself, if this *man*

ἐστιν ὁ Χριστός, ὁ τοῦ Θεοῦ ὁ ἐκλεκτός."
is the Christ, the - [2]of [3]God - [1]elect."
Messiah, chosen."

36 Ἐνέπαιξον δὲ αὐτῷ καὶ οἱ στρατιῶται,
[5]mocked [1]And [6]Him [4]also [2]the [3]soldiers,

προσερχόμενοι καὶ ὄξος προσφέροντες αὐτῷ, **37** καὶ
approaching and [3]sour [4]wine [1]offering [2]Him, and

λέγοντες, "Εἰ σὺ εἶ ὁ Βασιλεὺς τῶν Ἰουδαίων, σῶσον
saying, "If You are the King of the Jews, save

σεαυτόν." **38** Ἦν δὲ καὶ ἐπιγραφὴ γεγραμμένη[l] ἐπ'
Yourself." [5]was [1]And [2]also [3]a [4]superscription [6]written over

αὐτῷ, γράμμασιν Ἑλληνικοῖς καὶ Ῥωμαϊκοῖς καὶ
Him, in [6]letters [1]Greek [2]and [3]Latin [4]and

Ἑβραϊκοῖς·[m]
[5]Hebrew:

ΟΥΤΟΣ ΕΣΤΙΝ Ο ΒΑΣΙΛΕΥΣ ΤΩΝ ΙΟΥΔΑΙΩΝ.
THIS IS THE KING OF THE JEWS.

39 Εἷς δὲ τῶν κρεμασθέντων κακούργων ἐβλασφήμει
one ˜ And of the [2]being [3]hanged [1]evildoers blasphemed
criminals who was hanged

αὐτόν, λέγων, "Εἰ σὺ εἶ ὁ Χριστός,[n] σῶσον σεαυτὸν καὶ
Him, saying, "If You are the Christ, save Yourself and
Messiah,

ἡμᾶς."
us."

40 Ἀποκριθεὶς δὲ ὁ ἕτερος ἐπετίμα αὐτῷ, λέγων,
[5]answering [1]And [2]the [3]other [4]*one* rebuked him, saying,

"Οὐδὲ φοβῇ σὺ τὸν Θεόν, ὅτι ἐν τῷ αὐτῷ
"[3]not [4]even [1]Do [5]fear [2]you - God, because [3]in [4]the [5]same
under

κρίματι εἶ? **41** Καὶ ἡμεῖς μὲν δικαίως, ἄξια
[6]condemnation [1]you [2]are? And we indeed justly, [5]*things* [6]worthy

γὰρ ὧν ἐπράξαμεν ἀπολαμβάνομεν· οὗτος δὲ
[1]for [7]of [8]which [9]we [10]did [2]we [3]are [4]receiving; [12]this [13]*Man* [11]but
of what

οὐδὲν ἄτοπον ἔπραξε." **42** Καὶ ἔλεγε τῷ Ἰησοῦ, "Μνήσθητί
[15]nothing [16]wrong [14]did." And he said - to Jesus, "Remember

μου, Κύριε,[o] ὅταν ἔλθῃς ἐν τῇ βασιλείᾳ σου."
me, Lord, when You come in - kingdom ˜ Your."

43 Καὶ εἶπεν αὐτῷ ὁ Ἰησοῦς,[p] "Ἀμὴν λέγω σοι,
And [2]said [3]to [4]Him - [1]Jesus, "Amen I say to you,
"Assuredly

σήμερον μετ' ἐμοῦ ἔσῃ ἐν τῷ Παραδείσῳ."
today [4]with [5]Me [1]you [2]will [3]be in - Paradise."

Jesus Dies on the Cross

(Matt. 27:45–56; Mark 15:33–41; John 19:28–30)

44 Ἦν δὲ ὡσεὶ ὥρα ἕκτη, καὶ σκότος ἐγένετο ἐφ'
[2]*it* [3]was [1]And about *the* hour ˜ sixth, and darkness came upon

know what they do." And they divided His garments and cast lots.
35 And the people stood looking on. But even the rulers with them sneered, saying, "He saved others; let Him save Himself if He is the Christ, the chosen of God."
36 The soldiers also mocked Him, coming and offering Him sour wine,
37 and saying, "If You are the King of the Jews, save Yourself."
38 And an inscription also was written over Him in letters of Greek, Latin, and Hebrew:

THIS IS THE KING
OF THE JEWS.

39 Then one of the criminals who were hanged blasphemed Him, saying, "If You are the Christ, save Yourself and us."
40 But the other, answering, rebuked him, saying, "Do you not even fear God, seeing you are under the same condemnation?
41 "And we indeed justly, for we receive the due reward of our deeds; but this Man has done nothing wrong."
42 Then he said to Jesus, "Lord, remember me when You come into Your kingdom."
43 And Jesus said to him, "Assuredly, I say to you, today you will be with Me in Paradise."
44 Now it was about the sixth hour, and there was darkness

---

[j]**(23:34)** NU brackets Ο δε Ιησους through ποιουσι, *And Jesus* through *they are doing*, as doubtful.
[k]**(23:35)** NU omits συν αυτοις, *with them.*
[l]**(23:38)** NU omits γεγραμμενη, *written.*
[m]**(23:38)** NU omits γραμμασι Ελληνικοις και Ρωμαικοις και Εβραικοις, *in Greek and Latin and Hebrew letters.*
[n]**(23:39)** NU reads ουχι συ ει ο Χριστος, *are You not the Christ?* [o]**(23:42)** For τω Ιησου μνησθητι μου, Κυριε, *to Jesus, "Remember me, Lord,* NU reads Ιησου, μνησθητι μου, *"Jesus, remember me.*
[p]**(23:43)** NU omits ο Ιησους, *Jesus.*

***(23:35)** ἐκμυκτηρίζω (*ekmyktērizō*). Verb compounded from ἐκ, *from,* and μυκτήρ, *nose,* hence mean-

over all the earth until the ninth hour.
45 Then the sun was darkened, and the veil of the temple was torn in two.
46 And when Jesus had cried out with a loud voice, He said, "Father, *'into Your hands I commit My spirit.'"* Having said this, He breathed His last.
47 So when the centurion saw what had happened, he glorified God, saying, "Certainly this was a righteous Man!"
48 And the whole crowd who came together to that sight, seeing what had been done, beat their breasts and returned.
49 But all His acquaintances, and the women who followed Him from Galilee, stood at a distance, watching these things.
50 Now behold, *there was* a man named Joseph, a council member, a good and just man.
51 He had not consented to their decision and deed. *He was* from Arimathea, a city of the Jews, who himself was also waiting for the kingdom of God.
52 This man went to Pilate and asked for the body of Jesus.
53 Then he took it down, wrapped it in linen, and laid it in

[q](23:45) NU reads *του ηλιου εκλιποντος, the sun being eclipsed* (or *having failed*).
[r](23:46) NU reads *παρατιθεμαι, I commit.*
[s](23:46) For *και ταυτα, and these (things),* NU reads *τουτο δε, and this.*

ing to turn up the nose at someone, and thus *to sneer, mock,* or *treat with contempt.* Here it describes the rulers *sneering at* Christ on the cross, and in Luke 16:14 it is used of the Pharisees *deriding* Christ. The simpler form *μυκτηρίζω* appears in Gal. 6:7, where the intended sense is probably that because God is God, people who try to mock Him will not get away with it.

ὅλην τὴν γῆν ἕως ὥρας ἐνάτης. **45** Καὶ ἐσκοτίσθη ὁ
whole ˜ the land until *the* hour ˜ ninth. And [3]was [4]darkened [1]the

ἥλιος,[q] καὶ ἐσχίσθη τὸ καταπέτασμα τοῦ ναοῦ
[2]sun, and [6]was [7]split [1]the [2]veil [3]of [4]the [5]temple

μέσον.
in the middle.

46 Καὶ φωνήσας φωνῇ μεγάλῃ ὁ Ἰησοῦς εἶπε,
And calling with a voice ˜ great (loud) - Jesus said,

"Πάτερ, «εἰς χεῖράς σου παραθήσομαι[r] τὸ πνεῦμά μου.»" Καὶ
"Father, «into hands ˜ Your I will commit - spirit ˜ My.»" And

ταῦτα[s] εἰπὼν ἐξέπνευσεν.
these *things* saying (after He said these things,) He expired.

47 Ἰδὼν δὲ ὁ ἑκατόνταρχος τὸ γενόμενον ἐδόξασε
[4]seeing [1]And [2]the [3]centurion the *thing* happening (what had happened) glorified

τὸν Θεόν, λέγων, "Ὄντως ὁ ἄνθρωπος οὗτος δίκαιος ἦν."
- God, saying, "Certainly - man ˜ this righteous ˜ was."

48 Καὶ πάντες οἱ συμπαραγενόμενοι ὄχλοι ἐπὶ τὴν θεωρίαν
And all the [2]coming [3]together (which came) [1]crowds for - spectacle ˜

ταύτην, θεωροῦντες τὰ γενόμενα, τύπτοντες ἑαυτῶν
this, seeing (when they) the *things* (saw what) being done, (had happened,) beating (beat) [3]of [4]themselves (their own)

τὰ στήθη ὑπέστρεφον. **49** Εἱστήκεισαν δὲ πάντες οἱ
[1]the [2]chests (chests and) returned. [5]stood [1]And [2]all -

γνωστοὶ αὐτοῦ μακρόθεν καὶ γυναῖκες αἱ
[4]acquaintances [3]His at a distance and *the* women the *ones* (who)

συνακολουθήσασαι αὐτῷ ἀπὸ τῆς Γαλιλαίας, ὁρῶσαι
having followed (followed) Him from - Galilee, watching

ταῦτα.
these *things.*

Jesus Is Buried in Joseph's Tomb
(Matt. 27:57–61; Mark 15:42–47; John 19:38–42)

50 Καὶ ἰδού, ἀνὴρ ὀνόματι Ἰωσήφ, βουλευτὴς ὑπάρχων,
And behold, a man by name (named) Joseph, [2]a [3]counselor [1]being,

ἀνὴρ ἀγαθὸς καὶ δίκαιος **51** (οὗτος οὐκ ἦν
[4]a [8]man [5]good [6]and [7]righteous (this *man* not ˜ was (had not)

συγκατατεθειμένος τῇ βουλῇ καὶ τῇ πράξει αὐτῶν), ἀπὸ
agreed with (agreed to) - [2]decision [3]and - [4]deed [1]their), from

Ἀριμαθαίας πόλεως τῶν Ἰουδαίων, ὃς καὶ προσεδέχετο
Arimathea a city of the Jews, who indeed (himself) [2]was [4]waiting [5]for (was also)

καὶ αὐτὸς τὴν βασιλείαν τοῦ Θεοῦ, **52** οὗτος προσελθὼν
[3]also [1]he (waiting for) the kingdom - of God, this *man* coming to (approached)

τῷ Πιλάτῳ ᾐτήσατο τὸ σῶμα τοῦ Ἰησοῦ. **53** Καὶ
- Pilate (Pilate and) asked for the body - of Jesus. And

καθελὼν αὐτὸ ἐνετύλιξεν αὐτὸ σινδόνι, καὶ ἔθηκεν
having taken down ˜ it he wrapped it in a linen cloth, and put

αὐτὸ ἐν μνήματι λαξευτῷ, οὗ οὐκ ἦν οὐδέπω οὐδεὶς
it in a tomb cut out of rock, where not was not yet no one
no one had ever lain.

κείμενος. 54 Καὶ ἡμέρα ἦν Παρασκευή·[t] σάββατον
lying. And *the* day was *the* Preparation; *the* Sabbath

ἐπέφωσκε. 55 Κατακολουθήσασαι δὲ γυναῖκες, αἵτινες
was drawing near. [12]following [13]after [1]And [2]*the* [3]women, [4]who
followed after and

ἦσαν συνεληλυθυῖαι αὐτῷ ἐκ τῆς Γαλιλαίας, ἐθεάσαντο τὸ
[5]were [6]having [7]come [8]with [9]Him [10]from - [11]Galilee, observed the
had come

μνημεῖον καὶ ὡς ἐτέθη τὸ σῶμα αὐτοῦ.
tomb and how [3]was [4]placed - [2]body [1]His.

56 Ὑποστρέψασαι δὲ ἡτοίμασαν ἀρώματα καὶ μύρα.
returning ˜ And they prepared spices and perfumes.

The Open Tomb: He Is Risen
(Matt. 28:1–8; Mark 16:1–8; John 20:1–10)

24 1 Καὶ τὸ μὲν σάββατον ἡσύχασαν κατὰ τὴν
And *on* the indeed ˜ Sabbath they rested according to the

ἐντολήν. Τῇ δὲ μιᾷ τῶν σαββάτων, ὄρθρου
commandment. on ˜ But *the* first *day* of the week, at dawn ˜
very early

βαθέως, ἦλθον ἐπὶ τὸ μνῆμα φέρουσαι ἃ
deep, they came to the tomb bearing [3]which
in the morning,

ἡτοίμασαν ἀρώματα, καί τινες σὺν αὐταῖς.[a]
[4]they [5]prepared [1]*the* [2]spices, and certain *other women* with them.
had prepared

2 Εὗρον δὲ τὸν λίθον ἀποκεκυλισμένον ἀπὸ τοῦ
[2]they [3]found [1]And the stone having been rolled away from the

μνημείου. 3 Καὶ εἰσελθοῦσαι οὐχ εὗρον τὸ σῶμα τοῦ
tomb. And going in [3]not [1]they [2]did find the body of the

Κυρίου Ἰησοῦ. 4 Καὶ ἐγένετο ἐν τῷ διαπορεῖσθαι[b]*
Lord Jesus. And it happened in - to be greatly perplexed
as they were greatly perplexed

αὐτὰς περὶ τούτου, καὶ ἰδού, ἄνδρες δύο ἐπέστησαν αὐταῖς ἐν
them about this, and behold, men ˜ two stood by them in
that

ἐσθήσεσιν ἀστραπτούσαις. 5 Ἐμφόβων δὲ γενομένων αὐτῶν
clothing ˜ gleaming. [4]afraid [1]And [3]becoming [2]them
when they became

καὶ κλινουσῶν τὸ πρόσωπον εἰς τὴν γῆν, εἶπον πρὸς
and bending the face to the ground, they said to
bowed their faces

αὐτάς, "Τί ζητεῖτε τὸν ζῶντα μετὰ τῶν νεκρῶν? 6 Οὐκ
them, "Why do you seek the living *One* among the dead? [3]not

ἔστιν ὧδε, ἀλλ' ἠγέρθη! Μνήσθητε ὡς ἐλάλησεν ὑμῖν
[1]He [2]is here, but was raised! Remember how He spoke to you
is risen!

ἔτι ὢν ἐν τῇ Γαλιλαίᾳ, 7 λέγων ὅτι δεῖ τὸν
still being in - Galilee, saying that it is necessary *for* the
while He was still was

Υἱὸν τοῦ Ἀνθρώπου παραδοθῆναι εἰς χεῖρας ἀνθρώπων
Son - of Man to be handed over into *the* hands of men ˜
delivered

ἁμαρτωλῶν, καὶ σταυρωθῆναι, καὶ τῇ τρίτῃ ἡμέρᾳ
sinful, and to be crucified, and on the third day

a tomb *that was* hewn out of the rock, where no one had ever lain before.
54 That day was the Preparation, and the Sabbath drew near.
55 And the women who had come with Him from Galilee followed after, and they observed the tomb and how His body was laid.
56 Then they returned and prepared spices and fragrant oils. And they rested on the Sabbath according to the commandment.
24 Now on the first *day* of the week, very early in the morning, they, and certain *other women* with them, came to the tomb bringing the spices which they had prepared.
2 But they found the stone rolled away from the tomb.
3 Then they went in and did not find the body of the Lord Jesus.
4 And it happened, as they were greatly perplexed about this, that behold, two men stood by them in shining garments.
5 Then, as they were afraid and bowed *their* faces to the earth, they said to them, "Why do you seek the living among the dead?
6 "He is not here, but is risen! Remember how He spoke to you when He was still in Galilee,
7 "saying, 'The Son of Man must be delivered into the hands of sinful men, and be crucified, and the third day rise

---

[t]**(23:54)** NU reads *παρασκευης, of preparation.*
[a]**(24:1)** NU omits *και τινες συν αυταις, and certain (other women) with them.*
[b]**(24:4)** NU reads *απορεισθαι, to be perplexed.*

***(24:4)** *διαπορέω (diaporeō); ἀπορέω (aporeō).* Verbs meaning *be at a loss, perplexed. διαπορέω* is the intensive form of *ἀπορέω,* and is here best translated as *greatly perplexed. ἀπορέω* occurs only in the middle voice in the NT. It may involve being *uncertain* as to how to proceed (Acts 25:20) or as to the meaning of some statement (John 13:22) or event (as with *διαπορέω* here in Luke 24:4). Cf. also the cognate noun *ἀπορία, perplexity* (Luke 21:25).

again.'"
8 And they remembered His words.
9 Then they returned from the tomb and told all these things to the eleven and to all the rest.
10 It was Mary Magdalene, Joanna, Mary *the mother* of James, and the other *women* with them, who told these things to the apostles.
11 And their words seemed to them like idle tales, and they did not believe them.
12 But Peter arose and ran to the tomb; and stooping down, he saw the linen cloths lying by themselves; and he departed, marveling to himself at what had happened.
13 Now behold, two of them were traveling that same day to a village called Emmaus, which was seven miles from Jerusalem.
14 And they talked together of all these things which had happened.
15 So it was, while they conversed and reasoned, that Jesus Himself drew near and went with them.
16 But their eyes were restrained, so that they did not know Him.
17 And He said to them, "What kind of conversation *is* this that you have with one another as you walk and are sad?"

ἀναστῆναι." **8** Καὶ ἐμνήσθησαν τῶν ῥημάτων αὐτοῦ.
to rise again." And they remembered - words ~ His.

9 Καὶ ὑποστρέψασαι ἀπὸ τοῦ μνημείου, ἀπήγγειλαν
And returning from the tomb, they reported

ταῦτα πάντα τοῖς ἕνδεκα καὶ πᾶσι τοῖς λοιποῖς.
[2]these [3]*things* [1]all to the eleven and to all the rest.

10 Ἦσαν δὲ ἡ Μαγδαληνὴ Μαρία καὶ Ἰωάννα καὶ
[2]they [3]were [1]Now - Magdalene ~ Mary and Joanna and

Μαρία Ἰακώβου, καὶ αἱ λοιπαὶ σὺν αὐταῖς, αἳ[c] ἔλεγον
Mary *the mother* of James, and the rest with them, who told

πρὸς τοὺς ἀποστόλους ταῦτα. **11** Καὶ ἐφάνησαν ἐνώπιον
[3]to [4]the [5]apostles [1]these [2]*things.* And [3]seemed [4]before
in their

αὐτῶν ὡσεὶ λῆρος τὰ ῥήματα αὐτῶν,[d] καὶ ἠπίστουν
[5]them [6]like [7]nonsense - [2]words [1]their, and they disbelieved
view

αὐταῖς. **12** Ὁ δὲ Πέτρος ἀναστὰς ἔδραμεν ἐπὶ τὸ μνημεῖον,
them. - But Peter arising ran to the tomb,
rose up and

καὶ παρακύψας βλέπει τὰ ὀθόνια κείμενα[e] μόνα· καὶ
and stooping to look *in* he sees the linen strips lying alone; and
saw

ἀπῆλθε πρὸς ἑαυτὸν θαυμάζων τὸ γεγονός.
he went off [2]to [3]himself [1]marveling [4]at the *thing* having happened.
departed what had happened.

The Road to Emmaus

(Mark 16:12, 13)

13 Καὶ ἰδού, δύο ἐξ αὐτῶν ἦσαν πορευόμενοι ἐν αὐτῇ τῇ
And behold, two of them were traveling on very ~ the
that

ἡμέρᾳ εἰς κώμην ἀπέχουσαν σταδίους ἑξήκοντα ἀπὸ
day to a village being distant stadia ~ sixty from
which was about

Ἱερουσαλήμ, ᾗ ὄνομα Ἐμμαοῦς. **14** Καὶ αὐτοὶ
Jerusalem, to which *was the* name Emmaus. And they
called

ὡμίλουν πρὸς ἀλλήλους περὶ πάντων τῶν
were conversing with one another about all -

συμβεβηκότων τούτων. **15** Καὶ ἐγένετο ἐν τῷ
[3]having [4]come [5]about [1]these [2]*things.* And it happened in -
which had happened as they

ὁμιλεῖν αὐτοὺς καὶ συζητεῖν, καὶ αὐτὸς ὁ Ἰησοῦς
[2]to [3]converse [1]them and to discuss, and Himself ~ - Jesus
were conversing discussing, that

ἐγγίσας συνεπορεύετο αὐτοῖς. **16** Οἱ δὲ ὀφθαλμοὶ αὐτῶν
having drawn near traveled with them. - But eyes ~ their
drew near and started to travel

ἐκρατοῦντο τοῦ μὴ ἐπιγνῶναι αὐτόν.
were restrained from the not to recognize Him.
so that they did not

17 Εἶπε δὲ πρὸς αὐτούς, "Τίνες οἱ λόγοι οὗτοι οὓς
[2]He [3]said [1]And to them, "What *are* - words ~ these which

ἀντιβάλλετε πρὸς ἀλλήλους περιπατοῦντες, καὶ ἐστε[f]
you are exchanging with one another walking, and you are
as you walk,

σκυθρωποί?"
with a gloomy look?"
have

[c](24:10) NU omits αι, *who.* [d](24:11) NU reads ταυτα, *these.* [e](24:12) NU omits κειμενα, *lying.* [f](24:17) NU reads εσταθησαν, *they stood (there).*

18 Ἀποκριθεὶς δὲ ὁ εἷς ᾧ ὄνομα Κλεοπᾶς,
[10]answering [1]And [2]the [3]one [4]to [5]whom [6]*the* [7]name [8]*was* [9]Cleopas,
whose name

εἶπε πρὸς αὐτόν, "Σὺ μόνος παροικεῖς
said to Him, "[2]You [3]alone [1]Are living as a stranger
the only One so strange

Ἰερουσαλήμ, καὶ οὐκ ἔγνως τὰ γενόμενα ἐν αὐτῇ ἐν
in Jerusalem, and not ˜ did know the *things* having happened in it in
do what has happened

ταῖς ἡμέραις ταύταις?"
- days ˜ these?"

19 Καὶ εἶπεν αὐτοῖς, "Ποῖα?"
And He said to them, "What kind of *things?*"

Οἱ δὲ εἶπον αὐτῷ, "Τὰ περὶ Ἰησοῦ τοῦ
[2]the [3]*ones* [1]And said to Him, "The *things* concerning Jesus the
they

Ναζωραίου, ὃς ἐγένετο ἀνὴρ προφήτης δυνατὸς ἐν
Nazarene, who became a man *who was* a prophet mighty in
proved to be

ἔργῳ καὶ λόγῳ ἐναντίον τοῦ Θεοῦ καὶ παντὸς τοῦ λαοῦ,
deed and word before - God and all the people,

20 ὅπως τε παρέδωκαν αὐτὸν οἱ ἀρχιερεῖς καὶ οἱ ἄρχοντες
how ˜ and [6]handed [8]over [7]Him - [2]chief [3]priests [4]and - [5]rulers

ἡμῶν εἰς κρίμα θανάτου, καὶ ἐσταύρωσαν αὐτόν.
[1]our to a judgment of death, and they crucified Him.
be condemned to

21 Ἡμεῖς δὲ ἠλπίζομεν ὅτι αὐτός ἐστιν ὁ μέλλων
we ˜ But were hoping that He is the *One* being about
was who would

λυτροῦσθαι τὸν Ἰσραήλ. Ἀλλά γε σὺν πᾶσι τούτοις
to redeem - Israel. But - with all these *things*
besides this,

τρίτην ταύτην ἡμέραν ἄγει σήμερον[g] ἀφ' οὗ ταῦτα
[4]third [3]this [5]day [2]brings [1]today from which these *things*
the is since

ἐγένετο. 22 Ἀλλὰ καὶ γυναῖκές τινες ἐξ ἡμῶν ἐξέστησαν
happened. But also women ˜ certain from us astonished
Moreover of our group

ἡμᾶς, γενόμεναι ὄρθριαι ἐπὶ τὸ μνημεῖον. 23 Καὶ μὴ
us, coming early at the tomb. And not
after they arrived

εὑροῦσαι τὸ σῶμα αὐτοῦ, ἦλθον λέγουσαι καὶ ὀπτασίαν
finding - body ˜ His, they came saying also [4]a [5]vision

ἀγγέλων ἑωρακέναι, οἳ λέγουσιν αὐτὸν ζῆν. 24 Καὶ
[6]of [7]angels [1]to [2]have [3]seen, who say Him to live. And
that they had said that He was alive.

ἀπῆλθόν τινες τῶν σὺν ἡμῖν ἐπὶ τὸ μνημεῖον καὶ
[7]went [8]off [1]certain [2]of [3]the [4]*ones* [5]with [6]us to the tomb and
of those

εὗρον οὕτω καθὼς καὶ αἱ γυναῖκες εἶπον· αὐτὸν δὲ οὐκ
found *it* thus just as also the women said; [6]Him [1]but [4]not
had said;

εἶδον."
[2]they [3]did [5]see."

25 Καὶ αὐτὸς εἶπε πρὸς αὐτούς, "Ὦ ἀνόητοι καὶ βραδεῖς
And He said to them, "O foolish *ones* and slow

τῇ καρδίᾳ τοῦ πιστεύειν ἐπὶ πᾶσιν οἷς ἐλάλησαν οἱ
in the heart - to believe on all *things* which [3]spoke [1]the
of in

18 Then the one whose name was Cleopas answered and said to Him, "Are You the only stranger in Jerusalem, and have You not known the things which happened there in these days?"
19 And He said to them, "What things?" So they said to Him, "The things concerning Jesus of Nazareth, who was a Prophet mighty in deed and word before God and all the people,
20 "and how the chief priests and our rulers delivered Him to be condemned to death, and crucified Him.
21 "But we were hoping that it was He who was going to redeem Israel. Indeed, besides all this, today is the third day since these things happened.
22 "Yes, and certain women of our company, who arrived at the tomb early, astonished us.
23 "When they did not find His body, they came saying that they had also seen a vision of angels who said He was alive.
24 "And certain of those *who were* with us went to the tomb and found *it* just as the women had said; but Him they did not see."
25 Then He said to them, "O foolish ones, and slow of heart to believe in all that the prophets have spoken!

[g](24:21) NU omits σημερον, *today.*

26 "Ought not the Christ to
have suffered these things and
to enter into His glory?"
27 And beginning at Moses
and all the Prophets, He ex-
pounded to them in all the
Scriptures the things concerning Himself.
28 Then they drew near to the
village where they were going,
and He indicated that He would
have gone farther.
29 But they constrained Him,
saying, "Abide with us, for it is
toward evening, and the day is
far spent." And He went in to
stay with them.
30 Now it came to pass, as He
sat at the table with them, that
He took bread, blessed and
broke *it*, and gave it to them.
31 Then their eyes were
opened and they knew Him;
and He vanished from their
sight.
32 And they said to one another, "Did not our heart burn
within us while He talked with
us on the road, and while He
opened the Scriptures to us?"
33 So they rose up that very
hour and returned to Jerusalem, and found the eleven and
those *who were* with them gathered together,
34 saying, "The Lord is risen
indeed, and has appeared to Simon!"
35 And they told about the
things *that had happened* on the
road, and how He was known
to them in the breaking of
bread.

προφῆται! **26** Οὐχὶ ταῦτα ἔδει παθεῖν
[2]prophets! [3]not [10]these [11]*things* [1]Was [2]it [4]necessary [5]*for* [8]to [9]suffer

τὸν Χριστὸν καὶ εἰσελθεῖν εἰς τὴν δόξαν αὐτοῦ?" **27** Καὶ
[6]the [7]Christ and to enter into - glory ˜ His?" And
Messiah

ἀρξάμενος ἀπὸ Μωσέως καὶ ἀπὸ πάντων τῶν προφητῶν,
beginning from Moses and from all the Prophets,
at

διηρμήνευεν αὐτοῖς ἐν πάσαις ταῖς Γραφαῖς τὰ περὶ
He explained to them in all the Scriptures the *things* concerning

ἑαυτοῦ.
Himself.

28 Καὶ ἤγγισαν εἰς τὴν κώμην οὗ ἐπορεύοντο,
And they drew near to the village where they were going,
to which

καὶ αὐτὸς προσεποιεῖτο πορρωτέρω πορεύεσθαι. **29** Καὶ
and He made as though [3]farther [1]to [2]go. And
He was going.

παρεβιάσαντο αὐτόν, λέγοντες, "Μεῖνον μεθ' ἡμῶν, ὅτι
they constrained Him, saying, "Stay with us, because

πρὸς ἑσπέραν ἐστί, καὶ κέκλικεν[h] ἡ ἡμέρα." Καὶ
[3]toward [4]evening [1]it [2]is, and [3]has [4]declined [1]the [2]day." And
is far spent

εἰσῆλθε τοῦ μεῖναι σὺν αὐτοῖς. **30** Καὶ ἐγένετο ἐν τῷ
He went in - to stay with them. And it happened in -
while He

κατακλιθῆναι αὐτὸν μετ' αὐτῶν, λαβὼν τὸν ἄρτον
to recline *to eat* Him with them, having taken - bread
was reclining to eat

εὐλόγησε, καὶ κλάσας ἐπεδίδου αὐτοῖς. **31** Αὐτῶν δὲ
He blessed *it*, and having broken *it* He gave *it* to them. their ˜ And

διηνοίχθησαν οἱ ὀφθαλμοὶ καὶ ἐπέγνωσαν αὐτόν· καὶ αὐτὸς
[2]were [3]opened - [1]eyes and they knew Him; and He
recognized

ἄφαντος ἐγένετο ἀπ' αὐτῶν. **32** Καὶ εἶπον πρὸς ἀλλήλους,
invisible ˜ became from them. And they said to one another,
to

"Οὐχὶ ἡ καρδία ἡμῶν καιομένη ἦν ἐν ἡμῖν ὡς
"[2]not - [4]heart [3]our [5]burning [1]Was within us while

ἐλάλει ἡμῖν ἐν τῇ ὁδῷ, καὶ ὡς διήνοιγεν ἡμῖν
He was speaking to us on the road, and while He was opening up to us
interpreting

τὰς Γραφάς?" **33** Καὶ ἀναστάντες αὐτῇ τῇ ὥρᾳ ὑπέστρεψαν
the Scriptures?" And rising up very ˜ the hour they returned
that

εἰς Ἰερουσαλήμ, καὶ εὗρον συνηθροισμένους τοὺς ἕνδεκα
to Jerusalem, and they found [8]gathered [9]together [1]the [2]eleven

καὶ τοὺς σὺν αὐτοῖς, **34** λέγοντας ὅτι "Ἠγέρθη ὁ Κύριος
[3]and [4]the [5]*ones* [6]with [7]them, saying - "[3]is [4]risen [1]The [2]Lord
those who said

ὄντως καὶ ὤφθη Σίμωνι!" **35** Καὶ αὐτοὶ ἐξηγοῦντο τὰ
indeed and He appeared to Simon!" And they described the *things*
has appeared

ἐν τῇ ὁδῷ, καὶ ὡς ἐγνώσθη αὐτοῖς ἐν τῇ κλάσει τοῦ
on the road, and how He was known to them in the breaking -

ἄρτου.
of bread.

---

[h](**24:29**) NU adds ηδη, *already*.

Jesus Appears to His Disciples
(Mark 16:14; John 20:19, 20)

36 Ταῦτα δὲ αὐτῶν λαλούντων, αὐτὸς ὁ Ἰησοῦς[i]
[4]these [5]*things* [1]And [2]them [3]speaking, Himself ˜ - Jesus
as they spoke,

ἔστη ἐν μέσῳ αὐτῶν, καὶ λέγει αὐτοῖς, "Εἰρήνη ὑμῖν."
stood in midst ˜ their, and says to them, "Peace to you."
said

37 Πτοηθέντες δὲ καὶ ἔμφοβοι γενόμενοι ἐδόκουν πνεῦμα
[2]being [3]alarmed [1]But and fearful ˜ becoming they thought [3]a [4]spirit

θεωρεῖν. 38 Καὶ εἶπεν αὐτοῖς, "Τί τεταραγμένοι* ἐστέ?
[1]to [2]see. And He said to them, "Why [3]troubled [1]are [2]you?
they saw.

Καὶ διὰ τί διαλογισμοὶ ἀναβαίνουσιν ἐν ταῖς καρδίαις
And on account of what doubts ˜ do arise in - hearts ˜
why

ὑμῶν? 39 Ἴδετε τὰς χεῖράς μου καὶ τοὺς πόδας μου, ὅτι αὐτὸς
your? See - hands ˜ My and - feet ˜ My, that [4]Myself

ἐγώ εἰμι. Ψηλαφήσατέ με καὶ ἴδετε, ὅτι πνεῦμα σάρκα
[3]I [1]I [2]am. Handle Me and see, because a spirit [4]flesh
it is.

καὶ ὀστέα οὐκ ἔχει, καθὼς ἐμὲ θεωρεῖτε ἔχοντα." 40 Καὶ
[5]and [6]bones [2]not [1]does [3]have, as [3]Me [1]you [2]see having." And
you see that I have."

τοῦτο εἰπὼν ἐπέδειξεν αὐτοῖς τὰς χεῖρας καὶ τοὺς πόδας.
this ˜ saying He showed them the hands and the feet.
His His

41 Ἔτι δὲ ἀπιστούντων αὐτῶν ἀπὸ τῆς χαρᾶς καὶ
still ˜ But disbelieving ˜ them from - joy and
But as they still disbelieved for

θαυμαζόντων, εἶπεν αὐτοῖς, "Ἔχετέ τι βρώσιμον ἐνθάδε?"
marveling, He said to them, "Do you have any eatable *thing* here?"
marveled, food

42 Οἱ δὲ ἐπέδωκαν αὐτῷ ἰχθύος ὀπτοῦ μέρος, καὶ
[2]the [3]*ones* [1]And gave Him [2]of [3]a [5]fish [4]broiled [1]part, and
they

ἀπὸ μελισσίου κηρίου.[j] 43 Καὶ λαβὼν ἐνώπιον αὐτῶν
[3]from [4]a [5]beehive [1]a [2]honeycomb. And taking *it* [4]before [5]them
in their sight

ἔφαγεν.
[1]He [2]ate [3]*it*.

Jesus Opens the Scriptures

44 Εἶπε δὲ αὐτοίς, "Οὗτοι οἱ λόγοι[k] οὓς ἐλάλησα
[2]He [3]said [1]And to them, "These *are* the words which I spoke

πρὸς ὑμᾶς ἔτι ὢν σὺν ὑμῖν, ὅτι δεῖ
to you still being with you, because it is necessary
while I was still

πληρωθῆναι πάντα τὰ γεγραμμένα ἐν τῷ Νόμῳ
to be fulfilled all the *things* having been written in the Law
that all things be fulfilled which are

Μωσέως καὶ Προφήταις καὶ Ψαλμοῖς περὶ ἐμοῦ." 45 Τότε
of Moses and *the* Prophets and *the* Psalms concerning Me." Then

διήνοιξεν αὐτῶν τὸν νοῦν τοῦ συνιέναι τὰς Γραφάς.
He opened their - understanding - to comprehend the Scriptures.

46 Καὶ εἶπεν αὐτοῖς ὅτι "Οὕτω γέγραπται, καὶ οὕτως
And He said to them - "Thus it is written and thus

ἔδει[l] παθεῖν τὸν Χριστὸν καὶ ἀναστῆναι ἐκ
it was necessary *for* [3]to [4]suffer [1]the [2]Christ and to rise from

36 Now as they said these things, Jesus Himself stood in the midst of them, and said to them, "Peace to you."
37 But they were terrified and frightened, and supposed they had seen a spirit.
38 And He said to them, "Why are you troubled? And why do doubts arise in your hearts?
39 "Behold My hands and My feet, that it is I Myself. Handle Me and see, for a spirit does not have flesh and bones as you see I have."
40 When He had said this, He showed them His hands and His feet.
41 But while they still did not believe for joy, and marveled, He said to them, "Have you any food here?"
42 So they gave Him a piece of a broiled fish and some honeycomb.
43 And He took *it* and ate in their presence.
44 Then He said to them, "These *are* the words which I spoke to you while I was still with you, that all things must be fulfilled which were written in the Law of Moses and *the* Prophets and *the* Psalms concerning Me."
45 And He opened their understanding, that they might comprehend the Scriptures.
46 Then He said to them, "Thus it is written, and thus it was necessary for the Christ to suffer and to rise from the dead

[i]**(24:36)** NU omits ο Ιησους, *Jesus.* [j]**(24:42)** NU omits και απο μελισσιου κηριου, *and from a beehive a honeycomb.*
[k]**(24:44)** NU adds μου, *My.*
[l]**(24:46)** NU omits και ουτως εδει, *and thus it was necessary.*

***(24:38)** ταράσσω *(tarassō).* Verb meaning *shake, stir up, disturb, trouble.* In the NT this verb can be used literally of disturbing some object (water in John 5:4). Otherwise, it usually indicates mental or emotional agitation or troubling, and the confusion that such disturbance may cause (as here in Luke 24:38; cf. Acts 15:24; John 11:33). Often this involves (in the passive voice) the meaning *be frightened, terrified* (Matt. 14:26). Cf. the cognate nouns ταραχή, *disturbance, perplexity, tumult,* and τάραχος, *(mental)*

the third day,
47 "and that repentance and remission of sins should be preached in His name to all nations, beginning at Jerusalem.
48 "And you are witnesses of these things.
49 "Behold, I send the Promise of My Father upon you; but tarry in the city of Jerusalem until you are endued with power from on high."
50 And He led them out as far as Bethany, and He lifted up His hands and blessed them.
51 Now it came to pass, while He blessed them, that He was parted from them and carried up into heaven.
52 And they worshiped Him, and returned to Jerusalem with great joy,
53 and were continually in the temple praising and blessing God. Amen.

νεκρῶν τῇ τρίτῃ ἡμέρᾳ, **47** καὶ κηρυχθῆναι ἐπὶ τῷ
the dead on the third day, and *that* [6]to [7]be [8]proclaimed [9]in -
be preached

ὀνόματι αὐτοῦ μετάνοιαν καὶ[m] ἄφεσιν ἁμαρτιῶν εἰς πάντα
[11]name [10]His [1]repentance [2]and [3]forgiveness [4]of [5]sins to all

τὰ ἔθνη, ἀρξάμενον ἀπὸ Ἰερουσαλήμ. **48** Ὑμεῖς δέ ἐστε
the nations, beginning from Jerusalem. you ˜ And are
Gentiles, at

μάρτυρες τούτων. **49** Καὶ ἰδού, ἐγὼ ἀποστέλλω τὴν
witnesses of these *things*. And behold, I am sending the

ἐπαγγελίαν τοῦ Πατρός μου ἐφ' ὑμᾶς· ὑμεῖς δὲ καθίσατε ἐν
Promise - of Father ˜ My upon you; you ˜ but sit in
wait

τῇ πόλει Ἰερουσαλὴμ[n] ἕως οὗ ἐνδύσησθε δύναμιν ἐξ
the city of Jerusalem until - you are clothed with power from
endued

ὕψους."
the height."
on high."

Jesus Ascends to Heaven

(Mark 16:19, 20; Acts 1:9–11)

50 Ἐξήγαγε δὲ αὐτοὺς ἔξω ἕως εἰς Βηθανίαν, καὶ
[2]He [3]led [1]And them out as far as to Bethany, and

ἐπάρας τὰς χεῖρας αὐτοῦ εὐλόγησεν αὐτούς. **51** Καὶ ἐγένετο
lifting up - hands ˜ His He blessed them. And it happened

ἐν τῷ εὐλογεῖν αὐτὸν αὐτούς, διέστη ἀπ' αὐτῶν καὶ
in - [2]to [3]bless [1]Him them, He parted from them and
as He blessed

ἀνεφέρετο εἰς τὸν οὐρανόν. **52** Καὶ αὐτοὶ προσκυνήσαντες
was carried up into - heaven. And they worshiping
after they had worshiped

αὐτόν, ὑπέστρεψαν εἰς Ἰερουσαλὴμ μετὰ χαρᾶς μεγάλης,
Him, returned to Jerusalem with joy ˜ great,
Him, they

53 καὶ ἦσαν διὰ παντὸς ἐν τῷ ἱερῷ* αἰνοῦντες καὶ[o]
and they were through every *time* in the temple praising and
continually

εὐλογοῦντες τὸν Θεόν. Ἀμήν.[p]
blessing - God. Amen.
So be it.

[m](24:47) NU reads εις, *for.*
[n](24:49) NU omits Ιερουσαλημ, *of Jerusalem.*
[o](24:53) NU omits αινουντες και, *praising and.*
[p](24:53) NU omits Αμην, *Amen.*

agitation, consternation, commotion.

*(24:53) *ἱερόν (hieron).* Noun meaning *temple,* originally a substantival use of the adjective *ἱερός, holy,* thus literally meaning *a holy place.* Whereas *ναός, temple, shrine,* usually indicates the main temple building (see *ναός* at 1 Cor. 3:16) or inner sanctuary, *ἱερόν* typically includes the entire temple complex (Luke 21:5). Here Jesus' followers were assembling not in the temple proper but in one of its courts (cf. Acts 2:46 and the reference to Solomon's portico in Acts 3:11). Cf. the cognate noun *ἱερεύς, priest.*

The Gospel According to
JOHN

ΚΑΤΑ ΙΩΑΝΝΗΝ
ACCORDING TO JOHN

In the Beginning Was the Word

1 **1** Ἐν ἀρχῇ ἦν ὁ Λόγος,* καὶ ὁ Λόγος ἦν πρὸς
In *the* beginning was the Word, and the Word was with

τὸν Θεόν, καὶ Θεὸς ἦν ὁ Λόγος. **2** Οὗτος ἦν ἐν ἀρχῇ
- God, and [4]God [3]was [1]the [2]Word. This *One* was in *the* beginning
He

πρὸς τὸν Θεόν. **3** Πάντα δι' αὐτοῦ ἐγένετο, καὶ χωρὶς
with - God. All *things* through Him came to be, and without

αὐτοῦ ἐγένετο οὐδὲ ἕν ὃ γέγονεν. **4** Ἐν αὐτῷ
Him came to be not even one *thing* which has come to be. In Him

ζωὴ ἦν, καὶ ἡ ζωὴ ἦν τὸ φῶς τῶν ἀνθρώπων. **5** Καὶ τὸ φῶς
life ˜ was, and the life was the light - of men. And the light

ἐν τῇ σκοτίᾳ φαίνει, καὶ ἡ σκοτία αὐτὸ οὐ κατέλαβεν.
[2]in [3]the [4]darkness [1]shines, and the darkness [4]it [2]not [1]did [3]apprehend.

John Sent to Witness

6 Ἐγένετο ἄνθρωπος ἀπεσταλμένος παρὰ Θεοῦ, ὄνομα
There was a man having been sent from God, *the* name
sent whose

αὐτῷ Ἰωάννης. **7** Οὗτος ἦλθεν εἰς μαρτυρίαν, ἵνα
to him *was* John. This *man* came for a testimony, so that
name

μαρτυρήσῃ περὶ τοῦ φωτός, ἵνα πάντες πιστεύσωσι δι'
he might testify about the Light, so that all *people* might believe through

αὐτοῦ. **8** Οὐκ ἦν ἐκεῖνος τὸ φῶς ἀλλ' ἵνα
him. [4]not [3]was [1]That [2]*man* the Light but *was sent* so that

μαρτυρήσῃ περὶ τοῦ φωτός. **9** Ἦν τὸ φῶς τὸ ἀληθινὸν
he might testify about the Light. He was the Light ˜ - true

ὃ φωτίζει πάντα ἄνθρωπον ἐρχόμενον εἰς τὸν κόσμον.
which gives light to every man coming into the world.

10 Ἐν τῷ κόσμῳ ἦν, καὶ ὁ κόσμος δι' αὐτοῦ
[3]in [4]the [5]world [1]He [2]was, and the world through Him

ἐγένετο, καὶ ὁ κόσμος αὐτὸν οὐκ ἔγνω. **11** Εἰς τὰ
came to be, and the world [4]Him [2]not [1]did [3]know. To -

ἴδια ἦλθε, καὶ οἱ ἴδιοι αὐτὸν οὐ παρέλαβον.
His own *things* He came, and - His own *people* [4]Him [2]not [1]did [3]receive.

12 Ὅσοι δὲ ἔλαβον αὐτόν, ἔδωκεν αὐτοῖς ἐξουσίαν
[2]as [3]many [4]as [1]But received Him, He gave to them *the* right

τέκνα Θεοῦ γενέσθαι, τοῖς πιστεύουσιν εἰς τὸ ὄνομα
[3]children [4]of [5]God [1]to [2]become, to the *ones* believing in - name ˜
to those who believe

αὐτοῦ· **13** οἳ οὐκ ἐξ αἱμάτων, οὐδὲ ἐκ θελήματος σαρκός,
His; who not of blood, nor of *the* will of flesh,

οὐδὲ ἐκ θελήματος ἀνδρός, ἀλλ' ἐκ Θεοῦ ἐγεννήθησαν.
nor of *the* will of man, but of God were born.

1 In the beginning was the Word, and the Word was with God, and the Word was God.
2 He was in the beginning with God.
3 All things were made through Him, and without Him nothing was made that was made.
4 In Him was life, and the life was the light of men.
5 And the light shines in the darkness, and the darkness did not comprehend it.
6 There was a man sent from God, whose name *was* John.
7 This man came for a witness, to bear witness of the Light, that all through him might believe.
8 He was not that Light, but *was sent* to bear witness of that Light.
9 That was the true Light which gives light to every man coming into the world.
10 He was in the world, and the world was made through Him, and the world did not know Him.
11 He came to His own, and His own did not receive Him.
12 But as many as received Him, to them He gave the right to become children of God, to those who believe in His name:
13 who were born, not of blood, nor of the will of the flesh, nor of the will of man, but of God.

***(1:1)** λόγος *(logos).* Noun having the basic meaning *word.* λόγος has many specific meanings which fall into three groups. (1) The first relates to speaking, either generally (*statement,* Luke 20:20; *question,* Matt. 21:24; *subject* of discussion, Acts 8:21) or specifically about revelation by God (John 8:55; Rom. 9:6) and through Christ and the apostles (Titus 1:3; Acts 4:29; *the Gospel,* Luke 5:1). The noun ῥῆμα, *word, saying,* is synonymous with this

14 And the Word became flesh and dwelt among us, and we beheld His glory, the glory as of the only begotten of the Father, full of grace and truth.
15 John bore witness of Him and cried out, saying, "This was He of whom I said, 'He who comes after me is preferred before me, for He was before me.'"
16 And of His fullness we have all received, and grace for grace.
17 For the law was given through Moses, *but* grace and truth came through Jesus Christ.
18 No one has seen God at any time. The only begotten Son, who is in the bosom of the Father, He has declared *Him.*
19 Now this is the testimony of John, when the Jews sent priests and Levites from Jerusalem to ask him, "Who are you?"
20 He confessed, and did not deny, but confessed, "I am not the Christ."
21 And they asked him, "What then? Are you Elijah?" He said, "I am not." "Are you the Prophet?" And he answered, "No."
22 Then they said to him, "Who are you, that we may

The Word Becomes Flesh

14 Καὶ ὁ Λόγος σὰρξ ἐγένετο καὶ ἐσκήνωσεν* ἐν ἡμῖν,
And the Word flesh ˜ became and dwelt among us,

καὶ ἐθεασάμεθα τὴν δόξαν αὐτοῦ, δόξαν ὡς
and we beheld - glory ˜ His, glory as

μονογενοῦς παρὰ Πατρός, πλήρης χάριτος καὶ
of *the* only begotten *One* from *the* Father, full of grace and

ἀληθείας. **15** Ἰωάννης μαρτυρεῖ περὶ αὐτοῦ καὶ κέκραγε
truth. John testifies about Him and has cried out
testified

λέγων, "Οὗτος ἦν ὃν εἶπον, 'Ὁ ὀπίσω μου
saying, "This was *the One about* whom I said, 'The *One* [2]after [3]me
'He

ἐρχόμενος ἔμπροσθέν μου γέγονεν, ὅτι πρῶτός μου
[1]coming [8]before [9]me [4]has [5]come [6]to [7]be, because [3]first [4]of [5]me
who comes before me

ἦν.' **16** Καὶ[a] ἐκ τοῦ πληρώματος αὐτοῦ ἡμεῖς πάντες
[1]He [2]was.' And out of - fullness ˜ His we all

ἐλάβομεν, καὶ χάριν ἀντὶ χάριτος. **17** Ὅτι ὁ νόμος
received, even grace in place of grace. Because the law
replacing

διὰ Μωσέως ἐδόθη, ἡ χάρις καὶ ἡ ἀλήθεια διὰ
through Moses was given, - *but* grace and - truth through

Ἰησοῦ Χριστοῦ ἐγένετο. **18** Θεὸν οὐδεὶς ἑώρακε πώποτε.
Jesus Christ came to be. [6]God [1]No [2]one [3]has [5]seen [4]ever.

Ὁ μονογενὴς Υἱός,[b] ὁ ὢν εἰς τὸν κόλπον τοῦ
The only begotten Son, the *One* being in the bosom of the
unique He who is

Πατρός, ἐκεῖνος ἐξηγήσατο."
Father, that *One* explained *Him.*"
He

John the Baptist Prepares the Way

19 Καὶ αὕτη ἐστὶν ἡ μαρτυρία τοῦ Ἰωάννου ὅτε
And this is the testimony - of John when

ἀπέστειλαν[c] οἱ Ἰουδαῖοι ἐξ Ἱεροσολύμων ἱερεῖς καὶ
[3]sent [1]the [2]Jews [7]from [8]Jerusalem [4]priests [5]and

Λευίτας ἵνα ἐρωτήσωσιν αὐτόν, "Σὺ τίς εἶ?"
[6]Levites so that they might ask him, "[3]you [1]Who [2]are?"

20 Καὶ ὡμολόγησε, καὶ οὐκ ἠρνήσατο, καὶ ὡμολόγησεν ὅτι
And he confessed, and not ˜ did deny, and he confessed -

"Οὐκ εἰμὶ ἐγὼ ὁ Χριστός."
"[3]not [2]am [1]I the Christ."
Messiah."

21 Καὶ ἠρώτησαν αὐτόν, "Τί οὖν? Ἠλίας εἶ σύ?"
And they asked him, "What then? [3]Elijah [1]are [2]you?"

Καὶ λέγει, "Οὐκ εἰμί."
And he says, "[3]not [1]I [2]am."
said,

"Ὁ Προφήτης εἶ σύ?"
"[3]the [4]Prophet [1]Are [2]you?"

Καὶ ἀπεκρίθη, "Οὔ."
And he answered, "No."

22 Εἶπον οὖν αὐτῷ, "Τίς εἶ, ἵνα ἀπόκρισιν
[2]they [3]said [1]Therefore to him, "Who are you, so that [4]an [5]answer

---

[a](**1:16**) NU reads Οτι, *For.*
[b](**1:18**) NU reads Θεος, *God.* [c](**1:19**) NU adds προς αυτον, *to him.*

---

group. (2) The second group relates to *reckoning* of accounts (cf. Rom. 14:12; Matt. 18:23), and by extension *reason,* or *motive* (Acts 10:29; Matt. 5:32). The cognate verb λογίζομαι, *reckon, calculate,* and noun λογεία, *collection* of money (1 Cor. 16:1, 2), belong to this group. Finally, the name ὁ Λόγος, *the Word,* (here in John 1 and in 1 John 1:1) is a specialized use of the term. Whether it refers to Jesus as the content of God's revelation (first group) or to Jesus as the organizing principle or *Reason* behind the universe (second group) is debated by scholars.

***(1:14)** σκηνόω *(skēnoō).* Verb meaning *live, dwell,* sharing the root of σκηνή, *tent, dwelling.* Because the σκηνή was often a tent or other temporary dwelling,

δῶμεν τοῖς πέμψασιν ἡμᾶς? Τί λέγεις περὶ
[1]we [2]may [3]give to the ones having sent us? What do you say about
those who sent

σεαυτοῦ?"
yourself?"

23 Ἔφη,
He said,

"Ἐγὼ «φωνὴ βοῶντος·
"I am «*the* voice of *one* crying:

'Ἐν τῇ ἐρήμῳ εὐθύνατε τὴν ὁδὸν Κυρίου,'»[d]
'In the wilderness make straight the way of *the* Lord,'»

καθὼς εἶπεν Ἡσαΐας ὁ προφήτης."
just as [4]said [1]Isaiah [2]the [3]prophet."

24 Καὶ οἱ ἀπεσταλμένοι ἦσαν ἐκ τῶν Φαρισαίων.
And the ones having been sent were from the Pharisees.
those who had

25 Καὶ ἠρώτησαν αὐτὸν καὶ εἶπον αὐτῷ, "Τί οὖν βαπτίζεις
And they asked him and said to him, "Why then do you baptize

εἰ σὺ οὐκ εἶ ὁ Χριστὸς οὔτε Ἠλίας οὔτε ὁ Προφήτης?"
if you not ~ are the Christ nor Elijah nor the Prophet?"

26 Ἀπεκρίθη αὐτοῖς ὁ Ἰωάννης λέγων, "Ἐγὼ βαπτίζω ἐν
[2]answered [3]them - [1]John saying, "I baptize in
with

ὕδατι, μέσος δὲ ὑμῶν ἕστηκεν ὃν ὑμεῖς οὐκ οἴδατε.
water, among ~ but you has stood *One* whom you not ~ do know.
stands

27 Αὐτός ἐστιν[e] ὁ ὀπίσω μου ἐρχόμενος, ὃς ἔμπροσθέν
He is the *One* [2]after [3]me [1]coming, who [5]before
who comes,

μου γέγονεν,[f] οὗ ἐγὼ οὐκ εἰμὶ ἄξιος ἵνα λύσω
[6]me [1]has [2]come [3]to [4]be, of whom I not ~ am worthy that I should loose

αὐτοῦ τὸν ἱμάντα τοῦ ὑποδήματος." 28 Ταῦτα ἐν Βηθανίᾳ
[4]His [1]the [2]strap - [3]of [5]sandal." These *things* [2]in [3]Bethany

ἐγένετο πέραν τοῦ Ἰορδάνου, ὅπου ἦν Ἰωάννης βαπτίζων.
[1]happened beyond the Jordan, where was ~ John baptizing.

Behold the Lamb of God

29 Τῇ ἐπαύριον βλέπει τὸν Ἰησοῦν ἐρχόμενον πρὸς
On the next day he sees - Jesus coming toward
saw

αὐτὸν καὶ λέγει, "Ἴδε ὁ Ἀμνὸς τοῦ Θεοῦ ὁ αἴρων
him and says, "Behold the Lamb - of God the One taking away
said, who takes

τὴν ἁμαρτίαν τοῦ κόσμου! 30 Οὗτός ἐστι περὶ οὗ ἐγὼ
the sin of the world! This is *the One* about whom I

εἶπον, 'Ὀπίσω μου ἔρχεται ἀνὴρ ὃς ἔμπροσθέν μου
said, 'After me comes a man who [3]before [4]me

γέγονεν, ὅτι πρῶτός μου ἦν.' 31 Κἀγὼ οὐκ
[1]has [2]become, because [3]first [4]of [5]me [1]He [2]was.' And I not ~
ranks, before me

ᾔδειν αὐτόν· ἀλλ' ἵνα φανερωθῇ τῷ Ἰσραήλ,
did know Him; but that He should be revealed - to Israel,

διὰ τοῦτο ἦλθον ἐγὼ ἐν τῷ ὕδατι βαπτίζων." 32 Καὶ
on account of this came ~ I [2]in - [3]water [1]baptizing." And
therefore with

ἐμαρτύρησεν Ἰωάννης λέγων ὅτι "Τεθέαμαι τὸ Πνεῦμα
testified ~ John saying - "I have observed the Spirit

καταβαῖνον ὡσεὶ περιστερὰν ἐξ οὐρανοῦ, καὶ ἔμεινεν ἐπ'
coming down like a dove from heaven, and He remained upon

give an answer to those who sent us? What do you say about yourself?"
23 He said: "I *am*

'The voice of one crying in the wilderness:
"Make straight the way of the LORD,*" '*

as the prophet Isaiah said."
24 Now those who were sent were from the Pharisees.
25 And they asked him, saying, "Why then do you baptize if you are not the Christ, nor Elijah, nor the Prophet?"
26 John answered them, saying, "I baptize with water, but there stands One among you whom you do not know.
27 "It is He who, coming after me, is preferred before me, whose sandal strap I am not worthy to loose."
28 These things were done in Bethabara beyond the Jordan, where John was baptizing.
29 The next day John saw Jesus coming toward him, and said, "Behold! The Lamb of God who takes away the sin of the world!
30 "This is He of whom I said, 'After me comes a Man who is preferred before me, for He was before me.'
31 "I did not know Him; but that He should be revealed to Israel, therefore I came baptizing with water."
32 And John bore witness, saying, "I saw the Spirit descending from heaven like a dove, and He remained upon

---

[d](**1:23**) Is. 40:3
[e](**1:27**) NU omits Αυτος εστιν, *He is.*
[f](**1:27**) NU omits ος εμπροσθεν μου γεγονεν, *who has come to be before me.*

the meaning here is probably "dwelt temporarily among us." Additionally, since in the LXX σκηνή was used of the tent of the holy tabernacle (cf. Heb. 9:2), some interpreters suggest an implied reference to Jesus as the spiritual "holy of holies" where God is revealed to His people. In Revelation the idea of temporariness is not present, just as it need not be with the cognate σκηνή (as Luke 16:9). Both the verb and the noun occur in Rev. 13:6; 21:3. The expression "dwell over them" in Rev. 7:15 sug-

Him.
33 "I did not know Him, but He who sent me to baptize with water said to me, 'Upon whom you see the Spirit descending, and remaining on Him, this is He who baptizes with the Holy Spirit.'
34 "And I have seen and testified that this is the Son of God."
35 Again, the next day, John stood with two of his disciples.
36 And looking at Jesus as He walked, he said, "Behold the Lamb of God!"
37 The two disciples heard him speak, and they followed Jesus.
38 Then Jesus turned, and seeing them following, said to them, "What do you seek?" They said to Him, "Rabbi" (which is to say, when translated, Teacher), "where are You staying?"
39 He said to them, "Come and see." They came and saw where He was staying, and remained with Him that day (now it was about the tenth hour).
40 One of the two who heard John *speak,* and followed Him, was Andrew, Simon Peter's brother.
41 He first found his own brother Simon, and said to him, "We have found the Messiah"

αὐτόν. **33** Κἀγὼ οὐκ ᾔδειν αὐτόν, ἀλλ' ὁ πέμψας με
Him. And I not ˜ did know Him, but the *One* having sent me
(the One who sent)

βαπτίζειν ἐν ὕδατι, ἐκεῖνός μοι εἶπεν, "Ἐφ' ὃν ἂν
to baptize in (with) water, that *One* (He) [2]to [3]me [1]said, 'Upon whom ever

ἴδῃς τὸ Πνεῦμα καταβαῖνον καὶ μένον ἐπ' αὐτόν, οὗτός
you see the Spirit coming down and remaining on Him, this

ἐστιν ὁ βαπτίζων ἐν Πνεύματι Ἁγίῳ.' **34** Κἀγὼ ἑώρακα
is the *One* (He who) baptizing (baptizes) in (with) *the* Spirit ˜ Holy.' And I have seen

καὶ μεμαρτύρηκα ὅτι οὗτός ἐστιν ὁ Υἱὸς τοῦ Θεοῦ."
and have testified that this is the Son - of God."

Jesus Calls His First Disciples

35 Τῇ ἐπαύριον πάλιν εἱστήκει ὁ Ἰωάννης καὶ ἐκ τῶν
On the next day again stood ˜ - John and [2]of -

μαθητῶν αὐτοῦ δύο. **36** Καὶ ἐμβλέψας τῷ Ἰησοῦ
[4]disciples [3]his [1]two. And looking at (when he looked at) - Jesus

περιπατοῦντι, λέγει, "Ἴδε ὁ Ἀμνὸς τοῦ Θεοῦ!" **37** Καὶ
walking, he says (said), "Behold the Lamb - of God!" And

ἤκουσαν αὐτοῦ οἱ δύο μαθηταὶ λαλοῦντος, καὶ ἠκολούθησαν
[4]heard [5]him [1]the [2]two [3]disciples speaking, and they followed

τῷ Ἰησοῦ.
- Jesus.

38 Στραφεὶς δὲ ὁ Ἰησοῦς καὶ θεασάμενος* αὐτοὺς
[3]turning (turned) [1]And - [2]Jesus and observing (observed) them

ἀκολουθοῦντας, λέγει αὐτοῖς, "Τί ζητεῖτε?"
following, He says (and said) to them, "What are you seeking?"

Οἱ δὲ εἶπον αὐτῷ, "Ῥαββί" (ὃ λέγεται
[2]the [3]*ones* (they) [1]And said to Him, "Rabbi" (which is said (means)

ἑρμηνευόμενον Διδάσκαλε), "ποῦ μένεις?"
being translated Teacher), "where are You staying?"

39 Λέγει αὐτοῖς, "Ἔρχεσθε καὶ ἴδετε."[g] Ἦλθον καὶ
He says (said) to them, "Come and see." They came and

εἶδον ποῦ μένει, καὶ παρ' αὐτῷ ἔμειναν τὴν ἡμέραν
saw where He stays (was staying), and with Him they stayed - day ˜

ἐκείνην. Ὥρα ἦν ὡς δεκάτη.
that. [6]hour [1]It [2]was [3]about [4]*the* [5]tenth.

40 Ἦν Ἀνδρέας ὁ ἀδελφὸς Σίμωνος Πέτρου εἷς ἐκ τῶν
[7]was [1]Andrew [2]the [3]brother [4]of [5]Simon [6]Peter one of the

δύο τῶν ἀκουσάντων παρὰ Ἰωάννου καὶ ἀκολουθησάντων αὐτῷ.
two - hearing (who heard) from John and following (followed) Him.

41 Εὑρίσκει οὗτος πρῶτος τὸν ἀδελφὸν τὸν ἴδιον Σίμωνα,
[4]finds (found) [1]This [2]*one* [3]first - [7]brother - [5]his [6]own Simon,

καὶ λέγει αὐτῷ, "Εὑρήκαμεν τὸν Μεσίαν" (ὅ ἐστι
and says (said) to him, "We have found the Messiah" (which is (means)

---

g(1:39) NU reads οψεσθε, *you will see.*

gests that God shelters the martyrs from further harm. See σκῆνος at 2 Cor. 5:1.

*(1:38) θεάομαι *(theaomai).* Verb meaning *see, behold, look at, view, perceive.* Less common in the NT than the synonyms βλέπω and ὁράω, θεάομαι often carries with it the idea of deliberate observation, usually with the physical eyes, as here. In John 1:14, 32 (cf. 1 John 1:1), the perception may include something more than just the outward appearance. It may also mean "see" in the same way English *see* is used to mean *visit, greet* (as Rom. 15:24; Matt. 22:11). In the passive voice it may mean *be noticed, attract attention* (as Matt. 6:1; 23:5).

μεθερμηνευόμενον Χριστός). **42** Καὶ[h] ἤγαγεν αὐτὸν πρὸς τὸν
being translated Christ). And he led him to -
Anointed One).

Ἰησοῦν.
Jesus.

Ἐμβλέψας αὐτῷ ὁ Ἰησοῦς εἶπε, "Σὺ εἶ Σίμων ὁ υἱὸς
Looking at him - Jesus He said, "You are Simon the son of
When Jesus looked at him,

Ἰωνᾶ.[i] Σὺ κληθήσῃ Κηφᾶς." (ὃ ἑρμηνεύεται Πέτρος).
Jonah. You shall be called Cephas." (which is translated Peter).
means a stone).

Jesus Calls Philip and Nathanael

43 Τῇ ἐπαύριον ἠθέλησεν ἐξελθεῖν εἰς τὴν Γαλιλαίαν,
On the next day He wanted to go to - Galilee,

καὶ εὑρίσκει Φίλιππον καὶ λέγει αὐτῷ ὁ Ἰησοῦς, "Ἀκολούθει
and He finds Philip and [2]says [3]to [4]him - [1]Jesus, "Follow
found said

μοι." **44** Ἦν δὲ ὁ Φίλιππος ἀπὸ Βηθσαϊδά, ἐκ τῆς πόλεως
me." [3]was [1]Now - [2]Philip from Bethsaida, of the city

Ἀνδρέου καὶ Πέτρου.
of Andrew and Peter.

45 Εὑρίσκει Φίλιππος τὸν Ναθαναὴλ καὶ λέγει αὐτῷ,
finds ~ Philip - Nathanael and says to him,
found said

"Ὃν ἔγραψε Μωσῆς ἐν τῷ Νόμῳ καὶ οἱ
"*The One about* whom wrote ~ Moses in the Law and the

Προφῆται εὑρήκαμεν — Ἰησοῦν τὸν υἱὸν τοῦ Ἰωσὴφ τὸν
Prophets we have found — Jesus the son - of Joseph the *One*

ἀπὸ Ναζαρέτ."
from Nazareth."

46 Καὶ εἶπεν αὐτῷ Ναθαναήλ, "Ἐκ Ναζαρὲτ δύναταί
And [2]said [3]to [4]him [1]Nathanael, "Out of Nazareth is it possible
"Can anything good

τι ἀγαθὸν εἶναι?"
for anything good to be?"
come out of Nazareth?"

Λέγει αὐτῷ Φίλιππος, "Ἔρχου καὶ ἴδε."
[2]says [3]to [4]him [1]Philip, "Come and see."
said

47 Εἶδεν ὁ Ἰησοῦς τὸν Ναθαναὴλ ἐρχόμενον πρὸς αὐτὸν
saw ~ - Jesus - Nathaniel coming toward Him

καὶ λέγει περὶ αὐτοῦ, "Ἴδε ἀληθῶς Ἰσραηλίτης ἐν ᾧ
and says about him, "Behold truly an Israelite in whom
said

δόλος οὐκ ἔστι!"
[4]deceit [3]not [1]*there* [2]is!"

48 Λέγει αὐτῷ Ναθαναήλ, "Πόθεν με γινώσκεις?"
[2]says [3]to [4]Him [1]Nathaniel, "From where [4]me [1]do [2]You [3]know?"
said

Ἀπεκρίθη Ἰησοῦς καὶ εἶπεν αὐτῷ, "Πρὸ τοῦ σε
answered ~ Jesus and said to him, "Before - you
Philip

Φίλιππον φωνῆσαι, ὄντα ὑπὸ τὴν συκῆν, εἶδόν σε."
Philip to call, being under the fig tree, I saw you."
called you, while you were

49 Ἀπεκρίθη Ναθαναὴλ καὶ λέγει[j] αὐτῷ, "Ῥαββί, σὺ εἶ
answered ~ Nathaniel and says to Him, "Rabbi, You are
said

(which is translated, the
Christ).
42 And he brought him to Jesus. Now when Jesus looked at
him, He said, "You are Simon
the son of Jonah. You shall be
called Cephas" (which is translated, A Stone).
43 The following day Jesus
wanted to go to Galilee, and He
found Philip and said to him,
"Follow Me."
44 Now Philip was from Bethsaida, the city of Andrew and
Peter.
45 Philip found Nathanael and
said to him, "We have found
Him of whom Moses in the law,
and also the prophets, wrote—
Jesus of Nazareth, the son of
Joseph."
46 And Nathanael said to him,
"Can anything good come out of
Nazareth?" Philip said to him,
"Come and see."
47 Jesus saw Nathanael coming toward Him, and said of
him, "Behold, an Israelite indeed, in whom is no deceit!"
48 Nathanael said to Him,
"How do You know me?" Jesus
answered and said to him, "Before Philip called you, when you
were under the fig tree, I saw
you."
49 Nathanael answered and
said to Him, "Rabbi, You are

---

[h](**1:42**) NU omits Και, *And.* [i](**1:42**) NU reads Ιωαννου, *John.* [j](**1:49**) NU omits και λεγει, *and said.*

the Son of God! You are the
King of Israel!"
50 Jesus answered and said to
him, "Because I said to you, 'I
saw you under the fig tree,' do
you believe? You will see
greater things than these."
51 And He said to him, "Most
assuredly, I say to you, hereafter you shall see heaven
open, and the angels of God ascending and descending upon
the Son of Man."
2 On the third day there
was a wedding in Cana of
Galilee, and the mother of Jesus was there.
2 Now both Jesus and His
disciples were invited to the
wedding.
3 And when they ran out of
wine, the mother of Jesus said
to Him, "They have no wine."
4 Jesus said to her, "Woman,
what does your concern have to
do with Me? My hour has not
yet come."
5 His mother said to the servants, "Whatever He says to
you, do *it*."
6 Now there were set there
six waterpots of stone, according to the manner of purification
of the Jews, containing twenty
or thirty gallons apiece.
7 Jesus said to them, "Fill
the waterpots with water." And
they filled them up to the brim.
8 And He said to them,
"Draw *some* out now, and take
it to the master of the feast."
And they took *it*.
9 When the master of the
feast had tasted the water that

ὁ Υἱὸς τοῦ Θεοῦ! Σὺ εἶ ὁ Βασιλεὺς τοῦ Ἰσραήλ!"
the Son - of God! You are the King - of Israel!"

50 Ἀπεκρίθη Ἰησοῦς καὶ εἶπεν αὐτῷ, "Ὅτι εἶπόν σοι,
answered ˜ Jesus and said to him, "Because I said to you,

'Εἶδόν σε ὑποκάτω τῆς συκῆς,' πιστεύεις? Μείζω
'I saw you under the fig tree,' do you believe? Greater *than*

τούτων ὄψει." **51** Καὶ λέγει αὐτῷ, "Ἀμὴν ἀμὴν
these *things* you will see." And He says to him, "Amen amen
said "Most assuredly

λέγω ὑμῖν, ἀπ' ἄρτι[k] ὄψεσθε τὸν οὐρανὸν ἀνεῳγότα καὶ
I say to you, from now *on* you shall see - heaven opened and

τοὺς ἀγγέλους τοῦ Θεοῦ ἀναβαίνοντας καὶ καταβαίνοντας ἐπὶ
the angels - of God ascending and descending upon

τὸν Υἱὸν τοῦ Ἀνθρώπου."
the Son - of Man."

Jesus Turns Water to Wine

2 **1** Καὶ τῇ ἡμέρᾳ τῇ τρίτῃ γάμος ἐγένετο ἐν Κανὰ
And on the day ˜ - third [3]a [4]wedding [1]*there* [2]was in Cana

τῆς Γαλιλαίας, καὶ ἦν ἡ μήτηρ τοῦ Ἰησοῦ ἐκεῖ.
- of Galilee, and [5]was [1]the [2]mother - [3]of [4]Jesus there.

2 Ἐκλήθη δὲ καὶ ὁ Ἰησοῦς καὶ οἱ μαθηταὶ αὐτοῦ εἰς τὸν
[7]was [8]called [1]Now [2]both - [3]Jesus [4]and - [6]disciples [5]His to the
were invited

γάμον. **3** Καὶ ὑστερήσαντος οἴνου, λέγει ἡ μήτηρ τοῦ
wedding. And lacking ˜ wine, [5]says [1]the [2]mother -
when the wine had given out, said

Ἰησοῦ πρὸς αὐτόν, "Οἶνον οὐκ ἔχουσι."
[3]of [4]Jesus to Him, "[5]wine [3]not [1]They [2]do [4]have."

4 Λέγει[a] αὐτῇ ὁ Ἰησοῦς, "Τί ἐμοὶ καὶ
[2]says [3]to [4]her - [1]Jesus, "What to Me and
said "What does your concern have to do

σοί, γύναι? Οὔπω ἥκει ἡ ὥρα μου."
to you, woman? [4]not [5]yet [3]has [6]come - [2]hour [1]My."
with Me,

5 Λέγει ἡ μήτηρ αὐτοῦ τοῖς διακόνοις, "Ὅ τι ἂν
[3]says - [2]mother [1]His to the servants, - "What ever
said

λέγῃ ὑμῖν, ποιήσατε." **6** Ἦσαν δὲ ἐκεῖ ὑδρίαι
He says to you, do." [2]*there* [3]were [1]Now [9]there [6]water [7]jars

λίθιναι ἓξ κείμεναι κατὰ τὸν καθαρισμὸν τῶν Ἰουδαίων,
[5]stone [4]six [8]lying according to the purification of the Jews,
standing purification rites

χωροῦσαι ἀνὰ μετρητὰς δύο ἢ τρεῖς.
holding ˜ each [4]measures [1]two [2]or [3]three.

7 Λέγει αὐτοῖς ὁ Ἰησοῦς, "Γεμίσατε τὰς ὑδρίας
[2]says [3]to [4]them - [1]Jesus, "Fill the water jars
said

ὕδατος." Καὶ ἐγέμισαν αὐτὰς ἕως ἄνω. **8** Καὶ λέγει
with water." And they filled them up to *the* top. Then He says
said

αὐτοῖς, "Ἀντλήσατε νῦν, καὶ φέρετε τῷ ἀρχιτρικλίνῳ." Καὶ
to them, "Draw out now, and carry *some* to the head steward." And

ἤνεγκαν.
they brought *it*.

9 Ὡς δὲ ἐγεύσατο ὁ ἀρχιτρίκλινος τὸ ὕδωρ οἶνον
when ˜ Now [4]tasted [1]the [2]head [3]steward the water [3]wine

---

k(1:51) NU omits απ αρτι.
a(2:4) NU adds Και, *And*.

γεγενημένον, καὶ οὐκ ᾔδει πόθεν ἐστίν (οἱ δὲ
[1]having [2]become, and not ˜ did know from where it is (the ˜ but
which had was

διάκονοι ᾔδεισαν οἱ ἠντληκότες τὸ ὕδωρ), φωνεῖ τὸν
servants knew the *ones* having drawn the water), [4]calls [5]the
who had called

νυμφίον ὁ ἀρχιτρίκλινος 10 καὶ λέγει αὐτῷ, "Πᾶς
[6]bridegroom [1]the [2]head [3]steward and says to him, "Every
said

ἄνθρωπος πρῶτον τὸν καλὸν οἶνον τίθησι, καὶ ὅταν
man first [3]the [4]good [5]wine [1]sets [2]out, and when
serves,

μεθυσθῶσι, τότε[b] τὸν ἐλάσσω· σὺ τετήρηκας τὸν καλὸν
they have well drunk, then the inferior; you have kept the good

οἶνον ἕως ἄρτι." 11 Ταύτην ἐποίησε τὴν ἀρχὴν τῶν
wine until now." This [6]did - [1]beginning [2]of [3]the

σημείων ὁ Ἰησοῦς ἐν Κανὰ τῆς Γαλιλαίας καὶ ἐφανέρωσε τὴν
[4]signs - [5]Jesus in Cana - of Galilee and He revealed -

δόξαν* αὐτοῦ, καὶ ἐπίστευσαν εἰς αὐτὸν οἱ μαθηταὶ αὐτοῦ.
glory ˜ His, and [3]believed [4]in [5]Him - [2]disciples [1]His.

12 Μετὰ τοῦτο κατέβη εἰς Καπερναοὺμ, αὐτὸς καὶ ἡ
After this He went down to Capernaum, He and -

μήτηρ αὐτοῦ καὶ οἱ ἀδελφοὶ αὐτοῦ καὶ οἱ μαθηταὶ αὐτοῦ· καὶ
mother ˜ His and - brothers ˜ His and - disciples ˜ His; and

ἐκεῖ ἔμειναν οὐ πολλὰς ἡμέρας.
there they remained not many days.

Jesus Cleanses the Temple

13 Καὶ ἐγγὺς ἦν τὸ Πάσχα τῶν Ἰουδαίων, καὶ
And [7]near [6]was [1]the [2]Passover [3]of [4]the [5]Jews, and

ἀνέβη εἰς Ἱεροσόλυμα ὁ Ἰησοῦς. 14 Καὶ εὗρεν ἐν τῷ
[2]went [3]up [4]to [5]Jerusalem - [1]Jesus. And He found in the

ἱερῷ τοὺς πωλοῦντας βόας καὶ πρόβατα καὶ περιστεράς,
temple the *ones* selling oxen and sheep and doves,
those who sold

καὶ τοὺς κερματιστὰς καθημένους. 15 Καὶ ποιήσας
and the money changers sitting *there*. And having made

φραγέλλιον ἐκ σχοινίων, πάντας ἐξέβαλεν ἐκ τοῦ ἱεροῦ,
a whip out of cords, [3]all [1]He [2]drove out of the temple,

τά τε πρόβατα καὶ τοὺς βόας, καὶ τῶν κολλυβιστῶν
the ˜ both sheep and the oxen, and [5]of [6]the [7]money [8]changers

ἐξέχεε τὸ κέρμα, καὶ τὰς τραπέζας ἀνέστρεψε. 16 Καὶ
[1]He [2]scattered [3]the [4]coins, and the tables He overturned. And

τοῖς τὰς περιστερὰς πωλοῦσιν εἶπεν, "Ἄρατε ταῦτα
to the *ones* [2]the [3]doves [1]selling He said, "Take away these *things*

ἐντεῦθεν! Μὴ ποιεῖτε τὸν οἶκον τοῦ Πατρός μου οἶκον
from here! not ˜ Do make the house of Father ˜ My a house

ἐμπορίου!" 17 Ἐμνήσθησαν δὲ οἱ μαθηταὶ αὐτοῦ ὅτι
of *the* market!" [4]remembered [1]Then - [3]disciples [2]His that
merchandise!"

γεγραμμένον ἐστίν, «Ὁ ζῆλος τοῦ οἴκου σου καταφάγεταί
[3]written [1]it [2]is, «The zeal - of house ˜ Your will consume
had been, for

με.»[c]
Me.»

18 Ἀπεκρίθησαν οὖν οἱ Ἰουδαῖοι καὶ εἶπον αὐτῷ,
[4]answered [1]Therefore [2]the [3]Jews and said to Him,

was made wine, and did not know where it came from (but the servants who had drawn the water knew), the master of the feast called the bridegroom.
10 And he said to him, "Every man at the beginning sets out the good wine, and when the *guests* have well drunk, then the inferior. You have kept the good wine until now!"
11 This beginning of signs Jesus did in Cana of Galilee, and manifested His glory; and His disciples believed in Him.
12 After this He went down to Capernaum, He, His mother, His brothers, and His disciples; and they did not stay there many days.
13 Now the Passover of the Jews was at hand, and Jesus went up to Jerusalem.
14 And He found in the temple those who sold oxen and sheep and doves, and the money changers doing business.
15 When He had made a whip of cords, He drove them all out of the temple, with the sheep and the oxen, and poured out the changers' money and overturned the tables.
16 And He said to those who sold doves, "Take these things away! Do not make My Father's house a house of merchandise!"
17 Then His disciples remembered that it was written, *"Zeal for Your house has eaten Me up."*
18 So the Jews answered and

---

[b](**2:10**) NU omits τοτε, *then*. [c](**2:17**) Ps. 69:9

*(**2:11**) δόξα *(doxa)*. Common noun often translated *glory* (as here), but with a variety of meanings. Originally the word referred to *opinion, estimation,* then to *fame, honor, praise* (as 1 Thess. 2:6, where it may mean a monetary expression of honor); *magnificence, splendor* (as Matt. 4:8); *brightness, radiance* (as Acts 22:11). Being with God in the afterlife can be called a state of "glory" (Luke 24:26; 1 Pet. 5:10). In 2 Pet. 2:10 "the glories" might mean angels ("angelic majesties," NASB) or humans ("dignitaries," NKJV). Cf. the cognate verb δοξάζω, *honor* (1 Cor. 12:26), *glorify* (1 Pet. 4:16).

said to Him, "What sign do You
show to us, since You do these
things?"
19 Jesus answered and said to
them, "Destroy this temple,
and in three days I will raise it
up."
20 Then the Jews said, "It has
taken forty-six years to build
this temple, and will You raise it
up in three days?"
21 But He was speaking of the
temple of His body.
22 Therefore, when He had
risen from the dead, His disciples remembered that He had
said this to them; and they believed the Scripture and the
word which Jesus had said.
23 Now when He was in Jerusalem at the Passover, during
the feast, many believed in His
name when they saw the signs
which He did.
24 But Jesus did not commit
Himself to them, because He
knew all *men*,
25 and had no need that anyone should testify of man, for
He knew what was in man.
3 There was a man of the
Pharisees named Nicode-
mus, a ruler of the Jews.
2 This man came to Jesus by
night and said to Him, "Rabbi,
we know that You are a teacher
come from God; for no one can
do these signs that You do unless God is with him."
3 Jesus answered and said to
him, "Most assuredly, I say to

"Τί σημεῖον δεικνύεις ἡμῖν, ὅτι ταῦτα ποιεῖς?"
"What sign do You show to us, since [3]these [4]*things* [1]You [2]do?"

19 Ἀπεκρίθη Ἰησοῦς καὶ εἶπεν αὐτοῖς "Λύσατε τὸν ναὸν
answered ~ Jesus and said to them "Destroy - temple ~
τοῦτον, καὶ ἐν τρισὶν ἡμέραις ἐγερῶ αὐτόν."
this, and in three days I will raise it."

20 Εἶπον οὖν οἱ Ἰουδαῖοι, "Τεσσαράκοντα καὶ ἓξ
[4]said [1]Therefore [2]the [3]Jews, "Forty and six
ἔτεσιν ᾠκοδομήθη ὁ ναὸς οὗτος, καὶ σὺ ἐν τρισὶν ἡμέραις
years [3]was [4]built - [2]temple [1]this, and You in three days
in building
ἐγερεῖς αὐτόν?" **21** Ἐκεῖνος δὲ ἔλεγε περὶ τοῦ ναοῦ τοῦ
will raise it?" [2]that [3]*One* [1]But was speaking about the temple -
He
σώματος αὐτοῦ. **22** Ὅτε οὖν ἠγέρθη ἐκ νεκρῶν,
of body ~ His. when ~ Therefore He was raised from *the* dead,
ἐμνήσθησαν οἱ μαθηταὶ αὐτοῦ ὅτι τοῦτο ἔλεγε, καὶ
[3]remembered - [2]disciples [1]His that [3]this [4]*thing* [1]He [2]spoke, and
ἐπίστευσαν τῇ Γραφῇ καὶ τῷ λόγῳ ᾧ εἶπεν ὁ Ἰησοῦς.
they believed the Scripture and the word which said ~ - Jesus.

Jesus Knows All People

23 Ὡς δὲ ἦν ἐν τοῖς Ἱεροσολύμοις ἐν τῷ Πάσχα, ἐν
when ~ Now He was in - Jerusalem at the Passover, at
τῇ ἑορτῇ, πολλοὶ ἐπίστευσαν εἰς τὸ ὄνομα αὐτοῦ, θεωροῦντες
the feast, many believed in - name ~ His, observing
αὐτοῦ τὰ σημεῖα ἃ ἐποίει. **24** Αὐτὸς δὲ ὁ Ἰησοῦς
His - signs which He was doing. [3]Himself [1]But - [2]Jesus
οὐκ ἐπίστευεν ἑαυτὸν αὐτοῖς διὰ τὸ αὐτὸν γινώσκειν
[5]not [4]did [6]commit Himself to them because - Him to know
He knew
πάντας, **25** καὶ ὅτι οὐ χρείαν εἶχεν ἵνα τις
all *men*, and because [3]not [5]need [1]He [2]did [4]have that anyone
μαρτυρήσῃ περὶ τοῦ ἀνθρώπου, αὐτὸς γὰρ ἐγίνωσκε τί
should testify about - man, [2]He [3]Himself [1]for knew what
ἦν ἐν τῷ ἀνθρώπῳ.
was in - man.

You Must Be Born Again

3 **1** Ἦν δὲ ἄνθρωπος ἐκ τῶν Φαρισαίων,
[2]*there* [3]was [1]Now a man of the Pharisees,
Νικόδημος ὄνομα αὐτῷ, ἄρχων τῶν Ἰουδαίων. **2** Οὗτος
[5]*was* [6]Nicodemus [1]a [2]name [3]to [4]him, a ruler of the Jews. This *man*
whose name,
ἦλθε πρὸς αὐτὸν νυκτὸς καὶ εἶπεν αὐτῷ, "Ῥαββί, οἴδαμεν ὅτι
came to Him by night and said to Him, "Rabbi, we know that
ἀπὸ Θεοῦ ἐλήλυθας διδάσκαλος, οὐδεὶς γὰρ ταῦτα τὰ
[4]from [5]God [1]You [2]have [3]come *as* a teacher, [2]no [3]one [1]for [8]these -
σημεῖα δύναται ποιεῖν ἃ σὺ ποιεῖς ἐὰν μὴ ᾖ ὁ Θεὸς μετ'
[9]signs [4]is [5]able [6]to [7]do which You do if not is ~ - God with
unless
αὐτοῦ."
him."

3 Ἀπεκρίθη ὁ Ἰησοῦς καὶ εἶπεν αὐτῷ, "Ἀμὴν ἀμὴν
answered ~ - Jesus and said to him, "Amen amen
"Most assuredly

λέγω σοι, ἐὰν μή τις γεννηθῇ ἄνωθεν, οὐ δύναται
I say to you, if not someone is born again, [3]not [1]he [2]is able
unless

ἰδεῖν τὴν βασιλείαν τοῦ Θεοῦ."
to see the kingdom - of God."

4 Λέγει πρὸς αὐτὸν ὁ Νικόδημος, "Πῶς δύναται ἄνθρωπος
[2]says [3]to [4]Him - [1]Nicodemus, "How [1]is [4]able [2]a [3]man
said

γεννηθῆναι γέρων ὤν? Μὴ δύναται εἰς τὴν κοιλίαν τῆς
to be born old ~ being? [3]not [1]He [2]is [4]able [7]into [8]the [9]womb -
when he is old?

μητρὸς αὐτοῦ δεύτερον εἰσελθεῖν καὶ γεννηθῆναι?"
[10]of [12]mother [11]his [13]a [14]second [15]time [5]to [6]enter and be born, *is he?*"

5 Ἀπεκρίθη Ἰησοῦς, "Ἀμὴν ἀμὴν λέγω σοι, ἐὰν μή
answered ~ Jesus, "Amen amen I say to you, if not
"Most assuredly unless

τις γεννηθῇ ἐξ ὕδατος καὶ Πνεύματος,* οὐ δύναται
someone is born of water and of Spirit, [3]not [1]he [2]is able

εἰσελθεῖν εἰς τὴν βασιλείαν τοῦ Θεοῦ. 6 Τὸ
to enter into the kingdom - of God. The *thing*
That which

γεγεννημένον ἐκ τῆς σαρκὸς σάρξ ἐστι, καὶ τὸ
having been born of the flesh flesh ~ is, and the *thing*
has that which

γεγεννημένον ἐκ τοῦ Πνεύματος πνεῦμά ἐστι. 7 Μὴ θαυμάσῃς
having been born of the Spirit spirit ~ is. not ~ Do marvel
has

ὅτι εἶπόν σοι, 'Δεῖ ὑμᾶς γεννηθῆναι ἄνωθεν.'
that I said to you, 'It is necessary *for* you to be born again.'

8 Τὸ πνεῦμα ὅπου θέλει πνεῖ, καὶ τὴν φωνὴν αὐτοῦ
The wind [2]where [3]it [4]wishes [1]blows, and - [4]sound [3]its

ἀκούεις, ἀλλ' οὐκ οἶδας πόθεν ἔρχεται καὶ ποῦ
[1]you [2]hear, but [3]not [1]you [2]do know from where it comes and where

ὑπάγει. Οὕτως ἐστὶ πᾶς ὁ γεγεννημένος ἐκ τοῦ
it goes. So is every - *one* having been born of the
everyone who has

Πνεύματος."
Spirit."

9 Ἀπεκρίθη Νικόδημος καὶ εἶπεν αὐτῷ, "Πῶς δύναται
answered ~ Nicodemus and said to Him, "How [1]are [4]able

ταῦτα γενέσθαι?"
[2]these [3]*things* to be?"

10 Ἀπεκρίθη Ἰησοῦς καὶ εἶπεν αὐτῷ, "Σὺ εἶ ὁ
answered ~ Jesus and said to him, "You are the

διδάσκαλος τοῦ Ἰσραὴλ καὶ ταῦτα οὐ γινώσκεις?
teacher - of Israel and [5]these [6]*things* [3]not [1]you [2]do [4]know?

11 Ἀμὴν ἀμὴν λέγω σοι ὅτι ὃ οἴδαμεν λαλοῦμεν καὶ
Amen amen I say to you that what We know We speak and
Most assuredly

ὃ ἑωράκαμεν μαρτυροῦμεν, καὶ τὴν μαρτυρίαν ἡμῶν οὐ
what We have seen We testify, and - testimony ~ Our [3]not

λαμβάνετε. 12 Εἰ τὰ ἐπίγεια εἶπον ὑμῖν καὶ οὐ
[1]you [2]do receive. If - [3]earthly [4]*things* [1]I [2]said to you and [3]not

πιστεύετε, πῶς ἐὰν εἴπω ὑμῖν τὰ ἐπουράνια
[1]you [2]do believe, how if I should say to you - heavenly *things*

πιστεύσετε? 13 Καὶ οὐδεὶς ἀναβέβηκεν εἰς τὸν οὐρανὸν εἰ
will you believe? And no one has gone up into - heaven if

you, unless one is born again, he cannot see the kingdom of God."

4 Nicodemus said to Him, "How can a man be born when he is old? Can he enter a second time into his mother's womb and be born?"

5 Jesus answered, "Most assuredly, I say to you, unless one is born of water and the Spirit, he cannot enter the kingdom of God.

6 "That which is born of the flesh is flesh, and that which is born of the Spirit is spirit.

7 "Do not marvel that I said to you, 'You must be born again.'

8 "The wind blows where it wishes, and you hear the sound of it, but cannot tell where it comes from and where it goes. So is everyone who is born of the Spirit."

9 Nicodemus answered and said to Him, "How can these things be?"

10 Jesus answered and said to him, "Are you the teacher of Israel, and do not know these things?

11 "Most assuredly, I say to you, We speak what We know and testify what We have seen, and you do not receive Our witness.

12 "If I have told you earthly things and you do not believe, how will you believe if I tell you heavenly things?

13 "No one has ascended to

***(3:5)** πνεῦμα *(pneuma)*. A very common noun having the same double meaning, *wind* or *spirit*, as does Hebrew *rûach* in the OT. Jesus' play on words here in John 3:5–8 uses πνεῦμα in both meanings: the *wind* blowing where it wills is as unexplainable as being born from above by the *Spirit*. Related to πνέω, *blow, breathe*, πνεῦμα moves from a root meaning of *breeze, wind* to the *breath* (Rev. 11:11; 13:15). By extension then it refers also to the *spirit* as the life principle, that which gives life to the body (Luke 8:55; Acts 7:59; James 2:26). πνεῦμα is also the *spirit* as part of the human personality, the inner aspect as opposed to σάρξ, the outer aspect (2 Cor. 7:1; Col. 2:5). In the NT πνεῦμα is often either the human *spirit*, that part of individuals that is capable of responding to God (John 4:23; Rom. 1:9; 8:16), heaven but He who came down from heaven, *that is,* the Son of Man who is in heaven.

14 "And as Moses lifted up the serpent in the wilderness, even so must the Son of Man be lifted up,

15 "that whoever believes in Him should not perish but have eternal life.

16 "For God so loved the world that He gave His only begotten Son, that whoever believes in Him should not perish but have everlasting life.

17 "For God did not send His Son into the world to condemn the world, but that the world through Him might be saved.

18 "He who believes in Him is not condemned; but he who does not believe is condemned already, because he has not believed in the name of the only begotten Son of God.

19 "And this is the condemnation, that the light has come into the world, and men loved darkness rather than light, because their deeds were evil.

20 "For everyone practicing evil hates the light and does not come to the light, lest his deeds should be exposed.

21 "But he who does the truth comes to the light, that his deeds may be clearly seen, that they have been done in God."

μὴ ὁ ἐκ τοῦ οὐρανοῦ καταβάς, ὁ Υἱὸς τοῦ
not the *One* [4]out [5]of - [6]heaven [1]having [2]come [3]down, the Son -
except from who came

Ἀνθρώπου ὁ ὢν ἐν τῷ οὐρανῷ.[a] 14 Καὶ καθὼς Μωσῆς
of Man the *One* being in - heaven. And just as Moses
who is

ὕψωσε τὸν ὄφιν ἐν τῇ ἐρήμῳ, οὕτως ὑψωθῆναι
lifted up the serpent in the wilderness, so [9]to [10]be [11]lifted [12]up

δεῖ τὸν Υἱὸν τοῦ Ἀνθρώπου, 15 ἵνα πᾶς ὁ
[1]it [2]is [3]necessary [4]*for* [5]the [6]Son - [7]of [8]Man, that every - *one*
everyone who

πιστεύων εἰς αὐτὸν μὴ ἀπόληται ἀλλ'[b] ἔχῃ ζωὴν
believing in Him not ˜ should perish but should have life ˜
believes

αἰώνιον.
eternal.

16 "Οὕτω γὰρ ἠγάπησεν ὁ Θεὸς τὸν κόσμον ὥστε τὸν Υἱὸν
"[3]thus [1]For [4]loved - [2]God the world that - [6]Son

αὐτοῦ[c] τὸν μονογενῆ ἔδωκεν, ἵνα πᾶς ὁ πιστεύων εἰς
[3]His - [4]only [5]begotten [1]He [2]gave, that every - *one* believing in
unique everyone who believes

αὐτὸν μὴ ἀπόληται ἀλλ' ἔχῃ ζωὴν αἰώνιον. 17 Οὐ γὰρ
Him not ˜ should perish but should have life ˜ eternal. [4]not [1]For

ἀπέστειλεν ὁ Θεὸς τὸν Υἱὸν αὐτοῦ[d] εἰς τὸν κόσμον ἵνα
[3]did [5]send - [2]God - Son ˜ His into the world so that

κρίνῃ τὸν κόσμον ἀλλ' ἵνα σωθῇ ὁ
He might condemn the world but so that [3]might [4]be [5]saved [1]the

κόσμος δι' αὐτοῦ. 18 Ὁ πιστεύων εἰς αὐτὸν οὐ
[2]world through Him. The *one* believing in Him not ˜
who believes

κρίνεται, ὁ δὲ μὴ πιστεύων ἤδη
is being condemned, [2]the [3]*one* [1]but not believing already
who does not believe

κέκριται ὅτι μὴ πεπίστευκεν εἰς τὸ ὄνομα τοῦ
has been condemned because [3]not [1]he [2]has believed in the name of the

μονογενοῦς Υἱοῦ τοῦ Θεοῦ. 19 Αὕτη δέ ἐστιν ἡ κρίσις,*
only begotten Son - of God. this ˜ And is the judgment,
unique condemnation,

ὅτι τὸ φῶς ἐλήλυθεν εἰς τὸν κόσμον, καὶ ἠγάπησαν οἱ
that the light has come into the world, and loved ˜ -

ἄνθρωποι μᾶλλον τὸ σκότος ἢ τὸ φῶς, ἦν γὰρ πονηρὰ
men [3]more [1]the [2]darkness than the light, [4]were [1]for [5]evil

αὐτῶν τὰ ἔργα. 20 Πᾶς γὰρ ὁ φαῦλα πράσσων μισεῖ τὸ
[2]their - [3]works. every ˜ For - *one* evil ˜ practicing hates the
deeds. everyone who practices

φῶς καὶ οὐκ ἔρχεται πρὸς τὸ φῶς, ἵνα μὴ ἐλεγχθῇ τὰ
light and not ˜ does come to the light, that not [3]be [4]exposed -
lest

ἔργα αὐτοῦ. 21 Ὁ δὲ ποιῶν τὴν ἀλήθειαν ἔρχεται
[2]works [1]his. [2]the [3]*one* [1]But doing the truth comes
deeds who does

πρὸς τὸ φῶς ἵνα φανερωθῇ αὐτοῦ τὰ ἔργα ὅτι ἐν Θεῷ
to the light so that [3]may [4]be [5]revealed [1]his - [2]works that in God
deeds they have

ἐστιν εἰργασμένα."
they are worked."
been done in God."

---

[a](3:13) NU omits ο ων εν τω ουρανω, *the One who is in heaven.* [b](3:15) NU omits μη αποληται αλλ, *should not perish but.* [c](3:16) NU omits αυτου, *His.* [d](3:17) NU omits αυτου, *His.*

---

or the divine *Spirit* (Rom. 8:9; 1 Cor. 2:12).

*(3:19) κρίσις *(krisis).* Noun, a general legal term with the base meaning *judgment.* It can mean *court* (Matt. 5:21, 22; cf. κριτήριον), and is used to name the decisions of courts both in terms of *verdicts* and *punishments.* It is extended to apply to judgments made by persons outside formal legal contexts (John 7:24). Often in the NT, however, it refers to activities by God or the Messiah, especially on the Day of *Judgment* (2 Pet. 2:9). It can name the result of the process of judging (2 Thess. 1:5), and the *condemnation* of guilt (John 12:31) and *punishment* imposed (Rev. 18:10). Here in John 3:19 it describes the basis or reason for the condemnation is-

John the Baptist Exalts Christ

22 Μετὰ ταῦτα ἦλθεν ὁ Ἰησοῦς καὶ οἱ μαθηταὶ
After these *things* came ˜ - Jesus and - disciples ˜
along with

αὐτοῦ εἰς τὴν Ἰουδαίαν γῆν, καὶ ἐκεῖ διέτριβε μετ'
His into the Judean country, and there He was spending time with

αὐτῶν καὶ ἐβάπτιζεν. **23** Ἦν δὲ καὶ Ἰωάννης βαπτίζων
them and He was baptizing. [3]was [1]Now [4]also [2]John [5]baptizing

ἐν Αἰνὼν ἐγγὺς τοῦ Σαλήμ, ὅτι ὕδατα πολλὰ ἦν ἐκεῖ. Καὶ
in Aenon near - Salem, because water ˜ much was there. And

παρεγίνοντο καὶ ἐβαπτίζοντο. **24** Οὔπω γὰρ ἦν
they were coming and were being baptized. [4]not [5]yet [1]For [3]was
had

βεβλημένος εἰς τὴν φυλακὴν ὁ Ἰωάννης. **25** Ἐγένετο
[6]thrown [7]into - [8]prison - [2]John. [2]*there* [3]came [4]to [5]be
been thrown

οὖν ζήτησις ἐκ τῶν μαθητῶν Ἰωάννου μετὰ Ἰουδαίου
[1]Therefore a dispute from the disciples of John with a Jew

περὶ καθαρισμοῦ. **26** Καὶ ἦλθον πρὸς τὸν Ἰωάννην καὶ
about purification. And they came to - John and
purification rites.

εἶπον αὐτῷ, "Ῥαββί, ὃς ἦν μετὰ σοῦ πέραν τοῦ
said to him, "Rabbi, *He* who was with you beyond the

Ἰορδάνου, ᾧ σὺ μεμαρτύρηκας — ἴδε οὗτος
Jordan, to whom you have testified — behold this *man*

βαπτίζει, καὶ πάντες ἔρχονται πρὸς αὐτόν."
is baptizing, and all *men* are coming to Him."

27 Ἀπεκρίθη Ἰωάννης καὶ εἶπεν, "Οὐ δύναται ἄνθρωπος
answered ˜ John and said, "[4]not [3]is [5]able [1]A [2]man
"A man can receive

λαμβάνειν οὐδὲν ἐὰν μὴ ᾖ δεδομένον αὐτῷ ἐκ τοῦ
to receive nothing if not it is given to him from -
nothing unless it has been given

οὐρανοῦ. **28** Αὐτοὶ ὑμεῖς[e] μαρτυρεῖτε ὅτι εἶπον, 'Οὐκ εἰμὶ
heaven. yourselves ˜ You testify that I said, '[2]not [3]am

ἐγὼ ὁ Χριστός,' ἀλλ' ὅτι 'Ἀπεσταλμένος εἰμὶ ἔμπροσθεν
[1]I the Christ,' but - '[3]sent [1]I [2]am before
Messiah,' 'I have been sent

ἐκείνου.' **29** Ὁ ἔχων τὴν νύμφην νυμφίος ἐστίν·
that *One*.' The *one* having the bride [2]*the* [3]bridegroom [1]is;
Him.' He who has

ὁ δὲ φίλος τοῦ νυμφίου, ὁ ἑστηκὼς καὶ ἀκούων
the ˜ but friend of the bridegroom, the *one* standing and hearing
who stands hears

αὐτοῦ, χαρᾷ χαίρει διὰ τὴν φωνὴν τοῦ νυμφίου. Αὕτη
him, with joy rejoices because of the voice of the bridegroom. this ˜

οὖν ἡ χαρὰ ἡ ἐμὴ πεπλήρωται. **30** Ἐκεῖνον
Therefore - joy ˜ - my has been fulfilled. [5]that [6]*One*
Him

δεῖ αὐξάνειν, ἐμὲ δὲ ἐλαττοῦσθαι.
[1]It [2]is [3]necessary [4]*for* to increase, [2]for [3]me [1]but to decrease.

31 "Ὁ ἄνωθεν ἐρχόμενος ἐπάνω πάντων ἐστίν.
"The *One* [2]from [3]above [1]coming [5]above [6]all [4]is.
"He who comes

Ὁ ὢν ἐκ τῆς γῆς, ἐκ τῆς γῆς ἐστι καὶ ἐκ τῆς
The *one* being from the earth, [2]from [3]the [4]earth [1]is and [2]from [3]the
He who is

22 After these things Jesus and His disciples came into the land of Judea, and there He remained with them and baptized.
23 Now John also was baptizing in Aenon near Salim, because there was much water there. And they came and were baptized.
24 For John had not yet been thrown into prison.
25 Then there arose a dispute between *some* of John's disciples and the Jews about purification.
26 And they came to John and said to him, "Rabbi, He who was with you beyond the Jordan, to whom you have testified—behold, He is baptizing, and all are coming to Him!"
27 John answered and said, "A man can receive nothing unless it has been given to him from heaven.
28 "You yourselves bear me witness, that I said, 'I am not the Christ,' but, 'I have been sent before Him.'
29 "He who has the bride is the bridegroom; but the friend of the bridegroom, who stands and hears him, rejoices greatly because of the bridegroom's voice. Therefore this joy of mine is fulfilled.
30 "He must increase, but I *must* decrease.
31 "He who comes from above is above all; he who is of the earth is earthly and speaks

e(3:28) NU adds *μοι, (testify of) me.*

sued. The word can also mean those things required by *justice* or *righteousness* (Luke 11:42). Cf. the synonym *κρίμα*; the cognates *κριτής, a judge; κριτικός, able to judge;* and *κρίνω, judge, condemn.*

of the earth. He who comes
from heaven is above all.
32 "And what He has seen and
heard, that He testifies; and no
one receives His testimony.
33 "He who has received His
testimony has certified that
God is true.
34 "For He whom God has
sent speaks the words of God,
for God does not give the Spirit
by measure.
35 "The Father loves the Son,
and has given all things into His
hand.
36 "He who believes in the
Son has everlasting life; and he
who does not believe the Son
shall not see life, but the wrath
of God abides on him."
4 Therefore, when the Lord
knew that the Pharisees
had heard that Jesus made and
baptized more disciples than
John
2 (though Jesus Himself did
not baptize, but His disciples),
3 He left Judea and departed
again to Galilee.
4 But He needed to go
through Samaria.
5 So He came to a city of Samaria which is called Sychar,
near the plot of ground that Jacob gave to his son Joseph.
6 Now Jacob's well was
there. Jesus therefore, being
wearied from *His* journey, sat
thus by the well. It was about
the sixth hour.
7 A woman of Samaria came

γῆς λαλεῖ. Ὁ ἐκ τοῦ οὐρανοῦ ἐρχόμενος ἐπάνω
[4]earth [1]speaks. The *One* [2]from - [3]heaven [1]coming [5]above
He who comes

πάντων ἐστί. **32** Καί[f] ὃ ἑώρακε καὶ ἤκουσε, τοῦτο
[6]all [4]is. And what He has seen and heard, this

μαρτυρεῖ· καὶ τὴν μαρτυρίαν αὐτοῦ οὐδεὶς λαμβάνει.
He testifies; and - [5]testimony [4]His [1]no [2]one [3]receives.

33 Ὁ λαβὼν αὐτοῦ τὴν μαρτυρίαν ἐσφράγισεν ὅτι ὁ
The *one* receiving His - testimony has sealed that -
who receives certified

Θεὸς ἀληθής ἐστιν. **34** Ὃν γὰρ ἀπέστειλεν ὁ Θεὸς τὰ
God true ˜ is. [2]*He* [3]whom [1]For sent ˜ - God [2]the

ῥήματα τοῦ Θεοῦ λαλεῖ, οὐ γὰρ ἐκ μέτρου δίδωσιν ὁ
[3]sayings - [4]of [5]God [1]speaks, [9]not [6]for [13]by [14]measure [8]does [10]give -
words

Θεὸς[g] τὸ Πνεῦμα. **35** Ὁ Πατὴρ ἀγαπᾷ τὸν Υἱὸν καὶ
[7]God [11]the [12]Spirit. The Father loves the Son and

πάντα δέδωκεν ἐν τῇ χειρὶ αὐτοῦ. **36** Ὁ πιστεύων
[4]all [5]*things* [1]He [2]has [3]given into - hand ˜ His. The *one* believing
who believes

εἰς τὸν Υἱὸν ἔχει ζωὴν αἰώνιον· ὁ δὲ ἀπειθῶν τῷ Υἱῷ
in the Son has life ˜ eternal; [2]the [3]*one* [1]but disobeying the Son
who disobeys

οὐκ ὄψεται τὴν ζωήν, ἀλλ' ἡ ὀργὴ τοῦ Θεοῦ μένει ἐπ'
not ˜ will see - life, but the wrath - of God abides on

αὐτόν."
him."

Jesus Witnesses to a Samaritan Woman

4 **1** Ὡς οὖν ἔγνω ὁ Κύριος[a] ὅτι ἤκουσαν οἱ
when ˜ Therefore [3]knew [1]the [2]Lord that [3]heard [1]the
had heard

Φαρισαῖοι ὅτι Ἰησοῦς πλείονας μαθητὰς ποιεῖ καὶ
[2]Pharisees that Jesus [6]more [7]disciples [1]is [2]making [3]and
was

βαπτίζει ἢ Ἰωάννης **2** (καίτοιγε Ἰησοῦς αὐτὸς οὐκ
[4]is [5]baptizing than John (although Jesus Himself not ˜
was

ἐβάπτιζεν, ἀλλ' οἱ μαθηταὶ αὐτοῦ), **3** ἀφῆκε τὴν Ἰουδαίαν καὶ
was baptizing, but - disciples ˜ His), He left - Judea and

ἀπῆλθεν[b] εἰς τὴν Γαλιλαίαν. **4** Ἔδει δὲ αὐτὸν
went away into - Galilee. [2]it [3]was [4]necessary [5]*for* [1]But Him

διέρχεσθαι διὰ τῆς Σαμαρείας. **5** Ἔρχεται οὖν εἰς
to go through - Samaria. [2]He [3]comes [1]Therefore to
came

πόλιν τῆς Σαμαρείας λεγομένην Συχάρ, πλησίον τοῦ
a city - of Samaria being called Sychar, near the
called

χωρίου ὃ ἔδωκεν Ἰακὼβ Ἰωσὴφ τῷ υἱῷ αὐτοῦ. **6** Ἦν
piece of land which gave ˜ Jacob to Joseph - son ˜ his. [6]was

δὲ ἐκεῖ πηγὴ τοῦ Ἰακώβ. Ὁ οὖν Ἰησοῦς,
[1]Now [7]there [2]a [3]fountain - [4]of [5]Jacob. - Therefore Jesus,
the well

κεκοπιακὼς ἐκ τῆς ὁδοιπορίας, ἐκαθέζετο οὕτως ἐπὶ τῇ
having become tired from the journey, was sitting thus by the

πηγῇ. Ὥρα ἦν ὡσεὶ ἕκτη. **7** Ἔρχεται γυνὴ ἐκ τῆς
fountain. [6]hour [1]It [2]was [3]about [4]*the* [5]sixth. [5]comes [1]A [2]woman [3]of -
well. came

---

f(**3:32**) NU omits Και, *And.*
g(**3:34**) NU omits ο Θεος, *God.*
a(**4:1**) NU reads Ιησους, *Jesus.*
b(**4:3**) NU adds παλιν, *again.*

Σαμαρείας ἀντλῆσαι ὕδωρ. Λέγει αὐτῇ ὁ Ἰησοῦς, "Δός μοι
[4]Samaria to draw water. [2]says [3]to [4]her - [1]Jesus, "Give Me
said

πιεῖν." 8 Οἱ γὰρ μαθηταὶ αὐτοῦ ἀπεληλύθεισαν εἰς τὴν πόλιν
to drink." - For disciples ~ His had gone away into the city
a drink."

ἵνα τροφὰς ἀγοράσωσι.
so that [4]food [1]they [2]might [3]buy.

9 Λέγει οὖν αὐτῷ ἡ γυνὴ ἡ Σαμαρεῖτις, "Πῶς
[5]says [1]Therefore [6]to [7]Him [2]the [4]woman - [3]Samaritan, "How
said

σύ, Ἰουδαῖος ὤν, παρ' ἐμοῦ πιεῖν αἰτεῖς, οὔσης γυναικὸς
[2]You, [4]a [5]Jew [3]being, [9]from [10]me [7]to [8]drink [1]do [6]ask, being a woman ~
for a

Σαμαρείτιδος?" Οὐ γὰρ συγχρῶνται* Ἰουδαῖοι Σαμαρείταις.
Samaritan?" [4]not [1]For [3]do [5]associate [2]Jews with Samaritans.

10 Ἀπεκρίθη Ἰησοῦς καὶ εἶπεν αὐτῇ, "Εἰ ᾔδεις τὴν
answered ~ Jesus and said to her, "If you knew the

δωρεὰν τοῦ θεοῦ καὶ τίς ἐστιν ὁ λέγων σοι, 'Δός μοι
gift - of God and who is the *One* saying to you, 'Give Me

πιεῖν,' σὺ ἂν ᾔτησας αὐτὸν καὶ ἔδωκεν ἄν
to drink,' you - would have asked Him and He would have given -
a

σοι ὕδωρ ζῶν."
to you water ~ living."

11 Λέγει αὐτῷ ἡ γυνή, "Κύριε, οὔτε ἄντλημα
[3]says [4]to [5]Him [1]The [2]woman, "Sir, [3]no [4]bucket
said

ἔχεις καὶ τὸ φρέαρ ἐστὶ βαθύ. Πόθεν οὖν ἔχεις
[1]You [2]have and the well is deep. how ~ Therefore do You have

τὸ ὕδωρ τὸ ζῶν? 12 Μὴ σὺ μείζων εἶ τοῦ πατρὸς
the water ~ - living? *Surely* [3]not [1]You [4]greater [2]are - [7]father

ἡμῶν Ἰακὼβ ὃς ἔδωκεν ἡμῖν τὸ φρέαρ καὶ αὐτὸς ἐξ
[5]*than* [6]our Jacob, *are You* who gave us the well and he [2]from

αὐτοῦ ἔπιε καὶ οἱ υἱοὶ αὐτοῦ καὶ τὰ θρέμματα
[3]it [1]drank and - sons ~ his and - [2]domesticated [3]animals
flock

αὐτοῦ?"
[1]his?"

13 Ἀπεκρίθη Ἰησοῦς καὶ εἶπεν αὐτῇ, "Πᾶς ὁ πίνων
answered ~ Jesus and said to her, "Every - *one* drinking
"Everyone who drinks

ἐκ τοῦ ὕδατος τούτου διψήσει πάλιν, 14 ὃς δ' ἂν πίῃ
from - water ~ this will thirst again, who ~ But ever drinks

ἐκ τοῦ ὕδατος οὗ ἐγὼ δώσω αὐτῷ οὐ μὴ διψήσῃ εἰς
from the water which I shall give him [2]not [3]not [1]will [4]thirst into
will by no means ever

τὸν αἰῶνα. Ἀλλὰ τὸ ὕδωρ ὃ δώσω αὐτῷ γενήσεται ἐν
the age. But the water which I shall give to him will become in
thirst again.

αὐτῷ πηγὴ ὕδατος ἁλλομένου εἰς ζωὴν αἰώνιον."
him a fountain of water springing up into life ~ eternal."

15 Λέγει πρὸς αὐτὸν ἡ γυνή, "Κύριε, δός μοι τοῦτο τὸ
[3]says [4]to [5]Him [1]The [2]woman, "Sir, give me this -
said

ὕδωρ ἵνα μὴ διψῶ μηδὲ ἔρχωμαι ἐνθάδε ἀντλεῖν."
water so that [3]not [1]I [2]may thirst nor come here to draw."

to draw water. Jesus said to her, "Give Me a drink."

8 For His disciples had gone away into the city to buy food.

9 Then the woman of Samaria said to Him, "How is it that You, being a Jew, ask a drink from me, a Samaritan woman?" For Jews have no dealings with Samaritans.

10 Jesus answered and said to her, "If you knew the gift of God, and who it is who says to you, 'Give Me a drink,' you would have asked Him, and He would have given you living water."

11 The woman said to Him, "Sir, You have nothing to draw with, and the well is deep. Where then do You get that living water?

12 "Are You greater than our father Jacob, who gave us the well, and drank from it himself, as well as his sons and his livestock?"

13 Jesus answered and said to her, "Whoever drinks of this water will thirst again,

14 "but whoever drinks of the water that I shall give him will never thirst. But the water that I shall give him will become in him a fountain of water springing up into everlasting life."

15 The woman said to Him, "Sir, give me this water, that I may not thirst, nor come here to draw."

***(4:9)** *συγχράομαι (synchraomai).* Verb, a compound form from *σύν, with* and *χράομαι, use,* hence to *join in using.* Here it may express the fact that Jews and Samaritans did not *share* the same drinking vessels. Most interpreters believe, however, that it has the broader, metaphorical use *associate* or *have dealings with,* even in this context.

16 Jesus said to her, "Go, call your husband, and come here."
17 The woman answered and said, "I have no husband." Jesus said to her, "You have well said, 'I have no husband,'
18 "for you have had five husbands, and the one whom you now have is not your husband; in that you spoke truly."
19 The woman said to Him, "Sir, I perceive that You are a prophet.
20 "Our fathers worshiped on this mountain, and you *Jews* say that in Jerusalem is the place where one ought to worship."
21 Jesus said to her, "Woman, believe Me, the hour is coming when you will neither on this mountain, nor in Jerusalem, worship the Father.
22 "You worship what you do not know; we know what we worship, for salvation is of the Jews.
23 "But the hour is coming, and now is, when the true worshipers will worship the Father in spirit and truth; for the Father is seeking such to worship Him.
24 "God *is* Spirit, and those who worship Him must worship in spirit and truth."
25 The woman said to Him, "I know that Messiah is coming" (who is called Christ). "When

16 Λέγει αὐτῇ ὁ Ἰησοῦς,[c] "Ὕπαγε, φώνησον τὸν ἄνδρα
[2]says (said) [3]to [4]her - [1]Jesus, "Go, call - husband ˜
σου καὶ ἐλθὲ ἐνθάδε."
your and come here."

17 Ἀπεκρίθη ἡ γυνὴ καὶ εἶπεν,[d] "Οὐκ ἔχω
[3]answered [1]The [2]woman and said, "[3]not [1]I [2]do have
ἄνδρα."
a husband."

Λέγει αὐτῇ ὁ Ἰησοῦς, "Καλῶς εἶπας ὅτι 'Ἄνδρα οὐκ
[2]says (said) [3]to [4]her - [1]Jesus, "[7]well [5]You [6]said - 'A husband [3]not
ἔχω,' **18** πέντε γὰρ ἄνδρας ἔσχες, καὶ νῦν
[1]I [2]do have,' [5]five [1]for [6]husbands [2]you [3]have [4]had, and [6]now
ὃν ἔχεις οὐκ ἔστι σου ἀνήρ· τοῦτο ἀληθὲς
[1]*the* [2]*one* [3]whom [4]you [5]have [8]not [7]is your husband; this [4]truly
εἴρηκας."
[1]you [2]have [3]said."

19 Λέγει αὐτῷ ἡ γυνή, "Κύριε, θεωρῶ ὅτι προφήτης
[3]says (said) [4]to [5]Him [1]The [2]woman, "Sir, I perceive that [3]a [4]prophet
εἶ σύ. **20** Οἱ πατέρες ἡμῶν ἐν τῷ ὄρει τούτῳ
[2]are [1]You. - fathers ˜ Our [2]on - [4]mountain [3]this
προσεκύνησαν, καὶ ὑμεῖς λέγετε ὅτι ἐν Ἱεροσολύμοις ἐστὶν
[1]worshiped, and you *Jews* say that in Jerusalem is
ὁ τόπος ὅπου δεῖ προσκυνεῖν."
the place where it is necessary to worship."

21 Λέγει αὐτῇ ὁ Ἰησοῦς, "Γύναι, πίστευσόν μοι ὅτι
[2]says (said) [3]to [4]her - [1]Jesus, "Woman, believe Me that
ἔρχεται ὥρα ὅτε οὔτε ἐν τῷ ὄρει τούτῳ οὔτε ἐν
[3]is [4]coming [1]an [2]hour (the time) when neither on - mountain ˜ this nor in
Ἱεροσολύμοις προσκυνήσετε τῷ Πατρί. **22** Ὑμεῖς προσκυνεῖτε
Jerusalem will you worship the Father. You worship
ὃ οὐκ οἴδατε· ἡμεῖς προσκυνοῦμεν ὃ οἴδαμεν,
what [3]not [1]you [2]do know; we *Jews* worship what we know,
ὅτι ἡ σωτηρία ἐκ τῶν Ἰουδαίων ἐστίν. **23** Ἀλλ' ἔρχεται
because - salvation [2]from [3]the [4]Jews [1]is. But [3]is [4]coming
ὥρα καὶ νῦν ἐστιν, ὅτε οἱ ἀληθινοὶ προσκυνηταὶ
[1]an [2]hour (the time) and now is, when the true worshipers
προσκυνήσουσι τῷ Πατρὶ ἐν πνεύματι καὶ ἀληθείᾳ· καὶ γὰρ
will worship the Father in spirit and truth; indeed ˜ for
ὁ Πατὴρ τοιούτους ζητεῖ τοὺς προσκυνοῦντας αὐτόν.
the Father [3]such [1]is [2]seeking - *ones* worshiping (to worship) Him.

24 Πνεῦμα ὁ Θεός, καὶ τοὺς προσκυνοῦντας αὐτὸν ἐν
[2]*is* [3]Spirit - [1]God, and [5]the [6]*ones* (those) [7]worshiping (who worship) [8]Him [11]in
πνεύματι καὶ ἀληθείᾳ δεῖ προσκυνεῖν."
[12]spirit [13]and [14]truth [1]it [2]is [3]necessary [4]*for* [9]to [10]worship."

25 Λέγει αὐτῷ ἡ γυνή, "Οἶδα ὅτι Μεσίας* ἔρχεται"
[3]says (said) [4]to [5]Him [1]The [2]woman, "I know that Messiah is coming"
(ὁ λεγόμενος Χριστός). "Ὅταν ἔλθῃ ἐκεῖνος,
(the *One* being called (called) Christ (Anointed One)). "When [3]comes [1]that [2]*One,*

[c](4:16) NU omits ο Ιησους, *Jesus.* [d](4:17) NU adds αυτω, *to him.*

*(4:25) Μεσίας *(Mesias).* Noun, a transliteration of the Hebrew and Aramaic words for *anointed one,* which has been hellenized by ending in sigma as do Greek masculine nouns of first declension. Μεσίας appears only here and in John 1:41 in the NT. The Samaritans were ethnically half Jewish, so a Samaritan woman could have been familiar with this word. In both instances it is parenthetically translated by the Greek form Χριστός, *Christ, Anointed One.*

ἀναγγελεῖ ἡμῖν πάντα."
He will proclaim to us all *things*."

26 Λέγει αὐτῇ ὁ Ἰησοῦς, "Ἐγώ εἰμι, ὁ λαλῶν
[2]says [3]to [4]her - [1]Jesus, "I am *He*, the *One* speaking
said

σοι."
to you."

The Disciples View the Whitened Harvest

27 Καὶ ἐπὶ τούτῳ ἦλθον οἱ μαθηταὶ αὐτοῦ καὶ ἐθαύμασαν
And upon this came - disciples ˜ His and marveled
at this point

ὅτι μετὰ γυναικὸς ἐλάλει· οὐδεὶς μέντοι εἶπε, "Τί
that with a woman He was speaking; no one however said, "What

ζητεῖς?" ἢ "Τί λαλεῖς μετ' αὐτῆς?"
do You seek?" or "Why are You speaking with her?"

28 Ἀφῆκεν οὖν τὴν ὑδρίαν αὐτῆς ἡ γυνὴ καὶ
[4]left [1]Then - [6]water [7]jar [5]her [2]the [3]woman and

ἀπῆλθεν εἰς τὴν πόλιν καὶ λέγει τοῖς ἀνθρώποις, 29 "Δεῦτε,
went away into the city and says to the men, "Come,
said

ἴδετε ἄνθρωπον ὃς εἶπέ μοι πάντα ὅσα ἐποίησα. Μήτι
see a man who told me all *things* as many as I did. [3]not
everything I ever did.

οὗτός ἐστιν ὁ Χριστός?" 30 Ἐξῆλθον ἐκ τῆς πόλεως καὶ
[1]This [2]is [4]the [5]Christ, *is it?*" They went out of the city and

ἤρχοντο πρὸς αὐτόν.
were coming to Him.

31 Ἐν δὲ τῷ μεταξὺ ἠρώτων αὐτὸν οἱ μαθηταί,
in ˜ But the meantime [3]were [4]requesting [5]*of* [6]Him [1]the [2]disciples,

λέγοντες, "Ῥαββί, φάγε."
saying, "Rabbi, eat."

32 Ὁ δὲ εἶπεν αὐτοῖς, "Ἐγὼ βρῶσιν ἔχω φαγεῖν
[2]the [3]*One* [1]But said to them, "I food ˜ have to eat
He

ἣν ὑμεῖς οὐκ οἴδατε."
which you not ˜ do know."

33 Ἔλεγον οὖν οἱ μαθηταὶ πρὸς ἀλλήλους, "Μή
[4]were [5]saying [1]Therefore [2]the [3]disciples to one another, "[3]not

τις ἤνεγκεν αὐτῷ φαγεῖν?"
[1]Someone [2]has [4]brought Him *something* to eat, *has he?*"

34 Λέγει αὐτοῖς ὁ Ἰησοῦς, "Ἐμὸν βρῶμά ἐστιν ἵνα
[2]says [3]to [4]them - [1]Jesus, "My food is that
said

ποιῶ[e] τὸ θέλημα τοῦ πέμψαντός με καὶ τελειώσω αὐτοῦ
I may do the will of the *One* having sent Me and finish His
Him who

τὸ ἔργον. 35 Οὐχ ὑμεῖς λέγετε ὅτι 'Ἔτι τετράμηνός ἐστι
- work. [3]not [2]you [1]Do [4]say - '[3]still [4]four [5]months [1]*There* [2]are

καὶ ὁ θερισμὸς ἔρχεται'? Ἰδού, λέγω ὑμῖν, ἐπάρατε τοὺς
and the harvest comes'? Behold, I say to you, lift up -

ὀφθαλμοὺς ὑμῶν καὶ θεάσασθε τὰς χώρας, ὅτι λευκαί εἰσι
eyes ˜ your and observe the fields, that [4]white [1]they [2]are

πρὸς θερισμὸν ἤδη! 36 Καὶ ὁ θερίζων μισθὸν λαμβάνει
[5]for [6]harvest [3]already! And the *one* reaping wages ˜ receives

καὶ συνάγει καρπὸν εἰς ζωὴν αἰώνιον, ἵνα καὶ ὁ
and gathers fruit for life ˜ eternal, so that also the *one*

He comes, He will tell us all things."
26 Jesus said to her, "I who speak to you am *He*."
27 And at this *point* His disciples came, and they marveled that He talked with a woman; yet no one said, "What do You seek?" or, "Why are You talking with her?"
28 The woman then left her waterpot, went her way into the city, and said to the men,
29 "Come, see a Man who told me all things that I ever did. Could this be the Christ?"
30 Then they went out of the city and came to Him.
31 In the meantime His disciples urged Him, saying, "Rabbi, eat."
32 But He said to them, "I have food to eat of which you do not know."
33 Therefore the disciples said to one another, "Has anyone brought Him *anything* to eat?"
34 Jesus said to them, "My food is to do the will of Him who sent Me, and to finish His work.
35 "Do you not say, 'There are still four months and *then* comes the harvest'? Behold, I say to you, lift up your eyes and look at the fields, for they are already white for harvest!
36 "And he who reaps receives wages, and gathers fruit for eternal life, that both he

[e](4:34) NU reads ποιησω, *I should do.*

who sows and he who reaps
may rejoice together.
37 "For in this the saying is
true: 'One sows and another
reaps.'
38 "I sent you to reap that for
which you have not labored;
others have labored, and you
have entered into their labors."
39 And many of the Samaritans of that city believed in Him
because of the word of the
woman who testified, "He told
me all that I *ever* did."
40 So when the Samaritans
had come to Him, they urged
Him to stay with them; and He
stayed there two days.
41 And many more believed
because of His own word.
42 Then they said to the
woman, "Now we believe, not
because of what you said, for
we ourselves have heard *Him*
and we know that this is indeed
the Christ, the Savior of the
world."
43 Now after the two days He
departed from there and went
to Galilee.
44 For Jesus Himself testified
that a prophet has no honor in
his own country.
45 So when He came to Galilee, the Galileans received
Him, having seen all the things
He did in Jerusalem at the
feast; for they also had gone to
the feast.
46 So Jesus came again to

σπείρων ὁμοῦ χαίρῃ καὶ ὁ θερίζων. **37** Ἐν γὰρ
sowing [7]together [5]may [6]rejoice [1]and [2]the [3]*one* [4]reaping. in ˜ For

τούτῳ ὁ λόγος ἐστὶν ὁ ἀληθινὸς ὅτι '"Ἄλλος ἐστὶν ὁ
this the word (saying) is - true - 'Another ('One) is (sows) the *one*

σπείρων καὶ ἄλλος ὁ θερίζων.' **38** Ἐγὼ ἀπέστειλα ὑμᾶς
sowing and another the *one* reaping.' (reaps.') I sent you

θερίζειν ὃ οὐχ ὑμεῖς κεκοπιάκατε· ἄλλοι
to reap that *for which* [3]not [1]you [2]have labored; others

κεκοπιάκασι, καὶ ὑμεῖς εἰς τὸν κόπον αὐτῶν εἰσεληλύθατε."
have labored, and you [3]into - [5]work [4]their [1]have [2]entered."

Samaritans Accept Jesus as Savior of the World

39 Ἐκ δὲ τῆς πόλεως ἐκείνης πολλοὶ ἐπίστευσαν εἰς
from ˜ And - city ˜ that many [4]believed [5]in

αὐτὸν τῶν Σαμαρειτῶν διὰ τὸν λόγον τῆς γυναικὸς
[6]Him [1]of [2]the [3]Samaritans because of the word of the woman

μαρτυρούσης ὅτι "Εἶπέ μοι πάντα ὅσα ἐποίησα."
testifying - "He told me all *things* (everything) as many as (I ever) I did." (did.")

40 Ὡς οὖν ἦλθον πρὸς αὐτὸν οἱ Σαμαρεῖται,
when ˜ Therefore [3]came [4]to [5]Him [1]the [2]Samaritans,

ἠρώτων αὐτὸν μεῖναι παρ' αὐτοῖς· καὶ ἔμεινεν ἐκεῖ δύο
they were asking Him to stay with them; and He stayed there two

ἡμέρας. **41** Καὶ πολλῷ πλείους ἐπίστευσαν διὰ τὸν λόγον
days. And by many (many) more (more) they believed (believed) because of - word ˜

αὐτοῦ, **42** τῇ τε γυναικὶ ἔλεγον ὅτι "Οὐκέτι
His, [2]to [3]the [1]And woman they were saying - "No longer

διὰ τὴν σὴν λαλιὰν πιστεύομεν, αὐτοὶ γὰρ
because of - your speech do we believe, [3]ourselves [1]for

ἀκηκόαμεν καὶ οἴδαμεν ὅτι οὗτός ἐστιν ἀληθῶς ὁ Σωτὴρ
[2]we have heard and know that this is truly the Savior

τοῦ κόσμου, ὁ Χριστός."[f]
of the world, the Christ." (Messiah.")

Galileans Welcome Jesus

43 Μετὰ δὲ τὰς δύο ἡμέρας ἐξῆλθεν ἐκεῖθεν καὶ
after ˜ And - two days He went out from there and

ἀπῆλθεν[g] εἰς τὴν Γαλιλαίαν. **44** Αὐτὸς γὰρ ὁ Ἰησοῦς
went away into - Galilee. [3]Himself [1]For - [2]Jesus

ἐμαρτύρησεν ὅτι προφήτης ἐν τῇ ἰδίᾳ πατρίδι τιμὴν οὐκ
testified that a prophet [5]in - [6]his [7]own [8]country [4]honor [2]not

ἔχει. **45** Ὅτε οὖν ἦλθεν εἰς τὴν Γαλιλαίαν,
[1]does [3]have. when ˜ Therefore He came into - Galilee,

ἐδέξαντο αὐτὸν οἱ Γαλιλαῖοι, πάντα ἑωρακότες ἃ
[3]received [4]Him [1]the [2]Galileans, [7]all [8]*the* [9]*things* [5]having [6]seen which

ἐποίησεν ἐν Ἱεροσολύμοις ἐν τῇ ἑορτῇ· καὶ αὐτοὶ γὰρ ἦλθον
He did in Jerusalem at the feast; [3]also [2]they [1]for went (had gone)

εἰς τὴν ἑορτήν.
to the feast.

Jesus Heals a Nobleman's Son

46 Ἦλθεν οὖν πάλιν ὁ Ἰησοῦς[h] εἰς τὴν Κανὰ τῆς
[3]came [1]Then [4]again - [2]Jesus into - Cana -

f(4:42) NU omits ο Χριστος, *the Christ.*
g(4:43) NU omits και απηλθεν, *and went away.*
h(4:46) NU omits ο Ιησους, *Jesus.*

Γαλιλαίας ὅπου ἐποίησε τὸ ὕδωρ οἶνον. Καὶ ἦν τις
of Galilee where He made the water wine. And *there* was a certain
βασιλικὸς οὗ ὁ υἱὸς ἠσθένει ἐν Καπερναούμ. **47** Οὗτος
royal official whose - son was sick in Capernaum. This *man*
ἀκούσας ὅτι Ἰησοῦς ἥκει ἐκ τῆς Ἰουδαίας εἰς τὴν
having heard that Jesus has (had) come out of - Judea into -
Γαλιλαίαν, ἀπῆλθε πρὸς αὐτὸν καὶ ἠρώτα αὐτὸν[i] ἵνα
Galilee, went to Him and asked Him that
καταβῇ καὶ ἰάσηται αὐτοῦ τὸν υἱόν, ἔμελλε γὰρ
He might come down and heal his - son, [2]he [3]was [4]about [1]for
ἀποθνῄσκειν.
to die.

48 Εἶπεν οὖν ὁ Ἰησοῦς πρὸς αὐτόν, "Ἐὰν μὴ σημεῖα
[3]said [1]Then - [2]Jesus to him, "If not ("Unless) [4]signs
καὶ τέρατα ἴδητε, οὐ μὴ πιστεύσητε."
[5]and [6]wonders [1]you [2]*people* [3]see, [9]not [10]not (by no means) [7]you [8]will [11]believe."

49 Λέγει πρὸς αὐτὸν ὁ βασιλικός, "Κύριε, κατάβηθι
[4]says (said) [5]to [6]Him [1]The [2]royal [3]official, "Sir, come down
πρὶν ἀποθανεῖν τὸ παιδίον μου!"
before [3]to [4]die (dies) - [2]child ~ [1]my!"

50 Λέγει αὐτῷ ὁ Ἰησοῦς, "Πορεύου· ὁ υἱός σου ζῇ." Καὶ
[2]says (said) [3]to [4]him - [1]Jesus, "Go; - son ~ your lives." And
ἐπίστευσεν ὁ ἄνθρωπος τῷ λόγῳ ᾧ εἶπεν αὐτῷ ὁ
[3]believed [1]the [2]man the word which [2]said [3]to [4]him -
Ἰησοῦς, καὶ ἐπορεύετο.
[1]Jesus, and he was departing (set out on his journey).

51 Ἤδη δὲ αὐτοῦ καταβαίνοντος, οἱ δοῦλοι αὐτοῦ
already ~ And him (as he) going (was going) down, - servants ~ his
ἀπήντησαν αὐτῷ καὶ ἀπήγγειλαν,[j] λέγοντες ὅτι "Ὁ παῖς
met him and reported, saying - - "child ~
σου[k] ζῇ!" **52** Ἐπύθετο οὖν παρ' αὐτῶν τὴν ὥραν ἐν
Your lives!" [2]he [3]inquired [1]Therefore from them the hour at
ᾗ κομψότερον ἔσχε. Καὶ εἶπον αὐτῷ ὅτι "Χθὲς
which [4]better (he got better) [1]he [2]had [3]*it*. And they said to him - "Yesterday
ὥραν ἑβδόμην ἀφῆκεν αὐτὸν ὁ πυρετός." **53** Ἔγνω
at the hour ~ seventh [3]left [4]him [1]the [2]fever." [4]knew
οὖν ὁ πατὴρ ὅτι ἐν ἐκείνῃ τῇ ὥρᾳ ἐν ᾗ εἶπεν
[1]Therefore [2]the [3]father that *it was* at that - hour in which [2]said
αὐτῷ ὁ Ἰησοῦς ὅτι "Ὁ υἱός σου ζῇ." Καὶ ἐπίστευσεν αὐτὸς
[3]to [4]him - [1]Jesus - - "son ~ Your lives." And believed ~ he
καὶ ἡ οἰκία αὐτοῦ ὅλη. **54** Τοῦτο πάλιν δεύτερον σημεῖον
and - [3]household [1]his [2]whole. This again *is the* second sign
ἐποίησεν ὁ Ἰησοῦς, ἐλθὼν ἐκ τῆς Ἰουδαίας εἰς τὴν
did ~ - Jesus, coming (after He had come) out of - Judea into -
Γαλιλαίαν.
Galilee.

Cana of Galilee where He had made the water wine. And there was a certain nobleman whose son was sick at Capernaum.
47 When he heard that Jesus had come out of Judea into Galilee, he went to Him and implored Him to come down and heal his son, for he was at the point of death.
48 Then Jesus said to him, "Unless you *people* see signs and wonders, you will by no means believe."
49 The nobleman said to Him, "Sir, come down before my child dies!"
50 Jesus said to him, "Go your way; your son lives." So the man believed the word that Jesus spoke to him, and he went his way.
51 And as he was now going down, his servants met him and told *him,* saying, "Your son lives!"
52 Then he inquired of them the hour when he got better. And they said to him, "Yesterday at the seventh hour the fever left him."
53 So the father knew that *it was* at the same hour in which Jesus said to him, "Your son lives." And he himself believed, and his whole household.
54 This again *is* the second sign Jesus did when He had come out of Judea into Galilee.

[i](**4:47**) NU omits *αυτον, Him.* [j](**4:51**) NU omits *και απηγγειλαν, and reported.* [k](**4:51**) NU reads *αυτου, his.*

5 After this there was a
feast of the Jews, and Jesus went up to Jerusalem.
2 Now there is in Jerusalem
by the Sheep *Gate* a pool, which
is called in Hebrew, Bethesda,
having five porches.
3 In these lay a great multitude of sick people, blind, lame,
paralyzed, waiting for the moving of the water.
4 For an angel went down at
a certain time into the pool and
stirred up the water; then whoever stepped in first, after the
stirring of the water, was made
well of whatever disease he
had.
5 Now a certain man was
there who had an infirmity
thirty-eight years.
6 When Jesus saw him lying
there, and knew that he already
had been *in that condition* a
long time, He said to him, "Do
you want to be made well?"
7 The sick man answered
Him, "Sir, I have no man to put
me into the pool when the water is stirred up; but while I am
coming, another steps down
before me."
8 Jesus said to him, "Rise,
take up your bed and walk."
9 And immediately the man
was made well, took up his bed,

[a](5:2) NU reads Βηθζαθα, *Bethzatha.* [b](5:3) NU omits πολυ, *great.* [c](5:3) NU omits the rest of v. 3. [d](5:4) NU omits v. 4. [e](5:5) NU adds αυτου, *his.*

*(5:2) στοά *(stoa).* Noun meaning a *portico.* It describes a covered walkway bounded on one side by an exterior wall of a building or structure and on the other by a row of columns. Often such structures extended around all sides of an open courtyard, like a cloister in a monastery.

Jesus Heals a Man at the Pool of Bethesda

5 1 Μετὰ ταῦτα ἦν ἡ ἑορτὴ τῶν Ἰουδαίων, καὶ
After these *things there* was the feast of the Jews, and
ἀνέβη ὁ Ἰησοῦς εἰς Ἱεροσόλυμα. 2 Ἔστι δὲ ἐν τοῖς
[2]went [3]up - [1]Jesus to Jerusalem. [2]*there* [3]is [1]Now in -
Ἱεροσολύμοις ἐπὶ τῇ Προβατικῇ κολυμβήθρα ἡ
Jerusalem at the Sheep *Gate* a pool the *one*
which
ἐπιλεγομένη Ἑβραϊστὶ Βηθεσδά,[a] πέντε στοὰς* ἔχουσα.
being called in Hebrew Bethesda, [2]five [3]porticos [1]having.
is
3 Ἐν ταύταις κατέκειτο πλῆθος πολὺ[b] τῶν
In these *porticos* was lying a multitude ˜ great of the *ones*
sick
ἀσθενούντων, τυφλῶν, χωλῶν, ξηρῶν,[c] ἐκδεχομένων τὴν τοῦ
ailing, blind, lame, withered, waiting for the [2]of [3]the
people, paralyzed,
ὕδατος κίνησιν. 4 Ἄγγελος γὰρ κατὰ καιρὸν κατέβαινεν
[4]water [1]moving. [2]an [3]angel [1]For at a *certain* time would go down
ἐν τῇ κολυμβήθρᾳ καὶ ἐτάρασσε τὸ ὕδωρ· ὁ οὖν
in the pool and he would stir up the water; the ˜ therefore
πρῶτος ἐμβὰς μετὰ τὴν ταραχὴν τοῦ ὕδατος ὑγιὴς
first *one* having gone in after the stirring up of the water well ˜
ἐγίνετο ᾧ δήποτε κατείχετο νοσήματι.[d] 5 Ἦν
became - of whatever [2]he [3]was [4]held [5]fast [6]by [1]disease. [2]*there* [3]was
suffering
δέ τις ἄνθρωπος ἐκεῖ τριάκοντα καὶ ὀκτὼ ἔτη ἔχων ἐν
[1]Now a certain man there thirty and eight years having in
who had
τῇ ἀσθενείᾳ.[e]
the sickness.
an ailment.

6 Τοῦτον ἰδὼν ὁ Ἰησοῦς κατακείμενον, καὶ γνοὺς
[3]this [4]*man* [2]seeing - [1]Jesus lying *there,* and knowing
When Jesus saw knew
ὅτι πολὺν ἤδη χρόνον ἔχει, λέγει αὐτῷ,
that [6]much [2]already [7]time [1]he [3]has [4]*that* [5]*condition,* says to him,
a long had He said
"Θέλεις ὑγιὴς γενέσθαι?"
"Do you wish [3]well [1]to [2]become?"

7 Ἀπεκρίθη αὐτῷ ὁ ἀσθενῶν, "Κύριε, ἄνθρωπον οὐκ
[4]answered [5]Him [1]The [2]*one* [3]ailing, "Sir, [5]a [6]man [3]not
sick man,
ἔχω ἵνα, ὅταν ταραχθῇ τὸ ὕδωρ, βάλῃ με
[1]I [2]do [4]have so that, whenever [3]is [4]stirred [5]up [1]the [2]water, he may put me
εἰς τὴν κολυμβήθραν, ἐν ᾧ δὲ ἔρχομαι ἐγώ, ἄλλος
into the pool, [2]in [3]which [4]*time* [1]but [6]am [7]coming [5]I, another
while
πρὸ ἐμοῦ καταβαίνει."
before me goes down."

8 Λέγει αὐτῷ ὁ Ἰησοῦς, "Ἔγειραι, ἆρον τὸν κράββατόν
[2]says [3]to [4]him - [1]Jesus, "Arise, take up - pallet ˜
said
σου καὶ περιπάτει." 9 Καὶ εὐθέως ἐγένετο ὑγιὴς ὁ
your and walk." And immediately [3]became [4]well [1]the
ἄνθρωπος καὶ ἦρε τὸν κράββατον αὐτοῦ καὶ περιεπάτει.
[2]man and took up - pallet ˜ his and was walking.
began to walk.

10 Ἦν δὲ σάββατον ἐν ἐκείνῃ τῇ ἡμέρᾳ.
[2]it [3]was [1]Now a Sabbath on that - day.

Ἔλεγον οὖν οἱ Ἰουδαῖοι τῷ τεθεραπευμένῳ,
[4]said [1]Therefore [2]the [3]Jews to the *one* having been healed,
man who had

"Σάββατόν ἐστιν· οὐκ ἔξεστί σοι ἆραι τὸν
"[3]*the* [4]Sabbath [1]It [2]is; [7]not [5]it [6]is lawful for you to carry the
your

κράββατον."[f]
pallet."

11 Ἀπεκρίθη αὐτοῖς, "Ὁ ποιήσας με ὑγιῆ, ἐκεῖνός
He answered them, "The *One* having made me well, that *One*
who He

μοι εἶπεν, 'Ἆρον τὸν κράββατόν σου καὶ περιπάτει.' "
[2]to [3]me [1]said, 'Take up - pallet ~ your and walk.' "

12 Ἠρώτησαν οὖν αὐτόν, "Τίς ἐστιν ὁ ἄνθρωπος ὁ
[2]they [3]asked [1]Then him, "Who is the man the *one*
who

εἰπών σοι, 'Ἆρον τὸν κράββατόν σου[g] καὶ περιπάτει'?"
saying to you, 'Take up - pallet ~ your and walk'?"
said

13 Ὁ δὲ ἰαθεὶς οὐκ ᾔδει τίς ἐστιν, ὁ γὰρ
[2]the [3]one [1]But having been healed not ~ did know who He is, - for
man who was was,

Ἰησοῦς ἐξένευσεν, ὄχλου ὄντος ἐν τῷ τόπῳ.
Jesus withdrew, a crowd being in the place.
while a crowd was

14 Μετὰ ταῦτα εὑρίσκει αὐτὸν ὁ Ἰησοῦς ἐν τῷ ἱερῷ
After these *things* [2]finds [3]him - [1]Jesus in the temple
found

καὶ εἶπεν αὐτῷ, "Ἴδε ὑγιὴς γέγονας. Μηκέτι
and said to him, "See [4]well [1]you [2]have [3]become. No longer

ἁμάρτανε ἵνα μὴ χεῖρόν τί σοι γένηται."
sin so that [4]not [2]worse [1]something [6]to [7]you [3]may [5]happen."
lest

15 Ἀπῆλθεν ὁ ἄνθρωπος καὶ ἀνήγγειλε τοῖς Ἰουδαίοις ὅτι
[3]went [4]away [1]The [2]man and reported to the Jews that

Ἰησοῦς ἐστιν ὁ ποιήσας αὐτὸν ὑγιῆ.
Jesus is the *One* having made him well.
was who

Honor the Son Like the Father

16 Καὶ διὰ τοῦτο ἐδίωκον τὸν Ἰησοῦν οἱ
And because of this [3]were [4]persecuting - [5]Jesus [1]the

Ἰουδαῖοι καὶ ἐζήτουν αὐτὸν ἀποκτεῖναι,[h] ὅτι ταῦτα
[2]Jews and were seeking [3]Him [1]to [2]kill, because these *things*

ἐποίει ἐν σαββάτῳ.
He was doing on *the* Sabbath.

17 Ὁ δὲ Ἰησοῦς ἀπεκρίνατο αὐτοῖς, "Ὁ Πατήρ μου ἕως
- But Jesus answered them, - "Father ~ My until

ἄρτι ἐργάζεται κἀγὼ ἐργάζομαι." 18 Διὰ τοῦτο οὖν
now is working and I am working." Because of this therefore
has been

μᾶλλον ἐζήτουν αὐτὸν οἱ Ἰουδαῖοι ἀποκτεῖναι ὅτι
[5]all [6]the [7]more [3]were [4]seeking [10]Him [1]the [2]Jews [8]to [9]kill because

οὐ μόνον ἔλυε τὸ σάββατον ἀλλὰ καὶ Πατέρα
not only was He breaking the Sabbath but also [9]Father

and walked. And that day was the Sabbath.
10 The Jews therefore said to him who was cured, "It is the Sabbath; it is not lawful for you to carry your bed."
11 He answered them, "He who made me well said to me, 'Take up your bed and walk.' "
12 Then they asked him, "Who is the Man who said to you, 'Take up your bed and walk'?"
13 But the one who was healed did not know who it was, for Jesus had withdrawn, a multitude being in *that* place.
14 Afterward Jesus found him in the temple, and said to him, "See, you have been made well. Sin no more, lest a worse thing come upon you."
15 The man departed and told the Jews that it was Jesus who had made him well.
16 For this reason the Jews persecuted Jesus, and sought to kill Him, because He had done these things on the Sabbath.
17 But Jesus answered them, "My Father has been working until now, and I have been working."
18 Therefore the Jews sought all the more to kill Him, because He not only broke the Sabbath, but also said that God

---

f(**5:10**) NU adds σου, *your.*
g(**5:12**) NU omits τον κραββατον σου, *your pallet.*
h(**5:16**) NU omits και εζητουν αυτον αποκτειναι, *and were seeking to kill him.*

was His Father, making Himself equal with God.
19 Then Jesus answered and said to them, "Most assuredly, I say to you, the Son can do nothing of Himself, but what He sees the Father do; for whatever He does, the Son also does in like manner.
20 "For the Father loves the Son, and shows Him all things that He Himself does; and He will show Him greater works than these, that you may marvel.
21 "For as the Father raises the dead and gives life to *them,* even so the Son gives life to whom He will.
22 "For the Father judges no one, but has committed all judgment to the Son,
23 "that all should honor the Son just as they honor the Father. He who does not honor the Son does not honor the Father who sent Him.
24 "Most assuredly, I say to you, he who hears My word and believes in Him who sent Me has everlasting life, and shall not come into judgment, but has passed from death into life.
25 "Most assuredly, I say to you, the hour is coming, and now is, when the dead will hear the voice of the Son of God; and those who hear will live.
26 "For as the Father has life in Himself, so He has granted

ἴδιον ἔλεγε τὸν Θεόν, ἴσον ἑαυτὸν ποιῶν τῷ
[7]His [8]own [1]He [2]was [3]saying - [4]God [5]*to* [6]*be,* [12]equal [11]Himself [10]making -
that God was,

Θεῷ.
with God.

19 Ἀπεκρίνατο οὖν ὁ Ἰησοῦς καὶ εἶπεν αὐτοῖς, "Ἀμὴν
[3]answered [1]Then - [2]Jesus and said to them, "Amen
"Most

ἀμὴν λέγω ὑμῖν, οὐ δύναται ὁ Υἱὸς ποιεῖν ἀφ' ἑαυτοῦ
amen I say to you, [4]not [3]is [5]able [1]the [2]Son to do [2]of [3]Himself
assuredly

οὐδὲν ἐὰν μή τι βλέπῃ τὸν Πατέρα ποιοῦντα·
[1]nothing if not something He sees the Father doing;
anything except

ἃ γὰρ ἂν ἐκεῖνος ποιῇ, ταῦτα καὶ ὁ Υἱὸς
[2]*the* [3]*things* [4]which [1]for - that *One* does, these *things* also the Son
He

ὁμοίως ποιεῖ. 20 Ὁ γὰρ Πατὴρ φιλεῖ τὸν Υἱὸν καὶ πάντα
likewise does. the ~ For Father loves the Son and [5]all [6]*things*

δείκνυσιν αὐτῷ ἃ αὐτὸς ποιεῖ· καὶ μείζονα τούτων
[1]He [2]shows [3]to [4]Him which Himself ~ He does; and greater [2]*than* [3]these

δείξει αὐτῷ ἔργα, ἵνα ὑμεῖς θαυμάζητε. 21 Ὥσπερ
[4]He [5]will [6]show [7]Him [1]works, so that you may marvel. as ~
deeds,

γὰρ ὁ Πατὴρ ἐγείρει τοὺς νεκροὺς καὶ ζωοποιεῖ, οὕτω καὶ ὁ
For the Father raises the dead and gives life, thus also the

Υἱὸς οὓς θέλει ζωοποιεῖ. 22 Οὐδὲ γὰρ ὁ Πατὴρ
Son [3]to [4]whom [5]He [6]wills [1]gives [2]life. neither ~ For [2]the [3]Father

κρίνει οὐδένα ἀλλὰ τὴν κρίσιν πᾶσαν δέδωκε τῷ
[1]does [4]judge no one but - judgment ~ all He has given to the
anyone

Υἱῷ, 23 ἵνα πάντες τιμῶσι τὸν Υἱὸν καθὼς τιμῶσι τὸν
Son, so that all may honor the Son just as they honor the

Πατέρα. Ὁ μὴ τιμῶν τὸν Υἱὸν οὐ τιμᾷ τὸν Πατέρα
Father. The *one* not honoring the Son not ~ does honor the Father

τὸν πέμψαντα αὐτόν.
the *One* having sent Him.
who sent

Life and Judgment Are Through the Son

24 "Ἀμὴν ἀμὴν λέγω ὑμῖν ὅτι ὁ τὸν λόγον μου
"Amen amen I say to you that the *one* - [3]word [2]My
"Most assuredly

ἀκούων καὶ πιστεύων τῷ πέμψαντί με, ἔχει ζωὴν*
[1]hearing and believing in the *One* having sent Me, has life ~
who hears believes who

αἰώνιον, καὶ εἰς κρίσιν οὐκ ἔρχεται ἀλλὰ μεταβέβηκεν ἐκ
eternal, and into judgment not ~ does come but he has passed out of

τοῦ θανάτου εἰς τὴν ζωήν. 25 Ἀμὴν ἀμὴν λέγω ὑμῖν ὅτι
- death into - life. Amen amen I say to you that
Most assuredly

ἔρχεται ὥρα καὶ νῦν ἐστιν, ὅτε οἱ νεκροὶ ἀκούσονται τῆς
[3]is [4]coming [1]an [2]hour and now is, when the dead will hear the
a time

φωνῆς τοῦ Υἱοῦ τοῦ Θεοῦ, καὶ οἱ ἀκούσαντες ζήσονται.
voice of the Son - of God, and the *ones* hearing will live.
those who have heard

26 Ὥσπερ γὰρ ὁ Πατὴρ ἔχει ζωὴν ἐν ἑαυτῷ, οὕτως ἔδωκε
[2]just [3]as [1]For the Father has life in Himself, so He gave

***(5:24)** *ζωή (zōē).* Noun used often in the NT, meaning *life.* It ranges in meaning from the ordinary human life (as Acts 17:25; James 4:14) to eternal, spiritual life (as here and frequently in John). In this latter sense it comes close to being a synonym for salvation itself (1 John 5:11, 12). It is in this sense that Jesus speaks of Himself as *life* (John 14:6). Cf. the cognate verb *ζάω, live* (used metaphorically in Luke 10:28).

καὶ τῷ Υἱῷ ζωὴν ἔχειν ἐν ἑαυτῷ, 27 καὶ ἐξουσίαν ἔδωκεν
also to the Son [3]life [1]to [2]have in Himself, and [5]authority [1]He [2]gave

αὐτῷ καὶ κρίσιν ποιεῖν, ὅτι Υἱὸς Ἀνθρώπου ἐστί.
[3]to [4]Him also [3]judgment [1]to [2]make, because [3]*the* [4]Son [5]of [6]Man [1]He [2]is.

28 Μὴ θαυμάζετε τοῦτο· ὅτι ἔρχεται ὥρα ἐν ᾗ
not ˜ Do marvel *at* this; because [3]is [4]coming [1]an [2]hour (a time) in which

πάντες οἱ ἐν τοῖς μνημείοις ἀκούσονται τῆς φωνῆς αὐτοῦ
all the *ones* (those) in the tombs will hear - voice ˜ His

29 καὶ ἐκπορεύσονται — οἱ τὰ ἀγαθὰ ποιήσαντες,
and will come out — [1]the [2]*ones* (those) - [5]good [6]*things* [3]having [4]done, (who have done good,)

εἰς ἀνάστασιν ζωῆς, οἱ δὲ τὰ φαῦλα
to *the* resurrection of life, [2]the [3]*ones* (those) [1]but - [6]evil [7]*things* (who have done)

πράξαντες, εἰς ἀνάστασιν κρίσεως.
[4]having [5]practiced, (evil,) to *the* resurrection of judgment. (condemnation.)

30 "Οὐ δύναμαι ἐγὼ ποιεῖν ἀπ' ἐμαυτοῦ οὐδέν. Καθὼς
"[3]not [2]am [4]able [1]I to do [2]of [3]Myself [1]nothing. (anything.) Just as

ἀκούω, κρίνω, καὶ ἡ κρίσις ἡ ἐμὴ δικαία ἐστίν, ὅτι οὐ
I hear, I judge, and - judgment ˜ - My righteous ˜ is, because [3]not

ζητῶ τὸ θέλημα τὸ ἐμὸν ἀλλὰ τὸ θέλημα τοῦ πέμψαντός
[1]I [2]do seek - will ˜ - My but the will of the [2]having [3]sent (who)

με Πατρός.[i]
[4]Me [1]Father.

The Fourfold Witness to Jesus

31 "Ἐὰν ἐγὼ μαρτυρῶ περὶ ἐμαυτοῦ, ἡ μαρτυρία μου οὐκ
"If I testify about Myself, - testimony ˜ My not ˜

ἔστιν ἀληθής. 32 Ἄλλος ἐστὶν ὁ μαρτυρῶν περὶ ἐμοῦ,
is true. (valid.) Another is the *One* testifying about Me,

καὶ οἶδα ὅτι ἀληθής ἐστιν ἡ μαρτυρία ἣν μαρτυρεῖ
and I know that [9]true (valid) [8]is [1]the [2]testimony [3]which [4]He [5]testifies

περὶ ἐμοῦ. 33 Ὑμεῖς ἀπεστάλκατε πρὸς Ἰωάννην, καὶ
[6]about [7]Me. You have sent to John, and

μεμαρτύρηκε τῇ ἀληθείᾳ. 34 Ἐγὼ δὲ οὐ παρὰ ἀνθρώπου
he has testified to the truth. I ˜ But [2]not [6]from [7]man

τὴν μαρτυρίαν λαμβάνω, ἀλλὰ ταῦτα λέγω ἵνα ὑμεῖς
[4]the [5]testimony [1]do [3]receive, but these *things* I say so that you

σωθῆτε. 35 Ἐκεῖνος ἦν ὁ λύχνος ὁ καιόμενος καὶ
may be saved. That *one* (He) was the [4]lamp - [1]burning [2]and

φαίνων, ὑμεῖς δὲ ἠθελήσατε ἀγαλλιαθῆναι πρὸς ὥραν ἐν τῷ
[3]shining, you ˜ and wanted (were minded) to rejoice for an hour (a while) in -

φωτὶ αὐτοῦ. 36 Ἐγὼ δὲ ἔχω τὴν μαρτυρίαν μείζω τοῦ
light ˜ his. I ˜ But have the (a) testimony greater *than* the *one* (that)

Ἰωάννου· τὰ γὰρ ἔργα ἃ ἔδωκέ[j] μοι ὁ Πατὴρ ἵνα
of John; the ˜ for works (deeds) which [3]gave [4]to [5]Me [1]the [2]Father that

the Son to have life in Himself,
27 "and has given Him authority to execute judgment also, because He is the Son of Man.
28 "Do not marvel at this; for the hour is coming in which all who are in the graves will hear His voice
29 "and come forth—those who have done good, to the resurrection of life, and those who have done evil, to the resurrection of condemnation.
30 "I can of Myself do nothing. As I hear, I judge; and My judgment is righteous, because I do not seek My own will but the will of the Father who sent Me.
31 "If I bear witness of Myself, My witness is not true.
32 "There is another who bears witness of Me, and I know that the witness which He witnesses of Me is true.
33 "You have sent to John, and he has borne witness to the truth.
34 "Yet I do not receive testimony from man, but I say these things that you may be saved.
35 "He was the burning and shining lamp, and you were willing for a time to rejoice in his light.
36 "But I have a greater witness than John's; for the works which the Father has given Me

[i](**5:30**) NU omits Πατρος, *Father.* [j](**5:36**) NU reads δεδωκεν, *has given.*

to finish—the very works that I do—bear witness of Me, that the Father has sent Me.
37 "And the Father Himself, who sent Me, has testified of Me. You have neither heard His voice at any time, nor seen His form.
38 "But you do not have His word abiding in you, because whom He sent, Him you do not believe.
39 "You search the Scriptures, for in them you think you have eternal life; and these are they which testify of Me.
40 "But you are not willing to come to Me that you may have life.
41 "I do not receive honor from men.
42 "But I know you, that you do not have the love of God in you.
43 "I have come in My Father's name, and you do not receive Me; if another comes in his own name, him you will receive.
44 "How can you believe, who receive honor from one another, and do not seek the honor that *comes* from the only God?
45 "Do not think that I shall accuse you to the Father; there is *one* who accuses you—Moses, in whom you trust.
46 "For if you believed Moses, you would believe Me; for he wrote about Me.
47 "But if you do not believe his writings, how will you believe My words?"

τελειώσω αὐτά, αὐτὰ τὰ ἔργα ἃ ἐγὼ ποιῶ, μαρτυρεῖ
I might finish them, [3]themselves [1]the [2]works which I do, testify
these very works

περὶ ἐμοῦ ὅτι ὁ Πατήρ με ἀπέσταλκε. **37** Καὶ ὁ πέμψας
about Me that the Father [3]Me [1]has [2]sent. And the [2]having [3]sent
who

με Πατήρ, αὐτὸς μεμαρτύρηκε περὶ ἐμοῦ. Οὔτε φωνὴν
[4]Me [1]Father, Himself has testified about Me. Neither [5]voice

αὐτοῦ ἀκηκόατε πώποτε οὔτε εἶδος αὐτοῦ ἑωράκατε.
[4]His [1]have [2]you [3]heard at any time nor [5]form [4]His [1]have [2]you [3]seen.

38 Καὶ τὸν λόγον αὐτοῦ οὐκ ἔχετε μένοντα ἐν ὑμῖν,
And - [6]word [5]His [3]not [1]you [2]do [4]have remaining in you,
abiding

ὅτι ὃν ἀπέστειλεν ἐκεῖνος, τούτῳ ὑμεῖς οὐ
because *Him* whom [3]sent [1]that [2]*One*, this *One* you not ˜
He, Him

πιστεύετε. **39** Ἐρευνᾶτε τὰς Γραφάς, ὅτι ὑμεῖς δοκεῖτε ἐν
do believe. You search the Scriptures, because you think *that* in

αὐταῖς ζωὴν αἰώνιον ἔχειν, καὶ ἐκεῖναί εἰσιν αἱ
them [4]life [3]eternal [1]to [2]have, and those are the *ones*
you

μαρτυροῦσαι περὶ ἐμοῦ. **40** Καὶ οὐ θέλετε ἐλθεῖν πρός
testifying about Me. And [3]not [1]you [2]are [4]willing to come to

με ἵνα ζωὴν ἔχητε. **41** Δόξαν παρὰ ἀνθρώπων οὐ
Me so that [4]life [1]you [2]may [3]have. [5]glory [6]from [7]men [3]not

λαμβάνω. **42** Ἀλλ' ἔγνωκα ὑμᾶς, ὅτι τὴν ἀγάπην τοῦ
[1]I [2]do [4]receive. But I have known you, that [5]the [6]love -
come to know

Θεοῦ οὐκ ἔχετε ἐν ἑαυτοῖς. **43** Ἐγὼ ἐλήλυθα ἐν τῷ
[7]of [8]God [3]not [1]you [2]do [4]have in yourselves. I have come in the

ὀνόματι τοῦ Πατρός μου, καὶ οὐ λαμβάνετέ με· ἐὰν ἄλλος
name - of Father ˜ My, and [3]not [1]you [2]do receive Me; if another

ἔλθῃ ἐν τῷ ὀνόματι τῷ ἰδίῳ, ἐκεῖνον λήψεσθε. **44** Πῶς
comes in - [3]name - [1]his [2]own, that *one* you will receive. How
him

δύνασθε ὑμεῖς πιστεῦσαι, δόξαν παρὰ ἀλλήλων
are able ˜ you to believe, [2]glory [3]from [4]one [5]another

λαμβάνοντες, καὶ τὴν δόξαν τὴν παρὰ τοῦ μόνου Θεοῦ οὐ
[1]receiving, and the glory the *one* from the only God [3]not
who receive, which is

ζητεῖτε? **45** Μὴ δοκεῖτε ὅτι ἐγὼ κατηγορήσω ὑμῶν πρὸς
[1]you [2]do seek? not ˜ Do think that I will accuse you to

τὸν Πατέρα· ἔστιν ὁ κατηγορῶν ὑμῶν, Μωσῆς, εἰς ὃν
the Father; *there* is the *one* accusing you, Moses, in whom
one who accuses

ὑμεῖς ἠλπίκατε. **46** Εἰ γὰρ ἐπιστεύετε Μωσεῖ, ἐπιστεύετε
you have hoped. if ˜ For you believed Moses, you would believe
set your hope.

ἂν ἐμοί, περὶ γὰρ ἐμοῦ ἐκεῖνος ἔγραψεν. **47** Εἰ δὲ τοῖς
- Me, about ˜ for Me that *one* wrote. if ˜ But the
he his

ἐκείνου γράμμασιν οὐ πιστεύετε, πῶς τοῖς ἐμοῖς
[2]of [3]that [4]*one* [1]writings [7]not [5]you [6]do believe, how - [4]My

ῥήμασι πιστεύσετε?"
[5]words [1]will [2]you [3]believe?"

Jesus Feeds about 5000 Men

(Matt. 14:13–21; Mark 6:30–44; Luke 9:10–17)

6 **1** Μετὰ ταῦτα ἀπῆλθεν ὁ Ἰησοῦς πέραν τῆς
After these *things* [2]went [3]away - [1]Jesus beyond the

θαλάσσης τῆς Γαλιλαίας, τῆς Τιβεριάδος. **2** Καὶ
Sea - of Galilee, the *one* of Tiberias. And
that is

ἠκολούθει αὐτῷ ὄχλος πολύς, ὅτι ἑώρων αὐτοῦ[a]
[4]was [5]following [6]Him [1]a [3]crowd [2]large, because they were seeing His

τὰ σημεῖα ἃ ἐποίει ἐπὶ τῶν ἀσθενούντων.
- signs which He was doing upon the *ones* ailing.
for those who were sick.

3 Ἀνῆλθε δὲ εἰς τὸ ὄρος ὁ Ἰησοῦς, καὶ ἐκεῖ ἐκάθητο
[3]went [4]up [1]And [5]to [6]the [7]mountain - [2]Jesus, and there He sat down

μετὰ τῶν μαθητῶν αὐτοῦ. **4** Ἦν δὲ ἐγγὺς τὸ Πάσχα, ἡ
with - disciples ˜ His. [9]was [1]Now [10]near [2]the [3]Passover, [4]the

ἑορτὴ τῶν Ἰουδαίων. **5** Ἐπάρας οὖν ὁ Ἰησοῦς τοὺς
[5]feast [6]of [7]the [8]Jews. [3]raising [1]Then - [2]Jesus the
His

ὀφθαλμούς, καὶ θεασάμενος ὅτι πολὺς ὄχλος ἔρχεται πρὸς
eyes, and observing that a large crowd is coming toward
was

αὐτόν, λέγει πρὸς τὸν Φίλιππον, "Πόθεν ἀγοράσομεν ἄρτους
Him, says to - Philip, "Where shall we buy bread
said

ἵνα φάγωσιν οὗτοι?" **6** Τοῦτο δὲ ἔλεγε πειράζων*
so that [3]may [4]eat [1]these [2]*people?*" this ˜ Now He said testing
to test

αὐτόν, αὐτὸς γὰρ ᾔδει τί ἔμελλε ποιεῖν.
him, [2]He [3]Himself [1]for knew what He was intending to do.

7 Ἀπεκρίθη αὐτῷ Φίλιππος, "Διακοσίων δηναρίων
[2]answered [3]Him [1]Philip, "Two hundred denarii *worth of*

ἄρτοι οὐκ ἀρκοῦσιν αὐτοῖς, ἵνα ἕκαστος αὐτῶν
loaves of bread [2]not [1]are [3]enough for them, that each of them

βραχύ τι λάβῃ."
[4]little [5]*piece* [3]some [1]might [2]receive."

8 Λέγει αὐτῷ εἷς ἐκ τῶν μαθητῶν αὐτοῦ, Ἀνδρέας ὁ
[11]says [12]to [13]Him [1]One [2]of - [4]disciples [3]His, [5]Andrew [6]the
said

ἀδελφὸς Σίμωνος Πέτρου, **9** "Ἔστι παιδάριον ἓν ὧδε ὃ
[7]brother [8]of [9]Simon [10]Peter, "There is [2]little [3]boy [1]one here who
a

ἔχει πέντε ἄρτους κριθίνους καὶ δύο ὀψάρια, ἀλλὰ ταῦτα
has five loaves of bread ˜ barley and two small fish, but [3]these

τί ἐστιν εἰς τοσούτους?"
[1]what [2]are for so many?"

10 Εἶπε δὲ ὁ Ἰησοῦς, "Ποιήσατε τοὺς ἀνθρώπους
[3]said [1]And - [2]Jesus, "Make the men
people

ἀναπεσεῖν." Ἦν δὲ χόρτος πολὺς ἐν τῷ τόπῳ.
to recline." [2]*there* [3]was [1]Now [5]grass [4]much in the place.
that

Ἀνέπεσον οὖν οἱ ἄνδρες τὸν ἀριθμὸν ὡσεὶ
[9]reclined [1]Therefore [2]the [3]men - [7]*in* [8]number [4]about

πεντακισχίλιοι. **11** Ἔλαβε δὲ τοὺς ἄρτους ὁ Ἰησοῦς,
[5]five [6]thousand. [3]took [1]And [4]the [5]loaves [6]of [7]bread - [2]Jesus,

καὶ εὐχαριστήσας διέδωκε τοῖς μαθηταῖς, οἱ δὲ
and having given thanks He distributed *them* to the disciples, the ˜ and

6 After these things Jesus went over the Sea of Galilee, which is *the Sea* of Tiberias.
2 Then a great multitude followed Him, because they saw His signs which He performed on those who were diseased.
3 And Jesus went up on the mountain, and there He sat with His disciples.
4 Now the Passover, a feast of the Jews, was near.
5 Then Jesus lifted up *His* eyes, and seeing a great multitude coming toward Him, He said to Philip, "Where shall we buy bread, that these may eat?"
6 But this He said to test him, for He Himself knew what He would do.
7 Philip answered Him, "Two hundred denarii worth of bread is not sufficient for them, that every one of them may have a little."
8 One of His disciples, Andrew, Simon Peter's brother, said to Him,
9 "There is a lad here who has five barley loaves and two small fish, but what are they among so many?"
10 Then Jesus said, "Make the people sit down." Now there was much grass in the place. So the men sat down, in number about five thousand.
11 And Jesus took the loaves, and when He had given thanks He distributed *them* to the

---

[a](6:2) NU omits αυτου, *His,* thus *the signs.*

*(6:6) πειράζω *(peirazō).* Verb meaning *try, attempt* (as Acts 9:26), but usually *test* (as here in John 6:6), or even *examine* (2 Cor. 13:5). Such testing may involve painful trial (as Heb. 11:37), and may be imposed by God, who desires the person's successful completion, or by one, like Satan, who desires the person's downfall. This negative sense leads to the meaning *tempt* in the sense *entice to sin* (Gal. 6:1). Consequently Satan can be called "the tempter" (Matt. 4:3; cf. also James 1:13, 14). God can be "tested" by men (Acts 15:10), always a presumptuous sin. Cf. the cognate noun πειρασμός, *testing,*

disciples, and the disciples to
those sitting down; and likewise
of the fish, as much as they
wanted.
12 So when they were filled,
He said to His disciples,
"Gather up the fragments that
remain, so that nothing is lost."
13 Therefore they gathered
them up, and filled twelve baskets with the fragments of the
five barley loaves which were
left over by those who had
eaten.
14 Then those men, when
they had seen the sign that Jesus did, said, "This is truly the
Prophet who is to come into the
world."
15 Therefore when Jesus perceived that they were about to
come and take Him by force to
make Him king, He departed
again to the mountain by Himself alone.
16 Now when evening came,
His disciples went down to the
sea,
17 got into the boat, and went
over the sea toward Capernaum. And it was already dark,
and Jesus had not come to
them.
18 Then the sea arose be-
cause a great wind was blowing.
19 So when they had rowed
about three or four miles, they
saw Jesus walking on the sea

μαθηταὶ[b] τοῖς ἀνακειμένοις· ὁμοίως καὶ ἐκ τῶν
disciples to the *ones* reclining; likewise also of the
those who were

ὀψαρίων ὅσον ἤθελον. **12** Ὡς δὲ ἐνεπλήσθησαν,
fish as much as they wanted. when ˜ And they were full,

λέγει τοῖς μαθηταῖς αὐτοῦ, "Συναγάγετε τὰ περισσεύσαντα
He says - to disciples ˜ His, "Gather up the remaining
said leftover

κλάσματα, ἵνα μή τι ἀπόληται."
fragments, in order that not anything might be lost."
lest

13 Συνήγαγον οὖν καὶ ἐγέμισαν δώδεκα
[2]they [3]gathered [4]*them* [5]up [1]Therefore and they filled twelve

κοφίνους κλασμάτων ἐκ τῶν πέντε ἄρτων τῶν κριθίνων
baskets of fragments from the five loaves of bread ˜ - barley

ἃ ἐπερίσσευσε τοῖς βεβρωκόσιν. **14** Οἱ οὖν
which were left over by the *ones* having eaten. the ˜ Therefore
those who had

ἄνθρωποι ἰδόντες ὃ ἐποίησε σημεῖον ὁ Ἰησοῦς,[c]
men seeing [3]which [5]did [1]*the* [2]sign - [4]Jesus,
people when they saw

ἔλεγον ὅτι "Οὗτός ἐστιν ἀληθῶς ὁ Προφήτης ὁ
were saying - "This is truly the Prophet the *One*
who

ἐρχόμενος εἰς τὸν κόσμον."
coming into the world."
is to come

Jesus Walks on the Sea
(Matt. 14:22–33; Mark 6:45–52)

15 Ἰησοῦς οὖν γνοὺς ὅτι μέλλουσιν ἔρχεσθαι
Jesus ˜ Therefore knowing that they intend to come
when He perceived intended

καὶ ἁρπάζειν αὐτὸν ἵνα ποιήσωσιν αὐτὸν βασιλέα,
and to seize Him so that they might make Him king,

ἀνεχώρησεν εἰς τὸ ὄρος αὐτὸς μόνος.
withdrew to the mountain Himself alone.
by Himself.

16 Ὡς δὲ ὀψία ἐγένετο, κατέβησαν οἱ μαθηταὶ αὐτοῦ
when ˜ Now evening came, [3]went [4]down - [2]disciples [1]His

ἐπὶ τὴν θάλασσαν, **17** καὶ ἐμβάντες εἰς τὸ πλοῖον,
to the sea, and stepping in into the boat,
getting in

ἤρχοντο πέραν τῆς θαλάσσης εἰς Καπερναούμ. Καὶ
they were going across the sea to Capernaum. And

σκοτία ἤδη ἐγεγόνει, καὶ οὐκ ἐληλύθει πρὸς αὐτοὺς ὁ
darkness already ˜ had come, and [3]not [2]had [4]come [5]to [6]them -

Ἰησοῦς. **18** Ἡ τε θάλασσα ἀνέμου μεγάλου πνέοντος
[1]Jesus. the ˜ And sea [3]by [4]a [7]wind [5]great [6]blowing
strong

διηγείρετο. **19** Ἐληλακότες οὖν ὡς σταδίους εἴκοσι
[1]was [2]aroused. [2]having [3]rowed [1]Therefore about [5]stadia [1]twenty-
tossed.

πέντε ἢ τριάκοντα, θεωροῦσι τὸν Ἰησοῦν περιπατοῦντα ἐπὶ
[2]five [3]or [4]thirty, they see - Jesus walking upon
saw

---

[b](6:11) NU omits τοις μαθηταις, οι δε μαθηται, *to the disciples, and the disciples.* [c](6:14) NU omits ο Ιησους, *Jesus.*

trial (1 Pet. 4:12) or *temptation* (Luke 4:13).

τῆς θαλάσσης καὶ ἐγγὺς τοῦ πλοίου γινόμενον, καὶ
the sea and near the boat becoming, and
drawing near to the boat,

ἐφοβήθησαν.
they were afraid.

20 Ὁ δὲ λέγει αὐτοῖς, "Ἐγώ εἰμι· μὴ φοβεῖσθε."
[2]the [3]*One* [1]And says to them, "I am; not ˜ do be afraid."
He said "It is I;

21 Ἤθελον οὖν λαβεῖν αὐτὸν εἰς τὸ πλοῖον, καὶ
[2]they [3]wanted [1]Then to receive Him into the boat, and

εὐθέως τὸ πλοῖον ἐγένετο ἐπὶ τῆς γῆς εἰς ἣν
immediately the boat came to be at the land to which
arrived

ὑπῆγον.
they were going.

Jesus Discourses on the Bread of Life

22 Τῇ ἐπαύριον ὁ ὄχλος ὁ ἑστηκὼς πέραν
On the next day the crowd the *one* standing across
which had remained on the other

τῆς θαλάσσης, ἰδὼν ὅτι πλοιάριον ἄλλο οὐκ ἦν
the sea, seeing that [2]little [3]boat [1]another [5]not [4]was
side of the sea, when they saw

ἐκεῖ εἰ μὴ ἓν ἐκεῖνο εἰς ὃ ἐνέβησαν οἱ μαθηταὶ
there if not one ˜ that in which [3]embarked - [2]disciples
except had embarked

αὐτοῦ,[d] καὶ ὅτι οὐ συνεισῆλθε τοῖς μαθηταῖς αὐτοῦ
[1]His, and that [3]not [2]did [4]enter [9]together - [10]with [12]disciples [11]His
had not entered

ὁ Ἰησοῦς εἰς τὸ πλοιάριον ἀλλὰ μόνοι οἱ μαθηταὶ αὐτοῦ
- [1]Jesus [5]into [6]the [7]little [8]boat but only - disciples ˜ His

ἀπῆλθον — 23 ἄλλα δὲ ἦλθε πλοιάρια ἐκ Τιβεριάδος ἐγγὺς
went away — other ˜ and [3]came [1]little [2]boats from Tiberias near
had gone

τοῦ τόπου ὅπου ἔφαγον τὸν ἄρτον, εὐχαριστήσαντος τοῦ
the place where they ate the bread, [3]having [4]given [5]thanks [1]the
after the Lord had

Κυρίου — 24 ὅτε οὖν εἶδεν ὁ ὄχλος ὅτι Ἰησοῦς οὐκ
[2]Lord — when therefore [3]saw [1]the [2]crowd that Jesus not ˜
given thanks —

ἔστιν ἐκεῖ, οὐδὲ οἱ μαθηταὶ αὐτοῦ, ἐνέβησαν αὐτοὶ εἰς τὰ
is there, nor - disciples ˜ His, stepped in they into the
was got

πλοῖα καὶ ἦλθον εἰς Καπερναούμ, ζητοῦντες τὸν Ἰησοῦν.
boats and came to Capernaum, seeking - Jesus.

25 Καὶ εὑρόντες αὐτὸν πέραν τῆς θαλάσσης, εἶπον
And finding Him across the sea, they said
on the other side of

αὐτῷ, "Ῥαββί, πότε ὧδε γέγονας?"
to Him, "Rabbi, when [4]here [1]have [2]You [3]come?"
did You get?"

26 Ἀπεκρίθη αὐτοῖς ὁ Ἰησοῦς καὶ εἶπεν, "Ἀμὴν ἀμὴν
[2]answered [3]them - [1]Jesus and said, "Amen amen
"Most assuredly

λέγω ὑμῖν, ζητεῖτέ με, οὐχ ὅτι εἴδετε σημεῖα,* ἀλλ'
I say to you, you seek Me, not because you saw signs, but

ὅτι ἐφάγετε ἐκ τῶν ἄρτων καὶ ἐχορτάσθητε.
because you ate from the loaves of bread and were filled.

and drawing near the boat; and they were afraid.
20 But He said to them, "It is I; do not be afraid."
21 Then they willingly received Him into the boat, and immediately the boat was at the land where they were going.
22 On the following day, when the people who were standing on the other side of the sea saw that there was no other boat there, except that one which His disciples had entered, and that Jesus had not entered the boat with His disciples, but His disciples had gone away alone —
23 however, other boats came from Tiberias, near the place where they ate bread after the Lord had given thanks —
24 when the people therefore saw that Jesus was not there, nor His disciples, they also got into boats and came to Capernaum, seeking Jesus.
25 And when they found Him on the other side of the sea, they said to Him, "Rabbi, when did You come here?"
26 Jesus answered them and said, "Most assuredly, I say to you, you seek Me, not because you saw the signs, but because you ate of the loaves and were filled.

---

[d](6:22) NU omits *οτι, εκεινο εις ο ενεβησαν μαθηται αυτου, that in which His disciples had embarked.*

***(6:26)** *σημεῖον (sēmeion).* Noun meaning *sign.* In its broadest sense, a *σημεῖον* is any *mark* or *indicator* by which something is known. It can be a mark of genuineness (2 Thess. 3:17), a prearranged signal (Matt. 26:48), or even a warning (Luke 11:29, 30). *σημεῖον* often refers to an event with some special meaning, particularly *miracles* or *portents* in the skies which signify the approach of the Last Days. It often appears in such contexts with *δύναμις, miracle, work of power,* and *τέρας, omen, wonder* (as in Acts 2:22). Here in John 6:26 the emphasis is not on the miraculous act itself, but on understanding the underlying reality which it signifies.

27 "Do not labor for the food
which perishes, but for the food
which endures to everlasting
life, which the Son of Man will
give you, because God the Father has set His seal on Him."
28 Then they said to Him,
"What shall we do, that we may
work the works of God?"
29 Jesus answered and said to
them, "This is the work of God,
that you believe in Him whom
He sent."
30 Therefore they said to
Him, "What sign will You perform then, that we may see it
and believe You? What work
will You do?
31 "Our fathers ate the manna
in the desert; as it is written,
*'He gave them bread from
heaven to eat.'"*
32 Then Jesus said to them,
"Most assuredly, I say to you,
Moses did not give you the
bread from heaven, but My Father gives you the true bread
from heaven.
33 "For the bread of God is
He who comes down from
heaven and gives life to the
world."
34 Then they said to Him,
"Lord, give us this bread always."
35 And Jesus said to them, "I
am the bread of life. He who
comes to Me shall never hunger, and he who believes in Me
shall never thirst.

27 Ἐργάζεσθε μὴ τὴν βρῶσιν τὴν ἀπολλυμένην ἀλλὰ
Do work ˜ not for the food the *one* perishing but
which perishes

τὴν βρῶσιν τὴν μένουσαν εἰς ζωὴν αἰώνιον, ἣν ὁ Υἱὸς
for the food the *one* enduring to life ˜ eternal which the Son
which endures

τοῦ Ἀνθρώπου ὑμῖν δώσει· τοῦτον γὰρ ὁ Πατὴρ
\- of Man [3]to [4]you [1]will [2]give; [6]*upon* [7]this [8]One [5]For [10]the [11]Father

ἐσφράγισεν ὁ Θεός."
[12]has [13]set [14]*His* [15]seal - [9]God."

28 Εἶπον οὖν πρὸς αὐτόν, "Τί ποιῶμεν ἵνα
[2]they [3]said [1]Then to Him, "What should we do so that

ἐργαζώμεθα τὰ ἔργα τοῦ Θεοῦ?"
we may work the works - of God?"

29 Ἀπεκρίθη Ἰησοῦς καὶ εἶπεν αὐτοῖς, "Τοῦτό ἐστι τὸ
answered ˜ Jesus and said to them, "This is the

ἔργον τοῦ Θεοῦ, ἵνα πιστεύσητε εἰς ὃν ἀπέστειλεν
work - of God, that you may believe in *the One* whom [3]sent
He

ἐκεῖνος."
[1]that [2]One."
has sent."

30 Εἶπον οὖν αὐτῷ, "Τί οὖν ποιεῖς σὺ σημεῖον
[2]they [3]said [1]Therefore to Him, "What [2]then [3]do [5]do [4]You [1]sign

ἵνα ἴδωμεν καὶ πιστεύσωμέν σοι? Τί ἐργάζῃ?
so that we may see *it* and believe You? What do You work?
What work do You perform?

31 Οἱ πατέρες ἡμῶν τὸ μάννα ἔφαγον ἐν τῇ ἐρήμῳ· καθὼς
\- fathers ˜ Our - manna ˜ ate in the wilderness; just as

ἐστι γεγραμμένον, «Ἄρτον ἐκ τοῦ οὐρανοῦ ἔδωκεν αὐτοῖς
it is written, «[4]bread [5]out [6]of - [7]heaven [1]He [2]gave [3]them

φαγεῖν.»"[e]
to eat.»"

32 Εἶπεν οὖν αὐτοῖς ὁ Ἰησοῦς, "Ἀμὴν ἀμὴν λέγω
[3]said [1]Then [4]to [5]them - [2]Jesus, "Amen amen I say
"Most assuredly

ὑμῖν, οὐ Μωσῆς δέδωκεν ὑμῖν τὸν ἄρτον ἐκ τοῦ οὐρανοῦ,
to you, [3]not [1]Moses [2]has given you the bread out of - heaven,
Moses did not give

ἀλλ' ὁ Πατήρ μου δίδωσιν ὑμῖν τὸν ἄρτον ἐκ τοῦ οὐρανοῦ
but - Father ˜ My gives you the [2]bread [3]out [4]of - [5]heaven

τὸν ἀληθινόν. **33** Ὁ γὰρ ἄρτος τοῦ Θεοῦ ἐστιν ὁ
\- [1]true. the ˜ For bread - of God is the *One*
that which

καταβαίνων ἐκ τοῦ οὐρανοῦ καὶ ζωὴν διδοὺς τῷ κόσμῳ."
coming down out of - heaven and life ˜ giving to the world."
comes gives

34 Εἶπον οὖν πρὸς αὐτόν, "Κύριε, πάντοτε δὸς ἡμῖν τὸν
[2]they [3]said [1]Then to Him, "Lord, always give us -

ἄρτον τοῦτον."
bread ˜ this."

35 Εἶπε δὲ αὐτοῖς ὁ Ἰησοῦς, "Ἐγώ εἰμι ὁ ἄρτος τῆς
[3]said [1]And [4]to [5]them - [2]Jesus, "I am the bread -

ζωῆς. Ὁ ἐρχόμενος πρός με οὐ μὴ πεινάσῃ, καὶ
of life. The *one* coming to Me [2]not [3]not [1]shall [4]hunger, and
who comes never

ὁ πιστεύων εἰς ἐμὲ οὐ μὴ διψήσῃ πώποτε. **36** Ἀλλ'
the *one* believing in Me [2]not [3]not [1]shall [5]thirst [4]ever. But
who believes shall never thirst.

[e](**6:31**) Ex. 16:4; Neh. 9:15; Ps. 78:24.

εἶπον ὑμῖν ὅτι καὶ ἑωράκατέ με καὶ οὐ πιστεύετε.
I told you that [3]both [1]you [2]have seen Me and [3]not [1]you [2]do believe.

37 Πᾶν ὃ δίδωσί μοι ὁ Πατὴρ πρὸς ἐμὲ ἥξει,
Every*one* whom [3]gives [4]to [5]Me [1]the [2]Father [8]to [9]Me [6]will [7]come,

καὶ τὸν ἐρχόμενον πρὸς με οὐ μὴ ἐκβάλω ἔξω.
and the *one* coming to Me [3]not [4]not [1]I [2]will [5]cast out.
who comes never

38 Ὅτι καταβέβηκα ἐκ τοῦ οὐρανοῦ, οὐχ ἵνα ποιῶ
Because I have come down out of - heaven, not that I might do

τὸ θέλημα τὸ ἐμὸν ἀλλὰ τὸ θέλημα τοῦ πέμψαντός με.
- will ˜ - My but the will of the *One* having sent Me.
who

39 Τοῦτο δέ ἐστι τὸ θέλημα τοῦ πέμψαντός με Πατρός,[f]
this ˜ Now is the will of the [2]having [3]sent [4]Me [1]Father,
who

ἵνα πᾶν ὃ δέδωκέ μοι μὴ ἀπολέσω ἐξ αὐτοῦ
so that all which He has given to Me [3]not [1]I [2]should lose from it
I might lose no one from those whom He has given Me

ἀλλὰ ἀναστήσω αὐτὸν τῇ ἐσχάτῃ ἡμέρᾳ. **40** Τοῦτο δὲ
but I might raise up ˜ him on the last day. this ˜ And

ἐστι τὸ θέλημα τοῦ πέμψαντός με,[g] ἵνα πᾶς ὁ
is the will of the *One* having sent Me, that every - *one*
who everyone who

θεωρῶν τὸν Υἱὸν καὶ πιστεύων εἰς αὐτὸν ἔχῃ ζωὴν αἰώνιον,
seeing the Son and believing in Him may have life ˜ eternal,
sees believes

καὶ ἀναστήσω αὐτὸν ἐγὼ τῇ ἐσχάτῃ ἡμέρᾳ."
and [2]will [3]raise [5]up [4]him [1]I on the last day."

The Jews React Against His Teaching

41 Ἐγόγγυζον οὖν οἱ Ἰουδαῖοι περὶ αὐτοῦ ὅτι
[4]were [5]murmuring [1]Therefore [2]the [3]Jews about Him because
complaining

εἶπεν, "Ἐγώ εἰμι ὁ ἄρτος ὁ καταβὰς ἐκ τοῦ
He said, "I am the bread the *one* having come down out of -
which came

οὐρανοῦ." **42** Καὶ ἔλεγον, "Οὐχ οὗτός ἐστιν Ἰησοῦς ὁ
heaven." And they were saying, "[2]not [3]this [1]Is Jesus the

υἱὸς Ἰωσήφ, οὗ ἡμεῖς οἴδαμεν τὸν πατέρα καὶ τὴν μητέρα?
son of Joseph, whose [4]we [5]know - [1]father [2]and - [3]mother?

Πῶς οὖν λέγει οὗτος ὅτι 'Ἐκ τοῦ οὐρανοῦ
How then does [3]say [1]this [2]*man* - 'Out of - heaven

καταβέβηκα'?"
I have come down'?"

43 Ἀπεκρίθη οὖν ὁ Ἰησοῦς καὶ εἶπεν αὐτοῖς, "Μὴ
[3]answered [1]Therefore - [2]Jesus and said to them, "not ˜
"Stop

γογγύζετε μετ' ἀλλήλων. **44** Οὐδεὶς δύναται ἐλθεῖν πρός με
Do murmur with one another. No one is able to come to Me
complaining among yourselves.

ἐὰν μὴ ὁ Πατὴρ ὁ πέμψας με ἑλκύσῃ αὐτόν, καὶ
if not the Father the *One* having sent Me should draw him, and
unless who sent

ἐγὼ ἀναστήσω αὐτὸν ἐν τῇ ἐσχάτῃ ἡμέρᾳ. **45** Ἔστι
I will raise up ˜ him on the last day. It is

γεγραμμένον ἐν τοῖς Προφήταις, «Καὶ ἔσονται πάντες διδακτοὶ
written in the Prophets, «And [2]will [3]be [1]all taught

36 "But I said to you that you have seen Me and yet do not believe.
37 "All that the Father gives Me will come to Me, and the one who comes to Me I will by no means cast out.
38 "For I have come down from heaven, not to do My own will, but the will of Him who sent Me.
39 "This is the will of the Father who sent Me, that of all He has given Me I should lose nothing, but should raise it up at the last day.
40 "And this is the will of Him who sent Me, that everyone who sees the Son and believes in Him may have everlasting life; and I will raise him up at the last day."
41 The Jews then complained about Him, because He said, "I am the bread which came down from heaven."
42 And they said, "Is not this Jesus, the son of Joseph, whose father and mother we know? How is it then that He says, 'I have come down from heaven'?"
43 Jesus therefore answered and said to them, "Do not murmur among yourselves.
44 "No one can come to Me unless the Father who sent Me draws him; and I will raise him up at the last day.
45 "It is written in the prophets, *'And they shall all be taught*

f(**6:39**) NU omits Πατρος, *Father.* g(**6:40**) For του πεμψαντος με, *the (One) having sent Me,* NU reads του Πατρος μου, *My Father.*

by God.' Therefore everyone
who has heard and learned from
the Father comes to Me.
46 "Not that anyone has seen
the Father, except He who is
from God; He has seen the Father.
47 "Most assuredly, I say to
you, he who believes in Me has
everlasting life.
48 "I am the bread of life.
49 "Your fathers ate the
manna in the wilderness, and
are dead.
50 "This is the bread which
comes down from heaven, that
one may eat of it and not die.
51 "I am the living bread
which came down from heaven.
If anyone eats of this bread, he
will live forever; and the bread
that I shall give is My flesh,
which I shall give for the life of
the world."
52 The Jews therefore quar-
reled among themselves, saying, "How can this Man give us
His flesh to eat?"
53 Then Jesus said to them,
"Most assuredly, I say to you,
unless you eat the flesh of the
Son of Man and drink His blood,
you have no life in you.
54 "Whoever eats My flesh
and drinks My blood has eternal
life, and I will raise him up at
the last day.
55 "For My flesh is food indeed, and My blood is drink
indeed.
56 "He who eats My flesh and

Θεοῦ.»[h] Πᾶς οὖν ὁ ἀκούων παρὰ τοῦ Πατρὸς καὶ
of God.» every ˜ Therefore - *one* hearing from the Father and
Therefore everyone who hears

μαθὼν[i] ἔρχεται πρός με. 46 Οὐχ ὅτι τὸν Πατέρα τις
having learned comes to Me. Not that [4]the [5]Father [1]anyone
has

ἑώρακεν, εἰ μὴ ὁ ὢν παρὰ τοῦ Θεοῦ, οὗτος ἑώρακε
[2]has [3]seen, if not the *One* being from - God, this One has seen
except who is He

τὸν Πατέρα. 47 Ἀμὴν ἀμὴν λέγω ὑμῖν, ὁ πιστεύων εἰς
the Father. Amen amen I say to you, the *one* believing in
Most assuredly who believes

ἐμὲ[j] ἔχει ζωὴν αἰώνιον. 48 Ἐγώ εἰμι ὁ ἄρτος τῆς ζωῆς.
Me has life ˜ eternal. I am the bread - of life.

49 Οἱ πατέρες ὑμῶν ἔφαγον τὸ μάννα ἐν τῇ ἐρήμῳ, καὶ
- fathers ˜ Your ate the manna in the wilderness, and

ἀπέθανον. 50 Οὗτός ἐστιν ὁ ἄρτος ὁ ἐκ τοῦ οὐρανοῦ
they died. This is the bread the *one* out of - heaven
which comes down from

καταβαίνων, ἵνα τις ἐξ αὐτοῦ φάγῃ καὶ μὴ ἀποθάνῃ.
coming down, so that anyone [3]of [4]it [1]may [2]eat and not die.
heaven,

51 Ἐγώ εἰμι ὁ ἄρτος ὁ ζῶν ὁ ἐκ τοῦ οὐρανοῦ
I am the bread ˜ - living the *one* out of - heaven
which came down from

καταβάς. Ἐάν τις φάγῃ ἐκ τούτου τοῦ ἄρτου,
having come down. If anyone eats from this - bread,
heaven.

ζήσεται εἰς τὸν αἰῶνα. Καὶ ὁ ἄρτος δὲ ὃν ἐγὼ
he will live into the age. [2]indeed [3]the [4]bread [1]And which I
forever.

δώσω ἡ σάρξ μού ἐστιν ἣν ἐγὼ δώσω[k] ὑπὲρ τῆς
shall give - [3]flesh [2]My [1]is which I shall give in behalf of the

τοῦ κόσμου ζωῆς."
[2]of [3]the [4]world [1]life."

52 Ἐμάχοντο οὖν πρὸς ἀλλήλους οἱ Ἰουδαῖοι
[4]were [5]fighting [1]Therefore [6]with [7]one [8]another [2]the [3]Jews

λέγοντες, "Πῶς δύναται οὗτος ἡμῖν δοῦναι τὴν σάρκα
saying, "How is [3]able [1]this [2]*man* [6]us [4]to [5]give the flesh
His

φαγεῖν?"
to eat?"

53 Εἶπεν οὖν αὐτοῖς ὁ Ἰησοῦς, "Ἀμὴν ἀμὴν λέγω
[3]said [1]Then [4]to [5]them - [2]Jesus, "Amen amen I say
"Most assuredly

ὑμῖν, ἐὰν μὴ φάγητε τὴν σάρκα τοῦ Υἱοῦ τοῦ Ἀνθρώπου
to you, if not you eat the flesh of the Son - of Man
unless

καὶ πίητε αὐτοῦ τὸ αἷμα, οὐκ ἔχετε ζωὴν ἐν ἑαυτοῖς.
and drink His - blood, [3]not [1]you [2]do have life in yourselves.

54 Ὁ τρώγων μου τὴν σάρκα καὶ πίνων μου τὸ αἷμα ἔχει
The *one* eating My - flesh and drinking My - blood has
who eats drinks

ζωὴν αἰώνιον, καὶ ἐγὼ ἀναστήσω αὐτὸν τῇ ἐσχάτῃ ἡμέρᾳ.
life ˜ eternal, and I will raise up ˜ him on the last day.

55 Ἡ γὰρ σάρξ μου ἀληθῶς[l] ἐστι βρῶσις, καὶ τὸ αἷμά μου
- For flesh ˜ My truly is food, and - blood ˜ My

ἀληθῶς[m] ἐστι πόσις. 56 Ὁ τρώγων μου τὴν σάρκα καὶ
truly is drink. The *one* eating My - flesh and
who eats

---

[h](6:45) Is. 54:13
[i](6:45) TR, NU read *ακουσας, having heard* or *has heard.*
[j](6:47) NU omits *εις εμε, in Me.* [k](6:51) NU omits *ην εγω δωσω, which I shall give.* [l](6:55) NU reads *αληθης, true (food).*
[m](6:55) NU reads *αληθης, true (drink).*

πίνων μου τὸ αἷμα ἐν ἐμοὶ μένει κἀγὼ ἐν αὐτῷ. **57** Καθὼς
drinking My - blood [2]in [3]Me [1]abides and I in him. Just as
drinks

ἀπέστειλέ με ὁ ζῶν Πατήρ, κἀγὼ ζῶ διὰ τὸν
[4]sent [5]Me [1]the [2]living [3]Father, and I live because of the

Πατέρα, καὶ ὁ τρώγων με, κἀκεῖνος ζήσεται
Father, so also the *one* eating Me, that one also will live
who feeds on

δι' ἐμέ. **58** Οὗτός ἐστιν ὁ ἄρτος ὁ ἐκ τοῦ
because of Me. This *One* is the bread the *one* out of -
which came down

οὐρανοῦ καταβάς, οὐ καθὼς ἔφαγον οἱ πατέρες ὑμῶν τὸ
heaven having come down, not as [3]ate - [2]fathers [1]our the
from heaven,

μάννα [n] καὶ ἀπέθανον. Ὁ τρώγων τοῦτον τὸν ἄρτον
manna and died. The *one* eating this - bread
who feeds on

ζήσεται εἰς τὸν αἰῶνα." **59** Ταῦτα εἶπεν ἐν
will live into the age." These *things* He said in
forever."

συναγωγῇ διδάσκων ἐν Καπερναούμ.
the synagogue teaching in Capernaum.
as He taught

Many Disciples Turn Away from Jesus

60 Πολλοὶ οὖν ἀκούσαντες ἐκ τῶν μαθητῶν αὐτοῦ
many ~ Therefore [4]having [5]heard [1]from - [3]disciples [2]His
when they heard

εἶπον, "Σκληρός ἐστιν οὗτος ὁ λόγος· τίς δύναται αὐτοῦ
said, "[4]hard [3]is [1]This - [2]word; who is able [4]it
message;

ἀκούειν?"
[1]to [2]listen [3]to?"
accept."

61 Εἰδὼς δὲ ὁ Ἰησοῦς ἐν ἑαυτῷ ὅτι γογγύζουσι
[3]knowing [1]And - [2]Jesus in Himself that [3]are [4]murmuring
And because Jesus knew were complaining

περὶ τούτου οἱ μαθηταὶ αὐτοῦ, εἶπεν αὐτοῖς, "Τοῦτο ὑμᾶς
[5]about [6]this - [2]disciples [1]His, He said to them, "This you ~
"Does this

σκανδαλίζει? **62** Ἐὰν οὖν θεωρῆτε τὸν Υἱὸν τοῦ
causes to fall? [2]*what* [3]if [1]Then you should see the Son -
offend you?

Ἀνθρώπου ἀναβαίνοντα ὅπου ἦν τὸ πρότερον? **63** Τὸ
of Man ascending where He was - before? The

Πνεῦμά ἐστι τὸ ζῳοποιοῦν· ἡ σὰρξ οὐκ ὠφελεῖ
Spirit is the *One* making alive; the flesh not ~ does benefit
who makes alive;

οὐδέν. Τὰ ῥήματα ἃ ἐγὼ λαλῶ ὑμῖν πνεῦμά ἐστι καὶ ζωή
nothing. The words which I speak to you spirit ~ are and life ~
at all.

ἐστιν. **64** Ἀλλ' εἰσὶν ἐξ ὑμῶν τινες οἳ οὐ
they are. But *there* are from *among* you some who not ~

πιστεύουσιν." Ἤδει γὰρ ἐξ ἀρχῆς ὁ Ἰησοῦς τίνες εἰσὶν
do believe." [3]knew [1]For [4]from [5]*the* [6]beginning - [2]Jesus who are
were

οἱ μὴ πιστεύοντες καὶ τίς ἐστιν ὁ παραδώσων
the *ones* not believing and who is the *one* handing over ~
the ones who did not believe was the one who would betray

drinks My blood abides in Me, and I in him.
57 "As the living Father sent Me, and I live because of the Father, so he who feeds on Me will live because of Me.
58 "This is the bread which came down from heaven—not as your fathers ate the manna, and are dead. He who eats this bread will live forever."
59 These things He said in the synagogue as He taught in Capernaum.
60 Therefore many of His disciples, when they heard *this,* said, "This is a hard saying; who can understand it?"
61 When Jesus knew in Himself that His disciples complained about this, He said to them, "Does this offend you?
62 "*What* then if you should see the Son of Man ascend where He was before?
63 "It is the Spirit who gives life; the flesh profits nothing. The words that I speak to you are spirit, and *they* are life.
64 "But there are some of you who do not believe." For Jesus knew from the beginning who they were who did not believe,

---

n(**6:58**) NU omits *υμων το μαννα, our (fathers ate) the manna;* thus *the fathers ate and.*

and who would betray Him.
65 And He said, "Therefore I
have said to you that no one can
come to Me unless it has been
granted to him by My Father."
66 From that *time* many of His
disciples went back and walked
with Him no more.
67 Then Jesus said to the
twelve, "Do you also want to
go away?"
68 But Simon Peter answered
Him, "Lord, to whom shall we
go? You have the words of
eternal life.
69 "Also we have come to believe and know that You are the
Christ, the Son of the living
God."
70 Jesus answered them, "Did
I not choose you, the twelve,
and one of you is a devil?"
71 He spoke of Judas Iscariot,
the son of Simon, for it was he
who would betray Him, being
one of the twelve.
7 After these things Jesus
walked in Galilee; for He
did not want to walk in Judea,
because the Jews sought to kill
Him.
2 Now the Jews' Feast of
Tabernacles was at hand.
3 His brothers therefore said
to Him, "Depart from here and
go into Judea, that Your disciples also may see the works
that You are doing.
4 "For no one does anything
in secret while he himself seeks
to be known openly. If You do

αὐτόν. **65** Καὶ ἔλεγε, "Διὰ τοῦτο εἴρηκα ὑμῖν ὅτι
Him. And He said, "Because of this I have said to you that

οὐδεὶς δύναται ἐλθεῖν πρός με ἐὰν μὴ ᾖ δεδομένον αὐτῷ
no one is able to come to Me if not it be given to him
unless it has been granted

ἐκ τοῦ Πατρός μου."[o]
from - Father ~ My."

66 Ἐκ τούτου πολλοὶ ἀπῆλθον τῶν μαθητῶν αὐτοῦ εἰς
From this *time* many [4]went [5]away - [1]of [3]disciples [2]His to
turned back

τὰ ὀπίσω καὶ οὐκέτι μετ' αὐτοῦ περιεπάτουν.
the *things* behind and no longer [4]with [5]Him [1]were [2]they [3]walking.
would walk.

67 Εἶπεν οὖν ὁ Ἰησοῦς τοῖς δώδεκα, "Μὴ καὶ ὑμεῖς
[3]said [1]Therefore - [2]Jesus to the twelve, "[3]not [4]also [1]You

θέλετε ὑπάγειν?"
[2]do [5]want to go away, *do you?*"

68 Ἀπεκρίθη οὖν αὐτῷ Σίμων Πέτρος, "Κύριε, πρὸς
[4]answered [1]Therefore [5]Him [2]Simon [3]Peter, "Lord, to

τίνα ἀπελευσόμεθα? Ῥήματα ζωῆς αἰωνίου ἔχεις.
whom shall we go? [3]*the* [4]sayings [5]of [7]life [6]eternal [1]You [2]have.

69 Καὶ ἡμεῖς πεπιστεύκαμεν καὶ ἐγνώκαμεν ὅτι σὺ εἶ ὁ
And we have believed and have known that You are the
come to believe come to know

Χριστός, ὁ Υἱὸς τοῦ Θεοῦ τοῦ ζῶντος."[p]
Christ, the Son of the God ~ - living."
Messiah,

70 Ἀπεκρίθη αὐτοῖς,[q] "Οὐκ ἐγὼ ὑμᾶς τοὺς δώδεκα
He answered them, "[3]not [2]I [5]you - [6]twelve

ἐξελεξάμην, καὶ ἐξ ὑμῶν εἷς διάβολός ἐστιν?"
[1]Did [4]choose, and [2]of [3]you [1]one [5]a [6]devil [4]is?"

71 Ἔλεγε δὲ τὸν Ἰούδαν Σίμωνος
[2]He [3]was [4]speaking [1]Now - *about* Judas [2]*the* [3]*son* [4]of [5]Simon

Ἰσκαριώτην, οὗτος γὰρ ἔμελλεν αὐτὸν παραδιδόναι, εἷς
[1]Iscariot, [7]this [8]*one* [6]for was intending [3]Him [1]to [2]hand [4]over, [6]one
he betray,

ὢν ἐκ τῶν δώδεκα.
[5]being of the twelve.
though he was

Jesus' Brothers Disbelieve

7 **1** Καὶ περιεπάτει ὁ Ἰησοῦς μετὰ ταῦτα ἐν τῇ
And [5]was [6]walking - [4]Jesus [1]after [2]these [3]*things* in -

Γαλιλαίᾳ· οὐ γὰρ ἤθελεν ἐν τῇ Ἰουδαίᾳ περιπατεῖν
Galilee; [4]not [1]for [2]He [3]did [5]wish [8]in - [9]Judea [6]to [7]walk

ὅτι ἐζήτουν αὐτὸν οἱ Ἰουδαῖοι ἀποκτεῖναι. **2** Ἦν δὲ
because [3]were [4]seeking [7]Him [1]the [2]Jews [5]to [6]kill. [8]was [1]And

ἐγγὺς ἡ ἑορτὴ τῶν Ἰουδαίων ἡ Σκηνοπηγία.
[9]near [2]the [3]feast [4]of [5]the [6]Jews - [7]Tabernacles.
Jewish Feast of Tabernacles.

3 Εἶπον οὖν πρὸς αὐτὸν οἱ ἀδελφοὶ αὐτοῦ, "Μετάβηθι
[4]said [1]Therefore [5]to [6]Him - [3]brothers [2]His, "Depart

ἐντεῦθεν καὶ ὕπαγε εἰς τὴν Ἰουδαίαν, ἵνα καὶ οἱ μαθηταί
from here and go into - Judea, so that [3]also - [2]disciples

σου θεωρήσωσι τὰ ἔργα σου ἃ ποιεῖς. **4** Οὐδεὶς γὰρ
[1]Your may see - works ~ Your which You are doing. [2]no [3]one [1]For

ἐν κρυπτῷ τι ποιεῖ καὶ ζητεῖ αὐτὸς ἐν παρρησίᾳ
[6]in [7]secret [5]anything [4]does and seeks himself [3]in [4]openness
known publicly.

---

[o](6:65) NU omits μου, *My,* thus *the Father.*
[p](6:69) For ο Χριστος, ο Υιος του Θεου του ζωντος, *the Christ, the Son of the living God,* NU reads ο αγιος του Θεου, *the Holy (One) of God.*
[q](6:70) NU, TR add ο Ιησους, *Jesus (answered).*

εἶναι. Εἰ ταῦτα ποιεῖς, φανέρωσον σεαυτὸν τῷ
[1]to [2]be. If [3]these [4]*things* [1]You [2]do, show Yourself to the

κόσμῳ." 5 Οὐδὲ γὰρ οἱ ἀδελφοὶ αὐτοῦ ἐπίστευον εἰς αὐτόν.
world." [2]not [3]even [1]For - [5]brothers [4]His believed in Him.

6 Λέγει οὖν αὐτοῖς ὁ Ἰησοῦς, "Ὁ καιρὸς ὁ ἐμὸς
[3]says [1]Therefore [4]to [5]them - [2]Jesus, - "time ˜ - My
said

οὔπω πάρεστιν, ὁ δὲ καιρὸς ὁ ὑμέτερος πάντοτέ ἐστιν
[2]not [3]yet [1]is [4]present, - but time ˜ - your always ˜ is

ἕτοιμος. 7 Οὐ δύναται ὁ κόσμος μισεῖν ὑμᾶς, ἐμὲ δὲ μισεῖ
ready. [4]not [3]is [5]able [1]The [2]world to hate you, Me ˜ but it hates

ὅτι ἐγὼ μαρτυρῶ περὶ αὐτοῦ ὅτι τὰ ἔργα αὐτοῦ πονηρά
because I testify about it that - works ˜ its evil ˜

ἐστιν. 8 Ὑμεῖς ἀνάβητε εἰς τὴν ἑορτὴν ταύτην. Ἐγὼ οὔπω[a]
are. You go up to - feast ˜ this. I [2]not [3]yet

ἀναβαίνω εἰς τὴν ἑορτὴν ταύτην ὅτι ὁ καιρὸς ὁ ἐμὸς
[1]am [4]going [5]up to - feast ˜ this because - time ˜ - My

οὔπω πεπλήρωται." 9 Ταῦτα δὲ εἰπὼν αὐτοῖς,
[2]not [3]yet [1]has [4]been [5]fulfilled." these *things* And saying to them,
When He had said these things

ἔμεινεν ἐν τῇ Γαλιλαίᾳ.
He remained in - Galilee.

Jesus Teaches at the Feast of Tabernacles

10 Ὡς δὲ ἀνέβησαν οἱ ἀδελφοὶ αὐτοῦ, τότε καὶ αὐτὸς
when ˜ But [3]went [4]up - [2]brothers [1]His, then also Himself ˜

ἀνέβη εἰς τὴν ἑορτήν, οὐ φανερῶς, ἀλλ' ὡς ἐν
He went up to the feast, not openly, but as *it were* in

κρυπτῷ. 11 Οἱ οὖν Ἰουδαῖοι ἐζήτουν αὐτὸν ἐν τῇ ἑορτῇ
secret. the ˜ Then Jews were seeking Him at the feast

καὶ ἔλεγον, "Ποῦ ἐστιν ἐκεῖνος?" 12 Καὶ γογγυσμὸς* πολὺς
and they said, "Where is that *man?*" And [4]complaining [3]much

περὶ αὐτοῦ ἦν ἐν τοῖς ὄχλοις, οἱ
[5]concerning [6]Him [1]*there* [2]was among the crowds, the *ones*
some

μὲν ἔλεγον ὅτι "Ἀγαθός ἐστιν," ἄλλοι
on the one hand were saying - "[3]a [4]good [5]*man* [1]He [2]is," others

ἔλεγον, "Οὔ, ἀλλὰ πλανᾷ τὸν ὄχλον." 13 Οὐδεὶς
were saying, "No, but He deceives the crowd." No one
on the contrary

μέντοι παρρησίᾳ ἐλάλει περὶ αὐτοῦ διὰ τὸν
however [3]with [4]openness [1]was [2]speaking about Him because of the
openly

φόβον τῶν Ἰουδαίων.
fear of the Jews.

14 Ἤδη δὲ τῆς ἑορτῆς μεσούσης, ἀνέβη ὁ Ἰησοῦς
now ˜ But the feast being in the middle, [2]went [3]up - [1]Jesus
in the middle of the feast,

εἰς τὸ ἱερὸν καὶ ἐδίδασκε. 15 Καὶ ἐθαύμαζον οἱ
into the temple and taught. And [3]were [4]marveling [1]the
began to teach.

Ἰουδαῖοι λέγοντες, "Πῶς οὗτος γράμματα οἶδε, μὴ
[2]Jews saying, "How this *man* letters ˜ knows, not
is this man learned, since He

μεμαθηκώς?"
having learned?"
has not been educated?"

16 Ἀπεκρίθη οὖν[b] αὐτοῖς ὁ Ἰησοῦς καὶ εἶπεν, "Ἡ ἐμὴ
[3]answered [1]Therefore [4]them - [2]Jesus and said, - "My

these things, show Yourself to the world."
5 For even His brothers did not believe in Him.
6 Then Jesus said to them, "My time has not yet come, but your time is always ready.
7 "The world cannot hate you, but it hates Me because I testify of it that its works are evil.
8 "You go up to this feast. I am not yet going up to this feast, for My time has not yet fully come."
9 When He had said these things to them, He remained in Galilee.
10 But when His brothers had gone up, then He also went up to the feast, not openly, but as it were in secret.
11 Then the Jews sought Him at the feast, and said, "Where is He?"
12 And there was much complaining among the people concerning Him. Some said, "He is good"; others said, "No, on the contrary, He deceives the people."
13 However, no one spoke openly of Him for fear of the Jews.
14 Now about the middle of the feast Jesus went up into the temple and taught.
15 And the Jews marveled, saying, "How does this Man know letters, having never studied?"
16 Jesus answered them and said, "My doctrine is not Mine,

[a](7:8) NU reads ουκ, *not.*
[b](7:16) TR omits ουν, *Therefore.*

***(7:12)** γογγυσμός *(gongysmos).* Noun meaning *complaint, murmuring,* from γογγύζω, *murmur.* Like the English words *murmur, grumble,* the Greek word is an example of onomatopoeia, a word which sounds like the action it represents. As here, γογγυσμός suggests the grumbling undertones of complaint. Paul commands Christians to "do all things without *complaining* and disputing" (Phil. 2:14), and Peter tells us to "be hospitable to one another without *grumbling*" (1 Pet. 4:9). Cf. the cognate noun γογγυστής, *grumbler* (Jude 16); and the strenghened verb διαγογγύζω, *grumble (aloud), complain* (Luke 15:2; 19:7).

but His who sent Me.
17 "If anyone wills to do His
will, he shall know concerning
the doctrine, whether it is from
God or *whether* I speak on My
own *authority.*
18 "He who speaks from himself seeks his own glory; but
He who seeks the glory of the
One who sent Him is true, and
no unrighteousness is in Him.
19 "Did not Moses give you
the law, yet none of you keeps
the law? Why do you seek to
kill Me?"
20 The people answered and
said, "You have a demon. Who
is seeking to kill You?"
21 Jesus answered and said to
them, "I did one work, and you
all marvel.
22 "Moses therefore gave you
circumcision (not that it is from
Moses, but from the fathers),
and you circumcise a man on
the Sabbath.
23 "If a man receives circumcision on the Sabbath, so that
the law of Moses should not be
broken, are you angry with Me
because I made a man com-
pletely well on the Sabbath?
24 "Do not judge according to
appearance, but judge with
righteous judgment."
25 Now some of them from
Jerusalem said, "Is this not He
whom they seek to kill?
26 "But look! He speaks
boldly, and they say nothing to
Him. Do the rulers know indeed that this is truly the

διδαχὴ οὐκ ἔστιν ἐμὴ ἀλλὰ τοῦ πέμψαντός με.
teaching not ˜ is Mine but of the One having sent Me.
belongs to Him who

17 Ἐάν τις θέλῃ τὸ θέλημα αὐτοῦ ποιεῖν, γνώσεται περὶ
If anyone wills - [4]will [3]His [1]to [2]do, he will know about

τῆς διδαχῆς, πότερον ἐκ τοῦ Θεοῦ ἐστιν ἢ ἐγὼ ἀπ'
the teaching, whether [3]from - [4]God [1]it [2]is or *whether* I [3]from

ἐμαυτοῦ λαλῶ. **18** Ὁ ἀφ' ἑαυτοῦ λαλῶν, τὴν
[4]Myself [1]am [2]speaking. The *one* [2]from [3]himself [1]speaking, -
who speaks,

δόξαν τὴν ἰδίαν ζητεῖ, ὁ δὲ ζητῶν τὴν δόξαν
[5]glory - [3]his [4]own [1]is [2]seeking, [7]the [8]*One* [6]but seeking the glory
who seeks

τοῦ πέμψαντος αὐτόν, οὗτος ἀληθής ἐστι, καὶ
of the *One* having sent Him, this *One* true ˜ is, and
of Him who

ἀδικία ἐν αὐτῷ οὐκ ἔστιν. **19** Οὐ Μωσῆς δέδωκεν
[4]unrighteousness [5]in [6]Him [3]not [1]*there* [2]is. [2]not [3]Moses [1]Has [4]given

ὑμῖν τὸν νόμον, καὶ οὐδεὶς ἐξ ὑμῶν ποιεῖ τὸν νόμον? Τί
you the law, and yet no one of you does the law? Why
keeps

με ζητεῖτε ἀποκτεῖναι?"
[6]Me [1]are [2]you [3]seeking [4]to [5]kill?"

20 Ἀπεκρίθη ὁ ὄχλος καὶ εἶπε, "Δαιμόνιον ἔχεις.
[3]answered [1]The [2]crowd and said, "[3]a [4]demon [1]You [2]have.

Τίς σε ζητεῖ ἀποκτεῖναι?"
Who [5]You [1]is [2]seeking [3]to [4]kill?"

21 Ἀπεκρίθη Ἰησοῦς καὶ εἶπεν αὐτοῖς, "Ἓν ἔργον
answered ˜ Jesus and said to them, "[3]one [4]work

ἐποίησα, καὶ πάντες θαυμάζετε. **22** Διὰ τοῦτο Μωσῆς
[1]I [2]did, and *you* all marvel. Because of this Moses

δέδωκεν ὑμῖν τὴν περιτομήν (οὐχ ὅτι ἐκ τοῦ Μωσέως ἐστὶν
has given you - circumcision (not that [3]from - [4]Moses [1]it [2]is

ἀλλ' ἐκ τῶν πατέρων), καὶ ἐν σαββάτῳ περιτέμνετε
but from the fathers), and on a Sabbath you circumcise

ἄνθρωπον. **23** Εἰ περιτομὴν λαμβάνει ἄνθρωπος ἐν σαββάτῳ,
a man. If [4]circumcision [3]receives [1]a [2]man on a Sabbath,

ἵνα μὴ λυθῇ ὁ νόμος Μωσέως, ἐμοὶ
so that [6]not [5]should [7]be [8]broken [1]the [2]law [3]of [4]Moses, [12]with [13]Me

χολᾶτε ὅτι ὅλον ἄνθρωπον ὑγιῆ ἐποίησα ἐν
[9]are [10]you [11]angry because [3]a [4]whole [5]man [6]well [1]I [2]made on

σαββάτῳ? **24** Μὴ κρίνετε κατ' ὄψιν, ἀλλὰ τὴν
a Sabbath? not ˜ Do judge according to appearance, but -

δικαίαν κρίσιν κρίνατε."
[2]with [3]righteous [4]judgment [1]judge."

Could This Be the Christ?

25 Ἔλεγον οὖν τινες ἐκ τῶν Ἱεροσολυμιτῶν, "Οὐχ
[6]were [7]saying [1]Therefore [2]some [3]of [4]the [5]Jerusalemites, "[10]not
people of Jerusalem,

οὗτός ἐστιν ὃν ζητοῦσιν ἀποκτεῖναι? **26** Καὶ ἴδε!
[9]this [8]Is *the One* whom they are seeking to kill? And look!

Παρρησίᾳ λαλεῖ, καὶ οὐδὲν αὐτῷ λέγουσι.
[4]in [5]openness [1]He [2]is [3]speaking, and [4]nothing [5]to [6]Him [1]they [2]are [3]saying.
publicly

Μήποτε ἀληθῶς ἔγνωσαν οἱ ἄρχοντες ὅτι οὗτός ἐστιν
Perhaps [3]really [4]knew [1]the [2]rulers that this *man* is
Can it be that the rulers have really come to know

ἀληθῶς[c] ὁ Χριστός? 27 Ἀλλὰ τοῦτον οἴδαμεν πόθεν
truly the Christ? But [3]this [4]*man* [1]we [2]know from where
Messiah? we know where this man

ἐστίν· ὁ δὲ Χριστὸς ὅταν ἔρχηται, οὐδεὶς γινώσκει
He is; [3]the [1]but [4]Christ [2]whenever comes, no one knows
is from; Messiah

πόθεν ἐστίν."
from where He is."
where He is from."

28 Ἔκραξεν οὖν ἐν τῷ ἱερῷ διδάσκων ὁ Ἰησοῦς καὶ
[3]cried [4]out [1]Therefore [5]in [6]the [7]temple [8]teaching - [2]Jesus and

λέγων, "Κἀμὲ οἴδατε, καὶ οἴδατε πόθεν εἰμί· καὶ
saying, "And Me you know, and you know from where I am; and
"You both know Me, where I am from;

ἀπ' ἐμαυτοῦ οὐκ ἐλήλυθα, ἀλλ' ἔστιν ἀληθινὸς ὁ
[5]from [6]Myself [3]not [1]I [2]have [4]come, but [6]is [7]true [1]the [2]*One*
on My own He

πέμψας με, ὃν ὑμεῖς οὐκ οἴδατε. 29 Ἐγὼ[d] οἶδα αὐτὸν
[3]having [4]sent [5]Me, whom you not ~ do know. I know Him
who

ὅτι παρ' αὐτοῦ εἰμι, κἀκεῖνός με ἀπέστειλεν."
because [3]from [4]Him [1]I [2]am, and that One Me ~ sent."
He

30 Ἐζήτουν οὖν αὐτὸν πιάσαι. Καὶ οὐδεὶς
[2]they [3]were [4]seeking [1]Therefore [7]Him [5]to [6]arrest. And no one

ἐπέβαλεν ἐπ' αὐτὸν τὴν χεῖρα ὅτι οὔπω ἐληλύθει ἡ ὥρα
laid [3]on [4]Him [1]the [2]hand because [4]not [5]yet [3]had [6]come - [2]hour
a

αὐτοῦ. 31 Πολλοὶ δὲ ἐκ τοῦ ὄχλου ἐπίστευσαν εἰς αὐτὸν καὶ
[1]His. many ~ But of the crowd believed in Him and

ἔλεγον ὅτι "Ὁ Χριστὸς ὅταν ἔλθῃ, μήτι πλείονα
were saying - "The Christ whenever He comes, [3]no [4]more
Messiah

σημεῖα τούτων ποιήσει ὧν οὗτος ἐποίησεν?"
[5]signs [6]*than* [7]these [1]will [2]do which this *man* did, *will He?*"

Leaders Seek to Arrest Jesus

32 Ἤκουσαν οἱ Φαρισαῖοι τοῦ ὄχλου γογγύζοντος περὶ
[3]heard [1]The [2]Pharisees the crowd murmuring [3]about

αὐτοῦ ταῦτα, καὶ ἀπέστειλαν ὑπηρέτας οἱ Φαρισαῖοι καὶ
[4]Him [1]these [2]*things,* and [7]sent [8]attendants [1]the [2]Pharisees [3]and

οἱ ἀρχιερεῖς ἵνα πιάσωσιν αὐτόν.
[4]the [5]chief [6]priests so that they might arrest Him.

33 Εἶπεν οὖν[e] ὁ Ἰησοῦς, "Ἔτι μικρὸν χρόνον μεθ' ὑμῶν
[3]said [1]Then - [2]Jesus, "Yet a little time [3]with [4]you

εἰμι, καὶ ὑπάγω πρὸς τὸν πέμψαντά με. 34 Ζητήσετέ
[1]I [2]am, and *then* I go to the *One* having sent Me. You will seek
Him who

με καὶ οὐχ εὑρήσετε,[f] καὶ ὅπου εἰμὶ ἐγὼ ὑμεῖς οὐ
Me and [3]not [1]you [2]will find *Me,* and where am ~ I you not ~

δύνασθε ἐλθεῖν."
are able to come."

35 Εἶπον οὖν οἱ Ἰουδαῖοι πρὸς ἑαυτούς, "Ποῦ
[4]said [1]Therefore [2]the [3]Jews to themselves, "Where
among

οὗτος μέλλει πορεύεσθαι ὅτι ἡμεῖς οὐχ εὑρήσομεν
[2]this [3]*man* [1]does [4]intend to go that we not ~ will find

Christ?
27 "However, we know where this Man is from; but when the Christ comes, no one knows where He is from."
28 Then Jesus cried out, as He taught in the temple, saying, "You both know Me, and you know where I am from; and I have not come of Myself, but He who sent Me is true, whom you do not know.
29 "But I know Him, for I am from Him, and He sent Me."
30 Therefore they sought to take Him; but no one laid a hand on Him, because His hour had not yet come.
31 And many of the people believed in Him, and said, "When the Christ comes, will He do more signs than these which this *Man* has done?"
32 The Pharisees heard the crowd murmuring these things concerning Him, and the Pharisees and the chief priests sent officers to take Him.
33 Then Jesus said to them, "I shall be with you a little while longer, and *then* I go to Him who sent Me.
34 "You will seek Me and not find *Me,* and where I am you cannot come."
35 Then the Jews said among themselves, "Where does He intend to go that we shall not

---

c(**7:26**) NU omits αληθως, *truly.* d(**7:29**) TR adds δε, *But.* e(**7:33**) TR adds αυτοις, *to them.* f(**7:34**) NU adds in brackets με, *Me.*

find Him? Does He intend to go
to the Dispersion among the
Greeks and teach the Greeks?
36 "What is this thing that He
said, 'You will seek Me and not
find Me, and where I am you
cannot come'?"
37 On the last day, that great
day of the feast, Jesus stood
and cried out, saying, "If anyone thirsts, let him come to Me
and drink.
38 "He who believes in Me, as
the Scripture has said, out of
his heart will flow rivers of living water."
39 But this He spoke concerning the Spirit, whom those believing in Him would receive;
for the Holy Spirit was not yet
given, because Jesus was not
yet glorified.
40 Therefore many from the
crowd, when they heard this
saying, said, "Truly this is the
Prophet."
41 Others said, "This is the
Christ." But some said, "Will
the Christ come out of Galilee?
42 "Has not the Scripture said
that the Christ comes from the
seed of David and from the
town of Bethlehem, where David was?"
43 So there was a division
among the people because of
Him.
44 Now some of them wanted

αὐτόν? Μὴ εἰς τὴν διασποράν τῶν Ἑλλήνων*
Him? [3]not [7]into [8]the [9]dispersion [10]of [11]the [12]Greeks
among

μέλλει πορεύεσθαι καὶ διδάσκειν τοὺς Ἕλληνας?
[1]He [2]does [4]intend [5]to [6]go and to teach the Greeks, *does He?*

36 *Τίς ἐστιν οὗτος ὁ λόγος ὃν εἶπε, 'Ζητήσετέ με καὶ*
What is this - word which He said, 'You will seek Me and
thing

οὐχ εὑρήσετε,[g] καὶ ὅπου εἰμὶ ἐγὼ ὑμεῖς οὐ δύνασθε
[3]not [1]you [2]will find *Me,* and where am ˜ I you not ˜ are able

ἐλθεῖν'?"
to come'?"

Jesus Promises the Holy Spirit

37 *Ἐν δὲ τῇ ἐσχάτῃ ἡμέρᾳ τῇ μεγάλῃ τῆς ἑορτῆς*
on ˜ Now the last day the great *day* of the feast

εἱστήκει ὁ Ἰησοῦς καὶ ἔκραξε, λέγων, "Ἐάν τις διψᾷ,
stood ˜ - Jesus and cried out, saying, "If anyone thirsts,

ἐρχέσθω πρός με καὶ πινέτω. **38** *Ὁ πιστεύων εἰς*
let him come to Me and let him drink. The *one* believing in
who believes

ἐμέ, καθὼς εἶπεν ἡ Γραφή, ποταμοὶ ἐκ τῆς κοιλίας
Me, just as [3]said [1]the [2]Scripture, rivers [6]out [7]of - [9]belly

αὐτοῦ ῥεύσουσιν ὕδατος ζῶντος." **39** *(Τοῦτο δὲ εἶπε*
[8]his [4]will [5]flow [1]of [3]water [2]living." (this ˜ But He spoke

περὶ τοῦ Πνεύματος, οὗ ἔμελλον λαμβάνειν οἱ
concerning the Spirit, whom [6]were [7]about [8]to [9]receive [1]the [2]*ones*
those who

πιστεύοντες[h] εἰς αὐτόν, οὔπω γὰρ ἦν Πνεῦμα
[3]believing [4]in [5]Him, [15]not [16]yet [17]*given* [10]for [14]was [11]*the* [13]Spirit
believe

Ἅγιον[i] ὅτι Ἰησοῦς οὐδέπω ἐδοξάσθη.)
[12]Holy because Jesus [2]not [3]yet [1]was [4]glorified.)

The People Divided Over Jesus

40 *Πολλοὶ[j] οὖν ἐκ τοῦ ὄχλου ἀκούσαντες τὸν λόγον*
many ˜ Therefore from the crowd hearing the word
when they heard this saying

ἔλεγον, "Οὗτός ἐστιν ἀληθῶς ὁ Προφήτης."
said, "This is truly the Prophet."

41 *Ἄλλοι ἔλεγον, "Οὗτός ἐστιν ὁ Χριστός."*
Others said, "This is the Christ."
Messiah."

Ἄλλοι ἔλεγον, "Μὴ γὰρ ἐκ τῆς Γαλιλαίας ὁ Χριστὸς
Others said, "[5]not [1]For [7]out [8]of - [9]Galilee [2]the [3]Christ
But

ἔρχεται? **42** *Οὐχὶ ἡ Γραφὴ εἶπεν ὅτι ἐκ τοῦ*
[4]is [6]coming, *is He?* [2]not [3]the [4]Scripture [1]Did [5]say that from the

σπέρματος Δαβίδ, καὶ ἀπὸ Βηθλέεμ τῆς κώμης ὅπου ἦν
seed of David, and from Bethlehem the village from where was ˜
descendants where

Δαβὶδ ὁ Χριστὸς ἔρχεται?" **43** *Σχίσμα οὖν ἐν τῷ*
David the Christ is coming?" [2]a [3]division [1]Therefore [7]in [8]the
Messiah

ὄχλῳ ἐγένετο δι' αὐτόν. **44** *Τινὲς δὲ ἤθελον ἐξ*
[9]crowd [4]came [5]to [6]be because of Him. some ˜ Now [3]wished [1]of
occurred

---

g(7:36) NU adds in brackets *με, Me.* h(7:39) NU reads *πιστευσαντες, having believed* or *who believed.* i(7:39) NU omits *Αγιον, Holy.* j(7:40) NU omits *Πολλοι, Many;* therefore *some from.*

*(7:35) *διασπορά (diaspora).* Noun meaning *dispersion, diaspora.* It is used literally here of the dispersion of the Jews among the Gentile nations, but elsewhere metaphorically of Christians as pilgrims in the evil world (James 1:1; 1 Pet. 1:1). It is derived from the verb *διασπείρω, scatter, disperse,* which is used in Acts to refer to the scattering of the Christians from Jerusalem as a result of persecution (Acts 8:1; 11:19).

αὐτῶν πιάσαι αὐτόν, ἀλλ' οὐδεὶς ἐπέβαλεν ἐπ' αὐτὸν τὰς
[2]them to arrest Him, but no one laid [3]on [4]Him [1]the
a

χεῖρας.
[2]hand.

The Rulers Reject Jesus' Claims

45 Ἦλθον οὖν οἱ ὑπηρέται πρὸς τοὺς ἀρχιερεῖς καὶ
[4]came [1]Then [2]the [3]attendants to the chief priests and

Φαρισαίους, καὶ εἶπον αὐτοῖς ἐκεῖνοι, "Διὰ τί οὐκ
Pharisees, and [3]said [4]to [5]them [1]those [2]*men*, "Because of what [3]not
who "Why

ἠγάγετε αὐτόν?"
[1]did [2]you bring Him?"

46 Ἀπεκρίθησαν οἱ ὑπηρέται, "Οὐδέποτε οὕτως ἐλάλησεν
[3]answered [1]The [2]attendants, "[3]never [5]thus [4]spoke
"No man ever

ἄνθρωπος ὡς[k] οὗτος ὁ ἄνθρωπος!"
[1]A [2]man like this - man!"
spoke

47 Ἀπεκρίθησαν οὖν αὐτοῖς οἱ Φαρισαῖοι, "Μὴ καὶ
[4]answered [1]Therefore [5]them [2]the [3]Pharisees, "[8]not [9]also

ὑμεῖς πεπλάνησθε? 48 Μή τις ἐκ τῶν
[6]You [7]have [10]been deceived, *have you?* Not anyone of the
No one

ἀρχόντων ἐπίστευσεν εἰς αὐτὸν ἢ ἐκ τῶν Φαρισαίων?
rulers believed in Him nor of the Pharisees, *have they?*
has believed

49 Ἀλλ' ὁ ὄχλος οὗτος ὁ μὴ γινώσκων τὸν νόμον
But - crowd ˜ this the *one* not knowing the law
which does not know

ἐπικατάρατοί εἰσι."
accursed ˜ are."
is."

50 Λέγει Νικόδημος πρὸς αὐτούς (ὁ ἐλθὼν νυκτὸς[l]
says ˜ Nicodemus to them (the *one* having come *by* night
said (the one who came

πρὸς αὐτόν,[m] εἷς ὢν ἐξ αὐτῶν), 51 "Μὴ ὁ νόμος ἡμῶν
to Him, one ˜ being of them), "[4]not - [2]law [1]Our

κρίνει τὸν ἄνθρωπον ἐὰν μὴ ἀκούσῃ παρ' αὐτοῦ πρότερον
[3]does [5]judge - a man if not it hears from him first
unless

καὶ γνῷ τί ποιεῖ?"
and knows what he is doing, *does it?*"

52 Ἀπεκρίθησαν καὶ εἶπον αὐτῷ, "Μὴ καὶ σὺ ἐκ τῆς
They answered and said to him, "[3]not [4]also [1]You [5]from -

Γαλιλαίας εἶ? Ἐρεύνησον καὶ ἴδε, ὅτι προφήτης
[6]Galilee [2]are, *are you?* Search and see, because a prophet

ἐκ τῆς Γαλιλαίας οὐκ ἐγήγερται."[n]
[4]out [5]of - [6]Galilee [2]not [1]has [3]arisen."

An Adulteress Before the Light of the World

53 Καὶ[o] ἀπῆλθεν ἕκαστος εἰς τὸν οἶκον αὐτοῦ.
And [3]went [4]out [1]each [2]*one* to - [3]house [1]his [2]*own*.

8 1 Καὶ ὁ Ἰησοῦς ἐπορεύθη εἰς τὸ Ὄρος τῶν Ἐλαιῶν.
And - Jesus went to the Mount - of Olives.

2 Ὄρθρου δὲ πάλιν βαθέως[a] ἦλθεν ὁ Ἰησοῦς εἰς τὸ
[2]*at* [4]dawn [1]And [7]again [3]deep [6]came - [5]Jesus into the
And very early in the morning Jesus came again

to take Him, but no one laid hands on Him.
45 Then the officers came to the chief priests and Pharisees, who said to them, "Why have you not brought Him?"
46 The officers answered, "No man ever spoke like this Man!"
47 Then the Pharisees answered them, "Are you also deceived?
48 "Have any of the rulers or the Pharisees believed in Him?
49 "But this crowd that does not know the law is accursed."
50 Nicodemus (he who came to Jesus by night, being one of them) said to them,
51 "Does our law judge a man before it hears him and knows what he is doing?"
52 They answered and said to him, "Are you also from Galilee? Search and look, for no prophet has arisen out of Galilee."
53 And everyone went to his *own* house.

8 But Jesus went to the Mount of Olives.
2 Now early in the morning He came again into the temple,

---

[k](7:46) NU omits ως ουτος ο ανθρωπος, *like this man.*
[l](7:50) NU omits νυκτος, *(by) night.*
[m](7:50) NU adds το προτερον, *before.*
[n](7:52) NU reads εγειρεται, *is to rise.*
[o](7:53) NU brackets 7:53—8:11 as not original.
[a](8:2) NU, TR omit βαθεως, *deep.*

and all the people came to Him; and He sat down and taught them.

3 Then the scribes and Pharisees brought to Him a woman caught in adultery. And when they had set her in the midst,

4 they said to Him, "Teacher, this woman was caught in adultery, in the very act.

5 "Now Moses, in the law, commanded us that such should be stoned. But what do You say?"

6 This they said, testing Him, that they might have *something* of which to accuse Him. But Jesus stooped down and wrote on the ground with *His* finger, as though He did not hear.

7 So when they continued asking Him, He raised Himself up and said to them, "He who is without sin among you, let him throw a stone at her first."

8 And again He stooped down and wrote on the ground.

9 Then those who heard *it*, being convicted by *their* conscience, went out one by one, beginning with the oldest *even* to the last. And Jesus was left alone, and the woman standing in the midst.

10 When Jesus had raised Himself up and saw no one but the woman, He said to her, "Woman, where are those accusers of yours? Has no one condemned you?"

11 She said, "No one, Lord." And Jesus said to her, "Neither do I condemn you; go and sin no more."

ἱερόν, καὶ πᾶς ὁ λαὸς ἤρχετο πρὸς αὐτόν· καὶ
temple, and all the people was coming to Him; and
were

καθίσας ἐδίδασκεν αὐτούς.
having sat down He was teaching them.
began to teach

3 Ἄγουσι δὲ οἱ γραμματεῖς καὶ οἱ Φαρισαῖοι πρὸς
[7]bring [1]And [2]the [3]scribes [4]and [5]the [6]Pharisees to
brought

αὐτὸν γυναῖκα ἐπὶ μοιχείᾳ κατειλημμένην, καὶ στήσαντες
Him a woman in adultery having been caught, and having stood
who had been

αὐτὴν ἐν τῷ μέσῳ, 4 εἶπον αὐτῷ, "Διδάσκαλε, ταύτην
her in the midst, they said to Him, "Teacher, [3]this [4]*woman*

εὕρομεν[b] ἐπ' αὐτοφώρῳ μοιχευομένην. 5 Ἐν δὲ τῷ
[1]we [2]found [7]in [8]the [9]very [10]act [5]committing [6]adultery. in ˜ Now -

νόμῳ ἡμῶν[c] Μωσῆς ἐνετείλατο τὰς τοιαύτας λιθάζειν. Σὺ
law ˜ our Moses commanded - [3]such [4]*women* [1]to [2]stone. [8]You

οὖν τί λέγεις περὶ αὐτῆς?"[d] 6 Τοῦτο δὲ ἔλεγον
[5]Therefore [6]what [7]do [9]say about her?" this ˜ And they said

πειράζοντες αὐτόν, ἵνα ἔχωσι κατηγορίαν κατ'
testing Him, so that they might have an accusation against

αὐτοῦ.
Him.

Ὁ δὲ Ἰησοῦς κάτω κύψας, τῷ δακτύλῳ ἔγραφεν εἰς
- But Jesus down ˜ stooping, with the finger was writing into
His began to write on

τὴν γῆν.[e] 7 Ὡς δὲ ἐπέμενον ἐπερωτῶντες αὐτόν,
the ground. while ˜ And they were continuing questioning Him,

ἀναβλέψας[f] εἶπεν αὐτοῖς, "Ὁ ἀναμάρτητος ὑμῶν
looking up He said to them, "The *one* without sin of you
He looked up and "He who is among

πρῶτος λίθον βαλέτω ἐπ' αὐτήν." 8 Καὶ πάλιν κάτω
[8]first [4]a [5]stone [1]let [2]him [3]throw [6]at [7]her." And again down ˜
He stooped

κύψας ἔγραφεν εἰς τὴν γῆν. 9 Οἱ δὲ ἀκούσαντες
stooping He wrote into the ground. [2]the [3]*ones* [1]And hearing
down and on those who heard

ἐξήρχοντο εἷς καθ' εἷς, ἀρξάμενοι ἀπὸ τῶν πρεσβυτέρων
were going out one by one, beginning from the older *ones*
began to go out

ἕως τῶν ἐσχάτων.[g] Καὶ κατελείφθη μόνος ὁ Ἰησοῦς, καὶ ἡ
until the last *ones*. And [3]was [4]left [1]only - [2]Jesus, and the

γυνὴ ἐν μέσῳ οὖσα. 10 Ἀνακύψας δὲ ὁ Ἰησοῦς εἶδεν
woman in *the* midst being. [2]standing [3]up [1]And - Jesus saw
who was in the midst.

αὐτὴν καὶ[h] εἶπεν, "Γύναι, ποῦ εἰσιν οἱ κατήγοροί σου?[i]
her and said, "Woman, where are - accusers ˜ your?

Οὐδείς σε κατέκρινεν?"
[2]no [3]one [5]you [1]Did [4]condemn?"

11 Ἡ δὲ εἶπεν, "Οὐδείς, Κύριε."
[2]the [3]*one* [1]And said, "No one, Lord."
she

Εἶπε δὲ αὐτῇ ὁ Ἰησοῦς, "Οὐδὲ ἐγώ σε κατακρίνω·
[3]said [1]And [4]to [5]her - [2]Jesus, "Neither [2]I [4]you [1]do [3]condemn;

πορεύου καὶ ἀπὸ τοῦ νῦν[j] μηκέτι ἁμάρτανε."
go and from - now *on* [2]no [3]longer [1]sin."
no more

---

[b](8:4) For ταυτην ευρομεν, *we found this (woman)*, NU, TR read αυτη η γυνη κατειληπται, *this woman has been caught* (TR κατεληφθη, *was caught*). [c](8:5) NU, TR read ημιν, *(Moses commanded) us.* [d](8:5) NU, TR omit περι αυτης, *about her.* [e](8:6) TR adds μη προσποιουμενος, *not taking notice.* [f](8:7) TR reads ανακυψας, *rising up.* [g](8:9) NU omits εως των εσχατων, *until the last (ones).* [h](8:10) NU omits ειδεν αυτην και, *saw her and;* TR reads και μηδενα θεασαμενος πλην της γυναικος, *and saw no one but the woman.* [i](8:10) TR adds εκεινοι, *those.* [j](8:11) TR omits απο του νυν, *from now on.*

12 Πάλιν οὖν αὐτοῖς ὁ Ἰησοῦς ἐλάλησε λέγων, "Ἐγώ
[6]again [1]Then [4]to [5]them - [2]Jesus [3]spoke saying, "I

εἰμι τὸ φῶς* τοῦ κόσμου. Ὁ ἀκολουθῶν ἐμοὶ οὐ μὴ
am the light of the world. The *one* following Me [2]not [3]not
by no means

περιπατήσῃ ἐν τῇ σκοτίᾳ ἀλλ' ἕξει τὸ φῶς τῆς ζωῆς."
[1]shall [4]walk in - darkness but will have the light - of life."

Jesus Defends His Self-Witness

13 Εἶπον οὖν αὐτῷ οἱ Φαρισαῖοι, "Σὺ περὶ
[4]said [1]Therefore [5]to [6]Him [2]the [3]Pharisees, "You [2]about

σεαυτοῦ μαρτυρεῖς· ἡ μαρτυρία σου οὐκ ἔστιν ἀληθής."
[3]Yourself [1]testify; - testimony ~ Your not ~ is true."
valid."

14 Ἀπεκρίθη Ἰησοῦς καὶ εἶπεν αὐτοῖς, "Κἂν ἐγὼ
answered ~ Jesus and said to them, "Even if I

μαρτυρῶ περὶ ἐμαυτοῦ, ἀληθής ἐστιν ἡ μαρτυρία μου,
should testify about Myself, [4]true [3]is - [2]testimony [1]My,
valid

ὅτι οἶδα πόθεν ἦλθον καὶ ποῦ ὑπάγω, ὑμεῖς δὲ οὐκ
because I know from where I came and where I am going, you ~ but not ~

οἴδατε πόθεν ἔρχομαι καὶ ποῦ ὑπάγω. 15 Ὑμεῖς
do know from where I come and where I am going. You

κατὰ τὴν σάρκα κρίνετε· ἐγὼ οὐ κρίνω οὐδένα.
[2]according [3]to [4]the [5]flesh [1]judge; I not ~ do judge no one.
anyone.

16 Καὶ ἐὰν κρίνω δὲ ἐγώ, ἡ κρίσις ἡ ἐμὴ ἀληθής ἐστιν·
[2]even [3]if [5]judge [1]But [4]I, - judgment ~ - My true ~ is;
valid

ὅτι μόνος οὐκ εἰμί, ἀλλ' ἐγὼ καὶ ὁ πέμψας με Πατήρ.
because [4]alone [3]not [1]I [2]am, but I and the [2]sending [3]Me [1]Father.
who sent

17 Καὶ ἐν τῷ νόμῳ δὲ τῷ ὑμετέρῳ γέγραπται ὅτι δύο
[2]also [3]in - [5]law [1]But - [4]your it is written that [3]of [4]two

ἀνθρώπων ἡ μαρτυρία ἀληθής ἐστιν. 18 Ἐγώ εἰμι ὁ
[5]men [1]the [2]testimony true ~ is. I am the *One*
valid

μαρτυρῶν περὶ ἐμαυτοῦ, καὶ μαρτυρεῖ περὶ ἐμοῦ ὁ πέμψας
testifying about Myself, and [5]testifies [6]about [7]Me [1]the [3]sending
who sent

με Πατήρ."
[4]Me [2]Father."

19 Ἔλεγον οὖν αὐτῷ, "Ποῦ ἐστιν ὁ Πατήρ σου?"
[2]they [3]said [1]Then to Him, "Where is - Father ~ Your?"

Ἀπεκρίθη Ἰησοῦς, "Οὔτε ἐμὲ οἴδατε οὔτε τὸν Πατέρα
answered ~ Jesus, "[3]neither [4]Me [1]You [2]know nor - Father ~

μου. Εἰ ἐμὲ ᾔδειτε, καὶ τὸν Πατέρα μου ᾔδειτε ἄν."
My. If [3]Me [1]you [2]knew, also - Father ~ My you would know." -

20 Ταῦτα τὰ ῥήματα ἐλάλησεν ὁ Ἰησοῦς ἐν τῷ γαζοφυλακίῳ,
These - sayings spoke ~ - Jesus in the treasury,

διδάσκων ἐν τῷ ἱερῷ· καὶ οὐδεὶς ἐπίασεν αὐτόν, ὅτι
teaching in the temple; and no one seized Him, because
while teaching

οὔπω ἐληλύθει ἡ ὥρα αὐτοῦ.
[4]not [5]yet [3]had [6]come - [2]hour [1]His.
time

12 Then Jesus spoke to them again, saying, "I am the light of the world. He who follows Me shall not walk in darkness, but have the light of life."
13 The Pharisees therefore said to Him, "You bear witness of Yourself; Your witness is not true."
14 Jesus answered and said to them, "Even if I bear witness of Myself, My witness is true, for I know where I came from and where I am going; but you do not know where I come from and where I am going.
15 "You judge according to the flesh; I judge no one.
16 "And yet if I do judge, My judgment is true; for I am not alone, but I *am* with the Father who sent Me.
17 "It is also written in your law that the testimony of two men is true.
18 "I am One who bears witness of Myself, and the Father who sent Me bears witness of Me."
19 Then they said to Him, "Where is Your Father?" Jesus answered, "You know neither Me nor My Father. If you had known Me, you would have known My Father also."
20 These words Jesus spoke in the treasury, as He taught in the temple; and no one laid hands on Him, for His hour had not yet come.

***(8:12)** φῶς *(phōs).* Common noun meaning *light,* which may be used either literally (John 11:9) or metaphorically (as here in 8:12). It may also be used, by metonymy, of that which gives light, again literally (as Acts 16:29) or metaphorically (as Matt. 5:14). Eph. 5:13 appears to use it in the sense of that which is illuminated by light. The NT uses it especially of spiritual light and enlightenment, in contrast to spiritual darkness, a point also involved here in John 8:12 (cf. 1 John 1:7). Indeed, God is light (1 John 1:5). Cf. the cognate noun φωτισμός, *illumination, enlightenment, light* (only in 2 Cor. 4:4). See φωστήρ at Rev. 21:11.

21 Then Jesus said to them again, "I am going away, and you will seek Me, and will die in your sin. Where I go you cannot come."
22 So the Jews said, "Will He kill Himself, because He says, 'Where I go you cannot come'?"
23 And He said to them, "You are from beneath; I am from above. You are of this world; I am not of this world.
24 "Therefore I said to you that you will die in your sins; for if you do not believe that I am *He,* you will die in your sins."
25 Then they said to Him, "Who are You?" And Jesus said to them, "Just what I have been saying to you from the beginning.
26 "I have many things to say and to judge concerning you, but He who sent Me is true; and I speak to the world those things which I heard from Him."
27 They did not understand that He spoke to them of the Father.
28 Then Jesus said to them, "When you lift up the Son of Man, then you will know that I am *He,* and *that* I do nothing of Myself; but as My Father taught Me, I speak these things.
29 "And He who sent Me is with Me. The Father has not left Me alone, for I always do those things that please Him."

***(8:28)** ὑψόω *(hypsoō).* Verb meaning *lift up, raise, exalt,* used both literally and figuratively in the NT. While the word is used once in John in its most literal sense ("Moses *lifted up* the serpent," 3:14a), elsewhere in John it refers to Jesus' being *lifted up* on the cross as the moment of His exaltation (3:14b; here in 8:28; 12:32). The figurative meaning *exalt* is used both of Christ (Acts 2:33) and persons (Luke 1:52). This "exalting" may be misguided, as when one exalts himself (Matt. 23:12a) as opposed to when God exalts someone (23:12b; James 4:10). Cf. the cognate noun ὕψος, *height, high position* (and synonym ὕψωμα); and the adjective ὕψιστος, *highest, most exalted,* used substantively to refer to "the Most High (God)" (as Mark 5:7).

Jesus Predicts His Departure to the Father

21 Εἶπεν οὖν πάλιν αὐτοῖς ὁ Ἰησοῦς, "Ἐγὼ ὑπάγω,
[3]said [1]Then [6]again [4]to [5]them - [2]Jesus, "I am going away,
καὶ ζητήσετέ με, καὶ ἐν τῇ ἁμαρτίᾳ ὑμῶν ἀποθανεῖσθε.
and you will seek Me, and in - sin ˜ your you will die.
Ὅπου ἐγὼ ὑπάγω ὑμεῖς οὐ δύνασθε ἐλθεῖν."
Where I am going you not ˜ are able to come."
22 Ἔλεγον οὖν οἱ Ἰουδαῖοι, "Μήτι ἀποκτενεῖ
[4]said [1]Therefore [2]the [3]Jews, "[5]*Surely* [8]not [6]He [7]will [9]kill
ἑαυτόν, ὅτι λέγει, 'Ὅπου ἐγὼ ὑπάγω ὑμεῖς οὐ
Himself, *will He,* since He says, 'Where I am going you not ˜
δύνασθε ἐλθεῖν'?"
are able to come'?"
23 Καὶ εἶπεν αὐτοῖς, "Ὑμεῖς ἐκ τῶν κάτω ἐστέ, ἐγὼ
And He said to them, "You [2]from - [3]below [1]are, I
ἐκ τῶν ἄνω εἰμί. Ὑμεῖς ἐκ τοῦ κόσμου τούτου ἐστέ, ἐγὼ
[2]from - [3]above [1]am. You [2]from - [4]world [3]this [1]are, I
οὐκ εἰμὶ ἐκ τοῦ κόσμου τούτου. 24 Εἶπον οὖν ὑμῖν ὅτι
not ˜ am from - world ˜ this. [2]I [3]said [1]Therefore to you that
ἀποθανεῖσθε ἐν ταῖς ἁμαρτίαις ὑμῶν· ἐὰν γὰρ μὴ
you will die in - sins ˜ your; if ˜ for [3]not
πιστεύσητε ὅτι ἐγώ εἰμι, ἀποθανεῖσθε ἐν ταῖς ἁμαρτίαις
[1]you [2]do believe that I am *He,* you will die in - sins ˜
ὑμῶν."
your."
25 Ἔλεγον οὖν αὐτῷ, "Σὺ τίς εἶ?"
[2]they [3]said [1]Then to Him, "[3]You [1]Who [2]are?"
Καὶ εἶπεν αὐτοῖς ὁ Ἰησοῦς, "Τὴν ἀρχὴν ὅ τι
And [2]said [3]to [4]them - [1]Jesus, "[12]*from* [13]the [14]beginning - [6]what
καὶ λαλῶ ὑμῖν. 26 Πολλὰ ἔχω περὶ
[5]Even [7]I [8]am [9]speaking [10]to [11]you. [3]many [4]*things* [1]I [2]have [10]concerning
ὑμῶν λαλεῖν καὶ κρίνειν, ἀλλ' ὁ πέμψας με ἀληθής ἐστι,
[11]you [5]to [6]say [7]and [8]to [9]judge, but the *One* sending Me true ˜ is,
κἀγὼ ἃ ἤκουσα παρ' αὐτοῦ, ταῦτα λέγω εἰς
and [4]I [1]*the* [2]*things* [3]which heard from Him, these *things* I say to
τὸν κόσμον." 27 Οὐκ ἔγνωσαν ὅτι τὸν Πατέρα
the world." [3]not [1]They [2]did know that [6]*about* [7]the [8]Father
αὐτοῖς ἔλεγεν. 28 Εἶπεν οὖν αὐτοῖς ὁ Ἰησοῦς,
[4]to [5]them [1]He [2]was [3]speaking. [3]said [1]Therefore [4]to [5]them - [2]Jesus,
"Ὅταν ὑψώσητε* τὸν Υἱὸν τοῦ Ἀνθρώπου, τότε γνώσεσθε
"Whenever you lift up the Son - of Man, then you will know
ὅτι ἐγώ εἰμι καὶ ἀπ' ἐμαυτοῦ ποιῶ οὐδέν, ἀλλὰ καθὼς
that I am *He* and from Myself I do nothing, but just as
ἐδίδαξέ με ὁ Πατήρ μου, ταῦτα λαλῶ. 29 Καὶ ὁ
[3]taught [4]Me - [2]Father [1]My, these *things* I speak. And the *One*
πέμψας με μετ' ἐμοῦ ἐστιν. Οὐκ ἀφῆκέ με μόνον ὁ
having sent Me [2]with [3]Me [1]is. [7]not [6]has [8]left [9]Me [10]alone [4]The
Πατήρ, ὅτι ἐγὼ τὰ ἀρεστὰ αὐτῷ ποιῶ πάντοτε."
[5]Father, because I [3]the [4]*things* [5]pleasing [6]to [7]Him [2]do [1]always."

The Truth Shall Make You Free

30 Ταῦτα αὐτοῦ λαλοῦντος, πολλοὶ ἐπίστευσαν εἰς
[3]these [4]*things* [1]Him [2]saying, many believed in
While He spoke,

αὐτόν.
Him.

31 Ἔλεγεν οὖν ὁ Ἰησοῦς πρὸς τοὺς πεπιστευκότας αὐτῷ
[3]said [1]Then - [2]Jesus to the [2]having [3]believed [4]Him
who had

Ἰουδαίους, "Ἐὰν ὑμεῖς μείνητε ἐν τῷ λόγῳ τῷ ἐμῷ, ἀληθῶς
[1]Jews, "If you abide in - word ˜ - My, truly

μαθηταί μού ἐστε. 32 Καὶ γνώσεσθε τὴν ἀλήθειαν, καὶ ἡ
[4]disciples [3]My [1]you [2]are. And you will know the truth, and the

ἀλήθεια ἐλευθερώσει ὑμᾶς."
truth will make free ˜ you."

33 Ἀπεκρίθησαν αὐτῷ, "Σπέρμα Ἀβραάμ ἐσμεν καὶ
They answered Him, "[3]*the* [4]seed [5]of [6]Abraham [1]We [2]are and
descendants

οὐδενὶ δεδουλεύκαμεν πώποτε. Πῶς σὺ λέγεις ὅτι
to no one have we [2]been [3]enslaved [1]ever. How *can* You say -

'Ἐλεύθεροι γενήσεσθε'?"
'[4]free [1]You [2]will [3]become'?"

34 Ἀπεκρίθη αὐτοῖς ὁ Ἰησοῦς, "Ἀμὴν ἀμὴν λέγω ὑμῖν,
[2]answered [3]them - [1]Jesus, "Amen amen I say to you,
"Most assuredly

ὅτι πᾶς ὁ ποιῶν τὴν ἁμαρτίαν δοῦλός ἐστι τῆς
that every - *one* doing - sin [2]a [3]slave [1]is -
everyone who commits

ἁμαρτίας. 35 Ὁ δὲ δοῦλος οὐ μένει ἐν τῇ οἰκίᾳ εἰς
of sin. the ˜ But slave not ˜ does remain in the house into
a forever,

τὸν αἰῶνα, ὁ υἱὸς μένει εἰς τὸν αἰῶνα. 36 Ἐὰν οὖν
the age, the son remains into the age. if ˜ Therefore
forever.

ὁ Υἱὸς ὑμᾶς ἐλευθερώσῃ, ὄντως ἐλεύθεροι ἔσεσθε.
the Son you ˜ makes free, [4]truly [5]free [1]you [2]will [3]be.

Abraham's Seed and Satan's

37 "Οἶδα ὅτι σπέρμα Ἀβραάμ ἐστε, ἀλλὰ ζητεῖτέ
"I know that [3]*the* [4]seed [5]of [6]Abraham [1]you [2]are, but you seek
descendants

με ἀποκτεῖναι ὅτι ὁ λόγος ὁ ἐμὸς οὐ χωρεῖ ἐν ὑμῖν.
[3]Me [1]to [2]kill because - word ˜ - My no ˜ finds place in you.

38 Ἐγὼ ὃ ἑώρακα παρὰ τῷ Πατρί μου, λαλῶ, καὶ ὑμεῖς
I ˜ What have seen from - Father ˜ My, I speak, and you ˜

οὖν ὃ ἑωράκατε[k] παρὰ τῷ πατρὶ ὑμῶν ποιεῖτε."
therefore [2]what [3]you [4]have [5]seen [6]from - [8]father [7]your [1]do."

39 Ἀπεκρίθησαν καὶ εἶπον αὐτῷ, "Ὁ πατὴρ ἡμῶν
They answered and said to Him, - "[4]father [3]our

Ἀβραάμ ἐστι."
[1]Abraham [2]is."

Λέγει αὐτοῖς ὁ Ἰησοῦς, "Εἰ τέκνα τοῦ Ἀβραὰμ
[2]says [3]to [4]them - [1]Jesus, "If [3]children - [4]of [5]Abraham
said

ἦτε, τὰ ἔργα τοῦ Ἀβραὰμ ἐποιεῖτε. 40 Νῦν δὲ
[1]you [2]were, the works - of Abraham you would do. now ˜ But

ζητεῖτέ με ἀποκτεῖναι, ἄνθρωπον ὃς τὴν ἀλήθειαν ὑμῖν
you seek [3]Me [1]to [2]kill, a man who [3]the [4]truth [5]to [6]you

30 As He spoke these words, many believed in Him.
31 Then Jesus said to those Jews who believed Him, "If you abide in My word, you are My disciples indeed.
32 "And you shall know the truth, and the truth shall make you free."
33 They answered Him, "We are Abraham's descendants, and have never been in bondage to anyone. How *can* You say, 'You will be made free'?"
34 Jesus answered them, "Most assuredly, I say to you, whoever commits sin is a slave of sin.
35 "And a slave does not abide in the house forever, *but* a son abides forever.
36 "Therefore if the Son makes you free, you shall be free indeed.
37 "I know that you are Abraham's descendants, but you seek to kill Me, because My word has no place in you.
38 "I speak what I have seen with My Father, and you do what you have seen with your father."
39 They answered and said to Him, "Abraham is our father." Jesus said to them, "If you were Abraham's children, you would do the works of Abraham.
40 "But now you seek to kill Me, a Man who has told you

[k](8:38) NU reads ηκουσατε, *heard from.*

the truth which I heard from
God. Abraham did not do this.
41 "You do the deeds of your
father." Then they said to Him,
"We were not born of fornication; we have one Father—
God."
42 Jesus said to them, "If God
were your Father, you would
love Me, for I proceeded forth
and came from God; nor have I
come of Myself, but He sent
Me.
43 "Why do you not under-
stand My speech? Because you
are not able to listen to My
word.
44 "You are of *your* father the
devil, and the desires of your
father you want to do. He was a
murderer from the beginning,
and does not stand in the truth,
because there is no truth in
him. When he speaks a lie, he
speaks from his own *resources,*
for he is a liar and the father of
it.
45 "But because I tell the
truth, you do not believe Me.
46 "Which of you convicts Me
of sin? And if I tell the truth,
why do you not believe Me?
47 "He who is of God hears
God's words; therefore you do
not hear, because you are not
of God."

λελάληκα ἣν ἤκουσα παρὰ τοῦ Θεοῦ. Τοῦτο Ἀβραὰμ οὐκ
[1]has [2]spoken which I heard from - God. [5]this [1]Abraham [3]not

ἐποίησεν. 41 Ὑμεῖς ποιεῖτε τὰ ἔργα τοῦ πατρὸς ὑμῶν."
[2]did [4]do. You do the works - of father ˜ your."
deeds

Εἶπον οὖν αὐτῷ, "Ἡμεῖς ἐκ πορνείας οὐ
[2]they [3]said [1]Then to Him, "We [5]of [6]fornication [2]not

γεγεννήμεθα, ἕνα Πατέρα ἔχομεν — τὸν Θεόν."
[1]have [3]been [4]born, [9]one [10]Father [7]we [8]have — - God."

42 Εἶπεν οὖν αὐτοῖς ὁ Ἰησοῦς, "Εἰ ὁ Θεὸς Πατὴρ
[3]said [1]Therefore [4]to [5]them - [2]Jesus, "If - God [3]Father

ὑμῶν ἦν, ἠγαπᾶτε ἂν ἐμέ, ἐγὼ γὰρ ἐκ τοῦ Θεοῦ
[2]your [1]was, you would love - Me, I ˜ for from - God
were,

ἐξῆλθον καὶ ἥκω· οὐδὲ γὰρ ἀπ' ἐμαυτοῦ ἐλήλυθα, ἀλλ'
came forth and have come; not ˜ for from Myself have I come, but
proceeded

ἐκεῖνός με ἀπέστειλε. 43 Διὰ τί τὴν λαλιὰν
that *One* Me ˜ sent. On account of what - [6]speech
He Why do you not

τὴν ἐμὴν οὐ γινώσκετε? Ὅτι οὐ δύνασθε
- [5]My [3]not [1]do [2]you [4]know? Because [3]not [1]you [2]are able
understand what I say?

ἀκούειν τὸν λόγον τὸν ἐμόν. 44 Ὑμεῖς ἐκ τοῦ πατρὸς τοῦ
to listen to - word ˜ - My. You [2]from [3]the [4]father [5]the
your

διαβόλου ἐστέ, καὶ τὰς ἐπιθυμίας τοῦ πατρὸς ὑμῶν θέλετε
[6]devil [1]are, and the desires - of father ˜ your you want

ποιεῖν. Ἐκεῖνος ἀνθρωποκτόνος ἦν ἀπ' ἀρχῆς καὶ ἐν τῇ
to do. That *one* [2]a [3]murderer [1]was from *the* beginning and [4]in [5]the
He

ἀληθείᾳ οὐχ ἕστηκεν, ὅτι οὐκ ἔστιν ἀλήθεια ἐν αὐτῷ.
[6]truth [2]not [1]has [3]stood, because [3]not [1]*there* [2]is truth in him.
stayed,

Ὅταν λαλῇ τὸ ψεῦδος, ἐκ τῶν ἰδίων λαλεῖ,
Whenever he speaks the lie, from - his own *things* he speaks,
tells a

ὅτι ψεύστης ἐστὶ καὶ ὁ πατὴρ αὐτοῦ. 45 Ἐγὼ δὲ
because [3]a [4]liar [1]he [2]is and the father of it. [3]I [1]But
lies.

ὅτι τὴν ἀλήθειαν λέγω, οὐ πιστεύετέ μοι. 46 Τίς
[2]because [5]the [6]truth [4]speak, [9]not [7]you [8]do [10]believe Me. Who
Which

ἐξ ὑμῶν ἐλέγχει με περὶ ἁμαρτίας? Εἰ δὲ ἀλήθειαν
from you convicts Me concerning sin? if ˜ But [4]truth
of of

λέγω, διὰ τί ὑμεῖς οὐ πιστεύετέ μοι?
[1]I [2]am [3]speaking, on account of what [2]you [3]not [1]do [4]believe Me?
why

47 Ὁ ὢν ἐκ τοῦ Θεοῦ τὰ ῥήματα τοῦ Θεοῦ ἀκούει·
The *one* being from - God [2]the [3]sayings - [4]of [5]God [1]hears;
who is words

διὰ τοῦτο ὑμεῖς οὐκ ἀκούετε, ὅτι ἐκ τοῦ Θεοῦ
on account of this you not ˜ do hear *them,* because [4]from - [5]God
therefore

οὐκ ἐστέ."
[3]not [1]you [2]are."

Before Abraham Was, I AM

48 Ἀπεκρίθησαν οὖν οἱ Ἰουδαῖοι καὶ εἶπον αὐτῷ, "Οὐ
4answered 1Then 2the 3Jews and said to Him, "3not

καλῶς λέγομεν ἡμεῖς ὅτι Σαμαρείτης εἶ σὺ καὶ δαιμόνιον
5well 1Are 4saying 2we that 3a 4Samaritan 2are 1You and 3a 4demon
correctly

ἔχεις?"
1You 2have?"

49 Ἀπεκρίθη Ἰησοῦς, "Ἐγὼ δαιμόνιον οὐκ ἔχω, ἀλλὰ
answered ˜ Jesus, "I 4a 5demon 2not 1do 3have, but

τιμῶ τὸν Πατέρα μου, καὶ ὑμεῖς ἀτιμάζετέ με. 50 Ἐγὼ δὲ
I honor - Father ˜ My, and you dishonor Me. I ˜ But

οὐ ζητῶ τὴν δόξαν μου· ἔστιν ὁ ζητῶν καὶ
not ˜ am seeking - glory ˜ My; *there* is the One seeking *it* and
One who seeks it

κρίνων. 51 Ἀμὴν ἀμὴν λέγω ὑμῖν, ἐάν τις τὸν λόγον
judging. Amen amen I say to you, if anyone - 3word
who judges. Most assuredly

τὸν ἐμὸν τηρήσῃ, θάνατον οὐ μὴ θεωρήσῃ εἰς τὸν
- 2My 1keeps, 9death 6not 7not 4he 5shall 8see into the
he shall by no means experience death."

αἰῶνα."
age."

52 Εἶπον οὖν αὐτῷ οἱ Ἰουδαῖοι, "Νῦν ἐγνώκαμεν
4said 1Therefore 5to 6Him 2the 3Jews, "Now we have known
know

ὅτι δαιμόνιον ἔχεις! Ἀβραὰμ ἀπέθανε καὶ οἱ προφῆται,
that 3a 4demon 1You 2have! Abraham 4died 1and 2the 3prophets,

καὶ σὺ λέγεις, 'Ἐάν τις τὸν λόγον μου τηρήσῃ οὐ μὴ
and You say, 'If anyone - 3word 2My 1keeps 6not 7not
he shall

γεύσηται θανάτου εἰς τὸν αἰῶνα.'? 53 Μὴ σὺ
4he 5shall 8taste death into the age.'? 3not 1You
by no means ever experience death.'?

μείζων εἶ τοῦ πατρὸς ἡμῶν Ἀβραάμ, ὅστις ἀπέθανε?
4greater 5*than* 2are - father ˜ our Abraham, who died, *are You?*

Καὶ οἱ προφῆται ἀπέθανον. Τίνα σεαυτὸν σὺ
Also the prophets died. Whom 4Yourself 2You

ποιεῖς?"
1do 3make 5*out* 6*to* 7*be?"*

54 Ἀπεκρίθη Ἰησοῦς, "Ἐὰν ἐγὼ δοξάζω ἐμαυτόν, ἡ δόξα
answered ˜ Jesus, "If I glorify Myself, - glory ˜

μου οὐδέν ἐστιν. Ἔστιν ὁ Πατήρ μου ὁ δοξάζων με,
My nothing ˜ is. It is - Father ˜ My the One glorifying Me,
who glorifies

ὃν ὑμεῖς λέγετε ὅτι 'Θεὸς ἡμῶν ἐστι.' 55 Καὶ οὐκ
of whom you say - '4God 3our 1He 2is.' And yet 3not

ἐγνώκατε αὐτόν, ἐγὼ δὲ οἶδα αὐτόν. Καὶ ἐὰν εἴπω
1you 2have known Him, I ˜ but know Him. And if I would say

ὅτι οὐκ οἶδα αὐτόν, ἔσομαι ὅμοιος ὑμῶν, ψεύστης, ἀλλ'
that 3not 1I 2do know Him, I will be like you, a liar, but
would

οἶδα αὐτὸν καὶ τὸν λόγον αὐτοῦ τηρῶ. 56 Ἀβραὰμ ὁ
I do know Him and - 4word 3His 1I 2keep. Abraham -

πατὴρ ὑμῶν ἠγαλλιάσατο ἵνα ἴδῃ τὴν ἡμέραν τὴν
father ˜ your rejoiced that he should see - day ˜ -

ἐμήν, καὶ εἶδε καὶ ἐχάρη."
My, and he saw *it* and he was glad."

48 Then the Jews answered and said to Him, "Do we not say rightly that You are a Samaritan and have a demon?"
49 Jesus answered, "I do not have a demon; but I honor My Father, and you dishonor Me.
50 "And I do not seek My *own* glory; there is One who seeks and judges.
51 "Most assuredly, I say to you, if anyone keeps My word he shall never see death."
52 Then the Jews said to Him, "Now we know that You have a demon! Abraham is dead, and the prophets; and You say, 'If anyone keeps My word he shall never taste death.'
53 "Are You greater than our father Abraham, who is dead? And the prophets are dead. Who do You make Yourself out to be?"
54 Jesus answered, "If I honor Myself, My honor is nothing. It is My Father who honors Me, of whom you say that He is your God.
55 "Yet you have not known Him, but I know Him. And if I say, 'I do not know Him,' I shall be a liar like you; but I do know Him and keep His word.
56 "Your father Abraham rejoiced to see My day, and he saw *it* and was glad."

57 Then the Jews said to Him,
"You are not yet fifty years old,
and have You seen Abraham?"
58 Jesus said to them, "Most
assuredly, I say to you, before
Abraham was, I AM."
59 Then they took up stones
to throw at Him; but Jesus hid
Himself and went out of the
temple, going through the
midst of them, and so passed
by.
9 Now as *Jesus* passed by,
He saw a man who was
blind from birth.
2 And His disciples asked
Him, saying, "Rabbi, who
sinned, this man or his parents,
that he was born blind?"
3 Jesus answered, "Neither
this man nor his parents sinned,
but that the works of God
should be revealed in him.
4 "I must work the works of
Him who sent Me while it is
day; *the* night is coming when
no one can work.
5 "As long as I am in the
world, I am the light of the
world."
6 When He had said these
things, He spat on the ground
and made clay with the saliva;
and He anointed the eyes of the
blind man with the clay.
7 And He said to him, "Go,
wash in the pool of Siloam"
(which is translated, Sent). So
he went and washed, and came
back seeing.
8 Therefore the neighbors
and those who previously had

---

[l](8:59) NU omits the rest of this verse. [a](9:4) NU reads ημας, *we*.

*(9:4) ἐργάζομαι (*ergazomai*). Verb meaning *work* (intransitive), or *do, perform, accomplish* (transitive). Compared to synonyms like ποιέω, *do*, or πράσσω, *act, accomplish*, ἐργάζομαι is generally stronger, implying a considerable expenditure of effort to accomplish or produce something. Most often ἐργάζομαι and the cognate noun ἔργον, *work, deed*, are used in a positive sense, as here (cf. John 3:21; Rom. 2:10; James 2:17ff), but both may also refer to working/works unsuccessfully offered to God for salvation (as Rom. 4:2–6). The words are also general occupational terms used to indicate "working" for one's

57 Εἶπον οὖν οἱ Ἰουδαῖοι πρὸς αὐτόν, "Πεντήκοντα ἔτη
[4]said [1]Then [2]the [3]Jews to Him, "Fifty years
"You are

οὔπω ἔχεις, καὶ Ἀβραὰμ ἑώρακας?"
not yet You have, and [4]Abraham [1]have [2]You [3]seen?"
not yet fifty years old,

58 Εἶπεν αὐτοῖς ὁ Ἰησοῦς, "Ἀμὴν ἀμὴν λέγω ὑμῖν,
[2]said [3]to [4]them - [1]Jesus, "Amen amen I say to you,
"Most assuredly

πρὶν Ἀβραὰμ γενέσθαι, ἐγώ εἰμι." **59** Ἦραν οὖν
before Abraham to be, I am." [2]they [3]picked [4]up [1]Therefore
was,

λίθους ἵνα βάλωσιν ἐπ' αὐτόν· Ἰησοῦς δὲ ἐκρύβη
stones so that they might throw *them* on Him; Jesus ˜ but was hidden
at

καὶ ἐξῆλθεν ἐκ τοῦ ἱεροῦ,[l] διελθὼν διὰ μέσου αὐτῶν· καὶ
and went out of the temple, having gone through midst ˜ their; and

παρῆγεν οὕτως.
passed by thus.
in this way.

Jesus Heals a Man Born Blind

9 **1** Καὶ παράγων εἶδεν ἄνθρωπον τυφλὸν ἐκ γενετῆς.
And passing by He saw a man blind from birth.

2 Καὶ ἠρώτησαν αὐτὸν οἱ μαθηταὶ αὐτοῦ λέγοντες, "Ῥαββί,
And [3]asked [4]Him - [2]disciples [1]His saying, "Rabbi,

τίς ἥμαρτεν, οὗτος ἢ οἱ γονεῖς αὐτοῦ, ἵνα τυφλὸς
who sinned, this *man* or - parents ˜ his, that [4]blind

γεννηθῇ?"
[1]he [2]was [3]born?"

3 Ἀπεκρίθη Ἰησοῦς, "Οὔτε οὗτος ἥμαρτεν οὔτε οἱ
answered ˜ Jesus, "Neither this *man* sinned nor -

γονεῖς αὐτοῦ, ἀλλ' ἵνα φανερωθῇ τὰ ἔργα τοῦ
parents ˜ his, but so that [5]should [6]be [7]revealed [1]the [2]works -

Θεοῦ ἐν αὐτῷ. **4** Ἐμὲ[a] δεῖ ἐργάζεσθαι* τὰ
[3]of [4]God in him. [5]Me [1]It [2]is [3]necessary [4]*for* to work the

ἔργα* τοῦ πέμψαντός με ἕως ἡμέρα ἐστίν· ἔρχεται νὺξ
works of the *One* having sent Me while [3]day [1]it [2]is; [5]is [6]coming [4]night
of Him who

ὅτε οὐδεὶς δύναται ἐργάζεσθαι. **5** Ὅταν ἐν τῷ κόσμῳ ὦ,
when no one is able to work. When [3]in [4]the [5]world [1]I [2]am,

φῶς εἰμι τοῦ κόσμου." **6** Ταῦτα εἰπών, ἔπτυσε
[8]*the* [9]light [6]I [7]am of the world." [3]these [4]*things* [1]Having [2]said, He spat
When He had

χαμαὶ καὶ ἐποίησε πηλὸν ἐκ τοῦ πτύσματος, καὶ
on the ground and made clay from the saliva, and

ἐπέχρισε τὸν πηλὸν ἐπὶ τοὺς ὀφθαλμοὺς τοῦ τυφλοῦ. **7** Καὶ
smeared the clay on the eyes of the blind *man*. And

εἶπεν αὐτῷ, "Ὕπαγε νίψαι εἰς τὴν κολυμβήθραν τοῦ Σιλωάμ"
He said to him, "Go wash in the pool - of Siloam"

(ὅ ἑρμηνεύεται, Ἀπεσταλμένος). Ἀπῆλθεν οὖν καὶ ἐνίψατο,
(which is translated Having Been Sent). [2]he [3]went [1]So and washed,

καὶ ἦλθε βλέπων.
and he came seeing.

8 Οἱ οὖν γείτονες καὶ οἱ θεωροῦντες αὐτὸν τὸ
the ˜ Therefore neighbors and the *ones* seeing him -
those who previously saw

πρότερον ὅτι τυφλὸς[b] ἦν, ἔλεγον, "Οὐχ οὗτός ἐστιν
formerly that 3blind 1he 2was, were saying, "3not 2this 1is
him

ὁ καθήμενος καὶ προσαιτῶν?"
the man sitting and begging?"
he who was

9 Ἄλλοι ἔλεγον ὅτι "Οὗτός ἐστιν."
Others were saying - "This is he."

Ἄλλοι δὲ ὅτι[c] "Ὅμοιος αὐτῷ ἐστιν."
others ~ But - "3similar 4to 5him 1He 2is."
"He looks like him."

Ἐκεῖνος ἔλεγεν ὅτι "Ἐγώ εἰμι."
That *man* was saying - "I am *he*."
He kept

10 Ἔλεγον οὖν αὐτῷ, "Πῶς ἀνεῴχθησάν σου
2they 3were 4saying 1Therefore to him, "How were 3opened 1your
kept

οἱ ὀφθαλμοί?"
- 2eyes?"

11 Ἀπεκρίθη ἐκεῖνος καὶ εἶπεν, "Ἄνθρωπος λεγόμενος
3answered 1That 2*man* and said, "A man being called
He called

Ἰησοῦς πηλὸν ἐποίησε καὶ ἐπέχρισέ μου τοὺς ὀφθαλμοὺς καὶ
Jesus clay ~ made and anointed my - eyes and

εἶπέ μοι, 'Ὕπαγε εἰς τὴν κολυμβήθραν τοῦ[d] Σιλωὰμ καὶ
said to me, 'Go to the pool - of Siloam and

νίψαι.' Ἀπελθὼν δὲ καὶ νιψάμενος, ἀνέβλεψα."
wash.' 2having 3gone 1Then and having washed, I received *my* sight."
When I had gone and washed,

12 Εἶπον οὖν αὐτῷ, "Ποῦ ἐστιν ἐκεῖνος?"
2they 3said 1Then to him, "Where is that *man*?"
He?"

Λέγει, "Οὐκ οἶδα."
He says, "3not 1I 2do know."
said,

The Pharisees Excommunicate the Healed Man

13 Ἄγουσιν αὐτὸν πρὸς τοὺς Φαρισαίους τόν ποτε
They bring him 5to 6the 7Pharisees 1the 2*one* 3formerly
brought who was

τυφλόν. 14 Ἦν δὲ σάββατον ὅτε[e] τὸν πηλὸν ἐποίησεν ὁ
4blind. 2it 3was 1And a Sabbath when 3the 4clay 2made -

Ἰησοῦς καὶ ἀνέῳξεν αὐτοῦ τοὺς ὀφθαλμούς. 15 Πάλιν οὖν
1Jesus and opened his - eyes. again ~ Then

ἠρώτων αὐτὸν καὶ οἱ Φαρισαῖοι πῶς ἀνέβλεψεν.
4were 5asking 6him 3also 1the 2Pharisees how he received *his* sight.

Ὁ δὲ εἶπεν αὐτοῖς, "Πηλὸν ἐπέθηκέ μου ἐπὶ τοὺς
2the 3*one* 1And said to them, "3clay 1He 2put my ~ on -
he

ὀφθαλμούς, καὶ ἐνιψάμην, καὶ βλέπω."
eyes, and I washed, and I see."

16 Ἔλεγον οὖν ἐκ τῶν Φαρισαίων τινές, "Οὗτος ὁ
6were 7saying 1Therefore 3of 4the 5Pharisees 2some, "This -

ἄνθρωπος οὐκ ἔστι παρὰ τοῦ Θεοῦ, ὅτι τὸ σάββατον οὐ
man not ~ is from - God, because 5the 6Sabbath 3not

τηρεῖ."
1He 2does 4keep."

Ἄλλοι ἔλεγον, "Πῶς δύναται ἄνθρωπος ἁμαρτωλὸς
Others were saying, "How is 4able 1a 3man 2sinful

seen that he was blind said, "Is not this he who sat and begged?"
9 Some said, "This is he." Others *said,* "He is like him." He said, "I am *he.*"
10 Therefore they said to him, "How were your eyes opened?"
11 He answered and said, "A Man called Jesus made clay and anointed my eyes and said to me, 'Go to the pool of Siloam and wash.' So I went and washed, and I received sight."
12 Then they said to him, "Where is He?" He said, "I do not know."
13 They brought him who formerly was blind to the Pharisees.
14 Now it was a Sabbath when Jesus made the clay and opened his eyes.
15 Then the Pharisees also asked him again how he had received his sight. He said to them, "He put clay on my eyes, and I washed, and I see."
16 Therefore some of the Pharisees said, "This Man is not from God, because He does not keep the Sabbath." Others said, "How can a man who is a

[b](9:8) NU reads προσαιτης, *a beggar.* [c](9:9) For δε οτι, *But,* NU reads ελεγον ουχι, αλλα, *said, "No, but.* [d](9:11) NU omits την κολυμβηθραν του, *the pool of.* [e](9:14) NU reads εν η ημερα, *on which day (He made).*

livelihood (as 1 Cor. 4:12; 2 Thess. 3:8).

sinner do such signs?" And there was a division among them.
17 They said to the blind man again, "What do you say about Him because He opened your eyes?" He said, "He is a prophet."
18 But the Jews did not believe concerning him, that he had been blind and received his sight, until they called the parents of him who had received his sight.
19 And they asked them, saying, "Is this your son, who you say was born blind? How then does he now see?"
20 His parents answered them and said, "We know that this is our son, and that he was born blind;
21 "but by what means he now sees we do not know, or who opened his eyes we do not know. He is of age; ask him. He will speak for himself."
22 His parents said these *things* because they feared the Jews, for the Jews had agreed already that if anyone confessed *that* He *was* Christ, he would be put out of the synagogue.
23 Therefore his parents said, "He is of age; ask him."
24 So they again called the man who was blind, and said to him, "Give God the glory! We know that this Man is a sinner."
25 He answered and said, "Whether He is a sinner *or not* I do not know. One thing I

τοιαῦτα σημεῖα ποιεῖν?" Καὶ σχίσμα ἦν ἐν αὐτοῖς.
[7]such [8]signs [5]to [6]do?" And [3]a [4]division [1]*there* [2]was among them.

17 Λέγουσι τῷ τυφλῷ πάλιν, "Σὺ τί λέγεις περὶ
They say to the blind *man* again, "[3]you [1]What [2]do say about
said

αὐτοῦ ὅτι ἤνοιξέ σου τοὺς ὀφθαλμούς?"
Him because He opened your - eyes?"

Ὁ δὲ εἶπεν ὅτι "Προφήτης ἐστίν." 18 Οὐκ
[2]the [3]*one* [1]And said - "[3]a [4]prophet [1]He [2]is." [5]not
he

ἐπίστευσαν οὖν οἱ Ἰουδαῖοι περὶ αὐτοῦ, ὅτι τυφλὸς
[4]did [6]believe [1]Therefore [2]the [3]Jews about him, that [3]blind

ἦν καὶ ἀνέβλεψεν, ἕως ὅτου ἐφώνησαν τοὺς γονεῖς
[1]he [2]was and received *his* sight, until - they called the parents

αὐτοῦ τοῦ ἀναβλέψαντος. 19 Καὶ ἠρώτησαν αὐτοὺς
of him the *one* receiving *his* sight. And they asked them
who had received

λέγοντες, "Οὗτός ἐστιν ὁ υἱὸς ὑμῶν, ὃν ὑμεῖς λέγετε ὅτι
saying, "this ˜ Is - son ˜ your, whom you say that

τυφλὸς ἐγεννήθη? Πῶς οὖν ἄρτι βλέπει?"
[4]blind [1]he [2]was [3]born? How then [3]now [1]does [2]he [4]see?"

20 Ἀπεκρίθησαν δὲ αὐτοῖς οἱ γονεῖς αὐτοῦ καὶ εἶπον,
[4]answered [1]And [5]them - [3]parents [2]his and said,

"Οἴδαμεν ὅτι οὗτός ἐστιν ὁ υἱὸς ἡμῶν καὶ ὅτι τυφλὸς
"We know that this is - son ˜ our and that [4]blind

ἐγεννήθη· 21 πῶς δὲ νῦν βλέπει οὐκ οἴδαμεν, ἢ τίς
[1]he [2]was [3]born; how ˜ but now ˜ he sees [3]not [1]we [2]do know, or who

ἤνοιξεν αὐτοῦ τοὺς ὀφθαλμοὺς ἡμεῖς οὐκ οἴδαμεν. Αὐτὸς
opened his - eyes we not ˜ do know. He

ἡλικίαν ἔχει, αὐτὸν ἐρωτήσατε. Αὐτὸς περὶ ἑαυτοῦ λαλήσει."
age ˜ has, him ˜ ask. He [3]about [4]himself [1]will [2]speak."
is of age, for

22 Ταῦτα εἶπον οἱ γονεῖς αὐτοῦ ὅτι ἐφοβοῦντο τοὺς
These *things* [3]said - [2]parents [1]his because they feared the

Ἰουδαίους, ἤδη γὰρ συνετέθειντο οἱ Ἰουδαῖοι ἵνα ἐάν τις
Jews, [5]already [1]for [4]had [6]agreed [2]the [3]Jews that if anyone

αὐτὸν ὁμολογήσῃ Χριστόν, ἀποσυνάγωγος
[3]Him [1]should [2]confess *as the* Christ, [4]expelled [5]from [6]the [7]synagogue
Messiah, excommunicated

γένηται. 23 Διὰ τοῦτο οἱ γονεῖς αὐτοῦ εἶπον ὅτι
[1]he [2]would [3]be. On account of this - parents ˜ his said -
Therefore

"Ἡλικίαν ἔχει, αὐτὸν ἐρωτήσατε."
"[3]age [1]He [2]has, him ˜ ask."
"He is of age,

24 Ἐφώνησαν οὖν ἐκ δευτέρου τὸν ἄνθρωπον ὃς
[2]they [3]called [1]Therefore from a second the man who
a second time

ἦν τυφλὸς καὶ εἶπον αὐτῷ, "Δὸς δόξαν τῷ Θεῷ! Ἡμεῖς
was blind and said to him, "Give glory - to God! We

οἴδαμεν ὅτι ὁ ἄνθρωπος οὗτος ἁμαρτωλός ἐστιν."
know that - man ˜ this [2]a [3]sinner [1]is."

25 Ἀπεκρίθη οὖν ἐκεῖνος καὶ εἶπεν, "Εἰ
[4]answered [1]Therefore [2]that [3]*one* and said, "Whether
he

ἁμαρτωλός ἐστιν, οὐκ οἶδα. Ἓν οἶδα, ὅτι
[3]a [4]sinner [1]He [2]is, [7]not [5]I [6]do [8]know. One *thing* I do know, that

τυφλὸς ὤν, ἄρτι βλέπω."
blind ~ being now I see."
although I was blind

26 Εἶπον δὲ αὐτῷ πάλιν,[f] "Τί ἐποίησέ σοι? Πῶς
[2]they [3]said [1]And to him again, "What did He do to you? How

ἤνοιξέ σου τοὺς ὀφθαλμούς?"
did He open your - eyes?"

27 Ἀπεκρίθη αὐτοῖς, "Εἶπον ὑμῖν ἤδη, καὶ οὐκ
He answered them, "I told you already, and [3]not

ἠκούσατε. Τί πάλιν θέλετε ἀκούειν? Μὴ καὶ ὑμεῖς
[1]you [2]did listen. Why [7]again [1]do [2]you [3]want [4]to [5]hear [6]*it?* [10]not [11]also [8]You

θέλετε αὐτοῦ μαθηταὶ γενέσθαι?"
[9]do [12]want [15]His [16]disciples [13]to [14]become, *do you?*"

28 Ἐλοιδόρησαν αὐτὸν καὶ εἶπον, "Σὺ εἶ μαθητὴς
They reviled him and said, "You are a disciple

ἐκείνου, ἡμεῖς δὲ τοῦ Μωσέως ἐσμὲν μαθηταί. 29 Ἡμεῖς
of that *One,* we ~ but - [3]of [4]Moses [1]are [2]disciples. We

οἴδαμεν ὅτι Μωσεῖ λελάληκεν ὁ Θεός· τοῦτον δὲ
know that [4]to [5]Moses [2]has [3]spoken - [1]God; [9]this [10]*man* [6]but [7]*as* [8]*for*

οὐκ οἴδαμεν πόθεν ἐστίν."
[13]not [11]we [12]do [14]know from where He is."
where He is from."

30 Ἀπεκρίθη ὁ ἄνθρωπος καὶ εἶπεν αὐτοῖς, "Ἐν γὰρ
[3]answered [1]The [2]man and said to them, "in ~ For

τούτῳ θαυμαστόν ἐστιν, ὅτι ὑμεῖς οὐκ οἴδατε πόθεν
this [3]a [4]remarkable [5]*thing* [1]*there* [2]is that you not ~ do know from where
where He

ἐστί, καὶ ἀνέῳξέ μου τοὺς ὀφθαλμούς. 31 Οἴδαμεν δὲ ὅτι
He is, yet He opened my - eyes. [2]we [3]know [1]But that
is from,

ἁμαρτωλῶν ὁ Θεὸς οὐκ ἀκούει, ἀλλ' ἐάν τις
[6]sinners - [1]God [3]not [2]does [4]listen [5]to, but if anyone

θεοσεβὴς ᾖ καὶ τὸ θέλημα αὐτοῦ ποιῇ, τούτου ἀκούει.
God-fearing ~ is and - [3]will [2]His [1]does, [6]this [7]*one* [4]He [5]hears.

32 Ἐκ τοῦ αἰῶνος οὐκ ἠκούσθη ὅτι ἤνοιξέ τις
From the age [3]not [1]it [2]was [4]heard that opened ~ anyone
Since the world began, it has been unheard of

ὀφθαλμοὺς τυφλοῦ γεγεννημένου. 33 Εἰ μὴ ἦν οὗτος
the eyes [1]of [2]*one* [6]blind [3]having [4]been [5]born. If [4]not [3]was [1]this [2]*man*
were

παρὰ Θεοῦ, οὐκ ἠδύνατο ποιεῖν οὐδέν."
from God, [3]not [1]He [2]would [4]be [5]able to do nothing."
anything."

34 Ἀπεκρίθησαν καὶ εἶπον αὐτῷ, "Ἐν ἁμαρτίαις σὺ
They answered and said to him, "[5]in [6]sins [1]You

ἐγεννήθης ὅλος, καὶ σὺ διδάσκεις ἡμᾶς?" Καὶ ἐξέβαλον
[2]were [4]born [3]wholly, and you ~ do teach us?" And they cast

αὐτὸν ἔξω.
him out.

The Man's Belief and the Pharisees' Blindness

35 Ἤκουσεν ὁ Ἰησοῦς ὅτι ἐξέβαλον αὐτὸν ἔξω· καὶ
heard ~ - Jesus that they cast him out; and

εὑρὼν αὐτόν, εἶπεν αὐτῷ, "Σὺ πιστεύεις εἰς τὸν Υἱὸν
finding him, He said to him, "you ~ Do believe in the Son
when He found

τοῦ Θεοῦ?"[g]
- of God?"

know: that though I was blind, now I see."
26 Then they said to him again, "What did He do to you? How did He open your eyes?"
27 He answered them, "I told you already, and you did not listen. Why do you want to hear *it* again? Do you also want to become His disciples?"
28 Then they reviled him and said, "You are His disciple, but we are Moses' disciples.
29 "We know that God spoke to Moses; *as for* this *fellow,* we do not know where He is from."
30 The man answered and said to them, "Why, this is a marvelous thing, that you do not know where He is from; yet He has opened my eyes!
31 "Now we know that God does not hear sinners; but if anyone is a worshiper of God and does His will, He hears him.
32 "Since the world began it has been unheard of that anyone opened the eyes of one who was born blind.
33 "If this Man were not from God, He could do nothing."
34 They answered and said to him, "You were completely born in sins, and are you teaching us?" And they cast him out.
35 Jesus heard that they had cast him out; and when He had found him, He said to him, "Do you believe in the Son of God?"

---

[f](**9:26**) NU omits παλιν, *again.* [g](**9:35**) NU reads *ανθρωπον, (Son of) Man.*

36 He answered and said, "Who is He, Lord, that I may believe in Him?"
37 And Jesus said to him, "You have both seen Him and it is He who is talking with you."
38 Then he said, "Lord, I believe!" And he worshiped Him.
39 And Jesus said, "For judgment I have come into this world, that those who do not see may see, and that those who see may be made blind."
40 Then *some* of the Pharisees who were with Him heard these words, and said to Him, "Are we blind also?"
41 Jesus said to them, "If you were blind, you would have no sin; but now you say, 'We see.' Therefore your sin remains.

10 "Most assuredly, I say to you, he who does not enter the sheepfold by the door, but climbs up some other way, the same is a thief and a robber.
2 "But he who enters by the door is the shepherd of the sheep.
3 "To him the doorkeeper opens, and the sheep hear his voice; and he calls his own sheep by name and leads them out.
4 "And when he brings out his own sheep, he goes before

36 Ἀπεκρίθη ἐκεῖνος καὶ εἶπε, "Καὶ τίς ἐστι, Κύριε, ἵνα
[3]answered [1]That [2]*one* and said, "And who is He, Lord, that
He

πιστεύσω εἰς αὐτόν?"
I may believe in Him?"

37 Εἶπε δὲ αὐτῷ ὁ Ἰησοῦς, "Καὶ ἑώρακας αὐτὸν
[3]said [1]And [4]to [5]him - [2]Jesus, "[3]both [1]You [2]have seen Him

καὶ ὁ λαλῶν μετὰ σοῦ ἐκεῖνός ἐστιν."
and the *One* speaking with you [2]that [3]*One* [1]is."

38 Ὁ δὲ ἔφη, "Πιστεύω, Κύριε!" Καὶ προσεκύνησεν
[2]the [3]*one* [1]And said, "I believe, Lord!" And he worshiped
He

αὐτῷ.
Him.

39 Καὶ εἶπεν ὁ Ἰησοῦς, "Εἰς κρίμα ἐγὼ εἰς τὸν κόσμον
And said ˜ - Jesus, "For judgment I [2]into - [4]world

τοῦτον ἦλθον, ἵνα οἱ μὴ βλέποντες βλέπωσι, καὶ
[3]this [1]came, so that the *ones* not seeing may see, and
those who do not see

οἱ βλέποντες τυφλοὶ γένωνται."
the *ones* seeing [3]blind [1]may [2]become."
those who see

40 Καὶ ἤκουσαν ἐκ τῶν Φαρισαίων ταῦτα
And [10]heard [1]*some* [2]of [3]the [4]Pharisees [11]these [12]*things*

οἱ ὄντες μετ' αὐτοῦ καὶ εἶπον αὐτῷ, "Μὴ καὶ ἡμεῖς
[5]the [6]*ones* [7]being [8]with [9]Him and they said to Him, "[3]not [5]also [1]We
who were

τυφλοί ἐσμεν?"
[4]blind [2]are, *are we?*"

41 Εἶπεν αὐτοῖς ὁ Ἰησοῦς, "Εἰ τυφλοὶ ἦτε, οὐκ ἂν
[2]said [3]to [4]them - [1]Jesus, "If [3]blind [1]you [2]were, [6]not -

εἴχετε ἁμαρτίαν,* νῦν δὲ λέγετε ὅτι 'Βλέπομεν.' Ἡ
[4]you [5]would [7]have sin, now ˜ but you say - 'We see.' -

οὖν[h] ἁμαρτία ὑμῶν μένει.
Therefore sin ˜ your remains.

Jesus Is the True Shepherd

10 **1** "Ἀμὴν ἀμὴν λέγω ὑμῖν, ὁ μὴ εἰσερχόμενος
"Amen amen I say to you, the *one* not entering
"Most assuredly he who does not enter

διὰ τῆς θύρας εἰς τὴν αὐλὴν τῶν προβάτων, ἀλλὰ
through the door into the fold of the sheep, but
sheepfold,

ἀναβαίνων ἀλλαχόθεν, ἐκεῖνος κλέπτης ἐστὶ καὶ λῃστής.
going up another way, that *one* [2]a [3]thief [1]is and a robber.
goes

2 Ὁ δὲ εἰσερχόμενος διὰ τῆς θύρας ποιμήν ἐστι
[2]the [3]*one* [1]But entering through the door [2]*the* [3]shepherd [1]is
he who enters

τῶν προβάτων. **3** Τούτῳ ὁ θυρωρὸς ἀνοίγει, καὶ τὰ
of the sheep. To this *one* the doorkeeper opens, and the
him

πρόβατα τῆς φωνῆς αὐτοῦ ἀκούει· καὶ τὰ ἴδια πρόβατα
sheep - [3]voice [2]his [1]hear; and - [3]his [4]own [5]sheep

καλεῖ κατ' ὄνομα καὶ ἐξάγει αὐτά. **4** Καὶ ὅταν τὰ
[1]he [2]calls by name and he leads out ˜ them. And whenever -

ἴδια πρόβατα ἐκβάλῃ, ἔμπροσθεν αὐτῶν πορεύεται,
[4]his [5]own [6]sheep [1]he [2]brings [3]out, [9]before [10]them [7]he [8]goes,

---

[h](9:41) NU omits ουν, *Therefore.*

*(9:41) ἁμαρτία *(hamartia).* Noun meaning *sin.* The most common sense of ἁμαρτία in the NT is the act of violating the will or law of God (1 John 5:17). The less frequent ἁμάρτημα (Rom. 3:25) is synonymous. ἁμαρτία can also designate a continuing state of sinfulness as an inherent aspect of one's character (John 9:34). Here in 9:41 the emphasis is on the moral consequences and *guilt* that result from having sinned (cf. 1 John 1:7, 8). In Paul's letters and Hebrews, the concept of *sin* is that of a power which controls people (Rom. 7:20; Heb. 3:13). Cf. the cognate verb ἁμαρτάνω, *sin;* the noun ἁμαρτωλός, *sinner;* and the adjective ἁμαρτωλός, *sinful.*

καὶ τὰ πρόβατα αὐτῷ ἀκολουθεῖ, ὅτι οἴδασι τὴν φωνὴν
and the sheep him ˜ follow, because they know - voice ˜

αὐτοῦ. 5 Ἀλλοτρίῳ δὲ οὐ μὴ ἀκολουθήσωσιν ἀλλὰ
his. [2]a [3]stranger [1]But [6]not [7]not [4]they [5]would [8]follow but
they will by no means follow

φεύξονται ἀπ' αὐτοῦ, ὅτι οὐκ οἴδασι τῶν
they will flee from him, because [3]not [1]they [2]do [4]know [7]of [8]the

ἀλλοτρίων τὴν φωνήν." 6 Ταύτην τὴν παροιμίαν εἶπεν
[9]strangers [5]the [6]voice." This - figure of speech [2]spoke
illustration

αὐτοῖς ὁ Ἰησοῦς, ἐκεῖνοι δὲ οὐκ ἔγνωσαν τίνα ἦν
[3]to [4]them - [1]Jesus, [6]those [7]*ones* [5]but not ˜ did know what [3]were
they understand

ἃ ἐλάλει αὐτοῖς.
[1]*the* [2]*things* which He was speaking to them.

Jesus Is the Good Shepherd

7 Εἶπεν οὖν πάλιν αὐτοῖς ὁ Ἰησοῦς, "Ἀμὴν ἀμὴν
[3]said [1]Then [6]again [4]to [5]them - [2]Jesus, "Amen amen
"Most assuredly

λέγω ὑμῖν ὅτι ἐγώ εἰμι ἡ θύρα τῶν προβάτων. 8 Πάντες
I say to you that I am the door of the sheep. All

ὅσοι ἦλθον[a] κλέπται εἰσὶ καὶ λῃσταί, ἀλλ' οὐκ ἤκουσαν
as many as came thieves ˜ are and robbers, but [4]not [3]did [5]hear
who

αὐτῶν τὰ πρόβατα. 9 Ἐγώ εἰμι ἡ θύρα. Δι' ἐμοῦ ἐάν
[6]them [1]the [2]sheep. I am the door. [4]through [5]Me [1]If

τις εἰσέλθῃ, σωθήσεται, καὶ εἰσελεύσεται καὶ
[2]anyone [3]enters, he will be saved, and will go in and

ἐξελεύσεται καὶ νομὴν εὑρήσει. 10 Ὁ κλέπτης οὐκ ἔρχεται
will go out and [3]pasture [1]will [2]find. The thief not ˜ does come

εἰ μὴ ἵνα κλέψῃ καὶ θύσῃ καὶ ἀπολέσῃ. Ἐγὼ ἦλθον
if not that he may steal and may kill and may destroy. I came
except to steal to kill to destroy.

ἵνα ζωὴν ἔχωσι καὶ περισσὸν ἔχωσιν.
so that [4]life [1]they [2]may [3]have and [5]abundantly [1]they [2]may [3]have [4]*it.*

11 Ἐγώ εἰμι ὁ ποιμὴν ὁ καλός. Ὁ ποιμὴν ὁ καλὸς τὴν
I am the shepherd ˜ - good. The shepherd ˜ - good -

ψυχὴν αὐτοῦ τίθησιν ὑπὲρ τῶν προβάτων. 12 Ὁ
[4]life [3]His [1]lays [2]down in behalf of the sheep. [2]the

μισθωτὸς δέ, καὶ οὐκ ὢν ποιμήν, οὗ οὐκ εἰσὶ
[3]hired [4]hand [1]But, and not being a shepherd, of whom [4]not [3]are
the one who is not who does not

τὰ πρόβατα ἴδια, θεωρεῖ τὸν λύκον ἐρχόμενον καὶ ἀφίησι
[1]the [2]sheep his own, sees the wolf coming and leaves
own the sheep,

τὰ πρόβατα καὶ φεύγει· καὶ ὁ λύκος ἁρπάζει αὐτὰ καὶ
the sheep and flees; and the wolf snatches them and

σκορπίζει τὰ πρόβατα. 13 Ὁ δὲ μισθωτὸς φεύγει ὅτι
scatters the sheep. the ˜ And hired hand flees because

μισθωτός ἐστι καὶ οὐ μέλει αὐτῷ περὶ τῶν προβάτων.
[3]a [4]hired [5]hand [1]he [2]is and [3]not [1]it [2]is a care to him about the sheep.
he does not care

14 Ἐγώ εἰμι ὁ ποιμὴν ὁ καλός, καὶ γινώσκω τὰ ἐμά, καὶ
I am the shepherd ˜ - good, and I know - My *own,* and

γινώσκομαι ὑπὸ τῶν ἐμῶν.[b] 15 Καθὼς γινώσκει με ὁ
I am known by - My *own.* Just as [3]knows [4]Me [1]the

Πατήρ, κἀγὼ γινώσκω τὸν Πατέρα, καὶ τὴν ψυχήν μου
[2]Father, I also know the Father, and - [5]life [4]My

them; and the sheep follow
him, for they know his voice.
5 "Yet they will by no means
follow a stranger, but will flee
from him, for they do not know
the voice of strangers."
6 Jesus used this illustration,
but they did not understand the
things which He spoke to them.
7 Then Jesus said to them
again, "Most assuredly, I say to
you, I am the door of the
sheep.
8 "All who *ever* came before
Me are thieves and robbers,
but the sheep did not hear
them.
9 "I am the door. If anyone
enters by Me, he will be saved,
and will go in and out and find
pasture.
10 "The thief does not come
except to steal, and to kill, and
to destroy. I have come that
they may have life, and that
they may have *it* more abundantly.
11 "I am the good shepherd.
The good shepherd gives His
life for the sheep.
12 "But a hireling, *he who is*
not the shepherd, one who
does not own the sheep, sees
the wolf coming and leaves the
sheep and flees; and the wolf
catches the sheep and scatters
them.
13 "The hireling flees because
he is a hireling and does not
care about the sheep.
14 "I am the good shepherd;
and I know My *sheep,* and am
known by My own.
15 "As the Father knows Me,
even so I know the Father; and

[a](**10:8**) NU adds in brackets *προ εμου, before Me.*
[b](**10:14**) For *γινωσκομαι υπο των εμων, I am known by My (own),* NU reads *γινωσκουσι με τα εμα, My (own) know Me.*

I lay down My life for the sheep.
16 "And other sheep I have which are not of this fold; them also I must bring, and they will hear My voice; and there will be one flock *and* one shepherd.
17 "Therefore My Father loves Me, because I lay down My life that I may take it again.
18 "No one takes it from Me, but I lay it down of Myself. I have power to lay it down, and I have power to take it again. This command I have received from My Father."
19 Therefore there was a division again among the Jews because of these sayings.
20 And many of them said, "He has a demon and is mad. Why do you listen to Him?"
21 Others said, "These are not the words of one who has a demon. Can a demon open the eyes of the blind?"
22 Now it was the Feast of Dedication in Jerusalem, and it was winter.
23 And Jesus walked in the temple, in Solomon's porch.
24 Then the Jews surrounded Him and said to Him, "How long do You keep us in doubt? If You are the Christ, tell us plainly."
25 Jesus answered them, "I told you, and you do not believe. The works that I do in My Father's name, they bear witness of Me.
26 "But you do not believe, because you are not of My

τίθημι ὑπὲρ τῶν προβάτων. **16** *Καὶ ἄλλα πρόβατα*
[1]I [2]lay [3]down in behalf of the sheep. And other sheep

ἔχω ἃ οὐκ ἔστιν ἐκ τῆς αὐλῆς ταύτης· κἀκεῖνά με
I have which not ˜ are of - fold ˜ this; [8]those [9]*sheep* [10]also [5]Me

δεῖ ἀγαγεῖν, καὶ τῆς φωνῆς μου ἀκούσουσι·
[1]it [2]is [3]necessary [4]*for* [6]to [7]bring, and - [5]voice [4]My [1]they [2]will [3]hear;

καὶ γενήσεται μία ποίμνη, εἷς ποιμήν. **17** *Διὰ τοῦτο*
and *there* will be one flock, one shepherd. On account of this
Therefore

ὁ Πατήρ με ἀγαπᾷ, ὅτι ἐγὼ τίθημι τὴν ψυχήν μου
the Father Me ˜ loves, because I lay down - life ˜ My

ἵνα πάλιν λάβω αὐτήν. **18** *Οὐδεὶς αἴρει αὐτὴν ἀπ' ἐμοῦ,*
so that again I may take it *up*. No one takes it from Me,

ἀλλ' ἐγὼ τίθημι αὐτὴν ἀπ' ἐμαυτοῦ. Ἐξουσίαν ἔχω
but I lay down ˜ it of Myself. [3]power [1]I [2]have

θεῖναι αὐτήν, καὶ ἐξουσίαν ἔχω πάλιν λαβεῖν αὐτήν.
to lay down ˜ it, and [3]power [1]I [2]have [8]again [4]to [5]take [6]it [7]*up*.

Ταύτην τὴν ἐντολὴν ἔλαβον παρὰ τοῦ Πατρός μου."
This - command I received from - Father ˜ My."

19 *Σχίσμα οὖν πάλιν ἐγένετο ἐν τοῖς Ἰουδαίοις*
[2]a [3]division [1]Therefore again came to be among the Jews
occurred

διὰ τοὺς λόγους τούτους. **20** *Ἔλεγον δὲ πολλοὶ ἐξ*
because of - words ˜ these. [5]were [6]saying [1]And [2]many [3]of

αὐτῶν, "Δαιμόνιον ἔχει καὶ μαίνεται. Τί αὐτοῦ
[4]them, "[9]a [10]demon [7]He [8]has and is raving mad. Why [4]to [5]Him

ἀκούετε?"
[1]do [2]you [3]listen?"

21 *Ἄλλοι ἔλεγον, "Ταῦτα τὰ ῥήματα οὐκ ἔστι*
Others were saying, "These - sayings not ˜ are
words

δαιμονιζομένου. Μὴ δαιμόνιον δύναται
of *one* being demon-possessed. [3]not [5]*for* [6]a [7]demon [1]It [2]is [4]possible

τυφλῶν ὀφθαλμοὺς ἀνοίγειν?"
[12]of [13]blind [14]*people* [10]*the* [11]eyes [8]to [9]open, *is it?*"

Jesus Claims to Be Christ at the Feast of Hanukkah

22 *Ἐγένετο δὲ τὰ Ἐγκαίνια ἐν Ἱεροσολύμοις καὶ*
[2]it [3]was [1]Now the Feast of Dedication in Jerusalem and

χειμὼν ἦν. **23** *Καὶ περιεπάτει ὁ Ἰησοῦς ἐν τῷ ἱερῷ ἐν τῇ*
[3]winter [1]it [2]was. And [2]was [3]walking - [1]Jesus in the temple in the

Στοᾷ Σολομῶνος. **24** *Ἐκύκλωσαν οὖν αὐτὸν οἱ Ἰουδαῖοι*
Portico of Solomon. [4]surrounded [1]Therefore [5]Him [2]the [3]Jews

καὶ ἔλεγον αὐτῷ, "Ἕως πότε τὴν ψυχὴν ἡμῶν αἴρεις?
and said to Him, "Until when - [6]life [5]our [1]do [2]You [3]hold [4]up?
"How long will You keep us in suspense?

Εἰ σὺ εἶ ὁ Χριστός, εἰπὲ ἡμῖν παρρησίᾳ."
If You are the Christ, tell us in openness."
Messiah, plainly."

25 *Ἀπεκρίθη αὐτοῖς ὁ Ἰησοῦς, "Εἶπον ὑμῖν, καὶ οὐ*
[2]answered [3]them - [1]Jesus, "I told you, and [3]not

πιστεύετε. Τὰ ἔργα ἃ ἐγὼ ποιῶ ἐν τῷ ὀνόματι τοῦ
[1]you [2]do believe. The works which I do in the name -

Πατρός μου, ταῦτα μαρτυρεῖ περὶ ἐμοῦ. **26** *Ἀλλ' ὑμεῖς*
of Father ˜ My, these *things* testify about Me. But you

οὐ πιστεύετε, οὐ γάρ ἐστε ἐκ τῶν προβάτων τῶν ἐμῶν,
not ˜ do believe, [4]not [1]for [2]you [3]are of - sheep ˜ - My,

καθὼς εἶπον ὑμῖν.[c] 27 Τὰ πρόβατα τὰ ἐμὰ τῆς φωνῆς μου
just as I said to you. - sheep ~ - My - [3]voice [2]My

ἀκούει, κἀγὼ γινώσκω* αὐτά, καὶ ἀκολουθοῦσί μοι. 28 Κἀγὼ
[1]hear, and I know them, and they follow Me. And I

ζωὴν αἰώνιον δίδωμι αὐτοῖς, καὶ οὐ μὴ ἀπόλωνται εἰς
[3]life [2]eternal [1]give to them, and not not they shall perish into
they shall never ever

τὸν αἰῶνα, καὶ οὐχ ἁρπάσει τις αὐτὰ ἐκ τῆς χειρός
the age, and [3]not [2]will [4]snatch [1]anyone them out of - hand ~
perish, no one will snatch

μου. 29 Ὁ Πατήρ μου ὃς δέδωκέ μοι, μείζων
My. - Father ~ My who has given *them* to Me, [2]greater [3]*than*

πάντων[d] ἐστί· καὶ οὐδεὶς δύναται ἁρπάζειν ἐκ τῆς χειρὸς
[4]all [1]is; and no one is able to snatch *them* out of the hand

τοῦ Πατρός μου. 30 Ἐγὼ καὶ ὁ Πατὴρ ἕν ἐσμεν."
- of Father ~ My. I and the Father one ~ are."

Renewed Efforts to Stone Jesus

31 Ἐβάστασαν οὖν πάλιν λίθους οἱ Ἰουδαῖοι ἵνα
[5]took [6]up [1]Therefore [4]again [7]stones [2]the [3]Jews so that

λιθάσωσιν αὐτόν.
they might stone Him.

32 Ἀπεκρίθη αὐτοῖς ὁ Ἰησοῦς, "Πολλὰ καλὰ ἔργα ἔδειξα
[2]answered [3]them - [1]Jesus, "Many good works I showed

ὑμῖν ἐκ τοῦ Πατρός μου. Διὰ ποῖον αὐτῶν ἔργον
you from - Father ~ My. On account of which [2]of [3]them [1]work

λιθάζετέ με?"
do you stone Me?"

33 Ἀπεκρίθησαν αὐτῷ οἱ Ἰουδαῖοι λέγοντες, "Περὶ καλοῦ
[3]answered [4]Him [1]The [2]Jews saying, "About a good
"For

ἔργου οὐ λιθάζομέν σε, ἀλλὰ περὶ βλασφημίας, καὶ ὅτι
work [3]not [1]we [2]do [4]stone You, but about blasphemy, and because
for

σύ, ἄνθρωπος ὤν, ποιεῖς σεαυτὸν Θεόν."
You, [2]a [3]man [1]being, make Yourself God."

34 Ἀπεκρίθη αὐτοῖς ὁ Ἰησοῦς, "Οὐκ ἔστι γεγραμμένον ἐν
[2]answered [3]them - [1]Jesus, "[6]not [4]Is [5]it written in

τῷ νόμῳ ὑμῶν, «Ἐγὼ εἶπα, θεοί ἐστε»?[e] 35 Εἰ ἐκείνους
- law ~ your, «I said, [3]gods [1]you [2]are»? If [3]those [4]*ones*

εἶπε Θεούς, πρὸς οὓς ὁ λόγος τοῦ Θεοῦ ἐγένετο (καὶ
[1]He [2]called gods, to whom the word - of God came to be (and
came

οὐ δύναται λυθῆναι ἡ Γραφή), 36 ὃν ὁ
[4]not [3]is [5]able [6]to [7]be [8]broken [1]the [2]Scripture), [4]*of* [5]*the* [6]*One* [7]whom [8]the

Πατὴρ ἡγίασε καὶ ἀπέστειλεν εἰς τὸν κόσμον ὑμεῖς
[9]Father [10]sanctified [11]and [12]sent [13]into [14]the [15]world [2]you

λέγετε ὅτι 'βλασφημεῖς,' ὅτι εἶπον, 'Υἱὸς τοῦ
[1]do [3]say - 'You are blaspheming,' because I said, '[3]*the* [4]Son [5]of -

Θεοῦ εἰμι'? 37 Εἰ οὐ ποιῶ τὰ ἔργα τοῦ Πατρός μου,
[6]God [1]I [2]am'? If [3]not [1]I [2]am doing the works - of Father ~ My,

μὴ πιστεύετέ μοι. 38 Εἰ δὲ ποιῶ, κἂν ἐμοὶ μὴ
not ~ do believe Me. if ~ But I am doing *them,* even if [5]Me [3]not

πιστεύητε, τοῖς ἔργοις πιστεύσατε, ἵνα γνῶτε καὶ
[1]you [2]do [4]believe, [7]in [8]the [9]works [6]believe, so that you may know and

πιστεύσητε[f] ὅτι ἐν ἐμοὶ ὁ Πατὴρ κἀγὼ ἐν αὐτῷ."
may believe that [4]in [5]Me [1]the [2]Father [3]*is* and I in Him."

sheep, as I said to you.
27 "My sheep hear My voice, and I know them, and they follow Me.
28 "And I give them eternal life, and they shall never perish; neither shall anyone snatch them out of My hand.
29 "My Father, who has given *them* to Me, is greater than all; and no one is able to snatch *them* out of My Father's hand.
30 "I and *My* Father are one."
31 Then the Jews took up stones again to stone Him.
32 Jesus answered them, "Many good works I have shown you from My Father. For which of those works do you stone Me?"
33 The Jews answered Him, saying, "For a good work we do not stone You, but for blasphemy, and because You, being a Man, make Yourself God."
34 Jesus answered them, "Is it not written in your law, *'I said, "You are gods"'*?
35 "If He called them gods, to whom the word of God came (and the Scripture cannot be broken),
36 "do you say of Him whom the Father sanctified and sent into the world, 'You are blaspheming,' because I said, 'I am the Son of God'?
37 "If I do not do the works of My Father, do not believe Me;
38 "but if I do, though you do not believe Me, believe the works, that you may know and believe that the Father *is* in Me, and I in Him."

---

[c](**10:26**) NU omits καθως ειπον υμιν, *as I said to you.* [d](**10:29**) For ος . . . μειζων παντων, *who (has given them to Me is) greater (than) all,* NU reads ο . . . παντων μειζον, *What (my Father has given me is) greater than all.*
[e](**10:34**) Ps. 82:6
[f](**10:38**) NU reads γινωσκητε, *may understand.*

***(10:27)** γινώσκω (*ginōskō*). Common verb meaning *know,* appearing frequently in John's writings. The synonym οἶδα is based on perception, literally meaning *I have seen (and therefore know).* γινώσκω includes the idea of grasping and *understanding* the object perceived and thus often indicates the point when knowledge begins: *I come to know, learn.* It also often

39 Therefore they sought again to seize Him, but He escaped out of their hand.

40 And He went away again beyond the Jordan to the place where John was baptizing at first, and there He stayed.

41 Then many came to Him and said, "John performed no sign, but all the things that John spoke about this Man were true."

42 And many believed in Him there.

11 Now a certain *man* was sick, Lazarus of Bethany, the town of Mary and her sister Martha.

2 It was *that* Mary who anointed the Lord with fragrant oil and wiped His feet with her hair, whose brother Lazarus was sick.

3 Therefore the sisters sent to Him, saying, "Lord, behold, he whom You love is sick."

4 When Jesus heard *that,* He said, "This sickness is not unto death, but for the glory of God, that the Son of God may be glorified through it."

5 Now Jesus loved Martha and her sister and Lazarus.

6 So, when He heard that he was sick, He stayed two more days in the place where He was.

7 Then after this He said to *the* disciples, "Let us go to Judea again."

implies an experiential relationship between the knower and the object or person known, as in its euphemistic use for sexual intercourse (Matt. 1:25). Therefore it is especially appropriate to indicate knowledge of God (as John 17:3) or other personal relatonships, as here in John 10:27. Its meaning ranges from *understand, perceive,* to *acknowledge, recognize.* Cf. the cognate noun γνῶσις, *knowledge* (Rom. 2:20); and verb γνωρίζω, *make known* (Phil. 1:22).

39 Ἐζήτουν οὖν πάλιν αὐτὸν πιάσαι, καὶ
[2]they [3]were [4]seeking [1]Therefore again [3]Him [1]to [2]seize, and

ἐξῆλθεν ἐκ τῆς χειρὸς αὐτῶν.
He went out from - hand ˜ their.

Many Beyond Jordan Believe in Jesus

40 Καὶ ἀπῆλθε πάλιν πέραν τοῦ Ἰορδάνου εἰς τὸν
And He went away again beyond the Jordan to the

τόπον ὅπου ἦν Ἰωάννης τὸ πρῶτον βαπτίζων, καὶ ἔμεινεν
place where was ˜ John - first baptizing, and He stayed

ἐκεῖ. **41** Καὶ πολλοὶ ἦλθον πρὸς αὐτὸν καὶ ἔλεγον ὅτι
there. And many came to Him and said -

"Ἰωάννης μὲν σημεῖον ἐποίησεν οὐδέν, πάντα δὲ
"John indeed [3]sign [1]did [2]no, [5]all [6]*things* [4]but
performed but everything

ὅσα εἶπεν Ἰωάννης περὶ τούτου ἀληθῆ ἦν." **42** Καὶ
as many as said ˜ John about this *man* true ˜ were." And
which was."

ἐπίστευσαν πολλοὶ ἐκεῖ εἰς αὐτόν.
believed ˜ many there in Him.

Lazarus Dies at Bethany

11 **1** Ἦν δέ τις ἀσθενῶν, Λάζαρος ἀπὸ
[2]*there* [3]was [1]Now a certain *man* ailing, Lazarus from
who was sick,

Βηθανίας, ἐκ τῆς κώμης Μαρίας καὶ Μάρθας τῆς ἀδελφῆς
Bethany, of the village of Mary and Martha - sister ˜

αὐτῆς. **2** Ἦν δὲ Μαρία ἡ ἀλείψασα τὸν Κύριον
her. [2]it [3]was [1]Now Mary the *one* having anointed the Lord
who had

μύρῳ καὶ ἐκμάξασα τοὺς πόδας αὐτοῦ ταῖς θριξὶν αὐτῆς,
with myrrh and having wiped - feet ˜ His - with hair ˜ her,
had

ἧς ὁ ἀδελφὸς Λάζαρος ἠσθένει. **3** Ἀπέστειλαν οὖν αἱ
whose - brother Lazarus was sick. [4]sent [1]Therefore [2]the

ἀδελφαὶ πρὸς αὐτὸν λέγουσαι, "Κύριε, ἴδε ὃν φιλεῖς
[3]sisters to Him saying, "Lord, behold *he* whom You love

ἀσθενεῖ."
is sick."

4 Ἀκούσας δὲ ὁ Ἰησοῦς εἶπεν, "Αὕτη ἡ ἀσθένεια οὐκ
hearing ˜ And - Jesus said, "This - sickness not ˜
And when He heard,

ἔστι πρὸς θάνατον ἀλλ' ὑπὲρ τῆς δόξης τοῦ Θεοῦ, ἵνα
is unto death but for the glory - of God, so that

δοξασθῇ ὁ Υἱὸς τοῦ Θεοῦ δι' αὐτῆς." **5** Ἠγάπα
[5]may [6]be [7]glorified [1]the [2]Son - [3]of [4]God through it." [3]loved

δὲ ὁ Ἰησοῦς τὴν Μάρθαν καὶ τὴν ἀδελφὴν αὐτῆς καὶ τὸν
[1]And - [2]Jesus - Martha and - sister ˜ her and -

Λάζαρον. **6** Ὡς οὖν ἤκουσεν ὅτι ἀσθενεῖ, τότε μὲν
Lazarus. when ˜ Therefore He heard that he is sick, then -
was

ἔμεινεν ἐν ᾧ ἦν τόπῳ δύο ἡμέρας. **7** Ἔπειτα
He stayed in [3]in [4]which [5]He [6]was [1]*the* [2]place *for* two days. Then

μετὰ τοῦτο λέγει τοῖς μαθηταῖς, "Ἄγωμεν εἰς τὴν Ἰουδαίαν
after this He says to the disciples, "Let us go into - Judea
said

πάλιν."
again."

8 Λέγουσιν αὐτῷ οἱ μαθηταί, "Ῥαββί, νῦν
[3]say [4]to [5]Him [1]The [2]disciples, "Rabbi, *just* now
said

ἐζήτουν σε λιθάσαι οἱ Ἰουδαῖοι, καὶ πάλιν ὑπάγεις
[3]were [4]seeking [7]You [5]to [6]stone [1]the [2]Jews, and [5]again [1]are [2]You [3]going

ἐκεῖ?"
[4]there?"

9 Ἀπεκρίθη Ἰησοῦς, "Οὐχὶ δώδεκά εἰσιν ὧραι τῆς
answered ˜ Jesus, "[3]not [4]twelve [1]Are [2]*there* hours of the
in

ἡμέρας? Ἐάν τις περιπατῇ ἐν τῇ ἡμέρᾳ οὐ
day? If anyone walks in the day [3]not

προσκόπτει, ὅτι τὸ φῶς τοῦ κόσμου τούτου βλέπει.
[1]he [2]does [4]stumble, because [3]the [4]light - [5]of [7]world [6]this [1]he [2]sees.

10 Ἐὰν δέ τις περιπατῇ ἐν τῇ νυκτὶ προσκόπτει, ὅτι
if ˜ But anyone walks in the night he stumbles, because

τὸ φῶς οὐκ ἔστιν ἐν αὐτῷ." 11 Ταῦτα εἶπε, καὶ μετὰ
the light not ˜ is in him." These *things* He said, and after

τοῦτο λέγει αὐτοῖς, "Λάζαρος ὁ φίλος ἡμῶν κεκοίμηται,
this He says to them, "Lazarus - friend ˜ our has fallen asleep,
said

ἀλλὰ πορεύομαι ἵνα ἐξυπνίσω αὐτόν."
but I am going so that I may awaken him."

12 Εἶπον οὖν οἱ μαθηταὶ αὐτοῦ,[a] "Κύριε, εἰ
[4]said [1]Then - [3]disciples [2]His, "Lord, if

κεκοίμηται σωθήσεται." 13 Εἰρήκει δὲ ὁ Ἰησοῦς
he has fallen asleep he will be saved." [3]had [4]spoken [1]But - [2]Jesus
get well."

περὶ τοῦ θανάτου αὐτοῦ, ἐκεῖνοι δὲ ἔδοξαν ὅτι περὶ τῆς
about - death ˜ his, those ˜ but thought that about the
they

κοιμήσεως τοῦ ὕπνου λέγει.
resting - of sleep He is speaking.
was

14 Τότε οὖν εἶπεν αὐτοῖς ὁ Ἰησοῦς παρρησίᾳ,* "Λάζαρος
then ˜ So [2]said [3]to [4]them - [1]Jesus in openness, "Lazarus
plainly,

ἀπέθανε. 15 Καὶ χαίρω δι' ὑμᾶς, ἵνα πιστεύσητε,
died. And I rejoice on account of you, so that you may believe,
is dead. for your sake,

ὅτι οὐκ ἤμην ἐκεῖ. Ἀλλὰ ἄγωμεν πρὸς αὐτόν."
that [3]not [1]I [2]was there. But let us go to him."

16 Εἶπεν οὖν Θωμᾶς, ὁ λεγόμενος Δίδυμος, τοῖς
[8]said [1]Then [2]Thomas, [3]the [4]*one* [5]being [6]called [7]Twin, to the
called his

συμμαθηταῖς, "Ἄγωμεν καὶ ἡμεῖς ἵνα ἀποθάνωμεν μετ'
fellow disciples, "Let go also ˜ us so that we may die with
"Let us also go

αὐτοῦ."
Him."

Jesus Is the Resurrection and the Life

17 Ἐλθὼν οὖν ὁ Ἰησοῦς εὗρεν αὐτὸν
coming ˜ Therefore - Jesus found him
Therefore when He had come, that he had

τέσσαρας ἡμέρας ἤδη ἔχοντα ἐν τῷ μνημείῳ. 18 Ἦν δὲ
[6]four [7]days [1]already [2]having [3]in [4]the [5]tomb. [3]was [1]Now
been

8 *The* disciples said to Him, "Rabbi, lately the Jews sought to stone You, and are You going there again?"
9 Jesus answered, "Are there not twelve hours in the day? If anyone walks in the day, he does not stumble, because he sees the light of this world.
10 "But if one walks in the night, he stumbles, because the light is not in him."
11 These things He said, and after that He said to them, "Our friend Lazarus sleeps, but I go that I may wake him up."
12 Then His disciples said, "Lord, if he sleeps he will get well."
13 However, Jesus spoke of his death, but they thought that He was speaking about taking rest in sleep.
14 Then Jesus said to them plainly, "Lazarus is dead.
15 "And I am glad for your sakes that I was not there, that you may believe. Nevertheless let us go to him."
16 Then Thomas, who is called the Twin, said to his fellow disciples, "Let us also go, that we may die with Him."
17 So when Jesus came, He found that he had already been in the tomb four days.
18 Now Bethany was near Je-

---

[a](**11:12**) NU reads αυτω, *to Him.*

***(11:14)** παρρησία (*parrēsia*). Noun originally meaning *plainness of speech, outspokenness.* In the Gospels (as John 10:24 and here), the expression "with plainness of speech" often carries the adverbial sense "plainly, openly" and stands in contrast to speaking in parables (John 16:29). From this meaning there developed other senses like *public openness* (John 11:54; Col. 2:15), *boldness* or *confidence* (Heb. 4:16; 10:19; 1 John 2:28), and *fearlessness* (Eph. 6:19). Cf. the cognate verb παρρησιάζομαι, *speak freely, openly, or publicly* (Acts 18:26).

rusalem, about two miles away.
19 And many of the Jews had
joined the women around Martha and Mary, to comfort them
concerning their brother.
20 Then Martha, as soon as
she heard that Jesus was coming, went and met Him, but
Mary was sitting in the house.
21 Now Martha said to Jesus,
"Lord, if You had been here,
my brother would not have
died.
22 "But even now I know that
whatever You ask of God, God
will give You."
23 Jesus said to her, "Your
brother will rise again."
24 Martha said to Him, "I
know that he will rise again in
the resurrection at the last
day."
25 Jesus said to her, "I am the
resurrection and the life. He
who believes in Me, though he
may die, he shall live.
26 "And whoever lives and
believes in Me shall never die.
Do you believe this?"
27 She said to Him, "Yes,
Lord, I believe that You are the
Christ, the Son of God, who is
to come into the world."
28 And when she had said
these things, she went her way
and secretly called Mary her

ἡ Βηθανία ἐγγὺς τῶν Ἱεροσολύμων, ὡς ἀπὸ σταδίων
- [2]Bethany near - Jerusalem, about from stadia ˜
fifteen stadia

δεκαπέντε. **19** Καὶ πολλοὶ ἐκ τῶν Ἰουδαίων ἐληλύθεισαν
fifteen. And many from the Jews had come
away.

πρὸς τὰς περὶ[b] Μάρθαν καὶ Μαρίαν, ἵνα
to the *women* around Martha and Mary, so that

παραμυθήσωνται αὐτὰς περὶ τοῦ ἀδελφοῦ αὐτῶν. **20** Ἡ
they might comfort them concerning - brother ˜ their. -

οὖν Μάρθα, ὡς ἤκουσεν ὅτι Ἰησοῦς ἔρχεται, ὑπήντησεν
Then Martha, when she heard that Jesus is coming, met
was

αὐτῷ, Μαρία δὲ ἐν τῷ οἴκῳ ἐκαθέζετο.
Him, Mary ˜ but [3]in [4]the [5]house [1]was [2]sitting.

21 Εἶπεν οὖν Μάρθα πρὸς τὸν Ἰησοῦν, "Κύριε, εἰ ἦς
[3]said [1]Then [2]Martha to - Jesus, "Lord, if You were
had been

ὧδε, ὁ ἀδελφός μου οὐκ ἂν ἐτεθνήκει. **22** Ἀλλὰ καὶ νῦν
here, - brother ˜ my not ˜ - would have died. But even now

οἶδα ὅτι ὅσα ἂν αἰτήσῃ τὸν Θεόν, δώσει σοι ὁ
I know that as many *things* soever You ask - God, [2]will [3]give [4]You -
whatever

Θεός."
[1]God."

23 Λέγει αὐτῇ ὁ Ἰησοῦς, "Ἀναστήσεται ὁ ἀδελφός σου."
[2]says [3]to [4]her - [1]Jesus, "[7]will [8]rise [9]again - [6]brother [5]Your."
said

24 Λέγει αὐτῷ Μάρθα, "Οἶδα ὅτι ἀναστήσεται ἐν τῇ
[2]says [3]to [4]Him [1]Martha, "I know that he will rise again in the
said

ἀναστάσει ἐν τῇ ἐσχάτῃ ἡμέρᾳ."
resurrection in the last day."

25 Εἶπεν αὐτῇ ὁ Ἰησοῦς, "Ἐγώ εἰμι ἡ ἀνάστασις καὶ ἡ
[2]said [3]to [4]her - [1]Jesus, "I am the resurrection and the

ζωή. Ὁ πιστεύων εἰς ἐμέ, κἂν ἀποθάνῃ, ζήσεται.
life. The *one* believing in Me, even though he may die, he will live.
who believes

26 Καὶ πᾶς ὁ ζῶν καὶ πιστεύων εἰς ἐμὲ οὐ μὴ
And every - *one* living and believing in Me [2]not [3]not
everyone who lives believes shall never

ἀποθάνῃ εἰς τὸν αἰῶνα. Πιστεύεις τοῦτο?"
[1]shall [4]die into the age. Do you believe this?"
ever die.

27 Λέγει αὐτῷ, "Ναί, Κύριε, ἐγὼ πεπίστευκα ὅτι σὺ εἶ
She says to Him, "Yes, Lord, I have believed that You are
said come to believe

ὁ Χριστός, ὁ Υἱὸς τοῦ Θεοῦ, ὁ εἰς τὸν κόσμον
the Christ, the Son - of God, the *One* [2]into [3]the [4]world
Messiah, who is

ἐρχόμενος."
[1]coming."
to come."

Jesus Shares the Sorrow of Death

28 Καὶ ταῦτα εἰποῦσα, ἀπῆλθε καὶ ἐφώνησε
And [2]these [3]*things* [1]saying, she went out and called
when she had said,

---

[b](**11:19**) NU omits τας περι, *the (women) around.*

Μαρίαν τὴν ἀδελφὴν αὐτῆς λάθρα, εἰποῦσα, "Ὁ διδάσκαλος
Mary - sister ˜ her secretly, saying, "The teacher

πάρεστι καὶ φωνεῖ σε." 29 Ἐκείνη ὡς ἤκουσεν,
is here and is calling you." That *woman* when she heard,
She

ἐγείρεται ταχὺ καὶ ἔρχεται πρὸς αὐτόν. 30 Οὔπω δὲ
arises quickly and comes to Him. [4]not [5]yet [1]Now
arose came

ἐληλύθει ὁ Ἰησοῦς εἰς τὴν κώμην, ἀλλ' ἦν[c] ἐν τῷ τόπῳ ὅπου
[3]had [6]come - [2]Jesus into the village, but was in the place where

ὑπήντησεν αὐτῷ ἡ Μάρθα. 31 Οἱ οὖν Ἰουδαῖοι οἱ ὄντες
[2]met [3]Him - [1]Martha. the ˜ Then Jews the *ones* being
who were

μετ' αὐτῆς ἐν τῇ οἰκίᾳ καὶ παραμυθούμενοι αὐτήν, ἰδόντες
with her in the house and comforting her, seeing
when they saw

τὴν Μαρίαν ὅτι ταχέως ἀνέστη καὶ ἐξῆλθεν, ἠκολούθησαν
- Mary that [3]quickly [1]she [2]arose and went out, followed

αὐτῇ, λέγοντες[d] ὅτι "Ὑπάγει εἰς τὸ μνημεῖον ἵνα
her, saying - "She is going to the tomb so that

κλαύσῃ ἐκεῖ."
she may weep there."

32 Ἡ οὖν Μαρία, ὡς ἦλθεν ὅπου ἦν ὁ Ἰησοῦς,
- Then Mary, when she came where was ˜ - Jesus,

ἰδοῦσα αὐτόν, ἔπεσεν αὐτοῦ εἰς τοὺς πόδας, λέγουσα αὐτῷ,
seeing Him, fell His ˜ at - feet, saying to Him,

"Κύριε, εἰ ἦς ὧδε, οὐκ ἂν ἀπέθανέ μου ὁ ἀδελφός."
"Lord, if You were here, [4]not - [3]would [5]have [6]died [1]my - [2]brother."
had been

33 Ἰησοῦς οὖν ὡς εἶδεν αὐτὴν κλαίουσαν καὶ τοὺς
Jesus ˜ Therefore when He saw her weeping and the

συνελθόντας αὐτῇ Ἰουδαίους κλαίοντας, ἐνεβριμήσατο
[2]having [3]come [4]with [5]her [1]Jews weeping, groaned
who had come along with was

τῷ πνεύματι καὶ ἐτάραξεν ἑαυτόν. 34 Καὶ εἶπε, "Ποῦ
in the spirit and troubled Himself. And He said, "Where
moved deeply was troubled.

τεθείκατε αὐτόν?"
have you put him?"

Λέγουσιν αὐτῷ, "Κύριε, ἔρχου καὶ ἴδε."
They say to Him, "Lord, come and see."
said

35 Ἐδάκρυσεν ὁ Ἰησοῦς.
wept ˜ - Jesus.

36 Ἔλεγον οὖν οἱ Ἰουδαῖοι, "Ἴδε πῶς ἐφίλει
[4]were [5]saying [1]Therefore [2]the [3]Jews, "See how He loved

αὐτόν!"
him!"

37 Τινὲς δὲ ἐξ αὐτῶν εἶπον, "Οὐκ ἠδύνατο οὗτος,
some ˜ But of them said, "[2]not [1]Was [15]able [3]this [4]*man,*

ὁ ἀνοίξας τοὺς ὀφθαλμοὺς τοῦ τυφλοῦ,
[5]the [6]*One* [7]having [8]opened [9]the [10]eyes [11]of [12]the [13]blind [14]*man,*
who opened

ποιῆσαι ἵνα καὶ οὗτος μὴ ἀποθάνῃ?"
to do *something* so that also this *man* not ˜ might have died?"

sister, saying, "The Teacher has come and is calling for you."
29 As soon as she heard *that,* she arose quickly and came to Him.
30 Now Jesus had not yet come into the town, but was in the place where Martha met Him.
31 Then the Jews who were with her in the house, and comforting her, when they saw that Mary rose up quickly and went out, followed her, saying, "She is going to the tomb to weep there."
32 Then, when Mary came where Jesus was, and saw Him, she fell down at His feet, saying to Him, "Lord, if You had been here, my brother would not have died."
33 Therefore, when Jesus saw her weeping, and the Jews who came with her weeping, He groaned in the spirit and was troubled.
34 And He said, "Where have you laid him?" They said to Him, "Lord, come and see."
35 Jesus wept.
36 Then the Jews said, "See how He loved him!"
37 And some of them said, "Could not this Man, who opened the eyes of the blind, also have kept this man from dying?"

[c](11:30) NU adds ετι, *still.*
[d](11:31) NU reads δοξαντες, *supposing (that she was going).*

38 Then Jesus, again groaning in Himself, came to the tomb. It was a cave, and a stone lay against it.
39 Jesus said, "Take away the stone." Martha, the sister of him who was dead, said to Him, "Lord, by this time there is a stench, for he has been *dead* four days."
40 Jesus said to her, "Did I not say to you that if you would believe you would see the glory of God?"
41 Then they took away the stone *from the place* where the dead man was lying. And Jesus lifted up *His* eyes and said, "Father, I thank You that You have heard Me.
42 "And I know that You always hear Me, but because of the people who are standing by I said *this,* that they may believe that You sent Me."
43 Now when He had said these things, He cried with a loud voice, "Lazarus, come forth!"
44 And he who had died came out bound hand and foot with graveclothes, and his face was wrapped with a cloth. Jesus said to them, "Loose him, and let him go."
45 Then many of the Jews who had come to Mary, and had seen the things Jesus did, believed in Him.
46 But some of them went

Jesus Raises Lazarus from the Dead

38 Ἰησοῦς οὖν πάλιν ἐμβριμώμενος* ἐν ἑαυτῷ ἔρχεται
Jesus ˜ Then again groaning in Himself comes
being moved deeply came

εἰς τὸ μνημεῖον. Ἦν δὲ σπήλαιον, καὶ λίθος ἐπέκειτο
to the tomb. [2]*it* [3]was [1]Now a cave, and a stone was lying

ἐπ' αὐτῷ. **39** Λέγει ὁ Ἰησοῦς, "Ἄρατε τὸν λίθον."
upon it. says ˜ - Jesus, "Take away the stone."
said

Λέγει αὐτῷ ἡ ἀδελφὴ τοῦ τεθνηκότος Μάρθα,
[9]says [10]to [11]Him [2]the [3]sister [4]of [5]the [6]*one* [7]having [8]died [1]Martha,
said

"Κύριε, ἤδη ὄζει, τεταρταῖος γάρ ἐστι."
"Lord, already he stinks, [4]a [5]fourth [6]day [1]for [2]it [3]is."
for he has been dead for four days."

40 Λέγει αὐτῇ ὁ Ἰησοῦς, "Οὐκ εἶπόν σοι ὅτι ἐὰν
[2]says [3]to [4]her - [1]Jesus, "[7]not [5]Did [6]I say to you that if
said

πιστεύσῃς ὄψει τὴν δόξαν τοῦ Θεοῦ?" **41** Ἦραν
you believe you will see the glory - of God?" [2]they [3]took [4]away

οὖν τὸν λίθον οὗ ἦν ὁ τεθνηκὼς κείμενος.[e] Ὁ
[1]Then the stone from where [5]was [1]the [2]*one* [3]having [4]died lying. -
the dead man

δὲ Ἰησοῦς ἦρε τοὺς ὀφθαλμοὺς ἄνω καὶ εἶπε, "Πάτερ,
And Jesus lifted the eyes upward and said, "Father,
His

εὐχαριστῶ σοι ὅτι ἤκουσάς μου. **42** Ἐγὼ δὲ ᾔδειν ὅτι
I thank You that You heard Me. I ˜ And knew that

πάντοτέ μου ἀκούεις, ἀλλὰ διὰ τὸν ὄχλον τὸν
[2]always [4]Me [1]You [3]hear, but because of the crowd -

περιεστῶτα εἶπον, ἵνα πιστεύσωσιν ὅτι σύ με
standing around I said *this,* so that they may believe that You Me ˜

ἀπέστειλας." **43** Καὶ ταῦτα εἰπών, φωνῇ
sent." And [2]these [3]*things* [1]saying, [7]with [8]a [10]voice
after He had said,

μεγάλῃ ἐκραύγασε, "Λάζαρε, δεῦρο ἔξω!" **44** Καὶ ἐξῆλθεν
[9]great [4]He [5]cried [6]out, "Lazarus, come out!" And [5]came [6]out
loud

ὁ τεθνηκώς, δεδεμένος τοὺς πόδας καὶ τὰς χεῖρας
[1]the [2]*one* [3]having [4]died, having been bound - feet and - hands
the dead man, bound

κειρίαις, καὶ ἡ ὄψις αὐτοῦ σουδαρίῳ περιεδέδετο.
with grave clothes, and - face ˜ his [3]in [4]a [5]facecloth [1]was [2]wrapped.
handkerchief

Λέγει αὐτοῖς ὁ Ἰησοῦς, "Λύσατε αὐτὸν καὶ ἄφετε ὑπάγειν."
[7]says [8]to [9]them - [6]Jesus, "Loose him and allow *him* to go."
said

Chief Priests and Pharisees Plot to Kill Jesus

45 Πολλοὶ οὖν ἐκ τῶν Ἰουδαίων οἱ ἐλθόντες πρὸς
many ˜ Therefore of the Jews the *ones* coming to
who had come

τὴν Μαρίαν καὶ θεασάμενοι ἃ ἐποίησεν ὁ Ἰησοῦς,
- Mary and seeing what did ˜ - Jesus,
who had seen

ἐπίστευσαν εἰς αὐτόν. **46** Τινὲς δὲ ἐξ αὐτῶν ἀπῆλθον πρὸς
believed in Him. some ˜ But of them went away to

---

[e](11:41) NU omits *ου ην ο τεθνηκως κειμενος, from where the dead man was lying.*

*(11:38) ἐμβριμάομαι *(embrimaomai).* Verb meaning *to express* or *feel deep emotion.* Elsewhere in the NT it apparently means to express the opposite of tolerance or sympathy, thus to *reprimand* (Mark 14:5) or *sternly warn* (Matt. 9:30). Here in John 11:38 (cf. v. 33) it carries the idea *be deeply moved,* but commentators differ whether Jesus was deeply troubled over the loss of Lazarus (to Himself or His friends), or moved with indignation either at the power of death or possibly at the unbelief and hopelessness of the mourners.

τοὺς Φαρισαίους καὶ εἶπον αὐτοῖς ἃ ἐποίησεν ὁ
the Pharisees and told them *the things* which did ˜ -
Ἰησοῦς.
Jesus.

47 Συνήγαγον οὖν οἱ ἀρχιερεῖς καὶ οἱ Φαρισαῖοι
[8]gathered [1]Therefore [2]the [3]chief [4]priests [5]and [6]the [7]Pharisees
συνέδριον, καὶ ἔλεγον, "Τί ποιοῦμεν? Ὅτι οὗτος ὁ
a council, and said, "What are we doing? Because this -
ἄνθρωπος πολλὰ σημεῖα ποιεῖ. **48** Ἐὰν ἀφῶμεν αὐτὸν
man [2]many [3]signs [1]does. If we leave *alone* ˜ Him
οὕτω, πάντες πιστεύσουσιν εἰς αὐτόν, καὶ ἐλεύσονται οἱ
thus, all will believe in Him, and [3]will [4]come [1]the
in this way,
Ῥωμαῖοι καὶ ἀροῦσιν ἡμῶν καὶ τὸν τόπον καὶ τὸ ἔθνος."
[2]Romans and will take away our ˜ both - place and - nation."

49 Εἷς δέ τις ἐξ αὐτῶν, Καϊάφας, ἀρχιερεὺς ὢν
[4]one [1]And [2]a [3]certain of them, Caiaphas, [2]high [3]priest [1]being
τοῦ ἐνιαυτοῦ ἐκείνου, εἶπεν αὐτοῖς, "Ὑμεῖς οὐκ οἴδατε οὐδέν,
- year ˜ that, said to them, "You not ˜ do know nothing,
anything,
50 οὐδὲ διαλογίζεσθε ὅτι συμφέρει ἡμῖν[f] ἵνα εἷς
nor do you consider that it is advantageous for us that one
ἄνθρωπος ἀποθάνῃ ὑπὲρ τοῦ λαοῦ, καὶ μὴ ὅλον τὸ ἔθνος
man should die in behalf of the people, and [5]not [2]whole [1]the [3]nation
ἀπόληται." **51** Τοῦτο δὲ ἀφ' ἑαυτοῦ οὐκ εἶπεν, ἀλλὰ
[4]should [6]perish." this ˜ And [5]from [6]himself [3]not [1]he [2]did [4]say, but
on his own
ἀρχιερεὺς ὢν τοῦ ἐνιαυτοῦ ἐκείνου προεφήτευσεν ὅτι
[2]high [3]priest [1]being - year ˜ that he prophesied that
ἔμελλεν Ἰησοῦς ἀποθνήσκειν ὑπὲρ τοῦ ἔθνους, **52** καὶ
[2]was [3]about [1]Jesus to die in behalf of the nation, and
οὐχ ὑπὲρ τοῦ ἔθνους μόνον, ἀλλ' ἵνα καὶ τὰ τέκνα τοῦ
not in behalf of the nation only, but so that [3]also [7]the [8]children -
Θεοῦ τὰ διεσκορπισμένα συναγάγῃ εἰς
[9]of [10]God [11]the [12]*ones* [13]having [14]been [15]scattered [1]He [2]might [4]gather [5]into
who were scattered abroad
ἕν. **53** Ἀπ' ἐκείνης οὖν τῆς ἡμέρας συνεβουλεύσαντο
[6]one. [2]from [3]that [1]Therefore - day *on* they plotted
ἵνα ἀποκτείνωσιν αὐτόν.
so that they might kill Him.

54 Ἰησοῦς οὖν οὐκέτι παρρησίᾳ περιεπάτει
Jesus ˜ Therefore [2]no [3]longer [6]in [7]openness [1]would [4]walk [5]about
openly
ἐν τοῖς Ἰουδαίοις, ἀλλὰ ἀπῆλθεν ἐκεῖθεν εἰς τὴν χώραν
among the Jews, but He went away from there into the country
ἐγγὺς τῆς ἐρήμου, εἰς Ἐφραὶμ λεγομένην πόλιν. Κἀκεῖ
near the wilderness, to [5]Ephraim [3]being [4]called [1]a [2]city. And there
called
διέτριβε μετὰ τῶν μαθητῶν αὐτοῦ. **55** Ἦν δὲ ἐγγὺς τὸ
He stayed with - disciples ˜ His. [7]was [1]And [8]near [2]the
Πάσχα τῶν Ἰουδαίων, καὶ ἀνέβησαν πολλοὶ εἰς
[3]Passover [4]of [5]the [6]Jews, and [2]went [3]up [1]many to
Ἱεροσόλυμα ἐκ τῆς χώρας πρὸ τοῦ Πάσχα ἵνα
Jerusalem out of the country before the Passover so that
ἁγνίσωσιν ἑαυτούς. **56** Ἐζήτουν οὖν τὸν Ἰησοῦν
they might purify themselves. [2]they [3]were [4]seeking [1]Then - Jesus
καὶ ἔλεγον μετ' ἀλλήλων ἐν τῷ ἱερῷ ἑστηκότες,
and they were speaking with one another [2]in [3]the [4]temple [1]standing,

away to the Pharisees and told
them the things Jesus did.
47 Then the chief priests and
the Pharisees gathered a council and said, "What shall we do?
For this Man works many
signs.
48 "If we let Him alone like
this, everyone will believe in
Him, and the Romans will come
and take away both our place
and nation."
49 And one of them, Caia-
phas, being high priest that
year, said to them, "You know
nothing at all,
50 "nor do you consider that it
is expedient for us that one man
should die for the people, and
not that the whole nation should
perish."
51 Now this he did not say on
his own *authority;* but being
high priest that year he prophesied that Jesus would die for the
nation,
52 and not for that nation only,
but also that He would gather
together in one the children of
God who were scattered
abroad.
53 Then, from that day on,
they plotted to put Him to
death.
54 Therefore Jesus no longer
walked openly among the Jews,
but went from there into the
country near the wilderness, to
a city called Ephraim, and there
remained with His disciples.
55 And the Passover of the
Jews was near, and many went
from the country up to Jerusalem before the Passover, to purify themselves.
56 Then they sought Jesus,
and spoke among themselves
as they stood in the temple,

f(**11:50**) NU reads υμιν, *you.*

"What do you think—that He will not come to the feast?"
57 Now both the chief priests and the Pharisees had given a command, that if anyone knew where He was, he should report *it,* that they might seize Him.

12 Then, six days before the Passover, Jesus came to Bethany, where Lazarus was who had been dead, whom He had raised from the dead.
2 There they made Him a supper; and Martha served, but Lazarus was one of those who sat at the table with Him.
3 Then Mary took a pound of very costly oil of spikenard, anointed the feet of Jesus, and wiped His feet with her hair. And the house was filled with the fragrance of the oil.
4 But one of His disciples, Judas Iscariot, Simon's *son,* who would betray Him, said,
5 "Why was this fragrant oil not sold for three hundred denarii and given to the poor?"
6 This he said, not that he cared for the poor, but because he was a thief, and had the money box; and he used to take what was put in it.
7 But Jesus said, "Let her alone; she has kept this for the day of My burial.
8 "For the poor you have

"Τί δοκεῖ ὑμῖν — ὅτι οὐ μὴ ἔλθῃ εἰς τὴν
"What does it seem to you — that [3]not [4]not [1]He [2]would [5]come to the
do you think — He will definitely not come

ἑορτήν?" 57 Δεδώκεισαν δὲ καὶ οἱ ἀρχιερεῖς καὶ οἱ
feast?" [9]had [10]given [1]Now [2]both [3]the [4]chief [5]priests [6]and [7]the

Φαρισαῖοι ἐντολήν, ἵνα ἐάν τις γνῷ ποῦ ἐστι,
[8]Pharisees a command, that if anyone knew where He is,
was,

μηνύσῃ, ὅπως πιάσωσιν αὐτόν.
he should report *it,* so that they might seize Him.

Mary Anoints Jesus at Bethany

12 1 Ὁ οὖν Ἰησοῦς, πρὸ ἓξ ἡμερῶν τοῦ Πάσχα, ἦλθεν
- Then Jesus, [3]before [1]six [2]days the Passover, went

εἰς Βηθανίαν, ὅπου ἦν Λάζαρος ὁ τεθνηκώς,[a] ὃν
to Bethany, where was ˜ Lazarus the *one* having died, whom
who had died,

ἤγειρεν ἐκ νεκρῶν.[b] 2 Ἐποίησαν οὖν αὐτῷ δεῖπνον ἐκεῖ·
He raised from *the* dead. [2]they [3]made [1]Then for Him a dinner there;

καὶ ἡ Μάρθα διηκόνει, ὁ δὲ Λάζαρος εἷς ἦν τῶν
and - Martha was serving, - and Lazarus one ˜ was of the *ones*

ἀνακειμένων σὺν αὐτῷ. 3 Ἡ οὖν Μαρία λαβοῦσα λίτραν
reclining *to eat* with Him. - Then Mary having taken a pound

μύρου νάρδου πιστικῆς πολυτίμου, ἤλειψε τοὺς πόδας τοῦ
of perfume of [4]nard [3]pure [1]very [2]costly, anointed the feet -

Ἰησοῦ, καὶ ἐξέμαξε ταῖς θριξὶν αὐτῆς τοὺς πόδας αὐτοῦ. Ἡ
of Jesus, and wiped - [3]with [5]hair [4]her - [2]feet [1]His. the ˜

δὲ οἰκία ἐπληρώθη ἐκ τῆς ὀσμῆς τοῦ μύρου.
And house was filled from the fragrance of the perfume.
with

4 Λέγει οὖν εἷς ἐκ τῶν μαθητῶν αὐτοῦ, Ἰούδας
[19]says [1]Then [2]one [3]of - [5]disciples [4]His, [6]Judas
said

Σίμωνος[c] Ἰσκαριώτης, ὁ μέλλων αὐτὸν
[8]*son* [9]of [10]Simon [7]Iscariot, [11]the [12]*one* [13]being [14]about [17]Him
who was about to betray

παραδιδόναι, 5 "Διὰ τί τοῦτο τὸ μύρον οὐκ
[15]to [16]hand [18]over, "On account of what [2]this - [3]perfume [4]not
Him, "Why

ἐπράθη τριακοσίων δηναρίων καὶ ἐδόθη πτωχοῖς?"
[1]was [5]sold for three hundred denarii and given to poor *people?"*

6 Εἶπε δὲ τοῦτο, οὐχ ὅτι περὶ τῶν πτωχῶν
[2]he [3]said [1]Now this, not because [7]about [8]the [9]poor

ἔμελεν αὐτῷ, ἀλλὰ ὅτι κλέπτης ἦν καὶ τὸ
[1]it [2]was [3]a [4]care [5]to [6]him, but because [3]a [4]thief [1]he [2]was and [3]the
he cared,

γλωσσόκομον* εἶχε, καὶ τὰ βαλλόμενα
[4]money [5]box [1]he [2]had, and [4]the [5]*things* [6]being [7]put [8]in
he used to pilfer the things which

ἐβάσταζεν.
[1]he [2]was [3]removing.
were placed in it.

7 Εἶπεν οὖν ὁ Ἰησοῦς, "Ἄφες αὐτήν· εἰς τὴν ἡμέραν
[3]said [1]Then - [2]Jesus, "Let be ˜ her; for the day

τοῦ ἐνταφιασμοῦ μου τετήρηκεν αὐτό.[d] 8 Τοὺς πτωχοὺς γὰρ
- of burial ˜ My she has kept it. [5]the [6]poor [1]For

---

[a](12:1) NU omits ο τεθνηκως, *who had died.*
[b](12:1) NU adds Ιησους, *(whom) Jesus (raised).*
[c](12:4) NU omits Σιμωνος, *(son) of Simon.*
[d](12:7) NU adds ινα, *in order that,* before εις, *for,* and reads τηρηση, thus *in order that she may keep (it).*

*(12:6) γλωσσόκομον *(glōssokomon).* Noun, a general term for any *case* or *container.* All of its uses in the NT refer to a money box or bag. In the LXX at 2 Chron. 24:8, 10 it is used for the chest that King Joash set up to collect money for temple repairs.

πάντοτε ἔχετε μεθ' ἑαυτῶν, ἐμὲ δὲ οὐ πάντοτε
³always ²you ⁴have with yourselves, ⁷Me ¹but ⁴not ⁵always
you,

ἔχετε."
²you ³do ⁶have."

The Jews Plot to Kill Lazarus

9 Ἔγνω οὖν ὄχλος πολὺς ἐκ τῶν Ἰουδαίων ὅτι ἐκεῖ
⁸knew ¹So ⁴crowd ²a ³large ⁵from ⁶the ⁷Jews that ³there

ἐστι· καὶ ἦλθον, οὐ διὰ τὸν Ἰησοῦν μόνον, ἀλλ'
¹He ²is; and they came, not on account of - Jesus only, but
was;

ἵνα καὶ τὸν Λάζαρον ἴδωσιν, ὃν ἤγειρεν ἐκ
so that ³also - ⁵Lazarus ¹they ²might ⁴see, whom He raised from

νεκρῶν. 10 Ἐβουλεύσαντο δὲ οἱ ἀρχιερεῖς ἵνα καὶ τὸν
the dead. ⁵decided ¹But ²the ³chief ⁴priests that ³also -

Λάζαρον ἀποκτείνωσιν, 11 ὅτι πολλοὶ
⁵Lazarus ¹they ²should ⁴put ⁶to ⁷death, because ⁵many

δι' αὐτὸν ὑπῆγον τῶν Ἰουδαίων καὶ
¹on ²account ³of ⁴him ⁹were ¹⁰going ¹¹*away* ⁶of ⁷the ⁸Jews and

ἐπίστευον εἰς τὸν Ἰησοῦν.
were believing in - Jesus.

Jesus Enters Jerusalem in Triumph
(Matt. 21:1–11; Mark 11:1–11; Luke 19:28–40)

12 Τῇ ἐπαύριον ὄχλος πολὺς ὁ ἐλθὼν εἰς τὴν
On the next day ³crowd ¹a ²large the *one* coming to the
which was

ἑορτήν, ἀκούσαντες ὅτι ἔρχεται Ἰησοῦς εἰς Ἱεροσόλυμα,
feast, hearing that ²is ³coming ¹Jesus to Jerusalem,
when they heard was

13 ἔλαβον τὰ βαΐα τῶν φοινίκων καὶ ἐξῆλθον εἰς
took the branches of the palm trees and went out for
in order

ὑπάντησιν αὐτῷ καὶ ἔκραζον,
a meeting with Him and they were crying out,
to meet Him

"«Ὡσαννά!
"«Hosanna!

Εὐλογημένος ὁ ἐρχόμενος ἐν ὀνόματι Κυρίου,»[e]
Blessed *is* the *One* coming in *the* name of *the* Lord,»
who comes

Βασιλεὺς[f] τοῦ Ἰσραήλ!"
The King - of Israel!"

14 Εὑρὼν δὲ ὁ Ἰησοῦς ὀνάριον, ἐκάθισεν ἐπ'
³having ⁴found ¹And - ²Jesus a young donkey, He sat on
And when Jesus found

αὐτό· καθώς ἐστι γεγραμμένον,
it; just as it is written,

15 «Μὴ φοβοῦ, θύγατερ Σιών·
«not ˜ Do fear, daughter of Zion;

Ἰδού, ὁ βασιλεύς σου ἔρχεται,
Behold, - King ˜ your is coming,

Καθήμενος ἐπὶ πῶλον ὄνου.»[g]
Sitting on *the* colt of a donkey.»

16 Ταῦτα δὲ οὐκ ἔγνωσαν οἱ μαθηταὶ αὐτοῦ τὸ πρῶτον·
⁷these ⁸*things* ¹But ⁵not ⁴did ⁶know - ³disciples ²His - *at* first;
understand

with you always, but Me you do not have always."
9 Now a great many of the Jews knew that He was there; and they came, not for Jesus' sake only, but that they might also see Lazarus, whom He had raised from the dead.
10 But the chief priests plotted to put Lazarus to death also,
11 because on account of him many of the Jews went away and believed in Jesus.
12 The next day a great multitude that had come to the feast, when they heard that Jesus was coming to Jerusalem,
13 took branches of palm trees and went out to meet Him, and cried out:

"Hosanna!
'Blessed is He who comes in the name of the LORD!*'*
The King of Israel!"

14 Then Jesus, when He had found a young donkey, sat on it; as it is written:

15 *"Fear not, daughter of Zion;*
Behold, your King is coming,
Sitting on a donkey's colt."

16 His disciples did not understand these things at first; but

[e](12:13) Ps. 118:25, 26
[f](12:13) NU adds Καὶ ὁ, *Even the (King).*
[g](12:15) Zech. 9:9

when Jesus was glorified, then they remembered that these things were written about Him and *that* they had done these things to Him.
17 Therefore the people, who were with Him when He called Lazarus out of his tomb and raised him from the dead, bore witness.
18 For this reason the people also met Him, because they heard that He had done this sign.
19 The Pharisees therefore said among themselves, "You see that you are accomplishing nothing. Look, the world has gone after Him!"
20 Now there were certain Greeks among those who came up to worship at the feast.
21 Then they came to Philip, who was from Bethsaida of Galilee, and asked him, saying, "Sir, we wish to see Jesus."
22 Philip came and told Andrew, and in turn Andrew and Philip told Jesus.
23 But Jesus answered them, saying, "The hour has come that the Son of Man should be glorified.
24 "Most assuredly, I say to you, unless a grain of wheat falls into the ground and dies, it remains alone; but if it dies, it

ἀλλ' ὅτε ἐδοξάσθη ὁ Ἰησοῦς, τότε ἐμνήσθησαν ὅτι
but when [2]was [3]glorified - [1]Jesus, then they remembered that

ταῦτα ἦν ἐπ' αὐτῷ γεγραμμένα καὶ ταῦτα
these *things* were (had been) [2]about [3]Him [1]written and [3]these [4]*things*

ἐποίησαν αὐτῷ. 17 Ἐμαρτύρει οὖν ὁ ὄχλος ὁ
[1]they [2]did to Him. [23]was [24]testifying [1]Therefore [2]the [3]crowd [4]the [5]*one* (which)

ὢν μετ' αὐτοῦ ὅτε τὸν Λάζαρον ἐφώνησεν ἐκ τοῦ
[6]being (was) [7]with [8]Him [9]when - [12]Lazarus [10]He [11]called [13]out [14]of [15]the

μνημείου καὶ ἤγειρεν αὐτὸν ἐκ νεκρῶν. 18 Διὰ
[16]tomb [17]and [18]raised [19]him [20]from [21]*the* [22]dead. On account of (Therefore)

τοῦτο καὶ ὑπήντησεν αὐτῷ ὁ ὄχλος, ὅτι ἤκουσε τοῦτο
this [3]also [4]met [5]Him [1]the [2]crowd, because it (they) heard [5]this

αὐτὸν πεποιηκέναι τὸ σημεῖον.
[1]Him (that) [2]to [3]have [4]done (He had done) - sign.

19 Οἱ οὖν Φαρισαῖοι εἶπον πρὸς ἑαυτούς, "Θεωρεῖτε
the ~ Therefore Pharisees said to (among) themselves, "You see

ὅτι οὐκ ὠφελεῖτε οὐδέν. Ἴδε ὁ κόσμος ὀπίσω αὐτοῦ
that [3]not [1]you [2]do benefit (you are not doing) nothing (any good). Look the world [3]after [4]Him

ἀπῆλθεν!"
[1]went [2]off!" (has gone)

Jesus, the Fruitful Grain of Wheat

20 Ἦσαν δὲ τινες Ἕλληνες ἐκ τῶν ἀναβαινόντων
[2]*there* [3]were [1]And some Greeks from the *ones* (those) *going up* (who went up)

ἵνα προσκυνήσωσιν ἐν τῇ ἑορτῇ. 21 Οὗτοι οὖν
so that they might worship at the feast. [2]these [3]*people* [1]Then

προσῆλθον Φιλίππῳ τῷ ἀπὸ Βηθσαϊδὰ τῆς Γαλιλαίας, καὶ
approached Philip the *one* (who was) from Bethsaida - of Galilee, and

ἠρώτων αὐτὸν λέγοντες, "Κύριε, θέλομεν τὸν Ἰησοῦν
they were asking him saying, "Sir, we wish - [3]Jesus

ἰδεῖν." 22 Ἔρχεται Φίλιππος καὶ λέγει τῷ Ἀνδρέᾳ, καὶ
[1]to [2]see." comes ~ (came) Philip and says (spoke) - to Andrew, and

πάλιν Ἀνδρέας καὶ Φίλιππος λέγουσι τῷ Ἰησοῦ.
again Andrew and Philip say (spoke) - to Jesus.

23 Ὁ δὲ Ἰησοῦς ἀπεκρίνατο αὐτοῖς λέγων, "Ἐλήλυθεν ἡ
- But Jesus answered them saying, "[3]has [4]come [1]the

ὥρα ἵνα δοξασθῇ ὁ Υἱὸς τοῦ Ἀνθρώπου. 24 Ἀμὴν
[2]hour (time) that [5]should [6]be [7]glorified [1]the [2]Son - [3]of [4]Man. Amen (Most)

ἀμὴν λέγω ὑμῖν, ἐὰν μὴ ὁ κόκκος τοῦ σίτου πεσὼν
amen (assuredly) I say to you, if (unless) not the (a) grain - of wheat having fallen (falls)

εἰς τὴν γῆν ἀποθάνῃ, αὐτὸς μόνος μένει· ἐὰν δὲ ἀποθάνῃ,
into the ground dies, (and dies,) it alone ~ remains; if ~ but it dies,

πολὺν καρπὸν φέρει. **25** Ὁ φιλῶν τὴν ψυχὴν αὐτοῦ
[3]much [4]fruit [1]it [2]bears. The *one* loving - life ˜ his
who loves

ἀπολέσει[h] αὐτήν, καὶ ὁ μισῶν τὴν ψυχὴν αὐτοῦ ἐν τῷ
will lose it, and the *one* hating - life ˜ his in -
who hates

κόσμῳ τούτῳ εἰς ζωὴν αἰώνιον φυλάξει αὐτήν. **26** Ἐὰν ἐμοὶ
world ˜ this [4]for [6]life [5]eternal [1]will [2]keep [3]it. If [3]Me

διακονῇ τις, ἐμοὶ ἀκολουθείτω,* καὶ ὅπου εἰμὶ ἐγώ, ἐκεῖ
[2]serves [1]anyone, [7]Me [4]let [5]him [6]follow, and where am ˜ I, there

καὶ ὁ διάκονος ὁ ἐμὸς ἔσται. Καὶ ἐάν τις ἐμοὶ διακονῇ,
also - servant ˜ - My will be. And if anyone Me ˜ serves,

τιμήσει αὐτὸν ὁ Πατήρ.
[3]will [4]honor [5]him [1]the [2]Father.

Jesus Predicts His Death by Crucifixion

27 "Νῦν ἡ ψυχή μου τετάρακται, καὶ τί εἴπω?
"Now - soul ˜ My has become troubled, and what should I say?

'Πάτερ, σῶσόν με ἐκ τῆς ὥρας ταύτης'? Ἀλλὰ διὰ
'Father, save Me from - hour ˜ this'? But on account of
for this

τοῦτο ἦλθον εἰς τὴν ὥραν ταύτην. **28** Πάτερ, δόξασόν σου τὸ
this I came to - hour ˜ this. Father, glorify Your -
reason

ὄνομα."
name."

Ἦλθεν οὖν φωνὴ ἐκ τοῦ οὐρανοῦ, "Καὶ ἐδόξασα
[4]came [1]Then [2]a [3]voice out of - heaven, "[3]both [1]I [2]have glorified *it*

καὶ πάλιν δοξάσω."
and again I will glorify *it.*"

29 Ὁ οὖν ὄχλος ὁ ἑστὼς καὶ ἀκούσας
the ˜ Therefore crowd the *one* standing and hearing
which was standing heard

ἔλεγε βροντὴν γεγονέναι. Ἄλλοι ἔλεγον, "Ἄγγελος
were saying thunder to have happened. Others were saying, "An angel
that it had thundered.

αὐτῷ λελάληκεν."
[3]to [4]Him [1]has [2]spoken."

30 Ἀπεκρίθη ὁ Ἰησοῦς καὶ εἶπεν, "Οὐ δι' ἐμὲ αὕτη
answered ˜ - Jesus and said, "Not on account of Me this
for My sake

ἡ φωνὴ γέγονεν ἀλλὰ δι' ὑμᾶς. **31** Νῦν
- voice has come about but on account of you. Now
for your sake.

κρίσις ἐστὶ τοῦ κόσμου τούτου· νῦν ὁ ἄρχων τοῦ κόσμου
[2]*the* [3]judgment [1]is - of world ˜ this; now the ruler - of world ˜

τούτου ἐκβληθήσεται ἔξω. **32** Κἀγώ, ἐὰν ὑψωθῶ ἐκ τῆς
this will be cast out. And I, if I am lifted up from the

γῆς, πάντας ἑλκύσω πρὸς ἐμαυτόν." **33** Τοῦτο δὲ
earth, [4]all [5]*peoples* [1]I [2]shall [3]draw to Myself." [4]this [1]But

ἔλεγε, σημαίνων ποίῳ θανάτῳ ἔμελλεν
[2]He [3]said, signifying by what kind of death He was about

ἀποθνῄσκειν.
to die.

34 Ἀπεκρίθη αὐτῷ ὁ ὄχλος, "Ἡμεῖς ἠκούσαμεν ἐκ τοῦ
[3]answered [4]Him [1]The [2]crowd, "We heard from the

νόμου ὅτι ὁ Χριστὸς μένει εἰς τὸν αἰῶνα· καὶ πῶς σὺ
law that the Christ remains into the age; and so how You ˜
Messiah forever;

produces much grain.
25 "He who loves his life will lose it, and he who hates his life in this world will keep it for eternal life.
26 "If anyone serves Me, let him follow Me; and where I am, there My servant will be also. If anyone serves Me, him *My* Father will honor.
27 "Now My soul is troubled, and what shall I say? 'Father, save Me from this hour'? But for this purpose I came to this hour.
28 "Father, glorify Your name." Then a voice came from heaven, *saying,* "I have both glorified *it* and will glorify *it* again."
29 Therefore the people who stood by and heard *it* said that it had thundered. Others said, "An angel has spoken to Him."
30 Jesus answered and said, "This voice did not come because of Me, but for your sake.
31 "Now is the judgment of this world; now the ruler of this world will be cast out.
32 "And I, if I am lifted up from the earth, will draw all *peoples* to Myself."
33 This He said, signifying by what death He would die.
34 The people answered Him, "We have heard from the law that the Christ remains forever;

---

h(12:25) NU reads *απολλυει, loses.*

***(12:26)** ἀκολουθέω *(akoloutheō).* Common verb meaning *follow,* either literally *to follow after* or *accompany* (as Matt. 21:9; Mark 14:13), or frequently in the NT figuratively *to follow as a disciple,* suggesting the teacher-pupil relationship (as Luke 9:49). The figurative meaning often carries the implicit idea of emulating, even obeying (as probably here in John 12:26; cf. Matt. 19:27, 28).

and how *can* You say, 'The Son of Man must be lifted up'? Who is this Son of Man?"
35 Then Jesus said to them, "A little while longer the light is with you. Walk while you have the light, lest darkness overtake you; he who walks in darkness does not know where he is going.
36 "While you have the light, believe in the light, that you may become sons of light." These things Jesus spoke, and departed, and was hidden from them.
37 But although He had done so many signs before them, they did not believe in Him,
38 that the word of Isaiah the prophet might be fulfilled, which he spoke:

"Lord, who has believed our report?
And to whom has the arm of the LORD been revealed?"

39 Therefore they could not believe, because Isaiah said again:

40 *"He has blinded their eyes and hardened their hearts,*
Lest they should see with their eyes,
Lest they should understand with their hearts and turn,
So that I should heal them."

41 These things Isaiah said when he saw His glory and spoke of Him.

λέγεις, 'Δεῖ ὑψωθῆναι τὸν Υἱὸν τοῦ 'Ανθρώπου'?
do say, 'It is necessary *for* [5]to [6]be [7]lifted [8]up [1]the [2]Son - [3]of [4]Man'?

Τίς ἐστιν οὗτος ὁ Υἱὸς τοῦ 'Ανθρώπου?"
Who is this - Son - of Man?"

35 Εἶπεν οὖν αὐτοῖς ὁ 'Ιησοῦς, "Ἔτι μικρὸν χρόνον
[3]said [1]Therefore [4]to [5]them - [2]Jesus, "*For* yet a little time

τὸ φῶς μεθ' ὑμῶν ἐστι. Περιπατεῖτε ἕως τὸ φῶς ἔχετε
the light [2]with [3]you [1]is. Walk while [3]the [4]light [1]you [2]have

ἵνα μὴ σκοτία ὑμᾶς καταλάβῃ, καὶ ὁ περιπατῶν ἐν τῇ
so that not ˜ darkness you ˜ overtake, and the *one* walking in the
lest / who walks

σκοτίᾳ οὐκ οἶδε ποῦ ὑπάγει. **36** Ἕως τὸ φῶς
darkness not ˜ does know where he is going. While [3]the [4]light

ἔχετε, πιστεύετε εἰς τὸ φῶς, ἵνα υἱοὶ φωτὸς
[1]you [2]have, believe in the light, so that [4]sons [5]of [6]light

γένησθε."
[1]you [2]may [3]become."

Who Has Believed Our Report?

Ταῦτα ἐλάλησεν ὁ 'Ιησοῦς, καὶ ἀπελθὼν ἐκρύβη
[3]these [4]*things* [2]spoke - [1]Jesus, and departing He was hidden

ἀπ' αὐτῶν. **37** Τοσαῦτα δὲ αὐτοῦ σημεῖα πεποιηκότος
from them. [5]so [6]many [1]But [2]Him [7]signs [3]having [4]done
even though / He had done

ἔμπροσθεν αὐτῶν, οὐκ ἐπίστευον εἰς αὐτόν, **38** ἵνα ὁ
before them, [3]not [1]they [2]did believe in Him, that the
in their presence,

λόγος 'Ησαΐου τοῦ προφήτου πληρωθῇ, ὃν εἶπε,
word of Isaiah the prophet might be fulfilled, which he said,

«Κύριε, τίς ἐπίστευσε τῇ ἀκοῇ ἡμῶν?
«Lord, who believed - report ˜ our?
has believed

Καὶ ὁ βραχίων Κυρίου τίνι ἀπεκαλύφθη?»[i]
And the arm of *the* Lord to whom was it revealed?»
has it been

39 Διὰ τοῦτο οὐκ ἠδύναντο πιστεύειν, ὅτι πάλιν
On account of this [3]not [1]they [2]were able to believe, because again
Therefore

εἶπεν 'Ησαΐας,
said ˜ Isaiah,

40 «Τετύφλωκεν αὐτῶν τοὺς ὀφθαλμούς,
«He has blinded their - eyes,

Καὶ πεπώρωκεν αὐτῶν τὴν καρδίαν,
And He has hardened their - heart,

Ἵνα μὴ ἴδωσι τοῖς ὀφθαλμοῖς,
In order that [3]not [1]they [2]should see with the eyes,
Lest / their

Καὶ νοήσωσι τῇ καρδίᾳ καὶ ἐπιστραφῶσι,
And should understand with the heart and they should turn,
their

Καὶ ἰάσωμαι αὐτούς.»[j]
And I would heal them.»

41 Ταῦτα εἶπεν 'Ησαΐας ὅτε[k] εἶδε τὴν δόξαν αὐτοῦ καὶ
These *things* said ˜ Isaiah when he saw - glory ˜ His and

ἐλάλησε περὶ αὐτοῦ.
spoke about Him.

---

[i] **(12:38)** Is. 53:1
[j] **(12:40)** Is. 6:10
[k] **(12:41)** NU reads οτι, *because.*

Believers Should Walk in the Light

42 Ὅμως μέντοι καὶ ἐκ τῶν ἀρχόντων πολλοὶ
All the same however even out of the rulers many
from among

ἐπίστευσαν εἰς αὐτόν, ἀλλὰ διὰ τοὺς Φαρισαίους οὐχ
believed in Him, but because of the Pharisees [3]not

ὡμολόγουν, ἵνα μὴ ἀποσυνάγωγοι
[1]they [2]were confessing *Him,* so that [3]not [5]expelled [6]from [7]the [8]synagogue
lest excommunicated

γένωνται. 43 Ἠγάπησαν γὰρ τὴν δόξαν τῶν ἀνθρώπων
[1]they [2]should [4]be. [2]they [3]loved [1]For the glory - of men
praise

μᾶλλον ἤπερ τὴν δόξαν τοῦ Θεοῦ.
more than the glory - of God.
praise

44 Ἰησοῦς δὲ ἔκραξε καὶ εἶπεν, "Ὁ πιστεύων εἰς ἐμὲ
Jesus ˜ But cried out and said, "The *one* believing in Me
who believes

οὐ πιστεύει εἰς ἐμὲ ἀλλ' εἰς τὸν πέμψαντά με. 45 Καὶ
not ˜ believes in Me but in the *One* having sent Me. And
who

ὁ θεωρῶν ἐμὲ θεωρεῖ τὸν πέμψαντά με. 46 Ἐγὼ
the *one* seeing Me sees the *One* having sent Me. I
who sees who

φῶς εἰς τὸν κόσμον ἐλήλυθα, ἵνα πᾶς ὁ
[3]*as* [4]a [5]light [6]into [7]the [8]world [1]have [2]come, so that every - *one*
no one who

πιστεύων εἰς ἐμὲ ἐν τῇ σκοτίᾳ μὴ μείνῃ. 47 Καὶ ἐάν
believing in Me [4]in [5]the [6]darkness [2]not [1]should [3]abide. And if
believes should abide.

τις μου ἀκούσῃ τῶν ῥημάτων καὶ μὴ πιστεύσῃ,[l] ἐγὼ οὐ
anyone My ˜ hears - sayings and not ˜ does believe, I not ˜

κρίνω αὐτόν, οὐ γὰρ ἦλθον ἵνα κρίνω τὸν κόσμον,
do judge him, [4]not [1]for [2]I [3]did come so that I may judge the world,

ἀλλ' ἵνα σώσω τὸν κόσμον. 48 Ὁ ἀθετῶν ἐμὲ καὶ
but so that I may save the world. The *one* rejecting Me and
who rejects

μὴ λαμβάνων τὰ ῥήματά μου ἔχει τὸν κρίνοντα αὐτόν —
not receiving - sayings ˜ My has the *one* judging him —
does not receive that which judges

ὁ λόγος ὃν ἐλάλησα, ἐκεῖνος κρινεῖ αὐτὸν ἐν τῇ ἐσχάτῃ
the word which I spoke, that *word* will judge him on the last

ἡμέρᾳ. 49 Ὅτι ἐγὼ ἐξ ἐμαυτοῦ οὐκ ἐλάλησα, ἀλλ' ὁ
day. Because I from Myself not ˜ did speak, but the
on My own

πέμψας με Πατήρ, αὐτός μοι ἐντολὴν ἔδωκε, τί
[2]having [3]sent [4]Me [1]Father, He [4]to [5]Me [2]a [3]command [1]gave, what
who

εἴπω καὶ τί λαλήσω. 50 Καὶ οἶδα ὅτι ἡ ἐντολὴ
I should say and what I should speak. And I know that - command ˜

αὐτοῦ ζωὴ αἰώνιός ἐστιν. Ἃ οὖν λαλῶ ἐγώ,
His [3]life [2]eternal [1]is. [5]*the* [6]*things* [7]which [4]Therefore [9]speak [8]I,

καθὼς εἴρηκέ μοι ὁ Πατήρ, οὕτω λαλῶ."
just as [3]has [4]told [5]Me [1]the [2]Father, thus I speak."

Jesus Washes His Disciples' Feet

13 1 Πρὸ δὲ τῆς ἑορτῆς τοῦ Πάσχα, εἰδὼς ὁ
before ˜ Now the Feast of the Passover, knowing ˜ -
when Jesus

42 Nevertheless even among
the rulers many believed in
Him, but because of the Pharisees they did not confess *Him,*
lest they should be put out of
the synagogue;
43 for they loved the praise of
men more than the praise of
God.
44 Then Jesus cried out and
said, "He who believes in Me,
believes not in Me but in Him
who sent Me.
45 "And he who sees Me sees
Him who sent Me.
46 "I have come *as* a light into
the world, that whoever believes in Me should not abide in
darkness.
47 "And if anyone hears My
words and does not believe, I
do not judge him; for I did not
come to judge the world but to
save the world.
48 "He who rejects Me, and
does not receive My words,
has that which judges him — the
word that I have spoken will
judge him in the last day.
49 "For I have not spoken on
My own *authority;* but the Father who sent Me gave Me a
command, what I should say
and what I should speak.
50 "And I know that His command is everlasting life. Therefore, whatever I speak, just as
the Father has told Me, so I
speak."
13 Now before the Feast
of the Passover, when

[l](12:47) NU reads φυλαξῃ, *keep them.*

Jesus knew that His hour had
come that He should depart
from this world to the Father,
having loved His own who were
in the world, He loved them to
the end.
2 And supper being ended,
the devil having already put it
into the heart of Judas Iscariot,
Simon's *son,* to betray Him,
3 Jesus, knowing that the Father had given all things into
His hands, and that He had
come from God and was going
to God,
4 rose from supper and laid
aside His garments, took a
towel and girded Himself.
5 After that, He poured water into a basin and began to
wash the disciples' feet, and to
wipe *them* with the towel with
which He was girded.
6 Then He came to Simon
Peter. And *Peter* said to Him,
"Lord, are You washing my
feet?"
7 Jesus answered and said to
him, "What I am doing you do
not understand now, but you
will know after this."
8 Peter said to Him, "You
shall never wash my feet!" Jesus answered him, "If I do not
wash you, you have no part
with Me."
9 Simon Peter said to Him,
"Lord, not my feet only, but

Ἰησοῦς ὅτι ἐλήλυθεν αὐτοῦ ἡ ὥρα ἵνα μεταβῇ ἐκ τοῦ
Jesus that [3]has [4]come [1]His - [2]hour that He should depart from -
knew had time

κόσμου τούτου πρὸς τὸν Πατέρα, ἀγαπήσας τοὺς ἰδίους
world ˜ this to the Father, having loved - His own

τοὺς ἐν τῷ κόσμῳ, εἰς τέλος ἠγάπησεν αὐτούς. **2** Καὶ
the *ones* in the world, to *the* end He loved them. And
who were

δείπνου γενομένου,[a] τοῦ διαβόλου ἤδη βεβληκότος εἰς
supper having taken place, the devil already having put into
after supper,

τὴν καρδίαν Ἰούδα Σίμωνος Ἰσκαριώτου ἵνα αὐτὸν
the heart of Judas *the son* of Simon Iscariot that [4]Him

παραδῷ, **3** εἰδὼς ὁ Ἰησοῦς[b] ὅτι πάντα
[1]he [2]should [3]hand [5]over, knowing ˜ - Jesus that [5]all [6]things
betray, because Jesus knew

δέδωκεν αὐτῷ ὁ Πατὴρ εἰς τὰς χεῖρας, καὶ ὅτι ἀπὸ Θεοῦ
[3]has [4]given [7]to [8]Him [1]the [2]Father into the hands, and that from God
had His

ἐξῆλθε καὶ πρὸς τὸν Θεὸν ὑπάγει, **4** ἐγείρεται ἐκ τοῦ
He came and to - God He goes, He rises from the
had come was going, He rose

δείπνου καὶ τίθησι τὰ ἱμάτια, καὶ λαβὼν λέντιον
supper and lays *aside* the garments, and having taken a towel
laid aside His

διέζωσεν ἑαυτόν. **5** Εἶτα βάλλει ὕδωρ εἰς τὸν νιπτῆρα καὶ
He tied *it* around Himself. Then He puts water into the basin and
wrapped poured

ἤρξατο νίπτειν τοὺς πόδας τῶν μαθητῶν καὶ ἐκμάσσειν
began to wash the feet of the disciples and to dry *them*

τῷ λεντίῳ ᾧ ἦν διεζωσμένος. **6** Ἔρχεται οὖν
with the towel with which He was tied around. [2]He [3]comes [1]Then
had been wrapped. Then He came

πρὸς Σίμωνα Πέτρον· καὶ λέγει αὐτῷ ἐκεῖνος,[c] "Κύριε, σύ
to Simon Peter; and [3]says [4]to [5]Him [1]that [2]*one,* "Lord, [2]You
said he

μου νίπτεις τοὺς πόδας?"
[4]my [1]are [3]washing - feet?"

7 Ἀπεκρίθη Ἰησοῦς καὶ εἶπεν αὐτῷ, "Ὃ ἐγὼ ποιῶ σὺ
answered ˜ Jesus and said to him, "What I am doing you

οὐκ οἶδας ἄρτι, γνώσῃ δὲ μετὰ ταῦτα."
not ˜ do know now, [2]you [3]will [4]know [1]but after these *things.*"
understand understand

8 Λέγει αὐτῷ Πέτρος, "Οὐ μὴ νίψῃς τοὺς
[2]says [3]to [4]Him [1]Peter, "[7]not [8]not [5]You [6]shall [9]wash -
said never

πόδας μου εἰς τὸν αἰῶνα!"
feet ˜ my into the age!"
ever!"

Ἀπεκρίθη αὐτῷ ὁ Ἰησοῦς, "Ἐὰν μὴ νίψω σε, οὐκ
[2]answered [3]him - [1]Jesus, "If [3]not [1]I [2]do wash you, [3]not
"Unless

ἔχεις μέρος μετ' ἐμοῦ."
[1]you [2]do have a part with me."
share

9 Λέγει αὐτῷ Σίμων Πέτρος, "Κύριε, μὴ τοὺς πόδας μου
[3]says [4]to [5]Him [1]Simon [2]Peter, "Lord, not - feet ˜ my
said

---

[a](**13:2**) NU reads γινομενου, *during (supper).*
[b](**13:3**) NU omits ο Ιησους, *Jesus.* [c](**13:6**) NU omits εκεινος, *that one.*

μόνον, ἀλλὰ καὶ τὰς χεῖρας καὶ τὴν κεφαλήν!"
only, but also the hands and the head!"
my my

10 Λέγει αὐτῷ ὁ Ἰησοῦς, "Ὁ λελουμένος* οὐ
[2]says [3]to [4]him - [1]Jesus, "The *one* having been bathed [2]not
said who has

χρείαν ἔχει ἢ τοὺς πόδας νίψασθαι, ἀλλ' ἔστι
[4]need [1]does [3]have except *for* the feet to be washed, but he is
his

καθαρὸς ὅλος· καὶ ὑμεῖς καθαροί ἐστε, ἀλλ' οὐχὶ πάντες."
clean wholly; and you clean ˜ are, but not all *of you.*"
completely;

11 Ἤδει γὰρ τὸν παραδιδόντα αὐτόν· διὰ τοῦτο
[2]He [3]knew [1]For the *one* handing over ˜ Him; on account of this
who would betray therefore

εἶπεν, "Οὐχὶ πάντες καθαροί ἐστε."
He said, "[3]not [4]all [5]clean [1]You [2]are."

Jesus Explains His Example

12 Ὅτε οὖν ἔνιψε τοὺς πόδας αὐτῶν καὶ ἔλαβε
when ˜ Therefore He washed - feet ˜ their and took
had washed had taken

τὰ ἱμάτια αὐτοῦ, ἀναπεσὼν πάλιν, εἶπεν αὐτοῖς, "Γινώσκετε
- garments ˜ His, falling back again, He said to them, "Do you know
He reclined and understand

τί πεποίηκα ὑμῖν? 13 Ὑμεῖς φωνεῖτέ με 'Ὁ Διδάσκαλος,'
what I have done to you? You call Me - 'Teacher,'

καὶ 'Ὁ Κύριος,' καὶ καλῶς λέγετε, εἰμὶ γάρ. 14 Εἰ οὖν
and - 'Lord,' and [3]well [1]you [2]say, [5]I [6]am [4]for. if ˜ Therefore
correctly

ἐγὼ ἔνιψα ὑμῶν τοὺς πόδας, ὁ Κύριος καὶ ὁ Διδάσκαλος,
I washed your - feet, the Lord and the Teacher,
your your

καὶ ὑμεῖς ὀφείλετε ἀλλήλων νίπτειν τοὺς πόδας.
also ˜ you ought [5]of [6]one [7]another [1]to [2]wash [3]the [4]feet.

15 Ὑπόδειγμα γὰρ ἔδωκα ὑμῖν ἵνα καθὼς ἐγὼ ἐποίησα ὑμῖν
[5]an [6]example [1]For [2]I [3]gave [4]you that just as I did to you

καὶ ὑμεῖς ποιῆτε. 16 Ἀμὴν ἀμὴν λέγω ὑμῖν, οὐκ ἔστι
also ˜ you should do. Amen amen I say to you, [4]not [3]is
Most assuredly

δοῦλος μείζων τοῦ κυρίου αὐτοῦ, οὐδὲ ἀπόστολος μείζων
[1]a [2]slave greater *than* - master ˜ his, nor a messenger greater *than*
servant

τοῦ πέμψαντος αὐτόν. 17 Εἰ ταῦτα οἴδατε, μακάριοί
the *one* having sent him. If [3]these [4]*things* [1]you [2]know, [7]blessed
who

ἐστε ἐὰν ποιῆτε αὐτά. 18 Οὐ περὶ πάντων ὑμῶν
[5]you [6]are if you do them. [3]not [5]concerning [6]all [7]of [8]you

λέγω. Ἐγὼ οἶδα οὓς ἐξελεξάμην· ἀλλ' ἵνα ἡ
[1]I [2]do [4]speak. I know *those* whom I chose; but so that the

Γραφὴ πληρωθῇ, «Ὁ τρώγων μετ' ἐμοῦ τὸν ἄρτον[d]
Scripture may be fulfilled, «The *one* eating [2]with [3]Me - [1]bread
«He who eats

ἐπῆρεν ἐπ' ἐμὲ τὴν πτέρναν αὐτοῦ.»[e] 19 Ἀπ' ἄρτι λέγω
lifted up upon Me - heel ˜ his.» From now *on* I tell
against

ὑμῖν πρὸ τοῦ γενέσθαι, ἵνα ὅταν γένηται, πιστεύσητε ὅτι
you before - to happen, so that when it happens, you may believe that
it happens,

also *my* hands and *my* head!"
10 Jesus said to him, "He who is bathed needs only to wash *his* feet, but is completely clean; and you are clean, but not all of you."
11 For He knew who would betray Him; therefore He said, "You are not all clean."
12 So when He had washed their feet, taken His garments, and sat down again, He said to them, "Do you know what I have done to you?
13 "You call Me Teacher and Lord, and you say well, for *so* I am.
14 "If I then, *your* Lord and Teacher, have washed your feet, you also ought to wash one another's feet.
15 "For I have given you an example, that you should do as I have done to you.
16 "Most assuredly, I say to you, a servant is not greater than his master; nor is he who is sent greater than he who sent him.
17 "If you know these things, blessed are you if you do them.
18 "I do not speak concerning all of you. I know whom I have chosen; but that the Scripture may be fulfilled, *'He who eats bread with Me has lifted up his heel against Me.'*
19 "Now I tell you before it comes, that when it does come to pass, you may believe that

---

[d]**(13:18)** For μετ εμου, *with me,* NU reads μου, *My (bread).* [e]**(13:18)** Ps. 41:9

***(13:10)** λούω *(louō).* Verb meaning *wash, bathe,* usually implying the whole body, as here (in contrast with a subsequent washing of the feet). It may be used of a person (Acts 16:33), animal (2 Pet. 2:22), or corpse (Acts 9:37). It may refer to washings with religious significance as in the possible reference to baptism in Heb. 10:22 and in Jesus' *washing* "us from our sins in His own blood" (Rev. 1:5). Cf. the cognate noun λουτρόν, *bath, washing* (Eph. 5:26; Titus 3:5); and the compound verb ἀπολούω, *wash (away),* used of baptism in Acts 22:16.

I am *He.*
20 "Most assuredly, I say to
you, he who receives whomever I send receives Me; and
he who receives Me receives
Him who sent Me."
21 When Jesus had said these
things, He was troubled in
spirit, and testified and said,
"Most assuredly, I say to you,
one of you will betray Me."
22 Then the disciples looked
at one another, perplexed about
whom He spoke.
23 Now there was leaning on
Jesus' bosom one of His disciples, whom Jesus loved.
24 Simon Peter therefore motioned to him to ask who it was
of whom He spoke.
25 Then, leaning back on Jesus' breast, he said to Him,
"Lord, who is it?"
26 Jesus answered, "It is he
to whom I shall give a piece of
bread when I have dipped *it.*"
And having dipped the bread,
He gave *it* to Judas Iscariot, *the*
son of Simon.
27 Now after the piece of
bread, Satan entered him. Then
Jesus said to him, "What you
do, do quickly."
28 But no one at the table
knew for what reason He said
this to him.
29 For some thought, because

ἐγώ εἰμι. **20** Ἀμὴν ἀμὴν λέγω ὑμῖν, ὁ λαμβάνων
I am *He.* Amen amen I say to you the *one* receiving
Most assuredly who receives

ἐάν τινα πέμψω ἐμὲ λαμβάνει· ὁ δὲ ἐμὲ
if anyone I send Me ~ receives; [2]the [3]*one* [1]and Me ~
whomever who

λαμβάνων λαμβάνει τὸν πέμψαντά με."
receiving receives the *One* having sent Me."
receives Me who

Jesus Predicts Judas' Betrayal
(Matt. 26:20–25; Mark 14:17–21; Luke 22:21–23)

21 Ταῦτα εἰπὼν ὁ Ἰησοῦς ἐταράχθη τῷ
these *things* saying - Jesus He was troubled in the
When Jesus had said these things, His

πνεύματι καὶ ἐμαρτύρησε καὶ εἶπεν, "Ἀμὴν ἀμὴν λέγω
spirit and testified and said, "Amen amen I say
"Most assuredly

ὑμῖν ὅτι εἷς ἐξ ὑμῶν παραδώσει με." **22** Ἔβλεπον
to you that one of you will hand over ~ Me." [4]were [5]looking
betray

οὖν εἰς ἀλλήλους οἱ μαθηταί, ἀπορούμενοι περὶ τίνος
[1]Therefore [6]at [7]one [8]another [2]the [3]disciples, being at a loss about whom

λέγει. **23** Ἦν δὲ ἀνακείμενος εἷς τῶν μαθητῶν αὐτοῦ
He speaks. [6]was [1]Now [7]reclining [2]one - [3]of [5]disciples [4]His
was speaking.

ἐν τῷ κόλπῳ τοῦ Ἰησοῦ, ὃν ἠγάπα ὁ Ἰησοῦς.
on the bosom - of Jesus, *the one* whom loved ~ - Jesus.

24 Νεύει οὖν τούτῳ Σίμων Πέτρος πυθέσθαι τίς ἂν
[4]nods [1]Therefore [5]to [6]this [7]*one* [2]Simon [3]Peter to inquire who -
motioned

εἴη περὶ οὗ λέγει.
it might be about whom He speaks.
was speaking.

25 Ἐπιπεσὼν δὲ ἐκεῖνος οὕτως[f] ἐπὶ τὸ στῆθος τοῦ
[4]falling [5]back [1]And [2]that [3]*one* thus on the chest -
leaning

Ἰησοῦ, λέγει αὐτῷ, "Κύριε, τίς ἐστιν?"
of Jesus, says to Him, "Lord, who is it?"
said

26 Ἀποκρίνεται ὁ Ἰησοῦς, "Ἐκεῖνός ἐστιν ᾧ ἐγὼ
answers ~ - Jesus, "[3]that [4]*one* [1]It [2]is to whom I
answered

βάψας τὸ ψωμίον ἐπιδώσω."[g] Καὶ ἐμβάψας τὸ
having dipped the piece of bread will give *it.*" And having dipped the
after dipping after dipping

ψωμίον,[h] δίδωσιν Ἰούδα Σίμωνος Ἰσκαριώτῃ.
piece of bread, He gives *it* to Judas [2]*the* [3]*son* [4]of [5]Simon [1]Iscariot.
gave

27 Καὶ μετὰ τὸ ψωμίον, τότε εἰσῆλθεν εἰς ἐκεῖνον ὁ
And after the piece of bread, then [2]entered [3]into [4]that [5]*man* -

Σατανᾶς. Λέγει οὖν αὐτῷ ὁ Ἰησοῦς, "Ὃ ποιεῖς, ποίησον
[1]Satan. [8]says [6]Then [9]to [10]him - [7]Jesus, "What you do, do
said

τάχιον." **28** Τοῦτο δὲ οὐδεὶς ἔγνω τῶν ἀνακειμένων
quickly." [16]this [1]But [2]no [3]one [10]knew [4]of [5]the [6]*ones* [7]reclining [8]*to* [9]*eat*

πρὸς τί εἶπεν αὐτῷ. **29** Τινὲς γὰρ ἐδόκουν
[11]for [12]what [13]*purpose* [14]He [15]said to him. some ~ For were thinking

---

[f](13:25) TR omits ουτως, *thus.* [g](13:26) For βαψας το ψωμιον επιδωσω, *after dipping the piece of bread will give (it),* NU reads βαψω το ψωμιον και δωσω αυτω, *will dip the piece of bread and will give (it) to him.* [h](13:26) NU adds in brackets λαμβανει και, *He takes (it) and.*

ἐπεὶ τὸ γλωσσόκομον εἶχεν ὁ Ἰούδας, ὅτι λέγει αὐτῷ
since [3]the [4]money [5]box [2]had - [1]Judas, that [2]is [3]saying [4]to [5]him
used to hold was

ὁ Ἰησοῦς, "Ἀγόρασον ὧν χρείαν ἔχομεν εἰς τὴν
- [1]Jesus, "Buy *the things* of which [3]need [1]we [2]have for the

ἑορτήν," ἢ τοῖς πτωχοῖς ἵνα τι δῷ.
feast," or [6]to [7]the [8]poor [1]that [5]something [2]he [3]should [4]give.

30 Λαβὼν οὖν τὸ ψωμίον ἐκεῖνος,
[4]having [5]received [1]Therefore [6]the [7]piece [8]of [9]bread [2]that [3]*one,*

εὐθέως ἐξῆλθεν. Ἦν δὲ νύξ.
immediately ˜ he went out. [2]it [3]was [1]And night.

The New Commandment: Love as Christ Loved

31 Ὅτε ἐξῆλθε, λέγει ὁ Ἰησοῦς, "Νῦν ἐδοξάσθη ὁ
When he went out, says ˜ - Jesus, "Now [5]was [6]glorified [1]the
had gone said has been

Υἱὸς τοῦ Ἀνθρώπου, καὶ ὁ Θεὸς ἐδοξάσθη ἐν αὐτῷ. 32 Εἰ ὁ
[2]Son - [3]of [4]Man, and - God was glorified in Him. If -
has been

Θεὸς ἐδοξάσθη ἐν αὐτῷ, καὶ ὁ Θεὸς δοξάσει αὐτὸν ἐν ἑαυτῷ,
God was glorified in Him, also ˜ - God will glorify Him in Himself,
has been

καὶ εὐθὺς δοξάσει αὐτόν. 33 Τεκνία, ἔτι
and immediately He will glorify Him. Little children, *for* yet

μικρὸν μεθ' ὑμῶν εἰμι. Ζητήσετέ με, καὶ καθὼς εἶπον
a little *time* [3]with [4]you [1]I [2]am. You will seek Me, and just as I said

τοῖς Ἰουδαίοις ὅτι "Ὅπου ὑπάγω ἐγώ, ὑμεῖς οὐ δύνασθε
to the Jews - 'Where [2]am [3]going [1]I, you not ˜ are able

ἐλθεῖν,' καὶ ὑμῖν λέγω ἄρτι. 34 Ἐντολὴν
to come,' and so [4]to [5]you [1]I [2]am [3]saying now. A commandment ˜

καινὴν* δίδωμι ὑμῖν, ἵνα ἀγαπᾶτε ἀλλήλους· καθὼς ἠγάπησα
new I give to you, that you love one another; just as I loved

ὑμᾶς, ἵνα καὶ ὑμεῖς ἀγαπᾶτε ἀλλήλους. 35 Ἐν τούτῳ
you, that also ˜ you love one another. By this

γνώσονται πάντες ὅτι ἐμοὶ μαθηταί ἐστε, ἐὰν ἀγάπην
[2]will [3]know [1]all that [4]to [5]Me [3]disciples [1]you [2]are, if [3]love
My disciples

ἔχητε ἐν ἀλλήλοις."
[1]you [2]have with one another."
for

Jesus Predicts Peter's Denial
(Matt. 26:31–35; Mark 14:27–31; Luke 22:31–34)

36 Λέγει αὐτῷ Σίμων Πέτρος, "Κύριε, ποῦ ὑπάγεις?"
[3]says [4]to [5]Him [1]Simon [2]Peter, "Lord, where are You going?"
said

Ἀπεκρίθη αὐτῷ ὁ Ἰησοῦς, "Ὅπου ὑπάγω οὐ δύνασαί
[2]answered [3]him - [1]Jesus, "Where I am going [3]not [1]you [2]are [4]able

μοι νῦν ἀκολουθῆσαι, ὕστερον δὲ ἀκολουθήσεις μοι."
[7]Me [8]now [5]to [6]follow, later ˜ but you will follow Me."

37 Λέγει αὐτῷ Πέτρος, "Κύριε, διὰ τί οὐ
[2]says [3]to [4]Him [1]Peter, "Lord, on account of what [3]not
said why

δύναμαί σοι ἀκολουθῆσαι ἄρτι? Τὴν ψυχήν μου ὑπὲρ
[1]am [2]I [4]able [7]You [5]to [6]follow now? - [6]life [5]my [7]in [8]behalf [9]of
for Your

σοῦ θήσω."
[10]You [1]I [2]will [3]lay [4]down."
sake

Judas had the money box, that Jesus had said to him, "Buy *those things* we need for the feast," or that he should give something to the poor.
30 Having received the piece of bread, he then went out immediately. And it was night.
31 So, when he had gone out, Jesus said, "Now the Son of Man is glorified, and God is glorified in Him.
32 "If God is glorified in Him, God will also glorify Him in Himself, and glorify Him immediately.
33 "Little children, I shall be with you a little while longer. You will seek Me; and as I said to the Jews, 'Where I am going, you cannot come,' so now I say to you.
34 "A new commandment I give to you, that you love one another; as I have loved you, that you also love one another.
35 "By this all will know that you are My disciples, if you have love for one another."
36 Simon Peter said to Him, "Lord, where are You going?" Jesus answered him, "Where I am going you cannot follow Me now, but you shall follow Me afterward."
37 Peter said to Him, "Lord, why can I not follow You now? I will lay down my life for Your sake."

***(13:34)** *καινός (kainos).* Adjective meaning *new,* either qualitatively (in contrast to "old") or temporally (not existing before), as with the synonym *νέος, new.* While *καινός* and *νέος* may be used interchangeably in the NT (cf. Mark 2:22), *καινός* is especially qualitative and often points to what is different and better. That nuance is present here in John 13:34 and in passages like Heb. 8:8 (new covenant), Rev. 21:1 (new heaven and earth), and Eph. 4:24 (new man). Cf. the cognate noun *καινότης, newness* (Rom. 7:6), where the same qualitative emphasis is in focus.

38 Jesus answered him, "Will you lay down your life for My sake? Most assuredly, I say to you, the rooster shall not crow till you have denied Me three times.

14 "Let not your heart be troubled; you believe in God, believe also in Me.

2 "In My Father's house are many mansions; if *it were* not *so,* I would have told you. I go to prepare a place for you.

3 "And if I go and prepare a place for you, I will come again and receive you to Myself; that where I am, *there* you may be also.

4 "And where I go you know, and the way you know."

5 Thomas said to Him, "Lord, we do not know where You are going, and how can we know the way?"

6 Jesus said to him, "I am the way, the truth, and the life. No one comes to the Father except through Me.

7 "If you had known Me, you would have known My Father also; and from now on you know Him and have seen Him."

8 Philip said to Him, "Lord, show us the Father, and it is sufficient for us."

9 Jesus said to him, "Have I been with you so long, and yet you have not known Me,

38 Ἀπεκρίθη αὐτῷ ὁ Ἰησοῦς, "Τὴν ψυχήν σου ὑπὲρ
[2]answered [3]him - [1]Jesus, - "[6]life [5]your [7]in [8]behalf [9]of
for My

ἐμοῦ θήσεις? Ἀμὴν ἀμὴν λέγω σοι, οὐ μὴ
[10]Me [1]Will [2]you [3]lay [4]down? Amen amen I say to you, [4]not [5]not
sake Most assuredly a rooster

ἀλέκτωρ φωνήσῃ ἕως οὗ ἀπαρνήσῃ με τρίς.
[1]a [2]rooster [3]will [6]sound till - you deny Me three times.
shall by no means crow

Jesus Is the Way, the Truth, and the Life

14 1 "Μὴ ταρασσέσθω ὑμῶν ἡ καρδία· πιστεύετε εἰς
"[2]not [1]Do [3]let [6]be [7]troubled [4]your - [5]heart; you believe in

τὸν Θεόν, καὶ εἰς ἐμὲ πιστεύετε. **2** Ἐν τῇ οἰκίᾳ τοῦ Πατρός
- God, [2]also [3]in [4]Me [1]believe. In the house - of Father ˜

μου μοναὶ πολλαί εἰσιν, εἰ δὲ μή, εἶπον ἂν
My [3]dwelling [4]places [2]many [1]are, if ˜ and not *so,* I would have told -

ὑμῖν.[a] Πορεύομαι ἑτοιμάσαι τόπον ὑμῖν. **3** Καὶ ἐὰν πορευθῶ
you. I go to prepare a place for you. And if I go

καὶ ἑτοιμάσω ὑμῖν τόπον, πάλιν ἔρχομαι καὶ παραλήψομαι
and prepare for you a place, again I am coming and I will take

ὑμᾶς πρὸς ἐμαυτόν, ἵνα ὅπου εἰμὶ ἐγὼ καὶ ὑμεῖς ἦτε.
you to Myself, so that where am ˜ I [4]also [1]you [2]may [3]be.

4 Καὶ ὅπου ἐγὼ ὑπάγω οἴδατε, καὶ τὴν ὁδὸν οἴδατε."[b]
And where I am going you know, and the way you know."

5 Λέγει αὐτῷ Θωμᾶς, "Κύριε, οὐκ οἴδαμεν ποῦ
[2]says [3]to [4]Him [1]Thomas, "Lord, [3]not [1]we [2]do know where
said

ὑπάγεις, καὶ πῶς δυνάμεθα τὴν ὁδὸν εἰδέναι?"
You are going, and how are we able [3]the [4]way [1]to [2]know?"

6 Λέγει αὐτῷ ὁ Ἰησοῦς, "Ἐγώ εἰμι ἡ ὁδὸς καὶ ἡ
[2]says [3]to [4]him - [1]Jesus, "I am the way and the
said

ἀλήθεια καὶ ἡ ζωή. Οὐδεὶς ἔρχεται πρὸς τὸν Πατέρα εἰ μὴ
truth and the life. No one comes to the Father if not
except

δι' ἐμοῦ.
through Me.

Jesus Reveals the Father

7 "Εἰ ἐγνώκειτέ με, καὶ τὸν Πατέρα μου
"If you had known Me, [7]also - [6]Father [5]My

ἐγνώκειτε ἄν·[c] καὶ ἀπ' ἄρτι γινώσκετε αὐτὸν καὶ
[1]you [2]would [3]have [4]known; - and from now *on* you know Him and

ἑωράκατε αὐτόν."
you have seen Him."

8 Λέγει αὐτῷ Φίλιππος, "Κύριε, δεῖξον ἡμῖν τὸν Πατέρα
[2]says [3]to [4]Him [1]Philip, "Lord, show us the Father
said

καὶ ἀρκεῖ ἡμῖν."
and it is sufficient for us."

9 Λέγει αὐτῷ ὁ Ἰησοῦς, "Τοσοῦτον χρόνον μεθ' ὑμῶν
[2]says [3]to [4]him - [1]Jesus, "For so long a time [3]with [4]you
said

εἰμι καὶ οὐκ ἔγνωκάς με, Φίλιππε? Ὁ
[1]I [2]am and yet [3]not [1]you [2]have known Me Philip? The *one*
have I been

[a](14:2) NU adds ὀτι, thus either *(would I have told you) that (I go . . . ?)* or *(told you;) for (I go).*

[b](14:4) For και την οδον οιδατε, *and the way you know,* NU reads την οδον, *(where I am going you know) the way.*

[c](14:7) For εγνωκειτε αν, *you would have known,* NU reads γνωσεσθε, *you will know.*

ἑωρακὼς ἐμὲ ἑώρακε τὸν Πατέρα· καὶ πῶς σὺ λέγεις,
having seen Me has seen the Father; and so how you ˜ do say,
who has

'Δεῖξον ἡμῖν τὸν Πατέρα'? 10 Οὐ πιστεύεις ὅτι ἐγὼ ἐν τῷ
'Show us the Father'? [3]not [1]Do [2]you believe that I *am* in the

Πατρὶ καὶ ὁ Πατὴρ ἐν ἐμοί ἐστι? Τὰ ῥήματα ἃ ἐγὼ λαλῶ
Father and the Father [2]in [3]Me [1]is? The sayings which I speak

ὑμῖν ἀπ' ἐμαυτοῦ οὐ λαλῶ, ὁ δὲ Πατὴρ ὁ ἐν
to you [5]from [6]Myself [3]not [1]I [2]do [4]speak, the ˜ but Father the *One* in
on My own who

ἐμοὶ μένων, αὐτὸς[d] ποιεῖ τὰ ἔργα. 11 Πιστεύετέ μοι ὅτι ἐγὼ
Me abiding, He does the works. Believe Me that I *am*
abides,

ἐν τῷ Πατρὶ καὶ ὁ Πατὴρ ἐν ἐμοί, εἰ δὲ μή, διὰ τὰ
in the Father and the Father *is* in Me, if ˜ but not, because of the

ἔργα αὐτὰ πιστεύετέ μοι.
works themselves believe Me.

Prayer in Jesus' Name

12 "Ἀμὴν ἀμὴν λέγω ὑμῖν, ὁ πιστεύων εἰς ἐμέ, τὰ
"Amen amen I say to you, the *one* believing in Me, the
"Most assuredly who believes

ἔργα ἃ ἐγὼ ποιῶ κἀκεῖνος ποιήσει, καὶ μείζονα
works which I do that *one* also will do, and greater *works*
he

τούτων ποιήσει, ὅτι ἐγὼ πρὸς τὸν Πατέρα μου[e]
than these he will do, because I [3]to - [5]Father [4]My

πορεύομαι. 13 Καὶ ὅ τι ἂν αἰτήσητε ἐν τῷ ὀνόματί μου,
[1]am [2]going. And - what ever you may ask in - name ˜ My,

τοῦτο ποιήσω, ἵνα δοξασθῇ ὁ Πατὴρ ἐν τῷ Υἱῷ.
this I will do, so that [3]may [4]be [5]glorified [1]the [2]Father in the Son.

14 Ἐάν τι αἰτήσητε[f] ἐν τῷ ὀνόματί μου, ἐγὼ
If [4]anything [1]you [2]should [3]ask in - name ˜ My, I

ποιήσω. 15 Ἐὰν ἀγαπᾶτέ με, τὰς ἐντολὰς τὰς ἐμὰς
will do *it*. If you love Me, - [3]commandments - [2]My

τηρήσατε.[g]
[1]keep.

Jesus Promises Another Advocate

16 "Καὶ ἐγὼ ἐρωτήσω τὸν Πατέρα, καὶ ἄλλον Παράκλητον
"And I will ask the Father, and [5]another [6]Advocate
Helper

δώσει ὑμῖν, ἵνα μένῃ μεθ' ὑμῶν εἰς τὸν
[1]He [2]will [3]give [4]you, so that He may abide with you into the
forever,

αἰῶνα, 17 τὸ Πνεῦμα τῆς ἀληθείας, ὃ ὁ κόσμος οὐ
age, the Spirit - of truth, whom the world not ˜

δύναται λαβεῖν ὅτι οὐ θεωρεῖ αὐτὸ οὐδὲ γινώσκει
is able to receive because [3]not [1]it [2]does see It nor know
Him

αὐτό· ὑμεῖς δὲ γινώσκετε αὐτό, ὅτι παρ' ὑμῖν μένει καὶ
It; you ˜ but know It, because [3]with [4]you [1]He [2]abides and
Him; Him,

ἐν ὑμῖν ἔσται. 18 Οὐκ ἀφήσω ὑμᾶς ὀρφανούς· ἔρχομαι
[3]in [4]you [1]He [2]is. [3]not [1]I [2]will leave you orphans; I am coming

πρὸς ὑμᾶς.
to you.

Philip? He who has seen Me has seen the Father; so how can you say, 'Show us the Father'?
10 "Do you not believe that I am in the Father, and the Father in Me? The words that I speak to you I do not speak on My own *authority;* but the Father who dwells in Me does the works.
11 "Believe Me that I *am* in the Father and the Father in Me, or else believe Me for the sake of the works themselves.
12 "Most assuredly, I say to you, he who believes in Me, the works that I do he will do also; and greater *works* than these he will do, because I go to My Father.
13 "And whatever you ask in My name, that I will do, that the Father may be glorified in the Son.
14 "If you ask anything in My name, I will do *it.*
15 "If you love Me, keep My commandments.
16 "And I will pray the Father, and He will give you another Helper, that He may abide with you forever—
17 "the Spirit of truth, whom the world cannot receive, because it neither sees Him nor knows Him; but you know Him, for He dwells with you and will be in you.
18 "I will not leave you orphans; I will come to you.

[d]**(14:10)** NU reads αυτου, *(does) His (works).*
[e]**(14:12)** NU omits μου, *My,* thus *the Father.*
[f]**(14:14)** NU adds με, *Me.*
[g]**(14:15)** NU reads τηρησετε, *you will keep.*

19 "A little while longer and the world will see Me no more, but you will see Me. Because I live, you will live also.

20 "At that day you will know that I *am* in My Father, and you in Me, and I in you.

21 "He who has My commandments and keeps them, it is he who loves Me. And he who loves Me will be loved by My Father, and I will love him and manifest Myself to him."

22 Judas (not Iscariot) said to Him, "Lord, how is it that You will manifest Yourself to us, and not to the world?"

23 Jesus answered and said to him, "If anyone loves Me, he will keep My word; and My Father will love him, and We will come to him and make Our home with him.

24 "He who does not love Me does not keep My words; and the word which you hear is not Mine but the Father's who sent Me.

25 "These things I have spoken to you while being present with you.

26 "But the Helper, the Holy Spirit, whom the Father will send in My name, He will teach you all things, and bring to your remembrance all things that I said to you.

27 "Peace I leave with you, My peace I give to you; not as the world gives do I give to

The Indwelling of the Father and the Son

19 "Ἔτι μικρὸν καὶ ὁ κόσμος με οὐκέτι θεωρεῖ,
"Yet a little *while* and the world [4]Me [1]no [2]longer [3]sees,
"A little while longer

ὑμεῖς δὲ θεωρεῖτέ με. Ὅτι ἐγὼ ζῶ, καὶ ὑμεῖς ζήσεσθε.
you ˜ but see Me. Because I live, also ˜ you will live.

20 Ἐν ἐκείνῃ τῇ ἡμέρᾳ γνώσεσθε ὑμεῖς ὅτι ἐγὼ ἐν τῷ Πατρί
In that - day [2]will [3]know [1]you that I *am* in - Father ˜

μου, καὶ ὑμεῖς ἐν ἐμοί, κἀγὼ ἐν ὑμῖν. **21** Ὁ ἔχων τὰς
My, and you in Me, and I in you. The *one* having -
who has

ἐντολάς μου καὶ τηρῶν αὐτάς, ἐκεῖνός ἐστιν ὁ
commandments ˜ My and keeping them, that *one* is the *one*
keeps

ἀγαπῶν με. Ὁ δὲ ἀγαπῶν με ἀγαπηθήσεται ὑπὸ τοῦ
loving Me. [2]the [3]*one* [1]And loving Me will be loved by -
who loves who loves

Πατρός μου, καὶ ἐγὼ ἀγαπήσω αὐτὸν καὶ ἐμφανίσω* αὐτῷ
Father ˜ My, and I will love him and will manifest [2]to [3]him

ἐμαυτόν."
[1]Myself."

22 Λέγει αὐτῷ Ἰούδας (οὐχ ὁ Ἰσκαριώτης), "Κύριε, καὶ
[4]says [5]to [6]him [1]Judas ([2]not - [3]Iscariot), "Lord, and
said

τί γέγονεν ὅτι ἡμῖν μέλλεις ἐμφανίζειν σεαυτὸν
what has happened that [7]to [8]us [1]You [2]are [3]about [4]to [5]manifest [6]Yourself

καὶ οὐχὶ τῷ κόσμῳ?"
and not to the world?"

23 Ἀπεκρίθη Ἰησοῦς καὶ εἶπεν αὐτῷ, "Ἐάν τις ἀγαπᾷ
answered ˜ Jesus and said to him, "If anyone loves

με, τὸν λόγον μου τηρήσει. Καὶ ὁ Πατήρ μου ἀγαπήσει
Me, - [5]word [4]My [1]he [2]will [3]keep. And - Father ˜ My will love

αὐτόν, καὶ πρὸς αὐτὸν ἐλευσόμεθα καὶ μονὴν παρ' αὐτῷ
him, and [4]to [5]him [1]We [2]will [3]come and [4]*Our* [5]abode [6]with [7]him

ποιήσομεν. **24** Ὁ μὴ ἀγαπῶν με, τοὺς λόγους μου
[1]We [2]will [3]make. The *one* not loving Me, - [5]words [4]My
who does not love

οὐ τηρεῖ· καὶ ὁ λόγος ὃν ἀκούετε οὐκ ἔστιν ἐμός,
[2]not [1]does [3]keep; and the word which you hear not ˜ is Mine,

ἀλλὰ τοῦ πέμψαντός με Πατρός.
but *is* of the [2]having [3]sent [4]Me [1]Father.
who

The Gift of His Peace

25 "Ταῦτα λελάληκα ὑμῖν παρ' ὑμῖν μένων.
"These *things* I have spoken to you [2]with [3]you [1]remaining.
while I remain.

26 Ὁ δὲ Παράκλητος, τὸ Πνεῦμα τὸ Ἅγιον, ὃ πέμψει
the ˜ But Advocate, the Spirit ˜ - Holy, whom [3]will [4]send
Helper,

ὁ Πατὴρ ἐν τῷ ὀνόματί μου, ἐκεῖνος ὑμᾶς διδάξει πάντα
[1]the [2]Father in - name ˜ My, that One [3]you [1]will [2]teach all *things*
He

καὶ ὑπομνήσει ὑμᾶς πάντα ἃ εἶπον ὑμῖν.
and will remind you *of* all *things* which I said to you.

27 "Εἰρήνην ἀφίημι ὑμῖν, εἰρήνην τὴν ἐμὴν δίδωμι
"Peace I leave with you, peace ˜ - My I give

ὑμῖν· οὐ καθὼς ὁ κόσμος δίδωσιν, ἐγὼ δίδωμι ὑμῖν. Μὴ
to you; not as the world gives, I ˜ do give to you. [2]not

***(14:21)** ἐμφανίζω *(emphanizō)*. Verb meaning *make visible*, thus *reveal, manifest* (as here and v. 22; Matt. 27:53), *show* (as Heb. 11:14), *make known, explain, inform* (as "suggest" in Acts 23:15; cf. 23:22), and even *present charges (against)* (as Acts 24:1; 25:2, 15). Cf. the cognate adjective ἐμφανής, *visible* (Acts 10:40; Rom. 10:20).

ταρασσέσθω ὑμῶν ἡ καρδία, μηδὲ δειλιάτω.
[1]Do [3]let [6]be [7]troubled [4]your - [5]heart, nor let it be fearful.

28 Ἠκούσατε ὅτι ἐγὼ εἶπον ὑμῖν, ‘Ὑπάγω καὶ
You heard that I said to you, ‘I am going away and

ἔρχομαι πρὸς ὑμᾶς.’ Εἰ ἠγαπᾶτέ με, ἐχάρητε ἂν
I am coming *back* to you.’ If you loved Me, you would rejoice -

ὅτι εἶπον,[h] ‘Πορεύομαι πρὸς τὸν Πατέρα,’ ὅτι ὁ Πατήρ
because I said, ‘I am going to the Father,’ because - Father ~

μου μείζων μού ἐστι. **29** Καὶ νῦν εἴρηκα ὑμῖν πρὶν
My [2]greater [3]*than* [4]Me [1]is. And now I have told you before
I

γενέσθαι, ἵνα ὅταν γένηται, πιστεύσητε.
to happen, so that whenever it may happen, you may believe.
it happens,

30 Οὐκέτι πολλὰ λαλήσω μεθ’ ὑμῶν, ἔρχεται γὰρ
[3]no [4]longer [6]many [7]*things* [1]I [2]will [5]speak with you, [7]is [8]coming [1]for

ὁ τοῦ κόσμου[i] ἄρχων, καὶ ἐν ἐμοὶ οὐκ ἔχει οὐδέν.
[2]the [4]of [5]the [6]world [3]ruler, and in Me [3]not [1]he [2]has nothing.
he does not have anything.

31 Ἀλλ’ ἵνα γνῷ ὁ κόσμος ὅτι ἀγαπῶ τὸν Πατέρα,
But so that [3]may [4]know [1]the [2]world that I love the Father,

καὶ καθὼς ἐνετείλατό μοι ὁ Πατήρ, οὕτω ποιῶ. Ἐγείρεσθε,
and just as [3]commanded [4]Me [1]the [2]Father, so I do. Arise,

ἄγωμεν ἐντεῦθεν.
let us go from here.

The True Vine and Its Branches

15 **1** “Ἐγώ εἰμι ἡ ἄμπελος ἡ ἀληθινή, καὶ ὁ Πατήρ μου
“I am the vine ~ - true, and - Father ~ My

ὁ γεωργός ἐστι. **2** Πᾶν κλῆμα ἐν ἐμοὶ μὴ φέρον
[2]the [3]farmer [1]is. Every branch in Me not bearing
vinedresser which does not bear

καρπόν, αἴρει* αὐτό· καὶ πᾶν τὸ καρπὸν
fruit, He takes away ~ it; and every *branch* the *one* fruit ~
which bears

φέρον, καθαίρει αὐτὸ ἵνα πλείονα καρπὸν φέρῃ.
bearing, He prunes it so that [4]more [5]fruit [1]it [2]may [3]bear.
fruit,

3 Ἤδη ὑμεῖς καθαροί ἐστε διὰ τὸν λόγον ὃν
already ~ You clean ~ are because of the word which

λελάληκα ὑμῖν. **4** Μείνατε ἐν ἐμοί, κἀγὼ ἐν ὑμῖν. Καθὼς τὸ
I have spoken to you. Abide in Me, and I in you. Just as the

κλῆμα οὐ δύναται καρπὸν φέρειν ἀφ’ ἑαυτοῦ, ἐὰν μὴ
branch not ~ is able [3]fruit [1]to [2]bear from itself, if not ~
on its own, unless

μείνῃ ἐν τῇ ἀμπέλῳ, οὕτως οὐδὲ ὑμεῖς ἐὰν μὴ ἐν ἐμοὶ
it abides in the vine, so neither *can* you if not [3]in [4]Me
unless

μείνητε. **5** Ἐγώ εἰμι ἡ ἄμπελος, ὑμεῖς τὰ κλήματα. Ὁ
[1]you [2]abide. I am the vine, you *are* the branches. The *one*

μένων ἐν ἐμοὶ κἀγὼ ἐν αὐτῷ, οὗτος φέρει καρπὸν πολύν·
abiding in Me and I in him, this *one* bears fruit ~ much;
who abides

ὅτι χωρὶς ἐμοῦ οὐ δύνασθε ποιεῖν οὐδέν. **6** Ἐὰν μή
because apart from Me [3]not [1]you [2]are able to do nothing. If [3]not
anything.

τις μείνῃ ἐν ἐμοί, ἐβλήθη ἔξω ὡς τὸ κλῆμα καὶ
[1]anyone [2]does abide in Me, he was thrown out like the branch and
is a

you. Let not your heart be troubled, neither let it be afraid.
28 “You have heard Me say to you, ‘I am going away and coming *back* to you.’ If you loved Me, you would rejoice because I said, ‘I am going to the Father,’ for My Father is greater than I.
29 “And now I have told you before it comes, that when it does come to pass, you may believe.
30 “I will no longer talk much with you, for the ruler of this world is coming, and he has nothing in Me.
31 “But that the world may know that I love the Father, and as the Father gave Me commandment, so I do. Arise, let us go from here.
15 “I am the true vine, and My Father is the vinedresser.
2 “Every branch in Me that does not bear fruit He takes away; and every *branch* that bears fruit He prunes, that it may bear more fruit.
3 “You are already clean because of the word which I have spoken to you.
4 “Abide in Me, and I in you. As the branch cannot bear fruit of itself, unless it abides in the vine, neither can you, unless you abide in Me.
5 “I am the vine, you *are* the branches. He who abides in Me, and I in him, bears much fruit; for without Me you can do nothing.
6 “If anyone does not abide in Me, he is cast out as a

---

[h]**(14:28)** NU omits *ειπον, I said;* thus *because I am going.* [i]**(14:30)** TR adds *τουτου, this (world).*

***(15:2)** *αἴρω (airō).* Verb meaning *lift up, carry away.* It most often refers to lifting some literal object (branches here; stones, John 8:59; cf. the synonymous verb *ἀναλαμβάνω*). It may also refer to raising something figuratively (eyes in prayer, John 11:41). The meaning *take away* may be used euphemistically to indicate the destruction of things (the temple, John 11:48) or people (thus *execute,* Luke 23:18; cf. the use of *ἀπάγω* in Acts 12:19). *αἴρω* is used in two idioms. To *lift up* or *take up* the cross (*τὸν σταυρόν,* Mark 8:34)

branch and is withered; and they gather them and throw *them* into the fire, and they are burned.
7 "If you abide in Me, and My words abide in you, you will ask what you desire, and it shall be done for you.
8 "By this My Father is glorified, that you bear much fruit; so you will be My disciples.
9 "As the Father loved Me, I also have loved you; abide in My love.
10 "If you keep My commandments, you will abide in My love, just as I have kept My Father's commandments and abide in His love.
11 "These things I have spoken to you, that My joy may remain in you, and *that* your joy may be full.
12 "This is My commandment, that you love one another as I have loved you.
13 "Greater love has no one than this, than to lay down one's life for his friends.
14 "You are My friends if you do whatever I command you.
15 "No longer do I call you servants, for a servant does not know what his master is doing; but I have called you friends, for all things that I heard from My Father I have made known to you.
16 "You did not choose Me, but I chose you and appointed you that you should go and bear fruit, and *that* your fruit should remain, that whatever you ask the Father in My name He may give you.
17 "These things I command you, that you love one another.

---

[a](15:7) NU reads the command αιτησασθε, *ask*.
[b](15:8) NU reads γενησθε, *be* or *become (my disciples)*.
[c](15:11) NU reads η, *may be*.

means *to endure suffering or death*. To *lift up* or *hold up* someone's life (τὴν ψυχὴν, John 10:24) is *to keep them in suspense*. The verb αἴρω is also a technical term for *withdrawing* money from a bank (Luke 19:21).

***(15:14)** φίλος *(philos)*. Adjective derived from the verb φιλέω, *love, have affection for*, and having either a passive (*beloved, dear*) or active (*loving, devoted*) sense. However, with the possible exception of Acts 19:31, all of the NT occurrences are

ἐξηράνθη· καὶ συνάγουσιν αὐτὰ καὶ εἰς τὸ πῦρ
was dried up; and they gather them and [4]into [5]the [6]fire
dries up;

βάλλουσι, καὶ καίεται. **7** Ἐὰν μείνητε ἐν ἐμοὶ καὶ
[1]they [2]throw [3]*them*, and they are burned. If you abide in Me and

τὰ ῥήματά μου ἐν ὑμῖν μείνῃ, ὃ ἐὰν θέλητε
- sayings ˜ My [2]in [3]you [1]abide, [7]what [8]ever [9]you [10]may [11]desire

αἰτήσεσθε,[a] καὶ γενήσεται ὑμῖν. **8** Ἐν τούτῳ ἐδοξάσθη ὁ
[4]you [5]will [6]ask, and it will happen for you. By this [3]was [4]glorified -
is

Πατήρ μου, ἵνα καρπὸν πολὺν φέρητε· καὶ γενήσεσθε[b]
[2]Father [1]My, that [5]fruit [4]much [1]you [2]may [3]bear; and you will become

ἐμοὶ μαθηταί.
to Me disciples.
My

Love as He Loved

9 "Καθὼς ἠγάπησέ με ὁ Πατήρ, κἀγὼ ἠγάπησα ὑμᾶς·
"Just as [3]loved [4]Me [1]the [2]Father, I also loved you;

μείνατε ἐν τῇ ἀγάπῃ τῇ ἐμῇ. **10** Ἐὰν τὰς ἐντολάς μου
abide in - love ˜ - My. If - [4]commandments [3]My

τηρήσητε, μενεῖτε ἐν τῇ ἀγάπῃ μου, καθὼς ἐγὼ τὰς
[1]you [2]keep, you will abide in - love ˜ My, just as I [3]the

ἐντολὰς τοῦ Πατρός μου τετήρηκα καὶ μένω αὐτοῦ ἐν τῇ
[4]commandments - [5]of [7]Father [6]My [1]have [2]kept and I abide His ˜ in -

ἀγάπῃ. **11** Ταῦτα λελάληκα ὑμῖν ἵνα ἡ χαρὰ ἡ ἐμὴ
love. These *things* I have spoken to you so that - joy ˜ - My

ἐν ὑμῖν μείνῃ[c] καὶ ἡ χαρὰ ὑμῶν πληρωθῇ. **12** Αὕτη
[3]in [4]you [1]may [2]abide and - joy ˜ your may be made full. This

ἐστὶν ἡ ἐντολὴ ἡ ἐμή, ἵνα ἀγαπᾶτε ἀλλήλους καθὼς
is - commandment ˜ - My, that you love one another just as

ἠγάπησα ὑμᾶς. **13** Μείζονα ταύτης ἀγάπην οὐδεὶς ἔχει, ἵνα
I loved you. [4]greater [6]*than* [7]this [5]love [1]No [2]one [3]has, that

τις τὴν ψυχὴν αὐτοῦ θῇ ὑπὲρ φίλων αὐτοῦ.
someone - [5]life [4]his [1]should [2]lay [3]down in behalf of friends ˜ his.

14 Ὑμεῖς φίλοι* μού ἐστε ἐὰν ποιῆτε ὅσα ἐγὼ
You [3]friends [2]My [1]are if you do as many *things* as I
what

ἐντέλλομαι ὑμῖν. **15** Οὐκέτι ὑμᾶς λέγω δούλους, ὅτι ὁ
command you. No longer [4]you [1]do [2]I [3]call slaves, because the
servants, a

δοῦλος οὐκ οἶδε τί ποιεῖ αὐτοῦ ὁ κύριος· ὑμᾶς δὲ
slave not ˜ does know what [3]is [4]doing [1]his - [2]master; you ˜ but
servant

εἴρηκα φίλους, ὅτι πάντα ἃ ἤκουσα παρὰ τοῦ
I have called friends, because all *things* which I heard from -

Πατρός μου ἐγνώρισα ὑμῖν. **16** Οὐχ ὑμεῖς με ἐξελέξασθε,
Father ˜ My I made known to you. [3]not [1]You [5]Me [2]did [4]choose,

ἀλλ' ἐγὼ ἐξελεξάμην ὑμᾶς καὶ ἔθηκα ὑμᾶς ἵνα ὑμεῖς
but I chose you and appointed you that you

ὑπάγητε καὶ καρπὸν φέρητε, καὶ ὁ καρπὸς ὑμῶν
should go and [3]fruit [1]should [2]bear, and - fruit ˜ your

μένῃ· ἵνα ὅ τι ἂν αἰτήσητε τὸν Πατέρα ἐν τῷ
should remain; so that - what ever you may ask the Father in -

ὀνόματί μου, δώῃ ὑμῖν. **17** Ταῦτα ἐντέλλομαι ὑμῖν,
name ˜ My, He may give to you. These *things* I command you,

ἵνα ἀγαπᾶτε ἀλλήλους.
that you may love one another.

The Master Forewarns of Persecution

18 “Εἰ ὁ κόσμος ὑμᾶς μισεῖ, γινώσκετε ὅτι ἐμὲ πρῶτον
“If the world you ˜ hates, you know that [4]Me [5]before

ὑμῶν μεμίσηκεν. 19 Εἰ ἐκ τοῦ κόσμου ἦτε, ὁ κόσμος
[6]you [1]it [2]has [3]hated. If [3]of [4]the [5]world [1]you [2]were, the world

ἂν τὸ ἴδιον ἐφίλει. Ὅτι δὲ ἐκ τοῦ κόσμου οὐκ
- - [3]its [4]own [1]would [2]love. because ˜ But [4]of [5]the [6]world [3]not

ἐστέ, ἀλλ’ ἐγὼ ἐξελεξάμην ὑμᾶς ἐκ τοῦ κόσμου, διὰ
[1]you [2]are, but I chose you out of the world, because of

τοῦτο μισεῖ ὑμᾶς ὁ κόσμος. 20 Μνημονεύετε τοῦ λόγου οὗ
this [3]hates [4]you [1]the [2]world. Remember the word which

ἐγὼ εἶπον ὑμῖν, ‘Οὐκ ἔστι δοῦλος μείζων τοῦ κυρίου
I said to you, ‘[4]not [3]is [1]A [2]slave [5]greater [6]*than* - [8]master
servant

αὐτοῦ.’ Εἰ ἐμὲ ἐδίωξαν, καὶ ὑμᾶς διώξουσιν. Εἰ
[7]his.’ If [3]Me [1]they [2]persecuted, [6]also [8]you [4]they [5]will [7]persecute. If

τὸν λόγον μου ἐτήρησαν, καὶ τὸν ὑμέτερον τηρήσουσιν.
- [4]word [3]My [1]they [2]kept, also - [4]yours [1]they [2]will [3]keep.

21 Ἀλλὰ ταῦτα πάντα ποιήσουσιν ὑμῖν διὰ τὸ
But [2]these [3]*things* [1]all they will do to you because of -
for My

ὄνομά μου ὅτι οὐκ οἴδασι τὸν πέμψαντά με. 22 Εἰ
name ˜ My because [3]not [1]they [2]do know the *One* having sent Me. If
name's sake who

μὴ ἦλθον καὶ ἐλάλησα αὐτοῖς, ἁμαρτίαν οὐκ
not I came and spoke to them, [5]sin [3]not
I had not come spoken they would

εἶχον, νῦν δὲ πρόφασιν οὐκ ἔχουσι περὶ τῆς
[1]they [2]were [4]having, now ˜ but [4]excuse [3]no [1]they [2]have concerning -
not have sin,

ἁμαρτίας αὐτῶν. 23 Ὁ ἐμὲ μισῶν, καὶ τὸν Πατέρα μου
sin ˜ their. The *one* Me ˜ hating, [4]also - [3]Father [2]My
who hates,

μισεῖ. 24 Εἰ τὰ ἔργα μὴ ἐποίησα ἐν αὐτοῖς ἃ οὐδεὶς
[1]hates. If [5]the [6]works [3]not [1]I [2]did [4]do among them which no one ˜
I had not done

ἄλλος πεποίηκεν, ἁμαρτίαν οὐχ εἶχον· νῦν δὲ καὶ
other has done, [5]sin [3]not [1]they [2]were [4]having; now ˜ but [3]both
else They would not have sin;

ἑωράκασι καὶ μεμισήκασι καὶ ἐμὲ καὶ τὸν Πατέρα μου.
[1]they [2]have [4]seen and they have hated both Me and - Father ˜ My.

25 Ἀλλ’ ἵνα πληρωθῇ ὁ λόγος ὁ
But *this was* so that [3]might [4]be [5]fulfilled [1]the [2]word the *one*
which

γεγραμμένος ἐν τῷ νόμῳ αὐτῶν ὅτι «Ἐμίσησάν με
having been written in - law ˜ their - «They hated Me
was written

δωρεάν.» [d]
without cause.»

Future Witness and Rejection

26 “Ὅταν δὲ ἔλθῃ ὁ Παράκλητος, ὃν ἐγὼ πέμψω
“when ˜ But [3]comes [1]the [2]Advocate, whom I will send
Helper,

ὑμῖν παρὰ τοῦ Πατρός, τὸ Πνεῦμα τῆς ἀληθείας ὃ παρὰ
to you from the Father, the Spirit of truth who [3]from

τοῦ Πατρὸς ἐκπορεύεται, ἐκεῖνος μαρτυρήσει περὶ ἐμοῦ.
[4]the [5]Father [1]goes [2]out, that *One* will testify about Me.
proceeds, He

18 “If the world hates you, you know that it hated Me before *it hated* you.
19 “If you were of the world, the world would love its own. Yet because you are not of the world, but I chose you out of the world, therefore the world hates you.
20 “Remember the word that I said to you, ‘A servant is not greater than his master.’ If they persecuted Me, they will also persecute you. If they kept My word, they will keep yours also.
21 “But all these things they will do to you for My name’s sake, because they do not know Him who sent Me.
22 “If I had not come and spoken to them, they would have no sin, but now they have no excuse for their sin.
23 “He who hates Me hates My Father also.
24 “If I had not done among them the works which no one else did, they would have no sin; but now they have seen and also hated both Me and My Father.
25 “But *this happened* that the word might be fulfilled which is written in their law, *‘They hated Me without a cause.’*
26 “But when the Helper comes, whom I shall send to you from the Father, the Spirit of truth who proceeds from the Father, He will testify of Me.

---

[d](**15:25**) Ps. 69:4

substantives with the meaning *friend.* The word was a common form of familiar address (Luke 14:10) and sometimes implies no more than close association (“friends and neighbors,” Luke 15:6). In other cases, it denotes a special relationship between persons, as here in John 15:14, 15 between Jesus and His disciples, as the “friend of the bridegroom” (akin to the modern “best man”) in John 3:29, and as Abraham being called “a friend of God” in James 2:23. The feminine substantive φίλη is used to refer to “woman friends” (Luke 15:9).

27 "And you also will bear witness, because you have been with Me from the beginning.

16 "These things I have spoken to you, that you should not be made to stumble.
2 "They will put you out of the synagogues; yes, the time is coming that whoever kills you will think that he offers God service.
3 "And these things they will do to you because they have not known the Father nor Me.
4 "But these things I have told you, that when the time comes, you may remember that I told you of them. And these things I did not say to you at the beginning, because I was with you.
5 "But now I go away to Him who sent Me, and none of you asks Me, 'Where are You going?'
6 "But because I have said these things to you, sorrow has filled your heart.
7 "Nevertheless I tell you the truth. It is to your advantage that I go away; for if I do not go away, the Helper will not come to you; but if I depart, I will send Him to you.
8 "And when He has come, He will convict the world of sin, and of righteousness, and of judgment:
9 "of sin, because they do not believe in Me;
10 "of righteousness, because I go to My Father and you see Me no more;
11 "of judgment, because the ruler of this world is judged.
12 "I still have many things to say to you, but you cannot bear *them* now.

27 Καὶ ὑμεῖς δὲ μαρτυρεῖτε ὅτι ἀπ' ἀρχῆς μετ' ἐμοῦ
[3]also [2]you [1]But testify because from *the* beginning [3]with [4]Me
will testify

ἐστε.
[1]you [2]are.
have been.

16 1 "Ταῦτα λελάληκα ὑμῖν ἵνα μὴ
"These *things* I have spoken to you so that [3]not

σκανδαλισθῆτε. 2 Ἀποσυναγώγους
[1]you [2]may be made to stumble. [5]expelled [6]from [7]the [8]synagogue
They will

ποιήσουσιν ὑμᾶς· ἀλλ' ἔρχεται ὥρα ἵνα πᾶς ὁ
[1]They [2]will [3]make [4]you; but [3]is [4]coming [1]an [2]hour that every - *one*
excommunicate you; a time is coming when everyone who

ἀποκτείνας ὑμᾶς δόξῃ λατρείαν προσφέρειν τῷ Θεῷ.
killing you will think [3]a [4]service [1]to [2]offer - to God.
kills that he is offering

3 Καὶ ταῦτα ποιήσουσιν[a] ὅτι οὐκ ἔγνωσαν τὸν
And these *things* they will do because [3]not [1]they [2]did know the

Πατέρα οὐδὲ ἐμέ. 4 Ἀλλὰ ταῦτα λελάληκα ὑμῖν, ἵνα
Father nor Me. But these *things* I have spoken to you so that

ὅταν ἔλθῃ ἡ ὥρα,[b] μνημονεύητε αὐτῶν ὅτι ἐγὼ εἶπον
whenever [3]comes [1]the [2]hour, you may remember them that I told
time,

ὑμῖν. Ταῦτα δὲ ὑμῖν ἐξ ἀρχῆς οὐκ εἶπον
you. [2]these [3]*things* [1]But [8]to [9]you [10]from [11]*the* [12]beginning [6]not [4]I [5]did [7]say

ὅτι μεθ' ὑμῶν ἤμην.
because [3]with [4]you [1]I [2]was.

The Work of the Holy Spirit

5 "Νῦν δὲ ὑπάγω πρὸς τὸν πέμψαντά με, καὶ οὐδεὶς
"now ˜ But I am going to the *One* having sent Me, and no one
Him who

ἐξ ὑμῶν ἐρωτᾷ με, 'Ποῦ ὑπάγεις?' 6 Ἀλλ' ὅτι
of you asks Me, 'Where are You going?' But because

ταῦτα λελάληκα ὑμῖν, ἡ λύπη πεπλήρωκεν ὑμῶν τὴν
[4]these [5]*things* [1]I [2]have [3]spoken to you, - sorrow has filled your -

καρδίαν. 7 Ἀλλ' ἐγὼ τὴν ἀλήθειαν λέγω ὑμῖν. Συμφέρει ὑμῖν
heart. But I [2]the [3]truth [1]speak to you. It benefits you

ἵνα ἐγὼ ἀπέλθω· ἐὰν γὰρ ἐγὼ μὴ ἀπέλθω, ὁ Παράκλητος
that I go away; if ˜ for I not ˜ do go away, the Advocate
Helper

οὐκ ἐλεύσεται πρὸς ὑμᾶς· ἐὰν δὲ πορευθῶ, πέμψω αὐτὸν
not ˜ will come to you; if ˜ but I go, I will send Him

πρὸς ὑμᾶς. 8 Καὶ ἐλθὼν ἐκεῖνος ἐλέγξει τὸν κόσμον
to you. And having come that *One* will convict the world
when He comes, He

περὶ ἁμαρτίας καὶ περὶ δικαιοσύνης καὶ περὶ κρίσεως· 9 περὶ
about sin and about righteousness and about judgment; about

ἁμαρτίας μέν, ὅτι οὐ πιστεύουσιν εἰς ἐμέ· 10 περὶ
sin, - because [3]not [1]they [2]do believe in Me; about

δικαιοσύνης δέ, ὅτι πρὸς τὸν Πατέρα μου[c] ὑπάγω καὶ
righteousness, - because to - Father ˜ My I am going and

οὐκέτι θεωρεῖτέ με· 11 περὶ δὲ κρίσεως, ὅτι ὁ ἄρχων
[4]no [5]longer [1]you [2]see [3]Me; about - judgment, because the ruler

τοῦ κόσμου τούτου κέκριται. 12 Ἔτι πολλὰ ἔχω
- of world ˜ this has been judged. [2]still [4]many [5]*things* [1]I [3]have

λέγειν ὑμῖν, ἀλλ' οὐ δύνασθε βαστάζειν ἄρτι.
to say to you, but [3]not [1]you [2]are able to bear *them* now.

---

[a](16:3) TR adds υμιν, *to you*. [b](16:4) NU adds αυτων, *their (hour)*. [c](16:10) NU omits μου, *My*.

13 Ὅταν δὲ ἔλθῃ ἐκεῖνος, τὸ Πνεῦμα τῆς ἀληθείας,
whenever ~ But [3]comes [1]that [2]*One*, the Spirit - of truth,
He,

ὁδηγήσει ὑμᾶς εἰς πᾶσαν τὴν ἀλήθειαν· οὐ γὰρ
He will guide you into all - truth; [4]not [1]for

λαλήσει ἀφ' ἑαυτοῦ, ἀλλ' ὅσα ἂν ἀκούσῃ
[2]He [3]will [5]speak from Himself, but as many *things* as - He hears
on His own, whatever

λαλήσει· καὶ τὰ ἐρχόμενα ἀναγγελεῖ ὑμῖν.
He will speak; and [6]the [8]*things* [7]coming [1]He [2]will [3]announce [4]to [5]you.

14 Ἐκεῖνος ἐμὲ δοξάσει, ὅτι ἐκ τοῦ ἐμοῦ λήψεται
That *One* [3]Me [1]will [2]glorify, because from the *thing* of Me He will take
He what is Mine

καὶ ἀναγγελεῖ ὑμῖν. 15 Πάντα ὅσα ἔχει ὁ Πατὴρ
and He will announce *it* to you. All *things* as many as [3]has [1]the [2]Father
which

ἐμά ἐστι. Διὰ τοῦτο εἶπον ὅτι ἐκ τοῦ ἐμοῦ
[5]Mine [4]are. On account of this I said that from the *thing* of Me
Therefore what is Mine

λαμβάνει[d] καὶ ἀναγγελεῖ ὑμῖν.
He takes and will announce *it* to you.

Sorrow Will Turn To Joy

16 "Μικρὸν καὶ οὐ[e] θεωρεῖτέ με, καὶ πάλιν μικρὸν
"A little *while* and [3]not [1]you [2]do see Me, and again a little *while*

καὶ ὄψεσθέ με, ὅτι ὑπάγω πρὸς τὸν Πατέρα."
and you will see Me, because I am going to the Father."

17 Εἶπον οὖν ἐκ τῶν μαθητῶν αὐτοῦ πρὸς ἀλλήλους,
[6]said [1]Then [2]*some* [3]of - [5]disciples [4]His to one another,

"Τί ἐστι τοῦτο ὃ λέγει ἡμῖν, 'Μικρὸν καὶ οὐ
"What is this which He says to us, 'A little *while* and [3]not

θεωρεῖτέ με, καὶ πάλιν μικρὸν καὶ ὄψεσθέ με,' καὶ ὅτι
[1]you [2]do see Me, and again a little *while* and you will see Me,' and -

'Ἐγὼ ὑπάγω πρὸς τὸν Πατέρα'?" 18 Ἔλεγον οὖν, "Τοῦτο
'I am going to the Father'?" [2]they [3]said [1]Therefore, "[6]this

τί ἐστιν ὃ λέγει, 'Τὸ μικρόν'? Οὐκ οἴδαμεν τί
[4]What [5]is which He says, 'The little *while*'? [3]not [1]We [2]do know what
understand

λαλεῖ."
He is saying."

19 Ἔγνω οὖν ὁ Ἰησοῦς ὅτι ἤθελον αὐτὸν
[3]knew [1]Therefore - [2]Jesus that they were desiring [3]Him

ἐρωτᾶν, καὶ εἶπεν αὐτοῖς, "Περὶ τούτου ζητεῖτε μετ'
[1]to [2]ask, and He said to them, "About this are you inquiring with

ἀλλήλων ὅτι εἶπον, 'Μικρὸν καὶ οὐ θεωρεῖτέ με, καὶ
one another that I said, 'A little *while* and [3]not [1]you [2]do see Me, and

πάλιν μικρὸν καὶ ὄψεσθέ με'? 20 Ἀμὴν ἀμὴν λέγω
again a little *while* and you will see Me'? Amen amen I say
Most assuredly

ὑμῖν ὅτι κλαύσετε καὶ θρηνήσετε ὑμεῖς, ὁ δὲ κόσμος
to you that you will weep and [2]will [3]lament [1]you, the ~ but world

χαρήσεται· ὑμεῖς δὲ λυπηθήσεσθε, ἀλλ' ἡ λύπη ὑμῶν εἰς
will rejoice; you ~ and will be grieved, but - sorrow ~ your [3]into

χαρὰν γενήσεται. 21 Ἡ γυνὴ ὅταν τίκτῃ λύπην
[4]joy [1]will [2]become. The woman whenever she gives birth sorrow ~
turn. A

ἔχει, ὅτι ἦλθεν ἡ ὥρα αὐτῆς· ὅταν δὲ γεννήσῃ τὸ
has, because [3]came - [2]hour [1]her; whenever ~ but [3]is [4]born [1]the
time has come

13 "However, when He, the Spirit of truth, has come, He will guide you into all truth; for He will not speak on His own *authority,* but whatever He hears He will speak; and He will tell you things to come.
14 "He will glorify Me, for He will take of what is Mine and declare *it* to you.
15 "All things that the Father has are Mine. Therefore I said that He will take of Mine and declare *it* to you.
16 "A little while, and you will not see Me; and again a little while, and you will see Me, because I go to the Father."
17 Then *some* of His disciples said among themselves, "What is this that He says to us, 'A little while, and you will not see Me; and again a little while, and you will see Me'; and, 'because I go to the Father'?"
18 They said therefore, "What is this that He says, 'A little while'? We do not know what He is saying."
19 Now Jesus knew that they desired to ask Him, and He said to them, "Are you inquiring among yourselves about what I said, 'A little while, and you will not see Me; and again a little while, and you will see Me'?
20 "Most assuredly, I say to you that you will weep and lament, but the world will rejoice; and you will be sorrowful, but your sorrow will be turned into joy.
21 "A woman, when she is in labor, has sorrow because her hour has come; but as soon as

[d](16:15) TR reads λήψεται, *He will take.*
[e](16:16) NU reads οὐκέτι, *no longer.*

she has given birth to the child,
she no longer remembers the
anguish, for joy that a human
being has been born into the
world.
22 "Therefore you now have
sorrow; but I will see you again
and your heart will rejoice, and
your joy no one will take from
you.
23 "And in that day you will
ask Me nothing. Most as-
suredly, I say to you, whatever
you ask the Father in My name
He will give you.
24 "Until now you have asked
nothing in My name. Ask, and
you will receive, that your joy
may be full.
25 "These things I have spoken to you in figurative language; but the time is coming
when I will no longer speak to
you in figurative language, but I
will tell you plainly about the
Father.
26 "In that day you will ask in
My name, and I do not say to
you that I shall pray the Father
for you;
27 "for the Father Himself
loves you, because you have
loved Me, and have believed
that I came forth from God.
28 "I came forth from the Father and have come into the
world. Again, I leave the world
and go to the Father."
29 His disciples said to Him,
"See, now You are speaking
plainly, and using no figure of
speech!
30 "Now we are sure that You
know all things, and have no

παιδίον, οὐκέτι μνημονεύει τῆς θλίψεως, διὰ τὴν
[2]child, [6]no [7]longer [5]she [8]remembers the anguish, on account of the

χαρὰν ὅτι ἐγεννήθη ἄνθρωπος εἰς τὸν κόσμον. **22** Καὶ
joy that [3]was [4]born [1]a [2]man into the world. [3]also
a human being has been born

ὑμεῖς οὖν λύπην μὲν νῦν ἔχετε· πάλιν δὲ ὄψομαι ὑμᾶς,
[2]you [1]Therefore [6]sorrow - [4]now [5]have; again ~ but I will see you

καὶ χαρήσεται ὑμῶν ἡ καρδία, καὶ τὴν χαρὰν ὑμῶν οὐδεὶς
and [3]will [4]rejoice [1]your - [2]heart, and - [5]joy [4]your [1]no [2]one

αἴρει ἀφ' ὑμῶν. **23** Καὶ ἐν ἐκείνῃ τῇ ἡμέρᾳ ἐμὲ οὐκ
[3]takes from you. And in that - day [5]Me [3]not
will take

ἐρωτήσετε οὐδέν. Ἀμὴν ἀμὴν λέγω ὑμῖν ὅτι
[1]you [2]will [3]ask nothing. Amen amen I say to you that
anything. Most assuredly

ὅσα ἂν αἰτήσητε τὸν Πατέρα ἐν τῷ ὀνοματί μου
as many *things* as - you ask the Father in - name ~ My
whatever

δώσει ὑμῖν. **24** Ἕως ἄρτι οὐκ ᾐτήσατε οὐδὲν ἐν τῷ
He will give to you. Until now [3]not [1]you [2]did ask nothing in -
you have not asked anything

ὀνόματί μου. Αἰτεῖτε καὶ λήψεσθε, ἵνα ἡ χαρὰ ὑμῶν
name ~ My. Ask and you will receive, so that - joy ~ your

ᾖ πεπληρωμένη.
may be filled.
full.

Jesus Christ Has Overcome the World

25 "Ταῦτα ἐν παροιμίαις λελάληκα ὑμῖν, ἀλλ'
"These *things* [6]in [7]figures [8]of [9]speech [1]I [2]have [3]spoken [4]to [5]you, but

ἔρχεται ὥρα ὅτε οὐκέτι ἐν παροιμίαις λαλήσω
[3]is [4]coming [1]an [2]hour when [3]no [4]longer [8]in [9]figures [10]of [11]speech [1]I [2]will [5]speak
a time

ὑμῖν, ἀλλὰ παρρησίᾳ περὶ τοῦ Πατρὸς ἀναγγελῶ ὑμῖν.
[6]to [7]you, but [5]in [6]openness [7]about [8]the [9]Father [1]I [2]will [3]tell [4]you.
plainly

26 Ἐν ἐκείνῃ τῇ ἡμέρᾳ ἐν τῷ ὀνόματί μου αἰτήσεσθε, καὶ οὐ
At that - day in - name ~ My you will ask, and [3]not
time

λέγω ὑμῖν ὅτι ἐγὼ ἐρωτήσω τὸν Πατέρα περὶ ὑμῶν.
[1]I [2]do say to you that I will ask the Father for you.

27 Αὐτὸς γὰρ ὁ Πατὴρ φιλεῖ ὑμᾶς, ὅτι ὑμεῖς ἐμὲ
[4]Himself [1]For [2]the [3]Father loves you, because you [3]Me

πεφιλήκατε, καὶ πεπιστεύκατε ὅτι ἐγὼ παρὰ τοῦ Θεοῦ
[1]have [2]loved, and you have believed that I [3]from - [4]God

ἐξῆλθον. **28** Ἐξῆλθον παρὰ τοῦ Πατρὸς καὶ ἐλήλυθα εἰς
[1]came [2]forth. I came forth from the Father and I have come into

τὸν κόσμον. Πάλιν ἀφίημι τὸν κόσμον καὶ πορεύομαι πρὸς
the world. Again I am leaving the world and I am going to

τὸν Πατέρα."
the Father."

29 Λέγουσιν αὐτῷ οἱ μαθηταὶ αὐτοῦ, "Ἴδε, νῦν παρρησίᾳ
[3]say [4]to [5]Him - [2]disciples [1]His, "See, now [4]in [5]openness
said plainly

λαλεῖς καὶ παροιμίαν οὐδεμίαν λέγεις. **30** Νῦν
[1]You [2]are [3]speaking and [5]figure [6]of [7]speech [3]not [4]one [1]You [2]speak. Now
You are using no figure of speech.

οἴδαμεν ὅτι οἶδας πάντα καὶ οὐ χρείαν ἔχεις ἵνα
we know that You know all *things* and [3]not [5]need [1]You [2]do [4]have that

τίς σε ἐρωτᾷ. Ἐν τούτῳ πιστεύομεν ὅτι ἀπὸ Θεοῦ
anyone [3]You [1]should [2]question. By this we believe that [4]from [5]God
ἐξῆλθες."
[1]You [2]came [3]forth."

31 Ἀπεκρίθη αὐτοῖς ὁ Ἰησοῦς, "Ἄρτι πιστεύετε?
[2]answered [3]them - [1]Jesus, "Now do you believe?

32 Ἰδού, ἔρχεται ὥρα καὶ νῦν[f] ἐλήλυθεν, ἵνα
See, [3]is [4]coming [1]an [2]hour and now has come, that
a time

σκορπισθῆτε ἕκαστος εἰς τὰ ἴδια, καὶ ἐμὲ μόνον
you will be scattered each to - his own *things,* and [4]Me [5]alone

ἀφῆτε. Καὶ οὐκ εἰμὶ μόνος, ὅτι ὁ Πατὴρ μετ' ἐμοῦ
[1]you [2]will [3]leave. Yet [3]not [1]I [2]am alone, because the Father [2]with [3]Me

ἐστι. 33 Ταῦτα λελάληκα ὑμῖν ἵνα ἐν ἐμοὶ εἰρήνην
[1]is. These *things* I have spoken to you so that in Me [4]peace

ἔχητε. Ἐν τῷ κόσμῳ θλῖψιν* ἔχετε·[g] ἀλλὰ
[1]you [2]may [3]have. In the world [3]tribulation [1]you [2]have; but

θαρσεῖτε, ἐγὼ νενίκηκα τὸν κόσμον."
have courage, I have overcome the world."

Jesus Prays for Himself

17 1 Ταῦτα ἐλάλησεν ὁ Ἰησοῦς καὶ ἐπῆρε τοὺς
[3]these [4]*things* [2]spoke ~ - [1]Jesus and raised -

ὀφθαλμοὺς αὐτοῦ εἰς τὸν οὐρανὸν καὶ εἶπε, "Πάτερ, ἐλήλυθεν
eyes ~ His to - heaven and said, "Father, [3]has [4]come

ἡ ὥρα. Δόξασόν σου τὸν Υἱόν, ἵνα καὶ ὁ Υἱός σου
[1]the [2]hour. Glorify Your - Son, so that [3]also - [2]Son [1]Your
time.

δοξάσῃ σέ, 2 καθὼς ἔδωκας αὐτῷ ἐξουσίαν πάσης σαρκός,
may glorify You, just as You gave to Him authority *over* all flesh,

ἵνα πᾶν ὃ δέδωκας αὐτῷ, δώσει[a] αὐτοῖς ζωὴν
so that *to* all that You have given to Him, He will give to them life ~

αἰώνιον. 3 Αὕτη δέ ἐστιν ἡ αἰώνιος ζωή, ἵνα γινώσκωσί σε
eternal. this ~ And is - eternal life, that they may know You

τὸν μόνον ἀληθινὸν Θεόν, καὶ ὃν ἀπέστειλας Ἰησοῦν
the only true God, and *the One* whom You sent Jesus

Χριστόν. 4 Ἐγώ σε ἐδόξασα ἐπὶ τῆς γῆς. Τὸ ἔργον
Christ. I You ~ glorified on the earth. [3]the [4]work

ἐτελείωσα ὃ δέδωκάς μοι ἵνα ποιήσω. 5 Καὶ νῦν
[1]I [2]finished which You have given to Me that I should do. And now

δόξασόν με σύ, Πάτερ, παρὰ σεαυτῷ τῇ δόξῃ ᾗ
[2]glorify [3]Me [1]You, Father, *along* with Yourself with the glory which

εἶχον πρὸ τοῦ τὸν κόσμον εἶναι παρὰ σοί.
I had [3]before - [4]the [5]world [6]to [7]be [1]with [2]You.
existed

Jesus Prays for His Disciples

6 "Ἐφανέρωσά σου τὸ ὄνομα τοῖς ἀνθρώποις οὓς
"I manifested Your - name to the men whom

δέδωκάς μοι ἐκ τοῦ κόσμου. Σοὶ ἦσαν, καὶ
You have given to Me out of the world. [3]to [4]You [1]They [2]were and
Yours

ἐμοὶ αὐτοὺς δέδωκας, καὶ τὸν λόγον σου
[5]to [6]Me [4]them [1]You [2]have [3]given, and - [5]word [4]Your

τετηρήκασι. 7 Νῦν ἔγνωκαν ὅτι πάντα ὅσα
[1]they [2]have [3]kept. Now they have known that all *things* as many as

need that anyone should question You. By this we believe that You came forth from God."
31 Jesus answered them, "Do you now believe?
32 "Indeed the hour is coming, yes, has now come, that you will be scattered, each to his own, and will leave Me alone. And yet I am not alone, because the Father is with Me.
33 "These things I have spoken to you, that in Me you may have peace. In the world you will have tribulation; but be of good cheer, I have overcome the world."
17 Jesus spoke these words, lifted up His eyes to heaven, and said: "Father, the hour has come. Glorify Your Son, that Your Son also may glorify You,
2 "as You have given Him authority over all flesh, that He should give eternal life to as many as You have given Him.
3 "And this is eternal life, that they may know You, the only true God, and Jesus Christ whom You have sent.
4 "I have glorified You on the earth. I have finished the work which You have given Me to do.
5 "And now, O Father, glorify Me together with Yourself, with the glory which I had with You before the world was.
6 "I have manifested Your name to the men whom You have given Me out of the world. They were Yours, You gave them to Me, and they have kept Your word.
7 "Now they have known

---

[f](16:32) NU omits *νυν, now.* [g](16:33) TR reads *εξετε, will have.* [a](17:2) NU, TR read *δωση, He should give.*

*(16:33) *θλίψις (thlipsis).* Noun literally meaning *pressure,* but in the NT used only figuratively to identify *oppression, affliction, tribulation, trouble.* This figurative usage may focus either on outward circumstances, as might be caused by persecution (as here; 2 Thess. 1:6), or on the inner distress of spirit that results from such oppression (as 2 Cor. 2:4). In Rev. 7:14, "the great tribulation" (understood by many to reflect Matt. 24:21, 29) is a time of severe affliction and distressing trouble. Cf. the cognate verb *θλίβω, press upon, crowd* (as Mark 3:9),

that all things which You have given Me are from You.
8 "For I have given to them the words which You have given Me; and they have received *them,* and have known surely that I came forth from You; and they have believed that You sent Me.
9 "I pray for them. I do not pray for the world but for those whom You have given Me, for they are Yours.
10 "And all Mine are Yours, and Yours are Mine, and I am glorified in them.
11 "Now I am no longer in the world, but these are in the world, and I come to You. Holy Father, keep through Your name those whom You have given Me, that they may be one as We *are.*
12 "While I was with them in the world, I kept them in Your name. Those whom You gave Me I have kept; and none of them is lost except the son of perdition, that the Scripture might be fulfilled.
13 "But now I come to You, and these things I speak in the world, that they may have My joy fulfilled in themselves.
14 "I have given them Your word; and the world has hated them because they are not of the world, just as I am not of the world.
15 "I do not pray that You should take them out of the world, but that You should keep them from the evil one.
16 "They are not of the world, just as I am not of the world.
17 "Sanctify them by Your truth. Your word is truth.
18 "As You sent Me into the world, I also have sent them into the world.

δέδωκάς μοι παρὰ σοῦ ἐστιν. 8 Ὅτι τὰ ῥήματα ἃ
You have given to Me [2]from [3]You [1]is. Because the sayings which
are.

δέδωκάς μοι δέδωκα αὐτοῖς· καὶ αὐτοὶ ἔλαβον καὶ
You have given to Me I have given to them; and they received *them* and

ἔγνωσαν ἀληθῶς ὅτι παρὰ σοῦ ἐξῆλθον, καὶ ἐπίστευσαν
they knew truly that [4]from [5]You [1]I [2]came [3]forth, and they believed

ὅτι σύ με ἀπέστειλας. 9 Ἐγὼ περὶ αὐτῶν ἐρωτῶ. Οὐ
that You Me ˜ sent. I [4]concerning [5]them [2]am [3]asking. Not
praying.

περὶ τοῦ κόσμου ἐρωτῶ ἀλλὰ περὶ ὧν
concerning the world am I asking but concerning *those* whom
praying

δέδωκάς μοι, ὅτι σοί εἰσι. 10 Καὶ τὰ
You have given to Me, because [3]to [4]You [1]they [2]are. And [2]the [3]*things*
Yours all

ἐμὰ πάντα σά ἐστι, καὶ τὰ σὰ
[4]*which* [5]*are* [6]Mine [1]all [8]Yours [7]are, and the *things* *which are* Yours
Mine Yours

ἐμά, καὶ δεδόξασμαι ἐν αὐτοῖς. 11 Καὶ οὐκέτι εἰμὶ
are Mine, and I have been glorified in them. And [3]no [4]longer [1]I [2]am

ἐν τῷ κόσμῳ, καὶ οὗτοι ἐν τῷ κόσμῳ εἰσί, καὶ ἐγὼ πρός σε
in the world, yet these [2]in [3]the [4]world [1]are, and I [3]to [4]You

ἔρχομαι. Πάτερ ἅγιε, τήρησον αὐτοὺς ἐν τῷ ὀνόματί σου,
[1]am [2]coming. Father ˜ Holy, keep them in - name ˜ Your,

ᾧ[b] δέδωκάς μοι, ἵνα ὦσιν ἓν καθὼς ἡμεῖς.
which You have given to Me, that they may be one just as We *are.*

12 Ὅτε ἤμην μετ' αὐτῶν ἐν τῷ κόσμῳ,[c] ἐγὼ ἐτήρουν
When I was with them in the world, I was keeping
kept

αὐτοὺς ἐν τῷ ὀνόματί σου. Οὓς δέδωκάς μοι
them in - name ˜ Your. *Those* whom You have given to Me

ἐφύλαξα,[d] καὶ οὐδεὶς ἐξ αὐτῶν ἀπώλετο εἰ μὴ ὁ υἱὸς τῆς
I guarded, and no one of them was lost if not the son of
not one except

ἀπωλείας, ἵνα ἡ Γραφὴ πληρωθῇ. 13 Νῦν δὲ πρός
destruction, so that the Scripture might be fulfilled. now ˜ But to
perdition,

σε ἔρχομαι, καὶ ταῦτα λαλῶ ἐν τῷ κόσμῳ ἵνα
You I am coming, and these *things* I speak in the world so that

ἔχωσι τὴν χαρὰν τὴν ἐμὴν πεπληρωμένην ἐν αὐτοῖς.
they may have - joy ˜ - My having been fulfilled in them.
made complete

14 Ἐγὼ δέδωκα αὐτοῖς τὸν λόγον σου, καὶ ὁ κόσμος
I have given to them - word ˜ Your, and the world

ἐμίσησεν αὐτοὺς ὅτι οὐκ εἰσὶν ἐκ τοῦ κόσμου καθὼς ἐγὼ
hated them because [3]not [1]they [2]are of the world just as I

οὐκ εἰμὶ ἐκ τοῦ κόσμου. 15 Οὐκ ἐρωτῶ ἵνα ἄρῃς
not ˜ am of the world. [3]not [1]I [2]do ask that You should take

αὐτοὺς ἐκ τοῦ κόσμου, ἀλλ' ἵνα τηρήσῃς αὐτοὺς ἐκ τοῦ
them out of the world, but that You should keep them from the

πονηροῦ. 16 Ἐκ τοῦ κόσμου οὐκ εἰσὶ καθὼς ἐγὼ ἐκ τοῦ
evil *one.* [4]of [5]the [6]world [3]not [1]They [2]are just as I [3]of [4]the

κόσμου οὐκ εἰμί. 17 Ἁγίασον αὐτοὺς ἐν τῇ ἀληθείᾳ σου.[e] Ὁ
[5]world [2]not [1]am. Sanctify them by - truth ˜ Your. -

λόγος ὁ σὸς ἀλήθειά ἐστι. 18 Καθὼς ἐμὲ ἀπέστειλας εἰς τὸν
word ˜ - Your truth ˜ is. Just as [3]Me [1]You [2]sent into the

κόσμον, κἀγὼ ἀπέστειλα αὐτοὺς εἰς τὸν κόσμον. 19 Καὶ
world, I also sent them into the world. And

---

[b](17:11) TR reads ους, *(those) whom.*
[c](17:12) NU omits εν τω κοσμω, *in the world.*
[d](17:12) For Ους δεδωκας μοι, *(Those) whom You have given to Me,* NU reads ω δεδωκας μοι, και, *(name) which You have given to Me; and (I guarded).*
[e](17:17) NU omits σου, *Your;* thus *the truth.*

oppress, afflict (as 2 Thess. 1:6, 7).

ὑπὲρ αὐτῶν ἐγὼ ἁγιάζω ἐμαυτόν, ἵνα καὶ αὐτοὶ ὦσιν
in behalf of them I sanctify Myself, so that also ˜ they may be

ἡγιασμένοι ἐν ἀληθείᾳ.
sanctified by truth.

Jesus Prays for All Believers

20 "Οὐ περὶ τούτων δὲ ἐρωτῶ μόνον, ἀλλὰ καὶ
"[3]not [5]concerning [6]these - [1]I [2]am [4]asking alone, but also
praying

περὶ τῶν πιστευόντων[f] διὰ τοῦ λόγου αὐτῶν εἰς
concerning the *ones* believing [3]through - [5]word [4]their [1]in
who believe

ἐμέ· 21 ἵνα πάντες ἓν ὦσι, καθὼς σύ, Πάτερ,
[2]Me; so that [2]all [5]one [1]they [3]may [4]be, just as You, Father,

ἐν ἐμοὶ κἀγὼ ἐν σοί· ἵνα καὶ αὐτοὶ ἐν ἡμῖν ἓν[g] ὦσιν
are in Me and I in You; so that also ˜ they [4]in [5]Us [3]one [1]may [2]be

ἵνα ὁ κόσμος πιστεύσῃ ὅτι σύ με ἀπέστειλας. 22 Καὶ
so that the world may believe that You Me ˜ sent. And

ἐγὼ τὴν δόξαν ἣν δέδωκάς μοι δέδωκα αὐτοῖς
I [3]the [4]glory [5]which [6]You [7]have [8]given [9]to [10]Me [1]have [2]given to them

ἵνα ὦσιν ἓν καθὼς ἡμεῖς ἕν ἐσμεν· 23 ἐγὼ ἐν
so that they may be one just as We one ˜ are; I in

αὐτοῖς, καὶ σὺ ἐν ἐμοί, ἵνα ὦσι τετελειωμένοι εἰς
them, and You in Me, so that they may be perfected in

ἕν, καὶ ἵνα γινώσκῃ ὁ κόσμος ὅτι σύ με ἀπέστειλας
one, and so that [3]may [4]know [1]the [2]world that You Me ˜ sent
unity,

καὶ ἠγάπησας αὐτοὺς καθὼς ἐμὲ ἠγάπησας. 24 Πάτερ,
and You loved them just as [3]Me [1]You [2]loved. Father,

οὓς δέδωκάς μοι, θέλω ἵνα ὅπου εἰμὶ ἐγὼ κἀκεῖνοι
those whom You have given to Me, I desire that where am ˜ I those also
they

ὦσι μετ' ἐμοῦ ἵνα θεωρῶσι τὴν δόξαν τὴν ἐμὴν ἣν
may be with Me so that they may see - glory ˜ - My which

ἔδωκάς μοι, ὅτι ἠγάπησάς με πρὸ καταβολῆς
You gave to Me, because You loved Me before *the* foundation

κόσμου. 25 Πάτερ δίκαιε, καὶ ὁ κόσμος σε οὐκ
of *the* world. Father ˜ Righteous indeed the world [4]You [2]not

ἔγνω, ἐγὼ δέ σε ἔγνων, καὶ οὗτοι ἔγνωσαν ὅτι σύ με
[1]did [3]know, [6]I [5]yet [8]You [7]knew, and these knew that You Me ˜

ἀπέστειλας. 26 Καὶ ἐγνώρισα αὐτοῖς τὸ ὄνομά σου καὶ
sent. And I made known to them - name ˜ Your and

γνωρίσω, ἵνα ἡ ἀγάπη ἣν ἠγάπησάς με ἐν
I will make *it* known, so that the love *with* which You loved Me [3]in

αὐτοῖς ᾖ κἀγὼ ἐν αὐτοῖς."
[4]them [1]may [2]be and I in them."

Jesus Betrayed and Arrested in Gethsemane
(Matt. 26:47–56; Mark 14:43–50; Luke 22:47–53)

18 1 Ταῦτα εἰπὼν ὁ Ἰησοῦς ἐξῆλθε σὺν τοῖς
[3]these [4]*things* [1]Having [2]said - Jesus went out with -
After saying

μαθηταῖς αὐτοῦ πέραν τοῦ χειμάρρου τῶν Κέδρων, ὅπου
disciples ˜ His across the Wadi - Kidron, where
winter stream

ἦν κῆπος εἰς ὃν εἰσῆλθεν αὐτὸς καὶ οἱ μαθηταὶ αὐτοῦ.
there was a garden into which [5]entered [1]He [2]and - [4]disciples [3]His.

19 "And for their sakes I sanctify Myself, that they also may be sanctified by the truth.
20 "I do not pray for these alone, but also for those who will believe in Me through their word;
21 "that they all may be one, as You, Father, *are* in Me, and I in You; that they also may be one in Us, that the world may believe that You sent Me.
22 "And the glory which You gave Me I have given them, that they may be one just as We are one:
23 "I in them, and You in Me; that they may be made perfect in one, and that the world may know that You have sent Me, and have loved them as You have loved Me.
24 "Father, I desire that they also whom You gave Me may be with Me where I am, that they may behold My glory which You have given Me; for You loved Me before the foundation of the world.
25 "O righteous Father! The world has not known You, but I have known You; and these have known that You sent Me.
26 "And I have declared to them Your name, and will declare *it,* that the love with which You loved Me may be in them, and I in them."

18 When Jesus had spoken these words, He went out with His disciples over the Brook Kidron, where there was a garden, which He and His disciples entered.

---

f(**17:20**) TR reads *πιστευσοντων, who will believe.* g(**17:21**) NU omits *εν, one.*

2 And Judas, who betrayed Him, also knew the place; for Jesus often met there with His disciples.
3 Then Judas, having received a detachment *of troops,* and officers from the chief priests and Pharisees, came there with lanterns, torches, and weapons.
4 Jesus therefore, knowing all things that would come upon Him, went forward and said to them, "Whom are you seeking?"
5 They answered Him, "Jesus of Nazareth." Jesus said to them, "I am *He.*" And Judas, who betrayed Him, also stood with them.
6 Now when He said to them, "I am *He,*" they drew back and fell to the ground.
7 Then He asked them again, "Whom are you seeking?" And they said, "Jesus of Nazareth."
8 Jesus answered, "I have told you that I am *He.* Therefore, if you seek Me, let these go their way,"
9 that the saying might be fulfilled which He spoke, "Of those whom You gave Me I have lost none."
10 Then Simon Peter, having a sword, drew it and struck the high priest's servant, and cut off his right ear. The servant's name was Malchus.
11 So Jesus said to Peter, "Put your sword into the sheath. Shall I not drink the cup which My Father has given Me?"

2 Ἤιδει δὲ καὶ Ἰούδας, ὁ παραδιδοὺς αὐτόν, τὸν
[9]knew [1]Now [8]also [2]Judas, [3]the [4]*one* [5]handing [7]over [6]Him, the
betraying

τόπον· ὅτι πολλάκις συνήχθη καὶ ὁ Ἰησοῦς ἐκεῖ μετὰ τῶν
place; because [2]often [3]gathered [5]also - [1]Jesus [4]there with -

μαθητῶν αὐτοῦ. **3** Ὁ οὖν Ἰούδας, λαβὼν τὴν
disciples ˜ His. - Then Judas, having taken the

σπεῖραν, καὶ ἐκ τῶν ἀρχιερέων καὶ Φαρισαίων
detachment *of soldiers,* and [2]from [3]the [4]chief [5]priests [6]and [7]Pharisees

ὑπηρέτας, ἔρχεται ἐκεῖ μετὰ φανῶν καὶ λαμπάδων καὶ ὅπλων.
[1]attendants, comes there with lanterns and torches and weapons.
came

4 Ἰησοῦς οὖν, εἰδὼς πάντα τὰ ἐρχόμενα ἐπ'
Jesus ˜ Therefore, knowing all the *things* coming upon

αὐτόν, ἐξελθὼν εἶπεν αὐτοῖς, "Τίνα ζητεῖτε?"
Him, going out He said to them, "Whom are you seeking?"
went out and

5 Ἀπεκρίθησαν αὐτῷ, "Ἰησοῦν τὸν Ναζωραῖον."
They answered Him, "Jesus the Nazarene."

Λέγει αὐτοῖς ὁ Ἰησοῦς, "Ἐγώ εἰμι." Εἱστήκει δὲ καὶ
[2]says [3]to [4]them - [1]Jesus, "I am *He.*" [9]stood [1]Now [8]also
said was standing

Ἰούδας ὁ παραδιδοὺς αὐτὸν μετ' αὐτῶν. **6** Ὡς οὖν
[2]Judas [3]the [4]*one* [5]handing [7]over [6]Him with them. when ˜ Therefore
betraying

εἶπεν αὐτοῖς ὅτι "Ἐγώ εἰμι," ἀπῆλθον εἰς τὰ
He said to them - "I am *He,*" they went away into the *things*
they stepped back

ὀπίσω καὶ ἔπεσον χαμαί. **7** Πάλιν οὖν αὐτοὺς
behind and fell to the ground. again ˜ Therefore [3]them

ἐπηρώτησε, "Τίνα ζητεῖτε?"
[1]He [2]asked, "Whom are you seeking?"

Οἱ δὲ εἶπον, "Ἰησοῦν τὸν Ναζωραῖον."
[2]the [3]*ones* [1]And said, "Jesus the Nazarene."
they

8 Ἀπεκρίθη Ἰησοῦς, "Εἶπον ὑμῖν ὅτι ἐγώ εἰμι. Εἰ
answered ˜ Jesus, "I told you that I am *He.* if ˜

οὖν ἐμὲ ζητεῖτε, ἄφετε τούτους ὑπάγειν," **9** ἵνα
Therefore [4]Me [1]you [2]are [3]seeking, allow these *men* to go," so that

πληρωθῇ ὁ λόγος ὃν εἶπεν ὅτι "Οὓς
[6]might [7]be [8]fulfilled [1]the [2]word [3]which [4]He [5]said - "*Those* whom

δέδωκάς μοι οὐκ ἀπώλεσα ἐξ αὐτῶν οὐδένα." **10** Σίμων
You have given Me [3]not [1]I [2]did [4]lose [7]of [8]them [5]no [6]one." Simon ˜
any one."

οὖν Πέτρος ἔχων μάχαιραν εἵλκυσεν αὐτὴν καὶ ἔπαισε τὸν
Then Peter having a sword drew it and struck the

τοῦ ἀρχιερέως δοῦλον καὶ ἀπέκοψεν αὐτοῦ τὸ ὠτίον τὸ
[2]of [3]the [4]high [5]priest [1]slave and cut off his - ear ˜ -
servant

δεξιόν. Ἦν δὲ ὄνομα τῷ δούλῳ Μάλχος. **11** Εἶπεν
right. [7]was [1]And [2]*the* [3]name [4]to [5]the [6]slave Malchus. [3]said
the servant's name

οὖν ὁ Ἰησοῦς τῷ Πέτρῳ, "Βάλε τὴν μάχαιράν σου εἰς
[1]Therefore - [2]Jesus - to Peter, "Put - sword ˜ your into

τὴν θήκην. Τὸ ποτήριον ὃ δέδωκέ μοι ὁ Πατήρ, οὐ
the sheath. The cup which [3]has [4]given [5]Me [1]the [2]Father, [8]not

μὴ πίω αὐτό?"
[9]not [6]shall [7]I [10]drink it?"
surely

Jesus Appears Before the High Priest

12 Ἡ οὖν σπεῖρα καὶ ὁ χιλίαρχος καὶ οἱ
the ˜ Then detachment *of soldiers* and the chiliarch and the
captain

ὑπηρέται τῶν Ἰουδαίων συνέλαβον τὸν Ἰησοῦν καὶ ἔδησαν
attendants of the Jews arrested - Jesus and bound

αὐτόν. **13** Καὶ ἀπήγαγον αὐτὸν πρὸς Ἄνναν πρῶτον, ἦν
Him. And they led away ˜ Him to Annas first, [2]he [3]was

γὰρ πενθερὸς τοῦ Καϊάφα ὃς ἦν ἀρχιερεὺς τοῦ ἐνιαυτοῦ
[1]for *the* father-in-law - of Caiaphas who was high priest - year ˜

ἐκείνου. **14** Ἦν δὲ Καϊάφας ὁ συμβουλεύσας τοῖς
that. [3]was [1]Now [2]Caiaphas the *one* having advised the

Ἰουδαίοις ὅτι συμφέρει ἕνα ἄνθρωπον ἀπολέσθαι ὑπὲρ
Jews that it is expedient *for* one man to perish in behalf
was

τοῦ λαοῦ.
of the people.

Peter Denies His Lord

(Matt. 26:58, 69, 70; Mark 14:54, 66–68; Luke 22:54–57)

15 Ἠκολούθει δὲ τῷ Ἰησοῦ Σίμων Πέτρος, καὶ ὁ[a]
[4]was [5]following [1]Now - [6]Jesus [2]Simon [3]Peter, and so the
as was

ἄλλος μαθητής. Ὁ δὲ μαθητὴς ἐκεῖνος ἦν γνωστὸς τῷ
other disciple. - Now disciple ˜ that was known to the

ἀρχιερεῖ καὶ συνεισῆλθε τῷ Ἰησοῦ εἰς τὴν αὐλὴν τοῦ
high priest and entered with - Jesus into the courtyard of the

ἀρχιερέως. **16** Ὁ δὲ Πέτρος εἱστήκει πρὸς τῇ θύρᾳ ἔξω.
high priest. - Now Peter was standing at the door outside.

Ἐξῆλθεν οὖν ὁ μαθητὴς ὁ ἄλλος ὃς ἦν γνωστὸς
[12]went [13]out [1]Therefore [2]the [4]disciple - [3]other [5]who [6]was [7]known

τῷ ἀρχιερεῖ καὶ εἶπε τῇ θυρωρῷ, καὶ εἰσήγαγε
[8]to [9]the [10]high [11]priest and spoke to the *girl* doorkeeper, and brought in

τὸν Πέτρον.
- Peter.

17 Λέγει οὖν ἡ παιδίσκη ἡ θυρωρὸς τῷ Πέτρῳ,
[7]says [1]Then [2]the [3]servant [4]girl [5]the [6]doorkeeper - to Peter,
said who kept the door

"Μὴ καὶ σὺ ἐκ τῶν μαθητῶν εἶ τοῦ ἀνθρώπου
"[3]not [4]also [1]You [5]*one* [6]of [7]the [8]disciples [2]are - [9]of [11]man

τούτου?"
[10]this, *are you?*"

Λέγει ἐκεῖνος, "Οὐκ εἰμί." **18** Εἱστήκεισαν δὲ οἱ
[3]says [1]That [2]*one*, "[6]not [4]I [5]am." [12]stood [13]*there* [1]Now [2]the
He said, were standing

δοῦλοι καὶ οἱ ὑπηρέται ἀνθρακιὰν πεποιηκότες, ὅτι ψῦχος
[3]slaves [4]and [5]the [6]attendants [9]a [10]coal [11]fire [7]having [8]made, because [3]cold

ἦν, καὶ ἐθερμαίνοντο. Ἦν δὲ[b] μετ' αὐτῶν ὁ
[1]it [2]was, and they were warming themselves. [3]was [1]Now [5]with [6]them -

Πέτρος ἑστὼς καὶ θερμαινόμενος.
[2]Peter [4]standing and warming himself.

Jesus Questioned by the High Priest

19 Ὁ οὖν ἀρχιερεὺς ἠρώτησε τὸν Ἰησοῦν περὶ τῶν
the ˜ Then high priest asked - Jesus about -

μαθητῶν αὐτοῦ καὶ περὶ τῆς διδαχῆς αὐτοῦ.
disciples ˜ His and about - teaching ˜ His.

12 Then the detachment *of troops* and the captain and the officers of the Jews arrested Jesus and bound Him.
13 And they led Him away to Annas first, for he was the father-in-law of Caiaphas who was high priest that year.
14 Now it was Caiaphas who advised the Jews that it was expedient that one man should die for the people.
15 And Simon Peter followed Jesus, and so *did* another disciple. Now that disciple was known to the high priest, and went with Jesus into the courtyard of the high priest.
16 But Peter stood at the door outside. Then the other disciple, who was known to the high priest, went out and spoke to her who kept the door, and brought Peter in.
17 Then the servant girl who kept the door said to Peter, "You are not also *one* of this Man's disciples, are you?" He said, "I am not."
18 Now the servants and officers who had made a fire of coals stood there, for it was cold, and they warmed themselves. And Peter stood with them and warmed himself.
19 The high priest then asked Jesus about His disciples and His doctrine.

---

[a]**(18:15)** NU omits ὁ, *the (other disciple),* thus *another (disciple).*
[b]**(18:18)** NU adds καὶ, *also.*

20 Jesus answered him, "I
spoke openly to the world. I always taught in synagogues and
in the temple, where the Jews
always meet, and in secret I
have said nothing.
21 "Why do you ask Me? Ask
those who have heard Me what
I said to them. Indeed they
know what I said."
22 And when He had said
these things, one of the officers
who stood by struck Jesus with
the palm of his hand, saying,
"Do You answer the high priest
like that?"
23 Jesus answered him, "If I
have spoken evil, bear witness
of the evil; but if well, why do
you strike Me?"
24 Then Annas sent Him
bound to Caiaphas the high
priest.
25 Now Simon Peter stood
and warmed himself. Therefore
they said to him, "You are not
also *one* of His disciples, are
you?" He denied *it* and said, "I
am not!"
26 One of the servants of the
high priest, a relative *of him*
whose ear Peter cut off, said,
"Did I not see you in the garden
with Him?"
27 Peter then denied again;
and immediately a rooster
crowed.

20 Ἀπεκρίθη αὐτῷ ὁ Ἰησοῦς, "Ἐγὼ παρρησίᾳ ἐλάλησα
[2]answered [3]him - [1]Jesus, "I [2]in [3]openness [1]spoke
openly

τῷ κόσμῳ. Ἐγὼ πάντοτε ἐδίδαξα ἐν συναγωγῇ καὶ ἐν τῷ
to the world. I always taught in synagogue and in the
synagogues

ἱερῷ ὅπου πάντοτε[c] οἱ Ἰουδαῖοι συνέρχονται, καὶ ἐν
temple where [3]always [1]the [2]Jews come together, and in

κρυπτῷ ἐλάλησα οὐδέν. **21** Τί με ἐπερωτᾷς? Ἐπερώτησον
secret I spoke nothing. Why [4]Me [1]do [2]you [3]ask? Ask

τοὺς ἀκηκοότας τί ἐλάλησα αὐτοῖς. Ἴδε, οὗτοι οἴδασιν
the *ones* having heard what I spoke to them. Look, these *people* know
who have

ἃ εἶπον ἐγώ."
what said ~ I."

22 Ταῦτα δὲ αὐτοῦ εἰπόντος, εἷς τῶν ὑπηρετῶν
[5]these [6]*things* [1]And [2]Him [3]having [4]said, one of the attendants
when He had said,

παρεστηκὼς ἔδωκε ῥάπισμα τῷ Ἰησοῦ, εἰπών, "Οὕτως
standing alongside gave a slap - to Jesus, saying, "Thus
who stood by slapped "In this way

ἀποκρίνῃ τῷ ἀρχιερεῖ?"
do You answer the high priest?"

23 Ἀπεκρίθη αὐτῷ ὁ Ἰησοῦς, "Εἰ κακῶς ἐλάλησα,
[2]answered [3]him - [1]Jesus, "If [3]badly [1]I [2]spoke,

μαρτύρησον περὶ τοῦ κακοῦ, εἰ δὲ καλῶς, τί με
testify concerning the bad *thing,* if ~ but well, why [4]Me

δέρεις?" **24** Ἀπέστειλεν αὐτὸν ὁ Ἄννας δεδεμένον
[1]do [2]you [3]beat?" [2]sent [3]Him - [1]Annas having been bound
bound

πρὸς Καϊάφαν τὸν ἀρχιερέα.
to Caiaphas the high priest.

Peter Denies His Lord Twice More
(Matt. 26:71–75; Mark 14:69–72; Luke 22:58–62)

25 Ἦν δὲ Σίμων Πέτρος ἑστὼς καὶ θερμαινόμενος.
[4]was [1]Now [2]Simon [3]Peter standing and warming himself.

Εἶπον οὖν αὐτῷ, "Μὴ καὶ σὺ ἐκ τῶν μαθητῶν
[2]they [3]said [1]Therefore to him, "[3]not [4]also [1]You [5]*one* [6]of - [8]disciples

αὐτοῦ εἶ?"
[7]His [2]are, *are you?*"

Ἠρνήσατο οὖν ἐκεῖνος καὶ εἶπεν, "Οὐκ εἰμί."
[4]denied [5]*it* [1]Then [2]that [3]*one* and said, "[3]not [1]I [2]am."
he

26 Λέγει εἷς ἐκ τῶν δούλων τοῦ ἀρχιερέως, συγγενὴς
[19]says [1]One [2]of [3]the [4]slaves [5]of [6]the [7]high [8]priest, [10]a [11]relative
said servants

ὢν οὗ ἀπέκοψε Πέτρος τὸ ὠτίον, "Οὐκ ἐγώ σε
[9]being [12]of [13]whom [17]cut [18]off [16]Peter [14]the [15]ear, "[22]not [21]I [24]you
him whose

εἶδον ἐν τῷ κήπῳ μετ' αὐτοῦ?"
[20]did [23]see in the garden with Him?"

27 Πάλιν οὖν ἠρνήσατο ὁ Πέτρος, καὶ εὐθέως ἀλέκτωρ
[4]again [1]Then [3]denied - [2]Peter, and immediately a rooster

ἐφώνησεν.
sounded.
crowed.

---

[c](18:20) NU reads παντες, *(where) all (the Jews come).*

Jesus Appears Before Pilate

(Matt. 27:1, 2, 11–14; Mark 15:1–5; Luke 23:1–5)

28 Ἄγουσιν οὖν τὸν Ἰησοῦν ἀπὸ τοῦ Καϊάφα εἰς τὸ
[2]they [3]lead [1]Then - Jesus from - Caiaphas into the
led
πραιτώριον·* ἦν δὲ πρωΐ. Καὶ αὐτοὶ οὐκ
Praetorium; [2]it [3]was [1]and early morning. And [2]themselves [4]not
εἰσῆλθον εἰς τὸ πραιτώριον ἵνα μὴ μιανθῶσιν,
[1]they [3]did [5]enter into the Praetorium so that [3]not [1]they [2]might be defiled
lest
ἀλλ' ἵνα φάγωσι τὸ Πάσχα.
but so that they might eat the Passover.
29 Ἐξῆλθεν οὖν ὁ Πιλάτος πρὸς αὐτοὺς καὶ εἶπε, "Τίνα
[3]went [4]out [1]Then - [2]Pilate to them and said, "What
κατηγορίαν φέρετε κατὰ τοῦ ἀνθρώπου τούτου?"
accusation do you bring against - man ˜ this?"
30 Ἀπεκρίθησαν καὶ εἶπον αὐτῷ, "Εἰ μὴ ἦν οὗτος
They answered and said to him, "If [4]not [3]were [1]this [2]*man*
κακοποιός, οὐκ ἄν σοι παρεδώκαμεν αὐτόν."
an evil doer, [3]not - [8]to [9]you [1]we [2]would [4]have [5]handed [7]over [6]Him."
a criminal, delivered
31 Εἶπεν οὖν αὐτοῖς ὁ Πιλᾶτος, "Λάβετε αὐτὸν ὑμεῖς καὶ
[3]said [1]Then [4]to [5]them - [2]Pilate, "[7]take [8]Him [6]You and
κατὰ τὸν νόμον ὑμῶν κρίνατε αὐτόν."
according to - law ˜ your judge Him."
Εἶπον οὖν αὐτῷ οἱ Ἰουδαῖοι, "Ἡμῖν οὐκ ἔξεστιν
[4]said [1]Therefore [5]to [6]him [2]the [3]Jews, "For us [3]not [1]it [2]is lawful
ἀποκτεῖναι οὐδένα," **32** ἵνα ὁ λόγος τοῦ Ἰησοῦ
to kill no one," so that the word - of Jesus
anyone," saying
πληρωθῇ, ὃν εἶπε, σημαίνων ποίῳ θανάτῳ
might be fulfilled, which He said, signifying by what sort of death
ἤμελλεν ἀποθνῄσκειν.
He was about to die.
33 Εἰσῆλθεν οὖν εἰς τὸ πραιτώριον πάλιν ὁ Πιλᾶτος καὶ
[3]entered [1]Then [4]into [5]the [6]Praetorium [7]again - [2]Pilate and
ἐφώνησε τὸν Ἰησοῦν καὶ εἶπεν αὐτῷ, "Σὺ εἶ ὁ Βασιλεὺς
called - Jesus and said to Him, "You ˜ Are the King
τῶν Ἰουδαίων?"
of the Jews?"
34 Ἀπεκρίθη αὐτῷ ὁ Ἰησοῦς, "Ἀφ' ἑαυτοῦ σὺ τοῦτο
[2]answered [3]him - [1]Jesus, "From yourself [2]you [4]this
"For
λέγεις, ἢ ἄλλοι σοι εἶπον περὶ ἐμοῦ?"
[1]do [3]say, or [2]others [4]you [1]did [3]tell about Me?"
35 Ἀπεκρίθη ὁ Πιλᾶτος, "Μήτι ἐγὼ Ἰουδαῖός εἰμι? Τὸ
answered ˜ - Pilate, "[3]not [1]I [4]a [5]Jew [2]am, *am I?* -
ἔθνος τὸ σὸν καὶ οἱ ἀρχιερεῖς παρέδωκάν σε ἐμοί. Τί
nation ˜ - Your and the chief priests handed over ˜ You to me. What
delivered
ἐποίησας?"
did You do?"
have You done?"
36 Ἀπεκρίθη Ἰησοῦς, "Ἡ βασιλεία ἡ ἐμὴ οὐκ ἔστιν ἐκ
answered ˜ Jesus, - "kingdom ˜ - My not ˜ is of
τοῦ κόσμου τούτου. Εἰ ἐκ τοῦ κόσμου τούτου ἦν ἡ βασιλεία ἡ
- world ˜ this. If [4]of - [6]world [5]this [3]was - [2]kingdom -
were

28 Then they led Jesus from Caiaphas to the Praetorium, and it was early morning. But they themselves did not go into the Praetorium, lest they should be defiled, but that they might eat the Passover.
29 Pilate then went out to them and said, "What accusation do you bring against this Man?"
30 They answered and said to him, "If He were not an evildoer, we would not have delivered Him up to you."
31 Then Pilate said to them, "You take Him and judge Him according to your law." Therefore the Jews said to him, "It is not lawful for us to put anyone to death,"
32 that the saying of Jesus might be fulfilled which He spoke, signifying by what death He would die.
33 Then Pilate entered the Praetorium again, called Jesus, and said to Him, "Are You the King of the Jews?"
34 Jesus answered him, "Are you speaking for yourself about this, or did others tell you this concerning Me?"
35 Pilate answered, "Am I a Jew? Your own nation and the chief priests have delivered You to me. What have You done?"
36 Jesus answered, "My kingdom is not of this world. If My kingdom were of this world,

---

***(18:28)** *πραιτώριον (praitōrion).* Greek transliteration of the Latin *Praetorium,* a noun properly referring in NT times to the official residence of a Roman governor. Whether the Praetorium mentioned in the Gospels was the former Palace of Herod in the western section of Jerusalem or the fortress Antonia adjacent to the temple is disputed. The one mentioned in Acts 23:35 was clearly Herod's palace in Caesarea. The only other NT occurrence of *πραιτώριον* (Phil. 1:13) might refer to such a residence or to *the Praetorian, the imperial guard* (the emperor's bodyguard), depending on whether Philippians was written in Rome or in some other location.

My servants would fight, so
that I should not be delivered to
the Jews; but now My kingdom
is not from here."
37 Pilate therefore said to
Him, "Are You a king then?"
Jesus answered, "You say
rightly that I am a king. For this
cause I was born, and for this
cause I have come into the
world, that I should bear witness to the truth. Everyone
who is of the truth hears My
voice."
38 Pilate said to Him, "What is
truth?" And when he had said
this, he went out again to the
Jews, and said to them, "I find
no fault in Him at all.
39 "But you have a custom
that I should release someone
to you at the Passover. Do you
therefore want me to release to
you the King of the Jews?"
40 Then they all cried again,
saying, "Not this Man, but Barabbas!" Now Barabbas was a
robber.
19 So then Pilate took Jesus and scourged *Him.*
2 And the soldiers twisted a
crown of thorns and put *it* on
His head, and they put on Him a
purple robe.
3 Then they said, "Hail, King

ἐμή, οἱ ὑπηρέται ἂν οἱ ἐμοὶ ἠγωνίζοντο, ἵνα μὴ
[1]My, - servants ˜ - - My would fight, so that [3]not

παραδοθῶ τοῖς Ἰουδαίοις· νῦν δὲ ἡ βασιλεία ἡ
[1]I [2]might be handed over to the Jews; now ˜ but - kingdom ˜ -
delivered

ἐμὴ οὐκ ἔστιν ἐντεῦθεν."
My not ˜ is from here."

37 Εἶπεν οὖν αὐτῷ ὁ Πιλᾶτος, "Οὐκοῦν βασιλεὺς εἶ
[3]said [1]Therefore [4]to [5]Him - [2]Pilate, "So then [3]a [4]king [1]are

σύ?"
[2]You?"

Ἀπεκρίθη Ἰησοῦς, "Σὺ λέγεις ὅτι βασιλεύς εἰμι ἐγώ. Ἐγὼ
answered ˜ Jesus, "You say that [3]a [4]king [2]am [1]I. [8]I

εἰς τοῦτο γεγέννημαι, καὶ εἰς τοῦτο ἐλήλυθα εἰς τὸν
[5]for [6]this [7]*reason* have been born, and for this *reason* I have come into the

κόσμον, ἵνα μαρτυρήσω τῇ ἀληθείᾳ. Πᾶς ὁ ὢν ἐκ
world, so that I should testify to the truth. Every - *one* being of
Everyone who is

τῆς ἀληθείας ἀκούει μου τῆς φωνῆς."
the truth hears My - voice."

38 Λέγει αὐτῷ ὁ Πιλᾶτος, "Τί ἐστιν ἀλήθεια?"
[2]says [3]to [4]Him - [1]Pilate, "What is truth?"
said

Barabbas Chosen over Jesus
(Matt. 27:15–21; Mark 15:6–11; Luke 23:13–19)

Καὶ τοῦτο εἰπών, πάλιν ἐξῆλθε πρὸς τοὺς Ἰουδαίους
And [3]this [1]having [2]said, again he went out to the Jews

καὶ λέγει αὐτοῖς, "Ἐγὼ οὐδεμίαν αἰτίαν εὑρίσκω ἐν αὐτῷ.
and says to them, "I [2]no [3]charge [1]find in Him.
said crime

39 Ἔστι δὲ συνήθεια ὑμῖν ἵνα ἕνα ὑμῖν
[2]*there* [3]is [1]But a custom to you that [4]one [5]*person* [6]to [7]you
But you have a custom

ἀπολύσω ἐν τῷ Πάσχα. Βούλεσθε οὖν ὑμῖν
[1]I [2]should [3]release at the Passover. [2]do [3]you [4]wish [1]Therefore [9]to [10]you

ἀπολύσω τὸν Βασιλέα τῶν Ἰουδαίων?"
[5]*that* [6]I [7]should [8]release the King of the Jews?"

40 Ἐκραύγασαν οὖν πάλιν πάντες,[d] λέγοντες, "Μὴ
[2]they [4]cried [5]out [1]Then [6]again [3]all, saying, "Not

τοῦτον, ἀλλὰ τὸν Βαραββᾶν!" Ἦν δὲ ὁ Βαραββᾶς
this *man,* but - Barabbas!" [3]was [1]Now - [2]Barabbas

λῃστής.
a bandit.
an insurrectionist.

Jesus Mocked and Crowned with Thorns
(Matt. 27:27–31; Mark 15:16–20)

19 1 Τότε οὖν ἔλαβεν ὁ Πιλᾶτος τὸν Ἰησοῦν καὶ
then ˜ So took ˜ - Pilate - Jesus and

ἐμαστίγωσε. 2 Καὶ οἱ στρατιῶται πλέξαντες στέφανον ἐξ
flogged *Him.* And the soldiers having plaited a crown out of

ἀκανθῶν ἐπέθηκαν αὐτοῦ τῇ κεφαλῇ, καὶ ἱμάτιον πορφυροῦν
thorns put *it* on His - head, and [3]a [5]robe [4]purple

περιέβαλον αὐτόν. 3 Καὶ[a] ἔλεγον, "Χαῖρε, ὁ
[1]they [2]put [6]around Him. And they were saying, "Rejoice, -
kept saying, "Hail,

[d]**(18:40)** NU omits παντες, *(they) all.* [a]**(19:3)** NU adds ηρχοντο προς αυτον και, *they came up to Him and.*

Βασιλεὺς τῶν Ἰουδαίων!" Καὶ ἐδίδουν αὐτῷ ῥαπίσματα.
King of the Jews!" And they were giving Him slaps.
kept

4 Ἐξῆλθεν οὖν πάλιν ἔξω ὁ Πιλᾶτος καὶ λέγει αὐτοῖς, "Ἴδε,
[3]went [1]Then [5]again [4]out - [2]Pilate and says to them, "Look,
said

ἄγω ὑμῖν αὐτὸν ἔξω ἵνα γνῶτε ὅτι ἐν αὐτῷ
I am bringing [3]to [4]you [1]Him [2]out so that you may know that in Him

οὐδεμίαν αἰτίαν εὑρίσκω."
[3]no [4]charge [1]I [2]find."
crime

Pilate Persuaded to Crucify Jesus
(Matt. 27:22–26; Mark 15:12–15; Luke 23:20–25)

5 Ἐξῆλθεν οὖν ὁ Ἰησοῦς ἔξω, φορῶν τὸν ἀκάνθινον
[3]came [1]Then - [2]Jesus out, wearing the thorny

στέφανον καὶ τὸ πορφυροῦν ἱμάτιον. Καὶ λέγει αὐτοῖς,
crown and the purple robe. And he says to them,
Pilate said

"Ἴδε, ὁ ἄνθρωπος!"
"Behold, the man!"

6 Ὅτε οὖν εἶδον αὐτὸν οἱ ἀρχιερεῖς καὶ οἱ
when ˜ Therefore [7]saw [8]Him [1]the [2]chief [3]priests [4]and [5]the

ὑπηρέται, ἐκραύγασαν λέγοντες, "Σταύρωσον, σταύρωσον
[6]attendants, they cried out saying, "Crucify, crucify

αὐτόν!"
Him!"

Λέγει αὐτοῖς ὁ Πιλᾶτος, "Λάβετε αὐτὸν ὑμεῖς καὶ
[2]says [3]to [4]them - [1]Pilate, "[6]take [7]Him [5]You and
said

σταυρώσατε, ἐγὼ γὰρ οὐχ εὑρίσκω ἐν αὐτῷ αἰτίαν."
crucify *Him,* I ˜ for not ˜ do find in Him *any* charge."
crime."

7 Ἀπεκρίθησαν αὐτῷ οἱ Ἰουδαῖοι, "Ἡμεῖς νόμον ἔχομεν,
[3]answered [4]him [1]the [2]Jews, "We [2]a [3]law [1]have,

καὶ κατὰ τὸν νόμον ἡμῶν[b] ὀφείλει ἀποθανεῖν, ὅτι
and according to - law ˜ our He ought to die, because

ἑαυτὸν Θεοῦ Υἱὸν ἐποίησεν."
[3]Himself [6]of [7]God [4]*the* [5]Son [1]He [2]made."

8 Ὅτε οὖν ἤκουσεν ὁ Πιλᾶτος τοῦτον τὸν λόγον,
when ˜ Therefore heard ˜ - Pilate this - word,
saying,

μᾶλλον ἐφοβήθη, 9 καὶ εἰσῆλθεν εἰς τὸ πραιτώριον πάλιν
[3]more [1]he [2]was afraid, and he entered into the Praetorium again

καὶ λέγει τῷ Ἰησοῦ, "Πόθεν εἶ σύ?" Ὁ δὲ Ἰησοῦς
and says - to Jesus, "From where are You?" - But Jesus
said "Where are You from?"

ἀπόκρισιν οὐκ ἔδωκεν αὐτῷ. 10 Λέγει οὖν αὐτῷ ὁ Πιλᾶτος,
[4]an [5]answer [2]not [1]did [3]give to him. [3]says [1]Then [4]to [5]Him - [2]Pilate,
said

"Ἐμοὶ οὐ λαλεῖς? Οὐκ οἶδας ὅτι ἐξουσίαν
"[10]to [11]me [8]not [6]Are [7]You [9]speaking? [14]not [12]Do [13]You [15]know that [3]authority

ἔχω σταυρῶσαί σε καὶ ἐξουσίαν ἔχω ἀπολῦσαί σε?"
[1]I [2]have to crucify You and [3]authority [1]I [2]have to release You?"

11 Ἀπεκρίθη Ἰησοῦς, "Οὐκ εἶχες ἐξουσίαν
answered ˜ Jesus, "[3]not [1]You [2]were having authority ˜
"You would have no authority

of the Jews!" And they struck Him with their hands.
4 Pilate then went out again, and said to them, "Behold, I am bringing Him out to you, that you may know that I find no fault in Him."
5 Then Jesus came out, wearing the crown of thorns and the purple robe. And *Pilate* said to them, "Behold the Man!"
6 Therefore, when the chief priests and officers saw Him, they cried out, saying, "Crucify *Him,* crucify *Him!*" Pilate said to them, "You take Him and crucify *Him,* for I find no fault in Him."
7 The Jews answered him, "We have a law, and according to our law He ought to die, because He made Himself the Son of God."
8 Therefore, when Pilate heard that saying, he was the more afraid,
9 and went again into the Praetorium, and said to Jesus, "Where are You from?" But Jesus gave him no answer.
10 Then Pilate said to Him, "Are You not speaking to me? Do You not know that I have power to crucify You, and power to release You?"
11 Jesus answered, "You could have no power at all

---

[b](19:7) NU-Text omits ημων, *our,* thus *the law.*

against Me unless it had been
given you from above. Therefore the one who delivered Me
to you has the greater sin."
12 From then on Pilate sought
to release Him, but the Jews
cried out, saying, "If you let
this Man go, you are not Caesar's friend. Whoever makes
himself a king speaks against
Caesar."
13 When Pilate therefore
heard that saying, he brought
Jesus out and sat down in the
judgment seat in a place that is
called *the* Pavement, but in
Hebrew, Gabbatha.
14 Now it was the Preparation
Day of the Passover, and about
the sixth hour. And he said to
the Jews, "Behold your King!"
15 But they cried out, "Away
with *Him,* away with *Him!* Crucify Him!" Pilate said to them,
"Shall I crucify your King?" The
chief priests answered, "We
have no king but Caesar!"
16 Then he delivered Him to
them to be crucified. So they
took Jesus and led *Him* away.
17 And He, bearing His cross,
went out to a place called *the*
Place of a Skull, which is called
in Hebrew, Golgotha,

οὐδεμίαν κατ' ἐμοῦ εἰ μὴ ἦν σοι δεδομένον
no against Me if not it was [2]to [3]you [1]given
at all unless it had been

ἄνωθεν.* Διὰ τοῦτο ὁ παραδιδούς μέ σοι μείζονα
from above. Because of this the *one* handing over ˜ Me to you [2]a [3]greater
who betrayed

ἁμαρτίαν ἔχει." **12** Ἐκ τούτου ἐζήτει ὁ Πιλᾶτος
[4]sin [1]has." From this *point* [2]was [3]seeking - [1]Pilate

ἀπολῦσαι αὐτόν.
to release Him.

Οἱ δὲ Ἰουδαῖοι ἔκραζον λέγοντες, "Ἐὰν τοῦτον
the ˜ But Jews were crying out saying, "If [3]this [4]*man*
kept

ἀπολύσῃς, οὐκ εἶ φίλος τοῦ Καίσαρος. Πᾶς ὁ
[1]you [2]release, [7]not [5]you [6]are a friend - of Caesar. Every - *one*
Everyone who

βασιλέα ἑαυτὸν ποιῶν ἀντιλέγει τῷ Καίσαρι." **13** Ὁ
[3]a [4]king [2]himself [1]making speaks against - Caesar." -
makes

οὖν Πιλᾶτος ἀκούσας τοῦτον τὸν λόγον ἤγαγεν ἔξω
Therefore Pilate having heard this - word led outside ˜
saying

τὸν Ἰησοῦν καὶ ἐκάθισεν ἐπὶ τοῦ βήματος εἰς τόπον
- Jesus and sat down on the judgment seat in a place

λεγόμενον Λιθόστρωτον, Ἑβραϊστὶ δὲ Γαββαθᾶ. **14** Ἦν
being called *the* Pavement, [2]in [3]Hebrew [1]but Gabbatha. [2]it [3]was
called

δὲ Παρασκευὴ τοῦ Πάσχα, ὥρα δὲ ὡσεὶ
[1]Now *the* Preparation *Day* of the Passover, [7]hour [1]and [2]*it* [3]*was* [4]about

ἕκτη. Καὶ λέγει τοῖς Ἰουδαίοις, "Ἴδε, ὁ Βασιλεὺς ὑμῶν!"
[5]*the* [6]sixth. And he says to the Jews, "Behold, - King ˜ your!"
said

15 Οἱ δὲ ἐκραύγασαν, "Ἆρον, ἆρον!
[2]the [3]*ones* [1]But cried out, "Away *with Him,* away *with Him!*
they

Σταύρωσον αὐτόν!"
Crucify Him!"

Λέγει αὐτοῖς ὁ Πιλᾶτος, "Τὸν βασιλέα ὑμῶν
[2]says [3]to [4]them - [1]Pilate, - "[9]King [8]your
said

σταυρώσω?"
[5]Shall [6]I [7]crucify?"

Ἀπεκρίθησαν οἱ ἀρχιερεῖς, "Οὐκ ἔχομεν βασιλέα
[4]answered [1]the [2]chief [3]priests, "[7]not [5]we [6]do [8]have a king

εἰ μὴ Καίσαρα!" **16** Τότε οὖν παρέδωκεν αὐτὸν
if not Caesar!" then ˜ Therefore he handed over ˜ Him
except

αὐτοῖς ἵνα σταυρωθῇ.
to them so that He might be crucified.

Jesus Is Crucified

(Matt. 27:32–44; Mark 15:21–32; Luke 23:26–43)

Παρέλαβον δὲ τὸν Ἰησοῦν καὶ ἤγαγον.[c] **17** Καὶ
[2]they [3]took [4]along [1]And - Jesus and led *Him away.* And

βαστάζων τὸν σταυρὸν αὐτοῦ[d] ἐξῆλθεν εἰς τόπον λεγόμενον
carrying - cross ˜ His He went out to a place being called
called

Κρανίου Τόπον, ὃς λέγεται Ἑβραϊστὶ Γολγοθᾶ, **18** ὅπου
[2]of [3]a [4]Skull [1]Place, which is called in Hebrew Golgotha, where

---

[c](19:16) NU omits *και ηγαγον, and led Him away.*
[d](19:17) NU reads *εαυτω, (carrying the cross) by Himself.*

*(19:11) ἄνωθεν (anōthen). Adverb, formed from ἄνω, *above,* and the suffix -θεν indicating origin. Its basic use is to describe an action as originating *from above,* either literally as "woven *from the top*" (John 19:23) or figuratively as *from heaven* (here in 19:11; cf. 3:31). It may have a temporal nuance in the sense of either *from the beginning* (Luke 1:3) or *for a long time* (Acts 26:5). ἄνωθεν is also a common synonym for πάλιν, *again.* This overlap of the meanings *from above* and *again* plays an important role in Jesus' discussion with Nicodemus in John 3:3–8. Whereas Nicodemus emphasized the meaning *again* ("a second time," v. 4), Jesus emphasized the origins of the new birth as being *from above* or "from the Spirit" (vv. 6, 7).

αὐτὸν ἐσταύρωσαν, καὶ μετ' αὐτοῦ ἄλλους δύο, ἐντεῦθεν καὶ
[3]Him [1]they [2]crucified, and with Him others ˜ two, from here and
one on each

ἐντεῦθεν, μέσον δὲ τὸν Ἰησοῦν. 19 Ἔγραψε δὲ καὶ
from there, [3]in [4]the [5]middle [1]and - [2]Jesus. [4]wrote [1]And [3]also
side,

τίτλον ὁ Πιλᾶτος, καὶ ἔθηκεν ἐπὶ τοῦ σταυροῦ. Ἦν δὲ
[5]a [6]notice - [2]Pilate, and he put *it* on the cross. [2]it [3]was [1]And
title

γεγραμμένον,
written,

ΙΗΣΟΥΣ Ο ΝΑΖΩΡΑΙΟΣ Ο ΒΑΣΙΛΕΥΣ ΤΩΝ
JESUS THE NAZARENE THE KING OF THE

ΙΟΥΔΑΙΩΝ
JEWS

20 Τοῦτον οὖν τὸν τίτλον πολλοὶ ἀνέγνωσαν τῶν
[7]this [1]Therefore - [8]notice [2]many [6]read [3]of [4]the
title

Ἰουδαίων, ὅτι ἐγγὺς ἦν ὁ τόπος τῆς πόλεως ὅπου
[5]Jews, because [4]near [3]was [1]the [2]place of the city where
to

ἐσταυρώθη ὁ Ἰησοῦς· καὶ ἦν γεγραμμένον Ἑβραϊστί,
[2]was [3]crucified - [1]Jesus; and it was written in Hebrew,

Ἑλληνιστί, Ῥωμαϊστί.
in Greek, *and* in Latin.

21 Ἔλεγον οὖν τῷ Πιλάτῳ οἱ ἀρχιερεῖς τῶν
[8]said [1]Therefore - [9]to [10]Pilate [2]the [3]chief [4]priests [5]of [6]the

Ἰουδαίων, "Μὴ γράφε, 'Ὁ Βασιλεὺς τῶν Ἰουδαίων,' ἀλλ' ὅτι
[7]Jews, "not ˜ Do write, 'The King of the Jews,' but -

"Ἐκεῖνος εἶπε, "Βασιλεύς εἰμι τῶν Ἰουδαίων." ' "
'That One said, "[3]*the* [4]King [1]I [2]am of the Jews." ' "
'He

22 Ἀπεκρίθη ὁ Πιλᾶτος, "Ὃ γέγραφα, γέγραφα."
answered ˜ - Pilate, "What I have written, I have written."

23 Οἱ οὖν στρατιῶται, ὅτε ἐσταύρωσαν τὸν Ἰησοῦν,
the ˜ Then soldiers, when they crucified - Jesus,

ἔλαβον τὰ ἱμάτια αὐτοῦ καὶ ἐποίησαν τέσσαρα μέρη,
took - garments ˜ His and made four parts,

ἑκάστῳ στρατιώτῃ μέρος, καὶ τὸν χιτῶνα. Ἦν δὲ ὁ χιτὼν
to each soldier a part, also the tunic. [4]was [1]Now [2]the [3]tunic

ἄραφος, ἐκ τῶν ἄνωθεν ὑφαντὸς δι' ὅλου. **24** Εἶπον
seamless, from the top woven through *the* whole. [2]they [3]said

οὖν πρὸς ἀλλήλους, "Μὴ σχίσωμεν αὐτὸν ἀλλὰ
[1]Therefore to one another, "[3]not [1]Let [2]us [4]tear it but

λάχωμεν περὶ αὐτοῦ, τίνος ἔσται," ἵνα ἡ Γραφὴ
let us cast lots for it, whose it will be," so that the Scripture

πληρωθῇ ἡ λέγουσα,
might be fulfilled the *one* saying,
which says,

«Διεμερίσαντο τὰ ἱμάτιά μου ἑαυτοῖς,
«They divided - garments ˜ My among themselves,
them,

Καὶ ἐπὶ τὸν ἱματισμόν μου ἔβαλον κλῆρον.»[e]
And upon - clothing ˜ My they cast a lot.»

Οἱ μὲν οὖν στρατιῶται ταῦτα ἐποίησαν.
[3]the [1]So [2]then soldiers [2]these [3]*things* [1]did.

18 where they crucified Him, and two others with Him, one on either side, and Jesus in the center.
19 Now Pilate wrote a title and put *it* on the cross. And the writing was:

JESUS OF NAZARETH, THE KING OF THE JEWS.

20 Then many of the Jews read this title, for the place where Jesus was crucified was near the city; and it was written in Hebrew, Greek, *and* Latin.
21 Therefore the chief priests of the Jews said to Pilate, "Do not write, 'The King of the Jews,' but, 'He said, "I am the King of the Jews." ' "
22 Pilate answered, "What I have written, I have written."
23 Then the soldiers, when they had crucified Jesus, took His garments and made four parts, to each soldier a part, and also the tunic. Now the tunic was without seam, woven from the top in one piece.
24 They said therefore among themselves, "Let us not tear it, but cast lots for it, whose it shall be," that the Scripture might be fulfilled which says:

"They divided My
garments among them,
And for My clothing they
cast lots."

Therefore the soldiers did these things.

[e](**19:24**) Ps. 22:18

25 Now there stood by the
cross of Jesus His mother, and
His mother's sister, Mary the
wife of Clopas, and Mary Magdalene.
26 When Jesus therefore saw
His mother, and the disciple
whom He loved standing by,
He said to His mother,
"Woman, behold your son!"
27 Then He said to the disciple, "Behold your mother!"
And from that hour that disciple
took her to his own *home.*
28 After this, Jesus, knowing
that all things were now accomplished, that the Scripture
might be fulfilled, said, "I
thirst!"
29 Now a vessel full of sour
wine was sitting there; and
they filled a sponge with sour
wine, put *it* on hyssop, and put
it to His mouth.
30 So when Jesus had re-
ceived the sour wine, He said,
"It is finished!" And bowing His
head, He gave up His spirit.
31 Therefore, because it was
the Preparation *Day,* that the
bodies should not remain on the
cross on the Sabbath (for that
Sabbath was a high day), the
Jews asked Pilate that their
legs might be broken, and *that*
they might be taken away.
32 Then the soldiers came and
broke the legs of the first and of

Jesus Provides for His Mother

25 Εἱστήκεισαν δὲ παρὰ τῷ σταυρῷ τοῦ Ἰησοῦ ἡ μήτηρ
[2]*there* [3]stood [1]Now by the cross - of Jesus - mother ˜

αὐτοῦ, καὶ ἡ ἀδελφὴ τῆς μητρὸς αὐτοῦ, Μαρία ἡ τοῦ
His, and the sister - of mother ˜ His, Mary the *wife* of

Κλωπᾶ, καὶ Μαρία ἡ Μαγδαληνή. **26** Ἰησοῦς οὖν ἰδὼν
Clopas, and Mary - Magdalene. Jesus ˜ Therefore seeing

τὴν μητέρα, καὶ τὸν μαθητὴν παρεστῶτα ὃν ἠγάπα, λέγει
the mother, and the disciple [4]standing [5]by [1]whom [2]He [3]loved, says
His said

τῇ μητρὶ αὐτοῦ, "Γύναι, ἴδε ὁ υἱός σου!" **27** Εἶτα λέγει
- to mother ˜ His, "Woman, behold - son ˜ your!" Then He says
said

τῷ μαθητῇ, "Ἰδοὺ ἡ μήτηρ σου!" Καὶ ἀπ' ἐκείνης τῆς
to the disciple, "Behold - mother ˜ your!" And from that -

ὥρας ἔλαβεν ὁ μαθητὴς αὐτὴν εἰς τὰ ἴδια.
hour [3]took [1]the [2]disciple her into - his own *things*.
care.

It Is Finished
(Matt. 27:45–56; Mark 15:33–41; Luke 23:44–49)

28 Μετὰ τοῦτο ἰδὼν[f] ὁ Ἰησοῦς ὅτι πάντα ἤδη
After this seeing ˜ - Jesus that all *things* already

τετέλεσται, ἵνα τελειωθῇ ἡ Γραφή, λέγει,
has been fulfilled, so that [3]might [4]be [5]fulfilled [1]the [2]Scripture, He says,
had said,

"Διψῶ!" **29** Σκεῦος οὖν ἔκειτο ὄξους μεστόν· οἱ
"I thirst!" [2]a [3]vessel [1]Now was set [2]of [3]sour [4]wine [1]full; [6]the [7]*ones*
they

δέ, πλήσαντες σπόγγον ὄξους, καὶ ὑσσώπῳ
[5]and, having filled a sponge with sour wine, and [5]a [6]hyssop

περιθέντες, προσήνεγκαν αὐτοῦ τῷ στόματι. **30** Ὅτε
[1]having [2]put [3]*it* [4]around, they brought *it* His ˜ - to mouth. when ˜
held

οὖν ἔλαβε τὸ ὄξος ὁ Ἰησοῦς, εἶπε,
Therefore [2]received [3]the [4]sour [5]wine - [1]Jesus, He said,

"Τετέλεσται!" Καὶ κλίνας τὴν κεφαλήν,
"It has been accomplished!" And having bowed the head,
His

παρέδωκε τὸ πνεῦμα.
He gave over the spirit.
gave up His

A Soldier Pierces Jesus' Side

31 Οἱ οὖν Ἰουδαῖοι, ἵνα μὴ μείνῃ ἐπὶ τοῦ
the ˜ Therefore Jews, so that [4]not [3]should [5]remain [6]on [7]the

σταυροῦ τὰ σώματα ἐν τῷ σαββάτῳ, ἐπεὶ Παρασκευὴ
[8]cross [1]the [2]bodies on the Sabbath, since [3]*the* [4]Preparation [5]*Day*

ἦν (ἦν γὰρ μεγάλη ἡ ἡμέρα ἐκείνου τοῦ
[1]it [2]was ([12]was [6]for [13]a [14]great [15]*one* [7]the [8]day [9]of [10]that -
high

σαββάτου), ἠρώτησαν τὸν Πιλᾶτον ἵνα κατεαγῶσιν αὐτῶν
[11]Sabbath), asked - Pilate that [3]might [4]be [5]broken [1]their

τὰ σκέλη, καὶ ἀρθῶσιν. **32** Ἦλθον οὖν οἱ
- [2]legs, and they might be taken away. [4]came [1]Then [2]the

στρατιῶται καὶ τοῦ μὲν πρώτου κατέαξαν τὰ σκέλη καὶ
[3]soldiers and [5]of [6]the - [7]first [8]*man* [1]they [2]broke [3]the [4]legs and

f(**19:28**) NU, TR read ειδως, *knowing.*

τοῦ ἄλλου τοῦ συσταυρωθέντος αὐτῷ. 33 Ἐπὶ δὲ τὸν
of the other the *one* having been crucified with Him. [3]upon [1]But -
who was to

Ἰησοῦν ἐλθόντες, ὡς εἶδον αὐτὸν ἤδη τεθνηκότα, οὐ
[4]Jesus [2]coming, when they saw Him already having died, [3]not
that He had already died,

κατέαξαν αὐτοῦ τὰ σκέλη. 34 Ἀλλ᾽ εἷς τῶν στρατιωτῶν
[1]they [2]did break His - legs. But one of the soldiers

λόγχῃ αὐτοῦ τὴν πλευρὰν ἔνυξε, καὶ εὐθέως ἐξῆλθεν
with a spear [2]His - [3]side [1]pierced, and immediately [4]came [5]out

αἷμα καὶ ὕδωρ. 35 Καὶ ὁ ἑωρακὼς μεμαρτύρηκε, καὶ
[1]blood [2]and [3]water. And the *one* having seen has testified, and
who saw

ἀληθινὴ ἐστιν αὐτοῦ ἡ μαρτυρία, κἀκεῖνος οἶδεν ὅτι
[4]true [3]is [1]his - [2]testimony, and that *one* knows that
he

ἀληθῆ λέγει, ἵνα ὑμεῖς πιστεύσητε. 36 Ἐγένετο γὰρ
[3]true [4]*things* [1]he [2]says, so that you may believe. [4]happened [1]For
he tells the truth,

ταῦτα ἵνα ἡ Γραφὴ πληρωθῇ, «Ὀστοῦν οὐ
[2]these [3]*things* so that the Scripture might be fulfilled, «[2]a [3]bone [1]Not

συντριβήσεται αὐτοῦ.»[g] 37 Καὶ πάλιν ἑτέρα Γραφὴ λέγει,
[6]shall [7]be [8]broken [4]of [5]Him.» And again a different Scripture says,
another

«Ὄψονται εἰς ὃν ἐξεκέντησαν.»[h]
«They shall look at *Him* whom they pierced.

Joseph and Nicodemus Bury Jesus
(Matt. 27:57–61; Mark 15:42–47; Luke 23:50–56)

38 Μετὰ ταῦτα ἠρώτησε τὸν Πιλᾶτον ὁ Ἰωσὴφ ὁ
After these *things* [22]asked - [23]Pilate - [1]Joseph [2]the [3]*one*

ἀπὸ Ἀριμαθαίας, ὢν μαθητὴς τοῦ Ἰησοῦ,
[4]from [5]Arimathea, [6]being [7]a [8]disciple - [9]of [10]Jesus,

κεκρυμμένος δὲ διὰ τὸν φόβον τῶν
[12]having [13]been [14]hidden [11]but [15]because [16]of [17]the [18]fear [19]of [20]the
secretly

Ἰουδαίων, ἵνα ἄρῃ τὸ σῶμα τοῦ Ἰησοῦ· καὶ
[21]Jews, that he might take away the body - of Jesus; and

ἐπέτρεψεν ὁ Πιλᾶτος. Ἦλθεν οὖν καὶ ἦρε τὸ
[2]gave [3]permission - [1]Pilate. [5]he [6]came [4]Therefore and took away the

σῶμα τοῦ Ἰησοῦ.[i] 39 Ἦλθε δὲ καὶ Νικόδημος, ὁ
body - of Jesus. [14]came [1]And [13]also [2]Nicodemus, [3]the [4]*one*
who

ἐλθὼν πρὸς τὸν Ἰησοῦν[j] νυκτὸς τὸ πρῶτον, φέρων
[5]having [6]come [9]to - [10]Jesus [11]by [12]night - [7]*at* [8]first, bringing
had come

μίγμα σμύρνης καὶ ἀλόης ὡς λίτρας* ἑκατόν.
a mixture of myrrh and aloes about [3]pounds [1]a [2]hundred.

40 Ἔλαβον οὖν τὸ σῶμα τοῦ Ἰησοῦ καὶ ἔδησαν αὐτὸ ἐν
[2]they [3]took [1]Then the body - of Jesus and bound it in

ὀθονίοις μετὰ τῶν ἀρωμάτων, καθὼς ἔθος ἐστὶ τοῖς
linen strips with the spices, just as *the* custom is for the

Ἰουδαίοις ἐνταφιάζειν. 41 Ἦν δὲ ἐν τῷ τόπῳ ὅπου
Jews to bury. [2]*there* [3]was [1]Now in the place where

ἐσταυρώθη κῆπος, καὶ ἐν τῷ κήπῳ μνημεῖον καινὸν ἐν
He was crucified a garden, and in the garden a tomb ~ new in

ᾧ οὐδέπω οὐδεὶς ἐτέθη. 42 Ἐκεῖ οὖν διὰ τὴν
which not yet no one was buried. there ~ So on account of the
no one had yet been buried.

the other who was crucified with Him.

33 But when they came to Jesus and saw that He was already dead, they did not break His legs.

34 But one of the soldiers pierced His side with a spear, and immediately blood and water came out.

35 And he who has seen has testified, and his testimony is true; and he knows that he is telling the truth, so that you may believe.

36 For these things were done that the Scripture should be fulfilled, *"Not one of His bones shall be broken."*

37 And again another Scripture says, *"They shall look on Him whom they pierced."*

38 After this, Joseph of Arimathea, being a disciple of Jesus, but secretly, for fear of the Jews, asked Pilate that he might take away the body of Jesus; and Pilate gave *him* permission. So he came and took the body of Jesus.

39 And Nicodemus, who at first came to Jesus by night, also came, bringing a mixture of myrrh and aloes, about a hundred pounds.

40 Then they took the body of Jesus, and bound it in strips of linen with the spices, as the custom of the Jews is to bury.

41 Now in the place where He was crucified there was a garden, and in the garden a new tomb in which no one had yet been laid.

42 So there they laid Jesus,

[g]**(19:36)** Ex. 12:46; Num. 9:12; Ps. 34:20

[h]**(19:37)** Zech. 12:10

[i]**(19:38)** For του Ιησου, *of Jesus,* NU reads αυτου, *His.*

[j]**(19:39)** For τον Ιησουν, *Jesus,* NU reads αυτον, *Him.*

***(19:39)** λίτρα *(litra).* Noun, a unit of weight equal to a Roman *pound* (12 ounces or about 325 grams). The λίτρα was used to measure both weight and capacity.

because of the Jews' Preparation *Day,* for the tomb was nearby.

20 Now on the first *day* of the week Mary Magdalene went to the tomb early, while it was still dark, and saw *that* the stone had been taken away from the tomb.
2 Then she ran and came to Simon Peter, and to the other disciple, whom Jesus loved, and said to them, "They have taken away the Lord out of the tomb, and we do not know where they have laid Him."
3 Peter therefore went out, and the other disciple, and were going to the tomb.
4 So they both ran together, and the other disciple outran Peter and came to the tomb first.
5 And he, stooping down and looking in, saw the linen cloths lying *there;* yet he did not go in.
6 Then Simon Peter came, following him, and went into the tomb; and he saw the linen cloths lying *there,*
7 and the handkerchief that had been around His head, not lying with the linen cloths, but folded together in a place by itself.
8 Then the other disciple, who came to the tomb first, went in also; and he saw and believed.
9 For as yet they did not know the Scripture, that He

Παρασκευὴν τῶν Ἰουδαίων, ὅτι ἐγγὺς ἦν τὸ μνημεῖον,
Preparation *Day* of the Jews, because [4]near [3]was [1]the [2]tomb,

ἔθηκαν τὸν Ἰησοῦν.
they put - Jesus.

Peter and John See the Empty Tomb
(Matt. 28:1–8; Mark 16:1–8; Luke 24:1–12)

20 1 Τῇ δὲ μιᾷ τῶν σαββάτων Μαρία ἡ
[2]on [3]the [1]And first *day* of the week Mary -

Μαγδαληνὴ ἔρχεται πρωΐ, σκοτίας ἔτι οὔσης, εἰς τὸ
Magdalene comes early, dark still being, to the
came while it was still dark,

μνημεῖον καὶ βλέπει τὸν λίθον ἠρμένον ἐκ τοῦ
tomb and sees the stone having been taken away from the
saw that had

μνημείου. 2 Τρέχει οὖν καὶ ἔρχεται πρὸς Σίμωνα
tomb. [2]she [3]runs [1]Therefore and comes to Simon
ran came

Πέτρον καὶ πρὸς τὸν ἄλλον μαθητὴν ὃν ἐφίλει ὁ Ἰησοῦς,
Peter and to the other disciple whom loved ~ - Jesus,

καὶ λέγει αὐτοῖς, "Ἦραν τὸν Κύριον ἐκ τοῦ μνημείου,
and she says to them, "They took the Lord out of the tomb,
said have taken

καὶ οὐκ οἴδαμεν ποῦ ἔθηκαν αὐτόν." 3 Ἐξῆλθεν οὖν
and [3]not [1]we [2]do know where they laid Him." [7]went [8]out [1]Therefore
have laid

ὁ Πέτρος καὶ ὁ ἄλλος μαθητὴς καὶ ἤρχοντο εἰς τὸ
- [2]Peter [3]and [4]the [5]other [6]disciple and were going to the

μνημεῖον. 4 Ἔτρεχον δὲ οἱ δύο ὁμοῦ, καὶ ὁ ἄλλος
tomb. [4]were [5]running [1]And [2]the [3]two together, and the other

μαθητὴς προέδραμε τάχιον τοῦ Πέτρου καὶ ἦλθε πρῶτος
disciple ran ahead more quickly - *than* Peter and he came first

εἰς τὸ μνημεῖον. 5 Καὶ παρακύψας βλέπει κείμενα τὰ
to the tomb. And stooping to look *in* he sees lying *there* the
saw

ὀθόνια,* οὐ μέντοι εἰσῆλθεν. 6 Ἔρχεται οὖν[a] Σίμων
linen strips, [4]not [1]however [2]he [3]did [5]go [6]in. [4]comes [1]Then [2]Simon
came

Πέτρος ἀκολουθῶν αὐτῷ, καὶ εἰσῆλθεν εἰς τὸ μνημεῖον, καὶ
[3]Peter following him, and entered into the tomb, and

θεωρεῖ τὰ ὀθόνια κείμενα, 7 καὶ τὸ σουδάριον ὃ ἦν
he sees the linen strips lying *there,* and the facecloth which was
saw had been

ἐπὶ τῆς κεφαλῆς αὐτοῦ, οὐ μετὰ τῶν ὀθονίων κείμενον,
on - head ~ His, not [2]with [3]the [4]linen [5]strips [1]lying,

ἀλλὰ χωρὶς ἐντετυλιγμένον εἰς ἕνα τόπον. 8 Τότε οὖν
but apart from *them* having been rolled up in one place. then ~ So

εἰσῆλθε καὶ ὁ ἄλλος μαθητὴς ὁ ἐλθὼν πρῶτος
[13]went [14]in [12]also [1]the [2]other [3]disciple [4]the [5]*one* [6]having [7]come [8]first
who came

εἰς τὸ μνημεῖον, καὶ εἶδε καὶ ἐπίστευσεν. 9 Οὐδέπω γὰρ
[9]to [10]the [11]tomb, and he saw and believed. [4]not [5]yet [1]For

ᾔδεισαν τὴν Γραφὴν ὅτι δεῖ αὐτὸν ἐκ
[2]they [3]did [6]know the Scripture that it is necessary *for* Him [4]from
was

---

[a](20:6) NU adds και, *also.*

*(20:5) ὀθόνιον *(othonion).* Noun meaning *linen cloth.* In the NT the word always refers to the cloths used as a burial wrapping for the body of Jesus. The custom of the time called for a corpse to be wound with long strips of linen cloth, with spices interspersed between the layers to disguise the odor of decay. Cf. the cognate noun ὀθόνη, *linen cloth, sheet,* used in the NT only of the sheet Peter saw lowered from heaven (Acts 10:11; 11:5).

νεκρῶν ἀναστῆναι. 10 Ἀπῆλθον οὖν πάλιν πρὸς
[5]*the* [6]dead [1]to [2]rise [3]again. [4]went [5]away [1]Then [6]again [7]to

ἑαυτοὺς οἱ μαθηταί.
[8]themselves [2]the [3]disciples.
their own homes

Mary Magdalene Sees the Risen Lord
(Mark 16:9–11)

11 Μαρία δὲ εἱστήκει πρὸς τὸ μνημεῖον κλαίουσα
Mary ˜ But stood [2]toward [3]the [4]tomb [5]weeping
facing

ἔξω. Ὡς οὖν ἔκλαιε, παρέκυψεν εἰς τὸ
[1]outside. as ˜ Therefore she was weeping, she stooped to look into the

μνημεῖον. 12 Καὶ θεωρεῖ δύο ἀγγέλους ἐν λευκοῖς
tomb. And she sees two angels in white
saw

καθεζομένους, ἕνα πρὸς τῇ κεφαλῇ καὶ ἕνα πρὸς τοῖς ποσίν,
sitting, one at the head and one at the feet,

ὅπου ἔκειτο τὸ σῶμα τοῦ Ἰησοῦ.
where [5]was [6]lying [1]the [2]body - [3]of [4]Jesus.
had lain

13 Καὶ λέγουσιν αὐτῇ ἐκεῖνοι, "Γύναι, τί
And [3]say [4]to [5]her [1]those [2]*ones*, "Woman, why
said they,

κλαίεις?"
are you weeping?"

Λέγει αὐτοῖς, "Ὅτι ἦραν τὸν Κύριόν μου, καὶ
She says to them, "Because they took away - Lord ˜ my, and
said have taken

οὐκ οἶδα ποῦ ἔθηκαν αὐτόν." 14 Καὶ ταῦτα
[3]not [1]I [2]do know where they put Him." And [3]these [4]*things*

εἰποῦσα ἐστράφη εἰς τὰ ὀπίσω καὶ θεωρεῖ τὸν Ἰησοῦν
[1]having [2]said she turned to the *things* behind and sees - Jesus
back saw

ἑστῶτα καὶ οὐκ ᾔδει ὅτι Ἰησοῦς ἐστι.
standing *there* and [3]not [1]she [2]did know that [3]Jesus [1]it [2]is.
was.

15 Λέγει αὐτῇ ὁ Ἰησοῦς, "Γύναι, τί κλαίεις? Τίνα
[2]says [3]to [4]her - [1]Jesus, "Woman, why are you weeping? Whom
said

ζητεῖς?"
do you seek?"

Ἐκείνη, δοκοῦσα ὅτι ὁ κηπουρός ἐστι, λέγει αὐτῷ,
That *woman*, supposing that [3]the [4]gardener [1]He [2]is, says to Him,
She, was, said

"Κύριε, εἰ σὺ ἐβάστασας αὐτόν, εἰπέ μοι ποῦ ἔθηκας αὐτόν,
"Sir, if You carried away ˜ Him, tell me where You put Him,

κἀγὼ αὐτὸν ἀρῶ."
and I [3]Him [1]will [2]take away."

16 Λέγει αὐτῇ ὁ Ἰησοῦς, "Μαρία!"
[2]says [3]to [4]her - [1]Jesus, "Mary!"
said

Στραφεῖσα ἐκείνη, λέγει αὐτῷ,[b] "Ῥαββουνί!" (ὃ
[3]having [4]turned [1]That [2]*woman*, she says to Him. "Rabboni!" (which
After she had turned, she said

λέγεται, Διδάσκαλε).
is called, Teacher).
means,

must rise again from the dead.
10 Then the disciples went away again to their own homes.
11 But Mary stood outside by the tomb weeping, and as she wept she stooped down *and looked* into the tomb.
12 And she saw two angels in white sitting, one at the head and the other at the feet, where the body of Jesus had lain.
13 Then they said to her, "Woman, why are you weeping?" She said to them, "Because they have taken away my Lord, and I do not know where they have laid Him."
14 Now when she had said this, she turned around and saw Jesus standing *there,* and did not know that it was Jesus.
15 Jesus said to her, "Woman, why are you weeping? Whom are you seeking?" She, supposing Him to be the gardener, said to Him, "Sir, if You have carried Him away, tell me where You have laid Him, and I will take Him away."
16 Jesus said to her, "Mary!" She turned and said to Him, "Rabboni!" (which is to say, Teacher).

[b]**(20:16)** NU adds Εβραιστι, *in Hebrew.*

17 Jesus said to her, "Do not cling to Me, for I have not yet ascended to My Father; but go to My brethren and say to them, 'I am ascending to My Father and your Father, and *to* My God and your God.'"
18 Mary Magdalene came and told the disciples that she had seen the Lord, and *that* He had spoken these things to her.
19 Then, the same day at evening, being the first *day* of the week, when the doors were shut where the disciples were assembled, for fear of the Jews, Jesus came and stood in the midst, and said to them, "Peace *be* with you."
20 When He had said this, He showed them *His* hands and His side. Then the disciples were glad when they saw the Lord.
21 So Jesus said to them again, "Peace to you! As the Father has sent Me, I also send you."
22 And when He had said this, He breathed on *them,* and said to them, "Receive the Holy Spirit.
23 "If you forgive the sins of any, they are forgiven them; if you retain the *sins* of any, they are retained."
24 Now Thomas, called the Twin, one of the twelve, was not with them when Jesus came.
25 The other disciples therefore said to him, "We have seen the Lord." So he said to them,

17 Λέγει αὐτῇ ὁ Ἰησοῦς, "Μή μου ἅπτου, οὔπω
[2]says [3]to [4]her - [1]Jesus, "[6]not [9]Me [5]Do [7]hold [8]to, [13]not [14]yet
said cling to,

γὰρ ἀναβέβηκα πρὸς τὸν Πατέρα μου·[c] πορεύου δὲ πρὸς
[10]for [11]I [12]have ascended to - Father ˜ My; go ˜ but to

τοὺς ἀδελφούς μου καὶ εἰπὲ αὐτοῖς, "Ἀναβαίνω πρὸς τὸν
- brothers ˜ My and say to them, 'I am ascending to -

Πατέρα μου καὶ Πατέρα ὑμῶν, καὶ Θεόν μου καὶ Θεὸν
Father ˜ My and Father ˜ your, and *to* God ˜ My and God ˜

ὑμῶν.'" **18** Ἔρχεται Μαρία ἡ Μαγδαληνὴ ἀπαγγέλλουσα τοῖς
your.'" [3]goes [1]Mary - [2]Magdalene reporting to the
went

μαθηταῖς ὅτι ἑώρακε[d] τὸν Κύριον, καὶ ταῦτα εἶπεν
disciples that she has seen the Lord, and *that* [3]these [4]*things* [1]He [2]said
had

αὐτῇ.
to her.

The Disciples Are Commissioned
(Matt. 28:16–20; Mark 16:14–18; Luke 24:36–49)

19 Οὔσης οὖν ὀψίας, τῇ ἡμέρᾳ ἐκείνῃ τῇ μιᾷ τῶν
[2]*it* [3]being [1]Then evening, - on day ˜ that the first *day* of the
when it was

σαββάτων, καὶ τῶν θυρῶν κεκλεισμένων ὅπου ἦσαν οἱ
week, and the doors having been closed where [3]were [1]the

μαθηταὶ συνηγμένοι[e] διὰ τὸν φόβον τῶν Ἰουδαίων,
[2]disciples assembled because of - fear of the Jews,

ἦλθεν ὁ Ἰησοῦς καὶ ἔστη εἰς τὸ μέσον καὶ λέγει αὐτοῖς,
came ˜ - Jesus and stood in the midst and says to them,
said

"Εἰρήνη ὑμῖν." **20** Καὶ τοῦτο εἰπὼν ἔδειξεν αὐτοῖς τὰς
"Peace to you." And [3]this [1]having [2]said He showed them -

χεῖρας καὶ τὴν πλευρὰν αὐτοῦ. Ἐχάρησαν οὖν οἱ μαθηταὶ
[2]hands [3]and - [4]side [1]His. [8]rejoiced [5]Then [6]the [7]disciples

ἰδόντες τὸν Κύριον. **21** Εἶπεν οὖν αὐτοῖς ὁ Ἰησοῦς
having seen the Lord. [3]said [1]Therefore [4]to [5]them - [2]Jesus
when they saw

πάλιν, "Εἰρήνη ὑμῖν. Καθὼς ἀπέσταλκέ* με ὁ Πατήρ,
again, "Peace to you. Just as [3]has [4]sent [5]Me [1]the [2]Father,

κἀγὼ πέμπω ὑμᾶς." **22** Καὶ τοῦτο εἰπὼν ἐνεφύσησε
I also send you." And [3]this [1]having [2]said He breathed on *them*

καὶ λέγει αὐτοῖς, "Λάβετε Πνεῦμα Ἅγιον. **23** Ἄν τινων
and says to them, "Receive *the* Spirit ˜ Holy. [3]ever [1]Of [2]whom
said

ἀφῆτε τὰς ἁμαρτίας, ἀφίενται αὐτοῖς, ἄν τινων
you forgive the sins, they are forgiven them, [3]ever [1]of [2]whom

κρατῆτε, κεκράτηνται."
you retain *the sins,* they have been retained."

Thomas Sees and Believes

24 Θωμᾶς δέ, εἷς ἐκ τῶν δώδεκα, ὁ λεγόμενος
Thomas ˜ But, one of the twelve, the *one* being called
called

Δίδυμος, οὐκ ἦν μετ' αὐτῶν ὅτε ἦλθεν ὁ Ἰησοῦς. **25** Ἔλεγον
Twin, not ˜ was with them when came ˜ - Jesus. [5]said

οὖν αὐτῷ οἱ ἄλλοι μαθηταί, "Ἑωράκαμεν τὸν Κύριον."
[1]Therefore [6]to [7]him [2]the [3]other [4]disciples, "We have seen the Lord."

---

[c](20:17) NU omits μου, *My,* thus *to the Father.*
[d](20:18) NU reads εωρακα, *I have seen.*
[e](20:19) NU omits συνηγμενοι, *assembled.*

*(20:21) ἀποστέλλω *(apostellō).* Common verb in the NT compounded from ἀπό, *from,* and στέλλω, *send,* thus meaning *send, send out, send away.* It is sometimes used as an auxiliary verb to indicate that an action was performed by others at someone's direction (cf. ἀποστείλας ἀνεῖλε, *sending he killed,* Matt. 2:16). Like the synonym πέμπω, *send,* ἀποστέλλω often implies the sending on a mission or to represent the sender (as here in John

Ὁ δὲ εἶπεν αὐτοῖς, "Ἐὰν μὴ ἴδω ἐν ταῖς χερσὶν
[2]the [3]*one* [1]But said to them, "If not I see in - hands ˜
he "Unless

αὐτοῦ τὸν τύπον τῶν ἥλων καὶ βάλω τὸν δάκτυλόν μου εἰς τὸν
His the mark of the nails and put - finger ˜ my into the

τύπον τῶν ἥλων καὶ βάλω τὴν χεῖρά μου εἰς τὴν πλευρὰν
mark of the nails and put - hand ˜ my into - side ˜

αὐτοῦ, οὐ μὴ πιστεύσω."
His, [3]not [4]not [1]I [2]will [5]believe."
by no means

26 Καὶ μεθ' ἡμέρας ὀκτὼ πάλιν ἦσαν ἔσω οἱ μαθηταὶ
And after days ˜ eight again [3]were [4]inside - [2]disciples

αὐτοῦ καὶ Θωμᾶς μετ' αὐτῶν. Ἔρχεται ὁ Ἰησοῦς, τῶν θυρῶν
[1]His and Thomas with them. comes ˜ - Jesus, the doors
came

κεκλεισμένων, καὶ ἔστη εἰς τὸ μέσον καὶ εἶπεν, "Εἰρήνη
having been closed, and He stood in the midst and said, "Peace

ὑμῖν." 27 Εἶτα λέγει τῷ Θωμᾷ, "Φέρε τὸν δάκτυλόν σου
to you." Then He says - to Thomas, "Bring - finger ˜ your
said

ὧδε καὶ ἴδε τὰς χεῖράς μου· καὶ φέρε τὴν χεῖρά σου καὶ βάλε
here and see - hands ˜ My; and bring - hand ˜ your and put *it*

εἰς τὴν πλευράν μου. Καὶ μὴ γίνου ἄπιστος ἀλλὰ πιστός."
into - side ˜ My. And not ˜ do be unbelieving but believing."

28 Καὶ ἀπεκρίθη Θωμᾶς καὶ εἶπεν αὐτῷ, "Ὁ Κύριός μου
And answered ˜ Thomas and said to Him, - "Lord ˜ My

καὶ ὁ Θεός μου!"
and - God ˜ my!"

29 Λέγει αὐτῷ ὁ Ἰησοῦς, "Ὅτι ἑώρακάς με,[f]
[2]says [3]to [4]him - [1]Jesus, "Because you have seen Me,
said

πεπίστευκας. Μακάριοι οἱ μὴ ἰδόντες, καὶ
you have believed. Blessed *are* the *ones* not having seen yet
those who have not

πιστεύσαντες."
having believed."
have

These Are Written that You May Believe

30 Πολλὰ μὲν οὖν καὶ ἄλλα σημεῖα ἐποίησεν ὁ Ἰησοῦς
[5]many - [1]Now [3]also [6]other [7]signs [4]did - [2]Jesus

ἐνώπιον τῶν μαθητῶν αὐτοῦ ἃ οὐκ ἔστι γεγραμμένα
in the presence - of disciples ˜ His which not ˜ are written

ἐν τῷ βιβλίῳ τούτῳ. 31 Ταῦτα δὲ γέγραπται ἵνα
in - book ˜ this. these ˜ But have been written so that

πιστεύσητε ὅτι Ἰησοῦς ἐστιν ὁ Χριστός, ὁ Υἱὸς τοῦ Θεοῦ,
you may believe that Jesus is the Christ, the Son - of God,

καὶ ἵνα πιστεύοντες ζωὴν ἔχητε ἐν τῷ ὀνόματι αὐτοῦ.
and so that believing [4]life [1]you [2]may [3]have in - name His.
by believing

The Miraculous Catch of Fish

21 1 Μετὰ ταῦτα ἐφανέρωσεν ἑαυτὸν πάλιν ὁ Ἰησοῦς
After these *things* [2]revealed [3]Himself [4]again - [1]Jesus

τοῖς μαθηταῖς ἐπὶ τῆς θαλάσσης τῆς Τιβεριάδος,
to the disciples on the Sea of Tiberias,
at

"Unless I see in His hands the print of the nails, and put my finger into the print of the nails, and put my hand into His side, I will not believe."
26 And after eight days His disciples were again inside, and Thomas with them. Jesus came, the doors being shut, and stood in the midst, and said, "Peace to you!"
27 Then He said to Thomas, "Reach your finger here, and look at My hands; and reach your hand *here,* and put *it* into My side. Do not be unbelieving, but believing."
28 And Thomas answered and said to Him, "My Lord and my God!"
29 Jesus said to him, "Thomas, because you have seen Me, you have believed. Blessed *are* those who have not seen and *yet* have believed."
30 And truly Jesus did many other signs in the presence of His disciples, which are not written in this book;
31 but these are written that you may believe that Jesus is the Christ, the Son of God, and that believing you may have life in His name.
21 After these things Jesus showed Himself again to the disciples at the Sea

---

f(**20:29**) TR adds Θωμα, *Thomas.*

20:21). Cf. the cognate noun ἀπόστολος, *one sent, apostle.* While it can be used of a lesser "messenger, representative" (2 Cor. 8:23), ἀπόστολος typically means *apostle* in the official NT sense. Cf. also the cognate noun ἀποστολή, *apostleship* (as Acts 1:25; 1 Cor. 9:2).

of Tiberias, and in this way He
showed *Himself:*
2 Simon Peter, Thomas
called the Twin, Nathanael of
Cana in Galilee, the *sons* of
Zebedee, and two others of His
disciples were together.
3 Simon Peter said to them,
"I am going fishing." They said
to him, "We are going with you
also." They went out and immediately got into the boat, and
that night they caught nothing.
4 But when the morning had
now come, Jesus stood on the
shore; yet the disciples did not
know that it was Jesus.
5 Then Jesus said to them,
"Children, have you any food?"
They answered Him, "No."
6 And He said to them, "Cast
the net on the right side of the
boat, and you will find *some*."
So they cast, and now they
were not able to draw it in because of the multitude of fish.
7 Therefore that disciple
whom Jesus loved said to Peter, "It is the Lord!" Now when
Simon Peter heard that it was
the Lord, he put on *his* outer
garment (for he had removed
it), and plunged into the sea.
8 But the other disciples
came in the little boat (for they

ἐφανέρωσε δὲ οὕτως. **2** Ἦσαν ὁμοῦ Σίμων
[2]He [3]revealed [4]*Himself* [1]and thus. *There* were together Simon
in this manner.

Πέτρος, καὶ Θωμᾶς ὁ λεγόμενος Δίδυμος, καὶ Ναθαναὴλ
Peter, and Thomas the *one* being called Twin, and Nathanael
called

ὁ ἀπὸ Κανὰ τῆς Γαλιλαίας, καὶ οἱ τοῦ Ζεβεδαίου, καὶ
the *one* from Cana of Galilee, and the *sons* of Zebedee, and

ἄλλοι ἐκ τῶν μαθητῶν αὐτοῦ δύο. **3** Λέγει αὐτοῖς Σίμων
[2]others [3]of - [5]disciples [4]His [1]two. [3]says [4]to [5]them [1]Simon
said

Πέτρος, "Ὑπάγω ἁλιεύειν."
[2]Peter, "I am going to fish."
fishing."

Λέγουσιν αὐτῷ, "Ἐρχόμεθα καὶ ἡμεῖς σὺν σοί."
They say to him, "[2]are [3]coming [6]also [1]We [4]with [5]you."
said

Ἐξῆλθον καὶ ἐνέβησαν εἰς τὸ πλοῖον εὐθύς,[a] καὶ ἐν
They went out and stepped in into the boat immediately, and in
got

ἐκείνῃ τῇ νυκτὶ ἐπίασαν οὐδέν. **4** Πρωΐας δὲ ἤδη
that - night they caught nothing. [2]early [3]morning [1]But already
But as daybreak had

γενομένης, ἔστη ὁ Ἰησοῦς εἰς τὸν αἰγιαλόν· οὐ μέντοι
having become, stood ˜ - Jesus upon the shore; [5]not [1]however
already come,

ᾔδεισαν οἱ μαθηταὶ ὅτι Ἰησοῦς ἐστι.
[4]did [6]know [2]the [3]disciples that [3]Jesus [1]it [2]is.
was.

5 Λέγει οὖν αὐτοῖς ὁ Ἰησοῦς, "Παιδία, μή τι
[3]says [1]Then [4]to [5]them - [2]Jesus, "Children, not any
said you do not

προσφάγιον ἔχετε?"
fish you have?"
have any fish, do you?"

Ἀπεκρίθησαν αὐτῷ, "Οὔ."
They answered Him, "No."

6 Ὁ δὲ εἶπεν αὐτοῖς, "Βάλετε εἰς τὰ δεξιὰ μέρη
[2]the [3]*One* [1]But said to them, "Cast [3]to [4]the [5]right [6]parts
He on side

τοῦ πλοίου τὸ δίκτυον, καὶ εὑρήσετε." Ἔβαλον
[7]of [8]the [9]boat [1]the [2]net, and you will find *some*." [2]they [3]cast

οὖν, καὶ οὐκέτι αὐτὸ ἑλκύσαι ἴσχυσαν ἀπὸ
[1]Therefore, and [3]no [4]longer [8]it [6]to [7]haul [9]in [1]they [2]were [5]able from
because of

τοῦ πλήθους τῶν ἰχθύων.
the multitude of the fish.

7 Λέγει οὖν ὁ μαθητὴς ἐκεῖνος ὃν ἠγάπα ὁ
[7]says [1]Therefore - [3]disciple [2]that [4]whom [6]loved -
said

Ἰησοῦς τῷ Πέτρῳ, "Ὁ Κύριός ἐστι!" Σίμων Πέτρος,
[5]Jesus to Peter, "[3]the [4]Lord [1]It [2]is!" Simon Peter,

ἀκούσας ὅτι ὁ Κύριός ἐστι, τὸν ἐπενδύτην
hearing that [3]the [4]Lord [1]it [2]is, [7]the [8]outer [9]garment
when he heard was, he put on his

διεζώσατο (ἦν γὰρ γυμνός) καὶ ἔβαλεν ἑαυτὸν εἰς
[5]he [6]tied [10]around ([12]he [13]was [11]for stripped) and he threw himself into
outer garment without it) plunged

τὴν θάλασσαν. **8** Οἱ δὲ ἄλλοι μαθηταὶ τῷ πλοιαρίῳ
the sea. the ˜ But other disciples [2]in [3]the [4]little [5]boat

[a](21:3) NU omits ευθυς, *immediately.*

ἦλθον (οὐ γὰρ ἦσαν μακρὰν ἀπὸ τῆς γῆς, ἀλλ' ὡς ἀπὸ
[1]came ([9]not [6]for [7]they [8]were far from the land, but about from
two

πηχῶν διακοσίων), σύροντες τὸ δίκτυον τῶν ἰχθύων. 9 Ὡς
[3]cubits [1]two [2]hundred), dragging the net - of fish. as ˜
hundred cubits away),

οὖν ἀπέβησαν εἰς τὴν γῆν, βλέπουσιν ἀνθρακιὰν κειμένην
Then they got off to the land, they see a charcoal fire lying
onto saw laid there

καὶ ὀψάριον ἐπικείμενον, καὶ ἄρτον.
and fish lying on *it,* and bread.
placed

10 Λέγει αὐτοῖς ὁ Ἰησοῦς, "Ἐνέγκατε ἀπὸ τῶν ὀψαρίων
[2]says [3]to [4]them - [1]Jesus, "Bring *some* from the fish
said of

ὧν ἐπιάσατε νῦν." 11 Ἀνέβη Σίμων Πέτρος καὶ εἵλκυσε τὸ
which you caught ˜ now." [3]went [4]up [1]Simon [2]Peter and hauled the

δίκτυον ἐπὶ τῆς γῆς, μεστὸν ἰχθύων μεγάλων ἑκατὸν
net onto the land, full of [5]fish [4]large [1]one [2]hundred

πεντηκοντατριῶν· καὶ τοσούτων ὄντων, οὐκ ἐσχίσθη
[3]fifty-three; and [2]so [3]many [1]being, [7]not [6]was [8]torn
although there were,

τὸ δίκτυον. 12 Λέγει αὐτοῖς ὁ Ἰησοῦς, "Δεῦτε
[4]the [5]net. [2]says [3]to [4]them - [1]Jesus, "Come
said

ἀριστήσατε." Οὐδεὶς δὲ ἐτόλμα τῶν μαθητῶν ἐξετάσαι
and eat breakfast." [2]not [3]one [1]But [7]dared [4]of [5]the [6]disciples to question

αὐτόν, "Σὺ τίς εἶ?" — εἰδότες ὅτι ὁ Κύριός ἐστιν.
Him, "[3]You [1]Who [2]are?" — knowing that [3]the [4]Lord [1]it [2]is.
was.

13 Ἔρχεται οὖν ὁ Ἰησοῦς καὶ λαμβάνει τὸν ἄρτον καὶ
[3]comes [1]Then - [2]Jesus and takes the bread and
came took

δίδωσιν αὐτοῖς, καὶ τὸ ὀψάριον ὁμοίως. 14 Τοῦτο ἤδη
gives *it* to them, and the fish likewise. This *was* now
gave

τρίτον ἐφανερώθη ὁ Ἰησοῦς τοῖς μαθηταῖς αὐτοῦ,[b]
a third *time* [2]was [3]revealed - [1]Jesus to disciples ˜ His,

ἐγερθεὶς ἐκ νεκρῶν.
having been raised from *the* dead.
after He was

Jesus Reinstates Peter

15 Ὅτε οὖν ἠρίστησαν, λέγει τῷ Σίμωνι Πέτρῳ ὁ
when ˜ Therefore they ate breakfast, [2]says [3]to [4]Simon [5]Peter -
had eaten said

Ἰησοῦς, "Σίμων Ἰωνᾶ,[c] ἀγαπᾷς με πλεῖον τούτων?"
[1]Jesus, "Simon *son* of Jonah, do you love Me more *than* these?"

Λέγει αὐτῷ, "Ναί, Κύριε, σὺ οἶδας ὅτι φιλῶ σε."
He says to Him, "Yes, Lord, You know that I love You."
said

Λέγει αὐτῷ, "Βόσκε τὰ ἀρνία μου." 16 Λέγει αὐτῷ πάλιν
He says to him, "Feed - lambs ˜ My." He says to him again
said said

δεύτερον, "Σίμων Ἰωνᾶ,[d] ἀγαπᾷς με?"
a second *time,* "Simon *son* of Jonah, do you love Me?"

Λέγει αὐτῷ, "Ναί, Κύριε, σὺ οἶδας ὅτι φιλῶ σε."
He says to Him, "Yes, Lord, You know that I love You."
said

were not far from land, but about two hundred cubits), dragging the net with fish.
9 Then, as soon as they had come to land, they saw a fire of coals there, and fish laid on it, and bread.
10 Jesus said to them, "Bring some of the fish which you have just caught."
11 Simon Peter went up and dragged the net to land, full of large fish, one hundred and fifty-three; and although there were so many, the net was not broken.
12 Jesus said to them, "Come *and* eat breakfast." Yet none of the disciples dared ask Him, "Who are You?"—knowing that it was the Lord.
13 Jesus then came and took the bread and gave it to them, and likewise the fish.
14 This *is* now the third time Jesus showed Himself to His disciples after He was raised from the dead.
15 So when they had eaten breakfast, Jesus said to Simon Peter, "Simon, *son* of Jonah, do you love Me more than these?" He said to Him, "Yes, Lord; You know that I love You." He said to him, "Feed My lambs."
16 He said to him again a second time, "Simon, *son* of Jonah, do you love Me?" He said to Him, "Yes, Lord; You know

[b](**21:14**) NU omits *αυτου, His,* thus *the disciples.*
[c](**21:15**) NU reads *Ιωαννου, (son) of John.*
[d](**21:16**) NU reads *Ιωαννου, (son) of John.*

that I love You." He said to
him, "Tend My sheep."
17 He said to him the third
time, "Simon, *son* of Jonah, do
you love Me?" Peter was
grieved because He said to him
the third time, "Do you love
Me?" And he said to Him,
"Lord, You know all things;
You know that I love You." Jesus said to him, "Feed My
sheep.
18 "Most assuredly, I say to
you, when you were younger,
you girded yourself and walked
where you wished; but when
you are old, you will stretch out
your hands, and another will
gird you and carry *you* where
you do not wish."
19 This He spoke, signifying
by what death he would glorify
God. And when He had spoken
this, He said to him, "Follow
Me."
20 Then Peter, turning
around, saw the disciple whom
Jesus loved following, who also
had leaned on His breast at the
supper, and said, "Lord, who is
the one who betrays You?"
21 Peter, seeing him, said to
Jesus, "But Lord, what *about*
this man?"
22 Jesus said to him, "If I will
that he remain till I come, what
is that to you? You follow Me."
23 Then this saying went out
among the brethren that this
disciple would not die. Yet Jesus did not say to him that he

Λέγει αὐτῷ, "Ποίμαινε τὰ πρόβατά μου." **17** Λέγει αὐτῷ
He says to him, "Shepherd - sheep ˜ My." He says to him
said said

τὸ τρίτον, "Σίμων Ἰωνᾶ,[e] φιλεῖς με?"
the third *time,* "Simon *son* of Jonah, do you love Me?"

Ἐλυπήθη ὁ Πέτρος ὅτι εἶπεν αὐτῷ τὸ τρίτον,
[2]was [3]grieved - [1]Peter because He said to him the third *time,*
distressed

"Φιλεῖς με?" Καὶ εἶπεν αὐτῷ, "Κύριε, σὺ πάντα οἶδας.
"Do you love Me?" And he said to Him, "Lord, You [2]all [3]*things* [1]know.

Σὺ γινώσκεις ὅτι φιλῶ σε."
You know that I love You."

Λέγει αὐτῷ ὁ Ἰησοῦς, "Βόσκε τὰ πρόβατά μου. **18** Ἀμὴν
[2]says [3]to [4]him - [1]Jesus, "Feed - sheep ˜ My. Amen
said Most

ἀμὴν λέγω σοι, ὅτε ἦς νεώτερος, ἐζώννυες σεαυτὸν
amen I say to you, when you were younger, you girded yourself
assuredly used to dress

καὶ περιεπάτεις ὅπου ἤθελες· ὅταν δὲ γηράσῃς,
and walked where you wished; when ˜ but you grow old,
used to walk

ἐκτενεῖς τὰς χεῖράς σου καὶ ἄλλος σε ζώσει καὶ
you will stretch out - hands ˜ your and another [3]you [1]will [2]gird and
dress

οἴσει ὅπου οὐ θέλεις." **19** Τοῦτο δὲ εἶπε,
will carry *you* where [3]not [1]you [2]do [4]wish." this ˜ But He said,

σημαίνων ποίῳ θανάτῳ δοξάσει τὸν Θεόν. Καὶ τοῦτο
signifying by what kind of death he will glorify - God. And [3]this
would

εἰπὼν λέγει αὐτῷ, "Ἀκολούθει μοι."
[1]having [2]said He says to him, "Follow Me."
said

The Beloved Disciple and His Book

20 Ἐπιστραφεὶς δὲ ὁ Πέτρος βλέπει τὸν μαθητὴν ὃν
[3]turning [4]around [1]But - [2]Peter sees the disciple whom
saw

ἠγάπα ὁ Ἰησοῦς ἀκολουθοῦντα, ὃς καὶ ἀνέπεσεν ἐν τῷ
loved ˜ - Jesus following, *the one* who also reclined at the

δείπνῳ ἐπὶ τὸ στῆθος αὐτοῦ καὶ εἶπε, "Κύριε, τίς ἐστιν ὁ
supper on - chest ˜ His and said, "Lord, who is the *one*

παραδιδούς σε?" **21** Τοῦτον ἰδὼν ὁ Πέτρος λέγει τῷ Ἰησοῦ,
handing over ˜ You?" [3]this [4]*one* [2]seeing - [1]Peter says to Jesus,
who will betray him said

"Κύριε, οὗτος δὲ τί?"
"[2]Lord, [5]this [6]*man* [1]But [3]what [4]*about?*"

22 Λέγει αὐτῷ ὁ Ἰησοῦς, "Ἐὰν αὐτὸν θέλω μένειν ἕως
[2]says [3]to [4]him - [1]Jesus, "If [3]him [1]I [2]want to remain till
said

ἔρχομαι, τί πρὸς σέ? Σὺ ἀκολούθει μοι." **23** Ἐξῆλθεν
I come, what *is that* to you? You follow Me." [4]went [5]out

οὖν ὁ λόγος οὗτος εἰς τοὺς ἀδελφοὺς ὅτι ὁ μαθητὴς
[1]Therefore - [3]word [2]this to the brothers that - disciple ˜
saying among

ἐκεῖνος οὐκ ἀποθνῄσκει. Καὶ οὐκ εἶπεν αὐτῷ ὁ Ἰησοῦς ὅτι
that not ˜ does die. Yet [3]not [2]did [4]say [5]to [6]him - [1]Jesus that
would

---

[e](21:17) NU reads Ιωαννου, *(son) of John.*

οὐκ ἀποθνῄσκει, ἀλλ', "Ἐὰν αὐτὸν θέλω μένειν ἕως
[3]not [1]he [2]does die, but, "If [3]him [1]I [2]want to remain till
would

ἔρχομαι, τί πρὸς σέ?"
I come, what *is that* to you?"

24 Οὗτός ἐστιν ὁ μαθητὴς ὁ μαρτυρῶν περὶ τούτων
This is the disciple the *one* testifying about these *things*
who testifies

καὶ γράψας ταῦτα· καὶ οἴδαμεν ὅτι ἀληθής ἐστιν ἡ
and having written these *things;* and we know that [4]true [3]is -
wrote

μαρτυρία αὐτοῦ.
[2]testimony [1]his.

25 Ἔστι δὲ καὶ ἄλλα πολλὰ ὅσα ἐποίησεν ὁ
[2]*there* [3]is [1]And also [2]other [3]*things* [1]many which did ~ -
are

Ἰησοῦς, ἅτινα ἐὰν γράφηται καθ' ἕν, οὐδὲ αὐτὸν
Jesus, which if they were written by one, [3]not [4]even [7]itself
one by one,

οἶμαι τὸν κόσμον χωρῆσαι τὰ γραφόμενα βιβλία.
[1]I [2]suppose [5]the [6]world to have room for the [2]being [3]written [1]books.
would which would be

Ἀμήν.
Amen.
So be it.

would not die, but, "If I will that he remain till I come, what *is that* to you?"
24 This is the disciple who testifies of these things, and wrote these things; and we know that his testimony is true.
25 And there are also many other things that Jesus did, which if they were written one by one, I suppose that even the world itself could not contain the books that would be written. Amen.

THE ACTS

of the Apostles

ΠΡΑΞΕΙΣ ΑΠΟΣΤΟΛΩΝ
***THE* ACTS OF *THE* APOSTLES**

1 The former account I made, O Theophilus, of all that Jesus began both to do and teach,
2 until the day in which He was taken up, after He through the Holy Spirit had given commandments to the apostles whom He had chosen,
3 to whom He also presented Himself alive after His suffering by many infallible proofs, being seen by them during forty days and speaking of the things pertaining to the kingdom of God.
4 And being assembled together with *them,* He commanded them not to depart from Jerusalem, but to wait for the Promise of the Father, "which," *He said,* "you have heard from Me;
5 "for John truly baptized with water, but you shall be baptized with the Holy Spirit not many days from now."
6 Therefore, when they had come together, they asked Him, saying, "Lord, will You at this time restore the kingdom to Israel?"
7 And He said to them, "It is not for you to know times or seasons which the Father has put in His own authority.

Prologue

1 **1** Τὸν μὲν πρῶτον λόγον ἐποιησάμην περὶ πάντων, ὦ
The - former account I made concerning all *things,* O

Θεόφιλε, ὧν ἤρξατο ὁ Ἰησοῦς ποιεῖν τε καὶ διδάσκειν
Theophilus, which began ˜ - Jesus [2]to [3]do [1]both and to teach

2 ἄχρι ἧς ἡμέρας, ἐντειλάμενος τοῖς ἀποστόλοις διὰ
until [3]*in* [4]which [1]*the* [2]day, having commanded [5]the [6]apostles [1]by
after He

Πνεύματος Ἁγίου οὓς ἐξελέξατο, ἀνελήφθη· **3** οἷς
[2]*the* [4]Spirit [3]Holy whom He had chosen, He was taken up; to whom

καὶ παρέστησεν ἑαυτὸν ζῶντα μετὰ τὸ παθεῖν αὐτὸν ἐν
also He presented Himself living after - to suffer Him by
alive He suffered

πολλοῖς τεκμηρίοις, δι' ἡμερῶν τεσσαράκοντα
many convincing proofs, during days ˜ forty

ὀπτανόμενος αὐτοῖς καὶ λέγων τὰ περὶ τῆς
appearing to them and speaking of the *things* concerning the

βασιλείας τοῦ Θεοῦ.
kingdom - of God.

Jesus Promises to Send the Holy Spirit

4 Καὶ συναλιζόμενος παρήγγειλεν αὐτοῖς ἀπὸ
And assembling together with *them* He commanded them [4]from
as He assembled

Ἱεροσολύμων μὴ χωρίζεσθαι, ἀλλὰ περιμένειν τὴν
[5]Jerusalem [1]not [2]to [3]withdraw, but to await the

ἐπαγγελίαν τοῦ Πατρός, "ἣν ἠκούσατέ μου· **5** ὅτι
promise of the Father, "which you heard from Me; because

Ἰωάννης μὲν ἐβάπτισεν ὕδατι, ὑμεῖς δὲ βαπτισθήσεσθε ἐν
John - baptized in water, you ˜ but will be baptized in
with with

Πνεύματι Ἁγίῳ οὐ μετὰ πολλὰς ταύτας ἡμέρας."
the Spirit ˜ Holy not after many these days."
not many days from now."

6 Οἱ μὲν οὖν συνελθόντες ἐπηρώτων αὐτὸν
- - Then having come together they were asking Him
when they came

λέγοντες, "Κύριε, εἰ ἐν τῷ χρόνῳ τούτῳ ἀποκαθιστάνεις τὴν
saying, "Lord, - at - time ˜ this are You restoring the
going to restore

βασιλείαν τῷ Ἰσραήλ?"
kingdom - to Israel?"

7 Εἶπε δὲ πρὸς αὐτούς, "Οὐχ ὑμῶν ἐστι γνῶναι
[2]He [3]said [1]But to them, "[3]not [4]of [5]you [1]It [2]is to know
for

χρόνους ἢ καιροὺς οὓς ὁ Πατὴρ ἔθετο ἐν τῇ ἰδίᾳ
times or seasons which the Father has placed in - His own

ἐξουσίᾳ. 8 Ἀλλὰ λήψεσθε δύναμιν,* ἐπελθόντος τοῦ
authority. But you will receive power, [4]having [5]come [1]the
when the Holy

Ἁγίου Πνεύματος ἐφ' ὑμᾶς, καὶ ἔσεσθέ μοι[a] μάρτυρες ἔν
[2]Holy [3]Spirit upon you, and you will be [2]to [3]Me [1]witnesses in ˜
Spirit comes

τε Ἰερουσαλὴμ καὶ ἐν πάσῃ τῇ Ἰουδαίᾳ καὶ Σαμαρείᾳ, καὶ
both Jerusalem and in all - Judea and Samaria, and

ἕως ἐσχάτου τῆς γῆς."
to *the* last *part* of the earth."
end

Jesus Ascends to Heaven
(Mark 16:19, 20; Luke 24:50–53)

9 Καὶ ταῦτα εἰπών, βλεπόντων αὐτῶν,
And these *things* having said, seeing ˜ them,
after He said these things, while they were observing,

ἐπήρθη, καὶ νεφέλη ὑπέλαβεν αὐτὸν ἀπὸ τῶν
He was carried up, and a cloud took up ˜ Him from -

ὀφθαλμῶν αὐτῶν.
eyes ˜ their.

10 Καὶ ὡς ἀτενίζοντες ἦσαν εἰς τὸν οὐρανόν,
And as [3]looking [4]intently [1]they [2]were into - heaven,

πορευομένου αὐτοῦ, καὶ ἰδοὺ ἄνδρες δύο παρειστήκεισαν
going ˜ Him, - behold men ˜ two stood alongside
while He was going,

αὐτοῖς ἐν ἐσθῆτι λευκῇ, 11 οἳ καὶ εἶπον, "Ἄνδρες Γαλιλαῖοι,
them in clothing ˜ white, who also said, "Men Galileans,

τί ἑστήκατε ἐμβλέποντες εἰς τὸν οὐρανόν? Οὗτος ὁ Ἰησοῦς
why do you stand looking up into - heaven? This - Jesus

ὁ ἀναληφθεὶς ἀφ' ὑμῶν εἰς τὸν οὐρανὸν οὕτως
the *One* being taken up from you into - heaven in this manner
who was

ἐλεύσεται ὃν τρόπον ἐθεάσασθε αὐτὸν πορευόμενον εἰς τὸν
will come which manner you beheld Him going into -
as

οὐρανόν."
heaven."

The Upper Room Prayer Meeting

12 Τότε ὑπέστρεψαν εἰς Ἰερουσαλὴμ ἀπὸ ὄρους τοῦ
Then they returned to Jerusalem from *the* mountain the *one*
which is

καλουμένου Ἐλαιῶνος, ὅ ἐστιν ἐγγὺς Ἰερουσαλήμ,
being called *the Mount* of Olives, which is near Jerusalem,
called

σαββάτου ἔχον ὁδόν. 13 Καὶ ὅτε εἰσῆλθον,
of a Sabbath having a journey. And when they entered *Jerusalem,*
being a Sabbath day's journey away.

ἀνέβησαν εἰς τὸ ὑπερῷον οὗ ἦσαν καταμένοντες, ὅ
they went up into the upper room where they were staying, -

τε Πέτρος καὶ Ἰάκωβος καὶ Ἰωάννης καὶ Ἀνδρέας, Φίλιππος
both Peter and James and John and Andrew, Philip

καὶ Θωμᾶς, Βαρθολομαῖος καὶ Ματθαῖος, Ἰάκωβος
and Thomas, Bartholomew and Matthew, James

Ἀλφαίου καὶ Σίμων ὁ Ζηλωτής, καὶ Ἰούδας
the son of Alphaeus and Simon the Zealot, and Judas

Ἰακώβου. 14 Οὗτοι πάντες ἦσαν προσκαρτεροῦντες
the son of James. These all were continuing

8 "But you shall receive power when the Holy Spirit has come upon you; and you shall be witnesses to Me in Jerusalem, and in all Judea and Samaria, and to the end of the earth."
9 Now when He had spoken these things, while they watched, He was taken up, and a cloud received Him out of their sight.
10 And while they looked steadfastly toward heaven as He went up, behold, two men stood by them in white apparel,
11 who also said, "Men of Galilee, why do you stand gazing up into heaven? This *same* Jesus, who was taken up from you into heaven, will so come in like manner as you saw Him go into heaven."
12 Then they returned to Jerusalem from the mount called Olivet, which is near Jerusalem, a Sabbath day's journey.
13 And when they had entered, they went up into the upper room where they were staying: Peter, James, John, and Andrew; Philip and Thomas; Bartholomew and Matthew; James *the son* of Alphaeus and Simon the Zealot; and Judas *the son* of James.
14 These all continued with

---

[a](1:8) NU reads μου, *my.*

*(1:8) δύναμις *(dynamis).* Noun meaning *power,* deriving from *ability* or *strength* (natural or, as here, supernatural), as compared to the synonym ἐξουσία, *power,* deriving from *authority.* δύναμις is the "power" that is associated with working miracles (as Mark 6:14), so that the word itself may mean a "work of power," a *miracle* (as Heb. 2:4). It may also identify a powerful being (as Rom. 8:38; 1 Pet. 3:22), even God (Matt. 26:64). On occasion, when referring to language, it may be translated *meaning* (1 Cor. 14:11). Cf. the cognate verb δύναμαι, *to be able.*

one accord in prayer and supplication, with the women and Mary the mother of Jesus, and with His brothers.

15 And in those days Peter stood up in the midst of the disciples (altogether the number of names was about a hundred and twenty), and said,

16 "Men *and* brethren, this Scripture had to be fulfilled, which the Holy Spirit spoke before by the mouth of David concerning Judas, who became a guide to those who arrested Jesus;

17 "for he was numbered with us and obtained a part in this ministry."

18 (Now this man purchased a field with the wages of iniquity; and falling headlong, he burst open in the middle and all his entrails gushed out.

19 And it became known to all those dwelling in Jerusalem; so that field is called in their own language, Akel Dama, that is, Field of Blood.)

20 "For it is written in the Book of Psalms:

> *'Let his dwelling place be desolate,*
> *And let no one live in it';*

and,

> *'Let another take his office.'*

21 "Therefore, of these men who have accompanied us all the time that the Lord Jesus went in and out among us,

22 "beginning from the bap-

---

[b](**1:14**) NU omits *και τη δεησει, and petition.* [c](**1:15**) NU reads *αδελφων, brothers.* [d](**1:16**) NU omits *ταυτην, this,* thus *the Scripture.* [e](**1:20**) Ps. 69:25 [f](**1:20**) Ps. 109:8

***(1:20)** *ἐπισκοπή (episkopē).* Noun from the preposition *ἐπί, over,* and the noun *σκοπή, a watchtower,* thus used for the office of an *overseer.* Whether Judas's *ἐπισκοπή* here in 1:20 was apostleship or bishopric is disputed. Scholars hesitate to deduce a close relationship between apostles and bishops (cf. 1 Tim. 3:1). The other NT occurrences are unrelated to church office. *ἐπισκοπή* may also refer to a *visitation,* which involves demonstrations of divine power, either

---

ὁμοθυμαδὸν τῇ προσευχῇ καὶ τῇ δεήσει,[b] σὺν γυναιξὶ
with one mind - in prayer and - petition, together with *the* women

καὶ Μαρίᾳ τῇ μητρὶ τοῦ Ἰησοῦ, καὶ σὺν τοῖς ἀδελφοῖς αὐτοῦ.
and Mary the mother - of Jesus, and with - bothers ˜ His.

Matthias Chosen as the Twelfth Apostle

15 Καὶ ἐν ταῖς ἡμέραις ταύταις ἀναστὰς Πέτρος ἐν μέσῳ
And in - days ˜ these rising ˜ Peter in *the* midst
stood up

τῶν μαθητῶν[c] εἶπεν (ἦν τε ὄχλος ὀνομάτων ἐπὶ
of the disciples said (was and a congregation of names upon
and said (and the number of persons

τὸ αὐτὸ ὡς ἑκατὸν εἴκοσιν), **16** "Ἄνδρες ἀδελφοί,
the same as a hundred *and* twenty), "Men brothers,
assembled was about

ἔδει πληρωθῆναι τὴν Γραφὴν ταύτην[d] ἣν
it was necessary *for* ³to ⁴be ⁵fulfilled - ²Scripture ¹this which

προεῖπε τὸ Πνεῦμα τὸ Ἅγιον διὰ στόματος Δαβὶδ περὶ
⁴spoke ⁵before ¹the ³Spirit - ²Holy by *the* mouth of David about

Ἰούδα τοῦ γενομένου ὁδηγοῦ τοῖς συλλαβοῦσι τὸν
Judas the *one* having become a guide to the *ones* arresting -
who became those who arrested

Ἰησοῦν, **17** ὅτι κατηριθμημένος ἦν σὺν ἡμῖν καὶ
Jesus, because ³numbered ¹he ²was with us and
had been

ἔλαχεν τὸν κλῆρον τῆς διακονίας ταύτης." **18** (Οὗτος μὲν οὖν
obtained the portion - of ministry ˜ this." (This *one* - then
his

ἐκτήσατο χωρίον ἐκ μισθοῦ τῆς ἀδικίας, καὶ
purchased a field by means of *the* wages - of *his* unrighteousness, and

πρηνὴς γενόμενος ἐλάκησε μέσος, καὶ ἐξεχύθη
headfirst becoming he burst open in the middle, and ⁴were ⁵spilled ⁶out
falling headlong

πάντα τὰ σπλάγχνα αὐτοῦ. **19** Καὶ γνωστὸν ἐγένετο πᾶσι
¹all - ³entrails ²his. And ³known ¹it ²became to all

τοῖς κατοικοῦσιν Ἰερουσαλήμ, ὥστε κληθῆναι τὸ χωρίον
the *ones* dwelling *in* Jerusalem, so that ³to ⁴be ⁵called - ²field
is

ἐκεῖνο τῇ ἰδίᾳ διαλέκτῳ αὐτῶν Ἀκελδαμά, τοῦτ' ἔστι,
¹that - in ²own ³language ¹their Akel Dama, this is,
that

Χωρίον Αἵματος.) **20** "Γέγραπται γὰρ ἐν Βίβλῳ Ψαλμῶν,
Field of Blood.) "²it ³is ⁴written ¹For in *the* Book of Psalms,

«Γενηθήτω ἡ ἔπαυλις αὐτοῦ ἔρημος,
«Let ³become - ²residence ¹his deserted,

Καὶ μὴ ἔστω ὁ κατοικῶν ἐν αὐτῇ,»[e]
And ²not ¹let ⁵be ³the ⁴*one* dwelling in it,»
let no one dwell

καί,
and,

«Τὴν ἐπισκοπὴν* αὐτοῦ λάβοι ἕτερος.»[f]
- «⁵office ⁶of ⁷overseer ⁴his ¹May ³take ²another.»

21 Δεῖ οὖν τῶν συνελθόντων ἡμῖν ἀνδρῶν
²it ³is ⁴necessary ¹Therefore of the ²having ³gone ⁴with ⁵us ¹men
who accompanied

ἐν παντὶ χρόνῳ ἐν ᾧ εἰσῆλθε καὶ ἐξῆλθεν ἐφ' ἡμᾶς ὁ
in every time in which ⁴came ⁵in ⁶and ⁷went ⁸out ⁹among ¹⁰us ¹the

Κύριος Ἰησοῦς, **22** ἀρξάμενος ἀπὸ τοῦ βαπτίσματος Ἰωάννου
²Lord ³Jesus, beginning from the baptism of John

ἕως τῆς ἡμέρας ἧς ἀνελήφθη ἀφ' ἡμῶν, μάρτυρα τῆς
until the day of which He was taken up from us, [7]a [8]witness -
in

ἀναστάσεως αὐτοῦ γενέσθαι σὺν ἡμῖν ἕνα τούτων."
[11]of [13]resurrection [12]His [5]to [6]become [9]with [10]us [1]*for* [2]one [3]of [4]these."

23 Καὶ ἔστησαν δύο, Ἰωσὴφ τὸν καλούμενον
And they put forward two, Joseph the *one* being called
who is

Βαρσαβᾶν, ὃς ἐπεκλήθη Ἰοῦστος, καὶ Ματθίαν.
Barsabas, who was called Justus, and Matthias.
surnamed

24 Καὶ προσευξάμενοι εἶπον, "Σὺ Κύριε, καρδιογνῶστα
And having prayed they said, "You Lord, knower of the hearts
they prayed and

πάντων, ἀνάδειξον ὃν ἐξελέξω ἐκ τούτων τῶν δύο
of all, make manifest [6]whom [7]You [8]chose [3]of [4]these - [5]two
have chosen

ἕνα **25** λαβεῖν τὸν κλῆρον[g] τῆς διακονίας ταύτης καὶ
[1]*the* [2]one to receive the portion - of ministry ˜ this and

ἀποστολῆς, ἐξ ἧς παρέβη Ἰούδας πορευθῆναι εἰς τὸν
apostleship, from which [2]turned [3]aside [1]Judas to go to -

τόπον τὸν ἴδιον." **26** Καὶ ἔδωκαν κλήρους αὐτῶν,[h] καὶ
[3]place - [1]his [2]own." And they gave lots ˜ their, and
cast

ἔπεσεν ὁ κλῆρος ἐπὶ Ματθίαν, καὶ συγκατεψηφίσθη μετὰ
[3]fell [1]the [2]lot on Matthias, and he was added together with

τῶν ἕνδεκα ἀποστόλων.
the eleven apostles.

The Holy Spirit Comes at Pentecost

2 **1** Καὶ ἐν τῷ συμπληροῦσθαι τὴν ἡμέραν τῆς
And in - [5]to [6]be [7]fulfilled [1]the [2]Day -
when had come

Πεντηκοστῆς, ἦσαν ἅπαντες ὁμοθυμαδὸν[a] ἐπὶ τὸ αὐτό.
[3]of [4]Pentecost, they were all of one mind upon the same.
together.

2 Καὶ ἐγένετο ἄφνω ἐκ τοῦ οὐρανοῦ ἦχος ὥσπερ
And *there* was suddenly from - heaven a sound as

φερομένης πνοῆς βιαίας, καὶ ἐπλήρωσεν ὅλον τὸν
[5]being [6]borne [7]along [1]of [2]a [4]wind [3]violent, and it filled all the
of a rushing strong wind,

οἶκον οὗ ἦσαν καθήμενοι. **3** Καὶ ὤφθησαν αὐτοῖς
house where they were sitting. And *there* appeared to them

διαμεριζόμεναι γλῶσσαι ὡσεὶ πυρός, ἐκάθισέ τε ἐφ' ἕνα
[5]being [6]divided [1]tongues [2]as [3]of [4]fire, [8]it [9]sat [7]and on one ˜
distributed

ἕκαστον αὐτῶν. **4** Καὶ ἐπλήσθησαν ἅπαντες Πνεύματος
each of them. And they were filled ˜ all of *the* Spirit ˜
with

Ἁγίου, καὶ ἤρξαντο λαλεῖν ἑτέραις γλώσσαις καθὼς τὸ
Holy, and they began to speak with other tongues just as the
different languages

Πνεῦμα ἐδίδου αὐτοῖς ἀποφθέγγεσθαι.
Spirit was giving to them to speak out.
them utterance.

The Crowds at Pentecost Respond

5 Ἦσαν δὲ ἐν Ἰερουσαλὴμ κατοικοῦντες Ἰουδαῖοι,
[2]*there* [3]were [1]Now [5]in [6]Jerusalem [4]dwelling Jews,

---

tism of John to that day when He was taken up from us, one of these must become a witness with us of His resurrection."

23 And they proposed two: Joseph called Barsabas, who was surnamed Justus, and Matthias.

24 And they prayed and said, "You, O Lord, who know the hearts of all, show which of these two You have chosen

25 "to take part in this ministry and apostleship from which Judas by transgression fell, that he might go to his own place."

26 And they cast their lots, and the lot fell on Matthias. And he was numbered with the eleven apostles.

2 When the Day of Pentecost had fully come, they were all with one accord in one place.

2 And suddenly there came a sound from heaven, as of a rushing mighty wind, and it filled the whole house where they were sitting.

3 Then there appeared to them divided tongues, as of fire, and *one* sat upon each of them.

4 And they were all filled with the Holy Spirit and began to speak with other tongues, as the Spirit gave them utterance.

5 And there were dwelling in Jerusalem Jews, devout men,

---

[g](**1:25**) NU reads τοπον, *(the) place.*
[h](**1:26**) NU reads αυτοις, *for them.* [a](**2:1**) NU reads ομου, *together.*

in mercy (Luke 19:44) or possibly in judgment (1 Pet. 2:12).

from every nation under heaven.
6 And when this sound occurred, the multitude came together, and were confused, because everyone heard them speak in his own language.
7 Then they were all amazed and marveled, saying to one another, "Look, are not all these who speak Galileans?
8 "And how *is it that* we hear, each in our own language in which we were born?
9 "Parthians and Medes and Elamites, those dwelling in Mesopotamia, Judea and Cappadocia, Pontus and Asia,
10 "Phrygia and Pamphylia, Egypt and the parts of Libya adjoining Cyrene, visitors from Rome, both Jews and proselytes,
11 "Cretans and Arabs—we hear them speaking in our own tongues the wonderful works of God."
12 So they were all amazed and perplexed, saying to one another, "Whatever could this mean?"
13 Others mocking said, "They are full of new wine."
14 But Peter, standing up with the eleven, raised his voice and said to them, "Men of Judea and all who dwell in Jerusalem, let this be known to you, and heed my words.
15 "For these are not drunk,

ἄνδρες εὐλαβεῖς ἀπὸ παντὸς ἔθνους τῶν ὑπὸ τὸν
men ~ devout from every nation of the *ones* under -
those

οὐρανόν. 6 Γενομένης δὲ τῆς φωνῆς ταύτης, συνῆλθε τὸ
heaven. [4]taking [5]place [1]And - [3]sound [2]this, [8]came [9]together [6]the
And when this sound occurred,

πλῆθος καὶ συνεχύθη, ὅτι ἤκουον εἷς ἕκαστος
[7]multitude and was confounded, because they were [3]hearing [2]one [1]each

τῇ ἰδίᾳ διαλέκτῳ λαλούντων αὐτῶν. 7 Ἐξίσταντο
- [6]in [7]his [8]own [9]language [5]speaking [4]them. [2]they [3]were [4]amazed

δὲ καὶ ἐθαύμαζον, λέγοντες πρὸς ἀλλήλους,[b] "Οὐχ ἰδοὺ
[1]And and were marveling, saying to one another, "[3]not [1]Behold

πάντες οὗτοί εἰσιν οἱ λαλοῦντες Γαλιλαῖοι? 8 Καὶ
[4]all [5]these [2]are the *ones* speaking Galileans? And
who are

πῶς ἡμεῖς ἀκούομεν ἕκαστος τῇ ἰδίᾳ διαλέκτῳ ἡμῶν
how *is it that* we hear ~ each - in [2]own [3]language [1]our

ἐν ᾗ ἐγεννήθημεν? 9 Πάρθοι καὶ Μῆδοι καὶ Ἐλαμῖται, καὶ
in which we were born? Parthians and Medes and Elamites, and

οἱ κατοικοῦντες τὴν Μεσοποταμίαν, Ἰουδαίαν τε καὶ
the *ones* dwelling - *in* Mesopotamia, Judea and

Καππαδοκίαν, Πόντον καὶ τὴν Ἀσίαν, 10 Φρυγίαν τε καὶ
Cappadocia, Pontus and - Asia, Phrygia and

Παμφυλίαν, Αἴγυπτον καὶ τὰ μέρη τῆς Λιβύης τῆς κατὰ
Pamphylia, Egypt and the parts - of Libya the *one* toward
which is

Κυρήνην, καὶ οἱ ἐπιδημοῦντες Ῥωμαῖοι, Ἰουδαῖοί τε καὶ
Cyrene, and the visiting Romans, Jews ~ both and
visitors from Rome,

προσήλυτοι, 11 Κρῆτες καὶ Ἄραβες, ἀκούομεν λαλούντων
proselytes, Cretans and Arabians, we hear speaking ~

αὐτῶν ταῖς ἡμετέραις γλώσσαις τὰ μεγαλεῖα* τοῦ Θεοῦ."
them - in our tongues the mighty *deeds* - of God."
languages

12 Ἐξίσταντο δὲ πάντες καὶ διηπόρουν, ἄλλος πρὸς
[2]they [3]were [5]amazed [1]And [4]all and were perplexed, [2]other [3]to
one

ἄλλον λέγοντες, "Τί ἂν θέλοι τοῦτο εἶναι?"
[4]other [1]saying, "What - would this to be?"
another might this mean?"

13 Ἕτεροι δὲ χλευάζοντες ἔλεγον ὅτι "Γλεύκους
others ~ But mocking were saying - "[4]of [5]sweet [6]wine
were mocking and saying, "They are

μεμεστωμένοι εἰσί."
[3]filled [1]They [2]are."
full of new wine."

Peter Preaches at Pentecost

14 Σταθεὶς δὲ Πέτρος σὺν τοῖς ἕνδεκα, ἐπῆρε τὴν φωνὴν
[3]standing [1]But [2]Peter with the eleven, lifted up - voice ~
standing up

αὐτοῦ καὶ ἀπεφθέγξατο αὐτοῖς, "Ἄνδρες Ἰουδαῖοι καὶ οἱ
his and spoke out to them, "Men Jews and [2]the [3]*ones*
who

κατοικοῦντες Ἱερουσαλὴμ ἅπαντες, τοῦτο ὑμῖν γνωστὸν
[4]dwelling [5]of [6]Jerusalem [1]all, [8]this [11]to [12]you [10]known
dwell in

ἔστω καὶ ἐνωτίσασθε τὰ ῥήματά μου. 15 Οὐ γάρ, ὡς ὑμεῖς
[7]let [9]be and give ear to - words ~ my. [4]not [1]For, [6]as [7]you

[b](2:7) NU omits προς αλληλους, *to one another.*

*(2:11) μεγαλεῖος (*megaleios*). Adjective meaning *magnificent, grand, mighty.* The substantival plural used here apparently means "the mighty deeds," although some interpreters suggest "the great and good deeds" (cf. Luke 1:49) or "the praises" (cf. the use of μεγαλύνω, *praise, glorify,* in Luke 1:47). See the cognate noun μεγαλειότης, *majesty, magnificence,* at Luke 9:43; and the cognate verb μεγαλύνω, *magnify,* at Phil. 1:20.

ὑπολαμβάνετε, οὗτοι μεθύουσιν, ἔστι γὰρ ὥρα τρίτη
[8]suppose, [2]these [3]are [5]drunk, [10]it [11]is [9]for *just the* hour ˜ third

τῆς ἡμέρας. 16 Ἀλλὰ τοῦτό ἐστι τὸ εἰρημένον διὰ
of the day. But this is the *thing* having been spoken by
what was

τοῦ προφήτου Ἰωήλ,
the prophet Joel,

17 «Καὶ ἔσται ἐν ταῖς ἐσχάταις ἡμέραις, λέγει ὁ Θεός,
«And it shall be in the last days, says - God, *that*

Ἐκχεῶ ἀπὸ τοῦ Πνεύματός μου ἐπὶ πᾶσαν σάρκα,
I will pour out from - Spirit ˜ My upon all flesh,

Καὶ προφητεύσουσιν οἱ υἱοὶ ὑμῶν καὶ αἱ θυγατέρες
And [6]shall [7]prophesy - [2]sons [1]your [3]and - [5]daughters

ὑμῶν,
[4]your,

Καὶ οἱ νεανίσκοι ὑμῶν ὁράσεις ὄψονται,
And - [2]young [3]men [1]your [6]visions [4]shall [5]see,

Καὶ οἱ πρεσβύτεροι ὑμῶν ἐνυπνίῳ ἐνυπνιασθήσονται·
And - [2]old [3]men [1]your [6]a [7]dream [4]shall [5]dream;

18 Καί γε ἐπὶ τοὺς δούλους μου καὶ ἐπὶ τὰς δούλας
And - on - [2]male [3]slaves [1]My and on - [2]female [3]slaves
servants servants

μου
[1]My

Ἐν ταῖς ἡμέραις ἐκείναις ἐκχεῶ ἀπὸ τοῦ Πνεύματός
In - days ˜ those I will pour out from - Spirit ˜

μου,
My,

Καὶ προφητεύσουσι.
And they shall prophesy.

19 Καὶ δώσω τέρατα* ἐν τῷ οὐρανῷ ἄνω
And I will give wonders in - heaven above
show

Καὶ σημεῖα ἐπὶ τῆς γῆς κάτω,
And signs on the earth below,

Αἷμα καὶ πῦρ καὶ ἀτμίδα καπνοῦ·
Blood and fire and vapor of smoke;

20 Ὁ ἥλιος μεταστραφήσεται εἰς σκότος
The sun shall be changed into darkness

Καὶ ἡ σελήνη εἰς αἷμα
And the moon into blood

Πρὶν ἢ ἐλθεῖν τὴν ἡμέραν Κυρίου τὴν μεγάλην καὶ
Before [9]to [10]come [1]the [5]day [6]of [7]*the* [8]Lord - [2]great [3]and
comes

ἐπιφανῆ.
[4]glorious.

21 Καὶ ἔσται, πᾶς ὃς ἂν ἐπικαλέσηται τὸ ὄνομα
And it shall be, *that* every*one* who - calls on the name

Κυρίου σωθήσεται.»[c]
of *the* Lord shall be saved.»

22 "Ἄνδρες Ἰσραηλῖται, ἀκούσατε τοὺς λόγους τούτους·
"Men Israelites, hear - words ˜ these;
of Israel,

Ἰησοῦν τὸν Ναζωραῖον, ἄνδρα ἀπὸ τοῦ Θεοῦ
Jesus the Nazarene, a man [4]by - [5]God

ἀποδεδειγμένον εἰς ὑμᾶς δυνάμεσι καὶ τέρασι καὶ σημείοις
[1]having [2]been [3]attested to you by miracles and wonders and signs
who was

as you suppose, since it is *only* the third hour of the day.
16 "But this is what was spoken by the prophet Joel:

17 *'And it shall come to pass*
in the last days, says God,
That I will pour out of My Spirit on all flesh;
Your sons and your daughters shall prophesy,
Your young men shall see visions,
Your old men shall dream dreams.
18 *And on My menservants and on My maidservants*
I will pour out My Spirit in those days;
And they shall prophesy.
19 *I will show wonders in heaven above*
And signs in the earth beneath:
Blood and fire and vapor of smoke.
20 *The sun shall be turned into darkness,*
And the moon into blood,
Before the coming of the great and awesome day of the Lord.
21 *And it shall come to pass*
That whoever calls on the name of the Lord
Shall be saved.'

22 "Men of Israel, hear these words: Jesus of Nazareth, a Man attested by God to you by miracles, wonders, and signs

[c](**2:17–21**) Joel 2:28–32

(2:19) τέρας *(teras).* Noun meaning *wonder,* often used alongside σημεῖον, *sign,* (as here) and/or δύναμις, *miracle,* referring especially to the mighty works of Jesus or the apostles (see also Heb. 2:4; 2 Cor. 12:12). Whereas δύναμις views a miracle as a manifestation of power and σημεῖον as a pointer with significance, the term τέρας emphasizes the function of producing wonder or a sense of portent, perhaps even fear. See σημεῖον at John 6:26.

which God did through Him in your midst, as you yourselves also know—
23 "Him, being delivered by the determined purpose and foreknowledge of God, you have taken by lawless hands, have crucified, and put to death;
24 "whom God raised up, having loosed the pains of death, because it was not possible that He should be held by it.
25 "For David says concerning Him:

'I foresaw the LORD *always before my face,*
For He is at my right hand, that I may not be shaken.
26 *Therefore my heart rejoiced, and my tongue was glad;*
Moreover my flesh also will rest in hope.
27 *For You will not leave my soul in Hades,*
Nor will You allow Your Holy One to see corruption.
28 *You have made known to me the ways of life;*
You will make me full of joy in Your presence.'

29 "Men *and* brethren, let *me* speak freely to you of the patriarch David, that he is both dead and buried, and his tomb is with us to this day.
30 "Therefore, being a prophet, and knowing that God had sworn with an oath to him that of the fruit of his body, according to the flesh, He would raise up the Christ to sit on his throne,
31 "he, foreseeing this, spoke concerning the resurrection of the Christ, that His soul was

οἷς ἐποίησε δι᾽ αὐτοῦ ὁ Θεὸς ἐν μέσῳ ὑμῶν, καθὼς καὶ
which [2]performed [3]by [4]Him - [1]God in midst ˜ your, just as [3]also
αὐτοὶ οἴδατε, **23** τοῦτον τῇ ὡρισμένῃ
[2]yourselves [1]you know, this *One* [3]by [4]the [6]having [7]been [8]determined
defined
βουλῇ καὶ προγνώσει τοῦ Θεοῦ ἔκδοτον λαβόντες,[d]
[5]purpose [9]and [10]foreknowledge - [11]of [12]God [1]delivered [2]up taking,
purpose you took and,
διὰ χειρῶν ἀνόμων προσπήξαντες ἀνείλατε· **24** ὃν ὁ
by hands ˜ lawless nailing *Him* to *a cross* you killed *Him;* whom -
Θεὸς ἀνέστησε λύσας τὰς ὠδῖνας τοῦ θανάτου,
God raised *thus* doing away with the labor pains - of death,
καθότι οὐκ ἦν δυνατὸν κρατεῖσθαι αὐτὸν ὑπ᾽ αὐτοῦ.
because [3]not [1]it [2]was possible [3]to [4]be [5]held [1]*for* [2]Him by it.
25 Δαβὶδ γὰρ λέγει εἰς αὐτόν,
David ˜ For says in reference to Him,
«Προωρώμην τὸν Κύριον ἐνώπιόν μου διὰ παντός,
«I saw the Lord before me through all,
always,
Ὅτι ἐκ δεξιῶν μού ἐστιν ἵνα μὴ σαλευθῶ.
Because [3]at [5]right [6]*parts* [4]my [1]He [2]is that [3]not [1]I [2]may be shaken.
on right side
26 Διὰ τοῦτο εὐφράνθη ἡ καρδία μου
Because of this [3]was [4]glad - [2]heart [1]my
Therefore
Καὶ ἠγαλλιάσατο ἡ γλῶσσά μου,
And [3]rejoiced - [2]tongue [1]my,
Ἔτι δὲ καὶ ἡ σάρξ μου κατασκηνώσει ἐπ᾽ ἐλπίδι·
yet ˜ And [3]also - [2]flesh [1]my will dwell in hope;
27 Ὅτι οὐκ ἐγκαταλείψεις τὴν ψυχήν μου εἰς Ἅιδου,
Because [3]not [1]You [2]will abandon - soul ˜ my in Hades,
Οὐδὲ δώσεις τὸν Ὅσιόν σου ἰδεῖν διαφθοράν.
Nor will you give - [2]Holy [3]One [1]Your to see corruption.
allow
28 Ἐγνώρισάς μοι ὁδοὺς ζωῆς,
You have made known to me *the* ways of life,
Πληρώσεις με εὐφροσύνης μετὰ τοῦ προσώπου σου.»[e]
You will fill me of gladness with - face ˜ Your.»
with presence
29 "Ἄνδρες ἀδελφοί, ἐξὸν εἰπεῖν μετὰ
"Men brothers, it is permitted *to me* to speak with
παρρησίας πρὸς ὑμᾶς περὶ τοῦ πατριάρχου Δαβίδ, ὅτι καὶ
boldness to you about the patriarch David, that both ˜
ἐτελεύτησε καὶ ἐτάφη, καὶ τὸ μνῆμα αὐτοῦ ἐστιν ἐν ἡμῖν
he died and was buried, and - tomb ˜ his is with us
ἄχρι τῆς ἡμέρας ταύτης. **30** Προφήτης οὖν ὑπάρχων, καὶ
until - day ˜ this. [3]a [4]prophet [1]Therefore [2]being, and
εἰδὼς ὅτι ὅρκῳ ὤμοσεν αὐτῷ ὁ Θεὸς ἐκ καρποῦ τῆς
knowing that with an oath [2]swore [3]to [4]him - [1]God of *the* fruit -
had sworn
ὀσφύος αὐτοῦ, τὸ κατὰ σάρκα, ἀναστήσειν τὸν Χριστὸν[f]
of loins ˜ his, - according to *the* flesh, to raise up the Christ
Messiah
καθίσαι ἐπὶ τοῦ θρόνου αὐτοῦ, **31** προϊδὼν ἐλάλησε περὶ
to seat *Him* on - throne ˜ his, foreseeing *this* he spoke about
τῆς ἀναστάσεως* τοῦ Χριστοῦ ὅτι
the resurrection of the Christ that
Messiah

---

d(**2:23**) NU omits λαβοντες, *taking.*
e(**2:25–28**) Ps. 16:8–11
f(**2:30**) NU omits το κατα σαρκα, αναστησειν τον Χριστον, *according to (the) flesh, to raise up the Messiah.*

***(2:31)** ἀνάστασις *(anastasis).* Noun from the preposition ἀνά, *up,* and the noun στάσις, *a standing,* thus literally meaning a *rise* (Luke 2:34). Most often in the NT it refers to a *resurrection* from the dead, especially of Jesus (as here in Acts 2:31) and of Christians (as 1 Cor. 15:21). Cf. the cognate verb ἀνίστημι, *raise up* (as Acts 9:41), *stand up, arise* either

«Οὐ κατελείφθη ἡ ψυχὴ αὐτοῦ[g] εἰς ῞Αιδου,
«[4]not [3]was [5]left - [2]soul [1]His in Hades,

Οὐδὲ ἡ σὰρξ αὐτοῦ εἶδε διαφθοράν.»[h]
Nor - [3]flesh [2]His [1]did see corruption.»

32 Τοῦτον τὸν Ἰησοῦν ἀνέστησεν ὁ Θεός, οὗ πάντες ἡμεῖς
This - Jesus raised ˜ - God, of which all ˜ we

ἐσμεν μάρτυρες. 33 Τῇ δεξιᾷ οὖν τοῦ Θεοῦ
are witnesses. [5]to [6]the [7]right [8]*hand* [1]Therefore - [9]of [10]God

ὑψωθείς, τήν τε ἐπαγγελίαν τοῦ Ἁγίου
[2]having [3]being [4]exalted, [14]the [11]and [15]promise [16]of [17]the [18]Holy

Πνεύματος λαβὼν παρὰ τοῦ Πατρός, ἐξέχεε τοῦτο
[19]Spirit [12]having [13]received from the Father, He poured out this

ὃ νῦν[i] ὑμεῖς βλέπετε καὶ ἀκούετε. 34 Οὐ γὰρ Δαβὶδ
which now ˜ you see and hear. [4]not [1]For [2]David

ἀνέβη εἰς τοὺς οὐρανούς, λέγει δὲ αὐτός,
[3]did ascend into the heavens, [2]he [4]says [1]but [3]himself,

«Εἶπεν ὁ Κύριος τῷ Κυρίῳ μου,
«[3]said [1]The [2]Lord - to Lord ˜ my,

‘Κάθου ἐκ δεξιῶν μου
‘Sit at [2]right [3]*parts* [1]My
hand

35 Ἕως ἂν θῶ τοὺς ἐχθρούς σου ὑποπόδιον τῶν ποδῶν
Till - I put - enemies ˜ Your *as* a footstool - of feet ˜
for

σου.’»[j]
Your.’»

36 Ἀσφαλῶς οὖν γινωσκέτω πᾶς οἶκος Ἰσραὴλ ὅτι
[9]assuredly [1]Therefore [2]let [8]know [3]all [4]*the* [5]house [6]of [7]Israel that

καὶ Κύριον καὶ Χριστὸν αὐτὸν ὁ Θεὸς ἐποίησε τοῦτον τὸν
[4]both [5]Lord [6]and [7]Christ [3]Him - [1]God [2]made this -
Messiah

Ἰησοῦν ὃν ὑμεῖς ἐσταυρώσατε."
Jesus whom you crucified."

Peter Concludes His Appeal

37 Ἀκούσαντες δὲ κατενύγησαν τῇ καρδίᾳ, εἶπόν
[2]hearing [3]*this* [1]Now they were cut in the heart, [2]they [3]said
when they heard to

τε πρὸς τὸν Πέτρον καὶ τοὺς λοιποὺς ἀποστόλους, "Τί
[1]and to - Peter and the remaining apostles, "What
rest of the

ποιήσωμεν,[k] ἄνδρες ἀδελφοί?"
shall we do, men *and* brothers?"

38 Πέτρος δὲ ἔφη πρὸς αὐτούς, "Μετανοήσατε καὶ
Peter ˜ And said to them, "Repent and

βαπτισθήτω ἕκαστος ὑμῶν ἐπὶ τῷ ὀνόματι Ἰησοῦ Χριστοῦ
let [4]be [5]baptized [1]each [2]of [3]you in the name of Jesus Christ

εἰς ἄφεσιν ἁμαρτιῶν,[l] καὶ λήψεσθε τὴν δωρεὰν τοῦ
for *the* forgiveness of sins, and you will receive the gift of the

Ἁγίου Πνεύματος. 39 Ὑμῖν γάρ ἐστιν ἡ ἐπαγγελία καὶ
Holy Spirit. [5]for [6]you [1]For [4]is [2]the [3]promise and

τοῖς τέκνοις ὑμῶν, καὶ πᾶσι τοῖς εἰς μακράν, ὅσους
- for children ˜ your, and for all the *ones* to far away, as many as
afar off,

ἂν προσκαλέσηται Κύριος ὁ Θεὸς ἡμῶν." 40 Ἑτέροις τε
- [5]will [6]call [1]*the* [2]Lord - [4]God [3]our." [4]other [1]And

λόγοις πλείοσι διεμαρτύρετο καὶ παρεκάλει λέγων, "Σώθητε
[5]words [2]with [3]many he testified and exhorted *them* saying, "Be saved

not left in Hades, nor did His
flesh see corruption.
32 "This Jesus God has raised
up, of which we are all witnesses.
33 "Therefore being exalted
to the right hand of God, and
having received from the Father the promise of the Holy
Spirit, He poured out this which
you now see and hear.
34 "For David did not ascend
into the heavens, but he says
himself:

*'The LORD said to my
Lord,
"Sit at My right hand,*
35 *Till I make Your enemies
Your footstool." '*

36 "Therefore let all the
house of Israel know assuredly
that God has made this Jesus,
whom you crucified, both Lord
and Christ."
37 Now when they heard *this,*
they were cut to the heart, and
said to Peter and the rest of the
apostles, "Men *and* brethren,
what shall we do?"
38 Then Peter said to them,
"Repent, and let every one of
you be baptized in the name of
Jesus Christ for the remission
of sins; and you shall receive
the gift of the Holy Spirit.
39 "For the promise is to you
and to your children, and to all
who are afar off, as many as the
Lord our God will call."
40 And with many other
words he testified and exhorted
them, saying, "Be saved from

---

[g]**(2:31)** NU omits η ψυχη αυτου, *His soul.*
[h]**(2:31)** Ps. 16:10
[i]**(2:33)** NU omits νυν, *now.*
[j]**(2:34, 35)** Ps. 110:1
[k]**(2:37)** TR reads ποιησομεν, *(What) will we do?*
[l]**(2:38)** NU adds υμων, *your.*

literally (as Matt. 26:62) or figuratively from the dead (as Eph. 5:14), or to rise *to take office* (as Acts 7:18), or to rise against *to oppose* (as Mark 3:26).

this perverse generation."
41 Then those who gladly received his word were baptized;
and that day about three thousand souls were added *to them.*
42 And they continued steadfastly in the apostles' doctrine
and fellowship, in the breaking
of bread, and in prayers.
43 Then fear came upon every
soul, and many wonders and
signs were done through the
apostles.
44 Now all who believed were
together, and had all things in
common,
45 and sold their possessions
and goods, and divided them
among all, as anyone had need.
46 So continuing daily with
one accord in the temple, and
breaking bread from house to
house, they ate their food with
gladness and simplicity of heart,
47 praising God and having favor with all the people. And the
Lord added to the church daily
those who were being saved.
3 Now Peter and John went
up together to the temple
at the hour of prayer, the ninth
hour.
2 And a certain man lame
from his mother's womb was
carried, whom they laid daily at

ἀπὸ τῆς γενεᾶς τῆς σκολιᾶς ταύτης."
from - [3]generation - [2]crooked [1]this."

A Vital Church Grows in Numbers

41 Οἱ μὲν οὖν ἀσμένως[m] ἀποδεξάμενοι τὸν λόγον
[2]the [3]*ones* - [1]Then gladly receiving - word ˜
those who received

αὐτοῦ ἐβαπτίσθησαν, καὶ προσετέθησαν τῇ ἡμέρᾳ ἐκείνῃ
his were baptized, and [5]were [6]added - [7]on [9]day [8]that

ψυχαὶ ὡσεὶ τρισχίλιαι. **42** Ἦσαν δὲ προσκαρτεροῦντες
[4]souls [1]about [2]three [3]thousand. [2]they [3]were [1]And continuing
persons

τῇ διδαχῇ τῶν ἀποστόλων καὶ τῇ κοινωνίᾳ,* καὶ τῇ
in the teaching of the apostles and - in fellowship, and in the

κλάσει τοῦ ἄρτου καὶ ταῖς προσευχαῖς.
breaking of the bread and - in prayers.

43 Ἐγένετο δὲ πάσῃ ψυχῇ φόβος, πολλά τε τέρατα
[3]came [4]to [5]be [1]And [6]in [7]every [8]soul [2]fear, many ˜ and wonders
person

καὶ σημεῖα διὰ τῶν ἀποστόλων ἐγίνετο. **44** Πάντες
and signs [4]by [5]the [6]apostles [1]were [2]taking [3]place. all ˜

δὲ οἱ πιστεύοντες ἦσαν ἐπὶ τὸ αὐτὸ καὶ εἶχον
And the *ones* believing were upon the same and they had
together

ἅπαντα κοινά, **45** καὶ τὰ κτήματα καὶ τὰς ὑπάρξεις
all *things* *in* common, and - *their* possessions and - belongings

ἐπίπρασκον καὶ διεμέριζον αὐτὰ πᾶσι καθότι ἄν
they were selling and were dividing them to all to the degree that -
would sell distribute

τις χρείαν εἶχε. **46** Καθ' ἡμέραν τε
anyone [2]a [3]need [1]had. [2]according [3]to [4]a [5]day [1]And
daily

προσκαρτεροῦντες ὁμοθυμαδὸν ἐν τῷ ἱερῷ, κλῶντές τε
continuing with one mind in the temple, breaking ˜ and

κατ' οἶκον ἄρτον, μετελάμβανον τροφῆς ἐν
[2]according [3]to [4]a [5]house [1]bread, they were sharing food with
from house to house

ἀγαλλιάσει καὶ ἀφελότητι καρδίας, **47** αἰνοῦντες τὸν Θεὸν καὶ
joy and simplicity of heart, praising - God and
generosity

ἔχοντες χάριν πρὸς ὅλον τὸν λαόν. Ὁ δὲ Κύριος προσετίθει
having favor with all the people. the ˜ And Lord was adding

τοὺς σῳζομένους καθ' ἡμέραν τῇ
[8]the [9]*ones* [10]being [11]saved [1]according [2]to [3]a [4]day [5]to [6]the
those who were daily

ἐκκλησίᾳ.[n]
[7]church.

Peter and John Heal a Lame Man

3 **1** Ἐπὶ τὸ αὐτὸ δὲ Πέτρος καὶ Ἰωάννης ἀνέβαινον
[8]upon [9]the [10]same [1]And [2]Peter [3]and [4]John [5]were [6]going [7]up
together

εἰς τὸ ἱερὸν ἐπὶ τὴν ὥραν τῆς προσευχῆς τὴν
to the temple at the hour - of prayer *which was* the

ἐνάτην. **2** Καί τις ἀνὴρ χωλὸς ἐκ κοιλίας μητρὸς αὐτοῦ
ninth *hour.* And a man [2]lame [3]from [4]*the* [5]womb [6]of [8]mother [7]his

ὑπάρχων ἐβαστάζετο, ὃν ἐτίθουν καθ' ἡμέραν
[1]being was carried *there,* whom they would lay according to a day
who had been each day

---

m**(2:41)** NU omits ασμενως, *gladly.* n**(2:47)** For τη εκκλησια, *to the church,* NU reads επι το αυτο, *together.*

***(2:42)** κοινωνία *(koinōnia).* Noun meaning *fellowship, communion* and *sharing in common.* Here it is one of the four staples of the NT church, along with the apostles' doctrine, prayer, and the breaking of bread. The ritual act of "breaking of bread" is the κοινωνία ("communion") of the body and blood of Christ (1 Cor. 10:16). We can have κοινωνία with God the Father, with His Son Jesus Christ, and with the apostles (1 John 1:3), with one another (1 John 1:7), with the Spirit (Phil. 2:1), and with Christ's sufferings (Phil. 3:10). Even such mundane things as money and goods become κοινωνία when shared for Christ's sake, making the *contribution* itself "fellowship" (Rom. 15:26). See the cognate noun κοινωνός, *partaker, partner,* at Luke 5:10.

πρὸς τὴν θύραν τοῦ ἱεροῦ τὴν λεγομένην Ὡραίαν τοῦ
at the gate of the temple the *one* being called Beautiful - *for him*
which was called

αἰτεῖν ἐλεημοσύνην παρὰ τῶν εἰσπορευομένων εἰς τὸ
to ask alms from the *ones* entering into the
those who entered

ἱερόν, **3** ὃς ἰδὼν Πέτρον καὶ Ἰωάννην μέλλοντας
temple, who seeing Peter and John being about
when he saw about

εἰσιέναι εἰς τὸ ἱερόν, ἠρώτα ἐλεημοσύνην.
to enter into the temple, was asking *for* alms.
began

4 Ἀτενίσας δὲ Πέτρος εἰς αὐτὸν σὺν τῷ
[2]looking [3]intently [1]And [9]Peter [4]on [5]him [6]together [7]with -

Ἰωάννῃ, εἶπε, "Βλέψον εἰς ἡμᾶς." **5** Ὁ δὲ ἐπεῖχεν
[8]John, said, "Look at us." - And he fixed *his* attention

αὐτοῖς, προσδοκῶν τι παρ' αὐτῶν λαβεῖν. **6** Εἶπε δὲ
on them, expecting [3]something [4]from [5]them [1]to [2]receive. [3]said [1]But

Πέτρος, "Ἀργύριον καὶ χρυσίον οὐχ ὑπάρχει μοι, ὃ
[2]Peter, "Silver and gold not ˜ do belong to me, [2]*that* [3]which
I do not have,

δὲ ἔχω, τοῦτό σοι δίδωμι. Ἐν τῷ ὀνόματι Ἰησοῦ Χριστοῦ
[1]but I have, this [3]to [4]you [1]I [2]give. In the name of Jesus Christ

τοῦ Ναζωραίου, ἔγειρε καὶ περιπάτει." **7** Καὶ πιάσας αὐτὸν
the Nazarene, rise and walk." And taking hold of him

τῆς δεξιᾶς χειρὸς ἤγειρε· παραχρῆμα δὲ
of the right hand he raised *him;* immediately ˜ and
by his

ἐστερεώθησαν αὐτοῦ αἱ βάσεις καὶ τὰ σφυρά. **8** Καὶ
[5]were [6]strengthened [1]his - [2]feet [3]and - [4]ankles. And

ἐξαλλόμενος ἔστη καὶ περιεπάτει, καὶ εἰσῆλθε σὺν αὐτοῖς
leaping up he stood and walked, and he entered with them

εἰς τὸ ἱερόν, περιπατῶν καὶ ἁλλόμενος καὶ αἰνῶν τὸν Θεόν.
into the temple, walking and leaping and praising - God.

9 Καὶ εἶδεν αὐτὸν πᾶς ὁ λαὸς περιπατοῦντα καὶ αἰνοῦντα
And [4]saw [5]him [1]all [2]the [3]people walking and praising

τὸν Θεόν. **10** Ἐπεγίνωσκόν τε αὐτὸν ὅτι οὗτος ἦν ὁ
- God. [2]they [3]recognized [1]And him that this was the *one*

πρὸς τὴν ἐλεημοσύνην καθήμενος ἐπὶ τῇ Ὡραίᾳ Πύλῃ τοῦ
[2]for [3]the [4]alms [1]sitting at the Beautiful Gate of the

ἱεροῦ, καὶ ἐπλήσθησαν θάμβους καὶ ἐκστάσεως ἐπὶ
temple, and they were filled with astonishment and amazement at
because of

τῷ συμβεβηκότι αὐτῷ.
the *thing* having happened to him.
that which had happened

Peter Preaches in Solomon's Portico

11 Κρατοῦντος δὲ τοῦ ἰαθέντος χωλοῦ[a] τὸν
holding on to And the being healed lame *man* -
And while the lame man who had been healed held on to

Πέτρον καὶ Ἰωάννην, συνέδραμε πρὸς αὐτοὺς πᾶς ὁ λαὸς
Peter and John, [4]ran [5]together [6]to [7]them [1]all [2]the [3]people

ἐπὶ τῇ στοᾷ τῇ καλουμένῃ Σολομῶντος, ἔκθαμβοι.
in the portico the *one* being called Solomon's, utterly astonished.
which is called

12 Ἰδὼν δὲ Πέτρος ἀπεκρίνατο πρὸς τὸν λαόν,
seeing And Peter *this* he replied to the people,
And when Peter saw

the gate of the temple which is called Beautiful, to ask alms from those who entered the temple;
3 who, seeing Peter and John about to go into the temple, asked for alms.
4 And fixing his eyes on him, with John, Peter said, "Look at us."
5 So he gave them his attention, expecting to receive something from them.
6 Then Peter said, "Silver and gold I do not have, but what I do have I give you: In the name of Jesus Christ of Nazareth, rise up and walk."
7 And he took him by the right hand and lifted *him* up, and immediately his feet and ankle bones received strength.
8 So he, leaping up, stood and walked and entered the temple with them—walking, leaping, and praising God.
9 And all the people saw him walking and praising God.
10 Then they knew that it was he who sat begging alms at the Beautiful Gate of the temple; and they were filled with wonder and amazement at what had happened to him.
11 Now as the lame man who was healed held on to Peter and John, all the people ran together to them in the porch which is called Solomon's, greatly amazed.
12 So when Peter saw *it,* he responded to the people: "Men

---

[a](3:11) For *του ιαθεντος χωλου, the lame (man) who had been healed,* NU reads *αυτου, he.*

of Israel, why do you marvel at
this? Or why look so intently at
us, as though by our own
power or godliness we had
made this man walk?
13 "The God of Abraham,
Isaac, and Jacob, the God of our
fathers, glorified His Servant
Jesus, whom you delivered up
and denied in the presence of
Pilate, when he was determined to let *Him* go.
14 "But you denied the Holy
One and the Just, and asked for
a murderer to be granted to
you,
15 "and killed the Prince of
life, whom God raised from the
dead, of which we are witnesses.
16 "And His name, through
faith in His name, has made this
man strong, whom you see and
know. Yes, the faith which
comes through Him has given
him this perfect soundness in
the presence of you all.
17 "Yet now, brethren, I
know that you did *it* in ignorance, as *did* also your rulers.
18 "But those things which
God foretold by the mouth of all
His prophets, that the Christ
would suffer, He has thus fulfilled.
19 "Repent therefore and be
converted, that your sins may
be blotted out, so that times of
refreshing may come from the
presence of the Lord,
20 "and that He may send Jesus Christ, who was preached
to you before,
21 "whom heaven must re-
ceive until the times of restora-

"Ἄνδρες Ἰσραηλῖται, τί θαυμάζετε ἐπὶ τούτῳ? Ἢ ἡμῖν τί
"Men Israelites, why do you marvel at this? Or [6]at [7]us [1]why
of Israel,

ἀτενίζετε ὡς ἰδίᾳ δυνάμει ἢ εὐσεβείᾳ
[2]do [3]you [4]look [5]intently as though by our own power or piety

πεποιηκόσι τοῦ περιπατεῖν αὐτόν? 13 Ὁ Θεὸς Ἀβραὰμ καὶ
having made - [2]to [3]walk [1]him? The God of Abraham and
we have made

Ἰσαὰκ καὶ Ἰακώβ, ὁ Θεὸς τῶν πατέρων ἡμῶν, ἐδόξασε τὸν
Isaac and Jacob, the God - of fathers ˜ our, glorified -

Παῖδα αὐτοῦ Ἰησοῦν, ὃν ὑμεῖς μὲν παρεδώκατε καὶ
Servant ˜ His Jesus, whom you - handed over and
delivered

ἠρνήσασθε αὐτὸν κατὰ πρόσωπον Πιλάτου, κρίναντος ἐκείνου
denied Him to the face of Pilate, judging that One
in the presence when he had decided to

ἀπολύειν. 14 Ὑμεῖς δὲ τὸν Ἅγιον καὶ Δίκαιον ἠρνήσασθε,
to release. you ˜ But [2]the [3]Holy [4]and [5]Just [6]*One* [1]denied,
release Him.

καὶ ᾐτήσασθε ἄνδρα φονέα χαρισθῆναι ὑμῖν, 15 τὸν δὲ
and asked for a man a murderer to be granted to you, the ˜ and
a murderer

Ἀρχηγὸν* τῆς ζωῆς ἀπεκτείνατε, ὃν ὁ Θεὸς ἤγειρεν ἐκ
Prince - of life you killed, whom - God raised from

νεκρῶν, οὗ ἡμεῖς μάρτυρές ἐσμεν. 16 Καὶ ἐπὶ τῇ
the dead, of which we witnesses ˜ are. And upon -
on the basis of

πίστει τοῦ ὀνόματος αὐτοῦ, τοῦτον ὃν θεωρεῖτε καὶ
faith - of name ˜ His, [5]this [6]*one* [7]whom [8]you [9]observe [10]and
in

οἴδατε ἐστερέωσε τὸ ὄνομα αὐτοῦ. Καὶ ἡ πίστις ἡ δι'
[11]know [3]made [4]strong - [2]name [1]His. And the faith the *one* by
which is

αὐτοῦ ἔδωκεν αὐτῷ τὴν ὁλοκληρίαν ταύτην ἀπέναντι πάντων
Him gave to him - wholeness ˜ this before all ˜
has given

ὑμῶν. 17 Καὶ νῦν, ἀδελφοί, οἶδα ὅτι κατὰ ἄγνοιαν
you. And now, brothers, I know that according to ignorance

ἐπράξατε, ὥσπερ καὶ οἱ ἄρχοντες ὑμῶν. 18 Ὁ δὲ Θεὸς
you did *this,* as indeed also - rulers ˜ your. - But [4]God

ἃ προκατήγγειλε διὰ στόματος πάντων τῶν
[1]*the* [2]*things* [3]which announced beforehand by *the* mouth of all -

προφητῶν αὐτοῦ, παθεῖν τὸν Χριστόν, ἐπλήρωσεν οὕτως.
prophets ˜ His, [4]to [5]suffer [1]*for* [2]the [3]Christ, He fulfilled ˜ thus.
that the Messiah would suffer,

19 Μετανοήσατε οὖν καὶ ἐπιστρέψατε, εἰς τὸ
repent ˜ Therefore and turn back, for -
that

ἐξαλειφθῆναι ὑμῶν τὰς ἁμαρτίας, ὅπως ἂν ἔλθωσι
[3]to [4]be [5]wiped [6]away [1]your - [2]sins, in order that - [4]may [5]come
may

καιροὶ ἀναψύξεως ἀπὸ προσώπου τοῦ Κυρίου 20 καὶ
[1]seasons [2]of [3]relaxation from *the* face of the Lord and
presence

ἀποστείλῃ τὸν προκεχειρισμένον[b] ὑμῖν Χριστὸν
that He may send the *One* having been appointed for you *as* Christ
He who had been ordained to be your Messiah,

Ἰησοῦν, 21 ὃν δεῖ οὐρανὸν μὲν δέξασθαι ἄχρι
Jesus, whom it is necessary *for* heaven - to receive until
Jesus,

---

b(3:20) TR reads προκεκηρυγμενον, *having been proclaimed before.*

*(3:15) αρχηγός (archēgos). Noun meaning *one who leads* or *originates* something. No single English word expresses its meaning in all of its contexts. In the LXX it is used for the chief of a family or tribe (Num. 13:2). In Hebrews the word is used to describe Jesus as the *founder* or *originator* of both salvation (Heb. 2:10) and faith (Heb. 12:2). Jesus' title as Ἀρχηγὸν τῆς ζωῆς here in Acts 3:15 is somewhat ambiguous. It may mean that He is the "Ruler of life" or the "Originator of life" (cf. Acts 5:31). Cf. the cognate verb ἄρχω, *rule, begin;* and the noun ἀρχή, *beginning, ruler.*

χρόνων ἀποκαταστάσεως πάντων ὧν ἐλάλησεν ὁ Θεὸς
the times of *the* restoration of all *things* of which spoke ˜ - God

διὰ στόματος πάντων[c] τῶν ἁγίων αὐτοῦ προφητῶν ἀπ'
by *the* mouth of all - holy ˜ His prophets from
since the

αἰῶνος. **22** Μωσῆς μὲν γὰρ πρὸς τοὺς πατέρας[d] εἶπεν ὅτι
age. Moses ˜ - For [2]to [3]the [4]fathers [1]said -
earliest time.

«Προφήτην ὑμῖν ἀναστήσει Κύριος ὁ Θεὸς ἡμῶν[e] ἐκ
«[10]a [11]Prophet [8]for [9]you [5]will [6]raise [7]up [1]*The* [2]Lord - [4]God [3]our from

τῶν ἀδελφῶν ὑμῶν ὡς ἐμέ. Αὐτοῦ ἀκούσεσθε κατὰ πάντα
- brothers ˜ your like me. Him you shall hear in all *things*
everything

ὅσα ἂν λαλήσῃ πρὸς ὑμᾶς. **23** Ἔσται δέ, πᾶσα
as many as - He speaks to you. [2]it [3]will [4]be [1]And, *that* every
which

ψυχὴ ἥτις ἐὰν μὴ ἀκούσῃ τοῦ Προφήτου ἐκείνου
soul who - not ˜ does hear - Prophet ˜ that
person

ἐξολοθρευθήσεται ἐκ τοῦ λαοῦ.»[f] **24** Καὶ πάντες δὲ οἱ
shall be utterly destroyed from the people.» [2]also [3]all [1]And the

προφῆται ἀπὸ Σαμουὴλ καὶ τῶν καθεξῆς, ὅσοι
prophets from Samuel and the *ones* in order, as many as
his successors, who

ἐλάλησαν, καὶ κατήγγειλαν[g] τὰς ἡμέρας ταύτας. **25** Ὑμεῖς
spoke, also proclaimed - days ˜ these. You
have spoken, have proclaimed

ἐστε υἱοὶ τῶν προφητῶν καὶ τῆς διαθήκης ἧς διέθετο ὁ
are sons of the prophets and of the covenant which made ˜ -

Θεὸς πρὸς τοὺς πατέρας ἡμῶν,[h] λέγων πρὸς Ἀβραάμ, «Καὶ
God with - fathers ˜ our, saying to Abraham, «And

ἐν τῷ σπέρματί σου ἐνευλογηθήσονται πᾶσαι αἱ πατριαὶ
in - seed ˜ your [7]shall [8]be [9]blessed [1]all [2]the [3]families
offspring

τῆς γῆς.»[i] **26** Ὑμῖν πρῶτον ὁ Θεός, ἀναστήσας τὸν
[4]of [5]the [6]earth.» To you first - God, raising -
having raised

Παῖδα αὐτοῦ Ἰησοῦν,[j] ἀπέστειλεν αὐτὸν εὐλογοῦντα ὑμᾶς, ἐν
Servant ˜ His Jesus, sent Him blessing you, in
to bless by

τῷ ἀποστρέφειν ἕκαστον ἀπὸ τῶν πονηριῶν ὑμῶν."
- to turn away each *one* from - iniquities ˜ your."
turning each of you away

Peter and John Are Arrested

4 **1** Λαλούντων δὲ αὐτῶν πρὸς τὸν λαόν, ἐπέστησαν
[3]speaking [1]Now [2]them to the people, [12]came [13]upon
Now while they were speaking

αὐτοῖς οἱ ἱερεῖς καὶ ὁ στρατηγὸς τοῦ ἱεροῦ καὶ οἱ
[14]them [1]the [2]priests [3]and [4]the [5]captain [6]of [7]the [8]temple [9]and [10]the

Σαδδουκαῖοι, **2** διαπονούμενοι διὰ τὸ διδάσκειν αὐτοὺς
[11]Sadducees, being greatly disturbed because of - to teach them
because they were teaching

τὸν λαὸν καὶ καταγγέλλειν ἐν τῷ Ἰησοῦ τὴν ἀνάστασιν τῶν
the people and to proclaim in - Jesus the resurrection of the
proclaiming

νεκρῶν. **3** Καὶ ἐπέβαλον αὐτοῖς τὰς χεῖρας καὶ ἔθεντο εἰς
dead. And they laid [2]on [3]them - [1]hands and put *them* in

tion of all things, which God has spoken by the mouth of all His holy prophets since the world began.
22 "For Moses truly said to the fathers, *'The* L*ORD* *your God will raise up for you a Prophet like me from your brethren. Him you shall hear in all things, whatever He says to you.*
23 *'And it shall be that every soul who will not hear that Prophet shall be utterly destroyed from among the people.'*
24 "Yes, and all the prophets, from Samuel and those who follow, as many as have spoken, have also foretold these days.
25 "You are sons of the prophets, and of the covenant which God made with our fathers, saying to Abraham, *'And in your seed all the families of the earth shall be blessed.'*
26 "To you first, God, having raised up His Servant Jesus, sent Him to bless you, in turning away every one *of you* from your iniquities."

4 Now as they spoke to the people, the priests, the captain of the temple, and the Sadducees came upon them,
2 being greatly disturbed that they taught the people and preached in Jesus the resurrection from the dead.
3 And they laid hands on them, and put *them* in custody

[c](**3:21**) NU omits παντων, *all.* [d](**3:22**) NU omits γαρ προς τους πατερας, *For (Moses said) to the fathers.* [e](**3:22**) NU, TR read υμων, *your.* [f](**3:22, 23**) Deut. 18:15, 18, 19
[g](**3:24**) TR reads προκατηγγειλαν, *previously announced.*
[h](**3:25**) NU reads υμων, *your.* [i](**3:25**) Gen. 22:18; 26:4; 28:14
[j](**3:26**) NU omits Ιησουν, *Jesus.*

until the next day, for it was already evening.
4 However, many of those who heard the word believed; and the number of the men came to be about five thousand.
5 And it came to pass, on the next day, that their rulers, elders, and scribes,
6 as well as Annas the high priest, Caiaphas, John, and Alexander, and as many as were of the family of the high priest, were gathered together at Jerusalem.
7 And when they had set them in the midst, they asked, "By what power or by what name have you done this?"
8 Then Peter, filled with the Holy Spirit, said to them, "Rulers of the people and elders of Israel:
9 "If we this day are judged for a good deed *done* to a helpless man, by what means he has been made well,
10 "let it be known to you all, and to all the people of Israel, that by the name of Jesus Christ of Nazareth, whom you crucified, whom God raised from the dead, by Him this man stands here before you whole.
11 "This is the *'stone which was rejected by you builders, which has become the chief cornerstone.'*
12 "Nor is there salvation in

τήρησιν εἰς τὴν αὔριον, ἦν γὰρ ἑσπέρα ἤδη. 4 Πολλοὶ
custody for the next day, [2]it [3]was [1]for evening ˜ already. many ˜
until

δὲ τῶν ἀκουσάντων τὸν λόγον ἐπίστευσαν, καὶ
But of the *ones* hearing the word believed, and
those who heard message

ἐγενήθη ὁ ἀριθμὸς τῶν ἀνδρῶν ὡσεὶ χιλιάδες πέντε.
[6]came [7]to [8]be [1]the [2]number [3]of [4]the [5]men about thousand ˜ five.

Peter and John Testify to the Sanhedrin

5 Ἐγένετο δὲ ἐπὶ τὴν αὔριον συναχθῆναι αὐτῶν
[2]it [3]came [4]to [5]pass [1]Now on the next day to be assembled their
that their rulers and

τοὺς ἄρχοντας καὶ πρεσβυτέρους καὶ γραμματεῖς εἰς
- rulers and elders and scribes in
elders and scribes were assembled

Ἰερουσαλήμ, 6 καὶ Ἄνναν τὸν ἀρχιερέα καὶ Καϊάφαν καὶ
Jerusalem, and Annas the high priest and Caiaphas and

Ἰωάννην καὶ Ἀλέξανδρον καὶ ὅσοι ἦσαν ἐκ γένους
John and Alexander and as many as were of stock ˜
descent

ἀρχιερατικοῦ. 7 Καὶ στήσαντες αὐτοὺς ἐν μέσῳ
high-priestly. And standing them in *the* midst
they brought them forward and

ἐπυνθάνοντο, "Ἐν ποίᾳ δυνάμει ἢ ἐν ποίῳ
they were inquiring, "By what sort of miracle or in what kind of
began to inquire,

ὀνόματι ἐποιήσατε τοῦτο ὑμεῖς?"
name did [2]do [3]this [1]you?"

8 Τότε Πέτρος πλησθεὶς Πνεύματος Ἁγίου εἶπε
Then Peter having been filled with *the* Spirit ˜ Holy said

πρὸς αὐτούς, "Ἄρχοντες τοῦ λαοῦ καὶ πρεσβύτεροι τοῦ
to them, "Rulers of the people and elders -

Ἰσραήλ,[a] 9 εἰ ἡμεῖς σήμερον ἀνακρινόμεθα ἐπὶ εὐεργεσίᾳ
of Israel, if we today are being judged for a good work

ἀνθρώπου ἀσθενοῦς, ἐν τίνι οὗτος σέσωσται,
of a man ˜ weak, by what *means* this *man* has been saved,
to made well,

10 γνωστὸν ἔστω πᾶσιν ὑμῖν καὶ παντὶ τῷ λαῷ Ἰσραὴλ
[4]known [1]let [2]it [3]be to all ˜ you and to all the people of Israel

ὅτι ἐν τῷ ὀνόματι Ἰησοῦ Χριστοῦ τοῦ Ναζωραίου, ὃν ὑμεῖς
that by the name of Jesus Christ the Nazarene, whom you

ἐσταυρώσατε, ὃν ὁ Θεὸς ἤγειρεν ἐκ νεκρῶν, ἐν τούτῳ
crucified, whom - God raised from *the* dead, by this *name*

οὗτος παρέστηκεν ἐνώπιον ὑμῶν ὑγιής. 11 Οὗτός ἐστιν
this *man* stands before you whole. This is

«Ὁ λίθος ὁ ἐξουθενηθεὶς ὑφ' ὑμῶν τῶν
«The stone the *one* having been rejected by you the *ones*
which was who are

οἰκοδομούντων,
building,
the builders,

Ὁ γενόμενος εἰς κεφαλὴν γωνίας.»[b]
The *one* becoming for *the* head of *the* corner.»
Which became the chief cornerstone.»

12 Καὶ οὐκ ἔστιν ἐν ἄλλῳ οὐδενὶ ἡ σωτηρία, οὔτε γὰρ
And not *there* is in other no - salvation, neither ˜ for
there is salvation in no one else,

[a](4:8) NU omits *του Ισραηλ, of Israel.*
[b](4:11) Ps. 118:22

ὄνομά ἐστιν ἕτερον ὑπὸ τὸν οὐρανὸν τὸ δεδομένον
[4]name [1]is [2]*there* [3]another under - heaven the *one* having been given
which has

ἐν ἀνθρώποις ἐν ᾧ δεῖ σωθῆναι ἡμᾶς."
among men by which it is necessary *for* [2]to [3]be [4]saved [1]us."
we must be saved."

The Sanhedrin Forbids Teaching in the Name of Jesus

13 Θεωροῦντες δὲ τὴν τοῦ Πέτρου παρρησίαν καὶ
observing ˜ And the - [2]of [3]Peter [1]boldness and
And when they observed

Ἰωάννου, καὶ καταλαβόμενοι ὅτι ἄνθρωποι ἀγράμματοί*
John, and understanding that [6]men [3]uneducated
understood

εἰσι καὶ ἰδιῶται, ἐθαύμαζον, ἐπεγίνωσκόν τε αὐτοὺς
[1]they [2]are [4]and [5]unskilled, they marveled, [2]they [3]recognized [1]and them
were

ὅτι σὺν τῷ Ἰησοῦ ἦσαν. 14 Τὸν δὲ ἄνθρωπον
that [3]with - [4]Jesus [1]they [2]were. [3]the [1]But [4]man
had been. But because they saw

βλέποντες σὺν αὐτοῖς ἑστῶτα τὸν τεθεραπευμένον, οὐδὲν
[2]seeing [6]with [7]them [5]standing the *one* having been healed, [3]nothing
standing with them the man who had been

εἶχον ἀντειπεῖν. 15 Κελεύσαντες δὲ αὐτοὺς ἔξω
[1]they [2]had to say against *them.* commanding ˜ And them [4]outside
they commanded

τοῦ συνεδρίου ἀπελθεῖν συνέβαλλον πρὸς ἀλλήλους,
[5]the [6]council [1]to [2]go [3]away they were conferring to one another,
and began to confer among themselves,

16 λέγοντες, "Τί ποιήσωμεν τοῖς ἀνθρώποις τούτοις? Ὅτι
saying, "What shall we do - to men ˜ these? that ˜

μὲν γὰρ γνωστὸν σημεῖον γέγονε δι' αὐτῶν, πᾶσι
- For a known sign has come to pass by them, [3]to [4]all

τοῖς κατοικοῦσιν Ἱερουσαλὴμ φανερόν, καὶ οὐ
[5]the [6]*ones* [7]dwelling [8]*in* [9]Jerusalem [1]*is* [2]evident and [3]not
those who are

δυνάμεθα ἀρνήσασθαι. 17 Ἀλλ' ἵνα μὴ ἐπὶ πλεῖον
[1]we [2]are able to deny *it.* But that [2]not [5]to [6]more
lest further

διανεμηθῇ εἰς τὸν λαόν, ἀπειλῇ[c] ἀπειλησώμεθα αὐτοῖς
[1]it [3]be [4]spread among the people, with a threat let us threaten them

μηκέτι λαλεῖν ἐπὶ τῷ ὀνόματι τούτῳ μηδενὶ ἀνθρώπων."
[3]no [4]longer [1]to [2]speak in - name ˜ this to no one of men."
to any person at all."

18 Καὶ καλέσαντες αὐτούς, παρήγγειλαν αὐτοῖς τὸ καθόλου
And summoning them, they commanded them - [4]completely
at all

μὴ φθέγγεσθαι μηδὲ διδάσκειν ἐπὶ τῷ ὀνόματι τοῦ Ἰησοῦ.
[1]not [2]to [3]speak nor to teach in the name - of Jesus.

19 Ὁ δὲ Πέτρος καὶ Ἰωάννης ἀποκριθέντες πρὸς αὐτοὺς
- But Peter and John answering to them
answered them and

εἶπον, "Εἰ δίκαιόν ἐστιν ἐνώπιον τοῦ Θεοῦ ὑμῶν ἀκούειν
said, "If [3]right [1]it [2]is before - God [3]you [1]to [2]hear

μᾶλλον ἢ τοῦ Θεοῦ, κρίνατε. 20 Οὐ δυνάμεθα γὰρ ἡμεῖς,
rather than - God, you judge. [4]not [3]are [5]able [1]For [2]we,

ἃ εἴδομεν καὶ ἠκούσαμεν, μὴ λαλεῖν."
the things which we saw and heard, not to speak about *them.*"

any other, for there is no other name under heaven given among men by which we must be saved."
13 Now when they saw the boldness of Peter and John, and perceived that they were uneducated and untrained men, they marveled. And they realized that they had been with Jesus.
14 And seeing the man who had been healed standing with them, they could say nothing against it.
15 But when they had commanded them to go aside out of the council, they conferred among themselves,
16 saying, "What shall we do to these men? For, indeed, that a notable miracle has been done through them *is* evident to all who dwell in Jerusalem, and we cannot deny *it.*
17 "But so that it spreads no further among the people, let us severely threaten them, that from now on they speak to no man in this name."
18 So they called them and commanded them not to speak at all nor teach in the name of Jesus.
19 But Peter and John answered and said to them, "Whether it is right in the sight of God to listen to you more than to God, you judge.
20 "For we cannot but speak the things which we have seen and heard."

---

c(4:17) NU omits απειλη, *with a threat.*

---

*(4:13) ἀγράμματος (*agrammatos*). Adjective, occurring only here in the NT, a compound of α, *not,* and γράμμα, *letter,* meaning *illiterate.* Here it probably has its more general meaning *uneducated,* possibly with specific reference to a lack of formal training in interpreting the Jewish law.

21 So when they had further threatened them, they let them go, finding no way of punishing them, because of the people, since they all glorified God for what had been done.

22 For the man was over forty years old on whom this miracle of healing had been performed.

23 And being let go, they went to their own *companions* and reported all that the chief priests and elders had said to them.

24 So when they heard that, they raised their voice to God with one accord and said: "Lord, You *are* God, who made heaven and earth and the sea, and all that is in them,

25 "who by the mouth of Your servant David have said:

'Why did the nations rage,
And the people plot vain things?

26 *The kings of the earth took their stand,*
And the rulers were gathered together
Against the Lord *and against His Christ.'*

27 "For truly against Your holy Servant Jesus, whom You anointed, both Herod and Pontius Pilate, with the Gentiles and the people of Israel, were gathered together

21 Οἱ δὲ προσαπειλησάμενοι ἀπέλυσαν αὐτούς, μηδὲν
\- And having threatened *them* further they released them, nothing ˜
no way

εὑρίσκοντες τὸ πῶς κολάσονται αὐτούς, διὰ τὸν λαόν,
finding - how they will punish them, on account of the people,
to punish

ὅτι πάντες ἐδόξαζον τὸν Θεὸν ἐπὶ τῷ
because all ˜ they were glorifying - God over the *thing*
that which

γεγονότι. **22** Ἐτῶν γὰρ ἦν πλειόνων τεσσαράκοντα
having happened. [8]of [9]years [1]For [4]was [5]more [6]than [7]forty
had occurred. years old

ὁ ἄνθρωπος ἐφ' ὃν ἐγεγόνει τὸ σημεῖον τοῦτο τῆς
[2]the [3]man on whom had come about - sign ˜ this -

ἰάσεως.*
of healing.

The Believers Pray for Boldness

23 Ἀπολυθέντες δὲ ἦλθον πρὸς τοὺς ἰδίους καὶ
[2]being [3]released [1]And they came to - their own and

ἀπήγγειλαν ὅσα πρὸς αὐτοὺς οἱ ἀρχιερεῖς καὶ οἱ
reported as many *things* as [9]to [10]them [1]the [2]chief [3]priests [4]and [5]the
all that

πρεσβύτεροι εἶπον. **24** Οἱ δὲ ἀκούσαντες ὁμοθυμαδὸν
[6]elders [7]had [8]said. - And hearing with one mind
when they heard,

ἦραν φωνὴν πρὸς τὸν Θεὸν καὶ εἶπον, "Δέσποτα, σὺ
they lifted *their* voice to - God and said, "Master, You *are*

ὁ Θεὸς[d] ὁ ποιήσας τὸν οὐρανὸν καὶ τὴν γῆν καὶ τὴν
the God the *One* making - heaven and the earth and the
who made

θάλασσαν καὶ πάντα τὰ ἐν αὐτοῖς, **25** ὁ διὰ[e]
sea and all the *things* in them, the *One* by
who

στόματος Δαβὶδ παιδός σου εἰπών,
the mouth of David servant ˜ Your saying,
said,

«Ἱνατί ἐφρύαξαν ἔθνη,
«Why did [3]snort [1]*the* [2]Gentiles,
rage

Καὶ λαοὶ ἐμελέτησαν κενά?
And *the* people conspired vain *things*?

26 Παρέστησαν οἱ βασιλεῖς τῆς γῆς,
[6]took [7]a [8]stand [1]The [2]kings [3]of [4]the [5]earth,

Καὶ οἱ ἄρχοντες συνήχθησαν ἐπὶ τὸ αὐτὸ
And the rulers were assembled upon the same
together

Κατὰ τοῦ Κυρίου καὶ κατὰ τοῦ Χριστοῦ αὐτοῦ.»[f]
Against the Lord and against - Christ ˜ His.»
Messiah

27 "Συνήχθησαν γὰρ ἐπ' ἀληθείας[g] ἐπὶ τὸν ἅγιον
"[4]*there* [5]were [6]assembled [1]For [2]in [3]truth against - [2]holy
truly

Παῖδά σου Ἰησοῦν, ὃν ἔχρισας, Ἡρῴδης τε καὶ
[3]Servant [1]Your Jesus, whom You anointed, Herod ˜ both and

Πόντιος Πιλᾶτος, σὺν ἔθνεσι καὶ λαοῖς Ἰσραήλ,
Pontius Pilate, together with *the* Gentiles and *the* people of Israel,

---

[d]**(4:24)** NU omits ο Θεος, *the God.* [e]**(4:25)** For δια, *by,* NU reads του πατρος ημων δια πνευματος αγιου στοματος, thus *(who), by the Holy Spirit, through the mouth of our father (David).* [f]**(4:25, 26)** Ps. 2:1, 2 [g]**(4:27)** NU adds εν τη πολει ταυτη, *in this city.*

***(4:22)** ἴασις *(iasis).* Noun meaning *healing, cure,* used only here and in v. 30 in the NT. Cf. the cognate verb ἰάομαι, *heal,* which could be used literally for healing a sickness (Luke 5:17 and often) or figuratively for deliverance, restoration, healing of various ills, including sin or spiritual infirmity (as Matt. 13:15; James 5:16; Heb. 12:13). Cf. also the cognate noun ἰατρός, *physician.*

28 ποιῆσαι ὅσα ἡ χείρ σου καὶ ἡ βουλή σου
to do as many *things* as - hand ~ Your and - counsel ~ Your
all that

προώρισε γενέσθαι. **29** Καὶ τὰ νῦν, Κύριε,
foreordained to come to pass. And the *things* now, Lord,
now transpiring,

ἔπιδε ἐπὶ τὰς ἀπειλὰς αὐτῶν, καὶ δὸς τοῖς δούλοις σου
look upon - threats ~ their, and give - to slaves ~ Your
servants

μετὰ παρρησίας πάσης λαλεῖν τὸν λόγον σου, **30** ἐν τῷ
that with boldness ~ all to speak - word ~ Your, in -
they may message by

τὴν χεῖρά σου ἐκτείνειν σε εἰς ἴασιν, καὶ σημεῖα καὶ
- hand ~ Your [2]to [3]extend [1]You for healing, and *that* signs and
extending Your hand to heal,

τέρατα γίνεσθαι διὰ τοῦ ὀνόματος τοῦ ἁγίου Παιδός σου
wonders to occur through the name - of [2]holy [3]Servant [1]Your
may occur

Ἰησοῦ." **31** Καὶ δεηθέντων αὐτῶν, ἐσαλεύθη ὁ τόπος
Jesus." And petitioning them, [8]was [9]shaken [1]the [2]place
when they had made petition,

ἐν ᾧ ἦσαν συνηγμένοι, καὶ ἐπλήσθησαν ἅπαντες
[3]in [4]which [5]they [6]were [7]gathered, and they [2]were [3]filled [1]all

Πνεύματος Ἁγίου, καὶ ἐλάλουν τὸν λόγον τοῦ Θεοῦ μετὰ
with *the* Spirit ~ Holy, and they spoke the word - of God with
message

παρρησίας.
boldness.

The Believers Have All Things Common

32 Τοῦ δὲ πλήθους τῶν πιστευσάντων ἦν ἡ
[7]of [8]the [1]Now [9]multitude [10]of [11]the [12]*ones* [13]believing [14]was [2]the
of those who had believed

καρδία καὶ ἡ ψυχὴ μία, καὶ οὐδὲ εἷς τι τῶν
[3]heart [4]and [5]the [6]soul one, and not one [3]anything [4]of [5]the [6]*things*
that anything

ὑπαρχόντων αὐτῶν ἔλεγεν ἴδιον εἶναι, ἀλλ' ἦν
[7]belonging [8]of [9]them [1]was [2]saying [12]their [13]own [10]to [11]be, but [3]were
belonging to him was his own,

αὐτοῖς ἅπαντα κοινά.* **33** Καὶ μεγάλῃ δυνάμει
[5]to [6]them [1]all [2]*things* [4]common. And with great power

ἀπεδίδουν τὸ μαρτύριον οἱ ἀπόστολοι τῆς
[3]were [4]giving [5]forth [6]the [7]witness [1]the [2]apostles of the
their

ἀναστάσεως τοῦ Κυρίου Ἰησοῦ, χάρις τε μεγάλη ἦν ἐπὶ
resurrection of the Lord Jesus, [3]grace [1]and [2]great was on
favor

πάντας αὐτούς. **34** Οὐδὲ γὰρ ἐνδεής τις ὑπῆρχεν ἐν
all ~ them. [5]not [1]For [3]needy [2]anyone [4]was among

αὐτοῖς· ὅσοι γὰρ κτήτορες χωρίων ἢ οἰκιῶν ὑπῆρχον,
them; [2]as [3]many [4]as [1]for [6]owners [7]of [8]lands [9]or [10]houses [5]were,
all who

πωλοῦντες ἔφερον τὰς τιμὰς τῶν
selling *them* they were bringing the prices of the *things*
proceeds

πιπρασκομένων **35** καὶ ἐτίθουν παρὰ τοὺς πόδας τῶν
having been sold and were placing *them* beside the feet of the
which had been

28 "to do whatever Your hand and Your purpose determined before to be done.
29 "Now, Lord, look on their threats, and grant to Your servants that with all boldness they may speak Your word,
30 "by stretching out Your hand to heal, and that signs and wonders may be done through the name of Your holy Servant Jesus."
31 And when they had prayed, the place where they were assembled together was shaken; and they were all filled with the Holy Spirit, and they spoke the word of God with boldness.
32 Now the multitude of those who believed were of one heart and one soul; neither did anyone say that any of the things he possessed was his own, but they had all things in common.
33 And with great power the apostles gave witness to the resurrection of the Lord Jesus. And great grace was upon them all.
34 Nor was there anyone among them who lacked; for all who were possessors of lands or houses sold them, and brought the proceeds of the things that were sold,
35 and laid *them* at the apos-

***(4:32)** *κοινός (koinos).* Adjective meaning *common.* It can have a technical sense describing something as ritually defiled or unclean, for example "unwashed hands" (Mark 7:2) or nonkosher food (Acts 10:14). A more positive meaning of *κοινός* is the sense "widely shared." The very name of the language in which the NT was written is *ἡ κοινὴ διάλεκτος*, "the *common* dialect." The earliest Christians shared "all things in *common*" (Acts 2:44; here in 4:32), a technical phrase referring to sharing for the community good and not to communally owned property. Paul called Titus "a true son in our *common* faith" (Titus 1:4), and Jude wrote to the saints about "our *common* salvation" (Jude 3).

tles' feet; and they distributed
to each as anyone had need.
36 And Joses, who was also
named Barnabas by the apostles (which is translated Son of
Encouragement), a Levite of
the country of Cyprus,
37 having land, sold *it,* and
brought the money and laid *it* at
the apostles' feet.
5 But a certain man named
Ananias, with Sapphira his
wife, sold a possession.
2 And he kept back *part* of
the proceeds, his wife also being aware *of it,* and brought a
certain part and laid *it* at the
apostles' feet.
3 But Peter said, "Ananias,
why has Satan filled your heart
to lie to the Holy Spirit and
keep back *part* of the price of
the land for yourself?
4 "While it remained, was it
not your own? And after it was
sold, was it not in your own
control? Why have you conceived this thing in your heart?
You have not lied to men but to
God."
5 Then Ananias, hearing
these words, fell down and
breathed his last. So great fear
came upon all those who heard
these things.
6 And the young men arose
and wrapped him up, carried
him out, and buried *him.*

ἀποστόλων. Διεδίδοτο δὲ ἑκάστῳ καθότι ἄν
apostles. [2]they [3]were [4]distributing [1]And to each to the degree that -
would distribute

τις χρείαν εἶχεν.
anyone [2]a [3]need [1]had.

36 Ἰωσῆς[h] δὲ ὁ ἐπικληθεὶς Βαρναβᾶς ἀπὸ τῶν
Joses ˜ And the *one* being named Barnabas by the
who was surnamed

ἀποστόλων (ὅ ἐστι μεθερμηνευόμενον "Υἱὸς
apostles (which is being translated "Son
means

παρακλήσεως"), Λευίτης, Κύπριος τῷ γένει, **37** ὑπάρχοντος
of encouragement"), a Levite, a Cyprian - by nation, being
who

αὐτῷ ἀγροῦ, πωλήσας ἤνεγκε τὸ χρῆμα καὶ ἔθηκε παρὰ
to him a field, selling brought the money and placed *it* beside
possessing sold it and

τοὺς πόδας τῶν ἀποστόλων.
the feet of the apostles.

Ananias and Sapphira Lie to the Holy Spirit

5 **1** Ἀνὴρ δέ τις Ἀνανίας ὀνόματι, σὺν
[2]a [4]man [1]Now [3]certain Ananias by name, together with

Σαπφείρῃ τῇ γυναικὶ αὐτοῦ, ἐπώλησε κτῆμα **2** καὶ
Sapphira - wife ˜ his, sold a possession and

ἐνοσφίσατο ἀπὸ τῆς τιμῆς, συνειδυίας καὶ τῆς
kept back for himself from the price, [4]being [5]aware [6]*of* [7]*it* [3]also -

γυναικὸς αὐτοῦ, καὶ ἐνέγκας μέρος τι παρὰ τοὺς πόδας
[2]wife [1]his, and bringing [1]a [3]part [2]certain [7]beside [8]the [9]feet
brought

τῶν ἀποστόλων ἔθηκεν.
[10]of [11]the [12]apostles [4]*and* [5]placed [6]*it.*

3 Εἶπε δὲ Πέτρος, "Ἀνανία, διὰ τί ἐπλήρωσεν ὁ
[3]said [1]But [2]Peter, "Ananias, because of what has filled ˜ -
why

Σατανᾶς τὴν καρδίαν σου ψεύσασθαί σε τὸ Πνεῦμα τὸ Ἅγιον
Satan - heart ˜ your *for* [2]to [3]lie [4]to [1]you the Spirit ˜ - Holy

καὶ νοσφίσασθαί σε ἀπὸ τῆς τιμῆς τοῦ χωρίου?
and *for* [2]to [3]keep [4]back [5]for [6]yourself [1]you from the price of the land?

4 Οὐχὶ μένον σοὶ ἔμενε καὶ πραθὲν ἐν
not Remaining to you did it remain and being sold [4]in
While it remained unsold, did it not remain yours after it was sold,

τῇ σῇ ἐξουσίᾳ ὑπῆρχε? Τί ὅτι ἔθου ἐν τῇ καρδίᾳ
- [5]your [6]power [1]was [2]it [3]*not?* Why *is it* that you put in - heart ˜
control

σου τὸ πρᾶγμα τοῦτο? Οὐκ ἐψεύσω ἀνθρώποις ἀλλὰ τῷ
your - thing ˜ this? [3]not [1]You [2]did lie to men but -

Θεῷ." **5** Ἀκούων δὲ ὁ Ἀνανίας τοὺς λόγους τούτους,
to God." [3]hearing [1]And - [2]Ananias - words ˜ these,
And Ananias, while he was hearing

πεσὼν ἐξέψυξε. Καὶ ἐγένετο φόβος μέγας ἐπὶ πάντας
falling expired. And [3]came [4]to [5]be [2]fear [1]great on all
fell down and died.

τοὺς ἀκούοντας ταῦτα.[a] **6** Ἀναστάντες δὲ οἱ
the *ones* hearing these *things.* [5]rising [6]up [1]And [2]the
those who were rose up and

νεώτεροι συνέστειλαν αὐτὸν καὶ ἐξενέγκαντες ἔθαψαν.
[3]young [4]men covered up ˜ him and carrying *him* out buried *him.*
carried him out and

---

[h](4:36) NU reads Ιωσηφ, *Joseph.* [a](5:5) NU omits ταυτα, *these (things).*

7 Ἐγένετο δὲ ὡς ὡρῶν τριῶν διάστημα, καὶ ἡ
[2]it [3]happened [1]And about [3]of [5]hours [4]three [1]an [2]interval, and -
three hours later, that

γυνὴ αὐτοῦ μὴ εἰδυῖα τὸ γεγονὸς εἰσῆλθεν.
wife ˜ his not having known the *thing* having occurred came in.
what had transpired

8 Ἀπεκρίθη δὲ αὐτῇ ὁ Πέτρος, "Εἰπέ μοι, εἰ τοσούτου
[3]answered [1]And [4]her - [2]Peter, "Tell me, whether of so much
for

τὸ χωρίον ἀπέδοσθε?"
[3]the [4]land [1]you [2]sold?"

Ἡ δὲ εἶπε, "Ναί, τοσούτου."
[2]the [3]*one* [1]And said, "Yes, of so much."
she for

9 Ὁ δὲ Πέτρος εἶπεν πρὸς αὐτήν, "Τί ὅτι
- And Peter said to her, "Why *is it* that

συνεφωνήθη ὑμῖν πειράσαι τὸ Πνεῦμα Κυρίου? Ἰδού, οἱ
it was agreed by you to tempt the Spirit of *the* Lord? Behold, the

πόδες τῶν θαψάντων τὸν ἄνδρα σου ἐπὶ τῇ θύρᾳ καὶ
feet of the *ones* burying - husband ˜ your *are* at the door and
those who buried

ἐξοίσουσί σε." 10 Ἔπεσε δὲ παραχρῆμα παρὰ τοὺς
they will carry out ˜ you." [2]she [3]fell [1]And immediately beside -

πόδας αὐτοῦ καὶ ἐξέψυξεν. Εἰσελθόντες δὲ οἱ νεανίσκοι
feet ˜ his and expired. [5]entering [1]And [2]the [3]young [4]men
entered and

εὗρον αὐτὴν νεκράν, καὶ ἐξενέγκαντες ἔθαψαν πρὸς τὸν
found her dead, and carrying *her* out they buried *her* with -
they carried her out and

ἄνδρα αὐτῆς. 11 Καὶ ἐγένετο φόβος μέγας ἐφ' ὅλην τὴν
husband ˜ her. And [3]came [4]to [5]be [2]fear [1]great on all the

ἐκκλησίαν καὶ ἐπὶ πάντας τοὺς ἀκούοντας ταῦτα.
church and on all the *ones* hearing these *things*.
those who were

The Church Experiences Continuing Power

12 Διὰ δὲ τῶν χειρῶν τῶν ἀποστόλων ἐγίνετο σημεῖα
by ˜ Now the hands of the apostles [5]took [6]place [2]signs

καὶ τέρατα ἐν τῷ λαῷ πολλά. Καὶ ἦσαν ὁμοθυμαδὸν
[3]and [4]wonders [7]among [8]the [9]people [1]many. And they [2]were [3]of [4]one [5]mind

ἅπαντες ἐν τῇ Στοᾷ Σολομῶντος. 13 Τῶν δὲ λοιπῶν οὐδεὶς
[1]all in the Portico of Solomon. [2]of [3]the [1]But rest no one

ἐτόλμα κολλᾶσθαι αὐτοῖς, ἀλλ' ἐμεγάλυνεν αὐτοὺς ὁ
dared to join himself to them, but [3]was [4]magnifying [5]them [1]the
were

λαός. 14 Μᾶλλον δὲ προσετίθεντο πιστεύοντες τῷ
[2]people. [2]more [3]than [4]ever [1]And [7]were [8]added [5]believing [6]*ones* to the
believers

Κυρίῳ, πλήθη ἀνδρῶν τε καὶ γυναικῶν, 15 ὥστε κατὰ
Lord, multitudes [2]of [3]men [1]both and of women, so that [11]along

τὰς πλατείας ἐκφέρειν τοὺς ἀσθενεῖς καὶ τιθέναι
[12]the [13]streets [1]to [2]bring [3]out [4]the [5]sick [6]*people* [7]and [8]to [9]place [10]*them*
they were bringing placing

ἐπὶ κλινῶν καὶ κραββάτων, ἵνα ἐρχομένου Πέτρου κἂν
on couches and pallets, so that coming Peter at least
as Peter was passing

ἡ σκιὰ ἐπισκιάσῃ τινὶ αὐτῶν.
the shadow might overshadow someone of them.
his

7 Now it was about three hours later when his wife came in, not knowing what had happened.
8 And Peter answered her, "Tell me whether you sold the land for so much?" She said, "Yes, for so much."
9 Then Peter said to her, "How is it that you have agreed together to test the Spirit of the Lord? Look, the feet of those who have buried your husband *are* at the door, and they will carry you out."
10 Then immediately she fell down at his feet and breathed her last. And the young men came in and found her dead, and carrying *her* out, buried *her* by her husband.
11 So great fear came upon all the church and upon all who heard these things.
12 And through the hands of the apostles many signs and wonders were done among the people. And they were all with one accord in Solomon's Porch.
13 Yet none of the rest dared join them, but the people esteemed them highly.
14 And believers were increasingly added to the Lord, multitudes of both men and women,
15 so that they brought the sick out into the streets and laid *them* on beds and couches, that at least the shadow of Peter passing by might fall on some of them.

16 Also a multitude gathered from the surrounding cities to Jerusalem, bringing sick people and those who were tormented by unclean spirits, and they were all healed.
17 Then the high priest rose up, and all those who *were* with him (which is the sect of the Sadducees), and they were filled with indignation,
18 and laid their hands on the apostles and put them in the common prison.
19 But at night an angel of the Lord opened the prison doors and brought them out, and said,
20 "Go, stand in the temple and speak to the people all the words of this life."
21 And when they heard *that,* they entered the temple early in the morning and taught. But the high priest and those with him came and called the council together, with all the elders of the children of Israel, and sent to the prison to have them brought.
22 But when the officers came and did not find them in the prison, they returned and reported,
23 saying, "Indeed we found the prison shut securely, and the guards standing outside before the doors; but when we opened them, we found no one inside!"
24 Now when the high priest, the captain of the temple, and the chief priests heard these

---

[b](5:16) NU omits *εις, to,* thus *from the cities surrounding Jerusalem.*
[c](5:23) TR adds *εξω, outside.*

---

*(5:21) *συνέδριον (synedrion).* Noun from the preposition *σύν, together,* and the noun *ἕδρα, seat,* literally meaning *a council, the Sanhedrin.* In Jewish community structure, each local synagogue provided for a council of elders to pass judgments and order discipline in religious matters. The great Sanhedrin at Jerusalem—including priests, elders, and scribal scholars, and presided over by the high priest—served similar functions for Jews in general and especially for those in Palestine. Most of the NT references, as here in Acts, are to this latter body. Matt. 10:17 and the parallel Mark 13:9 refer to the local councils.

16 *Συνήρχετο δὲ καὶ τὸ πλῆθος τῶν*
[3]*there* [4]was [5]coming [6]together [1]And [2]also the multitude from the

πέριξ πόλεων εἰς[b] *Ἰερουσαλήμ, φέροντες ἀσθενεῖς καὶ*
[2]all [3]around [1]cities into Jerusalem, bringing *ones* sick and

ὀχλουμένους ὑπὸ πνευμάτων ἀκαθάρτων, οἵτινες
ones being disturbed by spirits ˜ unclean, who

ἐθεραπεύοντο ἅπαντες.
were [2]being [3]healed [1]all.

The Imprisoned Apostles Escape and Witness

17 *Ἀναστὰς δὲ ὁ ἀρχιερεὺς καὶ πάντες οἱ σὺν*
[5]rising [6]up [1]Now [2]the [3]high [4]priest and all the *ones* with
rose up ... those

αὐτῷ, ἡ οὖσα αἵρεσις τῶν Σαδδουκαίων, ἐπλήσθησαν
him, the being ˜ sect of the Sadducees, they were filled
that is

ζήλου **18** *καὶ ἐπέβαλον τὰς χεῖρας αυτῶν ἐπὶ τοὺς*
of jealousy and put - hands ˜ their on the
with

ἀποστόλους καὶ ἔθεντο αὐτοὺς ἐν τηρήσει δημοσίᾳ.
apostles and placed them in custody ˜ public.

19 *Ἄγγελος δὲ Κυρίου διὰ τῆς νυκτὸς ἤνοιξε τὰς θύρας*
[2]an [3]angel [1]But of *the* Lord during the night opened the doors

τῆς φυλακῆς, ἐξαγαγών τε αὐτοὺς εἶπε, **20** *"Πορεύεσθε, καὶ*
of the prison, [2]leading [4]out [1]and [3]them said, "Go, and

σταθέντες λαλεῖτε ἐν τῷ ἱερῷ τῷ λαῷ πάντα τὰ ῥήματα
standing speak in the temple to the people all the words
stand and

τῆς ζωῆς ταύτης." **21** *Ἀκούσαντες δὲ εἰσῆλθον ὑπὸ τὸν*
- of life ˜ this." hearing ˜ And they entered under the
when they heard, ... about

ὄρθρον εἰς τὸ ἱερὸν καὶ ἐδίδασκον.
dawn into the temple and were teaching.
daybreak

The Apostles Again Face the Sanhedrin

Παραγενόμενος δὲ ὁ ἀρχιερεὺς καὶ οἱ σὺν αὐτῷ,
arriving ˜ Now the high priest and the *ones* with him,
Now when the high priest and those with him arrived,

συνεκάλεσαν τὸ συνέδριον καὶ πᾶσαν τὴν γερουσίαν*
they called together the council even all the council of elders

τῶν υἱῶν Ἰσραήλ, καὶ ἀπέστειλαν εἰς τὸ δεσμωτήριον
of the sons of Israel, and sent to the prison

ἀχθῆναι αὐτούς. **22** *Οἱ δὲ ὑπηρέται παραγενόμενοι*
for [2]to [3]be [4]brought [1]them. the ˜ But attendants arriving *there*
when they arrived

οὐχ εὗρον αὐτοὺς ἐν τῇ φυλακῇ, ἀναστρέψαντες δὲ
not ˜ did find them in the jail, returning ˜ and
they returned

ἀπήγγειλαν, **23** *λέγοντες ὅτι "Τὸ μὲν δεσμωτήριον εὕρομεν*
they announced, saying - "The - prison we found
and

κεκλεισμένον ἐν πάσῃ ἀσφαλείᾳ καὶ τοὺς φύλακας[c] *ἑστῶτας*
having been shut in all security and the guards standing

πρὸ τῶν θυρῶν, ἀνοίξαντες δέ, ἔσω οὐδένα
before the doors, opening ˜ but, [5]within [3]no [4]one
when we opened them,

εὕρομεν!" **24** *Ὡς δὲ ἤκουσαν τοὺς λόγους τούτους ὅ τε*
[1]we [2]found!" when ˜ Now they heard - words ˜ these the ˜ both

ἱερεὺς καὶ ὁ[d] στρατηγὸς τοῦ ἱεροῦ καὶ οἱ ἀρχιερεῖς,
priest and the captain of the temple and the chief priests,

διηπόρουν περὶ αὐτῶν τί ἂν
they were greatly perplexed about them *as to* what -

γένοιτο τοῦτο.
[2]might [3]come [4]to [5]be [1]this.

25 Παραγενόμενος δέ τις ἀπήγγειλεν αὐτοῖς[e] ὅτι
arriving ˜ And someone reported to them -
And one arrived and

"Ἰδού, οἱ ἄνδρες οὓς ἔθεσθε ἐν τῇ φυλακῇ εἰσὶν ἐν τῷ
"Behold, the men whom you put in the jail are [2]in [3]the

ἱερῷ ἑστῶτες καὶ διδάσκοντες τὸν λαόν!" 26 Τότε ἀπελθὼν
[4]temple [1]standing and teaching the people!" Then [3]departing
departed

ὁ στρατηγὸς σὺν τοῖς ὑπηρέταις ἤγαγεν αὐτούς,
[1]the [2]captain together with the attendants brought them,
and brought

οὐ μετὰ βίας, ἐφοβοῦντο γὰρ τὸν λαόν, ἵνα μὴ
not with violence, [2]they [3]were [4]afraid [5]of [1]for the people, that not ˜
without lest

λιθασθῶσιν. 27 Ἀγαγόντες δὲ αὐτοὺς ἔστησαν ἐν τῷ
they be stoned. bringing ˜ And them they stood *them* in the
And they brought and set

συνεδρίῳ.
council.

Καὶ ἐπηρώτησεν αὐτοὺς ὁ ἀρχιερεύς, 28 λέγων, "Οὐ
And [4]asked [5]them [1]the [2]high [3]priest, saying, "[3]not

παραγγελίᾳ παρηγγείλαμεν ὑμῖν μὴ διδάσκειν ἐπὶ τῷ
[4]with [5]a [6]command [1]Did [2]we [7]command you not to teach in -

ὀνόματι τούτῳ? Καὶ ἰδοὺ πεπληρώκατε τὴν Ἰερουσαλὴμ τῆς
name ˜ this? And behold you have filled - Jerusalem -

διδαχῆς ὑμῶν καὶ βούλεσθε ἐπαγαγεῖν ἐφ' ἡμᾶς τὸ αἷμα
of teaching ˜ your and you want to bring on us the blood
with

τοῦ ἀνθρώπου τούτου."
- of man ˜ this."

29 Ἀποκριθεὶς δὲ Πέτρος καὶ οἱ ἀπόστολοι εἶπον,
[6]answering [1]But [2]Peter [3]and [4]the [5]apostles said,
answered and said,

"Πειθαρχεῖν δεῖ Θεῷ μᾶλλον ἢ ἀνθρώποις.
"[4]*for* [5]*us* [6]to [7]obey [1]It [2]is [3]necessary God rather than men.
"We must obey

30 Ὁ Θεὸς τῶν πατέρων ἡμῶν ἤγειρεν Ἰησοῦν, ὃν ὑμεῖς
The God - of fathers ˜ our raised Jesus, whom you

διεχειρίσασθε κρεμάσαντες ἐπὶ ξύλου. 31 Τοῦτον ὁ Θεὸς
laid violent hands on hanging *Him* upon a cross. This *One* - God
murdered by hanging

Ἀρχηγὸν καὶ Σωτῆρα ὕψωσε τῇ δεξιᾷ αὐτοῦ, δοῦναι
[2]*as* [3]Prince [4]and [5]Savior [1]exalted to [2]right [3]*hand* [1]His, to give

μετάνοιαν τῷ Ἰσραὴλ καὶ ἄφεσιν ἁμαρτιῶν. 32 Καὶ ἡμεῖς
repentance - to Israel and forgiveness of sins. And we

ἐσμεν αὐτοῦ[f] μάρτυρες τῶν ῥημάτων τούτων, καὶ τὸ Πνεῦμα
are His witnesses - of words ˜ these, [2]also [3]the [5]Spirit

δὲ τὸ Ἅγιον ὃ ἔδωκεν ὁ Θεὸς τοῖς πειθαρχοῦσιν
[1]and - [4]Holy whom gave ˜ - God to the *ones* obeying
those who obey

αὐτῷ."
Him."

things, they wondered what the outcome would be.
25 So one came and told them, saying, "Look, the men whom you put in prison are standing in the temple and teaching the people!"
26 Then the captain went with the officers and brought them without violence, for they feared the people, lest they should be stoned.
27 And when they had brought them, they set *them* before the council. And the high priest asked them,
28 saying, "Did we not strictly command you not to teach in this name? And look, you have filled Jerusalem with your doctrine, and intend to bring this Man's blood on us!"
29 But Peter and the *other* apostles answered and said: "We ought to obey God rather than men.
30 "The God of our fathers raised up Jesus whom you murdered by hanging on a tree.
31 "Him God has exalted to His right hand *to be* Prince and Savior, to give repentance to Israel and forgiveness of sins.
32 "And we are His witnesses to these things, and *so* also *is* the Holy Spirit whom God has given to those who obey Him."

---

[d]**(5:24)** NU omits ιερευς και ο, *priest and the.*
[e]**(5:25)** TR adds λεγων, *saying.* [f]**(5:32)** NU omits αυτου, *His.*

33 When they heard *this,* they
were furious and plotted to kill
them.
34 Then one in the council
stood up, a Pharisee named Gamaliel, a teacher of the law held
in respect by all the people, and
commanded them to put the
apostles outside for a little
while.
35 And he said to them: "Men
of Israel, take heed to yourselves what you intend to do
regarding these men.
36 "For some time ago Theudas rose up, claiming to be
somebody. A number of men,
about four hundred, joined him.
He was slain, and all who
obeyed him were scattered and
came to nothing.
37 "After this man, Judas of
Galilee rose up in the days of
the census, and drew away
many people after him. He also
perished, and all who obeyed
him were dispersed.
38 "And now I say to you,
keep away from these men and
let them alone; for if this plan or
this work is of men, it will come
to nothing;
39 "but if it is of God, you cannot overthrow it—lest you
even be found to fight against
God."
40 And they agreed with him,
and when they had called for

Gamaliel Gives Good Advice

33 Οἱ δὲ ἀκούσαντες διεπρίοντο καὶ ἐβουλεύοντο[g]
[2]the [3]*ones* [1]But hearing were infuriated and were resolving
But when they heard this, they

ἀνελεῖν αὐτούς. **34** Ἀναστὰς δέ τις ἐν τῷ συνεδρίῳ
to kill them. [6]standing [1]But [2]someone [3]in [4]the [5]council
stood up,

Φαρισαῖος ὀνόματι Γαμαλιήλ, νομοδιδάσκαλος τίμιος
a Pharisee by name Gamaliel, a teacher of *the* law held in honor
named

παντὶ τῷ λαῷ, ἐκέλευσεν ἔξω βραχύ τι τοὺς
by all the people, commanded [5]outside [7]short [8]*time* [6]a [3]the
and commanded

ἀποστόλους[h] ποιῆσαι.
[4]apostles [1]to [2]put.

35 Εἶπέ τε πρὸς αὐτούς, "Ἄνδρες Ἰσραηλῖται,
[2]he [3]said [1]And to them, "Men Israelites,
of Israel,

προσέχετε ἑαυτοῖς ἐπὶ τοῖς ἀνθρώποις τούτοις τί
take heed to yourselves with - men ~ these *as to* what

μέλλετε πράσσειν. **36** Πρὸ γὰρ τούτων τῶν ἡμερῶν
you are about to do. before ~ For these - days

ἀνέστη Θευδᾶς, λέγων εἶναί τινα ἑαυτόν, ᾧ
arose ~ Theudas, saying [2]to [3]be [4]someone [1]himself, to whom
claiming

προσεκλήθη ἀριθμὸς ἀνδρῶν ὡσεὶ τετρακοσίων· ὃς
was called a number of men about four hundred; who

ἀνῃρέθη, καὶ πάντες ὅσοι ἐπείθοντο αὐτῷ
was done away with, and all as many as were persuaded by him
who

διελύθησαν καὶ ἐγένοντο εἰς οὐδέν. **37** Μετὰ τοῦτον ἀνέστη
were scattered and became as nothing. After this [4]arose

Ἰούδας ὁ Γαλιλαῖος ἐν ταῖς ἡμέραις τῆς ἀπογραφῆς καὶ
[1]Judas [2]the [3]Galilean in the days of the registration and
census

ἀπέστησε λαὸν ἱκανὸν ὀπίσω αὐτοῦ.
caused [6]to [7]revolt [1]a [5]people [2]considerable [3]*number* [4]*of* after him.

Κἀκεῖνος ἀπώλετο, καὶ πάντες ὅσοι ἐπείθοντο αὐτῷ
That *one* also perished, and all as many as were persuaded by him
who

διεσκορπίσθησαν. **38** Καὶ τὰ νῦν λέγω ὑμῖν,
were dispersed. And *as for* the *things* now I say to you,
the present matter

ἀπόστητε ἀπὸ τῶν ἀνθρώπων τούτων καὶ ἐάσατε αὐτούς·
withdraw from - men ~ these and leave alone ~ them;

ὅτι ἐὰν ᾖ ἐξ ἀνθρώπων ἡ βουλὴ[i] ἢ τὸ ἔργον τοῦτο,
because if [6]is [7]of [8]men [1]the [2]counsel [3]or - [5]work [4]this,

καταλυθήσεται· **39** εἰ δὲ ἐκ Θεοῦ ἐστιν, οὐ δύνασθε
it will be abolished. if ~ But [3]of [4]God [1]it [2]is, [7]not [5]you [6]are [8]able
fail.

καταλῦσαι αὐτό,[j] μήποτε καὶ θεομάχοι
to abolish it, lest [2]also [5]*to* [6]*be* [7]fighting [8]against [9]God

εὑρεθῆτε."
[1]you [3]be [4]found."

40 Ἐπείσθησαν δὲ αὐτῷ, καὶ προσκαλεσάμενοι
[2]they [3]were [4]persuaded [1]And by him, and summoning
when they called

[g](**5:33**) NU reads εβουλοντο, *were wanting.*
[h](**5:34**) NU reads ανθρωπους, *men.*
[i](**5:38**) NU, TR add αυτη, *this.* [j](**5:39**) For δυνασθε . . . αυτο, NU reads δυνησεσθε . . . αυτους, *you will (not) be able (to overthrow) them.*

τοὺς ἀποστόλους, δείραντες παρήγγειλαν μὴ λαλεῖν ἐπὶ
the apostles, beating *them* they commanded *them* not to speak in
and beat

τῷ ὀνόματι τοῦ Ἰησοῦ, καὶ ἀπέλυσαν αὐτούς. **41** Οἱ μὲν
the name - of Jesus, and released them. [2]the [3]*ones* -
they

οὖν ἐπορεύοντο χαίροντες ἀπὸ προσώπου τοῦ συνεδρίου
[1]Then departed [7]rejoicing [1]from [2]*the* [3]face [4]of [5]the [6]council
presence

ὅτι ὑπὲρ τοῦ ὀνόματος τοῦ Ἰησοῦ[k]
because in behalf of the name - of Jesus

κατηξιώθησαν ἀτιμασθῆναι. **42** Πᾶσάν τε ἡμέραν, ἐν
they were counted worthy to be dishonored. every ~ And day, in

τῷ ἱερῷ καὶ κατ' οἶκον, οὐκ ἐπαύοντο
the temple and according to a house, [3]not [1]they [2]were ceasing
from house to house,

διδάσκοντες καὶ εὐαγγελιζόμενοι Ἰησοῦν τὸν Χριστόν.
from teaching and proclaiming the gospel of Jesus the Christ.
Messiah.

The Disciples Choose Seven to Serve

6 **1** Ἐν δὲ ταῖς ἡμέραις ταύταις, πληθυνόντων τῶν
in ~ And - days ~ these, multiplying the
as the disciples were

μαθητῶν, ἐγένετο γογγυσμὸς τῶν Ἑλληνιστῶν
disciples, *there* arose a murmuring of the Hellenists
increasing in number, complaint from the Greek-speaking Jews

πρὸς τοὺς Ἑβραίους ὅτι παρεθεωροῦντο ἐν τῇ
against the Hebrews because [3]were [4]being [5]overlooked [6]in [7]the
Aramaic-speaking Jews

διακονίᾳ τῇ καθημερινῇ αἱ χῆραι αὐτῶν.
[9]service [10]*of* [11]*food* - [8]daily - [2]widows [1]their.
distribution

2 Προσκαλεσάμενοι δὲ οἱ δώδεκα τὸ πλῆθος
[4]summoning [1]And [2]the [3]twelve the multitude
summoned whole congregation

τῶν μαθητῶν, εἶπον, "Οὐκ ἀρεστόν ἐστιν ἡμᾶς,
of the disciples, said, "[3]not [4]pleasing [1]It [2]is *to* us,
and said,

καταλείψαντας τὸν λόγον τοῦ Θεοῦ, διακονεῖν τραπέζαις.
forsaking the word - of God, to serve at tables.
that we should forsake

3 Ἐπισκέψασθε οὖν, ἀδελφοί, ἄνδρας ἐξ ὑμῶν
[3]look [4]for [1]Therefore, [2]brothers, [6]men [7]from [8]you
select from among

μαρτυρουμένους ἑπτά, πλήρεις Πνεύματος Ἁγίου[a] καὶ
[9]being [10]witnessed [5]seven, full of *the* Spirit ~ Holy and
of good reputation

σοφίας, οὓς καταστήσωμεν ἐπὶ τῆς χρείας ταύτης. **4** Ἡμεῖς
wisdom, whom we may appoint for - need ~ this. we ~

δὲ τῇ προσευχῇ καὶ τῇ διακονίᾳ τοῦ λόγου
But - in prayer and in the service of the word

προσκαρτερήσομεν." **5** Καὶ ἤρεσεν ὁ λόγος ἐνώπιον
will faithfully engage." And [3]was [4]pleasing [1]the [2]word before
continue." statement

παντὸς τοῦ πλήθους, καὶ ἐξελέξαντο Στέφανον, ἄνδρα
all the multitude, and they chose Stephen, a man
congregation,

πλήρης πίστεως καὶ Πνεύματος Ἁγίου, καὶ Φίλιππον καὶ
full of faith and of *the* Spirit ~ Holy, and Philip and

the apostles and beaten *them,*
they commanded that they
should not speak in the name of
Jesus, and let them go.
41 So they departed from the
presence of the council, rejoicing that they were counted
worthy to suffer shame for His
name.
42 And daily in the temple,
and in every house, they did
not cease teaching and preaching Jesus *as* the Christ.
6 Now in those days, when
the number of the disciples
was multiplying, there arose a
complaint against the Hebrews
by the Hellenists, because their
widows were neglected in the
daily distribution.
2 Then the twelve sum-
moned the multitude of the disciples and said, "It is not
desirable that we should leave
the word of God and serve tables.
3 "Therefore, brethren,
seek out from among you seven
men of *good* reputation, full of
the Holy Spirit and wisdom,
whom we may appoint over this
business;
4 "but we will give ourselves
continually to prayer and to the
ministry of the word."
5 And the saying pleased the
whole multitude. And they
chose Stephen, a man full of
faith and the Holy Spirit, and

[k]**(5:41)** NU omits του Ιησου, *of Jesus;* TR reads αυτου, *His (name).*
[a]**(6:3)** NU omits Αγιου, *Holy,* thus *(full of) spirit* or *the Spirit.*

Philip, Prochorus, Nicanor, Timon, Parmenas, and Nicolas, a proselyte from Antioch,
6 whom they set before the apostles; and when they had prayed, they laid hands on them.
7 Then the word of God spread, and the number of the disciples multiplied greatly in Jerusalem, and a great many of the priests were obedient to the faith.
8 And Stephen, full of faith and power, did great wonders and signs among the people.
9 Then there arose some from what is called the Synagogue of the Freedmen (Cyrenians, Alexandrians, and those from Cilicia and Asia), disputing with Stephen.
10 And they were not able to resist the wisdom and the Spirit by which he spoke.
11 Then they secretly induced men to say, "We have heard him speak blasphemous words against Moses and God."
12 And they stirred up the people, the elders, and the scribes; and they came upon *him,* seized him, and brought *him* to the council.
13 They also set up false witnesses who said, "This man does not cease to speak blasphemous words against this holy place and the law;
14 "for we have heard him say that this Jesus of Nazareth will

Πρόχορον καὶ Νικάνορα καὶ Τίμωνα καὶ Παρμενᾶν καὶ
Prochorus and Nicanor and Timon and Parmenas and

Νικόλαον προσήλυτον* Ἀντιοχέα, **6** οὓς ἔστησαν ἐνώπιον
Nicholas a proselyte of Antioch, whom they set before

τῶν ἀποστόλων, καὶ προσευξάμενοι ἐπέθηκαν αὐτοῖς τὰς
the apostles, and praying (when they prayed) they laid [3]on [4]them [1]the (their)

χεῖρας.
[2]hands.

7 Καὶ ὁ λόγος τοῦ Θεοῦ ηὔξανε, καὶ
And the word - of God was growing, and

ἐπληθύνετο ὁ ἀριθμὸς τῶν μαθητῶν ἐν Ἱερουσαλὴμ
[8]was [9]being [10]multiplied (increasing) [1]the [2]number [3]of [4]the [5]disciples [6]in [7]Jerusalem

σφόδρα, πολύς τε ὄχλος τῶν ἱερέων ὑπήκουον τῇ
exceedingly, [3]great [1]and [2]a crowd of the priests were obeying the

πίστει.
faith.

False Witnesses Accuse Stephen of Blasphemy

8 Στέφανος δὲ πλήρης πίστεως[b] καὶ δυνάμεως
Stephen ˜ And full of faith and power

ἐποίει τέρατα καὶ σημεῖα μεγάλα ἐν τῷ λαῷ.
was performing wonders and signs ˜ great among the people.

9 Ἀνέστησαν δέ τινες τῶν ἐκ τῆς Συναγωγῆς τῆς
[2]*there* [3]rose [4]up [1]But some of the *ones* from the Synagogue the *one* (which)

λεγομένης Λιβερτίνων καὶ Κυρηναίων καὶ Ἀλεξανδρέων
being called (is) of *the* Freedmen both of *the* Cyrenians and of *the* Alexandrians

καὶ τῶν ἀπὸ Κιλικίας καὶ Ἀσίας συζητοῦντες τῷ
and of the *ones* (those) from Cilicia and Asia debating -

Στεφάνῳ. **10** Καὶ οὐκ ἴσχυον ἀντιστῆναι τῇ σοφίᾳ καὶ
with Stephen. And [3]not [1]they [2]were able to withstand the wisdom and

τῷ Πνεύματι ᾧ ἐλάλει.
the Spirit with which he spoke.

11 Τότε ὑπέβαλον ἄνδρας λέγοντας ὅτι
Then they secretly instigated men *to be* saying -

"Ἀκηκόαμεν αὐτοῦ λαλοῦντος ῥήματα βλάσφημα εἰς
"We have heard him speaking words ˜ blasphemous against

Μωσῆν καὶ τὸν Θεόν." **12** Συνεκίνησάν τε τὸν λαὸν καὶ τοὺς
Moses and - God." [2]they [3]aroused [1]And the people and the

πρεσβυτέρους καὶ τοὺς γραμματεῖς, καὶ ἐπιστάντες
elders and the scribes, and coming upon *him* (they came against him)

συνήρπασαν αὐτὸν καὶ ἤγαγον εἰς τὸ συνέδριον,
they (and) seized him and led *him* to the council,

13 ἔστησάν τε μάρτυρας ψευδεῖς λέγοντας, "Ὁ
[2]they [3]put [4]forward [1]and witnesses ˜ false saying, -

ἄνθρωπος οὗτος οὐ παύεται ῥήματα βλάσφημα[c] λαλῶν
"man ˜ This not ˜ does cease [3]words [2]blasphemous [1]speaking

κατὰ τοῦ τόπου τοῦ ἁγίου[d] καὶ τοῦ νόμου· **14** ἀκηκόαμεν
against the place ˜ - holy and the law; [2]we [3]have [4]heard

γὰρ αὐτοῦ λέγοντος ὅτι Ἰησοῦς ὁ Ναζωραῖος οὗτος
[1]for him saying that [2]Jesus [3]the [4]Nazarene [1]this

---

[b](**6:8**) NU reads *χαριτος, of grace.* [c](**6:13**) NU omits *βλασφημα, blasphemous.* [d](**6:13**) NU (in brackets) and TR add *τουτου, this (holy place).*

*(**6:5**) *προσήλυτος (prosēlytos).* Noun from *πρός, to,* and *ἔρχομαι, come,* meaning *proselyte, convert.* In the NT the word refers to Gentiles converted to Judaism, many of whom were especially open to the gospel of Christ. The word was apparently not applied to those non-Jews, called "devout" or "God-fearers" (*σεβόμενος τὸν θεόν*), who did not submit to circumcision but participated in synagogue worship and observed basic Jewish laws. Thus, the expression "devout proselytes" in Acts 13:43 is curious and may emphasize fully worshiping proselytes.

καταλύσει τὸν τόπον τοῦτον καὶ ἀλλάξει τὰ ἔθη ἃ
will destroy - place ˜ this and will change the customs which

παρέδωκεν ἡμῖν Μωσῆς." 15 Καὶ ἀτενίσαντες εἰς αὐτὸν
[2]handed [3]down [4]to [5]us [1]Moses." And looking intently on him
at

ἅπαντες οἱ καθεζόμενοι ἐν τῷ συνεδρίῳ εἶδον τὸ
all the *ones* sitting in the council saw -
those who sat

πρόσωπον αὐτοῦ ὡσεὶ πρόσωπον ἀγγέλου.
face ˜ his like *the* face of an angel.

Stephen Recounts the Call of Abraham

7 1 Εἶπε δὲ ὁ ἀρχιερεύς, "Εἰ ἄρα ταῦτα οὕτως
[5]said [1]And [2]the [3]high [4]priest, - "Then these *things* thus ˜
"Are these things

ἔχει?"
have?"
so?"

2 Ὁ δὲ ἔφη, "Ἄνδρες ἀδελφοὶ καὶ πατέρες,
[2]the [3]*one* [1]And said, "Men brothers and fathers,
he

ἀκούσατε. Ὁ Θεὸς τῆς δόξης ὤφθη τῷ πατρὶ ἡμῶν
listen. The God - of glory appeared - to father ˜ our

Ἀβραὰμ ὄντι ἐν τῇ Μεσοποταμίᾳ πρὶν ἢ κατοικῆσαι
Abraham being in - Mesopotamia before to dwell
while he was he

αὐτὸν ἐν Χαρράν, 3 καὶ εἶπε πρὸς αὐτόν, «Ἔξελθε ἐκ τῆς
him in Haran, and said to him, «Go out from -
dwelled

γῆς σου καὶ ἐκ τῆς συγγενείας σου, καὶ δεῦρο εἰς γῆν ἣν
land ˜ your and from - relationship ˜ your, and come to a land which
relatives

ἄν σοι δείξω.»[a] 4 Τότε ἐξελθὼν ἐκ γῆς
- [4]you [1]I [2]will [3]show.» Then going forth from *the* land
he went forth

Χαλδαίων κατῴκησεν ἐν Χαρράν. Κἀκεῖθεν, μετὰ τὸ
of *the* Chaldeans he settled down in Haran. And from there, after -
and

ἀποθανεῖν τὸν πατέρα αὐτοῦ, μετῴκισεν αὐτὸν εἰς τὴν γῆν
[3]to [4]die - [2]father [1]his, He removed him to - land ˜
was dead

ταύτην εἰς ἣν ὑμεῖς νῦν κατοικεῖτε, 5 καὶ οὐκ ἔδωκεν
this in which you now dwell, and [3]not [1]He [2]did give

αὐτῷ κληρονομίαν ἐν αὐτῇ οὐδὲ βῆμα ποδός, καὶ
him an inheritance in it not even a step of a foot, and
a place to put his foot on,

ἐπηγγείλατο δοῦναι αὐτῷ εἰς κατάσχεσιν αὐτὴν καὶ τῷ
He promised to give [2]to [3]him [4]for [5]a [6]possession [1]it and -

σπέρματι αὐτοῦ μετ' αὐτόν, οὐκ ὄντος αὐτῷ τέκνου.
to seed ˜ his after him, not being to him a child.
descendants though he had no child.

6 Ἐλάλησε δὲ οὕτως ὁ Θεός, ὅτι ἔσται τὸ σπέρμα αὐτοῦ
[3]spoke [1]But [4]thus - [2]God, that [3]will [4]be - [2]seed [1]his
in this way would offspring

πάροικον ἐν γῇ ἀλλοτρίᾳ, καὶ δουλώσουσιν αὐτὸ καὶ
a stranger in a land foreign, and they will enslave it and
would enslave them

κακώσουσιν ἔτη τετρακόσια. 7 'Καὶ τὸ ἔθνος, ᾧ
they will treat *them* badly [3]years [1]four [2]hundred. 'And the nation, which
would

destroy this place and change the customs which Moses delivered to us."
15 And all who sat in the council, looking steadfastly at him, saw his face as the face of an angel.
7 Then the high priest said, "Are these things so?"
2 And he said, "Brethren and fathers, listen: The God of glory appeared to our father Abraham when he was in Mesopotamia, before he dwelt in Haran,
3 "and said to him, *'Get out of your country and from your relatives, and come to a land that I will show you.'*
4 "Then he came out of the land of the Chaldeans and dwelt in Haran. And from there, when his father was dead, He moved him to this land in which you now dwell.
5 "And *God* gave him no inheritance in it, not even *enough* to set his foot on. But even when *Abraham* had no child, He promised to give it to him for a possession, and to his descendants after him.
6 "But God spoke in this way: that his descendants would dwell in a foreign land, and that they would bring them into bondage and oppress *them* four hundred years.
7 *'And the nation to whom they will be in bondage I will judge,'* said God, *'and after that they shall come out and serve Me in this place.'*

[a](7:3) Gen. 12:1

8 "Then He gave him the covenant of circumcision; and so *Abraham* begot Isaac and circumcised him on the eighth day; and Isaac *begot* Jacob, and Jacob *begot* the twelve patriarchs.

9 "And the patriarchs, becoming envious, sold Joseph into Egypt. But God was with him

10 "and delivered him out of all his troubles, and gave him favor and wisdom in the presence of Pharaoh, king of Egypt; and he made him governor over Egypt and all his house.

11 "Now a famine and great trouble came over all the land of Egypt and Canaan, and our fathers found no sustenance.

12 "But when Jacob heard that there was grain in Egypt, he sent out our fathers first.

13 "And the second *time* Joseph was made known to his brothers, and Joseph's family became known to the Pharaoh.

14 "Then Joseph sent and called his father Jacob and all his relatives to *him*, seventy-five people.

15 "So Jacob went down to Egypt; and he died, he and our fathers.

16 "And they were carried back to Shechem and laid in the tomb that Abraham bought for a sum of money from the sons of Hamor, *the father* of Shechem.

ἐὰν δουλεύσωσιν, κρινῶ ἐγώ,' εἶπεν ὁ Θεός, 'καὶ μετὰ
- they will serve, [2]will [3]judge [1]I,' said - God, 'and after

ταῦτα ἐξελεύσονται καὶ λατρεύσουσί μοι ἐν τῷ τόπῳ
these *things* they will come out and will serve Me in - place ˜

τούτῳ.' 8 Καὶ ἔδωκεν αὐτῷ διαθήκην περιτομῆς· καὶ οὕτως
this.' And He gave him a covenant of circumcision; and so

ἐγέννησε τὸν Ἰσαὰκ καὶ περιέτεμεν αὐτὸν τῇ ἡμέρᾳ τῇ
he begot - Isaac and circumcised him on the day ˜ -

ὀγδόῃ, καὶ ὁ Ἰσαὰκ τὸν Ἰακώβ, καὶ ὁ Ἰακὼβ τοὺς δώδεκα
eighth, and - Isaac *begot* - Jacob, and - Jacob *begot* the twelve

πατριάρχας.
patriarchs.

The Patriarchs Go Down to Egypt

9 "Καὶ οἱ πατριάρχαι ζηλώσαντες τὸν Ἰωσὴφ ἀπέδοντο
"And the patriarchs being jealous of - Joseph sold *him*
became and sold

εἰς Αἴγυπτον· καὶ ἦν ὁ Θεὸς μετ' αὐτοῦ, 10 καὶ ἐξείλετο
into Egypt; and was ˜ - God with him, and He delivered

αὐτὸν ἐκ πασῶν τῶν θλίψεων αὐτοῦ, καὶ ἔδωκεν αὐτῷ χάριν
him out of all - afflictions ˜ his, and He gave him favor

καὶ σοφίαν ἐναντίον Φαραὼ βασιλέως Αἰγύπτου, καὶ
and wisdom before Pharaoh king of Egypt, and

κατέστησεν αὐτὸν ἡγούμενον ἐπ' Αἴγυπτον καὶ ὅλον τὸν
he appointed him a ruler over Egypt and [2]whole -

οἶκον αὐτοῦ. 11 Ἦλθε δὲ λιμὸς ἐφ' ὅλην τὴν γῆν
[3]house [1]his. [4]came [1]And [2]a [3]famine on whole ˜ the land

Αἰγύπτου[b] καὶ Χαναάν, καὶ θλῖψις μεγάλη, καὶ οὐχ
of Egypt and Canaan, and a(n) affliction ˜ great, and [4]not

εὕρισκον χορτάσματα οἱ πατέρες ἡμῶν. 12 Ἀκούσας δὲ
[3]were [5]finding [6]food - [2]fathers [1]our. [3]hearing [1]And
provisions heard that

Ἰακὼβ ὄντα σῖτα ἐν Αἰγύπτῳ ἐξαπέστειλε τοὺς πατέρας
[2]Jacob being ˜ wheat in Egypt sent out - fathers ˜
there was wheat and sent

ἡμῶν πρῶτον. 13 Καὶ ἐν τῷ δευτέρῳ ἀνεγνωρίσθη Ἰωσὴφ
our first. And on the second *visit* [2]was [3]known [4]again [1]Joseph

τοῖς ἀδελφοῖς αὐτοῦ, καὶ φανερὸν ἐγένετο τῷ Φαραὼ τὸ
- to brothers ˜ his, and [6]known [5]became [7]to [8]Pharaoh [1]the

γένος τοῦ Ἰωσήφ. 14 Ἀποστείλας δὲ Ἰωσὴφ μετεκαλέσατο
[2]family - [3]of [4]Joseph. [3]sending [1]And [2]Joseph summoned
sent and

τὸν πατέρα αὐτοῦ Ἰακὼβ καὶ πᾶσαν τὴν συγγένειαν, ἐν ψυχαῖς
- father ˜ his Jacob and all the relationship, [3]in [4]souls
his relatives, persons

ἑβδομήκοντα πέντε. 15 Κατέβη δὲ Ἰακὼβ εἰς Αἴγυπτον.
[1]seventy- [2]five. [3]went [4]down [1]And [2]Jacob to Egypt.

Καὶ ἐτελεύτησεν αὐτὸς καὶ οἱ πατέρες ἡμῶν, 16 καὶ
and he died he and - fathers ˜ our, and

μετετέθησαν εἰς Συχὲμ καὶ ἐτέθησαν ἐν τῷ μνήματι ὃ
they were conveyed to Shechem and were placed in the tomb which
brought back

ὠνήσατο Ἀβραὰμ τιμῆς ἀργυρίου παρὰ τῶν υἱῶν Ἑμμὸρ
bought ˜ Abraham of a price of silver from the sons of Hamor
for

τοῦ[c] Συχέμ.
- *father* of Shechem.

[b](7:11) For γην Αιγυπτου, *land of Egypt,* NU reads Αιγυπτου, *Egypt.*

[c](7:16) NU reads εν, *(the sons of Hamor) in (Shechem).*

God Delivers Israel through Moses

17 "Καθὼς δὲ ἤγγιζεν ὁ χρόνος τῆς ἐπαγγελίας*
"as ˜ Now [6]drew [7]near [1]the [2]time [3]of [4]the [5]promise
"when

ἧς ὤμοσεν[d] ὁ Θεὸς τῷ Ἀβραάμ, ηὔξησεν ὁ λαὸς καὶ
which swore ˜ - God - to Abraham, [3]increased [1]the [2]people and

ἐπληθύνθη ἐν Αἰγύπτῳ, 18 ἄχρις οὗ ἀνέστη βασιλεὺς
multiplied in Egypt, until - *there* arose a king ˜

ἕτερος[e] ὃς οὐκ ᾔδει τὸν Ἰωσήφ. 19 Οὗτος
different who not ˜ did know - Joseph. This *king*

κατασοφισάμενος τὸ γένος ἡμῶν ἐκάκωσε τοὺς πατέρας
taking advantage of - race ˜ our mistreated - fathers ˜
took and oppressed

ἡμῶν τοῦ ποιεῖν ἔκθετα τὰ βρέφη αὐτῶν εἰς τὸ μὴ
our - to make [3]exposed - [2]babies [1]their for - not
in order that they

ζωογονεῖσθαι. 20 Ἐν ᾧ καιρῷ ἐγεννήθη Μωσῆς
to keep *them* alive. In which time [2]was [3]born [1]Moses
might not preserve their lives. At this

καὶ ἦν ἀστεῖος τῷ Θεῷ· ὃς ἀνετράφη μῆνας τρεῖς
and he was well pleasing - to God; who was brought up months ˜ three

ἐν τῷ οἴκῳ τοῦ πατρός. 21 Ἐκτεθέντα δὲ αὐτὸν ἀνείλετο
in the house of the father. [2]being [3]exposed [1]But [9]him [8]took [10]up
his when he was

ἡ θυγάτηρ Φαραὼ καὶ ἀνεθρέψατο αὐτὸν ἑαυτῇ εἰς
[4]the [5]daughter [6]of [7]Pharaoh and brought up ˜ him for herself as

υἱόν. 22 Καὶ ἐπαιδεύθη Μωσῆς πάσῃ σοφίᾳ
a son. And [2]was [3]educated [1]Moses in all *the* wisdom

Αἰγυπτίων, ἦν δὲ δυνατὸς ἐν λόγοις καὶ ἔργοις.[f]
of *the* Egyptians, [2]he [3]was [1]and mighty in words and deeds.

23 Ὡς δὲ ἐπληροῦτο αὐτῷ τεσσαρακονταετὴς χρόνος,
when ˜ Now was fulfilled for him a forty-year time,
he had turned forty years old,

ἀνέβη ἐπὶ τὴν καρδίαν αὐτοῦ ἐπισκέψασθαι τοὺς ἀδελφοὺς
it came up in - heart ˜ his to visit - brothers ˜
entered his mind

αὐτοῦ τοὺς υἱοὺς Ἰσραήλ. 24 Καὶ ἰδών τινα
his the sons of Israel. And seeing someone
when he saw

ἀδικούμενον ἠμύνατο καὶ ἐποίησεν ἐκδίκησιν τῷ
being wronged he retaliated and did vengeance for the *one*
avenged

καταπονουμένῳ πατάξας τὸν Αἰγύπτιον. 25 Ἐνόμιζε δὲ
being oppressed striking the Egyptian. [2]he [3]supposed [1]Now
and struck

συνιέναι τοὺς ἀδελφοὺς αὐτοῦ ὅτι ὁ Θεὸς διὰ χειρὸς
[3]to [4]understand - [2]brothers [1]his that - God by hand ˜
that his brothers understood

αὐτοῦ δίδωσιν αὐτοῖς σωτηρίαν, οἱ δὲ οὐ συνῆκαν.
his gives to them deliverance, [2]the [3]*ones* [1]but not ˜ did understand.
was giving they

26 Τῇ τε ἐπιούσῃ ἡμέρᾳ ὤφθη αὐτοῖς
[2]on [3]the [1]And next day he appeared to them

μαχομένοις, καὶ συνήλασεν αὐτοὺς εἰς εἰρήνην, εἰπών,
fighting, and reconciled them to peace, saying,
as they were striving,

'Ἄνδρες, ἀδελφοί ἐστε ὑμεῖς! Ἱνατί ἀδικεῖτε ἀλλήλους?'
'Men, [3]brothers [2]are [1]you! Why do you wrong one another?'

17 "But when the time of the promise drew near which God had sworn to Abraham, the people grew and multiplied in Egypt
18 "till another king arose who did not know Joseph.
19 "This man dealt treacherously with our people, and oppressed our forefathers, making them expose their babies, so that they might not live.
20 "At this time Moses was born, and was well pleasing to God; and he was brought up in his father's house for three months.
21 "But when he was set out, Pharaoh's daughter took him away and brought him up as her own son.
22 "And Moses was learned in all the wisdom of the Egyptians, and was mighty in words and deeds.
23 "Now when he was forty years old, it came into his heart to visit his brethren, the children of Israel.
24 "And seeing one of *them* suffer wrong, he defended and avenged him who was oppressed, and struck down the Egyptian.
25 "For he supposed that his brethren would have understood that God would deliver them by his hand, but they did not understand.
26 "And the next day he appeared to two of them as they were fighting, and *tried to* reconcile them, saying, 'Men, you are brethren; why do you wrong one another?'

---

[d](7:17) NU reads *ωμολογησεν, promised.*
[e](7:18) NU adds in brackets *επ Αιγυπτον, over Egypt.*
[f](7:22) NU adds *αυτου, his.*

***(7:17)** ἐπαγγελία *(epangelia).* Common noun in the NT, originally meaning *announcement* but always in the NT meaning *promise.* Here it may approach the original meaning in the sense of a *pledge.* The NT occurrences most often refer to God's promises, primarily to the promise itself (as Rom. 9:9) but also to its content (the thing promised, as 1 John 2:25; Gal. 3:14). As in Gal. 3:14, the NT frequently links "the promise" with the Holy Spirit, especially in Luke and Acts (cf. Acts 2:33). Cf. the cognate verb ἐπαγγέλλομαι, *promise*

27 "But he who did his neighbor wrong pushed him away, saying, *'Who made you a ruler and a judge over us?*
28 *'Do you want to kill me as you did the Egyptian yesterday?'*
29 "Then, at this saying, Moses fled and became a dweller in the land of Midian, where he had two sons.
30 "And when forty years had passed, an Angel of the Lord appeared to him in a flame of fire in a bush, in the wilderness of Mount Sinai.
31 "When Moses saw *it,* he marveled at the sight; and as he drew near to observe, the voice of the Lord came to him,
32 *"saying, 'I am the God of your fathers — the God of Abraham, the God of Isaac, and the God of Jacob.'* And Moses trembled and dared not look.
33 *'Then the* LORD *said to him, "Take your sandals off your feet, for the place where you stand is holy ground.*
34 *"I have surely seen the oppression of My people who are in Egypt; I have heard their groaning and have come down to deliver them. And now come, I will send you to Egypt."'*
35 "This Moses whom they rejected, saying, *'Who made you a ruler and a judge?'* is the one God sent *to be* a ruler and a deliverer by the hand of the Angel who appeared to him in the bush.
36 "He brought them out, after he had shown wonders and signs in the land of Egypt, and in the Red Sea, and in the wil-

27 "Ὁ δὲ ἀδικῶν τὸν πλησίον ἀπώσατο αὐτὸν
"[2]the [3]*one* [1]But wronging the neighbor pushed away ˜ him
his

εἰπών, «Τίς σε κατέστησεν ἄρχοντα καὶ δικαστὴν ἐφ'
saying, «'Who you ˜ appointed a ruler and a judge over

ἡμᾶς? **28** Μὴ ἀνελεῖν με σὺ θέλεις ὃν τρόπον
us? [3]not [5]to [6]kill [7]me [1]You [2]do [4]desire, *do you* what manner
in the way that

ἀνεῖλες χθὲς τὸν Αἰγύπτιον?'»[g] **29** Ἔφυγε δὲ Μωσῆς ἐν
you killed [3]yesterday [1]the [2]Egyptian?'» [3]fled [1]Now [2]Moses at

τῷ λόγῳ τούτῳ, καὶ ἐγένετο πάροικος ἐν γῇ Μαδιάμ, οὗ
- word ˜ this, and he became a stranger in *the* land of Midian, where

ἐγέννησεν υἱοὺς δύο.
he begot sons ˜ two.

30 "Καὶ πληρωθέντων ἐτῶν τεσσαράκοντα, ὤφθη
"And [3]having [4]been [5]fulfilled [2]years [1]forty, *there* appeared
after another forty years,

αὐτῷ ἐν τῇ ἐρήμῳ τοῦ Ὄρους Σινᾶ ἄγγελος Κυρίου[h] ἐν
to him in the wilderness - of Mount Sinai an angel of *the* Lord in

φλογὶ πυρὸς βάτου. **31** Ὁ δὲ Μωσῆς ἰδὼν ἐθαύμαζε
a flame of fire of a bush. - And Moses seeing *it* marveled at
in when he saw

τὸ ὅραμα· προσερχομένου δὲ αὐτοῦ κατανοῆσαι,
the sight; approaching and him to observe closely,
and as he approached it

ἐγένετο φωνὴ Κυρίου πρὸς αὐτόν,[i] **32** «Ἐγὼ ὁ Θεὸς
[6]came [1]*the* [2]voice [3]of [4]*the* [5]Lord to him, «'I *am* the God

τῶν πατέρων σου, ὁ Θεὸς Ἀβραὰμ καὶ ὁ Θεὸς[j] Ἰσαὰκ
- of fathers ˜ your, the God of Abraham and the God of Isaac

καὶ ὁ Θεὸς Ἰακώβ.'»[k] Ἔντρομος δὲ γενόμενος Μωσῆς οὐκ
and the God of Jacob.'» trembling And becoming Moses not ˜
And Moses was trembling and was not

ἐτόλμα κατανοῆσαι. **33** «Εἶπε δὲ αὐτῷ ὁ Κύριος,
did dare to look closely. «[4]said [1]And [5]to [6]him [2]the [3]Lord,
bold enough

'Λῦσον τὸ ὑπόδημα τῶν ποδῶν σου, ὁ γὰρ τόπος ἐν ᾧ
'Remove the sandal - of feet ˜ your, the ˜ for place on which

ἕστηκας γῆ ἁγία ἐστίν. **34** Ἰδὼν εἶδον τὴν
you stand [3]ground [2]holy [1]is. Seeing I saw the
I have certainly seen

κάκωσιν τοῦ λαοῦ μου τοῦ ἐν Αἰγύπτῳ, καὶ τοῦ
mistreatment - of people ˜ My - in Egypt, and -

στεναγμοῦ αὐτῶν ἤκουσα, καὶ κατέβην ἐξελέσθαι αὐτούς·
groaning ˜ their I heard, and I came down to deliver them;
have heard, have come

καὶ νῦν δεῦρο, ἀποστελῶ σε εἰς Αἴγυπτον.'»[l] **35** Τοῦτον τὸν
and now come, I will send you to Egypt.'» This -

Μωσῆν ὃν ἠρνήσαντο εἰπόντες, «'Τίς σε κατέστησεν
Moses whom they denied saying, «'Who you ˜ appointed

ἄρχοντα καὶ δικαστήν?'»[m] Τοῦτον ὁ Θεὸς ἄρχοντα καὶ
a ruler and a judge?'» This *man* - God [2]*as* [3]a [4]ruler [5]and

λυτρωτὴν ἀπέστειλεν ἐν χειρὶ ἀγγέλου τοῦ ὀφθέντος αὐτῷ
[6]redeemer [1]sent by *the* hand of *the* angel the *one* appearing to him
who appeared

ἐν τῇ βάτῳ. **36** Οὗτος ἐξήγαγεν αὐτοὺς ποιήσας τέρατα καὶ
in the bush. This *man* led out ˜ them doing wonders and
and did

σημεῖα ἐν γῇ Αἰγύπτῳ καὶ ἐν Ἐρυθρᾷ θαλάσσῃ καὶ ἐν τῇ
signs in *the* land of Egypt and at *the* Red Sea and in the

[g](**7:27, 28**) Gen. 15:14
[h](**7:30**) NU omits Κυριου, *of the Lord.* [i](**7:31**) NU omits προς αυτον, *to him.*
[j](**7:32**) NU omits ο Θεος before both Ισαακ, *of Isaac,* and Ιακωβ, *of Jacob,* thus *the God of Abraham and Isaac and Jacob.*
[k](**7:32**) Ex. 3:6, 15
[l](**7:33, 34**) Ex. 3:5, 7, 8, 10
[m](**7:35**) Ex. 2:14

(Mark 14:11); and the noun ἐπάγγελμα, *promise* (2 Pet. 1:4; 3:13).

ἐρήμῳ ἔτη τεσσαράκοντα.
wilderness years ˜ forty.

Israel Rebels Against God

37 "Οὗτός ἐστιν ὁ Μωσῆς ὁ εἰπὼν τοῖς υἱοῖς
"This is the Moses the *one* saying to the sons
who said

Ἰσραήλ, «Προφήτην ὑμῖν ἀναστήσει Κύριος[n] ὁ Θεὸς
of Israel, «[10]a [11]Prophet [8]to [9]you [5]will [6]raise [7]up [1]*The* [2]Lord - [4]God

ἡμῶν[o] ἐκ τῶν ἀδελφῶν ὑμῶν ὡς ἐμέ.»[p] **38** Οὗτός ἐστιν
[3]our from - brothers ˜ your like me.» This is

ὁ γενόμενος ἐν τῇ ἐκκλησίᾳ ἐν τῇ ἐρήμῳ μετὰ τοῦ
the *one* being in the assembly in the wilderness with the
who was

ἀγγέλου τοῦ λαλοῦντος αὐτῷ ἐν τῷ Ὄρει Σινᾶ
angel the *one* speaking to him on - Mount Sinai
who was

καὶ τῶν πατέρων ἡμῶν, ὃς ἐδέξατο λόγια ζῶντα
and *who was with* - fathers ˜ our, who received sayings ˜ living

δοῦναι ἡμῖν, **39** ᾧ οὐκ ἠθέλησαν ὑπήκοοι γενέσθαι οἱ
to give to us, to whom [4]not [3]did [5]desire [8]obedient [6]to [7]be -

πατέρες ἡμῶν ἀλλ' ἀπώσαντο καὶ ἐστράφησαν τῇ καρδίᾳ
[2]fathers [1]our but they rejected *him* and returned - in heart ˜

αὐτῶν εἰς Αἴγυπτον, **40** εἰπόντες τῷ Ἀαρών, «Ποίησον ἡμῖν
their to Egypt, saying - to Aaron, «Make for us

θεοὺς οἳ προπορεύσονται ἡμῶν· ὁ γὰρ Μωσῆς οὗτος, ὃς
gods who will go before us; - for Moses ˜ this, who

ἐξήγαγεν ἡμᾶς ἐκ γῆς Αἰγύπτου, οὐκ οἴδαμεν τί
led out ˜ us from *the* land of Egypt, [3]not [1]we [2]do know what

γέγονεν αὐτῷ.»[q] **41** Καὶ ἐμοσχοποίησαν ἐν ταῖς ἡμέραις
has happened to him.» And they made a calf in - days ˜

ἐκείναις καὶ ἀνήγαγον θυσίαν τῷ εἰδώλῳ, καὶ εὐφραίνοντο
those and offered a sacrifice to the idol, and were rejoicing

ἐν τοῖς ἔργοις τῶν χειρῶν αὐτῶν. **42** Ἔστρεψε δὲ ὁ Θεὸς
in the works - of hands ˜ their. [3]turned [4]away [1]But - [2]God

καὶ παρέδωκεν αὐτοὺς λατρεύειν τῇ στρατιᾷ τοῦ οὐρανοῦ,
and gave over ˜ them to serve the host - of heaven,

καθὼς γέγραπται ἐν Βίβλῳ τῶν Προφητῶν,
just as it is written in *the* Book of the Prophets,

«Μὴ σφάγια καὶ θυσίας προσηνέγκατέ
«[3]not [5]slaughtered [6]animals [7]and [8]sacrifices [1]You [2]did [4]offer

μοι
to Me, *did you*

Ἔτη τεσσαράκοντα ἐν τῇ ἐρήμῳ, οἶκος
While you were years ˜ forty in the wilderness, *O* house

Ἰσραήλ?
of Israel?

43 Καὶ ἀνελάβετε τὴν σκηνὴν τοῦ Μολὸχ
Indeed you carried up the tabernacle - of Moloch

Καὶ τὸ ἄστρον τοῦ θεοῦ ὑμῶν Ῥεμφάν,
And the star - of god ˜ your Remphan,

Τοὺς τύπους οὓς ἐποιήσατε προσκυνεῖν αὐτοῖς·
The images which you made to worship them;

Καὶ μετοικιῶ ὑμᾶς ἐπέκεινα Βαβυλῶνος.»[r]
And I will relocate you beyond Babylon.»

derness forty years.

37 "This is that Moses who said to the children of Israel, *'The* L*ORD* *your God will raise up for you a Prophet like me from your brethren. Him you shall hear.'*

38 "This is he who was in the congregation in the wilderness with the Angel who spoke to him on Mount Sinai, and *with* our fathers, the one who received the living oracles to give to us,

39 "whom our fathers would not obey, but rejected. And in their hearts they turned back to Egypt,

40 "saying to Aaron, *'Make us gods to go before us; as for this Moses who brought us out of the land of Egypt, we do not know what has become of him.'*

41 "And they made a calf in those days, offered sacrifices to the idol, and rejoiced in the works of their own hands.

42 "Then God turned and gave them up to worship the host of heaven, as it is written in the book of the Prophets:

'Did you offer Me
slaughtered animals and
sacrifices during forty
years in the wilderness,
O house of Israel?
43 *You also took up the*
tabernacle of Moloch,
And the star of your god
Remphan,
Images which you made
to worship;
And I will carry you away
beyond Babylon.'

---

[n](**7:37**) NU omits Κυριος, *the Lord.* [o](**7:37**) NU omits *ημων, our,* TR reads *υμων, your.* [p](**7:37**) Deut. 18:15; TR adds *αυτου ακουσεσθε, Him you shall hear.*
[q](**7:40**) Ex. 32:1, 23
[r](**7:42, 43**) Amos 5:25–27

44 "Our fathers had the tabernacle of witness in the wilderness, as He appointed, instructing Moses to make it according to the pattern that he
had seen,
45 "which our fathers, having
received it in turn, also brought
with Joshua into the land possessed by the Gentiles, whom
God drove out before the face
of our fathers until the days of
David,
46 "who found favor before
God and asked to find a dwelling for the God of Jacob.
47 "But Solomon built Him a
house.
48 "However, the Most High
does not dwell in temples made
with hands, as the prophet
says:

49 *'Heaven is My throne,*
And earth is My footstool.
What house will you build
for Me? says the LORD,
Or what is the place of
My rest?
50 *Has My hand not made all*
these things?'

51 "*You* stiff-necked and uncircumcised in heart and ears!
You always resist the Holy
Spirit; as your fathers *did,* so
do you.
52 "Which of the prophets did
your fathers not persecute?
And they killed those who foretold the coming of the Just One,
of whom you now have become
the betrayers and murderers,
53 "who have received the
law by the direction of angels
and have not kept *it.*"

God's True Tabernacle

44 "Ἡ σκηνὴ τοῦ μαρτυρίου ἦν τοῖς πατράσιν ἡμῶν ἐν
"The tabernacle of the testimony was with fathers ˜ our in
tent

τῇ ἐρήμῳ, καθὼς διετάξατο ὁ λαλῶν τῷ Μωσῇ
the wilderness, just as [6]commanded [7]*him* [1]the [2]*One* [3]speaking - [4]to [5]Moses

ποιῆσαι αὐτὴν κατὰ τὸν τύπον ὃν ἑωράκει, **45** ἣν
to make it according to the pattern which he had seen, which

καὶ εἰσήγαγον διαδεξάμενοι οἱ πατέρες ἡμῶν μετὰ
also [7]brought [8]in [3]having [4]received [5]in [6]turn - [2]fathers [1]our with

Ἰησοῦ ἐν τῇ κατασχέσει τῶν ἐθνῶν ὧν ἐξῶσεν ὁ Θεὸς
Joshua into the possession of the Gentiles whom [2]drove [3]out - [1]God
when they dispossessed the

ἀπὸ προσώπου τῶν πατέρων ἡμῶν ἕως τῶν ἡμερῶν Δαβίδ,
from *the* face - of fathers ˜ our until the days of David,
presence

46 ὃς εὗρε χάριν ἐνώπιον τοῦ Θεοῦ καὶ ᾐτήσατο
who found favor before - God and asked

εὑρεῖν σκήνωμα τῷ Θεῷ Ἰακώβ. **47** Σολομῶν
opportunity to find a dwelling place for the God of Jacob. Solomon ˜

δὲ ᾠκοδόμησεν αὐτῷ οἶκον. **48** Ἀλλ' οὐχ ὁ Ὕψιστος ἐν
And built for Him a house. But [5]not [1]the [2]Most [3]High [7]in

χειροποιήτοις ναοῖς [s] κατοικεῖ· καθὼς ὁ προφήτης λέγει,
[8]handmade [9]sanctuaries [4]does [6]dwell; just as the prophet says,
said,

49 «Ὁ οὐρανός μοι θρόνος,
- «Heaven *is* My throne,

Ἡ δὲ γῆ ὑποπόδιον τῶν ποδῶν μου·
the ˜ And earth a footstool - of feet ˜ My;
for

Ποῖον οἶκον οἰκοδομήσετέ μοι, λέγει Κύριος,
What kind of house will you build for Me, says *the* Lord,

Ἢ τίς τόπος τῆς καταπαύσεώς μου?
Or what *is the* place - of rest ˜ My?
for

50 Οὐχὶ ἡ χείρ μου ἐποίησε ταῦτα πάντα?» [t]
[2]not - [4]hand [3]My [1]Did [5]make [7]these [8]*things* [6]all?»

Stephen Accuses Israel of Resisting the Holy Spirit

51 "Σκληροτράχηλοι καὶ ἀπερίτμητοι τῇ καρδίᾳ καὶ τοῖς
"Stiff-necked and uncircumcised - in heart and -

ὠσίν! Ὑμεῖς ἀεὶ τῷ Πνεύματι τῷ Ἁγίῳ ἀντιπίπτετε, ὡς οἱ
ears! You always [2]the [4]Spirit - [3]Holy [1]resist, as -

πατέρες ὑμῶν καὶ ὑμεῖς. **52** Τίνα τῶν προφητῶν οὐκ
fathers ˜ your *did* also ˜ you *do.* Whom of the prophets [4]not

ἐδίωξαν οἱ πατέρες ὑμῶν? Καὶ ἀπέκτειναν τοὺς
[1]did [5]persecute - [3]fathers [2]your? And they killed the *ones*
those who

προκαταγγείλαντας περὶ τῆς ἐλεύσεως τοῦ Δικαίου
announcing beforehand about the coming of the Righteous One
foretold

οὗ νῦν ὑμεῖς προδόται καὶ φονεῖς γεγένησθε,
of whom [3]now [1]you [5]betrayers [6]and [7]murderers [2]have [4]become,

53 οἵτινες ἐλάβετε τὸν νόμον εἰς διαταγὰς ἀγγέλων, καὶ οὐκ
who received the law as *the* ordinances of angels, and [3]not

ἐφυλάξατε."
[1]you [2]did keep *it.*"

---

[s](**7:48**) NU omits *ναοις, sanctuaries,* thus *houses* must be supplied (see v. 47). [t](**7:49, 50**) Is. 66:1, 2

Stephen Is Martyred

54 Ἀκούοντες δὲ ταῦτα διεπρίοντο ταῖς καρδίαις
hearing ˜ Now these *things* they were infuriated - in hearts ˜
Now as they heard

αὐτῶν καὶ ἔβρυχον τοὺς ὀδόντας ἐπ' αὐτόν. 55 Ὑπάρχων
their and were gnashing the teeth against him. being ˜
their

δὲ πλήρης Πνεύματος Ἁγίου, ἀτενίσας εἰς τὸν οὐρανόν,
But full of *the* Spirit ˜ Holy, looking intently into - heaven,
he looked

εἶδε δόξαν Θεοῦ καὶ Ἰησοῦν ἑστῶτα ἐκ δεξιῶν τοῦ
he saw *the* glory of God and Jesus standing at *the* right *parts* -
and hand

Θεοῦ, 56 καὶ εἶπεν, "Ἰδού, θεωρῶ τοὺς οὐρανοὺς
of God, and he said, "Behold, I see the heavens

ἀνεῳγμένους καὶ τὸν Υἱὸν τοῦ Ἀνθρώπου ἐκ δεξιῶν
having been opened and the Son - of Man [2]at [3]*the* [4]right [5]*parts*
hand

ἑστῶτα τοῦ Θεοῦ!" 57 Κράξαντες δὲ φωνῇ μεγάλῃ,
[1]standing - of God!" [2]crying [3]out [1]And with a voice ˜ great,
they cried out loud,

συνέσχον τὰ ὦτα αὐτῶν καὶ ὥρμησαν ὁμοθυμαδὸν ἐπ'
they stopped - ears ˜ their and ran with one purpose at

αὐτόν, 58 καὶ ἐκβαλόντες ἔξω τῆς πόλεως, ἐλιθοβόλουν. Καὶ
him, and casting *him* outside the city, they stoned *him.* And
they cast and

οἱ μάρτυρες ἀπέθεντο τὰ ἱμάτια παρὰ τοὺς πόδας
the witnesses laid down the cloaks beside the feet
their

νεανίου καλουμένου Σαύλου. 59 Καὶ ἐλιθοβόλουν τὸν
of a young man being called Saul. And they stoned -
named

Στέφανον ἐπικαλούμενον καὶ λέγοντα, "Κύριε Ἰησοῦ, δέξαι τὸ
Stephen calling on *God* and saying, "Lord Jesus, receive -

πνεῦμά μου." 60 Θεὶς δὲ τὰ γόνατα, ἔκραξε φωνῇ
spirit ˜ my." putting ˜ And the knees, he cried out with a voice ˜
Then he knelt down and

μεγάλῃ, "Κύριε, μὴ στήσῃς αὐτοῖς τὴν ἁμαρτίαν
great, "Lord, not ˜ do hold against them - sin ˜
loud,

ταύτην." Καὶ τοῦτο εἰπὼν ἐκοιμήθη.
this." And [3]this [1]having [2]said he fell asleep.

Saul Persecutes the Church

8 1 Σαῦλος δὲ ἦν συνευδοκῶν τῷ ἀναιρέσει αὐτοῦ.
Saul ˜ Now was agreeing with *them* - in murder ˜ his.

Ἐγένετο δὲ ἐν ἐκείνῃ τῇ ἡμέρᾳ διωγμὸς μέγας ἐπὶ
[2]*there* [3]arose [1]And in that - day a persecution ˜ great against

τὴν ἐκκλησίαν τὴν ἐν Ἱεροσολύμοις· πάντες δὲ
the church the *one* in Jerusalem; all ˜ and
which was

διεσπάρησαν κατὰ τὰς χώρας τῆς Ἰουδαίας καὶ Σαμαρείας
were scattered throughout the regions - of Judea and Samaria

πλὴν τῶν ἀποστόλων. 2 Συνεκόμισαν δὲ τὸν Στέφανον
except the apostles. [4]buried [1]And - [5]Stephen

ἄνδρες εὐλαβεῖς καὶ ἐποιήσαντο κοπετὸν μέγαν ἐπ' αὐτῷ.
[3]men [2]pious and made lamentation ˜ great over him.

54 When they heard these things they were cut to the heart, and they gnashed at him with *their* teeth.
55 But he, being full of the Holy Spirit, gazed into heaven and saw the glory of God, and Jesus standing at the right hand of God,
56 and said, "Look! I see the heavens opened and the Son of Man standing at the right hand of God!"
57 Then they cried out with a loud voice, stopped their ears, and ran at him with one accord;
58 and they cast *him* out of the city and stoned *him.* And the witnesses laid down their clothes at the feet of a young man named Saul.
59 And they stoned Stephen as he was calling on *God* and saying, "Lord Jesus, receive my spirit."
60 Then he knelt down and cried out with a loud voice, "Lord, do not charge them with this sin." And when he had said this, he fell asleep.

8 Now Saul was consenting to his death. At that time a great persecution arose against the church which was at Jerusalem; and they were all scattered throughout the regions of Judea and Samaria, except the apostles.
2 And devout men carried Stephen *to his burial,* and made great lamentation over him.

3 As for Saul, he made havoc
of the church, entering every
house, and dragging off men
and women, committing *them* to
prison.
4 Therefore those who were
scattered went everywhere
preaching the word.
5 Then Philip went down to
the city of Samaria and
preached Christ to them.
6 And the multitudes with
one accord heeded the things
spoken by Philip, hearing and
seeing the miracles which he
did.
7 For unclean spirits, crying
with a loud voice, came out of
many who were possessed; and
many who were paralyzed and
lame were healed.
8 And there was great joy in
that city.
9 But there was a certain
man called Simon, who previously practiced sorcery in the
city and astonished the people
of Samaria, claiming that he
was someone great,
10 to whom they all gave
heed, from the least to the
greatest, saying, "This man is
the great power of God."
11 And they heeded him because he had astonished them
with his sorceries for a long
time.
12 But when they believed

---

[a](**8:10**) NU, TR add *παντες, (they) all.* [b](**8:10**) NU adds *καλουμενη, that is called (Great).*

***(8:3)** *ἐκκλησια (ekklēsia).* Noun from *ἐκκαλέω, call out.* The normal Greek usage refers to a regularly experienced *assembly* (Acts 19:32, 39, 41). In the LXX it is used to translate *qāhāl, congregation,* and in this sense it is used in the NT of Israel (Acts 7:38). Jesus used the word to speak of building His church (Matt. 16:18), meaning the whole body of believers (cf. Eph. 1:22). The most common NT usage is of local Christian communities or congregations (Acts 8:3; 1 Cor. 16:19), including those that met in houses (Col. 4:15; Philem. 2).

3 *Σαῦλος δὲ ἐλυμαίνετο τὴν ἐκκλησίαν,* κατὰ τοὺς*
Saul ~ But was doing injury to the church, [3]according [4]to [5]the
from house to

οἴκους εἰσπορευόμενος, σύρων τε ἄνδρας καὶ γυναῖκας
[6]houses [1]going [2]in, dragging away both men and women
house

παρεδίδου εἰς φυλακήν.
he was handing *them* over to prison.
and committing them

Philip Preaches Christ in Samaria

4 *Οἱ μὲν οὖν διασπαρέντες διῆλθον*
[2]the [3]*ones* - [1]Therefore being scattered went about
those who were

εὐαγγελιζόμενοι τὸν λόγον. **5** *Φίλιππος δὲ κατελθὼν εἰς*
preaching the good news of the word. Philip ~ And going down to
went

πόλιν τῆς Σαμαρείας, ἐκήρυσσεν αὐτοῖς τὸν Χριστόν.
a city - of Samaria, was preaching to them the Christ.
Messiah.

6 *Προσεῖχόν τε οἱ ὄχλοι τοῖς λεγομένοις ὑπὸ τοῦ*
[7]gave [8]heed [1]And [2]the [3]crowds [9]to [10]the [11]*things* [12]being [13]said [14]by -

Φιλίππου ὁμοθυμαδὸν ἐν τῷ ἀκούειν αὐτοὺς καὶ βλέπειν τὰ
[15]Philip [4]with [5]one [6]accord in - [2]to [3]hear [1]them and to see the
as they were hearing and seeing

σημεῖα ἃ ἐποίει. **7** *Πολλῶν γὰρ τῶν ἐχόντων*
signs which he was doing. [2]of [3]many [1]For of the *ones* having
from those who had

πνεύματα ἀκάθαρτα βοῶντα φωνῇ μεγάλῃ
spirits ~ unclean *the spirits* crying out with a voice ~ great
loud

ἐξήρχετο, πολλοὶ δὲ παραλελυμένοι καὶ χωλοὶ
came out, many ~ and having been paralyzed and lame
paralytics

ἐθεραπεύθησαν. **8** *Καὶ ἐγένετο χαρὰ μεγάλη ἐν τῇ πόλει*
were healed. And *there* was joy ~ great in - city ~

ἐκείνῃ.
that.

Simon Is Converted and Baptized

9 *Ἀνὴρ δέ τις ὀνόματι Σίμων προϋπῆρχεν ἐν τῇ*
[2]a [4]man [1]Now [3]certain by name Simon was previously in the
named

πόλει μαγεύων καὶ ἐξιστῶν τὸ ἔθνος τῆς Σαμαρείας,
city practicing magic and astounding the people - of Samaria,

λέγων εἶναί τινα ἑαυτὸν μέγαν, **10** *ᾧ προσεῖχον*[a]
saying [2]to [3]be [4]someone [1]himself great, to whom they *all* gave heed
claiming

ἀπὸ μικροῦ ἕως μεγάλου, λέγοντες, "Οὗτός ἐστιν ἡ δύναμις
from small to great, saying, "This *one* is the [2]power
the least the greatest,

τοῦ Θεοῦ ἡ[b] *μεγάλη."* **11** *Προσεῖχον δὲ αὐτῷ διὰ*
- [3]of [4]God - [1]great." [2]they [3]gave [4]heed [1]But to him because of

τὸ ἱκανῷ χρόνῳ ταῖς μαγείαις ἐξεστακέναι
the considerable time [5]with [6]the [7]magic [8]arts [1]to [2]have [3]astounded
that he had

αὐτούς. **12** *Ὅτε δὲ ἐπίστευσαν τῷ Φιλίππῳ*
[4]them. when ~ But they believed - Philip

εὐαγγελιζομένῳ τὰ περὶ τῆς βασιλείας τοῦ Θεοῦ
preaching the good news of the *things* about the kingdom - of God
as he preached

καὶ τοῦ ὀνόματος Ἰησοῦ Χριστοῦ, ἐβαπτίζοντο ἄνδρες τε
and the name of Jesus Christ, they were baptized men ˜ both

καὶ γυναῖκες. **13** Ὁ δὲ Σίμων καὶ αὐτὸς ἐπίστευσε, καὶ
and women. - And Simon also ˜ himself believed, and

βαπτισθεὶς ἦν προσκαρτερῶν τῷ Φιλίππῳ, θεωρῶν
having been baptized he was continuing - with Philip, observing ˜

τε δυνάμεις[c] καὶ σημεῖα γινόμενα, ἐξίστατο.
and miracles and signs occurring, he was astounded.

Simon Sins Grievously

14 Ἀκούσαντες δὲ οἱ ἐν Ἱεροσολύμοις ἀπόστολοι ὅτι
[6]hearing [1]Now [2]the [4]in [5]Jerusalem [3]apostles that
Now when the apostles in Jerusalem heard

δέδεκται ἡ Σαμάρεια τὸν λόγον τοῦ Θεοῦ, ἀπέστειλαν πρὸς
[2]has [3]received - [1]Samaria the word - of God, they sent to
had

αὐτοὺς τὸν Πέτρον καὶ Ἰωάννην, **15** οἵτινες καταβάντες
them - Peter and John, who coming down
came down and

προσηύξαντο περὶ αὐτῶν ὅπως λάβωσι
prayed concerning them in order that they might receive

Πνεῦμα Ἅγιον· **16** οὔπω γὰρ ἦν ἐπ' οὐδενὶ αὐτῶν
the Spirit ˜ Holy; [4]not [5]yet [1]for [2]He [3]was [7]upon [8]no [9]one [10]of [11]them
had any

ἐπιπεπτωκός, μόνον δὲ βεβαπτισμένοι ὑπῆρχον εἰς τὸ
[6]fallen, [15]only [12]but [16]baptized [13]they [14]were in the
but they had only been baptized

ὄνομα τοῦ Χριστοῦ[d] Ἰησοῦ. **17** Τότε ἐπετίθουν τὰς χεῖρας
name - of Christ ˜ Jesus. Then they laid the hands
their

ἐπ' αὐτούς, καὶ ἐλάμβανον Πνεῦμα Ἅγιον.
upon them, and they received *the* Spirit ˜ Holy.

18 Θεασάμενος δὲ ὁ Σίμων ὅτι διὰ τῆς ἐπιθέσεως τῶν
[3]observing [1]Now - [2]Simon that by the laying on of the
Now when Simon observed

χειρῶν τῶν ἀποστόλων δίδοται τὸ Πνεῦμα τὸ Ἅγιον,[e]
hands of the apostles [4]is [5]given [1]the [3]Spirit - [2]Holy,
was

προσήνεγκεν αὐτοῖς χρήματα, **19** λέγων, "Δότε κἀμοὶ τὴν
he offered to them means, saying, "Give to me also -
money,

ἐξουσίαν ταύτην ἵνα ᾧ ἐὰν ἐπιθῶ τὰς χεῖρας λαμβάνῃ
power ˜ this that on whom ever I lay the hands he may receive
my

Πνεῦμα Ἅγιον."
the Spirit ˜ Holy."

20 Πέτρος δὲ εἶπε πρὸς αὐτόν, "Τὸ ἀργύριόν σου σὺν σοὶ
Peter ˜ But said to him, - "[3]silver [2]your [5]with [6]you

εἴη εἰς ἀπώλειαν, ὅτι τὴν δωρεὰν τοῦ Θεοῦ
[1]May [4]be in perdition, because [5]the [6]gift - [7]of [8]God

ἐνόμισας διὰ χρημάτων κτᾶσθαι! **21** Οὐκ ἔστι σοι
[1]you [2]thought [9]through [10]means [3]to [4]acquire! [3]not [1]*There* [2]is to you
money You have neither

μερὶς οὐδὲ κλῆρος ἐν τῷ λόγῳ τούτῳ. Ἡ γὰρ καρδία σου οὐκ
part nor portion in - word ˜ this. - For heart ˜ your not ˜

Philip as he preached the things concerning the kingdom of God and the name of Jesus Christ, both men and women were baptized.
13 Then Simon himself also believed; and when he was baptized he continued with Philip, and was amazed, seeing the miracles and signs which were done.
14 Now when the apostles who were at Jerusalem heard that Samaria had received the word of God, they sent Peter and John to them,
15 who, when they had come down, prayed for them that they might receive the Holy Spirit.
16 For as yet He had fallen upon none of them. They had only been baptized in the name of the Lord Jesus.
17 Then they laid hands on them, and they received the Holy Spirit.
18 And when Simon saw that through the laying on of the apostles' hands the Holy Spirit was given, he offered them money,
19 saying, "Give me this power also, that anyone on whom I lay hands may receive the Holy Spirit."
20 But Peter said to him, "Your money perish with you, because you thought that the gift of God could be purchased with money!
21 "You have neither part nor portion in this matter, for your heart is not right in the

---

[c]**(8:13)** NU, TR add μεγαλας, *great (miracles).* [d]**(8:16)** NU, TR read Κυριου, *Lord.* [e]**(8:18)** NU omits το Αγιον, *Holy.*

sight of God.
22 "Repent therefore of this
your wickedness, and pray God
if perhaps the thought of your
heart may be forgiven you.
23 "For I see that you are poisoned by bitterness and bound
by iniquity."
24 Then Simon answered and
said, "Pray to the Lord for me,
that none of the things which
you have spoken may come
upon me."
25 So when they had testified
and preached the word of the
Lord, they returned to Jerusalem, preaching the gospel in
many villages of the Samaritans.
26 Now an angel of the Lord
spoke to Philip, saying, "Arise
and go toward the south along
the road which goes down from
Jerusalem to Gaza." This is
desert.
27 So he arose and went. And
behold, a man of Ethiopia, a eunuch of great authority under
Candace the queen of the Ethiopians, who had charge of all
her treasury, and had come to
Jerusalem to worship,
28 was returning. And sitting
in his chariot, he was reading
Isaiah the prophet.
29 Then the Spirit said to
Philip, "Go near and overtake
this chariot."
30 So Philip ran to him, and
heard him reading the prophet
Isaiah, and said, "Do you
understand what you are reading?"

ἔστιν εὐθεῖα ἐνώπιον τοῦ Θεοῦ. **22** Μετανόησον οὖν ἀπὸ
is straight before - God. Repent therefore from
right

τῆς κακίας σου ταύτης, καὶ δεήθητι τοῦ Θεοῦ[f] εἰ
- [3]wickedness [2]your [1]this, and make petition to - God if

ἄρα ἀφεθήσεταί σοι ἡ ἐπίνοια τῆς καρδίας σου. **23** Εἰς
then [6]will [7]be [8]forgiven [9]you [1]the [2]intent - [3]of [5]heart [4]your. [6]in

γὰρ χολὴν πικρίας καὶ σύνδεσμον ἀδικίας
[1]For [7]*the* [8]gall [9]of [10]bitterness [11]and [12]*the* [13]bond [14]of [15]unrighteousness

ὁρῶ σε ὄντα."
[2]I [3]see [4]you [5]being."
that you are."

24 Ἀποκριθεὶς δὲ ὁ Σίμων εἶπε, "Δεήθητε ὑμεῖς
[3]answering [1]And - [2]Simon said, "[2]make [3]petition [1]You
answered and

ὑπὲρ ἐμοῦ πρὸς τὸν Κύριον ὅπως μηδὲν ἐπέλθῃ ἐπ' ἐμὲ
in behalf of me to the Lord that not any [8]may [9]come [10]on [11]me

ὧν εἰρήκατε."
[1]of [2]*the* [3]*things* [4]which [5]you [6]have [7]said."

25 Οἱ μὲν οὖν διαμαρτυράμενοι καὶ λαλήσαντες τὸν
- - Then solemnly bearing witness to and speaking the
when they had solemnly borne spoken

λόγον τοῦ Κυρίου, ὑπέστρεψαν εἰς Ἱερουσαλήμ, πολλάς τε
word of the Lord, they returned to Jerusalem, [7]many [1]and

κώμας τῶν Σαμαρειτῶν εὐηγγελίσαντο.
[8]villages [9]of [10]the [11]Samaritans [2]they [3]preached [4]the [5]gospel [6]to.

Philip Preaches Christ to an Ethiopian Eunuch

26 Ἄγγελος δὲ Κυρίου ἐλάλησε πρὸς Φίλιππον, λέγων,
[2]an [3]angel [1]Now of *the* Lord spoke to Philip, saying,

"Ἀνάστηθι καὶ πορεύου κατὰ μεσημβρίαν ἐπὶ τὴν ὁδὸν τὴν
"Get up and go toward *the* south on the road the *one*
which

καταβαίνουσαν ἀπὸ Ἱερουσαλὴμ εἰς Γάζαν· αὕτη ἐστὶν
going down from Jerusalem to Gaza; this is
goes

ἔρημος." **27** Καὶ ἀναστὰς ἐπορεύθη· καὶ ἰδού, ἀνὴρ Αἰθίοψ
desolate." And arising he went; and behold, a man an Ethiopian
a desert." he arose and of Ethiopia

εὐνοῦχος δυνάστης Κανδάκης τῆς βασιλίσσης Αἰθιόπων,
a eunuch a court official of Candace the queen of *the* Ethiopians,

ὃς ἦν ἐπὶ πάσης τῆς γάζης αὐτῆς, ὃς ἐληλύθει
who was over all - treasury ˜ her, who had come

προσκυνήσων εἰς Ἱερουσαλήμ, **28** ἦν τε ὑποστρέφων καὶ
[3]worshiping [1]to [2]Jerusalem, [2]he [3]was [1]and returning and
to worship

καθήμενος ἐπὶ τοῦ ἅρματος αὐτοῦ, καὶ ἀνεγίνωσκε* τὸν
sitting upon - chariot ˜ his, and he was reading the

προφήτην Ἠσαΐαν. **29** Εἶπε δὲ τὸ Πνεῦμα τῷ Φιλίππῳ,
prophet Isaiah. [4]said [1]And [2]the [3]Spirit - to Philip,

"Πρόσελθε καὶ κολλήθητι τῷ ἅρματι τούτῳ."
"Approach and join - with chariot ˜ this."

30 Προσδραμὼν δὲ ὁ Φίλιππος ἤκουσεν αὐτοῦ
[3]running [4]up [5]to [6]*it* [1]And - [2]Philip heard him
And Philip ran up to it and

ἀναγινώσκοντος τὸν προφήτην Ἠσαΐαν, καὶ εἶπεν, "Ἆρά γε
reading the prophet Isaiah, and he said, "Then -

γινώσκεις ἃ ἀναγινώσκεις?"
do you know what you are reading?"

---

f(**8:22**) NU reads Κυριου, *Lord.*

*(**8:28**) ἀναγινώσκω *(anaginōskō).* Verb meaning *read, read publicly.* Since the ancients generally read aloud even when alone, the eunuch was probably doing so here (see v. 30). Often the precise meaning of the word relates to formal, public reading (as Col. 4:16). Cf. the cognate noun ἀνάγνωσις, *a reading,* definitely *a public reading* in Acts 13:15.

31 Ὁ δὲ εἶπε, "Πῶς γὰρ ἂν δυναίμην ἐὰν μή τις
- And he said, "how ˜ For - could I if not someone
unless

ὁδηγήσῃ με?" Παρεκάλεσέ τε τὸν Φίλιππον ἀναβάντα
guides me?" [2]he [3]urged [1]And - Philip coming up
to come up

καθίσαι σὺν αὐτῷ. 32 Ἡ δὲ περιοχὴ τῆς Γραφῆς ἣν
to sit with him. the ˜ Now portion of the Scripture which
and sit

ἀνεγίνωσκεν ἦν αὕτη·
he was reading was this:

«Ὡς πρόβατον ἐπὶ σφαγὴν ἤχθη,
«As a sheep for slaughter He was led,

Καὶ ὡς ἀμνὸς ἐναντίον τοῦ κείραντος αὐτὸν ἄφωνος,
And as a lamb before the *one* shearing it *is* dumb,

Οὕτως οὐκ ἀνοίγει τὸ στόμα αὐτοῦ.
Thus [3]not [1]He [2]does open - mouth ˜ His.

33 Ἐν τῇ ταπεινώσει αὐτοῦ ἡ κρίσις αὐτοῦ ἤρθη·
In - humiliation ˜ His - judgment ˜ [1]His was taken away;
justice

Τὴν δὲ γενεὰν αὐτοῦ τίς διηγήσεται?
- And generation ˜ His who will recount?

Ὅτι αἴρεται ἀπὸ τῆς γῆς ἡ ζωὴ αὐτοῦ.»[g]
Because [3]is [4]taken [5]away [6]from [7]the [8]earth - [2]life [1]His.»

34 Ἀποκριθεὶς δὲ ὁ εὐνοῦχος τῷ Φιλίππῳ εἶπε,
[4]answering [1]And [2]the [3]eunuch - Philip said,
answered and said,

"Δέομαί σου, περὶ τίνος ὁ προφήτης λέγει τοῦτο? Περὶ
"I ask you, about whom [2]the [3]prophet [1]does [4]say this? About

ἑαυτοῦ ἢ περὶ ἑτέρου τινός?" 35 Ἀνοίξας δὲ ὁ Φίλιππος
himself or about other ˜ some *person?*" [3]opening [1]And - [2]Philip
opened

τὸ στόμα αὐτοῦ καὶ ἀρξάμενος ἀπὸ τῆς Γραφῆς ταύτης,
- mouth ˜ his and beginning from - Scripture ˜ this,
began at

εὐηγγελίσατο αὐτῷ τὸν Ἰησοῦν. 36 Ὡς δὲ
he preached the good news [3]to [4]him - [1]*about* [2]Jesus. as ˜ Now
and

ἐπορεύοντο κατὰ τὴν ὁδόν, ἦλθον ἐπί τι ὕδωρ, καί
they were going down the road, they came upon some water, and

φησιν ὁ εὐνοῦχος, "Ἰδού, ὕδωρ· τί κωλύει με
[3]said [1]the [2]eunuch, "Behold, *here is* water: what prevents me

βαπτισθῆναι?"[h] 38 Καὶ ἐκέλευσε στῆναι τὸ ἅρμα, καὶ
to be baptized?" And he ordered [3]to [4]stop [1]the [2]chariot, and
from being

κατέβησαν ἀμφότεροι εἰς τὸ ὕδωρ, ὅ τε Φίλιππος καὶ ὁ
they [2]went [3]down [1]both into the water, - both Philip and the

εὐνοῦχος, καὶ ἐβάπτισεν αὐτόν. 39 Ὅτε δὲ ἀνέβησαν ἐκ
eunuch, and he baptized him. when ˜ Now they went up out of

τοῦ ὕδατος, Πνεῦμα Κυρίου ἥρπασε τὸν Φίλιππον, καὶ οὐκ
the water, *the* Spirit of *the* Lord caught up ˜ - Philip, and [4]not

εἶδεν αὐτὸν οὐκέτι ὁ εὐνοῦχος· ἐπορεύετο γὰρ τὴν
[3]did [5]see [6]him [7]no [8]longer [1]the [2]eunuch; [10]he [11]went [12]*on* [9]for -
any

ὁδὸν αὐτοῦ χαίρων. 40 Φίλιππος δὲ εὑρέθη εἰς Ἄζωτον, καὶ
way ˜ his rejoicing. Philip ˜ And was found at Azotus, and

διερχόμενος εὐηγγελίζετο τὰς πόλεις πάσας ἕως τοῦ
going through he preached the gospel to [2]the [3]cities [1]all until -
as he passed

31 And he said, "How can I, unless someone guides me?" And he asked Philip to come up and sit with him.
32 The place in the Scripture which he read was this:

"He was led as a sheep to the slaughter;
And as a lamb before its shearer is silent,
So He opened not His mouth.
33 *In His humiliation His justice was taken away,*
And who will declare His generation?
For His life is taken from the earth."

34 So the eunuch answered Philip and said, "I ask you, of whom does the prophet say this, of himself or of some other man?"
35 Then Philip opened his mouth, and beginning at this Scripture, preached Jesus to him.
36 Now as they went down the road, they came to some water. And the eunuch said, "See, *here is* water. What hinders me from being baptized?"
37 Then Philip said, "If you believe with all your heart, you may." And he answered and said, "I believe that Jesus Christ is the Son of God."
38 So he commanded the chariot to stand still. And both Philip and the eunuch went down into the water, and he baptized him.
39 Now when they came up out of the water, the Spirit of the Lord caught Philip away, so that the eunuch saw him no more; and he went on his way rejoicing.
40 But Philip was found at Azotus. And passing through, he preached in all the cities till

---

g(**8:32, 33**) Is. 53:7, 8
h(**8:37**) TR adds v. 37: Ειπε δε ο Φιλιππος, Ει πιστευεις εξ ολης της καρδιας, εξσεστιν. Αποκριθεις δε ειρε, Πιστευω τον Υιον του Θεου ειναι τον Ιησουν Χριστον (see NKJV translation).

he came to Caesarea.
9 Then Saul, still breathing
threats and murder
against the disciples of the
Lord, went to the high priest
2 and asked letters from him
to the synagogues of Damascus, so that if he found any who
were of the Way, whether men
or women, he might bring them
bound to Jerusalem.
3 As he journeyed he came
near Damascus, and suddenly a
light shone around him from
heaven.
4 Then he fell to the ground,
and heard a voice saying to him,
"Saul, Saul, why are you persecuting Me?"
5 And he said, "Who are
You, Lord?" Then the Lord
said, "I am Jesus, whom you
are persecuting. It *is* hard for
you to kick against the goads."
6 So he, trembling and astonished, said, "Lord, what do You
want me to do?" Then the Lord
said to him, "Arise and go into
the city, and you will be told
what you must do."
7 And the men who jour-
neyed with him stood speechless, hearing a voice but seeing
no one.
8 Then Saul arose from the
ground, and when his eyes
were opened he saw no one.
But they led him by the hand
and brought *him* into Damascus.
9 And he was three days
without sight, and neither ate
nor drank.

ἐλθεῖν αὐτὸν εἰς Καισάρειαν.
[2]to [3]come [1]him to Caesarea.
he came

Saul Is Converted on the Damascus Road

9 1 Ὁ δὲ Σαῦλος ἔτι ἐμπνέων ἀπειλῆς καὶ φόνου εἰς
- Now Saul still breathing threat and murder against
murderous threats

τοὺς μαθητὰς τοῦ Κυρίου, προσελθὼν τῷ ἀρχιερεῖ,
the disciples of the Lord, coming to the high priest,
came

2 ᾐτήσατο παρ᾽ αὐτοῦ ἐπιστολὰς εἰς Δαμασκὸν πρὸς
requested from him letters *of authority* to Damascus to
and requested

τὰς συναγωγάς, ὅπως ἐάν τινας εὕρῃ τῆς Ὁδοῦ
the synagogues, that if [4]any [1]he [2]should [3]find [6]of [7]the [8]Way

ὄντας, ἄνδρας τε καὶ γυναῖκας, δεδεμένους
[5]being, men ˜ both and women, [5]having [6]been [7]bound
who were,

ἀγάγῃ εἰς Ἰερουσαλήμ. 3 Ἐν δὲ τῷ
[1]he [2]might [3]bring [4]*them* to Jerusalem. in ˜ And -
And as he was

πορεύεσθαι, ἐγένετο αὐτὸν ἐγγίζειν τῇ Δαμασκῷ, καὶ
to go, it came about *for* him to draw near - to Damascus, and
going, that he drew

ἐξαίφνης περιήστραψεν αὐτὸν φῶς ἀπὸ τοῦ οὐρανοῦ, 4 καὶ
suddenly [3]shone [4]around [5]him [1]a [2]light from - heaven, and

πεσὼν ἐπὶ τὴν γῆν, ἤκουσε φωνὴν λέγουσαν αὐτῷ, "Σαούλ,
falling on the ground, he heard, a voice saying to him, "Saul,
he fell and

Σαούλ, τί με διώκεις?"
Saul, why [4]Me [1]are [2]you [3]persecuting?"

5 Εἶπε δέ, "Τίς εἶ, Κύριε?"
[2]he [3]said [1]And, "Who are You, Lord?"

Ὁ δὲ Κύριος εἶπεν,[a] "Ἐγώ εἰμι Ἰησοῦς ὃν σὺ
the ˜ And Lord said, "I am Jesus whom you

διώκεις.[b] 6 Ἀλλὰ ἀνάστηθι καὶ εἴσελθε εἰς τὴν πόλιν, καὶ
are persecuting. But stand up and enter into the city, and

λαληθήσεταί σοι τί σε δεῖ ποιεῖν." 7 Οἱ δὲ
it will be spoken to you what *for* you it is necessary to do." the ˜ And
you must do."

ἄνδρες οἱ συνοδεύοντες αὐτῷ εἱστήκεισαν ἐνεοί,
men the *ones* traveling with him stood speechless,
who were

ἀκούοντες μὲν τῆς φωνῆς, μηδένα δὲ θεωροῦντες. 8 Ἠγέρθη
hearing - the voice, [3]no [4]one [1]but [2]seeing. [3]arose

δὲ ὁ Σαῦλος ἀπὸ τῆς γῆς, ἀνεῳγμένων τε τῶν
[1]And - [2]Saul from the ground, having been opened and -
and although his eyes

ὀφθαλμῶν αὐτοῦ, οὐδένα ἔβλεπε· χειραγωγοῦντες δὲ αὐτὸν
eyes ˜ his, [3]no [4]one [1]he [2]saw; [6]leading [8]by [9]the [10]hand [5]and [7]him
were open,

εἰσήγαγον εἰς Δαμασκόν. 9 Καὶ ἦν ἡμέρας τρεῖς μὴ
they brought *him* into Damascus. And he was days ˜ three not

βλέπων, καὶ οὐκ ἔφαγεν οὐδὲ ἔπιεν.
seeing, and [3]not [1]he [2]did eat nor did he drink.

---

[a](9:5) NU omits Κυριος ειπεν, *the Lord said,* thus *and He.* [b](9:5, 6) TR adds σκληρον σοι προς κεντρα λακτιζειν. Τρεμων τε και θαμβων ειπε, Κυριε, τι με θελεις ποιησαι? Και ο Κυριος προς αυτον (see NKJV translation) and omits Αλλα, *But,* of v. 6.

Ananias Baptizes Saul

10 Ἦν δέ τις μαθητὴς ἐν Δαμασκῷ ὀνόματι
[2]*there* [3]was [1]Now certain ˜ a disciple in Damascus by name
named

Ἀνανίας, καὶ εἶπε πρὸς αὐτὸν ὁ Κύριος ἐν ὁράματι,
Ananias, and [3]said [4]to [5]him [1]the [2]Lord in a vision,

"Ἀνανία!"
"Ananias!"

Ὁ δὲ εἶπεν, "Ἰδοὺ ἐγώ, Κύριε."
- And he said, "Behold I *am here,* Lord."

11 Ὁ δὲ Κύριος πρὸς αὐτόν, "Ἀναστὰς πορεύθητι ἐπὶ
the ˜ And Lord *said* to him, "Arising go to
"Arise and

τὴν ῥύμην τὴν καλουμένην Εὐθεῖαν καὶ ζήτησον ἐν οἰκίᾳ
the street the *one* being called Straight and seek out in *the* house
which is

Ἰούδα Σαῦλον ὀνόματι, Ταρσέα· ἰδοὺ γὰρ προσεύχεται,
of Judas Saul by name, of Tarsus; behold ˜ for he is praying,
a man named Saul,

12 καὶ εἶδεν ἐν ὁράματι ἄνδρα ὀνόματι Ἀνανίαν εἰσελθόντα
and he saw in a vision a man by name Ananias coming in
has seen named

καὶ ἐπιθέντα αὐτῷ χεῖρα ὅπως ἀναβλέψῃ."
and putting on him *his* hand in order that he might see again."

13 Ἀπεκρίθη δὲ Ἀνανίας, "Κύριε, ἀκήκοα ἀπὸ πολλῶν
[3]answered [1]But [2]Ananias, "Lord, I have heard from many

περὶ τοῦ ἀνδρὸς τούτου, ὅσα κακὰ ἐποίησε τοῖς
about - man ˜ this, as many [3]as [1]wicked [2]*things* he did -
how many has done

ἁγίοις σου ἐν Ἱερουσαλήμ· 14 καὶ ὧδε ἔχει ἐξουσίαν παρὰ
to saints ˜ Your in Jerusalem; and here he has authority from

τῶν ἀρχιερέων δῆσαι πάντας τοὺς ἐπικαλουμένους τὸ ὄνομά
the chief priests to bind all the *ones* calling on - name ˜
who are

σου."
Your."

15 Εἶπε δὲ πρὸς αὐτὸν ὁ Κύριος, "Πορεύου, ὅτι
[4]said [1]But [5]to [6]him [2]the [3]Lord, "Go *your way,* because

σκεῦος ἐκλογῆς μοί ἐστιν οὗτος τοῦ βαστάσαι τὸ ὄνομά
[4]a [5]vessel [6]of [7]election [8]to [9]Me [3]is [1]this [2]*one* - to bear - name ˜
a chosen vessel

μου ἐνώπιον ἐθνῶν καὶ βασιλέων, υἱῶν τε Ἰσραήλ·
My before Gentiles and kings, [2]*the* [3]sons [1]and of Israel;

16 ἐγὼ γὰρ ὑποδείξω αὐτῷ ὅσα δεῖ αὐτὸν
I ˜ for will show to him as many *things* as it is necessary *for* him
all the things that he must

ὑπὲρ τοῦ ὀνόματός μου παθεῖν."
in behalf of - name My to suffer."
suffer for the sake of My name."

17 Ἀπῆλθε δὲ Ἀνανίας καὶ εἰσῆλθεν εἰς τὴν οἰκίαν, καὶ
[3]departed [1]And [2]Ananias and entered into the house, and

ἐπιθεὶς ἐπ' αὐτὸν τὰς χεῖρας εἶπε, "Σαοὺλ ἀδελφέ, ὁ Κύριος
putting [3]on [4]him [1]the [2]hands he said, "Saul ˜ Brother, the Lord
he put his and

ἀπέσταλκέ με,[c] ὁ ὀφθείς σοι ἐν τῇ ὁδῷ ᾗ
has sent me, the *One* appearing to you in the way which
who appeared

ἤρχου, ὅπως ἀναβλέψῃς καὶ πλησθῇς Πνεύματος
you were coming, so that you may see again and be filled with *the* Spirit ˜

10 Now there was a certain disciple at Damascus named Ananias; and to him the Lord said in a vision, "Ananias." And he said, "Here I am, Lord."
11 So the Lord *said* to him, "Arise and go to the street called Straight, and inquire at the house of Judas for *one* called Saul of Tarsus, for behold, he is praying.
12 "And in a vision he has seen a man named Ananias coming in and putting *his* hand on him, so that he might receive his sight."
13 Then Ananias answered, "Lord, I have heard from many about this man, how much harm he has done to Your saints in Jerusalem.
14 "And here he has authority from the chief priests to bind all who call on Your name."
15 But the Lord said to him, "Go, for he is a chosen vessel of Mine to bear My name before Gentiles, kings, and the children of Israel.
16 "For I will show him how many things he must suffer for My name's sake."
17 And Ananias went his way and entered the house; and laying his hands on him he said, "Brother Saul, the Lord Jesus, who appeared to you on the road as you came, has sent me that you may receive your sight and be filled with the Holy Spirit."

[c](**9:17**) NU, TR add Ιησους, *Jesus.*

18 Immediately there fell from
his eyes *something* like scales,
and he received his sight at
once; and he arose and was
baptized.
19 So when he had received
food, he was strengthened.
Then Saul spent some days
with the disciples at Damascus.
20 Immediately he preached
the Christ in the synagogues,
that He is the Son of God.
21 Then all who heard were
amazed, and said, "Is this not
he who destroyed those who
called on this name in Jerusalem, and has come here for that
purpose, so that he might bring
them bound to the chief
priests?"
22 But Saul increased all the
more in strength, and confounded the Jews who dwelt in
Damascus, proving that this *Jesus* is the Christ.
23 Now after many days were
past, the Jews plotted to kill
him.
24 But their plot became
known to Saul. And they
watched the gates day and
night, to kill him.
25 Then the disciples took him
by night and let *him* down
through the wall in a large basket.
26 And when Saul had come to
Jerusalem, he tried to join the

Ἁγίου." **18** Καὶ εὐθέως ἀπέπεσον ἀπὸ τῶν ὀφθαλμῶν
Holy." And immediately *there* fell away from - eyes ˜

αὐτοῦ ὡσεὶ λεπίδες, ἀνέβλεψέ τε[d] καὶ ἀναστὰς
his *something* like scales, [2]he [3]saw [4]again [1]and and arising
he stood

ἐβαπτίσθη, **19** καὶ λαβὼν τροφὴν ἐνίσχυσεν.
he was baptized, and taking food he was strengthened.
and when he received

Saul Preaches Christ in Damascus

Ἐγένετο δὲ ὁ Σαῦλος[e] μετὰ τῶν ἐν Δαμασκῷ μαθητῶν
[3]was [1]Now - [2]Saul with the [2]in [3]Damascus [1]disciples

ἡμέρας τινάς. **20** Καὶ εὐθέως ἐν ταῖς συναγωγαῖς
days ˜ three. And immediately in the synagogues

ἐκήρυσσε τὸν Χριστὸν[f] ὅτι οὗτός ἐστιν ὁ Υἱὸς τοῦ
he was proclaiming - Christ that this *One* is the Son -
the Messiah

Θεοῦ.
of God.

21 Ἐξίσταντο δὲ πάντες οἱ ἀκούοντες καὶ
[6]were [7]astounded [1]And [2]all [3]the [4]*ones* [5]hearing and
those who heard

ἔλεγον, "Οὐχ οὗτός ἐστιν ὁ πορθήσας ἐν Ἱερουσαλὴμ
were saying, "[3]not [2]this [1]Is the *one* destroying [7]in [8]Jerusalem
who destroyed

τοὺς ἐπικαλουμένους τὸ ὄνομα τοῦτο, καὶ ὧδε εἰς τοῦτο
[1]the [2]*ones* [3]calling [4]on - [6]name [5]this, and here for this *purpose*
those who called

ἐλήλυθε ἵνα δεδεμένους αὐτοὺς ἀγάγῃ ἐπὶ τοὺς
has come that [5]having [6]been [7]bound [4]them [1]he [2]might [3]take to the

ἀρχιερεῖς?" **22** Σαῦλος δὲ μᾶλλον ἐνεδυναμοῦτο καὶ
chief priests?" Saul ˜ But *all the* more was growing strong and

συνέχυνε τοὺς Ἰουδαίους τοὺς κατοικοῦντας ἐν
was confounding the Jews the *ones* dwelling in
who were

Δαμασκῷ, συμβιβάζων ὅτι οὗτός ἐστιν ὁ Χριστός.
Damascus, proving that this *One* is the Christ.
Messiah.

Saul Escapes Death

23 Ὡς δὲ ἐπληροῦντο ἡμέραι ἱκαναί,
when ˜ Now [3]were [4]fulfilled [2]days [1]considerable,
many,

συνεβουλεύσαντο οἱ Ἰουδαῖοι ἀνελεῖν αὐτόν· **24** ἐγνώσθη
[7]plotted [5]the [6]Jews to kill him; [4]was [5]known

δὲ τῷ Σαύλῳ ἡ ἐπιβουλὴ αὐτῶν. Παρετήρουν τε τὰς
[1]but - [6]to [7]Saul - [3]plot [2]their. [9]they [10]closely [11]watched [8]And the

πύλας ἡμέρας τε καὶ νυκτὸς ὅπως αὐτὸν ἀνέλωσι·
city gates day ˜ both and night in order that [4]him [1]they [2]might [3]kill;

25 λαβόντες δὲ αὐτὸν οἱ μαθηταὶ νυκτός, καθῆκαν
[4]taking [1]but [5]him [2]the [3]disciples of night, they let him down
took by night and

διὰ τοῦ τείχους, χαλάσαντες ἐν σπυρίδι.
through the wall, lowering *him* in a basket.

Barnabas Introduces Saul at Jerusalem

26 Παραγενόμενος δὲ ὁ Σαῦλος[g] ἐν Ἱερουσαλήμ,
arriving Now - Saul in Jerusalem,
Now when Saul arrived

[d]**(9:18)** TR adds παραχρημα, *immediately.*
[e]**(9:19)** NU omits ο Σαυλος, *Saul,* thus *he was.*
[f]**(9:20)** NU reads Ιησουν, *Jesus.* [g]**(9:26)** NU omits ο Σαυλος, *Saul,* thus *he had come.*

ἐπειράτο κολλᾶσθαι τοῖς μαθηταῖς· καὶ πάντες
he tried to join himself to the disciples; and all ~
ἐφοβοῦντο αὐτόν, μὴ πιστεύοντες ὅτι ἐστὶ μαθητής.
they were afraid of him, not believing that he is a disciple.
was

27 Βαρναβᾶς δὲ ἐπιλαβόμενος αὐτὸν ἤγαγε πρὸς τοὺς
Barnabas ~ But taking hold of him brought *him* to the
took and brought
ἀποστόλους, καὶ διηγήσατο αὐτοῖς πῶς ἐν τῇ ὁδῷ εἶδε τὸν
apostles, and related to them how on the way he saw the
had seen
Κύριον καὶ ὅτι ἐλάλησεν αὐτῷ, καὶ πῶς ἐν Δαμασκῷ
Lord and that He spoke to him, and how in Damascus
had spoken
ἐπαρρησιάσατο ἐν τῷ ὀνόματι τοῦ Ἰησοῦ. **28** Καὶ ἦν μετ'
he spoke openly in the name - of Jesus. And he was [2]with
had spoken
αὐτῶν εἰσπορευόμενος[h] εἰς Ἱερουσαλήμ, **29** καὶ
[3]them [1]entering into Jerusalem, and
παρρησιαζόμενος ἐν τῷ ὀνόματι τοῦ Κυρίου Ἰησοῦ,[i]
speaking openly in the name of the Lord Jesus,
ἐλάλει τε καὶ συνεζήτει πρὸς τοὺς Ἑλληνιστάς·
[2]he [3]was [4]speaking [1]and and was disputing with the Hellenists;
Greek-speaking Jews;
οἱ δὲ ἐπεχείρουν αὐτὸν ἀνελεῖν. **30** Ἐπιγνόντες δὲ οἱ
- but they were attempting [3]him [1]to [2]kill. [4]learning [1]But [2]the
learned about it
ἀδελφοὶ κατήγαγον αὐτὸν εἰς Καισάρειαν καὶ ἐξαπέστειλαν
[3]brothers brought down ~ him to Caesarea and sent off ~
and brought
αὐτὸν εἰς Ταρσόν.
him to Tarsus.

The Church at Peace and Growing

31 Αἱ μὲν οὖν ἐκκλησίαι καθ' ὅλης τῆς Ἰουδαίας
the ~ - Then churches throughout whole ~ the Judea
all
καὶ Γαλιλαίας καὶ Σαμαρείας εἶχον[j] εἰρήνην
and Galilee and Samaria had peace
οἰκοδομούμεναι,* καὶ πορευόμεναι τῷ φόβῳ τοῦ Κυρίου καὶ
being edified, and going in the fear of the Lord and
and were living
τῇ παρακλήσει τοῦ Ἁγίου Πνεύματος ἐπληθύνοντο.
in the encouragement of the Holy Spirit were multiplying.

Peter Heals Aeneas

32 Ἐγένετο δὲ Πέτρον διερχόμενον διὰ
[2]it [3]happened [4]*that* [1]Now Peter going through
as Peter went
πάντων κατελθεῖν καὶ πρὸς τοὺς ἁγίους τοὺς
all *those parts* to go down also to the saints the *ones*
he went who were
κατοικοῦντας Λύδδαν. **33** Εὗρε δὲ ἐκεῖ ἄνθρωπόν τινα
dwelling at Lydda. [2]he [3]found [1]And there a man ~ certain
Αἰνέαν ὀνόματι ἐξ ἐτῶν ὀκτὼ κατακείμενον ἐπὶ κραββάτῳ,
Aeneas by name of years eight lying on a pallet,
named Aeneas who had been confined to a bed for eight years,
ὃς ἦν παραλελυμένος. **34** Καὶ εἶπεν αὐτῷ ὁ Πέτρος,
who was paralyzed. And [2]said [3]to [4]him - [1]Peter,

disciples; but they were all afraid of him, and did not believe that he was a disciple.
27 But Barnabas took him and brought *him* to the apostles. And he declared to them how he had seen the Lord on the road, and that He had spoken to him, and how he had preached boldly at Damascus in the name of Jesus.
28 So he was with them at Jerusalem, coming in and going out.
29 And he spoke boldly in the name of the Lord Jesus and disputed against the Hellenists, but they attempted to kill him.
30 When the brethren found out, they brought him down to Caesarea and sent him out to Tarsus.
31 Then the churches throughout all Judea, Galilee, and Samaria had peace and were edified. And walking in the fear of the Lord and in the comfort of the Holy Spirit, they were multiplied.
32 Now it came to pass, as Peter went through all *parts of the country,* that he also came down to the saints who dwelt in Lydda.
33 There he found a certain man named Aeneas, who had been bedridden eight years and was paralyzed.
34 And Peter said to him,

---

[h]**(9:28)** NU, TR add *και εκπορευομενος, and going out.* [i]**(9:29)** NU omits *Ιησου, Jesus.*
[j]**(9:31)** NU reads the singular *Η . . . εκκλησια . . . ειχεν, the . . . church . . . was having.*

***(9:31)** *οἰκοδομέω (oikodomeō).* Verb meaning *build, edify,* originally meaning *construct* or *build* an edifice (as in Luke 6:48 and often). It may mean *build* in a figurative sense, as when Jesus said He would "build" His church (Matt. 16:18). The term has a secondary meaning of *build up, strengthen, establish, edify,* referring in the NT to the spiritual development and character growth of Christians or, more often, of the Christian community in general (as here in Acts 9:31 and 1 Thess. 5:11). Cf. the cognate noun *οἰκοδομή, building:* either the activity of construction or the edifice itself, and again either literally or figuratively (cf. 1 Cor.

"Aeneas, Jesus the Christ heals you. Arise and make your bed." Then he arose immediately.
35 So all who dwelt at Lydda and Sharon saw him and turned to the Lord.
36 At Joppa there was a certain disciple named Tabitha, which is translated Dorcas. This woman was full of good works and charitable deeds which she did.
37 But it happened in those days that she became sick and died. When they had washed her, they laid *her* in an upper room.
38 And since Lydda was near Joppa, and the disciples had heard that Peter was there, they sent two men to him, imploring *him* not to delay in coming to them.
39 Then Peter arose and went with them. When he had come, they brought *him* to the upper room. And all the widows stood by him weeping, showing the tunics and garments which Dorcas had made while she was with them.
40 But Peter put them all out, and knelt down and prayed. And turning to the body he said, "Tabitha, arise." And she opened her eyes, and when she saw Peter she sat up.
41 Then he gave her *his* hand

"Αἰνέα, ἰᾶταί σε Ἰησοῦς ὁ Χριστός· ἀνάστηθι καὶ στρῶσον
"Aeneas, [4]heals [5]you [1]Jesus [2]the [3]Christ; arise and spread out
make

σεαυτῷ." Καὶ εὐθέως ἀνέστη. **35** Καὶ εἶδον αὐτὸν
for yourself." And immediately he stood up. And [9]saw [10]him
your bed."

πάντες οἱ κατοικοῦντες Λύδδαν καὶ τὸν Ἀσσάρωνα,
[1]all [2]the [3]*ones* [4]dwelling [5]at [6]Lydda [7]and - [8]Sharon,
those who were

οἵτινες ἐπέστρεψαν ἐπὶ τὸν Κύριον.
who turned to the Lord.
and they

Peter Restores Dorcas to Life

36 Ἐν Ἰόππῃ δέ τις ἦν μαθήτρια ὀνόματι
[2]in [3]Joppa [1]Now [7]certain [4]*there* [5]was [6]a [8]disciple by name
named

Ταβιθά, ἣ διερμηνευομένη λέγεται Δορκάς· αὕτη ἦν
Tabitha, which being translated is called Dorcas; this *woman* was

πλήρης ἀγαθῶν ἔργων καὶ ἐλεημοσυνῶν ὧν ἐποίει.
full of good works and charitable giving which she was doing.

37 Ἐγένετο δὲ ἐν ταῖς ἡμέραις ἐκείναις ἀσθενήσασαν
[2]it [3]came [4]about [1]But in - days ˜ those taking sick
that she

αὐτὴν ἀποθανεῖν· λούσαντες δὲ αὐτὴν ἔθηκαν ἐν
for her to die; washing ˜ and her they put *her* in
took sick and died; and they washed and

ὑπερῴῳ. **38** Ἐγγὺς δὲ οὔσης Λύδδης τῇ Ἰόππῃ, οἱ
an upper room. near Now being Lydda - to Joppa, the
Now since Lydda was near Joppa,

μαθηταὶ ἀκούσαντες ὅτι Πέτρος ἐστὶν ἐν αὐτῇ ἀπέστειλαν[k]
disciples having heard that Peter is in it sent
when they was Joppa

πρὸς αὐτὸν παρακαλοῦντες μὴ ὀκνῆσαι διελθεῖν ἕως αὐτῶν.[l]
to him urging *him* not to delay to come to them.

39 Ἀναστὰς δὲ Πέτρος συνῆλθεν αὐτοῖς· ὃν
[3]arising [1]And [2]Peter went with them; whom
rose and

παραγενόμενον ἀνήγαγον εἰς τὸ ὑπερῷον, καὶ παρέστησαν
arriving they took up into the upper room, and [4]stood [5]beside
when he arrived

αὐτῷ πᾶσαι αἱ χῆραι κλαίουσαι καὶ ἐπιδεικνύμεναι χιτῶνας
[6]him [1]all [2]the [3]widows weeping and showing *him* tunics

καὶ ἱμάτια ὅσα ἐποίει μετ' αὐτῶν οὖσα ἡ
and cloaks as many as [2]was [3]making [5]with [6]them [4]being -
which while she was

Δορκάς.
[1]Dorcas.

40 Ἐκβαλὼν δὲ ἔξω πάντας ὁ Πέτρος θεὶς τὰ
[2]having [3]put [1]And [6]outside [4]*them* [5]all - Peter placing the
kneeled and

γόνατα προσηύξατο, καὶ ἐπιστρέψας πρὸς τὸ σῶμα εἶπε,
knees prayed, and turning to the body he said,

"Ταβιθά, ἀνάστηθι." Ἡ δὲ ἤνοιξε τοὺς ὀφθαλμοὺς αὐτῆς,
"Tabitha, arise." - And she opened - eyes ˜ her,

καὶ ἰδοῦσα τὸν Πέτρον, ἀνεκάθισε. **41** Δοὺς δὲ αὐτῇ
and seeing - Peter she sat up. giving ˜ And to her
when she saw

[k](9:38) NU, TR add δυο ανδρας, *two men*.
[l](9:38) NU reads οκνησης . . . ημων, *"Do (not) delay (coming to) us."*

3:9, where either meaning is possible).

χεῖρα, ἀνέστησεν αὐτήν, φωνήσας δὲ τοὺς ἁγίους καὶ τὰς
a hand, he raised up ˜ her, calling ˜ and the saints and the
his when he called

χήρας, παρέστησεν αὐτὴν ζῶσαν. **42** Γνωστὸν δὲ ἐγένετο
widows, he presented her living. [4]known [1]And [2]it [3]became
alive.

καθ' ὅλης τῆς Ἰόππης, καὶ πολλοὶ ἐπίστευσαν ἐπὶ τὸν
throughout whole ˜ the of Joppa, and many believed on the
all

Κύριον. **43** Ἐγένετο δὲ ἡμέρας ἱκανὰς μεῖναι αὐτὸν
Lord. [2]it [3]came [4]about [1]And [10]days [9]considerable [7]to [8]stay [5]*for* [6]him
that he stayed many days

ἐν Ἰόππῃ παρά τινι Σίμωνι βυρσεῖ.
in Joppa with one Simon a tanner.

Cornelius Sends a Delegation to Peter

10 **1** Ἀνὴρ δέ τις ἦν ἐν Καισαρείᾳ ὀνόματι
[6]a [8]man [1]Now [7]certain [2]*there* [3]was [4]in [5]Caesarea by name
named

Κορνήλιος, ἑκατοντάρχης ἐκ σπείρης τῆς καλουμένης
Cornelius, a centurion of *the* cohort the *one* being called
regiment which is called

Ἰταλικῆς, **2** εὐσεβὴς καὶ φοβούμενος τὸν Θεὸν
the Italian *Regiment,* pious and fearing - God

σὺν παντὶ τῷ οἴκῳ αὐτοῦ, ποιῶν τε ἐλεημοσύνας
together with all - house ˜ his, doing ˜ and alms ˜
household who often gave

πολλὰς τῷ λαῷ καὶ δεόμενος τοῦ Θεοῦ διὰ παντός.
many to the people and making petition - of God through every*thing*.
alms who made to God always.

3 Εἶδεν ἐν ὁράματι φανερῶς ὡσεὶ ὥραν ἐνάτην τῆς
He saw in a vision clearly about *the* hour ˜ ninth of the

ἡμέρας ἄγγελον τοῦ Θεοῦ εἰσελθόντα πρὸς αὐτὸν καὶ εἰπόντα
day an angel - of God coming to him and saying

αὐτῷ, "Κορνήλιε!"
to him, "Cornelius!"

4 Ὁ δὲ ἀτενίσας αὐτῷ καὶ ἔμφοβος γενόμενος εἶπε,
- And looking intently at him and fearful ˜ becoming he said,
when he looked he became fearful and

"Τί ἐστι, Κύριε?"
"What is it, Lord?"

Εἶπε δὲ αὐτῷ, "Αἱ προσευχαί σου καὶ αἱ ἐλεημοσύναι
[2]he [3]said [1]And to him, - "prayers ˜ Your and - alms ˜

σου ἀνέβησαν εἰς μνημόσυνον ἐνώπιον τοῦ Θεοῦ. **5** Καὶ νῦν
your came up for a memorial before - God. And now
have come

πέμψον εἰς Ἰόππην ἄνδρας καὶ μετάπεμψαι Σίμωνα τὸν
send to Joppa men and send *them* for Simon the *one*
who

ἐπικαλούμενον Πέτρον· **6** οὗτος ξενίζεται παρά τινι
being called Peter; this *man* is staying as a guest with one
is surnamed he

Σίμωνι βυρσεῖ, ᾧ ἐστιν οἰκία παρὰ θάλασσαν."[a]
Simon a tanner, to whom is a house beside *the* sea."
whose house is

7 Ὡς δὲ ἀπῆλθεν ὁ ἄγγελος ὁ λαλῶν τῷ
when ˜ Now [8]departed [1]the [2]angel [3]the [4]*one* [5]speaking -
had departed who had been speaking

and lifted her up; and when he
had called the saints and widows, he presented her alive.
42 And it became known
throughout all Joppa, and many
believed on the Lord.
43 So it was that he stayed
many days in Joppa with Simon,
a tanner.
10 There was a certain
man in Caesarea called
Cornelius, a centurion of what
was called the Italian Regiment,
2 a devout *man* and one who
feared God with all his household, who gave alms generously
to the people, and prayed to
God always.
3 About the ninth hour of the
day he saw clearly in a vision an
angel of God coming in and saying to him, "Cornelius!"
4 And when he observed
him, he was afraid, and said,
"What is it, lord?" So he said to
him, "Your prayers and your
alms have come up for a memorial before God.
5 "Now send men to Joppa,
and send for Simon whose surname is Peter.
6 "He is lodging with Simon,
a tanner, whose house is by the
sea. He will tell you what you
must do."
7 And when the angel who
spoke to him had departed,

[a](**10:6**) TR adds *ουτος λαλησει σοι τι σε δει ποιειν*, *This (one) will tell you what it is necessary for you to do.*

Cornelius called two of his
household servants and a devout soldier from among those
who waited on him continually.
8 So when he had explained
all *these* things to them, he sent
them to Joppa.
9 The next day, as they went
on their journey and drew near
the city, Peter went up on the
housetop to pray, about the
sixth hour.
10 Then he became very hungry and wanted to eat; but
while they made ready, he fell
into a trance
11 and saw heaven opened
and an object like a great sheet
bound at the four corners, descending to him and let down to
the earth.
12 In it were all kinds of four-
footed animals of the earth,
wild beasts, creeping things,
and birds of the air.
13 And a voice came to him,
"Rise, Peter; kill and eat."
14 But Peter said, "Not so,
Lord! For I have never eaten
anything common or unclean."
15 And a voice *spoke* to him
again the second time, "What
God has cleansed you must not
call common."
16 This was done three times.
And the object was taken up
into heaven again.

Κορνηλίῳ,[b] φωνήσας δύο τῶν οἰκετῶν αὐτοῦ καὶ
[6]to [7]Cornelius, calling two - of [2]household [3]servants [1]his and
he called

στρατιώτην εὐσεβῆ τῶν προσκαρτερούντων αὐτῷ,
a soldier ˜ pious of the *ones* continuing with him,
from among those who waited on

8 καὶ ἐξηγησάμενος αὐτοῖς ἅπαντα, ἀπέστειλεν αὐτοὺς εἰς
and explaining to them all things, he sent them to
explained everything, and

τὴν Ἰόππην.
- Joppa.

Peter Sees a Vision on the Housetop

9 Τῇ δὲ ἐπαύριον, ὁδοιπορούντων ἐκείνων καὶ
[2]on [3]the [1]Now next day, traveling those *ones* and
as they were traveling

τῇ πόλει ἐγγιζόντων, ἀνέβη Πέτρος ἐπὶ τὸ δῶμα
[3]to [4]the [5]city [1]drawing [2]near, [7]went [8]up [6]Peter on the housetop

προσεύξασθαι περὶ ὥραν ἕκτην. 10 Ἐγένετο δὲ
to pray *at* about [3]hour [1]*the* [2]sixth. [2]he [3]became [1]And

πρόσπεινος καὶ ἤθελε γεύσασθαι· παρασκευαζόντων δὲ
hungry and wanted to eat; preparing but
but while they

ἐκείνων, ἐπέπεσεν ἐπ' αὐτὸν ἔκστασις,* 11 καὶ θεωρεῖ τὸν
those, [3]fell [4]on [5]him [1]a [2]trance, and he saw -
were preparing,

οὐρανὸν ἀνεῳγμένον, καὶ καταβαῖνον ἐπ' αὐτὸν σκεῦός
heaven having been opened, and descending to him a vessel ˜

τι ὡς ὀθόνην μεγάλην, τέσσαρσιν ἀρχαῖς
certain like a sheet ˜ great, [4]at [5]*the* [6]four [7]corners

δεδεμένον, καὶ[c] καθιέμενον ἐπὶ τῆς γῆς, 12 ἐν ᾧ
[1]having [2]been [3]bound, and being let down upon the ground, in which

ὑπῆρχε πάντα τὰ τετράποδα τῆς γῆς καὶ τὰ θηρία
were all the four-footed *animals* of the earth and the wild animals

καὶ τὰ ἑρπετὰ καὶ τὰ πετεινὰ τοῦ οὐρανοῦ.
and the reptiles and the birds of the heaven.
sky.

13 Καὶ ἐγένετο φωνὴ πρὸς αὐτόν, "Ἀναστάς, Πέτρε,
And *there* came a voice to him, "Arising, Peter,
"Stand up,

θῦσον καὶ φάγε!"
slaughter and eat!"

14 Ὁ δὲ Πέτρος εἶπε, "Μηδαμῶς, Κύριε! Ὅτι οὐδέποτε
- But Peter said, "Not at all, Lord! For never

ἔφαγον πᾶν κοινὸν ἢ ἀκάθαρτον."
did I eat any*thing* common or unclean."
ritually impure

15 Καὶ φωνὴ πάλιν ἐκ δευτέρου πρὸς αὐτόν,
And a voice *spoke* again of a second *time* to him,
the

"Ἃ ὁ Θεὸς ἐκαθάρισε, σὺ μὴ κοίνου."
"*The things* which - God made clean, you not ˜ must make common."
has made ceremonially impure."

16 Τοῦτο δὲ ἐγένετο ἐπὶ τρίς, καὶ πάλιν ἀνελήφθη
this ˜ And happened - three times, and again [3]was [4]taken [5]up

τὸ σκεῦος εἰς τὸν οὐρανόν.
[1]the [2]vessel into - heaven.

[b](10:7) For τω Κορνηλιω, *to Cornelius,* NU reads αυτω, *to him.* [c](10:11) NU omits δεδεμενον και, *having been bound and,* thus *being let down by (the) four corners.*

*(10:10) ἔκστασις (*ekstasis*). Noun from the preposition ἐκ, *out of,* and the noun στάσις, *a standing,* thus literally meaning *a standing out of.* It refers in some sense to being "beside oneself," thus meaning a state of *astonishment, amazement* (Mark 5:42), *terror* (Luke 5:26; Acts 3:10), or *trance* (as here in Acts 10:10). Cf. the cognate verb ἐξίστημι, *be amazed, astonished, astounded, out of one's senses* (literally *stand outside oneself;* Mark 3:21; Luke 2:47); and the English derivative *ecstasy.*

Cornelius' Delegates Summon Peter

17 Ὡς δὲ ἐν ἑαυτῷ διηπόρει ὁ Πέτρος
as ~ Now [5]within [6]himself [2]was [3]very [4]perplexed - [1]Peter

τί ἂν εἴη τὸ ὅραμα ὃ εἶδε, καὶ ἰδού, οἱ
as to what - [6]might [7]be [1]the [2]vision [3]which [4]he [5]saw, - behold, the
mean had seen,

ἄνδρες οἱ ἀπεσταλμένοι ἀπὸ τοῦ Κορνηλίου
men the *ones* having been sent from - Cornelius
who had

διερωτήσαντες τὴν οἰκίαν Σίμωνος, ἐπέστησαν ἐπὶ τὸν
having found by inquiry the house of Simon, stood at the

πυλῶνα, 18 καὶ φωνήσαντες ἐπυνθάνοντο εἰ Σίμων
gateway, and calling they were inquiring whether Simon
they called out and inquired

ὁ ἐπικαλούμενος Πέτρος ἐνθάδε ξενίζεται.
the *one* being called Peter [3]here [1]is [2]staying as a guest.
who is surnamed was staying there

19 Τοῦ δὲ Πέτρου διενθυμουμένου περὶ τοῦ ὁράματος,
- Now Peter pondering about the vision,
while Peter pondered

εἶπεν αὐτῷ τὸ Πνεῦμα, "Ἰδού, ἄνδρες[d] ζητοῦσί σε.
[3]said [4]to [5]him [1]the [2]Spirit, "Behold, men are seeking you.

20 Ἀλλὰ ἀναστὰς κατάβηθι καὶ πορεύου σὺν αὐτοῖς μηδὲν
Moreover arising go down and go with them nothing
rise and with no

διακρινόμενος, διότι ἐγὼ ἀπέσταλκα αὐτούς."
doubting, for I have sent them."
wavering,

21 Καταβὰς δὲ Πέτρος πρὸς τοὺς ἄνδρας,[e] εἶπεν,
[3]going [4]down [1]And [2]Peter to the men, said,
went and said,

"Ἰδού, ἐγώ εἰμι ὃν ζητεῖτε· τίς ἡ αἰτία
"Behold, I am *the one* whom you are seeking; What *is* the reason

δι' ἣν πάρεστε?"
on account of which you are here?"
for

22 Οἱ δὲ εἶπον, "Κορνήλιος ἑκατοντάρχης, ἀνὴρ
[2]the [3]*ones* [1]And said, "Cornelius a centurion, a man ~
they

δίκαιος καὶ φοβούμενος τὸν Θεόν, μαρτυρούμενός τε ὑπὸ
just and fearing - God, [2]being [3]witnessed [1]and by
having a good reputation with

ὅλου τοῦ ἔθνους τῶν Ἰουδαίων, ἐχρηματίσθη ὑπὸ
whole ~ the nation of the Jews, was given a revelation by
all the directed

ἀγγέλου ἁγίου μεταπέμψασθαί σε εἰς τὸν οἶκον αὐτοῦ καὶ
a(n) angel ~ holy to send for you to - house ~ his and

ἀκοῦσαι ῥήματα παρὰ σοῦ." 23 Εἰσκαλεσάμενος οὖν
to hear words from you." [2]inviting [4]in [1]Therefore
he invited

αὐτοὺς ἐξένισε.
[3]them he received *them* as guests.
them in and

Peter Meets Cornelius

Τῇ δὲ ἐπαύριον ὁ Πέτρος[f] ἐξῆλθε σὺν αὐτοῖς, καί
[2]on [3]the [1]Now next day - Peter went forth with them, and

τινες τῶν ἀδελφῶν τῶν ἀπὸ Ἰόππης συνῆλθον αὐτῷ. 24 Καὶ
some of the brothers - from Joppa went with him. And

17 Now while Peter wondered within himself what this vision which he had seen meant, behold, the men who had been sent from Cornelius had made inquiry for Simon's house, and stood before the gate.
18 And they called and asked whether Simon, whose surname was Peter, was lodging there.
19 While Peter thought about the vision, the Spirit said to him, "Behold, three men are seeking you.
20 "Arise therefore, go down and go with them, doubting nothing; for I have sent them."
21 Then Peter went down to the men who had been sent to him from Cornelius, and said, "Yes, I am he whom you seek. For what reason have you come?"
22 And they said, "Cornelius *the* centurion, a just man, one who fears God and has a good reputation among all the nation of the Jews, was divinely instructed by a holy angel to summon you to his house, and to hear words from you."
23 Then he invited them in and lodged *them*. On the next day Peter went away with them, and some brethren from Joppa accompanied him.
24 And the following day they

---

[d]**(10:19)** NU, TR add τρεις, *three.* [e]**(10:21)** TR adds *τους απεσταλμενους απο του Κορνηλιου προς αυτον, the (ones) having been sent from Cornelius to him.* [f]**(10:23)** NU omits *ο Πετρος, Peter,* and adds *αναστας*, thus *After waking the next day, he (went away).*

entered Caesarea. Now Cornelius was waiting for them, and had called together his relatives and close friends.
25 As Peter was coming in, Cornelius met him and fell down at his feet and worshiped *him.*
26 But Peter lifted him up, saying, "Stand up; I myself am also a man."
27 And as he talked with him, he went in and found many who had come together.
28 Then he said to them, "You know how unlawful it is for a Jewish man to keep company with or go to one of another nation. But God has shown me that I should not call any man common or unclean.
29 "Therefore I came without objection as soon as I was sent for. I ask, then, for what reason have you sent for me?"
30 So Cornelius said, "Four days ago I was fasting until this hour; and at the ninth hour I prayed in my house, and behold, a man stood before me in bright clothing,
31 "and said, 'Cornelius, your prayer has been heard, and your alms are remembered in the sight of God.
32 'Send therefore to Joppa and call Simon here, whose surname is Peter. He is lodging in the house of Simon, a tanner, by the sea. When he comes, he will speak to you.'
33 "So I sent to you immediately, and you have done well

τῇ ἐπαύριον εἰσῆλθον εἰς τὴν Καισάρειαν. Ὁ δὲ
on the next day they entered into - Caesarea. - And

Κορνήλιος ἦν προσδοκῶν αὐτούς, συγκαλεσάμενος τοὺς
Cornelius was waiting for them, having called together -

συγγενεῖς αὐτοῦ καὶ τοὺς ἀναγκαίους φίλους. 25 Ὡς δὲ
relatives ˜ his and - close friends. when ˜ Now

ἐγένετο τοῦ εἰσελθεῖν τὸν Πέτρον, συναντήσας αὐτῷ ὁ
it happened - to enter - Peter, meeting him -
that Peter entered, Cornelius met him,

Κορνήλιος, πεσὼν ἐπὶ τοὺς πόδας, προσεκύνησεν.
Cornelius, falling at the feet, worshiped *him.*
fell his and worshiped

26 Ὁ δὲ Πέτρος ἤγειρεν αὐτόν, λέγων, "Ἀνάστηθι! Κἀγὼ
- But Peter raised up ˜ him, saying, "Stand up! I [3]also

αὐτὸς ἄνθρωπός εἰμι." 27 Καὶ συνομιλῶν αὐτῷ εἰσῆλθε, καὶ
[1]myself [4]a [5]man [2]am." And conversing with him he went in, and
as he conversed

εὑρίσκει συνεληλυθότας πολλούς, 28 ἔφη τε πρὸς αὐτούς,
he found [2]having [3]gathered [1]many, [2]he [3]said [1]and to them,

"Ὑμεῖς ἐπίστασθε ὡς ἀθέμιτόν ἐστιν ἀνδρὶ Ἰουδαίῳ
"You know how unlawful it is for a man a Jew
a Jewish man

κολλᾶσθαι ἢ προσέρχεσθαι ἀλλοφύλῳ· καὶ ἐμοὶ ὁ Θεὸς
to associate with or to approach a Gentile; and yet to me - God

ἔδειξε μηδένα κοινὸν ἢ ἀκάθαρτον λέγειν ἄνθρωπον·
showed no one common or unclean to call a man;
has shown that I should call no man ceremonially impure or unclean;

29 διὸ καὶ ἀναντιρρήτως ἦλθον μεταπεμφθείς.
therefore also without objecting I came having been sent for.
when I was

Πυνθάνομαι οὖν, τίνι λόγῳ μετεπέμψασθέ με?"
I inquire therefore, for what reason did you send for me?"

30 Καὶ ὁ Κορνήλιος ἔφη, "Ἀπὸ τετάρτης ἡμέρας μέχρι
And - Cornelius said, "From *the* fourth day until
"Four days ago

ταύτης τῆς ὥρας ἤμην νηστεύων, καὶ[g] τὴν ἐνάτην ὥραν
this - hour I was fasting, and the ninth hour

προσευχόμενος ἐν τῷ οἴκῳ μου, καὶ ἰδού, ἀνὴρ ἔστη
I was praying in - house ˜ my, and behold, a man stood

ἐνώπιόν μου ἐν ἐσθῆτι λαμπρᾷ 31 καὶ φησί, 'Κορνήλιε,
before me in clothing ˜ shining and said, 'Cornelius,

εἰσηκούσθη σου ἡ προσευχὴ καὶ αἱ ἐλεημοσύναι σου
[3]was [4]heard [1]your - [2]prayer and - alms ˜ your
has been

ἐμνήσθησαν ἐνώπιον τοῦ Θεοῦ. 32 Πέμψον οὖν εἰς
were remembered before - God. Send therefore to
have been

Ἰόππην καὶ μετακάλεσαι Σίμωνα ὃς ἐπικαλεῖται Πέτρος·
Joppa and summon Simon who is called Peter;
surnamed

οὗτος ξενίζεται ἐν οἰκίᾳ Σίμωνος βυρσέως παρὰ
this *man* is staying as a guest in *the* house of Simon a tanner beside

θάλασσαν·[h] ὃς παραγενόμενος λαλήσει σοι.' 33 Ἐξαυτῆς
the sea; who arriving will speak to you.' Immediately
will come and

οὖν ἔπεμψα πρὸς σέ, σύ τε καλῶς ἐποίησας
therefore I sent to you, you ˜ and well ˜ did
have done

[g](10:30) NU omits νηστευων, και, *fasting, and,* thus *I was praying at the ninth hour.*
[h](10:32) NU omits the rest of v. 32.

παραγενόμενος. Νῦν οὖν πάντες ἡμεῖς ἐνώπιον τοῦ Θεοῦ
arriving. Now then all ˜ we [3]before - [4]God
well to come.

πάρεσμεν ἀκοῦσαι πάντα τὰ προστεταγμένα σοι ὑπὸ
[1]are [2]present to hear all the *things* having been commanded you by

τοῦ Θεοῦ."[i]
- God."

Peter Preaches Peace to Cornelius' House

34 Ἀνοίξας δὲ Πέτρος τὸ στόμα εἶπεν, "Ἐπ' ἀληθείας
[3]opening [1]And [2]Peter the mouth said, "In truth
opened his and said,

καταλαμβάνομαι ὅτι οὐκ ἔστι προσωπολήπτης* ὁ Θεός,
I comprehend that [3]not [2]is [4]One [5]to [6]show [7]partiality - [1]God,

35 ἀλλ' ἐν παντὶ ἔθνει ὁ φοβούμενος αὐτὸν καὶ
but in every nation the *one* fearing Him and

ἐργαζόμενος δικαιοσύνην δεκτὸς αὐτῷ ἐστι. 36 Τὸν λόγον
working righteousness [2]acceptable [3]to [4]Him [1]is. The word
message

ὃν ἀπέστειλε τοῖς υἱοῖς Ἰσραήλ, εὐαγγελιζόμενος
which He sent to the sons of Israel, preaching the good news of

εἰρήνην διὰ Ἰησοῦ Χριστοῦ — οὗτός ἐστι πάντων
peace through Jesus Christ — this *One* is [2]of [3]all

Κύριος — 37 ὑμεῖς οἴδατε, τὸ γενόμενον ῥῆμα καθ'
[1]Lord — you know, the [2]coming [3]to [4]be [1]word throughout
which was

ὅλης τῆς Ἰουδαίας, ἀρξάμενον ἀπὸ τῆς Γαλιλαίας μετὰ τὸ
whole ˜ the of Judea, beginning from - Galilee after the
all

βάπτισμα ὃ ἐκήρυξεν Ἰωάννης, Ἰησοῦν τὸν ἀπὸ Ναζαρέτ,
baptism which proclaimed ˜ John, Jesus - from Nazareth,

38 ὡς ἔχρισεν αὐτὸν ὁ Θεὸς Πνεύματι Ἁγίῳ καὶ δυνάμει,
how [2]anointed [3]Him - [1]God with *the* Spirit ˜ Holy and power,

ὃς διῆλθεν εὐεργετῶν καὶ ἰώμενος πάντας τοὺς
who went about doing good and healing all the *ones*
those who

καταδυναστευομένους ὑπὸ τοῦ διαβόλου, ὅτι ὁ Θεὸς ἦν μετ'
being oppressed by the devil, because - God was with
were

αὐτοῦ. 39 Καὶ ἡμεῖς ἐσμεν μάρτυρες πάντων ὧν
Him. And we are witnesses of all *the things* which

ἐποίησεν ἔν τε τῇ χώρᾳ τῶν Ἰουδαίων καὶ ἐν Ἱερουσαλήμ·
He did in ˜ both the country of the Jews and in Jerusalem;

ὃν καὶ[j] ἀνεῖλον κρεμάσαντες ἐπὶ ξύλου. 40 Τοῦτον ὁ
whom also ˜ they killed hanging *Him* on a tree. This *One* -
when they hanged

Θεὸς ἤγειρε τῇ τρίτῃ ἡμέρᾳ καὶ ἔδωκεν αὐτὸν ἐμφανῆ
God raised on the third day and gave Him [3]visible
granted

γενέσθαι, 41 οὐ παντὶ τῷ λαῷ, ἀλλὰ μάρτυσι τοῖς
[1]to [2]become, not to all the people, but to witnesses the *ones*
who

προκεχειροτονημένοις ὑπὸ τοῦ Θεοῦ, ἡμῖν, οἵτινες
having been chosen beforehand by God, to us, who
had been

συνεφάγομεν καὶ συνεπίομεν αὐτῷ μετὰ τὸ ἀναστῆναι
ate together and drank together with Him after - [2]to [3]arise
He

to come. Now therefore, we are all present before God, to hear all the things commanded you by God."
34 Then Peter opened *his* mouth and said: "In truth I perceive that God shows no partiality.
35 "But in every nation whoever fears Him and works righteousness is accepted by Him.
36 "The word which *God* sent to the children of Israel, preaching peace through Jesus Christ — He is Lord of all —
37 "that word you know, which was proclaimed throughout all Judea, and began from Galilee after the baptism which John preached:
38 "how God anointed Jesus of Nazareth with the Holy Spirit and with power, who went about doing good and healing all who were oppressed by the devil, for God was with Him.
39 "And we are witnesses of all things which He did both in the land of the Jews and in Jerusalem, whom they killed by hanging on a tree.
40 "Him God raised up on the third day, and showed Him openly,
41 "not to all the people, but to witnesses chosen before by God, *even* to us who ate and drank with Him after He arose

---

[i]**(10:33)** NU reads Κυριου, *Lord.* [j]**(10:39)** TR omits και, *also.*

***(10:34)** προσωπολήπτης *(prosōpolēptēs).* Noun used only here in the NT, meaning *one who shows partiality, a respecter of persons.* The word is a compound from πρόσωπον, *face, person,* and λῆμψις, *a receiving,* literally meaning to receive someone because of his wealth, position, or appearance. Here it is noted that God is not characterized as practicing such partiality or making such distinctions. See the cognate προσωπολημψία, *partiality,* at James 2:1.

from the dead.
42 "And He commanded us to
preach to the people, and to
testify that it is He who was ordained by God *to be* Judge of the
living and the dead.
43 "To Him all the prophets
witness that, through His
name, whoever believes in Him
will receive remission of sins."
44 While Peter was still
speaking these words, the Holy
Spirit fell upon all those who
heard the word.
45 And those of the circumcision who believed were astonished, as many as came with
Peter, because the gift of the
Holy Spirit had been poured out
on the Gentiles also.
46 For they heard them speak
with tongues and magnify God.
Then Peter answered,
47 "Can anyone forbid water,
that these should not be baptized who have received the
Holy Spirit just as we *have?*"
48 And he commanded them
to be baptized in the name of
the Lord. Then they asked him
to stay a few days.
11 Now the apostles and
brethren who were in
Judea heard that the Gentiles
had also received the word of
God.
2 And when Peter came up

αὐτὸν ἐκ νεκρῶν. **42** Καὶ παρήγγειλεν ἡμῖν κηρύξαι τῷ
[1]Him from *the* dead. And He commanded us to proclaim to the
arose

λαῷ καὶ διαμαρτύρασθαι ὅτι αὐτός ἐστιν ὁ
people and to testify solemnly that He is the *One*

ὡρισμένος ὑπὸ τοῦ Θεοῦ Κριτὴς ζώντων καὶ
having been appointed by - God *to be* Judge of *the* living and
ordained

νεκρῶν. **43** Τούτῳ πάντες οἱ προφῆται μαρτυροῦσιν,
of *the* dead. To this *One* all the prophets bear witness, *that*

ἄφεσιν ἁμαρτιῶν λαβεῖν διὰ τοῦ ὀνόματος αὐτοῦ
[8]forgiveness [9]of [10]sins [6]to [7]receive [11]through - [13]name [12]His
will

πάντα τὸν πιστεύοντα* εἰς αὐτόν."
[1]every - [2]*one* [3]believing [4]in [5]Him."
everyone who believes

The Holy Spirit Falls on Gentiles

44 Ἔτι λαλοῦντος τοῦ Πέτρου τὰ ῥήματα ταῦτα, ἐπέπεσε
[2]yet [3]speaking - [1]Peter - words ~ these, [4]fell
While Peter was still speaking

τὸ Πνεῦμα τὸ Ἅγιον ἐπὶ πάντας τοὺς ἀκούοντας τὸν
[1]the [3]Spirit - [2]Holy on all the *ones* hearing the
those who heard

λόγον. **45** Καὶ ἐξέστησαν οἱ ἐκ περιτομῆς
word. And [7]were [8]astounded [1]the [4]of [5]*the* [6]circumcision
message.

πιστοὶ ὅσοι συνῆλθον τῷ Πέτρῳ, ὅτι καὶ ἐπὶ
[2]believing [3]*ones* as many as came with - Peter, because [14]also [11]on
believers had come

τὰ ἔθνη ἡ δωρεὰ τοῦ Ἁγίου Πνεύματος
[12]the [13]Gentiles [1]the [2]gift [3]of [4]the [5]Holy [6]Spirit

ἐκκέχυται. **46** Ἤκουον γὰρ αὐτῶν λαλούντων
[7]has [8]been [9]poured [10]out. [2]they [3]heard [1]For them speaking
had

γλώσσαις καὶ μεγαλυνόντων τὸν Θεόν.
in tongues and magnifying - God.

Τότε ἀπεκρίθη ὁ Πέτρος, **47** "Μήτι τὸ ὕδωρ κωλῦσαι
Then answered ~ - Peter, "[3]not - [7]water [5]to [6]forbid
"Surely no one can forbid

δύναταί τις τοῦ μὴ βαπτισθῆναι τούτους οἵτινες τὸ
[2]is [4]able, [7]*is* [8]*he* [1]Anyone - *for* [2]not [3]to [4]be [5]baptized [1]these who [2]the
water, can he, that these should not be baptized

Πνεῦμα τὸ Ἅγιον ἔλαβον καθὼς καὶ ἡμεῖς?" **48** Προσέταξέ
[4]Spirit - [3]Holy [1]received just as also ~ we *did?*" [2]he [3]commanded

τε αὐτοὺς βαπτισθῆναι ἐν τῷ ὀνόματι τοῦ Κυρίου.[k] Τότε
[1]And them to be baptized in the name of the Lord. Then

ἠρώτησαν αὐτὸν ἐπιμεῖναι ἡμέρας τινάς.
they asked him to stay *for* days ~ some.

Peter Defends God's Grace at Jerusalem

11 **1** Ἤκουσαν δὲ οἱ ἀπόστολοι καὶ οἱ ἀδελφοὶ
[12]heard [1]Now [2]the [3]apostles [4]and [5]the [6]brothers

οἱ ὄντες κατὰ τὴν Ἰουδαίαν ὅτι καὶ τὰ ἔθνη
[7]the [8]*ones* [9]being [10]throughout - [11]Judea that even the Gentiles
who were

ἐδέξαντο τὸν λόγον τοῦ Θεοῦ. **2** Καὶ ὅτε ἀνέβη Πέτρος εἰς
received the word - of God. And when [2]came [3]up [1]Peter to
had received

---

k(**10:48**) For *του Κυριου, of the Lord,* NU reads *Ιησου Χριστου, of Jesus Christ.*

***(10:43)** *πιστευω (pisteuō).* Verb occurring frequently in the NT, meaning *believe, have faith, trust, put confidence in.* As here, it most often refers to faith in God or Christ, or, frequently in John, to belief in things Christ taught. It can also mean to believe any kind of claim, as in Acts 9:26 when some did not *believe* that Paul was a disciple. Occasionally (as Luke 16:11) it can mean *to entrust* someone with something. Cf. the cognate noun *πίστις, faith, confidence, trust;* sometimes, especially with the article, *the faith,* as the body of Christian belief (2 Tim. 4:7). Sometimes the meaning may be *faithfulness* (as possibly Rom. 3:3); cf. the cognate adjective *πιστός* which often means *faithful* (as Rev. 2:10).

Ἱεροσόλυμα, διεκρίνοντο πρὸς αὐτὸν οἱ ἐκ
Jerusalem, [6]were [7]contending [8]with [9]him [1]the [2]*ones* [3]of
those

περιτομῆς, 3 λέγοντες ὅτι "Πρὸς ἄνδρας ἀκροβυστίαν
[4]*the* [5]circumcision, saying - "To men foreskin ~
uncircumcised

ἔχοντας εἰσῆλθες καὶ συνέφαγες αὐτοῖς."
having you went in and ate with them."

4 Ἀρξάμενος δὲ ὁ Πέτρος ἐξετίθετο αὐτοῖς καθεξῆς
[3]beginning [1]But - [2]Peter was setting forth to them in order
began and explained

λέγων, 5 "Ἐγὼ ἤμην ἐν πόλει Ἰόππῃ προσευχόμενος καὶ
saying, "I was in *the* city Joppa praying and

εἶδον ἐν ἐκστάσει ὅραμα, καταβαῖνον σκεῦός τι ὡς
I saw in a trance a vision, [4]coming [5]down [1]a [3]vessel [2]certain like

ὀθόνην μεγάλην τέσσαρσιν ἀρχαῖς καθιεμένην ἐκ τοῦ
a sheet ~ great [3]by [4]*the* [5]four [6]corners [1]being [2]lowered from -

οὐρανοῦ, καὶ ἦλθεν ἄχρις ἐμοῦ· 6 εἰς ἣν ἀτενίσας
heaven, and it came as far as me; on which looking intently
when I looked intently

κατενόουν καὶ εἶδον τὰ τετράποδα τῆς γῆς καὶ τὰ
I was contemplating and I saw the four-footed *animals* of the earth and the
and contemplated,

θηρία καὶ τὰ ἑρπετὰ καὶ τὰ πετεινὰ τοῦ οὐρανοῦ.
wild beasts and the reptiles and the birds of the heaven.
sky.

7 Ἤκουσα δὲ φωνῆς λεγούσης μοι, 'Ἀναστάς, Πέτρε,
[2]I [3]heard [1]And a voice saying to me, 'Rising, Peter,
'Arise,

θῦσον καὶ φάγε!' 8 Εἶπον δέ, 'Μηδαμῶς, Κύριε! Ὅτι
slaughter and eat!' [2]I [3]said [1]But, 'By no means, Lord! For

πᾶν κοινὸν ἢ ἀκάθαρτον οὐδέποτε εἰσῆλθεν εἰς
every *thing* common or unclean never entered into
nothing ceremonially impure has ever

τὸ στόμα μου.' 9 Ἀπεκρίθη δέ μοι[a] φωνὴ ἐκ δευτέρου
- mouth ~ my.' [4]answered [1]But [5]me [2]a [3]voice of second *time*
a

ἐκ τοῦ οὐρανοῦ, 'Ἃ ὁ Θεὸς ἐκαθάρισε σὺ μὴ
from - heaven, '*The things* which - God made clean you not ~
has made

κοίνου.' 10 Τοῦτο δὲ ἐγένετο ἐπὶ τρίς, καὶ
must make common.' this ~ And took place - three times, and
ceremonially impure.'

πάλιν ἀνεσπάσθη ἅπαντα εἰς τὸν οὐρανόν. 11 Καὶ ἰδού,
again [3]were [4]drawn [5]up [1]all [2]*things* into - heaven. And behold,

ἐξαυτῆς τρεῖς ἄνδρες ἐπέστησαν ἐπὶ τὴν οἰκίαν ἐν ᾗ
immediately three men stood before the house in which

ἤμην, ἀπεσταλμένοι ἀπὸ Καισαρείας πρός με. 12 Εἶπε δέ
I was, having been sent from Caesarea to me. [4]said [1]And

μοι τὸ Πνεῦμα συνελθεῖν αὐτοῖς μηδὲν διακρινόμενον.[b]
[5]to [6]me [2]the [3]Spirit to go with them nothing wavering.
without any hesitating.

Ἦλθον δὲ σὺν ἐμοὶ καὶ οἱ ἓξ ἀδελφοὶ οὗτοι, καὶ
[6]went [1]Now [7]with [8]me [5]also - [3]six [4]brothers [2]these, and

εἰσήλθομεν εἰς τὸν οἶκον τοῦ ἀνδρός. 13 Ἀπήγγειλέ τε
we entered into the house of the man. [2]he [3]related [1]And

ἡμῖν πῶς εἶδε τὸν ἄγγελον ἐν τῷ οἴκῳ αὐτοῦ σταθέντα καὶ
to us how he saw the angel in - house ~ his standing and
had seen

to Jerusalem, those of the circumcision contended with him,
3 saying, "You went in to uncircumcised men and ate with them!"
4 But Peter explained *it* to them in order from the beginning, saying:
5 "I was in the city of Joppa praying; and in a trance I saw a vision, an object descending like a great sheet, let down from heaven by four corners; and it came to me.
6 "When I observed it intently and considered, I saw four-footed animals of the earth, wild beasts, creeping things, and birds of the air.
7 "And I heard a voice saying to me, 'Rise, Peter; kill and eat.'
8 "But I said, 'Not so, Lord! For nothing common or unclean has at any time entered my mouth.'
9 "But the voice answered me again from heaven, 'What God has cleansed you must not call common.'
10 "Now this was done three times, and all were drawn up again into heaven.
11 "At that very moment, three men stood before the house where I was, having been sent to me from Caesarea.
12 "Then the Spirit told me to go with them, doubting nothing. Moreover these six brethren accompanied me, and we entered the man's house.
13 "And he told us how he had seen an angel standing in his

---

[a]**(11:9)** NU omits *μοι, me.*
[b]**(11:12)** NU reads *διακριναντα, making (no) distinction between us.*

house, who said to him, 'Send
men to Joppa, and call for Simon whose surname is Peter,
14 'who will tell you words by
which you and all your household will be saved.'
15 "And as I began to speak,
the Holy Spirit fell upon them,
as upon us at the beginning.
16 "Then I remembered the
word of the Lord, how He said,
'John indeed baptized with water, but you shall be baptized
with the Holy Spirit.'
17 "If therefore God gave
them the same gift as *He gave*
us when we believed on the
Lord Jesus Christ, who was I
that I could withstand God?"
18 When they heard these
things they became silent; and
they glorified God, saying,
"Then God has also granted to
the Gentiles repentance to
life."
19 Now those who were scattered after the persecution that
arose over Stephen traveled as
far as Phoenicia, Cyprus, and
Antioch, preaching the word to
no one but the Jews only.
20 But some of them were
men from Cyprus and Cyrene,
who, when they had come to
Antioch, spoke to the Hellenists, preaching the Lord Jesus.
21 And the hand of the Lord
was with them, and a great

εἰπόντα αὐτῷ, "Ἀπόστειλον εἰς Ἰόππην ἄνδρας καὶ
saying to him, 'Send [2]to [3]Joppa [1]men and

μετάπεμψαι Σίμωνα τὸν ἐπικαλούμενον Πέτρον, **14** ὃς
send for Simon the *one* being called Peter, who
who is surnamed

λαλήσει ῥήματα πρὸς σὲ ἐν οἷς σωθήσῃ σὺ καὶ πᾶς ὁ
will speak words to you by which [2]will [3]be [4]saved [1]you and all -

οἶκός σου.' **15** Ἐν δὲ τῷ ἄρξασθαί με λαλεῖν, ἐπέπεσε τὸ
house ~ your.' in ~ And - to begin me to speak, [4]fell [1]the
And when I began

Πνεῦμα τὸ Ἅγιον ἐπ' αὐτοὺς ὥσπερ καὶ ἐφ' ἡμᾶς ἐν
[3]Spirit - [2]Holy on them as also on us in

ἀρχῇ. **16** Ἐμνήσθην δὲ τοῦ ῥήματος Κυρίου, ὡς
the beginning. [2]I [3]remembered [1]And the word of *the* Lord, how

ἔλεγεν, "Ἰωάννης μὲν ἐβάπτισεν ὕδατι, ὑμεῖς δὲ
He said, 'John - baptized in water, you ~ but
with

βαπτισθήσεσθε ἐν Πνεύματι Ἁγίῳ.' **17** Εἰ οὖν τὴν ἴσην
will be baptized in *the* Spirit ~ Holy.' If then [5]the [6]equal
with same

δωρεὰν ἔδωκεν αὐτοῖς ὁ Θεὸς ὡς καὶ ἡμῖν
[7]gift [2]gave [3]to [4]them - [1]God as *He* also *gave* to us
has given

πιστεύσασιν ἐπὶ τὸν Κύριον Ἰησοῦν Χριστόν, ἐγὼ δὲ τίς
believing on the Lord Jesus Christ, [3]I - [1]who
when we believed

ἤμην δυνατὸς κωλῦσαι τὸν Θεόν?" **18** Ἀκούσαντες δὲ
[2]was *to be* able to hinder - God?" hearing ~ And
when they heard

ταῦτα ἡσύχασαν καὶ ἐδόξαζον τὸν Θεόν, λέγοντες,
these *things* they remained silent and glorified - God, saying,

"Ἄραγε καὶ τοῖς ἔθνεσιν ὁ Θεὸς τὴν μετάνοιαν ἔδωκεν
"Indeed then even to the Gentiles - God - repentance ~ gave
has granted

εἰς ζωήν."
to life."

Barnabas and Saul Minister to the Church at Antioch

19 Οἱ μὲν οὖν διασπαρέντες ἀπὸ τῆς θλίψεως
[2]the [3]*ones* - [1]Then being scattered from the tribulation
who were because of

τῆς γενομένης ἐπὶ Στεφάνῳ διῆλθον ἕως Φοινίκης καὶ
the *one* coming about over Stephen went about as far as Phoenicia and
which came

Κύπρου καὶ Ἀντιοχείας, μηδενὶ λαλοῦντες τὸν λόγον εἰ
Cyprus and Antioch, [4]to [5]no [6]one [1]speaking [2]the [3]word if
message

μὴ μόνον Ἰουδαίοις. **20** Ἦσαν δέ τινες ἐξ αὐτῶν ἄνδρες
not only ~ Jews. [5]were [1]But [2]some [3]of [4]them men
except

Κύπριοι καὶ Κυρηναῖοι, οἵτινες εἰσελθόντες εἰς Ἀντιόχειαν
Cypriots and Cyrenians, who entering into Antioch
Cypriots when they entered

ἐλάλουν πρὸς τοὺς Ἑλληνιστάς, εὐαγγελιζόμενοι τὸν
spoke to the Hellenists, preaching the good news of the
Greek-speaking Jews,

Κύριον Ἰησοῦν. **21** Καὶ ἦν χεὶρ Κυρίου μετ' αὐτῶν,
Lord Jesus. And [6]was [1]*the* [2]hand [3]of [4]*the* [5]Lord with them,

πολύς τε ἀριθμὸς πιστεύσας ἐπέστρεψεν ἐπὶ τὸν Κύριον.
[2]a [3]great [1]and number believing turned to the Lord.
believed and

22 Ἠκούσθη δὲ ὁ λόγος εἰς τὰ ὦτα τῆς ἐκκλησίας
[6]was [7]heard [1]And [2]the [3]word [8]in [9]the [10]ears [11]of [12]the [13]church

τῆς ἐν Ἱεροσολύμοις περὶ αὐτῶν, καὶ ἐξαπέστειλαν
- [14]in [15]Jerusalem [4]about [5]them, and they sent forth

Βαρναβᾶν διελθεῖν ἕως Ἀντιοχείας· 23 ὃς παραγενόμενος
Barnabas to go as far as Antioch; who arriving
when he arrived

καὶ ἰδὼν τὴν χάριν τοῦ Θεοῦ ἐχάρη καὶ παρεκάλει πάντας
and seeing the grace - of God was glad and encouraged *them* all
saw

τῇ προθέσει τῆς καρδίας προσμένειν τῷ Κυρίῳ,
- with purpose - of heart to continue with the Lord,

24 ὅτι ἦν ἀνὴρ ἀγαθὸς καὶ πλήρης Πνεύματος Ἁγίου
because he was a man ˜ good and full of *the* Spirit ˜ Holy

καὶ πίστεως. Καὶ προσετέθη ὄχλος ἱκανὸς τῷ Κυρίῳ.
and of faith. And [4]was [5]added [1]a [3]crowd [2]considerable to the Lord.
number

25 Ἐξῆλθε δὲ εἰς Ταρσὸν ὁ Βαρναβᾶς[c] ἀναζητῆσαι
[3]went [4]forth [1]And [5]to [6]Tarsus - [2]Barnabas to seek out

Σαῦλον, 26 καὶ εὑρὼν ἤγαγεν αὐτὸν εἰς Ἀντιόχειαν.
Saul, and finding *him* he brought him to Antioch.
when he found

Ἐγένετο δὲ αὐτοὺς ἐνιαυτὸν ὅλον συναχθῆναι τῇ
[2]it [3]came [4]about [1]And *for* them a year ˜ whole to be gathered with the
that for they assembled

ἐκκλησίᾳ καὶ διδάξαι ὄχλον ἱκανόν, χρηματίσαι τε
church and to instruct a crowd ˜ considerable, [4]to [5]call [1]and
instructed many people, were called

πρῶτον ἐν Ἀντιοχείᾳ τοὺς μαθητὰς Χριστιανούς.*
[7]first [8]in [9]Antioch [2]the [3]disciples [6]Christians.

Antioch Sends Famine Relief to Judea

27 Ἐν ταύταις δὲ ταῖς ἡμέραις κατῆλθον ἀπὸ
[2]in [3]these [1]Now - days [2]went [3]down [4]from

Ἱεροσολύμων προφῆται εἰς Ἀντιόχειαν. 28 Ἀναστὰς δὲ εἷς
[5]Jerusalem [1]prophets to Antioch. [2]rising [3]up [1]And one

ἐξ αὐτῶν ὀνόματι Ἄγαβος, ἐσήμανε διὰ τοῦ Πνεύματος
of them by name Agabus, foretold by the Spirit
named

λιμὸν μέγαν μέλλειν ἔσεσθαι ἐφ᾽ ὅλην τὴν οἰκουμένην·
of a famine ˜ great to be about to be in whole ˜ the world;
about to happen all

ὅστις καὶ ἐγένετο ἐπὶ Κλαυδίου Καίσαρος.[d] 29 Τῶν
which also came to pass in the time of Claudius Caesar. [3]of [4]the

δὲ μαθητῶν καθὼς εὐπορεῖτό τις, ὥρισαν ἕκαστος
[1]And [5]disciples [6]as [7]he [8]had [9]plenty [2]anyone, determined each

αὐτῶν εἰς διακονίαν πέμψαι τοῖς κατοικοῦσιν ἐν τῇ Ἰουδαίᾳ
of them for service to send to the [2]dwelling [3]in - [4]Judea
as a ministry

ἀδελφοῖς· 30 ὃ καὶ ἐποίησαν ἀποστείλαντες πρὸς τοὺς
[1]brothers; which also ˜ they did sending *it* to the
and sent

πρεσβυτέρους διὰ χειρὸς Βαρναβᾶ καὶ Σαύλου.
elders by *the* hand of Barnabas and Saul.

number believed and turned to
the Lord.
22 Then news of these things
came to the ears of the church
in Jerusalem, and they sent out
Barnabas to go as far as Antioch.
23 When he came and had
seen the grace of God, he was
glad, and encouraged them all
that with purpose of heart they
should continue with the Lord.
24 For he was a good man, full
of the Holy Spirit and of faith.
And a great many people were
added to the Lord.
25 Then Barnabas departed
for Tarsus to seek Saul.
26 And when he had found
him, he brought him to Antioch.
So it was that for a whole year
they assembled with the church
and taught a great many people.
And the disciples were first
called Christians in Antioch.
27 And in these days prophets
came from Jerusalem to Antioch.
28 Then one of them, named
Agabus, stood up and showed
by the Spirit that there was going
to be a great famine
throughout all the world, which
also happened in the days of
Claudius Caesar.
29 Then the disciples, each
according to his ability, determined
to send relief to the
brethren dwelling in Judea.
30 This they also did, and sent
it to the elders by the hands of
Barnabas and Saul.

---

[c](**11:25**) NU omits ο Βαρναβας, *Barnabas,* thus *he departed.*

[d](**11:28**) NU omits Καισαρος, *Caesar.*

***(11:26)** Χριστιανός *(Christianos).* Noun from Χριστός, *Christ,* and a Latin suffix suggesting "belonging to," thus meaning one who is identified with or devoted to Christ, *a Christian.* Here in Acts 11:26 is the indication that the word was coined in Antioch, and it may have first been used by critics to ridicule the disciples. See also Acts 26:28, where Agrippa possibly uses it in scorn, and 1 Pet. 4:16, the only other occurrences in the NT.

12 Now about that time
Herod the king
stretched out *his* hand to harass
some from the church.
2 Then he killed James the
brother of John with the sword.
3 And because he saw that it
pleased the Jews, he proceeded
further to seize Peter also.
Now it was *during* the Days of
Unleavened Bread.
4 So when he had arrested
him, he put *him* in prison, and
delivered *him* to four squads of
soldiers to keep him, intending
to bring him before the people
after Passover.
5 Peter was therefore kept
in prison, but constant prayer
was offered to God for him by
the church.
6 And when Herod was
about to bring him out, that
night Peter was sleeping,
bound with two chains between
two soldiers; and the guards
before the door were keeping
the prison.
7 Now behold, an angel of
the Lord stood by *him,* and a
light shone in the prison; and he
struck Peter on the side and
raised him up, saying, "Arise
quickly!" And his chains fell off
his hands.
8 Then the angel said to him,
"Gird yourself and tie on your
sandals"; and so he did. And he
said to him, "Put on your garment and follow me."
9 So he went out and fol-
lowed him, and did not know
that what was done by the an-

Herod Kills James and Imprisons Peter

12 1 Κατ' ἐκεῖνον δὲ τὸν καιρὸν ἐπέβαλεν Ἡρῴδης ὁ
[2]at [3]that [1]And - time [4]put [1]Herod [2]the
set

βασιλεὺς τὰς χεῖρας κακῶσαί τινας τῶν ἀπὸ τῆς ἐκκλησίας.
[3]king the hands to harm some - from the church.
his

2 Ἀνεῖλε δὲ Ἰάκωβον τὸν ἀδελφὸν Ἰωάννου μαχαίρᾳ.
[2]he [3]killed [1]And James the brother of John with *the* sword.

3 Καὶ ἰδὼν ὅτι ἀρεστόν ἐστι τοῖς Ἰουδαίοις,
And seeing that [3]pleasing [1]it [2]is to the Jews,
when he saw was

προσέθετο συλλαβεῖν καὶ Πέτρον (ἦσαν δὲ αἱ
he proceeded further to arrest also ˜ Peter ([2]*then* [3]were [1]and the

ἡμέραι τῶν ἀζύμων), 4 ὃν καὶ πιάσας ἔθετο εἰς
Days - of Unleavened Bread), whom also seizing he put in
he had seized and put

φυλακήν, παραδοὺς τέσσαρσι τετραδίοις στρατιωτῶν
prison, handing *him* over to four four-man squads of soldiers
and delivered

φυλάσσειν αὐτόν, βουλόμενος μετὰ τὸ Πάσχα ἀναγαγεῖν
to guard him, planning after the Passover to bring again ˜

αὐτὸν τῷ λαῷ.
him to the people.

An Angel Delivers Peter from Prison

5 Ὁ μὲν οὖν Πέτρος ἐτηρεῖτο ἐν τῇ φυλακῇ·
- - Therefore Peter was kept in the prison;

προσευχὴ δὲ ἦν ἐκτενὴς[a] γινομένη ὑπὸ τῆς ἐκκλησίας
[3]prayer [1]but [4]was [2]earnest being made by the church

πρὸς τὸν Θεὸν ὑπὲρ αὐτοῦ. 6 Ὅτε δὲ ἔμελλεν αὐτὸν
to - God in behalf of him. when ˜ But [2]was [3]about [6]him

προάγειν ὁ Ἡρῴδης, τῇ νυκτὶ ἐκείνῃ ἦν ὁ Πέτρος
[4]to [5]bring [7]forth - [1]Herod, - on night ˜ that was ˜ - Peter

κοιμώμενος μεταξὺ δύο στρατιωτῶν δεδεμένος ἁλύσεσι
sleeping between two soldiers having been bound with chains ˜

δυσί, φύλακές τε πρὸ τῆς θύρας ἐτήρουν τὴν φυλακήν.
two, guards ˜ and before the door were keeping the prison.

7 Καὶ ἰδού, ἄγγελος Κυρίου ἐπέστη, καὶ φῶς
And behold, an angel of *the* Lord stood *there,* and a light

ἔλαμψεν ἐν τῷ οἰκήματι· πατάξας δὲ τὴν πλευρὰν τοῦ
shined in the prison room; striking ˜ and the side -
he struck

Πέτρου, ἤγειρεν αὐτὸν λέγων, "Ἀνάστα ἐν τάχει." Καὶ
of Peter, he roused him saying, "Stand up with quickness." And
and quickly."

ἐξέπεσον αὐτοῦ αἱ ἁλύσεις ἐκ τῶν χειρῶν. 8 Εἶπέ τε ὁ
[3]fell [4]away [1]his - [2]chains from the hands. [4]said [1]And [2]the
his

ἄγγελος πρὸς αὐτόν, "Περίζωσαι καὶ ὑπόδησαι τὰ σανδάλιά
[3]angel to him, "Gird yourself and put on - sandals ˜

σου." Ἐποίησε δὲ οὕτω. Καὶ λέγει αὐτῷ, "Περιβαλοῦ τὸ
your." [2]he [3]did [1]And so. And he said to him, "Put on *yourself* -

ἱμάτιόν σου καὶ ἀκολούθει μοι." 9 Καὶ ἐξελθὼν ἠκολούθει
cloak ˜ your and follow me." And going out he was following
he went out and followed

αὐτῷ, καὶ οὐκ ᾔδει ὅτι ἀληθές ἐστι τὸ γινόμενον διὰ
him, and not ˜ did know that [9]true [8]is [1]the [2]*thing* [3]taking [4]place [5]by
was

[a](12:5) NU reads εκτενως, *earnestly.*

τοῦ ἀγγέλου, ἐδόκει δὲ ὅραμα βλέπειν.
[6]the [7]angel, [11]he [12]was [13]thinking [10]but [16]a [17]vision [14]to [15]see.
that he was seeing.

10 Διελθόντες δὲ πρώτην φυλακὴν καὶ δευτέραν, ἦλθον
[2]going [3]through [1]And *the* first guard and second, they came
when they passed

ἐπὶ τὴν πύλην τὴν σιδηρᾶν τὴν φέρουσαν εἰς τὴν πόλιν,
to the gate ˜ - iron the *one* leading into the city,
which leads

ἥτις αὐτομάτη ἠνοίχθη αὐτοῖς, καὶ ἐξελθόντες προῆλθον
which by itself was opened to them, and going out they went forward
they exited and

ῥύμην μίαν, καὶ εὐθέως ἀπέστη ὁ ἄγγελος ἀπ' αὐτοῦ.
street ˜ one, and immediately [3]withdrew [1]the [2]angel from him.

11 Καὶ ὁ Πέτρος, γενόμενος ἐν ἑαυτῷ, εἶπε, "Νῦν οἶδα
And - Peter, coming to be in himself, said, "Now I know
having come to

ἀληθῶς ὅτι ἐξαπέστειλε Κύριος τὸν ἄγγελον αὐτοῦ καὶ
truly that [3]sent [4]forth [1]*the* [2]Lord - angel ˜ His and

ἐξείλετό με ἐκ χειρὸς Ἡρῴδου καὶ πάσης τῆς προσδοκίας
delivered me from *the* hand of Herod and from all the expectation

τοῦ λαοῦ τῶν Ἰουδαίων." 12 Συνιδών τε ἦλθεν ἐπὶ
of the people of the Jews." [2]realizing [3]*this* [1]And he came to
when he realized

τὴν οἰκίαν Μαρίας τῆς μητρὸς Ἰωάννου τοῦ ἐπικαλουμένου
the house of Mary the mother of John the *one* being called
who is surnamed

Μάρκου, οὗ ἦσαν ἱκανοὶ συνηθροισμένοι καὶ
Mark, where [4]were [1]*a* [2]considerable [3]*number* gathered and

προσευχόμενοι. 13 Κρούσαντος δὲ τοῦ Πέτρου[b] τὴν θύραν
were praying. knocking on And - Peter the door
And when Peter knocked on

τοῦ πυλῶνος, προσῆλθε παιδίσκη ὑπακοῦσαι, ὀνόματι
of the gate, [4]came [5]to [6]*it* [1]a [2]servant [3]girl to answer, by name
named

Ῥόδη. 14 Καὶ ἐπιγνοῦσα τὴν φωνὴν τοῦ Πέτρου, ἀπὸ
Rhoda. And recognizing the voice - of Peter, from
when she recognized because

τῆς χαρᾶς οὐκ ἤνοιξε τὸν πυλῶνα, εἰσδραμοῦσα δὲ
- joy [3]not [1]she [2]did open the gate, [2]running [3]in [1]but
of she ran in

ἀπήγγειλεν ἑστάναι τὸν Πέτρον πρὸ τοῦ πυλῶνος.
she announced [2]to [3]stand - [1]Peter before the gate.
and that Peter stood

15 Οἱ δὲ πρὸς αὐτὴν εἶπον, "Μαίνῃ!" Ἡ δὲ
[2]the [3]*ones* [1]But [5]to [6]her [4]said, "You are mad!" [2]the [3]*one* [1]But
they she

διϊσχυρίζετο οὕτως ἔχειν. Οἱ δὲ ἔλεγον, "Ὁ ἄγγελος
was insisting thus to have. [2]the [3]*ones* [1]And said, - "[4]angel
kept insisting that it was so. And they

αὐτοῦ ἐστιν." 16 Ὁ δὲ Πέτρος ἐπέμενε κρούων·
[3]his [1]It [2]is." - But Peter was continuing knocking;

ἀνοίξαντες δὲ εἶδον αὐτὸν καὶ ἐξέστησαν.
[2]opening [3]*the* [4]*door* [1]and they saw him and were astounded.
when they opened

17 Κατασείσας δὲ αὐτοῖς τῇ χειρὶ σιγᾶν,
motioning ˜ And to them with the hand to be silent,
his

gel was real, but thought he
was seeing a vision.
10 When they were past the
first and the second guard
posts, they came to the iron
gate that leads to the city,
which opened to them of its
own accord; and they went out
and went down one street, and
immediately the angel departed
from him.
11 And when Peter had come
to himself, he said, "Now I
know for certain that the Lord
has sent His angel, and has delivered me from the hand of
Herod and *from* all the expectation of the Jewish people."
12 So, when he had considered *this,* he came to the house
of Mary, the mother of John
whose surname was Mark,
where many were gathered together praying.
13 And as Peter knocked at
the door of the gate, a girl
named Rhoda came to answer.
14 When she recognized Peter's voice, because of *her* gladness she did not open the gate,
but ran in and announced that
Peter stood before the gate.
15 But they said to her, "You
are beside yourself!" Yet she
kept insisting that it was so. So
they said, "It is his angel."
16 Now Peter continued
knocking; and when they
opened *the door* and saw him,
they were astonished.
17 But motioning to them with
his hand to keep silent, he de-

---

[b](**12:13**) For του Πετρου, *Peter,* NU reads αυτου, *he.*

clared to them how the Lord
had brought him out of the
prison. And he said, "Go, tell
these things to James and to
the brethren." And he departed
and went to another place.
18 Then, as soon as it was
day, there was no small stir
among the soldiers about what
had become of Peter.
19 But when Herod had
searched for him and not found
him, he examined the guards
and commanded that *they*
should be put to death. And he
went down from Judea to Caesarea, and stayed *there.*
20 Now Herod had been very
angry with the people of Tyre
and Sidon; but they came to
him with one accord, and having made Blastus the king's
personal aide their friend, they
asked for peace, because their
country was supplied with food
by the king's *country.*
21 So on a set day Herod, arrayed in royal apparel, sat on
his throne and gave an oration
to them.
22 And the people kept shout-
ing, "The voice of a god and not
of a man!"
23 Then immediately an angel
of the Lord struck him, because
he did not give glory to God.
And he was eaten by worms
and died.
24 But the word of God grew
and multiplied.

διηγήσατο αὐτοῖς πῶς ὁ Κύριος αὐτὸν ἐξήγαγεν ἐκ τῆς
he related to them how the Lord him ˜ led forth out of the
had led

φυλακῆς. Εἶπε δέ, "'Απαγγείλατε 'Ιακώβῳ καὶ τοῖς
prison. [2]he [3]said [1]And, "Tell to James and the

ἀδελφοῖς ταῦτα." Καὶ ἐξελθὼν ἐπορεύθη εἰς ἕτερον τόπον.
brothers these *things.*" And going out he went to another place.
he departed and

18 Γενομένης δὲ ἡμέρας, ἦν τάραχος οὐκ ὀλίγος
becoming ˜ And day, *there* was [4]disturbance [1]not [2]a [3]little
when it became no small

ἐν τοῖς στρατιώταις, τί ἄρα ὁ Πέτρος ἐγένετο.
among the soldiers, *as to* what then - Peter became.
had become of Peter.

19 Ἡρῴδης δὲ ἐπιζητήσας αὐτὸν καὶ μὴ εὑρών,
Herod ˜ And seeking for him and not finding *him,*
after he sought did not find him,

ἀνακρίνας τοὺς φύλακας, ἐκέλευσεν ἀπαχθῆναι. Καὶ
examining the guards, commanded *them* to be led away. And
he examined and commanded that they be executed.

κατελθὼν ἀπὸ τῆς 'Ιουδαίας εἰς τὴν Καισάρειαν
going down from - Judea to - Caesarea

διέτριβεν.
he was spending time *there.*

The Enemy of God's Word Is Smitten

20 Ἦν δὲ ὁ Ἡρῴδης θυμομαχῶν Τυρίοις καὶ
[3]was [1]Now - [2]Herod very angry with the Tyrians and

Σιδωνίοις· ὁμοθυμαδὸν* δὲ παρῆσαν πρὸς αὐτόν, καὶ
Sidonians [2]with [3]one [4]purpose [1]and they came to him, and

πείσαντες Βλάστον τὸν ἐπὶ τοῦ κοιτῶνος τοῦ
persuading Blastus the *one* over the bedroom of the
after winning over

βασιλέως, ᾐτοῦντο εἰρήνην, διὰ τὸ τρέφεσθαι αὐτῶν
king, they asked for peace, because of - [3]to [4]be [5]fed [1]their
because was fed

τὴν χώραν ἀπὸ τῆς βασιλικῆς. 21 Τακτῇ δὲ ἡμέρᾳ ὁ
- [2]country from the royal *country.* [2]on [3]an [4]appointed [1]And day -
king's

Ἡρῴδης ἐνδυσάμενος ἐσθῆτα βασιλικὴν καὶ καθίσας ἐπὶ
Herod clothing himself with clothing ˜ royal and sitting at
clothed took his seat

τοῦ βήματος, ἐδημηγόρει πρὸς αὐτούς.
the judicial bench, was delivering an address to them.
and delivered

22 Ὁ δὲ δῆμος ἐπεφώνει, "Φωνὴ θεοῦ καὶ
the ˜ And populace was calling out, "*This is the* voice of a god and

οὐκ ἀνθρώπου!" 23 Παραχρῆμα δὲ ἐπάταξεν αὐτὸν ἄγγελος
not of a man!" [2]at [3]once [1]And [9]struck [10]him [4]an [5]angel

Κυρίου ἀνθ' ὧν οὐκ ἔδωκε[c] δόξαν τῷ Θεῷ, καὶ
[6]of [7]*the* [8]Lord against which [3]not [1]he [2]did give glory - to God, and
because

γενόμενος σκωληκόβρωτος, ἐξέψυξεν.
becoming eaten by worms, he expired.
he was and died.

24 Ὁ δὲ λόγος τοῦ Θεοῦ ηὔξανε καὶ ἐπληθύνετο.
the ˜ But word - of God was growing and being multiplied.

---

[c](12:23) NU, TR add *την, the (glory).*

*(12:20) ὁμοθυμαδόν *(homothymadon).* Adverb from the adjective ὁμός, *same,* and the noun θυμός, *mind* or *will* (a meaning not attested in the NT), thus meaning *of one accord, with one mind or purpose.* In all of the occurrences in Acts the meaning is something like *by joint or unanimous agreement* (as here; cf. 1:14; 2:1, 46). Luke uses the word to show the unanimity both of the early church and of its opponents (Acts 4:24; 7:57; 8:6; 18:12). Cf. Paul's use of ὁμοθυμαδόν in an admonition for unity in Rom. 15:6. It is suggested that in some contexts the word is perhaps weakened to mean simply *together* (possibly Acts 5:12).

Barnabas and Saul Separated for the Work of God

25 Βαρναβᾶς δὲ καὶ Σαῦλος ὑπέστρεψαν εἰς[d]
Barnabas ~ And and Saul returned to

Ἰερουσαλήμ, πληρώσαντες τὴν διακονίαν, συμπαραλαβόντες
Jerusalem, having fulfilled the ministry, taking along with *them*
their and took

καὶ Ἰωάννην τὸν ἐπικληθέντα Μᾶρκον.
also John the *one* being called Mark.
who was surnamed

13 1 Ἦσαν δέ τινες ἐν Ἀντιοχείᾳ κατὰ τὴν οὖσαν
[2]*there* [3]were [1]Now some [5]in [6]Antioch [1]in [2]the [4]being
that was

ἐκκλησίαν προφῆται καὶ διδάσκαλοι, ὅ τε Βαρναβᾶς καὶ
[3]church *who were* prophets and teachers, - both Barnabas and

Συμεὼν ὁ καλούμενος Νίγερ, καὶ Λούκιος ὁ Κυρηναῖος,
Simeon the *one* being called Niger, and Lucius the Cyrenian,
who was called

Μαναήν τε Ἡρῴδου τοῦ τετράρχου σύντροφος, καὶ
Manaen ~ and [4]Herod [5]the [6]tetrarch [1]brought [2]up [3]with, and

Σαῦλος.
Saul.

2 Λειτουργούντων δὲ αὐτῶν τῷ Κυρίῳ καὶ
performing service Now them to the Lord and
Now as they were ministering

νηστευόντων, εἶπε τὸ Πνεῦμα τὸ Ἅγιον, "Ἀφορίσατε δή
fasting, [4]said [1]the [3]Spirit - [2]Holy, "Set apart now

μοι τὸν Βαρναβᾶν καὶ τὸν Σαῦλον εἰς τὸ ἔργον ὃ
to me - Barnabas and - Saul for the work which

προσκέκλημαι αὐτούς." 3 Τότε νηστεύσαντες καὶ
I have called to ~ them." Then fasting and
after fasting

προσευξάμενοι καὶ ἐπιθέντες τὰς χεῖρας αὐτοῖς,
praying and laying the hands on them,
their

ἀπέλυσαν.
they sent *them* away.

Saul, Barnabas, and John Mark Preach in Cyprus

4 Οὗτοι μὲν οὖν, ἐκπεμφθέντες ὑπὸ τοῦ
These *two* - therefore, having been sent forth by the

Πνεύματος τοῦ Ἁγίου, κατῆλθον εἰς τὴν Σελεύκειαν. Ἐκεῖθεν
Spirit ~ - Holy, went down to - Seleucia. [2]from [3]there

δὲ ἀπέπλευσαν εἰς τὴν Κύπρον, 5 καὶ γενόμενοι ἐν
[1]And they sailed away to - Cyprus, and arriving in
when they arrived

Σαλαμῖνι, κατήγγελλον τὸν λόγον τοῦ Θεοῦ ἐν ταῖς
Salamis, they proclaimed the word - of God in the

συναγωγαῖς τῶν Ἰουδαίων· εἶχον δὲ καὶ Ἰωάννην
synagogues of the Jews; [2]they [3]had [1]and also John

ὑπηρέτην. 6 Διελθόντες δὲ τὴν[a] νῆσον ἄχρι
as an assistant. [2]going [3]across [1]And the island as far as
when they had crossed to

Πάφου, εὗρόν τινα μάγον ψευδοπροφήτην Ἰουδαῖον,
Paphos, they found certain ~ a magician a false prophet a Jew,
sorcerer

ᾧ ὄνομα Βαριησοῦν, 7 ὃς ἦν σὺν τῷ ἀνθυπάτῳ Σεργίῳ
whose name *was* Bar-Jesus, who was with the proconsul Sergius

25 And Barnabas and Saul returned from Jerusalem when they had fulfilled *their* ministry, and they also took with them John whose surname was Mark.

13 Now in the church that was at Antioch there were certain prophets and teachers: Barnabas, Simeon who was called Niger, Lucius of Cyrene, Manaen who had been brought up with Herod the tetrarch, and Saul.
2 As they ministered to the Lord and fasted, the Holy Spirit said, "Now separate to Me Barnabas and Saul for the work to which I have called them."
3 Then, having fasted and prayed, and laid hands on them, they sent *them* away.
4 So, being sent out by the Holy Spirit, they went down to Seleucia, and from there they sailed to Cyprus.
5 And when they arrived in Salamis, they preached the word of God in the synagogues of the Jews. They also had John as *their* assistant.
6 Now when they had gone through the island to Paphos, they found a certain sorcerer, a false prophet, a Jew whose name *was* Bar-Jesus,
7 who was with the proconsul, Sergius Paulus, an intelli-

[d]**(12:25)** TR reads εξ, *from.*
[a]**(13:6)** NU reads ολην την, *the whole.*

gent man. This man called for
Barnabas and Saul and sought
to hear the word of God.
8 But Elymas the sorcerer
(for so his name is translated)
withstood them, seeking to
turn the proconsul away from
the faith.
9 Then Saul, who also *is*
called Paul, filled with the Holy
Spirit, looked intently at him
10 and said, "O full of all deceit and all fraud, *you* son of the
devil, *you* enemy of all righteousness, will you not cease
perverting the straight ways of
the Lord?
11 "And now, indeed, the
hand of the Lord *is* upon you,
and you shall be blind, not seeing the sun for a time." And immediately a dark mist fell on
him, and he went around seeking someone to lead him by the
hand.
12 Then the proconsul be-
lieved, when he saw what had
been done, being astonished at
the teaching of the Lord.
13 Now when Paul and his
party set sail from Paphos, they
came to Perga in Pamphylia;
and John, departing from them,
returned to Jerusalem.
14 But when they departed
from Perga, they came to Antioch in Pisidia, and went into
the synagogue on the Sabbath

Παύλῳ, ἀνδρὶ συνετῷ. Οὗτος προσκαλεσάμενος Βαρναβᾶν
Paulus, a(n) man ˜ intelligent. This *man* summoning Barnabas
summoned

καὶ Σαῦλον ἐπεζήτησεν ἀκοῦσαι τὸν λόγον τοῦ Θεοῦ.
and Saul sought to hear the word - of God.
and sought

8 Ἀνθίστατο δὲ αὐτοῖς Ἐλύμας ὁ μάγος* (οὕτω γὰρ
[5]resisted [1]But [6]them [2]Elymas [3]the [4]magician (so ˜ for
sorcerer

μεθερμηνεύεται τὸ ὄνομα αὐτοῦ), ζητῶν διαστρέψαι τὸν
[3]is [4]translated - [2]name [1]his), seeking to turn away the

ἀνθύπατον ἀπὸ τῆς πίστεως.
proconsul from the faith.

9 Σαῦλος δέ, ὁ καὶ Παῦλος, πλησθεὶς
Saul ˜ But the *one* also *named* Paul, being filled
was

Πνεύματος Ἁγίου καὶ ἀτενίσας εἰς αὐτὸν 10 εἶπεν, "Ὦ
with *the* Spirit ˜ Holy and looking intently on him said, "O
looked and said,

πλήρης παντὸς δόλου καὶ πάσης ῥᾳδιουργίας, υἱὲ διαβόλου,
full of all deceit and all fraud, *you* son of *the* devil,

ἐχθρὲ πάσης δικαιοσύνης! Οὐ παύσῃ διαστρέφων τὰς
you enemy of all righteousness! [3]not [1]Will [2]you cease perverting the

ὁδοὺς Κυρίου τὰς εὐθείας? 11 Καὶ νῦν ἰδού, χεὶρ
[2]ways [3]of [4]*the* [5]Lord - [1]straight? And now behold, *the* hand

Κυρίου ἐπὶ σέ, καὶ ἔσῃ τυφλός, μὴ βλέπων τὸν ἥλιον
of *the* Lord *is* on you, and you will be blind, not seeing the sun

ἄχρι καιροῦ." Παραχρῆμα δὲ ἐπέπεσεν ἐπ' αὐτὸν
until a season *has passed*." immediately ˜ And [5]fell [6]on [7]him

ἀχλὺς καὶ σκότος, καὶ περιάγων ἐζήτει
[1]a [2]mistiness [3]and [4]darkness, and going around he was seeking
a dark mist, feeling his way about

χειραγωγούς. 12 Τότε ἰδὼν ὁ ἀνθύπατος τὸ
some to lead him by the hand. Then seeing the proconsul the *thing*
when the proconsul saw what

γεγονὸς ἐπίστευσεν, ἐκπλησσόμενος ἐπὶ τῇ διδαχῇ
having taken place he believed, being amazed at the teaching
had occurred,

τοῦ Κυρίου.
of the Lord.

Paul Preaches at Pisidian Antioch

13 Ἀναχθέντες δὲ ἀπὸ τῆς Πάφου οἱ περὶ τὸν
putting to sea Now from - Paphos the *ones* about -
Now Paul and his companions put to sea from Paphos

Παῦλον ἦλθον εἰς Πέργην τῆς Παμφυλίας. Ἰωάννης δὲ
Paul came to Perga - of Pamphylia. John ˜ But
and

ἀποχωρήσας ἀπ' αὐτῶν ὑπέστρεψεν εἰς Ἱεροσόλυμα. 14 Αὐτοὶ
departing from them returned to Jerusalem. they ˜
deserted them and

δὲ διελθόντες ἀπὸ τῆς Πέργης, παρεγένοντο εἰς Ἀντιόχειαν
But going on from - Perga, arrived in Antioch
went and arrived

τῆς Πισιδίας, καὶ εἰσελθόντες εἰς τὴν συναγωγὴν τῇ ἡμέρᾳ
- of Pisidia, and entering into the synagogue on the day
they entered on the

*(13:8) μάγος (*magos*). Noun, *wise man*, used of certain eastern (especially Persian or Babylonian) specialists in astrology, the interpretation of dreams, and other occult arts—a *magician* in the most basic sense of that word. Those who visited the child Jesus are therefore often appropriately called "Magi" (Matt. 2:1). The only other occurrence in the NT is here in Acts 13:6, 8, referring to the *sorcerer* Bar-Jesus (or "Elymas," apparently the Arabic equivalent of "magician") who practiced black magic. Cf. the cognate verb μαγεύω, *practice magic or sorcery* and noun μαγεία, *magic, sorcery*, both used only in Acts 8:9, 11 of Simon Magus.

τῶν σαββάτων, ἐκάθισαν.
of the Sabbath, they sat down.
Sabbath day, and

15 Μετὰ δὲ τὴν ἀνάγνωσιν τοῦ Νόμου καὶ τῶν
after ˜ Now the reading of the Law and the

Προφητῶν, ἀπέστειλαν οἱ ἀρχισυνάγωγοι πρὸς αὐτούς,
Prophets, [4]sent [1]the [2]synagogue [3]leaders to them,

λέγοντες, "Ἄνδρες ἀδελφοί, εἰ ἔστι λόγος ἐν ὑμῖν
saying, "Men brothers, if *there* is [3]a [4]word [1]by [2]you

παρακλήσεως πρὸς τὸν λαόν, λέγετε."
of encouragement for the people, speak."

16 Ἀναστὰς δὲ Παῦλος, καὶ κατασείσας τῇ χειρί,
[3]arising [1]And [2]Paul, and motioning with the hand,
rose his

εἶπεν, "Ἄνδρες Ἰσραηλῖται καὶ οἱ φοβούμενοι τὸν Θεόν,
said, "Men Israelites and the *ones* fearing - God,
you who fear

ἀκούσατε. 17 Ὁ Θεὸς τοῦ λαοῦ τούτου[b] ἐξελέξατο τοὺς
listen. The God - of people ˜ this chose -

πατέρας ἡμῶν, καὶ τὸν λαὸν ὕψωσεν ἐν τῇ παροικίᾳ ἐν
fathers ˜ our, and [3]the [4]people [1]lifted [2]up in the sojourn in
during their

γῇ Αἰγύπτῳ, καὶ μετὰ βραχίονος ὑψηλοῦ ἐξήγαγεν αὐτοὺς
the land of Egypt, and with a(n) arm ˜ high brought out ˜ them
uplifted

ἐξ αὐτῆς. 18 Καὶ ὡς τεσσαρακονταετῆ χρόνον
from it. And *for* about a forty-year time

ἐτροποφόρησεν αὐτοὺς ἐν τῇ ἐρήμῳ. 19 Καὶ
put up with them in the wilderness. And

καθελὼν ἔθνη ἑπτὰ ἐν γῇ Χαναάν,
destroying nations ˜ seven in *the* land of Canaan,
when He had destroyed

κατεκληρονόμησεν[c] αὐτοῖς τὴν γῆν αὐτῶν. 20 Καὶ μετὰ
He gave as an inheritance to them - land ˜ their. And after

ταῦτα,[d] ὡς ἔτεσι τετρακοσίοις καὶ πεντήκοντα,[e]
these *things, for* about [5]years [1]four [2]hundred [3]and [4]fifty,

ἔδωκε κριτὰς ἕως Σαμουὴλ τοῦ προφήτου.
He gave *them* judges until *the time of* Samuel the prophet.

21 Κἀκεῖθεν ᾐτήσαντο βασιλέα, καὶ ἔδωκεν αὐτοῖς ὁ Θεὸς
And then they asked for a king, and [2]gave [3]them - [1]God

τὸν Σαοὺλ υἱὸν Κίς, ἄνδρα ἐκ φυλῆς Βενιαμίν, ἔτη
- Saul *the* son of Kish, a man of *the* tribe of Benjamin, *for* years ˜

τεσσαράκοντα. 22 Καὶ μεταστήσας αὐτὸν ἤγειρεν αὐτοῖς
forty. And removing him He raised up for them
when He removed

τὸν Δαβὶδ εἰς βασιλέα, ᾧ καὶ εἶπε μαρτυρήσας,
- David as king, to whom also ˜ He said bearing witness,

«Εὗρον Δαβὶδ τὸν τοῦ Ἰεσσαὶ ἄνδρα κατὰ
«'I found David the *son* - of Jesse *to be* a man in accordance with
have found

τὴν καρδίαν μου,»[f] ὃς ποιήσει πάντα τὰ θελήματά μου.'
- heart ˜ My,» who will do all - wishes ˜ My.'
will

23 Τούτου ὁ Θεὸς ἀπὸ τοῦ σπέρματος κατ'
[5]of [6]this [7]*man* - [1]God [2]from [3]the [4]seed according to
descendants

ἐπαγγελίαν ἤγαγε[g] τῷ Ἰσραὴλ σωτηρίαν,[h]
His promise brought - to Israel salvation,
has brought

day and sat down.
15 And after the reading of the Law and the Prophets, the rulers of the synagogue sent to them, saying, "Men *and* brethren, if you have any word of exhortation for the people, say on."
16 Then Paul stood up, and motioning with *his* hand said, "Men of Israel, and you who fear God, listen:
17 "The God of this people Israel chose our fathers, and exalted the people when they dwelt as strangers in the land of Egypt, and with an uplifted arm He brought them out of it.
18 "Now for a time of about forty years He put up with their ways in the wilderness.
19 "And when He had destroyed seven nations in the land of Canaan, He distributed their land to them by allotment.
20 "After that He gave *them* judges for about four hundred and fifty years, until Samuel the prophet.
21 "And afterward they asked for a king; so God gave them Saul the son of Kish, a man of the tribe of Benjamin, for forty years.
22 "And when He had removed him, He raised up for them David as king, to whom also He gave testimony and said, *'I have found David* the *son* of Jesse, *a man after My own heart,* who will do all My will.'
23 "From this man's seed, according to *the* promise, God raised up for Israel a Savior—Jesus—

---

[b]**(13:17)** NU, TR add Ισραηλ, *Israel.*
[c]**(13:19)** TR reads κατεκληροδοτησεν, *He distributed.*
[d]**(13:20)** NU omits Και μετα ταυτα, *And after these (things),* thus as an inheritance for about four hundred and fifty years.
[e]**(13:20)** NU adds Και μετα ταυτα, *And after these (things He gave).*
[f]**(13:22)** 1 Sam. 13:14; Ps. 89:20 [g]**(13:23)** TR reads ηγειρε, *raised up.*
[h]**(13:23)** NU, TR read σωτηρα Ιησουν, *a savior, Jesus.*

24 "after John had first
preached, before His coming,
the baptism of repentance to all
the people of Israel.
25 "And as John was finishing
his course, he said, 'Who do
you think I am? I am not *He.*
But behold, there comes One
after me, the sandals of whose
feet I am not worthy to loose.'
26 "Men *and* brethren, sons
of the family of Abraham, and
those among you who fear God,
to you the word of this salvation
has been sent.
27 "For those who dwell in Jerusalem, and their rulers, because they did not know Him,
nor even the voices of the
Prophets which are read every
Sabbath, have fulfilled *them* in
condemning *Him.*
28 "And though they found no
cause for death *in Him,* they
asked Pilate that He should be
put to death.
29 "Now when they had fulfilled all that was written concerning Him, they took *Him*
down from the tree and laid
Him in a tomb.
30 "But God raised Him from
the dead.
31 "He was seen for many
days by those who came up
with Him from Galilee to Jerusalem, who are His witnesses
to the people.
32 "And we declare to you
glad tidings—that promise
which was made to the fathers.
33 "God has fulfilled this for us
their children, in that He has
raised up Jesus. As it is also

24 προκηρύξαντος Ἰωάννου πρὸ προσώπου τῆς εἰσόδου
[2]proclaiming [3]before [1]John before *the* face - of entrance ~
after John had first proclaimed before His coming

αὐτοῦ βάπτισμα μετανοίας τῷ Ἰσραήλ.[i] **25** Ὡς δὲ
His a baptism of repentance - to Israel. as ~ Now

ἐπλήρου ὁ Ἰωάννης τὸν δρόμον, ἔλεγε, 'Τίνα με
[2]was [3]finishing - [1]John the course, he said, 'Whom [4]me
his

ὑπονοεῖτε εἶναι? Οὐκ εἰμὶ ἐγώ. Ἀλλ' ἰδού, ἔρχεται
[1]do [2]you [3]suppose to be? [3]not [2]am [1]I *He.* But behold, *there* comes

μετ' ἐμὲ οὗ οὐκ εἰμὶ ἄξιος τὸ ὑπόδημα τῶν ποδῶν
after me *One* of whom [3]not [1]I [2]am worthy [3]the [4]sandal [5]of [6]the [7]feet
His

λῦσαι.'
[1]to [2]loosen.'

26 "Ἄνδρες ἀδελφοί, υἱοὶ γένους Ἀβραὰμ καὶ οἱ
"Men brothers, sons of *the* stock of Abraham and the *ones*
people those

ἐν ὑμῖν φοβούμενοι τὸν Θεόν, ὑμῖν[j] ὁ λόγος τῆς
among you fearing - God, to you the word -
who fear message

σωτηρίας ταύτης ἀπεστάλη. **27** Οἱ γὰρ κατοικοῦντες
of salvation ~ this was sent. [2]the [3]*ones* [1]For dwelling
has been

Ἱερουσαλὴμ καὶ οἱ ἄρχοντες αὐτῶν, τοῦτον ἀγνοήσαντες, καὶ
in Jerusalem and - rulers ~ their, [3]this [4]*One* [1]not [2]knowing, and

τὰς φωνὰς τῶν προφητῶν τὰς κατὰ πᾶν σάββατον
the voices of the prophets the *ones* [3]according [4]to [5]every [6]Sabbath
which are each

ἀναγινωσκομένας, κρίναντες ἐπλήρωσαν. **28** Καὶ
[1]being [2]read, condemning *Him* they fulfilled *them.* And
when they condemned

μηδεμίαν αἰτίαν θανάτου εὑρόντες, ᾐτήσαντο Πιλᾶτον
[2]no [3]cause [4]of [5]death [1]finding, they asked Pilate
though they found,

ἀναιρεθῆναι αὐτόν. **29** Ὡς δὲ ἐτέλεσαν πάντα τὰ
to be destroyed Him. when ~ And they finished all the *things*
that He be executed. had finished

περὶ αὐτοῦ γεγραμμένα, καθελόντες ἀπὸ τοῦ ξύλου,
[4]about [5]Him [1]having [2]been [3]written, taking *Him* down from the tree,
they took cross,

ἔθηκαν εἰς μνημεῖον. **30** Ὁ δὲ Θεὸς ἤγειρεν αὐτὸν ἐκ
they put *Him* in a tomb. - But God raised Him from
and

νεκρῶν· **31** ὃς ὤφθη ἐπὶ ἡμέρας πλείους τοῖς
the dead; who appeared for *some* days more to the *ones*

συναναβᾶσιν αὐτῷ ἀπὸ τῆς Γαλιλαίας εἰς Ἱερουσαλήμ, οἵτινές
going up with Him from - Galilee to Jerusalem, who
who had gone

εἰσι μάρτυρες αὐτοῦ πρὸς τὸν λαόν. **32** Καὶ ἡμεῖς ὑμᾶς
are witnesses ~ His to the people. And we [2]*to* [3]you

εὐαγγελιζόμεθα τὴν πρὸς τοὺς πατέρας ἐπαγγελίαν
[1]proclaim the good news of the [3]to [4]the [5]fathers [1]promise

γενομένην, **33** ὅτι ταύτην ὁ Θεὸς ἐκπεπλήρωκε τοῖς
[2]being, that [4]this [5]*promise* - [1]God [2]has [3]fulfilled -
which was made,

τέκνοις αὐτῶν ἡμῖν, ἀναστήσας Ἰησοῦν, ὡς καὶ ἐν τῷ
[8]to [10]children [9]their [6]for [7]us, raising up Jesus, as also in the
when He raised

---

[i](13:24) For τω Ισραηλ, *to Israel,* NU, TR read παντι τω λαω Ισραηλ, *to all the people of Israel.*
[j](13:26) NU reads ημιν, *to us.*

ψαλμῷ τῷ δευτέρῳ γέγραπται·
Psalm ˜ - second it is written:

«Υἱός μου εἶ σύ,
«[4]Son [3]My [2]are [1]You,

Ἐγὼ σήμερον γεγέννηκά σε.» [k]
I ˜ Today have begotten You.»

34 Ὅτι δὲ ἀνέστησεν αὐτὸν ἐκ νεκρῶν, μηκέτι μέλλοντα
that ˜ And He raised Him from *the* dead, no longer being about
has raised subject

ὑποστρέφειν εἰς διαφθοράν, οὕτως εἴρηκεν ὅτι
to return to corruption, thus He has said -

«Δώσω ὑμῖν τὰ ὅσια Δαβὶδ τὰ
«I will give to you the holy *things* [5]of [6]David [1]*and* [2]the
sure decrees of God concerning

πιστά.» [l]
[3]faithful [4]*things.*»
David.»

35 Διὸ καὶ ἐν ἑτέρῳ λέγει,
Therefore also in another *place* He says,
said,

«Οὐ δώσεις τὸν Ὅσιόν σου ἰδεῖν διαφθοράν.» [m]
«[3]not [1]You [2]will give - [2]Holy [3]*One* [1]Your to see corruption.»

36 Δαβὶδ μὲν γὰρ ἰδίᾳ γενεᾷ ὑπηρετήσας τῇ τοῦ
[2]David [3]indeed [1]For in his own generation having served by the -
after he had

Θεοῦ βουλῇ ἐκοιμήθη, καὶ προσετέθη πρὸς τοὺς πατέρας
[2]of [3]God [1]purpose fell asleep, and was added to - fathers ˜
died, was buried with

αὐτοῦ καὶ εἶδε διαφθοράν, 37 ὃν δὲ ὁ Θεὸς ἤγειρεν
his and saw corruption, [2]*He* [3]whom [1]but - God raised

οὐκ εἶδε διαφθοράν. 38 Γνωστὸν οὖν ἔστω ὑμῖν,
not ˜ did see corruption. [5]known [1]Therefore [2]let [3]it [4]be to you,

ἄνδρες ἀδελφοί, ὅτι διὰ τούτου ὑμῖν ἄφεσις ἁμαρτιῶν
men brothers, that by this *One* [6]to [7]you [1]forgiveness [2]of [3]sins

καταγγέλλεται, 39 καὶ ἀπὸ πάντων ὧν οὐκ
[4]is [5]proclaimed, and from all *the things* from which [3]not

ἠδυνήθητε ἐν τῷ νόμῳ Μωσέως δικαιωθῆναι,* ἐν τούτῳ
[1]you [2]were able by the law of Moses to be justified, by this *One*

πᾶς ὁ πιστεύων δικαιοῦται. 40 Βλέπετε οὖν μὴ
every - *one* believing is justified. Watch therefore lest
everyone who believes

ἐπέλθῃ ἐφ' ὑμᾶς τὸ εἰρημένον ἐν τοῖς προφήταις,
there come on you the *thing* having been spoken in the prophets,
that which has

41 «Ἴδετε, οἱ καταφρονηταί,
«Look, the despisers,
you

Καὶ θαυμάσατε καὶ ἀφανίσθητε,
And marvel and perish,

Ὅτι ἔργον ἐγὼ ἐργάζομαι ἐν ταῖς ἡμέραις ὑμῶν, [n]
For [4]a [5]work [1]I [2]will [3]work in - days ˜ your,
during

Ὃ οὐ μὴ πιστεύσητε
Which not not you will believe
by no means

Ἐάν τις ἐκδιηγῆται ὑμῖν.»" [o]
Though someone relates *it* to you.»"

written in the second Psalm:

'You are My Son,
Today I have begotten
You.'

34 "And that He raised Him from the dead, no more to return to corruption, He has spoken thus:

'I will give you the sure
mercies of David.'

35 "Therefore He also says in another *Psalm:*

'You will not allow Your
Holy One to see
corruption.'

36 "For David, after he had served his own generation by the will of God, fell asleep, was buried with his fathers, and saw corruption;
37 "but He whom God raised up saw no corruption.
38 "Therefore let it be known to you, brethren, that through this Man is preached to you the forgiveness of sins;
39 "and by Him everyone who believes is justified from all things from which you could not be justified by the law of Moses.
40 "Beware therefore, lest what has been spoken in the prophets come upon you:

41 *'Behold, you despisers,*
Marvel and perish!
For I work a work in your
days,
A work which you will by
no means believe,
Though one were to
declare it to you.'"

[k](13:33) Ps. 2:7
[l](13:34) Is. 55:3
[m](13:35) Ps. 16:10
[n](13:41) NU, TR add εργον, *A work (which).*
[o](13:41) Hab. 1:5

***(13:39)** δικαιόω *(dikaioō).* Verb meaning *justify.* The basic idea is of *vindicating* a person, either in a positive (Matt. 11:19) or a negative sense (Luke 10:29, "to justify" one's actions). In the NT the word is most often a technical term for God's activity (Rom. 8:33) whereby a person is *pronounced to be* and *treated as righteous* (δίκαιος). In a similar sense God may be "justified" or *declared* righteous (Luke 7:29; 1 Tim. 3:16). The one who is *justified* by God re-

42 So when the Jews went out
of the synagogue, the Gentiles
begged that these words might
be preached to them the next
Sabbath.
43 Now when the congrega-
tion had broken up, many of the
Jews and devout proselytes followed Paul and Barnabas, who,
speaking to them, persuaded
them to continue in the grace of
God.
44 On the next Sabbath almost the whole city came together to hear the word of God.
45 But when the Jews saw the
multitudes, they were filled
with envy; and contradicting
and blaspheming, they opposed
the things spoken by Paul.
46 Then Paul and Barnabas
grew bold and said, "It was
necessary that the word of God
should be spoken to you first;
but since you reject it, and
judge yourselves unworthy of
everlasting life, behold, we turn
to the Gentiles.
47 "For so the Lord has commanded us:

'I have set you as a light
to the Gentiles,
That you should be for
salvation to the ends of
the earth.'"

48 Now when the Gentiles
heard this, they were glad and
glorified the word of the Lord.
And as many as had been appointed to eternal life believed.
49 And the word of the Lord

---

p(13:42) Εξιοντων . . . εθνη, *going out . . . Gentiles,* NU reads Εξιοντων δε αυτων παρεκαλουν, *Now as they were going forth, they were urging.*
q(13:44) NU reads Κυριου, *Lord.* r(13:47) Is. 49:6

ceives forgiveness for sins (as here in Acts 13:38, 39). God's activity in *justifying* people may be associated with various intermediary means such as God's "grace" (Rom. 3:24), and a person's "faith" (3:28) or "works" (James 2:24). Cf. the cognate adjective δίκαιος, *just, righteous* (Rom. 2:13); and noun δικαιοσύνη, *righteousness* at Rom. 1:17.

Blessing and Conflict at Pisidian Antioch

42 Ἐξιόντων δὲ ἐκ τῆς συναγωγῆς τῶν Ἰουδαίων,
going out Now of the synagogue the Jews,
Now as the Jews were going out of the synagogue,

παρεκάλουν[p] τὰ ἔθνη εἰς τὸ μεταξὺ σάββατον
[3]were [4]urging [1]the [2]Gentiles for [8]the [9]next [10]Sabbath
began that

λαληθῆναι αὐτοῖς τὰ ῥήματα ταῦτα. **43** Λυθείσης
[3]to [4]be [5]spoken [6]to [7]them - [2]words [1]these. being broken up
be And when the

δὲ τῆς συναγωγῆς, ἠκολούθησαν πολλοὶ τῶν
And the synagogue, [10]followed [1]many [2]of [3]the
synagogue service was dismissed,

Ἰουδαίων καὶ τῶν σεβομένων προσηλύτων τῷ Παύλῳ καὶ τῷ
[4]Jews [5]and [6]of [7]the [8]worshiping [9]proselytes - Paul and -

Βαρναβᾷ, οἵτινες προσλαλοῦντες ἔπειθον αὐτοὺς ἐπιμένειν
Barnabas, who speaking to *them* persuaded them to continue

τῇ χάριτι τοῦ Θεοῦ.
in the grace - of God.

44 Τῷ τε ἐρχομένῳ σαββάτῳ σχεδὸν πᾶσα ἡ πόλις
[2]on [3]the [1]And coming Sabbath almost all the city

συνήχθη ἀκοῦσαι τὸν λόγον τοῦ Θεοῦ.[q] **45** Ἰδόντες δὲ οἱ
was assembled to hear the word - of God. seeing But the
But when the Jews

Ἰουδαῖοι τοὺς ὄχλους ἐπλήσθησαν ζήλου καὶ ἀντέλεγον
Jews the crowds they were filled of jealousy and spoke against
saw with

τοῖς ὑπὸ τοῦ Παύλου λεγομένοις, ἀντιλέγοντες καὶ
the *things* [3]by - [4]Paul [1]being [2]said, contradicting and

βλασφημοῦντες.
blaspheming.

46 Παρρησιασάμενοι δὲ ὁ Παῦλος καὶ ὁ Βαρναβᾶς
[5]speaking [6]boldly [1]But - [2]Paul [3]and - [4]Barnabas
spoke out and

εἶπον, "Ὑμῖν ἦν ἀναγκαῖον πρῶτον λαληθῆναι τὸν
said, "[12]to [13]you [1]It [2]was [3]necessary [14]first [9]to [10]be [11]spoken *[4]for* [5]the

λόγον τοῦ Θεοῦ. Ἐπειδὴ δὲ ἀπωθεῖσθε αὐτὸν καὶ οὐκ ἀξίους
[6]word - [7]of [8]God. since ˜ But you reject it and [2]not [5]worthy

κρίνετε ἑαυτοὺς τῆς αἰωνίου ζωῆς, ἰδοὺ στρεφόμεθα εἰς τὰ
[1]do [3]judge [4]yourselves - of eternal life, behold we turn to the

ἔθνη. **47** Οὕτω γὰρ ἐντέταλται ἡμῖν ὁ Κύριος,
Gentiles. so ˜ For [3]has [4]commanded [5]us [1]the [2]Lord,

«Τέθεικά σε εἰς φῶς ἐθνῶν
«I have set you for a light of *the* nations
to be

Τοῦ εἶναί σε εἰς σωτηρίαν ἕως ἐσχάτου τῆς
- [2]to [3]be [1]You for salvation to *the* end of the
That you should be

γῆς.»"[r]
earth.»"

48 Ἀκούοντα δὲ τὰ ἔθνη ἔχαιρε, καὶ ἐδόξαζον τὸν
hearing Now the Gentiles they rejoiced, and glorified the
Now when the Gentiles heard this,

λόγον τοῦ Κυρίου, καὶ ἐπίστευσαν ὅσοι ἦσαν
word of the Lord, and [9]believed [1]as [2]many [3]as [4]were

τεταγμένοι εἰς ζωὴν αἰώνιον. **49** Διεφέρετο δὲ ὁ
[5]appointed [6]for [8]life [7]eternal. [7]was [8]being [9]spread [1]And [2]the

λόγος τοῦ Κυρίου δι' ὅλης τῆς χώρας. 50 Οἱ δὲ
[3]word [4]of [5]the [6]Lord throughout whole ˜ the region. the ˜ But
all the

Ἰουδαῖοι παρώτρυναν τὰς σεβομένας γυναῖκας καὶ τὰς
Jews incited the worshiping women and the

εὐσχήμονας καὶ τοὺς πρώτους τῆς πόλεως καὶ ἐπήγειραν
prominent *women* and the first *men* of the city and raised up
leading

διωγμὸν ἐπὶ τὸν Παῦλον καὶ τὸν Βαρναβᾶν, καὶ ἐξέβαλον
a persecution against - Paul and - Barnabas, and cast out ˜

αὐτοὺς ἀπὸ τῶν ὁρίων αὐτῶν. 51 Οἱ δὲ ἐκτιναξάμενοι τὸν
them from - borders ˜ their. - But shaking off the
region they shook off

κονιορτὸν τῶν ποδῶν αὐτῶν ἐπ' αὐτούς, ἦλθον εἰς Ἰκόνιον.
dust - of feet ˜ their against them, they went to Iconium.
from and

52 Οἱ δὲ μαθηταὶ ἐπληροῦντο χαρᾶς καὶ Πνεύματος Ἁγίου.
the ˜ And disciples were filled with joy and *the* Spirit ˜ Holy.

Jews and Gentiles Assault Paul and Barnabas in Iconium

14 1 Ἐγένετο δὲ ἐν Ἰκονίῳ, κατὰ τὸ αὐτὸ
[2]it [3]came [4]to [5]pass [1]And in Iconium, according to the same
that they went

εἰσελθεῖν αὐτοὺς εἰς τὴν συναγωγὴν τῶν Ἰουδαίων, καὶ
to enter them into the synagogue of the Jews, and
in together

λαλῆσαι οὕτως ὥστε πιστεῦσαι Ἰουδαίων τε καὶ
to speak thus so that [10]to [11]believe [5]of [6]Jews [4]both [7]and
that they spoke in a way believed

Ἑλλήνων πολὺ πλῆθος. 2 Οἱ δὲ ἀπειθοῦντες Ἰουδαῖοι
[8]of [9]Greeks [1]a [2]great [3]multitude. the ˜ But disbelieving Jews

ἐπήγειραν καὶ ἐκάκωσαν τὰς ψυχὰς τῶν ἐθνῶν κατὰ τῶν
aroused and embittered the souls of the Gentiles against the
attitudes

ἀδελφῶν. 3 Ἱκανὸν μὲν οὖν χρόνον διέτριψαν
brothers. [4]a [5]considerable - [1]Therefore [6]time [2]they [3]spent [7]*there*

παρρησιαζόμενοι ἐπὶ τῷ Κυρίῳ τῷ μαρτυροῦντι τῷ λόγῳ
speaking boldly in the Lord the *one* bearing witness to the word
who was

τῆς χάριτος* αὐτοῦ, διδόντι σημεῖα καὶ τέρατα γίνεσθαι διὰ
- of grace ˜ His, giving signs and wonders to take place by
be done

τῶν χειρῶν αὐτῶν. 4 Ἐσχίσθη δὲ τὸ πλῆθος τῆς
- hands ˜ their. [7]was [8]divided [1]And [2]the [3]multitude [4]of [5]the

πόλεως, καὶ οἱ μὲν ἦσαν σὺν τοῖς Ἰουδαίοις, οἱ δὲ
[6]city, and the *ones* - were with the Jews, [2]the [3]*ones* [1]and
some others

σὺν τοῖς ἀποστόλοις. 5 Ὡς δὲ ἐγένετο ὁρμὴ τῶν
with the apostles. when ˜ And [3]came [4]about [1]an [2]impulse of [2]the
an attempt was made by

ἐθνῶν τε καὶ Ἰουδαίων σὺν τοῖς ἄρχουσιν αὐτῶν,
[3]Gentiles [1]both and *the* Jews together with - rulers ˜ their,

ὑβρίσαι καὶ λιθοβολῆσαι αὐτούς, 6 συνιδόντες
to mistreat and to stone them, becoming aware *of it*
they became aware of it

κατέφυγον εἰς τὰς πόλεις τῆς Λυκαονίας, Λύστραν καὶ Δέρβην,
they fled to the cities - of Lycaonia, Lystra and Derbe,
and

was being spread throughout all the region.
50 But the Jews stirred up the devout and prominent women and the chief men of the city, raised up persecution against Paul and Barnabas, and expelled them from their region.
51 But they shook off the dust from their feet against them, and came to Iconium.
52 And the disciples were filled with joy and with the Holy Spirit.

14 Now it happened in Iconium that they went together to the synagogue of the Jews, and so spoke that a great multitude both of the Jews and of the Greeks believed.
2 But the unbelieving Jews stirred up the Gentiles and poisoned their minds against the brethren.
3 Therefore they stayed there a long time, speaking boldly in the Lord, who was bearing witness to the word of His grace, granting signs and wonders to be done by their hands.
4 But the multitude of the city was divided: part sided with the Jews, and part with the apostles.
5 And when a violent attempt was made by both the Gentiles and Jews, with their rulers, to abuse and stone them,
6 they became aware of it and fled to Lystra and Derbe,

***(14:3)** *χάρις (charis).* Noun meaning *favor, grace.* To a Greek, anything of beauty, favor, or delight in which a person could rejoice spoke of *χάρις* (cf. Col. 4:6). Most often in the NT it designates the general favor or grace which God and Christ show to humanity (as here in Acts 14:3; cf. 15:11). The word became a formulaic way to express God's goodness (cf. Rom. 1:7). This divine grace was conceived both as a *state of grace* in which believers live (Rom. 5:2) and as specific *acts of grace* which they receive (Gal. 1:6). The word is also used of specific abilities given by God ("apostleship" in Rom. 1:5; cf. 12:3) and of gratitude to God for such gifts (1 Tim. 1:12). Between persons, the word is used of "finding" favor (cf. Luke 1:30), of "asking for" a favor (Acts 25:3), or "performing" a favor for someone else

cities of Lycaonia, and to the surrounding region.
7 And they were preaching the gospel there.
8 And in Lystra a certain man without strength in his feet was sitting, a cripple from his mother's womb, who had never walked.
9 *This* man heard Paul speaking. Paul, observing him intently and seeing that he had faith to be healed,
10 said with a loud voice, "Stand up straight on your feet!" And he leaped and walked.
11 Now when the people saw what Paul had done, they raised their voices, saying in the Lycaonian *language,* "The gods have come down to us in the likeness of men!"
12 And Barnabas they called Zeus, and Paul, Hermes, because he was the chief speaker.
13 Then the priest of Zeus, whose temple was in front of their city, brought oxen and garlands to the gates, intending to sacrifice with the multitudes.
14 But when the apostles Barnabas and Paul heard this, they tore their clothes and ran in among the multitude, crying out
15 and saying, "Men, why are you doing these things? We also are men with the same nature as you, and preach to you that you should turn from these useless things to the living God, who made the heaven, the earth, the sea, and all

---

[a](**14:13**) NU omits *αυτων, their.*

(1 Cor. 16:3). Cf. the related verbs *χαίρω, rejoice* (Phil. 3:1); *χαρίζομαι, freely give* (Rom. 8:32); *χαριτόω, highly favor* (Luke 1:28); and the noun *χάρισμα, gift* (1 Cor. 1:7).

***(14:15)** *μάταιος (mataios).* Adjective meaning *worthless, empty, useless, meaningless, vain* (whether as cause or effect). Here it is used substantivally to mean *meaningless* or *fallacious (things), vanities.* The NT usage suggests the meaning *empty of the truth or meaning* (which something would otherwise be thought to have), especially of false, ineffective religion (Titus 3:9; James 1:26). Cf. the cognate noun *ματαιότης, emptiness, futility,* suggesting worldliness (only Eph. 4:17; 2 Pet. 2:18); and the verb *ματαιόω, render worthless* (only Rom.

καὶ τὴν περίχωρον, **7** *κἀκεῖ ἦσαν εὐαγγελιζόμενοι.*
and the surrounding region, and there they were preaching the gospel.

Paul and Barnabas Taken for Gods in Lystra

8 *Καί τις ἀνὴρ ἐν Λύστροις ἀδύνατος τοῖς ποσὶν*
And certain ˜ a man in Lystra powerless in the (his) feet

ἐκάθητο, χωλὸς ἐκ κοιλίας μητρὸς αὐτοῦ ὑπάρχων, ὃς
was sitting, lame (being crippled) from (since) *the* womb (before) of mother ˜ his (his) being, (birth,) who

οὐδέποτε περιπεπατήκει. **9** *Οὗτος ἤκουσε τοῦ Παύλου*
never had walked. This *man* heard - Paul

λαλοῦντος· ὃς ἀτενίσας αὐτῷ καὶ ἰδὼν ὅτι πίστιν ἔχει
speaking; who looking intently on him and seeing that [3]faith [1]he [2]has (had)

τοῦ σωθῆναι, **10** *εἶπε μεγάλῃ τῇ φωνῇ, "Ἀνάστηθι ἐπὶ*
- to be saved, (cured,) said [3]great (with a) [1]with [2]the (loud) voice, "Stand up [2]on

τοὺς πόδας σου ὀρθός." Καὶ ἥλλετο καὶ περιεπάτει.
- [4]feet [3]your [1]straight." And he was (began) jumping and walking about.

11 *Οἱ δὲ ὄχλοι, ἰδόντες ὃ ἐποίησεν ὁ Παῦλος,*
the ˜ And crowds, seeing (when they saw) what did ˜ (had done) - Paul,

ἐπῆραν τὴν φωνὴν αὐτῶν Λυκαονιστὶ λέγοντες,
raised - voice ˜ their [2]in [3]*the* [4]Lycaonian [5]*language* [1]saying,

"Οἱ θεοὶ ὁμοιωθέντες ἀνθρώποις κατέβησαν πρὸς ἡμᾶς!"
"The gods being (have been) made like men came (and come) down to us!"

12 *Ἐκάλουν τε τὸν μὲν Βαρναβᾶν Δία, τὸν δὲ Παῦλον*
[2]they [3]called [1]And - - Barnabas Zeus, - and Paul

Ἑρμῆν, ἐπειδὴ αὐτὸς ἦν ὁ ἡγούμενος τοῦ λόγου.
Hermes, since he was the *one* (the) leading (leader) of (in) the word. (speaking.)

13 *Ὁ δὲ ἱερεὺς τοῦ Διὸς τοῦ ὄντος πρὸ τῆς πόλεως*
the ˜ And priest - of Zeus the *one* (whose) being (temple was) before - city ˜

αὐτῶν,[a] *ταύρους καὶ στέμματα ἐπὶ τοὺς πυλῶνας ἐνέγκας,*
their, [2]bulls [3]and [4]garlands [5]to [6]the [7]gates [1]bearing,

σὺν τοῖς ὄχλοις ἤθελεν θύειν.
together with the crowds was desiring to sacrifice *to them.*

14 *Ἀκούσαντες δὲ οἱ ἀπόστολοι Βαρναβᾶς καὶ*
hearing But the apostles Barnabas and (But when the apostles, Barnabas and Paul, heard)

Παῦλος, διαρρήξαντες τὰ ἱμάτια αὐτῶν, εἰσεπήδησαν εἰς τὸν
Paul, (this,) tearing (they tore) - garments ˜ their, they (and) rushed in to the

ὄχλον, κράζοντες **15** *καὶ λέγοντες, "Ἄνδρες! Τί ταῦτα*
crowd, crying out and saying, "Men! Why [4]these [5]*things*

ποιεῖτε? Καὶ ἡμεῖς ὁμοιοπαθεῖς ἐσμεν ὑμῖν
[1]are [2]you [3]doing? also ˜ We [3]of [4]the [5]same [6]nature [1]are [7]with [8]you

ἄνθρωποι, εὐαγγελιζόμενοι ὑμᾶς ἀπὸ τούτων τῶν
[2]men, preaching the gospel you (that you) [3]from (must) [4]these (turn) - (away)

ματαίων ἐπιστρέφειν ἐπὶ τὸν Θεὸν τὸν ζῶντα, «ὃς*
[5]useless [6]*things* (from) [1]to [2]turn (idols) to - [3]God [1]the [2]living, «who

ἐποίησε τὸν οὐρανὸν καὶ τὴν γῆν καὶ τὴν θάλασσαν καὶ
made the heaven and the earth and the sea and

πάντα τὰ ἐν αὐτοῖς·»[b] 16 ὃς ἐν ταῖς παρῳχημέναις
all the *things* in them;» who in the [2]having [3]gone [4]by
during past

γενεαῖς εἴασε πάντα τὰ ἔθνη πορεύεσθαι ταῖς ὁδοῖς
[1]generations permitted all the Gentiles to walk - in ways ˜

αὐτῶν. 17 Καίτοιγε οὐκ ἀμάρτυρον ἑαυτὸν ἀφῆκεν
their. And yet [3]not [6]without [7]witness [5]Himself [1]He [2]did [4]leave

ἀγαθοποιῶν, οὐρανόθεν ὑμῖν[c] ὑετοὺς διδοὺς καὶ καιροὺς
doing good, from heaven [2]to [3]you [4]rains [1]giving and seasons ˜

καρποφόρους, ἐμπιπλῶν τροφῆς καὶ εὐφροσύνης τὰς καρδίας
fruitbearing, filling [3]with [4]food [5]and [6]gladness - [2]hearts

ἡμῶν."[d] 18 Καὶ ταῦτα λέγοντες, μόλις κατέπαυσαν
[1]our." And [2]these [3]*things* [1]saying, scarcely ˜ they stopped
even saying,

τοὺς ὄχλους τοῦ μὴ θύειν αὐτοῖς.
the crowds - not to sacrifice to them.
from sacrificing

Paul Is Stoned but Escapes

19 Ἐπῆλθον δὲ ἀπὸ Ἀντιοχείας καὶ Ἰκονίου Ἰουδαῖοι,
[2]*there* [3]arrived [1]But from Antioch and Iconium Jews,

καὶ πείσαντες τοὺς ὄχλους καὶ λιθάσαντες τὸν Παῦλον,
and having persuaded the crowds and having stoned - Paul,

ἔσυρον ἔξω τῆς πόλεως, νομίσαντες αὐτὸν τεθνάναι.
they dragged *him* outside the city, supposing him to have died.

20 Κυκλωσάντων δὲ αὐτὸν τῶν μαθητῶν, ἀναστὰς
encircling But him the disciples, rising up
But when the disciples encircled him, he stood

εἰσῆλθεν εἰς τὴν πόλιν. Καὶ τῇ ἐπαύριον ἐξῆλθε
he entered into the city. And on the next day he went out
and

σὺν τῷ Βαρναβᾷ εἰς Δέρβην.
together with - Barnabas to Derbe.

Paul and Barnabas Strengthen Their Converts

21 Εὐαγγελισάμενοί τε τὴν πόλιν ἐκείνην καὶ
[2]having [3]preached [4]the [5]gospel [6]to [1]And - city ˜ that and

μαθητεύσαντες ἱκανούς, ὑπέστρεψαν εἰς τὴν Λύστραν καὶ
having made disciples ˜ considerable, they returned to - Lystra and
many,

Ἰκόνιον καὶ Ἀντιόχειαν, 22 ἐπιστηρίζοντες τὰς ψυχὰς τῶν
Iconium and Antioch, strengthening the souls of the
hearts

μαθητῶν, παρακαλοῦντες ἐμμένειν τῇ πίστει, καὶ ὅτι διὰ
disciples, urging *them* to continue in the faith, and that through

πολλῶν θλίψεων δεῖ ἡμᾶς εἰσελθεῖν εἰς τὴν
many afflictions it is necessary *for* us to enter into the
we must enter

βασιλείαν τοῦ Θεοῦ. 23 Χειροτονήσαντες δὲ αὐτοῖς
kingdom - of God. [2]installing [1]And [4]for [5]them
when they had installed

πρεσβυτέρους κατ' ἐκκλησίαν, προσευξάμενοι μετὰ
[3]elders at every church, having prayed with
in each

νηστειῶν, παρέθεντο αὐτοὺς τῷ Κυρίῳ εἰς ὃν
fastings, they commended them to the Lord in whom

πεπιστεύκεισαν. 24 Καὶ διελθόντες τὴν Πισιδίαν ἦλθον εἰς
they had believed. And having crossed - Pisidia they came to

things that are in them,
16 "who in bygone generations allowed all nations to walk in their own ways.
17 "Nevertheless He did not leave Himself without witness, in that He did good, gave us rain from heaven and fruitful seasons, filling our hearts with food and gladness."
18 And with these sayings they could scarcely restrain the multitudes from sacrificing to them.
19 Then Jews from Antioch and Iconium came there; and having persuaded the multitudes, they stoned Paul *and* dragged *him* out of the city, supposing him to be dead.
20 However, when the disciples gathered around him, he rose up and went into the city. And the next day he departed with Barnabas to Derbe.
21 And when they had preached the gospel to that city and made many disciples, they returned to Lystra, Iconium, and Antioch,
22 strengthening the souls of the disciples, exhorting *them* to continue in the faith, and saying, "We must through many tribulations enter the kingdom of God."
23 So when they had appointed elders in every church, and prayed with fasting, they commended them to the Lord in whom they had believed.
24 And after they had passed through Pisidia, they came to

---

b(**14:15**) Ps. 146:6
c(**14:17**) TR reads ημιν, *to us*. *d*(**14:17**) NU reads υμων, *your*.

1:21). Cf. also the synonym *κενός, empty, vain, ineffective,* used much more broadly in the NT.

Pamphylia.
25 Now when they had preached the word in Perga, they went down to Attalia.
26 From there they sailed to Antioch, where they had been commended to the grace of God for the work which they had completed.
27 Now when they had come and gathered the church together, they reported all that God had done with them, and that He had opened the door of faith to the Gentiles.
28 So they stayed there a long time with the disciples.

15 And certain *men* came down from Judea and taught the brethren, "Unless you are circumcised according to the custom of Moses, you cannot be saved."
2 Therefore, when Paul and Barnabas had no small dissension and dispute with them, they determined that Paul and Barnabas and certain others of them should go up to Jerusalem, to the apostles and elders, about this question.
3 So, being sent on their way by the church, they passed through Phoenicia and Samaria, describing the conversion of the Gentiles; and they caused great joy to all the brethren.
4 And when they had come to Jerusalem, they were received by the church and the apostles and the elders; and they reported all things that God had done with them.

Παμφυλίαν. **25** Καὶ λαλήσαντες ἐν Πέργῃ τὸν λόγον,
Pamphylia. And having spoken [3]in [4]Perga [1]the [2]word,

κατέβησαν εἰς Ἀττάλειαν. **26** Κἀκεῖθεν ἀπέπλευσαν εἰς
they went down to Attalia. And from there they sailed away to

Ἀντιόχειαν, ὅθεν ἦσαν παραδεδομένοι τῇ χάριτι τοῦ
Antioch, from where they were commended to the grace -
had been

Θεοῦ εἰς τὸ ἔργον ὃ ἐπλήρωσαν. **27** Παραγενόμενοι δὲ
of God for the work which they completed. arriving ~ Now
had completed. when they arrived

καὶ συναγαγόντες τὴν ἐκκλησίαν, ἀνήγγειλαν ὅσα
and gathering the church, they related as many *things* as
gathered all that

ἐποίησεν ὁ Θεὸς μετ' αὐτῶν καὶ ὅτι ἤνοιξε τοῖς ἔθνεσι
did ~ - God with them and that He opened for the Gentiles
God had done had opened

θύραν πίστεως. **28** Διέτριβον δὲ ἐκεῖ χρόνον οὐκ ὀλίγον σὺν
the door of faith. [2]they [3]spent [1]And there time not a little with
a long time

τοῖς μαθηταῖς.
the disciples.

The Conflict over Circumcision

15 **1** Καί τινες κατελθόντες ἀπὸ τῆς Ἰουδαίας
And certain *men* coming down from - Judea
came

ἐδίδασκον τοὺς ἀδελφοὺς ὅτι "Ἐὰν μὴ περιτέμνησθε τῷ
were teaching the brothers - "If [3]not [1]you [2]are circumcised in the
and taught

ἔθει Μωσέως, οὐ δύνασθε σωθῆναι." **2** Γενομένης
custom of Moses, [3]not [1]you [2]are able to be saved." arising ~
when there arose

οὖν στάσεως καὶ ζητήσεως* οὐκ ὀλίγης τῷ Παύλῳ καὶ τῷ
Therefore [4]dissension [5]and [6]debate [1]not [2]a [3]little - with Paul and -
a serious

Βαρναβᾷ πρὸς αὐτούς, ἔταξαν ἀναβαίνειν Παῦλον
Barnabas against them, they determined *that* [9]to [10]go [11]up [1]Paul
should

καὶ Βαρναβᾶν καί τινας ἄλλους ἐξ αὐτῶν πρὸς τοὺς
[2]and [3]Barnabas [4]and [5]some [6]others [7]of [8]them to the

ἀποστόλους καὶ πρεσβυτέρους εἰς Ἰερουσαλὴμ περὶ τοῦ
apostles and elders in Jerusalem about -

ζητήματος τούτου. **3** Οἱ μὲν οὖν, προπεμφθέντες ὑπὸ τῆς
issue ~ this. - - Therefore, being sent forth by the

ἐκκλησίας, διήρχοντο τὴν Φοινίκην καὶ Σαμάρειαν,
church, they were passing through - Phoenicia and Samaria,
they passed

ἐκδιηγούμενοι τὴν ἐπιστροφὴν τῶν ἐθνῶν, καὶ
telling in detail *about* the conversion of the Gentiles, and

ἐποίουν χαρὰν μεγάλην πᾶσι τοῖς ἀδελφοῖς.
they were causing joy ~ great to all the brothers.

4 Παραγενόμενοι δὲ εἰς Ἰερουσαλήμ, ἀπεδέχθησαν ὑπὸ
arriving ~ And in Jerusalem, they were received by
when they arrived

τῆς ἐκκλησίας καὶ τῶν ἀποστόλων καὶ τῶν πρεσβυτέρων,
the church and the apostles and the elders,

ἀνήγγειλάν τε ὅσα ὁ Θεὸς ἐποίησε μετ' αὐτῶν.
[2]they [3]related [1]and as many *things* as - God did with them.
all that had done

***(15:2)** ζήτησις (*zētēsis*). Noun literally meaning *a seeking,* thus *investigation, questioning, controversy, discussion, dispute.* It is used here and in v. 7 (as in John 3:25) with the sense of intense debate. Cf. the cognate noun ζήτημα, which is the *question at issue;* and the verb ζητέω, *seek,* which occurs frequently in the NT in a variety of senses.

5 Ἐξανέστησαν δέ τινες τῶν ἀπὸ τῆς αἱρέσεως
[14]rose [15]up [1]But [2]some [3]of [4]the [5]*ones* [6]from [7]the [8]sect
of those

τῶν Φαρισαίων πεπιστευκότες, λέγοντες ὅτι "Δεῖ
[9]of [10]the [11]Pharisees [12]having [13]believed, saying - "It is necessary
who had

περιτέμνειν αὐτούς, παραγγέλλειν τε τηρεῖν τὸν νόμον
to circumcise them, [2]to [3]command [4]*them* [1]and to keep the law

Μωσέως."
of Moses."

The Council at Jerusalem

6 Συνήχθησαν δὲ οἱ ἀπόστολοι καὶ οἱ πρεσβύτεροι
[7]gathered [1]And [2]the [3]apostles [4]and [5]the [6]elders

ἰδεῖν περὶ τοῦ λόγου τούτου.
to see about - word ˜ this.
saying

7 Πολλῆς δὲ συζητήσεως γενομένης, ἀναστὰς Πέτρος
much ˜ And debate being, rising ˜ Peter
And after much debate, Peter arose and

εἶπε πρὸς αὐτούς, "Ἄνδρες ἀδελφοί, ὑμεῖς ἐπίστασθε ὅτι ἀφ'
said to them, "Men brothers, you know that from
since

ἡμερῶν ἀρχαίων ὁ Θεὸς ἐν ἡμῖν[a] ἐξελέξατο διὰ τοῦ
the days ˜ ancient - God [2]among [3]us [1]chose [9]by -

στόματός μου ἀκοῦσαι τὰ ἔθνη τὸν λόγον τοῦ
[11]mouth [10]my [7]to [8]hear [4]*for* [5]the [6]Gentiles the word of the

εὐαγγελίου καὶ πιστεῦσαι. **8** Καὶ ὁ καρδιογνώστης Θεὸς
gospel and to believe. And the knower of hearts God
God who knows the heart

ἐμαρτύρησεν αὐτοῖς δοὺς αὐτοῖς τὸ Πνεῦμα τὸ Ἅγιον καθὼς
bore witness to them *by* giving to them the Spirit ˜ - Holy just as

καὶ ἡμῖν, **9** καὶ οὐδὲν διέκρινε μεταξὺ ἡμῶν τε καὶ
also *He did* to us, and nothing ˜ distinguished between us - and
made no distinction

αὐτῶν, τῇ πίστει καθαρίσας τὰς καρδίας αὐτῶν. **10** Νῦν
them, - [4]by [5]faith [1]purifying - [3]hearts [2]their. Now

οὖν τί πειράζετε τὸν Θεόν, ἐπιθεῖναι ζυγὸν ἐπὶ τὸν
therefore why do you test - God, to put a yoke upon the
by putting

τράχηλον τῶν μαθητῶν ὃν οὔτε οἱ πατέρες ἡμῶν οὔτε
neck of the disciples which neither - fathers ˜ our nor

ἡμεῖς ἰσχύσαμεν βαστάσαι? **11** Ἀλλὰ διὰ τῆς χάριτος τοῦ
we were able to bear? But through the grace of the

Κυρίου Ἰησοῦ[b] πιστεύομεν σωθῆναι καθ' ὃν τρόπον
Lord Jesus we believe to be saved according to which manner
that we will be saved in the same manner

κἀκεῖνοι."
also those."
as they."

12 Ἐσίγησε δὲ πᾶν τὸ πλῆθος, καὶ ἤκουον
[5]stopped [6]speaking [1]And [2]all [3]the [4]multitude, and listened to

Βαρναβᾶ καὶ Παύλου ἐξηγουμένων ὅσα ἐποίησεν ὁ Θεὸς
Barnabas and Paul telling as many [4]as [6]did - [5]God
had done

σημεῖα καὶ τέρατα ἐν τοῖς ἔθνεσι δι' αὐτῶν.
[1]signs [2]and [3]wonders among the Gentiles by them.

5 But some of the sect of the
Pharisees who believed rose
up, saying, "It is necessary to
circumcise them, and to command *them* to keep the law of
Moses."
6 Now the apostles and elders came together to consider
this matter.
7 And when there had been
much dispute, Peter rose up
and said to them: "Men and
brethren, you know that a good
while ago God chose among us,
that by my mouth the Gentiles
should hear the word of the
gospel and believe.
8 "So God, who knows the
heart, acknowledged them by
giving them the Holy Spirit, just
as *He did* to us,
9 "and made no distinction
between us and them, purifying
their hearts by faith.
10 "Now therefore, why do
you test God by putting a yoke
on the neck of the disciples
which neither our fathers nor
we were able to bear?
11 "But we believe that
through the grace of the Lord
Jesus Christ we shall be saved
in the same manner as they."
12 Then all the multitude kept
silent and listened to Barnabas
and Paul declaring how many
miracles and wonders God had
worked through them among
the Gentiles.

[a](**15:7**) NU reads υμιν, *you.*
[b](**15:11**) TR adds Χριστου, *Christ.*

13 And after they had become silent, James answered, saying, "Men *and* brethren, listen to me:
14 "Simon has declared how God at the first visited the Gentiles to take out of them a people for His name.
15 "And with this the words of the prophets agree, just as it is written:

16 *'After this I will return*
And will rebuild the tabernacle of David, which has fallen down;
I will rebuild its ruins,
And I will set it up;
17 *So that the rest of mankind may seek the* LORD,
Even all the Gentiles who are called by My name,
Says the LORD *who does all these things.'*

18 "Known to God from eternity are all His works.
19 "Therefore I judge that we should not trouble those from among the Gentiles who are turning to God,
20 "but that we write to them to abstain from things polluted by idols, *from* sexual immorality, *from* things strangled, and *from* blood.
21 "For Moses has had throughout many generations those who preach him in every

13 Μετὰ δὲ τὸ σιγῆσαι αὐτούς, ἀπεκρίθη Ἰάκωβος
after ~ Now - to stop speaking them, answered ~ James
they had finished speaking,

λέγων, 14 "Ἄνδρες ἀδελφοί, ἀκούσατέ μου. Συμεὼν
saying, "Men brothers, listen to me. Simeon
Simon

ἐξηγήσατο καθὼς πρῶτον ὁ Θεὸς ἐπεσκέψατο λαβεῖν ἐξ
told how first ~ - God visited *them* to take from
had declared

ἐθνῶν λαὸν ἐπὶ τῷ ὀνόματι αὐτοῦ. 15 Καὶ τούτῳ
the Gentiles a people for - name ~ His. And with this

συμφωνοῦσιν οἱ λόγοι τῶν προφητῶν, καθὼς γέγραπται,
[6]agree [1]the [2]words [3]of [4]the [5]prophets, just as it is written,

16 «Μετὰ ταῦτα ἀναστρέψω,
«After these *things* I will return,

Καὶ ἀνοικοδομήσω τὴν σκηνὴν Δαβὶδ τὴν
And I will build again the tabernacle of David the *one*
which

πεπτωκυῖαν,
having fallen,
has

Καὶ τὰ κατεσκαμμένα αὐτῆς ἀνοικοδομήσω
And the *things* having been ruined of it I will rebuild
its ruins

Καὶ ἀνορθώσω αὐτήν,
And I will restore it,

17 Ὅπως ἂν ἐκζητήσωσιν οἱ κατάλοιποι τῶν
In order that - [6]may [7]seek [8]out [1]the [2]remaining [3]*ones* -
rest

ἀνθρώπων τὸν Κύριον,
[4]of [5]men the Lord,

Καὶ πάντα τὰ ἔθνη ἐφ' οὓς ἐπικέκληται τὸ ὄνομά
And all the Gentiles on whom [3]has [4]been [5]called - [2]name

μου ἐπ' αὐτούς,
[1]My on them,

Λέγει Κύριος ὁ ποιῶν ταῦτα πάντα.»[c]
Says *the* Lord the *One* doing [2]these [3]*things* [1]all.»
who does

18 Γνωστὰ ἀπ' αἰῶνός[d] ἐστι τῷ Θεῷ πάντα τὰ ἔργα
Known from *the* age [3]are - [1]to [2]God all - works ~
forever

αὐτοῦ.
His.

19 Διὸ ἐγὼ κρίνω μὴ παρενοχλεῖν τοῖς ἀπὸ τῶν
Therefore I judge not to cause difficulty for the *ones* [2]from [3]the
that we must not those who are

ἐθνῶν ἐπιστρέφουσιν ἐπὶ τὸν Θεόν, 20 ἀλλὰ ἐπιστεῖλαι
[4]Gentiles [1]turning to - God, but to write
that we write

αὐτοῖς τοῦ ἀπέχεσθαι ἀπὸ τῶν ἀλισγημάτων τῶν εἰδώλων καὶ
to them - to abstain from the pollutions - of idols and
things polluted by

τῆς πορνείας καὶ τοῦ πνικτοῦ καὶ τοῦ αἵματος.
- *from* fornication and *from* the strangled *thing* and - *from* blood.
sexual immorality

21 Μωσῆς γὰρ ἐκ γενεῶν ἀρχαίων κατὰ πόλιν
Moses ~ For from generations ~ ancient according to a city
in each city

---

c(15:16, 17) Amos 9:11, 12; NU omits παντα, *all.*
d(15:18) NU omits the rest of v. 18 and reads Γνωστα απ αιωνος with v. 17: *Says the Lord who makes these things known from eternity.*

τοὺς κηρύσσοντας αὐτὸν ἔχει, ἐν ταῖς συναγωγαῖς
[2]the [3]*ones* [4]proclaiming [5]him [1]has, [8]in [9]the [10]synagogues
those who are

κατὰ πᾶν σάββατον ἀναγινωσκόμενος."
[11]according [12]to [13]every [14]Sabbath [6]being [7]read."
from one Sabbath to another

The Jerusalem Decree

22 Τότε ἔδοξε τοῖς ἀποστόλοις καὶ τοῖς
Then it seemed best to the apostles and the

πρεσβυτέροις σὺν ὅλῃ τῇ ἐκκλησίᾳ, ἐκλεξαμένους
elders together with whole ˜ the church, [4]being [5]chosen
all the

ἄνδρας ἐξ αὐτῶν πέμψαι εἰς Ἀντιόχειαν σὺν Παύλῳ
[3]men [6]from [7]them [1]to [2]send to Antioch together with Paul

καὶ Βαρναβᾷ, Ἰούδαν τὸν ἐπικαλούμενον Βαρσαββᾶν, καὶ
and Barnabas, Judas the *one* being called Barsabbas, and
who was surnamed

Σιλᾶν, ἄνδρας ἡγουμένους ἐν τοῖς ἀδελφοῖς, **23** γράψαντες
Silas, men leaders among the brothers, writing
leading men and they wrote

διὰ χειρὸς αὐτῶν τάδε·
by hand ˜ their these *things:*

Οἱ ἀπόστολοι καὶ οἱ πρεσβύτεροι καὶ οἱ ἀδελφοί,
The apostles and the elders and the brothers,

Τοῖς κατὰ τὴν Ἀντιόχειαν καὶ Συρίαν καὶ Κιλικίαν
To the [2]in - [3]Antioch [4]and [5]Syria [6]and [7]Cilicia

ἀδελφοῖς τοῖς ἐξ ἐθνῶν·
[1]brothers the *ones* of *the* Gentiles:
who are

Χαίρειν.
Greetings.

24 Ἐπειδὴ ἠκούσαμεν ὅτι τινὲς ἐξ ἡμῶν ἐξελθόντες
Since we heard that some from us going out
went forth from us and

ἐτάραξαν ὑμᾶς λόγοις, ἀνασκευάζοντες τὰς ψυχὰς
troubled you with words, unsettling - souls ˜
hearts

ὑμῶν, λέγοντες[e] περιτέμνεσθαι καὶ τηρεῖν τὸν νόμον,
your, saying to be circumcised and to keep the law,
that you must be keep

οἷς οὐ διεστειλάμεθα, **25** ἔδοξεν ἡμῖν
to whom [3]not [1]we [2]did give *such* orders, it seemed best to us

γενομένοις ὁμοθυμαδόν, ἐκλεξαμένους ἄνδρας
having come to be of the same mind, [4]being [5]chosen [3]men

πέμψαι πρὸς ὑμᾶς σὺν τοῖς ἀγαπητοῖς ἡμῶν Βαρναβᾷ
[1]to [2]send to you with - beloved ˜ our Barnabas

καὶ Παύλῳ, **26** ἀνθρώποις παραδεδωκόσι τὰς ψυχὰς
and Paul, men having given over - lives ˜
who have

αὐτῶν ὑπὲρ τοῦ ὀνόματος τοῦ Κυρίου ἡμῶν Ἰησοῦ
their for the sake of the name - of Lord ˜ our Jesus

Χριστοῦ. **27** Ἀπεστάλκαμεν οὖν Ἰούδαν καὶ Σιλᾶν,
Christ. We have sent therefore Judas and Silas,

καὶ αὐτοὺς διὰ λόγου ἀπαγγέλλοντας τὰ αὐτά.
also them by word telling the same *things.*
who will also tell you the same things by word.

28 Ἔδοξε γὰρ τῷ Ἁγίῳ Πνεύματι, καὶ ἡμῖν,
[2]it [3]seemed [4]best [1]For to the Holy Spirit, and to us,

city, being read in the synagogues every Sabbath."
22 Then it pleased the apostles and elders, with the whole church, to send chosen men of their own company to Antioch with Paul and Barnabas, *namely,* Judas who was also named Barsabas, and Silas, leading men among the brethren.
23 They wrote this *letter* by them:

The apostles, the elders, and the brethren,

To the brethren who are of the Gentiles in Antioch, Syria, and Cilicia:

Greetings.

24 Since we have heard that some who went out from us have troubled you with words, unsettling your souls, saying, "*You must* be circumcised and keep the law"—to whom we gave no *such* commandment—
25 it seemed good to us, being assembled with one accord, to send chosen men to you with our beloved Barnabas and Paul,
26 men who have risked their lives for the name of our Lord Jesus Christ.
27 We have therefore sent Judas and Silas, who will also report the same things by word of mouth.
28 For it seemed good to the Holy Spirit, and to us, to

[e](**15:24**) NU omits λεγοντες περιτεμνεσθαι και τηρειν τον νομον, *saying that you must be circumcised and keep the law.*

lay upon you no greater
burden than these
necessary things:
29 that you abstain from
things offered to idols,
from blood, from things
strangled, and from sexual
immorality. If you keep
yourselves from these,
you will do well.

Farewell.

30 So when they were sent
off, they came to Antioch; and
when they had gathered the
multitude together, they delivered the letter.
31 When they had read it,
they rejoiced over its encouragement.
32 Now Judas and Silas, themselves being prophets also, exhorted and strengthened the
brethren with many words.
33 And after they had stayed
there for a time, they were sent
back with greetings from the
brethren to the apostles.
34 However, it seemed good
to Silas to remain there.
35 Paul and Barnabas also remained in Antioch, teaching and
preaching the word of the Lord,
with many others also.
36 Then after some days Paul
said to Barnabas, "Let us now
go back and visit our brethren
in every city where we have
preached the word of the Lord,
and see how they are doing."
37 Now Barnabas was determined to take with them John
called Mark.
38 But Paul insisted that they
should not take with them the
one who had departed from

μηδὲν πλέον ἐπιτίθεσθαι ὑμῖν βάρος, πλὴν τῶν
no more [2]to [3]be [4]put [5]on [6]you [1]burden, except for -
to put on you no greater burden,

ἐπάναγκες τούτων, **29** ἀπέχεσθαι
[2]necessary [3]*things* [1]these, to abstain
that you

εἰδωλοθύτων καὶ αἵματος καὶ
from meat offered to idols and from blood and

πνικτοῦ καὶ πορνείας· ἐξ ὧν
from *anything* strangled and from fornication; from which
sexual immorality;

διατηροῦντες ἑαυτούς, εὖ πράξετε.
keeping back ˜ yourselves, [4]well [1]you [2]will [3]do.

Ἔρρωσθε.
Farewell.

The Aftermath of the Jerusalem Decision

30 Οἱ μὲν οὖν ἀπολυθέντες ἦλθον εἰς Ἀντιόχειαν,
- - Then having been dismissed they came to Antioch,

καὶ συναγαγόντες τὸ πλῆθος, ἐπέδωκαν τὴν ἐπιστολήν.
and having gathered the multitude, they delivered the letter.

31 Ἀναγνόντες δὲ ἐχάρησαν ἐπὶ τῇ παρακλήσει.
[2]reading [3]*it* [1]And they rejoiced for the encouragement.
when they had read

32 Ἰούδας τε καὶ Σιλᾶς, καὶ αὐτοὶ προφῆται ὄντες, διὰ
Judas ˜ And and Silas, [4]also [1]themselves [3]prophets [2]being, by

λόγου πολλοῦ παρεκάλεσαν τοὺς ἀδελφοὺς καὶ ἐπεστήριξαν.
word ˜ much encouraged the brothers and strengthened *them.*
many words

33 Ποιήσαντες δὲ χρόνον, ἀπελύθησαν μετ' εἰρήνης ἀπὸ
having made And time, they were dismissed with peace from
And when time had passed,

τῶν ἀδελφῶν πρὸς τοὺς ἀποστόλους.[f] **35** Παῦλος δὲ καὶ
the brothers to the apostles. Paul ˜ But and

Βαρναβᾶς διέτριβον ἐν Ἀντιοχείᾳ διδάσκοντες καὶ
Barnabas spent time in Antioch teaching and

εὐαγγελιζόμενοι μετὰ καὶ ἑτέρων πολλῶν τὸν λόγον
preaching [5]the [6]good [7]news [8]of [1]with [4]also [3]others [2]many the word

τοῦ Κυρίου.
of the Lord.

Paul and Barnabas Part over John Mark

36 Μετὰ δέ τινας ἡμέρας εἶπε Παῦλος πρὸς Βαρναβᾶν,
after ˜ Now some days said ˜ Paul to Barnabas,

"Ἐπιστρέψαντες δὴ ἐπισκεψώμεθα τοὺς ἀδελφοὺς ἡμῶν
"Returning now let us visit - brothers ˜ our
"Let us return and

κατὰ πᾶσαν πόλιν ἐν αἷς κατηγγείλαμεν τὸν λόγον τοῦ
according to every city in which we proclaimed the word of the
in each

Κυρίου, πῶς ἔχουσι." **37** Βαρναβᾶς δὲ ἐβουλεύσατο
Lord, *to see* how they have *it*." Barnabas ˜ And desired
they are doing."

συμπαραλαβεῖν τὸν Ἰωάννην τὸν καλούμενον Μᾶρκον.
to take along with *them* - John the *one* being called Mark.
who was called

38 Παῦλος δὲ ἠξίου, τὸν ἀποστάντα ἀπ'
Paul ˜ But considered it fitting, *as to* the *one* withdrawing from
insisted, as to him who had withdrawn

---

f(**15:33, 34**) NU reads τους αποστειλαντας αυτους, *those who had sent them;* TR adds v. 34: εδοξε δε τω Σιλα επιμειναι αυτου, *But it seemed best to Silas to remain there.*

αὐτῶν ἀπὸ Παμφυλίας καὶ μὴ συνελθόντα αὐτοῖς εἰς τὸ
them from Pamphylia and not going together with them to the
who had not gone

ἔργον, μὴ συμπαραλαβεῖν τοῦτον. 39 Ἐγένετο οὖν
work, not to take along with *them* this *one*. [5]arose [1]Therefore
that they not

παροξυσμὸς ὥστε ἀποχωρισθῆναι αὐτοὺς ἀπ᾽
[2]a [3]sharp [4]disagreement so that to be separated them from
they were separated

ἀλλήλων, τόν τε Βαρναβᾶν παραλαβόντα τὸν Μᾶρκον
one another, - and Barnabas taking along - Mark
took

ἐκπλεῦσαι εἰς Κύπρον. 40 Παῦλος δὲ ἐπιλεξάμενος Σιλᾶν
to sail away to Cyprus. Paul ~ But choosing Silas
and sailed

ἐξῆλθε παραδοθεὶς τῇ χάριτι τοῦ Θεοῦ[g] ὑπὸ τῶν
went out being given over to the grace - of God by the

ἀδελφῶν. 41 Διήρχετο δὲ τὴν Συρίαν καὶ Κιλικίαν
brothers. [2]he [3]passed [4]through [1]And - Syria and Cilicia

ἐπιστηρίζων τὰς ἐκκλησίας.
strengthening the churches.

Timothy Joins Paul and Silas

16 1 Κατήντησε δὲ εἰς Δέρβην καὶ Λύστραν. Καὶ ἰδού,
[2]he [3]arrived [1]Now at Derbe and Lystra. And behold,

μαθητής τις ἦν ἐκεῖ ὀνόματι Τιμόθεος, υἱὸς γυναικός
a disciple ~ certain was there by name Timothy, son of a [3]woman
named

τινος Ἰουδαίας πιστῆς, πατρὸς δὲ Ἕλληνος, 2 ὃς
[1]certain [2]Jewish believing, [2]of [3]a [5]father [1]but [4]Greek, who
who believed,

ἐμαρτυρεῖτο ὑπὸ τῶν ἐν Λύστροις καὶ Ἰκονίῳ ἀδελφῶν.
was borne witness of by the [2]in [3]Lystra [4]and [5]Iconium [1]brothers.
had a good testimony

3 Τοῦτον ἠθέλησεν ὁ Παῦλος σὺν αὐτῷ ἐξελθεῖν, καὶ λαβὼν
This *one* desired ~ - Paul [4]with [5]him [1]to [2]go [3]out, and taking
he took

περιέτεμεν αὐτὸν διὰ τοὺς Ἰουδαίους τοὺς ὄντας ἐν
he circumcised him because of the Jews the *ones* being in
and who were

τοῖς τόποις ἐκείνοις, ᾔδεισαν γὰρ ἅπαντες τὸν πατέρα αὐτοῦ
- places ~ those, [2]they [4]knew [1]for [3]all - father ~ his

ὅτι Ἕλλην ὑπῆρχεν. 4 Ὡς δὲ διεπορεύοντο τὰς
that [3]a [4]Greek [1]he [2]was. as ~ And they were going through the

πόλεις, παρεδίδουν αὐτοῖς φυλάσσειν τὰ δόγματα τὰ
cities, they were delivering to them [3]to [4]keep [1]the [2]decrees the *ones*
which

κεκριμένα ὑπὸ τῶν ἀποστόλων καὶ τῶν πρεσβυτέρων τῶν
having been decided by the apostles and the elders -
had

ἐν Ἱερουσαλήμ. 5 Αἱ μὲν οὖν ἐκκλησίαι
in Jerusalem. the ~ - Therefore churches

ἐστερεοῦντο τῇ πίστει καὶ ἐπερίσσευον τῷ ἀριθμῷ
were being strengthened - in faith and were growing - in number

καθ᾽ ἡμέραν.
according to a day.
each day.

them in Pamphylia, and had not gone with them to the work.
39 Then the contention became so sharp that they parted from one another. And so Barnabas took Mark and sailed to Cyprus;
40 but Paul chose Silas and departed, being commended by the brethren to the grace of God.
41 And he went through Syria and Cilicia, strengthening the churches.

16 Then he came to Derbe and Lystra. And behold, a certain disciple was there, named Timothy, *the* son of a certain Jewish woman who believed, but his father *was* Greek.
2 He was well spoken of by the brethren who were at Lystra and Iconium.
3 Paul wanted to have him go on with him. And he took *him* and circumcised him because of the Jews who were in that region, for they all knew that his father was Greek.
4 And as they went through the cities, they delivered to them the decrees to keep, which were determined by the apostles and elders at Jerusalem.
5 So the churches were strengthened in the faith, and increased in number daily.

g(**15:40**) NU reads Κυριου, *Lord.*

6 Now when they had gone through Phrygia and the region of Galatia, they were forbidden by the Holy Spirit to preach the word in Asia.
7 After they had come to Mysia, they tried to go into Bithynia, but the Spirit did not permit them.
8 So passing by Mysia, they came down to Troas.
9 And a vision appeared to Paul in the night. A man of Macedonia stood and pleaded with him, saying, "Come over to Macedonia and help us."
10 Now after he had seen the vision, immediately we sought to go to Macedonia, concluding that the Lord had called us to preach the gospel to them.
11 Therefore, sailing from Troas, we ran a straight course to Samothrace, and the next *day* came to Neapolis,
12 and from there to Philippi, which is the foremost city of that part of Macedonia, a colony. And we were staying in that city for some days.
13 And on the Sabbath day we went out of the city to the riverside, where prayer was customarily made; and we sat down and spoke to the women who met *there.*
14 Now a certain woman named Lydia heard *us.* She was a seller of purple from the city of Thyatira, who worshiped God. The Lord opened her

[a](16:7) NU adds Ιησου, *of Jesus.* [b](16:10) NU reads Θεος, *God.*
[c](16:13) NU reads πυλης, *gate.*
[d](16:13) For ενομιζετο προσευχη, *prayer was customarily,* NU reads ενομιζομεν προσευχην, *(where) we supposed a place of prayer (to be).*

***(16:12)** κολωνεία *(kolōneia).* Noun, a Latin loanword meaning *colony.* Philippi was reorganized as a military colony by Augustus after the battle of Actium (31 B.C.). It was composed of veterans settled in various cities, usually along the coast. Citizens of such colonies had full Roman legal rights, were under the direct laws and jurisdiction of Rome, and were free from poll tax and tribute.

Paul Hears the Macedonian Call

6 Διελθόντες δὲ τὴν Φρυγίαν καὶ τὴν Γαλατικὴν
[2]going [3]through [1]Now - Phrygia and the Galatian
when they had gone

χώραν, κωλυθέντες ὑπὸ τοῦ Ἁγίου Πνεύματος λαλῆσαι τὸν
region, being forbidden by the Holy Spirit to speak the
they were from speaking

λόγον ἐν τῇ Ἀσίᾳ, **7** ἐλθόντες κατὰ τὴν Μυσίαν ἐπείραζον
word in - Asia, having come to - Mysia they attempted

κατὰ τὴν Βιθυνίαν πορεύεσθαι, καὶ οὐκ εἴασεν αὐτοὺς τὸ
[3]to - [4]Bithynia [1]to [2]go, and [4]not [3]did [5]permit [6]them [1]the

Πνεῦμα·[a] **8** παρελθόντες δὲ τὴν Μυσίαν κατέβησαν εἰς
[2]Spirit; [2]going [3]along [4]by [1]and - Mysia they went down to
they bypassed and

Τρῳάδα.
Troas.

9 Καὶ ὅραμα διὰ τῆς νυκτὸς ὤφθη τῷ Παύλῳ, ἀνήρ
And a vision during the night appeared - to Paul, a man ˜

τις ἦν Μακεδὼν ἑστώς, παρακαλῶν αὐτὸν καὶ λέγων,
certain [3]was [1]of [2]Macedonia standing, urging him and saying,

"Διαβὰς εἰς Μακεδονίαν, βοήθησον ἡμῖν!" **10** Ὡς δὲ
"Coming across to Macedonia, help us!" when ˜ Now
"Come and help

τὸ ὅραμα εἶδεν, εὐθέως ἐζητήσαμεν ἐξελθεῖν εἰς τὴν
[3]the [4]vision [1]he [2]saw, immediately we sought to go out to -

Μακεδονίαν, συμβιβάζοντες ὅτι προσκέκληται ἡμᾶς ὁ
Macedonia, concluding that [3]had [4]called [5]us [1]the

Κύριος[b] εὐαγγελίσασθαι αὐτούς.
[2]Lord to preach the gospel to them.

Lydia Is Baptized at Philippi

11 Ἀναχθέντες οὖν ἀπὸ τῆς Τρῳάδος,
[2]putting [3]to [4]sea [1]Therefore from - Troas,

εὐθυδρομήσαμεν εἰς Σαμοθρᾴκην, τῇ τε ἐπιούσῃ εἰς
we ran a straight course to Samothrace, [2]on [3]the [1]and next *day* to

Νεάπολιν, **12** ἐκεῖθέν τε εἰς Φιλίππους, ἥτις ἐστὶ πρώτη
Neapolis, [2]from [3]there [1]and to Philippi, which is a first
chief

τῆς μερίδος τῆς Μακεδονίας πόλις, κολωνεία.* Ἦμεν
[2]of [3]the [4]part - [5]of [6]Macedonia [1]city, a *Roman* colony. [2]we [3]were
of that

δὲ ἐν αὐτῇ τῇ πόλει διατρίβοντες ἡμέρας τινάς. **13** Τῇ
[1]And [7]in [9]very [8]the [10]city [4]spending [6]days [5]some. [2]on [3]the
that

τε ἡμέρᾳ τῶν σαββάτων ἐξήλθομεν ἔξω τῆς πόλεως[c]
[1]And day of the Sabbath we went outside the city
Sabbath day

παρὰ ποταμόν, οὗ ἐνομίζετο προσευχὴ[d] εἶναι, καὶ
beside a river, where [2]was [3]customarily [1]prayer to be, and
made,

καθίσαντες ἐλαλοῦμεν ταῖς συνελθούσαις γυναιξί.
having sat down we spoke to the [2]having [3]come [4]together [5]*there* [1]women.
who assembled

14 Καί τις γυνὴ ὀνόματι Λυδία, πορφυρόπωλις
And certain ˜ a woman by name Lydia, a dealer in purple cloth
named

πόλεως Θυατείρων, σεβομένη τὸν Θεόν, ἤκουεν, ἧς ὁ
of *the* city of Thyatira, worshiping - God, heard *us,* whose [2]the
who worshiped

Κύριος διήνοιξε τὴν καρδίαν προσέχειν τοῖς λαλουμένοις
[3]Lord [4]opened - [1]heart to give heed to the *things* being spoken

ὑπὸ τοῦ Παύλου. 15 Ὡς δὲ ἐβαπτίσθη, καὶ ὁ οἶκος
by - Paul. when ˜ And she was baptized, and - house ˜

αὐτῆς, παρεκάλεσε λέγουσα, "Εἰ κεκρίκατέ με πιστὴν
her, she urged *us* saying, "If you have judged me [3]faithful

τῷ Κυρίῳ εἶναι, εἰσελθόντες εἰς τὸν οἶκόν μου, μείνατε.
[4]to [5]the [6]Lord [1]to [2]be, coming in to - house ˜ my, stay."
come and stay."

Καὶ παρεβιάσατο ἡμᾶς.
And she prevailed upon us.
persuaded

Paul and Silas Imprisoned

16 Ἐγένετο δὲ πορευομένων ἡμῶν εἰς προσευχήν,
[2]it [3]came [4]to [5]pass [1]Now going ˜ us to prayer,
as we went

παιδίσκην τινὰ ἔχουσαν πνεῦμα Πύθωνος ἀπαντῆσαι
that a [2]slave [3]girl [1]certain having a spirit of Python to meet
who had of divination met

ἡμῖν, ἥτις ἐργασίαν πολλὴν παρεῖχε τοῖς κυρίοις αὐτῆς
us, who [3]profit [2]much [1]brought - to masters ˜ her

μαντευομένη. 17 Αὕτη κατακολουθήσασα τῷ Παύλῳ καὶ
by giving oracles. This *girl* following after - Paul and
followed

ἡμῖν, ἔκραζε λέγουσα, "Οὗτοι οἱ ἄνθρωποι δοῦλοι τοῦ
us, was crying out saying, "These - men [2]slaves -
and cried servants

Θεοῦ τοῦ Ὑψίστου εἰσίν, οἵτινες καταγγέλλουσιν ἡμῖν[e]
[3]of [7]God [4]the [5]Most [6]High [1]are, who proclaim to us

ὁδὸν σωτηρίας." 18 Τοῦτο δὲ ἐποίει ἐπὶ πολλὰς ἡμέρας.
the way of salvation." this ˜ And she did for many days.

Διαπονηθεὶς δὲ ὁ Παῦλος καὶ ἐπιστρέψας, τῷ
[3]being [4]greatly [5]annoyed [1]And - [2]Paul and turning around, [2]to [3]the
was turned

πνεύματι εἶπε, "Παραγγέλλω σοι ἐν τῷ ὀνόματι Ἰησοῦ
[4]spirit [1]said, "I command you in the name of Jesus
and said,

Χριστοῦ ἐξελθεῖν ἀπ' αὐτῆς!" Καὶ ἐξῆλθεν αὐτῇ τῇ ὥρᾳ.
Christ to come out from her!" And it came out [3]very [1]in [2]the hour.
that

19 Ἰδόντες δὲ οἱ κύριοι αὐτῆς ὅτι ἐξῆλθεν ἡ ἐλπὶς τῆς
seeing And - masters her that [6]was [7]gone [1]the [2]hope -
And when her masters saw

ἐργασίας αὐτῶν, ἐπιλαβόμενοι τὸν Παῦλον καὶ τὸν Σιλᾶν,
[3]of [5]profit [4]their, taking hold of - Paul and - Silas,
they took

εἵλκυσαν εἰς τὴν ἀγορὰν* ἐπὶ τοὺς ἄρχοντας, 20 καὶ
they dragged *them* to the marketplace to the rulers, and
and

προσαγαγόντες αὐτοὺς τοῖς στρατηγοῖς εἶπον, "Οὗτοι οἱ
bringing them to the magistrates they said, "These -

ἄνθρωποι ἐκταράσσουσιν ἡμῶν τὴν πόλιν, Ἰουδαῖοι
men [3]are [4]agitating [5]our - [6]city, [2]Jews

ὑπάρχοντες, 21 καὶ καταγγέλλουσιν ἔθη ἃ οὐκ ἔξεστιν
[1]being, and they are proclaiming customs which not ˜ are lawful

ἡμῖν παραδέχεσθαι οὐδὲ ποιεῖν, Ῥωμαίοις οὖσι." 22 Καὶ
for us to receive nor to do, Romans ˜ being." And
or since we are."

heart to heed the things spoken by Paul.
15 And when she and her household were baptized, she begged *us,* saying, "If you have judged me to be faithful to the Lord, come to my house and stay." So she persuaded us.
16 Now it happened, as we went to prayer, that a certain slave girl possessed with a spirit of divination met us, who brought her masters much profit by fortune-telling.
17 This girl followed Paul and us, and cried out, saying, "These men are the servants of the Most High God, who proclaim to us the way of salvation."
18 And this she did for many days. But Paul, greatly annoyed, turned and said to the spirit, "I command you in the name of Jesus Christ to come out of her." And he came out that very hour.
19 But when her masters saw that their hope of profit was gone, they seized Paul and Silas and dragged *them* into the marketplace to the authorities.
20 And they brought them to the magistrates, and said, "These men, being Jews, exceedingly trouble our city;
21 "and they teach customs which are not lawful for us, being Romans, to receive or observe."
22 Then the multitude rose up

---

[e]**(16:17)** NU reads *υμιν, to you.*

***(16:19)** *ἀγορά (agora).* Noun *market, marketplace,* a public place where people often gathered for some public event (here and Mark 6:56) or to seek work opportunities (Matt. 20:3) or even for children to play (Matt. 11:16). The *ἀγορά* of Athens mentioned in Acts 17:17 was the center of public life. See the cognate adjective *ἀγοραῖος, pertaining to a market,* used substantivally in 17:5 to refer to *idlers* or *rabble* who crowded the marketplace. See also the cognate verb *ἀγοράζω, buy, purchase,* at Rev. 5:9.

together against them; and the
magistrates tore off their
clothes and commanded *them* to
be beaten with rods.
23 And when they had laid
many stripes on them, they
threw *them* into prison, commanding the jailer to keep them
securely.
24 Having received such a
charge, he put them into the inner prison and fastened their
feet in the stocks.
25 But at midnight Paul and
Silas were praying and singing
hymns to God, and the prisoners were listening to them.
26 Suddenly there was a great
earthquake, so that the foundations of the prison were
shaken; and immediately all the
doors were opened and everyone's chains were loosed.
27 And the keeper of the
prison, awaking from sleep and
seeing the prison doors open,
supposing the prisoners had
fled, drew his sword and was
about to kill himself.
28 But Paul called with a loud
voice, saying, "Do yourself no
harm, for we are all here."
29 Then he called for a light,
ran in, and fell down trembling
before Paul and Silas.
30 And he brought them out

συνεπέστη ὁ ὄχλος κατ' αὐτῶν, καὶ οἱ στρατηγοὶ
[3]rose [4]up [5]together [1]the [2]crowd against them, and the magistrates

περιρρήξαντες αὐτῶν τὰ ἱμάτια ἐκέλευον
having torn their - garments were ordering
tore and ordered

ῥαβδίζειν. **23** Πολλάς τε ἐπιθέντες αὐτοῖς
the lictors to beat *them* with rods. [3]many [1]And [2]laying [5]on [6]them
when they laid

πληγὰς ἔβαλον εἰς φυλακήν, παραγγείλαντες τῷ
[4]strokes they cast *them* into prison, commanding the
and commanded

δεσμοφύλακι ἀσφαλῶς τηρεῖν αὐτούς· **24** ὅς, παραγγελίαν
prison keeper [4]securely [1]to [2]keep [3]them; who, [4]a [5]command

τοιαύτην εἰληφώς, ἔβαλεν αὐτοὺς εἰς τὴν ἐσωτέραν
[3]such [1]having [2]received, cast them into the inner

φυλακὴν καὶ τοὺς πόδας αὐτῶν ἠσφαλίσατο εἰς τὸ ξύλον.
prison and - [3]feet [2]their [1]made secure in the wood.
stocks.

The Philippian Jailer Is Saved

25 Κατὰ δὲ τὸ μεσονύκτιον Παῦλος καὶ Σιλᾶς
about ˜ Now - midnight Paul and Silas

προσευχόμενοι ὕμνουν τὸν Θεόν, ἐπηκροῶντο
praying were singing hymns *to* - God, [4]were [5]listening [6]to
were praying and

δὲ αὐτῶν οἱ δέσμιοι· **26** ἄφνω δὲ σεισμὸς ἐγένετο
[1]and [7]them [2]the [3]prisoners; suddenly ˜ and [3]a(n) [5]earthquake [1]*there* [2]was

μέγας ὥστε σαλευθῆναι τὰ θεμέλια τοῦ δεσμωτηρίου,
[4]great so that [6]to [7]be [8]shaken [1]the [2]foundations [3]of [4]the [5]prison,
were

ἀνεῴχθησάν τε παραχρῆμα αἱ θύραι πᾶσαι, καὶ πάντων
[14]were [15]opened [9]and [10]immediately [12]the [13]doors [11]all, and [3]of [4]all

τὰ δεσμὰ ἀνέθη. **27** Ἔξυπνος δὲ γενόμενος ὁ
[1]the [2]bonds were loosed. awake And becoming the
And when the prison keeper awoke

δεσμοφύλαξ καὶ ἰδὼν ἀνεῳγμένας τὰς θύρας τῆς φυλακῆς,
prison keeper and seeing [6]opened [1]the [2]doors [3]of [4]the [5]prison,
saw

σπασάμενος μάχαιραν, ἔμελλεν ἑαυτὸν ἀναιρεῖν,
drawing a sword, he was about [3]himself [1]to [2]kill,
he drew and

νομίζων ἐκπεφευγέναι τοὺς δεσμίους.
supposing *that* [3]to [4]have [5]escaped [1]the [2]prisoners.
had

28 Ἐφώνησεν δὲ φωνῇ μεγάλῃ ὁ Παῦλος λέγων,
[3]called [4]out [1]But [5]with [6]a [8]voice [7]great - [2]Paul saying,
loud

"Μηδὲν πράξῃς σεαυτῷ κακόν, ἅπαντες γάρ ἐσμεν
"nothing ˜ Do [2]to [3]yourself [1]bad, [7]all [4]for [5]we [6]are

ἐνθάδε."
here."

29 Αἰτήσας δὲ φῶτα εἰσεπήδησε, καὶ ἔντρομος
[2]asking [3]for [1]And a light he rushed in, and trembling ˜
he asked and he came

γενόμενος προσέπεσε τῷ Παύλῳ καὶ τῷ Σιλᾷ, **30** καὶ
coming he fell before - Paul and - Silas, and
trembling and

προαγαγὼν αὐτοὺς ἔξω ἔφη, "Κύριοι, τί με
bringing forth ˜ them outside he said, "Sirs, what [5]me
he brought and

δεῖ ποιεῖν ἵνα σωθῶ?"
[1]is [2]it [3]necessary [4]*for* to do in order that I may be saved?"
must I

31 Οἱ δὲ εἶπον, "Πίστευσον ἐπὶ τὸν Κύριον Ἰησοῦν
[2]the [3]*ones* [1]And said, "Believe on the Lord Jesus
they

Χριστόν,[f] καὶ σωθήσῃ σὺ καὶ ὁ οἶκός σου." **32** Καὶ
Christ, and you will be saved you and - house ˜ your." And
household

ἐλάλησαν αὐτῷ τὸν λόγον τοῦ Κυρίου καὶ πᾶσι τοῖς ἐν τῇ
they spoke to him the word of the Lord and to all - in -

οἰκίᾳ αὐτοῦ. **33** Καὶ παραλαβὼν αὐτοὺς ἐν ἐκείνῃ τῇ ὥρᾳ
house ˜ his. And taking along ˜ them in that - hour
he took them aside

τῆς νυκτὸς ἔλουσεν ἀπὸ τῶν πληγῶν, καὶ ἐβαπτίσθη αὐτὸς
of the night he washed - the wounds, and he was baptized he
and their

καὶ οἱ αὐτοῦ πάντες παραχρῆμα. **34** Ἀναγαγών τε
and [2]the [3]*ones* [4]of [5]him [1]all immediately. [2]bringing [4]up [1]And
his family when he brought

αὐτοὺς εἰς τὸν οἶκον αὐτοῦ παρέθηκε τράπεζαν, καὶ
[3]them into - house ˜ his he put before *them* a table, and
he set a meal before them,

ἠγαλλίατο πανοικὶ πεπιστευκὼς τῷ Θεῷ.
he rejoiced with his whole house having believed - in God.

Paul Refuses to Depart Secretly

35 Ἡμέρας δὲ γενομένης, ἀπέστειλαν οἱ στρατηγοὶ
day ˜ Now becoming, [3]sent [1]the [2]magistrates
Now when it became day,

τοὺς ῥαβδούχους λέγοντες, "Ἀπόλυσον τοὺς ἀνθρώπους
the lictors saying, "Release - men ˜

ἐκείνους."
those."

36 Ἀπήγγειλε δὲ ὁ δεσμοφύλαξ τοὺς λόγους τούτους
[5]announced [1]And [2]the [3]prison [4]keeper - words ˜ these

πρὸς τὸν Παῦλον, ὅτι "Ἀπεστάλκασιν οἱ στρατηγοὶ ἵνα
to - Paul, - "[3]have [4]sent [1]The [2]magistrates so that

ἀπολυθῆτε· νῦν οὖν ἐξελθόντες πορεύεσθε ἐν
you may be released: now therefore going out go in
depart and

εἰρήνῃ."
peace."

37 Ὁ δὲ Παῦλος ἔφη πρὸς αὐτούς, "Δείραντες ἡμᾶς
- But Paul said to them, "Beating us
"They beat

δημοσίᾳ, ἀκατακρίτους, ἀνθρώπους Ῥωμαίους ὑπάρχοντας,
publicly, uncondemned, men Romans being,
although we were uncondemned Romans,

ἔβαλον εἰς φυλακήν, καὶ νῦν λάθρᾳ ἡμᾶς ἐκβάλλουσιν?
they cast *us* into prison, and [3]now [7]secretly [5]us [1]do [2]they [4]cast [6]out?
and

Οὐ γάρ! Ἀλλὰ ἐλθόντες αὐτοὶ ἐξαγαγέτωσαν."
no ˜ For! But coming themselves let them bring *us* out."
No indeed! let them come themselves and lead us out."

and said, "Sirs, what must I do to be saved?"
31 So they said, "Believe on the Lord Jesus Christ, and you will be saved, you and your household."
32 Then they spoke the word of the Lord to him and to all who were in his house.
33 And he took them the same hour of the night and washed *their* stripes. And immediately he and all his family were baptized.
34 Now when he had brought them into his house, he set food before them; and he rejoiced, having believed in God with all his household.
35 And when it was day, the magistrates sent the officers, saying, "Let those men go."
36 So the keeper of the prison reported these words to Paul, saying, "The magistrates have sent to let you go. Now therefore depart, and go in peace."
37 But Paul said to them, "They have beaten us openly, uncondemned Romans, *and* have thrown *us* into prison. And now do they put us out secretly? No indeed! Let them come themselves and get us out."

---

f(**16:31**) NU omits Χριστον, *Christ.*

38 And the officers told these words to the magistrates, and they were afraid when they heard that they were Romans.
39 Then they came and pleaded with them and brought *them* out, and asked *them* to depart from the city.
40 So they went out of the prison and entered *the house of* Lydia; and when they had seen the brethren, they encouraged them and departed.
17 Now when they had passed through Amphipolis and Apollonia, they came to Thessalonica, where there was a synagogue of the Jews.
2 Then Paul, as his custom was, went in to them, and for three Sabbaths reasoned with them from the Scriptures,
3 explaining and demonstrating that the Christ had to suffer and rise again from the dead, and *saying,* "This Jesus whom I preach to you is the Christ."
4 And some of them were persuaded; and a great multitude of the devout Greeks, and not a few of the leading women, joined Paul and Silas.
5 But the Jews who were not persuaded, becoming envious, took some of the evil men from the marketplace, and gathering a mob, set all the city in an up-

38 Ἀπήγγειλαν δὲ τοῖς στρατηγοῖς οἱ ῥαβδοῦχοι τὰ
[4]related [1]And [5]to [6]the [7]magistrates [2]the [3]lictors -

ῥήματα ταῦτα. Καὶ ἐφοβήθησαν ἀκούσαντες ὅτι Ῥωμαῖοί
words ˜ these. And they were afraid hearing that [3]Romans
when they heard

εἰσι, **39** καὶ ἐλθόντες παρεκάλεσαν αὐτούς, καὶ
[1]they [2]are, and coming they appealed to them, and
were, they came and

ἐξαγαγόντες ἠρώτων ἐξελθεῖν τῆς πόλεως.
bringing them out they asked *them* to depart of the city.
they led them out and from

40 Ἐξελθόντες δὲ ἐκ τῆς φυλακῆς εἰσῆλθον πρὸς
[2]coming [3]out [1]And from the prison they entered to
they departed and

τὴν Λυδίαν, καὶ ἰδόντες τοὺς ἀδελφούς,
- *the house of* Lydia, and seeing the brothers,
when they saw

παρεκάλεσαν αὐτοὺς καὶ ἐξῆλθον.
they encouraged them and departed.

Paul Preaches Christ in Thessalonica

17 **1** Διοδεύσαντες δὲ τὴν Ἀμφίπολιν καὶ
[2]traveling [3]through [1]Now - Amphipolis and
when they had traveled

Ἀπολλωνίαν, ἦλθον εἰς Θεσσαλονίκην, ὅπου ἦν ἡ
Apollonia, they came to Thessalonica, where [6]was [1]the

συναγωγὴ τῶν Ἰουδαίων. **2** Κατὰ δὲ τὸ εἰωθὸς τῷ
[2]synagogue [3]of [4]the [5]Jews. [2]according [3]to [1]And the custom -

Παύλῳ εἰσῆλθε πρὸς αὐτοὺς καὶ ἐπὶ σάββατα τρία διελέξατο
with Paul he entered with them and for Sabbaths ˜ three discussed

αὐτοῖς ἀπὸ τῶν Γραφῶν, **3** διανοίγων καὶ παρατιθέμενος ὅτι
with them from the Scriptures, opening and pointing out that
interpreting

τὸν Χριστὸν ἔδει παθεῖν καὶ ἀναστῆναι ἐκ
[5]the [6]Christ [1]it [2]was [3]necessary [4]*for* to suffer and to arise from
Messiah

νεκρῶν, καὶ ὅτι "Οὗτός ἐστιν ὁ Χριστός, Ἰησοῦς, ὃν ἐγὼ
the dead, and that "This *One* is the Christ, Jesus, whom I
Messiah,

καταγγέλλω ὑμῖν." **4** Καί τινες ἐξ αὐτῶν ἐπείσθησαν καὶ
proclaim to you." And some of them were persuaded and

προσεκληρώθησαν τῷ Παύλῳ καὶ τῷ Σιλᾷ, τῶν τε
were joined - with Paul and - Silas, [2]of [3]the [1]both

σεβομένων Ἑλλήνων πολὺ πλῆθος, γυναικῶν τε τῶν πρώτων
worshiping Greeks a great multitude, [2]of [5]women [1]and [3]the [4]first
chief

οὐκ ὀλίγαι.
not a few.

Unbelieving Jews Assault Jason's House

5 Προσλαβόμενοι δὲ οἱ Ἰουδαῖοι οἱ
[7]taking [8]along [1]And [2]the [3]Jews [4]the [5]*ones*
took who did not

ἀπειθοῦντες[a] τῶν ἀγοραίων* τινὰς ἄνδρας
[6]disobeying [12]of [13]the [14]marketplace [15]people [9]some [11]men
believe rabble

πονηρούς, καὶ ὀχλοποιήσαντες, ἐθορύβουν τὴν πόλιν,
[10]wicked, and forming a mob, threw [3]into [4]disorder [1]the [2]city,

---

[a](17:5) For Προσλαβομενοι . . . απειθουντες, *taking along . . . disobeying,* NU reads Ζηλωσαντες δε οι Ιουδαιοι και προσλαβομενοι, *And the Jews, becoming envious and taking along;* TR reads Ζηλωσαντες δε οι απειθουντες Ιουδαιοι, και προσλαβομενοι, *And the Jews who were unpersuaded, becoming envious and taking along.*

*(17:5) ἀγοραῖος (*agoraios*). Adjective meaning *pertaining to a market.* In the NT it is used only as a substantive designating persons or things associated with the ἀγορά, *market, marketplace,* the center of Greek urban life. Here it is used in a negative sense for the rabble that would crowd the ἀγορά with nothing to do, thus *idlers.* In Acts 19:38 the word has a technical legal sense: ἀγοραῖοι ἄγονται meaning "the courts are in session." See ἀγορά at 16:19.

ἐπιστάντες τε τῇ οἰκίᾳ Ἰάσονος, ἐζήτουν αὐτοὺς ἀγαγεῖν εἰς
[6]coming [7]upon [5]and the house of Jason, sought [3]them [1]to [2]bring to
they came and sought

τὸν δῆμον. 6 Μὴ εὑρόντες δὲ αὐτούς, ἔσυρον τὸν
the people. not finding But them, they dragged -
But when they did not find

Ἰάσονα καί τινας ἀδελφοὺς ἐπὶ τοὺς πολιτάρχας, βοῶντες ὅτι
Jason and some brothers to the politarchs, crying out -

"Οἱ τὴν οἰκουμένην ἀναστατώσαντες, οὗτοι καὶ ἐνθάδε
"The *ones* the world upsetting, these also [3]here
"The men who have upset the whole world,

πάρεισιν, 7 οὓς ὑποδέδεκται Ἰάσων· καὶ οὗτοι πάντες
[1]are [2]present, whom [2]has [3]received [1]Jason; and these all

ἀπέναντι τῶν δογμάτων Καίσαρος πράσσουσι, Βασιλέα
[2]contrary [3]to [4]the [5]decrees [6]of [7]Caesar [1]practice, [12]King

λέγοντες ἕτερον εἶναι, Ἰησοῦν." 8 Ἐτάραξαν δὲ τὸν
[8]saying [11]another [9]to [10]be, Jesus." [2]they [3]troubled [1]And the
there is,

ὄχλον καὶ τοὺς πολιτάρχας ἀκούοντας ταῦτα. 9 Καὶ
crowd and the politarchs hearing these *things.* And
when they heard

λαβόντες τὸ ἱκανὸν παρὰ τοῦ Ἰάσονος καὶ τῶν λοιπῶν,
having taken the sufficient *thing* from - Jason and the rest,
security bond

ἀπέλυσαν αὐτούς.
they released them.

Paul Ministers at Berea

10 Οἱ δὲ ἀδελφοὶ εὐθέως διὰ τῆς νυκτὸς ἐξέπεμψαν
the ˜ And brothers immediately during the night sent [5]away

τόν τε Παῦλον καὶ τὸν Σιλᾶν εἰς Βέροιαν, οἵτινες
- [1]both [2]Paul [3]and - [4]Silas to Berea, who

παραγενόμενοι εἰς τὴν συναγωγὴν ἀπῄεσαν τῶν Ἰουδαίων.
arriving [2]into [3]the [4]synagogue [1]went of the Jews.
when they arrived

11 Οὗτοι δὲ ἦσαν εὐγενέστεροι τῶν ἐν
these ˜ And were more noble-minded *than* the *ones* in

Θεσσαλονίκῃ, οἵτινες ἐδέξαντο τὸν λόγον μετὰ πάσης
Thessalonica, who received the word with all

προθυμίας, τὸ καθ' ἡμέραν ἀνακρίνοντες τὰς Γραφὰς
readiness, - according to a day examining the Scriptures
each day

εἰ ἔχοι ταῦτα οὕτως. 12 Πολλοὶ μὲν
to see whether might have these *things* thus. many ˜ -
these things might be so.

οὖν ἐξ αὐτῶν ἐπίστευσαν, καὶ τῶν Ἑλληνίδων γυναικῶν
Therefore of them believed, and of the [2]Greek [3]women

τῶν εὐσχημόνων καὶ ἀνδρῶν οὐκ ὀλίγοι. 13 Ὡς δὲ
- [1]prominent and men not a few. when ˜ Now

ἔγνωσαν οἱ ἀπὸ τῆς Θεσσαλονίκης Ἰουδαῖοι ὅτι καὶ ἐν τῇ
[5]learned [1]the [3]from - [4]Thessalonica [2]Jews that also in -

Βεροίᾳ κατηγγέλη ὑπὸ τοῦ Παύλου ὁ λόγος τοῦ Θεοῦ,
Berea [5]was [6]proclaimed [7]by - [8]Paul [1]the [2]word - [3]of [4]God,

ἦλθον κἀκεῖ σαλεύοντες[b] τοὺς ὄχλους. 14 Εὐθέως δὲ
they came ˜ also there shaking the crowds. immediately ˜ And
agitating

τότε τὸν Παῦλον ἐξαπέστειλαν οἱ ἀδελφοὶ πορεύεσθαι ὡς ἐπὶ
then - [4]Paul [3]sent [5]away [1]the [2]brothers to go as by

roar and attacked the house of
Jason, and sought to bring them
out to the people.
6 But when they did not find
them, they dragged Jason and
some brethren to the rulers of
the city, crying out, "These
who have turned the world up-
side down have come here too.
7 "Jason has harbored them,
and these are all acting contrary
to the decrees of Caesar, saying there is another king—
Jesus."
8 And they troubled the
crowd and the rulers of the city
when they heard these things.
9 So when they had taken security from Jason and the rest,
they let them go.
10 Then the brethren immediately sent Paul and Silas away
by night to Berea. When they
arrived, they went into the synagogue of the Jews.
11 These were more fair-
minded than those in Thessalonica, in that they received the
word with all readiness, and
searched the Scriptures daily *to
find out* whether these things
were so.
12 Therefore many of them
believed, and also not a few of
the Greeks, prominent women
as well as men.
13 But when the Jews from
Thessalonica learned that the
word of God was preached by
Paul at Berea, they came there
also and stirred up the crowds.
14 Then immediately the
brethren sent Paul away, to go

---

[b](17:13) NU adds *και ταρασσοντες, and inciting.*

to the sea; but both Silas and
Timothy remained there.
15 So those who conducted
Paul brought him to Athens;
and receiving a command for Silas and Timothy to come to him
with all speed, they departed.
16 Now while Paul waited for
them at Athens, his spirit was
provoked within him when he
saw that the city was given
over to idols.
17 Therefore he reasoned in
the synagogue with the Jews
and with the *Gentile* worshipers, and in the marketplace
daily with those who happened
to be there.
18 Then certain Epicurean
and Stoic philosophers encountered him. And some said,
"What does this babbler want
to say?" Others said, "He
seems to be a proclaimer of foreign gods," because he
preached to them Jesus and the
resurrection.
19 And they took him and
brought him to the Areopagus,
saying, "May we know what
this new doctrine *is* of which
you speak?
20 "For you are bringing some
strange things to our ears.
Therefore we want to know
what these things mean."
21 For all the Athenians and

τὴν θάλασσαν· ὑπέμενον δὲ ὅ τε Σιλᾶς καὶ ὁ Τιμόθεος
the sea; [6]remained [1]but - [2]both [3]Silas [4]and - [5]Timothy

ἐκεῖ. 15 Οἱ δὲ καθιστῶντες τὸν Παῦλον, ἤγαγον αὐτὸν
there. [2]the [3]*ones* [1]And conducting - Paul, brought him

ἕως Ἀθηνῶν, καὶ λαβόντες ἐντολὴν πρὸς τὸν Σιλᾶν καὶ
to Athens, and receiving a command for - Silas and

Τιμόθεον ἵνα ὡς τάχιστα ἔλθωσι πρὸς αὐτόν,
Timothy that as most quickly they should come to him,
quickly as possible

ἐξῄεσαν.
they went away.

Paul Encounters Philosophers at Athens

16 Ἐν δὲ ταῖς Ἀθήναις ἐκδεχομένου αὐτοὺς τοῦ Παύλου,
in ˜ And - Athens waiting for them - Paul,
while Paul waited for them,

παρωξύνετο τὸ πνεῦμα αὐτοῦ ἐν αὐτῷ θεωροῦντι
[3]was [4]provoked - [2]spirit [1]his within him observing
when he saw that

κατείδωλον οὖσαν τὴν πόλιν. 17 Διελέγετο μὲν οὖν ἐν
[4]full [5]of [6]idols [3]being [1]the [2]city. [2]he [3]reasoned - [1]Therefore in
was

τῇ συναγωγῇ τοῖς Ἰουδαίοις καὶ τοῖς σεβομένοις, καὶ ἐν
the synagogue with the Jews and the worshiping *Gentiles,* and in

τῇ ἀγορᾷ κατὰ πᾶσαν ἡμέραν πρὸς τοὺς
the marketplace according to every day with the
daily

παρατυγχάνοντας. 18 Τινὲς δὲ καὶ[c] τῶν Ἐπικουρείων καὶ
ones coming by. some ˜ And also of the Epicurean and

τῶν Στοϊκῶν φιλοσόφων συνέβαλλον αὐτῷ.
of the Stoic philosophers were conversing with him.

Καί τινες ἔλεγον, "Τί ἂν θέλοι ὁ σπερμολόγος*
And some were saying, "What - could [6]wish - [2]*one* [3]picking [4]up [5]seeds
babbler

οὗτος λέγειν?"
[1]this to say?"

Οἱ δέ, "Ξένων δαιμονίων δοκεῖ καταγγελεὺς
[2]the [3]*ones* [1]But, "[10]of [11]strange [12]demons [4]He [5]seems [8]a [9]proclaimer
others foreign deities

εἶναι" — ὅτι τὸν Ἰησοῦν καὶ τὴν ἀνάστασιν
[6]to [7]be" — because - [8]Jesus [9]and [10]the [11]resurrection

εὐηγγελίζετο. 19 Ἐπιλαβόμενοί τε αὐτοῦ
[1]he [2]was [3]preaching [4]the [5]good [6]news [7]of. [2]having [3]taken [1]And him
they took

ἐπὶ τὸν Ἄρειον Πάγον ἤγαγον λέγοντες, "Δυνάμεθα
[4]to [5]the [7]of [8]Ares [6]Hill [1]they [2]led [3]*him* saying, "Are we able
Areopagus and

γνῶναι τίς ἡ καινὴ αὕτη ἡ ὑπὸ σοῦ λαλουμένη
to know what [10]*is* - [2]new [1]this [4]the [5]*one* [8]by [9]you [6]being [7]spoken
which is spoken of

διδαχή? 20 Ξενίζοντα γάρ τινα εἰσφέρεις εἰς τὰς
[3]teaching? [6]surprising [7]*things* [1]For [5]some [2]you [3]are [4]bringing to -

ἀκοὰς ἡμῶν· βουλόμεθα οὖν γνῶναι τί ἂν θέλοι
ears ˜ our; [2]we [3]desire [1]therefore to know what - might wish
these

ταῦτα εἶναι." 21 Ἀθηναῖοι δὲ πάντες καὶ οἱ
these *things* to be." [3]Athenians [1]Now [2]all and the
things might mean."

c(17:18) TR omits και, *also.*

*(17:18) σπερμολόγος (*spermologos*). Adjective meaning *picking up seeds,* used as a substantive. Literally it referred to a bird that picks up seeds, such as a crow. It was applied figuratively to a person who "picked up" scraps of conversations or information, a *babbler* or *gossip.* Here it is probably used as an insult against Paul as one who had no unified system of philosophy, but rather took bits and pieces from various systems.

ἐπιδημοῦντες ξένοι εἰς οὐδὲν ἕτερον
[2]staying [3]*there* [4]as [5]visitors [1]strangers [9]for [10]nothing [11]other

εὐκαίρουν ἢ λέγειν τι καὶ ἀκούειν καινότερον.
[6]spent [7]their [8]time than to say [4]something [1]and [2]to [3]hear [5]newer.

Paul Addresses the Areopagus

22 Σταθεὶς δὲ ὁ Παῦλος ἐν μέσῳ τοῦ Ἀρείου Πάγου
[3]standing [1]And - [2]Paul in *the* midst of the [2]of [3]Ares [1]Hill
stood Areopagus

ἔφη, "Ἄνδρες Ἀθηναῖοι, κατὰ πάντα ὡς
said, "Men Athenians, according to all things [4]as [5]*being*
and said, in every way

δεισιδαιμονεστέρους ὑμᾶς θεωρῶ. 23 Διερχόμενος γὰρ καὶ
[6]very [7]religious [3]you [1]I [2]perceive. [2]passing [3]by [1]For and
superstitious as I passed

ἀναθεωρῶν τὰ σεβάσματα ὑμῶν, εὗρον καὶ βωμὸν ἐν ᾧ
considering the objects of worship ˜ your, I found also an altar on which
considered

ἐπεγέγραπτο, 'Ἀγνώστῳ Θεῷ.' Ὃν οὖν
had been inscribed, 'To *the* unknown God.' [2]*Him* [3]whom [1]Therefore

ἀγνοοῦντες εὐσεβεῖτε, τοῦτον ἐγὼ καταγγέλλω ὑμῖν. 24 Ὁ
being ignorant of you worship, this *One* I announce to you. The

Θεὸς ὁ ποιήσας τὸν κόσμον καὶ πάντα τὰ ἐν αὐτῷ,
God the *One* making the world and all the *things* in it,
who made

οὗτος, οὐρανοῦ καὶ γῆς Κύριος ὑπάρχων, οὐκ ἐν
this *One,* [3]of [4]heaven [5]and [6]earth [2]Lord [1]being, [8]not [10]in

χειροποιήτοις ναοῖς κατοικεῖ 25 οὐδὲ ὑπὸ
[12]made [13]by [14]human [15]hands [11]sanctuaries [7]does [9]dwell nor by

χειρῶν ἀνθρώπων[d] θεραπεύεται, προσδεόμενός
the hands of men is He served, *as though* needing more ˜

τινος, αὐτὸς διδοὺς πᾶσι ζωὴν καὶ πνοὴν κατὰ
something, He giving to all life and breath with respect to
for He gives in

πάντα· 26 ἐποίησέ τε ἐξ ἑνὸς αἵματος[e] πᾶν ἔθνος
all *things;* [2]He [3]made [1]and from one blood every nation

ἀνθρώπων κατοικεῖν ἐπὶ πᾶν τὸ πρόσωπον τῆς γῆς,
of men to dwell upon all the face of the earth,

ὁρίσας προστεταγμένους καιροὺς καὶ τὰς
determining [2]having [3]been [4]fixed [5]*for* [6]*them* [1]times and the
and He ordained

ὁροθεσίας τῆς κατοικίας αὐτῶν, 27 ζητεῖν τὸν
boundaries - of dwellings ˜ their, *in order for them* to seek the

Κύριον,[f] εἰ ἄρα γε ψηλαφήσειαν* αὐτὸν καὶ εὕροιεν,
Lord, if perhaps indeed they might grope for Him and find *Him,*

καί γε οὐ μακρὰν ἀπὸ ἑνὸς ἑκάστου ἡμῶν ὑπάρχοντα.
and yet [2]indeed [3]not [4]far [5]from [6]one [7]of [8]each [9]of [10]us [1]being.
any one He is.

28 "Ἐν αὐτῷ γὰρ ζῶμεν καὶ κινούμεθα καὶ ἐσμέν·' ὡς καί
'[2]in [3]Him [1]For we live and move and exist;' as also

τινες τῶν καθ' ὑμᾶς ποιητῶν εἰρήκασιν, 'Τοῦ γὰρ καὶ
some of the [2]among [3]you [1]poets have said, '[5]of [6]the [1]For [4]also
your own poets His

γένος ἐσμέν.' 29 Γένος οὖν ὑπάρχοντες τοῦ Θεοῦ, οὐκ
[7]race [2]we [3]are.' [3]*the* [4]race [1]Therefore [2]being - of God, [3]not
since we are

ὀφείλομεν νομίζειν χρυσῷ ἢ ἀργύρῳ ἢ λίθῳ,
[1]we [2]ought to suppose *that* [6]gold [7]or [8]silver [9]or [10]stone,

the foreigners who were there spent their time in nothing else but either to tell or to hear some new thing.
22 Then Paul stood in the midst of the Areopagus and said, "Men of Athens, I perceive that in all things you are very religious;
23 "for as I was passing through and considering the objects of your worship, I even found an altar with this inscription:

TO THE UNKNOWN GOD.

Therefore, the One whom you worship without knowing, Him I proclaim to you:
24 "God, who made the world and everything in it, since He is Lord of heaven and earth, does not dwell in temples made with hands.
25 "Nor is He worshiped with men's hands, as though He needed anything, since He gives to all life, breath, and all things.
26 "And He has made from one blood every nation of men to dwell on all the face of the earth, and has determined their preappointed times and the boundaries of their dwellings,
27 "so that they should seek the Lord, in the hope that they might grope for Him and find Him, though He is not far from each one of us;
28 "for in Him we live and move and have our being, as also some of your own poets have said, 'For we are also His offspring.'
29 "Therefore, since we are the offspring of God, we ought not to think that the Divine Nature is like gold or silver or

[d](**17:25**) NU reads *ανθρωπινων, human.* [e](**17:26**) NU omits *αιματος, blood.* [f](**17:27**) NU reads *Θεον, God.*

***(17:27)** *ψηλαφάω (psēlaphaō).* Verb meaning *touch, handle, feel about for, grope after,* referring here to people's efforts to "feel about for" God in hopes of finding Him. In other instances (Luke 24:39; 1 John 1:1; Heb. 12:18) the touching indicates contact with physical substance.

stone, something shaped by art
and man's devising.
30 "Truly, these times of ignorance God overlooked, but
now commands all men everywhere to repent,
31 "because He has appointed
a day on which He will judge the
world in righteousness by the
Man whom He has ordained.
He has given assurance of this
to all by raising Him from the
dead."
32 And when they heard of
the resurrection of the dead,
some mocked, while others
said, "We will hear you again on
this *matter.*"
33 So Paul departed from
among them.
34 However, some men
joined him and believed, among
them Dionysius the Areopagite,
a woman named Damaris, and
others with them.
18 After these things Paul
departed from Athens
and went to Corinth.
2 And he found a certain Jew
named Aquila, born in Pontus,
who had recently come from Italy with his wife Priscilla (because Claudius had commanded
all the Jews to depart from
Rome); and he came to them.
3 So, because he was of the
same trade, he stayed with
them and worked; for by occu-
pation they were tentmakers.

χαράγματι τέχνης καὶ ἐνθυμήσεως ἀνθρώπου, τὸ θεῖον
[11]in [12]an [13]image [14]of [15]skill [16]and [17]reflection [18]of [19]man, [1]the [2]Deity
shaped by

εἶναι ὅμοιον. **30** Τοὺς μὲν οὖν χρόνους τῆς ἀγνοίας
[3]to [4]be [5]like. [3]the [1]So [2]then times - of ignorance
is

ὑπεριδὼν ὁ Θεός, τὰ νῦν παραγγέλλει τοῖς ἀνθρώποις πᾶσι
overlooking ˜ - God, the now He commands - men ˜ all
overlooked but

πανταχοῦ μετανοεῖν, **31** διότι ἔστησεν ἡμέραν ἐν ᾗ
everywhere to repent, because He appointed a day in which
has appointed

μέλλει κρίνειν τὴν οἰκουμένην ἐν δικαιοσύνῃ ἐν ἀνδρὶ ᾧ
He is going to judge the world in righteousness by a man whom

ὥρισε, πίστιν παρασχὼν πᾶσιν, ἀναστήσας αὐτὸν ἐκ
He appointed, [3]proof [1]having [2]given to all, *by* raising Him from
ordained,

νεκρῶν."
the dead."

32 Ἀκούσαντες δὲ ἀνάστασιν νεκρῶν, οἱ μὲν
hearing ˜ But *the* resurrection of *the* dead, the *ones* -
when they heard about some

ἐχλεύαζον, οἱ δὲ εἶπον, "Ἀκουσόμεθά σου πάλιν περὶ
were scoffing, [2]the [3]*ones* [1]but said, "We will hear you again about
others

τούτου." **33** Καὶ οὕτως ὁ Παῦλος ἐξῆλθεν ἐκ μέσου αὐτῶν.
this." And thus - Paul went forth from midst ˜ their.

34 Τινὲς δὲ ἄνδρες κολληθέντες αὐτῷ, ἐπίστευσαν, ἐν
some ˜ But men being joined to him, believed, among
were and believed

οἷς καὶ Διονύσιος ὁ Ἀρεοπαγίτης καὶ γυνὴ ὀνόματι
whom *were* also Dionysius the Areopagite and a woman by name
named

Δάμαρις καὶ ἕτεροι σὺν αὐτοῖς.
Damaris and others with them.

Paul Ministers in Corinth

18 **1** Μετὰ δὲ ταῦτα χωρισθεὶς ὁ Παῦλος ἐκ τῶν
after ˜ Now these *things* having departed - [3]Paul [1]from -

Ἀθηνῶν ἦλθεν εἰς Κόρινθον. **2** Καὶ εὑρών τινα Ἰουδαῖον
[2]Athens came to Corinth. And finding certain ˜ a Jew
he found

ὀνόματι Ἀκύλαν, Ποντικὸν τῷ γένει, προσφάτως ἐληλυθότα
by name Aquila, from Pontus - by people, recently having come
named a native of Pontus,

ἀπὸ τῆς Ἰταλίας, καὶ Πρίσκιλλαν γυναῖκα αὐτοῦ, διὰ τὸ
from - Italy, and Priscilla wife ˜ his, because of -
because

τεταχέναι Κλαύδιον χωρίζεσθαι πάντας τοὺς Ἰουδαίους
[2]to [3]have [4]ordered [1]Claudius [8]to [9]depart [5]all [6]the [7]Jews
had

ἐκ τῆς Ῥώμης, προσῆλθεν αὐτοῖς, **3** καὶ διὰ τὸ
from - Rome, he came to them, and because of -
and because

ὁμότεχνον εἶναι, ἔμενε παρ' αὐτοῖς καὶ
[3]practicing [4]the [5]same [6]trade [1]to [2]be, he remained with them and
he was,

εἰργάζετο· ἦσαν γὰρ σκηνοποιοὶ* τὴν τέχνην.
worked; [2]they [3]were [1]for tentmakers - *by* trade.

*(18:3) σκηνοποιός (*skēnopoios*). Noun occurring only here in the NT, meaning *tentmaker,* a compound of σκῆνος, *tent,* and ποιέω, *make, do.* Paul's trade as a tentmaker may have derived from his rearing in Tarsus of Cilicia where the cloth of goat's hair used in making tents was a main product.

4 Διελέγετο δὲ ἐν τῇ συναγωγῇ κατὰ πᾶν
[2]he [3]was [4]discussing [1]And in the synagogue according to every
debating each

σάββατον, ἔπειθέ τε Ἰουδαίους καὶ Ἕλληνας.
Sabbath, [2]he [3]was [4]persuading [1]and Jews and Greeks.
Sabbath,

5 Ὡς δὲ κατῆλθον ἀπὸ τῆς Μακεδονίας ὅ τε Σιλᾶς
when ˜ Now [5]came [6]down [7]from - [8]Macedonia - [1]both [2]Silas

καὶ ὁ Τιμόθεος, συνείχετο τῷ Πνεύματι[a] ὁ Παῦλος,
[3]and - [4]Timothy, [10]was [11]absorbed [12]in [13]the [14]Spirit - [9]Paul,

διαμαρτυρόμενος τοῖς Ἰουδαίοις τὸν Χριστὸν Ἰησοῦν.
solemnly bearing witness to the Jews *that* [3]the [4]Christ [1]Jesus [2]*is.*
Messiah

6 Ἀντιτασσομένων δὲ αὐτῶν καὶ βλασφημούντων,
opposing But them and blaspheming,
But because they were opposing

ἐκτιναξάμενος τὰ ἱμάτια εἶπε πρὸς αὐτούς, "Τὸ αἷμα ὑμῶν
having shaken off the clothes he said to them, - "blood ˜ Your *be*
he shook off his and

ἐπὶ τὴν κεφαλὴν ὑμῶν· καθαρὸς ἐγώ· ἀπὸ τοῦ νῦν εἰς τὰ
on - head ˜ your; [3]clean [1]I [2]*am;* from the now [4]to [5]the
innocent now on

ἔθνη πορεύσομαι." 7 Καὶ μεταβὰς ἐκεῖθεν ἦλθεν εἰς
[6]Gentiles [1]I [2]will [3]go." And having gone over from there he went into

οἰκίαν τινὸς ὀνόματι[b] Ἰούστου, σεβομένου τὸν Θεόν,
the house of a certain *one* by name Justus, worshiping - God,
named who worshiped

οὗ ἡ οἰκία ἦν συνομοροῦσα τῇ συναγωγῇ. 8 Κρίσπος δὲ
whose - house was being next door to the synagogue. Crispus ˜ And

ὁ ἀρχισυνάγωγος ἐπίστευσε τῷ Κυρίῳ σὺν ὅλῳ τῷ
the synagogue leader believed in the Lord together with all -

οἴκῳ αὐτοῦ, καὶ πολλοὶ τῶν Κορινθίων ἀκούοντες
household ˜ his, and many of the Corinthians hearing
when they heard

ἐπίστευον καὶ ἐβαπτίζοντο.
were believing and were being baptized.

9 Εἶπε δὲ ὁ Κύριος δι' ὁράματος ἐν νυκτὶ τῷ Παύλῳ,
[4]said [1]Now [2]the [3]Lord by a vision in *the* night - to Paul,

"Μὴ φοβοῦ, ἀλλὰ λάλει καὶ μὴ σιωπήσῃς, 10 διότι
"not ˜ Do be afraid, but speak and not ˜ do keep silent, because

ἐγώ εἰμι μετὰ σοῦ καὶ οὐδεὶς ἐπιθήσεταί σοι τοῦ κακῶσαί σε,
I am with you and no one will attack you - to harm you,

διότι λαός ἐστί μοι πολὺς ἐν τῇ πόλει ταύτῃ."
because a [2]people [3]is [4]to [5]me [1]much in - city ˜ this."
I have many people

11 Ἐκάθισέ τε ἐνιαυτὸν καὶ μῆνας ἓξ διδάσκων ἐν
[2]he [3]settled [4]*there* [1]And a year and months ˜ six teaching [5]among

αὐτοῖς τὸν λόγον τοῦ Θεοῦ.
[6]them [1]the [2]word - [3]of [4]God.

12 Γαλλίωνος δὲ ἀνθυπατεύοντος τῆς Ἀχαΐας,
Gallio ˜ Now being proconsul - of Achaia,
Now while Gallio was

κατεπέστησαν ὁμοθυμαδὸν οἱ Ἰουδαῖοι τῷ Παύλῳ καὶ
[6]rose [7]up [8]against [3]with [4]one [5]purpose [1]the [2]Jews - Paul and

ἤγαγον αὐτὸν ἐπὶ τὸ βῆμα, 13 λέγοντες ὅτι "Παρὰ
brought him before the judicial bench, saying - "[8]contrary [9]to

4 And he reasoned in the synagogue every Sabbath, and persuaded both Jews and Greeks.
5 When Silas and Timothy had come from Macedonia, Paul was compelled by the Spirit, and testified to the Jews *that* Jesus *is* the Christ.
6 But when they opposed him and blasphemed, he shook *his* garments and said to them, "Your blood *be* upon your *own* heads; I *am* clean. From now on I will go to the Gentiles."
7 And he departed from there and entered the house of a certain *man* named Justus, *one* who worshiped God, whose house was next door to the synagogue.
8 Then Crispus, the ruler of the synagogue, believed on the Lord with all his household. And many of the Corinthians, hearing, believed and were baptized.
9 Now the Lord spoke to Paul in the night by a vision, "Do not be afraid, but speak, and do not keep silent;
10 "for I am with you, and no one will attack you to hurt you; for I have many people in this city."
11 And he continued *there* a year and six months, teaching the word of God among them.
12 When Gallio was proconsul of Achaia, the Jews with one accord rose up against Paul and brought him to the judgment seat,
13 saying, "This *fellow* per-

a(18:5) NU reads λογω, *(absorbed in) the word.*
b(18:7) NU adds Τιτιου, *Titius.*

suades men to worship God contrary to the law."
14 And when Paul was about to open *his* mouth, Gallio said to the Jews, "If it were a matter of wrongdoing or wicked crimes, O Jews, there would be reason why I should bear with you.
15 "But if it is a question of words and names and your own law, look *to it* yourselves; for I do not want to be a judge of such *matters.*"
16 And he drove them from the judgment seat.
17 Then all the Greeks took Sosthenes, the ruler of the synagogue, and beat *him* before the judgment seat. But Gallio took no notice of these things.
18 So Paul still remained a good while. Then he took leave of the brethren and sailed for Syria, and Priscilla and Aquila *were* with him. He had *his* hair cut off at Cenchrea, for he had taken a vow.
19 And he came to Ephesus, and left them there; but he himself entered the synagogue and reasoned with the Jews.
20 When they asked *him* to stay a longer time with them, he did not consent,
21 but took leave of them, saying, "I must by all means keep this coming feast in Jerusalem; but I will return again to

τὸν νόμον οὗτος ἀναπείθει τοὺς ἀνθρώπους σέβεσθαι τὸν
[10]the [11]law [1]This [2]*man* [3]persuades - [4]men [5]to [6]worship -

Θεόν."
[7]God."

14 Μέλλοντος δὲ τοῦ Παύλου ἀνοίγειν τὸ στόμα, εἶπεν ὁ
being about And - Paul to open the mouth, said ~ -
And when Paul was about his

Γαλλίων πρὸς τοὺς Ἰουδαίους, "Εἰ μὲν οὖν ἦν ἀδίκημά τι
Gallio to the Jews, "If - then it was misdeed ~ some

ἢ ῥᾳδιούργημα πονηρόν, ὦ Ἰουδαῖοι, κατὰ λόγον ἂν
or crime ~ wicked, O Jews, according to reason -

ἠνεσχόμην ὑμῶν· **15** εἰ δὲ ζήτημά ἐστι περὶ λόγου
I would bear with you; if ~ but [3]a [4]question [1]it [2]is about a word
accept your complaint; issue

καὶ ὀνομάτων καὶ νόμου τοῦ καθ' ὑμᾶς, ὄψεσθε
and names and law the *one* according to you, see *to it*
your own law,

αὐτοί· κριτὴς γὰρ ἐγὼ τούτων οὐ βούλομαι
yourselves; [8]a [9]judge [1]for [2]I [10]of [11]these [12]*things* [4]not [3]do [5]wish

εἶναι." **16** Καὶ ἀπήλασεν αὐτοὺς ἀπὸ τοῦ βήματος.
[6]to [7]be." And he drove away ~ them from the judicial bench.

17 Ἐπιλαβόμενοι δὲ πάντες οἱ Ἕλληνες[c] Σωσθένην τὸν
[5]taking [6]hold [7]of [1]And [2]all [3]the [4]Greeks Sosthenes the
took

ἀρχισυνάγωγον ἔτυπτον ἔμπροσθεν τοῦ βήματος. Καὶ
synagogue leader were beating *him* before the judicial bench. And
and beat

οὐδὲν τούτων τῷ Γαλλίωνι ἔμελλεν.
none of these *things* - [4]to [5]Gallio [1]was [2]a [3]concern.

Paul Returns to Antioch in Syria

18 Ὁ δὲ Παῦλος ἔτι προσμείνας ἡμέρας ἱκανάς,
- Now Paul still remaining *there* days ~ considerable,
remained there a good while,

τοῖς ἀδελφοῖς ἀποταξάμενος, ἐξέπλει εἰς τὴν Συρίαν, καὶ
[3]to [4]the [5]brothers [1]bidding [2]farewell, sailed away for - Syria, and
then bid farewell to the brothers, and

σὺν αὐτῷ Πρίσκιλλα καὶ Ἀκύλας, κειράμενος τὴν
together with him Priscilla and Aquila, having cut the
his

κεφαλὴν ἐν Κεγχρεαῖς, εἶχε γὰρ εὐχήν. **19** Κατήντησε[d]
head in Cenchrea, [2]he [3]had [1]for a vow. [2]he [3]arrived
hair had taken

δὲ εἰς Ἔφεσον, καὶ ἐκείνους κατέλιπεν αὐτοῦ, αὐτὸς δὲ
[1]And in Ephesus, and [3]those [4]*two* [1]he [2]left there, he ~ but

εἰσελθὼν εἰς τὴν συναγωγὴν διελέχθη τοῖς Ἰουδαίοις.
having entered into the synagogue discussed with the Jews.
debated

20 Ἐρωτώντων δὲ αὐτῶν ἐπὶ πλείονα χρόνον μεῖναι παρ'
asking And them [3]for [4]more [5]time [1]to [2]remain with
And when they asked him a longer

αὐτοῖς,[e] οὐκ ἐπένευσεν, **21** ἀλλ' ἀπετάξατο αὐτοῖς εἰπών,
them, [3]not [1]he [2]did consent, but bid farewell to them saying,

"Δεῖ[f] με πάντως τὴν ἑορτὴν τὴν ἐρχομένην
"It is necessary *for* me by all means [3]the [4]feast [5]the [6]*one* [7]coming
"I must which is

ποιῆσαι εἰς Ἱεροσόλυμα. Πάλιν δὲ ἀνακάμψω πρὸς ὑμᾶς,
[1]to [2]make in Jerusalem. [5]again [1]But [2]I [3]will [4]return to you,
keep

---

[c](18:17) NU omits οι Ελληνες, *the Greeks.*
[d](18:19) NU reads Κατηντησαν, *they came.*
[e](18:20) NU omits παρ αυτοις, *with them.*
[f](18:21) NU omits Δει . . . Ιεροσολυμα, *It is neccessary (for) . . . Jerusalem.*

τοῦ Θεοῦ θέλοντος." Καὶ ἀνήχθη ἀπὸ τῆς Ἐφέσου. 22 Καὶ
- God willing." And he put to sea from - Ephesus. And
if God wills."

κατελθὼν εἰς Καισάρειαν, ἀναβὰς καὶ
having gone down to Caesarea, *and* having gone up and

ἀσπασάμενος τὴν ἐκκλησίαν, κατέβη εἰς Ἀντιόχειαν.
having greeted the church, he went down to Antioch.

23 Καὶ ποιήσας χρόνον τινὰ ἐξῆλθε, διερχόμενος
And having done time ˜ some *there* he went out, going through
spent

καθεξῆς τὴν Γαλατικὴν χώραν καὶ Φρυγίαν, ἐπιστηρίζων
in order the Galatian region and Phrygian *region,* strengthening

πάντας τοὺς μαθητάς.
all the disciples.

Apollos Preaches in Ephesus

24 Ἰουδαῖος δέ τις Ἀπολλὼς ὀνόματι, Ἀλεξανδρεὺς τῷ
[2]a [4]Jew [1]Now [3]certain Apollos by name, an Alexandrian -
named Apollos, a native of

γένει, ἀνὴρ λόγιος, κατήντησεν εἰς Ἔφεσον, δυνατὸς
by people, a(n) man ˜ eloquent, arrived in Ephesus, mighty ˜
Alexandria, had arrived

ὢν ἐν ταῖς Γραφαῖς. 25 Οὗτος ἦν κατηχημένος τὴν
being in the Scriptures. This *man* was instructed *in* the
had been

ὁδὸν τοῦ Κυρίου, καὶ ζέων* τῷ Πνεύματι ἐλάλει
way of the Lord, and being fervent in the Spirit he was speaking

καὶ ἐδίδασκεν ἀκριβῶς τὰ περὶ τοῦ Κυρίου,[g]
and teaching accurately the *things* about the Lord,

ἐπιστάμενος μόνον τὸ βάπτισμα Ἰωάννου. 26 Οὗτός τε
knowing only the baptism of John. [2]this [3]*man* [1]And
although he knew

ἤρξατο παρρησιάζεσθαι ἐν τῇ συναγωγῇ. Ἀκούσαντες δὲ
began to speak boldly in the synagogue. hearing And
And when Aquila

αὐτοῦ Ἀκύλας καὶ Πρίσκιλλα, προσελάβοντο αὐτὸν καὶ
him Aquila and Priscilla, they took aside ˜ him and
and Priscilla heard him,

ἀκριβέστερον αὐτῷ ἐξέθεντο τὴν τοῦ Θεοῦ ὁδόν.
[4]more [5]accurately [2]to [3]him [1]explained the - [2]of [3]God [1]way.

27 Βουλομένου δὲ αὐτοῦ διελθεῖν εἰς τὴν Ἀχαΐαν,
desiring And him to go across to - Achaia,
And when he desired

προτρεψάμενοι οἱ ἀδελφοὶ ἔγραψαν τοῖς μαθηταῖς
having urged *him* on the brothers wrote to the disciples *there*

ἀποδέξασθαι αὐτόν· ὃς παραγενόμενος συνεβάλετο πολὺ
to receive him; who arriving assisted much
when he arrived greatly

τοῖς πεπιστευκόσιν διὰ τῆς χάριτος· 28 εὐτόνως γὰρ
with the *ones* having believed by - grace; [4]vigorously [1]for
with those who had

τοῖς Ἰουδαίοις διακατηλέγχετο δημοσίᾳ, ἐπιδεικνὺς διὰ τῶν
[6]the [7]Jews [2]he [3]was [5]refuting publicly, demonstrating by the

Γραφῶν εἶναι τὸν Χριστὸν Ἰησοῦν.
Scriptures *that* [2]to [3]be [4]the [5]Christ [1]Jesus.
was Messiah

you, God willing." And he sailed from Ephesus.
22 And when he had landed at Caesarea, and gone up and greeted the church, he went down to Antioch.
23 After he had spent some time *there,* he departed and went over the region of Galatia and Phrygia in order, strengthening all the disciples.
24 Now a certain Jew named Apollos, born at Alexandria, an eloquent man *and* mighty in the Scriptures, came to Ephesus.
25 This man had been instructed in the way of the Lord; and being fervent in spirit, he spoke and taught accurately the things of the Lord, though he knew only the baptism of John.
26 So he began to speak boldly in the synagogue. When Aquila and Priscilla heard him, they took him aside and explained to him the way of God more accurately.
27 And when he desired to cross to Achaia, the brethren wrote, exhorting the disciples to receive him; and when he arrived, he greatly helped those who had believed through grace;
28 for he vigorously refuted the Jews publicly, showing from the Scriptures that Jesus is the Christ.

---

[g](**18:25**) NU reads Ιησου, *Jesus.*

***(18:25)** *ζέω (zeō).* Verb literally meaning *boil,* used only twice in the NT with the figurative meaning *be fervent.* Both times it is linked with "in spirit" or "in the Spirit" and so refers to spiritual fervor or warmth and thus to zeal (here and Rom. 12:11). Cf. the cognate adjective *ζεστός, boiling, hot,* used only in Rev. 3:15, 16 of the spiritual condition that the Lord recommended to the Laodiceans.

19 And it happened, while
Apollos was at Cor-
inth, that Paul, having passed
through the upper regions,
came to Ephesus. And finding
some disciples
2 he said to them, "Did you
receive the Holy Spirit when
you believed?" So they said to
him, "We have not so much as
heard whether there is a Holy
Spirit."
3 And he said to them, "Into
what then were you baptized?"
So they said, "Into John's baptism."
4 Then Paul said, "John indeed baptized with a baptism of
repentance, saying to the people that they should believe on
Him who would come after him,
that is, on Christ Jesus."
5 When they heard *this*, they
were baptized in the name of
the Lord Jesus.
6 And when Paul had laid
hands on them, the Holy Spirit
came upon them, and they
spoke with tongues and prophesied.
7 Now the men were about
twelve in all.
8 And he went into the synagogue and spoke boldly for
three months, reasoning and
persuading concerning the
things of the kingdom of God.
9 But when some were hardened and did not believe, but
spoke evil of the Way before
the multitude, he departed from
them and withdrew the disci-

Paul Instructs Twelve Disciples of John

19 1 Ἐγένετο δὲ ἐν τῷ τὸν Ἀπολλῶ εἶναι ἐν
[2]it [3]came [4]about [1]And in - - Apollos to be in
while was

Κορίνθῳ, Παῦλον διελθόντα τὰ ἀνωτερικὰ μέρη ἐλθεῖν
Corinth, Paul having gone through the interior parts to come
that Paul, regions came

εἰς Ἔφεσον, καὶ εὑρῶν τινας μαθητὰς 2 εἶπε πρὸς αὐτούς, "Εἰ
to Ephesus, and finding some disciples said to them, "If
"Did

Πνεῦμα Ἅγιον ἐλάβετε πιστεύσαντες?"
[3]*the* [5]Spirit [4]Holy [1]you [2]received having believed?"
you receive

Οἱ δὲ εἶπον πρὸς αὐτόν, "Ἀλλ' οὐδὲ εἰ
[2]the [3]*ones* [1]But said to him, "But [3]not [4]even [6]whether
they even heard

Πνεῦμα Ἅγιόν ἐστιν ἠκούσαμεν."
[9]a [11]Spirit [10]Holy [7]*there* [8]is [1]we [2]did [5]hear."
we have not."

3 Εἶπέ τε πρὸς αὐτούς, "Εἰς τί οὖν ἐβαπτίσθητε?"
[2]he [3]said [1]And to them, "Into what then were you baptized?"

Οἱ δὲ εἶπον, "Εἰς τὸ Ἰωάννου βάπτισμα."
[2]the [3]*ones* [1]And said, "Into the [2]of [3]John [1]baptism."
they

4 Εἶπε δὲ Παῦλος, "Ἰωάννης μὲν ἐβάπτισε βάπτισμα
[3]said [1]But [2]Paul, "John - baptized with a baptism

μετανοίας, τῷ λαῷ λέγων εἰς τὸν ἐρχόμενον μετ'
of repentance, [2]to [3]the [4]people [1]saying [9]in [10]the [11]*One* [12]coming [13]after

αὐτὸν ἵνα πιστεύσωσι, τοῦτ' ἔστιν, εἰς τὸν Χριστὸν[a]
[14]him [5]that [6]they [7]should [8]believe, that is, in - Christ

Ἰησοῦν." 5 Ἀκούσαντες δὲ ἐβαπτίσθησαν εἰς τὸ ὄνομα
Jesus." hearing ˜ And they were baptized in the name
when they heard this,

τοῦ Κυρίου Ἰησοῦ. 6 Καὶ ἐπιθέντος αὐτοῖς τοῦ Παύλου τὰς
of the Lord Jesus. And placing on them - Paul the
when Paul laid on them his

χεῖρας, ἦλθε τὸ Πνεῦμα τὸ Ἅγιον ἐπ' αὐτούς, ἐλάλουν τε
hands, [4]came [1]the [3]Spirit - [2]Holy upon them, [2]they [3]spoke [1]and

γλώσσαις καὶ προεφήτευον. 7 Ἦσαν δὲ οἱ πάντες ἄνδρες
in tongues and prophesied. [5]were [1]Now [3]the [2]all [4]men
totaled

ὡσεὶ δεκαδύο.
about twelve.

Paul Preaches Two Years in Ephesus

8 Εἰσελθὼν δὲ εἰς τὴν συναγωγὴν ἐπαρρησιάζετο, ἐπὶ
entering ˜ And into the synagogue he was speaking boldly, for
he entered and spoke

μῆνας τρεῖς διαλεγόμενος καὶ πείθων τὰ περὶ τῆς
months ˜ three discussing and persuading the *things* concerning the
debating

βασιλείας τοῦ Θεοῦ. 9 Ὡς δὲ τινες ἐσκληρύνοντο καὶ
kingdom - of God. when ˜ But some became hardened and

ἠπείθουν, κακολογοῦντες τὴν Ὁδὸν ἐνώπιον τοῦ πλήθους,
disobedient, speaking against the Way before the multitude,
disbelieving,

ἀποστὰς ἀπ' αὐτῶν ἀφώρισε τοὺς μαθητάς, καθ'
withdrawing from them he separated the disciples, according to
he withdrew and each

---

[a](19:4) NU omits Χριστον, *Christ.*

ἡμέραν διαλεγόμενος ἐν τῇ σχολῇ Τυράννου τινός.
a day discussing in the school of a Tyrannus ~ certain.
day debating

10 Τοῦτο δὲ ἐγένετο ἐπὶ ἔτη δύο, ὥστε πάντας τοὺς
this ~ Now took place for years ~ two, so that all the *ones*
who were

κατοικοῦντας τὴν Ἀσίαν ἀκοῦσαι τὸν λόγον τοῦ Κυρίου
dwelling in - Asia to hear the word of the Lord
heard

Ἰησοῦ,[b] Ἰουδαίους τε καὶ Ἕλληνας.
Jesus, Jews ~ both and Greeks.

Miracles Magnify the Name of Jesus

11 Δυνάμεις τε οὐ τὰς τυχούσας ἐποίει ὁ Θεὸς
[5]miracles [1]And [6]not [7]the [8]common [9]*ones* [3]was [4]doing - [2]God
which were extraordinary

διὰ τῶν χειρῶν Παύλου, 12 ὥστε καὶ ἐπὶ τοὺς
by the hands of Paul, so that even [10]to [11]the [12]*ones*
those who

ἀσθενοῦντας ἐπιφέρεσθαι ἀπὸ τοῦ χρωτὸς αὐτοῦ σουδάρια ἢ
[13]being [14]sick [7]to [8]be [9]bringing [2]from - [4]skin [3]his [1]facecloths [5]or
were were brought

σιμικίνθια, καὶ ἀπαλλάσσεσθαι ἀπ' αὐτῶν τὰς νόσους, τά
[6]aprons, and [3]to [4]be [5]leaving [6]from [7]them [1]the [2]diseases, the ~
left,

τε πνεύματα τὰ πονηρὰ ἐξέρχεσθαι ἀπ' αὐτῶν.
and spirits ~ - unclean to be going out from them.
went

13 Ἐπεχείρησαν δέ τινες ἀπὸ τῶν περιερχομένων Ἰουδαίων
[9]attempted [1]But [2]some [3]from [4]the [5]going [6]about [7]Jewish
itinerant

ἐξορκιστῶν ὀνομάζειν ἐπὶ τοὺς ἔχοντας τὰ πνεύματα τὰ
[8]exorcists to name [7]over [8]the [9]*ones* [10]having [11]the [13]spirits -

πονηρὰ τὸ ὄνομα* τοῦ Κυρίου Ἰησοῦ, λέγοντες,
[12]evil [1]the [2]name [3]of [4]the [5]Lord [6]Jesus, saying,

"Ὁρκίζομεν[c] ὑμᾶς τὸν Ἰησοῦν ὃν ὁ Παῦλος κηρύσσει."
"We adjure you - *by* Jesus whom - Paul preaches."

14 Ἦσαν δέ τινες υἱοὶ Σκευᾶ Ἰουδαίου ἀρχιερέως ἑπτὰ
[2]*there* [3]were [1]Now some sons of Sceva a Jewish high priest seven

οἱ τοῦτο ποιοῦντες.
the *ones* this ~ doing.
who were

15 Ἀποκριθὲν δὲ τὸ πνεῦμα τὸ πονηρὸν εἶπε "Τὸν
[5]answering [1]But [2]the [4]spirit - [3]evil said -
answered and

Ἰησοῦν γινώσκω καὶ τὸν Παῦλον ἐπίσταμαι, ὑμεῖς δὲ
"Jesus I know and - Paul I am acquainted with, [4]you [1]but

τίνες ἐστέ?" 16 Καὶ ἐφαλλόμενος ἐπ' αὐτοὺς ὁ ἄνθρωπος
[2]who [3]are?" And [9]leaping [10]upon [11]them [1]the [2]man
lept

ἐν ᾧ ἦν τὸ πνεῦμα τὸ πονηρόν, καὶ κατακυριεύσαν[d]
[3]in [4]whom [5]was [6]the [8]spirit - [7]evil, and having subdued

αὐτῶν ἴσχυσε κατ' αὐτῶν, ὥστε γυμνοὺς καὶ
them prevailed against them, so that [3]naked [4]and

τετραυματισμένους ἐκφυγεῖν ἐκ τοῦ οἴκου ἐκείνου. 17 Τοῦτο
[5]having [6]been [7]wounded [1]to [2]flee from - house ~ that. this ~
they fled

ples, reasoning daily in the school of Tyrannus.
10 And this continued for two years, so that all who dwelt in Asia heard the word of the Lord Jesus, both Jews and Greeks.
11 Now God worked unusual miracles by the hands of Paul,
12 so that even handkerchiefs or aprons were brought from his body to the sick, and the diseases left them and the evil spirits went out of them.
13 Then some of the itinerant Jewish exorcists took it upon themselves to call the name of the Lord Jesus over those who had evil spirits, saying, "We exorcise you by the Jesus whom Paul preaches."
14 Also there were seven sons of Sceva, a Jewish chief priest, who did so.
15 And the evil spirit answered and said, "Jesus I know, and Paul I know; but who are you?"
16 Then the man in whom the evil spirit was leaped on them, overpowered them, and prevailed against them, so that they fled out of that house naked and wounded.
17 This became known both

[b]**(19:10)** NU omits Ιησου, *Jesus.* [c]**(19:13)** NU reads Ορκιζω, *I adjure.* [d]**(19:16)** NU, TR read *κατακυριευσας, overpowering* (modifying the man rather than the evil spirit); NU adds *αμφοτερων, (overpowering) all (of them).*

***(19:13)** *ὄνομα (onoma).* The common NT noun meaning *name,* used most often of one's personal name. While that is the meaning here, the exorcists used Jesus' name as representing the power associated with it (cf. Acts 4:7; 16:18). The ancients took seriously the idea that one's name represented his/her person and/or character. Indeed *ὄνομα* can equal *person,* as in Acts 1:15; Rev. 3:4. Especially when used of God or Christ, it suggests His identity and all that He represents; thus one may "bear His name" (as Acts 9:15) or "call on His name" (James 5:14). The phrase "in the name of" is an idiomatic expression meaning *by the authority of. ὄνομα* may also mean *reputation* (as Mark

to all Jews and Greeks dwelling
in Ephesus; and fear fell on
them all, and the name of the
Lord Jesus was magnified.
18 And many who had be-
lieved came confessing and telling their deeds.
19 Also, many of those who
had practiced magic brought
their books together and
burned *them* in the sight of all.
And they counted up the value
of them, and *it* totaled fifty
thousand *pieces* of silver.
20 So the word of the Lord
grew mightily and prevailed.
21 When these things were
accomplished, Paul purposed in
the Spirit, when he had passed
through Macedonia and Achaia,
to go to Jerusalem, saying, "After I have been there, I must
also see Rome."
22 So he sent into Macedonia
two of those who ministered to
him, Timothy and Erastus, but
he himself stayed in Asia for a
time.
23 And about that time there
arose a great commotion about
the Way.
24 For a certain man named
Demetrius, a silversmith, who
made silver shrines of Diana,

δὲ ἐγένετο γνωστὸν πᾶσιν Ἰουδαίοις τε καὶ Ἕλλησι τοῖς
Now became known to all Jews ˜ both and Greeks the *ones*
who were

κατοικοῦσι τὴν Ἔφεσον, καὶ ἐπέπεσε φόβος ἐπὶ πάντας
dwelling in - Ephesus, and fell ˜ fear upon all ˜

αὐτούς, καὶ ἐμεγαλύνετο τὸ ὄνομα τοῦ Κυρίου Ἰησοῦ.
them, and they were praising the name of the Lord Jesus.

18 Πολλοί τε τῶν πεπιστευκότων ἤρχοντο
many ˜ And of the *ones* having believed were coming
those who had

ἐξομολογούμενοι καὶ ἀναγγέλλοντες τὰς πράξεις αὐτῶν.
confessing and disclosing - actions ˜ their.
evil deeds

19 Ἱκανοὶ δὲ τῶν τὰ
[2]a [3]considerable [4]*number* [1]And of the *ones* [2]the [3]*things*
those who were

περίεργα πραξάντων συνενέγκαντες τὰς βίβλους
[4]belonging [5]to [6]magic [1]practicing bringing together the books
practicing magic brought together their

κατέκαιον ἐνώπιον πάντων· καὶ συνεψήφισαν τὰς τιμὰς
were burning them up before all; and they counted up the prices
and burnt totaled

αὐτῶν καὶ εὗρον ἀργυρίου μυριάδας πέντε.
of them and found *it to be* [4]*pieces* [5]of [6]silver [2]ten [3]thousands [1]five.
fifty thousand.

20 Οὕτω κατὰ κράτος ὁ λόγος τοῦ Κυρίου ηὔξανε καὶ
Thus toward power the word of the Lord was growing and
powerfully

ἴσχυεν.
becoming mighty.

Demetrius Foments the Ephesian Riot

21 Ὡς δὲ ἐπληρώθη ταῦτα, ἔθετο ὁ Παῦλος ἐν
when ˜ Now [3]were [4]fulfilled [1]these [2]*things,* resolved ˜ - Paul in

τῷ Πνεύματι, διελθὼν τὴν Μακεδονίαν καὶ Ἀχαΐαν,
the Spirit, having gone through - Macedonia and Achaia,

πορεύεσθαι εἰς Ἱερουσαλήμ, εἰπὼν ὅτι "Μετὰ τὸ γενέσθαι με
to go to Jerusalem, saying - "After - to be me
I have been

ἐκεῖ, δεῖ με καὶ Ῥώμην ἰδεῖν." **22** Ἀποστείλας
there, it is necessary *for* me also [3]Rome [1]to [2]see." [2]having [3]sent

δὲ εἰς τὴν Μακεδονίαν δύο τῶν διακονούντων αὐτῷ,
[1]And to - Macedonia two of the *ones* ministering to him,
those who were

Τιμόθεον καὶ Ἔραστον, αὐτὸς ἐπέσχε χρόνον εἰς τὴν
Timothy and Erastus, himself ˜ he stayed on *for* a time in -

Ἀσίαν.
Asia.

23 Ἐγένετο δὲ κατὰ τὸν καιρὸν ἐκεῖνον τάραχος οὐκ
[2]*there* [3]arose [1]Now during - time ˜ that [4]disturbance [1]not
a

ὀλίγος περὶ τῆς Ὁδοῦ. **24** Δημήτριος γάρ τις
[2]a [3]small concerning the Way. [7]Demetrius [1]For [2]a [3]certain [4]*man*
serious

ὀνόματι, ἀργυροκόπος, ποιῶν ναοὺς ἀργυροῦς Ἀρτέμιδος,
[5]by [6]name, a silversmith, making shrines ˜ silver of Artemis,
named, who made

6:14). Cf. the cognate verb *ὀνομάζω, name, give a name, call by name.*

παρείχετο τοῖς τεχνίταις ἐργασίαν οὐκ ὀλίγην, 25 οὓς
was getting for the craftsmen [4]trade [1]not [2]a [3]little, whom
a large amount of,

συναθροίσας, καὶ τοὺς περὶ τὰ τοιαῦτα ἐργάτας, εἶπεν,
gathering, and the [2]with - [3]such [4]*trades* [1]workers, said,
he gathered, and said,

"Ἄνδρες, ἐπίστασθε ὅτι ἐκ ταύτης τῆς ἐργασίας ἡ εὐπορία
"Men, you know that [4]from [5]this - [6]trade - [2]prosperity

ἡμῶν ἐστι. 26 Καὶ θεωρεῖτε καὶ ἀκούετε ὅτι οὐ μόνον
[1]our [3]is. And you observe and hear that not only

Ἐφέσου ἀλλὰ σχεδὸν πάσης τῆς Ἀσίας ὁ Παῦλος οὗτος
of Ephesus but almost of all - Asia - Paul ~ this
in in

πείσας μετέστησεν ἱκανὸν ὄχλον, λέγων ὅτι οὐκ
having persuaded turned away a considerable crowd, saying that [3]not
has persuaded and

εἰσὶ θεοὶ οἱ διὰ χειρῶν γινόμενοι. 27 Οὐ μόνον
[1]they [2]are gods the *ones* by *human* hands being produced. [2]not [3]only
which are made by human hands.

δὲ τοῦτο κινδυνεύει ἡμῖν τὸ μέρος εἰς ἀπελεγμὸν ἐλθεῖν,
[1]And this ~ is [4]in [5]danger [2]to [3]us - [1]part [8]to [9]disrepute [6]to [7]come,
business of ours

ἀλλὰ καὶ τὸ τῆς μεγάλης θεᾶς ἱερὸν Ἀρτέμιδος εἰς
but also the [2]of [3]the [4]great [5]goddess [1]temple Artemis [4]for
as

οὐθὲν λογισθῆναι, μέλλειν δὲ καὶ καθαιρεῖσθαι
[5]nothing [1]to [2]be [3]considered, [10]to [11]be [12]about [6]and [7]also [13]to [14]be [15]destroyed
will

τὴν μεγαλειότητα[e] αὐτῆς, ἣν ὅλη ἡ Ἀσία καὶ ἡ
- [9]magnificence [8]her, *she* whom all - Asia and the

οἰκουμένη σέβεται."
world worships."

28 Ἀκούσαντες δὲ καὶ γενόμενοι πλήρεις θυμοῦ,
hearing ~ And and becoming full of anger,
And when they heard, they became

ἔκραζον λέγοντες, "Μεγάλη ἡ Ἄρτεμις Ἐφεσίων!"
they were crying out saying, "Great *is* - Artemis of *the* Ephesians!"
and cried

29 Καὶ ἐπλήσθη ἡ πόλις ὅλη[f] τῆς συγχύσεως,
And [4]was [5]filled [6]with [1]the [3]city [2]whole the confusion,

ὥρμησάν τε ὁμοθυμαδὸν εἰς τὸ θέατρον, συναρπάσαντες
[2]they [3]rushed [1]and with one purpose into the theater, having seized

Γάϊον καὶ Ἀρίσταρχον Μακεδόνας, συνεκδήμους Παύλου.
Gaius and Aristarchus Macedonians, traveling companions of Paul.

30 Τοῦ δὲ Παύλου βουλομένου εἰσελθεῖν εἰς τὸν
- Now Paul desiring to enter into the
when Paul desired

δῆμον, οὐκ εἴων αὐτὸν οἱ μαθηταί.
popular assembly, [4]not [3]were [5]permitting [6]him [1]the [2]disciples.
people, would not permit

31 Τινὲς δὲ καὶ τῶν Ἀσιαρχῶν, ὄντες αὐτῷ φίλοι,
[3]some [1]And [2]also of the Asiarchs, being [2]with [3]him [1]friends,
officials of Asia,

πέμψαντες πρὸς αὐτόν, παρεκάλουν μὴ δοῦναι ἑαυτὸν εἰς
sending to him, were urging *him* not to present himself in
sent word and urged

τὸ θέατρον. 32 Ἄλλοι μὲν οὖν ἄλλο τι
the theater. others ~ - Then [5]different [4]something

ἔκραζον, ἦν γὰρ ἡ ἐκκλησία συγκεχυμένη, καὶ οἱ
[1]were [2]calling [3]out, [9]was [6]for [7]the [8]assembly confused, and the

brought no small profit to the
craftsmen.
25 He called them together
with the workers of similar oc-
cupation, and said: "Men, you
know that we have our prosperity by this trade.
26 "Moreover you see and
hear that not only at Ephesus,
but throughout almost all Asia,
this Paul has persuaded and
turned away many people, saying that they are not gods which
are made with hands.
27 "So not only is this trade of
ours in danger of falling into dis-
repute, but also the temple of
the great goddess Diana may
be despised and her magnificence destroyed, whom all Asia
and the world worship."
28 Now when they heard *this,*
they were full of wrath and
cried out, saying, "Great *is* Diana of the Ephesians!"
29 So the whole city was filled
with confusion, and rushed into
the theater with one accord,
having seized Gaius and Aristarchus, Macedonians, Paul's
travel companions.
30 And when Paul wanted to
go in to the people, the disciples would not allow him.
31 Then some of the officials
of Asia, who were his friends,
sent to him pleading that he
would not venture into the theater.
32 Some therefore cried one
thing and some another, for the
assembly was confused, and

[e](**19:27**) NU reads της μεγαλειοτητος, *(she be destroyed) from her magnificence.*
[f](**19:29**) NU omits ολη, *whole.*

most of them did not know why
they had come together.
33 And they drew Alexander
out of the multitude, the Jews
putting him forward. And Alexander motioned with his hand,
and wanted to make his defense
to the people.
34 But when they found out
that he was a Jew, all with one
voice cried out for about two
hours, "Great *is* Diana of the
Ephesians!"
35 And when the city clerk
had quieted the crowd, he said:
"Men of Ephesus, what man is
there who does not know that
the city of the Ephesians is
temple guardian of the great
goddess Diana, and of the *image* which fell down from Zeus?
36 "Therefore, since these
things cannot be denied, you
ought to be quiet and do nothing rashly.
37 "For you have brought
these men here who are neither robbers of temples nor
blasphemers of your goddess.
38 "Therefore, if Demetrius
and his fellow craftsmen have a
case against anyone, the courts
are open and there are procon-
suls. Let them bring charges
against one another.
39 "But if you have any other
inquiry to make, it shall be determined in the lawful assembly.
40 "For we are in danger of
being called in question for today's uproar, there being no
reason which we may give to
account for this disorderly gathering."
41 And when he had said
these things, he dismissed the
assembly.

πλείους οὐκ ᾔδεισαν τίνος ἕνεκεν συνεληλύθεισαν.
majority not ˜ did know of what on account of they had come together.
for what reason

33 Ἐκ δὲ τοῦ ὄχλου προεβίβασαν[g] Ἀλέξανδρον,
from ˜ And the crowd they brought forward Alexander,

προβαλόντων αὐτὸν τῶν Ἰουδαίων. Ὁ δὲ Ἀλέξανδρος,
[3]putting [5]forward [4]him [1]the [2]Jews. - And Alexander,

κατασείσας τὴν χεῖρα, ἤθελεν ἀπολογεῖσθαι τῷ
motioning *with* the hand, desired to make a defense to the
motioned his and desired

δήμῳ. 34 Ἐπιγνόντες δὲ ὅτι Ἰουδαῖός ἐστι, φωνὴ
popular assembly. recognizing ˜ But that [3]a [4]Jew [1]he [2]is, [8]voice
people. was,

ἐγένετο μία ἐκ πάντων ὡς ἐπὶ ὥρας δύο κραζόντων,
[5]*there* [6]arose [7]one from *them* all as for hours ˜ two calling out,

"Μεγάλη ἡ Ἄρτεμις Ἐφεσίων!"
"Great *is* - Artemis of *the* Ephesians!"

35 Καταστείλας δὲ ὁ γραμματεὺς τὸν ὄχλον φησίν,
[2]having [3]quieted [1]And [6]the [7]city [8]clerk [4]the [5]crowd said,

"Ἄνδρες Ἐφέσιοι, τίς γάρ ἐστιν ἄνθρωπος ὃς οὐ
"Men Ephesians, what ˜ for [2]is [3]*there* [1]man who not ˜

γινώσκει τὴν Ἐφεσίων πόλιν νεωκόρον οὖσαν
does know *that* the [2]of [3]*the* [4]Ephesians [1]city [6]*the* [7]temple [8]keeper [5]being
is

τῆς μεγάλης θεᾶς[h] Ἀρτέμιδος καὶ τοῦ Διοπετοῦς?
of the great goddess Artemis and of the *image* fallen from heaven?

36 Ἀναντιρρήτων οὖν ὄντων τούτων, δέον
[5]undeniable [1]Therefore [4]being [2]these [3]*things*, [8]necessary [9]*for*
since these things are,

ἐστὶν ὑμᾶς κατεσταλμένους ὑπάρχειν καὶ μηδὲν προπετὲς
[6]it [7]is you [3]quieted [1]to [2]be and [3]nothing [4]rash

πράσσειν. 37 Ἠγάγετε γὰρ τοὺς ἄνδρας τούτους, οὔτε
[1]to [2]do. [2]you [3]brought [1]For - men ˜ these, neither

ἱεροσύλους οὔτε βλασφημοῦντας τὴν θεὸν ὑμῶν.[i] 38 Εἰ
temple thieves nor *ones* blaspheming - goddess ˜ your. If
blasphemers of

μὲν οὖν Δημήτριος καὶ οἱ σὺν αὐτῷ τεχνῖται ἔχουσι πρός
- then Demetrius and the [2]with [3]him [1]craftsmen have [3]against

τινα λόγον, ἀγοραῖοι ἄγονται, καὶ ἀνθύπατοί εἰσιν·
[4]anyone [1]a [2]word, *the* courts lead, and [3]proconsuls [1]*there* [2]are;
complaint, are in session,

ἐγκαλείτωσαν ἀλλήλοις. 39 Εἰ δέ τι περὶ
let them accuse one another. if ˜ But [6]anything [7]about
bring charges against

ἑτέρων ἐπιζητεῖτε, ἐν τῇ ἐννόμῳ ἐκκλησίᾳ
[8]other [9]*matters* [1]you [2]are [3]wanting [4]to [5]know, [14]by [15]the [16]lawful [17]assembly

ἐπιλυθήσεται. 40 Καὶ γὰρ κινδυνεύομεν ἐγκαλεῖσθαι
[10]it [11]will [12]be [13]determined. [3]also [1]For [2]we are in danger to be accused
of being

στάσεως περὶ τῆς σήμερον, μηδενὸς αἰτίου ὑπάρχοντος
of a riot concerning - today, [3]no [4]cause [1]*there* [2]being

περὶ οὗ οὐ δυνησόμεθα δοῦναι λόγον τῆς
[6]about [7]which [5]not we will be able to give a word -
for at all an explanation

συστροφῆς ταύτης." 41 Καὶ ταῦτα εἰπών, ἀπέλυσε
of commotion ˜ this." And [3]these [4]*things* [1]having [2]said, he dismissed

τὴν ἐκκλησίαν.
the assembly.

---

[g](19:33) NU reads *συνεβίβασαν, instructed.*
[h](19:35) NU omits *θεας, goddess.*
[i](19:37) NU reads *ημων, our.*

Paul Travels in Greece

20 1 Μετὰ δὲ τὸ παύσασθαι τὸν θόρυβον,
after ~ Now - [3]to [4]cease [1]the [2]disturbance,
had ceased

προσκαλεσάμενος ὁ Παῦλος τοὺς μαθητὰς καὶ[a] ἀσπασάμενος,
summoning ~ - Paul the disciples and greeting *them,*
summoned greeted them and

ἐξῆλθε πορευθῆναι εἰς τὴν Μακεδονίαν. 2 Διελθὼν δὲ
went out to go to - Macedonia. [2]going [3]through [1]And
when he had gone

τὰ μέρη ἐκεῖνα καὶ παρακαλέσας αὐτοὺς λόγῳ πολλῷ,
- parts ~ those and encouraging them with word ~ much,
encouraged many words,

ἦλθεν εἰς τὴν Ἑλλάδα. 3 Ποιήσας τε μῆνας τρεῖς,
he came to - Greece. [2]having [3]made [1]And months ~ three *there,*
spent

γενομένης αὐτῷ ἐπιβουλῆς ὑπὸ τῶν Ἰουδαίων μέλλοντι
[3]having [4]become [5]*against* [6]him [1]a [2]plot by the Jews being about
been developed as he was

ἀνάγεσθαι εἰς τὴν Συρίαν, ἐγένετο γνώμη τοῦ
to put to sea for - Syria, [3]came [4]about [1]a [2]decision -
was made

ὑποστρέφειν διὰ Μακεδονίας. 4 Συνείπετο δὲ αὐτῷ
to return through Macedonia. [5]was [6]accompanying [1]And [7]him

ἄχρι τῆς Ἀσίας[b] Σώπατρος[c] Βεροιαῖος, Θεσσαλονικέων
[8]to - [9]Asia [2]Sopater [3]a [4]Berean, [11]of [12]*the* [13]Thessalonians

δὲ Ἀρίσταρχος καὶ Σεκοῦνδος, καὶ Γάϊος Δερβαῖος, καὶ
[10]and Aristarchus and Secundus, and Gaius of Derbe, and

Τιμόθεος, Ἀσιανοὶ δὲ Τυχικὸς καὶ Τρόφιμος. 5 Οὗτοι
Timothy, [2]*the* [3]Asians [1]and Tychichus and Trophimus. These *men*

προσελθόντες ἔμενον ἡμᾶς ἐν Τρῳάδι. 6 Ἡμεῖς δὲ
having gone ahead were waiting for us in Troas. we ~ And

ἐξεπλεύσαμεν μετὰ τὰς ἡμέρας τῶν ἀζύμων ἀπὸ
sailed away after the Days of the Unleavened Bread from

Φιλίππων, καὶ ἤλθομεν πρὸς αὐτοὺς εἰς τὴν Τρῳάδα ἄχρις
Philippi, and we came to them in - Troas within

ἡμερῶν πέντε, οὗ διετρίψαμεν ἡμέρας ἑπτά.
days ~ five, where we spent days ~ seven.

Paul Ministers at Troas

7 Ἐν δὲ τῇ μιᾷ τῶν σαββάτων, συνηγμένων τῶν
on ~ Now the first *day* of the week, being assembled the
when the disciples were

μαθητῶν[d] κλάσαι ἄρτον, ὁ Παῦλος διελέγετο αὐτοῖς,
disciples to break bread, - Paul was discussing with them,
assembled

μέλλων ἐξιέναι τῇ ἐπαύριον, παρέτεινέ τε τὸν λόγον
being about to leave on the next day, [2]he [3]extended [1]and the word
message

μέχρι μεσονυκτίου. 8 Ἦσαν δὲ λαμπάδες
until midnight. [2]*there* [3]were [1]And [8]lamps

ἱκαναὶ ἐν τῷ ὑπερῴῳ οὗ ἦμεν[e]
[4]a [5]considerable [6]*number* [7]*of* in the upper room where we were

συνηγμένοι. 9 Καθήμενος δέ τις νεανίας ὀνόματι
assembled. [9]sitting [1]And [3]certain [2]a [4]young [5]man [6]by [7]name
sat named

Εὔτυχος ἐπὶ τῆς θυρίδος, καταφερόμενος ὕπνῳ βαθεῖ,
[8]Eutychus in the window, being overwhelmed by a sleep ~ deep,

20 After the uproar had
ceased, Paul called the
disciples to *himself,* embraced
them, and departed to go to
Macedonia.
2 Now when he had gone
over that region and encouraged them with many words,
he came to Greece
3 and stayed three months.
And when the Jews plotted
against him as he was about to
sail to Syria, he decided to return through Macedonia.
4 And Sopater of Berea accompanied him to Asia—also
Aristarchus and Secundus of
the Thessalonians, and Gaius of
Derbe, and Timothy, and Tychicus and Trophimus of Asia.
5 These men, going ahead,
waited for us at Troas.
6 But we sailed away from
Philippi after the Days of Unleavened Bread, and in five
days joined them at Troas,
where we stayed seven days.
7 Now on the first *day* of the
week, when the disciples came
together to break bread, Paul,
ready to depart the next day,
spoke to them and continued
his message until midnight.
8 There were many lamps in
the upper room where they
were gathered together.
9 And in a window sat a certain young man named Euty-
chus, who was sinking into a
deep sleep. He was overcome

---

[a](**20:1**) NU adds *παρακαλεσας, after encouraging them.*
[b](**20:4**) NU omits *αχρι της Ασιας, to Asia.*
[c](**20:4**) NU adds *Πυρρου, son of Pyrrhus.*
[d](**20:7**) For *των μαθητων, the disciples,* NU reads *ημων, we.* [e](**20:8**) TR reads *ησαν, they were.*

by sleep; and as Paul continued speaking, he fell down from the third story and was taken up dead.
10 But Paul went down, fell on him, and embracing *him* said, "Do not trouble yourselves, for his life is in him."
11 Now when he had come up, had broken bread and eaten, and talked a long while, even till daybreak, he departed.
12 And they brought the young man in alive, and they were not a little comforted.
13 Then we went ahead to the ship and sailed to Assos, there intending to take Paul on board; for so he had given orders, intending himself to go on foot.
14 And when he met us at Assos, we took him on board and came to Mitylene.
15 We sailed from there, and the next *day* came opposite Chios. The following *day* we arrived at Samos and stayed at Trogyllium. The next *day* we came to Miletus.
16 For Paul had decided to sail past Ephesus, so that he would not have to spend time in Asia; for he was hurrying to be at Jerusalem, if possible, on the Day of Pentecost.

f(20:15) NU omits *και μειναντες εν Τρωγυλλιω, and remaining in Trogyllium.*

διαλεγομένου τοῦ Παύλου ἐπὶ πλεῖον, κατενεχθεὶς
discussing ˜ - Paul for more, having been overwhelmed
while Paul was speaking a while longer,

ἀπὸ τοῦ ὕπνου ἔπεσεν ἀπὸ τοῦ τριστέγου κάτω καὶ ἤρθη
by - sleep he fell [2]from [3]the [4]third [5]story [1]down and was taken up
picked

νεκρός.
dead.

10 *Καταβὰς δὲ ὁ Παῦλος ἐπέπεσεν αὐτῷ, καὶ*
[3]going [4]down [1]But - [2]Paul fell upon him, and
went bent over

συμπεριλαβὼν εἶπε, "Μὴ θορυβεῖσθε, ἡ γὰρ ψυχὴ αὐτοῦ ἐν
embracing *him* said, "not ˜ Do be troubled, - for life ˜ his [2]in

αὐτῷ ἐστιν." **11** *Ἀναβὰς δὲ καὶ κλάσας ἄρτον καὶ*
[3]him [1]is." [2]going [3]up [1]And and breaking bread and
when he had gone broken

γευσάμενος, ἐφ' ἱκανόν τε ὁμιλήσας ἄχρις αὐγῆς,
eating, [3]for [4]a [5]considerable [6]*time* [1]and [2]talking until daybreak,
eaten, talked

οὕτως ἐξῆλθεν. **12** *Ἤγαγον δὲ τὸν παῖδα ζῶντα, καὶ*
thus he departed. [2]they [3]brought [1]And the boy living, and

παρεκλήθησαν οὐ μετρίως.
they were encouraged not moderately.
greatly.

From Troas to Miletus

13 *Ἡμεῖς δέ, προσελθόντες ἐπὶ τὸ πλοῖον, ἀνήχθημεν*
we ˜ Now, having gone ahead on the ship, put to sea

εἰς τὴν Ἄσσον, ἐκεῖθεν μέλλοντες ἀναλαμβάνειν τὸν
for - Assos, from there intending to take [2]on [3]board -

Παῦλον, οὕτω γὰρ ἦν διατεταγμένος, μέλλων αὐτὸς
[1]Paul, thus ˜ for it was arranged, intending himself
had been since he intended to go

πεζεύειν. **14** *Ὡς δὲ συνέβαλεν ἡμῖν εἰς τὴν Ἄσσον,*
to walk. when ˜ And he met us in - Assos,
by land.

ἀναλαβόντες αὐτὸν ἤλθομεν εἰς Μιτυλήνην.
having taken aboard ˜ him we came to Mitylene.

15 *Κἀκεῖθεν ἀποπλεύσαντες, τῇ ἐπιούσῃ κατηντήσαμεν*
And from there having sailed away, on the next *day* we arrived

ἀντικρὺ Χίου, τῇ δὲ ἑτέρᾳ παρεβάλομεν εἰς Σάμον· καὶ
opposite Chios, [2]on [3]the [1]and other *day* we approached to Samos; and
next

μείναντες ἐν Τρωγυλλίῳ,[f] *τῇ ἐχομένῃ ἤλθομεν εἰς*
remaining in Trogyllium, on the following *day* we came to
remained

Μίλητον. **16** *Ἔκρινε γὰρ ὁ Παῦλος παραπλεῦσαι τὴν*
Miletus. [3]decided [1]For - [2]Paul to sail by -
had decided

Ἔφεσον, ὅπως μὴ γένηται αὐτῷ
Ephesus, in order that [3]not [1]it [2]might happen to him
develop that he would have

χρονοτριβῆσαι ἐν τῇ Ἀσίᾳ, ἔσπευδε γάρ, εἰ δυνατὸν
to spend time in - Asia, [2]he [3]was [4]hurrying [1]for, if [3]possible

ἦν αὐτῷ, τὴν ἡμέραν τῆς Πεντηκοστῆς γενέσθαι εἰς
[1]it [2]was for him, [5]*for* [6]the [7]Day - [8]of [9]Pentecost [1]to [2]be [3]in

Ἱεροσόλυμα.
[4]Jerusalem.

Paul Exhorts the Ephesian Elders

17 Ἀπὸ δὲ τῆς Μιλήτου πέμψας εἰς Ἔφεσον
from ~ Now - Miletus having sent to Ephesus

μετεκαλέσατο τοὺς πρεσβυτέρους τῆς ἐκκλησίας. **18** Ὡς
he summoned the elders of the church. when ~

δὲ παρεγένοντο πρὸς αὐτόν, εἶπεν αὐτοῖς, "Ὑμεῖς
And they were present with him, he said to them, "You

ἐπίστασθε ἀπὸ πρώτης ἡμέρας ἀφ' ἧς ἐπέβην εἰς τὴν
know from *the* first day from which I arrived in -

Ἀσίαν, πῶς μεθ' ὑμῶν τὸν πάντα χρόνον ἐγενόμην,
Asia, how [3]with [4]you [5]the [6]all [7]time [1]I [2]was,
whole

19 δουλεύων τῷ Κυρίῳ μετὰ πάσης ταπεινοφροσύνης* καὶ
serving the Lord with all humility and

πολλῶν δακρύων καὶ πειρασμῶν τῶν συμβάντων μοι ἐν
many tears and trials the *ones* happening to me by
which happened

ταῖς ἐπιβουλαῖς τῶν Ἰουδαίων· **20** ὡς οὐδὲν ὑπεστειλάμην
the plots of the Jews; how [4]nothing [1]I [2]drew [3]back
I did not shrink from

τῶν συμφερόντων τοῦ μὴ ἀναγγεῖλαι ὑμῖν καὶ
of the *things* profiting *you* - not to declare to you and
declaring to you any of the things profitable to you or from

διδάξαι ὑμᾶς δημοσίᾳ καὶ κατ' οἴκους,
to teach you publicly and according to houses,
teaching from house to house,

21 διαμαρτυρόμενος Ἰουδαίοις τε καὶ Ἕλλησι τὴν
solemnly bearing witness [2]to [3]Jews [1]both and to Greeks *about* the

εἰς τὸν Θεὸν μετάνοιαν καὶ πίστιν τὴν εἰς τὸν Κύριον
[2]toward - [3]God [1]repentance and *the* faith - toward - Lord ~

ἡμῶν Ἰησοῦν.[g] **22** Καὶ νῦν ἰδού, ἐγὼ δεδεμένος τῷ
our Jesus. And now behold, I having been bound in the
my

πνεύματι πορεύομαι εἰς Ἱερουσαλήμ, τὰ ἐν αὐτῇ
spirit am going to Jerusalem, [3]the [4]*things* [7]in [8]it
that will happen

συναντήσοντά μοι μὴ εἰδώς, **23** πλὴν ὅτι τὸ Πνεῦμα τὸ
[5]meeting [6]me [1]not [2]knowing, except that the Spirit ~ -
to me there

Ἅγιον κατὰ πόλιν διαμαρτύρεται λέγον ὅτι δεσμά
Holy according to a city is solemnly bearing witness saying that bonds
in each city

με καὶ θλίψεις μένουσιν. **24** Ἀλλ' οὐδενὸς
[6]me [1]and [2]tribulations [3]are [4]waiting [5]for [7]*there.* But [6]of [7]nothing
I count

λόγον ποιοῦμαι, οὐδὲ ἔχω τὴν ψυχήν μου τιμίαν
[4]an [5]account [1]I [2]make [3]myself, nor do I have - life ~ my *as* valuable
myself as nothing, regard

ἐμαυτῷ,[h] ὡς τελειῶσαι τὸν δρόμον μου μετὰ χαρᾶς,[i]
to myself, so to complete - course ~ my with joy,
in order that I may

καὶ τὴν διακονίαν ἣν ἔλαβον παρὰ τοῦ Κυρίου Ἰησοῦ
and the ministry which I received from the Lord Jesus

διαμαρτύρασθαι τὸ εὐαγγέλιον τῆς χάριτος τοῦ Θεοῦ.
to bear solemn testimony to the gospel of the grace - of God.

25 "Καὶ νῦν ἰδού, ἐγὼ οἶδα ὅτι οὐκέτι ὄψεσθε τὸ
"And now behold, I know that [14]no [15]longer [13]will [16]see -

πρόσωπόν μου ὑμεῖς πάντες ἐν οἷς διῆλθον
[18]face [17]my [1]you [2]all [3]among [4]whom [5]I [6]passed [7]through

17 From Miletus he sent to Ephesus and called for the elders of the church.
18 And when they had come to him, he said to them: "You know, from the first day that I came to Asia, in what manner I always lived among you,
19 "serving the Lord with all humility, with many tears and trials which happened to me by the plotting of the Jews;
20 "how I kept back nothing that was helpful, but proclaimed it to you, and taught you publicly and from house to house,
21 "testifying to Jews, and also to Greeks, repentance toward God and faith toward our Lord Jesus Christ.
22 "And see, now I go bound in the spirit to Jerusalem, not knowing the things that will happen to me there,
23 "except that the Holy Spirit testifies in every city, saying that chains and tribulations await me.
24 "But none of these things move me; nor do I count my life dear to myself, so that I may finish my race with joy, and the ministry which I received from the Lord Jesus, to testify to the gospel of the grace of God.
25 "And indeed, now I know that you all, among whom I

---

[g](**20:21**) TR adds Χριστον, *Christ.* [h](**20:24**) For Αλλ . . . εμαυτω, *But . . . to myself,* NU reads Αλλ ουδενος λογου ποιουμαι την ψυχην τιμιαν εμαυτω, *But I do not count (my) life of any account (as) valuable to myself.*
[i](**20:24**) NU omits μετα χαρας, *with joy.*

***(20:19)** ταπεινοφροσύνη *(tapeinophrosynē).* Noun meaning *humility,* from ταπεινός, *low, humble,* and φρονέω, *think.* Humility is thus regarding oneself as of less importance both in the sight of God and before others. Consequently, one who is humble is willing to serve. The word is often compared to the synonym πραΰτης, *meekness,* which indicates relating submissively toward God or others as a result of a humble view of oneself. See πραΰτης at 2 Cor. 10:1. The ancient Greeks thought humility indicated a craven or servile spirit, a sense that may be seen in Col. 2:18, 23.

have gone preaching the kingdom of God, will see my face no more.

26 "Therefore I testify to you this day that I *am* innocent of the blood of all *men*.

27 "For I have not shunned to declare to you the whole counsel of God.

28 "Therefore take heed to yourselves and to all the flock, among which the Holy Spirit has made you overseers, to shepherd the church of God which He purchased with His own blood.

29 "For I know this, that after my departure savage wolves will come in among you, not sparing the flock.

30 "Also from among yourselves men will rise up, speaking perverse things, to draw away the disciples after themselves.

31 "Therefore watch, and remember that for three years I did not cease to warn everyone night and day with tears.

32 "So now, brethren, I commend you to God and to the word of His grace, which is able to build you up and give you an inheritance among all those who are sanctified.

33 "I have coveted no one's silver or gold or apparel.

34 "Yes, you yourselves know that these hands have provided for my necessities, and for those who were with me.

35 "I have shown you in every way, by laboring like this, that you must support the weak. And remember the words of the Lord Jesus, that He said, 'It is more blessed to give than to receive.' "

κηρύσσων τὴν βασιλείαν τοῦ Θεοῦ.[j] **26** Διὸ μαρτύρομαι
[8]preaching [9]the [10]kingdom - [11]of [12]God. Therefore I testify

ὑμῖν ἐν τῇ σήμερον ἡμέρᾳ ὅτι καθαρὸς ἐγὼ ἀπὸ τοῦ αἵματος
to you on the today ˜ day that [3]pure [1]I [2]*am* from the blood
this very day innocent

πάντων. **27** Οὐ γὰρ ὑπεστειλάμην τοῦ μὴ ἀναγγεῖλαι ὑμῖν
of all. [4]not [1]For [2]I [3]did draw back - not to declare to you
from declaring

πᾶσαν τὴν βουλὴν τοῦ Θεοῦ. **28** Προσέχετε οὖν
all the counsel - of God. [2]take [3]heed [1]Therefore

ἑαυτοῖς καὶ παντὶ τῷ ποιμνίῳ, ἐν ᾧ ὑμᾶς τὸ Πνεῦμα τὸ
to yourselves and to all the flock, in which [5]you [1]the [3]Spirit -

Ἅγιον ἔθετο ἐπισκόπους, ποιμαίνειν τὴν ἐκκλησίαν τοῦ
[2]Holy [4]set *as* overseers, to shepherd the church of the
bishops,

Κυρίου καὶ[k] Θεοῦ, ἣν περιεποιήσατο διὰ τοῦ ἰδίου
Lord and of God, which He acquired through - His own

αἵματος. **29** Ἐγὼ γὰρ οἶδα τοῦτο, ὅτι εἰσελεύσονται μετὰ τὴν
blood. I ˜ For know this, that [3]will [4]come [5]in [8]after -

ἄφιξίν μου λύκοι βαρεῖς εἰς ὑμᾶς, μὴ φειδόμενοι τοῦ
[10]departure [9]my [2]wolves [1]savage [6]to [7]you, not sparing the

ποιμνίου, **30** καὶ ἐξ ὑμῶν αὐτῶν ἀναστήσονται
flock, and from among you yourselves will arise

ἄνδρες λαλοῦντες διεστραμμένα τοῦ ἀποσπᾶν
men speaking *things* having been distorted - *in order* to draw away

τοὺς μαθητὰς ὀπίσω αὐτῶν. **31** Διὸ γρηγορεῖτε,
the disciples after them. Therefore be alert,

μνημονεύοντες ὅτι τριετίαν νύκτα καὶ ἡμέραν οὐκ
remembering that *for* three years night and day [3]not

ἐπαυσάμην μετὰ δακρύων νουθετῶν ἕνα ἕκαστον.
[1]I [2]did cease with tears exhorting one ˜ each.

32 "Καὶ τὰ νῦν παρατίθεμαι ὑμᾶς, ἀδελφοί,[l] τῷ
"And the *things* now I entrust you, brothers, -
for the present

Θεῷ καὶ τῷ λόγῳ τῆς χάριτος αὐτοῦ τῷ δυναμένῳ
to God and to the word - of grace ˜ His the *one* being able
which is

ἐποικοδομῆσαι καὶ δοῦναι ὑμῖν κληρονομίαν ἐν τοῖς
to build *you* up and to give you an inheritance among [2]the [3]*ones*
those who

ἡγιασμένοις πᾶσιν. **33** Ἀργυρίου ἢ χρυσίου ἢ
[4]having [5]been [6]sanctified [1]all. [3]*the* [4]silver [5]or [6]gold [7]or
have

ἱματισμοῦ οὐδενὸς ἐπεθύμησα. **34** Αὐτοὶ γινώσκετε ὅτι
[8]clothes [9]of [10]no [11]one [1]I [2]desired. yourselves ˜ You know that

ταῖς χρείαις μου καὶ τοῖς οὖσι μετ' ἐμοῦ
- [5]to [7]needs [6]my [8]and [9]to [10]the [11]*ones* [12]being [13]with [14]me
those who were

ὑπηρέτησαν αἱ χεῖρες αὗται. **35** Πάντα ὑπέδειξα ὑμῖν
[3]rendered [4]service - [2]hands [1]these. By all *things* I showed to you
In every way

ὅτι οὕτω κοπιῶντας δεῖ ἀντιλαμβάνεσθαι τῶν
that thus laboring it is necessary to help the *ones*

ἀσθενούντων, μνημονεύειν τε τῶν λόγων τοῦ Κυρίου Ἰησοῦ
being weak, [2]to [3]remember [1]and the words of the Lord Jesus

ὅτι αὐτὸς εἶπε, 'Μακάριόν ἐστι μᾶλλον διδόναι ἢ
that He said, '[4]blessed [1]It [2]is [3]more to give than

λαμβάνειν.' "
to receive.' "

---

[j](**20:25**) NU omits *του Θεου, of God.* [k](**20:28**) NU, TR omit *Κυριου και, the Lord and.* [l](**20:32**) NU omits *αδελφοι, brothers.*

Elsewhere in the NT, however, it is a virtue which makes possible Christian unity. Cf. the cognate adjective *ταπεινόφρων, humble,* used only in 1 Pet. 3:8 (in NU; M, TR have *φιλόφρων*). See *ταπεινόω* at Luke 14:11.

36 Καὶ ταῦτα εἰπών, θεὶς τὰ γόνατα αὐτοῦ,
And [3]these [4]*things* [1]having [2]said, placing - knees ˜ his,
he knelt down,

σὺν πᾶσιν αὐτοῖς προσηύξατο. 37 Ἱκανὸς δὲ
together with all ˜ them he prayed. [4]considerable [1]And
and

ἐγένετο κλαυθμὸς πάντων, καὶ ἐπιπεσόντες ἐπὶ τὸν τράχηλον
[2]*there* [3]was weeping of all, and falling on the neck
by they fell

τοῦ Παύλου κατεφίλουν αὐτόν, 38 ὀδυνώμενοι
- of Paul they were affectionately kissing him, feeling pain
and

μάλιστα ἐπὶ τῷ λόγῳ ᾧ εἰρήκει ὅτι οὐκέτι
most over the word which he had said that [8]no [9]longer
words

μέλλουσι τὸ πρόσωπον αὐτοῦ θεωρεῖν. Προέπεμπον
[1]they [2]are [3]about - [7]face [6]his [4]to [5]see. [11]they [12]accompanied
were

δὲ αὐτὸν εἰς τὸ πλοῖον.
[10]And him to the ship.

Warnings on the Journey to Jerusalem

21 1 Ὡς δὲ ἐγένετο ἀναχθῆναι ἡμᾶς
when ˜ Now it came about to put to sea us
that we had put to sea

ἀποσπασθέντας ἀπ' αὐτῶν, εὐθυδρομήσαντες ἤλθομεν εἰς
having withdrawn from them, running a straight course we came to
we ran a straight course and

τὴν Κῶν, τῇ δὲ ἑξῆς εἰς τὴν Ῥόδον, κἀκεῖθεν εἰς
- Coos, [2]on [3]the [1]and next *day* to - Rhodes, and from there to

Πάταρα· 2 καὶ εὑρόντες πλοῖον διαπερῶν εἰς Φοινίκην,
Patara; and having found a ship crossing over to Phoenicia,

ἐπιβάντες ἀνήχθημεν. 3 Ἀναφάνεντες δὲ τὴν Κύπρον
boarding *it* we put to sea. sighting ˜ And - Cyprus
we boarded it and And when we had sighted

καὶ καταλιπόντες αὐτὴν εὐώνυμον, ἐπλέομεν εἰς Συρίαν, καὶ
and leaving behind ˜ it *on the* left, we sailed to Syria, and
had left it behind

κατήχθημεν εἰς Τύρον, ἐκεῖσε γὰρ ἦν τὸ πλοῖον
we put in to harbor in Tyre, there ˜ for [3]was [1]the [2]ship

ἀποφορτιζόμενον τὸν γόμον. 4 Καὶ ἀνευρόντες μαθητάς,[a]
unloading the cargo. And having discovered disciples,

ἐπεμείναμεν αὐτοῦ ἡμέρας ἑπτά, οἵτινες τῷ Παύλῳ ἔλεγον
we stayed there days ˜ seven, who - [2]to [3]Paul [1]said
they

διὰ τοῦ Πνεύματος μὴ ἀναβαίνειν εἰς Ἱερουσαλήμ. 5 Ὅτε
through the Spirit not to go up to Jerusalem. when ˜

δὲ ἐγένετο ἡμᾶς ἐξαρτίσαι τὰς ἡμέρας, ἐξελθόντες
But it came about us to finish the days *there,* having gone out
that we had completed

ἐπορευόμεθα, προπεμπόντων ἡμᾶς πάντων σὺν
we departed, [4]accompanying [5]us [1]all [2]*of* [3]*them* together with

γυναιξὶ καὶ τέκνοις ἕως ἔξω τῆς πόλεως, καὶ θέντες
their wives and children until *we were* outside the city, and placing
kneeling

τὰ γόνατα ἐπὶ τὸν αἰγιαλὸν προσηυξάμεθα. 6 Καὶ
the knees on the shore we prayed. And

36 And when he had said
these things, he knelt down and
prayed with them all.
37 Then they all wept freely,
and fell on Paul's neck and
kissed him,
38 sorrowing most of all for
the words which he spoke, that
they would see his face no
more. And they accompanied
him to the ship.
21 Now it came to pass,
that when we had de-
parted from them and set sail,
running a straight course we
came to Cos, the following *day*
to Rhodes, and from there to
Patara.
2 And finding a ship sailing
over to Phoenicia, we went
aboard and set sail.
3 When we had sighted Cy-
prus, we passed it on the left,
sailed to Syria, and landed at
Tyre; for there the ship was to
unload her cargo.
4 And finding disciples, we
stayed there seven days. They
told Paul through the Spirit not
to go up to Jerusalem.
5 When we had come to the
end of those days, we departed
and went on our way; and they
all accompanied us, with wives
and children, till *we were* out of
the city. And we knelt down on
the shore and prayed.
6 When we had taken our

[a](21:4) NU adds τους, *the (disciples).*

leave of one another, we
boarded the ship, and they returned home.
7 And when we had finished
our voyage from Tyre, we
came to Ptolemais, greeted the
brethren, and stayed with them
one day.
8 On the next *day* we who
were Paul's companions departed and came to Caesarea,
and entered the house of Philip
the evangelist, who was *one* of
the seven, and stayed with him.
9 Now this man had four virgin daughters who prophesied.
10 And as we stayed many
days, a certain prophet named
Agabus came down from Judea.
11 When he had come to us,
he took Paul's belt, bound his
own hands and feet, and said,
"Thus says the Holy Spirit, 'So
shall the Jews at Jerusalem bind
the man who owns this belt,
and deliver *him* into the hands
of the Gentiles.'"
12 Now when we heard these
things, both we and those from
that place pleaded with him not
to go up to Jerusalem.
13 Then Paul answered,
"What do you mean by weeping
and breaking my heart? For I
am ready not only to be bound,
but also to die at Jerusalem for

ἀσπασάμενοι ἀλλήλους, ἐπέβημεν εἰς τὸ πλοῖον, ἐκεῖνοι
having greeted one another, we went up into the ship, those ˜
boarded they

δὲ ὑπέστρεψαν εἰς τὰ ἴδια.
and returned to - their own *homes.*

7 Ἡμεῖς δέ, τὸν πλοῦν διανύσαντες ἀπὸ Τύρου,
we ˜ Now, [3]the [4]voyage [1]having [2]completed from Tyre,

κατηντήσαμεν εἰς Πτολεμαΐδα, καὶ ἀσπασάμενοι τοὺς
we arrived in Ptolemais, and having greeted the

ἀδελφοὺς ἐμείναμεν ἡμέραν μίαν παρ' αὐτοῖς. 8 Τῇ δὲ
brothers *there* we remained day ˜ one with them. [2]on [3]the [1]But
stayed

ἐπαύριον ἐξελθόντες οἱ περὶ τὸν Παῦλον ἦλθον[b] εἰς
next day [5]going [6]forth [1]the [2]*ones* [3]about - [4]Paul came to
those accompanying Paul went forth and

Καισάρειαν· καὶ εἰσελθόντες εἰς τὸν οἶκον Φιλίππου τοῦ
Caesarea; and entering into the house of Philip the

εὐαγγελιστοῦ, ὄντος ἐκ τῶν ἑπτά, ἐμείναμεν παρ' αὐτῷ.
evangelist, being of the seven, we remained with him.
who was one stayed

9 Τούτῳ δὲ ἦσαν θυγατέρες παρθένοι τέσσαρες
[2]to [3]this [4]*man* [1]And were daughters virgins four
And he had four virgin daughters who

προφητεύουσαι. 10 Ἐπιμενόντων δὲ ἡμῶν ἡμέρας
prophesying. remaining ˜ And us *there* days ˜
prophesied. And while we remained

πλείους, κατῆλθέ τις ἀπὸ τῆς Ἰουδαίας προφήτης
more, [9]came [10]down [2]certain [4]from - [5]Judea [1]a [3]prophet
several,

ὀνόματι Ἄγαβος.
[6]by [7]name [8]Agabus.
named

11 Καὶ ἐλθὼν πρὸς ἡμᾶς καὶ ἄρας τὴν ζώνην τοῦ
And coming to us and taking the belt -
when he came took

Παύλου, δήσας τε αὐτοῦ τοὺς πόδας καὶ τὰς χεῖρας εἶπε,
of Paul, binding ˜ and his - feet and - hands he said,
bound

"Τάδε λέγει τὸ Πνεῦμα τὸ Ἅγιον, 'Τὸν ἄνδρα οὗ
"These *things* [4]says [1]the [3]Spirit - [2]Holy, 'The man whose
"This is what

ἐστιν ἡ ζώνη αὕτη οὕτω δήσουσιν ἐν Ἰερουσαλὴμ οἱ
[3]is - [1]belt [2]this [8]in [9]this [10]way [6]will [7]bind [11]in [12]Jerusalem [4]the

Ἰουδαῖοι καὶ παραδώσουσιν εἰς χεῖρας ἐθνῶν.'"
[5]Jews and they will hand *him* over into *the* hands of *the* Gentiles.'"

12 Ὡς δὲ ἠκούσαμεν ταῦτα, παρεκαλοῦμεν ἡμεῖς τε
when ˜ Now we heard these *things,* [7]urged [2]we [1]both

καὶ οἱ ἐντόπιοι τοῦ μὴ ἀναβαίνειν αὐτὸν εἰς
[3]and [4]the [5]local [6]residents - [9]not [10]to [11]go [12]up [8]him to

Ἰερουσαλήμ.
Jerusalem.

13 Ἀπεκρίθη τε ὁ Παῦλος, "Τί ποιεῖτε κλαίοντες
[3]answered [1]And - [2]Paul, "What are you doing weeping

καὶ συνθρύπτοντές μου τὴν καρδίαν? Ἐγὼ γὰρ οὐ μόνον
and breaking my - heart? I ˜ For [3]not [4]only

δεθῆναι ἀλλὰ καὶ ἀποθανεῖν εἰς Ἰερουσαλὴμ ἑτοίμως ἔχω
[5]to [6]be [7]bound [8]but [9]also [10]to [11]die [12]at [13]Jerusalem [2]ready [1]have
am

---

[b](21:8) NU reads ηλθομεν, *we came,* omitting οι περι τον Παυλον, *those accompanying Paul.*

ὑπὲρ τοῦ ὀνόματος τοῦ Κυρίου Ἰησοῦ."
in behalf of the name of the Lord Jesus."

14 Μὴ πειθομένου δὲ αὐτοῦ, ἡσυχάσαμεν
not being persuaded And him, we were silent
And when he remained unpersuaded,

εἰπόντες, "Τὸ θέλημα τοῦ Κυρίου γενέσθω."
saying, "[2]the [3]will [4]of [5]the [6]Lord [1]Let [7]be [8]done."
and said,

Paul Is Urged to Conciliate His Critics

15 Μετὰ δὲ τὰς ἡμέρας ταύτας ἐπισκευασάμενοι
after ~ Now - days ~ these having prepared

ἀνεβαίνομεν εἰς Ἱερουσαλήμ. 16 Συνῆλθον δὲ καὶ
we went up to Jerusalem. [9]came [10]together [1]And [2]also

τῶν μαθητῶν ἀπὸ Καισαρείας σὺν ἡμῖν, ἄγοντες παρ'
[3]*some* [4]of [5]the [6]disciples [7]from [8]Caesarea with us, bringing *us* [9]with

ᾧ ξενισθῶμεν, Μνάσωνί τινι Κυπρίῳ,
[10]whom [11]we [12]would [13]stay [14]as [15]guest, [1]to [2]Mnason [4]certain [3]a [5]Cypriot,

ἀρχαίῳ μαθητῇ.
[6]an [7]original [8]disciple.
a longstanding

17 Γενομένων δὲ ἡμῶν εἰς Ἱεροσόλυμα, ἀσμένως ἐδέξαντο
arriving And us in Jerusalem, [5]gladly [3]received
And when we arrived

ἡμᾶς οἱ ἀδελφοί. 18 Τῇ δὲ ἐπιούσῃ εἰσῄει ὁ
[4]us [1]the [2]brothers. [2]on [3]the [1]And next day [2]was [3]going [4]in -

Παῦλος σὺν ἡμῖν πρὸς Ἰάκωβον, πάντες τε παρεγένοντο οἱ
[1]Paul with us to James, all ~ and [3]were [4]present [1]the

πρεσβύτεροι. 19 Καὶ ἀσπασάμενος αὐτούς, ἐξηγεῖτο
[2]elders. And having greeted them, he reported

καθ' ἓν ἕκαστον ὧν ἐποίησεν ὁ Θεὸς ἐν
according to one ~ each *the things* which did ~ - God among
one by one had done

τοῖς ἔθνεσι διὰ τῆς διακονίας αὐτοῦ.
the Gentiles through - ministry ~ his.

20 Οἱ δὲ ἀκούσαντες ἐδόξαζον τὸν Κύριον,[c]
- And hearing *this* they were glorifying the Lord,
when they heard

εἰπόντες αὐτῷ, "Θεωρεῖς, ἀδελφέ, πόσαι μυριάδες
saying to him, "You see, brother, how many tens of thousands

εἰσὶν Ἰουδαίων τῶν πεπιστευκότων, καὶ πάντες ζηλωταὶ
there are of Jews the *ones* having believed, and [3]all [4]zealots
who have

τοῦ νόμου ὑπάρχουσι. 21 Κατηχήθησαν δὲ περὶ
[5]of [6]the [7]law [1]they [2]are. [2]they [3]have [4]been [5]informed [1]And about
for

σοῦ ὅτι ἀποστασίαν διδάσκεις ἀπὸ Μωσέως τοὺς κατὰ
you that [4]defection [1]you [2]are [3]teaching from Moses *to* [2]the [4]among

τὰ ἔθνη πάντας Ἰουδαίους, λέγων μὴ περιτέμνειν αὐτοὺς
[5]the [6]Gentiles [1]all [3]Jews, saying [3]not [4]to [5]circumcise [1]*for* [2]them

τὰ τέκνα μηδὲ τοῖς ἔθεσι περιπατεῖν. 22 Τί οὖν ἐστι?
the children nor [3]in [4]the [5]customs [1]to [2]walk. What then is it?
their our

Πάντως δεῖ πλῆθος συνελθεῖν·[d] ἀκούσονται
[3]certainly [1]It [2]is necessary *for* an assembly to come together; [2]they [3]will [4]hear

γὰρ ὅτι ἐλήλυθας. 23 Τοῦτο οὖν ποίησον ὅ σοι
[1]for that you have come. [3]this [1]Therefore [2]do which [3]to [4]you

the name of the Lord Jesus."
14 So when he would not be persuaded, we ceased, saying, "The will of the Lord be done."
15 And after those days we packed and went up to Jerusalem.
16 Also some of the disciples from Caesarea went with us and brought with them a certain Mnason of Cyprus, an early disciple, with whom we were to lodge.
17 And when we had come to Jerusalem, the brethren received us gladly.
18 On the following *day* Paul went in with us to James, and all the elders were present.
19 When he had greeted them, he told in detail those things which God had done among the Gentiles through his ministry.
20 And when they heard *it*, they glorified the Lord. And they said to him, "You see, brother, how many myriads of Jews there are who have believed, and they are all zealous for the law;
21 "but they have been informed about you that you teach all the Jews who are among the Gentiles to forsake Moses, saying that they ought not to circumcise *their* children nor to walk according to the customs.
22 "What then? The assembly must certainly meet, for they will hear that you have come.
23 "Therefore do what we tell

---

[c](**21:20**) NU reads Θεον, *God.* [d](**21.22**) NU omits δει πληθος συνελθειν, *It is necessary for an assembly to come together;* thus reading *They will certainly hear.*

you: We have four men who
have taken a vow.
24 "Take them and be purified
with them, and pay their ex-
penses so that they may shave
their heads, and that all may
know that those things of which
they were informed concerning
you are nothing, but *that* you
yourself also walk orderly and
keep the law.
25 "But concerning the Gentiles who believe, we have written *and* decided that they
should observe no such thing,
except that they should keep
themselves from *things* offered
to idols, from blood, from
things strangled, and from sexual immorality."
26 Then Paul took the men,
and the next day, having been
purified with them, entered the
temple to announce the expira-
tion of the days of purification,
at which time an offering should
be made for each one of them.
27 Now when the seven days
were almost ended, the Jews
from Asia, seeing him in the
temple, stirred up the whole
crowd and laid hands on him,
28 crying out, "Men of Israel,
help! This is the man who
teaches all *men* everywhere
against the people, the law, and
this place; and furthermore he

λέγομεν· εἰσὶν ἡμῖν ἄνδρες τέσσαρες εὐχὴν ἔχοντες
[1]we [2]say: *there* are with us men ˜ four [2]a [3]vow [1]having
who have taken

ἐφ' ἑαυτῶν. **24** Τούτους παραλαβὼν ἁγνίσθητι σὺν αὐτοῖς
upon themselves. these ˜ Taking purify yourself with them
Take them and

καὶ δαπάνησον ἐπ' αὐτοῖς ἵνα ξυρήσωνται τὴν
and pay for them that they may have [3]shaved - [1]the
their

κεφαλήν, καὶ γνῶσι πάντες ὅτι ὧν
[2]head and [2]may [3]know [1]all that *the things* which

κατήχηνται περὶ σοῦ οὐδέν ἐστιν, ἀλλὰ
they have been informed about you nothing ˜ are, but *that*

στοιχεῖς καὶ αὐτὸς τὸν νόμον φυλάσσων.
you are agreeing with and yourself [2]the [3]law [1]keeping.

25 Περὶ δὲ τῶν πεπιστευκότων ἐθνῶν ἡμεῖς
concerning ˜ But the [2]having [3]believed [1]Gentiles we
who have

ἐπεστείλαμεν, κρίναντες μηδὲν τοιοῦτο τηρεῖν αὐτούς, εἰ
wrote, having judged [4]nothing [5]such [2]to [3]keep [1]them, if
that they must keep no such thing,

μὴ [e] φυλάσσεσθαι αὐτοὺς τό τε
not [2]to [3]guard [4]from [1]them [6]the [7]*thing* [5]both
except that they keep themselves from both that which has been

εἰδωλόθυτον καὶ τὸ αἷμα καὶ πνικτὸν καὶ
offered to idols and *from* - blood and *from anything* strangled and

πορνείαν."
from fornication."
sexual immorality."

Paul Is Arrested in the Temple

26 Τότε ὁ Παῦλος παραλαβὼν τοὺς ἄνδρας, τῇ ἐχομένῃ
Then - Paul having taken the men, on the coming

ἡμέρᾳ σὺν αὐτοῖς ἁγνισθεὶς εἰσῄει εἰς τὸ ἱερόν,
day [4]with [5]them [1]having [2]been [3]purified entered into the temple,

διαγγέλλων τὴν ἐκπλήρωσιν τῶν ἡμερῶν τοῦ ἁγνισμοῦ
thus giving notice of the completion of the days of the purification

ἕως οὗ προσηνέχθη ὑπὲρ ἑνὸς ἑκάστου αὐτῶν
until *the time* when [3]was [4]offered [5]in [6]behalf [7]of [9]one [8]each [10]of [11]them

ἡ προσφορά.
[1]the [2]offering.

27 Ὡς δὲ ἔμελλον αἱ ἑπτὰ ἡμέραι συντελεῖσθαι, οἱ
when ˜ Now [4]were [5]about [1]the [2]seven [3]days to be completed, the

ἀπὸ τῆς Ἀσίας Ἰουδαῖοι, θεασάμενοι αὐτὸν ἐν τῷ ἱερῷ,
[2]from - [3]Asia [1]Jews, seeing him in the temple,
when they saw

συνέχεον πάντα τὸν ὄχλον καὶ ἐπέβαλον τὰς χεῖρας ἐπ'
were stirring up all the crowd and put the hands on
their

αὐτόν, **28** κράζοντες, "Ἄνδρες Ἰσραηλῖται, βοηθεῖτε! Οὗτός
him, crying out, "Men Israelites, help! This

ἐστιν ὁ ἄνθρωπος ὁ κατὰ τοῦ λαοῦ καὶ τοῦ νόμου καὶ
is the man the *one* against the people and the law and
who

τοῦ τόπου τούτου πάντας πανταχοῦ διδάσκων, ἔτι τε καὶ
- place ˜ this [3]all [4]*people* [5]everywhere [1]*is* [2]teaching, yet ˜ and [3]also
further

---

[e]**(21:25)** NU omits *μηδεν τοιουτο τηρειν αυτους, ει μη, that they must keep no such thing, except.*

Ἕλληνας εἰσήγαγεν εἰς τὸ ἱερὸν καὶ κεκοίνωκεν τὸν
[5]Greeks [1]he [2]has [4]brought into the temple and has made common -
ceremonially impure

ἅγιον τόπον τοῦτον!" 29 Ἦσαν γὰρ ἑωρακότες[f] Τρόφιμον
[2]holy [3]place [1]this!" [2]they [3]were [1]For having seen Trophimus
had seen

τὸν Ἐφέσιον ἐν τῇ πόλει σὺν αὐτῷ, ὃν ἐνόμιζον ὅτι εἰς
the Ephesian in the city with him, whom they supposed that [4]into

τὸ ἱερὸν εἰσήγαγεν ὁ Παῦλος. 30 Ἐκινήθη τε ἡ πόλις
[5]the [6]temple [2]had [3]brought - [1]Paul. [5]was [6]aroused [1]And [2]the [4]city

ὅλη καὶ ἐγένετο συνδρομὴ τοῦ λαοῦ, καὶ ἐπιλαβόμενοι
[3]whole and *there* was a running together of the people, and taking hold
mob forming they seized

τοῦ Παύλου εἷλκον αὐτὸν ἔξω τοῦ ἱεροῦ, καὶ
- of Paul they were dragging him outside the temple, and
Paul and

εὐθέως ἐκλείσθησαν αἱ θύραι. 31 Ζητούντων δὲ αὐτὸν
immediately [3]were [4]shut [1]the [2]doors. seeking ˜ And [3]him

ἀποκτεῖναι, ἀνέβη φάσις τῷ χιλιάρχῳ τῆς σπείρης ὅτι
[1]to [2]kill, [6]went [7]up [4]a [5]report to the chiliarch of the cohort that
commander garrison

ὅλη συγκέχυται Ἰερουσαλήμ, 32 ὃς ἐξαυτῆς
whole [2]has [3]been [4]stirred [5]up [1]Jerusalem, who immediately
all had

παραλαβὼν στρατιώτας καὶ ἑκατοντάρχους, κατέδραμεν
having taken along soldiers and centurions, ran down

ἐπ' αὐτούς· οἱ δέ, ἰδόντες τὸν χιλίαρχον καὶ τοὺς
among them; - and, seeing the chiliarch and the
when they saw commander

στρατιώτας, ἐπαύσαντο τύπτοντες τὸν Παῦλον. 33 Ἐγγίσας
soldiers, they stopped beating - Paul. [4]approaching
approached

δὲ ὁ χιλίαρχος ἐπελάβετο αὐτοῦ καὶ ἐκέλευσε δεθῆναι
[1]And [2]the [3]chiliarch took hold of him and ordered *him* to be bound
commander that he

ἁλύσεσι δυσί, καὶ ἐπυνθάνετο τίς ἂν εἴη καὶ τί
with chains ˜ two, and he was inquiring who - he might be and what

ἐστι πεποιηκώς. 34 Ἄλλοι δὲ ἄλλο τι ἐβόων
he is having done. others ˜ But [8]other [9]*thing* [7]some [4]were [5]crying [6]out
had

ἐν τῷ ὄχλῳ· μὴ δυνάμενος δὲ γνῶναι τὸ ἀσφαλὲς
[1]among [2]the [3]crowd; [11]not [12]being [13]able [10]and to learn the certain *thing*
and because he was unable truth

διὰ τὸν θόρυβον, ἐκέλευσεν ἄγεσθαι αὐτὸν εἰς τὴν
because of the noise, he commanded [2]to [3]be [4]brought [1]him into the
that he be brought

παρεμβολήν. 35 Ὅτε δὲ ἐγένετο ἐπὶ τοὺς ἀναβαθμούς,
barracks. when ˜ But he arrived at the stairs,

συνέβη βαστάζεσθαι αὐτὸν ὑπὸ τῶν στρατιωτῶν διὰ
it happened [2]to [3]be [4]carried [1]him by the soldiers because of
that he was being carried

τὴν βίαν τοῦ ὄχλου. 36 Ἠκολούθει γὰρ τὸ πλῆθος τοῦ
the force of the crowd. [7]was [8]following [1]For [2]the [3]multitude [4]of [5]the
violence

λαοῦ κρᾶζον, "Αἶρε αὐτόν!"
[6]people calling out, "Take away ˜ him!"

also brought Greeks into the temple and has defiled this holy place."
29 (For they had previously seen Trophimus the Ephesian with him in the city, whom they supposed that Paul had brought into the temple.)
30 And all the city was disturbed; and the people ran together, seized Paul, and dragged him out of the temple; and immediately the doors were shut.
31 Now as they were seeking to kill him, news came to the commander of the garrison that all Jerusalem was in an uproar.
32 He immediately took soldiers and centurions, and ran down to them. And when they saw the commander and the soldiers, they stopped beating Paul.
33 Then the commander came near and took him, and commanded *him* to be bound with two chains; and he asked who he was and what he had done.
34 And some among the multitude cried one thing and some another. So when he could not ascertain the truth because of the tumult, he commanded him to be taken into the barracks.
35 When he reached the stairs, he had to be carried by the soldiers because of the violence of the mob.
36 For the multitude of the people followed after, crying out, "Away with him!"

---

f(**21:29**) NU, TR read *προεωρακοτες*, *having previously seen.*

37 Then as Paul was about to
be led into the barracks, he said
to the commander, "May I
speak to you?" He replied,
"Can you speak Greek?
38 "Are you not the Egyptian
who some time ago stirred up a
rebellion and led the four thousand assassins out into the wilderness?"
39 But Paul said, "I am a Jew
from Tarsus, in Cilicia, a citizen
of no mean city; and I implore
you, permit me to speak to the
people."
40 So when he had given him
permission, Paul stood on the
stairs and motioned with his
hand to the people. And when
there was a great silence, he
spoke to *them* in the Hebrew
language, saying,
22 "Brethren and fathers,
hear my defense be-
fore you now."
2 And when they heard that
he spoke to them in the Hebrew language, they kept all
the more silent. Then he said:
3 "I am indeed a Jew, born in
Tarsus of Cilicia, but brought
up in this city at the feet of Gamaliel, taught according to the
strictness of our fathers' law,
and was zealous toward God as
you all are today.
4 "I persecuted this Way to

[g](21:37) NU, TR add τι, *(to say) something.*

Paul Addresses the Jerusalem Mob

37 Μέλλων τε εἰσάγεσθαι εἰς τὴν παρεμβολὴν ὁ
[2]being [3]about [1]And to be led into the barracks -

Παῦλος λέγει τῷ χιλιάρχῳ, "Εἰ ἔξεστί μοι εἰπεῖν[g]
Paul says to the chiliarch, "If it is permitted for me to speak
said commander, "Is it

πρὸς σέ?"
to you?"

Ὁ δὲ ἔφη, "Ἑλληνιστὶ γινώσκεις? **38** Οὐκ ἄρα σὺ
- And he said, "[4]Greek [1]Do [2]you [3]know? [3]not [4]then [2]you

εἶ ὁ Αἰγύπτιος ὁ πρὸ τούτων τῶν ἡμερῶν
[1]Are the Egyptian the *one* [3]before [4]these - [5]days
who

ἀναστατώσας καὶ ἐξαγαγὼν εἰς τὴν ἔρημον τοὺς
[1]rising [2]up and leading forth into the wilderness the
rose led

τετρακισχιλίους ἄνδρας τῶν σικαρίων?"
four thousand men of the assassins?"

39 Εἶπε δὲ ὁ Παῦλος, "Ἐγὼ ἄνθρωπος μέν εἰμι Ἰουδαῖος,
[3]said [1]But - [2]Paul, "I [2]a [3]man - [1]am a Jew,

Ταρσεὺς τῆς Κιλικίας, οὐκ ἀσήμου πόλεως πολίτης·
from Tarsus - of Cilicia, [5]not [3]of [4]a(n) [6]obscure [7]city [1]a [2]citizen;

δέομαι δέ σου, ἐπίτρεψόν μοι λαλῆσαι πρὸς τὸν λαόν."
[9]I [10]request [8]and of you, permit me to speak to the people."

40 Ἐπιτρέψαντος δὲ αὐτοῦ, ὁ Παῦλος ἑστὼς ἐπὶ τῶν
permitting ˜ And him, - Paul standing on the
stood

ἀναβαθμῶν κατέσεισε τῇ χειρὶ τῷ λαῷ· πολλῆς
steps motioned with the hand to the people; much ˜
his and when

δὲ σιγῆς γενομένης, προσεφώνησε τῇ Ἑβραΐδι
and silence taking place, he addressed *them* in the Hebrew
there was a great silence,

διαλέκτῳ λέγων,
language saying,

22 **1** "Ἄνδρες ἀδελφοὶ καὶ πατέρες, ἀκούσατέ μου τῆς
"Men brothers and fathers, hear [2]my -

πρὸς ὑμᾶς νυνὶ ἀπολογίας."
[4]to [5]you [1]now [3]defense."

2 Ἀκούσαντες δὲ ὅτι τῇ Ἑβραΐδι διαλέκτῳ
hearing ˜ And that in the Hebrew language
when they heard

προσεφώνει αὐτοῖς, μᾶλλον παρέσχον ἡσυχίαν.
he is addressing them, [4]more [1]they [2]granted [3]*him* silence.
was they were all the more silent.

Καὶ φησίν,
And he said,

3 "Ἐγὼ μέν εἰμι ἀνὴρ Ἰουδαῖος, γεγεννημένος ἐν Ταρσῷ
"I - am a man a Jew, having been born in Tarsus

τῆς Κιλικίας, ἀνατεθραμμένος δὲ ἐν τῇ πόλει ταύτῃ,
- of Cilicia, [2]having [3]been [4]brought [5]up [1]but in - city ˜ this,

παρὰ τοὺς πόδας Γαμαλιήλ, πεπαιδευμένος κατὰ
at the feet of Gamaliel, having been educated according to

ἀκρίβειαν τοῦ πατρῴου νόμου, ζηλωτὴς ὑπάρχων τοῦ
the exactness of the [2]of [3]our [4]forefathers [1]law, [6]a [7]zealot [5]being -

Θεοῦ, καθὼς πάντες ὑμεῖς ἐστε σήμερον· **4** ὃς ταύτην τὴν
of God, just as all ˜ you are today; *I* who [2]this -
for

Ὁδὸν ἐδίωξα ἄχρι θανάτου, δεσμεύων καὶ παραδιδοὺς εἰς
[3]Way [1]persecuted to death, binding and handing over to

φυλακὰς ἄνδρας τε καὶ γυναῖκας, **5** ὡς καὶ ὁ ἀρχιερεὺς
prisons men ˜ both and women, as also the high priest

μαρτυρεῖ μοι καὶ πᾶν τὸ πρεσβυτέριον· παρ' ὧν καὶ
testifies of me and all the council of elders; from whom also
along with

ἐπιστολὰς δεξάμενος πρὸς τοὺς ἀδελφούς, εἰς Δαμασκὸν
letters ˜ receiving to the brothers, [4]to [5]Damascus
I received

ἐπορευόμην, ἄξων καὶ τοὺς ἐκεῖσε ὄντας
[1]I [2]was [3]going, having brought also the *ones* there ˜ being
and went, in order to bring those who were

δεδεμένους εἰς Ἰερουσαλήμ, ἵνα τιμωρηθῶσιν.
having been bound to Jerusalem, so that they might be punished.

6 Ἐγένετο δέ μοι πορευομένῳ καὶ ἐγγίζοντι τῇ
[2]it [3]happened [1]And for me going and approaching -
as I was

Δαμασκῷ, περὶ μεσημβρίαν, ἐξαίφνης ἐκ τοῦ οὐρανοῦ
Damascus, about midday, suddenly from - heaven

περιαστράψαι φῶς ἱκανὸν περὶ ἐμέ. **7** Ἔπεσά τε εἰς
[4]to [5]shine [6]around [3]light [1]a [2]considerable about me. [2]I [3]fell [1]And to
shone

τὸ ἔδαφος καὶ ἤκουσα φωνῆς λεγούσης μοι, 'Σαούλ, Σαούλ,
the ground and heard a voice saying to me, 'Saul, Saul,

τί με διώκεις?' **8** Ἐγὼ δὲ ἀπεκρίθην, 'Τίς εἶ,
why [4]Me [1]are [2]you [3]persecuting?' I ˜ And answered, 'Who are You,

Κύριε?' Εἶπέ τε πρός με, 'Ἐγώ εἰμι Ἰησοῦς ὁ Ναζωραῖος
Lord?' [2]He [3]said [1]And to me, 'I am Jesus the Nazarene

ὃν σὺ διώκεις.' **9** Οἱ δὲ σὺν ἐμοὶ ὄντες τὸ μὲν
whom you are persecuting.' [2]the [3]*ones* [1]And [5]with [6]me [4]being [8]the -
those who were

φῶς ἐθεάσαντο, καὶ ἔμφοβοι ἐγένοντο·[a] τὴν δὲ φωνὴν οὐκ
[9]light [7]observed, and terrified ˜ became; [6]the [1]but [7]voice [4]not

ἤκουσαν τοῦ λαλοῦντός μοι. **10** Εἶπον δέ, 'Τί
[2]they [3]did [5]hear of the *One* speaking to me. [2]I [3]said [1]And, 'What

ποιήσω, Κύριε?' Ὁ δὲ Κύριος εἶπε πρός με, 'Ἀναστὰς
shall I do, Lord?' the ˜ And Lord said to me, 'Arising
'Arise and

πορεύου εἰς Δαμασκόν, κἀκεῖ σοι λαληθήσεται περὶ
go into Damascus, and there [5]to [6]you [1]it [2]will [3]be [4]told about

πάντων ὧν τέτακταί σοι ποιῆσαι.' **11** Ὡς δὲ
all *the things* which it has been appointed for you to do.' when ˜ And

οὐκ ἐνέβλεπον ἀπὸ τῆς δόξης τοῦ φωτὸς ἐκείνου,
[3]not [1]I [2]was seeing from the glory - of light ˜ that,
because of brightness

χειραγωγούμενος ὑπὸ τῶν συνόντων μοι, ἦλθον εἰς
being led by the hand by the *ones* being with me, I came to
those who were

Δαμασκόν. **12** Ἀνανίας δέ τις, ἀνὴρ εὐλαβὴς
Damascus. [4]Ananias [1]And [2]a [3]certain, a man ˜ devout

κατὰ τὸν νόμον, μαρτυρούμενος ὑπὸ πάντων τῶν
according to the law, being testified of by all the

κατοικούντων ἐν Δαμασκῷ[b] Ἰουδαίων, **13** ἐλθὼν πρός με καὶ
[2]dwelling [3]in [4]Damascus [1]Jews, coming to me and
came

ἐπιστὰς εἶπέ μοι, 'Σαοὺλ ἀδελφέ, ἀνάβλεψον.' Κἀγὼ αὐτῇ
standing said to me, 'Saul ˜ Brother, see again.' And I in same ˜
stood and that

the death, binding and delivering into prisons both men and
women,
5 "as also the high priest
bears me witness, and all the
council of the elders, from
whom I also received letters to
the brethren, and went to Damascus to bring in chains even
those who were there to Jerusalem to be punished.
6 "Now it happened, as I
journeyed and came near Damascus at about noon, suddenly
a great light from heaven shone
around me.
7 "And I fell to the ground
and heard a voice saying to me,
'Saul, Saul, why are you persecuting Me?'
8 "So I answered, 'Who are
You, Lord?' And He said to me,
'I am Jesus of Nazareth, whom
you are persecuting.'
9 "And those who were with
me indeed saw the light and
were afraid, but they did not
hear the voice of Him who
spoke to me.
10 "So I said, 'What shall I do,
Lord?' And the Lord said to
me, 'Arise and go into Damascus, and there you will be told
all things which are appointed
for you to do.'
11 "And since I could not see
for the glory of that light, being
led by the hand of those who
were with me, I came into Damascus.
12 "Then a certain Ananias, a
devout man according to the
law, having a good testimony
with all the Jews who dwelt
there,
13 "came to me; and he stood
and said to me, 'Brother Saul,
receive your sight.' And at that

[a](22:9) NU omits *και εμφοβοι εγενοντο, and became terrified.*
[b](22:12) NU, TR omit *εν Δαμασκω, in Damascus.*

same hour I looked up at him.
14 "Then he said, 'The God of
our fathers has chosen you that
you should know His will, and
see the Just One, and hear the
voice of His mouth.
15 'For you will be His witness to all men of what you
have seen and heard.
16 'And now why are you
waiting? Arise and be baptized,
and wash away your sins, calling on the name of the Lord.'
17 "Now it happened, when I
returned to Jerusalem and was
praying in the temple, that I
was in a trance
18 "and saw Him saying to
me, 'Make haste and get out of
Jerusalem quickly, for they will
not receive your testimony concerning Me.'
19 "So I said, 'Lord, they
know that in every synagogue I
imprisoned and beat those who
believe on You.
20 'And when the blood of
Your martyr Stephen was shed,
I also was standing by consenting to his death, and guarding
the clothes of those who were
killing him.'
21 "Then He said to me, 'Depart, for I will send you far from
here to the Gentiles.'"
22 And they listened to him
until this word, and *then* they
raised their voices and said,
"Away with such a *fellow* from
the earth, for he is not fit to
live!"
23 Then, as they cried out and

τῇ ὥρᾳ ἀνέβλεψα εἰς αὐτόν. 14 Ὁ δὲ εἶπε, 'Ὁ Θεὸς τῶν
the hour looked up at him. - And he said, 'The God -
very

πατέρων ἡμῶν προεχειρίσατό σε γνῶναι τὸ θέλημα αὐτοῦ καὶ
of fathers ~ our has chosen you to know - will ~ His and

ἰδεῖν τὸν δίκαιον καὶ ἀκοῦσαι φωνὴν ἐκ τοῦ στόματος
to see the righteous *One* and to hear a voice from - mouth ~

αὐτοῦ. 15 Ὅτι ἔσῃ μάρτυς αὐτῷ πρὸς πάντας ἀνθρώπους
His. For you will be a witness to Him to all men

ὧν ἑώρακας καὶ ἤκουσας. 16 Καὶ νῦν τί
of *the things* which you have seen and heard. And now what

μέλλεις? Ἀναστὰς βάπτισαι καὶ ἀπόλουσαι τὰς
are you going *to do?* Arising be baptized and wash away -
Arise,

ἁμαρτίας σου ἐπικαλεσάμενος τὸ ὄνομα τοῦ Κυρίου.'[c]
sins ~ your calling on the name of the Lord.'

17 Ἐγένετο δέ μοι ὑποστρέψαντι εἰς Ἰερουσαλὴμ καὶ
[2]it [3]happened [1]And to me having returned to Jerusalem and
when I had

προσευχομένου μου ἐν τῷ ἱερῷ, γενέσθαι με ἐν ἐκστάσει
praying ~ me in the temple, to become me in a trance
while I was praying that I came to be

18 καὶ ἰδεῖν αὐτὸν λέγοντά μοι, 'Σπεῦσον καὶ ἔξελθε ἐν
and to see Him saying to me, 'Hurry and go out with
saw

τάχει ἐξ Ἰερουσαλήμ, διότι οὐ παραδέξονταί σου τὴν
quickness from Jerusalem, because [3]not [1]they [2]will receive your -
quickly

μαρτυρίαν περὶ ἐμοῦ.' 19 Κἀγὼ εἶπον, 'Κύριε, αὐτοὶ
witness about Me.' And I said, 'Lord, they

ἐπίστανται ὅτι ἐγὼ ἤμην φυλακίζων καὶ δέρων κατὰ τὰς
know that I was imprisoning and beating according to the
in each

συναγωγὰς τοὺς πιστεύοντας ἐπὶ σέ· 20 καὶ ὅτε ἐξεχεῖτο
synagogues the *ones* believing on You; and when [7]was [8]shed
synagogue

τὸ αἷμα Στεφάνου τοῦ μάρτυρός σου, καὶ αὐτὸς ἤμην
[1]the [2]blood [3]of [4]Stephen - [6]witness [5]Your, [10]also [11]myself [9]I [12]was

ἐφεστὼς καὶ συνευδοκῶν τῇ ἀναιρέσει αὐτοῦ,[d] φυλάσσων
standing by and agreeing with *them* - in murder ~ his, guarding
consenting to

τὰ ἱμάτια τῶν ἀναιρούντων αὐτόν.' 21 Καὶ εἶπεν πρός
the clothes of the *ones* murdering him.' And He said to

με, 'Πορεύου, ὅτι ἐγὼ εἰς ἔθνη μακρὰν ἐξαποστελῶ
me, 'Go, because I [6]to [7]*the* [8]Gentiles [4]far [5]away [1]will [2]send

σε.'"
[3]you.'"

Roman Citizenship Aids Paul

22 Ἤκουον δὲ αὐτοῦ ἄχρι τούτου τοῦ λόγου, καὶ
[2]they [3]were [4]hearing [1]Now him until this - word, and
listening to statement,

ἐπῆραν τὴν φωνὴν αὐτῶν λέγοντες, "Αἶρε ἀπὸ τῆς γῆς
they lifted - voice ~ their saying, "Take away from the earth

τὸν τοιοῦτον, οὐ γὰρ καθῆκεν αὐτὸν ζῆν!" 23 Κραζόντων
- such a *man,* [4]not [1]for [2]it [3]is [5]fitting *for* him to live!" crying out
And as they

[c](22:16) For του Κυριου, *of the Lord,* NU reads αυτου, *His (name).*
[d](22:20) NU omits τη αναιρεσει αυτου, *to his murder.*

δὲ αὐτῶν καὶ ῥιπτούντων τὰ ἱμάτια, καὶ κονιορτὸν
And them and throwing off the clothes, and dust ˜
were crying out their

βαλλόντων εἰς τὸν ἀέρα, 24 ἐκέλευσεν αὐτὸν ὁ χιλίαρχος
throwing in the air, [3]ordered [4]him [1]the [2]chiliarch
commander

ἄγεσθαι εἰς τὴν παρεμβολήν, εἰπὼν μάστιξιν
to be brought into the barracks, saying [8]with [9]lashes
and said

ἀνετάζεσθαι αὐτὸν ἵνα ἐπιγνῷ δι' ἣν αἰτίαν
[3]to [4]be [5]given [6]a [7]hearing [1]*for* [2]him so that he might learn for which cause
interrogated why

οὕτως ἐπεφώνουν αὐτῷ.
thus they were crying out against him.

25 Ὡς δὲ προέτεινεν αὐτὸν τοῖς ἱμᾶσιν, εἶπεν
as ˜ But they were stretching out ˜ him with the thongs, [2]said

πρὸς τὸν ἑστῶτα ἑκατόνταρχον ὁ Παῦλος, "Εἰ
[3]to [4]the [6]standing [7]*there* [5]centurion - [1]Paul, -

ἄνθρωπον Ῥωμαῖον καὶ ἀκατάκριτον ἔξεστιν ὑμῖν
"[8]a [9]man [10]*who* [11]*is* [12]a [13]Roman [14]and [15]uncondemned [1]Is [2]it [3]lawful [4]for [5]you

μαστίζειν?"
[6]to [7]scourge?"

26 Ἀκούσας δὲ ὁ ἑκατόντορχος, προσελθὼν
[4]hearing [5]*this* [1]And [2]the [3]centurion, going to
And when the centurion heard this, he approached

ἀπήγγειλε τῷ χιλιάρχῳ λέγων, "Ὅρα[e] τί μέλλεις
he reported to the chiliarch saying, "Watch what you are about
and commander

ποιεῖν· ὁ γὰρ ἄνθρωπος οὗτος Ῥωμαῖός ἐστι." 27 Προσελθὼν
to do; - for man ˜ this [2]a [3]Roman [1]is." [4]approaching
approached and

δὲ ὁ χιλίαρχος εἶπεν αὐτῷ, "Λέγε μοι, εἰ σὺ Ῥωμαῖος
[1]And [2]the [3]chiliarch said to him, "Tell me, - [2]you [3]a [4]Roman
commander

εἶ?"
[1]are?"

Ὁ δὲ ἔφη, "Ναί."
- And he said, "Yes."

28 Ἀπεκρίθη τε ὁ χιλίαρχος, "Ἐγὼ πολλοῦ
[4]answered [1]And [2]the [3]chiliarch, "I [4]with [5]much
commander,

κεφαλαίου τὴν πολιτείαν ταύτην ἐκτησάμην."
[6]money - [3]citizenship [2]this [1]acquired."

Ὁ δὲ Παῦλος ἔφη, "Ἐγὼ δὲ καὶ γεγέννημαι."
- And Paul said, "I ˜ But indeed have been born *a citizen.*"
was

29 Εὐθέως οὖν ἀπέστησαν ἀπ' αὐτοῦ οἱ μέλλοντες
Immediately then [10]withdrew [11]from [12]him [1]the [2]*ones* [3]being [4]about
who were

αὐτὸν ἀνετάζειν. Καὶ ὁ χιλίαρχος δὲ ἐφοβήθη,
[7]him [5]to [6]give [8]a [9]hearing. [14]even [15]the [16]chiliarch [13]And was afraid,
interrogate. commander

ἐπιγνοὺς ὅτι Ῥωμαῖός ἐστι καὶ ὅτι ἦν αὐτὸν
having learned that [3]a [4]Roman [1]he [2]is and that he was [3]him
was had

δεδεκώς.
[1]having [2]bound.
bound.

tore off *their* clothes and threw dust into the air,
24 the commander ordered him to be brought into the barracks, and said that he should be examined under scourging, so that he might know why they shouted so against him.
25 And as they bound him with thongs, Paul said to the centurion who stood by, "Is it lawful for you to scourge a man who is a Roman, and uncondemned?"
26 When the centurion heard *that,* he went and told the commander, saying, "Take care what you do, for this man is a Roman."
27 Then the commander came and said to him, "Tell me, are you a Roman?" He said, "Yes."
28 The commander answered, "With a large sum I obtained this citizenship." And Paul said, "But I was born *a citizen.*"
29 Then immediately those who were about to examine him withdrew from him; and the commander was also afraid after he found out that he was a Roman, and because he had bound him.

[e](22:26) NU omits Ορα, *Watch,* thus *What are you about to do?*

30 The next day, because he
wanted to know for certain why
he was accused by the Jews, he
released him from *his* bonds,
and commanded the chief
priests and all their council to
appear, and brought Paul down
and set him before them.
23 Then Paul, looking
earnestly at the coun-
cil, said, "Men *and* brethren, I
have lived in all good conscience before God until this
day."
2 And the high priest Ananias
commanded those who stood
by him to strike him on the
mouth.
3 Then Paul said to him,
"God will strike you, *you* whitewashed wall! For you sit to
judge me according to the law,
and do you command me to be
struck contrary to the law?"
4 And those who stood by
said, "Do you revile God's high
priest?"
5 Then Paul said, "I did not
know, brethren, that he was
the high priest; for it is written,
*'You shall not speak evil of a
ruler of your people.'*"
6 But when Paul perceived
that one part were Sadducees
and the other Pharisees, he
cried out in the council, "Men
and brethren, I am a Pharisee,
the son of a Pharisee; concerning the hope and resurrection of
the dead I am being judged!"
7 And when he had said this,

Paul Divides the Sanhedrin

30 Τῇ δὲ ἐπαύριον βουλόμενος γνῶναι τὸ ἀσφαλὲς
[2]on [3]the [1]Now next day desiring to know the certain *thing*
truth

τὸ τί κατηγορεῖται παρὰ τῶν Ἰουδαίων, ἔλυσεν αὐτὸν
\- *as to* why he is accused by the Jews, he released him
was

ἀπὸ τῶν δεσμῶν,[f] καὶ ἐκέλευσεν ἐλθεῖν τοὺς ἀρχιερεῖς καὶ
from the bonds, and ordered [8]to [9]come [1]the [2]chief [3]priests [4]and

ὅλον τὸ συνέδριον αὐτῶν, καὶ καταγαγὼν τὸν Παῦλον
[6]whole - [7]council [5]their, and bringing down ~ - Paul
he brought

ἔστησεν εἰς αὐτούς.
he set *him* to them.
and presented

23 1 Ἀτενίσας δὲ ὁ Παῦλος τῷ συνεδρίῳ εἶπεν,
[3]looking [4]intently [1]And - [2]Paul at the council said,
looked and said,

"Ἄνδρες ἀδελφοί, ἐγὼ πάσῃ συνειδήσει ἀγαθῇ πεπολίτευμαι*
"Men brothers, I with all conscience ~ good have lived

τῷ Θεῷ ἄχρι ταύτης τῆς ἡμέρας." 2 Ὁ δὲ ἀρχιερεὺς
\- with God until this - day." the ~ But high priest

Ἀνανίας ἐπέταξε τοῖς παρεστῶσιν αὐτῷ τύπτειν αὐτοῦ τὸ
Ananias commanded the *ones* standing by him to strike his -

στόμα. 3 Τότε ὁ Παῦλος πρὸς αὐτὸν εἶπε, "Τύπτειν σε
mouth. Then - Paul [2]to [3]him [1]said, "[7]to [8]strike [9]you

μέλλει ὁ Θεός, τοῖχε κεκονιαμένε! Καὶ σὺ κάθῃ
[5]is [6]about - [4]God, *you* wall having been whitewashed! And you ~ do sit
you whitewashed wall!

κρίνων με κατὰ τὸν νόμον, καὶ παρανομῶν
judging me according to the law, and breaking the law
contrary to

κελεύεις με τύπτεσθαι?"
do you command me to be struck? "
that I

4 Οἱ δὲ παρεστῶτες εἶπον, "Τὸν ἀρχιερέα τοῦ
[2]the [3]*ones* [1]But standing by said, "[4]the [5]high [6]priest -

Θεοῦ λοιδορεῖς?"
[7]of [8]God [1]Do [2]you [3]revile?"

5 Ἔφη τε ὁ Παῦλος, "Οὐκ ᾔδειν, ἀδελφοί, ὅτι ἐστὶ
[3]said [1]And - [2]Paul, "[6]not [4]I [5]did [7]know, brothers, that he is

ἀρχιερεύς· γέγραπται γάρ, «Ἄρχοντα τοῦ λαοῦ σου
the high priest; [2]it [3]is [4]written [1]for, «[11]a [12]ruler - [13]of [15]people [14]your

οὐκ ἐρεῖς κακῶς.»"[a] 6 Γνοὺς δὲ ὁ Παῦλος
[7]not [5]You [6]shall [8]speak [10]of [9]badly.»" [3]knowing [1]But - [2]Paul
wickedly.»" But when Paul perceived

ὅτι τὸ ἓν μέρος ἐστὶ Σαδδουκαίων, τὸ δὲ ἕτερον
that the one part is of *the* Sadducees, the ~ and other
was

Φαρισαίων, ἔκραξεν ἐν τῷ συνεδρίῳ, "Ἄνδρες ἀδελφοί,
of *the* Pharisees, was crying out in the council, "Men brothers
he cried

ἐγὼ Φαρισαῖός εἰμι, υἱὸς Φαρισαίου· περὶ ἐλπίδος καὶ
I [2]a [3]Pharisee [1]am, a son of a Pharisee; concerning *the* hope and

ἀναστάσεως νεκρῶν ἐγὼ κρίνομαι!" 7 Τοῦτο δὲ
resurrection of *the* dead I am being judged!" this And
And when he

---

f(22:30) NU omits απο των δεσμων, *from the bonds.*
a(23:5) Ex. 22:28

*(23:1) πολιτεύομαι (*politeuomai*). Verb originally meaning *live as a citizen, have one's citizenship* in a city-state (the πόλις). The word also had the broader meaning *conduct oneself, live one's life,* as here and in Phil. 1:27. In these NT occurrences, the idea of living in a manner appropriate for a citizen of the kingdom of heaven may be implicit. Cf. the cognate nouns πολίτευμα, *commonwealth, state* (Phil. 3:20); πολιτεία, *citizenship, commonwealth* (Acts 22:28; Eph. 2:12); and πολίτης, *(fellow) citizen* (Acts 21:39; Luke 15:15; Heb. 8:11).

αὐτοῦ λαλήσαντος, ἐγένετο στάσις τῶν Φαρισαίων
him speaking, *there* came to be a discord of the Pharisees
had spoken this, dispute between

καὶ τῶν Σαδδουκαίων, καὶ ἐσχίσθη τὸ πλῆθος.
and the Sadducees, and [3]was [4]divided [1]the [2]assembly.

8 Σαδδουκαῖοι μὲν γὰρ λέγουσι μὴ εἶναι ἀνάστασιν μηδὲ
Sadducees ˜ - For say not to be resurrection nor
that there is no

ἄγγελον μήτε πνεῦμα, Φαρισαῖοι δὲ ὁμολογοῦσι τὰ
angel nor spirit, Pharisees ˜ but confess [2]the [3]*things*
all these

ἀμφότερα.
[1]both.
things.

9 Ἐγένετο δὲ κραυγὴ μεγάλη, καὶ ἀναστάντες
[2]*there* [3]came [4]to [5]be [1]And a(n) outcry ˜ great, and [9]standing [10]up
stood up

οἱ γραμματεῖς[b] τοῦ μέρους τῶν Φαρισαίων
[1]the [2]scribes [3]of [4]the [5]part [6]of [7]the [8]Pharisees
Pharisees' party

διεμάχοντο λέγοντες, "Οὐδὲν κακὸν εὑρίσκομεν ἐν τῷ
were contending sharply saying, "[3]nothing [4]wrong [1]We [2]find in -
and contended

ἀνθρώπῳ τούτῳ· εἰ δὲ πνεῦμα ἐλάλησεν αὐτῷ ἢ ἄγγελος,
man ˜ this; if ˜ but a spirit [4]spoke [5]to [6]him [1]or [2]an [3]angel,
has spoken

μὴ θεομαχῶμεν."[c] 10 Πολλῆς δὲ γενομένης στάσεως,
[9]not [7]let [8]us fight against God." much ˜ And becoming ˜ discord,
And when much dissension developed,

εὐλαβηθεὶς ὁ χιλίαρχος μὴ διασπασθῇ ὁ Παῦλος ὑπ' αὐτῶν,
[3]being [4]afraid [1]the [2]chiliarch lest [2]be [3]torn [4]apart - [1]Paul by them,
commander might be

ἐκέλευσε τὸ στράτευμα καταβῆναι καὶ ἁρπάσαι αὐτὸν
commanded the detachment of soldiers to go down and to seize him

ἐκ μέσου αὐτῶν, ἄγειν τε εἰς τὴν παρεμβολήν.
from *the* midst of them, [2]to [3]bring [4]*him* [1]and into the barracks.

Paul's Nephew Exposes a Plot

11 Τῇ δὲ ἐπιούσῃ νυκτὶ ἐπιστὰς αὐτῷ ὁ Κύριος
[2]on [3]the [1]Now next night [3]standing [4]by [5]him [1]the [2]Lord
stood

εἶπε, "Θάρσει, Παῦλε,[d] ὡς γὰρ διεμαρτύρω
said, "Take courage, Paul, as ˜ for you solemnly testified about
and said,

τὰ περὶ ἐμοῦ εἰς Ἱερουσαλήμ, οὕτω σε
the *things* concerning Me in Jerusalem, so [5]you
you

δεῖ καὶ εἰς Ῥώμην μαρτυρῆσαι."
[1]it [2]is [3]necessary [4]*for* also [3]in [4]Rome [1]to [2]testify."
must testify."

12 Γενομένης δὲ ἡμέρας, ποιήσαντές τινες τῶν
becoming ˜ Now day, [5]making [1]some [2]of [3]the
Now when it was joined in

Ἰουδαίων[e] συστροφήν, ἀνεθεμάτισαν ἑαυτούς, λέγοντες
[4]Jews a conspiracy, bound [2]by [3]a [4]curse [1]themselves, saying
and bound

μήτε φαγεῖν μήτε πιεῖν ἕως οὗ ἀποκτείνωσι τὸν Παῦλον.
neither to eat nor to drink until - they would kill - Paul.
would they eat drink

a dissension arose between the Pharisees and the Sadducees; and the assembly was divided.
8 For Sadducees say that there is no resurrection—and no angel or spirit; but the Pharisees confess both.
9 Then there arose a loud outcry. And the scribes of the Pharisees' party arose and protested, saying, "We find no evil in this man; but if a spirit or an angel has spoken to him, let us not fight against God."
10 Now when there arose a great dissension, the commander, fearing lest Paul might be pulled to pieces by them, commanded the soldiers to go down and take him by force from among them, and bring *him* into the barracks.
11 But the following night the Lord stood by him and said, "Be of good cheer, Paul; for as you have testified for Me in Jerusalem, so you must also bear witness at Rome."
12 And when it was day, some of the Jews banded together and bound themselves under an oath, saying that they would neither eat nor drink till they had killed Paul.

---

[b]**(23:9)** For οι γραμματεις, *the scribes,* NU reads τινες των γραμματων, *certain of the scribes.*
[c]**(23:9)** NU omits μη θεομαχωμεν, *let us not fight against God.*
[d]**(23:11)** NU omits Παυλε, *Paul.* [e]**(23:12)** For τινες των Ιουδαιων, *some of the Jews,* NU reads οι Ιουδαιοι, *the Jews.*

13 Now there were more than
forty who had formed this conspiracy.
14 They came to the chief
priests and elders, and said,
"We have bound ourselves under a great oath that we will eat
nothing until we have killed
Paul.
15 "Now you, therefore, together with the council, suggest to the commander that he
be brought down to you tomorrow, as though you were going
to make further inquiries concerning him; but we are ready
to kill him before he comes
near."
16 So when Paul's sister's son
heard of their ambush, he went
and entered the barracks and
told Paul.
17 Then Paul called one of the
centurions to *him* and said,
"Take this young man to the
commander, for he has something to tell him."
18 So he took him and brought
him to the commander and
said, "Paul the prisoner called
me to *him* and asked *me* to
bring this young man to you.
He has something to say to
you."
19 Then the commander took
him by the hand, went aside,

13 Ἦσαν δὲ πλείους τεσσαράκοντα οἱ ταύτην τὴν
[2]*there* [3]were [1]And over four hundred the *ones* [3]this -
who

συνωμοσίαν πεποιηκότες· **14** οἵτινες προσελθόντες τοῖς
[4]plot [1]having [2]made; who coming to the
had came

ἀρχιερεῦσι καὶ τοῖς πρεσβυτέροις εἶπον, "Ἀναθέματι
chief priests and to the elders said, "[6]with [7]a [8]curse
and said,

ἀνεθεματίσαμεν ἑαυτοὺς μηδενὸς γεύσασθαι ἕως οὗ
[1]We [2]bound [4]by [5]oath [3]ourselves [11]nothing [9]to [10]taste until -
have bound

ἀποκτείνωμεν τὸν Παῦλον. **15** Νῦν οὖν ὑμεῖς ἐμφανίσατε
we kill - Paul. Now therefore ˜ you [5]inform
suggest to

τῷ χιλιάρχῳ σὺν τῷ συνεδρίῳ ὅπως αὔριον[f] αὐτὸν
[6]the [7]chiliarch [1]together [2]with [3]the [4]council so that tomorrow [4]him
commander

καταγάγῃ πρὸς ὑμᾶς ὡς μέλλοντας διαγινώσκειν
[1]he [2]may [3]bring [5]down to you as being about to determine
as though you are going

ἀκριβέστερον τὰ περὶ αὐτοῦ· ἡμεῖς δέ, πρὸ τοῦ
more accurately the *things* concerning him; we ˜ but, before -

ἐγγίσαι αὐτόν, ἕτοιμοί ἐσμεν τοῦ ἀνελεῖν αὐτόν."
to come near him, prepared ˜ are - to kill him."
he comes near,

16 Ἀκούσας δὲ ὁ υἱὸς τῆς ἀδελφῆς Παύλου τὸ ἔνεδρον
hearing But the son of the sister of Paul the ambush
But when Paul's sister's son heard about

παραγενόμενος καὶ εἰσελθὼν εἰς τὴν παρεμβολήν, ἀπήγγειλε
coming and entering into the barracks, he told *this*
he came entered and

τῷ Παύλῳ.
- to Paul.

17 Προσκαλεσάμενος δὲ ὁ Παῦλος ἕνα τῶν
[3]summoning [1]And - [2]Paul one of the
summoned

ἑκατοντάρχων ἔφη, "Τὸν νεανίαν τοῦτον ἀπάγαγε πρὸς
centurions said, - "[3]young [4]man [2]this [1]Lead [5]away to
and said,

τὸν χιλίαρχον, ἔχει γάρ τι ἀπαγγεῖλαι αὐτῷ."
the chiliarch, [2]he [3]has [1]for something to tell him."
commander,

18 Ὁ μὲν οὖν παραλαβὼν αὐτὸν ἤγαγε πρὸς τὸν
- - Therefore taking along ˜ him he brought *him* to the

χιλίαρχον καὶ φησίν, "Ὁ δέσμιος Παῦλος προσκαλεσάμενός
chiliarch and said, "The prisoner Paul having summoned
commander

με ἠρώτησε τοῦτον τὸν νεανίαν ἀγαγεῖν πρὸς σέ, ἔχοντά
me asked *me* [3]this - [4]young [5]man [1]to [2]bring to you, having
for he has

τι λαλῆσαί σοι."
something to say to you."

19 Ἐπιλαβόμενος δὲ τῆς χειρὸς αὐτοῦ ὁ χιλίαρχος καὶ
[4]taking [5]*him* [6]by [1]And - [8]hand [7]his [2]the [3]chiliarch and
took commander

---

f(**23:15**) NU omits αυριον, *tomorrow*.

ἀναχωρήσας κατ' ἰδίαν ἐπυνθάνετο, "Τί ἐστιν ὃ
withdrawing to his own he was inquiring, "What is it that
withdrew a private place and inquired,

ἔχεις ἀπαγγεῖλαί μοι?"
you have to tell me?"

20 Εἶπε δὲ ὅτι "Οἱ Ἰουδαῖοι συνέθεντο τοῦ ἐρωτῆσαί
[2]he [3]said [1]And - "The Jews agreed - to ask
have agreed

σε ὅπως αὔριον εἰς τὸ συνέδριον καταγάγῃς τὸν Παῦλον
you that tomorrow [5]to [6]the [7]council [1]you [2]bring [4]down - [3]Paul

ὡς μέλλοντά τι ἀκριβέστερον πυνθάνεσθαι
as being about [3]something [4]more [5]accurate [1]to [2]learn
as though they are going

περὶ αὐτοῦ. 21 Σὺ οὖν μὴ πεισθῇς αὐτοῖς·
concerning him. You therefore not ˜ do be persuaded by them;

ἐνεδρεύουσι γὰρ αὐτὸν ἐξ αὐτῶν ἄνδρες πλείους
[9]are [10]lying [11]in [12]wait [13]for [1]for [14]him [7]of [8]them [6]men [2]more [3]than

τεσσαράκοντα, οἵτινες ἀνεθεμάτισαν ἑαυτοὺς μήτε φαγεῖν
[4]four [5]hundred, who bound [2]by [3]a [4]curse [1]themselves neither to eat
have bound

μήτε πιεῖν ἕως οὗ ἀνέλωσιν αὐτόν, καὶ νῦν ἕτοιμοί εἰσι
nor to drink until - they kill him, and now [3]prepared [1]they [2]are

προσδεχόμενοι τὴν ἀπὸ σοῦ ἐπαγγελίαν." 22 Ὁ μὲν οὖν
waiting for the [2]from [3]you [1]promise." the ˜ - Then

χιλίαρχος ἀπέλυσε τὸν νεανίαν, παραγγείλας, "Μηδενὶ
chiliarch dismissed the young man, commanding *him*, "[2]no [3]one
commander and commanded

ἐκλαλῆσαι ὅτι ταῦτα ἐνεφάνισας πρός με."
[1]Tell that [3]these [4]*things* [1]you [2]made [3]known to me."
have made

Paul Is Sent to Felix

23 Καὶ προσκαλεσάμενος δύο τινὰς τῶν ἑκατοντάρχων
And having summoned two - of the centurions

εἶπεν, "Ἑτοιμάσατε στρατιώτας διακοσίους ὅπως
he said, "Make ready [3]soldiers [1]two [2]hundred in order that

πορευθῶσιν ἕως Καισαρείας, καὶ ἱππεῖς ἑβδομήκοντα καὶ
they may go to Caesarea, and horsemen ˜ seventy and

δεξιολάβους διακοσίους, ἀπὸ τρίτης ὥρας τῆς νυκτός,
[3]bowmen [1]two [2]hundred, from *the* third hour of the night,
to leave at

24 κτήνη τε παραστῆσαι, ἵνα ἐπιβιβάσαντες
[4]animals [1]and [2]to [3]place [5]at [6]*their* [7]disposal in order that putting [2]on [3]*them*
mounts place they may put

τὸν Παῦλον διασώσωσι πρὸς Φήλικα τὸν ἡγεμόνα,"
- [1]Paul they may bring *him* safely to Felix the governor,"
and

25 γράψας ἐπιστολὴν περιέχουσαν τὸν τύπον τοῦτον·
and writing a letter containing - content ˜ this:
he wrote which contained

26 Κλαύδιος Λυσίας,
Claudius Lysias,

Τῷ κρατίστῳ ἡγεμόνι Φήλικι·
To the most excellent governor Felix:

Χαίρειν.
To greet.
Greetings.

27 Τὸν ἄνδρα τοῦτον συλληφθέντα ὑπὸ τῶν Ἰουδαίων
- man ˜ This having been arrested by the Jews

and asked privately, "What is it that you have to tell me?"
20 And he said, "The Jews have agreed to ask that you bring Paul down to the council tomorrow, as though they were going to inquire more fully about him.
21 "But do not yield to them, for more than forty of them lie in wait for him, men who have bound themselves by an oath that they will neither eat nor drink till they have killed him; and now they are ready, waiting for the promise from you."
22 So the commander let the young man depart, and commanded *him,* "Tell no one that you have revealed these things to me."
23 And he called for two centurions, saying, "Prepare two hundred soldiers, seventy horsemen, and two hundred spearmen to go to Caesarea at the third hour of the night;
24 "and provide mounts to set Paul on, and bring *him* safely to Felix the governor."
25 He wrote a letter in the following manner:

26 Claudius Lysias,

To the most excellent governor Felix:

Greetings.

27 This man was seized by the Jews and was about

to be killed by them.
Coming with the troops I
rescued him, having
learned that he was a
Roman.
28 And when I wanted to
know the reason they
accused him, I brought
him before their council.
29 I found out that he was
accused concerning
questions of their law, but
had nothing charged
against him deserving of
death or chains.
30 And when it was told me
that the Jews lay in wait
for the man, I sent him
immediately to you, and
also commanded his
accusers to state before
you the charges against
him.

Farewell.

31 Then the soldiers, as they
were commanded, took Paul
and brought *him* by night to Antipatris.
32 The next day they left the
horsemen to go on with him,
and returned to the barracks.
33 When they came to Caesarea and had delivered the letter
to the governor, they also presented Paul to him.
34 And when the governor
had read *it,* he asked what
province he was from. And
when he understood that *he
was* from Cilicia,
35 he said, "I will hear you
when your accusers also have

καὶ μέλλοντα ἀναιρεῖσθαι ὑπ' αὐτῶν, ἐπιστὰς σὺν
and being about to be killed by them, coming upon *them* with
I came

τῷ στρατεύματι ἐξειλόμην αὐτόν, μαθὼν ὅτι
the detachment of soldiers I rescued him, having learned that
and

Ῥωμαῖός ἐστι. 28 Βουλόμενος δὲ γνῶναι τὴν αἰτίαν δι'
[3]a [4]Roman [1]he [2]is. desiring ˜ And to know the cause for

ἣν ἐνεκάλουν αὐτῷ, κατήγαγον αὐτὸν εἰς τὸ
which they were accusing him, I took down ˜ him to -

συνέδριον αὐτῶν· 29 ὃν εὗρον ἐγκαλούμενον
council ˜ their; whom I found being accused
and I found that he was

περὶ ζητημάτων τοῦ νόμου αὐτῶν, μηδὲν ἄξιον θανάτου
about questions - of law ˜ their, *but* [2]no [6]worthy [7]of [8]death

ἢ δεσμῶν ἔγκλημα ἔχοντα.
[9]or [10]bonds [3]accusation [4]*against* [5]*him* [1]having.
chains had.

30 Μηνυθείσης δέ μοι ἐπιβουλῆς εἰς τὸν ἄνδρα
[2]becoming [3]known [1]And to me of a plot against the man
when it became that

μέλλειν[g] ἔσεσθαι ὑπὸ τῶν Ἰουδαίων,[h] ἐξαυτῆς
[4]to [5]be [6]about [7]to [8]be [1]by [2]the [3]Jews, at once
was about to happen

ἔπεμψα πρὸς σέ, παραγγείλας καὶ τοῖς
I sent *him* to you, commanding ˜ also the
and also commanded

κατηγόροις λέγειν τὰ πρὸς αὐτὸν ἐπὶ σοῦ.
accusers to say the *things* against him before you.
state the charges

Ἔρρωσο.[i]
Be strong.
Farewell.

31 Οἱ μὲν οὖν στρατιῶται, κατὰ τὸ
the ˜ - Then soldiers, according to the *thing*
as it

διατεταγμένον αὐτοῖς, ἀναλαβόντες τὸν Παῦλον, ἤγαγον
having been commanded them, taking up - Paul, brought *him*
had been took and brought

διὰ τῆς νυκτὸς εἰς τὴν Ἀντιπατρίδα. 32 Τῇ δὲ ἐπαύριον
during the night to - Antipatris. [2]on [3]the [1]And next day

ἐάσαντες τοὺς ἱππεῖς πορεύεσθαι σὺν αὐτῷ, ὑπέστρεψαν εἰς
leaving the horsemen to go on with him, they returned to
they left and

τὴν παρεμβολήν· 33 οἵτινες εἰσελθόντες εἰς τὴν Καισάρειαν
the barracks; who entering into - Caesarea
when they entered

καὶ ἀναδόντες τὴν ἐπιστολὴν τῷ ἡγεμόνι, παρέστησαν καὶ
and delivering the letter to the governor, presented ˜ also
delivered

τὸν Παῦλον αὐτῷ.
- Paul to him.

34 Ἀναγνοὺς δὲ ὁ ἡγεμὼν[j] καὶ ἐπερωτήσας
[4]reading [5]the [6]letter [1]And [2]the [3]governor and asking
And when the governor read the letter asked

ἐκ ποίας ἐπαρχίας ἐστὶ καὶ πυθόμενος ὅτι ἀπὸ
from what province he is and learning that *he was* from
was learned

Κιλικίας, 35 "Διακούσομαί σου," ἔφη, "ὅταν καὶ οἱ
Cilicia, "I will give [2]a [3]hearing [1]you," he said, "whenever [3]also -

g(23:30) NU omits μελλειν, *to be about.*
h(23:30) NU omits υπο των Ιουδαιων, *by the Jews.*
i(23:30) NU omits Ερρωσο, *Farewell.*
j(23:34) NU omits ο ηγεμων, *the governor.*

κατήγοροί σου παραγένωνται." Ἐκέλευσέ τε αὐτὸν ἐν τῷ
[2]accusers [1]your arrive." [2]he [3]ordered [1]And him [4]in [5]the

πραιτωρίῳ Ἡρῴδου φυλάσσεσθαι.
[6]Praetorium [7]of [8]Herod [1]to [2]be [3]guarded.

Tertullus Accuses Paul of Sedition

24 1 Μετὰ δὲ πέντε ἡμέρας κατέβη ὁ ἀρχιερεὺς
after ˜ Now five days [5]came [6]down [1]the [2]high [3]priest

Ἀνανίας μετὰ τῶν[a] πρεσβυτέρων καὶ ῥήτορος
[4]Ananias with the elders and a(n) [2]advocate
attorney

Τερτύλλου τινός, οἵτινες ἐνεφάνισαν τῷ ἡγεμόνι
[3]*named* [4]Tertullus [1]certain, who made known to the governor

κατὰ τοῦ Παύλου.
the charges against - Paul.

2 Κληθέντος δὲ αὐτοῦ, ἤρξατο κατηγορεῖν ὁ
being called And him, [2]began [3]to [4]accuse [5]*him* -
And when he had been called,

Τέρτυλλος λέγων, "Πολλῆς εἰρήνης τυγχάνοντες διὰ σοῦ καὶ
[1]Tertullus saying, "[2]much [3]peace [1]Attaining by you and
"Since we are attaining great peace

κατορθωμάτων[b] γινομένων τῷ ἔθνει τούτῳ διὰ τῆς σῆς
successes coming about - for nation ˜ this by - your
prosperity is coming about

προνοίας, 3 πάντῃ τε καὶ πανταχοῦ ἀποδεχόμεθα,
foresight, [2]in [3]every [4]*thing* [1]both and everywhere we accept *it,*

κράτιστε Φῆλιξ, μετὰ πάσης εὐχαριστίας. 4 Ἵνα δὲ μὴ
most excellent Felix, with all thanksgiving. that ˜ But [2]not

ἐπὶ πλεῖόν σε ἐγκόπτω, παρακαλῶ ἀκοῦσαί σε ἡμῶν
[5]for [6]more [4]you [1]I [3]weary I request [2]to [3]hear [1]you us
any longer

συντόμως τῇ σῇ ἐπιεικείᾳ. 5 Εὑρόντες γὰρ τὸν ἄνδρα
briefly - in your graciousness. [2]having [3]found [1]For - man ˜

τοῦτον λοιμὸν καὶ κινοῦντα στάσιν πᾶσι τοῖς Ἰουδαίοις
this *to be* a plague and *one* causing discord with all the Jews
public menace among

τοῖς κατὰ τὴν οἰκουμένην, πρωτοστάτην τε τῆς τῶν
- throughout the world, [2]a [3]leader [1]and of the [2]of [3]the
Roman Empire,

Ναζωραίων αἱρέσεως, 6 ὃς καὶ τὸ ἱερὸν ἐπείρασε
[4]Nazarenes [1]sect, who also [4]the [5]temple [1]attempted

βεβηλῶσαι, ὃν καὶ ἐκρατήσαμεν,[c] 8 παρ' οὗ
[2]to [3]profane, whom also we arrested, from whom

δυνήσῃ, αὐτὸς ἀνακρίνας, περὶ πάντων
you will be able, [4]yourself [1]having [2]judged [3]*him,* [7]about [8]all

τούτων ἐπιγνῶναι ὧν ἡμεῖς κατηγοροῦμεν αὐτοῦ."
[9]these [10]*things* [5]to [6]learn of which we are accusing him."

9 Συνεπέθεντο[d] δὲ καὶ οἱ Ἰουδαῖοι, φάσκοντες
[5]joined [6]in [7]the [8]attack [1]And [4]also [2]the [3]Jews, asserting *that*

ταῦτα οὕτως ἔχειν.
these *things* [3]thus [1]to [2]have.
were so

Paul Defends Himself Before Felix

10 Ἀπεκρίθη δὲ ὁ Παῦλος, νεύσαντος αὐτῷ τοῦ
[3]answered [1]But - [2]Paul, [6]having [7]nodded [8]for [9]him [4]the

come." And he commanded him
to be kept in Herod's Praetorium.
24 Now after five days
Ananias the high priest
came down with the elders and
a certain orator *named* Tertullus. These gave evidence to the
governor against Paul.
2 And when he was called
upon, Tertullus began his accusation, saying: "Seeing that
through you we enjoy great
peace, and prosperity is being
brought to this nation by your
foresight,
3 "we accept *it* always and in
all places, most noble Felix,
with all thankfulness.
4 "Nevertheless, not to be
tedious to you any further, I
beg you to hear, by your courtesy, a few words from us.
5 "For we have found this
man a plague, a creator of dissension among all the Jews
throughout the world, and a
ringleader of the sect of the
Nazarenes.
6 "He even tried to profane
the temple, and we seized him,
and wanted to judge him according to our law.
7 "But the commander Lys-
ias came by and with great violence took *him* out of our
hands,
8 "commanding his accusers
to come to you. By examining
him yourself you may ascertain
all these things of which we accuse him."
9 And the Jews also as-
sented, maintaining that these
things were so.
10 Then Paul, after the governor had nodded to him to

[a](**24:1**) NU reads *τινων, certain (of the elders).*
[b](**24:2**) NU reads *διορθωματων, reforms.*
[c](**24:6–8**) TR adds vv. 6b–8a: *και κατα τον ημετερον νομον ηθελησαμεν κρινειν.* (v. 7) *Παρελθων δε Λυσιας ο χιλιαρχος μετα πολλης βιας εκ των χειρων ημων απηγαγε,* (v. 8) *κελευσας τους κατηγορους αυτου ερχεσθαι επι σε* (see NKJV translation).
[d](**24:9**) TR reads *Συνεθεντο, agreed.*

speak, answered: "Inasmuch as
I know that you have been for
many years a judge of this nation, I do the more cheerfully
answer for myself,
11 "because you may ascertain that it is no more than
twelve days since I went up to
Jerusalem to worship.
12 "And they neither found
me in the temple disputing with
anyone nor inciting the crowd,
either in the synagogues or in
the city.
13 "Nor can they prove the
things of which they now accuse me.
14 "But this I confess to you,
that according to the Way
which they call a sect, so I worship the God of my fathers, believing all things which are
written in the Law and in the
Prophets.
15 "I have hope in God, which
they themselves also accept,
that there will be a resurrection
of *the* dead, both of *the* just and
the unjust.
16 "This *being* so, I myself always strive to have a conscience without offense toward
God and men.
17 "Now after many years I
came to bring alms and offerings to my nation,
18 "in the midst of which
some Jews from Asia found me
purified in the temple, neither
with a mob nor with tumult.
19 "They ought to have been

ἡγεμόνος λέγειν, "Ἐκ πολλῶν ἐτῶν ὄντα σε κριτὴν τῷ
[5]governor to say, "[9]of [10]many [11]years [3]being [2]you [4]a [5]judge -
speak, "for that you have been

ἔθνει τούτῳ ἐπιστάμενος, εὐθυμότερον τὰ
[6]for [8]nation [7]this [1]Knowing, the more cheerfully [3]the [4]*things*

περὶ ἐμαυτοῦ ἀπολογοῦμαι, **11** δυναμένου σου γνῶναι
[5]concerning [6]myself [1]I [2]defend, [2]being [3]able [1]you to know
because you are able

ὅτι οὐ πλείους εἰσί μοι ἡμέραι δεκαδύο, ἀφ' ἧς
that [3]not [4]more [5]*than* [1]*there* [2]are [8]to [9]me [7]days [6]twelve, from which
it has not been more than twelve days since

ἀνέβην προσκυνήσων ἐν Ἱερουσαλήμ, **12** καὶ οὔτε ἐν τῷ
I went up worshiping in Jerusalem, and neither [8]in [9]the
to worship

ἱερῷ εὗρόν με πρός τινα διαλεγόμενον ἢ
[10]temple [1]did [2]they [3]find [4]me [6]with [7]anyone [5]discussing or
disputing

ἐπισύστασιν ποιοῦντα ὄχλου, οὔτε ἐν ταῖς συναγωγαῖς,
[2]an [3]uprising [1]making of a crowd, neither in the synagogues,
inciting a crowd to rise up, either

οὔτε κατὰ τὴν πόλιν. **13** Οὔτε παραστῆσαί με[e]
nor in the city. Nor [4]to [5]prove [6]*against* [7]me
or

δύνανται περὶ ὧν νῦν κατηγοροῦσί μου.
[1]are [2]they [3]able concerning which *things* [3]now [1]they [2]are accusing me.
the things about which

14 Ὁμολογῶ δὲ τοῦτό σοι ὅτι κατὰ τὴν ὁδὸν ἣν
[2]I [3]confess [1]But this to you that according to the way which

λέγουσιν αἵρεσιν, οὕτω λατρεύω τῷ
they call a sect, thus I am worshiping the

πατρῴῳ Θεῷ, πιστεύων πᾶσι τοῖς
[2]belonging [3]to [4]*my* [5]forefathers [1]God, believing in all the *things*

κατὰ τὸν Νόμον καὶ τοῖς Προφήταις γεγραμμένοις,
[4]throughout [5]the [6]Law [7]and [8]the [9]Prophets [1]having [2]been [3]written,
in which have

15 ἐλπίδα ἔχων εἰς τὸν Θεόν, ἣν καὶ αὐτοὶ οὗτοι
hope ˜ having in - God, which even [3]themselves [1]these [2]*ones*
they

προσδέχονται, ἀνάστασιν μέλλειν ἔσεσθαι νεκρῶν,[f]
are waiting for, a resurrection to be about to be of *the* dead,
that there is going to be a resurrection

δικαίων τε καὶ ἀδίκων. **16** Ἐν τούτῳ δὲ
[2]of [3]righteous [4]*ones* [1]both and of unrighteous *ones.* [2]in [3]this [1]And

αὐτὸς ἀσκῶ, ἀπρόσκοπον συνείδησιν ἔχων πρὸς τὸν
myself ˜ I am engaging, [3]blameless [2]a [4]conscience [1]having toward -

Θεὸν καὶ τοὺς ἀνθρώπους διὰ παντός. **17** Δι' ἐτῶν δὲ
God and - men through every*thing*. [2]through [4]years [1]Now
always. And after many

πλειόνων παρεγενόμην ἐλεημοσύνας ποιήσων εἰς τὸ
[3]more I arrived [5]alms [1]being [2]about [3]to [4]make [8]to -
years to bring

ἔθνος μου καὶ προσφοράς, **18** ἐν οἷς εὗρόν με
[10]nation [9]my [6]and [7]offerings, among whom [5]found [6]me

ἡγνισμένον ἐν τῷ ἱερῷ, οὐ μετὰ ὄχλου οὐδὲ
[7]having [8]been [9]purified [10]in [11]the [12]temple, [13]not [14]with [15]a [16]crowd [17]nor

μετὰ θορύβου, τινὲς ἀπὸ τῆς Ἀσίας Ἰουδαῖοι· **19** οὓς
[18]with [19]turmoil, [1]some [3]from - [4]Asia [2]Jews; *for* whom
who

e(24:13) NU reads σοι, *(to prove) to you.*
f(24:15) NU omits νεκρων, *of (the) dead.*

δεῖ ἐπὶ σοῦ παρεῖναι καὶ κατηγορεῖν εἴ
it is necessary [4]before [5]you [1]to [2]be [3]present and to make accusation if
ought

τι ἔχοιεν πρός με. 20 Ἢ αὐτοὶ οὗτοι
[4]anything [1]they [2]might [3]have against me. Or [3]themselves [2]these

εἰπάτωσαν τί[g] εὗρον ἐν ἐμοὶ ἀδίκημα, στάντος μου ἐπὶ
[1]let say what [2]they [3]found [4]in [5]me [1]wrong, standing ˜ me before
when I stood

τοῦ συνεδρίου, 21 ἢ περὶ μιᾶς ταύτης φωνῆς ἧς
the council, or *it is* because of one ˜ this voice which
unless statement

ἔκραξα ἑστὼς ἐν αὐτοῖς, ὅτι 'Περὶ ἀναστάσεως
I cried out standing among them, - 'Concerning *the* resurrection
when I stood

νεκρῶν ἐγὼ κρίνομαι σήμερον ὑφ' ὑμῶν.' "
of *the* dead I am being judged [3]today [1]by [2]you.' "

Felix Procrastinates

22 Ἀκούσας δὲ ταῦτα[h] ὁ Φῆλιξ ἀνεβάλετο αὐτούς,
hearing ˜ And these *things* - Felix adjourned them,
when he heard

ἀκριβέστερον εἰδὼς τὰ περὶ τῆς Ὁδοῦ, εἰπών,
[2]more [3]accurately [1]knowing the *things* concerning the Way, saying,
since he knew and said,

"Ὅταν Λυσίας ὁ χιλίαρχος καταβῇ, διαγνώσομαι τὰ
"When Lysias the chiliarch comes down, I will decide the *things*
commander your

καθ' ὑμᾶς," 23 διαταξάμενός τε τῷ ἑκατοντάρχῃ
according to you," ordering ˜ and the centurion
case," he ordered

τηρεῖσθαι τὸν Παῦλον, ἔχειν τε ἄνεσιν, καὶ
to keep watch over - Paul, [2]*for* [3]*him* [4]to [5]have [1]and freedom, and
some liberty,

μηδένα κωλύειν τῶν ἰδίων αὐτοῦ ὑπηρετεῖν ἢ
[3]no [4]one [1]to [2]forbid - of [2]own [3]*people* [1]his to serve or

προσέρχεσθαι[i] αὐτῷ.
to come to him.

24 Μετὰ δὲ ἡμέρας τινάς, παραγενόμενος ὁ Φῆλιξ σὺν
after ˜ Now days ˜ some, arriving ˜ - Felix with
when Felix arrived

Δρουσίλλῃ τῇ γυναικί, οὔσῃ Ἰουδαίᾳ, μετεπέμψατο τὸν
Drusilla the wife, being a Jewess, he sent for -
his who was

Παῦλον, καὶ ἤκουσεν αὐτοῦ περὶ τῆς εἰς Χριστὸν[j]
Paul, and heard of him concerning the [2]in [3]Christ
from

πίστεως.
[1]faith.

25 Διαλεγομένου δὲ αὐτοῦ περὶ δικαιοσύνης καὶ
discussing And him about righteousness and
And as he reasoned

ἐγκρατείας καὶ τοῦ κρίματος τοῦ μέλλοντος ἔσεσθαι,
self-control and the judgment the *one* being about to be,
which is going

ἔμφοβος γενόμενος ὁ Φῆλιξ ἀπεκρίθη, "Τὸ νῦν ἔχον
[3]afraid [2]becoming - [1]Felix answered, "The now having
became and answered, "For the present

πορεύου, καιρὸν δὲ μεταλαβὼν μετακαλέσομαί σε"·
go, [3]a [4]time [1]but [2]receiving I will summon you";
but when I have opportunity

here before you to object if they had anything against me.
20 "Or else let those who are *here* themselves say if they found any wrongdoing in me while I stood before the council,
21 "unless *it is* for this one statement which I cried out, standing among them, 'Concerning the resurrection of the dead I am being judged by you this day.' "
22 But when Felix heard these things, having more accurate knowledge of *the* Way, he adjourned the proceedings and said, "When Lysias the commander comes down, I will make a decision on your case."
23 So he commanded the centurion to keep Paul and to let *him* have liberty, and told him not to forbid any of his friends to provide for or visit him.
24 And after some days, when Felix came with his wife Drusilla, who was Jewish, he sent for Paul and heard him concerning the faith in Christ.
25 Now as he reasoned about righteousness, self-control, and the judgment to come, Felix was afraid and answered, "Go away for now; when I have a convenient time I will call for you."

---

[g](24:20) TR reads ει τι, *if any*, thus *if (they found) any (wrong in me)*.
[h](24:22) NU omits Ακουσας ταυτα, *when he heard these things*.
[i](24:23) NU omits η προσερχεσθαι, *or to come to*. [j](24:24) NU adds Ιησουν, *Jesus*.

26 Meanwhile he also hoped
that money would be given him
by Paul, that he might release
him. Therefore he sent for him
more often and conversed with
him.
27 But after two years Por-
cius Festus succeeded Felix;
and Felix, wanting to do the
Jews a favor, left Paul bound.
25 Now when Festus had
come to the province,
after three days he went up
from Caesarea to Jerusalem.
2 Then the high priest and
the chief men of the Jews informed him against Paul; and
they petitioned him,
3 asking a favor against him,
that he would summon him to
Jerusalem—while *they* lay in
ambush along the road to kill
him.
4 But Festus answered that
Paul should be kept at Caesarea, and that he himself was going *there* shortly.
5 "Therefore," he said, "let
those who have authority
among you go down with *me*
and accuse this man, to see if
there is any fault in him."
6 And when he had remained
among them more than ten
days, he went down to Caesarea. And the next day, sitting
on the judgment seat, he commanded Paul to be brought.

26 ἅμα καὶ ἐλπίζων ὅτι χρήματα δοθήσεται αὐτῷ
at the same time also hoping that money will be given to him
he also hoped would

ὑπὸ τοῦ Παύλου, ὅπως λύσῃ αὐτόν·[k] διὸ καὶ
by - Paul, that he might release him; therefore also

πυκνότερον αὐτὸν μεταπεμπόμενος ὡμίλει αὐτῷ.
[4]more [5]often [3]him [1]sending [2]for he was conversing with him.

27 Διετίας δὲ πληρωθείσης, ἔλαβε
[2]a [3]two-year [4]period [1]And being fulfilled, [2]received
And after two years had passed,

διάδοχον ὁ Φῆλιξ Πόρκιον Φῆστον· θέλων τε χάριτας
[5]*as* [6]*his* [7]successor - [1]Felix [3]Porcius [4]Festus; desiring ~ and [3]favors

καταθέσθαι τοῖς Ἰουδαίοις ὁ Φῆλιξ κατέλιπε τὸν Παῦλον
[1]to [2]grant to the Jews - Felix left - Paul

δεδεμένον.
having been bound.
imprisoned.

Festus Agrees to Send Paul to Caesar

25 **1** Φῆστος οὖν ἐπιβὰς τῇ ἐπαρχείᾳ, μετὰ τρεῖς
Festus ~ Then setting foot in in the province, after three
When Festus had set

ἡμέρας ἀνέβη εἰς Ἱεροσόλυμα ἀπὸ Καισαρείας.
days he went up to Jerusalem from Caesarea.

2 Ἐνεφάνισαν δὲ αὐτῷ ὁ ἀρχιερεὺς[a] καὶ οἱ
[12]made [13]known [1]And [14]to [15]him [2]the [3]high [4]priest [5]and [6]the

πρῶτοι τῶν Ἰουδαίων κατὰ τοῦ Παύλου, καὶ
[7]foremost [8]*men* [9]of [10]the [11]Jews *the case* against - Paul, and
prominent

παρεκάλουν αὐτόν, **3** αἰτούμενοι χάριν κατ' αὐτοῦ
they were appealing to him, asking for favor against him
support

ὅπως μεταπέμψηται αὐτὸν εἰς Ἰερουσαλήμ, ἐνέδραν
that he would summon him to Jerusalem, [2]an [3]ambush

ποιοῦντες ἀνελεῖν αὐτὸν κατὰ τὴν ὁδόν. **4** Ὁ μὲν οὖν Φῆστος
[1]making to kill him along the way. - - Then Festus
planning

ἀπεκρίθη τηρεῖσθαι τὸν Παῦλον ἐν Καισαρείᾳ, ἑαυτὸν
answered *that* [2]to [3]be [4]kept - [1]Paul in Caesarea, [4]himself
should

δὲ μέλλειν ἐν τάχει ἐκπορεύεσθαι. **5** "Οἱ
[1]and [2]*that* [3]*he* to be about [5]in [6]quickness [1]to [2]go [3]out [4]*there.* "the ~
was shortly

οὖν δυνατοὶ ἐν ὑμῖν," φησί, "συγκαταβάντες, εἴ
Therefore powerful *ones* among you," he said, "going down with *me,* if
prominent men "let them go

τί ἐστιν ἐν τῷ ἀνδρὶ τούτῳ,[b] κατηγορείτωσαν αὐτοῦ."
[3]anything [1]*there* [2]is in - man ~ this, let them accuse him."

6 Διατρίψας δὲ ἐν αὐτοῖς ἡμέρας πλείους[c] ἢ
spending ~ And among them [4]days [1]more [2]than
when he had stayed

δέκα, καταβὰς εἰς Καισάρειαν, τῇ ἐπαύριον καθίσας ἐπὶ
[3]ten, going down to Caesarea, on the next day sitting at
he went he sat

τοῦ βήματος ἐκέλευσε τὸν Παῦλον ἀχθῆναι.
the judicial bench he commanded - Paul to be brought.
and

---

k(24:26) NU omits *οπως λυση αυτον, that he might release him.*
a(25:2) NU reads *οι αρχιερεις, the chief priests.*
b(25:5) NU reads *ατοπον, (if there is anything) improper (in this man).*
c(25:6) NU adds *οκτω, (more than) eight or (ten days).*

7 Παραγενομένου δὲ αὐτοῦ, περιέστησαν[d] οἱ ἀπὸ
arriving And him, [8]stood [9]around [10]*him* [1]the [6]from
And when he arrived,

Ἱεροσολύμων καταβεβηκότες Ἰουδαῖοι, πολλὰ καὶ βαρέα
[7]Jerusalem [3]having [4]come [5]down [2]Jews, [12]many [13]and [14]heavy
who came serious

αἰτιώματα φέροντες κατὰ τοῦ Παύλου ἃ οὐκ ἴσχυον
[15]accusations [11]bringing against - Paul which [3]not [1]they [2]were able

ἀποδεῖξαι, **8** ἀπολογουμένου αὐτοῦ ὅτι "Οὔτε εἰς τὸν
to prove, defending himself him - *saying* "Neither against the
while he defended himself

νόμον τῶν Ἰουδαίων οὔτε εἰς τὸ ἱερὸν οὔτε εἰς Καίσαρά
law of the Jews nor against the temple nor against Caesar

τι ἥμαρτον."
[4]any [1]did [2]I [3]commit sin."

9 Ὁ Φῆστος δὲ τοῖς Ἰουδαίοις θέλων χάριν
- Festus ˜ But [6]to [7]the [8]Jews [1]desiring [4]a [5]favor

καταθέσθαι, ἀποκριθεὶς τῷ Παύλῳ εἶπε, "Θέλεις εἰς
[2]to [3]grant, answering - Paul said, "Are you willing [3]to
answered and said,

Ἱεροσόλυμα ἀναβάς, ἐκεῖ περὶ τούτων κρίνεσθαι
[4]Jerusalem [1]going [2]up, there [6]concerning [7]these [8]*things* [1]to [2]be [3]judged
to go

ἐπ' ἐμοῦ?"
[4]before [5]me?"

10 Εἶπε δὲ ὁ Παῦλος, "Ἐπὶ τοῦ βήματος Καίσαρος
[3]said [1]But - [2]Paul, "Before the judicial bench of Caesar

ἑστώς εἰμι, οὗ με δεῖ κρίνεσθαι·
[3]standing [1]I [2]am, of whom [5]me [1]it [2]is [3]necessary [4]*for* to be judged;
by

Ἰουδαίους οὐδὲν ἠδίκησα, ὡς καὶ σὺ κάλλιον ἐπιγινώσκεις.
[3]*the* [4]Jews [5]nothing [1]I [2]wronged, as also you [2]very [3]well [1]know.
I have done no wrong to the Jews,

11 Εἰ μὲν γὰρ ἀδικῶ καὶ ἄξιον θανάτου πέπραχά
if ˜ - For I am doing wrong and [4]worthy [5]of [6]death [1]have [2]done

τι, οὐ παραιτοῦμαι τὸ ἀποθανεῖν· εἰ δὲ οὐδέν
[3]anything, [9]not [7]I [8]am [10]avoiding - to die; if ˜ but [3]nothing
trying to escape a death sentence;

ἐστιν ὧν οὗτοι κατηγοροῦσί μου, οὐδείς με
[1]*there* [2]is of *the things* which these *people* are accusing me, no one [5]me
to

δύναται αὐτοῖς χαρίσασθαι. Καίσαρα ἐπικαλοῦμαι."
[1]is [2]able [6]to [7]them [3]to [4]give. [11]Caesar [8]I [9]appeal [10]to."
deliver.

12 Τότε ὁ Φῆστος συλλαλήσας μετὰ τοῦ συμβουλίου
Then - Festus having talked together with - the council
his

ἀπεκρίθη, "Καίσαρα ἐπικέκλησαι? Ἐπὶ Καίσαρα
answered, "[5]Caesar [1]Have [2]you [3]appealed [4]to? Before Caesar

πορεύσῃ!"
you shall go!"

Paul Brought Before Agrippa and Bernice

13 Ἡμερῶν δὲ διαγενομένων τινῶν, Ἀγρίππας ὁ
days Now passing by some, Agrippa the
Now when some days had passed,

7 When he had come, the Jews who had come down from Jerusalem stood about and laid many serious complaints against Paul, which they could not prove,
8 while he answered for himself, "Neither against the law of the Jews, nor against the temple, nor against Caesar have I offended in anything at all."
9 But Festus, wanting to do the Jews a favor, answered Paul and said, "Are you willing to go up to Jerusalem and there be judged before me concerning these things?"
10 So Paul said, "I stand at Caesar's judgment seat, where I ought to be judged. To the Jews I have done no wrong, as you very well know.
11 "For if I am an offender, or have committed anything deserving of death, I do not object to dying; but if there is nothing in these things of which these men accuse me, no one can deliver me to them. I appeal to Caesar."
12 Then Festus, when he had conferred with the council, answered, "You have appealed to Caesar? To Caesar you shall go!"
13 And after some days King Agrippa and Bernice came to

---

[d](25:7) NU adds *αυτον*, *(stood around) him.*

Caesarea to greet Festus.
14 When they had been there
many days, Festus laid Paul's
case before the king, saying:
"There is a certain man left a
prisoner by Felix,
15 "about whom the chief
priests and the elders of the
Jews informed *me,* when I was
in Jerusalem, asking for a judgment against him.
16 "To them I answered, 'It is
not the custom of the Romans
to deliver any man to destruction before the accused meets
the accusers face to face, and
has opportunity to answer for
himself concerning the charge
against him.'
17 "Therefore when they had
come together, without any delay, the next day I sat on the
judgment seat and commanded
the man to be brought in.
18 "When the accusers stood
up, they brought no accusation
against him of such things as I
supposed,
19 "but had some questions
against him about their own religion and about a certain Jesus,
who had died, whom Paul affirmed to be alive.
20 "And because I was uncertain of such questions, I asked
whether he was willing to go to
Jerusalem and there be judged
concerning these matters.

βασιλεὺς καὶ Βερνίκη κατήντησαν εἰς Καισάρειαν
king and Bernice arrived in Caesarea

ἀσπασάμενοι τὸν Φῆστον.
greeting - Festus.
and greeted

14 *Ὡς δὲ πλείους ἡμέρας διέτριβεν*[e] *ἐκεῖ, ὁ Φῆστος*
as ˜ And [4]more [5]days [1]he [2]was [3]spending there, - Festus
many

τῷ βασιλεῖ ἀνέθετο τὰ κατὰ τὸν Παῦλον, λέγων,
[3]the [4]king [1]laid [2]before the *things* against - Paul, saying,
charges

"Ἀνήρ τίς ἐστι καταλελειμμένος ὑπὸ Φήλικος
"[3]a [5]man [4]certain [1]*There* [2]is having been left [3]by [4]Felix
who was

δέσμιος, **15** *περὶ οὗ, γενομένου μου εἰς Ἱεροσόλυμα,*
[1]a [2]prisoner, about whom, being ˜ me in Jerusalem,
when I was

ἐνεφάνισαν οἱ ἀρχιερεῖς καὶ οἱ πρεσβύτεροι τῶν
[10]informed [11]*me* [1]the [2]chief [3]priests [4]and [5]the [6]elders [7]of [8]the

Ἰουδαίων, αἰτούμενοι κατ' αὐτοῦ δίκην· **16** *πρὸς οὓς*
[9]Jews, asking for [2]against [3]him [1]punishment; to whom

ἀπεκρίθην ὅτι οὐκ ἔστιν ἔθος Ῥωμαίοις χαρίζεσθαί τινα
I answered that [3]not [1]it [2]is a custom with Romans to give any
deliver

ἄνθρωπον εἰς ἀπώλειαν[f] *πρὶν ἢ ὁ κατηγορούμενος*
man to destruction before - the *one* being accused

κατὰ πρόσωπον ἔχοι τοὺς κατηγόρους, τόπον
[5]according [6]to [7]face [1]may [2]have [3]the [4]accusers, [11]an [12]opportunity
face to may meet his

τε ἀπολογίας λάβοι περὶ τοῦ ἐγκλήματος.
[8]and [13]of [14]defense [9]may [10]receive concerning the charge.
for

17 *Συνελθόντων οὖν αὐτῶν ἐνθάδε, ἀναβολὴν μηδεμίαν*
assembling Therefore them here, [4]delay [3]no
Therefore when they had assembled

ποιησάμενος, τῇ ἑξῆς καθίσας ἐπὶ τοῦ βήματος,
[1]having [2]made, on the next *day* sitting at the judicial bench,
I took my seat

ἐκέλευσα ἀχθῆναι τὸν ἄνδρα· **18** *περὶ οὗ*
I commanded [3]to [4]be [5]brought [1]the [2]man; concerning whom
and

σταθέντες οἱ κατήγοροι οὐδεμίαν αἰτίαν ἐπέφερον
standing the accusers [2]no [3]accusation [1]brought
when the accusers stood, they brought

ὧν ὑπενόουν ἐγώ,[g] **19** *ζητήματα δέ τινα*
of *the things* which [2]was [3]supposing [1]I, [5]questions [1]but [4]some

περὶ τῆς ἰδίας δεισιδαιμονίας εἶχον πρὸς αὐτὸν καὶ
[6]about - [7]their [8]own [9]religion [2]they [3]had against him and

περί τινος Ἰησοῦ τεθνηκότος, ὃν ἔφασκεν ὁ Παῦλος
about a certain Jesus having died, whom claimed ˜ - Paul
who had

ζῆν. **20** *Ἀπορούμενος δὲ ἐγὼ τὴν περὶ*
to be living. [3]being [4]at [5]a [6]loss [1]And [2]I *as to* the [2]concerning
And since I was uncertain

τούτου ζήτησιν, ἔλεγον εἰ βούλοιτο πορεύεσθαι εἰς
[3]this [1]investigation, I said whether he was willing to go to
asked

Ἱερουσαλὴμ κἀκεῖ κρίνεσθαι περὶ τούτων. **21** *Τοῦ*
Jerusalem and there to be judged concerning these *things.* -
charges.

---

[e](25:14) NU, TR read *διετριβον, they were spending.*
[f](25:16) NU omits *εις απωλειαν, to destruction.*
[g](25:18) NU adds *πονηρων, (of the) crimes (which I was supposing).*

δὲ Παύλου ἐπικαλεσαμένου τηρηθῆναι αὐτὸν εἰς τὴν τοῦ
But Paul appealing [2]to [3]be [4]kept [1]him for the -
But when Paul appealed that he be kept

Σεβαστοῦ διάγνωσιν, ἐκέλευσα τηρεῖσθαι
[2]of [3]His [4]Majesty [5]the [6]Emperor [1]decision, I commanded [2]to [3]be [4]kept
that he be

αὐτὸν ἕως οὗ πέμψω αὐτὸν πρὸς Καίσαρα."
[1]him until - I may send him to Caesar."
kept

22 Ἀγρίππας δὲ πρὸς τὸν Φῆστον ἔφη, "Ἐβουλόμην καὶ
Agrippa ˜ And [2]to - [3]Festus [1]said, "I [3]was [4]wishing [2]also

αὐτὸς τοῦ ἀνθρώπου ἀκοῦσαι."
[1]myself [7]the [8]man [5]to [6]hear."

Ὁ δέ, "Αὔριον," φησίν, "ἀκούσῃ αὐτοῦ."
[2]the [3]*one* [1]And, "[5]Tomorrow," [4]said, "you will hear him."
he

23 Τῇ οὖν ἐπαύριον, ἐλθόντος τοῦ Ἀγρίππα
[2]on [3]the [1]Therefore next day, [4]coming - [1]Agrippa
when Agrippa and

καὶ τῆς Βερνίκης μετὰ πολλῆς φαντασίας καὶ εἰσελθόντων
[2]and - [3]Bernice with all pomp and entering
Bernice had come entered

εἰς τὸ ἀκροατήριον, σύν τε τοῖς χιλιάρχοις καὶ
into the auditorium, [2]together [3]with [1]and the chiliarchs and
commanders

ἀνδράσι τοῖς κατ' ἐξοχὴν οὖσι τῆς πόλεως, καὶ
men the *ones* [2]according [3]to [4]excellence [1]being of the city, and
who were most prominent in

κελεύσαντος τοῦ Φήστου, ἤχθη ὁ Παῦλος.
commanding ˜ - Festus, [2]was [3]brought - [1]Paul.
when Festus had commanded,

24 Καί φησιν ὁ Φῆστος, "Ἀγρίππα βασιλεῦ καὶ πάντες οἱ
And said ˜ - Festus, "Agrippa ˜ King and all the

συμπαρόντες ἡμῖν ἄνδρες, θεωρεῖτε τοῦτον περὶ οὗ πᾶν τὸ
[2]being [3]with [4]us [1]men, observe this *man* about whom all the
who are

πλῆθος τῶν Ἰουδαίων ἐνέτυχόν μοι ἔν τε Ἱεροσολύμοις καὶ
number of the Jews petitioned me in ˜ both Jerusalem and
people

ἐνθάδε, ἐπιβοῶντες μὴ δεῖν ζῆν αὐτὸν
here, crying against *him* [3]not [1]to [2]be [4]fitting [5]*for* [7]to [8]live [6]him
that it is

μηκέτι. **25** Ἐγὼ δὲ καταλαβόμενος μηδὲν ἄξιον θανάτου
no longer. I ˜ But understanding [5]nothing [6]worthy [7]of [8]death
any But when I came to understand

αὐτὸν πεπραχέναι, καὶ αὐτοῦ δὲ τούτου ἐπικαλεσαμένου
[1]him [2]to [3]have [4]done, [10]also [13]himself [9]and [11]this [12]*one* appealing to
he had appealed

τὸν Σεβαστόν, ἔκρινα πέμπειν αὐτόν. **26** Περὶ
- His Majesty the Emperor, I decided to send him. About

οὗ ἀσφαλές τι γράψαι τῷ κυρίῳ οὐκ ἔχω.
whom [6]certain [5]anything [7]to [8]write [9]to [10]the [11]lord [3]not [1]I [2]do [4]have.
my

Διὸ προήγαγον αὐτὸν ἐφ' ὑμῶν καὶ μάλιστα ἐπὶ σοῦ,
Therefore I brought him before you and especially before you,
have brought

Βασιλεῦ Ἀγρίππα, ὅπως τῆς ἀνακρίσεως γενομένης
King Agrippa, in order that the hearing taking place
when this hearing has finished

21 "But when Paul appealed to be reserved for the decision of Augustus, I commanded him to be kept till I could send him to Caesar."
22 Then Agrippa said to Festus, "I also would like to hear the man myself." "Tomorrow," he said, "you shall hear him."
23 So the next day, when Agrippa and Bernice had come with great pomp, and had entered the auditorium with the commanders and the prominent men of the city, at Festus' command Paul was brought in.
24 And Festus said: "King Agrippa and all the men who are here present with us, you see this man about whom the whole assembly of the Jews petitioned me, both at Jerusalem and here, crying out that he was not fit to live any longer.
25 "But when I found that he had committed nothing deserving of death, and that he himself had appealed to Augustus, I decided to send him.
26 "I have nothing certain to write to my lord concerning him. Therefore I have brought him out before you, and especially before you, King Agrippa, so that after the examination has taken place I may have

something to write.
27 "For it seems to me unreasonable to send a prisoner and
not to specify the charges
against him."
26 Then Agrippa said to
Paul, "You are permit-
ted to speak for yourself." So
Paul stretched out his hand and
answered for himself:
2 "I think myself happy, King
Agrippa, because today I shall
answer for myself before you
concerning all the things of
which I am accused by the
Jews,
3 "especially because you
are expert in all customs and
questions which have to do with
the Jews. Therefore I beg you
to hear me patiently.
4 "My manner of life from
my youth, which was spent
from the beginning among my
own nation at Jerusalem, all the
Jews know.
5 "They knew me from the
first, if they were willing to testify, that according to the strictest sect of our religion I lived a
Pharisee.
6 "And now I stand and am
judged for the hope of the
promise made by God to our fathers.
7 "To this *promise* our
twelve tribes, earnestly serving
God night and day, hope to attain. For this hope's sake, King
Agrippa, I am accused by the
Jews.
8 "Why should it be thought
incredible by you that God
raises the dead?
9 "Indeed, I myself thought I
must do many things contrary

σχῶ τι γράψαι. **27** Ἄλογον γάρ μοι δοκεῖ
I may have something to write. [4]unreasonable [1]For [5]to [6]me [2]it [3]seems

πέμποντα δέσμιον, μὴ καὶ τὰς κατ' αὐτοῦ αἰτίας
sending a prisoner, not [3]also [4]the [6]against [7]him [5]accusations
to send

σημᾶναι."
[1]to [2]signify."

Paul Defends His Pre-Conversion Life

26 **1** Ἀγρίππας δὲ πρὸς τὸν Παῦλον ἔφη, "Ἐπιτρέπεταί
Agrippa ˜ And [2]to - [3]Paul [1]said, "It is permitted

σοι ὑπὲρ σεαυτοῦ λέγειν."
for you [3]in [4]behalf [5]of [6]yourself [1]to [2]speak."

Τότε ὁ Παῦλος ἀπελογεῖτο, ἐκτείνας τὴν
Then - Paul spoke in his own defense, having extended the
his

χεῖρα, **2** "Περὶ πάντων ὧν ἐγκαλοῦμαι ὑπὸ
hand, "Concerning all *the things* of which I am accused by

Ἰουδαίων, Βασιλεῦ Ἀγρίππα, ἥγημαι ἐμαυτὸν μακάριον
the Jews, King Agrippa, I have considered myself fortunate

ἐπὶ σοῦ μέλλων ἀπολογεῖσθαι σήμερον,
[9]before [10]you [1]being [2]about [3]to [4]speak [5]in [6]my [7]own [8]defense today,
to be

3 μάλιστα γνώστην ὄντα σὲ πάντων τῶν κατὰ
especially [3]an [4]expert [2]being [1]you [6]*in* [7]all [8]the [12]in [13]relation [14]to
since you are well versed

Ἰουδαίους ἠθῶν τε καὶ ζητημάτων· διὸ δέομαί σου,
[15]*the* [16]Jews [9]customs [5]both [10]and [11]questions; therefore I beg you,

μακροθύμως ἀκοῦσαί μου. **4** Τὴν μὲν οὖν βίωσίν μου
[4]patiently [1]to [2]hear [3]me. - - Therefore [2]way [3]of [4]life [1]my

τὴν ἐκ νεότητος τὴν ἀπ' ἀρχῆς γενομένην ἐν τῷ
- from *my* youth the one from *the* beginning being among -
which was spent

ἔθνει μου ἐν Ἱεροσολύμοις, ἴσασι πάντες οἱ Ἰουδαῖοι,
nation ˜ my in Jerusalem, [4]know [1]all [2]the [3]Jews,

5 προγινώσκοντές με ἄνωθεν, ἐὰν θέλωσι
knowing beforehand ˜ me for a long time, if they are willing
since they have known

μαρτυρεῖν, ὅτι κατὰ τὴν ἀκριβεστάτην αἵρεσιν τῆς
to testify, that according to the strictest sect -

ἡμετέρας θρησκείας* ἔζησα Φαρισαῖος. **6** Καὶ νῦν ἐπ' ἐλπίδι
of our religion I lived *as* a Pharisee. And now for *the* hope

τῆς πρὸς τοὺς πατέρας ἐπαγγελίας γενομένης ὑπὸ τοῦ
of the [7]to [8]the [9]fathers [1]promise [2]having [3]been [4]made [5]by -
our

Θεοῦ ἕστηκα κρινόμενος, **7** εἰς ἣν τὸ δωδεκάφυλον
[6]God I stand being judged, *a promise* to which - [2]twelve [3]tribes

ἡμῶν ἐν ἐκτενείᾳ νύκτα καὶ ἡμέραν λατρεῦον ἐλπίζει
[1]our in earnestness [3]night [4]and [5]day [1]serving [2]*God* hope
as they earnestly serve

καταντῆσαι. Περὶ ἧς ἐλπίδος ἐγκαλοῦμαι, Βασιλεῦ
to attain. Concerning which hope I am accused, King

Ἀγρίππα,[a] ὑπὸ Ἰουδαίων. **8** Τί ἄπιστον
Agrippa, by *the* Jews. Why [4]an [5]unbelievable [6]*thing*

κρίνεται παρ' ὑμῖν, εἰ ὁ Θεὸς νεκροὺς ἐγείρει?
[1]is [2]it [3]considered by you *people,* if - God [2]*the* [3]dead [1]raises?

9 Ἐγὼ μὲν οὖν ἔδοξα ἐμαυτῷ πρὸς τὸ ὄνομα Ἰησοῦ
I ˜ - Therefore thought in myself [9]against [10]the [11]name [12]of [13]Jesus

---

[a](26:7) NU omits Αγριππα, *Agrippa*.

*(26:5) θρησκεία (*thrēskeia*). Noun meaning *religion* in the sense of *outward duties of one's belief.* Here it is used for the sect of Judaism, elsewhere for the cult of angel worship (Col. 2:18) and for the essentials of true religion, the charity that is motivated by the love of God (James 1:26, 27). Cf. the cognate adjective θρῆσκος, *religious,* used to describe those who are careful to practice the visible things pertaining to serving God (James 1:26).

τοῦ Ναζωραίου δεῖν πολλὰ ἐναντία πρᾶξαι·
[14]the [15]Nazarene [1]to [2]be [3]necessary [6]many [8]*things* [7]hostile [4]to [5]do;
that it was

10 ὃ καὶ ἐποίησα ἐν Ἱεροσολύμοις, καὶ πολλοὺς τῶν
which also I did in Jerusalem, and many of the

ἁγίων ἐγὼ φυλακαῖς κατέκλεισα, τὴν παρὰ τῶν ἀρχιερέων
saints I [3]in [4]prisons [1]shut [2]up, [7]the [9]from [10]the [11]chief [12]priests

ἐξουσίαν λαβών, ἀναιρουμένων τε αὐτῶν
[8]authority [5]having [6]received, [15]being [16]put [17]to [18]death [13]and [14]them
when they were

κατήνεγκα ψῆφον. **11** Καὶ κατὰ πάσας τὰς συναγωγὰς
I cast [3]against [4]*them* [1]a [2]pebble. And [4]in [5]all [6]the [7]synagogues
my vote.

πολλάκις τιμωρῶν αὐτούς, ἠνάγκαζον βλασφημεῖν,
[3]often [1]punishing [2]them, I was compelling *them* to blaspheme,
I punished and compelled

περισσῶς τε ἐμμαινόμενος αὐτοῖς, ἐδίωκον
[3]exceedingly [1]and [2]being enraged against them, I persecuted *them*

ἕως καὶ εἰς τὰς ἔξω πόλεις.
[2]as [3]far [4]as [1]even to the outer cities.
foreign

Paul Recounts His Conversion

(Acts 9:1–19; 22:6–16)

12 "Ἐν οἷς καὶ πορευόμενος εἰς τὴν Δαμασκὸν
"In which *pursuits* also traveling to - Damascus
as I traveled

μετ' ἐξουσίας καὶ ἐπιτροπῆς τῆς παρὰ τῶν ἀρχιερέων,
with authority and a commission - from the chief priests,

13 ἡμέρας μέσης, κατὰ τὴν ὁδὸν εἶδον, βασιλεῦ,
[4]of [5]*the* [6]day [1]in [2]the [3]middle, along the way I saw, *O* king,

οὐρανόθεν ὑπὲρ τὴν λαμπρότητα τοῦ ἡλίου,
[3]from [4]heaven [5]more [6]than [7]the [8]brightness [9]of [10]the [11]sun,

περιλάμψαν με φῶς καὶ τοὺς σὺν ἐμοὶ πορευομένους.
[12]shining [13]around [14]me [1]a [2]light and the *ones* [2]with [3]me [1]traveling.
which shone

14 Πάντων δὲ καταπεσόντων ἡμῶν εἰς τὴν γῆν,
all And falling down us to the ground,
And when we had all fallen down

ἤκουσα φωνὴν λαλοῦσαν πρός με καὶ λέγουσαν τῇ Ἑβραΐδι
I heard a voice speaking to me and saying in the Hebrew

διαλέκτῳ, 'Σαούλ, Σαούλ, τί με διώκεις? Σκληρόν
language, 'Saul, Saul, why [4]Me [1]are [2]you [3]persecuting? *It is* hard

σοι πρὸς κέντρα λακτίζειν.' **15** Ἐγὼ δὲ εἶπον, 'Τίς
for you [3]against [4]*the* [5]goads [1]to [2]kick.' I ˜ And said, 'Who

εἶ, Κύριε?' Ὁ δὲ[b] εἶπεν, 'Ἐγώ εἰμι Ἰησοῦς ὃν σὺ
are You, Lord?' [2]the [3]*One* [1]And said, 'I am Jesus whom you
He

διώκεις. **16** Ἀλλὰ ἀνάστηθι καὶ στῆθι ἐπὶ τοὺς πόδας
are persecuting. But arise and stand on - feet ˜

σου· εἰς τοῦτο γὰρ ὤφθην σοι, προχειρίσασθαί σε
your; [2]for [3]this *purpose* [1]for I appeared to you, to appoint you
have appeared

ὑπηρέτην καὶ μάρτυρα ὧν τε εἶδές[c]
a servant and a witness [2]of [3]*the* [4]*things* [5]which [1]both you saw
minister have seen

ὧν τε ὀφθήσομαί σοι, **17** ἐξαιρούμενός σε
[2]of [3]*the* [4]*things* [5]*in* [6]which [1]and I will appear to you, delivering you

to the name of Jesus of Nazareth.
10 "This I also did in Jerusalem, and many of the saints I
shut up in prison, having received authority from the chief
priests; and when they were
put to death, I cast my vote
against *them.*
11 "And I punished them often
in every synagogue and compelled *them* to blaspheme; and
being exceedingly enraged
against them, I persecuted
them even to foreign cities.
12 "While thus occupied, as I
journeyed to Damascus with
authority and commission from
the chief priests,
13 "at midday, O king, along
the road I saw a light from
heaven, brighter than the sun,
shining around me and those
who journeyed with me.
14 "And when we all had fallen
to the ground, I heard a voice
speaking to me and saying in
the Hebrew language, 'Saul,
Saul, why are you persecuting
Me? *It is* hard for you to kick
against the goads.'
15 "So I said, 'Who are You,
Lord?' And He said, 'I am Jesus, whom you are persecuting.
16 'But rise and stand on your
feet; for I have appeared to you
for this purpose, to make you a
minister and a witness both of
the things which you have seen
and of the things which I will
yet reveal to you.
17 'I will deliver you from the

---

[b]**(26:15)** NU adds Κυριος, *(the) Lord.*
[c]**(26:16)** NU adds in brackets με, *(you have seen about) me.*

Jewish people, as well as *from* the Gentiles, to whom I now send you,
18 'to open their eyes, *in order* to turn *them* from darkness to light, and *from* the power of Satan to God, that they may receive forgiveness of sins and an inheritance among those who are sanctified by faith in Me.'
19 "Therefore, King Agrippa, I was not disobedient to the heavenly vision,
20 "but declared first to those in Damascus and in Jerusalem, and throughout all the region of Judea, and *then* to the Gentiles, that they should repent, turn to God, and do works befitting repentance.
21 "For these reasons the Jews seized me in the temple and tried to kill *me*.
22 "Therefore, having obtained help from God, to this day I stand, witnessing both to small and great, saying no other things than those which the prophets and Moses said would come—
23 "that the Christ would suffer, that He would be the first to rise from the dead, and would proclaim light to the *Jewish* people and to the Gentiles."
24 Now as he thus made his defense, Festus said with a loud voice, "Paul, you are beside yourself! Much learning is driving you mad!"

---

d(26:17) TR adds *νυν*, *now*.

*(26:20) *μετανοέω* (*metanoeō*). Verb compounded from *μετά*, *after*, and *νοέω*, *perceive*, *think*, meaning *change one's mind*, *feel regret*, *repent*. Although associated with the idea of "turning to God" (as here), the primary meaning of *μετανοέω* relates to the turning away "from evil" (Acts 8:22; cf. Rev. 9:20, 21). It may imply not only ceasing evil acts, but also beginning good ones ("fruit in keeping with repentance," Matt. 3:8). John the Baptist preached to Israel, "Repent, for the kingdom of heaven is at hand" (Matt. 3:2; cf. 4:17), and this call was continued in the preaching of the apostles (cf. Acts 2:38). God leads us to repentance (Rom. 2:4) and desires that all should "come to repentance" (2 Pet. 3:9). Cf. the near synonym *μεταμέλομαι*, *have remorse* (Matt. 27:3; 2 Cor. 7:8); and the cognate noun *μετάνοια*, *repentance* (Acts 20:21).

ἐκ τοῦ λαοῦ καὶ τῶν ἐθνῶν, εἰς οὓς ἐγὼ[d] σε
from the people and from the Gentiles, to whom I [3]you

ἀποστέλλω 18 ἀνοῖξαι ὀφθαλμοὺς αὐτῶν τοῦ ὑποστρέψαι
[1]am [2]sending to open eyes ˜ their - *in order* to turn *them*

ἀπὸ σκότους εἰς φῶς καὶ τῆς ἐξουσίας τοῦ Σατανᾶ ἐπὶ τὸν
from darkness to light and from the authority - of Satan to -

Θεόν, τοῦ λαβεῖν αὐτοὺς ἄφεσιν ἁμαρτιῶν καὶ
God, - *in order for* [2]to [3]receive [1]them forgiveness of sins and

κλῆρον ἐν τοῖς ἡγιασμένοις πίστει τῇ εἰς ἐμέ.'
an inheritance among the *ones* having been sanctified by faith - in Me.'

Paul Defends His Post-Conversion Life

19 "Ὅθεν, Βασιλεῦ Ἀγρίππα, οὐκ ἐγενόμην
"For which reason, King Agrippa, [3]not [1]I [2]was

ἀπειθὴς τῇ οὐρανίῳ ὀπτασίᾳ, 20 ἀλλὰ τοῖς ἐν
disobedient to the heavenly vision, but [2]to [3]the [4]*ones* [5]in

Δαμασκῷ πρῶτον καὶ Ἱεροσολύμοις, εἰς πᾶσάν τε τὴν
[6]Damascus [1]first and Jerusalem, [2]into [3]all [1]and the

χώραν τῆς Ἰουδαίας καὶ τοῖς ἔθνεσιν, ἀπαγγέλλων
region - of Judea and to the Gentiles, proclaiming *for them*
proclaimed that they

μετανοεῖν* καὶ ἐπιστρέφειν ἐπὶ τὸν Θεόν, ἄξια τῆς
to repent and to turn to - God, [3]worthy [4]of [5]the
must repent turn this

μετανοίας ἔργα πράσσοντας. 21 Ἕνεκα τούτων με
[6]repentance [2]works [1]doing. Because of these *things* [4]me
and do.

οἱ Ἰουδαῖοι συλλαβόμενοι ἐν τῷ ἱερῷ ἐπειρῶντο
[1]the [2]Jews [3]arresting in the temple were attempting
arrested and attempted

διαχειρίσασθαι. 22 Ἐπικουρίας οὖν τυχὼν
to lay violent hands on *me*. [4]help [1]Therefore [2]having [3]obtained
kill

τῆς παρὰ τοῦ Θεοῦ, ἄχρι τῆς ἡμέρας ταύτης ἕστηκα
- from - God, until - day ˜ this I stand

μαρτυρόμενος μικρῷ τε καὶ μεγάλῳ, οὐδὲν ἐκτὸς
bearing witness [2]to [3]small [4]*people* [1]both and to great *people,* [2]nothing [3]except
common

λέγων ὧν τε οἱ προφῆται ἐλάλησαν μελλόντων
[1]saying *the things* which both the prophets [3]spoke [4]of [5]*as* [6]being [7]about

γίνεσθαι καὶ Μωσῆς, 23 εἰ παθητὸς ὁ Χριστός,
[8]to [9]happen [1]and [2]Moses, that [4]subject [5]to [6]suffering [1]the [2]Christ [3]*was,*
to suffer Messiah

εἰ πρῶτος ἐξ ἀναστάσεως νεκρῶν φῶς μέλλει
that *as the* first from resurrection from *the* dead [6]a [7]light [1]He [2]is [3]about
to rise was

καταγγέλλειν τῷ λαῷ καὶ τοῖς ἔθνεσι."
[4]to [5]proclaim to the *Jewish* people and to the Gentiles."

Agrippa Parries Paul's Appeal

24 Ταῦτα δὲ αὐτοῦ ἀπολογουμένου, ὁ Φῆστος
these *things* Now him speaking in his defense, - Festus
Now as he spoke these things

μεγάλῃ τῇ φωνῇ ἔφη, "Μαίνῃ, Παῦλε! Τὰ πολλά
[4]great - [2]with [3]a [5]voice [1]said, "You are mad, Paul! The many
loud Your higher

σε γράμματα εἰς μανίαν περιτρέπει."
[4]you [1]writings [5]to [6]madness [2]are [3]turning."
learning is driving."

25 Ὁ δέ,[e] "Οὐ μαίνομαι," φησί, "κράτιστε Φῆστε,
[2]the [3]*one* [1]But "[7]not [5]I [6]am [8]mad," [4]said, "most excellent Festus,
he

ἀλλὰ ἀληθείας καὶ σωφροσύνης ῥήματα ἀποφθέγγομαι.
but [5]of [6]truth [7]and [8]reasonableness [4]words [1]I [2]boldly [3]declare.

26 Ἐπίσταται γὰρ περὶ τούτων ὁ βασιλεύς, πρὸς ὃν
[4]knows [1]For [5]about [6]these [7]*things* [2]the [3]king, to whom

καὶ παρρησιαζόμενος λαλῶ· λανθάνειν γὰρ αὐτόν
also speaking freely I speak; [12]to [13]escape [15]notice [1]for [14]him
freely escapes

τι τούτων οὐ πείθομαι οὐδέν, οὐ γάρ
[7]*that* [8]any [9]of [10]these [11]*things* [4]not [2]I [3]am [5]persuaded [6]nothing, [19]not [16]for
none I am persuaded,

ἐν γωνίᾳ πεπραγμένον τοῦτο. **27** Πιστεύεις, Βασιλεῦ
[22]in [23]a [24]corner [18]having [20]been [21]done [17]this. Do you believe, King
has

Ἀγρίππα, τοῖς προφήταις? Οἶδα ὅτι πιστεύεις."
Agrippa, the prophets? I know that you believe."

28 Ὁ δὲ Ἀγρίππας πρὸς τὸν Παῦλον ἔφη, "Ἐν ὀλίγῳ
- And Agrippa [2]to - [3]Paul [1]said, "In a little
short time

με πείθεις Χριστιανὸν γενέσθαι!"
[4]me [1]you [2]are [3]persuading [7]a [8]Christian [5]to [6]become!"

29 Ὁ δὲ Παῦλος εἶπεν, "Εὐξαίμην ἂν τῷ Θεῷ, καὶ ἐν
- But Paul said, "I would pray - - to God, both in

ὀλίγῳ καὶ ἐν πολλῷ οὐ μόνον σὲ ἀλλὰ καὶ πάντας τοὺς
a little and in much not only you but also *for* all the *ones*
short time a long time who are

ἀκούοντάς μου σήμερον γενέσθαι τοιούτους ὁποῖος κἀγώ εἰμι,
hearing me today to become such kind as I also am,
would

παρεκτὸς τῶν δεσμῶν τούτων."
except for - bonds ~ these."
chains

30 Καὶ ταῦτα εἰπόντος αὐτοῦ,[f] ἀνέστη ὁ βασιλεὺς
And [3]these [4]*things* [2]saying [1]him, [7]stood [5]the [6]king
when he had said,

καὶ ὁ ἡγεμών, ἥ τε Βερνίκη, καὶ οἱ συγκαθήμενοι
and the governor, - and Bernice, and the *ones* sitting together

αὐτοῖς, **31** καὶ ἀναχωρήσαντες ἐλάλουν πρὸς
with them, and withdrawing they were speaking to
when they withdrew among

ἀλλήλους, λέγοντες ὅτι "Οὐδὲν θανάτου ἄξιον ἢ δεσμῶν
one another, saying - "[4]nothing [6]of [7]death [5]worthy [8]or [9]bonds
themselves, chains

πράσσει ὁ ἄνθρωπος οὗτος."
[3]practices - [2]man [1]This."

32 Ἀγρίππας δὲ τῷ Φήστῳ ἔφη, "Ἀπολελύσθαι
Agrippa ~ And [2]to [3]Festus [1]said, "[8]to [9]have [10]been [11]released
"could have been

ἐδύνατο ὁ ἄνθρωπος οὗτος εἰ μὴ ἐπεκέκλητο Καίσαρα."
[6]was [7]able - [5]man [4]This if [3]not [1]he [2]had appealed to Caesar."
released

Paul Begins the Voyage to Rome

27 **1** Ὡς δὲ ἐκρίθη τοῦ ἀποπλεῖν ἡμᾶς εἰς τὴν
when ~ Now it was decided - [2]to [3]sail [4]away [1]us to -
that we should sail away

25 But he said, "I am not mad, most noble Festus, but speak the words of truth and reason.
26 "For the king, before whom I also speak freely, knows these things; for I am convinced that none of these things escapes his attention, since this thing was not done in a corner.
27 "King Agrippa, do you believe the prophets? I know that you do believe."
28 Then Agrippa said to Paul, "You almost persuade me to become a Christian."
29 And Paul said, "I would to God that not only you, but also all who hear me today, might become both almost and altogether such as I am, except for these chains."
30 When he had said these things, the king stood up, as well as the governor and Bernice and those who sat with them;
31 and when they had gone aside, they talked among themselves, saying, "This man is doing nothing deserving of death or chains."
32 Then Agrippa said to Festus, "This man might have been set free if he had not appealed to Caesar."
27 And when it was decided that we should

e(26:25) NU adds Παυλος, *Paul (said).*
f(26:30) NU omits Και ταυτα ειποντος αυτου, *And when he had said these (things).*

sail to Italy, they delivered Paul
and some other prisoners to
one named Julius, a centurion of
the Augustan Regiment.
2 So, entering a ship of Adramyttium, we put to sea, meaning to sail along the coasts of
Asia. Aristarchus, a Macedonian of Thessalonica, was with
us.
3 And the next *day* we landed
at Sidon. And Julius treated
Paul kindly and gave *him* liberty
to go to his friends and receive
care.
4 When we had put to sea
from there, we sailed under *the*
shelter of Cyprus, because the
winds were contrary.
5 And when we had sailed
over the sea which is off Cilicia
and Pamphylia, we came to
Myra, *a city* of Lycia.
6 There the centurion found
an Alexandrian ship sailing to
Italy, and he put us on board.
7 When we had sailed slowly
many days, and arrived with
difficulty off Cnidus, the wind
not permitting us to proceed,
we sailed under *the shelter of*
Crete off Salmone.
8 Passing it with difficulty,
we came to a place called Fair
Havens, near the city *of* Lasea.
9 Now when much time had
been spent, and sailing was

Ἰταλίαν, παρεδίδουν τόν τε Παῦλον καί τινας ἑτέρους
Italy, they handed over - both Paul and certain other

δεσμώτας ἑκατοντάρχῃ ὀνόματι Ἰουλίῳ, σπείρης Σεβαστῆς.
prisoners to a centurion by name Julius, of the cohort of Augustus.
named Augustan Regiment.

2 Ἐπιβάντες δὲ πλοίῳ Ἀδραμυττηνῷ, μέλλοντες πλεῖν
[2]having [3]boarded [1]And a ship of Adramyttium, being about to sail to
scheduled

τοὺς κατὰ τὴν Ἀσίαν τόπους, ἀνήχθημεν, ὄντος σὺν
the [2]along - [3]Asia [1]places, we put to sea, *there* being with
ports along the Asian coast,

ἡμῖν Ἀριστάρχου Μακεδόνος Θεσσαλονικέως. 3 Τῇ τε
us Aristarchus a Macedonian from Thessalonica. [2]on [3]the [1]And

ἑτέρᾳ κατήχθημεν εἰς Σιδῶνα, φιλανθρώπως τε ὁ
other *day* we put in to harbor into Sidon, [5]kindly [1]and -
next

Ἰούλιος τῷ Παύλῳ χρησάμενος ἐπέτρεψε πρὸς τοὺς φίλους
[2]Julius - [4]Paul [3]treating permitted *him* [5]to [6]the [7]friends
treated and permitted his

πορευθέντα ἐπιμελείας τυχεῖν. 4 Κἀκεῖθεν ἀναχθέντες
[4]going [3]care [1]to [2]find. And from there having put to sea
by going

ὑπεπλεύσαμεν τὴν Κύπρον διὰ τὸ τοὺς
we sailed under the sheltered side of - Cyprus because of - the
because

ἀνέμους εἶναι ἐναντίους. 5 Τό τε πέλαγος τὸ κατὰ τὴν
winds to be against *us*. [5]the [1]And [6]sea - [7]along -
were which is off

Κιλικίαν καὶ Παμφυλίαν διαπλεύσαντες, κατήλθομεν εἰς
[8]Cilicia [9]and [10]Pamphylia [2]having [3]sailed [4]across, we came down to
docked at

Μύρα τῆς Λυκίας. 6 Κἀκεῖ εὑρὼν ὁ ἑκατόνταρχος πλοῖον
Myra - of Lycia. And there [3]finding [1]the [2]centurion a ship
in found an

Ἀλεξανδρῖνον πλέον εἰς τὴν Ἰταλίαν, ἐνεβίβασεν ἡμᾶς εἰς
of Alexandria sailing for - Italy, he put aboard ˜ us in
Alexandrian ship and

αὐτό. 7 Ἐν ἱκαναῖς δὲ ἡμέραις
it. [4]during [5]a [6]considerable [7]*number* [8]*of* [1]And [9]days

βραδυπλοοῦντες καὶ μόλις γενόμενοι κατὰ τὴν Κνίδον,
[2]sailing [3]slowly and with difficulty arriving down off - Cnidus,

μὴ προσεῶντος ἡμᾶς τοῦ ἀνέμου,
[3]not [4]permitting [6]to [7]go [8]forward [5]us [1]the [2]wind,
since the wind would not permit us to go on,

ὑπεπλεύσαμεν τὴν Κρήτην κατὰ Σαλμώνην,
we sailed under the sheltered side of - Crete down off Salmone,

8 μόλις τε παραλεγόμενοι αὐτὴν ἤλθομεν εἰς τόπον
[2]with [3]difficulty [1]and sailing past it we came to a place ˜

τινὰ καλούμενον Καλοὺς Λιμένας, ᾧ ἐγγὺς ἦν πόλις
certain being called Fair Havens, [2]to [3]which [1]near was *the* city
called

Λασαία.
Lasea.

Paul's Warning Is Ignored

9 Ἱκανοῦ δὲ χρόνου διαγενομένου καὶ
[2]a [3]considerable [4]*amount* [1]Now of time having passed and

ὄντος ἤδη ἐπισφαλοῦς τοῦ πλοὸς διὰ τὸ καὶ τὴν
[4]being [3]already [5]dangerous [1]the [2]voyage because of - [5]also [1]the
having already become because

Νηστείαν ἤδη παρεληλυθέναι, παρῄνει ὁ Παῦλος
[2]Fast [6]already [3]to [4]have [7]gone [8]by, recommended ˜ - Paul

10 λέγων αὐτοῖς, "Ἄνδρες, θεωρῶ ὅτι μετὰ ὕβρεως καὶ
saying to them, "Men I perceive that with hardship and

πολλῆς ζημίας, οὐ μόνον τοῦ φορτίου καὶ τοῦ πλοίου ἀλλὰ
much loss, not only of the cargo and of the ship but

καὶ τῶν ψυχῶν ἡμῶν, μέλλειν ἔσεσθαι τὸν πλοῦν." 11 Ὁ
also - of lives ˜ our, [3]to [4]be [5]about [6]to [7]be [1]the [2]voyage." the ˜
is going

δὲ ἑκατοντάρχης τῷ κυβερνήτῃ καὶ τῷ ναυκλήρῳ
But centurion [3]by [4]the [5]steersman [6]and [7]the [8]shipowner

ἐπείθετο μᾶλλον ἢ τοῖς ὑπὸ τοῦ Παύλου
[1]was [2]persuaded rather than by the *things* [3]by - [4]Paul

λεγομένοις. 12 Ἀνευθέτου δὲ τοῦ λιμένος ὑπάρχοντος πρὸς
[1]being [2]said. [5]unsuitable [1]And [2]the [3]harbor [4]being for
And since the harbor was unsuitable

παραχειμασίαν, οἱ πλείους ἔθεντο βουλὴν ἀναχθῆναι
wintering, the majority gave counsel to put to sea

κἀκεῖθεν, εἴ πως δύναιντο καταντήσαντες εἰς Φοίνικα
from there, if perhaps they might be able arriving in Phoenix
to get to

παραχειμάσαι, λιμένα τῆς Κρήτης βλέποντα κατὰ
to spend the winter *there,* a harbor - of Crete looking down
open to the

λίβα καὶ κατὰ χῶρον.
southwest and down northwest.
to the

Paul's Ship Is Caught in a Tempest

13 Ὑποπνεύσαντος δὲ νότου, δόξαντες τῆς
blowing gently And a south wind, supposing [4]the
And when a south wind blew gently, their

προθέσεως κεκρατηκέναι, ἄραντες ἆσσον
[5]purpose [1]to [2]have [3]attained, taking up closer
they had they weighed anchor and sailed

παρελέγοντο τὴν Κρήτην. 14 Μετ' οὐ πολὺ δὲ ἔβαλε
they sailed along - Crete. [4]after [2]not [3]much [1]But *there* rushed
along close inshore to long

κατ' αὐτῆς ἄνεμος τυφωνικὸς ὁ καλούμενος
down from it a wind like a whirlwind the *one* being called
hurricane which is called

Εὐροκλύδων·[a] 15 συναρπασθέντος δὲ τοῦ πλοίου, καὶ μὴ
Euroclydon; being seized *by it* and the ship, and not
and when the ship was seized by it,

δυναμένου ἀντοφθαλμεῖν τῷ ἀνέμῳ, ἐπιδόντες
being able to face into the wind, giving in *to the wind*

ἐφερόμεθα. 16 Νησίον δέ τι
we were being driven along. [8]a [10]little [11]island [1]And [9]certain

ὑποδραμόντες καλούμενον Κλαύδην[b]
[2]running [3]under [4]the [5]sheltered [6]side [7]of being called Clauda
called

μόλις ἰσχύσαμεν περικρατεῖς γενέσθαι τῆς σκάφης,
with difficulty we were able [3]in [4]command [1]to [2]be of the skiff,

17 ἣν ἄραντες, βοηθείαις ἐχρῶντο, ὑποζωννύντες τὸ
which having taken *it* up, [3]supports [1]they [2]used, *for* undergirding the
hoisted cables

now dangerous because the
Fast was already over, Paul advised them,
10 saying, "Men, I perceive
that this voyage will end with
disaster and much loss, not
only of the cargo and ship, but
also our lives."
11 Nevertheless the centurion
was more persuaded by the
helmsman and the owner of the
ship than by the things spoken
by Paul.
12 And because the harbor
was not suitable to winter in,
the majority advised to set sail
from there also, if by any
means they could reach Phoenix, a harbor of Crete opening
toward the southwest and
northwest, *and* winter *there.*
13 When the south wind blew
softly, supposing that they had
obtained *their* desire, putting
out to sea, they sailed close by
Crete.
14 But not long after, a tem-
pestuous head wind arose,
called Euroclydon.
15 So when the ship was
caught, and could not head into
the wind, we let *her* drive.
16 And running under *the shelter of* an island called Clauda,
we secured the skiff with difficulty.
17 When they had taken it on
board, they used cables to

---

[a](27:14) NU reads Ευρακυλων, *Euraquilo.*
[b](27:16) NU reads Καυδα, *Cauda.*

undergird the ship; and fearing
lest they should run aground on
the Syrtis *Sands,* they struck
sail and so were driven.
18 And because we were exceedingly tempest-tossed, the
next *day* they lightened the
ship.
19 On the third *day* we threw
the ship's tackle overboard with
our own hands.
20 Now when neither sun nor
stars appeared for many days,
and no small tempest beat on
us, all hope that we would be
saved was finally given up.
21 But after long abstinence
from food, then Paul stood in
the midst of them and said,
"Men, you should have listened
to me, and not have sailed from
Crete and incurred this disaster
and loss.
22 "And now I urge you to
take heart, for there will be no
loss of life among you, but only
of the ship.
23 "For there stood by me
this night an angel of the God to
whom I belong and whom I
serve,
24 "saying, 'Do not be afraid,
Paul; you must be brought before Caesar; and indeed God
has granted you all those who
sail with you.'
25 "Therefore take heart,
men, for I believe God that it
will be just as it was told me.
26 "However, we must run
aground on a certain island."

πλοῖον· φοβούμενοί τε μὴ εἰς τὴν Σύρτην[c]
ship; [2]being [3]afraid [1]and lest [4]in [5]the [6]Syrtes [7]*Shallows*

ἐκπέσωσι, χαλάσαντες τὸ σκεῦος, οὕτως
[1]they [2]run [3]aground, letting down the driving anchor, thus
they let

ἐφέροντο. **18** Σφοδρῶς δὲ
they were being driven along *by the wind.* [4]violently [1]And

χειμαζομένων ἡμῶν, τῇ ἑξῆς ἐκβολὴν
[3]being [5]tossed [6]by [7]the [8]storm, [2]us, on the next *day* [3]a [4]jettisoning
were because we, they began casting

ἐποιοῦντο, **19** καὶ τῇ τρίτῃ αὐτόχειρες τὴν
[1]they [2]made, and on the third *day* with our own hands [3]the
things overboard,

σκευὴν τοῦ πλοίου ἐρρίψαμεν.[d] **20** Μήτε δὲ ἡλίου
[4]equipment [6]of [7]the [8]ship [1]we [2]threw [5]off. neither ˜ And *the* sun

μήτε ἄστρων ἐπιφαινόντων ἐπὶ πλείονας ἡμέρας, χειμῶνός τε
nor stars having appeared for more days, [4]storm [1]and
many

οὐκ ὀλίγου ἐπικειμένου, λοιπὸν περιῃρεῖτο πᾶσα ἐλπὶς
[2]no [3]small pressing on *us,* finally [8]was [9]taken [10]away [1]every [2]hope

τοῦ σῴζεσθαι ἡμᾶς.
- [5]to [6]be [7]saved [3]*for* [4]us.

21 Πολλῆς δὲ ἀσιτίας ὑπαρχούσης, τότε σταθεὶς ὁ
much ˜ Now lack of appetite being, then standing ˜ -
Now when they had abstained from food a long time, stood

Παῦλος ἐν μέσῳ αὐτῶν εἶπεν, "Ἔδει μέν, ὦ ἄνδρες,
Paul in *the* midst of them said, "It was needful, - O men,
and said, "Men, you should have followed

πειθαρχήσαντάς μοι μὴ ἀνάγεσθαι ἀπὸ τῆς Κρήτης,
obeying me not to put to sea from - Crete,
my advice and put

κερδῆσαί τε τὴν ὕβριν ταύτην καὶ τὴν ζημίαν.
[2]to [3]spare [4]*yourselves* [1]and - hardship ˜ this and - loss.

22 Καὶ τὰ νῦν παραινῶ ὑμᾶς εὐθυμεῖν,
And the *things* now I urge you to keep up *your* courage,
for the present

ἀποβολὴ γὰρ ψυχῆς οὐδεμία ἔσται ἐξ ὑμῶν, πλὴν
[5]loss [1]for [6]of [9]life [7]not [8]one [2]*there* [3]will [4]be from you, only
among

τοῦ πλοίου. **23** Παρέστη γάρ μοι ταύτῃ τῇ νυκτὶ ἄγγελος
of the ship. [2]*there* [3]stood [4]by [1]For me this - night an angel

τοῦ Θεοῦ οὗ εἰμι, ᾧ καὶ λατρεύω, **24** λέγων, 'Μὴ
- of God of whom I am, whom also I serve, saying, 'not ˜
to whom I belong,

φοβοῦ, Παῦλε· Καίσαρί σε δεῖ
Do be afraid, Paul; [9]Caesar [5]you [1]it [2]is [3]necessary [4]*for*

παραστῆναι, καὶ ἰδού, κεχάρισταί σοι ὁ Θεὸς πάντας
[6]to [7]stand [8]before, and behold, [2]has [3]granted [4]you - [1]God all

τοὺς πλέοντας μετὰ σοῦ.' **25** Διὸ εὐθυμεῖτε,
the *ones* sailing with you.' Therefore keep up *your* courage,

ἄνδρες· πιστεύω γὰρ τῷ Θεῷ ὅτι οὕτως ἔσται καθ' ὃν
men; [2]I [3]believe [1]for - God that thus it will be according to what
in the very

τρόπον λελάληταί μοι. **26** Εἰς νῆσον δέ τινα
manner it has been spoken to me. [10]on [11]a(n) [13]island [1]But [12]certain
way

δεῖ ἡμᾶς ἐκπεσεῖν."
[2]it [3]is [4]necessary [5]*for* [6]us [7]to [8]run [9]aground."

---

[c](**27:17**) NU, TR read Συρτιν, *Syrtis.*
[d](**27:19**) NU reads ερριψαν, *they threw off.*

27 Ὡς δὲ τεσσαρεσκαιδεκάτη νὺξ ἐγένετο,
when ˜ Now [3]*the* [4]fourteenth [5]night [1]it [2]was,

διαφερομένων ἡμῶν ἐν τῷ Ἀδρίᾳ, κατὰ μέσον τῆς
[7]being [8]carried [9]about [6]us in the Adriatic Sea, in *the* middle of the
as we were driven about

νυκτὸς ὑπενόουν οἱ ναῦται προσάγειν τινὰ
night [3]were [4]suspecting [1]the [2]sailors [7]to [8]be [9]approaching [5]some
sensed that was

αὐτοῖς χώραν. 28 Καὶ βολίσαντες εὗρον
[10]to [11]them [6]land. And having taken a sounding they found *it to be*
them

ὀργυιὰς εἴκοσι, βραχὺ δὲ διαστήσαντες, καὶ πάλιν
fathoms ˜ twenty, [4]a [5]little [6]farther [1]and [2]going [3]along, also again
when they had gone

βολίσαντες, εὗρον ὀργυιὰς δεκαπέντε·
having taken a sounding, they found *it to be* fathoms ˜ fifteen;
and found

29 φοβούμενοί τε μήπως εἰς τραχεῖς τόπους
[2]being [3]afraid [1]and lest perhaps [4]on [5]rocky [6]places

ἐκπέσωμεν, ἐκ πρύμνης ῥίψαντες ἀγκύρας τέσσαρας,
[1]we [2]run [3]aground, [11]from [12]*the* [13]stern [7]throwing [8]out [10]anchors [9]four,
they threw

ηὔχοντο ἡμέραν γενέσθαι.
they were praying *for* day to become.
and to come.

30 Τῶν δὲ ναυτῶν ζητούντων φυγεῖν ἐκ τοῦ πλοίου καὶ
the ˜ Now sailors seeking to flee from the ship and
Now as the sailors were seeking

χαλασάντων τὴν σκάφην εἰς τὴν θάλασσαν, προφάσει ὡς
letting down the skiff into the sea, in pretense as though
let

ἐκ πρῴρας μελλόντων ἀγκύρας ἐκτείνειν, 31 εἶπεν ὁ
from *the* prow being about [4]anchors [1]to [2]spread [3]out, said ˜ -
they were

Παῦλος τῷ ἑκατοντάρχῃ καὶ τοῖς στρατιώταις, "Ἐὰν μὴ
Paul to the centurion and to the soldiers, "If [4]not

οὗτοι μείνωσιν ἐν τῷ πλοίῳ, ὑμεῖς σωθῆναι οὐ
[1]these [2]*men* [3]do [5]remain in the ship, you [4]to [5]be [6]saved [2]not
will

δύνασθε." 32 Τότε οἱ στρατιῶται ἀπέκοψαν τὰ σχοινία τῆς
[1]are [3]able." Then the soldiers cut off the ropes of the
not be

σκάφης καὶ εἴασαν αὐτὴν ἐκπεσεῖν.
skiff and let it to fall off.
fall

33 Ἄχρι δὲ οὗ ἤμελλεν ἡμέρα γίνεσθαι,
until ˜ And *the time* when it was about [3]day [1]to [2]be,

παρεκάλει ὁ Παῦλος ἅπαντας μεταλαβεῖν τροφῆς, λέγων,
[5]was [6]urging - [4]Paul *them* all to receive *their* share of food, saying,

"Τεσσαρεσκαιδεκάτην σήμερον ἡμέραν προσδοκῶντες
"[2]*is* [3]*the* [4]fourteenth [1]Today day [3]waiting

ἄσιτοι διατελεῖτε, μηδὲν προσλαβόμενοι. 34 Διὸ
[4]without [5]eating [1]you [2]continue, [8]nothing [6]having [7]taken. Therefore

παρακαλῶ ὑμᾶς προσλαβεῖν τροφῆς, τοῦτο γὰρ πρὸς τῆς
I urge you to take food, this ˜ for [2]for -

ὑμετέρας σωτηρίας ὑπάρχει· οὐδενὸς γὰρ ὑμῶν θρὶξ
[3]your [4]deliverance [1]is; [11]of [12]no [13]one [5]for [14]of [15]you [6]a [7]hair

ἐκ τῆς κεφαλῆς πεσεῖται."[e] 35 Εἰπὼν δὲ ταῦτα
[8]from [9]the [10]head will fall." [2]having [3]said [1]And these *things*

27 Now when the fourteenth
night had come, as we were
driven up and down in the Adriatic *Sea,* about midnight the
sailors sensed that they were
drawing near some land.
28 And they took soundings
and found *it* to be twenty fathoms; and when they had gone a
little farther, they took soundings again and found *it* to be fifteen fathoms.
29 Then, fearing lest we
should run aground on the
rocks, they dropped four anchors from the stern, and
prayed for day to come.
30 And as the sailors were
seeking to escape from the
ship, when they had let down
the skiff into the sea, under
pretense of putting out anchors
from the prow,
31 Paul said to the centurion
and the soldiers, "Unless these
men stay in the ship, you cannot be saved."
32 Then the soldiers cut away
the ropes of the skiff and let it
fall off.
33 And as day was about to
dawn, Paul implored *them* all to
take food, saying, "Today is the
fourteenth day you have waited
and continued without food, and
eaten nothing.
34 "Therefore I urge you to
take nourishment, for this is for
your survival, since not a hair
will fall from the head of any of
you."
35 And when he had said

[e](**27:34**) NU reads *απολειται, will perish.*

these things, he took bread and
gave thanks to God in the presence of them all; and when he
had broken *it* he began to eat.
36 Then they were all encouraged, and also took food themselves.
37 And in all we were two
hundred and seventy-six persons on the ship.
38 So when they had eaten
enough, they lightened the ship
and threw out the wheat into
the sea.
39 When it was day, they did
not recognize the land; but they
observed a bay with a beach,
onto which they planned to run
the ship if possible.
40 And they let go the anchors
and left *them* in the sea, meanwhile loosing the rudder ropes;
and they hoisted the mainsail to
the wind and made for shore.
41 But striking a place where
two seas met, they ran the ship
aground; and the prow stuck
fast and remained immovable,
but the stern was being broken
up by the violence of the
waves.
42 And the soldiers' plan was
to kill the prisoners, lest any of
them should swim away and escape.
43 But the centurion, wanting
to save Paul, kept them from
their purpose, and commanded
that those who could swim
should jump *overboard* first and
get to land,

καὶ λαβὼν ἄρτον, εὐχαρίστησε τῷ Θεῷ ἐνώπιον
and having taken bread, he gave thanks - to God before
in the presence of

πάντων, καὶ κλάσας ἤρξατο ἐσθίειν. **36** Εὔθυμοι δὲ
all, and having broken *it* he began to eat. cheerful And
And they all

γενόμενοι πάντες καὶ αὐτοὶ προσελάβοντο τροφῆς.
becoming all [2]also [5]themselves [1]they [3]took [4]food.
became cheerful and

37 Ἦμεν δὲ ἐν τῷ πλοίῳ αἱ πᾶσαι ψυχαί, διακόσιαι
[2]we [3]were [1]Now [7]in [8]the [9]ship [5]the [4]all [6]souls, two hundred
persons,

ἑβδομήκοντα ἕξ. **38** Κορεσθέντες δὲ τῆς τροφῆς
seventy- six. [2]having [3]enough [1]And of the food

ἐκούφιζον τὸ πλοῖον ἐκβαλλόμενοι τὸν σῖτον εἰς τὴν
they were lightening the ship throwing out the wheat into the
began

θάλασσαν.
sea.

Paul and Company Are Shipwrecked Off Malta

39 Ὅτε δὲ ἡμέρα ἐγένετο, τὴν γῆν οὐκ
when ˜ Now [3]day [1]it [2]became, [8]the [9]land [6]not

ἐπεγίνωσκον, κόλπον δέ τινα κατενόουν ἔχοντα
[4]they [5]did [7]recognize, [13]a [15]bay [10]but [14]certain [11]they [12]noticed having
which had

αἰγιαλόν, εἰς ὃν ἐβουλεύσαντο, εἰ δυνατόν, ἐξῶσαι τὸ
a beach, on which they resolved, if possible, to run [3]ashore [1]the

πλοῖον. **40** Καὶ τὰς ἀγκύρας περιελόντες εἴων εἰς
[2]ship. And [3]the [4]anchors [1]casting [2]off they were leaving *them* in
they cast off and left

τὴν θάλασσαν, ἅμα ἀνέντες τὰς ζευκτηρίας τῶν
the sea, at the same time loosening the ropes of the

πηδαλίων, καὶ ἐπάραντες τὸν ἀρτέμονα τῇ πνεούσῃ
rudders, and having raised the foresail to the blowing *wind*

κατεῖχον εἰς τὸν αἰγιαλόν. **41** Περιπεσόντες δὲ εἰς
they were steering for the beach. having fallen But onto
began But they struck

τόπον διθάλασσον ἐπώκειλαν τὴν ναῦν, καὶ ἡ
a place with the sea on both sides they ran [3]aground [1]the [2]vessel, and the
a reef and

μὲν πρῷρα ἐρείσασα ἔμεινεν ἀσάλευτος, ἡ δὲ πρύμνα
- prow jamming fast remained unmoved, the ˜ but stern
became stuck and

ἐλύετο ὑπὸ τῆς βίας τῶν κυμάτων. **42** Τῶν δὲ
was being broken up by the violence of the waves. [6]of [7]the [1]And

στρατιωτῶν βουλὴ ἐγένετο ἵνα τοὺς δεσμώτας
[8]soldiers [4]*the* [5]decision [2]it [3]was that [4]the [5]prisoners

ἀποκτείνωσι, μή τις ἐκκολυμβήσας διαφύγῃ. **43** Ὁ δὲ
[1]they [2]would [3]kill, lest any swimming away should escape. the ˜ But
should swim away and

ἑκατόνταρχος, βουλόμενος διασῶσαι τὸν Παῦλον, ἐκώλυσεν
centurion, wanting to rescue - Paul, hindered

αὐτοὺς τοῦ βουλήματος, ἐκέλευσέ τε τοὺς δυναμένους
them of the intention, commanded ˜ and the *ones* being able
in their those who were

κολυμβᾶν ἀπορρίψαντας πρώτους ἐπὶ τὴν γῆν
to swim throwing *themselves* down first [3]toward [4]the [5]land
to jump in

ἐξιέναι, **44** καὶ τοὺς λοιπούς, οὓς μὲν ἐπὶ σανίσιν, οὓς
[1]to [2]go, and the rest, the ones - on boards, [2]the [3]ones
some others

δὲ ἐπί τινων τῶν ἀπὸ τοῦ πλοίου. Καὶ οὕτως
[1]and on some of the *things* from the ship. And in this way

ἐγένετο πάντας διασωθῆναι ἐπὶ τὴν γῆν.
it came about *for* all to be rescued on the land.
that all were brought safely to

Paul and Luke are Honored on Malta

28 **1** Καὶ διασωθέντες, τότε ἐπέγνωσαν[a] ὅτι Μελίτη ἡ
And being rescued, then they learned that [5]Malta [1]the
when they were

νῆσος καλεῖται. **2** Οἵ δὲ βάρβαροι παρεῖχον οὐ τὴν
[2]island [3]is [4]called. the ˜ And foreigners were showing [3]not [1]the
was non-Greek natives

τυχοῦσαν φιλανθρωπίαν* ἡμῖν, ἀνάψαντες γὰρ πυράν,
[4]being [5]common [2]kindness to us, [2]having [3]kindled [1]for a fire,
extraordinary

προσελάβοντο πάντας ἡμᾶς, διὰ τὸν ὑετὸν
they accepted [3]into [4]*their* [5]society [2]all [1]us, because of the rain

τὸν ἐφεστῶτα καὶ διὰ τὸ ψῦχος. **3** Συστρέψαντος δὲ
the *one* having arrived and because of the cold. [3]gathering [1]But
which had begun But when Paul

τοῦ Παύλου φρυγάνων πλῆθος καὶ ἐπιθέντος ἐπὶ τὴν
- [2]Paul [6]of [7]dry [8]sticks [4]a [5]number and putting *them* on the
had gathered a large bundle of sticks put

πυράν, ἔχιδνα ἐκ τῆς θέρμης διεξελθοῦσα καθῆψε
fire, a viper [4]because [5]of [6]the [7]heat [1]having [2]come [3]out took hold of
which came fastened on

τῆς χειρὸς αὐτοῦ.
- hand ˜ his.

4 Ὡς δὲ εἶδον οἱ βάρβαροι κρεμάμενον τὸ θηρίον
when ˜ And [3]saw [1]the [2]foreigners [6]hanging [4]the [5]animal
natives snake

ἐκ τῆς χειρὸς αὐτοῦ, ἔλεγον πρὸς ἀλλήλους, "Πάντως
from - hand ˜ his, they said to one another, "Certainly

φονεύς ἐστιν ὁ ἄνθρωπος οὗτος, ὃν διασωθέντα ἐκ τῆς
[4]a [5]murderer [3]is - [2]man [1]this, whom being rescued from the
though he was

θαλάσσης ἡ Δίκη ζῆν οὐκ εἴασεν." **5** Ὁ μὲν οὖν,
sea - Justice [4]to [5]live [2]not [1]did [3]permit." - - Then,
continue living

ἀποτινάξας τὸ θηρίον εἰς τὸ πῦρ, ἔπαθεν οὐδὲν κακόν.
having shaken off the animal into the fire, he suffered nothing bad.
snake harmful.

6 Οἱ δὲ προσεδόκων αὐτὸν μέλλειν πίμπρασθαι ἢ
- And they were expecting him to be about to swell up or

καταπίπτειν ἄφνω νεκρόν. Ἐπὶ πολὺ δὲ αὐτῶν
to fall down suddenly ˜ dead. for much *time* But them
But after they waited for a long

προσδοκώντων καὶ θεωρούντων μηδὲν ἄτοπον εἰς αὐτὸν
waiting and observing nothing out of place [2]to [3]him
time observed unusual

γινόμενον, μεταβαλλόμενοι ἔλεγον θεὸν αὐτὸν εἶναι.
[1]happening, changing *their* minds they said [4]a [5]god [1]him [2]to [3]be.
that he was.

7 Ἐν δὲ τοῖς περὶ τὸν τόπον ἐκεῖνον ὑπῆρχε
in ˜ Now the *areas* around - place ˜ that were

44 and the rest, some on boards and some on *parts* of the ship. And so it was that they all escaped safely to land.

28 Now when they had escaped, they then found out that the island was called Malta.
2 And the natives showed us unusual kindness; for they kindled a fire and made us all welcome, because of the rain that was falling and because of the cold.
3 But when Paul had gathered a bundle of sticks and laid *them* on the fire, a viper came out because of the heat, and fastened on his hand.
4 So when the natives saw the creature hanging from his hand, they said to one another, "No doubt this man is a murderer, whom, though he has escaped the sea, yet justice does not allow to live."
5 But he shook off the creature into the fire and suffered no harm.
6 However, they were expecting that he would swell up or suddenly fall down dead. But after they had looked for a long time and saw no harm come to him, they changed their minds and said that he was a god.
7 In that region there was an

[a](**28:1**) NU reads *επεγνωμεν, we learned.*

***(28:2)** *φιλανθρωπία (philanthrōpia).* Noun meaning *kindness* or *love for humanity.* It is a compound from the adjective *φίλος, loving, affectionate,* and the noun *ἄνθρωπος, man,* and is the source of the English *philanthropy.* Here in Acts 28:2 it refers to the *hospitality* extended to the victims of a shipwreck. In Titus 3:4 the word appears with its earliest sense of the love for and kindness extended to humanity by God. The cognate adverb *φιλανθρώπως, kindly, benevolently,* occurs in the NT only at Acts 27:3.

estate of the leading citizen of
the island, whose name was
Publius, who received us and
entertained us courteously for
three days.
8 And it happened that the
father of Publius lay sick of a
fever and dysentery. Paul went
in to him and prayed, and he
laid his hands on him and healed
him.
9 So when this was done, the
rest of those on the island who
had diseases also came and
were healed.
10 They also honored us in
many ways; and when we departed, they provided such
things as were necessary.
11 After three months we
sailed in an Alexandrian ship
whose figurehead was the Twin
Brothers, which had wintered
at the island.
12 And landing at Syracuse,
we stayed three days.
13 From there we circled
round and reached Rhegium.
And after one day the south
wind blew; and the next day we
came to Puteoli,
14 where we found brethren,
and were invited to stay with
them seven days. And so we
went toward Rome.
15 And from there, when the
brethren heard about us, they
came to meet us as far as Appii
Forum and Three Inns. When
Paul saw them, he thanked God

χωρία τῷ πρώτῳ τῆς νήσου, ὀνόματι
pieces of land *belonging* to the foremost *citizen* of the island, by name
named

Ποπλίῳ, ὃς ἀναδεξάμενος ἡμᾶς τρεῖς ἡμέρας φιλοφρόνως
Publius, who welcoming us [6]*for* [7]three [8]days [3]hospitably
welcomed

ἐξένισεν. **8** Ἐγένετο δὲ τὸν πατέρα τοῦ
[1]received [2]*us* [4]as [5]guests. [2]it [3]came [4]to [5]pass [1]And *for* the father -
and received that

Ποπλίου πυρετοῖς καὶ δυσεντερίᾳ συνεχόμενον
of Publius [7]attacks [8]of [9]fever [10]and [11]dysentery [5]suffering [6]from

κατακεῖσθαι, πρὸς ὃν ὁ Παῦλος εἰσελθὼν καὶ
[1]to [2]be [3]lying [4]down, to whom - Paul coming in and
was came

προσευξάμενος, ἐπιθεὶς τὰς χεῖρας αὐτῷ, ἰάσατο αὐτόν.
praying, laying the hands on him, healed him.
prayed, and his

9 Τούτου οὖν γενομένου, καὶ οἱ λοιποὶ οἱ ἔχοντες
this ˜ Then happening, also the rest the *ones* having
Then after this happened, who were

ἀσθενείας ἐν τῇ νήσῳ προσήρχοντο καὶ ἐθεραπεύοντο,
sicknesses on the island were coming to *him* and were being healed,
ill

10 οἳ καὶ πολλαῖς τιμαῖς ἐτίμησαν ἡμᾶς, καὶ ἀναγομένοις
who also [3]with [4]many [5]honors [1]honored [2]us, and putting to sea
when we put

ἐπέθεντο τὰ πρὸς τὴν χρείαν.
they gave *us* the *things* for the need.
that we needed.

Paul Reaches Rome

11 Μετὰ δὲ τρεῖς μῆνας ἀνήχθημεν ἐν πλοίῳ
after ˜ Now three months we put to sea in a ship

παρακεχειμακότι ἐν τῇ νήσῳ, Ἀλεξανδρίνῳ,
having wintered on the island, *belonging* to Alexandria,
that had

παρασήμῳ Διοσκούροις. **12** Καὶ καταχθέντες εἰς
marked by *the* Dioscuri. And putting in to harbor at
with the figurehead of the Twin Brothers.

Συρακούσας ἐπεμείναμεν ἡμέρας τρεῖς, **13** ὅθεν
Syracuse we stayed *there* days ˜ three, from where

περιελθόντες[b] κατηντήσαμεν εἰς Ῥήγιον. Καὶ μετὰ μίαν
having gone around we arrived at Rhegium. And after one
sailed

ἡμέραν ἐπιγενομένου νότου, δευτεραῖοι ἤλθομεν εἰς
day [4]coming [5]on [1]a [2]south [3]wind, on the second day we came to
arose

Ποτιόλους, **14** οὗ εὑρόντες ἀδελφούς, παρεκλήθημεν ἐπ᾽
Puteoli, where having found brothers, we were urged by

αὐτοῖς ἐπιμεῖναι ἡμέρας ἑπτά· καὶ οὕτως εἰς τὴν Ῥώμην
them to stay for days ˜ seven; and so [3]to - [4]Rome

ἤλθομεν. **15** Κἀκεῖθεν οἱ ἀδελφοὶ ἀκούσαντες τὰ
[1]we [2]came. And from there the brothers hearing the *things*
when they heard about our

περὶ ἡμῶν, ἐξῆλθον εἰς ἀπάντησιν ἡμῖν ἄχρις
concerning us, came out for a meeting with us as far as
circumstances, to meet

Ἀππίου Φόρου καὶ Τριῶν Ταβερνῶν, οὓς ἰδὼν ὁ Παῦλος,
Appii Forum and Three Taverns, whom seeing ˜ - Paul,
when Paul saw,

---

[b](**28:13**) NU reads *περιελοντες, having weighed anchor.*

εὐχαριστήσας τῷ Θεῷ, ἔλαβε θάρσος.
giving thanks - to God, he took, courage.
he gave and

16 Ὅτε δὲ ἤλθομεν εἰς Ῥώμην, ὁ ἑκατόνταρχος
when ~ Now we came to Rome, the centurion

παρέδωκε τοὺς δεσμίους τῷ στρατοπεδάρχῳ·[c] τῷ δὲ
handed over the prisoners to the commandant of the camp; - but

Παύλῳ ἐπετράπη μένειν καθ᾽ ἑαυτόν, σὺν τῷ
[4]for [5]Paul [1]it [2]was [3]permitted to stay by himself, with the
Paul was allowed

φυλάσσοντι αὐτὸν στρατιώτῃ.
[2]guarding [3]him [1]soldier.

Paul Witnesses to the Roman Jews

17 Ἐγένετο δὲ μετὰ ἡμέρας τρεῖς συγκαλέσασθαι
[2]it [3]came [4]about [1]Now after days ~ three [2]to [3]call [4]together
that Paul

τὸν Παῦλον[d] τοὺς ὄντας τῶν Ἰουδαίων πρώτους·
- [1]Paul the *ones* being [2]of [3]the [4]Jews [1]foremost;
called together those who were prominent among the Jews;

συνελθόντων δὲ αὐτῶν, ἔλεγε πρὸς αὐτούς, "Ἄνδρες
[7]coming [8]together [5]and [6]them, he said to them, "Men
and when they had come together,

ἀδελφοί, ἐγὼ οὐδὲν ἐναντίον ποιήσας τῷ λαῷ ἢ τοῖς
brothers, I [3]nothing [4]against [1]having [2]done the people or the
though I had

ἔθεσι τοῖς πατρῴοις, δέσμιος ἐξ
customs - belonging to *our* forefathers, [5]as [6]a [7]prisoner [8]from

Ἱεροσολύμων παρεδόθην εἰς τὰς χεῖρας τῶν Ῥωμαίων,
[9]Jerusalem [1]I [2]was [3]handed [4]over into the hands of the Romans,

18 οἵτινες ἀνακρίναντές με ἐβούλοντο ἀπολῦσαι
who examining me were wanting to release *me*
when they had examined

διὰ τὸ μηδεμίαν αἰτίαν θανάτου ὑπάρχειν ἐν ἐμοί.
because of - [3]no [4]charge of death [1]to [2]be in me.
because cause for there was my case.

19 Ἀντιλεγόντων δὲ τῶν Ἰουδαίων, ἠναγκάσθην
[3]speaking [4]against [1]But [2]the [3]Jews, I was compelled
But when the Jews spoke in opposition,

ἐπικαλέσασθαι Καίσαρα, οὐχ ὡς τοῦ ἔθνους μου ἔχων τι
to appeal to Caesar, not as - [8]nation [7]my [1]having [2]anything
if I had

κατηγορῆσαι. 20 Διὰ ταύτην οὖν τὴν αἰτίαν
[3]*of* [4]*which* [5]to [6]accuse. [2]because [3]of [4]this [1]Therefore - reason

παρεκάλεσα ὑμᾶς ἰδεῖν καὶ προσλαλῆσαι, ἕνεκεν γὰρ τῆς
I requested [3]you [1]to [2]see and to speak to *you,* [2]because [3]of [1]for the

ἐλπίδος τοῦ Ἰσραὴλ τὴν ἅλυσιν ταύτην περίκειμαι."
hope - of Israel - [5]chain [4]this [1]I [2]am [3]wearing."

21 Οἱ δὲ πρὸς αὐτὸν εἶπον, "Ἡμεῖς οὔτε γράμματα
[2]the [3]*ones* [1]And [5]to [6]him [4]said, "We neither [2]letters
they

περὶ σοῦ ἐδεξάμεθα ἀπὸ τῆς Ἰουδαίας, οὔτε
[3]concerning [4]you [1]received from - Judea, nor

παραγενόμενός τις τῶν ἀδελφῶν ἀπήγγειλεν ἢ ἐλάλησέ
[6]arriving [2]anyone [3]of [4]the [5]brothers [1]did [7]report or spoke
who arrived speak

τι περὶ σοῦ πονηρόν. 22 Ἀξιοῦμεν δὲ παρὰ
anything [2]about [3]you [1]evil. [2]we [3]consider [4]it [5]fitting [1]But [8]from
request

and took courage.
16 Now when we came to
Rome, the centurion delivered
the prisoners to the captain of
the guard; but Paul was permitted
to dwell by himself with the
soldier who guarded him.
17 And it came to pass after
three days that Paul called the
leaders of the Jews together.
So when they had come together,
he said to them: "Men
and brethren, though I have
done nothing against our people
or the customs of our fathers,
yet I was delivered as a prisoner
from Jerusalem into the
hands of the Romans,
18 "who, when they had examined
me, wanted to let *me*
go, because there was no cause
for putting me to death.
19 "But when the Jews spoke
against *it,* I was compelled to
appeal to Caesar, not that I had
anything of which to accuse my
nation.
20 "For this reason therefore
I have called for you, to see *you*
and speak with *you,* because for
the hope of Israel I am bound
with this chain."
21 Then they said to him, "We
neither received letters from
Judea concerning you, nor have
any of the brethren who came
reported or spoken any evil of
you.
22 "But we desire to hear
from you what you think; for

[c](28:16) NU omits ο εκατονταρχος παρεδωκε τους δεσμιους τω στρατοπεδαρχω, *the centurion handed over the prisoners to the commandant of the camp.*
[d](28:17) For τον Παυλον, *Paul,* NU reads αυτον, *he (called together).*

concerning this sect, we know
that it is spoken against everywhere."
23 So when they had ap-
pointed him a day, many came
to him at *his* lodging, to whom
he explained and solemnly testified of the kingdom of God, persuading them concerning Jesus
from both the Law of Moses
and the Prophets, from morning till evening.
24 And some were persuaded
by the things which were spoken, and some disbelieved.
25 So when they did not agree
among themselves, they departed after Paul had said one
word: "The Holy Spirit spoke
rightly through Isaiah the
prophet to our fathers,
26 "saying,

'Go to this people and say:
"Hearing you will hear, and
shall not understand;
And seeing you will see,
and not perceive;
27 *For the hearts of this*
people have grown dull.
Their ears are hard of
hearing,
And their eyes they have
closed,
Lest they should see with
their eyes and hear with
their ears,
Lest they should
understand with their
hearts and turn,

σοῦ ἀκοῦσαι ἃ φρονεῖς, περὶ μὲν γὰρ τῆς
[9]you [6]to [7]hear *the things* which you think, concerning ˜ - for -

αἱρέσεως ταύτης γνωστόν ἐστιν ἡμῖν ὅτι πανταχοῦ
sect ˜ this [3]known [1]it [2]is to us that everywhere

ἀντιλέγεται."
it is spoken against."

23 Ταξάμενοι δὲ αὐτῷ ἡμέραν, ἧκον πρὸς αὐτὸν εἰς
[2]having [3]appointed [1]And for him a day, [2]came [3]to [4]him [5]in

τὴν ξενίαν πλείονες, οἷς ἐξετίθετο
[6]the [7]lodging [8]place [1]more, to whom he was explaining
his many,

διαμαρτυρόμενος τὴν βασιλείαν τοῦ Θεοῦ, πείθων τε
solemnly testifying to the kingdom - of God, persuading ˜ and
and solemnly

αὐτοὺς τὰ περὶ τοῦ Ἰησοῦ ἀπό τε τοῦ Νόμου
them *of* the *things* concerning - Jesus from ˜ both the Law

Μωσέως καὶ τῶν Προφητῶν ἀπὸ πρωῒ ἕως ἑσπέρας.
of Moses and from the Prophets from morning till evening.

24 Καὶ οἱ μὲν ἐπείθοντο τοῖς λεγομένοις,
And the *ones* - were persuaded by the *things* being said,
some

οἱ δὲ ἠπίστουν.
[2]the [3]*ones* [1]but refused to believe.
others

25 Ἀσύμφωνοι δὲ ὄντες πρὸς ἀλλήλους ἀπελύοντο,
[3]not [4]harmonious [1]And [2]being with one another they went away
in disagreement

εἰπόντος τοῦ Παύλου ῥῆμα ἕν, ὅτι "Καλῶς τὸ Πνεῦμα τὸ
saying ˜ - Paul word ˜ one, - "[5]well [1]The [3]Spirit -
after Paul had said rightly

Ἅγιον ἐλάλησε διὰ Ἠσαΐου τοῦ προφήτου πρὸς τοὺς
[2]Holy [4]spoke through Isaiah the prophet to -

πατέρας ἡμῶν,[e] **26** λέγον,
fathers ˜ our, saying,

«Πορεύθητι πρὸς τὸν λαὸν τοῦτον καὶ εἰπόν,
«Go to - people ˜ this and say,

"Ἀκοῇ ἀκούσετε καὶ οὐ μὴ συνῆτε,
'In hearing you shall hear and not not understand,
by no means

Καὶ βλέποντες βλέψετε καὶ οὐ μὴ ἴδητε·
And seeing you shall see and not not perceive;
by no means

27 Ἐπαχύνθη γὰρ ἡ καρδία τοῦ λαοῦ τούτου,
[7]became [8]dull [1]For [2]the [3]heart - [4]of [6]people [5]this,
has become

Καὶ τοῖς ὠσὶ βαρέως ἤκουσαν,
And with the ears heavily they heard,
their ears are hard of hearing,

Καὶ τοὺς ὀφθαλμοὺς αὐτῶν ἐκάμμυσαν·
And - eyes ˜ their they closed;
have closed;

Μήποτε ἴδωσι τοῖς ὀφθαλμοῖς
Lest they should see with the eyes
their

Καὶ τοῖς ὠσὶν ἀκούσωσι
And with the ears they should hear
their

Καὶ τῇ καρδίᾳ συνῶσι καὶ ἐπιστρέψωσι,
And with the heart they should understand and turn back,
their

[e](28:25) NU reads υμων, *your.*

Καὶ ἰάσομαι αὐτούς.'»[f]
And I shall heal them.'»
should

28 Γνωστὸν οὖν ἔστω ὑμῖν ὅτι τοῖς ἔθνεσιν
[5]known [1]Therefore [2]let [3]it [4]be to you that [7]to [8]the [9]Gentiles

ἀπεστάλη τὸ σωτήριον τοῦ Θεοῦ, αὐτοὶ καὶ ἀκούσονται."
[5]was [6]sent [1]the [2]salvation - [3]of [4]God, they ~ and will hear *it.*"
has been

29 Καὶ[g] ταῦτα αὐτοῦ εἰπόντος, ἀπῆλθον οἱ Ἰουδαῖοι,
And [3]these [4]*things* [1]him [2]saying, [7]went [8]away [5]the [6]Jews,
when he had said,

πολλὴν ἔχοντες ἐν ἑαυτοῖς συζήτησιν.
[11]much [9]having [13]among [14]themselves [10]a [12]dispute.
great

Paul's Ministry Continues Unhindered

30 Ἔμεινε δὲ ὁ Παῦλος διετίαν ὅλην ἐν
[3]remained [1]Now - [2]Paul [4]*for* [5]a [7]two-year [8]period [6]whole in
two full years

ἰδίῳ μισθώματι, καὶ ἀπεδέχετο πάντας τοὺς
his own rented house, and he was receiving all the *ones*
those who were

εἰσπορευομένους πρὸς αὐτόν, 31 κηρύσσων τὴν βασιλείαν τοῦ
coming to him, preaching the kingdom -

Θεοῦ καὶ διδάσκων τὰ περὶ τοῦ Κυρίου Ἰησοῦ
of God and teaching the *things* concerning the Lord Jesus

Χριστοῦ μετὰ πάσης παρρησίας, ἀκωλύτως.
Christ with all boldness, without hindrance.

So that I should heal
them." '

28 "Therefore let it be known to you that the salvation of God has been sent to the Gentiles, and they will hear it!"
29 And when he had said these words, the Jews departed and had a great dispute among themselves.
30 Then Paul dwelt two whole years in his own rented house, and received all who came to him,
31 preaching the kingdom of God and teaching the things which concern the Lord Jesus Christ with all confidence, no one forbidding him.

f(**28:26, 27**) Is. 6:9, 10
g(**28:29**) NU omits v. 29.

The Epistle of Paul the Apostle to the
ROMANS

ΠΡΟΣ ΡΩΜΑΙΟΥΣ
TO *THE* ROMANS

1 Paul, a bondservant of Jesus Christ, called *to be* an apostle, separated to the gospel of God
2 which He promised before through His prophets in the Holy Scriptures,
3 concerning His Son Jesus Christ our Lord, who was born of the seed of David according to the flesh,
4 *and* declared *to be* the Son of God with power according to the Spirit of holiness, by the resurrection from the dead.
5 Through Him we have received grace and apostleship for obedience to the faith among all nations for His name,
6 among whom you also are the called of Jesus Christ;

7 To all who are in Rome, beloved of God, called *to be* saints:

Grace to you and peace from God our Father and the Lord Jesus Christ.

8 First, I thank my God through Jesus Christ for you all, that your faith is spoken of throughout the whole world.
9 For God is my witness, whom I serve with my spirit in the gospel of His Son, that without ceasing I make mention

---

[a](1:1) NU reads Χριστου Ιησου, *Christ Jesus.*

*(1:3) σπέρμα (sperma). Common noun meaning *seed,* used either of the seed of plants (as Matt. 13:32) or of a person's *offspring, descendants, posterity* (as John 8:37), even including spiritual posterity (Gal. 3:29). References to Jesus as being of the "seed" of David would belong to this category (as here and John 7:42). In 1 John 3:9 the reference is apparently to the "germ" of life planted in believers at regeneration by the Holy

Paul Greets the Saints in Rome

1 1 Παῦλος, δοῦλος Ἰησοῦ Χριστοῦ,[a] κλητὸς
Paul, a bondservant of Jesus Christ, a called
ἀπόστολος, ἀφωρισμένος εἰς εὐαγγέλιον Θεοῦ, 2 ὃ
apostle, having been separated to *the* gospel of God, which
προεπηγγείλατο διὰ τῶν προφητῶν αὐτοῦ ἐν Γραφαῖς
He promised before through - prophets ~ His in *the* Scriptures ~
Ἁγίαις, 3 περὶ τοῦ Υἱοῦ αὐτοῦ, τοῦ γενομένου ἐκ
Holy, concerning - Son ~ His, the *One* coming of
who came
σπέρματος* Δαβὶδ κατὰ σάρκα, 4 τοῦ ὁρισθέντος
the seed of David according to *the* flesh, the *One* being declared
Υἱοῦ Θεοῦ ἐν δυνάμει κατὰ Πνεῦμα ἁγιωσύνης ἐξ
Son of God in power according to *the* Spirit of holiness by
with
ἀναστάσεως νεκρῶν, Ἰησοῦ Χριστοῦ τοῦ Κυρίου ἡμῶν,
the resurrection of dead *ones,* Jesus Christ - Lord ~ our,
5 δι' οὗ ἐλάβομεν χάριν καὶ ἀποστολὴν εἰς ὑπακοὴν
through whom we received grace and apostleship for obedience
πίστεως ἐν πᾶσι τοῖς ἔθνεσιν ὑπὲρ τοῦ ὀνόματος αὐτοῦ,
of faith among all the nations on behalf of - name ~ His,
6 ἐν οἷς ἐστε καὶ ὑμεῖς κλητοὶ Ἰησοῦ Χριστοῦ·
among whom [3]are [2]also [1]you called of Jesus Christ:
7 Πᾶσι τοῖς οὖσιν ἐν Ῥώμῃ ἀγαπητοῖς Θεοῦ, κλητοῖς
To all the *ones* being in Rome beloved of God, called
those who are
ἁγίοις·
saints:

Χάρις ὑμῖν καὶ εἰρήνη ἀπὸ Θεοῦ Πατρὸς ἡμῶν καὶ Κυρίου
Grace to you and peace from God Father ~ our and *the* Lord
Ἰησοῦ Χριστοῦ.
Jesus Christ.

Paul Desires to Visit Rome

8 Πρῶτον μὲν εὐχαριστῶ τῷ Θεῷ μου διὰ Ἰησοῦ
First indeed I thank - God ~ my through Jesus
Χριστοῦ ὑπὲρ πάντων ὑμῶν ὅτι ἡ πίστις ὑμῶν καταγγέλλεται
Christ for all ~ you that - faith ~ your is proclaimed
well known
ἐν ὅλῳ τῷ κόσμῳ. 9 Μάρτυς γάρ μού ἐστιν ὁ Θεός, ᾧ
in whole ~ the world. [5]witness [1]For [4]my [3]is - [2]God, whom
λατρεύω ἐν τῷ πνεύματί μου ἐν τῷ εὐαγγελίῳ τοῦ Υἱοῦ
I serve in - spirit ~ my in the gospel - of Son ~
with
αὐτοῦ, ὡς ἀδιαλείπτως μνείαν ὑμῶν ποιοῦμαι, πάντοτε ἐπὶ
His, how unceasingly [3]mention [4]of [5]you [1]I [2]make, always at

τῶν προσευχῶν μου 10 δεόμενος εἴ πως ἤδη ποτὲ
- prayers ˜ my requesting if somehow already at sometime
now

εὐοδωθήσομαι ἐν τῷ θελήματι τοῦ Θεοῦ ἐλθεῖν πρὸς ὑμᾶς.
I shall succeed in the will - of God to come to you.

11 Ἐπιποθῶ γὰρ ἰδεῖν ὑμᾶς ἵνα τι μεταδῶ χάρισμα
[2]I [3]long [1]For to see you so that [4]some [1]I [2]may [3]impart [6]gift

ὑμῖν πνευματικὸν εἰς τὸ στηριχθῆναι ὑμᾶς, 12 τοῦτο δέ
[7]to [8]you [5]spiritual for - to be established you, this ˜ and
that you may be established, that

ἐστι, συμπαρακληθῆναι ἐν ὑμῖν διὰ τῆς ἐν ἀλλήλοις
is, to be encouraged together among you through the [2]in [3]one [4]another
that I may

πίστεως ὑμῶν τε καὶ ἐμοῦ. 13 Οὐ θέλω δὲ ὑμᾶς
[1]faith [6]of [7]you [5]both and of me. [4]not [2]I [3]do [5]want [1]But you

ἀγνοεῖν, ἀδελφοί, ὅτι πολλάκις προεθέμην ἐλθεῖν πρὸς
to be unaware, brothers, that often I planned to come to

ὑμᾶς (καὶ ἐκωλύθην ἄχρι τοῦ δεῦρο), ἵνα τινὰ καρπὸν
you (and I was hindered until the present), that [4]some [5]fruit

σχῶ καὶ ἐν ὑμῖν, καθὼς καὶ ἐν τοῖς λοιποῖς
[1]I [2]may [3]have also among you, just as also among the remaining

ἔθνεσιν. 14 Ἕλλησί τε καὶ βαρβάροις, σοφοῖς τε καὶ
Gentiles. [2]to [3]Greeks [1]Both and barbarians, [2]to [3]wise [1]both and

ἀνοήτοις ὀφειλέτης εἰμί. 15 Οὕτω τὸ κατ' ἐμὲ
to unintelligent [3]a [4]debtor [1]I [2]am. So the according to me
as much as is in me

πρόθυμον καὶ ὑμῖν τοῖς ἐν Ῥώμῃ εὐαγγελίσασθαι.
I am eager [5]also [6]to [7]you [8]the [9]*ones* [10]in [11]Rome [1]to [2]preach [3]the [4]gospel.
who are

The Just Live by Faith

16 Οὐ γὰρ ἐπαισχύνομαι τὸ εὐαγγέλιον τοῦ Χριστοῦ,[b]
[4]not [1]For [2]I [3]am [5]ashamed of the gospel - of Christ,

δύναμις γὰρ Θεοῦ ἐστιν εἰς σωτηρίαν παντὶ τῷ
[4]*the* [5]power [1]for [6]of [7]God [2]it [3]is for salvation to every - *one*

πιστεύοντι, Ἰουδαίῳ τε πρῶτον καὶ Ἕλληνι.
believing, [2]to [3]*the* [4]Jew [1]both first and to *the* Greek.
who believes,

17 Δικαιοσύνη* γὰρ Θεοῦ ἐν αὐτῷ ἀποκαλύπτεται ἐκ
[2]a [3]righteousness [1]For of God in it is revealed from

πίστεως εἰς πίστιν, καθὼς γέγραπται, «Ὁ δὲ δίκαιος ἐκ
faith to faith, just as it is written, «the ˜ But righteous *one* by

πίστεως ζήσεται.»[c]
faith shall live.»

God's Wrath Is Revealed Against Unrighteousness

18 Ἀποκαλύπτεται γὰρ ὀργὴ Θεοῦ ἀπ' οὐρανοῦ ἐπὶ
[6]is [7]revealed [1]For [2]*the* [3]wrath [4]of [5]God from heaven upon

πᾶσαν ἀσέβειαν καὶ ἀδικίαν ἀνθρώπων τῶν τὴν
all ungodliness and unrighteousness of men the *ones* [2]the
who

ἀλήθειαν ἐν ἀδικίᾳ κατεχόντων. 19 Διότι τὸ
[3]truth [4]in [5]unrighteousness [1]suppressing. For this reason the *thing*
suppress.

γνωστὸν τοῦ Θεοῦ φανερόν ἐστιν ἐν αὐτοῖς, ὁ γὰρ Θεὸς
known - of God manifest ˜ is in them, - for God

αὐτοῖς ἐφανέρωσε. 20 Τὰ γὰρ ἀόρατα αὐτοῦ ἀπὸ
[3]to [4]them [1]manifested [2]*it*. the ˜ For invisible *things* of Him from

of you always in my prayers,
10 making request if, by some means, now at last I may find a way in the will of God to come to you.
11 For I long to see you, that I may impart to you some spiritual gift, so that you may be established—
12 that is, that I may be encouraged together with you by the mutual faith both of you and me.
13 Now I do not want you to be unaware, brethren, that I often planned to come to you (but was hindered until now), that I might have some fruit among you also, just as among the other Gentiles.
14 I am a debtor both to Greeks and to barbarians, both to wise and to unwise.
15 So, as much as is in me, *I am* ready to preach the gospel to you who are in Rome also.
16 For I am not ashamed of the gospel of Christ, for it is the power of God to salvation for everyone who believes, for the Jew first and also for the Greek.
17 For in it the righteousness of God is revealed from faith to faith; as it is written, *"The just shall live by faith."*
18 For the wrath of God is revealed from heaven against all ungodliness and unrighteousness of men, who suppress the truth in unrighteousness,
19 because what may be known of God is manifest in them, for God has shown *it* to them.
20 For since the creation of the world His invisible *attributes*

---

b(1:16) NU omits *του Χριστου, of Christ.*
c(1:17) Hab. 2:4

Spirit. Cf. the cognate verb *σπείρω, sow (seed),* either literally (as Matt. 6:26) or figuratively (as Matt. 25:24), but also of sowing the word of God (as Mark 4:14), and even the human body at burial (1 Cor. 15:42ff).

*(1:17) *δικαιοσύνη (dikaiosynē).* Noun used often in the NT to mean *righteousness, uprightness, justice.* It derives its meaning from judicial contexts whether as the characteristic of a judge (especially God, as Acts 17:31), or as what is required

are clearly seen, being understood by the things that are made, *even* His eternal power and Godhead, so that they are without excuse,
21 because, although they knew God, they did not glorify *Him* as God, nor were thankful, but became futile in their thoughts, and their foolish hearts were darkened.
22 Professing to be wise, they became fools,
23 and changed the glory of the incorruptible God into an image made like corruptible man—and birds and four-footed animals and creeping things.
24 Therefore God also gave them up to uncleanness, in the lusts of their hearts, to dishonor their bodies among themselves,
25 who exchanged the truth of God for the lie, and worshiped and served the creature rather than the Creator, who is blessed forever. Amen.
26 For this reason God gave them up to vile passions. For even their women exchanged the natural use for what is against nature.
27 Likewise also the men, leaving the natural use of the woman, burned in their lust for one another, men with men committing what is shameful, and receiving in themselves the penalty of their error which was due.
28 And even as they did not like to retain God in *their* knowledge, God gave them over to a debased mind, to do those things which are not fitting;
29 being filled with all unrigh-

---

of a person by God (as Phil. 3:6). The latter sense leads to the meaning *right standing (with God),* as often in Paul's writings including here in Romans. The meaning of the phrase "the righteousness of God" is debated. It may refer to being right (found guiltless) *before* God, or to right standing provided *by* God (through faith in Christ), or perhaps even both. Cognates include the verb δικαιόω, *show (or do) justice, justify* (Rom. 5:1); adjective δίκαιος, *righteous, just, upright;* adverb δικαίως, *justly, uprightly;* and noun δικαίωσις, *justification, acquital* (only Rom. 4:25; 5:18).

κτίσεως κόσμου τοῖς ποιήμασι νοούμενα
the creation of *the* world [6]by [7]the [8]things [9]made [4]being [5]understood

καθορᾶται, ἥ τε ἀΐδιος αὐτοῦ δύναμις καὶ θειότης, εἰς
[1]are [2]clearly [3]seen, - both eternal ~ His power and divinity, for
so

τὸ εἶναι αὐτοὺς ἀναπολογήτους. **21** Διότι γνόντες τὸν
- to be them without excuse. For this reason knowing -
that they are

Θεόν, οὐχ ὡς Θεὸν ἐδόξασαν ἢ εὐχαρίστησαν, ἀλλ'
God, [3]not [6]as [7]God [1]they [2]did [4]glorify [5]*Him* or give thanks, but

ἐματαιώθησαν ἐν τοῖς διαλογισμοῖς αὐτῶν καὶ ἐσκοτίσθη ἡ
they became futile in - reasonings ~ their and [4]was [5]darkened -

ἀσύνετος αὐτῶν καρδία. **22** Φάσκοντες εἶναι σοφοὶ
[2]senseless [1]their [3]heart. Professing to be wise

ἐμωράνθησαν, **23** καὶ ἤλλαξαν τὴν δόξαν τοῦ ἀφθάρτου
they became fools, and changed the glory of the incorruptible

Θεοῦ ἐν ὁμοιώματι εἰκόνος φθαρτοῦ ἀνθρώπου καὶ
God in a likeness of an image of corruptible man and
for

πετεινῶν καὶ τετραπόδων καὶ ἑρπετῶν.
of birds and of quadrupeds and of reptiles.

24 Διὸ καὶ παρέδωκεν αὐτοὺς ὁ Θεὸς ἐν ταῖς
Therefore [2]also [3]gave [5]over [4]them - [1]God in the

ἐπιθυμίαις τῶν καρδιῶν αὐτῶν εἰς ἀκαθαρσίαν, τοῦ
lusts - of hearts ~ their to uncleanness, -

ἀτιμάζεσθαι τὰ σώματα αὐτῶν ἐν ἑαυτοῖς, **25** οἵτινες
to dishonor - bodies ~ their among themselves, who

μετήλλαξαν τὴν ἀλήθειαν τοῦ Θεοῦ ἐν τῷ ψεύδει καὶ
exchanged the truth - of God in the lie and
for

ἐσεβάσθησαν καὶ ἐλάτρευσαν τῇ κτίσει παρὰ τὸν
worshiped and served the creature rather than the

Κτίσαντα, ὅς ἐστιν εὐλογητὸς εἰς τοὺς αἰῶνας. Ἀμήν.
One having created, who is blessed to the ages. Amen.
Creator, forever. So be it.

26 Διὰ τοῦτο παρέδωκεν αὐτοὺς ὁ Θεὸς εἰς πάθη
On account of this [2]gave [4]over [3]them - [1]God to passions

ἀτιμίας· αἵ τε γὰρ θήλειαι αὐτῶν μετήλλαξαν τὴν φυσικὴν
of dishonor; - even ~ for females ~ their exchanged the natural

χρῆσιν εἰς τὴν παρὰ φύσιν, **27** ὁμοίως τε καὶ οἱ ἄρρενες,
use for the *use* against nature, likewise ~ and also the males,

ἀφέντες τὴν φυσικὴν χρῆσιν τῆς θηλείας, ἐξεκαύθησαν ἐν τῇ
leaving the natural use of the female, were inflamed by -

ὀρέξει αὐτῶν εἰς ἀλλήλους, ἄρσενες ἐν ἄρσεσι τὴν
lust ~ their for one another, males with males -

ἀσχημοσύνην κατεργαζόμενοι, καὶ τὴν ἀντιμισθίαν ἣν
shamelessness ~ committing, and [4]the [5]penalty [6]which

ἔδει τῆς πλάνης αὐτῶν ἐν ἑαυτοῖς ἀπολαμβάνοντες.
[7]was [8]fitting - [9]*for* [11]error [10]their [3]in [4]themselves [1]getting [2]back.

28 Καὶ καθὼς οὐκ ἐδοκίμασαν τὸν Θεὸν ἔχειν ἐν
And just as [3]not [1]they [2]did [4]see [5]fit - [8]God [6]to [7]have in
wish

ἐπιγνώσει, παρέδωκεν αὐτοὺς ὁ Θεὸς εἰς ἀδόκιμον νοῦν,
their knowledge, [2]gave [4]over [3]them - [1]God to a disapproved mind,
debased

ποιεῖν τὰ μὴ καθήκοντα, **29** πεπληρωμένους πάσῃ
to do the *things* not being proper, having been filled with all
suitable,

ἀδικίᾳ, πορνείᾳ,[d] πονηρίᾳ, πλεονεξίᾳ, κακίᾳ·
unrighteousness, sexual immorality, evil, greed, malice;

μεστοὺς φθόνου, φόνου, ἔριδος, δόλου, κακοηθείας·
full of envy, murder, strife, deceit, maliciousness;

ψιθυριστάς,* **30** καταλάλους, θεοστυγεῖς, ὑβριστάς,
they are whisperers, slanderers, haters of God, insolent men,

ὑπερηφάνους, ἀλαζόνας, ἐφευρετὰς κακῶν, γονεῦσιν
haughty, braggarts, inventors of bad *things,* [2]to [3]parents

ἀπειθεῖς, **31** ἀσυνέτους, ἀσυνθέτους, ἀστόργους, ἀσπόνδους,[e]
[1]disobedient, senseless, untrustworthy, unloving, unforgiving,

ἀνελεήμονας· **32** οἵτινες τὸ δικαίωμα τοῦ Θεοῦ
unmerciful; who [3]the [4]righteous [5]judgment - [6]of [7]God

ἐπιγνόντες, ὅτι οἱ τὰ τοιαῦτα πράσσοντες ἄξιοι
[1]having [2]known, that the *ones* - [2]such [3]*things* [1]practicing [5]deserving

θανάτου εἰσίν, οὐ μόνον αὐτὰ ποιοῦσιν ἀλλὰ καὶ
[6]of [7]death [4]are, not only them ˜ do but also

συνευδοκοῦσι τοῖς πράσσουσι.
approve of the *ones* practicing *them.*
those who practice

God Judges by Righteous Principles

2 **1** Διὸ ἀναπολόγητος εἶ, ὦ ἄνθρωπε πᾶς ὁ
Therefore, [3]inexcusable [1]you [2]are, O man every - *one*
everyone who

κρίνων, ἐν ᾧ γὰρ κρίνεις τὸν ἕτερον, σεαυτὸν κατακρίνεις,
judging, [2]in [3]what [1]for you judge the other, [3]yourself [1]you [2]condemn,
judges, another,

τὰ γὰρ αὐτὰ πράσσεις ὁ κρίνων.
[11]the [4]for [12]same [13]*things* [5]you [9]are [10]practicing [6]the [7]*one* [8]judging.
who judge.

2 Οἴδαμεν δὲ ὅτι τὸ κρίμα τοῦ Θεοῦ ἐστι κατὰ
[2]we [3]know [1]But that the judgment - of God is according to

ἀλήθειαν ἐπὶ τοὺς τὰ τοιαῦτα πράσσοντας. **3** Λογίζῃ
truth on the *ones* - [2]such [3]*things* [1]practicing. [2]do [3]you [4]think

δὲ τοῦτο, ὦ ἄνθρωπε ὁ κρίνων τοὺς τὰ τοιαῦτα
[1]But this, O man the *one* judging the *ones* - [2]such [3]*things*
you who judge

πράσσοντας καὶ ποιῶν αὐτά, ὅτι σὺ ἐκφεύξῃ τὸ κρίμα τοῦ
[1]practicing yet doing them, that you will escape the judgment -

Θεοῦ? **4** Ἢ τοῦ πλούτου τῆς χρηστότητος αὐτοῦ καὶ τῆς
of God? Or [4]the [5]riches - [6]of [8]kindness [7]His [9]and -

ἀνοχῆς καὶ τῆς μακροθυμίας καταφρονεῖς, ἀγνοῶν ὅτι
[10]forbearance [11]and - [12]longsuffering [1]do [2]you [3]despise, not knowing that

τὸ χρηστὸν τοῦ Θεοῦ εἰς μετάνοιάν σε ἄγει? **5** Κατὰ
the kindness - of God [3]to [4]repentance [2]you [1]leads? [2]according [3]to

δὲ τὴν σκληρότητά σου καὶ ἀμετανόητον καρδίαν
[1]But - hardness ˜ your and impenitent heart

θησαυρίζεις σεαυτῷ ὀργὴν ἐν ἡμέρᾳ ὀργῆς καὶ
you are treasuring up for yourself wrath in *the* day of wrath and

ἀποκαλύψεως καὶ[a] δικαιοκρισίας τοῦ Θεοῦ, **6** ὃς
revelation and of *the* righteous judgment - of God, who

ἀποδώσει ἑκάστῳ κατὰ τὰ ἔργα αὐτοῦ,[b] **7** τοῖς
will pay back to each *one* according to works ˜ his, to the *ones*

μὲν καθ' ὑπομονὴν ἔργου ἀγαθοῦ δόξαν καὶ τιμὴν
on the one hand *who* by endurance of work ˜ good [3]glory [4]and [5]honor

καὶ ἀφθαρσίαν ζητοῦσι, ζωὴν αἰώνιον· **8** τοῖς
[6]and [7]incorruption [1]are [2]seeking, life ˜ eternal; to the *ones*

teousness, sexual immorality,
wickedness, covetousness, maliciousness; full of envy, murder, strife, deceit, evil-
mindedness; *they are* whisperers,
30 backbiters, haters of God,
violent, proud, boasters, inventors of evil things, disobedient
to parents,
31 undiscerning, untrustworthy, unloving, unforgiving, unmerciful;
32 who, knowing the righ-
teous judgment of God, that
those who practice such things
are deserving of death, not only
do the same but also approve of
those who practice them.
2 Therefore you are inex-
cusable, O man, whoever
you are who judge, for in whatever you judge another you
condemn yourself; for you who
judge practice the same things.
2 But we know that the judgment of God is according to
truth against those who practice such things.
3 And do you think this,
O man, you who judge those
practicing such things, and doing the same, that you will escape the judgment of God?
4 Or do you despise the
riches of His goodness, forbearance, and longsuffering,
not knowing that the goodness
of God leads you to repentance?
5 But in accordance with
your hardness and your impenitent heart you are treasuring up
for yourself wrath in the day of
wrath and revelation of the
righteous judgment of God,
6 who *"will render to each
one according to his deeds"*:
7 eternal life to those who by
patient continuance in doing
good seek for glory, honor, and
immortality;
8 but to those who are self-

[d](**1:29**) NU omits πορνεια, *sexual immorality.*
[e](**1:31**) NU omits ασπονδους, *unforgiving.*
[a](**2:5**) TR, NU omit και, *and.* [b](**2:6**) Ps. 62:12; Prov. 24:12

***(1:29)** ψιθυριστής *(psithyristēs).* Noun meaning *whisperer, gossiper,* appearing only here in the NT. It is an example of onomatopoeia, a word sounding like what it represents: the "ps," "th," and "s" sounds all suggest whispering. The word has a negative connotation of

seeking and do not obey the truth, but obey unrighteousness—indignation and wrath,
9 tribulation and anguish, on every soul of man who does evil, of the Jew first and also of the Greek;
10 but glory, honor, and peace to everyone who works what is good, to the Jew first and also to the Greek.
11 For there is no partiality with God.
12 For as many as have sinned without law will also perish without law, and as many as have sinned in the law will be judged by the law
13 (for not the hearers of the law *are* just in the sight of God, but the doers of the law will be justified;
14 for when Gentiles, who do not have the law, by nature do the things in the law, these, although not having the law, are a law to themselves,
15 who show the work of the law written in their hearts, their conscience also bearing witness, and between themselves *their* thoughts accusing or else excusing *them*)
16 in the day when God will judge the secrets of men by Jesus Christ, according to my gospel.
17 Indeed you are called a Jew, and rest on the law, and make your boast in God,
18 and know *His* will, and approve the things that are excellent, being instructed out of the law,
19 and are confident that you yourself are a guide to the blind, a light to those who are in darkness,
20 an instructor of the foolish,

δὲ ἐξ ἐριθείας, καὶ ἀπειθοῦσι μὲν τῇ
on the other hand *who are* of selfish ambition, and *are* disobeying - the

ἀληθείᾳ, πειθομένοις δὲ τῇ ἀδικίᾳ, θυμὸς καὶ ὀργή,
truth, obeying ˜ but - unrighteousness, wrath and anger,

9 θλῖψις καὶ στενοχωρία, ἐπὶ πᾶσαν ψυχὴν ἀνθρώπου τοῦ
tribulation and anguish, upon every soul of man -

κατεργαζομένου τὸ κακόν, Ἰουδαίου τε πρῶτον καὶ Ἕλληνος·
working - evil, [2]of [3]a [4]Jew [1]both first and of a Greek;

10 δόξα δὲ καὶ τιμὴ καὶ εἰρήνη παντὶ τῷ ἐργαζομένῳ τὸ
glory ˜ but and honor and peace to every*one* - working -

ἀγαθόν, Ἰουδαίῳ τε πρῶτον καὶ Ἕλληνι. 11 Οὐ γάρ
good, [2]to [3]a [4]Jew [1]both first and to a Greek. [4]not [1]For

ἐστι προσωποληψία παρὰ τῷ Θεῷ. 12 Ὅσοι γὰρ
[2]*there* [3]is partiality with - God. [2]as [3]many [4]as [1]For

ἀνόμως ἥμαρτον, ἀνόμως καὶ ἀπολοῦνται· καὶ ὅσοι ἐν
without law sinned, without law also ˜ will perish; and as many as in

νόμῳ ἥμαρτον, διὰ νόμου κριθήσονται. 13 Οὐ γὰρ οἱ
law sinned, through *the* law will be judged. not ˜ For the
by

ἀκροαταὶ τοῦ νόμου δίκαιοι παρὰ τῷ Θεῷ, ἀλλ' οἱ
hearers of the law *are* righteous with - God, but the

ποιηταὶ τοῦ νόμου δικαιωθήσονται. 14 Ὅταν γὰρ ἔθνη
doers of the law will be justified. whenever ˜ For Gentiles

τὰ μὴ νόμον ἔχοντα φύσει τὰ τοῦ νόμου
the *ones* not law ˜ having by nature [2]the [3]*things* [4]of [5]the [6]law
who do not have law

ποιῇ, οὗτοι, νόμον μὴ ἔχοντες, ἑαυτοῖς εἰσι νόμος·
[1]do, these, [3]law [1]not [2]having, [7]to [8]themselves [4]are [5]a [6]law;

15 οἵτινες ἐνδείκνυνται τὸ ἔργον τοῦ νόμου γραπτὸν ἐν ταῖς
who show the work of the law written in -

καρδίαις αὐτῶν, συμμαρτυρούσης αὐτῶν τῆς συνειδήσεως,
hearts ˜ their, [3]witnessing [4]with [5]*them* [1]their - [2]conscience,

καὶ μεταξὺ ἀλλήλων τῶν λογισμῶν κατηγορούντων ἢ καὶ
and between themselves the thoughts accusing or even
among their accuse

ἀπολογουμένων, 16 ἐν ἡμέρᾳ ὅτε κρινεῖ ὁ Θεὸς τὰ κρυπτὰ
defending *them,* in *the* day when judges ˜ - God the secrets
defend

τῶν ἀνθρώπων κατὰ τὸ εὐαγγέλιόν μου διὰ Ἰησοῦ
- of men according to - gospel ˜ my through Jesus

Χριστοῦ.[c]
Christ.

The Jews Are as Guilty as the Gentiles They Judge

17 Ἴδε[d] σὺ Ἰουδαῖος ἐπονομάζῃ καὶ ἐπαναπαύῃ τῷ νόμῳ
Look, you [3]a [4]Jew [1]are [2]named and rest on the law

καὶ καυχᾶσαι ἐν Θεῷ 18 καὶ γινώσκεις τὸ θέλημα καὶ
and boast in God and know the will and
His

δοκιμάζεις τὰ διαφέροντα κατηχούμενος ἐκ τοῦ νόμου,
approve the *things* excelling being instructed from the law,
by

19 πέποιθάς τε σεαυτὸν ὁδηγὸν εἶναι τυφλῶν,
[2]you [3]have [4]been [5]persuaded [1]and yourself a guide to be of *the* blind,
are confident that you are a guide to

φῶς τῶν ἐν σκότει, 20 παιδευτὴν ἀφρόνων,
a light of the *ones* in darkness, a corrector of foolish *ones,*

c(2:16) NU reads Χριστου Ιησου, *Christ Jesus.*
d(2:17) NU reads Ει δε, *But if.*

whispering *slander.* However, it is differentiated from καταλάλος, *slanderer* (v. 30), in that whispering or talebearing is done behind someone's back. Cf. the cognate noun ψιθυρισμός, *whispering, secret gossip* (2 Cor. 12:20).

διδάσκαλον νηπίων, ἔχοντα τὴν μόρφωσιν τῆς
a teacher of immature *ones,* having the form -

γνώσεως καὶ τῆς ἀληθείας ἐν τῷ νόμῳ. **21** Ὁ οὖν
of knowledge and of the truth in the law. The *one* therefore
You

διδάσκων ἕτερον, σεαυτὸν οὐ διδάσκεις? Ὁ κηρύσσων
teaching another, [5]yourself [3]not [1]do [2]you [4]teach? The *one* preaching
who teach You who preach

μὴ κλέπτειν, κλέπτεις? **22** Ὁ λέγων μὴ
not to steal, do you steal? The *one* saying not
You who say, "Do

μοιχεύειν, μοιχεύεις? Ὁ βδελυσσόμενος τὰ
to commit adultery, do you commit adultery? The *one* abhorring -
not commit adultery," You who abhor

εἴδωλα, ἱεροσυλεῖς? **23** Ὃς ἐν νόμῳ καυχᾶσαι, διὰ
idols, do you rob temples? [2]who [4]in [5]*the* [6]law [1]You [3]boast, through

τῆς παραβάσεως* τοῦ νόμου τὸν Θεὸν ἀτιμάζεις?
the transgression of the law - [4]God [1]do [2]you [3]dishonor?

24 «Τὸ γὰρ ὄνομα τοῦ Θεοῦ δι' ὑμᾶς βλασφημεῖται ἐν
«the ˜ For name - of God through you is blasphemed among

τοῖς ἔθνεσι,» [e] καθὼς γέγραπται.
the Gentiles,» just as it is written.

Circumcision *Per Se* Is of No Avail

25 Περιτομὴ μὲν γὰρ ὠφελεῖ ἐὰν νόμον πράσσῃς,
[3]circumcision [2]indeed [1]For profits if [3]*the* [4]law [1]you [2]practice,
keep,

ἐὰν δὲ παραβάτης νόμου ᾖς, ἡ περιτομή σου
if ˜ but [3]a [4]transgressor [5]of [6]law [1]you [2]are, - circumcision ˜ your

ἀκροβυστία γέγονεν. **26** Ἐὰν οὖν ἡ ἀκροβυστία τὰ
[3]uncircumcision [1]has [2]become. if ˜ Therefore the uncircumcision [2]the
a Gentile

δικαιώματα τοῦ νόμου φυλάσσῃ, οὐχὶ ἡ
[3]righteous [4]requirements [5]of [6]the [7]law [1]keeps, [9]not -

ἀκροβυστία αὐτοῦ εἰς περιτομὴν λογισθήσεται? **27** Καὶ
[11]uncircumcision [10]his [14]for [15]circumcision [8]will [12]be [13]counted? And

κρινεῖ ἡ ἐκ φύσεως ἀκροβυστία, τὸν νόμον τελοῦσα, σὲ
[8]will [9]judge [1]the [3]by [4]nature [2]uncircumcision, [6]the [7]law [5]fulfilling, you
the one physically uncircumcised, who fulfills,

τὸν διὰ γράμματος καὶ περιτομῆς παραβάτην νόμου?
the [4]along [5]with [6]*your* [7]letter [8]and [9]circumcision [1]transgressor [2]of [3]law?
written code

28 Οὐ γὰρ ὁ ἐν τῷ φανερῷ Ἰουδαῖός ἐστιν, οὐδὲ ἡ ἐν τῷ
[4]not [1]For [5]the [7]in [8]the [9]open [6]Jew [2]he [3]is, nor *is* the [2]in [3]the
outwardly

φανερῷ ἐν σαρκὶ περιτομή· **29** ἀλλ' ὁ ἐν τῷ κρυπτῷ
[4]open [5]in [6]flesh [1]circumcision; but the [3]in [4]the [5]secret
outwardly inwardly

Ἰουδαῖος, καὶ περιτομὴ καρδίας ἐν πνεύματι, οὐ
[1]Jew [2]*is,* and circumcision *is* of *the* heart in spirit, not

γράμματι, οὗ ὁ ἔπαινος οὐκ ἐξ ἀνθρώπων ἀλλ' ἐκ τοῦ Θεοῦ.
in letter, whose - praise *is* not of men but of - God.

Paul Answers an Objection

3 **1** Τί οὖν τὸ περισσὸν τοῦ Ἰουδαίου, ἢ τίς ἡ
What then *is* the advantage of the Jew, or what *is* the

ὠφέλεια τῆς περιτομῆς? **2** Πολὺ κατὰ πάντα τρόπον!
profit - of circumcision? Much according to every way!
in

a teacher of babes, having the
form of knowledge and truth in
the law.
21 You, therefore, who teach
another, do you not teach yourself? You who preach that a
man should not steal, do you
steal?
22 You who say, "Do not commit adultery," do you commit
adultery? You who abhor idols,
do you rob temples?
23 You who make your boast
in the law, do you dishonor God
through breaking the law?
24 For *"the name of God is
blasphemed among the Gentiles
because of you,"* as it is written.
25 For circumcision is indeed
profitable if you keep the law;
but if you are a breaker of the
law, your circumcision has become uncircumcision.
26 Therefore, if an uncircumcised man keeps the righteous
requirements of the law, will
not his uncircumcision be
counted as circumcision?
27 And will not the physically
uncircumcised, if he fulfills the
law, judge you who, *even* with
your written *code* and circumcision, *are* a transgressor of the
law?
28 For he is not a Jew who *is
one* outwardly, nor *is* circumcision that which *is* outward in
the flesh;
29 but *he is* a Jew who *is one*
inwardly; and circumcision *is
that* of the heart, in the Spirit,
not in the letter; whose praise
is not from men but from God.
3 What advantage then has
the Jew, or what *is* the
profit of circumcision?
2 Much in every way! Chiefly

---

[e](2:24) Is. 52:5; Ezek. 36:22

*(2:23) παράβασις *(parabasis).* Noun meaning *transgression.* It is derived from the verb παραβαίνω, literally *go* or *turn aside* (as Acts 1:25), but used figuratively with terms such as "law" or "tradition" to mean *transgress* (Matt. 15:2). It is in this latter sense that the noun παράβασις refers to a violation of an established, known law. As here in Rom. 2:23, the "law" which is violated may be a general rather than a specific one. Cf. also the cognate noun παραβάτης, *transgressor* (Rom. 2:25), used of those who customarily violate the law.

because to them were committed the oracles of God.
3 For what if some did not believe? Will their unbelief make the faithfulness of God without effect?
4 Certainly not! Indeed, let God be true but every man a liar. As it is written:

"That You may be justified
in Your words,
And may overcome when
You are judged."

5 But if our unrighteousness demonstrates the righteousness of God, what shall we say? *Is* God unjust who inflicts wrath? (I speak as a man.)
6 Certainly not! For then how will God judge the world?
7 For if the truth of God has increased through my lie to His glory, why am I also still judged as a sinner?
8 And *why* not *say,* "Let us do evil that good may come"?—as we are slanderously reported and as some affirm that we say. Their condemnation is just.
9 What then? Are we better *than they?* Not at all. For we have previously charged both Jews and Greeks that they are all under sin.
10 As it is written:

"There is none righteous,
no, not one;
11 *There is none who*
understands;
There is none who seeks
after God.

Πρῶτον μὲν γὰρ ὅτι ἐπιστεύθησαν τὰ λόγια τοῦ
[3]first [2]indeed [1]For because they were entrusted with the oracles -

Θεοῦ. 3 Τί γὰρ εἰ ἠπίστησάν τινες? Μὴ ἡ ἀπιστία
of God. what ˜ For if disbelieved ˜ some? [1]*Surely* [5]not - [3]unbelief

αὐτῶν τὴν πίστιν τοῦ Θεοῦ καταργήσει? 4 Μὴ γένοιτο!
[2]their [7]the [8]faithfulness - [9]of [10]God [4]will [6]nullify? [3]not [1]May [2]it [4]be!

Γινέσθω δὲ ὁ Θεὸς ἀληθής, πᾶς δὲ ἄνθρωπος ψεύστης,
[6]let [8]be [5]But - [7]God true, every ˜ but man a liar,

καθὼς γέγραπται,
just as it is written,

«Ὅπως ἂν δικαιωθῇς ἐν τοῖς λόγοις σου
«So that - You may be justified in - words ˜ your

Καὶ νικήσῃς[a] ἐν τῷ κρίνεσθαί σε.»[b]
And You may overcome in - to be judged You.»
when You are judged.»

5 Εἰ δὲ ἡ ἀδικία ἡμῶν Θεοῦ δικαιοσύνην
if ˜ But - unrighteousness ˜ our [4]of [5]God [2]*the* [3]righteousness

συνίστησι, τί ἐροῦμεν? Μὴ ἄδικος ὁ Θεὸς
[1]demonstrates, what shall we say? [1]*Surely* [8]not [7]*is* [9]unrighteous - [2]God

ὁ ἐπιφέρων τὴν ὀργήν? (Κατὰ ἄνθρωπον
[3]the [4]*One* [5]inflicting - [6]wrath, [10]*is* [11]*He?* (According to a man
who inflicts (I speak as a

λέγω.) 6 Μὴ γένοιτο! Ἐπεὶ πῶς κρινεῖ ὁ Θεὸς τὸν
I say.) [3]not [1]May [2]it [4]be! For otherwise how will judge ˜ - God the
man.)

κόσμον? 7 Εἰ γὰρ ἡ ἀλήθεια τοῦ Θεοῦ ἐν τῷ ἐμῷ ψεύσματι
world? if ˜ For the truth - of God by - my lie

ἐπερίσσευσεν εἰς τὴν δόξαν αὐτοῦ, τί ἔτι κἀγὼ ὡς
abounded to - glory ˜ His, why [4]still [2]I [3]also [6]as

ἁμαρτωλὸς κρίνομαι? 8 Καὶ μὴ καθὼς βλασφημούμεθα καὶ
[7]a [8]sinner [1]am [5]judged? And *why* not just as we are blasphemed and
slandered

καθώς φασί τινες ἡμᾶς λέγειν ὅτι "Ποιήσωμεν τὰ κακὰ
just as say ˜ some us to say - "Let us do - bad *things*
some affirm that we say

ἵνα ἔλθῃ τὰ ἀγαθά"? Ὧν τὸ κρίμα
so that [3]may [4]come - [1]good [2]*things*"? Of whom the judgment
whose condemnation

ἔνδικόν ἐστι.
just ˜ is.

All Have Sinned

9 Τί οὖν? Προεχόμεθα? Οὐ πάντως.
What then? Are we *any* better? Not at all.

Προῃτιασάμεθα γὰρ Ἰουδαίους τε καὶ Ἕλληνας πάντας
[2]we [3]previously [4]charged [1]For Jews ˜ both and Greeks all
that

ὑφ' ἁμαρτίαν εἶναι. 10 Καθὼς γέγραπται ὅτι
under sin to be. Just as it is written -
they are all under sin.

«Οὐκ ἔστι δίκαιος οὐδὲ εἷς,
«[3]not [1]*There* [2]is a righteous *person* not even one,

11 Οὐκ ἔστιν ὁ συνιών,
[3]not [1]*There* [2]is - *one* understanding,
who understands,

Οὐκ ἔστιν ὁ ἐκζητῶν τὸν Θεόν.
[3]not [1]*There* [2]is - *one* seeking - God.
who seeks

---

[a](3:4) NU reads νικησεις, *you will overcome.*
[b](3:4) Ps. 51:4

12 Πάντες ἐξέκλιναν,
All *have* turned aside,
῞Αμα ἠχρειώθησαν·
Together they became unprofitable;
Οὐκ ἔστι ποιῶν χρηστότητα,
[3]not [1]*There* [2]is *one* doing kindness,
Οὐκ ἔστιν ἕως ἑνός.»[c]
[3]not [1]*There* [2]is so much as one.»

13 «Τάφος ἀνεῳγμένος ὁ λάρυγξ αὐτῶν,
«[4]a(n) [6]grave [5]opened - [2]throat [1]Their [3]*is,*
Ταῖς γλώσσαις αὐτῶν ἐδολιοῦσαν.»[d]
- With tongues ˜ their they deceived.»
«Ἰὸς ἀσπίδων ὑπὸ τὰ χείλη αὐτῶν.»[e]
«Poison of asps (vipers) *is* under - lips ˜ their.»

14 «῟Ων τὸ στόμα ἀρᾶς καὶ πικρίας γέμει.»[f]
«Whose - mouth [3]of [4]cursing [5]and [6]bitterness [1]is [2]full.»

15 «Ὀξεῖς οἱ πόδες αὐτῶν ἐκχέαι αἷμα,
«Swift *are* - feet ˜ their to shed blood,

16 Σύντριμμα καὶ ταλαιπωρία ἐν ταῖς ὁδοῖς αὐτῶν,
Ruin and misery *are* in - ways ˜ their,

17 Καὶ ὁδὸν εἰρήνης οὐκ ἔγνωσαν.»[g]
And *the* way of peace [3]not [1]they [2]did [4]know.»

18 «Οὐκ ἔστι φόβος Θεοῦ ἀπέναντι τῶν ὀφθαλμῶν
«[3]not [1]*There* [2]is a fear of God before - eyes ˜
αὐτῶν.»[h]
their.»

19 Οἴδαμεν δὲ ὅτι ὅσα ὁ νόμος λέγει, τοῖς
[2]we [3]know [1]Now that as many *things* as the law says, to the *ones*
ἐν τῷ νόμῳ λαλεῖ, ἵνα πᾶν στόμα φραγῇ καὶ
in (under) the law it speaks, so that every mouth may be stopped and
ὑπόδικος γένηται πᾶς ὁ κόσμος τῷ Θεῷ. 20 Διότι
[6]accountable [4]may [5]become [1]all [2]the [3]world - to God. Therefore
ἐξ ἔργων νόμου οὐ δικαιωθήσεται πᾶσα σὰρξ ἐνώπιον αὐτοῦ,
by works of law not ˜ will be justified all flesh before Him,
(no flesh will be justified)
διὰ γὰρ νόμου ἐπίγνωσις ἁμαρτίας.
through ˜ for law *is the* knowledge of sin.

God's Righteousness Is Through Faith

21 Νυνὶ δὲ χωρὶς νόμου δικαιοσύνη Θεοῦ
now ˜ But apart from law a righteousness of God
πεφανέρωται, μαρτυρουμένη ὑπὸ τοῦ νόμου καὶ τῶν
has been revealed, being (which is) witnessed to by the law and the
προφητῶν, 22 δικαιοσύνη δὲ Θεοῦ διὰ πίστεως
prophets, a righteousness furthermore of God through faith
Ἰησοῦ Χριστοῦ εἰς πάντας καὶ ἐπὶ πάντας[i] τοὺς
of (in) Jesus Christ to all and upon all the *ones* (believers.)
πιστεύοντας. Οὐ γάρ ἐστι διαστολή· 23 πάντες γὰρ
believing. [4]not [1]For [2]*there* [3]is a difference; all ˜ for
ἥμαρτον καὶ ὑστεροῦνται τῆς δόξης τοῦ Θεοῦ,
sinned and are lacking of the glory - of God,
24 δικαιούμενοι δωρεὰν τῇ αὐτοῦ χάριτι διὰ τῆς
being justified as a gift (freely) - His ˜ by grace through the

12 *They have all turned*
aside;
They have together
become unprofitable;
There is none who does
good, no, not one."
13 *"Their throat is an open*
tomb;
With their tongues they
have practiced deceit";
"The poison of asps is
under their lips";
14 *"Whose mouth is full of*
cursing and bitterness."
15 *"Their feet are swift to*
shed blood;
16 *Destruction and misery*
are in their ways;
17 *And the way of peace*
they have not known."
18 *"There is no fear of God*
before their eyes."

19 Now we know that what-
ever the law says, it says to
those who are under the law,
that every mouth may be
stopped, and all the world may
become guilty before God.
20 Therefore by the deeds of
the law no flesh will be justified
in His sight, for by the law *is*
the knowledge of sin.
21 But now the righteousness
of God apart from the law is revealed, being witnessed by the
Law and the Prophets,
22 even the righteousness of
God, through faith in Jesus
Christ, to all and on all who believe. For there is no difference;
23 for all have sinned and fall
short of the glory of God,
24 being justified freely by His
grace through the redemption

[c](**3:12**) Ps. 14:1–3; 53:1–3; Eccl. 7:20 [d](**3:13**) Ps. 5:9
[e](**3:13**) Ps. 140:3
[f](**3:14**) Ps. 10:7
[g](**3:17**) Is. 59:7, 8
[h](**3:18**) Ps. 36:1
[i](**3:22**) NU omits *και επι παντας, and upon all.*

that is in Christ Jesus,
25 whom God set forth *as* a
propitiation by His blood,
through faith, to demonstrate
His righteousness, because in
His forbearance God had
passed over the sins that were
previously committed,
26 to demonstrate at the
present time His righteousness, that He might be just and
the justifier of the one who has
faith in Jesus.
27 Where *is* boasting then? It
is excluded. By what law? Of
works? No, but by the law of
faith.
28 Therefore we conclude
that a man is justified by faith
apart from the deeds of the law.
29 Or *is He* the God of the
Jews only? *Is He* not also the
God of the Gentiles? Yes, of
the Gentiles also,
30 since *there is* one God who
will justify the circumcised by
faith and the uncircumcised
through faith.
31 Do we then make void the
law through faith? Certainly
not! On the contrary, we establish the law.
4 What then shall we say
that Abraham our father
has found according to the flesh?
2 For if Abraham was justified by works, he has *something*
to boast about, but not before
God.
3 For what does the Scripture say? *"Abraham believed
God, and it was accounted to
him for righteousness."*
4 Now to him who works,
the wages are not counted as
grace but as debt.
5 But to him who does not

---

[a](**4:1**) NU reads προπατορα, *forefather.*
[b](**4:3**) Gen. 15:6
[c](**4:4**) TR adds το, *the.*

*(**3:24**) ἀπολύτρωσις (*apolytrōsis*). Noun meaning *redemption,* literally the buying back or freeing (of a slave) by payment of the redemption price. Its NT occurrences emphasize both the price (Jesus' blood in Eph. 1:7; Col. 1:14) and the resulting freedom. The use of ἀπολύτρωσις and its cognates in salvation contexts implies the complete liberation of those redeemed by Christ from their former slavery. Cf. the simple λύτρωσις with essentially the same meaning (Luke 1:68; 2:38); and the cognate verb

ἀπολυτρώσεως* τῆς ἐν Χριστῷ Ἰησοῦ, **25** ὃν προέθετο ὁ
redemption - in Christ Jesus, whom [2]set [3]forth -

Θεὸς ἱλαστήριον διὰ τῆς πίστεως ἐν τῷ αὐτοῦ αἵματι, εἰς
[1]God *as* a propitiation through - faith in - His blood, for

ἔνδειξιν τῆς δικαιοσύνης αὐτοῦ διὰ τὴν πάρεσιν
a demonstration - of righteousness ˜ His through the passing over

τῶν προγεγονότων ἁμαρτημάτων, ἐν τῇ ἀνοχῇ
of the [2]having [3]previously [4]occurred [1]sins, in the forbearance

τοῦ Θεοῦ, **26** πρὸς ἔνδειξιν τῆς δικαιοσύνης αὐτοῦ ἐν
- of God, for a demonstration - of righteousness ˜ His in

τῷ νῦν καιρῷ, εἰς τὸ εἶναι αὐτὸν δίκαιον καὶ δικαιοῦντα
the now season, for - to be Him righteous and declaring righteous
present time, that He might be

τὸν ἐκ πίστεως Ἰησοῦ.
the *one* of *the* faith of Jesus.
who has faith in Jesus.

Boasting Is Excluded

27 Ποῦ οὖν ἡ καύχησις? Ἐξεκλείσθη. Διὰ ποίου
Where then *is* the boasting? It was shut out. Through what
is excluded.

νόμου? Τῶν ἔργων? Οὐχί, ἀλλὰ διὰ νόμου πίστεως.
law? - Of works? No, but through a law of faith.

28 Λογιζόμεθα οὖν πίστει δικαιοῦσθαι ἄνθρωπον
We consider therefore *that* [6]by [7]faith [3]to [4]be [5]justified [1]a [2]man
is person

χωρὶς ἔργων νόμου. **29** Ἢ Ἰουδαίων ὁ Θεὸς μόνον?
apart from works of law. Or [5]of [6]Jews [3]the [1]*is* [2]*He* [4]God only?

Οὐχὶ δὲ καὶ ἐθνῶν? Ναί, καὶ ἐθνῶν, **30** ἐπείπερ
[4]not [1]But [2]*is* [3]*He* also of Gentiles? Yes, also of Gentiles, since

εἷς ὁ Θεός, ὃς δικαιώσει περιτομὴν ἐκ πίστεως καὶ
there is one - God, who will justify circumcision by faith and

ἀκροβυστίαν διὰ τῆς πίστεως. **31** Νόμον οὖν
uncircumcision through the faith. [5]law [1]Therefore

καταργοῦμεν διὰ τῆς πίστεως? Μὴ γένοιτο! Ἀλλὰ
[2]do [3]we [4]nullify through - faith? [3]not [1]May [2]it [4]be! But
On the contrary

νόμον ἱστῶμεν.
[3]law [1]we [2]establish.

Abraham Was Justified by Faith

4 **1** Τί οὖν ἐροῦμεν Ἀβραὰμ τὸν πατέρα[a] ἡμῶν
What then shall we say *that* Abraham - father ˜ our

εὑρηκέναι κατὰ σάρκα? **2** Εἰ γὰρ Ἀβραὰμ ἐξ ἔργων
to have found according to *the* flesh? if ˜ For Abraham by works
has

ἐδικαιώθη, ἔχει καύχημα, ἀλλ' οὐ πρὸς τὸν Θεόν. **3** Τί
was justified, he has a boast, but not with - God. what ˜

γὰρ ἡ Γραφὴ λέγει? «Ἐπίστευσε δὲ Ἀβραὰμ τῷ Θεῷ,
For [2]the [3]Scripture [1]does [4]say? «[7]believed [5]And [6]Abraham - God,

καὶ ἐλογίσθη αὐτῷ εἰς δικαιοσύνην.»[b] **4** Τῷ δὲ
and it was accounted to him for righteousness.» [2]to [3]the [4]*one* [1]Now

ἐργαζομένῳ ὁ μισθὸς οὐ λογίζεται κατὰ χάριν ἀλλὰ
working the reward not ˜ is accounted according to grace but
who works

κατὰ[c] ὀφείλημα.* **5** Τῷ δὲ μὴ ἐργαζομένῳ,
according to debt. [2]to [3]the [4]*one* [1]But not working,
who does not work,

πιστεύοντι δὲ ἐπὶ τὸν δικαιοῦντα τὸν ἀσεβῆ, λογίζεται ἡ
believing ˜ but on the *One* justifying the ungodly, [3]is [4]accounted -
believes

πίστις αὐτοῦ εἰς δικαιοσύνην.
[2]faith [1]his for righteousness.

David Celebrates the Same Truth

6 Καθάπερ καὶ Δαβὶδ λέγει τὸν μακαρισμὸν τοῦ
Just as also David says the blessing of the
speaks of

ἀνθρώπου ᾧ ὁ Θεὸς λογίζεται δικαιοσύνην χωρὶς
man to whom - God accounts righteousness apart from

ἔργων,
works,

7 «Μακάριοι ὧν ἀφέθησαν αἱ ἀνομίαι,
«Blessed *are they* whose [3]were [4]forgiven - [1]lawless [2]deeds,
have been

Καὶ ὧν ἐπεκαλύφθησαν αἱ ἁμαρτίαι.
And whose [2]were [3]covered [4]over - [1]sins.

8 Μακάριος ἀνὴρ ᾧ οὐ μὴ λογίσηται Κύριος
Blessed *is* a man to whom [4]not [5]not [3]shall [6]impute [1]*the* [2]Lord
by no means

ἁμαρτίαν.» [d]
sin.»

Abraham Was Justified Long Before Circumcision

9 Ὁ μακαρισμὸς οὖν οὗτος ἐπὶ τὴν περιτομήν, ἢ
- *Does* [3]blessing [1]then [2]this *come* upon the circumcision, or

καὶ ἐπὶ τὴν ἀκροβυστίαν? Λέγομεν γὰρ ὅτι «Ἐλογίσθη τῷ
also upon the uncircumcision? [2]we [3]say [1]For that «[3]was [4]accounted -

Ἀβραὰμ ἡ πίστις εἰς δικαιοσύνην.» [e] **10** Πῶς οὖν
[5]to [6]Abraham [1]The [2]faith for righteousness.» How then
His

ἐλογίσθη? Ἐν περιτομῇ ὄντι ἢ ἐν ἀκροβυστίᾳ? Οὐκ
was it accounted? In circumcision being or in uncircumcision? Not
While he was circumcised

ἐν περιτομῇ ἀλλ' ἐν ἀκροβυστίᾳ. **11** Καὶ σημεῖον ἔλαβε
in circumcision but in uncircumcision. And [3]a [4]sign [1]he [2]received

περιτομῆς, σφραγῖδα τῆς δικαιοσύνης τῆς πίστεως τῆς
of circumcision, a seal of the righteousness of the faith the *one*
which

ἐν τῇ ἀκροβυστίᾳ, εἰς τὸ εἶναι αὐτὸν πατέρα
he had while in - uncircumcision, for - to be him father
so that he should be

πάντων τῶν πιστευόντων δι' ἀκροβυστίας, εἰς τὸ
of all the *ones* believing through uncircumcision, for -
although uncircumcised, so that

λογισθῆναι καὶ αὐτοῖς τὴν δικαιοσύνην, **12** καὶ πατέρα
to be imputed also to them the righteousness, and a father
righteousness should also be imputed to them,

περιτομῆς τοῖς οὐκ ἐκ περιτομῆς μόνον, ἀλλὰ καὶ
of circumcision to the *ones* not of circumcision only, but also

τοῖς στοιχοῦσι τοῖς ἴχνεσι τῆς πίστεως τῆς
to the *ones* following in the steps of the faith [5]the [6]*one*
which

ἐν τῇ ἀκροβυστίᾳ τοῦ πατρὸς ἡμῶν Ἀβραάμ.
[7]*he* [8]*had* [9]*while* [10]in - [11]uncircumcision - [1]of [3]father [2]our [4]Abraham.

work but believes on Him who justifies the ungodly, his faith is accounted for righteousness,

6 just as David also describes the blessedness of the man to whom God imputes righteousness apart from works:

7 *"Blessed are those whose*
lawless deeds are
forgiven,
And whose sins are
covered;
8 *Blessed is the man to*
whom the L*ORD* *shall*
not impute sin."

9 *Does* this blessedness then *come* upon the circumcised *only,* or upon the uncircumcised also? For we say that faith was accounted to Abraham for righteousness.

10 How then was it accounted? While he was circumcised, or uncircumcised? Not while circumcised, but while uncircumcised.

11 And he received the sign of circumcision, a seal of the righteousness of the faith which *he had while still* uncircumcised, that he might be the father of all those who believe, though they are uncircumcised, that righteousness might be imputed to them also,

12 and the father of circumcision to those who not only *are* of the circumcision, but who also walk in the steps of the faith which our father Abraham *had while still* uncircumcised.

---

[d]**(4:7, 8)** Ps. 32:1, 2
[e]**(4:9)** Gen. 15:6

λυτρόω, *free by paying ransom, redeem* (1 Pet. 1:18); and noun λύτρον, *ransom price* (only in Matt. 20:28; Mark 10:45).

***(4:4)** ὀφείλημα *(opheilēma).* Noun, used only twice in the NT, meaning *what is owed, one's due,* thus *debt.* Here the wages for which one works are considered *owed* because they have been earned; they are not an undeserved favor. In the Lord's Prayer the word is used figuratively of *liability for wrongdoing* (Matt. 6:12; the parallel Luke 11:4 reads "sins"). Cf. the cognate verb ὀφειλω, *owe, be obligated, sin* (1 Cor. 7:3). See ὀφειλέτης at Luke 13:4.

13 For the promise that he would be the heir of the world *was* not to Abraham or to his seed through the law, but through the righteousness of faith.
14 For if those who are of the law *are* heirs, faith is made void and the promise made of no effect,
15 because the law brings about wrath; for where there is no law *there is* no transgression.
16 Therefore *it is* of faith that *it might be* according to grace, so that the promise might be sure to all the seed, not only to those who are of the law, but also to those who are of the faith of Abraham, who is the father of us all
17 (as it is written, *"I have made you a father of many nations"*) in the presence of Him whom he believed—God, who gives life to the dead and calls those things which do not exist as though they did;
18 who, contrary to hope, in hope believed, so that he became the father of many nations, according to what was spoken, *"So shall your descendants be."*
19 And not being weak in faith, he did not consider his own body, already dead (since he was about a hundred years old), and the deadness of Sarah's womb.
20 He did not waver at the promise of God through unbelief, but was strengthened in faith, giving glory to God,
21 and being fully convinced that what He had promised He was also able to perform.
22 And therefore *"it was accounted to him for righteousness."*
23 Now it was not written for his sake alone that it was imputed to him,
24 but also for us. It shall be imputed to us who believe in

The Promise Was Granted Through Faith

13 Οὐ γὰρ διὰ νόμου ἡ ἐπαγγελία τῷ Ἀβραὰμ ἢ τῷ
not~ For through law *was* the promise - to Abraham or -

σπέρματι αὐτοῦ, τὸ κληρονόμον αὐτὸν εἶναι τοῦ κόσμου,
to seed~ his, the heir him to be of the world,
that he should be heir

ἀλλὰ διὰ δικαιοσύνης πίστεως. **14** Εἰ γὰρ οἱ ἐκ
but through a righteousness of faith. if~ For the *ones* of
those who are

νόμου κληρονόμοι, κεκένωται ἡ πίστις καὶ
law *are* heirs, [2]has [3]been [4]emptied - [1]faith and

κατήργηται ἡ ἐπαγγελία· **15** ὁ γὰρ νόμος ὀργὴν
[3]has [4]been [5]nullified [1]the [2]promise; the~ for law wrath~

κατεργάζεται· οὗ γὰρ οὐκ ἔστι νόμος, οὐδὲ
produces; where~ for [3]not [1]*there* [2]is law, neither *is there*

παράβασις. **16** Διὰ τοῦτο ἐκ πίστεως ἵνα
transgression. On account of this *it is* of faith so that *it may be*

κατὰ χάριν, εἰς τὸ εἶναι βεβαίαν τὴν ἐπαγγελίαν παντὶ
according to grace, for - to be sure the promise to all
so that the promise might be sure

τῷ σπέρματι, οὐ τῷ ἐκ τοῦ νόμου μόνον, ἀλλὰ καὶ
the seed, not to the *one* of the law only, but also

τῷ ἐκ πίστεως Ἀβραάμ, ὅς ἐστι πατὴρ πάντων ἡμῶν
to the *one* of *the* faith of Abraham, who is father of all of us

17 (καθὼς γέγραπται ὅτι «Πατέρα πολλῶν ἐθνῶν τέθεικά
(just as it is written - «A father of many nations I have appointed

σε»)·[f] κατέναντι οὗ ἐπίστευσε Θεοῦ, τοῦ ζῳοποιοῦντος
you»); before [2]whom [3]he [4]believed [1]God, the *One* giving life to

τοὺς νεκροὺς καὶ καλοῦντος τὰ μὴ ὄντα ὡς
the dead *ones* and calling the *things* not being as though
which do not exist

ὄντα. **18** Ὃς παρ' ἐλπίδα ἐπ' ἐλπίδι ἐπίστευσεν, εἰς τὸ
being. Who beyond hope [2]on [3]hope [1]believed, for -
they existed. so that

γενέσθαι αὐτὸν «πατέρα πολλῶν ἐθνῶν,» κατὰ τὸ
to become him «a father of many nations,» according to the *thing*
he should become

εἰρημένον, «Οὕτως ἔσται τὸ σπέρμα σου.»[g] **19** Καὶ μὴ
having been spoken, «So [3]shall [4]be - [2]seed [1]your.» And not

ἀσθενήσας τῇ πίστει, οὐ[h] κατενόησε τὸ ἑαυτοῦ σῶμα
weakening - in faith, [3]not [1]he [2]did [4]consider - his own body

ἤδη νενεκρωμένον, ἑκατονταέτης που ὑπάρχων, καὶ
already having been worn out, [3]a [4]hundred [5]years [6]*old* [2]about [1]being, and

τὴν νέκρωσιν τῆς μήτρας Σάρρας, **20** εἰς δὲ τὴν ἐπαγγελίαν
the deadness of the womb of Sarah, at~ and the promise

τοῦ Θεοῦ οὐ διεκρίθη τῇ ἀπιστίᾳ ἀλλ' ἐνεδυναμώθη τῇ
- of God [3]not [1]he [2]did [4]waver - in unbelief but was empowered -

πίστει, δοὺς δόξαν τῷ Θεῷ, **21** καὶ πληροφορηθεὶς ὅτι ὃ
by faith, giving glory - to God, and being fully convinced that what

ἐπήγγελται δυνατός ἐστι καὶ ποιῆσαι. **22** Διὸ καὶ
He had promised [4]able [1]He [2]is [3]also to do. Therefore also

«ἐλογίσθη αὐτῷ εἰς δικαιοσύνην.»[i] **23** Οὐκ ἐγράφη
«it was accounted to him for righteousness.» [4]not [2]it [3]was [5]written

δὲ δι' αὐτὸν μόνον ὅτι ἐλογίσθη αὐτῷ, **24** ἀλλὰ
[1]Now on account of him only that it was accounted to him, but

καὶ δι' ἡμᾶς οἷς μέλλει λογίζεσθαι, τοῖς
also on account of us to whom it is about to be imputed, the *ones*
it was going

---

[f](**4:17**) Gen. 17:5
[g](**4:18**) Gen. 15:5
[h](**4:19**) NU omits *ου, not.*
[i](**4:22**) Gen. 15:6

πιστεύουσιν ἐπὶ τὸν ἐγείραντα Ἰησοῦν τὸν Κύριον ἡμῶν
believing on the One having raised Jesus - Lord ˜ our
Him who raised

ἐκ νεκρῶν, 25 ὃς παρεδόθη διὰ τὰ
from *the* dead, who was delivered over on account of -

παραπτώματα ἡμῶν καὶ ἠγέρθη διὰ τὴν δικαίωσιν
transgressions ˜ our and was raised on account of - justification ˜

ἡμῶν.
our.

Faith Triumphs in Trouble

5 1 Δικαιωθέντες οὖν ἐκ πίστεως, εἰρήνην ἔχομεν
Having been justified therefore by faith, [3]peace [1]we [2]have

πρὸς τὸν Θεὸν διὰ τοῦ Κυρίου ἡμῶν Ἰησοῦ Χριστοῦ,
with - God through - Lord ˜ our Jesus Christ,

2 δι' οὗ καὶ τὴν προσαγωγὴν ἐσχήκαμεν τῇ πίστει[a]
through whom also - [4]access [1]we [2]have [3]had - by faith

εἰς τὴν χάριν ταύτην ἐν ᾗ ἑστήκαμεν, καὶ καυχώμεθα ἐπ'
into - grace ˜ this in which we stand, and we boast on
in

ἐλπίδι τῆς δόξης τοῦ Θεοῦ. 3 Οὐ μόνον δέ, ἀλλὰ καὶ
hope of the glory - of God. [2]not [3]only [1]And [4]*so,* but also ˜

καυχώμεθα ἐν ταῖς θλίψεσιν, εἰδότες ὅτι ἡ θλῖψις ὑπομονὴν
we boast in - tribulations, knowing that - tribulation endurance ˜

κατεργάζεται, 4 ἡ δὲ ὑπομονὴ δοκιμήν, ἡ δὲ δοκιμὴ ἐλπίδα.
works, - and endurance character, - and character hope.

5 Ἡ δὲ ἐλπὶς οὐ καταισχύνει, ὅτι ἡ ἀγάπη τοῦ Θεοῦ
- And hope not ˜ does put to shame, because the love - of God
disappoint,

ἐκκέχυται ἐν ταῖς καρδίαις ἡμῶν διὰ Πνεύματος
has been poured out in - hearts ˜ our through *the* Spirit ˜

Ἁγίου τοῦ δοθέντος ἡμῖν.
Holy the *One* having been given to us.
who was given

Justified by His Death; Saved by His Life

6 Ἔτι γὰρ Χριστός, ὄντων ἡμῶν ἀσθενῶν,[b] κατὰ
yet ˜ For Christ, being ˜ us weak, according to
when we were weak, at the right

καιρὸν ὑπὲρ ἀσεβῶν ἀπέθανε. 7 Μόλις γὰρ ὑπὲρ
a season on behalf of *the* ungodly died. scarcely ˜ For on behalf of
time

δικαίου τις ἀποθανεῖται, ὑπὲρ γὰρ τοῦ ἀγαθοῦ
a righteous *person* anyone ˜ will die, [2]on [3]behalf [4]of [1]for the good

τάχα τις καὶ τολμᾷ ἀποθανεῖν. 8 Συνίστησι δὲ τὴν
perhaps someone even dares to die. [3]demonstrates [1]But [4]the

ἑαυτοῦ ἀγάπην εἰς ἡμᾶς ὁ Θεός, ὅτι ἔτι ἁμαρτωλῶν ὄντων
[6]of [7]Himself [5]love [8]to [9]us - [2]God, that still sinners being
His own while we were still

ἡμῶν, Χριστὸς ὑπὲρ ἡμῶν ἀπέθανε. 9 Πολλῷ οὖν
us, Christ [2]on [3]behalf [4]of [5]us [1]died. Much then ˜
sinners,

μᾶλλον, δικαιωθέντες νῦν ἐν τῷ αἵματι αὐτοῦ,
more, having been justified now by - blood ˜ His,

σωθησόμεθα δι' αὐτοῦ ἀπὸ τῆς ὀργῆς. 10 Εἰ γὰρ ἐχθροὶ
we shall be saved through Him from - wrath. if ˜ For enemies ˜

ὄντες κατηλλάγημεν* τῷ Θεῷ διὰ τοῦ θανάτου τοῦ Υἱοῦ
being we were reconciled - to God through the death - of Son ˜

Him who raised up Jesus our Lord from the dead,
25 who was delivered up because of our offenses, and was raised because of our justification.

5 Therefore, having been justified by faith, we have peace with God through our Lord Jesus Christ,
2 through whom also we have access by faith into this grace in which we stand, and rejoice in hope of the glory of God.
3 And not only *that,* but we also glory in tribulations, knowing that tribulation produces perseverance;
4 and perseverance, character; and character, hope.
5 Now hope does not disappoint, because the love of God has been poured out in our hearts by the Holy Spirit who was given to us.
6 For when we were still without strength, in due time Christ died for the ungodly.
7 For scarcely for a righteous man will one die; yet perhaps for a good man someone would even dare to die.
8 But God demonstrates His own love toward us, in that while we were still sinners, Christ died for us.
9 Much more then, having now been justified by His blood, we shall be saved from wrath through Him.
10 For if when we were enemies we were reconciled to God through the death of His

---

[a](5:2) NU brackets *τῃ πιστει, by faith.*
[b](5:6) NU adds *ετι, yet.*

***(5:10)** *καταλλάσσω (katallassō).* Verb meaning *reconcile,* whether of husband and wife (1 Cor. 7:11) or of God and man (here and 2 Cor. 5:20). As applied to divine-human relations, the word indicates a change in relationship, the restoration of a broken relationship between God and persons at God's initiative. Cf. the cognate noun *καταλλαγή, reconciliation,* which occurs only in the same contexts (Rom. 5:11; 11:15; 2 Cor. 5:18, 19). The English *atonement* carries the same idea of "oneness."

Son, much more, having been
reconciled, we shall be saved
by His life.
11 And not only *that,* but we
also rejoice in God through our
Lord Jesus Christ, through
whom we have now received
the reconciliation.
12 Therefore, just as through
one man sin entered the world,
and death through sin, and thus
death spread to all men, because all sinned—
13 (For until the law sin was in
the world, but sin is not imputed when there is no law.
14 Nevertheless death
reigned from Adam to Moses,
even over those who had not
sinned according to the likeness
of the transgression of Adam,
who is a type of Him who was
to come.
15 But the free gift *is* not like
the offense. For if by the one
man's offense many died, much
more the grace of God and the
gift by the grace of the one
Man, Jesus Christ, abounded to
many.
16 And the gift *is* not like *that
which came* through the one
who sinned. For the judgment
which came from one *offense resulted* in condemnation, but the
free gift *which came* from many
offenses *resulted* in justification.
17 For if by the one man's offense death reigned through the
one, much more those who receive abundance of grace and of
the gift of righteousness will
reign in life through the One,
Jesus Christ.)
18 Therefore, as through one
man's offense *judgment* came to

αὐτοῦ, πολλῷ μᾶλλον καταλλαγέντες σωθησόμεθα ἐν τῇ
His, much more having been reconciled we shall be saved by -

ζωῇ αὐτοῦ. 11 Οὐ μόνον δέ, ἀλλὰ καὶ καυχώμενοι ἐν τῷ
life ˜ His. [2]not [3]only [4]*so* [1]And, but also boasting in -
we rejoice

Θεῷ διὰ τοῦ Κυρίου ἡμῶν Ἰησοῦ Χριστοῦ, δι' οὗ νῦν
God through - Lord ˜ our Jesus Christ, through whom now

τὴν καταλλαγὴν ἐλάβομεν.
- [3]reconciliation [1]we [2]received.

Death Through Adam and Life Through Christ

12 Διὰ τοῦτο, ὥσπερ δι' ἑνὸς ἀνθρώπου ἡ
On account of this, just as through one man -
Therefore,

ἁμαρτία εἰς τὸν κόσμον εἰσῆλθε, καὶ διὰ τῆς ἁμαρτίας ὁ
sin [2]into [3]the [4]world [1]entered, and through - sin -

θάνατος, καὶ οὕτως εἰς πάντας ἀνθρώπους ὁ θάνατος διῆλθεν,
death, and thus to all men - death passed,

ἐφ' ᾧ πάντες ἥμαρτον. 13 Ἄχρι γὰρ νόμου ἁμαρτία ἦν ἐν
because all sinned. until ˜ For law sin was in

κόσμῳ, ἁμαρτία δὲ οὐκ ἐλλογεῖται, μὴ ὄντος νόμου.
the world, sin ˜ but not ˜ is imputed, not being ˜ law.
where there is no law.

14 Ἀλλ' ἐβασίλευσεν ὁ θάνατος ἀπὸ Ἀδὰμ μέχρι Μωϋσέως
But reigned ˜ - death from Adam until Moses

καὶ ἐπὶ τοὺς μὴ ἁμαρτήσαντας ἐπὶ τῷ ὁμοιώματι
even over the *ones* not sinning on the likeness
those who did not sin according to

τῆς παραβάσεως Ἀδάμ, ὅς ἐστι τύπος τοῦ μέλλοντος.
of the transgression of Adam, who is a type of the coming *One.*
of Him who was to come.

15 Ἀλλ' οὐχ ὡς τὸ παράπτωμα, οὕτω καὶ τὸ χάρισμα. Εἰ
But not as the offense, so also *is* the free gift. if ˜

γὰρ τῷ τοῦ ἑνὸς παραπτώματι οἱ πολλοὶ ἀπέθανον,
For by the [2]of [3]the [4]one [5]*man* [1]offense the many died,

πολλῷ μᾶλλον ἡ χάρις τοῦ Θεοῦ καὶ ἡ δωρεὰ ἐν χάριτι τῇ
much more the grace - of God and the gift by grace -

τοῦ ἑνὸς ἀνθρώπου Ἰησοῦ Χριστοῦ εἰς τοὺς πολλοὺς
of the one man Jesus Christ [2]to [3]the [4]many

ἐπερίσσευσε. 16 Καὶ οὐχ ὡς δι' ἑνὸς ἁμαρτήσαντος,
[1]abounded. And not as through one *man* sinning,

τὸ δώρημα· τὸ μὲν γὰρ κρίμα ἐξ
is the gift; [6]the [2]on [3]the [4]one [5]hand [1]for judgment *which came* from

ἑνὸς εἰς κατάκριμα, τὸ δὲ χάρισμα ἐκ
one *offense resulted* in condemnation, - on the other hand *the* gift *is* from

πολλῶν παραπτωμάτων εἰς δικαίωμα. 17 Εἰ γὰρ τῷ
many offenses *resulting* in justification. if ˜ For by [1]the

τοῦ ἑνὸς παραπτώματι ὁ θάνατος ἐβασίλευσε διὰ τοῦ
[3]of [4]the [5]one [6]*man* [2]offense - death reigned through the

ἑνός, πολλῷ μᾶλλον οἱ τὴν περισσείαν τῆς χάριτος
one *man,* much more the *ones* [2]the [3]abundance [4]of [5]the [6]grace

καὶ τῆς δωρεᾶς τῆς δικαιοσύνης λαμβάνοντες ἐν ζωῇ
[7]and [8]of [9]the [10]gift - [11]of [12]righteousness [1]receiving [15]in [16]life

βασιλεύσουσι διὰ τοῦ ἑνὸς Ἰησοῦ Χριστοῦ. 18 Ἄρα
[13]will [14]reign through the one *man* Jesus Christ. So

οὖν ὡς δι' ἑνὸς παραπτώματος εἰς πάντας
therefore as through one offense *judgment came* to all

ἀνθρώπους εἰς κατάκριμα, οὕτω καὶ δι' ἑνὸς
men *resulting* in condemnation, so also *the gift* through one
δικαιώματος εἰς πάντας ἀνθρώπους εἰς δικαίωσιν ζωῆς.
righteous act to all men *resulting* in justification of life.
19 Ὥσπερ γὰρ διὰ τῆς παρακοῆς* τοῦ ἑνὸς ἀνθρώπου
[2]just [3]as [1]For through the disobedience of the one man
ἁμαρτωλοὶ κατεστάθησαν οἱ πολλοί, οὕτω καὶ διὰ τῆς
[5]sinners [3]were [4]constituted [1]the [2]many, so also through the
ὑπακοῆς τοῦ ἑνὸς δίκαιοι κατασταθήσονται οἱ πολλοί.
obedience of the One [6]righteous [3]will [4]be [5]constituted [1]the [2]many.
20 Νόμος δὲ παρεισῆλθεν ἵνα πλεονάσῃ τὸ
law ˜ But came in alongside so that [3]might [4]abound [1]the
παράπτωμα. Οὗ δὲ ἐπλεόνασεν ἡ ἁμαρτία,
[2]offense. where ˜ But abounded ˜ - sin,
ὑπερεπερίσσευσεν ἡ χάρις, **21** ἵνα ὥσπερ ἐβασίλευσεν ἡ
superabounded ˜ - grace, so that just as ruled ˜ -
ἁμαρτία ἐν τῷ θανάτῳ, οὕτω καὶ ἡ χάρις βασιλεύσῃ διὰ
sin in - death, so also - grace might reign through
by
δικαιοσύνης εἰς ζωὴν αἰώνιον διὰ Ἰησοῦ Χριστοῦ τοῦ Κυρίου
righteousness to life ˜ eternal through Jesus Christ - Lord ˜
ἡμῶν.
our.

The Justified Are Dead to Sin and Alive to God

6 **1** Τί οὖν ἐροῦμεν? Ἐπιμένομεν τῇ ἁμαρτίᾳ ἵνα ἡ
What then shall we say? Shall we continue - in sin so that -
χάρις πλεονάσῃ? **2** Μὴ γένοιτο! Οἵτινες ἀπεθάνομεν τῇ
grace may abound? [3]not [1]May [2]it [4]be! who ˜ We died -
ἁμαρτίᾳ, πῶς ἔτι ζήσομεν ἐν αὐτῇ? **3** Ἢ ἀγνοεῖτε
to sin, how [4]longer [1]shall [2]we [3]live in it? Or do you not know
ὅτι ὅσοι ἐβαπτίσθημεν εἰς Χριστὸν Ἰησοῦν εἰς τὸν
that as many *of us* as were baptized into Christ Jesus [3]into -
θάνατον αὐτοῦ ἐβαπτίσθημεν? **4** Συνετάφημεν οὖν
[5]death [4]His [1]were [2]baptized? [2]we [3]were [4]buried [5]with [1]Therefore
αὐτῷ διὰ τοῦ βαπτίσματος εἰς τὸν θάνατον, ἵνα ὥσπερ
Him through - baptism into - death, so that just as
ἠγέρθη Χριστὸς ἐκ νεκρῶν διὰ τῆς δόξης τοῦ Πατρός,
[2]was [3]raised [1]Christ from *the* dead through the glory of the Father,
οὕτω καὶ ἡμεῖς ἐν καινότητι ζωῆς περιπατήσωμεν. **5** Εἰ γὰρ
so also we [3]in [4]newness [5]of [6]life [1]should [2]walk. if ˜ For
σύμφυτοι γεγόναμεν τῷ ὁμοιώματι τοῦ θανάτου
[4]united [5]together [1]we [2]have [3]become in the likeness - of death ˜
αὐτοῦ, ἀλλὰ καὶ τῆς ἀναστάσεως ἐσόμεθα·
His, but [3]also [5]*in* [6]*the* [7]*likeness* [8]of [9]the [10]resurrection [1]we [2]shall [4]be;
certainly His
6 τοῦτο γινώσκοντες, ὅτι ὁ παλαιὸς ἡμῶν ἄνθρωπος
this ˜ knowing, that - old ˜ our man
συνεσταυρώθη ἵνα καταργηθῇ τὸ σῶμα τῆς
was crucified so that [5]may [6]be [7]done [8]away [9]with [1]the [2]body -
ἁμαρτίας, τοῦ μηκέτι δουλεύειν ἡμᾶς τῇ ἁμαρτίᾳ. **7** Ὁ
[3]of [4]sin, - *that* no longer to serve us - sin. [2]the [3]*one*
we should no longer serve For he
γὰρ ἀποθανὼν δεδικαίωται ἀπὸ τῆς ἁμαρτίας. **8** Εἰ δὲ
[1]For having died has been justified from - sin. if ˜ But
who has died
ἀπεθάνομεν σὺν Χριστῷ, πιστεύομεν ὅτι καὶ συζήσομεν
we died with Christ, we believe that also we shall live together

all men, resulting in condemnation, even so through one Man's righteous act *the free gift came* to all men, resulting in justification of life.
19 For as by one man's disobedience many were made sinners, so also by one Man's obedience many will be made righteous.
20 Moreover the law entered that the offense might abound. But where sin abounded, grace abounded much more,
21 so that as sin reigned in death, even so grace might reign through righteousness to eternal life through Jesus Christ our Lord.
6 What shall we say then? Shall we continue in sin that grace may abound?
2 Certainly not! How shall we who died to sin live any longer in it?
3 Or do you not know that as many of us as were baptized into Christ Jesus were baptized into His death?
4 Therefore we were buried with Him through baptism into death, that just as Christ was raised from the dead by the glory of the Father, even so we also should walk in newness of life.
5 For if we have been united together in the likeness of His death, certainly we also shall be *in the likeness* of *His* resurrection,
6 knowing this, that our old man was crucified with *Him,* that the body of sin might be done away with, that we should no longer be slaves of sin.
7 For he who has died has been freed from sin.
8 Now if we died with Christ, we believe that we shall also

***(5:19)** *παρακοή (parakoē).* Noun meaning *disobedience.* It is derived from the verb *παρακούω,* literally *overhear* or *ignore* (as Mark 5:36), but extended to include the sense *refuse to listen, disobey* (Matt. 18:17). In both the OT and NT, disobedience is often portrayed as a refusal to listen (Jer. 35:17; Acts 7:57). Here in Rom. 5:19 *παρακοή* is the one man's disobedience through which sin entered the world. Cf. the antonyms *ὑπακοή, obedience* (also here) and *ὑπακούω, hear, obey* (Heb. 5:9).

live with Him,
9 knowing that Christ, having been raised from the dead,
dies no more. Death no longer
has dominion over Him.
10 For *the death* that He died,
He died to sin once for all; but
the life that He lives, He lives to
God.
11 Likewise you also, reckon
yourselves to be dead indeed to
sin, but alive to God in Christ
Jesus our Lord.
12 Therefore do not let sin
reign in your mortal body, that
you should obey it in its lusts.
13 And do not present your
members *as* instruments of unrighteousness to sin, but present yourselves to God as
being alive from the dead, and
your members *as* instruments
of righteousness to God.
14 For sin shall not have dominion over you, for you are
not under law but under grace.
15 What then? Shall we sin because we are not under law but
under grace? Certainly not!
16 Do you not know that to
whom you present yourselves
slaves to obey, you are that
one's slaves whom you obey,
whether of sin *leading* to death,
or of obedience *leading* to righteousness?
17 But God be thanked that
though you were slaves of sin,
yet you obeyed from the heart
that form of doctrine to which
you were delivered.
18 And having been set free
from sin, you became slaves of
righteousness.
19 I speak in human *terms* because of the weakness of your
flesh. For just as you presented
your members *as* slaves of uncleanness, and of lawlessness
leading to *more* lawlessness, so
now present your members *as*

αὐτῷ, **9** *εἰδότες ὅτι Χριστὸς ἐγερθεὶς ἐκ νεκρῶν*
with Him, knowing that Christ having been raised from *the* dead

οὐκέτι ἀποθνῄσκει· θάνατος αὐτοῦ οὐκέτι κυριεύει.
no longer dies; death [5]*over* [6]Him [2]no [3]longer [1]is [4]master.

10 *Ὃ γὰρ ἀπέθανε, τῇ ἁμαρτίᾳ ἀπέθανεν ἐφάπαξ·*
[2]what [3]*death* [1]For He died, - [3]to [4]sin [1]He [2]died once for all;

ὃ δὲ ζῇ, ζῇ τῷ Θεῷ. **11** *Οὕτω καὶ ὑμεῖς*
[2]what [3]*life* [1]but He lives, He lives - to God. Thus also you

λογίζεσθε ἑαυτοὺς νεκροὺς μὲν εἶναι τῇ ἁμαρτίᾳ, ζῶντας
consider yourselves [3]dead [4]indeed [1]to [2]be - to sin, living ~

δὲ τῷ Θεῷ ἐν Χριστῷ Ἰησοῦ τῷ Κυρίῳ ἡμῶν.[a]
but - to God in Christ Jesus - Lord ~ our.

12 *Μὴ οὖν βασιλευέτω ἡ ἁμαρτία ἐν τῷ θνητῷ ὑμῶν*
[3]not [1]Therefore [2]do [4]let [6]reign - [5]sin in - mortal ~ your

σώματι εἰς τὸ ὑπακούειν αὐτῇ ἐν[b] *ταῖς ἐπιθυμίαις αὐτοῦ,*
body - - to obey it in - desires ~ its,

13 *μηδὲ παριστάνετε τὰ μέλη ὑμῶν ὅπλα*
nor present - members ~ your *as* instruments

ἀδικίας τῇ ἁμαρτίᾳ, ἀλλὰ παραστήσατε ἑαυτοὺς τῷ
of unrighteousness - to sin, but present yourselves -

Θεῷ ὡς ἐκ νεκρῶν ζῶντας, καὶ τὰ μέλη ὑμῶν
to God as [2]from [3]*the* [4]dead [1]living, and - members ~ your

ὅπλα δικαιοσύνης τῷ Θεῷ. **14** *Ἁμαρτία γὰρ ὑμῶν*
as instruments of righteousness - to God. sin ~ For [5]*over* [6]you

οὐ κυριεύσει, οὐ γάρ ἐστε ὑπὸ νόμον, ἀλλ' ὑπὸ
[2]not [1]shall [3]be [4]master, [10]not [7]for [8]you [9]are under law, but under

χάριν.
grace.

From Slaves of Sin to Servants of God

15 *Τί οὖν? Ἁμαρτήσομεν ὅτι οὐκ ἐσμὲν ὑπὸ νόμον*
What then? Shall we sin because [3]not [1]we [2]are under law

ἀλλ' ὑπὸ χάριν? Μὴ γένοιτο! **16** *Οὐκ οἴδατε ὅτι*
but under grace? [3]not [1]May [2]it [4]be! [3]not [1]Do [2]you [4]know that

ᾧ παριστάνετε ἑαυτοὺς δούλους εἰς ὑπακοήν, δοῦλοί
to whom you present yourselves *as* slaves (obedient) for (slaves,) obedience, [3]slaves

ἐστε ᾧ ὑπακούετε, ἤτοι ἁμαρτίας εἰς θάνατον
[1]you [2]are to whom you obey, whether of sin *resulting* in death

ἢ ὑπακοῆς εἰς δικαιοσύνην? **17** *Χάρις δὲ τῷ Θεῷ*
or of obedience *resulting* in righteousness? thanks ~ But - *be* to God

ὅτι ἦτε δοῦλοι τῆς ἁμαρτίας, ὑπηκούσατε δὲ ἐκ*
that you used to be slaves - of sin, [2]you [3]obeyed [1]but out of (from)

καρδίας εἰς ὃν παρεδόθητε τύπον διδαχῆς.
your heart [5]to [6]which [7]you [8]were [9]delivered [1]*the* [2]form [3]of [4]teaching.

18 *Ἐλευθερωθέντες δὲ ἀπὸ τῆς ἁμαρτίας, ἐδουλώθητε*
[2]having [3]been [4]freed [1]And from - sin, you became enslaved

τῇ δικαιοσύνῃ. **19** *Ἀνθρώπινον λέγω διὰ τὴν*
- to righteousness. [3]humanly (on a human level) [1]I [2]speak on account of the

ἀσθένειαν τῆς σαρκὸς ὑμῶν. Ὥσπερ γὰρ παρεστήσατε τὰ
weakness - of flesh ~ your. [2]just [3]as [1]For you presented -

μέλη ὑμῶν δοῦλα τῇ ἀκαθαρσίᾳ, καὶ τῇ ἀνομίᾳ
members ~ your *as* slaves - to uncleanness, and to lawlessness

εἰς τὴν ἀνομίαν, οὕτω νῦν παραστήσατε τὰ
resulting in - *more* lawlessness, so now present -

---

[a](6:11) NU omits *τω κυριω ημων, our Lord.*
[b](6:12) NU omits *αυτη εν, it in.*

*(6:17) *ὑπακούω (hypakouō).* Verb from the preposition *ὑπό, under,* and the verb *ἀκούω, hear,* and so meaning to hear in submission, thus *obey, be in subjection to.* It is used of obedience to one's parents (Eph. 6:1), a master (Eph. 6:5), a husband (1 Pet. 3:6), the Lord (Heb. 5:9), or the teaching and preaching of the gospel (as here in Rom. 6:17; cf. Rom. 10:16; 2 Thess. 3:14). When one

μέλη ὑμῶν δοῦλα τῇ δικαιοσύνῃ εἰς ἁγιασμόν.
members ~ your *as* slaves - to righteousness *resulting* in sanctification.

20 Ὅτε γὰρ δοῦλοι ἦτε τῆς ἁμαρτίας, ἐλεύθεροι
when ~ For [3]slaves [1]you [2]were - of sin, [3]free

ἦτε τῇ δικαιοσύνῃ. **21** Τίνα οὖν καρπὸν
[1]you [2]were - *with reference* to righteousness. what ~ So fruit

εἴχετε τότε ἐφ' οἷς νῦν ἐπαισχύνεσθε? Τὸ γὰρ
did you have then over which *things* [3]now [1]you [2]are [4]ashamed? the ~ For
of

τέλος ἐκείνων θάνατος. **22** Νυνὶ δὲ ἐλευθερωθέντες ἀπὸ
end of those *things is* death. now ~ But having been freed from

τῆς ἁμαρτίας, δουλωθέντες δὲ τῷ Θεῷ, ἔχετε τὸν
- sin, [2]having [3]become [4]enslaved [1]but - to God, you have -

καρπὸν ὑμῶν εἰς ἁγιασμόν, τὸ δὲ τέλος ζωὴν αἰώνιον.
fruit ~ your *resulting* in sanctification, the ~ and end life ~ eternal.

23 Τὰ γὰρ ὀψώνια τῆς ἁμαρτίας θάνατος, τὸ δὲ χάρισμα
the ~ For wages - of sin *is* death, the ~ but gift

τοῦ Θεοῦ ζωὴ αἰώνιος ἐν Χριστῷ Ἰησοῦ τῷ Κυρίῳ ἡμῶν.
- of God *is* life ~ eternal in Christ Jesus - Lord ~ our.

Life in Christ Delivers from the Law

7 **1** Ἢ ἀγνοεῖτε, ἀδελφοί (γινώσκουσι γὰρ νόμον
Or do you not know, brothers ([4]to [5]*ones* [6]knowing [1]for [7]*the* [8]law

λαλῶ), ὅτι ὁ νόμος κυριεύει τοῦ ἀνθρώπου ἐφ' ὅσον
[2]I [3]speak), that the law has control - of a man for as long
as long

χρόνον ζῇ? **2** Ἡ γὰρ ὕπανδρος γυνὴ τῷ
a time as he lives? the ~ For [2]subject [3]to [4]a [5]man [1]woman [11]to [12]the
as who is under

ζῶντι ἀνδρὶ δέδεται νόμῳ. Ἐὰν δὲ ἀποθάνῃ ὁ
[13]living [14]husband [6]has [7]been [8]bound [9]by [10]law. if ~ But [3]should [4]die [1]the

ἀνήρ, κατήργηται ἀπὸ τοῦ νόμου τοῦ ἀνδρός. **3** Ἄρα οὖν,
[2]husband, she is released from the law of the husband. So then,

ζῶντος τοῦ ἀνδρός, μοιχαλὶς χρηματίσει ἐὰν
living the husband, [5]an [6]adulteress [1]she [2]will [3]be [4]called if
while the husband is living,

γένηται ἀνδρὶ ἑτέρῳ· ἐὰν δὲ ἀποθάνῃ ὁ
she becomes *married* to a husband ~ different; if ~ but [3]should [4]die [1]the
her

ἀνήρ, ἐλευθέρα ἐστὶν ἀπὸ τοῦ νόμου, τοῦ μὴ εἶναι αὐτὴν
[2]husband, [7]free [5]she [6]is from the law, - not to be her
so that she is not

μοιχαλίδα γενομένην ἀνδρὶ ἑτέρῳ. **4** Ὥστε,
an adulteress having become *married* to a husband ~ different. Therefore,

ἀδελφοί μου, καὶ ὑμεῖς ἐθανατώθητε τῷ νόμῳ διὰ τοῦ
brothers ~ my, also ~ you were put to death to the law through the

σώματος τοῦ Χριστοῦ εἰς τὸ γενέσθαι ὑμᾶς ἑτέρῳ,
body - of Christ for - to become you to another,
so that you may be married

τῷ ἐκ νεκρῶν ἐγερθέντι, ἵνα
to the *One* out of the dead having been raised, so that
to Him who was raised from the dead,

καρποφορήσωμεν τῷ Θεῷ. **5** Ὅτε γὰρ ἦμεν ἐν τῇ σαρκί,
we might bear fruit - to God. when ~ For we were in the flesh,

τὰ παθήματα τῶν ἁμαρτιῶν τὰ διὰ τοῦ νόμου
the passions - of sins - *aroused* through the law

ἐνηργεῖτο ἐν τοῖς μέλεσιν ἡμῶν εἰς τὸ καρποφορῆσαι τῷ
were at work in - members ~ our for - to bear fruit -
in order

slaves *of* righteousness for holiness.
20 For when you were slaves of sin, you were free in regard to righteousness.
21 What fruit did you have then in the things of which you are now ashamed? For the end of those things *is* death.
22 But now having been set free from sin, and having become slaves of God, you have your fruit to holiness, and the end, everlasting life.
23 For the wages of sin *is* death, but the gift of God *is* eternal life in Christ Jesus our Lord.

7 Or do you not know, brethren (for I speak to those who know the law), that the law has dominion over a man as long as he lives?
2 For the woman who has a husband is bound by the law to *her* husband as long as he lives. But if the husband dies, she is released from the law of *her* husband.
3 So then if, while *her* husband lives, she marries another man, she will be called an adulteress; but if her husband dies, she is free from that law, so that she is no adulteress, though she has married another man.
4 Therefore, my brethren, you also have become dead to the law through the body of Christ, that you may be married to another—to Him who was raised from the dead, that we should bear fruit to God.
5 For when we were in the flesh, the sinful passions which were aroused by the law were at work in our members to bear

"obeys" the truth, he submits to its authority. Cf. the cognate noun ὑπακοή, *obedience*.

fruit to death.
6 But now we have been delivered from the law, having died to what we were held by, so that we should serve in the newness of the Spirit and not *in* the oldness of the letter.
7 What shall we say then? *Is* the law sin? Certainly not! On the contrary, I would not have known sin except through the law. For I would not have known covetousness unless the law had said, *"You shall not covet."*
8 But sin, taking opportunity by the commandment, produced in me all *manner of evil* desire. For apart from the law sin *was* dead.
9 I was alive once without the law, but when the commandment came, sin revived and I died.
10 And the commandment, which *was* to *bring* life, I found to *bring* death.
11 For sin, taking occasion by the commandment, deceived me, and by it killed *me*.
12 Therefore the law *is* holy, and the commandment holy and just and good.
13 Has then what is good become death to me? Certainly not! But sin, that it might appear sin, was producing death in me through what is good, so that sin through the commandment might become exceedingly sinful.
14 For we know that the law is spiritual, but I am carnal, sold

θανάτῳ. 6 Νυνὶ δὲ κατηργήθημεν ἀπὸ τοῦ νόμου, ἀποθανόντες
to death. now ˜ But we were released from the law, having died

ἐν ᾧ κατειχόμεθα, ὥστε δουλεύειν ἡμᾶς ἐν
in *that* to which we were held fast, so that to serve as slaves us in
we should serve as slaves

καινότητι Πνεύματος, καὶ οὐ παλαιότητι γράμματος.
newness of *the* Spirit, and not oldness of *the* letter.

Sin Takes Advantage Through the Law

7 Τί οὖν ἐροῦμεν? Ὁ νόμος ἁμαρτία? Μὴ γένοιτο!
What then shall we say? *Is* the law sin? [3]not [1]May [2]it [4]be!

Ἀλλὰ τὴν ἁμαρτίαν οὐκ ἔγνων εἰ μὴ διὰ
But - [5]sin [3]not [1]I [2]did [4]know if not through
On the contrary I would not have known except

νόμου. Τήν τε γὰρ ἐπιθυμίαν οὐκ ᾔδειν εἰ μὴ
law. - also ˜ For [5]covetousness [3]not [1]I [2]had [4]known if not
I would not have known unless

ὁ νόμος ἔλεγεν, «Οὐκ ἐπιθυμήσεις.»[a] 8 Ἀφορμὴν δὲ
the law said, «[3]not [1]You [2]shall [4]desire.» [4]opportunity [1]But
had said, covet.»

λαβοῦσα ἡ ἁμαρτία διὰ τῆς ἐντολῆς κατειργάσατο ἐν
[3]taking - [2]sin through the commandment produced in

ἐμοὶ πᾶσαν ἐπιθυμίαν. Χωρὶς γὰρ νόμου ἁμαρτία
me every *kind of* desire. [2]apart [3]from [1]For law sin
covetousness.

νεκρά. 9 Ἐγὼ δὲ ἔζων χωρὶς νόμου ποτέ· ἐλθούσης δὲ
is dead. I ˜ But lived apart from law once; coming but
but when

τῆς ἐντολῆς, ἡ ἁμαρτία ἀνέζησεν, ἐγὼ δὲ ἀπέθανον.
the commandment, - sin revived, I ˜ but died.
the commandment came,

10 Καὶ εὑρέθη μοι ἡ ἐντολὴ
And [8]was [9]found [10]*with* [11]*reference* [12]to [13]me [1]the [2]commandment

ἡ εἰς ζωήν, αὕτη εἰς θάνατον. 11 Ἡ γὰρ
[3]the [4]*one* [5]*meant* [6]for [7]life, this *one to be* to death. - For

ἁμαρτία ἀφορμὴν λαβοῦσα διὰ τῆς ἐντολῆς ἐξηπάτησέ
sin opportunity ˜ taking through the commandment deceived

με, καὶ δι' αὐτῆς ἀπέκτεινεν. 12 Ὥστε ὁ μὲν νόμος
me, and through it killed *me*. Therefore the indeed ˜ law *is*

ἅγιος, καὶ ἡ ἐντολὴ ἁγία καὶ δικαία καὶ ἀγαθή.
holy, and the commandment *is* holy and righteous and good.

The Law Cannot Deliver from Indwelling Sin

13 Τὸ οὖν ἀγαθὸν ἐμοὶ γέγονε θάνατος? Μὴ
[3]the [1]Then [4]good [7]to [8]me [2]has [5]become [6]death? [11]not

γένοιτο! Ἀλλὰ ἡ ἁμαρτία, ἵνα φανῇ
[9]May [10]it [12]be! But - sin, so that it might appear
On the contrary

ἁμαρτία, διὰ τοῦ ἀγαθοῦ μοι κατεργαζομένη θάνατον,
sin, *was* through the good [3]to [4]me [1]producing [2]death,

ἵνα γένηται καθ' ὑπερβολὴν* ἁμαρτωλὸς ἡ
so that [5]might [6]become [7]according [8]to [9]extreme [10]sinful -
extremely

ἁμαρτία διὰ τῆς ἐντολῆς. 14 Οἴδαμεν γὰρ ὅτι ὁ
[1]sin [2]through [3]the [4]commandment. [2]we [3]know [1]For that the

νόμος πνευματικός ἐστιν· ἐγὼ δὲ σαρκικός εἰμι, πεπραμένος
law spiritual ˜ is; I ˜ but fleshly ˜ am, having been sold

---

[a](7:7) Ex. 20:17; Deut. 5:21

*(7:13) ὑπερβολή (*hyperbolē*). Noun from the preposition ὑπέρ, *beyond* and the noun βολή, *throwing,* hence figuratively meaning *excess, superiority,* or *excellence.* Here it is used in combination with καθ' to mean "according to excess" or "beyond measure, excessively" (cf. 1 Cor. 12:31; 2 Cor. 1:8; Gal 1:13). The heightened idiom καθ' ὑπερβολὴν εἰς ὑπερβολὴν means *far beyond all measure* (2 Cor. 4:17). Cf. the cognate verb ὑπερβάλλω, *go beyond, outdo, surpass* (2 Cor. 9:14); and English derivative *hyperbole.*

ὑπὸ τὴν ἁμαρτίαν. **15** Ὃ γὰρ κατεργάζομαι οὐ γινώσκω.
under - sin. what ˜ For I am doing [3]not [1]I [2]do [4]know.

Οὐ γὰρ ὃ θέλω τοῦτο πράσσω, ἀλλ' ὃ μισῶ τοῦτο ποιῶ.
not ˜ For what I will this I practice, but what I hate this I do.

16 Εἰ δὲ ὃ οὐ θέλω τοῦτο ποιῶ, σύμφημι τῷ νόμῳ
if ˜ But what [3]not [1]I [2]do [4]will this I do, I agree with the law

ὅτι καλός. **17** Νυνὶ δὲ οὐκέτι ἐγὼ κατεργάζομαι αὐτό,
that *it is* good. now ˜ But *it is* no longer I *who* am doing it,

ἀλλ' ἡ οἰκοῦσα ἐν ἐμοὶ ἁμαρτία. **18** Οἶδα γὰρ ὅτι οὐκ
but the [2]dwelling [3]in [4]me [1]sin. [2]I [3]know [1]For that [3]not

οἰκεῖ ἐν ἐμοί, τοῦτ' ἔστιν ἐν τῇ σαρκί μου, ἀγαθόν.
[1]*there* [2]does [4]dwell in me, this (that) is in - flesh ˜ my, *any* good.

Τὸ γὰρ θέλειν παράκειταί μοι, τὸ δὲ κατεργάζεσθαι τὸ
- For to will is present with me, - but to do the

καλὸν οὐχ εὑρίσκω. **19** Οὐ γὰρ ὃ θέλω ποιῶ ἀγαθόν, ἀλλ'
good [3]not [1]I [2]do [4]find. not ˜ For what [2]I [3]will [4]I [5]do [1]good, but

ὃ οὐ θέλω κακὸν τοῦτο πράσσω. **20** Εἰ δὲ ὃ οὐ
what [4]not [2]I [3]do [5]will [1]evil this I practice. if ˜ But what [3]not

θέλω ἐγὼ τοῦτο ποιῶ, οὐκέτι ἐγὼ κατεργάζομαι αὐτὸ
[1]I [2]do [4]will [6]I [5]this [7]do, *it is* no longer I *who* am doing it

ἀλλ' ἡ οἰκοῦσα ἐν ἐμοὶ ἁμαρτία. **21** Εὑρίσκω ἄρα τὸν νόμον
but the [2]dwelling [3]in [4]me [1]sin. I find then the law

τῷ θέλοντι ἐμοὶ ποιεῖν τὸ καλόν, ὅτι ἐμοὶ τὸ κακὸν
[3]the (who) [4]*one* [5]willing (wishes) [1]to [2]me to do the good, that with me the evil

παράκειται. **22** Συνήδομαι γὰρ τῷ νόμῳ τοῦ Θεοῦ κατὰ
is present. [2]I [3]delight [1]For in the law - of God according to

τὸν ἔσω ἄνθρωπον, **23** βλέπω δὲ ἕτερον νόμον ἐν τοῖς
the inner man, [2]I [3]see [1]but a different law in -

μέλεσί μου ἀντιστρατευόμενον τῷ νόμῳ τοῦ νοός μου,
members ˜ my waging war with the law - of mind ˜ my,

καὶ αἰχμαλωτίζοντά με ἐν τῷ νόμῳ τῆς ἁμαρτίας τῷ ὄντι
and capturing me by the law - of sin the *one* (which) being (is)

ἐν τοῖς μέλεσί μου. **24** Ταλαίπωρος ἐγὼ ἄνθρωπος! Τίς
in - members ˜ my. *What a* wretched [2]I [3]*am* [1]man! Who

με ῥύσεται ἐκ τοῦ σώματος τοῦ θανάτου τούτου?
[3]me [1]will [2]deliver from - [2]body - [3]of [4]death [1]this?

25 Εὐχαριστῶ[b] τῷ Θεῷ διὰ Ἰησοῦ Χριστοῦ τοῦ Κυρίου
I thank - God through Jesus Christ - Lord ˜

ἡμῶν! Ἄρα οὖν αὐτὸς ἐγὼ τῷ μὲν νοΐ
our! So then myself ˜ I [5]with [6]the [1]on [2]the [3]one [4]hand [7]mind

δουλεύω νόμῳ Θεοῦ, τῇ δὲ σαρκὶ νόμῳ
serve *the* law of God, [5]with [6]the [1]on [2]the [3]other [4]hand [7]flesh *the* law

ἁμαρτίας.
of sin.

Deliverance from Indwelling Sin Is by the Holy Spirit

8 **1** Οὐδὲν ἄρα νῦν κατάκριμα τοῖς ἐν
There is [3]no [1]therefore [2]now condemnation to the *ones* (those who are) in

Χριστῷ Ἰησοῦ,[a] μὴ κατὰ σάρκα περιπατοῦσιν
Christ Jesus, *who are* not [2]according [3]to [4]*the* [5]flesh [1]walking

ἀλλὰ κατὰ Πνεῦμα. **2** Ὁ γὰρ νόμος τοῦ Πνεύματος τῆς
but according to *the* Spirit. the ˜ For law of the Spirit -

ζωῆς ἐν Χριστῷ Ἰησοῦ ἠλευθέρωσέ* με[b] ἀπὸ τοῦ νόμου τῆς
of life in Christ Jesus freed me from the law -

under sin.
15 For what I am doing, I do not understand. For what I will to do, that I do not practice; but what I hate, that I do.
16 If, then, I do what I will not to do, I agree with the law that *it is* good.
17 But now, *it is* no longer I who do it, but sin that dwells in me.
18 For I know that in me (that is, in my flesh) nothing good dwells; for to will is present with me, but *how* to perform what is good I do not find.
19 For the good that I will *to do,* I do not do; but the evil I will not *to do,* that I practice.
20 Now if I do what I will not *to do,* it is no longer I who do it, but sin that dwells in me.
21 I find then a law, that evil is present with me, the one who wills to do good.
22 For I delight in the law of God according to the inward man.
23 But I see another law in my members, warring against the law of my mind, and bringing me into captivity to the law of sin which is in my members.
24 O wretched man that I am! Who will deliver me from this body of death?
25 I thank God—through Jesus Christ our Lord! So then, with the mind I myself serve the law of God, but with the flesh the law of sin.

8 *There is* therefore now no condemnation to those who are in Christ Jesus, who do not walk according to the flesh, but according to the Spirit.
2 For the law of the Spirit of life in Christ Jesus has made me free from the law of sin and

[b](**7:25**) NU reads Χαρις δε, *But thanks.*
[a](**8:1**) NU omits the rest of this verse. [b](**8:2**) NU reads σε, *you.*

*(**8:2**) ἐλευθερόω (*eleutheroō*). Verb meaning *set free, free, liberate.* In the NT it is used only in a spiritual sense to refer to believers' being freed from sin and death (here), corruption (Rom. 8:21), and the Mosaic law (Gal. 5:1). It can imply a freedom that is eschatological in its fullest experience (Rom. 8:21). Cf. the cognate noun ἐλευθερία, *freedom, liberty,* which occurs in some of these same contexts (as Rom. 8:21; Gal. 5:1). In James 1:25; 2:12, "the law of

death.
3 For what the law could not
do in that it was weak through
the flesh, God *did* by sending
His own Son in the likeness of
sinful flesh, on account of sin:
He condemned sin in the flesh,
4 that the righteous requirement of the law might be fulfilled in us who do not walk
according to the flesh but according to the Spirit.
5 For those who live according to the flesh set their minds
on the things of the flesh, but
those *who live* according to the
Spirit, the things of the Spirit.
6 For to be carnally minded
is death, but to be spiritually
minded *is* life and peace.
7 Because the carnal mind *is*
enmity against God; for it is not
subject to the law of God, nor
indeed can be.
8 So then, those who are in
the flesh cannot please God.
9 But you are not in the flesh
but in the Spirit, if indeed the
Spirit of God dwells in you.
Now if anyone does not have
the Spirit of Christ, he is not
His.
10 And if Christ *is* in you, the
body *is* dead because of sin, but
the Spirit *is* life because of righteousness.
11 But if the Spirit of Him who
raised Jesus from the dead
dwells in you, He who raised
Christ from the dead will also
give life to your mortal bodies
through His Spirit who dwells in
you.
12 Therefore, brethren, we
are debtors — not to the flesh,
to live according to the flesh.
13 For if you live according to

ἁμαρτίας καὶ τοῦ θανάτου. 3 Τὸ γὰρ ἀδύνατον τοῦ
of sin and - of death. [2]the [3]*thing* [1]For impossible *for* the

νόμου ἐν ᾧ ἠσθένει διὰ τῆς σαρκός, ὁ Θεὸς τὸν
law in that it was weak through the flesh, - God *did* [2]the

ἑαυτοῦ Υἱὸν πέμψας ἐν ὁμοιώματι σαρκὸς ἁμαρτίας καὶ
[4]of [5]Himself [3]Son [1]sending in *the* likeness of flesh of sin and
His own of sinful flesh

περὶ ἁμαρτίας κατέκρινε τὴν ἁμαρτίαν ἐν τῇ σαρκί,
concerning sin He condemned - sin in the flesh,

4 ἵνα τὸ δικαίωμα τοῦ νόμου πληρωθῇ ἐν
so that the righteous requirement of the law might be fulfilled in

ἡμῖν τοῖς μὴ κατὰ σάρκα περιπατοῦσιν ἀλλὰ
us the *ones* not [2]according [3]to [4]*the* [5]flesh [1]walking but
who do walk

κατὰ Πνεῦμα. 5 Οἱ γὰρ κατὰ σάρκα ὄντες
according to *the* Spirit. the *ones* For according to *the* flesh being
For those who are fleshly

τὰ τῆς σαρκὸς φρονοῦσιν, οἱ δὲ
[5]the [6]*things* [7]of [8]the [9]flesh [1]set [2]their [3]minds [4]on, [11]the [12]*ones* [10]but

κατὰ Πνεῦμα τὰ τοῦ Πνεύματος. 6 Τὸ γὰρ
according to *the* Spirit *on* the *things* of the Spirit. the ˜ For

φρόνημα τῆς σαρκὸς θάνατος, τὸ δὲ φρόνημα τοῦ
mind of the flesh *is* death, the ˜ but mind of the

Πνεύματος ζωὴ καὶ εἰρήνη. 7 Διότι τὸ φρόνημα τῆς
Spirit *is* life and peace. Therefore the mind of the

σαρκὸς ἔχθρα εἰς Θεόν, τῷ γὰρ νόμῳ τοῦ Θεοῦ οὐχ
flesh *is* enmity against God, [6]to [7]the [1]for [8]law - [9]of [10]God [4]not

ὑποτάσσεται, οὐδὲ γὰρ δύναται. 8 Οἱ δὲ ἐν σαρκὶ
[2]it [3]does [5]submit, nor indeed can it. [2]the [3]*ones* [1]And [5]in [6]*the* [7]flesh
those

ὄντες Θεῷ ἀρέσαι οὐ δύνανται. 9 Ὑμεῖς δὲ οὐκ ἐστὲ ἐν
[4]being [13]God [11]to [12]please [9]not [8]are [10]able. you ˜ But not ˜ are in
who are

σαρκὶ ἀλλ' ἐν Πνεύματι, εἴπερ Πνεῦμα Θεοῦ οἰκεῖ ἐν ὑμῖν.
the flesh but in *the* Spirit, if indeed *the* Spirit of God dwells in you.
since

Εἰ δέ τις Πνεῦμα Χριστοῦ οὐκ ἔχει, οὗτος οὐκ ἔστιν
if ˜ But anyone [4]*the* [5]Spirit [6]of [7]Christ [2]not [1]does [3]have, this *one* not ˜ is

αὐτοῦ. 10 Εἰ δὲ Χριστὸς ἐν ὑμῖν, τὸ μὲν σῶμα
His. if ˜ But Christ *is* in you, [5]the [1]on [2]the [3]one [4]hand [6]body

νεκρὸν διὰ ἁμαρτίαν, τὸ δὲ πνεῦμα ζωὴ
is dead through sin, [5]the [1]on [2]the [3]other [4]hand [6]spirit *is* life

διὰ δικαιοσύνην. 11 Εἰ δὲ τὸ Πνεῦμα τοῦ
on account of righteousness. if ˜ But the Spirit of the *One*
of Him who

ἐγείραντος Ἰησοῦν ἐκ νεκρῶν οἰκεῖ ἐν ὑμῖν, ὁ
having raised Jesus from *the* dead dwells in you, the *One*
raised He who

ἐγείρας τὸν Χριστὸν ἐκ νεκρῶν ζωοποιήσει καὶ τὰ
having raised - Christ from *the* dead [1]will [3]give [4]life [5]to [2]also -
raised

θνητὰ σώματα ὑμῶν διὰ τὸ ἐνοικοῦν αὐτοῦ Πνεῦμα ἐν ὑμῖν.
[7]mortal [8]bodies [6]your through - [3]indwelling [1]His [2]Spirit in you.

Sonship Is Realized Through the Same Spirit

12 Ἄρα οὖν, ἀδελφοί, ὀφειλέται ἐσμέν, οὐ τῇ σαρκί,
So then, brothers, [3]debtors [1]we [2]are, not to the flesh,

τοῦ κατὰ σάρκα ζῆν. 13 Εἰ γὰρ κατὰ σάρκα
- [3]according [4]to [5]*the* [6]flesh [1]to [2]live. if ˜ For according to *the* flesh

---

liberty" suggests that the Christian lives as a person free to perform God's will rather than as a slave to a ritualistic law. Cf. also the adjective ἐλεύθερος, *free,* which is used both in the sociopolitical (as Gal. 3:28) and the spiritual sense (as Rom. 6:20).

ζῆτε, μέλλετε ἀποθνήσκειν, εἰ δὲ Πνεύματι τὰς πράξεις
you live, you are going to die, if ˜ but by *the* Spirit the practices

τοῦ σώματος θανατοῦτε, ζήσεσθε. 14 Ὅσοι γὰρ
of the body you put to death, you will live. [2]as [3]many [4]as [1]For

Πνεύματι Θεοῦ ἄγονται, οὗτοί εἰσιν υἱοὶ Θεοῦ. 15 Οὐ γὰρ
by *the* Spirit of God are led, these are sons of God. [4]not [1]For

ἐλάβετε πνεῦμα δουλείας πάλιν εἰς φόβον, ἀλλ'
[2]you [3]did [5]receive a spirit of slavery again for fear, but

ἐλάβετε Πνεῦμα υἱοθεσίας ἐν ᾧ κράζομεν, "Ἀββα* ὁ
you received *the* Spirit of adoption by whom we cry out, "Abba, -

Πατήρ!" 16 Αὐτὸ τὸ Πνεῦμα συμμαρτυρεῖ τῷ πνεύματι
Father!" [3]Himself [1]The [2]Spirit bears witness with - spirit ˜

ἡμῶν ὅτι ἐσμὲν τέκνα Θεοῦ. 17 Εἰ δὲ τέκνα, καὶ
our that we are children of God. if ˜ And children, also

κληρονόμοι — κληρονόμοι μὲν Θεοῦ, συγκληρονόμοι
heirs — heirs on the one hand of God, fellow heirs

δὲ Χριστοῦ, εἴπερ συμπάσχομεν ἵνα καὶ
on the other hand of Christ, if indeed we suffer together so that [3]also
since

συνδοξασθῶμεν.
[1]we [2]may be glorified together.

From Suffering to Glory

18 Λογίζομαι γὰρ ὅτι οὐκ ἄξια τὰ παθήματα τοῦ
[2]I [3]consider [1]For that [7]*are* [8]not [9]worthy [1]the [2]sufferings [3]of [4]the

νῦν καιροῦ πρὸς τὴν μέλλουσαν δόξαν
[5]now [6]season *to be compared* with the coming glory
present time

ἀποκαλυφθῆναι εἰς ἡμᾶς. 19 Ἡ γὰρ ἀποκαραδοκία τῆς
to be revealed in us. the ˜ For eager expectation of the

κτίσεως τὴν ἀποκάλυψιν τῶν υἱῶν τοῦ Θεοῦ ἀπεκδέχεται.
creation [3]the [4]revelation [5]of [6]the [7]sons - [8]of [9]God [1]eagerly [2]awaits.

20 Τῇ γὰρ ματαιότητι ἡ κτίσις ὑπετάγη, οὐχ ἑκοῦσα,
- For [5]to [6]futility [1]the [2]creation [3]was [4]subjected, not willing,
willingly,

ἀλλὰ διὰ τὸν ὑποτάξαντα, ἐπ' ἐλπίδι, 21 ὅτι
but on account of the *One* subjecting *it*, upon hope, because
Him who subjected in

καὶ αὐτὴ ἡ κτίσις ἐλευθερωθήσεται ἀπὸ τῆς δουλείας τῆς
even [3]itself [1]the [2]creation will be freed from the slavery -

φθορᾶς εἰς τὴν ἐλευθερίαν τῆς δόξης τῶν τέκνων τοῦ
of corruption into the freedom of the glory of the children -

Θεοῦ. 22 Οἴδαμεν γὰρ ὅτι πᾶσα ἡ κτίσις συστενάζει καὶ
of God. [2]we [3]know [1]For that all the creation groans together and

συνωδίνει ἄχρι τοῦ νῦν. 23 Οὐ μόνον δέ, ἀλλὰ
labors in birth together until the now. [2]not [3]only [4]*so* [1]And, but
present.

καὶ αὐτοὶ τὴν ἀπαρχὴν τοῦ Πνεύματος ἔχοντες, καὶ
also *we* ourselves [2]the [3]firstfruit [4]of [5]the [6]Spirit [1]having, even

ἡμεῖς αὐτοὶ ἐν ἑαυτοῖς στενάζομεν, υἱοθεσίαν
we ourselves [2]in [3]ourselves [1]groan, [6]adoption

ἀπεκδεχόμενοι, τὴν ἀπολύτρωσιν τοῦ σώματος ἡμῶν. 24 Τῇ
[4]eagerly [5]awaiting, the redemption - of body ˜ our. [2]in [3]the
by this

γὰρ ἐλπίδι ἐσώθημεν, ἐλπὶς δὲ βλεπομένη οὐκ ἔστιν ἐλπίς·
[1]For hope we were saved, hope ˜ but being seen not ˜ is hope;

the flesh you will die; but if by the Spirit you put to death the deeds of the body, you will live.
14 For as many as are led by the Spirit of God, these are sons of God.
15 For you did not receive the spirit of bondage again to fear, but you received the Spirit of adoption by whom we cry out, "Abba, Father."
16 The Spirit Himself bears witness with our spirit that we are children of God,
17 and if children, then heirs—heirs of God and joint heirs with Christ, if indeed we suffer with *Him,* that we may also be glorified together.
18 For I consider that the sufferings of this present time are not worthy *to be compared* with the glory which shall be revealed in us.
19 For the earnest expectation of the creation eagerly waits for the revealing of the sons of God.
20 For the creation was subjected to futility, not willingly, but because of Him who subjected *it* in hope;
21 because the creation itself also will be delivered from the bondage of corruption into the glorious liberty of the children of God.
22 For we know that the whole creation groans and labors with birth pangs together until now.
23 Not only *that,* but we also who have the firstfruits of the Spirit, even we ourselves groan within ourselves, eagerly waiting for the adoption, the redemption of our body.
24 For we were saved in this hope, but hope that is seen is

***(8:15)** Ἀββᾶ *(Abba).* Noun meaning *father.* It is one of a handful of Aramaic expressions adopted by the Greek-speaking church. Originally a childhood word similar to our "Papa" or "Daddy," by NT times it had become a term of respect and endearment both for one's own father and for elders. In His agony in Gethsemane, Jesus used the term as an address to God in prayer (Mark 14:36), apparently in keeping with Jewish practice. The intimate family term fits the tender appeal to the Father in a crisis. In Rom. 8:15 Paul uses Ἀββᾶ as the natural address by the children of God to the One who has adopted them into His family. A similar usage in

not hope; for why does one still hope for what he sees?
25 But if we hope for what we do not see, we eagerly wait for *it* with perseverance.
26 Likewise the Spirit also helps in our weaknesses. For we do not know what we should pray for as we ought, but the Spirit Himself makes intercession for us with groanings which cannot be uttered.
27 Now He who searches the hearts knows what the mind of the Spirit *is,* because He makes intercession for the saints according to *the will of* God.
28 And we know that all things work together for good to those who love God, to those who are the called according to *His* purpose.
29 For whom He foreknew, He also predestined *to be* conformed to the image of His Son, that He might be the firstborn among many brethren.
30 Moreover whom He predestined, these He also called; whom He called, these He also justified; and whom He justified, these He also glorified.
31 What then shall we say to these things? If God *is* for us, who *can be* against us?
32 He who did not spare His own Son, but delivered Him up for us all, how shall He not with Him also freely give us all things?
33 Who shall bring a charge against God's elect? *It is* God who justifies.
34 Who *is* he who condemns? *It is* Christ who died, and furthermore is also risen, who is even at the right hand of God, who also makes intercession for us.
35 Who shall separate us from the love of Christ? *Shall* tribula-

ὃ γὰρ βλέπει τις, τί καὶ[c] ἐλπίζει? **25** Εἰ δὲ
[8]what [1]for [10]sees [9]one, [2]why [5]also [3]does [4]one [6]hope [7]for? if ˜ But
still

ὃ οὐ βλέπομεν ἐλπίζομεν, δι' ὑπομονῆς ἀπεκδεχόμεθα.
[4]what [7]not [5]we [6]do [8]see [1]we [2]hope [3]*for,* with endurance we eagerly await *it.*

26 Ὡσαύτως δὲ καὶ τὸ Πνεῦμα συναντιλαμβάνεται ταῖς
likewise ˜ And also the Spirit helps -

ἀσθενείαις ἡμῶν. Τὸ γὰρ τί προσευξόμεθα[d] καθὸ
in weaknesses ˜ our. - For what we shall pray as

δεῖ οὐκ οἴδαμεν, ἀλλ' αὐτὸ τὸ Πνεῦμα
it is necessary [3]not [1]we [2]do [4]know, but [3]Himself [1]the [2]Spirit
we ought

ὑπερεντυγχάνει ὑπὲρ ἡμῶν[e] στεναγμοῖς ἀλαλήτοις.
intercedes on behalf of us with groanings ˜ inexpressible.

27 Ὁ δὲ ἐρευνῶν τὰς καρδίας οἶδε τί τὸ φρόνημα
[2]the [3]*One* [1]And searching the hearts knows what the mind

τοῦ Πνεύματος, ὅτι κατὰ Θεὸν ἐντυγχάνει ὑπὲρ
of the Spirit *is,* because according to God He intercedes on behalf of

ἁγίων. **28** Οἴδαμεν δὲ ὅτι τοῖς ἀγαπῶσι τὸν Θεὸν
the saints. [2]we [3]know [1]And that to the *ones* loving - God
those who love

πάντα συνεργεῖ εἰς ἀγαθόν, τοῖς κατὰ
all *things* work together for good, to the *ones* [3]according [4]to
those who

πρόθεσιν κλητοῖς οὖσιν. **29** Ὅτι οὓς προέγνω, καὶ
[5]*His* [6]purpose [2]called [1]being. Because whom He foreknew, also ˜
are.

προώρισε συμμόρφους τῆς εἰκόνος τοῦ Υἱοῦ αὐτοῦ, εἰς τὸ
He predestined *to be* conformed of the image - of Son ˜ His, for -
to that He

εἶναι αὐτὸν πρωτότοκον ἐν πολλοῖς ἀδελφοῖς· **30** οὓς δὲ
to be Him firstborn among many brothers; whom ˜ and
should be

προώρισε, τούτους καὶ ἐκάλεσε· καὶ οὓς ἐκάλεσε, τούτους
He predestined, these also ˜ He called; and whom He called, these

καὶ ἐδικαίωσεν· οὓς δὲ ἐδικαίωσε, τούτους καὶ ἐδόξασε.
also ˜ He justified; whom ˜ and He justified, these also ˜ He glorified.

Nothing Can Separate Us From God's Love

31 Τί οὖν ἐροῦμεν πρὸς ταῦτα? Εἰ ὁ Θεὸς ὑπὲρ
What then shall we say to these *things?* If - God *is* for

ἡμῶν, τίς καθ' ἡμῶν? **32** Ὅς γε τοῦ ἰδίου Υἱοῦ
us, who *can be* against us? *He* who indeed - [4]His [5]own [6]Son

οὐκ ἐφείσατο, ἀλλ' ὑπὲρ ἡμῶν πάντων παρέδωκεν αὐτόν,
[2]not [1]did [3]spare, but on behalf of us all gave up ˜ Him,

πῶς οὐχὶ καὶ σὺν αὐτῷ τὰ πάντα ἡμῖν χαρίσεται?
how [3]not [4]also [5]with [6]Him - [11]all [12]*things* [9]to [10]us [1]shall [2]He [7]freely [8]give?

33 Τίς ἐγκαλέσει κατὰ ἐκλεκτῶν Θεοῦ? Θεὸς ὁ
Who shall bring a charge against *the* elect *ones* of God? God *is* the *One*
chosen

δικαιῶν. **34** Τίς ὁ κατακρινῶν? Χριστὸς ὁ
justifying. Who *is* the *one* condemning? Christ *is* the *One*

ἀποθανών, μᾶλλον δὲ καὶ ἐγερθείς, ὃς καί ἐστιν ἐν
having died, rather ˜ but also having been raised, who also is at

δεξιᾷ τοῦ Θεοῦ, ὃς καὶ ἐντυγχάνει ὑπὲρ ἡμῶν.
the right *hand* - of God, who also intercedes on behalf of us.

35 Τίς ἡμᾶς χωρίσει ἀπὸ τῆς ἀγάπης τοῦ Χριστοῦ?
Who [3]us [1]shall [2]separate from the love - of Christ?

---

[c](**8:24**) NU omits *τι και, why also.*
[d](**8:26**) NU reads *προσευξωμεθα, we should pray.* [e](**8:26**) NU omits *υπερ ημων, for us.*

Gal. 4:6 contrasts being a slave with the intimate fellowship a son or daughter has with the beloved Father.

Θλῖψις ἢ στενοχωρία ἢ διωγμὸς ἢ λιμὸς ἢ γυμνότης ἢ
Shall tribulation or distress or persecution or famine or nakedness or

κίνδυνος ἢ μάχαιρα? **36** Καθὼς γέγραπται ὅτι
danger or sword? Just as it is written -

«Ἕνεκέν σου θανατούμεθα ὅλην τὴν ἡμέραν,
«For sake ˜ Your we are put to death whole ˜ the day,

Ἐλογίσθημεν ὡς πρόβατα σφαγῆς.»[f]
We are accounted as sheep for slaughter.»

37 Ἀλλ' ἐν τούτοις πᾶσιν ὑπερνικῶμεν διὰ
But in [2]these [3]*things* [1]all we more than conquer through
are more than conquerors

τοῦ ἀγαπήσαντος ἡμᾶς. **38** Πέπεισμαι γὰρ ὅτι
the *One* having loved us. [2]I [3]have [4]been [5]persuaded [1]For that
Him who loved

οὔτε θάνατος οὔτε ζωὴ οὔτε ἄγγελοι οὔτε ἀρχαὶ οὔτε
neither death nor life nor angels nor principalities nor
rulers

δυνάμεις οὔτε ἐνεστῶτα οὔτε μέλλοντα **39** οὔτε ὕψωμα οὔτε
powers nor *things* present nor *things* coming nor height nor

βάθος οὔτε τις κτίσις ἑτέρα δυνήσεται ἡμᾶς χωρίσαι
depth nor any [2]created [3]thing [1]other shall be able [3]us [1]to [2]separate

ἀπὸ τῆς ἀγάπης τοῦ Θεοῦ τῆς ἐν Χριστῷ Ἰησοῦ τῷ Κυρίῳ
from the love - of God the *one* in Christ Jesus - Lord ˜
which is

ἡμῶν.
our.

Paul Bemoans Israel's Rejection of Christ

9 **1** Ἀλήθειαν λέγω ἐν Χριστῷ, οὐ ψεύδομαι,
[4]truth [1]I [2]am [3]speaking in Christ, [3]not [1]I [2]am [4]lying,

συμμαρτυρούσης μοι τῆς συνειδήσεώς μου ἐν Πνεύματι Ἁγίῳ,
[7]witnessing [8]with [9]me - [6]conscience [5]my in *the* Spirit ˜ Holy,

2 ὅτι λύπη μοί ἐστι μεγάλη καὶ ἀδιάλειπτος ὀδύνη τῇ
that sorrow to me *there* is great and unceasing pain -
I have great sorrow

καρδίᾳ μου. **3** Εὐχόμην γὰρ αὐτὸς ἐγὼ ἀνάθεμα* εἶναι
in heart ˜ my. [2]I [3]could [4]wish [1]For [6]myself [5]I [9]accursed [7]to [8]be

ἀπὸ τοῦ Χριστοῦ ὑπὲρ τῶν ἀδελφῶν μου, τῶν συγγενῶν
from - Christ on behalf of - brothers ˜ my, - countrymen ˜

μου κατὰ σάρκα, **4** οἵτινές εἰσιν Ἰσραηλῖται, ὧν
my according to *the* flesh, who are Israelites, of whom

ἡ υἱοθεσία καὶ ἡ δόξα καὶ αἱ διαθῆκαι καὶ ἡ νομοθεσία
are the adoption and the glory and the covenants and the law-giving

καὶ ἡ λατρεία καὶ αἱ ἐπαγγελίαι, **5** ὧν οἱ πατέρες
and the worship and the promises, of whom *are* the fathers

καὶ ἐξ ὧν ὁ Χριστὸς τὸ κατὰ σάρκα, ὁ ὢν
and from whom - Christ *came* - according to *the* flesh, the *One* being
He who is

ἐπὶ πάντων Θεὸς εὐλογητὸς εἰς τοὺς αἰῶνας. Ἀμήν.
[2]over [3]all [1]God blessed to the ages. Amen.
forever. So be it.

This Rejection Is Not Inconsistent with God's Word

6 Οὐχ οἷον δὲ ὅτι ἐκπέπτωκεν ὁ λόγος τοῦ
[2]*it* [3]*is* [4]not [5]as [6]though [1]But - [11]has [12]failed [7]the [8]word -

Θεοῦ. Οὐ γὰρ πάντες οἱ ἐξ Ἰσραήλ, οὗτοι
[9]of [10]God. not ˜ For all the *ones* of Israel, these *are of*

tion, or distress, or persecution, or famine, or nakedness, or peril, or sword?
36 As it is written:

"For Your sake we are
killed all day long;
We are accounted as
sheep for the
slaughter."

37 Yet in all these things we are more than conquerors through Him who loved us.
38 For I am persuaded that neither death nor life, nor angels nor principalities nor powers, nor things present nor things to come,
39 nor height nor depth, nor any other created thing, shall be able to separate us from the love of God which is in Christ Jesus our Lord.
9 I tell the truth in Christ, I am not lying, my conscience also bearing me witness in the Holy Spirit,
2 that I have great sorrow and continual grief in my heart.
3 For I could wish that I myself were accursed from Christ for my brethren, my countrymen according to the flesh,
4 who are Israelites, to whom *pertain* the adoption, the glory, the covenants, the giving of the law, the service *of God,* and the promises;
5 of whom *are* the fathers and from whom, according to the flesh, Christ *came,* who is over all, *the* eternally blessed God. Amen.
6 But it is not that the word of God has taken no effect. For they *are* not all Israel who *are* of

---

f(**8:36**) Ps. 44:22

***(9:3)** ἀνάθεμα *(anathema).* Noun originally meaning *that which has been devoted to God, a votive offering.* In the LXX at Josh. 6:17, 18 it carries a negative sense: *that which has been devoted to God for destruction, (a thing) accursed.* In the NT it is always used with a negative meaning (here in Rom. 9:3; Acts 23:14; 1 Cor. 12:3; 16:22; Gal. 1:9). The variant spelling ἀνάθημα in Luke 21:5 has a positive meaning, *a consecrated offering* (some mss. read ἀνάθεμα). Cf. the cognate verb ἀναθεματίζω, *bind with an oath* or *under a curse, pronounce a curse* (Acts 23:12, 14, 21; Mark 14:71);

Israel,
7 nor *are they* all children because they are the seed of Abraham; but, *"In Isaac your seed shall be called."*
8 That is, those who *are* the children of the flesh, these *are* not the children of God; but the children of the promise are counted as the seed.
9 For this *is* the word of promise: *"At this time I will come and Sarah shall have a son."*
10 And not only *this,* but when Rebecca also had conceived by one man, *even* by our father Isaac
11 (for *the children* not yet being born, nor having done any good or evil, that the purpose of God according to election might stand, not of works but of Him who calls),
12 it was said to her, *"The older shall serve the younger."*
13 As it is written, *"Jacob I have loved, but Esau I have hated."*
14 What shall we say then? *Is there* unrighteousness with God? Certainly not!
15 For He says to Moses, *"I will have mercy on whomever I will have mercy, and I will have compassion on whomever I will have compassion."*
16 So then *it is* not of him who wills, nor of him who runs, but of God who shows mercy.
17 For the Scripture says to the Pharaoh, *"For this very purpose I have raised you up, that I may show My power in you, and that My name may be declared in all the earth."*
18 Therefore He has mercy on whom He wills, and whom He wills He hardens.

Ἰσραήλ· **7** οὐδ' ὅτι εἰσὶ σπέρμα Ἀβραάμ, πάντες
Israel; neither because they are *the* seed of Abraham, *are they* all

τέκνα, ἀλλ' «Ἐν Ἰσαὰκ κληθήσεταί σοι σπέρμα.»[a]
children, but «In Isaac [4]shall [5]be [6]called [1]to [2]you [3]seed.»
your

8 Τοῦτ' ἔστιν, οὐ τὰ τέκνα τῆς σαρκός, ταῦτα τέκνα τοῦ
This is, not the children of the flesh, *are* these children -
That

Θεοῦ, ἀλλὰ τὰ τέκνα τῆς ἐπαγγελίας λογίζεται εἰς σπέρμα.
of God, but the children of the promise are counted for a seed.

9 Ἐπαγγελίας γὰρ ὁ λόγος οὗτος, «Κατὰ τὸν καιρὸν
[6]of [7]promise [1]For [4]the [5]word [2]this [3]*is,* «According to - season ˜
«At this time

τοῦτον ἐλεύσομαι, καὶ ἔσται τῇ Σάρρᾳ υἱός.»[b] **10** Οὐ
this I will come, and *there* shall be - to Sarah a son.» [2]not
Sarah shall have

μόνον δέ, ἀλλὰ καὶ Ῥεβέκκα ἐξ ἑνὸς κοίτην
[3]only [4]*so* [1]And, but also Rebecca [3]from [4]one [5]*man* [2]conception

ἔχουσα, Ἰσαὰκ τοῦ πατρὸς ἡμῶν· **11** μήπω γὰρ γεννηθέντων,
[1]having, Isaac - father ˜ our; [2]not [3]yet [1]for being born,

μηδὲ πραξάντων τι ἀγαθὸν ἢ κακόν,[c] ἵνα ἡ
nor practicing anything good or bad, so that the

κατ' ἐκλογὴν πρόθεσις τοῦ Θεοῦ μένῃ, οὐκ ἐξ
[4]according [5]to [6]election [1]purpose - [2]of [3]God might abide, not of

ἔργων ἀλλ' ἐκ τοῦ καλοῦντος, **12** ἐρρέθη αὐτῇ ὅτι «Ὁ
works but of the *One* calling, it was said to her - «The
Him who calls,

μείζων δουλεύσει τῷ ἐλάσσονι.»[d] **13** Καθὼς γέγραπται,
greater will serve the lesser.» Just as it is written,
older younger.»

«Τὸν Ἰακὼβ ἠγάπησα,
- «Jacob I loved,

Τὸν δὲ Ἠσαῦ ἐμίσησα.»[e]
- But Esau I hated.»

This Rejection Is Not Inconsistent with God's Justice

14 Τί οὖν ἐροῦμεν? Μὴ ἀδικία παρὰ
What then shall we say? *Surely there is* not unrighteousness with

τῷ Θεῷ? Μὴ γένοιτο! **15** Τῷ γὰρ Μωϋσῇ λέγει,
- God? [3]not [1]May [2]it [4]be! - For to Moses He says,

«Ἐλεήσω ὃν ἂν ἐλεῶ,
«I will have mercy on whom ever I have mercy,

Καὶ οἰκτιρήσω ὃν ἂν οἰκτείρω.»[f]
And I will have compassion on whom ever I have compassion.»

16 Ἄρα οὖν οὐ τοῦ θέλοντος, οὐδὲ τοῦ τρέχοντος,
So then *it is* not of the *one* willing, nor of the *one* running,
him who wills, him who runs,

ἀλλὰ τοῦ ἐλεοῦντος Θεοῦ. **17** Λέγει γὰρ ἡ Γραφὴ τῷ
but of the having mercy God. [4]says [1]For [2]the [3]Scripture -
God who shows mercy.

Φαραὼ ὅτι «Εἰς αὐτὸ τοῦτο ἐξήγειρά σε, ὅπως
to Pharaoh - «For [3]itself [1]this [2]*thing* I raised up ˜ you, that

ἐνδείξωμαι ἐν σοὶ τὴν δύναμίν μου, καὶ ὅπως διαγγελῇ
I might show in you - power ˜ My, and that [3]may [4]be [5]proclaimed

τὸ ὄνομά μου ἐν πάσῃ τῇ γῇ.»[g] **18** Ἄρα οὖν ὃν θέλει
- [2]name [1]My in all the earth.» So then *on* whom He wills

ἐλεεῖ, ὃν δὲ θέλει σκληρύνει.
He has mercy, whom ˜ and He wills He hardens.

---

[a](9:7) Gen. 21:12
[b](9:9) Gen. 18:10, 14
[c](9:11) NU reads φαῦλον, *evil.* [d](9:12) Gen. 25:23
[e](9:13) Mal. 1:2, 3
[f](9:15) Ex. 33:19
[g](9:17) Ex. 9:16

and the English derivative *anathema.*

19 Ἐρεῖς οὖν μοι, "Τί ἔτι μέμφεται? Τῷ γὰρ
[2]you [3]will [4]say [1]Then to me, "Why still does He find fault? - For
βουλήματι αὐτοῦ τίς ἀνθέστηκε?" 20 Μενοῦνγε, ὦ ἄνθρωπε,
[5]will [4]His [1]who [2]*ever* [3]resisted?" But indeed, O man,
σὺ τίς εἶ ὁ ἀνταποκρινόμενος τῷ Θεῷ? Μὴ
[3]you [1]who [2]are the *one* answering back - to God? *Surely* [5]not
ἐρεῖ τὸ πλάσμα τῷ πλάσαντι, "Τί με
[4]will [6]say [1]the [2]thing [3]formed to the *one* having formed *it,* "Why [4]me
ἐποίησας οὕτως?" 21 Ἢ οὐκ ἔχει ἐξουσίαν ὁ
[1]did [2]you [3]make like this?" Or [2]not [1]does [5]have [6]*the* [7]right [3]the
κεραμεὺς τοῦ πηλοῦ, ἐκ τοῦ αὐτοῦ φυράματος ποιῆσαι
[4]potter *over* the clay, out of the same lump to make
ὃ μὲν εἰς τιμὴν σκεῦος, ὃ δὲ εἰς ἀτιμίαν? 22 Εἰ δὲ
the one [2]for [3]honor [1]vessel, the other for dishonor? if ˜ But
θέλων ὁ Θεὸς ἐνδείξασθαι τὴν ὀργὴν καὶ γνωρίσαι τὸ
desiring ˜ - God to show the (His) wrath and to make known -
δυνατὸν αὐτοῦ, ἤνεγκεν ἐν πολλῇ μακροθυμίᾳ σκεύη ὀργῆς
power ˜ His, bore with much longsuffering vessels of wrath
κατηρτισμένα εἰς ἀπώλειαν, 23 καὶ ἵνα
having been prepared for destruction, and so that
γνωρίσῃ τὸν πλοῦτον τῆς δόξης αὐτοῦ ἐπὶ σκεύη
He might make known the riches - of glory ˜ His on vessels
ἐλέους,* ἃ προητοίμασεν εἰς δόξαν, 24 οὓς καὶ
of mercy, which He prepared beforehand for glory, whom also
ἐκάλεσεν ἡμᾶς οὐ μόνον ἐξ Ἰουδαίων, ἀλλὰ καὶ ἐξ ἐθνῶν?
He called us not only from Jews, but also from Gentiles?
25 Ὡς καὶ ἐν τῷ Ὡσηὲ λέγει,
As also in - Hosea He says,

«Καλέσω τὸν οὐ λαόν μου 'λαόν μου'
«I will call the *one* (those who are) not people ˜ My 'people ˜ My'
Καὶ τὴν οὐκ ἠγαπημένην 'ἠγαπημένην.'»[h]
And the *one* not beloved 'beloved.'»

26 «Καὶ ἔσται ἐν τῷ τόπῳ οὗ ἐρρέθη αὐτοῖς,
«And it shall be in the place where it was said to them,
'Οὐ λαός μου ὑμεῖς,'
'[3]not [5]people [4]My [1]You [2]*are,*'
Ἐκεῖ κληθήσονται υἱοὶ Θεοῦ ζῶντος.»[i]
There they shall be called sons of *the* God ˜ living.»

27 Ἠσαΐας δὲ κράζει ὑπὲρ τοῦ Ἰσραήλ,[j]
Isaiah ˜ And cries out concerning - Israel,
«Ἐὰν ᾖ ὁ ἀριθμὸς τῶν υἱῶν Ἰσραὴλ ὡς ἡ ἄμμος
«If [8]were [1]the [2]number [3]of [4]the [5]sons [6]of [7]Israel as the sand
τῆς θαλάσσης,
of the sea,
Τὸ κατάλειμμα σωθήσεται·
The remnant will be saved;

28 Λόγον γὰρ συντελῶν καὶ συντέμνων ἐν
[8]an [9]account [1]For [2]*He* [3]*is* [4]finishing [5]and [6]cutting [7]short in
δικαιοσύνῃ·
righteousness;
Ὅτι λόγον συντετμημένον[k] ποιήσει Κύριος
Because [5]an [6]account [7]having [8]been [9]cut [10]short (a short account) [3]will [4]make [1]*the* [2]Lord
ἐπὶ τῆς γῆς.»
upon the earth.»

19 You will say to me then, "Why does He still find fault? For who has resisted His will?"
20 But indeed, O man, who are you to reply against God? Will the thing formed say to him who formed *it,* "Why have you made me like this?"
21 Does not the potter have power over the clay, from the same lump to make one vessel for honor and another for dishonor?
22 *What* if God, wanting to show *His* wrath and to make His power known, endured with much longsuffering the vessels of wrath prepared for destruction,
23 and that He might make known the riches of His glory on the vessels of mercy, which He had prepared beforehand for glory,
24 *even* us whom He called, not of the Jews only, but also of the Gentiles?
25 As He says also in Hosea:

"I will call them My people, who were not My people,
And her beloved, who was not beloved."

26 *"And it shall come to pass in the place where it was said to them,*
'You are not My people,'
There they shall be called sons of the living God."

27 Isaiah also cries out concerning Israel:

"Though the number of the children of Israel be as the sand of the sea,
The remnant will be saved.

28 *For He will finish the work and cut it short in righteousness,*
Because the LORD *will make a short work upon the earth."*

---

[h](9:25) Hos. 2:23
[i](9:26) Hos. 1:10
[j](9:27) Is. 10:22, 23
[k](9:28) NU omits εν δικαιοσυνη οτι λογον συντετμημενον, thus reading *For, finishing (it) and cutting (it) short, the Lord will make an account upon . . .*

***(9:23)** ἔλεος *(eleos).* Noun meaning *mercy,* a manifestation of compassion—not merely a feeling, but an action—for one in distress. Whereas χάρις, *grace,* em-

29 And as Isaiah said before:

"Unless the LORD *of*
Sabaoth had left us a
seed,
We would have become
like Sodom,
And we would have been
made like Gomorrah."

30 What shall we say then?
That Gentiles, who did not pursue righteousness, have attained to righteousness, even
the righteousness of faith;
31 but Israel, pursuing the law
of righteousness, has not attained to the law of righteousness.
32 Why? Because *they did* not
seek it by faith, but as it were,
by the works of the law. For
they stumbled at that stumbling
stone.
33 As it is written:

"Behold, I lay in Zion a
stumbling stone and
rock of offense,
And whoever believes on
Him will not be put to
shame."

10 Brethren, my heart's desire and prayer to
God for Israel is that they may
be saved.
2 For I bear them witness
that they have a zeal for God,
but not according to knowledge.
3 For they being ignorant of
God's righteousness, and seeking to establish their own righteousness, have not submitted
to the righteousness of God.
4 For Christ *is* the end of the
law for righteousness to everyone who believes.
5 For Moses writes about

29 Καὶ καθὼς προείρηκεν Ἠσαΐας,
And just as predicted ˜ Isaiah,

«Εἰ μὴ Κύριος Σαβαὼθ ἐγκατέλιπεν ἡμῖν σπέρμα,
«If not *the* Lord of Sabaoth left us a seed,
«Unless Hosts had left

Ὡς Σόδομα ἂν ἐγενήθημεν,
Like Sodom - we would have become,

Καὶ ὡς Γόμορρα ἂν ὡμοιώθημεν.»[l]
And like Gomorrah - we would have been compared.»

The Present Condition of Israel

30 Τί οὖν ἐροῦμεν? Ὅτι ἔθνη, τὰ μὴ διώκοντα
What then shall we say? That Gentiles, the *ones* not pursuing

δικαιοσύνην, κατέλαβε δικαιοσύνην, δικαιοσύνην δὲ τὴν ἐκ
righteousness, attained to righteousness, [2]a [3]righteousness [1]even - of

πίστεως. **31** Ἰσραὴλ δέ, διώκων νόμον δικαιοσύνης, εἰς
faith. Israel ˜ But, pursuing a law of righteousness, to

νόμον δικαιοσύνης[m] οὐκ ἔφθασε. **32** Διὰ τί? Ὅτι
a law of righteousness not ˜ did attain. Why? Because

οὐκ ἐκ πίστεως, ἀλλ' ὡς ἐξ ἔργων νόμου.[n]
they did not *seek it* out of faith, but as out of works of law.
by by

Προσέκοψαν γὰρ τῷ λίθῳ τοῦ προσκόμματος. **33** Καθὼς
[2]they [3]stumbled [1]For at the stone - of stumbling. Just as

γέγραπται,
it is written,

«Ἰδοὺ τίθημι ἐν Σιὼν λίθον προσκόμματος καὶ πέτραν
«Behold I place in Zion a stone of stumbling and a rock
lay

σκανδάλου,
of offense,

Καὶ πᾶς ὁ πιστεύων ἐπ' αὐτῷ οὐ
And every - *one* believing on Him not ˜
no one who believes in Him

καταισχυνθήσεται.»[o]
will be put to shame.»

Israel Needs the Universal Message of Salvation

10 **1** Ἀδελφοί, ἡ μὲν εὐδοκία τῆς ἐμῆς καρδίας καὶ
Brothers, the - good pleasure - of my heart and
desire

ἡ δέησις ἡ πρὸς τὸν Θεὸν ὑπὲρ τοῦ Ἰσραήλ[a] ἐστιν εἰς
the supplication - to - God on behalf - of Israel is for
my

σωτηρίαν. **2** Μαρτυρῶ γὰρ αὐτοῖς ὅτι ζῆλον* Θεοῦ
salvation. [2]I [3]bear [4]witness [1]For to them that [3]a [4]zeal [5]of [6]God
for

ἔχουσιν, ἀλλ' οὐ κατ' ἐπίγνωσιν. **3** Ἀγνοοῦντες γὰρ
[1]they [2]have, but not according to full knowledge. [2]not [3]knowing [1]For

τὴν τοῦ Θεοῦ δικαιοσύνην καὶ τὴν ἰδίαν δικαιοσύνην[b]
the - [2]of [3]God [1]righteousness and - their own righteousness

ζητοῦντες στῆσαι, τῇ δικαιοσύνῃ τοῦ Θεοῦ οὐχ
seeking to establish, [5]to [6]the [7]righteousness - [8]of [9]God [3]not

ὑπετάγησαν. **4** Τέλος γὰρ νόμου Χριστὸς εἰς δικαιοσύνην
[1]they [2]did [4]submit. [4]*the* [5]end [1]For [6]of [7]law [2]Christ [3]*is* for righteousness

παντὶ τῷ πιστεύοντι. **5** Μωϋσῆς γὰρ γράφει τὴν
to every - *one* believing. Moses ˜ For writes *about* the
everyone who believes.

---

[l](9:29) Is. *1:9*
[m](9:31) NU omits δικαιοσυνης, *of righteousness.*
[n](9:32) NU omits νομου, *of law.* [o](9:33) Is. 8:14; 28:16
[a](10:1) NU reads αυτων, *them.* [b](10:3) NU brackets δικαιοσυνην, *righteousness.*

phasizes that favor is not deserved, ἔλεος emphasizes the misery that elicits response. The word may refer to mercy shown by human beings (as Luke 10:37), or by God to people in general (as

δικαιοσύνην τὴν ἐκ τοῦ νόμου, ὅτι «ὁ ποιήσας αὐτὰ
righteousness - of the law, - «The ^{2}doing ^{3}them

ἄνθρωπος ζήσεται ἐν αὐτοῖς.»[c] 6 Ἡ δὲ ἐκ πίστεως
^{1}man shall live by them.» the ~ But ^{2}of ^{3}faith

δικαιοσύνη οὕτω λέγει, «Μὴ εἴπῃς ἐν τῇ καρδίᾳ σου, 'Τίς
^{1}righteousness thus says, «not ~ Do say in - heart ~ your, 'Who

ἀναβήσεται εἰς τὸν οὐρανόν?'»[d] (τοῦτ' ἔστι Χριστὸν
will ascend into - heaven?'» (this is ^{3}Christ
(that

καταγαγεῖν) 7 ἤ, «'Τίς καταβήσεται εἰς τὴν ἄβυσσον?'»[e]
^{1}to ^{2}bring ^{4}down) or, «'Who will descend into the abyss?'»

(τοῦτ' ἔστι Χριστὸν ἐκ νεκρῶν ἀναγαγεῖν.) 8 'Αλλὰ τί
(this is ^{3}Christ ^{5}from ^{6}*the* ^{7}dead ^{1}to ^{2}bring ^{4}up.) But what
(that

λέγει?
does it say?

«'Εγγύς σου τὸ ῥῆμά ἐστιν,
«^{4}near ^{5}you ^{1}The ^{2}word ^{3}is,

'Εν τῷ στόματί σου καὶ ἐν τῇ καρδίᾳ σου» —[f]
In - mouth ~ your and in - heart ~ your» —

τοῦτ' ἔστι τὸ ῥῆμα τῆς πίστεως ὃ κηρύσσομεν, 9 ὅτι ἐὰν
this is the word - of faith which we proclaim, that if
that

ὁμολογήσῃς ἐν τῷ στόματί σου Κύριον 'Ιησοῦν καὶ πιστεύσῃς
you confess with - mouth ~ your *the* Lord Jesus and you believe

ἐν τῇ καρδίᾳ σου ὅτι ὁ Θεὸς αὐτὸν ἤγειρεν ἐκ νεκρῶν,
in - heart ~ your that - God Him ~ raised from *the* dead,

σωθήσῃ. 10 Καρδίᾳ γὰρ πιστεύεται εἰς
you will be saved. ^{2}with ^{3}*the* ^{4}heart ^{1}For it is believed *resulting* in
one believes

δικαιοσύνην, στόματι δὲ ὁμολογεῖται εἰς
righteousness, ^{2}with ^{3}*the* ^{4}mouth ^{1}and it is confessed *resulting* in
one confesses

σωτηρίαν. 11 Λέγει γὰρ ἡ Γραφή, «Πᾶς ὁ πιστεύων ἐπ'
salvation. ^{4}says ^{1}For ^{2}the ^{3}Scripture, «Every - *one* believing on
«No one who believes in

αὐτῷ οὐ καταισχυνθήσεται.»[g] 12 Οὐ γάρ ἐστι διαστολὴ
Him not ~ will be shamed.» ^{4}not ^{1}For ^{2}*there* ^{3}is a difference
Him will be put to shame.»

'Ιουδαίου τε καὶ Ἕλληνος, ὁ γὰρ αὐτὸς Κύριος πάντων,
between Jew and also Greek, the ~ for same Lord of all,

πλουτῶν εἰς πάντας τοὺς ἐπικαλουμένους αὐτόν.
being rich to all the *ones* calling upon Him.
is those who call

13 «Πᾶς γὰρ ὃς ἂν ἐπικαλέσηται τὸ ὄνομα Κυρίου
«^{2}every ^{3}*one* ^{1}For who ever shall call on the name of *the* Lord

σωθήσεται.»[h]
shall be saved.»

Israel Has Rejected the Universal Message of Salvation

14 Πῶς οὖν ἐπικαλέσονται εἰς ὃν οὐκ
How then shall they call on *the One* in whom ^{3}not

ἐπίστευσαν? Πῶς δὲ πιστεύσουσιν οὗ οὐκ
^{1}they ^{2}did ^{4}believe? how ~ And shall they believe *the One* whom ^{3}not

ἤκουσαν? Πῶς δὲ ἀκούσουσι χωρὶς κηρύσσοντος?
^{1}they ^{2}did ^{4}hear? how ~ And shall they hear without one proclaiming?
a preacher?

the righteousness which is of the law, *"The man who does those things shall live by them."*
6 But the righteousness of faith speaks in this way, *"Do not say in your heart, 'Who will ascend into heaven?' "* (that is, to bring Christ down *from above*)
7 or, *" 'Who will descend into the abyss?' "* (that is, to bring Christ up from the dead).
8 But what does it say? *"The word is near you, in your mouth and in your heart"* (that is, the word of faith which we preach):
9 that if you confess with your mouth the Lord Jesus and believe in your heart that God has raised Him from the dead, you will be saved.
10 For with the heart one believes unto righteousness, and with the mouth confession is made unto salvation.
11 For the Scripture says, *"Whoever believes on Him will not be put to shame."*
12 For there is no distinction between Jew and Greek, for the same Lord over all is rich to all who call upon Him.
13 For *"whoever calls on the name of the LORD shall be saved."*
14 How then shall they call on Him in whom they have not believed? And how shall they believe in Him of whom they have not heard? And how shall they hear without a preacher?

---

c(**10:5**) Lev. 18:5
d(**10:6**) Deut. 30:12
e(**10:7**) Deut. 30:13
f(**10:8**) Deut. 30:14
g(**10:11**) Is. 28:16
h(**10:13**) Joel 2:32

Luke 1:58) or in Christ for redemption (as Rom. 15:9). Cf. the cognate verb ἐλεέω, *show mercy, take pity;* adjective ἐλεήμων, *merciful;* and noun ἐλεημοσύνη, *act of mercy, almsgiving.*

***(10:2)** ζῆλος *(zēlos).* Noun used either positively meaning *zeal, ardor, earnestness* (as here and John 2:17), or negatively meaning *jealousy, envy* (as Rom. 13:13; James 3:14). Several of the positive uses in the NT have been influenced by the Jewish concept of "holy zeal" (cf. the phrase "zeal of God" in 2 Cor. 11:2). When plural in the negative sense, as in 2 Cor. 12:20; Gal. 5:20, the word refers to the various manifestations of jealousy.

15 And how shall they preach unless they are sent? As it is written:

"How beautiful are the feet
of those who preach
the gospel of peace,
Who bring glad tidings of
good things!"

16 But they have not all obeyed the gospel. For Isaiah says, *"LORD, who has believed our report?"*
17 So then faith *comes* by hearing, and hearing by the word of God.
18 But I say, have they not heard? Yes indeed:

"Their sound has gone out
to all the earth,
And their words to the
ends of the world."

19 But I say, did Israel not know? First Moses says:

"I will provoke you to
jealousy by those who
are not a nation,
I will move you to anger
by a foolish nation."

20 But Isaiah is very bold and says:

"I was found by those who
did not seek Me;
I was made manifest to
those who did not ask
for Me."

21 But to Israel he says:

"All day long I have
stretched out My hands
To a disobedient and
contrary people."

11 I say then, has God cast away His people?

15 Πῶς δὲ κηρύξουσιν ἐὰν μὴ ἀποσταλῶσι? Καθὼς
how ˜ And shall they proclaim if not they are sent? Just as
preach unless

γέγραπται,
it is written,

«Ὡς ὡραῖοι οἱ πόδες τῶν εὐαγγελιζομένων
«How beautiful *are* the feet of the *ones* announcing good news

εἰρήνην,[i]
of peace,

Τῶν εὐαγγελιζομένων τὰ ἀγαθά.»[j]
Of the *ones* announcing good news - *of* good *things*.»

16 Ἀλλ' οὐ πάντες ὑπήκουσαν τῷ εὐαγγελίῳ. Ἠσαΐας γὰρ
But not all obeyed the gospel. Isaiah ˜ For

λέγει, «Κύριε, τίς ἐπίστευσε τῇ ἀκοῇ ἡμῶν?»[k] **17** Ἄρα ἡ
says, «Lord, who believed - report ˜ our?» So -

πίστις ἐξ ἀκοῆς, ἡ δὲ ἀκοὴ διὰ ῥήματος Θεοῦ.[l]
faith *comes* from hearing, - and hearing through *the* word of God.

18 Ἀλλὰ λέγω, μὴ οὐκ ἤκουσαν?
But I say, *Surely it is* not *that* 3not 1they 2did 4hear?

Μενοῦνγε,
Indeed, yes *they did*,

«Εἰς πᾶσαν τὴν γῆν ἐξῆλθεν ὁ φθόγγος αὐτῶν,
«To all the earth went out - sound ˜ their,
voice

Καὶ εἰς τὰ πέρατα τῆς οἰκουμένης τὰ ῥήματα
And to the ends of the inhabited earth - words ˜

αὐτῶν.»[m]
their.»

19 Ἀλλὰ λέγω, μὴ οὐκ ἔγνω Ἰσραήλ?
But I say, *surely it is* not *that* 3not 2did 4know 1Israel?

Πρῶτος Μωϋσῆς λέγει,
First Moses says,

«Ἐγὼ παραζηλώσω ὑμᾶς ἐπ' οὐκ ἔθνει,
«I will provoke 2to 3jealousy 1you on *those who are* not a nation,
by

Ἐπὶ ἔθνει ἀσυνέτῳ παροργιῶ ὑμᾶς.»[n]
On a(n) nation ˜ unintelligent I will anger you.»
By

20 Ἠσαΐας δὲ ἀποτολμᾷ καὶ λέγει,
Isaiah ˜ But is very bold and says,

«Εὑρέθην τοῖς ἐμὲ μὴ ζητοῦσιν,
«I was found by the *ones* 3Me 1not 2seeking,
those who did not seek Me,

Ἐμφανὴς ἐγενόμην τοῖς ἐμὲ μὴ ἐπερωτῶσι.»[o]
3manifest 1I 2became to the *ones* 4Me 1not 2asking 3for.»
those who did not ask for Me.»

21 Πρὸς δὲ τὸν Ἰσραὴλ λέγει, «Ὅλην τὴν ἡμέραν
to ˜ But - Israel he says, «whole ˜ The day

ἐξεπέτασα τὰς χεῖράς μου πρὸς λαὸν ἀπειθοῦντα
I stretched out - hands ˜ My to a people disobeying
a disobedient and

καὶ ἀντιλέγοντα.»[p]
and contradicting.»
contradictory people.»

The Remnant: Israel's Rejection Is Not Total

11 **1** Λέγω οὖν, μὴ ἀπώσατο ὁ Θεὸς τὸν λαὸν
I say then, *surely* 3not 2did 4put 5away - 1God - people ˜
reject

---

[i](**10:15**) NU omits των ευαγγελιζομενων ειρηνην, *of the ones announcing good news of peace.*
[j](**10:15**) Is. 52:7; Nah. 1:15
[k](**10:16**) Is. 53:1
[l](**10:17**) NU reads Χριστου, *of Christ.* [m](**10:18**) Ps. 19:4
[n](**10:19**) Deut. 32:21
[o](**10:20**) Is. 65:1
[p](**10:21**) Is. 65:2

Cf. the cognate verb ζηλόω, which may also be the positive *strive earnestly, be zealous for* (Gal. 4:18) or the negative *be filled with envy or jealousy* (Acts 17:5). Cf. also the cognate noun ζηλωτής, *zealot* (Luke 6:15).

αὐτοῦ? Μὴ γένοιτο! Καὶ γὰρ ἐγὼ Ἰσραηλίτης εἰμί, ἐκ
His? [3]not [1]May [2]it [4]be! [7]also [5]For [6]I [9]an [10]Israelite [8]am, of

σπέρματος Ἀβραάμ, φυλῆς Βενιαμίν. 2 Οὐκ ἀπώσατο
the seed of Abraham, of *the* tribe of Benjamin. [3]not [2]did [4]cast [5]away
reject

ὁ Θεὸς τὸν λαὸν αὐτοῦ ὃν προέγνω. Ἢ οὐκ οἴδατε
- [1]God - people ˜ His whom He foreknew. Or [3]not [1]do [2]you [4]know

ἐν Ἠλίᾳ τί λέγει ἡ Γραφή? Ὡς ἐντυγχάνει
in *the passage about* Elijah what [3]says [1]the [2]Scripture? How he pleads

τῷ Θεῷ κατὰ τοῦ Ἰσραήλ, λέγων,[a] 3 «Κύριε, τοὺς
- with God against - Israel, saying, «Lord, -

προφήτας σου ἀπέκτειναν καὶ τὰ θυσιαστήριά σου
prophets ˜ Your they killed and - altars ˜ Your

κατέσκαψαν, κἀγὼ ὑπελείφθην μόνος, καὶ ζητοῦσι τὴν
they tore down, and I am left alone, and they are seeking -

ψυχήν μου.»[b] 4 Ἀλλὰ τί λέγει αὐτῷ ὁ χρηματισμός?
life ˜ my.» But what [1]does [5]say [6]to [7]him [2]the [3]divine [4]response?

«Κατέλιπον ἐμαυτῷ ἑπτακισχιλίους ἄνδρας οἵτινες οὐκ
«I left for Myself seven thousand men who not ˜
have

ἔκαμψαν γόνυ τῇ Βάαλ.»[c] 5 Οὕτως οὖν καὶ ἐν τῷ νῦν
did bend a knee - to Baal.» So then also in the now
not bent present

καιρῷ λεῖμμα κατ' ἐκλογὴν χάριτος γέγονεν.
season [4]a [5]remnant [6]according [7]to [8]*the* [9]election [10]of [11]grace [1]*there* [2]has [3]been.
time

6 Εἰ δὲ χάριτι, οὐκέτι ἐξ ἔργων, ἐπεὶ ἡ χάρις
if ˜ And by grace, *it is* no longer of works, since - grace
otherwise

οὐκέτι γίνεται χάρις.[d] Εἰ δὲ ἐξ ἔργων, οὐκέτι ἐστὶ χάρις,
no longer becomes grace. if ˜ But of works, [3]no [4]longer [1]it [2]is grace,

ἐπεὶ τὸ ἔργον οὐκέτι ἐστὶν ἔργον. 7 Τί οὖν? Ὃ
since - work no longer is work. What then? What
otherwise

ἐπιζητεῖ Ἰσραήλ, τοῦτο οὐκ ἐπέτυχεν, ἡ δὲ ἐκλογὴ
seeks ˜ Israel, this [3]not [1]it [2]did [4]obtain, the ˜ but election
elect

ἐπέτυχεν· οἱ δὲ λοιποὶ ἐπωρώθησαν. 8 Καθὼς γέγραπται,
did obtain; the ˜ but rest were hardened. Just as it is written,

«Ἔδωκεν αὐτοῖς ὁ Θεὸς πνεῦμα κατανύξεως,
«[2]gave [3]them - [1]God a spirit of stupor,

Ὀφθαλμοὺς τοῦ μὴ βλέπειν
Eyes - not to see

Καὶ ὦτα τοῦ μὴ ἀκούειν,
And ears - not to hear,

Ἕως τῆς σήμερον ἡμέρας.»[e]
Until the today ˜ day.»
this very day.»

9 Καὶ Δαβὶδ λέγει,
And David says,

«Γενηθήτω ἡ τράπεζα αὐτῶν εἰς παγίδα καὶ εἰς θήραν
«[1]Let [4]become - [3]table [2]their for a snare and for a trap

Καὶ εἰς σκάνδαλον καὶ εἰς ἀνταπόδομα* αὐτοῖς·
And for an offense and for a recompense to them;

10 Σκοτισθήτωσαν οἱ ὀφθαλμοὶ αὐτῶν τοῦ μὴ βλέπειν,
[1]Let [4]be [5]darkened - [3]eyes [2]their - not to see,

Καὶ τὸν νῶτον αὐτῶν διὰ παντὸς σύγκαμψον.»[f]
And - back ˜ their through all be bent.»
always be bowed down.»

Certainly not! For I also am an Israelite, of the seed of Abraham, *of* the tribe of Benjamin.
2 God has not cast away His people whom He foreknew. Or do you not know what the Scripture says of Elijah, how he pleads with God against Israel, saying,
3 *"Lord, they have killed Your prophets and torn down Your altars, and I alone am left, and they seek my life"?*
4 But what does the divine response say to him? *"I have reserved for Myself seven thousand men who have not bowed the knee to Baal."*
5 Even so then, at this present time there is a remnant according to the election of grace.
6 And if by grace, then *it is* no longer of works; otherwise grace is no longer grace. But if *it is* of works, it is no longer grace; otherwise work is no longer work.
7 What then? Israel has not obtained what it seeks; but the elect have obtained it, and the rest were blinded.
8 Just as it is written:

"God has given them a spirit of stupor,
Eyes that they should not see
And ears that they should not hear,
To this very day."

9 And David says:

"Let their table become a snare and a trap,
A stumbling block and a recompense to them.
10 *Let their eyes be darkened, so that they do not see,*
And bow down their back always."

---

[a](**11:2**) NU omits λεγων, *saying.* [b](**11:3**) 1 Kings 19:10, 14 [c](**11:4**) 1 Kings 19:18 [d](**11:6**) NU omits the rest of v. 6.
[e](**11:8**) Deut. 29:4; Is. 29:10
[f](**11:10**) Ps. 69:22, 23

***(11:9)** *ἀνταπόδομα (antapodoma).* Noun meaning *repayment.* The nuance of the word may be either positive (*reward*), negative (*retribution*), or neutral (*recompense*). Here Paul quotes Ps. 68:23 of the LXX (= English 69:22) where the word has its negative sense indicating that unbelieving Israelites, in contrast to the

11 I say then, have they stumbled that they should fall? Certainly not! But through their fall, to provoke them to jealousy, salvation *has come* to the Gentiles.
12 Now if their fall *is* riches for the world, and their failure riches for the Gentiles, how much more their fullness!
13 For I speak to you Gentiles; inasmuch as I am an apostle to the Gentiles, I magnify my ministry,
14 if by any means I may provoke to jealousy *those who are* my flesh and save some of them.
15 For if their being cast away *is* the reconciling of the world, what *will* their acceptance *be* but life from the dead?
16 For if the firstfruit *is* holy, the lump *is* also *holy;* and if the root *is* holy, so *are* the branches.
17 And if some of the branches were broken off, and you, being a wild olive tree, were grafted in among them, and with them became a partaker of the root and fatness of the olive tree,
18 do not boast against the branches. But if you do boast, *remember that* you do not support the root, but the root supports you.
19 You will say then, "Branches were broken off that I might be grafted in."
20 Well *said.* Because of unbelief they were broken off, and you stand by faith. Do not be haughty, but fear.
21 For if God did not spare the natural branches, He may not spare you either.
22 Therefore consider the goodness and severity of God: on those who fell, severity; but toward you, goodness, if you

[g](11:19) TR adds οι, *the.*
[h](11:22) NU reads χρηστοτης Θεου, *kindness of God.*

godly remnant, will be punished for their unbelief. In Luke 14:12–14 Jesus warns of inviting only people who can return your invitation so that you will "get a *reward.*" He tells His people to show charity to the unfortunate; then they will "be repaid (ἀνταποδίδωμι) at the resurrection of the just." Cf. the cognate verb ἀνταποδίδωμι, *repay, return* (Rom. 11:35; 1 Thess. 3:9); and noun ἀνταπόδοσις, *reward* (Col. 3:24).

The Restoration: Israel's Rejection Is Not Final

11 Λέγω οὖν, μὴ ἔπταισαν ἵνα
I say then, *surely it is* not *that* they stumbled in order that

πέσωσι? Μὴ γένοιτο! Ἀλλὰ τῷ αὐτῶν παραπτώματι ἡ
they might fall? [3]not [1]May [2]it [4]be! But - by their transgression -

σωτηρία τοῖς ἔθνεσιν, εἰς τὸ παραζηλῶσαι αὐτούς.
salvation *came* to the Gentiles, for - to provoke [2]to [3]jealousy [1]them.
in order

12 Εἰ δὲ τὸ παράπτωμα αὐτῶν πλοῦτος κόσμου καὶ τὸ
if ˜ But - transgression ˜ their *is the* riches of *the* world and -

ἥττημα αὐτῶν πλοῦτος ἐθνῶν, πόσῳ μᾶλλον τὸ
defeat ˜ their *is the* riches of *the* Gentiles, how much more -

πλήρωμα αὐτῶν!
fullness ˜ their!

13 Ὑμῖν γὰρ λέγω τοῖς ἔθνεσιν. Ἐφ' ὅσον μέν εἰμι
[2]to [3]you [1]For I say to the Gentiles. Inasmuch as indeed am ˜

ἐγὼ ἐθνῶν ἀπόστολος, τὴν διακονίαν μου δοξάζω, **14** εἴ
I [3]of [4]Gentiles [1]an [2]apostle, - [4]ministry [3]my [1]I [2]glorify, if

πως παραζηλώσω μου τὴν σάρκα καὶ σώσω
somehow I may provoke to jealousy my - flesh and I may save
fellow Jews

τινὰς ἐξ αὐτῶν. **15** Εἰ γὰρ ἡ ἀποβολὴ αὐτῶν
some of them. if ˜ For the casting away of them

καταλλαγὴ κόσμου, τίς ἡ πρόσληψις, εἰ μὴ
means reconciliation *for the* world, what *will be* the acceptance, if not
their

ζωὴ ἐκ νεκρῶν? **16** Εἰ δὲ ἡ ἀπαρχὴ ἁγία, καὶ τὸ φύραμα·
life from *the* dead? if ˜ But the firstfruit *is* holy, also the lump;

καὶ εἰ ἡ ῥίζα ἁγία, καὶ οἱ κλάδοι.
and if the root *is* holy, also the branches.

17 Εἰ δέ τινες τῶν κλάδων ἐξεκλάσθησαν, σὺ δὲ
if ˜ But some of the branches were broken off, you ˜ and

ἀγριέλαιος ὢν ἐνεκεντρίσθης ἐν αὐτοῖς, καὶ
[2]a [3]wild [4]olive [5]tree [1]being were grafted in them, and
who are

συγκοινωνὸς τῆς ῥίζης καὶ τῆς πιότητος τῆς
[2]a [3]partaker [4]of [5]the [6]root [7]and [8]of [9]the [10]fatness [11]of [12]the

ἐλαίας ἐγένου, **18** μὴ κατακαυχῶ τῶν κλάδων. Εἰ δὲ
[13]olive [14]tree [1]became, not ˜ do boast of the branches. if ˜ But
against

κατακαυχᾶσαι, οὐ σὺ τὴν ῥίζαν βαστάζεις, ἀλλ' ἡ ῥίζα
you do boast, *remember* [3]not [1]you [5]the [6]root [2]do [4]support, but the root

σέ. **19** Ἐρεῖς οὖν, "Ἐξεκλάσθησαν[g] κλάδοι ἵνα ἐγὼ
you. You will say then, "[2]were [3]broken [4]off [1]branches so that I

ἐγκεντρισθῶ." **20** Καλῶς. Τῇ ἀπιστίᾳ ἐξεκλάσθησαν,
might be grafted in." Well *said.* - By unbelief they were broken off,

σὺ δὲ τῇ πίστει ἕστηκας. Μὴ ὑψηλοφρόνει, ἀλλὰ φοβοῦ.
you ˜ but - by faith stand. not ˜ Do be haughty, but fear.

21 Εἰ γὰρ ὁ Θεὸς τῶν κατὰ φύσιν κλάδων οὐκ ἐφείσατο,
if ˜ For - God [4]the [6]according [7]to [8]nature [5]branches [2]not [1]did [3]spare,
natural branches

μή πως οὐδὲ σοῦ φείσεται. **22** Ἴδε οὖν χρηστότητα
perhaps neither [4]you [1]will [2]He [3]spare. See therefore *the* kindness

καὶ ἀποτομίαν Θεοῦ· ἐπὶ μὲν τοὺς πεσόντας,
and severity of God; upon on the one hand the *ones* having fallen,
those who fell,

ἀποτομίαν· ἐπὶ δὲ σέ, χρηστότητα,[h] ἐὰν
severity; upon [2]on [3]the [4]other [5]hand [1]you, kindness, if

ἐπιμείνῃς τῇ χρηστότητι. Ἐπεὶ καὶ σὺ ἐκκοπήσῃ. 23 Καὶ
you remain in the kindness. Since also ˜ you will be cut out. [2]also
His

ἐκεῖνοι δέ, ἐὰν μὴ ἐπιμείνωσι τῇ ἀπιστίᾳ,
[3]those [1]And, if [3]not [1]they [2]do [4]remain - in unbelief,

ἐγκεντρισθήσονται, δυνατὸς γὰρ ἐστιν ὁ Θεὸς πάλιν
they will be grafted in, [4]able [1]for [3]is - [2]God again

ἐγκεντρίσαι αὐτούς. 24 Εἰ γὰρ σὺ ἐκ τῆς κατὰ
to graft in ˜ them. if ˜ For you [3]out [4]of [5]the [9]according [10]to
by

φύσιν ἐξεκόπης ἀγριελαίου, καὶ παρὰ φύσιν ἐνεκεντρίσθης
[11]nature [1]were [2]cut [6]wild [7]olive [8]tree, and against nature you were grafted

εἰς καλλιέλαιον, πόσῳ μᾶλλον οὗτοι, οἱ κατὰ
into a cultivated olive tree, how much more these, the *ones* according to
the natural

φύσιν, ἐγκεντρισθήσονται τῇ ἰδίᾳ ἐλαίᾳ?
nature, will be grafted into - their own olive tree?
ones,

25 Οὐ γὰρ θέλω ὑμᾶς ἀγνοεῖν, ἀδελφοί, τὸ
[4]not [1]For [2]I [3]do [5]desire you to be ignorant, brothers, -

μυστήριον τοῦτο, ἵνα μὴ ἦτε παρ' ἑαυτοῖς
of mystery ˜ this, in order that not ˜ you be by yourselves
lest in your own opinion

φρόνιμοι, ὅτι πώρωσις ἀπὸ μέρους τῷ Ἰσραὴλ γέγονεν
wise, that hardening from part - to Israel has happened
in

ἄχρις οὗ τὸ πλήρωμα τῶν ἐθνῶν εἰσέλθῃ. 26 Καὶ οὕτω πᾶς
until the fullness of the Gentiles comes in. And thus all

Ἰσραὴλ σωθήσεται, καθὼς γέγραπται,
Israel will be saved, just as it is written,

«Ἥξει ἐκ Σιὼν ὁ Ῥυόμενος,
«[4]will [5]come [6]out [7]of [8]Zion [1]The [2]*One* [3]delivering,
The Deliverer,

Καὶ ἀποστρέψει ἀσεβείας* ἀπὸ Ἰακώβ·
And He will turn away ungodliness from Jacob;

27 Καὶ αὕτη αὐτοῖς ἡ παρ' ἐμοῦ διαθήκη,»
And this *is* [5]with [6]them [1]the [3]from [4]Me [2]covenant,»

«Ὅταν ἀφέλωμαι τὰς ἁμαρτίας αὐτῶν.» [i]
«When I take away - sins ˜ their.»

28 Κατὰ μὲν τὸ εὐαγγέλιον ἐχθροὶ
[5]according [6]to [1]On [2]the [3]one [4]hand the gospel *they are* enemies

δι' ὑμᾶς, κατὰ δὲ τὴν ἐκλογὴν
because of you, [5]according [6]to [1]on [2]the [3]other [4]hand the election

ἀγαπητοὶ διὰ τοὺς πατέρας. 29 Ἀμεταμέλητα γὰρ
they are beloved on account of the fathers. [9]*are* [10]irrevocable [1]For

τὰ χαρίσματα καὶ ἡ κλῆσις τοῦ Θεοῦ. 30 Ὥσπερ γὰρ
[2]the [3]gifts [4]and [5]the [6]calling - [7]of [8]God. [2]just [3]as [1]For

καὶ ὑμεῖς ποτε ἠπειθήσατε τῷ Θεῷ, νῦν δὲ
also ˜ you once disobeyed - God, now ˜ but

ἠλεήθητε τῇ τούτων ἀπειθείᾳ, 31 οὕτω καὶ
you were shown mercy by the [2]of [3]these [1]disobedience, so also
their

οὗτοι νῦν ἠπείθησαν, τῷ ὑμετέρῳ ἐλέει ἵνα καὶ
these now disobeyed, - by your mercy in order that also ˜
the mercy shown to you

αὐτοὶ ἐλεηθῶσι. 32 Συνέκλεισε γὰρ ὁ Θεὸς τοὺς
they might be shown mercy. [3]shut [4]up [1]For - [2]God -

πάντας εἰς ἀπείθειαν ἵνα τοὺς πάντας ἐλεήσῃ.
all to disobedience so that - [5]to [6]all [1]He [2]might [3]show [4]mercy.

continue in *His* goodness. Otherwise you also will be cut off.
23 And they also, if they do not continue in unbelief, will be grafted in, for God is able to graft them in again.
24 For if you were cut out of the olive tree which is wild by nature, and were grafted contrary to nature into a cultivated olive tree, how much more will these, who *are* natural *branches,* be grafted into their own olive tree?
25 For I do not desire, brethren, that you should be ignorant of this mystery, lest you should be wise in your own opinion, that blindness in part has happened to Israel until the fullness of the Gentiles has come in.
26 And so all Israel will be saved, as it is written:

"The Deliverer will come
out of Zion,
And He will turn away
ungodliness from Jacob;
27 *For this is My covenant*
with them,
When I take away their
sins."

28 Concerning the gospel *they are* enemies for your sake, but concerning the election *they are* beloved for the sake of the fathers.
29 For the gifts and the calling of God *are* irrevocable.
30 For as you were once disobedient to God, yet have now obtained mercy through their disobedience,
31 even so these also have now been disobedient, that through the mercy shown you they also may obtain mercy.
32 For God has committed them all to disobedience, that He might have mercy on all.

---

[i]**(11:27)** Is. 59:20, 21

***(11:26)** *ἀσέβεια (asebeia).* Noun meaning *ungodliness, impiety.* It is derived from the verb ἀσεβέω, an α- negative compound of σέβω *(reverence, worship),* hence meaning *to act impiously* (2 Pet. 2:6) or *commit impious deeds* (Jude 15). The noun ἀσέβεια is used to describe the irreligious attitudes and conduct of unbelievers (Rom. 1:18). It designates irreligion in general (as here in Rom. 11:26). Cf. the cognate adjective ἀσεβής, *impious, godless* (2 Pet. 3:7; often a substan-

33 Oh, the depth of the riches
both of the wisdom and knowledge of God! How unsearchable
are His judgments and His ways
past finding out!

34 *"For who has known the*
mind of the LORD?
Or who has become His
counselor?"
35 *"Or who has first given to*
Him
And it shall be repaid to
him?"

36 For of Him and through
Him and to Him *are* all things,
to whom *be* glory forever.
Amen.

12 I beseech you there-
fore, brethren, by the
mercies of God, that you present your bodies a living sacrifice, holy, acceptable to God,
which is your reasonable service.
2 And do not be conformed
to this world, but be transformed by the renewing of your
mind, that you may prove what
is that good and acceptable and
perfect will of God.
3 For I say, through the
grace given to me, to everyone
who is among you, not to think
of himself more highly than he
ought to think, but to think soberly, as God has dealt to each
one a measure of faith.
4 For as we have many
members in one body, but all
the members do not have the
same function,
5 so we, *being* many, are one
body in Christ, and individually
members of one another.

33 Ὦ βάθος πλούτου καὶ σοφίας καὶ γνώσεως
O *the* depth of *the* riches and of *the* wisdom and of *the* knowledge

Θεοῦ! Ὡς ἀνεξερεύνητα τὰ κρίματα αὐτοῦ καὶ ἀνεξιχνίαστοι
of God! How unsearchable *are* - judgments ˜ His and untraceable

αἱ ὁδοὶ αὐτοῦ!
- ways ˜ His!

34 «Τίς γὰρ ἔγνω νοῦν Κυρίου?
«who ˜ For knew *the* mind of *the* Lord?

Ἢ τίς σύμβουλος αὐτοῦ ἐγένετο?»[j]
Or who [3]counselor [2]His [1]became?»

35 «Ἢ τίς προέδωκεν αὐτῷ,
«Or who gave beforehand to Him,

Καὶ ἀνταποδοθήσεται αὐτῷ?»[k]
And it shall be repaid to him?»

36 Ὅτι ἐξ αὐτοῦ καὶ δι' αὐτοῦ καὶ εἰς αὐτὸν τὰ πάντα·
Because of Him and through Him and to Him *are* - all *things;*

αὐτῷ ἡ δόξα εἰς τοὺς αἰῶνας. Ἀμήν.
to Him *be* the glory to the ages. Amen.
forever. So be it.

Live in the Will of God

12 1 Παρακαλῶ οὖν ὑμᾶς, ἀδελφοί, διὰ τῶν
I urge therefore ˜ you, brothers, through the

οἰκτιρμῶν τοῦ Θεοῦ, παραστῆσαι τὰ σώματα ὑμῶν θυσίαν
compassions - of God, to present - bodies ˜ your a sacrifice ˜

ζῶσαν, ἁγίαν, εὐάρεστον τῷ Θεῷ, τὴν λογικὴν λατρείαν
living, holy, well pleasing - to God, - [2]reasonable [3]service

ὑμῶν. 2 Καὶ μὴ συσχηματίζεσθε τῷ αἰῶνι τούτῳ, ἀλλὰ
[1]your. And not ˜ do be conformed - to age ˜ this, but

μεταμορφοῦσθε τῇ ἀνακαινώσει τοῦ νοὸς ὑμῶν,[a] εἰς τὸ
be transformed by the renewing - of mind ˜ your, for -
so that

δοκιμάζειν ὑμᾶς τί τὸ θέλημα τοῦ Θεοῦ, τὸ ἀγαθὸν καὶ
to prove you what *is* the will - of God, the good and
you may prove

εὐάρεστον καὶ τέλειον.
well pleasing and perfect.

Serve God with Spiritual Gifts

3 Λέγω γάρ, διὰ τῆς χάριτος τῆς δοθείσης
[2]I [3]say [1]For, through the grace the *one* having been given
given

μοι, παντὶ τῷ ὄντι ἐν ὑμῖν, μὴ ὑπερφρονεῖν παρ'
to me, to every - *one* being among you, not to think too highly beyond
everyone who is

ὃ δεῖ φρονεῖν, ἀλλὰ φρονεῖν εἰς τὸ σωφρονεῖν,
what it is necessary to think, but to think - - to be reasonable,
you should think,

ἑκάστῳ ὡς ὁ Θεὸς ἐμέρισε μέτρον πίστεως. 4 Καθάπερ γὰρ
to each as - God apportioned a measure of faith. [2]just [3]as [1]For

ἐν ἑνὶ σώματι μέλη πολλὰ ἔχομεν, τὰ δὲ μέλη πάντα
in one body [4]members [3]many [1]we [2]have, [7]the [5]but [8]members [6]all

οὐ τὴν αὐτὴν ἔχει πρᾶξιν, 5 οὕτως οἱ πολλοὶ ἕν
[10]not [12]the [13]same [9]do [11]have use, so - *being* many [3]one

σῶμά ἐσμεν ἐν Χριστῷ ὁ δὲ καθ' εἷς ἀλλήλων
[4]body [1]we [2]are in Christ - and by one [2]of [3]one [4]another
individually

---

j(**11:34**) Is. 40:13; Jer. 23:18
k(**11:35**) Job 41:11
a(**12:2**) NU omits υμων, *your.*

tive as in 1 Tim. 1:9); and the antonym εὐσέβεια, *godliness, religion* (2 Pet. 1:3).

μέλη. 6 Ἔχοντες δὲ χαρίσματα κατὰ τὴν χάριν τὴν
[1]members. Having then gifts [2]according [3]to [4]the [5]grace -

δοθεῖσαν ἡμῖν διάφορα, εἴτε προφητείαν,*
[6]having [7]been [8]given [9]to [10]us [1]differing, whether prophecy,

κατὰ τὴν ἀναλογίαν τῆς πίστεως· 7 εἴτε διακονίαν, ἐν
according to the proportion - of faith; whether ministry, in

τῇ διακονίᾳ· εἴτε ὁ διδάσκων, ἐν τῇ διδασκαλίᾳ· 8 εἴτε
the ministry; whether - teaching, in the teaching; whether
our

ὁ παρακαλῶν, ἐν τῇ παρακλήσει· ὁ μεταδιδούς, ἐν
the *one* exhorting, in the exhortation; the *one* sharing, with

ἁπλότητι· ὁ προϊστάμενος, ἐν σπουδῇ· ὁ
simplicity; the *one* leading, with diligence; the *one*

ἐλεῶν, ἐν ἱλαρότητι.
showing mercy, with cheerfulness.

Behave Like a Christian

9 Ἡ ἀγάπη ἀνυπόκριτος. Ἀποστυγοῦντες τὸ πονηρόν,
- *Let* love *be* unhypocritical. Abhorring the evil,

κολλώμενοι τῷ ἀγαθῷ. 10 Τῇ φιλαδελφίᾳ εἰς ἀλλήλους
clinging to the good. - With brotherly love for one another

φιλόστοργοι, τῇ τιμῇ ἀλλήλους προηγούμενοι, 11 τῇ
warmly affectionate, - in honor [2]one [3]another [1]preferring, -

σπουδῇ μὴ ὀκνηροί, τῷ πνεύματι ζέοντες, τῷ Κυρίῳ
in diligence not lagging, - in spirit boiling, [2]the [3]Lord
glowing,

δουλεύοντες, 12 τῇ ἐλπίδι χαίροντες, τῇ θλίψει
[1]serving, - in hope rejoicing, - in tribulation

ὑπομένοντες, τῇ προσευχῇ προσκαρτεροῦντες, 13 ταῖς
bearing up, - in prayer continuing steadfastly, [2]in [3]the

χρείαις τῶν ἁγίων κοινωνοῦντες, τὴν φιλοξενίαν διώκοντες.
[4]needs [5]of [6]the [7]saints [1]sharing, - hospitality ˜ pursuing.

14 Εὐλογεῖτε τοὺς διώκοντας ὑμᾶς, εὐλογεῖτε καὶ μὴ
Bless the *ones* persecuting you, bless and not ˜
those who persecute

καταρᾶσθε. 15 Χαίρειν μετὰ χαιρόντων καὶ κλαίειν μετὰ
do curse. To rejoice with rejoicing *ones* and to weep with
Rejoice weep

κλαιόντων. 16 Τὸ αὐτὸ εἰς ἀλλήλους φρονοῦντες. Μὴ
weeping *ones.* [2]the [3]same [4]*thing* [5]to [6]one [7]another [1]Minding. Not

τὰ ὑψηλὰ φρονοῦντες, ἀλλὰ τοῖς ταπεινοῖς
[2]the [3]high [4]*things* [1]minding, but [2]with [3]the [4]humble [5]*people*

συναπαγόμενοι. Μὴ γίνεσθε φρόνιμοι παρ' ἑαυτοῖς.
[1]associating. not ˜ Do become wise by yourselves.
in your own opinion.

17 Μηδενὶ κακὸν ἀντὶ κακοῦ ἀποδιδόντες. Προνοούμενοι
[2]to [3]no [4]one [5]evil [6]for [7]evil [1]Repaying. Having regard for

καλὰ ἐνώπιον πάντων ἀνθρώπων. 18 Εἰ δυνατόν, τὸ
noble *things* before all men. If possible, the *thing*
as much as

ἐξ ὑμῶν, μετὰ πάντων ἀνθρώπων εἰρηνεύοντες. 19 Μὴ
of you, [3]with [4]all [5]men [1]keeping [2]peace. Not
depends on

ἑαυτοὺς ἐκδικοῦντες, ἀγαπητοί, ἀλλὰ δότε τόπον τῇ ὀργῇ·
yourselves ˜ avenging, beloved *ones,* but give place - to wrath;

6 Having then gifts differing according to the grace that is given to us, *let us use them:* if prophecy, *let us prophesy* in proportion to our faith;
7 or ministry, *let us use it* in *our* ministering; he who teaches, in teaching;
8 he who exhorts, in exhortation; he who gives, with liberality; he who leads, with diligence; he who shows mercy, with cheerfulness.
9 *Let* love *be* without hypocrisy. Abhor what is evil. Cling to what is good.
10 *Be* kindly affectionate to one another with brotherly love, in honor giving preference to one another;
11 not lagging in diligence, fervent in spirit, serving the Lord;
12 rejoicing in hope, patient in tribulation, continuing steadfastly in prayer;
13 distributing to the needs of the saints, given to hospitality.
14 Bless those who persecute you; bless and do not curse.
15 Rejoice with those who rejoice, and weep with those who weep.
16 Be of the same mind toward one another. Do not set your mind on high things, but associate with the humble. Do not be wise in your own opinion.
17 Repay no one evil for evil. Have regard for good things in the sight of all men.
18 If it is possible, as much as depends on you, live peaceably with all men.
19 Beloved, do not avenge yourselves, but *rather* give place to wrath; for it is written,

***(12:6)** *προφητεία (prophēteia).* Noun meaning *prophecy.* The word may imply prophetic activity (as Rev. 11:6), the prophetic utterance (as 2 Pet. 1:20), or the gift of prophesying (as here in Rom. 12:6; cf. 1 Cor. 12:10). The terms in this word group are derived from a compound of the preposition *πρό, before,* and the verb *φημί, speak.* Thus the cognate noun *προφήτης, prophet,* is one who speaks before and for God, giving God's revealed word to others (whether for the future or for the present). Cf. also the cognate verb *προφητεύω, prophesy.*

"Vengeance is Mine, I will repay," says the Lord.
20 Therefore

> *"If your enemy is hungry,*
> *feed him;*
> *If he is thirsty, give him a*
> *drink;*
> *For in so doing you will*
> *heap coals of fire on his*
> *head."*

21 Do not be overcome by evil, but overcome evil with good.

13 Let every soul be subject to the governing authorities. For there is no authority except from God, and the authorities that exist are appointed by God.
2 Therefore whoever resists the authority resists the ordinance of God, and those who resist will bring judgment on themselves.
3 For rulers are not a terror to good works, but to evil. Do you want to be unafraid of the authority? Do what is good, and you will have praise from the same.
4 For he is God's minister to you for good. But if you do evil, be afraid; for he does not bear the sword in vain; for he is God's minister, an avenger to *execute* wrath on him who practices evil.
5 Therefore *you* must be subject, not only because of wrath but also for conscience' sake.
6 For because of this you also pay taxes, for they are God's ministers attending continually to this very thing.
7 Render therefore to all their due: taxes to whom taxes *are due,* customs to whom customs, fear to whom fear, honor

γέγραπται γάρ, «Ἐμοὶ ἐκδίκησις, ἐγὼ ἀνταποδώσω,» [b]
[2]it [3]is [4]written [1]for, «To Me *is* vengeance, I will repay,»
«Vengeance is Mine,

λέγει Κύριος.
says *the* Lord.

20 «Ἐὰν οὖν [c] πεινᾷ ὁ ἐχθρός σου, ψώμιζε αὐτόν·
«If therefore [3]hungers - [2]enemy [1]your, feed him;
Ἐὰν διψᾷ, πότιζε αὐτόν·
If he thirsts, give [2]a [3]drink [1]him;
Τοῦτο γὰρ ποιῶν, ἄνθρακας πυρὸς σωρεύσεις
[3]this [1]For [2]doing, [8]coals [9]of [10]fire [4]you [5]will [6]be [7]heaping
ἐπὶ τὴν κεφαλὴν αὐτοῦ.» [d]
on - head ˜ his.»

21 Μὴ νικῶ ὑπὸ τοῦ κακοῦ, ἀλλὰ νίκα ἐν τῷ
not ˜ Do be overcome by - evil, but overcome [2]by -
ἀγαθῷ τὸ κακόν.
[3]good - [1]evil.

Submit to Government

13 **1** Πᾶσα ψυχὴ ἐξουσίαις ὑπερεχούσαις ὑποτασσέσθω.
[2]every [3]soul [5]to [8]authorities [6]*the* [7]governing [1]Let [4]submit.
Οὐ γάρ ἐστιν ἐξουσία εἰ μὴ ὑπὸ Θεοῦ, αἱ δὲ οὖσαι
[12]not [9]For [10]*there* [11]is an authority if not by God, the ˜ and being ˜
except that exist
ἐξουσίαι [a] ὑπὸ τοῦ Θεοῦ τεταγμέναι εἰσίν. **2** Ὥστε ὁ
authorities [3]by - [4]God [2]instituted [1]are. Consequently the *one*
ἀντιτασσόμενος τῇ ἐξουσίᾳ, τῇ τοῦ Θεοῦ διαταγῇ
resisting the authority, [3]the - [5]of [6]God [4]ordinance
ἀνθέστηκεν, οἱ δὲ ἀνθεστηκότες ἑαυτοῖς κρίμα
[1]has [2]opposed, [8]the [9]*ones* [7]and [10]opposing [14]to [15]themselves [13]judgment
λήμψονται. **3** Οἱ γὰρ ἄρχοντες οὐκ εἰσὶ φόβος τῶν ἀγαθῶν
[11]will [12]receive. - For rulers not ˜ are a fear - of good
ἔργων ἀλλὰ τῶν κακῶν. Θέλεις δὲ μὴ φοβεῖσθαι τὴν
works but - of bad *ones.* [2]do [3]you [4]wish [1]And not to fear the
ἐξουσίαν? Τὸ ἀγαθὸν ποίει καὶ ἕξεις ἔπαινον ἐξ αὐτῆς·
authority? [2]the [3]good [1]Do and you will have praise from it;
4 Θεοῦ γὰρ διάκονός ἐστι σοὶ εἰς τὸ ἀγαθόν. Ἐὰν δὲ τὸ
[6]of [7]God [1]for [4]a [5]servant [2]it [3]is to you for - good. if ˜ But -
κακὸν ποιῇς, φοβοῦ, οὐ γὰρ εἰκῇ τὴν μάχαιραν
[3]bad [1]you [2]do, fear, [4]not [1]for [8]in [9]vain [6]the [7]sword
φορεῖ· Θεοῦ γὰρ διάκονός ἐστιν, ἔκδικος εἰς ὀργὴν
[2]it [3]does [5]bear; [15]of [16]God [10]for [13]a [14]servant [11]it [12]is, an avenger for wrath
τῷ τὸ κακὸν πράσσοντι. **5** Διὸ ἀνάγκη
to the *one* - bad ˜ practicing. Therefore *it is* necessary
ὑποτάσσεσθαι, οὐ μόνον διὰ τὴν ὀργήν, ἀλλὰ καὶ
to be subject, not only on account of - wrath, but also
διὰ τὴν συνείδησιν. **6** Διὰ τοῦτο γὰρ καὶ
on account of - conscience. [2]on [3]account [4]of [5]this [1]For also
φόρους τελεῖτε, λειτουργοὶ γὰρ Θεοῦ εἰσιν εἰς αὐτὸ
[3]taxes [1]you [2]pay, [7]ministers [4]for [8]of [9]God [5]they [6]are to itself
this
τοῦτο προσκαρτεροῦντες. **7** Ἀπόδοτε οὖν πᾶσι τὰς
this *thing* attending continually. Render therefore to all the
very thing their
ὀφειλάς· τῷ τὸν φόρον τὸν φόρον, τῷ τὸ
dues; to the *one* - taxes *are due* - taxes, to the *one* -
τέλος τὸ τέλος, τῷ τὸν φόβον τὸν φόβον,
customs *are due* - customs, to the *one* - fear *is due* - fear,

[b](12:19) Deut. 32:35
[c](12:20) NU reads Αλλα εαν, *But if.*
[d](12:20) Prov. 25:21, 22
[a](13:1) NU omits εξουσιαι, *authorities.*

τῷ τὴν τιμὴν τὴν τιμήν.
to the *one* - honor *is due* - honor.

Love Your Neighbor

8 Μηδενὶ μηδὲν ὀφείλετε εἰ μὴ τὸ ἀγαπᾶν
[3]to [4]no [5]one [2]nothing [1]Owe if not - to love
anyone except

ἀλλήλους, ὁ γὰρ ἀγαπῶν τὸν ἕτερον, νόμον πεπλήρωκε.
one another, [2]the [3]*one* [1]for loving the other, [3]*the* [4]law [1]has [2]fulfilled.

9 Τὸ γάρ, «Οὐ μοιχεύσεις,» «Οὐ φονεύσεις,» «Οὐ
- For, «[3]not [1]You [2]shall commit adultery,» «[3]not [1]You [2]shall kill,» «[3]not

κλέψεις,»[b] «Οὐκ ἐπιθυμήσεις,»[c] καὶ εἴ τις ἑτέρα
[1]You [2]shall steal,» «[3]not [1]You [2]shall covet,» and if *there is* any different
other

ἐντολή, ἐν τούτῳ τῷ λόγῳ ἀνακεφαλαιοῦται, ἐν τῷ,
commandment, in this - word it is summed up, in the,
this,

«Ἀγαπήσεις τὸν πλησίον σου ὡς σεαυτόν.»[d] 10 Ἡ ἀγάπη
«You shall love - neighbor ˜ your as yourself.» - Love

τῷ πλησίον κακὸν οὐκ ἐργάζεται· πλήρωμα οὖν
[5]to [6]a [7]neighbor [4]bad [2]not [1]does [3]work; [11]*the* [12]fulfillment [8]therefore
harm

νόμου ἡ ἀγάπη.
[13]of [14]law - [9]love [10]*is*.

Put On Christ; Put Off Carnality

11 Καὶ τοῦτο, εἰδότες τὸν καιρόν, ὅτι ὥρα ἡμᾶς[e]
And *do* this, knowing the season, that [1]*it* [2]*is* [4]*the* [5]hour [6]for [7]us
time, time

ἤδη ἐξ ὕπνου ἐγερθῆναι, νῦν γὰρ ἐγγύτερον ἡμῶν ἡ
[3]already [11]out [12]of [13]sleep [8]to [9]be [10]raised, now ˜ for [4]nearer [1]our -

σωτηρία ἢ ὅτε ἐπιστεύσαμεν. 12 Ἡ νὺξ προέκοψεν, ἡ
[2]salvation [3]*is* than when we *first* believed. The night advanced, the ˜
is far spent,

δὲ ἡμέρα ἤγγικεν. Ἀποθώμεθα οὖν τὰ ἔργα τοῦ
and day has drawn near. Let us put off therefore the works -

σκότους, καὶ ἐνδυσώμεθα τὰ ὅπλα τοῦ φωτός. 13 Ὡς ἐν
of darkness, and let us put on the weapons of the light. As in

ἡμέρᾳ, εὐσχημόνως περιπατήσωμεν, μὴ κώμοις καὶ
the day, [4]properly [1]let [2]us [3]walk, not in revelries and

μέθαις, μὴ κοίταις καὶ ἀσελγείαις, μὴ ἔριδι καὶ ζήλῳ.
drinking bouts, not in orgies and debaucheries, not in strife and jealousy.

14 Ἀλλ' ἐνδύσασθε τὸν Κύριον Ἰησοῦν Χριστόν, καὶ τῆς
But put on the Lord Jesus Christ, and [5]*for* [6]the

σαρκὸς* πρόνοιαν μὴ ποιεῖσθε εἰς ἐπιθυμίας.
[7]flesh [4]provision [2]not [1]do [3]make for *its* lusts.

The Law of Liberty

14 1 Τὸν δὲ ἀσθενοῦντα τῇ πίστει
[3]the [4]*one* [1]Now [5]being [6]weak [7]in [8]the [9]faith

προσλαμβάνεσθε, μὴ εἰς διακρίσεις διαλογισμῶν. 2 Ὃς μὲν
[2]receive, not for disputes of reasonings. One indeed
over opinions.

πιστεύει φαγεῖν πάντα, ὁ δὲ ἀσθενῶν
believes *he is allowed* to eat all *things*, [2]the [3]*one* [1]but being weak

λάχανα ἐσθίει. 3 Ὁ ἐσθίων τὸν μὴ ἐσθίοντα μὴ
vegetables ˜ eats. [3]the [4]*one* [5]eating [7]the [8]*one* [9]not [10]eating [2]not

to whom honor.
8 Owe no one anything except to love one another, for he who loves another has fulfilled the law.
9 For the commandments, *"You shall not commit adultery," "You shall not murder," "You shall not steal," "You shall not bear false witness," "You shall not covet,"* and if *there is* any other commandment, are *all* summed up in this saying, namely, *"You shall love your neighbor as yourself."*
10 Love does no harm to a neighbor; therefore love *is* the fulfillment of the law.
11 And *do* this, knowing the time, that now *it is* high time to awake out of sleep; for now our salvation *is* nearer than when we *first* believed.
12 The night is far spent, the day is at hand. Therefore let us cast off the works of darkness, and let us put on the armor of light.
13 Let us walk properly, as in the day, not in revelry and drunkenness, not in lewdness and lust, not in strife and envy.
14 But put on the Lord Jesus Christ, and make no provision for the flesh, to *fulfill its* lusts.
14 Receive one who is weak in the faith, *but* not to disputes over doubtful things.
2 For one believes he may eat all things, but he who is weak eats *only* vegetables.
3 Let not him who eats despise him who does not eat, and

---

b(13:9) TR adds *ου ψευδομαρτυρησεις, You shall not bear false witness.*
c(13:9) Ex. 20:13–15, 17; Deut. 5:17–19, 21
d(13:9) Lev. 19:18
e(13:11) NU reads *υμας, for you.*

*(13:14) σάρξ *(sarx)*. Very common noun meaning *flesh*. In its literal sense, the word refers to the substance of the body, whether of animals or persons (1 Cor. 15:39; 1 Pet. 4:1). In its idiomatic use, it indicates the human race or personhood (Matt. 24:22; 1 Pet. 1:24). In an ethical and spiritual sense, σαρξ is the lower nature of a person, the seat and vehicle of sinful desires (Rom. 7:25; 8:4–9; and here; Gal. 5:16, 17). Cf. the cognate adjectives σαρκικός

let not him who does not eat
judge him who eats; for God
has received him.
4 Who are you to judge another's servant? To his own
master he stands or falls. Indeed, he will be made to stand,
for God is able to make him
stand.
5 One person esteems *one*
day above another; another esteems every day *alike.* Let
each be fully convinced in his
own mind.
6 He who observes the day,
observes *it* to the Lord; and he
who does not observe the day,
to the Lord he does not observe *it.* He who eats, eats to
the Lord, for he gives God
thanks; and he who does not
eat, to the Lord he does not
eat, and gives God thanks.
7 For none of us lives to himself, and no one dies to himself.
8 For if we live, we live to
the Lord; and if we die, we die
to the Lord. Therefore,
whether we live or die, we are
the Lord's.
9 For to this end Christ died
and rose and lived again, that
He might be Lord of both the
dead and the living.
10 But why do you judge your
brother? Or why do you show
contempt for your brother? For
we shall all stand before the
judgment seat of Christ.
11 For it is written:

"As I live, says the LORD,
Every knee shall bow to
Me,
And every tongue shall
confess to God."

12 So then each of us shall
give account of himself to God.
13 Therefore let us not judge
one another anymore, but

ἐξουθενείτω, καὶ ὁ μὴ ἐσθίων τὸν ἐσθίοντα μὴ
[1]Let [6]despise, and [3]the [4]*one* [5]not [6]eating [8]the [9]*one* [10]eating [2]not

κρινέτω, ὁ Θεὸς γὰρ αὐτὸν προσελάβετο. **4** Σὺ τίς εἶ
[1]let [7]judge, - God ˜ for him ˜ received. [3]you [1]Who [2]are

ὁ κρίνων ἀλλότριον οἰκέτην? Τῷ
the *one* judging [4]belonging [5]to [6]another [1]a [2]household [3]servant? -

ἰδίῳ κυρίῳ στήκει ἢ πίπτει. Σταθήσεται δέ, δυνατὸς
To his own master he stands or he falls. [2]he [3]will [4]stand [1]But, [8]able

γάρ ἐστιν ὁ Θεὸς[a] στῆσαι αὐτόν. **5** Ὃς μὲν κρίνει
[5]for [7]is - [6]God to make stand ˜ him. One indeed judges

ἡμέραν παρ' ἡμέραν, ὃς δὲ κρίνει πᾶσαν ἡμέραν.
a day above a day, one ˜ (another) but judges every day *the same.*

Ἕκαστος ἐν τῷ ἰδίῳ νοῒ πληροφορείσθω. **6** Ὁ
[2]each [6]in - [7]his [8]own [9]mind [1]Let [3]be [4]fully [5]convinced. The *one*

φρονῶν τὴν ἡμέραν, Κυρίῳ φρονεῖ·[b] καὶ ὁ μὴ
being intent on (observing) the day, to *the* Lord he is intent on *it;* (observes) and the *one* not

φρονῶν τὴν ἡμέραν, Κυρίῳ οὐ φρονεῖ. Καὶ
being intent on (observing) the day, to *the* Lord [3]not [1]he [2]is intent on *it.* (does observe) And

ὁ ἐσθίων, Κυρίῳ ἐσθίει, εὐχαριστεῖ γὰρ τῷ Θεῷ·
the *one* eating, [2]to [3]*the* [4]Lord [1]eats, [6]he [7]gives [8]thanks [5]for - to God;

καὶ ὁ μὴ ἐσθίων Κυρίῳ οὐκ ἐσθίει, καὶ εὐχαριστεῖ
and the *one* not eating to *the* Lord [2]not [1]does [3]eat, and he gives thanks

τῷ Θεῷ. **7** Οὐδεὶς γὰρ ἡμῶν ἑαυτῷ ζῇ καὶ οὐδεὶς
- to God. [2]no [3]one [1]For of us [2]to [3]himself [1]lives and no one

ἑαυτῷ ἀποθνήσκει. **8** Ἐάν τε γὰρ ζῶμεν, τῷ Κυρίῳ
[2]to [3]himself [1]dies. whether ˜ For we live, to the Lord

ζῶμεν, ἐάν τε ἀποθνήσκωμεν, τῷ Κυρίῳ ἀποθνήσκομεν.
we live, whether we die, to the Lord we die.

Ἐάν τε οὖν ζῶμεν, ἐάν τε ἀποθνήσκωμεν, τοῦ Κυρίου
Whether therefore we live, whether we die, [3]of [4]the [5]Lord

ἐσμέν. **9** Εἰς τοῦτο γὰρ Χριστὸς καὶ ἀπέθανε καὶ
[1]we [2]are. [2]for [3]this [4]*reason* [1]For Christ also died and

ἀνέστη[c] καὶ ἔζησεν, ἵνα καὶ νεκρῶν καὶ ζώντων
rose and lived *again,* so that both of *the* dead and of *the* living

κυριεύσῃ. **10** Σὺ δὲ τί κρίνεις τὸν ἀδελφόν σου? Ἢ
He might be Lord. [4]you [1]But [2]why [3]do [5]judge - brother ˜ your? Or

καὶ σὺ τί ἐξουθενεῖς τὸν ἀδελφόν σου? Πάντες γὰρ
also [3]you [1]why [2]do [4]despise - brother ˜ your? [3]all [1]For

παραστησόμεθα τῷ βήματι τοῦ Χριστοῦ.[d]
[2]we shall stand before the judgment seat - of Christ.

11 Γέγραπται γάρ,
[2]it [3]is [4]written [1]For,

«Ζῶ ἐγώ, λέγει Κύριος,
«*As* live ˜ I, says *the* Lord,

Ὅτι ἐμοὶ κάμψει πᾶν γόνυ,
- [5]to [6]Me [3]shall [4]bend [1]Every [2]knee,

Καὶ πᾶσα γλῶσσα ἐξομολογήσεται τῷ Θεῷ.»[e]
And every tongue shall confess - to God.»

12 Ἄρα οὖν ἕκαστος ἡμῶν περὶ ἑαυτοῦ λόγον
So then each of us [5]concerning [6]himself [3]an [4]account

δώσει τῷ Θεῷ.
[1]shall [2]give - to God.

13 Μηκέτι οὖν ἀλλήλους κρίνωμεν, ἀλλὰ τοῦτο
[4]no [5]longer [1]Therefore [7]one [8]another [2]let [3]us [6]judge, but this ˜

[a](**14:4**) NU reads ο Κυριος, *the Lord.* [b](**14:6**) NU omits the rest of this sentence. [c](**14:9**) NU omits και ανεστη, *and rose.* [d](**14:10**) NU reads Θεου, *of God.* [e](**14:11**) Is. 45:23

and σαρκινος, both meaning *fleshly.*

κρίνατε μᾶλλον, τὸ μὴ τιθέναι πρόσκομμα τῷ ἀδελφῷ
judge rather, - not to put a stumbling block to the brother
before our

ἢ σκάνδαλον.
or an offense.

The Law of Love

14 Οἶδα καὶ πέπεισμαι ἐν Κυρίῳ Ἰησοῦ ὅτι οὐδὲν
I know and have been persuaded in *the* Lord Jesus that nothing
am convinced

κοινὸν δι' αὐτοῦ, εἰ μὴ τῷ λογιζομένῳ τι
is common through itself, if not to the *one* considering anything
by except

κοινὸν εἶναι, ἐκείνῳ κοινόν. 15 Εἰ δὲ διὰ
[3]common [1]to [2]be, to that *one* *it is* common. if ~ But on account of

βρῶμα ὁ ἀδελφός σου λυπεῖται, οὐκέτι κατὰ ἀγάπην
food - brother ~ your is grieved, [3]no [4]longer [6]according [7]to [8]love

περιπατεῖς. Μὴ τῷ βρώματί σου ἐκεῖνον ἀπόλλυε,
[1]you [2]are [5]walking. [10]not - [12]with [14]food [13]your [15]that [16]*one* [9]Do [11]destroy,

ὑπὲρ οὗ Χριστὸς ἀπέθανε. 16 Μὴ βλασφημείσθω
on behalf of whom Christ died. [3]not [2]do [4]let [7]be [8]blasphemed
slandered

οὖν ὑμῶν τὸ ἀγαθόν. 17 Οὐ γάρ ἐστιν ἡ βασιλεία τοῦ
[1]Therefore [5]your - [6]good. [7]not [1]For [6]is [2]the [3]kingdom -

Θεοῦ βρῶσις καὶ πόσις, ἀλλὰ δικαιοσύνη καὶ εἰρήνη καὶ
[4]of [5]God eating and drinking, but righteousness and peace and

χαρὰ ἐν Πνεύματι Ἁγίῳ. 18 Ὁ γὰρ ἐν τούτοις[f]
joy in *the* Spirit ~ Holy. [2]the [3]*one* [1]For [6]in [7]these [8]*things*

δουλεύων* τῷ Χριστῷ, εὐάρεστος τῷ Θεῷ καὶ δόκιμος τοῖς
[4]serving - [5]Christ, *is* well pleasing - to God and approved -

ἀνθρώποις. 19 Ἄρα οὖν τὰ τῆς εἰρήνης
by men. So therefore [4]the [5]*things* - [6]of [7]peace

διώκωμεν καὶ τὰ τῆς οἰκοδομῆς τῆς εἰς ἀλλήλους.
[1]let [2]us [3]pursue and the *things* - of edification - for one another.

20 Μὴ ἕνεκεν βρώματος κατάλυε τὸ ἔργον τοῦ
[2]not [3]for [4]the [5]sake [6]of [7]food [1]Do [8]tear [9]down the work -

Θεοῦ. Πάντα μὲν καθαρά, ἀλλὰ κακὸν τῷ ἀνθρώπῳ τῷ
of God. All *things* indeed *are* clean, but *are* evil to the man -

διὰ προσκόμματος ἐσθίοντι. 21 Καλὸν τὸ μὴ φαγεῖν κρέα
[2]with [3]offense [1]eating. *It is* good - not to eat meat

μηδὲ πιεῖν οἶνον μηδὲ ἐν ᾧ ὁ ἀδελφός σου
nor to drink wine nor *to do anything* by which - brother ~ your

προσκόπτει ἢ σκανδαλίζεται ἢ ἀσθενεῖ.[g] 22 Σὺ πίστιν
stumbles or is offended or becomes weak. [2]you [4]faith

ἔχεις? Κατὰ σεαυτὸν ἔχε ἐνώπιον τοῦ Θεοῦ. Μακάριος
[1]Do [3]have? By yourself have *it* before - God. Blessed *is*

ὁ μὴ κρίνων ἑαυτὸν ἐν ᾧ δοκιμάζει. 23 Ὁ δὲ
the *one* not judging himself in what he approves. [2]the [3]*one* [1]But
But he who

διακρινόμενος, ἐὰν φάγῃ, κατακέκριται, ὅτι οὐκ
doubting, if he eats, he is condemned, because *he does* not *eat*
doubts,

ἐκ πίστεως· πᾶν δὲ ὃ οὐκ ἐκ πίστεως ἁμαρτία
from faith; every*thing* ~ and which *is* not of faith sin ~

ἐστίν.
is.

rather resolve this, not to put a stumbling block or a cause to fall in *our* brother's way.
14 I know and am convinced by the Lord Jesus that *there is* nothing unclean of itself; but to him who considers anything to be unclean, to him *it is* unclean.
15 Yet if your brother is grieved because of *your* food, you are no longer walking in love. Do not destroy with your food the one for whom Christ died.
16 Therefore do not let your good be spoken of as evil;
17 for the kingdom of God is not eating and drinking, but righteousness and peace and joy in the Holy Spirit.
18 For he who serves Christ in these things *is* acceptable to God and approved by men.
19 Therefore let us pursue the things *which make* for peace and the things by which one may edify another.
20 Do not destroy the work of God for the sake of food. All things indeed *are* pure, but *it is* evil for the man who eats with offense.
21 *It is* good neither to eat meat nor drink wine nor *do anything* by which your brother stumbles or is offended or is made weak.
22 Do you have faith? Have *it* to yourself before God. Happy *is* he who does not condemn himself in what he approves.
23 But he who doubts is condemned if he eats, because *he does* not *eat* from faith; for whatever *is* not from faith is sin.

---

f(**14:18**) NU-Text reads *τουτω, this.*
g(**14:21**) NU omits *η σκανδαλιζεται η ασθενει, or is offended or becomes weak.*

***(14:18)** *δουλεύω (douleuō).* Verb meaning *be a (bond)slave, perform the service of a slave, serve.* The cognate noun *δοῦλος, slave, (bond)servant,* is often used in the NT to refer to the believer's relationship to God or Christ (Phil. 1:1; James 1:1). Christians belong to God/Christ. They happily give to Him, their master, unconditional obedience as His due and their obligation (cf. Luke 17:7–10). In Greco-Roman society it was both a great honor and privileged opportunity to be slaves of an important master. Slaves

15 We then who are strong ought to bear with the scruples of the weak, and not to please ourselves.

2 Let each of us please *his* neighbor for *his* good, leading to edification.

3 For even Christ did not please Himself; but as it is written, *"The reproaches of those who reproached You fell on Me."*

4 For whatever things were written before were written for our learning, that we through the patience and comfort of the Scriptures might have hope.

5 Now may the God of patience and comfort grant you to be like-minded toward one another, according to Christ Jesus,

6 that you may with one mind *and* one mouth glorify the God and Father of our Lord Jesus Christ.

7 Therefore receive one another, just as Christ also re-

Soli Deo Gloria

24 Τῷ[h] δὲ δυναμένῳ ὑμᾶς στηρίξαι κατὰ τὸ
[2]to [3]the [4]*One* [1]Now being able [3]you [1]to [2]establish according to -
Him who is

εὐαγγέλιόν μου καὶ τὸ κήρυγμα Ἰησοῦ Χριστοῦ, κατὰ
gospel ˜ my and the proclamation of Jesus Christ, according to

ἀποκάλυψιν μυστηρίου χρόνοις αἰωνίοις σεσιγημένου,
the revelation of *the* mystery in times ˜ eternal having been kept silent,

25 φανερωθέντος δὲ νῦν, διά τε Γραφῶν προφητικῶν,
[3]manifested [1]but [2]now, through ˜ and Scriptures ˜ prophetic,

κατ' ἐπιταγὴν τοῦ αἰωνίου Θεοῦ, εἰς ὑπακοὴν
according to *the* commandment of the eternal God, [7]for [8]obedience

πίστεως εἰς πάντα τὰ ἔθνη γνωρισθέντος, **26** μόνῳ σοφῷ
[9]of [10]faith [3]to [4]all [5]the [6]nations [1]made [2]known, to *the* only wise

Θεῷ, διὰ Ἰησοῦ Χριστοῦ, ᾧ ἡ δόξα εἰς τοὺς
God, through Jesus Christ, to whom *be* the glory to the
forever.

αἰῶνας. Ἀμήν.
ages. Amen.
So be it.

Please Your Brethren, Not Yourself

15 **1** Ὀφείλομεν δὲ ἡμεῖς οἱ δυνατοὶ τὰ
[5]are [6]obligated [2]then [1]We [3]the [4]strong [10]the
who are

ἀσθενήματα τῶν ἀδυνάτων βαστάζειν καὶ μὴ ἑαυτοῖς
[11]infirmities [12]of [13]the [14]weak [7]to [8]bear [9]with and not [3]ourselves

ἀρέσκειν. **2** Ἕκαστος[a] ἡμῶν τῷ πλησίον ἀρεσκέτω εἰς τὸ
[1]to [2]please. [2]each [3]of [4]us [6]the [7]neighbor [1]Let [5]please for -
his

ἀγαθὸν πρὸς οἰκοδομήν. **3** Καὶ γὰρ ὁ Χριστὸς οὐχ ἑαυτῷ
good toward edification. even ˜ For - Christ [2]not [4]Himself

ἤρεσεν, ἀλλά, καθὼς γέγραπται, «Οἱ ὀνειδισμοὶ τῶν
[1]did [3]please, but, just as it is written, «The reproaches of the *ones*

ὀνειδιζόντων σε ἐπέπεσον ἐπ' ἐμέ.»[b] **4** Ὅσα γὰρ
reproaching You fell on Me.» [2]as [3]many [4]*things* [1]For

προεγράφη, εἰς τὴν ἡμετέραν διδασκαλίαν
as were previously written, [4]for - [5]our [6]own [7]teaching

προεγράφη,[c] ἵνα διὰ τῆς ὑπομονῆς καὶ
[1]were [2]previously [3]written, in order that through the patience and

διὰ τῆς παρακλήσεως τῶν Γραφῶν τὴν ἐλπίδα
through the encouragement of the Scriptures - [4]hope

ἔχωμεν. **5** Ὁ δὲ Θεὸς τῆς ὑπομονῆς καὶ τῆς
[1]we [2]may [3]have. [3]the [1]But [2]*may* [4]God - of patience and -

παρακλήσεως δῴη ὑμῖν τὸ αὐτὸ φρονεῖν ἐν
of encouragement give you [3]the [4]same [5]*thing* [1]to [2]mind among
grant to be like-minded

ἀλλήλοις κατὰ Χριστὸν Ἰησοῦν, **6** ἵνα ὁμοθυμαδὸν
one another according to Christ Jesus, so that with one accord

ἐν ἑνὶ στόματι δοξάζητε τὸν Θεὸν καὶ Πατέρα τοῦ Κυρίου
with one mouth you may glorify the God and Father - of Lord ˜

ἡμῶν Ἰησοῦ Χριστοῦ.
our Jesus Christ.

Glorify God Together

7 Διὸ προσλαμβάνεσθε ἀλλήλους, καθὼς καὶ ὁ
Therefore receive one another, just as also -

---

[h](**14:24**) TR puts 14:24–26 after Rom. 16:24; NU brackets it after 16:23, omitting 16:24.
[a](**15:2**) TR adds γαρ, *for.*
[b](**15:3**) Ps. 69:9
[c](**15:4**) NU reads εγραφη, *were written.*

gained benefits and status from the authority delegated to them. Christians are also admonished to offer such service to one another (Gal. 5:13). Cf. the cognate noun δουλεία, *servitude, slavery;* and verb δουλόω, *enslave, bring into bondservice.*

Χριστὸς προσελάβετο ὑμᾶς,[d] εἰς δόξαν Θεοῦ. **8** Λέγω
Christ received you, to *the* glory of God. [2]I [3]say [4]*that*

δὲ Χριστὸν Ἰησοῦν[e] διάκονον γεγενῆσθαι περιτομῆς
[1]Now Christ Jesus [4]a [5]servant [1]to [2]have [3]become of *the* circumcision
became

ὑπὲρ ἀληθείας Θεοῦ, εἰς τὸ βεβαιῶσαι τὰς ἐπαγγελίας
on behalf of *the* truth of God, for - to confirm the promises
in order

τῶν πατέρων, **9** τὰ δὲ ἔθνη ὑπὲρ ἐλέους δοξάσαι
of the fathers, the ~ and Gentiles [4]on [5]behalf [6]of [7]mercy [1]to [2]glorify
to

τὸν Θεόν, καθὼς γέγραπται,
- [3]God, just as it is written,

«Διὰ τοῦτο ἐξομολογήσομαί σοι ἐν ἔθνεσι
«For this *reason* I will confess to You among Gentiles

Καὶ τῷ ὀνόματί σου ψαλῶ.»[f]
And - to name ~ Your I will sing praise.»

10 Καὶ πάλιν λέγει,
And again he says,

«Εὐφράνθητε, ἔθνη, μετὰ τοῦ λαοῦ αὐτοῦ.»[g]
«Rejoice, *O* Gentiles, with - people ~ His.»

11 Καὶ πάλιν,
And again,

«Αἰνεῖτε τὸν Κύριον, πάντα τὰ ἔθνη,
«Praise the Lord, all the Gentiles,
you

Καὶ ἐπαινέσατε[h] αὐτόν, πάντες οἱ λαοί.»[i]
And praise Him, all the peoples.»
you

12 Καὶ πάλιν, Ἠσαΐας λέγει,
And again, Isaiah says,

«Ἔσται ἡ ῥίζα τοῦ Ἰεσσαί,
«*There* shall be the root - of Jesse,

Καὶ ὁ ἀνιστάμενος ἄρχειν ἐθνῶν·
And the *One* rising up to rule Gentiles;

Ἐπ' αὐτῷ ἔθνη ἐλπιοῦσιν.»[j]
On Him Gentiles shall hope.»

13 Ὁ δὲ Θεὸς τῆς ἐλπίδος πληρώσαι ὑμᾶς πάσης
[3]the [1]Now [2]*may* God - of hope fill you with all

χαρᾶς καὶ εἰρήνης ἐν τῷ πιστεύειν, εἰς τὸ περισσεύειν ὑμᾶς
joy and peace in - to believe, for - to abound you
believing, so that you may abound

ἐν τῇ ἐλπίδι ἐν δυνάμει Πνεύματος Ἁγίου.
in - hope by *the* power of *the* Spirit ~ Holy.

Paul's Mission from Jerusalem to Illyricum

14 Πέπεισμαι δέ, ἀδελφοί μου, καὶ αὐτὸς ἐγὼ
[2]I [3]have [4]been [5]persuaded [1]Now, brothers ~ my, even myself ~ I
am confident

περὶ ὑμῶν, ὅτι καὶ αὐτοὶ μεστοί ἐστε ἀγαθωσύνης,
concerning you, that also [2]yourselves [4]full [1]you [3]are of goodness,

πεπληρωμένοι πάσης γνώσεως, δυνάμενοι καὶ ἄλλους[k]
having been filled with all knowledge, being able also [3]others

νουθετεῖν. **15** Τολμηρότερον δὲ ἔγραψα ὑμῖν, ἀδελφοί,[l]
[1]to [2]admonish. [2]more [3]daringly [1]And I wrote to you, brothers,
write

ἀπὸ μέρους, ὡς ἐπαναμιμνήσκων ὑμᾶς, διὰ τὴν χάριν
from part, as reminding you, because of the grace
in

ceived us, to the glory of God.
8 Now I say that Jesus Christ has become a servant to the circumcision for the truth of God, to confirm the promises *made* to the fathers,
9 and that the Gentiles might glorify God for *His* mercy, as it is written:

"For this reason I will confess to You among the Gentiles,
And sing to Your name."

10 And again he says:

"Rejoice, O Gentiles, with His people!"

11 And again:

"Praise the LORD, all you Gentiles!
Laud Him, all you peoples!"

12 And again, Isaiah says:

"There shall be a root of Jesse;
And He who shall rise to reign over the Gentiles,
In Him the Gentiles shall hope."

13 Now may the God of hope fill you with all joy and peace in believing, that you may abound in hope by the power of the Holy Spirit.
14 Now I myself am confident concerning you, my brethren, that you also are full of goodness, filled with all knowledge, able also to admonish one another.
15 Nevertheless, brethren, I have written more boldly to you on *some* points, as reminding you, because of the grace given

---

[d]**(15:7)** TR reads ημας, *us.*
[e]**(15:8)** TR reads Ιησουν Χριστον, *Jesus Christ;* NU reads Χριστον, *Christ.*
[f]**(15:9)** 2 Sam. 22:50; Ps. 18:49 [g]**(15:10)** Deut. 32:43
[h]**(15:11)** NU reads επαινεσατωσαν, *let (all peoples) praise.*
[i]**(15:11)** Ps. 117:1
[j]**(15:12)** Is. 11:10
[k]**(15:14)** TR, NU read αλληλους, *one another.*
[l]**(15:15)** NU omits αδελφοι, *brothers.*

to me by God,
16 that I might be a minister
of Jesus Christ to the Gentiles,
ministering the gospel of God,
that the offering of the Gentiles
might be acceptable, sanctified
by the Holy Spirit.
17 Therefore I have reason to
glory in Christ Jesus in the
things *which pertain* to God.
18 For I will not dare to
speak of any of those things
which Christ has not accomplished through me, in word
and deed, to make the Gentiles
obedient—
19 in mighty signs and wonders, by the power of the Spirit
of God, so that from Jerusalem
and round about to Illyricum I
have fully preached the gospel
of Christ.
20 And so I have made it my
aim to preach the gospel, not
where Christ was named, lest I
should build on another man's
foundation,
21 but as it is written:

"To whom He was not
announced, they shall
see;
And those who have not
heard shall
understand."

22 For this reason I also have
been much hindered from coming to you.
23 But now no longer having a
place in these parts, and having
a great desire these many
years to come to you,
24 whenever I journey to
Spain, I shall come to you. For
I hope to see you on my journey, and to be helped on my
way there by you, if first I may
enjoy your *company* for a while.
25 But now I am going to Jerusalem to minister to the
saints.
26 For it pleased those from
Macedonia and Achaia to make

τὴν δοθεῖσάν μοι ὑπὸ τοῦ Θεοῦ, **16** εἰς τὸ εἶναί με
- having been given to me by - God, for - to be me
that I should be

λειτουργὸν Ἰησοῦ Χριστοῦ εἰς τὰ ἔθνη, ἱερουργοῦντα
a minister of Jesus Christ to the Gentiles, [1]ministering [6]as [7]a [8]priest

τὸ εὐαγγέλιον τοῦ Θεοῦ, ἵνα γένηται ἡ προσφορὰ τῶν
[2]the [3]gospel - [4]of [5]God, so that [6]may [7]be [1]the [2]offering [3]of [4]the

ἐθνῶν εὐπρόσδεκτος, ἡγιασμένη ἐν Πνεύματι Ἁγίῳ.
[5]Gentiles acceptable, sanctified by *the* Spirit ˜ Holy.

17 Ἔχω οὖν καύχησιν ἐν Χριστῷ Ἰησοῦ
[2]I [3]have [1]Therefore a boasting in Christ Jesus
something to boast of

τὰ πρὸς τὸν Θεόν. **18** Οὐ γὰρ τολμήσω λαλεῖν
in the *things* pertaining to - God. [4]not [1]For [2]I [3]will [5]dare to speak

τι ὧν οὐ κατειργάσατο Χριστὸς δι' ἐμοῦ
anything of *the things* which [3]not [2]did [4]work [5]out [1]Christ through me
accomplish

εἰς ὑπακοὴν ἐθνῶν, λόγῳ καὶ ἔργῳ, **19** ἐν δυνάμει
for *the* obedience of Gentiles, in word and in work, by *the* power

σημείων καὶ τεράτων, ἐν δυνάμει Πνεύματος Θεοῦ· ὥστε
of signs and wonders, by *the* power of *the* Spirit of God; so that

με ἀπὸ Ἱερουσαλὴμ καὶ κύκλῳ μέχρι τοῦ Ἰλλυρικοῦ
me from Jerusalem and around as far as - Illyricum
I as far as

πεπληρωκέναι τὸ εὐαγγέλιον τοῦ Χριστοῦ, **20** οὕτω δὲ
to have fulfilled the gospel - of Christ, so ˜ and
have fully preached

φιλοτιμούμενον* εὐαγγελίζεσθαι, οὐχ ὅπου ὠνομάσθη
eagerly striving to evangelize, [4]not [1]where [3]was [5]named

Χριστός, ἵνα μὴ ἐπ' ἀλλότριον θεμέλιον
[2]Christ, in order that [3]not [5]upon [8]belonging [9]to [10]another [6]a [7]foundation
lest

οἰκοδομῶ, **21** ἀλλὰ καθὼς γέγραπται,
[1]I [2]should [4]build, but just as it is written,

«Οἷς οὐκ ἀνηγγέλη περὶ αὐτοῦ ὄψονται·
«To whom [3]not [1]it [2]was [4]announced about Him they shall see;

Καὶ οἳ οὐκ ἀκηκόασι συνήσουσι.»[m]
And those who not ˜ have heard shall understand.»

Paul Plans to Visit Rome

22 Διὸ καὶ ἐνεκοπτόμην τὰ πολλὰ τοῦ ἐλθεῖν πρὸς
Therefore also ˜ I was hindered - many *things* - to come to
much

ὑμᾶς. **23** Νυνὶ δὲ μηκέτι τόπον ἔχων ἐν τοῖς κλίμασι τούτοις,
you. now ˜ But no longer place ˜ having in - regions ˜ these,

ἐπιποθίαν δὲ ἔχων τοῦ ἐλθεῖν πρὸς ὑμᾶς ἀπὸ πολλῶν ἐτῶν,
[3]a [4]longing [1]and [2]having - to come to you from many years,
for

24 ὡς ἐὰν πορεύωμαι εἰς τὴν Σπανίαν, ἐλεύσομαι πρὸς
when ever I travel to - Spain, I shall come to

ὑμᾶς.[n] Ἐλπίζω γὰρ διαπορευόμενος θεάσασθαι ὑμᾶς, καὶ
you. [2]I [3]hope [1]For *while* traveling through to see you, and

ὑφ' ὑμῶν προπεμφθῆναι ἐκεῖ ἐὰν ὑμῶν πρῶτον ἀπὸ
by you to be sent forward there if [7]*from* [8]you [9]first [5]from
in

μέρους ἐμπλησθῶ. **25** Νυνὶ δὲ πορεύομαι εἰς Ἱερουσαλὴμ
[6]part [1]I [2]may [3]be [4]filled. now ˜ But I am traveling to Jerusalem

διακονῶν τοῖς ἁγίοις. **26** Εὐδόκησαν γὰρ Μακεδονία καὶ
ministering to the saints. [5]thought [6]it [7]good [1]For [2]Macedonia [3]and

---

m(**15:21**) Is. 52:15
n(**15:24**) NU omits ελευσομαι προς υμας, *I shall come to you.*

*(**15:20**) φιλοτιμέομαι (*philotimeomai*). Compound verb from φιλέω, *to love*, and τιμή, *value, honor*, thus meaning *to love honor, be ambitious.* In the NT it is used in the positive sense of *to consider it an honor, aspire.* In 2 Cor. 5:9 Paul speaks of what he *aspires* to achieve, and in 1 Thess.

'Αχαΐα κοινωνίαν τινὰ ποιήσασθαι εἰς τοὺς πτωχοὺς τῶν
[4]Achaia [11]fellowship [10]some [8]to [9]make for the poor of the
contribution

ἁγίων τῶν ἐν 'Ιερουσαλήμ. 27 Εὐδόκησαν γάρ, καὶ
saints - in Jerusalem. [2]they [3]thought [4]it [5]good [1]For, and

ὀφειλέται αὐτῶν εἰσιν. Εἰ γὰρ τοῖς πνευματικοῖς αὐτῶν
[4]debtors [3]their [1]they [2]are. if ˜ For - [4]in [6]spiritual [7]*things* [5]their

ἐκοινώνησαν τὰ ἔθνη, ὀφείλουσι καὶ ἐν τοῖς σαρκικοῖς
[3]shared [1]the [2]Gentiles, they are obligated also in the fleshly *things*
material

λειτουργῆσαι αὐτοῖς. 28 Τοῦτο οὖν ἐπιτελέσας καὶ
to minister to them. [4]this [1]Therefore [2]having [3]finished and

σφραγισάμενος αὐτοῖς τὸν καρπὸν τοῦτον, ἀπελεύσομαι
having sealed to them - fruit ˜ this, I shall go away

δι' ὑμῶν εἰς τὴν Σπανίαν. 29 Οἶδα δὲ ὅτι ἐρχόμενος
by way of you to - Spain. [2]I [3]know [1]But that coming

πρὸς ὑμᾶς, ἐν πληρώματι εὐλογίας τοῦ εὐαγγελίου[o] τοῦ
to you, in *the* fullness of *the* blessing of the gospel -

Χριστοῦ ἐλεύσομαι.
of Christ I shall come.

30 Παρακαλῶ δὲ ὑμᾶς, ἀδελφοί, διὰ τοῦ Κυρίου ἡμῶν
[2]I [3]beg [1]Now [4]you, brothers, through - Lord ˜ our

'Ιησοῦ Χριστοῦ, καὶ διὰ τῆς ἀγάπης τοῦ Πνεύματος,
Jesus Christ, and through the love of the Spirit,

συναγωνίσασθαί μοι ἐν ταῖς προσευχαῖς ὑπὲρ ἐμοῦ
to strive together with me in - prayers on behalf of me

πρὸς τὸν Θεόν, 31 ἵνα ῥυσθῶ ἀπὸ τῶν
to - God, that I may be delivered from the *ones*
those who

ἀπειθούντων ἐν τῇ 'Ιουδαίᾳ καὶ ἵνα ἡ διακονία μου ἡ εἰς
disbelieving in - Judea and that - service ˜ my - for
do not believe

'Ιερουσαλὴμ εὐπρόσδεκτος γένηται τοῖς ἁγίοις, 32 ἵνα
Jerusalem [3]acceptable [1]may [2]become to the saints, so that

ἐν χαρᾷ ἔλθω πρὸς ὑμᾶς διὰ θελήματος Θεοῦ καὶ
in joy I may come to you through *the* will of God and

συναναπαύσωμαι ὑμῖν. 33 'Ο δὲ Θεὸς τῆς εἰρήνης
I may be refreshed together with you. the ˜ And God - of peace

μετὰ πάντων ὑμῶν. 'Αμήν.
be with all ˜ you. Amen.
So be it.

Paul Commends Sister Phoebe

16 1 Συνίστημι δὲ ὑμῖν Φοίβην τὴν ἀδελφὴν ἡμῶν,
[2]I [3]commend [1]Now to you Phoebe - sister ˜ our,

οὖσαν διάκονον τῆς ἐκκλησίας τῆς ἐν Κεγχρεαῖς, 2 ἵνα
being a servant of the church - in Cenchrea, so that
who is

αὐτὴν προσδέξησθε ἐν Κυρίῳ ἀξίως τῶν ἁγίων, καὶ
[4]her [1]you [2]may [3]receive in *the* Lord worthily of the saints, and

παραστῆτε αὐτῇ ἐν ᾧ ἂν ὑμῶν χρήζῃ
you may stand by her in what ever [5]from [6]you [2]she [3]may [4]need

πράγματι, καὶ γὰρ αὐτὴ προστάτις πολλῶν ἐγενήθη καὶ
[1]thing, indeed ˜ for she [2]a [3]helper [4]of [5]many [1]became and
proved to be

αὐτοῦ ἐμοῦ.
[3]myself [1]of [2]me.

a certain contribution for the poor among the saints who are in Jerusalem.
27 It pleased them indeed, and they are their debtors. For if the Gentiles have been partakers of their spiritual things, their duty is also to minister to them in material things.
28 Therefore, when I have performed this and have sealed to them this fruit, I shall go by way of you to Spain.
29 But I know that when I come to you, I shall come in the fullness of the blessing of the gospel of Christ.
30 Now I beg you, brethren, through the Lord Jesus Christ, and through the love of the Spirit, that you strive together with me in prayers to God for me,
31 that I may be delivered from those in Judea who do not believe, and that my service for Jerusalem may be acceptable to the saints,
32 that I may come to you with joy by the will of God, and may be refreshed together with you.
33 Now the God of peace *be* with you all. Amen.

16 I commend to you Phoebe our sister, who is a servant of the church in Cenchrea,
2 that you may receive her in the Lord in a manner worthy of the saints, and assist her in whatever business she has need of you; for indeed she has been a helper of many and of myself also.

---

[o](**15:29**) NU omits *του ευαγγελιου του, of the gospel.*

4:11, he urges his readers to *aspire* to a quiet life. Here in Rom. 15:20 it may also refer to Paul's desire to preach the gospel, or it may express the idea that he considers it an honor to take the gospel to new regions.

3 Greet Priscilla and Aquila, my fellow workers in Christ Jesus,
4 who risked their own necks for my life, to whom not only I give thanks, but also all the churches of the Gentiles.
5 Likewise *greet* the church that is in their house. Greet my beloved Epaenetus, who is the firstfruits of Achaia to Christ.
6 Greet Mary, who labored much for us.
7 Greet Andronicus and Junia, my countrymen and my fellow prisoners, who are of note among the apostles, who also were in Christ before me.
8 Greet Amplias, my beloved in the Lord.
9 Greet Urbanus, our fellow worker in Christ, and Stachys, my beloved.
10 Greet Apelles, approved in Christ. Greet those who are of the *household* of Aristobulus.
11 Greet Herodion, my countryman. Greet those who are of the *household* of Narcissus who are in the Lord.
12 Greet Tryphena and Tryphosa, who have labored in the Lord. Greet the beloved Persis, who labored much in the Lord.

Paul Greets Various Roman Saints

3 Ἀσπάσασθε Πρίσκαν[a] καὶ Ἀκύλαν τοὺς συνεργούς
Greet Prisca and Aquila - [2]fellow [3]workers

μου ἐν Χριστῷ Ἰησοῦ, **4** οἵτινες ὑπὲρ τῆς ψυχῆς μου τὸν
[1]my in Christ Jesus, who for - life ˜ my -

ἑαυτῶν τράχηλον ὑπέθηκαν, οἷς οὐκ ἐγὼ μόνος
[2]their [3]own [4]neck [1]risked, to whom not I ˜ only

εὐχαριστῶ, ἀλλὰ καὶ πᾶσαι αἱ ἐκκλησίαι τῶν ἐθνῶν, **5** καὶ
give thanks, but also all the churches of the Gentiles, and

τὴν κατ' οἶκον αὐτῶν ἐκκλησίαν.
the [2]at [4]house [3]their [1]church.

Ἀσπάσασθε Ἐπαίνετον τὸν ἀγαπητόν μου, ὅς ἐστιν
Greet Epaenetus - beloved ˜ my, who is

ἀπαρχὴ τῆς Ἀχαΐας[b] εἰς Χριστόν.
the firstfruit - of Achaia for Christ.

6 Ἀσπάσασθε Μαριάμ, ἥτις πολλὰ ἐκοπίασεν εἰς
Greet Mary, who [2]many [3]*things* [1]labored for
much

ἡμᾶς.[c]
us.

7 Ἀσπάσασθε Ἀνδρόνικον καὶ Ἰουνίαν τοὺς συγγενεῖς
Greet Andronicus and Junia - countrymen ˜
relatives

μου καὶ συναιχμαλώτους μου, οἵτινές εἰσιν ἐπίσημοι ἐν τοῖς
my and [2]fellow [3]captives [1]my, who are notable among the

ἀποστόλοις, οἳ καὶ πρὸ ἐμοῦ γεγόνασιν ἐν Χριστῷ.
apostles, who also [7]before [8]me [1]have [2]come [3]to [4]be [5]in [6]Christ.
were

8 Ἀσπάσασθε Ἀμπλίαν[d] τὸν ἀγαπητόν μου ἐν Κυρίῳ.
Greet Amplias - beloved ˜ my in *the* Lord.

9 Ἀσπάσασθε Οὐρβανὸν τὸν συνεργὸν ἡμῶν ἐν
Greet Urbanus - [2]fellow [3]worker [1]our in

Χριστῷ, καὶ Στάχυν τὸν ἀγαπητόν μου.
Christ, and Stachys - beloved ˜ my.

10 Ἀσπάσασθε Ἀπελλῆν τὸν δόκιμον ἐν Χριστῷ.
Greet Apelles the *one* approved in Christ.

Ἀσπάσασθε τοὺς ἐκ τῶν Ἀριστοβούλου.
Greet the *ones* from the *household* of Aristobulus.

11 Ἀσπάσασθε Ἡρῳδίωνα τὸν συγγενῆ μου.
Greet Herodion - countryman ˜ my.
relative

Ἀσπάσασθε τοὺς ἐκ τῶν Ναρκίσσου τοὺς
Greet the *ones* from the *household* of Narcissus the *ones*
who

ὄντας ἐν Κυρίῳ.
being in *the* Lord.
are

12 Ἀσπάσασθε Τρύφαιναν καὶ Τρυφῶσαν τὰς
Greet Tryphena and Tryphosa the ones
who have

κοπιώσας ἐν Κυρίῳ.
laboring in *the* Lord.
labored

Ἀσπάσασθε Περσίδα τὴν ἀγαπητήν, ἥτις πολλὰ
Greet [3]Persis [1]the [2]beloved, who [2]many [3]things
much

ἐκοπίασεν ἐν Κυρίῳ.
[1]labored in *the* Lord.

---

[a](**16:3**) TR reads Πρισκιλλαν, *Priscilla.*
[b](**16:5**) NU reads Ασιας, *Asia.* [c](**16:6**) NU reads υμας, *you.*
[d](**16:8**) NU reads Αμπλιατον, *Ampliatus.*

13 Ἀσπάσασθε Ῥοῦφον τὸν ἐκλεκτὸν ἐν Κυρίῳ, καὶ τὴν
Greet Rufus the elect (chosen one) in *the* Lord, and -

μητέρα αὐτοῦ καὶ ἐμοῦ.
mother ˜ his and mine.

14 Ἀσπάσασθε Ἀσύγκριτον, Φλέγοντα, Ἑρμᾶν, Πατροβᾶν,
Greet Asyncritus, Phlegon, Hermas, Patrobas,

Ἑρμῆν,[e] καὶ τοὺς σὺν αὐτοῖς ἀδελφούς.
Hermes, and the [2]with [3]them [1]brothers.

15 Ἀσπάσασθε Φιλόλογον καὶ Ἰουλίαν, Νηρέα καὶ τὴν
Greet Philologus and Julia, Nereus and -

ἀδελφὴν αὐτοῦ, καὶ Ὀλυμπᾶν, καὶ τοὺς σὺν αὐτοῖς πάντας
sister ˜ his, and Olympas, and [2]the [4]with [5]them [1]all

ἁγίους.
[3]saints.

16 Ἀσπάσασθε ἀλλήλους ἐν φιλήματι ἁγίῳ.
Greet one another with a kiss ˜ holy.

Ἀσπάζονται ὑμᾶς αἱ ἐκκλησίαι[f] τοῦ Χριστοῦ.
[5]greet [6]you [1]The [2]churches - [3]of [4]Christ.

Paul Warns of Those Who Cause Divisions and Offenses

17 Παρακαλῶ δὲ ὑμᾶς, ἀδελφοί, σκοπεῖν τοὺς τὰς
[2]I [3]urge [1]Now you, brothers, to look out for the *ones* -

διχοστασίας καὶ τὰ σκάνδαλα παρὰ τὴν διδαχὴν ἣν
[2]divisions [3]and - [4]offenses [5]contrary [6]to [7]the [8]teaching [9]which

ὑμεῖς ἐμάθετε ποιοῦντας, καὶ ἐκκλίνατε ἀπ' αὐτῶν. 18 Οἱ γὰρ
[10]you [11]learned [1]making, and turn away from them. - For

τοιοῦτοι τῷ Κυρίῳ ἡμῶν Ἰησοῦ[g] Χριστῷ οὐ δουλεύουσιν
such *people* - [5]Lord [4]our [6]Jesus [7]Christ [2]not [1]do [3]serve

ἀλλὰ τῇ ἑαυτῶν κοιλίᾳ, καὶ διὰ τῆς χρηστολογίας καὶ
but - their own belly, and through - smooth speech and

εὐλογίας ἐξαπατῶσι τὰς καρδίας τῶν ἀκάκων. 19 Ἡ γὰρ
flattering speech they deceive the hearts of the guileless. - For

ὑμῶν ὑπακοὴ εἰς πάντας ἀφίκετο. Χαίρω οὖν τὸ
your obedience [2]to [3]all [1]reached (has become known). I rejoice therefore -

ἐφ' ὑμῖν, θέλω δὲ ὑμᾶς σοφοὺς μὲν εἶναι εἰς τὸ
over you, [2]I [3]wish [1]but you [7]wise [1]on [2]the [3]one [4]hand [5]to [6]be to the

ἀγαθόν, ἀκεραίους δὲ εἰς τὸ κακόν. 20 Ὁ δὲ
good, [5]innocent [1]on [2]the [3]other [4]hand to the evil. the ˜ And

Θεὸς τῆς εἰρήνης συντρίψει τὸν Σατανᾶν ὑπὸ τοὺς πόδας
God - of peace will crush - Satan under - feet ˜

ὑμῶν ἐν τάχει.
your in swiftness (shortly).

Ἡ χάρις τοῦ Κυρίου ἡμῶν Ἰησοῦ Χριστοῦ[h] μεθ' ὑμῶν.
The grace - of Lord ˜ our Jesus Christ *be* with you.

21 Ἀσπάζονται ὑμᾶς Τιμόθεος ὁ συνεργός μου, καὶ
There greet you Timothy - [2]fellow [3]worker [1]my, and

Λούκιος καὶ Ἰάσων καὶ Σωσίπατρος οἱ συγγενεῖς μου.
Lucius and Jason and Sosipater - countrymen (relatives) ˜ my.

22 Ἀσπάζομαι ὑμᾶς ἐγὼ Τέρτιος ὁ γράψας τὴν
[3]greet [4]you [1]I [2]Tertius the *one* writing (who wrote) the

ἐπιστολὴν ἐν Κυρίῳ.
epistle in *the* Lord.

13 Greet Rufus, chosen in the Lord, and his mother and mine.
14 Greet Asyncritus, Phlegon, Hermas, Patrobas, Hermes, and the brethren who are with them.
15 Greet Philologus and Julia, Nereus and his sister, and Olympas, and all the saints who are with them.
16 Greet one another with a holy kiss. The churches of Christ greet you.
17 Now I urge you, brethren, note those who cause divisions and offenses, contrary to the doctrine which you learned, and avoid them.
18 For those who are such do not serve our Lord Jesus Christ, but their own belly, and by smooth words and flattering speech deceive the hearts of the simple.
19 For your obedience has become known to all. Therefore I am glad on your behalf; but I want you to be wise in what is good, and simple concerning evil.
20 And the God of peace will crush Satan under your feet shortly. The grace of our Lord Jesus Christ *be* with you. Amen.
21 Timothy, my fellow worker, and Lucius, Jason, and Sosipater, my countrymen, greet you.
22 I, Tertius, who wrote *this* epistle, greet you in the Lord.

---

[e](**16:14**) NU transposes Ερμαν and Ερμην, *Hermas* and *Hermes*.
[f](**16:16**) NU adds πασαι, *all*.
[g](**16:18**) NU omits Ιησου, *Jesus*.
[h](**16:20**) NU omits Χριστου, *Christ*.

23 Gaius, my host and *the host* of the whole church, greets you. Erastus, the treasurer of the city, greets you, and Quartus, a brother.
24 The grace of our Lord Jesus Christ *be* with you all. Amen.
25 Now to Him who is able to establish you according to my gospel and the preaching of Jesus Christ, according to the revelation of the mystery kept secret since the world began
26 but now made manifest, and by the prophetic Scriptures made known to all nations, according to the commandment of the everlasting God, for obedience to the faith—
27 to God, alone wise, *be* glory through Jesus Christ forever. Amen.

23 Ἀσπάζεται ὑμᾶς Γάϊος ὁ ξένος μου καὶ τῆς ἐκκλησίας ὅλης.
[2]greets [3]you [1]Gaius - host ˜ my and of the church ˜ whole.

Ἀσπάζεται ὑμᾶς Ἔραστος ὁ οἰκονόμος τῆς πόλεως, καὶ Κούαρτος ὁ ἀδελφός.
[2]greets [3]you [1]Erastus the treasurer of the city, and Quartus the brother.

24 Ἡ χάρις τοῦ Κυρίου ἡμῶν Ἰησοῦ Χριστοῦ μετὰ πάντων ὑμῶν. Ἀμήν.[i]
The grace - of Lord ˜ our Jesus Christ *be* with all ˜ you. Amen.
So be it.

[i](**16:24**) NU, TR add vv. 25–27 which are found in M at 14:24–26; NU omits 16:24 and brackets 16:25–27.

The First Epistle of Paul the Apostle to the CORINTHIANS

ΠΡΟΣ ΚΟΡΙΝΘΙΟΥΣ Α
TO *THE* CORINTHIANS 1

Paul Greets the Corinthians

1 1 Παῦλος, κλητὸς ἀπόστολος Ἰησοῦ Χριστοῦ διὰ
Paul, called *to be* an apostle of Jesus Christ through

θελήματος Θεοῦ, καὶ Σωσθένης ὁ ἀδελφός,
the will of God, and Sosthenes the brother,
our

2 Τῇ ἐκκλησίᾳ τοῦ Θεοῦ τῇ οὔσῃ ἐν Κορίνθῳ,
To the church - of God the *one* being at Corinth,
which is

ἡγιασμένοις ἐν Χριστῷ Ἰησοῦ, κλητοῖς ἁγίοις,
to *ones* having been sanctified in Christ Jesus, called *to be* saints,
to those who have

σὺν πᾶσι τοῖς ἐπικαλουμένοις τὸ ὄνομα τοῦ Κυρίου
with all the *ones* calling upon the name - of Lord ~
those who are calling on

ἡμῶν Ἰησοῦ Χριστοῦ ἐν παντὶ τόπῳ, αὐτῶν τε καὶ ἡμῶν·
our Jesus Christ in every place, theirs ~ both and ours:

3 Χάρις ὑμῖν καὶ εἰρήνη ἀπὸ Θεοῦ Πατρὸς ἡμῶν καὶ
Grace to you and peace from God Father ~ our and

Κυρίου Ἰησοῦ Χριστοῦ.
the Lord Jesus Christ.

Paul Thanks God for Their Spiritual Gifts

4 Εὐχαριστῶ τῷ θεῷ μου πάντοτε περὶ ὑμῶν ἐπὶ τῇ
I thank - God ~ my always concerning you for the

χάριτι τοῦ Θεοῦ τῇ δοθείσῃ ὑμῖν ἐν Χριστῷ Ἰησοῦ, 5 ὅτι ἐν
grace - of God - being given to you by Christ Jesus, that in
which was

παντὶ ἐπλουτίσθητε ἐν αὐτῷ ἐν παντὶ λόγῳ καὶ πάσῃ
every*thing* you were enriched by Him in all utterance and all
speech

γνώσει, 6 καθὼς τὸ μαρτύριον τοῦ Χριστοῦ ἐβεβαιώθη ἐν
knowledge, just as the testimony - of Christ was confirmed in

ὑμῖν, 7 ὥστε ὑμᾶς μὴ ὑστερεῖσθαι ἐν μηδενὶ χαρίσματι,*
you, so that you not to be coming short in no gift,
are not any

ἀπεκδεχομένους τὴν ἀποκάλυψιν τοῦ Κυρίου ἡμῶν Ἰησοῦ
awaiting the revelation - of Lord ~ our Jesus

Χριστοῦ, 8 ὃς καὶ βεβαιώσει ὑμᾶς ἕως τέλους,
Christ, who also will confirm you until *the* end,

ἀνεγκλήτους ἐν τῇ ἡμέρᾳ τοῦ Κυρίου ἡμῶν Ἰησοῦ
that you may be blameless in the day - of Lord ~ our Jesus

Χριστοῦ. 9 Πιστὸς ὁ Θεός, δι' οὗ ἐκλήθητε εἰς
Christ. [2]*is* [3]faithful - [1]God, by whom you were called into

κοινωνίαν τοῦ Υἱοῦ αὐτοῦ Ἰησοῦ Χριστοῦ τοῦ Κυρίου ἡμῶν.
the fellowship - of Son ~ His Jesus Christ - Lord ~ our.

1 Paul, called *to be* an apostle of Jesus Christ through the will of God, and Sosthenes *our* brother,

2 To the church of God which is at Corinth, to those who are sanctified in Christ Jesus, called *to be* saints, with all who in every place call on the name of Jesus Christ our Lord, both theirs and ours:

3 Grace to you and peace from God our Father and the Lord Jesus Christ.

4 I thank my God always concerning you for the grace of God which was given to you by Christ Jesus,
5 that you were enriched in everything by Him in all utterance and all knowledge,
6 even as the testimony of Christ was confirmed in you,
7 so that you come short in no gift, eagerly waiting for the revelation of our Lord Jesus Christ,
8 who will also confirm you to the end, *that you may be* blameless in the day of our Lord Jesus Christ.
9 God *is* faithful, by whom you were called into the fellowship of His Son, Jesus Christ our Lord.

***(1:7)** *χάρισμα (charisma).* Noun meaning *gift (freely given)* or a *gift of grace,* cf. the cognate *χάρις, grace.* In the NT *χάρισμα* is limited to gifts given by God and may refer to a variety of things ranging from deliverance from mortal danger (2 Cor. 1:11) to the gift of celibacy (1 Cor. 7:7) to eternal life (Rom. 6:23). Perhaps all the uses in 1 Corinthians are to special gifts of the Spirit for ministry called "spiritual gifts." Cf. the English *charismatic;* and see *πνευματικός* at 1 Cor. 2:13).

10 Now I plead with you,
brethren, by the name of our
Lord Jesus Christ, that you all
speak the same thing, and *that*
there be no divisions among
you, but *that* you be perfectly
joined together in the same
mind and in the same judgment.
11 For it has been declared to
me concerning you, my brethren, by those of Chloe's *household,* that there are contentions
among you.
12 Now I say this, that each of
you says, "I am of Paul," or "I
am of Apollos," or "I am of Cephas," or "I am of Christ."
13 Is Christ divided? Was Paul
crucified for you? Or were you
baptized in the name of Paul?
14 I thank God that I baptized
none of you except Crispus and
Gaius,
15 lest anyone should say that
I had baptized in my own name.
16 Yes, I also baptized the
household of Stephanas. Besides, I do not know whether I
baptized any other.
17 For Christ did not send me
to baptize, but to preach the
gospel, not with wisdom of
words, lest the cross of Christ
should be made of no effect.
18 For the message of the
cross is foolishness to those
who are perishing, but to us
who are being saved it is the
power of God.
19 For it is written:

"I will destroy the wisdom
of the wise,
And bring to nothing the
understanding of the
prudent."

20 Where *is* the wise? Where
is the scribe? Where *is* the
disputer of this age? Has not
God made foolish the wisdom of

Sectarianism Is Sin

10 Παρακαλῶ δὲ ὑμᾶς, ἀδελφοί, διὰ τοῦ ὀνόματος τοῦ
[2]I [3]appeal [4]to [1]Now you, brothers, by the name -

Κυρίου ἡμῶν Ἰησοῦ Χριστοῦ, ἵνα τὸ αὐτὸ λέγητε
of Lord ˜ our Jesus Christ, that [4]the [5]same [6]*thing* [1]you [3]speak

πάντες, καὶ μὴ ᾖ ἐν ὑμῖν σχίσματα, ἦτε δὲ
[2]all, and not ˜ *there* be [2]among [3]you [1]divisions, [5]you [6]be [4]but

κατηρτισμένοι ἐν τῷ αὐτῷ νοΐ καὶ ἐν τῇ αὐτῇ γνώμῃ.
restored in the same mind and in the same purpose.
made complete

11 Ἐδηλώθη γάρ μοι περὶ ὑμῶν, ἀδελφοί μου, ὑπὸ
[2]it [3]was [4]shown [1]For to me concerning you, brothers ˜ my, by

τῶν Χλόης, ὅτι ἔριδες ἐν ὑμῖν εἰσι.
the *ones* of Chloe, that [3]contentions [4]among [5]you [1]*there* [2]are.
those of Chloe's household,

12 Λέγω δὲ τοῦτο, ὅτι ἕκαστος ὑμῶν λέγει, "Ἐγὼ μέν εἰμι
[2]I [3]say [1]Now this, that each of you says, "I - am

Παύλου," "Ἐγὼ δὲ Ἀπολλῶ," "Ἐγὼ δὲ Κηφᾶ," "Ἐγὼ
of Paul," "I - *am* of Apollos," "I - *am* of Cephas," "I

δὲ Χριστοῦ." **13** Μεμέρισται ὁ Χριστός? Μὴ Παῦλος
- *am* of Christ." Has [2]been [3]divided - [1]Christ? [6]not [4]Paul

ἐσταυρώθη ὑπὲρ ὑμῶν, ἢ εἰς τὸ ὄνομα Παύλου
[5]was [7]crucified for you, *was he,* or [4]in [5]the [6]name [7]of [8]Paul

ἐβαπτίσθητε? **14** Εὐχαριστῶ τῷ Θεῷ ὅτι οὐδένα ὑμῶν
[1]were [2]you [3]baptized? I thank - God that [3]none [4]of [5]you

ἐβάπτισα εἰ μὴ Κρίσπον καὶ Γάϊον, **15** ἵνα μή τις
[1]I [2]baptized if not Crispus and Gaius, that not anyone
except lest

εἴπῃ ὅτι εἰς τὸ ἐμὸν ὄνομα ἐβάπτισα.[a] **16** Ἐβάπτισα δὲ
should say that [3]in - [4]my [5]name [1]I [2]baptized. [2]I [4]baptized [1]And

καὶ τὸν Στεφανᾶ οἶκον. Λοιπὸν οὐκ οἶδα εἴ
[3]also the [2]of [3]Stephanas [1]household. Beyond that, [3]not [1]I [2]do know whether

τινα ἄλλον ἐβάπτισα. **17** Οὐ γὰρ ἀπέστειλέ με Χριστὸς
[3]anyone [4]else [1]I [2]baptized. [4]not [1]For [3]did [5]send [6]me [2]Christ

βαπτίζειν, ἀλλ' εὐαγγελίζεσθαι, οὐκ ἐν σοφίᾳ λόγου, ἵνα μὴ
to baptize, but to preach the gospel, not in wisdom of word, that not
eloquent wisdom, lest

κενωθῇ ὁ σταυρὸς τοῦ Χριστοῦ.
[5]should [6]be [7]rendered [8]invalid [1]the [2]cross - [3]of [4]Christ.

Christ Is the Power and Wisdom of God

18 Ὁ λόγος γὰρ ὁ τοῦ σταυροῦ τοῖς μὲν
[2]the [3]word [1]For - of the cross [3]to [4]the [5]*ones* -
message those who are

ἀπολλυμένοις μωρία ἐστί, τοῖς δὲ σωζομένοις ἡμῖν
[6]perishing [2]foolishness [1]is, [10]the [11]*ones* [7]but [12]being [13]saved [8]to [9]us
who are

δύναμις Θεοῦ ἐστι. **19** Γέγραπται γάρ,
[16]*the* [17]power [18]of [19]God [14]it [15]is. [2]it [3]is [4]written [1]For,

«Ἀπολῶ τὴν σοφίαν τῶν σοφῶν,
«I will destroy the wisdom of the wise,

Καὶ τὴν σύνεσιν τῶν συνετῶν ἀθετήσω.»[b]
And the intelligence of the intelligent I will reject.»

20 Ποῦ σοφός? Ποῦ γραμματεύς? Ποῦ συζητητὴς
Where *is the* wise *person?* Where *is the* scribe? Where *is the* disputer

τοῦ αἰῶνος τούτου? Οὐχὶ ἐμώρανεν ὁ Θεὸς τὴν σοφίαν τοῦ
- of age ˜ this? [2]not [1]Did [4]make [5]foolish - [3]God the wisdom -

---

[a](1:15) NU reads ἐβαπτίσθητε, *you were baptized.* [b](1:19) Is. 29:14

κόσμου τούτου? **21** Ἐπειδὴ γὰρ ἐν τῇ σοφίᾳ τοῦ Θεοῦ οὐκ
of world ˜ this? since ˜ For in the wisdom - of God [6]not

ἔγνω ὁ κόσμος διὰ τῆς σοφίας τὸν Θεόν, εὐδόκησεν
[5]did [7]know [1]the [2]world [3]through - [4]wisdom - God, [2]was [3]pleased

ὁ Θεὸς διὰ τῆς μωρίας τοῦ κηρύγματος σῶσαι τοὺς
- [1]God through the foolishness of the preaching to save the *ones*
our

πιστεύοντας. **22** Ἐπειδὴ καὶ Ἰουδαῖοι σημεῖον αἰτοῦσι καὶ
believing. Indeed also Jews [2]a [3]sign [1]request and

Ἕλληνες σοφίαν ζητοῦσιν, **23** ἡμεῖς δὲ κηρύσσομεν Χριστὸν
Greeks wisdom ˜ seek, we ˜ but preach Christ

ἐσταυρωμένον, Ἰουδαίοις μὲν σκάνδαλον, Ἕλλησι[c] δὲ
having been crucified, to Jews - a stumbling block, [2]to [3]Greeks [1]and
an offense,

μωρίαν, **24** αὐτοῖς δὲ τοῖς κλητοῖς, Ἰουδαίοις τε καὶ
foolishness, [2]to [3]them [1]but the *ones* called, Jews ˜ both and
who are

Ἕλλησι, Χριστὸν Θεοῦ δύναμιν καὶ Θεοῦ σοφίαν.
Greeks, Christ [3]of [4]God [1]*the* [2]power and [3]of [4]God [1]*the* [2]wisdom.

25 Ὅτι τὸ μωρὸν τοῦ Θεοῦ σοφώτερον τῶν ἀνθρώπων
Because the foolish *thing* - of God [2]wiser - [3]*than* [4]men
foolishness

ἐστί, καὶ τὸ ἀσθενὲς τοῦ Θεοῦ ἰσχυρότερον τῶν ἀνθρώπων
[1]is, and the weak *thing* - of God [2]stronger - [3]*than* [4]men
weakness

ἐστί.
[1]is.

Glory Only in the Lord

26 Βλέπετε γὰρ τὴν κλῆσιν ὑμῶν, ἀδελφοί, ὅτι οὐ πολλοὶ
[2]you [3]see [1]For - calling ˜ your, brothers, that not many

σοφοὶ κατὰ σάρκα, οὐ πολλοὶ δυνατοί, οὐ πολλοὶ
wise according to *the* flesh, not many powerful, not many

εὐγενεῖς·* **27** ἀλλὰ τὰ μωρὰ τοῦ κόσμου
noble *are called;* but [3]the [4]foolish [5]*things* [6]of [7]the [8]world

ἐξελέξατο ὁ Θεὸς ἵνα τοὺς σοφοὺς
[2]chose - [1]God in order that [6]the [7]wise

καταισχύνῃ, καὶ τὰ ἀσθενῆ τοῦ κόσμου
[1]He [2]might [3]put [4]to [5]shame, and the weak *things* of the world
humiliate

ἐξελέξατο ὁ Θεὸς ἵνα καταισχύνῃ τὰ ἰσχυρά.
chose ˜ - God in order that He might put to shame the strong *things*.
humiliate

28 Καὶ τὰ ἀγενῆ τοῦ κόσμου καὶ τὰ
And [3]the [4]base [5]*things* [6]of [7]the [8]world [9]and [10]the [11]*things*

ἐξουθενημένα ἐξελέξατο ὁ Θεός, καὶ τὰ μὴ
[12]having [13]been [14]despised [2]chose - [1]God, and the *things* not
which

ὄντα, ἵνα τὰ ὄντα καταργήσῃ, **29** ὅπως
being, in order that [4]the [5]*things* [6]being [1]He [2]might [3]nullify, that
are not, which are

μὴ καυχήσηται πᾶσα σὰρξ ἐνώπιον τοῦ Θεοῦ.[d] **30** Ἐξ
[4]not [3]may [5]boast [1]all [2]flesh before - God. [2]from

αὐτοῦ δὲ ὑμεῖς ἐστε ἐν Χριστῷ Ἰησοῦ, ὃς ἐγενήθη ἡμῖν
[3]Him [1]But you are in Christ Jesus, who became for us

σοφία ἀπὸ Θεοῦ, δικαιοσύνη τε καὶ ἁγιασμὸς καὶ
wisdom from God, righteousness ˜ and and sanctification and

this world?
21 For since, in the wisdom of God, the world through wisdom did not know God, it pleased God through the foolishness of the message preached to save those who believe.
22 For Jews request a sign, and Greeks seek after wisdom;
23 but we preach Christ crucified, to the Jews a stumbling block and to the Greeks foolishness,
24 but to those who are called, both Jews and Greeks, Christ the power of God and the wisdom of God.
25 Because the foolishness of God is wiser than men, and the weakness of God is stronger than men.
26 For you see your calling, brethren, that not many wise according to the flesh, not many mighty, not many noble, *are called.*
27 But God has chosen the foolish things of the world to put to shame the wise, and God has chosen the weak things of the world to put to shame the things which are mighty;
28 and the base things of the world and the things which are despised God has chosen, and the things which are not, to bring to nothing the things that are,
29 that no flesh should glory in His presence.
30 But of Him you are in Christ Jesus, who became for us wisdom from God—and righteousness and sanctification

[c]**(1:23)** NU reads *εθνεσιν, Gentiles.* [d]**(1:29)** TR reads *αυτου, Him.*

***(1:26)** εὐγενής *(eugenēs).* Adjective meaning *well-born,* from *εὐ, well,* and *γένος, family, race.* When used literally, it refers to a person from a *noble* family (as here and Luke 19:12). In Acts 17:11 it appears in its comparative form, *εὐγενέστερος,* and carries the figurative meaning "more noble- (or open-) minded."

and redemption—
31 that, as it is written, *"He who glories, let him glory in the LORD."*

2 And I, brethren, when I came to you, did not come with excellence of speech or of wisdom declaring to you the testimony of God.
2 For I determined not to know anything among you except Jesus Christ and Him crucified.
3 I was with you in weakness, in fear, and in much trembling.
4 And my speech and my preaching *were* not with persuasive words of human wisdom, but in demonstration of the Spirit and of power,
5 that your faith should not be in the wisdom of men but in the power of God.
6 However, we speak wisdom among those who are mature, yet not the wisdom of this age, nor of the rulers of this age, who are coming to nothing.
7 But we speak the wisdom of God in a mystery, the hidden *wisdom* which God ordained before the ages for our glory,
8 which none of the rulers of this age knew; for had they known, they would not have crucified the Lord of glory.
9 But as it is written:

"Eye has not seen, nor ear heard,
Nor have entered into the heart of man

ἀπολύτρωσις· 31 ἵνα καθὼς γέγραπται, «Ὁ καυχώμενος,
redemption; that as it is written, «The *one* boasting,
who boasts,

ἐν Κυρίῳ καυχάσθω.»[e]
[4]in [5]*the* [6]Lord [1]let [2]him [3]boast.»

Paul's Proclamation: Christ Crucified

2 1 Κἀγὼ ἐλθὼν πρὸς ὑμᾶς, ἀδελφοί, ἦλθον οὐ
And I having come to you, brothers, came not
when I came

καθ' ὑπεροχὴν λόγου ἢ σοφίας καταγγέλλων ὑμῖν τὸ
according to excellence of speech or of wisdom declaring to you the

μαρτύριον[a] τοῦ Θεοῦ. 2 Οὐ γὰρ ἔκρινα τοῦ εἰδέναι
testimony - of God. [4]not [1]For [2]I [3]determined - to know

τι ἐν ὑμῖν εἰ μὴ Ἰησοῦν Χριστὸν καὶ τοῦτον
anything among you if not Jesus Christ and this one
except Him

ἐσταυρωμένον. 3 Καὶ ἐγὼ ἐν ἀσθενείᾳ καὶ ἐν φόβῳ καὶ ἐν
crucified. And I [4]in [5]weakness [6]and [7]in [8]fear [9]and [10]in

τρόμῳ πολλῷ ἐγενόμην πρὸς ὑμᾶς. 4 Καὶ ὁ λόγος μου
[12]trembling [11]much [1]was [2]with [3]you. And - message ˜ my

καὶ τὸ κήρυγμά μου οὐκ ἐν πειθοῖς ἀνθρωπίνης[b] σοφίας
and - preaching ˜ my *were* not with persuasive [2]of [3]human [4]wisdom

λόγοις, ἀλλ' ἐν ἀποδείξει Πνεύματος καὶ δυνάμεως,
[1]words, but in demonstration of *the* Spirit and of power,

5 ἵνα ἡ πίστις ὑμῶν μὴ ᾖ ἐν σοφίᾳ
in order that - faith ˜ your not ˜ should be in *the* wisdom

ἀνθρώπων ἀλλ' ἐν δυνάμει Θεοῦ.
of men but in *the* power of God.

God's Wisdom Is for the Spiritual

6 Σοφίαν δὲ λαλοῦμεν ἐν τοῖς τελείοις,
[4]wisdom [1]But [2]we [3]speak among the mature *ones*,
those who are mature,

σοφίαν δὲ οὐ τοῦ αἰῶνος τούτου, οὐδὲ τῶν ἀρχόντων τοῦ
[3]*the* [4]wisdom [1]but [2]not - of age ˜ this, nor of the rulers -

αἰῶνος τούτου, τῶν καταργουμένων· 7 ἀλλὰ λαλοῦμεν
of age ˜ this, the *ones* being destroyed; but we speak
who are

σοφίαν Θεοῦ ἐν μυστηρίῳ, τὴν ἀποκεκρυμμένην, ἣν
the wisdom of God in a mystery, the *wisdom* having been hidden, which

προώρισεν ὁ Θεὸς πρὸ τῶν αἰώνων εἰς δόξαν ἡμῶν, 8 ἣν
foreordained ˜ - God before the ages for glory ˜ our, which

οὐδεὶς τῶν ἀρχόντων τοῦ αἰῶνος τούτου ἔγνωκεν· εἰ γὰρ
none of the rulers - of age ˜ this knew; if ˜ for

ἔγνωσαν, οὐκ ἂν τὸν Κύριον τῆς δόξης
they had known, [3]not - [6]the [7]Lord - [8]of [9]glory

ἐσταύρωσαν. 9 Ἀλλὰ καθὼς γέγραπται,
[1]they [2]would [4]have [5]crucified. But just as it is written,

«Ἃ ὀφθαλμὸς οὐκ εἶδε καὶ οὖς οὐκ
«*The things* which an eye not ˜ saw and an ear not ˜
has not seen has

ἤκουσε,»[c]
heard,»
not heard,»

Καὶ ἐπὶ καρδίαν ἀνθρώπου οὐκ ἀνέβη,
And [4]into [5]*the* [6]heart [7]of [8]man [2]not [1]did [3]enter,
has not entered,

[e](1:31) Jer. 9:24
[a](2:1) NU reads μυστηριον, *mystery.* [b](2:4) NU omits ανθρωπινης, *human.*
[c](2:9) Is. 64:4

Ἃ ἡτοίμασεν ὁ Θεὸς τοῖς ἀγαπῶσιν
Things which [2]has [3]prepared - [1]God for the *ones* loving (who love)

αὐτόν.
Him.

10 Ἡμῖν δὲ ὁ Θεὸς ἀπεκάλυψε διὰ τοῦ Πνεύματος αὐτοῦ.
[5]to [6]us [1]But - [2]God [3]revealed [4]*them* through - Spirit ~ His.

Τὸ γὰρ Πνεῦμα πάντα ἐρευνᾷ, καὶ τὰ βάθη τοῦ Θεοῦ.
the ~ For Spirit [2]all [3]*things* [1]searches, even the deep *things* - of God.

11 Τίς γὰρ οἶδεν ἀνθρώπων τὰ τοῦ ἀνθρώπου εἰ μὴ
who ~ For [3]knows [1]of (among) [2]men the *things* - of a man if not (except)

τὸ πνεῦμα τοῦ ἀνθρώπου τὸ ἐν αὐτῷ? Οὕτω καὶ τὰ
the spirit of the man the *one* (which is) in him? So also [4]the [5]*things*

τοῦ Θεοῦ οὐδεὶς οἶδεν εἰ μὴ τὸ Πνεῦμα τοῦ Θεοῦ.
- [6]of [7]God [1]no [2]one [3]knows if not (except) the Spirit - of God.

12 Ἡμεῖς δὲ οὐ τὸ πνεῦμα τοῦ κόσμου ἐλάβομεν, ἀλλὰ
we ~ Now [2]not [4]the [5]spirit [6]of [7]the [8]world [1]did [3]receive, but

τὸ Πνεῦμα τὸ ἐκ τοῦ Θεοῦ, ἵνα εἰδῶμεν
the Spirit the *One* (who is) from - God, in order that we might know

τὰ ὑπὸ τοῦ Θεοῦ χαρισθέντα ἡμῖν· 13 ἃ καὶ
the *things* [6]by - [7]God [1]having (which have) [2]been [3]given [4]to [5]us; which also ~

λαλοῦμεν, οὐκ ἐν διδακτοῖς ἀνθρωπίνης σοφίας λόγοις, ἀλλ᾽ ἐν
we speak, not in [2]taught [3]of (by) [4]human [5]wisdom [1]words, but in

διδακτοῖς Πνεύματος Ἁγίου,[d] πνευματικοῖς*
words taught of (by) *the* Spirit ~ Holy, [4]with [5]spiritual [6]*things* [7]*or* [8]*persons*

πνευματικὰ συγκρίνοντες. 14 Ψυχικὸς δὲ ἄνθρωπος οὐ
[2]spiritual [3]*things* [1]comparing. [3]natural [1]But [2]a man not ~

δέχεται τὰ τοῦ Πνεύματος τοῦ Θεοῦ, μωρία γὰρ
receives the *things* of the Spirit - of God, [4]foolishness [1]for

αὐτῷ ἐστι, καὶ οὐ δύναται γνῶναι, ὅτι
[5]to [6]him [2]they [3]are, and [3]not [1]he [2]is able to know *them,* because

πνευματικῶς ἀνακρίνεται. 15 Ὁ δὲ πνευματικὸς
[3]spiritually [1]they [2]are discerned. the ~ But spiritual *person*

ἀνακρίνει μὲν πάντα, αὐτὸς δὲ ὑπ᾽ οὐδενὸς ἀνακρίνεται.
examines - all *things,* [3]himself [1]but [6]by [7]no [8]one [2]he [4]is [5]examined.

16 «Τίς γὰρ ἔγνω νοῦν Κυρίου,
«who ~ For knew (has known) *the* mind of *the* Lord,

Ὃς συμβιβάσει αὐτόν?»[e]
Who (That) will (he may) instruct Him?»

Ἡμεῖς δὲ νοῦν Χριστοῦ ἔχομεν.
we ~ But [2]*the* [3]mind [4]of [5]Christ [1]have.

Sectarianism Is Carnal

3 1 Καὶ ἐγώ, ἀδελφοί, οὐκ ἠδυνήθην ὑμῖν λαλῆσαι ὡς
And I, brothers, not ~ was able [3]to [4]you [1]to [2]speak as

πνευματικοῖς ἀλλ᾽ ὡς σαρκικοῖς, ὡς νηπίοις ἐν Χριστῷ.
to spiritual *people* but as to carnal *people,* as to babes in Christ.

2 Γάλα ὑμᾶς ἐπότισα καὶ οὐ βρῶμα, οὔπω γὰρ
[4]milk [3]you [1]I [2]gave to drink and not solid food, [4]not [5]yet [1]for

The things which God has prepared for those who love Him."

10 But God has revealed *them* to us through His Spirit. For the Spirit searches all things, yes, the deep things of God.
11 For what man knows the things of a man except the spirit of the man which is in him? Even so no one knows the things of God except the Spirit of God.
12 Now we have received, not the spirit of the world, but the Spirit who is from God, that we might know the things that have been freely given to us by God.
13 These things we also speak, not in words which man's wisdom teaches but which the Holy Spirit teaches, comparing spiritual things with spiritual.
14 But the natural man does not receive the things of the Spirit of God, for they are foolishness to him; nor can he know *them,* because they are spiritually discerned.
15 But he who is spiritual judges all things, yet he himself is *rightly* judged by no one.
16 For *"who has known the mind of the* LORD *that he may instruct Him?"* But we have the mind of Christ.

3 And I, brethren, could not speak to you as to spiritual *people* but as to carnal, as to babes in Christ.
2 I fed you with milk and not

---

[d](2:13) NU omits Αγιου, *Holy.* [e](2:16) Is. 40:13

*(2:13) πνευματικός *(pneumatikos).* Adjective from πνεῦμα, *spirit,* thus meaning *pertaining to the spirit, spiritual.* Often πνευματικός is used in contrast to that which is σαρκικός, *fleshly* or *carnal* (as 1 Cor. 3:1), or that which is ψυχικός, *natural* or *unspiritual* (as here, cf. v. 14; see ψυχικός at 1 Cor. 15:46). What is thus *spiritual* requires the enlightening or regenerating work (the endowment) of the Spirit upon the human spirit for there to be meaning and life. In the neuter plural, the adjective may be used substantivally with the special sense *spiritual gifts* (as 1 Cor. 12:1; 14:1), that is, Spirit-given endowments for ministering.

with solid food; for until now
you were not able *to receive it,*
and even now you are still not
able;
3 for you are still carnal. For
where *there are* envy, strife,
and divisions among you, are
you not carnal and behaving like
mere men?
4 For when one says, "I am
of Paul," and another, "I *am* of
Apollos," are you not carnal?
5 Who then is Paul, and who
is Apollos, but ministers
through whom you believed, as
the Lord gave to each one?
6 I planted, Apollos watered,
but God gave the increase.
7 So then neither he who
plants is anything, nor he who
waters, but God who gives the
increase.
8 Now he who plants and he
who waters are one, and each
one will receive his own reward
according to his own labor.
9 For we are God's fellow
workers; you are God's field,
you are God's building.
10 According to the grace of
God which was given to me, as
a wise master builder I have
laid the foundation, and another
builds on it. But let each one
take heed how he builds on it.
11 For no other foundation
can anyone lay than that which
is laid, which is Jesus Christ.
12 Now if anyone builds on
this foundation *with* gold, silver,
precious stones, wood, hay,
straw,
13 each one's work will become clear; for the Day will declare it, because it will be
revealed by fire; and the fire
will test each one's work, of
what sort it is.

ἐδύνασθε. Ἀλλ' οὔτε ἔτι νῦν δύνασθε, **3** ἔτι γὰρ
[2]you [3]were able. Indeed neither [4]yet [3]now [1]are [2]you [5]able, [4]still [1]for

σαρκικοί ἐστε. Ὅπου γὰρ ἐν ὑμῖν ζῆλος καὶ
[5]carnal [2]you [3]are. where ~ (insofar as) For [8]among [9]you [1]*there* [2]*are* [3]envy [4]and

ἔρις καὶ διχοστασίαι,[a] οὐχὶ σαρκικοί ἐστε καὶ
[5]strife [6]and [7]divisions, [12]not [13]carnal [10]are [11]you and

κατὰ ἄνθρωπον περιπατεῖτε? **4** Ὅταν γὰρ λέγῃ
[2]according [3]to [4]man (human principles) [1]walking? whenever ~ For says ~

τις, "Ἐγὼ μέν εἰμι Παύλου," ἕτερος δέ, "Ἐγὼ Ἀπολλῶ,"
someone, "I - am of Paul," another ~ and, "I *am* of Apollos,"

οὐχὶ σαρκικοί[b] ἐστε?
[3]not [4]carnal [1]are [2]you?

The Ministry: Watering, Working, Warning

5 Τίς οὖν ἐστι Παῦλος, τίς δὲ Ἀπολλώς, ἀλλ' ἢ
Who then is Paul, who ~ and *is* Apollos, but -

διάκονοι δι' ὧν ἐπιστεύσατε, καὶ ἑκάστῳ ὡς ὁ Κύριος
ministers through whom you believed, and to each *one* as the Lord

ἔδωκεν? **6** Ἐγὼ ἐφύτευσα, Ἀπολλὼς ἐπότισεν, ἀλλ' ὁ Θεὸς
gave? (has given?) I planted, Apollos watered, but - God

ηὔξανεν. **7** Ὥστε οὔτε ὁ φυτεύων ἐστί τι,
caused *you* to grow. So then neither the *one* planting (who plants) is anything,

οὔτε ὁ ποτίζων, ἀλλ' ὁ αὐξάνων Θεός.
nor the *one* watering, (who waters,) but [2]the [3]*One* (who) [4]causing (causes) [5]*you* [6]to [7]grow [1]God.

8 Ὁ φυτεύων δὲ καὶ ὁ ποτίζων ἕν εἰσιν,
[2]the [3]*one* [4]planting (who plants) [1]Now and the *one* watering (who waters) one ~ are,

ἕκαστος δὲ τὸν ἴδιον μισθὸν λήψεται κατὰ τὸν
each ~ and - [3]his [4]own [5]reward [1]will [2]receive according to -

ἴδιον κόπον. **9** Θεοῦ γάρ ἐσμεν συνεργοί· Θεοῦ
his own labor. [5]of [6]God [1]For [2]we [3]are [4]coworkers; [11]of [12]God

γεώργιον, Θεοῦ οἰκοδομή ἐστε.
[9]*the* [10]field, [15]of [16]God [13]*the* [14]building [7]you [8]are.

10 Κατὰ τὴν χάριν τοῦ Θεοῦ τὴν δοθεῖσάν μοι, ὡς
According to the grace - of God the *one* (which) being (was) given to me, as

σοφὸς ἀρχιτέκτων θεμέλιον τέθεικα, ἄλλος δὲ
a wise master builder [4]a [5]foundation [1]I [2]have [3]laid, another ~ but

ἐποικοδομεῖ. Ἕκαστος δὲ βλεπέτω πῶς ἐποικοδομεῖ.
builds on *it.* [3]each [1]But [2]let take care how he builds on *it.*

11 Θεμέλιον γὰρ ἄλλον οὐδεὶς δύναται θεῖναι παρὰ τὸν
[9]foundation [1]For [8]another [2]no [3]one [4]is [5]able [6]to [7]lay other than the *one*

κείμενον, ὅς ἐστιν Ἰησοῦς Χριστός. **12** Εἰ δέ τις
being (which is) laid, which is Jesus Christ. if ~ Now anyone

ἐποικοδομεῖ ἐπὶ τὸν θεμέλιον τοῦτον χρυσόν, ἄργυρον, λίθους
builds upon - foundation ~ this with gold, silver, stones ~

τιμίους, ξύλα, χόρτον, καλάμην, **13** ἑκάστου τὸ ἔργον
precious, wood, hay, straw, [3]of [4]each [5]*one* [1]the [2]work

φανερὸν γενήσεται· ἡ γὰρ ἡμέρα δηλώσει, ὅτι ἐν πυρὶ
[8]evident [6]will [7]become: the ~ for Day will reveal *it,* because [4]by [5]fire

ἀποκαλύπτεται· καὶ ἑκάστου τὸ ἔργον ὁποῖόν
[1]it [2]is (will be) [3]revealed; and [7]of [8]each [9]*one* [5]the [6]work [10]*as* [11]*to* [12]what [13]sort

---

[a](3:3) NU omits και διχοστασιαι, *and divisions.*
[b](3:4) NU reads ανθρωποι, *(merely) men.*

ἐστι τὸ πῦρ[c] δοκιμάσει. **14** Εἴ τινος τὸ ἔργον μένει
[14]it [15]is [1]the [2]fire [3]will [4]test. If [3]of [4]anyone [1]the [2]work [8]remains
ὃ ἐποικοδόμησε, μισθὸν λήψεται. **15** Εἴ τινος
[5]which [6]he [7]built, [12]a [13]reward [9]he [10]will [11]receive. If [3]of [4]anyone
τὸ ἔργον κατακαήσεται, ζημιωθήσεται· αὐτὸς δὲ
[1]the [2]work is burned down, he will suffer damage; [3]himself [1]but
σωθήσεται, οὕτω δὲ ὡς διὰ πυρός.
[2]he will be saved, so ˜ but as through fire.

16 Οὐκ οἴδατε ὅτι ναὸς* Θεοῦ ἐστε καὶ τὸ
[3]not [1]Do [2]you know that [3]*the* [4]temple [5]of [6]God [1]you [2]are and the
Πνεῦμα τοῦ Θεοῦ οἰκεῖ ἐν ὑμῖν? **17** Εἴ τις τὸν ναὸν τοῦ
Spirit - of God dwells in you? If anyone [2]the [3]temple -
Θεοῦ φθείρει, φθερεῖ τοῦτον ὁ Θεός. Ὁ γὰρ ναὸς τοῦ
[4]of [5]God [1]destroys, [7]will [8]destroy [9]this [10]*one* - [6]God. the ˜ For temple -
him
Θεοῦ ἅγιός ἐστιν, οἵτινές ἐστε ὑμεῖς.
of God holy ˜ is, which are ˜ you.

Shun Worldly Wisdom

18 Μηδεὶς ἑαυτὸν ἐξαπατάτω. Εἴ τις δοκεῖ σοφὸς εἶναι
[2]no [3]one [5]himself [1]Let [4]deceive. If anyone [3]seems [6]wise [4]to [5]be
ἐν ὑμῖν ἐν τῷ αἰῶνι τούτῳ, μωρὸς γενέσθω ἵνα
[1]among [2]you in - age ˜ this, [4]foolish [1]let [2]him [3]become in order that
γένηται σοφός. **19** Ἡ γὰρ σοφία τοῦ κόσμου τούτου
he may become wise. the ˜ For wisdom - of world ˜ this
μωρία παρὰ τῷ θεῷ ἐστι. Γέγραπται γάρ, «Ὁ
[2]foolishness [3]with - [4]God [1]is. [6]it [7]is [8]written [5]For, «The *One*
«He
δρασσόμενος τοὺς σοφοὺς ἐν τῇ πανουργίᾳ αὐτῶν»·[d] **20** καὶ
catching the wise in - craftiness ˜ their»; and
catches
πάλιν, «Κύριος γινώσκει τοὺς διαλογισμοὺς τῶν σοφῶν, ὅτι
again, «*The* Lord knows the reasonings of the wise, that
εἰσὶ μάταιοι.»[e] **21** Ὥστε μηδεὶς καυχάσθω ἐν ἀνθρώποις·
they are useless.» So then [2]no [3]one [1]let boast in men:
πάντα γὰρ ὑμῶν ἐστιν, **22** εἴτε Παῦλος εἴτε Ἀπολλῶς
[2]all [3]*things* [1]for yours ˜ are, whether Paul or Apollos
εἴτε Κηφᾶς εἴτε κόσμος εἴτε ζωὴ εἴτε θάνατος εἴτε ἐνεστῶτα
or Cephas or *the* world or life or death or *things* present
εἴτε μέλλοντα, πάντα ὑμῶν ἐστιν, **23** ὑμεῖς δὲ Χριστοῦ,
or *things* coming, all *things* yours ˜ are, you ˜ and *are* of Christ,
Χριστὸς δὲ Θεοῦ.
Christ ˜ and *is* of God.

The Ministers: Stewards of the Mysteries

4 **1** Οὕτως ἡμᾶς λογιζέσθω ἄνθρωπος ὡς ὑπηρέτας Χριστοῦ
[4]so [6]us [1]Let [5]consider [2]a [3]man as servants of Christ
καὶ οἰκονόμους μυστηρίων Θεοῦ. **2** Ὃ δὲ λοιπὸν
and stewards of *the* mysteries of God. [3]what [1]Now [2]furthermore
ζητεῖται ἐν τοῖς οἰκονόμοις ἵνα πιστός τις εὑρεθῇ.
is demanded among the stewards *is* that [4]faithful [1]one [2]be [3]found.
required
3 Ἐμοὶ δὲ εἰς ἐλάχιστόν ἐστιν ἵνα ὑφ' ὑμῶν
[2]to [3]me [1]But [6]as [7]a [8]very [9]small [10]*thing* [4]it [5]is that [5]by [6]you
ἀνακριθῶ ἢ ὑπὸ ἀνθρωπίνης ἡμέρας· ἀλλ' οὐδὲ
[1]I [2]should [3]be [4]judged or by a human day; indeed [3]not [4]even
court;

14 If anyone's work which he has built on *it* endures, he will receive a reward.
15 If anyone's work is burned, he will suffer loss; but he himself will be saved, yet so as through fire.
16 Do you not know that you are the temple of God and *that* the Spirit of God dwells in you?
17 If anyone defiles the temple of God, God will destroy him. For the temple of God is holy, which *temple* you are.
18 Let no one deceive himself. If anyone among you seems to be wise in this age, let him become a fool that he may become wise.
19 For the wisdom of this world is foolishness with God. For it is written, *"He catches the wise in their own craftiness"*;
20 and again, *"The* LORD *knows the thoughts of the wise, that they are futile."*
21 Therefore let no one boast in men. For all things are yours:
22 whether Paul or Apollos or Cephas, or the world or life or death, or things present or things to come—all are yours.
23 And you *are* Christ's, and Christ *is* God's.

4 Let a man so consider us, as servants of Christ and stewards of the mysteries of God.
2 Moreover it is required in stewards that one be found faithful.
3 But with me it is a very small thing that I should be judged by you or by a human court. In fact, I do not even

---

[c]**(3:13)** NU adds in brackets αυτο, *itself.*
[d]**(3:19)** Job 5:13
[e]**(3:20)** Ps. 94:11

***(3:16)** ναός *(naos).* Noun meaning *temple, shrine,* used in the NT especially for the temple of God, but also for a pagan temple or shrine (Acts 17:24). Most often it is the Jewish temple in Jerusalem (as Luke 1:21), but it is also used of the heavenly *sanctuary* (Rev. 14:15). When used figuratively, ναός refers to Christians either corporately (as probably here in 1 Cor. 3:16) or individually (as 1 Cor. 6:19) as a "spiritual" temple, God's true dwelling place. When distinguished from ἱερόν, *temple,* ναός usually indi-

judge myself.
4 For I know of nothing against myself, yet I am not justified by this; but He who judges me is the Lord.
5 Therefore judge nothing before the time, until the Lord comes, who will both bring to light the hidden things of darkness and reveal the counsels of the hearts. Then each one's praise will come from God.
6 Now these things, brethren, I have figuratively transferred to myself and Apollos for your sakes, that you may learn in us not to think beyond what is written, that none of you may be puffed up on behalf of one against the other.
7 For who makes you differ *from another?* And what do you have that you did not receive? Now if you did indeed receive *it,* why do you boast as if you had not received *it?*
8 You are already full! You are already rich! You have reigned as kings without us—and indeed I could wish you did reign, that we also might reign with you!
9 For I think that God has displayed us, the apostles, last, as men condemned to death; for we have been made a spectacle to the world, both to angels and to men.
10 We *are* fools for Christ's sake, but you *are* wise in Christ! We *are* weak, but you *are* strong! You *are* distinguished, but we *are* dishonored!
11 To the present hour we both hunger and thirst, and we are poorly clothed, and beaten, and homeless.
12 And we labor, working

ἐμαυτὸν ἀνακρίνω. 4 Οὐδὲν γὰρ ἐμαυτῷ σύνοιδα, ἀλλ'
[6]myself [1]I [2]do [5]judge. [6]nothing [1]For [4]with [5]myself [2]I [3]know, but
I am conscious of,

οὐκ ἐν τούτῳ δεδικαίωμαι· ὁ δὲ ἀνακρίνων με
[3]not [6]by [7]this [1]I [2]have [4]been [5]justified; [12]the [13]*One* [8]but [14]judging [15]me
who judges

Κύριός ἐστιν. 5 Ὥστε μὴ πρὸ καιροῦ τι κρίνετε,
[9]*the* [10]Lord [11]is. So then [2]not [5]before [6]*the* [7]time [4]anything [1]do [3]judge,

ἕως ἂν ἔλθῃ ὁ Κύριος, ὃς καὶ φωτίσει τὰ κρυπτὰ
until - [3]comes [1]the [2]Lord, who also will bring to light the *things* hidden

τοῦ σκότους καὶ φανερώσει τὰς βουλὰς τῶν καρδιῶν· καὶ
of the darkness and will make clear the purposes of the hearts; and
by

τότε ὁ ἔπαινος γενήσεται ἑκάστῳ ἀπὸ τοῦ Θεοῦ.
then the praise will be to each *one* from - God.

The Apostles Are Fools for Christ's Sake

6 Ταῦτα δέ, ἀδελφοί, μετεσχημάτισα εἰς ἐμαυτὸν
[2]these [3]*things* [1]Now, brothers, I have transformed to myself
figuratively applied

καὶ Ἀπολλὼ δι' ὑμᾶς, ἵνα ἐν ἡμῖν μάθητε
and Apollos for the sake of you, in order that in us you may learn
your sakes,

τὸ μὴ ὑπὲρ ὃ γέγραπται φρονεῖν,[a] ἵνα μὴ εἷς
- not [3]beyond [4]what [5]is [6]written [1]to [2]think, so that not ˜ one
certainly

ὑπὲρ τοῦ ἑνὸς μὴ φυσιοῦσθε κατὰ τοῦ ἑτέρου. 7 Τίς
[5]in [6]behalf [7]of - [8]one [1]not [2]be [3]puffed [4]up against the other. who ˜

γάρ σε διακρίνει? Τί δὲ ἔχεις ὃ οὐκ ἔλαβες?
For you ˜ makes differ? what ˜ And do you have that [3]not [1]you [2]did receive?

Εἰ δὲ καὶ ἔλαβες, τί καυχᾶσαι ὡς μὴ
if ˜ And indeed ˜ you received *what you have,* why do you boast as not
though

λαβών? 8 Ἤδη κεκορεσμένοι ἐστέ, ἤδη
receiving *it?* Already [3]satiated [1]you [2]are, already
you did not receive it? full

ἐπλουτήσατε, χωρὶς ἡμῶν ἐβασιλεύσατε· καὶ ὄφελόν γε
you became rich, without us you reigned *as kings;* and I wish *that* indeed
have become have reigned

ἐβασιλεύσατε, ἵνα καὶ ἡμεῖς ὑμῖν
you did reign, in order that also ˜ we [4]with [5]you

συμβασιλεύσωμεν! 9 Δοκῶ γὰρ ὅτι ὁ Θεὸς ἡμᾶς τοὺς
[1]might [2]reign [3]together! [2]I [3]think [1]For that - God [2]us [3]the

ἀποστόλους ἐσχάτους ἀπέδειξεν ὡς ἐπιθανατίους· ὅτι
[4]apostles [5]*to* [6]*be* [7]last [1]displayed as condemned to death; because

θέατρον* ἐγενήθημεν τῷ κόσμῳ καὶ ἀγγέλοις καὶ
[3]a [4]spectacle [1]we [2]became to the world and to angels and

ἀνθρώποις. 10 Ἡμεῖς μωροὶ διὰ Χριστόν, ὑμεῖς δὲ
to men. We *are* fools for the sake of Christ, you ˜ but

φρόνιμοι ἐν Χριστῷ! Ἡμεῖς ἀσθενεῖς, ὑμεῖς δὲ ἰσχυροί!
are wise in Christ! We *are* weak, you ˜ but *are* strong!

Ὑμεῖς ἔνδοξοι, ἡμεῖς δὲ ἄτιμοι! 11 Ἄχρι τῆς ἄρτι
You *are* honored, we ˜ but *are* dishonored! Until the present

ὥρας καὶ πεινῶμεν καὶ διψῶμεν καὶ γυμνητεύομεν καὶ
hour both ˜ we hunger and thirst and are poorly clothed and
time

κολαφιζόμεθα καὶ ἀστατοῦμεν 12 καὶ κοπιῶμεν ἐργαζόμενοι
are beaten and are homeless and we labor working

---

[a](4:6) NU omits *φρονειν, to think.*

cates the inner sanctuary and ἱερόν the entire temple complex; see ἱερόν at Luke 24:53.

*(4:9) *θέατρον (theatron).* Noun meaning an open, public *theater,* such as at Ephesus (Acts 19:29, 31). The word could also refer to what was seen at such a theater, a *play* or other *spectacle.* It is in this sense that Paul uses it (ironically) here at 1 Cor. 4:9, presenting himself as a public spectacle for people to gape at. Cf. the cognate verb *θεατρίζω, put to shame, expose publicly*

ταῖς ἰδίαις χερσί. Λοιδορούμενοι εὐλογοῦμεν,
\- with our own hands. Being reviled we bless,

διωκόμενοι ἀνεχόμεθα, **13** βλασφημούμενοι[b]
being persecuted we endure, being defamed

παρακαλοῦμεν· ὡς περικαθάρματα τοῦ κόσμου ἐγενήθημεν,
we encourage; [3]as [4]*the* [5]filthy [6]things [7]of [8]the [9]world [1]we [2]became,
refuse have become,

πάντων περίψημα ἕως ἄρτι.
[12]of [13]all [14]*things* [10]*the* [11]offscourings until now.
dirt

Paul's Paternal Care

14 Οὐκ ἐντρέπων ὑμᾶς γράφω ταῦτα, ἀλλ' ὡς τέκνα
[5]not [6]shaming [7]you [1]I [2]write [3]these [4]*things,* but as [3]children
to shame

μου ἀγαπητὰ νουθετῶ. **15** Ἐὰν γὰρ μυρίους
[1]my [2]beloved I admonish *you.* if ˜ For [4]ten [5]thousand
although

παιδαγωγοὺς ἔχητε ἐν Χριστῷ, ἀλλ' οὐ
[6]guides [1]you [2]might [3]have in Christ, yet *you do* not *have*

πολλοὺς πατέρας· ἐν γὰρ Χριστῷ Ἰησοῦ διὰ τοῦ
many fathers: in ˜ for Christ Jesus [4]through [5]the

εὐαγγελίου ἐγὼ ὑμᾶς ἐγέννησα. **16** Παρακαλῶ οὖν ὑμᾶς,
[6]gospel [1]I [3]you [2]begot. [2]I [3]urge [1]Therefore you,

μιμηταί μου γίνεσθε. **17** Διὰ τοῦτο ἔπεμψα ὑμῖν
[2]imitators [3]of [4]me [1]be. Because of this I sent [2]to [3]you

Τιμόθεον, ὅς ἐστι τέκνον μου ἀγαπητὸν καὶ πιστὸν ἐν
[1]Timothy, who is [5]child [1]my [2]beloved [3]and [4]faithful in

Κυρίῳ, ὃς ὑμᾶς ἀναμνήσει τὰς ὁδούς μου τὰς ἐν Χριστῷ,
the Lord, who [3]you [1]will [2]remind of - ways ˜ my - in Christ,

καθὼς πανταχοῦ ἐν πάσῃ ἐκκλησίᾳ διδάσκω. **18** Ὡς μὴ
as [3]everywhere [4]in [5]every [6]church [1]I [2]teach. [6]as [8]not
each as though I were

ἐρχομένου δέ μου πρὸς ὑμᾶς ἐφυσιώθησάν τινες.
[9]coming [1]Now [7]me [10]to [11]you [3]were [4]puffed [5]up [2]some.
not coming

19 Ἐλεύσομαι δὲ ταχέως πρὸς ὑμᾶς, ἐὰν ὁ Κύριος θελήσῃ,
[2]I [3]will [4]come [1]But [7]shortly [5]to [6]you, if the Lord wills,

καὶ γνώσομαι, οὐ τὸν λόγον τῶν πεφυσιωμένων, ἀλλὰ τὴν
and I will know, not the word of the *ones* being puffed up, but the
those who are

δύναμιν. **20** Οὐ γὰρ ἐν λόγῳ ἡ βασιλεία τοῦ Θεοῦ ἀλλ'
power. [6]*is* [7]not [1]For [8]in [9]word [2]the [3]kingdom - [4]of [5]God but

ἐν δυνάμει. **21** Τί θέλετε? Ἐν ῥάβδῳ ἔλθω πρὸς
in power. What do you desire? [6]with [7]a [8]rod [1]Shall [2]I [3]come [4]to

ὑμᾶς, ἢ ἐν ἀγάπῃ πνεύματί τε πραότητος?
[5]you, or in love [2]in [3]a [4]spirit [1]and of meekness?

Immorality Defiles the Church

5 **1** Ὅλως ἀκούεται ἐν ὑμῖν
[3]actually [1]It [2]is [4]heard [10]among [11]you [5]*that* [6]*there* [7]*is*

πορνεία, καὶ τοιαύτη πορνεία ἥτις οὐδὲ ἐν
[8]sexual [9]immorality, and such sexual immorality which [2]not [3]even [5]among

τοῖς ἔθνεσιν ὀνομάζεται,[a] ὥστε γυναῖκά τινα τοῦ
[6]the [7]Gentiles [1]is [4]named, so that [4]*the* [5]wife [1]someone [6]of [7]the
his

with our own hands. Being reviled, we bless; being persecuted, we endure;
13 being defamed, we en-
treat. We have been made as
the filth of the world, the off-
scouring of all things until now.
14 I do not write these things
to shame you, but as my beloved children I warn *you.*
15 For though you might have
ten thousand instructors in
Christ, yet *you do* not *have*
many fathers; for in Christ Jesus I have begotten you
through the gospel.
16 Therefore I urge you, imitate me.
17 For this reason I have sent
Timothy to you, who is my beloved and faithful son in the
Lord, who will remind you of
my ways in Christ, as I teach
everywhere in every church.
18 Now some are puffed up,
as though I were not coming to
you.
19 But I will come to you
shortly, if the Lord wills, and I
will know, not the word of
those who are puffed up, but
the power.
20 For the kingdom of God *is*
not in word but in power.
21 What do you want? Shall I
come to you with a rod, or in
love and a spirit of gentleness?
5 It is actually reported *that*
there is sexual immorality
among you, and such sexual immorality as is not even named
among the Gentiles—that a

---

[b](**4:13**) NU reads *δυσφημουμενοι, being slandered.* [a](**5:1**) NU omits *ονομαζεται, named.*

(Heb. 10:33), just as a drama in a theater is a public performance.

man has his father's wife!
2 And you are puffed up, and have not rather mourned, that he who has done this deed might be taken away from among you.
3 For I indeed, as absent in body but present in spirit, have already judged (as though I were present) him who has so done this deed.
4 In the name of our Lord Jesus Christ, when you are gathered together, along with my spirit, with the power of our Lord Jesus Christ,
5 deliver such a one to Satan for the destruction of the flesh, that his spirit may be saved in the day of the Lord Jesus.
6 Your glorying *is* not good. Do you not know that a little leaven leavens the whole lump?
7 Therefore purge out the old leaven, that you may be a new lump, since you truly are unleavened. For indeed Christ, our Passover, was sacrificed for us.
8 Therefore let us keep the feast, not with old leaven, nor with the leaven of malice and wickedness, but with the unleavened *bread* of sincerity and truth.
9 I wrote to you in my epistle not to keep company with sexually immoral people.
10 Yet *I* certainly *did* not *mean* with the sexually immoral people of this world, or with the covetous, or extortioners, or idolaters, since then you would need to go out of the world.
11 But now I have written to

πατρὸς ἔχειν! **2** Καὶ ὑμεῖς πεφυσιωμένοι ἐστέ, καὶ οὐχὶ
[8]father [2]to [3]have! And you [2]puffed [3]up [1]are, and [2]not
has!

μᾶλλον ἐπενθήσατε,* ἵνα ἐξαρθῇ ἐκ μέσου
[3]rather [1]have [4]grieved, so that [7]would [8]be [9]taken [10]out [11]from [13]midst
removed

ὑμῶν ὁ τὸ ἔργον τοῦτο ποιήσας. **3** Ἐγὼ μὲν γὰρ ὡς
[12]your [1]the [2]*one* - [6]deed [5]this [3]having [4]done. [2]I [3]indeed [1]For as
he who did.

ἀπὼν τῷ σώματι, παρὼν δὲ τῷ πνεύματι, ἤδη
being absent - in body, [2]being [3]present [1]but - in spirit, already

κέκρικα ὡς παρῶν τὸν οὕτω τοῦτο
have judged as though being present the *one* so [2]this [3]*deed*
I were present him who has done this deed

κατεργασάμενον, **4** ἐν τῷ ὀνόματι τοῦ Κυρίου ἡμῶν Ἰησοῦ
[1]doing, in the name - of Lord ˜ our Jesus
in this way,

Χριστοῦ,[b] συναχθέντων ὑμῶν καὶ τοῦ ἐμοῦ πνεύματος,
Christ, [2]being [3]gathered [1]you and - my spirit *is with you,*
when you are assembled

σὺν τῇ δυνάμει τοῦ Κυρίου ἡμῶν Ἰησοῦ Χριστοῦ,[b]
with the power - of Lord ˜ our Jesus Christ,

5 παραδοῦναι τὸν τοιοῦτον τῷ Σατανᾷ εἰς ὄλεθρον τῆς
to hand over - such a one - to Satan for *the* destruction of the

σαρκός, ἵνα τὸ πνεῦμα σωθῇ ἐν τῇ ἡμέρᾳ τοῦ
flesh, in order that the spirit may be saved in the day of the
his

Κυρίου Ἰησοῦ.[c]
Lord Jesus.

6 Οὐ καλὸν τὸ καύχημα ὑμῶν. Οὐκ οἴδατε ὅτι
[4]not [3]*is* [5]good - [2]boasting [1]Your. [8]not [6]Do [7]you [9]know that

μικρὰ ζύμη ὅλον τὸ φύραμα ζυμοῖ? **7** Ἐκκαθάρατε
a little leaven [3]whole [2]the [4]batch [5]of [6]dough [1]leavens? Clean out

τὴν παλαιὰν ζύμην, ἵνα ἦτε νέον φύραμα,
the old leaven, in order that you may be a new batch of dough,

καθώς ἐστε ἄζυμοι. Καὶ γὰρ τὸ Πάσχα ἡμῶν
since you are unleavened. indeed ˜ For - Passover ˜ our

ὑπὲρ ἡμῶν[d] ἐτύθη, Χριστός. **8** Ὥστε
[4]in [5]behalf [6]of [7]us [2]was [3]sacrificed, [1]Christ. So then

ἑορτάζωμεν, μὴ ἐν ζύμῃ παλαιᾷ, μηδὲ ἐν ζύμῃ
let us observe the feast, not with leaven ˜ old, nor with leaven

κακίας καὶ πονηρίας, ἀλλ' ἐν ἀζύμοις εἰλικρινείας καὶ
of malice and wickedness, but with unleavened *loaves* of sincerity and

ἀληθείας.
of truth.

Immorality Must Be Judged

9 Ἔγραψα ὑμῖν ἐν τῇ ἐπιστολῇ μὴ συναναμίγνυσθαι
I wrote to you in the letter not to associate with
my

πόρνοις, **10** καὶ οὐ πάντως τοῖς
sexually immoral people, and yet *I did* not *mean* certainly with the

πόρνοις τοῦ κόσμου τούτου ἢ τοῖς πλεονέκταις,
sexually immoral people - of world ˜ this or with the covetous people,

ἢ ἅρπαξιν, ἢ εἰδωλολάτραις, ἐπεὶ ὀφείλετε ἄρα
or with swindlers, or with idolaters, since you are obligated then

ἐκ τοῦ κόσμου ἐξελθεῖν! **11** Νυνὶ δὲ ἔγραψα ὑμῖν μὴ
[3]out [4]of [5]the [6]world [1]to [2]go! now ˜ But I wrote to you not
write

---

[b](5:4) NU omits Χριστου, *Christ.* [c](5:5) NU omits Ιησου, *Jesus.*
[d](5:7) NU omits υπερ ημων, *in behalf of us.*

---

*(5:2) πενθέω *(pentheō).* Verb meaning *grieve, mourn (over),* in contrast with gladness or joy, often implying both inward sorrow and outward expression. It may refer to grieving over one's own sins (James 4:9) or the sins of others (as here in 1 Cor. 5:2 and 2 Cor. 12:21), as well as other matters (Mark 16:10). In Matt. 5:4 some interpreters think the mourning is over personal sin, but others that it is over

συναναμίγνυσθαι ἐάν τις ἀδελφὸς ὀνομαζόμενος ᾖ
to associate with [6]if [1]anyone [4]a [5]brother [2]being [3]named he should be

πόρνος ἢ πλεονέκτης ἢ εἰδωλολάτρης ἢ
a sexually immoral person or covetous person or idolater or

λοίδορος ἢ μέθυσος ἢ ἅρπαξ — τῷ τοιούτῳ
abusive person or drunkard or swindler — - [5]with [6]such [7]a [8]person

μηδὲ συνεσθίειν. 12 Τί γάρ μοι καὶ τοὺς
[1]not [2]even [3]to [4]eat. what ˜ For to me also the *ones*
have I to do with judging those

ἔξω κρίνειν? Οὐχὶ τοὺς ἔσω ὑμεῖς κρίνετε?
outside to be judging? [3]not [5]the [6]*ones* [7]inside [2]you [1]Do [4]judge?
who are outside?

13 Τοὺς δὲ ἔξω ὁ Θεὸς κρινεῖ. «Καὶ ἐξαρεῖτε τὸν
[2]the [3]*ones* [1]But outside - God will judge. «And take away the
remove

πονηρὸν ἐξ ὑμῶν αὐτῶν.»[e]
wicked person from you yourselves.»

Christians Must Not Sue Fellow Christians

6 1 Τολμᾷ τις ὑμῶν πρᾶγμα ἔχων πρὸς τὸν
Does [10]dare [1]anyone [2]of [3]you [5]a [6]lawsuit [4]having [7]against [8]the
who has

ἕτερον κρίνεσθαι ἐπὶ τῶν ἀδίκων καὶ οὐχὶ ἐπὶ τῶν
[9]other to go to court before the unrighteous and not before the

ἁγίων? 2 Οὐκ οἴδατε ὅτι οἱ ἅγιοι τὸν κόσμον κρινοῦσι?
saints? [3]not [1]Do [2]you know that the saints [3]the [4]world [1]will [2]judge?

Καὶ εἰ ἐν ὑμῖν κρίνεται ὁ κόσμος, ἀνάξιοί ἐστε
And if [6]by [7]you [3]is [4]being [5]judged [1]the [2]world, [10]unworthy [8]are [9]you
will be

κριτηρίων ἐλαχίστων? 3 Οὐκ οἴδατε ὅτι ἀγγέλους
[11]of [14]tribunals [12]very [13]small? [3]not [1]Do [2]you know that [4]angels
to judge

κρινοῦμεν? Μήτι γε βιωτικά! 4 Βιωτικὰ μὲν οὖν
[1]we [2]will [3]judge? Let alone - ordinary *matters!* [5]ordinary - [2]then

κριτήρια ἐὰν ἔχητε, τοὺς ἐξουθενημένους ἐν τῇ
[6]lawsuits [1]If [3]you [4]have, the *ones* being disdained within the
those who are

ἐκκλησίᾳ, τούτους καθίζετε. 5 Πρὸς ἐντροπὴν ὑμῖν
church, [3]these [1]you [2]appoint *to judge.* [4]for [5]shame [6]to [7]you
your shame

λέγω. Οὕτως οὐκ ἔνι ἐν ὑμῖν σοφὸς οὐδὲ εἷς ὃς
[1]I [2]say [3]*this.* So [3]not [1]is [2]there among you *a* wise *man* not even one who

δυνήσεται διακρῖναι ἀνὰ μέσον τοῦ ἀδελφοῦ αὐτοῦ?
will be able to judge - between - [2]brother [3]*and* [4]*another* [1]his?

6 Ἀλλὰ ἀδελφὸς μετὰ ἀδελφοῦ κρίνεται, καὶ τοῦτο ἐπὶ
But brother [4]against [5]brother [1]goes [2]to [3]court, and this before

ἀπίστων. 7 Ἤδη μὲν οὖν ὅλως ἥττημα ὑμῖν
unbelieving *ones.* Already - therefore [3]actually [4]a [5]defeat [6]for [7]you

ἐστιν ὅτι κρίματα ἔχετε μεθ' ἑαυτῶν. Διὰ τί
[1]it [2]is that [3]lawsuits [1]you [2]have against yourselves. On account of what
one another. Why

οὐχὶ μᾶλλον ἀδικεῖσθε? Διὰ τί οὐχὶ μᾶλλον
not rather be wronged? On account of what not rather
accept wrong? Why

ἀποστερεῖσθε? 8 Ἀλλὰ ὑμεῖς ἀδικεῖτε καὶ ἀποστερεῖτε,
be defrauded? But you wrong and defraud,
accept being defrauded?

καὶ ταῦτα ἀδελφούς! 9 Ἢ οὐκ οἴδατε ὅτι
and these *things* *to your* brothers! Or [3]not [1]do [2]you know that

you not to keep company with
anyone named a brother, who
is sexually immoral, or covetous, or an idolater, or a re-
viler, or a drunkard, or an
extortioner—not even to eat
with such a person.
12 For what *have* I *to do* with
judging those also who are outside? Do you not judge those
who are inside?
13 But those who are outside
God judges. Therefore *"put
away from yourselves the evil
person."*
6 Dare any of you, having a
matter against another,
go to law before the unrighteous, and not before the
saints?
2 Do you not know that the
saints will judge the world? And
if the world will be judged by
you, are you unworthy to judge
the smallest matters?
3 Do you not know that we
shall judge angels? How much
more, things that pertain to this
life?
4 If then you have judgments
concerning things pertaining to
this life, do you appoint those
who are least esteemed by the
church to judge?
5 I say this to your shame. Is
it so, that there is not a wise
man among you, not even one,
who will be able to judge between his brethren?
6 But brother goes to law
against brother, and that before
unbelievers!
7 Now therefore, it is already an utter failure for you
that you go to law against one
another. Why do you not rather
accept wrong? Why do you not
rather *let yourselves* be
cheated?
8 No, you yourselves do
wrong and cheat, and *you do*
these things *to your* brethren!
9 Do you not know that the

---

e(5:13) Deut. 17:7; 19:19; 22:21, 24; 24:7

the wicked who oppress the righteous. Cf. the cognate noun πένθος, *grief, mourning* (James 4:9; Rev. 18:7, 8; 21:4).

unrighteous will not inherit the kingdom of God? Do not be deceived. Neither fornicators, nor idolaters, nor adulterers, nor homosexuals, nor sodomites,
10 nor thieves, nor covetous, nor drunkards, nor revilers, nor extortioners will inherit the kingdom of God.
11 And such were some of you. But you were washed, but you were sanctified, but you were justified in the name of the Lord Jesus and by the Spirit of our God.
12 All things are lawful for me, but all things are not helpful. All things are lawful for me, but I will not be brought under the power of any.
13 Foods for the stomach and the stomach for foods, but God will destroy both it and them. Now the body *is* not for sexual immorality but for the Lord, and the Lord for the body.
14 And God both raised up the Lord and will also raise us up by His power.
15 Do you not know that your bodies are members of Christ? Shall I then take the members of Christ and make *them* members of a harlot? Certainly not!
16 Or do you not know that he who is joined to a harlot is one body *with her?* For *"the two,"* He says, *"shall become one flesh."*
17 But he who is joined to the Lord is one spirit *with Him.*
18 Flee sexual immorality. Every sin that a man does is outside the body, but he who commits sexual immorality sins against his own body.
19 Or do you not know that your body is the temple of the Holy Spirit *who is* in you, whom you have from God, and you

ἄδικοι βασιλείαν Θεοῦ οὐ κληρονομήσουσι? Μὴ
the unrighteous [4]*the* [5]kingdom [6]of [7]God [2]not [1]will [3]inherit? not ˜

πλανᾶσθε! Οὔτε πόρνοι οὔτε εἰδωλολάτραι οὔτε
Do be deceived! Neither sexually immoral people nor idolaters nor

μοιχοὶ οὔτε μαλακοὶ* οὔτε ἀρσενοκοῖται* **10** οὔτε
adulterers nor homosexuals nor sodomites nor

πλεονέκται οὔτε κλέπται οὔτε μέθυσοι, οὐ λοίδοροι, οὐχ
covetous persons nor thieves nor drunkards, nor abusive people, nor

ἅρπαγες βασιλείαν Θεοῦ οὐ κληρονομήσουσι. **11** Καὶ
swindlers [4]*the* [5]kingdom [6]of [7]God [2]not [1]will [3]inherit. And
ever

ταῦτά τινες ἦτε! Ἀλλὰ ἀπελούσασθε, ἀλλὰ
these some of you were! But you were washed, but

ἡγιάσθητε, ἀλλ' ἐδικαιώθητε ἐν τῷ ὀνόματι τοῦ
you were sanctified, but you were justified in the name of the

Κυρίου Ἰησοῦ[a] καὶ ἐν τῷ Πνεύματι τοῦ Θεοῦ ἡμῶν.
Lord Jesus and by the Spirit - of God ˜ our.

Glorify God in Body and Spirit

12 Πάντα μοι ἔξεστιν, ἀλλ' οὐ πάντα συμφέρει.
All *things* [3]for [4]me [1]are [2]lawful, but [4]not [1]all [2]*things* [3]are [5]profitable.

Πάντα μοι ἔξεστιν, ἀλλ' οὐκ ἐγὼ ἐξουσιασθήσομαι ὑπό
All *things* [3]for [4]me [1]are [2]lawful, but [3]not [1]I [2]will be mastered by

τινος. **13** Τὰ βρώματα τῇ κοιλίᾳ καὶ ἡ κοιλία τοῖς
anything. - Foods for the stomach and the stomach -

βρώμασιν, ὁ δὲ Θεὸς καὶ ταύτην καὶ ταῦτα
for foods, - but God [3]both [4]this [5]*stomach* [6]and [7]these [8]*foods*

καταργήσει. Τὸ δὲ σῶμα οὐ τῇ πορνείᾳ ἀλλὰ
[1]will [2]destroy. the ˜ Now body *is* not - for sexual immorality but

τῷ Κυρίῳ, καὶ ὁ Κύριος τῷ σώματι. **14** Ὁ δὲ Θεὸς καὶ
for the Lord, and the Lord for the body. - But God both

τὸν Κύριον ἤγειρε καὶ ἡμᾶς ἐξεγερεῖ διὰ τῆς δυνάμεως αὐτοῦ.
[2]the [3]Lord [1]raised and [3]us [1]will [2]raise by - power ˜ His.

15 Οὐκ οἴδατε ὅτι τὰ σώματα ὑμῶν μέλη Χριστοῦ
[3]not [1]Do [2]you know that - bodies ˜ your [2]members [3]of [4]Christ

ἐστιν? Ἄρας οὖν τὰ μέλη τοῦ Χριστοῦ ποιήσω
[1]are? taking ˜ Then the members - of Christ shall I make *them*
Then shall I take and

πόρνης μέλη? Μὴ γένοιτο! **16** Οὐκ οἴδατε ὅτι
[2]of [3]a [4]harlot [1]members? [7]not [5]May [6]it [8]be! [3]not [1]Do [2]you know that
Certainly not!

ὁ κολλώμενος τῇ πόρνῃ ἓν σῶμά ἐστιν?
the *one* being united with the harlot [2]one [3]body [4]*with* [5]*her* [1]is?

«Ἔσονται» γάρ, φησίν, «οἱ δύο εἰς σάρκα μίαν.»[b]
«[11]shall [12]be» [6]For, [7]He [8]says, «[9]The [10]two for flesh ˜ one.»

17 Ὁ δὲ κολλώμενος τῷ Κυρίῳ ἓν πνεῦμά
[2]the [3]*one* [1]But being united with the Lord [2]one [3]spirit [4]*with* [5]*Him*

ἐστι. **18** Φεύγετε τὴν πορνείαν. Πᾶν ἁμάρτημα ὃ ἐὰν
[1]is. Flee from - sexual immorality. Every sin that -

ποιήσῃ ἄνθρωπος ἐκτὸς τοῦ σώματός ἐστιν, ὁ δὲ
[3]may [4]do [1]a [2]man [6]outside [7]the [8]body [5]is, [10]the [11]*one* [9]but

πορνεύων εἰς τὸ ἴδιον σῶμα ἁμαρτάνει.
committing sexual immorality [2]against - [3]his [4]own [5]body [1]sins.

19 Ἢ οὐκ οἴδατε ὅτι τὸ σῶμα ὑμῶν ναὸς τοῦ ἐν
Or [3]not [1]do [2]you know that - body ˜ your [2]a [3]temple [4]of [5]the [8]within

ὑμῖν Ἁγίου Πνεύματός ἐστιν, οὗ ἔχετε ἀπὸ Θεοῦ, καὶ οὐκ
[9]you [6]Holy [7]Spirit [1]is, whom you have from God, and [3]not

---

[a](6:11) NU adds Χριστου, *Christ.* [b](6:16) Gen. 2:24

*(6:9) μαλακός *(malakos).* Adjective meaning *soft.* Its normal use is to describe things, such as "soft garments" (Luke 7:25). Here it is used substantivally to mean *effeminate ones,* the passive partners in homosexual intercourse. See ἀρσενοκοίτης at 1 Cor. 6:9.

*(6:9) ἀρσενοκοίτης *(arsenokoitēs).* Noun used only here and in 1 Tim. 1:10, derived from the adjective ἄρσην, *male,* and the noun κοίτη, *bed, coitus,* thus meaning a *male homosexual.* Specifically, it refers to the male homosexual partner who takes the active role

ἐστὲ ἑαυτῶν? **20** Ἠγοράσθητε γὰρ τιμῆς· δοξάσατε
[1]you [2]are of yourselves? [2]you [3]were [4]bought [1]For at a price; glorify ˜
your own?

δὴ τὸν Θεὸν ἐν τῷ σώματι ὑμῶν[c] καὶ ἐν τῷ πνεύματι
therefore - God in - body ˜ your and in - spirit ˜

ὑμῶν, ἅτινά ἐστι τοῦ Θεοῦ.
your, which are - of God.
belong to

Christian Principles of Marriage

7 **1** Περὶ δὲ ὧν ἐγράψατέ μοι, καλὸν
concerning ˜ Now *the things* about which you wrote to me, *it is* good

ἀνθρώπῳ γυναικὸς μὴ ἅπτεσθαι. **2** Διὰ δὲ τὰς
for a man [4]a [5]woman [1]not [2]to [3]touch. [2]because [3]of [1]But -

πορνείας ἕκαστος τὴν ἑαυτοῦ γυναῖκα ἐχέτω καὶ
sexual immoralities [2]each [3]*man* [5]the [7]of [8]himself [6]wife [1]let [4]have and
his own

ἑκάστη τὸν ἴδιον ἄνδρα ἐχέτω. **3** Τῇ γυναικὶ ὁ
[2]each [3]*woman* - [5]her [6]own [7]husband [1]let [4]have. [9]to [10]the [11]wife [2]the
his

ἀνὴρ τὴν ὀφειλομένην εὔνοιαν[a] ἀποδιδότω, ὁμοίως δὲ καὶ
[3]husband [5]the [7]being [8]owed [6]affection [1]Let [4]render, likewise ˜ and also
conjugal rights

ἡ γυνὴ τῷ ἀνδρί. **4** Ἡ γυνὴ τοῦ ἰδίου σώματος
the wife to the husband. The wife - [5]over [6]her [7]own [8]body
her

οὐκ ἐξουσιάζει ἀλλ' ὁ ἀνήρ, ὁμοίως δὲ καὶ ὁ
[2]not [1]does [3]have [4]authority but the husband *does,* likewise ˜ and also the

ἀνὴρ τοῦ ἰδίου σώματος οὐκ ἐξουσιάζει ἀλλ'
husband - [5]over [6]his [7]own [8]body [2]not [1]does [3]have [4]authority rather

ἡ γυνή. **5** Μὴ ἀποστερεῖτε ἀλλήλους, εἰ μήτι ἂν ἐκ
the wife *does.* not ˜ Do deprive one another, if not - by
except

συμφώνου πρὸς καιρὸν ἵνα σχολάζητε τῇ νηστείᾳ
agreement for a time that you may devote yourselves - to fasting

καὶ[b] τῇ προσευχῇ καὶ πάλιν ἐπὶ τὸ αὐτὸ συνέρχησθε[c] ἵνα
and - to prayer and again in the same come together that
come together lest

μὴ πειράζῃ ὑμᾶς ὁ Σατανᾶς διὰ τὴν ἀκρασίαν*
not [2]tempt [3]you - [1]Satan because of - [2]lack [3]of [4]self-control

ὑμῶν. **6** Τοῦτο δὲ λέγω κατὰ συγγνώμην, οὐ κατ'
[1]your. [4]this [1]But [2]I [3]say according to a concession, not according to
as as

ἐπιταγήν. **7** Θέλω γὰρ πάντας ἀνθρώπους εἶναι ὡς καὶ
a command. [2]I [3]desire [1]For all men to be as even

ἐμαυτόν. Ἀλλ' ἕκαστος ἴδιον χάρισμα ἔχει ἐκ Θεοῦ, ὃς
myself. But each *one* [2]his [3]own [4]gift [1]has from God, one

μὲν οὕτως, ὃς δὲ οὕτως.
- thus, one ˜ and thus.
in this way, another in that.

8 Λέγω δὲ τοῖς ἀγάμοις καὶ ταῖς χήραις, καλὸν
[2]I [3]say [1]Now to the unmarried *ones* and to the widows, [3]good

αὐτοῖς ἐστιν ἐὰν μείνωσιν ὡς κἀγώ. **9** Εἰ δὲ οὐκ
[4]for [5]them [1]it [2]is if they should remain as I also *remain.* if ˜ But [3]not

ἐγκρατεύονται, γαμησάτωσαν, κρεῖσσον γάρ ἐστι
[1]they [2]are exercising self-control, let them marry, [4]better [1]for [2]it [3]is

γαμῆσαι ἢ πυροῦσθαι.
to marry than to burn.
be sexually aroused.

are not your own?
20 For you were bought at a price; therefore glorify God in your body and in your spirit, which are God's.

7 Now concerning the things of which you wrote to me: *It is* good for a man not to touch a woman.
2 Nevertheless, because of sexual immorality, let each man have his own wife, and let each woman have her own husband.
3 Let the husband render to his wife the affection due her, and likewise also the wife to her husband.
4 The wife does not have authority over her own body, but the husband *does.* And likewise the husband does not have authority over his own body, but the wife *does.*
5 Do not deprive one another except with consent for a time, that you may give yourselves to fasting and prayer; and come together again so that Satan does not tempt you because of your lack of self-control.
6 But I say this as a concession, not as a commandment.
7 For I wish that all men were even as I myself. But each one has his own gift from God, one in this manner and another in that.
8 But I say to the unmarried and to the widows: It is good for them if they remain even as I am;
9 but if they cannot exercise self-control, let them marry. For it is better to marry than to burn *with passion.*

---

[c](6:20) NU omits the rest of v. 20.
[a](7:3) For οφειλομενην ευνοιαν, *affection being owed,* NU reads οφειλην, *debt.* [b](7:5) NU omits τη νηστεια και, *to fasting and.* [c](7:5) NU reads ητε, *be.*

in distinction from the μαλακός, the passive partner. See μαλακός at 1 Cor. 6:9.

*(7:5) ἀκρασία *(akrasia).* Noun meaning *lack of self-control, self-indulgence.* The word is formed from the α- negative prefix and the root of κρατέω, *take hold, hold fast,* thus suggesting a lack of holding in control. Here Paul apparently refers to a lack of self-restraint that might result from unnecessary and prolonged abstinence from marital relations. Cf. the cognate adjective ἀκρατής, *without self-control* (2 Tim. 3:3).

10 Now to the married I command, *yet* not I but the Lord: A wife is not to depart from *her* husband.
11 But even if she does depart, let her remain unmarried or be reconciled to *her* husband. And a husband is not to divorce *his* wife.
12 But to the rest I, not the Lord, say: If any brother has a wife who does not believe, and she is willing to live with him, let him not divorce her.
13 And a woman who has a husband who does not believe, if he is willing to live with her, let her not divorce him.
14 For the unbelieving husband is sanctified by the wife, and the unbelieving wife is sanctified by the husband; otherwise your children would be unclean, but now they are holy.
15 But if the unbeliever departs, let him depart; a brother or a sister is not under bondage in such *cases*. But God has called us to peace.
16 For how do you know, O wife, whether you will save *your* husband? Or how do you know, O husband, whether you will save *your* wife?
17 But as God has distributed to each one, as the Lord has called each one, so let him walk. And so I ordain in all the churches.
18 Was anyone called while circumcised? Let him not be-

Paul's Command to the Married

10 Τοῖς δὲ γεγαμηκόσι παραγγέλλω, οὐκ ἐγὼ ἀλλ'
[2]to [3]the [4]*ones* [1]Now having married I command, not I but
who have

ὁ Κύριος, γυναῖκα ἀπὸ ἀνδρὸς μὴ χωρισθῆναι
the Lord, [4]a [5]wife [8]from [9]a [10]husband [2]not [1]do [3]let [6]be [7]separated

11 — ἐὰν δὲ καὶ χωρισθῇ, μενέτω ἄγαμος ἢ τῷ
— [3]if [1]and [2]even she separates, let her remain unmarried or [3]to [4]the
her

ἀνδρὶ καταλλαγήτω — καὶ ἄνδρα γυναῖκα μὴ
[5]husband [1]be [2]reconciled — and [3]a [4]husband [7]a [8]wife [2]not

ἀφιέναι. **12** Τοῖς δὲ λοιποῖς ἐγὼ λέγω, οὐχ ὁ Κύριος,
[1]let [5]send [6]away. [2]to [3]the [1]And rest I speak, not the Lord,
divorce.

εἴ τις ἀδελφὸς γυναῖκα ἔχει ἄπιστον καὶ αὐτὴ συνευδοκεῖ
if any brother [2]an [4]wife [1]has [3]unbelieving and she consents

οἰκεῖν μετ' αὐτοῦ, μὴ ἀφιέτω αὐτήν. **13** Καὶ γυνὴ
to dwell with him, not ˜ do let him send away ˜ her. And a wife
live divorce

ἥτις ἔχει ἄνδρα ἄπιστον καὶ αὐτὸς συνευδοκεῖ οἰκεῖν
who has a(n) husband ˜ unbelieving and he consents to dwell
live

μετ' αὐτῆς, μὴ ἀφιέτω αὐτόν.[d]
with her, not ˜ do let her send away ˜ him.
divorce

14 Ἡγίασται γὰρ ὁ ἀνὴρ ὁ ἄπιστος ἐν τῇ γυναικὶ
[5]has [6]been [7]sanctified [1]For [2]the [4]husband - [3]unbelieving by the wife

καὶ ἡγίασται ἡ γυνὴ ἡ ἄπιστος ἐν τῷ ἀνδρί·[e] ἐπεὶ
and [4]has [5]been [6]sanctified [1]the [3]wife - [2]unbelieving by the husband; for

ἄρα τὰ τέκνα ὑμῶν ἀκάθαρτά ἐστι, νῦν δὲ ἅγιά
otherwise - children ˜ your unclean ˜ are, now ˜ but [3]holy
would be,

ἐστιν. **15** Εἰ δὲ ὁ ἄπιστος χωρίζεται,
[1]they [2]are. if ˜ But the unbelieving *spouse* separates,

χωριζέσθω. Οὐ δεδούλωται ὁ ἀδελφὸς ἢ ἡ
let *him or her* separate. [7]not [6]has [8]been [9]bound [1]The [2]brother [3]or [4]the

ἀδελφὴ ἐν τοῖς τοιούτοις· ἐν δὲ εἰρήνῃ κέκληκεν ἡμᾶς[f] ὁ
[5]sister in - such *cases;* [6]to [1]but [7]peace [3]has [4]called [5]us -

Θεός. **16** Τί γὰρ οἶδας, γύναι, εἰ τὸν ἄνδρα
[2]God. how ˜ For do you know, wife, whether [4]the [5]husband
your

σώσεις? Ἢ τί οἶδας, ἄνερ, εἰ τὴν γυναῖκα
[1]you [2]will [3]save? Or how do you know, husband, whether [4]the [5]wife
your

σώσεις?
[1]you [2]will [3]save?

Live as the Lord Has Called You

17 Εἰ μὴ ἑκάστῳ ὡς ἐμέρισεν ὁ Θεός, ἕκαστον
If not [4]to [5]each [6]*one* [1]as [3]distributed - [2]God, [12]each [13]*one*
Otherwise

ὡς κέκληκεν ὁ Κύριος, οὕτω περιπατείτω. Καὶ οὕτως ἐν
[7]as [10]has [11]called [8]the [9]Lord, so let him walk. And so [3]in
live.

ταῖς ἐκκλησίαις πάσαις διατάσσομαι. **18** Περιτετμημένος
[5]the [6]churches [4]all [1]I [2]command. [4]having [5]been [6]circumcised
who had

---

[d](7:13) NU reads τον ανδρα, *the husband.*
[e](7:14) NU reads αδελφω, *brother.* [f](7:15) NU reads υμας, *you.*

τις ἐκλήθη? Μὴ ἐπισπάσθω. Ἐν
[2]anyone [1]Was [3]called? [9]not [7]Let [8]him [10]become [11]uncircumcised. [15]in
while

ἀκροβυστίᾳ τις ἐκλήθη? Μὴ περιτεμνέσθω.
[16]uncircumcision [13]anyone [12]Was [14]called? [19]not [17]Let [18]him be circumcised.
uncircumcised

19 Ἡ περιτομὴ οὐδέν ἐστι καὶ ἡ ἀκροβυστία οὐδέν ἐστιν,
- Circumcision nothing ˜ is and - uncircumcision nothing ˜ is,

ἀλλὰ τήρησις ἐντολῶν Θεοῦ. 20 Ἕκαστος ἐν
but keeping *the* commandments of God *is something.* Each *one* in

τῇ κλήσει ᾗ ἐκλήθη, ἐν ταύτῃ μενέτω.
the calling in which he was called, [4]in [5]this [6]*calling* [1]let [2]him [3]remain.
that

21 Δοῦλος ἐκλήθης? Μή σοι
[4]*as* [5]a [6]slave [1]Were [2]you [3]called? [8]not [14]to [15]you

μελέτω, ἀλλ' εἰ καὶ δύνασαι ἐλεύθερος
[7]do [9]let [10]it [11]be [12]a [13]concern, but if also you are able [3]free

γενέσθαι, μᾶλλον χρῆσαι. 22 Ὁ γὰρ ἐν Κυρίῳ
[1]to [2]become, rather make use of *it.* [2]the [3]*one* [1]For [7]in [8]*the* [9]Lord

κληθεὶς δοῦλος, ἀπελεύθερος Κυρίου ἐστίν.
[4]having [5]been [6]called *as* a slave, [2]*the* [3]free [4]*man* [5]of [6]*the* [7]Lord [1]is.
who was

Ὁμοίως καὶ ὁ ἐλεύθερος κληθείς, δοῦλός ἐστι
Likewise also the *one* [3]*as* [4]a [5]free [6]*man* [1]being [2]called, [8]a [9]slave [7]is
who was

Χριστοῦ. 23 Τιμῆς ἠγοράσθητε· μὴ γίνεσθε δοῦλοι
[10]of [11]Christ. [4]at [5]a [6]price [1]You [2]were [3]bought; not ˜ do become slaves

ἀνθρώπων. 24 Ἕκαστος ἐν ᾧ ἐκλήθη, ἀδελφοί,
of men. Each *one* in *the state* in which he was called, brothers,

ἐν τούτῳ μενέτω παρὰ Θεῷ.
in this *circumstance* let him remain with God.

Paul's Advice to the Unmarried and Widows

25 Περὶ δὲ τῶν παρθένων ἐπιταγὴν Κυρίου οὐκ
concerning ˜ Now the virgins [5]a [6]command [7]of [8]*the* [9]Lord [3]not

ἔχω, γνώμην δὲ δίδωμι ὡς ἠλεημένος ὑπὸ
[1]I [2]do [4]have, [13]an [14]opinion [10]but [11]I [12]give as having been shown mercy by

Κυρίου πιστὸς εἶναι. 26 Νομίζω οὖν τοῦτο καλὸν
the Lord [3]faithful [1]to [2]be. [2]I [3]consider [1]Therefore this [3]good
trustworthy

ὑπάρχειν διὰ τὴν ἐνεστῶσαν ἀνάγκην, ὅτι καλὸν
[1]to [2]be because of the present distress, that *it is* good

ἀνθρώπῳ τὸ οὕτως εἶναι. 27 Δέδεσαι γυναικί? Μὴ
for a man - [3]thus [1]to [2]be. Have you been bound to a wife? not ˜
as he is

ζήτει λύσιν. Λέλυσαι ἀπὸ γυναικός? Μὴ ζήτει
Do seek release. Have you been released from a wife? not ˜ Do seek

γυναῖκα. 28 Ἐὰν δὲ καὶ γήμῃς, οὐχ ἥμαρτες·
a wife. [3]if [1]But [2]even you should marry, [3]not [1]you [2]have sinned;

καὶ ἐὰν γήμῃ ἡ παρθένος, οὐχ ἥμαρτε.
and if [3]should [4]marry [1]the [2]virgin, [7]not [5]she [6]has [8]sinned.

Θλῖψιν δὲ τῇ σαρκὶ ἕξουσιν οἱ τοιοῦτοι, ἐγὼ δὲ
[13]tribulation [9]But [14]in [15]the [16]flesh [11]will [12]have - [10]such, I ˜ and

ὑμῶν φείδομαι. 29 Τοῦτο δέ φημι, ἀδελφοί, ὁ καιρὸς
you ˜ spare. [4]this [1]But [2]I [3]say, brothers, the time
would spare.

συνεσταλμένος· τὸ λοιπόν ἐστιν ἵνα καὶ οἱ
having been shortened; the remaining *thing* it is that even the *ones*
has from now on

come uncircumcised. Was anyone called while uncircumcised?
Let him not be circumcised.
19 Circumcision is nothing and
uncircumcision is nothing, but
keeping the commandments of
God *is what matters.*
20 Let each one remain in the
same calling in which he was
called.
21 Were you called *while* a
slave? Do not be concerned
about it; but if you can be made
free, rather use *it.*
22 For he who is called in the
Lord *while* a slave is the Lord's
freedman. Likewise he who is
called *while* free is Christ's
slave.
23 You were bought at a
price; do not become slaves of
men.
24 Brethren, let each one remain with God in that *state* in
which he was called.
25 Now concerning virgins: I
have no commandment from
the Lord; yet I give judgment
as one whom the Lord in His
mercy *has made* trustworthy.
26 I suppose therefore that
this is good because of the present distress—that *it is* good
for a man to remain as he is:
27 Are you bound to a wife?
Do not seek to be loosed. Are
you loosed from a wife? Do not
seek a wife.
28 But even if you do marry,
you have not sinned; and if a
virgin marries, she has not
sinned. Nevertheless such will
have trouble in the flesh, but I
would spare you.
29 But this I say, brethren,
the time *is* short, so that from
now on even those who have

wives should be as though they had none,
30 those who weep as though they did not weep, those who rejoice as though they did not rejoice, those who buy as though they did not possess,
31 and those who use this world as not misusing *it.* For the form of this world is passing away.
32 But I want you to be without care. He who is unmarried cares for the things of the Lord—how he may please the Lord.
33 But he who is married cares about the things of the world—how he may please *his* wife.
34 There is a difference between a wife and a virgin. The unmarried woman cares about the things of the Lord, that she may be holy both in body and in spirit. But she who is married cares about the things of the world—how she may please *her* husband.
35 And this I say for your own profit, not that I may put a leash on you, but for what is proper, and that you may serve the Lord without distraction.
36 But if any man thinks he is behaving improperly toward his virgin, if she is past the flower of youth, and thus it must be, let him do what he wishes. He does not sin; let them marry.
37 Nevertheless he who stands steadfast in his heart, having no necessity, but has power over his own will, and has so determined in his heart that he will keep his virgin, does well.
38 So then he who gives *her* in marriage does well, but he who

ἔχοντες γυναῖκας ὡς μὴ ἔχοντες ὦσι, **30** καὶ
having wives [3]as [4]not [5]having [6]*wives* [1]should [2]be, and
as though they did not have

οἱ κλαίοντες ὡς μὴ κλαίοντες, καὶ οἱ χαίροντες ὡς μὴ
the *ones* weeping as not weeping, and the *ones* rejoicing as not

χαίροντες, καὶ οἱ ἀγοράζοντες ὡς μὴ κατέχοντες, **31** καὶ
rejoicing, and the *ones* buying as not possessing, and
owning,

οἱ χρώμενοι τῷ κόσμῳ τούτῳ ὡς μὴ καταχρώμενοι.
the *ones* using - world ˜ this as not using *it* up.

Παράγει γὰρ τὸ σχῆμα τοῦ κόσμου τούτου. **32** Θέλω
[7]is [8]passing [9]away [1]For [2]the [3]form - [4]of [6]world [5]this. [2]I [3]want

δὲ ὑμᾶς ἀμερίμνους εἶναι. Ὁ ἄγαμος μεριμνᾷ
[1]And you [3]without [4]anxiety [1]to [2]be. The unmarried man cares about

τὰ τοῦ Κυρίου, πῶς ἀρέσει τῷ Κυρίῳ.
the *things* of the Lord, *about* how he may please the Lord.

33 Ὁ δὲ γαμήσας μεριμνᾷ τὰ τοῦ κόσμου,
[2]the [3]*man* [1]But having married cares about the *things* of the world,

πῶς ἀρέσει τῇ γυναικί. **34** Μεμέρισται[g] καὶ ἡ
about how he may please the wife. [7]have [8]been [9]divided [1]And [2]the
his are different

γυνὴ καὶ ἡ παρθένος. Ἡ ἄγαμος μεριμνᾷ τὰ
[3]wife [4]and [5]the [6]virgin. The unmarried woman cares about the *things*

τοῦ Κυρίου, ἵνα ᾖ ἁγία καὶ σώματι καὶ πνεύματι,
of the Lord, that she may be holy both in body and in spirit,

ἡ δὲ γαμήσασα μεριμνᾷ τὰ τοῦ κόσμου,
[2]the [3]*woman* [1]but having married cares about the *things* of the world,

πῶς ἀρέσει τῷ ἀνδρί. **35** Τοῦτο δὲ πρὸς τὸ ὑμῶν
about how she may please the husband. [4]this [1]And [5]for [6]the [8]of [9]you
her your own

αὐτῶν συμφέρον λέγω, οὐχ ἵνα βρόχον ὑμῖν
[10]yourselves [7]profit [2]I [3]say, not that [6]a [7]snare [5]you

ἐπιβάλω, ἀλλὰ πρὸς τὸ εὔσχημον καὶ
[1]I [2]may [3]put [4]upon, but for the proper *thing* and *for*
that which is proper

εὐπρόσεδρον τῷ Κυρίῳ ἀπερισπάστως.
constancy to the Lord without distraction.

36 Εἰ δέ τις ἀσχημονεῖν ἐπὶ τὴν
if ˜ Now anyone [2]to [3]be [4]behaving [5]improperly [6]toward -
that he is

παρθένον αὐτοῦ νομίζει, ἐὰν ᾖ ὑπέρακμος, καὶ οὕτως
[8]virgin [7]his [1]thinks, if she is past her prime, and so

ὀφείλει γίνεσθαι, ὃ θέλει ποιείτω· οὐχ
it is obligated to happen, [4]what [5]he [6]desires [1]let [2]him [3]do; [9]not
must happen,

ἁμαρτάνει· γαμείτωσαν. **37** Ὃς δὲ ἕστηκεν ἑδραῖος ἐν
[7]he [8]does [10]sin; let them marry. [2]*he* [3]who [1]But has stood firm in
stands

τῇ καρδίᾳ, μὴ ἔχων ἀνάγκην, ἐξουσίαν δὲ ἔχει περὶ τοῦ
the heart, not having necessity, [3]power [1]and [2]has concerning -
his over

ἰδίου θελήματος, καὶ τοῦτο κέκρικεν ἐν τῇ καρδίᾳ αὐτοῦ τοῦ
his own desire, and [3]this [1]has [2]decided in - heart ˜ his -

τηρεῖν τὴν ἑαυτοῦ παρθένον, καλῶς ποιεῖ.[h] **38** Ὥστε καὶ
to keep the [2]of [3]himself [1]virgin, well ˜ does. So also
his own

ὁ ἐκγαμίζων[i] καλῶς ποιεῖ,[j] ὁ δὲ μὴ
the *one* giving in marriage well ˜ does, [2]the [3]*one* [1]but not
who gives

[g](7:34) NU adds και, *also.*
[h](7:37) NU reads ποιησει, *will do.* [i](7:38) NU adds την εαυτου παρθενον, *his own virgin.*
[j](7:38) NU reads ποιησει, *will do.*

ἐκγαμίζων κρεῖσσον ποιεῖ.
giving in marriage better ˜ does.

39 Γυνὴ δέδεται νόμῳ[k] ἐφ' ὅσον χρόνον ζῇ ὁ
A wife has been bound by *the* law for as much time [3]lives -
(as long as)

ἀνὴρ αὐτῆς, ἐὰν δὲ καὶ κοιμηθῇ ὁ ἀνήρ, ἐλευθέρα
[2]husband [1]her, if ˜ but [3]also [4]sleeps [1]the [2]husband, [7]free
(dies) (her)

ἐστὶν ᾧ θέλει γαμηθῆναι, μόνον ἐν Κυρίῳ.
[5]she [6]is [11]to [12]whom [13]she [14]desires [8]to [9]be [10]married, only in *the* Lord.

40 Μακαριωτέρα δέ ἐστιν ἐὰν οὕτω μείνῃ, κατὰ
[4]more [5]blessed [1]But [2]she [3]is if [3]thus [1]she [2]remains, according to
(in)

τὴν ἐμὴν γνώμην· δοκῶ δὲ κἀγὼ Πνεῦμα Θεοῦ ἔχειν.
- my opinion; [2]I [3]think [1]and I also [3]*the* [4]Spirit [5]of [6]God [1]to [2]have.
(have.)

Be Sensitive to Conscience

8 1 Περὶ δὲ τῶν εἰδωλοθύτων, οἴδαμεν ὅτι πάντες
concerning ˜ Now the *things* offered to idols, we know that [2]all

γνῶσιν ἔχομεν. Ἡ γνῶσις φυσιοῖ, ἡ δὲ ἀγάπη οἰκοδομεῖ.
[4]knowledge [1]we [3]have. - Knowledge puffs up, - but love edifies.

2 Εἰ δέ τις δοκεῖ εἰδέναι τι, οὐδέπω οὐδὲν
if ˜ And anyone thinks to know anything, [7]yet [6]nothing
(that he knows)

ἔγνωκε καθὼς δεῖ γνῶναι. 3 Εἰ δέ τις
[1]he [2]has [3]come [4]to [5]know as it is necessary to know. if ˜ But anyone
(he ought)

ἀγαπᾷ τὸν Θεόν, οὗτος ἔγνωσται ὑπ' αὐτοῦ. 4 Περὶ
loves - God, this *one* has been known by Him. [2]concerning
(he)

τῆς βρώσεως οὖν τῶν εἰδωλοθύτων οἴδαμεν ὅτι
[3]the [4]eating [1]Therefore of the *things* offered to idols we know that

οὐδὲν εἴδωλον ἐν κόσμῳ καὶ ὅτι οὐδεὶς Θεὸς ἕτερος[a]
[3]*is* [4]nothing [1]an [2]idol in *the* world and that *there is* no God ˜ other

εἰ μὴ εἷς. 5 Καὶ γὰρ εἴπερ εἰσὶ λεγόμενοι "θεοὶ"
if not one. even ˜ For if they are being called "gods"
(except for)

εἴτε ἐν οὐρανῷ εἴτε ἐπὶ γῆς (ὥσπερ εἰσὶ "θεοὶ" πολλοὶ
whether in heaven or on earth (just as *there* are "gods" ˜ many

καὶ "κύριοι" πολλοί), 6 ἀλλ' ἡμῖν εἷς Θεὸς ὁ Πατήρ, ἐξ
and "lords" ˜ many), yet for us *there is* one God the Father, of

οὗ τὰ πάντα καὶ ἡμεῖς εἰς αὐτόν, καὶ εἷς Κύριος Ἰησοῦς
whom - *are* all *things* and we for Him, and one Lord Jesus

Χριστός, δι' οὗ τὰ πάντα καὶ ἡμεῖς δι' αὐτοῦ.
Christ, through whom - *are* all *things* and we *live* through Him.

7 Ἀλλ' οὐκ ἐν πᾶσιν ἡ γνῶσις, τινὲς δὲ τῇ
But [3]*is* [4]not [5]in [6]all [7]*people* [1]the [2]knowledge, some ˜ rather -
(this)

συνειδήσει[b] τοῦ εἰδώλου ἕως ἄρτι ὡς
with consciousness of the idol until now [3]as

εἰδωλόθυτον ἐσθίουσι, καὶ ἡ συνείδησις αὐτῶν
[4]*something* [5]offered [6]to [7]idols [1]eat [2]*it*, and - conscience ˜ their

ἀσθενὴς οὖσα μολύνεται. 8 Βρῶμα δὲ ἡμᾶς οὐ παρίστησι
weak ˜ being is defiled. food ˜ But [4]us [2]not [1]does [3]present

τῷ Θεῷ, οὔτε γὰρ ἐὰν φάγωμεν περισσεύομεν, οὔτε ἐὰν
- to God, neither ˜ for if we eat do we have more, nor if

does not give *her* in marriage
does better.
39 A wife is bound by law as
long as her husband lives; but if
her husband dies, she is at liberty to be married to whom she
wishes, only in the Lord.
40 But she is happier if she remains as she is, according to
my judgment—and I think I
also have the Spirit of God.

8 Now concerning things offered to idols: We know
that we all have knowledge.
Knowledge puffs up, but love
edifies.
2 And if anyone thinks that
he knows anything, he knows
nothing yet as he ought to
know.
3 But if anyone loves God,
this one is known by Him.
4 Therefore concerning the
eating of things offered to idols,
we know that an idol *is* nothing
in the world, and that *there is* no
other God but one.
5 For even if there are so-
called gods, whether in heaven
or on earth (as there are many
gods and many lords),
6 yet for us *there is* one God,
the Father, of whom *are* all
things, and we for Him; and one
Lord Jesus Christ, through
whom *are* all things, and
through whom we *live*.
7 However, *there is* not in
everyone that knowledge; for
some, with consciousness of
the idol, until now eat *it* as a
thing offered to an idol; and
their conscience, being weak, is
defiled.
8 But food does not com-
mend us to God; for neither if
we eat are we the better, nor if
we do not eat are we the

[k](7:39) NU omits νομῳ, *by (the) law.* [a](8:4) NU omits ετερος, *other.*
[b](8:7) NU reads συνηθεια, *with custom* (that is, *being accustomed to*).

worse.
9 But beware lest somehow
this liberty of yours become a
stumbling block to those who
are weak.
10 For if anyone sees you who
have knowledge eating in an
idol's temple, will not the conscience of him who is weak be
emboldened to eat those things
offered to idols?
11 And because of your
knowledge shall the weak
brother perish, for whom
Christ died?
12 But when you thus sin
against the brethren, and
wound their weak conscience,
you sin against Christ.
13 Therefore, if food makes
my brother stumble, I will
never again eat meat, lest I
make my brother stumble.
9 Am I not an apostle? Am I
not free? Have I not seen
Jesus Christ our Lord? Are you
not my work in the Lord?
2 If I am not an apostle to
others, yet doubtless I am to
you. For you are the seal of my
apostleship in the Lord.
3 My defense to those who
examine me is this:
4 Do we have no right to eat
and drink?
5 Do we have no right to
take along a believing wife, as
do also the other apostles, the
brothers of the Lord, and Cephas?
6 Or *is it* only Barnabas and I
who have no right to refrain
from working?
7 Who ever goes to war at

μὴ φάγωμεν ὑστερούμεθα. **9** Βλέπετε δὲ μή πως ἡ ἐξουσία
[3]not [1]we [2]do eat do we lack. watch ~ But not how - [2]right
beware lest liberty

ὑμῶν αὕτη πρόσκομμα γένηται τοῖς ἀσθενοῦσιν.
[3]of [4]yours [1]this [6]a [7]stumbling [8]block [5]become to the *ones* being weak.
those who are

10 Ἐὰν γάρ τις ἴδῃ σε τὸν ἔχοντα γνῶσιν ἐν
if ~ For anyone should see you the *one* having knowledge [2]in
who has

εἰδωλείῳ κατακείμενον, οὐχὶ ἡ συνείδησις αὐτοῦ,
[3]an [4]idol's [5]temple [1]dining, [7]not - [9]conscience [8]his,

ἀσθενοῦς ὄντος, οἰκοδομηθήσεται εἰς τὸ τὰ
[11]weak [10]being, [6]will [12]be [13]built [14]up for - [3]the [4]*things*
strengthened so that they eat

εἰδωλόθυτα ἐσθίειν? **11** Καὶ ἀπολεῖται ὁ ἀσθενῶν
[5]offered [6]to [7]idols [1]to [2]eat? And [1]shall [13]perish [2]the [4]being [5]weak
foods offered to idols? weak

ἀδελφὸς ἐπὶ τῇ σῇ γνώσει, δι' ὃν
[3]brother [14]because [15]of - [16]your [17]knowledge, [6]for [7]the [8]sake [9]of [10]whom
brother

Χριστὸς ἀπέθανεν? **12** Οὕτω δὲ ἁμαρτάνοντες εἰς τοὺς
[11]Christ [12]died? thus But sinning against the
But when you thus sin

ἀδελφοὺς καὶ τύπτοντες αὐτῶν τὴν συνείδησιν ἀσθενοῦσαν
brothers and wounding their - conscience being weak
wound weak conscience

εἰς Χριστὸν ἁμαρτάνετε. **13** Διόπερ εἰ βρῶμα
[3]against [4]Christ [1]you [2]sin. Wherefore if food

σκανδαλίζει τὸν ἀδελφόν μου, οὐ μὴ φάγω κρέα
causes [3]to [4]stumble - [2]brother [1]my, not not will I eat meat
by no means

εἰς τὸν αἰῶνα, ἵνα μὴ τὸν ἀδελφόν μου σκανδαλίσω.
into the age, that not - [4]brother [3]my [1]I [2]cause [5]to [6]stumble.
forever, lest

Paul's Pattern of Self-Denial

9 **1** Οὐκ εἰμὶ ἀπόστολος? Οὐκ εἰμὶ ἐλεύθερος? Οὐχὶ
[3]not [1]Am [2]I an apostle? [3]not [1]Am [2]I free? [3]not

Ἰησοῦν Χριστὸν[a] τὸν Κύριον ἡμῶν ἑώρακα? Οὐ τὸ ἔργον
[5]Jesus [6]Christ - [8]Lord [7]our [1]Have [2]I [4]seen? [11]not - [13]work

μου ὑμεῖς ἐστε ἐν Κυρίῳ? **2** Εἰ ἄλλοις οὐκ εἰμὶ ἀπόστολος,
[12]my [10]you [9]Are in the Lord? If to others [3]not [1]I [2]am an apostle,

ἀλλά γε ὑμῖν εἰμι. Ἡ γὰρ σφραγὶς τῆς ἐμῆς
yet indeed [3]to [4]you [1]I [2]am. [8]the [5]For [9]seal - [10]of [11]my

ἀποστολῆς ὑμεῖς ἐστε ἐν Κυρίῳ. **3** Ἡ ἐμὴ ἀπολογία τοῖς
[12]apostleship [6]you [7]are in *the* Lord. - My defense to the *ones*

ἐμὲ ἀνακρίνουσιν αὕτη ἐστί. **4** Μὴ οὐκ ἔχομεν ἐξουσίαν
me ~ examining this ~ is. - [3]not [1]Do [2]we have a right

φαγεῖν καὶ πιεῖν? **5** Μὴ οὐκ ἔχομεν ἐξουσίαν ἀδελφὴν
to eat and to drink? - [3]not [1]Do [2]we have a right [8]a [9]sister

γυναῖκα περιάγειν, ὡς καὶ οἱ λοιποὶ ἀπόστολοι καὶ
[4]a [5]wife [6]*who* [7]*is* [1]to [2]take [3]about, as also the remaining apostles and
other

οἱ ἀδελφοὶ τοῦ Κυρίου, καὶ Κηφᾶς? **6** Ἢ μόνος ἐγὼ καὶ
the brothers of the Lord, and Cephas? Or [2]only [3]I [4]and

Βαρναβᾶς οὐκ ἔχομεν ἐξουσίαν τοῦ μὴ ἐργάζεσθαι? **7** Τίς
[5]Barnabas [6]not [1]do [7]have a right - not to work? Who
to forego working?

[a](9:1) NU omits Χριστον, *Christ*.

στρατεύεται ἰδίοις ὀψωνίοις ποτέ? Τίς φυτεύει ἀμπελῶνα
serves as a soldier at his own wages ever? Who plants a vineyard
expense

καὶ ἐκ τοῦ καρποῦ αὐτοῦ οὐκ ἐσθίει? Ἢ τίς ποιμαίνει
and [4]from - [6]fruit [5]its [2]not [1]does [3]eat? Or who shepherds

ποίμνην καὶ ἐκ τοῦ γάλακτος τῆς ποίμνης οὐκ ἐσθίει?
a flock and [4]from [5]the [6]milk [7]of [8]the [9]flock [2]not [1]does [3]eat?

8 Μὴ κατὰ ἄνθρωπον ταῦτα λαλῶ? Ἢ οὐχὶ
[3]not [7]according [8]to [9]a [10]man [5]these [6]*things* [1]I [2]do [4]speak, *do I?* Or [2]not
by human standards

καὶ ὁ νόμος ταῦτα λέγει? **9** Ἐν γὰρ τῷ Μωϋσέως
[5]also [3]the [4]law [7]these [8]*things* [1]does [6]say? in ˜ For the [2]of [3]Moses

νόμῳ γέγραπται, «Οὐ φιμώσεις βοῦν ἀλοῶντα.»[b] Μὴ
[1]law it is written, «[3]not [1]You [2]shall muzzle an ox threshing.» [3]not
while it threshes.» God

τῶν βοῶν μέλει τῷ Θεῷ? **10** Ἢ
[8]for [9]the [10]oxen [1]It [2]is [4]a [5]concern - [6]to [7]God, *is it?* Or
is not really concerned about the oxen, is He?

δι' ἡμᾶς πάντως λέγει? Δι'
[6]for [7]the [8]sake [9]of [10]us [3]certainly [1]does [2]He [4]say [5]*this?* [15]for [16]the [17]sake [18]of
for our sakes for our

ἡμᾶς γὰρ ἐγράφη, ὅτι ἐπ' ἐλπίδι ὀφείλει ὁ
[19]us [11]For [12]it [13]was [14]written, that [7]in [8]hope [4]ought [1]the [2]*one*
sakes

ἀροτριῶν ἀροτριᾶν καὶ ὁ ἀλοῶν τῆς ἐλπίδος αὐτοῦ
[3]plowing [5]to [6]plow and the *one* threshing - [6]of [8]hope [7]his
who plows who threshes

μετέχειν ἐπ' ἐλπίδι. **11** Εἰ ἡμεῖς ὑμῖν τὰ
[3]*ought* [4]to [5]partake [1]in [2]hope. If we [2]to [3]you [4]the

πνευματικὰ ἐσπείραμεν, μέγα εἰ ἡμεῖς ὑμῶν τὰ
[5]spiritual [6]*things* [1]sowed, *is it* a great *thing* if we [2]your -

σαρκικὰ θερίσομεν? **12** Εἰ ἄλλοι τῆς ἐξουσίας ὑμῶν
[3]material [4]*things* [1]reap? If others [2]of [3]the [4]right [5]over [6]you
this

μετέχουσιν, οὐ μᾶλλον ἡμεῖς?
[1]partake, *do* not more ˜ we?

Ἀλλ' οὐκ ἐχρησάμεθα τῇ ἐξουσίᾳ ταύτῃ, ἀλλὰ πάντα
But [3]not [1]we [2]did use - right ˜ this, but [3]all [4]*things*

στέγομεν ἵνα μὴ ἐγκοπήν τινα δῶμεν τῷ εὐαγγελίῳ τοῦ
[1]we [2]bear that [2]not [5]hindrance [4]any [1]we [3]give to the gospel -
lest

Χριστοῦ. **13** Οὐκ οἴδατε ὅτι οἱ τὰ ἱερὰ
of Christ. [3]not [1]Do [2]you know that the *ones* [2]the [3]sacred [4]*things*

ἐργαζόμενοι ἐκ τοῦ ἱεροῦ ἐσθίουσιν, οἱ τῷ
[1]working [6]from [7]the [8]temple [5]eat, *and* the *ones* [2]at [3]the
who minister

θυσιαστηρίῳ προσεδρεύοντες τῷ θυσιαστηρίῳ
[4]altar [1]serving [8]in [9]the [10]altar
who serve

συμμερίζονται? **14** Οὕτω καὶ ὁ Κύριος διέταξε τοῖς τὸ
[5]have [6]a [7]share? Thus also the Lord commanded the *ones* [2]the

εὐαγγέλιον καταγγέλλουσιν ἐκ τοῦ εὐαγγελίου ζῆν.
[3]gospel [1]proclaiming [6]from [7]the [8]gospel [4]to [5]live.
who proclaim

15 Ἐγὼ δὲ οὐδενὶ ἐχρησάμην τούτων. Οὐκ ἔγραψα
I ˜ But none ˜ used of these *things*. [4]not [2]I [3]have [5]written

δὲ ταῦτα ἵνα οὕτω γένηται ἐν ἐμοί, καλὸν γάρ
[1]Now these *things* that [4]thus [1]it [2]should [3]become in me, [2]*it* [3]*is* good [1]for
for

his own expense? Who plants a vineyard and does not eat of its fruit? Or who tends a flock and does not drink of the milk of the flock?
8 Do I say these things as a *mere* man? Or does not the law say the same also?
9 For it is written in the law of Moses, *"You shall not muzzle an ox while it treads out the grain."* Is it oxen God is concerned about?
10 Or does He say *it* altogether for our sakes? For our sakes, no doubt, *this* is written, that he who plows should plow in hope, and he who threshes in hope should be partaker of his hope.
11 If we have sown spiritual things for you, *is it* a great thing if we reap your material things?
12 If others are partakers of *this* right over you, *are* we not even more? Nevertheless we have not used this right, but endure all things lest we hinder the gospel of Christ.
13 Do you not know that those who minister the holy things eat *of the things* of the temple, and those who serve at the altar partake of *the offerings of* the altar?
14 Even so the Lord has commanded that those who preach the gospel should live from the gospel.
15 But I have used none of these things, nor have I written these things that it should be

[b](9:9) Deut. 25:4

done so to me; for it *would be*
better for me to die than that
anyone should make my boasting void.
16 For if I preach the gospel, I
have nothing to boast of, for necessity is laid upon me; yes,
woe is me if I do not preach the
gospel!
17 For if I do this willingly, I
have a reward; but if against my
will, I have been entrusted with
a stewardship.
18 What is my reward then?
That when I preach the gospel,
I may present the gospel of
Christ without charge, that I
may not abuse my authority in
the gospel.
19 For though I am free from
all *men,* I have made myself a
servant to all, that I might win
the more;
20 and to the Jews I became
as a Jew, that I might win Jews;
to those *who are* under the law,
as under the law, that I might
win those *who are* under the
law;
21 to those *who are* without
law, as without law (not being
without law toward God, but
under law toward Christ), that I
might win those *who are* without law;
22 to the weak I became as
weak, that I might win the
weak. I have become all things
to all *men,* that I might by all
means save some.
23 Now this I do for the gospel's sake, that I may be partaker of it with *you.*
24 Do you not know that
those who run in a race all run,

μοι μᾶλλον ἀποθανεῖν ἤ τὸ καύχημά μου ἵνα τις
for me rather to die than - [5]boasting [4]my [1]that [2]anyone

κενώσῃ. 16 Ἐὰν γὰρ εὐαγγελίζωμαι, οὐκ ἔστι μοι
[3]make [6]empty. if ~ For I preach the gospel, [3]not [1]*there* [2]is for me
nothing

καύχημα, ἀνάγκη γάρ μοι ἐπίκειται. Οὐαὶ δέ μοί
boasting, compulsion ~ for [4]me [1]is [2]pressed [3]on. woe ~ But [2]to [3]me
to boast about,

ἐστιν ἐὰν μὴ εὐαγγελίζωμαι! 17 Εἰ γὰρ ἑκὼν τοῦτο
[1]is if [3]not [1]I [2]do preach the gospel! if ~ For [4]willingly [3]this

πράσσω, μισθὸν ἔχω· εἰ δὲ ἄκων, οἰκονομίαν
[1]I [2]do, [7]a [8]reward [5]I [6]have; if ~ but unwillingly, [6]a [7]commission

πεπίστευμαι. 18 Τίς οὖν μοί ἐστιν ὁ μισθός?
[1]I [2]have [3]been [4]entrusted [5]with. What then my ~ is - reward?

Ἵνα εὐαγγελιζόμενος ἀδάπανον θήσω τὸ
That preaching the gospel [8]without [9]charge [1]I [2]may [3]present [4]the
when I preach

εὐαγγέλιον τοῦ Χριστοῦ,[c] εἰς τὸ μὴ καταχρήσασθαι τῇ
[5]gospel - [6]of [7]Christ, for - not to make full use of -
so as not to exploit

ἐξουσίᾳ μου ἐν τῷ εὐαγγελίῳ.
right ~ my in the gospel.
rights

Paul's Pattern of Serving All Men

19 Ἐλεύθερος γὰρ ὢν ἐκ πάντων, πᾶσιν ἐμαυτὸν
[3]free [1]For [2]being from all *men,* [4]to [5]all [6]*men* [3]myself

ἐδούλωσα ἵνα τοὺς πλείονας κερδήσω. 20 Καὶ
[1]I [2]enslaved in order that [4]the [5]more [1]I [2]might [3]win. And

ἐγενόμην τοῖς Ἰουδαίοις ὡς Ἰουδαῖος, ἵνα Ἰουδαίους
I became to the Jews as a Jew, in order that [4]Jews

κερδήσω· τοῖς ὑπὸ νόμον ὡς ὑπὸ νόμον,[d] ἵνα
[1]I [2]might [3]win; to the *ones* under law as under law, in order that

τοὺς ὑπὸ νόμον κερδήσω· 21 τοῖς ἀνόμοις ὡς
[4]the [5]*ones* [6]under [7]law [1]I [2]might [3]win; to the *ones* without law as
outside the

ἄνομος (μὴ ὢν ἄνομος Θεῷ[e] ἀλλ' ἔννομος
one without law (not being without law toward God but subject to law
outside the outside the

Χριστῷ),[f] ἵνα κερδήσω ἀνόμους. 22 Ἐγενόμην
toward Christ), in order that I might win *those* without law. I became
outside the

τοῖς ἀσθενέσιν ὡς[g] ἀσθενής, ἵνα τοὺς ἀσθενεῖς
to the *ones* being weak as weak, in order that [4]the [5]weak [6]*ones*
the weak

κερδήσω. Τοῖς πᾶσι γέγονα τὰ πάντα
[1]I [2]might [3]win. - [6]to [7]all [8]*people* [1]I [2]have [3]become - [4]all [5]*things*

ἵνα πάντως τινὰς σώσω. 23 Τοῦτο[h] δὲ ποιῶ
in order that certainly [4]some [1]I [2]might [3]save. [4]this [1]And [2]I [3]do

διὰ τὸ εὐαγγέλιον, ἵνα συγκοινωνὸς
for the sake of the gospel, in order that [4]a [5]sharer

αὐτοῦ γένωμαι.
[6]of [7]it [8]*with* [9]*you* [1]I [2]may [3]become.

Paul's Pattern in Striving for a Crown

24 Οὐκ οἴδατε ὅτι οἱ ἐν σταδίῳ τρέχοντες
[3]not [1]Do [2]you know that the *ones* [2]in [3]a [4]stadium [1]running
race

---

c(9:18) NU omits του Χριστου, *of Christ.*
d(9:20) NU adds μη ων αυτος υπο νομον, *not being myself under law.*
e(9:21) NU reads θεου, *(without the law) of God.*
f(9:21) NU reads Χριστου, *(subject to the law) of Christ.* g(9:22) NU omits ως, *as.* h(9:23) NU reads Παντα, *all (things).*

πάντες μὲν τρέχουσιν, εἷς δὲ λαμβάνει τὸ βραβεῖον? Οὕτω
all - run, one ˜ but receives the prize? So

τρέχετε ἵνα καταλάβητε. 25 Πᾶς δὲ ὁ
run in order that you may win. every ˜ And - *one*
everyone who

ἀγωνιζόμενος πάντα ἐγκρατεύεται. Ἐκεῖνοι μὲν
competing [3]*in* [4]all [5]*things* [1]exercises [2]self-control. [7]those [8]*compete* -
competes they

οὖν ἵνα φθαρτὸν στέφανον λάβωσιν, ἡμεῖς δὲ
[6]Now in order that [4]a [5]perishable [6]crown [1]they [2]may [3]receive, we ˜ but

ἄφθαρτον. 26 Ἐγὼ τοίνυν οὕτω τρέχω ὡς οὐκ
compete for an imperishable *crown*. I ˜ So thus ˜ run as ˜ not

ἀδήλως, οὕτω πυκτεύω ὡς οὐκ ἀέρα δέρων. 27 Ἀλλ'
uncertainly, thus I box as ˜ not [2]*the* [3]air [1]beating. But
without a goal,

ὑπωπιάζω μου τὸ σῶμα καὶ δουλαγωγῶ, μή πως
I treat [3]roughly [1]my - [2]body and I bring *it* into subjection, not how
lest

ἄλλοις κηρύξας, αὐτὸς ἀδόκιμος* γένωμαι.
[3]to [4]others [1]having [2]preached, [7]myself [9]disqualified [5]I [6]should [8]become.

Learn from Old Testament Examples

10 1 Οὐ θέλω δὲ ὑμᾶς ἀγνοεῖν, ἀδελφοί, ὅτι
[4]not [2]I [3]do [5]desire [1]Now *for* you to be ignorant, brothers, that

οἱ πατέρες ἡμῶν πάντες ὑπὸ τὴν νεφέλην ἦσαν καὶ πάντες
- [3]fathers [2]our [1]all [5]under [6]the [7]cloud [4]were and all

διὰ τῆς θαλάσσης διῆλθον 2 καὶ πάντες εἰς τὸν Μωϋσῆν
[2]through [3]the [4]sea [1]passed and all [3]into - [4]Moses

ἐβαπτίσαντο ἐν τῇ νεφέλῃ καὶ ἐν τῇ θαλάσσῃ 3 καὶ πάντες
[1]were [2]baptized in the cloud and in the sea and all

τὸ αὐτὸ βρῶμα πνευματικὸν ἔφαγον 4 καὶ πάντες τὸ αὐτὸ
[2]the [3]same [5]food [4]spiritual [1]ate and all [2]the [3]same

πόμα πνευματικὸν ἔπιον. Ἔπινον γὰρ ἐκ
[5]drink [4]spiritual [1]drank. [7]they [8]were [9]drinking [6]For from

πνευματικῆς ἀκολουθούσης πέτρας, ἡ δὲ πέτρα ἦν ὁ
a spiritual [2]following [3]*them* [1]rock, the ˜ and rock was -
that followed

Χριστός. 5 Ἀλλ' οὐκ ἐν τοῖς πλείοσιν αὐτῶν εὐδόκησεν ὁ
Christ. But [3]not [5]with [6]the [7]majority [8]of [9]them [2]was [4]pleased -

Θεός, κατεστρώθησαν γὰρ ἐν τῇ ἐρήμῳ.
[1]God, [11]they [12]were [13]scattered [14]on [15]the [16]ground [10]for in the wilderness.
laid low

6 Ταῦτα δὲ τύποι ἡμῶν ἐγενήθησαν εἰς τὸ μὴ
[2]these [3]*things* [1]Now [5]examples [6]for [7]us [4]became for - [2]not
in order that we

εἶναι ἡμᾶς ἐπιθυμητὰς κακῶν καθὼς κἀκεῖνοι
[3]to [4]be [1]us those who desire of evil *things* just as those also
should not be desirous

ἐπεθύμησαν. 7 Μηδὲ εἰδωλολάτραι γίνεσθε καθώς τινες
desired. Nor idolaters ˜ be just as some

αὐτῶν· ὥσπερ γέγραπται, «Ἐκάθισεν ὁ λαὸς φαγεῖν καὶ
of them; as it is written, «[3]sat [4]down [1]The [2]people to eat and

πιεῖν, καὶ ἀνέστησαν παίζειν.»[a] 8 Μηδὲ
to drink, and arose to play.» Nor

πορνεύωμεν καθώς τινες αὐτῶν
let us commit sexual immorality just as some of them

ἐπόρνευσαν, καὶ ἔπεσον ἐν μιᾷ ἡμέρᾳ εἴκοσι τρεῖς
committed sexual immorality, and [4]fell [5]in [6]one [7]day [1]twenty [2]three

but one receives the prize? Run
in such a way that you may obtain *it*.
25 And everyone who competes *for the prize* is temperate
in all things. Now they *do it* to
obtain a perishable crown, but
we *for* an imperishable *crown*.
26 Therefore I run thus: not
with uncertainty. Thus I fight:
not as *one who* beats the air.
27 But I discipline my body
and bring *it* into subjection,
lest, when I have preached to
others, I myself should become
disqualified.
10 Moreover, brethren, I
do not want you to be
unaware that all our fathers
were under the cloud, all
passed through the sea,
2 all were baptized into Moses in the cloud and in the sea,
3 all ate the same spiritual
food,
4 and all drank the same spiritual drink. For they drank of
that spiritual Rock that followed
them, and that Rock was
Christ.
5 But with most of them God
was not well pleased, for *their
bodies* were scattered in the
wilderness.
6 Now these things became
our examples, to the intent that
we should not lust after evil
things as they also lusted.
7 And do not become idolaters as *were* some of them. As
it is written, *"The people sat
down to eat and drink, and rose
up to play."*
8 Nor let us commit sexual
immorality, as some of them
did, and in one day twenty-

[a](10:7) Ex. 32:6

*(9:27) ἀδόκιμος (*adokimos*). Adjective derived from δόκιμος, *tried, proved, approved,* negated by the α-prefix, thus meaning *disapproved, rejected.* The idea is that one has failed in some testing and is therefore *disqualified* (as here) from the athletic contest Paul is using as an analogy for the Christian life and ministry. It may refer to things (Heb. 6:8) or people, where its sense is often extended to mean *worthless, debased* (Rom. 1:28).

three thousand fell;
9 nor let us tempt Christ, as
some of them also tempted,
and were destroyed by serpents;
10 nor complain, as some of
them also complained, and
were destroyed by the de-
stroyer.
11 Now all these things happened to them as examples,
and they were written for our
admonition, upon whom the
ends of the ages have come.
12 Therefore let him who
thinks he stands take heed lest
he fall.
13 No temptation has overtaken you except such as is
common to man; but God *is*
faithful, who will not allow you
to be tempted beyond what you
are able, but with the temptation will also make the way of
escape, that you may be able to
bear *it*.
14 Therefore, my beloved,
flee from idolatry.
15 I speak as to wise men;
judge for yourselves what I
say.
16 The cup of blessing which
we bless, is it not the communion of the blood of Christ? The
bread which we break, is it not
the communion of the body of
Christ?
17 For we, *though* many, are
one bread *and* one body; for we
all partake of that one bread.
18 Observe Israel after the
flesh: Are not those who eat of
the sacrifices partakers of the
altar?
19 What am I saying then?
That an idol is anything, or
what is offered to idols is anything?
20 Rather, that the things
which the Gentiles sacrifice
they sacrifice to demons and
not to God, and I do not want
you to have fellowship with demons.
21 You cannot drink the cup of
the Lord and the cup of de-

χιλιάδες. **9** Μηδὲ ἐκπειράζωμεν τὸν Χριστὸν καθὼς καί τινες
[3]thousand. Nor let us tempt - Christ just as also some

αὐτῶν ἐπείρασαν, καὶ ὑπὸ τῶν ὄφεων ἀπώλοντο.
of them tempted *Him*, and [3]by [4]the [5]serpents [1]were [2]destroyed.

10 Μηδὲ γογγύζετε καθὼς καί τινες αὐτῶν ἐγόγγυσαν, καὶ
Nor grumble just as also some of them grumbled, and

ἀπώλοντο ὑπὸ τοῦ ὀλοθρευτοῦ. **11** Ταῦτα δὲ πάντα[b]
were destroyed by the destroyer. [3]these [4]*things* [1]Now [2]all

τύποι συνέβαινον ἐκείνοις, ἐγράφη δὲ
[9]*as* [10]examples [5]happened [6]to [7]those [8]*people*, [12]they [13]were [14]written [11]and

πρὸς νουθεσίαν ἡμῶν εἰς οὓς τὰ τέλη τῶν αἰώνων
for instruction ˜ our to whom the ends of the ages

κατήντησεν. **12** Ὥστε ὁ δοκῶν ἑστάναι βλεπέτω μὴ
have come. So then the *one* thinking to stand let him watch not
(who thinks he stands ... lest)

πέσῃ! **13** Πειρασμὸς ὑμᾶς οὐκ εἴληφεν εἰ μὴ
he should fall! Temptation [4]you [2]not [1]has [3]taken if not
(No temptation has overtaken you except such as)

ἀνθρώπινος, πιστὸς δὲ ὁ Θεὸς ὃς οὐκ ἐάσει ὑμᾶς
a human *one*, [3]*is* [4]faithful [1]but - [2]God who not ˜ will permit you
(is common to man,)

πειρασθῆναι ὑπὲρ ὃ δύνασθε, ἀλλὰ ποιήσει σὺν
to be tempted beyond what you are able, but He will make together with

τῷ πειρασμῷ καὶ τὴν ἔκβασιν τοῦ δύνασθαι ὑμᾶς
the temptation also the way out - [3]to [4]be [5]able [1]*for* [2]you

ὑπενεγκεῖν.
to bear *it*.

Flee from Idolatry

14 Διόπερ, ἀγαπητοί μου, φεύγετε ἀπὸ τῆς
Wherefore, [2]beloved [3]*ones*, [1]my, flee from -

εἰδωλολατρείας. **15** Ὡς φρονίμοις λέγω· κρίνατε ὑμεῖς ὅ
idolatry. [3]as [4]to [5]wise [6]*men* [1]I [2]speak: judge ˜ you what

φημι. **16** Τὸ ποτήριον τῆς εὐλογίας ὃ εὐλογοῦμεν, οὐχὶ
I say. The cup - of blessing which we bless, [3]not

κοινωνία τοῦ αἵματος τοῦ Χριστοῦ ἐστι? Τὸν ἄρτον ὃν
[4]*the* [5]fellowship [6]of [7]the [8]blood - [9]of [10]Christ [1]is [2]it? The bread which

κλῶμεν, οὐχὶ κοινωνία τοῦ σώματος τοῦ Χριστοῦ ἐστιν?
we break, [3]not [4]*the* [5]fellowship [6]of [7]the [8]body - [9]of [10]Christ [1]is [2]it?

17 Ὅτι εἷς ἄρτος, ἓν σῶμα οἱ πολλοί ἐσμεν· οἱ γὰρ
Because [5]one [6]bread, [7]one [8]body [2]the [3]many [1]we [4]are; - for

πάντες ἐκ τοῦ ἑνὸς ἄρτου μετέχομεν. **18** Βλέπετε τὸν
[2]all [4]from [5]the [6]one [7]bread [1]we [3]partake. Look at -

Ἰσραὴλ κατὰ σάρκα. Οὐχὶ οἱ ἐσθίοντες τὰς θυσίας
Israel according to *the* flesh. [2]not [3]the [4]*ones* [5]eating [6]the [7]sacrifices
(after ... who ate)

κοινωνοὶ τοῦ θυσιαστηρίου εἰσί? **19** Τί οὖν φημι?
[8]partners [9]of [10]the [11]altar [1]Are? What then am I saying?

Ὅτι εἴδωλόν τί ἐστιν ἢ ὅτι εἰδωλόθυτόν τί
That an idol anything ˜ is or that *something* offered to idols anything ˜

ἐστιν? **20** Ἀλλ᾽ ὅτι ἃ θύει τὰ ἔθνη,[c]
is? *No*, but that *the things* which [3]sacrifice [1]the [2]Gentiles,

δαιμονίοις θύει καὶ οὐ Θεῷ. Οὐ θέλω δὲ ὑμᾶς
[6]to [7]demons [4]they [5]sacrifice and not to God. [4]not [2]I [3]do [5]desire [1]And *for* you

κοινωνοὺς τῶν δαιμονίων γίνεσθαι. **21** Οὐ δύνασθε
[3]partners [4]of [5]the [6]demons [1]to [2]be. [3]not [1]You [2]are [4]able

ποτήριον Κυρίου πίνειν καὶ ποτήριον δαιμονίων· οὐ
[7]*the* [8]cup [9]of [10]*the* [11]Lord [5]to [6]drink and *the* cup of demons; [3]not

---

[b](**10:11**) NU omits παντα, *all*. [c](**10:20**) NU omits τα εθνη, *the Gentiles*.

δύνασθε τραπέζης Κυρίου μετέχειν καὶ τραπέζης
[1]you [2]are [4]able [7]of [8]*the* [9]table [10]of [11]*the* [12]Lord [5]to [6]partake and of *the* table

δαιμονίων. 22 Ἢ παραζηλοῦμεν τὸν Κύριον? Μὴ
of demons. Or do we provoke [3]to [4]jealousy [1]the [2]Lord? [7]not

ἰσχυρότεροι αὐτοῦ ἐσμεν?
[8]stronger [9]*than* [10]Him [5]We [6]are, *are we?*
He

Do All to the Glory of God

23 Πάντα μοι[d] ἔξεστιν, ἀλλ᾽ οὐ πάντα συμφέρει.
All *things* [3]for [4]me [1]are [2]lawful, but not all *things* are profitable.

Πάντα μοι[d] ἔξεστιν, ἀλλ᾽ οὐ πάντα οἰκοδομεῖ.
All *things* [3]for [4]me [1]are [2]lawful, but not all *things* build up.
edify.

24 Μηδεὶς τὸ ἑαυτοῦ ζητείτω ἀλλὰ τὸ τοῦ
[2]no [3]one [5]the [6]*thing* [7]of [8]himself [1]Let [4]seek but [3]the [4]*thing* [5]of [6]the
his own concerns another's concern

ἑτέρου ἕκαστος. 25 Πᾶν τὸ ἐν μακέλλῳ
[7]other [1]each [2]*one*. [2]every [3]the [4]*thing* [7]in [8]*the* [9]meat [10]market
everything

πωλούμενον ἐσθίετε, μηδὲν ἀνακρίνοντες διὰ τὴν
[5]being [6]sold [1]Eat, nothing ˜ questioning for the sake of the

συνείδησιν. 26 «Τοῦ γὰρ Κυρίου ἡ γῆ καὶ τὸ
conscience. «[5]of [6]the [1]For [7]Lord [2]the [3]earth [4]*is* and -

πλήρωμα αὐτῆς.»[e] 27 Εἰ δέ τις καλεῖ ὑμᾶς τῶν
fullness ˜ its.» if ˜ And someone [5]invites [6]you [1]of [2]the

ἀπίστων, καὶ θέλετε πορεύεσθαι, πᾶν τὸ
[3]unbelieving [4]*ones,* and you desire to go, [2]anything -

παρατιθέμενον ὑμῖν ἐσθίετε, μηδὲν ἀνακρίνοντες
[3]being [4]placed [5]before [6]you [1]eat, nothing ˜ questioning

διὰ τὴν συνείδησιν. 28 Ἐὰν δέ τις ὑμῖν
for the sake of the conscience. if ˜ But someone [3]to [4]you

εἴπῃ, "Τοῦτο εἰδωλόθυτόν ἐστι," μὴ ἐσθίετε
[1]should [2]say, "This [2]*something* [3]offered [4]to [5]idols [1]is," not ˜ do eat *it*

δι᾽ ἐκεῖνον τὸν μηνύσαντα καὶ τὴν συνείδησιν,[f] «Τοῦ
because of that *one* - revealing and the conscience, «[5]of [6]the
who told you his

γὰρ Κυρίου ἡ γῆ καὶ τὸ πλήρωμα αὐτῆς.»[g]
[1]For [7]Lord [2]the [3]earth [4]*is* and - fullness ˜ its.»

29 Συνείδησιν δὲ λέγω, οὐχὶ τὴν ἑαυτοῦ ἀλλὰ τὴν
[4]conscience [1]Now [2]I [3]say, not the *one* of yourself but the *one*
your own that

τοῦ ἑτέρου. Ἵνα τί γὰρ ἡ ἐλευθερία μου κρίνεται ὑπὸ
of the other. - why ˜ For - [3]freedom [2]my [1]is judged by

ἄλλης συνειδήσεως? 30 Εἰ ἐγὼ χάριτι μετέχω, τί
[3]of [4]another [1]*the* [2]conscience? If I [2]with [3]thanks [1]partake, why

βλασφημοῦμαι ὑπὲρ οὗ ἐγὼ εὐχαριστῶ? 31 Εἴτε
am I defamed for *that* of which I give thanks? whether ˜

οὖν ἐσθίετε εἴτε πίνετε, εἴτε τι ποιεῖτε, πάντα
Therefore you eat or you drink, or [3]anything [1]you [2]do, [5]all [6]*things*

εἰς δόξαν Θεοῦ ποιεῖτε. 32 Ἀπρόσκοποι γίνεσθε καὶ
[7]for [8]*the* [9]glory [10]of [11]God [4]do. [2]without [3]offense [1]Be both

Ἰουδαίοις καὶ Ἕλλησι καὶ τῇ ἐκκλησίᾳ τοῦ Θεοῦ,
toward Jews and toward Greeks and toward the church - of God,

33 καθὼς κἀγὼ πάντα πᾶσιν ἀρέσκω, μὴ ζητῶν τὸ
just as I also [5]*in* [6]all [7]*things* [3]to [4]all [1]am [2]pleasing, not seeking the
my

mons; you cannot partake of the Lord's table and of the table of demons.
22 Or do we provoke the Lord to jealousy? Are we stronger than He?
23 All things are lawful for me, but not all things are helpful; all things are lawful for me, but not all things edify.
24 Let no one seek his own, but each one the other's *well-being.*
25 Eat whatever is sold in the meat market, asking no questions for conscience' sake;
26 for *"the earth is the* LORD'*s, and all its fullness."*
27 If any of those who do not believe invites you *to dinner,* and you desire to go, eat whatever is set before you, asking no question for conscience' sake.
28 But if anyone says to you, "This was offered to idols," do not eat it for the sake of the one who told you, and for conscience' sake; for *"the earth is the* LORD'*s, and all its fullness."*
29 "Conscience," I say, not your own, but that of the other. For why is my liberty judged by another *man's* conscience?
30 But if I partake with thanks, why am I evil spoken of for *the food* over which I give thanks?
31 Therefore, whether you eat or drink, or whatever you do, do all to the glory of God.
32 Give no offense, either to the Jews or to the Greeks or to the church of God,
33 just as I also please all *men* in all *things,* not seeking my

[d](**10:23**) NU omits μοι, *for me.* [e](**10:26**) Ps. 24:1; 50:12; 89:11
[f](**10:28**) NU omits the rest of v. 28. [g](**10:28**) Ps. 24:1; 50:12; 89:11

own profit, but the *profit* of
many, that they may be saved.
11 Imitate me, just as I
also *imitate* Christ.
2 Now I praise you, brethren, that you remember me in
all things and keep the traditions just as I delivered *them* to
you.
3 But I want you to know
that the head of every man is
Christ, the head of woman *is*
man, and the head of Christ *is*
God.
4 Every man praying or
prophesying, having *his* head
covered, dishonors his head.
5 But every woman who
prays or prophesies with *her*
head uncovered dishonors her
head, for that is one and the
same as if her head were
shaved.
6 For if a woman is not covered, let her also be shorn. But
if it is shameful for a woman to
be shorn or shaved, let her be
covered.
7 For a man indeed ought not
to cover *his* head, since he is
the image and glory of God; but
woman is the glory of man.
8 For man is not from
woman, but woman from man.
9 Nor was man created for
the woman, but woman for the
man.
10 For this reason the woman
ought to have *a symbol of* authority on *her* head, because of
the angels.
11 Nevertheless, neither *is*
man independent of woman,
nor woman independent of
man, in the Lord.
12 For as woman *came* from

ἐμαυτοῦ συμφέρον ἀλλὰ τὸ τῶν πολλῶν, ἵνα
[2]of [3]myself [1]profit but the *profit* of the many, in order that
own

σωθῶσι.
they may be saved.

11 1 Μιμηταί μου γίνεσθε καθὼς κἀγὼ Χριστοῦ.
[2]imitators [3]of [4]me [1]Be just as I also *am* of Christ.

The Meaning of Head Coverings

2 Ἐπαινῶ δὲ ὑμᾶς, ἀδελφοί,[a] ὅτι πάντα μου
[2]I [3]praise [1]Now you, brothers, because [4]*in* [5]all [6]*things* [3]me

μέμνησθε, καὶ καθὼς παρέδωκα ὑμῖν, τὰς παραδόσεις
[1]you [2]remember, and just as I handed down to you, [4]the [5]traditions

κατέχετε. 3 Θέλω δὲ ὑμᾶς εἰδέναι ὅτι παντὸς ἀνδρὸς
[1]you [2]hold [3]fast. [2]I [3]want [1]But you to know that [5]of [6]every [7]man

ἡ κεφαλὴ ὁ Χριστός ἐστι, κεφαλὴ δὲ γυναικὸς ὁ
[3]the [4]head - [1]Christ [2]is, [12]*the* [13]head [8]and [14]of [15]*the* [16]woman [9]the

ἀνήρ, κεφαλὴ δὲ Χριστοῦ ὁ Θεός. 4 Πᾶς ἀνὴρ
[10]man [11]*is,* [20]*the* [21]head [17]and [22]of [23]Christ - [18]God [19]*is.* Every man

προσευχόμενος ἢ προφητεύων κατὰ κεφαλῆς ἔχων
praying or prophesying [3]upon [4]*his* [5]head [1]having [2]*something*
who prays who prophesies with his head covered

καταισχύνει τὴν κεφαλὴν αὐτοῦ. 5 Πᾶσα δὲ γυνὴ
dishonors - head ˜ his. every ˜ But woman

προσευχομένη ἢ προφητεύουσα ἀκατακαλύπτῳ τῇ
praying or prophesying [4]uncovered [1]with [2]the
who prays who prophesies her

κεφαλῇ καταισχύνει τὴν κεφαλὴν ἑαυτῆς, ἓν γάρ ἐστι καὶ
[3]head dishonors the head of herself, [4]one [1]for [2]it [3]is and
her own head,

τὸ αὐτὸ τῇ ἐξυρημένῃ. 6 Εἰ γὰρ οὐ
the same *thing* with the *head* being shaved. if ˜ For [4]not

κατακαλύπτεται γυνή, καὶ κειράσθω. Εἰ δὲ
[3]is [5]covered [1]a [2]woman, [8]also [6]let [7]her have her hair cut. if ˜ But

αἰσχρὸν γυναικὶ τὸ κείρασθαι ἢ ξυρᾶσθαι,
it is a shameful *thing* for a woman - to have her hair cut or to be shaved,

κατακαλυπτέσθω. 7 Ἀνὴρ μὲν γὰρ οὐκ ὀφείλει
let her be covered. [2]a [3]man - [1]For not ˜ ought

κατακαλύπτεσθαι τὴν κεφαλήν, εἰκὼν καὶ δόξα Θεοῦ
to cover the head, [2]*the* [3]image [4]and [5]glory [6]of [7]God
his

ὑπάρχων· γυνὴ δὲ δόξα ἀνδρός ἐστιν. 8 Οὐ γάρ ἐστιν
[1]being; woman ˜ but [2]*the* [3]glory [4]of [5]man [1]is. [4]not [1]For [3]is
since he is;

ἀνὴρ ἐκ γυναικός, ἀλλὰ γυνὴ ἐξ ἀνδρός. 9 Καὶ γὰρ οὐκ
[2]man from woman, but woman *is* from man. also ˜ For [3]not

ἐκτίσθη ἀνὴρ διὰ τὴν γυναῖκα, ἀλλὰ γυνὴ
[2]was [4]created [1]man for the sake of the woman, but woman

διὰ τὸν ἄνδρα. 10 Διὰ τοῦτο ὀφείλει ἡ γυνὴ
for the sake of the man. Because of this [3]ought [1]the [2]woman

ἐξουσίαν ἔχειν ἐπὶ τῆς κεφαλῆς διὰ τοὺς
[6]*a* [7]*symbol* [8]*of* [9]authority [4]to [5]have upon the head because of the
her

ἀγγέλους. 11 Πλὴν οὔτε ἀνὴρ χωρὶς γυναικός,
angels. Nevertheless neither *is* man apart from woman,
independent of

οὔτε γυνὴ χωρὶς ἀνδρός, ἐν Κυρίῳ. 12 Ὥσπερ γὰρ ἡ
nor woman apart from man, in *the* Lord. as ˜ For the
independent of

---

[a](11:2) NU omits αδελφοι, *brothers*.

γυνὴ ἐκ τοῦ ἀνδρός, οὕτω καὶ ὁ ἀνὴρ διὰ τῆς γυναικός,
woman *is* from the man, so also the man *is* by the woman,

τὰ δὲ πάντα ἐκ τοῦ Θεοῦ. 13 Ἐν ὑμῖν αὐτοῖς
- but all *things are* from - God. [2]among [3]you [4]yourselves

κρίνατε. Πρέπον ἐστὶ γυναῖκα ἀκατακάλυπτον τῷ Θεῷ
[1]Judge. [7]proper [5]Is [6]it *for* a woman [5]uncovered [3]to [4]God

προσεύχεσθαι? 14 Ἢ οὐδὲ αὐτὴ ἡ φύσις διδάσκει ὑμᾶς ὅτι
[1]to [2]pray? Or [2]not [4]itself - [3]nature [1]does [5]teach you that

ἀνὴρ μὲν ἐὰν κομᾷ, ἀτιμία αὐτῷ ἐστι?
[2]a [3]man - [1]if should wear long hair, [3]a [4]dishonor [5]to [6]him [1]it [2]is?

15 Γυνὴ δὲ ἐὰν κομᾷ, δόξα αὐτῇ ἐστιν·
[2]a [3]woman [1]But [2]if should wear long hair, [3]a [4]glory [5]for [6]her [1]it [2]is;

ὅτι ἡ κόμη ἀντὶ περιβολαίου δέδοται.[b]
because the (her) long hair [6]in [7]place [8]of [9]a [10]covering [1]has [2]been [3]given [4]*to* [5]*her.*

16 Εἰ δέ τις δοκεῖ φιλόνεικος εἶναι, ἡμεῖς τοιαύτην
if ˜ But anyone seems [3]contentious [1]to [2]be, we [4]such

συνήθειαν οὐκ ἔχομεν, οὐδὲ αἱ ἐκκλησίαι τοῦ Θεοῦ.
[5]a [6]custom [2]not [1]do [3]have, nor *do* the churches - of God.

Improper Conduct at the Lord's Supper

17 Τοῦτο δὲ παραγγέλλων οὐκ ἐπαινῶ, ὅτι οὐκ
[3]this (Now) [1]Now [2]instructing (giving this instruction) [6]not [4]I [5]do praise *you,* because [3]not

εἰς τὸ κρεῖττον ἀλλ' εἰς τὸ ἧττον συνέρχεσθε.
[6]for [7]the [8]better [9]but [10]for [11]the [12]worse [1]you [2]are [4]coming [5]together.

18 Πρῶτον μὲν γὰρ συνερχομένων ὑμῶν ἐν ἐκκλησίᾳ, ἀκούω
first ˜ - For [2]coming [3]together [1]you (when you come together) in church, I hear

σχίσματα ἐν ὑμῖν ὑπάρχειν, καὶ μέρος τι πιστεύω.
[3]divisions [4]among [5]you [1]to [2]be, (that there are,) and *in* part ˜ some I believe *it.*

19 Δεῖ γὰρ καὶ αἱρέσεις* ἐν ὑμῖν εἶναι,
[2]it [3]is [4]necessary [1]For [7]also [8]factions [9]among [10]you [5]to [6]be, (that there be,)

ἵνα οἱ δόκιμοι φανεροὶ γένωνται ἐν ὑμῖν.
in order that the approved *ones* [3]clear (recognized) [1]may [2]become among you.

20 Συνερχομένων οὖν ὑμῶν ἐπὶ τὸ αὐτό, οὐκ ἔστι
coming together Therefore you (Therefore when you assemble) in the same *place,* [3]not [1]it [2]is

Κυριακὸν Δεῖπνον φαγεῖν. 21 Ἕκαστος γὰρ τὸ ἴδιον
[6]*the* [7]Lord's [8]Supper [4]to [5]eat. [5]each [6]*one* [1]For - [9]his [10]own

δεῖπνον προλαμβάνει ἐν τῷ φαγεῖν, καὶ ὃς μὲν πεινᾷ,
[11]supper [7]takes [8]first [2]in - [3]to [4]eat, (when you eat,) and one - goes hungry,

ὃς δὲ μεθύει. 22 Μὴ γὰρ οἰκίας οὐκ ἔχετε εἰς τὸ
one ˜ (another) and is drunk. - For [5]houses [3]not [1]do [2]you [4]have for -

ἐσθίειν καὶ πίνειν? Ἢ τῆς ἐκκλησίας τοῦ Θεοῦ
to eat (eating) and to drink? (drinking?) Or [4]the [5]church - [6]of [7]God

καταφρονεῖτε, καὶ καταισχύνετε τοὺς μὴ ἔχοντας? Τί
[1]do [2]you [3]despise, and do you disgrace the *ones* not having? (those who do not have?) What

ὑμῖν εἴπω? Ἐπαινέσω ὑμᾶς ἐν τούτῳ? Οὐκ
[4]to [5]you [1]shall [2]I [3]say? Shall I praise you in this? [3]not

ἐπαινῶ!
[1]I [2]do praise *you!*

man, even so man also *comes* through woman; but all things are from God.
13 Judge among yourselves. Is it proper for a woman to pray to God with her head uncovered?
14 Does not even nature itself teach you that if a man has long hair, it is a dishonor to him?
15 But if a woman has long hair, it is a glory to her; for *her* hair is given to her for a covering.
16 But if anyone seems to be contentious, we have no such custom, nor *do* the churches of God.
17 Now in giving these instructions I do not praise *you,* since you come together not for the better but for the worse.
18 For first of all, when you come together as a church, I hear that there are divisions among you, and in part I believe it.
19 For there must also be factions among you, that those who are approved may be recognized among you.
20 Therefore when you come together in one place, it is not to eat the Lord's Supper.
21 For in eating, each one takes his own supper ahead of *others;* and one is hungry and another is drunk.
22 What! Do you not have houses to eat and drink in? Or do you despise the church of God and shame those who have nothing? What shall I say to you? Shall I praise you in this? I do not praise *you.*

---

[b](11:15) NU, TR add *αυτη, to her.*

***(11:19)** *αἵρεσις (hairesis).* Noun with a variety of meanings. Apparently it originally meant a *choice, opinion,* and then a *sect, faction,* or *party* identified by distinctive views (as Acts 5:17; 15:5; 26:5), and ultimately a *divisive (heretical) opinion or sect, heresy.* Sometimes it is difficult to decide whether to translate *heresy* or *faction,* as here in 1 Cor. 11:19 or Gal. 5:20; 2 Pet. 2:1. The Jews regarded Christians as a *heretical sect* (Acts 24:5, 14; 28:22). Cf. the cognate adjective *αἱρετικός, factious, heretical* (Titus 3:10).

23 For I received from the
Lord that which I also delivered
to you: that the Lord Jesus on
the *same* night in which He was
betrayed took bread;
24 and when He had given
thanks, He broke *it* and said,
"Take, eat; this is My body
which is broken for you; do this
in remembrance of Me."
25 In the same manner *He*
also *took* the cup after supper,
saying, "This cup is the new
covenant in My blood. This do,
as often as you drink *it,* in remembrance of Me."
26 For as often as you eat this
bread and drink this cup, you
proclaim the Lord's death till
He comes.
27 Therefore whoever eats
this bread or drinks *this* cup of
the Lord in an unworthy manner will be guilty of the body
and blood of the Lord.
28 But let a man examine himself, and so let him eat of the
bread and drink of the cup.
29 For he who eats and drinks
in an unworthy manner eats and
drinks judgment to himself, not
discerning the Lord's body.
30 For this reason many *are*
weak and sick among you, and
many sleep.
31 For if we would judge ourselves, we would not be
judged.
32 But when we are judged,
we are chastened by the Lord,
that we may not be condemned
with the world.

Institution of the Lord's Supper

(Matt. 26:26–30; Mark 14:22–26; Luke 22:14–20)

23 Ἐγὼ γὰρ παρέλαβον ἀπὸ τοῦ Κυρίου ὃ καὶ
I ˜ For received from the Lord what also ˜
παρέδωκα ὑμῖν, ὅτι ὁ Κύριος Ἰησοῦς ἐν τῇ νυκτὶ ᾗ
I handed down to you, that the Lord Jesus during the night in which
παρεδίδοτο ἔλαβεν ἄρτον. **24** Καὶ εὐχαριστήσας
He was handed over took bread. And having given thanks
betrayed
ἔκλασε καὶ εἶπε, "Λάβετε, φάγετε·[c] τοῦτό μού ἐστι τὸ
He broke *it* and said, "Take, eat: this My ˜ is -
σῶμα τὸ ὑπὲρ ὑμῶν κλώμενον·[d] τοῦτο ποιεῖτε εἰς
body the *one* [3]in [4]behalf [5]of [6]you [1]being [2]broken; this ˜ do in
which has been broken for your sakes;
τὴν ἐμὴν ἀνάμνησιν." **25** Ὡσαύτως καὶ τὸ ποτήριον μετὰ τὸ
- My remembrance." Likewise also the cup after -
δειπνῆσαι, λέγων, "Τοῦτο τὸ ποτήριον ἡ καινὴ διαθήκη
to eat supper, saying, "This - cup [2]the [3]new [4]covenant
supper,
ἐστὶν ἐν τῷ ἐμῷ αἵματι. Τοῦτο ποιεῖτε, ὁσάκις ἂν πίνητε,
[1]is in - My blood. This do, as often as - you drink *it,*
εἰς τὴν ἐμὴν ἀνάμνησιν." **26** Ὁσάκις γὰρ ἂν ἐσθίητε τὸν
in - My remembrance." [2]as [3]often [4]as [1]For - you eat -
ἄρτον τοῦτον, καὶ τὸ ποτήριον τοῦτο πίνητε, τὸν θάνατον τοῦ
bread ˜ this, and - [3]cup [2]this [1]drink, [6]the [7]death [8]of [9]the
Κυρίου καταγγέλλετε ἄχρις οὗ ἂν ἔλθῃ.
[10]Lord [4]you [5]proclaim until - - He comes.

Examine Yourself Before Partaking

27 Ὥστε ὃς ἂν ἐσθίῃ τὸν ἄρτον τοῦτον ἢ πίνῃ τὸ
So then whoever - eats - bread ˜ this or drinks the
ποτήριον τοῦ Κυρίου ἀναξίως τοῦ Κυρίου[e] ἔνοχος ἔσται
cup of the Lord unworthily [7]of [8]the [9]Lord [3]guilty [1]will [2]be
τοῦ σώματος καὶ τοῦ[f] αἵματος τοῦ Κυρίου. **28** Δοκιμαζέτω
[4]of [5]the [6]body and of the blood of the Lord. [2]let [5]examine
δὲ ἄνθρωπος ἑαυτόν, καὶ οὕτως ἐκ τοῦ ἄρτου ἐσθιέτω
[1]But [3]a [4]man himself, and thus [4]from [5]the [6]bread [1]let [2]him [3]eat
in this way
καὶ ἐκ τοῦ ποτηρίου πινέτω. **29** Ὁ γὰρ ἐσθίων καὶ
and [4]from [5]the [6]cup [1]let [2]him [3]drink. [2]the [3]*one* [1]For eating and
who eats
πίνων ἀναξίως,[g] κρίμα ἑαυτῷ ἐσθίει καὶ πίνει, μὴ
drinking unworthily, [4]judgment [5]to [6]himself [1]eats [2]and [3]drinks, not
who drinks
διακρίνων τὸ σῶμα τοῦ Κυρίου.[h] **30** Διὰ τοῦτο
judging correctly the body of the Lord. Because of this
ἐν ὑμῖν πολλοὶ ἀσθενεῖς καὶ ἄρρωστοι, καὶ κοιμῶνται
[2]among [3]you [1]many *are* weak and sick, and sleep
many
ἱκανοί. **31** Εἰ γὰρ ἑαυτοὺς διεκρίνομεν, οὐκ ἂν
in large numbers. if ˜ For [3]ourselves [1]we [2]judge [4]correctly, [7]not -
have died.
ἐκρινόμεθα. **32** Κρινόμενοι δέ, ὑπὸ Κυρίου
[5]we [6]would [8]be [9]judged. [2]being [3]judged [1]But, [7]by [8]*the* [9]Lord
when we are
παιδευόμεθα, ἵνα μὴ σὺν τῷ κόσμῳ
[4]we [5]are [6]disciplined, in order that [3]not [6]with [7]the [8]world

---

c(**11:24**) NU omits Λαβετε, φαγετε, *Take, eat.*
d(**11:24**) NU omits κλωμενον, *being broken.*
e(**11:27**) NU, TR omit του Κυριου, *of the Lord.*
f(**11:27**) TR omits του, *of the.* g(**11:29**) NU omits αναξιως, *unworthily.*
h(**11:29**) NU omits του Κυριου, *of the Lord.*

κατακριθῶμεν. 33 Ὥστε, ἀδελφοί μου, συνερχόμενοι
[1]we [2]may [4]be [5]condemned. So then, brothers ~ my, coming together
when you come

εἰς τὸ φαγεῖν, ἀλλήλους ἐκδέχεσθε. 34 Εἰ δέ τις
for - to eat, [3]one [4]another [1]wait [2]for. if ~ But anyone
together

πεινᾷ, ἐν οἴκῳ ἐσθιέτω, ἵνα μὴ εἰς κρίμα
is hungry, [4]at [5]home [1]let [2]him [3]eat, that not [4]for [5]judgment
lest

συνέρχησθε. Τὰ δὲ λοιπὰ ὡς ἂν ἔλθω
[1]you [2]come [3]together. the ~ And remaining *things* whenever - I come
rest

διατάξομαι.
I will order.
put in order.

Spiritual Gifts: Unity in Diversity

12 1 Περὶ δὲ τῶν πνευματικῶν, ἀδελφοί, οὐ
concerning ~ Now - spiritual *gifts,* brothers, [3]not

θέλω ὑμᾶς ἀγνοεῖν. 2 Οἴδατε ὅτι ὅτε[a] ἔθνη
[1]I [2]do want you to be ignorant. You know that when [3]Gentiles

ἦτε, πρὸς τὰ εἴδωλα τὰ ἄφωνα ὡς ἂν ἤγεσθε
[1]you [2]were, [11]to [12]the [14]idols - [13]speechless [4]how - [5]you [6]were [7]led

ἀπαγόμενοι. 3 Διὸ γνωρίζω ὑμῖν ὅτι οὐδεὶς ἐν
[8]being [9]carried [10]away. Therefore I make known to you that no one [2]by

Πνεύματι Θεοῦ λαλῶν λέγει ἀνάθεμα Ἰησοῦν, καὶ οὐδεὶς
[3]*the* [4]Spirit [5]of [6]God [1]speaking says accursed thing Jesus, and no one
Jesus be cursed,

δύναται εἰπεῖν Κύριον Ἰησοῦν εἰ μὴ ἐν Πνεύματι Ἁγίῳ.
is able to say Lord Jesus if not by *the* Spirit ~ Holy.
except

4 Διαιρέσεις δὲ χαρισμάτων εἰσί, τὸ δὲ αὐτὸ
[4]varieties [1]Now [5]of [6]spiritual [7]*gifts* [2]*there* [3]are, the ~ but same

Πνεῦμα. 5 Καὶ διαιρέσεις διακονιῶν εἰσι, καὶ ὁ αὐτὸς
Spirit. And [3]varieties [4]of [5]ministries [1]*there* [2]are, and the same

Κύριος. 6 Καὶ διαιρέσεις ἐνεργημάτων εἰσίν, ὁ δὲ αὐτός
Lord. And [3]varieties [4]of [5]activities [1]*there* [2]are, the ~ but same

ἐστι Θεὸς ὁ ἐνεργῶν τὰ πάντα ἐν πᾶσιν. 7 Ἑκάστῳ
is ~ God the *One* working - all *things* in all *things.* [2]to [3]each [4]*one*

δὲ δίδοται ἡ φανέρωσις τοῦ Πνεύματος πρὸς τὸ
[1]But is given the manifestation of the Spirit for the

συμφέρον. 8 Ὧι μὲν γὰρ διὰ τοῦ Πνεύματος δίδοται
profiting *of all.* [2]to [3]one - [1]For [10]by [11]the [12]Spirit [4]is [5]given
profit

λόγος σοφίας,* ἄλλῳ δὲ λόγος γνώσεως κατὰ
[6]a [7]word [8]of [9]wisdom, [14]to [15]another [13]and a word of knowledge according to

τὸ αὐτὸ Πνεῦμα, 9 ἑτέρῳ δὲ πίστις ἐν τῷ αὐτῷ
the same Spirit, [2]to [3]another [1]and faith by the same

Πνεύματι, ἄλλῳ δὲ χαρίσματα ἰαμάτων ἐν τῷ αὐτῷ[b]
Spirit, [2]to [3]another [1]and gifts of healings by the same

Πνεύματι, 10 ἄλλῳ δὲ ἐνεργήματα δυνάμεων, ἄλλῳ
Spirit, [2]to [3]another [1]and activities of miracles, [2]to [3]another

δὲ προφητεία, ἄλλῳ δὲ διακρίσεις πνευμάτων, ἑτέρῳ
[1]and prophecy, [2]to [3]another [1]and discernings of spirits, [2]to [3]another

δὲ γένη γλωσσῶν, ἄλλῳ δὲ ἑρμηνεία γλωσσῶν.
[1]and kinds of tongues, [2]to [3]another [1]and interpretation of tongues.

11 Πάντα δὲ ταῦτα ἐνεργεῖ τὸ ἓν καὶ τὸ αὐτὸ
[9]all [1]But [10]these [11]*things* [8]works [2]the [3]one [4]and [5]the [6]same

33 Therefore, my brethren, when you come together to eat, wait for one another.

34 But if anyone is hungry, let him eat at home, lest you come together for judgment. And the rest I will set in order when I come.

12 Now concerning spiritual *gifts,* brethren, I do not want you to be ignorant:

2 You know that you were Gentiles, carried away to these dumb idols, however you were led.

3 Therefore I make known to you that no one speaking by the Spirit of God calls Jesus accursed, and no one can say that Jesus is Lord except by the Holy Spirit.

4 There are diversities of gifts, but the same Spirit.

5 There are differences of ministries, but the same Lord.

6 And there are diversities of activities, but it is the same God who works all in all.

7 But the manifestation of the Spirit is given to each one for the profit *of all:*

8 for to one is given the word of wisdom through the Spirit, to another the word of knowledge through the same Spirit,

9 to another faith by the same Spirit, to another gifts of healings by the same Spirit,

10 to another the working of miracles, to another prophecy, to another discerning of spirits, to another *different* kinds of tongues, to another the interpretation of tongues.

11 But one and the same

---

[a](12:2) TR omits *οτε, when.*
[b](12:9) NU reads *ενι, one.*

***(12:8)** *σοφια (sophia).* Noun common in the NT, meaning *wisdom,* typically as a spiritual or intellectual capacity of human beings (Luke 2:52) or even of God (Rom. 11:33). More abstractly, it can mean something like a body of learning or instruction (Acts 7:22) and be very practical (James 1:5; cf. 3:17). It can also be personified, perhaps reflecting the OT Proverbs (as Matt. 11.19). Paul often used the word to represent unspiritual, worldly wisdom that believers must reject (as 1 Cor. 1:17, 19), but here in 12:8 it refers to the wisdom that God imparts as a spiri-

Spirit works all these things,
distributing to each one individually as He wills.
12 For as the body is one and
has many members, but all the
members of that one body, being many, are one body, so also
is Christ.
13 For by one Spirit we were
all baptized into one body—
whether Jews or Greeks,
whether slaves or free—and
have all been made to drink into
one Spirit.
14 For in fact the body is not
one member but many.
15 If the foot should say, "Because I am not a hand, I am not
of the body," is it therefore not
of the body?
16 And if the ear should say,
"Because I am not an eye, I am
not of the body," is it therefore
not of the body?
17 If the whole body *were* an
eye, where *would be* the hearing? If the whole *were* hearing,
where *would be* the smelling?
18 But now God has set the
members, each one of them, in
the body just as He pleased.
19 And if they *were* all one
member, where *would* the body
be?
20 But now indeed *there are*
many members, yet one body.
21 And the eye cannot say to
the hand, "I have no need of
you"; nor again the head to the
feet, "I have no need of you."
22 No, much rather, those
members of the body which
seem to be weaker are necessary.
23 And those *members* of the
body which we think to be less
honorable, on these we bestow
greater honor; and our unpre-

Πνεῦμα, διαιροῦν ἰδίᾳ ἑκάστῳ καθὼς βούλεται.
[7]Spirit, distributing [3]his [4]own [1]to [2]each just as He wills.

Unity and Diversity in One Body

12 Καθάπερ γὰρ τὸ σῶμα ἕν ἐστι καὶ μέλη ἔχει πολλά,
[2]just [3]as [1]For the body one ˜ is and [3]parts [1]has [2]many,
πάντα δὲ τὰ μέλη τοῦ σώματος τοῦ ἑνός,[c] πολλὰ ὄντα, ἕν
all ˜ but the parts of the body ˜ - one, many ˜ being, one ˜
ἐστι σῶμα, οὕτω καὶ ὁ Χριστός. 13 Καὶ γὰρ ἐν ἑνὶ
are body, so also *is* - Christ. also ˜ For by one
Πνεύματι ἡμεῖς πάντες εἰς ἓν σῶμα ἐβαπτίσθημεν, εἴτε
Spirit we all [3]into [4]one [5]body [1]were [2]baptized, whether
Ἰουδαῖοι εἴτε Ἕλληνες, εἴτε δοῦλοι εἴτε ἐλεύθεροι, καὶ
Jews or Greeks, whether slaves or free, and
πάντες εἰς[d] ἓν Πνεῦμα ἐποτίσθημεν. 14 Καὶ γὰρ
[3]all [7]into [8]one [9]Spirit [1]we [2]were [4]given [5]to [6]drink. also ˜ For
τὸ σῶμα οὐκ ἔστιν ἓν μέλος ἀλλὰ πολλά. 15 Ἐὰν εἴπῃ ὁ
the body not ˜ is one part but many. If [3]says [1]the
πούς, "Ὅτι οὐκ εἰμὶ χείρ, οὐκ εἰμὶ ἐκ τοῦ σώματος," οὐ
[2]foot, "Because [3]not [1]I [2]am a hand, [3]not [1]I [2]am of the body," not
it is
παρὰ τοῦτο οὐκ ἔστιν ἐκ τοῦ σώματος. 16 Καὶ ἐὰν εἴπῃ τὸ
because of this [3]not [1]is [2]it of the body. And if [3]says [1]the
not any less a part
οὖς, "Ὅτι οὐκ εἰμὶ ὀφθαλμός, οὐκ εἰμὶ ἐκ τοῦ σώματος,"
[2]ear, "Because [3]not [1]I [2]am an eye, [3]not [1]I [2]am of the body,"
οὐ παρὰ τοῦτο οὐκ ἔστιν ἐκ τοῦ σώματος. 17 Εἰ ὅλον τὸ
not because of this [3]not [1]is [2]it of the body. If whole ˜ the
it is not any less a part
σῶμα ὀφθαλμός, ποῦ ἡ ἀκοή? Εἰ ὅλον ἀκοή,
body *were* an eye, where *would be* the hearing? If *the* whole *were* hearing,
ποῦ ἡ ὄσφρησις? 18 Νυνὶ δὲ ὁ Θεὸς ἔθετο τὰ
where *would be* the sense of smell? now ˜ But - God set the
has set
μέλη ἓν ἕκαστον αὐτῶν ἐν τῷ σώματι καθὼς ἠθέλησεν.
parts one ˜ each of them in the body just as He desired.
19 Εἰ δὲ ἦν τὰ πάντα ἓν μέλος, ποῦ τὸ σῶμα?
if ˜ And [3]were - [1]all [2]*parts* one part, where *would be* the body?
20 Νῦν δὲ πολλὰ μὲν μέλη, ἓν δὲ σῶμα.
now ˜ But *there are* many - parts, one ˜ but body.
21 Οὐ δύναται δὲ ὁ ὀφθαλμὸς εἰπεῖν τῇ χειρί,
[5]not [4]is [6]able [1]But [2]the [3]eye to say to the hand,
"Χρείαν σου οὐκ ἔχω," ἢ πάλιν ἡ κεφαλὴ τοῖς ποσί,
"[5]need [6]of [7]you [3]not [1]I [2]do [4]have," or again the head to the feet,
"Χρείαν ὑμῶν οὐκ ἔχω." 22 Ἀλλὰ πολλῷ μᾶλλον τὰ
"[5]need [6]of [7]you [3]not [1]I [2]do [4]have." But by much more the
to a greater degree
δοκοῦντα μέλη τοῦ σώματος ἀσθενέστερα ὑπάρχειν
[5]seeming [1]parts [2]of [3]the [4]body [8]weaker [6]to [7]be
which seem
ἀναγκαῖά ἐστι. 23 Καὶ ἃ δοκοῦμεν ἀτιμότερα
[10]necessary [9]are. And *the parts* [4]which [5]we [6]consider [9]less [10]honorable
εἶναι τοῦ σώματος, τούτοις τιμὴν περισσοτέραν
[7]to [8]be [1]of [2]the [3]body, to these [4]honor [3]greater
περιτίθεμεν· καὶ τὰ ἀσχήμονα ἡμῶν εὐσχημοσύνην
[1]we [2]bestow; and - [2]unpresentable [3]*parts* [1]our [6]propriety
presentability

[c]**(12:12)** NU omits του ενος, *(of the) one (body).*
[d]**(12:13)** NU omits εις, *into.*

tual gift. Cf. the cognate adjective σοφός, *wise;* and the verb σοφίζω, *make wise, instruct* in the active voice (only 2 Tim. 3:15) or *craftily devise* in the passive voice (only 2 Pet. 1:16).

περισσοτέραν ἔχει. 24 Τὰ δὲ εὐσχήμονα ἡμῶν οὐ χρείαν
5greater 4have. - But 2presentable 3*parts* 1our 5not 7need

ἔχει. 'Αλλ' ὁ Θεὸς συνεκέρασε τὸ σῶμα, τῷ
4do 6have. But - God united the body, 4to 5the 6*part*

ὑστεροῦντι περισσοτέραν δοὺς τιμὴν 25 ἵνα μὴ ᾖ
7being 8inferior 2greater 1giving 3honor that not *there* be
lest

σχίσματα ἐν τῷ σώματι, ἀλλὰ τὸ αὐτὸ ὑπὲρ ἀλλήλων
divisions in the body, but 4the 5same 6for 7each 8other

μεριμνῶσι τὰ μέλη. 26 Καὶ εἴτε πάσχει ἓν μέλος,
3care 1the 2parts. And if 3suffers 1one 2part,

συμπάσχει πάντα τὰ μέλη· εἴτε δοξάζεται ἓν μέλος,
7suffer 8together 4all 5the 6parts; or if 3is 4honored 1one 2part,

συγχαίρει πάντα τὰ μέλη.
8rejoice 9together 5all 6the 7parts.

27 Ὑμεῖς δέ ἐστε σῶμα Χριστοῦ καὶ μέλη ἐκ
you ˜ Now are *the* body of Christ and parts from
members individually.

μέρους. 28 Καὶ οὓς μὲν ἔθετο ὁ Θεὸς ἐν τῇ ἐκκλησίᾳ
each part. And *those* whom - set ˜ - God in the church *are:*
has set

πρῶτον ἀποστόλους, δεύτερον προφήτας, τρίτον διδασκάλους,
first apostles, second prophets, third teachers,

ἔπειτα δυνάμεις, εἶτα χαρίσματα ἰαμάτων, ἀντιλήψεις,
then miracles, then gifts of healings, helps,

κυβερνήσεις,* γένη γλωσσῶν. 29 Μὴ πάντες ἀπόστολοι?
administrations, kinds of tongues. 3not 1All 2*are* apostles, *are they?*

Μὴ πάντες προφῆται? Μὴ πάντες διδάσκαλοι? Μὴ
3not 1All 2*are* prophets, *are they?* 3not 1All 2*are* teachers, *are they?* 3not

πάντες δυνάμεις? 30 Μὴ πάντες χαρίσματα
1All 2*are workers of* miracles, *are they?* 3not 1All 5gifts

ἔχουσιν ἰαμάτων? Μὴ πάντες γλώσσαις
2do 4have of healings, *do they?* 3not 1All 5with 6tongues

λαλοῦσι? Μὴ πάντες διερμηνεύουσι? 31 Ζηλοῦτε δὲ
2do 4speak, *do they?* 3not 1All 2do interpret, *do they?* 2strive 3for 1But

τὰ χαρίσματα τὰ κρείττονα.[e] Καὶ ἔτι καθ'
the gifts ˜ - better. And yet 6according 7to
a much

ὑπερβολὴν ὁδὸν ὑμῖν δείκνυμι.
8a 9more 10excellent 11way 4to 5you 1I 2make 3known.
better

Paul's Paean of Praise to Love

13 1 'Εὰν ταῖς γλώσσαις τῶν ἀνθρώπων λαλῶ καὶ
If 3with 4the 5tongues - 6of 7men 1I 2speak and

τῶν ἀγγέλων, ἀγάπην δὲ μὴ ἔχω, γέγονα χαλκὸς
- of angels, 5love 1but 3not 2do 4have, I have become *as* brass ˜

ἠχῶν ἢ κύμβαλον ἀλαλάζον. 2 Καὶ ἐὰν ἔχω προφητείαν
sounding or a cymbal ˜ clashing. And if I have *the gift of* prophecy

καὶ εἰδῶ τὰ μυστήρια πάντα καὶ πᾶσαν τὴν γνῶσιν, καὶ ἐὰν
and know - mysteries ˜ all and all - knowledge, and if

ἔχω πᾶσαν τὴν πίστιν ὥστε ὄρη μεθιστάνειν, ἀγάπην
I have all - faith so as 3mountains 1to 2remove, 8love

δὲ μὴ ἔχω, οὐθέν εἰμι. 3 Καὶ ἐὰν ψωμίσω πάντα
4but 6not 5do 7have, 11nothing 9I 10am. And if I dole out all

τὰ ὑπάρχοντά μου, καὶ ἐὰν παραδῶ τὸ σῶμά μου ἵνα
the *things* belonging of me, and if I hand over - body ˜ my that
my possessions,

sentable *parts* have greater
modesty,
24 but our presentable *parts*
have no need. But God composed the body, having given
greater honor to that *part* which
lacks it,
25 that there should be no
schism in the body, but *that* the
members should have the same
care for one another.
26 And if one member suffers,
all the members suffer with *it;*
or if one member is honored, all
the members rejoice with *it.*
27 Now you are the body of
Christ, and members individually.
28 And God has appointed
these in the church: first apostles, second prophets, third
teachers, after that miracles,
then gifts of healings, helps, administrations, varieties of
tongues.
29 *Are* all apostles? *Are* all
prophets? *Are* all teachers? *Are*
all workers of miracles?
30 Do all have gifts of healings? Do all speak with
tongues? Do all interpret?
31 But earnestly desire the
best gifts. And yet I show you a
more excellent way.
13 Though I speak with
the tongues of men
and of angels, but have not
love, I have become sounding
brass or a clanging cymbal.
2 And though I have *the gift
of* prophecy, and understand all
mysteries and all knowledge,
and though I have all faith, so
that I could remove mountains,
but have not love, I am nothing.
3 And though I bestow all my
goods to feed *the poor,* and
though I give my body to be

[e](12:31) NU reads μειζονα, *greater.*

*(12:28) κυβερνήσις (*kybernēsis*). Noun, occurring only here in the NT, originally meaning the *steering, piloting* performed by a ship's helmsman. Here it refers metaphorically to the *guidance* or *governance* ("administration") exercised by a church leader. The precise function is uncertain. Cf. the cognate noun κυβερνήτης, *helmsman,* used literally in Acts 27:11; Rev. 18:17.

burned, but have not love, it profits me nothing.
4 Love suffers long *and* is kind; love does not envy; love does not parade itself, is not puffed up;
5 does not behave rudely, does not seek its own, is not provoked, thinks no evil;
6 does not rejoice in iniquity, but rejoices in the truth;
7 bears all things, believes all things, hopes all things, endures all things.
8 Love never fails. But whether *there are* prophecies, they will fail; whether *there are* tongues, they will cease; whether *there is* knowledge, it will vanish away.
9 For we know in part and we prophesy in part.
10 But when that which is perfect has come, then that which is in part will be done away.
11 When I was a child, I spoke as a child, I understood as a child, I thought as a child; but when I became a man, I put away childish things.
12 For now we see in a mirror, dimly, but then face to face. Now I know in part, but then I shall know just as I also am known.
13 And now abide faith, hope, love, these three; but the greatest of these *is* love.
14 Pursue love, and desire spiritual *gifts*, but especially that you may prophesy.
2 For he who speaks in a tongue does not speak to men but to God, for no one under-

[a](13:3) NU reads καυχησωμαι, *I may boast.*

***(14:2)** λαλέω *(laleō).* Common verb meaning *speak.* It may stress the idea of speaking as the utterance of sound, especially by the speech organs, while a synonym like λέγω, *say, speak,* (with which it is often interchangeable) implies that what is spoken is rational communication. Thus λαλέω is perhaps more suitable than λέγω when the speech is not understandable, as here. The verb can also be used figuratively (Heb. 12:24) or even of inanimate things (Rev. 10:4). Cf. the cognate noun λαλιά, *speech* as what is said (John 4:42) or *way of speaking* (John 8:43; Matt. 26:73).

καυθήσωμαι,[a] ἀγάπην δὲ μὴ ἔχω, οὐδὲν ὠφελοῦμαι.
I may be burned, [5]love [1]but [3]not [2]do [4]have, [9]nothing [6]I [7]am [8]profited.

4 Ἡ ἀγάπη μακροθυμεῖ, χρηστεύεται, ἡ ἀγάπη οὐ
\- Love is patient, is kind, - love not ˜

ζηλοῖ, ἡ ἀγάπη οὐ περπερεύεται, οὐ φυσιοῦται, 5 οὐκ
does envy, - love not ˜ does boast, not ˜ is puffed up, not ˜

ἀσχημονεῖ, οὐ ζητεῖ τὰ ἑαυτῆς, οὐ
does behave disgracefully, not ˜ seeks the *things* of itself, not ˜
its own thing,

παροξύνεται, οὐ λογίζεται τὸ κακόν· 6 οὐ χαίρει
is provoked to anger, not ˜ does reckon - evil; not ˜ does rejoice
plan

ἐπὶ τῇ ἀδικίᾳ, συγχαίρει δὲ τῇ ἀληθείᾳ, 7 πάντα
over - unrighteousness, [2]rejoices [3]with [1]but the truth, [2]all [3]*things*

στέγει, πάντα πιστεύει, πάντα ἐλπίζει, πάντα
[1]bears, [5]all [6]*things* [4]believes, [8]all [9]*things* [7]hopes, [11]all [12]*things*

ὑπομένει.
[10]endures.

8 Ἡ ἀγάπη οὐδέποτε ἐκπίπτει. Εἴτε δὲ
\- Love never fails. whether ˜ But

προφητεῖαι, καταργηθήσονται· εἴτε γλῶσσαι, παύσονται·
there are prophecies, they will pass away; or tongues, they will cease;

εἴτε γνῶσις, καταργηθήσεται. 9 Ἐκ μέρους δὲ γινώσκομεν
or knowledge, it will pass away. [4]by [5]part [1]Now [2]we [3]know

καὶ ἐκ μέρους προφητεύομεν. 10 Ὅταν δὲ ἔλθῃ τὸ
and [3]by [4]part [1]we [2]prophesy. when ˜ But [4]comes [1]the

τέλειον, τότε τὸ ἐκ μέρους καταργηθήσεται.
[2]complete [3]*thing,* then the *thing* out of part shall pass away.
which is partial

11 Ὅτε ἤμην νήπιος, ὡς νήπιος ἐλάλουν, ὡς
When I was a young child, [3]as [4]a [5]young [6]child [1]I [2]spoke, [9]as

νήπιος ἐφρόνουν, ὡς νήπιος ἐλογιζόμην· ὅτε
[10]a [11]young [12]child [7]I [8]thought, [15]as [16]a [17]young [18]child [13]I [14]reasoned; when ˜

δὲ γέγονα ἀνὴρ κατήργηκα τὰ τοῦ νηπίου.
but I have become a man I have set aside the *things* of the young child.
became put away

12 Βλέπομεν γὰρ ἄρτι δι' ἐσόπτρου ἐν αἰνίγματι, τότε
[3]we [4]see [1]For [2]now by means of a mirror by reflection, then ˜
indirectly,

δὲ πρόσωπον πρὸς πρόσωπον. Ἄρτι γινώσκω ἐκ μέρους, τότε
but face to face. Now I know by part, then ˜

δὲ ἐπιγνώσομαι καθὼς καὶ ἐπεγνώσθην. 13 Νυνὶ δὲ μένει
but I will know just as also I was known. now ˜ And remains

πίστις, ἐλπίς, ἀγάπη, τὰ τρία ταῦτα· μείζων δὲ τούτων
faith, hope, love, - three ˜ these; [2]*the* [3]greatest [1]but of these

ἡ ἀγάπη.
\- *is* love.

Comparing Prophecy and Tongues

14 1 Διώκετε τὴν ἀγάπην, ζηλοῦτε δὲ τὰ πνευματικά,
Pursue - love, desire ˜ and the spiritual *gifts,*

μᾶλλον δὲ ἵνα προφητεύητε. 2 Ὁ γὰρ λαλῶν* γλώσσῃ
rather ˜ but that you may prophesy. [2]the [3]*one* [1]For speaking in a tongue

οὐκ ἀνθρώποις λαλεῖ ἀλλὰ τῷ Θεῷ, οὐδεὶς γὰρ ἀκούει·
[2]not [3]to [4]men [1]speaks but - to God, [2]no [3]one [1]for hears *him;*
understands

πνεύματι δὲ λαλεῖ μυστήρια. 3 Ὁ δὲ προφητεύων
[2]in [3]*the* [4]spirit [1]but he speaks mysteries. [2]the [3]*one* [1]But prophesying
who prophesies

ἀνθρώποις λαλεῖ οἰκοδομὴν καὶ παράκλησιν καὶ παραμυθίαν.
[2]to [3]men [1]speaks *for* edification and exhortation and comfort.

4 Ὁ λαλῶν γλώσσῃ ἑαυτὸν οἰκοδομεῖ, ὁ δὲ
The *one* speaking in a tongue himself ˜ edifies, [2]the [3]*one* [1]but

προφητεύων ἐκκλησίαν οἰκοδομεῖ. 5 Θέλω δὲ πάντας ὑμᾶς
prophesying [2]*the* [3]church [1]edifies. [2]I [3]want [1]Now all ˜ you
who prophesies

λαλεῖν γλώσσαις, μᾶλλον δὲ ἵνα προφητεύητε·
to speak in tongues, [2]even [3]more [1]but that you should prophesy;

μείζων γὰρ[a] ὁ προφητεύων ἢ ὁ λαλῶν
[5]*is* [6]greater [1]for [2]the [3]*one* [4]prophesying than the *one* speaking
who prophesies

γλώσσαις, ἐκτὸς εἰ μὴ διερμηνεύει, ἵνα ἡ ἐκκλησία
in tongues, without if not he interprets, in order that the church
unless

οἰκοδομὴν λάβῃ.
[3]edification [1]may [2]receive.

Tongues Need to Be Translated

6 Νυνὶ δέ, ἀδελφοί, ἐὰν ἔλθω πρὸς ὑμᾶς γλώσσαις
now ˜ But, brothers, if I come to you [2]in [3]tongues

λαλῶν, τί ὑμᾶς ὠφελήσω, ἐὰν μὴ ὑμῖν λαλήσω ἢ
[1]speaking, what [4]you [1]will [2]I [3]profit, if not [3]to [4]you [1]I [2]speak either
unless

ἐν ἀποκαλύψει ἢ ἐν γνώσει ἢ ἐν προφητείᾳ ἢ ἐν
with a revelation or with knowledge or with a prophecy or with

διδαχῇ? 7 Ὅμως τὰ ἄψυχα φωνὴν διδόντα, εἴτε
a teaching? Likewise the lifeless *things* [2]a [3]sound [1]giving, whether
when they make,

αὐλὸς εἴτε κιθάρα, ἐὰν διαστολὴν τοῖς φθόγγοις μὴ
flute or harp, if [5]a [6]distinction [7]in [8]the [9]tones [3]not

διδῷ, πῶς γνωσθήσεται τὸ αὐλούμενον ἢ
[1]they [2]do [4]give, how will it be known the *thing* being played on the flute or
make, what is

τὸ κιθαριζόμενον? 8 Καὶ γὰρ ἐὰν ἄδηλον φωνὴν
the *thing* being played on the harp? also ˜ For if [4]an [5]indistinct [6]sound
what is

σάλπιγξ δῷ, τίς παρασκευάσεται εἰς πόλεμον? 9 Οὕτω καὶ
[1]a [2]trumpet [3]gives, who will prepare for battle? So also

ὑμεῖς διὰ τῆς γλώσσης ἐὰν μὴ εὔσημον λόγον δῶτε, πῶς
[2]you [9]by [10]the [11]tongue [1]if [4]not [7]clear [6]a [8]word [3]do [5]give, how

γνωσθήσεται τὸ λαλούμενον? Ἔσεσθε γὰρ εἰς ἀέρα
will it be known the *thing* being spoken? [2]you [3]will [4]be [1]For [6]into [7]*the* [8]air
what is

λαλοῦντες. 10 Τοσαῦτα, εἰ τύχοι, γένη φωνῶν
[5]speaking. [7]so [8]many, [3]if [4]it [5]should [6]be, [9]kinds [10]of [11]sounds
perhaps,

ἐστιν ἐν κόσμῳ, καὶ οὐδὲν αὐτῶν[b] ἄφωνον. 11 Ἐὰν
[1]*There* [2]are in *the* world, and none of them without sound. If
meaning.

οὖν μὴ εἰδῶ τὴν δύναμιν τῆς φωνῆς, ἔσομαι τῷ
then [3]not [1]I [2]do know the power of the sound, I will be to the *one*
meaning

λαλοῦντι βάρβαρος καὶ ὁ λαλῶν ἐν ἐμοὶ
speaking *as* a barbarian and the *one* speaking *will be* with me
foreigner

stands *him;* however, in the
spirit he speaks mysteries.
3 But he who prophesies
speaks edification and exhortation and comfort to men.
4 He who speaks in a tongue
edifies himself, but he who
prophesies edifies the church.
5 I wish you all spoke with
tongues, but even more that
you prophesied; for he who
prophesies *is* greater than he
who speaks with tongues, unless indeed he interprets, that
the church may receive edification.
6 But now, brethren, if I
come to you speaking with
tongues, what shall I profit you
unless I speak to you either by
revelation, by knowledge, by
prophesying, or by teaching?
7 Even things without life,
whether flute or harp, when
they make a sound, unless they
make a distinction in the
sounds, how will it be known
what is piped or played?
8 For if the trumpet makes
an uncertain sound, who will
prepare for battle?
9 So likewise you, unless you
utter by the tongue words easy
to understand, how will it be
known what is spoken? For you
will be speaking into the air.
10 There are, it may be, so
many kinds of languages in the
world, and none of them *is*
without significance.
11 Therefore, if I do not know
the meaning of the language, I
shall be a foreigner to him who
speaks, and he who speaks *will
be* a foreigner to me.

[a](**14:5**) NU reads δε, *and.*
[b](**14:10**) NU omits αυτων, *of them.*

12 Even so you, since you are zealous for spiritual *gifts, let it be* for the edification of the church *that* you seek to excel.
13 Therefore let him who speaks in a tongue pray that he may interpret.
14 For if I pray in a tongue, my spirit prays, but my understanding is unfruitful.
15 What is *the conclusion* then? I will pray with the spirit, and I will also pray with the understanding. I will sing with the spirit, and I will also sing with the understanding.
16 Otherwise, if you bless with the spirit, how will he who occupies the place of the uninformed say "Amen" at your giving of thanks, since he does not understand what you say?
17 For you indeed give thanks well, but the other is not edified.
18 I thank my God I speak with tongues more than you all;
19 yet in the church I would rather speak five words with my understanding, that I may teach others also, than ten thousand words in a tongue.
20 Brethren, do not be children in understanding; however, in malice be babes, but in understanding be mature.
21 In the law it is written:

"With men of other
tongues and other lips
I will speak to this
people;
And yet, for all that, they
will not hear Me,"

says the Lord.
22 Therefore tongues are for a sign, not to those who believe

βάρβαρος. **12** Οὕτω καὶ ὑμεῖς, ἐπεὶ ζηλωταί ἐστε
as a barbarian. So also you, since [3]zealots [1]you [2]are
foreigner.

πνευμάτων, πρὸς τὴν οἰκοδομὴν τῆς ἐκκλησίας ζητεῖτε
of spiritual *gifts,* [6]to [7]the [8]edification [9]of [10]the [11]church [1]seek

ἵνα περισσεύητε. **13** Διόπερ ὁ λαλῶν γλώσσῃ
[2]that [3]you [4]may [5]abound. Therefore [2]the [3]*one* [4]speaking [5]in [6]a [7]tongue

προσευχέσθω ἵνα διερμηνεύῃ. **14** Ἐὰν γὰρ προσεύχωμαι
[1]let [8]pray that he may interpret. if ˜ For I pray

γλώσσῃ, τὸ πνεῦμά μου προσεύχεται, ὁ δὲ νοῦς μου
in a tongue, - spirit ˜ my prays, - but mind ˜ my

ἄκαρπός ἐστι. **15** Τί οὖν ἐστι? Προσεύξομαι τῷ
unfruitful ˜ is. What [3]then [1]is [2]it? I will pray with the

πνεύματι, προσεύξομαι δὲ καὶ τῷ νοΐ. Ψαλῶ τῷ
spirit, [2]I [3]will [5]pray [1]but [4]also with the mind. I will sing with the

πνεύματι, ψαλῶ δὲ καὶ τῷ νοΐ. **16** Ἐπεὶ ἐὰν
spirit, [2]I [3]will [5]sing [1]but [4]also with the mind. Otherwise if

εὐλογήσῃς τῷ πνεύματι, ὁ ἀναπληρῶν τὸν τόπον
you bless with the spirit, [3]the [4]*one* [5]filling [6]the [7]place
sitting in

τοῦ ἰδιώτου πῶς ἐρεῖ τὸ "Ἀμὴν" ἐπὶ τῇ σῇ
[8]of [9]the [10]uninformed [1]how [2]will [11]say - "Amen" at - your
when you give

εὐχαριστίᾳ, ἐπειδὴ τί λέγεις οὐκ οἶδε?
thanksgiving, since [5]what [6]you [7]are [8]saying [3]not [1]he [2]does [4]know?
thanks,

17 Σὺ μὲν γὰρ καλῶς εὐχαριστεῖς, ἀλλ' ὁ ἕτερος οὐκ
you ˜ - For [3]well [1]give [2]thanks, but the other *person* not ˜

οἰκοδομεῖται. **18** Εὐχαριστῶ τῷ Θεῷ μου,[c] πάντων ὑμῶν
is edified. I thank - God ˜ my, [7]all [5]*than* [6]you

μᾶλλον γλώσσαις λαλῶν, **19** ἀλλ' ἐν ἐκκλησίᾳ θέλω πέντε
[4]more [2]in [3]tongues [1]speaking, but in *the* church I desire [3]five

λόγους διὰ τοῦ νοός μου λαλῆσαι, ἵνα καὶ ἄλλους
[4]words [5]by - [7]mind [6]my [1]to [2]speak, in order that [5]also [4]others

κατηχήσω, ἢ μυρίους λόγους ἐν γλώσσῃ.
[1]I [2]may [3]instruct, rather than ten thousand words in a tongue.

Tongues Are a Sign for Unbelievers

20 Ἀδελφοί, μὴ παιδία γίνεσθε ταῖς φρεσίν· ἀλλὰ τῇ
Brothers, [2]not [4]children [1]do [3]be in the thoughts; rather -
your

κακίᾳ νηπιάζετε, ταῖς δὲ φρεσὶ τέλειοι* γίνεσθε. **21** Ἐν
in malice be children, - but in thoughts mature ˜ be. In

τῷ νόμῳ γέγραπται ὅτι
the law it is written that

«Ἐν ἑτερογλώσσοις
«With *ones* speaking foreign languages

Καὶ ἐν χείλεσιν ἑτέροις
And by lips ˜ other
strange

Λαλήσω τῷ λαῷ τούτῳ,
I will speak - to people ˜ this,

Καὶ οὐδ' οὕτως εἰσακούσονταί μου,»[d]
And yet not even in this way will they hear Me,»

λέγει Κύριος. **22** Ὥστε αἱ γλῶσσαι εἰς σημεῖόν εἰσιν οὐ
says *the* Lord. So then the tongues [2]for [3]a [4]sign [1]are not

---

c(**14:18**) NU omits *μου, my.*
d(**14:21**) Is. 28:11, 12; Deut. 28:49

***(14:20)** *τέλειος (teleios).* Frequent adjective meaning *complete, perfect, mature, full-grown.* It is derived from the noun *τέλος, end, goal,* and so basically means *reaching the end designed for,* with the precise sense depending on the given context. Thus, here the meaning is *full-grown, adult, mature,* as opposed to "children" (cf. 1 Cor. 2:6). In James 1:4, the "perfect work" is the *completed* or *finished* work, and "perfect and complete" means *fully developed and*

τοῖς πιστεύουσιν ἀλλὰ τοῖς ἀπίστοις· ἡ δὲ
to the *ones* believing but to the unbelieving *ones;* - but
who believe

προφητεία οὐ τοῖς ἀπίστοις ἀλλὰ τοῖς
prophecy *is* not for the unbelieving *ones* but for the *ones*

πιστεύουσιν. **23** Ἐὰν οὖν συνέλθῃ ἡ ἐκκλησία ὅλη
believing. If then [4]comes [5]together [1]the [3]church [2]whole
who believe.

ἐπὶ τὸ αὐτὸ καὶ πάντες γλώσσαις λαλῶσιν, εἰσέλθωσι δὲ
at the same *place* and all [2]in [3]tongues [1]speak, [10]come [11]in [4]and
in

ἰδιῶται ἢ ἄπιστοι, οὐκ ἐροῦσιν ὅτι
[5]uninformed [6]*ones* [7]or [8]unbelieving [9]*ones,* [14]not [12]will [13]they [15]say that

μαίνεσθε? **24** Ἐὰν δὲ πάντες προφητεύωσιν,
you are out of your mind? if ˜ But all prophesy,

εἰσέλθῃ δέ τις ἄπιστος ἢ ἰδιώτης, ἐλέγχεται ὑπὸ
[6]comes [7]in [1]and [2]someone [3]unbelieving [4]or [5]uninformed, he is reproved by

πάντων, ἀνακρίνεται ὑπὸ πάντων. **25** Καὶ οὕτω[e] τὰ
all, he is called to account by all. And so the

κρυπτὰ τῆς καρδίας αὐτοῦ φανερὰ γίνεται, καὶ οὕτω πεσὼν
hidden *things* - of heart ˜ his clear ˜ become, and so falling

ἐπὶ πρόσωπον προσκυνήσει τῷ Θεῷ, ἀπαγγέλλων ὅτι "Ὁ Θεὸς
on *his* face he will worship - God, reporting - - "God

ὄντως ἐν ὑμῖν ἐστι!"
truly [2]among [3]you [1]is!"

Proper Order in the Church Meeting

26 Τί οὖν ἐστιν, ἀδελφοί? Ὅταν συνέρχησθε,
What [3]then [1]is [2]it, brothers? Whenever you come together,

ἕκαστος ὑμῶν[f] ψαλμὸν ἔχει, διδαχὴν ἔχει, γλῶσσαν ἔχει,
each of you [2]a [3]song [1]has, [5]a [6]teaching [4]has, [8]a [9]tongue [7]has,

ἀποκάλυψιν ἔχει, ἑρμηνείαν ἔχει. Πάντα πρὸς
[11]a [12]revelation [10]has, [14]an [15]interpretation [13]has. [17]all [18]*things* [20]for

οἰκοδομὴν γινέσθω. **27** Εἴτε γλώσσῃ τις λαλεῖ, κατὰ
[21]edification [16]Let [19]be. If [3]in [4]a [5]tongue [1]anyone [2]speaks, *let it be* by

δύο ἢ τὸ πλεῖστον τρεῖς, καὶ ἀνὰ μέρος, καὶ εἷς
two or *at* the most three, and by part, and one ˜
turns,

διερμηνευέτω. **28** Ἐὰν δὲ μὴ ᾖ διερμηνευτής,
let interpret. if ˜ And [3]not [1]*there* [2]is an interpreter,

σιγάτω ἐν ἐκκλησίᾳ, ἑαυτῷ δὲ λαλείτω καὶ τῷ
let him be silent in *the* church, [5]to [6]himself [1]but [2]let [3]him [4]speak and -

Θεῷ. **29** Προφῆται δὲ δύο ἢ τρεῖς λαλείτωσαν, καὶ οἱ
to God. [6]prophets [1]And [3]two [4]or [5]three [2]let [7]speak, and [2]the

ἄλλοι διακρινέτωσαν. **30** Ἐὰν δὲ ἄλλῳ
[3]others [1]let [4]pass [5]judgment. if ˜ But [4]to [5]another

ἀποκαλυφθῇ καθημένῳ, ὁ πρῶτος σιγάτω.
[1]*something* [2]is [3]revealed sitting, [2]the [3]first [1]let be silent.
who sits by,

31 Δύνασθε γὰρ καθ' ἕνα πάντες προφητεύειν ἵνα
[2]you [3]are [5]able [1]For [8]*one* [9]by [10]one [4]all [6]to [7]prophesy in order that

πάντες μανθάνωσι καὶ πάντες παρακαλῶνται. **32** Καὶ
all may learn and all may be encouraged. And

πνεύματα προφητῶν προφήταις ὑποτάσσεται. **33** Οὐ γὰρ
the spirits of prophets [3]to [4]prophets [1]are [2]subject. [4]not [1]For

ἐστιν ἀκαταστασίας ὁ Θεὸς ἀλλὰ εἰρήνης.
[3]is [5]of [6]confusion - [2]God but of peace.

but to unbelievers; but prophesying is not for unbelievers but for those who believe.
23 Therefore if the whole church comes together in one place, and all speak with tongues, and there come in *those who are* uninformed or unbelievers, will they not say that you are out of your mind?
24 But if all prophesy, and an unbeliever or an uninformed person comes in, he is convinced by all, he is convicted by all.
25 And thus the secrets of his heart are revealed; and so, falling down on *his* face, he will worship God and report that God is truly among you.
26 How is it then, brethren? Whenever you come together, each of you has a psalm, has a teaching, has a tongue, has a revelation, has an interpretation. Let all things be done for edification.
27 If anyone speaks in a tongue, *let there be* two or at the most three, *each* in turn, and let one interpret.
28 But if there is no interpreter, let him keep silent in church, and let him speak to himself and to God.
29 Let two or three prophets speak, and let the others judge.
30 But if *anything* is revealed to another who sits by, let the first keep silent.
31 For you can all prophesy one by one, that all may learn and all may be encouraged.
32 And the spirits of the prophets are subject to the prophets.
33 For God is not *the author* of confusion but of peace, as in all

[e]**(14:25)** NU omits Και ουτω, *And so.* [f]**(14:26)** NU omits υμων, *of you.*

whole (ὁλόκληρος). In Matt. 5:48 τέλειος is used of both human beings and God. See the cognate verb τελειόω at Heb. 12:23.

the churches of the saints.
34 Let your women keep silent in the churches, for they are not permitted to speak; but *they are* to be submissive, as the law also says.
35 And if they want to learn something, let them ask their own husbands at home; for it is shameful for women to speak in church.
36 Or did the word of God come *originally* from you? Or *was it* you only that it reached?
37 If anyone thinks himself to be a prophet or spiritual, let him acknowledge that the things which I write to you are the commandments of the Lord.
38 But if anyone is ignorant, let him be ignorant.
39 Therefore, brethren, desire earnestly to prophesy, and do not forbid to speak with tongues.
40 Let all things be done decently and in order.
15 Moreover, brethren, I declare to you the gospel which I preached to you, which also you received and in which you stand,
2 by which also you are saved, if you hold fast that word which I preached to you—unless you believed in vain.
3 For I delivered to you first of all that which I also received: that Christ died for our sins according to the Scriptures,
4 and that He was buried, and that He rose again the third day according to the Scriptures,
5 and that He was seen by Cephas, then by the twelve.
6 After that He was seen by

Women Must Keep Silent in the Church

Ὡς ἐν πάσαις ταῖς ἐκκλησίαις τῶν ἁγίων, 34 αἱ γυναῖκες
As in all the churches of the saints, - [3]women

ὑμῶν[g] ἐν ταῖς ἐκκλησίαις σιγάτωσαν, οὐ γὰρ
[2]your [6]in [7]the [8]churches [1]let [4]be [5]silent, [12]not [9]for

ἐπιτέτραπται αὐταῖς λαλεῖν, ἀλλ' ὑποτάσσεσθαι,
[10]it [11]has [13]been [14]permitted for them to speak, but to be in subjection,

καθὼς καὶ ὁ νόμος λέγει. 35 Εἰ δέ τι μαθεῖν
just as also the law says. if ˜ And [5]anything [3]to [4]learn

θέλουσιν, ἐν οἴκῳ τοὺς ἰδίους ἄνδρας ἐπερωτάτωσαν,
[1]they [2]desire, [12]at [13]home - [9]their [10]own [11]husbands [6]let [7]them [8]ask,

αἰσχρὸν γάρ ἐστι γυναιξὶν ἐν ἐκκλησίᾳ λαλεῖν.
[17]a [18]shameful [19]*thing* [14]for [15]it [16]is for women [3]in [4]church [1]to [2]speak.

36 Ἢ ἀφ' ὑμῶν ὁ λόγος τοῦ Θεοῦ ἐξῆλθεν? Ἢ εἰς
Or [8]from [9]you [2]the [3]word - [4]of [5]God [1]did [6]go [7]forth? Or [4]to

ὑμᾶς μόνους κατήντησεν?
[5]you [6]only [1]did [2]it [3]come?

37 Εἴ τις δοκεῖ προφήτης εἶναι ἢ πνευματικός,
If anyone thinks [3]a [4]prophet [1]to [2]be (that he is) or a spiritual *person,*

ἐπιγινωσκέτω ἃ γράφω ὑμῖν ὅτι Κυρίου
let him recognize *the things* which I am writing to you that [4]of [5]*the* [6]Lord

εἰσὶν ἐντολαί. 38 Εἰ δέ τις ἀγνοεῖ,
[1]they [2]are [3]commandments. if ˜ But anyone is ignorant,

ἀγνοείτω.[h]
let him be ignorant.

Let All Be Done Decently and in Order

39 Ὥστε, ἀδελφοί,[i] ζηλοῦτε τὸ προφητεύειν, καὶ τὸ
So then, brothers, seek - to prophesy, and -

λαλεῖν γλώσσαις μὴ κωλύετε. 40 Πάντα εὐσχημόνως καὶ
[4]to [5]speak [6]in [7]tongues [2]not [1]do [3]forbid. [2]all [3]*things* [6]properly [7]and

κατὰ τάξιν γινέσθω.
[8]according [9]to [10]order [1]Let [4]be [5]done.

Christ Risen Is Fundamental to the Faith

15 1 Γνωρίζω δὲ ὑμῖν, ἀδελφοί, τὸ εὐαγγέλιον
[2]I [3]make [4]known [1]Now to you, brothers, the gospel

ὃ εὐηγγελισάμην ὑμῖν, ὃ καὶ παρελάβετε, ἐν ᾧ
which I preached to you, which also ˜ you received, in which

καὶ ἑστήκατε, 2 δι' οὗ καὶ σῴζεσθε, τίνι λόγῳ
also ˜ you stand, through which also ˜ you are saved, [5]to [6]which [7]word (that word which)

εὐηγγελισάμην ὑμῖν, εἰ κατέχετε, ἐκτὸς εἰ μὴ εἰκῇ
[8]I [9]preached [10]to [11]you, [1]if [2]you [3]hold [4]fast, without if not (unless) [3]in [4]vain

ἐπιστεύσατε. 3 Παρέδωκα γὰρ ὑμῖν ἐν πρώτοις ὃ
[1]you [2]believed. [2]I [3]handed [4]down [1]For to you among first *things* (first) what

καὶ παρέλαβον, ὅτι Χριστὸς ἀπέθανεν ὑπὲρ τῶν ἁμαρτιῶν
also ˜ I received, that Christ died in behalf of - sins ˜

ἡμῶν κατὰ τὰς Γραφάς, 4 καὶ ὅτι ἐτάφη, καὶ ὅτι
our according to the Scriptures, and that He was buried, and that

ἐγήγερται τῇ τρίτῃ ἡμέρᾳ κατὰ τὰς Γραφάς,
He has been (was) raised on the third day according to the Scriptures,

5 καὶ ὅτι ὤφθη Κηφᾷ, εἶτα τοῖς δώδεκα. 6 Ἔπειτα
and that He appeared to Cephas, then to the twelve. Thereafter

[g](14:34) NU omits υμων, *your.* [h](14:38) NU reads αγνοειται, *he is not known* or *(If anyone does not recognize this,) he is not recognized.*
[i](14:39) NU adds in brackets μου, *my.*

ὤφθη ἐπάνω πεντακοσίοις ἀδελφοῖς ἐφάπαξ, ἐξ
He appeared [2]more [3]than [1]to [4]five [5]hundred brothers at one time, of

ὧν οἱ πλείους μένουσιν ἕως ἄρτι, τινὲς δὲ καὶ
whom the majority remain until now, some ˜ but also

ἐκοιμήθησαν. 7 Ἔπειτα ὤφθη Ἰακώβῳ, εἶτα τοῖς
fell asleep. Thereafter He appeared to James, then to [2]the
died.

ἀποστόλοις πᾶσιν. 8 Ἔσχατον δὲ πάντων, ὡσπερεὶ τῷ
[3]apostles [1]all. last ˜ And of all, as though to the

ἐκτρώματι, ὤφθη κἀμοί. 9 Ἐγὼ γάρ εἰμι ὁ
one untimely born He appeared to me also. I ˜ For am the

ἐλάχιστος τῶν ἀποστόλων, ὃς οὐκ εἰμὶ ἱκανὸς καλεῖσθαι
least of the apostles, who not ˜ am qualified to be called
worthy

ἀπόστολος διότι ἐδίωξα τὴν ἐκκλησίαν τοῦ Θεοῦ.
an apostle because I persecuted the church - of God.

10 Χάριτι δὲ Θεοῦ εἰμι ὅ εἰμι, καὶ ἡ χάρις αὐτοῦ
[2]by [3]*the* [4]grace [1]But of God I am what I am, and - grace ˜ His

ἡ εἰς ἐμὲ οὐ κενὴ ἐγενήθη, ἀλλὰ περισσότερον
the *one* to me [2]not [4]vain [1]did [3]become, but more
toward has

αὐτῶν πάντων ἐκοπίασα, οὐκ ἐγὼ δέ, ἀλλ' ἡ χάρις τοῦ
than them all I toiled, [2]not [3]I [1]and, but the grace -

Θεοῦ ἡ σὺν ἐμοί. 11 Εἴτε οὖν ἐγὼ εἴτε ἐκεῖνοι, οὕτω
of God - with me. whether ˜ Therefore I or those, so
they,

κηρύσσομεν καὶ οὕτως ἐπιστεύσατε.
we preach and so you believed.

Christ Risen Is Fundamental to Our Hope

12 Εἰ δὲ Χριστὸς κηρύσσεται ὅτι ἐκ νεκρῶν
if ˜ Now Christ is being preached that [5]from [6]*the* [7]dead
as

ἐγήγερται, πῶς λέγουσί τινες ἐν ὑμῖν ὅτι
[1]He [2]has [3]been [4]raised, how do [4]say [1]some [2]among [3]you that
being

ἀνάστασις νεκρῶν οὐκ ἔστιν? 13 Εἰ δὲ ἀνάστασις
[4]resurrection [5]of [6]*the* [7]dead [3]no [1]*there* [2]is? if ˜ But [4]resurrection

νεκρῶν οὐκ ἔστιν, οὐδὲ Χριστὸς ἐγήγερται. 14 Εἰ δὲ
[5]of [6]*the* [7]dead [3]no [1]*there* [2]is, neither Christ ˜ has been raised. if ˜ And

Χριστὸς οὐκ ἐγήγερται, κενὸν ἄρα τὸ κήρυγμα ἡμῶν,
Christ not ˜ has been raised, [4]*is* [5]vain [1]then - [3]preaching [2]our,

κενὴ δὲ καὶ ἡ πίστις ὑμῶν! 15 Εὑρισκόμεθα δὲ καὶ
[10]*is* [11]vain [6]and [9]also - [8]faith [7]your! [2]we [4]are [5]found [1]And [3]also

ψευδομάρτυρες τοῦ Θεοῦ ὅτι ἐμαρτυρήσαμεν κατὰ τοῦ
to be false witnesses - of God because we bore witness against -
testified concerning

Θεοῦ ὅτι ἤγειρε τὸν Χριστόν, ὃν οὐκ ἤγειρεν εἴπερ
God that He raised - Christ, whom [3]not [1]He [2]did raise if indeed
it should

ἄρα νεκροὶ οὐκ ἐγείρονται. 16 Εἰ γὰρ νεκροὶ οὐκ
then *the* dead not ˜ are raised. if ˜ For *the* dead not ˜
be true that

ἐγείρονται, οὐδὲ Χριστὸς ἐγήγερται. 17 Εἰ δὲ Χριστὸς
are raised, neither Christ ˜ has been raised. if ˜ And Christ

οὐκ ἐγήγερται, ματαία ἡ πίστις ὑμῶν· ἔτι ἐστὲ ἐν
not ˜ has been raised, [3]*is* [4]worthless - [2]faith [1]your; [7]still [5]you [6]are in

over five hundred brethren at once, of whom the greater part remain to the present, but some have fallen asleep.
7 After that He was seen by James, then by all the apostles.
8 Then last of all He was seen by me also, as by one born out of due time.
9 For I am the least of the apostles, who am not worthy to be called an apostle, because I persecuted the church of God.
10 But by the grace of God I am what I am, and His grace toward me was not in vain; but I labored more abundantly than they all, yet not I, but the grace of God *which was* with me.
11 Therefore, whether *it was* I or they, so we preach and so you believed.
12 Now if Christ is preached that He has been raised from the dead, how do some among you say that there is no resurrection of the dead?
13 But if there is no resurrection of the dead, then Christ is not risen.
14 And if Christ is not risen, then our preaching *is* empty and your faith *is* also empty.
15 Yes, and we are found false witnesses of God, because we have testified of God that He raised up Christ, whom He did not raise up—if in fact the dead do not rise.
16 For if *the* dead do not rise, then Christ is not risen.
17 And if Christ is not risen, your faith *is* futile; you are still

in your sins!
18 Then also those who have fallen asleep in Christ have perished.
19 If in this life only we have hope in Christ, we are of all men the most pitiable.
20 But now Christ is risen from the dead, *and* has become the firstfruits of those who have fallen asleep.
21 For since by man *came* death, by Man also *came* the resurrection of the dead.
22 For as in Adam all die, even so in Christ all shall be made alive.
23 But each one in his own order: Christ the firstfruits, afterward those *who are* Christ's at His coming.
24 Then *comes* the end, when He delivers the kingdom to God the Father, when He puts an end to all rule and all authority and power.
25 For He must reign till He has put all enemies under His feet.
26 The last enemy *that* will be destroyed *is* death.
27 For *"He has put all things under His feet."* But when He says "all things are put under Him," *it is* evident that He who put all things under Him is excepted.
28 Now when all things are made subject to Him, then the Son Himself will also be subject to Him who put all things under Him, that God may be all in all.
29 Otherwise, what will they do who are baptized for the

---

[a](15:20) NU omits εγενετο, *He became.*
[b](15:27) Ps. 8:6

*(15:23) ἀπαρχή (aparchē). Noun meaning *firstling, firstfruits,* a compound from ἀπό, *from,* and ἀρχή, *beginning, first cause.* In the LXX and some other Greek writers, the word was a technical term for a sacrificial *firstfruits* that must be offered to a deity before the rest could be put to ordinary use. In the NT the word probably continues to bear this sense of being consecrated to God. Often, however, it also carries a sense of expectation—as here of Christ in the resurrection order; of early converts in an area (Rom. 16:5; 1 Cor. 16:15; cf. Rev. 14:4); and of the Holy Spirit regarded as

ταῖς ἁμαρτίαις ὑμῶν! **18** *Ἄρα καὶ οἱ κοιμηθέντες ἐν*
\- sins ˜ your! Then also the *ones* falling asleep in
those who have died

Χριστῷ ἀπώλοντο. **19** *Εἰ ἐν τῇ ζωῇ ταύτῃ ἠλπικότες ἐσμὲν*
Christ perished. If [8]in - [10]life [9]this [4]having [5]hoped [1]we [2]are
have perished. we have only

ἐν Χριστῷ μόνον, ἐλεεινότεροι πάντων ἀνθρώπων ἐσμέν!
[6]in [7]Christ [3]only, [16]most [17]pitiable [13]of [14]all [15]men [11]we [12]are!
hoped in Christ,

Christ Risen Assures the Resurrection of All

20 *Νυνὶ δὲ Χριστὸς ἐγήγερται ἐκ νεκρῶν,*
now ˜ But Christ has been raised from *the* dead, *and*

ἀπαρχὴ τῶν κεκοιμημένων ἐγένετο. [a]
[3]*the* [4]firstfruits [5]of [6]the [7]*ones* [8]having [9]fallen [10]asleep [1]He [2]became.
died

21 *Ἐπειδὴ γὰρ δι' ἀνθρώπου ὁ θάνατος, καὶ δι' ἀνθρώπου*
since ˜ For by a man - death *came,* also by a man

ἀνάστασις νεκρῶν. **22** *Ὥσπερ γὰρ ἐν τῷ Ἀδὰμ*
comes the resurrection of *the* dead. as ˜ For in - Adam

πάντες ἀποθνήσκουσιν οὕτω καὶ ἐν τῷ Χριστῷ πάντες
all die so also in - Christ all

ζῳοποιηθήσονται. **23** *Ἕκαστος δὲ ἐν τῷ ἰδίῳ τάγματι·*
will be made alive. each ˜ But in - his own order:
group:

ἀπαρχὴ Χριστός, ἔπειτα οἱ τοῦ Χριστοῦ ἐν τῇ*
[2]*the* [3]firstfruits [1]Christ, then the *ones* - of Christ at -
those who belong to

παρουσίᾳ αὐτοῦ. **24** *Εἶτα τὸ τέλος, ὅταν παραδῷ τὴν*
coming ˜ His. Then *will be* the end, when He hands over the

βασιλείαν τῷ Θεῷ καὶ Πατρί, ὅταν καταργήσῃ πᾶσαν
kingdom - to God even *the* Father, when He abolishes every

ἀρχὴν καὶ πᾶσαν ἐξουσίαν καὶ δύναμιν. **25** *Δεῖ*
ruler and every authority and power. [2]it [3]is [4]necessary [5]*for*

γὰρ αὐτὸν βασιλεύειν ἄχρις οὗ ἂν θῇ πάντας τοὺς ἐχθροὺς
[1]For Him to reign until - - He puts all the enemies
His

ὑπὸ τοὺς πόδας αὐτοῦ. **26** *Ἔσχατος ἐχθρὸς καταργεῖται ὁ*
under - feet ˜ His. *The* last enemy being abolished - *is*
that will be

θάνατος. **27** *«Πάντα γὰρ ὑπέταξεν ὑπὸ τοὺς πόδας*
death. «[4]all [5]*things* [1]For [2]He [3]subjected under - feet ˜

αὐτοῦ.» [b] *Ὅταν δὲ εἴπῃ ὅτι πάντα ὑποτέτακται,*
His.» when ˜ But He says that all *things* have been subjected,

δῆλον ὅτι ἐκτὸς τοῦ ὑποτάξαντος αὐτῷ τὰ
it is evident that *this is* except for the *One* subjecting [3]to [4]Him -
Him who subjected

πάντα. **28** *Ὅταν δὲ ὑποταγῇ αὐτῷ τὰ πάντα, τότε*
[1]all [2]*things.* when ˜ Now [3]are [4]subjected [5]to [6]Him - [1]all [2]*things,* then

καὶ αὐτὸς ὁ Υἱὸς ὑποταγήσεται τῷ ὑποτάξαντι αὐτῷ
also [3]Himself [1]the [2]Son will be subjected to the *One* subjecting [3]to [4]Him
to Him who subjected

τὰ πάντα, ἵνα ᾖ ὁ Θεὸς τὰ πάντα ἐν πᾶσιν.
\- [1]all [2]*things,* in order that [2]may [3]be - [1]God - all in all.

The Consequences of Denying the Resurrection

29 *Ἐπεὶ τί ποιήσουσιν οἱ βαπτιζόμενοι ὑπὲρ τῶν*
Otherwise what will they do the *ones* being baptized for the
who are

νεκρῶν? Εἰ ὅλως νεκροὶ οὐκ ἐγείρονται, τί καὶ
dead? If [6]at [7]all [1]*the* [2]dead [4]not [3]are [5]raised, why [3]also

βαπτίζονται ὑπὲρ τῶν νεκρῶν?[c] 30 Τί καὶ ἡμεῖς
[1]are [2]they baptized for the dead? Why [3]also [2]we

κινδυνεύομεν πᾶσαν ὥραν? 31 Καθ' ἡμέραν ἀποθνήσκω,
[1]are in danger every hour? According to a day I die,
Daily

νὴ τὴν ὑμετέραν καύχησιν,[d] ἣν ἔχω ἐν Χριστῷ
I affirm by - your boasting, which I have in Christ
my boasting in you,

Ἰησοῦ τῷ Κυρίῳ ἡμῶν. 32 Εἰ κατὰ ἄνθρωπον
Jesus - Lord ˜ our. If according to man
for human purposes

ἐθηριομάχησα ἐν Ἐφέσῳ, τί μοι τὸ ὄφελος? Εἰ
I fought with wild beasts in Ephesus, what *is* [3]to [4]me [1]the [2]benefit? If

νεκροὶ οὐκ ἐγείρονται,
the dead not ˜ are raised,

«Φάγωμεν καὶ πίωμεν,
«Let us eat and drink,

Αὔριον γὰρ ἀποθνήσκομεν.»[e]
tomorrow ˜ For we die.»

33 Μὴ πλανᾶσθε· "Φθείρουσιν ἤθη χρηστὰ ὁμιλίαι
not ˜ Do be deceived: "[3]corrupt [5]habits [4]good [2]associations

κακαί." 34 Ἐκνήψατε δικαίως καὶ μὴ ἁμαρτάνετε,
[1]Evil." Be sober uprightly and not ˜ do sin,
Awake as you ought

ἀγνωσίαν γὰρ Θεοῦ τινες ἔχουσι. Πρὸς ἐντροπὴν ὑμῖν
[4]ignorance [1]for [5]of [6]God [2]some [3]have. [9]for [10]shame [11]to [12]you
no knowledge about your shame

λέγω.
[7]I [8]speak.

The Resurrection Body Will Be Glorious

35 Ἀλλ' ἐρεῖ τις, "Πῶς ἐγείρονται οἱ νεκροί?
But [2]will [3]say [1]someone, "How are [3]raised [1]the [2]dead?

Ποίῳ δὲ σώματι ἔρχονται?" 36 Ἄφρον, σὺ
[5]with [6]what [7]sort [8]of [4]And body do they come?" Fool, you ˜

ὃ σπείρεις οὐ ζωοποιεῖται ἐὰν μὴ ἀποθάνῃ. 37 Καὶ ὃ
what sow not ˜ is made alive if not it dies. And what
unless

σπείρεις, οὐ τὸ σῶμα τὸ γενησόμενον σπείρεις, ἀλλὰ
you sow, [3]not [5]the [6]body [7]the [8]*one* [9]going [10]to [11]be [1]you [2]do [4]sow, but
that will be

γυμνὸν κόκκον, εἰ τύχοι, σίτου ἤ τινος τῶν
a bare grain, if it should be, of wheat or of some of the
perhaps

λοιπῶν. 38 Ὁ δὲ Θεὸς αὐτῷ δίδωσι σῶμα καθὼς
remaining *grains*. - But God [2]to [3]it [1]gives a body just as
other

ἠθέλησε, καὶ ἑκάστῳ τῶν σπερμάτων τὸ ἴδιον σῶμα. 39 Οὐ
He desired, and to each of the seeds - its own body. [4]not

πᾶσα σὰρξ ἡ αὐτὴ σάρξ, ἀλλὰ ἄλλη[f] μὲν
[1]All [2]flesh [3]*is* the same flesh, but *there is* a different *kind* - *of flesh*

ἀνθρώπων, ἄλλη δὲ σὰρξ κτηνῶν, ἄλλη δὲ ἰχθύων,
of men, another ˜ and flesh of beasts, another ˜ and of fish,
for for for

ἄλλη δὲ πτηνῶν. 40 Καὶ σώματα ἐπουράνια, καὶ
another ˜ and of birds. And *there are* bodies ˜ heavenly, and
for celestial,

dead, if the dead do not rise at all? Why then are they baptized for the dead?
30 And why do we stand in jeopardy every hour?
31 I affirm, by the boasting in you which I have in Christ Jesus our Lord, I die daily.
32 If, in the manner of men, I have fought with beasts at Ephesus, what advantage *is it* to me? If *the* dead do not rise, *"Let us eat and drink, for tomorrow we die!"*
33 Do not be deceived: "Evil company corrupts good habits."
34 Awake to righteousness, and do not sin; for some do not have the knowledge of God. I speak *this* to your shame.
35 But someone will say, "How are the dead raised up? And with what body do they come?"
36 Foolish one, what you sow is not made alive unless it dies.
37 And what you sow, you do not sow that body that shall be, but mere grain—perhaps wheat or some other *grain.*
38 But God gives it a body as He pleases, and to each seed its own body.
39 All flesh *is* not the same flesh, but *there is* one *kind of* flesh of men, another flesh of animals, another of fish, *and* another of birds.
40 *There are* also celestial

---

[c](15:29) For *των νεκρων, the dead,* NU reads *αυτων, them.* [d](15:31) NU adds in brackets *αδελφοι, brothers.* [e](15:32) Is. 22:13 [f](15:39) TR adds *σαρξ, flesh.*

the firstfruit that promises final redemption (Rom. 8:23).

bodies and terrestrial bodies;
but the glory of the celestial *is*
one, and the *glory* of the terrestrial *is* another.
41 *There is* one glory of the
sun, another glory of the moon,
and another glory of the stars;
for *one* star differs from *another*
star in glory.
42 So also *is* the resurrection
of the dead. *The body* is sown in
corruption, it is raised in incorruption.
43 It is sown in dishonor, it is
raised in glory. It is sown in
weakness, it is raised in power.
44 It is sown a natural body, it
is raised a spiritual body. There
is a natural body, and there is a
spiritual body.
45 And so it is written, *"The
first man Adam became a living
being."* The last Adam *became* a
life-giving spirit.
46 However, the spiritual is
not first, but the natural, and
afterward the spiritual.
47 The first man *was* of the
earth, *made* of dust; the second
Man *is* the Lord from heaven.
48 As *was* the *man* of dust, so
also *are* those *who are made* of
dust; and as *is* the heavenly
Man, so also *are* those *who are*
heavenly.
49 And as we have borne the
image of the *man* of dust, we
shall also bear the image of the
heavenly *Man.*
50 Now this I say, brethren,
that flesh and blood cannot inherit the kingdom of God; nor
does corruption inherit incorruption.
51 Behold, I tell you a mys-

σώματα ἐπίγεια, ἀλλ' ἑτέρα μὲν ἡ τῶν ἐπουρανίων
bodies ~ earthly, but [7]*is* [8]one - [1]the [3]of [4]the [5]heavenly [6]*bodies*
terrestrial, celestial

δόξα, ἑτέρα δὲ ἡ τῶν ἐπιγείων.
[2]glory, [16]*is* [17]another [9]and [10]the [11]*glory* [12]of [13]the [14]earthly [15]*bodies.*
brightness, terrestrial

41 Ἄλλη δόξα ἡλίου, καὶ ἄλλη δόξα σελήνης,
There is one glory of *the* sun, and another glory of *the* moon,
brightness brightness

καὶ ἄλλη δόξα ἀστέρων, ἀστὴρ γὰρ ἀστέρος
and another glory of *the* stars, [2]*one* [3]star [1]for [5]from [6]*another* [7]star
brightness

διαφέρει ἐν δόξῃ.
[4]differs in glory.
brightness.

42 Οὕτω καὶ ἡ ἀνάστασις τῶν νεκρῶν. Σπείρεται ἐν
Thus also *is* the resurrection of the dead. It is sown in
The body

φθορᾷ, ἐγείρεται ἐν ἀφθαρσίᾳ. **43** Σπείρεται ἐν ἀτιμίᾳ,
corruption, it is raised in incorruption. It is sown in dishonor,

ἐγείρεται ἐν δόξῃ. Σπείρεται ἐν ἀσθενείᾳ, ἐγείρεται ἐν
it is raised in glory. It is sown in weakness, it is raised in

δυνάμει. **44** Σπείρεται σῶμα ψυχικόν, ἐγείρεται σῶμα
power. It is sown a body ~ natural, it is raised a body ~

πνευματικόν. Ἔστι[g] σῶμα ψυχικὸν καὶ ἔστι σῶμα
spiritual. *There* is a body ~ natural and *there* is a body ~

πνευματικόν. **45** Οὕτω καὶ γέγραπται, «Ἐγένετο ὁ πρῶτος
spiritual. Thus also it is written, «[5]became [1]The [2]first

ἄνθρωπος Ἀδὰμ εἰς ψυχὴν ζῶσαν»·[h] ὁ ἔσχατος Ἀδὰμ
[3]man [4]Adam - a soul ~ living»; the last Adam *became*

εἰς πνεῦμα ζῳοποιοῦν. **46** Ἀλλ' οὐ πρῶτον τὸ
- a spirit making alive. But [4]*is* [5]not [6]first [1]the
a life-giving spirit. that which

πνευματικόν, ἀλλὰ τὸ ψυχικόν,* ἔπειτα τὸ
[2]spiritual [3]*thing,* but the natural *thing,* then the
is spiritual, that which is natural, that which

πνευματικόν. **47** Ὁ πρῶτος ἄνθρωπος ἐκ γῆς, χοϊκός·
spiritual *thing.* The first man *was* from earth, made of dust;
is spiritual.

ὁ δεύτερος ἄνθρωπος ὁ Κύριος[i] ἐξ οὐρανοῦ. **48** Οἷος
the second man *is* the Lord from heaven. Like

ὁ χοϊκός, τοιοῦτοι καὶ οἱ χοϊκοί, καὶ οἷος
the *one* made of dust, such also *are* the *ones* made of dust, and like

ὁ ἐπουράνιος, τοιοῦτοι καὶ οἱ ἐπουράνιοι. **49** Καὶ καθὼς
the heavenly *One,* such also *will be* the heavenly *ones.* And just as

ἐφορέσαμεν τὴν εἰκόνα τοῦ χοϊκοῦ, φορέσωμεν[j] καὶ
we bore the image of the *one* made of dust, let us bear ~ also
have borne

τὴν εἰκόνα τοῦ ἐπουρανίου.
the image of the heavenly *One.*

The Coming of Christ Is Our Final Victory over Death

50 Τοῦτο δέ φημι, ἀδελφοί, ὅτι σὰρξ καὶ αἷμα
[4]this [1]Now [2]I [3]say, brothers, that flesh and blood

βασιλείαν Θεοῦ κληρονομῆσαι οὐ δύνανται, οὐδὲ ἡ
[6]*the* [7]kingdom [8]of [9]God [4]to [5]inherit [2]not [1]are [3]able, nor -
cannot inherit,

φθορὰ τὴν ἀφθαρσίαν κληρονομεῖ. **51** Ἰδού, μυστήριον
[2]corruption - [4]incorruption [1]will [3]inherit. Behold, [4]a [5]mystery

---

[g](15:44) NU reads Ει εστιν, *If (there) is.*
[h](15:45) Gen. 2:7
[i](15:47) NU omits ο Κυριος, *the Lord.* [j](15:49) NU, TR read φορεσομεν, *we will bear.*

*(15:46) ψυχικός (*psychikos*). Adjective, cognate to the noun ψυχή, *soul, self,* literally meaning *of (or pertaining to) the soul, life.* It may be translated *natural* or *unspiritual,* even *sensual,* in contrast with the supernatural or spiritual. It generally stands in contrast (whether stated or implied) with πνευματικός, *spiritual,* and thus indicates one who is animated solely by the natural, human psyche and not by the spirit as regenerated by the Holy Spirit (1 Cor. 2:14; James 3:15; Jude 19). See ψυχή at Luke 21:19.

ὑμῖν λέγω· Πάντες μὲν οὐ κοιμηθησόμεθα, πάντες δὲ
[3]you [1]I [2]tell: [4]all - [3]not [1]We [2]shall [5]sleep, [9]all [6]but
die,

ἀλλαγησόμεθα 52 ἐν ἀτόμῳ, ἐν ῥιπῇ ὀφθαλμοῦ, ἐν
[7]we [8]shall [10]be [11]changed in a moment, in *the* twinkling of an eye, at

τῇ ἐσχάτῃ σάλπιγγι. Σαλπίσει γάρ, καὶ οἱ νεκροὶ
the last trumpet. [2]a [3]trumpet [4]will [5]sound [1]For, and the dead

ἐγερθήσονται ἄφθαρτοι, καὶ ἡμεῖς ἀλλαγησόμεθα.
will be raised incorruptible, and we shall be changed.

53 Δεῖ γὰρ τὸ φθαρτὸν τοῦτο ἐνδύσασθαι
[2]it [3]is [4]necessary [5]*for* [1]For - [2]corruptible [3]*thing* [1]this to put on

ἀφθαρσίαν καὶ τὸ θνητὸν τοῦτο ἐνδύσασθαι ἀθανασίαν.
incorruption and *for* - [2]mortal [3]*thing* [1]this to put on immortality.

54 Ὅταν δὲ τὸ φθαρτὸν τοῦτο ἐνδύσηται ἀφθαρσίαν
when ˜ And - [2]corruptible [3]*thing* [1]this should put on incorruption

καὶ τὸ θνητὸν τοῦτο ἐνδύσηται ἀθανασίαν, τότε
and - [2]mortal [3]*thing* [1]this should put on immortality, then

γενήσεται ὁ λόγος ὁ γεγραμμένος,
will come to pass the word the *one* having been written,
which was

«Κατεπόθη ὁ θάνατος εἰς νῖκος.»[k]
«[2]was [3]swallowed [4]up - [1]Death in victory.»

55 «Ποῦ σου, θάνατε, τὸ κέντρον?[l]
«[2]where [3]*is* [4]your, [1]Death, - sting?

Ποῦ σου, Ἅιδη,[m] τὸ νῖκος?»[n]
[2]where [3]*is* [4]your, [1]Hades, - victory?»

56 Τὸ δὲ κέντρον τοῦ θανάτου ἡ ἁμαρτία, ἡ δὲ δύναμις
the ˜ Now sting - of death *is* - sin, - the ˜ and power

τῆς ἁμαρτίας ὁ νόμος. 57 Τῷ δὲ Θεῷ χάρις τῷ
- of sin *is* the law. - But [3]to [4]God [1]thanks [2]*be* to the *One*
who is

διδόντι ἡμῖν τὸ νῖκος διὰ τοῦ Κυρίου ἡμῶν Ἰησοῦ Χριστοῦ!
giving us the victory through - Lord ˜ our Jesus Christ!

58 Ὥστε, ἀδελφοί μου ἀγαπητοί, ἑδραῖοι γίνεσθε,
So then, [3]brothers [1]my [2]beloved, steadfast ˜ be,

ἀμετακίνητοι, περισσεύοντες ἐν τῷ ἔργῳ τοῦ Κυρίου πάντοτε,
immovable, abounding in the work of the Lord always,

εἰδότες ὅτι ὁ κόπος ὑμῶν οὐκ ἔστι κενὸς ἐν Κυρίῳ.
knowing that - labor ˜ your not ˜ is vain in *the* Lord.
in vain

The Collection for the Saints

16 1 Περὶ δὲ τῆς λογίας τῆς εἰς τοὺς ἁγίους,
concerning ˜ Now the collection the *one* for the saints,
which is

ὥσπερ διέταξα ταῖς ἐκκλησίαις τῆς Γαλατίας, οὕτω καὶ ὑμεῖς
as I directed to the churches - of Galatia, so also you

ποιήσατε. 2 Κατὰ μίαν σαββάτων ἕκαστος ὑμῶν
do. According to *the* first *day* of *the* week [2]each [3]of [4]you
must do. On

παρ' ἑαυτῷ τιθέτω, θησαυρίζων ὅ τι ἂν
[7]beside [8]himself [1]let [5]put [6]*something,* storing up what something -
aside whatever

εὐοδῶται, ἵνα μὴ ὅταν ἔλθω τότε λογίαι
he may prosper, in order that [6]not [1]when [2]I [3]come [9]then [8]collections

γίνωνται. 3 Ὅταν δὲ παραγένωμαι, οὓς ἐὰν
[4]*there* [5]may [7]be. when ˜ But I arrive, *those* whom ever

tery: We shall not all sleep, but we shall all be changed—
52 in a moment, in the twinkling of an eye, at the last trumpet. For the trumpet will sound, and the dead will be raised incorruptible, and we shall be changed.
53 For this corruptible must put on incorruption, and this mortal *must* put on immortality.
54 So when this corruptible has put on incorruption, and this mortal has put on immortality, then shall be brought to pass the saying that is written: *"Death is swallowed up in victory."*

55 *"O Death, where is your sting?*
O Hades, where is your victory?"

56 The sting of death *is* sin, and the strength of sin *is* the law.
57 But thanks *be* to God, who gives us the victory through our Lord Jesus Christ.
58 Therefore, my beloved brethren, be steadfast, immovable, always abounding in the work of the Lord, knowing that your labor is not in vain in the Lord.

16 Now concerning the collection for the saints, as I have given orders to the churches of Galatia, so you must do also:
2 On the first *day* of the week let each one of you lay something aside, storing up as he may prosper, that there be no collections when I come.
3 And when I come, whom-

[k](15:54) Is. 25:8
[l](15:55) NU reads νικος, *victory.* [m](15:55) NU reads θανατε, *Death* (in both lines of v. 55).
[n](15:55) Hos. 13:14; NU reads κεντρον, *sting.*

ever you approve by *your* letters I will send to bear your gift
to Jerusalem.
4 But if it is fitting that I go
also, they will go with me.
5 Now I will come to you
when I pass through Macedonia
(for I am passing through Macedonia).
6 And it may be that I will remain, or even spend the winter
with you, that you may send me
on my journey, wherever I go.
7 For I do not wish to see
you now on the way; but I hope
to stay a while with you, if the
Lord permits.
8 But I will tarry in Ephesus
until Pentecost.
9 For a great and effective
door has opened to me, and
there are many adversaries.
10 And if Timothy comes, see
that he may be with you without fear; for he does the work
of the Lord, as I also *do*.
11 Therefore let no one despise him. But send him on his
journey in peace, that he may
come to me; for I am waiting
for him with the brethren.
12 Now concerning *our*
brother Apollos, I strongly
urged him to come to you with
the brethren, but he was quite
unwilling to come at this time;
however, he will come when he
has a convenient time.
13 Watch, stand fast in the
faith, be brave, be strong.
14 Let all *that* you *do* be done
with love.
15 I urge you, brethren—you
know the household of Stephanas, that it is the firstfruits of

δοκιμάσητε δι' ἐπιστολῶν, τούτους πέμψω ἀπενεγκεῖν τὴν
you approve by letters, these I will send to carry -

χάριν ὑμῶν εἰς Ἰερουσαλήμ. **4** Ἐὰν δὲ ᾖ ἄξιον τοῦ
[2]gracious [3]gift [1]your to Jerusalem. if ˜ But it is fitting -
that

κἀμὲ πορεύεσθαι, σὺν ἐμοὶ πορεύσονται.
me also to go, [4]with [5]me [1]they [2]will [3]go.
I go also,

Paul's Personal Plans

5 Ἐλεύσομαι δὲ πρὸς ὑμᾶς ὅταν Μακεδονίαν
[2]I [3]will [4]come [1]Now to you when [4]Macedonia

διέλθω, Μακεδονίαν γὰρ διέρχομαι. **6** Πρὸς ὑμᾶς
[1]I [2]go [3]through, [10]Macedonia [5]for [6]I [7]am [8]coming [9]through. [6]with [7]you

δὲ τυχὸν παραμενῶ, ἢ καὶ παραχειμάσω, ἵνα ὑμεῖς με
[1]And [2]perhaps [3]I [4]will [5]remain, or even spend the winter, that you [3]me

προπέμψητε οὗ ἐὰν πορεύωμαι. **7** Οὐ θέλω γὰρ ὑμᾶς
[1]may [2]send forth where ever I may go. [4]not [2]I [3]do [5]wish [1]For [8]you

ἄρτι ἐν παρόδῳ ἰδεῖν, ἐλπίζω δὲ χρόνον τινὰ ἐπιμεῖναι
[9]now [10]in [11]passing [6]to [7]see, [13]I [14]hope [12]but [18]time [17]some [15]to [16]remain
spend

πρὸς ὑμᾶς ἐὰν ὁ Κύριος ἐπιτρέπῃ. **8** Ἐπιμενῶ δὲ ἐν
with you if the Lord permits. [2]I [3]will [4]remain [1]But in

Ἐφέσῳ ἕως τῆς Πεντηκοστῆς. **9** Θύρα γάρ μοι
Ephesus until - Pentecost. [2]a [3]door [1]For [6]to [7]me

ἀνέῳγε μεγάλη καὶ ἐνεργής, καὶ ἀντικείμενοι
[4]has [5]opened *that is* great and effective, and *there are* opponents ˜

πολλοί. **10** Ἐὰν δὲ ἔλθῃ Τιμόθεος, βλέπετε ἵνα ἀφόβως
many. if ˜ Now comes ˜ Timothy, watch that [6]without [7]fear
see to it

γένηται πρὸς ὑμᾶς, τὸ γὰρ ἔργον Κυρίου ἐργάζεται
[1]he [2]may [3]be [4]with [5]you, [11]the [8]for [12]work [13]of [14]*the* [15]Lord [9]he [10]works
performs

ὡς καὶ ἐγώ. **11** Μή τις οὖν αὐτὸν ἐξουθενήσῃ.
as also I *do*. [3]not [5]anyone [1]Therefore [7]him [2]do [4]let [6]despise.

Προπέμψατε δὲ αὐτὸν ἐν εἰρήνῃ, ἵνα ἔλθῃ πρός με,
[9]send [11]away [8]And [10]him in peace, that he may come to me,

ἐκδέχομαι γὰρ αὐτὸν μετὰ τῶν ἀδελφῶν.
[2]I [3]wait [4]for [1]for him with the brothers.

12 Περὶ δὲ Ἀπολλῶ τοῦ ἀδελφοῦ, πολλὰ
concerning ˜ Now Apollos the brother, [4]many [5]*things*
our much

παρεκάλεσα αὐτὸν ἵνα ἔλθῃ πρὸς ὑμᾶς μετὰ τῶν ἀδελφῶν,
[1]I [2]urged [3]him that he come to you with the brothers,

καὶ πάντως οὐκ ἦν θέλημα ἵνα νῦν ἔλθῃ· ἐλεύσεται
and [4]at [5]all [3]not [1]it [2]was *his* will that [3]now [1]he [2]come; [5]he [6]will [7]come

δὲ ὅταν εὐκαιρήσῃ.
[4]but whenever he has an opportunity.

Paul's Final Exhortations

13 Γρηγορεῖτε, στήκετε ἐν τῇ πίστει, ἀνδρίζεσθε,
Watch, stand fast in the faith, be courageous,

κραταιοῦσθε. **14** Πάντα ὑμῶν ἐν ἀγάπῃ γινέσθω.
be strong. [2]all [4]*deeds* [3]your [6]in [7]love [1]Let [5]be.

15 Παρακαλῶ δὲ ὑμᾶς, ἀδελφοί (οἴδατε τὴν οἰκίαν
[2]I [3]urge [1]Now you, brothers (you know the household

Στεφανᾶ, ὅτι ἐστὶν ἀπαρχὴ τῆς Ἀχαΐας, καὶ εἰς διακονίαν
of Stephanas, that it is *the* firstfruits - of Achaia, and [4]to [5]service

τοῖς ἁγίοις ἔταξαν ἑαυτούς), 16 ἵνα καὶ ὑμεῖς
[6]to [7]the [8]saints [1]they [2]assigned [3]themselves), that also ˜ you
have devoted

ὑποτάσσησθε τοῖς τοιούτοις καὶ παντὶ τῷ συνεργοῦντι
subject yourselves - to such *people* and to every - *one* working together
everyone who works

καὶ κοπιῶντι. 17 Χαίρω δὲ ἐπὶ τῇ παρουσίᾳ Στεφανᾶ
and laboring. [2]I [3]rejoice [1]Now over the coming of Stephanas
labors.

καὶ Φουρτουνάτου καὶ Ἀχαϊκοῦ, ὅτι τὸ ὑμῶν
and Fortunatus and Achaicus, because the [2]of [3]you
what was lacking

ὑστέρημα οὗτοι ἀνεπλήρωσαν. 18 Ἀνέπαυσαν γὰρ τὸ ἐμὸν
[1]lack these filled up. [2]they [3]refreshed [1]For - my
on your part they have supplied.

πνεῦμα καὶ τὸ ὑμῶν· ἐπιγινώσκετε οὖν τοὺς τοιούτους.
spirit and - yours; [2]give [3]recognition [4]to [1]therefore - such *people*.

His Greeting and Farewell

19 Ἀσπάζονται ὑμᾶς αἱ ἐκκλησίαι τῆς Ἀσίας.
[5]greet [6]you [1]The [2]churches - [3]of [4]Asia.

Ἀσπάζονται ὑμᾶς ἐν Κυρίῳ πολλὰ Ἀκύλας καὶ
[10]greet [11]you [14]in [15]*the* [16]Lord [12]many [13]*things* [7]Aquila [8]and
warmly

Πρίσκιλλα, σὺν τῇ κατ' οἶκον αὐτῶν ἐκκλησίᾳ.
[9]Priscilla, together with the [2]in [4]house [3]their [1]church.

20 Ἀσπάζονται ὑμᾶς οἱ ἀδελφοὶ πάντες. Ἀσπάσασθε
[4]greet [5]you [2]the [3]brothers [1]All. Greet

ἀλλήλους ἐν φιλήματι ἁγίῳ.
one another with a kiss ˜ holy.

21 Ὁ ἀσπασμὸς τῇ ἐμῇ χειρὶ Παύλου. 22 Εἴ τις
The greeting *is* - by my *own* hand of Paul. If anyone

οὐ φιλεῖ τὸν Κύριον Ἰησοῦν Χριστόν,[a] ἤτω ἀνάθεμα.
not ˜ does love the Lord Jesus Christ, let him be accursed.

Μαρανα θα!* 23 Ἡ χάρις τοῦ Κυρίου Ἰησοῦ Χριστοῦ[b] μεθ'
Marana tha! The grace of the Lord Jesus Christ *be* with
Our Lord, come!

ὑμῶν. 24 Ἡ ἀγάπη μου μετὰ πάντων ὑμῶν ἐν Χριστῷ
you. - love ˜ My *be* with all ˜ you in Christ

Ἰησοῦ. Ἀμήν.[c]
Jesus. Amen.
So be it.

Achaia, and *that* they have devoted themselves to the ministry of the saints—
16 that you also submit to such, and to everyone who works and labors with *us.*
17 I am glad about the coming of Stephanas, Fortunatus, and Achaicus, for what was lacking on your part they supplied.
18 For they refreshed my spirit and yours. Therefore acknowledge such men.
19 The churches of Asia greet you. Aquila and Priscilla greet you heartily in the Lord, with the church that is in their house.
20 All the brethren greet you. Greet one another with a holy kiss.
21 The salutation with my own hand—Paul's.
22 If anyone does not love the Lord Jesus Christ, let him be accursed. O Lord, come!
23 The grace of our Lord Jesus Christ *be* with you.
24 My love *be* with you all in Christ Jesus. Amen.

[a]**(16:22)** NU omits Ιησουν Χριστον, *Jesus Christ.* [b]**(16:23)** NU omits Χριστου, *Christ.* [c]**(16:24)** NU omits Αμην, *Amen.*

***(16:22)** Μαρὰνα θά *(Marana tha).* Christian Aramaic expression used only here in the NT, *Marana* meaning *the (our) Lord,* and *tha* being an imperative plea *come!* While the phrase refers to Christ's "coming," there is disagreement as to which coming of the Lord is intended. The difference arises from differing ways of dividing the Greek transliteration into Aramaic words. The church fathers divided it as Μαρὰν αθά, "Our Lord has come." Most modern scholars prefer Μαράνα θά (as here), "Our Lord *comes* or *is coming,*" though some consider θα as a plea, "Come."

The Second Epistle of Paul the Apostle to the
CORINTHIANS

1 Paul, an apostle of Jesus
Christ by the will of God,
and Timothy *our* brother,

To the church of God
which is at Corinth, with all the
saints who are in all Achaia:

2 Grace to you and peace
from God our Father and the
Lord Jesus Christ.

3 Blessed *be* the God and Father of our Lord Jesus Christ,
the Father of mercies and God
of all comfort,
4 who comforts us in all our
tribulation, that we may be able
to comfort those who are in any
trouble, with the comfort with
which we ourselves are comforted by God.
5 For as the sufferings of
Christ abound in us, so our consolation also abounds through
Christ.
6 Now if we are afflicted, *it is*
for your consolation and salvation, which is effective for enduring the same sufferings
which we also suffer. Or if we
are comforted, *it is* for your
consolation and salvation.
7 And our hope for you *is*
steadfast, because we know

---

[a](1:6, 7) NU omits και σωτηριας, *and salvation,* and uses a different order of major clauses in vv. 6, 7.

ΠΡΟΣ ΚΟΡΙΝΘΙΟΥΣ Β
TO *THE* CORINTHIANS 2

1 1 Παῦλος, ἀπόστολος Ἰησοῦ Χριστοῦ διὰ θελήματος
Paul, an apostle of Jesus Christ by *the* will
Θεοῦ, καὶ Τιμόθεος ὁ ἀδελφός,
of God, and Timothy the (our) brother,

Τῇ ἐκκλησίᾳ τοῦ Θεοῦ τῇ οὔσῃ ἐν Κορίνθῳ,
To the church - of God the *one* (which) being (is) at Corinth,
σὺν τοῖς ἁγίοις πᾶσι τοῖς οὖσιν ἐν ὅλῃ τῇ Ἀχαΐᾳ·
together with [2]the [3]saints [1]all the *ones* (who) being (are) in whole (all) ~ the Achaia;

2 Χάρις ὑμῖν καὶ εἰρήνη ἀπὸ Θεοῦ Πατρὸς ἡμῶν καὶ
Grace to you and peace from God Father ~ our and
Κυρίου Ἰησοῦ Χριστοῦ.
the Lord Jesus Christ.

God's Comfort in Suffering

3 Εὐλογητὸς ὁ Θεὸς καὶ Πατὴρ τοῦ Κυρίου ἡμῶν Ἰησοῦ
Blessed *be* the God and Father - of Lord ~ our Jesus
Χριστοῦ, ὁ Πατὴρ τῶν οἰκτιρμῶν καὶ Θεὸς πάσης
Christ, the Father - of mercies and God of all (utmost)
παρακλήσεως, 4 ὁ παρακαλῶν ἡμᾶς ἐπὶ πάσῃ τῇ
comfort, the *One* comforting us in all -
θλίψει ἡμῶν, εἰς τὸ δύνασθαι ἡμᾶς παρακαλεῖν τοὺς
tribulation ~ our, for (in order for) - [2]to [3]be [4]able [1]us to comfort the *ones*
ἐν πάσῃ θλίψει διὰ τῆς παρακλήσεως ἧς
in any affliction by means of the comfort *with* which
παρακαλούμεθα αὐτοὶ ὑπὸ τοῦ Θεοῦ. 5 Ὅτι καθὼς
we [2]are [3]comforted [1]ourselves by - God. Because just as
περισσεύει τὰ παθήματα τοῦ Χριστοῦ εἰς ἡμᾶς, οὕτω διὰ
[5]abound [1]the [2]sufferings - [3]of [4]Christ in us, thus [5]through
τοῦ Χριστοῦ περισσεύει καὶ ἡ παράκλησις ἡμῶν. 6 Εἴτε δὲ
- [6]Christ [4]abounds [3]also - [2]consolation [1]our. if ~ Now
θλιβόμεθα, ὑπὲρ τῆς ὑμῶν παρακλήσεως καὶ
we are afflicted, *it is* for the sake of - your consolation and
σωτηρίας, τῆς ἐνεργουμένης ἐν ὑπομονῇ τῶν αὐτῶν
salvation, the *one* (which) being (is) effective in *the* endurance of the same
παθημάτων ὧν καὶ ἡμεῖς πάσχομεν. 7 Καὶ ἡ ἐλπὶς ἡμῶν
sufferings which also ~ we are suffering. And - hope ~ our
βεβαία ὑπὲρ ὑμῶν, εἴτε παρακαλούμεθα, ὑπὲρ τῆς
is firm (steadfast) concerning you, if we are comforted, for the sake of -
ὑμῶν παρακλήσεως καὶ σωτηρίας,[a] εἰδότες ὅτι ὥσπερ
your consolation and salvation, knowing that as indeed

κοινωνοί ἐστε τῶν παθημάτων, οὕτω καὶ τῆς
[3]sharers [1]you [2]are of the sufferings, thus also *you will share* of the

παρακλήσεως.
consolation.

God's Deliverance from Suffering

8 Οὐ γὰρ θέλομεν ὑμᾶς ἀγνοεῖν, ἀδελφοί,
[4]not [1]For [2]we [3]do [5]desire you to be ignorant, brothers,

ὑπὲρ τῆς θλίψεως ἡμῶν τῆς γενομένης ἡμῖν[b] ἐν τῇ
concerning - affliction ˜ our the *one* having happened to us in -
which happened

Ἀσίᾳ, ὅτι καθ' ὑπερβολὴν ἐβαρήθημεν ὑπὲρ
Asia, that [4]to [5]an [6]extraordinary [7]degree [1]we [2]were [3]burdened beyond
beyond measure

δύναμιν, ὥστε ἐξαπορηθῆναι ἡμᾶς καὶ τοῦ ζῆν.
ability, so that [2]to [3]despair [1]us even - to live.
our strength, we despaired of living.

9 Ἀλλὰ αὐτοὶ ἐν ἑαυτοῖς τὸ ἀπόκριμα τοῦ θανάτου
But [2]ourselves [9]in [10]ourselves [5]the [6]sentence - [7]of [8]death

ἐσχήκαμεν, ἵνα μὴ πεποιθότες ὦμεν ἐφ'
[1]we [3]have [4]had, in order that [3]not [5]having [6]confidence [1]we [2]may [4]be in
we should not trust

ἑαυτοῖς ἀλλ' ἐπὶ τῷ Θεῷ τῷ ἐγείροντι τοὺς νεκρούς, 10 ὃς
ourselves but in - God the *One* raising the dead *ones,* who
who raises

ἐκ τηλικούτου θανάτου ἐρρύσατο ἡμᾶς καὶ ῥύεται,[c] εἰς
from so great a death delivered us and is delivering *us,* in

ὃν ἠλπίκαμεν ὅτι καὶ ἔτι ῥύσεται,
whom we have put hope that also [3]still [1]He [2]will deliver *us,*

11 συνυπουργούντων καὶ ὑμῶν ὑπὲρ ἡμῶν τῇ δεήσει,
[3]joining [4]in [5]helping [2]also [1]you in behalf of us in the entreaty,
prayer,

ἵνα ἐκ πολλῶν προσώπων τὸ εἰς ἡμᾶς χάρισμα διὰ
that [5]by [6]many [7]persons [12]*for* [13]the [16]to [17]us [14]gift [15]*given* [17]through

πολλῶν εὐχαριστηθῇ ὑπὲρ ὑμῶν.[d]
[18]many [1]thanks [2]may [3]be [4]given [8]in [9]behalf [10]of [11]you.
in your behalf.

Paul Defends His Sincerity

12 Ἡ γὰρ καύχησις ἡμῶν αὕτη ἐστί, τὸ μαρτύριον τῆς
- For boasting ˜ our this ˜ is, the testimony -

συνειδήσεως ἡμῶν, ὅτι ἐν ἁπλότητι καὶ εἰλικρινείᾳ Θεοῦ, οὐκ
of conscience ˜ our, that in simplicity and sincerity of God, not
openness godly sincerity,

ἐν σοφίᾳ σαρκικῇ ἀλλ' ἐν χάριτι Θεοῦ, ἀνεστράφημεν
in wisdom ˜ fleshly but in *the* grace of God, we conducted ourselves
have conducted

ἐν τῷ κόσμῳ, περισσοτέρως δὲ πρὸς ὑμᾶς. 13 Οὐ γὰρ
in the world, especially ˜ but toward you. [4]not [1]For

ἄλλα γράφομεν ὑμῖν ἀλλ' ἢ ἃ
[6]other [7]*things* [2]we [3]do [5]write to you rather than *things* which
except

ἀναγινώσκετε ἢ καὶ ἐπιγινώσκετε, ἐλπίζω δὲ ὅτι καὶ ἕως
you read or also understand, [2]I [3]hope [1]and that also until

τέλους ἐπιγνώσεσθε, 14 καθὼς καὶ ἐπέγνωτε ἡμᾶς
the end you will understand *them,* just as also you understood us
have understood

that as you are partakers of the sufferings, so also *you will partake* of the consolation.
8 For we do not want you to be ignorant, brethren, of our trouble which came to us in Asia: that we were burdened beyond measure, above strength, so that we despaired even of life.
9 Yes, we had the sentence of death in ourselves, that we should not trust in ourselves but in God who raises the dead,
10 who delivered us from so great a death, and does deliver us; in whom we trust that He will still deliver *us,*
11 you also helping together in prayer for us, that thanks may be given by many persons on our behalf for the gift *granted* to us through many.
12 For our boasting is this: the testimony of our conscience that we conducted ourselves in the world in simplicity and godly sincerity, not with fleshly wisdom but by the grace of God, and more abundantly toward you.
13 For we are not writing any other things to you than what you read or understand. Now I trust you will understand, even to the end
14 (as also you have under-

[b](1:8) NU omits ημιν, *to us.*
[c](1:10) NU reads ρυσεται, *will deliver.*
[d](1:11) NU, TR read ημων, *us.*

stood us in part), that we are
your boast as you also *are* ours,
in the day of the Lord Jesus.
15 And in this confidence I intended to come to you before,
that you might have a second
benefit—
16 to pass by way of you to
Macedonia, to come again from
Macedonia to you, and be
helped by you on my way to Judea.
17 Therefore, when I was
planning this, did I do it lightly?
Or the things I plan, do I plan
according to the flesh, that with
me there should be Yes, Yes,
and No, No?
18 But *as* God *is* faithful, our
word to you was not Yes and
No.
19 For the Son of God, Jesus
Christ, who was preached
among you by us—by me, Silvanus, and Timothy—was not
Yes and No, but in Him was
Yes.
20 For all the promises of God
in Him *are* Yes, and in Him
Amen, to the glory of God
through us.
21 Now He who establishes
us with you in Christ and has
anointed us *is* God,
22 who also has sealed us and
given us the Spirit in our hearts
as a guarantee.
23 Moreover I call God as witness against my soul, that to

ἀπὸ μέρους, ὅτι καύχημα ὑμῶν ἐσμεν, καθάπερ καὶ ὑμεῖς
from part, because [4]boasting [3]your [1]we [2]are, as indeed also you *are*
in

ἡμῶν, ἐν τῇ ἡμέρᾳ τοῦ Κυρίου[e] Ἰησοῦ.
ours, in the day of the Lord Jesus.

Paul Defends His Change of Plans

15 Καὶ ταύτῃ τῇ πεποιθήσει ἐβουλόμην ἐλθεῖν πρὸς ὑμᾶς
And in this - confidence I willed to come to you
intended

τὸ πρότερον, ἵνα δευτέραν χάριν ἔχητε, 16 καὶ
- earlier, that [4]a [5]second [6]grace [1]you [2]might [3]have, and
benefit

δι' ὑμῶν διελθεῖν εἰς Μακεδονίαν, καὶ πάλιν ἀπὸ
through you to pass into Macedonia, and again from
by way of

Μακεδονίας ἐλθεῖν πρὸς ὑμᾶς, καὶ ὑφ' ὑμῶν προπεμφθῆναι
Macedonia to come to you, and by you to be sent on

εἰς τὴν Ἰουδαίαν. 17 Τοῦτο οὖν βουλευόμενος, μήτι ἄρα
into - Judea. [3]this [1]Therefore [2]deciding, [6]not [7]then
when I decided, I did

τῇ ἐλαφρίᾳ ἐχρησάμην? Ἢ ἃ βουλεύομαι,
- [9]lightness [4]I [5]did [8]use, *did I?* Or *the things* which I decide,
not do it lightly,

κατὰ σάρκα βουλεύομαι, ἵνα ᾖ παρ' ἐμοὶ τὸ
[4]according [5]to [6]*the* [7]flesh [1]do [2]I [3]decide, that *there* may be with me the

"Ναί, ναί" καὶ τὸ "Οὔ, οὔ"? 18 Πιστὸς δὲ ὁ Θεός, ὅτι ὁ
"Yes, yes" and the "No, no"? [4]faithful [1]But - [2]God [3]*is,* because -

λόγος ἡμῶν ὁ πρὸς ὑμᾶς οὐκ ἐγένετο[f] "Ναὶ καὶ οὔ." 19 Ὁ
word ˜ our - to you not ˜ was "Yes and no." the ˜
message

γὰρ τοῦ Θεοῦ Υἱός, Ἰησοῦς Χριστός, ὁ ἐν ὑμῖν δι'
For - [2]of [3]God [1]Son, Jesus Christ, the *One* [3]among [4]you [5]by
who

ἡμῶν κηρυχθείς — δι' ἐμοῦ καὶ Σιλουανοῦ καὶ Τιμοθέου —
[6]us [1]being [2]preached — by me and Silvanus and Timothy —
was

οὐκ ἐγένετο "Ναὶ καὶ οὔ," ἀλλὰ "Ναὶ" ἐν αὐτῷ γέγονεν.
not ˜ was "Yes and no," but [3]"Yes" [4]in [5]Him [1]has [2]become.

20 Ὅσαι γὰρ ἐπαγγελίαι Θεοῦ, ἐν αὐτῷ τὸ "Ναί"
[2]as [3]many [5]as [1]For [4]promises *are* of God, in Him *are* the "Yes"

καὶ ἐν αὐτῷ τὸ "Ἀμὴν" τῷ Θεῷ πρὸς δόξαν δι'
and in Him *are* the "Amen" - [4]to [5]God [1]to [2]*the* [3]glory through
of

ἡμῶν. 21 Ὁ δὲ βεβαιῶν ἡμᾶς σὺν ὑμῖν εἰς
us. [2]the [3]*One* [1]Now establishing us together with you in
He who establishes

Χριστόν, καὶ χρίσας ἡμᾶς, Θεός, 22 ὁ καὶ
Christ, and anointing us, *is* God, the *One* also
who has anointed who

σφραγισάμενος ἡμᾶς καὶ δοὺς τὸν ἀρραβῶνα* τοῦ
sealing us and giving *us* the pledge of the
has sealed given down payment

Πνεύματος ἐν ταῖς καρδίαις ἡμῶν.
Spirit in - hearts ˜ our.

23 Ἐγὼ δὲ μάρτυρα τὸν Θεὸν ἐπικαλοῦμαι ἐπὶ τὴν
I ˜ Now [4]*as* [5]*a* [6]witness - [3]God [1]call [2]upon against -

---

e(**1:14**) NU adds in brackets *ημων, our.*
f(**1:18**) NU reads *εστιν, is.*

***(1:22)** *ἀρραβών (arrabōn).* Noun meaning *deposit, pledge.* All of the NT occurrences are figurative and refer to the Holy Spirit as God's *guarantee, down payment* given to certify His promises to us (as here). These promises include our resurrected body (2 Cor. 5:5) and eternal inheritance (Eph. 1:14). In the Greek world of the day, such an *ἀρραβών* made a contract binding and guaranteed future delivery.

ἐμὴν ψυχὴν ὅτι φειδόμενος ὑμῶν οὐκέτι ἦλθον εἰς
my soul that sparing you [3]no [4]more [1]I [2]came to
in order to spare

Κόρινθον. 24 Οὐχ ὅτι κυριεύομεν ὑμῶν τῆς πίστεως, ἀλλὰ
Corinth. Not that we lord it over your - faith, but

συνεργοί ἐσμεν τῆς χαρᾶς ὑμῶν, τῇ γὰρ πίστει ἑστήκατε.
[3]fellow [4]workers [1]we [2]are - of joy ˜ your, - for by faith you stand.

2 1 Ἔκρινα δὲ ἐμαυτῷ τοῦτο, τὸ μὴ πάλιν ἐν λύπῃ
[2]I [3]judged [1]But [5]within [6]myself [4]this, - not [5]again [6]in [7]sorrow
determined

πρὸς ὑμᾶς ἐλθεῖν. 2 Εἰ γὰρ ἐγὼ λυπῶ ὑμᾶς, καὶ
[3]to [4]you [1]to [2]come. if ˜ For I make sorrowful ˜ you, then ˜

τίς ἐστιν ὁ εὐφραίνων με εἰ μὴ ὁ λυπούμενος
who is the *one* making glad ˜ me if not the *one* being made sorrowful

ἐξ ἐμοῦ?
by me?

Forgive and Encourage the Offender

3 Καὶ ἔγραψα ὑμῖν[a] τοῦτο αὐτὸ ἵνα μὴ ἐλθὼν
And I wrote [4]to [5]you [1]this [2]same [3]*thing* that not coming
lest, when I came,

λύπην ἔχω ἀφ᾽ ὧν ἔδει με
[3]sorrow [1]I [2]have from *those* from whom it is necessary *for* me
should have I ought

χαίρειν, πεποιθὼς ἐπὶ πάντας ὑμᾶς ὅτι ἡ ἐμὴ χαρὰ
to rejoice, having confidence in all ˜ you that - my joy

πάντων ὑμῶν ἐστιν. 4 Ἐκ γὰρ πολλῆς θλίψεως καὶ
[4]of [6]all [5]you [1]is [2]*the* [3]*joy.* [2]out [3]of [1]For much affliction and

συνοχῆς καρδίας ἔγραψα ὑμῖν διὰ πολλῶν δακρύων, οὐχ
distress of heart I wrote to you through many tears, not

ἵνα λυπηθῆτε, ἀλλὰ τὴν ἀγάπην
in order that you might be made sorrowful, but [9]the [10]love

ἵνα γνῶτε ἣν ἔχω περισσοτέρως
[1]in [2]order [3]that [4]you [5]might [6]come [7]to [8]know which I have especially

εἰς ὑμᾶς.
for you.

5 Εἰ δέ τις λελύπηκεν, οὐκ ἐμὲ
if ˜ Now anyone has caused sorrow, [3]not [5]me

λελύπηκεν, ἀλλὰ ἀπὸ μέρους, ἵνα μὴ ἐπιβαρῶ
[1]he [2]has [4]caused [6]sorrow, but from part, that not I burden
in lest

πάντας ὑμᾶς. 6 Ἱκανὸν τῷ τοιούτῳ ἡ ἐπιτιμία αὕτη
all ˜ you. Sufficient - to such a person - *is* punishment ˜ this

ἡ ὑπὸ τῶν πλειόνων, 7 ὥστε τοὐναντίον μᾶλλον
the *one inflicted* by the majority, so that on the other hand [3]rather
which was

ὑμᾶς χαρίσασθαι καὶ παρακαλέσαι, μή πως τῇ
[1]you [2]*ought* to forgive and to comfort *him,* not how by the
lest somehow

περισσοτέρᾳ λύπῃ καταποθῇ ὁ τοιοῦτος. 8 Διὸ
excessive sorrow [4]be [5]swallowed [6]up - [1]such [2]a [3]person. Therefore
overwhelmed

παρακαλῶ ὑμᾶς κυρῶσαι εἰς αὐτὸν ἀγάπην. 9 Εἰς τοῦτο γὰρ
I appeal to you to confirm to him *your* love. [2]to [3]this [4]*end* [1]For
reaffirm

καὶ ἔγραψα ἵνα γνῶ τὴν δοκιμὴν ὑμῶν, εἰ εἰς
also ˜ I wrote so that I might know the character of you, *to see* if in
put you to the test,

spare you I came no more to Corinth.
24 Not that we have dominion over your faith, but are fellow workers for your joy; for by faith you stand.

2 But I determined this within myself, that I would not come again to you in sorrow.
2 For if I make you sorrowful, then who is he who makes me glad but the one who is made sorrowful by me?
3 And I wrote this very thing to you, lest, when I came, I should have sorrow over those from whom I ought to have joy, having confidence in you all that my joy is *the joy* of you all.
4 For out of much affliction and anguish of heart I wrote to you, with many tears, not that you should be grieved, but that you might know the love which I have so abundantly for you.
5 But if anyone has caused grief, he has not grieved me, but all of you to some extent—not to be too severe.
6 This punishment which *was inflicted* by the majority *is* sufficient for such a man,
7 so that, on the contrary, you *ought* rather to forgive and comfort *him,* lest perhaps such a one be swallowed up with too much sorrow.
8 Therefore I urge you to reaffirm *your* love to him.
9 For to this end I also wrote, that I might put you to the test, whether you are obe-

[a](2:3) NU omits *υμιν, to you.*

dient in all things.

10 Now whom you forgive anything, I also *forgive.* For if indeed I have forgiven anything, I have forgiven that one for your sakes in the presence of Christ,

11 lest Satan should take advantage of us; for we are not ignorant of his devices.

12 Furthermore, when I came to Troas to *preach* Christ's gospel, and a door was opened to me by the Lord,

13 I had no rest in my spirit, because I did not find Titus my brother; but taking my leave of them, I departed for Macedonia.

14 Now thanks *be* to God who always leads us in triumph in Christ, and through us diffuses the fragrance of His knowledge in every place.

15 For we are to God the fragrance of Christ among those who are being saved and among those who are perishing.

16 To the one *we are* the aroma of death *leading* to death, and to the other the aroma of life *leading* to life. And who *is* sufficient for these things?

17 For we are not, as so many, peddling the word of God; but as of sincerity, but as from God, we speak in the sight of God in Christ.

3 Do we begin again to commend ourselves? Or do we need, as some *others,* epistles of commendation to

---

[b](2:10) For ει τι, *if anything,* NU reads ο, *what.*
[c](2:10) For ω, *(the one) whom,* NU reads ει τι, *if anything.* [d](2:17) NU, TR read πολλοι, *many.*

*(2:14) θριαμβεύω (thriambeuō). Verb meaning *lead as a captive in a triumphal procession.* The word describes an ancient custom for a victorious general returning home. In Col. 2:15 (the only other NT occurrence) Jesus "triumphs over" the forces of evil and leads them, subjugated, in His victory march (cf. the ideas in Eph. 4:8). Here in 2 Cor. 2:14 the same picture is apparently involved. Paul sees himself marching in Christ's triumphal procession (whether as a captive or as a participant in the victory is debated by interpreters), while the incense of the knowledge of

πάντα ὑπήκοοί ἐστε. **10** Ὧι δέ τι χαρίζεσθε,
all *things* [3]obedient [1]you [2]are. [2]to [3]whom [1]And [6]anything [4]you [5]forgive,

καὶ ἐγώ· καὶ γὰρ ἐγὼ εἴ τι[b] κεχάρισμαι,
also ~ I *forgive;* indeed ~ for I ~ if [3]anything [1]have [2]forgiven,

ᾧ[c] κεχάρισμαι, δι' ὑμᾶς ἐν
the one whom I have forgiven, *I have done so* for the sake of you in
for your sakes

προσώπῳ Χριστοῦ, **11** ἵνα μὴ πλεονεκτηθῶμεν ὑπὸ τοῦ
the presence of Christ, that not ~ we be taken advantage of by -
lest

Σατανᾶ, οὐ γὰρ αὐτοῦ τὰ νοήματα ἀγνοοῦμεν.
Satan, [4]not [1]for [7]his - [8]plots [2]we [3]are [5]ignorant [6]of.
devices

Triumph in Christ

12 Ἐλθὼν δὲ εἰς τὴν Τρῳάδα εἰς τὸ εὐαγγέλιον τοῦ
coming ~ Now to - Troas for the gospel of
when I went

Χριστοῦ, καὶ θύρας μοι ἀνεῳγμένης ἐν Κυρίῳ, **13** οὐκ
Christ, and a door [4]to [5]me [1]having [2]been [3]opened by *the* Lord, [3]not
was I

ἔσχηκα ἄνεσιν τῷ πνεύματί μου, τῷ μὴ εὑρεῖν με
[1]I [2]have [4]had rest - in spirit ~ my, by the not to find me
had no relief because I did not find

Τίτον τὸν ἀδελφόν μου, ἀλλὰ ἀποταξάμενος αὐτοῖς ἐξῆλθον εἰς
Titus - brother ~ my, but taking leave of them I departed for
saying farewell to

Μακεδονίαν.
Macedonia.

14 Τῷ δὲ Θεῷ χάρις τῷ πάντοτε θριαμβεύοντι*
- Now [3]to [4]God [1]thanks [2]*be* the *One* always leading [2]in [3]triumph

ἡμᾶς ἐν τῷ Χριστῷ καὶ τὴν ὀσμὴν τῆς γνώσεως αὐτοῦ
[1]us in - Christ and [5]the [6]fragrance [7]of [8]the [9]knowledge [10]of [11]Him

φανεροῦντι δι' ἡμῶν ἐν παντὶ τόπῳ. **15** Ὅτι Χριστοῦ
[1]making [2]known [3]through [4]us in every place. Because [5]of [6]Christ

εὐωδία ἐσμὲν τῷ Θεῷ ἐν τοῖς σῳζομένοις καὶ ἐν
[3]*the* [4]aroma [1]we [2]are - to God among the *ones* being saved and among

τοῖς ἀπολλυμένοις, **16** οἷς μὲν ὀσμὴ θανάτου
the *ones* perishing, to the ones - *it is the* fragrance of death
some

εἰς θάνατον, οἷς δὲ ὀσμὴ ζωῆς εἰς
leading to death, [2]to [3]the [4]ones [1]but *the* fragrance of life *leading* to
others

ζωήν. Καὶ πρὸς ταῦτα τίς ἱκανός? **17** Οὐ γάρ ἐσμεν
life. And [4]for [5]these [6]*things* [1]who [2]*is* [3]sufficient? [4]not [1]For [2]we [3]are

ὡς οἱ λοιποί,[d] καπηλεύοντες τὸν λόγον τοῦ Θεοῦ, ἀλλ' ὡς
as the rest, peddling the word - of God, but as
adulterating for gain

ἐξ εἰλικρινείας, ἀλλ' ὡς ἐκ Θεοῦ, κατενώπιον τοῦ Θεοῦ, ἐν
out of sincerity, but as from God, [3]before - [4]God, [5]in

Χριστῷ λαλοῦμεν.
[6]Christ [1]we [2]speak.

You Are Christ's Epistle

3 **1** Ἀρχόμεθα πάλιν ἑαυτοὺς συνιστάνειν? Εἰ μὴ
Do we begin again [3]ourselves [1]to [2]recommend? - [3]not
commend?

χρῄζομεν, ὥς τινες, συστατικῶν ἐπιστολῶν πρὸς ὑμᾶς
[1]We [2]do [4]need, as some *do,* [2]of [3]recommendation [1]letters to you

ἢ ἐξ ὑμῶν συστατικῶν?[a] **2** Ἡ ἐπιστολὴ
or [4]from [5]you [1]*letters* [2]of [3]recommendation, *do we?* - [4]letter

ἡμῶν ὑμεῖς ἐστε, ἐγγεγραμμένη ἐν ταῖς καρδίαις ἡμῶν,
[3]our [1]you [2]are, having been written in - hearts ˜ our,

γινωσκομένη καὶ ἀναγινωσκομένη ὑπὸ πάντων ἀνθρώπων·
being known and being read by all men;

3 φανερούμενοι ὅτι ἐστὲ ἐπιστολὴ Χριστοῦ διακονηθεῖσα
being made known that you are *the* letter of Christ being ministered (which was)

ὑφ' ἡμῶν, ἐγγεγραμμένη οὐ μέλανι, ἀλλὰ Πνεύματι
by us, having been written not with ink, but with *the* Spirit

Θεοῦ ζῶντος, οὐκ ἐν πλαξὶ λιθίναις, ἀλλ' ἐν πλαξὶ
of *the* God ˜ living, not in tablets *made* of stone, but in tablets

καρδίαις σαρκίναις.
[4]*namely* [5]in [6]hearts [1]*made* [2]of [3]flesh.

The Spirit, Not the Letter

4 Πεποίθησιν δὲ τοιαύτην ἔχομεν διὰ τοῦ Χριστοῦ
[5]trust [1]And [4]such [2]we [3]have through - Christ

πρὸς τὸν Θεόν. **5** Οὐχ ὅτι ἱκανοί ἐσμεν ἀφ' ἑαυτῶν
toward - God. Not that [3]sufficient [1]we [2]are from (in) ourselves

λογίσασθαί τι ὡς ἐξ ἑαυτῶν, ἀλλ' ἡ ἱκανότης ἡμῶν
to consider anything as from ourselves, but - sufficiency ˜ our

ἐκ τοῦ Θεοῦ, **6** ὃς καὶ ἱκάνωσεν ἡμᾶς διακόνους
is from - God, who also made sufficient ˜ us *to be* ministers

καινῆς διαθήκης, οὐ γράμματος, ἀλλὰ Πνεύματος· τὸ γὰρ
of a new covenant, not of *the* letter, but of *the* Spirit; the ˜ for

γράμμα ἀποκτένει, τὸ δὲ Πνεῦμα ζῳοποιεῖ.
letter kills, the ˜ but Spirit makes alive.

The Glory of the New Covenant

7 Εἰ δὲ ἡ διακονία τοῦ θανάτου ἐν γράμμασιν
if ˜ Now the ministry - of death [4]in [5]letters

ἐντετυπωμένη ἐν λίθοις ἐγενήθη ἐν δόξῃ, ὥστε μὴ
[1]having [2]been [3]engraved on stones came to be with glory, so that [5]not (could)

δύνασθαι ἀτενίσαι τοὺς υἱοὺς Ἰσραὴλ εἰς τὸ
[6]to [7]be [8]able [9]to [10]look [11]intently (not) [1]the [2]sons (children) [3]of [4]Israel into the

πρόσωπον Μωϋσέως διὰ τὴν δόξαν τοῦ προσώπου αὐτοῦ,
face of Moses because of the glory - of face ˜ his,

τὴν καταργουμένην, **8** πῶς οὐχὶ μᾶλλον ἡ
the *glory which was* passing away, how [7]not [9]more [2]the

διακονία τοῦ Πνεύματος ἔσται ἐν δόξῃ? **9** Εἰ γὰρ ἡ
[3]ministry [4]of [5]the [6]Spirit [1]will [8]be with glory? (glorious?) if ˜ For the

διακονίᾳ τῆς κατακρίσεως δόξα, πολλῷ μᾶλλον περισσεύει
ministry - of condemnation *had* glory, by much more [5]abounds (exceeds)

ἡ διακονία τῆς δικαιοσύνης ἐν δόξῃ. **10** Καὶ γὰρ οὐ
[1]the [2]ministry - [3]of [4]righteousness in glory. even ˜ For [7]not

δεδόξασται τὸ δεδοξασμένον ἐν τούτῳ τῷ μέρει,
[6]has [8]been [9]glorified [1]the [2]*thing* (that which) [3]having (has) [4]been [5]glorified in this - part, (respect,)

ἕνεκεν τῆς ὑπερβαλλούσης δόξης. **11** Εἰ γὰρ τὸ
on account of the surpassing glory. if ˜ For the *thing* (what is)

you or *letters* of commendation
from you?
2 You are our epistle written
in our hearts, known and read
by all men;
3 clearly *you are* an epistle of
Christ, ministered by us, written not with ink but by the
Spirit of the living God, not on
tablets of stone but on tablets
of flesh, *that is,* of the heart.
4 And we have such trust
through Christ toward God.
5 Not that we are sufficient
of ourselves to think of anything as *being* from ourselves,
but our sufficiency *is* from God,
6 who also made us sufficient
as ministers of the new covenant, not of the letter but of
the Spirit; for the letter kills,
but the Spirit gives life.
7 But if the ministry of death,
written *and* engraved on
stones, was glorious, so that
the children of Israel could not
look steadily at the face of Moses because of the glory of his
countenance, which *glory* was
passing away,
8 how will the ministry of the
Spirit not be more glorious?
9 For if the ministry of condemnation *had* glory, the ministry of righteousness exceeds
much more in glory.
10 For even what was made
glorious had no glory in this respect, because of the glory that
excels.
11 For if what is passing away

[a](3:1) NU omits *συστατικων, (letters) of recommendation.*

Christ (preached by him) fills the air. Burning incense was part of the custom of such victory parades.

was glorious, what remains *is*
much more glorious.
12 Therefore, since we have
such hope, we use great boldness of speech—
13 unlike Moses, *who* put a
veil over his face so that the
children of Israel could not look
steadily at the end of what was
passing away.
14 But their minds were
blinded. For until this day the
same veil remains unlifted in
the reading of the Old Testament, because the *veil* is taken
away in Christ.
15 But even to this day, when
Moses is read, a veil lies on
their heart.
16 Nevertheless when one
turns to the Lord, the veil is
taken away.
17 Now the Lord is the Spirit;
and where the Spirit of the
Lord *is,* there *is* liberty.
18 But we all, with unveiled
face, beholding as in a mirror
the glory of the Lord, are being
transformed into the same image from glory to glory, just as
by the Spirit of the Lord.
4 Therefore, since we have
this ministry, as we have
received mercy, we do not lose
heart.
2 But we have renounced the
hidden things of shame, not
walking in craftiness nor han-
dling the word of God deceit-

καταργούμενον διὰ δόξης, πολλῷ μᾶλλον τὸ
passing away *was* through glory, by much more the *thing*
with what is

μένον ἐν δόξῃ.
remaining *is* with glory.
glorious.

12 Ἔχοντες οὖν τοιαύτην ἐλπίδα, πολλῇ
Having therefore such a hope, [3]great

παρρησίᾳ χρώμεθα, 13 καὶ οὐ καθάπερ Μωϋσῆς
[4]boldness [5]of [6]speech [1]we [2]use, and not as Moses

ἐτίθει κάλυμμα ἐπὶ τὸ πρόσωπον ἑαυτοῦ πρὸς τὸ μὴ
was putting a veil over - face ˜ his for - [5]not
who put so that could

ἀτενίσαι τοὺς υἱοὺς Ἰσραὴλ εἰς τὸ τέλος τοῦ
[6]to [7]look [8]intently [1]the [2]sons [3]of [4]Israel toward the end of the *thing*
not at what was

καταργουμένου. 14 Ἀλλ᾽ ἐπωρώθη τὰ νοήματα αὐτῶν.
passing away. But [3]were [4]hardened - [2]minds [1]their.

Ἄχρι γὰρ τῆς σήμερον[b] τὸ αὐτὸ κάλυμμα ἐπὶ τῇ
until ˜ For - today the same veil [5]during [6]the

ἀναγνώσει τῆς Παλαιᾶς Διαθήκης μένει μὴ
[7]reading [8]of [9]the [10]Old [11]Testament [1]remains [2]not
unlifted,

ἀνακαλυπτόμενον, ὅτι ἐν Χριστῷ καταργεῖται. 15 Ἀλλ᾽ ἕως
[3]being [4]unveiled, because in Christ it passes away. But until
is removed.

σήμερον, ἡνίκα ἀναγινώσκεται Μωϋσῆς, κάλυμμα ἐπὶ τὴν
today, when [2]is [3]read [1]Moses, a veil [2]upon -

καρδίαν αὐτῶν κεῖται. 16 Ἡνίκα δ᾽ ἂν ἐπιστρέψῃ πρὸς
[4]heart [3]their [1]lies. whenever ˜ But - he turns to
one

Κύριον, περιαιρεῖται τὸ κάλυμμα. 17 Ὁ δὲ Κύριος τὸ
the Lord, [3]is [4]taken [5]away [1]the [2]veil. the ˜ Now Lord [2]the

Πνεῦμά ἐστιν· οὗ δὲ τὸ Πνεῦμα Κυρίου, ἐκεῖ[c]
[3]Spirit [1]is; where ˜ and the Spirit of *the* Lord *is,* there *is*

ἐλευθερία. 18 Ἡμεῖς δὲ πάντες, ἀνακεκαλυμμένῳ
freedom. we ˜ And all, [4]having [5]been [6]unveiled
liberty.

προσώπῳ τὴν δόξαν Κυρίου κατοπτριζόμενοι,
[1]with [2]a [3]face [12]the [13]glory [14]of [15]*the* [16]Lord [7]beholding [8]as [9]in [10]a [11]mirror,
contemplating,

τὴν αὐτὴν εἰκόνα μεταμορφούμεθα ἀπὸ δόξης εἰς
[21]the [22]same [23]image [17]are [18]being [19]transformed [20]into from glory to

δόξαν, καθάπερ ἀπὸ Κυρίου Πνεύματος.
glory, just as by [3]of [4]*the* [5]Lord [1]*the* [2]Spirit.

The Light of Christ's Gospel

4 1 Διὰ τοῦτο, ἔχοντες τὴν διακονίαν ταύτην, καθὼς
Because of this, having - ministry ˜ this, as
since we have

ἠλεήθημεν, οὐκ ἐκκακοῦμεν, 2 ἀλλὰ ἀπειπάμεθα
we received mercy, [3]not [1]we [2]do [4]lose [5]heart, but we have renounced
despair,

τὰ κρυπτὰ τῆς αἰσχύνης, μὴ περιπατοῦντες ἐν πανουργίᾳ
the hidden *things* - of shame, not walking in craftiness

μηδὲ δολοῦντες τὸν λόγον τοῦ Θεοῦ, ἀλλὰ τῇ φανερώσει
nor falsifying the word - of God, but by the disclosure
announcement

[b](3:14) NU adds ημερας, *(the) day (today),* thus *this very day.* [c](3:17) NU omits εκει, *there (is).*

τῆς ἀληθείας συνιστῶντες ἑαυτοὺς πρὸς πᾶσαν συνείδησιν
of the truth recommending ourselves to every conscience
commending the conscience

ἀνθρώπων ἐνώπιον τοῦ Θεοῦ. 3 Εἰ δὲ καὶ ἔστι
of men before - God. [3]if [1]But [2]even [6]is
of every man

κεκαλυμμένον τὸ εὐαγγέλιον ἡμῶν, ἐν τοῖς
[7]hidden - [5]gospel [4]our, [11]among [12]the [13]*ones*
those who are

ἀπολλυμένοις ἐστὶ κεκαλυμμένον, 4 ἐν οἷς ὁ Θεὸς τοῦ
[14]perishing [8]it [9]is [10]hidden, among whom the god -

αἰῶνος τούτου ἐτύφλωσε τὰ νοήματα τῶν ἀπίστων εἰς
of age ˜ this blinded the minds of the unbelieving *ones* for
has blinded unbelievers so that

τὸ μὴ αὐγάσαι αὐτοῖς[a] τὸν φωτισμὸν τοῦ εὐαγγελίου
- [11]not [12]to [13]shine [14]on [15]them [1]the [2]light [3]of [4]the [5]gospel
should not

τῆς δόξης τοῦ Χριστοῦ, ὅς ἐστιν εἰκὼν τοῦ Θεοῦ. 5 Οὐ
[6]of [7]the [8]glory - [9]of [10]Christ, who is *the* image - of God. [4]not

γὰρ ἑαυτοὺς κηρύσσομεν, ἀλλὰ Χριστὸν Ἰησοῦν Κύριον,
[1]For [6]ourselves [2]we [3]do [5]preach, but Christ Jesus *the* Lord,

ἑαυτοὺς δὲ δούλους ὑμῶν διὰ Ἰησοῦν. 6 Ὅτι ὁ
ourselves ˜ and bondservants ˜ your for the sake of Jesus. Because -
slaves

Θεὸς ὁ εἰπὼν ἐκ σκότους φῶς λάμψαι, ὃς ἔλαμψεν
God the *One* saying *for* [4]from [5]darkness [1]light [2]to [3]shine, who shined
who said

ἐν ταῖς καρδίαις ἡμῶν πρὸς φωτισμὸν τῆς γνώσεως τῆς
in - hearts ˜ our to *the* illumination of the knowledge of the
light

δόξης τοῦ Θεοῦ ἐν προσώπῳ Ἰησοῦ Χριστοῦ.
glory - of God in *the* face of Jesus Christ.

Cast Down but Unconquered

7 Ἔχομεν δὲ τὸν θησαυρὸν τοῦτον ἐν ὀστρακίνοις
[2]we [3]have [1]But - treasure ˜ this in clay

σκεύεσιν, ἵνα ἡ ὑπερβολὴ τῆς δυνάμεως ᾖ
vessels, so that the extraordinary character of the power may be

τοῦ Θεοῦ καὶ μὴ ἐξ ἡμῶν· 8 ἐν παντὶ θλιβόμενοι, ἀλλ᾽
- of God and not of us; in every*thing* being oppressed, but

οὐ στενοχωρούμενοι· ἀπορούμενοι, ἀλλ᾽ οὐκ ἐξαπορούμενοι·
not being restricted; being at a loss, but not despairing;
being crushed; being perplexed,

9 διωκόμενοι, ἀλλ᾽ οὐκ ἐγκαταλειπόμενοι· καταβαλλόμενοι,
being persecuted, but not being forsaken; being struck down,

ἀλλ᾽ οὐκ ἀπολλύμενοι· 10 πάντοτε τὴν νέκρωσιν τοῦ
but not perishing; always [6]the [7]putting [8]to [9]death [10]of [11]the

Κυρίου[b] Ἰησοῦ ἐν τῷ σώματι περιφέροντες, ἵνα καὶ ἡ
[12]Lord [13]Jesus [3]in [4]the [5]body [1]carrying [2]about, so that also the

ζωὴ τοῦ Ἰησοῦ ἐν τῷ σώματι ἡμῶν φανερωθῇ. 11 Ἀεὶ
life - of Jesus [4]in - [6]body [5]our [1]may [2]be [3]revealed. always ˜

γὰρ ἡμεῖς οἱ ζῶντες εἰς θάνατον παραδιδόμεθα
For we the *ones* living [4]to [5]death [1]are [2]handed [3]over
who are

διὰ Ἰησοῦν, ἵνα καὶ ἡ ζωὴ τοῦ Ἰησοῦ
for the sake of Jesus, that [6]also [1]the [2]life - [3]of [4]Jesus

φανερωθῇ ἐν τῇ θνητῇ σαρκὶ ἡμῶν. 12 Ὥστε ὁ μὲν
[5]may [7]be [8]revealed in - [2]mortal [3]flesh [1]our. So then - -

fully, but by manifestation of
the truth commending our-
selves to every man's conscience in the sight of God.
3 But even if our gospel is
veiled, it is veiled to those who
are perishing,
4 whose minds the god of
this age has blinded, who do not
believe, lest the light of the
gospel of the glory of Christ,
who is the image of God, should
shine on them.
5 For we do not preach ourselves, but Christ Jesus the
Lord, and ourselves your bondservants for Jesus' sake.
6 For it is the God who commanded light to shine out of
darkness, who has shone in our
hearts to *give* the light of the
knowledge of the glory of God
in the face of Jesus Christ.
7 But we have this treasure
in earthen vessels, that the excellence of the power may be of
God and not of us.
8 *We are* hard-pressed on every side, yet not crushed; *we
are* perplexed, but not in despair;
9 persecuted, but not forsaken; struck down, but not
destroyed—
10 always carrying about in
the body the dying of the Lord
Jesus, that the life of Jesus also
may be manifested in our body.
11 For we who live are always
delivered to death for Jesus'
sake, that the life of Jesus also
may be manifested in our mortal flesh.
12 So then death is working in

[a](**4:4**) NU omits *αυτοις, on them.* [b](**4:10**) NU omits *Κυριου, the Lord.*

us, but life in you.
13 And since we have the
same spirit of faith, according
to what is written, *"I believed
and therefore I spoke,"* we also
believe and therefore speak,
14 knowing that He who
raised up the Lord Jesus will
also raise us up with Jesus, and
will present *us* with you.
15 For all things *are* for your
sakes, that grace, having
spread through the many, may
cause thanksgiving to abound to
the glory of God.
16 Therefore we do not lose
heart. Even though our outward man is perishing, yet the
inward *man* is being renewed
day by day.
17 For our light affliction,
which is but for a moment, is
working for us a far more exceeding *and* eternal weight of
glory,
18 while we do not look at the
things which are seen, but at
the things which are not seen.
For the things which are seen
are temporary, but the things
which are not seen *are* eternal.
5 For we know that if our
earthly house, *this* tent, is
destroyed, we have a building
from God, a house not made
with hands, eternal in the heavens.
2 For in this we groan, ear-

θάνατος ἐν ἡμῖν ἐνεργεῖται, ἡ δὲ ζωὴ ἐν ὑμῖν.* **13** *Ἔχοντες*
death [4]in [5]us [1]is [2]at [3]work, - but life in you. having ˜
since we have

δὲ τὸ αὐτὸ πνεῦμα τῆς πίστεως, κατὰ τὸ
But the same spirit - of faith, according to the *thing*
that which

γεγραμμένον, «Ἐπίστευσα, διὸ ἐλάλησα,» [c] *καὶ ἡμεῖς*
having been written, «I believed, therefore I spoke,» also ˜ we
is

πιστεύομεν, διὸ καὶ λαλοῦμεν, **14** *εἰδότες ὅτι ὁ*
believe, therefore also ˜ we speak, knowing that the *One*
He

ἐγείρας τὸν Κύριον Ἰησοῦν, καὶ ἡμᾶς διὰ [d] *Ἰησοῦ ἐγερεῖ*
raising the Lord Jesus, [2]also [4]us [5]by [6]Jesus [1]will [3]raise
who raised

καὶ παραστήσει σὺν ὑμῖν. **15** *Τὰ γὰρ πάντα*
and will present *us* together with you. - For all *things are*

δι' ὑμᾶς, ἵνα ἡ χάρις πλεονάσασα διὰ τῶν
for the sake of you, so that - grace increasing through the
having spread

πλειόνων τὴν εὐχαριστίαν περισσεύσῃ εἰς τὴν δόξαν
more - [3]thanksgiving [1]may [2]cause [4]to [5]abound to the glory
many

τοῦ Θεοῦ.
- of God.

Seeing the Invisible

16 *Διὸ οὐκ ἐκκακοῦμεν, ἀλλ' εἰ καὶ ὁ ἔξω ἡμῶν*
Therefore [3]not [1]we [2]do [4]lose [5]heart, but if ˜ even - outer ˜ our
despair,

ἄνθρωπος διαφθείρεται, ἀλλ' ὁ ἔσωθεν [e] *ἀνακαινοῦται*
man is being destroyed, yet the inner *man* is being renewed

ἡμέρᾳ καὶ ἡμέρᾳ. **17** *Τὸ γὰρ παραυτίκα ἐλαφρὸν τῆς*
day and day. the ˜ For momentary lightness -
by insignificant

θλίψεως ἡμῶν καθ' ὑπερβολὴν εἰς ὑπερβολὴν αἰώνιον
of tribulation ˜ our [11]to [12]excess [13]to [14]excess [6]an [7]eternal
affliction far beyond all measure

βάρος δόξης κατεργάζεται ἡμῖν, **18** *μὴ σκοπούντων*
[8]weight [9]of [10]glory [1]is [2]working [3]out [4]for [5]us, not looking at
while we do not look

ἡμῶν τὰ βλεπόμενα, ἀλλὰ τὰ μὴ βλεπόμενα·
us the *things* being seen, but the *things* not being seen;
at

τὰ γὰρ βλεπόμενα πρόσκαιρα, τὰ δὲ μὴ
[2]the [3]*things* [1]for being seen *are* temporary, [2]the [3]*things* [1]but not

βλεπόμενα αἰώνια.
being seen *are* eternal.

The Reassurance of the Resurrection

5 **1** *Οἴδαμεν γὰρ ὅτι ἐὰν ἡ ἐπίγειος ἡμῶν οἰκία τοῦ*
[2]we [3]know [1]For that if - earthly ˜ our house of the
this

σκήνους καταλυθῇ, οἰκοδομὴν ἐκ Θεοῦ ἔχομεν, οἰκίαν*
tent is destroyed, [3]a [4]building [5]from [6]God [1]we [2]have, a house

ἀχειροποίητον, αἰώνιον ἐν τοῖς οὐρανοῖς. **2** *Καὶ γὰρ ἐν τούτῳ*
not made by hand, eternal in the heavens. also ˜ For in this *tent*

---

[c](4:13) Ps. 116:10
[d](4:14) NU reads *συν, with.*
[e](4:16) NU reads *εσω ημων, our inner (man).*

***(4:12)** *ἐνεργέω (energeō).* Verb from the preposition *ἐν, in,* and the noun *ἔργον, work,* meaning *work in, be at work, effectively work, produce.* The word is used often in the NT of God's working within (or among) believers to produce desired effects (as Phil. 2:13; cf. God's word in 1 Thess. 2:13), but can also be used of the working of evil spiritual beings (as Eph. 2:2) or of impersonal forces (as here in 2 Cor. 4:12). Cf. the cognate noun *ἐνέργεια, working, operation, activity,* also used for the influence of God (Eph. 1:19) or Satan (2 Thess. 2:9). The cognate adjective *ἐνεργής* means *effective, active, powerful* (Heb. 4:12; 1 Cor. 16:9).

***(5:1)** *σκῆνος (skēnos).* Noun, synonymous with *σκηνή, tent, dwelling.* Here

στενάζομεν, τὸ οἰκητήριον ἡμῶν τὸ ἐξ οὐρανοῦ
we groan, - [7]habitation [6]our [8]the [9]*one* [10]from [11]heaven
which is

ἐπενδύσασθαι ἐπιποθοῦντες. **3** Εἴ γε καὶ ἐνδυσάμενοι
[3]to [4]put [5]on [1]earnestly [2]desiring. If indeed also having been clothed

οὐ γυμνοὶ εὑρεθησόμεθα. **4** Καὶ γὰρ οἱ ὄντες ἐν τῷ
[3]not [6]naked [1]we [2]will [4]be [5]found. also ~ For [2]the [3]*ones* [4]being [5]in [6]the
who are this

σκήνει στενάζομεν βαρούμενοι, ἐφ' ᾧ οὐ θέλομεν
[7]tent [1]we [8]groan being burdened, upon which [3]not [1]we [2]do desire
inasmuch as

ἐκδύσασθαι, ἀλλ' ἐπενδύσασθαι, ἵνα καταποθῇ
to be stripped, but to put on *clothing,* that [4]may [5]be [6]swallowed [7]up

τὸ θνητὸν ὑπὸ τῆς ζωῆς. **5** Ὁ δὲ
[1]the [2]*thing* [3]mortal by - life. [2]the [3]*One* [1]Now
that which is He

κατεργασάμενος ἡμᾶς εἰς αὐτὸ τοῦτο Θεός, ὁ καὶ δοὺς
preparing us for same ~ this *thing is* God, the *One* also giving
who prepared who gave

ἡμῖν τὸν ἀρραβῶνα τοῦ Πνεύματος. **6** Θαρροῦντες
to us the pledge of the Spirit. [2]being [3]confident
down payment

οὖν πάντοτε καὶ εἰδότες ὅτι ἐνδημοῦντες ἐν τῷ σώματι
[1]Therefore always and knowing that being at home in the body
while we are

ἐκδημοῦμεν ἀπὸ τοῦ Κυρίου — **7** διὰ πίστεως γὰρ
we are away from home from the Lord — [4]by [5]faith [1]for

περιπατοῦμεν, οὐ διὰ εἴδους — **8** θαρροῦμεν δὲ καὶ
[2]we [3]walk, not by sight — [2]we [3]are [4]confident [1]but and

εὐδοκοῦμεν μᾶλλον ἐκδημῆσαι ἐκ τοῦ σώματος καὶ
consider *it* good rather to be away from home from the body and
prefer

ἐνδημῆσαι πρὸς τὸν Κύριον.
to be at home with the Lord.

The Judgment Seat of Christ

9 Διὸ καὶ φιλοτιμούμεθα, εἴτε ἐνδημοῦντες εἴτε
Therefore also we aspire, whether being at home or
have as our ambition,

ἐκδημοῦντες, εὐάρεστοι αὐτῷ εἶναι. **10** Τοὺς γὰρ
being away from home, [3]pleasing [4]to [5]Him [1]to [2]be. - For
acceptable

πάντας ἡμᾶς φανερωθῆναι δεῖ ἔμπροσθεν τοῦ
[6]all [5]us [7]to [8]appear [1]it [2]is [3]necessary [4]*for* before the
we must all appear

βήματος τοῦ Χριστοῦ, ἵνα κομίσηται ἕκαστος τὰ
judicial bench - of Christ, that [3]may [4]receive [1]each [2]one the *things*

διὰ τοῦ σώματος, πρὸς ἃ ἔπραξεν,
through the body, in accordance with *the things* which he did,
done in

εἴτε ἀγαθὸν εἴτε κακόν.
whether good or bad.

11 Εἰδότες οὖν τὸν φόβον τοῦ Κυρίου ἀνθρώπους
Knowing therefore the fear of the Lord [3]men

πείθομεν, Θεῷ δὲ πεφανερώμεθα. Ἐλπίζω
[1]we [2]persuade, [10]to [11]God [4]but [5]we [6]have [7]been [8]made [9]known. [13]I [14]hope
I expect

δὲ καὶ ἐν ταῖς συνειδήσεσιν ὑμῶν πεφανερῶσθαι.
[12]And also in - consciences ~ your to have been made known.

nestly desiring to be clothed with our habitation which is from heaven,
3 if indeed, having been clothed, we shall not be found naked.
4 For we who are in *this* tent groan, being burdened, not because we want to be unclothed, but further clothed, that mortality may be swallowed up by life.
5 Now He who has prepared us for this very thing *is* God, who also has given us the Spirit as a guarantee.
6 So *we are* always confident, knowing that while we are at home in the body we are absent from the Lord.
7 For we walk by faith, not by sight.
8 We are confident, yes, well pleased rather to be absent from the body and to be present with the Lord.
9 Therefore we make it our aim, whether present or absent, to be well pleasing to Him.
10 For we must all appear before the judgment seat of Christ, that each one may receive the things *done* in the body, according to what he has done, whether good or bad.
11 Knowing, therefore, the terror of the Lord, we persuade men; but we are well known to God, and I also trust are well known in your consciences.

(and in v. 4) the word is used metaphorically to refer to the body. Because the tent was a temporary dwelling within Greek culture, the idea of transitoriness is implicit in the future. These temporary, "earthen" bodies will be replaced by permanent, glorious ones. The cognate noun σκήνωμα, *tent, dwelling,* is used in the same figurative way as σκῆνος (2 Pet. 1:13), and for the temple David wished to build as God's dwelling place (Acts 7:46). See σκηνόω at John 1:14.

12 For we do not commend ourselves again to you, but give you opportunity to boast on our behalf, that you may have *an answer* for those who boast in appearance and not in heart.
13 For if we are beside ourselves, *it is* for God; or if we are of sound mind, *it is* for you.
14 For the love of Christ compels us, because we judge thus: that if One died for all, then all died;
15 and He died for all, that those who live should live no longer for themselves, but for Him who died for them and rose again.
16 Therefore, from now on, we regard no one according to the flesh. Even though we have known Christ according to the flesh, yet now we know *Him thus* no longer.
17 Therefore, if anyone *is* in Christ, *he is* a new creation; old things have passed away; behold, all things have become new.
18 Now all things *are* of God, who has reconciled us to Himself through Jesus Christ, and has given us the ministry of reconciliation,
19 that is, that God was in Christ reconciling the world to Himself, not imputing their trespasses to them, and has committed to us the word of reconciliation.
20 Now then, we are ambassadors for Christ, as though God were pleading through us: we implore *you* on Christ's be-

Be Reconciled to God

12 Οὐ γὰρ πάλιν ἑαυτοὺς συνιστάνομεν ὑμῖν, ἀλλὰ
[4]not [1]For [9]again [6]ourselves [2]we [3]do [5]recommend [7]to [8]you, but
commend

ἀφορμὴν διδόντες ὑμῖν καυχήματος ὑπὲρ ἡμῶν, ἵνα
[4]an [5]occasion [1]giving [2]to [3]you of boasting in behalf of us, so that
opportunity give

ἔχητε πρὸς τοὺς ἐν προσώπῳ καυχωμένους καὶ
you may have *an answer* for the *ones* [2]in [3]face [1]boasting and
appearance

οὐ καρδίᾳ. 13 Εἴτε γὰρ ἐξέστημεν, Θεῷ·
not in heart. if ˜ For we were out of *our* senses, *it was* for God;
beside ourselves,

εἴτε σωφρονοῦμεν, ὑμῖν. 14 Ἡ γὰρ ἀγάπη τοῦ
if we are of sound mind, *it is* for you. the ˜ For love -

Χριστοῦ συνέχει ἡμᾶς, κρίναντας τοῦτο, ὅτι εἰ[a] εἷς ὑπὲρ
of Christ compels us, judging this, that if One [2]for
having concluded

πάντων ἀπέθανεν, ἄρα οἱ πάντες ἀπέθανον. 15 Καὶ ὑπὲρ
[3]all [1]died, then - all died. And [3]for

πάντων ἀπέθανεν ἵνα οἱ ζῶντες μηκέτι ἑαυτοῖς
[4]all [1]He [2]died so that the *ones* living [3]no [4]longer [5]for [6]themselves
they who live

ζῶσιν, ἀλλὰ τῷ ὑπὲρ αὐτῶν ἀποθανόντι καὶ
[1]should [2]live, but for the *One* [4]for [5]them [1]dying [2]and
who died

ἐγερθέντι. 16 Ὥστε ἡμεῖς ἀπὸ τοῦ νῦν οὐδένα οἴδαμεν
[3]arising. Therefore we from the now [2]no [3]one [1]know
arose. now on

κατὰ σάρκα· εἰ δὲ καὶ ἐγνώκαμεν κατὰ σάρκα
according to *the* flesh; [3]if [1]and [2]even we have known [2]according [3]to [4]*the* [5]flesh

Χριστόν, ἀλλὰ νῦν οὐκέτι γινώσκομεν. 17 Ὥστε εἴ
[1]Christ, yet now no longer do we know *Him thus.* Therefore if

τις ἐν Χριστῷ, καινὴ κτίσις· τὰ ἀρχαῖα παρῆλθεν,
anyone *is* in Christ, *he is* a new creation; the old *things* passed away,

ἰδοὺ γέγονε καινὰ τὰ πάντα.[b] 18 Τὰ δὲ πάντα ἐκ
behold [3]have [4]become [5]new - [1]all [2]*things.* - And all *things are* of

τοῦ Θεοῦ τοῦ καταλλάξαντος ἡμᾶς ἑαυτῷ διὰ Ἰησοῦ[c]
- God the *One* reconciling us to Himself through Jesus
who reconciled

Χριστοῦ καὶ δόντος ἡμῖν τὴν διακονίαν τῆς καταλλαγῆς,
Christ and giving to us the ministry of the reconciliation,
who gave this

19 ὡς ὅτι Θεὸς ἦν ἐν Χριστῷ κόσμον καταλλάσσων
as that God was in Christ [2]*the* [3]world [1]reconciling
that is,

ἑαυτῷ, μὴ λογιζόμενος αὐτοῖς τὰ παραπτώματα αὐτῶν, καὶ
to Himself, not reckoning to them - transgressions ˜ their, and
imputing

θέμενος ἐν ἡμῖν τὸν λόγον τῆς καταλλαγῆς.
putting in us the word of the reconciliation.
committing to message of this

20 Ὑπὲρ Χριστοῦ οὖν πρεσβεύομεν,* ὡς τοῦ
In behalf of Christ therefore we serve as ambassadors, as -
though

Θεοῦ παρακαλοῦντος δι' ἡμῶν· δεόμεθα ὑπὲρ
of God appealing through us: we beg *you* in behalf of
God were appealing

---

[a](5:14) NU omits ει, *if.*
[b](5:17) NU omits τα παντα, *all (things).*
[c](5:18) NU omits Ιησου, *Jesus.*

***(5:20)** *πρεσβεύω (presbeuō).* Verb meaning *to serve* or *travel as an ambassador* or *emissary.* This technical usage is derived from the precedence of and representative role of elders within Greek society. Paul uses the term figuratively here (cf. Eph. 6:20) to describe his missionary activity as *serving as an ambassador* on Christ's behalf. The cognate noun *πρεσβεία, embassy,* refers to the bearers of the message, not to a building, as today (Luke 14:32; 19:14).

Χριστοῦ, καταλλάγητε τῷ Θεῷ. **21** Τὸν γὰρ μὴ
Christ, be reconciled - to God. [4]the [5]*One* [1]For [6]not
Him who did

γνόντα ἁμαρτίαν, ὑπὲρ ἡμῶν ἁμαρτίαν ἐποίησεν, ἵνα ἡμεῖς
[7]knowing [8]sin, [12]for [13]us [9]*to* [10]*be* [11]sin [2]He [3]made, so that we
not know

γενώμεθα δικαιοσύνη Θεοῦ ἐν αὐτῷ.
might become *the* righteousness of God in Him.

The Minister's Authentication

6 **1** Συνεργοῦντες δὲ καὶ παρακαλοῦμεν μὴ εἰς
[2]working [3]together [4]*with* [5]*Him* [1]And also ˜ we urge [2]not [9]in

κενὸν τὴν χάριν τοῦ Θεοῦ δέξασθαι ὑμᾶς — **2** λέγει γάρ,
[10]vain [5]the [6]grace - [7]of [8]God [3]to [4]receive [1]you — [2]He [3]says [1]for,
receive that you —

«Καιρῷ δεκτῷ ἐπήκουσά σου,
«[4]In [5]a(n) [7]time [6]acceptable I heard you,

Καὶ ἐν ἡμέρᾳ σωτηρίας ἐβοήθησά σοι.» [a]
And in a day of salvation I helped you.»

Ἰδού, νῦν «καιρὸς εὐπρόσδεκτος,» ἰδού, νῦν
Behold, now *is the* «time ˜ acceptable,» behold, now *is the*

«ἡμέρα σωτηρίας» — **3** μηδεμίαν ἐν μηδενὶ διδόντες
«day of salvation» — [2]no [6]in [7]nothing [1]giving
at all we give

προσκοπήν, ἵνα μὴ μωμηθῇ ἡ διακονία, **4** ἀλλ' ἐν
[3]occasion [4]for [5]offense, that [3]not [4]be [5]blamed [1]the [2]ministry, but in
lest

παντὶ συνιστῶντες ἑαυτοὺς ὡς Θεοῦ διάκονοι, ἐν ὑπομονῇ
every*thing* recommending ourselves as [2]of [3]God [1]ministers, in endurance ˜
commending

πολλῇ, ἐν θλίψεσιν, ἐν ἀνάγκαις, ἐν στενοχωρίαις, **5** ἐν
much, in afflictions, in calamities, in distresses, in
hardships,

πληγαῖς, ἐν φυλακαῖς, ἐν ἀκαταστασίαις, ἐν κόποις, ἐν
strokes, in imprisonments, in disturbances, in labors, in

ἀγρυπνίαις, ἐν νηστείαις, **6** ἐν ἁγνότητι, ἐν γνώσει, ἐν
sleepless nights, in fastings, in purity, in knowledge, in

μακροθυμίᾳ, ἐν χρηστότητι, ἐν Πνεύματι Ἁγίῳ, ἐν ἀγάπῃ
patience, in kindness, in *the* Spirit ˜ Holy, in love ˜

ἀνυποκρίτῳ, **7** ἐν λόγῳ ἀληθείας, ἐν δυνάμει Θεοῦ, διὰ
unhypocritical, in *the* word of truth, in *the* power of God, through

τῶν ὅπλων τῆς δικαιοσύνης τῶν δεξιῶν καὶ ἀριστερῶν,
the weapons - of righteousness of the right *parts* and of *the* left *parts*,
on the right hand on the left hand,

8 διὰ δόξης καὶ ἀτιμίας, διὰ δυσφημίας καὶ εὐφημίας·
through glory and dishonor, through ill repute and good repute;

ὡς πλάνοι καὶ ἀληθεῖς, **9** ὡς ἀγνοούμενοι καὶ
as deceivers and yet true, as being not known and
unknown

ἐπιγινωσκόμενοι,* ὡς ἀποθνῄσκοντες καὶ ἰδού, ζῶμεν, ὡς
being well known, as dying and behold, we live, as

παιδευόμενοι καὶ μὴ θανατούμενοι, **10** ὡς λυπούμενοι
being disciplined and not being put to death, as being sorrowful

ἀεὶ δὲ χαίροντες, ὡς πτωχοὶ πολλοὺς δὲ πλουτίζοντες, ὡς
always ˜ but rejoicing, as poor [3]many [1]but [2]making [4]rich, as

μηδὲν ἔχοντες καὶ πάντα κατέχοντες.
nothing ˜ having and [2]all [3]*things* [1]possessing.

half, be reconciled to God.
21 For He made Him who
knew no sin *to be* sin for us, that
we might become the righ-
teousness of God in Him.

6 We then, *as* workers together *with Him* also
plead with *you* not to receive
the grace of God in vain.
2 For He says:

"In an acceptable time I
have heard you,
And in the day of
salvation I have helped
you."

Behold, now *is* the accepted
time; behold, now *is* the day of
salvation.
3 We give no offense in anything, that our ministry may not
be blamed.
4 But in all *things* we commend ourselves as ministers of
God: in much patience, in tribulations, in needs, in distresses,
5 in stripes, in imprisonments, in tumults, in labors, in
sleeplessness, in fastings;
6 by purity, by knowledge, by
longsuffering, by kindness, by
the Holy Spirit, by sincere love,
7 by the word of truth, by
the power of God, by the armor
of righteousness on the right
hand and on the left,
8 by honor and dishonor, by
evil report and good report; as
deceivers, and *yet* true;
9 as unknown, and *yet* well
known; as dying, and behold we
live; as chastened, and *yet* not
killed;
10 as sorrowful, yet always
rejoicing; as poor, yet making
many rich; as having nothing,
and *yet* possessing all things.

---

[a](**6:2**) Is. 49:8

***(6:9)** *ἐπιγινώσκω (epiginōskō).* Verb, common in the NT with a variety of meanings, especially *know, understand, recognize.* Here the form is intensive, suggesting *know exactly, completely* (as also 1 Cor. 13:12). Sometimes the verb means *recognize* (as Luke 24:16) or *acknowledge* (as 1 Cor. 16:18), sometimes *learn, find out* (as Luke 7:37) or *come to know* (2 Pet. 2:21). Cf. the cognate noun *ἐπίγνωσις, knowledge.* Some interpreters have suggested that in the Pastorals (1 Tim. 2:4; 4:3; 2 Tim. 2:25; 3:7; Titus 1:1) and 2 Peter (2 Pet. 1:2, 3, 8: 2:20, 21) these words reflect Christian

11 O Corinthians! We have spoken openly to you, our heart is wide open.
12 You are not restricted by us, but you are restricted by your *own* affections.
13 Now in return for the same (I speak as to children), you also be open.
14 Do not be unequally yoked together with unbelievers. For what fellowship has righteousness with lawlessness? And what communion has light with darkness?
15 And what accord has Christ with Belial? Or what part has a believer with an unbeliever?
16 And what agreement has the temple of God with idols? For you are the temple of the living God. As God has said:

"I will dwell in them
And walk among them.
I will be their God,
And they shall be My people."

17 Therefore

"Come out from among them
And be separate, says the Lord.
Do not touch what is unclean,
And I will receive you."
18 *"I will be a Father to you,*
And you shall be My sons and daughters,
Says the LORD Almighty."

7 Therefore, having these promises, beloved, let us cleanse ourselves from all filthiness of the flesh and spirit, per-

---

[b](**6:16**) NU reads Ημεις, we. [c](**6:16**) Lev. 26:12; Jer. 32:38; Ezek. 37:27
[d](**6:17**) Is. 52:11; Ezek. 20:34, 41 [e](**6:18**) 2 Sam. 7:14; Is. 43:6; Jer. 31:9

---

reaction against incipient Gnosticism and imply the true knowledge of Christ as opposed to false claims of knowledge.

The Unequal Yoke: Be Holy

11 Τὸ στόμα ἡμῶν ἀνέῳγε πρὸς ὑμᾶς, Κορίνθιοι, ἡ
- mouth ˜ Our has opened to you, *O* Corinthians, -

καρδία ἡμῶν πεπλάτυνται. **12** Οὐ στενοχωρεῖσθε ἐν
heart ˜ our has been opened wide. [3]not [1]You [2]are restricted by

ἡμῖν, στενοχωρεῖσθε δὲ ἐν τοῖς σπλάγχνοις ὑμῶν.
us, [2]you [3]are [4]restricted [1]but by - [3]inward [4]parts [1]your [2]*own*.
affections

13 Τὴν δὲ αὐτὴν ἀντιμισθίαν — ὡς τέκνοις λέγω —
[2]*in* [3]the [1]Now same exchange — [3]as [4]to [5]children [1]I [2]speak —
Now in return for the same —

πλατύνθητε καὶ ὑμεῖς.
[8]be [9]opened [10]wide [7]also [6]you.

14 Μὴ γίνεσθε ἑτεροζυγοῦντες ἀπίστοις· τίς γὰρ
not ˜ Do be unevenly yoked with unbelieving *ones*; what ˜ for
mismated with unbelievers;

μετοχὴ δικαιοσύνῃ καὶ ἀνομίᾳ? Τίς δὲ
sharing *is there* for righteousness and lawlessness? what ˜ And
participation with

κοινωνία φωτὶ πρὸς σκότος? **15** Τίς δὲ
fellowship *is there* for light with darkness? what ˜ And
communion

συμφώνησις Χριστῷ πρὸς Βελιάρ? Ἢ τίς μερὶς
agreement *is there* for Christ with Belial? Or what part *is there*

πιστῷ μετὰ ἀπίστου? **16** Τίς δὲ
for a believing *one* with an unbelieving *one*? what ˜ And
believer unbeliever?

συγκατάθεσις ναῷ Θεοῦ μετὰ εἰδώλων? Ὑμεῖς[b] γὰρ
union *is there* for *the* temple of God with idols? you ˜ For

ναὸς Θεοῦ ἐστε ζῶντος, καθὼς εἶπεν ὁ Θεὸς ὅτι
[2]*the* [3]temple [4]of [5]*the* [7]God [1]are [6]living, just as said ˜ - God -

«Ἐνοικήσω ἐν αὐτοῖς καὶ ἐμπεριπατήσω,
«I will dwell in them and walk among *them*,

Καὶ ἔσομαι αὐτῶν Θεός,
And I will be their God,

Καὶ αὐτοὶ ἔσονταί μοι λαός.»[c]
And they will be to Me a people.»
My

17 Διὸ «Ἐξέλθετε ἐκ μέσου αὐτῶν
Therefore «Come out from *the* midst of them

Καὶ ἀφορίσθητε,» λέγει Κύριος,
And be separated,» says *the* Lord,

«Καὶ ἀκαθάρτου μὴ ἅπτεσθε·
«And [4]*anything* [5]unclean [2]not [1]do [3]touch;
ceremonially impure

Κἀγὼ εἰσδέξομαι ὑμᾶς.»[d]
And I will receive you.»

18 Καὶ «Ἔσομαι ὑμῖν εἰς Πατέρα,
And «I will be to you for a Father,
as

Καὶ ὑμεῖς ἔσεσθέ μοι εἰς υἱοὺς καὶ θυγατέρας, λέγει
And you will be to Me for sons and daughters, says
as

Κύριος Παντοκράτωρ.»[e]
the Lord Almighty.»

7 **1** Ταύτας οὖν ἔχοντες τὰς ἐπαγγελίας, ἀγαπητοί,
[3]these [1]Therefore [2]having - promises, beloved *ones*,

καθαρίσωμεν ἑαυτοὺς ἀπὸ παντὸς μολυσμοῦ σαρκὸς καὶ
let us cleanse ourselves from all defilement of flesh and

πνεύματος, ἐπιτελοῦντες ἁγιωσύνην ἐν φόβῳ Θεοῦ.
of spirit, completing holiness in *the* fear of God.
perfecting

Paul Rejoices Over the Corinthians' Repentance

2 Χωρήσατε ἡμᾶς· οὐδένα ἠδικήσαμεν, οὐδένα
Make room for us *in your hearts;* [3]no [4]one [1]we [2]wronged, [7]no [8]one

ἐφθείραμεν, οὐδένα ἐπλεονεκτήσαμεν. 3 Οὐ πρὸς
[5]we [6]corrupted, [13]no [14]one [9]we [10]took [11]advantage [12]of. [3]not [5]for
to

κατάκρισιν λέγω, προείρηκα γὰρ ὅτι ἐν ταῖς
[6]*your* [7]condemnation [1]I [2]do [4]speak, [9]I [10]have [11]said [12]before [8]for that [3]in -
condemn you

καρδίαις ἡμῶν ἐστε εἰς τὸ συναποθανεῖν καὶ συζῆν.
[5]hearts [4]our [1]you [2]are for - to die together and to live together.
so that we we

4 Πολλή μοι παρρησία πρὸς ὑμᾶς, πολλή μοι καύχησις
Much to me *is* confidence toward you, much to me *is* boasting
Great is my great is my

ὑπὲρ ὑμῶν· πεπλήρωμαι τῇ παρακλήσει,
concerning you; I have been filled - with comfort,

ὑπερπερισσεύομαι τῇ χαρᾷ ἐπὶ πάσῃ τῇ θλίψει ἡμῶν.
I am overflowing - with joy in all - tribulation ˜ our.

5 Καὶ γὰρ ἐλθόντων ἡμῶν εἰς Μακεδονίαν οὐδεμίαν
indeed ˜ For coming ˜ we into Macedonia [4]no
when we came

ἔσχηκεν ἄνεσιν ἡ σάρξ ἡμῶν, ἀλλ' ἐν παντὶ θλιβόμενοι·
[3]had [5]rest - [2]flesh [1]our, but in every*thing* being afflicted;
we were

ἔξωθεν μάχαι, ἔσωθεν φόβοι. 6 Ἀλλ' ὁ
outside *were* disputes, inside *were* fears. But the *One*

παρακαλῶν τοὺς ταπεινοὺς παρεκάλεσεν ἡμᾶς, ὁ Θεός, ἐν τῇ
comforting the lowly comforted us, - God, by the
who comforts

παρουσίᾳ Τίτου· 7 οὐ μόνον δὲ ἐν τῇ παρουσίᾳ αὐτοῦ,
coming of Titus; [2]not [3]only [1]and by - coming ˜ his,

ἀλλὰ καὶ ἐν τῇ παρακλήσει ᾗ παρεκλήθη ἐφ' ὑμῖν,
but also by the consolation with which he was comforted over you,

ἀναγγέλλων ἡμῖν τὴν ὑμῶν ἐπιπόθησιν, τὸν ὑμῶν ὀδυρμόν, τὸν
reporting to us - your longing, - your mourning, -
as he reported

ὑμῶν ζῆλον ὑπὲρ ἐμοῦ, ὥστε με μᾶλλον χαρῆναι.
your zeal in behalf of me, so that me [3]more [1]to [2]rejoice.
I rejoiced even more.

8 Ὅτι εἰ καὶ ἐλύπησα ὑμᾶς ἐν τῇ ἐπιστολῇ, οὐ
Because if ˜ even I caused sorrow ˜ you in the letter, [3]not

μεταμέλομαι,* εἰ καὶ μετεμελόμην. βλέπω γὰρ ὅτι ἡ
[1]I [2]do regret *it,* if ˜ even I did regret *it.* [2]I [3]see [1]For that -

ἐπιστολὴ ἐκείνη, εἰ καὶ πρὸς ὥραν, ἐλύπησεν ὑμᾶς.
letter ˜ that, if ˜ even for an hour, caused sorrow ˜ you.
a while,

9 Νῦν χαίρω, οὐχ ὅτι ἐλυπήθητε, ἀλλ' ὅτι
Now I rejoice, not because you were caused sorrow, but because

ἐλυπήθητε εἰς μετάνοιαν· ἐλυπήθητε γὰρ
you were caused sorrow to repentance; [2]you [3]were [4]caused [5]sorrow [1]for

κατὰ Θεόν, ἵνα ἐν μηδενὶ ζημιωθῆτε ἐξ ἡμῶν.
according to God, that in nothing you might suffer loss from us.
in a godly manner,

fecting holiness in the fear of God.
2 Open *your hearts* to us. We have wronged no one, we have corrupted no one, we have cheated no one.
3 I do not say *this* to condemn; for I have said before that you are in our hearts, to die together and to live together.
4 Great *is* my boldness of speech toward you, great *is* my boasting on your behalf. I am filled with comfort. I am exceedingly joyful in all our tribulation.
5 For indeed, when we came to Macedonia, our bodies had no rest, but we were troubled on every side. Outside *were* conflicts, inside *were* fears.
6 Nevertheless God, who comforts the downcast, comforted us by the coming of Titus,
7 and not only by his coming, but also by the consolation with which he was comforted in you, when he told us of your earnest desire, your mourning, your zeal for me, so that I rejoiced even more.
8 For even if I made you sorry with my letter, I do not regret it; though I did regret it. For I perceive that the same epistle made you sorry, though only for a while.
9 Now I rejoice, not that you were made sorry, but that your sorrow led to repentance. For you were made sorry in a godly manner, that you might suffer loss from us in nothing.

***(7:8)** *μεταμέλομαι (metamelomai).* Verb meaning *regret, have remorse.* It may be compared to the near synonym *μετανοέω, repent,* which the NT always uses of repentance to salvation. Whereas *μετανοέω* literally indicates a change (*μετά*) in one's way of thinking (*νοέω*), *μεταμέλομαι* views it more as a change in one's feelings, cares, or concerns (*μέλω*). The terms, however, are essentially synonymous, and can just as surely indicate genuine change. Matthew uses the word of Judas (Matt. 21:29, 32; 27:3), and it is used once of God (Heb. 7:21).

10 For godly sorrow produces repentance *leading* to salvation, not to be regretted; but the sorrow of the world produces death.
11 For observe this very thing, that you sorrowed in a godly manner: What diligence it produced in you, *what* clearing *of yourselves, what* indignation, *what* fear, *what* vehement desire, *what* zeal, *what* vindication! In all *things* you proved yourselves to be clear in this matter.
12 Therefore, although I wrote to you, *I did* not *do it* for the sake of him who had done the wrong, nor for the sake of him who suffered wrong, but that our care for you in the sight of God might appear to you.
13 Therefore we have been comforted in your comfort. And we rejoiced exceedingly more for the joy of Titus, because his spirit has been refreshed by you all.
14 For if in anything I have boasted to him about you, I am not ashamed. But as we spoke all things to you in truth, even so our boasting to Titus was found true.
15 And his affections are greater for you as he remembers the obedience of you all, how with fear and trembling you received him.
16 Therefore I rejoice that I have confidence in you in everything.

---

[a](7:11) NU omits υμας, *you.* [b](7:13) NU reads ημων, *our.*

10 Ἡ γὰρ κατὰ Θεὸν λύπη μετάνοιαν εἰς σωτηρίαν
the ~ For [2]according [3]to [4]God [1]sorrow [6]repentance [7]to [8]salvation
godly sorrow

ἀμεταμέλητον κατεργάζεται· ἡ δὲ τοῦ κόσμου λύπη
[9]without [10]regret [5]produces; the ~ but [2]of [3]the [4]world [1]sorrow
worldly sorrow

θάνατον κατεργάζεται. **11** Ἰδοὺ γὰρ αὐτὸ τοῦτο, τὸ
death ~ produces. behold ~ For very ~ this *thing,* -
that

κατὰ Θεὸν λυπηθῆναι ὑμᾶς,[a] πόσην
according to God to be caused sorrow you, how much
you were caused sorrow in a godly manner,

κατειργάσατο ὑμῖν σπουδήν, ἀλλὰ ἀπολογίαν, ἀλλὰ
[2]it [3]produced [4]in [5]you [1]diligence, even a defense *of yourselves,* even
an eagerness to defend

ἀγανάκτησιν, ἀλλὰ φόβον, ἀλλὰ ἐπιπόθησιν, ἀλλὰ ζῆλον,
indignation, even fear, even longing, even zeal,

ἀλλὰ ἐκδίκησιν. Ἐν παντὶ συνεστήσατε ἑαυτοὺς ἁγνοὺς
even vengeance. In every*thing* you demonstrated yourselves [3]pure

εἶναι ἐν τῷ πράγματι. **12** Ἄρα εἰ καὶ ἔγραψα ὑμῖν, οὐχ
[1]to [2]be in the matter. Then if ~ even I wrote to you, *it was* not
this

εἵνεκεν τοῦ ἀδικήσαντος, οὐδὲ εἵνεκεν τοῦ
for the sake of the *one* doing wrong, nor for the sake of the *one*
him who did the him who

ἀδικηθέντος, ἀλλ' εἵνεκεν τοῦ φανερωθῆναι τὴν
being wronged, but for the sake of - [7]to [8]be [9]made [10]known -
was so that might

σπουδὴν ὑμῶν τὴν ὑπὲρ ἡμῶν πρὸς ὑμᾶς ἐνώπιον τοῦ
[2]diligence [1]your - [3]in [4]behalf [5]of [6]us to you before -

Θεοῦ. **13** Διὰ τοῦτο παρακεκλήμεθα.
God. Because of this we have been comforted.

Paul Rejoices Over the Joy of Titus

Ἐπὶ δὲ τῇ παρακλήσει ὑμῶν[b] περισσοτέρως μᾶλλον
in ~ And - comfort ~ your [3]exceedingly [4]more

ἐχάρημεν ἐπὶ τῇ χαρᾷ Τίτου, ὅτι ἀναπέπαυται τὸ
[1]we [2]rejoiced over the joy of Titus, because [3]has [4]been [5]refreshed -

πνεῦμα αὐτοῦ ἀπὸ πάντων ὑμῶν. **14** Ὅτι εἴ τι αὐτῷ
[2]spirit [1]his by all ~ you. Because if [5]anything [8]to [9]him

ὑπὲρ ὑμῶν κεκαύχημαι, οὐ κατῃσχύνθην,
[6]concerning [7]you [1]I [2]have [3]boasted [4]about, [12]not [10]I [11]was [13]put [14]to [15]shame,

ἀλλ' ὡς πάντα ἐν ἀληθείᾳ ἐλαλήσαμεν ὑμῖν, οὕτω καὶ ἡ
but as [3]all [4]*things* [7]in [8]truth [1]we [2]spoke [5]to [6]you, thus also -

καύχησις ἡμῶν ἡ ἐπὶ Τίτου ἀλήθεια ἐγενήθη. **15** Καὶ τὰ
boasting ~ our - to Titus truth ~ became. And -

σπλάγχνα αὐτοῦ περισσοτέρως εἰς ὑμᾶς ἐστιν,
[2]inward [3]parts [1]his [5]far [6]greater [7]toward [8]you [4]are,
affections

ἀναμιμνησκομένου τὴν πάντων ὑμῶν ὑπακοήν, ὡς μετὰ φόβου
remembering the [2]of [4]all [3]you [1]obedience, how with fear
as he remembers

καὶ τρόμου ἐδέξασθε αὐτόν. **16** Χαίρω ὅτι ἐν παντὶ
and trembling you received him. I rejoice that in every*thing*

θαρρῶ ἐν ὑμῖν.
I am confident in you.
about

Excel in the Grace of Giving

8 1 Γνωρίζομεν δὲ ὑμῖν, ἀδελφοί, τὴν χάριν τοῦ Θεοῦ
[2]we [3]make [4]known [1]Now to you, brothers, the grace - of God

τὴν δεδομένην ἐν ταῖς ἐκκλησίαις τῆς Μακεδονίας,
the *one* having been given in the churches - of Macedonia,
which has to

2 ὅτι ἐν πολλῇ δοκιμῇ θλίψεως ἡ περισσεία τῆς χαρᾶς
that in much ~ a test of affliction the abundance - of joy ~
a great trial

αὐτῶν καὶ ἡ κατὰ βάθους πτωχεία αὐτῶν ἐπερίσσευσεν εἰς
their and - [3]down [4]to [5]a [6]depth [2]poverty [1]their abounded to
extremely deep poverty

τὸν πλοῦτον τῆς ἁπλότητος αὐτῶν. 3 Ὅτι κατὰ
the riches - of generosity ~ their. Because according to

δύναμιν, μαρτυρῶ, καὶ ὑπὲρ δύναμιν αὐθαίρετοι,
their ability, I bear witness, and beyond *their* ability of *their* own accord,
they were freely willing,

4 μετὰ πολλῆς παρακλήσεως δεόμενοι ἡμῶν τὴν χάριν καὶ
with much appeal begging us *for* the grace and

τὴν κοινωνίαν τῆς διακονίας τῆς εἰς τοὺς ἁγίους[a] — 5 καὶ
the fellowship of the ministry - to the saints — and

οὐ καθὼς ἠλπίσαμεν, ἀλλ' ἑαυτοὺς ἔδωκαν πρῶτον τῷ
not as we hoped, but [3]themselves [1]they [2]gave first to the

Κυρίῳ καὶ ἡμῖν διὰ θελήματος Θεοῦ, 6 εἰς τὸ παρακαλέσαι
Lord and to us by *the* will of God, for - [2]to [3]urge
so that we

ἡμᾶς Τίτον, ἵνα καθὼς προενήρξατο, οὕτω καὶ ἐπιτελέσῃ
[1]us Titus, that just as he previously began, thus [3]also [1]he [2]would finish
urged had begun before,

εἰς ὑμᾶς καὶ τὴν χάριν ταύτην. 7 Ἀλλ' ὥσπερ ἐν παντὶ
in you [3]also - [2]grace [1]this. But as indeed in every*thing*

περισσεύετε, πίστει καὶ λόγῳ καὶ γνώσει καὶ πάσῃ
you abound, in faith and in word and in knowledge and in all

σπουδῇ καὶ τῇ ἐξ ὑμῶν ἐν ἡμῖν[b] ἀγάπῃ, ἵνα καὶ ἐν
diligence and in the [2]from [3]you [4]to [5]us [1]love, *see* that also in
your love for us,

ταύτῃ τῇ χάριτι περισσεύητε.
this - grace you abound.

Christ: Our Pattern for Generous Giving

8 Οὐ κατ' ἐπιταγὴν λέγω, ἀλλὰ διὰ τῆς
[3]not [4]by [5]a [6]command [1]I [2]speak, but by means of the

ἑτέρων σπουδῆς καὶ τὸ τῆς ὑμετέρας ἀγάπης γνήσιον
[2]of [3]others [1]diligence also [2]the - [4]of [5]your [6]love [3]genuineness

δοκιμάζων. 9 Γινώσκετε γὰρ τὴν χάριν τοῦ Κυρίου ἡμῶν
[1]testing. [2]you [3]know [1]For the grace - of Lord ~ our
I am testing.

Ἰησοῦ Χριστοῦ, ὅτι δι' ὑμᾶς ἐπτώχευσε, πλούσιος
Jesus Christ, that for the sake of you He became poor, rich ~
although

ὤν, ἵνα ὑμεῖς τῇ ἐκείνου πτωχείᾳ
being, in order that you by the [2]of [3]that [4]one [1]poverty
He was rich, His

πλουτήσητε. 10 Καὶ γνώμην ἐν τούτῳ δίδωμι. Τοῦτο γὰρ
might become rich. And [3]*my* [4]opinion [5]in [6]this [1]I [2]give. this ~ For

ὑμῖν συμφέρει, οἵτινες οὐ μόνον τὸ ποιῆσαι ἀλλὰ καὶ τὸ
[3]for [4]you [1]is [2]profitable, who not only - [3]to [4]do [5]*this* [6]but [7]also -
doing

8 Moreover, brethren, we make known to you the grace of God bestowed on the churches of Macedonia:
2 that in a great trial of affliction the abundance of their joy and their deep poverty abounded in the riches of their liberality.
3 For I bear witness that according to *their* ability, yes, and beyond *their* ability, *they were* freely willing,
4 imploring us with much urgency that we would receive the gift and the fellowship of the ministering to the saints.
5 And not *only* as we had hoped, but they first gave themselves to the Lord, and *then* to us by the will of God.
6 So we urged Titus, that as he had begun, so he would also complete this grace in you as well.
7 But as you abound in everything—in faith, in speech, in knowledge, in all diligence, and in your love for us—*see* that you abound in this grace also.
8 I speak not by commandment, but I am testing the sincerity of your love by the diligence of others.
9 For you know the grace of our Lord Jesus Christ, that though He was rich, yet for your sakes He became poor, that you through His poverty might become rich.
10 And in this I give advice: It is to your advantage not only to be doing what you began and

---

[a](8:4) TR adds δεξασθαι ημας, *that we would receive (the grace and the fellowship).*

[b](8:7) For υμων εν ημιν, *(from) you to us,* NU reads ημων εν υμιν, *(from) us to you.*

were desiring to do a year ago;
11 but now you also must complete the doing *of it;* that as *there was* a readiness to desire *it,* so *there* also *may be* a completion out of what *you* have.
12 For if there is first a willing mind, *it is* accepted according to what one has, *and* not according to what he does not have.
13 For *I do* not *mean* that others should be eased and you burdened;
14 but by an equality, *that* now at this time your abundance *may supply* their lack, that their abundance also may supply your lack—that there may be equality.
15 As it is written, *"He who gathered much had nothing left over, and he who gathered little had no lack."*
16 But thanks *be* to God who puts the same earnest care for you into the heart of Titus.
17 For he not only accepted the exhortation, but being more diligent, he went to you of his own accord.
18 And we have sent with him the brother whose praise *is* in the gospel throughout all the churches,
19 and not only *that,* but who was also chosen by the churches to travel with us with this gift, which is administered by us to the glory of the Lord Himself and *to show* your ready mind,
20 avoiding this: that anyone should blame us in this lavish

θέλειν προενήρξασθε ἀπὸ πέρυσι. **11** Νυνὶ δὲ καὶ τὸ
[8]to [9]desire [1]previously [2]began from last year. now ˜ And also -
desired to since

ποιῆσαι ἐπιτελέσατε, ὅπως καθάπερ ἡ προθυμία τοῦ
[2]to [3]do [4]*it* [1]complete, that as indeed *there was* the readiness -
doing

θέλειν, οὕτω καὶ τὸ ἐπιτελέσαι ἐκ τοῦ ἔχειν.
to desire *it,* thus also *there may be* - to complete out of - to have.
the completion from what you have.

12 Εἰ γὰρ ἡ προθυμία πρόκειται, καθὸ ἐὰν ἔχῃ τις,
if ˜ For the readiness is present, according as - has ˜ anyone,
is set forth,

εὐπρόσδεκτος, οὐ καθὸ οὐκ ἔχει. **13** Οὐ
it is acceptable, not according as [3]not [1]he [2]does have. [2]*I* [3]*do* [4]not [5]*mean*

γὰρ ἵνα ἄλλοις ἄνεσις, ὑμῖν δὲ θλῖψις·
[1]For that for others *to have* relief, [2]for [3]you [1]and affliction;
difficult circumstances;

14 ἀλλ' ἐξ ἰσότητος, ἐν τῷ νῦν καιρῷ τὸ ὑμῶν
but *that* from equality, at the now time - your
by way of present

περίσσευμα εἰς τὸ ἐκείνων ὑστέρημα, ἵνα καὶ τὸ ἐκείνων
abundance *may be* for the [2]of [3]those [1]need, that also the [2]of [3]those
their their

περίσσευμα γένηται εἰς τὸ ὑμῶν ὑστέρημα, ὅπως
[1]abundance may come to be for - your need, in order that

γένηται ἰσότης· **15** καθὼς γέγραπται,
there may be equality; just as it is written,

«Ὁ τὸ πολὺ οὐκ ἐπλεόνασε,
«The *one who gathered* - much not ˜ did have too much,

Καὶ ὁ τὸ ὀλίγον οὐκ ἠλαττόνησε.»[c]
And the *one who gathered* - little not ˜ did have too little.»

The Collection for the Saints in Judea

16 Χάρις δὲ τῷ Θεῷ τῷ διδόντι[d] τὴν αὐτὴν
thanks ˜ Now - *be* to God the One giving the same
who gives

σπουδὴν ὑπὲρ ὑμῶν ἐν τῇ καρδίᾳ Τίτου. **17** Ὅτι τὴν
earnestness concerning you in the heart of Titus. Because [3]the
my

μὲν παράκλησιν ἐδέξατο, σπουδαιότερος δὲ ὑπάρχων,
- [4]appeal [1]he [2]received, [7]more [8]earnest [5]but [6]being,
accepted, diligent

αὐθαίρετος ἐξῆλθε πρὸς ὑμᾶς. **18** Συνεπέμψαμεν δὲ μετ'
of *his* own accord he came to you. [2]we [3]sent [4]together [1]And with

αὐτοῦ τὸν ἀδελφὸν οὗ ὁ ἔπαινος ἐν τῷ εὐαγγελίῳ διὰ
him the brother whose - praise *is* in the gospel through

πασῶν τῶν ἐκκλησιῶν **19** — οὐ μόνον δέ, ἀλλὰ καὶ
all the churches — [2]not [3]only [4]*so* [1]and, but [3]also

χειροτονηθεὶς ὑπὸ τῶν ἐκκλησιῶν συνέκδημος ἡμῶν
[1]having [2]been [4]chosen by the churches *as* [2]traveling [3]companion [1]our
who was

σὺν τῇ χάριτι ταύτῃ τῇ διακονουμένῃ ὑφ' ἡμῶν πρὸς τὴν
with - grace ˜ this the *one* being served by us to the
gift which is ministered

αὐτοῦ τοῦ Κυρίου δόξαν καὶ προθυμίαν ἡμῶν —
[5]Himself [2]of [3]the [4]Lord [1]glory and *to show* readiness ˜ our —

20 στελλόμενοι τοῦτο, μή τις ἡμᾶς μωμήσηται ἐν τῇ
avoiding this, lest anyone [3]us [1]should [2]blame in -

---

[c](8:15) Ex. 16:18
[d](8:16) NU reads δοντι, *having given,* thus *(who) gave.*

ἁδρότητι ταύτῃ τῇ διακονουμένῃ ὑφ᾽ ἡμῶν·
abundance ~ this the *one* being served by us;
which is ministered

21 προνοούμενοι[e] καλὰ οὐ μόνον ἐνώπιον Κυρίου ἀλλὰ
having regard for good *things* not only before *the* Lord but
honorable

καὶ ἐνώπιον ἀνθρώπων. 22 Συνεπέμψαμεν δὲ αὐτοῖς τὸν
also before men. [2]we [3]sent [4]together [1]And with them -

ἀδελφὸν ἡμῶν ὃν ἐδοκιμάσαμεν ἐν πολλοῖς πολλάκις
brother ~ our whom we [2]approved [5]in [6]many [7]*things* [1]often

σπουδαῖον ὄντα, νυνὶ δὲ πολὺ σπουδαιότερον,
[4]diligent [3]being, now ~ but *being* much more diligent,
as being,

πεποιθήσει πολλῇ τῇ εἰς ὑμᾶς. 23 Εἴτε ὑπὲρ
by *his* confidence ~ great - in you. If *anyone asks* concerning

Τίτου, κοινωνὸς ἐμὸς καὶ εἰς ὑμᾶς συνεργός· εἴτε ἀδελφοὶ
Titus, *he is* partner ~ my and [3]for [4]you [1]fellow [2]worker; or brothers ~

ἡμῶν, ἀπόστολοι ἐκκλησιῶν, δόξα Χριστοῦ. 24 Τὴν
our, *they are* messengers of *the* churches, *the* glory of Christ. [5]the

οὖν ἔνδειξιν τῆς ἀγάπης ὑμῶν, καὶ ἡμῶν καυχήσεως
[1]Therefore [6]proof - [7]of [9]love [8]your, [10]and [12]our [11]of [13]boasting

ὑπὲρ ὑμῶν, εἰς αὐτοὺς ἐνδείξασθε[f] εἰς πρόσωπον τῶν
[14]concerning [15]you, [3]to [4]them [2]show in *the* face of the
before

ἐκκλησιῶν.
churches.

Faithful Brethren Administer the Gift

9 1 Περὶ μὲν γὰρ τῆς διακονίας τῆς εἰς τοὺς ἁγίους
concerning ~ - For the ministry - to the saints

περισσόν μοί ἐστι τὸ γράφειν ὑμῖν. 2 Οἶδα γὰρ τὴν
[3]unnecessary [4]for [5]me [1]it [2]is - to write to you. [2]I [3]know [1]For -

προθυμίαν ὑμῶν ἣν ὑπὲρ ὑμῶν καυχῶμαι
readiness ~ your which [3]concerning [4]you [1]I [2]boast

Μακεδόσιν, ὅτι Ἀχαΐα παρεσκεύασται ἀπὸ πέρυσι, καὶ
to *the* Macedonians, that Achaia has been prepared from last year, and
since

ὁ ἐξ ὑμῶν ζῆλος ἠρέθισε τοὺς πλείονας. 3 Ἔπεμψα δὲ
the [2]from [3]you [1]zeal aroused the majority. [2]I [3]sent [1]And
your zeal has aroused

τοὺς ἀδελφούς, ἵνα μὴ τὸ καύχημα ἡμῶν τὸ ὑπὲρ ὑμῶν
the brothers, that not - boasting ~ our - about you
lest

κενωθῇ ἐν τῷ μέρει τούτῳ, ἵνα καθὼς ἔλεγον,
be made empty in - matter ~ this, that just as I said,
lose its justification

παρεσκευασμένοι ἦτε, 4 μή πως, ἐὰν ἔλθωσι σὺν
[4]prepared [1]you [2]may [3]be, lest perhaps, if *some* [2]come [3]with

ἐμοὶ Μακεδόνες καὶ εὕρωσιν ὑμᾶς ἀπαρασκευάστους,
[4]me [1]Macedonians and find you unprepared,

καταισχυνθῶμεν ἡμεῖς (ἵνα μὴ λέγωμεν[a] ὑμεῖς!) ἐν τῇ
[2]should [3]be [4]ashamed [1]we (that [3]not [1]we [2]would say you!) in -
(not to mention

ὑποστάσει ταύτῃ τῆς καυχήσεως.[b] 5 Ἀναγκαῖον οὖν
confidence this - of boasting. [5]necessary [1]Therefore
this confident boasting.

ἡγησάμην παρακαλέσαι τοὺς ἀδελφούς, ἵνα
[2]I [3]considered [4]it to urge the brothers, that

gift which is administered by us—
21 providing honorable things, not only in the sight of the Lord, but also in the sight of men.
22 And we have sent with them our brother whom we have often proved diligent in many things, but now much more diligent, because of the great confidence which *we have* in you.
23 If *anyone inquires* about Titus, *he is* my partner and fellow worker concerning you. Or if our brethren *are inquired about, they are* messengers of the churches, the glory of Christ.
24 Therefore show to them, and before the churches the proof of your love and of our boasting on your behalf.

9 Now concerning the ministering to the saints, it is superfluous for me to write to you;
2 for I know your willingness, about which I boast of you to the Macedonians, that Achaia was ready a year ago; and your zeal has stirred up the majority.
3 Yet I have sent the brethren, lest our boasting of you should be in vain in this respect, that, as I said, you may be ready;
4 lest if *some* Macedonians come with me and find you unprepared, we (not to mention you!) should be ashamed of this confident boasting.
5 Therefore I thought it necessary to exhort the brethren

[e](8:21) NU reads *προνοουμεν γαρ, For we have regard for.*
[f](8:24) TR adds *και, and.*
[a](9:4) NU reads *λεγω, I would (not) say.*
[b](9:4) NU omits *της καυχησεως, of boasting.*

to go to you ahead of time, and
prepare your generous gift beforehand, which *you had* previously promised, that it may be
ready as *a matter of* generosity
and not as a grudging obligation.
6 But this *I say:* He who
sows sparingly will also reap
sparingly, and he who sows
bountifully will also reap bountifully.
7 *So let* each one *give* as he
purposes in his heart, not
grudgingly or of necessity; for
God loves a cheerful giver.
8 And God *is* able to make all
grace abound toward you, that
you, always having all sufficiency in all *things,* may have an
abundance for every good
work.
9 As it is written:

"He has dispersed abroad,
He has given to the poor;
His righteousness endures
forever."

10 Now may He who supplies
seed to the sower, and bread
for food, supply and multiply
the seed you have *sown* and increase the fruits of your righteousness,
11 while *you are* enriched in
everything for all liberality,
which causes thanksgiving
through us to God.
12 For the administration of
this service not only supplies
the needs of the saints, but also
is abounding through many
thanksgivings to God,
13 while, through the proof of
this ministry, they glorify God
for the obedience of your con-

προέλθωσιν εἰς ὑμᾶς καὶ προκαταρτίσωσι τὴν
they should go before *me* to you and should arrange in advance -

προκατηγγελμένην εὐλογίαν ὑμῶν, ταύτην ἑτοίμην
[3]having [4]been [5]previously [6]promised [2]blessing [1]your, *that* this [3]ready
which you bountiful gift

εἶναι, οὕτως ὡς εὐλογίαν καὶ μὴ ὡς πλεονεξίαν.
[1]to [2]be, thus as a blessing and not as greediness.
would bountiful gift grudgingly given.

God Loves a Cheerful Giver

6 Τοῦτο δέ, ὁ σπείρων φειδομένως, φειδομένως
this ˜ Now *I say,* the *one* sowing sparingly, [4]sparingly
who sows

καὶ θερίσει, καὶ ὁ σπείρων ἐπ' εὐλογίαις, ἐπ' εὐλογίαις
[2]also [1]will [3]reap, and the *one* sowing for a blessing, [4]for [5]a [6]blessing
who sows bounty, bounty

καὶ θερίσει. 7 Ἕκαστος καθὼς προαιρεῖται τῇ καρδίᾳ,
[2]also [1]will [3]reap. *Let* each *one give* just as he decides in the heart,
his

μὴ ἐκ λύπης ἢ ἐξ ἀνάγκης, ἱλαρὸν γὰρ δότην ἀγαπᾷ ὁ
not of grief or of necessity, [4]a [5]cheerful [1]for [6]giver [3]loves -

Θεός. 8 Δυνατὸς δὲ ὁ Θεὸς πᾶσαν χάριν περισσεῦσαι εἰς
[2]God. [4]able [1]And - [2]God [3]*is* [7]all [8]grace [5]to [6]make [9]abound to
every

ὑμᾶς, ἵνα ἐν παντὶ πάντοτε πᾶσαν αὐτάρκειαν ἔχοντες
you, that in every*thing* always [2]all [3]sufficiency [1]having

περισσεύητε εἰς πᾶν ἔργον ἀγαθόν, 9 καθὼς γέγραπται,
you may abound for every work ˜ good, just as it is written,

«Ἐσκόρπισεν, ἔδωκε τοῖς πένησιν·
«He dispersed, He gave to the poor *people;*
has dispersed, He has given

Ἡ δικαιοσύνη αὐτοῦ μένει εἰς τὸν αἰῶνα.»[c]
- righteousness ˜ His remains into the age.»
forever.»

10 Ὁ δὲ ἐπιχορηγῶν σπέρμα τῷ σπείροντι καὶ
[2]the [3]*One* [1]Now supplying seed to the *one* sowing also
who supplies who sows

ἄρτον εἰς βρῶσιν χορηγήσαι,[d] καὶ πληθύναι[e] τὸν σπόρον
[4]bread [5]for [6]food [1]may [2]He [3]supply, and may He multiply - seed ˜

ὑμῶν καὶ αὐξήσαι τὰ γενήματα τῆς δικαιοσύνης ὑμῶν·
your and increase the fruits - of righteousness ˜ your;

11 ἐν παντὶ πλουτιζόμενοι εἰς πᾶσαν ἁπλότητα, ἥτις
in every*thing* being made rich to all generosity, which

κατεργάζεται δι' ἡμῶν εὐχαριστίαν τῷ Θεῷ. 12 Ὅτι ἡ
produces through us thanksgiving - to God. Because the

διακονία τῆς λειτουργίας ταύτης οὐ μόνον ἐστὶ
ministry - of service ˜ this not only is

προσαναπληροῦσα τὰ ὑστερήματα τῶν ἁγίων, ἀλλὰ καὶ
supplying the needs of the saints, but also

περισσεύουσα διὰ πολλῶν εὐχαριστιῶν τῷ Θεῷ,
is abounding by means of many thanksgivings - to God,

13 διὰ τῆς δοκιμῆς τῆς διακονίας ταύτης
through the proof - of ministry ˜ this
while through approved character

δοξάζοντες τὸν Θεὸν ἐπὶ τῇ ὑποταγῇ τῆς ὁμολογίας ὑμῶν εἰς
glorifying - God for the obedience - of confession ˜ your to
they glorify

c(9:9) Ps. 112:9
d(9:10) NU reads χορηγησει, *will supply.*
e(9:10) NU reads πληθυνει, *will multiply.*

τὸ εὐαγγέλιον τοῦ Χριστοῦ, καὶ ἁπλότητι τῆς κοινωνίας
the gospel - of Christ, and *for the* generosity of the sharing
your

εἰς αὐτοὺς καὶ εἰς πάντας, **14** καὶ αὐτῶν δεήσει ὑπὲρ
toward them and toward all, and their prayer in behalf of

ὑμῶν ἐπιποθούντων ὑμᾶς διὰ τὴν ὑπερβάλλουσαν χάριν
you longing for you because of the surpassing grace
as they long

τοῦ Θεοῦ ἐφ' ὑμῖν. **15** Χάρις δὲ τῷ Θεῷ ἐπὶ τῇ
- of God in you. thanks ˜ And - *be* to God for -

ἀνεκδιηγήτῳ αὐτοῦ δωρεᾷ!
indescribable ˜ His gift!

Paul Defends His Authority

10 **1** Αὐτὸς δὲ ἐγὼ Παῦλος παρακαλῶ ὑμᾶς διὰ τῆς
[4]myself [1]Now [2]I [3]Paul appeal to you by the

πραότητος* καὶ ἐπιεικείας τοῦ Χριστοῦ, ὃς κατὰ
meekness and gentleness - of Christ, *I* who according to
face to

πρόσωπον μὲν ταπεινὸς ἐν ὑμῖν, ἀπὼν δὲ θαρρῶ
face - *am* subservient among you, [2]being [3]absent [1]but am bold
when I am away

εἰς ὑμᾶς. **2** Δέομαι δέ, τὸ μὴ παρὼν θαρρῆσαι
toward you. [2]I [3]plead [1]Now, - *that* [4]not [1]being [2]present [3]to [5]be [6]bold
when I am present I may

τῇ πεποιθήσει ᾗ λογίζομαι τολμῆσαι ἐπί
with the confidence with which I consider to be courageous toward
plan

τινας τοὺς λογιζομένους ἡμᾶς ὡς κατὰ σάρκα
some the *ones* considering us as [2]according [3]to [4]*the* [5]flesh
who consider

περιπατοῦντας. **3** Ἐν σαρκὶ γὰρ περιπατοῦντες, οὐ
[1]walking. [3]in [4]*the* [5]flesh [1]For [2]walking, [8]not
though we walk,

κατὰ σάρκα στρατευόμεθα, **4** τὰ γὰρ ὅπλα
[12]according [13]to [14]*the* [15]flesh [6]we [7]do [9]serve [10]in [11]war, the ˜ For weapons

τῆς στρατείας ἡμῶν οὐ σαρκικά, ἀλλὰ δυνατὰ τῷ Θεῷ
- of campaign ˜ our *are* not fleshly, but powerful - in God
warfare

πρὸς καθαίρεσιν ὀχυρωμάτων, **5** λογισμοὺς καθαιροῦντες καὶ
to *the* destruction of strongholds, reasonings ˜ destroying and

πᾶν ὕψωμα ἐπαιρόμενον κατὰ τῆς γνώσεως τοῦ Θεοῦ, καὶ
every exaltation being lifted up against the knowledge - of God, and
high thing exalting itself

αἰχμαλωτίζοντες πᾶν νόημα εἰς τὴν ὑπακοὴν τοῦ Χριστοῦ,
taking into captivity every thought into the obedience - of Christ,
under

6 καὶ ἐν ἑτοίμῳ ἔχοντες ἐκδικῆσαι πᾶσαν παρακοήν,
and in readiness having to punish all disobedience,
being ready every act of

ὅταν πληρωθῇ ὑμῶν ἡ ὑπακοή.
whenever [3]is [4]completed [1]your - [2]obedience.

The Reality of Paul's Authority

7 Τὰ κατὰ πρόσωπον βλέπετε? Εἴ τις
[5]the [6]*things* [7]according [8]to [9]face [1]Do [2]you [3]look [4]at? If anyone
things as they appear

fession to the gospel of Christ,
and for *your* liberal sharing with
them and all *men,*
14 and by their prayer for you,
who long for you because of the
exceeding grace of God in you.
15 Thanks *be* to God for His
indescribable gift!
10 Now I, Paul, myself
am pleading with you
by the meekness and gentleness of Christ—who in presence *am* lowly among you, but
being absent am bold toward
you.
2 But I beg *you* that when I
am present I may not be bold
with that confidence by which I
intend to be bold against some,
who think of us as if we walked
according to the flesh.
3 For though we walk in the
flesh, we do not war according
to the flesh.
4 For the weapons of our
warfare *are* not carnal but
mighty in God for pulling down
strongholds,
5 casting down arguments
and every high thing that exalts
itself against the knowledge of
God, bringing every thought
into captivity to the obedience
of Christ,
6 and being ready to punish
all disobedience when your obedience is fulfilled.
7 Do you look at things according to the outward appearance? If anyone is convinced in

***(10:1)** *πραΰτης (praytēs); πραότης (praotēs).* Noun meaning *gentleness, meekness, courtesy,* perhaps even *submissiveness.* The basic sense is a meek submitting to the treatment one receives, especially from God, but also from others because one is submitted to God. This virtue arises from one's "humility" (see *ταπεινοφροσύνη* at Acts 20:19), a proper sense of oneself as of less importance before God. Here in 2 Cor. 10:1 Christ is our example of "meekness and gentleness" (*ἐπιείκεια*). We are to show meekness to all men (Titus 3:2). Cf. the cognate adjective *πραΰς (πρᾶος), meek, gentle, considerate, unassuming* (Matt. 11:29; 1 Pet. 3:4).

himself that he is Christ's, let
him again consider this in himself, that just as he *is* Christ's,
even so we *are* Christ's.
8 For even if I should boast
somewhat more about our authority, which the Lord gave us
for edification and not for your
destruction, I shall not be
ashamed—
9 lest I seem to terrify you
by letters.
10 "For *his* letters," they say,
"*are* weighty and powerful, but
his bodily presence *is* weak,
and *his* speech contemptible."
11 Let such a person consider
this, that what we are in word
by letters when we are absent,
such *we will* also *be* in deed
when we are present.
12 For we dare not class ourselves or compare ourselves
with those who commend
themselves. But they, measuring themselves by themselves,
and comparing themselves
among themselves, are not
wise.
13 We, however, will not
boast beyond measure, but
within the limits of the sphere
which God appointed us—a
sphere which especially includes you.
14 For we are not overex-
tending ourselves (as though
our authority did not extend to
you), for it was to you that we
came with the gospel of Christ;
15 not boasting of things beyond measure, *that is,* in other

πέποιθεν ἑαυτῷ Χριστοῦ εἶναι, τοῦτο λογιζέσθω πάλιν
has persuaded himself [3]of [4]Christ [1]to [2]be, [9]this [5]let [6]him [8]consider [7]again
that he is Christ's,

ἀφ' ἑαυτοῦ, ὅτι καθὼς αὐτὸς Χριστοῦ, οὕτω καὶ ἡμεῖς
based on himself, that just as he *is* of Christ, so also we *are*
to

Χριστοῦ.[a] **8** Ἐάν τε γὰρ καὶ περισσότερόν τι
of Christ. [3]if - [1]For [2]even [7]more [6]something
somewhat

καυχήσωμαι περὶ τῆς ἐξουσίας ἡμῶν, ἧς ἔδωκεν ὁ
[4]I [5]boast concerning - authority ~ our, which [3]gave [1]the

Κύριος ἡμῖν[b] εἰς οἰκοδομὴν καὶ οὐκ εἰς καθαίρεσιν ὑμῶν, οὐκ
[2]Lord us for edification and not for destruction ~ your, [3]not

αἰσχυνθήσομαι, **9** ἵνα μὴ δόξω ὡς ἂν ἐκφοβεῖν ὑμᾶς διὰ τῶν
[1]I [2]will be ashamed, that not I seem as if to terrify you by the
lest my

ἐπιστολῶν. **10** Ὅτι, "Αἱ μὲν ἐπιστολαί," φησί, "βαρεῖαι
letters. Because, "The - letters," they say, "*are* difficult
"His severe

καὶ ἰσχυραί, ἡ δὲ παρουσία τοῦ σώματος ἀσθενὴς καὶ ὁ
and strong, the ~ but presence of the body *is* weak and the
but his bodily presence his

λόγος ἐξουθενημένος." **11** Τοῦτο λογιζέσθω ὁ τοιοῦτος,
word being despised." [6]this [1]Let [5]consider - [2]such [3]a [4]person,
speech amounts to nothing."

ὅτι οἷοί ἐσμεν τῷ λόγῳ δι' ἐπιστολῶν ἀπόντες,
that of what sort we are - in word by letters being absent,
when we are

τοιοῦτοι καὶ παρόντες τῷ ἔργῳ!
of such a kind also being present - *we will be* in deed!
when we are

The Extent of Paul's Authority

12 Οὐ γὰρ τολμῶμεν ἐγκρῖναι ἢ συγκρῖναι ἑαυτούς
[4]not [1]For [2]we [3]do [5]dare to class or to compare ourselves

τισι τῶν ἑαυτοὺς συνιστανόντων, ἀλλὰ αὐτοί, ἐν
with any of the *ones* themselves ~ recommending, but they, [3]by
of those who commend,

ἑαυτοῖς ἑαυτοὺς μετροῦντες καὶ συγκρίνοντες ἑαυτοὺς
[4]themselves [2]themselves [1]measuring and comparing themselves
when they measure

ἑαυτοῖς, οὐ συνιοῦσιν. **13** Ἡμεῖς δὲ οὐχὶ εἰς τὰ
with themselves, not ~ do understand. we ~ But [2]not [4]to [5]the
beyond

ἄμετρα καυχησόμεθα, ἀλλὰ κατὰ τὸ μέτρον
[6]immeasurable [7]*things* [1]will [3]boast, but according to the measure
limits

τοῦ κανόνος οὗ ἐμέρισεν ἡμῖν ὁ Θεὸς μέτρου,
of the sphere *of influence* which [2]assigned [3]to [4]us - [1]God *as* a measure,

ἐφικέσθαι ἄχρι καὶ ὑμῶν. **14** Οὐ γὰρ ὡς μὴ
to reach [2]as [3]far [4]as [1]even you. [4]not [1]For [7]as [8]though [9]not
we

ἐφικνούμενοι εἰς ὑμᾶς ὑπερεκτείνομεν ἑαυτούς, ἄχρι
[10]reaching [11]to [12]you [2]we [3]are [5]overextending [6]ourselves, [15]as [16]far [17]as
did not reach

γὰρ καὶ ὑμῶν ἐφθάσαμεν ἐν τῷ εὐαγγελίῳ τοῦ Χριστοῦ·
[13]for [14]even you we came with the gospel - of Christ;

15 οὐκ εἰς τὰ ἄμετρα καυχώμενοι ἐν ἀλλοτρίοις
not [2]to [3]the [4]immeasurable [5]*things* [1]boasting in [3]of [4]others
beyond the limits

---

[a](**10:7**) NU omits Χριστου, *of Christ.* [b](**10:8**) NU omits ημιν, *us.*

κόποις, ἐλπίδα δὲ ἔχοντες, αὐξανομένης τῆς πίστεως
[1]*the* [2]labors, [7]hope [5]but [6]having, being increased the faith
that as your faith

ὑμῶν, ἐν ὑμῖν μεγαλυνθῆναι κατὰ τὸν
of you, [4]by [5]you [1]to [2]be [3]enlarged according to -
is increased, we shall

κανόνα ἡμῶν εἰς περισσείαν, 16 εἰς τὰ
[2]sphere [3]*of* [4]*influence* [1]our to abundance, [5]to [6]the [7]*regions*
greatly,

ὑπερέκεινα ὑμῶν εὐαγγελίσασθαι, οὐκ ἐν ἀλλοτρίῳ
[8]beyond [9]you [1]to [2]preach [3]the [4]gospel, *and* not [7]in [12]of [13]others

κανόνι εἰς τὰ ἕτοιμα καυχήσασθαι.
[8]*the* [9]sphere [10]*of* [11]*influence* [3]in [4]the [5]*things* [6]prepared [1]to [2]boast.
done

17 «Ὁ δὲ καυχώμενος, ἐν Κυρίῳ καυχάσθω.»[c] 18 Οὐ
«[2]the [3]*one* [1]Now boasting, in *the* Lord let him boast.» [9]not
who boasts,

γὰρ ὁ ἑαυτὸν συνιστῶν, ἐκεῖνός ἐστι δόκιμος, ἀλλ'
[1]For [2]the [3]*one* [5]himself [4]recommending, [6]that [7]*one* [8]is approved, but
he who commends,

ὃν ὁ Κύριος συνίστησιν.
the one whom the Lord recommends.
commends.

Paul's Concern for Believers' Fidelity

11 1 Ὄφελον ἀνείχεσθέ μου μικρὸν τῇ ἀφροσύνῃ·
O that you would bear with me a little in the foolishness;
my

ἀλλὰ καὶ ἀνέχεσθέ μου. 2 Ζηλῶ γὰρ ὑμᾶς
but indeed you do bear with me. [2]I [3]am [4]zealous [5]for [1]For you

Θεοῦ ζήλῳ, ἡρμοσάμην γὰρ ὑμᾶς ἑνὶ ἀνδρὶ
[4]of [5]God [1]with [2]*the* [3]zeal, [7]I [8]betrothed [6]for you to one husband

παρθένον ἁγνὴν παραστῆσαι τῷ Χριστῷ. 3 Φοβοῦμαι δὲ
[4]*as* [5]a [7]virgin [6]pure [1]to [2]present [3]*you* - to Christ. [2]I [3]am [4]afraid [1]But

μή πως ὡς ὁ ὄφις Εὔαν ἐξηπάτησεν ἐν τῇ πανουργίᾳ
lest perhaps as the serpent Eve ˜ deceived by - craftiness ˜

αὐτοῦ, οὕτω φθαρῇ τὰ νοήματα ὑμῶν ἀπὸ τῆς
his, so [3]may [4]be [5]corrupted - [2]minds [1]your from the

ἁπλότητος[a] τῆς εἰς τὸν Χριστόν. 4 Εἰ μὲν γὰρ ὁ
simplicity the *one* in - Christ. if ˜ - For the *one*
which is he who

ἐρχόμενος ἄλλον Ἰησοῦν κηρύσσει ὃν οὐκ ἐκηρύξαμεν,
coming *to you* [2]another [3]Jesus [1]preaches whom [3]not [1]we [2]did [4]preach,
comes

ἢ πνεῦμα ἕτερον λαμβάνετε ὃ οὐκ ἐλάβετε, ἢ
or *if* [4]spirit [3]another [1]you [2]receive which [3]not [1]you [2]did receive, or

εὐαγγέλιον ἕτερον ὃ οὐκ ἐδέξασθε, καλῶς
gospel ˜ another which [3]not [1]you [2]did [4]receive, [7]well
accept, you may

ἀνείχεσθε.
[5]you [6]would [8]bear [9]*with* [10]*him*.
well put up with him.

Paul Contrasted with False Apostles

5 Λογίζομαι γὰρ μηδὲν ὑστερηκέναι τῶν
[2]I [3]consider [4]*myself* [1]For *in* nothing to have been inferior of the
to the

men's labors, but having hope,
that as your faith is increased,
we shall be greatly enlarged by
you in our sphere,
16 to preach the gospel in the
regions beyond you, *and* not to
boast in another man's sphere
of accomplishment.
17 But *"he who glories, let
him glory in the* LORD.*"*
18 For not he who commends
himself is approved, but whom
the Lord commends.
11 Oh, that you would
bear with me in a little
folly—and indeed you do bear
with me.
2 For I am jealous for you
with godly jealousy. For I have
betrothed you to one husband,
that I may present *you as* a
chaste virgin to Christ.
3 But I fear, lest somehow,
as the serpent deceived Eve by
his craftiness, so your minds
may be corrupted from the simplicity that is in Christ.
4 For if he who comes
preaches another Jesus whom
we have not preached, or *if* you
receive a different spirit which
you have not received, or a different gospel which you have
not accepted—you may well
put up with it!
5 For I consider that I am
not at all inferior to the most

[c](10:17) Jer. 9:24
[a](11:3) NU adds in brackets *και της αγνοτητος, and the purity.*

eminent apostles.

6 Even though *I am* untrained in speech, yet *I am* not in knowledge. But we have been thoroughly manifested among you in all things.

7 Did I commit sin in humbling myself that you might be exalted, because I preached the gospel of God to you free of charge?

8 I robbed other churches, taking wages *from them* to minister to you.

9 And when I was present with you, and in need, I was a burden to no one, for what I lacked the brethren who came from Macedonia supplied. And in everything I kept myself from being burdensome to you, and so I will keep *myself.*

10 As the truth of Christ is in me, no one shall stop me from this boasting in the regions of Achaia.

11 Why? Because I do not love you? God knows!

12 But what I do, I will also continue to do, that I may cut off the opportunity from those who desire an opportunity to be regarded just as we are in the things of which they boast.

13 For such *are* false apostles, deceitful workers, transforming themselves into apostles of Christ.

14 And no wonder! For Satan himself transforms himself into an angel of light.

15 Therefore *it is* no great thing if his ministers also transform themselves into ministers of righteousness, whose end will be according to their works.

ὑπερλίαν ἀποστόλων. **6** *Εἰ δὲ καὶ ἰδιώτης τῷ λόγῳ,*
exceedingly apostles. [3]if [1]But [2]even *I am* unskilled - in word,
super speech,

ἀλλ' οὐ τῇ γνώσει, ἀλλ' ἐν παντὶ
yet *I am* not *inferior* - in knowledge, but in every *way*

φανερωθέντες[b] *ἐν πᾶσιν εἰς ὑμᾶς.* **7** *Ἢ ἁμαρτίαν*
being made known [3]in [4]all [5]*things* [1]to [2]you. Or [4]sin
I was

ἐποίησα ἐμαυτὸν ταπεινῶν ἵνα ὑμεῖς ὑψωθῆτε,
[1]did [2]I [3]commit [7]myself [5]*in* [6]humbling in order that you might be exalted,

ὅτι δωρεὰν τὸ τοῦ Θεοῦ εὐαγγέλιον*
because [9]without [10]payment [3]the - [5]of [6]God [4]gospel

εὐηγγελισάμην ὑμῖν? **8** *Ἄλλας ἐκκλησίας ἐσύλησα λαβὼν*
[1]I [2]preached [7]to [8]you? [3]other [4]churches [1]I [2]robbed taking

ὀψώνιον πρὸς τὴν ὑμῶν διακονίαν, **9** *καὶ παρὼν*
wages *from them* for - your ministry, and being present
to minister to you, when I was

πρὸς ὑμᾶς καὶ ὑστερηθείς, οὐ κατενάρκησα οὐδενός· τὸ γὰρ
with you and lacking, [3]not [1]I [2]did burden no one; - for
in need, anyone;

ὑστέρημά μου προσανεπλήρωσαν οἱ ἀδελφοί, ἐλθόντες ἀπὸ
[5]need [4]my [3]supplied [1]the [2]brothers, coming from
who came

Μακεδονίας. Καὶ ἐν παντὶ ἀβαρῆ ὑμῖν ἐμαυτὸν
Macedonia. And in every*thing* [4]not [5]burdensome [6]to [7]you [3]myself
from being a burden

ἐτήρησα καὶ τηρήσω. **10** *Ἔστιν ἀλήθεια Χριστοῦ ἐν*
[1]I [2]kept and so I will keep *myself.* [5]is [1]*The* [2]truth [3]of [4]Christ in

ἐμοὶ ὅτι ἡ καύχησις αὕτη οὐ φραγήσεται εἰς ἐμὲ ἐν τοῖς
me that - boasting ~ this not ~ will be stopped for me in the

κλίμασι τῆς Ἀχαΐας. **11** *Διὰ τί? Ὅτι οὐκ ἀγαπῶ*
regions - of Achaia. Because of what? Because [3]not [1]I [2]do love
Why?

ὑμᾶς? Ὁ Θεὸς οἶδεν! **12** *Ὃ δὲ ποιῶ, καὶ ποιήσω, ἵνα*
you? - God knows! what ~ But I am doing, also I will do, that

ἐκκόψω τὴν ἀφορμὴν τῶν θελόντων ἀφορμήν, ἵνα ἐν
I may cut off the opportunity of the *ones* desiring an opportunity, that in
those who desire

ᾧ καυχῶνται εὑρεθῶσι καθὼς καὶ ἡμεῖς. **13** *Οἱ γὰρ*
what they boast they may be found just as also we *are.* - For

τοιοῦτοι ψευδαπόστολοι, ἐργάται δόλιοι, μετασχηματιζόμενοι
such *ones are* false apostles, workers ~ deceitful, transforming themselves
disguising

εἰς ἀποστόλους Χριστοῦ. **14** *Καὶ οὐ θαυμαστόν! Αὐτὸς γὰρ ὁ*
into apostles of Christ. And no wonder! [3]himself [1]For -

Σατανᾶς μετασχηματίζεται εἰς ἄγγελον φωτός. **15** *Οὐ*
[2]Satan transforms himself into an angel of light. *It is* not
disguises himself as

μέγα οὖν εἰ καὶ οἱ διάκονοι αὐτοῦ μετασχηματίζονται
a great *thing* therefore if also - ministers ~ his transform themselves
disguise

ὡς διάκονοι δικαιοσύνης, ὧν τὸ τέλος ἔσται κατὰ τὰ
as ministers of righteousness, whose - end is according to -
will be

ἔργα αὐτῶν.
works ~ their.

[b](11:6) NU reads *φανερωσαντες, revealing (this).*

*(11:7) *δωρεάν (dōrean).* Adverb usually meaning *as a gift, freely* (as Matt. 10:8; Rom. 3:24; here at 2 Cor. 11:7). The word may also have a negative nuance as in the meaning *without cause, undeservedly* (John 15:25) or *for nothing, for no reason* (Gal. 2:21). Cf. also the cognate verb *δωρέομαι, (freely) give* (Mark 15:45; 2 Pet. 1:3); and the nouns *δωρεά, δώρημα* and *δῶρον*, all meaning *gift, present.*

Paul Reluctantly Decides to Boast

16 Πάλιν λέγω, μή τίς με δόξῃ ἄφρονα εἶναι.
Again I say, [2]not [3]anyone [5]me [1]let [4]think [8]foolish [6]to [7]be.
no one

Εἰ δὲ μή γε, κἂν ὡς ἄφρονα δέξασθέ με, ἵνα κἀγὼ
if ˜ And not, - at least [3]as [4]foolish [1]receive [2]me, that I also
Otherwise, a fool

μικρόν τι καυχήσωμαι. **17** Ὃ λαλῶ, οὐ λαλῶ
[3]a [4]little [5]something [1]may [2]boast. What I speak, [3]not [1]I [2]do speak
in a small way

κατὰ Κύριον, ἀλλ' ὡς ἐν ἀφροσύνῃ, ἐν ταύτῃ τῇ
according to *the* Lord, but as in foolishness, in this -

ὑποστάσει τῆς καυχήσεως. **18** Ἐπεὶ πολλοὶ καυχῶνται
confidence - of boasting. Since many are boasting

κατὰ τὴν σάρκα, κἀγὼ καυχήσομαι. **19** Ἡδέως γὰρ
according to the flesh, I also will boast. [8]gladly [1]For

ἀνέχεσθε τῶν ἀφρόνων, φρόνιμοι ὄντες.
[2]you [3]bear [4]with [5]the [6]foolish [7]*ones*, wise ˜ being *yourselves*.
fools,

20 Ἀνέχεσθε γὰρ εἴ τις ὑμᾶς καταδουλοῖ, εἴ
[2]you [3]bear [4]with [5]*him* [1]For if someone you ˜ enslaves, if

τις κατεσθίει, εἴ τις λαμβάνει, εἴ τις
someone devours *you*, if someone takes *from you*, if someone

ἐπαίρεται, εἴ τις ὑμᾶς εἰς πρόσωπον δέρει.
lifts *himself* up, if someone [2]you [3]in [4]*the* [5]face [1]strikes.
is presumptuous,

21 Κατὰ ἀτιμίαν λέγω, ὡς ὅτι ἡμεῖς ἠσθενήσαμεν. Ἐν
According to shame I say, - that we were weak *for that*. [2]in
To our too weak

ᾧ δ' ἄν τις τολμᾷ (ἐν ἀφροσύνῃ λέγω), τολμῶ
[3]what [1]But ever anyone should dare (in foolishness I say), dare ˜
is bold (foolishly am bold

κἀγώ.
I also.

Paul's Unsurpassed Sufferings for Christ

22 Ἑβραῖοί εἰσι? Κἀγώ. Ἰσραηλῖταί εἰσι?
[3]Hebrews [1]Are [2]they? I also *am*. [3]Israelites [1]Are [2]they?

Κἀγώ. Σπέρμα Ἀβραάμ εἰσι? Κἀγώ. **23** Διάκονοι
I also *am*. [3]*the* [4]seed [5]of [6]Abraham [1]Are [2]they? I also *am*. [3]ministers

Χριστοῦ εἰσι? (Παραφρονῶν λαλῶ!) Ὑπὲρ ἐγώ.
[4]of [5]Christ [1]Are [2]they? (Being beside myself I speak!) [3]even [4]more [1]I [2]*am*.
(Irrationally

Ἐν κόποις περισσοτέρως, ἐν πληγαῖς ὑπερβαλλόντως, ἐν
In labors far more, in beatings immeasurably, in

φυλακαῖς περισσοτέρως, ἐν θανάτοις πολλάκις. **24** Ὑπὸ
imprisonments far more, in deaths often. By

Ἰουδαίων πεντάκις τεσσαράκοντα παρὰ μίαν ἔλαβον.
Jews five times [3]forty [4]*lashes* [5]less [6]one [1]I [2]received.
minus

25 Τρὶς ἐραβδίσθην, ἅπαξ ἐλιθάσθην, τρὶς
Three times I was beaten with rods, once I was stoned, three times

ἐναυάγησα, νυχθήμερον ἐν τῷ βυθῷ
I was shipwrecked, a night and day [4]in [5]the [6]depth [7]*of* [8]*the* [9]*sea*

πεποίηκα. **26** Ὁδοιπορίαις πολλάκις, κινδύνοις ποταμῶν,
[1]I [2]have [3]spent. In journeys often, in dangers of rivers,

κινδύνοις λῃστῶν, κινδύνοις ἐκ γένους, κινδύνοις ἐξ ἐθνῶν,
in dangers of robbers, in dangers from *my* race, in dangers from Gentiles,

16 I say again, let no one think me a fool. If otherwise, at least receive me as a fool, that I also may boast a little.
17 What I speak, I speak not according to the Lord, but as it were, foolishly, in this confidence of boasting.
18 Seeing that many boast according to the flesh, I also will boast.
19 For you put up with fools gladly, since you *yourselves* are wise!
20 For you put up with it if one brings you into bondage, if one devours *you*, if one takes *from you*, if one exalts himself, if one strikes you on the face.
21 To *our* shame I say that we were too weak for that! But in whatever anyone is bold—I speak foolishly—I am bold also.
22 Are they Hebrews? So *am* I. Are they Israelites? So *am* I. Are they the seed of Abraham? So *am* I.
23 Are they ministers of Christ?—I speak as a fool—I *am* more: in labors more abundant, in stripes above measure, in prisons more frequently, in deaths often.
24 From the Jews five times I received forty *stripes* minus one.
25 Three times I was beaten with rods; once I was stoned; three times I was shipwrecked; a night and a day I have been in the deep;
26 *in* journeys often, *in* perils of waters, *in* perils of robbers, *in* perils of *my own* countrymen, *in* perils of the Gentiles,

in perils in the city, *in* perils in
the wilderness, *in* perils in the
sea, *in* perils among false
brethren;
27 in weariness and toil, in
sleeplessness often, in hunger
and thirst, in fastings often, in
cold and nakedness—
28 besides the other things,
what comes upon me daily: my
deep concern for all the
churches.
29 Who is weak, and I am not
weak? Who is made to stumble,
and I do not burn *with indigna-*
tion?
30 If I must boast, I will boast
in the things which concern my
infirmity.
31 The God and Father of our
Lord Jesus Christ, who is
blessed forever, knows that I
am not lying.
32 In Damascus the governor,
under Aretas the king, was
guarding the city of the Dama-
scenes with a garrison, desiring
to arrest me;
33 but I was let down in a basket through a window in the
wall, and escaped from his
hands.
12 It is doubtless not
profitable for me to
boast. I will come to visions and
revelations of the Lord:
2 I know a man in Christ who
fourteen years ago—whether
in the body I do not know, or
whether out of the body I do
not know, God knows—such a
one was caught up to the third
heaven.
3 And I know such a man—
whether in the body or out of
the body I do not know, God
knows—
4 how he was caught up into
Paradise and heard inexpress-

κινδύνοις ἐν πόλει, κινδύνοις ἐν ἐρημίᾳ, κινδύνοις ἐν
in dangers in *the* city, in dangers in *the* wilderness, in dangers in

θαλάσσῃ, κινδύνοις ἐν ψευδαδέλφοις, **27** ἐν κόπῳ καὶ
the sea, in dangers among false brothers, in labor and

μόχθῳ, ἐν ἀγρυπνίαις πολλάκις, ἐν λιμῷ καὶ δίψει, ἐν
hardship, in sleepless nights often, in hunger and thirst, in

νηστείαις πολλάκις, ἐν ψύχει καὶ γυμνότητι. **28** Χωρὶς
fastings often, in cold and nakedness. Apart from
lack of clothing.

τῶν παρεκτός, ἡ ἐπισύστασίς[c] μου ἡ καθ'
the *things* besides, - disturbance ˜ my the *one* according to
what I leave unmentioned, what comes against me daily,

ἡμέραν, ἡ μέριμνα πασῶν τῶν ἐκκλησιῶν. **29** Τίς ἀσθενεῖ,
a day, the care of all the churches. Who is weak,
anxiety for

καὶ οὐκ ἀσθενῶ? Τίς σκανδαλίζεται, καὶ οὐκ ἐγὼ
and [3]not [1]I [2]am weak? Who is caused to stumble, and [3]not [1]I
led to sin,

πυροῦμαι? **30** Εἰ καυχᾶσθαι δεῖ,
[2]do burn *with indignation?* If [4]to [5]boast [1]it [2]is [3]necessary,

τὰ τῆς ἀσθενείας μου καυχήσομαι. **31** Ὁ Θεὸς
[10]the [11]*things* - [12]of [14]weakness [13]my [6]I [7]will [8]boast [9]about. The God

καὶ Πατὴρ τοῦ Κυρίου[d] Ἰησοῦ Χριστοῦ[e] οἶδεν, ὁ ὢν
and Father of the Lord Jesus Christ knows, the *One* being
who is

εὐλογητὸς εἰς τοὺς αἰῶνας, ὅτι οὐ ψεύδομαι. **32** Ἐν
blessed into the ages, that [3]not [1]I [2]am lying. In
forever,

Δαμασκῷ ὁ ἐθνάρχης Ἀρέτα τοῦ βασιλέως ἐφρούρει τὴν
Damascus the ethnarch of Aretas the king was guarding the
governor under

Δαμασκηνῶν πόλιν, πιάσαι με θέλων,[f] **33** καὶ διὰ
[2]of [3]*the* [4]Damascenes [1]city, [6]to [7]arrest [8]me [5]desiring, and [8]through

θυρίδος ἐν σαργάνῃ ἐχαλάσθην διὰ τοῦ τείχους καὶ
[9]a [10]window [5]in [6]a [7]basket [1]I [2]was [3]let [4]down through the wall and
in

ἐξέφυγον τὰς χεῖρας αὐτοῦ.
I escaped - hands ˜ his.

Paul's Sublime Vision of Paradise

12 1 Καυχᾶσθαι δὴ[a] οὐ συμφέρει[b] μοι. Ἐλεύσομαι
To boast indeed not ˜ is profitable for me. [2]I [3]will [4]come

γὰρ εἰς ὀπτασίας καὶ ἀποκαλύψεις Κυρίου. **2** Οἶδα
[1]For to visions and revelations of *the* Lord. I know

ἄνθρωπον ἐν Χριστῷ πρὸ ἐτῶν δεκατεσσάρων — εἴτε ἐν
a man in Christ before years fourteen — whether in
fourteen years ago —

σώματι οὐκ οἶδα, εἴτε ἐκτὸς τοῦ σώματος οὐκ οἶδα,
the body [3]not [1]I [2]do know, or outside the body [3]not [1]I [2]do know,

ὁ Θεὸς οἶδεν — ἁρπαγέντα τὸν τοιοῦτον ἕως τρίτου
- God knows — [4]being [5]snatched - [1]such [2]a [3]one to *the* third
was caught up

οὐρανοῦ. **3** Καὶ οἶδα τὸν τοιοῦτον ἄνθρωπον — εἴτε ἐν
heaven. And I know - such a man — whether in

σώματι, εἴτε ἐκτὸς[c] τοῦ σώματος οὐκ οἶδα, ὁ Θεὸς
the body, or outside the body [3]not [1]I [2]do know, - God

οἶδεν — **4** ὅτι ἡρπάγη εἰς τὸν Παράδεισον καὶ ἤκουσεν
knows — that he was snatched into - Paradise and heard
caught up

---

c(11:28) NU reads επιστασις, *pressure.*
d(11:31) TR adds ημων, *our (Lord).* e(11:31) NU omits Χριστου, *Christ.*
f(11:32) NU omits θελων, *desiring.* a(12:1) NU reads δει, *is necessary.*
b(12:1) For συμφερει μοι, *is (not) profitable for me,* NU reads συμφερον μεν, *though it is (not) profitable.*
c(12:3) NU reads χωρις, *apart.*

ἄρρητα ῥήματα ἃ οὐκ ἐξὸν ἀνθρώπῳ λαλῆσαι.
inexpressible words which [3]not [1]it [2]is permitted for a man to speak.

5 Ὑπὲρ τοῦ τοιούτου καυχήσομαι, ὑπὲρ δὲ ἐμαυτοῦ
Concerning - such a one I will boast, concerning ˜ but myself

οὐ καυχήσομαι εἰ μὴ ἐν ταῖς ἀσθενείαις μου.[d] 6 Ἐὰν
[3]not [1]I [2]will boast if not in - weaknesses ˜ my. if ˜
except

γὰρ θελήσω καυχήσασθαι, οὐκ ἔσομαι ἄφρων, ἀλήθειαν
For I should desire to boast, [3]not [1]I [2]will be foolish, [5]truth

γὰρ ἐρῶ· φείδομαι δέ, μή τις εἰς ἐμὲ
[1]for [2]I [3]will [4]speak; [7]I [8]spare [9]*you* [6]but, lest anyone [2]in [3]reference [4]to [5]me
me to be

λογίσηται ὑπὲρ ὃ βλέπει με ἢ ἀκούει τι ἐξ
[1]consider beyond what he sees me *to be* or hears something from

ἐμοῦ.
me.

Paul's Thorn in the Flesh

7 Καὶ τῇ ὑπερβολῇ τῶν ἀποκαλύψεων ἵνα
And [6]by [7]*the* [8]extraordinary [9]quality [10]of [11]the [12]revelations [1]that
lest

μὴ ὑπεραίρωμαι, ἐδόθη μοι σκόλοψ* τῇ σαρκί,
[3]not [2]I [4]exalt [5]myself, [18]was [19]given [20]to [21]me [13]a [14]thorn [15]in [16]the [17]flesh,

ἄγγελος Σατᾶν ἵνα με κολαφίζῃ, ἵνα μὴ ὑπεραίρωμαι.
a messenger of Satan that [4]me [1]it [2]might [3]beat, that not ˜ I exalt myself.
lest

8 Ὑπὲρ τούτου τρὶς τὸν Κύριον παρεκάλεσα ἵνα
Concerning this three times [3]the [4]Lord [1]I [2]implored that

ἀποστῇ ἀπ' ἐμοῦ. 9 Καὶ εἴρηκέ μοι, "Ἀρκεῖ σοι ἡ
it leave from me. And He has said to me, "[3]is [4]sufficient [5]for [6]you -
depart

χάρις μου, ἡ γὰρ δύναμίς μου[e] ἐν ἀσθενείᾳ τελειοῦται."
[2]grace [1]My, - for strength ˜ My [4]in [5]weakness [1]is [2]made [3]perfect."

Ἥδιστα οὖν μᾶλλον καυχήσομαι ἐν ταῖς ἀσθενείαις μου,
gladly ˜ Therefore [3]rather [1]I [2]will boast in - weaknesses ˜ my,

ἵνα ἐπισκηνώσῃ ἐπ' ἐμὲ ἡ δύναμις τοῦ Χριστοῦ.
in order that [5]may [6]dwell [7]upon [8]me [1]the [2]power - [3]of [4]Christ.

10 Διὸ εὐδοκῶ ἐν ἀσθενείαις, ἐν ὕβρεσιν, ἐν ἀνάγκαις, ἐν
Therefore I delight in weaknesses, in insults, in calamities, in

διωγμοῖς, ἐν στενοχωρίαις, ὑπὲρ Χριστοῦ. Ὅταν γὰρ
persecutions, in distresses, in behalf of Christ. whenever ˜ For

ἀσθενῶ, τότε δυνατός εἰμι.
I am weak, then [3]strong [1]I [2]am.

The Signs of an Apostle

11 Γέγονα ἄφρων καυχώμενος·[f] ὑμεῖς με
I have become foolish *in* boasting; you me ˜

ἠναγκάσατε! Ἐγὼ γὰρ ὤφειλον ὑφ' ὑμῶν συνίστασθαι.
compelled! I ˜ For ought [4]by [5]you [1]to [2]be [3]recommended.
commended.

Οὐδὲν γὰρ ὑστέρησα τῶν ὑπερλίαν ἀποστόλων, εἰ
[7]*in* [8]nothing [6]For have I been inferior of the exceedingly apostles, if ˜
to the super

καὶ οὐδέν εἰμι. 12 Τὰ μὲν σημεῖα τοῦ ἀποστόλου
even [3]nothing [1]I [2]am. The - signs of the apostle

κατειργάσθη ἐν ὑμῖν ἐν πάσῃ ὑπομονῇ, ἐν σημείοις καὶ
were worked among you with all perseverance, in signs and

ible words, which it is not lawful for a man to utter.
5 Of such a one I will boast; yet of myself I will not boast, except in my infirmities.
6 For though I might desire to boast, I will not be a fool; for I will speak the truth. But I refrain, lest anyone should think of me above what he sees me *to be* or hears from me.
7 And lest I should be exalted above measure by the abundance of the revelations, a thorn in the flesh was given to me, a messenger of Satan to buffet me, lest I be exalted above measure.
8 Concerning this thing I pleaded with the Lord three times that it might depart from me.
9 And He said to me, "My grace is sufficient for you, for My strength is made perfect in weakness." Therefore most gladly I will rather boast in my infirmities, that the power of Christ may rest upon me.
10 Therefore I take pleasure in infirmities, in reproaches, in needs, in persecutions, in distresses, for Christ's sake. For when I am weak, then I am strong.
11 I have become a fool in boasting; you have compelled me. For I ought to have been commended by you; for in nothing was I behind the most eminent apostles, though I am nothing.
12 Truly the signs of an apostle were accomplished among you with all perseverance, in

---

[d](12:5) NU omits *μου, my.*
[e](12:9) NU omits *μου, My.*
[f](12:11) NU omits *καυχωμενος, (in) boasting.*

---

*(12:7) *σκόλοψ (skolops).* Noun originally meaning anything pointed, such as a *stake,* but later used to mean a *thorn* (as in Num. 33:55 of the LXX). Here Paul uses the word metaphorically to describe a sharp and painful condition, probably physical (cf. Gal. 4:13). The precise nature of this malady is unknown, although physical disfigurement (cf. Acts 14:19) and eye trouble (cf. Gal. 6:11) are among the more common guesses.

signs and wonders and mighty
deeds.
13 For what is it in which you
were inferior to other
churches, except that I myself
was not burdensome to you?
Forgive me this wrong!
14 Now *for* the third time I am
ready to come to you. And I will
not be burdensome to you; for I
do not seek yours, but you. For
the children ought not to lay up
for the parents, but the parents
for the children.
15 And I will very gladly spend
and be spent for your souls;
though the more abundantly I
love you, the less I am loved.
16 But be that *as it may,* I did
not burden you. Nevertheless,
being crafty, I caught you by
cunning!
17 Did I take advantage of you
by any of those whom I sent to
you?
18 I urged Titus, and sent our
brother with *him.* Did Titus
take advantage of you? Did we
not walk in the same spirit? Did
we not *walk* in the same steps?
19 Again, do you think that we
excuse ourselves to you? We
speak before God in Christ. But
we do all things, beloved, for
your edification.
20 For I fear lest, when I
come, I shall not find you such
as I wish, and *that* I shall be
found by you such as you do not
wish; lest *there be* contentions,
jealousies, outbursts of wrath,
selfish ambitions, backbitings,
whisperings, conceits, tumults;
21 lest, when I come again,
my God will humble me among

τέρασι καὶ δυνάμεσι. **13** Τί γάρ ἐστιν ὅ ἡττήθητε
wonders and miracles. what ˜ For is it *in* which you were inferior

ὑπὲρ τὰς λοιπὰς ἐκκλησίας, εἰ μὴ ὅτι αὐτὸς ἐγὼ οὐ
more than the remaining churches, if not that myself ˜ I not ˜
rest of the except

κατενάρκησα ὑμῶν? Χαρίσασθέ μοι τὴν ἀδικίαν ταύτην!
did burden you? Forgive me - wrong ˜ this!

Paul's Unselfish Concern for the Corinthians

14 Ἰδού, τρίτον ἑτοίμως ἔχω ἐλθεῖν πρὸς ὑμᾶς, καὶ
Behold, a third time readily I have to come to you, and
I am ready

οὐ καταναρκήσω ὑμῶν.[g] Οὐ γὰρ ζητῶ τὰ ὑμῶν,
[3]not [1]I [2]will burden you. [4]not [1]For [2]I [3]do [5]seek the *things* of you,
what is yours,

ἀλλὰ ὑμᾶς. Οὐ γὰρ ὀφείλει τὰ τέκνα τοῖς γονεῦσι
but you. [5]not [1]For [4]ought [2]the [3]children [9]for [10]the [11]parents

θησαυρίζειν, ἀλλ' οἱ γονεῖς τοῖς τέκνοις. **15** Ἐγὼ δὲ ἥδιστα
[6]to [7]store [8]up, but the parents for the children. I ˜ And gladly

δαπανήσω καὶ ἐκδαπανηθήσομαι ὑπὲρ τῶν ψυχῶν ὑμῶν,
will spend and be expended for the sake of - souls ˜ your,

εἰ καὶ περισσοτέρως ὑμᾶς ἀγαπῶν, ἧττον ἀγαπῶμαι.
if even *the* more you ˜ loving, *the* less I am loved.
although I love,

16 Ἔστω δέ, ἐγὼ οὐ κατεβάρησα ὑμᾶς. Ἀλλ'
[2]let [3]*that* [4]be [1]But, I not ˜ did burden you. But
But be that as it may,

ὑπάρχων πανοῦργος,* δόλῳ ὑμᾶς ἔλαβον! **17** Μή
being crafty, [4]with [5]deceit [3]you [1]I [2]took! [11]not

τινα ὧν ἀπέσταλκα πρὸς ὑμᾶς, δι' αὐτοῦ
[1]*By* [2]anyone [3]whom [4]I [5]have [6]sent [7]to [8]you, [16]by [17]him

ἐπλεονέκτησα ὑμᾶς? **18** Παρεκάλεσα Τίτον καὶ
[9]I [10]did [12]take [13]advantage [14]of [15]you, *did I?* I urged Titus and

συναπέστειλα τὸν ἀδελφόν. Μήτι ἐπλεονέκτησεν ὑμᾶς
I sent with *him* the brother. [3]not [2]did [4]take [5]advantage [6]of [7]you

Τίτος? Οὐ τῷ αὐτῷ Πνεύματι περιεπατήσαμεν?
[1]Titus, [8]*did* [9]*he?* [12]not [14]in [15]the [16]same [17]Spirit [10]Did [11]we [13]walk?

Οὐ τοῖς αὐτοῖς ἴχνεσι?
Did we not *walk* in the same footprints?

19 Πάλιν[h] δοκεῖτε ὅτι ὑμῖν ἀπολογούμεθα?
Again do you think that [5]to [6]you [1]we [2]are [3]defending [4]ourselves?

Κατενώπιον τοῦ Θεοῦ ἐν Χριστῷ λαλοῦμεν. Τὰ δὲ
Before - God [4]in [5]Christ [1]we [2]are [3]speaking. - And

πάντα, ἀγαπητοί, ὑπὲρ τῆς ὑμῶν οἰκοδομῆς.
all *things,* beloved *ones, we do* for the sake of - your edification.

20 Φοβοῦμαι γὰρ μή πως ἐλθὼν οὐχ οἵους
[2]I [3]am [4]afraid [1]For lest perhaps coming [5]not [6]of [7]what [8]sort
when I come as

θέλω εὕρω ὑμᾶς, κἀγὼ εὑρεθῶ ὑμῖν οἷον οὐ
[9]I [10]desire [1]I [2]will [3]find [4]you, and I will be found by you of what sort [3]not
as

θέλετε, μή πως ἔρεις,[i] ζῆλοι,
[1]you [2]do desire, lest perhaps *there be* contentions, jealousies,

θυμοί, ἐριθεῖαι, καταλαλιαί, ψιθυρισμοί, φυσιώσεις,
rages, disputes, slanders, gossipings, conceits,
outbursts of wrath, pride,

ἀκαταστασίαι· **21** μὴ πάλιν ἐλθόντα με ταπεινώσει ὁ Θεός
disorders; lest again coming [5]me [3]will [4]humble - [2]God
when I come

[g](12:14) NU omits υμων, *you.* [h](12:19) NU reads Παλαι and punctuates as a statement rather than a question, *For a long time (you have been thinking).* [i](12:20) NU reads ερις, *strife.*

*(12:16) πανοῦργος *(panourgos).* Compound adjective from πᾶς, *all, any,* and ἔργον, *work,* thus suggesting one who is ready and able to do anything, therefore *clever, crafty, sly.* It and its cognate noun πανουργία, *craftiness, deceitful cunning* (Luke 20:23; 2 Cor. 11:3) always have a negative nuance in the NT. Here (as often in this section of 2 Corinthians) Paul is ironically accepting

μου πρὸς ὑμᾶς, καὶ πενθήσω πολλοὺς τῶν
[1]my among you, and I will mourn for many of the *ones*
who have

προημαρτηκότων καὶ μὴ μετανοησάντων ἐπὶ τῇ ἀκαθαρσίᾳ
sinning before and not repenting for the impurity
previously sinned repented

καὶ πορνείᾳ καὶ ἀσελγείᾳ ᾗ ἔπραξαν.
and fornication and sensuality which they practiced.
sexual immorality

Paul Will Come with Authority

13 1 Τρίτον τοῦτο ἔρχομαι πρὸς ὑμᾶς.
[4]*the* [5]third [6]time [1]This [2]*will* [3]*be* I am coming to you.

«Ἐπὶ στόματος δύο μαρτύρων καὶ τριῶν
«By *the* mouth of two witnesses and three
«On the basis of the testimony or

σταθήσεται πᾶν ῥῆμα.»[a] 2 Προείρηκα καὶ
shall [3]be [4]established [1]every [2]word.» I have previously said and
each

προλέγω, ὡς παρὼν τὸ δεύτερον, καὶ ἀπὼν νῦν
I say beforehand, as being present the second *time,* and being absent now

γράφω[b] τοῖς προημαρτηκόσι καὶ τοῖς λοιποῖς πᾶσιν,
I write to the *ones* having sinned before and [1]to [3]the [4]rest [2]all,
those who had

ὅτι ἐὰν ἔλθω εἰς τὸ πάλιν, οὐ φείσομαι, 3 ἐπεὶ δοκιμὴν
that if I come - - again, [3]not [1]I [2]will spare *you,* since [4]proof

ζητεῖτε τοῦ ἐν ἐμοὶ λαλοῦντος Χριστοῦ, ὃς εἰς
[1]you [2]are [3]seeking of the [3]in [4]me [2]speaking [1]Christ, who [4]toward

ὑμᾶς οὐκ ἀσθενεῖ, ἀλλὰ δυνατεῖ ἐν ὑμῖν. 4 Καὶ γὰρ εἰ[c]
[5]you [2]not [1]is [3]weak, but is strong in you. even ˜ For if
For although

ἐσταυρώθη ἐξ ἀσθενείας, ἀλλὰ ζῇ ἐκ δυνάμεως Θεοῦ.
He was crucified out of weakness, yet He lives by *the* power of God.

Καὶ γὰρ ἡμεῖς ἀσθενοῦμεν ἐν αὐτῷ, ἀλλὰ ζησόμεθα σὺν αὐτῷ
[3]also [1]For [2]we are weak in Him, yet we shall live with Him

ἐκ δυνάμεως Θεοῦ εἰς ὑμᾶς. 5 Ἑαυτοὺς πειράζετε
by *the* power of God toward you. yourselves ˜ Put to the test
Test

εἰ ἐστὲ ἐν τῇ πίστει, ἑαυτοὺς δοκιμάζετε. Ἢ οὐκ
whether you are in the faith, yourselves ˜ examine. Or [3]not

ἐπιγινώσκετε ἑαυτοὺς ὅτι Ἰησοῦς Χριστὸς ἐν ὑμῖν ἐστιν — εἰ
[1]do [2]you know yourselves that Jesus Christ [2]in [3]you [1]is — if

μήτι ἀδόκιμοί ἐστε? 6 Ἐλπίζω δὲ ὅτι γνώσεσθε ὅτι
[3]not [4]unqualified [1]you [2]are? [2]I [3]hope [1]But that you will know that
unless you do not stand the test?

ἡμεῖς οὐκ ἐσμὲν ἀδόκιμοι.
we not ˜ are unqualified.
did stand the test.

Paul Prefers Not to Press His Authority

7 Εὔχομαι[d] δὲ πρὸς τὸν Θεὸν μὴ ποιῆσαι ὑμᾶς κακὸν
[2]I [3]pray [1]Now to - God [2]not [3]to [4]do [1]you bad ˜
that you do no evil

μηδέν, οὐχ ἵνα ἡμεῖς δόκιμοι φανῶμεν, ἀλλ' ἵνα ὑμεῖς τὸ
nothing, not that we [3]approved [1]may [2]appear, but that you [3]the
at all, that

καλὸν ποιῆτε, ἡμεῖς δὲ ὡς ἀδόκιμοι ὦμεν.
[4]good [5]*thing* [1]may [2]do, we ˜ but [3]as [4]unqualified [1]may [2]be.
which is good though we may seem as not standing the test.

you, and I shall mourn for many
who have sinned before and
have not repented of the uncleanness, fornication, and
lewdness which they have practiced.

13 This *will be* the third
time I am coming to
you. *"By the mouth of two or
three witnesses every word
shall be established."*
2 I have told you before, and
foretell as if I were present the
second time, and now being absent I write to those who have
sinned before, and to all the
rest, that if I come again I will
not spare—
3 since you seek a proof of
Christ speaking in me, who is
not weak toward you, but
mighty in you.
4 For though He was crucified in weakness, yet He lives
by the power of God. For we
also are weak in Him, but we
shall live with Him by the
power of God toward you.
5 Examine yourselves *as to*
whether you are in the faith.
Test yourselves. Do you not
know yourselves, that Jesus
Christ is in you?—unless indeed you are disqualified.
6 But I trust that you will
know that we are not disqualified.
7 Now I pray to God that you
do no evil, not that we should
appear approved, but that you
should do what is honorable,
though we may seem disqualified.

---

[a](**13:1**) Deut. 19:15
[b](**13:2**) NU omits γραφω, *I write.* [c](**13:4**) NU omits ει, *if.* [d](**13:7**) NU reads ευχομεθα, *we pray.*

what his critics have said about him.

8 For we can do nothing against the truth, but for the truth.
9 For we are glad when we are weak and you are strong. And this also we pray, that you may be made complete.
10 Therefore I write these things being absent, lest being present I should use sharpness, according to the authority which the Lord has given me for edification and not for destruction.
11 Finally, brethren, farewell. Become complete. Be of good comfort, be of one mind, live in peace; and the God of love and peace will be with you.
12 Greet one another with a holy kiss.
13 All the saints greet you.
14 The grace of the Lord Jesus Christ, and the love of God, and the communion of the Holy Spirit *be* with you all. Amen.

8 Οὐ γὰρ δυνάμεθά τι κατὰ τῆς ἀληθείας, ἀλλ'
[4]not [1]For [2]we [3]are [5]able *to do* anything against the truth, but

ὑπὲρ τῆς ἀληθείας. **9** Χαίρομεν γὰρ ὅταν ἡμεῖς
in behalf of the truth. [2]we [3]rejoice [1]For whenever we

ἀσθενῶμεν, ὑμεῖς δὲ δυνατοὶ ἦτε. Τοῦτο δὲ καὶ εὐχόμεθα, τὴν
are weak, you ˜ but strong ˜ are. this ˜ And also we pray for, -

ὑμῶν κατάρτισιν. **10** Διὰ τοῦτο ταῦτα ἀπὼν
your completion. Because of this [3]these [4]*things* [5]being [6]absent

γράφω, ἵνα παρὼν μὴ ἀποτόμως χρήσωμαι,
[1]I [2]write, in order that being present [3]not [5]severely [1]I [2]may [4]act,
when I am present I may not deal sharply with you,

κατὰ τὴν ἐξουσίαν ἣν ἔδωκέ μοι ὁ Κύριος εἰς
according to the authority which [3]gave [4]me [1]the [2]Lord for

οἰκοδομὴν καὶ οὐκ εἰς καθαίρεσιν.
edification and not for destruction.

Greetings and Benediction

11 Λοιπόν, ἀδελφοί, χαίρετε, καταρτίζεσθε,
For the rest, brothers, rejoice, restore *yourselves,*
Finally, farewell,

παρακαλεῖσθε, τὸ αὐτὸ φρονεῖτε, εἰρηνεύετε, καὶ ὁ
comfort *yourselves,* [2]the [3]same [4]*thing* [1]think, be at peace, and the
be in agreement,

Θεὸς τῆς ἀγάπης καὶ εἰρήνης ἔσται μεθ' ὑμῶν.
God - of love and peace will be with you.

12 Ἀσπάσασθε ἀλλήλους ἐν ἁγίῳ φιλήματι.
Greet one another with a holy kiss.

13 Ἀσπάζονται ὑμᾶς οἱ ἅγιοι πάντες.
[4]greet [5]you [2]the [3]saints [1]All.

Ἡ χάρις τοῦ Κυρίου Ἰησοῦ Χριστοῦ καὶ ἡ ἀγάπη τοῦ
The grace of the Lord Jesus Christ and the love -

Θεοῦ καὶ ἡ κοινωνία τοῦ Ἁγίου Πνεύματος μετὰ πάντων
of God and the fellowship of the Holy Spirit *be* with all ˜

ὑμῶν. Ἀμήν.[e]
you. Amen.
So be it.

[e](**13:13**) NU omits Αμην, *Amen.*

The Epistle of Paul the Apostle to the
GALATIANS

ΠΡΟΣ ΓΑΛΑΤΑΣ
TO *THE* GALATIANS

Paul Greets the Galatians with Grace

1 **1** Παῦλος, ἀπόστολος (οὐκ ἀπ' ἀνθρώπων οὐδὲ δι'
Paul, an apostle (not from men nor through
ἀνθρώπου, ἀλλὰ διὰ Ἰησοῦ Χριστοῦ, καὶ Θεοῦ Πατρὸς
man, but through Jesus Christ, and God *the* Father
τοῦ ἐγείραντος αὐτὸν ἐκ νεκρῶν), **2** καὶ οἱ σὺν ἐμοὶ
the *One* raising (who raised) Him from *the* dead), and [2]the [4]with [5]me
πάντες ἀδελφοί,
[1]all [3]brothers,

Ταῖς ἐκκλησίαις τῆς Γαλατίας·
To the churches - of Galatia:

3 Χάρις ὑμῖν καὶ εἰρήνη ἀπὸ Θεοῦ Πατρὸς καὶ Κυρίου
Grace to you and peace from God *the* Father and Lord ˜
ἡμῶν Ἰησοῦ Χριστοῦ **4** τοῦ δόντος ἑαυτὸν περὶ τῶν
our Jesus Christ the *One* giving (who gave) Himself for -
ἁμαρτιῶν ἡμῶν ὅπως ἐξέληται ἡμᾶς ἐκ τοῦ ἐνεστῶτος
sins ˜ our so that He might deliver us from the [3]being [4]present (present)
αἰῶνος πονηροῦ, κατὰ τὸ θέλημα τοῦ Θεοῦ καὶ Πατρὸς
[2]age [1]evil, (evil age,) according to the will - of [2]God [3]and [4]Father
ἡμῶν, **5** ᾧ ἡ δόξα εἰς τοὺς αἰῶνας τῶν αἰώνων.
[1]our, to whom *be* the glory for the ages of the ages. (forever and ever.)
Ἀμήν.
Amen. (So be it.)

There Is Only One Gospel

6 Θαυμάζω ὅτι οὕτω ταχέως μετατίθεσθε ἀπὸ τοῦ
I marvel that so quickly you are turning from the *One* (Him who)
καλέσαντος ὑμᾶς ἐν χάριτι Χριστοῦ εἰς ἕτερον* εὐαγγέλιον,
calling (called) you in *the* grace of Christ to a different gospel,
7 ὃ οὐκ ἔστιν ἄλλο·* εἰ μή τινές εἰσιν οἱ
which not ˜ is another; if not certain are the *ones* (except there are certain people)
ταράσσοντες ὑμᾶς καὶ θέλοντες μεταστρέψαι τὸ εὐαγγέλιον
troubling (who trouble) you and wishing (wish) to change (to pervert) the gospel
τοῦ Χριστοῦ. **8** Ἀλλὰ καὶ ἐὰν ἡμεῖς ἢ ἄγγελος ἐξ οὐρανοῦ
- of Christ. But even if we or an angel from heaven
εὐαγγελίζεται ὑμῖν παρ' ὃ εὐηγγελισάμεθα ὑμῖν,
preach a gospel to you than (other than) what we preached to you,

---

1 Paul, an apostle (not from
men nor through man, but
through Jesus Christ and God
the Father who raised Him
from the dead),
2 and all the brethren who
are with me,

To the churches of Galatia:

3 Grace to you and peace
from God the Father and our
Lord Jesus Christ,
4 who gave Himself for our
sins, that He might deliver us
from this present evil age, according to the will of our God
and Father,
5 to whom *be* glory forever
and ever. Amen.

6 I marvel that you are turning away so soon from Him who
called you in the grace of
Christ, to a different gospel,
7 which is not another; but
there are some who trouble
you and want to pervert the
gospel of Christ.
8 But even if we, or an angel
from heaven, preach any other
gospel to you than what we
have preached to you, let him

***(1:6, 7)** ἄλλος *(allos);* ἕτερος *(heteros).* Adjectives, both meaning *another,* but when used precisely ἄλλος means another of the *same* kind and ἕτερος means another of a *different* kind. Here the Galatians' legalism represents a *different* sort of gospel, not another of the same kind. Jesus promised the Holy Spirit as ἄλλον Παράκλητον, *another Helper,* that would be *like* Him (John 14:16). Compounds with ἑτερο- tend to stress the "different" aspect as well. Cf. ἑτεροδιδασκαλέω, *to teach a different doctrine* (that is, "heretical"; 1 Tim. 1:3); and ἑτεροζυγέω, *to unevenly yoke,* used of animals that need yokes of a different kind, and of persons who are mismated be-

be accursed.
9 As we have said before, so
now I say again, if anyone
preaches any other gospel to
you than what you have received, let him be accursed.
10 For do I now persuade
men, or God? Or do I seek to
please men? For if I still
pleased men, I would not be a
bondservant of Christ.
11 But I make known to you,
brethren, that the gospel which
was preached by me is not according to man.
12 For I neither received it
from man, nor was I taught *it,*
but *it came* through the revelation of Jesus Christ.
13 For you have heard of my
former conduct in Judaism, how
I persecuted the church of God
beyond measure and *tried to* destroy it.
14 And I advanced in Judaism
beyond many of my contempo-
raries in my own nation, being
more exceedingly zealous for
the traditions of my fathers.
15 But when it pleased God,
who separated me from my
mother's womb and called *me*
through His grace,
16 to reveal His Son in me,
that I might preach Him among
the Gentiles, I did not immediately confer with flesh and
blood,
17 nor did I go up to Jerusalem to those *who were* apostles
before me; but I went to Arabia, and returned again to Damascus.

ἀνάθεμα ἔστω. **9** Ὡς προειρήκαμεν, καὶ ἄρτι πάλιν
[4]accursed [1]let [2]him [3]be. As we have said before, and [4]just [5]now [3]again

λέγω, εἴ τις ὑμᾶς εὐαγγελίζεται παρ' ὃ
[1]I [2]say, if anyone [4]*to* [5]you [1]preaches [2]a [3]gospel than what
other than

παρελάβετε, ἀνάθεμα ἔστω. **10** Ἄρτι γὰρ ἀνθρώπους
you received, [4]accursed [1]let [2]him [3]be. [4]just [5]now [1]For [7]men

πείθω, ἢ τὸν Θεόν? Ἢ ζητῶ ἀνθρώποις ἀρέσκειν? Εἰ
[2]do [3]I [6]persuade, or - God? Or do I seek [3]men [1]to [2]please? if ˜

γὰρ ἔτι ἀνθρώποις ἤρεσκον, Χριστοῦ δοῦλος οὐκ ἂν
For [2]still [4]men [1]I [3]pleased, [11]of [12]Christ [9]a [10]bondservant [7]not -
slave

ἤμην.
[5]I [6]would [8]be.

Paul's Call to Apostleship

11 Γνωρίζω δὲ ὑμῖν, ἀδελφοί, τὸ εὐαγγέλιον τὸ
[2]I [3]make [4]known [1]Now to you, brothers, the gospel -

εὐαγγελισθὲν ὑπ' ἐμοῦ ὅτι οὐκ ἔστι κατὰ ἄνθρωπον.
preached by me that [3]not [1]it [2]is according to man.
because

12 Οὐδὲ γὰρ ἐγὼ παρὰ ἀνθρώπου παρέλαβον αὐτό, οὔτε
[3]neither [1]For [2]I [6]from [7]man [4]received [5]it, nor

ἐδιδάχθην, ἀλλὰ δι' ἀποκαλύψεως Ἰησοῦ Χριστοῦ.
was I taught *it,* but through a revelation of Jesus Christ.

13 Ἠκούσατε γὰρ τὴν ἐμὴν ἀναστροφήν ποτε ἐν τῷ
[2]you [3]heard [4]of [1]For - my conduct at one time in -

Ἰουδαϊσμῷ, ὅτι καθ' ὑπερβολὴν ἐδίωκον τὴν
Judaism, that according to excess I was persecuting the
beyond measure I used to persecute

ἐκκλησίαν τοῦ Θεοῦ καὶ ἐπόρθουν αὐτήν, **14** καὶ
church - of God and I was devastating it, and

προέκοπτον ἐν τῷ Ἰουδαϊσμῷ ὑπὲρ πολλοὺς συνηλικιώτας
I was advancing in - Judaism above many my own age

ἐν τῷ γένει μου, περισσοτέρως ζηλωτὴς ὑπάρχων τῶν
among - race ˜ my, [2]far [3]more [4]a [5]zealot [1]being for the

πατρικῶν μου παραδόσεων. **15** Ὅτε δὲ εὐδόκησεν ὁ
[2]of [4]forefathers [3]my [1]traditions. when ˜ But [2]was [3]pleased -

Θεός,[a] ὁ ἀφορίσας με ἐκ κοιλίας μητρός μου καὶ
[1]God, the *One* separating me from *the* womb of mother ˜ my and
who separated

καλέσας διὰ τῆς χάριτος αὐτοῦ, **16** ἀποκαλύψαι τὸν Υἱὸν
calling *me* through - grace ˜ His, to reveal - Son ˜
called

αὐτοῦ ἐν ἐμοί ἵνα εὐαγγελίζωμαι αὐτὸν ἐν τοῖς
His in me so that I might preach the gospel about Him among the
by

ἔθνεσιν, εὐθέως οὐ προσανεθέμην σαρκὶ καὶ αἵματι,
Gentiles, immediately [3]not [1]I [2]did [4]consult with flesh and blood,

17 οὐδὲ ἀνῆλθον εἰς Ἱεροσόλυμα πρὸς τοὺς πρὸ
neither did I go up to Jerusalem to the [2]before
those who were

ἐμοῦ ἀποστόλους, ἀλλὰ ἀπῆλθον εἰς Ἀραβίαν καὶ πάλιν
[3]me [1]apostles, but I went off to Arabia and [3]again

ὑπέστρεψα εἰς Δαμασκόν.
[1]I [2]returned to Damascus.

---

[a](1:15) NU brackets ο Θεος, *God.*

☞ ———

cause of different beliefs (2 Cor. 6:14).

Paul's Contacts at Jerusalem

18 Ἔπειτα μετὰ ἔτη τρία ἀνῆλθον εἰς Ἱεροσόλυμα
Then after years ˜ three I went up to Jerusalem

ἱστορῆσαι Πέτρον,[b] καὶ ἐπέμεινα πρὸς αὐτὸν ἡμέρας
to visit Peter, and I stayed with him days ˜

δεκαπέντε. 19 Ἕτερον δὲ τῶν ἀποστόλων οὐκ εἶδον
fifteen. [6]*any* [7]other [1]But [8]of [9]the [10]apostles [4]not [2]I [3]did [5]see

εἰ μὴ Ἰάκωβον τὸν ἀδελφὸν τοῦ Κυρίου. 20 Ἃ δὲ
if not James the brother of the Lord. what ˜ Now
except

γράφω ὑμῖν, ἰδοὺ ἐνώπιον τοῦ Θεοῦ, ὅτι οὐ ψεύδομαι.
I write to you, behold before - God, - [3]not [1]I [2]do [4]lie.

21 Ἔπειτα ἦλθον εἰς τὰ κλίματα τῆς Συρίας καὶ τῆς Κιλικίας.
Then I went into the regions - of Syria and - of Cilicia.

22 Ἤμην δὲ ἀγνοούμενος τῷ προσώπῳ ταῖς ἐκκλησίαις τῆς
[2]I [3]was [1]And being unknown - by face to the churches -
unknown

Ἰουδαίας ταῖς ἐν Χριστῷ. 23 Μόνον δὲ ἀκούοντες
of Judea the *ones* in Christ. [5]only [1]But [4]hearing
which are they

ἦσαν ὅτι "Ὁ διώκων ἡμᾶς ποτε νῦν
[2]they [3]were that "The *one* persecuting us at one time now
heard "He who persecuted

εὐαγγελίζεται τὴν πίστιν ἥν ποτε ἐπόρθει."
preaches the gospel *of* the faith which at one time he was devastating."

24 Καὶ ἐδόξαζον ἐν ἐμοὶ τὸν Θεόν.
And they glorified [2]in [3]me - [1]God.
by means of

Paul Defends His Gospel at Jerusalem

2 1 Ἔπειτα διὰ δεκατεσσάρων ἐτῶν πάλιν ἀνέβην εἰς
Then through fourteen years again I went up to
after

Ἱεροσόλυμα μετὰ Βαρναβᾶ, συμπαραλαβὼν καὶ Τίτον.
Jerusalem with Barnabas, taking along also Titus.

2 Ἀνέβην δὲ κατὰ ἀποκάλυψιν καὶ ἀνεθέμην αὐτοῖς τὸ
[2]I [3]went [4]up [1]And by revelation and I set before them the

εὐαγγέλιον ὃ κηρύσσω ἐν τοῖς ἔθνεσι, κατ' ἰδίαν δὲ
gospel which I preach among the Gentiles, privately ˜ but

τοῖς δοκοῦσι, μή πως εἰς κενὸν τρέχω ἢ
to the *ones* being influential, lest somehow [5]for [6]nothing [1]I [2]run [3]or
to those with influence, might run

ἔδραμον. 3 Ἀλλ' οὐδὲ Τίτος ὁ σὺν ἐμοί, Ἕλλην
[4]ran. But not even Titus the *one* with me, [2]a [3]Greek
had run. who was

ὤν, ἠναγκάσθη περιτμηθῆναι· 4 διὰ
[1]being, was compelled to be circumcised; [2]*that* [3]*was* [4]because [5]of
although he was,

δὲ τοὺς παρεισάκτους ψευδαδέλφους — οἵτινες
[1]And the [3]secretly [4]brought [5]in [1]false [2]brothers — who

παρεισῆλθον κατασκοπῆσαι τὴν ἐλευθερίαν ἡμῶν ἣν ἔχομεν
slipped in to spy out - freedom ˜ our which we have

ἐν Χριστῷ Ἰησοῦ, ἵνα ἡμᾶς καταδουλώσωνται —
in Christ Jesus, so that [4]us [1]they [2]might [3]reduce [5]to [6]slavery —

5 οἷς οὐδὲ πρὸς ὥραν εἴξαμεν τῇ ὑποταγῇ, ἵνα ἡ
to whom not even for an hour did we yield - in subjection, that the

ἀλήθεια τοῦ εὐαγγελίου διαμείνῃ πρὸς ὑμᾶς. 6 Ἀπὸ δὲ
truth of the gospel might remain with you. from ˜ But

18 Then after three years I went up to Jerusalem to see Peter, and remained with him fifteen days.
19 But I saw none of the other apostles except James, the Lord's brother.
20 (Now *concerning* the things which I write to you, indeed, before God, I do not lie.)
21 Afterward I went into the regions of Syria and Cilicia.
22 And I was unknown by face to the churches of Judea which *were* in Christ.
23 But they were hearing only, "He who formerly persecuted us now preaches the faith which he once *tried to* destroy."
24 And they glorified God in me.

2 Then after fourteen years I went up again to Jerusalem with Barnabas, and also took Titus with *me.*
2 And I went up by revelation, and communicated to them that gospel which I preach among the Gentiles, but privately to those who were of reputation, lest by any means I might run, or had run, in vain.
3 Yet not even Titus who *was* with me, being a Greek, was compelled to be circumcised.
4 And *this occurred* because of false brethren secretly brought in (who came in by stealth to spy out our liberty which we have in Christ Jesus, that they might bring us into bondage),
5 to whom we did not yield submission even for an hour, that the truth of the gospel might continue with you.
6 But from those who

[b](1:18) NU reads Κηφαν, *Cephas.*

seemed to be something—
whatever they were, it makes
no difference to me; God shows
personal favoritism to no
man—for those who seemed *to
be something* added nothing to
me.
7 But on the contrary, when
they saw that the gospel for the
uncircumcised had been committed to me, as *the gospel* for
the circumcised *was* to Peter
8 (for He who worked effectively in Peter for the apostleship to the circumcised also
worked effectively in me toward the Gentiles),
9 and when James, Cephas,
and John, who seemed to be pillars, perceived the grace that
had been given to me, they
gave me and Barnabas the right
hand of fellowship, that we
should go to the Gentiles and
they to the circumcised.
10 *They desired* only that we
should remember the poor, the
very thing which I also was eager to do.
11 Now when Peter had come
to Antioch, I withstood him to
his face, because he was to be
blamed;
12 for before certain men
came from James, he would eat
with the Gentiles; but when
they came, he withdrew and
separated himself, fearing
those who were of the circumcision.
13 And the rest of the Jews
also played the hypocrite with
him, so that even Barnabas
was carried away with their

τῶν δοκούντων εἶναί τι — ὁποῖοί ποτε ἦσαν
the *ones* seeming to be something — whatever sort then they were
those who seemed

οὐδέν μοι διαφέρει· πρόσωπον Θεὸς ἀνθρώπου οὐ
nothing to me it makes a difference; [5]*the* [6]face [1]God [7]of [8]a [9]man [3]not
it makes no difference to me; God shows no partiality

λαμβάνει — ἐμοὶ γὰρ οἱ δοκοῦντες οὐδὲν
[2]does [4]receive — [11]to [12]me [10]so the *ones* being influential nothing
to a man — those with influence

προσανέθεντο, 7 ἀλλὰ τοὐναντίον, ἰδόντες ὅτι
contributed, but on the contrary, seeing that
when they saw

πεπίστευμαι τὸ εὐαγγέλιον τῆς ἀκροβυστίας
I have been entrusted *with* the gospel - of uncircumcision
had for the uncircumcised

καθὼς Πέτρος τῆς περιτομῆς 8 (ὁ γὰρ
just as Peter *with the gospel* - of circumcision ([2]the [3]*One* [1]for
for the circumcised (for He who

ἐνεργήσας Πέτρῳ εἰς ἀποστολὴν τῆς περιτομῆς, ἐνήργησε
working with Peter in *the* apostleship of the circumcision, worked
worked for the circumcised,

καὶ ἐμοὶ εἰς τὰ ἔθνη), 9 καὶ γνόντες τὴν χάριν τὴν
also with me in *that for* the Gentiles), and perceiving the grace the *one*
perceived which

δοθεῖσάν μοι, Ἰάκωβος καὶ Κηφᾶς καὶ Ἰωάννης, οἱ
having been given to me, James and Cephas and John, the *ones*
was given who

δοκοῦντες στῦλοι εἶναι, δεξιὰς ἔδωκαν ἐμοὶ καὶ
seeming [3]pillars [1]to [2]be, [8]*their* [9]right [10]*hands* [4]gave [5]me [6]and
seemed

Βαρναβᾷ κοινωνίας, ἵνα ἡμεῖς εἰς τὰ ἔθνη, αὐτοὶ δὲ εἰς
[7]Barnabas of fellowship, that we *should go* to the Gentiles, they ˜ and to

τὴν περιτομήν· 10 μόνον τῶν πτωχῶν ἵνα
the circumcision; only *they desired* [5]the [6]poor [1]that

μνημονεύωμεν, ὃ καὶ ἐσπούδασα αὐτὸ τοῦτο
[2]we [3]should [4]remember, which indeed I made every effort [4]very [3]this [5]*thing*

ποιῆσαι.
[1]to [2]do.

Paul Resists a Return to the Law

11 Ὅτε δὲ ἦλθε Πέτρος[a] εἰς Ἀντιόχειαν, κατὰ
when ˜ But came ˜ Peter to Antioch, [4]to [5]*his*

πρόσωπον αὐτῷ ἀντέστην ὅτι κατεγνωσμένος ἦν.
[6]face [3]him [1]I [2]withstood because [3]condemned [1]he [2]was.
opposed blameworthy

12 Πρὸ τοῦ γὰρ ἐλθεῖν τινας ἀπὸ Ἰακώβου, μετὰ τῶν
before ˜ - For [3]to [4]come [1]certain [2]*men* from James, [5]with [6]the
came

ἐθνῶν συνήσθιεν· ὅτε δὲ ἦλθον ὑπέστελλε
[7]Gentiles [1]he [2]would [3]eat [4]together; when ˜ but they came he drew back
began to draw back

καὶ ἀφώριζεν ἑαυτόν, φοβούμενος τοὺς ἐκ
and separated himself, fearing the *ones* from
began to separate those of the

περιτομῆς. 13 Καὶ συνυπεκρίθησαν αὐτῷ καὶ οἱ λοιποὶ
the circumcision. And [7]joined [9]in [10]hypocrisy [8]him [1]also [2]the [3]rest
circumcision party.

Ἰουδαῖοι ὥστε καὶ Βαρναβᾶς συναπήχθη αὐτῶν τῇ
[4]of [5]*the* [6]Jews so that even Barnabas was carried away with their -

---

[a](2:11) NU reads Κηφας, *Cephas*.

ὑποκρίσει.* **14** Ἀλλ' ὅτε εἶδον ὅτι οὐκ ὀρθοποδοῦσι
hypocrisy. But when I saw that [3]not [1]they [2]did act rightly

πρὸς τὴν ἀλήθειαν τοῦ εὐαγγελίου, εἶπον τῷ Πέτρῳ[b]
with respect to the truth of the gospel, I said - to Peter

ἔμπροσθεν πάντων, "Εἰ σύ, Ἰουδαῖος ὑπάρχων,
before *them* all, "If you, [2]a [3]Jew [1]being,

ἐθνικῶς ζῇς καὶ οὐκ Ἰουδαϊκῶς, τί[c] τὰ ἔθνη
[5]in [6]Gentile [7]fashion [4]live and not in Jewish fashion, why [4]the [5]Gentiles

ἀναγκάζεις Ἰουδαΐζειν? **15** Ἡμεῖς φύσει Ἰουδαῖοι, καὶ
[1]do [2]you [3]compel to live as a Jew? We *who are* by nature Jews, and

οὐκ ἐξ ἐθνῶν ἁμαρτωλοί, **16** εἰδότες ὅτι οὐ δικαιοῦται
not [2]of [3]*the* [4]Gentiles [1]sinners, knowing that [4]not [3]is [5]justified

ἄνθρωπος ἐξ ἔργων νόμου ἐὰν μὴ διὰ πίστεως Ἰησοῦ
[1]a [2]man by *the* works of *the* law if not through faith of Jesus
but in

Χριστοῦ, καὶ ἡμεῖς εἰς Χριστὸν Ἰησοῦν ἐπιστεύσαμεν ἵνα
Christ, even we [2]in [3]Christ [4]Jesus [1]believed so that

δικαιωθῶμεν ἐκ πίστεως Χριστοῦ καὶ οὐκ ἐξ ἔργων
we might be justified by faith of Christ and not by *the* works
in

νόμου, διότι οὐ δικαιωθήσεται ἐξ ἔργων νόμου
of *the* law, because [4]not [3]will [5]be [6]justified [7]by [8]*the* [9]works [10]of [11]*the* [12]law
no flesh will be justified by the works of

πᾶσα σάρξ. **17** Εἰ δὲ ζητοῦντες δικαιωθῆναι ἐν Χριστῷ
[1]all [2]flesh. if ˜ But seeking to be justified in Christ
the law. by seeking

εὑρέθημεν καὶ αὐτοὶ ἁμαρτωλοί, ἆρα Χριστὸς ἁμαρτίας
[1]we [4]were [5]found [3]also [2]ourselves sinners, then *is* Christ [3]of [4]sin

διάκονος? Μὴ γένοιτο! **18** Εἰ γὰρ ἃ κατέλυσα,
[1]a [2]servant? [7]not [5]Let [6]it [8]be! if ˜ For *the things* which I destroyed,

ταῦτα πάλιν οἰκοδομῶ, παραβάτην ἐμαυτὸν συνίστημι.
these *things* [3]again [1]I [2]build, [8]a [9]transgressor [6]myself [7]*as* [4]I [5]present.

19 Ἐγὼ γὰρ διὰ νόμου νόμῳ ἀπέθανον ἵνα Θεῷ
I ˜ For through *the* law [2]to [3]*the* [4]law [1]died that [4]to [5]God

ζήσω. **20** Χριστῷ συνεσταύρωμαι· ζῶ δὲ οὐκέτι
[1]I [2]might [3]live. With Christ I have been crucified; [5]live [1]and [3]no [4]longer
am

ἐγώ, ζῇ δὲ ἐν ἐμοὶ Χριστός· ὃ δὲ νῦν ζῶ ἐν
[2]I, [8]lives [6]but [9]in [10]me [7]Christ; [12]*that* [13]which [11]and [15]now [14]I [16]live in

σαρκί, ἐν πίστει ζῶ τῇ τοῦ Υἱοῦ τοῦ Θεοῦ τοῦ
the flesh, [3]in [4]faith [1]I [2]live in the Son - of God the *One*
by who

ἀγαπήσαντός με καὶ παραδόντος ἑαυτὸν ὑπὲρ ἐμοῦ. **21** Οὐκ
loving me and giving Himself for me. [3]not
loved gave

ἀθετῶ τὴν χάριν τοῦ Θεοῦ· εἰ γὰρ διὰ νόμου
[1]I [2]do annul the grace - of God; if ˜ for [3]through [4]*the* [5]law

δικαιοσύνη, ἄρα Χριστὸς δωρεὰν ἀπέθανεν."
[1]righteousness [2]*comes,* then Christ [2]for [3]nothing [1]died."

Justification Is by Faith

3 **1** Ὦ ἀνόητοι Γαλάται! Τίς ὑμᾶς ἐβάσκανε τῇ ἀληθείᾳ
O foolish Galatians! Who you ˜ bewitched [4]the [5]truth

μὴ πείθεσθαι,[a] οἷς κατ' ὀφθαλμοὺς Ἰησοῦς Χριστὸς
[1]not [2]to [3]obey, to whom toward eyes Jesus Christ
that you should not obey, before whose

προεγράφη ἐν ὑμῖν[b] ἐσταυρωμένος? **2** Τοῦτο
was portrayed publicly among you having been crucified? This
as

hypocrisy.
14 But when I saw that they
were not straightforward about
the truth of the gospel, I said to
Peter before *them* all, "If you,
being a Jew, live in the manner
of Gentiles and not as the Jews,
why do you compel Gentiles to
live as Jews?
15 "We *who are* Jews by nature, and not sinners of the
Gentiles,
16 "knowing that a man is not
justified by the works of the law
but by faith in Jesus Christ,
even we have believed in Christ
Jesus, that we might be justified by faith in Christ and not by
the works of the law; for by the
works of the law no flesh shall
be justified.
17 "But if, while we seek to
be justified by Christ, we ourselves also are found sinners, *is*
Christ therefore a minister of
sin? Certainly not!
18 "For if I build again those
things which I destroyed, I
make myself a transgressor.
19 "For I through the law died
to the law that I might live to
God.
20 "I have been crucified with
Christ; it is no longer I who
live, but Christ lives in me; and
the *life* which I now live in the
flesh I live by faith in the Son of
God, who loved me and gave
Himself for me.
21 "I do not set aside the
grace of God; for if righteousness *comes* through the law,
then Christ died in vain."
3 O foolish Galatians! Who
has bewitched you that
you should not obey the truth,
before whose eyes Jesus Christ
was clearly portrayed among
you as crucified?
2 This only I want to learn

---

[b]**(2:14)** NU reads Κηφα, *to Cephas.* [c]**(2:14)** NU reads πως, *how (is it).*
[a]**(3:1)** NU omits τη αληθεια μη πειθεσθαι, *not to obey the truth.* [b]**(3:1)** NU omits εν υμιν, *among you.*

***(2:13)** ὑπόκρισις *(hypokrisis).* Noun meaning *hypocrisy, pretense.* It is derived from the verb ὑποκρίνομαι, *playact, pretend* (only Luke 20:20 in the NT). The word was commonly used in Koine Greek of playing a role in a stage production. The meaning of the noun ὑπόκρισις was extended to include *acting insincerely,*

from you: Did you receive the
Spirit by the works of the law,
or by the hearing of faith?
3 Are you so foolish? Having
begun in the Spirit, are you now
being made perfect by the
flesh?
4 Have you suffered so many
things in vain—if indeed *it was*
in vain?
5 Therefore He who supplies
the Spirit to you and works miracles among you, *does He do it*
by the works of the law, or by
the hearing of faith?—
6 just as Abraham *"believed
God, and it was accounted to
him for righteousness."*
7 Therefore know that *only*
those who are of faith are sons
of Abraham.
8 And the Scripture, foreseeing that God would justify
the Gentiles by faith, preached
the gospel to Abraham beforehand, *saying, "In you all the nations shall be blessed."*
9 So then those who *are* of
faith are blessed with believing
Abraham.
10 For as many as are of the
works of the law are under the
curse; for it is written, *"Cursed
is everyone who does not continue in all things which are
written in the book of the law,
to do them."*
11 But that no one is justified
by the law in the sight of God *is*
evident, for *"the just shall live
by faith."*
12 Yet the law is not of faith,
but *"the man who does them
shall live by them."*
13 Christ has redeemed us

μόνον θέλω μαθεῖν ἀφ' ὑμῶν· Ἐξ ἔργων νόμου τὸ
only do I wish to learn from you: [6]by [7]*the* [8]works [9]of [10]*the* [11]law [4]the

Πνεῦμα ἐλάβετε ἢ ἐξ ἀκοῆς πίστεως? **3** Οὕτως
[5]Spirit [1]Did [2]you [3]receive or by *the* hearing of faith? [3]so
in

ἀνόητοί ἐστε? Ἐναρξάμενοι Πνεύματι, νῦν σαρκὶ
[4]foolish [1]Are [2]you? Beginning in *the* Spirit, [3]now [6]in [7]*the* [8]flesh
After you have begun by by

ἐπιτελεῖσθε? **4** Τοσαῦτα ἐπάθετε εἰκῇ?
[1]will [2]you [4]be [5]completed? [4]so [5]many [6]*things* [1]Have [2]you [3]suffered in vain?

Εἴ γε καὶ εἰκῇ. **5** Ὁ οὖν ἐπιχορηγῶν
If [3]really [1]indeed [2]*they* [4]*were* in vain. [2]the [3]*One* [1]Therefore supplying
He who supplies

ὑμῖν τὸ Πνεῦμα καὶ ἐνεργῶν δυνάμεις ἐν ὑμῖν,
[3]to [4]you [1]the [2]Spirit and working miracles among you, *does He*
works

ἐξ ἔργων νόμου ἢ ἐξ ἀκοῆς πίστεως? **6** Καθὼς
do it by *the* works of *the* law or by *the* hearing of faith? Just as
in

Ἀβραὰμ «ἐπίστευσε τῷ Θεῷ, καὶ ἐλογίσθη αὐτῷ εἰς
Abraham «believed - God, and it was accounted to him for
as

δικαιοσύνην.»[c] **7** Γινώσκετε ἄρα ὅτι οἱ ἐκ
righteousness.» Know therefore that the *ones* of
those who are

πίστεως, οὗτοί εἰσιν υἱοὶ Ἀβραάμ. **8** Προϊδοῦσα δὲ ἡ
faith, these are sons of Abraham. [4]foreseeing [1]And [2]the

Γραφὴ ὅτι ἐκ πίστεως δικαιοῖ τὰ ἔθνη ὁ Θεός,
[3]Scripture that [5]by [6]faith [2]justifies [3]the [4]nations - [1]God,
would justify Gentiles

προευηγγελίσατο τῷ Ἀβραὰμ ὅτι
preached the gospel beforehand - to Abraham *saying* that

«Ἐνευλογηθήσονται ἐν σοὶ πάντα τὰ ἔθνη.»[d] **9** Ὥστε
«[4]will [5]be [6]blessed [7]in [8]you [1]All [2]the [3]nations.» Therefore
by Gentiles.»

οἱ ἐκ πίστεως εὐλογοῦνται σὺν τῷ πιστῷ Ἀβραάμ.
the *ones* of faith are blessed with - believing Abraham.
those who are

The Law Brings a Curse

10 Ὅσοι γὰρ ἐξ ἔργων νόμου εἰσίν, ὑπὸ
[2]as [3]many [4]as [1]For [6]of [7]*the* [8]works [9]of [10]*the* [11]law [5]are, [13]under

κατάραν εἰσί· γέγραπται γάρ, «Ἐπικατάρατος πᾶς ὃς
[14]a [15]curse [12]are; [17]it [18]is [19]written [16]for, «Cursed *is* every *one* who

οὐκ ἐμμένει ἐν πᾶσι τοῖς γεγραμμένοις ἐν τῷ βιβλίῳ
not ˜ does remain in all the *things* having been written in the book

τοῦ νόμου τοῦ ποιῆσαι αὐτά.»[e] **11** Ὅτι δὲ ἐν νόμῳ
of the law - to do them.» that ˜ Now [7]by [8]*the* [9]law

οὐδεὶς δικαιοῦται παρὰ τῷ Θεῷ δῆλον, ὅτι «Ὁ
[1]no [2]one [3]is [4]justified [5]before - [6]God *is* evident, because «the

δίκαιος ἐκ πίστεως ζήσεται.»[f] **12** Ὁ δὲ νόμος
righteous *person* by faith shall live.» the ˜ But law
person who is righteous

οὐκ ἔστιν ἐκ πίστεως, ἀλλ' «Ὁ ποιήσας αὐτὰ ἄνθρωπος[g]
not ˜ is of faith, but «The [2]doing [3]them [1]man
who does

ζήσεται ἐν αὐτοῖς.»[h] **13** Χριστὸς ἡμᾶς ἐξηγόρασεν ἐκ τῆς
shall live by them.» Christ us ˜ redeemed from the

---

[c](3:6) Gen. 15:6
[d](3:8) Gen. 12:3; 18:18; 22:18; 26:4; 28:14
[e](3:10) Deut. 27:26
[f](3:11) Hab. 2:4
[g](3:12) NU omits ανθρωπος, *man.* [h](3:12) Lev. 18:5

---

hypocrisy. Here in Gal. 2:13 Paul accused Peter and other Jewish believers of hypocrisy for eating with Gentile believers but then ceasing to do so when others arrived from Jerusalem who might have criticized this violation of Jewish custom. Cf. the cognate noun ὑποκριτής, *hypocrite, playactor* (Matt. 6:16).

κατάρας τοῦ νόμου γενόμενος ὑπὲρ ἡμῶν κατάρα, γέγραπται
curse of the law *by* becoming [3]for [4]us [1]a [2]curse, [6]it [7]is [8]written

γάρ, «Ἐπικατάρατος πᾶς ὁ κρεμάμενος ἐπὶ ξύλου» [i] —
[5]for, «Cursed *is* every - *one* hanging on a tree» —
everyone who hangs

14 ἵνα εἰς τὰ ἔθνη ἡ εὐλογία τοῦ Ἀβραὰμ γένηται
so that [7]to [8]the [9]nations [1]the [2]blessing - [3]of [4]Abraham [5]might [6]come
Gentiles

ἐν Χριστῷ Ἰησοῦ, ἵνα τὴν ἐπαγγελίαν τοῦ Πνεύματος
in Christ Jesus, that [4]the [5]promise [6]of [7]the [8]Spirit
by

λάβωμεν διὰ τῆς πίστεως.
[1]we [2]might [3]receive through - faith.

The Promise to Abraham Is Changeless

15 Ἀδελφοί, κατὰ ἄνθρωπον λέγω· Ὅμως
Brothers, [3]according [4]to [5]man [1]I [2]speak: Nevertheless
in human fashion Though

ἀνθρώπου κεκυρωμένην διαθήκην οὐδεὶς ἀθετεῖ ἢ
[3]*is* [4]of [5]a [6]man [7]*yet* [8]having [9]been [10]confirmed [1]a [2]covenant no one annuls or

ἐπιδιατάσσεται. 16 Τῷ δὲ Ἀβραὰμ ἐρρέθησαν αἱ
adds to *it.* - Now [5]to [6]Abraham [3]were [4]spoken [1]the

ἐπαγγελίαι καὶ τῷ σπέρματι αὐτοῦ. Οὐ λέγει, "Καὶ τοῖς
[2]promises and - to Seed ˜ his. [3]not [1]He [2]does [4]say, "And -

σπέρμασιν," ὡς ἐπὶ πολλῶν, ἀλλ' ὡς ἐφ' ἑνός, «Καὶ τῷ
to seeds," as to many, but as to one, «And -

σπέρματί σου,» [j] ὅς ἐστι Χριστός. 17 Τοῦτο δὲ λέγω,
to Seed ˜ your,» who is Christ. this ˜ And I say,

διαθήκην προκεκυρωμένην ὑπὸ τοῦ Θεοῦ εἰς Χριστὸν [k] ὁ
[13]a [14]covenant [15]previously [16]confirmed [17]by - [18]God [19]to [20]Christ [1]the
for

μετὰ ἔτη τετρακόσια καὶ τριάκοντα γεγονὼς νόμος οὐκ
[4]after [9]years [5]four [6]hundred [7]and [8]thirty [3]made [2]law [11]not

ἀκυροῖ, εἰς τὸ καταργῆσαι τὴν ἐπαγγελίαν. 18 Εἰ
[10]does [12]annul, for - to make of no effect the promise. if ˜
so that it makes the promise of no effect.

γὰρ ἐκ νόμου ἡ κληρονομία, οὐκέτι ἐξ ἐπαγγελίας·
For [4]by [5]*the* [6]law [1]the [2]inheritance [3]*comes, it is* no longer by promise;

τῷ δὲ Ἀβραὰμ δι' ἐπαγγελίας κεχάρισται ὁ Θεός.
- but [5]to [6]Abraham [7]by [8]promise [2]has [3]given [4]*it* - [1]God.

The Purpose of the Law

19 Τί οὖν ὁ νόμος? Τῶν παραβάσεων χάριν
Why then *was* the law *given?* - [7]transgressions [4]on [5]account [6]of

προσετέθη ἄχρις οὗ ἔλθῃ τὸ σπέρμα ᾧ
[1]It [2]was [3]added until - [3]should [4]come [1]the [2]Seed to whom

ἐπήγγελται, διαταγεὶς δι' ἀγγέλων ἐν χειρὶ
it was promised, *and* being commanded through angels by *the* hand
had been it was

μεσίτου. 20 Ὁ δὲ μεσίτης ἑνὸς οὐκ ἔστιν, ὁ δὲ
of a mediator. the ˜ Now mediator [3]of [4]one [2]not [1]is, - but
for one person

Θεὸς εἷς ἐστιν. 21 Ὁ οὖν νόμος κατὰ τῶν
God one ˜ is. [3]the [1]Therefore [2]*is* [4]law against the

ἐπαγγελιῶν τοῦ Θεοῦ? Μὴ γένοιτο! Εἰ γὰρ ἐδόθη νόμος
promises - of God? [3]not [1]Let [2]it [4]be! if ˜ For [3]was [4]given [1]a [2]law
had been

from the curse of the law, having become a curse for us (for it
is written, *"Cursed is everyone
who hangs on a tree"*),
14 that the blessing of Abraham might come upon the Gentiles in Christ Jesus, that we
might receive the promise of
the Spirit through faith.
15 Brethren, I speak in the
manner of men: Though *it is*
only a man's covenant, yet *if it
is* confirmed, no one annuls or
adds to it.
16 Now to Abraham and his
Seed were the promises made.
He does not say, "And to
seeds," as of many, but as of
one, *"And to your Seed,"* who
is Christ.
17 And this I say, *that* the law,
which was four hundred and
thirty years later, cannot annul
the covenant that was confirmed before by God in Christ,
that it should make the promise
of no effect.
18 For if the inheritance *is* of
the law, *it is* no longer of promise; but God gave *it* to Abraham
by promise.
19 What purpose then *does*
the law *serve?* It was added because of transgressions, till the
Seed should come to whom the
promise was made; *and it was*
appointed through angels by the
hand of a mediator.
20 Now a mediator does not
mediate for one *only,* but God is
one.
21 *Is* the law then against the
promises of God? Certainly not!
For if there had been a law

---

[i](3:13) Deut. 21:23
[j](3:16) Gen. 12:7; 13:15; 24:7 [k](3:17) NU omits εις Χριστον, *for Christ.*

given which could have given
life, truly righteousness would
have been by the law.
22 But the Scripture has confined all under sin, that the
promise by faith in Jesus Christ
might be given to those who
believe.
23 But before faith came, we
were kept under guard by the
law, kept for the faith which
would afterward be revealed.
24 Therefore the law was our
tutor *to bring us* to Christ, that
we might be justified by faith.
25 But after faith has come,
we are no longer under a tutor.
26 For you are all sons of God
through faith in Christ Jesus.
27 For as many of you as
were baptized into Christ have
put on Christ.
28 There is neither Jew nor
Greek, there is neither slave
nor free, there is neither male
nor female; for you are all one
in Christ Jesus.
29 And if you *are* Christ's,
then you are Abraham's seed,
and heirs according to the
promise.
4 Now I say *that* the heir, as
long as he is a child, does
not differ at all from a slave,
though he is master of all,
2 but is under guardians and
stewards until the time appointed by the father.
3 Even so we, when we
were children, were in bondage
under the elements of the
world.

ὁ δυνάμενος ζῳοποιῆσαι, ὄντως ἂν ἐκ νόμου ἦν ἡ
the *one* being able to give life, truly - [4]by [5]*the* [6]law [2]would [3]be -
which was able

δικαιοσύνη. **22** Ἀλλὰ συνέκλεισεν ἡ Γραφὴ τὰ πάντα
[1]righteousness. But [3]confined [1]the [2]Scripture - all *things*
has confined

ὑπὸ ἁμαρτίαν ἵνα ἡ ἐπαγγελία ἐκ πίστεως Ἰησοῦ
under sin so that the promise [4]by [5]faith [6]of [7]Jesus
in

Χριστοῦ δοθῇ τοῖς πιστεύουσι.
[8]Christ [1]might [2]be [3]given to the *ones* believing.
those who believe.

23 Πρὸ τοῦ δὲ ἐλθεῖν τὴν πίστιν, ὑπὸ νόμον
before ˜ - But [2]to [3]come - [1]faith, [7]under [8]*the* [9]law
came

ἐφρουρούμεθα,* συγκεκλεισμένοι εἰς τὴν μέλλουσαν πίστιν
[4]we [5]were [6]guarded, having been confined for the [2]being [3]about [1]faith
hemmed in which was

ἀποκαλυφθῆναι. **24** Ὥστε ὁ νόμος παιδαγωγὸς ἡμῶν
to be revealed. Therefore the law [4]custodian [3]our
tutor

γέγονεν εἰς Χριστόν, ἵνα ἐκ πίστεως
[1]has [2]become *leading us* to Christ, so that [5]by [6]faith

δικαιωθῶμεν. **25** Ἐλθούσης δὲ τῆς πίστεως, οὐκέτι
[1]we [2]might [3]be [4]justified. coming But - faith, [3]no [4]longer
But since faith came,

ὑπὸ παιδαγωγόν ἐσμεν.
[5]under [6]a [7]custodian [1]we [2]are.
tutor

Sons and Heirs

26 Πάντες γὰρ υἱοὶ Θεοῦ ἐστε διὰ τῆς πίστεως ἐν
[4]all [1]For [5]sons [6]of [7]God [2]you [3]are through - faith in

Χριστῷ Ἰησοῦ. **27** Ὅσοι γὰρ εἰς Χριστὸν
Christ Jesus. [2]as [3]many [4]*of* [5]*you* [6]as [1]For [9]into [10]Christ

ἐβαπτίσθητε, Χριστὸν ἐνεδύσασθε. **28** Οὐκ ἔνι
[7]were [8]baptized, [14]Christ [11]were [12]clothed [13]in. [3]no [1]There [2]is

Ἰουδαῖος οὐδὲ Ἕλλην, οὐκ ἔνι δοῦλος οὐδὲ ἐλεύθερος, οὐκ
Jew nor Greek, [3]no [1]there [2]is slave nor free *man,* [3]no

ἔνι ἄρσεν καὶ θῆλυ· πάντες γὰρ ὑμεῖς εἷς ἐστε ἐν
[1]there [2]is male and female; [4]all [1]for [2]you [5]one [3]are in

Χριστῷ Ἰησοῦ. **29** Εἰ δὲ ὑμεῖς Χριστοῦ, ἄρα τοῦ Ἀβραὰμ
Christ Jesus. if ˜ And you *are* of Christ, then - [5]of [6]Abraham

σπέρμα ἐστὲ καὶ κατ' ἐπαγγελίαν κληρονόμοι.
[3]a [4]seed [1]you [2]are and [2]according [3]to [4]*the* [5]promise [1]heirs.

Sons Versus Slaves

4 **1** Λέγω δέ, ἐφ' ὅσον χρόνον ὁ κληρονόμος
[2]I [3]say [1]Now, for as much as ˜ time the heir

νήπιός ἐστιν, οὐδὲν διαφέρει δούλου, κύριος πάντων
[2]a [3]minor [1]is, [6]nothing [4]he [5]differs from a slave, master of all
he does not differ at all though he is master

ὤν, **2** ἀλλὰ ὑπὸ ἐπιτρόπους ἐστὶ καὶ οἰκονόμους ἄχρι τῆς
being, but [3]under [4]guardians [1]he [2]is and stewards until the
of all,

προθεσμίας τοῦ πατρός. **3** Οὕτω καὶ ἡμεῖς, ὅτε ἦμεν
appointed time of the father. So also we, when we were

νήπιοι, ὑπὸ τὰ στοιχεῖα τοῦ κόσμου ἦμεν δεδουλωμένοι.
minors, [4]by [5]the [6]elements [7]of [8]the [9]world [1]we [2]were [3]enslaved.

***(3:23)** φρουρέω *(phroureō).* Verb, a military term meaning *keep under guard, garrison.* In 2 Cor. 11:32 Paul uses the word literally to describe how the governor of Damascus guarded the city to prevent his escape. Elsewhere in the NT φρουρέω is used figuratively of God's guarding believers by His power for salvation (1 Pet. 1:5); of God's peace guarding believers' hearts and minds (Phil. 4:7); and here in Gal. 3:23 of believers being kept in protective custody by the law until the coming of faith.

4 Ὅτε δὲ ἦλθε τὸ πλήρωμα τοῦ χρόνου, ἐξαπέστειλεν ὁ
when ˜ But [6]came [1]the [2]fullness [3]of [4]the [5]time, [8]sent [9]forth -

Θεὸς τὸν Υἱὸν αὐτοῦ, γενόμενον ἐκ γυναικός, γενόμενον ὑπὸ
[7]God - Son ˜ His, being born of a woman, being born under

νόμον, 5 ἵνα τοὺς ὑπὸ νόμον ἐξαγοράσῃ, ἵνα
the law, so that [4]the [5]*ones* [6]under [7]*the* [8]law [1]He [2]might [3]redeem, so that

τὴν υἱοθεσίαν* ἀπολάβωμεν. 6 Ὅτι δέ ἐστε υἱοί,
[4]the [5]adoption [1]we [2]might [3]receive. because ˜ And you are sons,

ἐξαπέστειλεν ὁ Θεὸς τὸ Πνεῦμα τοῦ Υἱοῦ αὐτοῦ εἰς τὰς
[2]sent [3]forth - [1]God the Spirit - of Son ˜ His into -

καρδίας ὑμῶν,[a] κρᾶζον, "Ἀββᾶ ὁ Πατήρ!" 7 Ὥστε
hearts ˜ your, crying, "Abba, - Father!" Therefore

οὐκέτι εἶ δοῦλος ἀλλ' υἱός, εἰ δὲ υἱός, καὶ κληρονόμος
[3]no [4]longer [1]you [2]are a slave but a son, if ˜ and a son, also an heir

Θεοῦ[b] διὰ Χριστοῦ.
of God through Christ.

Paul Fears for the Galatians' Spiritual Welfare

8 Ἀλλὰ τότε μέν, οὐκ εἰδότες Θεόν,
But at one time indeed, not knowing God,
when you did not know

ἐδουλεύσατε τοῖς μὴ φύσει οὖσι θεοῖς. 9 Νῦν δέ,
you were slaves to the *ones* not by nature being gods. now ˜ But,
to those who by nature were not

γνόντες Θεόν, μᾶλλον δὲ γνωσθέντες ὑπὸ Θεοῦ,
knowing God, rather ˜ but being known by God,
since you know since you became known

πῶς ἐπιστρέφετε πάλιν ἐπὶ τὰ ἀσθενῆ καὶ πτωχὰ στοιχεῖα
how do you turn again to the weak and beggarly elements

οἷς πάλιν ἄνωθεν δουλεύειν θέλετε? 10 Ἡμέρας
to which again anew [3]to [4]be [5]slaves [1]you [2]wish? [3]days
once again

παρατηρεῖσθε καὶ μῆνας καὶ καιροὺς καὶ ἐνιαυτούς.
[1]You [2]observe and months and seasons and years.

11 Φοβοῦμαι ὑμᾶς μή πως εἰκῇ κεκοπίακα εἰς
I am afraid for you lest somehow [7]in [8]vain [1]I [2]have [3]worked [4]hard [5]for

ὑμᾶς.
[6]you.

12 Γίνεσθε ὡς ἐγώ, ὅτι κἀγὼ ὡς ὑμεῖς, ἀδελφοί,
Become as I *am,* because I also *am* as you *are,* brothers,

δέομαι ὑμῶν. Οὐδέν με ἠδικήσατε. 13 Οἴδατε δὲ ὅτι
I beseech you. nothing me You have wronged. [2]you [3]know [1]But that
You have not wronged me at all.

δι' ἀσθένειαν τῆς σαρκὸς εὐηγγελισάμην ὑμῖν τὸ
because of weakness of the flesh I preached the gospel to you the
in

πρότερον. 14 Καὶ τὸν πειρασμόν μου[c] τὸν ἐν τῇ σαρκί
former *time.* And - trial ˜ my the *one* in - flesh ˜
which was

μου οὐκ ἐξουθενήσατε οὐδὲ ἐξεπτύσατε, ἀλλ' ὡς ἄγγελον
my [3]not [1]you [2]did despise nor disdain, but as an angel

Θεοῦ ἐδέξασθέ με, ὡς Χριστὸν Ἰησοῦν. 15 Τίς[d] οὖν ἦν[e] ὁ
of God you received me, as Christ Jesus. What then was -

μακαρισμὸς ὑμῶν? Μαρτυρῶ γὰρ ὑμῖν ὅτι, εἰ δυνατόν,
blessing ˜ your? [2]I [3]bear [4]witness [1]For to you that, if possible,

τοὺς ὀφθαλμοὺς ὑμῶν ἐξορύξαντες ἂν ἐδώκατέ
- [4]eyes [3]your [1]tearing [2]out - you would have given *them*
you would have torn out your eyes and

4 But when the fullness of the time had come, God sent forth His Son, born of a woman, born under the law,

5 to redeem those who were under the law, that we might receive the adoption as sons.

6 And because you are sons, God has sent forth the Spirit of His Son into your hearts, crying out, "Abba, Father!"

7 Therefore you are no longer a slave but a son, and if a son, then an heir of God through Christ.

8 But then, indeed, when you did not know God, you served those which by nature are not gods.

9 But now after you have known God, or rather are known by God, how *is it that* you turn again to the weak and beggarly elements, to which you desire again to be in bondage?

10 You observe days and months and seasons and years.

11 I am afraid for you, lest I have labored for you in vain.

12 Brethren, I urge you to become like me, for I *became* like you. You have not injured me at all.

13 You know that because of physical infirmity I preached the gospel to you at the first.

14 And my trial which was in my flesh you did not despise or reject, but you received me as an angel of God, *even* as Christ Jesus.

15 What then was the blessing you *enjoyed?* For I bear you witness that, if possible, you would have plucked out your own eyes and given them to

---

[a](**4:6**) NU reads ημων, *our.* [b](**4:7**) For Θεου δια Χριστου, *of God through Christ,* NU reads δια Θεος, *through God.* [c](**4:14**) NU reads υμων, *your.* [d](**4:15**) NU reads που, *where.* [e](**4:15**) NU omits ην, *was.*

---

*(**4:5**) *υἱοθεσία (huiothesia).* Noun, a compound from *υἱος, son,* and *θέσις, a placing,* thus meaning *adoption.* The word was a legal technical term for a father's declaration that his natural-born child was officially a son or daughter, with all the rights and privileges that this included. In the NT it is used only in a religious sense. *υἱοθεσία* indicates that believers are accepted by God

me.
16 Have I therefore become your enemy because I tell you the truth?
17 They zealously court you, *but* for no good; yes, they want to exclude you, that you may be zealous for them.
18 But it is good to be zealous in a good thing always, and not only when I am present with you.
19 My little children, for whom I labor in birth again until Christ is formed in you,
20 I would like to be present with you now and to change my tone; for I have doubts about you.
21 Tell me, you who desire to be under the law, do you not hear the law?
22 For it is written that Abraham had two sons: the one by a bondwoman, the other by a freewoman.
23 But he *who was* of the bondwoman was born according to the flesh, and he of the freewoman through promise,
24 which things are symbolic. For these are the two covenants: the one from Mount Sinai which gives birth to bondage, which is Hagar—
25 for this Hagar is Mount Sinai in Arabia, and corresponds to Jerusalem which now is, and is in bondage with her children—
26 but the Jerusalem above is free, which is the mother of us all.
27 For it is written:

"Rejoice, O barren,
You who do not bear!
Break forth and shout,
You who are not in labor!

---

f(**4:19**) NU reads *τεκνα*, *children.* g(**4:24**) TR adds *αι*, *the.* h(**4:26**) NU omits *παντων*, *all.*

---

as His sons. The Holy Spirit gives the realization that one is a son (or daughter) of God (Rom. 8:15). Completed sonship includes the future redemption of the body (Rom. 8:23). Israel as a nation is called God's "son" in the OT (Ex. 4:22), and thus collectively is said to possess the adoption (Rom. 9:4).

***(4:24)** ἀλληγορέω *(allēgoreō).* Verb, used only here, from ἄλλος, *other,* and ἀγορεύω, *speak* (in the

μοι. **16** Ὥστε ἐχθρὸς ὑμῶν γέγονα ἀληθεύων
to me. Therefore [5]enemy [4]your [1]have [2]I [3]become *by* speaking truth

ὑμῖν? **17** Ζηλοῦσιν ὑμᾶς οὐ καλῶς· ἀλλὰ
to you? They are zealous about you not well; but
in the wrong way;

ἐκκλεῖσαι ὑμᾶς θέλουσιν ἵνα αὐτοὺς
[3]to [4]shut [6]out [5]you [1]they [2]wish so that [6]them

ζηλοῦτε. **18** Καλὸν δὲ τὸ ζηλοῦσθαι ἐν
[1]you [2]may [3]be [4]zealous [5]about. [4]good [1]But [2]*it* [3]*is* - to be zealous in

καλῷ πάντοτε, καὶ μὴ μόνον ἐν τῷ παρεῖναί με πρὸς
a good thing always, and not only in - to be present me with
when I am present

ὑμᾶς. **19** Τεκνία[f] μου, οὓς πάλιν ὠδίνω ἄχρις οὗ
you. [2]little [3]children [1]My, for whom again I labor in birth until -

μορφωθῇ Χριστὸς ἐν ὑμῖν! **20** Ἤθελον δὲ παρεῖναι
[2]has [3]been [4]formed [1]Christ in you! [2]I [3]wanted [1]And to be present
is

πρὸς ὑμᾶς ἄρτι καὶ ἀλλάξαι τὴν φωνήν μου, ὅτι
with you just now and to change - voice ˜ my, because
tone

ἀποροῦμαι ἐν ὑμῖν.
I am uncertain in you.
about

Sarah and Hagar: Two Covenants

21 Λέγετέ μοι, οἱ ὑπὸ νόμον θέλοντες εἶναι, τὸν
Tell me, the *ones* [4]under [5]*the* [6]law [1]wishing [2]to [3]be, [11]the
you who wish

νόμον οὐκ ἀκούετε? **22** Γέγραπται γὰρ ὅτι Ἀβραὰμ δύο
[12]law [9]not [7]do [8]you [10]hear? [2]it [3]is [4]written [1]For that Abraham [2]two

υἱοὺς ἔσχεν, ἕνα ἐκ τῆς παιδίσκης καὶ ἕνα ἐκ τῆς ἐλευθέρας.
[3]sons [1]had, one by the servant girl and one by the free *woman.*

23 Ἀλλ' ὁ μὲν ἐκ τῆς παιδίσκης κατὰ
But [4]the [5]*one* [1]to [2]be [3]sure by the servant girl [4]according [5]to

σάρκα γεγέννηται, ὁ δὲ ἐκ τῆς ἐλευθέρας διὰ
[6]*the* [7]flesh [1]has [2]been [3]born, [9]the [10]*one* [8]but by the free *woman* through
was

τῆς ἐπαγγελίας, **24** ἅτινά ἐστιν ἀλληγορούμενα.* Αὗται
the promise, which *things* is speaking allegorically. these ˜
are

γάρ εἰσιν[g] δύο διαθῆκαι, μία μὲν ἀπὸ Ὄρους Σινᾶ, εἰς
For are two covenants, one in fact from Mount Sinai, [3]into

δουλείαν γεννῶσα, ἥτις ἐστὶν Ἁγάρ. **25** Τὸ γὰρ Ἁγὰρ
[4]slavery [1]bearing [2]*children,* which is Hagar. - For Hagar

Σινᾶ Ὄρος ἐστὶν ἐν τῇ Ἀραβίᾳ, συστοιχεῖ δὲ τῇ νῦν
[3]Sinai [2]Mount [1]is in - Arabia, corresponds ˜ and to the now
present

Ἰερουσαλήμ, δουλεύει δὲ μετὰ τῶν τέκνων αὐτῆς. **26** Ἡ
Jerusalem, [2]is [3]in [4]slavery [1]and with - children ˜ her. the ˜

δὲ ἄνω Ἰερουσαλὴμ ἐλευθέρα ἐστίν, ἥτις ἐστὶ μήτηρ
But above ˜ Jerusalem free ˜ is, which is *the* mother

πάντων[h] ἡμῶν. **27** Γέγραπται γάρ,
of all of us. [2]it [3]is [4]written [1]For,

«Εὐφράνθητι, στεῖρα ἡ οὐ τίκτουσα·
«Rejoice, barren *one* the *one* not giving birth;
who does give

Ῥῆξον καὶ βόησον ἡ οὐκ ὠδίνουσα·
Break forth and shout the *one* not having birth pangs;
who does have

Ὅτι πολλὰ τὰ τέκνα τῆς ἐρήμου
Because 7*are* 8many 1the 2children 3of 4the 5desolate 6*woman*
Μᾶλλον ἢ τῆς ἐχούσης τὸν ἄνδρα.»[i]
More than *those* of the *one* having the husband.»
her who has a

28 Ἡμεῖς[j] δέ, ἀδελφοί, κατὰ Ἰσαάκ, ἐπαγγελίας τέκνα
we ˜ But, brothers, like Isaac, 3of 4promise 2children
ἐσμέν.[k] 29 Ἀλλ' ὥσπερ τότε ὁ κατὰ σάρκα
1are. But just as then the *one* 3according 4to 5*the* 6flesh
γεννηθεὶς ἐδίωκε τὸν κατὰ Πνεῦμα, οὕτω καὶ
1being 2born persecuted the *one born* according to *the* Spirit, so *it is* also
who was
νῦν. 30 Ἀλλὰ τί λέγει ἡ Γραφή? «Ἔκβαλε τὴν
now. But what does 3say 1the 2Scripture? «Cast out the
παιδίσκην καὶ τὸν υἱὸν αὐτῆς, οὐ γὰρ μὴ κληρονομήσῃ
servant girl and - son ˜ her, 9not 1for 10not 8will 11inherit
certainly
ὁ υἱὸς τῆς παιδίσκης μετὰ τοῦ υἱοῦ»[l] τῆς ἐλευθέρας.
2the 3son 4of 5the 6servant 7girl with the son» of the free *woman*.
31 Ἄρα, ἀδελφοί, οὐκ ἐσμὲν παιδίσκης τέκνα
So then, brothers, 3not 1we 2are 5of 6a 7servant 8girl 4children
ἀλλὰ τῆς ἐλευθέρας.
but of the free *woman*.

Maintaining Christian Liberty

5 1 Τῇ ἐλευθερίᾳ οὖν[a] ᾗ Χριστὸς ἡμᾶς
2in 3the 4freedom 1Therefore in which Christ us ˜
ἠλευθέρωσε, στήκετε,[b] καὶ μὴ πάλιν ζυγῷ δουλείας
freed, stand fast, and 2not 6again 8a 9yoke 10of 11slavery
ἐνέχεσθε.
1do 3be 4loaded 5down 7with.
2 Ἴδε, ἐγὼ Παῦλος λέγω ὑμῖν ὅτι ἐὰν περιτέμνησθε,
Look, I Paul say to you that if you get circumcised,
Χριστὸς ὑμᾶς οὐδὲν ὠφελήσει. 3 Μαρτύρομαι δὲ πάλιν
Christ 3you 4nothing 1will 2profit. 2I 3testify 1But again
παντὶ ἀνθρώπῳ περιτεμνομένῳ ὅτι ὀφειλέτης ἐστὶν ὅλον
to every man being circumcised that 3a 4debtor 1he 2is 8whole
who gets circumcised
τὸν νόμον ποιῆσαι. 4 Κατηργήθητε ἀπὸ τοῦ Χριστοῦ,
7the 9law 5to 6do. You have become estranged from - Christ,
οἵτινες ἐν νόμῳ δικαιοῦσθε· τῆς χάριτος ἐξεπέσετε.
you who 3by 4*the* 5law 1are 2justified; - 4grace 1you 2fell 3from.
have fallen
5 Ἡμεῖς γὰρ Πνεύματι ἐκ πίστεως ἐλπίδα δικαιοσύνης
we ˜ For by *the* Spirit 7by 8faith 3*the* 4hope 5of 6righteousness
ἀπεκδεχόμεθα. 6 Ἐν γὰρ Χριστῷ Ἰησοῦ οὔτε περιτομή
1eagerly 2await. in ˜ For Christ Jesus neither circumcision
τι ἰσχύει οὔτε ἀκροβυστία, ἀλλὰ πίστις δι' ἀγάπης
4anything 3means 1nor 2uncircumcision, but faith 2through 3love
has any power
ἐνεργουμένη.
1working.

Resuming the Christian Race

7 Ἐτρέχετε καλῶς· τίς ὑμᾶς ἐνέκοψεν τῇ ἀληθείᾳ
You were running well; who you ˜ hindered 4the 5truth

For the desolate has
many more children
Than she who has a
husband."

28 Now we, brethren, as Isaac *was,* are children of promise.
29 But, as he who was born according to the flesh then persecuted him *who was born* according to the Spirit, even so *it is* now.
30 Nevertheless what does the Scripture say? *"Cast out the bondwoman and her son, for the son of the bondwoman shall not be heir with the son of the freewoman."*
31 So then, brethren, we are not children of the bondwoman but of the free.
5 Stand fast therefore in the liberty by which Christ has made us free, and do not be entangled again with a yoke of bondage.
2 Indeed I, Paul, say to you that if you become circumcised, Christ will profit you nothing.
3 And I testify again to every man who becomes circumcised that he is a debtor to keep the whole law.
4 You have become estranged from Christ, you who *attempt to* be justified by law; you have fallen from grace.
5 For we through the Spirit eagerly wait for the hope of righteousness by faith.
6 For in Christ Jesus neither circumcision nor uncircumcision avails anything, but faith working through love.
7 You ran well. Who hindered you from obeying the truth?

---

i**(4:27)** Is. 54:1
j**(4:28)** NU reads Υμεις, *you.* k**(4:28)** NU reads εστε, *(you) are.*
l**(4:30)** Gen. 21:10
a**(5:1)** NU omits ουν η, *therefore in which.*
b**(5:1)** NU adds ουν, *therefore.*

agora, or marketplace), hence meaning *to allegorize, speak in a symbolic manner.* The biblical allegory here does not deny the literal meaning of the OT events nor the priority of history. Rather it is a literary genre that looks for deeper spiritual truth illustrated in OT events.

8 This persuasion does not *come* from Him who calls you.

9 A little leaven leavens the whole lump.

10 I have confidence in you, in the Lord, that you will have no other mind; but he who troubles you shall bear his judgment, whoever he is.

11 And I, brethren, if I still preach circumcision, why do I still suffer persecution? Then the offense of the cross has ceased.

12 I could wish that those who trouble you would even cut themselves off!

13 For you, brethren, have been called to liberty; only do not *use* liberty as an opportunity for the flesh, but through love serve one another.

14 For all the law is fulfilled in one word, *even* in this: *"You shall love your neighbor as yourself."*

15 But if you bite and devour one another, beware lest you be consumed by one another!

16 I say then: Walk in the Spirit, and you shall not fulfill the lust of the flesh.

17 For the flesh lusts against the Spirit, and the Spirit against the flesh; and these are contrary to one another, so that you do not do the things that you wish.

18 But if you are led by the Spirit, you are not under the law.

μὴ πείθεσθαι? **8** Ἡ πεισμονὴ οὐκ ἐκ τοῦ
[1]not [2]to [3]obey? The persuasion *does* not *come* from the *One*
from obeying? This Him who

καλοῦντος ὑμᾶς. **9** Μικρὰ ζύμη ὅλον τὸ φύραμα ζυμοῖ.
calling you. A little leaven [3]whole [2]the [4]lump [5]of [6]dough [1]leavens.
calls

10 Ἐγὼ πέποιθα εἰς ὑμᾶς ἐν Κυρίῳ ὅτι οὐδὲν ἄλλο
I am persuaded in you in *the* Lord that [6]nothing [7]other
have confidence else

φρονήσετε· ὁ δὲ ταράσσων ὑμᾶς βαστάσει τὸ
[1]you [2]will [3]be [4]intent [5]on; [9]the [10]*one* [8]but troubling you will bear the
he who troubles his

κρίμα, ὅστις ἂν ᾖ. **11** Ἐγὼ δέ, ἀδελφοί, εἰ
judgment, who ever he may be. I ˜ And, brothers, if

περιτομὴν ἔτι κηρύσσω, τί ἔτι διώκομαι? Ἄρα
[4]circumcision [2]still [1]I [3]preach, why [3]still [1]am [2]I [4]persecuted? Then
In that case

κατήργηται τὸ σκάνδαλον τοῦ σταυροῦ.
[6]has [7]been [8]done [9]away [10]with [1]the [2]offense [3]of [4]the [5]cross.

12 Ὄφελον καὶ ἀποκόψονται οἱ
O that [6]even [5]would [7]cut [8]themselves [9]off [1]the [2]*ones*
castrate themselves those who

ἀναστατοῦντες ὑμᾶς!
[3]disturbing [4]you!
disturb

13 Ὑμεῖς γὰρ ἐπ' ἐλευθερίᾳ ἐκλήθητε, ἀδελφοί· μόνον
you ˜ For [3]to [4]freedom [1]were [2]called, brothers; only

μὴ τὴν ἐλευθερίαν εἰς ἀφορμὴν τῇ σαρκί, ἀλλὰ
do not *use* the freedom for an opportunity for the flesh, but

διὰ τῆς ἀγάπης δουλεύετε ἀλλήλοις. **14** Ὁ γὰρ πᾶς
through - love serve as slaves to one another. [3]the [1]For [2]all

νόμος ἐν ἑνὶ λόγῳ πληροῦται,[c] ἐν τῷ,
law [3]in [4]one [5]word [1]is [2]fulfilled, in the *one which says,*
command

«Ἀγαπήσεις τὸν πλησίον σου ὡς σεαυτόν.»[d] **15** Εἰ δὲ
«You shall love - neighbor ˜ your as yourself.» if ˜ But

ἀλλήλους δάκνετε καὶ κατεσθίετε, βλέπετε μὴ ὑπὸ
[5]one [6]another [1]you [2]bite [3]and [4]devour, watch out not by
that you

ἀλλήλων ἀναλωθῆτε.
one another you be consumed.
are not consumed by one another.

The Spirit and the Flesh

16 Λέγω δέ, Πνεύματι περιπατεῖτε καὶ ἐπιθυμίαν
I say then, [2]by [3]*the* [4]Spirit [1]walk and [7]*the* [8]desire

σαρκὸς οὐ μὴ τελέσητε. **17** Ἡ γὰρ σὰρξ
[9]of [10]*the* [11]flesh [3]not [4]not [1]you [2]will [5]carry [6]out. the ˜ For flesh
certainly not

ἐπιθυμεῖ κατὰ τοῦ Πνεύματος, τὸ δὲ Πνεῦμα κατὰ
desires contrary to the Spirit, the ˜ and Spirit contrary to

τῆς σαρκός, ταῦτα δὲ ἀντίκειται ἀλλήλοις, ἵνα μὴ
the flesh, [2]these [3]*things* [1]and oppose each other, so that not
in order that

ἃ ἂν θέλητε, ταῦτα ποιῆτε. **18** Εἰ δὲ Πνεύματι
what ever you wish, these *things* you may do. if ˜ But [4]by [5]*the* [6]Spirit
you may not do whatever things you wish.

ἄγεσθε, οὐκ ἐστὲ ὑπὸ νόμον.
[1]you [2]are [3]led, [9]not [7]you [8]are under *the* law.

---

[c](**5:14**) NU reads πεπλήρωται, *has been fulfilled.* [d](**5:14**) Lev. 19:18

19 Φανερὰ δέ ἐστι τὰ ἔργα τῆς σαρκός, ἅτινά ἐστι·
[8]manifest [1]Now [7]are [2]the [3]works [4]of [5]the [6]flesh, which is:
are:

μοιχεία,[e] πορνεία, ἀκαθαρσία, ἀσέλγεια, 20 εἰδωλολατρεία,
adultery, fornication, immorality, licentiousness, idolatry,

φαρμακεία, ἔχθραι, ἔρεις, ζῆλοι, θυμοί,
sorcery, enmities, contentions, jealousies, outbursts of wrath,

ἐριθεῖαι, διχοστασίαι, αἱρέσεις, 21 φθόνοι, φόνοι,[f]
selfish ambitions, dissensions, factions, envies, murders,

μέθαι, κῶμοι, καὶ τὰ ὅμοια τούτοις· ἃ
drinking bouts, revelries, and the *things* like these; which

προλέγω ὑμῖν καθὼς καὶ προεῖπον ὅτι οἱ τὰ
I tell beforehand ˜ you just as also ˜ I told *you* before that the ones -
those who

τοιαῦτα πράσσοντες βασιλείαν Θεοῦ οὐ κληρονομήσουσιν.
such *things* practicing [4]*the* [5]kingdom [6]of [7]God [2]not [1]will [3]inherit.
do such things

22 Ὁ δὲ καρπὸς τοῦ Πνεύματός ἐστιν ἀγάπη, χαρά,
the ˜ But fruit of the Spirit is love, joy,

εἰρήνη, μακροθυμία, χρηστότης, ἀγαθωσύνη, πίστις,
peace, longsuffering, kindness, goodness, faithfulness,

23 πραότης, ἐγκράτεια* — κατὰ τῶν τοιούτων οὐκ ἔστι
gentleness, self-control — against - such *things* [3]not [1]*there* [2]is
no

νόμος. 24 Οἱ δὲ τοῦ Χριστοῦ τὴν σάρκα ἐσταύρωσαν
a law. [2]the [3]*ones* [1]And - of Christ [2]the [3]flesh [1]crucified
law. those who are Christ's have crucified

σὺν τοῖς παθήμασι καὶ ταῖς ἐπιθυμίαις.
with the passions and the desires.
its its

25 Εἰ ζῶμεν Πνεύματι, Πνεύματι καὶ στοιχῶμεν.
If we live by *the* Spirit, [7]with [8]*the* [9]Spirit [3]also [1]let [2]us [4]keep [5]in [6]line.

26 Μὴ γινώμεθα κενόδοξοι, ἀλλήλους προκαλούμενοι,
[3]not [1]Let [2]us become conceited, [2]one [3]another [1]provoking,

ἀλλήλοις φθονοῦντες.
[5]one [6]another [4]envying.

19 Now the works of the flesh are evident, which are: adultery, fornication, uncleanness, lewdness,
20 idolatry, sorcery, hatred, contentions, jealousies, outbursts of wrath, selfish ambitions, dissensions, heresies,
21 envy, murders, drunkenness, revelries, and the like; of which I tell you beforehand, just as I also told *you* in time past, that those who practice such things will not inherit the kingdom of God.
22 But the fruit of the Spirit is love, joy, peace, longsuffering, kindness, goodness, faithfulness,
23 gentleness, self-control. Against such there is no law.
24 And those *who are* Christ's have crucified the flesh with its passions and desires.
25 If we live in the Spirit, let us also walk in the Spirit.
26 Let us not become conceited, provoking one another, envying one another.

Bear and Share the Burdens

6 1 Ἀδελφοί, ἐὰν καὶ προληφθῇ ἄνθρωπος ἔν τινι
Brothers, if ˜ even [3]is [4]overtaken [1]a [2]man in some
any

παραπτώματι, ὑμεῖς οἱ πνευματικοὶ καταρτίζετε τὸν τοιοῦτον
trespass, you the spiritual *ones* restore the such *one*
who are spiritual such a person

ἐν πνεύματι πραότητος, σκοπῶν σεαυτὸν μὴ καὶ σὺ
with a spirit of gentleness, looking out for yourself lest also ˜ you

πειρασθῇς. 2 Ἀλλήλων τὰ βάρη βαστάζετε, καὶ οὕτως
be tempted. [4]of [5]one [6]another [2]the [3]burdens [1]Bear, and thus

ἀναπληρώσατε[a] τὸν νόμον τοῦ Χριστοῦ. 3 Εἰ γὰρ δοκεῖ
fulfill the law - of Christ. if ˜ For thinks ˜

τις εἶναί τι, μηδὲν ὤν, ἑαυτὸν φρεναπατᾷ.
anyone to be something, nothing ˜ being, [3]himself [1]he [2]deceives.
that he is when he is nothing,

4 Τὸ δὲ ἔργον ἑαυτοῦ δοκιμαζέτω ἕκαστος, καὶ τότε εἰς
- But [7]work [5]his [6]own [1]let [4]examine [2]each [3]*person,* and then [5]in

ἑαυτὸν μόνον τὸ καύχημα ἕξει καὶ οὐκ εἰς τὸν
[6]himself [7]alone - [4]boasting [1]he [2]will [3]have and not in the

ἕτερον. 5 Ἕκαστος γὰρ τὸ ἴδιον φορτίον βαστάσει.
other *fellow.* each ˜ For - [3]his [4]own [5]load [1]shall [2]bear.

6 Brethren, if a man is overtaken in any trespass, you who *are* spiritual restore such a one in a spirit of gentleness, considering yourself lest you also be tempted.
2 Bear one another's burdens, and so fulfill the law of Christ.
3 For if anyone thinks himself to be something, when he is nothing, he deceives himself.
4 But let each one examine his own work, and then he will have rejoicing in himself alone, and not in another.
5 For each one shall bear his own load.

---

[e](**5:19**) NU omits *μοιχεια, adultery.* [f](**5:21**) NU omits *φονοι, murders.*
[a](**6:2**) NU reads *αναπληρωσετε, you will fulfill.*

***(5:23)** *ἐγκράτεια (enkrateia).* Noun meaning *self-control, self-discipline, self-denial.* The word is derived from the preposition *ἐν, in,* and the verb *κρατέω, hold,* hence suggesting a holding oneself in. Here self-control is made possible for the Christian through the fruit of the Spirit of God. It is one of the virtues necessary for spiritual progress in the Christian life (2 Pet. 1:6). Cf. the cognate verb *ἐγκρατεύομαι, exercise self-control* (1 Cor. 7:9; 9:25, where the example of the athlete is in-

6 Let him who is taught the word share in all good things with him who teaches.
7 Do not be deceived, God is not mocked; for whatever a man sows, that he will also reap.
8 For he who sows to his flesh will of the flesh reap corruption, but he who sows to the Spirit will of the Spirit reap everlasting life.
9 And let us not grow weary while doing good, for in due season we shall reap if we do not lose heart.
10 Therefore, as we have opportunity, let us do good to all, especially to those who are of the household of faith.
11 See with what large letters I have written to you with my own hand!
12 As many as desire to make a good showing in the flesh, these *would* compel you to be circumcised, only that they may not suffer persecution for the cross of Christ.
13 For not even those who are circumcised keep the law, but they desire to have you circumcised that they may boast in your flesh.
14 But God forbid that I should boast except in the cross of our Lord Jesus Christ, by whom the world has been crucified to me, and I to the world.
15 For in Christ Jesus neither circumcision nor uncircumcision avails anything, but a new creation.
16 And as many as walk according to this rule, peace and

---

[b](6:13) NU reads περιτεμνομενοι, *(the ones) being circumcised.*
[c](6:13) TR reads ημετερα, *our.* [d](6:15) NU omits εν, *in,* and Χριστος Ιησου, *Christ Jesus,* and reads ουτε γαρ, *for neither.*
[e](6:15) NU reads εστιν, *is.*

---

structive); and adjective ἐγκρατής, *self-controlled* (only Titus 1:8).

***(6:14)** σταυρόω *(stauroō).* Common verb meaning *crucify.* Originally it meant *to fence by driving stakes;* then, as the σταυρός, *stake,* became an instrument of execution, σταυρόω described the action of executing by affixing a person to a stake, or cross (see σταυρός at Mark 8:34). In the NT it is used lit-

Be Generous and Do Good

6 Κοινωνείτω δὲ ὁ κατηχούμενος τὸν λόγον
[2]let [9]share [1]Now [3]the [4]*one* [5]being [6]taught [7]the [8]word
him who is taught

τῷ κατηχοῦντι ἐν πᾶσιν ἀγαθοῖς. 7 Μὴ πλανᾶσθε,
with the *one* teaching in all good *things.* not ˜ Do be deceived,
him who teaches

Θεὸς οὐ μυκτηρίζεται· ὃ γὰρ ἐὰν σπείρῃ ἄνθρωπος, τοῦτο
God not ˜ is mocked; what ˜ for ever [3]sows [1]a [2]man, this

καὶ θερίσει. 8 Ὅτι ὁ σπείρων εἰς τὴν σάρκα ἑαυτοῦ
also he will reap. Because the *one* sowing to - [3]flesh [1]his [2]own
he who sows

ἐκ τῆς σαρκὸς θερίσει φθοράν, ὁ δὲ σπείρων εἰς τὸ
of the flesh will reap corruption, [2]the [3]*one* [1]but sowing to the
from he who sows

Πνεῦμα ἐκ τοῦ Πνεύματος θερίσει ζωὴν αἰώνιον. 9 Τὸ δὲ
Spirit of the Spirit will reap life ˜ eternal. [3]the [1]And
from And while

καλὸν ποιοῦντες μὴ ἐκκακῶμεν, καιρῷ γὰρ
[4]good [5]*thing* [2]doing [8]not [6]let [7]us [9]lose [10]heart, [12]in [15]season [11]for
we do good,

ἰδίῳ θερίσομεν, μὴ ἐκλυόμενοι. 10 Ἄρα οὖν ὡς
[13]its [14]own we will reap, not becoming weary. So then as
due if we do not become

καιρὸν ἔχομεν, ἐργαζώμεθα τὸ ἀγαθὸν πρὸς πάντας,
[3]opportunity [1]we [2]have, let us work the good *thing* toward all,
what is good

μάλιστα δὲ πρὸς τοὺς οἰκείους τῆς πίστεως.
especially ˜ but toward the householders of the faith.
members of the household of

Glory Only in the Cross

11 Ἴδετε πηλίκοις ὑμῖν γράμμασιν ἔγραψα τῇ
See with what large [4]to [5]you [1]letters [2]I [3]wrote with -

ἐμῇ χειρί! 12 Ὅσοι θέλουσιν εὐπροσωπῆσαι ἐν
my *own* hand! As many as wish to make a good showing in

σαρκί, οὗτοι ἀναγκάζουσιν ὑμᾶς περιτέμνεσθαι, μόνον ἵνα
the flesh, these compel you to get circumcised, only so that

μὴ τῷ σταυρῷ τοῦ Χριστοῦ διώκωνται.
[3]not [6]for [7]the [8]cross - [9]of [10]Christ [1]they [2]should [4]be [5]persecuted.

13 Οὐδὲ γὰρ οἱ περιτετμημένοι[b] αὐτοὶ νόμον
[2]not [3]even [1]For the *ones* having been circumcised [4]themselves [2]*the* [3]law
those who are circumcised

φυλάσσουσιν, ἀλλὰ θέλουσιν ὑμᾶς περιτέμνεσθαι ἵνα ἐν τῇ
[1]keep, but they wish you to be circumcised so that [4]in -

ὑμετέρᾳ[c] σαρκὶ καυχήσωνται. 14 Ἐμοὶ δὲ μὴ γένοιτο
[5]your [6]flesh [1]they [2]may [3]boast. [6]for [7]me [1]But [4]not [2]let [3]it [5]be

καυχᾶσθαι εἰ μὴ ἐν τῷ σταυρῷ τοῦ Κυρίου ἡμῶν Ἰησοῦ
to boast if not in the cross - of Lord ˜ our Jesus
except

Χριστοῦ, δι' οὗ ἐμοὶ κόσμος ἐσταύρωται* κἀγὼ
Christ, through whom [6]to [7]me [1]*the* [2]world [3]has [4]been [5]crucified and I

τῷ κόσμῳ. 15 Ἐν γὰρ Χριστῷ Ἰησοῦ οὔτε[d] περιτομή
to the world. in ˜ For Christ Jesus neither circumcision

τι ἰσχύει[e] οὔτε ἀκροβυστία, ἀλλὰ καινὴ κτίσις. 16 Καὶ
anything ˜ means nor uncircumcision, but a new creation. And
has any power

ὅσοι τῷ κανόνι τούτῳ στοιχήσουσιν, εἰρήνη ἐπ' αὐτοὺς
as many as - [6]rule [4]with [5]this [1]keep [2]in [3]line, peace *be* upon them

καὶ ἔλεος, καὶ ἐπὶ τὸν Ἰσραὴλ τοῦ Θεοῦ.
and mercy, and upon the Israel - of God.

Paul's Farewell of Grace

17 Τοῦ λοιποῦ, κόπους μοι μηδεὶς παρεχέτω, ἐγὼ γὰρ
For the rest, [6]labors [5]me [2]no [3]one [1]let [4]cause, I ˜ for
Finally, trouble

τὰ στίγματα τοῦ Κυρίου[f] Ἰησοῦ ἐν τῷ σώματί μου
[5]the [6]marks [7]of [8]the [9]Lord [10]Jesus [2]in - [4]body [3]my

βαστάζω.
[1]bear.

18 Ἡ χάρις τοῦ Κυρίου ἡμῶν Ἰησοῦ Χριστοῦ μετὰ τοῦ
The grace - of Lord ˜ our Jesus Christ *be* with -

πνεύματος ὑμῶν, ἀδελφοί. Ἀμήν.
spirit ˜ your, brothers. Amen.
So be it.

mercy *be* upon them, and upon the Israel of God.
17 From now on let no one trouble me, for I bear in my body the marks of the Lord Jesus.
18 Brethren, the grace of our Lord Jesus Christ *be* with your spirit. Amen.

---

[f](**6:17**) NU omits Κυριου, *Lord.*

erally of the crucifixion of Jesus (Matt. 20:19; 27:38) and of others (Matt. 23:34), and also figuratively (as here in Gal. 6:14) to consider as dead those features of life which are worldly, carnal, or Satan-inspired (cf. Gal. 5:24; and the cognate *συσταυρόω*, *crucify with* (Rom. 6:6).

The Epistle of Paul the Apostle to the

EPHESIANS

ΠΡΟΣ ΕΦΕΣΙΟΥΣ
TO *THE* EPHESIANS

1 Paul, an apostle of Jesus Christ by the will of God,

To the saints who are in Ephesus, and faithful in Christ Jesus:

2 Grace to you and peace from God our Father and the Lord Jesus Christ.

3 Blessed *be* the God and Father of our Lord Jesus Christ, who has blessed us with every spiritual blessing in the heavenly *places* in Christ,
4 just as He chose us in Him before the foundation of the world, that we should be holy and without blame before Him in love,
5 having predestined us to adoption as sons by Jesus Christ to Himself, according to the good pleasure of His will,
6 to the praise of the glory of His grace, by which He made us accepted in the Beloved.
7 In Him we have redemption through His blood, the forgiveness of sins, according to the riches of His grace
8 which He made to abound toward us in all wisdom and prudence,
9 having made known to us the mystery of His will, according to His good pleasure which He purposed in Himself,
10 that in the dispensation of

---

[a](1:6) For εν η, *by which*, NU reads ης, *which*.

---

*(1:4) ἐκλέγομαι (eklegomai). Verb meaning *choose, select,* from the preposition ἐκ, *out,* and the verb λέγω, *say, call, name.* The consistent use of the middle voice in the NT usually implies choosing for oneself. It often refers, as here, to the *election* of be-

Paul Greets the Saints in Ephesus

1 1 Παῦλος, ἀπόστολος Ἰησοῦ Χριστοῦ διὰ θελήματος
Paul, an apostle of Jesus Christ by *the* will

Θεοῦ,
of God,

Τοῖς ἁγίοις τοῖς οὖσιν ἐν Ἐφέσῳ καὶ πιστοῖς ἐν
To the saints the *ones* being in Ephesus and *who are* faithful in
who are at

Χριστῷ Ἰησοῦ·
Christ Jesus:

2 Χάρις ὑμῖν καὶ εἰρήνη ἀπὸ Θεοῦ Πατρὸς ἡμῶν καὶ
Grace to you and peace from God Father ˜ our and

Κυρίου Ἰησοῦ Χριστοῦ.
the Lord Jesus Christ.

To the Praise of His Glory

3 Εὐλογητὸς ὁ Θεὸς καὶ Πατὴρ τοῦ Κυρίου ἡμῶν Ἰησοῦ
Blessed *be* the God and Father - of Lord ˜ our Jesus

Χριστοῦ, ὁ εὐλογήσας ἡμᾶς ἐν πάσῃ εὐλογίᾳ πνευματικῇ
Christ, the *one* blessing us with every blessing ˜ spiritual
who blessed

ἐν τοῖς ἐπουρανίοις ἐν Χριστῷ, 4 καθὼς ἐξελέξατο* ἡμᾶς ἐν
in the heavenly *realms* in Christ, just as He chose us in

αὐτῷ πρὸ καταβολῆς κόσμου, εἶναι ἡμᾶς ἁγίους καὶ
Him before *the* foundation of *the* world, to be us holy and
that we should be

ἀμώμους κατενώπιον αὐτοῦ ἐν ἀγάπῃ 5 προορίσας ἡμᾶς
blameless before Him in love having predestined us

εἰς υἱοθεσίαν διὰ Ἰησοῦ Χριστοῦ εἰς αὐτόν, κατὰ τὴν
to adoption as sons by Jesus Christ to Him, according to the
Himself,

εὐδοκίαν τοῦ θελήματος αὐτοῦ, 6 εἰς ἔπαινον δόξης τῆς
good pleasure - of will ˜ His, to *the* praise of *the* glory -

χάριτος αὐτοῦ ἐν[a] ᾗ ἐχαρίτωσεν ἡμᾶς ἐν τῷ
of grace ˜ His by which He bestowed favor upon us in the

ἠγαπημένῳ, 7 ἐν ᾧ ἔχομεν τὴν ἀπολύτρωσιν διὰ τοῦ
Beloved *One,* in whom we have the redemption through -

αἵματος αὐτοῦ, τὴν ἄφεσιν τῶν παραπτωμάτων, κατὰ
blood ˜ His, the forgiveness - of transgressions, according to

τὸν πλοῦτον τῆς χάριτος αὐτοῦ 8 ἧς ἐπερίσσευσεν εἰς
the riches - of grace ˜ His which He made to abound toward

ἡμᾶς ἐν πάσῃ σοφίᾳ καὶ φρονήσει 9 γνωρίσας ἡμῖν τὸ
us in all wisdom and insight having made known to us the

μυστήριον τοῦ θελήματος αὐτοῦ, κατὰ τὴν εὐδοκίαν
mystery - of will ˜ His, according to - [2]good [3]pleasure

αὐτοῦ ἣν προέθετο ἐν αὐτῷ 10 εἰς οἰκονομίαν τοῦ
[1]His which He purposed in Him for an administration of the
Himself

πληρώματος τῶν καιρῶν, ἀνακεφαλαιώσασθαι τὰ πάντα ἐν
fullness of the times, to sum up - all *things* in
bring together

τῷ Χριστῷ, τὰ[b] ἐπὶ τοῖς οὐρανοῖς καὶ τὰ ἐπὶ τῆς
- Christ, the *things* in the heavens and the *things* on the
heaven

γῆς· ἐν αὐτῷ, 11 ἐν ᾧ καὶ ἐκληρώθημεν
earth: in Him, in whom also we were appointed by lot

προορισθέντες κατὰ πρόθεσιν τοῦ τὰ πάντα
being predestined according to *the* purpose of the *one* - [2]all [3]*things*

ἐνεργοῦντος κατὰ τὴν βουλὴν τοῦ θελήματος αὐτοῦ, 12 εἰς
[1]working according to the counsel - of will ~ His, for
so

τὸ εἶναι ἡμᾶς εἰς ἔπαινον δόξης αὐτοῦ τοὺς
- [2]to [3]be [1]us to *the* praise of glory ~ His the *ones*
that we should be we who

προηλπικότας ἐν τῷ Χριστῷ· 13 ἐν ᾧ καὶ ὑμεῖς,
having hoped before in the Christ; in whom also you,
were first to hope Messiah;

ἀκούσαντες τὸν λόγον τῆς ἀληθείας, τὸ εὐαγγέλιον τῆς
hearing the word of the truth, the gospel -
when you heard message

σωτηρίας ὑμῶν, ἐν ᾧ καὶ πιστεύσαντες ἐσφραγίσθητε
of salvation ~ your, in whom also believing you were sealed
when you believed

τῷ Πνεύματι τῆς ἐπαγγελίας τῷ Ἁγίῳ, 14 ὅς[c] ἐστιν
with the [2]Spirit - [3]of [4]promise - [1]Holy, who is

ἀρραβὼν τῆς κληρονομίας ἡμῶν, εἰς ἀπολύτρωσιν τῆς
the deposit - of inheritance ~ our, for *the* redemption of the
until

περιποιήσεως, εἰς ἔπαινον τῆς δόξης αὐτοῦ.
possession, to *the* praise - of glory ~ His.

Paul Prays for the Ephesians' Spiritual Perception

15 Διὰ τοῦτο κἀγώ, ἀκούσας τὴν καθ' ὑμᾶς
Because of this I also, hearing the [2]according [3]to [4]you
after I heard of of each of

πίστιν ἐν τῷ Κυρίῳ Ἰησοῦ καὶ τὴν ἀγάπην τὴν εἰς
[1]faith in the Lord Jesus and the love the *one* towards
your which is

πάντας τοὺς ἁγίους, 16 οὐ παύομαι εὐχαριστῶν ὑπὲρ
all the saints, [3]not [1]I [2]do cease giving thanks concerning

ὑμῶν, μνείαν ὑμῶν[d] ποιούμενος ἐπὶ τῶν προσευχῶν μου,
you, [2]mention [3]of [4]you [1]making in - prayers ~ my,

17 ἵνα ὁ Θεὸς τοῦ Κυρίου ἡμῶν Ἰησοῦ Χριστοῦ, ὁ Πατὴρ
that the God - of Lord ~ our Jesus Christ, the Father

τῆς δόξης, δώῃ ὑμῖν πνεῦμα σοφίας καὶ ἀποκαλύψεως ἐν
- of glory, may give you *the* spirit of wisdom and revelation in

ἐπιγνώσει αὐτοῦ, 18 πεφωτισμένους τοὺς ὀφθαλμοὺς
the knowledge of Him, [6]having [7]been [8]enlightened [1]the [2]eyes

τῆς καρδίας[e] ὑμῶν εἰς τὸ εἰδέναι ὑμᾶς τίς ἐστιν ἡ ἐλπὶς
- [3]of [5]heart [4]your for - [2]to [3]know [1]you what is the hope
that you may know

τῆς κλήσεως αὐτοῦ καὶ τίς ὁ πλοῦτος τῆς δόξης τῆς
- of calling ~ His and what *is* the riches of the glory -

κληρονομίας αὐτοῦ ἐν τοῖς ἁγίοις 19 καὶ τί τὸ
of inheritance ~ His in the saints and what *is* the
among

the fullness of the times He
might gather together in one all
things in Christ, both which are
in heaven and which are on
earth—in Him.
11 In Him also we have obtained an inheritance, being
predestined according to the
purpose of Him who works all
things according to the counsel
of His will,
12 that we who first trusted in
Christ should be to the praise of
His glory.
13 In Him you also *trusted,* after you heard the word of truth,
the gospel of your salvation; in
whom also, having believed,
you were sealed with the Holy
Spirit of promise,
14 who is the guarantee of our
inheritance until the redemption
of the purchased possession, to
the praise of His glory.
15 Therefore I also, after I
heard of your faith in the Lord
Jesus and your love for all the
saints,
16 do not cease to give thanks
for you, making mention of you
in my prayers:
17 that the God of our Lord
Jesus Christ, the Father of
glory, may give to you the spirit
of wisdom and revelation in the
knowledge of Him,
18 the eyes of your understanding being enlightened; that
you may know what is the hope
of His calling, what are the
riches of the glory of His inheritance in the saints,
19 and what *is* the exceeding

[b](**1:10**) TR adds τε, *both.* [c](**1:14**) NU reads ο, *which.* [d](**1:16**) NU omits υμων, *of you.* [e](**1:18**) TR reads διανοιας, *understanding.*

lievers by God, in Christ, to salvation. The same use applies to the cognate noun ἐκλογή, *choice, selection, election* (as 2 Pet. 1:10), although at times the choosing can be merely human (as Luke 14:7). Cf. also the cognate adjective ἐκλεκτός, *chosen, select* (1 Pet. 1:1).

greatness of His power toward
us who believe, according to
the working of His mighty
power
20 which He worked in Christ
when He raised Him from the
dead and seated *Him* at His
right hand in the heavenly
places,
21 far above all principality
and power and might and dominion, and every name that is
named, not only in this age but
also in that which is to come.
22 And He put all *things* under
His feet, and gave Him *to be*
head over all *things* to the
church,
23 which is His body, the fullness of Him who fills all in all.
2 And you *He made alive,*
who were dead in tres-
passes and sins,
2 in which you once walked
according to the course of this
world, according to the prince
of the power of the air, the
spirit who now works in the
sons of disobedience,
3 among whom also we all
once conducted ourselves in
the lusts of our flesh, fulfilling
the desires of the flesh and of
the mind, and were by nature
children of wrath, just as the
others.
4 But God, who is rich in
mercy, because of His great
love with which He loved us,
5 even when we were dead
in trespasses, made us alive together with Christ (by grace

ὑπερβάλλον μέγεθος τῆς δυνάμεως αὐτοῦ εἰς ἡμᾶς τοὺς
exceeding greatness - of power ˜ His toward us the *ones*
who

πιστεύοντας κατὰ τὴν ἐνέργειαν τοῦ κράτους τῆς
believing according to the working of the might -
believe

ἰσχύος αὐτοῦ **20** ἣν ἐνήργησεν ἐν τῷ Χριστῷ ἐγείρας
of strength ˜ His which He worked in - Christ raising
when He raised

αὐτὸν ἐκ τῶν νεκρῶν, καὶ ἐκάθισας ἐν δεξιᾷ αὐτοῦ
Him from the dead, and seating at [2]right [3]*hand* [1]His
when He seated Him

ἐν τοῖς ἐπουρανίοις **21** ὑπεράνω πάσης ἀρχῆς καὶ ἐξουσίας
in the heavenly *realms* above every ruler and authority

καὶ δυνάμεως καὶ κυριότητος καὶ παντὸς ὀνόματος
and power and lordship and every name
dominion

ὀνομαζομένου οὐ μόνον ἐν τῷ αἰῶνι τούτῳ ἀλλὰ καὶ ἐν τῷ
being named not only in - age ˜ this but also in the
that is

μέλλοντι. **22** Καὶ πάντα ὑπέταξεν ὑπὸ τοὺς πόδας αὐτοῦ,
coming *age.* And [3]all [4]*things* [1]He [2]subjected under - feet ˜ His,

καὶ αὐτὸν ἔδωκε κεφαλὴν ὑπὲρ πάντα τῇ ἐκκλησίᾳ,
and [3]Him [1]He [2]gave *to be* head over all *things* to the church,

23 ἥτις ἐστὶ τὸ σῶμα αὐτοῦ, τὸ πλήρωμα τοῦ τὰ
which is - body ˜ His, the fullness of the *One* -

πάντα ἐν πᾶσι πληρουμένου.
[2]all [3]*things* [4]in [5]all [6]*things* [1]filling.

You Are Saved by Grace Through Faith

2 **1** Καὶ ὑμᾶς ὄντας νεκροὺς τοῖς παραπτώμασι καὶ ταῖς
And you being dead - in transgressions and -
were

ἁμαρτίαις,[a] **2** ἐν αἷς ποτε περιεπατήσατε κατὰ τὸν
sins, in which once ˜ you walked according to the

αἰῶνα τοῦ κόσμου τούτου, κατὰ τὸν ἄρχοντα τῆς
age - of world ˜ this, according to the ruler of the

ἐξουσίας τοῦ ἀέρος, τοῦ πνεύματος τοῦ νῦν ἐνεργοῦντος
domain of the air, the spirit the *one* now working
which is

ἐν τοῖς υἱοῖς τῆς ἀπειθείας· **3** ἐν οἷς καὶ ἡμεῖς
in the sons - of disobedience; among whom also we
among

πάντες ἀνεστράφημέν ποτε ἐν ταῖς ἐπιθυμίαις τῆς σαρκὸς
all [2]conducted [3]ourselves [1]once in the lusts - of flesh ˜

ἡμῶν, ποιοῦντες τὰ θελήματα τῆς σαρκὸς καὶ τῶν διανοιῶν,
our, doing the desires of the flesh and of the senses,

καὶ ἦμεν τέκνα φύσει ὀργῆς ὡς καὶ οἱ λοιποί· **4** ὁ δὲ
and we were children [3]by [4]nature [1]of [2]wrath as also the rest; - but

Θεός, πλούσιος ὢν ἐν ἐλέει, διὰ τὴν πολλὴν ἀγάπην
God, rich ˜ being in mercy, because of - [2]much [3]love
great

αὐτοῦ ἣν ἠγάπησεν ἡμᾶς, **5** καὶ ὄντας ἡμᾶς νεκροὺς
[1]His *with* which He loved us, and being ˜ us dead
when we were

τοῖς παραπτώμασι* συνεζωοποίησε τῷ Χριστῷ —
- in transgressions He made *us* alive together - with Christ —

---

[a](2:1) NU adds υμων, *your.*

*(2:5) παράπτωμα (*paraptōma*). Noun meaning literally a *fall beside, misstep,* but used in the NT only with the figurative sense *trespass, sin.* While it may indicate transgressions against other people (Matt. 6:14), usually it refers specifically to sins against God. Most often it appears in the plural (as here in Eph. 2:5). It may have a specific or collective sense when used in the singular (Adam's sin, Rom. 5:15–18; Israel's unbelief, 11:11, 12). As compared to the synonym ἁμαρτία, *sin,* παράπτωμα may imply unpremeditated violations of God's law (see ἁμαρτία at John 9:41).

χάριτί ἐστε σεσῳσμένοι — 6 καὶ συνήγειρε καὶ
by grace you are having been saved — and He raised *us* together and
you have been

συνεκάθισεν ἐν τοῖς ἐπουρανίοις ἐν Χριστῷ Ἰησοῦ, 7 ἵνα
seated *us* together in the heavenly *realms* in Christ Jesus, so that

ἐνδείξηται ἐν τοῖς αἰῶσι τοῖς ἐπερχομένοις τὸν ὑπερβάλλοντα
He might show in the ages ˜ - coming the exceeding

πλοῦτον τῆς χάριτος αὐτοῦ ἐν χρηστότητι ἐφ' ἡμᾶς ἐν
riches - of grace ˜ His in *His* kindness toward us in

Χριστῷ Ἰησοῦ. 8 Τῇ γὰρ χάριτί ἐστε σεσῳσμένοι διὰ
Christ Jesus. - For by grace you are having been saved through
you have been

τῆς πίστεως· καὶ τοῦτο οὐκ ἐξ ὑμῶν, Θεοῦ τὸ
- faith; and this *is* not of you, *but is* [3]of [4]God [1]the
yourselves,

δῶρον· 9 οὐκ ἐξ ἔργων, ἵνα μή τις καυχήσηται. 10 Αὐτοῦ
[2]gift; not of works, that not anyone should boast. [4]His
lest

γάρ ἐσμεν ποίημα, κτισθέντες ἐν Χριστῷ Ἰησοῦ ἐπὶ ἔργοις
[1]For [2]we [3]are creation, created in Christ Jesus for works ˜

ἀγαθοῖς οἷς προητοίμασεν ὁ Θεὸς ἵνα ἐν αὐτοῖς
good which [2]prepared [3]beforehand - [1]God that [4]in [5]them

περιπατήσωμεν.
[1]we [2]should [3]walk.

Brought Near by the Blood of Christ

11 Διὸ μνημονεύετε ὅτι ὑμεῖς ποτὲ τὰ ἔθνη ἐν
Therefore remember that you once *were* the Gentiles in

σαρκί — οἱ λεγόμενοι ἀκροβυστία ὑπὸ τῆς λεγομένης
the flesh — the *ones* being called uncircumcision by the *one* being called
who are called called

περιτομῆς ἐν σαρκὶ χειροποιήτου — 12 ὅτι ἦτε
circumcision [5]in [6]*the* [7]flesh [1]made [2]by [3]*human* [4]hands — that you were

ἐν τῷ καιρῷ ἐκείνῳ χωρὶς Χριστοῦ, ἀπηλλοτριωμένοι τῆς
in - time ˜ that apart from Christ, being estranged from the

πολιτείας τοῦ Ἰσραὴλ καὶ ξένοι τῶν διαθηκῶν τῆς
citizenship - of Israel and strangers of the covenants -
to

ἐπαγγελίας, ἐλπίδα μὴ ἔχοντες καὶ ἄθεοι ἐν τῷ κόσμῳ.
of promise, [3]hope [1]not [2]having and godless in the world.

13 Νυνὶ δὲ ἐν Χριστῷ Ἰησοῦ ὑμεῖς οἵ ποτε ὄντες μακρὰν
now ˜ But in Christ Jesus you the *ones* once being far away
who were

ἐγγὺς ἐγενήθητε ἐν τῷ αἵματι τοῦ Χριστοῦ.
[5]near [1]have [2]come [3]to [4]be by the blood - of Christ.

Christ Is Our Peace and Cornerstone

14 Αὐτὸς γάρ ἐστιν ἡ εἰρήνη ἡμῶν, ὁ ποιήσας τὰ
He ˜ For is - peace ˜ our, the *one* making -
who made

ἀμφότερα ἓν καὶ τὸ μεσότοιχον τοῦ φραγμοῦ λύσας,
both one and [2]the [3]dividing [4]wall [5]of [6]the [7]hedge [1]destroying,
who destroyed the dividing wall of separation,

15 τὴν ἔχθραν, ἐν τῇ σαρκὶ αὐτοῦ, τὸν νόμον τῶν
[6]the [7]enmity, [3]in - [5]flesh [4]His, [8]the [9]law [10]of [11]the
by means of

ἐντολῶν ἐν δόγμασιν καταργήσας, ἵνα
[12]commandments [13]*contained* [14]in [15]ordinances [1]having [2]abolished, that *from*

you have been saved),
6 and raised *us* up together,
and made *us* sit together in the
heavenly *places* in Christ Jesus,
7 that in the ages to come He
might show the exceeding
riches of His grace in *His* kindness toward us in Christ Jesus.
8 For by grace you have
been saved through faith, and
that not of yourselves; *it is* the
gift of God,
9 not of works, lest anyone
should boast.
10 For we are His workman-
ship, created in Christ Jesus for
good works, which God prepared beforehand that we
should walk in them.
11 Therefore remember that
you, once Gentiles in the
flesh — who are called Uncircumcision by what is called the
Circumcision made in the flesh
by hands —
12 that at that time you were
without Christ, being aliens
from the commonwealth of Israel and strangers from the
covenants of promise, having
no hope and without God in the
world.
13 But now in Christ Jesus
you who once were far off have
been brought near by the blood
of Christ.
14 For He Himself is our
peace, who has made both one,
and has broken down the middle wall of separation,
15 having abolished in His
flesh the enmity, *that is,* the
law of commandments *con-
tained* in ordinances, so as to

create in Himself one new man
from the two, *thus* making
peace,
16 and that He might reconcile
them both to God in one body
through the cross, thereby putting to death the enmity.
17 And He came and preached
peace to you who were afar off
and to those who were near.
18 For through Him we both
have access by one Spirit to the
Father.
19 Now, therefore, you are no
longer strangers and foreigners, but fellow citizens with the
saints and members of the
household of God,
20 having been built on the
foundation of the apostles and
prophets, Jesus Christ Himself
being the chief corner*stone,*
21 in whom the whole building, being fitted together,
grows into a holy temple in the
Lord,
22 in whom you also are being
built together for a dwelling
place of God in the Spirit.
3 For this reason I, Paul,
the prisoner of Christ Jesus for you Gentiles—
2 if indeed you have heard of
the dispensation of the grace of
God which was given to me for
you,
3 how that by revelation He
made known to me the mystery
(as I have briefly written already,
4 by which, when you read,
you may understand my knowledge in the mystery of Christ),
5 which in other ages was
not made known to the sons of
men, as it has now been revealed by the Spirit to His holy
apostles and prophets:

τοὺς δύο κτίσῃ ἐν ἑαυτῷ εἰς ἕνα καινὸν ἄνθρωπον,
the two He might create in Himself for one new man,

ποιῶν εἰρήνην, **16** *καὶ ἀποκαταλλάξῃ τοὺς ἀμφοτέρους ἐν*
making peace, and *that* He might reconcile - both in

ἑνὶ σώματι τῷ Θεῷ διὰ τοῦ σταυροῦ, ἀποκτείνας τὴν ἔχθραν
one body - to God by the cross, putting to death the enmity

ἐν αὐτῷ. **17** *Καὶ ἐλθὼν εὐηγγελίσατο εἰρήνην ὑμῖν*
in Him. And coming He preached peace to you
Himself. when He came

τοῖς μακρὰν καὶ[b] *τοῖς ἐγγύς.* **18** *Ὅτι δι' αὐτοῦ*
the *ones* far away and to the *ones* near. Because through Him
who were

ἔχομεν τὴν προσαγωγὴν οἱ ἀμφότεροι ἐν ἑνὶ Πνεύματι πρὸς
[1]we [3]have [4]the [5]access - [2]both by one Spirit to

τὸν Πατέρα. **19** *Ἄρα οὖν οὐκέτι ἐστὲ ξένοι καὶ*
the Father. then ˜ Therefore no longer are you strangers and
So

πάροικοι, ἀλλὰ[c] *συμπολῖται τῶν ἁγίων καὶ*
aliens, but fellow citizens of the saints and

οἰκεῖοι τοῦ Θεοῦ, **20** *ἐποικοδομηθέντες ἐπὶ τῷ*
members of the household - of God, being built upon the

θεμελίῳ τῶν ἀποστόλων καὶ προφητῶν, ὄντος
foundation of the apostles and prophets, [4]being

ἀκρογωνιαίου αὐτοῦ Ἰησοῦ Χριστοῦ, **21** *ἐν ᾧ πᾶσα*
[5]at [6]*the* [7]extreme [8]corner [3]Himself [1]Jesus [2]Christ, in whom all
the chief cornerstone the

οἰκοδομὴ συναρμολογουμένη αὔξει εἰς ναὸν ἅγιον ἐν
the building being joined together grows into a temple ˜ holy in
whole building

Κυρίῳ, **22** *ἐν ᾧ καὶ ὑμεῖς συνοικοδομεῖσθε εἰς*
the Lord, in whom also ˜ you are being built together for
as

κατοικητήριον τοῦ Θεοῦ ἐν Πνεύματι.
a habitation - of God in *the* Spirit.

Revelation of the Mystery

3 **1** *Τούτου χάριν ἐγὼ Παῦλος, ὁ δέσμιος τοῦ Χριστοῦ*
[3]this [1]Because [2]of I Paul, the prisoner - of Christ

Ἰησοῦ ὑπὲρ ὑμῶν τῶν ἐθνῶν **2** *— εἴ γε ἠκούσατε τὴν*
Jesus in behalf of you - Gentiles — if indeed you heard of the
have heard

οἰκονομίαν τῆς χάριτος τοῦ Θεοῦ τῆς δοθείσης μοι εἰς
stewardship of the grace - of God the *one* being given to me for
which was

ὑμᾶς, **3** *ὅτι κατὰ ἀποκάλυψιν ἐγνώρισέ μοι τὸ*
you, that by revelation He made known to me the

μυστήριον, καθὼς προέγραψα ἐν ὀλίγῳ, **4** *πρὸς ὃ*
mystery, just as I wrote before in a little, with reference to which
briefly,

δύνασθε ἀναγινώσκοντες νοῆσαι τὴν σύνεσίν μου ἐν τῷ
[2]you [3]are [4]able [1]reading to understand - insight ˜ my in the
when you read

μυστηρίῳ τοῦ Χριστοῦ, **5** *ὃ ἑτέραις γενεαῖς οὐκ*
mystery - of Christ, which in other generations not ˜

ἐγνωρίσθη τοῖς υἱοῖς τῶν ἀνθρώπων, ὡς νῦν
was made known to the sons - of men, as now

ἀπεκαλύφθη τοῖς ἁγίοις ἀποστόλοις αὐτοῦ καὶ προφήταις
it has been revealed to [2]holy [3]apostles [1]His and prophets

[b](**2:17**) NU adds *ειρηνην, peace.* [c](**2:19**) NU adds *εστε, you are.*

ἐν Πνεύματι, **6** εἶναι τὰ ἔθνη συγκληρονόμα καὶ
in *the* Spirit, *that* [3]to [4]be [1]the [2]Gentiles fellow heirs and
by should

σύσσωμα καὶ συμμέτοχα τῆς ἐπαγγελίας αὐτοῦ [a] ἐν τῷ
of the same body and sharing together - of promise ˜ His in -
participants in

Χριστῷ διὰ τοῦ εὐαγγελίου, **7** οὗ ἐγενόμην διάκονος
Christ by the gospel, of which I became a servant
minister

κατὰ τὴν δωρεὰν τῆς χάριτος τοῦ Θεοῦ, τὴν δοθεῖσάν
according to the free gift of the grace - of God, the *one* being given
which was

μοι κατὰ τὴν ἐνέργειαν τῆς δυνάμεως αὐτοῦ.
to me according to the working - of power ˜ His.

Purpose of the Mystery

8 Ἐμοὶ τῷ ἐλαχιστοτέρῳ πάντων ἁγίων ἐδόθη ἡ χάρις
To me the very least of all *the* saints was given - grace ˜

αὕτη, ἐν τοῖς ἔθνεσιν εὐαγγελίσασθαι τὸν ἀνεξιχνίαστον
this, [3]among [4]the [5]Gentiles [1]to [2]preach the incomprehensible

πλοῦτον τοῦ Χριστοῦ, **9** καὶ φωτίσαι πάντας τίς ἡ
riches - of Christ, and to enlighten all *as to* what *is* the

οἰκονομία [b] τοῦ μυστηρίου τοῦ ἀποκεκρυμμένου ἀπὸ τῶν
administration of the mystery the *one* having been hidden from the
which had

αἰώνων ἐν τῷ Θεῷ τῷ τὰ πάντα κτίσαντι διὰ Ἰησοῦ
ages in - God the *One* - [2]all [3]*things* [1]creating through Jesus
who created

Χριστοῦ, [c] **10** ἵνα γνωρισθῇ νῦν ταῖς ἀρχαῖς
Christ, that [6]might [7]be [8]made [9]known [13]now [14]to [15]the [16]rulers

καὶ ταῖς ἐξουσίαις ἐν τοῖς ἐπουρανίοις διὰ τῆς
[17]and [18]to [19]the [20]authorities [21]in [22]the [23]heavenly [24]*realms* [10]by [11]the

ἐκκλησίας ἡ πολυποίκιλος σοφία τοῦ Θεοῦ, **11** κατὰ
[12]church [1]the [2]many-sided [3]wisdom - [4]of [5]God, according to
manifold

πρόθεσιν τῶν αἰώνων ἣν ἐποίησεν ἐν Χριστῷ Ἰησοῦ τῷ
the purpose of the ages which He made in Christ Jesus -

Κυρίῳ ἡμῶν, **12** ἐν ᾧ ἔχομεν τὴν παρρησίαν καὶ τὴν
Lord ˜ our, in whom we have the boldness and the

προσαγωγὴν ἐν πεποιθήσει διὰ τῆς πίστεως αὐτοῦ.
access with confidence through - faith of Him.
in

13 Διὸ αἰτοῦμαι μὴ ἐκκακεῖν ἐν ταῖς θλίψεσί μου
Therefore I ask *you* not to lose heart at - afflictions ˜ my

ὑπὲρ ὑμῶν, ἥτις ἐστὶ δόξα ὑμῶν.
on behalf of you, which is glory ˜ your.

Appreciation of the Mystery

14 Τούτου χάριν κάμπτω τὰ γόνατά μου πρὸς τὸν
[3]this [1]Because [2]of I bend - knees ˜ my to the

Πατέρα τοῦ Κυρίου ἡμῶν Ἰησοῦ Χριστοῦ, [d] **15** ἐξ οὗ
Father - of Lord ˜ our Jesus Christ, from whom

πᾶσα πατριὰ ἐν οὐρανοῖς καὶ ἐπὶ γῆς ὀνομάζεται, **16** ἵνα
every family in heavens and upon earth is named, that
heaven takes its name,

δώῃ ὑμῖν, κατὰ τὸν πλοῦτον τῆς δόξης αὐτοῦ,
He would give you, according to the riches - of glory ˜ His,
grant

6 that the Gentiles should be
fellow heirs, of the same body,
and partakers of His promise in
Christ through the gospel,
7 of which I became a minister according to the gift of the
grace of God given to me by the
effective working of His power.
8 To me, who am less than
the least of all the saints, this
grace was given, that I should
preach among the Gentiles the
unsearchable riches of Christ,
9 and to make all see what *is*
the fellowship of the mystery,
which from the beginning of the
ages has been hidden in God
who created all things through
Jesus Christ;
10 to the intent that now the
manifold wisdom of God might
be made known by the church
to the principalities and powers
in the heavenly *places,*
11 according to the eternal
purpose which He accom-
plished in Christ Jesus our
Lord,
12 in whom we have boldness
and access with confidence
through faith in Him.
13 Therefore I ask that you do
not lose heart at my tribulations
for you, which is your glory.
14 For this reason I bow my
knees to the Father of our Lord
Jesus Christ,
15 from whom the whole family in heaven and earth is
named,
16 that He would grant you,
according to the riches of His

---

[a](**3:6**) NU omits αυτου, *His.*
[b](**3:9**) TR reads κοινωνια, *fellowship.*
[c](**3:9**) NU omits δια Ιησου Χριστου, *through Jesus Christ.* [d](**3:14**) NU omits του Κυριου ημων Ιησου Χριστου, *of our Lord Jesus Christ.*

glory, to be strengthened with
might through His Spirit in the
inner man,
17 that Christ may dwell in
your hearts through faith; that
you, being rooted and grounded
in love,
18 may be able to comprehend
with all the saints what *is* the
width and length and depth and
height—
19 to know the love of Christ
which passes knowledge; that
you may be filled with all the
fullness of God.
20 Now to Him who is able to
do exceedingly abundantly
above all that we ask or think,
according to the power that
works in us,
21 to Him *be* glory in the
church by Christ Jesus to all
generations, forever and ever.
Amen.
4 I, therefore, the prisoner
of the Lord, beseech you
to walk worthy of the calling
with which you were called,
2 with all lowliness and gentleness, with longsuffering,
bearing with one another in
love,
3 endeavoring to keep the
unity of the Spirit in the bond of
peace.
4 *There is* one body and one
Spirit, just as you were called in
one hope of your calling;
5 one Lord, one faith, one
baptism;
6 one God and Father of all,
who *is* above all, and through
all, and in you all.

---

a(4:6) NU omits ημιν, *us;* TR reads υμιν, *you.*

***(3:18)** *καταλαμβάνω (katalambanō).* Verb with a variety of meanings, all growing out of the basic idea *take hold of, grasp,* from the preposition *κατά, down,* and the verb *λαμβάνω, take, receive.* It may mean *make one's own, attain* (as 1 Cor. 9:24; Phil. 3:12); *come upon, overtake,* often with hostile intent (as Mark 9:18; 1 Thess. 5:4); and thus *catch, seize, take* (as John 8:3). The word is also applied to mental activities in the sense of *grasp, comprehend, understand* (as here in Eph. 3:18). Commentators debate which of these meanings is predominant in John 1:5.

δυνάμει κραταιωθῆναι διὰ τοῦ Πνεύματος αὐτοῦ εἰς τὸν
[4]with [5]power [1]to [2]be [3]strengthened by - Spirit ˜ His in the

ἔσω ἄνθρωπον, **17** κατοικῆσαι τὸν Χριστὸν διὰ τῆς
inward man, [3]to [4]dwell - [1]*for* [2]Christ through -
that Christ may dwell

πίστεως ἐν ταῖς καρδίαις ὑμῶν, ἐν ἀγάπῃ ἐρριζωμένοι καὶ
faith in - hearts ˜ your, in love having been rooted and
being

τεθεμελιωμένοι, **18** ἵνα ἐξισχύσητε καταλαβέσθαι* σὺν
having been founded, that you may be able to grasp with
being comprehend

πᾶσι τοῖς ἁγίοις τί τὸ πλάτος καὶ μῆκος καὶ βάθος καὶ
all the saints what *is* the breadth and length and depth and

ὕψος, **19** γνῶναί τε τὴν ὑπερβάλλουσαν τῆς γνώσεως
height, [2]to [3]know [1]and the [4]surpassing - [5]knowledge
which surpasses

ἀγάπην τοῦ Χριστοῦ, ἵνα πληρωθῆτε εἰς πᾶν τὸ πλήρωμα
[1]love - [2]of [3]Christ, that you may be filled to all the fullness

τοῦ Θεοῦ.
- of God.

20 Τῷ δὲ δυναμένῳ ὑπὲρ πάντα ποιῆσαι
[2]to [3]the [4]*One* [1]Now being able beyond all *things* to do
Him who is able to do exceedingly more than

ὑπερεκπερισσοῦ ὧν αἰτούμεθα ἢ νοοῦμεν, κατὰ τὴν
exceedingly more which we ask or think, according to the
all the things

δύναμιν τὴν ἐνεργουμένην ἐν ἡμῖν, **21** αὐτῷ ἡ δόξα ἐν
power the *one* working in us, to Him *be* the glory in
which is

τῇ ἐκκλησίᾳ ἐν Χριστῷ Ἰησοῦ εἰς πάσας τὰς γενεὰς τοῦ
the church in Christ Jesus to all - generations of the
forever

αἰῶνος τῶν αἰώνων. Ἀμήν.
age of the ages. Amen.
and ever. So be it.

Walk in Unity

4 **1** Παρακαλῶ οὖν ὑμᾶς ἐγώ, ὁ δέσμιος ἐν Κυρίῳ,
[2]I [3]urge [1]Therefore you I, the prisoner in *the* Lord,
of

ἀξίως περιπατῆσαι τῆς κλήσεως ἧς ἐκλήθητε,
[3]worthily [1]to [2]walk of the calling *with* which you were called,

2 μετὰ πάσης ταπεινοφροσύνης καὶ πραότητος, μετὰ
with all humility and meekness, with
utmost

μακροθυμίας, ἀνεχόμενοι ἀλλήλων ἐν ἀγάπῃ, **3** σπουδάζοντες
longsuffering, bearing with one another in love, being diligent
patience,

τηρεῖν τὴν ἑνότητα τοῦ Πνεύματος ἐν τῷ συνδέσμῳ τῆς
to keep the unity of the Spirit in the bond -

εἰρήνης. **4** Ἓν σῶμα καὶ ἓν Πνεῦμα, καθὼς καὶ
of peace. *There is* one body and one Spirit, just as also

ἐκλήθητε ἐν μιᾷ ἐλπίδι τῆς κλήσεως ὑμῶν· **5** εἷς Κύριος,
you were called in one hope - of calling ˜ your; one Lord,

μία πίστις, ἓν βάπτισμα, **6** εἷς Θεὸς καὶ Πατὴρ πάντων,
one faith, one baptism, one God and Father of all,

ὁ ἐπὶ πάντων καὶ διὰ πάντων καὶ ἐν πᾶσιν ἡμῖν.[a]
the *One* over all and through all and in all ˜ us.
who is

Each Believer Has a Spiritual Gift

7 Ἑνὶ δὲ ἑκάστῳ ἡμῶν ἐδόθη ἡ χάρις κατὰ τὸ
[2]to [4]one [1]But [3]each of us was given - grace according to the

μέτρον τῆς δωρεᾶς τοῦ Χριστοῦ. **8** Διὸ λέγει,
measure of the free gift - of Christ. Therefore He says,
it

«Ἀναβὰς εἰς ὕψος ᾐχμαλώτευσεν αἰχμαλωσίαν
«Ascending on a height He led captive ˜ captivity
«When He ascended high prisoners of war

Καὶ ἔδωκε δόματα τοῖς ἀνθρώποις.»[b]
And He gave gifts - to men.»

9 Τὸ δὲ «Ἀνέβη,» τί ἐστιν εἰ μὴ ὅτι καὶ
the ˜ Now «He went up,» what is it if not that also ˜
this, does it mean except

κατέβη πρῶτον[c] εἰς τὰ κατώτερα μέρη τῆς γῆς?
He descended first into the lower parts of the earth?

10 Ὁ καταβάς, αὐτός ἐστι καὶ ὁ ἀναβὰς
The *One* descending, He is also the *One* ascending
who descended, who ascended

ὑπεράνω πάντων τῶν οὐρανῶν, ἵνα πληρώσῃ τὰ
above all the heavens, in order that He might fill -

πάντα. **11** Καὶ αὐτὸς ἔδωκε τοὺς μὲν ἀποστόλους, τοὺς
all *things*. And He gave the *ones* - *as* apostles, [2]the [3]*others*
some some

δὲ προφήτας, τοὺς δὲ εὐαγγελιστάς, τοὺς δὲ
[1]and *as* prophets, [2]the [3]*others* [1]and *as* evangelists, [2]the [3]*others* [1]and
some some

ποιμένας καὶ διδασκάλους, **12** πρὸς τὸν καταρτισμὸν* τῶν
as shepherds and teachers, for the equipping of the
pastors

ἁγίων εἰς ἔργον διακονίας εἰς οἰκοδομὴν τοῦ σώματος τοῦ
saints for a work of service for *the* edification of the body -
ministry building up

Χριστοῦ, **13** μέχρι καταντήσωμεν οἱ πάντες εἰς τὴν ἑνότητα
of Christ, until we arrive ˜ - all in the unity

τῆς πίστεως καὶ τῆς ἐπιγνώσεως τοῦ Υἱοῦ τοῦ Θεοῦ, εἰς
of the faith and of the knowledge of the Son - of God, to

ἄνδρα τέλειον, εἰς μέτρον ἡλικίας τοῦ πληρώματος τοῦ
a man ˜ complete, to *the* measure of *the* stature of the fullness -
mature,

Χριστοῦ, **14** ἵνα μηκέτι ὦμεν νήπιοι,
of Christ, that [3]no [4]longer [1]we [2]may [5]be infants,

κλυδωνιζόμενοι καὶ περιφερόμενοι παντὶ ἀνέμῳ τῆς
being tossed as by waves and being carried about by every wind -

διδασκαλίας, ἐν τῇ κυβείᾳ τῶν ἀνθρώπων, ἐν πανουργίᾳ,
of teaching, by the trickery - of men, by craftiness,

πρὸς τὴν μεθοδείαν τῆς πλάνης, **15** ἀληθεύοντες
in regard to the scheming - of deception, [3]telling [4]the [5]truth
in the interest of deceitful scheming,

δὲ ἐν ἀγάπῃ αὐξήσωμεν εἰς αὐτὸν τὰ πάντα, ὅς
[1]but [2]*that* in love we may grow [4]into [5]Him - [1]*in* [2]all [3]*things,* who

ἐστιν ἡ κεφαλή, ὁ Χριστός, **16** ἐξ οὗ πᾶν τὸ σῶμα
is the head, - Christ, from whom all the body

συναρμολογούμενον καὶ συμβιβαζόμενον διὰ πάσης ἁφῆς
being fitted together and being brought together through every joint
held by what every

τῆς ἐπιχορηγίας, κατ' ἐνέργειαν ἐν μέτρῳ ἑνὸς
of the supply, according to *the* working in a measure of one
joint supplies, of the measure of each

7 But to each one of us grace was given according to the measure of Christ's gift.
8 Therefore He says:

> *"When He ascended on high,*
> *He led captivity captive,*
> *And gave gifts to men."*

9 (Now this, *"He ascended"*—what does it mean but that He also first descended into the lower parts of the earth?
10 He who descended is also the One who ascended far above all the heavens, that He might fill all things.)
11 And He Himself gave some *to be* apostles, some prophets, some evangelists, and some pastors and teachers,
12 for the equipping of the saints for the work of ministry, for the edifying of the body of Christ,
13 till we all come to the unity of the faith and of the knowledge of the Son of God, to a perfect man, to the measure of the stature of the fullness of Christ;
14 that we should no longer be children, tossed to and fro and carried about with every wind of doctrine, by the trickery of men, in the cunning craftiness of deceitful plotting,
15 but, speaking the truth in love, may grow up in all things into Him who is the head—Christ—
16 from whom the whole body, joined and knit together by what every joint supplies, according to the effective work-

---

[b]**(4:8)** Ps. 68:18
[c]**(4:9)** NU omits πρωτον, *first.*

***(4:12)** καταρτισμός *(katartismos).* Noun meaning *equipping,* occurring only here in the NT. Other possible meanings include *completion, training* (see the cognate verb καταρτίζω at Heb. 11:3). The basic idea is "making fit" or "preparing fully," thus enabling someone (or something) to be what he (it) was designed to be. Consequently, the word generally carries a functional connotation, as does the cognate noun κατάρτισις,

ing by which every part does its
share, causes growth of the
body for the edifying of itself in
love.
17 This I say, therefore, and
testify in the Lord, that you
should no longer walk as the
rest of the Gentiles walk, in the
futility of their mind,
18 having their understanding
darkened, being alienated from
the life of God, because of the
ignorance that is in them, because of the blindness of their
heart;
19 who, being past feeling,
have given themselves over to
lewdness, to work all uncleanness with greediness.
20 But you have not so
learned Christ,
21 if indeed you have heard
Him and have been taught by
Him, as the truth is in Jesus:
22 that you put off, concerning
your former conduct, the old
man which grows corrupt according to the deceitful lusts,
23 and be renewed in the
spirit of your mind,
24 and that you put on the
new man which was created according to God, in true righteousness and holiness.
25 Therefore, putting away
lying, *"Let each one of you
speak truth with his neighbor,"*
for we are members of one another.
26 *"Be angry, and do not sin"*:
do not let the sun go down on
your wrath,

ἑκάστου μέρους, τὴν αὔξησιν τοῦ σώματος ποιεῖται εἰς
of each part, [2]the [3]growth [4]of [5]the [6]body [1]causes to
individual

οἰκοδομὴν ἑαυτοῦ ἐν ἀγάπῃ.
edification of itself in love.
the building up

Put on the New Man

17 Τοῦτο οὖν λέγω καὶ μαρτύρομαι ἐν Κυρίῳ, μηκέτι
This [3]therefore [1]I [2]say and testify in *the* Lord, no longer

ὑμᾶς περιπατεῖν καθὼς καὶ τὰ λοιπὰ[d] ἔθνη περιπατεῖ
are you to walk just as also the rest *of* *the* Gentiles walk

ἐν ματαιότητι τοῦ νοὸς αὐτῶν, 18 ἐσκοτισμένοι τῇ
in *the* futility - of mind ˜ their, having been darkened -

διανοίᾳ, ὄντες ἀπηλλοτριωμένοι τῆς ζωῆς τοῦ Θεοῦ,
in understanding, being estranged from the life - of God,

διὰ τὴν ἄγνοιαν τὴν οὖσαν ἐν αὐτοῖς, διὰ τὴν
because of the ignorance the *one* being in them, because of the
which is

πώρωσιν τῆς καρδίας αὐτῶν, 19 οἵτινες ἀπηλγηκότες
hardening - of heart ˜ their, who having become callous
because they had

ἑαυτοὺς παρέδωκαν τῇ ἀσελγείᾳ εἰς ἐργασίαν
themselves ˜ gave over - to debauchery for *the* working

ἀκαθαρσίας πάσης ἐν πλεονεξίᾳ. 20 Ὑμεῖς δὲ οὐχ οὕτως
of uncleanness ˜ all with greediness. you ˜ But [2]not [3]thus
utmost

ἐμάθετε τὸν Χριστόν, 21 εἴ γε αὐτὸν ἠκούσατε καὶ ἐν αὐτῷ
[1]did [4]learn - Christ, if indeed [3]Him [1]you [2]heard and [3]in [4]Him

ἐδιδάχθητε, καθώς ἐστιν ἀλήθεια ἐν τῷ Ἰησοῦ, 22 ἀποθέσθαι
[1]were [2]taught, just as is ˜ truth in - Jesus, to put off
that you

ὑμᾶς, κατὰ τὴν προτέραν ἀναστροφήν, τὸν παλαιὸν
you, with respect to the former way of life, the old
put off, concerning your

ἄνθρωπον τὸν φθειρόμενον κατὰ τὰς ἐπιθυμίας τῆς
man the *one* being corrupted according to the lusts -
which is deceitful lusts,

ἀπάτης, 23 ἀνανεοῦσθαι δὲ τῷ πνεύματι τοῦ νοὸς ὑμῶν,
of deceit, [2]to [3]be [4]renewed [1]and in the spirit - of mind ˜ your,
that you be

24 καὶ ἐνδύσασθαι τὸν καινὸν ἄνθρωπον τὸν κατὰ
and to put on the new man the *one* [3]according [4]to
that you which was in the likeness of

Θεὸν κτισθέντα ἐν δικαιοσύνῃ καὶ ὁσιότητι τῆς ἀληθείας.
[5]God [1]being [2]created in righteousness and holiness of the truth.
created

Do Not Grieve the Spirit of God

25 Διὸ ἀποθέμενοι τὸ ψεῦδος, «λαλεῖτε ἀλήθειαν
Therefore putting off the lie, «[1]Let [4]speak [5]truth

ἕκαστος μετὰ τοῦ πλησίον αὐτοῦ,»[e] ὅτι ἐσμὲν
[2]each [3]one with - neighbor ˜ his,» because we are

ἀλλήλων μέλη. 26 «Ὀργίζεσθε καὶ μὴ
[2]of [3]one [4]another [1]members. «Be angry and not ˜

ἁμαρτάνετε»·[f] ὁ ἥλιος μὴ ἐπιδυέτω ἐπὶ τῷ παροργισμῷ
do sin»: [4]the [5]sun [2]not [1]Do [3]let [6]set on - anger ˜

---

[d](4:17) NU omits λοιπα, *rest (of)*. [e](4:25) Zech. 8:16
[f](4:26) Ps. 4:4

---

completion (only at 2 Cor. 13:9).

ὑμῶν, **27** μηδὲ δίδοτε τόπον τῷ διαβόλῳ. **28** Ὁ
your, nor give place to the devil. [2]the [3]*one*
opportunity him who

κλέπτων μηκέτι κλεπτέτω, μᾶλλον δὲ κοπιάτω,
[4]stealing [6]no [7]longer [1]Let [5]steal, rather ˜ but let him labor,
stole

ἐργαζόμενος τὸ ἀγαθὸν ταῖς[g] χερσίν, ἵνα
working the good *thing* with the hands, in order that
that which is good with his

ἔχῃ μεταδιδόναι τῷ χρείαν ἔχοντι. **29** Πᾶς
he may have *something* to share with the *one* need ˜ having. any
him who has. Let no

λόγος σαπρὸς ἐκ τοῦ στόματος ὑμῶν μὴ ἐκπορευέσθω,
word ˜ decayed out of - mouth your not ˜ Let proceed,
corrupt word proceed from your mouth,

ἀλλ' εἴ τις ἀγαθὸς πρὸς οἰκοδομὴν τῆς χρείας, ἵνα
but if anything *is* good for edification of the need, that
only what as needed,

δῷ χάριν τοῖς ἀκούουσι. **30** Καὶ μὴ λυπεῖτε τὸ
it may give grace to the *ones* hearing. And not ˜ do grieve the
those who hear.

Πνεῦμα τὸ Ἅγιον τοῦ Θεοῦ, ἐν ᾧ ἐσφραγίσθητε εἰς
Spirit ˜ - Holy - of God, by whom you were sealed for

ἡμέραν ἀπολυτρώσεως. **31** Πᾶσα πικρία καὶ θυμὸς καὶ ὀργὴ
the day of redemption. [2]all [3]bitterness [4]and [5]wrath [6]and [7]anger

καὶ κραυγὴ καὶ βλασφημία ἀρθήτω ἀφ' ὑμῶν, σὺν
[8]and [9]clamor [10]and [11]blasphemy [1]Let [12]be [13]removed from you, with

πάσῃ κακίᾳ. **32** Γίνεσθε δὲ εἰς ἀλλήλους χρηστοί,
all malice. be ˜ And [2]to [3]one [4]another [1]kind,

εὔσπλαγχνοι, χαριζόμενοι ἑαυτοῖς, καθὼς καὶ ὁ Θεὸς ἐν
tenderhearted, forgiving one another, just as also - God in

Χριστῷ ἐχαρίσατο ὑμῖν.[h]
Christ forgave you.

Walk in Love

5 **1** Γίνεσθε οὖν μιμηταὶ* τοῦ Θεοῦ, ὡς τέκνα
be ˜ Therefore imitators - of God, as children ˜

ἀγαπητά, **2** καὶ περιπατεῖτε ἐν ἀγάπῃ, καθὼς καὶ ὁ Χριστὸς
beloved, and walk in love, just as also - Christ

ἠγάπησεν ἡμᾶς καὶ παρέδωκεν ἑαυτὸν ὑπὲρ ἡμῶν
loved us and gave Himself in behalf of us

προσφορὰν καὶ θυσίαν τῷ Θεῷ εἰς ὀσμὴν εὐωδίας.
as an offering and a sacrifice - to God for an odor of fragrance.
a fragrant aroma.

3 Πορνεία δὲ καὶ πᾶσα ἀκαθαρσία ἢ πλεονεξία μηδὲ
[5]fornication [1]But [6]and [7]all [8]uncleanness [9]or [10]covetousness [3]not
sexual immorality any unclean thing greed

ὀνομαζέσθω ἐν ὑμῖν, καθὼς πρέπει ἁγίοις, **4** καὶ
[2]do [4]let [11]be [12]named among you, just as it is fitting for saints, also
neither

αἰσχρότης καὶ μωρολογία ἢ εὐτραπελία, τὰ οὐκ
wickedness and foolish talk or coarse jesting, the *things* not
which are

ἀνήκοντα, ἀλλὰ μᾶλλον εὐχαριστία. **5** Τοῦτο γὰρ ἐστε[a]
proper, but rather thanksgiving. this ˜ For you are
you

γινώσκοντες ὅτι πᾶς πόρνος ἢ ἀκάθαρτος ἢ
knowing that every fornicator or unclean *person* or
know no sexually immoral person

27 nor give place to the devil.
28 Let him who stole steal no
longer, but rather let him labor,
working with *his* hands what is
good, that he may have something to give him who has need.
29 Let no corrupt word proceed out of your mouth, but
what is good for necessary edification, that it may impart
grace to the hearers.
30 And do not grieve the Holy
Spirit of God, by whom you
were sealed for the day of redemption.
31 Let all bitterness, wrath,
anger, clamor, and evil speaking be put away from you, with
all malice.
32 And be kind to one an-
other, tenderhearted, forgiving
one another, even as God in
Christ forgave you.
5 Therefore be imitators of
God as dear children.
2 And walk in love, as Christ
also has loved us and given
Himself for us, an offering and a
sacrifice to God for a sweet-
smelling aroma.
3 But fornication and all uncleanness or covetousness, let
it not even be named among
you, as is fitting for saints;
4 neither filthiness, nor foolish talking, nor coarse jesting,
which are not fitting, but rather
giving of thanks.
5 For this you know, that no
fornicator, unclean person, nor

---

[g](4:28) NU adds ιδιαις, *his own.* [h](4:32) NU, TR read υμιν, *you.* [a](5:5) NU reads ιστε, *know (this).*

***(5:1)** μιμητής *(mimētēs).* Noun meaning *imitator, emulator.* This Greek word does not have the negative connotation or artificial sense conveyed by the English words *imitate* or *mimic.* It suggests, basically, the repetition of a pattern already established by another (as 1 Thess. 1:6; 2:14). Paul invited his readers to be "imitators" both of himself (1 Cor. 4:16; 11:1) and of God (here in Eph. 5:1). Cf. the cognate verb μιμέομαι, *imitate, emulate.*

covetous man, who is an idolater, has any inheritance in the kingdom of Christ and God.
6 Let no one deceive you with empty words, for because of these things the wrath of God comes upon the sons of disobedience.
7 Therefore do not be partakers with them.
8 For you were once darkness, but now *you are* light in the Lord. Walk as children of light
9 (for the fruit of the Spirit *is* in all goodness, righteousness, and truth),
10 finding out what is acceptable to the Lord.
11 And have no fellowship with the unfruitful works of darkness, but rather expose *them.*
12 For it is shameful even to speak of those things which are done by them in secret.
13 But all things that are exposed are made manifest by the light, for whatever makes manifest is light.
14 Therefore He says:

"Awake, you who sleep,
Arise from the dead,
And Christ will give you light."

15 See then that you walk circumspectly, not as fools but as wise,
16 redeeming the time, because the days are evil.
17 Therefore do not be unwise, but understand what the

πλεονέκτης, ὅς ἐστιν εἰδωλολάτρης, οὐκ ἔχει
covetous person, who is an idolater, not ˜ does have
has

κληρονομίαν ἐν τῇ βασιλείᾳ τοῦ Χριστοῦ καὶ Θεοῦ. **6** Μηδεὶς
an inheritance in the kingdom - of Christ and God. [2]no [3]one

ὑμᾶς ἀπατάτω κενοῖς λόγοις, διὰ ταῦτα γὰρ
[5]you [1]Let [4]deceive with empty words, [2]because [3]of [4]these [5]*things* [1]for

ἔρχεται ἡ ὀργὴ τοῦ Θεοῦ ἐπὶ τοὺς υἱοὺς τῆς ἀπειθείας.
[10]comes [6]the [7]wrath - [8]of [9]God upon the sons - of disobedience.

7 Μὴ οὖν γίνεσθε συμμέτοχοι αὐτῶν. **8** Ἦτε γάρ
[3]not [1]Therefore [2]do [4]be sharers with them. [2]you [3]were [1]For
participants

ποτε σκότος, νῦν δὲ φῶς ἐν Κυρίῳ.
once darkness, now ˜ but *you are* light in *the* Lord.

Walk in Light

Ὡς τέκνα φωτὸς περιπατεῖτε — **9** ὁ γὰρ καρπὸς τοῦ
As children of light walk — the ˜ for fruit of the

Πνεύματος[b] ἐν πάσῃ ἀγαθωσύνῃ καὶ δικαιοσύνῃ καὶ
Spirit *is* in all goodness and righteousness and
the utmost

ἀληθείᾳ — **10** δοκιμάζοντες τί ἐστιν εὐάρεστον τῷ Κυρίῳ.
truth — proving what is pleasing to the Lord.

11 Καὶ μὴ συγκοινωνεῖτε τοῖς ἔργοις τοῖς ἀκάρποις τοῦ
And not ˜ do participate in the works ˜ - unfruitful -

σκότους, μᾶλλον δὲ καὶ ἐλέγχετε. **12** Τὰ
of darkness, rather ˜ but also expose *them.* [9]the [10]*things*

γὰρ κρυφῇ γινόμενα ὑπ' αὐτῶν αἰσχρόν ἐστι καὶ
[1]For [15]in [16]secret [11]taking [12]place [13]by [14]them [4]shameful [2]it [3]is [5]even
being done

λέγειν. **13** Τὰ δὲ πάντα ἐλεγχόμενα ὑπὸ τοῦ φωτὸς
[6]to [7]speak [8]of. - But all *things* being exposed by the light
that are

φανεροῦται, πᾶν γὰρ τὸ φανερούμενον φῶς ἐστι.
are made manifest, [2]every [3]*thing* [1]for - being made manifest light ˜ is.

14 Διὸ λέγει,
Therefore He says,
it

"Ἔγειρε, ὁ καθεύδων,
"Get up, the *one* sleeping,
"Awake, you who are

Καὶ ἀνάστα ἐκ τῶν νεκρῶν,
And arise from the dead,

Καὶ ἐπιφαύσει σοι ὁ Χριστός."
And [2]will [3]shine [4]on [5]you - [1]Christ."
the Messiah."

Walk in Wisdom

15 Βλέπετε οὖν πῶς ἀκριβῶς περιπατεῖτε, μὴ ὡς
Watch therefore how [3]carefully [1]you [2]walk, not as
that

ἄσοφοι, ἀλλ' ὡς σοφοί, **16** ἐξαγοραζόμενοι τὸν καιρόν,
unwise, but as wise, buying up the time,
redeeming opportunity,

ὅτι αἱ ἡμέραι πονηραί εἰσι. **17** Διὰ τοῦτο μὴ
because the days evil ˜ are. Because of this not ˜

γίνεσθε ἄφρονες, ἀλλὰ συνιέντες τί τὸ θέλημα τοῦ
do be foolish, but understanding what the will of the
understand

[b](5:9) NU reads φωτος, *light.*

Κυρίου. 18 Καὶ μὴ μεθύσκεσθε οἴνῳ, ἐν ᾧ ἐστιν
Lord *is.* And not ˜ do get drunk with wine, in which is

ἀσωτία, ἀλλὰ πληροῦσθε ἐν Πνεύματι, 19 λαλοῦντες
dissipation, but be filled with *the* Spirit, speaking

ἑαυτοῖς ψαλμοῖς* καὶ ὕμνοις καὶ ᾠδαῖς πνευματικαῖς,
to yourselves with psalms and hymns and songs ˜ spiritual,
one another

ᾄδοντες καὶ ψάλλοντες* ἐν τῇ καρδίᾳ ὑμῶν τῷ Κυρίῳ,
singing and singing praises in - heart ˜ your to the Lord,
making melody

20 εὐχαριστοῦντες πάντοτε ὑπὲρ πάντων ἐν ὀνόματι τοῦ
giving thanks always concerning all *things* in *the* name -

Κυρίου ἡμῶν Ἰησοῦ Χριστοῦ τῷ Θεῷ καὶ Πατρί,
of Lord ˜ our Jesus Christ - to *our* God and Father,

21 ὑποτασσόμενοι ἀλλήλοις ἐν φόβῳ Θεοῦ.[c]
subjecting yourselves to one another in *the* fear of God.

Husbands and Wives Depict Christ and the Church

22 Αἱ γυναῖκες, τοῖς ἰδίοις ἀνδράσιν ὑποτάσσεσθε,[d]
- Wives, - to your own husbands subject yourselves,

ὡς τῷ Κυρίῳ, 23 ὅτι ἀνήρ ἐστι κεφαλὴ τῆς
as to the Lord, because *the* husband is *the* head of the

γυναικός ὡς καὶ ὁ Χριστὸς κεφαλὴ τῆς ἐκκλησίας, καὶ αὐτός
wife as also - Christ *is the* head of the church, and He

ἐστι Σωτὴρ τοῦ σώματος. 24 Ἀλλ᾽ ὥσπερ ἡ ἐκκλησία
is *the* Savior of the body. But just as the church

ὑποτάσσεται τῷ Χριστῷ, οὕτω καὶ αἱ γυναῖκες τοῖς
is subjected - to Christ, so also the wives *must be* -

ἰδίοις[e] ἀνδράσιν ἐν παντί.
to their own husbands in every*thing.*

25 Οἱ ἄνδρες, ἀγαπᾶτε τὰς γυναῖκας ἑαυτῶν, καθὼς
- Husbands, love the wives of yourselves, just as
your own wives,

καὶ ὁ Χριστὸς ἠγάπησε τὴν ἐκκλησίαν καὶ ἑαυτὸν παρέδωκεν
also - Christ loved the church and Himself ˜ gave

ὑπὲρ αὐτῆς, 26 ἵνα αὐτὴν ἁγιάσῃ,
in behalf of her, in order that [4]her [1]He [2]might [3]sanctify,

καθαρίσας τῷ λουτρῷ τοῦ ὕδατος ἐν ῥήματι, 27 ἵνα
cleansing *her* by the washing - of water by *the* word, that

παραστήσῃ αὐτὴν ἑαυτῷ ἔνδοξον τὴν ἐκκλησίαν, μὴ
He might present her to Himself glorious ˜ the church, not

ἔχουσαν σπίλον ἢ ῥυτίδα ἤ τι τῶν τοιούτων, ἀλλ᾽ ἵνα
having spot or wrinkle or any - of such *things,* but that

ᾖ ἁγία καὶ ἄμωμος. 28 Οὕτως ὀφείλουσιν οἱ
she should be holy and blameless. So [3]ought [1]the

ἄνδρες ἀγαπᾶν τὰς ἑαυτῶν γυναῖκας ὡς τὰ
[2]husbands to love the [2]of [3]themselves [1]wives as the
their own their

ἑαυτῶν σώματα. Ὁ ἀγαπῶν τὴν ἑαυτοῦ γυναῖκα
[2]of [3]themselves [1]bodies. The *one* loving the [2]of [3]himself [1]wife
own who loves his own

ἑαυτὸν ἀγαπᾷ. 29 Οὐδεὶς γάρ ποτε τὴν ἑαυτοῦ σάρκα
[5]himself [4]loves. [2]no [3]one [1]For ever [2]the [4]of [5]himself [3]flesh
his own

ἐμίσησεν, ἀλλ᾽ ἐκτρέφει καὶ θάλπει αὐτήν, καθὼς καὶ ὁ
[1]hated, but nourishes and cherishes her, just as also the
it,

will of the Lord *is.*
18 And do not be drunk with
wine, in which is dissipation;
but be filled with the Spirit,
19 speaking to one another in
psalms and hymns and spiritual
songs, singing and making melody in your heart to the Lord,
20 giving thanks always for all
things to God the Father in the
name of our Lord Jesus Christ,
21 submitting to one another
in the fear of God.
22 Wives, submit to your own
husbands, as to the Lord.
23 For the husband is head of
the wife, as also Christ is head
of the church; and He is the
Savior of the body.
24 Therefore, just as the
church is subject to Christ, so
let the wives *be* to their own
husbands in everything.
25 Husbands, love your
wives, just as Christ also loved
the church and gave Himself for
her,
26 that He might sanctify and
cleanse her with the washing of
water by the word,
27 that He might present her
to Himself a glorious church,
not having spot or wrinkle or
any such thing, but that she
should be holy and without
blemish.
28 So husbands ought to love
their own wives as their own
bodies; he who loves his wife
loves himself.
29 For no one ever hated his
own flesh, but nourishes and
cherishes it, just as the Lord

---

c(**5:21**) NU reads Χριστου, *of Christ.*
d(**5:22**) NU omits υποτασσεσθε, *subject yourselves.*
e(**5:24**) NU omits ιδιοις, *own.*

***(5:19)** ψαλμός *(psalmos);* ψάλλω *(psallō).* The verb (ψάλλω) means *sing a psalm, sing praise* (Rom. 15:9; 1 Cor. 14:15; James 5:13), originally implying the accompaniment of a harp. For Jews, this would mean singing an OT psalm; the NT usage may include Christian songs of praise. The cognate noun (ψαλμός) means *psalm, song of praise,* either specifically from the OT Book of Psalms (Luke 20:42; Acts 1:20; 13:33) or perhaps a Christian song of praise (1 Cor. 14:26; here in Eph. 5:19; parallel Col. 3:16). It is not possible to make precise distinctions between the

does the church.
30 For we are members of His body, of His flesh and of His bones.
31 *"For this reason a man shall leave his father and mother and be joined to his wife, and the two shall become one flesh."*
32 This is a great mystery, but I speak concerning Christ and the church.
33 Nevertheless let each one of you in particular so love his own wife as himself, and let the wife *see* that she respects *her* husband.
6 Children, obey your parents in the Lord, for this is right.
2 *"Honor your father and mother,"* which is the first commandment with promise:
3 *"that it may be well with you and you may live long on the earth."*
4 And you, fathers, do not provoke your children to wrath, but bring them up in the training and admonition of the Lord.
5 Bondservants, be obedient to those who are your masters according to the flesh, with fear and trembling, in sincerity of heart, as to Christ;
6 not with eyeservice, as men-pleasers, but as bondservants of Christ, doing the will of God from the heart,
7 with goodwill doing service, as to the Lord, and not to men,
8 knowing that whatever good anyone does, he will receive the same from the Lord,

Κύριος τὴν ἐκκλησίαν. **30** Ὅτι μέλη ἐσμὲν τοῦ σώματος
Lord *does* the church. For [3]members [1]we [2]are - of body ˜

αὐτοῦ,[f] ἐκ τῆς σαρκὸς αὐτοῦ καὶ ἐκ τῶν ὀστέων αὐτοῦ.
His, of - flesh ˜ His and of - bones ˜ His.

31 «Ἀντὶ τούτου καταλείψει ἄνθρωπος τὸν πατέρα αὐτοῦ καὶ
«For this *reason* [3]shall [4]leave [1]a [2]man - father ˜ his and

τὴν μητέρα, καὶ προσκολληθήσεται πρὸς τὴν γυναῖκα αὐτοῦ,
- mother, and shall be joined to - wife ˜ his,

καὶ ἔσονται οἱ δύο εἰς σάρκα μίαν.»[g] **32** Τὸ μυστήριον
and [3]shall [4]be [1]the [2]two for flesh ˜ one.» - mystery ˜

τοῦτο μέγα ἐστίν, ἐγὼ δὲ λέγω εἰς Χριστὸν καὶ
This great ˜ is, I ˜ but speak in reference to Christ and

εἰς τὴν ἐκκλησίαν. **33** Πλὴν καὶ ὑμεῖς οἱ
in reference to the church. Nevertheless also you -

καθ' ἕνα, ἕκαστος τὴν ἑαυτοῦ γυναῖκα οὕτως ἀγαπάτω
each one, [2]each [3]one [6]the [8]of [9]himself [7]wife [4]so [1]let [5]love
individually, his own

ὡς ἑαυτόν, ἡ δὲ γυνὴ ἵνα φοβῆται τὸν ἄνδρα.
as himself, the ˜ and wife *see* that she respect the husband.
her

Filial Honor and Fatherly Nurture

6 **1** Τὰ τέκνα, ὑπακούετε τοῖς γονεῦσιν ὑμῶν ἐν Κυρίῳ,
- Children, obey - parents ˜ your in *the* Lord,

τοῦτο γάρ ἐστι δίκαιον. **2** «Τίμα τὸν πατέρα σου καὶ τὴν
this ˜ for is right. «Honor - father ˜ your and -

μητέρα,» ἥτις ἐστὶν ἐντολὴ πρώτη ἐν ἐπαγγελίᾳ,
mother,» which is [3]commandment [1]*the* [2]first with a promise,

3 «ἵνα εὖ σοι γένηται καὶ ἔσῃ μακροχρόνιος
«that [4]well [5]with [6]you [1]it [2]may [3]be and *that* you may be long-lived

ἐπὶ τῆς γῆς.»[a] **4** Καὶ οἱ πατέρες, μὴ παροργίζετε τὰ
upon the earth.» And - fathers, [2]not [1]do [3]make [6]angry -

τέκνα ὑμῶν, ἀλλ' ἐκτρέφετε αὐτὰ ἐν παιδείᾳ καὶ νουθεσίᾳ
[5]children [4]your, but nourish them in *the* discipline and instruction

Κυρίου.
of *the* Lord.

Servants, Masters, and the Master

5 Οἱ δοῦλοι, ὑπακούετε τοῖς κυρίοις κατὰ σάρκα
- Bondservants, obey the masters according to *the* flesh
Slaves, your

μετὰ φόβου καὶ τρόμου, ἐν ἁπλότητι τῆς καρδίας ὑμῶν, ὡς
with fear and trembling, in simplicity - of heart ˜ your, as
the openness

τῷ Χριστῷ, **6** μὴ κατ' ὀφθαλμοδουλείαν ὡς
- to Christ, not in accordance with eyeservice as
with

ἀνθρωπάρεσκοι, ἀλλ' ὡς δοῦλοι τοῦ Χριστοῦ ποιοῦντες τὸ
pleasers of men, but as bondservants - of Christ doing the
slaves

θέλημα τοῦ Θεοῦ ἐκ ψυχῆς, **7** μετ' εὐνοίας δουλεύοντες
will - of God from *the* soul, with goodwill doing service
wholeheartedly,

ὡς τῷ Κυρίῳ καὶ οὐκ ἀνθρώποις, **8** εἰδότες ὅτι ἐάν τι
as to the Lord and not to men, knowing that if [4]any

ἕκαστος ποιήσῃ ἀγαθόν, τοῦτο κομιεῖται παρὰ τοῦ
[1]each [2]one [3]does good *thing,* this he will receive back from the

---

f(**5:30**) NU omits the rest of v. 30. g(**5:31**) Gen. 2:24
a(**6:2, 3**) Ex. 20:12; Deut. 5:16

"psalms," "hymns," and "spiritual songs" mentioned here.

Κυρίου, εἴτε δοῦλος εἴτε ἐλεύθερος.
Lord, whether *he is* a bondservant or a free *person.*
slave

9 Καὶ οἱ κύριοι, τὰ αὐτὰ ποιεῖτε πρὸς αὐτούς,
And - masters, [2]the [3]same [4]*things* [1]do to them,

ἀνιέντες τὴν ἀπειλήν, εἰδότες ὅτι καὶ ὑμῶν αὐτῶν[b] ὁ
giving up - threatening, knowing that [6]also [3]of [4]you [5]yourselves [1]the
your own Master

Κύριός ἐστιν ἐν οὐρανοῖς, καὶ προσωποληψία οὐκ ἔστι παρ'
[2]Master is in *the* heavens, and partiality not ˜ is with
heaven, there is no partiality

αὐτῷ.
Him.

Put on the Panoply of God

10 Τὸ λοιπόν, ἀδελφοί μου, ἐνδυναμοῦσθε ἐν Κυρίῳ καὶ
For the rest, brothers ˜ my, be strong in *the* Lord and
Finally,

ἐν τῷ κράτει τῆς ἰσχύος αὐτοῦ. 11 Ἐνδύσασθε τὴν
in the might - of strength ˜ His. Put on the

πανοπλίαν τοῦ Θεοῦ πρὸς τὸ δύνασθαι ὑμᾶς στῆναι πρὸς
full armor - of God so that - [2]to [3]be [4]able [1]you to stand up against
may

τὰς μεθοδείας τοῦ διαβόλου. 12 Ὅτι οὐκ ἔστιν
the cunning strategems of the devil. Because [6]not [5]is

ἡμῖν ἡ πάλη πρὸς αἷμα καὶ σάρκα, ἀλλὰ πρὸς τὰς
[3]with [4]us [1]the [2]struggle against blood and flesh, but against the
our

ἀρχάς, πρὸς τὰς ἐξουσίας, πρὸς τοὺς κοσμοκράτορας* τοῦ
rulers, against the authorities, against the world-rulers of the

σκότους τοῦ αἰῶνος[c] τούτου, πρὸς τὰ πνευματικὰ τῆς
darkness - of age ˜ this, against the spiritual *forces* -

πονηρίας ἐν τοῖς ἐπουρανίοις. 13 Διὰ τοῦτο ἀναλάβετε
of evil in the heavenly *realms.* Because of this take up

τὴν πανοπλίαν τοῦ Θεοῦ, ἵνα δυνηθῆτε ἀντιστῆναι
the full armor - of God, in order that you may be able to withstand

ἐν τῇ ἡμέρᾳ τῇ πονηρᾷ, καὶ ἅπαντα κατεργασάμενοι στῆναι.
in the day ˜ - evil, and [2]all [3]*things* [1]accomplishing to stand.
having accomplished

14 Στῆτε οὖν περιζωσάμενοι τὴν ὀσφὺν ὑμῶν ἐν ἀληθείᾳ,
Stand therefore girding - waist ˜ your with truth,
having girded

καὶ ἐνδυσάμενοι τὸν θώρακα τῆς δικαιοσύνης, 15 καὶ
and putting on the breastplate - of righteousness, and
having put on

ὑποδησάμενοι τοὺς πόδας ἐν ἑτοιμασίᾳ τοῦ εὐαγγελίου τῆς
binding under the feet with *the* preparation of the gospel -
having shod your

εἰρήνης, 16 ἐπὶ πᾶσιν ἀναλαβόντες τὸν θυρεὸν
of peace, to all *these things* taking up the shield
in addition to

τῆς πίστεως, ἐν ᾧ δυνήσεσθε πάντα τὰ βέλη τοῦ
- of faith, with which you will be able [3]all [4]the [5]arrows [10]of [11]the
flaming

πονηροῦ τὰ πεπυρωμένα σβέσαι· 17 καὶ τὴν
[12]evil [13]*one* - [6]having [7]been [8]set [9]afire [1]to [2]quench; and [3]the
arrows

περικεφαλαίαν τοῦ σωτηρίου δέξασθαι, καὶ τὴν μάχαιραν
[4]helmet - [5]of [6]salvation [1]to [2]receive, and the sword

whether *he is* a slave or free.
9 And you, masters, do the same things to them, giving up threatening, knowing that your own Master also is in heaven, and there is no partiality with Him.
10 Finally, my brethren, be strong in the Lord and in the power of His might.
11 Put on the whole armor of God, that you may be able to stand against the wiles of the devil.
12 For we do not wrestle against flesh and blood, but against principalities, against powers, against the rulers of the darkness of this age, against spiritual *hosts* of wickedness in the heavenly *places.*
13 Therefore take up the whole armor of God, that you may be able to withstand in the evil day, and having done all, to stand.
14 Stand therefore, having girded your waist with truth, having put on the breastplate of righteousness,
15 and having shod your feet with the preparation of the gospel of peace;
16 above all, taking the shield of faith with which you will be able to quench all the fiery darts of the wicked one.
17 And take the helmet of salvation, and the sword of the

---

[b](6:9) For *και υμων αυτων* NU reads *και αυτων και υμων*, *both their (Master) and yours.*
[c](6:12) NU omits *του αιωνος*, *of the age.*

***(6:12)** *κοσμοκράτωρ (kosmokratōr).* Noun meaning *world-ruler.* It is a compound word formed from the noun *κόσμος*, *world,* and the verb *κρατέω*, *to rule* (a meaning not directly attested in the NT). These "cosmic rulers" are evil forces with which believers have to contend. Here the word is associated with a variety of terms that commonly designated evil supernatural beings which influence human affairs: "rulers" (*ἀρχή*), "authorities" (*ἐξουσία*), and "spiritual forces of evil" (*πνευματικὰ τῆς πονηρίας*). It is not possible to distinguish the specific nuances of these words. Although the terms have uses in the realm of human governance, such meanings are unlikely here since Paul explicitly states

Spirit, which is the word of God;
18 praying always with all prayer and supplication in the Spirit, being watchful to this end with all perseverance and supplication for all the saints—
19 and for me, that utterance may be given to me, that I may open my mouth boldly to make known the mystery of the gospel,
20 for which I am an ambassador in chains; that in it I may speak boldly, as I ought to speak.
21 But that you also may know my affairs *and* how I am doing, Tychicus, a beloved brother and faithful minister in the Lord, will make all things known to you;
22 whom I have sent to you for this very purpose, that you may know our affairs, and *that* he may comfort your hearts.
23 Peace to the brethren, and love with faith, from God the Father and the Lord Jesus Christ.
24 Grace *be* with all those who love our Lord Jesus Christ in sincerity. Amen.

τοῦ Πνεύματος, ὅ ἐστι ῥῆμα Θεοῦ, **18** διὰ πάσης
of the Spirit, which is *the* word of God, through every

προσευχῆς καὶ δεήσεως προσευχόμενοι ἐν παντὶ καιρῷ ἐν
prayer and petition praying in every season in

Πνεύματι, καὶ εἰς αὐτὸ τοῦτο ἀγρυπνοῦντες ἐν πάσῃ
the Spirit, and to same ˜ this *end* being awake with all
watchful

προσκαρτερήσει καὶ δεήσει περὶ πάντων τῶν ἁγίων,
perseverance and petition concerning all the saints,
for

19 καὶ ὑπὲρ ἐμοῦ, ἵνα μοι δοθῇ λόγος ἐν ἀνοίξει
and in behalf of me, that to me may be given speech in *the* opening

τοῦ στόματός μου ἐν παρρησίᾳ γνωρίσαι τὸ μυστήριον
- of mouth ˜ my in boldness to make known the mystery
boldly

τοῦ εὐαγγελίου **20** ὑπὲρ οὗ πρεσβεύω ἐν
of the gospel for the sake of which I serve as an ambassador in

ἁλύσει, ἵνα ἐν αὐτῷ παρρησιάσωμαι ὡς δεῖ με
a chain, that in it I may speak boldly as it is necessary *for* me
chains, I must

λαλῆσαι.
to speak.
speak.

Paul's Greeting of Grace

21 Ἵνα δὲ εἰδῆτε καὶ ὑμεῖς τὰ κατ' ἐμέ,
that ˜ Now [3]may [4]know [2]also [1]you the *things* with respect to me,
my circumstances,

τί πράσσω, πάντα ὑμῖν γνωρίσει Τυχικὸς ὁ
what I am doing, [16]all [17]*things* [14]to [15]you [11]will [12]make [13]known [1]Tychicus [2]the
how my

ἀγαπητὸς ἀδελφὸς καὶ πιστὸς διάκονος ἐν Κυρίῳ, **22** ὃν
[3]beloved [4]brother [5]and [6]faithful [7]servant [8]in [9]*the* [10]Lord, whom

ἔπεμψα πρὸς ὑμᾶς εἰς αὐτὸ τοῦτο, ἵνα γνῶτε
I sent to you for same ˜ this *purpose*, that you may come to know

τὰ περὶ ἡμῶν καὶ παρακαλέσῃ τὰς καρδίας ὑμῶν.
the *things* about us and *that* he may encourage - hearts ˜ your.
our situation comfort

23 Εἰρήνη τοῖς ἀδελφοῖς καὶ ἀγάπη μετὰ πίστεως ἀπὸ
Peace to the brothers and love with faith from

Θεοῦ Πατρὸς καὶ Κυρίου Ἰησοῦ Χριστοῦ. **24** Ἡ χάρις μετὰ
God *the* Father and *the* Lord Jesus Christ. - Grace *be* with

πάντων τῶν ἀγαπώντων τὸν Κύριον ἡμῶν Ἰησοῦν Χριστὸν
all the *ones* loving - Lord ˜ our Jesus Christ
those who love

ἐν ἀφθαρσίᾳ. Ἀμήν.
in incorruptibility. Amen.
with an incorruptible love. So be it.

that the struggle is not against "flesh and blood," and specifically locates at least some of these evil forces "in the heavenly places."

The Epistle of Paul the Apostle to the
PHILIPPIANS

ΠΡΟΣ ΦΙΛΙΠΠΗΣΙΟΥΣ
TO *THE* PHILIPPIANS

Paul Greets the Saints in Philippi

1 **1** Παῦλος καὶ Τιμόθεος, δοῦλοι Ἰησοῦ Χριστοῦ,
Paul and Timothy, bondservants of Jesus Christ,
slaves

Πᾶσι τοῖς ἁγίοις ἐν Χριστῷ Ἰησοῦ τοῖς οὖσιν ἐν
To all the saints in Christ Jesus the *ones* being in
who are at

Φιλίπποις, σὺν ἐπισκόποις καὶ διακόνοις·
Philippi, together with *the* overseers and deacons:

2 Χάρις ὑμῖν καὶ εἰρήνη ἀπὸ Θεοῦ Πατρὸς ἡμῶν καὶ
Grace to you and peace from God Father ˜ our and

Κυρίου Ἰησοῦ Χριστοῦ.
the Lord Jesus Christ.

Paul Thanks and Praises God for the Philippians

3 Εὐχαριστῶ τῷ Θεῷ μου ἐπὶ πάσῃ τῇ μνείᾳ ὑμῶν,
I thank - God ˜ my upon every - remembrance of you,
mention

4 πάντοτε ἐν πάσῃ δεήσει μου ὑπὲρ πάντων ὑμῶν μετὰ
always in [2]every [3]prayer [1]my in behalf of all of you [4]with
petition

χαρᾶς τὴν δέησιν ποιούμενος, **5** ἐπὶ τῇ κοινωνίᾳ ὑμῶν εἰς τὸ
[5]joy [2]the [3]prayer [1]making, for - fellowship ˜ your in the
petition partnership

εὐαγγέλιον ἀπὸ πρώτης ἡμέρας ἄχρι τοῦ νῦν,
gospel from *the* first day until - now,
the present,

6 πεποιθὼς αὐτὸ τοῦτο, ὅτι ὁ ἐναρξάμενος
having been persuaded of [2]same [3]*thing* [1]this, that the *one* having begun
very He who began

ἐν ὑμῖν ἔργον ἀγαθὸν ἐπιτελέσει ἄχρις ἡμέρας Χριστοῦ
in you a work ˜ good will complete *it* until *the* day of Christ

Ἰησοῦ· **7** καθώς ἐστι δίκαιον ἐμοὶ τοῦτο φρονεῖν ὑπὲρ
Jesus; just as it is right for me [3]this [1]to [2]think concerning

πάντων ὑμῶν, διὰ τὸ ἔχειν με ἐν τῇ καρδίᾳ ὑμᾶς, ἔν τε
all of you, because - to have me in the heart you, in ˜ both
I have you in my heart,

τοῖς δεσμοῖς μου καὶ ἐν τῇ ἀπολογίᾳ καὶ βεβαιώσει τοῦ
- bonds ˜ my and in the defense and confirmation of the

εὐαγγελίου, συγκοινωνούς μου τῆς χάριτος πάντας ὑμᾶς ὄντας.
gospel, [4]partakers [5]with [6]me - [7]of [8]grace [2]all [1]you [3]being.
are.

8 Μάρτυς γάρ μού ἐστιν ὁ Θεός, ὡς ἐπιποθῶ πάντας ὑμᾶς ἐν
[3]witness [1]For [2]my is - God, how I long for all ˜ you in
yearn after with

σπλάγχνοις Ἰησοῦ Χριστοῦ. **9** Καὶ τοῦτο προσεύχομαι, ἵνα ἡ
the inward parts of Jesus Christ. And this I pray, that -
the affection

1 Paul and Timothy, bondservants of Jesus Christ,

To all the saints in Christ Jesus who are in Philippi, with the bishops and deacons:

2 Grace to you and peace from God our Father and the Lord Jesus Christ.

3 I thank my God upon every remembrance of you,
4 always in every prayer of mine making request for you all with joy,
5 for your fellowship in the gospel from the first day until now,
6 being confident of this very thing, that He who has begun a good work in you will complete *it* until the day of Jesus Christ;
7 just as it is right for me to think this of you all, because I have you in my heart, inasmuch as both in my chains and in the defense and confirmation of the gospel, you all are partakers with me of grace.
8 For God is my witness, how greatly I long for you all with the affection of Jesus Christ.
9 And this I pray, that your

love may abound still more and more in knowledge and all discernment,
10 that you may approve the things that are excellent, that you may be sincere and without offense till the day of Christ,
11 being filled with the fruits of righteousness which *are* by Jesus Christ, to the glory and praise of God.
12 But I want you to know, brethren, that the things *which happened* to me have actually turned out for the furtherance of the gospel,
13 so that it has become evident to the whole palace guard, and to all the rest, that my chains are in Christ;
14 and most of the brethren in the Lord, having become confident by my chains, are much more bold to speak the word without fear.
15 Some indeed preach Christ even from envy and strife, and some also from goodwill:
16 The former preach Christ from selfish ambition, not sincerely, supposing to add affliction to my chains;
17 but the latter out of love, knowing that I am appointed for the defense of the gospel.
18 What then? Only *that* in every way, whether in pretense or in truth, Christ is preached; and in this I rejoice, yes, and will rejoice.
19 For I know that this will turn out for my deliverance

ἀγάπη ὑμῶν ἔτι μᾶλλον καὶ μᾶλλον περισσεύῃ ἐν ἐπιγνώσει
love ˜ your [3]yet [4]more [5]and [6]more [1]may [2]abound in knowledge

καὶ πάσῃ αἰσθήσει, **10** εἰς τὸ δοκιμάζειν ὑμᾶς τὰ
and all (the utmost) perception, for (so) - [2]to [3]approve (that you may) [1]you (approve) the *things*

διαφέροντα, ἵνα ἦτε εἰλικρινεῖς καὶ ἀπρόσκοποι
differing, (excelling,) in order that you may be sincere and without offense

εἰς ἡμέραν Χριστοῦ, **11** πεπληρωμένοι καρπῶν[a]
to (till) *the* day of Christ, having been filled with *the* fruits

δικαιοσύνης τῶν διὰ Ἰησοῦ Χριστοῦ εἰς δόξαν καὶ
of righteousness the *ones* (which are) by Jesus Christ to *the* glory and

ἔπαινον Θεοῦ.
praise of God.

Christ Is Being Preached

12 Γινώσκειν δὲ ὑμᾶς βούλομαι, ἀδελφοί, ὅτι τὰ
[5]to [6]know [1]Now [4]you [2]I [3]want, brothers, that the *things*

κατ' ἐμὲ μᾶλλον εἰς προκοπὴν τοῦ εὐαγγελίου
against me [3]more (rather) [4]for [5]*the* [6]advancement [7]of [8]the [9]gospel

ἐλήλυθεν, **13** ὥστε τοὺς δεσμούς μου φανεροὺς ἐν
[1]have [2]come, so that - (it) bonds ˜ (has become) my (evident) [3]evident (that my bonds) [4]in (are)

Χριστῷ γενέσθαι ἐν ὅλῳ τῷ πραιτωρίῳ καὶ τοῖς λοιποῖς
[5]Christ (in) [1]to [2]become (Christ) in (among) whole ˜ the praetorium (palace guard) and to [2]the [3]rest

πᾶσι, **14** καὶ τοὺς πλείονας τῶν ἀδελφῶν ἐν Κυρίῳ,
[1]all, and - most of the brothers in *the* Lord,

πεποιθότας τοῖς δεσμοῖς μου, περισσοτέρως τολμᾶν
having been persuaded - by bonds ˜ my, much more to be (are) bold

ἀφόβως τὸν λόγον λαλεῖν. **15** Τινὲς μὲν καὶ διὰ
[5]fearlessly [3]the [4]word [1]to [2]speak. Some indeed even because of

φθόνον καὶ ἔριν, τινὲς δὲ καὶ δι' εὐδοκίαν τὸν Χριστὸν
envy and strife, some ˜ but also because of good will - [3]Christ

κηρύσσουσιν· **16** οἱ μὲν ἐξ ἐριθείας τὸν
[1]are [2]preaching; the *former ones* indeed out of selfish ambition -

Χριστὸν καταγγέλλουσιν, οὐχ ἁγνῶς, οἰόμενοι θλῖψιν
Christ ˜ proclaim, not sincerely, (of pure motive,) supposing [3]affliction

ἐπιφέρειν[b] τοῖς δεσμοῖς μου,[c] **17** οἱ δὲ ἐξ
[1]to [2]add - to bonds ˜ my, [2]the [3]*latter* [4]*ones* [1]but out of

ἀγάπης, εἰδότες ὅτι εἰς ἀπολογίαν τοῦ εὐαγγελίου
love, knowing that for *the* defense of the gospel

κεῖμαι. **18** Τί γάρ? Πλὴν[d] παντὶ τρόπῳ, εἴτε
I am appointed. What then? Nevertheless in every way, whether

προφάσει εἴτε ἀληθείᾳ, Χριστὸς καταγγέλλεται, καὶ ἐν τούτῳ
in pretense or in truth, Christ is proclaimed, and in this

χαίρω, ἀλλὰ καὶ χαρήσομαι.
I rejoice, yet also I will rejoice.

To Live Is Christ

19 Οἶδα γὰρ ὅτι τοῦτό μοι ἀποβήσεται εἰς σωτηρίαν
[2]I [3]know [1]For that this [4]to [5]me [1]will [2]turn [3]out for deliverance

---

[a](1:11) NU reads καρπον, *fruit.* [b](1:16) NU reads εγειρειν, *to raise up.* [c](1:16, 17) NU transposes vv. 16 and 17. [d](1:18) For Πλην, *Nevertheless,* NU reads Πλην οτι, *Only that.*

διὰ τῆς ὑμῶν δεήσεως καὶ ἐπιχορηγίας τοῦ Πνεύματος
through - your prayer and *the* supply of the Spirit
petition

Ἰησοῦ Χριστοῦ, 20 κατὰ τὴν ἀποκαραδοκίαν καὶ ἐλπίδα
of Jesus Christ, according to - [2]earnest [3]expectation [4]and [5]hope

μου ὅτι ἐν οὐδενὶ αἰσχυνθήσομαι, ἀλλ' ἐν πάσῃ παρρησίᾳ,
[1]my that in nothing will I be ashamed, but with all boldness,
utmost

ὡς πάντοτε, καὶ νῦν, μεγαλυνθήσεται* Χριστὸς ἐν τῷ σώματί
as always, also now, [2]will [3]be [4]magnified [1]Christ in - body ˜

μου, εἴτε διὰ ζωῆς εἴτε διὰ θανάτου. 21 Ἐμοὶ γὰρ τὸ ζῆν
my, whether by life or by death. [2]to [3]me [1]For - to live

Χριστὸς καὶ τὸ ἀποθανεῖν κέρδος. 22 Εἰ δὲ τὸ ζῆν ἐν
is Christ and - to die *is* gain. if ˜ But - *I am* to live *on* in

σαρκί, τοῦτό μοι καρπὸς ἔργου· καὶ τί αἱρήσομαι
the flesh, this to me *will mean* fruit from labor; and what I will choose

οὐ γνωρίζω. 23 Συνέχομαι δὲ[e] ἐκ τῶν δύο, τὴν
[3]not [1]I [2]do make known. [2]I [3]am [4]hard-pressed [1]But by the two, [2]the

ἐπιθυμίαν ἔχων εἰς τὸ ἀναλῦσαι καὶ σὺν Χριστῷ εἶναι,
[3]desire [1]having - - to depart and [3]with [4]Christ [1]to [2]be,

πολλῷ μᾶλλον κρεῖσσον. 24 Τὸ δὲ ἐπιμένειν ἐν τῇ
which is by much more better. - But to remain in the
far

σαρκὶ ἀναγκαιότερον δι' ὑμᾶς. 25 Καὶ τοῦτο
flesh *is* more needful for the sake of you. And [5]this

πεποιθώς, οἶδα ὅτι μενῶ καὶ
[1]having [2]been [3]persuaded [4]of, I know that I will remain and

συμπαραμενῶ[f] πᾶσιν ὑμῖν εἰς τὴν ὑμῶν προκοπὴν καὶ
will continue together with all ˜ you for - your progress and

χαρὰν τῆς πίστεως, 26 ἵνα τὸ καύχημα ὑμῶν περισσεύῃ
joy of the faith, so that - boasting ˜ your may abound
in

ἐν Χριστῷ Ἰησοῦ ἐν ἐμοὶ διὰ τῆς ἐμῆς παρουσίας πάλιν πρὸς
in Christ Jesus in me by - my coming again to

ὑμᾶς.
you.

Striving and Suffering for Christ

27 Μόνον ἀξίως τοῦ εὐαγγελίου τοῦ Χριστοῦ
Only [3]worthily [4]of [5]the [6]gospel - [7]of [8]Christ

πολιτεύεσθε, ἵνα εἴτε ἐλθὼν καὶ ἰδὼν ὑμᾶς εἴτε
[1]conduct [2]yourselves, in order that whether coming and seeing you or
I come see

ἀπών, ἀκούσω[g] τὰ περὶ ὑμῶν, ὅτι στήκετε ἐν
being away, I may hear of the *things* about you, that you stand fast in
am absent, your affairs,

ἑνὶ πνεύματι, μιᾷ ψυχῇ συναθλοῦντες τῇ πίστει τοῦ
one spirit, with one soul striving together for the faith of the

εὐαγγελίου, 28 καὶ μὴ πτυρόμενοι ἐν μηδενὶ ὑπὸ τῶν
gospel, and not being terrified in nothing by the *ones*
anything your

ἀντικειμένων, ἥτις αὐτοῖς μέν ἐστιν ἔνδειξις ἀπωλείας,
being opposed, which to them indeed is a proof of destruction,
enemies, demonstration

ὑμῖν[h] δὲ σωτηρίας, καὶ τοῦτο ἀπὸ Θεοῦ. 29 Ὅτι ὑμῖν
[2]to [3]you [1]but of salvation, and this from God. Because to you

ἐχαρίσθη τὸ ὑπὲρ Χριστοῦ, οὐ μόνον τὸ εἰς αὐτὸν
it was granted - for the sake of Christ, not only - in Him

through your prayer and the supply of the Spirit of Jesus Christ,
20 according to my earnest expectation and hope that in nothing I shall be ashamed, but with all boldness, as always, so now also Christ will be magnified in my body, whether by life or by death.
21 For to me, to live *is* Christ, and to die *is* gain.
22 But if *I* live on in the flesh, this *will mean* fruit from *my* labor; yet what I shall choose I cannot tell.
23 For I am hard-pressed between the two, having a desire to depart and be with Christ, *which is* far better.
24 Nevertheless to remain in the flesh *is* more needful for you.
25 And being confident of this, I know that I shall remain and continue with you all for your progress and joy of faith,
26 that your rejoicing for me may be more abundant in Jesus Christ by my coming to you again.
27 Only let your conduct be worthy of the gospel of Christ, so that whether I come and see you or am absent, I may hear of your affairs, that you stand fast in one spirit, with one mind striving together for the faith of the gospel,
28 and not in any way terrified by your adversaries, which is to them a proof of perdition, but to you of salvation, and that from God.
29 For to you it has been granted on behalf of Christ, not

---

[e]**(1:23)** TR reads γαρ, *For.*
[f]**(1:25)** NU reads παραμενω, *will stay.* [g]**(1:27)** NU reads ακουω, *I hear.*
[h]**(1:28)** NU reads υμων, *your.*

***(1:20)** μεγαλύνω *(megalynō).* Verb meaning literally *to enlarge* something (tassels, Matt. 23:5), or figuratively *to magnify, exalt, praise* (God, Luke 1:46). The verb may also be used of persons (the apostles, Acts 5:13) with the sense *hold in high esteem.* When it appears in the passive voice (as here in Phil. 1:20 of Christ), it has the meaning *be praised* or *be glorified.* Cf. the cognate noun μεγαλωσύνη, *greatness, majesty,* used in Jude 25 in a doxology, and in Heb. 1:3; 8:1 as a name for God Himself (as a king may be called

only to believe in Him, but also
to suffer for His sake,
30 having the same conflict
which you saw in me and now
hear *is* in me.

2 Therefore if *there is* any
consolation in Christ, if
any comfort of love, if any fellowship of the Spirit, if any affection and mercy,
2 fulfill my joy by being like-
minded, having the same love,
being of one accord, of one
mind.
3 *Let* nothing *be done* through
selfish ambition or conceit, but
in lowliness of mind let each esteem others better than himself.
4 Let each of you look out
not only for his own interests,
but also for the interests of others.
5 Let this mind be in you
which was also in Christ Jesus,
6 who, being in the form of
God, did not consider it robbery to be equal with God,
7 but made Himself of no
reputation, taking the form of a
bondservant, *and* coming in the
likeness of men.
8 And being found in appearance as a man, He humbled
Himself and became obedient to
the point of death, even the
death of the cross.
9 Therefore God also has
highly exalted Him and given
Him the name which is above
every name,
10 that at the name of Jesus

πιστεύειν, ἀλλὰ καὶ τὸ ὑπὲρ αὐτοῦ πάσχειν, **30** τὸν
to believe, but also - for the sake of Him to suffer, [2]the

αὐτὸν ἀγῶνα ἔχοντες οἷον εἴδετε ἐν ἐμοὶ καὶ νῦν ἀκούετε ἐν
[3]same [4]struggle [1]having which you saw in me and now you hear *is* in

ἐμοί.
me.

Unity Through Humility

2 **1** Εἴ τις οὖν παράκλησις ἐν Χριστῷ, εἴ
[2]if [3]*there* [4]*is* [5]any [1]Therefore encouragement in Christ, if
consolation

τι παραμύθιον ἀγάπης, εἴ τις κοινωνία
there is any comfort of love, if *there is* any fellowship

Πνεύματος, εἴ τις σπλάγχνα καὶ οἰκτιρμοί,
of *the* Spirit, if *there are* any inward parts and mercies,
affections acts of compassion,

2 πληρώσατέ μου τὴν χαράν, ἵνα τὸ αὐτὸ φρονῆτε, τὴν
fulfill my - joy, that [3]the [4]same [5]*thing* [1]you [2]think, [8]the
you be like-minded,

αὐτὴν ἀγάπην ἔχοντες, σύμψυχοι, τὸ ἓν
[9]same [10]love [7]having, *being* united in spirit, the one *thing*
intending the same

φρονοῦντες, **3** μηδὲν κατὰ ἐριθείαν ἢ κενοδοξίαν,
thinking, *doing* nothing according to selfish ambition or conceit,
purpose,

ἀλλὰ τῇ ταπεινοφροσύνῃ ἀλλήλους ἡγούμενοι
but - in humility [2]one [3]another [1]regarding
with

ὑπερέχοντας ἑαυτῶν. **4** Μὴ τὰ ἑαυτῶν
as being better than yourselves. [6]not [7]*only* [9]the [10]*things* [11]of [12]yourselves
your own concerns

ἕκαστος σκοπεῖτε,[a] ἀλλὰ καὶ τὰ ἑτέρων
[2]each [3]*one* [1]Let [4]look [5]out [8]for, but [3]also [4]*for* [5]the [6]*things* [7]of [8]others
concerns

ἕκαστος.
[1]each [2]one.

The Example of the Humbled and Exalted Christ

5 Τοῦτο γὰρ φρονείσθω ἐν ὑμῖν ὃ καὶ ἐν
[6]this [1]Indeed [2]let [3]a [4]mind [5]be in you which *was* also in
Indeed, let this mind be

Χριστῷ Ἰησοῦ, **6** ὃς ἐν μορφῇ Θεοῦ ὑπάρχων, οὐχ
Christ Jesus, who [2]in [3]*the* [4]form [5]of [6]God [1]existing, [8]not

ἁρπαγμὸν ἡγήσατο τὸ εἶναι ἴσα Θεῷ, **7** ἀλλ'
[11]a [12]robbery [7]did [9]consider [10]*it* - to be equal with God, but
thing to be seized

ἑαυτὸν ἐκένωσε μορφὴν δούλου λαβών, ἐν
Himself ˜ emptied *of His privileges* [2]*the* [3]form [4]of [5]a [6]bondservant [1]taking, [10]in

ὁμοιώματι ἀνθρώπων γενόμενος. **8** Καὶ σχήματι
[11]*the* [12]likeness [13]of [14]men [7]coming [8]to [9]be. And [3]in [4]appearance

εὑρεθεὶς ὡς ἄνθρωπος, ἐταπείνωσεν ἑαυτὸν γενόμενος
[1]being [2]found as a man, He humbled Himself becoming

ὑπήκοος μέχρι θανάτου, θανάτου δὲ σταυροῦ. **9** Διὸ καὶ ὁ
obedient unto death, [2]a [3]death [1]and of a cross. Therefore also -

Θεὸς αὐτὸν ὑπερύψωσε καὶ ἐχαρίσατο αὐτῷ ὄνομα τὸ
God [3]Him [1]highly [2]exalted and graciously gave Him a name the *one*
which is

ὑπὲρ πᾶν ὄνομα, **10** ἵνα ἐν τῷ ὀνόματι Ἰησοῦ πᾶν γόνυ
above every name, that at the name of Jesus every knee

---

a(**2:4**) NU reads σκοπουντες, *looking out for.*

"Your/His Majesty"). See the cognate adjective μεγαλεῖος at Acts 2:11; and the cognate noun μεγαλειότης at Luke 9:43.

κάμψῃ ἐπουρανίων καὶ ἐπιγείων καὶ καταχθονίων,
may bow of heavenly *beings* and earthly *beings* and subterranean *beings*,

11 καὶ πᾶσα γλῶσσα ἐξομολογήσηται ὅτι Κύριος Ἰησοῦς
and *that* every tongue may confess that [3]*is* [4]Lord [1]Jesus

Χριστὸς εἰς δόξαν Θεοῦ Πατρός.
[2]Christ to *the* glory of God *the* Father.

Holding Fast the Word of Life

12 Ὥστε, ἀγαπητοί μου, καθὼς πάντοτε ὑπηκούσατε, μὴ
So then, beloved ˜ my, just as always you obeyed, not

ὡς ἐν τῇ παρουσίᾳ μου μόνον, ἀλλὰ νῦν πολλῷ μᾶλλον ἐν τῇ
as in - presence ˜ my only, but now by much more in -

ἀπουσίᾳ μου, μετὰ φόβου καὶ τρόμου τὴν ἑαυτῶν σωτηρίαν
absence ˜ my, with fear and trembling - [3]your [4]own [5]salvation

κατεργάζεσθε, **13** ὁ Θεὸς γάρ ἐστιν ὁ ἐνεργῶν ἐν ὑμῖν
[1]work [2]out, - God ˜ for is the *One* being at work in you

καὶ τὸ θέλειν καὶ τὸ ἐνεργεῖν ὑπὲρ τῆς
both - to desire and - to be at work for the sake of -

εὐδοκίας. **14** Πάντα ποιεῖτε χωρὶς γογγυσμῶν καὶ
His good pleasure. [2]all [3]*things* [1]Do without grumblings and

διαλογισμῶν, **15** ἵνα γένησθε ἄμεμπτοι καὶ
disputings, in order that you may come to be blameless and

ἀκέραιοι, τέκνα Θεοῦ ἀμώμητα ἐν μέσῳ γενεᾶς
innocent, children of God unblemished in *the* midst of a [4]generation
harmless, without fault

σκολιᾶς καὶ διεστραμμένης, ἐν οἷς φαίνεσθε ὡς
[1]crooked [2]and [3]perverted, among whom you shine as

φωστῆρες ἐν κόσμῳ, **16** λόγον ζωῆς ἐπέχοντες, εἰς
light bearers in *the* world, [3]*the* [4]word [5]of [6]life [1]holding [2]fast, as

καύχημα ἐμοὶ εἰς ἡμέραν Χριστοῦ, ὅτι οὐκ εἰς κενὸν
a ground of boasting for me in *the* day of Christ, that [3]not [5]for [6]nothing
my joy in vain

ἔδραμον οὐδὲ εἰς κενὸν ἐκοπίασα. **17** Ἀλλ' εἰ καὶ
[1]I [2]did [4]run nor [4]for [5]nothing [1]did [2]I [3]labor. But if ˜ even
in vain

σπένδομαι* ἐπὶ τῇ θυσίᾳ καὶ λειτουργίᾳ τῆς πίστεως
I am being poured out upon the sacrifice and service - of faith ˜

ὑμῶν, χαίρω καὶ συγχαίρω πᾶσιν ὑμῖν. **18** Τὸ δ'
your, I rejoice and I rejoice together with all ˜ you. the ˜ And
For

αὐτὸ καὶ ὑμεῖς χαίρετε καὶ συγχαίρετέ μοι.
same *reason* also you rejoice and rejoice together with me.

Paul Commends Timothy

19 Ἐλπίζω δὲ ἐν Κυρίῳ Ἰησοῦ Τιμόθεον ταχέως πέμψαι
[2]I [3]hope [1]Now in *the* Lord Jesus [3]Timothy [6]shortly [1]to [2]send
expect

ὑμῖν, ἵνα κἀγὼ εὐψυχῶ γνοὺς τὰ περὶ
[4]to [5]you, that I also may be encouraged knowing the *things* concerning
when I learn of your

ὑμῶν. **20** Οὐδένα γὰρ ἔχω ἰσόψυχον, ὅστις γνησίως
you. [4]no [5]one [1]For [2]I [3]have of like mind, who [3]genuinely
circumstances.

τὰ περὶ ὑμῶν μεριμνήσει. **21** Οἱ πάντες
[6]the [7]*things* [8]concerning [9]you [1]will [2]be [4]concerned [5]about. - all ˜
your circumstances

every knee should bow, of those in heaven, and of those on earth, and of those under the earth,

11 and *that* every tongue should confess that Jesus Christ *is* Lord, to the glory of God the Father.

12 Therefore, my beloved, as you have always obeyed, not as in my presence only, but now much more in my absence, work out your own salvation with fear and trembling;

13 for it is God who works in you both to will and to do for *His* good pleasure.

14 Do all things without complaining and disputing,

15 that you may become blameless and harmless, children of God without fault in the midst of a crooked and perverse generation, among whom you shine as lights in the world,

16 holding fast the word of life, so that I may rejoice in the day of Christ that I have not run in vain or labored in vain.

17 Yes, and if I am being poured out *as a drink offering* on the sacrifice and service of your faith, I am glad and rejoice with you all.

18 For the same reason you also be glad and rejoice with me.

19 But I trust in the Lord Jesus to send Timothy to you shortly, that I also may be encouraged when I know your state.

20 For I have no one likeminded, who will sincerely care for your state.

21 For all seek their own, not

***(2:17)** σπένδω *(spendō).* Verb meaning *offer a drink offering.* It occurs in the NT only in the passive voice and with the figurative sense *be offered (in sacrifice).* The ancient custom of pouring out the drink offering on or by the sacrifice apparently accounts for Paul's usage here and in 2 Tim. 4:6. Viewing his approaching death as such a libation, Paul could say that he was being "poured out as a drink offering." The drink offering was not an offering for sin but an offering of dedication and gratitude.

the things which are of Christ Jesus.
22 But you know his proven character, that as a son with *his* father he served with me in the gospel.
23 Therefore I hope to send him at once, as soon as I see how it goes with me.
24 But I trust in the Lord that I myself shall also come shortly.
25 Yet I considered it necessary to send to you Epaphroditus, my brother, fellow worker, and fellow soldier, but your messenger and the one who ministered to my need;
26 since he was longing for you all, and was distressed because you had heard that he was sick.
27 For indeed he was sick almost unto death; but God had mercy on him, and not only on him but on me also, lest I should have sorrow upon sorrow.
28 Therefore I sent him the more eagerly, that when you see him again you may rejoice, and I may be less sorrowful.
29 Receive him therefore in the Lord with all gladness, and hold such men in esteem;
30 because for the work of Christ he came close to death, not regarding his life, to supply what was lacking in your service toward me.

---

[b](2:30) NU reads παραβολευσαμενος, *risking.*

---

*(2:30) λειτουργία *(leitourgia).* Noun meaning *service.* The word was the usual term for service, often voluntary, to the state, but in the NT it always has a religious nuance. Here it is used of Epaphroditus's mission to bring gifts from the Philippians to Paul. Similarly it describes the gift from the Corinthians to the poor Christians at Jerusalem (2 Cor. 9:12). λειτουργία may also refer to ritual and cultic services, such as officiating as a priest (Luke 1:23). Cf. the cognate verb λειτουργέω, *serve* (Heb. 10:11); and noun λειτουργός, *servant* (Rom. 15:16), both particularly in a religious function.

γὰρ τὰ ἑαυτῶν ζητοῦσιν, οὐ τὰ Χριστοῦ
For [2]the [3]*things* [4]of [5]themselves [1]seek, not the *things* of Christ
their own interests

Ἰησοῦ. 22 Τὴν δὲ δοκιμὴν αὐτοῦ γινώσκετε, ὅτι ὡς
Jesus. - And proof ~ his you know, that as
approved character

πατρὶ τέκνον σὺν ἐμοὶ ἐδούλευσεν εἰς τὸ
[3]with [4]a [5]father [1]a [2]child [11]with [12]me [6]he [7]served [8]as [9]a [10]slave for the

εὐαγγέλιον. 23 Τοῦτον μὲν οὖν ἐλπίζω πέμψαι ὡς ἂν
gospel. This *one* - therefore I hope to send [3]when [4]ever
Him expect as soon as

ἀπίδω τὰ περὶ ἐμέ, ἐξαυτῆς.
[5]I [6]may [7]see [8]the [9]*things* [10]concerning [11]me, [1]at [2]once.
how my circumstances go,

24 Πέποιθα δὲ ἐν Κυρίῳ ὅτι καὶ αὐτὸς ταχέως
[2]I [3]have [4]been [5]persuaded [1]But in *the* Lord that [4]also [2]myself [6]shortly

ἐλεύσομαι.
[1]I [3]will [5]come.

Paul Praises Epaphroditus

25 Ἀναγκαῖον δὲ ἡγησάμην Ἐπαφρόδιτον, τὸν
[5]necessary [1]But [2]I [3]considered [4]*it* [10]Epaphroditus, -

ἀδελφὸν καὶ συνεργὸν καὶ συστρατιώτην μου, ὑμῶν δὲ
[12]brother [13]and [14]fellow [15]worker [16]and [17]fellow [18]soldier [11]my, [20]your [19]and

ἀπόστολον καὶ λειτουργὸν τῆς χρείας μου, πέμψαι πρὸς
[21]apostle [22]and [23]minister - [24]of [26]need [25]my, [6]to [7]send [8]to
messenger to

ὑμᾶς, 26 ἐπειδὴ ἐπιποθῶν ἦν πάντας ὑμᾶς, καὶ
[9]you, since [3]longing [4]for [1]he [2]was all ~ you, and

ἀδημονῶν διότι ἠκούσατε ὅτι ἠσθένησε. 27 Καὶ γὰρ
being distressed because you heard that he was sick. indeed ~ For
was had heard

ἠσθένησε παραπλήσιον θανάτῳ, ἀλλ' ὁ Θεὸς αὐτὸν
he was sick coming near to death, but - God him ~

ἠλέησεν, οὐκ αὐτὸν δὲ μόνον, ἀλλὰ καὶ ἐμέ, ἵνα μὴ
showed mercy, [2]not [3]him [1]and only, but also me, that [3]not
lest

λύπην ἐπὶ λύπην σχῶ. 28 Σπουδαιοτέρως οὖν
[5]sorrow [6]upon [7]sorrow [1]I [2]should [4]have. More eagerly therefore

ἔπεμψα αὐτόν, ἵνα ἰδόντες αὐτὸν πάλιν
I sent him, in order that seeing him again
when you see

χαρῆτε, κἀγὼ ἀλυπότερος ὦ. 29 Προσδέχεσθε
you may have joy, and I [3]less [4]anxious [1]may [2]be. Receive

οὖν αὐτὸν ἐν Κυρίῳ μετὰ πάσης χαρᾶς, καὶ τοὺς
therefore ~ him in *the* Lord with all joy, and -
the utmost

τοιούτους ἐντίμους ἔχετε, 30 ὅτι διὰ τὸ ἔργον τοῦ
[2]such [3]*ones* [4]in [5]honor [1]hold, because on account of the work -

Χριστοῦ μέχρι θανάτου ἤγγισε, παραβουλευσάμενος[b] τῇ
of Christ [4]unto [5]death [1]he [2]drew [3]near, being careless with the
his

ψυχῇ, ἵνα ἀναπληρώσῃ τὸ ὑμῶν ὑστέρημα τῆς πρός
life, in order that he might fill up - your deficiency - [3]to
that which was lacking

με λειτουργίας.*
[4]me [1]of [2]service.
in your

True Circumcision and False

3 1 Τὸ λοιπόν, ἀδελφοί μου, χαίρετε ἐν Κυρίῳ. Τὰ
For the rest, brothers ~ my, rejoice in *the* Lord. [3]the
Finally,

αὐτὰ γράφειν ὑμῖν ἐμοὶ μὲν οὐκ ὀκνηρόν, ὑμῖν
[4]same [5]*things* [1]To [2]write to you for me - *is* not troublesome, [2]for [3]you

δὲ τὸ ἀσφαλές. 2 Βλέπετε τοὺς κύνας, βλέπετε τοὺς
[1]but *it is* the safe *thing*. Watch the dogs, watch the
Beware of beware of

κακοὺς ἐργάτας, βλέπετε τὴν κατατομήν! 3 Ἡμεῖς γάρ ἐσμεν
evil workers, watch the mutilation! we ~ For are
beware of

ἡ περιτομή, οἱ Πνεύματι Θεοῦ[a] λατρεύοντες καὶ
the circumcision, the *ones* [2]in [3]*the* [4]Spirit [5]of [6]God [1]worshiping and
who are by

καυχώμενοι ἐν Χριστῷ Ἰησοῦ καὶ οὐκ ἐν σαρκὶ
boasting in Christ Jesus and not [3]in [4]*the* [5]flesh

πεποιθότες, 4 καίπερ ἐγὼ ἔχων πεποίθησιν καὶ ἐν
[1]having [2]confidence, although I *am* having confidence also in

σαρκί.
the flesh.

That I May Know Him

Εἴ τις δοκεῖ ἄλλος πεποιθέναι ἐν σαρκί, ἐγὼ
If any [3]thinks [1]other [2]*person* to have confidence in *the* flesh, I

μᾶλλον· 5 περιτομῇ ὀκταήμερος, ἐκ γένους Ἰσραήλ,
even more: in circumcision on the eighth day, of *the* nation of Israel,
circumcised when eight days old,

φυλῆς Βενιαμίν, Ἑβραῖος ἐξ Ἑβραίων, κατὰ νόμον
of *the* tribe of Benjamin, a Hebrew of Hebrews, with respect to *the* law

Φαρισαῖος, 6 κατὰ ζῆλον διώκων τὴν ἐκκλησίαν,
a Pharisee, with respect to zeal persecuting the church,

κατὰ δικαιοσύνην τὴν ἐν νόμῳ γενόμενος ἄμεμπτος.
with respect to righteousness the *one* in *the* law being blameless.
which is

7 Ἀλλ' ἅτινα ἦν μοι κέρδη, ταῦτα ἥγημαι
But such *things* as were to me gain, these *things* I have considered

διὰ τὸν Χριστὸν ζημίαν. 8 Ἀλλὰ μενοῦν καὶ
[2]for [3]the [4]sake [5]of - [6]Christ [1]loss. More than that also ~

ἡγοῦμαι πάντα ζημίαν εἶναι διὰ τὸ ὑπερέχον τῆς
I consider all *things* [3]loss [1]to [2]be for the sake of the excelling *thing* of the
excellence

γνώσεως Χριστοῦ Ἰησοῦ τοῦ Κυρίου μου, δι' ὃν τὰ
knowledge of Christ Jesus - Lord ~ my, for the sake of whom -

πάντα ἐζημιώθην, καὶ ἡγοῦμαι σκύβαλα εἶναι
[5]all [6]*things* [1]I [2]sustained [3]loss [4]of, and I consider *them* [3]rubbish [1]to [2]be

ἵνα Χριστὸν κερδήσω 9 καὶ εὑρεθῶ ἐν αὐτῷ, μὴ
in order that [4]Christ [1]I [2]may [3]gain and may be found in Him, not

ἔχων ἐμὴν δικαιοσύνην τὴν ἐκ νόμου, ἀλλὰ
having *as* my righteousness the *righteousness* of *the* law, but

τὴν διὰ πίστεως Χριστοῦ, τὴν ἐκ Θεοῦ
the *righteousness* by faith of Christ, the [2]*which* [3]*is* [4]from [5]God
in

δικαιοσύνην ἐπὶ τῇ πίστει· 10 τοῦ γνῶναι αὐτὸν καὶ
[1]righteousness on - faith; - *so as* to know Him and
on the basis of

τὴν δύναμιν τῆς ἀναστάσεως αὐτοῦ καὶ τὴν κοινωνίαν τῶν
the power - of resurrection ~ His and the fellowship -
sharing

3 Finally, my brethren, rejoice in the Lord. For me to write the same things to you *is* not tedious, but for you *it is* safe.
2 Beware of dogs, beware of evil workers, beware of the mutilation!
3 For we are the circumcision, who worship God in the Spirit, rejoice in Christ Jesus, and have no confidence in the flesh,
4 though I also might have confidence in the flesh. If anyone else thinks he may have confidence in the flesh, I more so:
5 circumcised the eighth day, of the stock of Israel, *of* the tribe of Benjamin, a Hebrew of the Hebrews; concerning the law, a Pharisee;
6 concerning zeal, persecuting the church; concerning the righteousness which is in the law, blameless.
7 But what things were gain to me, these I have counted loss for Christ.
8 Yet indeed I also count all things loss for the excellence of the knowledge of Christ Jesus my Lord, for whom I have suffered the loss of all things, and count them as rubbish, that I may gain Christ
9 and be found in Him, not having my own righteousness, which *is* from the law, but that which *is* through faith in Christ, the righteousness which is from God by faith;
10 that I may know Him and the power of His resurrection, and the fellowship of His suffer-

[a](3:3) TR reads Θεω, thus *worshiping God in the Spirit.*

ings, being conformed to His death,
11 if, by any means, I may attain to the resurrection from the dead.
12 Not that I have already attained, or am already perfected; but I press on, that I may lay hold of that for which Christ Jesus has also laid hold of me.
13 Brethren, I do not count myself to have apprehended; but one thing *I do,* forgetting those things which are behind and reaching forward to those things which are ahead,
14 I press toward the goal for the prize of the upward call of God in Christ Jesus.
15 Therefore let us, as many as are mature, have this mind; and if in anything you think otherwise, God will reveal even this to you.
16 Nevertheless, to *the degree* that we have already attained, let us walk by the same rule, let us be of the same mind.
17 Brethren, join in following my example, and note those who so walk, as you have us for a pattern.
18 For many walk, of whom I have told you often, and now tell you even weeping, *that they are* the enemies of the cross of Christ:
19 whose end *is* destruction, whose god *is their* belly, and *whose* glory *is* in their shame—who set their mind on earthly things.
20 For our citizenship is in heaven, from which we also eagerly wait for the Savior, the Lord Jesus Christ,
21 who will transform our lowly body that it may be con-

παθημάτων αὐτοῦ, συμμορφούμενος[b] *τῷ θανάτῳ αὐτοῦ,* **11** *εἴ*
of sufferings ~ His, being conformed - to death ~ His, if

πως καταντήσω εἰς τὴν ἐξανάστασιν τῶν νεκρῶν.
in some way I may arrive to the resurrection from the dead.
attain

Pressing On Toward the Goal

12 *Οὐχ ὅτι ἤδη ἔλαβον ἢ ἤδη τετελείωμαι,*
Not that already ~ I obtained or already have been made perfect,

διώκω δὲ εἰ καὶ καταλάβω ἐφ' ᾧ καὶ κατελήφθην
[2]I [3]pursue [1]but if also I may lay hold *of that* for which also I was laid hold of
press on

ὑπὸ τοῦ Χριστοῦ Ἰησοῦ. **13** *Ἀδελφοί, ἐγὼ ἐμαυτὸν οὐ*
by - Christ Jesus. Brothers, I [4]myself [2]not

λογίζομαι κατειληφέναι· ἓν δέ, τὰ μὲν ὀπίσω
[1]do [3]consider to have laid hold; [2]one [3]*thing* [1]but, [5]the [6]*things* - [7]behind

ἐπιλανθανόμενος, τοῖς δὲ ἔμπροσθεν ἐπεκτεινόμενος,
[4]forgetting, [12]the [13]*things* [8]and [14]ahead [9]reaching [10]out [11]for,

14 *κατὰ σκοπὸν διώκω ἐπὶ τὸ βραβεῖον τῆς ἄνω κλήσεως*
toward a goal I pursue for the prize of the upward call
press on

τοῦ Θεοῦ ἐν Χριστῷ Ἰησοῦ. **15** *Ὅσοι οὖν τέλειοι,*
- of God in Christ Jesus. [2]as [3]many [4]as [1]Therefore *are* perfect,
mature,

τοῦτο φρονῶμεν· καὶ εἴ τι ἑτέρως φρονεῖτε, καὶ
[4]this [5]*way* [1]let [2]us [3]think; and if [3]anything [4]otherwise [1]you [2]think, even

τοῦτο ὁ Θεὸς ὑμῖν ἀποκαλύψει. **16** *Πλὴν εἰς*
this - God [3]to [4]you [1]will [2]reveal. Nevertheless to
in reference to

ὃ ἐφθάσαμεν, τῷ αὐτῷ στοιχεῖν κανόνι,[c] *τὸ*
what we attained, [5]with [6]the [7]same [1]to [2]be [3]in [4]line rule, [3]the
have attained, keep be

αὐτὸ φρονεῖν.
[4]same [5]*thing* [1]to [2]think.
in agreement.

Our Citizenship Is in Heaven

17 *Συμμιμηταί μου γίνεσθε, ἀδελφοί, καὶ σκοπεῖτε*
[2]fellow [3]imitators [4]of [5]me [1]Be, brothers, and look out for

τοὺς οὕτω περιπατοῦντας καθὼς ἔχετε τύπον ἡμᾶς.
the *ones* thus walking just as you have [2]for [3]a [4]pattern [1]us.

18 *Πολλοὶ γὰρ περιπατοῦσιν, οὓς πολλάκις ἔλεγον*
many ~ For walk, whom often I was speaking of

ὑμῖν, νῦν δὲ καὶ κλαίων λέγω, τοὺς ἐχθροὺς τοῦ σταυροῦ
to you, now ~ and also weeping I speak of, the enemies of the cross

τοῦ Χριστοῦ, **19** *ὧν τὸ τέλος ἀπώλεια, ὧν ὁ Θεὸς ἡ*
- of Christ, whose - end *is* destruction, whose - God *is* the

κοιλία καὶ ἡ δόξα ἐν τῇ αἰσχύνῃ αὐτῶν, οἱ τὰ
belly and - *whose* glory *is* in - shame ~ their, the *ones* [2]the
who are mindful of

ἐπίγεια φρονοῦντες. **20** *Ἡμῶν γὰρ τὸ πολίτευμα ἐν*
[3]earthly [4]*things* [1]thinking. our ~ For - citizenship [2]in
the things of the earth. is

οὐρανοῖς ὑπάρχει, ἐξ οὗ καὶ Σωτῆρα ἀπεκδεχόμεθα,
[3]*the* [4]heavens [1]exists, from which also [4]a [5]Savior [1]we [2]eagerly [3]await,
in heaven,

Κύριον Ἰησοῦν Χριστόν, **21** *ὃς μετασχηματίσει τὸ σῶμα**
the Lord Jesus Christ, who will transform the body

---

[b](3:10) NU reads *συμμορφιζομενος, conforming.*
[c](3:16) NU omits *κανονι, rule,* and the rest of the verse.

---

*(3:21) *σῶμα (sōma).* Very common noun meaning *body,* either human or animal. It is the general term for referring to the physical aspect of a person, as contrasted with the nonmaterial *πνεῦμα, spirit* (James 2:26), and *ψυχή, soul* (Matt. 10:28). Consequently, *σῶμα* was often used for *dead bodies, corpses* (Matt. 27:58). Here in Phil. 3:21 Paul contrasts the "lowly" physical body

τῆς ταπεινώσεως ἡμῶν εἰς[d] τὸ γενέσθαι αὐτὸ σύμμορφον
- of humiliation ˜ our for - to become it similar in form
our lowly body so that it may become of the same

τῷ σώματι τῆς δόξης αὐτοῦ, κατὰ τὴν ἐνέργειαν
with the body - of glory ˜ His, according to the working
form as His glorious body,

τοῦ δύνασθαι αὐτὸν καὶ ὑποτάξαι ἑαυτῷ τὰ πάντα.
of the to be able Him also to subject to Himself - all *things*.
by which He is able

4 1 Ὥστε, ἀδελφοί μου ἀγαπητοὶ καὶ ἐπιπόθητοι, χαρὰ καὶ
So then, brothers ˜ my beloved and longed for, [2]joy [3]and

στέφανός μου, οὕτω στήκετε ἐν Κυρίῳ, ἀγαπητοί.
[4]crown [1]my, in this way stand fast in *the* Lord, beloved.

Be United, Joyful and in Prayer

2 Εὐοδίαν παρακαλῶ καὶ Συντύχην παρακαλῶ τὸ
Euodia I urge and Syntyche I urge [3]the
to

αὐτὸ φρονεῖν ἐν Κυρίῳ. 3 Ναί,[a] ἐρωτῶ καὶ σέ,
[4]same [5]*thing* [1]to [2]think in *the* Lord. Yes, I ask also ˜ you,
be in agreement

σύζυγε γνήσιε, συλλαμβάνου αὐταῖς, αἵτινες ἐν τῷ
yokefellow ˜ genuine, assist together with them, *women* who in the
true companion,

εὐαγγελίῳ συνήθλησάν μοι, μετὰ καὶ Κλήμεντος καὶ
gospel struggled together with me, with also ˜ Clement and

τῶν λοιπῶν συνεργῶν μου, ὧν τὰ ὀνόματα ἐν
the remaining of [2]fellow [3]workers [1]my, whose - names *are* in
rest

Βίβλῳ Ζωῆς.
the Book of Life.

4 Χαίρετε ἐν Κυρίῳ πάντοτε. Πάλιν ἐρῶ, χαίρετε! 5 Τὸ
Rejoice in *the* Lord always. Again I say, rejoice! -

ἐπιεικὲς ὑμῶν γνωσθήτω πᾶσιν ἀνθρώποις. Ὁ Κύριος
[3]gentleness [2]your [1]Let be known to all men. The Lord
forbearing spirit

ἐγγύς. 6 Μηδὲν μεριμνᾶτε, ἀλλ' ἐν παντὶ τῇ
is near. [4]nothing [1]Be [2]anxious [3]about, but in every *thing* -

προσευχῇ καὶ τῇ δεήσει μετὰ εὐχαριστίας τὰ αἰτήματα
with prayer and - petition along with thanksgiving - [3]requests
by means of

ὑμῶν γνωριζέσθω πρὸς τὸν Θεόν. 7 Καὶ ἡ εἰρήνη τοῦ
[2]your [1]let be made known to - God. And the peace -

Θεοῦ, ἡ ὑπερέχουσα πάντα νοῦν, φρουρήσει τὰς
of God, the *one* surpassing all understanding, will guard -
which is

καρδίας ὑμῶν καὶ τὰ νοήματα ὑμῶν ἐν Χριστῷ Ἰησοῦ.
hearts ˜ your and - minds ˜ your in Christ Jesus.
thoughts

Think on These Things

8 Τὸ λοιπόν, ἀδελφοί, ὅσα ἐστὶν ἀληθῆ,
For the rest, brothers, as many *things* as are true,
Finally,

ὅσα σεμνά, ὅσα δίκαια, ὅσα ἁγνά,
as many as *are* honorable, as many as *are* just, as many as *are* pure,

ὅσα προσφιλῆ, ὅσα εὔφημα — εἴ τις
as many as *are* pleasing, as many as *are* attractive — if *there is* any

formed to His glorious body, according to the working by which He is able even to subdue all things to Himself.

4 Therefore, my beloved and longed-for brethren, my joy and crown, so stand fast in the Lord, beloved.

2 I implore Euodia and I implore Syntyche to be of the same mind in the Lord.

3 And I urge you also, true companion, help these women who labored with me in the gospel, with Clement also, and the rest of my fellow workers, whose names *are* in the Book of Life.

4 Rejoice in the Lord always. Again I will say, rejoice!

5 Let your gentleness be known to all men. The Lord *is* at hand.

6 Be anxious for nothing, but in everything by prayer and supplication, with thanksgiving, let your requests be made known to God;

7 and the peace of God, which surpasses all understanding, will guard your hearts and minds through Christ Jesus.

8 Finally, brethren, whatever things are true, whatever things *are* noble, whatever things *are* just, whatever things *are* pure, whatever things *are* lovely, whatever things *are* of good report, if *there is* any vir-

---

[d]**(3:21)** NU omits *εις το γενεσθαι αυτο*, *for it to become.* [a]**(4:3)** TR reads *Και*, *And.*

which dies with the "glorious" resurrection body. When occurring with a moral or ethical nuance, the word was essentially synonymous with *σάρξ* in referring to humanity's sinful nature (Rom. 6:6; 8:11–13). The word became a common metaphor for referring to the church as "the body of Christ" of which He is the head (Col. 1:18). Cf. the cognate adjective *σωματικός*, *bodily, corporeal* (1 Tim. 4:8); and adverb *σωματικῶς*, *bodily, corporeally* (Col. 2:9).

tue and if *there is* anything
praiseworthy—meditate on
these things.
9 The things which you
learned and received and heard
and saw in me, these do, and
the God of peace will be with
you.
10 But I rejoiced in the Lord
greatly that now at last your
care for me has flourished
again; though you surely did
care, but you lacked opportunity.
11 Not that I speak in regard
to need, for I have learned in
whatever state I am, to be content:
12 I know how to be abased,
and I know how to abound.
Everywhere and in all things I
have learned both to be full and
to be hungry, both to abound
and to suffer need.
13 I can do all things through
Christ who strengthens me.
14 Nevertheless you have
done well that you shared in my
distress.
15 Now you Philippians know
also that in the beginning of the
gospel, when I departed from
Macedonia, no church shared
with me concerning giving and
receiving but you only.
16 For even in Thessalonica
you sent *aid* once and again for
my necessities.
17 Not that I seek the gift, but
I seek the fruit that abounds to
your account.
18 Indeed I have all and
abound. I am full, having re-

---

[b](**4:13**) NU omits Χριστω, *Christ*.

---

*(**4:15**) *κοινωνέω (koinōneō)*. Verb meaning *have a share in*. When used with a negative sense of *sharing in* the "sins" (1 Tim. 5:22) or "evil deeds" (2 John 11) of others, the word includes the idea of participation in, and equal responsibility for, those actions. Also the positive sense of *sharing in* the needs of others involves participation: *distributing* what is necessary to meet those needs (Rom. 12:13). Paul urged the Gentiles to so share with the Jews since the Gentiles themselves had shared in, or been *partakers of*, the Jews' spiritual blessings (Rom. 15:27). The idea of sharing through a *contribution* is also present here in Phil. 4:15 (cf. Gal. 6:6). Cf. the cognate nouns *κοινωνία*,

ἀρετὴ καὶ εἴ τις ἔπαινος — ταῦτα
virtue and if *there is* any praise — [2]these [3]*things*
moral excellence commendation —

λογίζεσθε. 9 Ἃ καὶ ἐμάθετε καὶ παρελάβετε καὶ
[1]ponder. *The things* which also you learned and received and
meditate on.

ἠκούσατε καὶ εἴδετε ἐν ἐμοί, ταῦτα πράσσετε· καὶ ὁ
heard and saw in me, [2]these [3]*things* [1]practice; and the

Θεὸς τῆς εἰρήνης ἔσται μεθ' ὑμῶν.
God - of peace will be with you.

Paul Is Thankful for the Philippians' Generosity

10 Ἐχάρην δὲ ἐν Κυρίῳ μεγάλως ὅτι ἤδη ποτὲ
[2]I [3]rejoiced [1]But in *the* Lord greatly that now once *again*

ἀνεθάλετε τὸ ὑπὲρ ἐμοῦ φρονεῖν, ἐφ' ᾧ καὶ
you revived - in behalf of me to think, upon which indeed
have revived your mindfulness on my behalf, inasmuch as

ἐφρονεῖτε, ἠκαιρεῖσθε δέ. 11 Οὐχ ὅτι
you were thinking, [2]you [3]were [4]lacking [5]opportunity [1]but. Not that
mindful,

καθ' ὑστέρησιν λέγω, ἐγὼ γὰρ ἔμαθον ἐν
[4]with [5]respect [6]to [7]lack [1]I [2]am [3]speaking, I ~ for learned in
need have learned

οἷς εἰμι αὐτάρκης εἶναι. 12 Οἶδα καὶ
the circumstances in which I am [3]content [1]to [2]be. I know *how* both

ταπεινοῦσθαι, οἶδα καὶ περισσεύειν. Ἐν παντὶ καὶ
to be abased, [2]I [3]know [4]how [1]and to abound. In every *place* and

ἐν πᾶσι μεμύημαι καὶ χορτάζεσθαι καὶ πεινᾶν,
in all *circumstances* I have learned both to be full and to be hungry,

καὶ περισσεύειν καὶ ὑστερεῖσθαι. 13 Πάντα ἰσχύω
both to abound and to be in need. All *things* I am able to do

ἐν τῷ ἐνδυναμοῦντί με Χριστῷ.[b] 14 Πλὴν
in [2]the [3]*One* [4]strengthening [5]me [1]Christ. Nevertheless
through who strengthens

καλῶς ἐποιήσατε συγκοινωνήσαντές μου τῇ θλίψει.
[3]well [1]you [2]did sharing with my - affliction.
trial.

15 Οἴδατε δὲ καὶ ὑμεῖς, Φιλιππήσιοι, ὅτι ἐν ἀρχῇ
[4]know [1]Now [3]also [2]you, Philippians, that in *the* beginning

τοῦ εὐαγγελίου, ὅτε ἐξῆλθον ἀπὸ Μακεδονίας, οὐδεμία
of the gospel, when I went out from Macedonia, no

μοι ἐκκλησία ἐκοινώνησεν* εἰς λόγον δόσεως καὶ
[3]with [4]me [1]church [2]shared in an accounting of giving and

λήψεως εἰ μὴ ὑμεῖς μόνοι. 16 Ὅτι καὶ ἐν Θεσσαλονίκῃ
receiving if not you only. Because even in Thessalonica
except

καὶ ἅπαξ καὶ δὶς εἰς τὴν χρείαν μοι ἐπέμψατε. 17 Οὐχ ὅτι
both once and twice [3]for - [5]need [4]my [1]you [2]sent. Not that
once and again

ἐπιζητῶ τὸ δόμα, ἀλλ' ἐπιζητῶ τὸν καρπὸν τὸν
I seek the gift, but I seek the fruit the *one*
which is

πλεονάζοντα εἰς λόγον ὑμῶν. 18 Ἀπέχω δὲ πάντα
increasing to account ~ your. [2]I [3]have [6]in [7]full [1]And [4]all [5]*things*

καὶ περισσεύω. Πεπλήρωμαι, δεξάμενος παρὰ
and I abound. I have been made full, receiving from
having received

'Επαφροδίτου τὰ παρ' ὑμῶν, ὀσμὴν εὐωδίας,
Epaphroditus the *things* from you, an odor of fragrance,
a fragrant aroma,

θυσίαν δεκτήν, εὐάρεστον τῷ Θεῷ. **19** Ὁ δὲ Θεός μου
a(n) sacrifice ˜ acceptable, well pleasing - to God. - And God ˜ my

πληρώσει πᾶσαν χρείαν ὑμῶν κατὰ τὸν πλοῦτον αὐτοῦ ἐν
will fill all need ˜ your according to - riches ˜ His in
supply

δόξῃ ἐν Χριστῷ 'Ιησοῦ. **20** Τῷ δὲ Θεῷ καὶ Πατρὶ ἡμῶν
glory in Christ Jesus. - Now to [2]God [3]and [4]Father [1]our

ἡ δόξα εἰς τοὺς αἰῶνας τῶν αἰώνων. 'Αμήν.
be the glory into the ages of the ages. Amen.
forever and ever. So be it.

Paul's Greeting of Grace

21 'Ασπάσασθε πάντα ἅγιον ἐν Χριστῷ 'Ιησοῦ.
Greet every saint in Christ Jesus.

'Ασπάζονται ὑμᾶς οἱ σὺν ἐμοὶ ἀδελφοί. **22** 'Ασπάζονται
[5]greet [6]you [1]The [3]with [4]me [2]brothers. [4]greet

ὑμᾶς πάντες οἱ ἅγιοι, μάλιστα δὲ οἱ ἐκ τῆς Καίσαρος
[5]you [1]All [2]the [3]saints, especially ˜ but the *ones* of the [2]of [3]Caesar

οἰκίας.
[1]household.

23 Ἡ χάρις τοῦ Κυρίου 'Ιησοῦ Χριστοῦ μετὰ πάντων
The grace of the Lord Jesus Christ *be* with all ˜

ὑμῶν.[c] 'Αμήν.[d]
you. Amen.
So be it.

ceived from Epaphroditus the things *sent* from you, a sweet-smelling aroma, an acceptable sacrifice, well pleasing to God.
19 And my God shall supply all your need according to His riches in glory by Christ Jesus.
20 Now to our God and Father *be* glory forever and ever. Amen.
21 Greet every saint in Christ Jesus. The brethren who are with me greet you.
22 All the saints greet you, but especially those who are of Caesar's household.
23 The grace of our Lord Jesus Christ be with you all. Amen.

---

[c]**(4:23)** NU reads *του πνευματος υμων, your spirit.* [d]**(4:23)** NU omits *Αμην, Amen.*

fellowship, at Acts 2:42, and *κοινωνός, partaker,* at Luke 5:10.

The Epistle of Paul the Apostle to the
COLOSSIANS

1 Paul, an apostle of Jesus Christ by the will of God, and Timothy our brother,

2 To the saints and faithful brethren in Christ *who are* in Colosse:

Grace to you and peace from God our Father and the Lord Jesus Christ.

3 We give thanks to the God and Father of our Lord Jesus Christ, praying always for you,
4 since we heard of your faith in Christ Jesus and of your love for all the saints;
5 because of the hope which is laid up for you in heaven, of which you heard before in the word of the truth of the gospel,
6 which has come to you, as *it has* also in all the world, and is bringing forth fruit, as *it is* also among you since the day you heard and knew the grace of God in truth;
7 as you also learned from Epaphras, our dear fellow servant, who is a faithful minister of Christ on your behalf,
8 who also declared to us your love in the Spirit.

---

[a](**1:2**) NU omits *και Κυριου Ιησου Χριστου, and the Lord Jesus Christ.*
[b](**1:6**) TR omits *και αυξανομενον, and growing.*

***(1:4)** *πίστις (pistis).* Common noun meaning *faith, trust.* The usage of the word falls into three general categories. First, *πίστις* refers to that quality possessed by someone which causes faith or trust: *faithfulness, reliability* (Rom. 3:3). Most often in the NT, however, it means the act of believing in God or Christ (as here in Col. 1:4). This acceptance of God's promises and truths is one of the foundational Christian virtues (1 Cor. 13:13). Paul also speaks of a special "gift of faith" (1 Cor. 12:9), an absolute confi-

ΠΡΟΣ ΚΟΛΑΣΣΑΕΙΣ
TO *THE* COLOSSIANS

Paul Greets His Brethren in Christ

1 1 Παῦλος, ἀπόστολος Ἰησοῦ Χριστοῦ διὰ θελήματος
Paul, an apostle of Jesus Christ through *the* will
by
Θεοῦ, καὶ Τιμόθεος ὁ ἀδελφός,
of God, and Timothy the brother,
2 Τοῖς ἐν Κολασσαῖς ἁγίοις καὶ πιστοῖς ἀδελφοῖς ἐν
To the [7]in [8]Colosse [1]holy [2]and [3]faithful [4]brothers [5]in
Χριστῷ·
[6]Christ:
Χάρις ὑμῖν καὶ εἰρήνη ἀπὸ Θεοῦ Πατρὸς ἡμῶν καὶ Κυρίου
Grace to you and peace from God Father ˜ our and *the* Lord
Ἰησοῦ Χριστοῦ.[a]
Jesus Christ.

He Thanks God for Their Faith in Christ

3 Εὐχαριστοῦμεν τῷ Θεῷ καὶ Πατρὶ τοῦ Κυρίου ἡμῶν
We give thanks to the God and Father - of Lord ˜ our
Ἰησοῦ Χριστοῦ πάντοτε περὶ ὑμῶν προσευχόμενοι,
Jesus Christ always [2]for [3]you [1]praying,
4 ἀκούσαντες τὴν πίστιν* ὑμῶν ἐν Χριστῷ Ἰησοῦ καὶ τὴν
hearing of - faith ˜ your in Christ Jesus and the
when we heard of your
ἀγάπην τὴν εἰς πάντας τοὺς ἁγίους, 5 διὰ τὴν
love the *one* towards all the saints, because of the
which is
ἐλπίδα τὴν ἀποκειμένην ὑμῖν ἐν τοῖς οὐρανοῖς, ἣν
hope - being laid up for you in the heavens, *of* which
προηκούσατε ἐν τῷ λόγῳ τῆς ἀληθείας τοῦ εὐαγγελίου
you heard before in the word of the truth of the gospel
6 τοῦ παρόντος εἰς ὑμᾶς, καθὼς καὶ ἐν παντὶ τῷ κόσμῳ, καί
- coming to you, just as also in all the world, and
which has come
ἐστι καρποφορούμενον καὶ αὐξανόμενον,[b] καθὼς καὶ ἐν
is bearing fruit and growing, just as also among
ὑμῖν, ἀφ' ἧς ἡμέρας ἠκούσατε καὶ ἐπέγνωτε τὴν χάριν τοῦ
you, from which day you heard and fully knew the grace -
the day which
Θεοῦ ἐν ἀληθείᾳ· 7 καθὼς καὶ ἐμάθετε ἀπὸ Ἐπαφρᾶ τοῦ
of God in truth; just as also you learned from Epaphras -
ἀγαπητοῦ συνδούλου ἡμῶν, ὅς ἐστι πιστὸς ὑπὲρ ὑμῶν
[2]beloved [3]fellow [4]bondservant [1]our, who is a faithful [4]for [5]you
διάκονος τοῦ Χριστοῦ, 8 ὁ καὶ δηλώσας ἡμῖν τὴν ὑμῶν
[1]servant - [2]of [3]Christ, the *one* also showing us - of your
minister who told
ἀγάπην ἐν Πνεύματι.
love in *the* Spirit.

Christ Preeminent

9 Διὰ τοῦτο καὶ ἡμεῖς, ἀφ' ἧς ἡμέρας
On account of this also ~ we, from which day
the day which

ἠκούσαμεν, οὐ παυόμεθα ὑπὲρ ὑμῶν προσευχόμενοι, καὶ
we heard, not ~ do cease [2]for [3]you [1]praying, and

αἰτούμενοι ἵνα πληρωθῆτε τὴν ἐπίγνωσιν τοῦ
asking that you may be filled *with* the full knowledge of

θελήματος αὐτοῦ ἐν πάσῃ σοφίᾳ καὶ συνέσει πνευματικῇ,
will ~ His in all wisdom and understanding ~ spiritual,

10 περιπατῆσαι ὑμᾶς ἀξίως τοῦ Κυρίου εἰς πᾶσαν
[2]to [3]walk [1]you worthily of the Lord to all
that you should walk please Him

ἀρεσκείαν, ἐν παντὶ ἔργῳ ἀγαθῷ καρποφοροῦντες καὶ
pleasing, in every work ~ good bearing fruit and
in all respects,

αὐξανόμενοι εἰς τὴν ἐπίγνωσιν τοῦ Θεοῦ, 11 ἐν πάσῃ
increasing in the full knowledge - of God, with all

δυνάμει δυναμούμενοι κατὰ τὸ κράτος τῆς δόξης αὐτοῦ
power being empowered according to the might - of glory ~ His

εἰς πᾶσαν ὑπομονὴν καὶ μακροθυμίαν μετὰ χαρᾶς,
for all endurance and longsuffering with joy,

12 εὐχαριστοῦντες τῷ Πατρὶ τῷ ἱκανώσαντι ἡμᾶς[c] εἰς τὴν
giving thanks to the Father - having qualified us for the
who has to

μερίδα τοῦ κλήρου τῶν ἁγίων ἐν τῷ φωτί, 13 ὃς
share of the inheritance of the saints in the light, who
share in

ἐρρύσατο ἡμᾶς ἐκ τῆς ἐξουσίας τοῦ σκότους καὶ
rescued us from the authority - of darkness and
dominion

μετέστησεν εἰς τὴν βασιλείαν τοῦ Υἱοῦ τῆς ἀγάπης αὐτοῦ,
transferred *us* into the kingdom of the Son - of love ~ His,

14 ἐν ᾧ ἔχομεν τὴν ἀπολύτρωσιν,[d] τὴν ἄφεσιν τῶν
in whom we have - redemption, the forgiveness -

ἁμαρτιῶν· 15 ὅς ἐστιν εἰκὼν τοῦ Θεοῦ τοῦ ἀοράτου,
of sins; who is *the* image of the God ~ - invisible,

πρωτότοκος πάσης κτίσεως, 16 ὅτι ἐν αὐτῷ ἐκτίσθη τὰ
the firstborn of all creation, because by Him were created -
over

πάντα, τὰ ἐν τοῖς οὐρανοῖς καὶ τὰ ἐπὶ τῆς γῆς, τὰ
all *things,* the *ones* in the heavens and the *ones* on the earth, the

ὁρατὰ καὶ τὰ ἀόρατα, εἴτε θρόνοι εἴτε κυριότητες
visible *things* and the invisible *things,* whether thrones or lordships
dominions

εἴτε ἀρχαὶ εἴτε ἐξουσίαι· τὰ πάντα δι' αὐτοῦ καὶ εἰς αὐτὸν
or rulers or authorities; - all *things* through Him and for Him

ἔκτισται, 17 καὶ αὐτός ἐστι πρὸ πάντων καὶ τὰ πάντα
have been created, and He is before all and - all *things*

ἐν αὐτῷ συνέστηκε. 18 Καὶ αὐτός ἐστιν ἡ κεφαλὴ τοῦ
in Him consisted. And He is the head of the
hold together.

σώματος, τῆς ἐκκλησίας· ὅς ἐστιν ἀρχή, πρωτότοκος ἐκ
body, the church; who is *the* beginning, *the* firstborn from

τῶν νεκρῶν, ἵνα γένηται ἐν πᾶσιν αὐτὸς πρωτεύων,
the dead, so that [2]may [3]be [7]in [8]all [9]*things* [1]He [4]having [5]first [6]place,
preeminent,

19 ὅτι ἐν αὐτῷ εὐδόκησεν πᾶν τὸ Πλήρωμα κατοικῆσαι,
because in Him [4]was [5]pleased [1]all [2]the [3]Fullness to dwell,

9 For this reason we also, since the day we heard it, do not cease to pray for you, and to ask that you may be filled with the knowledge of His will in all wisdom and spiritual understanding;
10 that you may walk worthy of the Lord, fully pleasing *Him,* being fruitful in every good work and increasing in the knowledge of God;
11 strengthened with all might, according to His glorious power, for all patience and longsuffering with joy;
12 giving thanks to the Father who has qualified us to be partakers of the inheritance of the saints in the light.
13 He has delivered us from the power of darkness and conveyed *us* into the kingdom of the Son of His love,
14 in whom we have redemption through His blood, the forgiveness of sins.
15 He is the image of the invisible God, the firstborn over all creation.
16 For by Him all things were created that are in heaven and that are on earth, visible and invisible, whether thrones or dominions or principalities or powers. All things were created through Him and for Him.
17 And He is before all things, and in Him all things consist.
18 And He is the head of the body, the church, who is the beginning, the firstborn from the dead, that in all things He may have the preeminence.
19 For it pleased *the Father that* in Him all the fullness should dwell,

---

c(**1:12**) NU reads *υμας, you.*
d(**1:14**) TR adds *δια του αιματος αυτου, through His blood.*

dence in God's ability to do the miraculous (cf. Matt. 17:20). Finally, *πίστις* was used to refer to the content of what one believed, *the Christian faith, doctrine* (Jude 3). See the cognate verb *πιστεύω, believe,* at Acts 10:43; and adjective *πιστός, faithful, believing,* at 2 Thess. 3:3.

20 and by Him to reconcile all things to Himself, by Him, whether things on earth or things in heaven, having made peace through the blood of His cross.
21 And you, who once were alienated and enemies in your mind by wicked works, yet now He has reconciled
22 in the body of His flesh through death, to present you holy, and blameless, and above reproach in His sight—
23 if indeed you continue in the faith, grounded and steadfast, and are not moved away from the hope of the gospel which you heard, which was preached to every creature under heaven, of which I, Paul, became a minister.
24 I now rejoice in my sufferings for you, and fill up in my flesh what is lacking in the afflictions of Christ, for the sake of His body, which is the church,
25 of which I became a minister according to the stewardship from God which was given to me for you, to fulfill the word of God,
26 the mystery which has been hidden from ages and from generations, but now has been revealed to His saints.
27 To them God willed to make known what are the riches of the glory of this mys-

20 *καὶ δι' αὐτοῦ ἀποκαταλλάξαι τὰ πάντα εἰς αὐτόν,*
and through Him to reconcile - all *things* to Him*self,*

εἰρηνοποιήσας διὰ τοῦ αἵματος τοῦ σταυροῦ αὐτοῦ, δι'
having made peace through the blood - of cross ˜ His, through

αὐτοῦ, εἴτε τὰ ἐπὶ τῆς γῆς εἴτε τὰ ἐπὶ τοῖς
Him, whether the *things* on the earth or the *things* in the

οὐρανοῖς.
heavens.

Reconciled Through Christ

21 *Καὶ ὑμᾶς ποτε ὄντας ἀπηλλοτριωμένους καὶ ἐχθροὺς*
And you once ˜ being alienated and enemies
who were

τῇ διανοίᾳ ἐν τοῖς ἔργοις τοῖς πονηροῖς, νυνὶ δὲ
in the mind by the works ˜ - wicked, now ˜ yet
your

ἀποκατήλλαξεν **22** *ἐν τῷ σώματι τῆς σαρκὸς αὐτοῦ διὰ τοῦ*
He reconciled in the body - of flesh ˜ His through -
has reconciled

θανάτου, παραστῆσαι ὑμᾶς ἁγίους καὶ ἀμώμους καὶ
death, to present you holy and blameless and

ἀνεγκλήτους κατενώπιον αὐτοῦ, **23** *εἴ γε ἐπιμένετε τῇ*
irreproachable before Him, if indeed you continue in the

πίστει τεθεμελιωμένοι καὶ ἑδραῖοι καὶ μὴ μετακινούμενοι
faith having been founded and firm and not drifting away

ἀπὸ τῆς ἐλπίδος τοῦ εὐαγγελίου οὗ ἠκούσατε, τοῦ
from the hope of the gospel which you heard, the *one*
which

κηρυχθέντος ἐν πάσῃ τῇ κτίσει τῇ ὑπὸ τὸν οὐρανόν, οὗ
being proclaimed in all - creation - under - heaven, of which
was

ἐγενόμην ἐγὼ Παῦλος διάκονος.
³became ¹I ²Paul a servant.
minister.

Paul's Sacrificial Service for Christ

24 *Νῦν χαίρω ἐν τοῖς παθήμασι ὑπὲρ ὑμῶν, καὶ*
Now I rejoice in the sufferings for you, and
my

ἀνταναπληρῶ τὰ ὑστερήματα τῶν θλίψεων τοῦ Χριστοῦ ἐν τῇ
I fill up the *things* lacking of the afflictions - of Christ in -
in

σαρκί μου ὑπὲρ τοῦ σώματος αὐτοῦ, ὅ ἐστιν ἡ ἐκκλησία,
flesh ˜ my for - body ˜ His, which is the church,

25 *ἧς ἐγενόμην ἐγὼ διάκονος κατὰ τὴν οἰκονομίαν*
of which became ˜ I a servant according to the stewardship
minister

τοῦ Θεοῦ τὴν δοθεῖσάν μοι εἰς ὑμᾶς πληρῶσαι τὸν
- of God the *one* having been given to me for you to fulfill the
which was

λόγον τοῦ Θεοῦ, **26** *τὸ μυστήριον τὸ ἀποκεκρυμμένον ἀπὸ*
word - of God, the mystery - having been hidden from

τῶν αἰώνων καὶ ἀπὸ τῶν γενεῶν — νυνὶ δὲ ἐφανερώθη τοῖς
the ages and from the generations — now ˜ but was revealed -

ἁγίοις αὐτοῦ, **27** *οἷς ἠθέλησεν ὁ Θεὸς γνωρίσαι τί*
to saints ˜ His, to whom willed ˜ - God to make known what

τὸ πλοῦτος τῆς δόξης τοῦ μυστηρίου τούτου ἐν τοῖς
the riches of the glory - of mystery ˜ this *are* among the

ἔθνεσιν, ὅς ἐστι Χριστὸς ἐν ὑμῖν, ἡ ἐλπὶς τῆς δόξης·
nations, who is Christ in you, the hope - of glory;

28 ὃν ἡμεῖς καταγγέλλομεν, νουθετοῦντες πάντα ἄνθρωπον
whom we proclaim, warning every man

καὶ διδάσκοντες πάντα ἄνθρωπον ἐν πάσῃ σοφίᾳ, ἵνα
and teaching every man in all wisdom, so that

παραστήσωμεν πάντα ἄνθρωπον τέλειον ἐν Χριστῷ Ἰησοῦ·
we may present every man perfect in Christ Jesus;

29 εἰς ὃ καὶ κοπιῶ, ἀγωνιζόμενος κατὰ τὴν ἐνέργειαν
for which also I labor, striving according to - working ˜

αὐτοῦ τὴν ἐνεργουμένην ἐν ἐμοὶ ἐν δυνάμει.
His the one (which is) working in me with power.

2 1 Θέλω γὰρ ὑμᾶς εἰδέναι ἡλίκον ἀγῶνα ἔχω
[2]I [3]want [1]For you to know how great a struggle I have

περὶ ὑμῶν καὶ τῶν ἐν Λαοδικείᾳ καὶ ὅσοι οὐχ
concerning you and the ones (those) in Laodicea and as many as not ˜

ἑωράκασι τὸ πρόσωπόν μου ἐν σαρκί, 2 ἵνα παρακληθῶσιν
have seen - face ˜ my in *the* flesh, that [3]may [4]be [5]encouraged

αἱ καρδίαι αὐτῶν, συμβιβασθέντων ἐν ἀγάπῃ, καὶ εἰς πάντα
- [2]hearts [1]their, being joined together (united) in love, and to all

πλοῦτον τῆς πληροφορίας τῆς συνέσεως, εἰς ἐπίγνωσιν
riches of the full assurance - of understanding, to a full knowledge

τοῦ μυστηρίου τοῦ Θεοῦ καὶ Πατρὸς καὶ τοῦ Χριστοῦ,[a]
of the mystery - of God both of *the* Father and - of Christ,

3 ἐν ᾧ εἰσι πάντες οἱ θησαυροὶ τῆς σοφίας καὶ τῆς
in whom [9]are [1]all [2]the [3]treasures - [4]of [5]wisdom [6]and -

γνώσεως ἀπόκρυφοι.
[7]of [8]knowledge [10]hidden.

Walk in Christ, Not Philosophy

4 Τοῦτο δὲ λέγω ἵνα μή τις ὑμᾶς
this ˜ Now I say in order that not (lest) someone [3]you

παραλογίζηται ἐν πιθανολογίᾳ. 5 Εἰ γὰρ καὶ τῇ
[1]may [2]deceive with persuasive speech. though ˜ For indeed [4]in [5]the

σαρκὶ ἄπειμι, ἀλλὰ τῷ πνεύματι σὺν ὑμῖν εἰμι, χαίρων
[6]flesh [1]I [2]am [3]absent, yet - [5]in [6]spirit [3]with [4]you [1]I [2]am, rejoicing

καὶ βλέπων ὑμῶν τὴν τάξιν καὶ τὸ στερέωμα τῆς εἰς
and seeing (to see) your - order (orderliness) and the firmness of [3]in

Χριστὸν πίστεως ὑμῶν.
[4]Christ [2]faith [1]your.

6 Ὡς οὖν παρελάβετε τὸν Χριστὸν Ἰησοῦν τὸν
As therefore you received - Christ Jesus the

Κύριον, ἐν αὐτῷ περιπατεῖτε, 7 ἐρριζωμένοι καὶ
Lord, in Him walk, having been rooted, and

ἐποικοδομούμενοι ἐν αὐτῷ καὶ βεβαιούμενοι ἐν τῇ πίστει,
being built up in Him and being established in the faith,

καθὼς ἐδιδάχθητε, περισσεύοντες ἐν αὐτῇ ἐν εὐχαριστίᾳ.
just as you were taught, abounding in it with thanksgiving.

8 Βλέπετε μή τις ὑμᾶς ἔσται ὁ συλαγωγῶν διὰ
Beware lest anyone [6]you [1]will [2]be [3]the [4]*one* [5]capturing (captures you) through

τῆς φιλοσοφίας καὶ κενῆς ἀπάτης, κατὰ τὴν παράδοσιν
- philosophy and empty deceit, according to the tradition

tery among the Gentiles: which
is Christ in you, the hope of
glory.
28 Him we preach, warning
every man and teaching every
man in all wisdom, that we may
present every man perfect in
Christ Jesus.
29 To this *end* I also labor,
striving according to His working which works in me mightily.
2 For I want you to know
what a great conflict I
have for you and those in Laodicea, and *for* as many as have
not seen my face in the flesh,
2 that their hearts may be
encouraged, being knit together in love, and *attaining* to
all riches of the full assurance of
understanding, to the knowledge of the mystery of God,
both of the Father and of
Christ,
3 in whom are hidden all the
treasures of wisdom and knowledge.
4 Now this I say lest anyone
should deceive you with persuasive words.
5 For though I am absent in
the flesh, yet I am with you in
spirit, rejoicing to see your
good order and the steadfastness of your faith in Christ.
6 As you therefore have received Christ Jesus the Lord,
so walk in Him,
7 rooted and built up in Him
and established in the faith, as
you have been taught, abounding in it with thanksgiving.
8 Beware lest anyone cheat
you through philosophy and
empty deceit, according to the

---

[a](2:2) NU omits *και Πατρος και του, both of the Father and.*

tradition of men, according to
the basic principles of the world,
and not according to Christ.
9 For in Him dwells all the
fullness of the Godhead bodily;
10 and you are complete in
Him, who is the head of all principality and power.
11 In Him you were also circumcised with the circumcision
made without hands, by putting
off the body of the sins of the
flesh, by the circumcision of
Christ,
12 buried with Him in baptism, in which you also were
raised with *Him* through faith in
the working of God, who raised
Him from the dead.
13 And you, being dead in
your trespasses and the uncircumcision of your flesh, He has
made alive together with Him,
having forgiven you all trespasses,
14 having wiped out the hand-
writing of requirements that
was against us, which was contrary to us. And He has taken it
out of the way, having nailed it
to the cross.
15 Having disarmed principalities and powers, He made a
public spectacle of them, triumphing over them in it.
16 So let no one judge you in
food or in drink, or regarding a
festival or a new moon or sabbaths,
17 which are a shadow of
things to come, but the substance is of Christ.
18 Let no one cheat you of
your reward, taking delight in
false humility and worship of angels, intruding into those things

---

[b](2:11) NU omits *των αμαρτιων, of the sins.*
[c](2:13) TR omits *υμας, you.*
[d](2:18) NU omits *μη, not.*

---

*(2:14) *χειρόγραφον* (*cheirographon*). Noun, used only here in the NT, from *χείρ, hand,* and *γράφω, write,* thus meaning *a (handwritten) document.* The word was a technical term referring to a signed *bill of indebtedness.* Such bonds were handwritten by the debtor so that they could not later be disputed. Thus, the word here implies a sense of awareness of one's sins and consequent indebtedness to God. The point is that this indebtedness has been canceled (for "wiped out," see *ἐξαλείφω* at Rev. 3:5) by its being nailed to the cross at Christ's crucifixion.

τῶν ἀνθρώπων, κατὰ τὰ στοιχεῖα τοῦ κόσμου καὶ οὐ
\- of men, according to the basic principles of the world and not

κατὰ Χριστόν. **9** *Ὅτι ἐν αὐτῷ κατοικεῖ πᾶν τὸ*
according to Christ. Because in Him dwells all the

Πλήρωμα τῆς Θεότητος σωματικῶς, **10** *καί ἐστε ἐν αὐτῷ*
Fullness of the Godhead bodily, and you are [2]in [3]Him

πεπληρωμένοι, ὅς ἐστιν ἡ κεφαλὴ πάσης ἀρχῆς καὶ
[1]completed, who is the head of every rule and

ἐξουσίας, **11** *ἐν ᾧ καὶ περιετμήθητε περιτομῇ*
authority, in whom also you were circumcised with *the* circumcision

ἀχειροποιήτῳ ἐν τῇ ἀπεκδύσει τοῦ σώματος τῶν
made without hands by the putting off of the body of the

ἁμαρτιῶν[b] *τῆς σαρκός, ἐν τῇ περιτομῇ τοῦ Χριστοῦ,*
sins of the flesh, by the circumcision - of Christ,

12 *συνταφέντες αὐτῷ ἐν τῷ βαπτίσματι, ἐν ᾧ*
having been buried together with Him in - baptism, in which

καὶ συνηγέρθητε διὰ τῆς πίστεως τῆς ἐνεργείας
also you were raised together through - faith of the working
in

τοῦ Θεοῦ τοῦ ἐγείραντος αὐτὸν ἐκ τῶν νεκρῶν. **13** *Καὶ*
\- of God the *One* having raised Him from the dead. And
who raised

ὑμᾶς, νεκροὺς ὄντας ἐν τοῖς παραπτώμασι καὶ τῇ ἀκροβυστίᾳ
you, dead ~ being in the trespasses and the uncircumcision
your

τῆς σαρκὸς ὑμῶν, συνεζωοποίησε ὑμᾶς[c] *σὺν αὐτῷ,*
\- of flesh ~ your, He made [2]alive [3]together [1]you with Him,

χαρισάμενος ἡμῖν πάντα τὰ παραπτώματα, **14** *ἐξαλείψας τὸ*
forgiving us all the trespasses, wiping out the
our

καθ' ἡμῶν χειρόγραφον τοῖς δόγμασιν ὃ ἦν*
[4]against [5]us [1]handwriting - [2]in [3]ordinances which was

ὑπεναντίον ἡμῖν, καὶ αὐτὸ ἦρκεν ἐκ τοῦ μέσου
contrary to us, and [3]it [1]has [2]taken out of the midst
way

προσηλώσας αὐτὸ τῷ σταυρῷ· **15** *ἀπεκδυσάμενος τὰς ἀρχὰς*
nailing it to the cross; having disarmed the rulers

καὶ τὰς ἐξουσίας ἐδειγμάτισεν ἐν παρρησίᾳ, θριαμβεύσας
and the authorities He exposed *them* with openness, triumphing over
powers He mocked them in public,

αὐτοὺς ἐν αὐτῷ.
them by it.

Follow Christ, Not Legalism

16 *Μὴ οὖν τις ὑμᾶς κρινέτω ἐν βρώσει ἢ ἐν*
[3]not [1]Therefore [5]anyone [7]you [2]do [4]let [6]judge in food or in

πόσει ἢ ἐν μέρει ἑορτῆς ἢ νουμηνίας ἢ σαββάτων,
drink or in *the* matter of a festival or of a new moon or of sabbaths,

17 *ἅ ἐστι σκιὰ τῶν μελλόντων, τὸ δὲ σῶμα*
which *things* is a shadow of the coming *things,* the ~ but body *is*
are

Χριστοῦ. **18** *Μηδεὶς ὑμᾶς καταβραβευέτω θέλων ἐν*
of Christ. [2]no [3]one [6]you [1]Let [4]rule [5]against desiring *to do so* in

ταπεινοφροσύνῃ καὶ θρησκείᾳ τῶν ἀγγέλων, ἃ
false humility and in worship of the angels, [3]*the* [4]*things* [5]which

μὴ[d] *ἑώρακεν ἐμβατεύων, εἰκῇ φυσιούμενος ὑπὸ τοῦ νοὸς*
[8]not [6]he [7]has [9]seen [1]intruding [2]into, in vain being puffed up by the mind
his carnal

τῆς σαρκὸς αὐτοῦ, 19 καὶ οὐ κρατῶν τὴν κεφαλήν, ἐξ
- of flesh ~ his, and not holding on to the head, from
mind,

οὗ πᾶν τὸ σῶμα, διὰ τῶν ἁφῶν καὶ συνδέσμων
which *is* all the body, through the joints and bonds
ligaments

ἐπιχορηγούμενον καὶ συμβιβαζόμενον, αὔξει τὴν αὔξησιν
supported and jointed together, grows *with* the growth

τοῦ Θεοῦ.
- of God.

20 Εἰ[e] ἀπεθάνετε σὺν Χριστῷ ἀπὸ τῶν στοιχείων τοῦ
If you died with Christ from the basic principles of the

κόσμου, τί, ὡς ζῶντες ἐν κόσμῳ, δογματίζεσθε,
world, why, as living in *the* world, do you submit to regulations,

21 "Μὴ ἅψῃ μηδὲ γεύσῃ μηδὲ θίγῃς," 22 ἅ ἐστι
"not ~ Do handle nor taste nor touch," which *things* is
are

πάντα εἰς φθορὰν τῇ ἀποχρήσει, κατὰ τὰ ἐντάλματα
all for corruption with the using, according to the commands

καὶ διδασκαλίας τῶν ἀνθρώπων? 23 Ἅτινά ἐστι λόγον
and teachings - of men? Which *things* is a word
indeed have a

μὲν ἔχοντα σοφίας ἐν ἐθελοθρησκίᾳ καὶ
indeed having of wisdom in self-imposed religion and
reputation

ταπεινοφροσύνῃ καὶ ἀφειδίᾳ σώματος, οὐκ ἐν τιμῇ τινι
false humility and severity *on the* body, *but* not in value ~ any
of

πρὸς πλησμονὴν τῆς σαρκός.
for indulgence of the flesh.
against

Seek Christ, Not Carnality

3 1 Εἰ οὖν συνηγέρθητε τῷ Χριστῷ, τὰ ἄνω
If therefore you were raised - with Christ, [2]the [3]*things* [4]above

ζητεῖτε, οὗ ὁ Χριστός ἐστιν ἐν δεξιᾷ τοῦ Θεοῦ
[1]seek, where - Christ is [2]at [3]*the* [4]right [5]*hand* - [6]of [7]God

καθήμενος. 2 Τὰ ἄνω φρονεῖτε, μὴ τὰ ἐπὶ τῆς
[1]sitting. [2]the [3]*things* [4]above [1]Mind, not the *things* on the

γῆς. 3 Ἀπεθάνετε γάρ, καὶ ἡ ζωὴ ὑμῶν κέκρυπται σὺν τῷ
earth. [2]you [3]died [1]For, and - life ~ your has been hidden with -
is

Χριστῷ ἐν τῷ Θεῷ. 4 Ὅταν ὁ Χριστὸς φανερωθῇ, ἡ ζωὴ
Christ in - God. Whenever - Christ is manifested, - life ~
appears,

ἡμῶν,[a] τότε καὶ ὑμεῖς σὺν αὐτῷ φανερωθήσεσθε ἐν δόξῃ.
our, then also ~ you with Him will be manifested in glory.
will appear

5 Νεκρώσατε οὖν τὰ μέλη ὑμῶν τὰ ἐπὶ τῆς γῆς·
Put to death therefore - members ~ your - on the earth:

πορνείαν, ἀκαθαρσίαν, πάθος, ἐπιθυμίαν κακήν, καὶ τὴν
sexual immorality, uncleanness, passion, desire ~ bad, and the

πλεονεξίαν* ἥτις ἐστὶν εἰδωλολατρεία, 6 δι' ἃ
greed which is idolatry, because of which *things*

ἔρχεται ἡ ὀργὴ τοῦ Θεοῦ ἐπὶ τοὺς υἱοὺς τῆς ἀπειθείας,
[5]is [6]coming [1]the [2]wrath - [3]of [4]God on the sons - of disobedience,

7 ἐν οἷς καὶ ὑμεῖς περιεπατήσατέ ποτε ὅτε ἐζῆτε ἐν
in which also you walked ~ once when you lived in

which he has not seen, vainly
puffed up by his fleshly mind,
19 and not holding fast to the
Head, from whom all the body,
nourished and knit together by
joints and ligaments, grows
with the increase *that is* from
God.
20 Therefore, if you died with
Christ from the basic principles
of the world, why, as *though*
living in the world, do you subject yourselves to regulations—
21 "Do not touch, do not
taste, do not handle,"
22 which all concern things
which perish with the using—
according to the command-
ments and doctrines of men?
23 These things indeed have
an appearance of wisdom in
self-imposed religion, *false* humility, and neglect of the body,
but are of no value against the
indulgence of the flesh.
3 If then you were raised
with Christ, seek those
things which are above, where
Christ is, sitting at the right
hand of God.
2 Set your mind on things
above, not on things on the earth.
3 For you died, and your life
is hidden with Christ in God.
4 When Christ *who is* our life
appears, then you also will appear with Him in glory.
5 Therefore put to death
your members which are on the
earth: fornication, uncleanness,
passion, evil desire, and covetousness, which is idolatry.
6 Because of these things
the wrath of God is coming
upon the sons of disobedience,
7 in which you yourselves
once walked when you lived in

---

e(2:20) TR adds *ουν, therefore.* *a*(3:4) NU reads *υμων, your.*

***(3:5)** *πλεονεξία (pleonexia).* Noun, from *πλέον, more,* and *ἔχω, have,* thus meaning the (inordinate) desire to have more, as seen in *covetousness, greed, avarice.* The word and its cognates appear always to imply a passion for gain at the expense of others. The NT links this sin with uncleanness (Eph. 4:19; 5:3) and identifies it as idolatry (here in Col. 3:5). In Mark 7:22 the word is plural, referring to various expressions of *greed.* In 2 Cor. 9:5 Paul refers to a gift given grudgingly because of one's *avarice.* Cf. the cognate noun

them.
8 But now you yourselves are to put off all these: anger, wrath, malice, blasphemy, filthy language out of your mouth.
9 Do not lie to one another, since you have put off the old man with his deeds,
10 and have put on the new *man* who is renewed in knowledge according to the image of Him who created him,
11 where there is neither Greek nor Jew, circumcised nor uncircumcised, barbarian, Scythian, slave *nor* free, but Christ *is* all and in all.
12 Therefore, as *the* elect of God, holy and beloved, put on tender mercies, kindness, humility, meekness, longsuffering;
13 bearing with one another, and forgiving one another, if anyone has a complaint against another; even as Christ forgave you, so you also *must do.*
14 But above all these things put on love, which is the bond of perfection.
15 And let the peace of God rule in your hearts, to which also you were called in one body; and be thankful.
16 Let the word of Christ dwell in you richly in all wisdom, teaching and admonishing one another in psalms and hymns and spiritual songs, singing with grace in your hearts to the Lord.
17 And *whatever* you do in word or deed, *do* all in the name of the Lord Jesus, giving thanks to God the Father through Him.

---

[b](3:13) NU reads ο Κυριος, *the Lord.* [c](3:15) NU reads Χριστου, *of Christ.* [d](3:16) NU reads Θεω, *God.*

πλεονέκτης, *greedy or covetous person* (1 Cor. 5:10, 11; Eph. 5:5); and the verb πλεονεκτέω, *take advantage of, cheat* (2 Cor. 2:11; 1 Thess. 4:6).

*(3:15) βραβεύω (*brabeuō*). Verb meaning *control, rule*. The basic sense of the word was *to award the prize* (βραβεῖον) in an athletic contest. This sense was broadened to include *judging* such contests and ultimately to *exercising control* over any situation. Here it is the control exercised by the "peace of God" over believers' thoughts that makes possible Christian unity. The noun βραβεῖον is used liter-

αὐτοῖς. 8 Νυνὶ δὲ ἀπόθεσθε καὶ ὑμεῖς τὰ πάντα· ὀργήν,
them. now ˜ But put off also ˜ you - all *things:* wrath,

θυμόν, κακίαν, βλασφημίαν, αἰσχρολογίαν ἐκ τοῦ στόματος
anger, malice, blasphemy, filthy language out of - mouth ˜
slander,

ὑμῶν. 9 Μὴ ψεύδεσθε εἰς ἀλλήλους, ἀπεκδυσάμενοι τὸν
your. not ˜ Do lie to one another, having stripped off the
since you have

παλαιὸν ἄνθρωπον σὺν ταῖς πράξεσιν αὐτοῦ, 10 καὶ
old man with - practices ˜ its, and

ἐνδυσάμενοι τὸν νέον τὸν ἀνακαινούμενον εἰς
having put on the new the *one which is* being renewed in
have

ἐπίγνωσιν κατ' εἰκόνα τοῦ κτίσαντος αὐτόν,
full knowledge according to *the* image of the One having created it,
Him who created

11 ὅπου οὐκ ἔνι Ἕλλην καὶ Ἰουδαῖος, περιτομὴ καὶ
where [3]not [1]there [2]is Greek and Jew, circumcision and

ἀκροβυστία, βάρβαρος, Σκύθης, δοῦλος, ἐλεύθερος, ἀλλὰ τὰ
uncircumcision, barbarian, Scythian, slave, free *person,* but -

πάντα καὶ ἐν πᾶσι Χριστός.
[3]all [4]*things* [5]and [6]in [7]all [8]*things* [1]Christ [2]*is.*

The Characteristics of Christ

12 Ἐνδύσασθε οὖν ὡς ἐκλεκτοὶ τοῦ Θεοῦ, ἅγιοι καὶ
Put on therefore as elect *ones* - of God, holy and

ἠγαπημένοι, σπλάγχνα οἰκτιρμοῦ, χρηστότητα,
beloved, bowels of compassion, kindness,

ταπεινοφροσύνην, πραότητα, μακροθυμίαν, 13 ἀνεχόμενοι
humility, meekness, longsuffering, putting up with
patience, forbearing

ἀλλήλων καὶ χαριζόμενοι ἑαυτοῖς ἐάν τις πρός τινα
one another and forgiving yourselves if anyone [5]against [6]anyone

ἔχῃ μομφήν· καθὼς καὶ ὁ Χριστὸς[b] ἐχαρίσατο ὑμῖν
[1]should [2]have [3]a [4]complaint; just as also - Christ forgave you

οὕτω καὶ ὑμεῖς· 14 ἐπὶ πᾶσι δὲ τούτοις τὴν ἀγάπην,
so also you *do;* [2]above [3]all [1]but these *things* - *put on* love,

ἥτις ἐστὶ σύνδεσμος τῆς τελειότητος. 15 Καὶ ἡ εἰρήνη τοῦ
which is *the* bond - of perfection. And [2]the [3]peace -
completeness.

Θεοῦ[c] βραβευέτω* ἐν ταῖς καρδίαις ὑμῶν, εἰς ἣν καὶ
[4]of [5]God [1]let [6]rule in - hearts ˜ your, to which also

ἐκλήθητε ἐν ἑνὶ σώματι· καὶ εὐχάριστοι γίνεσθε. 16 Ὁ
you were called in one body; and thankful ˜ be. [2]the

λόγος τοῦ Χριστοῦ ἐνοικείτω ἐν ὑμῖν πλουσίως, ἐν πάσῃ
[3]word - [4]of [5]Christ [1]Let [6]dwell in you richly, with all

σοφίᾳ διδάσκοντες καὶ νουθετοῦντες ἑαυτοὺς ψαλμοῖς καὶ
wisdom teaching and admonishing yourselves in psalms and

ὕμνοις καὶ ᾠδαῖς πνευματικαῖς ἐν χάριτι ᾄδοντες ἐν τῇ
hymns and songs ˜ spiritual [2]with [3]grace [1]singing in -

καρδίᾳ ὑμῶν τῷ Κυρίῳ.[d] 17 Καὶ πᾶν ὅ τι ἂν
heart ˜ your to the Lord. And every - *thing* what ever

ποιῆτε ἐν λόγῳ ἢ ἐν ἔργῳ, πάντα ἐν ὀνόματι Κυρίου
you may do in word or in work, *do* all *things* in *the* name of *the* Lord
deed,

Ἰησοῦ, εὐχαριστοῦντες τῷ Θεῷ καὶ Πατρὶ δι' αὐτοῦ.
Jesus, giving thanks to the God and Father through Him.

Serve Christ in Your Home

18 Αἱ γυναῖκες, ὑποτάσσεσθε τοῖς ἰδίοις ἀνδράσιν, ὡς
- Wives, subject yourselves - to your own husbands, as
ἀνῆκεν ἐν Κυρίῳ.
is fitting in *the* Lord.

19 Οἱ ἄνδρες, ἀγαπᾶτε τὰς γυναῖκας καὶ μὴ πικραίνεσθε
- Husbands, love the wives and not ˜ do be bitter
your
πρὸς αὐτάς.
toward them.

20 Τὰ τέκνα, ὑπακούετε τοῖς γονεῦσι κατὰ πάντα,
- Children, obey the parents with respect to all *things,*
your in
τοῦτο γάρ ἐστιν εὐάρεστον ἐν Κυρίῳ.
this ˜ for is well pleasing in *the* Lord.

21 Οἱ πατέρες, μὴ ἐρεθίζετε τὰ τέκνα ὑμῶν, ἵνα
- Fathers, not ˜ do provoke - children ˜ your, in order that
lest
μὴ ἀθυμῶσιν.
not they become discouraged.

22 Οἱ δοῦλοι, ὑπακούετε κατὰ πάντα τοῖς
- Bondservants, obey with respect to all *things* the
Slaves, in your
κατὰ σάρκα κυρίοις, μὴ ἐν ὀφθαλμοδουλείαις ὡς
[2]according [3]to [4]*the* [5]flesh [1]masters, not with eyeservice as
ἀνθρωπάρεσκοι, ἀλλ' ἐν ἁπλότητι καρδίας, φοβούμενοι τὸν
men-pleasers, but with singleness of heart, fearing -
sincerity
Θεόν.[e] 23 Καὶ πᾶν ὅ τι ἐὰν ποιῆτε, ἐκ ψυχῆς
God. And every - *thing* what ever you may do, from *your* soul
heartily
ἐργάζεσθε, ὡς τῷ Κυρίῳ καὶ οὐκ ἀνθρώποις, 24 εἰδότες ὅτι
work *it,* as to the Lord and not to men, knowing that
ἀπὸ Κυρίου λήψεσθε[f] τὴν ἀνταπόδοσιν τῆς κληρονομίας.
from *the* Lord you will receive the reward of the inheritance.
Τῷ γὰρ Κυρίῳ Χριστῷ δουλεύετε. 25 Ὁ δὲ ἀδικῶν
the ˜ For Lord Christ you serve. [2]the [3]*one* [1]But doing wrong
κομιεῖται ὃ ἠδίκησε, καὶ οὐκ ἔστι προσωποληψία.
will get back what he did wrong, and [3]not [1]*there* [2]is [4]partiality.

4 1 Οἱ κύριοι, τὸ δίκαιον καὶ τὴν ἰσότητα τοῖς δούλοις
- Masters, the just *thing* and the equality [2]to [3]the [4]slave
justice fairness to your
παρέχεσθε, εἰδότες ὅτι καὶ ὑμεῖς ἔχετε Κύριον ἐν οὐρανοῖς.
[1]provide, knowing that also ˜ you have a Master in *the* heavens.

Manifest Christlikeness

2 Τῇ προσευχῇ προσκαρτερεῖτε, γρηγοροῦντες ἐν αὐτῇ
- [3]in [4]prayer [1]Continue [2]earnestly, being vigilant in it
ἐν εὐχαριστίᾳ, 3 προσευχόμενοι ἅμα καὶ περὶ
with thanksgiving, praying at the same time also for
ἡμῶν, ἵνα ὁ Θεὸς ἀνοίξῃ ἡμῖν θύραν τοῦ λόγου, λαλῆσαι
us, that - God would open for us a door for the word, to speak
message,
τὸ μυστήριον τοῦ Χριστοῦ, δι' ὃ καὶ δέδεμαι,
the mystery - of Christ, because of which [3]also [1]I [2]have been bound,
am in chains,
4 ἵνα φανερώσω αὐτὸ ὡς δεῖ με λαλῆσαι.
that I may make manifest ˜ it as it is necessary *for* me to speak.
I ought

18 Wives, submit to your own husbands, as is fitting in the Lord.
19 Husbands, love your wives and do not be bitter toward them.
20 Children, obey your parents in all things, for this is well pleasing to the Lord.
21 Fathers, do not provoke your children, lest they become discouraged.
22 Bondservants, obey in all things your masters according to the flesh, not with eyeservice, as men-pleasers, but in sincerity of heart, fearing God.
23 And whatever you do, do it heartily, as to the Lord and not to men,
24 knowing that from the Lord you will receive the reward of the inheritance; for you serve the Lord Christ.
25 But he who does wrong will be repaid for what he has done, and there is no partiality.
4 Masters, give your bondservants what is just and fair, knowing that you also have a Master in heaven.
2 Continue earnestly in prayer, being vigilant in it with thanksgiving;
3 meanwhile praying also for us, that God would open to us a door for the word, to speak the mystery of Christ, for which I am also in chains,
4 that I may make it manifest, as I ought to speak.

---

[e](3:22) NU reads *τον Κυριον, the Lord.*
[f](3:24) NU reads *απολημψεσθε, you will get back.*

---

ally in 1 Cor. 9:24 for a prize in athletics, and figuratively in Phil. 3:14 for the Christian's reward for fulfilling God's call.

5 Walk in wisdom toward those *who are* outside, redeeming the time.
6 *Let* your speech always *be* with grace, seasoned with salt, that you may know how you ought to answer each one.
7 Tychicus, a beloved brother, faithful minister, and fellow servant in the Lord, will tell you all the news about me.
8 I am sending him to you for this very purpose, that he may know your circumstances and comfort your hearts,
9 with Onesimus, a faithful and beloved brother, who is *one* of you. They will make known to you all things which *are happening* here.
10 Aristarchus my fellow prisoner greets you, with Mark the cousin of Barnabas (about whom you received instructions: if he comes to you, welcome him),
11 and Jesus who is called Justus. These *are my* only fellow workers for the kingdom of God who are of the circumcision; they have proved to be a comfort to me.
12 Epaphras, who is *one* of you, a bondservant of Christ, greets you, always laboring fervently for you in prayers, that you may stand perfect and complete in all the will of God.
13 For I bear him witness that he has a great zeal for you, and

5 Ἐν σοφίᾳ περιπατεῖτε πρὸς τοὺς ἔξω, τὸν καιρὸν
In wisdom walk toward the *ones* outside, [3]the [4]season
outsiders, opportunity

ἐξαγοραζόμενοι. 6 Ὁ λόγος ὑμῶν πάντοτε ἐν χάριτι,
[1]buying [2]up. - *Let* word ˜ your always *be* with grace,

ἅλατι ἠρτυμένος, εἰδέναι πῶς δεῖ ὑμᾶς
[4]with [5]salt [1]having [2]been [3]seasoned, to know how it is necessary *for* you
seasoned, you ought

ἑνὶ ἑκάστῳ ἀποκρίνεσθαι.
[4]one [3]each [1]to [2]answer.

Servants of Christ Send Greetings

7 Τὰ κατ' ἐμὲ πάντα γνωρίσει ὑμῖν
the *things* with respect to me All [2]will [3]make [4]known [5]to [6]you
All my doings

Τυχικός, ὁ ἀγαπητὸς ἀδελφὸς καὶ πιστὸς διάκονος καὶ
[1]Tychicus, the beloved brother and faithful servant and

σύνδουλος ἐν Κυρίῳ, 8 ὃν ἔπεμψα πρὸς ὑμᾶς εἰς αὐτὸ
fellow slave in *the* Lord, whom I sent to you for itself ˜
am sending this very

τοῦτο, ἵνα γνῷ τὰ περὶ ὑμῶν[a] καὶ
this, that he may know the *things* concerning you and
thing,

παρακαλέσῃ τὰς καρδίας ὑμῶν, 9 σὺν Ὀνησίμῳ, τῷ πιστῷ
he may encourage - hearts ˜ your, with Onesimus, the faithful

καὶ ἀγαπητῷ ἀδελφῷ, ὅς ἐστιν ἐξ ὑμῶν. Πάντα ὑμῖν
and beloved brother, who is *one* of you. [7]all [5]to [6]you

γνωριοῦσι τὰ ὧδε.
[1]They [2]will [3]make [4]known the *things happening* here.

10 Ἀσπάζεται ὑμᾶς Ἀρίσταρχος ὁ συναιχμάλωτός μου, καὶ
[5]greets [6]you [1]Aristarchus - [3]fellow [4]prisoner [2]my, and

Μᾶρκος ὁ ἀνεψιὸς Βαρναβᾶ (περὶ οὗ ἐλάβετε ἐντολάς,
Mark the cousin of Barnabas (about whom you received orders,
instructions,

ἐὰν ἔλθῃ πρὸς ὑμᾶς, δέξασθε αὐτόν), 11 καὶ Ἰησοῦς ὁ
if he comes to you, receive him), and Jesus the *one*
welcome who is

λεγόμενος Ἰοῦστος, οἱ ὄντες ἐκ περιτομῆς· οὗτοι μόνοι
being called Justus, the *ones* being of *the* circumcision; these alone *are*
called who are

συνεργοὶ εἰς τὴν βασιλείαν τοῦ Θεοῦ, οἵτινες ἐγενήθησάν
fellow workers for the kingdom - of God, who became
proved to be

μοι παρηγορία. 12 Ἀσπάζεται ὑμᾶς Ἐπαφρᾶς ὁ ἐξ
to me a comfort. [2]greets [3]you [1]Epaphras, the *one* of
who is

ὑμῶν, δοῦλος Χριστοῦ, πάντοτε ἀγωνιζόμενος ὑπὲρ ὑμῶν
you, a bondservant of Christ, always struggling for you
slave

ἐν ταῖς προσευχαῖς, ἵνα στῆτε τέλειοι καὶ
in the prayers, that you may stand perfect and
his mature

πεπληρωμένοι[b] ἐν παντὶ θελήματι τοῦ Θεοῦ.
having been fulfilled in all *the* will - of God.
complete

13 Μαρτυρῶ γὰρ αὐτῷ ὅτι ἔχει ζῆλον[c] πολὺν ὑπὲρ
[2]I [3]bear [4]witness [1]For for him that he has zeal ˜ much for

---

[a](4:8) NU reads *γνωτε τα περι ημων, you may know the things concerning us.*
[b](4:12) NU reads *πεπληροφορημενοι, having been fully assured.*
[c](4:13) NU reads *πολυν πονον, much distress.*

ὑμῶν καὶ τῶν ἐν Λαοδικείᾳ καὶ τῶν ἐν Ἱεραπόλει.
you and the *ones* in Laodicea and the *ones* in Hierapolis.
those those

14 Ἀσπάζεται ὑμᾶς Λουκᾶς ὁ ἰατρὸς* ὁ ἀγαπητός, καὶ
[5]greets [6]you [1]Luke [2]the [4]physician - [3]beloved, also

Δημᾶς. 15 Ἀσπάσασθε τοὺς ἐν Λαοδικείᾳ ἀδελφοὺς καὶ
Demas. Greet the [2]in [3]Laodicea [1]brothers and

Νυμφᾶν καὶ τὴν κατ' οἶκον αὐτοῦ[d] ἐκκλησίαν. 16 Καὶ
Nymphas and the [2]in [4]house [3]his [1]church. And

ὅταν ἀναγνωσθῇ παρ' ὑμῖν ἡ ἐπιστολή, ποιήσατε ἵνα
whenever [3]is [4]read [5]before [6]you [1]the [2]letter, make that
this see

καὶ ἐν τῇ Λαοδικέων ἐκκλησίᾳ ἀναγνωσθῇ, καὶ τὴν
also in the [2]of [3]*the* [4]Laodiceans [1]church it is read, and [5]the [6]*one*

ἐκ Λαοδικείας ἵνα καὶ ὑμεῖς ἀναγνῶτε. 17 Καὶ εἴπατε
[7]from [8]Laodicea [1]that [3]also [2]you [4]read. And say

Ἀρχίππῳ, "Βλέπε τὴν διακονίαν ἣν παρέλαβες ἐν Κυρίῳ,
to Archippus, "See to the service which you received in *the* Lord,
ministry

ἵνα αὐτὴν πληροῖς."
that [3]it [1]you [2]fulfill."

18 Ὁ ἀσπασμὸς τῇ ἐμῇ χειρὶ Παύλου. Μνημονεύετέ
The greeting *is* - by my *own* hand of Paul. Remember

μου τῶν δεσμῶν. Ἡ χάρις μεθ' ὑμῶν. Ἀμήν.[e]
my - bonds. - Grace *be* with you. Amen.
chains. So be it.

those who are in Laodicea, and those in Hierapolis.
14 Luke the beloved physician and Demas greet you.
15 Greet the brethren who are in Laodicea, and Nymphas and the church that *is* in his house.
16 Now when this epistle is read among you, see that it is read also in the church of the Laodiceans, and that you likewise read the epistle from Laodicea.
17 And say to Archippus, "Take heed to the ministry which you have received in the Lord, that you may fulfill it."
18 This salutation by my own hand—Paul. Remember my chains. Grace *be* with you. Amen.

[d](**4:15**) NU reads αυτης, *her.* [e](**4:18**) NU omits Αμην, *Amen.*

***(4:14)** ἰατρός *(iatros).* Noun meaning *physician.* Although it appears in two proverbs (Mark 2:17; Luke 4:23), in the NT the word always has its literal sense of one who provides healing services. Here in Col. 4:14 it designates Luke's profession. Earlier attempts to show a preference for medical terminology in Luke-Acts, however, cannot be substantiated. Ignatius used the word figuratively of Christ as the "physician of body and soul" (ἰατρὸς σαρκικὸς καὶ πνευματικός, *Letter to the Ephesians* 7:2).

The First Epistle of Paul the Apostle to the
THESSALONIANS

ΠΡΟΣ ΘΕΣΣΑΛΟΝΙΚΕΙΣ Α
TO *THE* THESSALONIANS 1

Paul Greets the Thessalonian Church

1 Paul, Silvanus, and Timothy,

To the church of the Thessalonians in God the Father and the Lord Jesus Christ:

Grace to you and peace from God our Father and the Lord Jesus Christ.

2 We give thanks to God always for you all, making mention of you in our prayers,
3 remembering without ceasing your work of faith, labor of
love, and patience of hope in
our Lord Jesus Christ in the
sight of our God and Father,
4 knowing, beloved breth-
ren, your election by God.
5 For our gospel did not
come to you in word only, but
also in power, and in the Holy
Spirit and in much assurance,
as you know what kind of men
we were among you for your
sake.
6 And you became followers
of us and of the Lord, having
received the word in much affliction, with joy of the Holy
Spirit,
7 so that you became exam-

1 1 Παῦλος καὶ Σιλουανὸς καὶ Τιμόθεος,
Paul and Silvanus and Timothy,

Τῇ ἐκκλησίᾳ Θεσσαλονικέων ἐν Θεῷ Πατρὶ καὶ
To the church of *the* Thessalonians in God *the* Father and

Κυρίῳ Ἰησοῦ Χριστῷ·
the Lord Jesus Christ:

Χάρις ὑμῖν καὶ εἰρήνη[a] ἀπὸ Θεοῦ Πατρὸς ἡμῶν καὶ
Grace to you and peace from God Father ˜ our and

Κυρίου Ἰησοῦ Χριστοῦ.
the Lord Jesus Christ.

Paul Praises the Thessalonians' Example

2 Εὐχαριστοῦμεν τῷ Θεῷ πάντοτε περὶ πάντων
We give thanks - to God always concerning all ˜

ὑμῶν, μνείαν ὑμῶν ποιούμενοι ἐπὶ τῶν προσευχῶν ἡμῶν,
you, [2]mention [3]of [4]you [1]making in - prayers ˜ our,

3 ἀδιαλείπτως μνημονεύοντες ὑμῶν τοῦ ἔργου τῆς πίστεως καὶ
constantly remembering your - work - of faith and
mentioning

τοῦ κόπου τῆς ἀγάπης καὶ τῆς ὑπομονῆς τῆς ἐλπίδος τοῦ
- labor - of love and - perseverance - of hope -
endurance

Κυρίου ἡμῶν Ἰησοῦ Χριστοῦ ἔμπροσθεν τοῦ Θεοῦ καὶ
of Lord ˜ our Jesus Christ before - [2]God [3]and
in in the presence of

Πατρὸς ἡμῶν, 4 εἰδότες, ἀδελφοὶ ἠγαπημένοι ὑπὸ Θεοῦ, τὴν
[4]Father [1]our, knowing, brothers having been loved by God, -
who have

ἐκλογὴν ὑμῶν. 5 Ὅτι τὸ εὐαγγέλιον ἡμῶν οὐκ ἐγενήθη
election ˜ your. Because - gospel ˜ our not ˜ did come to be
selection did not come

εἰς ὑμᾶς ἐν λόγῳ μόνον, ἀλλὰ καὶ ἐν δυνάμει καὶ ἐν Πνεύματι
to you in word only, but also in power and in *the* Spirit ˜

Ἁγίῳ καὶ ἐν πληροφορίᾳ πολλῇ, καθὼς οἴδατε οἷοι
Holy and in [2]full [3]assurance [1]much, just as you know of what sort
with full conviction,

ἐγενήθημεν ἐν ὑμῖν δι' ὑμᾶς. 6 Καὶ ὑμεῖς μιμηταὶ
we were among you for the sake of you. And you [2]imitators
proved to be for your sake. followers

ἡμῶν ἐγενήθητε καὶ τοῦ Κυρίου, δεξάμενοι τὸν λόγον
[3]of [4]us [1]became and of the Lord, receiving the word
in that you received

ἐν θλίψει πολλῇ μετὰ χαρᾶς Πνεύματος Ἁγίου, 7 ὥστε
in affliction ˜ much with joy of *the* Spirit ˜ Holy, so that
during great trial

γενέσθαι ὑμᾶς τύπους[b] πᾶσι τοῖς πιστεύουσιν ἐν τῇ
[2]to [3]become [1]you examples to all the *ones* believing in -
you became patterns those who believe

[a](1:1) NU omits the rest of the verse. [b](1:7) NU reads *τυπον, an example.*

Μακεδονίᾳ καὶ τῇ Ἀχαΐᾳ. 8 Ἀφʼ ὑμῶν γὰρ
Macedonia and - Achaia. [2]from [3]you [1]For

ἐξήχηται ὁ λόγος τοῦ Κυρίου οὐ μόνον ἐν τῇ
[9]has [10]resounded [11]forth [4]the [5]word [6]of [7]the [8]Lord not only in -

Μακεδονίᾳ καὶ ἐν τῇ Ἀχαΐᾳ, ἀλλὰ καὶ ἐν παντὶ τόπῳ ἡ πίστις
Macedonia and in - Achaia, but also in every place - faith ˜

ὑμῶν ἡ πρὸς τὸν Θεὸν ἐξελήλυθεν, ὥστε μὴ χρείαν ἡμᾶς
your - toward - God has gone forth, so that [2]not [5]need [1]us
we have no

ἔχειν λαλεῖν τι. 9 Αὐτοὶ γὰρ περὶ ἡμῶν
[3]to [4]have to say anything. [3]themselves [1]For [5]about [6]us
need

ἀπαγγέλλουσιν ὁποίαν εἴσοδον ἔσχομεν πρὸς ὑμᾶς, καὶ
[2]they [4]report what kind of entrance we had to you, and

πῶς ἐπεστρέψατε πρὸς τὸν Θεὸν ἀπὸ τῶν εἰδώλων δουλεύειν
how you turned to - God from the idols to be a slave
serve

Θεῷ ζῶντι καὶ ἀληθινῷ, 10 καὶ ἀναμένειν τὸν Υἱὸν αὐτοῦ
to a [4]God [1]living [2]and [3]true, and to wait for - Son ˜ His
genuine,

ἐκ τῶν οὐρανῶν, ὃν ἤγειρεν ἐκ τῶν νεκρῶν,
out of the heavens, whom He raised out from the dead *ones*,
from heaven, from

Ἰησοῦν τὸν ῥυόμενον* ἡμᾶς ἀπὸ τῆς ὀργῆς τῆς ἐρχομένης.
Jesus the *One* delivering us from the wrath ˜ - coming.
who delivers

Paul's Conduct in Thessalonica

2 1 Αὐτοὶ γὰρ οἴδατε, ἀδελφοί, τὴν εἴσοδον
[3]yourselves [1]For [2]you know, brothers, - *regarding* entrance ˜

ἡμῶν τὴν πρὸς ὑμᾶς ὅτι οὐ κενὴ γέγονεν. 2 Ἀλλὰ[a]
our - to you that [3]not [7]vain [1]it [2]has [4]come [5]to [6]be. But

προπαθόντες καὶ ὑβρισθέντες, καθὼς οἴδατε,
suffering before and being insultingly treated, just as you know,
although we suffered before were

ἐν Φιλίπποις, ἐπαρρησιασάμεθα ἐν τῷ Θεῷ ἡμῶν λαλῆσαι
in Philippi, we made bold in - God ˜ our to speak
dared

πρὸς ὑμᾶς τὸ εὐαγγέλιον τοῦ Θεοῦ ἐν πολλῷ ἀγῶνι. 3 Ἡ
to you the gospel - of God in much struggle. -
with conflict.

γὰρ παράκλησις ἡμῶν οὐκ ἐκ πλάνης οὐδὲ ἐξ
For exhortation ˜ our *was* not from error nor from
urging

ἀκαθαρσίας οὔτε ἐν δόλῳ, 4 ἀλλὰ καθὼς δεδοκιμάσμεθα
uncleanness nor in deceit, but just as we have been approved
trickery,

ὑπὸ τοῦ Θεοῦ πιστευθῆναι τὸ εὐαγγέλιον οὕτω
by - God to be entrusted with the gospel thus
in this way

λαλοῦμεν, οὐχ ὡς ἀνθρώποις ἀρέσκοντες, ἀλλὰ τῷ Θεῷ τῷ
we speak, not as men ˜ pleasing, but - God the *One*
who is

δοκιμάζοντι τὰς καρδίας ἡμῶν. 5 Οὔτε γάρ ποτε ἐν λόγῳ
testing - hearts ˜ our. neither ˜ For ever [3]in [4]a [5]word
using flattering

κολακείας ἐγενήθημεν, καθὼς οἴδατε, οὔτε ἐν προφάσει
[6]of [7]flattery [1]were [2]we, just as you know, nor in a pretext
speech covering up

ples to all in Macedonia and
Achaia who believe.
8 For from you the word of
the Lord has sounded forth, not
only in Macedonia and Achaia,
but also in every place. Your
faith toward God has gone out,
so that we do not need to say
anything.
9 For they themselves de-
clare concerning us what manner of entry we had to you, and
how you turned to God from
idols to serve the living and
true God,
10 and to wait for His Son
from heaven, whom He raised
from the dead, *even* Jesus who
delivers us from the wrath to
come.
2 For you yourselves know,
brethren, that our coming
to you was not in vain.
2 But even after we had suffered before and were spitefully
treated at Philippi, as you
know, we were bold in our God
to speak to you the gospel of
God in much conflict.
3 For our exhortation *did* not
come from error or uncleanness, nor *was it* in deceit.
4 But as we have been ap-
proved by God to be entrusted
with the gospel, even so we
speak, not as pleasing men, but
God who tests our hearts.
5 For neither at any time
did we use flattering words, as
you know, nor a cloak for

---

[a](2:2) TR adds και, *even.*

***(1:10)** ῥύομαι *(rhyomai).* Verb with a variety of meaning ranging from *rescue, deliver* to *preserve, save.* ῥύομαι occurs infrequently in the NT, in contrast to the very common σώζω, *save* (see σώζω at Matt. 10:22). It often refers to deliverance from someone or something (cf. Matt. 6:13; 2 Tim. 4:17). Almost half of its NT occurrences are in quotations or allusions to the OT, in which God is the One who rescues or delivers (Matt. 27:43 and Ps. 22:8; Rom. 11:26 and Is. 59:20). It is used of deliverance that the Christian already enjoys (Col. 1:13), as well as that for which he hopes and waits (as here in 1 Thess. 1:10; also Rom. 11:26).

covetousness—God *is* witness.
6 Nor did we seek glory from
men, either from you or from
others, when we might have
made demands as apostles of
Christ.
7 But we were gentle among
you, just as a nursing *mother*
cherishes her own children.
8 So, affectionately longing
for you, we were well pleased
to impart to you not only the
gospel of God, but also our own
lives, because you had become
dear to us.
9 For you remember, brethren, our labor and toil; for laboring night and day, that we
might not be a burden to any of
you, we preached to you the
gospel of God.
10 You *are* witnesses, and
God *also,* how devoutly and
justly and blamelessly we be-
haved ourselves among you
who believe;
11 as you know how we ex-
horted, and comforted, and
charged every one of you, as a
father *does* his own children,
12 that you would walk worthy of God who calls you into
His own kingdom and glory.
13 For this reason we also
thank God without ceasing, because when you received the
word of God which you heard
from us, you welcomed *it* not *as*
the word of men, but as it is in
truth, the word of God, which

πλεονεξίας, Θεὸς μάρτυς, **6** οὔτε ζητοῦντες ἐξ
of covetousness, God *is our* witness, nor *were we* seeking [2]from
greed,

ἀνθρώπων δόξαν, οὔτε ἀφ' ὑμῶν οὔτε ἀπὸ ἄλλων,
[3]men [1]glory, neither from you nor from others,

δυνάμενοι ἐν βάρει εἶναι ὡς Χριστοῦ ἀπόστολοι,
being able in weight to be as [2]of [3]Christ [1]apostles,
even though we were able to carry weight

7 ἀλλ' ἐγενήθημεν ἤπιοι[b] ἐν μέσῳ ὑμῶν, ὡς ἂν τροφὸς
but we were gentle in midst ˜ your, as - a nurse
we proved to be nursing mother

θάλπῃ τὰ ἑαυτῆς τέκνα. **8** Οὕτως ὁμειρόμενοι ὑμῶν,
cherishes the [2]of [3]herself [1]children. Thus longing for you,
her own In this way

εὐδοκοῦμεν μεταδοῦναι ὑμῖν οὐ μόνον τὸ εὐαγγέλιον
we were well pleased to impart to you not only the gospel

τοῦ Θεοῦ, ἀλλὰ καὶ τὰς ἑαυτῶν ψυχάς, διότι ἀγαπητοὶ
- of God, but also the [2]of [3]ourselves [1]lives, because [4]beloved
our own selves, dear

ἡμῖν γεγένησθε.[c] **9** Μνημονεύετε γάρ, ἀδελφοί, τὸν κόπον
[5]to [6]us [1]you [2]had [3]become. [2]you [3]remember [1]For, brothers, - labor ˜

ἡμῶν καὶ τὸν μόχθον· νυκτὸς γὰρ καὶ ἡμέρας ἐργαζόμενοι
our and - toil; [3]of [4]night [1]for [5]and [6]day [2]working
by

πρὸς τὸ μὴ ἐπιβαρῆσαί τινα ὑμῶν, ἐκηρύξαμεν εἰς ὑμᾶς
so that - not to burden any of you, we proclaimed to you
we might not be a burden to

τὸ εὐαγγέλιον τοῦ Θεοῦ. **10** Ὑμεῖς μάρτυρες καὶ ὁ Θεός,
the gospel - of God. You *are* witnesses and *so is* - God,

ὡς ὁσίως καὶ δικαίως καὶ ἀμέμπτως ὑμῖν τοῖς
how devoutly and righteously and blamelessly [3]to [4]you [5]the [6]*ones*
justly who

πιστεύουσιν ἐγενήθημεν, **11** καθάπερ οἴδατε ὡς ἕνα
[7]believing [1]we [2]were, as indeed you know how one ˜
believe we proved to be,

ἕκαστον ὑμῶν ὡς πατὴρ τέκνα ἑαυτοῦ, παρακαλοῦντες ὑμᾶς
each of you as a father children of himself, exhorting you
his own children, we exhorted

καὶ παραμυθούμενοι καὶ μαρτυρόμενοι[d] **12** εἰς τὸ
and comforting *you* and imploring *you* for -
comforted that you

περιπατῆσαι ὑμᾶς ἀξίως τοῦ Θεοῦ τοῦ καλοῦντος ὑμᾶς
[2]to [3]walk [1]you worthily - of God the *One* calling you
would make your walk worthy who calls

εἰς τὴν ἑαυτοῦ βασιλείαν καὶ δόξαν.
into the [2]of [3]Himself [1]kingdom and glory.
His own

The Conversion of the Thessalonians

13 Διὰ τοῦτο καὶ ἡμεῖς εὐχαριστοῦμεν τῷ Θεῷ
Because of this also ˜ we give thanks - to God

ἀδιαλείπτως, ὅτι παραλαβόντες λόγον ἀκοῆς παρ' ἡμῶν
unceasingly, that receiving a word of hearing from us
regularly, when you received the word of God which you

τοῦ Θεοῦ, ἐδέξασθε οὐ λόγον ἀνθρώπων, ἀλλὰ καθὼς
- of God, you received not *the* word of men, but just as
heard from us,

ἐστιν ἀληθῶς, λόγον Θεοῦ, ὃς καὶ ἐνεργεῖται ἐν ὑμῖν
it is ˜ truly, *the* word of God, which also is at work in you
among

[b](2:7) NU reads νηπιοι, *infants.* [c](2:8) NU reads εγενηθητε, *you became.* [d](2:11) TR reads μαρτυρουμενοι, *bearing witness (to you).*

τοῖς πιστεύουσιν. 14 Ὑμεῖς γὰρ μιμηταὶ ἐγενήθητε,
the *ones* believing. you ~ For imitators ~ became,
who believe. followers

ἀδελφοί, τῶν ἐκκλησιῶν τοῦ Θεοῦ τῶν οὐσῶν ἐν τῇ
brothers, of the churches - of God the *ones* being in -
which are

Ἰουδαίᾳ ἐν Χριστῷ Ἰησοῦ, ὅτι τὰ αὐτὰ ἐπάθετε
Judea in Christ Jesus, because [3]the [4]same [5]*things* [1]you [2]suffered

καὶ ὑμεῖς ὑπὸ τῶν ἰδίων συμφυλετῶν καθὼς καὶ αὐτοὶ
even you by - your own fellow countrymen just as also they *did*

ὑπὸ τῶν Ἰουδαίων, 15 τῶν καὶ τὸν Κύριον ἀποκτεινάντων
by the Jews, the *ones* [2]both [3]the [4]Lord [1]killing
Judeans, who killed

Ἰησοῦν καὶ τοὺς ἰδίους[e] προφήτας, καὶ ἡμᾶς ἐκδιωξάντων,
Jesus and - their own prophets, and us ~ persecuting,
have persecuted,

καὶ Θεῷ μὴ ἀρεσκόντων, καὶ πᾶσιν ἀνθρώποις ἐναντίων,
and [3]God [1]not [2]pleasing, and *are* [2]all [3]men [1]against,
do not please,

16 κωλυόντων ἡμᾶς τοῖς ἔθνεσι λαλῆσαι ἵνα
forbidding us [3]to [4]the [5]Gentiles [1]to [2]speak so that
hindering from speaking

σωθῶσιν, εἰς τὸ ἀναπληρῶσαι αὐτῶν τὰς ἁμαρτίας
they may be saved, for - to fill up *the measure of* their - sins
so as

πάντοτε. Ἔφθασε δὲ ἐπ' αὐτοὺς ἡ ὀργὴ εἰς τέλος.
always. [6]came [1]But [7]upon [8]them [2]the [3]wrath [4]*of* [5]*God* to *the* end.
has come utmost.

Paul Longs to See the Thessalonians

17 Ἡμεῖς δέ, ἀδελφοί, ἀπορφανισθέντες ἀφ' ὑμῶν πρὸς
we ~ But brothers, being taken as orphans from you for
unwillingly separated

καιρὸν ὥρας, προσώπῳ οὐ καρδίᾳ, περισσοτέρως
a time of an hour, in face not in heart, [2]all [3]the [4]more
a short season, made

ἐσπουδάσαμεν τὸ πρόσωπον ὑμῶν ἰδεῖν ἐν πολλῇ ἐπιθυμίᾳ.
[1]were [5]eager - [4]face [3]your [1]to [2]see with much desire.
every effort

18 Διὸ[f] ἠθελήσαμεν ἐλθεῖν πρὸς ὑμᾶς, ἐγὼ μὲν Παῦλος
Therefore we desired to come to you, I - Paul

καὶ ἅπαξ καὶ δίς, καὶ ἐνέκοψεν* ἡμᾶς ὁ Σατανᾶς. 19 Τίς
both once and twice, and [2]hindered [3]us - [1]Satan. what ~
time and again, but

γὰρ ἡμῶν ἐλπὶς ἢ χαρὰ ἢ στέφανος καυχήσεως? Ἢ οὐχὶ
For *is* our hope or joy or crown of boasting? Or *are* not

καὶ ὑμεῖς, ἔμπροσθεν τοῦ Κυρίου ἡμῶν Ἰησοῦ[g] ἐν τῇ
even you, before - Lord ~ our Jesus at -
in the presence of

αὐτοῦ παρουσίᾳ? 20 Ὑμεῖς γάρ ἐστε ἡ δόξα ἡμῶν καὶ ἡ
His coming? you ~ For are - glory ~ our and -

χαρά.
joy.

Paul's Anxiety in Athens

3 1 Διὸ μηκέτι στέγοντες, εὐδοκήσαμεν
Therefore no longer enduring, we were well pleased
when we could no longer endure it,

also effectively works in you
who believe.
14 For you, brethren, became
imitators of the churches of
God which are in Judea in
Christ Jesus. For you also suffered the same things from
your own countrymen, just as
they *did* from the Judeans,
15 who killed both the Lord
Jesus and their own prophets,
and have persecuted us; and
they do not please God and are
contrary to all men,
16 forbidding us to speak to
the Gentiles that they may be
saved, so as always to fill up *the*
measure of their sins; but wrath
has come upon them to the uttermost.
17 But we, brethren, having
been taken away from you for a
short time in presence, not in
heart, endeavored more eagerly to see your face with
great desire.
18 Therefore we wanted to
come to you—even I, Paul,
time and again—but Satan hindered us.
19 For what *is* our hope, or
joy, or crown of rejoicing? *Is it*
not even you in the presence of
our Lord Jesus Christ at His
coming?
20 For you are our glory and
joy.
3 Therefore, when we
could no longer endure it,
we thought it good to be left in

---

[e](2:15) NU omits ιδιους, *their own,* thus reading *the prophets.* [f](2:18) NU reads Διοτι, *For.* [g](2:19) TR adds Χριστου, *Christ.*

*(2:18) ἐγκόπτω *(enkoptō).* Verb meaning *hinder, restrain, impede,* typically by an obstacle that might be overcome. Here and in Rom. 15:22 Paul was *hindered* from carrying out travel plans. In Gal. 5:7 someone *held back* the Galatians from continuing spiritual advancement. According to 1 Pet. 3:7, prayers may be *hindered* if husbands fail to honor their wives. The context in Acts 24:4 suggests the specialized meaning *to weary* found in the LXX, although it might possibly mean *delay.* Cf. the cognate noun ἐγκοπή, *hindrance, restraint* (only in 1 Cor. 9:12).

Athens alone,
2 and sent Timothy, our
brother and minister of God,
and our fellow laborer in the
gospel of Christ, to establish
you and encourage you concerning your faith,
3 that no one should be
shaken by these afflictions; for
you yourselves know that we
are appointed to this.
4 For, in fact, we told you
before when we were with you
that we would suffer tribulation,
just as it happened, and you
know.
5 For this reason, when I
could no longer endure it, I sent
to know your faith, lest by
some means the tempter had
tempted you, and our labor
might be in vain.
6 But now that Timothy has
come to us from you, and
brought us good news of your
faith and love, and that you always have good remembrance
of us, greatly desiring to see
us, as we also *to see* you—
7 therefore, brethren, in all
our affliction and distress we
were comforted concerning you
by your faith.
8 For now we live, if you
stand fast in the Lord.
9 For what thanks can we
render to God for you, for all
the joy with which we rejoice
for your sake before our God,
10 night and day praying exceedingly that we may see your

καταλειφθῆναι ἐν Ἀθήναις μόνοι, **2** καὶ ἐπέμψαμεν Τιμόθεον,
to be left behind in Athens alone, and we sent Timothy,

τὸν ἀδελφὸν ἡμῶν καὶ διάκονον[a] τοῦ Θεοῦ καὶ συνεργὸν
- brother ˜ our and servant - of God and [2]fellow [3]worker
minister

ἡμῶν ἐν τῷ εὐαγγελίῳ τοῦ Χριστοῦ, εἰς τὸ στηρίξαι ὑμᾶς
[1]our in the gospel - of Christ, for - to establish you
in order

καὶ παρακαλέσαι ὑμᾶς περὶ τῆς πίστεως ὑμῶν **3** τὸ
and to encourage you concerning - faith ˜ your - *that*

μηδένα σαίνεσθαι ἐν ταῖς θλίψεσι ταύταις. Αὐτοὶ γὰρ
no one to be disturbed by - afflictions ˜ these. [3]yourselves [1]For
should trials

οἴδατε ὅτι εἰς τοῦτο κείμεθα. **4** Καὶ γὰρ ὅτε πρὸς
[2]you [4]know that for this we are appointed. even ˜ For when [3]with

ὑμᾶς ἦμεν, προελέγομεν ὑμῖν ὅτι μέλλομεν
[4]you [1]we [2]were, we were telling [2]in [3]advance [1]you that we are going
were

θλίβεσθαι, καθὼς καὶ ἐγένετο καὶ οἴδατε. **5** Διὰ τοῦτο
to be afflicted, just as also it happened and you know. Because of this

κἀγὼ μηκέτι στέγων, ἔπεμψα εἰς τὸ γνῶναι
I also no longer enduring, sent for - to know
when I could no longer endure, in order to learn about

τὴν πίστιν ὑμῶν, μή πως ἐπείρασεν ὑμᾶς ὁ πειράζων
- faith ˜ your, lest somehow [4]tempted [5]you [1]the [2]*one* [3]tempting
the tempter

καὶ εἰς κενὸν γένηται ὁ κόπος ἡμῶν.
and [6]in [7]vain [3]come [4]to [5]be - [2]labor [1]our.
for nothing

Paul Is Encouraged Through Timothy

6 Ἄρτι δὲ ἐλθόντος Τιμοθέου πρὸς ἡμᾶς ἀφ' ὑμῶν καὶ
now ˜ But coming ˜ Timothy to us from you and
when Timothy came

εὐαγγελισαμένου ἡμῖν τὴν πίστιν καὶ τὴν ἀγάπην
bringing good news to us *regarding* - [2]faith [3]and - [4]love
brought

ὑμῶν, καὶ ὅτι ἔχετε μνείαν ἡμῶν ἀγαθὴν πάντοτε,
[1]your, and that you have [2]remembrance [3]of [4]us [1]good always,

ἐπιποθοῦντες ἡμᾶς ἰδεῖν καθάπερ καὶ ἡμεῖς ὑμᾶς,
longing [3]us [1]to [2]see as indeed also ˜ we *long to see* you,

7 διὰ τοῦτο παρεκλήθημεν, ἀδελφοί, ἐφ' ὑμῖν ἐπὶ
because of this we were encouraged, brothers, in regard to you in

πάσῃ τῇ θλίψει καὶ ἀνάγκῃ ἡμῶν διὰ τῆς ὑμῶν
all - [2]affliction [3]and [4]distress [1]our by means of - your

πίστεως. **8** Ὅτι νῦν ζῶμεν ἐὰν ὑμεῖς στήκετε ἐν Κυρίῳ.
faith. Because now we live if you stand firm in *the* Lord.

9 Τίνα γὰρ εὐχαριστίαν δυνάμεθα τῷ Θεῷ ἀνταποδοῦναι
what ˜ For thanksgiving are we able - [5]to [6]God [1]to [2]give [3]in [4]return
to render

περὶ ὑμῶν ἐπὶ πάσῃ τῇ χαρᾷ ᾗ χαίρομεν
concerning you for all the joy with which we are rejoicing

δι' ὑμᾶς ἔμπροσθεν τοῦ Θεοῦ ἡμῶν, **10** νυκτὸς καὶ
because of you before - God ˜ our, of night and
in the presence of by

ἡμέρας ὑπερεκπερισσοῦ δεόμενοι εἰς τὸ ἰδεῖν ὑμῶν τὸ
day beyond all measure praying for - to see your -
in order

---

[a](3:2) NU reads συνεργον, *fellow worker,* and omits the following και συνεργον ημων, *and our fellow worker.*

πρόσωπον καὶ καταρτίσαι τὰ ὑστερήματα τῆς πίστεως
face and to make complete the shortcomings - of faith ~
what is lacking in

ὑμῶν?
your?

Paul's Wish for the Thessalonians

11 Αὐτὸς δὲ ὁ Θεὸς καὶ Πατὴρ ἡμῶν, καὶ ὁ Κύριος
[7]Himself [1]Now [2]*may* - [4]God [5]and [6]Father [3]our, and - Lord ~

ἡμῶν Ἰησοῦς Χριστός,[b] κατευθύναι τὴν ὁδὸν ἡμῶν πρὸς
our Jesus Christ, make straight - way ~ our to
lead us directly

ὑμᾶς. 12 Ὑμᾶς δὲ ὁ Κύριος πλεονάσαι καὶ
you. [6]you [1]And [2]*may* [3]the [4]Lord [5]make to increase and

περισσεύσαι τῇ ἀγάπῃ εἰς ἀλλήλους καὶ εἰς πάντας, καθάπερ
to abound - in love for one another and for all *people,* as indeed

καὶ ἡμεῖς εἰς ὑμᾶς, 13 εἰς τὸ στηρίξαι ὑμῶν τὰς καρδίας
also ~ we *do* for you, for - to establish your - hearts
in order

ἀμέμπτους ἐν ἁγιωσύνῃ ἔμπροσθεν τοῦ Θεοῦ καὶ Πατρὸς
to be blameless in holiness before - [2]God [3]and [4]Father

ἡμῶν ἐν τῇ παρουσίᾳ τοῦ Κυρίου ἡμῶν Ἰησοῦ Χριστοῦ[c] μετὰ
[1]our at the coming - of Lord ~ our Jesus Christ with

πάντων τῶν ἁγίων αὐτοῦ.
all - saints ~ His.

Paul Pleads for Purity

4 1 Λοιπὸν οὖν, ἀδελφοί, ἐρωτῶμεν ὑμᾶς καὶ
For the rest then, brothers, we request of you and
Finally

παρακαλοῦμεν ἐν Κυρίῳ Ἰησοῦ καθὼς παρελάβετε παρ' ἡμῶν
exhort *you* in *the* Lord Jesus just as you received from us

τὸ πῶς δεῖ ὑμᾶς περιπατεῖν καὶ ἀρέσκειν Θεῷ,[a]
- how it is necessary *for* you to walk and to please God,
you ought

ἵνα περισσεύητε μᾶλλον. 2 Οἴδατε γὰρ τίνας παραγγελίας
that you should abound more. [2]you [3]know [1]For what commandments
instructions

ἐδώκαμεν ὑμῖν διὰ τοῦ Κυρίου Ἰησοῦ. 3 Τοῦτο γάρ ἐστι
we gave you through the Lord Jesus. this ~ For is

θέλημα τοῦ Θεοῦ, ὁ ἁγιασμὸς* ὑμῶν, ἀπέχεσθαι ὑμᾶς ἀπὸ
the will - of God, - sanctification ~ your, [2]to [3]abstain [1]you from
that you abstain

τῆς πορνείας, 4 εἰδέναι ἕκαστον ὑμῶν τὸ ἑαυτοῦ
- fornication, to know each *one* of you [3]the [5]of [6]himself
sexual immorality, that each of you know how to possess

σκεῦος κτᾶσθαι ἐν ἁγιασμῷ καὶ τιμῇ, 5 μὴ ἐν πάθει
[4]vessel [1]to [2]possess in sanctification and honor, not in *the* passion
his own vessel lustful

ἐπιθυμίας, καθάπερ καὶ τὰ ἔθνη τὰ μὴ εἰδότα τὸν Θεόν,
of desire, just as also the Gentiles the *ones* not knowing - God,
passion, who do not know

6 τὸ μὴ ὑπερβαίνειν καὶ πλεονεκτεῖν ἐν τῷ πράγματι τὸν
- *so as* not to overstep and to defraud [3]in [4]the [5]matter -
transgress against this

ἀδελφὸν αὐτοῦ, διότι ἔκδικος ὁ Κύριος περὶ πάντων
[2]brother [1]his, because [4]*the* [5]avenger [1]the [2]Lord [3]*is* concerning all

τούτων, καθὼς καὶ προείπαμεν ὑμῖν καὶ διεμαρτυράμεθα.
these *things,* just as also ~ we told before ~ you and solemnly testified.

face and perfect what is lacking in your faith?
11 Now may our God and Father Himself, and our Lord Jesus Christ, direct our way to you.
12 And may the Lord make you increase and abound in love to one another and to all, just as we *do* to you,
13 so that He may establish your hearts blameless in holiness before our God and Father at the coming of our Lord Jesus Christ with all His saints.
4 Finally then, brethren, we urge and exhort in the Lord Jesus that you should abound more and more, just as you received from us how you ought to walk and to please God;
2 for you know what commandments we gave you through the Lord Jesus.
3 For this is the will of God, your sanctification: that you should abstain from sexual immorality;
4 that each of you should know how to possess his own vessel in sanctification and honor,
5 not in passion of lust, like the Gentiles who do not know God;
6 that no one should take advantage of and defraud his brother in this matter, because the Lord *is* the avenger of all such, as we also forewarned you and testified.

---

b(3:11) NU omits Χριστος, *Christ.* c(3:13) NU omits Χριστος, *Christ.*
a(4:1) NU adds καθως και περιπατειτε, *just as indeed you do walk.*

***(4:3)** ἁγιασμός *(hagiasmos).* Noun meaning *sanctification.* It may refer to sanctification as the active work that brings about holiness (2 Thess. 2:13) or to the result of that work, in which case it might be translated *holiness* (Heb. 12:14). Interpreters debate which of these senses is found in particular occurrences in the NT. Cf. the cognate adjective ἅγιος, *holy;* verb ἁγιάζω, *sanctify, consecrate, make holy;* and noun ἁγιωσύνη, *holiness.* At the root of all of these words is the idea of being set apart or consecrated to God and thus peculiarly His. Separation from moral defilement is included in the meaning.

7 For God did not call us to
uncleanness, but in holiness.
8 Therefore he who rejects
this does not reject man, but
God, who has also given us His
Holy Spirit.
9 But concerning brotherly
love you have no need that I
should write to you, for you
yourselves are taught by God
to love one another;
10 and indeed you do so toward all the brethren who are in
all Macedonia. But we urge
you, brethren, that you increase more and more;
11 that you also aspire to lead
a quiet life, to mind your own
business, and to work with
your own hands, as we commanded you,
12 that you may walk properly
toward those who are outside,
and *that* you may lack nothing.
13 But I do not want you to be
ignorant, brethren, concerning
those who have fallen asleep,
lest you sorrow as others who
have no hope.
14 For if we believe that Jesus
died and rose again, even so
God will bring with Him those
who sleep in Jesus.
15 For this we say to you by
the word of the Lord, that we
who are alive *and* remain until
the coming of the Lord will by
no means precede those who
are asleep.

7 Οὐ γὰρ ἐκάλεσεν ἡμᾶς ὁ Θεὸς ἐπὶ ἀκαθαρσίᾳ, ἀλλ' ἐν
[5]not [1]For [3]called [4]us - [2]God for uncleanness, but in

ἁγιασμῷ. **8** Τοιγαροῦν ὁ ἀθετῶν οὐκ ἄνθρωπον
sanctification. Therefore the *one* rejecting *this* [2]not [4]a [5]man
holiness.

ἀθετεῖ, ἀλλὰ τὸν Θεὸν τὸν καὶ δόντα[b] τὸ Πνεῦμα
[1]is [3]rejecting, but - God the *One* also having given - [3]Spirit
who has

αὐτοῦ τὸ Ἅγιον εἰς ὑμᾶς.[c]
[1]His - [2]Holy to you.

A Brotherly and Orderly Life

9 Περὶ δὲ τῆς φιλαδελφίας οὐ χρείαν ἔχετε
concerning ˜ Now - brotherly love [3]not [5]need [1]you [2]do [4]have

γράφειν ὑμῖν, αὐτοὶ γὰρ ὑμεῖς θεοδίδακτοί ἐστε εἰς
for me to write to you, [3]yourselves [1]for [2]you [5]taught [6]by [7]God [4]are -

τὸ ἀγαπᾶν ἀλλήλους. **10** Καὶ γὰρ ποιεῖτε αὐτὸ εἰς
- to love one another. indeed ˜ For you are doing it toward

πάντας τοὺς ἀδελφοὺς τοὺς ἐν ὅλῃ τῇ Μακεδονίᾳ.
all the brothers - in whole ˜ the Macedonia.
all

Παρακαλοῦμεν δὲ ὑμᾶς, ἀδελφοί, περισσεύειν μᾶλλον,
[2]we [3]urge [1]But you, brothers, to increase more,

11 καὶ φιλοτιμεῖσθαι ἡσυχάζειν καὶ πράσσειν τὰ
and to have as your ambition to be quiet and to practice -
aspire mind your

ἴδια καὶ ἐργάζεσθαι ταῖς ἰδίαις χερσὶν ὑμῶν, καθὼς
your own *things* and to work - with [2]own [3]hands [1]your, just as
own affairs

ὑμῖν παρηγγείλαμεν, **12** ἵνα περιπατῆτε εὐσχημόνως
[3]you [1]we [2]commanded, in order that you may walk becomingly
decently

πρὸς τοὺς ἔξω καὶ μηδενὸς χρείαν ἔχητε.
toward the *ones* outside and [4]of [5]nothing [3]need [1]may [2]have.

The Comfort of Christ's Coming

13 Οὐ θέλομεν[d] δὲ ὑμᾶς ἀγνοεῖν, ἀδελφοί,
[4]not [2]we [3]do [5]desire [1]Now you to be ignorant, brothers,
uninformed,

περὶ τῶν κεκοιμημένων, ἵνα μὴ λυπῆσθε καθὼς
concerning the *ones* having fallen asleep, that not ˜ you be sorrowful as
those who have died, lest

καὶ οἱ λοιποὶ οἱ μὴ ἔχοντες ἐλπίδα. **14** Εἰ γὰρ
also the rest the *ones* not having hope. if ˜ For
who have no

πιστεύομεν ὅτι Ἰησοῦς ἀπέθανε καὶ ἀνέστη, οὕτω καὶ ὁ Θεὸς
we believe that Jesus died and rose, thus also - God

τοὺς κοιμηθέντας διὰ τοῦ Ἰησοῦ ἄξει σὺν αὐτῷ.
[3]the [4]*ones* [5]falling [6]asleep [7]through - [8]Jesus [1]will [2]bring with Him.
those who die in

15 Τοῦτο γὰρ ὑμῖν λέγομεν ἐν λόγῳ Κυρίου, ὅτι ἡμεῖς
this ˜ For [3]to [4]you [1]we [2]say by a word of *the* Lord, that we

οἱ ζῶντες οἱ περιλειπόμενοι εἰς τὴν παρουσίαν τοῦ
the *ones* living the *ones* remaining to the coming of the
who are who are

Κυρίου οὐ μὴ φθάσωμεν τοὺς κοιμηθέντας.
Lord not not will come before the *ones* falling asleep.
by no means will precede those who are dead.

---

[b](4:8) NU reads διδοντα, *(who also) is giving.*
[c](4:8) TR reads ημας, *us.*
[d](4:13) TR reads θελω, *I do (not) desire.*

16 Ὅτι αὐτὸς ὁ Κύριος ἐν κελεύσματι, ἐν φωνῇ
Because [3]Himself [1]the [2]Lord with a cry of command, with *the* voice
ἀρχαγγέλου καὶ ἐν σάλπιγγι Θεοῦ, καταβήσεται ἀπ᾽
of an archangel and with *the* trumpet of God, will descend from
οὐρανοῦ, καὶ οἱ νεκροὶ ἐν Χριστῷ ἀναστήσονται πρῶτον,
heaven, and the dead *ones* in Christ will rise first,
17 ἔπειτα ἡμεῖς οἱ ζῶντες οἱ περιλειπόμενοι, ἅμα
then we the *ones* living the *ones* remaining, [5]together
who are who are
σὺν αὐτοῖς ἁρπαγησόμεθα* ἐν νεφέλαις εἰς ἀπάντησιν τοῦ
[6]with [7]them [1]will [2]be [3]caught [4]up in *the* clouds for a meeting of the
to meet the
Κυρίου εἰς ἀέρα. Καὶ οὕτω πάντοτε σὺν Κυρίῳ
Lord in *the* air. And thus [3]always [5]with [6]*the* [7]Lord
in this way
ἐσόμεθα. 18 Ὥστε παρακαλεῖτε ἀλλήλους ἐν τοῖς λόγοις
[1]we [2]will [4]be. So then comfort one another with - words ˜
τούτοις.
these.

The Day of the Lord

5 1 Περὶ δὲ τῶν χρόνων καὶ τῶν καιρῶν, ἀδελφοί, οὐ
concerning ˜ Now the times and the seasons, brothers, [3]not
χρείαν ἔχετε ὑμῖν γράφεσθαι.
[5]need [1]you [2]do [4]have [11]to [12]you [6]*for* [7]*anything* [8]to [9]be [10]written.
2 Αὐτοὶ γὰρ ἀκριβῶς οἴδατε ὅτι ἡ ἡμέρα Κυρίου ὡς
[3]yourselves [1]For [5]accurately [2]you [4]know that the day of *the* Lord [3]as
κλέπτης ἐν νυκτὶ οὕτως ἔρχεται. 3 Ὅταν γὰρ λέγωσιν,
[4]a [5]thief [6]in [7]*the* [8]night [1]so [2]comes. when ˜ For they say,
"Εἰρήνη καὶ ἀσφάλεια," τότε αἰφνίδιος αὐτοῖς ἐφίσταται
"Peace and safety," then sudden [4]them [2]comes [3]upon
ὄλεθρος, ὥσπερ ἡ ὠδὶν τῇ ἐν γαστρὶ ἐχούσῃ,
[1]destruction, just as the pain of labor to the *one* in *the* womb having,
the woman who is pregnant,
καὶ οὐ μὴ ἐκφύγωσιν. 4 Ὑμεῖς δέ, ἀδελφοί, οὐκ ἐστὲ
and [3]not [4]not [1]they [2]will escape. you ˜ But, brothers, not ˜ are
by no means
ἐν σκότει, ἵνα ἡ ἡμέρα ὑμᾶς ὡς κλέπτης καταλάβῃ.
in darkness, so that the day [3]you [4]as [5]a [6]thief [1]should [2]overtake.
5 Πάντες ὑμεῖς υἱοὶ φωτός ἐστε καὶ υἱοὶ ἡμέρας. Οὐκ ἐσμὲν
all ˜ You [2]sons [3]of [4]light [1]are and sons of day. [3]not [1]We [2]are
νυκτὸς οὐδὲ σκότους. 6 Ἄρα οὖν μὴ καθεύδωμεν ὡς καὶ οἱ
of night nor of darkness. So then [3]not [1]let [2]us sleep as also the
λοιποί, ἀλλὰ γρηγορῶμεν καὶ νήφωμεν. 7 Οἱ γὰρ
rest, but let us be awake and let us be sober. [2]the [3]*ones* [1]For
watching
καθεύδοντες νυκτὸς καθεύδουσι, καὶ οἱ μεθυσκόμενοι
sleeping [2]of [3]night [1]sleep, and the *ones* getting drunk
at
νυκτὸς μεθύουσιν. 8 Ἡμεῖς δὲ ἡμέρας ὄντες,
[3]of [4]night [1]are [2]drunk. we ˜ But [2]of [3]day [1]being,
at since we are of the day,
νήφωμεν, ἐνδυσάμενοι θώρακα πίστεως καὶ ἀγάπης
let us be sober, putting on a breastplate of faith and love
clothing ourselves with
καὶ περικεφαλαίαν, ἐλπίδα σωτηρίας. 9 Ὅτι οὐκ ἔθετο
and *as* a helmet, *the* hope of salvation. Because [3]not [2]did [4]appoint
ἡμᾶς ὁ Θεὸς εἰς ὀργήν, ἀλλ᾽ εἰς περιποίησιν σωτηρίας διὰ
[5]us - [1]God to wrath, but to *the* obtaining of salvation through

16 For the Lord Himself will descend from heaven with a shout, with the voice of an archangel, and with the trumpet of God. And the dead in Christ will rise first.
17 Then we who are alive *and* remain shall be caught up together with them in the clouds to meet the Lord in the air. And thus we shall always be with the Lord.
18 Therefore comfort one another with these words.

5 But concerning the times and the seasons, brethren, you have no need that I should write to you.
2 For you yourselves know perfectly that the day of the Lord so comes as a thief in the night.
3 For when they say, "Peace and safety!" then sudden destruction comes upon them, as labor pains upon a pregnant woman. And they shall not escape.
4 But you, brethren, are not in darkness, so that this Day should overtake you as a thief.
5 You are all sons of light and sons of the day. We are not of the night nor of darkness.
6 Therefore let us not sleep, as others *do,* but let us watch and be sober.
7 For those who sleep, sleep at night, and those who get drunk are drunk at night.
8 But let us who are of the day be sober, putting on the breastplate of faith and love, and *as* a helmet the hope of salvation.
9 For God did not appoint us to wrath, but to obtain salvation

***(4:17)** ἁρπάζω *(harpazō).* Verb meaning *snatch, seize* (cf. Jude 23), also meaning *steal, plunder* (as the intensive form διαρπάζω in Matt. 12:29). It generally carries with it the idea of force (though not necessarily violence), and often implies suddenness so that there is no question of resistance (as here in 1 Thess. 4:17; cf. Acts 8:39). Cf. the cognate noun ἁρπαγμός, occurring only in the NT at Phil. 2:6 where its meaning, possibly *robbery* or *prize,* occasions much interpretive dispute.

through our Lord Jesus Christ,
10 who died for us, that
whether we wake or sleep, we
should live together with Him.
11 Therefore comfort each
other and edify one another,
just as you also are doing.
12 And we urge you, brethren, to recognize those who labor among you, and are over
you in the Lord and admonish
you,
13 and to esteem them very
highly in love for their work's
sake. Be at peace among yourselves.
14 Now we exhort you, brethren, warn those who are unruly, comfort the fainthearted,
uphold the weak, be patient
with all.
15 See that no one renders
evil for evil to anyone, but always pursue what is good both
for yourselves and for all.
16 Rejoice always,
17 pray without ceasing,
18 in everything give thanks;
for this is the will of God in
Christ Jesus for you.
19 Do not quench the Spirit.
20 Do not despise prophecies.
21 Test all things; hold fast
what is good.
22 Abstain from every form of
evil.
23 Now may the God of peace
Himself sanctify you com-

τοῦ Κυρίου ἡμῶν Ἰησοῦ Χριστοῦ, **10** τοῦ ἀποθανόντος
\- Lord ˜ our Jesus Christ, the *One* dying
who died

ὑπὲρ ἡμῶν, ἵνα εἴτε γρηγορῶμεν εἴτε
in behalf of us, in order that whether we are awake or

καθεύδωμεν,* ἅμα σὺν αὐτῷ ζήσωμεν. **11** Διὸ
we are sleeping, [4]together [5]with [6]Him [1]we [2]may [3]live. Therefore

παρακαλεῖτε ἀλλήλους καὶ οἰκοδομεῖτε εἷς τὸν ἕνα, καθὼς
comfort one another and build up one the one, just as
edify each one the other,

καὶ ποιεῖτε.
also ˜ you are doing.

Various Exhortations

12 Ἐρωτῶμεν δὲ ὑμᾶς, ἀδελφοί, εἰδέναι τοὺς
[2]we [3]request [4]of [1]Now you, brothers, to know the *ones*
recognize those who

κοπιῶντας ἐν ὑμῖν καὶ προϊσταμένους ὑμῶν ἐν Κυρίῳ καὶ
laboring among you and ruling you in *the* Lord and
labor have charge of

νουθετοῦντας ὑμᾶς, **13** καὶ ἡγεῖσθαι αὐτοὺς ὑπερεκπερισσοῦ ἐν
instructing you, and to regard them beyond all measure in
instruct

ἀγάπῃ διὰ τὸ ἔργον αὐτῶν. Εἰρηνεύετε ἐν ἑαυτοῖς.
love because of - work ˜ their. Be at peace among yourselves.

14 Παρακαλοῦμεν δὲ ὑμᾶς, ἀδελφοί, νουθετεῖτε τοὺς
[2]we [3]exhort [1]Now you, brothers, admonish the

ἀτάκτους, παραμυθεῖσθε τοὺς ὀλιγοψύχους, ἀντέχεσθε
disorderly *ones*, encourage the discouraged *ones*, hold up
be supportive of

τῶν ἀσθενῶν, μακροθυμεῖτε πρὸς πάντας. **15** Ὁρᾶτε μή
the weak *ones*, be patient toward all. See *that* not
no

τις κακὸν ἀντὶ κακοῦ τινι ἀποδῷ, ἀλλὰ
anyone [3]evil [4]in [5]place [6]of [7]evil [8]to [9]anyone [1]pays [2]back, but
one

πάντοτε τὸ ἀγαθὸν διώκετε καὶ εἰς ἀλλήλους καὶ εἰς
always [2]the [3]good [4]*thing* [1]pursue both for one another and for
that which is good

πάντας. **16** Πάντοτε χαίρετε! **17** Ἀδιαλείπτως προσεύχεσθε!
all. always ˜ Rejoice! unceasingly ˜ Pray!
regularly

18 Ἐν παντὶ εὐχαριστεῖτε! Τοῦτο γὰρ θέλημα Θεοῦ ἐν
In every*thing* give thanks! this ˜ For *is the* will of God in

Χριστῷ Ἰησοῦ εἰς ὑμᾶς. **19** Τὸ Πνεῦμα μὴ σβέννυτε,
Christ Jesus for you. [4]the [5]Spirit [2]not [1]Do [3]quench,

20 προφητείας μὴ ἐξουθενεῖτε. **21** Πάντα δὲ[a]
[4]prophecies [2]not [1]do [3]despise. [3]all [4]*things* [1]But
prophetic utterances

δοκιμάζετε, τὸ καλὸν κατέχετε. **22** Ἀπὸ παντὸς εἴδους
[2]test, the good *thing* hold fast. From every form
that which is good

πονηροῦ ἀπέχεσθε.
of evil abstain.

Paul's Greeting of Grace

23 Αὐτὸς δὲ ὁ Θεὸς τῆς εἰρήνης ἁγιάσαι ὑμᾶς
[7]Himself [1]Now [2]*may* [3]the [4]God - [5]of [6]peace sanctify you

---

[a](5:21) TR omits δε, *But.*

*(5:10) καθεύδω (*katheudō*). Verb meaning *sleep.* It usually refers to natural sleep (as Matt. 13:25; 25:5), but is used figuratively in 1 Thess. 5:6, 7 to indicate spiritual carelessness and indifference (cf. also Eph. 5:14). The meaning here in 1 Thess. 5:10 is problematic. If it is used figuratively of moral laxness, there is a paradox that moral action does not affect appropriation of salvation in Christ. Most interpreters therefore favor the euphemistic meaning *die* (possibly also in Mark 5:39 and parallels; cf. the synonym κοιμάομαι in 1 Thess. 4:13–15). Thus, "whether we wake or sleep" figuratively expresses the idea "whether we live or die, we should live with Him."

ὁλοτελεῖς, καὶ ὁλόκληρον ὑμῶν τὸ πνεῦμα καὶ ἡ ψυχὴ
quite complete, and *may* 9whole 1your - 2spirit 3and - 4soul

καὶ τὸ σῶμα ἀμέμπτως ἐν τῇ παρουσίᾳ τοῦ Κυρίου ἡμῶν
5and - 6body 10blamelessly 11at 12the 13coming - 14of 16Lord 15our
and blameless

Ἰησοῦ Χριστοῦ τηρηθείη. 24 Πιστὸς ὁ καλῶν ὑμᾶς,
17Jesus 18Christ 7be 8kept. 6faithful 1The 2*One* 3calling 4you 5*is*,
He who calls

ὃς καὶ ποιήσει.
who also will do *this*.

25 Ἀδελφοί, προσεύχεσθε[b] περὶ ἡμῶν.
Brothers, pray concerning us.

26 Ἀσπάσασθε τοὺς ἀδελφοὺς πάντας ἐν φιλήματι ἁγίῳ.
Greet 2the 3brothers 1all with a kiss ˜ holy.

27 Ὁρκίζω ὑμᾶς τὸν Κύριον ἀναγνωσθῆναι τὴν ἐπιστολὴν
I adjure by ˜ you the Lord *for* 3to 4be 5read 1the 2letter
this

πᾶσι τοῖς ἁγίοις[c] ἀδελφοῖς.
to all the holy brothers.

28 Ἡ χάρις τοῦ Κυρίου ἡμῶν Ἰησοῦ Χριστοῦ μεθ' ὑμῶν.
The grace - of Lord ˜ our Jesus Christ *be* with you.

Ἀμήν.[d]
Amen.
So be it.

pletely; and may your whole spirit, soul, and body be preserved blameless at the coming of our Lord Jesus Christ.
24 He who calls you *is* faithful, who also will do *it*.
25 Brethren, pray for us.
26 Greet all the brethren with a holy kiss.
27 I charge you by the Lord that this epistle be read to all the holy brethren.
28 The grace of our Lord Jesus Christ *be* with you. Amen.

[b](**5:25**) NU adds in brackets και, *(be praying) also.*
[c](**5:27**) NU omits αγιοις, *holy.* [d](**5:28**) NU omits Αμην, *Amen.*

The Second Epistle of Paul the Apostle to the

THESSALONIANS

1 Paul, Silvanus, and Timothy,

To the church of the Thessalonians in God our Father and the Lord Jesus Christ:

2 Grace to you and peace from God our Father and the Lord Jesus Christ.

3 We are bound to thank God always for you, brethren, as it is fitting, because your faith grows exceedingly, and the love of every one of you all abounds toward each other,
4 so that we ourselves boast of you among the churches of God for your patience and faith in all your persecutions and tribulations that you endure,
5 *which is* manifest evidence of the righteous judgment of God, that you may be counted worthy of the kingdom of God, for which you also suffer;
6 since *it is* a righteous thing with God to repay with tribulation those who trouble you,
7 and to *give* you who are troubled rest with us when the Lord Jesus is revealed from heaven with His mighty angels,
8 in flaming fire taking vengeance on those who do not know God, and on those who

ΠΡΟΣ ΘΕΣΣΑΛΟΝΙΚΕΙΣ Β
TO *THE* THESSALONIANS 2

Paul Greets the Thessalonian Church

1 1 Παῦλος καὶ Σιλουανὸς καὶ Τιμόθεος,
Paul and Silvanus and Timothy,

Τῇ ἐκκλησίᾳ Θεσσαλονικέων ἐν Θεῷ Πατρὶ ἡμῶν καὶ
To the church of *the* Thessalonians in God Father ˜ our and

Κυρίῳ Ἰησοῦ Χριστῷ·
the Lord Jesus Christ:

2 Χάρις ὑμῖν καὶ εἰρήνη ἀπὸ Θεοῦ Πατρὸς ἡμῶν καὶ
Grace to you and peace from God Father ˜ our and

Κυρίου Ἰησοῦ Χριστοῦ.
the Lord Jesus Christ.

God Will Judge the Persecutors

3 Εὐχαριστεῖν ὀφείλομεν τῷ Θεῷ πάντοτε περὶ
[3]to [4]give [5]thanks [1]We [2]ought - to God always concerning

ὑμῶν, ἀδελφοί, καθὼς ἄξιόν ἐστιν, ὅτι ὑπεραυξάνει ἡ
you, brothers, just as [3]fitting [1]it [2]is, because [3]grows [4]exceedingly -

πίστις ὑμῶν καὶ πλεονάζει ἡ ἀγάπη ἑνὸς ἑκάστου πάντων
[2]faith [1]your and [12]increases [1]the [2]love [3]of [5]one [4]each [6]of [8]all

ὑμῶν εἰς ἀλλήλους, 4 ὥστε ἡμᾶς αὐτοὺς ἐν ὑμῖν
[7]you [9]for [10]one [11]another, so that us (we) ourselves [3]in [4]you

καυχᾶσθαι ἐν ταῖς ἐκκλησίαις τοῦ Θεοῦ ὑπὲρ τῆς ὑπομονῆς
[1]to [2]boast (are boasting) among the churches - of God about - patience ˜

ὑμῶν καὶ πίστεως ἐν πᾶσι τοῖς διωγμοῖς ὑμῶν καὶ ταῖς
your and faith in all - persecutions ˜ your and -

θλίψεσιν αἷς ἀνέχεσθε, 5 ἔνδειγμα τῆς δικαίας
afflictions which you endure, *which is* evidence of the righteous

κρίσεως τοῦ Θεοῦ, εἰς τὸ καταξιωθῆναι ὑμᾶς τῆς
judgment - of God, for (so that) - [2]to [3]be [4]counted [5]worthy (you may be counted) [1]you (worthy) of the

βασιλείας τοῦ Θεοῦ, ὑπὲρ ἧς καὶ πάσχετε, 6 εἴπερ
kingdom - of God, in behalf of which also ˜ you suffer, since *it is*

δίκαιον παρὰ Θεῷ ἀνταποδοῦναι τοῖς θλίβουσιν ὑμᾶς
a righteous *thing* with God to repay [3]the [4]*ones* [5]afflicting [6]you

θλῖψιν 7 καὶ ὑμῖν τοῖς θλιβομένοις ἄνεσιν
[1]with [2]affliction and [3]to [4]you [5]the [6]*ones* (who are) [7]being [8]afflicted [1]with [2]rest

μεθ' ἡμῶν ἐν τῇ ἀποκαλύψει τοῦ Κυρίου Ἰησοῦ ἀπ'
along with us at the revelation of the Lord Jesus from

οὐρανοῦ μετ' ἀγγέλων δυνάμεως αὐτοῦ, 8 ἐν πυρὶ φλογός,
heaven with the angels (His angels) of power ˜ (powerful) His, (angels,) in fire (flaming) of flame, (fire,)

διδόντος ἐκδίκησιν τοῖς μὴ εἰδόσι Θεὸν καὶ τοῖς μὴ
giving (inflicting) vengeance on the *ones* not knowing God and on the *ones* not

ὑπακούουσι τῷ εὐαγγελίῳ τοῦ Κυρίου ἡμῶν Ἰησοῦ Χριστοῦ,[a]
obeying the gospel - of Lord ˜ our Jesus Christ,

9 οἵτινες δίκην τίσουσιν, ὄλεθρον* αἰώνιον ἀπὸ
who as such [3]a [4]penalty [1]will [2]pay, destruction ˜ eternal from

προσώπου τοῦ Κυρίου καὶ ἀπὸ τῆς δόξης τῆς ἰσχύος αὐτοῦ,
the face of the Lord and from the glory - of might ˜ His,

10 ὅταν ἔλθῃ ἐνδοξασθῆναι ἐν τοῖς ἁγίοις αὐτοῦ καὶ
whenever He comes to be glorified among - saints ˜ His and

θαυμασθῆναι ἐν πᾶσι τοῖς πιστεύσασιν,[b] ὅτι
to be marveled at among all the *ones* having believed, because
those who have

ἐπιστεύθη τὸ μαρτύριον ἡμῶν ἐφ᾽ ὑμᾶς, ἐν τῇ ἡμέρᾳ ἐκείνῃ.
[5]was [6]believed - [2]testimony [1]our [3]to [4]you, in - Day ˜ that.

11 Εἰς ὃ καὶ προσευχόμεθα πάντοτε περὶ ὑμῶν, ἵνα
For which also ˜ we pray always concerning you, that

ὑμᾶς ἀξιώσῃ τῆς κλήσεως ὁ Θεὸς ἡμῶν καὶ
[5]you [3]may [4]count [6]worthy [7]of [8]the [9]calling - [2]God [1]our and
this

πληρώσῃ πᾶσαν εὐδοκίαν ἀγαθωσύνης καὶ ἔργον
may fulfill all *the* good pleasure of *His* goodness and *the* work

πίστεως ἐν δυνάμει, **12** ὅπως ἐνδοξασθῇ τὸ ὄνομα
of faith with power, in order that [7]may [8]be [9]glorified [1]the [2]name

τοῦ Κυρίου ἡμῶν Ἰησοῦ[c] ἐν ὑμῖν, καὶ ὑμεῖς ἐν αὐτῷ,
- [3]of [5]Lord [4]our [6]Jesus in you, and you in Him,

κατὰ τὴν χάριν τοῦ Θεοῦ ἡμῶν καὶ Κυρίου Ἰησοῦ
according to the grace - of God ˜ our and Lord Jesus

Χριστοῦ.
Christ.

The Man of Sin and the Restrainer

2 **1** Ἐρωτῶμεν δὲ ὑμᾶς, ἀδελφοί, ὑπὲρ τῆς
[2]we [3]request [4]of [1]Now you, brothers, concerning the

παρουσίας τοῦ Κυρίου ἡμῶν Ἰησοῦ Χριστοῦ καὶ ἡμῶν
coming - of Lord ˜ our Jesus Christ and our

ἐπισυναγωγῆς ἐπ᾽ αὐτόν, **2** εἰς τὸ μὴ ταχέως σαλευθῆναι
assembling to Him, for - [2]not [5]hastily [3]to [4]be [6]shaken
that be

ὑμᾶς ἀπὸ τοῦ νοὸς μήτε θροεῖσθαι, μήτε διὰ πνεύματος
[1]you from the mind nor to be disturbed, neither by spirit
your composure be

μήτε διὰ λόγου μήτε δι᾽ ἐπιστολῆς ὡς δι᾽ ἡμῶν, ὡς ὅτι
nor by word nor by letter as through us, - that
from

ἐνέστηκεν ἡ ἡμέρα τοῦ Χριστοῦ.[a] **3** Μή τις ὑμᾶς
[5]has [6]come [1]the [2]Day - [3]of [4]Christ. [2]not [3]anyone [5]you
no one

ἐξαπατήσῃ κατὰ μηδένα τρόπον· ὅτι ἐὰν
[1]Let [4]deceive by no manner; because *that Day will not come* if
any means;

μὴ ἔλθῃ ἡ ἀποστασία πρῶτον καὶ ἀποκαλυφθῇ ὁ
not [3]comes [1]the [2]apostasy first and [5]is [6]revealed [1]the
unless rebellion

ἄνθρωπος τῆς ἁμαρτίας,[b] ὁ υἱὸς τῆς ἀπωλείας, **4** ὁ
[2]man - [3]of [4]sin, the son - of perdition, the *one*
who is

ἀντικείμενος καὶ ὑπεραιρόμενος ἐπὶ πάντα λεγόμενον θεὸν
opposing and exalting himself over every*thing* being called god

do not obey the gospel of our Lord Jesus Christ.
9 These shall be punished with everlasting destruction from the presence of the Lord and from the glory of His power,
10 when He comes, in that Day, to be glorified in His saints and to be admired among all those who believe, because our testimony among you was believed.
11 Therefore we also pray always for you that our God would count you worthy of *this* calling, and fulfill all the good pleasure of *His* goodness and the work of faith with power,
12 that the name of our Lord Jesus Christ may be glorified in you, and you in Him, according to the grace of our God and the Lord Jesus Christ.

2 Now, brethren, concerning the coming of our Lord Jesus Christ and our gathering together to Him, we ask you,
2 not to be soon shaken in mind or troubled, either by spirit or by word or by letter, as if from us, as though the day of Christ had come.
3 Let no one deceive you by any means; for *that Day will not come* unless the falling away comes first, and the man of sin is revealed, the son of perdition,
4 who opposes and exalts himself above all that is called

[a]**(1:8)** NU omits Χριστου, *Christ.* [b]**(1:10)** TR reads πιστευουσιν, *who are believing.* [c]**(1:12)** TR adds Χριστου, *Christ.*
[a]**(2:2)** NU reads του κυριου, *of the Lord.*
[b]**(2:3)** NU reads ανομιας, *of lawlessness.*

***(1:9)** ὄλεθρος *(olethros).* Noun meaning *destruction, ruin, death,* typically in the NT with spiritual and/or eschatological implications, as here where eternal destruction is in view. In 1 Cor. 5:5 interpreters debate whether it means physical death or some other bodily judgment. See the synonym (an etymological cousin) ἀπώλεια at Matt. 7:13.

God or that is worshiped, so
that he sits as God in the temple of God, showing himself
that he is God.
5 Do you not remember that
when I was still with you I told
you these things?
6 And now you know what is
restraining, that he may be revealed in his own time.
7 For the mystery of law-
lessness is already at work;
only He who now restrains *will
do so* until He is taken out of the
way.
8 And then the lawless one
will be revealed, whom the
Lord will consume with the
breath of His mouth and destroy with the brightness of His
coming.
9 The coming of the *lawless
one* is according to the working
of Satan, with all power, signs,
and lying wonders,
10 and with all unrighteous deception among those who perish, because they did not
receive the love of the truth,
that they might be saved.
11 And for this reason God
will send them strong delusion,
that they should believe the lie,
12 that they all may be condemned who did not believe the
truth but had pleasure in unrighteousness.
13 But we are bound to give
thanks to God always for you,
brethren beloved by the Lord,

ἢ σέβασμα, ὥστε αὐτὸν εἰς τὸν ναὸν τοῦ Θεοῦ
or *every* object of worship, so that him [4]in [5]the [6]temple - [7]of [8]God
he sanctuary

ὡς Θεὸν[c] καθίσαι, ἀποδεικνύντα ἑαυτὸν ὅτι ἐστὶ Θεός.
[9]as [10]God [1]to [2]sit [3]down, displaying himself that he is God.
takes his seat,

5 Οὐ μνημονεύετε ὅτι ἔτι ὢν πρὸς ὑμᾶς ταῦτα
[3]not [1]Do [2]you remember that yet being with you [5]these [6]*things*
while I was still

ἔλεγον ὑμῖν? **6** Καὶ νῦν τὸ κατέχον οἴδατε,
[1]I [2]was [3]telling [4]you? And now the *thing* holding back you know,
that which is restraining

εἰς τὸ ἀποκαλυφθῆναι αὐτὸν ἐν τῷ ἑαυτοῦ καιρῷ. **7** Τὸ
for - to be revealed him in the [2]of [3]himself [1]time. the ~
in order that he may be revealed his own

γὰρ μυστήριον ἤδη ἐνεργεῖται τῆς ἀνομίας· μόνον
For mystery [4]already [3]is [5]at [6]work - [1]of [2]lawlessness; only

ὁ κατέχων ἄρτι ἕως ἐκ μέσου
the *One* holding back *will continue* now until [3]from [4]*the* [5]midst
He who is restraining will continue until He is taken out of

γένηται. **8** Καὶ τότε ἀποκαλυφθήσεται ὁ ἄνομος, ὃν
[1]He [2]comes. And then [4]will [5]be [6]revealed [1]the [2]lawless [3]*one,* whom
the way.

ὁ Κύριος[d] ἀναλώσει[e] τῷ πνεύματι τοῦ στόματος αὐτοῦ
the Lord will consume with the breath - of mouth ~ His

καὶ καταργήσει τῇ ἐπιφανείᾳ τῆς παρουσίας αὐτοῦ,
and will abolish by the appearing - of coming ~ His,
brightness

9 οὗ ἐστιν ἡ παρουσία κατ' ἐνέργειαν τοῦ Σατανᾶ
of whom [3]is [1]the [2]coming according to *the* working - of Satan
whose coming is

ἐν πάσῃ δυνάμει καὶ σημείοις καὶ τέρασι ψεύδους **10** καὶ
with all power and signs and wonders of falsehood and
lying wonders

ἐν πάσῃ ἀπάτῃ τῆς ἀδικίας ἐν τοῖς
in all deception - of unrighteousness among the *ones*
those who

ἀπολλυμένοις, ἀνθ' ὧν τὴν ἀγάπην τῆς ἀληθείας οὐκ
perishing, because [5]the [6]love [7]of [8]the [9]truth [3]not
perish,

ἐδέξαντο εἰς τὸ σωθῆναι αὐτούς. **11** Καὶ διὰ
[1]they [2]did [4]receive for - [2]to [3]be [4]saved [1]them. And because of
in order that they might be saved.

τοῦτο πέμψει[f] αὐτοῖς ὁ Θεὸς ἐνέργειαν πλάνης εἰς τὸ
this [2]will [3]send [4]to [5]them - [1]God *the* working of delusion for -
in order for

πιστεῦσαι αὐτοὺς τῷ ψεύδει, **12** ἵνα κριθῶσι
[2]to [3]believe [1]them the lie, so that they [2]should [3]be [4]judged

πάντες οἱ μὴ πιστεύσαντες τῇ ἀληθείᾳ ἀλλ' εὐδοκήσαντες
[1]all the *ones* not believing the truth but taking pleasure
who did not believe took

ἐν τῇ ἀδικίᾳ.
in - unrighteousness.

Hold Fast to What You Were Taught

13 Ἡμεῖς δὲ ὀφείλομεν εὐχαριστεῖν τῷ Θεῷ πάντοτε
we ~ But ought to give thanks - to God always

περὶ ὑμῶν, ἀδελφοὶ ἠγαπημένοι ὑπὸ Κυρίου, ὅτι
concerning you, brothers having been loved by *the* Lord, because
who have

[c](2:4) NU omits ως Θεον, *as God.* [d](2:8) NU adds in brackets Ιησους, *(the Lord) Jesus.* [e](2:8) NU reads ανελει, *will destroy.* [f](2:11) NU reads πεμπει, *sends.*

εἵλετο ὑμᾶς ὁ Θεὸς ἀπ' ἀρχῆς[g] εἰς σωτηρίαν ἐν ἁγιασμῷ
[2]chose [3]you - [1]God from *the* beginning for salvation by sanctification

Πνεύματος καὶ πίστει ἀληθείας, 14 εἰς ὃ ἐκάλεσεν ὑμᾶς
of *the* Spirit and by faith of *the* truth, to which He called you
in

διὰ τοῦ εὐαγγελίου ἡμῶν, εἰς περιποίησιν δόξης τοῦ
through - gospel ~ our, for *the* obtaining of *the* glory -

Κυρίου ἡμῶν Ἰησοῦ Χριστοῦ. 15 Ἄρα οὖν, ἀδελφοί, στήκετε,
of Lord ~ our Jesus Christ. So then, brothers, stand firm,

καὶ κρατεῖτε τὰς παραδόσεις ἃς ἐδιδάχθητε, εἴτε διὰ
and hold to the traditions which you were taught, whether by

λόγου εἴτε δι' ἐπιστολῆς ἡμῶν.
word or by letter ~ our.

16 Αὐτὸς δὲ ὁ Κύριος ἡμῶν Ἰησοῦς Χριστός, καὶ ὁ
[7]Himself [1]Now [2]*may* - [4]Lord [3]our [5]Jesus [6]Christ, and -

Θεὸς καὶ Πατὴρ ἡμῶν, ὁ ἀγαπήσας ἡμᾶς καὶ δοὺς
[2]God [3]and [4]Father [1]our, the *One* loving us and giving *us*
who loved gave

παράκλησιν αἰωνίαν καὶ ἐλπίδα ἀγαθὴν ἐν χάριτι,
comfort ~ eternal and a hope ~ good by grace,

17 παρακαλέσαι ὑμῶν τὰς καρδίας καὶ στηρίξαι ὑμᾶς ἐν
comfort your - hearts and establish you in

παντὶ λόγῳ καὶ ἔργῳ ἀγαθῷ.
every [2]word [3]and [4]work [1]good.

Paul Asks Prayer for Spiritual Success and Safety

3 1 Τὸ λοιπόν, προσεύχεσθε, ἀδελφοί, περὶ ἡμῶν,
For the rest, pray, brothers, concerning us,
Finally,

ἵνα ὁ λόγος τοῦ Κυρίου τρέχῃ καὶ δοξάζηται καθὼς
that the word of the Lord may run and may be glorified just as

καὶ πρὸς ὑμᾶς, 2 καὶ ἵνα ῥυσθῶμεν ἀπὸ τῶν
also *it has been* with you, and that we may be delivered from -

ἀτόπων καὶ πονηρῶν ἀνθρώπων· οὐ γὰρ πάντων ἡ πίστις.
evil and wicked men; [4]*is* [5]not [1]for [6]of [7]all [2]the [3]faith.
for not all have faith.

3 Πιστὸς* δέ ἐστιν ὁ Κύριος, ὃς στηρίξει ὑμᾶς καὶ
faithful ~ But is the Lord, who will establish you and

φυλάξει ἀπὸ τοῦ πονηροῦ. 4 Πεποίθαμεν δὲ ἐν
will guard *you* from the evil *one.* [2]we [3]have [4]been [5]persuaded [1]And in

Κυρίῳ ἐφ' ὑμᾶς, ὅτι ἃ παραγγέλλομεν ὑμῖν καὶ
the Lord toward you, that *the things* which we command to you both

ποιεῖτε καὶ ποιήσετε. 5 Ὁ δὲ Κύριος κατευθύναι
you are doing and you will do *them.* [3]the [1]Now [4]Lord [2]may [5]direct

ὑμῶν τὰς καρδίας εἰς τὴν ἀγάπην τοῦ Θεοῦ καὶ εἰς τὴν
your - hearts into the love - of God and into the

ὑπομονὴν τοῦ Χριστοῦ.
patience - of Christ.

Paul Warns Against Idleness

6 Παραγγέλλομεν δὲ ὑμῖν, ἀδελφοί, ἐν ὀνόματι τοῦ
[2]we [3]command [1]Now you, brothers, in *the* name -

Κυρίου ἡμῶν Ἰησοῦ Χριστοῦ, στέλλεσθαι ὑμᾶς ἀπὸ παντὸς
of Lord ~ our Jesus Christ, [2]to [3]keep [4]away [1]you from every
that you withdraw

ἀδελφοῦ ἀτάκτως περιπατοῦντος καὶ μὴ κατὰ
brother [2]in [3]a [4]disorderly [5]way [1]walking and not according to
living in idleness

because God from the beginning chose you for salvation through sanctification by the Spirit and belief in the truth,
14 to which He called you by our gospel, for the obtaining of the glory of our Lord Jesus Christ.
15 Therefore, brethren, stand fast and hold the traditions which you were taught, whether by word or our epistle.
16 Now may our Lord Jesus Christ Himself, and our God and Father, who has loved us and given *us* everlasting consolation and good hope by grace,
17 comfort your hearts and establish you in every good word and work.

3 Finally, brethren, pray for us, that the word of the Lord may run *swiftly* and be glorified, just as *it is* with you,
2 and that we may be delivered from unreasonable and wicked men; for not all have faith.
3 But the Lord is faithful, who will establish you and guard *you* from the evil one.
4 And we have confidence in the Lord concerning you, both that you do and will do the things we command you.
5 Now may the Lord direct your hearts into the love of God and into the patience of Christ.
6 But we command you, brethren, in the name of our Lord Jesus Christ, that you withdraw from every brother who walks disorderly and not

---

[g](2:13) For απ αρχης, NU reads απαρχην, *as (the) firstfruits.*

***(3:3)** πιστός *(pistos).* Common adjective meaning *faithful* or *believing.* It is derived from the verb πιστεύω, *believe* (see πιστεύω at Acts 16:31), and may have either an active or passive nuance. In the active sense, it describes one who believes in God or Christ (Abraham in Gal. 3:9; cf. Timothy's mother in Acts 16:1). Its passive usage serves to describe either a person (Timothy in 1 Cor. 4:17) or God and Christ (as here in 2 Thess. 3:3) as being *faithful* and *dependable.* The word means *reliable* or *trustworthy* when applied to things such as words or sayings (as Titus 3:8; Rev. 21:5). See the cognate noun πίστις, *faith, trust,* at Col. 1:4.

according to the tradition which
he received from us.
7 For you yourselves know
how you ought to follow us, for
we were not disorderly among
you;
8 nor did we eat anyone's
bread free of charge, but
worked with labor and toil night
and day, that we might not be a
burden to any of you,
9 not because we do not
have authority, but to make
ourselves an example of how
you should follow us.
10 For even when we were
with you, we commanded you
this: If anyone will not work,
neither shall he eat.
11 For we hear that there are
some who walk among you in a
disorderly manner, not working
at all, but are busybodies.
12 Now those who are such
we command and exhort
through our Lord Jesus Christ
that they work in quietness and
eat their own bread.
13 But *as for* you, brethren,
do not grow weary *in* doing
good.
14 And if anyone does not
obey our word in this epistle,
note that person and do not
keep company with him, that he
may be ashamed.
15 Yet do not count *him* as an
enemy, but admonish *him* as a
brother.
16 Now may the Lord of
peace Himself give you peace
always in every way. The Lord
be with you all.
17 The salutation of Paul with
my own hand, which is a sign in
every epistle; so I write.
18 The grace of our Lord

τὴν παράδοσιν ἣν παρέλαβον[a] παρ' ἡμῶν. 7 Αὐτοὶ γὰρ
the tradition which they received from us. [3]yourselves [1]For

οἴδατε πῶς δεῖ μιμεῖσθαι ἡμᾶς, ὅτι οὐκ
[2]you know how it is necessary to imitate us, because [3]not
follow

ἠτακτήσαμεν ἐν ὑμῖν 8 οὐδὲ δωρεὰν ἄρτον
[1]we [2]were disorderly among you nor [7]without [8]paying [4]bread

ἐφάγομεν παρά τινος, ἀλλ' ἐν κόπῳ καὶ μόχθῳ νύκτα καὶ
[1]did [2]we [3]eat [5]from [6]anyone, but in labor and hardship night and

ἡμέραν ἐργαζόμενοι πρὸς τὸ μὴ ἐπιβαρῆσαί τινα ὑμῶν·
day working for - not to put a burden on any of you;
we worked in order to be

9 οὐχ ὅτι οὐκ ἔχομεν ἐξουσίαν, ἀλλ' ἵνα ἑαυτοὺς
not because [3]not [1]we [2]do have authority, but in order that [4]ourselves

τύπον δῶμεν ὑμῖν εἰς τὸ μιμεῖσθαι ἡμᾶς.
[5]*as* [6]a [7]pattern [1]we [2]may [3]give to you for - to imitate us.
so that you might follow

10 Καὶ γὰρ ὅτε ἦμεν πρὸς ὑμᾶς, τοῦτο παρηγγέλλομεν
even ˜ For when we were with you, this we commanded

ὑμῖν ὅτι εἴ τις οὐ θέλει ἐργάζεσθαι μηδὲ ἐσθιέτω!
you that if anyone not ˜ is willing to work neither let him eat!

11 Ἀκούομεν γάρ τινας περιπατοῦντας ἐν ὑμῖν
[2]we [3]hear [1]For *that* some *are* walking among you

ἀτάκτως, μηδὲν ἐργαζομένους, ἀλλὰ
in a disorderly way, [1]not [3]at [4]all [2]working, but

περιεργαζομένους. 12 Τοῖς δὲ τοιούτοις παραγγέλλομεν
doing unnecessary things. - And to such *ones* we command
being busybodies.

καὶ παρακαλοῦμεν διὰ τοῦ Κυρίου ἡμῶν[b] Ἰησοῦ Χριστοῦ ἵνα
and urge by - Lord ˜ our Jesus Christ that

μετὰ ἡσυχίας ἐργαζόμενοι τὸν ἑαυτῶν ἄρτον ἐσθίωσιν.
[2]with [3]quietness [1]working [6]the [8]of [9]themselves [7]bread [4]they [5]eat.
they work in quietness and eat their own bread.

13 Ὑμεῖς δέ, ἀδελφοί, μὴ ἐκκακήσητε καλοποιοῦντες. 14 Εἰ
you ˜ And, brothers, not ˜ do lose heart *for* doing good. if ˜

δέ τις οὐχ ὑπακούει τῷ λόγῳ ἡμῶν διὰ τῆς ἐπιστολῆς,
Now anyone not ˜ does obey - word ˜ our by the letter,
in this

τοῦτον σημειοῦσθε καὶ μὴ συναναμίγνυσθε αὐτῷ, ἵνα
[2]this [3]*one* [1]mark and not ˜ do mingle with him, so that
take note of him

ἐντραπῇ· 15 καὶ μὴ ὡς ἐχθρὸν ἡγεῖσθε,
he may be put to shame; and yet [2]not [5]as [6]an [7]enemy [1]do [3]consider [4]*him,*

ἀλλὰ νουθετεῖτε ὡς ἀδελφόν.
but admonish *him* as a brother.

Benediction of Grace

16 Αὐτὸς δὲ ὁ Κύριος τῆς εἰρήνης δῴη ὑμῖν τὴν
[7]Himself [1]Now [3]the [4]Lord - [5]of [6]peace [2]may [8]give you -

εἰρήνην διὰ παντὸς ἐν παντὶ τρόπῳ. Ὁ Κύριος μετὰ
peace through every *thing* in every manner. The Lord *be* with
always

πάντων ὑμῶν.
all ˜ you.

17 Ὁ ἀσπασμὸς τῇ ἐμῇ χειρὶ Παύλου, ὅ ἐστι
The greeting *is* - by my *own* hand of Paul, which is

σημεῖον ἐν πάσῃ ἐπιστολῇ· οὕτω γράφω· 18 ἡ χάρις τοῦ
a sign in every letter; so I write: the grace -

---

[a](3:6) TR reads παρελαβε, *he received.*
[b](3:12) For δια του Κυριου ημων, *by our Lord,* NU reads εν Κυριω, *in (the) Lord.*

Κυρίου ἡμῶν Ἰησοῦ Χριστοῦ μετὰ πάντων ὑμῶν. Ἀμήν.[c]
of Lord ~ our Jesus Christ *be* with all ~ you. Amen.
So be it.

Jesus Christ *be* with you all. Amen.

[c](**3:18**) NU omits Αμην, *Amen.*

The First Epistle of Paul the Apostle to

TIMOTHY

1 Paul, an apostle of Jesus
Christ, by the command-
ment of God our Savior and the
Lord Jesus Christ, our hope,

2 To Timothy, a true son in
the faith:

Grace, mercy, *and* peace
from God our Father and Jesus
Christ our Lord.

3 As I urged you when I
went into Macedonia—remain
in Ephesus that you may charge
some that they teach no other
doctrine,
4 nor give heed to fables and
endless genealogies, which
cause disputes rather than
godly edification which is in
faith.
5 Now the purpose of the
commandment is love from a
pure heart, *from* a good conscience, and *from* sincere faith,
6 from which some, having
strayed, have turned aside to
idle talk,
7 desiring to be teachers of
the law, understanding neither
what they say nor the things
which they affirm.
8 But we know that the law
is good if one uses it lawfully,
9 knowing this: that the law
is not made for a righteous person, but for *the* lawless and in-

ΠΡΟΣ ΤΙΜΟΘΕΟΝ Α
TO TIMOTHY 1

Paul Greets Timothy

1 **1** Παῦλος, ἀπόστολος Ἰησοῦ Χριστοῦ[a] κατ'
Paul, an apostle of Jesus Christ according to

ἐπιταγὴν Θεοῦ Σωτῆρος ἡμῶν καὶ Κυρίου Ἰησοῦ Χριστοῦ[b]
the command of God Savior ˜ our and *the* Lord Jesus Christ

τῆς ἐλπίδος ἡμῶν,
- hope ˜ our,

2 Τιμοθέῳ, γνησίῳ τέκνῳ ἐν πίστει·
To Timothy, a genuine child in *the* faith:

Χάρις, ἔλεος, εἰρήνη ἀπὸ Θεοῦ Πατρὸς ἡμῶν[c] καὶ Χριστοῦ
Grace, mercy, peace from God Father ˜ our and Christ

Ἰησοῦ τοῦ Κυρίου ἡμῶν.
Jesus - Lord ˜ our.

Paul Warns of False Doctrine

3 Καθὼς παρεκάλεσά σε προσμεῖναι ἐν Ἐφέσῳ
Just as I urged you to remain in Ephesus

πορευόμενος εἰς Μακεδονίαν, ἵνα παραγγείλῃς τισὶ
traveling (as I traveled) into Macedonia, that you should command certain *ones*

μὴ ἑτεροδιδασκαλεῖν **4** μηδὲ προσέχειν μύθοις καὶ
not to teach differently nor to pay attention to myths and

γενεαλογίαις ἀπεράντοις, αἵτινες ζητήσεις παρέχουσι μᾶλλον
genealogies ˜ endless, which disputes ˜ provide rather

ἢ οἰκονομίαν Θεοῦ τὴν ἐν πίστει· **5** τὸ δὲ τέλος τῆς
than edification of God the *one* (which is) in faith; the ˜ now end (goal) of the

παραγγελίας ἐστὶν ἀγάπη ἐκ καθαρᾶς καρδίας καὶ
command is love out of a pure heart and

συνειδήσεως ἀγαθῆς καὶ πίστεως ἀνυποκρίτου,
a conscience ˜ good and faith without hypocrisy (sincere faith),

6 ὧν τινες ἀστοχήσαντες ἐξετράπησαν εἰς
from which *things* certain *ones* having missed the mark (strayed) turned aside to

ματαιολογίαν, **7** θέλοντες εἶναι νομοδιδάσκαλοι, μὴ
futile talk, desiring to be teachers of *the* law, not

νοοῦντες μήτε ἃ λέγουσι μήτε περὶ τίνων
understanding neither (either) *the things* which they say nor (or) about what *things*

διαβεβαιοῦνται.
they affirm.

8 Οἴδαμεν δὲ ὅτι καλὸς ὁ νόμος ἐάν τις αὐτῷ
[2]we [3]know [1]But that [3]*is* [4]good [1]the [2]law if one [2]it

νομίμως χρῆται, **9** εἰδὼς τοῦτο, ὅτι δικαίῳ νόμος
[3]lawfully [1]uses, knowing this, that [6]for [7]a [8]righteous [9]*person* [1]law

οὐ κεῖται, ἀνόμοις δὲ καὶ ἀνυποτάκτοις,
[3]not [2]is [4]laid [5]down, [11]for [12]lawless [13]*people* [10]but and for insubordinate,

---

[a](1:1) NU reads Χριστου Ιησου, *Christ Jesus.*
[b](1:1) NU omits Κυριος, *Lord,* and reads Χριστου Ιησου, *Christ Jesus.*
[c](1:2) NU omits ημων, *our.*

ἀσεβέσι καὶ ἁμαρτωλοῖς, ἀνοσίοις καὶ βεβήλοις, πατρολῴαις
for ungodly and for sinners, for unholy and for profane, for patricides
killers of fathers

καὶ μητρολῴαις, ἀνδροφόνοις, **10** πόρνοις, ἀρσενοκοίταις,
and for matricides, for manslayers, for fornicators, for sodomites,
killers of mothers, for murderers,

ἀνδραποδισταῖς, ψεύσταις, ἐπιόρκοις, καὶ εἴ τι ἕτερον τῇ
for slave dealers, for liars, for perjurers, and if anything different -
kidnappers, else

ὑγιαινούσῃ* διδασκαλίᾳ ἀντίκειται, **11** κατὰ τὸ
[3]to [4]healthful [5]teaching [1]is [2]opposed, according to the
sound doctrine

εὐαγγέλιον τῆς δόξης τοῦ μακαρίου Θεοῦ, ὃ
gospel of the glory of the blessed God, *with* which

ἐπιστεύθην ἐγώ.
[2]was [3]entrusted [1]I.

Glory to God for His Grace

12 Καὶ χάριν ἔχω τῷ ἐνδυναμώσαντί με Χριστῷ
And [3]thanks [1]I [2]have to the *One* empowering me Christ
give who empowers

Ἰησοῦ τῷ Κυρίῳ ἡμῶν, ὅτι πιστόν με ἡγήσατο
Jesus - Lord ˜ our, because [4]faithful [3]me [1]He [2]considered

θέμενος εἰς διακονίαν, **13** τὸν πρότερον ὄντα βλάσφημον
putting *me* into service, the *one* formerly being a blasphemer
ministry, I who was formerly

καὶ διώκτην καὶ ὑβριστήν. Ἀλλὰ ἠλεήθην, ὅτι
and a persecutor and an insolent man. But I was shown mercy, because

ἀγνοῶν ἐποίησα ἐν ἀπιστίᾳ, **14** ὑπερεπλεόνασε δὲ ἡ
being ignorant I did *it* in unbelief, [7]superabounded [1]and [2]the

χάρις τοῦ Κυρίου ἡμῶν μετὰ πίστεως καὶ ἀγάπης τῆς ἐν
[3]grace - [4]of [6]Lord [5]our with faith and love - in

Χριστῷ Ἰησοῦ. **15** Πιστὸς ὁ λόγος καὶ πάσης ἀποδοχῆς
Christ Jesus. Faithful *is* the word and [2]of [3]all [4]acceptance
Trustworthy

ἄξιος, ὅτι Χριστὸς Ἰησοῦς ἦλθεν εἰς τὸν κόσμον ἁμαρτωλοὺς
[1]worthy, that Christ Jesus came into the world [3]sinners

σῶσαι, ὧν πρῶτός εἰμι ἐγώ. **16** Ἀλλὰ διὰ τοῦτο
[1]to [2]save, of whom [3]first [2]am [1]I. But because of this

ἠλεήθην, ἵνα ἐν ἐμοὶ πρώτῳ ἐνδείξηται Ἰησοῦς
I was shown mercy, so that in me first [3]might [4]show [5]forth [1]Jesus

Χριστὸς[d] τὴν πᾶσαν μακροθυμίαν, πρὸς ὑποτύπωσιν
[2]Christ the ˜ all longsuffering, as a pattern
His patience,

τῶν μελλόντων πιστεύειν ἐπ' αὐτῷ εἰς ζωὴν αἰώνιον.
for the *ones* coming to believe on Him for life ˜ eternal.
who are going

17 Τῷ δὲ Βασιλεῖ τῶν αἰώνων, ἀφθάρτῳ, ἀοράτῳ,
[2]to [3]the [1]Now King of the ages, incorruptible, invisible,
immortal,

μόνῳ σοφῷ[e] Θεῷ, τιμὴ καὶ δόξα εἰς τοὺς αἰῶνας τῶν
the only wise God, *be* honor and glory to the ages of the
forever and ever.

αἰώνων. Ἀμήν.
ages. Amen.
So be it.

subordinate, for *the* ungodly and
for sinners, for *the* unholy and
profane, for murderers of fathers and murderers of
mothers, for manslayers,
10 for fornicators, for sodomites, for kidnappers, for liars,
for perjurers, and if there is any
other thing that is contrary to
sound doctrine,
11 according to the glorious
gospel of the blessed God
which was committed to my
trust.
12 And I thank Christ Jesus
our Lord who has enabled me,
because He counted me faithful, putting *me* into the ministry,
13 although I was formerly a
blasphemer, a persecutor, and
an insolent man; but I obtained
mercy because I did *it* igno-
rantly in unbelief.
14 And the grace of our Lord
was exceedingly abundant, with
faith and love which are in
Christ Jesus.
15 This *is* a faithful saying and
worthy of all acceptance, that
Christ Jesus came into the
world to save sinners, of whom
I am chief.
16 However, for this reason I
obtained mercy, that in me first
Jesus Christ might show all
longsuffering, as a pattern to
those who are going to believe
on Him for everlasting life.
17 Now to the King eternal,
immortal, invisible, to God who
alone is wise, *be* honor and
glory forever and ever. Amen.

---

[d]**(1:16)** NU reads Χριστος Ιησους, *Christ Jesus.*
[e]**(1:17)** NU omits σοφω, *wise.*

***(1:10)** ὑγιαίνω *(hygiainō).* Verb meaning *to be in good physical health.* It is derived from the noun ὑγιής, *sound, whole, healthy,* which the LXX uses to translate the Hebrew *shālōm, soundness, welfare, peace.* The word expresses a key theme of the Pastoral Epistles where it is used figuratively for *being sound* in faith, love, and endurance (Titus 1:13; 2:2), and for *being correct* or *sound* in doctrine, described as healthy *teaching* (1 Tim. 1:10) and *words* (1 Tim. 6:3; 2 Tim. 1:13).

18 This charge I commit to you, son Timothy, according to the prophecies previously made concerning you, that by them you may wage the good warfare,

19 having faith and a good conscience, which some having rejected, concerning the faith have suffered shipwreck,

20 of whom are Hymenaeus and Alexander, whom I delivered to Satan that they may learn not to blaspheme.

2 Therefore I exhort first of all that supplications, prayers, intercessions, *and* giving of thanks be made for all men,

2 for kings and all who are in authority, that we may lead a quiet and peaceable life in all godliness and reverence.

3 For this *is* good and acceptable in the sight of God our Savior,

4 who desires all men to be saved and to come to the knowledge of the truth.

5 For *there is* one God and one Mediator between God and men, *the* Man Christ Jesus,

6 who gave Himself a ransom for all, to be testified in due time,

7 for which I was appointed a preacher and an apostle—I am speaking the truth in Christ *and* not lying—a teacher of the Gentiles in faith and truth.

8 I desire therefore that the men pray everywhere, lifting

Fight the Good Fight of Faith

18 Ταύτην τὴν παραγγελίαν παρατίθεμαί σοι, τέκνον
This - command I commit to you, *my* child
charge

Τιμόθεε, κατὰ τὰς προαγούσας ἐπὶ σε
Timothy, in accordance with the [2]preceding [3]concerning [4]you
previously made

προφητείας, ἵνα στρατεύῃ ἐν αὐταῖς τὴν καλὴν στρατείαν,
[1]prophecies, that you may war by them the good warfare,

19 ἔχων πίστιν καὶ ἀγαθὴν συνείδησιν, ἥν τινες
having faith and a good conscience, which certain *ones*

ἀπωσάμενοι περὶ τὴν πίστιν ἐναυάγησαν· 20 ὧν
thrusting away concerning the faith suffered shipwreck; of whom
rejecting

ἐστιν Ὑμέναιος καὶ Ἀλέξανδρος, οὓς παρέδωκα τῷ Σατανᾷ
is Hymenaeus and Alexander, whom I handed over to Satan
are

ἵνα παιδευθῶσι μὴ βλασφημεῖν.
so that they may be taught not to blaspheme.

Pray for All Men

2 1 Παρακαλῶ οὖν πρῶτον πάντων ποιεῖσθαι
I exhort therefore first of all [2]to [3]be [4]made
that supplications

δεήσεις, προσευχάς, ἐντεύξεις, εὐχαριστίας, ὑπὲρ
[1]supplications, prayers, intercessions, thanksgivings, on behalf of
be made,

πάντων ἀνθρώπων, 2 ὑπὲρ βασιλέων καὶ πάντων τῶν
all men, on behalf of kings and all the *ones*
those

ἐν ὑπεροχῇ ὄντων, ἵνα ἤρεμον καὶ ἡσύχιον βίον
in prominence being, so that a tranquil and quiet life
who are in authority,

διάγωμεν ἐν πάσῃ εὐσεβείᾳ καὶ σεμνότητι. 3 Τοῦτο γὰρ
we may lead in all godliness and dignity. this ˜ For *is*

καλὸν καὶ ἀπόδεκτον ἐνώπιον τοῦ Σωτῆρος ἡμῶν Θεοῦ, 4 ὅς
good and acceptable before - [3]Savior [2]our [1]God, who

πάντας ἀνθρώπους θέλει σωθῆναι καὶ εἰς ἐπίγνωσιν
[2]all [3]men [1]desires to be saved and [3]to [4]full [5]knowledge

ἀληθείας ἐλθεῖν. 5 Εἷς γὰρ Θεός, εἷς καὶ
[6]of [7]truth [1]to [2]come. [2]*there* [3]*is* [4]one [1]For God, one ˜ also

Μεσίτης Θεοῦ καὶ ἀνθρώπων, ἄνθρωπος Χριστὸς Ἰησοῦς,
Mediator *between* God and men, *the* man Christ Jesus,

6 ὁ δοὺς ἑαυτὸν ἀντίλυτρον ὑπὲρ πάντων, τὸ
the *One* having given Himself a ransom on behalf of all *people,* the
He who gave

μαρτύριον καιροῖς ἰδίοις· 7 εἰς ὃ ἐτέθην ἐγὼ
testimony in [3]seasons [1]its [2]own; to which [2]was [3]appointed [1]I
in due time;

κῆρυξ καὶ ἀπόστολος — ἀλήθειαν λέγω ἐν Χριστῷ,[a] οὐ
a herald and apostle — *the* truth I speak in Christ, [3]not

ψεύδομαι — διδάσκαλος ἐθνῶν ἐν πίστει καὶ ἀληθείᾳ.
[1]I [2]do [4]lie — a teacher of Gentiles in faith and truth.

Men and Women in the Church

8 Βούλομαι οὖν προσεύχεσθαι τοὺς ἄνδρας ἐν παντὶ
I desire therefore [3]to [4]pray [1]the [2]men in every

---

[a](2:7) NU omits εν Χριστω, *in Christ.*

τόπῳ, ἐπαίροντας ὁσίους χεῖρας χωρὶς ὀργῆς καὶ διαλογισμοῦ.
place, lifting up holy hands without wrath and doubting.

9 Ὡσαύτως καὶ τὰς γυναῖκας ἐν καταστολῇ κοσμίῳ μετὰ
Likewise also the women in apparel ˜ modest with

αἰδοῦς καὶ σωφροσύνης κοσμεῖν ἑαυτάς, μὴ ἐν πλέγμασιν
propriety and discretion to adorn themselves, not with braids

ἢ χρυσῷ ἢ μαργαρίταις ἢ ἱματισμῷ πολυτελεῖ, 10 ἀλλ' ὃ
or gold or pearls or clothing ˜ expensive, but which

πρέπει γυναιξὶν ἐπαγγελλομέναις θεοσέβειαν, δι'
is fitting for women professing godliness, by means of

ἔργων ἀγαθῶν. 11 Γυνὴ ἐν ἡσυχίᾳ μανθανέτω ἐν πάσῃ
works ˜ good. [2]a [3]woman [5]in [6]silence [1]Let [4]learn with all

ὑποταγῇ. 12 Γυναικὶ δὲ διδάσκειν οὐκ ἐπιτρέπω, οὐδὲ
submission. [6]a [7]woman [1]But [8]to [9]teach [4]not [2]I [3]do [5]permit, nor

αὐθεντεῖν ἀνδρός, ἀλλ' εἶναι ἐν ἡσυχίᾳ. 13 Ἀδὰμ γὰρ
to have authority over a man, but to be in silence. Adam ˜ For

πρῶτος ἐπλάσθη, εἶτα Εὔα. 14 Καὶ Ἀδὰμ οὐκ ἠπατήθη,
first was formed, then Eve. And Adam not ˜ was deceived,

ἡ δὲ γυνὴ ἀπατηθεῖσα ἐν παραβάσει γέγονε.
the ˜ but woman being deceived [5]in [6]transgression [1]has [2]come [3]to [4]be.
came

15 Σωθήσεται δὲ διὰ τῆς τεκνογονίας, ἐὰν μείνωσιν
[2]she [3]will [4]be [5]saved [1]But through - childbirth, if they remain

ἐν πίστει καὶ ἀγάπῃ καὶ ἁγιασμῷ μετὰ σωφροσύνης.
in faith and love and sanctification with self-control.

Qualifications of Bishops

3 1 Πιστὸς ὁ λόγος· εἴ τις ἐπισκοπῆς
[4]faithful [1]The [2]word [3]*is:* if anyone [3]*the* [4]position [5]of [6]overseer
trustworthy

ὀρέγεται, καλοῦ ἔργου ἐπιθυμεῖ. 2 Δεῖ οὖν τὸν
[1]aspires [2]to, a good work he desires. It is necessary therefore *for* the
an

ἐπίσκοπον ἀνεπίληπτον εἶναι, μιᾶς γυναικὸς ἄνδρα,
overseer [3]blameless [1]to [2]be, [6]of [7]one [8]wife [4]*the* [5]husband,

νηφάλεον, σώφρονα, κόσμιον, φιλόξενον, διδακτικόν,
temperate, prudent, well-behaved, loving strangers, skillful at teaching,
hospitable,

3 μὴ πάροινον, μὴ πλήκτην, μὴ αἰσχροκερδῆ,[a] ἀλλ'
not given to wine, not a bully, not greedy for base gain, but
violent,

ἐπιεικῆ, ἄμαχον, ἀφιλάργυρον, 4 τοῦ ἰδίου οἴκου
gentle, peaceable, not loving money, - [2]his [3]own [4]house
not quarrelsome, household

καλῶς προϊστάμενον, τέκνα ἔχοντα ἐν ὑποταγῇ, μετὰ πάσης
[5]well [1]ruling, children ˜ having in submission, with all

σεμνότητος· 5 (εἰ δέ τις τοῦ ἰδίου οἴκου προστῆναι οὐκ
reverence; (if ˜ but one - [7]his [8]own [9]house [5]to [6]rule [2]not
household

οἶδε, πῶς ἐκκλησίας Θεοῦ ἐπιμελήσεται?)
[1]does [3]know [4]*how,* how [6]a [7]church [8]of [9]God [1]will [2]he [3]take [4]care [5]of?)

6 μὴ νεόφυτον, ἵνα μὴ τυφωθεὶς εἰς κρίμα
not a neophyte, in order that not being puffed up [3]into [4]judgment
new convert, lest

ἐμπέσῃ τοῦ διαβόλου. 7 Δεῖ δὲ αὐτὸν καὶ
[1]he [2]fall of the devil. [2]it [3]is [4]necessary [1]And *for* him also

μαρτυρίαν καλὴν ἔχειν ἀπὸ τῶν ἔξωθεν, ἵνα μὴ
[3]a [5]testimony [4]good [1]to [2]have from the *ones* outside, in order that not
lest

up holy hands, without wrath
and doubting;
9 in like manner also, that
the women adorn themselves in
modest apparel, with propriety
and moderation, not with
braided hair or gold or pearls or
costly clothing,
10 but, which is proper for
women professing godliness,
with good works.
11 Let a woman learn in silence with all submission.
12 And I do not permit a
woman to teach or to have authority over a man, but to be in
silence.
13 For Adam was formed
first, then Eve.
14 And Adam was not de-
ceived, but the woman being
deceived, fell into transgression.
15 Nevertheless she will be
saved in childbearing if they
continue in faith, love, and holiness, with self-control.
3 This *is* a faithful saying: If
a man desires the position
of a bishop, he desires a good
work.
2 A bishop then must be
blameless, the husband of
one wife, temperate, sober-
minded, of good behavior, hospitable, able to teach;
3 not given to wine, not violent, not greedy for money, but
gentle, not quarrelsome, not
covetous;
4 one who rules his own
house well, having *his* children
in submission with all reverence
5 (for if a man does not know
how to rule his own house, how
will he take care of the church
of God?);
6 not a novice, lest being
puffed up with pride he fall into
the *same* condemnation as the
devil.
7 Moreover he must have a
good testimony among those
who are outside, lest he fall into

---

[a](3:3) NU omits *μη αισχροκερδη, not greedy for base gain.*

reproach and the snare of the
devil.
8 Likewise deacons *must be*
reverent, not double-tongued,
not given to much wine, not
greedy for money,
9 holding the mystery of the
faith with a pure conscience.
10 But let these also first be
tested; then let them serve as
deacons, being *found* blameless.
11 Likewise, *their* wives *must*
be reverent, not slanderers,
temperate, faithful in all things.
12 Let deacons be the husbands of one wife, ruling *their*
children and their own houses
well.
13 For those who have served
well as deacons obtain for
themselves a good standing and
great boldness in the faith
which is in Christ Jesus.
14 These things I write to
you, though I hope to come to
you shortly;
15 but if I am delayed, *I write*
so that you may know how you
ought to conduct yourself in the
house of God, which is the
church of the living God, the
pillar and ground of the truth.
16 And without controversy
great is the mystery of godliness:

God was manifested in
the flesh,
Justified in the Spirit,
Seen by angels,
Preached among the
Gentiles,
Believed on in the world,
Received up in glory.

εἰς ὀνειδισμὸν ἐμπέσῃ καὶ παγίδα τοῦ διαβόλου.
[3]into [4]reproach [1]he [2]fall and *the* snare of the devil.

Qualifications of Deacons

8 Διακόνους ὡσαύτως σεμνούς, μὴ
It is necessary for deacons likewise *to be* reverent, not

διλόγους, μὴ οἴνῳ πολλῷ προσέχοντας, μὴ
double-tongued, not [3]to [5]wine [4]much [1]being [2]given, not

αἰσχροκερδεῖς,* 9 ἔχοντας τὸ μυστήριον τῆς πίστεως ἐν
greedy for base gain, having (holding) the mystery of the faith with

καθαρᾷ συνειδήσει. 10 Καὶ οὗτοι δὲ δοκιμαζέσθωσαν
a pure conscience. [5]also [3]these [4]*men* [1]But [2]let [6]be [7]approved

πρῶτον, εἶτα διακονείτωσαν, ἀνέγκλητοι ὄντες.
first, then let them serve as deacons, irreproachable ˜ being.

11 Γυναῖκας ὡσαύτως σεμνάς, μὴ διαβόλους,
Their wives likewise *must be* reverent, not slanderers,

νηφαλέους, πιστὰς ἐν πᾶσι. 12 Διάκονοι ἔστωσαν μιᾶς
temperate, faithful in all *things.* deacons ˜ Let be [2]of [3]one

γυναικὸς ἄνδρες, τέκνων καλῶς προϊστάμενοι καὶ τῶν ἰδίων
[4]wife [1]husbands, [6]children [7]well [5]ruling and - their own

οἴκων. 13 Οἱ γὰρ καλῶς διακονήσαντες
houses (households). [2]the [3]*ones* [1]For [6]well [4]having [5]served [7]as [8]deacons

βαθμὸν ἑαυτοῖς καλὸν περιποιοῦνται καὶ πολλὴν
[10]a [12]standing [13]for [14]themselves [11]good [9]obtain and much

παρρησίαν ἐν πίστει τῇ ἐν Χριστῷ Ἰησοῦ.
boldness in *the* faith the *one* (which is) in Christ Jesus.

Magnum Mysterium

14 Ταῦτά σοι γράφω, ἐλπίζων ἐλθεῖν πρός σε
These *things* to you I write, hoping to come to you

τάχιον. 15 Ἐὰν δὲ βραδύνω, ἵνα εἰδῇς πῶς
shortly. if ˜ But I tarry (I am delayed), *I write* so that you may know how

δεῖ ἐν οἴκῳ Θεοῦ ἀναστρέφεσθαι, ἥτις ἐστὶν
it is necessary [4]in [5]*the* [6]house [7]of [8]God [1]to [2]conduct [3]oneself, which is

ἐκκλησία Θεοῦ ζῶντος, στῦλος καὶ ἑδραίωμα τῆς
the church of *the* God ˜ living, *the* pillar and bulwark of the

ἀληθείας. 16 Καὶ ὁμολογουμένως μέγα ἐστὶ τὸ τῆς εὐσεβείας
truth. And confessedly great is the - [2]of [3]godliness

μυστήριον·
[1]mystery:

Θεὸς[b] ἐφανερώθη ἐν σαρκί,
God was manifested in *the* flesh,

Ἐδικαιώθη ἐν Πνεύματι,
He was justified in *the* Spirit,

Ὤφθη ἀγγέλοις,
He was seen by angels,

Ἐκηρύχθη ἐν ἔθνεσιν,
He was proclaimed among Gentiles,

Ἐπιστεύθη ἐν κόσμῳ,
He was believed *on* in *the* world,

Ἀνελήφθη ἐν δόξῃ.
He was taken up in glory.

---

[b]**(3:16)** NU reads ὅς, *who.*

*__(3:8)__ αἰσχροκερδής *(aischrokerdēs)*. Adjective meaning *fond of* or *seeking dishonest gain,* occurring elsewhere only in 1 Tim. 3:3 (NU omits) and Titus 1:7. The word is a general synonym of "covetous" (see πλεονεξία at Col. 3:5). Cf. the cognate adverb αἰσχροκερδῶς, *for dishonest gain* (only in 1 Pet. 5:2).

Doctrines of Demons

4 1 Τὸ δὲ Πνεῦμα ῥητῶς λέγει ὅτι ἐν ὑστέροις καιροῖς
the ˜ Now Spirit explicity says that in later seasons
times

ἀποστήσονταί τινες τῆς πίστεως, προσέχοντες πνεύμασι
[2]will [3]depart [4]from [1]some the faith, giving heed to spirits ˜

πλάνοις καὶ διδασκαλίαις δαιμονίων, 2 ἐν ὑποκρίσει
deceitful and to teachings of demons, in hypocrisy

ψευδολόγων, κεκαυτηριασμένων τὴν ἰδίαν συνείδησιν,
of liars, having been seared *in* - their own conscience,

3 κωλυόντων γαμεῖν, ἀπέχεσθαι βρωμάτων ἃ ὁ
forbidding to marry, *commanding* to abstain from foods which -

Θεὸς ἔκτισεν εἰς μετάληψιν μετὰ εὐχαριστίας τοῖς
God created for *the* receiving with thanksgiving by the *ones*
to be received those

πιστοῖς καὶ ἐπεγνωκόσι τὴν ἀλήθειαν. 4 Ὅτι
who are faithful and have come to know the truth. Because
who are believers

πᾶν κτίσμα Θεοῦ καλόν, καὶ οὐδὲν ἀπόβλητον, μετὰ
every creature of God *is* good, and not one *is to be* rejected, with

εὐχαριστίας λαμβανόμενον, 5 ἁγιάζεται γὰρ διὰ λόγου
thanksgiving being received, [2]it [3]is [4]sanctified [1]for through *the* word

Θεοῦ καὶ ἐντεύξεως.
of God and petition.

A Good Servant of Jesus Christ

6 Ταῦτα ὑποτιθέμενος τοῖς ἀδελφοῖς καλὸς
[4]*in* [5]these [6]*things* [1]Instructing [2]the [3]brothers [10]a [11]good

ἔσῃ διάκονος Ἰησοῦ Χριστοῦ,[a] ἐντρεφόμενος τοῖς
[7]you [8]will [9]be servant of Jesus Christ, being nourished by the

λόγοις τῆς πίστεως καὶ τῆς καλῆς διδασκαλίας ᾗ
words of the faith and of the good teaching which

παρηκολούθηκας. 7 Τοὺς δὲ βεβήλους καὶ γραώδεις
you have carefully followed. - But profane and old womens'

μύθους παραιτοῦ. Γύμναζε* δὲ σεαυτὸν πρὸς εὐσέβειαν.
myths reject. exercise ˜ But yourself to godliness.
Rather

8 Ἡ γὰρ σωματικὴ γυμνασία πρὸς ὀλίγον ἐστὶν ὠφέλιμος, ἡ
- For bodily exercise for a little is profitable, -

δὲ εὐσέβεια πρὸς πάντα ὠφέλιμός ἐστιν, ἐπαγγελίαν ἔχουσα
but godliness for all *things* profitable ˜ is, promise ˜ having

ζωῆς τῆς νῦν καὶ τῆς μελλούσης. 9 Πιστὸς ὁ λόγος καὶ
of life of the now and of the coming *life*. Faithful *is* the word and
of the present life Trustworthy

πάσης ἀποδοχῆς ἄξιος. 10 Εἰς τοῦτο γὰρ καὶ κοπιῶμεν καὶ
[2]of [3]all [4]acceptance [1]worthy. [6]to [7]this [5]For also we labor and

ὀνειδιζόμεθα,[b] ὅτι ἠλπίκαμεν ἐπὶ Θεῷ ζῶντι, ὅς
suffer reproach, because we have set our hope on *the* God ˜ living, who

ἐστι Σωτὴρ πάντων ἀνθρώπων, μάλιστα πιστῶν.
is Savior of all men, especially of believers.

Take Heed to Yourself and Your Doctrine

11 Παράγγελλε ταῦτα καὶ δίδασκε. 12 Μηδείς σου
Command [3]these [4]*things* [1]and [2]teach. [2]no [3]one [5]your

τῆς νεότητος καταφρονείτω, ἀλλὰ τύπος γίνου τῶν
- [6]youth [1]Let [4]despise, but [2]a [3]pattern [1]become for the

4 Now the Spirit expressly
says that in latter times
some will depart from the faith,
giving heed to deceiving spirits
and doctrines of demons,
2 speaking lies in hypocrisy,
having their own conscience
seared with a hot iron,
3 forbidding to marry, *and*
commanding to abstain from
foods which God created to be
received with thanksgiving by
those who believe and know
the truth.
4 For every creature of God
is good, and nothing is to be refused if it is received with
thanksgiving;
5 for it is sanctified by the
word of God and prayer.
6 If you instruct the brethren
in these things, you will be a
good minister of Jesus Christ,
nourished in the words of faith
and of the good doctrine which
you have carefully followed.
7 But reject profane and old
wives' fables, and exercise
yourself toward godliness.
8 For bodily exercise profits
a little, but godliness is profitable for all things, having promise of the life that now is and of
that which is to come.
9 This *is* a faithful saying and
worthy of all acceptance.
10 For to this *end* we both labor and suffer reproach, because we trust in the living
God, who is *the* Savior of all
men, especially of those who
believe.
11 These things command and
teach.
12 Let no one despise your
youth, but be an example to the

---

[a]**(4:6)** NU reads Χριστος Ιησους, *Christ Jesus.*
[b]**(4:10)** NU reads αγωνιζομεθα, *we strive.*

***(4:7)** γυμνάζω *(gymnazō).* Verb meaning literally *to exercise naked* (from γυμνός, *naked, bare*), following the Greek practice of exercising in the nude. It then came to mean simply *to train,* either physically, mentally, or spiritually. Here it is training oneself in godliness. In Heb. 5:14 the senses are to be *trained* to differentiate between good and evil. The false teachers had *trained* their hearts in greed (2 Pet. 2:14).

believers in word, in conduct,
in love, in spirit, in faith, in purity.
13 Till I come, give attention
to reading, to exhortation, to
doctrine.
14 Do not neglect the gift that
is in you, which was given to
you by prophecy with the laying
on of the hands of the eldership.
15 Meditate on these things;
give yourself entirely to them,
that your progress may be evident to all.
16 Take heed to yourself and
to the doctrine. Continue in
them, for in doing this you will
save both yourself and those
who hear you.
5 Do not rebuke an older
man, but exhort *him* as a
father, younger men as
brothers,
2 older women as mothers,
younger women as sisters, with
all purity.
3 Honor widows who are really widows.
4 But if any widow has children or grandchildren, let them
first learn to show piety at
home and to repay their parents; for this is good and acceptable before God.
5 Now she who is really a
widow, and left alone, trusts in
God and continues in supplications and prayers night and day.
6 But she who lives in pleasure is dead while she lives.
7 And these things com-
mand, that they may be blameless.
8 But if anyone does not provide for his own, and especially
for those of his household, he

πιστῶν ἐν λόγῳ, ἐν ἀναστροφῇ, ἐν ἀγάπῃ, ἐν πνεύματι,[c] ἐν
faithful in word, in conduct, in love, in spirit, in
believers

πίστει, ἐν ἁγνείᾳ. 13 Ἕως ἔρχομαι πρόσεχε τῇ
faith, in purity. Until I come give attention -

ἀναγνώσει, τῇ παρακλήσει, τῇ διδασκαλίᾳ. 14 Μὴ
to *public* reading, - to exhortation, - to teaching. not ˜

ἀμέλει τοῦ ἐν σοὶ χαρίσματος, ὃ ἐδόθη σοι διὰ
Do neglect the [2]in [3]you [1]gift, which was given to you through
along with

προφητείας μετὰ ἐπιθέσεως τῶν χειρῶν τοῦ πρεσβυτερίου.
prophecy with laying on of the hands of the eldership.

15 Ταῦτα μελέτα, ἐν τούτοις ἴσθι, ἵνα σου ἡ
[3]these [4]*things* [1]Meditate [2]on, [6]in [7]these [8]*things* [5]be, so that your -

προκοπὴ φανερὰ ᾖ ἐν πᾶσιν. 16 Ἔπεχε σεαυτῷ
progress [3]evident [1]may [2]be among all. Take heed to yourself
to

καὶ τῇ διδασκαλίᾳ. Ἐπίμενε αὐτοῖς· τοῦτο γὰρ ποιῶν καὶ
and to the teaching. Continue in them; [4]this [1]for [2]*by* [3]doing both

σεαυτὸν σώσεις καὶ τοὺς ἀκούοντάς σου.
yourself you will save and the *ones* hearing you.
those who hear

How to Treat Other Believers

5 1 Πρεσβυτέρῳ μὴ ἐπιπλήξῃς, ἀλλὰ παρακάλει ὡς
[5]an [6]older [7]man [2]not [1]Do [3]rebuke [4]sharply, but exhort *him* as

πατέρα, νεωτέρους ὡς ἀδελφούς, 2 πρεσβυτέρας ὡς μητέρας,
a father, younger men as brothers, older women as mothers,

νεωτέρας ὡς ἀδελφάς, ἐν πάσῃ ἁγνείᾳ.
younger women as sisters, with all purity.

How to Honor True Widows

3 Χήρας τίμα τὰς ὄντως χήρας. 4 Εἰ δέ τις
widows ˜ Honor the *ones* really widows. if ˜ But a certain
who really are

χήρα τέκνα ἢ ἔκγονα ἔχει, μανθανέτωσαν πρῶτον τὸν
widow [2]children [3]or [4]grandchildren [1]has, let them learn first -

ἴδιον οἶκον εὐσεβεῖν καὶ ἀμοιβὰς ἀποδιδόναι
[5]their [6]own [7]house [1]to [2]show [3]piety [4]to and payments to give back
household to make repayment

τοῖς προγόνοις, τοῦτο γάρ ἐστιν[a] ἀπόδεκτον ἐνώπιον τοῦ
to the parents, this ˜ for is acceptable before -
their

Θεοῦ. 5 Ἡ δὲ ὄντως χήρα καὶ μεμονωμένη
God. [2]the [3]*one* [1]Now *who is* really a widow and having been left alone
she

ἤλπικεν ἐπὶ τὸν Θεὸν καὶ προσμένει ταῖς δεήσεσι
has set her hope on - God and continues - in supplications

καὶ ταῖς προσευχαῖς νυκτὸς καὶ ἡμέρας. 6 Ἡ δὲ
and - in prayers night and day. [2]the [3]*one* [1]But
she who is

σπαταλῶσα, ζῶσα τέθνηκε. 7 Καὶ ταῦτα
living for pleasure, living has died. And these *things*
is dead while she lives.

παράγγελλε, ἵνα ἀνεπίληπτοι ὦσιν. 8 Εἰ δέ τις
command, so that [4]blameless [1]they [2]may [3]be. if ˜ But anyone

τῶν ἰδίων καὶ μάλιστα τῶν οἰκείων οὐ προνοεῖ,
- [5]his [6]own [7]and [8]especially [9]the [10]householders [2]not [1]does [3]provide [4]for,
his

---

[c](4:12) NU omits εν πνευματι, *in spirit.*
[a](5:4) TR adds καλον και, *good and.*

τὴν πίστιν ἤρνηται καὶ ἔστιν ἀπίστου χείρων.
[14]the [15]faith [11]he [12]has [13]denied and is [2]*than* [3]*an* [4]unbeliever [1]worse.

9 Χήρα καταλεγέσθω μὴ ἔλαττον ἐτῶν ἑξήκοντα
[6]a [7]widow [5]Let be enrolled *if* not less than years ˜ sixty

γεγονυῖα, ἑνὸς ἀνδρὸς γυνή, **10** ἐν ἔργοις καλοῖς
having become, [3]of [4]one [5]man [1]*the* [2]wife, by works ˜ good
lived,

μαρτυρουμένη, εἰ ἐτεκνοτρόφησεν, εἰ ἐξενοδόχησεν, εἰ
being witnessed, if she brought up children, if she lodged strangers, if
approved,

ἁγίων πόδας ἔνιψεν, εἰ θλιβομένοις ἐπήρκεσεν, εἰ
[3]of [4]saints [1]*the* [2]feet she washed, if *the* afflicted *ones* she relieved, if

παντὶ ἔργῳ ἀγαθῷ ἐπηκολούθησε.
every work ˜ good she diligently followed.

Counsel for Younger Widows

11 Νεωτέρας δὲ χήρας παραιτοῦ· ὅταν γὰρ
[5]younger [1]But [6]widows [2]refuse [3]*to* [4]*enroll;* whenever ˜ for

καταστρηνιάσωσι τοῦ Χριστοῦ, γαμεῖν θέλουσιν,
they grow wanton *against* - Christ, [3]to [4]marry [1]they [2]desire,

12 ἔχουσαι κρίμα ὅτι τὴν πρώτην πίστιν ἠθέτησαν.
having judgment because the first *pledge of* faith they set aside.
their

13 Ἅμα δὲ καὶ ἀργαὶ μανθάνουσι,
[2]at [3]the [4]same [5]time [1]And also [5]idle [1]they [2]learn [3]*to* [4]*be,*
besides

περιερχόμεναι τὰς οἰκίας, οὐ μόνον δὲ ἀργαί, ἀλλὰ
going around the houses, [2]not [3]only [1]and idle, but
from house to house,

καὶ φλύαροι καὶ περίεργοι, λαλοῦσαι τὰ μὴ
also gossipy and busybodies, speaking the *things which are* not

δέοντα. **14** Βούλομαι οὖν νεωτέρας γαμεῖν,
proper. I desire therefore younger women to marry,

τεκνογονεῖν, οἰκοδεσποτεῖν, μηδεμίαν ἀφορμὴν διδόναι
to bear children, to manage the house, [3]no [4]opportunity [1]to [2]give

τῷ ἀντικειμένῳ λοιδορίας χάριν. **15** Ἤδη γάρ τινες
to the adversary [3]reproach [1]because [2]of. already ˜ For some

ἐξετράπησαν ὀπίσω τοῦ Σατανᾶ. **16** Εἴ τις πιστὸς ἢ[b]
turned aside after - Satan. If any believing man or

πιστὴ ἔχει χήρας, ἐπαρκείτω αὐταῖς, καὶ μὴ
believing woman has widows, let *that one* relieve them, and [2]not

βαρείσθω ἡ ἐκκλησία, ἵνα ταῖς ὄντως χήραις
[1]let [5]be [6]burdened [3]the [4]church, so that [4]the [5]*ones* [6]really [7]widows
those who are

ἐπαρκέσῃ.
[1]it [2]may [3]relieve.

How to Honor the Elders

17 Οἱ καλῶς προεστῶτες πρεσβύτεροι διπλῆς τιμῆς*
[2]the [6]well [4]having [5]ruled [3]elders [10]of [11]double [12]honor

ἀξιούσθωσαν, μάλιστα οἱ κοπιῶντες ἐν λόγῳ καὶ
[1]Let [7]be [8]counted [9]worthy, especially the *ones* laboring in word and

διδασκαλίᾳ. **18** Λέγει γὰρ ἡ Γραφή, «Βοῦν ἀλοῶντα
teaching. [4]says [1]For [2]the [3]Scripture, «[9]an [10]ox [11]threshing [12]*grain*

οὐ φιμώσεις,»[c] καί, «Ἄξιος ὁ ἐργάτης τοῦ μισθοῦ
[7]not [5]you [6]shall [8]muzzle,» and, «[4]worthy [1]The [2]worker [3]*is* - of wages ˜
A

has denied the faith and is worse than an unbeliever.
9 Do not let a widow under sixty years old be taken into the number, *and not unless* she has been the wife of one man,
10 well reported for good works: if she has brought up children, if she has lodged strangers, if she has washed the saints' feet, if she has relieved the afflicted, if she has diligently followed every good work.
11 But refuse *the* younger widows; for when they have begun to grow wanton against Christ, they desire to marry,
12 having condemnation because they have cast off their first faith.
13 And besides they learn *to be* idle, wandering about from house to house, and not only idle but also gossips and busybodies, saying things which they ought not.
14 Therefore I desire that *the* younger *widows* marry, bear children, manage the house, give no opportunity to the adversary to speak reproachfully.
15 For some have already turned aside after Satan.
16 If any believing man or woman has widows, let them relieve them, and do not let the church be burdened, that it may relieve those who are really widows.
17 Let the elders who rule well be counted worthy of double honor, especially those who labor in the word and doctrine.
18 For the Scripture says, *"You shall not muzzle an ox while it treads out the grain,"* and, "The laborer *is* worthy of

---

b**(5:16)** NU omits πιστος η, *believing man or.*
c**(5:18)** Deut. 25:4

***(5:17)** τιμή *(timē).* Noun, common in the NT, meaning *price, value* (as Acts 5:2), *honor, respect* (as 1 Tim. 6:1; John 4:4), or even *position of honor* (as Heb. 5:4). The word generally includes the recognition of the dignity or value of a given position. Here in 1 Tim. 5:17 it may designate a monetary expression of honor or value, thus an *honorarium.* Cf. the cognate verb τιμάω, *value, set a price on* (as Matt. 27:9), *honor, respect* (which may include obedience, as Eph. 6:2; 1 Pet. 2:17); and the adjective τίμιος, *valuable, precious, honored, respected.*

his wages."
19 Do not receive an accusation against an elder except
from two or three witnesses.
20 Those who are sinning rebuke in the presence of all, that
the rest also may fear.
21 I charge *you* before God
and the Lord Jesus Christ and
the elect angels that you observe these things without prej-
udice, doing nothing with
partiality.
22 Do not lay hands on anyone
hastily, nor share in other people's sins; keep yourself pure.
23 No longer drink only water, but use a little wine for
your stomach's sake and your
frequent infirmities.
24 Some men's sins are
clearly evident, preceding *them*
to judgment, but those of some
men follow later.
25 Likewise, the good works
of some are clearly evident, and
those that are otherwise cannot
be hidden.
6 Let as many bondservants
as are under the yoke
count their own masters worthy of all honor, so that the
name of God and *His* doctrine
may not be blasphemed.
2 And those who have be-
lieving masters, let them not
despise *them* because they are
brethren, but rather serve *them*
because those who are benefited are believers and beloved.
Teach and exhort these things.
3 If anyone teaches otherwise and does not consent to
wholesome words, *even* the

αὐτοῦ.»[d] **19** Κατὰ πρεσβυτέρου κατηγορίαν μὴ παραδέχου,
his.» Against an elder [4]an [5]accusation [2]not [1]do [3]receive,

ἐκτὸς εἰ μὴ ἐπὶ δύο ἢ τριῶν μαρτύρων. **20** Τοὺς
without if not on *the basis of* two or three witnesses. The *ones*
unless Those

ἁμαρτάνοντας ἐνώπιον πάντων ἔλεγχε, ἵνα καὶ οἱ λοιποὶ
sinning [2]before [3]all [1]rebuke, so that also the rest
who sin

φόβον ἔχωσι. **21** Διαμαρτύρομαι ἐνώπιον τοῦ Θεοῦ καὶ
[3]fear [1]may [2]have. I charge *you* before - God and

Κυρίου[e] Ἰησοῦ Χριστοῦ καὶ τῶν ἐκλεκτῶν ἀγγέλων, ἵνα
the Lord Jesus Christ and the elect angels, that

ταῦτα φυλάξῃς χωρὶς προκρίματος, μηδὲν ποιῶν
[3]these [4]*things* [1]you [2]observe without prejudgment, nothing ˜ doing

κατὰ πρόσκλησιν. **22** Χεῖρας ταχέως μηδενὶ ἐπιτίθει,
according to inclination. [2]hands [6]hastily [4]no [5]one [1]Lay [3]on,
partiality.

μηδὲ κοινώνει ἁμαρτίαις ἀλλοτρίαις. Σεαυτὸν ἁγνὸν τήρει.
nor share in sins of others. [2]yourself [3]pure [1]Keep.

23 Μηκέτι ὑδροπότει, ἀλλ' οἴνῳ ὀλίγῳ χρῶ διὰ τὸν
No longer drink water *only,* but [4]wine [2]a [3]little [1]use on account of -

στόμαχόν σου καὶ τὰς πυκνάς σου ἀσθενείας.
stomach ˜ your and - frequent ˜ your weaknesses.
illnesses.

24 Τινῶν ἀνθρώπων αἱ ἁμαρτίαι πρόδηλοί εἰσι,
[3]of [4]some [5]men [1]The [2]sins [7]evident [8]beforehand [6]are,

προάγουσαι εἰς κρίσιν, τισὶ δὲ καὶ ἐπακολουθοῦσιν.
preceding *them* to judgment, some ˜ but also follow after.

25 Ὡσαύτως καὶ τὰ καλὰ ἔργα πρόδηλά ἐστι,
Likewise also the good works *of some* [2]evident [3]beforehand [1]are,

καὶ τὰ ἄλλως ἔχοντα κρυβῆναι οὐ δύνανται.
and the *ones* otherwise ˜ having [4]to [5]be [6]hidden [2]not [1]are [3]able.
which are

How to Honor Masters

6 **1** Ὅσοι εἰσὶν ὑπὸ ζυγὸν δοῦλοι, τοὺς ἰδίους
As many as are [2]under [3]*the* [4]yoke [1]bondservants, - [8]their [9]own
slaves,

δεσπότας* πάσης τιμῆς ἀξίους ἡγείσθωσαν, ἵνα μὴ τὸ
[10]masters [12]of [13]all [14]honor [11]worthy [5]let [6]them [7]count, so that [9]not [1]the

ὄνομα τοῦ Θεοῦ καὶ ἡ διδασκαλία βλασφημῆται.
[2]name - [3]of [4]God [5]and [6]the [7]teaching [8]may be blasphemed.

2 Οἱ δὲ πιστοὺς ἔχοντες δεσπότας μὴ
[2]the [3]*ones* [1]And [5]believing [4]having [6]masters [9]not

καταφρονείτωσαν, ὅτι ἀδελφοί εἰσιν· ἀλλὰ μᾶλλον
[7]let [8]them [10]despise *them,* because [3]brothers [1]they [2]are; but rather

δουλευέτωσαν, ὅτι πιστοί εἰσι καὶ ἀγαπητοὶ οἱ
let them serve as slaves, because [8]believing [7]are [9]and [10]beloved [1]the [2]*ones*

τῆς εὐεργεσίας ἀντιλαμβανόμενοι.
[4]the [5]good [6]service [3]receiving.

Of False Doctrine and Human Greed

Ταῦτα δίδασκε καὶ παρακάλει. **3** Εἴ τις
[4]these [5]*things* [1]Teach [2]and [3]exhort. If anyone

ἑτεροδιδασκαλεῖ καὶ μὴ προσέρχεται ὑγιαίνουσιν λόγοις,
teaches differently and not ˜ does consent to healthy words,
sound

---

[d](5:18) Luke 10:7
[e](5:21) NU omits Κυριου, *Lord,* and reads Χριστου Ιησου, *Christ Jesus.*

*(6:1) δεσπότης (*despotēs*). Noun meaning *lord, master.* The word originally referred to the head of a household in his position as *owner* of its property (as 2 Tim. 2:21, metaphorically of God) and slaves (as here in 1 Tim. 6:1, 2). The Greeks also used δεσπόται to refer to their gods as a description of absolute power (cf. the Christian use of the title for God in Jude 4; Acts 4:24). A person who used this word would be admitting his total dependence upon God's majesty and power. Peter's reference to the false teachers who deny "the Lord (Δεσπότης) who bought

τοῖς τοῦ Κυρίου ἡμῶν Ἰησοῦ Χριστοῦ, καὶ τῇ κατ'
the *ones* - of Lord ~ our Jesus Christ, and to the [2]according [3]to
those doctrine

εὐσέβειαν διδασκαλίᾳ, 4 τετύφωται, μηδὲν
[4]godliness [1]teaching, he has been puffed up, nothing ~
which accords with godliness, he is proud,

ἐπιστάμενος, ἀλλὰ νοσῶν περὶ ζητήσεις καὶ
understanding, but being diseased concerning disputes and
morbidly concerned with

λογομαχίας, ἐξ ὧν γίνεται φθόνος, ἔρις, βλασφημίαι,
word battles, from which becomes envy, strife, blasphemies,
come slanders,

ὑπόνοιαι πονηραί, 5 διαπαρατριβαὶ[a] διεφθαρμένων
suspicions ~ evil, constant wranglings [3]having [4]been [5]corrupted
of men

ἀνθρώπων τὸν νοῦν καὶ ἀπεστερημένων τῆς
[1]of [2]men *with reference to* the mind and having been deprived of the
of corrupt minds

ἀληθείας, νομιζόντων πορισμὸν εἶναι τὴν εὐσέβειαν.
truth, supposing *that* [4]gain [2]to [3]be - [1]godliness.
is a means of profit

Ἀφίστασο[b] ἀπὸ τῶν τοιούτων. 6 Ἔστι δὲ πορισμὸς μέγας ἡ
Withdraw from - such *people.* [5]is [1]But [7]gain [6]great -

εὐσέβεια μετὰ αὐταρκείας. 7 Οὐδὲν γὰρ εἰσηνέγκαμεν εἰς
[2]godliness [3]with [4]contentment. [4]nothing [1]For [2]we [3]brought into

τὸν κόσμον, δῆλον[c] ὅτι οὐδὲ ἐξενεγκεῖν τι
the world, *and it is* certain that neither [4]to [5]carry [7]out [6]anything

δυνάμεθα! 8 Ἔχοντες δὲ διατροφὰς καὶ σκεπάσματα,
[1]are [2]we [3]able! having ~ But food and coverings,

τούτοις ἀρκεσθησόμεθα. 9 Οἱ δὲ βουλόμενοι
with these *things* we shall be content. [2]the [3]*ones* [1]But desiring

πλουτεῖν ἐμπίπτουσιν εἰς πειρασμὸν καὶ παγίδα καὶ ἐπιθυμίας
to be rich fall into temptation and a snare and [5]desires

πολλὰς ἀνοήτους καὶ βλαβεράς, αἵτινες βυθίζουσι τοὺς
[1]many [2]senseless [3]and [4]harmful, which sink -

ἀνθρώπους εἰς ὄλεθρον καὶ ἀπώλειαν. 10 Ῥίζα γὰρ πάντων
men into destruction and perdition. [7]a [8]root [1]For [9]of [10]all

τῶν κακῶν ἐστιν ἡ φιλαργυρία, ἧς τινες ὀρεγόμενοι
- [11]evils [6]is [2]the [3]love [4]of [5]money, of which some *by* aspiring

ἀπεπλανήθησαν ἀπὸ τῆς πίστεως καὶ ἑαυτοὺς περιέπειραν
have strayed away from the faith and [2]themselves [1]pierced [3]through

ὀδύναις πολλαῖς.
with pangs ~ many.

The Man of God

11 Σὺ δέ, ὦ ἄνθρωπε τοῦ Θεοῦ, ταῦτα φεῦγε.
You however, O man - of God, [2]these [3]*things* [1]flee.

Δίωκε δὲ δικαιοσύνην, εὐσέβειαν, πίστιν, ἀγάπην, ὑπομονήν,
pursue ~ But righteousness, godliness, faith, love, endurance,

πραότητα. 12 Ἀγωνίζου τὸν καλὸν ἀγῶνα τῆς πίστεως,
gentleness. Struggle the good struggle - of faith,

ἐπιλαβοῦ τῆς αἰωνίου ζωῆς, εἰς ἣν[d] ἐκλήθης καὶ
lay hold on - eternal life, to which you were called and

ὡμολόγησας τὴν καλὴν ὁμολογίαν ἐνώπιον πολλῶν μαρτύρων.
you confessed the good confession before many witnesses.

13 Παραγγέλλω σοι ἐνώπιον τοῦ Θεοῦ τοῦ ζωοποιοῦντος τὰ
I charge you before - God the *One* giving life to -
who gives

words of our Lord Jesus Christ,
and to the doctrine which accords with godliness,
4 he is proud, knowing nothing, but is obsessed with disputes and arguments over
words, from which come envy,
strife, reviling, evil suspicions,
5 useless wranglings of men
of corrupt minds and destitute
of the truth, who suppose that
godliness is a *means of* gain.
From such withdraw yourself.
6 Now godliness with con-
tentment is great gain.
7 For we brought nothing
into *this* world, *and it is* certain
we can carry nothing out.
8 And having food and clothing, with these we shall be content.
9 But those who desire to be
rich fall into temptation and a
snare, and *into* many foolish
and harmful lusts which drown
men in destruction and perdition.
10 For the love of money is a
root of all *kinds of* evil, for
which some have strayed from
the faith in their greediness,
and pierced themselves
through with many sorrows.
11 But you, O man of God,
flee these things and pursue
righteousness, godliness, faith,
love, patience, gentleness.
12 Fight the good fight of
faith, lay hold on eternal life, to
which you were also called and
have confessed the good confession in the presence of many
witnesses.
13 I urge you in the sight of
God who gives life to all things,

---

[a](**6:5**) TR reads παραδιατριβαι, *useless occupations.*
[b](**6:5**) NU omits this sentence. [c](**6:7**) NU omits δηλον, *(and it is) certain.*
[d](**6:12**) TR adds και, *also.*

them" (2 Pet. 2:1) refers to the redemption effected by Christ Jesus.

and *before* Christ Jesus who witnessed the good confession before Pontius Pilate,
14 that you keep *this* commandment without spot, blameless until our Lord Jesus
Christ's appearing,
15 which He will manifest in
His own time, *He who is* the
blessed and only Potentate, the
King of kings and Lord of lords,
16 who alone has immortality,
dwelling in unapproachable
light, whom no man has seen or
can see, to whom *be* honor and
everlasting power. Amen.
17 Command those who are
rich in this present age not to
be haughty, nor to trust in uncertain riches but in the living
God, who gives us richly all
things to enjoy.
18 *Let them* do good, that they
be rich in good works, ready to
give, willing to share,
19 storing up for themselves a
good foundation for the time to
come, that they may lay hold on
eternal life.
20 O Timothy! Guard what
was committed to your trust,
avoiding the profane *and* idle
babblings and contradictions
of what is falsely called
knowledge—
21 by professing it some have
strayed concerning the faith.
Grace *be* with you. Amen.

πάντα καὶ Χριστοῦ Ἰησοῦ τοῦ μαρτυρήσαντος ἐπὶ
all *things* and *before* Christ Jesus the *One* witnessing before
who witnessed

Ποντίου Πιλάτου τὴν καλὴν ὁμολογίαν, 14 τηρῆσαί σε τὴν
Pontius Pilate the good confession, to keep you the
that you keep

ἐντολὴν ἄσπιλον, ἀνεπίληπτον, μέχρι τῆς ἐπιφανείας
commandment without spot, blameless, until the appearing

τοῦ Κυρίου ἡμῶν Ἰησοῦ Χριστοῦ, 15 ἣν καιροῖς ἰδίοις
- of Lord ˜ our Jesus Christ, which [1]in [4]seasons [2]its [3]own
in His own time

δείξει ὁ μακάριος καὶ μόνος Δυνάστης, ὁ
He will show *He who is* the blessed and only Sovereign, the

Βασιλεὺς τῶν βασιλευόντων καὶ Κύριος τῶν
King of the *ones* ruling and Lord of the *ones*

κυριευόντων, 16 ὁ μόνος ἔχων ἀθανασίαν, φῶς οἰκῶν
exercising lordship, the only *One* having immortality, [4]light [1]dwelling [2]in

ἀπρόσιτον, ὃν εἶδεν οὐδεὶς ἀνθρώπων οὐδὲ ἰδεῖν
[3]unapproachable, whom [5]saw [1]no [2]one [3]of [4]men nor [3]to [4]see
has seen

δύναται· ᾧ τιμὴ καὶ κράτος αἰώνιον. Ἀμήν.
[1]is [2]able; to whom *be* honor and power ˜ eternal. Amen.
So be it.

Instructions to the Rich

17 Τοῖς πλουσίοις ἐν τῷ νῦν αἰῶνι παράγγελλε μὴ
To the rich in the now age command not
present

ὑψηλοφρονεῖν μηδὲ ἠλπικέναι ἐπὶ πλούτου
to be haughty nor to have put *their* hope on [3]of [4]riches

ἀδηλότητι, ἀλλ' ἐν τῷ Θεῷ τῷ ζῶντι,[e] τῷ παρέχοντι
[1]the [2]uncertainty, but in - [3]God [1]the [2]living, the *One* providing

ἡμῖν πάντα πλουσίως εἰς ἀπόλαυσιν, 18 ἀγαθοεργεῖν,
for us all *things* richly for enjoyment, to do good,

πλουτεῖν ἐν ἔργοις καλοῖς, εὐμεταδότους εἶναι, κοινωνικούς,
to be rich in works ˜ good, [3]generous [1]to [2]be, sharing,

19 ἀποθησαυρίζοντας ἑαυτοῖς θεμέλιον καλὸν εἰς τὸ
treasuring away for yourselves a foundation ˜ good for the

μέλλον, ἵνα ἐπιλάβωνται τῆς αἰνωίου[f] ζωῆς.
coming *time*, that they may lay hold of - eternal life.
future,

Guard Your Heritage

20 Ὦ Τιμόθεε, τὴν παραθήκην φύλαξον, ἐκτρεπόμενος τὰς
O Timothy, [2]the [3]deposit [1]guard, turning away from the

βεβήλους κενοφωνίας καὶ ἀντιθέσεις τῆς ψευδωνύμου
profane empty babblings and opposing views - of falsely called

"γνώσεως," 21 ἥν τινες ἐπαγγελλόμενοι περὶ τὴν
"knowledge," which some *by* professing *expertise* [4]concerning [5]the

πίστιν ἠστόχησαν.
[6]faith [1]missed [2]*their* [3]aim.

Ἡ χάρις μετὰ[g] σοῦ. Ἀμήν.[h]
- Grace *be* with you. Amen.
So be it.

---

[e](6:17) NU omits τῳ ζωντι, *the living.*
[f](6:19) NU reads οντως, *what is really (life).*
[g](6:21) NU reads μεθ υμων, *with you.*
[h](6:21) NU omits Αμην, *Amen.*

The Second Epistle of Paul the Apostle to
TIMOTHY

ΠΡΟΣ ΤΙΜΟΘΕΟΝ Β
TO TIMOTHY 2

Paul Greets Timothy

1 **1** Παῦλος, ἀπόστολος Χριστοῦ Ἰησοῦ[a] διὰ θελήματος
Paul, an apostle of Christ Jesus through *the* will

Θεοῦ κατ' ἐπαγγελίαν ζωῆς τῆς ἐν Χριστῷ Ἰησοῦ,
of God according to *the* promise of life - in Christ Jesus,

2 Τιμοθέῳ, ἀγαπητῷ τέκνῳ·
To Timothy, beloved child:

Χάρις, ἔλεος, εἰρήνη ἀπὸ Θεοῦ Πατρὸς καὶ Χριστοῦ Ἰησοῦ
Grace, mercy, peace from God *the* Father and Christ Jesus

τοῦ Κυρίου ἡμῶν.
- Lord ˜ our.

Paul Thanks God for Timothy and His Maternal Forebears

3 Χάριν ἔχω τῷ Θεῷ, ᾧ λατρεύω ἀπὸ
[3]thanks [1]I [2]have to God, whom I serve from
give have been serving as did

προγόνων ἐν καθαρᾷ συνειδήσει, ὡς ἀδιάλειπτον ἔχω τὴν
my forefathers with a pure conscience, as [3]unceasing [1]I [2]have -

περὶ σοῦ μνείαν ἐν ταῖς δεήσεσί μου νυκτὸς καὶ ἡμέρας,
[5]about [6]you [4]remembrance in - petitions ˜ my night and day,

4 ἐπιποθῶν σε ἰδεῖν, μεμνημένος σου τῶν δακρύων, ἵνα
longing [3]you [1]to [2]see, having recalled your - tears, so that

χαρᾶς πληρωθῶ, **5** ὑπόμνησιν λαμβάνων τῆς ἐν σοὶ
with joy I may be filled, recollection ˜ taking the [3]*that* [4]*is* [5]in [6]you
recollecting

ἀνυποκρίτου πίστεως, ἥτις ἐνῴκησε πρῶτον ἐν τῇ μάμμῃ
[1]unhypocritical [2]faith, which dwelt first in - grandmother ˜
unfeigned

σου Λωΐδι καὶ τῇ μητρί σου Εὐνίκῃ, πέπεισμαι
your Lois and - in mother ˜ your Eunice, [2]I [3]have [4]been [5]persuaded

δὲ ὅτι καὶ ἐν σοί. **6** Δι' ἣν αἰτίαν ἀναμιμνῄσκω σε
[1]and that also *is* in you. For which cause I remind you

ἀναζωπυρεῖν τὸ χάρισμα τοῦ Θεοῦ, ὅ ἐστιν ἐν σοὶ διὰ
to inflame the gift - of God, which is in you through

τῆς ἐπιθέσεως τῶν χειρῶν μου. **7** Οὐ γὰρ ἔδωκεν ἡμῖν ὁ
the laying on - of hands ˜ my. [4]not [1]For [3]did [5]give [6]us -

Θεὸς πνεῦμα δειλίας, ἀλλὰ δυνάμεως καὶ ἀγάπης καὶ
[2]God a spirit of cowardice, but of power and love and

σωφρονισμοῦ.*
of self-control.

Do Not Be Ashamed of the Gospel

8 Μὴ οὖν ἐπαισχυνθῇς τὸ μαρτύριον τοῦ Κυρίου
[3]not [1]Therefore [2]do be ashamed of the testimony - of Lord ˜

ἡμῶν μηδὲ ἐμὲ τὸν δέσμιον αὐτοῦ, ἀλλὰ συγκακοπάθησον τῷ
our nor of me - prisoner ˜ His, but endure hardship with the

1 Paul, an apostle of Jesus Christ by the will of God, according to the promise of life which is in Christ Jesus,

2 To Timothy, a beloved son:

Grace, mercy, *and* peace from God the Father and Christ Jesus our Lord.

3 I thank God, whom I serve with a pure conscience, as *my* forefathers *did,* as without ceasing I remember you in my prayers night and day,
4 greatly desiring to see you, being mindful of your tears, that I may be filled with joy,
5 when I call to remembrance the genuine faith that is in you, which dwelt first in your grandmother Lois and your mother Eunice, and I am persuaded is in you also.
6 Therefore I remind you to stir up the gift of God which is in you through the laying on of my hands.
7 For God has not given us a spirit of fear, but of power and of love and of a sound mind.
8 Therefore do not be ashamed of the testimony of our Lord, nor of me His prisoner, but share with me in the

---

[a](**1:1**) TR reads Ιησου Χριστου, *Jesus Christ.*

***(1:7)** *σωφρονισμός (sōphronismos).* Noun used only here in the NT, literally meaning *soundness of mind,* then *self-discipline* as the result. The word is one of a large group of cognates including the noun *σωφροσύνη, moderation, self-control, reason* (Acts 26:25; 1 Tim. 2:9, 15); adverb *σωφρόνως, soberly* (Titus 2:12); verb *σωφρονέω, be of sound mind, be reasonable, be serious* (Mark 5:15; Rom. 12:3; Titus 2:6);

sufferings for the gospel according to the power of God,
9 who has saved us and
called *us* with a holy calling, not
according to our works, but according to His own purpose and
grace which was given to us in
Christ Jesus before time began,
10 but has now been revealed
by the appearing of our Savior
Jesus Christ, *who* has abolished
death and brought life and immortality to light through the
gospel,
11 to which I was appointed a
preacher, an apostle, and a
teacher of the Gentiles.
12 For this reason I also suffer
these things; nevertheless I am
not ashamed, for I know whom
I have believed and am persuaded that He is able to keep
what I have committed to Him
until that Day.
13 Hold fast the pattern of
sound words which you have
heard from me, in faith and love
which are in Christ Jesus.
14 That good thing which was
committed to you, keep by the
Holy Spirit who dwells in us.
15 This you know, that all
those in Asia have turned away
from me, among whom are
Phygellus and Hermogenes.
16 The Lord grant mercy to
the household of Onesiphorus,
for he often refreshed me, and
was not ashamed of my chain;
17 but when he arrived in
Rome, he sought me out very
zealously and found *me*.
18 The Lord grant to him that

εὐαγγελίῳ κατὰ δύναμιν Θεοῦ, **9** τοῦ σώσαντος ἡμᾶς
gospel according to *the* power of God, the *One* having saved us
He who saved

καὶ καλέσαντος κλήσει ἁγίᾳ, οὐ κατὰ τὰ ἔργα
and having called *us* with a calling ˜ holy, not according to - works ˜
called

ἡμῶν, ἀλλὰ κατ' ἰδίαν πρόθεσιν καὶ χάριν, τὴν
our, but according to His own purpose and grace, the *one*
which

δοθεῖσαν ἡμῖν ἐν Χριστῷ Ἰησοῦ πρὸ χρόνων αἰωνίων,
having been given to us in Christ Jesus before times ˜ eternal,
was time began,

10 φανερωθεῖσαν δὲ νῦν διὰ τῆς ἐπιφανείας τοῦ
[2]having [3]been [4]manifested [1]but now through the appearance -

Σωτῆρος ἡμῶν Ἰησοῦ Χριστοῦ,[b] καταργήσαντος
of Savior ˜ our Jesus Christ, having nullified

μὲν τὸν θάνατον, φωτίσαντος δὲ
[2]on [3]the [4]one [5]hand - [1]death, having brought to light on the other

ζωὴν καὶ ἀφθαρσίαν διὰ τοῦ εὐαγγελίου, **11** εἰς ὃ
life and incorruption through the gospel, to which
immortality

ἐτέθην ἐγὼ κῆρυξ καὶ ἀπόστολος καὶ διδάσκαλος
[2]was [3]appointed [1]I a herald and apostle and teacher

ἐθνῶν.[c] **12** Δι' ἣν αἰτίαν καὶ ταῦτα πάσχω, ἀλλ' οὐκ
of Gentiles. For which cause also [3]these [4]*things* [1]I [2]suffer, but [3]not

ἐπαισχύνομαι, οἶδα γὰρ ᾧ πεπίστευκα καὶ
[1]I [2]am [4]ashamed, [6]I [7]know [5]for whom I have believed and

πέπεισμαι ὅτι δυνατός ἐστι τὴν παραθήκην μου
I have been persuaded that [3]able [1]He [2]is - [7]deposit [6]my

φυλάξαι εἰς ἐκείνην τὴν ἡμέραν.
[4]to [5]guard to that - day.

Be Loyal to the Faith

13 Ὑποτύπωσιν ἔχε ὑγιαινόντων λόγων ὧν παρ' ἐμοῦ
[2]a [3]pattern [1]Have of healthy words which [3]from [4]me
Hold to a pattern of sound

ἤκουσας, ἐν πίστει καὶ ἀγάπῃ τῇ ἐν Χριστῷ Ἰησοῦ. **14** Τὴν
[1]you [2]heard, in faith and love - in Christ Jesus. [2]the

καλὴν παραθήκην φύλαξον διὰ Πνεύματος Ἁγίου τοῦ
[3]good [4]deposit [1]Guard through *the* Spirit ˜ Holy -

ἐνοικοῦντος ἐν ἡμῖν.
dwelling in us.

15 Οἶδας τοῦτο, ὅτι ἀπεστράφησάν με πάντες οἱ
You know this, that [6]turned [7]away [8]from [9]me [1]all [2]the [3]*ones*
those

ἐν τῇ Ἀσίᾳ, ὧν ἐστι Φύγελος καὶ Ἑρμογένης.
[4]in - [5]Asia, of whom is Phygellus and Hermogenes.
are

16 Δῴη ἔλεος ὁ Κύριος τῷ Ὀνησιφόρου οἴκῳ,
[1]May [4]give [5]mercy [2]the [3]Lord to the [2]of [3]Onesiphorus [1]house,
grant household,

ὅτι πολλάκις με ἀνέψυξε καὶ τὴν ἅλυσίν μου οὐκ
because [2]often [4]me [1]he [3]refreshed and - [5]*of* [7]chain [6]my [3]not

ἐπαισχύνθη, **17** ἀλλὰ γενόμενος ἐν Ῥώμῃ
[1]he [2]was [4]ashamed, but coming to be in Rome
when he arrived

σπουδαιότερον[d] ἐζήτησέ με καὶ εὗρε. **18** Δῴη αὐτῷ ὁ
[2]more [3]zealously [1]he [4]sought [7]me [5]and [6]found. [1]May [4]give [5]him [2]the
very actively grant

---

b(**1:10**) NU reads Χριστου Ιησου, *Christ Jesus.*
c(**1:11**) NU omits εθνων, *of Gentiles.* *d*(**1:17**) NU reads σπουδαιως, *zealously.*

adjective σώφρων, *thoughtful, modest* (1 Tim. 3:2; Titus 2:2, 5); and verb σωφρονίζω, *urge, admonish* (Titus 2:4).

Κύριος εὑρεῖν ἔλεος παρὰ Κυρίου ἐν ἐκείνῃ τῇ ἡμέρᾳ! Καὶ
[3]Lord to find mercy from *the* Lord in that - day! And

ὅσα ἐν Ἐφέσῳ διηκόνησε,[e] βέλτιον σὺ γινώσκεις.
how many *ways* in Ephesus he served, [3]very [4]well [1]you [2]know.

Be Strong in Grace

2 1 Σὺ οὖν, τέκνον μου, ἐνδυναμοῦ ἐν τῇ χάριτι
You therefore, child ˜ my, be empowered by the grace

τῇ ἐν Χριστῷ Ἰησοῦ. 2 Καὶ ἃ ἤκουσας παρ'
the *one* in Christ Jesus. And *the things* which you heard from
which is

ἐμοῦ διὰ πολλῶν μαρτύρων, ταῦτα παράθου πιστοῖς
me through many witnesses, these *things* commit to faithful

ἀνθρώποις, οἵτινες ἱκανοὶ ἔσονται καὶ ἑτέρους διδάξαι.
men, who [3]competent [1]will [2]be also [3]others [1]to [2]teach.

3 Σὺ οὖν κακοπάθησον[a] ὡς καλὸς στρατιώτης Ἰησοῦ
You therefore endure hardship as a good soldier of Jesus

Χριστοῦ.[b] 4 Οὐδεὶς στρατευόμενος ἐμπλέκεται ταῖς τοῦ
Christ. No one serving as a soldier entangles *himself* in the -

βίου πραγματείαις, ἵνα τῷ
[2]of [3]*civilian* [4]life [1]affairs, in order that [4]the [5]*one*

στρατολογήσαντι ἀρέσῃ. 5 Ἐὰν δὲ καὶ
[6]having [7]enlisted [8]him [1]he [2]may [3]please. if ˜ And also

ἀθλῇ τις, οὐ στεφανοῦται ἐὰν μὴ
[2]competes [3]in [4]athletics [1]anyone, [7]not [5]he [6]is [8]crowned if not
unless according

νομίμως ἀθλήσῃ. 6 Τὸν κοπιῶντα γεωργὸν
lawfully he competes. [5]the [6]hardworking [7]farmer
to the rules

δεῖ πρῶτον τῶν καρπῶν μεταλαμβάνειν.
[1]It [2]is [3]necessary [4]*for to be* first [3]of [4]the [5]fruits [1]to [2]receive.
crops

7 Νόει ἃ λέγω· δῴη[c] γάρ σοι ὁ Κύριος
Consider *the things* which I say; [4]may [5]give [1]for [6]you [2]the [3]Lord

σύνεσιν ἐν πᾶσι.
understanding in all *things*.

8 Μνημόνευε Ἰησοῦν Χριστὸν ἐγηγερμένον ἐκ νεκρῶν,
Remember Jesus Christ having been raised from *the* dead,

ἐκ σπέρματος Δαβίδ, κατὰ τὸ εὐαγγέλιόν μου· 9 ἐν ᾧ
of *the* seed of David, according to - gospel ˜ my; in which

κακοπαθῶ μέχρι δεσμῶν ὡς κακοῦργος,* ἀλλ' ὁ λόγος τοῦ
I endure hardship unto bonds as an evildoer, but the word -
chains

Θεοῦ οὐ δέδεται. 10 Διὰ τοῦτο πάντα ὑπομένω
of God not ˜ has been bound. On account of this [3]all [4]*things* [1]I [2]endure
is chained.

διὰ τοὺς ἐκλεκτούς, ἵνα καὶ αὐτοὶ σωτηρίας
on account of the elect, so that [2]also [1]they [5]salvation

τύχωσιν τῆς ἐν Χριστῷ Ἰησοῦ μετὰ δόξης αἰωνίου.
[3]may [4]obtain the *one* in Christ Jesus with glory ˜ eternal.
which is

11 Πιστὸς ὁ λόγος·
Faithful *is* the word:
Trustworthy

Εἰ γὰρ συναπεθάνομεν,
if ˜ For we died with *Him*,

Καὶ συζήσομεν·
also ˜ We will live with *Him;*

he may find mercy from the Lord in that Day—and you know very well how many ways he ministered *to me* at Ephesus.

2 You therefore, my son, be strong in the grace that is in Christ Jesus.
2 And the things that you have heard from me among many witnesses, commit these to faithful men who will be able to teach others also.
3 You therefore must endure hardship as a good soldier of Jesus Christ.
4 No one engaged in warfare entangles himself with the affairs of *this* life, that he may please him who enlisted him as a soldier.
5 And also if anyone competes in athletics, he is not crowned unless he competes according to the rules.
6 The hardworking farmer must be first to partake of the crops.
7 Consider what I say, and may the Lord give you understanding in all things.
8 Remember that Jesus Christ, of the seed of David, was raised from the dead according to my gospel,
9 for which I suffer trouble as an evildoer, *even* to the point of chains; but the word of God is not chained.
10 Therefore I endure all things for the sake of the elect, that they also may obtain the salvation which is in Christ Jesus with eternal glory.
11 *This is* a faithful saying:

For if we died with *Him,*
We shall also live with *Him.*

---

[e]**(1:18)** The Vulgate and a few Greek mss. add *μοι, me.* [a]**(2:3)** NU reads *συγκακοπαθησον, endure hardship together.*
[b]**(2:3)** NU reads Χριστου Ιησου, *Christ Jesus.*
[c]**(2:7)** NU reads *δωσει, will give.*

***(2:9)** *κακοῦργος (kakourgos).* Adjective, used only substantivally in the NT, meaning *criminal.* The word is a compound form derived from the adjective *κακός, evil,* and the noun *ἔργον, deed,* thus literally meaning *evildoer.* Unlike its more general synonym *κακοποιός* (*evildoer,* 1 Pet. 2:12), *κακοῦργος* always has the more severe nuance of criminal actions. Both words convey the sense of one who

12 If we endure,
We shall also reign with
Him.
If we deny *Him,*
He also will deny us.
13 If we are faithless,
He remains faithful;
He cannot deny Himself.

14 Remind *them* of these
things, charging *them* before
the Lord not to strive about
words to no profit, to the ruin
of the hearers.
15 Be diligent to present
yourself approved to God, a
worker who does not need to
be ashamed, rightly dividing the
word of truth.
16 But shun profane *and* idle
babblings, for they will increase
to more ungodliness.
17 And their message will
spread like cancer. Hymenaeus
and Philetus are of this sort,
18 who have strayed concerning the truth, saying that the
resurrection is already past;
and they overthrow the faith of
some.
19 Nevertheless the solid
foundation of God stands, having this seal: "The Lord knows
those who are His," and, "Let
everyone who names the name
of Christ depart from iniquity."
20 But in a great house there
are not only vessels of gold and
silver, but also of wood and
clay, some for honor and some
for dishonor.

---

[d](2:13) NU adds γαρ, *for.*
[e](2:14) NU reads Θεου, *God.* [f](2:19) Num. 16:5
[g](2:19) TR reads Χριστου, *of Christ.*

---

habitually engages in evil or criminal acts. κακοῦργος is used literally of two criminals in Luke 23:32, 33, 39 (see λῃστής, *bandits,* in the parallel at Matt. 21:13), and figuratively of Paul here in 2 Tim. 2:9.

***(2:15)** *ὀρθοτομέω (orthotomeō).* Verb meaning *teach correctly.* The word appears in Greek literature prior to the time of 2 Timothy only in Prov. 3:6; 11:5 of the LXX. It is a compound word formed from the adjective ὀρθός, *straight,* and the verb τομέω, *cut.* In Proverbs it means *cut a line in a straight path,* but the emphasis is on the idea of "straight" and not "cutting." It is that nuance which is picked up here in 2 Tim. 2:15: dealings with the

12 Εἰ ὑπομένομεν,
If we endure,
Καὶ συμβασιλεύσομεν·
also ˜ We will reign with *Him;*
Εἰ ἀρνούμεθα,
If we deny *Him,*
Κἀκεῖνος ἀρνήσεται ἡμᾶς·
Also that One (He also) will deny us;

13 Εἰ ἀπιστοῦμεν,
If we disbelieve,
Ἐκεῖνος πιστὸς μένει·
That one (He) faithful ˜ remains;
Ἀρνήσασθαι[d] ἑαυτὸν οὐ δύναται.
[5]to [6]deny [7]Himself [3]not [1]He [2]is [4]able.

The Approved and Disapproved Workers

14 Ταῦτα ὑπομίμνῃσκε, διαμαρτυρόμενος ἐνώπιον τοῦ
[4]these [5]*things* [1]Remind [2]*them* [3]*of,* charging *them* before the
Κυρίου[e] μὴ λογομαχεῖν, εἰς οὐδὲν χρήσιμον, ἐπὶ
Lord not to dispute about words, [2]for [3]nothing [1]useful, for
καταστροφῇ τῶν ἀκουόντων. **15** Σπούδασον σεαυτὸν δόκιμον
the ruin of the *ones* hearing (hearers). Be eager [3]yourself [4]approved
παραστῆσαι τῷ Θεῷ, ἐργάτην ἀνεπαίσχυντον, ὀρθοτομοῦντα*
[1]to [2]present - to God, a worker unashamed, cutting straight (rightly dividing)
τὸν λόγον τῆς ἀληθείας. **16** Τὰς δὲ βεβήλους κενοφωνίας
the word - of truth. - But profane empty chatterings
περιΐστασο· ἐπὶ πλεῖον γὰρ προκόψουσιν ἀσεβείας,
shun; [5]to [6]more [1]for [2]they [3]will [4]advance of ungodliness,
17 καὶ ὁ λόγος αὐτῶν ὡς γάγγραινα νομὴν ἕξει·
and - word ˜ their like gangrene [3]a [4]spreading (will) [1]will [2]have (spread);
ὧν ἐστιν Ὑμέναιος καὶ Φίλητος, **18** οἵτινες περὶ τὴν
of whom is (are) Hymenaeus and Philetus, who concerning the
ἀλήθειαν ἠστόχησαν, λέγοντες τὴν ἀνάστασιν ἤδη
truth missed *their* aim (strayed), saying *that* the resurrection already (has)
γεγονέναι, καὶ ἀνατρέπουσι τήν τινων πίστιν. **19** Ὁ
to have occurred (already occurred), and they overturn the [2]of [3]some [1]faith. the ˜
μέντοι στερεὸς θεμέλιος τοῦ Θεοῦ ἕστηκεν, ἔχων τὴν
Nevertheless firm foundation - of God has stood (stands), having -
σφραγῖδα ταύτην· «Ἔγνω Κύριος τοὺς ὄντας αὐτοῦ,»[f]
seal ˜ this: «[3]knew («knows) [1]*The* [2]Lord the *ones* (those who) being (are) His,»
καί, "Ἀποστήτω ἀπὸ ἀδικίας πᾶς ὁ ὀνομάζων τὸ
and, "[1]Let [10]depart [11]from [12]unrighteousness [2]every - [3]*one* [4]naming [5]the
ὄνομα Κυρίου."[g] **20** Ἐν μεγάλῃ δὲ οἰκίᾳ οὐκ ἔστι
[6]name [7]of [8]*the* [9]Lord." [2]in [3]a [4]great [1]Now house [3]not [1]*there* [2]is (are)
μόνον σκεύη χρυσᾶ καὶ ἀργυρᾶ, ἀλλὰ καὶ ξύλινα καὶ
only vessels gold and silver, but also wood and
ὀστράκινα, καὶ ἃ μὲν εἰς τιμήν, ἃ δὲ εἰς ἀτιμίαν.
clay, and some indeed to honor, some ˜ and to dishonor.

21 Ἐὰν οὖν τις ἐκκαθάρῃ ἑαυτὸν ἀπὸ τούτων,
If therefore anyone cleanses himself from these *latter,*

ἔσται σκεῦος εἰς τιμήν, ἡγιασμένον καὶ εὔχρηστον
he will be a vessel for honor, having been consecrated and useful

τῷ Δεσπότῃ, εἰς πᾶν ἔργον ἀγαθὸν ἡτοιμασμένον.
to the Master, ^{4}for ^{5}every ^{7}work ^{6}good ^{1}having ^{2}been ^{3}prepared.

22 Τὰς δὲ νεωτερικὰς ἐπιθυμίας φεῦγε, δίωκε δὲ
- But ^{2}youthful ^{3}lusts ^{1}flee, pursue ˜ but

δικαιοσύνην, πίστιν, ἀγάπην, εἰρήνην, μετὰ τῶν
righteousness, faith, love, peace, with the *ones*

ἐπικαλουμένων τὸν Κύριον ἐκ καθαρᾶς καρδίας. 23 Τὰς δὲ
calling on the Lord out of a pure heart. - But

μωρὰς καὶ ἀπαιδεύτους ζητήσεις παραιτοῦ, εἰδὼς ὅτι
foolish and ignorant disputes reject, knowing that

γεννῶσι μάχας. 24 Δοῦλον δὲ Κυρίου οὐ δεῖ
they bring forth fights. ^{2}a ^{3}bondservant (slave) ^{1}And of *the* Lord not ˜ ought

μάχεσθαι, ἀλλ' ἤπιον εἶναι πρὸς πάντας, διδακτικόν,
to fight, but ^{3}gentle ^{1}to ^{2}be to all, skillful at teaching,

ἀνεξίκακον, 25 ἐν πραότητι παιδεύοντα τοὺς
forbearing, in meekness instructing the *ones*

ἀντιδιατιθεμένους, μήποτε δῷ αὐτοῖς ὁ Θεὸς μετάνοιαν
opposing, *if* perhaps ^{2}may ^{3}give ^{4}them - ^{1}God repentance

εἰς ἐπίγνωσιν ἀληθείας, 26 καὶ ἀνανήψωσιν
to a full knowledge of truth, and they regain their senses *and escape*

ἐκ τῆς τοῦ διαβόλου παγίδος, ἐζωγρημένοι ὑπ'
out of the ^{2}of ^{3}the ^{4}devil ^{1}snare, having been captured alive by

αὐτοῦ εἰς τὸ ἐκείνου θέλημα.
him for (to) the (do) ^{2}of ^{3}that ^{4}one (his) ^{1}will.

Perilous Times and Perilous Men

3 1 Τοῦτο δὲ γίνωσκε, ὅτι ἐν ἐσχάταις ἡμέραις
^{3}this ^{1}But ^{2}know, that in *the* last days

ἐνστήσονται καιροὶ χαλεποί. 2 Ἔσονται γὰρ οἱ ἄνθρωποι
^{3}will ^{4}set ^{5}in ^{2}seasons ^{1}perilous. ^{3}will ^{4}be ^{1}For - ^{2}men

φίλαυτοι, φιλάργυροι, ἀλαζόνες, ὑπερήφανοι, βλάσφημοι,
lovers of self, lovers of money, boasters, haughty, blasphemers,

γονεῦσιν ἀπειθεῖς, ἀχάριστοι, ἀνόσιοι,
^{2}to ^{3}parents ^{1}disobedient, unthankful, unholy,

3 ἄστοργοι, ἄσπονδοι, διάβολοι, ἀκρατεῖς,
without natural affections (unloving), unforgiving, slanderers, without self-control,

ἀνήμεροι, ἀφιλάγαθοι, 4 προδόται, προπετεῖς,
brutal, not loving *what is* good, traitors, headstrong,

τετυφωμένοι, φιλήδονοι μᾶλλον ἢ φιλόθεοι,
having been puffed up (proud), lovers of pleasure rather than lovers of God,

5 ἔχοντες μόρφωσιν εὐσεβείας, τὴν δὲ δύναμιν αὐτῆς
having a form of godliness, - but ^{3}power ^{2}its

ἠρνημένοι. Καὶ τούτους ἀποτρέπου. 6 Ἐκ τούτων γὰρ
^{1}denying. And ^{4}these ^{5}*people* ^{1}turn ^{2}away ^{3}from. ^{2}of ^{3}these ^{1}For

εἰσιν οἱ ἐνδύνοντες εἰς τὰς οἰκίας καὶ αἰχμαλωτεύοντες
are the *ones* creeping into - houses and captivating

γυναικάρια σεσωρευμένα ἁμαρτίαις, ἀγόμενα ἐπιθυμίαις
little women (gullible) having been loaded down with sins, being led (who are) by lusts ˜

21 Therefore if anyone cleanses himself from the latter, he will be a vessel for honor, sanctified and useful for the Master, prepared for every good work.
22 Flee also youthful lusts; but pursue righteousness, faith, love, peace with those who call on the Lord out of a pure heart.
23 But avoid foolish and ignorant disputes, knowing that they generate strife.
24 And a servant of the Lord must not quarrel but be gentle to all, able to teach, patient,
25 in humility correcting those who are in opposition, if God perhaps will grant them repentance, so that they may know the truth,
26 and *that* they may come to their senses *and escape* the snare of the devil, having been taken captive by him to *do* his will.

3 But know this, that in the last days perilous times will come:
2 For men will be lovers of themselves, lovers of money, boasters, proud, blasphemers, disobedient to parents, unthankful, unholy,
3 unloving, unforgiving, slanderers, without self-control, brutal, despisers of good,
4 traitors, headstrong, haughty, lovers of pleasure rather than lovers of God,
5 having a form of godliness but denying its power. And from such people turn away!
6 For of this sort are those who creep into households and make captives of gullible women loaded down with sins, led away by various lusts,

"word of truth" must be *correct* and *right.* The occurrences in Proverbs may also suggest here that it is only when Timothy's conduct is in keeping with the teaching that he can be "unashamed" before God.

7 always learning and never
able to come to the knowledge
of the truth.
8 Now as Jannes and Jam-
bres resisted Moses, so do
these also resist the truth: men
of corrupt minds, disapproved
concerning the faith;
9 but they will progress no
further, for their folly will be
manifest to all, as theirs also
was.
10 But you have carefully followed my doctrine, manner of
life, purpose, faith, longsuffering, love, perseverance,
11 persecutions, afflictions,
which happened to me at Antioch, at Iconium, at Lystra—
what persecutions I endured.
And out of *them* all the Lord delivered me.
12 Yes, and all who desire to
live godly in Christ Jesus will
suffer persecution.
13 But evil men and impostors
will grow worse and worse, deceiving and being deceived.
14 But you must continue in
the things which you have
learned and been assured of,
knowing from whom you have
learned *them,*
15 and that from childhood
you have known the Holy Scriptures, which are able to make
you wise for salvation through
faith which is in Christ Jesus.
16 All Scripture *is* given by inspiration of God, and *is* profitable for doctrine, for reproof,
for correction, for instruction

ποικίλαις, **7** πάντοτε μανθάνοντα καὶ μηδέποτε εἰς
various, always learning and never [5]to

ἐπίγνωσιν ἀληθείας ἐλθεῖν δυνάμενα. **8** Ὃν τρόπον
[6]a [7]full [8]knowledge [9]of [10]truth [3]to [4]come [1]being [2]able. [2]by [3]what [4]way
And in just

δὲ Ἰάννης καὶ Ἰαμβρῆς ἀντέστησαν Μωϋσεῖ, οὕτω καὶ
[1]And Jannes and Jambres resisted Moses, thus also
the way

οὗτοι ἀνθίστανται τῇ ἀληθείᾳ, ἄνθρωποι κατεφθαρμένοι
these resist the truth, men having been corrupted
corrupted

τὸν νοῦν, ἀδόκιμοι περὶ τὴν πίστιν. **9** Ἀλλ' οὐ
regarding the mind, unqualified regarding the faith. But [3]not
in disapproved

προκόψουσιν ἐπὶ πλεῖον, ἡ γὰρ ἄνοια αὐτῶν ἔκδηλος
[1]they [2]will progress toward more, - for folly ˜ their [3]very [4]clear
further,

ἔσται πᾶσιν, ὡς καὶ ἡ ἐκείνων ἐγένετο.
[1]will [2]be to all, as also the *one* of theirs became.
that

The Man of God and the Word of God

10 Σὺ δὲ παρηκολούθηκάς μου τῇ διδασκαλίᾳ, τῇ
You however have carefully followed my - teaching, -
doctrine,

ἀγωγῇ, τῇ προθέσει, τῇ πίστει, τῇ μακροθυμίᾳ, τῇ ἀγάπῃ, τῇ
conduct, - purpose, - faith, - longsuffering, - love, -
lifestyle, patience,

ὑπομονῇ, **11** τοῖς διωγμοῖς, τοῖς παθήμασιν, οἷά μοι
endurance, - persecutions, - sufferings, which [2]to [3]me

ἐγένετο ἐν Ἀντιοχείᾳ, ἐν Ἰκονίῳ, ἐν Λύστροις, οἵους
[1]happened in Antioch, in Iconium, in Lystra, what

διωγμοὺς ὑπήνεγκα. Καὶ ἐκ πάντων με ἐρρύσατο ὁ
persecutions I bore. And [5]out [6]of [7]*them* [8]all [4]me [3]rescued [1]the

Κύριος. **12** Καὶ πάντες δὲ οἱ θέλοντες εὐσεβῶς ζῆν
[2]Lord. Indeed all ˜ and the *ones* desiring [3]godly [1]to [2]live
Yes those who desire

ἐν Χριστῷ Ἰησοῦ διωχθήσονται. **13** Πονηροὶ δὲ ἄνθρωποι
in Christ Jesus will be persecuted. evil ˜ But men

καὶ γόητες προκόψουσιν ἐπὶ τὸ χεῖρον, πλανῶντες καὶ
and imposters will advance upon the worse, deceiving and
will get worse and worse,

πλανώμενοι. **14** Σὺ δὲ μένε ἐν οἷς ἔμαθες καὶ
being deceived. you ˜ But continue in *the things* which you learned and
have learned

ἐπιστώθης, εἰδὼς παρὰ τίνος[a] ἔμαθες, **15** καὶ ὅτι
were assured of, knowing from whom you learned *them,* and that
been

ἀπὸ βρέφους τὰ Ἱερὰ Γράμματα οἶδας, τὰ δυνάμενά
from a baby [3]the [4]Sacred [5]Letters [1]you [2]know, the *ones* being able
have known, which are

σε σοφίσαι εἰς σωτηρίαν διὰ πίστεως τῆς ἐν Χριστῷ
[3]you [1]to [2]make [4]wise to salvation through faith - in Christ

Ἰησοῦ. **16** Πᾶσα Γραφὴ θεόπνευστος καὶ ὠφέλιμος πρὸς
Jesus. All Scripture *is* God-breathed and beneficial for

διδασκαλίαν, πρὸς ἔλεγχον, πρὸς ἐπανόρθωσιν, πρὸς παιδείαν
teaching, for reproof, for correction, for instruction
doctrine,

---

[a](3:14) NU reads *τινων*, the plural form of *whom.*

τὴν ἐν δικαιοσύνῃ, **17** ἵνα ἄρτιος ᾖ ὁ τοῦ Θεοῦ
- in righteousness, so that [7]proficient [5]may [6]be [1]the - [3]of [4]God

ἄνθρωπος, πρὸς πᾶν ἔργον ἀγαθὸν ἐξηρτισμένος.
[2]man, for every work ˜ good having been thoroughly equipped.

Preach the Word

4 **1** Διαμαρτύρομαι οὖν ἐγὼ ἐνώπιον τοῦ Θεοῦ, καὶ τοῦ
[2]charge [3]therefore [1]I before - God, and the

Κυρίου Ἰησοῦ Χριστοῦ [a] τοῦ μέλλοντος κρίνειν ζῶντας
Lord Jesus Christ the *One* being about to judge *the ones* living
who is going

καὶ νεκροὺς κατὰ [b] τὴν ἐπιφάνειαν αὐτοῦ καὶ τὴν
and dead in accordance with - appearing ˜ His and -

βασιλείαν αὐτοῦ, **2** κήρυξον τὸν λόγον, ἐπίστηθι εὐκαίρως,
kingdom ˜ His, proclaim the word, stand by in good season,
be ready in season,

ἀκαίρως, ἔλεγξον, ἐπιτίμησον, παρακάλεσον, ἐν πάσῃ
out of season, reprove, admonish, exhort, with all

μακροθυμίᾳ καὶ διδαχῇ. **3** Ἔσται γὰρ καιρὸς ὅτε τῆς
longsuffering and teaching. [2]*there* [3]will [4]be [1]For a time when -
patience

ὑγιαινούσης διδασκαλίας οὐκ ἀνέξονται, ἀλλὰ
[7]healthy [8]teaching [3]not [1]they [2]will [4]put [5]up [6]with, but
sound doctrine

κατὰ τὰς ἐπιθυμίας τὰς ἰδίας ἑαυτοῖς
according to - [3]lusts - [1]their [2]own for themselves

ἐπισωρεύσουσι διδασκάλους, κνηθόμενοι τὴν ἀκοήν, **4** καὶ
they will heap up teachers, tickling the hearing, and
their ears,

ἀπὸ μὲν τῆς ἀληθείας τὴν ἀκοὴν
[5]from [1]on [2]the [3]one [4]hand the truth [5]the [6]hearing
their ears

ἀποστρέψουσιν, ἐπὶ δὲ τοὺς μύθους
[1]they [2]will [3]turn [4]away, [11]to [7]on [8]the [9]other [10]hand - myths

ἐκτραπήσονται. **5** Σὺ δὲ νῆφε ἐν πᾶσι,
they will be turned aside. You however be watchful in all *things,*

κακοπάθησον, ἔργον ποίησον εὐαγγελιστοῦ, τὴν διακονίαν
endure hardship, [2]*the* [3]work [1]do of an evangelist, - [3]ministry

σου πληροφόρησον.
[2]your [1]fulfill.

Paul's Valedictory

6 Ἐγὼ γὰρ ἤδη σπένδομαι, καὶ ὁ
[3]I [1]For [2]already am being poured out *as a drink offering,* and the

καιρὸς τῆς ἐμῆς ἀναλύσεως ἐφέστηκε. **7** Τὸν ἀγῶνα τὸν
time - of my departure has set in. The struggle ˜ -
arrived.

καλὸν ἠγώνισμαι,* τὸν δρόμον τετέλεκα, τὴν πίστιν
good I have struggled, the course I have finished, the faith
race

τετήρηκα. **8** Λοιπόν, ἀπόκειταί μοι ὁ τῆς
I have kept. *For the* rest, there is laid up for me the -
Finally,

δικαιοσύνης στέφανος, ὃν ἀποδώσει μοι ὁ Κύριος ἐν
[2]of [3]righteousness [1]garland, which [3]will [4]render [5]to [6]me [1]the [2]Lord in
crown,

ἐκείνῃ τῇ ἡμέρᾳ, ὁ δίκαιος Κριτής, οὐ μόνον δὲ ἐμοί,
that - day, the righteous Judge, [2]not [3]only [1]but to me,

---

in righteousness,

17 that the man of God may be complete, thoroughly equipped for every good work.

4 I charge *you* therefore before God and the Lord Jesus Christ, who will judge the living and the dead at His appearing and His kingdom:

2 Preach the word! Be ready in season *and* out of season. Convince, rebuke, exhort, with all longsuffering and teaching.

3 For the time will come when they will not endure sound doctrine, but according to their own desires, *because* they have itching ears, they will heap up for themselves teachers;

4 and they will turn *their* ears away from the truth, and be turned aside to fables.

5 But you be watchful in all things, endure afflictions, do the work of an evangelist, fulfill your ministry.

6 For I am already being poured out as a drink offering, and the time of my departure is at hand.

7 I have fought the good fight, I have finished the race, I have kept the faith.

8 Finally, there is laid up for me the crown of righteousness, which the Lord, the righteous Judge, will give to me on that Day, and not to me only but

---

[a] **(4:1)** NU omits του Κυριου, *the Lord,* and reads Χριστου Ιησου, *Christ Jesus.* [b] **(4:1)** NU reads και, *and.*

***(4:7)** ἀγωνίζομαι *(agōnizomai).* Verb meaning *engage in (an athletic) contest* (as 1 Cor. 9:25), often used more broadly to mean *struggle, strive, fight,* either figuratively (as here) or literally (as John 18:36). Generally the word implies that earnest effort is required in a contest (often against an opponent) toward a desired goal. Cf. the cognate noun ἀγών, *(athletic) contest* (Heb. 12:1), *struggle, conflict* (also here and in 1 Tim. 6:12). Even prayer can be viewed as "struggling" (Col. 4:12; cf. Rom. 15:30 where a compound of the same verb, συναγωνίζομαι, *struggle together,* is used).

also to all who have loved His
appearing.
9 Be diligent to come to me
quickly;
10 for Demas has forsaken
me, having loved this present
world, and has departed for
Thessalonica—Crescens for
Galatia, Titus for Dalmatia.
11 Only Luke is with me. Get
Mark and bring him with you,
for he is useful to me for ministry.
12 And Tychicus I have sent
to Ephesus.
13 Bring the cloak that I left
with Carpus at Troas when you
come—and the books, espe-
cially the parchments.
14 Alexander the coppersmith
did me much harm. May the
Lord repay him according to his
works.
15 You also must beware of
him, for he has greatly resisted
our words.
16 At my first defense no one
stood with me, but all forsook
me. May it not be charged
against them.
17 But the Lord stood with
me and strengthened me, so
that the message might be
preached fully through me, and
that all the Gentiles might hear.
Also I was delivered out of the
mouth of the lion.
18 And the Lord will deliver
me from every evil work and
preserve *me* for His heavenly
kingdom. To Him *be* glory forever and ever. Amen!

ἀλλὰ καὶ πᾶσι τοῖς ἠγαπηκόσι τὴν ἐπιφάνειαν αὐτοῦ.
but also to all the *ones* having loved - appearing ˜ His.
those who have

Timothy Is Urged to Come

9 Σπούδασον ἐλθεῖν πρός με ταχέως. 10 Δημᾶς γάρ με
Be diligent to come to me quickly. Demas ˜ For me ˜

ἐγκατέλιπεν, ἀγαπήσας τὸν νῦν αἰῶνα, καὶ ἐπορεύθη εἰς
forsook, loving the now age, and traveled to
present

Θεσσαλονίκην, Κρήσκης εἰς Γαλατίαν, Τίτος εἰς Δαλματίαν.
Thessalonica, Crescens to Galatia, Titus to Dalmatia.

11 Λουκᾶς ἐστι μόνος μετ' ἐμοῦ. Μᾶρκον ἀναλαβὼν ἄγε
Luke is ˜ alone with me. [3]Mark [1]Taking [2]along bring *him*

μετὰ σεαυτοῦ, ἔστι γάρ μοι εὔχρηστος εἰς διακονίαν.
with yourself, [2]he [3]is [1]for [5]to [6]me [4]useful for ministry.

12 Τυχικὸν δὲ ἀπέστειλα εἰς Ἔφεσον. 13 Τὸν φαιλόνην
Tychicus ˜ And I sent to Ephesus. The cloak

ὃν ἀπέλιπον ἐν Τρῳάδι παρὰ Κάρπῳ, ἐρχόμενος φέρε,
which I left in Troas with Carpus, coming bring,
bring when you come,

καὶ τὰ βιβλία, μάλιστα τὰς μεμβράνας. 14 Ἀλέξανδρος ὁ
and the books, especially the parchments. Alexander the

χαλκεὺς πολλά μοι κακὰ ἐνεδείξατο. Ἀποδῴη[c] αὐτῷ
coppersmith [2]many [4]*things* [5]to [6]me [3]bad [1]showed. [7]May [10]repay [11]him
did me much harm.

ὁ Κύριος κατὰ τὰ ἔργα αὐτοῦ· 15 ὃν καὶ σὺ
[8]the [9]Lord according to - works ˜ his; whom also ˜ you

φυλάσσου, λίαν γὰρ ἀνθέστηκε τοῖς ἡμετέροις
should guard against, [3]very [4]much [1]for [2]he resisted - our
greatly

λόγοις.
words.

The Lord Is Faithful

16 Ἐν τῇ πρώτῃ μου ἀπολογίᾳ οὐδείς μοι
In - first ˜ my defense no one with me

συμπαρεγένετο, ἀλλὰ πάντες με ἐγκατέλιπον — μὴ αὐτοῖς
came to help, but all me ˜ forsook — [3]not [6]to [7]them

λογισθείη! 17 Ὁ δὲ Κυριός μοι παρέστη καὶ
[1]may [2]it [4]be [5]reckoned! the ˜ But Lord [3]me [1]stood [2]by and

ἐνεδυνάμωσέ με, ἵνα δι' ἐμοῦ τὸ κήρυγμα
empowered me, so that through me the proclamation

πληροφορηθῇ καὶ ἀκούσῃ πάντα τὰ ἔθνη, καὶ
might be fulfilled and [4]might [5]hear [1]all [2]the [3]Gentiles, and

ἐρρύσθην ἐκ στόματος λέοντος. 18 Καὶ ῥύσεταί με ὁ
I was rescued out of *the* mouth of a lion. And [3]will [4]rescue [5]me [1]the

Κύριος ἀπὸ παντὸς ἔργου πονηροῦ καὶ σώσει εἰς τὴν
[2]Lord from every work ˜ evil and will preserve *me* for -

βασιλείαν αὐτοῦ τὴν ἐπουράνιον, ᾧ ἡ δόξα εἰς τοὺς
[3]kingdom [1]His - [2]heavenly, to whom *be* the glory to the
forever and

αἰῶνας τῶν αἰώνων. Ἀμήν.
ages of the ages. Amen.
ever. So be it.

---

[c](4:14) NU reads αποδωσει, *will repay.*

Personalia and Paul's Farewell

19 Ἄσπασαι Πρίσκαν καὶ Ἀκύλαν, καὶ τὸν Ὀνησιφόρου
Greet Prisca and Aquila, and the [2]of [3]Onesiphorus
οἶκον. 20 Ἔραστος ἔμεινεν ἐν Κορίνθῳ, Τρόφιμον δὲ
[1]house. Erastus stayed in Corinth, Trophimus ~ but
household.
ἀπέλιπον ἐν Μιλήτῳ ἀσθενοῦντα. 21 Σπούδασον πρὸ
I left in Miletus ailing. Be diligent [3]before
ill.
χειμῶνος ἐλθεῖν. Ἀσπάζεταί σε Εὔβουλος καὶ Πούδης
[4]winter [1]to [2]come. [6]greets [7]you [5]Eubulus and Pudens
as well as
καὶ Λίνος καὶ Κλαυδία καὶ οἱ ἀδελφοὶ πάντες.
and Linus and Claudia and [2]the [3]brothers [1]all.
22 Ὁ Κύριος Ἰησοῦς Χριστὸς[d] μετὰ τοῦ πνεύματός σου.
The Lord Jesus Christ *be* with - spirit ~ your.
Ἡ χάρις μεθ' ὑμῶν. Ἀμήν.[e]
- Grace *be* with you. Amen.
So be it.

19 Greet Prisca and Aquila, and the household of Onesiphorus.
20 Erastus stayed in Corinth, but Trophimus I have left in Miletus sick.
21 Do your utmost to come before winter. Eubulus greets you, as well as Pudens, Linus, Claudia, and all the brethren.
22 The Lord Jesus Christ be with your spirit. Grace be with you. Amen.

[d](4:22) NU omits Ιησους Χριστος, *Jesus Christ.*
[e](4:22) NU omits Αμην, *Amen.*

The Epistle of Paul the Apostle to
TITUS

ΠΡΟΣ ΤΙΤΟΝ
TO TITUS

1 Paul, a bondservant of God and an apostle of Jesus Christ, according to the faith of God's elect and the acknowledgment of the truth which accords with godliness,
2 in hope of eternal life which God, who cannot lie, promised before time began,
3 but has in due time manifested His word through preaching, which was committed to me according to the commandment of God our Savior;

4 To Titus, a true son in *our* common faith:

Grace, mercy, *and* peace from God the Father and the Lord Jesus Christ our Savior.
5 For this reason I left you in Crete, that you should set in order the things that are lacking, and appoint elders in every city as I commanded you—
6 if a man is blameless, the husband of one wife, having faithful children not accused of dissipation or insubordination.
7 For a bishop must be blameless, as a steward of God, not self-willed, not quick-tempered, not given to wine, not violent, not greedy for money,

Paul Greets Titus

1 **1** Παῦλος, δοῦλος Θεοῦ, ἀπόστολος δὲ Ἰησοῦ
Paul, a bondservant of God, apostle ˜ and of Jesus
slave

Χριστοῦ κατὰ πίστιν ἐκλεκτῶν Θεοῦ καὶ
Christ according to *the* faith of *the* elect *ones* of God and

ἐπίγνωσιν ἀληθείας τῆς κατ' εὐσέβειαν **2** ἐπ'
the full knowledge of *the* truth the *one* according to godliness upon
which is in

ἐλπίδι ζωῆς αἰωνίου, ἣν ἐπηγγείλατο ὁ ἀψευδὴς Θεὸς
hope of life ˜ eternal, which [4]promised [1]the [2]unlying [3]God
truthful

πρὸ χρόνων αἰωνίων, **3** ἐφανέρωσε δὲ καιροῖς ἰδίοις τὸν
before times ˜ eternal, [2]He [3]manifested [1]but [6]in [9]season [7]its [8]own -
time began, in due time

λόγον αὐτοῦ ἐν κηρύγματι ὃ ἐπιστεύθην ἐγὼ
[5]word [4]His in a proclamation *with* which [2]was [3]entrusted [1]I

κατ' ἐπιταγὴν τοῦ Σωτῆρος ἡμῶν Θεοῦ,
according to *the* command - of [3]Savior [2]our [1]God,

4 Τίτῳ, γνησίῳ τέκνῳ κατὰ κοινὴν πίστιν·
To Titus, a genuine child according to a common faith:

Χάρις, ἔλεος,[a] εἰρήνη ἀπὸ Θεοῦ Πατρὸς καὶ Κυρίου
Grace, mercy, peace from God *the* Father and *the* Lord

Ἰησοῦ Χριστοῦ[b] τοῦ Σωτῆρος ἡμῶν.
Jesus Christ - Savior ˜ our.

Qualified Elders Are Needed

5 Τούτου χάριν κατέλιπόν[c] σε ἐν Κρήτῃ, ἵνα
[3]of [4]this [1]On [2]account I left behind ˜ you in Crete, in order that
For this reason

τὰ λείποντα ἐπιδιορθώσῃ καὶ
[6]the [7]*things* [8]*that* [9]*are* [10]lacking [1]you [2]should [3]set [4]in [5]order and

καταστήσῃς κατὰ πόλιν πρεσβυτέρους, ὡς ἐγώ σοι
you should appoint *in* every city elders, as I you ˜

διεταξάμην· **6** εἴ τίς ἐστιν ἀνέγκλητος, μιᾶς γυναικὸς
commanded: if one is blameless, [3]of [4]one [5]wife

ἀνήρ, τέκνα ἔχων πιστά, μὴ ἐν κατηγορίᾳ ἀσωτίας
[1]*the* [2]husband, [8]children [6]having [7]believing, not in accusation of dissipation
faithful,

ἢ ἀνυπότακτα. **7** Δεῖ γὰρ τὸν ἐπίσκοπον*
or *who are* insubordinate. [2]it [3]is [4]necessary [1]For *for* the overseer
a bishop

ἀνέγκλητον εἶναι ὡς Θεοῦ οἰκονόμον, μὴ αὐθάδη, μὴ
[3]blameless [1]to [2]be as [3]of [4]God [1]a [2]steward, not self-willed, not

ὀργίλον, μὴ πάροινον, μὴ πλήκτην, μὴ αἰσχροκερδῆ,
quick-tempered, not given to wine, not a bully, not greedy for base gain,
violent,

---

[a](1:4) NU omits ελεος, *mercy,* and reads και, *and.* [b](1:4) NU omits Κυριου, *(the) Lord,* and reads Χριστου Ιησου, *Christ Jesus.* [c](1:5) NU reads απελιπον, *left (you) off.*

---

*(1:7) ἐπίσκοπος (episkopos). Noun meaning *overseer, bishop.* It is a compound of the preposition ἐπί, *over,* and the noun σκοπός, *one who watches* or *looks out,* thus meaning *overseer, guardian,* in the sense of "one who watches over (to protect)." The word designates persons who hold a definite function or office within a social group. In the NT it refers specifically

8 ἀλλὰ φιλόξενον, φιλάγαθον, σώφρονα, δίκαιον, ὅσιον,
but loving strangers, loving good, prudent, just, holy,
hospitable,

ἐγκρατῆ, 9 ἀντεχόμενον τοῦ κατὰ τὴν διδαχὴν πιστοῦ
self-controlled, holding on to [1]the [4]according [5]to [6]the [7]teaching [2]faithful
as he was taught

λόγου, ἵνα δυνατὸς ᾖ καὶ παρακαλεῖν ἐν τῇ
[3]word, in order that [4]able [1]he [2]may [3]be also to exhort by -

διδασκαλίᾳ τῇ ὑγιαινούσῃ καὶ τοὺς ἀντιλέγοντας
teaching ˜ - healthful and [3]the [4]*ones* [5]contradicting
sound doctrine those who oppose it

ἐλέγχειν.
[1]to [2]convince.

Problems Elders Must Face

10 Εἰσὶ γὰρ πολλοὶ καὶ ἀνυπότακτοι, ματαιολόγοι καὶ
[2]*there* [3]are [1]For [5]many [4]also insubordinate, idle talkers and

φρεναπάται, μάλιστα οἱ ἐκ περιτομῆς, 11 οὓς
deceivers, especially the *ones* of *the* circumcision, whom
those

δεῖ ἐπιστομίζειν, οἵτινες ὅλους οἴκους
it is necessary to shut *their* mouths, who [2]whole [3]houses
households

ἀνατρέπουσι διδάσκοντες ἃ μὴ δεῖ αἰσχροῦ
[1]overturn teaching *things* which [3]not [1]one [2]ought [8]base

κέρδους χάριν. 12 Εἶπέ τις ἐξ αὐτῶν, ἴδιος
[9]gain [4]for [5]the [6]sake [7]of. *There* said a certain one of them, [5]own

αὐτῶν προφήτης, "Κρῆτες ἀεὶ ψεῦσται, κακὰ θηρία,
[3]of [4]their [1]a [2]prophet, "Cretans *are* always liars, evil beasts,

γαστέρες ἀργαί." 13 Ἡ μαρτυρία αὕτη ἐστὶν ἀληθής. Δι' ἣν
bellies ˜ idle." - testimony ˜ This is true. For which
gluttons

αἰτίαν ἔλεγχε αὐτοὺς ἀποτόμως, ἵνα ὑγιαίνωσιν ἐν τῇ
cause rebuke them sharply, so that they may be healthy in the

πίστει, 14 μὴ προσέχοντες Ἰουδαϊκοῖς μύθοις καὶ ἐντολαῖς
faith, not giving heed to Jewish myths and to commands

ἀνθρώπων ἀποστρεφομένων τὴν ἀλήθειαν. 15 Πάντα μὲν[d]
of men turning away from the truth. All *things* indeed

καθαρὰ τοῖς καθαροῖς· τοῖς δὲ μεμιασμένοις καὶ
are pure to the pure; [2]to [3]the [4]*ones* [1]but having been defiled and
who are

ἀπίστοις οὐδὲν καθαρόν, ἀλλὰ μεμίανται αὐτῶν καὶ ὁ
unbelieving nothing *is* pure, but [6]have [7]been [8]defiled [2]their [1]both -
unfaithful

νοῦς καὶ ἡ συνείδησις. 16 Θεὸν ὁμολογοῦσιν εἰδέναι, τοῖς
[3]mind [4]and - [5]conscience. [5]God [1]They [2]profess [3]to [4]know, [7]in [8]the
their

δὲ ἔργοις ἀρνοῦνται, βδελυκτοὶ ὄντες καὶ ἀπειθεῖς καὶ πρὸς
[6]but [9]works they deny *Him*, abominable ˜ being and disobedient and for

πᾶν ἔργον ἀγαθὸν ἀδόκιμοι.
every work ˜ good disqualified.

Qualities of a Healthy Flock

2 1 Σὺ δὲ λάλει ἃ πρέπει τῇ ὑγιαινούσῃ
you ˜ But speak *the things* which suit - healthy
sound

διδασκαλίᾳ.
teaching.
doctrine.

8 but hospitable, a lover of
what is good, sober-minded,
just, holy, self-controlled,
9 holding fast the faithful
word as he has been taught,
that he may be able, by sound
doctrine, both to exhort and
convict those who contradict.
10 For there are many insubordinate, both idle talkers and
deceivers, especially those of
the circumcision,
11 whose mouths must be
stopped, who subvert whole
households, teaching things
which they ought not, for the
sake of dishonest gain.
12 One of them, a prophet of
their own, said, "Cretans *are*
always liars, evil beasts, lazy
gluttons."
13 This testimony is true.
Therefore rebuke them
sharply, that they may be
sound in the faith,
14 not giving heed to Jewish
fables and commandments of
men who turn from the truth.
15 To the pure all things are
pure, but to those who are defiled and unbelieving nothing is
pure; but even their mind and
conscience are defiled.
16 They profess to know God,
but in works they deny Him,
being abominable, disobedient,
and disqualified for every good
work.
2 But as for you, speak the
things which are proper
for sound doctrine:

[d](**1:15**) NU omits μεν, *indeed.*

to the *overseers* and *bishops* of the church (as here). In Acts 20:28 the elders (πρεσβυτέρος, cf. v. 17) are said to be "overseers" of the church. The epistle to the Philippians is addressed to saints in Philippi together with "the *bishops* and the deacons" (1:1). The use of ἐπίσκοπος in 1 Pet. 2:25 to describe Christ as the "*Overseer* of your souls" reflects a long-standing use of the term to describe divine figures as protectors and guardians.

2 that the older men be sober, reverent, temperate, sound in faith, in love, in patience;
3 the older women likewise, that they be reverent in behavior, not slanderers, not given to much wine, teachers of good things—
4 that they admonish the young women to love their husbands, to love their children,
5 to be discreet, chaste, homemakers, good, obedient to their own husbands, that the word of God may not be blasphemed.
6 Likewise, exhort the young men to be sober-minded,
7 in all things showing yourself *to be* a pattern of good works; in doctrine *showing* integrity, reverence, incorruptibility,
8 sound speech that cannot be condemned, that one who is an opponent may be ashamed, having nothing evil to say of you.
9 *Exhort* bondservants to be obedient to their own masters, to be well pleasing in all *things,* not answering back,
10 not pilfering, but showing all good fidelity, that they may adorn the doctrine of God our Savior in all things.
11 For the grace of God that brings salvation has appeared to all men,
12 teaching us that, denying ungodliness and worldly lusts, we should live soberly, righteously, and godly in the present age,

2 Πρεσβύτας νηφαλέους εἶναι, σεμνούς, σώφρονας,
Older men *are* [3]sober [1]to [2]be, serious, temperate,
ὑγιαίνοντας τῇ πίστει, τῇ ἀγάπῃ, τῇ ὑπομονῇ.
healthy (sound) in the faith, - in love, - in endurance.

3 Πρεσβύτιδας ὡσαύτως ἐν καταστήματι ἱεροπρεπεῖς,
Older women likewise in demeanor *are to be* reverent,
μὴ διαβόλους, μὴ οἴνῳ πολλῷ δεδουλωμένας,
not slanderers, [2]not [5]to [7]wine [6]much [1]having [3]been [4]enslaved,
καλοδιδασκάλους, **4** ἵνα σωφρονίζωσι τὰς νέας
teaching what is good, so that they may urge the young women
φιλάνδρους εἶναι, φιλοτέκνους, **5** σώφρονας,
[3]lovers [4]of [5]*their* [6]husbands [1]to [2]be, lovers of *their* children, temperate,
ἁγνάς, οἰκουρούς, ἀγαθάς, ὑποτασσομένας τοῖς ἰδίοις
pure, homemakers, good, submitting - to their own
ἀνδράσιν, ἵνα μὴ ὁ λόγος τοῦ Θεοῦ βλασφημῆται.
husbands, in order that not (lest) the word - of God be blasphemed.

6 Τοὺς νεωτέρους ὡσαύτως παρακάλει σωφρονεῖν,
[3]the [4]young [5]men [1]Likewise [2]exhort to be sensible,
7 περὶ πάντα σεαυτὸν παρεχόμενος τύπον καλῶν
concerning all *things* (in all respects) yourself ~ showing *to be* an example of good
ἔργων, ἐν τῇ διδασκαλίᾳ ἀδιαφθορίαν,[a] σεμνότητα,
works, in the (your) teaching integrity, dignity,
ἀφθαρσίαν,[b] **8** λόγον ὑγιῆ ἀκατάγνωστον, ἵνα ὁ
incorruptibility, (immortality,) [3]speech [1]healthy [2]irreprehensible, in order that the *one*
ἐξ ἐναντίας ἐντραπῇ, μηδὲν ἔχων περὶ ἡμῶν[c]
from *the* opposition may be put to shame, nothing ~ having [4]about [5]us
λέγειν φαῦλον.
[2]to [3]say [1]bad.

9 Δούλους ἰδίοις δεσπόταις ὑποτάσσεσθαι
Exhort bondservants (slaves) [4]to [5]their [6]own [7]masters [1]to [2]be [3]subject
ἐν πᾶσιν, εὐαρέστους εἶναι, μὴ ἀντιλέγοντας, **10** μὴ
in all *things,* [3]well [4]pleasing [1]to [2]be, not talking back, not
νοσφιζομένους, ἀλλὰ πίστιν πᾶσαν ἐνδεικνυμένους ἀγαθήν,
misappropriating, (embezzling,) but [4]faith [2]all [1]showing [3]good,
ἵνα τὴν διδασκαλίαν τοῦ Σωτῆρος ἡμῶν Θεοῦ κοσμῶσιν
so that [4]the [5]teaching (doctrine) - [6]of [9]Savior [8]our [7]God [1]they [2]may [3]adorn
ἐν πᾶσιν.
in all *things.*

Trained by Saving Grace

11 Ἐπεφάνη γὰρ ἡ χάρις τοῦ Θεοῦ ἡ σωτήριος πᾶσιν
[7]appeared (has appeared) [1]For [2]the [4]grace - [5]of [6]God - [3]saving to all
ἀνθρώποις, **12** παιδεύουσα ἡμᾶς ἵνα ἀρνησάμενοι τὴν
men, teaching us that denying -
ἀσέβειαν καὶ τὰς κοσμικὰς* ἐπιθυμίας σωφρόνως καὶ
ungodliness and - worldly lusts [4]soberly [5]and
δικαίως καὶ εὐσεβῶς ζήσωμεν ἐν τῷ νῦν αἰῶνι,
[6]righteously [7]and [8]godly [1]we [2]should [3]live in the now (present) age,

---

[a](**2:7**) NU reads αφθοριαν, *soundness.*
[b](**2:7**) NU omits αφθαρσιαν, *incorruptibility.*
[c](**2:8**) TR reads υμων, *you.*

***(2:12)** κοσμικός *(kosmikos).* Adjective meaning *worldly* in an ethical sense or *pertaining to this earth* in a morally neutral sense. Here it describes the "lusts" or strong desires we are taught to deny because they are opposed to God's desires. In Heb. 9:1 it describes "the *earthly* sanctuary" as opposed to the perfect and true heavenly sanctuary. Cf. the English derivative *cosmic.*

13 προσδεχόμενοι τὴν μακαρίαν ἐλπίδα καὶ ἐπιφάνειαν τῆς
expecting the blessed hope and appearing of the

δόξης τοῦ μεγάλου Θεοῦ καὶ Σωτῆρος ἡμῶν Ἰησοῦ Χριστοῦ,
glory - [1]of [3]great [4]God [5]and [6]Savior [2]our [7]Jesus [8]Christ,

14 ὃς ἔδωκεν ἑαυτὸν ὑπὲρ ἡμῶν, ἵνα λυτρώσηται ἡμᾶς
who gave Himself for us, so that He might redeem us

ἀπὸ πάσης ἀνομίας καὶ καθαρίσῃ ἑαυτῷ λαὸν
from all lawlessness and might purify for Himself a people

περιούσιον, ζηλωτὴν καλῶν ἔργων.
as His own possession, zealous of good works.

15 Ταῦτα λάλει καὶ παρακάλει καὶ ἔλεγχε μετὰ
[2]these [3]*things* [1]Speak and exhort and rebuke with

πάσης ἐπιταγῆς. Μηδείς σου περιφρονείτω.
all command. [2]no [3]one [5]you [1]Let [4]despise.
authority.

Gracious Virtues for the Recipients of Grace

3 1 Ὑπομίμνησκε αὐτοὺς ἀρχαῖς καὶ[a] ἐξουσίαις
Remind them [4]to [5]rulers [6]and [7]authorities

ὑποτάσσεσθαι, πειθαρχεῖν, πρὸς πᾶν ἔργον ἀγαθὸν ἑτοίμους
[1]to [2]be [3]subject, to be obedient, for every work ˜ good [3]ready

εἶναι, 2 μηδένα βλασφημεῖν, ἀμάχους εἶναι, ἐπιεικεῖς,
[1]to [2]be, [3]no [4]one [1]to [2]blaspheme, [7]uncontentious [5]to [6]be, gentle,
to slander,

πᾶσαν ἐνδεικνυμένους πραότητα πρὸς πάντας ἀνθρώπους.
all ˜ demonstrating meekness to all men.

3 Ἦμεν γάρ ποτε καὶ ἡμεῖς ἀνόητοι, ἀπειθεῖς, πλανώμενοι,
[3]were [1]For [5]once [4]also [2]we senseless, disobedient, being deceived,

δουλεύοντες ἐπιθυμίαις καὶ ἡδοναῖς ποικίλαις, ἐν κακίᾳ καὶ
being enslaved to [2]lusts [3]and [4]pleasures [1]various, [6]in [7]malice [8]and

φθόνῳ διάγοντες, στυγητοί, μισοῦντες ἀλλήλους. 4 Ὅτε δὲ
[9]envy [5]living, hateful, hating one another. when ˜ But

ἡ χρηστότης καὶ ἡ φιλανθρωπία ἐπεφάνη τοῦ Σωτῆρος
the kindness and the love for mankind [5]appeared - [1]of [4]Savior

ἡμῶν Θεοῦ, 5 οὐκ ἐξ ἔργων τῶν ἐν δικαιοσύνῃ ὧν
[3]our [2]God, not of works - in righteousness which

ἐποιήσαμεν ἡμεῖς ἀλλὰ κατὰ τὸν αὐτοῦ ἔλεον ἔσωσεν
did ˜ we but according to - His mercy He saved

ἡμᾶς διὰ λουτροῦ παλιγγενεσίας καὶ ἀνακαινώσεως
us through *the* bath of regeneration and renewing
washing

Πνεύματος Ἁγίου, 6 οὗ ἐξέχεεν ἐφ' ἡμᾶς πλουσίως
of *the* Spirit ˜ Holy, whom He poured out on us richly

διὰ Ἰησοῦ Χριστοῦ τοῦ Σωτῆρος ἡμῶν, 7 ἵνα
through Jesus Christ - Savior ˜ our, in order that

δικαιωθέντες τῇ ἐκείνου χάριτι κληρονόμοι
having been justified by the [2]of [3]that [4]*One* [1]grace [8]heirs
His grace

γενώμεθα κατ' ἐλπίδα ζωῆς αἰωνίου.
[5]we [6]might [7]become according to *the* hope of life ˜ eternal.

Do Good and Avoid Dissension

8 Πιστὸς ὁ λόγος, καὶ περὶ τούτων βούλομαί σε
Faithful *is* the word, and concerning these *things* I want you
Trustworthy

διαβεβαιοῦσθαι, ἵνα φροντίζωσι καλῶν ἔργων
to strongly affirm, so that [7]may [8]take [9]thought [12]good [13]works

13 looking for the blessed hope and glorious appearing of our great God and Savior Jesus Christ,
14 who gave Himself for us, that He might redeem us from every lawless deed and purify for Himself *His* own special people, zealous for good works.
15 Speak these things, exhort, and rebuke with all authority. Let no one despise you.

3 Remind them to be subject to rulers and authorities, to obey, to be ready for every good work,
2 to speak evil of no one, to be peaceable, gentle, showing all humility to all men.
3 For we ourselves were also once foolish, disobedient, deceived, serving various lusts and pleasures, living in malice and envy, hateful and hating one another.
4 But when the kindness and the love of God our Savior toward man appeared,
5 not by works of righteousness which we have done, but according to His mercy He saved us, through the washing of regeneration and renewing of the Holy Spirit,
6 whom He poured out on us abundantly through Jesus Christ our Savior,
7 that having been justified by His grace we should become heirs according to the hope of eternal life.
8 This is a faithful saying, and these things I want you to affirm constantly, that those who have believed in God should be careful to maintain good works.

[a](3:1) NU omits *καὶ, and.*

These things are good and profitable to men.
9 But avoid foolish disputes,
genealogies, contentions, and
strivings about the law; for they
are unprofitable and useless.
10 Reject a divisive man after
the first and second admonition,
11 knowing that such a person
is warped and sinning, being
self-condemned.
12 When I send Artemas to
you, or Tychicus, be diligent to
come to me at Nicopolis, for I
have decided to spend the winter there.
13 Send Zenas the lawyer and
Apollos on their journey with
haste, that they may lack nothing.
14 And let our *people* also
learn to maintain good works,
to *meet* urgent needs, that they
may not be unfruitful.
15 All who *are* with me greet
you. Greet those who love us in
the faith. Grace *be* with you all.
Amen.

προϊστασθαι οἱ πεπιστευκότες Θεῷ. Ταῦτά ἐστι τὰ
[10]to [11]maintain [1]the [2]*ones* [3]having [4]believed [5]in [6]God. These *things* is -
those who have ... are

καλὰ καὶ ὠφέλιμα τοῖς ἀνθρώποις. **9** *Μωρὰς δὲ ζητήσεις καὶ*
good and profitable to men. foolish ˜ But disputes and

γενεαλογίας καὶ ἔρεις καὶ μάχας νομικὰς περιΐστασο, εἰσὶ
genealogies and strifes and fights ˜ legal avoid, [2]they [3]are

γὰρ ἀνωφελεῖς καὶ μάταιοι. **10** *Αἱρετικὸν* ἄνθρωπον μετὰ*
[1]for unprofitable and futile. A divisive man after

μίαν καὶ δευτέραν νουθεσίαν παραιτοῦ, **11** *εἰδὼς ὅτι*
one and a second admonition reject, knowing that
a first

ἐξέστραπται ὁ τοιοῦτος καὶ ἁμαρτάνει, ὢν
[4]has [5]been [6]perverted - [1]such [2]*a* [3]*person* and is sinning, being

αὐτοκατάκριτος.
self-condemned.

Personalia and Paul's Farewell

12 *Ὅταν πέμψω Ἀρτεμᾶν πρὸς σὲ ἢ Τύχικον,*
Whenever I shall send Artemas to you or Tychicus,

σπούδασον ἐλθεῖν πρός με εἰς Νικόπολιν, ἐκεῖ γὰρ
hasten to come to me to Nicopolis, there ˜ for

κέκρικα παραχειμάσαι. **13** *Ζηνᾶν τὸν νομικὸν καὶ*
I have judged to spend the winter. Zenas the lawyer and
decided

Ἀπολλὼ σπουδαίως πρόπεμψον, ἵνα μηδὲν αὐτοῖς
Apollos speedily send forward, in order that nothing to them

λείπῃ. **14** *Μανθανέτωσαν δὲ καὶ οἱ ἡμέτεροι καλῶν*
may be lacking. [2]let [6]learn [1]And [5]also - [3]our [4]*people* [9]good

ἔργων προϊστασθαι εἰς τὰς ἀναγκαίας χρείας, ἵνα μὴ
[10]works [7]to [8]maintain for - urgent needs, in order that [3]not
lest

ὦσιν ἄκαρποι.
[1]they [2]may [4]be unfruitful.

15 *Ἀσπάζονταί σε οἱ μετ' ἐμοῦ πάντες.*
[8]greet [9]you [2]the [3]*ones* [4]*who* [5]*are* [6]with [7]me [1]All.

Ἄσπασαι τοὺς φιλοῦντας ἡμᾶς ἐν πίστει.
Greet the *ones* loving us in faith.
those who love

Ἡ χάρις μετὰ πάντων ὑμῶν. Ἀμήν. [b]
- Grace *be* with all of you. Amen.
So be it.

---

[b](3:15) NU omits Αμην, *Amen.*

*(3:10) *αἱρετικός (hairetikos).* Adjective meaning *divisive, factious,* appearing only here in the NT. The word is derived from the verb *αἱρετίζω, to choose.* Like the cognate noun *αἵρεσις, sect* (see *αἵρεσις* at 1 Cor. 11:19), this adjective was used to describe persons who associated with groups that were considered divisive. These groups were usually identified by their distinctive teachings. Thus, here in Titus 3:10 the word *αἱρετικός* may have the sense *heretical.*

The Epistle of Paul the Apostle to
PHILEMON

ΠΡΟΣ ΦΙΛΗΜΟΝΑ
TO PHILEMON

Paul Greets Philemon

1 Παῦλος, δέσμιος Χριστοῦ Ἰησοῦ, καὶ Τιμόθεος ὁ
Paul, a prisoner of Christ Jesus, and Timothy the

ἀδελφός,
brother,

Φιλήμονι τῷ ἀγαπητῷ καὶ συνεργῷ ἡμῶν **2** καὶ
To Philemon - [2]beloved [3]and [4]fellow [5]worker [1]our and

Ἀπφίᾳ τῇ ἀγαπητῇ [a] καὶ Ἀρχίππῳ τῷ συστρατιώτῃ ἡμῶν
to Apphia the beloved and to Archippus - [2]fellow [3]soldier [1]our

καὶ τῇ κατ' οἶκόν σου ἐκκλησίᾳ·
and to the [2]at [4]house [3]your [1]church:

3 Χάρις ὑμῖν καὶ εἰρήνη ἀπὸ Θεοῦ Πατρὸς ἡμῶν καὶ
Grace to you and peace from God Father ˜ our and

Κυρίου Ἰησοῦ Χριστοῦ.
the Lord Jesus Christ.

Paul Commends Philemon's Love and Faith

4 Εὐχαριστῶ τῷ Θεῷ μου πάντοτε μνείαν σου
I thank - God ˜ my always [2]mention [3]of [4]you

ποιούμενος ἐπὶ τῶν προσευχῶν μου, **5** ἀκούων σου τὴν
[1]making in - prayers ˜ my, hearing of your -

ἀγάπην καὶ τὴν πίστιν ἣν ἔχεις πρὸς τὸν Κύριον Ἰησοῦν
love and - faith which you have toward the Lord Jesus

καὶ εἰς πάντας τοὺς ἁγίους, **6** ὅπως ἡ κοινωνία τῆς
and toward all the saints, that the sharing -

πίστεώς σου ἐνεργὴς γένηται ἐν ἐπιγνώσει παντὸς
of faith ˜ your [3]effective [1]may [2]become in full knowledge of every

ἀγαθοῦ τοῦ ἐν ἡμῖν [b] εἰς Χριστὸν Ἰησοῦν. **7** Χάριν
good *thing* the *one* in us for Christ Jesus. [5]thanksgiving
which is

γὰρ ἔχομεν πολλὴν [c] καὶ παράκλησιν ἐπὶ τῇ ἀγάπῃ σου,
[1]For [2]we [3]have [4]much and encouragement over - love ˜ your,

ὅτι τὰ σπλάγχνα τῶν ἁγίων ἀναπέπαυται διὰ σοῦ,
because the inward parts of the saints have been refreshed through you,
affections

ἀδελφέ.
brother.

Paul Intercedes for Onesimus

8 Διό, πολλὴν ἐν Χριστῷ παρρησίαν ἔχων
Therefore, [2]much [4]in [5]Christ [3]boldness [1]having

ἐπιτάσσειν σοι τὸ ἀνῆκον, **9** διὰ τὴν ἀγάπην
to command you the fitting *thing,* on account of - love
what is fitting,

μᾶλλον παρακαλῶ, τοιοῦτος ὢν ὡς Παῦλος πρεσβύτης,
rather I appeal, [2]such [3]a [4]one [1]being as Paul an old man,

1 Paul, a prisoner of Christ Jesus, and Timothy *our* brother,

To Philemon our beloved *friend* and fellow laborer,
2 to the beloved Apphia, Archippus our fellow soldier, and to the church in your house:

3 Grace to you and peace from God our Father and the Lord Jesus Christ.

4 I thank my God, making mention of you always in my prayers,
5 hearing of your love and faith which you have toward the Lord Jesus and toward all the saints,
6 that the sharing of your faith may become effective by the acknowledgment of every good thing which is in you in Christ Jesus.
7 For we have great joy and consolation in your love, because the hearts of the saints have been refreshed by you, brother.
8 Therefore, though I might be very bold in Christ to command you what is fitting,
9 *yet* for love's sake I rather appeal *to you* — being such a one as Paul, the aged, and now also

[a](2) NU reads αδελφη, *sister.* [b](6) TR reads υμιν, *you.* [c](7) NU reads χαραν γαρ πολλην εσχον, *For I had much joy.*

a prisoner of Jesus Christ—
10 I appeal to you for my son Onesimus, whom I have begotten *while* in my chains,
11 who once was unprofitable to you, but now is profitable to you and to me.
12 I am sending him back. You therefore receive him, that is, my own heart,
13 whom I wished to keep with me, that on your behalf he might minister to me in my chains for the gospel.
14 But without your consent I wanted to do nothing, that your good deed might not be by compulsion, as it were, but voluntary.
15 For perhaps he departed for a while for this *purpose,* that you might receive him forever,
16 no longer as a slave but more than a slave—a beloved brother, especially to me but how much more to you, both in the flesh and in the Lord.
17 If then you count me as a partner, receive him as *you would* me.
18 But if he has wronged you or owes anything, put that on my account.
19 I, Paul, am writing with my own hand. I will repay—not to mention to you that you owe me even your own self besides.
20 Yes, brother, let me have joy from you in the Lord; refresh my heart in the Lord.
21 Having confidence in your obedience, I write to you, knowing that you will do even more than I say.
22 But, meanwhile, also prepare a guest room for me, for I trust that through your prayers I shall be granted to you.

νυνὶ δὲ καὶ δέσμιος Ἰησοῦ Χριστοῦ. **10** Παρακαλῶ σε
now ˜ but also a prisoner of Jesus Christ. I appeal to you

περὶ τοῦ ἐμοῦ τέκνου, ὃν ἐγέννησα ἐν τοῖς δεσμοῖς μου,
concerning - my child, whom I begot in - bonds ˜ my,

Ὀνήσιμον, **11** τόν ποτέ σοι ἄχρηστον, νυνὶ δὲ σοὶ καὶ
Onesimus, the *one* once to you unprofitable, now ˜ but to you and
who was

ἐμοὶ εὔχρηστον, **12** ὃν ἀνέπεμψα. Σὺ δὲ[d] αὐτόν, τοῦτ᾽ ἔστι
to me *is* useful, whom I sent back. You then [2]him, [3]this [4]is
am sending that

τὰ ἐμὰ σπλάγχνα, προσλαβοῦ·[e] **13** ὃν ἐγὼ ἐβουλόμην
- [5]my [6]inward [7]parts, [1]receive; whom I wished
very heart,

πρὸς ἐμαυτὸν κατέχειν, ἵνα ὑπὲρ σοῦ διακονῇ
with myself to retain, in order that on behalf of you he might serve

μοι ἐν τοῖς δεσμοῖς τοῦ εὐαγγελίου. **14** Χωρὶς δὲ τῆς σῆς
me in the bonds of the gospel. without ˜ But - your

γνώμης οὐδὲν ἠθέλησα ποιῆσαι, ἵνα μὴ ὡς κατὰ
consent [5]nothing [1]I [2]wished [3]to [4]do, in order that [4]not [6]as [7]by

ἀνάγκην τὸ ἀγαθόν σου ᾖ ἀλλὰ κατὰ ἑκούσιον.
[8]necessity - [2]good [1]your [3]might [5]be but by *being* voluntary.

15 Τάχα γὰρ διὰ τοῦτο ἐχωρίσθη πρὸς ὥραν
perhaps ˜ For on account of this he was taken away for an hour
a time

ἵνα αἰώνιον αὐτὸν ἀπέχῃς, **16** οὐκέτι ὡς δοῦλον
in order that [5]eternally [4]him [1]you [2]might [3]keep, no longer as a slave

ἀλλ᾽ ὑπὲρ δοῦλον, ἀδελφὸν ἀγαπητόν, μάλιστα ἐμοί,
but beyond a slave, a brother ˜ beloved, especially to me,

πόσῳ δὲ μᾶλλον σοὶ καὶ ἐν σαρκὶ καὶ ἐν Κυρίῳ.
[2]how [3]much [1]but [4]more to you both in *the* flesh and in *the* Lord.

Paul Encourages Philemon's Obedience

17 Εἰ οὖν με ἔχεις κοινωνόν, προσλαβοῦ αὐτὸν ὡς
If then [3]me [1]you [2]have *as* a partner, receive him as
count

ἐμέ. **18** Εἰ δέ τι ἠδίκησέ σε ἢ ὀφείλει, τοῦτο
me. if ˜ But *in* anything he wronged you or owes *anything,* [2]this

ἐμοὶ ἐλλόγει. **19** Ἐγὼ Παῦλος ἔγραψα τῇ ἐμῇ χειρί,
[3]to [4]me [1]charge. I Paul wrote - with my *own* hand,
am writing

"Ἐγὼ ἀποτίσω" — ἵνα μὴ λέγω σοι ὅτι καὶ σεαυτόν
"I will repay" — in order that not ˜ I say to you that even yourself
lest

μοι προσοφείλεις! **20** Ναί, ἀδελφέ, ἐγώ σου
[3]to [4]me [1]you [2]owe! Yes, brother, [2]I [5]from [6]you

ὀναίμην ἐν Κυρίῳ· ἀνάπαυσόν μου τὰ σπλάγχνα ἐν
[1]may [3]have [4]profit in *the* Lord; refresh my - inward parts in
affections

Κυρίῳ.[f]
the Lord.

21 Πεποιθὼς τῇ ὑπακοῇ σου ἔγραψά σοι,
Having been persuaded of - obedience ˜ your I wrote to you,
Being confident of I am writing

εἰδὼς ὅτι καὶ ὑπὲρ ὃ λέγω ποιήσεις. **22** Ἅμα δὲ
knowing that even beyond what I say you will do. meanwhile ˜ But

καὶ ἑτοίμαζέ μοι ξενίαν, ἐλπίζω γὰρ ὅτι διὰ τῶν
also prepare me a guest room, [2]I [3]hope [1]for that through -

προσευχῶν ὑμῶν χαρισθήσομαι ὑμῖν.
prayers ˜ your I will be graciously given to you.

---

[d](**12**) NU reads *σοι, to you,* for *συ δε,* thus adding to v. 12a: *whom I sent back to you.* [e](**12**) NU omits *προσλαβου, receive* (see previous note).
[f](**20**) NU reads *Χριστω, Christ.*

Paul's Farewell

23 Ἀσπάζονταί σε Ἐπαφρᾶς ὁ συναιχμάλωτός μου ἐν
There greet you Epaphras - [2]fellow [3]captive [1]my in
Χριστῷ Ἰησοῦ, 24 Μᾶρκος, Ἀρίσταρχος, Δημᾶς, Λουκᾶς, οἱ
Christ Jesus, Mark, Aristarchus, Demas, Luke, -
συνεργοί μου.
[2]fellow [3]workers [1]my.

25 Ἡ χάρις τοῦ Κυρίου ἡμῶν Ἰησοῦ Χριστοῦ μετὰ τοῦ
The grace - of Lord ˜ our Jesus Christ *be* with -
πνεύματος ὑμῶν. Ἀμήν.[g]
spirit ˜ your. Amen.
So be it.

23 Epaphras, my fellow prisoner in Christ Jesus, greets you,
24 *as do* Mark, Aristarchus, Demas, Luke, my fellow laborers.
25 The grace of our Lord Jesus Christ *be* with your spirit. Amen.

---

[g] **(25)** NU omits Αμην, *Amen.*

The Epistle to the

HEBREWS

ΠΡΟΣ ΕΒΡΑΙΟΥΣ
TO *THE* HEBREWS

1 God, who at various times
and in various ways spoke
in time past to the fathers by
the prophets,
2 has in these last days spoken to us by *His* Son, whom He
has appointed heir of all things,
through whom also He made
the worlds;
3 who being the brightness
of *His* glory and the express
image of His person, and upholding all things by the word of
His power, when He had by
Himself purged our sins, sat
down at the right hand of the
Majesty on high,
4 having become so much
better than the angels, as He
has by inheritance obtained a
more excellent name than they.
5 For to which of the angels
did He ever say:

"You are My Son,
Today I have begotten
You"?

And again:

"I will be to Him a Father,
And He shall be to Me a
Son"?

6 But when He again brings
the firstborn into the world, He
says:

The Son: God's Supreme Revelation

1 **1** Πολυμερῶς καὶ πολυτρόπως πάλαι ὁ Θεὸς λαλήσας
In many ways and in various ways long ago - God having spoken
who spoke

τοῖς πατράσιν ἐν τοῖς προφήταις, **2** ἐπ' ἐσχάτου τῶν ἡμερῶν
to the fathers by the prophets, in *the* last - of days ˜

τούτων ἐλάλησεν ἡμῖν ἐν Υἱῷ, ὃν ἔθηκε κληρονόμον
these spoke to us by a Son, whom He appointed an heir
has spoken

πάντων, δι' οὗ καὶ τοὺς αἰῶνας ἐποίησεν· **3** ὃς ὢν
of all *things,* through whom also [3]the [4]ages [1]He [2]made; who being
worlds

ἀπαύγασμα τῆς δόξης καὶ χαρακτὴρ* τῆς
the radiance of the glory and *the* exact representation -
His image

ὑποστάσεως αὐτοῦ, φέρων τε τὰ πάντα τῷ ῥήματι τῆς
of essence ˜ His, bearing ˜ and - all *things* by the word -
upholding

δυνάμεως αὐτοῦ, δι' ἑαυτοῦ [a] καθαρισμὸν ποιησάμενος τῶν
of power ˜ His, [2]by [3]Himself [5]purification [1]having [4]made -
when He had

ἁμαρτιῶν ἡμῶν, [b] ἐκάθισεν ἐν δεξιᾷ τῆς μεγαλωσύνης
for sins ˜ our, sat down on *the* right *hand* of the Majesty
at

ἐν ὑψηλοῖς, **4** τοσούτῳ κρείττων γενόμενος τῶν ἀγγέλων
on high, [3]as [4]much [5]better [1]having [2]become *than* the angels
so

ὅσῳ διαφορώτερον παρ' αὐτοὺς κεκληρονόμηκεν ὄνομα.
as [4]a [5]more [6]excellent [8]more [9]than [10]them [1]He [2]has [3]inherited [7]name.
they

The Son Exalted Above Angels

5 Τίνι γὰρ εἶπέ ποτε τῶν ἀγγέλων,
[2]to [3]which [1]For [7]did [8]He [10]say [9]ever [4]of [5]the [6]angels,

«Υἱός μου εἶ σύ,
«[4]Son [3]My [2]are [1]You,

Ἐγὼ σήμερον γεγέννηκά σε»? [c]
I ˜ Today have begotten You»?

καὶ πάλιν,
And again,

«Ἐγὼ ἔσομαι αὐτῷ εἰς Πατέρα,
«I will be to Him for a Father,

Καὶ αὐτὸς ἔσται μοι εἰς Υἱόν»? [d]
And He will be to Me for a Son»?

6 Ὅταν δὲ πάλιν εἰσαγάγῃ τὸν Πρωτότοκον εἰς τὴν
when ˜ But again ˜ He brings in the Firstborn into the

οἰκουμένην, λέγει,
world, He says,

---

[a](**1:3**) NU omits δι εαυτου, *by Himself.*
[b](**1:3**) NU omits ημων, *our.*
[c](**1:5**) Ps. 2:7 [d](**1:5**) 2 Sam. 7:14; 1 Chron. 17:13

---

*(**1:3**) χαρακτήρ (*charaktēr*). Noun meaning *representation,* derived from *χαράσσω, engrave.* In classical Greek the word was used to indicate an *impression, stamp, representation,* as of the impression of a person's likeness on a coin or seal. Here it is used metaphorically to express the complete similarity of the Son of

«Καὶ προσκυνησάτωσαν αὐτῷ πάντες ἄγγελοι Θεοῦ.»[e]
«And let [6]worship [7]Him [1]all [2]*the* [3]angels [4]of [5]God.»

7 Καὶ πρὸς μὲν τοὺς ἀγγέλους λέγει,
And [5]to [1]on [2]the [3]one [4]hand the angels He says,

«Ὁ ποιῶν τοὺς ἀγγέλους αὐτοῦ πνεύματα
«The *One* making - angels ~ His spirits
«He who makes

Καὶ τοὺς λειτουργοὺς αὐτοῦ πυρὸς φλόγα»·[f]
And - servants ~ His [2]of [3]fire [1]flames»:
ministers

8 πρὸς δὲ τὸν Υἱόν,
to ~ But the Son *He says,*

«Ὁ θρόνος σου, ὁ Θεός, εἰς τὸν αἰῶνα τοῦ αἰῶνος·
- «throne ~ Your, - *O* God, *is* to the age of the age;
forever and ever;

Ῥάβδος εὐθύτητος ἡ ῥάβδος τῆς βασιλείας σου.
A scepter of uprightness *is* the scepter - of kingdom ~ Your.

9 Ἠγάπησας δικαιοσύνην καὶ ἐμίσησας ἀνομίαν·
You loved righteousness and hated lawlessness;

Διὰ τοῦτο ἔχρισέ σε ὁ Θεός, ὁ Θεός σου,
On account of this [4]anointed [5]You - [1]God, - [3]God [2]Your,

Ἔλαιον ἀγαλλιάσεως παρὰ τοὺς μετόχους σου»·[g]
With oil of gladness beyond - companions ~ Your»:

10 καί,
and,

«Σὺ κατ' ἀρχάς, Κύριε, τὴν γῆν
«You [2]in [3]*the* [4]beginning, [1]Lord, [9]the [10]earth

ἐθεμελίωσας,
[5]laid [6]the [7]foundation [8]of,

Καὶ ἔργα τῶν χειρῶν σού εἰσιν οἱ οὐρανοί·
And [4]works - [5]of [7]hands [6]Your [3]are [1]the [2]heavens;

11 Αὐτοὶ ἀπολοῦνται, σὺ δὲ διαμένεις·
They will perish, You ~ but remain;

Καὶ πάντες ὡς ἱμάτιον παλαιωθήσονται,
And all *things* like a garment will become old,

12 Καὶ ὡσεὶ περιβόλαιον ἑλίξεις αὐτοὺς
And like a cloak You will roll up ~ them

Καὶ[h] ἀλλαγήσονται.
And they will be changed.

Σὺ δὲ ὁ αὐτὸς εἶ
You ~ But [2]the [3]same [1]are

Καὶ τὰ ἔτη σου οὐκ ἐκλείψουσι.»[i]
And - years ~ Your not ~ will fail.»

13 Πρὸς τίνα δὲ τῶν ἀγγέλων εἴρηκέ ποτε,
[2]to [3]which [1]But of the angels has He said ~ ever,

«Κάθου ἐκ δεξιῶν μου
«Sit at [2]right [3]*parts* [1]My
hand

Ἕως ἂν θῶ τοὺς ἐχθρούς σου ὑποπόδιον τῶν ποδῶν
Till - I put - enemies ~ Your *as* a footstool - of feet ~
for

σου»?[j]
Your»?

14 Οὐχὶ πάντες εἰσὶ λειτουργικὰ πνεύματα εἰς διακονίαν
[3]not [4]all [1]Are [2]they ministering spirits [4]for [5]ministry
to minister

"Let all the angels of God worship Him."

7 And of the angels He says:

"Who makes His angels spirits
And His ministers a flame of fire."

8 But to the Son *He says:*

"Your throne, O God, is forever and ever;
A scepter of righteousness is the scepter of Your kingdom.
9 *You have loved righteousness and hated lawlessness;*
Therefore God, Your God, has anointed You
With the oil of gladness more than Your companions."

10 And:

"You, LORD, in the beginning laid the foundation of the earth,
And the heavens are the work of Your hands.
11 *They will perish, but You remain;*
And they will all grow old like a garment;
12 *Like a cloak You will fold them up,*
And they will be changed.
But You are the same,
And Your years will not fail."

13 But to which of the angels has He ever said:

"Sit at My right hand,
Till I make Your enemies Your footstool"?

14 Are they not all ministering

---

e(**1:6**) Deut. 32:43 (LXX, DSS); Ps. 97:7
f(**1:7**) Ps. 104:4 *g*(**1:8, 9**) Ps. 45:6, 7 *h*(**1:12**) NU adds ὡς ἱμάτιον, *(And) like a garment.*
i(**1:10–12**) Ps. 102:25–27
j(**1:13**) Ps. 110:1

God to the Father, just as a coin exactly represents the type from which it is struck. This word also expresses the idea that Christ is the (only) *representation* of God's glory and essence available to humanity. Cf. the cognate nouns χάραξ, *an embankment* or *barricade* (Luke 19:43); and χάραγμα,

spirits sent forth to minister for
those who will inherit salvation?

2 Therefore we must give
the more earnest heed to
the things we have heard, lest
we drift away.
2 For if the word spoken
through angels proved steadfast, and every transgression
and disobedience received a
just reward,
3 how shall we escape if we
neglect so great a salvation,
which at the first began to be
spoken by the Lord, and was
confirmed to us by those who
heard *Him,*
4 God also bearing witness
both with signs and wonders,
with various miracles, and gifts
of the Holy Spirit, according to
His own will?
5 For He has not put the
world to come, of which we
speak, in subjection to angels.
6 But one testified in a certain place, saying:

*"What is man that You are
mindful of him,
Or the son of man that
You take care of him?*
7 *You have made him a little
lower than the angels;
You have crowned him
with glory and honor,
And set him over the
works of Your hands.*
8 *You have put all things in
subjection under his
feet."*

For in that He put all in subjection under him, He left nothing

ἀποστελλόμενα διὰ τοὺς μέλλοντας κληρονομεῖν
[1]being [2]sent [3]out for the sake of the *ones* being about to inherit
those who are

σωτηρίαν?
salvation?

First Warning: Do Not Neglect Salvation

2 1 Διά τοῦτο δεῖ περισσοτέρως ἡμᾶς
On account of this it is necessary *for* [5]so [6]much [7]more [1]us

προσέχειν τοῖς ἀκουσθεῖσι, μήποτε
[2]to [3]give [4]heed to the *things* having been heard, lest
we have

παραρρυῶμεν. 2 Εἰ γὰρ ὁ δι' ἀγγέλων
we should drift away. if ˜ For the [5]through [6]angels

λαληθεὶς λόγος ἐγένετο βέβαιος, καὶ πᾶσα παράβασις
[2]having [3]been [4]spoken [1]word became steadfast, and every transgression
which was

καὶ παρακοὴ ἔλαβεν ἔνδικον μισθαποδοσίαν, 3 πῶς ἡμεῖς
and disobedience received a just reward, how we ˜

ἐκφευξόμεθα τηλικαύτης ἀμελήσαντες σωτηρίας, ἥτις,
shall escape [2]so [3]great [1]neglecting a salvation, which,
if we neglect

ἀρχὴν λαβοῦσα λαλεῖσθαι διὰ τοῦ Κυρίου, ὑπὸ
[3]a [4]beginning [1]having [2]received to be spoken by the Lord, [6]by
in the beginning was

τῶν ἀκουσάντων εἰς ἡμᾶς ἐβεβαιώθη,
[7]the [8]*ones* [9]having [10]heard [11]*Him* [4]to [5]us [1]*and* [2]was [3]confirmed,
who

4 συνεπιμαρτυροῦντος τοῦ Θεοῦ σημείοις τε καὶ τέρασι καὶ
[2]also [3]bearing [4]witness - [1]God [6]with [7]signs [5]both and wonders and

ποικίλαις δυνάμεσι καὶ Πνεύματος Ἁγίου μερισμοῖς
various miracles and [2]of [3]*the* [5]Spirit [4]Holy [1]distributions
gifts

κατὰ τὴν αὐτοῦ θέλησιν?
according to - His will?

The Son Made Lower than Angels

5 Οὐ γὰρ ἀγγέλοις ὑπέταξε τὴν οἰκουμένην τὴν
[4]not [1]For [15]to [16]angels [2]He [3]did [5]subject [6]the [7]world [8]the [9]*one*
which is

μέλλουσαν, περὶ ἧς λαλοῦμεν. 6 Διεμαρτύρατο δέ
[10]coming, [11]concerning [12]which [13]we [14]speak. [4]testified [1]But
to come,

πού τις λέγων,
[3]somewhere [2]someone saying,

«Τί ἐστιν ἄνθρωπος ὅτι μιμνήσκῃ αὐτοῦ,
«What is man that You remember him,

Ἢ υἱὸς ἀνθρώπου ὅτι ἐπισκέπτῃ αὐτόν?
Or *the* son of man that You are concerned about him?

7 Ἠλάττωσας αὐτὸν βραχύ τι παρ' ἀγγέλους,
You made lower ˜ him for [2]short [3]*time* [1]some than *the* angels,
for a little while

Δόξῃ καὶ τιμῇ ἐστεφάνωσας αὐτόν,[a]
With glory and honor You crowned him,

8 Πάντα ὑπέταξας ὑποκάτω τῶν ποδῶν αὐτοῦ.»[b]
[3]all [4]*things* [1]You [2]subjected under - feet ˜ his.»
have subjected

---

[a](2:7) TR adds και κατεστησας αυτον επι τα εργα των χειρων σου, *and set him over the works of Your hands.*
[b](2:6–8) Ps. 8:4–6.

impress, mark (of the beast, Rev. 13:16) or an *image* (Acts 17:29).

Ἐν γὰρ τῷ ὑποτάξαι αὐτῷ τὰ πάντα οὐδὲν ἀφῆκεν αὐτῷ
in ~ For - to subject to him - all *things* [3]nothing [1]He [2]left [6]to [7]him
subjecting

ἀνυπότακτον. Νῦν δὲ οὔπω ὁρῶμεν αὐτῷ τὰ πάντα
[4]not [5]subjected. now ~ But [3]not [4]yet [1]we [2]do [5]see [11]to [12]him - [6]all [7]*things*

ὑποτεταγμένα. **9** Τὸν δὲ "βραχύ τι παρ'
[8]having [9]been [10]subjected. [4]the [5]*One* [1]But "[10]for [12]short [13]*time* [11]some [14]than
"for a little while

ἀγγέλους ἠλαττωμένον" βλέπομεν, Ἰησοῦν διὰ τὸ
[15]*the* [16]angels [6]having [7]been [8]made [9]lower" [2]we [3]see, Jesus through the
who was

πάθημα τοῦ θανάτου "δόξῃ καὶ τιμῇ ἐστεφανωμένον,"*
suffering - of death "[4]with [5]glory [6]and [7]honor [1]having [2]been [3]crowned,"

ὅπως χάριτι Θεοῦ ὑπὲρ παντὸς γεύσηται θανάτου.
so that by *the* grace of God [5]in [6]behalf [7]of [8]all [1]He [2]might [3]taste [4]death.

Bringing Many Sons to Glory

10 Ἔπρεπε γὰρ αὐτῷ, δι' ὃν τὰ πάντα
[2]it [3]was [4]fitting [1]For for Him, on account of whom - *are* all *things*

καὶ δι' οὗ τὰ πάντα, πολλοὺς υἱοὺς εἰς δόξαν
and through whom - *are* all *things,* [2]many [3]sons [4]to [5]glory

ἀγαγόντα, τὸν Ἀρχηγὸν τῆς σωτηρίας αὐτῶν διὰ
[1]bringing, [9]the [10]Originator - [11]of [13]salvation [12]their [14]through
in bringing,

παθημάτων τελειῶσαι. **11** Ὅ τε γὰρ ἁγιάζων καὶ
[15]sufferings [6]to [7]make [8]complete. [3]the [4]*One* [2]both [1]For sanctifying and
He who sanctifies

οἱ ἁγιαζόμενοι ἐξ ἑνὸς πάντες· δι'
the *ones* being sanctified *are* [2]out [3]of [4]one [1]all; on account of
those who are

ἣν αἰτίαν οὐκ ἐπαισχύνεται ἀδελφοὺς αὐτοὺς καλεῖν,
which reason [3]not [1]He [2]is [4]ashamed [8]brothers [7]them [5]to [6]call,

12 λέγων,
saying,

«Ἀπαγγελῶ τὸ ὄνομά σου τοῖς ἀδελφοῖς μου,
«I will announce - name ~ Your - to brothers ~ My,

Ἐν μέσῳ ἐκκλησίας ὑμνήσω σε»·[c]
In *the* midst of *the* congregation I will sing praise ~ You»;

13 καὶ πάλιν,
and again,

«Ἐγὼ ἔσομαι πεποιθὼς ἐπ' αὐτῷ»·[d]
«I will be having trusted in Him»;
will put trust

καὶ πάλιν,
and again,

«Ἰδοὺ ἐγὼ καὶ τὰ παιδία ἅ μοι ἔδωκεν ὁ Θεός.»[e]
«Behold I and the children whom [3]to [4]Me [2]gave - [1]God.»
has given

14 Ἐπεὶ οὖν τὰ παιδία κεκοινώνηκε σαρκὸς καὶ αἵματος,
since ~ Therefore the children have shared of flesh and blood,

καὶ αὐτὸς παραπλησίως μετέσχε τῶν αὐτῶν, ἵνα
also [2]Himself [3]likewise [1]He [4]shared the same *things,* in order that

διὰ τοῦ θανάτου καταργήσῃ τὸν τὸ κράτος ἔχοντα τοῦ
through - death He might destroy the *one* [2]the [3]power [1]having -

θανάτου, τοῦτ' ἔστι τὸν διάβολον, **15** καὶ ἀπαλλάξῃ
of death, that is the devil, and *that* He might release

τούτους, ὅσοι φόβῳ θανάτου διὰ παντὸς τοῦ ζῆν
these, as many as by fear of death through all of the *time* to live
of their lives

that is not put under him. But now we do not yet see all things put under him.

9 But we see Jesus, who was made a little lower than the angels, for the suffering of death crowned with glory and honor, that He, by the grace of God, might taste death for everyone.

10 For it was fitting for Him, for whom *are* all things and by whom *are* all things, in bringing many sons to glory, to make the captain of their salvation perfect through sufferings.

11 For both He who sanctifies and those who are being sanctified *are* all of one, for which reason He is not ashamed to call them brethren,

12 saying:

"I will declare Your name
to My brethren;
In the midst of the
assembly I will sing
praise to You."

13 And again:

"I will put My trust in
Him."

And again:

"Here am I and the
children whom God has
given Me."

14 Inasmuch then as the children have partaken of flesh and blood, He Himself likewise shared in the same, that through death He might destroy him who had the power of death, that is, the devil,

15 and release those who through fear of death were all

---

[c]**(2:12)** Ps. 22:22
[d]**(2:13)** 2 Sam. 22:3 LXX; Is. 8:17 LXX [e]**(2:13)** Is. 8:18

***(2:9)** στεφανόω *(stephanoō).* Verb literally meaning *to crown, award the victor's prize.* Often it is used figuratively (as here in Heb. 2:7, 9) to refer to the bestowing of some honor or reward. Cf. the cognate noun *στέφανος, crown,* which must be distinguished from *διάδημα, crown, diadem.* The latter is the royal crown (Rev. 19:12), whereas the στέφανος is the wreath placed on the head of a victorious general (Rev. 6:2) or athlete (1 Cor. 9:25) or other celebrant (1 Thess. 2:19). In passages like 2 Tim. 4:8 ("crown of righteousness"),

their lifetime subject to bondage.
16 For indeed He does not give aid to angels, but He does give aid to the seed of Abraham.
17 Therefore, in all things He had to be made like *His* brethren, that He might be a merciful and faithful High Priest in things *pertaining* to God, to make propitiation for the sins of the people.
18 For in that He Himself has suffered, being tempted, He is able to aid those who are tempted.
3 Therefore, holy brethren, partakers of the heavenly calling, consider the Apostle and High Priest of our confession, Christ Jesus,
2 who was faithful to Him who appointed Him, as Moses also *was faithful* in all His house.
3 For this One has been counted worthy of more glory than Moses, inasmuch as He who built the house has more honor than the house.
4 For every house is built by someone, but He who built all things *is* God.
5 And Moses indeed *was* faithful in all His house as a servant, for a testimony of those things which would be spoken *afterward,*
6 but Christ as a Son over His own house, whose house we are if we hold fast the confidence and the rejoicing of the hope firm to the end.

---

[a](3:1) NU omits Χριστον, *Christ.* [b](3:6) NU omits μεχρι τελους βεβαιαν, *firm until (the) end.*

---

1 Pet. 5:4 ("crown of glory"), and James 1:12 ("crown of life") the modifying nouns either characterize or identify the metaphorical victor's crowns (i.e, "glorious crown" or "crowned with glory").

***(3:1)** μέτοχος *(metochos).* Adjective meaning *having a share in, being a participant or partner with, being a companion of.* Used substantivally it means *partner, companion* (Heb. 1:9). A synonym of the more common κοινωνός which stresses the idea of "having in common," μέτοχος focuses more on the fact of "sharing." The writer of Hebrews views his readers as *sharing in* the heavenly calling (here in 3:1), Christ (3:14), the Holy Spirit (6:4), and the disci-

ἔνοχοι ἦσαν δουλείας. **16** Οὐ γὰρ δήπου ἀγγέλων
[2]subject [3]to [1]were [4]slavery. [5]not [1]For [2]surely [8]of [9]angels
to

ἐπιλαμβάνεται, ἀλλὰ σπέρματος Ἀβραὰμ ἐπιλαμβάνεται.
[3]He [4]does [6]take [7]hold, but [4]of [5]*the* [6]seed [7]of [8]Abraham [1]He [2]takes [3]hold.
give aid, to gives aid.

17 Ὅθεν ὤφειλε κατὰ πάντα τοῖς ἀδελφοῖς
Whence He was obligated [6]in [7]all [8]*respects* [4]the [5]brothers
His

ὁμοιωθῆναι, ἵνα ἐλεήμων γένηται καὶ πιστὸς
[1]to [2]become [3]like, in order that [4]a [5]merciful [1]He [2]might [3]become and faithful

ἀρχιερεὺς τὰ πρὸς τὸν Θεόν, εἰς τὸ
high priest *in* the *things* in regard to - God, for -
in order that He

ἱλάσκεσθαι τὰς ἁμαρτίας τοῦ λαοῦ. **18** Ἐν
to propitiate the sins of the people. [2]in
might make propitiation for

ᾧ γὰρ πέπονθεν αὐτὸς πειρασθείς, δύναται
[3]that [4]which [1]For [5]He [7]has [8]suffered [6]Himself being tempted, He is able

τοῖς πειραζομένοις βοηθῆσαι.
[3]the [4]*ones* [5]being [6]tempted [1]to [2]help.
those who are

The Son Was Faithful

3 **1** Ὅθεν, ἀδελφοὶ ἅγιοι, κλήσεως ἐπουρανίου
Therefore, brothers ˜ holy, [5]calling [2]of [3]*the* [4]heavenly

μέτοχοι,* κατανοήσατε τὸν Ἀπόστολον καὶ Ἀρχιερέα τῆς
[1]sharers, consider the Apostle and High Priest -

ὁμολογίας ἡμῶν Ἰησοῦν Χριστόν,[a] **2** πιστὸν ὄντα τῷ
of confession ˜ our Jesus Christ, faithful ˜ being to the *One*
who is

ποιήσαντι αὐτὸν ὡς καὶ Μωϋσῆς ἐν ὅλῳ τῷ οἴκῳ αὐτοῦ.
having made Him as also Moses *was* in [2]whole - [3]house [1]His.
who appointed all His house.

3 Πλείονος γὰρ δόξης οὗτος παρὰ Μωϋσῆν
[8]of [9]more [1]For [10]glory [2]this [3]*One* [11]than [12]Moses
He

ἠξίωται καθ' ὅσον πλείονα τιμὴν ἔχει
[4]has [5]been [6]counted [7]worthy by as much as [7]more [8]honor [6]has
inasmuch as

τοῦ οἴκου ὁ κατασκευάσας αὐτόν. **4** Πᾶς γὰρ
[9]*than* [10]the [11]house [1]the [2]*One* [3]having [4]prepared [5]it. every ˜ For

οἶκος κατασκευάζεται ὑπό τινος, ὁ δὲ τὰ πάντα
house is prepared by someone, [2]the [3]*One* [1]but - [6]all [7]*things*

κατασκευάσας Θεός. **5** Καὶ Μωϋσῆς μὲν πιστὸς ἐν ὅλῳ
[4]having [5]prepared *is* God. And Moses indeed *was* faithful in [2]whole
all

τῷ οἴκῳ αὐτοῦ ὡς θεράπων εἰς μαρτύριον τῶν
- [3]house [1]His as a servant for a testimony of the *things*
His house

λαληθησομένων, **6** Χριστὸς δὲ ὡς Υἱὸς ἐπὶ τὸν οἶκον αὐτοῦ,
being spoken, Christ ˜ but as a Son over - [3]house [1]His [2]*own,*
which would be

οὗ οἶκός ἐσμεν ἡμεῖς, ἐάνπερ τὴν παρρησίαν καὶ τὸ
whose house are ˜ we, if indeed [4]the [5]confidence [6]and [7]the

καύχημα τῆς ἐλπίδος μέχρι τέλους βεβαίαν[b] κατάσχωμεν.
[8]boast - [9]of [10]hope [12]until [13]*the* [14]end [11]firm [1]we [2]hold [3]fast.

Second Warning: Be Faithful

7 Διό, καθὼς λέγει τὸ Πνεῦμα τὸ Ἅγιον,
Therefore, just as [4]says [1]the [3]Spirit - [2]Holy,

«Σήμερον ἐὰν τῆς φωνῆς αὐτοῦ ἀκούσητε,
«Today if - [4]voice [3]His [1]you [2]hear,

8 Μὴ σκληρύνητε τὰς καρδίας ὑμῶν
not ˜ Do harden - hearts ˜ your

Ὡς ἐν τῷ παραπικρασμῷ,
As in the rebellion,

Κατὰ τὴν ἡμέραν τοῦ πειρασμοῦ ἐν τῇ ἐρήμῳ,
According to the day of the trial in the wilderness,
As in

9 Οὗ ἐπείρασάν με οἱ πατέρες ὑμῶν,
Of which *place* [3]tested [4]Me - [2]fathers [1]your,
Where

Ἐδοκίμασάν με[c] καὶ εἶδον τὰ ἔργα μου τεσσαράκοντα
They examined Me and saw - works ˜ My forty
tried

ἔτη.
years.

10 Διὸ προσώχθισα τῇ γενεᾷ ἐκείνῃ
Therefore I was angry - with generation ˜ that

Καὶ εἶπον, "Ἀεὶ πλανῶνται τῇ καρδίᾳ·
And I said, 'always ˜ They go astray in the heart;
their

Αὐτοὶ δὲ οὐκ ἔγνωσαν τὰς ὁδούς μου'·
they ˜ And not ˜ did know - ways ˜ My';
have not known

11 Ὡς ὤμοσα ἐν τῇ ὀργῇ μου,
As I swore in - wrath ˜ My,

'Εἰ εἰσελεύσονται εἰς τὴν κατάπαυσίν μου.'»[d]
'If they will enter into - rest ˜ My.'»
'They shall not

12 Βλέπετε, ἀδελφοί, μήποτε ἔσται ἔν τινι ὑμῶν
Look, brothers, lest *there* will be in anyone of you

καρδία πονηρὰ ἀπιστίας ἐν τῷ ἀποστῆναι ἀπὸ Θεοῦ
a(n) heart ˜ evil of unbelief in - to depart from *the* God ˜
departing

ζῶντος· 13 ἀλλὰ παρακαλεῖτε ἑαυτοὺς καθ' ἑκάστην
living; but exhort yourselves according to each
daily,

ἡμέραν, ἄχρις οὗ τὸ "σήμερον" καλεῖται, ἵνα μὴ
day, until which *time* - [4]"today" [1]it [2]is [3]called, in order that [4]not
while lest

σκληρυνθῇ ἐξ ὑμῶν τις ἀπάτῃ τῆς ἁμαρτίας.
[5]be [6]hardened [2]of [3]you [1]anyone by *the* deceitfulness - of sin.

14 Μέτοχοι γὰρ γεγόναμεν τοῦ Χριστοῦ, ἐάνπερ τὴν
[5]sharers [1]For [2]we [3]have [4]become - of Christ, if indeed [4]the

ἀρχὴν τῆς ὑποστάσεως* μέχρι τέλους βεβαίαν
[5]beginning [6]of [7]the [8]assurance [10]until [11]*the* [12]end [9]firm

κατάσχωμεν, 15 ἐν τῷ λέγεσθαι,
[1]we [2]hold [3]fast, in - to be said,
saying,

«Σήμερον ἐὰν τῆς φωνῆς αὐτοῦ ἀκούσητε,
«Today if - voice ˜ His you hear,

Μὴ σκληρύνητε τὰς καρδίας ὑμῶν
not ˜ Do harden - hearts ˜ your

Ὡς ἐν τῷ παραπικρασμῷ.»[e]
As in the rebellion.»

7 Therefore, as the Holy Spirit says:

"Today, if you will hear
His voice,
8 *Do not harden your hearts*
as in the rebellion,
In the day of trial in the
wilderness,
9 *Where your fathers tested*
Me, tried Me,
And saw My works forty
years.
10 *Therefore I was angry*
with that generation,
And said, 'They always go
astray in their heart,
And they have not known
My ways.'
11 *So I swore in My wrath,*
'They shall not enter My
rest.' "

12 Beware, brethren, lest there be in any of you an evil heart of unbelief in departing from the living God;
13 but exhort one another daily, while it is called *"Today,"* lest any of you be hardened through the deceitfulness of sin.
14 For we have become partakers of Christ if we hold the beginning of our confidence steadfast to the end,
15 while it is said:

"Today, if you will hear
His voice,
Do not harden your
hearts as in the
rebellion."

---

[c](3:9) For Εδοκιμασαν με, *They examined Me,* NU reads εν δοκιμασια, *(tested Me) with a test.*
[d](3:7–11) Ps. 95:7–11
[e](3:15) Ps. 95:7, 8

pline that identifies them as children of God (12:8). Cf. the cognate verb *μετέχω, share, participate, partake of* (1 Cor. 9:10; Heb. 2:14), and see *κοινωνέω* at Phil. 4:15.

***(3:14)** *ὑπόστασις (hypostasis).* Noun meaning either *substantial nature, essence, actual being, reality* (as in Heb. 1:3, where Jesus is the express representation of the "essence" of God), or *confidence, assurance* (as here in 3:14). In 2 Cor. 9:4; 11:17 it is used of Paul's "confident boasting." In Heb. 11:1 either meaning might fit: faith could be described as the *assurance* and *confidence* of things hoped for, or as the *substantial nature* and *reality* of those things.

16 For who, having heard, rebelled? Indeed, *was it* not all who came out of Egypt, *led* by Moses?
17 Now with whom was He angry forty years? *Was it* not with those who sinned, whose corpses fell in the wilderness?
18 And to whom did He swear that they would not enter His rest, but to those who did not obey?
19 So we see that they could not enter in because of unbelief.

4 Therefore, since a promise remains of entering His rest, let us fear lest any of you seem to have come short of it.
2 For indeed the gospel was preached to us as well as to them; but the word which they heard did not profit them, not being mixed with faith in those who heard *it*.
3 For we who have believed do enter that rest, as He has said:

> *"So I swore in My wrath,*
> *'They shall not enter My rest,'"*

although the works were finished from the foundation of the world.
4 For He has spoken in a certain place of the seventh *day* in this way: *"And God rested on the seventh day from all His*

16 Τίνες γὰρ ἀκούσαντες παρεπίκραναν? Ἀλλ' οὐ πάντες
who ˜ For having heard revolted? But *was it* not all

οἱ ἐξελθόντες ἐξ Αἰγύπτου διὰ Μωϋσέως?
the *ones* coming out of Egypt through Moses?
who came

17 Τίσι δὲ προσώχθισε τεσσαράκοντα ἔτη? Οὐχὶ
[2]with [3]whom [1]Now was He angry forty years? *Was it* not

τοῖς ἁμαρτήσασιν, ὧν τὰ κῶλα ἔπεσεν ἐν τῇ
with the *ones* having sinned, whose - corpses fell in the
who

ἐρήμῳ? **18** Τίσι δὲ ὤμοσε μὴ εἰσελεύσεσθαι
wilderness? [2]to [3]whom [1]And did He swear not to enter
that they would not enter

εἰς τὴν κατάπαυσιν αὐτοῦ εἰ μὴ τοῖς ἀπειθήσασι?
into - rest ˜ His if not to the *ones* having disobeyed?
except who

19 Καὶ βλέπομεν ὅτι οὐκ ἠδυνήθησαν εἰσελθεῖν δι'
And we see that [3]not [1]they [2]were able to enter on account of

ἀπιστίαν.
unbelief.

The Continuing Promise of Rest

4 **1** Φοβηθῶμεν οὖν, μήποτε καταλειπομένης
[2]let [3]us [4]fear [1]Therefore, lest [3]being [4]left
while the

ἐπαγγελίας εἰσελθεῖν εἰς τὴν κατάπαυσιν αὐτοῦ, δοκῇ
[1]*the* [2]promise to enter into - rest ˜ His, [4]seems
promise remains

τις ἐξ ὑμῶν ὑστερηκέναι. **2** Καὶ γάρ ἐσμεν
[1]anyone [2]of [3]you to have come short. indeed ˜ For we are
we have

εὐηγγελισμένοι καθάπερ κἀκεῖνοι, ἀλλ' οὐκ
having good news preached *to us* just as those also, but [6]not
had

ὠφέλησεν ὁ λόγος τῆς ἀκοῆς ἐκείνους, μὴ
[5]did [7]profit [1]the [2]word - [3]of [4]hearing those, not
which they heard because

συγκεκρασμένους τῇ πίστει τοῖς ἀκούσασιν.
having been mixed together - in faith with the *ones* having heard *it*.
they were not those who

3 Εἰσερχόμεθα γὰρ εἰς τὴν κατάπαυσιν οἱ
[2]we [7]enter [1]For [8]into [9]the [10]rest [3]the [4]*ones*
who

πιστεύσαντες, καθὼς εἴρηκεν,
[5]having [6]believed, just as He has said,
have

> «Ὡς ὤμοσα ἐν τῇ ὀργῇ μου,
> «As I swore in - wrath ˜ My,
>
> 'Εἰ εἰσελεύσονται εἰς τὴν κατάπαυσίν μου,'»[a]
> 'If they will enter into - rest ˜ My,'»
> 'They shall not

καίτοι τῶν ἔργων ἀπὸ καταβολῆς κόσμου γενηθέντων.
although the works [4]from [5]*the* [6]foundation [7]of [8]*the* [9]world [1]coming [2]to [3]be.
His were finished.

4 Εἴρηκε γάρ που περὶ τῆς ἑβδόμης οὕτω,
[2]He [3]has [4]said [1]For somewhere concerning the seventh *day* thus,

«Καὶ κατέπαυσεν ὁ Θεὸς ἐν τῇ ἡμέρᾳ τῇ ἑβδόμῃ ἀπὸ πάντων
«And rested ˜ - God on the day ˜ - seventh from all

---

[a](4:3) Ps. 95:11

τῶν ἔργων αὐτοῦ»·[b] 5 καὶ ἐν τούτῳ πάλιν, «Εἰ
- works ˜ His»; and in this *place* again, «If
«They

εἰσελεύσονται εἰς τὴν κατάπαυσίν μου.»[c] 6 Ἐπεὶ οὖν
they will enter into - rest ˜ My.» since ˜ Therefore
shall not

ἀπολείπεται τινὰς εἰσελθεῖν εἰς αὐτήν, καὶ οἱ πρότερον
it remains *for* some to enter into it, and the *ones* formerly

εὐαγγελισθέντες οὐκ εἰσῆλθον δι'
having good news preached *to them* not ˜ did enter on account of

ἀπείθειαν, 7 πάλιν τινὰ ὁρίζει ἡμέραν, «Σήμερον,» ἐν
disobedience, again [4]certain [1]He [2]appoints [3]a [5]day, «Today,» [2]in

Δαβὶδ λέγων μετὰ τοσοῦτον χρόνον, καθὼς εἴρηται,
[3]David [1]saying after such a time, just as it has been said,

«Σήμερον ἐὰν τῆς φωνῆς αὐτοῦ ἀκούσητε,
«Today if - [4]voice [3]His [1]you [2]hear,

Μὴ σκληρύνητε τὰς καρδίας ὑμῶν.»[d]
not ˜ Do harden - hearts your.»

8 Εἰ γὰρ αὐτοὺς Ἰησοῦς κατέπαυσεν, οὐκ ἂν περὶ
if ˜ For [3]them [1]Joshua [2]brought [4]to [5]rest, [8]not - [13]concerning
had given He would not

ἄλλης ἐλάλει μετὰ ταῦτα ἡμέρας. 9 Ἄρα
[14]another [6]He [7]was [9]speaking [10]after [11]these [12]*things* day. Then
have spoken afterward of another

ἀπολείπεται σαββατισμὸς τῷ λαῷ τοῦ Θεοῦ. 10 Ὁ
there remains a Sabbath rest for the people - of God. [2]the [3]*one*

γὰρ εἰσελθὼν εἰς τὴν κατάπαυσιν αὐτοῦ καὶ αὐτὸς
[1]For having entered into - rest ˜ His also himself ˜
who

κατέπαυσεν ἀπὸ τῶν ἔργων αὐτοῦ ὥσπερ ἀπὸ τῶν
rested from - works his as [3]from -

ἰδίων ὁ Θεός.
[4]His [5]own [6]*works* - [1]God [2]*rested.*

God's Word Discovers Our Condition

11 Σπουδάσωμεν οὖν εἰσελθεῖν εἰς ἐκείνην τὴν
[2]let [3]us [4]be [5]eager [1]Therefore to enter into that -

κατάπαυσιν, ἵνα μὴ ἐν τῷ αὐτῷ τις ὑποδείγματι
rest, in order that not [3]in [4]the [5]same [1]anyone [6]example
lest

πέσῃ τῆς ἀπειθείας.
[2]falls - of disobedience.

12 Ζῶν γὰρ ὁ λόγος τοῦ Θεοῦ καὶ ἐνεργὴς καὶ
[6]*is* [7]living [1]For [2]the [3]word - [4]of [5]God and powerful and

τομώτερος ὑπὲρ πᾶσαν μάχαιραν δίστομον καὶ διϊκνούμενος
sharper beyond every sword ˜ two-edged and piercing
any

ἄχρι μερισμοῦ ψυχῆς τε καὶ πνεύματος, ἁρμῶν τε καὶ
as far as *the* division of soul ˜ both and spirit, [2]of [3]joints [1]both and

μυελῶν, καὶ κριτικὸς ἐνθυμήσεων καὶ ἐννοιῶν
of marrows, and *is* able to discern *the* thoughts and intentions
marrow,

καρδίας. 13 Καὶ οὐκ ἔστι κτίσις ἀφανὴς ἐνώπιον αὐτοῦ,
of *the* heart. And [3]not [1]*there* [2]is a creature hidden before Him,

πάντα δὲ γυμνὰ καὶ τετραχηλισμένα τοῖς ὀφθαλμοῖς
[2]all [3]*things* [1]but *are* naked and having been laid open - to eyes ˜

αὐτοῦ, πρὸς ὃν ἡμῖν ὁ λόγος.
His, to whom for us *is* the account.
we must give an account.

works";
5 and again in this *place: "They shall not enter My rest."*
6 Since therefore it remains that some *must* enter it, and those to whom it was first preached did not enter because of disobedience,
7 again He designates a certain day, saying in David, *"Today,"* after such a long time, as it has been said:

"Today, if you will hear
His voice,
Do not harden your
hearts."

8 For if Joshua had given them rest, then He would not afterward have spoken of another day.
9 There remains therefore a rest for the people of God.
10 For he who has entered His rest has himself also ceased from his works as God *did* from His.
11 Let us therefore be diligent to enter that rest, lest anyone fall according to the same example of disobedience.
12 For the word of God *is* living and powerful, and sharper than any two-edged sword, piercing even to the division of soul and spirit, and of joints and marrow, and is a discerner of the thoughts and intents of the heart.
13 And there is no creature hidden from His sight, but all things *are* naked and open to the eyes of Him to whom we *must give* account.

---

[b](**4:4**) Gen. 2:2
[c](**4:5**) Ps. 95:11
[d](**4:7**) Ps. 95:7, 8

14 Seeing then that we have a great High Priest who has passed through the heavens, Jesus the Son of God, let us hold fast *our* confession.
15 For we do not have a High Priest who cannot sympathize with our weaknesses, but was in all *points* tempted as *we are, yet* without sin.
16 Let us therefore come boldly to the throne of grace, that we may obtain mercy and find grace to help in time of need.

5 For every high priest taken from among men is appointed for men in things *pertaining* to God, that he may offer both gifts and sacrifices for sins.
2 He can have compassion on those who are ignorant and going astray, since he himself is also subject to weakness.
3 Because of this he is required as for the people, so also for himself, to offer *sacrifices* for sins.
4 And no man takes this honor to himself, but he who is called by God, just as Aaron *was.*
5 So also Christ did not glorify Himself to become High Priest, *but it* was He who said to Him:

"You are My Son,
Today I have begotten
You."

6 As *He* also *says* in another *place:*

Our Compassionate High Priest

14 Ἔχοντες οὖν Ἀρχιερέα μέγαν διεληλυθότα
having ˜ Therefore a [2]High [3]Priest [1]great having gone through
who has

τοὺς οὐρανούς, Ἰησοῦν τὸν Υἱὸν τοῦ Θεοῦ, κρατῶμεν τῆς
the heavens, Jesus the Son - of God, let us hold fast the

ὁμολογίας. **15** Οὐ γὰρ ἔχομεν ἀρχιερέα μὴ δυνάμενον
confession. [4]not [1]For [2]we [3]do [5]have a high priest not being able
who cannot

συμπαθῆσαι ταῖς ἀσθενείαις ἡμῶν, πεπειραμένον δὲ
to sympathize with - weaknesses ˜ our, [2]having [3]been [4]tested [1]but

κατὰ πάντα καθ' ὁμοιότητα χωρὶς ἁμαρτίας.
in all *respects* according to similarities without sin.
in quite the same way

16 Προσερχώμεθα οὖν μετὰ παρρησίας τῷ θρόνῳ τῆς
[2]let [3]us [4]approach [1]Therefore with boldness to the throne -

χάριτος, ἵνα λάβωμεν ἔλεον καὶ χάριν εὕρωμεν
of grace, in order that we may receive mercy and [4]grace [1]we [2]may [3]find

εἰς εὔκαιρον βοήθειαν.
for well-timed help.
to help in time of need.

The Qualifications for High Priesthood

5 **1** Πᾶς γὰρ ἀρχιερεὺς ἐξ ἀνθρώπων λαμβανόμενος
every ˜ For high priest [3]out [4]of [5]men [1]being [2]taken

ὑπὲρ ἀνθρώπων καθίσταται τὰ πρὸς τὸν
[8]in [9]behalf [10]of [11]men [6]is [7]appointed *in* the *things in regard* to -

Θεόν, ἵνα προσφέρῃ δῶρά τε καὶ θυσίας ὑπὲρ
God, in order that he may offer gifts ˜ both and sacrifices in behalf of

ἁμαρτιῶν, **2** μετριοπαθεῖν δυνάμενος τοῖς ἀγνοοῦσι
sins, [3]to [4]deal [5]gently [1]being [2]able with the *ones* being ignorant
those who sin in ignorance

καὶ πλανωμένοις, ἐπεὶ καὶ αὐτὸς περίκειται ἀσθένειαν.
and going astray, since [4]also [2]himself [1]he [3]is [5]subject [6]to weakness.
go

3 Καὶ διὰ ταύτην ὀφείλει, καθὼς περὶ τοῦ
And on account of this he is obligated, just as concerning the

λαοῦ, οὕτω καὶ περὶ ἑαυτοῦ προσφέρειν ὑπὲρ ἁμαρτιῶν.
people, so also concerning himself to offer for sins.

4 Καὶ οὐχ ἑαυτῷ τις λαμβάνει τὴν τιμήν, ἀλλ' ὁ [a]
And [3]not [7]for [8]himself [1]someone [2]does [4]take [5]the [6]honor, but the *one*

καλούμενος ὑπὸ τοῦ Θεοῦ, καθάπερ καὶ Ἀαρών.
being called by - God, just as also Aaron *was.*
who is

Christ Is a Priest Forever

5 Οὕτω καὶ ὁ Χριστὸς οὐχ ἑαυτὸν ἐδόξασε γενηθῆναι
So also - Christ [2]not [4]Himself [1]did [3]glorify to become

ἀρχιερέα, ἀλλ' ὁ λαλήσας πρὸς αὐτόν,
high priest, but the *One* having spoken to Him,
it was He who said

«Υἱός μου εἶ σύ,
«[4]Son [3]My [2]are [1]You,

Ἐγὼ σήμερον γεγέννηκά σε»· [b]
I ˜ Today have begotten You»;

καθὼς καὶ ἐν ἑτέρῳ λέγει,
just as also in another *place* He says,

[a](5:4) NU omits ὁ, *the (one)*, thus *when being called.* [b](5:5) Ps. 2:7

6 «Σὺ ἱερεὺς εἰς τὸν αἰῶνα
«You *are* a priest into the age
forever

Κατὰ τὴν τάξιν Μελχισέδεκ»·[c]
According to the order of Melchizedek»;

7 ὃς ἐν ταῖς ἡμέραις τῆς σαρκὸς αὐτοῦ, δεήσεις τε καὶ
who in the days - of flesh ˜ His, [9]prayers [8]both [10]and

ἱκετηρίας πρὸς τὸν δυνάμενον σῴζειν αὐτὸν ἐκ
[11]supplications [12]to [13]the [14]*One* [15]being [16]able [17]to [18]save [19]Him [20]from
who was

θανάτου μετὰ κραυγῆς ἰσχυρᾶς καὶ δακρύων προσενέγκας, καὶ
[21]death [3]with [5]crying [4]strong [6]and [7]tears [1]having [2]offered, and
loud when He had

εἰσακουσθεὶς ἀπὸ τῆς εὐλαβείας, 8 καίπερ ὢν Υἱός,
being heard from the fear of God, although being a Son,
was because of His piety, He was

ἔμαθεν ἀφ' ὧν ἔπαθε τὴν ὑπακοήν. 9 Καὶ
He learned [2]from [3]which [4]*things* [5]He [6]suffered - [1]obedience. And

τελειωθεὶς ἐγένετο τοῖς ὑπακούουσιν αὐτῷ
having been made perfect He became to [2]the [3]*ones* [4]obeying [5]Him
those who obey

πᾶσιν αἴτιος σωτηρίας αἰωνίου, 10 προσαγορευθεὶς ὑπὸ
[1]all *the* source of salvation ˜ eternal, having been designated by

τοῦ Θεοῦ Ἀρχιερεὺς κατὰ τὴν τάξιν Μελχισέδεκ.
- God a High Priest according to the order of Melchizedek.

Spiritual Immaturity

11 Περὶ οὗ πολὺς ἡμῖν ὁ λόγος καὶ δυσερμήνευτος
Concerning whom much to us the word and hard to explain
we have much to say and it is hard

λέγειν, ἐπεὶ νωθροὶ γεγόνατε ταῖς ἀκοαῖς. 12 Καὶ
to say, since [4]dull [1]you [2]have [3]become - in hearing. indeed ˜
to explain, of

γὰρ ὀφείλοντες εἶναι διδάσκαλοι διὰ τὸν χρόνον, πάλιν
For being obligated to be teachers by the time, again
although you ought this

χρείαν ἔχετε τοῦ διδάσκειν ὑμᾶς τίνα τὰ στοιχεῖα
[3]need [1]you [2]have - *for someone* to teach you what *are* the elements

τῆς ἀρχῆς τῶν λογίων τοῦ Θεοῦ, καὶ γεγόνατε χρείαν
of the beginning of the oracles - of God, and you have become [3]need
come to

ἔχοντες γάλακτος, καὶ οὐ στερεᾶς τροφῆς. 13 Πᾶς γὰρ
[1]*ones* [2]having of milk, and not of solid food. every ˜ For
have need everyone

ὁ μετέχων γάλακτος ἄπειρος λόγου δικαιοσύνης,
- *one* partaking of milk *is* unacquainted with *the* word of righteousness,
who partakes

νήπιος γάρ ἐστι. 14 Τελείων δέ ἐστιν ἡ
[4]an [5]infant [1]for [2]he [3]is. [6]of [7]*the* [8]mature [9]*ones* [1]But [5]is [2]the
for those who are full-grown

στερεὰ τροφή, τῶν διὰ τὴν ἕξιν τὰ αἰσθητήρια
[3]solid [4]food, of the *ones* because of the practice [2]the [3]senses
for their their

γεγυμνασμένα ἐχόντων πρὸς διάκρισιν καλοῦ τε καὶ
[4]having [5]been [6]trained [1]having for *the* distinguishing of good ˜ both and
trained

κακοῦ.
bad.

"You are a priest forever
According to the order of
Melchizedek";

7 who, in the days of His flesh, when He had offered up prayers and supplications, with vehement cries and tears to Him who was able to save Him from death, and was heard because of His godly fear,
8 though He was a Son, *yet* He learned obedience by the things which He suffered.
9 And having been perfected, He became the author of eternal salvation to all who obey Him,
10 called by God as High Priest *"according to the order of Melchizedek,"*
11 of whom we have much to say, and hard to explain, since you have become dull of hearing.
12 For though by this time you ought to be teachers, you need *someone* to teach you again the first principles of the oracles of God; and you have come to need milk and not solid food.
13 For everyone who partakes *only* of milk *is* unskilled in the word of righteousness, for he is a babe.
14 But solid food belongs to those who are of full age, *that is,* those who by reason of use have their senses exercised to discern both good and evil.

[c](5:6) Ps. 110:4

6 Therefore, leaving the discussion of the elementary *principles* of Christ, let us go on to perfection, not laying again the foundation of repentance from dead works and of faith toward God,

2 of the doctrine of baptisms, of laying on of hands, of resurrection of the dead, and of eternal judgment.

3 And this we will do if God permits.

4 For *it is* impossible for those who were once enlightened, and have tasted the heavenly gift, and have become partakers of the Holy Spirit,

5 and have tasted the good word of God and the powers of the age to come,

6 if they fall away, to renew them again to repentance, since they crucify again for themselves the Son of God, and put *Him* to an open shame.

7 For the earth which drinks in the rain that often comes upon it, and bears herbs useful for those by whom it is cultivated, receives blessing from God;

8 but if it bears thorns and briers, *it is* rejected and near to being cursed, whose end *is* to be burned.

9 But, beloved, we are confident of better things concerning you, yes, things that accompany salvation, though we speak in this manner.

10 For God *is* not unjust to forget your work and labor of love which you have shown toward His name, *in that* you have ministered to the saints, and do minister.

---

[a](6:3) NU, TR read ποιησομεν, *we will do.*
[b](6:10) NU omits του κοπου, *the labor.*

---

*(6:5) γεύομαι *(geuomai).* Verb meaning *taste* (Matt. 27:34), *eat* (Acts 20:11), *partake of* or *experience* (Matt. 16:28; 1 Pet. 2:3). Compared to synonyms meaning "eat" (like ἐσθίω), γεύομαι emphasizes the sensation of taste and thus the experience. It is this nuance of *experience* in the sense of coming to know fully and personally that determines its meaning in such figurative uses as "taste death" (Heb. 2:9) and "having tasted the heavenly gift" and "good word of God" (here in Heb. 6:4, 5).

The Peril of Not Progressing

6 1 Διό, ἀφέντες τὸν τῆς ἀρχῆς τοῦ Χριστοῦ λόγον,
Therefore, leaving the [2]of [3]the [4]beginning - [5]of [6]Christ [1]word,
subject,

ἐπὶ τὴν τελειότητα φερώμεθα, μὴ πάλιν θεμέλιον
[11]to - [12]perfection [7]let [8]us [9]be [10]moved, not again [3]a [4]foundation

καταβαλλόμενοι μετανοίας ἀπὸ νεκρῶν ἔργων, καὶ πίστεως
[1]laying [2]down of repentance from dead works, and of faith

ἐπὶ Θεόν, 2 βαπτισμῶν διδαχῆς, ἐπιθέσεώς τε χειρῶν,
toward God, [3]of [4]baptisms [1]of [2]teaching, [6]of [7]laying [8]on [5]and of hands,

ἀναστάσεώς τε νεκρῶν, καὶ κρίματος αἰωνίου. 3 Καὶ
[2]of [3]resurrection [1]and of dead *ones,* and of judgment ˜ eternal. And

τοῦτο ποιήσωμεν[a] ἐάνπερ ἐπιτρέπῃ ὁ Θεός.
[4]this [1]let [2]us [3]do if indeed permits ˜ - God.

4 Ἀδύνατον γὰρ τοὺς ἅπαξ φωτισθέντας,
[2]*it* [3]*is* [4]impossible [1]For *for* the *ones* once having been enlightened,

γευσαμένους τε τῆς δωρεᾶς τῆς ἐπουρανίου καὶ μετόχους
[2]having [3]tasted [1]and of the gift ˜ - heavenly and [3]sharers

γενηθέντας Πνεύματος Ἁγίου 5 καὶ καλὸν γευσαμένους*
[1]having [2]become of *the* Spirit ˜ Holy and [3]*the* [4]good [1]having [2]tasted

Θεοῦ ῥῆμα δυνάμεις τε μέλλοντος αἰῶνος 6 καὶ
[6]of [7]God [5]word [9]*the* [10]powerful [11]deeds [8]and of *the* coming age and

παραπεσόντας, πάλιν ἀνακαινίζειν εἰς μετάνοιαν,
having fallen away, [4]again [1]to [2]renew [3]*them* to repentance,

ἀνασταυροῦντας ἑαυτοῖς τὸν Υἱὸν τοῦ Θεοῦ καὶ
crucifying again for themselves the Son - of God and
since they crucify

παραδειγματίζοντας. 7 Γῆ γὰρ ἡ πιοῦσα τὸν ἐπ'
holding *Him* up to contempt. [2]*the* [3]earth [1]For the *one* drinking the [4]upon
hold which drinks

αὐτῆς πολλάκις ἐρχόμενον ὑετόν, καὶ τίκτουσα βοτάνην
[5]it [2]often [3]coming [1]rain, and bearing vegetation ˜
bears

εὔθετον ἐκείνοις δι' οὓς καὶ γεωργεῖται,
suitable for those on account of whom indeed it is cultivated,

μεταλαμβάνει εὐλογίας ἀπὸ τοῦ Θεοῦ· 8 ἐκφέρουσα δὲ
receives a blessing from - God; [2]bringing [3]forth [1]but
if it brings

ἀκάνθας καὶ τριβόλους, ἀδόκιμος καὶ κατάρας ἐγγύς,
thorn plants and thistles, *it is* worthless and [2]a [3]curse [1]near,

ἧς τὸ τέλος εἰς καῦσιν.
of which the end *is* for burning.

A Better Estimate

9 Πεπείσμεθα δὲ περὶ ὑμῶν, ἀγαπητοί,
[2]we [3]have [4]been [5]persuaded [1]But concerning you, beloved *ones,*

τὰ κρείσσονα καὶ ἐχόμενα σωτηρίας, εἰ καὶ οὕτω
of the better *things* and having salvation, if indeed so
those pertaining to even though

λαλοῦμεν. 10 Οὐ γὰρ ἄδικος ὁ Θεὸς ἐπιλαθέσθαι τοῦ ἔργου
we speak. [4]not [1]For [5]unjust - [2]God [3]*is* to forget - work ˜

ὑμῶν καὶ τοῦ κόπου[b] τῆς ἀγάπης ἧς ἐνεδείξασθε εἰς τὸ
your and the labor - of love which you showed toward -
your have shown

ὄνομα αὐτοῦ, διακονήσαντες τοῖς ἁγίοις καὶ διακονοῦντες.
name ˜ His, having ministered to the saints and ministering.
in that you have do minister.

11 Ἐπιθυμοῦμεν δὲ ἕκαστον ὑμῶν τὴν αὐτὴν ἐνδείκνυσθαι
[2]we [3]desire [1]But *for* each of you [3]the [4]same [1]to [2]show

σπουδὴν πρὸς τὴν πληροφορίαν τῆς ἐλπίδος ἄχρι τέλους·
diligence to the full assurance of the hope until *the* end;

12 ἵνα μὴ νωθροὶ γένησθε, μιμηταὶ δὲ
in order that [2]not [4]dull [1]you [3]become, [7]imitators [5]but [6]*become*
lest

τῶν διὰ πίστεως καὶ μακροθυμίας κληρονομούντων τὰς
of the *ones* through faith and patience inheriting the
those who inherit

ἐπαγγελίας.
promises.

God's Infallible Purpose in Christ

13 Τῷ γὰρ Ἀβραὰμ ἐπαγγειλάμενος ὁ Θεός, ἐπεὶ κατ'
- For [5]to [6]Abraham [2]making [3]a [4]promise - [1]God, since [3]by
when God made a promise,

οὐδενὸς εἶχε μείζονος ὀμόσαι, ὤμοσε καθ' ἑαυτοῦ,
[4]no [5]one [1]He [2]had greater to swear, swore by Himself,

14 λέγων, «Ἦ μὴν εὐλογῶν εὐλογήσω σε καὶ πληθύνων
saying «Truly blessing I will bless you and multiplying

πληθυνῶ σε.»[c] **15** Καὶ οὕτω μακροθυμήσας ἐπέτυχε
I will multiply you.» And so having patience he obtained
after he had been patient,

τῆς ἐπαγγελίας. **16** Ἄνθρωποι μὲν γὰρ κατὰ τοῦ μείζονος
the promise. [2]men [3]indeed [1]For [5]by [6]the [7]greater

ὀμνύουσι, καὶ πάσης αὐτοῖς ἀντιλογίας πέρας εἰς
[4]swear, and [8]of [9]every [11]to [12]them [10]dispute [6]an [7]end [3]for

βεβαίωσιν ὁ ὅρκος, **17** ἐν ᾧ περισσότερον βουλόμενος
[4]confirmation [1]the [2]oath [5]*is,* in which [5]even [6]more [7]clearly [2]wanting

ὁ Θεὸς ἐπιδεῖξαι τοῖς κληρονόμοις τῆς ἐπαγγελίας τὸ
- [1]God [3]to [4]show to the heirs of the promise the

ἀμετάθετον τῆς βουλῆς αὐτοῦ ἐμεσίτευσεν ὅρκῳ,
unchangeableness - of resolution ˜ His guaranteed *it* by an oath,

18 ἵνα διὰ δύο πραγμάτων ἀμεταθέτων, ἐν οἷς
in order that through two things ˜ unchangeable, in which *it is*

ἀδύνατον ψεύσασθαι Θεόν, ἰσχυρὰν παράκλησιν
impossible [3]to [4]lie [1]*for* [2]God, [8]a [9]strong [10]encouragement

ἔχωμεν[d] οἱ καταφυγόντες κρατῆσαι τῆς
[5]we [6]might [7]have the *ones* having fled to take hold of the
who have

προκειμένης ἐλπίδος· **19** ἣν ὡς ἄγκυραν ἔχομεν
[2]being [3]set [4]before [5]*us* [1]hope; which *hope* [3]as [4]an [5]anchor [1]we [2]have

τῆς ψυχῆς, ἀσφαλῆ τε καὶ βεβαίαν καὶ εἰσερχομένην εἰς
of the soul, sure ˜ both and secure and entering into
which enters

τὸ ἐσώτερον τοῦ καταπετάσματος, **20** ὅπου Πρόδρομος
the inner *side* of the veil, where *the* Forerunner

ὑπὲρ ἡμῶν εἰσῆλθεν Ἰησοῦς, κατὰ τὴν τάξιν
in behalf of us entered *even* Jesus, [6]according [7]to [8]the [9]order

Μελχισέδεκ Ἀρχιερεὺς γενόμενος εἰς τὸν αἰῶνα.
[10]of [11]Melchizedek [3]a [4]High [5]Priest [1]having [2]become into the age.
forever.

Melchizedek, King of Righteousness

7 **1** Οὗτος γὰρ ὁ Μελχισέδεκ, βασιλεὺς Σαλήμ, ἱερεὺς τοῦ
this ˜ For - Melchizedek, king of Salem, priest -

11 And we desire that each one of you show the same diligence to the full assurance of hope until the end,
12 that you do not become sluggish, but imitate those who through faith and patience inherit the promises.
13 For when God made a promise to Abraham, because He could swear by no one greater, He swore by Himself,
14 saying, *"Surely blessing I will bless you, and multiplying I will multiply you."*
15 And so, after he had patiently endured, he obtained the promise.
16 For men indeed swear by the greater, and an oath for confirmation *is* for them an end of all dispute.
17 Thus God, determining to show more abundantly to the heirs of promise the immutability of His counsel, confirmed *it* by an oath,
18 that by two immutable things, in which it *is* impossible for God to lie, we might have strong consolation, who have fled for refuge to lay hold of the hope set before *us.*
19 This *hope* we have as an anchor of the soul, both sure and steadfast, and which enters the Presence *behind* the veil,
20 where the forerunner has entered for us, *even* Jesus, having become High Priest forever according to the order of Melchizedek.
7 For this Melchizedek, king of Salem, priest of

---

[c](6:14) Gen. 22:17
[d](6:18) Some mss. read εχομεν, *we have.*

the Most High God, who met
Abraham returning from the
slaughter of the kings and
blessed him,
2 to whom also Abraham
gave a tenth part of all, first being translated "king of righteousness," and then also king
of Salem, meaning "king of
peace,"
3 without father, without
mother, without genealogy,
having neither beginning of
days nor end of life, but made
like the Son of God, remains a
priest continually.
4 Now consider how great
this man *was,* to whom even
the patriarch Abraham gave a
tenth of the spoils.
5 And indeed those who are
of the sons of Levi, who receive the priesthood, have a
commandment to receive tithes
from the people according to
the law, that is, from their
brethren, though they have
come from the loins of Abraham;
6 but he whose genealogy is
not derived from them received
tithes from Abraham and
blessed him who had the promises.
7 Now beyond all contradiction the lesser is blessed by the
better.
8 Here mortal men receive
tithes, but there he *receives
them,* of whom it is witnessed
that he lives.
9 Even Levi, who receives
tithes, paid tithes through
Abraham, so to speak,
10 for he was still in the loins
of his father when Melchizedek
met him.

Θεοῦ τοῦ ὑψίστου, ὁ συναντήσας Ἀβραὰμ
[5]God [1]of [2]the [3]Most [4]High, the *one* having met Abraham
who met

ὑποστρέφοντι ἀπὸ τῆς κοπῆς τῶν βασιλέων καὶ εὐλογήσας
returning from the slaughter of the kings and having blessed
blessed

αὐτόν, 2 ᾧ καὶ δεκάτην ἀπὸ πάντων ἐμέρισεν Ἀβραάμ,
him, to whom also [3]a [4]tenth [5]from [6]all [2]divided [1]Abraham,

πρῶτον μὲν ἑρμηνευόμενος "βασιλεὺς δικαιοσύνης,"
first on one hand being interpreted "king of righteousness,"

ἔπειτα δὲ καὶ "βασιλεὺς Σαλήμ," ὅ ἐστι "βασιλεὺς
then on the other also "king of Salem," which is "king
means

εἰρήνης," 3 ἀπάτωρ, ἀμήτωρ, ἀγενεαλόγητος, μήτε
of peace," without father, without mother, without genealogy, [2]neither

ἀρχὴν ἡμερῶν μήτε ζωῆς τέλος ἔχων,
[3]beginning [4]of [5]days [6]nor [8]of [9]life [7]end [1]having,

ἀφωμοιωμένος δὲ τῷ Υἱῷ τοῦ Θεοῦ, μένει ἱερεὺς
[11]having [12]been [13]made [14]like [10]but to the Son - of God, remains a priest

εἰς τὸ διηνεκές.
in - continuous *time.*
continually.

4 Θεωρεῖτε δὲ πηλίκος οὗτος, ᾧ καὶ δεκάτην
observe ~ But how great this *man was,* to whom even [5]a [6]tenth

Ἀβραὰμ ἔδωκεν ἐκ τῶν ἀκροθινίων ὁ πατριάρχης. 5 Καὶ
[1]Abraham [4]gave [7]from [8]the [9]spoils [2]the [3]patriarch. And

οἱ μὲν ἐκ τῶν υἱῶν Λευὶ τὴν ἱερατείαν
[2]the [3]*ones* [1]indeed out of the sons of Levi [2]the [3]priesthood
those who are

λαμβάνοντες ἐντολὴν ἔχουσιν ἀποδεκατοῦν τὸν λαὸν
[1]receiving [5]a [6]commandment [4]have to collect tithes from the people
who receive

κατὰ τὸν νόμον, τοῦτ' ἔστι τοὺς ἀδελφοὺς αὐτῶν, καίπερ
according to the law, this is - *from* brothers ~ their, though
that

ἐξεληλυθότας ἐκ τῆς ὀσφύος Ἀβραάμ. 6 Ὁ δὲ μὴ
having come forth from the loins of Abraham. [2]the [3]*one* [1]But not
they have come

γενεαλογούμενος ἐξ αὐτῶν δεδεκάτωκεν τὸν Ἀβραάμ,
tracing *his* descent from them has received tithes from - Abraham,

καὶ τὸν ἔχοντα τὰς ἐπαγγελίας εὐλόγηκε. 7 Χωρὶς
and [4]the [5]*one* [6]having [7]the [8]promises [1]he [2]has [3]blessed. without ~

δὲ πάσης ἀντιλογίας τὸ ἔλαττον ὑπὸ τοῦ κρείττονος
But any contradiction the lesser [3]by [4]the [5]better

εὐλογεῖται. 8 Καὶ ὧδε μὲν δεκάτας ἀποθνήσκοντες
[1]is [2]blessed. And here on one hand [4]tithes [1]dying
mortal

ἄνθρωποι λαμβάνουσιν, ἐκεῖ δὲ
[2]men [3]receive, there on the other *one of whom*

μαρτυρούμενος ὅτι ζῇ. 9 Καὶ ὡς ἔπος εἰπεῖν, διὰ
being witnessed that he lives. And as a word to say, through
it is so to speak,

Ἀβραὰμ καὶ Λευὶ ὁ δεκάτας λαμβάνων δεδεκάτωται.
Abraham even Levi the *one* tithes ~ receiving has paid tithes.

10 Ἔτι γὰρ ἐν τῇ ὀσφύϊ τοῦ πατρὸς ἦν ὅτε
[4]still [1]For [5]in [6]the [7]loins [8]of [9]the [10]father [2]he [3]was when
his

συνήντησεν αὐτῷ ὁ Μελχισέδεκ.
[2]met [3]him - [1]Melchizedek.

The Need for a New Priesthood

11 Εἰ μὲν οὖν τελείωσις διὰ τῆς Λευιτικῆς
if ˜ - Therefore perfection [2]through [3]the [4]Levitical

ἱερωσύνης ἦν (ὁ λαὸς γὰρ ἐπ' αὐτῇ νενομοθέτητο),
[5]priesthood [1]was (7the [8]people [6]for under it have received the law),
were

τίς ἔτι χρεία κατὰ τὴν τάξιν Μελχισέδεκ ἕτερον
why *is there* yet a need according to the order of Melchizedek *for* another

ἀνίστασθαι ἱερέα καὶ οὐ κατὰ τὴν τάξιν Ἀαρὼν
[2]to [3]rise [1]priest and not [4]according [5]to [6]the [7]order [8]of [9]Aaron

λέγεσθαι? **12** Μετατιθεμένης γὰρ τῆς ἱερωσύνης, ἐξ ἀνάγκης
[1]to [2]be [3]called? [4]being [5]changed [1]For [2]the [3]priesthood, of necessity

καὶ νόμου μετάθεσις γίνεται. **13** Ἐφ' ὃν γὰρ
also [5]of [6]law [3]a [4]change [1]*there* [2]occurs. [3]on [2]*He* [4]whom [1]For
concerning

λέγεται ταῦτα, φυλῆς ἑτέρας μετέσχηκεν, ἀφ' ἧς
[7]are [8]said [5]these [6]*things*, [11]of [13]tribe [12]another [9]has [10]shared, from which
to belongs,

οὐδεὶς προσέσχηκε τῷ θυσιαστηρίῳ. **14** Πρόδηλον γὰρ
no one has devoted himself to the altar. [2]*it* [3]*is* [4]evident [1]For
officiated

ὅτι ἐξ Ἰούδα ἀνατέταλκεν ὁ Κύριος ἡμῶν, εἰς ἣν
that out of Judah [3]has [4]risen - [2]Lord [1]our, for which
regarding

φυλὴν οὐδὲν περὶ ἱερωσύνης[a] Μωϋσῆς ἐλάλησε. **15** Καὶ
tribe [3]nothing [4]concerning [5]priesthood [1]Moses [2]spoke. And

περισσότερον ἔτι κατάδηλόν ἐστιν, εἰ κατὰ τὴν
[4]even [5]more [3]yet [6]clearer [1]it [2]is, if according to the

ὁμοιότητα Μελχισέδεκ ἀνίσταται ἱερεὺς ἕτερος, **16** ὃς οὐ
likeness of Melchizedek *there* arises priest ˜ another, who [5]not

κατὰ νόμον ἐντολῆς σαρκικῆς
[6]according [7]to [8]*the* [9]law [10]of [11]a [13]commandment [12]fleshly

γέγονεν ἀλλὰ κατὰ δύναμιν ζωῆς
[1]has [2]become [3]*a* [4]*priest* but according to *the* power of a(n) life ˜

ἀκαταλύτου. **17** Μαρτυρεῖ[b] γὰρ ὅτι
indestructible. [2]He [3]witnesses [1]For -
endless.

«Σὺ ἱερεὺς εἰς τὸν αἰῶνα
«You *are* a priest into the age
forever

Κατὰ τὴν τάξιν Μελχισέδεκ.»[c]
According to the order of Melchizedek.»

18 Ἀθέτησις μὲν γὰρ γίνεται προαγούσης
[5]an [6]annulment [2]on [3]one [4]hand [1]For comes about [3]preceding

ἐντολῆς διὰ τὸ αὐτῆς ἀσθενὲς καὶ ἀνωφελές.
[1]of [2]*the* [4]commandment on account of - its weakness and uselessness.

19 Οὐδὲν γὰρ ἐτελείωσεν ὁ νόμος, ἐπεισαγωγὴ
[5]nothing [1]For [4]made [6]perfect [2]the [3]law, [10]a [11]bringing [12]in

δὲ κρείττονος ἐλπίδος, δι' ἧς ἐγγίζομεν τῷ
[7]but [8]*there* [9]*is* of a better hope, through which we draw near -

Θεῷ.
to God.

The Greatness of the New Priest

20 Καὶ καθ' ὅσον οὐ χωρὶς ὁρκωμοσίας,
And by as much as *it was* not without oath taking,
inasmuch as

11 Therefore, if perfection were through the Levitical priesthood (for under it the people received the law), what further need *was there* that another priest should rise according to the order of Melchizedek, and not be called according to the order of Aaron?
12 For the priesthood being changed, of necessity there is also a change of the law.
13 For He of whom these things are spoken belongs to another tribe, from which no man has officiated at the altar.
14 For *it is* evident that our Lord arose from Judah, of which tribe Moses spoke nothing concerning priesthood.
15 And it is yet far more evident if, in the likeness of Melchizedek, there arises another priest
16 who has come, not according to the law of a fleshly commandment, but according to the power of an endless life.
17 For He testifies:

"You are a priest forever
According to the order of
Melchizedek."

18 For on the one hand there is an annulling of the former commandment because of its weakness and unprofitableness,
19 for the law made nothing perfect; on the other hand, *there is the* bringing in of a better hope, through which we draw near to God.
20 And inasmuch as *He was* not *made priest* without an oath

[a](7:14) NU reads *ιερεων*, *priests*. [b](7:17) NU reads *μαρτυρειται*, *it is witnessed*.
[c](7:17) Ps. 110:4b

21 (for they have become priests without an oath, but He with an oath by Him who said to Him:

"The LORD *has sworn*
And will not relent,
'You are a priest forever
According to the order of
Melchizedek' "),

22 by so much more Jesus has become a surety of a better covenant.
23 Also there were many priests, because they were prevented by death from continuing.
24 But He, because He continues forever, has an unchangeable priesthood.
25 Therefore He is also able to save to the uttermost those who come to God through Him, since He always lives to make intercession for them.
26 For such a High Priest was fitting for us, *who is* holy, harmless, undefiled, separate from sinners, and has become higher than the heavens;
27 who does not need daily, as those high priests, to offer up sacrifices, first for His own sins and then for the people's, for this He did once for all when He offered up Himself.
28 For the law appoints as high priests men who have weakness, but the word of the

21 οἱ μὲν γὰρ χωρὶς ὁρκωμοσίας εἰσὶν
[6]the [7]*ones* [2]on [3]the [4]one [5]hand [1]for [11]without [12]oath [13]taking [8]are
they have

ἱερεῖς γεγονότες, ὁ δὲ μετὰ ὁρκωμοσίας διὰ
[10]priests [9]become, [15]the [16]*One* [14]But with oath taking through
He

τοῦ λέγοντος πρὸς αὐτόν,
the *One* saying to Him,
who says

«Ὤμοσε Κύριος
«[3]swore [1]*The* [2]Lord
«has sworn

Καὶ οὐ μεταμεληθήσεται,
And [3]not [1]He [2]will change *His* mind,

'Σὺ ἱερεὺς εἰς τὸν αἰῶνα [d]
'You *are* a priest into the age
forever

Κατὰ τὴν τάξιν Μελχισέδεκ,'» [e]
According to the order of Melchizedek,'»

22 κατὰ τοσοῦτον κρείττονος διαθήκης γέγονεν ἔγγυος
By so much of a better covenant [2]has [3]become [4]surety

Ἰησοῦς. **23** Καὶ οἱ μὲν πλείονές εἰσι γεγονότες
[1]Jesus. And [4]the [1]on [2]one [3]hand [8]many [6]are [7]become
have

ἱερεῖς διὰ τὸ θανάτῳ κωλύεσθαι παραμένειν.
[5]priests on account of - by death to be prevented to continue.
because they were prevented by death from continuing.

24 Ὁ δέ, διὰ τὸ μένειν αὐτὸν εἰς τὸν αἰῶνα,
[2]the [3]*One* [1]But, because of - [2]to [3]remain [1]Him into the age,
He because He remains forever,

ἀπαράβατον ἔχει τὴν ἱερωσύνην. **25** Ὅθεν καὶ σῴζειν εἰς
[2]an [3]unchangeable [1]has - priesthood. Therefore [3]also [5]to [6]save [7]to

τὸ παντελὲς δύναται τοὺς προσερχομένους δι'
[8]the [9]complete [10]*degree* [1]He [2]is [4]able the *ones* coming to [2]through
completely

αὐτοῦ τῷ Θεῷ, πάντοτε ζῶν εἰς τὸ ἐντυγχάνειν ὑπὲρ
[3]Him - [1]God, always living for - to intercede in behalf
since He always lives in order

αὐτῶν.
of them.

26 Τοιοῦτος γὰρ ἡμῖν ἔπρεπεν Ἀρχιερεύς, ὅσιος,
such ˜ For [6]for [7]us [4]was [5]fitting [1]a [2]High [3]Priest, holy,

ἄκακος, ἀμίαντος, κεχωρισμένος ἀπὸ τῶν ἁμαρτωλῶν, καὶ
innocent, undefiled, having been separated from - sinners, and

ὑψηλότερος τῶν οὐρανῶν γενόμενος· **27** ὃς οὐκ ἔχει
[2]higher [3]*than* [4]the [5]heavens [1]becoming; who not ˜ does have
has become;

καθ' ἡμέραν ἀνάγκην, ὥσπερ οἱ ἀρχιερεῖς, πρότερον
[2]according [3]to [4]a [5]day [1]need, as the high priests, [5]beforehand
daily

ὑπὲρ τῶν ἰδίων ἁμαρτιῶν θυσίας ἀναφέρειν,
[6]in [7]behalf [8]of - [9]His [10]own [11]sins [4]sacrifices [1]to [2]offer [3]up,

ἔπειτα τῶν τοῦ λαοῦ· τοῦτο γὰρ ἐποίησεν ἐφάπαξ
then *in behalf of* the *sins* of the people; this ˜ for He did once for all

ἑαυτὸν ἀνενέγκας. **28** Ὁ νόμος γὰρ ἀνθρώπους καθίστησιν
[3]Himself [1]offering [2]up. [2]the [3]law [1]For men ˜ appoints

ἀρχιερεῖς ἔχοντας ἀσθένειαν, ὁ λόγος δὲ τῆς
as high priests having weakness, [2]the [3]word [1]but of the
who have

[d](**7:21**) NU omits the rest of v. 21. [e](**7:21**) Ps. 110:4

ὁρκωμοσίας τῆς μετὰ τὸν νόμον Υἱὸν εἰς τὸν
oath the *one* after the law *appoints* a Son [4]into [5]the
which came forever

αἰῶνα τετελειωμένον.
[6]age [1]having [2]been [3]perfected.
who has

The New Priestly Service

8 1 Κεφάλαιον δὲ ἐπὶ τοῖς λεγομένοις·
[2]*this* [3]*is* [4]*the* [5]main [6]point [1]Now over the *things* being said:
of

τοιοῦτον ἔχομεν Ἀρχιερέα, ὃς ἐκάθισεν ἐν δεξιᾷ τοῦ
[3]such [1]we [2]have a High Priest, who sat at *the* right *hand* of the

θρόνου τῆς Μεγαλωσύνης ἐν τοῖς οὐρανοῖς, 2 τῶν ἁγίων
throne of the Majesty in the heavens, [3]of [4]the [5]holies
sanctuary

Λειτουργὸς καὶ τῆς σκηνῆς τῆς ἀληθινῆς, ἣν ἔπηξεν ὁ
[1]a [2]Minister and of the tabernacle ˜ - true, which [3]set [4]up [1]the

Κύριος, καὶ οὐκ ἄνθρωπος. 3 Πᾶς γὰρ ἀρχιερεὺς εἰς τὸ
[2]Lord, and not man. every ˜ For high priest [3]for -
in order

προσφέρειν δῶρά τε καὶ θυσίας καθίσταται· ὅθεν
[4]to [5]offer [7]gifts [6]both [8]and [9]sacrifices [1]is [2]appointed; therefore

ἀναγκαῖον ἔχειν τι καὶ τοῦτον ὃ
it is necessary [5]to [6]have [7]something [4]also [1]*for* [2]this [3]*One* which

προσενέγκῃ. 4 Εἰ μὲν γὰρ ἦν ἐπὶ γῆς, οὐδ' ἂν
He may offer. if ˜ - For He was on earth, [3]not -
were

ἦν ἱερεύς, ὄντων τῶν ἱερέων τῶν
[1]He [2]would [4]be a priest, being - priests the *ones*
since there are who

προσφερόντων κατὰ τὸν νόμον τὰ δῶρα· 5 οἵτινες
offering [3]according [4]to [5]the [6]law [1]the [2]gifts; who
offer

ὑποδείγματι καὶ σκιᾷ λατρεύουσι τῶν ἐπουρανίων, καθὼς
[2]a [3]copy [4]and [5]a [6]shadow [1]serve of the heavenly *things,* just as

κεχρημάτισται Μωϋσῆς μέλλων ἐπιτελεῖν τὴν σκηνήν,
[2]has [3]been [4]warned [1]Moses being about to complete the tabernacle,
had when he was

«Ὅρα,» γάρ φησι, «ποιήσεις πάντα κατὰ τὸν τύπον
«See,» for He says, «you shall make all *things* according to the pattern

τὸν δειχθέντα σοι ἐν τῷ ὄρει.»[a] 6 Νυνὶ δὲ
the *one* having been shown to you on the mountain.» now ˜ But

διαφορωτέρας τέτυχε λειτουργίας, ὅσῳ καὶ
[5]more [6]excellent [1]He [2]has [3]obtained [4]a [7]service, inasmuch as [3]also

κρείττονός ἐστι διαθήκης Μεσίτης, ἥτις ἐπὶ κρείττοσιν
[7]better [1]He [2]is [5]of [6]a [8]covenant [4]Mediator, which [4]upon [5]better

ἐπαγγελίαις νενομοθέτηται.
[6]promises [1]has [2]been [3]enacted.

A New Covenant

7 Εἰ γὰρ ἡ πρώτη ἐκείνη ἦν ἄμεμπτος,* οὐκ ἂν
if ˜ For - [2]first [3]*covenant* [1]that was faultless, [4]not -
were

δευτέρας ἐζητεῖτο τόπος. 8 Μεμφόμενος γὰρ
[7]*for* [8]a [9]second [3]would [5]be [6]sought [1]a [2]place. [2]finding [3]fault [4]*with* [1]For
have been

αὐτοῖς λέγει,
them He says,

oath, which came after the law,
appoints the Son who has been
perfected forever.
8 Now *this is* the main point
of the things we are say-
ing: We have such a High
Priest, who is seated at the
right hand of the throne of the
Majesty in the heavens,
2 a Minister of the sanctuary
and of the true tabernacle
which the Lord erected, and
not man.
3 For every high priest is appointed to offer both gifts and
sacrifices. Therefore *it is* necessary that this One also have
something to offer.
4 For if He were on earth,
He would not be a priest, since
there are priests who offer the
gifts according to the law;
5 who serve the copy and
shadow of the heavenly things,
as Moses was divinely in-
structed when he was about to
make the tabernacle. For He
said, *"See that you make all
things according to the pattern
shown you on the mountain."*
6 But now He has obtained a
more excellent ministry, inasmuch as He is also Mediator of
a better covenant, which was
established on better promises.
7 For if that first *covenant*
had been faultless, then no
place would have been sought
for a second.
8 Because finding fault with
them, He says: *"Behold, the*

---

a(**8:5**) Ex. 25:40

***(8:7)** ἄμεμπτος *(amemptos).* Adjective meaning *blameless, faultless,* from the α- negative plus the root of *μέμφομαι, find fault with, blame.* Here the word is applied to a thing, a "faultless" covenant. Elsewhere in the NT, the word is applied to persons (indirectly in 1 Thess. 3:13) to indicate a condition in which others cannot legitimately find reason to cast blame for moral failure. Cf. the cognate adverb ἀμέμπτως, *blamelessly* (1 Thess. 2:10).

days are coming, says the LORD, when I will make a new covenant with the house of Israel and with the house of Judah—

9 *"not according to the covenant that I made with their fathers in the day when I took them by the hand to lead them out of the land of Egypt; because they did not continue in My covenant, and I disregarded them, says the LORD.*

10 *"For this is the covenant that I will make with the house of Israel after those days, says the LORD: I will put My laws in their mind and write them on their hearts; and I will be their God, and they shall be My people.*

11 *"None of them shall teach his neighbor, and none his brother, saying, 'Know the LORD,' for all shall know Me, from the least of them to the greatest of them.*

12 *"For I will be merciful to their unrighteousness, and their sins and their lawless deeds I will remember no more."*

«'Ιδού, ἡμέραι ἔρχονται, λέγει Κύριος,
«Behold, days are coming, says *the* Lord,

Καὶ συντελέσω ἐπὶ τὸν οἶκον 'Ισραὴλ
And I will accomplish over the house of Israel
establish

Καὶ ἐπὶ τὸν οἶκον 'Ιούδα διαθήκην καινήν,
And over the house of Judah a covenant ˜ new,

9 Οὐ κατὰ τὴν διαθήκην ἣν ἐποίησα τοῖς
Not according to the covenant which I made -

πατράσιν αὐτῶν
with fathers ˜ their

'Εν ἡμέρᾳ ἐπιλαβομένου μου τῆς χειρὸς αὐτῶν
In *the* day taking ˜ Me - hand ˜ their
when I took

'Εξαγαγεῖν αὐτοὺς ἐκ γῆς Αἰγύπτου
To lead forth ˜ them out of *the* land of Egypt

῞Οτι αὐτοὶ οὐκ ἐνέμειναν ἐν τῇ διαθήκῃ μου,
Because they not ˜ did persevere in - covenant ˜ My,

Κἀγὼ ἠμέλησα αὐτῶν, λέγει Κύριος.
And I was unconcerned about them, says *the* Lord.
disregarded

10 ῞Οτι αὕτη ἡ διαθήκη ἣν διαθήσομαι τῷ οἴκῳ
Because this *is* the covenant which I shall covenant with the house

'Ισραὴλ
of Israel

Μετὰ τὰς ἡμέρας ἐκείνας, λέγει Κύριος,
After - days ˜ those, says *the* Lord,

Διδοὺς νόμους μου εἰς τὴν διάνοιαν αὐτῶν,
Giving laws ˜ My into the mind ˜ their,
I will put

Καὶ ἐπὶ καρδίας αὐτῶν ἐπιγράψω αὐτούς,
And upon hearts ˜ their I shall write them,

Καὶ ἔσομαι αὐτοῖς εἰς Θεὸν
And I will be to them for God

Καὶ αὐτοὶ ἔσονταί μοι εἰς λαόν.
And they will be to Me for a people.

11 Καὶ οὐ μὴ διδάξωσιν ἕκαστος τὸν πολίτην[b]
And not not will they teach each *one* - [2]fellow [3]citizen
by no means

αὐτοῦ
[1]his

Καὶ ἕκαστος τὸν ἀδελφὸν αὐτοῦ, λέγων,
And each *one* - brother ˜ his, saying,

'Γνῶθι τὸν Κύριον,'
'Know the Lord,'

῞Οτι πάντες εἰδήσουσί με
Because all will know Me

'Απὸ μικροῦ αὐτῶν ἕως μεγάλου αὐτῶν.
From *the* little *one* of them to *the* great *one* of them.
least greatest

12 ῞Οτι ἵλεως ἔσομαι ταῖς ἀδικίαις αὐτῶν,
Because [4]merciful [1]I [2]will [3]be to unrighteousness ˜ their,

Καὶ τῶν ἁμαρτιῶν αὐτῶν καὶ τῶν ἀνομιῶν αὐτῶν[c]
And - sins ˜ their and - [2]lawless [3]deeds [1]their

Οὐ μὴ μνησθῶ ἔτι.»[d]
Not not I will remember no more.»
By no means any

[b](8:11) TR reads πλησιον, *neighbor.*

[c](8:12) NU omits και των ανομιων αυτων, *and their lawless deeds.*

[d](8:8–12) Jer. 31:31–34

13 Ἐν τῷ λέγειν "καινὴν" πεπαλαίωκε τὴν πρώτην.
In - to say "new" He has made [3]old [1]the [2]first.
By saying obsolete

Τὸ δὲ παλαιούμενον καὶ γηράσκον ἐγγὺς ἀφανισμοῦ.
[5]the [6]*one* [4]And becoming old and growing old *is* near destruction.
obsolete ready to vanish.

The Features of the Earthly Sanctuary

9 **1** Εἶχε μὲν οὖν καὶ ἡ πρώτη [a] δικαιώματα
[7]had [2]indeed [1]Then [3]even [4]the [5]first [6]*covenant* ordinances

λατρείας τό τε ἅγιον κοσμικόν. **2** Σκηνὴ γὰρ
of service the ˜ and sanctuary ˜ earthly. [2]a [3]tabernacle [1]For

κατεσκευάσθη ἡ πρώτη ἐν ᾗ ἥ τε λυχνία καὶ ἡ
was prepared the first *part* in which *were* the ˜ both lampstand and the

τράπεζα καὶ ἡ πρόθεσις τῶν ἄρτων, ἥτις λέγεται
table and the presentation of the loaves, which is called

Ἅγια· **3** μετὰ δὲ τὸ δεύτερον καταπέτασμα σκηνὴ
the holy place; after ˜ and the second veil a tabernacle

ἡ λεγομένη Ἅγια Ἁγίων, **4** χρυσοῦν ἔχουσα θυμιατήριον
the *one* being called *the* Holy of Holies, [2]a [3]golden [1]having altar
which is

καὶ τὴν κιβωτὸν τῆς διαθήκης περικεκαλυμμένην πάντοθεν
and the ark of the covenant having been covered round on all sides

χρυσίῳ, ἐν ᾗ στάμνος χρυσῆ ἔχουσα τὸ μάννα καὶ ἡ
with gold, in which *were* a jar ˜ golden having the manna and the

ῥάβδος* Ἀαρὼν ἡ βλαστήσασα καὶ αἱ πλάκες τῆς
rod of Aaron the *one* having budded and the tablets of the
which

διαθήκης, **5** ὑπεράνω δὲ αὐτῆς Χερουβὶμ δόξης
covenant, above ˜ and it *were* cherubim of glory

κατασκιάζοντα τὸ ἱλαστήριον· περὶ ὧν οὐκ ἔστι
overshadowing the mercy seat; concerning which *things* [3]not [1]*there* [2]is
we cannot

νῦν λέγειν κατὰ μέρος.
now to speak according to part.
now speak in detail.

The Limitations of the Earthly Service

6 Τούτων δὲ οὕτω κατεσκευασμένων, εἰς μὲν
these *things* Now thus having been prepared, [7]into -
Now when these things had been thus prepared,

τὴν πρώτην σκηνὴν διὰ παντὸς εἰσίασιν οἱ ἱερεῖς τὰς
[8]the [9]first [10]tabernacle [3]through [4]all [5]go [6]in [1]the [2]priests [12]the
at all times

λατρείας ἐπιτελοῦντες, **7** εἰς δὲ τὴν δευτέραν ἅπαξ τοῦ
[13]services [11]accomplishing, into ˜ but the second once of the
during

ἐνιαυτοῦ μόνος ὁ ἀρχιερεύς, οὐ χωρὶς αἵματος, ὃ
year [5]alone [1]the [2]high [3]priest [4]*goes*, not without blood, which

προσφέρει ὑπὲρ ἑαυτοῦ καὶ τῶν τοῦ λαοῦ
he offers in behalf of himself and the [4]of [5]the [6]people

ἀγνοημάτων, **8** τοῦτο δηλοῦντος τοῦ Πνεύματος τοῦ Ἁγίου,
[1]sins [2]of [3]ignorance, [5]this [4]indicating [1]the [3]Spirit - [2]Holy,

μήπω πεφανερῶσθαι τὴν τῶν Ἁγίων ὁδόν,
that [8]not [9]yet [6]to [7]have [10]been [11]revealed [1]the [3]of [4]the [5]Holies [2]way,
was into

ἔτι τῆς πρώτης σκηνῆς ἐχούσης στάσιν, **9** ἥτις
while still the first tabernacle having an existence, which *was*
was standing,

13 In that He says, *"A new covenant,"* He has made the first obsolete. Now what is becoming obsolete and growing old is ready to vanish away.

9 Then indeed, even the first *covenant* had ordinances of divine service and the earthly sanctuary.
2 For a tabernacle was prepared: the first *part,* in which *was* the lampstand, the table, and the showbread, which is called the sanctuary;
3 and behind the second veil, the part of the tabernacle which is called the Holiest of All,
4 which had the golden censer and the ark of the covenant overlaid on all sides with gold, in which *were* the golden pot that had the manna, Aaron's rod that budded, and the tablets of the covenant;
5 and above it were the cherubim of glory overshadowing the mercy seat. Of these things we cannot now speak in detail.
6 Now when these things had been thus prepared, the priests always went into the first part of the tabernacle, performing *the services.*
7 But into the second part the high priest *went* alone once a year, not without blood, which he offered for himself and *for* the people's sins *committed* in ignorance;
8 the Holy Spirit indicating this, that the way into the Holiest of All was not yet made manifest while the first tabernacle was still standing.
9 It *was* symbolic for the

---

a(**9:1**) TR adds σκηνη, *tabernacle.*

***(9:4)** ῥάβδος *(rhabdos).* Noun meaning *stick, staff, rod.* It is used for a large staff, such as for walking (Matt. 10:10); a ruler's staff or scepter (Heb. 1:8) and symbolically of any firm governance ("rule with a *rod* of iron," Rev. 2:27); Aaron's rod (here in Heb. 9:4); and a rod or stick for punishing (1 Cor. 4:21). The verb form ῥαβδίζω is used in this last sense, *to beat with rods,* in Acts 16:22; 2 Cor. 11:25. Roman lictors *(ῥαβδουχοι, rod-bearers)* carried fasces (bundles of sticks) and were

present time in which both gifts and sacrifices are offered which cannot make him who performed the service perfect in regard to the conscience—
10 *concerned* only with foods and drinks, various washings, and fleshly ordinances imposed until the time of reformation.
11 But Christ came *as* High Priest of the good things to come, with the greater and more perfect tabernacle not made with hands, that is, not of this creation.
12 Not with the blood of goats and calves, but with His own blood He entered the Most Holy Place once for all, having obtained eternal redemption.
13 For if the blood of bulls and goats and the ashes of a heifer, sprinkling the unclean, sanctifies for the purifying of the flesh,
14 how much more shall the blood of Christ, who through the eternal Spirit offered Himself without spot to God, cleanse your conscience from dead works to serve the living God?
15 And for this reason He is the Mediator of the new covenant, by means of death, for the redemption of the transgressions under the first covenant, that those who are called may receive the promise of the eternal inheritance.

παραβολὴ εἰς τὸν καιρὸν τὸν ἐνεστηκότα, καθ᾽ ὃν
a figure for the time - having been present, according to which
symbol present time,

δῶρά τε καὶ θυσίαι προσφέρονται μὴ δυνάμεναι κατὰ
gifts ˜ both and sacrifices are being offered not being able according to
which are not able in respect to

συνείδησιν τελειῶσαι τὸν λατρεύοντα,
conscience to make perfect the *one* serving,
performing the service,

10 μόνον ἐπὶ βρώμασι καὶ πόμασι καὶ διαφόροις
concerned only on foods and drinks and different
with

βαπτισμοῖς καὶ δικαιώμασι σαρκός, μέχρι καιροῦ διορθώσεως
washings and ordinances of flesh, [3]until [4]a [5]time [6]of [7]reformation

ἐπικείμενα.
[1]being [2]imposed.
which are

Christ's Service in the Heavenly Sanctuary

11 Χριστὸς δὲ παραγενόμενος Ἀρχιερεὺς τῶν
Christ ˜ But arriving *as* a High Priest of the
came

μελλόντων[b] ἀγαθῶν διὰ τῆς μείζονος καὶ τελειοτέρας
[3]coming [1]good [2]*things* through the greater and more perfect
to come

σκηνῆς οὐ χειροποιήτου, τοῦτ᾽ ἔστιν, οὐ ταύτης τῆς κτίσεως,
tabernacle not made by hands, this is, not of this - creation,
that

12 οὐδὲ δι᾽ αἵματος τράγων καὶ μόσχων, διὰ δὲ τοῦ
not through blood of goats and of calves, through ˜ but -

ἰδίου αἵματος, εἰσῆλθεν ἐφάπαξ εἰς τὰ Ἅγια, αἰωνίαν
His own blood, entered once for all into the Holies, [3]eternal
and entered

λύτρωσιν εὑράμενος. 13 Εἰ γὰρ τὸ αἷμα ταύρων καὶ
[4]redemption [1]having [2]obtained. if ˜ For the blood of bulls and

τράγων καὶ σποδὸς δαμάλεως ῥαντίζουσα τοὺς
of goats and ashes of a heifer sprinkling the *ones*

κεκοινωμένους ἁγιάζει πρὸς τὴν τῆς σαρκὸς καθαρότητα,
having been defiled sanctifies for the [2]of [3]the [4]flesh [1]purity,

14 πόσῳ μᾶλλον τὸ αἷμα τοῦ Χριστοῦ, ὃς διὰ
by how much more the blood - of Christ, who through

Πνεύματος Αἰωνίου ἑαυτὸν προσήνεγκεν ἄμωμον τῷ Θεῷ,
the Spirit ˜ Eternal Himself ˜ offered unblemished - to God,

καθαριεῖ τὴν συνείδησιν ὑμῶν[c] ἀπὸ νεκρῶν ἔργων εἰς
will cleanse - conscience ˜ your from dead works for
in order that

τὸ λατρεύειν Θεῷ ζῶντι? 15 Καὶ διὰ τοῦτο
- to serve *the* God ˜ living? And on account of this
we might serve

διαθήκης καινῆς Μεσίτης ἐστίν, ὅπως, θανάτου
[5]of [6]a [8]covenant [7]new [3]*the* [4]Mediator [1]He [2]is, so that, a death
since a death

γενομένου εἰς ἀπολύτρωσιν τῶν ἐπὶ τῇ πρώτῃ
having occurred for redemption of the [2]at [3]the [4]first
has at the time of

διαθήκῃ παραβάσεων τὴν ἐπαγγελίαν λάβωσιν οἱ
[5]covenant [1]transgressions [13]the [14]promise [11]may [12]receive [6]the [7]*ones*

κεκλημένοι τῆς αἰωνίου κληρονομίας.
[8]having [9]been [10]called of the eternal inheritance.

---

[b](9:11) NU reads γενομενων, *that have come.* [c](9:14) NU reads ημων, *our.*

similar in role to modern policemen.

The Mediator's Death Is Necessary

16 Ὅπου γὰρ διαθήκη, θάνατον ἀνάγκη
where ˜ For *there is* a testament, [4]*for* [5]death [1]*there* [2]*is* [3]necessity

φέρεσθαι τοῦ διαθεμένου. **17** Διαθήκη γὰρ ἐπὶ
to be offered of the *one* making the testament. [2]a [3]testament [1]For over

νεκροῖς βεβαία, ἐπεὶ μήποτε ἰσχύει ὅτε ζῇ ὁ
dead *people is* permanent, since never ˜ it is valid when [6]lives [1]the [2]*one*
valid,

διαθέμενος. **18** Ὅθεν οὐδ' ἡ πρώτη χωρὶς
[3]making [4]the [5]testament. Therefore not even the first *covenant* without

αἵματος ἐγκεκαίνισται. **19** Λαληθείσης γὰρ
blood has been dedicated. having been spoken For
For when every commandment

πάσης ἐντολῆς κατὰ νόμον ὑπὸ Μωϋσέως παντὶ τῷ
every commandment [3]according [4]to [5]law [1]by [2]Moses to all the
had been spoken

λαῷ, λαβὼν τὸ αἷμα τῶν μόσχων καὶ τράγων μετὰ
people, having taken the blood of the calves and goats with
he took

ὕδατος καὶ ἐρίου κοκκίνου καὶ ὑσσώπου αὐτό τε τὸ βιβλίον
water and wool ˜ scarlet and hyssop [6]itself [3]both [4]the [5]scroll

καὶ πάντα τὸν λαὸν ἐρράντισε, **20** λέγων, «Τοῦτο τὸ αἷμα
[7]and [8]all [9]the [10]people [1]he [2]sprinkled, saying, «This *is* the blood
and

τῆς διαθήκης ἧς ἐνετείλατο πρὸς ὑμᾶς ὁ Θεός.»[d] **21** Καὶ
of the covenant which [2]commanded [3]to [4]you - [1]God.» [2]both

τὴν σκηνὴν δὲ καὶ πάντα τὰ σκεύη* τῆς λειτουργίας
[3]the [4]tabernacle [1]And and all the vessels of the service

τῷ αἵματι ὁμοίως ἐρράντισε. **22** Καὶ σχεδὸν ἐν αἵματι
[4]with [5]the [6]blood [1]likewise [2]he [3]sprinkled. And [5]almost [10]with [11]blood

πάντα καθαρίζεται κατὰ τὸν νόμον, καὶ χωρὶς
[6]all [7]*things* [8]are [9]cleansed [1]according [2]to [3]the [4]law, and without

αἱματεκχυσίας οὐ γίνεται ἄφεσις.
shedding of blood [3]no [1]*there* [2]is remission.

The Greatness of the Sacrifice of Christ

23 Ἀνάγκη οὖν τὰ μὲν ὑποδείγματα
[2]*it* [3]*was* [4]necessary [5]*for* [1]Therefore the - copies

τῶν ἐν τοῖς οὐρανοῖς, τούτοις καθαρίζεσθαι, αὐτὰ
of the *things* in the heavens, [4]by [5]these [1]to [2]be [3]cleansed, [10]themselves

δὲ τὰ ἐπουράνια κρείττοσι θυσίαις παρὰ ταύτας. **24** Οὐ
[6]but [7]the [8]heavenly [9]*things* by better sacrifices than these. [4]not

γὰρ εἰς χειροποίητα ἅγια εἰσῆλθεν ὁ Χριστός,
[1]For [6]into [9]made [10]by [11]hands [7]*the* [8]holies [3]did [5]enter - [2]Christ,

ἀντίτυπα τῶν ἀληθινῶν, ἀλλ' εἰς αὐτὸν τὸν
which are representations of the true *things*, but into itself ˜ -
copies

οὐρανόν, νῦν ἐμφανισθῆναι τῷ προσώπῳ τοῦ Θεοῦ ὑπὲρ
heaven, now to appear in the presence - of God in behalf of

ἡμῶν· **25** οὐδ' ἵνα πολλάκις προσφέρῃ ἑαυτόν, ὥσπερ
us; nor so that [5]often [1]He [2]should [3]offer [4]Himself, just as

ὁ ἀρχιερεὺς εἰσέρχεται εἰς τὰ Ἅγια κατ' ἐνιαυτὸν ἐν
the high priest enters into the Holies according to a year with
every year

αἵματι ἀλλοτρίῳ, **26** ἐπεὶ ἔδει αὐτὸν
blood belonging to another, since it was necessary *for* Him
would have been

16 For where there *is* a testament, there must also of necessity be the death of the testator.

17 For a testament *is* in force after men are dead, since it has no power at all while the testator lives.

18 Therefore not even the first *covenant* was dedicated without blood.

19 For when Moses had spoken every precept to all the people according to the law, he took the blood of calves and goats, with water, scarlet wool, and hyssop, and sprinkled both the book itself and all the people,

20 saying, *"This is the blood of the covenant which God has commanded you."*

21 Then likewise he sprinkled with blood both the tabernacle and all the vessels of the ministry.

22 And according to the law almost all things are purified with blood, and without shedding of blood there is no remission.

23 Therefore *it was* necessary that the copies of the things in the heavens should be purified with these, but the heavenly things themselves with better sacrifices than these.

24 For Christ has not entered the holy places made with hands, *which are* copies of the true, but into heaven itself, now to appear in the presence of God for us;

25 not that He should offer Himself often, as the high priest enters the Most Holy Place every year with blood of another—

26 He then would have had to

---

d**(9:20)** Ex. 24:8

***(9:21)** *σκεῦος (skeuos).* Noun, a general term for any *object, thing, household good,* or *equipment,* or more specifically any container, such as a *vessel, jar, dish.* It also has a broad range of figurative senses including *instrument* (Acts 9:15) and *human body* (2 Cor. 4:7). In 1 Thess. 4:4 the meaning could be "control his own *body*" with particular reference to its sexual practices. However, in keeping with the rabbinic usage

suffer often since the foundation of the world; but now, once
at the end of the ages, He has
appeared to put away sin by the
sacrifice of Himself.
27 And as it is appointed for
men to die once, but after this
the judgment,
28 so Christ was offered once
to bear the sins of many. To
those who eagerly wait for Him
He will appear a second time,
apart from sin, for salvation.
10 For the law, having a
shadow of the good
things to come, *and* not the
very image of the things, can
never with these same sacrifices, which they offer continually year by year, make those
who approach perfect.
2 For then would they not
have ceased to be offered? For
the worshipers, once purified,
would have had no more consciousness of sins.
3 But in those *sacrifices there
is* a reminder of sins every
year.
4 For *it is* not possible that
the blood of bulls and goats
could take away sins.
5 Therefore, when He came
into the world, He said:

"Sacrifice and offering You
did not desire,
But a body You have
prepared for Me.

πολλάκις παθεῖν ἀπὸ καταβολῆς κόσμου· νῦν δὲ ἅπαξ
[3]often [1]to [2]suffer from *the* foundation of *the* world; now ˜ but once

ἐπὶ συντελείᾳ τῶν αἰώνων εἰς ἀθέτησιν ἁμαρτίας διὰ
at *the* completion of the ages [5]for [6]*the* [7]removal [8]of [9]sin [10]through

τῆς θυσίας αὐτοῦ πεφανέρωται. **27** Καὶ καθ'
[11]the [12]sacrifice [13]of [14]Him [1]He [2]has [3]been [4]revealed. And by
Himself just

ὅσον ἀπόκειται τοῖς ἀνθρώποις ἅπαξ ἀποθανεῖν, μετὰ δὲ
as much as it is appointed - for men [3]once [1]to [2]die, after ˜ and
as

τοῦτο κρίσις, **28** οὕτω καὶ ὁ Χριστός, ἅπαξ προσενεχθεὶς
this judgment, so also - Christ, once having been offered

εἰς τὸ πολλῶν ἀνενεγκεῖν ἁμαρτίας, ἐκ δευτέρου χωρὶς
for - [5]of [6]many [1]to [2]bear [3]*the* [4]sins, from a second *time* without
in order

ἁμαρτίας ὀφθήσεται τοῖς αὐτὸν ἀπεκδεχομένοις εἰς
sin He will appear to the *ones* [4]Him [1]eagerly [2]waiting [3]for for

σωτηρίαν.
salvation.

Animal Sacrifices Are Insufficient

10 1 Σκιὰν γὰρ ἔχων ὁ νόμος τῶν μελλόντων
[5]a [6]shadow [1]For [4]having [2]the [3]law of the [3]coming
since the law has to come

ἀγαθῶν, οὐκ αὐτὴν τὴν εἰκόνα τῶν πραγμάτων,
[1]good [2]*things*, *and* not [3]itself [1]the [2]image of the things,

κατ' ἐνιαυτὸν ταῖς αὐταῖς θυσίαις ἃς
[9]according [10]to [11]a [12]year [5]with [6]the [7]same [8]sacrifices [13]which
every year

προσφέρουσιν εἰς τὸ διηνεκὲς οὐδέποτε δύνανται[a]
[14]they [15]offer [16]for - [17]continuous [18]*time* [3]never [1]they [2]are [4]able
continually

τοὺς προσερχομένους τελειῶσαι. **2** Ἐπεὶ οὐκ
[21]the [22]*ones* [23]approaching [19]to [20]make [24]perfect. Otherwise [3]not
those who approach would

ἂν ἐπαύσαντο προσφερόμεναι, διὰ τὸ μηδεμίαν
- [1]did [2]they [4]cease being offered, because of - [11]no
they not have ceased to be offered, because would

ἔχειν ἔτι συνείδησιν ἁμαρτιῶν τοὺς λατρεύοντας,
[8]to [9]have [10]yet [12]consciousness [13]of [14]sins [1]the [2]*ones* [3]serving,
have had no more the worshipers,

ἅπαξ κεκαθαρμένους? **3** Ἀλλ' ἐν αὐταῖς ἀνάμνησις
[4]once [5]having [6]been [7]cleansed? But in them *there is* a reminder

ἁμαρτιῶν κατ' ἐνιαυτόν. **4** Ἀδύνατον γὰρ αἷμα
of sins according to a year. [2]*it* [3]*is* [4]impossible [5]*for* [1]For *the* blood
yearly.

ταύρων καὶ τράγων ἀφαιρεῖν ἁμαρτίας.
of bulls and of goats to take away sins.

Christ's Death Fulfills God's Will

5 Διὸ εἰσερχόμενος εἰς τὸν κόσμον λέγει,
Therefore entering into the world He says,
when He entered said,

«Θυσίαν καὶ προσφορὰν οὐκ ἠθέλησας,
«Sacrifice and offering [3]not [1]You [2]did [4]wish,
desire,

Σῶμα δὲ κατηρτίσω μοι·
[2]a [3]body [1]But you did prepare for Me;
have prepared

---

[a](10:1) NU, TR read δυναται, *it is (never) able*, thus referring to the law.

of referring to a wife as a "vessel," another possibly is "acquire a wife" (cf. "the weaker *vessel*" in 1 Pet. 3:7).

6 Ὁλοκαυτώματα καὶ περὶ ἁμαρτίας οὐκ
With whole burnt offerings and *sacrifices* concerning sin [3]not

εὐδόκησας.
[1]You [2]were [4]well [5]pleased.

7 Τότε εἶπον, "Ἰδοὺ ἥκω,
Then I said, 'Behold I have come,

Ἐν κεφαλίδι βιβλίου γέγραπται περὶ ἐμοῦ,
In a roll of a scroll it is written concerning Me,

Τοῦ ποιῆσαι, ὁ Θεός, τὸ θέλημά σου.'»[b]
- To do, - *O* God, - will ˜ Your.'»

8 Ἀνώτερον λέγων ὅτι «Θυσίαν καὶ προσφορὰν καὶ
Earlier saying - «Sacrifice and offering and

ὁλοκαυτώματα καὶ περὶ ἁμαρτίας οὐκ
whole burnt offerings and *sacrifices* concerning sin [3]not

ἠθέλησας οὐδὲ εὐδόκησας» (αἵτινες
[1]You [2]did [4]wish nor were You well pleased *with them*» (which
desire

κατὰ τὸν νόμον προσφέρονται), 9 τότε εἴρηκεν, «Ἰδοὺ
[3]according [4]to [5]the [6]law [1]are [2]offered), then He has said, «Behold

ἥκω τοῦ ποιῆσαι, ὁ Θεός,[c] τὸ θέλημά σου.»
I have come - to do, - *O* God, - will ˜ Your.»

Ἀναιρεῖ τὸ πρῶτον ἵνα τὸ δεύτερον
He takes away the first in order that [4]the [5]second

στήσῃ, 10 Ἐν ᾧ θελήματι ἡγιασμένοι ἐσμὲν
[1]He [2]may [3]establish, By which will [3]sanctified [1]we [2]are

οἱ διὰ τῆς προσφορᾶς τοῦ σώματος Ἰησοῦ Χριστοῦ
the *ones* through the offering of the body of Jesus Christ

ἐφάπαξ.*
once for all.

Christ's Death Perfects the Sanctified

11 Καὶ πᾶς μὲν ἱερεὺς ἕστηκε καθ' ἡμέραν
And every - priest has stood [3]according [4]to [5]a [6]day
stands ministering daily

λειτουργῶν καὶ τὰς αὐτὰς πολλάκις προσφέρων θυσίας,
[1]performing [2]service and [2]the [3]same [5]often [1]offering [4]sacrifices,

αἵτινες οὐδέποτε δύνανται περιελεῖν ἁμαρτίας. 12 Αὐτὸς δὲ
which never ˜ are able to take away sins. [3]Himself [1]But

μίαν ὑπὲρ ἁμαρτιῶν προσενέγκας θυσίαν εἰς τὸ
[6]one [8]in [9]behalf [10]of [11]sins [4]having [5]offered [7]sacrifice [12]for -

διηνεκὲς ἐκάθισεν ἐν δεξιᾷ τοῦ Θεοῦ,
[13]uninterrupted [14]*time* [2]He [15]sat at *the* right *hand* - of God,
all

13 τὸ λοιπὸν ἐκδεχόμενος ἕως τεθῶσιν οἱ ἐχθροὶ αὐτοῦ
the remaining waiting till [3]are [4]put - [2]enemies [1]His
henceforth

ὑποπόδιον τῶν ποδῶν αὐτοῦ. 14 Μιᾷ γὰρ προσφορᾷ
as a footstool - of feet ˜ His. [2]by [3]one [1]For offering
for

τετελείωκεν εἰς τὸ διηνεκὲς τοὺς ἁγιαζομένους.
He has perfected for - uninterrupted *time* the *ones* being sanctified.
forever those who are

15 Μαρτυρεῖ δὲ ἡμῖν καὶ τὸ Πνεῦμα τὸ Ἅγιον· μετὰ
[6]witnesses [1]But [7]to [8]us [5]also [2]the [4]Spirit - [3]Holy; after ˜

γὰρ τὸ προειρηκέναι,
for - to have said before,
He had

6 *In burnt offerings and*
sacrifices for sin
You had no pleasure.
7 *Then I said, 'Behold, I*
have come—
In the volume of the book
it is written of Me—
To do Your will,
O God.' "

8 Previously saying, *"Sacrifice and offering, burnt offerings, and offerings for sin You did not desire, nor had pleasure in them"* (which are offered according to the law),
9 then He said, *"Behold, I have come to do Your will, O God."* He takes away the first that He may establish the second.
10 By that will we have been sanctified through the offering of the body of Jesus Christ once *for all.*
11 And every priest stands ministering daily and offering repeatedly the same sacrifices, which can never take away sins.
12 But this Man, after He had offered one sacrifice for sins forever, sat down at the right hand of God,
13 from that time waiting till His enemies are made His footstool.
14 For by one offering He has perfected forever those who are being sanctified.
15 But the Holy Spirit also witnesses to us; for after He had said before,

---

[b](**10:5–7**) Ps. 40:6–8
[c](**10:9**) NU omits ο Θεος, *O God.*

***(10:10)** ἐφάπαξ *(ephapax).* Adverb meaning *at one time* or *once for all,* a strengthened form of ἅπαξ, *once, once for all* (as in Heb. 9:26, 27; 6:4; 10:2). In 1 Cor. 15:6 it means *at one time.* Here in Heb. 10:10 and elsewhere the adverb describes Jesus' death and sacrifice of Himself for our sins as *once for all,* thus indicating the finished redemptive work of Christ.

16 *"This is the covenant that I will make with them after those days, says the* LORD: *I will put My laws into their hearts, and in their minds I will write them,"*
17 *then He adds, "Their sins and their lawless deeds I will remember no more."*
18 Now where there is remission of these, *there is* no longer an offering for sin.
19 Therefore, brethren, having boldness to enter the Holiest by the blood of Jesus,
20 by a new and living way which He consecrated for us, through the veil, that is, His flesh,
21 and *having* a High Priest over the house of God,
22 let us draw near with a true heart in full assurance of faith, having our hearts sprinkled from an evil conscience and our bodies washed with pure water.
23 Let us hold fast the confession of *our* hope without wavering, for He who promised *is* faithful.
24 And let us consider one another in order to stir up love and good works,
25 not forsaking the assembling of ourselves together, as *is* the manner of some, but exhorting *one another,* and so much the more as you see the Day approaching.

16 «Αὕτη ἡ διαθήκη ἣν διαθήσομαι πρὸς αὐτοὺς
«This *is* the covenant which I shall covenant with them

Μετὰ τὰς ἡμέρας ἐκείνας, λέγει Κύριος,
After - days ˜ those, says *the* Lord,

Διδοὺς νόμους μου ἐπὶ καρδίας αὐτῶν,
Giving laws ˜ My on hearts ˜ their,
I will put

Καὶ ἐπὶ τῶν διανοιῶν αὐτῶν ἐπιγράψω αὐτούς,
And on - minds ˜ their I will write them,

17 Καὶ τῶν ἁμαρτιῶν καὶ τῶν ἀνομιῶν αὐτῶν
And the sins and - [2]lawless [3]deeds [1]their
their

Οὐ μὴ μνησθῶ ἔτι.»[d]
Not not shall I remember no longer.»
By no means any

18 Ὅπου δὲ ἄφεσις τούτων, οὐκέτι προσφορὰ
where ˜ Now *there is* forgiveness of these, *there is* no longer an offering

περὶ ἁμαρτίας.
concerning sin.

Hold Fast the Confession of Your Hope

19 Ἔχοντες οὖν, ἀδελφοί, παρρησίαν εἰς τὴν εἴσοδον
[3]having [1]Therefore, [2]brothers, confidence for the entering
to enter

τῶν Ἁγίων ἐν τῷ αἵματι Ἰησοῦ, 20 ἣν ἐνεκαίνισεν
of the Holies by the blood of Jesus, [7]which [8]He [9]inaugurated

ἡμῖν ὁδὸν πρόσφατον καὶ ζῶσαν διὰ τοῦ
[10]for [11]us [1]by [2]a [6]way [3]new [4]and [5]living through the

καταπετάσματος, τοῦτ᾽ ἔστι, τῆς σαρκὸς αὐτοῦ, 21 καὶ
veil, this is, - flesh ˜ His, and *having*
that

ἱερέα μέγαν ἐπὶ τὸν οἶκον τοῦ Θεοῦ, 22 προσερχώμεθα
a priest ˜ great over the house - of God, let us approach
high

μετὰ ἀληθινῆς καρδίας ἐν πληροφορίᾳ πίστεως,
with a true heart in full assurance of faith,

ἐρραντισμένοι τὰς καρδίας ἀπὸ συνειδήσεως πονηρᾶς
having been sprinkled *as to* the hearts from a(n) conscience ˜ evil
our

καὶ λελουμένοι τὸ σῶμα ὕδατι καθαρῷ.
and having been washed *as to* the body with water ˜ clean.
our

23 Κατέχωμεν τὴν ὁμολογίαν τῆς ἐλπίδος ἀκλινῆ,
Let us hold fast the confession of the hope without wavering,

πιστὸς γὰρ ὁ ἐπαγγειλάμενος. 24 Καὶ κατανοῶμεν
[6]*is* [7]faithful [1]for [2]the [3]*One* [4]having [5]promised. And let us consider
He who

ἀλλήλους εἰς παροξυσμὸν ἀγάπης καὶ καλῶν ἔργων, 25 μὴ
one another for *the* stirring up of love and of good works, not
to stir up

ἐγκαταλείποντες τὴν ἐπισυναγωγὴν ἑαυτῶν, καθὼς
forsaking the assembling of ourselves, just as *is*

ἔθος τισίν, ἀλλὰ παρακαλοῦντες, καὶ τοσούτῳ μᾶλλον
the custom for some, but exhorting *one another,* and by as much more
all the

ὅσῳ βλέπετε ἐγγίζουσαν τὴν ἡμέραν.
as you see [3]drawing [4]near [1]the [2]day.

[d](10:16, 17) Jer. 31:33, 34

Fourth Warning: Do Not Cast Away Your Confidence

26 Ἑκουσίως γὰρ ἁμαρτανόντων ἡμῶν μετὰ τὸ λαβεῖν τὴν
[4]willfully [1]For [3]sinning [2]us after - to receive the
if we sin receiving

ἐπίγνωσιν τῆς ἀληθείας, οὐκέτι περὶ ἁμαρτιῶν
knowledge of the truth, [2]no [3]longer [7]concerning [8]sins

ἀπολείπεται θυσία, 27 φοβερὰ δέ τις ἐκδοχὴ
[1]*there* [4]remains [5]a [6]sacrifice, [4]fearful [1]but [3]certain [2]a(n) [5]expectation

κρίσεως καὶ πυρὸς ζῆλος ἐσθίειν μέλλοντος τοὺς
of judgment and [3]of [4]fire [1]of [2]zeal [7]to [8]devour [5]being [6]about the
of fiery zeal

ὑπεναντίους. 28 Ἀθετήσας τις νόμον Μωϋσέως χωρὶς
adversaries. disregarding ˜ Anyone *the* law of Moses without

οἰκτιρμῶν ἐπὶ δυσὶν ἢ τρισὶ μάρτυσιν ἀποθνῄσκει.
compassions on *the word of* two or three witnesses dies.

29 Πόσῳ, δοκεῖτε, χείρονος ἀξιωθήσεται
By how much, [3]do [4]you [5]think, [1]worse [6]he [7]will [8]be [9]deemed [10]worthy

τιμωρίας ὁ τὸν Υἱὸν τοῦ Θεοῦ καταπατήσας,
[2]punishment the *one* [3]the [4]Son - [5]of [6]God [1]having [2]trampled [7]underfoot
who has

καὶ τὸ αἷμα τῆς διαθήκης κοινὸν ἡγησάμενος ἐν ᾧ
and [5]the [6]blood [7]of [8]the [9]covenant [3]*as* [4]common [1]having [2]regarded by which
has

ἡγιάσθη, καὶ τὸ Πνεῦμα τῆς χάριτος ἐνυβρίσας?
he was sanctified, and [3]the [4]Spirit - [5]of [6]grace [1]having [2]insulted?
has

30 Οἴδαμεν γὰρ τὸν εἰπόντα,
[2]we [3]know [1]For the *One* having said,
Him who

«Ἐμοὶ ἐκδίκησις, ἐγὼ ἀνταποδώσω, λέγει Κύριος»·[e]
«[3]to [4]Me [1]Vengeance [2]*is,* I will repay, says *the* Lord»;
«Mine

καὶ πάλιν,
and again,

«Κύριος κρινεῖ τὸν λαὸν αὐτοῦ.»[f]
«*The* Lord will judge - people ˜ His.»

31 Φοβερὸν τὸ ἐμπεσεῖν εἰς χεῖρας Θεοῦ
It is a fearful *thing* - to fall into *the* hands of *the* God ˜

ζῶντος!
living!

32 Ἀναμιμνῄσκεσθε δὲ τὰς πρότερον ἡμέρας, ἐν αἷς
remember ˜ But the former days, in which

φωτισθέντες πολλὴν ἄθλησιν ὑπεμείνατε παθημάτων,
having been enlightened [3]a [4]great [5]struggle [1]you [2]endured of sufferings,
after you were

33 τοῦτο μὲν ὀνειδισμοῖς τε καὶ θλίψεσι
this *part* - [5]to [6]reproaches [4]both [7]and [8]to [9]afflictions
in part

θεατριζόμενοι, τοῦτο δὲ κοινωνοὶ τῶν οὕτως
[1]being [2]exposed [3]publicly, [11]this [12]*part* [10]but [15]sharers [16]of [17]the [18]*ones* [20]thus
in part treated

ἀναστρεφομένων γενηθέντες. 34 Καὶ γὰρ τοῖς δεσμοῖς
[19]living [13]having [14]become. indeed ˜ For - in bonds ˜
in this way

μου[g] συνεπαθήσατε καὶ τὴν ἁρπαγὴν τῶν
my you suffered with *me* and [3]the [4]plunder [5]of [6]the [7]*things*
sympathized your

26 For if we sin willfully after
we have received the knowledge of the truth, there no longer remains a sacrifice for sins,
27 but a certain fearful expectation of judgment, and fiery indignation which will devour the
adversaries.
28 Anyone who has rejected
Moses' law dies without mercy
on the testimony of two or
three witnesses.
29 Of how much worse pun-
ishment, do you suppose, will
he be thought worthy who has
trampled the Son of God underfoot, counted the blood of the
covenant by which he was sanctified a common thing, and insulted the Spirit of grace?
30 For we know Him who
said, *"Vengeance is Mine, I will
repay,"* says the Lord. And
again, *"The LORD will judge His
people."*
31 It is a fearful thing to fall
into the hands of the living God.
32 But recall the former days
in which, after you were illuminated, you endured a great
struggle with sufferings:
33 partly while you were
made a spectacle both by reproaches and tribulations, and
partly while you became companions of those who were so
treated;
34 for you had compassion on
me in my chains, and joyfully
accepted the plundering of your

---

e(**10:30**) Deut. 32:35
f(**10:30**) Deut. 32:36
g(**10:34**) For δεσμοις μου, *in my bonds,* NU reads δεσμιοις, *with the prisoners.*

goods, knowing that you have a
better and an enduring possession for yourselves in heaven.
35 Therefore do not cast away
your confidence, which has
great reward.
36 For you have need of endurance, so that after you have
done the will of God, you may
receive the promise:

37 *"For yet a little while,*
And He who is coming
will come and will not
tarry.
38 *Now the just shall live by*
faith;
But if anyone draws back,
My soul has no pleasure
in him."

39 But we are not of those
who draw back to perdition, but
of those who believe to the saving of the soul.
11 Now faith is the substance of things hoped
for, the evidence of things not
seen.
2 For by it the elders obtained a *good* testimony.
3 By faith we understand
that the worlds were framed by
the word of God, so that the
things which are seen were not
made of things which are visible.
4 By faith Abel offered to
God a more excellent sacrifice
than Cain, through which he obtained witness that he was righ-

ὑπαρχόντων ὑμῶν μετὰ χαρᾶς προσεδέξασθε, γινώσκοντες
[8]belonging [9]to [10]you [11]with [12]joy [1]you [2]received, knowing
possessions

ἔχειν ἑαυτοῖς κρείττονα ὕπαρξιν ἐν οὐρανοῖς[h] καὶ
to have for yourselves a better [3]possession [4]in [5]*the* [6]heavens [1]and
that you have heaven

μένουσαν.
[2]remaining.
enduring.

35 Μὴ ἀποβάλητε οὖν τὴν παρρησίαν ὑμῶν, ἥτις
[3]not [2]do [4]cast [5]away [1]Therefore - confidence ˜ your, which

ἔχει μισθαποδοσίαν μεγάλην. **36** Ὑπομονῆς γὰρ ἔχετε
has a recompense ˜ great. [5]of [6]endurance [1]For [2]you [3]have

χρείαν ἵνα τὸ θέλημα τοῦ Θεοῦ ποιήσαντες κομίσησθε
[4]need so that [3]the [4]will - [5]of [6]God [1]having [2]done you may receive

τὴν ἐπαγγελίαν.
the promise.

37 Ἔτι γὰρ «μικρὸν ὅσον ὅσον,
yet ˜ For «a little as long as long,
«a very little while,

Ὁ ἐρχόμενος ἥξει καὶ οὐ χρονιεῖ.
The *One* coming will come and not ˜ will delay.
He who is coming

38 Ὁ δὲ δίκαιος[i] ἐκ πίστεως ζήσεται,
the ˜ But righteous *one* [3]by [4]faith [1]shall [2]live,

Καὶ ἐὰν ὑποστείληται,
And if he withdraws,

Οὐκ εὐδοκεῖ ἡ ψυχή μου ἐν αὐτῷ.»[j]
[4]not [3]is [5]well [6]pleased - [2]soul [1]My with him.»

39 Ἡμεῖς δὲ οὐκ ἐσμὲν ὑποστολῆς εἰς ἀπώλειαν,
we ˜ But not ˜ are of *those* shrinking back to destruction,

ἀλλὰ πίστεως εἰς περιποίησιν ψυχῆς.
but of faith to *the* saving of *the* soul.

By Faith We Understand

11 **1** Ἔστι δὲ πίστις ἐλπιζομένων
[3]is [1]Now [2]faith [6]of [7]*things* [8]being [9]hoped [10]for

ὑπόστασις, πραγμάτων ἔλεγχος οὐ βλεπομένων. **2** Ἐν
[4]*the* [5]assurance, [13]of [14]things [11]*the* [12]proof not being seen. [2]by

ταύτῃ γὰρ ἐμαρτυρήθησαν οἱ πρεσβύτεροι. **3** Πίστει
[3]this [1]For [6]obtained [7]witness [4]the [5]elders. By faith

νοοῦμεν κατηρτίσθαι* τοὺς αἰῶνας ῥήματι Θεοῦ,
we understand [3]to [4]have [5]been [6]prepared [1]the [2]worlds by a word of God,

εἰς τὸ μὴ ἐκ φαινομένων τὰ βλεπόμενα
for - [7]not [10]out [11]of [12]*things* [13]being [14]visible [1]the [2]*things* [3]being [4]seen
in order that

γεγονέναι.
[5]to [6]have [8]been [9]made.
have

Faith at the Dawn of History

4 Πίστει πλείονα θυσίαν Ἄβελ παρὰ Κάϊν προσήνεγκε
By faith [5]a [6]greater [7]sacrifice [1]Abel [8]than [9]Cain [2]offered
better

τῷ Θεῷ, δι' ἧς ἐμαρτυρήθη εἶναι δίκαιος,
- [3]to [4]God, through which he obtained witness to be just,
that he was

---

[h](**10:34**) NU omits *εν ουρανοις, in (the) heavens.*
[i](**10:38**) NU adds *μου, my (righteous one).*
[j](**10:37, 38**) Hab. 2:3, 4 LXX

*(**11:3**) *καταρτίζω (katartizō).* Verb from the preposition *κατά, down* and the noun *ἄρτος, joint.* This word has many idiomatic translations in context, but the main ideas are *to make fit, equip, mend,* or *restore.* Here it means *make* or *create.* It can mean *to prepare,* as the body of Christ in the Virgin's womb (Heb. 10:5); *to complete* (2 Cor. 13:11); *to perfect* (1 Thess. 3:10); and *to mend* (nets, Matt. 4:21).

μαρτυροῦντος ἐπὶ τοῖς δώροις αὐτοῦ τοῦ Θεοῦ, καὶ δι'
[2]witnessing [3]to - [5]gifts ˜ [4]his - [1]God, and through
concerning

αὐτῆς ἀποθανὼν ἔτι λαλεῖται. **5** Πίστει Ἐνὼχ
it having died still ˜ he speaks. By faith Enoch
although he died

μετετέθη τοῦ μὴ ἰδεῖν θάνατον, καὶ «οὐχ εὑρίσκετο
was taken away - not to see death, and «[3]not [1]he [2]was found

διότι μετέθηκεν αὐτὸν ὁ Θεός»·[a] πρὸ γὰρ τῆς μεταθέσεως
because [2]took [4]away [3]him - [1]God»; before ˜ for - translation ˜
had taken

αὐτοῦ[b] μεμαρτύρηται εὐηρεστηκέναι τῷ Θεῷ.
his he has obtained witness to have been pleasing - to God.
that he was

6 Χωρὶς δὲ πίστεως ἀδύνατον εὐαρεστῆσαι, πιστεῦσαι
without ˜ But faith *it is* impossible to be pleasing, [10]to [11]believe

γὰρ δεῖ τὸν προσερχόμενον τῷ Θεῷ ὅτι ἔστι
[1]for [2]it [3]is [4]necessary [5]*for* [6]the [7]*one* [8]approaching - [9]God that He is

καὶ τοῖς ἐκζητοῦσιν αὐτὸν μισθαποδότης γίνεται.
and *that* [5]to [6]the [7]*ones* [8]seeking [9]Him [3]a [4]rewarder [1]He [2]becomes.
those who seek

7 Πίστει χρηματισθεὶς Νῶε περὶ τῶν
By faith having been warned *by God* [8]Noah [1]concerning [2]the [3]*things*

μηδέπω βλεπομένων, εὐλαβηθεὶς κατεσκεύασε κιβωτὸν εἰς
[4]not [5]yet [6]being [7]seen, being reverent prepared an ark for

σωτηρίαν τοῦ οἴκου αὐτοῦ, δι' ἧς κατέκρινε τὸν
the salvation - of household ˜ his, through which he condemned the

κόσμον, καὶ τῆς κατὰ πίστιν δικαιοσύνης ἐγένετο
world, and [4]of [5]the [7]according [8]to [9]faith [6]righteousness [1]became

κληρονόμος.
[2]an [3]heir.

Faithful Abraham

8 Πίστει καλούμενος Ἀβραὰμ ὑπήκουσεν ἐξελθεῖν εἰς τὸν
By faith being called Abraham obeyed to go forth to the
when he was

τόπον ὃν ἤμελλε λαμβάνειν εἰς κληρονομίαν. Καὶ
place which he was about to receive for an inheritance. And

ἐξῆλθε μὴ ἐπιστάμενος ποῦ ἔρχεται. **9** Πίστει
he went forth not understanding where he goes. By faith
was going.

παρῴκησεν εἰς γῆν τῆς ἐπαγγελίας ὡς ἀλλοτρίαν, ἐν
he migrated into a land - of promise as *in* a foreign *land*, [2]in

σκηναῖς κατοικήσας μετὰ Ἰσαὰκ καὶ Ἰακὼβ τῶν
[3]tents [1]dwelling with Isaac and Jacob the

συγκληρονόμων τῆς ἐπαγγελίας τῆς αὐτῆς. **10** Ἐξεδέχετο
fellow heirs of the promise ˜ - same. [2]he [3]waited [4]for

γὰρ τὴν τοὺς θεμελίους ἔχουσαν πόλιν, ἧς τεχνίτης* καὶ
[1]For the - [3]foundations [2]having [1]city, whose builder and

δημιουργὸς ὁ Θεός. **11** Πίστει καὶ αὐτὴ Σάρρα[c] δύναμιν εἰς
maker - *is* God. By faith [3]also [2]herself [1]Sarah [5]power [6]for

καταβολὴν σπέρματος ἔλαβε καὶ παρὰ καιρὸν ἡλικίας
[7]sowing [8]of [9]seed [4]received and beyond time of age
conception past the normal age

ἔτεκεν,[d] ἐπεὶ πιστὸν ἡγήσατο τὸν
she bore a child, since [3]*Him* [4]faithful [1]she [2]regarded the *One*
who

teous, God testifying of his
gifts; and through it he being
dead still speaks.
5 By faith Enoch was taken
away so that he did not see
death, *"and was not found, because God had taken him"*; for
before he was taken he had this
testimony, that he pleased God.
6 But without faith *it is* impossible to please *Him*, for he
who comes to God must believe
that He is, and *that* He is a
rewarder of those who diligently seek Him.
7 By faith Noah, being divinely warned of things not yet
seen, moved with godly fear,
prepared an ark for the saving
of his household, by which he
condemned the world and became heir of the righteousness
which is according to faith.
8 By faith Abraham obeyed
when he was called to go out to
the place which he would receive as an inheritance. And he
went out, not knowing where
he was going.
9 By faith he dwelt in the
land of promise as *in* a foreign
country, dwelling in tents with
Isaac and Jacob, the heirs with
him of the same promise;
10 for he waited for the city
which has foundations, whose
builder and maker *is* God.
11 By faith Sarah herself also
received strength to conceive
seed, and she bore a child when
she was past the age, because
she judged Him faithful who had

[a](**11:5**) Gen. 5:24
[b](**11:5**) NU omits αυτου, *his,* thus, *(before) the translation.*
[c](**11:11**) NU adds στειρα, *(was) barren,* thus making the verbs of v. 11 to refer to Abraham: *By faith—and Sarah herself (was) barren—he received power . . . he regarded.*
[d](**11:11**) NU omits ετεκεν, *she bore a child.*

***(11:10)** τεχνίτης *(technitēs).* Noun meaning *craftsman, designer,* related to the English *technician.* In other passages, the word refers to people possessing the skills of various trades or crafts (silversmiths, Acts 19:24). Here in Heb. 11:10 it refers to God as the *designer, architect* of the heavenly city. The word apparently emphasizes the specialized training and skill of craftsmanship. Cf. the cognate noun τέχνη, *skill, trade, craft* (Rev. 18:22, where both nouns occur).

promised.
12 Therefore from one man, and him as good as dead, were born *as many* as the stars of the sky in multitude—innumerable as the sand which is by the seashore.
13 These all died in faith, not having received the promises, but having seen them afar off were assured of them, embraced *them* and confessed that they were strangers and pilgrims on the earth.
14 For those who say such things declare plainly that they seek a homeland.
15 And truly if they had called to mind that *country* from which they had come out, they would have had opportunity to return.
16 But now they desire a better, that is, a heavenly *country*. Therefore God is not ashamed to be called their God, for He has prepared a city for them.
17 By faith Abraham, when he was tested, offered up Isaac, and he who had received the promises offered up his only begotten *son*,
18 of whom it was said, *"In Isaac your seed shall be called,"*
19 concluding that God *was* able to raise *him* up, even from the dead, from which he also received him in a figurative sense.
20 By faith Isaac blessed Jacob and Esau concerning things to come.
21 By faith Jacob, when he

ἐπαγγειλάμενον. **12** Διὸ καὶ ἀφ᾽ ἑνὸς ἐγεννήθησαν,
having promised. Therefore even from one *man* they were begotten,
had

καὶ ταῦτα νενεκρωμένου, καθὼς τὰ ἄστρα τοῦ
and *in* these *things* having been worn out, just as the stars of the
him as good as dead,

οὐρανοῦ τῷ πλήθει καὶ ὡς ἡ ἄμμος ἡ παρὰ τὸ χεῖλος
heaven in the quantity and [2]as [3]the [4]sand - [5]by [6]the [7]shore
in multitude

τῆς θαλάσσης ἡ ἀναρίθμητος.
[8]of [9]the [10]sea - [1]innumerable.

The Heavenly Hope of Faith

13 Κατὰ πίστιν ἀπέθανον οὗτοι πάντες, μὴ
According to faith [3]died [1]these [2]all, not

λαβόντες τὰς ἐπαγγελίας, ἀλλὰ πόρρωθεν αὐτὰς ἰδόντες[e]
having received the promises, but [4]from [5]afar [3]them [1]having [2]seen

καὶ ἀσπασάμενοι, καὶ ὁμολογήσαντες ὅτι ξένοι καὶ
and welcoming *them,* and confessing that [3]strangers [4]and

παρεπίδημοί εἰσιν ἐπὶ τῆς γῆς. **14** Οἱ γὰρ τοιαῦτα
[5]sojourners [1]they [2]are on the earth. [2]the [3]*ones* [1]For [5]such [6]*things*
were

λέγοντες ἐμφανίζουσιν ὅτι πατρίδα ἐπιζητοῦσι. **15** Καὶ εἰ
[4]saying make evident that [3]a [4]fatherland [1]they [2]seek. And if ˜

μὲν ἐκείνης ἐμνημόνευον ἀφ᾽ ἧς ἐξῆλθον,
indeed [4]that [5]*land* [1]they [2]were [3]remembering from which they went out,
had remembered

εἶχον ἂν καιρὸν ἀνακάμψαι. **16** Νῦν δὲ
they would have had - opportunity to turn back. now ˜ But

κρείττονος ὀρέγονται, τοῦτ᾽ ἔστιν, ἐπουρανίου. Διὸ οὐκ
a better *land* they aspire to, this is, a heavenly *one.* Therefore [3]not
that

ἐπαισχύνεται αὐτοὺς ὁ Θεὸς Θεὸς ἐπικαλεῖσθαι αὐτῶν,
[2]is [4]ashamed [5]*of* [6]them - [1]God [11]God [7]to [8]be [9]called [10]their,

ἡτοίμασε γὰρ αὐτοῖς πόλιν.
[13]He [14]prepared [12]for for them a city.

The Faith of the Patriarchs

17 Πίστει προσενήνοχεν Ἀβραὰμ τὸν Ἰσαὰκ πειραζόμενος,
By faith [2]has [3]offered [4]up [1]Abraham - Isaac being tested,
had when he was

καὶ τὸν μονογενῆ προσέφερεν ὁ τὰς ἐπαγγελίας
and [9]the [10]only [11]begotten [12]*son* [7]offered [8]up [1]the [2]*one* [5]the [6]promises
his

ἀναδεξάμενος, **18** πρὸς ὃν ἐλαλήθη ὅτι «Ἐν Ἰσαὰκ
[3]having [4]received, to whom it was spoken - «In Isaac
with regard to

κληθήσεταί σοι σπέρμα,»[f] **19** λογισάμενος ὅτι καὶ ἐκ
[4]shall [5]be [6]called [2]to [3]you [1]seed,» considering that even from
your seed,»

νεκρῶν ἐγείρειν δυνατὸς ὁ Θεός· ὅθεν αὐτὸν καὶ ἐν
the dead [4]to [5]raise [6]*him* [7]*up* [2]*was* [3]able - [1]God; from which [4]him [2]also [5]in
as

παραβολῇ ἐκομίσατο. **20** Πίστει περὶ μελλόντων
[6]a [7]figure [1]he [3]received. By faith concerning coming *things*
a type

εὐλόγησεν Ἰσαὰκ τὸν Ἰακὼβ καὶ τὸν Ἠσαῦ. **21** Πίστει Ἰακὼβ
blessed ˜ Isaac - Jacob and - Esau. By faith Jacob

---

[e](**11:13**) TR adds *και πεισθεντες, and being convinced (of them).*
[f](**11:18**) Gen. 21:12

ἀποθνῄσκων ἕκαστον τῶν υἱῶν Ἰωσὴφ εὐλόγησε, καὶ
dying [2]each [3]of [4]the [5]sons [6]of [7]Joseph [1]blessed, and
when he was dying

«προσεκύνησεν ἐπὶ τὸ ἄκρον τῆς ῥάβδου αὐτοῦ.»[g] 22 Πίστει
«worshiped on the top - of staff ˜ his.» By faith

Ἰωσὴφ τελευτῶν περὶ τῆς ἐξόδου τῶν υἱῶν
Joseph dying [2]concerning [3]the [4]exodus [5]of [6]the [7]sons
when he was dying

Ἰσραὴλ ἐμνημόνευσε, καὶ περὶ τῶν ὀστέων αὐτοῦ
[8]of [9]Israel [1]remembered, and [3]concerning - [5]bones [4]his

ἐνετείλατο.
[1]gave [2]orders.

The Faith of Moses

23 Πίστει Μωϋσῆς γεννηθεὶς ἐκρύβη τρίμηνον ὑπὸ
By faith Moses having been born was hidden three months by
when he was

τῶν πατέρων αὐτοῦ, διότι εἶδον ἀστεῖον τὸ παιδίον, καὶ
- parents ˜ his, because they saw beautiful ˜ the child, and
a

οὐκ ἐφοβήθησαν τὸ διάταγμα τοῦ βασιλέως. 24 Πίστει
[3]not [1]they [2]did [4]fear the edict of the king. By faith

Μωϋσῆς μέγας γενόμενος ἠρνήσατο λέγεσθαι υἱὸς
Moses [3]great [1]having [2]become refused to be called a son
when he was grown up

θυγατρὸς Φαραώ, 25 μᾶλλον ἑλόμενος συγκακουχεῖσθαι
of *the* daughter of Pharaoh, rather choosing to be mistreated with

τῷ λαῷ τοῦ Θεοῦ ἢ πρόσκαιρον ἔχειν ἁμαρτίας
the people - of God than [3]*the* [4]temporary [1]to [2]have [6]of [7]sin

ἀπόλαυσιν, 26 μείζονα πλοῦτον ἡγησάμενος τῶν
[5]pleasure, [6]greater [7]riches [1]regarding [8]*than* [9]the

Αἰγύπτου[h] θησαυρῶν τὸν ὀνειδισμὸν τοῦ Χριστοῦ,
[11]of [12]Egypt [10]treasures [2]the [3]reproach - [4]of [5]Christ,

ἀπέβλεπε γὰρ εἰς τὴν μισθαποδοσίαν.* 27 Πίστει
[14]he [15]was [16]looking [13]for to the reward. By faith

κατέλιπεν Αἴγυπτον, μὴ φοβηθεὶς τὸν θυμὸν τοῦ βασιλέως,
he left Egypt, not fearing the anger of the king,

τὸν γὰρ Ἀόρατον ὡς ὁρῶν ἐκαρτέρησε. 28 Πίστει
[6]the [1]for [7]Unseen [8]*One* [4]as [5]seeing [2]he [3]endured. By faith

πεποίηκε τὸ Πάσχα καὶ τὴν πρόσχυσιν τοῦ αἵματος,
he has made the Passover and the sprinkling of the blood,
kept

ἵνα μὴ ὁ ὀλοθρεύων τὰ πρωτότοκα θίγῃ
in order that [7]not [1]the [2]*one* [3]destroying [4]the [5]firstborn [6]should [8]touch
lest he who destroyed

αὐτῶν. 29 Πίστει διέβησαν τὴν Ἐρυθρὰν θάλασσαν ὡς
them. By faith they passed through the Red Sea as

διὰ ξηρᾶς, ἧς πεῖραν λαβόντες οἱ Αἰγύπτιοι
through dry *land,* which [4]an [5]attempt [3]taking [1]the [2]Egyptians
attempted to do and

κατεπόθησαν. 30 Πίστει τὰ τείχη Ἱεριχὼ ἔπεσε,
were swallowed. By faith the walls of Jericho fell,
drowned.

κυκλωθέντα ἐπὶ ἑπτὰ ἡμέρας.
having been encircled for seven days.

was dying, blessed each of the
sons of Joseph, and worshiped,
leaning on the top of his staff.
22 By faith Joseph, when he
was dying, made mention of the
departure of the children of Israel, and gave instructions concerning his bones.
23 By faith Moses, when he
was born, was hidden three
months by his parents, because
they saw *he was* a beautiful
child; and they were not afraid
of the king's command.
24 By faith Moses, when he
became of age, refused to be
called the son of Pharaoh's
daughter,
25 choosing rather to suffer
affliction with the people of God
than to enjoy the passing pleasures of sin,
26 esteeming the reproach of
Christ greater riches than the
treasures in Egypt; for he
looked to the reward.
27 By faith he forsook Egypt,
not fearing the wrath of the
king; for he endured as seeing
Him who is invisible.
28 By faith he kept the Passover and the sprinkling of
blood, lest he who destroyed
the firstborn should touch
them.
29 By faith they passed
through the Red Sea as by dry
land, whereas the Egyptians,
attempting *to do* so, were
drowned.
30 By faith the walls of Jericho
fell down after they were encircled for seven days.

---

[g]**(11:21)** Gen. 47:31 LXX
[h]**(11:26)** TR reads *εν Αιγυπτω, in Egypt.*

***(11:26)** *μισθαποδοσία (misthapodosia).* Noun literally meaning *payment of wages.* It is found only in Christian literature, and appears only in Hebrews in the NT. The word can have the positive sense of *reward,* particularly the eternal reward that awaits the believer (as here and in 10:35). *μισθαποδοσία* can also have the negative sense of *punishment, retribution* (Heb. 2:2). Cf. the cognate noun *μισθαποδοτής, rewarder* (Heb. 11:6); and *ἀνταπόδομα, repayment,* whether positive or negative (at Rom. 11:9).

31 By faith the harlot Rahab did not perish with those who did not believe, when she had received the spies with peace.
32 And what more shall I say? For the time would fail me to tell of Gideon and Barak and Samson and Jephthah, also *of* David and Samuel and the prophets:
33 who through faith subdued kingdoms, worked righteousness, obtained promises, stopped the mouths of lions,
34 quenched the violence of fire, escaped the edge of the sword, out of weakness were made strong, became valiant in battle, turned to flight the armies of the aliens.
35 Women received their dead raised to life again. Others were tortured, not accepting deliverance, that they might obtain a better resurrection.
36 Still others had trial of mockings and scourgings, yes, and of chains and imprisonment.
37 They were stoned, they were sawn in two, were tempted, were slain with the sword. They wandered about in sheepskins and goatskins, being destitute, afflicted, tormented—
38 of whom the world was not worthy. They wandered in deserts and mountains, *in* dens and caves of the earth.
39 And all these, having obtained a good testimony through faith, did not receive the promise,
40 God having provided some-

By Faith They Overcame

31 Πίστει Ῥαὰβ ἡ πόρνη οὐ συναπώλετο τοῖς
By faith Rahab the prostitute not ˜ did perish with the *ones*

ἀπειθήσασι, δεξαμένη τοὺς κατασκόπους μετ' εἰρήνης.
having disobeyed, receiving the spies with peace.
who disbelieved, when she received

32 Καὶ τί ἔτι λέγω? Ἐπιλείψει γάρ με διηγούμενον
And what more do I say? [4]will [5]fail [1]For [6]me [7]relating
should to tell

ὁ χρόνος περὶ Γεδεών, Βαράκ τε καὶ Σαμψὼν καὶ Ἰεφθάε,
[2]the [3]time about Gideon, Barak ˜ both and Samson and Jephthah,

Δαβίδ τε καὶ Σαμουὴλ καὶ τῶν προφητῶν, **33** οἳ διὰ
David ˜ both and Samuel and the prophets, who through

πίστεως κατηγωνίσαντο βασιλείας, εἰργάσαντο δικαιοσύνην,
faith overcame kingdoms, worked righteousness,

ἐπέτυχον ἐπαγγελιῶν, ἔφραξαν στόματα λεόντων, **34** ἔσβεσαν
obtained promises, stopped *the* mouths of lions, quenched

δύναμιν πυρός, ἔφυγον στόματα μαχαίρας, ἐνεδυναμώθησαν
the power of fire, escaped *the* mouths of *the* sword, were made strong
edge

ἀπὸ ἀσθενείας, ἐγενήθησαν ἰσχυροὶ ἐν πολέμῳ, παρεμβολὰς
from weakness, became mighty in battle, [4]*the* [5]armies

ἔκλιναν ἀλλοτρίων. **35** Ἔλαβον γυναῖκες ἐξ ἀναστάσεως
[1]turned [2]to [3]flight of foreigners. received ˜ Women [4]by [5]resurrection

τοὺς νεκροὺς αὐτῶν. Ἄλλοι δὲ ἐτυμπανίσθησαν, οὐ
- [2]dead [3]*ones* [1]their. others ˜ And were tortured, not

προσδεξάμενοι τὴν ἀπολύτρωσιν, ἵνα κρείττονος
accepting - deliverance, in order that [4]a [5]better

ἀναστάσεως τύχωσιν. **36** Ἕτεροι δὲ ἐμπαιγμῶν καὶ
[6]resurrection [1]they [2]might [3]obtain. others ˜ And [4]of [5]mockings [6]and
with

μαστίγων πεῖραν ἔλαβον, ἔτι δὲ δεσμῶν καὶ φυλακῆς.
[7]of [8]scourgings [2]a [3]trial [1]took, more ˜ and of bonds and of prison.
with had experiences, with with

37 Ἐλιθάσθησαν, ἐπρίσθησαν, ἐπειράσθησαν,[i] ἐν
They were stoned, they were sawn *in two,* they were tried, by

φόνῳ μαχαίρας ἀπέθανον. Περιῆλθον ἐν μηλωταῖς,
murder of sword they died. They went about in sheepskins,
being murdered with the

ἐν αἰγείοις δέρμασιν, ὑστερούμενοι, θλιβόμενοι,
in [2]of [3]a [4]goat [1]skins, being in want, being afflicted,
goatskins,

κακουχούμενοι, **38** ὧν οὐκ ἦν ἄξιος ὁ κόσμος, ἐν
being ill treated, of whom [4]not [3]was [5]worthy [1]the [2]world, [7]in

ἐρημίαις πλανώμενοι καὶ ὄρεσι καὶ σπηλαίοις καὶ ταῖς
[8]deserts [6]wandering and mountains and caves and the

ὀπαῖς τῆς γῆς.
holes of the earth.

We Also Are Heirs of Faith

39 Καὶ οὗτοι πάντες μαρτυρηθέντες διὰ τῆς πίστεως
And these all having obtained witness through the faith
their

οὐκ ἐκομίσαντο τὴν ἐπαγγελίαν, **40** τοῦ Θεοῦ περὶ ἡμῶν
not ˜ did receive the promise, - God [5]concerning [6]us

[i](11:37) NU omits *επειρασθησαν, they were tried.*

κρεῖττόν τι προβλεψαμένου ἵνα μὴ χωρὶς ἡμῶν
[4]better [3]something [1]having [2]provided so that [3]not [7]without [8]us

τελειωθῶσι.
[1]they [2]should [4]be [5]made [6]perfect.

Run the Race with Endurance

12 1 Τοιγαροῦν καὶ ἡμεῖς, τοσοῦτον ἔχοντες
So therefore also ˜ we, [2]so [3]great [1]having
since we have

περικείμενον ἡμῖν νέφος μαρτύρων, ὄγκον ἀποθέμενοι
[8]lying [9]around [10]us [4]a [5]cloud [6]of [7]witnesses, [14]impediment [11]laying [12]aside
let us lay

πάντα καὶ τὴν εὐπερίστατον ἁμαρτίαν, δι' ὑπομονῆς
[13]every and the easily ensnaring sin, through endurance

τρέχωμεν τὸν προκείμενον ἡμῖν ἀγῶνα, 2 ἀφορῶντες εἰς τὸν
let us run the [2]being [3]set [4]before [5]us [1]race, looking away to the
that is

τῆς πίστεως Ἀρχηγὸν καὶ Τελειωτὴν Ἰησοῦν, ὃς ἀντὶ
[4]of [5]the [6]faith [1]Originator [2]and [3]Perfecter Jesus, who because of
our

τῆς προκειμένης αὐτῷ χαρᾶς ὑπέμεινε σταυρόν, αἰσχύνης
the [2]being [3]set [4]before [5]Him [1]joy endured a cross, [2]*the* [3]shame

καταφρονήσας, ἐν δεξιᾷ τε τοῦ θρόνου τοῦ
[1]despising, [8]at [9]*the* [10]right [11]*hand* [4]and [12]of [13]the [14]throne -

Θεοῦ κεκάθικεν.
[15]of [16]God [5]has [6]sat [7]down.

Accept the Discipline of God

3 Ἀναλογίσασθε γὰρ τὸν τοιαύτην ὑπομεμενηκότα ὑπὸ
consider ˜ For the *One* [3]such [1]having [2]endured [5]by
Him who

τῶν ἁμαρτωλῶν εἰς αὐτὸν ἀντιλογίαν, ἵνα μὴ
- [6]sinners [7]against [8]Himself [4]hostility, in order that not ˜
lest

κάμητε ταῖς ψυχαῖς ὑμῶν ἐκλυόμενοι. 4 Οὔπω
you be weary - [3]in [5]souls [4]your [1]losing [2]courage. [3]not [4]yet

μέχρις αἵματος ἀντικατέστητε πρὸς τὴν ἁμαρτίαν
[6]until [7]blood [1]You [2]have [5]resisted [9]against - [10]sin
to the point of bloodshed

ἀνταγωνιζόμενοι. 5 Καὶ ἐκλέλησθε τῆς παρακλήσεως,
[8]struggling. And you have forgotten the exhortation,

ἥτις ὑμῖν ὡς υἱοῖς διαλέγεται,
which [2]to [3]you [4]as [5]to [6]sons [1]speaks,

«Υἱέ μου, μὴ ὀλιγώρει παιδείας* Κυρίου,
«son ˜ My, not ˜ do make light of *the* discipline of *the* Lord,

Μηδὲ ἐκλύου ὑπ' αὐτοῦ ἐλεγχόμενος·
Nor lose courage [3]by [4]Him [1]being [2]reproved;
when you are

6 Ὃν γὰρ ἀγαπᾷ Κύριος παιδεύει,
whom ˜ For [3]loves [1]*the* [2]Lord He disciplines,

Μαστιγοῖ δὲ πάντα υἱὸν ὃν παραδέχεται.» [a]
scourges ˜ And every son whom He receives.»

7 Εἰς[b] παιδείαν ὑπομένετε· ὡς υἱοῖς ὑμῖν
It is for discipline *that* you endure; [5]as [6]with [7]sons [4]you

προσφέρεται ὁ Θεός. Τίς γάρ ἐστιν υἱὸς ὃν οὐ
[2]deals [3]with - [1]God. what ˜ For [2]is [3]*there* [1]son whom [4]not

παιδεύει πατήρ? 8 Εἰ δὲ χωρίς ἐστε παιδείας ἧς
[3]does [5]discipline [1]a [2]father? if ˜ But [3]without [1]you [2]are discipline of which

thing better for us, that they should not be made perfect apart from us.

12 Therefore we also, since we are surrounded by so great a cloud of witnesses, let us lay aside every weight, and the sin which so easily ensnares *us*, and let us run with endurance the race that is set before us,

2 looking unto Jesus, the author and finisher of *our* faith, who for the joy that was set before Him endured the cross, despising the shame, and has sat down at the right hand of the throne of God.

3 For consider Him who endured such hostility from sinners against Himself, lest you become weary and discouraged in your souls.

4 You have not yet resisted to bloodshed, striving against sin.

5 And you have forgotten the exhortation which speaks to you as to sons:

"My son, do not despise
the chastening of the
LORD,
Nor be discouraged when
you are rebuked by
Him;

6 *For whom the LORD loves*
He chastens,
And scourges every son
whom He receives."

7 If you endure chastening, God deals with you as with sons; for what son is there whom a father does not chasten?

8 But if you are without chas-

---

[a](**12:5, 6**) Prov. 3:11, 12
[b](**12:7**) TR reads Εἰ, *If (you endure discipline).*

***(12:5)** παιδεία *(paideia).* Noun from παῖς, *child,* thus literally meaning *childrearing,* and from that *training, discipline* in general. The word may have the negative sense of discipline that is for *correction, chastisement* (as throughout Heb. 12). It can also have the positive sense of *training, instruction,* as in the training and admonition of children (Eph. 6:4; the idea of punishment or discipline may be included here), and of *training* in righteousness (2 Tim. 3:16). Cf. the cognate verb παιδεύω, *bring up, train, correct, chastise, discipline, educate* (as Acts 7:22; 22:3), even *scourge* (as Luke 23:16, 22).

tening, of which all have become partakers, then you are
illegitimate and not sons.
9 Furthermore, we have had
human fathers who corrected
us, and we paid *them* respect.
Shall we not much more readily
be in subjection to the Father of
spirits and live?
10 For they indeed for a few
days chastened *us* as seemed
best to them, but He for *our*
profit, that *we* may be partakers
of His holiness.
11 Now no chastening seems
to be joyful for the present, but
painful; nevertheless, afterward it yields the peaceable
fruit of righteousness to those
who have been trained by it.
12 Therefore strengthen the
hands which hang down, and
the feeble knees,
13 and make straight paths for
your feet, so that what is lame
may not be *dislocated,* but
rather be healed.
14 Pursue peace with all *people,* and holiness, without which
no one will see the Lord:
15 looking carefully lest anyone fall short of the grace of
God; lest any root of bitterness
springing up cause trouble, and
by this many become defiled;
16 lest there *be* any fornicator
or profane person like Esau,
who for one morsel of food sold
his birthright.
17 For you know that afterward, when he wanted to in-

μέτοχοι γεγόνασι πάντες, ἄρα νόθοι ἐστε καὶ οὐχ
[4]sharers [2]have [3]become [1]all, then [3]illegitimate [1]you [2]are and not

υἱοί. **9** Εἶτα τοὺς μὲν τῆς σαρκὸς ἡμῶν πατέρας
sons. Furthermore - - [5]of [6]the [7]flesh [3]our [4]fathers

εἴχομεν παιδευτὰς καὶ ἐνετρεπόμεθα. Οὐ πολλῷ μᾶλλον
[1]we [2]had *as* correctors and we respected *them.* [3]not [4]by [5]much [6]more
have had

ὑποταγησόμεθα τῷ Πατρὶ τῶν πνευμάτων καὶ ζήσομεν?
[1]Shall [2]we [7]be [8]subjected to the Father - of spirits and we shall live?

10 Οἱ μὲν γὰρ πρὸς ὀλίγας ἡμέρας κατὰ
[2]the [3]*ones* [4]indeed [1]For for a few days [4]according [5]to
they as

τὸ δοκοῦν αὐτοῖς ἐπαίδευον, ὁ δὲ
[6]the [7]*thing* [8]seeming [9]*good* [10]to [11]them [1]were [2]disciplining [3]*us,* [13]the [14]*One* [12]but
seemed best He

ἐπὶ τὸ συμφέρον εἰς τὸ μεταλαβεῖν τῆς ἁγιότητος αὐτοῦ.
for the profit for - to partake in - holiness ˜ His.
our in order

11 Πᾶσα δὲ παιδεία πρὸς μὲν τὸ παρὸν οὐ δοκεῖ χαρᾶς
all ˜ Now discipline for - the present not ˜ does seem [3]of [4]joy
joyful

εἶναι ἀλλὰ λύπης, ὕστερον δὲ καρπὸν εἰρηνικὸν τοῖς
[1]to [2]be but of grief, later ˜ but [4]*the* [6]fruit [5]peaceable [9]to [10]the [11]*ones*
painful, those who

δι' αὐτῆς γεγυμνασμένοις ἀποδίδωσι δικαιοσύνης.
[15]by [16]it [12]having [13]been [14]trained [1]it [2]gives [3]out [7]of [8]righteousness.
have yields

Renew Your Spiritual Vitality

12 Διὸ τὰς παρειμένας χεῖρας καὶ τὰ
Therefore [2]the [4]having [5]been [6]weakened [3]hands [7]and [8]the
which are

παραλελυμένα γόνατα ἀνορθώσατε, **13** καὶ τροχιὰς
[10]having [11]been [12]disabled [9]knees [1]straighten, and [3]paths
which are strengthen,

ὀρθὰς ποιήσατε τοῖς ποσὶν ὑμῶν, ἵνα μὴ τὸ χωλὸν
[2]straight [1]make - for feet ˜ your, so that [4]not [1]the [2]lame

ἐκτραπῇ, ἰαθῇ δὲ μᾶλλον.
[3]may [5]be [6]turned [7]aside, [10]may [11]be [12]healed [8]but [9]rather.

14 Εἰρήνην διώκετε μετὰ πάντων, καὶ τὸν ἁγιασμόν, οὗ
peace ˜ Pursue with all *people,* and the holiness, which ˜

χωρὶς οὐδεὶς ὄψεται τὸν Κύριον, **15** ἐπισκοποῦντες μή τις
without no one will see the Lord, taking care not anyone
lest

ὑστερῶν ἀπὸ τῆς χάριτος τοῦ Θεοῦ, μή τις ῥίζα πικρίας ἄνω
failing from the grace - of God, not any root of bitterness up ˜
fall lest

φύουσα ἐνοχλῇ καὶ διὰ ταύτης μιανθῶσι πολλοί, **16** μή
growing cause trouble and through this [2]be [3]defiled [1]many, not
lest

τις πόρνος ἢ βέβηλος ὡς Ἠσαῦ, ὃς
any fornicator or profane *person* as Esau, who
sexually immoral person

ἀντὶ βρώσεως μιᾶς ἀπέδοτο τὰ πρωτοτόκια αὐτοῦ.
in place of eating ˜ one gave up - birthright ˜ his.
in exchange for one meal

17 Ἴστε γὰρ ὅτι καὶ μετέπειτα θέλων
[2]you [3]know [1]For that indeed afterward wishing
when he wanted

κληρονομῆσαι τὴν εὐλογίαν ἀπεδοκιμάσθη, μετανοίας γὰρ
to inherit the blessing he was rejected, [8]*for* [9]repentance [1]for

τόπον οὐχ εὗρε, καίπερ μετὰ δακρύων ἐκζητήσας
[6]a [7]place [4]not [2]he [3]did [5]find, though [5]with [6]tears [1]having [2]sought [4]out
he

αὐτήν.
[3]it.

The Glorious Company

18 Οὐ γὰρ προσεληλύθατε ψηλαφωμένῳ ὄρει[c] καὶ
[4]not [1]For [2]you [3]have [5]come [6]to [9]being [10]touched [7]a [8]mountain and
that may be

κεκαυμένῳ πυρὶ καὶ γνόφῳ καὶ σκότῳ[d] καὶ
having been burned with fire and to blackness and to darkness and
that

θυέλλῃ 19 καὶ σάλπιγγος ἤχῳ καὶ φωνῇ
to a whirlwind and [4]of [5]a [6]trumpet [1]to [2]a [3]sound and to a voice

ῥημάτων, ἧς οἱ ἀκούσαντες παρῃτήσαντο μὴ
of words, which the *ones* having heard requested not
those who heard begged that

προστεθῆναι αὐτοῖς λόγον. 20 Οὐκ ἔφερον γὰρ
to be added to them a word. [4]not [2]they [3]were [5]bearing [1]For
no further word be spoken to them.

τὸ διαστελλόμενον, «Κἂν θηρίον θίγῃ τοῦ ὄρους,
the *thing* being commanded «If even a beast touches the mountain,
what was

λιθοβοληθήσεται.»[e] 21 Καί, οὕτω φοβερὸν ἦν τὸ
it shall be stoned.» And, so fearful was the *thing*
the

φανταζόμενον, Μωϋσῆς εἶπεν, «Ἔκφοβός εἰμι καὶ
appearing, Moses said, «[3]terrified [1]I [2]am and
spectacle,

ἔντρομος.»[f] 22 Ἀλλὰ προσεληλύθατε Σιὼν Ὄρει καὶ
trembling.» But you have come to Zion to *the* Mountain and

πόλει Θεοῦ ζῶντος, Ἱερουσαλὴμ ἐπουρανίῳ, καὶ μυριάσιν
city of [3]God [1]*the* [2]living, to a Jerusalem ˜ heavenly, and to myriads
thousands

ἀγγέλων, 23 πανηγύρει καὶ ἐκκλησίᾳ πρωτοτόκων ἐν
of angels, to a festal assembly and church of firstborn *ones* [4]in

οὐρανοῖς ἀπογεγραμμένων, καὶ Κριτῇ Θεῷ πάντων,
[5]*the* [6]heavens [1]having [2]been [3]enrolled, and [3]*the* [4]Judge [1]to [2]God of all *people,*

καὶ πνεύμασι δικαίων τετελειωμένων,* 24 καὶ
and to spirits of just *people* having been made perfect, and

διαθήκης νέας Μεσίτῃ Ἰησοῦ, καὶ αἵματι
[5]of [6]a [8]covenant [7]new [3]*the* [4]Mediator [1]to [2]Jesus, and to *the* blood

ῥαντισμοῦ κρεῖττον λαλοῦντι παρὰ τὸ Ἄβελ.
of sprinkling [2]a [3]better [4]*thing* [1]speaking than the *blood* of Abel.
which speaks better things

Final Warning: Hear the Heavenly Voice

25 Βλέπετε μὴ παραιτήσησθε τὸν λαλοῦντα. Εἰ γὰρ
See to it *that* [3]not [1]you [2]do refuse the *One* speaking. if ˜ For
Him who speaks.

ἐκεῖνοι οὐκ ἔφυγον, τὸν ἐπὶ γῆς παραιτησάμενοι
those *ones* not ˜ did escape, [3]the [4]*One* [7]on [8]earth [1]having [2]refused
they Him

χρηματίζοντα, πολλῷ μᾶλλον ἡμεῖς οἱ τὸν
[5]warning [6]*them,* how much more we the *ones* [4]the [5]*One* [6]*warning*
who warned who turn away from

herit the blessing, he was
rejected, for he found no place
for repentance, though he
sought it diligently with tears.
18 For you have not come to
the mountain that may be
touched and that burned with
fire, and to blackness and darkness and tempest,
19 and the sound of a trumpet
and the voice of words, so that
those who heard *it* begged that
the word should not be spoken
to them anymore.
20 (For they could not endure
what was commanded: *"And if
so much as a beast touches the
mountain, it shall be stoned or
shot with an arrow."*
21 And so terrifying was the
sight *that* Moses said, *"I am exceedingly afraid* and trembling.")
22 But you have come to
Mount Zion and to the city of
the living God, the heavenly Jerusalem, to an innumerable
company of angels,
23 to the general assembly
and church of the firstborn *who
are* registered in heaven, to
God the Judge of all, to the spirits of just men made perfect,
24 to Jesus the Mediator of
the new covenant, and to the
blood of sprinkling that speaks
better things than *that of* Abel.
25 See that you do not refuse
Him who speaks. For if they did
not escape who refused Him
who spoke on earth, much
more *shall we not escape* if we

---

[c](**12:18**) NU omits ορει, *a mountain.*
[d](**12:18**) NU reads ζοφω, *gloom.* [e](**12:20**) Ex. 19:12, 13; TR adds η βολιδι κατατοξευθησεται, *or shot with an arrow.*
[f](**12:21**) Deut. 9:19

***(12:23)** τελειόω *(teleioō).* Verb, common in the NT, from the root τέλος, *end, goal,* thus meaning *bring to (the intended) end/goal, complete, finish, make perfect.* The basic idea is of bringing something or someone to the place where it/he is in full measure what its/his designer intended. Here, then, the saints in the afterlife have arrived at that goal and are thus *perfected.* The verb may mean *complete* or *finish* a task (as John 4:34), *complete* or *perfect* a quality (1 John 2:5) or person (Heb. 10:1). Even Jesus as the God-*man* has been

turn away from Him who *speaks* from heaven,
26 whose voice then shook the earth; but now He has promised, saying, *"Yet once more I shake not only the earth, but also heaven."*
27 Now this, *"Yet once more,"* indicates the removal of those things that are being shaken, as of things that are made, that the things which cannot be shaken may remain.
28 Therefore, since we are receiving a kingdom which cannot be shaken, let us have grace, by which we may serve God acceptably with reverence and godly fear.
29 For our God *is* a consuming fire.

13 Let brotherly love continue.
2 Do not forget to entertain strangers, for by so *doing* some have unwittingly entertained angels.
3 Remember the prisoners as if chained with them — those who are mistreated — since you yourselves are in the body also.
4 Marriage *is* honorable among all, and the bed undefiled; but fornicators and adulterers God will judge.
5 *Let your* conduct *be* without covetousness; *be* content with such things as you have. For He Himself has said, *"I will never leave you nor forsake you."*
6 So we may boldly say:

ἀπ' οὐρανῶν ἀποστρεφόμενοι· **26** οὗ ἡ φωνὴ τὴν γῆν
[7]from [8]heavens [1]turning [2]away [3]from; whose - voice [3]the [4]earth
Him who warns from heaven;

ἐσάλευσε τότε, νῦν δὲ ἐπήγγελται λέγων, «Ἔτι ἅπαξ
[2]shook [1]then, now ˜ but He has promised saying, «Yet once more

ἐγὼ σείω[g] οὐ μόνον τὴν γῆν ἀλλὰ καὶ τὸν οὐρανόν.»[h]
I shake not only the earth but also the heaven.»

27 Τὸ δὲ "ἔτι ἅπαξ" δηλοῖ τῶν
[2]the [3]*phrase* [1]Now "yet once more" makes clear [3]of [4]the [5]*things*

σαλευομένων τὴν μετάθεσιν ὡς πεποιημένων, ἵνα
[6]being [7]shaken [1]the [2]removal as of *things* having been made, so that

μείνῃ τὰ μὴ σαλευόμενα. **28** Διὸ
[6]may [7]remain [1]the [2]*things* [3]not [4]being [5]shaken. Therefore
which cannot be

βασιλείαν ἀσάλευτον παραλαμβάνοντες ἔχωμεν χάριν,
[2]a(n) [4]kingdom [3]unshakable [1]receiving let us have grace,
since we are receiving

δι' ἧς λατρεύομεν[i] εὐαρέστως τῷ Θεῷ μετὰ αἰδοῦς[j]
through which we serve acceptably ˜ - God with reverence

καὶ εὐλαβείας. **29** Καὶ γὰρ ὁ Θεὸς ἡμῶν πῦρ
and godly fear. indeed ˜ For - God ˜ our *is* a fire ˜

καταναλίσκον.
consuming.

Concluding Moral Instructions

13 **1** Ἡ φιλαδελφία μενέτω. **2** Τῆς φιλοξενίας μὴ
- [2]brotherly [3]love [1]Let [4]remain. - [4]hospitality [2]not

ἐπιλανθάνεσθε, διὰ ταύτης γὰρ ἔλαθόν
[1]Do [3]forget, [6]through [7]this [5]for [9]were [10]hidden [11]*from* [12]*themselves*
without knowing it

τινες ξενίσαντες ἀγγέλους. **3** Μιμνῄσκεσθε τῶν δεσμίων
[8]some having entertained angels. Remember the prisoners
have

ὡς συνδεδεμένοι, τῶν κακουχουμένων ὡς καὶ
as having been bound with *them*, the *ones* being ill treated as also
as if those who are you

αὐτοὶ ὄντες ἐν σώματι. **4** Τίμιος ὁ γάμος ἐν πᾶσι
yourselves being in *the* body. [3]honorable - [1]Marriage [2]*is* among all
yourselves are also

καὶ ἡ κοίτη ἀμίαντος, πόρνους δὲ καὶ μοιχοὺς
and the bed undefiled, fornicators ˜ but and adulterers
sexually immoral persons

κρινεῖ ὁ Θεός. **5** Ἀφιλάργυρος ὁ τρόπος,
[2]will [3]judge - [1]God. [7]not [8]loving [9]money - [1]*Let* [2]*your* [3]way [4]of [5]life [6]*be*,
without covetousness

ἀρκούμενοι τοῖς παροῦσιν. Αὐτὸς γὰρ εἴρηκεν,
being satisfied with the *things* being present. [3]Himself [1]For [2]He has said,
what you have.

«Οὐ μή σε ἀνῶ,
«Not not [4]you [1]shall [2]I [3]desert,
«By no means

Οὐδ' οὐ μή σε ἐγκαταλείπω»·[a]
Nor not not [4]you [1]shall [2]I [3]forsake»;
in any way

6 ὥστε θαρροῦντας ἡμᾶς λέγειν,
so that being confident us to say,
we may

[g](12:26) NU reads σεισω, *shall shake.*
[h](12:26) Hag. 2:6
[i](12:28) NU, TR read λατρευωμεν, *we may serve.*
[j](12:28) NU reads δεους, *awe.* [a](13:5) Deut. 31:6, 8; Josh. 1:5

thus "perfected" (Heb. 2:10). Cf. the cognate nouns τελειότης and τελείωσις, either of which can mean *perfection, completeness, maturity, fulfillment;* and see the cognate adjective τέλειος at 1 Cor. 14:20.

«Κύριος ἐμοὶ βοηθός,
«*The* Lord *is* to me a helper,
my

Καὶ οὐ φοβηθήσομαι·
And [3]not [1]I [2]will fear;

Τί ποιήσει μοι ἄνθρωπος?» [b]
What will [2]do [3]to [4]me [1]man?»
can

Concluding Religious Instructions

7 Μνημονεύετε τῶν ἡγουμένων ὑμῶν, οἵτινες ἐλάλησαν
Remember - leaders ~ your, who spoke

ὑμῖν τὸν λόγον τοῦ Θεοῦ, ὧν ἀναθεωροῦντες τὴν ἔκβασιν
to you the word - of God, of whom looking at the result
considering

τῆς ἀναστροφῆς μιμεῖσθε τὴν πίστιν. **8** Ἰησοῦς Χριστὸς
of the conduct imitate the faith. Jesus Christ
their their

χθὲς καὶ σήμερον ὁ αὐτός, καὶ εἰς τοὺς αἰῶνας.
[4]yesterday [5]and [6]today [1]*is* [2]the [3]same, and to the ages.
forever.

9 Διδαχαῖς ποικίλαις καὶ ξέναις μὴ παραφέρεσθε. [c]
[6]with [10]teachings [7]various [8]and [9]strange [2]not [1]Do [3]be [4]carried [5]away.

Καλὸν γὰρ χάριτι βεβαιοῦσθαι τὴν καρδίαν,
[12]*it* [13]*is* [14]good [11]For [21]by [22]grace [18]to [19]be [20]established [15]*for* [16]the [17]heart,

οὐ βρώμασιν, ἐν οἷς οὐκ ὠφελήθησαν οἱ
not by foods, by which [6]not [5]were [7]profited [1]the [2]*ones*

περιπατήσαντες. **10** Ἔχομεν θυσιαστήριον* ἐξ οὗ φαγεῖν
[3]having [4]walked. We have an altar from which [11]to [12]eat
lived.

οὐκ ἔχουσιν ἐξουσίαν οἱ τῇ σκηνῇ λατρεύοντες.
[8]not [7]do [9]have [10]right [1]the [2]*ones* [4]in [5]the [6]tabernacle [3]serving.
those who serve.

11 Ὧν γὰρ εἰσφέρεται ζῴων τὸ αἷμα περὶ
[2]of [3]which [1]For [7]is [8]brought [9]in [4]animals [5]the [6]blood concerning

ἁμαρτίας εἰς τὰ Ἅγια διὰ τοῦ ἀρχιερέως, τούτων τὰ
sin into the Holies by the high priest, [3]of [4]these [5]*animals* [1]the

σώματα κατακαίεται ἔξω τῆς παρεμβολῆς. **12** Διὸ καὶ
[2]bodies are burned up outside the camp. Therefore also ~

Ἰησοῦς, ἵνα ἁγιάσῃ διὰ τοῦ ἰδίου αἵματος τὸν
Jesus, so that He might sanctify [3]through - [4]His [5]own [6]blood [1]the

λαόν, ἔξω τῆς πύλης ἔπαθε. **13** Τοίνυν ἐξερχώμεθα πρὸς
[2]people, [8]outside [9]the [10]gate [7]suffered. So let us go out to

αὐτὸν ἔξω τῆς παρεμβολῆς, τὸν ὀνειδισμὸν αὐτοῦ φέροντες.
Him outside the camp, - [3]reproach [2]His [1]bearing.

14 Οὐ γὰρ ἔχομεν ὧδε μένουσαν πόλιν, ἀλλὰ τὴν
[4]not [1]For [2]we [3]do [5]have here a continuing city, but [3]the [4]*one*
permanent

μέλλουσαν ἐπιζητοῦμεν. **15** Δι' αὐτοῦ οὖν
[5]coming [1]we [2]seek. [2]through [3]Him [1]Therefore
to come

ἀναφέρωμεν θυσίαν αἰνέσεως διὰ παντὸς τῷ Θεῷ, τοῦτ'
let us offer up a sacrifice of praise through all - to God, this
always that

ἔστι, καρπὸν χειλέων ὁμολογούντων τῷ ὀνόματι αὐτοῦ. **16** Τῆς
is, *the* fruit of lips confessing - to name ~ His. [5]the

δὲ εὐποιΐας καὶ κοινωνίας μὴ ἐπιλανθάνεσθε, τοιαύταις
[1]But [6]doing [7]of [8]good [9]and [10]generosity [3]not [2]do [4]forget, [12]with [13]such

"The LORD *is my helper;*
I will not fear.
What can man do to me?"

7 Remember those who rule over you, who have spoken the word of God to you, whose faith follow, considering the outcome of *their* conduct.
8 Jesus Christ *is* the same yesterday, today, and forever.
9 Do not be carried about with various and strange doctrines. For *it is* good that the heart be established by grace, not with foods which have not profited those who have been occupied with them.
10 We have an altar from which those who serve the tabernacle have no right to eat.
11 For the bodies of those animals, whose blood is brought into the sanctuary by the high priest for sin, are burned outside the camp.
12 Therefore Jesus also, that He might sanctify the people with His own blood, suffered outside the gate.
13 Therefore let us go forth to Him, outside the camp, bearing His reproach.
14 For here we have no continuing city, but we seek the one to come.
15 Therefore by Him let us continually offer the sacrifice of praise to God, that is, the fruit of *our* lips, giving thanks to His name.
16 But do not forget to do good and to share, for with

---

[b]**(13:6)** Ps. 118:6
[c]**(13:9)** TR reads *περιφεφερεσθε, Do (not) be carried about.*

***(13:10)** *θυσιαστήριον (thysiastērion).* Noun from *θυσία, sacrifice, offering,* thus literally meaning the *place of sacrifice, altar.* The word is used variously (but always positively) of the altar of burnt offering (as Matt. 5:23f), the altar of incense (Luke 1:11), the altar in heaven (as Rev. 6:9), one built by Abraham (James 2:21), and the general location of the altar (Rev. 14:18). The figurative use here in Heb. 13:10 is difficult to interpret. Scholars have offered various opinions regarding the author's specific identification of the "altar" that include Christ's cross; Christ's sacrifice (by metonymy); the communion table (cf. 1 Cor. 10:12, 18); and

such sacrifices God is well
pleased.
17 Obey those who rule over
you, and be submissive, for
they watch out for your souls,
as those who must give account. Let them do so with joy
and not with grief, for that
would be unprofitable for you.
18 Pray for us; for we are
confident that we have a good
conscience, in all things desiring to live honorably.
19 But I especially urge *you* to
do this, that I may be restored
to you the sooner.
20 Now may the God of peace
who brought up our Lord Jesus
from the dead, that great Shepherd of the sheep, through the
blood of the everlasting covenant,
21 make you complete in every good work to do His will,
working in you what is well
pleasing in His sight, through
Jesus Christ, to whom *be* glory
forever and ever. Amen.
22 And I appeal to you, brethren, bear with the word of exhortation, for I have written to
you in few words.
23 Know that *our* brother
Timothy has been set free,
with whom I shall see you if he
comes shortly.
24 Greet all those who rule
over you, and all the saints.
Those from Italy greet you.

γὰρ θυσίαις εὐαρεστεῖται ὁ Θεός.
[11]for sacrifices [2]is [3]pleased - [1]God.

17 Πείθεσθε τοῖς ἡγουμένοις ὑμῶν καὶ ὑπείκετε, αὐτοὶ
Obey - leaders ˜ your and yield to *them*, they ˜
submit

γὰρ ἀγρυπνοῦσιν ὑπὲρ τῶν ψυχῶν ὑμῶν ὡς λόγον
for keep watch over - souls ˜ your as [2]an [3]account

ἀποδώσοντες, ἵνα μετὰ χαρᾶς τοῦτο ποιῶσι καὶ μὴ
[1]giving, in order that [5]with [6]joy [4]this [1]they [2]may [3]do and not

στενάζοντες, ἀλυσιτελὲς γὰρ ὑμῖν τοῦτο.
groaning, [5]unprofitable [1]for [6]for [7]you [2]this [3]*would* [4]*be*.

The Writer Requests Prayer

18 Προσεύχεσθε περὶ ἡμῶν. Πεποίθαμεν γὰρ ὅτι
Pray concerning us. [2]we [3]are [4]persuaded [1]For that

καλὴν συνείδησιν ἔχομεν, ἐν πᾶσι καλῶς θέλοντες
[3]a [4]good [5]conscience [1]we [2]have, in all *things* [4]well [1]desiring
commendably

ἀναστρέφεσθαι. **19** Περισσοτέρως δὲ παρακαλῶ τοῦτο
[2]to [3]live. [2]even [3]more [1]But I urge *you* [3]this

ποιῆσαι, ἵνα τάχιον ἀποκατασταθῶ ὑμῖν.
[1]to [2]do, in order that [7]more [8]quickly [1]I [2]may [3]be [4]restored [5]to [6]you.

Benediction, Final Exhortation, and Farewell

20 Ὁ δὲ Θεὸς τῆς εἰρήνης, ὁ ἀναγαγὼν
[3]the [1]Now [2]*may* God - of peace, the *One* having brought up
who

ἐκ νεκρῶν τὸν Ποιμένα τῶν προβάτων τὸν μέγαν ἐν
[4]from [5]*the* [6]dead [7]the [9]Shepherd [10]of [11]the [12]sheep - [8]great [13]by

αἵματι διαθήκης αἰωνίου, τὸν Κύριον ἡμῶν Ἰησοῦν,
[14]*the* [15]blood [16]of [17]a(n) [19]covenant [18]eternal, - [2]Lord [1]our [3]Jesus,

21 καταρτίσαι ὑμᾶς ἐν παντὶ ἔργῳ[d] ἀγαθῷ εἰς τὸ
make complete ˜ you in every work ˜ good for -
in order

ποιῆσαι τὸ θέλημα αὐτοῦ, ποιῶν ἐν ὑμῖν[e] τὸ εὐάρεστον
to do - will ˜ His, doing in you the *thing* pleasing
working

ἐνώπιον αὐτοῦ, διὰ Ἰησοῦ Χριστοῦ, ᾧ ἡ δόξα εἰς
before Him, through Jesus Christ, to whom *be* the glory to
forever

τοὺς αἰῶνας τῶν αἰώνων. Ἀμήν.
the ages of the ages. Amen.
and ever. So be it.

22 Παρακαλῶ δὲ ὑμᾶς, ἀδελφοί, ἀνέχεσθε τοῦ λόγου τῆς
[2]I [3]appeal [4]to [1]And you, brothers, bear with the word -

παρακλήσεως, καὶ γὰρ διὰ βραχέων ἐπέστειλα ὑμῖν.
of exhortation, indeed ˜ for through few *words* I wrote to you.
briefly

23 Γινώσκετε τὸν ἀδελφὸν[f] Τιμόθεον ἀπολελυμένον, μεθ'
Know *that* the brother Timothy having been released, with
our has

οὗ, ἐὰν τάχιον ἔρχηται, ὄψομαι ὑμᾶς.
whom, if [3]quickly [1]he [2]comes, I will see you.

24 Ἀσπάσασθε πάντας τοὺς ἡγουμένους ὑμῶν καὶ πάντας
Greet all - leaders ˜ your and all

τοὺς ἁγίους. Ἀσπάζονται ὑμᾶς οἱ ἀπὸ τῆς Ἰταλίας.
the saints. [4]greet [5]you [1]The [2]*ones* [3]from - [4]Italy.
Those

---

[d](**13:21**) NU omits εργω, *work*, thus *in every good (thing)*. [e](**13:21**) NU reads ημιν, *us*. [f](**13:23**) NU adds ημων, *our*.

---

the altar in heaven. Cf. *βωμός, altar,* used in the NT (as in the LXX) only of a disapproved altar (Acts 17:23).

25 Ἡ χάρις μετὰ πάντων ὑμῶν. Ἀμήν.
- Grace *be* with all ~ you. Amen.
So be it.

25 Grace *be* with you all. Amen.

The Epistle of
JAMES

1 James, a bondservant of
God and of the Lord Jesus
Christ,

To the twelve tribes which
are scattered abroad:

Greetings.

2 My brethren, count it all
joy when you fall into various
trials,
3 knowing that the testing of
your faith produces patience.
4 But let patience have *its*
perfect work, that you may be
perfect and complete, lacking
nothing.
5 If any of you lacks wisdom,
let him ask of God, who gives
to all liberally and without reproach, and it will be given to
him.
6 But let him ask in faith,
with no doubting, for he who
doubts is like a wave of the sea
driven and tossed by the wind.
7 For let not that man suppose that he will receive anything from the Lord;
8 *he is* a double-minded man,
unstable in all his ways.
9 Let the lowly brother glory
in his exaltation,

ΙΑΚΩΒΟΥ
OF JAMES

James Greets the Twelve Tribes

1 1 Ἰάκωβος, Θεοῦ καὶ Κυρίου Ἰησοῦ Χριστοῦ
James, [3]of [4]God [5]and [6]of [7]*the* [8]Lord [9]Jesus [10]Christ
δοῦλος,
[1]a [2]bondservant,
slave,

Ταῖς δώδεκα φυλαῖς ταῖς ἐν τῇ Διασπορᾷ·
To the twelve tribes the *ones* in the Dispersion:
which are

Χαίρειν.
Greetings.

Profiting from Trials

2 Πᾶσαν χαρὰν ἡγήσασθε, ἀδελφοί μου, ὅταν πειρασμοῖς
[3]all [4]joy [1]Count [2]*it,* brothers ˜ my, when [5]trials
περιπέσητε ποικίλοις, 3 γινώσκοντες ὅτι τὸ δοκίμιον ὑμῶν
[1]you [2]fall [3]into [4]various, knowing that the testing of your
τῆς πίστεως κατεργάζεται ὑπομονήν. 4 Ἡ δὲ ὑπομονὴ
- faith produces endurance. - But [2]endurance
ἔργον τέλειον ἐχέτω, ἵνα ἦτε τέλειοι καὶ ὁλόκληροι,
[4]*its* [6]work [5]perfect [1]let [3]have, that you might be mature and complete,
ἐν μηδενὶ λειπόμενοι.
[2]in [3]nothing [1]lacking.
5 Εἰ δέ τις ὑμῶν λείπεται σοφίας, αἰτείτω παρὰ τοῦ
if ˜ But any of you lacks wisdom, let him ask from [2]the [3]*One*
who
διδόντος Θεοῦ πᾶσιν ἁπλῶς καὶ οὐκ ὀνειδίζοντος, καὶ
[4]giving [1]God to all generously and not reproaching, and
gives does not reproach,
δοθήσεται αὐτῷ. 6 Αἰτείτω δὲ ἐν πίστει, μηδὲν
it will be given to him. [2]let [3]him [4]ask [1]But in faith, nothing ˜
διακρινόμενος, ὁ γὰρ διακρινόμενος ἔοικε κλύδωνι
doubting, [2]the [3]*one* [1]for doubting is like a wave
for he who doubts
θαλάσσης ἀνεμιζομένῳ καὶ ῥιπιζομένῳ. 7 Μὴ γὰρ
of *the* sea being moved by wind and being blown *about.* [3]not [1]For
driven and tossed by the wind.
οἰέσθω ὁ ἄνθρωπος ἐκεῖνος ὅτι λήψεταί τι παρὰ
[2]let [6]suppose - [5]man [4]that that he will receive anything from
τοῦ Κυρίου. 8 Ἀνὴρ δίψυχος ἀκατάστατος ἐν πάσαις
the Lord. *He is* a man ˜ double-minded unstable in all
ταῖς ὁδοῖς αὐτοῦ.
- ways ˜ his.

The Perspective of Rich and Poor

9 Καυχάσθω δὲ ὁ ἀδελφὸς ὁ ταπεινὸς ἐν τῷ ὕψει
[2]let [6]boast [1]Now [3]the [5]brother - [4]lowly in - height ˜
high position

αὐτοῦ, 10 ὁ δὲ πλούσιος ἐν τῇ ταπεινώσει αὐτοῦ, ὅτι ὡς
his, the ˜ but rich *man* in - humiliation ˜ his, because as

ἄνθος χόρτου παρελεύσεται. 11 Ἀνέτειλε γὰρ ὁ ἥλιος
a flower of wild grass he will pass away. [4]arose [1]For [2]the [3]sun

σὺν τῷ καύσωνι καὶ ἐξήρανε τὸν χόρτον, καὶ τὸ ἄνθος αὐτοῦ
with - burning heat and withered the grass, and - flower ˜ its

ἐξέπεσε, καὶ ἡ εὐπρέπεια τοῦ προσώπου αὐτοῦ ἀπώλετο.
fell off, and the beauty - of face ˜ its perished.

Οὕτω καὶ ὁ πλούσιος ἐν ταῖς πορείαις αὐτοῦ μαρανθήσεται.
So [4]also [1]the [2]rich [3]*man* [8]in - [10]journeys [9]his [5]will [6]fade [7]away.
pursuits

Loving God under Trials

12 Μακάριος ἀνὴρ ὃς ὑπομένει πειρασμόν, ὅτι
Blessed *is the* man who endures temptation, because

δόκιμος γενόμενος λήψεται τὸν στέφανον τῆς ζωῆς ὃν
approved ˜ becoming he will receive the crown - of life which
when he is approved,

ἐπηγγείλατο ὁ Κύριος[a] τοῖς ἀγαπῶσιν αὐτόν.
[3]promised [1]the [2]Lord to the *ones* loving Him.
those who love

13 Μηδεὶς πειραζόμενος λεγέτω ὅτι "Ἀπὸ Θεοῦ πειράζομαι,"
[2]no [3]one [4]being [5]tempted [1]Let [6]say - "[4]by [5]God [1]I [2]am [3]tempted,"
when he is

ὁ γὰρ Θεὸς ἀπείραστός ἐστι κακῶν, πειράζει δὲ
- for God [2]without [3]temptation [1]is of evil, [2]He [4]tempts [1]and
cannot be tempted by

αὐτὸς οὐδένα. 14 Ἕκαστος δὲ πειράζεται, ὑπὸ τῆς ἰδίας
[3]Himself no one. [2]each [3]*one* [1]But is tempted, by - his own

ἐπιθυμίας ἐξελκόμενος καὶ δελεαζόμενος. 15 Εἶτα ἡ
lusts being drawn away and being enticed. Then -
when he is enticed.

ἐπιθυμία συλλαβοῦσα τίκτει ἁμαρτίαν, ἡ δὲ ἁμαρτία
lust conceiving gives birth *to* sin, - and sin
when it conceives

ἀποτελεσθεῖσα ἀποκύει θάνατον.
coming to completion bears death.
when it is full-grown

16 Μὴ πλανᾶσθε, ἀδελφοί μου ἀγαπητοί. 17 Πᾶσα
not ˜ Do be deceived, [3]brothers [1]my [2]beloved. Every

δόσις ἀγαθὴ καὶ πᾶν δώρημα τέλειον ἄνωθέν ἐστι,
gift ˜ good and every gift ˜ perfect [2]from [3]above [1]is,

καταβαῖνον ἀπὸ τοῦ Πατρὸς τῶν φώτων, παρ' ᾧ οὐκ ἔνι
coming down from the Father - of lights, with whom [3]no [1]there [2]is
and comes

παραλλαγὴ ἢ τροπῆς* ἀποσκίασμα. 18 Βουληθεὶς
variation or [2]of [3]turning [1]shadow. Exercising *His* will

ἀπεκύησεν ἡμᾶς λόγῳ ἀληθείας, εἰς τὸ εἶναι
He gave birth to us by *the* word of truth, for - [2]to [3]be
in order that we

ἡμᾶς ἀπαρχήν τινα τῶν αὐτοῦ κτισμάτων.
[1]us [7]firstfruits [4]a [5]kind [6]of - of His creatures.
might be

The Qualities Needed in Trials

19 Ὥστε,[b] ἀδελφοί μου ἀγαπητοί, ἔστω πᾶς ἄνθρωπος
So then, [3]brothers [1]my [2]beloved, [4]let [7]be [5]every [6]man

ταχὺς εἰς τὸ ἀκοῦσαι, βραδὺς εἰς τὸ λαλῆσαι, βραδὺς εἰς
quick - - to hear, slow - - to speak, slow to

10 but the rich in his humiliation, because as a flower of the
field he will pass away.
11 For no sooner has the sun
risen with a burning heat than it
withers the grass; its flower
falls, and its beautiful appearance perishes. So the rich man
also will fade away in his pursuits.
12 Blessed *is* the man who endures temptation; for when he
has been approved, he will receive the crown of life which
the Lord has promised to those
who love Him.
13 Let no one say when he is
tempted, "I am tempted by
God"; for God cannot be
tempted by evil, nor does He
Himself tempt anyone.
14 But each one is tempted
when he is drawn away by his
own desires and enticed.
15 Then, when desire has
conceived, it gives birth to sin;
and sin, when it is full-grown,
brings forth death.
16 Do not be deceived, my
beloved brethren.
17 Every good gift and every
perfect gift is from above, and
comes down from the Father of
lights, with whom there is no
variation or shadow of turning.
18 Of His own will He brought
us forth by the word of truth,
that we might be a kind of firstfruits of His creatures.
19 So then, my beloved brethren, let every man be swift to
hear, slow to speak, slow to

---

[a]**(1:12)** NU omits ο Κυριος, *the Lord.* [b]**(1:19)** NU reads Ιστε, *Know (this)* or *(This) you know.*

***(1:17)** *τροπή (tropē).* Noun, used only here in the NT, meaning a *turning,* especially a *revolution* of heavenly bodies. It is derived from the verb *τρέπω, turn.* James uses it in an extended metaphor showing that, unlike the changes observed in the light of the sun and moon, God never changes or varies.

wrath;
20 for the wrath of man does
not produce the righteousness
of God.
21 Therefore lay aside all filthiness and overflow of wickedness, and receive with
meekness the implanted word,
which is able to save your
souls.
22 But be doers of the word,
and not hearers only, deceiving
yourselves.
23 For if anyone is a hearer of
the word and not a doer, he is
like a man observing his natural
face in a mirror;
24 for he observes himself,
goes away, and immediately
forgets what kind of man he
was.
25 But he who looks into the
perfect law of liberty and continues *in it,* and is not a forgetful hearer but a doer of the
work, this one will be blessed in
what he does.
26 If anyone among you thinks
he is religious, and does not bridle his tongue but deceives his
own heart, this one's religion *is*
useless.
27 Pure and undefiled religion
before God and the Father is
this: to visit orphans and widows in their trouble, *and* to
keep oneself unspotted from
the world.
2 My brethren, do not hold
the faith of our Lord Jesus
Christ, *the Lord* of glory, with
partiality.
2 For if there should come

ὀργήν· **20** ὀργὴ γὰρ ἀνδρὸς δικαιοσύνην Θεοῦ οὐ
anger; [2]*the* [3]wrath [1]for of man [4]*the* [5]righteousness [6]of [7]God [2]not

κατεργάζεται.
[1]does [3]produce.

Practice Your Religion

21 Διὸ ἀποθέμενοι πᾶσαν ῥυπαρίαν καὶ περισσείαν
Therefore laying aside all filthiness and abundance

κακίας, ἐν πραΰτητι δέξασθε τὸν ἔμφυτον λόγον τὸν
of evil, in gentleness receive the implanted word the *one* (which)

δυνάμενον σῶσαι τὰς ψυχὰς ὑμῶν. **22** Γίνεσθε δὲ ποιηταὶ
being able (is able) to save - souls ˜ your. become ˜ But doers

λόγου καὶ μὴ μόνον ἀκροαταί, παραλογιζόμενοι ἑαυτούς.
of *the* word and not only ˜ hearers, deceiving yourselves.

23 Ὅτι εἴ τις ἀκροατὴς λόγου ἐστὶ καὶ οὐ ποιητής,
Because if anyone [2]a [3]hearer [4]of [5]*the* [6]word [1]is and not a doer,

οὗτος ἔοικεν ἀνδρὶ κατανοοῦντι τὸ πρόσωπον τῆς γενέσεως
this *one* is like a man observing the face (his natural) - of existence ˜

αὐτοῦ ἐν ἐσόπτρῳ· **24** κατενόησε γὰρ ἑαυτὸν καὶ ἀπελήλυθε
his (face) in a mirror; [2]he [3]observed [1]for himself and has gone away

καὶ εὐθέως ἐπελάθετο ὁποῖος ἦν. **25** Ὁ δὲ
and immediately forgot what sort of *man* he was. [2]the [3]*one* [1]But

παρακύψας εἰς νόμον τέλειον τὸν τῆς ἐλευθερίας καὶ
having looked (who looks) into *the* law ˜ perfect - - of liberty and

παραμείνας, οὗτος οὐκ ἀκροατὴς ἐπιλησμονῆς
having continued (continues in it), this *one* not (because he has not) [3]a [4]hearer [5]of [6]forgetfulness (become a)

γενόμενος ἀλλὰ ποιητὴς ἔργου, οὗτος μακάριος ἐν τῇ
[1]having [2]become (forgetful hearer) but a doer of *the* work, this *one* [3]blessed [4]in -

ποιήσει αὐτοῦ ἔσται.
[6]doing [5]his [1]will [2]be.

26 Εἴ τις δοκεῖ θρησκὸς εἶναι ἐν ὑμῖν,[c] μὴ
If anyone thinks [3]religious [1]to [2]be (that he is) among you, not

χαλιναγωγῶν γλῶσσαν αὐτοῦ ἀλλὰ ἀπατῶν καρδίαν αὐτοῦ,
bridling tongue ˜ his but deceiving heart ˜ his,

τούτου μάταιος ἡ θρησκεία. **27** Θρησκεία καθαρὰ καὶ
[3]of [4]this [5]*man* [6]*is* [7]useless [1]the [2]religion. [4]religion [1]Pure [2]and

ἀμίαντος παρὰ Θεῷ καὶ Πατρὶ αὕτη ἐστίν· ἐπισκέπτεσθαι
[3]undefiled before God and *the* Father this ˜ is: to look after (care for)

ὀρφανοὺς καὶ χήρας ἐν τῇ θλίψει αὐτῶν, ἄσπιλον ἑαυτὸν
orphans and widows in - affliction ˜ their, [4]unspotted [3]oneself

τηρεῖν ἀπὸ τοῦ κόσμου.
[1]to [2]keep from the world.

Beware of Personal Favoritism

2 **1** Ἀδελφοί μου, μὴ ἐν προσωποληψίαις* ἔχετε τὴν
brothers ˜ My, [2]not [13]with [14]partiality [1]do [3]have (hold) [4]the

πίστιν τοῦ Κυρίου ἡμῶν Ἰησοῦ Χριστοῦ τῆς δόξης. **2** Ἐὰν
[5]faith - [6]of [8]Lord [7]our [11]Jesus [12]Christ - [9]of [10]glory. if ˜

---

[c](**1:26**) NU omits εν υμιν, *among you.*

***(2:1)** προσωποληψία (*prosōpolēpsia*). Noun meaning *partiality.* The word is a compound from πρόσωπον, *face, person,* and λῆμψις, *a receiving,* thus meaning *respect of persons,* receiving of someone because of his social position, wealth (as here), or appearance. Its occurrences within the NT all specifically note that *partiality* is not a characteristic of God (cf. also Rom. 2:11; Eph. 6:9). Cf. the cognate verb προσωποληπτέω, *show partiality* (James 2:9); and the cognate noun προσωπολήπτης, *one who shows partiality* (Acts 10:34).

γὰρ εἰσέλθῃ εἰς τὴν συναγωγὴν ὑμῶν ἀνὴρ χρυσοδακτύλιος
For [3]enters [4]into - [6]assembly [5]your [1]a [2]man with a gold ring

ἐν ἐσθῆτι λαμπρᾷ, εἰσέλθῃ δὲ καὶ πτωχὸς ἐν ῥυπαρᾷ
in clothes ˜ bright, [2]*there* [3]enters [1]and also a poor *man* in dirty
fine,

ἐσθῆτι, **3** καὶ ἐπιβλέψητε ἐπὶ τὸν φοροῦντα τὴν ἐσθῆτα τὴν
clothes, and you look upon the *one* wearing the clothes ˜ -
who wears

λαμπρὰν καὶ εἴπητε αὐτῷ, "Σὺ κάθου ὧδε καλῶς," καὶ
bright and you say to him, "You sit here well," and
fine in a good seat,"

τῷ πτωχῷ εἴπητε, "Σὺ στῆθι ἐκεῖ" ἢ "Κάθου ὧδε ὑπὸ τὸ
to the poor *man* you say, "You stand there" or "Sit here under -

ὑποπόδιόν μου," **4** καὶ οὐ διεκρίθητε ἐν ἑαυτοῖς
footstool ˜ my," and so [3]not [1]did [2]you differentiate among yourselves

καὶ ἐγένεσθε κριταὶ διαλογισμῶν πονηρῶν?
and became judges of thoughts ˜ evil?
with corrupt decisions?

5 Ἀκούσατε, ἀδελφοί μου ἀγαπητοί. Οὐχ ὁ Θεὸς
Listen, [3]brothers [1]my [2]beloved. [6]not - [5]God

ἐξελέξατο τοὺς πτωχοὺς τοῦ κόσμου πλουσίους ἐν πίστει καὶ
[4]Did [7]choose the poor of the world *to be* rich in faith and

κληρονόμους τῆς βασιλείας ἧς ἐπηγγείλατο τοῖς
heirs of the kingdom which He promised to the *ones*

ἀγαπῶσιν αὐτόν? **6** Ὑμεῖς δὲ ἠτιμάσατε τὸν πτωχόν. Οὐχ
loving Him? you ˜ But dishonored the poor *man.* [2]not
who love

οἱ πλούσιοι καταδυναστεύουσιν ὑμῶν, καὶ αὐτοὶ ἕλκουσιν
[3]the [4]rich [1]Do [5]oppress you, and they drag

ὑμᾶς εἰς κριτήρια? **7** Οὐκ αὐτοὶ βλασφημοῦσι τὸ καλὸν ὄνομα
you into *the* courts? [3]not [2]they [1]Do [4]blaspheme the noble name

τὸ ἐπικληθὲν ἐφ' ὑμᾶς? **8** Εἰ μέντοι νόμον τελεῖτε
the *one* being called upon you? If [2]really [4]*the* [6]law [1]you [3]fulfill
by which you are called?

βασιλικὸν κατὰ τὴν Γραφήν, «Ἀγαπήσεις τὸν πλησίον
[5]royal according to the Scripture, «You shall love - neighbor ˜

σου ὡς σεαυτόν,»[a] καλῶς ποιεῖτε. **9** Εἰ δὲ
your as yourself,» [3]well [1]you [2]do. if ˜ But

προσωποληπτεῖτε, ἁμαρτίαν ἐργάζεσθε, ἐλεγχόμενοι ὑπὸ
you show partiality, [3]sin [1]you [2]accomplish, being convicted by
commit and are

τοῦ νόμου ὡς παραβάται. **10** Ὅστις γὰρ ὅλον τὸν νόμον
the law as transgressors. whoever ˜ For [4]whole [3]the [5]law

τηρήσει, πταίσει δὲ ἐν ἑνί, γέγονε πάντων ἔνοχος.
[1]will [2]keep, [7]will [8]stumble [6]but in one *point,* has become [2]of [3]all [1]guilty.

11 Ὁ γὰρ εἰπών, «Μὴ μοιχεύσεις,»[b] εἶπε
[2]the [3]*One* [1]For saying, «[3]not [1]You [2]shall [4]commit [5]adultery,» said ˜
who said,

καί, «Μὴ φονεύσεις.»[c] Εἰ δὲ οὐ μοιχεύσεις,
also, «[3]not [1]You [2]shall [4]murder.» if ˜ Now [3]not [1]you [2]do [4]commit [5]adultery,

φονεύσεις δέ, γέγονας παραβάτης νόμου.
[7]you [8]will [9]murder [6]but, you have become a transgressor of *the* law.

12 Οὕτω λαλεῖτε καὶ οὕτω ποιεῖτε ὡς διὰ νόμου ἐλευθερίας
So speak and so do as [7]by [8]*the* [9]law [10]of [11]liberty

μέλλοντες κρίνεσθαι. **13** Ἡ γὰρ κρίσις ἀνέλεος
[1]*the* [2]*ones* [3]going [4]to [5]be [6]judged. - For judgment *is* without mercy
those who will

into your assembly a man with
gold rings, in fine apparel, and
there should also come in a
poor man in filthy clothes,
3 and you pay attention to
the one wearing the fine clothes
and say to him, "You sit here in
a good place," and say to the
poor man, "You stand there,"
or, "Sit here at my footstool,"
4 have you not shown partiality among yourselves, and become judges with evil thoughts?
5 Listen, my beloved brethren: Has God not chosen the
poor of this world *to be* rich in
faith and heirs of the kingdom
which He promised to those
who love Him?
6 But you have dishonored
the poor man. Do not the rich
oppress you and drag you into
the courts?
7 Do they not blaspheme
that noble name by which you
are called?
8 If you really fulfill *the* royal
law according to the Scripture,
*"You shall love your neighbor
as yourself,"* you do well;
9 but if you show partiality,
you commit sin, and are convicted by the law as transgressors.
10 For whoever shall keep the
whole law, and yet stumble in
one *point,* he is guilty of all.
11 For He who said, *"Do not
commit adultery,"* also said,
"Do not murder." Now if you
do not commit adultery, but
you do murder, you have become a transgressor of the law.
12 So speak and so do as
those who will be judged by the
law of liberty.
13 For judgment is without

---

a(**2:8**) Lev. 19:18
b(**2:11**) Ex. 20:14; Deut. 5:18 *c*(**2:11**) Ex. 20:13; Deut. 5:17

mercy to the one who has
shown no mercy. Mercy triumphs over judgment.
14 What *does it* profit, my
brethren, if someone says he
has faith but does not have
works? Can faith save him?
15 If a brother or sister is naked and destitute of daily food,
16 and one of you says to
them, "Depart in peace, be
warmed and filled," but you do
not give them the things which
are needed for the body, what
does it profit?
17 Thus also faith by itself, if
it does not have works, is dead.
18 But someone will say,
"You have faith, and I have
works." Show me your faith
without your works, and I will
show you my faith by my
works.
19 You believe that there is
one God. You do well. Even the
demons believe—and tremble!
20 But do you want to know,
O foolish man, that faith without works is dead?
21 Was not Abraham our father justified by works when he
offered Isaac his son on the altar?
22 Do you see that faith was
working together with his
works, and by works faith was
made perfect?
23 And the Scripture was fulfilled which says, *"Abraham believed God, and it was*

τῷ μὴ ποιήσαντι ἔλεος. Κατακαυχᾶται ἔλεον κρίσεως.
to the *one* not doing mercy. [2]triumphs [3]over [1]Mercy judgment.
who does not show

Faith Without Works Is Dead

14 *Τί τὸ ὄφελος, ἀδελφοί μου, ἐὰν πίστιν λέγῃ τις*
What *is* the benefit, brothers ˜ my, if [5]faith [2]says [1]someone
profit,

ἔχειν, ἔργα δὲ μὴ ἔχῃ? Μὴ δύναται ἡ πίστις
[3]to [4]have, works ˜ but [3]not [1]he [2]does [4]have? [8]not [7]is [9]able [5]The [6]faith
he has, That

σῶσαι αὐτόν? **15** *Ἐὰν δὲ ἀδελφὸς ἢ ἀδελφὴ γυμνοὶ*
to save him, *is it?* if ˜ And a brother or sister naked ˜

ὑπάρχωσι καὶ λειπόμενοι ὦσι τῆς ἐφημέρου τροφῆς, **16** *εἴπῃ*
is and lacking ˜ is of the daily food, [5]says
destitute

δέ τις αὐτοῖς ἐξ ὑμῶν, "Ὑπάγετε ἐν εἰρήνῃ,
[1]and [2]someone [6]to [7]them [3]of [4]you, "Go in peace,

θερμαίνεσθε καὶ χορτάζεσθε," μὴ δῶτε δὲ αὐτοῖς τὰ
be warmed and filled," [4]not [2]you [3]do [5]give [1]but to them the

ἐπιτήδεια τοῦ σώματος, τί τὸ ὄφελος? **17** *Οὕτω καὶ*
necessary *things* of the body, what *is* the benefit? Thus also
profit?

ἡ πίστις, ἐὰν μὴ ἔργα ἔχῃ, νεκρά ἐστι καθ'
the faith, if [3]not [5]works [1]it [2]does [4]have, dead ˜ is *being* by
that

ἑαυτήν.
itself.

18 *Ἀλλ' ἐρεῖ τις, "Σὺ πίστιν ἔχεις, κἀγὼ ἔργα*
But [2]will [3]say [1]someone, "You faith ˜ have, and I works ˜

ἔχω." Δεῖξόν μοι τὴν πίστιν σου[d] *ἐκ τῶν ἔργων σου, κἀγὼ*
have." Show me - faith ˜ your from - works ˜ your, and I
without

δείξω σοι ἐκ τῶν ἔργων μου[e] *τὴν πίστιν μου.* **19** *Σὺ*
will show you [3]by - [5]works [4]my - [2]faith [1]my. You
by means of

πιστεύεις ὅτι ὁ Θεὸς εἷς ἐστί. Καλῶς ποιεῖς. Καὶ τὰ
believe that - God one ˜ is. [3]well [1]You [2]do. Even the

δαιμόνια πιστεύουσι — καὶ φρίσσουσι!
demons believe — and they shudder!

20 *Θέλεις δὲ γνῶναι, ὦ ἄνθρωπε κενέ, ὅτι ἡ πίστις*
[2]do [3]you [4]want [1]But to know, O man ˜ foolish, that - faith

χωρὶς τῶν ἔργων νεκρά[f] *ἐστιν?* **21** *Ἀβραὰμ ὁ πατὴρ ἡμῶν*
without - works dead ˜ is? [3]Abraham - [5]father [4]our

οὐκ ἐξ ἔργων ἐδικαιώθη ἀνενέγκας Ἰσαὰκ τὸν υἱὸν
[2]not [7]by [8]works [1]Was [6]justified offering Isaac - son ˜
by means of when he offered

αὐτοῦ ἐπὶ τὸ θυσιαστήριον? **22** *Βλέπεις ὅτι ἡ πίστις*
his on the altar? Do you see that - faith

συνήργει τοῖς ἔργοις αὐτοῦ, καὶ ἐκ τῶν
was working together - with works ˜ his, and by -
by means of

ἔργων ἡ πίστις ἐτελειώθη? **23** *Καὶ ἐπληρώθη ἡ*
works the faith was made complete? And [3]was [4]fulfilled [1]the
his

Γραφὴ ἡ λέγουσα, «Ἐπίστευσε δὲ Ἀβραὰμ τῷ Θεῷ,
[2]Scripture the *one* saying, «[3]believed [1]And [2]Abraham - God,
which says,

[d](2:18) NU omits *σου, your.*
[e](2:18) NU omits *μου, my.*
[f](2:20) NU reads *αργη, useless.*

καὶ ἐλογίσθη αὐτῷ εἰς δικαιοσύνην.»[g] Καὶ φίλος Θεοῦ
and it was accounted to him for righteousness.» And [4]a [5]friend [6]of [7]God

ἐκλήθη. 24 Ὁρᾶτε τοίνυν[h] ὅτι ἐξ ἔργων
[1]he [2]was [3]called. You see then that [5]by [6]works
by means of

δικαιοῦται ἄνθρωπος καὶ οὐκ ἐκ πίστεως μόνον. 25 Ὁμοίως
[3]is [4]justified [1]a [2]man and not by faith only. likewise ˜

δὲ καὶ Ῥαὰβ ἡ πόρνη οὐκ ἐξ ἔργων ἐδικαιώθη
And [6]also [3]Rahab [4]the [5]harlot [2]not [8]by [9]works [1]was [7]justified
by means of

ὑποδεξαμένη τοὺς ἀγγέλους καὶ ἑτέρᾳ ὁδῷ ἐκβαλοῦσα?
receiving the messengers and [4]another [5]way [1]sending [2]*them* [3]out?
when she received sent

26 Ὥσπερ γὰρ τὸ σῶμα χωρὶς πνεύματος νεκρόν ἐστιν, οὕτω
as ˜ For the body without *the* spirit dead ˜ is, so

καὶ ἡ πίστις χωρὶς τῶν ἔργων νεκρά ἐστι.
also - faith without - works dead ˜ is.

The Untamable Tongue

3 1 Μὴ πολλοὶ διδάσκαλοι γίνεσθε, ἀδελφοί μου,
[2]not [3]many [4]*of* [5]*you* [7]teachers [1]Let [6]become, brothers ˜ my,

εἰδότες ὅτι μεῖζον κρίμα ληψόμεθα. 2 Πολλὰ γὰρ
knowing that [4]greater [5]judgment [1]we [2]shall [3]receive. [5]*in* [6]many [7]*ways* [1]For
stricter

πταίομεν ἅπαντες. Εἴ τις ἐν λόγῳ οὐ πταίει,
[2]we [3]stumble [4]all. If anyone [4]in [5]word [2]not [1]does [3]stumble,

οὗτος τέλειος ἀνήρ, δυνατὸς χαλιναγωγῆσαι καὶ ὅλον τὸ
this *one is* perfect ˜ a man, able [2]to [3]bridle [1]also whole ˜ the
mature

σῶμα. 3 Ἴδε,[a] τῶν ἵππων τοὺς χαλινοὺς εἰς τὰ
body. See, - [7]of [8]horses - [3]bits [4]into [5]the
Consider that

στόματα βάλλομεν πρὸς τὸ πείθεσθαι αὐτοὺς ἡμῖν, καὶ ὅλον
[6]mouths [1]we [2]put for - [2]to [3]obey [1]them us, and [4]whole
that they may obey

τὸ σῶμα αὐτῶν μετάγομεν. 4 Ἰδού, καὶ τὰ πλοῖα, τηλικαῦτα
- [5]body [3]their [1]we [2]guide. See, also the ships, [2]so [3]large
Consider

ὄντα καὶ ὑπὸ σκληρῶν ἀνέμων ἐλαυνόμενα,
[1]being and [3]by [4]rough [5]winds [1]being [2]driven,
although they are fierce are

μετάγεται ὑπὸ ἐλαχίστου πηδαλίου ὅπου ἂν ἡ ὁρμὴ
they are guided by a very small rudder wherever - the impulse

τοῦ εὐθύνοντος βούληται. 5 Οὕτω καὶ ἡ γλῶσσα μικρὸν
of the *one* guiding straight desires. So also the tongue [3]small
pilot

μέλος ἐστὶ καὶ μεγαλαυχεῖ.
[2]a [4]member [1]is and it boasts great things.

Ἰδού, ὀλίγον[b] πῦρ ἡλίκην ὕλην ἀνάπτει! 6 Καὶ ἡ
See, [6]little [5]a [7]fire [1]how [2]great [3]a [4]forest kindles! And the

γλῶσσα πῦρ, ὁ κόσμος τῆς ἀδικίας. Οὕτως ἡ
tongue *is* a fire, the world - of unrighteousness. Thus the
a

γλῶσσα καθίσταται ἐν τοῖς μέλεσιν ἡμῶν, ἡ
tongue is set among - members ˜ our, the *thing*
as that which

σπιλοῦσα ὅλον τὸ σῶμα καὶ φλογίζουσα τὸν τροχὸν τῆς
defiling whole ˜ the body and setting on fire the course -
defiles sets

accounted to him for righteousness." And he was called the friend of God.
24 You see then that a man is justified by works, and not by faith only.
25 Likewise, was not Rahab the harlot also justified by works when she received the messengers and sent *them* out another way?
26 For as the body without the spirit is dead, so faith without works is dead also.
3 My brethren, let not many of you become teachers, knowing that we shall receive a stricter judgment.
2 For we all stumble in many things. If anyone does not stumble in word, he *is* a perfect man, able also to bridle the whole body.
3 Indeed, we put bits in horses' mouths that they may obey us, and we turn their whole body.
4 Look also at ships: although they are so large and are driven by fierce winds, they are turned by a very small rudder wherever the pilot desires.
5 Even so the tongue is a little member and boasts great things. See how great a forest a little fire kindles!
6 And the tongue *is* a fire, a world of iniquity. The tongue is so set among our members that it defiles the whole body, and sets on fire the course of na-

---

[g](2:23) Gen. 15:6
[h](2:24) NU omits τοινυν, *then.* [a](3:3) NU reads ει δε, *Now if.*
[b](3:5) NU reads ηλικον, *great.*

ture; and it is set on fire by hell.
7 For every kind of beast and
bird, of reptile and creature of
the sea, is tamed and has been
tamed by mankind.
8 But no man can tame the
tongue. *It is* an unruly evil, full
of deadly poison.
9 With it we bless our God
and Father, and with it we
curse men, who have been
made in the similitude of God.
10 Out of the same mouth
proceed blessing and cursing.
My brethren, these things
ought not to be so.
11 Does a spring send forth
fresh *water* and bitter from the
same opening?
12 Can a fig tree, my brethren, bear olives, or a grapevine
bear figs? Thus no spring yields
both salt water and fresh.
13 Who *is* wise and understanding among you? Let him
show by good conduct *that* his
works *are done* in the meekness of wisdom.
14 But if you have bitter envy
and self-seeking in your hearts,
do not boast and lie against the
truth.
15 This wisdom does not descend from above, but *is*
earthly, sensual, demonic.
16 For where envy and self-
seeking *exist,* confusion and every evil thing *are* there.
17 But the wisdom that is
from above is first pure, then

---

[c](3:12) For Ουτως ουδεμια πηγη αλυκον και, *Thus no spring . . . salt and,* NU reads Ουτε αλυκον, *Neither (is) salt (able to produce sweet).*

***(3:6)** *γέεννα (geenna).* Noun meaning *Gehenna, hell,* used several times in the Synoptic Gospels, but otherwise only here in the NT. It is a Greek approximation of the Hebrew words for *Valley of (the sons of) Hinnom* (as in Josh. 15:8; 18:16; Jer. 7:32). Originally a ravine south of Jerusalem, the name came to represent the eternal place of punishment in the afterlife to which the condemned are cast (as Matt. 5:29; 23:33), a place sometimes characterized by fire (Matt. 5:22; 18:9). James figuratively presents the ungoverned tongue as a flame set on fire from Gehenna or hell.

γενέσεως, καὶ φλογιζομένη ὑπὸ τῆς Γεέννης.* **7** Πᾶσα γὰρ
of nature, and being set on fire by - hell. every ~ For
is

φύσις θηρίων τε καὶ πετεινῶν, ἑρπετῶν τε καὶ
nature of beasts ~ both and of birds, [2]of [3]reptiles [1]both and
kind

ἐναλίων, δαμάζεται καὶ δεδάμασται τῇ φύσει τῇ
of sea creatures, is tamed and has been tamed by the species ~ -
race

ἀνθρωπίνῃ. **8** Τὴν δὲ γλῶσσαν οὐδεὶς δύναται ἀνθρώπων
[2]human. [10]the [1]But [11]tongue [2]no [3]one [6]is [7]able [4]of [5]men

δαμάσαι. Ἀκατάσχετον κακόν, μεστὴ ἰοῦ θανατηφόρου.
[8]to [9]tame. *It is* a restless evil *thing,* full of poison ~ deadly.

9 Ἐν αὐτῇ εὐλογοῦμεν τὸν Θεὸν καὶ Πατέρα, καὶ ἐν αὐτῇ
With it we bless the God and Father, and with it
our

καταρώμεθα τοὺς ἀνθρώπους τοὺς καθ' ὁμοίωσιν
we curse - men the *ones* [4]according [5]to [6]*the* [7]likeness
who

Θεοῦ γεγονότας. **10** Ἐκ τοῦ αὐτοῦ στόματος
[8]of [9]God [1]having [2]been [3]made. Out of the same mouth
are created.

ἐξέρχεται εὐλογία καὶ κατάρα. Οὐ χρή, ἀδελφοί μου,
come blessings and curses. [6]not [5]ought, [2]brothers [1]My,

ταῦτα οὕτω γίνεσθαι. **11** Μήτι ἡ πηγὴ ἐκ τῆς αὐτῆς
[3]these [4]*things* [9]so [7]to [8]be. [4]not [1]The [2]spring [7]from [8]the [9]same

ὀπῆς βρύει τὸ γλυκὺ καὶ τὸ πικρόν?
[10]opening [3]does [5]pour [6]forth the sweet and the bitter *water, does it?*

12 Μὴ δύναται, ἀδελφοί μου, συκῆ ἐλαίας ποιῆσαι
[3]not [1]It [2]is [4]possible, brothers ~ my, *for* a fig tree [3]olives [1]to [2]make

ἢ ἄμπελος σῦκα? Οὕτως οὐδεμία πηγὴ ἁλυκὸν καὶ[c] γλυκὺ
or a vine figs, *is it?* Thus no spring [5]*both* [6]salt [7]and [8]sweet

ποιῆσαι ὕδωρ.
[1]*is* [2]*able* [3]to [4]produce water.

Heavenly Versus Demonic Wisdom

13 Τίς σοφὸς καὶ ἐπιστήμων ἐν ὑμῖν?
Is there anyone wise and understanding among you?

Δειξάτω ἐκ τῆς καλῆς ἀναστροφῆς τὰ ἔργα αὐτοῦ ἐν
Let him show by the good conduct - *that* works ~ his *are* in
his

πραΰτητι σοφίας. **14** Εἰ δὲ ζῆλον πικρὸν ἔχετε καὶ
meekness of wisdom. if ~ But [4]jealousy [3]bitter [1]you [2]have and

ἐριθείαν ἐν τῇ καρδίᾳ ὑμῶν, μὴ κατακαυχᾶσθε καὶ ψεύδεσθε
strife in - heart ~ your, not ~ do boast and lie

κατὰ τῆς ἀληθείας. **15** Οὐκ ἔστιν αὕτη ἡ σοφία ἄνωθεν
against the truth. [4]not [3]is [1]This - [2]wisdom [7]from [8]above

κατερχομένη, ἀλλ' ἐπίγειος, ψυχική, δαιμονιώδης.
[5]coming [6]down, but *it is* earthly, natural, demonic.
that which comes down,

16 Ὅπου γὰρ ζῆλος καὶ ἐριθεία, ἐκεῖ ἀκαταστασία καὶ πᾶν
where ~ For jealousy and strife *exist,* there disorder and every

φαῦλον πρᾶγμα. **17** Ἡ δὲ ἄνωθεν σοφία πρῶτον μὲν
evil deed *exist.* the ~ Now [2]from [3]above [1]wisdom [5]first -

ἁγνή ἐστιν, ἔπειτα εἰρηνική, ἐπιεικής,* εὐπειθής, μεστὴ
[6]pure [4]is, then peaceable, gentle, compliant, full

ἐλέους καὶ καρπῶν ἀγαθῶν, ἀδιάκριτος καὶ ἀνυπόκριτος.
of mercy and fruits ~ good, without partiality and without hypocrisy.

18 Καρπὸς δὲ τῆς δικαιοσύνης ἐν εἰρήνῃ σπείρεται
[2]*the* [3]fruit [1]Now - of righteousness [3]in [4]peace [1]is [2]sown

τοῖς ποιοῦσιν εἰρήνην.
by the *ones* making peace.

Worldly Pride Produces Conflict

4 **1** Πόθεν πόλεμοι καὶ μάχαι ἐν ὑμῖν? Οὐκ
From where *come* wars and disputes among you? *Is it* not

ἐντεῦθεν, ἐκ τῶν ἡδονῶν ὑμῶν τῶν στρατευομένων ἐν
from here, from - pleasures ~ your the *ones* warring in
which war

τοῖς μέλεσιν ὑμῶν? **2** Ἐπιθυμεῖτε καὶ οὐκ ἔχετε·
- members ~ your? You desire and [3]not [1]you [2]do have;

φονεύετε καὶ ζηλοῦτε καὶ οὐ δύνασθε ἐπιτυχεῖν. Μάχεσθε
you murder and are jealous and [3]not [1]you [2]are able to obtain. You fight

καὶ πολεμεῖτε. Οὐκ ἔχετε[a] διὰ τὸ μὴ αἰτεῖσθαι
and make war. [3]not [1]You [2]do have on account of - not [2]to [3]ask
because you do not

ὑμᾶς. **3** Αἰτεῖτε καὶ οὐ λαμβάνετε διότι κακῶς
[1]you. You ask and not ~ do receive because [3]badly
ask. with wrong motives

αἰτεῖσθε, ἵνα ἐν ταῖς ἡδοναῖς ὑμῶν δαπανήσητε.
[1]you [2]ask, in order that in - pleasures ~ your you may spend *it*.
on

4 Μοιχοὶ καὶ[b] μοιχαλίδες! Οὐκ οἴδατε ὅτι ἡ φιλία
Adulterers and adulteresses! [3]not [1]Do [2]you know that - friendship

τοῦ κόσμου ἔχθρα τοῦ Θεοῦ ἐστιν? Ὃς ἂν οὖν
of the world [2]enmity - [3]of [4]God [1]is? Who ever therefore
with with

βουληθῇ φίλος εἶναι τοῦ κόσμου, ἐχθρὸς τοῦ Θεοῦ
wants [3]a [4]friend [1]to [2]be of the world, [3]an [4]enemy - [5]of [6]God

καθίσταται. **5** Ἢ δοκεῖτε ὅτι κενῶς ἡ Γραφὴ λέγει, Πρὸς
[1]is [2]constituted. Or do you think that in vain the Scripture says, [8]to

φθόνον ἐπιποθεῖ τὸ Πνεῦμα ὃ κατῴκησεν[c] ἐν ἡμῖν?
[9]envy [7]longs [1]the [2]Spirit [3]which [4]dwelt [5]in [6]us?
yearns jealously dwells

Μείζονα δὲ δίδωσι χάριν. Διὸ λέγει,
[13]greater [10]But [11]He [12]gives grace. Therefore He says,

6 «Ὁ Θεὸς ὑπερηφάνοις ἀντιτάσσεται,
- «God [2]proud [3]*people* [1]resists,

Ταπεινοῖς δὲ δίδωσι χάριν.»[d]
[2]to [3]humble [4]*people* [1]But He gives grace.»

Humility Cures Worldliness

7 Ὑποτάγητε οὖν τῷ Θεῷ, ἀντίστητε δὲ τῷ διαβόλῳ
submit ~ Therefore - to God, resist ~ and the devil

καὶ φεύξεται ἀφ' ὑμῶν. **8** Ἐγγίσατε τῷ Θεῷ καὶ
and he will flee from you. Draw near - to God and

ἐγγιεῖ ὑμῖν. Καθαρίσατε χεῖρας, ἁμαρτωλοί, καὶ
He will draw near to you. Cleanse *your* hands, *you* sinners, and

ἁγνίσατε καρδίας, δίψυχοι. **9** Ταλαιπωρήσατε καὶ
purify *your* hearts, *you* double-minded. Be distressed and

πενθήσατε καὶ κλαύσατε! Ὁ γέλως ὑμῶν εἰς πένθος
mourn and weep! - [3]laughter [2]your [5]into [6]mourning

peaceable, gentle, willing to
yield, full of mercy and good
fruits, without partiality and
without hypocrisy.
18 Now the fruit of righteousness is sown in peace by those
who make peace.
4 Where do wars and fights
come from among you? Do
they not *come* from your *desires*
for pleasure that war in your
members?
2 You lust and do not have.
You murder and covet and cannot obtain. You fight and war.
Yet you do not have because
you do not ask.
3 You ask and do not re-
ceive, because you ask amiss,
that you may spend *it* on your
pleasures.
4 Adulterers and adulter-
esses! Do you not know that
friendship with the world is enmity with God? Whoever therefore wants to be a friend of the
world makes himself an enemy
of God.
5 Or do you think that the
Scripture says in vain, "The
Spirit who dwells in us yearns
jealously"?
6 But He gives more grace.
Therefore He says:

"God resists the proud,
But gives grace to the
humble."

7 Therefore submit to God.
Resist the devil and he will flee
from you.
8 Draw near to God and He
will draw near to you. Cleanse
your hands, *you* sinners; and
purify *your* hearts, *you* double-
minded.
9 Lament and mourn and
weep! Let your laughter be
turned to mourning and *your*

---

[a](**4:2**) TR adds δε, *Yet (you do not have).*
[b](**4:4**) NU omits Μοιχοι και, *Adulterers and.*
[c](**4:5**) NU reads κατωκισεν, *which He made to dwell.*
[d](**4:6**) Prov. 3:34

***(3:17)** ἐπιεικής (epieikēs).* Adjective meaning *gentle.* In Phil. 4:5 it is used substantivally as equivalent to the cognate noun ἐπιείκεια, *gentleness, graciousness* (Acts 24:4; 2 Cor. 10:1). The word designates the quality that makes one amenable in dealings with others, not difficult to live and work with. Its meaning as a substantive would include *considerateness, mildness, kindness.*

joy to gloom.
10 Humble yourselves in the
sight of the Lord, and He will
lift you up.
11 Do not speak evil of one
another, brethren. He who
speaks evil of a brother and
judges his brother, speaks evil
of the law and judges the law.
But if you judge the law, you
are not a doer of the law but a
judge.
12 There is one Lawgiver,
who is able to save and to destroy. Who are you to judge another?
13 Come now, you who say,
"Today or tomorrow we will go
to such and such a city, spend a
year there, buy and sell, and
make a profit";
14 whereas you do not know
what *will happen* tomorrow.
For what *is* your life? It is even
a vapor that appears for a little
time and then vanishes away.
15 Instead you *ought* to say,
"If the Lord wills, we shall live
and do this or that."
16 But now you boast in your
arrogance. All such boasting is
evil.
17 Therefore, to him who
knows to do good and does not
do *it,* to him it is sin.
5 Come now, *you* rich,
weep and howl for your
miseries that are coming upon
you!
2 Your riches are corrupted,

μεταστραφήτω καὶ ἡ χαρὰ εἰς κατήφειαν. **10** Ταπεινώθητε
[1]Let [4]change and the joy into dejection. Be humbled
your

ἐνώπιον τοῦ Κυρίου καὶ ὑψώσει ὑμᾶς.
before the Lord and He will exult you.

Humility Does Not Judge a Brother

11 Μὴ καταλαλεῖτε* ἀλλήλων, ἀδελφοί. Ὁ
[2]not [1]Do [3]speak against one another, brothers. The *one*

καταλαλῶν ἀδελφοῦ καὶ κρίνων τὸν ἀδελφὸν αὐτοῦ
speaking against a brother and judging - brother ˜ his
who speaks judges

καταλαλεῖ νόμου καὶ κρίνει νόμον. Εἰ δὲ νόμον κρίνεις,
speaks against *the* law and judges *the* law. if ˜ And [3]*the* [4]law [1]you [2]judge,

οὐκ εἶ ποιητὴς νόμου ἀλλὰ κριτής. **12** Εἷς ἐστιν ὁ
[7]not [5]you [6]are a doer of *the* law but a judge. [3]one [1]*There* [2]is -

Νομοθέτης[e] ὁ δυνάμενος σῶσαι καὶ ἀπολέσαι. Σὺ δὲ
Lawgiver the *One* being able to save and to destroy. [4]you [1]But
who is

τίς[f] εἶ ὃς κρίνεις τὸν ἕτερον?[g]
[2]who [3]are who judges the other?

Humility Does Not Boast about Tomorrow

13 Ἄγε νῦν, οἱ λέγοντες, "Σήμερον καὶ αὔριον
Come now, the *ones* saying, "Today and tomorrow
Listen now, you who say,

πορευσώμεθα[h] εἰς τήνδε τὴν πόλιν καὶ ποιήσωμεν ἐκεῖ
let us travel to this - city and let us spend [3]there

ἐνιαυτὸν ἕνα καὶ ἐμπορευσώμεθα καὶ κερδήσωμεν," —
[2]year [1]one and let us trade and make gain," —

14 οἵτινες οὐκ ἐπίστασθε τὸ τῆς αὔριον.
you who not ˜ do know the *happening* of the *life* tomorrow.

Ποία γὰρ ἡ ζωὴ ὑμῶν? Ἀτμὶς γάρ ἔσται ἡ πρὸς
[2]what [3]sort [1]For *is* - life ˜ your? [5]a [6]vapor [1]For [2]it [3]will [4]be the *one* for
which

ὀλίγον φαινομένη, ἔπειτα δὲ καὶ ἀφανιζομένη. **15** Ἀντὶ
a little *time* appearing, then ˜ but also disappearing. Instead of
appears, disappears. Instead

τοῦ λέγειν ὑμᾶς· "Ἐὰν ὁ Κύριος θελήσῃ, καὶ ζήσωμεν καὶ
- [2]to [3]say [1]you: "If the Lord wills, [5]also [1]we [2]shall [3]live [4]and
you should say:

ποιήσωμεν τοῦτο ἢ ἐκεῖνο." **16** Νῦν δὲ καυχᾶσθε ἐν ταῖς
we shall do this or that." now ˜ But you boast in -

ἀλαζονείαις ὑμῶν. Πᾶσα καύχησις τοιαύτη πονηρά ἐστιν.
pretensions ˜ your. All boasting ˜ such evil ˜ is.

17 Εἰδότι οὖν καλὸν ποιεῖν καὶ μὴ ποιοῦντι,
[2]to [3]*the* [4]*one* [5]knowing [1]Therefore [8]good [6]to [7]do and not doing *it,*

ἁμαρτία αὐτῷ ἐστιν.
[5]sin [1]to [2]him [3]it [4]is.

Rich Oppressors Will Be Judged

5 **1** Ἄγε νῦν, οἱ πλούσιοι, κλαύσατε ὀλολύζοντες ἐπὶ ταῖς
Come now, - *you* rich, weep crying aloud at -
Listen and cry

ταλαιπωρίαις ὑμῶν ταῖς ἐπερχομέναις! **2** Ὁ πλοῦτος ὑμῶν
miseries ˜ your the *ones* coming upon *you!* - riches ˜ Your
which are

---

[e](4:12) NU adds *και κριτης, and Judge.*
[f](4:12) TR omits *δε τις, But who.* [g](4:12) NU reads *πλησιον, a neighbor.*
[h](4:13) TR reads *πορευσομεθα, we will travel.*

---

*(4:11) *καταλαλέω (katalaleō).* Compound verb from the preposition *κατά, against,* and the verb *λαλέω, speak,* thus meaning *speak against, speak evil of, defame, slander.* As its usage here indicates, it may be used either in reference to things (the law) or persons (fellow believers; cf. 1 Pet. 2:12). Cf. the cognate noun *καταλαλία, slander, defamation, evil speech* (2 Cor. 12:20; 1 Pet. 2:1); and the cognate adjective *κατάλαλος,* used substantivally as *slanderers* (Rom. 1:30).

σέσηπε καὶ τὰ ἱμάτια ὑμῶν σητόβρωτα γέγονεν. **3** Ὁ
have decayed and - garments ˜ your [3]moth-eaten [1]have [2]become. -

χρυσὸς ὑμῶν καὶ ὁ ἄργυρος κατίωται, καὶ ὁ ἰὸς
gold ˜ Your and - silver have become corroded, and - poison ˜

αὐτῶν εἰς μαρτύριον ὑμῖν ἔσται καὶ φάγεται τὰς σάρκας
their [3]for [4]a [5]witness [6]to [7]you [1]will [2]be and will eat - flesh ˜
against

ὑμῶν ὡς πῦρ. Ἐθησαυρίσατε ἐν ἐσχάταις ἡμέραις.
your as a fire. You stored up treasure in *the* last days.

4 Ἰδού, ὁ μισθὸς τῶν ἐργατῶν τῶν ἀμησάντων τὰς χώρας
See, the wages of the laborers the *ones* having reaped - fields ˜
who reaped

ὑμῶν, ὁ ἀπεστερημένος ἀφ᾽ ὑμῶν, κράζει, καὶ αἱ
your, the *wages* having been held back from you, cry out, and the
which were kept back by

βοαὶ τῶν θερισάντων εἰς τὰ ὦτα Κυρίου Σαβαὼθ*
cries of the reaping *ones* [3]into [4]the [5]ears [6]of [7]*the* [8]Lord [9]of [10]Sabaoth
reapers Hosts

εἰσεληλύθασιν. **5** Ἐτρυφήσατε ἐπὶ τῆς γῆς καὶ
[1]have [2]entered. You lived luxuriously upon the earth and

ἐσπαταλήσατε, ἐθρέψατε τὰς καρδίας ὑμῶν ὡς [a] ἐν ἡμέρᾳ
you lived riotously, you nourished - hearts ˜ your as in a day

σφαγῆς. **6** Κατεδικάσατε, ἐφονεύσατε τὸν δίκαιον. Οὐκ
of slaughter. You condemned, you murdered the righteous *one.* [3]not

ἀντιτάσσεται ὑμῖν.
[1]He [2]does resist you.

Be Patient and Persevering

7 Μακροθυμήσατε οὖν, ἀδελφοί, ἕως τῆς παρουσίας
Be patient therefore, brothers, until the coming

τοῦ Κυρίου. Ἰδού, ὁ γεωργὸς ἐκδέχεται τὸν τίμιον καρπὸν
of the Lord. See, the farmer awaits the precious fruit

τῆς γῆς, μακροθυμῶν ἐπ᾽ αὐτὸν ἕως λάβῃ ὑετὸν
of the earth, being patient on it until it receives [1]*the* [5]rain
for

πρώϊμον καὶ ὄψιμον. **8** Μακροθυμήσατε καὶ ὑμεῖς. Στηρίξατε
[2]early [3]and [4]late. [3]be [4]patient [2]also [1]You. Establish

τὰς καρδίας ὑμῶν, ὅτι ἡ παρουσία τοῦ Κυρίου
- hearts ˜ your, because the coming of the Lord

ἤγγικε. **9** Μὴ στενάζετε κατ᾽ ἀλλήλων, ἀδελφοί,
has drawn near. not ˜ Do murmur against one another, brothers,

ἵνα μὴ κριθῆτε. [b] Ἰδού, ὁ Κριτὴς πρὸ τῶν
in order that [3]not [1]you [2]may be judged. See, the Judge [3]before [4]the

θυρῶν ἕστηκεν. **10** Ὑπόδειγμα λάβετε, ἀδελφοί μου, τῆς
[5]doors [1]has [2]stood. [4]*as* [5]an [6]example [3]take, [2]brothers [1]My, -
stands.

κακοπαθείας καὶ τῆς μακροθυμίας τοὺς προφήτας οἳ
of evil suffering and - of longsuffering the prophets who

ἐλάλησαν τῷ ὀνόματι Κυρίου. **11** Ἰδού, μακαρίζομεν
spoke in the name of *the* Lord. See, we count as blessed

τοὺς ὑπομένοντας. Τὴν ὑπομονὴν Ἰὼβ ἠκούσατε, καὶ τὸ
the *ones* enduring. [4]the [5]endurance [6]of [7]Job [1]You [2]heard [3]of, and [3]the
those who endure. have heard

τέλος Κυρίου εἴδετε, ὅτι πολύσπλαγχνός ἐστι καὶ
[4]end [5]of [6]*the* [7]Lord [1]you [2]know, that [3]compassionate [1]He [2]is and

οἰκτίρμων.
merciful.

and your garments are moth-eaten.
3 Your gold and silver are corroded, and their corrosion will be a witness against you and will eat your flesh like fire. You have heaped up treasure in the last days.
4 Indeed the wages of the laborers who mowed your fields, which you kept back by fraud, cry out; and the cries of the reapers have reached the ears of the Lord of Sabaoth.
5 You have lived on the earth in pleasure and luxury; you have fattened your hearts as in a day of slaughter.
6 You have condemned, you have murdered the just; he does not resist you.
7 Therefore be patient, brethren, until the coming of the Lord. See *how* the farmer waits for the precious fruit of the earth, waiting patiently for it until it receives the early and latter rain.
8 You also be patient. Establish your hearts, for the coming of the Lord is at hand.
9 Do not grumble against one another, brethren, lest you be condemned. Behold, the Judge is standing at the door!
10 My brethren, take the prophets, who spoke in the name of the Lord, as an example of suffering and patience.
11 Indeed we count them blessed who endure. You have heard of the perseverance of Job and seen the end *intended by* the Lord—that the Lord is very compassionate and merciful.

---

[a](5:5) NU omits ως, *as.*
[b](5:9) TR reads *κατακριθητε, you may (not) be condemned.*

*(5:4) Σαβαώθ *(Sabaōth).* Noun used twice in the NT, meaning *Sabaoth, hosts, armies.* The word is a Greek transliteration of the plural of Hebrew *sābā', army, host* (cf. Rom. 9:29 quoting Is. 1:9), and so the *Lord of Sabaoth* is the *Lord of hosts* or *Lord of (heavenly) armies.* Such a characterization always emphasizes God's majesty and might as manifested in the myriad angelic host who fight for Him and do His bidding. James presents this picture to emphasize the coming judgment of the avenging God.

12 But above all, my brethren, do not swear, either by
heaven or by earth or with any
other oath. But let your "Yes"
be "Yes," and *your* "No," "No,"
lest you fall into judgment.
13 Is anyone among you suffering? Let him pray. Is anyone
cheerful? Let him sing psalms.
14 Is anyone among you sick?
Let him call for the elders of the
church, and let them pray over
him, anointing him with oil in
the name of the Lord.
15 And the prayer of faith will
save the sick, and the Lord will
raise him up. And if he has committed sins, he will be forgiven.
16 Confess *your* trespasses to
one another, and pray for one
another, that you may be
healed. The effective, fervent
prayer of a righteous man avails
much.
17 Elijah was a man with a nature like ours, and he prayed
earnestly that it would not rain;
and it did not rain on the land
for three years and six months.
18 And he prayed again, and
the heaven gave rain, and the
earth produced its fruit.
19 Brethren, if anyone among
you wanders from the truth,
and someone turns him back,
20 let him know that he who
turns a sinner from the error of
his way will save a soul from
death and cover a multitude of
sins.

Meeting Specific Needs

12 Πρὸ πάντων δέ, ἀδελφοί μου, μὴ ὀμνύετε, μήτε
[2]before [3]all [4]*things* [1]And, brothers ˜ my, not ˜ do swear, neither
above all

τὸν οὐρανὸν μήτε τὴν γῆν μήτε ἄλλον τινὰ ὅρκον. Ἤτω δὲ
by the heaven nor the earth nor other ˜ any oath. [2]let [5]be [1]But

ὑμῶν τὸ Ναὶ ναί καὶ τὸ Οὒ οὔ, ἵνα μὴ εἰς ὑπόκρισιν[c]
[3]your - [4]Yes [6]yes and the No no, so that [3]not [5]into [6]hypocrisy
your

πέσητε. **13** Κακοπαθεῖ τις ἐν ὑμῖν?
[1]you [2]may [4]fall. [1]Does [5]suffer [6]misfortune [2]anyone [3]among [4]you?

Προσευχέσθω. Εὐθυμεῖ τις? Ψαλλέτω. **14** Ἀσθενεῖ
Let him pray. [1]Is [3]cheerful [2]anyone? Let him sing. [1]Is [5]sick

τις ἐν ὑμῖν? Προσκαλεσάσθω τοὺς πρεσβυτέρους τῆς
[2]anyone [3]among [4]you? Let him call on the elders of the

ἐκκλησίας, καὶ προσευξάσθωσαν ἐπ' αὐτὸν, ἀλείψαντες αὐτὸν
church, and let them pray over him, anointing him

ἐλαίῳ ἐν τῷ ὀνόματι τοῦ Κυρίου. **15** Καὶ ἡ εὐχὴ τῆς
with oil in the name of the Lord. And the prayer of

πίστεως σώσει τὸν κάμνοντα, καὶ ἐγερεῖ αὐτὸν ὁ
faith will save the *one* being ill, and [3]will [4]raise [6]up [5]him [1]the
who is sick,

Κύριος. Κἂν ἁμαρτίας ᾖ πεποιηκώς, ἀφεθήσεται
[2]Lord. And if [5]a [6]sin [1]he [2]should [3]have [4]committed, it will be forgiven
has

αὐτῷ. **16** Ἐξομολογεῖσθε[d] ἀλλήλοις τὰ παραπτώματα[e]
him. Confess to one another the transgressions
your

καὶ εὔχεσθε ὑπὲρ ἀλλήλων, ὅπως ἰαθῆτε. Πολὺ
and pray in behalf of one another, so that you may be healed. [10]much
very

ἰσχύει δέησις δικαίου ἐνεργουμένη.
[9]is [11]powerful [1]A [2]prayer [3]of [4]a [5]righteous [6]*person* [7]being [8]effective.
The effective prayer of a righteous person.

17 Ἠλίας ἄνθρωπος ἦν ὁμοιοπαθὴς ἡμῖν, καὶ προσευχῇ
Elijah [2]a [3]man [1]was of similar nature to us, and with a prayer

προσηύξατο τοῦ μὴ βρέξαι, καὶ οὐκ ἔβρεξεν ἐπὶ τῆς γῆς
he prayed - not to rain, and [3]not [1]it [2]did rain upon the earth
for it not

ἐνιαυτοὺς τρεῖς καὶ μῆνας ἕξ. **18** Καὶ πάλιν προσηύξατο, καὶ
for years ˜ three and months ˜ six. And again he prayed, and

ὁ οὐρανὸς ὑετὸν ἔδωκε καὶ ἡ γῆ ἐβλάστησε τὸν καρπὸν
the heaven rain ˜ gave and the earth produced - fruit ˜

αὐτῆς.
its.

Bring Back the Erring One

19 Ἀδελφοί, ἐάν τις ἐν ὑμῖν πλανηθῇ ἀπὸ τῆς
Brothers, if anyone among you wanders away from the

ἀληθείας, καὶ ἐπιστρέψῃ τις αὐτόν, **20** γινωσκέτω ὅτι
truth, and [2]turns [4]back [1]anyone [3]him, let him know that

ὁ ἐπιστρέψας ἁμαρτωλὸν ἐκ πλάνης ὁδοῦ αὐτοῦ σώσει
the *one* [1]turning [4]back [2]a [3]sinner from *the* error of way ˜ his will save

ψυχὴν[f] ἐκ θανάτου καὶ καλύψει πλῆθος ἁμαρτιῶν.
a soul from death and will cover a multitude of sins.

---

c(5:12) TR reads υπο κρισιν, *under judgment.*
d(5:16) NU adds Ουν, *Therefore.*
e(5:16) NU reads τας αμαρτιας, *(your) sins.*
f(5:20) NU adds αυτου, *his (soul).*

The First Epistle of
PETER

ΠΕΤΡΟΥ Α
OF PETER 1

Peter Greets the Elect Pilgrims

1 1 Πέτρος, ἀπόστολος Ἰησοῦ Χριστοῦ,
Peter, an apostle of Jesus Christ,
Ἐκλεκτοῖς παρεπιδήμοις Διασπορᾶς Πόντου, Γαλατίας,
To the elect sojourners of the Dispersion of Pontus, Galatia,
Καππαδοκίας, Ἀσίας, καὶ Βιθυνίας, 2 κατὰ
Cappadocia, Asia, and Bithynia, according to
πρόγνωσιν Θεοῦ Πατρός, ἐν ἁγιασμῷ Πνεύματος, εἰς
the foreknowledge of God *the* Father, in *the* sanctification of *the* Spirit, for
ὑπακοὴν καὶ ῥαντισμὸν αἵματος Ἰησοῦ Χριστοῦ·
obedience and sprinkling of *the* blood of Jesus Christ:
Χάρις ὑμῖν καὶ εἰρήνη πληθυνθείη.
May grace to you and peace be multiplied.

New Life and Heavenly Inheritance

3 Εὐλογητὸς ὁ Θεὸς καὶ Πατὴρ τοῦ Κυρίου ἡμῶν Ἰησοῦ
Blessed *is* the God and Father - of Lord ˜ our Jesus
Χριστοῦ, ὁ κατὰ τὸ πολὺ αὐτοῦ ἔλεος
Christ, the *One* according to - great ˜ His mercy
who
ἀναγεννήσας ἡμᾶς εἰς ἐλπίδα ζῶσαν δι' ἀναστάσεως
having begotten again ˜ us to a hope ˜ living through *the* resurrection
has
Ἰησοῦ Χριστοῦ ἐκ νεκρῶν, 4 εἰς κληρονομίαν ἄφθαρτον καὶ
of Jesus Christ from *the* dead, into an inheritance incorruptible and
ἀμίαντον καὶ ἀμάραντον, τετηρημένην ἐν οὐρανοῖς εἰς ὑμᾶς
undefiled and unfading, having been kept in *the* heavens for you
being
5 τοὺς ἐν δυνάμει Θεοῦ φρουρουμένους διὰ πίστεως εἰς
the *ones* by *the* power of God *are* being guarded through faith for
who
σωτηρίαν ἑτοίμην ἀποκαλυφθῆναι ἐν καιρῷ ἐσχάτῳ. 6 Ἐν
the salvation ready to be revealed in *the* time ˜ last. In
ᾧ ἀγαλλιᾶσθε, ὀλίγον ἄρτι, εἰ δέον ἐστί,
which you rejoice, *though for* a little *while* now, if [3]necessary [1]it [2]is,
λυπηθέντες ἐν ποικίλοις πειρασμοῖς, 7 ἵνα τὸ
having been distressed by various trials, so that the
you have
δοκίμιον ὑμῶν τῆς πίστεως πολὺ τιμιώτερον χρυσίου
genuineness of your - faith *which is* much more precious *than* gold
τοῦ ἀπολλυμένου, διὰ πυρὸς δὲ δοκιμαζομένου,
the *one* perishing, [4]through [5]fire [1]but [2]being [3]tested,
which perishes,
εὑρεθῇ εἰς ἔπαινον καὶ τιμὴν καὶ εἰς δόξαν ἐν ἀποκαλύψει
may be found to praise and honor and to glory at *the* revelation
Ἰησοῦ Χριστοῦ. 8 Ὃν οὐκ εἰδότες[a] ἀγαπᾶτε, εἰς ὃν
of Jesus Christ. Whom not ˜ having known you love, in whom

1 Peter, an apostle of Jesus Christ,

To the pilgrims of the Dispersion in Pontus, Galatia, Cappadocia, Asia, and Bithynia,
2 elect according to the foreknowledge of God the Father, in sanctification of the Spirit, for obedience and sprinkling of the blood of Jesus Christ:

Grace to you and peace be multiplied.

3 Blessed *be* the God and Father of our Lord Jesus Christ, who according to His abundant mercy has begotten us again to a living hope through the resurrection of Jesus Christ from the dead,
4 to an inheritance incorruptible and undefiled and that does not fade away, reserved in heaven for you,
5 who are kept by the power of God through faith for salvation ready to be revealed in the last time.
6 In this you greatly rejoice, though now for a little while, if need be, you have been grieved by various trials,
7 that the genuineness of your faith, *being* much more precious than gold that perishes, though it is tested by fire, may be found to praise, honor, and glory at the revelation of Jesus Christ,
8 whom having not seen you

---

[a](1:8) NU reads ιδοντες, *having seen.*

love. Though now you do not
see *Him,* yet believing, you rejoice with joy inexpressible and
full of glory,
9 receiving the end of your
faith—the salvation of *your*
souls.
10 Of this salvation the prophets have inquired and searched
carefully, who prophesied of
the grace *that would come* to
you,
11 searching what, or what
manner of time, the Spirit of
Christ who was in them was indicating when He testified beforehand the sufferings of
Christ and the glories that
would follow.
12 To them it was revealed
that, not to themselves, but to
us they were ministering the
things which now have been reported to you through those
who have preached the gospel
to you by the Holy Spirit sent
from heaven—things which angels desire to look into.
13 Therefore gird up the loins
of your mind, be sober, and
rest *your* hope fully upon the
grace that is to be brought to
you at the revelation of Jesus
Christ;
14 as obedient children, not
conforming yourselves to the
former lusts, *as* in your ignorance;
15 but as He who called you *is*
holy, you also be holy in all *your*
conduct,
16 because it is written, *"Be
holy, for I am holy."*
17 And if you call on the Fa-

ἄρτι μὴ ὁρῶντες, πιστεύοντες δὲ ἀγαλλιᾶσθε χαρᾷ
now not seeing, believing ˜ but you rejoice [1]with [7]joy

ἀνεκλαλήτῳ καὶ δεδοξασμένῃ, **9** κομιζόμενοι τὸ
[2]inexpressible [3]and [4]having [5]been [6]glorified, obtaining for yourselves the
glorified,

τέλος τῆς πίστεως ὑμῶν, σωτηρίαν ψυχῶν.
outcome - [3]faith [1]of [2]your, *the* salvation *of your* souls.

10 Περὶ ἧς σωτηρίας ἐξεζήτησαν καὶ ἐξηρεύνησαν
Concerning which salvation [3]sought [4]out [5]and [6]inquired [7]carefully
this have sought

προφῆται οἱ περὶ τῆς εἰς ὑμᾶς χάριτος
[1]*the* [2]prophets the *ones* [3]about [4]the [6]*coming* [7]for [8]you [5]grace
who

προφητεύσαντες, **11** ἐρευνῶντες εἰς τίνα ἢ ποῖον καιρὸν
[1]having [2]prophesied, searching for who or what kind of time
prophesied,

ἐδήλου τὸ ἐν αὐτοῖς Πνεῦμα Χριστοῦ προμαρτυρόμενον
[7]was [8]revealing [1]the [5]in [6]them [2]Spirit [3]of [4]Christ testifying beforehand to
when He testified

τὰ εἰς Χριστὸν παθήματα καὶ τὰς μετὰ ταῦτα δόξας·
the [2]to [3]Christ [1]sufferings and the [2]after [3]these [4]*things* [1]glories:
of which were to follow

12 οἷς ἀπεκαλύφθη ὅτι οὐχ ἑαυτοῖς, ὑμῖν[b] δὲ
to them it was revealed that not to themselves, [2]to [3]you [1]but

διηκόνουν αὐτά, ἃ νῦν ἀνηγγέλη ὑμῖν
they were ministering these *things,* which *things* now were announced to you

διὰ τῶν εὐαγγελισαμένων ὑμᾶς ἐν Πνεύματι Ἁγίῳ
by the *ones* having proclaimed the gospel to you by *the* Spirit ˜ Holy
those who proclaimed

ἀποσταλέντι ἀπ' οὐρανοῦ, εἰς ἃ ἐπιθυμοῦσιν ἄγγελοι
having been sent from heaven, into which *things* desire ˜ angels
sent

παρακύψαι.
to look into.

Life in Relation to God Our Father

13 Διὸ ἀναζωσάμενοι τὰς ὀσφύας τῆς διανοίας ὑμῶν,
Therefore having girded up the loins - [3]mind [1]of [2]your,
gird up

νήφοντες, τελείως ἐλπίσατε ἐπὶ τὴν φερομένην ὑμῖν
being sober, completely ˜ hope upon the [2]being [3]borne [4]to [5]you
stay sober, put your hope fully in brought

χάριν ἐν ἀποκαλύψει Ἰησοῦ Χριστοῦ. **14** Ὡς τέκνα
[1]grace at *the* revelation of Jesus Christ. As children
obedient

ὑπακοῆς, μὴ συσχηματιζόμενοι ταῖς πρότερον
of obedience, not being conformed to the former
children, conforming yourselves

ἐν τῇ ἀγνοίᾳ ὑμῶν ἐπιθυμίαις,* **15** ἀλλὰ κατὰ
[2]*which* [3]*you* [4]*had* [5]in - [7]ignorance [6]your [1]lusts, but just as

τὸν καλέσαντα ὑμᾶς ἅγιον καὶ αὐτοὶ ἅγιοι ἐν πάσῃ
the *One* having called you *is* holy also ˜ you [3]holy [4]in [5]all
who

ἀναστροφῇ γενήθητε, **16** διότι γέγραπται, «Ἅγιοι
[6]manner [7]of [8]life [1]*should* [2]be, because it is written, «[4]holy

γίνεσθε, ὅτι ἐγὼ ἅγιός εἰμι.»[c] **17** Καὶ εἰ Πατέρα
[1]You [2]shall [3]be, because I holy ˜ am.» And if [4]*the* [5]Father

---

[b](**1:12**) TR reads ημιν, *to us.* [c](**1:16**) Lev. 11:44, 45; 19:2; 20:7

*(**1:14**) ἐπιθυμία *(epithymia).* Noun usually translated *lust* in the NT, meaning *strong desire, longing, craving.* Such desire is perhaps neutral in Mark 4:19; Rev. 18:14, and may be good, as in Phil. 1:23; 1 Thess. 2:17. Most often, as here in 1 Pet. 1:14, it is an evil desire for something forbidden (cf. Gal. 5:16; 1 John 2:16), whether sexual or otherwise. Cf. the cognate verb ἐπιθυμέω, *crave, desire, long for,* which can also be negative ("covet," Acts 20:33) but is more often positive in the NT (as 1 Tim. 3:1).

ἐπικαλεῖσθε τὸν ἀπροσωπολήμπτως κρίνοντα κατὰ τὸ
[1]you [2]call [3]on the *One* impartially ~ judging according to the
who judges

ἑκάστου ἔργον, ἐν φόβῳ τὸν τῆς παροικίας ὑμῶν
[2]of [3]each [4]*one* [1]work, [13]in [14]fear [7]*during* [8]the - [12]sojourn [10]of [11]your
temporary stay

χρόνον ἀναστράφητε, **18** εἰδότες ὅτι οὐ
[9]time [5]conduct [6]yourselves, knowing that [3]not

φθαρτοῖς, ἀργυρίῳ ἢ χρυσίῳ, ἐλυτρώθητε
[5]with [6]perishable [7]*things,* [8]*like* [9]silver [10]or [11]gold, [1]you [2]were [4]redeemed

ἐκ τῆς ματαίας ὑμῶν ἀναστροφῆς
from - futile ~ your way of life

πατροπαραδότου, **19** ἀλλὰ τιμίῳ αἵματι ὡς
handed down from *your* forefathers, but with *the* precious blood [3]as

ἀμνοῦ ἀμώμου καὶ ἀσπίλου Χριστοῦ, **20** προεγνωσμένου
[4]a [5]lamb [6]blameless [7]and [8]spotless [1]of [2]Christ, having been foreknown

μὲν πρὸ καταβολῆς κόσμου, φανερωθέντος
on the one hand before *the* foundation of *the* world, being revealed
He was made manifest

δὲ ἐπ' ἐσχάτων τῶν χρόνων δι' ὑμᾶς
on the other hand on *the* last - times for the sake of you
in these

21 τοὺς δι' αὐτοῦ πιστεύοντας εἰς Θεὸν τὸν ἐγείραντα
the *ones* through Him believing in God the *One* raising
who believe who raised

αὐτὸν ἐκ νεκρῶν καὶ δόξαν αὐτῷ δόντα, ὥστε τὴν πίστιν
Him from *the* dead and [2]glory [3]to [4]Him [1]giving, so that - faith ~
gave,

ὑμῶν καὶ ἐλπίδα εἶναι εἰς Θεόν.
your and hope to be in God.
are

Life in Relation to Our Brethren

22 Τὰς ψυχὰς ὑμῶν ἡγνικότες ἐν τῇ ὑπακοῇ τῆς
- [4]souls [3]your [1]Having [2]purified by - obedience of the
Since you have to

ἀληθείας διὰ Πνεύματος[d] εἰς φιλαδελφίαν
truth through *the* Spirit with reference to [2]brotherly [3]love

ἀνυπόκριτον, ἐκ καθαρᾶς καρδίας ἀλλήλους ἀγαπήσατε
[1]unhypocritical, [8]from [9]a [10]pure [11]heart [5]one [6]another [4]love

ἐκτενῶς, **23** ἀναγεγεννημένοι οὐκ ἐκ σπορᾶς φθαρτῆς
[7]fervently, having been born again not from seed ~ perishable
because you have

ἀλλὰ ἀφθάρτου, διὰ λόγου ζῶντος Θεοῦ καὶ
but rather *from* imperishable *seed,* through *the* word [3]living [1]of [2]God and
which lives

μένοντος εἰς τὸν αἰῶνα.[e] **24** Διότι
remaining into the age. For
abides forever.

«Πᾶσα σὰρξ ὡς χόρτος,
«All flesh *is* as grass,

Καὶ πᾶσα δόξα ἀνθρώπου[f] ὡς ἄνθος χόρτου.
And all *the* glory of man *is* as *the* flower of grass.

Ἐξηράνθη ὁ χόρτος,
[3]withered [1]The [2]grass,
withers

Καὶ τὸ ἄνθος αὐτοῦ ἐξέπεσε,
And - flower ~ its fell off,
falls

ther, who without partiality
judges according to each one's
work, conduct yourselves
throughout the time of your
stay *here* in fear;
18 knowing that you were not
redeemed with corruptible
things, *like* silver or gold, from
your aimless conduct *received*
by tradition from your fathers,
19 but with the precious blood
of Christ, as of a lamb without
blemish and without spot.
20 He indeed was fore-
ordained before the foundation
of the world, but was manifest
in these last times for you
21 who through Him believe in
God, who raised Him from the
dead and gave Him glory, so
that your faith and hope are in
God.
22 Since you have purified
your souls in obeying the truth
through the Spirit in sincere
love of the brethren, love one
another fervently with a pure
heart,
23 having been born again, not
of corruptible seed but incorruptible, through the word of
God which lives and abides forever,
24 because

"All flesh is as grass,
And all the glory of man
as the flower of the
grass.
The grass withers,
And its flower falls away,

[d](**1:22**) NU omits δια Πνευματος, *through the Spirit.* [e](**1:23**) NU omits εις τον αιωνα, *forever.*
[f](**1:24**) NU reads αυτης, *(all) its (glory).*

25 *But the word of the* LORD
endures forever."

Now this is the word which by the gospel was preached to you.

2 Therefore, laying aside all malice, all deceit, hypocrisy, envy, and all evil speaking,
2 as newborn babes, desire the pure milk of the word, that you may grow thereby,
3 if indeed you have tasted that the Lord *is* gracious.
4 Coming to Him *as to* a living stone, rejected indeed by men, but chosen by God *and* precious,
5 you also, as living stones, are being built up a spiritual house, a holy priesthood, to offer up spiritual sacrifices acceptable to God through Jesus Christ.
6 Therefore it is also contained in the Scripture,

"Behold, I lay in Zion
A chief cornerstone,
elect, precious,
And he who believes on
Him will by no means
be put to shame."

7 Therefore, to you who believe, *He is* precious; but to those who are disobedient,

"The stone which the
builders rejected
Has become the chief
cornerstone,"

8 and

"A stone of stumbling

Τὸ δὲ ῥῆμα Κυρίου μένει εἰς τὸν αἰῶνα.»[g]
the ˜ But word of *the* Lord remains into the age.»
forever.»

25 Τοῦτο δέ ἐστι τὸ ῥῆμα τὸ εὐαγγελισθὲν εἰς ὑμᾶς.
this ˜ But is the word the *one* preached to you.
which was proclaimed

The Chosen Stone and His Chosen People

2 1 Ἀποθέμενοι οὖν πᾶσαν κακίαν καὶ πάντα δόλον
[2]putting [3]away [1]Therefore all malice and all deceit
καὶ ὑποκρίσεις καὶ φθόνους καὶ πάσας καταλαλιάς, 2 ὡς
and hypocrisies and envies and all slanders, as
ἀρτιγέννητα βρέφη, τὸ λογικὸν ἄδολον γάλα
new born babies, [2]the [3]spiritual [4]unadulterated [5]milk
pure
ἐπιποθήσατε, ἵνα ἐν αὐτῷ αὐξηθῆτε,[a] 3 εἴπερ
[1]desire, in order that by it you may grow, if indeed
ἐγεύσασθε ὅτι χρηστὸς ὁ Κύριος. 4 Πρὸς ὃν
you tasted that [3]*is* [4]kind [1]the [2]Lord. Toward whom
have tasted
προσερχόμενοι, λίθον ζῶντα, ὑπὸ ἀνθρώπων
approaching, *as to* a stone ˜ living, [8]by [9]men
μὲν ἀποδεδοκιμασμένον, παρὰ
[1]on [2]the [3]one [4]hand [5]having [6]been [7]rejected, [17]before
δὲ Θεῷ ἐκλεκτὸν, ἔντιμον, 5 καὶ
[10]but [11]on [12]the [13]other [14]hand [18]God [15]chosen, [16]precious, also
αὐτοὶ ὡς λίθοι ζῶντες οἰκοδομεῖσθε οἶκος
[2]yourselves [6]as [8]stones [7]living [1]you [3]are [4]being [5]built *into* a house ˜
πνευματικός, ἱεράτευμα ἅγιον, ἀνενέγκαι πνευματικὰς θυσίας
spiritual, a priesthood ˜ holy, to offer up spiritual sacrifices
εὐπροσδέκτους τῷ Θεῷ διὰ Ἰησοῦ Χριστοῦ. 6 Διότι
acceptable to God through Jesus Christ. For
περιέχει ἐν τῇ Γραφῇ,
it is contained in the Scripture,

«Ἰδού, τίθημι ἐν Σιὼν
«Behold, I place in Zion
Λίθον ἀκρογωνιαῖον, ἐκλεκτόν, ἔντιμον,
A stone at the extreme corner, chosen, precious,
chief cornerstone,
Καὶ ὁ πιστεύων ἐπ' αὐτῷ οὐ μὴ
And the *one* believing on Him [2]not [3]not
he who believes by no means
καταισχυνθῇ.»[b]
[1]shall [4]be put to shame.»

7 Ὑμῖν οὖν ἡ τιμὴ τοῖς πιστεύουσιν,
[4]*is* [5]to [6]you [1]Therefore [2]the [3]honor the *ones* believing,
who believe,
ἀπειθοῦσι[c] δὲ,
[2]*to* [3]*the* [4]*ones* [5]disobeying [1]but,

«Λίθον ὃν ἀπεδοκίμασαν οἱ οἰκοδομοῦντες,
«*The* stone which [4]rejected [1]the [2]*ones* [3]building,
builders,
Οὗτος ἐγενήθη εἰς κεφαλὴν γωνίας»[d]
This *One* became for *the* head of the corner»
the chief cornerstone»

8 καὶ
and

«Λίθος προσκόμματος
«A stone of stumbling

[g](1:24) Is. 40:6–8
[a](2:2) NU adds εις σωτηριαν, *into salvation.*
[b](2:6) Is. 28:16
[c](2:7) NU reads απιστουσιν, *(to the ones) disbelieving.*
[d](2:7) Ps. 118:22

Καὶ πέτρα σκανδάλου»·[e]
And a rock of offense»;

οἳ προσκόπτουσι τῷ λόγῳ ἀπειθοῦντες, εἰς ὃ
those who stumble [3]to [4]the [5]word [1]being [2]disobedient, to which

καὶ ἐτέθησαν.
also ˜ they were appointed.

9 Ὑμεῖς δὲ «γένος ἐκλεκτόν, βασίλειον ἱεράτευμα,
[2]you [3]*are* [1]But «a race ˜ chosen, a royal priesthood,

ἔθνος ἅγιον, λαὸς εἰς περιποίησιν, ὅπως τὰς
a nation ˜ holy, a people for *God's own* possession, that [4]the

ἀρετὰς* ἐξαγγείλητε»[f] τοῦ ἐκ σκότους ὑμᾶς
[5]excellencies (excellent virtues) [1]you [2]may [3]proclaim» of the One (Him) [4]from [5]darkness [3]you

καλέσαντος εἰς τὸ θαυμαστὸν αὐτοῦ φῶς· 10 οἵ ποτε
[1]having [2]called (who called) into - marvelous ˜ His light; who formerly *were*

οὐ λαός, νῦν δὲ λαὸς Θεοῦ, οἱ οὐκ
not a people, now ˜ but *are the* people of God, the *ones* not

ἠλεημένοι, νῦν δὲ ἐλεηθέντες.
having received mercy, now ˜ but receiving mercy.

Life in Relation to the World

11 Ἀγαπητοί, παρακαλῶ ὡς παροίκους καὶ παρεπιδήμους
Beloved *ones,* I implore *you* as strangers (pilgrims) and sojourners

ἀπέχεσθαι τῶν σαρκικῶν ἐπιθυμιῶν, αἵτινες στρατεύονται
to abstain from the [2]of [3]the [4]flesh [1]lusts, which war

κατὰ τῆς ψυχῆς· 12 τὴν ἀναστροφὴν ὑμῶν ἔχοντες καλὴν
against the soul; - [3]manner [4]of [5]life [2]your [1]having noble

ἐν τοῖς ἔθνεσιν, ἵνα, ἐν ᾧ καταλαλοῦσιν ὑμῶν ὡς
among the Gentiles, so that, in which (whenever) they speak against you as

κακοποιῶν, ἐκ τῶν καλῶν ἔργων ἐποπτεύσαντες δοξάσωσι
evildoers, from (when) [3]the [4]noble [5]works [1]having [2]observed (they observe) they may glorify

τὸν Θεὸν ἐν ἡμέρᾳ ἐπισκοπῆς.
- God in *the* day of visitation.

Submission to Government

13 Ὑποτάγητε οὖν πάσῃ ἀνθρωπίνῃ κτίσει
[2]subject [3]yourselves [1]Therefore to every human creation (institution)

διὰ τὸν Κύριον· εἴτε βασιλεῖ ὡς ὑπερέχοντι,
on account of the Lord: whether to a king as *to one* having authority,

14 εἴτε ἡγεμόσιν ὡς δι' αὐτοῦ πεμπομένοις εἰς
or to governors as [5]by [6]him [1]*to* [2]*those* [3]being [4]sent for

ἐκδίκησιν κακοποιῶν, ἔπαινον δὲ ἀγαθοποιῶν.
the punishment of evildoers, [2]*for* [3]*the* [4]praise [1]and *of those* doing good.

15 Ὅτι οὕτως ἐστὶ τὸ θέλημα τοῦ Θεοῦ, ἀγαθοποιοῦντας
Because so is the will - of God, doing good

φιμοῦν τὴν τῶν ἀφρόνων ἀνθρώπων ἀγνωσίαν· 16 ὡς
to (you may) silence the - [2]of [3]foolish [4]men [1]ignorance: as

ἐλεύθεροι, καὶ μὴ ὡς ἐπικάλυμμα ἔχοντες τῆς κακίας τὴν
free *men,* and not [3]as [4]a [5]cover [1]having (using) [6]of (for) [7]wickedness -

ἐλευθερίαν, ἀλλ' ὡς δοῦλοι Θεοῦ. 17 Πάντας τιμήσατε.
[2]freedom, but as bondservants of God. all ˜ Honor.

And a rock of offense."

They stumble, being disobedient to the word, to which they also were appointed.

9 But you *are* a chosen generation, a royal priesthood, a holy nation, His own special people, that you may proclaim the praises of Him who called you out of darkness into His marvelous light;

10 who once *were* not a people but *are* now the people of God, who had not obtained mercy but now have obtained mercy.

11 Beloved, I beg *you* as sojourners and pilgrims, abstain from fleshly lusts which war against the soul,

12 having your conduct honorable among the Gentiles, that when they speak against you as evildoers, they may, by *your* good works which they observe, glorify God in the day of visitation.

13 Therefore submit yourselves to every ordinance of man for the Lord's sake, whether to the king as supreme,

14 or to governors, as to those who are sent by him for the punishment of evildoers and *for the* praise of those who do good.

15 For this is the will of God, that by doing good you may put to silence the ignorance of foolish men—

16 as free, yet not using liberty as a cloak for vice, but as bondservants of God.

17 Honor all *people.* Love the

---

[e](2:8) Is. 8:14
[f](2:9) Ex. 9:16; Is. 43:20

***(2:9)** ἀρετή *(aretē).* Noun meaning *excellence,* but in the NT only used of *moral excellence, virtue* (Phil. 4:8; 2 Pet. 1:3, 5). The meaning here in 1 Pet. 2:9 is problematic. Following the LXX practice of translating Hebrew *tehillāh, praise,* by ἀρετή, it may mean *praises* or *laudes.* Another possibility is the later meaning *manifestation of divine power* (cf. 2 Pet. 1:3).

brotherhood. Fear God. Honor
the king.
18 Servants, *be* submissive to
your masters with all fear, not
only to the good and gentle, but
also to the harsh.
19 For this *is* commendable, if
because of conscience toward
God one endures grief, suffering wrongfully.
20 For what credit *is it* if,
when you are beaten for your
faults, you take it patiently? But
when you do good and suffer, if
you take it patiently, this *is*
commendable before God.
21 For to this you were called,
because Christ also suffered for
us, leaving us an example, that
you should follow His steps:

22 *"Who committed no sin,*
Nor was deceit found in
His mouth";

23 who, when He was reviled,
did not revile in return; when
He suffered, He did not
threaten, but committed *Him-*
self to Him who judges righteously;
24 who Himself bore our sins
in His own body on the tree,
that we, having died to sins,
might live for righteousness —
by whose stripes you were
healed.
25 For you were like sheep
going astray, but have now returned to the Shepherd and
Overseer of your souls.

Τὴν ἀδελφότητα ἀγαπήσατε. Τὸν Θεὸν φοβεῖσθε. Τὸν βασιλέα
[2]the [3]brotherhood [1]Love. - God ˜ Fear. [2]the [3]king

τιμᾶτε.
[1]Honor.

Submission to Masters

18 Οἱ οἰκέται, ὑποτασσόμενοι ἐν παντὶ φόβῳ τοῖς
- Servants, subjecting yourselves with all fear to the
subject

δεσπόταις, οὐ μόνον τοῖς ἀγαθοῖς καὶ ἐπιεικέσιν, ἀλλὰ καὶ
masters, not only to the good and gentle, but also

τοῖς σκολιοῖς. 19 Τοῦτο γὰρ χάρις, εἰ διὰ συνείδησιν
to the crooked. this ˜ For *brings* favor, if because of conscience
harsh. is admirable,

Θεοῦ ὑποφέρει τις λύπας, πάσχων ἀδίκως. 20 Ποῖον
of God endures ˜ someone pain, suffering unjustly. [2]what [3]kind [4]of
toward

γὰρ κλέος εἰ ἁμαρτάνοντες καὶ κολαφιζόμενοι ὑπομενεῖτε?
[1]For credit *is it* if sinning and being beaten you endure?
when you sin are

Ἀλλ᾽ εἰ ἀγαθοποιοῦντες καὶ πάσχοντες ὑπομενεῖτε, τοῦτο
But if doing good and suffering *for it* you endure, this
when you do suffer

χάρις παρὰ Θεῷ. 21 Εἰς τοῦτο γὰρ ἐκλήθητε, ὅτι
brings favor before God. [2]to [3]this [1]For you were called, because
is admirable

καὶ Χριστὸς ἔπαθεν ὑπὲρ ἡμῶν,[g] ὑμῖν[h] ὑπολιμπάνων
also ˜ Christ suffered in behalf of us, [5]for [6]you [1]leaving [2]behind

ὑπογραμμὸν* ἵνα ἐπακολουθήσητε τοῖς ἴχνεσιν αὐτοῦ,
[3]an [4]example that you should follow - in footsteps ˜ His,

22 ὃς
who

«Ἁμαρτίαν οὐκ ἐποίησεν,
«[4]sin [2]not [1]Did [3]commit,

Οὐδὲ εὑρέθη δόλος ἐν τῷ στόματι αὐτοῦ»·[i]
Nor [1]was [3]found [2]deceit in - mouth ˜ His»;

23 ὃς λοιδορούμενος οὐκ ἀντελοιδόρει, πάσχων οὐκ
who being reviled not ˜ did revile in return, suffering not ˜
verbally abused return verbal insults,

ἠπείλει, παρεδίδου δὲ τῷ κρίνοντι δικαίως·
did threaten, [2]committed [3]*Himself* [1]but to the *One* judging righteously;
Him who judges

24 ὃς τὰς ἁμαρτίας ἡμῶν αὐτὸς ἀνήνεγκεν ἐν τῷ σώματι
who - [4]sins [3]our [1]Himself [2]bore in - body ˜

αὐτοῦ ἐπὶ τὸ ξύλον, ἵνα ταῖς ἁμαρτίαις ἀπογενόμενοι,
His upon the tree, in order that - [3]to [4]sins [1]having [2]died,

τῇ δικαιοσύνῃ ζήσωμεν· «οὗ τῷ μώλωπι αὐτοῦ
- [8]for [9]righteousness [5]we [6]might [7]live: «of whom - by wound ˜ His
wounds

ἰάθητε.»[j] 25 Ἦτε γὰρ ὡς πρόβατα πλανώμενα, ἀλλ᾽
you were healed.» [2]you [3]were [1]For like sheep going astray, but

ἐπεστράφητε νῦν ἐπὶ τὸν Ποιμένα καὶ Ἐπίσκοπον τῶν ψυχῶν
you turned back now to the Shepherd and Overseer - of souls ˜
have turned

ὑμῶν.
your.

---

[g](2:21) NU reads *υμων*, *you.* [h](2:21) TR reads *ημιν*, *for us.*
[i](2:22) Is. 53:9
[j](2:24) Is. 53:5

*(2:21) *ὑπογραμμός (hypogrammos).* Noun, used only here in the NT, meaning *pattern* or *example*. The word is derived from the compound verb *ὑπογράφω* (literally, *write under*) which was used to designate the practice of drawing guidelines on which students would practice writing letters. The noun originally meant a pattern or example to be followed by students learning to write or draw, but quickly took on the more general meaning of any pattern or example. Here the word designates Christ as the believer's example of suffering.

Submission to Husbands

3 1 Ὁμοίως, αἱ γυναῖκες, ὑποτασσόμεναι τοῖς ἰδίοις
Likewise, - wives, subjecting yourselves - to your own
subject

ἀνδράσιν, ἵνα καὶ εἴ τινες ἀπειθοῦσι τῷ λόγῳ,
husbands, so that even if some are disobedient to the word,

διὰ τῆς τῶν γυναικῶν ἀναστροφῆς ἄνευ λόγου
on account of the [2]of [3]the [4]wives [1]conduct without a word

κερδηθήσονται, 2 ἐποπτεύσαντες τὴν ἐν φόβῳ
they shall be gained *for Christ,* having observed - [4]with [5]fear
when they observe respect

ἁγνὴν ἀναστροφὴν ὑμῶν. 3 Ὧν ἔστω οὐχ ὁ ἔξωθεν
[2]chaste [3]conduct [1]your. Of whom let it be ˜ not the outward

ἐμπλοκῆς τριχῶν καὶ περιθέσεως χρυσίων ἢ ἐνδύσεως
[2]of [3]braiding [4]of [5]hairs [6]and [7]wearing [8]of [9]gold [10]or [11]of [12]putting [13]on
hair

ἱματίων κόσμος, 4 ἀλλ' ὁ κρυπτὸς τῆς καρδίας
[14]of [15]garments [1]adorning, rather, *let it be* the hidden [2]of [3]the [4]heart

ἄνθρωπος ἐν τῷ ἀφθάρτῳ τοῦ πραέος καὶ ἡσυχίου
[1]man with the incorruptible *attitude* of the gentle and quiet
person a

πνεύματος, ὅ ἐστιν ἐνώπιον τοῦ Θεοῦ πολυτελές. 5 Οὕτω
spirit, which is [3]before - [4]God [1]very [2]costly. thus ˜

γάρ ποτε καὶ αἱ ἅγιαι γυναῖκες αἱ ἐλπίζουσαι ἐπὶ
For formerly [9]also [1]the [2]holy [3]women [4]the [5]*ones* [6]hoping [7]on
who hoped

Θεὸν ἐκόσμουν ἑαυτάς, ὑποτασσόμεναι τοῖς ἰδίοις
[8]God adorned themselves, subjecting themselves - to their own

ἀνδράσιν, 6 ὡς Σάρρα ὑπήκουσε τῷ Ἀβραάμ, κύριον αὐτὸν
husbands, as Sarah obeyed - Abraham, [3]lord [2]him

καλοῦσα, ἧς ἐγενήθητε τέκνα, ἀγαθοποιοῦσαι καὶ μὴ
[1]calling, of whom you became children, doing good and not
when you do are

φοβούμεναι μηδεμίαν πτόησιν.
being afraid of no terror.
not afraid of any

A Word to Husbands

7 Οἱ ἄνδρες ὁμοίως, συνοικοῦντες κατὰ γνῶσιν ὡς
- Husbands likewise, living together according to knowledge as
live

ἀσθενεστέρῳ σκεύει τῷ γυναικείῳ, ἀπονέμοντες τιμὴν
with a weaker vessel with the feminine *one,* showing honor *to her*
wife,

ὡς καὶ συγκληρονόμοι χάριτος ζωῆς, εἰς τὸ μὴ
as also a fellow heir of *the* grace of life, for - [3]not
in order that may

ἐγκόπτεσθαι τὰς προσευχὰς ὑμῶν.
[4]to [5]be [6]hindered - [2]prayers [1]your.
not be hindered

Life in Relation to Suffering

8 Τὸ δὲ τέλος, πάντες ὁμόφρονες, συμπαθεῖς,
- And finally, all *be* likeminded, sympathetic,

φιλάδελφοι, εὔσπλαγχνοι, φιλόφρονες,[a] 9 μὴ ἀποδιδόντες
loving the brothers, compassionate, friendly, not returning

κακὸν ἀντὶ κακοῦ ἢ λοιδορίαν ἀντὶ λοιδορίας, τοὐναντίον
evil for evil or reviling for reviling, [2]on [3]the [4]contrary

3 Wives, likewise, *be* submissive to your own hus-
bands, that even if some do not
obey the word, they, without a
word, may be won by the conduct of their wives,
2 when they observe your
chaste conduct *accompanied* by
fear.
3 Do not let your adornment
be *merely* outward—arranging
the hair, wearing gold, or putting on *fine* apparel—
4 rather *let it be* the hidden
person of the heart, with the incorruptible *beauty* of a gentle
and quiet spirit, which is very
precious in the sight of God.
5 For in this manner, in former times, the holy women
who trusted in God also
adorned themselves, being submissive to their own husbands,
6 as Sarah obeyed Abraham,
calling him lord, whose daughters you are if you do good and
are not afraid with any terror.
7 Husbands, likewise, dwell
with *them* with understanding,
giving honor to the wife, as to
the weaker vessel, and as *being*
heirs together of the grace of
life, that your prayers may not
be hindered.
8 Finally, all *of you be* of one
mind, having compassion for
one another; love as brothers,
be tenderhearted, *be* courteous;
9 not returning evil for evil or
reviling for reviling, but on the

[a](3:8) NU reads ταπεινοφρονες, *humble.*

contrary blessing, knowing that you were called to this, that you may inherit a blessing.
10 For

"He who would love life
And see good days,
Let him refrain his tongue
from evil,
And his lips from speaking
deceit.
11 *Let him turn away from*
evil and do good;
Let him seek peace and
pursue it.
12 *For the eyes of the* LORD
are on the righteous,
And His ears are open to
their prayers;
But the face of the LORD
is against those who do
evil."

13 And who *is* he who will harm you if you become followers of what is good?
14 But even if you should suffer for righteousness' sake, *you are* blessed. *"And do not be afraid of their threats, nor be troubled."*
15 But sanctify the Lord God in your hearts, and always *be* ready to *give* a defense to everyone who asks you a reason for the hope that is in you, with meekness and fear;
16 having a good conscience, that when they defame you as evildoers, those who revile your good conduct in Christ may be ashamed.
17 For *it is* better, if it is the will of God, to suffer for doing good than for doing evil.
18 For Christ also suffered once for sins, the just for the unjust, that He might bring us

---

[b](3:10–12) Ps. 34:12–16
[c](3:14) Is. 8:12
[d](3:15) NU reads Χριστον, *Christ (as Lord).*
[e](3:18) TR reads ημας, *us.*

---

*(3:15) ἀπολογία *(apologia).* Noun meaning *defense, reply,* from the preposition ἀπό, *back,* and the noun λογία, *speech.* Most of the NT uses have a legal, or quasi-legal, context (as Acts 22:1), but Paul also used the word to speak of defense of the gospel (Phil. 1:7, 17). Here in 3:15 Peter may be speaking in the general sense of a response or specifically of a formal defense when questioned in the context of legal charges. Cf. the cognate verb ἀπολογέομαι, *speak in one's own*

δὲ εὐλογοῦντες, εἰδότες ὅτι εἰς τοῦτο ἐκλήθητε ἵνα
[1]but blessing, knowing that for this *purpose* you were called that

εὐλογίαν κληρονομήσητε.
[4]a [5]blessing [1]you [2]may [3]inherit.

10 «Ὁ γὰρ θέλων ζωὴν ἀγαπᾶν
«[2]the [3]*one* [1]For desiring [3]life [1]to [2]love
«he who desires

Καὶ ἰδεῖν ἡμέρας ἀγαθάς,
And to see days ˜ good,

Παυσάτω τὴν γλῶσσαν αὐτοῦ ἀπὸ κακοῦ
Let him stop - tongue ˜ his from evil

Καὶ χείλη αὐτοῦ τοῦ μὴ λαλῆσαι δόλον·
And lips ˜ his - not to speak deceit;
from speaking

11 Ἐκκλινάτω ἀπὸ κακοῦ καὶ ποιησάτω ἀγαθόν·
Let him turn away from evil and let him do good;

Ζητησάτω εἰρήνην καὶ διωξάτω αὐτήν.
Let him seek peace and pursue it.

12 Ὅτι ὀφθαλμοὶ Κυρίου ἐπὶ δικαίους
Because *the* eyes of the Lord *are* upon *the* righteous *ones*

Καὶ ὦτα αὐτοῦ εἰς δέησιν αὐτῶν,
And ears ˜ His *open* to prayer ˜ their,

Πρόσωπον δὲ Κυρίου ἐπὶ ποιοῦντας κακά.»[b]
[2]*the* [3]face [1]But of *the* Lord *is* against *the ones* doing evil *things.*»

13 Καὶ τίς ὁ κακώσων ὑμᾶς ἐὰν τοῦ ἀγαθοῦ
And who *is* the *one* harming you if [4]of [5]the [6]good
who will harm

μιμηταὶ γένησθε? **14** Ἀλλ' εἰ καὶ πάσχοιτε διὰ
[3]imitators [1]you [2]become But if ˜ even you should suffer on account of

δικαιοσύνην, μακάριοι. «Τὸν δὲ φόβον αὐτῶν μὴ
righteousness, *you are* blessed. - «But [5]fear [4]their [2]not

φοβηθῆτε μηδὲ ταραχθῆτε.»[c] **15** Κύριον δὲ τὸν Θεὸν[d]
[1]do [3]fear nor be troubled.» [3]*the* [4]Lord [1]But - [5]God

ἁγιάσατε ἐν ταῖς καρδίαις ὑμῶν, ἕτοιμοι δὲ ἀεὶ πρὸς
[2]sanctify in - hearts ˜ your, [3]*be* [4]prepared [1]and [2]always with

ἀπολογίαν* παντὶ τῷ αἰτοῦντι ὑμᾶς λόγον περὶ τῆς ἐν
a defense to every - *one* asking you a word concerning the [2]in
everyone who asks

ὑμῖν ἐλπίδος, μετὰ πραΰτητος καὶ φόβου, **16** συνείδησιν
[3]you [1]hope, with gentleness and respect, [2]a [4]conscience

ἔχοντες ἀγαθήν, ἵνα ἐν ᾧ καταλαλῶσιν ὑμῶν ὡς
[1]having [3]good, so that in what *thing* they speak against you as

κακοποιῶν, καταισχυνθῶσιν οἱ ἐπηρεάζοντες ὑμῶν
evildoers, [9]may [10]be [11]put [12]to [13]shame [1]the [2]*ones* [3]reviling [4]your

τὴν ἀγαθὴν ἐν Χριστῷ ἀναστροφήν.
- [5]good [7]in [8]Christ [6]conduct.

Suffering in Identification with Christ

17 Κρεῖττον γὰρ ἀγαθοποιοῦντας, εἰ θέλοι τὸ
[2]*it* [3]*is* [4]better [1]For [7]*for* [8]doing [9]good, [10]if [15]should [16]will [11]the

θέλημα τοῦ Θεοῦ, πάσχειν ἢ κακοποιοῦντας. **18** Ὅτι
[12]will - [13]of [14]God, [5]to [6]suffer than *for* doing evil. Because

καὶ Χριστὸς ἅπαξ περὶ ἁμαρτιῶν ἔπαθε, δίκαιος
also ˜ Christ [2]once [3]for [4]sins [1]suffered, *the* just
to atone for

ὑπὲρ ἀδίκων, ἵνα ὑμᾶς[e] προσαγάγῃ τῷ Θεῷ,
on behalf of *the* unjust, so that [4]you [1]He [2]might [3]bring to God,

θανατωθεὶς μὲν σαρκί, ζωοποιηθεὶς
being put to death on the one hand in the flesh, [2]being [3]made [4]alive

δὲ πνεύματι· 19 ἐν ᾧ καὶ τοῖς ἐν
[1]but [5]on [6]the [7]other [8]hand in the spirit; by whom also [2]to [3]the [5]in

φυλακῇ πνεύμασι πορευθεὶς ἐκήρυξεν, 20 ἀπειθήσασί
[6]prison [4]spirits [1]going He proclaimed, having disobeyed
He went and preached, who

ποτε, ὅτε ἀπεξεδέχετο[f] ἡ τοῦ Θεοῦ μακροθυμία ἐν
formerly, when [5]was [6]waiting [1]the - [3]of [4]God [2]patience in

ἡμέραις Νῶε, κατασκευαζομένης κιβωτοῦ, εἰς ἣν ὀλίγαι,
the days of Noah, [3]being [4]prepared [1]*the* [2]ark, into which a few,
when the ark was prepared,

τοῦτ' ἔστιν ὀκτὼ ψυχαί, διεσώθησαν δι' ὕδατος· 21 ὃ
that is eight souls, were saved through water; which
persons,

ἀντίτυπον νῦν καὶ ἡμᾶς σῴζει βάπτισμα, οὐ σαρκὸς
as an antitype [2]now [3]also [5]us [4]saves [1]baptism, not [5]of [6]*the* [7]flesh

ἀπόθεσις ῥύπου, ἀλλὰ συνειδήσεως ἀγαθῆς ἐπερώτημα
[1]the [2]removal [3]of [4]filth, but [8]conscience [5]*for* [6]a [7]good [1]an [2]appeal

εἰς Θεόν, δι' ἀναστάσεως Ἰησοῦ Χριστοῦ, 22 ὅς ἐστιν ἐν
[3]to [4]God, through *the* resurrection of Jesus Christ, who is at

δεξιᾷ τοῦ Θεοῦ, πορευθεὶς εἰς οὐρανόν, ὑποταγέντων
the right *hand* - of God, having gone into heaven, [6]being [7]subjected

αὐτῷ ἀγγέλων καὶ ἐξουσιῶν καὶ δυνάμεων.
[8]to [9]Him [1]angels [2]and [3]authorities [4]and [5]powers.

4

1 Χριστοῦ οὖν παθόντος ὑπὲρ ἡμῶν[a]
Christ ˜ Therefore having suffered in behalf of us
since Christ suffered

σαρκί, καὶ ὑμεῖς τὴν αὐτὴν ἔννοιαν ὁπλίσασθε,
in *the* flesh, also ˜ you [3]*with* [4]the [5]same [6]thought [1]arm [2]yourselves,

ὅτι ὁ παθὼν ἐν σαρκὶ πέπαυται ἁμαρτίας,
because the *one* suffering in *the* flesh has ceased of sin,
he who suffered from

2 εἰς τὸ μηκέτι ἀνθρώπων ἐπιθυμίαις, ἀλλὰ θελήματι
in order - no longer [12]of [13]men [9]for [10]*the* [11]lusts, [14]but [15]for [16]*the* [17]will

Θεοῦ τὸν ἐπίλοιπον ἐν σαρκὶ βιῶσαι χρόνον.
[18]of [19]God [3]the [4]remaining [6]in [7]*the* [8]flesh [1]to [2]live [5]time.

3 Ἀρκετὸς γὰρ ὑμῖν ὁ παρεληλυθὼς χρόνος τοῦ
[9]*is* [10]sufficient [1]For [11]for [12]you [2]the [6]having [7]passed [8]by [3]time -
lifetime that is

βίου[b] τὸ θέλημα τῶν ἐθνῶν κατεργάσασθαι,
[4]of [5]life [15]the [16]will [17]of [18]the [19]Gentiles [13]to [14]accomplish,
past

πεπορευμένους ἐν ἀσελγείαις, ἐπιθυμίαις, οἰνοφλυγίαις,
having walked in wantonness, lusts, drunkenness,

κώμοις, πότοις, καὶ ἀθεμίτοις εἰδωλολατρείαις. 4 Ἐν
revelries, drinking parties, and lawless idolatries. In
abominable

ᾧ ξενίζονται, μὴ συντρεχόντων ὑμῶν εἰς τὴν αὐτὴν
which they are surprised, not running together with you into the same

τῆς ἀσωτίας ἀνάχυσιν, βλασφημοῦντες· 5 οἳ
- [3]of [4]debauchery [1]pouring [2]out, reviling *you;* *these* who
flood,

ἀποδώσουσι λόγον τῷ ἑτοίμως ἔχοντι κρῖναι ζῶντας
will give up an account to the *One* readily having to judge *the* living
Him who is ready

καὶ νεκρούς. 6 Εἰς τοῦτο γὰρ καὶ νεκροῖς
and *the* dead. [2]for [3]this [4]*reason* [1]For also to *the* dead

to God, being put to death in the flesh but made alive by the Spirit,
19 by whom also He went and preached to the spirits in prison,
20 who formerly were disobedient, when once the Divine longsuffering waited in the days of Noah, while *the* ark was being prepared, in which a few, that is, eight souls, were saved through water.
21 There is also an antitype which now saves us—baptism (not the removal of the filth of the flesh, but the answer of a good conscience toward God), through the resurrection of Jesus Christ,
22 who has gone into heaven and is at the right hand of God, angels and authorities and powers having been made subject to Him.

4 Therefore, since Christ suffered for us in the flesh, arm yourselves also with the same mind, for he who has suffered in the flesh has ceased from sin,
2 that he no longer should live the rest of *his* time in the flesh for the lusts of men, but for the will of God.
3 For we *have spent* enough of our past lifetime in doing the will of the Gentiles—when we walked in lewdness, lusts, drunkenness, revelries, drinking parties, and abominable idolatries.
4 In regard to these, they think it strange that you do not run with *them* in the same flood of dissipation, speaking evil of *you.*
5 They will give an account to Him who is ready to judge the living and the dead.
6 For this reason the gospel was preached also to those who

---

[f](3:20) TR reads *απαξ εξεδεχετο, once waited.*
[a](4:1) NU omits *υπερ ημων, in behalf of us.*
[b](4:3) NU omits *του βιου, of life.*

defense, usually used for answering legal charges (Acts 24:10; 25:8).

are dead, that they might be
judged according to men in the
flesh, but live according to God
in the spirit.
7 But the end of all things is
at hand; therefore be serious
and watchful in your prayers.
8 And above all things have
fervent love for one another,
for *"love will cover a multitude*
of sins."
9 *Be* hospitable to one another without grumbling.
10 As each one has received a
gift, minister it to one another,
as good stewards of the manifold grace of God.
11 If anyone speaks, *let him*
speak as the oracles of God. If
anyone ministers, *let him do it*
as with the ability which God
supplies, that in all things God
may be glorified through Jesus
Christ, to whom belong the
glory and the dominion forever
and ever. Amen.
12 Beloved, do not think it
strange concerning the fiery
trial which is to try you, as
though some strange thing happened to you;
13 but rejoice to the extent
that you partake of Christ's sufferings, that when His glory is
revealed, you may also be glad
with exceeding joy.
14 If you are reproached for
the name of Christ, blessed *are*
you, for the Spirit of glory and
of God rests upon you. On their

εὐηγγελίσθη, ἵνα κριθῶσι
good news was proclaimed, in order that they might be judged

μὲν κατὰ ἀνθρώπους σαρκί, ζῶσι
on the one hand according to men in *the* flesh, [6]*that* [7]they [8]might [9]live

δὲ κατὰ Θεὸν πνεύματι.
[1]but [2]on [3]the [4]other [5]hand according to God in *the* spirit.

Serving for God's Glory

7 Πάντων δὲ τὸ τέλος ἤγγικε. Σωφρονήσατε
[4]of [5]all [6]*things* [1]Now [2]the [3]end has drawn near. [2]be [3]of [4]sound [5]mind

οὖν καὶ νήψατε εἰς τὰς προσευχάς. **8** Πρὸ
[1]Therefore and be self-controlled in the prayers. [2]above
(your)

πάντων δὲ τὴν εἰς ἑαυτοὺς ἀγάπην ἐκτενῆ ἔχοντες, ὅτι
[3]all [4]*things* [1]But - [8]for [9]yourselves [7]love [6]constant [5]having, because
(one another) (have,)

ἀγάπη καλύψει πλῆθος ἁμαρτιῶν· **9** φιλόξενοι εἰς
love will cover a multitude of sins; *be* hospitable *people* to

ἀλλήλους ἄνευ γογγυσμῶν· **10** ἕκαστος καθὼς ἔλαβε
one another without grumblings; [3]each [4]*one* [1]just [2]as received
(has received)

χάρισμα, εἰς ἑαυτοὺς αὐτὸ διακονοῦντες ὡς καλοὶ οἰκονόμοι
a gift, [2]to [3]yourselves [4]*with* [5]it [1]serving as good stewards
(one another) (minister)

ποικίλης χάριτος Θεοῦ. **11** Εἴ τις λαλεῖ, ὡς
of the manifold grace of God. If anyone speaks, *let him speak* as

λόγια Θεοῦ. Εἴ τις διακονεῖ, ὡς ἐξ ἰσχύος,
the utterances of God. If anyone serves, *let him serve* as from strength,

ὡς χορηγεῖ ὁ Θεός, ἵνα ἐν πᾶσι δοξάζηται ὁ Θεὸς
as supplies ˜ - God, so that in all *things* [2]may [3]be [4]glorified - [1]God

διὰ Ἰησοῦ Χριστοῦ, ᾧ ἐστιν ἡ δόξα καὶ τὸ κράτος
through Jesus Christ, to whom is the glory and the power

εἰς τοὺς αἰῶνας τῶν αἰώνων. Ἀμήν.
to the ages of the ages. Amen.
(forever and ever.) (So be it.)

Suffering for God's Glory

12 Ἀγαπητοί, μὴ ξενίζεσθε τῇ ἐν ὑμῖν πυρώσει
Beloved *ones,* not ˜ do be surprised by the [2]among [3]you [1]burning
(fiery trial)

πρὸς πειρασμὸν ὑμῖν γινομένῃ, ὡς ξένου ὑμῖν
[6]for [7]a [8]test [9]to [10]you [4]taking [5]place, as a strange *thing* [2]to [3]you
(to test) (you)

συμβαίνοντος, **13** ἀλλὰ καθὸ κοινωνεῖτε τοῖς τοῦ
[1]happening, but in so far as you participate in the -

Χριστοῦ παθήμασι, χαίρετε, ἵνα καὶ ἐν τῇ ἀποκαλύψει
[2]of [3]Christ [1]sufferings, rejoice, in order that also in the revelation of
(at)

τῆς δόξης αὐτοῦ χαρῆτε ἀγαλλιώμενοι. **14** Εἰ
- glory ˜ His you may rejoice being glad. If
(with great happiness.)

ὀνειδίζεσθε ἐν ὀνόματι Χριστοῦ, μακάριοι, ὅτι τὸ
you are reviled in *the* name of Christ, *you are* blessed, because the

τῆς δόξης καὶ τὸ τοῦ Θεοῦ Πνεῦμα ἐφ᾽ ὑμᾶς
[2]of [3]the [4]glory [5]and - - [6]of [7]God [1]Spirit [9]upon [10]you

ἀναπαύεται.[c] Κατὰ μὲν αὐτοὺς
[8]rests. [5]according [6]to [1]On [2]the [3]one [4]hand them

[c](4:14) NU omits the rest of v. 14.

βλασφημεῖται, κατὰ δὲ ὑμᾶς δοξάζεται.
He is blasphemed, [5]according [6]to [1]but [2]on [3]the [4]other you He is glorified.

15 Μὴ γάρ τις ὑμῶν πασχέτω ὡς φονεὺς ἢ κλέπτης ἢ
[3]not [1]For [4]anyone [5]of [6]you [2]let [7]suffer as a murderer or a thief or

κακοποιὸς ἢ ὡς ἀλλοτριοεπίσκοπος· **16** εἰ δὲ ὡς
an evildoer or as a meddler in others' affairs; if ~ but as

Χριστιανός, μὴ αἰσχυνέσθω, δοξαζέτω
a Christian *he suffers,* [3]not [1]let [2]him [4]be [5]put [6]to [7]shame, [9]let [10]him [11]glorify

δὲ τὸν Θεὸν ἐν τῷ μέρει[d] τούτῳ. **17** Ὅτι ὁ καιρὸς
[8]but - God in - matter ~ this. Because the time *has come*

τοῦ ἄρξασθαι τὸ κρίμα ἀπὸ τοῦ οἴκου τοῦ Θεοῦ· εἰ δὲ
- *for* [2]to [3]begin - [1]judgment from (at) the house - of God; if ~ but

πρῶτον ἀφ' ἡμῶν, τί τὸ τέλος τῶν ἀπειθούντων
first from (with) us, what *is* the end of the ones (those who) being (are) disobedient

τῷ τοῦ Θεοῦ εὐαγγελίῳ?
to the - [2]of [3]God [1]gospel?

18 Καὶ «Εἰ ὁ δίκαιος μόλις σῴζεται,
And «If the righteous *one* scarcely is saved,

Ὁ ἀσεβὴς καὶ ἁμαρτωλὸς ποῦ φανεῖται?»[e]
[3]the [4]godless [5]and [6]*the* [7]sinner [1]Where [2]will [8]appear?»

19 Ὥστε καὶ οἱ πάσχοντες κατὰ τὸ θέλημα τοῦ
So also the ones (those) suffering (who suffer) according to the will -

Θεοῦ ὡς πιστῷ Κτίστῃ παρατιθέσθωσαν τὰς ψυχὰς αὐτῶν
of God [6]as [7]to [8]a [9]faithful [10]Creator [1]let [2]them [3]entrust - [5]souls [4]their

ἐν ἀγαθοποιΐᾳ.
in doing good.

Elders Are to Pastor the Flock

5 **1** Πρεσβυτέρους τοὺς ἐν ὑμῖν παρακαλῶ ὁ
The elders the ones (who are) among you I encourage - *as*

συμπρεσβύτερος καὶ μάρτυς τῶν τοῦ Χριστοῦ παθημάτων, ὁ
a fellow elder and witness of the - [2]of [3]Christ [1]sufferings, the (a)

καὶ τῆς μελλούσης ἀποκαλύπτεσθαι δόξης κοινωνός·
[2]also [3]of (in) [4]the [6]being (that is) [7]about [8]to [9]be [10]revealed [5]glory [1]sharer;

2 ποιμάνατε τὸ ἐν ὑμῖν ποίμνιον τοῦ Θεοῦ,
shepherd the [4]among [5]you [1]flock - [2]of [3]God,

ἐπισκοποῦντες μὴ ἀναγκαστῶς, ἀλλ' ἑκουσίως,[a] μηδὲ
overseeing not by compulsion, but rather willingly, nor

αἰσχροκερδῶς, ἀλλὰ προθύμως, **3** μηδὲ ὡς
in fondness for dishonest gain, but rather eagerly, nor as

κατακυριεύοντες τῶν κλήρων, ἀλλὰ τύποι
being masters over the portions (flock) *under you,* but rather examples ~

γινόμενοι τοῦ ποιμνίου. **4** Καὶ φανερωθέντος τοῦ
being of (to) the flock. And appearing (when the) the (Chief)

Ἀρχιποίμενος, κομιεῖσθε τὸν ἀμαράντινον τῆς δόξης
Chief Shepherd, (Shepherd appears,) you will receive the unfading - [2]of [3]glory

στέφανον.
[1]crown.

part He is blasphemed, but on your part He is glorified.
15 But let none of you suffer as a murderer, a thief, an evildoer, or as a busybody in other people's matters.
16 Yet if *anyone suffers* as a Christian, let him not be ashamed, but let him glorify God in this matter.
17 For the time *has come* for judgment to begin at the house of God; and if *it begins* with us first, what will *be* the end of those who do not obey the gospel of God?
18 Now

> *"If the righteous one is*
> *scarcely saved,*
> *Where will the ungodly*
> *and the sinner appear?"*

19 Therefore let those who suffer according to the will of God commit their souls *to Him* in doing good, as to a faithful Creator.

5 The elders who are among you I exhort, I who am a fellow elder and a witness of the sufferings of Christ, and also a partaker of the glory that will be revealed:
2 Shepherd the flock of God which is among you, serving as overseers, not by compulsion but willingly, not for dishonest gain but eagerly;
3 nor as being lords over those entrusted to you, but being examples to the flock;
4 and when the Chief Shepherd appears, you will receive the crown of glory that does not fade away.

---

[d](**4:16**) NU reads *ονοματι, name.* [e](**4:18**) Prov. 11:31 LXX [a](**5:2**) NU adds *κατα Θεον, according to God.*

5 Likewise you younger people, submit yourselves to *your* elders. Yes, all of *you* be submissive to one another, and be clothed with humility, for

> "God resists the proud,
> But gives grace to the humble."

6 Therefore humble yourselves under the mighty hand of God, that He may exalt you in due time,
7 casting all your care upon Him, for He cares for you.
8 Be sober, be vigilant; because your adversary the devil walks about like a roaring lion, seeking whom he may devour.
9 Resist him, steadfast in the faith, knowing that the same sufferings are experienced by your brotherhood in the world.
10 But may the God of all grace, who called us to His eternal glory by Christ Jesus, after you have suffered a while, perfect, establish, strengthen, and settle *you*.
11 To Him *be* the glory and the dominion forever and ever. Amen.
12 By Silvanus, our faithful brother as I consider him, I have written to you briefly, ex-

Submit to God and Resist the Devil

5 Ὁμοίως, νεώτεροι, ὑποτάγητε πρεσβυτέροις.
Likewise, younger *people,* subject yourselves to *the* elders.

Πάντες δὲ ἀλλήλοις ὑποτασσόμενοι, τὴν
all ˜ And [3]to [4]one [5]another [1]subjecting [2]yourselves, -
be subject,

ταπεινοφροσύνην ἐγκομβώσασθε, ὅτι
with humility clothe yourselves, because

«Ὁ Θεὸς ὑπερηφάνοις ἀντιτάσσεται,
- «God [2]proud [3]*people* [1]resists,

Ταπεινοῖς δὲ δίδωσι χάριν.»[b]
[2]to [3]humble [4]*people* [1]But He gives grace.»

6 Ταπεινώθητε οὖν ὑπὸ τὴν κραταιὰν χεῖρα τοῦ
[2]humble [3]yourselves [1]Therefore under the mighty hand -

Θεοῦ, ἵνα ὑμᾶς ὑψώσῃ ἐν καιρῷ, **7** πᾶσαν τὴν
of God, so that [4]you [1]He [2]may [3]exalt in time, [2]all -
at the right time,

μέριμναν* ὑμῶν ἐπιρρίψαντες ἐπ' αὐτόν, ὅτι αὐτῷ
[4]anxiety [3]your [1]casting upon Him, because [5]to [6]Him
He

μέλει περὶ ὑμῶν.
[1]it [2]is [3]a [4]concern about you.
cares

8 Νήψατε, γρηγορήσατε![c] Ὁ ἀντίδικος ὑμῶν
Be self-controlled, be watchful! - adversary ˜ Your
sober,

διάβολος ὡς λέων ὠρυόμενος περιπατεῖ ζητῶν τίνα
the devil as a lion ˜ roaring walks about seeking someone

καταπίῃ· **9** ᾧ ἀντίστητε στερεοὶ τῇ πίστει,
he may devour; whom resist *being* steadfast in *your* faith,
resist him

εἰδότες τὰ αὐτὰ τῶν παθημάτων τῇ ἐν κόσμῳ ὑμῶν
knowing the same *things* - of sufferings - [7]in [8]*the* [9]world [5]your
sufferings

ἀδελφότητι ἐπιτελεῖσθαι. **10** Ὁ δὲ Θεὸς πάσης
[4]by [6]brotherhood [1]to [2]be [3]accomplished. the ˜ But God of all
are experienced.

χάριτος, ὁ καλέσας ὑμᾶς[d] εἰς τὴν αἰώνιον αὐτοῦ δόξαν
grace, the *One* having called you into - eternal ˜ His glory
who called

ἐν Χριστῷ Ἰησοῦ, ὀλίγον παθόντας αὐτὸς
in Christ Jesus, [3]a [4]little [5]*while* [1]having [2]suffered [8]Himself
after you have

καταρτίσαι[e] ὑμᾶς — στηρίξει, σθενώσει,
[6]may [7]He [9]make [11]complete [10]you — He will establish, strengthen, *and*

θεμελιώσει. **11** Αὐτῷ ἡ δόξα καὶ τὸ κράτος εἰς τοὺς
found *you.* To Him *be* the glory and the power to the
firmly ground forever and

αἰῶνας τῶν αἰώνων. Ἀμήν.
ages of the ages. Amen.
ever. So be it.

Peter's Farewell of Peace

12 Διὰ Σιλουανοῦ ὑμῖν τοῦ πιστοῦ ἀδελφοῦ, ὡς
By Silvanus [14]to [15]you [1]the [2]faithful [3]brother, [4]as

λογίζομαι, δι' ὀλίγων ἔγραψα, παρακαλῶν καὶ
[5]I [6]consider [7]*him,* [10]through [11]a [12]few [13]*words* [8]I [9]wrote, exhorting and
briefly have written,

---

[b](5:5) Prov. 3:34 LXX
[c](5:8) TR adds οτι, *because.*
[d](5:10) TR reads ημας, *us.*
[e](5:10) NU reads καταρτισει, *He will make (you) complete.*

---

*(5:7) *μέριμνα (merimna).* Noun meaning *care, anxiety, worry.* Cf. the cognate verb *μεριμνάω, to care, worry, be anxious.* Phil. 4:6 urges believers "to *be anxious* for nothing," which complements Peter's admonition here in 1 Pet. 5:7 to cast all worry and care on the Lord. This same kind of anxiety is also the theme of Matt. 6:25–34. However, in passages where *μέριμνα* expresses Paul's care regarding the spiritual welfare of others (Phil. 2:20; 2 Cor. 11:28), it may not carry the idea of "anxiety" (perhaps also 1 Cor. 7:33, 34).

ἐπιμαρτυρῶν ταύτην εἶναι ἀληθῆ χάριν τοῦ Θεοῦ εἰς ἣν
testifying this to be *the* true grace - of God in which

ἐστήκατε. 13 Ἀσπάζεται ὑμᾶς ἡ ἐν Βαβυλῶνι
you stand. [9]greets [10]you [1]The [2]*woman* [3]in [4]Babylon
She who is

συνεκλεκτή, καὶ Μᾶρκος ὁ υἱός μου.
[5]chosen [6]together [7]with [8]*you,* also Mark - son ˜ my.

14 Ἀσπάσασθε ἀλλήλους ἐν φιλήματι ἀγάπης.
Greet one another with a kiss of love.

Εἰρήνη ὑμῖν πᾶσι τοῖς ἐν Χριστῷ Ἰησοῦ. Ἀμήν.
Peace *be* to you all the *ones* in Christ Jesus. Amen.
who are So be it.

horting and testifying that this is the true grace of God in which you stand.
13 She who is in Babylon, elect together with *you,* greets you; and *so does* Mark my son.
14 Greet one another with a kiss of love. Peace to you all who are in Christ Jesus. Amen.

The Second Epistle of
PETER

ΠΕΤΡΟΥ Β
OF PETER 2

1 Simon Peter, a bondservant and apostle of Jesus Christ,

To those who have obtained like precious faith with us by the righteousness of our God and Savior Jesus Christ:

2 Grace and peace be multiplied to you in the knowledge of God and of Jesus our Lord,
3 as His divine power has given to us all things that *pertain* to life and godliness, through the knowledge of Him who called us by glory and virtue,
4 by which have been given to us exceedingly great and precious promises, that through these you may be partakers of the divine nature, having escaped the corruption *that is* in the world through lust.
5 But also for this very reason, giving all diligence, add to your faith virtue, to virtue knowledge,
6 to knowledge self-control, to self-control perseverance, to perseverance godliness,
7 to godliness brotherly kindness, and to brotherly kindness love.
8 For if these things are

Peter Greets the Faithful

1 **1** Συμεὼν Πέτρος, δοῦλος καὶ ἀπόστολος Ἰησοῦ
Simeon Peter, a bondservant and apostle of Jesus
slave

Χριστοῦ,
Christ,

Τοῖς ἰσότιμον ἡμῖν λαχοῦσι πίστιν ἐν
To the *ones* [4]of [5]the [6]same [7]kind [8]with [9]us [1]having [2]obtained [3]faith by
those who have

δικαιοσύνῃ τοῦ Θεοῦ ἡμῶν καὶ Σωτῆρος Ἰησοῦ Χριστοῦ·
the righteousness - of God ˜ our and Savior Jesus Christ:

2 Χάρις ὑμῖν καὶ εἰρήνη πληθυνθείη ἐν ἐπιγνώσει
May grace to you and peace be multiplied in *your* knowledge

τοῦ Θεοῦ καὶ Ἰησοῦ τοῦ Κυρίου ἡμῶν.
- of God and of Jesus - Lord ˜ our.

Fruitful Growth in the Faith

3 Ὡς πάντα ἡμῖν τῆς θείας δυνάμεως αὐτοῦ τὰ
As [8]all [6]to [7]us - [2]divine [3]power [1]His [9]things

πρὸς ζωὴν καὶ εὐσέβειαν δεδωρημένης, διὰ τῆς
[10]*pertaining* [11]to [12]life [13]and [14]godliness [4]having [5]given, through the
has granted,

ἐπιγνώσεως τοῦ καλέσαντος ἡμᾶς διὰ δόξης καὶ
knowledge of the *One* having called us by glory and
Him who

ἀρετῆς, **4** δι᾽ ὧν τὰ τίμια ἡμῖν καὶ μέγιστα
moral excellence, through which - precious [7]to [8]us [1]and [2]great

ἐπαγγέλματα δεδώρηται, ἵνα διὰ τούτων
[3]promises [4]have [5]been [6]given, so that through these *things*

γένησθε θείας κοινωνοὶ φύσεως, ἀποφυγόντες τῆς
we may become [2]of [3]*the* [4]divine [1]sharers nature, having escaped the

ἐν κόσμῳ ἐν ἐπιθυμίᾳ φθορᾶς. **5** Καὶ αὐτὸ
[2]*that* [3]*is* [4]in [5]*the* [6]world [7]by [8]lust [1]corruption. [2]also [3]*for* [5]very

τοῦτο δέ, σπουδὴν πᾶσαν παρεισενέγκαντες,
[4]this [6]*thing* [1]But, [10]diligence [9]all [7]bringing [8]in,
reason making every effort,

ἐπιχορηγήσατε* ἐν τῇ πίστει ὑμῶν τὴν ἀρετήν, ἐν δὲ τῇ
provide with - faith ˜ your - virtue, with ˜ and -

ἀρετῇ τὴν γνῶσιν, **6** ἐν δὲ τῇ γνώσει τὴν ἐγκράτειαν,
virtue - knowledge, with ˜ and - knowledge - self-control,

ἐν δὲ τῇ ἐγκρατείᾳ τὴν ὑπομονήν, ἐν δὲ τῇ ὑπομονῇ
with ˜ and - self-control - perseverance, with ˜ and - perseverance

τὴν εὐσέβειαν, **7** ἐν δὲ τῇ εὐσεβείᾳ τὴν φιλαδελφίαν, ἐν
- godliness, with ˜ and - godliness - brotherly love, with ˜

δὲ τῇ φιλαδελφίᾳ τὴν ἀγάπην. **8** Ταῦτα γὰρ ὑμῖν
and - brotherly love - love. [3]these [4]*things* [1]For [2]*if* [8]to [9]you

---

*(1:5) ἐπιχορηγέω (*epichorēgeō*). Verb meaning *provide, furnish,* or *support,* generally implying the idea of sparing no expense, thus fully (even lavishly) furnishing what is needed. Here in 2 Pet. 1:5 we are to *provide* with or *add* to our faith a complement of Christian graces. In so doing we assure that an entrance into Christ's kingdom will be *furnished* for or *granted* to us (v. 11). Paul uses the verb in its general sense of *providing* or *giving* what is needed (seed, 2 Cor. 9:10; the Spirit,

ὑπάρχοντα καὶ πλεονάζοντα, οὐκ ἀργοὺς οὐδὲ ἀκάρπους
[5]being [6]at [7]disposal and *are* increasing, [4]neither [5]useless [6]nor [7]unfruitful
belong barren

καθίστησιν εἰς τὴν τοῦ Κυρίου ἡμῶν Ἰησοῦ Χριστοῦ
[1]it [2]makes [3]*you* in the - [2]of [4]Lord [3]our [5]Jesus [6]Christ

ἐπίγνωσιν. 9 Ὧι γὰρ μὴ πάρεστι ταῦτα,
[1]knowledge. [2]*he* [3]in [4]whom [1]For [8]not [7]are [9]present [5]these [6]*things,*

τυφλός ἐστι, μυωπάζων, λήθην λαβὼν τοῦ
[11]blind [10]is, being shortsighted, forgetfulness ˜ receiving the
having forgotten

καθαρισμοῦ τῶν πάλαι αὐτοῦ ἁμαρτιῶν. 10 Διὸ
cleansing - [4]in [5]time [6]past [2]his [1]of [3]sins. Therefore
of his past sins.

μᾶλλον, ἀδελφοί, σπουδάσατε βεβαίαν ὑμῶν τὴν κλῆσιν
[3]even [4]more, [1]brothers, [2]be [5]eager [12]certain [8]your - [9]calling

καὶ ἐκλογὴν ποιεῖσθαι, ταῦτα γὰρ ποιοῦντες οὐ μὴ
[10]and [11]election [6]to [7]make, [15]these [16]*things* [13]for [14]practicing [19]not [20]not
if you do by no means

πταίσητέ ποτε. 11 Οὕτω γὰρ πλουσίως
[17]you [18]shall [21]stumble never. [2]in [3]this [4]way [1]For [12]richly
in any way.

ἐπιχορηγηθήσεται ὑμῖν ἡ εἴσοδος εἰς τὴν αἰώνιον
[7]will [8]be [9]supplied [10]to [11]you [5]the [6]entrance into the eternal

βασιλείαν τοῦ Κυρίου ἡμῶν καὶ Σωτῆρος Ἰησοῦ Χριστοῦ.
kingdom - of Lord ˜ our and Savior Jesus Christ.

Peter's Approaching Death

12 Διὸ οὐκ ἀμελήσω[a] ἀεὶ ὑμᾶς ὑπομιμνήσκειν
Therefore [3]not [1]I [2]shall [4]neglect [8]constantly [7]you [5]to [6]remind

περὶ τούτων, καίπερ εἰδότας, καὶ ἐστηριγμένους ἐν
concerning these *things,* although knowing, and having been established in
you know, have been

τῇ παρούσῃ ἀληθείᾳ. 13 Δίκαιον δὲ ἡγοῦμαι, ἐφʼ
the [2]being [3]present [1]truth. [5]right [1]But [2]I [3]consider [4]*it,* in
which is as

ὅσον εἰμὶ ἐν τούτῳ τῷ σκηνώματι, διεγείρειν ὑμᾶς ἐν
so far as I am in this - tent, to stir up ˜ you by
long as

ὑπομνήσει. 14 εἰδὼς ὅτι ταχινή ἐστιν ἡ ἀπόθεσις τοῦ
a reminder, knowing that [8]soon [7]is [1]the [2]putting [3]off -

σκηνώματός μου, καθὼς καὶ ὁ Κύριος ἡμῶν Ἰησοῦς Χριστὸς
[4]of [6]tent [5]my, just as even - Lord ˜ our Jesus Christ

ἐδήλωσέ μοι. 15 Σπουδάσω δὲ καὶ ἑκάστοτε
made clear to me. [2]I [3]will [4]make [5]an [6]effort [1]And also at any time
has made whenever necessary

ἔχειν ὑμᾶς μετὰ τὴν ἐμὴν ἔξοδον τὴν τούτων
[4]to [5]have [3]you [11]after - [12]my [13]departure - [8]of [9]these [10]*things*

μνήμην ποιεῖσθαι.
[6]a [7]reminder [1]to [2]make.
cause.

The Trustworthy Prophetic Word

16 Οὐ γὰρ σεσοφισμένοις μύθοις
not ˜ For [3]having [4]been [5]craftily [6]devised [2]fables
For we did not follow craftily devised

ἐξακολουθήσαντες ἐγνωρίσαμεν ὑμῖν τὴν τοῦ Κυρίου ἡμῶν
[1]following we made known to you the - [4]of [6]Lord [5]our
fables when

yours and abound, *you will be*
neither barren nor unfruitful in
the knowledge of our Lord Jesus Christ.
9 For he who lacks these
things is shortsighted, even to
blindness, and has forgotten
that he was cleansed from his
old sins.
10 Therefore, brethren, be
even more diligent to make
your call and election sure, for
if you do these things you will
never stumble;
11 for so an entrance will be
supplied to you abundantly into
the everlasting kingdom of our
Lord and Savior Jesus Christ.
12 For this reason I will not be
negligent to remind you always
of these things, though you
know and are established in the
present truth.
13 Yes, I think it is right, as
long as I am in this tent, to stir
you up by reminding *you,*
14 knowing that shortly I *must*
put off my tent, just as our Lord
Jesus Christ showed me.
15 Moreover I will be careful
to ensure that you always have
a reminder of these things after
my decease.
16 For we did not follow cun-
ningly devised fables when we
made known to you the power
and coming of our Lord Jesus

[a](1:12) For ουκ αμελησω, *I shall not neglect,* NU reads μελλησω, *I intend.*

Gal. 3:5). The figurative usage in Col. 2:19 (cf. Eph. 4:16) is more problematic. It may refer to the structural *support* of the body by ligaments ("*supported* and held together") or to what is *provided* to make growth possible ("nourished").

Christ, but were eyewitnesses
of His majesty.
17 For He received from God
the Father honor and glory
when such a voice came to Him
from the Excellent Glory: "This
is My beloved Son, in whom I
am well pleased."
18 And we heard this voice
which came from heaven when
we were with Him on the holy
mountain.
19 And so we have the prophetic word confirmed, which
you do well to heed as a light
that shines in a dark place, until
the day dawns and the morning
star rises in your hearts;
20 knowing this first, that no
prophecy of Scripture is of any
private interpretation,
21 for prophecy never came
by the will of man, but holy men
of God spoke *as they were*
moved by the Holy Spirit.
2 But there were also false
prophets among the peo-
ple, even as there will be false
teachers among you, who will
secretly bring in destructive
heresies, even denying the
Lord who bought them, *and*
bring on themselves swift destruction.
2 And many will follow their
destructive ways, because of
whom the way of truth will be
blasphemed.
3 By covetousness they will
exploit you with deceptive

Ἰησοῦ Χριστοῦ δύναμιν καὶ παρουσίαν, ἀλλ᾽ ἐπόπται
[7]Jesus [8]Christ [1]power [2]and [3]coming, but rather [3]eyewitnesses

γενηθέντες τῆς ἐκείνου μεγαλειότητος. **17** Λαβὼν
[1]having [2]become of the [2]of [3]that [4]*One* [1]majesty. [2]having [3]received
became His majesty. He

γὰρ παρὰ Θεοῦ Πατρὸς τιμὴν καὶ δόξαν, φωνῆς
[1]For from God *the* Father honor and glory, a voice
when a voice

ἐνεχθείσης αὐτῷ τοιᾶσδε ὑπὸ τῆς μεγαλοπρεποῦς δόξης,
being brought to Him such as this by the Magnificent Glory,
was

"Οὗτός ἐστιν ὁ Υἱός μου ὁ ἀγαπητός εἰς ὃν ἐγὼ
"This is - [3]Son [1]My - [2]beloved in whom I

εὐδόκησα" **18** — καὶ ταύτην τὴν φωνὴν ἡμεῖς ἠκούσαμεν
was well pleased." — and this - voice we heard
am

ἐξ οὐρανοῦ ἐνεχθεῖσαν, σὺν αὐτῷ ὄντες ἐν τῷ
[3]from [4]heaven [1]being [2]brought, [6]with [7]Him [5]being on the
uttered, when we were

ὄρει τῷ ἁγίῳ. **19** Καὶ ἔχομεν βεβαιότερον τὸν προφητικὸν
mountain ˜ - holy. And we have [4]more [5]certain [1]the [2]prophetic
confirmed

λόγον, ᾧ καλῶς ποιεῖτε προσέχοντες, ὡς λύχνῳ φαίνοντι ἐν
[3]word, which [3]well [1]you [2]do receiving, as a lamp shining in
to receive,

αὐχμηρῷ τόπῳ, ἕως οὗ ἡμέρα διαυγάσῃ καὶ φωσφόρος
a dark place, until which day dawns and *the* morning star
the

ἀνατείλῃ ἐν ταῖς καρδίαις ὑμῶν, **20** τοῦτο πρῶτον γινώσκοντες,
rises in - hearts ˜ your, [2]this [3]first [1]knowing,

ὅτι πᾶσα προφητεία Γραφῆς ἰδίας ἐπιλύσεως* οὐ
that every prophecy of Scripture [3]of [4]one's [5]own [6]interpretation [2]not
no

γίνεται. **21** Οὐ γὰρ θελήματι ἀνθρώπου ἠνέχθη ποτὲ
[1]occurs. [4]not [1]For [7]by [8]the [9]will [10]of [11]man [3]was [6]brought [5]ever
occurs.

προφητεία, ἀλλ᾽ ὑπὸ Πνεύματος Ἁγίου φερόμενοι
[2]prophecy, but rather [9]by [10]*the* [12]Spirit [11]Holy [6]being [7]brought [8]along
moved

ἐλάλησαν ἅγιοι[b] Θεοῦ ἄνθρωποι.
[5]spoke [1]holy [3]of [4]God [2]men.

Destructive Doctrines of False Teachers

2 **1** Ἐγένοντο δὲ καὶ ψευδοπροφῆται ἐν τῷ λαῷ, ὡς
[2]*there* [3]occurred [1]But also false prophets among the people, as ˜

καὶ ἐν ὑμῖν ἔσονται ψευδοδιδάσκαλοι, οἵτινες
even [6]among [7]you [1]*there* [2]will [3]be [4]false [5]teachers, who

παρεισάξουσιν αἱρέσεις ἀπωλείας, καὶ τὸν ἀγοράσαντα
will secretly bring in opinions of destruction, even [4]the [5]*One* [6]having [7]bought
destructive heresies, He who bought

αὐτοὺς Δεσπότην ἀρνούμενοι, ἐπάγοντες ἑαυτοῖς ταχινὴν
[8]them [2]*the* [3]Master [1]denying, bringing upon themselves swift

ἀπώλειαν. **2** Καὶ πολλοὶ ἐξακολουθήσουσιν αὐτῶν ταῖς
destruction. And many will follow after their -

ἀσελγείαις,[a] δι᾽ οὓς ἡ ὁδὸς τῆς ἀληθείας
debaucheries, because of whom the way - of truth

βλασφημηθήσεται. **3** Καὶ ἐν πλεονεξίᾳ πλαστοῖς λόγοις
will be blasphemed. And by covetousness with fabricated words

---

b(1:21) NU reads απο, *(men spoke) from (God).*
a(2:2) TR reads απωλειαις, *pernicious ways.*

*(1:20) ἐπίλυσις *(epilysis).* Noun used only here in the NT, meaning *interpretation, analysis.* The adjective ἴδιος which modifies ἐπίλυσις here refers to the interpreter of prophecies, thus indicating that Scripture is not for arbitrary or isolated interpretation. Cf. the cognate verb ἐπιλύω, *interpret, explain,* used only in the NT at Mark 4:34 and Acts 19:39. In the latter verse it apparently means *settle, decide* (but even there could mean *explain.*

ὑμᾶς ἐμπορεύσονται, οἷς τὸ κρίμα ἔκπαλαι οὐκ
[4]you [1]they [2]will [3]exploit, for whom the judgment for a long time not ˜
their has not

ἀργεῖ, καὶ ἡ ἀπώλεια αὐτῶν οὐ νυστάξει.[b]
is idle, and - destruction ˜ their not ˜ will sleep.
been

Doom of the False Teachers

4 Εἰ γὰρ ὁ Θεὸς ἀγγέλων ἁμαρτησάντων οὐκ ἐφείσατο,
if ˜ For - God [4]*the* [5]angels [6]having [7]sinned [2]not [1]did [3]spare,
when they

ἀλλὰ σειραῖς ζόφου ταρταρώσας
but rather [8]to [9]chains [10]of [11]darkness [1]confining [2]*them* [3]to [4]Tartarus

παρέδωκεν εἰς κρίσιν τηρουμένους, 5 καὶ ἀρχαίου
[5]gave [6]*them* [7]over [14]for [15]judgment [12]being [13]kept, and *the* ancient
reserved,

κόσμου οὐκ ἐφείσατο, ἀλλ' ὄγδοον Νῶε
world not ˜ did spare, but rather [3]*the* [4]eighth [5]*person* [2]Noah
with seven others

δικαιοσύνης κήρυκα ἐφύλαξε, κατακλυσμὸν κόσμῳ
[8]of [9]righteousness [6]a [7]herald [1]protected, [12]a [13]flood [15]*the* [17]world

ἀσεβῶν ἐπάξας, 6 καὶ πόλεις Σοδόμων καὶ
[16]ungodly [10]having [11]brought [14]upon, and [2]*the* [3]cities [4]of [5]Sodom [6]and
when He

Γομόρρας τεφρώσας καταστροφῇ κατέκρινεν,
[7]Gomorrah [1]reducing [8]to [9]ashes [13]to [14]destruction [10]He [11]condemned [12]*them,*

ὑπόδειγμα μελλόντων ἀσεβεῖν τεθεικώς,
[18]an [19]example [20]being [21]about [22]to [23]be [24]ungodly [15]having [16]made [17]*them,*
who were

7 καὶ δίκαιον Λώτ, καταπονούμενον ὑπὸ τῆς τῶν ἀθέσμων
and righteous Lot, being oppressed by the - [4]of [5]lawless [6]*men*
who was

ἐν ἀσελγείᾳ ἀναστροφῆς, ἐρρύσατο 8 (βλέμματι γὰρ καὶ
[2]in [3]debauchery [1]conduct, He rescued ([2]by [3]a [4]glance [1]for and
indecent conduct, what he saw

ἀκοῇ ὁ δίκαιος, ἐγκατοικῶν ἐν αὐτοῖς, ἡμέραν
by hearing the righteous *one,* dwelling among them, [5]day
what he heard that righteous man, while he lived

ἐξ ἡμέρας ψυχὴν δικαίαν ἀνόμοις ἔργοις
[6]by [7]day [4]soul [2]*his* [3]righteous [8]with [9]*their* [10]lawless [11]works
deeds

ἐβασάνιζεν)· 9 οἶδε Κύριος εὐσεβεῖς ἐκ πειρασμοῦ
[1]tormented); [3]knows [1]*the* [2]Lord [7]*the* [8]godly [9]from [10]temptation

ῥύεσθαι, ἀδίκους δὲ εἰς ἡμέραν κρίσεως
[4]*how* [5]to [6]deliver, [15]*the* [16]unjust [11]and [19]for [20]*the* [21]day [22]of [23]judgment

κολαζομένους τηρεῖν, 10 μάλιστα δὲ τοὺς ὀπίσω
[17]being [18]punished [12]*how* [13]to [14]keep, especially ˜ and the *ones* [2]after
under punishment those

σαρκὸς ἐν ἐπιθυμίᾳ μιασμοῦ πορευομένους, καὶ κυριότητος
[3]*the* [4]flesh [5]in [6]*the* [7]lust [8]of [9]pollution [1]walking, and lordship ˜
who walk, despise

καταφρονοῦντας.
despising.
authority.

Depravity of the False Teachers

Τολμηταί, αὐθάδεις, δόξας οὐ τρέμουσι
They are bold, self-willed, [7]glories [3]not [1]they [2]do [4]tremble [5]at
brazen, illustrious persons

words; for a long time their judgment has not been idle, and their destruction does not slumber.

4 For if God did not spare the angels who sinned, but cast *them* down to hell and delivered *them* into chains of darkness, to be reserved for judgment;

5 and did not spare the ancient world, but saved Noah, *one of* eight *people,* a preacher of righteousness, bringing in the flood on the world of the ungodly;

6 and turning the cities of Sodom and Gomorrah into ashes, condemned *them* to destruction, making *them* an example to those who afterward would live ungodly;

7 and delivered righteous Lot, *who was* oppressed by the filthy conduct of the wicked

8 (for that righteous man, dwelling among them, tormented *his* righteous soul from day to day by seeing and hearing *their* lawless deeds)—

9 *then* the Lord knows how to deliver the godly out of temptations and to reserve the unjust under punishment for the day of judgment,

10 and especially those who walk according to the flesh in the lust of uncleanness and despise authority. *They are* presumptuous, self-willed. They are not afraid to speak evil of dignitaries,

b(**2:3**) NU reads νυσταζει, *is (not) asleep.*

11 whereas angels, who are greater in power and might, do not bring a reviling accusation against them before the Lord.
12 But these, like natural brute beasts made to be caught and destroyed, speak evil of the things they do not understand, and will utterly perish in their own corruption,
13 *and* will receive the wages of unrighteousness, *as* those who count it pleasure to carouse in the daytime. *They are* spots and blemishes, carousing in their own deceptions while they feast with you,
14 having eyes full of adultery and that cannot cease from sin, enticing unstable souls. *They have* a heart trained in covetous practices, *and are* accursed children.
15 They have forsaken the right way and gone astray, following the way of Balaam the *son* of Beor, who loved the wages of unrighteousness;
16 but he was rebuked for his iniquity: a dumb donkey speaking with a man's voice restrained the madness of the prophet.
17 These are wells without water, clouds carried by a tempest, for whom is reserved the blackness of darkness forever.
18 For when they speak great swelling *words* of emptiness, they allure through the lusts of the flesh, through lewdness,

βλασφημοῦντες, **11** ὅπου ἄγγελοι, ἰσχύϊ καὶ δυνάμει
[6]blaspheming, where (whereas) angels, [3]in [4]might [5]and [6]in [7]power

μείζονες ὄντες, οὐ φέρουσι κατ' αὐτῶν παρὰ Κυρίῳ
[2]greater [1]being, not ~ do bring [4]against [5]them [6]before [7]*the* [8]Lord

βλάσφημον κρίσιν. **12** Οὗτοι δέ, ὡς ἄλογα ζῷα
[1]a [2]slanderous [3]judgment. these ~ But, as unreasoning animals ~

φυσικὰ γεγενημένα εἰς ἅλωσιν καὶ φθοράν, ἐν οἷς
natural having been born for capture and destruction, [2]in (at) [3]*things* [4]which

ἀγνοοῦσι βλασφημοῦντες, ἐν τῇ φθορᾷ αὐτῶν καὶ
[5]they [6]are [7]ignorant [8]of [1]blaspheming (blaspheme), [13]in - [15]destruction [14]their [9]and

καταφθαρήσονται,[c] **13** κομιούμενοι[d] μισθὸν ἀδικίας,
[10]will [11]be [12]destroyed, receiving *the* wages of unrighteousness,

ἡδονὴν ἡγούμενοι τὴν ἐν ἡμέρᾳ τρυφήν, σπῖλοι* καὶ
[3]a [4]pleasure [1]counting [2]*as* the (to) [2]in (in the) [3]*the* [4]day [1]reveling (revel ... daytime), *they are* spots and

μῶμοι, ἐντρυφῶντες ἐν ταῖς ἀπάταις αὐτῶν συνευωχούμενοι
blemishes, reveling in - deceptions ~ their feasting together (while they feast)

ὑμῖν, **14** ὀφθαλμοὺς ἔχοντες μεστοὺς μοιχαλίδος καὶ
with you, eyes ~ having full of an adulteress (adultery) and

ἀκαταπαύστους ἁμαρτίας, δελεάζοντες ψυχὰς ἀστηρίκτους,
unceasing (unable to cease) from sin, enticing souls ~ unstable,

καρδίαν γεγυμνασμένην πλεονεξίας ἔχοντες,
[2]a [3]heart [4]having [5]been [6]trained [7]of (in) [8]greediness [1]having,

κατάρας τέκνα, **15** καταλιπόντες εὐθεῖαν ὁδὸν
[9]*they* [10]*are* [12]of [13]a [14]curse (accursed) [11]children (children), having left behind *the* straight way

ἐπλανήθησαν, ἐξακολουθήσαντες τῇ ὁδῷ τοῦ Βαλαὰμ
they have gone astray, having followed after the way - of Balaam

τοῦ Βοσόρ,[e] ὃς μισθὸν ἀδικίας ἠγάπησεν,
the *son* of Bosor, who [2]*the* [3]wages [4]of [5]unrighteousness [1]loved,

16 ἔλεγξιν δὲ ἔσχεν ἰδίας παρανομίας· ὑποζύγιον
[4]a [5]rebuke (rebuked) [1]But [2]he [3]had (was) *for* his own lawlessness: [3]beast [4]of [5]burden (donkey)

ἄφωνον, ἐν ἀνθρώπου φωνῇ φθεγξάμενον, ἐκώλυσε τὴν
[1]a [2]dumb, [7]with [10]of [11]a [12]man [8]*the* [9]voice [6]speaking, restrained the

τοῦ προφήτου παραφρονίαν. **17** Οὗτοί εἰσι πηγαὶ ἄνυδροι,
[2]of [3]the [4]prophet [1]madness. These are springs (wells) ~ waterless,

νεφέλαι[f] ὑπὸ λαίλαπος ἐλαυνόμεναι, οἷς ὁ ζόφος τοῦ
clouds [3]by [4]a [5]storm [1]being [2]driven, for whom the gloom (darkness) of the

σκότους εἰς αἰῶνα[g] τετήρηται.
darkness (netherworld) [4]for [5]eternity (forever) [1]has [2]been [3]reserved.

Deceptions of the False Teachers

18 Ὑπέρογκα γὰρ ματαιότητος φθεγγόμενοι, δελεάζουσιν
[3]swollen (haughty) [4]*words* [1]For [5]of [6]emptiness [2]speaking (when they speak), they entice

ἐν ἐπιθυμίαις σαρκός, ἀσελγείαις, τοὺς ὄντως
with lusts of *the* flesh, with sensuality, the *ones* (those who) being (are)

---

[c](2:12) NU reads φθαρησονται, *will be ruined.* [d](2:13) NU reads αδικουμενοι, *suffering wrong (as).* [e](2:15) A few mss. read Βεωρ, *of Beor.* [f](2:17) For νεφελαι, *clouds,* NU reads και ομιχλαι, *and mists.* [g](2:17) NU omits εις αιωνα, *forever.*

*(2:13) σπίλος (*spilos*). Noun meaning *spot* or *stain.* Here it figuratively refers to lewd persons who have crept into the church. In Eph. 5:27 it refers to moral blemish. The feminine noun σπιλάς in Jude 12 has two divergent meanings. Often it means a *rock* or *reef* over which the sea washes. Thus in Jude it could represent those who are a "hidden danger" to the community as a hidden reef. However, as with σπίλος in 2 Peter, σπιλάς can also refer figura-

ἀποφυγόντας[h] τοὺς ἐν πλάνῃ ἀναστρεφομένους,
escaping from the *ones* [2]in [3]error [1]living,
those who are

19 ἐλευθερίαν αὐτοῖς ἐπαγγελλόμενοι, αὐτοὶ δοῦλοι
[2]freedom [3]to [4]them [1]promising, themselves slaves ˜
while they themselves

ὑπάρχοντες τῆς φθορᾶς· ᾧ γάρ τις ἥττηται,
being - of corruption; [2]by [3]whom [1]for anyone has been defeated,
are slaves

τούτῳ καὶ δεδούλωται. 20 Εἰ γὰρ ἀποφυγόντες τὰ
by this *one* also he has been enslaved. if ˜ For having escaped from the

μιάσματα τοῦ κόσμου ἐν ἐπιγνώσει τοῦ Κυρίου[i] καὶ
corruptions of the world by the knowledge of the Lord and

Σωτῆρος Ἰησοῦ Χριστοῦ, τούτοις δὲ πάλιν
Savior Jesus Christ, [2]by [3]these [1]yet again

ἐμπλακέντες ἡττῶνται, γέγονεν αὐτοῖς τὰ
having become entangled they are defeated, [4]have [5]become [7]for [8]them [1]the
has

ἔσχατα χείρονα τῶν πρώτων. 21 Κρεῖττον γὰρ ἦν
[2]last [3]*things* [6]worse *than* the first. [4]better [1]For [2]it [3]was
latter end

αὐτοῖς μὴ ἐπεγνωκέναι τὴν ὁδὸν τῆς δικαιοσύνης, ἢ
for them not to have known the way - of righteousness, than

ἐπιγνοῦσιν ἐπιστρέψαι ἐκ τῆς παραδοθείσης αὐτοῖς
knowing *it* to turn from the [3]having [4]been [5]handed [6]down [7]to [8]them
delivered

ἁγίας ἐντολῆς. 22 Συμβέβηκε δὲ αὐτοῖς
[1]holy [2]commandment. [2]it [3]has [4]happened [1]But to them *according to*

τὸ τῆς ἀληθοῦς παροιμίας,
the *saying* of the true proverb,

«Κύων ἐπιστρέψας ἐπὶ τὸ ἴδιον ἐξέραμα,»[j]
«A dog returning to - his own vomit,»
returns

καί,
and,

"Ὗς λουσαμένη εἰς κύλισμα βορβόρου."
"A sow having washed *returns* to a wallowing *in* mud."
her

God's Promise Is Not Slack

3 1 Ταύτην ἤδη, ἀγαπητοί, δευτέραν ὑμῖν γράφω
This already, beloved *ones, is the* second [4]to [5]you [2]I [3]write

ἐπιστολήν, ἐν αἷς διεγείρω ὑμῶν ἐν ὑπομνήσει τὴν
[1]letter, in *both of* which I stir up your [3]by [4]a [5]reminder -

εἰλικρινῆ διάνοιαν, 2 μνησθῆναι τῶν
[1]pure [2]mind, to remember the

προειρημένων ῥημάτων ὑπὸ τῶν ἁγίων προφητῶν,
[2]having [3]been [4]previously [5]spoken [1]words by the holy prophets,

καὶ τῆς τῶν ἀποστόλων ὑμῶν[a] ἐντολῆς τοῦ Κυρίου καὶ
and the - [2]of [4]apostles [3]your [1]commandment of the Lord and

Σωτῆρος· 3 τοῦτο πρῶτον γινώσκοντες, ὅτι ἐλεύσονται ἐπ'
Savior; [2]this [3]first [1]knowing, that [2]will [3]come [4]in

ἐσχάτου τῶν ἡμερῶν ἐμπαῖκται, κατὰ τὰς ἰδίας
[5]*the* [6]last [7]of [8]the [9]days [1]mockers, [11]according [12]to - [14]own

ἐπιθυμίας αὐτῶν πορευόμενοι, 4 καὶ λέγοντες, "Ποῦ ἐστιν ἡ
[15]desires [13]their [10]going, and saying, "Where is the
living,

the ones who have actually escaped from those who live in error.

19 While they promise them liberty, they themselves are slaves of corruption; for by whom a person is overcome, by him also he is brought into bondage.

20 For if, after they have escaped the pollutions of the world through the knowledge of the Lord and Savior Jesus Christ, they are again entangled in them and overcome, the latter end is worse for them than the beginning.

21 For it would have been better for them not to have known the way of righteousness, than having known *it,* to turn from the holy commandment delivered to them.

22 But it has happened to them according to the true proverb: *"A dog returns to his own vomit,"* and, "a sow, having washed, to her wallowing in the mire."

3 Beloved, I now write to you this second epistle (in *both of* which I stir up your pure minds by way of reminder),

2 that you may be mindful of the words which were spoken before by the holy prophets, and of the commandment of us, the apostles of the Lord and Savior,

3 knowing this first: that scoffers will come in the last days, walking according to their own lusts,

4 and saying, "Where is the

---

[h](**2:18**) For ουτως αποφυγοντας, *(those who) are escaping from,* NU reads ολιγως αποφευγοντας, *(the ones) barely escaping from.* [i](**2:20**) NU adds ημων, *our (Lord).* [j](**2:22**) Prov. 26:11 [a](**3:2**) TR reads ημων, *of us* (the apostles).

---

tively to evil persons who are "stains" or "blemishes" on the community.

promise of His coming? For
since the fathers fell asleep, all
things continue as *they were*
from the beginning of creation."
5 For this they willfully forget: that by the word of God
the heavens were of old, and
the earth standing out of water
and in the water,
6 by which the world *that*
then existed perished, being
flooded with water.
7 But the heavens and the
earth *which* are now preserved
by the same word, are re-
served for fire until the day of
judgment and perdition of ungodly men.
8 But, beloved, do not forget
this one thing, that with the
Lord one day *is* as a thousand
years, and a thousand years as
one day.
9 The Lord is not slack concerning *His* promise, as some
count slackness, but is longsuffering toward us, not willing
that any should perish but that
all should come to repentance.
10 But the day of the Lord will
come as a thief in the night, in
which the heavens will pass
away with a great noise, and
the elements will melt with fervent heat; both the earth and
the works that are in it will be
burned up.
11 Therefore, since all these
things will be dissolved, what
manner *of persons* ought you to
be in holy conduct and godliness,
12 looking for and hastening

---

[b](3:7) NU reads αυτω, *(the) same (word).*
[c](3:9) NU reads υμας, *you.*
[d](3:10) NU omits εν νυκτι, *in (the) night.*
[e](3:10) NU reads ευρεθησεται, *will be found,* understood as *will be laid bare* or *will be judged.*

---

*(3:10) ῥοιζηδόν *(rhoizēdon).* Adverb used only here in the NT, meaning *with (loud) hissing, with roaring speed,* perhaps *suddenly.* The word may suggest the noise and speed with which a rapidly thrown object flies through the air, or the roaring and crackling of the devouring flames. Some interpreters think Peter chose the word to emphasize power and speed.

ἐπαγγελία τῆς παρουσίας αὐτοῦ? Ἀφʼ ἧς γὰρ οἱ πατέρες
promise - of coming ˜ His? [2]from [3]which [1]For the fathers
since

ἐκοιμήθησαν, πάντα οὕτω διαμένει ἀπʼ ἀρχῆς
fell asleep, all *things* [2]in [3]this [4]manner [1]continue *as* from *the* beginning
died, the same

κτίσεως." 5 Λανθάνει γὰρ αὐτοὺς τοῦτο θέλοντας, ὅτι
of creation." [3]escapes [4]notice [1]For [5]*of* [6]them [2]this willingly, that
For this they forget

οὐρανοὶ ἦσαν ἔκπαλαι, καὶ γῆ ἐξ ὕδατος καὶ διʼ
the heavens were from of old, and *the* land [2]out [3]of [4]water [5]and [6]through

ὕδατος συνεστῶσα, τῷ τοῦ Θεοῦ λόγῳ, 6 διʼ ὧν ὁ
[7]water [1]existing, by the - [2]of [3]God [1]word, by which the

τότε κόσμος ὕδατι κατακλυσθεὶς ἀπώλετο· 7 οἱ δὲ
then ˜ world [4]by [5]water [2]being [3]flooded [1]perished; the ˜ but
at that time

νῦν οὐρανοὶ καὶ ἡ γῆ τῷ αὐτοῦ[b] *λόγῳ τεθησαυρισμένοι*
now heavens and - earth - [5]His [4]by [6]word [2]stored [3]up
present

εἰσὶ πυρί τηρούμενοι εἰς ἡμέραν κρίσεως καὶ ἀπωλείας
[1]are [9]for [10]fire [7]being [8]reserved to *the* day of judgment and destruction
until

τῶν ἀσεβῶν ἀνθρώπων.
- of ungodly men.

8 *Ἓν δὲ τοῦτο μὴ λανθανέτω ὑμᾶς, ἀγαπητοί, ὅτι*
in ˜ But this [3]not [1]let [2]it escape notice *of* you, beloved *ones,* that
let you not forget,

μία ἡμέρα παρὰ Κυρίῳ ὡς χίλια ἔτη καὶ χίλια ἔτη
one day with *the* Lord *is* as a thousand years and a thousand years

ὡς ἡμέρα μία. 9 Οὐ βραδύνει ὁ Κύριος τῆς ἐπαγγελίας, ὥς
as day ˜ one. [4]not [3]does [5]delay [1]The [2]Lord the promise, as
His

τινες βραδύτητα ἡγοῦνται, ἀλλὰ μακροθυμεῖ εἰς ἡμᾶς,[c]
some slowness ˜ regard, but rather is patient toward us,

μὴ βουλόμενός τινας ἀπολέσθαι, ἀλλὰ πάντας εἰς
not wanting anyone to perish, but rather all [4]for
to

μετάνοιαν χωρῆσαι.
[5]repentance [1]to [2]make [3]room.
come.

The Day of the Lord Shall Come

10 *Ἥξει δὲ ἡ ἡμέρα Κυρίου ὡς κλέπτης ἐν*
[7]will [8]come [1]But [2]the [3]day [4]of [5]*the* [6]Lord as a thief in

νυκτί,[d] *ἐν ᾗ οἱ οὐρανοὶ ῥοιζηδὸν* παρελεύσονται,*
the night, in which the heavens with a hissing noise will pass away,

στοιχεῖα δὲ καυσούμενα λυθήσονται, καὶ γῆ καὶ
[2]*the* [3]elements [1]and being burned up will be destroyed, both *the* earth and

τὰ ἐν αὐτῇ ἔργα κατακαήσεται.[e] 11 *Τούτων*
the [2]in [3]it [1]works will be completely burned up. [2]these [3]*things*
Therefore

οὖν πάντων λυομένων, ποταποὺς δεῖ
[1]Therefore all being destroyed, what sort of *people* it is necessary *for*
since all these things will be ought

ὑπάρχειν ὑμᾶς ἐν ἁγίαις ἀναστροφαῖς καὶ εὐσεβείαις,
[2]to [3]be [1]you in holy conduct and godliness,

12 *προσδοκῶντας καὶ σπεύδοντας τὴν παρουσίαν τῆς τοῦ*
looking for and hastening the coming of the -

Θεοῦ ἡμέρας, δι' ἣν οὐρανοὶ πυρούμενοι
[2]of [3]God [1]day, because of which *the* heavens being set on fire
λυθήσονται, καὶ στοιχεῖα καυσούμενα τήκεται?
will be destroyed, and *the* elements being burned up dissolve?
will dissolve?

13 Καινοὺς δὲ οὐρανοὺς καὶ γῆν καινὴν κατὰ τὸ
[9]new [1]But [10]heavens [11]and [12]a(n) [14]earth [13]new [2]according [3]to -
ἐπάγγελμα αὐτοῦ προσδοκῶμεν, ἐν οἷς δικαιοσύνη κατοικεῖ.
[5]promise [4]His [6]we [7]look [8]for, in which righteousness dwells.

Be Steadfast Till He Comes

14 Διό, ἀγαπητοί, ταῦτα προσδοκῶντες,
Therefore, beloved *ones,* [4]these [5]*things* [1]looking [2]forward [3]to,
σπουδάσατε ἄσπιλοι καὶ ἀμώμητοι αὐτῷ εὑρεθῆναι ἐν
be eager [8]unspotted [9]and [10]unblemished [4]by [5]him [1]to [2]be [3]found [6]in
εἰρήνῃ. 15 Καὶ τὴν τοῦ Κυρίου ἡμῶν μακροθυμίαν
[7]peace. And [2]the - [4]of [6]Lord [5]our [3]patience
σωτηρίαν ἡγεῖσθε, καθὼς καὶ ὁ ἀγαπητὸς ἡμῶν ἀδελφὸς
[7]*to* [8]*be* [9]salvation [1]consider, just as also - beloved ˜ our brother
Παῦλος κατὰ τὴν αὐτῷ δοθεῖσαν σοφίαν ἔγραψεν
Paul according to the [5]to [6]him [2]having [3]been [4]given [1]wisdom wrote
ὑμῖν, 16 ὡς καὶ ἐν πάσαις ταῖς ἐπιστολαῖς, λαλῶν ἐν αὐταῖς
to you, as also in all the letters, speaking in them
his
περὶ τούτων, ἐν οἷς ἐστι δυσνόητά τινα,
about these *things,* in which *there* are [3]hard [4]to [5]understand [1]some [2]*things,*
ἃ οἱ ἀμαθεῖς καὶ ἀστήρικτοι στρεβλοῦσιν, ὡς καὶ τὰς
which the unlearned and unstable twist, as *they do* also the
λοιπὰς Γραφάς, πρὸς τὴν ἰδίαν αὐτῶν ἀπώλειαν. 17 Ὑμεῖς
remaining Scriptures, to - own ˜ their destruction. You
rest of the
οὖν, ἀγαπητοί, προγινώσκοντες φυλάσσεσθε, ἵνα
therefore, beloved *ones,* knowing *this* beforehand be on guard, so that
μή, τῇ τῶν ἀθέσμων πλάνῃ συναπαχθέντες,
[2]not, [11]by [12]the [14]of [15]lawless [16]*people* [13]error [8]being [9]carried [10]away,
lest,
ἐκπέσητε τοῦ ἰδίου στηριγμοῦ. 18 Αὐξάνετε δὲ ἐν
[1]you [3]fall [4]from - [5]your [6]own [7]firmness. grow ˜ But in
steadfastness.
χάριτι καὶ γνώσει τοῦ Κυρίου ἡμῶν καὶ Σωτῆρος Ἰησοῦ
grace and knowledge - of Lord ˜ our and Savior Jesus
Χριστοῦ. Αὐτῷ ἡ δόξα καὶ νῦν καὶ εἰς ἡμέραν
Christ. To Him *be* the glory both now and to *the* day
forever.
αἰῶνος. Ἀμήν.
of eternity. Amen.
So be it.

the coming of the day of God,
because of which the heavens
will be dissolved, being on fire,
and the elements will melt with
fervent heat?
13 Nevertheless we, according to His promise, look for
new heavens and a new earth in
which righteousness dwells.
14 Therefore, beloved, looking forward to these things, be
diligent to be found by Him in
peace, without spot and blameless;
15 and consider *that* the longsuffering of our Lord *is*
salvation—as also our beloved
brother Paul, according to the
wisdom given to him, has written to you,
16 as also in all his epistles,
speaking in them of these
things, in which are some
things hard to understand,
which untaught and unstable
people twist to their own destruction, as *they do* also the
rest of the Scriptures.
17 You therefore, beloved,
since you know *this* beforehand, beware lest you also fall
from your own steadfastness,
being led away with the error of
the wicked;
18 but grow in the grace and
knowledge of our Lord and Savior Jesus Christ. To Him *be* the
glory both now and forever.
Amen.

The First Epistle of
JOHN

ΙΩΑΝΝΟΥ Α
OF JOHN 1

1 That which was from the
beginning, which we have
heard, which we have seen
with our eyes, which we have
looked upon, and our hands
have handled, concerning the
Word of life—
2 the life was manifested,
and we have seen, and bear
witness, and declare to you that
eternal life which was with the
Father and was manifested to
us—
3 that which we have seen
and heard we declare to you,
that you also may have fellowship with us; and truly our fellowship *is* with the Father and
with His Son Jesus Christ.
4 And these things we write
to you that your joy may be full.
5 This is the message which
we have heard from Him and
declare to you, that God is light
and in Him is no darkness at all.
6 If we say that we have fellowship with Him, and walk in
darkness, we lie and do not
practice the truth.
7 But if we walk in the light
as He is in the light, we have
fellowship with one another,
and the blood of Jesus Christ
His Son cleanses us from all
sin.
8 If we say that we have no
sin, we deceive ourselves, and

Prologue

1 1 Ὃ ἦν ἀπ᾿ ἀρχῆς, ὃ ἀκηκόαμεν,
That which was from *the* beginning, that which we have heard,

ὃ ἑωράκαμεν τοῖς ὀφθαλμοῖς ἡμῶν, ὃ
that which we have seen - with eyes ˜ our, that which

ἐθεασάμεθα, καὶ αἱ χεῖρες ἡμῶν ἐψηλάφησαν περὶ τοῦ
we looked upon, and - hands ˜ our handled concerning the

λόγου τῆς ζωῆς — 2 καὶ ἡ ζωὴ ἐφανερώθη, καὶ ἑωράκαμεν
word - of life — and the life was manifested, and we have seen

καὶ μαρτυροῦμεν καὶ ἀπαγγέλλομεν ὑμῖν τὴν ζωὴν τὴν
and we bear witness and we declare to you the life ˜ -

αἰώνιον ἥτις ἦν πρὸς τὸν Πατέρα καὶ ἐφανερώθη ἡμῖν —
eternal which was with the Father and was manifested to us —

3 ὃ ἑωράκαμεν καὶ ἀκηκόαμεν, ἀπαγγέλλομεν ὑμῖν,
that which we have seen and have heard, we declare to you,

ἵνα καὶ ὑμεῖς κοινωνίαν ἔχητε μεθ᾿ ἡμῶν. Καὶ ἡ
in order that also ˜ you [3]fellowship [1]may [2]have with us. [2]indeed -

κοινωνία δὲ ἡ ἡμετέρα μετὰ τοῦ Πατρὸς καὶ μετὰ τοῦ Υἱοῦ
[4]fellowship [1]And - [3]our *is* with the Father and with - Son ˜

αὐτοῦ Ἰησοῦ Χριστοῦ. 4 Καὶ ταῦτα γράφομεν ὑμῖν,
His Jesus Christ. And these *things* we write to you,

ἵνα ἡ χαρὰ ἡμῶν[a] ᾖ πεπληρωμένη.
in order that - joy ˜ our may be fulfilled.

Principles of Fellowship with Him

5 Καὶ ἔστιν αὕτη ἡ ἀγγελία ἣν ἀκηκόαμεν ἀπ᾿ αὐτοῦ
And is ˜ this the message which we have heard from Him

καὶ ἀναγγέλλομεν ὑμῖν, ὅτι ὁ Θεὸς φῶς ἐστι καὶ σκοτία
and we announce to you, that - God light ˜ is and [7]darkness
in Him

ἐν αὐτῷ οὐκ ἔστιν οὐδεμία. 6 Ἐὰν εἴπωμεν ὅτι
[1]in [2]Him [5]not [3]*there* [4]is [6]none. If we should say that
there is no darkness at all. claim

κοινωνίαν ἔχομεν μετ᾿ αὐτοῦ, καὶ ἐν τῷ σκότει
[3]fellowship [1]we [2]have with Him, and [4]in [5]the [6]darkness

περιπατῶμεν, ψευδόμεθα καὶ οὐ ποιοῦμεν τὴν ἀλήθειαν.
[1]we [2]are [3]walking, we are lying and [3]not [1]we [2]are doing the truth.
practicing

7 Ἐὰν δὲ ἐν τῷ φωτὶ περιπατῶμεν ὡς αὐτός ἐστιν ἐν τῷ
if ˜ But [4]in [5]the [6]light [1]we [2]are [3]walking as Himself ˜ He is in the

φωτί, κοινωνίαν ἔχομεν μετ᾿ ἀλλήλων, καὶ τὸ αἷμα Ἰησοῦ
light, [3]fellowship [1]we [2]have with one another, and the blood of Jesus

Χριστοῦ τοῦ Υἱοῦ αὐτοῦ καθαρίζει ἡμᾶς ἀπὸ πάσης ἁμαρτίας.
Christ - Son ˜ His cleanses us from all sin.

8 Ἐὰν εἴπωμεν ὅτι ἁμαρτίαν οὐκ ἔχομεν, ἑαυτοὺς
If we should say that [5]sin [3]not [1]we [2]do [4]have, [9]ourselves
claim

---

[a](1:4) TR reads υμων, *your.*

πλανῶμεν καὶ ἡ ἀλήθεια οὐκ ἔστιν ἐν ἡμῖν. **9** Ἐὰν
[6]we [7]are [8]deceiving and the truth not ˜ is in us. If

ὁμολογῶμεν τὰς ἁμαρτίας ἡμῶν, πιστός ἐστι καὶ δίκαιος ἵνα
we confess - sins ˜ our, [3]faithful [1]He [2]is and righteous that

ἀφῇ ἡμῖν τὰς ἁμαρτίας καὶ καθαρίσῃ ἡμᾶς ἀπὸ
He should forgive us the sins and cleanse us from
our

πάσης ἀδικίας. **10** Ἐὰν εἴπωμεν ὅτι οὐχ
all unrighteousness. If we should say that [3]not
claim

ἡμαρτήκαμεν, ψεύστην ποιοῦμεν αὐτὸν καὶ ὁ λόγος αὐτοῦ οὐκ
[1]we [2]have [4]sinned, [8]a [9]liar [5]we [6]make [7]Him and - word ˜ His not ˜

ἔστιν ἐν ἡμῖν.
is in us.

2 **1** Τεκνία μου, ταῦτα γράφω ὑμῖν ἵνα μὴ
[2]little [3]children [1]My, these *things* I write to you in order that [3]not

ἁμάρτητε. Καὶ ἐάν τις ἁμάρτῃ, Παράκλητον* ἔχομεν
[1]you [2]may [4]sin. And if someone should sin, [3]a [4]Paraclete [1]we [2]have
Helper

πρὸς τὸν Πατέρα, Ἰησοῦν Χριστὸν δίκαιον. **2** Καὶ
with the Father, Jesus Christ *the* righteous *One.* And

αὐτὸς ἱλασμός ἐστι περὶ τῶν ἁμαρτιῶν ἡμῶν, οὐ
[2]Himself [4]a [5]propitiation [1]He [3]is concerning - sins ˜ our, [2]not
satisfying sacrifice

περὶ τῶν ἡμετέρων δὲ μόνον ἀλλὰ καὶ περὶ
[3]concerning - [4]ours [1]and only but also concerning [1]*those*

ὅλου τοῦ κόσμου.
[4]whole [2]of [3]the [5]world.

Principles of Knowing Him

3 Καὶ ἐν τούτῳ γινώσκομεν ὅτι ἐγνώκαμεν αὐτόν, ἐὰν
And by this we know that we have known Him, if
come to know

τὰς ἐντολὰς αὐτοῦ τηρῶμεν. **4** Ὁ λέγων,
- [4]commandments [3]His [1]we [2]keep. The *one* saying,
who says,

"Ἔγνωκα αὐτόν," καὶ τὰς ἐντολὰς αὐτοῦ μὴ
"I have known Him," and - [4]commandments [3]His [1]not
"I have come to know does

τηρῶν, ψεύστης ἐστί, καὶ ἐν τούτῳ ἡ ἀλήθεια οὐκ ἔστιν.
[2]keeping, [6]a [7]liar [5]is, and [5]in [6]this [7]*one* [1]the [2]truth [4]not [3]is.
not keep, him

5 Ὃς δ' ἂν τηρῇ αὐτοῦ τὸν λόγον, ἀληθῶς ἐν τούτῳ ἡ
who ˜ But ever keeps His - word, truly in this *one* the
him

ἀγάπη τοῦ Θεοῦ τετελείωται. Ἐν τούτῳ γινώσκομεν ὅτι ἐν
love - of God has been perfected. By this we know that [3]in
reached completion.

αὐτῷ ἐσμεν. **6** Ὁ λέγων ἐν αὐτῷ μένειν ὀφείλει
[4]Him [1]we [2]are. The *one* saying [3]in [4]Him [1]to [2]abide ought
who claims

καθὼς ἐκεῖνος περιεπάτησε καὶ αὐτὸς οὕτω περιπατεῖν.
just as that *One* walked also himself thus to walk.

7 Ἀδελφοί,[a] οὐκ ἐντολὴν καινὴν γράφω
Brothers, [3]not [7]a [9]commandment [8]new [1]I [2]am [4]writing

ὑμῖν, ἀλλ' ἐντολὴν παλαιὰν ἣν εἴχετε ἀπ'
[5]to [6]you, but a(n) commandment ˜ old which you were having from
have had

the truth is not in us.
9 If we confess our sins, He
is faithful and just to forgive us
our sins and to cleanse us from
all unrighteousness.
10 If we say that we have not
sinned, we make Him a liar, and
His word is not in us.
2 My little children, these
things I write to you, so
that you may not sin. And if
anyone sins, we have an Advocate with the Father, Jesus
Christ the righteous.
2 And He Himself is the propitiation for our sins, and not
for ours only but also for the
whole world.
3 Now by this we know that
we know Him, if we keep His
commandments.
4 He who says, "I know
Him," and does not keep His
commandments, is a liar, and
the truth is not in him.
5 But whoever keeps His
word, truly the love of God is
perfected in him. By this we
know that we are in Him.
6 He who says he abides in
Him ought himself also to walk
just as He walked.
7 Brethren, I write no new
commandment to you, but an
old commandment which you
have had from the beginning.
The old commandment is the

---

[a](2:7) NU reads Αγαπητοι, *Beloved.*

***(2:1)** Παράκλητος *(Paraklētos).* Noun meaning *intercessor, helper.* It is derived from the preposition παρά, *beside,* and the verb καλέω, *call,* hence originally meaning in a passive sense *one who is called beside (to offer support).* This passive sense was gradually replaced by the more active meaning *mediator, intercessor.* Here in 1 John 2:1 Christ takes the role of an Intercessor for the person who sins. In John 14:16, 17 the Holy Spirit is called the Παράκλητος, there meaning *Helper.* Cf. also the cognate verb παρακαλέω, *summon, encourage* (Matt. 26:53; 1 Thess. 4:18); and the noun παράκλησις, *request, encouragement* (2 Cor. 8:4; Phil. 2:1).

word which you heard from the beginning.
8 Again, a new commandment I write to you, which thing is true in Him and in you, because the darkness is passing away, and the true light is already shining.
9 He who says he is in the light, and hates his brother, is in darkness until now.
10 He who loves his brother abides in the light, and there is no cause for stumbling in him.
11 But he who hates his brother is in darkness and walks in darkness, and does not know where he is going, because the darkness has blinded his eyes.
12 I write to you, little children,
Because your sins are forgiven you for His name's sake.
13 I write to you, fathers,
Because you have known Him *who is* from the beginning.
I write to you, young men,
Because you have overcome the wicked one.
I write to you, little children,
Because you have known the Father.
14 I have written to you, fathers,
Because you have known Him *who is* from the beginning.
I have written to you, young men,

ἀρχῆς. Ἡ ἐντολὴ ἡ παλαιά ἐστιν ὁ λόγος ὃν
the beginning. The commandment ˜ - old is the word which

ἠκούσατε ἀπ' ἀρχῆς.[b] **8** Πάλιν ἐντολὴν καινὴν
you heard from *the* beginning. Again [4]a [6]commandment [5]new

γράφω ὑμῖν, ὅ ἐστιν ἀληθὲς ἐν αὐτῷ καὶ ἐν ὑμῖν,
[1]I [2]am [3]writing [7]to [8]you, which is true in Him and in you,

ὅτι ἡ σκοτία παράγεται, καὶ τὸ φῶς τὸ ἀληθινὸν ἤδη
because the darkness is passing away, and the light ˜ - true already

φαίνει. **9** Ὁ λέγων ἐν τῷ φωτὶ εἶναι καὶ τὸν ἀδελφὸν
shines. The *one* saying [3]in [4]the [5]light [1]to [2]be and - [3]brother
who says that he is

αὐτοῦ μισῶν, ἐν τῇ σκοτίᾳ ἐστὶν ἕως ἄρτι. **10** Ὁ
[2]his [1]hating, [5]in [6]the [7]darkness [4]is until now. The *one*
hates,

ἀγαπῶν τὸν ἀδελφὸν αὐτοῦ ἐν τῷ φωτὶ μένει, καὶ
loving - brother ˜ his [2]in [3]the [4]light [1]abides, and
who loves

σκάνδαλον ἐν αὐτῷ οὐκ ἔστιν. **11** Ὁ δὲ μισῶν
[4]a [5]snare [6]in [7]him [3]not [1]*there* [2]is. [2]the [3]*one* [1]But hating
cause for stumbling who hates

τὸν ἀδελφὸν αὐτοῦ ἐν τῇ σκοτίᾳ ἐστὶ καὶ ἐν τῇ σκοτίᾳ
- brother ˜ his [2]in [3]the [4]darkness [1]is and [2]in [3]the [4]darkness

περιπατεῖ, καὶ οὐκ οἶδε ποῦ ὑπάγει, ὅτι ἡ σκοτία
[1]walks, and [3]not [1]he [2]knows where he is going, because the darkness

ἐτύφλωσε τοὺς ὀφθαλμοὺς αὐτοῦ.
blinded - eyes ˜ his.
has blinded

The Spiritual State of John's Readers

12 Γράφω ὑμῖν, τεκνία,
I am writing to you, little children,

Ὅτι ἀφέωνται ὑμῖν αἱ ἁμαρτίαι
Because [3]have [4]been [5]forgiven [6]you [1]the [2]sins
your

διὰ τὸ ὄνομα αὐτοῦ.
on account of - name ˜ His.

13 Γράφω ὑμῖν, πατέρες,
I am writing to you, fathers,

Ὅτι ἐγνώκατε τὸν ἀπ' ἀρχῆς.
Because you have known the *One who is* from *the* beginning.
come to know

Γράφω ὑμῖν, νεανίσκοι,
I am writing to you, young men,

Ὅτι νενικήκατε τὸν πονηρόν.
Because you have overcome the evil *one*.

Γράφω[c] ὑμῖν, παιδία,
I am writing to you, little children,

Ὅτι ἐγνώκατε τὸν Πατέρα.
Because you have known the Father.
come to know

14 Ἔγραψα ὑμῖν, πατέρες,
I wrote to you, fathers,

Ὅτι ἐγνώκατε τὸν ἀπ' ἀρχῆς.
Because you have known the *One who is* from *the* beginning.
come to know

Ἔγραψα ὑμῖν, νεανίσκοι,
I wrote to you, young men,

---

[b](2:7) NU omits απ αρχης, *from the beginning.*
[c](2:13) NU reads εγραψα, *I wrote.*

῞Οτι ἰσχυροί ἐστε καὶ ὁ λόγος τοῦ Θεοῦ ἐν
Because [3]strong [1]you [2]are and the word - of God [2]in

ὑμῖν μένει καὶ νενικήκατε τὸν πονηρόν.
[3]you [1]abides and you have overcome the evil *one.*

Because you are
strong, and the word
of God abides in you,
And you have overcome
the wicked one.

Do Not Love the World

15 Μὴ ἀγαπᾶτε τὸν κόσμον μηδὲ τὰ ἐν τῷ κόσμῳ.
not ˜ Do love the world nor the *things* in the world.

᾿Εάν τις ἀγαπᾷ τὸν κόσμον, οὐκ ἔστιν ἡ ἀγάπη* τοῦ
If anyone loves the world, [7]not [6]is [1]the [2]love [3]of [4]the

Πατρὸς ἐν αὐτῷ. **16** ῞Οτι πᾶν τὸ ἐν τῷ κόσμῳ — ἡ
[5]Father in him. Because every*thing* - in the world — the

ἐπιθυμία τῆς σαρκὸς καὶ ἡ ἐπιθυμία τῶν ὀφθαλμῶν καὶ ἡ
desire of the flesh and the desire of the eyes and the

ἀλαζονεία τοῦ βίου — οὐκ ἔστιν ἐκ τοῦ Πατρὸς ἀλλ᾿ ἐκ τοῦ
pride - of life — not ˜ is from the Father but [2]from [3]the

κόσμου ἐστί. **17** Καὶ ὁ κόσμος παράγεται καὶ ἡ ἐπιθυμία
[4]world [1]is. And the world is passing away and - desire ˜

αὐτοῦ, ὁ δὲ ποιῶν τὸ θέλημα τοῦ Θεοῦ μένει εἰς
its, [2]the [3]*one* [1]but doing the will - of God abides into
who does forever.

τὸν αἰῶνα.
the age.

15 Do not love the world or the things in the world. If anyone loves the world, the love of the Father is not in him.
16 For all that *is* in the world—the lust of the flesh, the lust of the eyes, and the pride of life—is not of the Father but is of the world.
17 And the world is passing away, and the lust of it; but he who does the will of God abides forever.

The Deceptions of the Last Hour

18 Παιδία, ἐσχάτη ὥρα ἐστί, καὶ καθὼς ἠκούσατε ὅτι
Little children, [3]*the* [4]last [5]hour [1]it [2]is, and just as you heard that

ὁ[d] ᾿Αντίχριστος ἔρχεται, καὶ νῦν ἀντίχριστοι πολλοὶ
the Antichrist is coming, even now antichrists ˜ many

γεγόνασιν, ὅθεν γινώσκομεν ὅτι ἐσχάτη ὥρα ἐστίν.
have become, from this we know that [3]*the* [4]last [5]hour [1]it [2]is.
have appeared;

19 ᾿Εξ ἡμῶν ἐξῆλθον, ἀλλ᾿ οὐκ ἦσαν ἐξ ἡμῶν, εἰ
Out from us they went, but [3]not [1]they [2]were from us, if ˜

γὰρ ἦσαν ἐξ ἡμῶν μεμενήκεισαν ἂν μεθ᾿ ἡμῶν,
for they were from us they would have remained - with us,

ἀλλ᾿ ἵνα φανερωθῶσιν ὅτι οὐκ
but *they went out* in order that they might be made manifest that [3]not

εἰσὶ πάντες ἐξ ἡμῶν. **20** Καὶ ὑμεῖς χρῖσμα ἔχετε ἀπὸ
[1]they [2]are all from us. And you [2]an [3]anointing [1]have from

τοῦ ῾Αγίου, καὶ οἴδατε πάντα.[e] **21** Οὐκ ἔγραψα ὑμῖν
the Holy *One,* and you know all *things.* [3]not [1]I [2]did [4]write to you

ὅτι οὐκ οἴδατε τὴν ἀλήθειαν, ἀλλ᾿ ὅτι οἴδατε
because [3]not [1]you [2]do [4]know the truth, but because you know

αὐτήν, καὶ ὅτι πᾶν ψεῦδος ἐκ τῆς ἀληθείας οὐκ ἔστι.
it, and because every lie [3]from [4]the [5]truth [2]not [1]is.
no lie is of the truth.

22 Τίς ἐστιν ὁ ψεύστης εἰ μὴ ὁ ἀρνούμενος ὅτι
Who is the liar if not the *one* denying that
who denies

᾿Ιησοῦς οὐκ ἔστιν ὁ Χριστός? Οὗτός ἐστιν ὁ ἀντίχριστος,
Jesus not is the Christ? This is the antichrist,
that Jesus is the Christ?

ὁ ἀρνούμενος τὸν Πατέρα καὶ τὸν Υἱόν. **23** Πᾶς ὁ
the *one* denying the Father and the Son. Every - *one*
the one who denies Everyone who

18 Little children, it is the last hour; and as you have heard that the Antichrist is coming, even now many antichrists have come, by which we know that it is the last hour.
19 They went out from us, but they were not of us; for if they had been of us, they would have continued with us; but *they went out* that they might be made manifest, that none of them were of us.
20 But you have an anointing from the Holy One, and you know all things.
21 I have not written to you because you do not know the truth, but because you know it, and that no lie is of the truth.
22 Who is a liar but he who denies that Jesus is the Christ? He is antichrist who denies the Father and the Son.
23 Whoever denies the Son

---

[d](2:18) NU omits ὁ, *the.*
[e](2:20) NU reads παντες, *you all;* thus, *you all know.*

***(2:15)** ἀγάπη (*agapē*). Noun meaning *love.* Although common in both the LXX and the NT, the word rarely occurs in existing secular Greek manuscripts of the period. Like its synonym φιλία (see φίλος at John 15:14), it designates love between persons (John 13:35), of people for God (as here in 1 John 2:15), of God for humanity (Rom. 5:8), and of God for Christ (John 17:26). Whereas φιλία emphasizes the idea of love arising from personal relationships, ἀγάπη is founded upon deep appreciation and high regard. It is perhaps for this reason that ἀγάπη is the love which God commands (cf. the use of the verb ἀγαπάω

does not have the Father either; he who acknowledges the
Son has the Father also.
24 Therefore let that abide in
you which you heard from the
beginning. If what you heard
from the beginning abides in
you, you also will abide in the
Son and in the Father.
25 And this is the promise that
He has promised us—eternal
life.
26 These things I have written to you concerning those
who *try to* deceive you.
27 But the anointing which
you have received from Him
abides in you, and you do not
need that anyone teach you;
but as the same anointing
teaches you concerning all
things, and is true, and is not a
lie, and just as it has taught
you, you will abide in Him.
28 And now, little children,
abide in Him, that when He appears, we may have confidence
and not be ashamed before Him
at His coming.
29 If you know that He is righteous, you know that everyone
who practices righteousness is
born of Him.
3 Behold what manner of
love the Father has be-
stowed on us, that we should
be called children of God!
Therefore the world does not
know us, because it did not
know Him.
2 Beloved, now we are children of God; and it has not yet
been revealed what we shall
be, but we know that when
He is revealed, we shall be
like Him, for we shall see Him

ἀρνούμενος τὸν Υἱὸν οὐδὲ τὸν Πατέρα ἔχει. **24** Ὑμεῖς
denying (denies) the Son neither [2]the [3]Father [1]has. You

οὖν ὃ ἠκούσατε ἀπ᾽ ἀρχῆς, ἐν ὑμῖν
therefore [2]that [3]which [4]you [5]heard [6]from [7]*the* [8]beginning, [10]in [11]you

μενέτω.
[1]let [9]abide.

Let the Truth Abide in You

Ἐὰν ἐν ὑμῖν μείνῃ ὃ ἀπ᾽ ἀρχῆς ἠκούσατε,
If [9]in [10]you [8]abides [1]that [2]which [5]from [6]*the* [7]beginning [3]you [4]heard,

καὶ ὑμεῖς ἐν τῷ Υἱῷ καὶ ἐν τῷ Πατρὶ μενεῖτε. **25** Καὶ αὕτη
also ˜ you [3]in [4]the [5]Son [6]and [7]in [8]the [9]Father [1]will [2]abide. And this

ἐστὶν ἡ ἐπαγγελία ἣν αὐτὸς ἐπηγγείλατο ἡμῖν, τὴν ζωὴν
is the promise which Himself ˜ He promised to you, - life ˜

τὴν αἰώνιον. **26** Ταῦτα ἔγραψα ὑμῖν περὶ τῶν
- eternal. These *things* I wrote to you concerning the *ones* (those)

πλανώντων ὑμᾶς. **27** Καὶ ὑμεῖς, τὸ χρῖσμα ὃ ἐλάβετε
deceiving (who deceive) you. And *as for* you, the anointing which you received

ἀπ᾽ αὐτοῦ ἐν ὑμῖν μένει, καὶ οὐ χρείαν ἔχετε ἵνα τις
from Him [2]in [3]you [1]abides, and [3]no [4]need [1]you [2]have that anyone

διδάσκῃ ὑμᾶς, ἀλλ᾽ ὡς τὸ αὐτὸ χρῖσμα διδάσκει ὑμᾶς
should teach you, but as the same anointing teaches you

περὶ πάντων, καὶ ἀληθές ἐστι, καὶ οὐκ ἔστι ψεῦδος, καὶ
concerning all *things,* and true ˜ is, and not ˜ is false, and

καθὼς ἐδίδαξεν ὑμᾶς, μενεῖτε[f] ἐν αὐτῷ.
just as it taught you, you will abide in Him.

The Children of God

28 Καὶ νῦν, τεκνία, μένετε ἐν αὐτῷ, ἵνα ὅταν[g]
And now, little children, abide in Him in order that whenever

φανερωθῇ, ἔχωμεν παρρησίαν καὶ μὴ αἰσχυνθῶμεν ἀπ᾽
He appears, we may have confidence and not be shamed from (due to)

αὐτοῦ ἐν τῇ παρουσίᾳ αὐτοῦ. **29** Ἐὰν εἰδῆτε ὅτι δίκαιός
Him at - coming ˜ His. If you know that [3]righteous

ἐστι, γινώσκετε ὅτι πᾶς ὁ ποιῶν τὴν δικαιοσύνην ἐξ
[1]He [2]is, you know that every (everyone) - *one* (who) doing (practices) - righteousness [4]of

αὐτοῦ γεγέννηται.
[5]Him [1]has [2]been [3]born.

3 **1** Ἴδετε ποταπὴν ἀγάπην δέδωκεν ἡμῖν ὁ Πατήρ,
Behold what manner of love [3]has [4]given [5]to [6]us [1]the [2]Father,

ἵνα τέκνα Θεοῦ κληθῶμεν.[a] Διὰ τοῦτο ὁ
that [5]children [6]of [7]God [1]we [2]should [3]be [4]called. On account of this the

κόσμος οὐ γινώσκει ὑμᾶς[b] ὅτι οὐκ ἔγνω αὐτόν.
world [2]not [1]does [3]know you because [3]not [1]it [2]did know Him.

2 Ἀγαπητοί, νῦν τέκνα Θεοῦ ἐσμεν, καὶ οὔπω
Beloved *ones,* [3]now [4]children [5]of [6]God [1]we [2]are, and [3]not [4]yet

ἐφανερώθη τί ἐσόμεθα. Οἴδαμεν δὲ ὅτι ἐὰν
[1]it [2]has [5]been [6]revealed what we shall be. [2]we [3]know [1]But that if (when)

φανερωθῇ, ὅμοιοι αὐτῷ ἐσόμεθα, ὅτι ὀψόμεθα αὐτὸν
He appears, [4]like [5]Him [1]we [2]shall [3]be, because we shall see Him

---

f(2:27) NU reads μενετε, *you abide.*
g(2:28) NU reads εαν, *if.*
a(3:1) NU adds και εσμεν, *and we are.*
b(3:1) NU reads ημας, *us.*

in John 13:34, 35). Cf. also the cognate adjective ἀγαπητός, *beloved* (Rom. 1:7).

καθώς ἐστι. **3** Καὶ πᾶς ὁ ἔχων τὴν ἐλπίδα ταύτην ἐπ'
just as He is. And every - *one* having - hope ˜ this upon
everyone who has in

αὐτῷ ἁγνίζει ἑαυτόν, καθὼς ἐκεῖνος ἁγνός ἐστι.
Him purifies himself, just as that *One* pure ˜ is.
He

Sin and the Child of God

4 Πᾶς ὁ ποιῶν τὴν ἁμαρτίαν καὶ τὴν ἀνομίαν
Every - *one* doing - sin also - lawlessness ˜
Everyone who practices

ποιεῖ, καὶ ἡ ἁμαρτία ἐστὶν ἡ ἀνομία.* **5** Καὶ οἴδατε ὅτι
does, and - sin is - lawlessness. And you know that
practices,

ἐκεῖνος ἐφανερώθη ἵνα τὰς ἁμαρτίας ἡμῶν ἄρῃ,
that *One* appeared that - [6]sins [5]our [1]He [2]might [3]take [4]away,
He

καὶ ἁμαρτία ἐν αὐτῷ οὐκ ἔστι. **6** Πᾶς ὁ ἐν αὐτῷ
and [6]sin [1]in [2]Him [5]not [3]*there* [4]is. Every - *one* [2]in [3]Him
Everyone who

μένων οὐχ ἁμαρτάνει· πᾶς ὁ ἁμαρτάνων οὐχ ἑώρακεν
[1]abiding [5]not [4]does [6]sin; every - *one* sinning [2]not [1]has [3]seen
abides everyone who sins

αὐτὸν οὐδὲ ἔγνωκεν αὐτόν.
Him nor has he known Him.

7 Τεκνία, μηδεὶς πλανάτω ὑμᾶς· ὁ ποιῶν
Little children, [2]no [3]one [1]let [4]deceive you; the *one* doing
who practices

τὴν δικαιοσύνην δίκαιός ἐστι, καθὼς ἐκεῖνος δίκαιός ἐστιν.
- righteousness righteous ˜ is, just as that *One* righteous ˜ is.
He

8 Ὁ ποιῶν τὴν ἁμαρτίαν ἐκ τοῦ διαβόλου ἐστίν,
The *one* doing - sin [2]from [3]the [4]devil [1]is,
who practices

ὅτι ἀπ' ἀρχῆς ὁ διάβολος ἁμαρτάνει. Εἰς τοῦτο
because from *the* beginning the devil sins. For this *reason*
has been sinning.

ἐφανερώθη ὁ Υἱὸς τοῦ Θεοῦ, ἵνα λύσῃ τὰ ἔργα
[5]appeared [1]the [2]Son - [3]of [4]God, that He might destroy the works

τοῦ διαβόλου. **9** Πᾶς ὁ γεγεννημένος ἐκ τοῦ Θεοῦ
of the devil. Every - *one* having been born of - God
No one who has

ἁμαρτίαν οὐ ποιεῖ, ὅτι σπέρμα αὐτοῦ ἐν αὐτῷ
[4]sin [2]not [1]does [3]do, because seed ˜ His [2]in [3]him
practices,

μένει, καὶ οὐ δύναται ἁμαρτάνειν, ὅτι ἐκ τοῦ Θεοῦ
[1]abides, and not he is able to sin, because of - God
he cannot sin,

γεγέννηται. **10** Ἐν τούτῳ φανερά ἐστι τὰ τέκνα τοῦ
he has been born. By this [12]manifest [11]are [1]the [2]children -

Θεοῦ καὶ τὰ τέκνα τοῦ διαβόλου.
[3]of [4]God [5]and [6]the [7]children [8]of [9]the [10]devil.

The Imperative of Love

Πᾶς ὁ μὴ ποιῶν δικαιοσύνην οὐκ ἔστιν ἐκ τοῦ
Every - *one* not doing righteousness not ˜ is of -
Everyone who does not practice

as He is.
3 And everyone who has this
hope in Him purifies himself,
just as He is pure.
4 Whoever commits sin also
commits lawlessness, and sin is
lawlessness.
5 And you know that He was
manifested to take away our
sins, and in Him there is no sin.
6 Whoever abides in Him
does not sin. Whoever sins has
neither seen Him nor known
Him.
7 Little children, let no one
deceive you. He who practices
righteousness is righteous, just
as He is righteous.
8 He who sins is of the devil,
for the devil has sinned from
the beginning. For this purpose
the Son of God was manifested,
that He might destroy the
works of the devil.
9 Whoever has been born of
God does not sin, for His seed
remains in him; and he cannot
sin, because he has been born
of God.
10 In this the children of God
and the children of the devil are
manifest: Whoever does not
practice righteousness is not of

---

*(3:4) ἀνομία *(anomia).* Noun literally meaning *lawlessness, breaking of the law,* from the α- negative and the noun νόμος, *law.* Thus here sin is seen essentially as transgression of law, especially of the law of God as His revealed will. Cf. the cognate adjective ἄνομος, *lawless, unlawful* (as Luke 22:37, lawless (ones) = transgressors); and adverb ἀνόμως, *without the law* (as twice in Rom. 2:12, its only NT usage).

God, nor *is* he who does not love his brother.
11 For this is the message that you heard from the beginning, that we should love one another,
12 not as Cain *who* was of the wicked one and murdered his brother. And why did he murder him? Because his works were evil and his brother's righteous.
13 Do not marvel, my brethren, if the world hates you.
14 We know that we have passed from death to life, because we love the brethren. He who does not love *his* brother abides in death.
15 Whoever hates his brother is a murderer, and you know that no murderer has eternal life abiding in him.
16 By this we know love, because He laid down His life for us. And we also ought to lay down *our* lives for the brethren.
17 But whoever has this world's goods, and sees his brother in need, and shuts up his heart from him, how does the love of God abide in him?
18 My little children, let us not love in word or in tongue, but in deed and in truth.
19 And by this we know that we are of the truth, and shall assure our hearts before Him.
20 For if our heart condemns

[c](3:14) NU omits αδελφον, *brother.* [d](3:19) NU reads γνωσομεθα, *we shall know.*

Θεοῦ, καὶ ὁ μὴ ἀγαπῶν τὸν ἀδελφὸν αὐτοῦ.
God, and the *one* not (who does) loving (not love) - brother ˜ his.

11 Ὅτι αὕτη ἐστὶν ἡ ἀγγελία ἣν ἠκούσατε ἀπ'
Because this is the message which you heard from

ἀρχῆς, ἵνα ἀγαπῶμεν ἀλλήλους, 12 οὐ καθὼς Κάϊν
the beginning, that we should love one another, not as Cain *who*

ἐκ τοῦ πονηροῦ ἦν καὶ ἔσφαξε τὸν ἀδελφὸν αὐτοῦ. Καὶ
[2]from [3]the [4]evil [5]*one* [1]was and slew - brother ˜ his. And

χάριν τίνος ἔσφαξεν αὐτόν? Ὅτι τὰ ἔργα αὐτοῦ πονηρὰ
[3]favor [1]of [2]what (for what reason) did he slay him? Because - works ˜ his evil ˜

ἦν, τὰ δὲ τοῦ ἀδελφοῦ αὐτοῦ δίκαια.
were, [2]the [3]*works* [1]and - of brother ˜ his *were* righteous.

13 Μὴ θαυμάζετε, ἀδελφοί μου, εἰ μισεῖ ὑμᾶς ὁ κόσμος.
not ˜ Do marvel, brothers ˜ my, if [3]hates [4]you [1]the [2]world.

14 Ἡμεῖς οἴδαμεν ὅτι μεταβεβήκαμεν ἐκ τοῦ θανάτου εἰς
We know that we have passed over from - death into

τὴν ζωήν, ὅτι ἀγαπῶμεν τοὺς ἀδελφούς. Ὁ μὴ
- life, because we love the brothers. The *one* not (who does)

ἀγαπῶν τὸν ἀδελφὸν[c] μένει ἐν τῷ θανάτῳ. 15 Πᾶς ὁ
loving (not love) the (his) brother abides in - death. Every (Everyone) - *one* (who)

μισῶν τὸν ἀδελφὸν αὐτοῦ ἀνθρωποκτόνος ἐστί, καὶ οἴδατε ὅτι
hating (hates) - brother ˜ his [2]a [3]murderer [1]is, and you know that

πᾶς ἀνθρωποκτόνος οὐκ ἔχει ζωὴν αἰώνιον ἐν ἑαυτῷ
every murderer not ˜ does have life ˜ eternal [2]in [3]him

μένουσαν.
[1]abiding.

The Outworking of Love

16 Ἐν τούτῳ ἐγνώκαμεν τὴν ἀγάπην, ὅτι ἐκεῖνος
By this we have known (come to know) - love, because that *One* (He)

ὑπὲρ ἡμῶν τὴν ψυχὴν αὐτοῦ ἔθηκε. Καὶ ἡμεῖς ὀφείλομεν
[5]in [7]behalf [6]our - [4]life [3]His [1]laid [2]down. And we ought

ὑπὲρ τῶν ἀδελφῶν τὰς ψυχὰς τιθέναι. 17 Ὃς δ'
[6]in [7]behalf [8]of [9]the (our) [10]brothers [4]the (our) [5]lives [1]to [2]lay [3]down. who ˜ But

ἂν ἔχῃ τὸν βίον τοῦ κόσμου καὶ θεωρῇ τὸν ἀδελφὸν αὐτοῦ
ever has the life of the world (world's goods) and sees - brother ˜ his

χρείαν ἔχοντα καὶ κλείσῃ τὰ σπλάγχνα αὐτοῦ ἀπ' αὐτοῦ,
need ˜ having and closes (shuts) - bowels ˜ (off) his (compassion) from (towards) him, (him,)

πῶς ἡ ἀγάπη τοῦ Θεοῦ μένει ἐν αὐτῷ?
how [2]the [3]love - [4]of [5]God [1]does [6]abide in him?

18 Τεκνία μου, μὴ ἀγαπῶμεν λόγῳ μηδὲ τῇ γλώσσῃ,
[2]little [3]children [1]My, [6]not [4]let [5]us [7]love in word nor - in tongue,

ἀλλ' ἐν ἔργῳ καὶ ἀληθείᾳ. 19 Καὶ ἐν τούτῳ γινώσκομεν[d] ὅτι
but in deed and truth. And in this we know that

ἐκ τῆς ἀληθείας ἐσμέν, καὶ ἔμπροσθεν αὐτοῦ πείσομεν
[3]from [4]the [5]truth [1]we [2]are, and before Him we shall persuade (assure)

τὰς καρδίας ἡμῶν, 20 ὅτι ἐὰν καταγινώσκῃ ἡμῶν ἡ
- hearts ˜ our, because if [3]condemns [4]*us* [1]our -

καρδία, ὅτι μείζων ἐστὶν ὁ Θεὸς τῆς καρδίας ἡμῶν καὶ
[2]heart, - [7]greater [6]is - [5]God [8]*than* - heart ˜ our and

γινώσκει πάντα.
He knows all *things*.

21 Ἀγαπητοί, ἐὰν ἡ καρδία ἡμῶν μὴ καταγινώσκῃ ἡμῶν,
Beloved *ones,* if - heart ˜ our [2]not [1]does [3]condemn us,

παρρησίαν ἔχομεν πρὸς τὸν Θεόν, 22 καὶ ὃ ἐὰν
[3]confidence [1]we [2]have toward - God, and what ever

αἰτῶμεν, λαμβάνομεν παρ' αὐτοῦ, ὅτι τὰς ἐντολὰς
we should ask, we receive from Him, because - [4]commandments

αὐτοῦ τηροῦμεν καὶ τὰ ἀρεστὰ ἐνώπιον αὐτοῦ ποιοῦμεν.
[3]His [1]we [2]keep and [3]the [4]*things* [5]pleasing [6]before [7]Him [1]we [2]do.

23 Καὶ αὕτη ἐστὶν ἡ ἐντολὴ αὐτοῦ, ἵνα πιστεύσωμεν
And this is - commandment ˜ His, that we should believe

τῷ ὀνόματι τοῦ Υἱοῦ αὐτοῦ Ἰησοῦ Χριστοῦ καὶ ἀγαπῶμεν
in the name - of Son ˜ His Jesus Christ and should love

ἀλλήλους, καθὼς ἔδωκεν ἐντολήν. [e]
one another, just as He gave commandment.

The Spirit of Truth and the Spirit of Error

24 Καὶ ὁ τηρῶν τὰς ἐντολὰς αὐτοῦ ἐν αὐτῷ
And the *one* keeping - commandments ˜ His [2]in [3]Him
who keeps

μένει καὶ αὐτὸς ἐν αὐτῷ. Καὶ ἐν τούτῳ γινώσκομεν ὅτι
[1]abides and He in him. And by this we know that

μένει ἐν ἡμῖν, ἐκ τοῦ Πνεύματος οὗ ἡμῖν ἔδωκεν.
He abides in us, from the Spirit whom [3]us [1]He [2]gave.

4 1 Ἀγαπητοί, μὴ παντὶ πνεύματι πιστεύετε, ἀλλὰ
Beloved *ones,* [2]not [4]every [5]spirit [1]do [3]believe, but

δοκιμάζετε τὰ πνεύματα εἰ ἐκ τοῦ Θεοῦ ἐστιν, ὅτι
test the spirits [1]if [4]from - [5]God [2]they [3]are because
whether

πολλοὶ ψευδοπροφῆται ἐξεληλύθασιν εἰς τὸν κόσμον. 2 Ἐν
many false prophets have gone out into the world. By

τούτῳ γινώσκεται τὸ Πνεῦμα τοῦ Θεοῦ· πᾶν πνεῦμα ὃ
this [5]is [6]known [1]the [2]Spirit - [3]of [4]God: every spirit which

ὁμολογεῖ Ἰησοῦν Χριστὸν ἐν σαρκὶ ἐληλυθότα ἐκ τοῦ
confesses *that* Jesus Christ [3]in [4]*the* [5]flesh [1]having [2]come [7]of -
has

Θεοῦ ἐστι, 3 καὶ πᾶν πνεῦμα ὃ μὴ ὁμολογεῖ [a] Ἰησοῦν
[8]God [6]is, and every spirit which not ˜ does confess *that* Jesus

Χριστὸν ἐν σαρκὶ ἐληλυθότα ἐκ τοῦ Θεοῦ οὐκ ἔστι. Καὶ
Christ [3]in [4]*the* [5]flesh [1]having [2]come [8]of - [9]God [7]not [6]is. And
has

τοῦτό ἐστι τὸ τοῦ Ἀντιχρίστου, ὃ ἀκηκόατε ὅτι
this is the *spirit* of the Antichrist, which you have heard that

ἔρχεται, καὶ νῦν ἐν τῷ κόσμῳ ἐστὶν ἤδη.
it is coming, and now [3]in [4]the [5]world [1]is [2]already.

4 Ὑμεῖς ἐκ τοῦ Θεοῦ ἐστε, τεκνία, καὶ
You [2]of - [3]God [1]are, little children, and

νενικήκατε αὐτούς, ὅτι μείζων ἐστὶν ὁ ἐν ὑμῖν
you have overcome them, because greater is the *One* in you

ἢ ὁ ἐν τῷ κόσμῳ. 5 Αὐτοὶ ἐκ τοῦ κόσμου εἰσί·
than the *one* in the world. They [2]of [3]the [4]world [1]are:

διὰ τοῦτο ἐκ τοῦ κόσμου λαλοῦσι, καὶ ὁ κόσμος
on account of this [3]of [4]the [5]world [1]they [2]speak, and the world

us, God is greater than our heart, and knows all things.

21 Beloved, if our heart does not condemn us, we have confidence toward God.

22 And whatever we ask we receive from Him, because we keep His commandments and do those things that are pleasing in His sight.

23 And this is His commandment: that we should believe on the name of His Son Jesus Christ and love one another, as He gave us commandment.

24 Now he who keeps His commandments abides in Him, and He in him. And by this we know that He abides in us, by the Spirit whom He has given us.

4 Beloved, do not believe every spirit, but test the spirits, whether they are of God; because many false prophets have gone out into the world.

2 By this you know the Spirit of God: Every spirit that confesses that Jesus Christ has come in the flesh is of God,

3 and every spirit that does not confess that Jesus Christ has come in the flesh is not of God. And this is the *spirit* of the Antichrist, which you have heard was coming, and is now already in the world.

4 You are of God, little children, and have overcome them, because He who is in you is greater than he who is in the world.

5 They are of the world. Therefore they speak *as* of the world, and the world hears them.

---

[e](**3:23**) NU adds *ημιν, to us.* [a](**4:3**) NU omits *Χριστον εν σαρκι εληλυθοτα, Christ having come in the flesh.*

6 We are of God. He who knows God hears us; he who is not of God does not hear us. By this we know the spirit of truth and the spirit of error.
7 Beloved, let us love one another, for love is of God; and everyone who loves is born of God and knows God.
8 He who does not love does not know God, for God is love.
9 In this the love of God was manifested toward us, that God has sent His only begotten Son into the world, that we might live through Him.
10 In this is love, not that we loved God, but that He loved us and sent His Son *to be* the propitiation for our sins.
11 Beloved, if God so loved us, we also ought to love one another.
12 No one has seen God at any time. If we love one another, God abides in us, and His love has been perfected in us.
13 By this we know that we abide in Him, and He in us, because He has given us of His Spirit.
14 And we have seen and testify that the Father has sent the Son *as* Savior of the world.
15 Whoever confesses that Jesus is the Son of God, God abides in him, and he in God.
16 And we have known and

αὐτῶν ἀκούει. **6** *Ἡμεῖς ἐκ τοῦ Θεοῦ ἐσμεν· ὁ γινώσκων*
them ~ hears. We [2]of - [3]God [1]are: the *one* knowing
who knows

τὸν Θεὸν ἀκούει ἡμῶν· ὃς οὐκ ἔστιν ἐκ τοῦ Θεοῦ οὐκ
- God hears us; *he* who not ~ is of - God not ~

ἀκούει ἡμῶν. Ἐκ τούτου γινώσκομεν τὸ πνεῦμα τῆς
does hear us. From this we know the spirit -

ἀληθείας καὶ τὸ πνεῦμα τῆς πλάνης.
of truth and the spirit - of error.

Knowing God Through Love

7 *Ἀγαπητοί, ἀγαπῶμεν ἀλλήλους, ὅτι ἡ ἀγάπη ἐκ τοῦ*
Beloved *ones,* let us love one another, because - love [2]of -

Θεοῦ ἐστι, καὶ πᾶς ὁ ἀγαπῶν ἐκ τοῦ Θεοῦ γεγέννηται
[3]God [1]is, and every - *one* loving [4]of - [5]God [1]has [2]been [3]born
everyone who loves

καὶ γινώσκει τὸν Θεόν. **8** *Ὁ μὴ ἀγαπῶν οὐκ ἔγνω*
and knows - God. The *one* not loving not ~ did know
who does not love

τὸν Θεόν, ὅτι ὁ Θεὸς ἀγάπη ἐστίν. **9** *Ἐν τούτῳ ἐφανερώθη*
- God, because - God love ~ is. By this [5]is [6]manifested

ἡ ἀγάπη τοῦ Θεοῦ ἐν ἡμῖν, ὅτι τὸν Υἱὸν αὐτοῦ τὸν
[1]the [2]love - [3]of [4]God in us, that - [6]Son [3]His -

μονογενῆ ἀπέσταλκεν ὁ Θεὸς εἰς τὸν κόσμον ἵνα
[4]only [5]begotten [2]sent - [1]God into the world in order that
unique

ζήσωμεν δι' αὐτοῦ. **10** *Ἐν τούτῳ ἐστὶν ἡ ἀγάπη, οὐχ ὅτι*
we might live through Him. In this is - love, not that

ἡμεῖς ἠγαπήσαμεν τὸν Θεόν, ἀλλ' ὅτι αὐτὸς ἠγάπησεν ἡμᾶς
we loved - God, but that He loved us

καὶ ἀπέστειλε τὸν Υἱὸν αὐτοῦ ἱλασμὸν περὶ τῶν*
and sent - Son ~ His *as* a propitiation concerning -
satisfying sacrifice

ἁμαρτιῶν ἡμῶν. **11** *Ἀγαπητοί, εἰ οὕτως ὁ Θεὸς ἠγάπησεν*
sins ~ our. Beloved *ones,* if in this way - God loved

ἡμᾶς, καὶ ἡμεῖς ὀφείλομεν ἀλλήλους ἀγαπᾶν.
us, indeed we ought [3]one [4]another [1]to [2]love.

Seeing God Through Love

12 *Θεὸν οὐδεὶς πώποτε τεθέαται. Ἐὰν ἀγαπῶμεν*
[6]God [1]No [2]one [4]ever [3]has [5]seen. If we love

ἀλλήλους, ὁ Θεὸς ἐν ἡμῖν μένει καὶ ἡ ἀγάπη αὐτοῦ
one another, - God [2]in [3]us [1]abides and - love ~ His

τετελειωμένη ἐστὶν ἐν ἡμῖν. **13** *(Ἐν τούτῳ γινώσκομεν ὅτι*
[2]being [3]perfected [1]is in us. (By this we know that
has been perfected

ἐν αὐτῷ μένομεν καὶ αὐτὸς ἐν ἡμῖν, ὅτι ἐκ τοῦ Πνεύματος
[3]in [4]Him [1]we [2]abide and He in us, because of - Spirit ~

αὐτοῦ δέδωκεν ἡμῖν.) **14** *Καὶ ἡμεῖς τεθεάμεθα καὶ*
His He has given us.) And we have seen and

μαρτυροῦμεν ὅτι ὁ Πατὴρ ἀπέσταλκε τὸν Υἱὸν Σωτῆρα τοῦ
we testify that the Father has sent the Son *as* Savior of the

κόσμου. **15** *Ὃς ἂν ὁμολογήσῃ ὅτι Ἰησοῦς ἐστιν ὁ Υἱὸς τοῦ*
world. Who ever confesses that Jesus is the Son -

Θεοῦ, ὁ Θεὸς ἐν αὐτῷ μένει, καὶ αὐτὸς ἐν τῷ Θεῷ. **16** *Καὶ*
of God, - God [2]in [3]him [1]abides, and he in - God. And

***(4:10)** *ἱλασμός (hilasmos).* Noun used only here and 1 John 2:2 in the NT, meaning *propitiation, expiation,* perhaps (indirectly) *sin offering.* The basic idea (though some interpreters disagree) is to appease wrath for an offense by means of sacrificial atonement. Thus Jesus satisfied the requirements of God's justice, His wrath, by giving Himself for our sins. Cf. the cognate noun *ἱλαστήριον, that which expiates* or *propitiates* (Rom. 3:25), and *the place of expiation* or *propitiation, the mercy seat* (Heb. 9:5); and the verb *ἱλάσκομαι, expiate, propitiate,* at Luke 18:13.

ἡμεῖς ἐγνώκαμεν καὶ πεπιστεύκαμεν τὴν ἀγάπην ἣν ἔχει ὁ
we have known and have believed the love which has ˜ -
have come to know and believe

Θεὸς ἐν ἡμῖν. Ὁ Θεὸς ἀγάπη ἐστί, καὶ ὁ μένων ἐν τῇ
God in us. - God love ˜ is, and the *one* abiding in -
who abides

ἀγάπῃ ἐν τῷ Θεῷ μένει, καὶ ὁ Θεὸς ἐν αὐτῷ μένει.
love [2]in - [3]God [1]abides, and - God [2]in [3]him [1]abides.

The Consummation of Love

17 Ἐν τούτῳ τετελείωται ἡ ἀγάπη μεθ' ἡμῶν,
By this [2]has [3]been [4]perfected - [1]love with us,
reached completion

ἵνα παρρησίαν ἔχωμεν ἐν τῇ ἡμέρᾳ τῆς κρίσεως,
in order that [4]confidence [1]we [2]may [3]have in the day - of judgment,

ὅτι καθὼς ἐκεῖνός ἐστι, καὶ ἡμεῖς ἐσμεν ἐν τῷ κόσμῳ
because just as that *One* is, also ˜ we are in - world ˜
He

τούτῳ. **18** Φόβος οὐκ ἔστιν ἐν τῇ ἀγάπῃ, ἀλλ' ἡ τελεία
this. [4]fear [3]not [1]*There* [2]is in - love, but - perfect
complete

ἀγάπη ἔξω βάλλει τὸν φόβον, ὅτι ὁ φόβος κόλασιν
love out ˜ casts - fear, because - fear punishment ˜

ἔχει. Ὁ δὲ φοβούμενος οὐ τετελείωται ἐν τῇ
has. [2]the [3]*one* [1]But fearing not ˜ has been perfected in -
involves. who fears made complete

ἀγάπῃ. **19** Ἡμεῖς ἀγαπῶμεν αὐτὸν[b] ὅτι αὐτὸς πρῶτος
love. We love Him because He first

ἠγάπησεν ἡμᾶς.
loved us.

Keeping God's Command by Faith

20 Ἐάν τις εἴπῃ ὅτι "Ἀγαπῶ τὸν Θεόν," καὶ τὸν
If anyone should say - "I love - God," and -
claims,

ἀδελφὸν αὐτοῦ μισῇ, ψεύστης ἐστίν· ὁ γὰρ μὴ
[3]brother [2]his [1]hates, [6]a [7]liar [4]he [5]is; [9]the [10]*one* [8]for not
who

ἀγαπῶν τὸν ἀδελφὸν αὐτοῦ ὃν ἑώρακε, τὸν Θεὸν ὃν
loving - brother ˜ his whom he has seen, - [9]God [10]whom
does not love

οὐχ ἑώρακε πῶς[c] δύναται ἀγαπᾶν? **21** Καὶ
[13]not [11]he [12]has [14]seen [1]how [2]is [3]it [4]possible [5]*for* [6]*him* [7]to [8]love? And

ταύτην τὴν ἐντολὴν ἔχομεν ἀπ' αὐτοῦ, ἵνα ὁ ἀγαπῶν
this - commandment we have from Him, that the *one* loving
who loves

τὸν Θεὸν ἀγαπᾷ καὶ τὸν ἀδελφὸν αὐτοῦ.
- God should love also - brother ˜ his.

5

1 Πᾶς ὁ πιστεύων ὅτι Ἰησοῦς ἐστιν ὁ Χριστός, ἐκ
Every - *one* believing that Jesus is the Christ, [4]of
Everyone who believes

τοῦ Θεοῦ γεγέννηται, καὶ πᾶς ὁ ἀγαπῶν τὸν
- [5]God [1]has [2]been [3]born, and every - *one* loving the *One*
everyone who loves

γεννήσαντα ἀγαπᾷ καὶ τὸν γεγεννημένον ἐξ αὐτοῦ. **2** Ἐν
having borne loves also the *one* having been born of Him. By
who bore who has

τούτῳ γινώσκομεν ὅτι ἀγαπῶμεν τὰ τέκνα τοῦ Θεοῦ, ὅταν
this we know that we love the children - of God, whenever

believed the love that God has
for us. God is love, and he who
abides in love abides in God,
and God in him.
17 Love has been perfected
among us in this: that we may
have boldness in the day of
judgment; because as He is, so
are we in this world.
18 There is no fear in love;
but perfect love casts out fear,
because fear involves torment.
But he who fears has not been
made perfect in love.
19 We love Him because He
first loved us.
20 If someone says, "I love
God," and hates his brother, he
is a liar; for he who does not
love his brother whom he has
seen, how can he love God
whom he has not seen?
21 And this commandment we
have from Him: that he who
loves God *must* love his brother
also.
5 Whoever believes that Jesus is the Christ is born of
God, and everyone who loves
Him who begot also loves him
who is begotten of Him.
2 By this we know that we
love the children of God, when

---

[b]**(4:19)** NU omits *αυτον*, *Him.* [c]**(4:20)** NU reads *ου*, *not,* instead of *πως*, *how;* thus, *he is not able to love God whom.*

we love God and keep His commandments.
3 For this is the love of God,
that we keep His command-
ments. And His command-
ments are not burdensome.
4 For whatever is born of
God overcomes the world. And
this is the victory that has overcome the world—our faith.
5 Who is he who overcomes
the world, but he who believes
that Jesus is the Son of God?
6 This is He who came by
water and blood—Jesus Christ;
not only by water, but by water
and blood. And it is the Spirit
who bears witness, because the
Spirit is truth.
7 For there are three that
bear witness in heaven: the Father, the Word, and the Holy
Spirit; and these three are one.
8 And there are three that
bear witness on earth: the
Spirit, the water, and the blood;
and these three agree as one.
9 If we receive the witness
of men, the witness of God is
greater; for this is the witness
of God which He has testified of
His Son.
10 He who believes in the Son
of God has the witness in himself; he who does not believe
God has made Him a liar, because he has not believed the
testimony that God has given of
His Son.
11 And this is the testimony:
that God has given us eternal
life, and this life is in His Son.
12 He who has the Son has
life; he who does not have the

---

[a](5:4) NU reads ημων, *our.*
[b](5:7, 8) NU, M read as above. Only four or five very late Greek manuscripts add: . . . *in heaven: the Father, the Word, and the Holy Spirit; and these three are one. And there are three that bear witness on earth . . .*
[c](5:9) NU reads οτι, *that.*

***(5:3)** τηρέω *(tēreō).* Verb with the basic meaning *keep.* The word appears frequently in the NT in a variety of closely related senses. It is used with respect to persons or things with the meanings *watch over, guard* (as Matt. 27:36, 54); *protect, keep safe* (as John 17:11, 15; Rev. 3:10); *hold, reserve, preserve* (as John 2:10; 1 Pet. 1:4). It has the specialized meaning *observe* when its object is some aspect of law or teaching (as here in

τὸν Θεὸν ἀγαπῶμεν καὶ τὰς ἐντολὰς αὐτοῦ τηρῶμεν.
- [3]God [1]we [2]love [4]and - [8]commandments [7]His [5]we [6]keep.

3 Αὕτη γάρ ἐστιν ἡ ἀγάπη τοῦ Θεοῦ, ἵνα τὰς ἐντολὰς
this ˜ For is the love - of God, that - [4]commandments

αὐτοῦ τηρῶμεν.* Καὶ αἱ ἐντολαὶ αὐτοῦ βαρεῖαι οὐκ
[3]His [1]we [2]keep. And - [2]commandments [1]His [5]burdensome [4]not

εἰσίν, **4** ὅτι πᾶν τὸ γεγεννημένον ἐκ τοῦ Θεοῦ
[3]are, because every*thing* - having been born of - God

νικᾷ τὸν κόσμον· καὶ αὕτη ἐστὶν ἡ νίκη ἡ
overcomes the world: and this is the victory the *one* (which)

νικήσασα τὸν κόσμον, ἡ πίστις ὑμῶν.[a] **5** Τίς ἐστιν ὁ
overcoming (has overcome) the world, - faith ˜ your. Who is the *one*

νικῶν τὸν κόσμον εἰ μὴ ὁ πιστεύων ὅτι Ἰησοῦς
overcoming (who overcomes) the world if not the *one* believing (who believes) that Jesus

ἐστιν ὁ Υἱὸς τοῦ Θεοῦ?
is the Son - of God?

The Certainty of God's Witness

6 Οὗτός ἐστιν ὁ ἐλθὼν δι' ὕδατος καὶ αἵματος,
This (He) is the *One* having come (who came) through water and blood,

Ἰησοῦς Χριστός, οὐκ ἐν τῷ ὕδατι μόνον, ἀλλ' ἐν τῷ ὕδατι καὶ
Jesus Christ, not in (by) the water only, but in (by) the water and

τῷ αἵματι. Καὶ τὸ Πνεῦμά ἐστι τὸ μαρτυροῦν, ὅτι τὸ
the blood. And the Spirit is the *One* witnessing (who witnesses), because the

Πνεῦμά ἐστιν ἡ ἀλήθεια. **7** Ὅτι τρεῖς εἰσιν οἱ
Spirit is the truth. Because three are the *ones*

μαρτυροῦντες·[b] **8** τὸ Πνεῦμα καὶ τὸ ὕδωρ καὶ τὸ αἷμα, καὶ
witnessing (who witness): the Spirit and the water and the blood, and

οἱ τρεῖς εἰς τὸ ἕν εἰσιν. **9** Εἰ τὴν μαρτυρίαν τῶν ἀνθρώπων
the three [2]into [3]the [4]one [1]are (agree as one). If [3]the [4]testimony - [5]of [6]men

λαμβάνομεν, ἡ μαρτυρία τοῦ Θεοῦ μείζων ἐστίν· ὅτι αὕτη
[1]we [2]receive, the testimony - of God greater ˜ is; because this

ἐστὶν ἡ μαρτυρία τοῦ Θεοῦ ἣν[c] μεμαρτύρηκε περὶ τοῦ
is the testimony - of God which He has testified concerning -

Υἱοῦ αὐτοῦ. **10** Ὁ πιστεύων εἰς τὸν Υἱὸν τοῦ Θεοῦ ἔχει
Son ˜ His. The *one* believing (who believes) in the Son - of God has

τὴν μαρτυρίαν ἐν αὑτῷ· ὁ μὴ πιστεύων τῷ Θεῷ
the testimony in him*self;* the *one* not believing (who does not believe) - God

ψεύστην πεποίηκεν αὐτόν, ὅτι οὐ πεπίστευκεν εἰς τὴν
[4]a [5]liar [1]has [2]made [3]Him, because [3]not [1]he [2]has [4]believed in the

μαρτυρίαν ἣν μεμαρτύρηκεν ὁ Θεὸς περὶ τοῦ Υἱοῦ
testimony which [2]has [3]testified - [1]God concerning - Son ˜

αὐτοῦ. **11** Καὶ αὕτη ἐστὶν ἡ μαρτυρία, ὅτι ζωὴν αἰώνιον
His. And this is the testimony, that [7]life [6]eternal

ἔδωκεν ἡμῖν ὁ Θεός, καὶ αὕτη ἡ ζωὴ ἐν τῷ Υἱῷ αὐτοῦ ἐστιν.
[2]has [3]given [4]to [5]us - [1]God, and this - life [2]in - [4]Son [3]His [1]is.

12 Ὁ ἔχων τὸν Υἱὸν ἔχει τὴν ζωήν· ὁ μὴ
The *one* having (who has) the Son has - life; the *one* not (who does)

ἔχων τὸν Υἱὸν τοῦ Θεοῦ τὴν ζωὴν οὐκ ἔχει.
having the Son - of God - [4]life [2]not [1]does [3]have.
not have

13 Ταῦτα ἔγραψα ὑμῖν τοῖς πιστεύουσιν εἰς τὸ
These *things* I wrote to you the *ones* believing in the
write who believe

ὄνομα τοῦ Υἱοῦ τοῦ Θεοῦ, ἵνα εἰδῆτε ὅτι ζωὴν
name of the Son - of God, in order that you may know that [4]life

αἰώνιον ἔχετε,[d] καὶ ἵνα πιστεύητε εἰς τὸ ὄνομα τοῦ Υἱοῦ
[3]eternal [1]you [2]have, and that you may believe in the name of the Son

τοῦ Θεοῦ.
- of God.

Confidence and Compassion in Prayer

14 Καὶ αὕτη ἐστὶν ἡ παρρησία ἣν ἔχομεν πρὸς αὐτόν,
And this is the confidence which we have toward Him,

ὅτι ἐάν τι αἰτώμεθα κατὰ τὸ θέλημα αὐτοῦ,
that if [4]anything [1]we [2]should [3]ask according to - will ˜ His,

ἀκούει ἡμῶν. 15 Καὶ ἐὰν οἴδαμεν ὅτι ἀκούει ἡμῶν, ὃ ἐὰν
He hears us. And if we know that He hears us, what ever

αἰτώμεθα, οἴδαμεν ὅτι ἔχομεν τὰ αἰτήματα ἃ
we may ask, we know that we have the requests which

ἠτήκαμεν παρ᾽ αὐτοῦ. 16 Ἐάν τις ἴδῃ τὸν ἀδελφὸν
we have requested from Him. If anyone sees - brother ˜

αὐτοῦ ἁμαρτάνοντα ἁμαρτίαν μὴ πρὸς θάνατον, αἰτήσει, καὶ
his sinning a sin not to death, he will ask and

δώσει αὐτῷ ζωὴν τοῖς ἁμαρτάνουσι μὴ πρὸς
He will give him life to the *ones* sinning not to
who do not sin

θάνατον. Ἔστιν ἁμαρτία πρὸς θάνατον· οὐ περὶ ἐκείνης
death. *There* is a sin to death: not concerning that *sin*

λέγω ἵνα ἐρωτήσῃ. 17 Πᾶσα ἀδικία ἁμαρτία
am I saying that he should ask. Every unrighteousness sin ˜

ἐστί, καὶ ἔστιν ἁμαρτία οὐ πρὸς θάνατον.
is, and *there* is a sin not to death.

Epilogue: Knowing Reality and Rejecting Idols

18 Οἴδαμεν ὅτι πᾶς ὁ γεγεννημένος ἐκ τοῦ Θεοῦ οὐχ
We know that every - *one* having been born of - God not ˜
everyone who has

ἁμαρτάνει, ἀλλ᾽ ὁ γεννηθεὶς ἐκ τοῦ Θεοῦ τηρεῖ
does sin, but the *one* having been born of - God keeps
who was

ἑαυτόν,[e] καὶ ὁ πονηρὸς οὐχ ἅπτεται αὐτοῦ.
himself, and the evil *one* not ˜ does touch him.

19 Οἴδαμεν ὅτι ἐκ τοῦ Θεοῦ ἐσμεν, καὶ ὁ κόσμος*
We know that [3]from - [4]God [1]we [2]are, and the world ˜

ὅλος ἐν τῷ πονηρῷ κεῖται.
whole [2]in [3]the [4]evil [5]*one* [1]lies.

20 Οἴδαμεν δὲ ὅτι ὁ Υἱὸς τοῦ Θεοῦ ἥκει καὶ δέδωκεν
[2]we [3]know [1]And that the Son - of God has come and has given

ἡμῖν διάνοιαν ἵνα γινώσκωμεν τὸν ἀληθινόν· καί ἐσμεν ἐν
us understanding that we might know the true *one;* and we are in

τῷ ἀληθινῷ, ἐν τῷ Υἱῷ αὐτοῦ Ἰησοῦ Χριστῷ. Οὗτός ἐστιν ὁ
the true *one,* in - Son ˜ His Jesus Christ. This One is the
He

ἀληθινὸς Θεὸς καὶ ἡ ζωὴ ἡ αἰώνιος.
true God and - life ˜ - eternal.

Son of God does not have life.
13 These things I have written to you who believe in the name of the Son of God, that you may know that you have eternal life, and that you may *continue to* believe in the name of the Son of God.
14 Now this is the confidence that we have in Him, that if we ask anything according to His will, He hears us.
15 And if we know that He hears us, whatever we ask, we know that we have the petitions that we have asked of Him.
16 If anyone sees his brother sinning a sin *which does* not *lead* to death, he will ask, and He will give him life for those who commit sin not *leading* to death. There is sin *leading* to death. I do not say that he should pray about that.
17 All unrighteousness is sin, and there is sin not *leading* to death.
18 We know that whoever is born of God does not sin; but he who has been born of God keeps himself, and the wicked one does not touch him.
19 We know that we are of God, and the whole world lies *under the sway of* the wicked one.
20 And we know that the Son of God has come and has given us an understanding, that we may know Him who is true; and we are in Him who is true, in His Son Jesus Christ. This is the true God and eternal life.

---

[d](5:13) NU omits the rest of this verse.
[e](5:18) NU reads *αυτον*, *him.*

---

1 John 5:3; John 9:16). Cf. the cognate noun *τήρησις*, *observance* (1 Cor. 7:19); *custody, imprisonment* (Acts 4:3; 5:18).

***(5:19)** *κόσμος (kosmos).* Noun meaning *adornment* (1 Pet. 3:3) or *order,* and by common extension the *ordered universe, world* (John 17:5; Acts 17:24). It is used in the NT almost exclusively in this latter sense, but with a wide range of nuances. It may refer to the planet Earth generally (Matt. 26:13), specifically in contrast to heaven (John 16:28), or as the place where humans live (1 Tim. 6:7). It is used of humanity generally (John 4:42), or with specific reference to believers (John 3:16, 17). Here in 1 John 5:19 *κόσμος* represents all the aspects of

21 Little children, keep yourselves from idols. Amen.

21 Τεκνία, φυλάξατε ἑαυτοὺς ἀπὸ τῶν εἰδώλων. Ἀμήν.
Little children, guard yourselves from - idols. Amen.
So be it.

---

the created order that are hostile to God and His purposes, all organized evil which the devil controls and directs (cf. 1 John 2:15). Cf. the verb *κοσμέω, put in order, adorn* (Matt. 23:29); and the adjective *κοσμικός, earthly, worldly* (Titus 2:12).

The Second Epistle of
JOHN

ΙΩΑΝΝΟΥ Β
OF JOHN 2

The Elder Greets the Elect Lady

1 Ὁ Πρεσβύτερος,
The Elder,

Ἐκλεκτῇ κυρίᾳ* καὶ τοῖς τέκνοις αὐτῆς, οὓς ἐγὼ ἀγαπῶ
To *the* elect lady and - children ~ her, whom I love

ἐν ἀληθείᾳ, καὶ οὐκ ἐγὼ μόνος, ἀλλὰ καὶ πάντες οἱ
in truth, and not I only, but also all the *ones*
those who

ἐγνωκότες τὴν ἀλήθειαν, **2** διὰ τὴν ἀλήθειαν
having known the truth, on account of the truth
have come to know

τὴν μένουσαν ἐν ἡμῖν καὶ μεθ' ἡμῶν ἔσται εἰς τὸν
the *one* abiding in us and [3]with [4]us [1]will [2]be into the
which abides forever.

αἰῶνα.
age.

3 Ἔσται μεθ' ἡμῶν[a] χάρις, ἔλεος, εἰρήνη παρὰ Θεοῦ
[5]will [6]be [7]with [8]us [1]Grace, [2]mercy, [3]*and* [4]peace from God

Πατρὸς καὶ παρὰ Κυρίου[b] Ἰησοῦ Χριστοῦ τοῦ Υἱοῦ τοῦ
the Father and from *the* Lord Jesus Christ the Son of the

Πατρός, ἐν ἀληθείᾳ καὶ ἀγάπῃ.
Father, in truth and love.

Walk in Christ's Commandments

4 Ἐχάρην λίαν ὅτι εὕρηκα ἐκ τῶν τέκνων σου
I rejoiced greatly that I have found *some* of - children ~ your

περιπατοῦντας ἐν ἀληθείᾳ, καθὼς ἐντολὴν ἐλάβομεν
walking in truth, just as [3]commandment [1]we [2]received

παρὰ τοῦ Πατρός. **5** Καὶ νῦν ἐρωτῶ σε, κυρία, οὐχ ὡς
from the Father. And now I ask you, lady, not as

ἐντολὴν γράφων σοι καινήν, ἀλλὰ ἣν
[2]a [4]commandment [1]writing [5]to [6]you [3]new, but *one* which

εἴχομεν ἀπ' ἀρχῆς, ἵνα ἀγαπῶμεν ἀλλήλους. **6** Καὶ
we were having from *the* beginning, that we should love one another. And
have had

αὕτη ἐστὶν ἡ ἀγάπη, ἵνα περιπατῶμεν κατὰ τὰς
this is - love, that we should walk according to -

ἐντολὰς αὐτοῦ. Αὕτη ἐστὶν ἡ ἐντολή, καθὼς
commandments ~ His. This is the commandment, just as

ἠκούσατε ἀπ' ἀρχῆς, ἵνα ἐν αὐτῇ περιπατῆτε.
you heard from *the* beginning, [1]that [5]in [6]it [2]you [3]should [4]walk.

Beware of Antichrist Deceivers

7 Ὅτι πολλοὶ πλάνοι εἰσῆλθον εἰς τὸν κόσμον, οἱ
Because many deceivers entered into the world, the *ones*
who do

1 The Elder,

To the elect lady and her children, whom I love in truth, and not only I, but also all those who have known the truth,
2 because of the truth which abides in us and will be with us forever:

3 Grace, mercy, *and* peace will be with you from God the Father and from the Lord Jesus Christ, the Son of the Father, in truth and love.

4 I rejoiced greatly that I have found *some* of your children walking in truth, as we received commandment from the Father.
5 And now I plead with you, lady, not as though I wrote a new commandment to you, but that which we have had from the beginning: that we love one another.
6 This is love, that we walk according to His commandments. This is the commandment, that as you have heard from the beginning, you should walk in it.
7 For many deceivers have gone out into the world who do

---

[a](3) TR reads υμων, *you.*
[b](3) NU omits Κυριου, *the Lord.*

***(v. 1)** κυρια *(kyria).* Feminine noun, used only in 2 John meaning *lady,* a title of respect (cf. κύριος, *lord, sir*). It is possible that here in 2 John κυρια is a proper name, Cyria ("Martha" is the Aramaic name with the same meaning). Another possibility is that it is a figure of speech personifying a church, and not an individual woman (the NT presents

not confess Jesus Christ *as*
coming in the flesh. This is a
deceiver and an antichrist.
8 Look to yourselves, that
we do not lose those things we
worked for, but *that* we may receive a full reward.
9 Whoever transgresses and
does not abide in the doctrine of
Christ does not have God. He
who abides in the doctrine of
Christ has both the Father and
the Son.
10 If anyone comes to you and
does not bring this doctrine, do
not receive him into your house
nor greet him;
11 for he who greets him
shares in his evil deeds.
12 Having many things to
write to you, I did not wish *to
do so* with paper and ink; but I
hope to come to you and speak
face to face, that our joy may be
full.
13 The children of your elect
sister greet you. Amen.

μὴ ὁμολογοῦντες Ἰησοῦν Χριστὸν ἐρχόμενον ἐν σαρκί. Οὗτός
not confessing Jesus Christ coming in *the* flesh. This
not confess Jesus Christ as

ἐστιν ὁ πλάνος καὶ ὁ ἀντίχριστος. **8** Βλέπετε ἑαυτούς,
is the deceiver and the antichrist. Look *to* yourselves,

ἵνα μὴ ἀπολέσωμεν[c] ἃ εἰργασάμεθα,
in order that [3]not [1]we [2]should [4]lose *the things for* which we worked,
lest

ἀλλὰ μισθὸν πλήρη ἀπολάβωμεν.[d]
but [4]a [6]reward [5]full [1]we [2]should [3]receive.

9 Πᾶς ὁ παραβαίνων[e] καὶ μὴ μένων ἐν τῇ
Every - *one* transgressing and not abiding in the
Everyone who transgresses does not abide

διδαχῇ τοῦ Χριστοῦ Θεὸν οὐκ ἔχει· ὁ μένων ἐν τῇ
teaching - of Christ [4]God [2]not [1]does [3]have; the *one* abiding in the
who abides

διδαχῇ τοῦ Χριστοῦ, οὗτος καὶ τὸν Πατέρα καὶ τὸν Υἱὸν
teaching - of Christ, [1]this [2]*one* [4]both [5]the [6]Father [7]and [8]the [9]Son

ἔχει. **10** Εἴ τις ἔρχεται πρὸς ὑμᾶς καὶ ταύτην τὴν διδαχὴν
[3]has. If anyone comes to you and [4]this - [5]teaching

οὐ φέρει, μὴ λαμβάνετε αὐτὸν εἰς οἰκίαν, καὶ
[2]not [1]does [3]bring, not ~ do receive him into *your* house, [1]and

"Χαίρειν" αὐτῷ μὴ λέγετε· **11** ὁ γὰρ λέγων αὐτῷ
[7]"Rejoice" [5]to [6]him [3]not [2]do [4]say; [2]the [3]*one* [1]For saying to him
do not greet him; who greets

"Χαίρειν" κοινωνεῖ τοῖς ἔργοις αὐτοῦ τοῖς πονηροῖς.
"Rejoice" [1]shares - [2]in [5]works [3]his - [4]evil.
him

John's Farewell Greeting

12 Πολλὰ ἔχων ὑμῖν γράφειν, οὐκ
many *things* Having to you to write, [3]not
Although I had many things to write to you,

ἐβουλήθην διὰ χάρτου καὶ μέλανος, ἀλλὰ ἐλπίζω
[1]I [2]did wish *to write* through paper and ink, but I hope
with

ἐλθεῖν πρὸς ὑμᾶς καὶ στόμα πρὸς στόμα λαλῆσαι, ἵνα
to come to you and [3]mouth [4]to [5]mouth [1]to [2]speak, in order that
face to face

ἡ χαρὰ ἡμῶν ᾖ πεπληρωμένη.
- joy ~ our may be fulfilled.

13 Ἀσπάζεταί σε τὰ τέκνα τῆς ἀδελφῆς σου τῆς
[7]greet [8]you [1]The [2]children - [3]of [6]sister [4]your -

ἐκλεκτῆς. Ἀμήν.[f]
[5]elect. Amen.
So be it.

---

[c](**8**) NU reads απολεσητε, *you should (not) lose.*
[d](**8**) NU reads απολαβητε, *you should receive.*
[e](**9**) NU reads προαγων, *going ahead.*
[f](**13**) NU omits Αμην, *Amen.*

the church as the bride of Christ).

The Third Epistle of
JOHN

ΙΩΑΝΝΟΥ Γ
OF JOHN 3

The Elder Greets Gaius

1 Ὁ Πρεσβύτερος,
The Elder,

Γαΐῳ τῷ ἀγαπητῷ, ὃν ἐγὼ ἀγαπῶ ἐν ἀληθείᾳ.
To Gaius the beloved, whom I love in truth.

2 Ἀγαπητέ, περὶ πάντων εὔχομαί σε εὐοδοῦσθαι καὶ
Beloved, concerning all *things* I pray you to prosper and

ὑγιαίνειν, καθὼς εὐοδοῦταί σου ἡ ψυχή. **3** Ἐχάρην γὰρ
to be healthy, just as [3]prospers [1]your - [2]soul. [2]I [3]rejoiced [1]For

λίαν, ἐρχομένων ἀδελφῶν καὶ μαρτυρούντων σου τῇ
greatly, coming ~ brothers and witnessing of you to
when brothers came and witnessed to the truth which is

ἀληθείᾳ, καθὼς σὺ ἐν ἀληθείᾳ περιπατεῖς. **4** Μειζοτέραν
truth, just as you [2]in [3]truth [1]walk. [6]greater [7]*than*
in you,

τούτων οὐκ ἔχω χαράν, ἵνα ἀκούω τὰ ἐμὰ τέκνα
[8]these [9]*things* [3]not [1]I [2]do [4]have [5]joy, that I hear - *that* my children

ἐν[a] ἀληθείᾳ περιπατοῦντα.
[3]in [4]truth [1]*are* [2]walking.

Gaius Is Commended for Generosity

5 Ἀγαπητέ, πιστὸν ποιεῖς ὃ ἐὰν ἐργάσῃ εἰς
Beloved, [3]a [4]faithful [5]*thing* [1]you [2]do what ever you work for
faithfully

τοὺς ἀδελφοὺς καὶ εἰς[b] τοὺς ξένους, **6** οἳ ἐμαρτύρησάν
the brothers and for the strangers, who gave testimony

σου τῇ ἀγάπῃ ἐνώπιον ἐκκλησίας, οὓς
your ~ - to love before *the* church, *with reference to* whom
concerning your love

καλῶς ποιήσεις προπέμψας ἀξίως τοῦ Θεοῦ.
[4]well [1]you [2]will [3]do sending forth worthily - of God.
if you send them forth in a manner worthy

7 Ὑπὲρ γὰρ τοῦ Ὀνόματος ἐξῆλθον, μηδὲν
[2]in [3]behalf [4]of [1]For the Name they went out, nothing ~

λαμβάνοντες ἀπὸ τῶν ἐθνῶν. **8** Ἡμεῖς οὖν ὀφείλομεν
taking from the nations. We therefore ought
pagans.

ἀπολαμβάνειν[c] τοὺς τοιούτους ἵνα συνεργοὶ
to receive - such *ones* in order that [4]fellow [5]workers

γινώμεθα τῇ ἀληθείᾳ.
[1]we [2]might [3]be with the truth.

Diotrephes Is Criticized and Demetrius Commended

9 Ἔγραψα τῇ ἐκκλησίᾳ, ἀλλ' ὁ φιλοπρωτεύων
I wrote to the church, but the *one* loving preeminence
Diotrephes who loves the

1 The Elder,

To the beloved Gaius,
whom I love in truth:

2 Beloved, I pray that you
may prosper in all things and be
in health, just as your soul pros-
pers.
3 For I rejoiced greatly when
brethren came and testified of
the truth *that is* in you, just as
you walk in the truth.
4 I have no greater joy than
to hear that my children walk in
truth.
5 Beloved, you do faithfully
whatever you do for the brethren and for strangers,
6 who have borne witness of
your love before the church. *If*
you send them forward on their
journey in a manner worthy of
God, you will do well,
7 because they went forth
for His name's sake, taking
nothing from the Gentiles.
8 We therefore ought to receive such, that we may become fellow workers for the
truth.
9 I wrote to the church, but
Diotrephes, who loves to have

---

[a](**4**) NU adds *τη, the (truth).* [b](**5**) NU reads *τουτο, this,* for *εις τους,* thus *and this (especially) to strangers.* [c](**8**) NU reads *υπολαμβανειν, to support.*

the preeminence among them, does not receive us.
10 Therefore, if I come, I will call to mind his deeds which he does, prating against us with malicious words. And not content with that, he himself does not receive the brethren, and forbids those who wish to, putting *them* out of the church.
11 Beloved, do not imitate what is evil, but what is good. He who does good is of God, but he who does evil has not seen God.
12 Demetrius has a *good* testimony from all, and from the truth itself. And we also bear witness, and you know that our testimony is true.
13 I had many things to write, but I do not wish to write to you with pen and ink;
14 but I hope to see you shortly, and we shall speak face to face. Peace to you. Our friends greet you. Greet the friends by name.

αὐτῶν Διοτρέφης οὐκ ἐπιδέχεται ἡμᾶς. **10** Διὰ
of them Diotrephes not ˜ does receive us. On account of
preeminence over them

τοῦτο, ἐὰν ἔλθω, ὑπομνήσω αὐτοῦ τὰ ἔργα ἃ ποιεῖ,
this, if I come, I will call to mind his - works which he does,

λόγοις πονηροῖς φλυαρῶν* ἡμᾶς. Καὶ μὴ ἀρκούμενος ἐπὶ
[3]with [5]words [4]evil [1]slandering [2]us. And not being content upon
with

τούτοις, οὔτε αὐτὸς ἐπιδέχεται τοὺς ἀδελφούς, καὶ τοὺς
these *things*, [3]not [1]he [2]does [4]receive the brothers, and the *ones*
that, those who

βουλομένους κωλύει, καὶ ἐκ τῆς ἐκκλησίας
desiring *to receive them* he hinders, and [4]out [5]of [6]the [7]church
desire

ἐκβάλλει.
[1]he [2]casts [3]*them*.

11 Ἀγαπητέ, μὴ μιμοῦ τὸ κακόν, ἀλλὰ τὸ ἀγαθόν.
Beloved, not ˜ do imitate the bad, but the good.

Ὁ ἀγαθοποιῶν ἐκ τοῦ Θεοῦ ἐστιν· ὁ[d] κακοποιῶν οὐχ
The *one* doing good [2]of - [3]God [1]is; the *one* doing evil [2]not
who does who does

ἑώρακε τὸν Θεόν. **12** Δημητρίῳ μεμαρτύρηται ὑπὸ
[1]has [3]seen - God. To Demetrius it has been witnessed by
Demetrius has a good testimony with

πάντων, καὶ ὑπ' αὐτῆς τῆς ἀληθείας. Καὶ ἡμεῖς δὲ
all, and [1]by [4]itself [2]the [3]truth. [7]also [6]we [5]And
everyone, of

μαρτυροῦμεν, καὶ οἴδατε ὅτι ἡ μαρτυρία ἡμῶν ἀληθής ἐστι.
testify, and you know that - testimony ˜ our true ˜ is.

John's Farewell Greeting

13 Πολλὰ εἶχον γράφειν, ἀλλ' οὐ θέλω διὰ
Many *things* I had to write, but [3]not [1]I [2]do [4]wish [9]through
with

μέλανος καὶ καλάμου σοι γράψαι. **14** Ἐλπίζω δὲ
[10]ink [11]and [12]pen [7]to [8]you [5]to [6]write. [2]I [3]wish [1]But

εὐθέως ἰδεῖν σε, καὶ στόμα πρὸς στόμα λαλήσομεν.
immediately to see you, and [4]mouth [5]to [6]mouth [1]we [2]shall [3]speak.
shortly face to face

Εἰρήνη σοι. Ἀσπάζονταί σε οἱ φίλοι. Ἀσπάζου τοὺς
Peace to you. [3]greet [4]you [1]The [2]friends. Greet the
Our our

φίλους κατ' ὄνομα.
friends by name.

---

[d](**11**) TR adds δε, *but (the one)*.

*(**v. 10**) φλυαρέω (*phlyareō*). Verb, used only here in the NT (from φλύω, *babble*), meaning either *to talk nonsense* or *bring unjustified charges against*. Cf. the cognate adjective φλύαρος, translated by some as *gossipy* or *foolish*, but perhaps used substantivally for *babblers* or even *idle accusers* (only in 1 Tim. 5:13).

The Epistle of
JUDE

ΙΟΥΔΑ
JUDE

Jude Greets the Called

1 Ἰούδας, Ἰησοῦ Χριστοῦ δοῦλος, ἀδελφὸς δὲ
Jude, [3]of [4]Jesus [5]Christ [1]a [2]bondservant, brother ~ and
slave,

Ἰακώβου,
of James,

Τοῖς ἐν Θεῷ Πατρὶ ἡγιασμένοις[a] καὶ
To *the ones* [5]by [6]God [7]*the* [8]Father [2]having [3]been [4]sanctified [9]and
those who are sanctified

Ἰησοῦ Χριστῷ τετηρημένοις κλητοῖς·
[13]in [14]Jesus [15]Christ [10]having [11]been [12]kept [1]called:
preserved

2 Ἔλεος ὑμῖν καὶ εἰρήνη καὶ ἀγάπη πληθυνθείη.
May mercy to you and peace and love be multiplied.

Jude's Reason for Writing

3 Ἀγαπητοί, πᾶσαν σπουδὴν ποιούμενος γράφειν ὑμῖν
Beloved *ones*, [2]all [3]diligence [1]making to write to you
while I was very diligent

περὶ τῆς κοινῆς[b] σωτηρίας, ἀνάγκην ἔσχον γράψαι ὑμῖν
about the common salvation, [3]a [4]necessity [1]I [2]had to write to you
our it became necessary

παρακαλῶν ἐπαγωνίζεσθαι τῇ ἅπαξ
exhorting *you* to contend earnestly for the [4]once [5]for [6]all

παραδοθείσῃ τοῖς ἁγίοις πίστει. 4 Παρεισέδυσαν
[2]having [3]been [7]delivered [8]to [9]the [10]saints [1]faith. [4]slipped [5]in [6]stealthily
which was have crept

γάρ τινες ἄνθρωποι, οἱ πάλαι προγεγραμμένοι εἰς
[1]For [2]certain [3]men, the *ones* long ago having been written before for
who were marked out

τοῦτο τὸ κρίμα, ἀσεβεῖς, τὴν τοῦ Θεοῦ ἡμῶν χάριν
this - condemnation, ungodly *men*, [2]the - [4]of [6]God [5]our [3]grace

μετατιθέντες εἰς ἀσέλγειαν* καὶ τὸν μόνον Δεσπότην Θεὸν[c]
[1]changing into licentiousness and [2]the [3]only [4]Master [5]God
perverting

καὶ Κύριον ἡμῶν Ἰησοῦν Χριστὸν ἀρνούμενοι.
[6]and [8]Lord [7]our [9]Jesus [10]Christ [1]denying.

Old and New Apostates

5 Ὑπομνῆσαι δὲ ὑμᾶς βούλομαι, εἰδότας ὑμᾶς ἅπαξ
[4]to [5]remind [1]But [6]you [2]I [3]desire, knowing ~ you once
though you once knew

τοῦτο, ὅτι ὁ Κύριος, λαὸν ἐκ γῆς Αἰγύπτου
this, that the Lord, [3]a [4]people [5]from [6]*the* [7]land [8]of [9]Egypt

σώσας, τὸ δεύτερον τοὺς μὴ πιστεύσαντας
[1]having [2]saved, the second *time* [2]the [3]*ones* [4]not [5]believing
afterward who did not believe

1 Jude, a bondservant of Jesus Christ, and brother of James,

To those who are called, sanctified by God the Father, and preserved in Jesus Christ:

2 Mercy, peace, and love be multiplied to you.

3 Beloved, while I was very diligent to write to you concerning our common salvation, I found it necessary to write to you exhorting you to contend earnestly for the faith which was once for all delivered to the saints.
4 For certain men have crept in unnoticed, who long ago were marked out for this condemnation, ungodly men, who turn the grace of our God into lewdness and deny the only Lord God and our Lord Jesus Christ.
5 But I want to remind you, though you once knew this, that the Lord, having saved the people out of the land of Egypt, afterward destroyed those who did not believe.

---

[a](1) NU reads ηγαπημενοις, *beloved.* [b](3) NU adds ημων, *our (common salvation).* [c](4) NU omits Θεον, *God.*

*(v. 4) ἀσέλγεια *(aselgeia).* Noun meaning *debauchery, sensuality.* The word is a comprehensive term for evil and perversion, but usually implies sexual *licentiousness.* It is usually found in NT vice lists alongside other words for sexual immorality (κοίται, *orgies,* in Rom. 13:13; μοιχεία, *adultery,* and πορνεία, *fornication,* in Gal. 5:19). Here in Jude 4 its meaning may include the *insolence* of the scoffer.

6 And the angels who did not
keep their proper domain, but
left their own abode, He has reserved in everlasting chains under darkness for the judgment
of the great day;
7 as Sodom and Gomorrah,
and the cities around them in a
similar manner to these, having
given themselves over to sexual immorality and gone after
strange flesh, are set forth as
an example, suffering the vengeance of eternal fire.
8 Likewise also these dreamers defile the flesh, reject authority, and speak evil of
dignitaries.
9 Yet Michael the archangel,
in contending with the devil,
when he disputed about the
body of Moses, dared not bring
against him a reviling accusation, but said, "The Lord rebuke you!"
10 But these speak evil of
whatever they do not know;
and whatever they know natu-
rally, like brute beasts, in these
things they corrupt them-
selves.
11 Woe to them! For they
have gone in the way of Cain,
have run greedily in the error of
Balaam for profit, and perished
in the rebellion of Korah.

ἀπώλεσεν. **6** Ἀγγέλους τε τοὺς μὴ τηρήσαντας τὴν
[1]destroyed. angels ˜ And the *ones* not having kept the
who did not keep their

ἑαυτῶν ἀρχήν, ἀλλὰ ἀπολιπόντας τὸ ἴδιον
[2]of [3]themselves [1]domain, but rather having left - their own
own

οἰκητήριον, εἰς κρίσιν μεγάλης ἡμέρας δεσμοῖς
habitation, [9]for [10]*the* [11]judgment [12]of [13]*the* [14]great [15]day [4]with [6]bonds
chains

ἀϊδίοις ὑπὸ ζόφον τετήρηκεν. **7** Ὡς Σόδομα καὶ
[5]eternal [7]under [8]darkness [1]He [2]has [3]kept. As Sodom and
the netherworld

Γόμορρα, καὶ αἱ περὶ αὐτὰς πόλεις, τὸν ὅμοιον τούτοις
Gomorrah, and the [2]around [3]them [1]cities, - similar to these
in a similar manner

τρόπον ἐκπορνεύσασαι καὶ ἀπελθοῦσαι
manner having indulged in sexual immorality and having gone
to these angels

ὀπίσω σαρκὸς ἑτέρας, πρόκεινται δεῖγμα, πυρὸς αἰωνίου
after flesh ˜ other, are exhibited *as* an example, [4]of [6]fire [5]eternal

δίκην ὑπέχουσαι.
[2]*the* [3]punishment [1]undergoing.
suffering.

8 Ὁμοίως μέντοι καὶ οὗτοι ἐνυπνιαζόμενοι σάρκα μὲν
Likewise indeed even these dreaming *ones* [2]*the* [3]flesh -
dreamers

μιαίνουσι, κυριότητα δὲ ἀθετοῦσι, δόξας δὲ βλασφημοῦσιν.
[1]defile, [6]lordship [4]and [5]reject, [9]glories [7]and [8]blaspheme.
authority

9 Ὁ δὲ Μιχαὴλ ὁ ἀρχάγγελος, ὅτε τῷ διαβόλῳ
- But Michael the archangel, when [3]with [4]the [5]devil

διακρινόμενος διελέγετο περὶ τοῦ Μωσέως σώματος, οὐκ
[1]taking [2]issue was arguing about the [2]of [3]Moses [1]body, not ˜
and

ἐτόλμησε κρίσιν ἐπενεγκεῖν βλασφημίας, ἀλλ' εἶπεν,
dared [3]a [4]judgment [1]to [2]bring of blasphemy, but rather said,
to bring a reviling accusation,

"Ἐπιτιμήσαι σοι Κύριος!"*
"[1]May [4]rebuke [5]you [2]*the* [3]Lord!"

10 Οὗτοι δὲ ὅσα μὲν οὐκ οἴδασι
these ˜ But [2]as [3]many [4]*things* [5]as - [8]not [6]they [7]do [9]know
understand

βλασφημοῦσιν, ὅσα δὲ φυσικῶς ὡς τὰ
[1]revile, [11]as [12]many [13]*things* [14]as [10]but [17]instinctively [18]like -

ἄλογα ζῷα ἐπίστανται, ἐν τούτοις
[19]unreasoning [20]animals [15]they [16]understand, by these *things*

φθείρονται. **11** Οὐαὶ αὐτοῖς!
they are corrupted. Woe to them!

Ὅτι τῇ ὁδῷ τοῦ Κάϊν ἐπορεύθησαν
Because [3]in [4]the [5]way - [6]of [7]Cain [1]they [2]went
have gone

Καὶ τῇ πλάνῃ τοῦ Βαλαὰμ μισθοῦ
And in the error - of Balaam [4]for [5]pay
they have

ἐξεχύθησαν
[1]they [2]abandoned [3]themselves
rushed for profit

Καὶ τῇ ἀντιλογίᾳ τοῦ Κόρε ἀπώλοντο.
And in the rebellion - of Korah they were destroyed.
have perished.

*(v. 9) κύριος (*kyrios*). Noun meaning *master, Lord.* In secular usage κύριος meant *owner* or *master,* and was particularly used of slaveholders (as Eph. 6:5; Col. 4:1). It was also a common term of respectful address ("sir," John 12:21; see κυρία, *lady,* at 2 John 1). In the LXX, Κύριος translates the Hebrew *'Adōnai, Lord,* and also stands for the personal name of God, *Yahweh.* The word is used of both God and Christ within the NT as a designation of deity (sometimes the specific reference is unclear, as in Acts 9:31). It is not always possible in the Gospels to know

The Apostates Are Depraved and Doomed

12 Οὗτοί εἰσιν ἐν ταῖς ἀγάπαις ὑμῶν σπιλάδες,
These are [2]in - [4]love [5]feasts [3]your [1]stains,

συνευωχούμενοι ἀφόβως, ἑαυτοὺς ποιμαίνοντες,
feasting together *with you* without fear, [3]themselves [1]caring [2]for,
while they feast

νεφέλαι ἄνυδροι ὑπὸ ἀνέμων παραφερόμεναι,[d] δένδρα
they are clouds ˜ waterless [4]by [5]winds [1]being [2]carried [3]along, [8]trees

φθινοπωρινά, ἄκαρπα, δὶς ἀποθανόντα, ἐκριζωθέντα,
[6]late [7]autumn, unfruitful, twice having died, having been uprooted,
dead, uprooted,

13 κύματα ἄγρια θαλάσσης ἐπαφρίζοντα τὰς ἑαυτῶν
waves ˜ wild of *the* sea casting up *the* foam of the of themselves
their own

αἰσχύνας, ἀστέρες πλανῆται οἷς ὁ ζόφος τοῦ σκότους
shame, stars ˜ wandering for whom the gloom of the darkness
darkness netherworld

εἰς αἰῶνα τετήρηται.
[4]for [5]eternity [1]has [2]been [3]reserved.
forever

14 Προεφήτευσε δὲ καὶ τούτοις ἕβδομος ἀπὸ
[7]prophesied [1]Now [11]also [8]about [9]these [10]*men* [3]*the* [4]seventh [5]from

Ἀδὰμ Ἐνώχ, λέγων, "Ἰδού, ἦλθε Κύριος ἐν ἁγίαις
[6]Adam [2]Enoch, saying, "Behold, [3]came [1]*the* [2]Lord with [2]holy
comes

μυριάσιν αὐτοῦ **15** ποιῆσαι κρίσιν κατὰ πάντων καὶ ἐλέγξαι
[3]myriads [1]His to perform judgment upon all and to convict
thousands

πάντας τοὺς ἀσεβεῖς αὐτῶν[e] περὶ πάντων τῶν ἔργων
all the ungodly among them about all - [3]deeds

ἀσεβείας αὐτῶν ὧν ἠσέβησαν, καὶ περὶ πάντων
[2]ungodly [1]their which they committed impiously, and about all

τῶν σκληρῶν ὧν ἐλάλησαν κατ' αὐτοῦ ἁμαρτωλοὶ
the harsh *words* which [3]spoke [4]against [5]Him [2]sinners
have spoken

ἀσεβεῖς."
[1]ungodly."

The Apostates Were Predicted

16 Οὗτοί εἰσι γογγυσταί, μεμψίμοιροι, κατὰ τὰς
These are grumblers, complainers, [2]according [3]to -

ἐπιθυμίας αὐτῶν πορευόμενοι, καὶ τὸ στόμα αὐτῶν λαλεῖ
[5]desires [4]their [1]walking, and - mouth ˜ their speaks

ὑπέρογκα, θαυμάζοντες πρόσωπα ὠφελείας χάριν.
puffed up *words*, marveling at faces [5]advantage [1]for [2]the [3]sake [4]of.
flattering people to gain.

17 Ὑμεῖς δέ, ἀγαπητοί, μνήσθητε τῶν ῥημάτων τῶν
you ˜ But, beloved *ones*, remember the words -

προειρημένων ὑπὸ τῶν ἀποστόλων τοῦ Κυρίου ἡμῶν
having been spoken beforehand by the apostles - of Lord ˜ our
which were

Ἰησοῦ Χριστοῦ, **18** ὅτι ἔλεγον ὑμῖν ὅτι ἐν ἐσχάτῳ χρόνῳ
Jesus Christ, that they told you that in *the* last time
how

ἔσονται ἐμπαῖκται κατὰ τὰς ἑαυτῶν ἐπιθυμίας
there shall be mockers [2]according [3]to [4]the [6]of [7]themselves [5]desires
their own

12 These are spots in your
love feasts, while they feast
with you without fear, serving
only themselves. *They are*
clouds without water, carried
about by the winds; late autumn
trees without fruit, twice dead,
pulled up by the roots;
13 raging waves of the sea,
foaming up their own shame;
wandering stars for whom is reserved the blackness of darkness forever.
14 Now Enoch, the seventh
from Adam, prophesied about
these men also, saying, "Behold, the Lord comes with ten
thousands of His saints,
15 "to execute judgment on
all, to convict all who are ungodly among them of all their
ungodly deeds which they have
committed in an ungodly way,
and of all the harsh things which
ungodly sinners have spoken
against Him."
16 These are grumblers, complainers, walking according to
their own lusts; and they mouth
great swelling *words,* flattering
people to gain advantage.
17 But you, beloved, remember the words which were spoken before by the apostles of
our Lord Jesus Christ:
18 how they told you that
there would be mockers in
the last time who would walk
according to their own ungodly

[d]**(12)** TR reads *περιφερομεναι, being carried about.*

[e]**(15)** For *παντας τους ασεβεις αυτων, all the ungodly among them,* NU reads *πασαν ψυχην, every soul.*

how a speaker intends the word as an address for Jesus. It sometimes clearly means "Lord" (John 20:28), sometimes clearly means "sir" (John 4:11), and other times is ambiguous (Matt. 8:2; cf. Acts 9:5).

lusts.
19 These are sensual persons, who cause divisions, not having the Spirit.
20 But you, beloved, building yourselves up on your most holy faith, praying in the Holy Spirit,
21 keep yourselves in the love of God, looking for the mercy of our Lord Jesus Christ unto eternal life.
22 And on some have compassion, making a distinction;
23 but others save with fear, pulling *them* out of the fire, hating even the garment defiled by the flesh.

24 Now to Him who is able
to keep you from
stumbling,
And to present *you*
faultless
Before the presence of
His glory with
exceeding joy,
25 To God our Savior,
Who alone is wise,
Be glory and majesty,
Dominion and power,
Both now and forever.
Amen.

πορευόμενοι τῶν ἀσεβειῶν.
[1]walking - of impieties.
for godlessness.

Maintain Your Spiritual Life

19 Οὗτοί εἰσιν οἱ ἀποδιορίζοντες, ψυχικοί, Πνεῦμα
These are the *ones* dividing, natural *men*, [3]*the* [4]Spirit
who cause division, worldly,

μὴ ἔχοντες.
[1]not [2]having.

20 Ὑμεῖς δέ, ἀγαπητοί, τῇ ἁγιωτάτῃ ὑμῶν πίστει
you ˜ But, beloved *ones*, in [2]most [3]holy [1]your faith

ἐποικοδομοῦντες ἑαυτούς, ἐν Πνεύματι Ἁγίῳ προσευχόμενοι,
building up ˜ yourselves, [2]in [3]*the* [5]Spirit [4]Holy [1]praying,
build pray,

21 ἑαυτοὺς ἐν ἀγάπῃ Θεοῦ τηρήσατε, προσδεχόμενοι τὸ
[2]yourselves [3]in [4]*the* [5]love [6]of [7]God [1]keep, waiting for the
anticipating

ἔλεος τοῦ Κυρίου ἡμῶν Ἰησοῦ Χριστοῦ εἰς ζωὴν αἰώνιον.
mercy - of Lord ˜ our Jesus Christ to life ˜ eternal.

22 Καὶ οὓς μὲν ἐλεεῖτε, διακρινόμενοι·[f] **23** οὓς
And [4]some - [1]have [2]mercy [3]on, making a distinction; others ˜

δὲ ἐν φόβῳ σῴζετε, ἐκ πυρὸς ἁρπάζοντες,[g] μισοῦντες
But [2]with [3]fear [1]save, [6]out [7]of [8]*the* [9]fire [4]snatching [5]*them*, hating

καὶ τὸν ἀπὸ τῆς σαρκὸς ἐσπιλωμένον χιτῶνα.
even the [5]by [6]the [7]flesh [2]having [3]been [4]stained [1]garment.

God Is Able

24 Τῷ δὲ δυναμένῳ φυλάξαι αὐτοὺς[h]
[2]to [3]the [4]*One* [1]Now being able to guard them
Him who is

ἀπταίστους,
without stumbling,
from

Καὶ στῆσαι κατενώπιον τῆς δόξης αὐτοῦ
And to make *you* stand before - glory ˜ His

Ἀμώμους ἐν ἀγαλλιάσει,
Blameless with exultation,

25 Μόνῳ σοφῷ[i] Θεῷ Σωτῆρι ἡμῶν,[j]
To *the* only wise God Savior ˜ our,

Δόξα καὶ μεγαλωσύνη,
Be glory and majesty,

Κράτος καὶ ἐξουσία,[k]
Sovereignty and power,

Καὶ νῦν καὶ εἰς πάντας τοὺς αἰῶνας! Ἀμήν.
Both now and to all the ages! Amen.
forever! So be it.

---

f(22) NU reads διακρινομενους, *(some) who are doubting.*
g(23) NU adds ους δε ελεατε εν φοβω, *and on some have mercy with fear,* and omits εν φοβω, *with fear,* in the first clause.
h(24) NU reads υμας, *you.*
i(25) NU omits σοφω, *wise.*
j(25) NU adds δια Ιησου Χριστου του κυριου ημων, *through Jesus Christ our Lord.*
k(25) NU adds προ παντος του αιωνος, *before all time.*

THE REVELATION

of Jesus Christ

ΑΠΟΚΑΛΥΨΙΣ
REVELATION

Introduction and Benediction

1 **1** Ἀποκάλυψις* Ἰησοῦ Χριστοῦ ἣν ἔδωκεν αὐτῷ ὁ
The Revelation of Jesus Christ which [2]gave [3]to [4]Him -

Θεὸς δεῖξαι τοῖς δούλοις αὐτοῦ ἃ δεῖ
[1]God to show - to bondservants ˜ His *the things* which it is necessary
slaves must

γενέσθαι ἐν τάχει. Καὶ ἐσήμανεν ἀποστείλας διὰ
to happen with swiftness. And He made *it* known *by* sending *it* through
occur shortly.

τοῦ ἀγγέλου αὐτοῦ τῷ δούλῳ αὐτοῦ Ἰωάννῃ, **2** ὃς
- angel ˜ His - to bondservant ˜ His John, who
slave

ἐμαρτύρησε τὸν λόγον τοῦ Θεοῦ καὶ τὴν μαρτυρίαν Ἰησοῦ
testified to the word - of God and the testimony of Jesus

Χριστοῦ, ὅσα εἶδε.
Christ, as many *things* as he saw.

3 Μακάριος ὁ ἀναγινώσκων, καὶ οἱ ἀκούοντες
Blessed *is* the *one* reading, and the *ones* hearing
he who reads, those who hear

τοὺς λόγους τῆς προφητείας καὶ τηροῦντες τὰ ἐν αὐτῇ
the words of the prophecy and keeping the *things* [4]in [5]it
who keep

γεγραμμένα· ὁ γὰρ καιρὸς ἐγγύς.
[1]having [2]been [3]written; the ˜ for time *is* near.

John Greets the Seven Churches of the Province of Asia

4 Ἰωάννης,
John,

Ταῖς ἑπτὰ ἐκκλησίαις ταῖς ἐν τῇ Ἀσίᾳ·
To the seven churches - in - Asia:

Χάρις ὑμῖν καὶ εἰρήνη ἀπὸ Θεοῦ,[a] ὁ ὢν καὶ ὁ
Grace to you and peace from God, the *One* being and the *One*
He who is He

ἦν καὶ ὁ ἐρχόμενος, καὶ ἀπὸ τῶν ἑπτὰ Πνευμάτων
He was and the *One* coming, and from the seven Spirits
who was who is

ἃ ἐνώπιον τοῦ θρόνου αὐτοῦ, **5** καὶ ἀπὸ Ἰησοῦ Χριστοῦ, ὁ
which *are* before - throne ˜ His, and from Jesus Christ, the
who

μάρτυς ὁ πιστός, ὁ πρωτότοκος τῶν νεκρῶν καὶ ὁ ἄρχων
witness ˜ - faithful, the firstborn of the dead *ones* and the ruler

τῶν βασιλέων τῆς γῆς.
of the kings of the earth.

Τῷ ἀγαπῶντι[b] ἡμᾶς
To the *One* loving us
Him who loves

1 The Revelation of Jesus Christ, which God gave Him to show His servants—things which must shortly take place. And He sent and signified *it* by His angel to His servant John,
2 who bore witness to the word of God, and to the testimony of Jesus Christ, to all things that he saw.
3 Blessed *is* he who reads and those who hear the words of this prophecy, and keep those things which are written in it; for the time *is* near.
4 John, to the seven churches which are in Asia:

Grace to you and peace from Him who is and who was and who is to come, and from the seven Spirits who are before His throne,
5 and from Jesus Christ, the faithful witness, the firstborn from the dead, and the ruler over the kings of the earth. To Him who loved us and washed

---

[a](**1:4**) TR reads του, *the (One).* [b](**1:5**) Many mss., TR read αγαπησαντι, *having loved.*

---

*(**1:1**) ἀποκάλυψις *(apokalypsis).* Noun from ἀπό, *from, away,* and κάλυμμα, *covering, veil,* thus meaning *an uncovering, revelation, disclosure,* especially of things previously hidden. In the NT the word is typically used of spiritual things, ranging from a specific vision to an individual (2 Cor. 12:1), to spiritual truth (Luke 2:32), to a large book (here in Rev. 1:1), to eschatological events (2 Thess. 1:7; Rom. 8:19). Generally, the implication is that things thus revealed could be known only by supernatural disclosure. The cognate verb ἀποκαλύπτω, *uncover, reveal,* has essentially the

us from our sins in His own
blood,
6 and has made us kings and
priests to His God and Father,
to Him *be* glory and dominion
forever and ever. Amen.
7 Behold, He is coming with
clouds, and every eye will see
Him, even they who pierced
Him. And all the tribes of the
earth will mourn because of
Him. Even so, Amen.
8 "I am the Alpha and the
Omega, *the* Beginning and *the*
End," says the Lord, "who is
and who was and who is to
come, the Almighty."
9 I, John, both your brother
and companion in the tribulation
and kingdom and patience of Jesus Christ, was on the island
that is called Patmos for the
word of God and for the testimony of Jesus Christ.
10 I was in the Spirit on the
Lord's Day, and I heard behind
me a loud voice, as of a trumpet,
11 saying, "I am the Alpha and
the Omega, the First and the
Last," and, "What you see,
write in a book and send *it* to
the seven churches which are
in Asia: to Ephesus, to Smyrna,

Καὶ λούσαντι[c] ἡμας ἀπὸ τῶν ἁμαρτιῶν ἡμῶν ἐν τῷ
And having washed us from - sins ˜ our in -
who washed

αἵματι αὐτοῦ,
blood ˜ His,

6 Καὶ ἐποίησεν ἡμᾶς βασιλείαν, ἱερεῖς τῷ Θεῷ καὶ
And He made us a kingdom, priests - [1]to [3]God [4]and

Πατρὶ αὐτοῦ,
[5]Father [2]His,

Αὐτῷ ἡ δόξα καὶ τὸ κράτος
To Him *be* the glory and the power
dominion

Εἰς τοὺς αἰῶνας τῶν αἰώνων. Ἀμήν.
To the ages of the ages. Amen.
Forever and ever. So be it.

7 «Ἰδού, ἔρχεται μετὰ τῶν νεφελῶν,»[d]
«Behold, He is coming with the clouds,»

Καὶ «ὄψεται αὐτὸν πᾶς ὀφθαλμός,
And «[3]will [4]see [5]Him [1]every [2]eye,

Καὶ οἵτινες αὐτὸν ἐξεκέντησαν.
And those who Him ˜ pierced.

Καὶ κόψονται ἐπ' αὐτὸν πᾶσαι αἱ φυλαὶ τῆς γῆς.»[e]
And [7]will [8]mourn [9]over [10]Him [1]all [2]the [3]tribes [4]of [5]the [6]earth.»
land.»

Ναί, ἀμήν!
Yes, amen!
so let it be!

8 "Ἐγώ εἰμι τὸ Ἄλφα καὶ τὸ Ὦ,"[f]
"I am the Alpha and the Omega,"

Λέγει Κύριος ὁ Θεός,[g]
Says *the* Lord - God,

"Ὁ ὢν καὶ ὁ ἦν καὶ ὁ ἐρχόμενος,
"The *One* being and the *One* He was and the *One* coming,
He who is He who was He who is to come,

Ὁ Παντοκράτωρ."
The Almighty."

John's Vision of the Son of Man

9 Ἐγὼ Ἰωάννης, ὁ ἀδελφὸς ὑμῶν καὶ κοινωνὸς[h] ἐν τῇ
I John, - brother ˜ your and partner in the

θλίψει καὶ βασιλείᾳ καὶ ὑπομονῇ ἐν Χριστῷ Ἰησοῦ,[i]
tribulation and kingdom and endurance in Christ Jesus,

ἐγενόμην ἐν τῇ νήσῳ τῇ καλουμένῃ Πάτμῳ διὰ τὸν
came to be in the island - being called Patmos on account of the
on

λόγον τοῦ Θεοῦ καὶ διὰ τὴν μαρτυρίαν Ἰησοῦ Χριστοῦ.
word - of God and on account of the testimony of Jesus Christ.

10 Ἐγενόμην ἐν Πνεύματι ἐν τῇ Κυριακῇ* ἡμέρᾳ
I came to be in *the* Spirit in the [2]belonging [3]to [4]the [5]Lord [1]day
on Lord's day

καὶ ἤκουσα φωνὴν ὀπίσω μου μεγάλην ὡς σάλπιγγος,
and I heard a voice behind me great as a trumpet,
loud

11 λεγούσης,[j] "Ὁ βλέπεις γράψον εἰς βιβλίον καὶ
saying, "That which you see write in a book and

πέμψον ταῖς ἑπτὰ ἐκκλησίαις·[k] εἰς Ἔφεσον καὶ εἰς Σμύρναν
send to the seven churches: to Ephesus and to Smyrna

---

c(1:5) NU reads λυσαντι, *having loosed.*
d(1:7) Dan. 7:13
e(1:7) Zech. 12:10
f(1:8) TR adds Αρχη και Τελος, *Beginning and End.*
g(1:8) TR reads ο Κυριος, *the Lord,* omitting ο Θεος, *God.* h(1:9) TR, NU read συγκοινωνος, *fellow partner.* i(1:9) TR reads Ιησου Χριστου, *Jesus Christ;* NU reads only Ιησου, *Jesus.*
j(1:11) TR adds εγω ειμι το Α και το Ω ο Πρωτος και ο Εσχατος και, *I am the Alpha and the Omega, the First and the Last.*
k(1:11) TR adds ταις εν Ασια, *which are in Asia.*

same range of meanings (cf. Gal. 1:16).

***(1:10)** κυριακός *(kyriakos).* Adjective, derived from κύριος, meaning *belonging to the Lord.* The word designates something as particularly belonging to or pertaining to the Lord. Here it refers to Sunday as "the Lord's day." It is used in 1 Cor. 11:20 of "the Lord's Supper" as the central act of Christian worship.

καὶ εἰς Πέργαμον καὶ εἰς Θυάτειρα καὶ εἰς Σάρδεις καὶ εἰς
and to Pergamos and to Thyatira and to Sardis and to
Pergamum

Φιλαδέλφειαν καὶ εἰς Λαοδίκειαν." 12 Καὶ ἐκεῖ ἐπέστρεψα
Philadelphia and to Laodicea." And there I turned

βλέπειν τὴν φωνὴν ἥτις ἐλάλει μετ' ἐμοῦ. Καὶ ἐπιστρέψας
to see the voice which was speaking with me. And having turned

εἶδον ἑπτὰ λυχνίας χρυσᾶς, 13 καὶ ἐν μέσῳ τῶν ἑπτὰ
I saw seven lampstands ˜ golden, and in *the* midst of the seven

λυχνιῶν ὅμοιον Υἱὸν Ἀνθρώπου, ἐνδεδυμένον
lampstands *Someone* like *the* Son of Man, having been clothed in

ποδήρη καὶ περιεζωσμένον πρὸς τοῖς μαστοῖς
a robe reaching to the feet and having been girded across the breasts

ζώνην χρυσῆν. 14 Ἡ δὲ κεφαλὴ αὐτοῦ καὶ αἱ τρίχες
with a belt ˜ golden. - And head ˜ His and the hairs
His hair

λευκαί, καὶ ὡς ἔριον λευκόν, ὡς χιών· καὶ οἱ ὀφθαλμοὶ
were white, and like wool ˜ white, like snow; and - eyes ˜

αὐτοῦ ὡς φλὸξ πυρός. 15 Καὶ οἱ πόδες αὐτοῦ ὅμοιοι
His *were* like a flame of fire. And - feet ˜ His *were* like

χαλκολιβάνῳ,* ὡς ἐν καμίνῳ πεπυρωμένοι, καὶ
chalkolibanon, as *if* [5]in [6]a [7]furnace [1]having [2]been [3]heated [4]thoroughly, and
fine brass,

ἡ φωνὴ αὐτοῦ ὡς φωνὴ ὑδάτων πολλῶν, 16 καὶ ἔχων ἐν
- voice ˜ His *was* like *the* sound of waters ˜ many, and having in
He had

τῇ δεξιᾷ αὐτοῦ χειρὶ ἀστέρας ἑπτά, καὶ ἐκ τοῦ στόματος
- right ˜ His hand stars ˜ seven, and out of - mouth ˜

αὐτοῦ ῥομφαία δίστομος ὀξεῖα ἐκπορευομένη, καὶ ἡ
His [1]a [4]sword [3]double-edged [2]sharp proceeding, and -

ὄψις αὐτοῦ ὡς ὁ ἥλιος φαίνει ἐν τῇ δυνάμει αὐτοῦ.
face ˜ His *was* as the sun shines in - strength ˜ its.
countenance

17 Καὶ ὅτε εἶδον αὐτόν, ἔπεσα πρὸς τοὺς πόδας αὐτοῦ ὡς
And when I saw Him, I fell at - feet ˜ His as *if*

νεκρός.
dead.

Καὶ ἔθηκε τὴν δεξιὰν αὐτοῦ ἐπ' ἐμέ, λέγων,[l] "Μὴ
And He put - [2]right [3]*hand* [1]His on me, saying, "not ˜

φοβοῦ· ἐγώ εἰμι ὁ Πρῶτος καὶ ὁ Ἔσχατος, 18 καὶ ὁ
Do fear; I am the First and the Last, and the *One*
He

ζῶν, καὶ ἐγενόμην νεκρός, καὶ ἰδού, ζῶν εἰμι εἰς τοὺς
living, and I became dead, and behold, [3]living [1]I [2]am to the
who lives, forever and

αἰῶνας τῶν αἰώνων. Ἀμήν.[m] Καὶ ἔχω τὰς κλεῖδας τοῦ
ages of the ages. Amen. And I have the keys -
ever. So be it.

Θανάτου καὶ τοῦ Ἅιδου. 19 Γράψον οὖν ἃ
of Death and - of Hades. Write therefore *the things* which

εἶδες, καὶ ἃ εἰσι, καὶ ἃ μέλλει
you saw, and *the things* which are, and *the things* which are about

γίνεσθαι μετὰ ταῦτα. 20 Τὸ μυστήριον τῶν ἑπτὰ
to happen after these *things*. The mystery of the seven

ἀστέρων ὧν εἶδες ἐπὶ τῆς δεξιᾶς μου, καὶ τὰς ἑπτὰ
stars which you saw on - [2]right [3]*hand* [1]My, and the seven

λυχνίας τὰς χρυσᾶς· Οἱ ἑπτὰ ἀστέρες ἄγγελοι τῶν ἑπτὰ
lampstands ˜ - golden: The seven stars [2]angels [3]of [4]the [5]seven

to Pergamos, to Thyatira, to Sardis, to Philadelphia, and to Laodicea."
12 Then I turned to see the voice that spoke with me. And having turned I saw seven golden lampstands,
13 and in the midst of the seven lampstands *One* like the Son of Man, clothed with a garment down to the feet and girded about the chest with a golden band.
14 His head and hair *were* white like wool, as white as snow, and His eyes like a flame of fire;
15 His feet *were* like fine brass, as if refined in a furnace, and His voice as the sound of many waters;
16 He had in His right hand seven stars, out of His mouth went a sharp two-edged sword, and His countenance *was* like the sun shining in its strength.
17 And when I saw Him, I fell at His feet as dead. But He laid His right hand on me, saying to me, "Do not be afraid; I am the First and the Last.
18 "I *am* He who lives, and was dead, and behold, I am alive forevermore. Amen. And I have the keys of Hades and of Death.
19 "Write the things which you have seen, and the things which are, and the things which will take place after this.
20 "The mystery of the seven stars which you saw in My right hand, and the seven golden lampstands: The seven stars are the angels of the seven

[l](1:17) TR adds μοι, *to me.*
[m](1:18) NU omits Αμην, *Amen.*

*(1:15) χαλκολίβανον *(chalkolibanon).* Noun representing the name of a metal or an alloy. Since the word does not occur outside of the Book of Revelation (here and Rev. 2:18), it is impossible to know exactly what type of metal is being described. It has been transliterated here as *chalkolibanon* and translated as *fine brass.* Other suggested translations are *gold ore* or *bronze.*

churches, and the seven lampstands which you saw are the
seven churches.

2 "To the angel of the
church of Ephesus write,
'These things says He who
holds the seven stars in His
right hand, who walks in the
midst of the seven golden lampstands:
2 "I know your works, your
labor, your patience, and that
you cannot bear those who are
evil. And you have tested those
who say they are apostles and
are not, and have found them
liars;
3 "and you have persevered
and have patience, and have labored for My name's sake and
have not become weary.
4 "Nevertheless I have *this*
against you, that you have left
your first love.
5 "Remember therefore
from where you have fallen; repent and do the first works, or
else I will come to you quickly
and remove your lampstand
from its place—unless you repent.
6 "But this you have, that
you hate the deeds of the Nicolaitans, which I also hate.
7 "He who has an ear, let
him hear what the Spirit says to
the churches. To him who
overcomes I will give to eat
from the tree of life, which is in
the midst of the Paradise of
God."'

ἐκκλησιῶν εἰσι, καὶ αἱ λυχνίαι αἱ ἑπτὰ ἑπτὰ[n] ἐκκλησίαι
[6]churches [1]are, and the lampstands ˜ - seven [2]seven [3]churches

εἰσί.
[1]are.

The Letter to Ephesus: The Loveless Church

2 1 "Τῷ ἀγγέλῳ τῆς ἐν Ἐφέσῳ ἐκκλησίας γράψον,
"To the angel of the [2]in [3]Ephesus [1]church write,

'Τάδε λέγει ὁ κρατῶν τοὺς ἑπτὰ ἀστέρας ἐν τῇ
'These *things* says the *One* holding the seven stars in -

δεξιᾷ αὐτοῦ, ὁ περιπατῶν ἐν μέσῳ τῶν ἑπτὰ
[2]right [3]*hand* [1]His, the *One* walking in *the* midst of the seven
who walks

λυχνιῶν τῶν χρυσῶν·
lampstands ˜ - golden:

2 'Οἶδα τὰ ἔργα σου καὶ τὸν κόπον σου καὶ τὴν
'I know - works ˜ your and - labor ˜ your and -

ὑπομονήν σου, καὶ ὅτι οὐ δύνῃ βαστάσαι κακούς. Καὶ
endurance ˜ your, and that [3]not [1]you [2]are [4]able to bear evil *people*. And

ἐπείρασας τοὺς λέγοντας ἑαυτοὺς ἀποστόλους εἶναι[a] καὶ
you tested the *ones* saying themselves [3]apostles [1]to [2]be and
those who say that they are apostles

οὐκ εἰσί, καὶ εὗρες αὐτοὺς ψευδεῖς· 3 καὶ ὑπομονὴν
[3]not [1]they [2]are, and you found them liars; and [3]endurance

ἔχεις καὶ ἐβάστασας διὰ τὸ ὄνομά μου καὶ οὐκ
[1]you [2]have and you bore patiently on account of - name ˜ My and [3]not
have borne

ἐκοπίασας.[b]
[1]you [2]did become weary.

4 "Ἀλλὰ ἔχω κατὰ σοῦ, ὅτι τὴν ἀγάπην σου τὴν
'But I have against you, that - [5]love [3]your -

πρώτην ἀφῆκας.
[4]first [1]you [2]left.
have left.

5 'Μνημόνευε οὖν πόθεν πέπτωκας καὶ
'Remember therefore from where you have fallen and

μετανόησον καὶ τὰ πρῶτα ἔργα ποίησον· εἰ δὲ μή,
repent and [2]the [3]first [4]works [1]do; if ˜ but not,

ἔρχομαί σοι ταχὺ[c] καὶ κινήσω τὴν λυχνίαν σου ἐκ
I am coming to you swiftly and I will remove - lampstand ˜ your out of

τοῦ τόπου αὐτῆς — ἐὰν μὴ μετανοήσῃς. 6 Ἀλλὰ τοῦτο
- place ˜ its — if [3]not [1]you [2]do repent. But this
unless

ἔχεις, ὅτι μισεῖς τὰ ἔργα τῶν Νικολαϊτῶν, ἃ κἀγὼ
you have, that you hate the works of the Nicolaitans, which *things* I also

μισῶ.
hate.

7 "Ὁ ἔχων οὖς ἀκουσάτω τί τὸ Πνεῦμα λέγει
'The *one* having an ear let him hear what the Spirit says
'He who has

ταῖς ἐκκλησίαις. Τῷ νικῶντι δώσω αὐτῷ φαγεῖν ἐκ
to the churches. To the *one* overcoming I will give to him to eat of
him who overcomes I will grant

τοῦ ξύλου τῆς ζωῆς, ὅ ἐστιν ἐν τῷ Παραδείσῳ[d] τοῦ Θεοῦ
the tree - of life, which is in the Paradise - of God ˜

μου.'[e]
My.'

---

[n](1:20) TR adds ας ειδες, *which you saw.*
[a](2:2) TR reads φασκοντας ειναι αποστολους, *declaring to be apostles.*
[b](2:3) TR reads κεκοπιακας και ου κεκμηκας, *you have labored and have not become weary.*
[c](2:5) NU omits ταχυ, *swiftly.* [d](2:7) Many mss., TR read μεσω του παραδεισου, *in the midst of the Paradise.*
[e](2:7) TR, NU omit μου, *my.*

The Letter to Smyrna: The Persecuted Church

8 "Καὶ τῷ ἀγγέλῳ τῆς ἐν Σμύρνῃ ἐκκλησίας γράψον,
"And to the angel of the [2]in [3]Smyrna [1]church write,

'Τάδε λέγει ὁ Πρῶτος καὶ ὁ Ἔσχατος, ὃς ἐγένετο
'These *things* says the First and the Last, who became

νεκρὸς καὶ ἔζησεν·
dead and lived;
came to life;

9 'Οἶδά σου τὰ ἔργα καὶ[f] τὴν θλῖψιν καὶ τὴν πτωχείαν
'I know your - works and the tribulation and the poverty
your your

(ἀλλὰ πλούσιος εἶ), καὶ τὴν βλασφημίαν ἐκ τῶν
(but [3]rich [1]you [2]are), and the blasphemy of the *ones*
slander those

λεγόντων Ἰουδαίους εἶναι ἑαυτοὺς καὶ οὐκ εἰσίν, ἀλλὰ
saying [4]Jews [2]to [3]be [1]themselves and [3]not [1]they [2]are, but *are*
who say they are Jews

συναγωγὴ τοῦ Σατανᾶ.
a synagogue - of Satan.
congregation

10 'Μηδὲν φοβοῦ ἃ μέλλεις παθεῖν. Ἰδοὺ
'nothing ˜ Fear *about the things* which you are about to suffer. Behold

δή, μέλλει βαλεῖν ὁ διάβολος ἐξ ὑμῶν εἰς φυλακήν,
indeed, [3]is [4]about [5]to [6]throw [1]the [2]devil *some* of you into prison,

ἵνα πειρασθῆτε, καὶ ἕξετε θλῖψιν ἡμέρας δέκα.
so that you may be tested, and you will have tribulation days ˜ ten.
trouble

Γίνου πιστὸς ἄχρι θανάτου, καὶ δώσω σοι τὸν στέφανον
Be faithful up to death, and I will give to you the crown

τῆς ζωῆς.
- of life.

11 ''Ὁ ἔχων οὖς ἀκουσάτω τί τὸ Πνεῦμα λέγει
'The *one* having an ear let him hear what the Spirit says
'He who has

ταῖς ἐκκλησίαις. Ὁ νικῶν οὐ μὴ ἀδικηθῇ ἐκ
to the churches. The *one* overcoming not not will be harmed by
He who overcomes by no means

τοῦ θανάτου τοῦ δευτέρου.'
the death ˜ - second.'

The Letter to Pergamos: The Compromising Church

12 "Καὶ τῷ ἀγγέλῳ τῆς ἐν Περγάμῳ ἐκκλησίας γράψον,
"And to the angel of the [2]in [3]Pergamos [1]church write,
Pergamum

'Τάδε λέγει ὁ ἔχων τὴν ῥομφαίαν τὴν δίστομον
'These *things* says the *One* having the [3]sword - [2]double-edged
He who has

τὴν ὀξεῖαν·
- [1]sharp:

13 'Οἶδα τὰ ἔργα σου καὶ[g] ποῦ κατοικεῖς, ὅπου ὁ
'I know - works ˜ your and where you are dwelling, where the

θρόνος τοῦ Σατανᾶ. Καὶ κρατεῖς τὸ ὄνομά μου, καὶ οὐκ
throne - of Satan *is*. And you hold fast to - name ˜ My, and [3]not

ἠρνήσω τὴν πίστιν μου[h] ἐν ταῖς ἡμέραις αἷς Ἀντίπας
[1]you [2]did deny - faith ˜ My in the days in which Antipas *was*
disown

8 "And to the angel of the
church in Smyrna write,
'These things says the
First and the Last, who was
dead, and came to life:
9 "I know your works, tribulation, and poverty (but you are
rich); and *I know* the blasphemy of those who say they
are Jews and are not, but *are* a
synagogue of Satan.
10 "Do not fear any of those
things which you are about to
suffer. Indeed, the devil is
about to throw *some* of you into
prison, that you may be tested,
and you will have tribulation ten
days. Be faithful until death,
and I will give you the crown of
life.
11 "He who has an ear, let
him hear what the Spirit says to
the churches. He who overcomes shall not be hurt by the
second death." '
12 "And to the angel of the
church in Pergamos write,
'These things says He who
has the sharp two-edged
sword:
13 "I know your works, and
where you dwell, where Satan's
throne *is*. And you hold fast to
My name, and did not deny My
faith even in the days in which

---

f(**2:9**) NU omits *τα εργα και, works and.*
g(**2:13**) NU omits *τα εργα σου και, your works and.*
h(**2:13**) NU, TR add *και, even.*

Antipas *was* My faithful martyr,
who was killed among you,
where Satan dwells.
14 "But I have a few things
against you, because you have
there those who hold the doctrine of Balaam, who taught Balak to put a stumbling block
before the children of Israel, to
eat things sacrificed to idols,
and to commit sexual immorality.
15 "Thus you also have those
who hold the doctrine of the
Nicolaitans, which thing I hate.
16 "Repent, or else I will
come to you quickly and will
fight against them with the
sword of My mouth.
17 "He who has an ear, let
him hear what the Spirit says to
the churches. To him who
overcomes I will give some of
the hidden manna to eat. And I
will give him a white stone, and
on the stone a new name written which no one knows except
him who receives *it*."'
18 "And to the angel of the
church in Thyatira write,
'These things says the Son
of God, who has eyes like a
flame of fire, and His feet like
fine brass:
19 "I know your works, love,
service, faith, and your patience; and *as* for your works,
the last *are* more than the first.
20 "Nevertheless I have a few
things against you, because you

ὁ μάρτυς μου ὁ πιστός, ὃς ἀπεκτάνθη παρ' ὑμῖν, ὅπου ὁ
- [3]witness [1]My - [2]faithful, who was killed <u>alongside</u> you, where -
among

Σατανᾶς κατοικεῖ.
Satan is dwelling.

14 "Ἀλλὰ ἔχω κατὰ σοῦ ὀλίγα, ὅτι ἔχεις ἐκεῖ
'But I have [4]against [5]you [1]a [2]few [3]*things,* because you have there

κρατοῦντας τὴν διδαχὴν Βαλαάμ, ὃς ἐδίδαξε τόν Βαλὰκ
some <u>holding</u> the teaching of Balaam, who taught - Balak
who hold

βαλεῖν σκάνδαλον ἐνώπιον τῶν υἱῶν Ἰσραὴλ καὶ φαγεῖν
to throw a stumbling block before the sons of Israel both to eat

εἰδωλόθυτα καὶ πορνεῦσαι. 15 Οὕτως ἔχεις καὶ
things sacrificed to idols and to commit fornication. Thus [3]have [2]also

σὺ κρατοῦντας τὴν διδαχὴν Νικολαϊτῶν ὁμοίως.[i]
[1]you *some* <u>holding</u> the teaching of *the* Nicolaitans likewise.
who hold

16 'Μετανόησον οὖν! Εἰ δὲ μή, ἔρχομαί σοι ταχὺ
'Repent therefore! if ~ But not, I am coming to you swiftly

καὶ πολεμήσω μετ' αὐτῶν ἐν τῇ ῥομφαίᾳ τοῦ στόματός
and I will make war with them with the sword - of mouth ~

μου.
My.

17 'Ὁ ἔχων οὖς ἀκουσάτω τί τὸ Πνεῦμα λέγει
<u>'The *one*</u> <u>having</u> an ear let him hear what the Spirit says
'He who has

ταῖς ἐκκλησίαις. Τῷ νικῶντι δώσω αὐτῷ[j] τοῦ
to the churches. To <u>the *one*</u> <u>overcoming</u> I will give to him of the
him who overcomes

μάννα τοῦ κεκρυμμένου. Καὶ δώσω αὐτῷ ψῆφον λευκήν,
manna - having been hidden. And I will give to him a pebble ~ white,

καὶ ἐπὶ τὴν ψῆφον ὄνομα καινὸν γεγραμμένον, ὃ οὐδεὶς
and on the pebble a name ~ new having been written, which no one

οἶδεν εἰ μὴ ὁ λαμβάνων.'
knows <u>if</u> <u>not</u> <u>the *one*</u> <u>receiving</u> *it.*'
except he who receives

The Letter to Thyatira: The Corrupt Church

18 "Καὶ τῷ ἀγγέλῳ τῆς ἐν Θυατείροις ἐκκλησίας
"And to the angel of the [2]in [3]Thyatira [1]church

γράψον,
write,

'Τάδε λέγει ὁ Υἱὸς τοῦ Θεοῦ, ὁ ἔχων τοὺς
'These *things* says the Son - of God, <u>the *One*</u> <u>having</u> -
He who has

ὀφθαλμοὺς αὐτοῦ ὡς φλόγα πυρός, καὶ οἱ πόδες αὐτοῦ ὅμοιοι
eyes ~ His like a flame of fire, and - feet ~ His similar

χαλκολιβάνῳ·*
to chalkolibanon:

19 'Οἶδά σου τὰ ἔργα καὶ τὴν ἀγάπην καὶ τὴν πίστιν καὶ
'I know your - works and - [2]love [3]and - [4]faith [5]and

τὴν διακονίαν καὶ τὴν ὑπομονήν σου· καὶ τὰ ἔργα σου τὰ
- [6]service [7]and - [8]endurance [1]your; and - [3]works [1]your -

ἔσχατα πλείονα τῶν πρώτων.
[2]last *are* greater *than* the first.

20 "Ἀλλὰ ἔχω κατὰ σοῦ[k] ὅτι ἀφεῖς τὴν γυναῖκά
'But I have against you that you tolerate - wife ~

---

[i](2:15) TR reads ο μισω, *which I hate.*
[j](2:17) TR adds φαγειν απο, *to eat from.*
[k](2:20) TR adds ολιγα, *a few things.*

*(2:18) χαλκολίβανον *(chalkolibanon).* See χαλκολίβανον at Rev. 1:15.

σου[l] Ἰεζάβελ, ἡ λέγει ἑαυτὴν προφῆτιν, καὶ
your Jezebel, *she* who says herself *to be* a prophetess, and
she is

διδάσκει καὶ πλανᾷ τοὺς ἐμοὺς δούλους πορνεῦσαι
teaches and deceives - My bondservants to commit fornication
slaves

καὶ φαγεῖν εἰδωλόθυτα. 21 Καὶ ἔδωκα αὐτῇ χρόνον
and to eat *things* sacrificed to idols. And I gave to her time

ἵνα μετανοήσῃ, καὶ οὐ θέλει μετανοῆσαι[m] ἐκ τῆς
so that she might repent, and 3not 1she 2does wish to repent of -

πορνείας αὐτῆς.[n] 22 Ἰδού, βάλλω αὐτὴν εἰς κλίνην, καὶ
fornication ˜ her. Behold, I am throwing her into a bed, and
sickbed,

τοὺς μοιχεύοντας μετ' αὐτῆς εἰς θλῖψιν μεγάλην, ἐὰν
the ones committing adultery with her into tribulation ˜ great, if
those who commit trouble

μὴ μετανοήσωσιν ἐκ τῶν ἔργων αὐτῆς.[o] 23 Καὶ τὰ τέκνα
3not 1they 2do repent of - works ˜ her. And - children ˜

αὐτῆς ἀποκτενῶ ἐν θανάτῳ. Καὶ γνώσονται πᾶσαι αἱ
her I will kill by death. And 4will 5know 1all 2the

ἐκκλησίαι ὅτι ἐγώ εἰμι ὁ ἐρευνῶν νεφροὺς καὶ καρδίας.
3churches that I am the *One* searching kidneys and hearts.
He who searches minds

Καὶ δώσω ὑμῖν ἑκάστῳ κατὰ τὰ ἔργα ὑμῶν.
And I will give to you to each *one* according to - works ˜ your.

24 ''Ὑμῖν δὲ λέγω, τοῖς λοιποῖς τοῖς ἐν Θυατείροις,
'2to 3you 1But I say, to the rest the *ones* in Thyatira,
who are

ὅσοι οὐκ ἔχουσι τὴν διδαχὴν ταύτην, οἵτινες οὐκ ἔγνωσαν
as many as not ˜ do have - teaching ˜ this, who not ˜ knew
have not known

τὰ βαθέα τοῦ Σατανᾶ, ὡς λέγουσιν, οὐ βάλλω[p] ἐφ' ὑμᾶς
the depths - of Satan, as they say, 3not 1I 2am putting on you

ἄλλο βάρος. 25 Πλὴν ὃ ἔχετε κρατήσατε ἄχρις οὗ ἂν
any other burden. Only what you have hold fast until -

ἥξω. 26 Καὶ ὁ νικῶν καὶ ὁ τηρῶν ἄχρι
I shall come. And the *one* overcoming and the *one* keeping until
he who overcomes he who keeps

τέλους τὰ ἔργα μου,
the end - works ˜ My,

«Δώσω αὐτῷ ἐξουσίαν ἐπὶ τῶν ἐθνῶν —
«I will give to him authority over the nations —

27 Καὶ ποιμανεῖ αὐτοὺς ἐν ῥάβδῳ σιδηρᾷ·
And he shall shepherd them with a(n) rod ˜ iron;
rule

Ὡς τὰ σκεύη τὰ κεραμικὰ συντριβήσεται» —[q]
Like - vessels ˜ - clay they shall be smashed» —

28 ὡς κἀγὼ εἴληφα παρὰ τοῦ Πατρός μου. Καὶ δώσω
as I also have received from - Father ˜ My. And I will give

αὐτῷ τὸν ἀστέρα τὸν πρωϊνόν.
to him the star ˜ - morning.

29 ''Ὁ ἔχων οὖς ἀκουσάτω τί τὸ Πνεῦμα λέγει
'The *one* having an ear let him hear what the Spirit says
'He who has

ταῖς ἐκκλησίαις.'
to the churches.'

allow that woman Jezebel, who calls herself a prophetess, to teach and seduce My servants to commit sexual immorality and eat things sacrificed to idols.
21 "And I gave her time to repent of her sexual immorality, and she did not repent.
22 "Indeed I will cast her into a sickbed, and those who commit adultery with her into great tribulation, unless they repent of their deeds.
23 "I will kill her children with death, and all the churches shall know that I am He who searches the minds and hearts. And I will give to each one of you according to your works.
24 "Now to you I say, and to the rest in Thyatira, as many as do not have this doctrine, who have not known the depths of Satan, as they say, I will put on you no other burden.
25 "But hold fast what you have till I come.
26 "And he who overcomes, and keeps My works until the end, to him I will give power over the nations—

27 *'He shall rule them with a rod of iron;*
They shall be dashed to pieces like the potter's vessels'—

as I also have received from My Father;
28 "and I will give him the morning star.
29 "He who has an ear, let him hear what the Spirit says to the churches." '

---

[l](2:20) TR, NU omit σου, *your,* reading την γυναικα, *that woman.*
[m](2:21) TR omits και ου θελει μετανοησαι, *and she does not wish to repent.*
[n](2:21) TR adds και ου μετενοησεν, *and she did not repent.*
[o](2:22) TR reads αυτων, *their.* [p](2:24) TR reads ου βαλω, *I will not put.*
[q](2:27) Ps. 2:8, 9

3 "And to the angel of the
church in Sardis write,
'These things says He who
has the seven Spirits of God
and the seven stars: "I know
your works, that you have a
name that you are alive, but
you are dead.
2 "Be watchful, and
strengthen the things which remain, that are ready to die, for
I have not found your works
perfect before God.
3 "Remember therefore how
you have received and heard;
hold fast and repent. Therefore
if you will not watch, I will come
upon you as a thief, and you will
not know what hour I will come
upon you.
4 "You have a few names
even in Sardis who have not defiled their garments; and they
shall walk with Me in white, for
they are worthy.
5 "He who overcomes shall
be clothed in white garments,
and I will not blot out his name
from the Book of Life; but I will
confess his name before My
Father and before His angels.
6 "He who has an ear, let
him hear what the Spirit says to
the churches."'
7 "And to the angel of the
church in Philadelphia write,
'These things says He who
is holy, He who is true, *"He*

---

[a](3:1) TR, NU read *οτι*, *that.*
[b](3:2) TR (*στηριξον*) and NU (*στηρισον*) read *strengthen.*
[c](3:2) TR reads *μελλει αποθανειν*, *which are about to die;* NU reads *εμελλον αποθανειν*, *which were about to die.*
[d](3:2) TR omits *μου*, *my.*
[e](3:3) NU omits *επι σε*, *upon you.* [f](3:5) NU reads *ουτως*, *thus.*

---

*(3:5) *ἐξαλείφω* (*exaleiphō*). Verb meaning *wipe away, erase, remove, obliterate.* In Rev. 7:17; 21:4 tears are *wiped away* as a metaphor for the end of human sorrow. Elsewhere in the NT, its usage reflects the practice of *blotting out* or *erasing* writing in legal documents to end their effects. Such "wiping out" is applied to our sins (as recorded against us; Acts 3:19), names in the Lamb's Book of Life (here in Rev. 3:5), and the signed bill of indebtedness to God for sin (Col. 2:14; see *χειρόγραφον* at Col. 2:14).

The Letter to Sardis: The Dead Church

3 1 "Καὶ τῷ ἀγγέλῳ τῆς ἐν Σάρδεσιν ἐκκλησίας γράψον,
"And to the angel of the [2]in [3]Sardis [1]church write,

'Τάδε λέγει ὁ ἔχων τὰ ἑπτὰ Πνεύματα τοῦ Θεοῦ
'These *things* says the *One* (He who) having (has) the seven Spirits - of God

καὶ τοὺς ἑπτὰ ἀστέρας·
and the seven stars:

'Οἶδά σου τὰ ἔργα, ὅτι ὄνομα ἔχεις, καὶ[a] ζῇς καὶ
'I know your - works, that [3]a [4]name [1]you [2]have, and (that) you live and

νεκρὸς εἶ. 2 Γίνου γρηγορῶν, καὶ τήρησον[b] τὰ
[3]dead [1]you [2]are. Be watching, (vigilant,) and keep the

λοιπὰ ἃ ἔμελλες ἀποβάλλειν,[c] οὐ γὰρ
remaining *things* which you were about to throw away, [4]not [1]for

εὕρηκά σου τὰ ἔργα πεπληρωμένα ἐνώπιον τοῦ Θεοῦ
[2]I [3]have [5]found your - works having been completed before - God ˜

μου.[d]
My.

3 'Μνημόνευε οὖν πῶς εἴληφας καὶ ἤκουσας,
'Remember therefore how you have received and you heard,

καὶ τήρει, καὶ μετανόησον. Ἐὰν οὖν μὴ
and hold fast, (keep holding fast,) and repent. If therefore [3]not

γρηγορήσῃς, ἥξω ἐπί σε[e] ὡς κλέπτης, καὶ οὐ μὴ
[1]you [2]will watch, I will come upon you like a thief, and [3]not [4]not (by no means)

γνώσῃ ποίαν ὥραν ἥξω ἐπί σε. 4 Ἀλλ' ὀλίγα
[1]you [2]shall know what hour I shall come upon you. But [3]a [4]few

ἔχεις ὀνόματα ἐν Σάρδεσιν ἃ οὐκ ἐμόλυναν τὰ ἱμάτια
[1]you [2]have names (individuals) in Sardis which (who) not ˜ did defile (have not defiled) - garments ˜

αὐτῶν· καὶ περιπατήσουσι μετ' ἐμοῦ ἐν λευκοῖς, ὅτι
their; and they will walk with Me in white *robes,* because

ἄξιοί εἰσιν. 5 Ὁ νικῶν, οὗτος[f] περιβαλεῖται ἐν
[3]worthy [1]they [2]are. The *one* (He who) overcoming, (overcomes,) this one will be clothed in

ἱματίοις λευκοῖς, καὶ οὐ μὴ ἐξαλείψω* τὸ ὄνομα αὐτοῦ
garments ˜ white, and [3]not [4]not (by no means) [1]I [2]shall wipe out - name ˜ his

ἐκ τῆς Βίβλου τῆς Ζωῆς, καὶ ὁμολογήσω τὸ ὄνομα αὐτοῦ
from the Book - of Life, and I will confess - name ˜ his

ἐνώπιον τοῦ Πατρός μου καὶ ἐνώπιον τῶν ἀγγέλων αὐτοῦ.
before - Father ˜ My and before - angels ˜ His.

6 "Ὁ ἔχων οὖς ἀκουσάτω τί τὸ Πνεῦμα λέγει
'The *one* ('He who) having (has) an ear let him hear what the Spirit says

ταῖς ἐκκλησίαις.'
to the churches.'

The Letter to Philadelphia: The Faithful Church

7 "Καὶ τῷ ἀγγέλῳ τῆς ἐν Φιλαδελφείᾳ ἐκκλησίας
"And to the angel of the [2]in [3]Philadelphia [1]church

γράψον,
write,

'Τάδε λέγει ὁ ἅγιος, ὁ ἀληθινός, ὁ ἔχων τὴν
'These *things* says the holy *One,* the true *One,* the *One* (He who) having (has) the

κλεῖν τοῦ Δαβίδ, ὁ ἀνοίγων καὶ οὐδεὶς κλείσει αὐτὴν
key - of David, the *One* opening and no one shall shut it
He who opens

εἰ μὴ ὁ ἀνοίγων, καὶ οὐδεὶς ἀνοίξει.[g]
if not the *One* opening, and no one shall open.
except

8 'Οἶδά σου τὰ ἔργα. Ἰδού, δέδωκα ἐνώπιόν σου θύραν
'I know your - works. Behold, I have given before you a door
granted

ἀνεῳγμένην, ἣν οὐδεὶς δύναται κλεῖσαι αὐτήν· ὅτι
having been opened, which no one is able to shut it; because

μικρὰν ἔχεις δύναμιν καὶ ἐτήρησάς μου τὸν λόγον καὶ οὐκ
[3]a [4]little [1]you [2]have strength and you kept My - word and [3]not
have kept you

ἠρνήσω τὸ ὄνομά μου. 9 Ἰδού, δίδωμι ἐκ τῆς
[1]you [2]did deny - name ˜ My. Behold, I am giving *those* of the
have not denied granting

συναγωγῆς τοῦ Σατανᾶ, τῶν λεγόντων ἑαυτοὺς Ἰουδαίους
synagogue - of Satan, the *ones* saying themselves [3]Jews
those who say they are Jews

εἶναι καὶ οὐκ εἰσίν, ἀλλὰ ψεύδονται — ἰδού, ποιήσω
[1]to [2]be and [3]not [1]they [2]are, but they are lying — behold, I will make

αὐτοὺς ἵνα ἥξωσι καὶ προσκυνήσωσιν ἐνώπιον τῶν
them so that they shall come and they shall do obeisance before -

ποδῶν σου καὶ γνῶσιν ὅτι ἠγάπησά σε. 10 Ὅτι
feet ˜ your and they shall know that I loved you. Because
have loved

ἐτήρησας τὸν λόγον τῆς ὑπομονῆς μου, κἀγώ σε τηρήσω ἐκ
you kept the word of endurance ˜ My, I also [3]you [1]will [2]keep from
have kept

τῆς ὥρας τοῦ πειρασμοῦ τῆς μελλούσης ἔρχεσθαι ἐπὶ τῆς
the hour - of trial the *one* being about to come upon the
temptation which is

οἰκουμένης ὅλης, πειράσαι τοὺς κατοικοῦντας ἐπὶ τῆς
[2]inhabited [3]earth [1]whole, to test the *ones* dwelling on the
those who dwell

γῆς.
earth.

11 'Ἔρχομαι[h] ταχύ. Κράτει ὃ ἔχεις, ἵνα μηδεὶς
'I am coming swiftly. Hold fast what you have, so that no one

λάβῃ τὸν στέφανόν σου. 12 Ὁ νικῶν, ποιήσω αὐτὸν
may take - crown ˜ your. The *one* overcoming, I will make him
He who overcomes,

στύλον ἐν τῷ ναῷ τοῦ Θεοῦ μου, καὶ ἔξω οὐ μὴ
a pillar in the shrine - of God ˜ My, and [6]out [3]not [4]not
by no means

ἐξέλθῃ ἔτι. Καὶ γράψω ἐπ' αὐτὸν τὸ ὄνομα τοῦ
[1]he [2]will [5]go *any* longer. And I will write on him the name -

Θεοῦ μου καὶ τὸ ὄνομα τῆς πόλεως τοῦ Θεοῦ μου, τῆς
of God ˜ My and the name of the city - of God ˜ My, the

καινῆς Ἰερουσαλήμ, ἣ καταβαίνει ἀπὸ τοῦ οὐρανοῦ ἀπὸ τοῦ
new Jerusalem, which comes down from - heaven from -

Θεοῦ μου, καὶ τὸ ὄνομά μου τὸ καινόν.
God ˜ My, and - [3]name [1]My - [2]new.

13 'Ὁ ἔχων οὖς ἀκουσάτω τί τὸ Πνεῦμα λέγει
'The *one* having an ear let him hear what the Spirit says
'He who has

ταῖς ἐκκλησίαις.'
to the churches.'

who has the key of David, He who opens and no one shuts, and shuts and no one opens":
8 "I know your works. See, I have set before you an open door, and no one can shut it; for you have a little strength, have kept My word, and have not denied My name.
9 "Indeed I will make *those* of the synagogue of Satan, who say they are Jews and are not, but lie—indeed I will make them come and worship before your feet, and to know that I have loved you.
10 "Because you have kept My command to persevere, I also will keep you from the hour of trial which shall come upon the whole world, to test those who dwell on the earth.
11 "Behold, I am coming quickly! Hold fast what you have, that no one may take your crown.
12 "He who overcomes, I will make him a pillar in the temple of My God, and he shall go out no more. I will write on him the name of My God and the name of the city of My God, the New Jerusalem, which comes down out of heaven from My God. And *I will write on him* My new name.
13 "He who has an ear, let him hear what the Spirit says to the churches."'

[g]**(3:7)** TR reads και ουδεις κλειει και κλειει και ουδεις ανοιγει, *and no one shuts, and shuts and no one opens;* NU reads και ουδεις κλεισει και κλειων και ουδεις ανοιγει, *and no one shall open and shutting and no one opens.*
[h]**(3:11)** TR adds ιδου, *behold.*

14 "And to the angel of the church of the Laodiceans write,
'These things says the Amen, the Faithful and True Witness, the Beginning of the creation of God:
15 "I know your works, that you are neither cold nor hot. I could wish you were cold or hot.
16 "So then, because you are lukewarm, and neither cold nor hot, I will vomit you out of My mouth.
17 "Because you say, 'I am rich, have become wealthy, and have need of nothing'—and do not know that you are wretched, miserable, poor, blind, and naked—
18 "I counsel you to buy from Me gold refined in the fire, that you may be rich; and white garments, that you may be clothed, *that* the shame of your nakedness may not be revealed; and anoint your eyes with eye salve, that you may see.
19 "As many as I love, I rebuke and chasten. Therefore be zealous and repent.
20 "Behold, I stand at the door and knock. If anyone hears My voice and opens the door, I will come in to him and dine with him, and he with Me.
21 "To him who overcomes I will grant to sit with Me on My throne, as I also overcame and sat down with My Father on His throne.
22 "He who has an ear, let him hear what the Spirit says to the churches."'"

The Letter to Laodicea: The Lukewarm Church

14 "Καὶ τῷ ἀγγέλῳ τῆς ἐν Λαοδικείᾳ ἐκκλησίας[i]
"And to the angel of the [2]in [3]Laodicea [1]church

γράψον,
write,

'Τάδε λέγει ὁ Ἀμήν, ὁ μάρτυς ὁ πιστὸς καὶ
'These *things* says the Amen, the [4]witness - [1]faithful [2]and

ἀληθινός, ἡ ἀρχὴ τῆς κτίσεως τοῦ Θεοῦ·
[3]true, the beginning of the creation - of God:

15 'Οἶδά σου τὰ ἔργα, ὅτι οὔτε ψυχρὸς εἶ οὔτε
'I know your - works, that [3]neither [4]cold [1]you [2]are nor

ζεστός. Ὄφελον ψυχρὸς ἦς ἢ ζεστός. **16** Οὕτως ὅτι
hot. I could wish [3]cold [1]you [2]were or hot. Thus because

χλιαρὸς εἶ, καὶ οὐ ζεστὸς οὔτε ψυχρός, μέλλω σε
[3]lukewarm [1]you [2]are, and not hot nor cold, I am about [3]you

ἐμέσαι ἐκ τοῦ στόματός μου. **17** Ὅτι λέγεις, "Πλούσιός
[1]to [2]vomit out of - mouth ˜ My. Because you say, "[3]wealthy

εἰμι, καὶ πεπλούτηκα, καὶ οὐδενὸς χρείαν ἔχω," καὶ
[1]I [2]am, and I have become rich, and [4]of [5]nothing [3]need [1]I [2]have," and

οὐκ οἶδας ὅτι σὺ εἶ ὁ ταλαίπωρος καὶ ὁ ἐλεεινὸς
[3]not [1]you [2]do know that you are the wretched *one* and the pitiable *one*

καὶ πτωχὸς καὶ τυφλὸς καὶ γυμνός, **18** συμβουλεύω σοι
and poor and blind and naked, I counsel you

ἀγοράσαι χρυσίον παρ' ἐμοῦ πεπυρωμένον ἐκ
to buy gold from Me having been heated thoroughly by
refined

πυρός, ἵνα πλουτήσῃς, καὶ ἱμάτια λευκά, ἵνα
fire, so that you may become rich, and robes ˜ white, so that

περιβάλῃ, καὶ μὴ φανερωθῇ ἡ αἰσχύνη τῆς
you may be clothed, and [7]not [6]may [8]appear [1]the [2]shame [3]of

γυμνότητός σου· καὶ κολλύριον ἵνα ἐγχρίσῃ τοὺς
[5]nakedness [4]your; and eye salve so that you may anoint -

ὀφθαλμούς σου, ἵνα βλέπῃς. **19** Ἐγὼ ὅσους ἐὰν
eyes ˜ your, in order that you may see. I as many as -

φιλῶ, ἐλέγχω καὶ παιδεύω. Ζήλευε οὖν καὶ μετανόησον.
I love, I rebuke and I chasten. Be zealous therefore and repent.
discipline.

20 'Ἰδού, ἕστηκα ἐπὶ τὴν θύραν καὶ κρούω. Ἐάν
'Behold, I stand at the door and I am knocking. If

τις ἀκούσῃ τῆς φωνῆς μου καὶ ἀνοίξῃ τὴν θύραν, καὶ[j]
anyone hears - voice ˜ My and opens the door, and
then

εἰσελεύσομαι πρὸς αὐτὸν καὶ δειπνήσω μετ' αὐτοῦ, καὶ αὐτὸς
I will come in to him and I will dine with him, and he

μετ' ἐμοῦ. **21** Ὁ νικῶν, δώσω αὐτῷ καθίσαι μετ'
with Me. The *one* overcoming, I will give to him to sit with
He who overcomes, I will grant

ἐμοῦ ἐν τῷ θρόνῳ μου, ὡς κἀγὼ ἐνίκησα καὶ ἐκάθισα μετὰ
Me in - throne ˜ My, as I also overcame and sat down with

τοῦ Πατρός μου ἐν τῷ θρόνῳ αὐτοῦ.
- Father ˜ My in - throne ˜ His.

22 'Ὁ ἔχων οὖς ἀκουσάτω τί τὸ Πνεῦμα λέγει
'The *one* having an ear let him hear what the Spirit says
'He who has

ταῖς ἐκκλησίαις.'"
to the churches.'"

---

i(**3:14**) TR reads *εκκλησιας Λαοδικεων, church of (the) Laodiceans.*
j(**3:20**) TR omits *και, and (then).*

John Sees the Throne Room of Heaven

4 **1** Μετὰ ταῦτα εἶδον, καὶ ἰδού, θύρα ἀνεῳγμένη
After these *things* I looked, and behold, a door having been opened
standing open

ἐν τῷ οὐρανῷ, καὶ ἡ φωνὴ ἡ πρώτη ἣν ἤκουσα ὡς
in the heaven, and the voice ˜ - first which I heard *was* like
sky,

σάλπιγγος λαλούσης μετ᾽ ἐμοῦ, λέγων, "Ἀνάβα ὧδε, καὶ
a trumpet speaking with me, saying, "Come up here, and

δείξω σοι ἃ δεῖ γενέσθαι μετὰ
I will show to you *the things* which it is necessary to happen after
must occur

ταῦτα." **2** Εὐθέως ἐγενόμην ἐν Πνεύματι, καὶ ἰδού,
these *things*." Immediately I came to be in *the* Spirit, and behold,

θρόνος ἔκειτο ἐν τῷ οὐρανῷ (καὶ ἐπὶ τὸν θρόνον καθήμενος)
a throne was set in the heaven (and on the throne *One* sitting)
situated sky

3 ὅμοιος[a] ὁράσει λίθῳ ἰάσπιδι καὶ σαρδίῳ, καὶ
similar in appearance to a stone ˜ jasper and sardius, and
carnelian,

ἶρις κυκλόθεν τοῦ θρόνου, ὁμοίως
there was a rainbow around the throne, likewise *there was the*

ὅρασις σμαραγδίνων. **4** Κυκλόθεν τοῦ θρόνου θρόνοι
appearance of emeralds. Around the throne *were* [3]thrones

εἴκοσι τέσσαρες, καὶ ἐπὶ τοὺς θρόνους[b] τοὺς εἴκοσι τέσσαρας
[1]twenty- [2]four, and on the thrones the twenty- four

πρεσβυτέρους καθημένους, περιβεβλημένους ἐν ἱματίοις
elders *were* sitting, having been clothed in robes ˜

λευκοῖς, καὶ[c] ἐπὶ τὰς κεφαλὰς αὐτῶν στεφάνους
white, and on - heads ˜ their *there were* crowns ˜

χρυσοῦς. **5** Καὶ ἐκ τοῦ θρόνου ἐκπορεύονται ἀστραπαὶ καὶ
golden. And from the throne proceed lightnings and
proceeded

φωναὶ καὶ βρονταί. Καὶ ἑπτὰ λαμπάδες πυρὸς καιόμεναι
voices and thunders. And seven torches of fire *were* burning

ἐνώπιον τοῦ θρόνου αὐτοῦ,[d] αἵ εἰσιν ἑπτὰ Πνεύματα τοῦ
before - throne ˜ His, which are seven Spirits -

Θεοῦ· **6** καὶ ἐνώπιον τοῦ θρόνου ὡς[e] θάλασσα
of God; and before the throne *was something* like a sea ˜

ὑαλίνη, ὁμοία κρυστάλλῳ. Καὶ ἐν μέσῳ τοῦ θρόνου καὶ
glass, similar to crystal. And in *the* midst of the throne and

κύκλῳ τοῦ θρόνου τέσσαρα ζῷα* γέμοντα ὀφθαλμῶν
around the throne *were* four living creatures being full of eyes

ἔμπροσθεν καὶ ὄπισθεν. **7** Καὶ τὸ ζῷον τὸ πρῶτον
in front and in back. And the [2]living [3]creature - [1]first

ὅμοιον λέοντι, καὶ τὸ δεύτερον ζῷον ὅμοιον μόσχῳ, καὶ
was like a lion, and the second living creature *was* like a calf, and

τὸ τρίτον ζῷον ἔχον πρόσωπον ἀνθρώπου, καὶ τὸ
the third living creature having a face of a man, and the
had

τέταρτον[f] ὅμοιον ἀετῷ πετομένῳ. **8** Καὶ τὰ τέσσαρα
fourth *one* *was* like a(n) eagle ˜ flying. And the four

ζῷα, ἓν καθ᾽ ἓν ἔχον ἀνὰ πτέρυγας ἕξ, κυκλόθεν
living creatures, one by one having [3]apiece [2]wings [1]six, around
each one

καὶ ἔσωθεν γέμουσιν ὀφθαλμῶν. Καὶ ἀνάπαυσιν οὐκ
and within are full of eyes. And [5]rest [3]not
were they never

4 After these things I
looked, and behold, a door
standing open in heaven. And
the first voice which I heard
was like a trumpet speaking
with me, saying, "Come up
here, and I will show you things
which must take place after
this."
2 Immediately I was in the
Spirit; and behold, a throne set
in heaven, and *One* sat on the
throne.
3 And He who sat there was
like a jasper and a sardius stone
in appearance; and *there was* a
rainbow around the throne, in
appearance like an emerald.
4 Around the throne *were*
twenty-four thrones, and on the
thrones I saw twenty-four elders sitting, clothed in white
robes; and they had crowns of
gold on their heads.
5 And from the throne proceeded lightnings, thunderings,
and voices. Seven lamps of fire
were burning before the throne,
which are the seven Spirits of
God.
6 Before the throne *there*
was a sea of glass, like crystal.
And in the midst of the throne,
and around the throne, *were*
four living creatures full of eyes
in front and in back.
7 The first living creature
was like a lion, the second living
creature like a calf, the third living creature had a face like a
man, and the fourth living creature *was* like a flying eagle.
8 *The* four living creatures,
each having six wings, were full
of eyes around and within. And
they do not rest day or night,

---

[a](**4:3**) TR precedes with *και ο καθημενος ην, and the One sitting was (similar);* NU with *και ο καθημενος, and the One sitting.* [b](**4:4**) TR adds *ειδον, I saw.* [c](**4:4**) TR adds *εσχον, they had.* [d](**4:5**) TR, NU omit *αυτου, His.* [e](**4:6**) TR omits *ως, like.* [f](**4:7**) TR, NU add *ζωον, living creature.*

---

*(**4:6**) *ζῷον (zōon).* Noun from the verb *ζάω, live,* thus meaning *living thing* or *creature.* The normal use of the word in Hellenistic Greek was to refer to animals (Heb. 13:11; 2 Pet. 2:12). Here in Rev. 4:6 and throughout

saying:

"Holy, holy, holy,
Lord God Almighty,
Who was and is and is to come!"

9 Whenever the living creatures give glory and honor and thanks to Him who sits on the throne, who lives forever and ever,
10 the twenty-four elders fall down before Him who sits on the throne and worship Him who lives forever and ever, and cast their crowns before the throne, saying:

11 "You are worthy, O Lord,
To receive glory and honor and power;
For You created all things,
And by Your will they exist and were created."

5 And I saw in the right *hand* of Him who sat on the throne a scroll written inside and on the back, sealed

ἔχουσιν ἡμέρας καὶ νυκτός, λέγοντες,
[1]they [2]do [4]have by day and by night, saying,
cease or

"Ἅγιος, ἅγιος, ἅγιος,
"Holy, holy, holy,

Ἅγιος, ἅγιος, ἅγιος,
Holy, holy, holy,

Ἅγιος, ἅγιος, ἅγιος,[g]
Holy, holy, holy,

Κύριος ὁ Θεὸς ὁ Παντοκράτωρ,
Lord - God the Almighty,

Ὁ ἦν καὶ ὁ ὢν καὶ ὁ
The *One who* was and the *One* being and the *One*
who is who

ἐρχόμενος!"
coming!"
is to come!"

9 Καὶ ὅταν δῶσι τὰ ζῷα δόξαν καὶ τιμὴν
And whenever [4]give [1]the [2]living [3]creatures glory and honor
ascribe

καὶ εὐχαριστίαν τῷ καθημένῳ ἐπὶ τοῦ θρόνου, τῷ
and thanksgiving to the *One* sitting on the throne, to the *One*
Him who sits Him

ζῶντι εἰς τοὺς αἰῶνας τῶν αἰώνων, 10 πεσοῦνται οἱ
living to the ages of the ages, [5]will [6]fall [7]down [1]the
who lives forever and ever,

εἴκοσι τέσσαρες πρεσβύτεροι ἐνώπιον τοῦ καθημένου ἐπὶ
[2]twenty- [3]four [4]elders before the *One* sitting on
Him who sits

τοῦ θρόνου καὶ προσκυνήσουσι τῷ ζῶντι εἰς τοὺς αἰῶνας
the throne and they will worship the *One* living to the ages
Him who lives forever and ever,

τῶν αἰώνων, καὶ βαλοῦσι τοὺς στεφάνους αὐτῶν ἐνώπιον
of the ages, and they will cast - crowns ˜ their before

τοῦ θρόνου, λέγοντες,
the throne, saying,

11 "Ἄξιος εἶ,
"[3]worthy [1]You [2]are,

Ὁ Κύριος καὶ ὁ Θεὸς ἡμῶν,
- [2]Lord [3]and - [4]God [1]Our,

Ὁ Ἅγιος,[h]
The Holy *One,*

Λαβεῖν τὴν δόξαν καὶ τὴν τιμὴν καὶ τὴν δύναμιν,
To receive the glory and the honor and the power,

Ὅτι σὺ ἔκτισας πάντα,
Because You created all *things,*

Καὶ διὰ τὸ θέλημά σου ἦσαν[i] καὶ
And on account of - will ˜ Your they were and
by existed

ἐκτίσθησαν!"
they were created!"

The Lamb Takes the Scroll

5 1 Καὶ εἶδον ἐπὶ τὴν δεξιὰν τοῦ καθημένου ἐπὶ τοῦ
And I saw on the right *hand* of the *One* sitting on the
in

θρόνου βιβλίον γεγραμμένον ἔσωθεν καὶ ἔξωθεν[a]
throne a scroll having been written inside and outside
book

---

[g](4:8) TR, NU read αγιος, *holy,* three times rather than nine.
[h](4:11) TR reads Κυριε, *O Lord,* for Κυριος, *Lord,* and omits και through Αγιος. NU omits Ο Αγιος, *The Holy (One).*
[i](4:11) TR reads εισιν, *they are.* [a](5:1) TR, NU read οπισθεν, *on back.*

Revelation the "living creatures" are neither genuinely animals nor human, but special beings who stand before God's throne to glorify Him (reminiscent of the cherubim in Ezek. 1:5ff). See the near synonym θηρίον, *wild beast,* at Rev. 6:8.

κατεσφραγισμένον σφραγῖσιν ἑπτά.
having been sealed with seals ˜ seven.

2 Καὶ εἶδον ἄγγελον ἰσχυρὸν κηρύσσοντα ἐν φωνῇ
And I saw a(n) angel ˜ strong proclaiming with a voice ˜

μεγάλῃ, "Τίς ἄξιος ἐστιν ἀνοῖξαι τὸ βιβλίον καὶ λῦσαι τὰς
great, "Who worthy ˜ is to open the scroll and to loose -
loud, book break

σφραγῖδας αὐτοῦ?" 3 Καὶ οὐδεὶς ἐδύνατο ἐν τῷ οὐρανῷ ἄνω[b]
seals ˜ its?" And no one was able in the heaven above

οὔτε ἐπὶ τῆς γῆς οὔτε ὑποκάτω τῆς γῆς ἀνοῖξαι[c] τὸ βιβλίον
nor on the earth nor underneath the earth to open the scroll
book

οὔτε βλέπειν αὐτό. 4 Καὶ ἐγὼ ἔκλαιον πολύ, ὅτι οὐδεὶς
nor to look at it. And I was weeping much, because no one
began to weep

ἄξιος εὑρέθη ἀνοῖξαι τὸ βιβλίον οὔτε βλέπειν αὐτό.
[3]worthy [1]was [2]found to open the scroll nor to look at it.
book

5 Καὶ εἷς ἐκ τῶν πρεσβυτέρων λέγει μοι, "Μὴ κλαῖε.
And one of the elders says to me, "not ˜ Do weep.
said "Stop weeping.

Ἰδού, ἐνίκησεν ὁ λέων ὁ ἐκ τῆς φυλῆς Ἰούδα, ἡ ῥίζα
Behold, [12]overcame [1]the [2]lion - [3]of [4]the [5]tribe [6]of [7]Judah, [8]the [9]root
has overcome

Δαβίδ, ὁ ἀνοίγων[d] τὸ βιβλίον καὶ[e] τὰς ἑπτὰ
[10]of [11]David, the *One* opening the scroll and - [2]seven
He who opens book

σφραγῖδας αὐτοῦ." 6 Καὶ εἶδον[f] ἐν μέσῳ τοῦ θρόνου καὶ
[3]seals [1]its." And I saw in *the* midst of the throne and

τῶν τεσσάρων ζῴων, καὶ ἐν μέσῳ τῶν
of the four living creatures, and in *the* midst of the

πρεσβυτέρων, Ἀρνίον ἑστηκὸς ὡς ἐσφαγμένον, ἔχον
elders, a Lamb standing as *if* having been slaughtered, having
slain,

κέρατα ἑπτὰ καὶ ὀφθαλμοὺς ἑπτά, ἅ εἰσι τὰ ἑπτὰ
horns ˜ seven and eyes ˜ seven, which are the seven

Πνεύματα τοῦ Θεοῦ ἀποστελλόμενα εἰς πᾶσαν τὴν γῆν. 7 Καὶ
Spirits of God being sent out into all the earth. And

ἦλθε καὶ εἴληφεν[g] ἐκ τῆς δεξιᾶς τοῦ καθημένου
He came and has taken out of the right *hand* of the *One* sitting
took

ἐπὶ τοῦ θρόνου.
on the throne.

Worthy Is the Lamb

8 Καὶ ὅτε ἔλαβε τὸ βιβλίον, τὰ τέσσαρα ζῷα
And when He took the scroll, the four living creatures
book,

καὶ οἱ εἴκοσι τέσσαρες πρεσβύτεροι ἔπεσον ἐνώπιον τοῦ
and the twenty- four elders fell down before the

Ἀρνίου, ἔχοντες ἕκαστος κιθάραν, καὶ φιάλας χρυσᾶς
Lamb, [3]having [1]each [2]*one* a harp, and bowls ˜ golden

γεμούσας θυμιαμάτων, αἵ εἰσι προσευχαὶ τῶν ἁγίων.
being filled with incenses, which are prayers of the saints.
incense,

9 Καὶ ᾄδουσιν ᾠδὴν καινήν, λέγοντες,
And they sing a song ˜ new, saying,
sang

with seven seals.
2 Then I saw a strong angel proclaiming with a loud voice, "Who is worthy to open the scroll and to loose its seals?"
3 And no one in heaven or on the earth or under the earth was able to open the scroll, or to look at it.
4 So I wept much, because no one was found worthy to open and read the scroll, or to look at it.
5 But one of the elders said to me, "Do not weep. Behold, the Lion of the tribe of Judah, the Root of David, has prevailed to open the scroll and to loose its seven seals."
6 And I looked, and behold, in the midst of the throne and of the four living creatures, and in the midst of the elders, stood a Lamb as though it had been slain, having seven horns and seven eyes, which are the seven Spirits of God sent out into all the earth.
7 Then He came and took the scroll out of the right hand of Him who sat on the throne.
8 Now when He had taken the scroll, the four living creatures and the twenty-four elders fell down before the Lamb, each having a harp, and golden bowls full of incense, which are the prayers of the saints.
9 And they sang a new song, saying:

---

[b](5:3) TR, NU omit *ανω, above.* [c](5:3) TR adds *και αναγνωναι, and to read.* [d](5:5) TR, NU read *ανοιξαι, to open.* [e](5:5) TR adds *λυσαι, to loose.* [f](5:6) TR adds *και ιδου, and behold.* [g](5:7) TR adds *το βιβλιον, the scroll.*

"You are worthy to take
the scroll,
And to open its seals;
For You were slain,
And have redeemed us to
God by Your blood
Out of every tribe and
tongue and people and
nation,
10 And have made us kings
and priests to our God;
And we shall reign on the
earth."

11 Then I looked, and I heard the voice of many angels around the throne, the living creatures, and the elders; and the number of them was ten thousand times ten thousand, and thousands of thousands,
12 saying with a loud voice:

"Worthy is the Lamb who
was slain
To receive power and
riches and wisdom,
And strength and honor
and glory and blessing!"

13 And every creature which is in heaven and on the earth and under the earth and such as are in the sea, and all that are in them, I heard saying:

"Blessing and honor and
glory and power
Be to Him who sits on
the throne,
And to the Lamb, forever
and ever!"

14 Then the four living creatures said, "Amen!" And the twenty-four elders fell down and worshiped Him who lives forever and ever.

"Ἄξιος εἶ λαβεῖν τὸ βιβλίον
"[3]worthy [1]You [2]are to take the scroll
book

Καὶ ἀνοῖξαι τὰς σφραγῖδας αὐτοῦ·
And to open - seals ˜ its;

Ὅτι ἐσφάγης,
Because You were slaughtered,
slain,

Καὶ ἠγόρασας* τῷ Θεῷ ἡμᾶς[h] ἐν τῷ αἵματί σου
And You bought - [2]to [3]God [1]us by - blood ˜ Your
redeemed

Ἐκ πάσης φυλῆς καὶ γλώσσης καὶ λαοῦ καὶ ἔθνους·
Out of every tribe and tongue and people and nation;
language

10 Καὶ ἐποίησας αὐτοὺς[i] τῷ Θεῷ ἡμῶν βασιλεῖς[j] καὶ
And You made them - [4]to [6]God [5]our [1]kings [2]and
have made

ἱερεῖς,
[3]priests,

Καὶ βασιλεύσουσιν[k] ἐπὶ τῆς γῆς."
And they will reign on the earth."

11 Καὶ εἶδον, καὶ ἤκουσα ὡς[l] φωνὴν ἀγγέλων πολλῶν
And I looked, and I heard as *it were* a voice of angels ˜ many

κύκλῳ τοῦ θρόνου καὶ τῶν ζῴων καὶ τῶν πρεσβυτέρων.
around the throne and the living creatures and the elders.

Καὶ ἦν ὁ ἀριθμὸς αὐτῶν μυριάδες μυριάδων, καὶ χιλιάδες
And [5]was [1]the [2]number [3]of [4]them myriads of myriads, and thousands
countless thousands,

χιλιάδων, **12** λέγοντες φωνῇ μεγάλῃ,
of thousands, saying with a voice ˜ great,
loud,

"Ἄξιόν ἐστι τὸ Ἀρνίον τὸ ἐσφαγμένον
"Worthy is the Lamb the *One* having been slaughtered
who was slain

Λαβεῖν τὴν δύναμιν καὶ τὸν πλοῦτον καὶ σοφίαν καὶ
To receive the power and the wealth and wisdom and

ἰσχὺν
strength

Καὶ τιμὴν καὶ δόξαν καὶ εὐλογίαν!"
And honor and glory and blessing!"

13 Καὶ πᾶν κτίσμα ὃ ἐν τῷ οὐρανῷ καὶ ἐπὶ τῆς γῆς
And every creature which [2]in - [3]heaven [4]and [5]on [6]the [7]earth

καὶ ὑποκάτω τῆς γῆς καὶ ἐπὶ τῆς θαλάσσης ἐστί, καὶ
[8]and [9]underneath [10]the [11]earth [12]and [13]on [14]the [15]sea [1]is, and

τὰ ἐν αὐτοῖς, πάντας ἤκουσα λέγοντας,
the *things* in them, [3]all [1]I [2]heard saying,

"Τῷ καθημένῳ ἐπὶ τῷ θρόνῳ,
"To the *One* sitting on the throne,

Καὶ τῷ Ἀρνίῳ,
And to the Lamb,

Ἡ εὐλογία καὶ ἡ τιμὴ καὶ ἡ δόξα καὶ τὸ κράτος
Be the blessing and the honor and the glory and the power

Εἰς τοὺς αἰῶνας τῶν αἰώνων. Ἀμήν!"[m]
To the ages of the ages. Amen!"
Forever and ever. So be it!"

14 — καὶ τὰ τέσσαρα ζῷα λέγοντα τὸ Ἀμήν.
— and the four living creatures *were* saying the Amen.

Καὶ οἱ[n] πρεσβύτεροι ἔπεσον καὶ προσεκύνησαν.[o]
And the elders fell down and worshiped.

---

[h](5:9) NU omits ημας, *us.*
[i](5:10) TR reads ημας, *us.*
[j](5:10) NU reads βασιλειαν, *a kingdom.*
[k](5:10) TR reads βασιλευσομεν, *we shall reign.* [l](5:11) TR, NU omit ως, *as.* [m](5:13) TR, NU omit Αμην, *Amen.*
[n](5:14) TR adds εικοσι τεσσαρες, *twenty-four.*
[o](5:14) TR adds ζωντι εις τους αιωνας των αιωνων, *the one* living forever and ever.

***(5:9)** ἀγοράζω *(agorazō).* Frequent verb in the NT meaning *buy, purchase.* It may be used literally for buying merchandise of any kind, as a field (Matt. 13:44) or food (Mark 6:37). More

First Seal: The Conqueror

6 1 Καὶ εἶδον ὅτι[a] ἤνοιξε τὸ Ἀρνίον μίαν ἐκ τῶν ἑπτὰ[b]
And I saw that ^{3}opened ^{1}the ^{2}Lamb one of the seven
the first

σφραγίδων, καὶ ἤκουσα ἑνὸς ἐκ τῶν τεσσάρων ζῴων
seals, and I heard one of the four living creatures

λέγοντος, ὡς φωνὴ βροντῆς, "Ἔρχου καὶ ἴδε." 2 Καὶ[c] ἰδού,
saying, like a voice of thunder, "Come and see." And behold,

ἵππος λευκός, καὶ ὁ καθήμενος ἐπ' αὐτὸν ἔχων τόξον.
a horse ˜ white, and the *One* sitting on it having a bow.
had

Καὶ ἐδόθη αὐτῷ στέφανος, καὶ ἐξῆλθε νικῶν, καὶ
And ^{3}was ^{4}given ^{5}to ^{6}him ^{1}a ^{2}crown, and he went out conquering, and

ἵνα νικήσῃ.
so that he might conquer.

Second Seal: Conflict on Earth

3 Καὶ ὅτε ἤνοιξε τὴν δευτέραν σφραγῖδα, ἤκουσα τοῦ
And when He opened the second seal, I heard the

δευτέρου ζῴου λέγοντος, "Ἔρχου!"[d] 4 Καὶ ἐξῆλθεν
second living creature saying, "Come!" And ^{3}went ^{4}out

ἄλλος ἵππος πυρός, καὶ τῷ καθημένῳ ἐπ' αὐτὸν
^{1}another ^{2}horse of fire, and to the *one* sitting on it
fiery red,

ἐδόθη αὐτῷ λαβεῖν τὴν εἰρήνην ἐκ τῆς γῆς, ἵνα
it was given to him to take - peace from the earth, so that
granted

ἀλλήλως σφάξωσι· καὶ ἐδόθη αὐτῷ μάχαιρα
^{4}each ^{5}other ^{1}they ^{2}might ^{3}slaughter; and ^{4}was ^{5}given ^{6}to ^{7}him ^{1}a ^{3}sword
slay;

μεγάλη.
^{2}great.
huge.

Third Seal: Scarcity on Earth

5 Καὶ ὅτε ἤνοιξε τὴν σφραγῖδα τὴν τρίτην, ἤκουσα τοῦ
And when He opened the seal ˜ - third, I heard the

τρίτου ζῴου λέγοντος, "Ἔρχου καὶ ἴδε."[e] Καὶ ἰδού,
third living creature saying, "Come and see." And behold,

ἵππος μέλας, καὶ ὁ καθήμενος ἐπ' αὐτὸν ἔχων ζυγὸν
a horse ˜ black, and the *one* sitting on it having a balance
had a pair of scales

ἐν τῇ χειρὶ αὐτοῦ.
in - hand ˜ his.

6 Καὶ ἤκουσα[f] φωνὴν ἐν μέσῳ τῶν τεσσάρων
And I heard a voice in *the* midst of the four

ζῴων λέγουσαν, "Χοῖνιξ σίτου δηναρίου, καὶ τρεῖς
living creatures saying, "A choenix of wheat for a denarius, and three

χοίνικες κριθῆς δηναρίου· καὶ τὸ ἔλαιον καὶ τὸν οἶνον μὴ
choenixes of barley for a denarius; and the olive oil and the wine not ˜
but

ἀδικήσῃς."
do harm."
disturb."

Fourth Seal: Widespread Death on Earth

7 Καὶ ὅτε ἤνοιξε τὴν σφραγῖδα τὴν τετάρτην,
And when He opened the seal ˜ - fourth,

6 Now I saw when the
Lamb opened one of the
seals; and I heard one of the
four living creatures saying with
a voice like thunder, "Come
and see."
2 And I looked, and behold, a
white horse. He who sat on it
had a bow; and a crown was
given to him, and he went out
conquering and to conquer.
3 When He opened the sec-
ond seal, I heard the second living creature saying, "Come and
see."
4 Another horse, fiery red,
went out. And it was granted to
the one who sat on it to take
peace from the earth, and that
people should kill one another;
and there was given to him a
great sword.
5 When He opened the third
seal, I heard the third living
creature say, "Come and see."
So I looked, and behold, a black
horse, and he who sat on it had
a pair of scales in his hand.
6 And I heard a voice in the
midst of the four living creatures saying, "A quart of wheat
for a denarius, and three quarts
of barley for a denarius; and do
not harm the oil and the wine."
7 When He opened the
fourth seal, I heard the voice of

---

[a](**6:1**) TR, NU read *οτε, when.* [b](**6:1**) TR omits *επτα, seven.*
[c](**6:2**) TR adds *βλεπε και ειδον και, see and I saw and (behold);* NU adds *ειδον και, I saw and.*
[d](**6:3**) TR adds *και βλεπε, and see.* [e](**6:5**) TR reads *βλεπε και ειδον, see and I saw;* NU reads *ειδον, I saw.*
[f](**6:6**) NU adds *ως, as (it were).*

interesting is the figurative use represented here in Rev. 5:9, probably based on the analogy with the slave market. Jesus Christ has *purchased* or *redeemed* people from enslavement to sin by the blood of His cross and made them to belong to God (1 Cor. 6:20; 2 Pet. 2:1). See the cognate noun ἀγορά at Acts 16:19.

the fourth living creature saying, "Come and see."
8 So I looked, and behold, a
pale horse. And the name of
him who sat on it was Death,
and Hades followed with him.
And power was given to them
over a fourth of the earth, to kill
with sword, with hunger, with
death, and by the beasts of the
earth.
9 When He opened the fifth
seal, I saw under the altar the
souls of those who had been
slain for the word of God and
for the testimony which they
held.
10 And they cried with a loud
voice, saying, "How long,
O Lord, holy and true, until
You judge and avenge our blood
on those who dwell on the
earth?"
11 Then a white robe was
given to each of them; and it
was said to them that they
should rest a little while longer,
until both *the number of* their
fellow servants and their brethren, who would be killed as
they *were,* was completed.
12 I looked when He opened
the sixth seal, and behold,
there was a great earthquake;
and the sun became black as

---

[g](6:7) TR, NU add φωνην, *(the) voice (of).*
[h](6:7) TR reads βλεπε και ειδον, *see and I saw;* NU reads ειδον, *I saw.*
[i](6:8) NU, TR read αυτοις, *to them.* [j](6:9) TR, NU omit του Αρνιου, *of the lamb.* [k](6:11) TR reads εδοθησαν εκαστοις στολαι λευκαι, *white robes were given to each.*
[l](6:11) NU, TR add μικρον, *a little.* [m](6:11) NU reads πληρωθωσιν, *should be completed (in number).*

***(6:8)** θηρίον *(thērion).* Common noun, usually meaning *wild animal* or *beast* (as Heb. 12:20), or more specifically *four-legged animals* (as James 3:7), especially dangerous ones (as here in Rev. 6:8). The word is also applied to the visionary "beasts" John sees later in Revelation that represent the two anti-Christian, evil powers (13:1f, 11f), especially "the beast" who is the personification of Satan (14:9; 20:10). While the near synonym ζῷον emphasizes the element of life, θηρίον emphasizes the bestial nature, making it a better word to represent evil (see

ἤκουσα[g] τοῦ τετάρτου ζῴου λέγοντος, "Ἔρχου καὶ
I heard the fourth living creature saying, "Come and

ἴδε."[h] **8** Καὶ ἰδού, ἵππος χλωρός, καὶ ὁ καθήμενος
see." And behold, a [3]horse [1]pale [2]green, and the *one* sitting
sickly pale,

ἐπάνω αὐτοῦ, ὄνομα αὐτῷ ὁ Θάνατος, καὶ ὁ Ἅιδης
on it, *the* name to him - *was* Death, and - Hades
whose name

ἠκολουθεῖ αὐτῷ. Καὶ ἐδόθη αὐτῷ[i] ἐξουσία ἐπὶ τὸ
was following him. And [2]was [3]given [4]to [5]him [1]authority over the
a

τέταρτον τῆς γῆς ἀποκτεῖναι ἐν ῥομφαίᾳ καὶ ἐν λιμῷ καὶ
fourth of the earth to kill with a sword and with famine and

ἐν θανάτῳ καὶ ὑπὸ τῶν θηρίων* τῆς γῆς.
with death and by the wild beasts of the earth.

Fifth Seal: The Cry of the Martyrs

9 Καὶ ὅτε ἤνοιξε τὴν πέμπτην σφραγῖδα, εἶδον
And when He opened the fifth seal, I saw

ὑποκάτω τοῦ θυσιαστηρίου τὰς ψυχὰς τῶν
underneath the altar the souls of the *ones*
those who

ἐσφαγμένων διὰ τὸν λόγον τοῦ Θεοῦ καὶ
having been slaughtered on account of the word - of God and
had been slain

διὰ τὴν μαρτυρίαν τοῦ Ἀρνίου[j] ἣν εἶχον.
on account of the testimony of the Lamb which they were having.
had.

10 Καὶ ἔκραξαν φωνῇ μεγάλῃ, λέγοντες, "Ἕως
And they cried out *with* a voice ˜ great, saying, "Until
loud, "How

πότε, ὁ Δεσπότης, ὁ ἅγιος καὶ ἀληθινός, οὐ κρίνεις
when, - O Master, the holy *One* and true *One,* [3]not [1]do [2]you [4]judge
long, Sovereign,

καὶ ἐκδικεῖς τὸ αἷμα ἡμῶν ἐκ τῶν κατοικούντων ἐπὶ τῆς
and avenge - blood ˜ our of the *ones* dwelling on the
on those who dwell

γῆς?" **11** Καὶ ἐδόθη αὐτοῖς στολὴ λευκή,[k] καὶ
earth?" And [5]was [6]given [7]to [8]them [1]a [2]long [4]robe [3]white, and

ἐρρέθη αὐτοῖς ἵνα ἀναπαύσωνται ἔτι χρόνον,[l] ἕως
it was said to them that they should rest yet a time, until
they were told a while,

πληρώσωσι[m] καὶ οἱ σύνδουλοι αὐτῶν καὶ
[20]should [21]complete [22]*their* [23]*course* [1]also - [3]fellow [4]bondservants [2]their [5]and
slaves

οἱ ἀδελφοὶ αὐτῶν καὶ οἱ μέλλοντες ἀποκτένεσθαι ὡς
- [7]brothers [6]their [8]and [9]the [10]*ones* [11]being [12]about [13]to [14]be [15]killed [16]as
those who were

καὶ αὐτοί.
[17]also [18]they [19]*were.*

Sixth Seal: Cosmic Disturbances

12 Καὶ εἶδον ὅτε ἤνοιξε τὴν σφραγῖδα τὴν ἕκτην, καὶ
And I saw when He opened the seal ˜ - sixth, and
that

σεισμὸς μέγας ἐγένετο· καὶ ὁ ἥλιος μέλας ἐγένετο ὡς
a(n) earthquake ˜ great occurred; and the sun black ˜ became as
severe

σάκκος τρίχινος, καὶ ἡ σελήνη ὅλη ἐγένετο ὡς αἷμα.
sackcloth of hair, and the moon ~ whole became like blood.

13 Καὶ οἱ ἀστέρες τοῦ οὐρανοῦ ἔπεσον εἰς τὴν γῆν ὡς
And the stars of the heaven fell to the earth like
sky

συκῆ βαλοῦσα[n] τοὺς ὀλύνθους αὐτῆς, ὑπὸ ἀνέμου μεγάλου
a fig tree casting - [2]late [3]figs [1]its, [6]by [7]a [9]wind [8]great
high

σειομένη. 14 Καὶ ὁ οὐρανὸς ἀπεχωρίσθη ὡς βιβλίον
[4]being [5]shaken. And the heaven was split like a scroll
sky

ἑλισσόμενος, καὶ πᾶν ὄρος καὶ νῆσος ἐκ τῶν τόπων
being rolled up, and every mountain and island [3]out [4]of - [6]places

αὐτῶν ἐκινήθησαν.
[5]their [1]were [2]moved.

15 Καὶ οἱ βασιλεῖς τῆς γῆς καὶ οἱ μεγιστᾶνες καὶ οἱ
And the kings of the earth and the magnates and the
great ones

χιλίαρχοι καὶ οἱ πλούσιοι καὶ οἱ ἰσχυροὶ καὶ πᾶς
chiliarchs and the rich and the mighty and every
high-ranking military men

δοῦλος καὶ[o] ἐλεύθερος ἔκρυψαν ἑαυτοὺς εἰς τὰ σπήλαια καὶ
slave and free *person* hid themselves in the caves and

εἰς τὰς πέτρας τῶν ὀρέων. 16 Καὶ λέγουσι τοῖς ὄρεσι
in the rocks of the mountains. And they say to the mountains
crags said

καὶ ταῖς πέτραις, "Πέσετε ἐφ' ἡμᾶς καὶ κρύψατε ἡμᾶς ἀπὸ
and to the rocks, "Fall on us and hide us from *the*
crags,

προσώπου τοῦ καθημένου ἐπὶ τῷ θρόνῳ καὶ ἀπὸ τῆς
face of the *One* sitting on the throne and from the
Him who sits

ὀργῆς τοῦ 'Αρνίου! 17 Ὅτι ἦλθεν ἡ ἡμέρα ἡ μεγάλη
wrath of the Lamb! Because [7]came [1]the [3]day - [2]great
has come

τῆς ὀργῆς αὐτοῦ,[p] καὶ τίς δύναται σταθῆναι?"
- [4]of [6]wrath [5]His, and who is able to stand?"

The Sealed of Israel

7 1 Καὶ μετὰ τοῦτο[a] εἶδον τέσσαρας ἀγγέλους ἑστῶτας ἐπὶ
And after this I saw four angels standing at

τὰς τέσσαρας γωνίας τῆς γῆς, κρατοῦντας τοὺς τέσσαρας
the four corners of the earth, holding the four

ἀνέμους τῆς γῆς, ἵνα μὴ πνέῃ ἄνεμος ἐπὶ τῆς γῆς,
winds of the earth, so that [4]not [3]should [5]blow [1]a [2]wind on the earth,

μήτε ἐπὶ τῆς θαλάσσης, μήτε ἐπὶ τι δένδρον. 2 Καὶ εἶδον
nor on the sea, nor on any tree. And I saw

ἄλλον ἄγγελον ἀναβαίνοντα ἀπὸ ἀνατολῆς ἡλίου, ἔχοντα
another angel coming up from *the* rising of the sun, having
the east,

σφραγῖδα Θεοῦ ζῶντος.
the seal of *the* God ~ living.

Καὶ ἔκραξε φωνῇ μεγάλῃ τοῖς τέσσαρσιν
And he cried out with a voice ~ great to the four
loud

ἀγγέλοις, οἷς ἐδόθη αὐτοῖς ἀδικῆσαι τὴν γῆν καὶ τὴν
angels, to whom it was given to them to harm the earth and the
it had been granted

sackcloth of hair, and the moon
became like blood.
13 And the stars of heaven fell
to the earth, as a fig tree drops
its late figs when it is shaken by
a mighty wind.
14 Then the sky receded as a
scroll when it is rolled up, and
every mountain and island was
moved out of its place.
15 And the kings of the earth,
the great men, the rich men,
the commanders, the mighty
men, every slave and every
free man, hid themselves in the
caves and in the rocks of the
mountains,
16 and said to the mountains
and rocks, "Fall on us and hide
us from the face of Him who
sits on the throne and from the
wrath of the Lamb!
17 "For the great day of His
wrath has come, and who is
able to stand?"
7 After these things I saw
four angels standing at the
four corners of the earth, holding the four winds of the earth,
that the wind should not blow
on the earth, on the sea, or on
any tree.
2 Then I saw another angel
ascending from the east, having
the seal of the living God. And
he cried with a loud voice to the
four angels to whom it was
granted to harm the earth and

---

[n](6:13) TR, NU read βαλλει, *casts.* [o](6:15) TR adds πας, *every.* [p](6:17) NU reads αυτων, *their.*
[a](7:1) TR reads ταυτα, *these (things).*

ζῷον at Rev. 4:6). Mark 1:13 does not mean Jesus was living in direct contact with wild animals but emphasizes the separation from human society.

the sea,
3 saying, "Do not harm the
earth, the sea, or the trees till
we have sealed the servants of
our God on their foreheads."
4 And I heard the number of
those who were sealed. One
hundred *and* forty-four thousand of all the tribes of the children of Israel *were* sealed:

5 of the tribe of Judah twelve thousand *were* sealed;
of the tribe of Reuben twelve thousand *were* sealed;
of the tribe of Gad twelve thousand *were* sealed;
6 of the tribe of Asher twelve thousand *were* sealed;
of the tribe of Naphtali twelve thousand *were* sealed;
of the tribe of Manasseh twelve thousand *were* sealed;
7 of the tribe of Simeon twelve thousand *were* sealed;
of the tribe of Levi twelve thousand *were* sealed;
of the tribe of Issachar twelve thousand *were* sealed;
8 of the tribe of Zebulun twelve thousand *were* sealed;
of the tribe of Joseph twelve thousand *were* sealed;
of the tribe of Benjamin twelve thousand *were* sealed.

9 After these things I looked,
and behold, a great multitude
which no one could number, of
all nations, tribes, peoples, and

θάλασσαν, **3** λέγων, "Μὴ ἀδικήσητε τὴν γῆν, μήτε τὴν
sea, saying, "not ˜ Do harm the earth, nor the

θάλασσαν, μήτε τὰ δένδρα, ἄχρις οὗ σφραγίσωμεν* τοὺς
sea, nor the trees, until - we shall seal the

δούλους τοῦ Θεοῦ ἡμῶν ἐπὶ τῶν μετώπων αὐτῶν." **4** Καὶ
bondservants - of God ˜ our on - foreheads ˜ their." And
slaves

ἤκουσα τὸν ἀριθμὸν τῶν ἐσφραγισμένων, ἑκατὸν καὶ
I heard the number of the *ones* having been sealed, one hundred and
those who were

τεσσεράκοντα τέσσαρες χιλιάδες ἐσφραγισμένων ἐκ πάσης
forty- four thousands having been sealed out of every
thousand

φυλῆς υἱῶν Ἰσραήλ·
tribe of *the* sons of Israel:

5 Ἐκ φυλῆς Ἰούδα δώδεκα χιλιάδες ἐσφραγισμέναι,
Out of *the* tribe of Judah twelve thousands having been sealed,
thousand

Ἐκ φυλῆς Ῥουβὶμ δώδεκα χιλιάδες,[b]
Out of *the* tribe of Reuben twelve thousands,
thousand,

Ἐκ φυλῆς Γὰδ δώδεκα χιλιάδες,
Out of *the* tribe of Gad twelve thousands,
thousand,

6 Ἐκ φυλῆς Ἀσὴρ δώδεκα χιλιάδες,
Out of *the* tribe of Asher twelve thousands,
thousand,

Ἐκ φυλῆς Νεφθαλεὶμ δώδεκα χιλιάδες,
Out of *the* tribe of Naphtali twelve thousands,
thousand,

Ἐκ φυλῆς Μανασσῆ δώδεκα χιλιάδες,
Out of *the* tribe of Manasseh twelve thousands,
thousand,

7 Ἐκ φυλῆς Συμεὼν δώδεκα χιλιάδες,
Out of *the* tribe of Simeon twelve thousands,
thousand,

Ἐκ φυλῆς Λευὶ δώδεκα χιλιάδες,
Out of *the* tribe of Levi twelve thousands,
thousand,

Ἐκ φυλῆς Ἰσαχὰρ δώδεκα χιλιάδες,
Out of *the* tribe of Issachar twelve thousands,
thousand,

8 Ἐκ φυλῆς Ζαβουλὼν δώδεκα χιλιάδες,
Out of *the* tribe of Zebulun twelve thousands,
thousand,

Ἐκ φυλῆς Ἰωσὴφ δώδεκα χιλιάδες,
Out of *the* tribe of Joseph twelve thousands,
thousand,

Ἐκ φυλῆς Βενιαμὶν δώδεκα χιλιάδες ἐσφραγισμέναι.
Out of *the* tribe of Benjamin twelve thousands, having been sealed.
thousand,

A Multitude from the Great Tribulation

9 Μετὰ ταῦτα εἶδον, καὶ ἰδού, ὄχλος πολὺς ὃν
After these *things* I looked, and behold, a crowd ˜ large which
great multitude

ἀριθμῆσαι[c] οὐδεὶς ἐδύνατο, ἐκ παντὸς ἔθνους καὶ φυλῶν
[5]to [6]number [1]no [2]one [3]was [4]able, out of every nation and *from* tribes

---

[b](7:5) TR adds εσφραγισμενοι, *having been sealed,* after each tribe. [c](7:9) NU, TR add αυτον, *it.*

---

*(7:3) σφραγίζω (*sphragizō*). Verb meaning *seal.* As is clear here, this sealing is more like that of a notary public than a sealing of an envelope in that it signifies a mark of identification or authentication. It was commonly used of the "impression" of an official's signet ring made in wax. The

καὶ λαῶν καὶ γλωσσῶν, ἑστῶτας ἐνώπιον τοῦ θρόνου καὶ
and peoples and tongues, standing before the throne and
languages,

ἐνώπιον τοῦ Ἀρνίου, περιβεβλημένους στολὰς λευκάς, καὶ
before the Lamb, having been clothed in long robes ~ white, and
with

φοίνικας ἐν ταῖς χερσὶν αὐτῶν. 10 Καὶ κράζουσι
palm branches in - hands ~ their. And they cry out
cried out

φωνῇ μεγάλῃ, λέγοντες,
with a voice ~ great, saying,
loud,

"Ἡ σωτηρία τῷ Θεῷ ἡμῶν
- "Salvation *belongs* - to God ~ our

Τῷ καθημένῳ ἐπὶ τῷ θρόνῳ,
To the *One* sitting on the throne,

Καὶ τῷ Ἀρνίῳ!"
And to the Lamb!"

11 Καὶ πάντες οἱ ἄγγελοι εἱστήκεισαν κύκλῳ τοῦ θρόνου
And all the angels stood around the throne

καὶ τῶν πρεσβυτέρων καὶ τῶν τεσσάρων ζῴων, καὶ
and the elders and the four living creatures, and

ἔπεσον ἐνώπιον τοῦ θρόνου αὐτοῦ[d] ἐπὶ τὰ πρόσωπα αὐτῶν
they fell down before - throne ~ His on - faces ~ their

καὶ προσεκύνησαν τῷ Θεῷ, 12 λέγοντες,
and they worshiped - God, saying,

"Ἀμήν! Ἡ εὐλογία καὶ ἡ δόξα καὶ ἡ σοφία
"Amen! - Blessing and - glory and - wisdom

Καὶ ἡ εὐχαριστία καὶ ἡ τιμὴ καὶ ἡ δύναμις καὶ ἡ ἰσχὺς
And - thanksgiving and - honor and - power and - might

Τῷ Θεῷ ἡμῶν εἰς τοὺς αἰῶνας τῶν αἰώνων.
- *Belong* to God ~ our to the ages of the ages.
forever and ever.

Ἀμήν."
Amen."
So be it."

13 Καὶ ἀπεκρίθη εἷς ἐκ τῶν πρεσβυτέρων, λέγων μοι,
And [5]answered [1]one [2]of [3]the [4]elders, saying to me,

"Οὗτοι οἱ περιβεβλημένοι τὰς στολὰς τὰς λευκάς,
"These the *ones* having been clothed in the long robes ~ - white,
who are

τίνες εἰσί, καὶ πόθεν ἦλθον?"
who are they, and from where did they come?"

14 Καὶ εἶπον αὐτῷ, "Κύριέ μου,[e] σὺ οἶδας."
And I said to him, "lord ~ My, you know."

Καὶ εἶπέ μοι,
And he said to me,

"Οὗτοί εἰσιν οἱ ἐρχόμενοι ἐκ τῆς θλίψεως τῆς
"These are the *ones* coming out of the tribulation ~ -

μεγάλης,
great,

Καὶ ἔπλυναν τὰς στολὰς αὐτῶν
And they washed - [2]long [3]robes [1]their
have washed

Καὶ ἐλεύκαναν[f] ἐν τῷ αἵματι τοῦ Ἀρνίου.
And they made *them* white in the blood of the Lamb.

15 Διὰ τοῦτό εἰσιν ἐνώπιον τοῦ θρόνου τοῦ Θεοῦ,
On account of this they are before the throne - of God,

tongues, standing before the
throne and before the Lamb,
clothed with white robes, with
palm branches in their hands,
10 and crying out with a loud
voice, saying, "Salvation *be-*
longs to our God who sits on
the throne, and to the Lamb!"
11 All the angels stood around
the throne and the elders and
the four living creatures, and
fell on their faces before the
throne and worshiped God,
12 saying:

"Amen! Blessing and glory
and wisdom,
Thanksgiving and honor
and power and might,
Be to our God forever
and ever.
Amen."

13 Then one of the elders answered, saying to me, "Who
are these arrayed in white
robes, and where did they
come from?"
14 And I said to him, "Sir, you
know." So he said to me,
"These are the ones who come
out of the great tribulation, and
washed their robes and made
them white in the blood of the
Lamb.
15 "Therefore they are before
the throne of God, and serve

[d](7:11) TR, NU omit *αυτου, His.* [e](7:14) TR omits *μου, my.* [f](7:14) TR adds *στολας αυτων, their robes;* NU adds *αυτας, them.*

legal custom led to a variety of specific nuances for the term: protection (as here), secrecy (Rev. 10:4), official security (Matt. 27:66), attestation (John 3:33). The Holy Spirit's indwelling serves to officially identify and certify the believer as God's child (Eph. 1:13; 4:30; 2 Cor. 1:22). Cf. the cognate noun *σφραγίς, seal,* which has the same range of meanings.

Him day and night in His temple. And He who sits on the
throne will dwell among them.
16 "They shall neither hunger
anymore nor thirst anymore;
the sun shall not strike them,
nor any heat;
17 "for the Lamb who is in the
midst of the throne will shepherd them and lead them to living fountains of waters. And
God will wipe away every tear
from their eyes."
8 When He opened the sev-
enth seal, there was si-
lence in heaven for about half an
hour.
2 And I saw the seven angels
who stand before God, and to
them were given seven trumpets.
3 Then another angel, having
a golden censer, came and
stood at the altar. He was given
much incense, that he should
offer *it* with the prayers of all
the saints upon the golden altar
which was before the throne.
4 And the smoke of the incense, with the prayers of the
saints, ascended before God
from the angel's hand.
5 Then the angel took the

Καὶ λατρεύουσιν αὐτῷ ἡμέρας καὶ νυκτὸς ἐν τῷ ναῷ
And they serve Him day and night in - shrine ˜

αὐτοῦ.
His.

Καὶ ὁ καθήμενος ἐπὶ τῷ θρόνῳ σκηνώσει ἐπ'
And the *One* sitting on the throne will dwell over
(dwell over: shelter)

αὐτούς.
them.

16 Οὐ πεινάσουσιν ἔτι,
[3]not [1]They [2]shall hunger *any* longer,

Οὐδὲ διψήσουσιν ἔτι,
Nor shall they thirst *any* longer,

Οὐδ' οὐ μὴ πέσῃ ἐπ' αὐτοὺς ὁ ἥλιος,
Nor not not [1]shall [4]fall [5]on [6]them [2]the [3]sun,
(not not: by any means; fall on: strike)

Οὐδὲ πᾶν καῦμα.
Nor any heat.

17 Ὅτι τὸ Ἀρνίον τὸ ἀνὰ μέσον τοῦ θρόνου
Because the Lamb the *One* in the midst of the throne
(the One: who is)

ποιμαίνει[g] αὐτοὺς
shepherds them

Καὶ ὁδηγεῖ[h] αὐτοὺς ἐπὶ ζωῆς[i] πηγὰς ὑδάτων.
And He leads them to [4]of [5]life [1]springs [2]of [3]waters.

Καὶ ἐξαλείψει ὁ Θεὸς πᾶν δάκρυον ἐκ τῶν
And [2]will [3]wipe [4]away - [1]God every tear from -

ὀφθαλμῶν αὐτῶν."
eyes ˜ their."

Seventh Seal: Prelude to the Seven Trumpets

8 1 Καὶ ὅτε ἤνοιξε τὴν σφραγῖδα τὴν ἑβδόμην, ἐγένετο
And when He opened the seal ˜ - seventh, occurred ˜

σιγὴ ἐν τῷ οὐρανῷ ὡς ἡμιώριον. 2 Καὶ εἶδον τοὺς ἑπτὰ
silence in - heaven *for* about a half hour. And I saw the seven

ἀγγέλους οἳ ἐνώπιον τοῦ Θεοῦ ἑστήκασι, καὶ ἐδόθησαν
angels who [2]before - [3]God [1]stood, and [3]were [4]given

αὐτοῖς ἑπτὰ σάλπιγγες.
[5]to [6]them [1]seven [2]trumpets.

3 Καὶ ἄλλος ἄγγελος ἦλθε καὶ ἐστάθη ἐπὶ τοῦ
And another angel came and stood upon the
(upon: at)

θυσιαστηρίου, ἔχων λιβανωτὸν χρυσοῦν. Καὶ ἐδόθη αὐτῷ
altar, having a censer ˜ golden. And [3]was [4]given [5]to [6]him

θυμιάματα πολλά, ἵνα δώσει ταῖς προσευχαῖς τῶν
[2]incenses [1]many, so that he will give *it* with the prayers of [2]the
(incenses many: much incense; will give: could offer)

ἁγίων πάντων ἐπὶ τὸ θυσιαστήριον τὸ χρυσοῦν τὸ ἐνώπιον
[3]saints [1]all upon the altar ˜ - golden the *one* before
(the one: which is)

τοῦ θρόνου. 4 Καὶ ἀνέβη ὁ καπνὸς τῶν θυμιαμάτων
the throne. And [6]went [7]up [1]the [2]smoke [3]of [4]the [5]incenses
(incenses: incense)

ταῖς προσευχαῖς τῶν ἁγίων ἐκ χειρὸς τοῦ ἀγγέλου
with the prayers of the saints out of *the* hand of the angel

ἐνώπιον τοῦ Θεοῦ. 5 Καὶ εἴληφεν ὁ ἄγγελος τὸν λιβανωτὸν
before - God. And [3]has [4]taken [1]the [2]angel the censer
(has taken: took)

---

[g](7:17) TR, NU read ποιμανει, *will shepherd.*
[h](7:17) TR, NU read οδηγησει, *will guide.*
[i](7:17) TR reads ζωτας, *living.*

καὶ ἐγέμισεν αὐτὸν ἐκ τοῦ πυρὸς τοῦ θυσιαστηρίου καὶ
and filled it from the fire of the altar and
with from

ἔβαλεν εἰς τὴν γῆν. Καὶ ἐγένοντο βρονταὶ καὶ φωναὶ καὶ
he threw *it* to the earth. And *there* occurred thunders and voices and

ἀστραπαὶ καὶ σεισμός.
lightnings and an earthquake.

6 *Καὶ οἱ ἑπτὰ ἄγγελοι οἱ ἔχοντες τὰς ἑπτὰ*
And the seven angels the *ones* having the seven
who had

σάλπιγγας ἡτοίμασαν ἑαυτοὺς ἵνα
trumpets prepared themselves so that
to

σαλπίσωσι.
they might sound the trumpets.
sound

First Trumpet: Vegetation Struck

7 *Καὶ ὁ πρῶτος*[a] *ἐσάλπισε, καὶ ἐγένετο*
And the first *one* sounded *his* trumpet, and *there* occurred

χάλαζα καὶ πῦρ μεμιγμένα ἐν αἵματι, καὶ ἐβλήθη
hail and fire having been mixed with blood, and they were thrown

εἰς τὴν γῆν· καὶ τὸ τρίτον τῆς γῆς κατεκάη[b] *καὶ τὸ*
to the earth; and the third of the earth was burned up and the
a a

τρίτον τῶν δένδρων κατεκάη καὶ πᾶς χόρτος χλωρὸς
third of the trees was burned up and all grass ˜ green

κατεκάη.
was burned up.

Second Trumpet: The Seas Struck

8 *Καὶ ὁ δεύτερος ἄγγελος ἐσάλπισε, καὶ*
And the second angel sounded *his* trumpet, and

ὡς ὄρος μέγα[c] *καιόμενον ἐβλήθη εἰς τὴν*
something like a [3]mountain [1]great [2]burning was thrown into the

θάλασσαν, καὶ ἐγένετο τὸ τρίτον τῆς θαλάσσης αἷμα.
sea, and [6]became [1]the [2]third [3]of [4]the [5]sea blood.
a

9 *Καὶ ἀπέθανε τὸ τρίτον τῶν κτισμάτων ἐν τῇ θαλάσσῃ,*
And [9]died [1]the [2]third [3]of [4]the [5]creatures [6]in [7]the [8]sea,
a

τὰ ἔχοντα ψυχάς. Καὶ τὸ τρίτον τῶν πλοίων διεφθάρη.
the *ones* having lives. And the third of the ships was destroyed.
those which had life. a

Third Trumpet: The Waters Struck

10 *Καὶ ὁ τρίτος ἄγγελος ἐσάλπισε, καὶ ἔπεσεν*
And the third angel sounded *his* trumpet, and [4]fell

ἐκ τοῦ οὐρανοῦ ἀστὴρ μέγας καιόμενος ὡς λαμπάς, καὶ
[5]out [6]of [7]the [8]heaven [1]a [3]star [2]great burning like a torch, and
sky

ἔπεσεν ἐπὶ τὸ τρίτον τῶν ποταμῶν καὶ ἐπὶ τὰς πηγὰς τῶν
it fell on the third of the rivers and on the springs -
a

ὑδάτων. 11 *Καὶ τὸ ὄνομα τοῦ ἀστέρος λέγεται ὁ Ἄψινθος.*
of waters. And the name of the star is called - Wormword.

Καὶ ἐγένετο τὸ τρίτον τῶν ὑδάτων εἰς ἄψινθον, καὶ πολλοὶ
And [6]became [1]the [2]third [3]of [4]the [5]waters into wormwood, and many
turned a

censer, filled it with fire from
the altar, and threw *it* to the
earth. And there were noises,
thunderings, lightnings, and an
earthquake.
6 So the seven angels who
had the seven trumpets prepared themselves to sound.
7 The first angel sounded:
And hail and fire followed, mingled with blood, and they were
thrown to the earth. And a third
of the trees were burned up,
and all green grass was burned
up.
8 Then the second angel
sounded: And *something* like a
great mountain burning with
fire was thrown into the sea,
and a third of the sea became
blood.
9 And a third of the living
creatures in the sea died, and a
third of the ships were destroyed.
10 Then the third angel
sounded: And a great star fell
from heaven, burning like a
torch, and it fell on a third of
the rivers and on the springs of
water.
11 The name of the star is
Wormwood. A third of the waters became wormwood, and

[a](8:7) TR adds *αγγελος*, *angel.* [b](8:7) TR omits *και το τριτον της γης κατεκαη*, *and the third of the earth was burned up.*
[c](8:8) TR, NU add *πυρι*, *with fire.*

many men died from the water,
because it was made bitter.
12 Then the fourth angel
sounded: And a third of the sun
was struck, a third of the moon,
and a third of the stars, so that
a third of them were darkened.
A third of the day did not shine,
and likewise the night.
13 And I looked, and I heard
an angel flying through the
midst of heaven, saying with a
loud voice, "Woe, woe, woe to
the inhabitants of the earth, because of the remaining blasts of
the trumpet of the three angels
who are about to sound!"
9 Then the fifth angel
sounded: And I saw a star
fallen from heaven to the earth.
To him was given the key to
the bottomless pit.
2 And he opened the bottomless pit, and smoke arose out of
the pit like the smoke of a great
furnace. So the sun and the air
were darkened because of the
smoke of the pit.
3 Then out of the smoke locusts came upon the earth. And
to them was given power, as
the scorpions of the earth have
power.
4 They were commanded not

τῶν ἀνθρώπων ἀπέθανον ἐκ τῶν ὑδάτων ὅτι
of the men died from the waters because

ἐπικράνθησαν.
they were made bitter.

Fourth Trumpet: The Heavens Struck

12 Καὶ ὁ τέταρτος ἄγγελος ἐσάλπισε, καὶ
And the fourth angel sounded *his* trumpet, and

ἐπλήγη τὸ τρίτον τοῦ ἡλίου καὶ τὸ τρίτον τῆς σελήνης
[6]was [7]struck [1]the [2]third [3]of [4]the [5]sun and the third of the moon
a a

καὶ τὸ τρίτον τῶν ἀστέρων, ἵνα σκοτισθῇ τὸ τρίτον
and the third of the stars, so that [5]was [6]darkened [1]the [2]third
a a

αὐτῶν καὶ τὸ τρίτον αὐτῆς μὴ φάνῃ ἡ ἡμέρα,
[3]of [4]them and [6]*for* [7]the [8]third [9]of [10]it [4]not [3]should [5]shine [1]the [2]day,
a

καὶ ἡ νὺξ ὁμοίως.
and the night likewise.

13 Καὶ εἶδον, καὶ ἤκουσα ἑνὸς ἀετοῦ[d] πετομένου ἐν
And I saw, and I heard one eagle flying in
an

μεσουρανήματι, λέγοντος φωνῇ μεγάλῃ, "Οὐαί, οὐαί,
midheaven, saying with a voice ~ great, "Alas, alas,
loud,

οὐαὶ τοὺς κατοικοῦντας ἐπὶ τῆς γῆς, ἐκ τῶν λοιπῶν
alas *for* the *ones* dwelling on the earth, from the remaining
those who dwell

φωνῶν τῆς σάλπιγγος τῶν τριῶν ἀγγέλων τῶν μελλόντων
sounds of the trumpet of the three angels the *ones* being about
blasts who are

σαλπίζειν!"
to sound *their* trumpets!"

The Fifth Trumpet: The Locusts from the Abyss

9 **1** Καὶ ὁ πέμπτος ἄγγελος ἐσάλπισε, καὶ εἶδον
And the fifth angel sounded *his* trumpet, and I saw

ἀστέρα ἐκ τοῦ οὐρανοῦ πεπτωκότα εἰς τὴν γῆν. Καὶ
a star [3]out [4]of [5]the [6]heaven [1]having [2]fallen to the earth. And
sky

ἐδόθη αὐτῷ ἡ κλεὶς τοῦ φρέατος τῆς ἀβύσσου.*
[9]was [10]given [11]to [12]Him [1]the [2]key [3]of [4]the [5]shaft [6]of [7]the [8]abyss.
bottomless pit.

2 Καὶ ἤνοιξε τὸ φρέαρ τῆς ἀβύσσου, καὶ ἀνέβη καπνὸς
And he opened the shaft of the abyss, and [2]went [3]up [1]smoke
bottomless pit,

ἐκ τοῦ φρέατος ὡς καπνὸς καμίνου καιομένης.[a] Καὶ
out of the shaft like *the* smoke of a furnace ~ burning. And

ἐσκοτίσθη ὁ ἥλιος καὶ ὁ ἀὴρ ἐκ τοῦ καπνοῦ τοῦ
[3]was [4]darkened [1]the [2]sun and the air from the smoke of the

φρέατος. **3** Καὶ ἐκ τοῦ καπνοῦ ἐξῆλθον ἀκρίδες εἰς τὴν
shaft. And out of the smoke came forth locusts to the

γῆν. Καὶ ἐδόθη αὐταῖς ἐξουσία, ὡς ἔχουσιν ἐξουσίαν οἱ
earth. And [2]was [3]given [4]to [5]them [1]power, as [5]have [6]power -

σκορπίοι τῆς γῆς. **4** Καὶ ἐρρέθη αὐταῖς ἵνα μὴ
[1]scorpions [2]of [3]the [4]earth. And it was said to them that [3]not
they were told

---

[d](**8:13**) Some mss., TR read αγγελος, *angel.*
[a](**9:2**) TR, NU read μεγαλης, *great.*

*(**9:1**) ἄβυσσος *(abyssos).* Noun meaning *depths, underworld.* It is derived from the α- intensive prefix and the Ionic form of βάθος, *depth,* thus meaning a *bottomless pit.* The word is used to designate the ocean deep (Gen. 1:2 LXX) and the realm of the dead (Rom. 10:7, paraphrasing Deut. 30:12 LXX). Most often in the NT it designates the dwelling place of evil supernatural beings, such as demons (here in Rev. 9:1; cf. Luke 8:31), Satan (Rev. 20:3), the "beast" (Rev. 11:7), and Abaddon who rules over the underworld (Rev. 9:11). Cf. the English cognate *abyss.*

ἀδικήσωσι τὸν χόρτον τῆς γῆς οὐδὲ πᾶν χλωρὸν οὐδὲ
[1]they [2]should harm the grass of the earth nor any green *thing* nor
plant

πᾶν δένδρον, εἰ μὴ τοὺς ἀνθρώπους[b] οἵτινες οὐκ ἔχουσι
any tree, if not the men who not ˜ do have
except

τὴν σφραγῖδα τοῦ Θεοῦ ἐπὶ τῶν μετώπων αὐτῶν. 5 Καὶ
the seal - of God on - foreheads ˜ their. And

ἐδόθη αὐταῖς ἵνα μὴ ἀποκτείνωσιν αὐτούς, ἀλλ' ἵνα
it was given to them that [3]not [1]they [2]should kill them, but that
they were not granted to kill

βασανισθῶσι μῆνας πέντε. Καὶ ὁ βασανισμὸς αὐτῶν
they should torment *them* months ˜ five. And - torment ˜ their

ὡς βασανισμὸς σκορπίου ὅταν παίσῃ ἄνθρωπον.
was like *the* torment of a scorpion whenever it strikes a man.

6 Καὶ ἐν ταῖς ἡμέραις ἐκείναις ζητήσουσιν οἱ ἄνθρωποι τὸν
And in - days ˜ those [2]will [3]seek - [1]men -

θάνατον καὶ οὐ μὴ εὑρήσουσιν αὐτόν· καὶ ἐπιθυμήσουσιν
death and not not will they find it; and they will desire
by no means be longing

ἀποθανεῖν, καὶ φεύξεται[c] ἀπ' αὐτῶν ὁ θάνατος. 7 Καὶ τὰ
to die, and [2]will [3]flee [4]from [5]them - [1]death. And the

ὁμοιώματα τῶν ἀκρίδων ὅμοια ἵπποις ἡτοιμασμένοις
appearances of the locusts *was* similar to horses having been prepared
shape

εἰς πόλεμον, καὶ ἐπὶ τὰς κεφαλὰς αὐτῶν ὡς
for battle, and on - heads ˜ their *were something* like

στέφανοι χρυσοῖ,[d] καὶ τὰ πρόσωπα αὐτῶν ὡς πρόσωπα
crowns ˜ golden, and - faces ˜ their *were* like faces

ἀνθρώπων. 8 Καὶ εἶχον τρίχας ὡς τρίχας γυναικῶν, καὶ οἱ
of men. And they had hairs like *the* hairs of women, and -
hair hair

ὀδόντες αὐτῶν ὡς λεόντων ἦσαν. 9 Καὶ εἶχον θώρακας
teeth ˜ their [2]like [3]*teeth* [4]of [5]lions [1]were. And they had breastplates

ὡς θώρακας σιδηροῦς, καὶ ἡ φωνὴ τῶν πτερύγων αὐτῶν
like breastplates ˜ iron, and the sound - of wings ˜ their

ὡς φωνὴ ἁρμάτων ἵππων πολλῶν τρεχόντων εἰς
was like *the* sound of chariots of horses ˜ many running into
with rushing

πόλεμον. 10 Καὶ ἔχουσιν οὐρὰς ὁμοίας σκορπίοις, καὶ κέντρα.
battle. And they have tails like scorpions, and stings.
had

Καὶ[e] ἐν ταῖς οὐραῖς αὐτῶν ἐξουσίαν ἔχουσι[f] τοῦ ἀδικῆσαι
And in - tails ˜ their [3]power [1]they [2]have - to harm

τοὺς ἀνθρώπους μῆνας πέντε, 11 ἔχουσαι βασιλέα ἐπ' αὐτῶν
- men months ˜ five, having *as* a king over them

ἄγγελον τῆς ἀβύσσου· ὄνομα αὐτῷ Ἑβραϊστὶ Ἀββαδών,
the angel of the abyss; *the* name to him in Hebrew *is* Abbadon,
bottomless pit; whose name

ἐν δὲ τῇ Ἑλληνικῇ ὄνομα ἔχει Ἀπολλύων.
in ˜ but - Greek [3]*the* [4]name [1]he [2]has [5]Apollyon.

12 Ἡ οὐαὶ ἡ μία ἀπῆλθεν. Ἰδού, ἔρχεται ἔτι δύο οὐαὶ
The woe ˜ - one passed away. Behold, [4]is [5]coming [1]yet [2]two [3]woes
first is past. are

μετὰ ταῦτα.
after these *things*.

to harm the grass of the earth, or any green thing, or any tree, but only those men who do not have the seal of God on their foreheads.
5 And they were not given *authority* to kill them, but to torment them *for* five months. Their torment *was* like the torment of a scorpion when it strikes a man.
6 In those days men will seek death and will not find it; they will desire to die, and death will flee from them.
7 The shape of the locusts was like horses prepared for battle. On their heads were crowns of something like gold, and their faces *were* like the faces of men.
8 They had hair like women's hair, and their teeth were like lions' *teeth.*
9 And they had breastplates like breastplates of iron, and the sound of their wings *was* like the sound of chariots with many horses running into battle.
10 They had tails like scorpions, and there were stings in their tails. Their power *was* to hurt men five months.
11 And they had as king over them the angel of the bottomless pit, whose name in Hebrew *is* Abaddon, but in Greek he has the name Apollyon.
12 One woe is past. Behold, still two more woes are coming after these things.

---

[b](**9:4**) TR adds μονους, *only.*
[c](**9:6**) NU reads φευγει, *flees.* [d](**9:7**) TR, NU read ομοιοι χρυσω, *like gold.*
[e](**9:10**) TR reads ην, *was.*
[f](**9:10**) TR, NU omit εχουσι, *they have.*

13 Then the sixth angel
sounded: And I heard a voice
from the four horns of the
golden altar which is before God,
14 saying to the sixth angel
who had the trumpet, "Release
the four angels who are bound
at the great river Euphrates."
15 So the four angels, who
had been prepared for the hour
and day and month and year,
were released to kill a third of
mankind.
16 Now the number of the
army of the horsemen *was* two
hundred million; I heard the
number of them.
17 And thus I saw the horses
in the vision: those who sat on
them had breastplates of fiery
red, hyacinth blue, and sulfur
yellow; and the heads of the
horses *were* like the heads of lions; and out of their mouths
came fire, smoke, and brimstone.
18 By these three *plagues* a
third of mankind was killed—by
the fire and the smoke and the
brimstone which came out of
their mouths.
19 For their power is in their
mouth and in their tails; for
their tails *are* like serpents,
having heads; and with them
they do harm.
20 But the rest of mankind,
who were not killed by these
plagues, did not repent of the

Sixth Trumpet: The Angels from the Euphrates

13 Καὶ ὁ ἕκτος ἄγγελος ἐσάλπισε, καὶ ἤκουσα
And the sixth angel sounded *his* trumpet, and I heard

φωνὴν μίαν ἐκ τῶν τεσσάρων κεράτων τοῦ θυσιαστηρίου
voice ˜ one from the four horns of the altar ˜
a

τοῦ χρυσοῦ τοῦ ἐνώπιον τοῦ Θεοῦ, **14** λέγοντος τῷ ἕκτῳ
- golden the *one* before - God, saying to the sixth
which is

ἀγγέλῳ, ὁ ἔχων τὴν σάλπιγγα, "Λῦσον τοὺς τέσσαρας
angel, the *one* having the trumpet, "Loose the four
he who had "Release

ἀγγέλους τοὺς δεδεμένους ἐπὶ τῷ ποταμῷ τῷ μεγάλῳ
angels the *ones* having been tied up at the river ˜ - great
who are

Εὐφράτῃ." **15** Καὶ ἐλύθησαν οἱ τέσσαρες ἄγγελοι οἱ
Euphrates." And [4]were [5]loosed [1]the [2]four [3]angels the *ones*
released who

ἡτοιμασμένοι εἰς τὴν ὥραν καὶ εἰς τὴν ἡμέραν καὶ μῆνα
having been prepared for the hour and for the day and month
had

καὶ ἐνιαυτόν, ἵνα ἀποκτείνωσι τὸ τρίτον τῶν ἀνθρώπων.
and year, so that they might kill the third - of men.
a

16 Καὶ ὁ ἀριθμὸς τῶν στρατευμάτων τοῦ ἵππου μυριάδες[g]
And the number of the troops of the horse *was* myriads
cavalry was countless

μυριάδων· ἤκουσα τὸν ἀριθμὸν αὐτῶν. **17** Καὶ οὕτως εἶδον τοὺς
of myriads; I heard the number of them. And thus I saw the
thousands;

ἵππους ἐν τῇ ὁράσει καὶ τοὺς καθημένους ἐπ᾽ αὐτῶν,
horses in the vision and the *ones* sitting on them,
those who rode

ἔχοντας θώρακας πυρίνους καὶ ὑακινθίνους καὶ θειώδεις.
having breastplates *of* fiery *red* and hyacinth *blue* and sulfurous *yellow.*

Καὶ αἱ κεφαλαὶ τῶν ἵππων ὡς κεφαλαὶ λεόντων, καὶ
And the heads of the horses *were* like heads of lions, and

ἐκ τῶν στομάτων αὐτῶν ἐκπορεύεται πῦρ καὶ καπνὸς καὶ
out of - mouths ˜ their proceed fire and smoke and

θεῖον. **18** Ὑπὸ τῶν τριῶν πληγῶν τούτων ἀπεκτάνθησαν τὸ
sulfur. By - [2]three [3]plagues [1]these [8]were [9]killed [4]the
brimstone. a

τρίτον τῶν ἀνθρώπων, ἀπὸ τοῦ πυρὸς καὶ τοῦ καπνοῦ καὶ τοῦ
[5]third [6]of [7]men, from the fire and the smoke and the
humankind,

θείου τοῦ ἐκπορευομένου ἐκ τῶν στομάτων αὐτῶν. **19** Ἡ
sulfur - proceeding out of - mouths ˜ their. the ˜

γὰρ ἐξουσία τῶν ἵππων[h] ἐν τῷ στόματι αὐτῶν ἐστι καὶ ἐν
For power of the horses [2]in - [4]mouth [3]their [1]is and in

ταῖς οὐραῖς αὐτῶν· αἱ γὰρ οὐραὶ αὐτῶν ὅμοιαι ὄφεων ἔχουσαι
- tails ˜ their; - for tails ˜ their *are* like serpents having

κεφαλάς, καὶ ἐν αὐταῖς ἀδικοῦσι.
heads, and with them they do harm.

20 Καὶ οἱ λοιποὶ τῶν ἀνθρώπων, οἳ οὐκ
And the rest - of men, those who not ˜
humankind,

ἀπεκτάνθησαν ἐν ταῖς πληγαῖς ταύταις, οὐ μετενόησαν ἐκ
were killed by - plagues ˜ these, not ˜ did repent from

---

g(**9:16**) TR adds δυο, *two;* NU reads δισμυριαδες, *a double myriad* (20,000), which times the myriad (10,000) would be two hundred million.

h(**9:19**) TR reads Αι γαρ εξουσιαι αυτων, *for their powers (are).*

τῶν ἔργων τῶν χειρῶν αὐτῶν, ἵνα μὴ προσκυνήσωσι τὰ
the works - of hands ˜ their, that [3]not [1]they [2]should worship -

δαιμόνια, καὶ τὰ εἴδωλα τὰ χρυσᾶ καὶ τὰ ἀργυρᾶ καὶ τὰ
demons, and - idols - of gold and - of silver and -

χαλκᾶ καὶ τὰ λίθινα καὶ τὰ ξύλινα, ἃ οὔτε βλέπειν
of bronze and - of stone and - of wood, which neither [3]to [4]see

δύναται οὔτε ἀκούειν οὔτε περιπατεῖν· **21** καὶ οὐ
[1]are [2]able nor to hear nor to walk; and [3]not

μετενόησαν ἐκ τῶν φόνων αὐτῶν οὔτε ἐκ τῶν φαρμάκων[i]*
[1]they [2]did repent of - murders ˜ their nor of - drugs ˜

αὐτῶν οὔτε ἐκ τῆς πορνείας αὐτῶν οὔτε ἐκ τῶν κλεμμάτων
their nor of - fornication ˜ their nor of - thefts ˜

αὐτῶν.
their.

The Mighty Angel with the Scroll

10 **1** Καὶ εἶδον[a] ἄγγελον ἰσχυρὸν καταβαίνοντα ἐκ τοῦ
And I saw a(n) angel ˜ strong coming down out of -
from the

οὐρανοῦ, περιβεβλημένον νεφέλην, καὶ ἡ ἶρις ἐπὶ τῆς
heaven, having been clothed with a cloud, and the rainbow on -
sky,

κεφαλῆς αὐτοῦ, καὶ τὸ πρόσωπον αὐτοῦ ὡς ὁ ἥλιος, καὶ οἱ
head ˜ his, and - face ˜ his like the sun, and -

πόδες αὐτοῦ ὡς στύλοι πυρός, **2** καὶ ἔχων ἐν τῇ χειρὶ αὐτοῦ
feet ˜ his like pillars of fire, and having in - hand ˜ his

βιβλίον ἀνεῳγμένον. Καὶ ἔθηκε τὸν πόδα αὐτοῦ τὸν δεξιὸν
a scroll having been opened. And he put - [3]foot [1]his - [2]right

ἐπὶ τῆς θαλάσσης, τὸν δὲ εὐώνυμον ἐπὶ τῆς γῆς, **3** καὶ
on the sea, the ˜ but left *one* on the earth, and

ἔκραξε φωνῇ μεγάλῃ ὥσπερ λέων μυκᾶται. Καὶ ὅτε
he cried out with a voice ˜ great just like a lion roars. And when
loud

ἔκραξεν, ἐλάλησαν αἱ ἑπτὰ βρονταὶ τὰς ἑαυτῶν φωνάς.
he cried out, [4]spoke [1]the [2]seven [3]thunders - their own voices.
uttered

4 Καὶ ὅτε ἐλάλησαν αἱ ἑπτὰ βρονταί,[b] ἔμελλον γράφειν.
And when [4]spoke [1]the [2]seven [3]thunders, I was about to write.

Καὶ ἤκουσα φωνὴν ἐκ τοῦ οὐρανοῦ, λέγουσαν,[c]
And I heard a voice out of - heaven, saying,
from the sky,

"Σφράγισον ἃ ἐλάλησαν αἱ ἑπτὰ βρονταί, καὶ μὴ
"Seal up *the things* which [4]spoke [1]the [2]seven [3]thunders, and [2]not
uttered

αὐτὰ γράψῃς." **5** Καὶ ὁ ἄγγελος ὃν εἶδον ἑστῶτα ἐπὶ τῆς
[4]them [1]do [3]write." And the angel whom I saw standing on the

θαλάσσης καὶ ἐπὶ τῆς γῆς ἦρε τὴν χεῖρα αὐτοῦ τὴν δεξιὰν[d]
sea and on the earth raised - [3]hand [1]his - [2]right
land

εἰς τὸν οὐρανὸν **6** καὶ ὤμοσε τῷ ζῶντι εἰς τοὺς αἰῶνας
to - heaven and swore by the *One* living to the ages
the sky Him who lives forever and ever,

τῶν αἰώνων, ὃς ἔκτισε τὸν οὐρανὸν καὶ τὰ ἐν αὐτῷ, καὶ
of the ages, who created the heaven and the *things* in it, and

τὴν γῆν καὶ τὰ ἐν αὐτῇ, καὶ τὴν θάλασσαν καὶ τὰ
the earth and the *things* in it, and the sea and the *things*

ἐν αὐτῇ, ὅτι χρόνος οὐκέτι ἔσται· **7** ἀλλ' ἐν ταῖς
in it, because time no longer shall be; but in the
there shall be no more delay;

works of their hands, that they should not worship demons, and idols of gold, silver, brass, stone, and wood, which can neither see nor hear nor walk.
21 And they did not repent of their murders or their sorceries or their sexual immorality or their thefts.

10 I saw still another mighty angel coming down from heaven, clothed with a cloud. And a rainbow *was* on his head, his face *was* like the sun, and his feet like pillars of fire.
2 He had a little book open in his hand. And he set his right foot on the sea and *his* left *foot* on the land,
3 and cried with a loud voice, as *when* a lion roars. When he cried out, seven thunders uttered their voices.
4 Now when the seven thunders uttered their voices, I was about to write; but I heard a voice from heaven saying to me, "Seal up the things which the seven thunders uttered, and do not write them."
5 The angel whom I saw standing on the sea and on the land raised up his hand to heaven
6 and swore by Him who lives forever and ever, who created heaven and the things that are in it, the earth and the things that are in it, and the sea and the things that are in it, that there should be delay no longer,
7 but in the days of the

---

[i](9:21) TR reads *φαρμακειων, sorceries.* [a](10:1) TR, NU add *αλλον, another.* [b](10:4) TR adds *τας φωνας εαυτων, their own voices.* [c](10:4) TR adds *μοι, to me.* [d](10:5) TR omits *την δεξιαν, the right.*

***(9:21)** *φαρμακεία (pharmakeia).* Noun meaning *sorcery, magic, witchcraft.* The word is derived from the noun *φάρμακον* (as here), which ranges in meaning from *poison* or *magic potion* to *medicine, drug* (this latter sense is the source of English *pharmacy*). It is distinguished from the near synonym *μαγεία, magic,* in that *φαρμακεία* emphasizes the mixing and use of such potions, especially with incantations and charms in the practice of witchcraft. Cf. the cognate noun *φαρ-*

sounding of the seventh angel,
when he is about to sound, the
mystery of God would be finished, as He declared to His
servants the prophets.
8 Then the voice which I
heard from heaven spoke to me
again and said, "Go, take the
little book which is open in the
hand of the angel who stands on
the sea and on the earth."
9 So I went to the angel and
said to him, "Give me the little
book." And he said to me,
"Take and eat it; and it will
make your stomach bitter, but
it will be as sweet as honey in
your mouth."
10 Then I took the little book
out of the angel's hand and ate
it, and it was as sweet as honey
in my mouth. But when I had
eaten it, my stomach became
bitter.
11 And he said to me, "You
must prophesy again about
many peoples, nations,
tongues, and kings."
11 Then I was given a
reed like a measuring
rod. And the angel stood, saying, "Rise and measure the
temple of God, the altar, and
those who worship there.
2 "But leave out the court
which is outside the temple,

ἡμέραις τῆς φωνῆς τοῦ ἑβδόμου ἀγγέλου, ὅταν μέλλῃ
days of the voice of the seventh angel, whenever he is about

σαλπίζειν, καὶ ἐτελέσθη[e] τὸ μυστήριον τοῦ Θεοῦ, ὡς
to sound *his* trumpet, and [5]is [6]finished [1]the [2]mystery - [3]of [4]God, as

εὐηγγέλισε τοὺς δούλους αὐτοῦ τοὺς προφήτας.
He told the good news - *to* bondservants ~ His the prophets.
slaves

John Consumes the Scroll

8 Καὶ ἡ φωνὴ ἣν ἤκουσα ἐκ τοῦ οὐρανοῦ, πάλιν
And the voice which I heard out of - heaven, again
from the sky,

λαλοῦσα μετ' ἐμοῦ καὶ λέγουσα, "Ὕπαγε, λάβε τὸ
was speaking with me and saying, "Go, take the

βιβλιδάριον τὸ ἀνεῳγμένον ἐν τῇ χειρὶ τοῦ ἀγγέλου
little scroll the *one* having been opened in the hand of the angel
which was open

τοῦ ἑστῶτος ἐπὶ τῆς θαλάσσης καὶ ἐπὶ τῆς γῆς." **9** Καὶ
- standing on the sea and on the earth." And
land."

ἀπῆλθον πρὸς τὸν ἄγγελον, λέγων αὐτῷ δοῦναί[f] μοι τὸ
I went out to the angel, saying to him to give to me the
telling him

βιβλιδάριον.
little scroll.

Καὶ λέγει μοι, "Λάβε καὶ κατάφαγε αὐτό· καὶ
And he says to me, "Take and eat up ~ it; and
said devour it;

πικρανεῖ σου τὴν κοιλίαν, ἀλλ' ἐν τῷ στόματί σου
it will make [3]bitter [1]your - [2]belly, but in - mouth ~ your

ἔσται γλυκὺ ὡς μέλι." **10** Καὶ ἔλαβον τὸ βιβλίον ἐκ τῆς
it will be *as* sweet as honey." And I took the scroll out of the

χειρὸς τοῦ ἀγγέλου καὶ κατέφαγον αὐτό, καὶ ἦν ἐν τῷ
hand of the angel and ate up ~ it, and it was in -
devoured it,

στόματί μου ὡς μέλι γλυκύ. Καὶ ὅτε ἔφαγον αὐτό,
mouth ~ my [2]as [3]honey [1]sweet. And when I ate it,

ἐπικράνθη ἡ κοιλία μου.
[3]was [4]made [5]bitter - [2]belly [1]my.

11 Καὶ λέγουσί[g] μοι, "Δεῖ σε πάλιν
And they say to me, "It is necessary *for* you again
said "You must

προφητεῦσαι ἐπὶ λαοῖς καὶ ἐπὶ ἔθνεσι καὶ γλώσσαις καὶ
to prophesy over [2]peoples [3]and [4]over [5]nations [6]and [7]tongues [8]and
prophesy languages

βασιλεῦσι πολλοῖς."
[9]kings [1]many."

God Empowers His Two Witnesses

11 **1** Καὶ ἐδόθη μοι κάλαμος ὅμοιος ῥάβδῳ, λέγων
And [3]was [4]given [5]to [6]me [1]a [2]reed like a rod, saying

"Ἔγειρε καὶ μέτρησον τὸν ναὸν τοῦ Θεοῦ καὶ τὸ
"Rise and measure the shrine - of God and the

θυσιαστήριον καὶ τοὺς προσκυνοῦντας ἐν αὐτῷ. **2** Καὶ τὴν
altar and the *ones* worshiping in it. And the
those who worship But

αὐλὴν τὴν ἔξωθεν τοῦ ναοῦ ἔκβαλε ἔξω, καὶ μὴ αὐτὴν
court ~ - outer of the shrine leave out, and [2]not [4]it

---

[e](10:7) TR reads τελεσθη, *would be finished.*
[f](10:9) TR reads δος, *give.*
[g](10:11) TR reads λεγει, *he says.*

μακεύς (or φάρμακος), *sorcerer, magician* (Rev. 21:8; 22:15). See μάγος, *wise man,* at Acts 13:8.

μετρήσῃς, ὅτι ἐδόθη τοῖς ἔθνεσι. Καὶ τὴν πόλιν
[1]Do [3]measure, because it was given to the nations. And [4]the [6]city
has been granted

τὴν ἁγίαν* πατήσουσι μῆνας τεσσαράκοντα καὶ δύο.
- [5]holy [1]they [2]will [3]trample [10]months [7]forty [8]and [9]two.

3 Καὶ δώσω τοῖς δυσὶ μάρτυσί μου, καὶ προφητεύσουσιν
And I will give - to [2]two [3]witnesses [1]My, and they will prophesy
grant that

ἡμέρας χιλίας διακοσίας ἑξήκοντα περιβεβλημένοι
[6]days [1]a [2]thousand [3]two [4]hundred [5]sixty having been clothed in

σάκκους."
sackcloth."

4 Οὗτοί εἰσιν αἱ δύο ἐλαῖαι καὶ αἱ δύο λυχνίαι αἱ
These are the two olive trees and the two lampstands the *ones*
which

ἐνώπιον τοῦ Κυρίου[a] τῆς γῆς ἑστῶτες. 5 Καὶ εἴ τις
[3]before [4]the [5]Lord [6]of [7]the [8]earth [1]*are* [2]standing. And if anyone

αὐτοὺς θέλει ἀδικῆσαι, πῦρ ἐκπορεύεται ἐκ τοῦ στόματος
[4]them [1]wants [2]to [3]harm, fire proceeds out of - mouth ˜

αὐτῶν καὶ κατεσθίει τοὺς ἐχθροὺς αὐτῶν. Καὶ εἴ τις θέλει
their and eats up - enemies ˜ their. And if anyone wants
devours

αὐτοὺς ἀδικῆσαι, οὕτως δεῖ αὐτὸν ἀποκτανθῆναι.
[3]them [1]to [2]harm, in this way it is necessary *for* him to be killed.
he must

6 Οὗτοι ἔχουσι τὸν οὐρανὸν ἐξουσίαν κλεῖσαι, ἵνα μὴ
These *men* have - [5]heaven [1]power [2]to [3]shut [4]up, so that [3]not
the sky no

ὑετὸς βρέχῃ τὰς ἡμέρας τῆς προφητείας αὐτῶν· καὶ
[5]a [6]rain [1]it [2]does [4]rain *during* the days of prophecy ˜ their; and
rain falls

ἐξουσίαν ἔχουσιν ἐπὶ τῶν ὑδάτων στρέφειν αὐτὰ εἰς αἷμα,
[3]authority [1]they [2]have over the waters to turn them into blood,

καὶ πατάξαι τὴν γῆν ὁσάκις ἐὰν θελήσωσιν ἐν πάσῃ
and to strike the earth as often as - they may want with every

πληγῇ.
plague.

The Beast Kills the Witnesses

7 Καὶ ὅταν τελέσωσι τὴν μαρτυρίαν αὐτῶν, τὸ
And whenever they may finish - testimony ˜ their, the

Θηρίον τὸ ἀναβαῖνον ἐκ τῆς ἀβύσσου ποιήσει μετ'
Beast the *one* going up out of the abyss will make [2]with
who ascends bottomless pit

αὐτῶν πόλεμον καὶ νικήσει αὐτοὺς καὶ ἀποκτενεῖ αὐτούς.
[3]them [1]war and will overcome them and will kill them.
conquer

8 Καὶ τὸ πτῶμα[b] αὐτῶν ἐπὶ τῆς πλατείας τῆς πόλεως
And - corpse ˜ their *will lie* on the street of the city ˜

τῆς μεγάλης ἥτις καλεῖται πνευματικῶς Σόδομα καὶ Αἴγυπτος,
- great which is called spiritually Sodom and Egypt,
figuratively

ὅπου καὶ ὁ Κύριος αὐτῶν[c] ἐσταυρώθη.
where also - Lord ˜ their was crucified.

9 Καὶ βλέπουσιν[d] ἐκ τῶν λαῶν καὶ φυλῶν καὶ
And [11]see [1]*some* [2]of [3]the [4]peoples [5]and [6]tribes [7]and
saw

and do not measure it, for it has been given to the Gentiles. And they will tread the holy city underfoot *for* forty-two months.
3 "And I will give *power* to my two witnesses, and they will prophesy one thousand two hundred and sixty days, clothed in sackcloth."
4 These are the two olive trees and the two lampstands standing before the God of the earth.
5 And if anyone wants to harm them, fire proceeds from their mouth and devours their enemies. And if anyone wants to harm them, he must be killed in this manner.
6 These have power to shut heaven, so that no rain falls in the days of their prophecy; and they have power over waters to turn them to blood, and to strike the earth with all plagues, as often as they desire.
7 When they finish their testimony, the beast that ascends out of the bottomless pit will make war against them, overcome them, and kill them.
8 And their dead bodies *will lie* in the street of the great city which spiritually is called Sodom and Egypt, where also our Lord was crucified.
9 Then *those* from the peoples, tribes, tongues, and na-

---

[a](**11:4**) TR reads Θεου, *God.*
[b](**11:8**) TR reads τα πτωματα, *(their) corpses.*
[c](**11:8**) TR reads ημων, *our.*
[d](**11:9**) TR reads βλεψουσιν, *shall see.*

***(11:2)** ἅγιος *(hagios).* Adjective meaning *holy, sacred.* The fundamental idea is *separation,* and thus to be *consecrated* and *dedicated to God* and to His service. It may describe both things (the "holy city" here; the temple as the "holy place," Matt. 24:15) or people. Christians are to be dedicated to God and thus *holy* (1 Pet. 1:16). Describing deity, it is used of the "Holy Spirit" (Matt. 1:18), "Holy Father" (John 17:11), and of the "holy Servant Jesus" (Acts 4:27). The word also occurs as a noun. In the masculine singular it designates God (1 John 2:20) or Christ (Mark 1:24) as *the Holy One.* The plural ἅγιοι is used for Christians as *saints* (Phil. 1:1). The neuter form τὸ ἅγιον is used of the *sanctuary* (Heb. 9:1) and of *sacrifi-*

tions will see their dead bodies
three-and-a-half days, and not
allow their dead bodies to be
put into graves.
10 And those who dwell on
the earth will rejoice over
them, make merry, and send
gifts to one another, because
these two prophets tormented
those who dwell on the earth.
11 Now after the three-and-a-
half days the breath of life from
God entered them, and they
stood on their feet, and great
fear fell on those who saw
them.
12 And they heard a loud
voice from heaven saying to
them, "Come up here." And
they ascended to heaven in a
cloud, and their enemies saw
them.
13 In the same hour there was
a great earthquake, and a tenth
of the city fell. In the earthquake seven thousand people
were killed, and the rest were
afraid and gave glory to the God
of heaven.
14 The second woe is past.
Behold, the third woe is coming
quickly.
15 Then the seventh angel
sounded: And there were loud

γλωσσῶν καὶ ἐθνῶν τὸ πτῶμα[e] αὐτῶν ἡμέρας τρεῖς
[8]tongues [9]and [10]nations - corpse ˜ their [5]days [1]three [2]*and*
languages

ἥμισυ, καὶ τὰ πτώματα αὐτῶν οὐκ ἀφήσουσι[f] τεθῆναι εἰς
[3]one [4]half, and - [6]corpses [5]their [3]not [1]they [2]will [4]allow to be put into

μνῆμα.[g] 10 Καὶ οἱ κατοικοῦντες ἐπὶ τῆς γῆς χαίρουσιν[h]
a tomb. And the *ones* dwelling on the earth rejoice
those who dwell

ἐπ' αὐτοῖς καὶ εὐφρανθήσονται[i] καὶ δῶρα δώσουσιν[j]
over them and they will be glad and [4]gifts [1]they [2]will [3]give

ἀλλήλοις, ὅτι οὗτοι οἱ δύο προφῆται ἐβασάνισαν τοὺς
to one another, because these - two prophets tormented the *ones*
those

κατοικοῦντας ἐπὶ τῆς γῆς.
dwelling on the earth.
who dwell

The Witnesses Are Resurrected

11 Καὶ μετὰ τὰς τρεῖς ἡμέρας καὶ ἥμισυ, πνεῦμα ζωῆς
And after the three [4]days [1]and [2]one [3]half, a breath of life
spirit

ἐκ τοῦ Θεοῦ εἰσῆλθεν εἰς αὐτούς, καὶ ἔστησαν ἐπὶ τοὺς
from - God entered into them, and they stood on -

πόδας αὐτῶν, καὶ φόβος μέγας ἔπεσεν ἐπὶ τοὺς
feet ˜ their, and fear ˜ great fell on the *ones*
those who were

θεωροῦντας αὐτούς.
watching them.

12 Καὶ ἤκουσα[k] φωνὴν μεγάλην ἐκ τοῦ οὐρανοῦ,
And I heard a voice ˜ great out of - heaven,
loud from the sky,

λέγουσαν αὐτοῖς, "Ἀνάβητε ὧδε." Καὶ ἀνέβησαν εἰς τὸν
saying to them, "Come up here." And they went up to -

οὐρανὸν ἐν τῇ νεφέλῃ, καὶ ἐθεώρησαν αὐτοὺς οἱ ἐχθροὶ
heaven in the cloud, and [3]watched [4]them - [2]enemies

αὐτῶν. 13 Ἐν ἐκείνῃ τῇ ἡμέρᾳ[l] ἐγένετο σεισμὸς
[1]their. In that - day [4]occurred [1]a(n) [3]earthquake

μέγας, καὶ τὸ δέκατον τῆς πόλεως ἔπεσε, καὶ ἀπεκτάνθησαν
[2]great, and the tenth of the city fell, and [6]were [7]killed
severe, a

ἐν τῷ σεισμῷ ὀνόματα ἀνθρώπων, χιλιάδες ἑπτά. Καὶ οἱ
[8]in [9]the [10]earthquake [3]names [4]of [5]men, [2]thousand [1]seven. And the
individuals

λοιποὶ ἔμφοβοι ἐγένοντο καὶ ἔδωκαν δόξαν τῷ Θεῷ τοῦ
rest fearful ˜ became and gave glory to the God -

οὐρανοῦ.
of heaven.

14 Ἡ οὐαὶ ἡ δευτέρα ἀπῆλθεν. Ἡ οὐαὶ ἡ τρίτη, ἰδού,
The woe ˜ - second passed away. The woe ˜ - third, behold,
is over.

ἔρχεται ταχύ.
is coming swiftly.
shortly.

Seventh Trumpet: The Kingdom Proclaimed

15 Καὶ ὁ ἕβδομος ἄγγελος ἐσάλπισε, καὶ
And the seventh angel sounded *his* trumpet, and

---

[e](**11:9**) TR reads *τα πρωματα, (their) corpses.*
[f](**11:9**) NU reads *αφιουσιν, they do (not) allow.*
[g](**11:9**) TR reads *μνηματα, tombs.* [h](**11:10**) TR reads *χαρουσιν, will rejoice.*
[i](**11:10**) NU reads *ευφραινονται, are glad.*
[j](**11:10**) NU, TR read *πεμψουσιν, they will send.*
[k](**11:12**) NU, TR read *ηκουσαν, they heard.*
[l](**11:13**) NU, TR read *ωρα, hour.*

---

cial meat (Matt. 7:6). Cf. the cognate verb *ἁγιάζω, consecrate* (Matt. 23:17), and see the noun *ἁγιασμός, holiness,* at 1 Thess. 4:3.

ἐγένοντο φωναὶ μεγάλαι ἐν τῷ οὐρανῷ, λέγοντες,
there occurred voices ˜ great in - heaven, saying,
loud

"Ἐγένετο ἡ βασιλεία[m] τοῦ κόσμου,
"6became 1The 2kingdom 3of 4the 5world,
"has become

Τοῦ Κυρίου ἡμῶν καὶ τοῦ Χριστοῦ αὐτοῦ,
- *The kingdom* of Lord ˜ our and - of Christ ˜ His,

Καὶ βασιλεύσει εἰς τοὺς αἰῶνας τῶν αἰώνων!"
And He shall reign to the ages of the ages!"
forever and ever!"

16 Καὶ οἱ εἴκοσι τέσσαρες πρεσβύτεροι οἱ ἐνώπιον τοῦ
And the twenty- four elders the *ones* before the

θρόνου[n] τοῦ Θεοῦ οἳ κάθηνται ἐπὶ τοὺς θρόνους αὐτῶν,
throne - of God who sit on - thrones ˜ their,

ἔπεσον ἐπὶ τὰ πρόσωπα αὐτῶν καὶ προσεκύνησαν τῷ Θεῷ,
fell on - faces ˜ their and worshiped - God,

17 λέγοντες,
saying,

"Εὐχαριστοῦμέν σοι,
"We thank You,

Κύριε ὁ Θεὸς ὁ Παντοκράτωρ,
Lord - God the Almighty,

Ὁ ὢν καὶ ὁ ἦν,[o]
The *One* being and the *One* was,
who is who

Ὅτι εἴληφας τὴν δύναμίν σου τὴν μεγάλην καὶ
Because You have taken - 3power 1Your - 2great and

ἐβασίλευσας.
You reigned.
have begun to reign.

18 Καὶ τὰ ἔθνη ὠργίσθησαν,
And the nations were angry,

Καὶ ἦλθεν ἡ ὀργή σου,
And 3came - 2wrath 1Your,

Καὶ ὁ καιρὸς τῶν νεκρῶν κριθῆναι,
And the time of the dead to be judged,

Καὶ δοῦναι τὸν μισθὸν τοῖς δούλοις* σου τοῖς
And to give the reward - to bondservants ˜ Your the
slaves

προφήταις
prophets

Καὶ τοῖς ἁγίοις καὶ τοῖς φοβουμένοις τὸ ὄνομά σου,
And to the saints and to the *ones* fearing - name ˜ Your,
those who fear

Τοῖς μικροῖς καὶ τοῖς μεγάλοις,
To the small and to the great,

Καὶ διαφθεῖραι τοὺς διαφθείροντας τὴν γῆν."
And to destroy the *ones* destroying the earth."
those who destroy

19 Καὶ ἠνοίχθη ὁ ναὸς τοῦ Θεοῦ ἐν τῷ οὐρανῷ, καὶ
And 5was 6opened 1the 2shrine - 3of 4God in - heaven, and

ὤφθη ἡ κιβωτὸς τῆς διαθήκης τοῦ Κυρίου[p] ἐν τῷ
9was 10seen 1the 2ark 3of 4the 5covenant 6of 7the 8Lord in -
appeared

voices in heaven, saying, "The
kingdoms of this world have become *the kingdoms* of our Lord
and of His Christ, and He shall
reign forever and ever!"
16 And the twenty-four elders
who sat before God on their
thrones fell on their faces and
worshiped God,
17 saying:

"We give You thanks,
O Lord God Almighty,
The One who is and who
was and who is to
come,
Because You have taken
Your great power and
reigned.
18 The nations were angry,
and Your wrath has
come,
And the time of the dead,
that they should be
judged,
And that You should
reward Your servants
the prophets and the
saints,
And those who fear Your
name, small and great,
And should destroy those
who destroy the earth."

19 Then the temple of God
was opened in heaven, and the
ark of His covenant was seen in

[m]**(11:15)** TR reads *εγενοντο αι βασιλειαι, the kingdoms have become.*
[n]**(11:16)** NU, TR omit *του θρονου, the throne.*
[o]**(11:17)** TR adds *και ο ερχομενος, and the (One) coming.* [p]**(11:19)** TR, NU read *αυτου, His.*

***(11:18)** δοῦλος *(doulos).* Very common noun meaning *servant, bondservant, slave.* It is derived from the verb *δέω, bind,* and is frequently used of literal servitude, especially in the Gospels. The word is commonly used to express metaphorically that one's will is determined by some other person or thing whom or which one serves, such as Christ (Jude 1); God (Titus 1:1); sin (Rom. 6:17); or corruption (2 Pet. 2:19). See the cognate verb *δουλεύω, serve,* at Rom. 14:18.

His temple. And there were
lightnings, noises, thunderings,
an earthquake, and great hail.
12 Now a great sign ap-
peared in heaven: a
woman clothed with the sun,
with the moon under her feet,
and on her head a garland of
twelve stars.
2 Then being with child, she
cried out in labor and in pain to
give birth.
3 And another sign appeared
in heaven: behold, a great, fiery
red dragon having seven heads
and ten horns, and seven diadems on his heads.
4 His tail drew a third of the
stars of heaven and threw them
to the earth. And the dragon
stood before the woman who
was ready to give birth, to devour her Child as soon as it was
born.
5 She bore a male Child who
was to rule all nations with a
rod of iron. And her Child was
caught up to God and His
throne.
6 Then the woman fled into
the wilderness, where she has
a place prepared by God, that
they should feed her there one
thousand two hundred and sixty
days.
7 And war broke out in
heaven: Michael and his angels
fought with the dragon; and the

ναῷ αὐτοῦ. Καὶ ἐγένοντο ἀστραπαὶ καὶ φωναὶ καὶ βρονταὶ
shrine ˜ His. And *there* occurred lightnings and voices and thunders

καὶ χάλαζα μεγάλη.
and hail ˜ great.
huge.

The Woman, the Child and the Dragon

12 1 Καὶ σημεῖον μέγα ὤφθη ἐν τῷ οὐρανῷ· γυνὴ
And a sign ˜ great was seen in - heaven; a woman
appeared the sky;

περιβεβλημένη τὸν ἥλιον, καὶ ἡ σελήνη ὑποκάτω τῶν
having been clothed with the sun, and the moon underneath -
with

ποδῶν αὐτῆς, καὶ ἐπὶ τῆς κεφαλῆς αὐτῆς στέφανος ἀστέρων
feet ˜ her, and on - head ˜ her a crown of stars ˜

δώδεκα. 2 Καὶ ἐν γαστρὶ ἔχουσα, ἔκραζεν ὠδίνουσα
twelve. And in a womb having, she was crying out being in labor
being pregnant,

καὶ βασανιζομένη τεκεῖν. 3 Καὶ ὤφθη ἄλλο σημεῖον
and being in great pain to give birth. And [3]was [4]seen [1]another [2]sign
appeared

ἐν τῷ οὐρανῷ· καὶ ἰδού, δράκων πυρὸς μέγας ἔχων κεφαλὰς
in - heaven; and behold, [1]a [3]dragon [4]of [5]fire [2]great having heads ˜
the sky; a huge, fiery dragon

ἑπτὰ καὶ κέρατα δέκα, καὶ ἐπὶ τὰς κεφαλὰς αὐτοῦ ἑπτὰ
seven and horns ˜ ten, and on - heads ˜ his seven

διαδήματα. 4 Καὶ ἡ οὐρὰ αὐτοῦ σύρει τὸ τρίτον τῶν ἀστέρων
diadems. And - tail ˜ his draws the third of the stars
crowns. drew a

τοῦ οὐρανοῦ καὶ ἔβαλεν αὐτοὺς εἰς τὴν γῆν. Καὶ ὁ δράκων
- of heaven and threw them to the earth. And the dragon
of the sky

ἕστηκεν ἐνώπιον τῆς γυναικὸς τῆς μελλούσης τεκεῖν,
stood before the woman the *one* being about to give birth,
who was

ἵνα ὅταν τέκῃ, τὸ Τέκνον αὐτῆς
so that whenever she might give birth, - [6]Child [5]her

καταφάγῃ. 5 Καὶ ἔτεκεν Υἱὸν ἄρρενα ὃς μέλλει
[1]he [2]might [3]eat [4]up. And she gave birth to a Son a male who is about
devour. would

ποιμαίνειν πάντα τὰ ἔθνη ἐν ῥάβδῳ σιδηρᾷ. Καὶ
to shepherd all the nations with a(n) rod ˜ iron. And
Gentiles

ἡρπάσθη τὸ Τέκνον αὐτῆς πρὸς τὸν Θεὸν καὶ πρὸς τὸν
[3]was [4]snatched [5]up - [2]Child [1]her to - God and to -

θρόνον αὐτοῦ. 6 Καὶ ἡ γυνὴ ἔφυγεν εἰς τὴν ἔρημον ὅπου
throne ˜ His. And the woman fled into the wilderness where

ἔχει ἐκεῖ τόπον ἡτοιμασμένον ὑπὸ τοῦ Θεοῦ, ἵνα ἐκεῖ
she has there a place having been prepared by - God, so that there

ἐκτρέφωσιν αὐτὴν ἡμέρας χιλίας διακοσίας ἑξήκοντα.
they may nourish her [7]days [1]a [2]thousand [3]two [4]hundred [5]*and* [6]sixty.

Satan Thrown Out of Heaven

7 Καὶ ἐγένετο πόλεμος ἐν τῷ οὐρανῷ· ὁ Μιχαὴλ καὶ οἱ
And occurred ˜ war in - heaven; - Michael and -
took place

ἄγγελοι αὐτοῦ πολεμῆσαι μετὰ τοῦ δράκοντος· καὶ ὁ δράκων
angels ˜ his to wage war with the dragon; and the dragon
waging

ἐπολέμησε, καὶ οἱ ἄγγελοι αὐτοῦ, 8 καὶ οὐκ
made war, and - angels ˜ his, and [3]not
he

ἴσχυσεν,[a] οὐδὲ τόπος εὑρέθη αὐτῷ[b] ἔτι ἐν
[1]he [2]was strong *enough*, nor [2]a [3]place [1]was [4]found for him *any* longer in
did not win out,

τῷ οὐρανῷ. 9 Καὶ ἐβλήθη ὁ δράκων ὁ μέγας, ὁ
- heaven. And [4]was [5]thrown [6]*down* [1]the [3]dragon - [2]great, the

ὄφις ὁ ἀρχαῖος, ὁ καλούμενος Διάβολος καὶ Σατανᾶς,
serpent ˜ - ancient, the *one* being called Slanderer and Satan,
he who is called Devil

ὁ πλανῶν* τὴν οἰκουμένην ὅλην· ἐβλήθη εἰς τὴν
the *one* deceiving the [2]inhabited [3]world [1]whole; he was thrown to the
he who deceives

γῆν, καὶ οἱ ἄγγελοι αὐτοῦ μετ' αὐτοῦ ἐβλήθησαν.
earth, and - angels ˜ his with him were thrown *down*.

10 Καὶ ἤκουσα φωνὴν μεγάλην ἐν τῷ οὐρανῷ λέγουσαν,
And I heard a voice ˜ great in - heaven saying,
loud the sky

"Ἄρτι ἐγένετο ἡ σωτηρία καὶ ἡ δύναμις
"Now came the salvation and the power
have come

Καὶ ἡ βασιλεία τοῦ Θεοῦ ἡμῶν
And the kingdom - of God ˜ our

Καὶ ἡ ἐξουσία τοῦ Χριστοῦ αὐτοῦ,
And the authority - of Christ ˜ His,

Ὅτι ἐβλήθη[c] ὁ κατήγορος τῶν ἀδελφῶν
Because [6]was [7]thrown [8]*out* [1]the [2]accuser - [3]of [5]brothers
has been

ἡμῶν,
[4]our,

Ὁ κατηγορῶν αὐτῶν ἐνώπιον τοῦ Θεοῦ ἡμῶν ἡμέρας
The *one* accusing them before - God ˜ our day
Who accused

καὶ νυκτός.
and night.

11 Καὶ αὐτοὶ ἐνίκησαν αὐτὸν διὰ τὸ αἷμα τοῦ Ἀρνίου
And they overcame him by the blood of the Lamb
conquered

Καὶ διὰ τὸν λόγον τῆς μαρτυρίας αὐτῶν,
And by the word - of testimony ˜ their,
message

Καὶ οὐκ ἠγάπησαν τὴν ψυχὴν αὐτῶν ἄχρι θανάτου.
And [3]not [1]they [2]did love - life ˜ their up to death.

12 Διὰ τοῦτο εὐφραίνεσθε, οὐρανοί,
On account of this be glad, *O* heavens,

Καὶ οἱ ἐν αὐτοῖς σκηνοῦντες!
And the *ones* [2]in [3]them [1]dwelling!
you who dwell!

Οὐαὶ[d] τῇ γῇ καὶ τῇ θαλάσσῃ!
Woe to the earth and to the sea!

Ὅτι κατέβη ὁ διάβολος πρὸς ὑμᾶς, ἔχων
Because [3]was [4]thrown [5]down [1]the [2]devil to you, having

θυμὸν μέγαν,
wrath ˜ great,

Εἰδὼς ὅτι ὀλίγον καιρὸν ἔχει."
Knowing that [3]a [4]little [5]time [1]he [2]has."

dragon and his angels fought,
8 but they did not prevail,
nor was a place found for them
in heaven any longer.
9 So the great dragon was
cast out, that serpent of old,
called the Devil and Satan, who
deceives the whole world; he
was cast to the earth, and his
angels were cast out with him.
10 Then I heard a loud voice
saying in heaven, "Now salvation, and strength, and the
kingdom of our God, and the
power of His Christ have come,
for the accuser of our brethren,
who accused them before our
God day and night, has been
cast down.
11 "And they overcame him
by the blood of the Lamb and by
the word of their testimony,
and they did not love their lives
to the death.
12 "Therefore rejoice, O
heavens, and you who dwell in
them! Woe to the inhabitants of
the earth and the sea! For the
devil has come down to you,
having great wrath, because he
knows that he has a short
time."

---

[a](**12:8**) TR reads ουκ ισχυσαν, *they were not strong (enough).*
[b](**12:8**) TR, NU read αυτων, *for them.*
[c](**12:10**) TR reads κατεβληθη, *thrown down.*
[d](**12:12**) TR adds τοις κατοικουσι, *to those dwelling in.*

---

*(**12:9**) πλανάω *(planaō).* Verb meaning *deceive, lead astray,* implying the misleading of another, causing someone to wander or err from the truth (cf. James 5:19). Here in Rev. 12:9 Satan is the one who has led the world astray. The passive means *go astray, wander, err, be misled,* and can be literal (as Matt. 18:12, of straying sheep) or figurative (as 2 Pet. 2:15). The idea of an agent of deception may be present (as Matt. 24:24) or may not (as Heb. 5:2). Cf. the cognate noun πλάνη, *wandering, error, deception.* The unbeliever lives in such error (Rom. 1:27; Eph. 4:14).

13 Now when the dragon saw that he had been cast to the earth, he persecuted the woman who gave birth to the male *Child.*

14 But the woman was given two wings of a great eagle, that she might fly into the wilderness to her place, where she is nourished for a time and times and half a time, from the presence of the serpent.

15 So the serpent spewed water out of his mouth like a flood after the woman, that he might cause her to be carried away by the flood.

16 But the earth helped the woman, and the earth opened its mouth and swallowed up the flood which the dragon had spewed out of his mouth.

17 And the dragon was enraged with the woman, and he went to make war with the rest of her offspring, who keep the commandments of God and have the testimony of Jesus Christ.

13 Then I stood on the sand of the sea. And I saw a beast rising up out of the sea, having seven heads and ten horns, and on his horns ten crowns, and on his heads a blasphemous name.

2 Now the beast which I saw was like a leopard, his feet were like *the feet of* a bear, and his mouth like the mouth of a lion. The dragon gave him his power, his throne, and great authority.

3 And *I saw* one of his heads

e(12:14) TR, NU read οπου τρεφεται, *where she is nourished.*
f(12:17) TR reads του Ιησου Χριστου, *of Jesus Christ.*
a(13:1) NU reads εσταθη, *he stood.* b(13:1) TR reads ονομα, *a name;* NU brackets the plural *names.*

The Dragon Persecutes the Woman and Her Seed

13 Καὶ ὅτε εἶδεν ὁ δράκων ὅτι ἐβλήθη εἰς τὴν γῆν,
And when [3]saw [1]the [2]dragon that he was thrown to the earth,

ἐδίωξε τὴν γυναῖκα ἥτις ἔτεκε τὸν ἄρρενα. **14** Καὶ
he persecuted the woman who gave birth to the male. And

ἐδόθησαν τῇ γυναικὶ δύο πτέρυγες τοῦ ἀετοῦ τοῦ
[7]were [8]given [9]to [10]the [11]woman [1]two [2]wings [3]of [4]the [6]eagle -
a

μεγάλου, ἵνα πέτηται εἰς τὴν ἔρημον εἰς τὸν τόπον
[5]great, so that she might fly into the desert to - place ˜

αὐτῆς, ὅπως[e] τρέφηται ἐκεῖ καιρὸν καὶ καιροὺς καὶ
her, so that she might be nourished there a time and times and

ἥμισυ καιροῦ, ἀπὸ προσώπου τοῦ ὄφεως. **15** Καὶ ἔβαλεν ὁ
half of a time, from *the* face of the serpent. And [3]cast [1]the
spewed

ὄφις ἐκ τοῦ στόματος αὐτοῦ ὀπίσω τῆς γυναικὸς ὕδωρ ὡς
[2]serpent out of - mouth ˜ his [5]after [6]the [7]woman [1]water [2]like

ποταμόν, ἵνα αὐτὴν ποταμοφόρητον
[3]a [4]river, so that [4]her [5]*to* [6]*be* [7]carried [8]off [9]by [10]the [11]river

ποιήσῃ. **16** Καὶ ἐβοήθησεν ἡ γῆ τῇ γυναικί, καὶ
[1]he [2]might [3]make. And [3]helped [1]the [2]earth the woman, and

ἤνοιξεν ἡ γῆ τὸ στόμα αὐτῆς καὶ κατέπιε τὸν ποταμὸν
[3]opened [1]the [2]earth - mouth ˜ its and drank up the river

ὃν ἔβαλεν ὁ δράκων ἐκ τοῦ στόματος αὐτοῦ. **17** Καὶ
which [3]cast [1]the [2]dragon out of - mouth ˜ his. And
had cast

ὠργίσθη ὁ δράκων ἐπὶ τῇ γυναικί, καὶ ἀπῆλθε ποιῆσαι
[3]was [4]angry [1]the [2]dragon over the woman, and he went off to make

πόλεμον μετὰ τῶν λοιπῶν τοῦ σπέρματος αὐτῆς τῶν
war with the rest - of seed ˜ her the *ones*
who

τηρούντων τὰς ἐντολὰς τοῦ Θεοῦ καὶ ἐχόντων τὴν μαρτυρίαν
keeping the commands - of God and having the testimony
keep have

Ἰησοῦ.[f]
of Jesus.

The Beast from the Sea

13 **1** Καὶ ἐστάθην[a] ἐπὶ τὴν ἄμμον τῆς θαλάσσης. Καὶ
And I stood on the sand of the sea. And
seashore.

εἶδον ἐκ τῆς θαλάσσης Θηρίον ἀναβαῖνον, ἔχον κέρατα
I saw [5]out [6]of [7]the [8]sea [1]a [2]Beast [3]coming [4]up, having horns ˜

δέκα καὶ κεφαλὰς ἑπτά, καὶ ἐπὶ τῶν κεράτων αὐτοῦ δέκα
ten and heads ˜ seven, and on - horns ˜ his ten

διαδήματα, καὶ ἐπὶ τὰς κεφαλὰς αὐτοῦ ὀνόματα[b] βλασφημίας.
diadems, and on - heads ˜ his names of blasphemy.
crowns, blasphemous names.

2 Καὶ τὸ Θηρίον ὃ εἶδον ἦν ὅμοιον παρδάλει καὶ οἱ
And the Beast which I saw was similar to a leopard and -

πόδες αὐτοῦ ὡς ἄρκου καὶ τὸ στόμα αὐτοῦ ὡς
feet ˜ his *were* like *those* of a bear and - mouth ˜ his *was* like

στόμα λέοντος. Καὶ ἔδωκεν αὐτῷ ὁ δράκων τὴν δύναμιν
the mouth of a lion. And [3]gave [4]to [5]him [1]the [2]dragon - power ˜

αὐτοῦ καὶ τὸν θρόνον αὐτοῦ καὶ ἐξουσίαν μεγάλην. **3** Καὶ μίαν
his and - throne ˜ his and authority ˜ great. And one

ἐκ τῶν κεφαλῶν αὐτοῦ ὡσεὶ ἐσφαγμένην εἰς θάνατον,
of - horns ˜ his *was* as *if* having been slaughtered to death,
slain

καὶ ἡ πληγὴ τοῦ θανάτου αὐτοῦ ἐθεραπεύθη. Καὶ ἐθαύμασεν
and - ²wound - ³of ⁴death ¹his was healed. And ⁴marveled
mortal wound

ὅλη ἡ γῆ ὀπίσω τοῦ Θηρίου.
²whole ¹the ³earth after the Beast.

4 Καὶ προσεκύνησαν τῷ δράκοντι τῷ δεδωκότι τὴν
And they worshiped the dragon the *one* having given the
who had

ἐξουσίαν τῷ Θηρίῳ· καὶ προσεκύνησαν τῷ Θηρίῳ, λέγοντες,
authority to the Beast; and they worshiped the Beast, saying,

"Τίς ὅμοιος τῷ Θηρίῳ? Τίς δύνατος πολεμῆσαι μετ' αὐτοῦ?"
"Who *is* like the Beast? Who is able to make war with him?"

5 Καὶ ἐδόθη αὐτῷ στόμα λαλοῦν μεγάλα καὶ
And ³was ⁴given ⁵to ⁶him ¹a ²mouth speaking great *things* and

βλασφημίαν,[c] καὶ ἐδόθη αὐτῷ ἐξουσία πόλεμον[d]
blasphemy, and ²was ³given ⁴to ⁵him ¹authority ⁸war

ποιῆσαι μῆνας τεσσαράκοντα δύο. 6 Καὶ ἤνοιξε τὸ στόμα
⁶to ⁷make ¹¹months ⁹forty- ¹⁰two. And he opened - mouth ˜

αὐτοῦ εἰς βλασφημίαν πρὸς τὸν Θεόν, βλασφημῆσαι τὸ
his in blasphemy against - God, to blaspheme -

ὄνομα αὐτοῦ καὶ τὴν σκηνὴν αὐτοῦ, τοὺς ἐν τῷ οὐρανῷ
name ˜ His and - dwelling ˜ His, the *ones* ²in - ³heaven
those

σκηνοῦντας. 7 Καὶ ἐδόθη αὐτῷ ποιῆσαι πόλεμον μετὰ τῶν
¹dwelling. And it was given to him to make war with the
who dwell. granted

ἁγίων καὶ νικῆσαι αὐτούς. Καὶ ἐδόθη αὐτῷ ἐξουσία ἐπὶ
saints and to overcome them. And ²was ³given ⁴to ⁵him ¹authority over
conquer

πᾶσαν φυλὴν καὶ λαὸν[e] καὶ γλῶσσαν καὶ ἔθνος. 8 Καὶ
every tribe and people and tongue and nation. And
language

προσκυνήσουσιν αὐτὸν πάντες οἱ κατοικοῦντες ἐπὶ τῆς
⁸shall ⁹worship ¹⁰him ¹all ²the ³*ones* ⁴dwelling ⁵on ⁶the
those who dwell

γῆς, ὧν οὐ γέγραπται τὸ ὄνομα ἐν τῷ Βιβλίῳ
⁷earth, of whom ⁴not ³has ⁵been ⁶written ¹the ²name in the Book
whose name is not written

τῆς Ζωῆς τοῦ Ἀρνίου τοῦ ἐσφαγμένου ἀπὸ καταβολῆς
of Life of the Lamb - having been slaughtered from *the* foundation
slain

κόσμου.
of the world.

9 Εἴ τις ἔχει οὖς, ἀκουσάτω.
If anyone has an ear, let him hear.

10 Εἴ τις ἔχει αἰχμαλωσίαν, ὑπάγει·[f]
If anyone has captivity, he goes away;
will go

Εἴ τις ἐν μαχαίρᾳ, δεῖ αὐτὸν
If anyone *is* with *the* sword, it is necessary *for* him
he must

ἀποκτανθῆναι.[g]
to be killed.

Ὧδέ ἐστιν ἡ ὑπομονὴ καὶ ἡ πίστις τῶν ἁγίων.
Here is the endurance and the faith of the saints.

as if it had been mortally wounded, and his deadly wound was healed. And all the world marveled and followed the beast.
4 So they worshiped the dragon who gave authority to the beast; and they worshiped the beast, saying, "Who *is* like the beast? Who is able to make war with him?"
5 And he was given a mouth speaking great things and blasphemies, and he was given authority to continue for forty-two months.
6 Then he opened his mouth in blasphemy against God, to blaspheme His name, His tabernacle, and those who dwell in heaven.
7 It was granted to him to make war with the saints and to overcome them. And authority was given him over every tribe, tongue, and nation.
8 All who dwell on the earth will worship him, whose names have not been written in the Book of Life of the Lamb slain from the foundation of the world.
9 If anyone has an ear, let him hear.
10 He who leads into captivity shall go into captivity; he who kills with the sword must be killed with the sword. Here is the patience and the faith of the saints.

---

[c] **(13:5)** NU, TR read βλασφημιας, *blasphemies.* [d] **(13:5)** NU omits πολεμον, *war.* [e] **(13:7)** TR omits και λαον, *and people.* [f] **(13:10)** TR reads Ει τις αιχμαλωσιαν συναγει εις αιχμαλωσιαν υπαγει, *If anyone leads into captivity, into captivity he goes;* NU reads Ει τις εις αιχμαλωσιαν εις αιχμαλωσιαν υπαγει, *If anyone (is to go) into captivity, into captivity he goes.* [g] **(13:10)** TR reads Ει τις εν μαχαιρα αποκτενει δει αυτον εν μαχαιρα αποκτανθηναι, *If anyone will kill with a sword, he must be killed with a sword;* NU reads Ει τις εν μαχαιρη αποκτανθηναι αυτον εν μαχαιρη αποκτανθηναι, *If anyone is to be killed with a sword, with a sword he will be killed.*

11 Then I saw another beast coming up out of the earth, and he had two horns like a lamb and spoke like a dragon.
12 And he exercises all the authority of the first beast in his presence, and causes the earth and those who dwell in it to worship the first beast, whose deadly wound was healed.
13 He performs great signs, so that he even makes fire come down from heaven on the earth in the sight of men.
14 And he deceives those who dwell on the earth by those signs which he was granted to do in the sight of the beast, telling those who dwell on the earth to make an image to the beast who was wounded by the sword and lived.
15 He was granted *power* to give breath to the image of the beast, that the image of the beast should both speak and cause as many as would not worship the image of the beast to be killed.
16 He causes all, both small and great, rich and poor, free and slave, to receive a mark on their right hand or on their foreheads,
17 and that no one may buy or sell except one who has the mark or the name of the beast, or the number of his name.
18 Here is wisdom. Let him who has understanding calculate the number of the beast,

The Beast from the Land

11 Καὶ εἶδον ἄλλο θηρίον ἀναβαῖνον ἐκ τῆς γῆς, καὶ
And I saw another beast coming up out of the earth, and

εἶχε κέρατα δύο ὅμοια ἀρνίῳ καὶ ἐλάλει ὡς δράκων.
he had horns ˜ two similar to a lamb and he spoke like a dragon.

12 Καὶ τὴν ἐξουσίαν τοῦ πρώτου Θηρίου πᾶσαν ποιεῖ
And [4]the [5]authority [6]of [7]the [8]first [9]Beast [3]all [1]he [2]does
exercises

ἐνώπιον αὐτοῦ, καὶ ἐποίει τὴν γῆν καὶ τοὺς ἐν αὐτῇ
before him, and he was making the earth and the *ones* [2]in [3]it
those who

κατοικοῦντας ἵνα προσκυνήσωσι τὸ Θηρίον τὸ πρῶτον,
[1]dwelling that they should worship the Beast ˜ - first,
dwell

οὗ ἐθεραπεύθη ἡ πληγὴ τοῦ θανάτου αὐτοῦ. **13** Καὶ
of whom [5]was [6]healed - [2]wound - [3]of [4]death [1]his. And
whose mortal wound was healed.

ποιεῖ σημεῖα μεγάλα, καὶ πῦρ ἵνα ἐκ τοῦ οὐρανοῦ
he does signs ˜ great, [3]even [4]fire [1]so [2]that [8]out [9]of - [10]heaven

καταβαίνῃ ἐπὶ τὴν γῆν ἐνώπιον τῶν ἀνθρώπων. **14** Καὶ
[5]should [6]come [7]down on the earth before - men. And

πλανᾷ τοὺς ἐμοὺς[h] τοὺς κατοικοῦντας ἐπὶ τῆς γῆς διὰ
he deceives the *ones* my *own* the *ones* dwelling on the earth by
my own people who dwell

τὰ σημεῖα ἃ ἐδόθη αὐτῷ ποιῆσαι ἐνώπιον τοῦ Θηρίου,
the signs which were given to him to do before the Beast,

λέγων τοῖς κατοικοῦσιν ἐπὶ τῆς γῆς ποιῆσαι εἰκόνα τῷ
saying to the *ones* dwelling on the earth to make an image to the
those who dwell

Θηρίῳ ὃ εἶχε πληγὴν — καὶ ἔζησεν! — ἀπὸ τῆς
Beast who had *the* wound — and came to life! — from the

μαχαίρας. **15** Καὶ ἐδόθη αὐτῷ πνεῦμα δοῦναι τῇ εἰκόνι
sword. And it was given to him [3]breath [1]to [2]give to the image
granted

τοῦ Θηρίου, ἵνα καὶ λαλήσῃ ἡ εἰκὼν τοῦ Θηρίου
of the Beast, so that [6]both [7]should [8]speak [1]the [2]image [3]of [4]the [5]Beast

καὶ ποιήσῃ ὅσοι ἐὰν μὴ προσκυνήσωσι τῇ εἰκόνι τοῦ
and should make as many as - not ˜ would worship the image of the

Θηρίου ἀποκτανθῶσι. **16** Καὶ ποιεῖ πάντας, τοὺς
Beast *that* they should be killed. And he makes all *people,* the

μικροὺς καὶ τοὺς μεγάλους, καὶ τοὺς πλουσίους καὶ τοὺς
small and the great, and the rich and the

πτωχούς, καὶ τοὺς ἐλευθέρους καὶ τοὺς δούλους, ἵνα
poor, and the free *men* and the slaves, so that

δώσωσιν[i] αὐτοῖς χαράγματα[j] ἐπὶ τῆς χειρὸς αὐτῶν τῆς
they should give to them marks on - [3]hand [1]their -

δεξιᾶς ἢ ἐπὶ τὸ μέτωπον[k] αὐτῶν, **17** καὶ ἵνα μή τις
[2]right or on - forehead ˜ their, and so that not anyone
lest

δύναται ἀγοράσαι ἢ πωλῆσαι εἰ μὴ ὁ ἔχων τὸ
would be able to buy or to sell if not the *one* having the
except he who has

χάραγμα,[l] τὸ ὄνομα τοῦ Θηρίου ἢ τὸν ἀριθμὸν τοῦ
mark, the name of the Beast or the number -

ὀνόματος αὐτοῦ. **18** Ὧδε ἡ σοφία ἐστίν. Ὁ ἔχων
of name ˜ his. Here - wisdom ˜ is. The *one* having
He who has

νοῦν ψηφισάτω τὸν ἀριθμὸν τοῦ Θηρίου, ἀριθμὸς
understanding let him calculate the number of the Beast, [4]*the* [5]number

---

h(13:14) TR, NU omit τους εμους, *my own (people).*
i(13:16) TR reads δωση, *he should give.*
j(13:16) TR, NU read χαραγμα, *a mark.*
k(13:16) TR reads των μετωπων, *(their) foreheads.*
l(13:17) TR adds η, *or.*

γὰρ ἀνθρώπου ἐστίν. Ὁ ἀριθμὸς αὐτοῦ, χξς΄.
[1]for [6]of [7]*a* [8]man [2]it [3]is. - number ˜ His, 666.

The Lamb and the 144,000 on Mount Zion

14 1 Καὶ εἶδον, καὶ ἰδού, τὸ Ἀρνίον ἑστηκὸς ἐπὶ τὸ
And I saw, and behold, the Lamb standing on -

Ὄρος Σιών, καὶ μετ᾽ αὐτοῦ ἀριθμός,[a] ρμδ΄ χιλιάδες, ἔχουσαι
Mount Zion, and with Him a number, 144 thousands, having
thousand,

τὸ ὄνομα αὐτοῦ καὶ[b] τὸ ὄνομα τοῦ Πατρὸς αὐτοῦ
- name ˜ His and the name - of Father ˜ His

γεγραμμένον ἐπὶ τῶν μετώπων αὐτῶν. 2 Καὶ ἤκουσα φωνὴν
having been written on - foreheads ˜ their. And I heard a voice

ἐκ τοῦ οὐρανοῦ, ὡς φωνὴν ὑδάτων πολλῶν, καὶ ὡς
out of - heaven, like *the* sound of waters ˜ many, and like
from the sky,

φωνὴν βροντῆς μεγάλης. Καὶ ἡ φωνὴ ἣν ἤκουσα ὡς
the sound of thunder ˜ great. And the sound which I heard *was* as
loud.

κιθαρῳδῶν κιθαριζόντων ἐν ταῖς κιθάραις αὐτῶν. 3 Καὶ
of harpists harping with - harps ˜ their. And
playing on

ᾄδουσιν ᾠδὴν καινὴν ἐνώπιον τοῦ θρόνου καὶ ἐνώπιον τῶν
they sing a song ˜ new before the throne and before the
sang

τεσσάρων ζῴων καὶ τῶν πρεσβυτέρων· καὶ οὐδεὶς
four living creatures and the elders; and no one

ἐδύνατο μαθεῖν τὴν ᾠδὴν εἰ μὴ αἱ ρμδ΄ χιλιάδες οἱ
was able to learn the song if not the 144 thousands the *ones*
except thousand who had

ἠγορασμένοι ἀπὸ τῆς γῆς. 4 Οὗτοί εἰσιν οἳ μετὰ
having been redeemed from the earth. These are *those* who [4]with
been bought

γυναικῶν οὐκ ἐμολύνθησαν, παρθένοι γάρ εἰσιν. Οὗτοί εἰσιν
[5]women [2]not [1]were [3]defiled, [9]virgins [6]for [7]they [8]are. These are

οἱ ἀκολουθοῦντες τῷ Ἀρνίῳ ὅπου ἐὰν ὑπάγῃ. Οὗτοι ὑπὸ
the *ones* following the Lamb where ever He may go. These [3]by
those who follow

Ἰησοῦ[c] ἠγοράσθησαν ἀπὸ τῶν ἀνθρώπων, ἀπαρχὴ τῷ
[4]Jesus [1]were [2]redeemed from *among* - men, firstfruits -
bought

Θεῷ καὶ τῷ Ἀρνίῳ. 5 Καὶ οὐχ εὑρέθη ἐν τῷ στόματι
to God and to the Lamb. And [4]not [3]was [5]found [6]in - [8]mouth

αὐτῶν ψεῦδος,[d] ἄμωμοι γάρ εἰσι.[e]
[7]their [1]a [2]lie, [12]blameless [9]for [10]they [11]are.

The Proclamations of Three Angels

6 Καὶ εἶδον[f] ἄγγελον πετόμενον ἐν μεσουρανήματι,
And I saw an angel flying in midheaven,

ἔχοντα εὐαγγέλιον αἰώνιον εὐαγγελίσαι τοὺς καθημένους[g]
having a(n) gospel ˜ eternal to preach to the *ones* sitting
everlasting good news to proclaim to those who dwell

ἐπὶ τῆς γῆς, καὶ ἐπὶ πᾶν ἔθνος καὶ φυλὴν καὶ γλῶσσαν καὶ
on the earth, and on every nation and tribe and tongue and
language

λαόν, 7 λέγων ἐν φωνῇ μεγάλῃ, "Φοβήθητε τὸν Κύριον[h]
people, saying with a voice ˜ great "Fear the Lord
loud

for it is the number of a man:
His number *is* 666.

14 Then I looked, and behold, a Lamb standing
on Mount Zion, and with Him
one hundred *and* forty-four
thousand, having His Father's
name written on their foreheads.
2 And I heard a voice from
heaven, like the voice of many
waters, and like the voice of
loud thunder. And I heard the
sound of harpists playing their
harps.
3 They sang as it were a new
song before the throne, before
the four living creatures, and
the elders; and no one could
learn that song except the hundred
and forty-four thousand
who were redeemed from the
earth.
4 These are the ones who
were not defiled with women,
for they are virgins. These are
the ones who follow the Lamb
wherever He goes. These
were redeemed from *among*
men, *being* firstfruits to God
and to the Lamb.
5 And in their mouth was
found no deceit, for they are
without fault before the throne
of God.
6 Then I saw another angel
flying in the midst of heaven,
having the everlasting gospel to
preach to those who dwell on
the earth—to every nation,
tribe, tongue, and people—
7 saying with a loud voice,
"Fear God and give glory to

[a](**14:1**) TR, NU omit αριθμος, *a number.*
[b](**14:1**) TR omits το ονομα αυτου και, *His name and.*
[c](**14:4**) TR, NU omit υπο Ιησου, *by Jesus.*
[d](**14:5**) TR reads δολος, *deceit.* [e](**14:5**) TR adds ενωπιον του θρονου του Θεου, *before the throne of God.* [f](**14:6**) TR, NU add αλλον, *another.*
[g](**14:6**) TR reads κατοικουντας, *dwelling.*
[h](**14:7**) TR, NU read Θεον, *God.*

Him, for the hour of His judgment has come; and worship
Him who made heaven and
earth, the sea and springs of
water."
8 And another angel fol-
lowed, saying, "Babylon is
fallen, is fallen, that great city,
because she has made all nations drink of the wine of the
wrath of her fornication."
9 Then a third angel followed
them, saying with a loud voice,
"If anyone worships the beast
and his image, and receives *his*
mark on his forehead or on his
hand,
10 "he himself shall also drink
of the wine of the wrath of God,
which is poured out full
strength into the cup of His indignation. He shall be tormented with fire and brimstone
in the presence of the holy angels and in the presence of the
Lamb.
11 "And the smoke of their
torment ascends forever and
ever; and they have no rest day
or night, who worship the beast
and his image, and whoever receives the mark of his name."
12 Here is the patience of the
saints; here *are* those who keep
the commandments of God and
the faith of Jesus.
13 Then I heard a voice from
heaven saying to me, "Write:
'Blessed *are* the dead who die
in the Lord from now on.'"
"Yes," says the Spirit, "that
they may rest from their la-

καὶ δότε αὐτῷ δόξαν, ὅτι ἦλθεν ἡ ὥρα τῆς κρίσεως
and give [2]to [3]Him [1]glory, because [6]came [1]the [2]hour - [3]of [5]judgment
has come

αὐτοῦ, καὶ προσκυνήσατε αὐτὸν τὸν ποιήσαντα τὸν οὐρανὸν
[4]His, and you shall worship Him the *One* having made the heaven
who made sky

καὶ τὴν γῆν καὶ τὴν θάλασσαν καὶ πηγὰς ὑδάτων."
and the earth and the sea and springs of waters."
water."

8 Καὶ ἄλλος δεύτερος[i] ἄγγελος ἠκολούθησε, λέγων,
And another [2]a [3]second [1]angel followed, saying,

"Ἔπεσε Βαβυλὼν[j] ἡ μεγάλη. Ἐκ τοῦ οἴνου τοῦ θυμοῦ
"[4]Fell [1]Babylon [2]the [3]great. From the wine of the wrath

τῆς πορνείας αὐτῆς πεπότικε πάντα τὰ ἔθνη."
- of fornication ˜ her she has made [4]to [5]drink [1]all [2]the [3]nations."

9 Καὶ ἄλλος[k] ἄγγελος τρίτος ἠκολούθησεν αὐτοῖς, λέγων
And another angel a third followed them, saying

ἐν φωνῇ μεγάλῃ, "Εἴ τις προσκυνεῖ τὸ Θηρίον καὶ τὴν
with a voice ˜ great, "If anyone worships the Beast and -
loud,

εἰκόνα αὐτοῦ, καὶ λαμβάνει χάραγμα ἐπὶ τοῦ μετώπου αὐτοῦ
image ˜ his, and receives a mark on - forehead ˜ his

ἢ ἐπὶ τὴν χεῖρα αὐτοῦ, **10** καὶ αὐτὸς πίεται ἐκ τοῦ οἴνου
or on - hand ˜ his, and he shall drink of the wine
then

τοῦ θυμοῦ τοῦ Θεοῦ, τοῦ κεκερασμένου ἀκράτου ἐν τῷ
of the wrath of God, the *one* having been mixed undiluted in the
which is

ποτηρίῳ τῆς ὀργῆς αὐτοῦ. Καὶ βασανισθήσεται ἐν πυρὶ
cup - of wrath ˜ His. And they will be tormented with fire

καὶ θείῳ ἐνώπιον τῶν ἁγίων ἀγγέλων καὶ ἐνώπιον τοῦ
and brimstone before the holy angels and before the
sulfur

Ἀρνίου. **11** Καὶ ὁ καπνὸς τοῦ βασανισμοῦ αὐτῶν εἰς
Lamb. And the smoke - of torment ˜ their [3]to
forever

αἰῶνας αἰώνων ἀναβαίνει· καὶ οὐκ ἔχουσιν ἀνάπαυσιν
[4]*the* [5]ages [6]of [7]ages [1]goes [2]up; and [3]not [1]they [2]do have rest
and ever

ἡμέρας καὶ νυκτός, οἱ προσκυνοῦντες τὸ Θηρίον καὶ τὴν
day and night, the *ones* worshiping the Beast and -
those who worship

εἰκόνα αὐτοῦ, καὶ εἴ τις λαμβάνει τὸ χάραγμα τοῦ
image ˜ his, and if anyone receives the mark -
anyone who

ὀνόματος αὐτοῦ."
of name ˜ his."

12 Ὧδε ἡ ὑπομονὴ τῶν ἁγίων ἐστίν, οἱ τηροῦντες
Here [2]the [3]endurance [4]of [5]the [6]saints [1]is, the *ones* keeping
those who keep

τὰς ἐντολὰς τοῦ Θεοῦ καὶ τὴν πίστιν Ἰησοῦ. **13** Καὶ ἤκουσα
the commands - of God and the faith of Jesus. And I heard

φωνῆς ἐκ τοῦ οὐρανοῦ λεγούσης,[l] "Γράψον· 'Μακάριοι οἱ
a voice out of - heaven saying, "Write: 'Blessed *are* the
from the sky

νεκροὶ οἱ ἐν Κυρίῳ ἀποθνῄσκοντες ἀπ' ἄρτι,' λέγει ναὶ
dead the *ones* [2]in [3]*the* [4]Lord [1]dying from now *on*,' says ˜ yes
who die

τὸ Πνεῦμα, 'ἵνα ἀναπαύσωνται ἐκ τῶν κόπων αὐτῶν, τὰ
the Spirit, 'so that they may rest from - labors ˜ their, -

---

[i](**14:8**) TR omits δευτερος, *second.* [j](**14:8**) TR adds η πολις, *the city.*
[k](**14:9**) TR omits αλλος, *another.* [l](**14:13**) TR adds μοι, *to me.*

δὲ ἔργα αὐτῶν ἀκολουθεῖ μετ' αὐτῶν.' "
and works ~ their follow along with them.' "

Reaping the Earth's Harvest

14 Καὶ εἶδον, καὶ ἰδού, νεφέλη λευκή, καὶ ἐπὶ τὴν
And I saw, and behold, a cloud ~ white, and on the

νεφέλην καθήμενον ὅμοιον Υἱὸν Ἀνθρώπου, ἔχων ἐπὶ τῆς
cloud *One* sitting like *the* Son of Man, having on -

κεφαλῆς αὐτοῦ στέφανον χρυσοῦν, καὶ ἐν τῇ χειρὶ αὐτοῦ
head ~ His a crown ~ golden, and in - hand ~ His

δρέπανον ὀξύ.
a sickle ~ sharp.

15 Καὶ ἄλλος ἄγγελος ἐξῆλθεν ἐκ τοῦ ναοῦ κράζων ἐν
And another angel came out of the shrine crying out with

φωνῇ μεγάλῃ τῷ καθημένῳ ἐπὶ τῆς νεφέλης, "Πέμψον
a voice ~ great to the *One* sitting on the cloud, "Send
loud "Thrust in

τὸ δρέπανόν σου καὶ θέρισον, ὅτι ἦλθεν[m] ἡ ὥρα θερίσαι,
- sickle ~ Your and reap, because [3]came [1]the [2]hour to reap,
has come time

ὅτι ἐξηράνθη ὁ θερισμὸς τῆς γῆς." **16** Καὶ ἔβαλεν
because [6]was [7]dried [8]up [1]the [2]harvest [3]of [4]the [5]earth." And [7]swung
has withered

ὁ καθήμενος ἐπὶ τὴν νεφέλην τὸ δρέπανον αὐτοῦ ἐπὶ
[1]the [2]*One* [3]sitting [4]on [5]the [6]cloud - sickle ~ His onto

τὴν γῆν, καὶ ἐθερίσθη ἡ γῆ.
the earth, and [3]was [4]reaped [1]the [2]earth.
harvested

Reaping the Grapes of Wrath

17 Καὶ ἄλλος ἄγγελος ἐξῆλθεν ἐκ τοῦ ναοῦ τοῦ ἐν τῷ
And another angel came out of the shrine - in -

οὐρανῷ, ἔχων καὶ αὐτὸς δρέπανον ὀξύ.
heaven, [3]having [2]also [1]he a sickle ~ sharp.

18 Καὶ ἄλλος ἄγγελος ἐξῆλθεν ἐκ τοῦ θυσιαστηρίου,
And another angel came out from the altar,

ἔχων ἐξουσίαν ἐπὶ τοῦ πυρός, καὶ ἐφώνησεν ἐν κραυγῇ
having authority over the fire, and he called with a cry ~

μεγάλῃ τῷ ἔχοντι τὸ δρέπανον τὸ ὀξύ, λέγων, "Πέμψον
great to the *one* having the sickle ~ - sharp, saying, "Send
loud who had "Thrust in

σου τὸ δρέπανον τὸ ὀξὺ καὶ τρύγησον τοὺς βότρυας τῆς
your - sickle ~ - sharp and gather the grape clusters of the

ἀμπέλου τῆς γῆς, ὅτι ἤκμασεν ἡ σταφυλὴ τῆς
vine of the earth, because [8]was [9]ripe [1]the [2]bunch [3]of [4]grapes [5]of [6]the
is

γῆς."[n] **19** Καὶ ἐξέβαλεν ὁ ἄγγελος τὸ δρέπανον αὐτοῦ εἰς
[7]earth." And [3]threw [4]out [1]the [2]angel - sickle ~ his to

τὴν γῆν καὶ ἐτρύγησε τὴν ἄμπελον τῆς γῆς, καὶ ἔβαλεν
the earth and gathered the vine of the earth, and he threw *it*

εἰς τὴν ληνὸν τοῦ θυμοῦ τοῦ Θεοῦ τὸν μέγαν. **20** Καὶ
into the [2]winepress [3]of [4]the [5]wrath - [6]of [7]God - [1]great. And

ἐπατήθη ἡ ληνὸς ἔξωθεν τῆς πόλεως, καὶ ἐξῆλθεν
[3]was [4]trampled [1]the [2]winepress outside the city, and [2]came [3]out

αἷμα ἐκ τῆς ληνοῦ ἄχρι τῶν χαλινῶν τῶν ἵππων, ἀπὸ
[1]blood of the winepress up to the bridles of the horses, about

σταδίων* χιλίων ἑξακοσίων.
[5]stadia [1]a [2]thousand [3]six [4]hundred.

bors, and their works follow them."
14 Then I looked, and behold, a white cloud, and on the cloud sat *One* like the Son of Man, having on His head a golden crown, and in His hand a sharp sickle.
15 And another angel came out of the temple, crying with a loud voice to Him who sat on the cloud, "Thrust in Your sickle and reap, for the time has come for You to reap, for the harvest of the earth is ripe."
16 So He who sat on the cloud thrust in His sickle on the earth, and the earth was reaped.
17 Then another angel came out of the temple which is in heaven, he also having a sharp sickle.
18 And another angel came out from the altar, who had power over fire, and he cried with a loud cry to him who had the sharp sickle, saying, "Thrust in your sharp sickle and gather the clusters of the vine of the earth, for her grapes are fully ripe."
19 So the angel thrust his sickle into the earth and gathered the vine of the earth, and threw *it* into the great winepress of the wrath of God.
20 And the winepress was trampled outside the city, and blood came out of the winepress, up to the horses' bridles, for one thousand six hundred furlongs.

---

m(**14:15**) TR adds σοι, *for you.* n(**14:18**) TR, NU read αι σταφυλαι αυτης, *its grapes.*

***(14:20)** *σταδιον (stadion).* Noun meaning a *stade,* a measure of distance equal to about 200 yards or 185 meters (Luke 24:13). It was the length of the running course at Mt. Olympia, and the word came to be used for the *arena* or *stadium* where footraces and other athletic events were held. The emphasis of the word, however, was always on the competition itself and not on the physical structure. Thus, Paul's metaphor in 1 Cor. 9:24 of "running in a stadium" is perhaps better translated as "running in a race."

15 Then I saw another
sign in heaven, great
and marvelous: seven angels
having the seven last plagues,
for in them the wrath of God is
complete.
2 And I saw *something* like a
sea of glass mingled with fire,
and those who have the victory
over the beast, over his image
and over his mark *and* over the
number of his name, standing
on the sea of glass, having
harps of God.
3 They sing the song of Moses,
the servant of God, and
the song of the Lamb, saying:

"Great and marvelous *are*
Your works,
Lord God Almighty!
Just and true *are* Your
ways,
O King of the saints!
4 Who shall not fear You,
O Lord, and glorify
Your name?
For *You* alone *are* holy.
For all nations shall come
and worship before
You,
For Your judgments have
been manifested."

5 After these things I looked,
and behold, the temple of the
tabernacle of the testimony in
heaven was opened.
6 And out of the temple came
the seven angels having the
seven plagues, clothed in pure
bright linen, and having their
chests girded with golden
bands.
7 Then one of the four living

Prelude to the Bowl Judgments

15 1 Καὶ εἶδον ἄλλο σημεῖον ἐν τῷ οὐρανῷ μέγα καὶ
And I saw another sign in - heaven great and
the sky

θαυμαστόν· ἀγγέλους ἑπτὰ ἔχοντας πληγὰς ἑπτὰ τὰς ἐσχάτας,
marvelous: angels ˜ seven having [4]plagues [2]seven [1]the [3]last,

ὅτι ἐν αὐταῖς ἐτελέσθη ὁ θυμὸς τοῦ Θεοῦ.
because in them [5]was [6]completed [1]the [2]wrath - [3]of [4]God.
has been

2 Καὶ εἶδον ὡς θάλασσαν ὑαλίνην μεμιγμένην πυρί,
And I saw like a sea ˜ glassy having been mixed with fire,

καὶ τοὺς νικῶντας ἐκ τοῦ Θηρίου καὶ ἐκ τῆς εἰκόνος
and the *ones* overcoming from the Beast and from - image ˜
those who prevailed over over

αὐτοῦ καὶ[a] ἐκ τοῦ ἀριθμοῦ τοῦ ὀνόματος αὐτοῦ, ἑστῶτας ἐπὶ
his and from the number - of name ˜ his, standing on
over

τὴν θάλασσαν τὴν ὑαλίνην, ἔχοντας τὰς κιθάρας τοῦ Θεοῦ.
the sea ˜ - glassy, having the harps - of God.

3 Καὶ ᾄδουσι τὴν ᾠδὴν Μωϋσέως, τοῦ δούλου τοῦ Θεοῦ,
And they sing the song of Moses, the bondservant - of God,
sang slave

καὶ τὴν ᾠδὴν τοῦ Ἀρνίου, λέγοντες,
and the song of the Lamb, saying,

"Μεγάλα καὶ θαυμαστὰ τὰ ἔργα σου,
"Great and marvelous *are* - works ˜ Your,

Κύριε ὁ Θεὸς ὁ Παντοκράτωρ!
Lord - God the Almighty!

Δίκαιαι καὶ ἀληθιναὶ αἱ ὁδοί σου,
Righteous and true *are* - ways ˜ Your,

Ὁ Βασιλεὺς τῶν ἐθνῶν![b]
The King of the nations!
O

4 Τίς οὐ μὴ φοβηθῇ σε, Κύριε,
Who not not fear You, Lord,
shall

Καὶ δοξάσῃ τὸ ὄνομά σου?
And glorify - name ˜ Your?

Ὅτι μόνος ἅγιος·
Because *You* alone *are* holy;

Ὅτι πάντες[c] ἥξουσι καὶ προσκυνήσουσιν ἐνώπιόν
Because all *nations* will come and will worship before

σου·
You;

Ὅτι τὰ δικαιώματά σου ἐφανερώθησαν."
Because - [2]righteous [3]judgments [1]Your were manifested."
have been

5 Καὶ μετὰ ταῦτα εἶδον, καὶ[d] ἠνοίγη ὁ ναὸς
And after these *things* I saw, and [9]was [10]opened [1]the [2]shrine

τῆς σκηνῆς τοῦ μαρτυρίου ἐν τῷ οὐρανῷ. 6 Καὶ ἐξῆλθον
[3]of [4]the [5]tent [6]of [7]the [8]testimony in - heaven. And [4]went [5]out
tabernacle

οἱ ἑπτὰ ἄγγελοι οἱ ἔχοντες τὰς ἑπτὰ πληγὰς[e] οἳ ἦσαν
[1]the [2]seven [3]angels the *ones* having the seven plagues who were

ἐνδεδυμένοι λίνον καθαρὸν λαμπρόν, καὶ περιεζωσμένοι περὶ
dressed in [3]linen [1]pure [2]bright, and girded around

τὰ στήθη ζώνας χρυσᾶς. 7 Καὶ ἓν ἐκ τῶν τεσσάρων
the chests *with* belts ˜ golden. And one of the four

---

[a](15:2) TR adds εκ του χαραγματος αυτου, *over his mark.* [b](15:3) TR reads αγιων, *saints.* [c](15:4) TR, NU read παντα τα εθνη, *all the nations.* [d](15:5) TR adds ιδου, *behold.* [e](15:6) TR, NU add εκ του ναου, *from the shrine.*

ζῴων ἔδωκε τοῖς ἑπτὰ ἀγγέλοις ἑπτὰ φιάλας χρυσᾶς
living creatures gave to the seven angels seven bowls ˜ golden

γεμούσας τοῦ θυμοῦ τοῦ Θεοῦ τοῦ ζῶντος εἰς τοὺς
being filled with the wrath - of God the *One* living to the
who lives forever and

αἰῶνας τῶν αἰώνων. 8 Καὶ ἐγεμίσθη ὁ ναὸς ἐκ τοῦ καπνοῦ
ages of the ages. And [3]was [4]filled [1]the [2]shrine by the smoke
ever.

ἐκ τῆς δόξης τοῦ Θεοῦ καὶ ἐκ τῆς δυνάμεως αὐτοῦ, καὶ
from the glory - of God and from - power ˜ His, and

οὐδεὶς ἐδύνατο εἰσελθεῖν εἰς τὸν ναὸν ἄχρι τελεσθῶσιν αἱ
no one was able to enter into the shrine until [8]were [9]ended [1]the

ἑπτὰ πληγαὶ τῶν ἑπτὰ ἀγγέλων.
[2]seven [3]plagues [4]of [5]the [6]seven [7]angels.

16 1 Καὶ ἤκουσα φωνῆς μεγάλης ἐκ τοῦ ναοῦ λεγούσης
And I heard a voice ˜ great from the shrine saying
loud

τοῖς ἑπτὰ ἀγγέλοις, "Ὑπάγετε καὶ ἐκχέατε τὰς ἑπτὰ[a]
to the seven angels, "Go and pour out the seven

φιάλας τοῦ θυμοῦ* τοῦ Θεοῦ εἰς τὴν γῆν."
bowls of the wrath - of God to the earth."
on

First Bowl: Malignant Sores

2 Καὶ ἀπῆλθεν ὁ πρῶτος καὶ ἐξέχεε τὴν φιάλην
And [4]went [5]off [1]the [2]first [3]*one* and poured out - bowl ˜

αὐτοῦ εἰς τὴν γῆν, καὶ ἐγένετο ἕλκος κακὸν καὶ πονηρὸν
his to the earth, and [6]came [1]a(n) [5]ulcer [2]bad [3]and [4]evil
on malignant

ἐπὶ τοὺς ἀνθρώπους τοὺς ἔχοντας τὸ χάραγμα τοῦ Θηρίου καὶ
on the men - having the mark of the Beast and

τοὺς προσκυνοῦντας τῇ εἰκόνι αὐτοῦ.
the *ones* worshiping - image ˜ his.
those who worshiped

Second Bowl: The Sea Turns to Blood

3 Καὶ ὁ δεύτερος ἄγγελος ἐξέχεε τὴν φιάλην αὐτοῦ εἰς
And the second angel poured out - bowl ˜ his into

τὴν θάλασσαν, καὶ ἐγένετο αἷμα ὡς νεκροῦ· καὶ πᾶσα
the sea, and it became blood as of a dead *man;* and all
turned into every

ψυχὴ ἀπέθανεν ἐν τῇ θαλάσσῃ.
life [4]died [1]in [2]the [3]sea.
living thing

Third Bowl: The Waters Turn to Blood

4 Καὶ ὁ τρίτος[b] ἐξέχεε τὴν φιάλην αὐτοῦ εἰς τοὺς
And the third *one* poured out - bowl ˜ his into the

ποταμοὺς καὶ εἰς τὰς πηγὰς τῶν ὑδάτων, καὶ ἐγένετο
rivers and into the springs - of waters, and it became
water, they turned into

αἷμα.
blood.

5 Καὶ ἤκουσα τοῦ ἀγγέλου τῶν ὑδάτων λέγοντος,
And I heard the angel of the waters saying,

"Δίκαιος[c] εἶ,
"[3]righteous [1]You [2]are,

creatures gave to the seven angels seven golden bowls full of the wrath of God who lives forever and ever.
8 The temple was filled with smoke from the glory of God and from His power, and no one was able to enter the temple till the seven plagues of the seven angels were completed.
16 Then I heard a loud voice from the temple saying to the seven angels, "Go and pour out the bowls of the wrath of God on the earth."
2 So the first went and poured out his bowl upon the earth, and a foul and loathsome sore came upon the men who had the mark of the beast and those who worshiped his image.
3 Then the second angel poured out his bowl on the sea, and it became blood as of a dead *man;* and every living creature in the sea died.
4 Then the third angel poured out his bowl on the rivers and springs of water, and they became blood.
5 And I heard the angel of the waters saying:

"You are righteous,
O Lord,

[a](16:1) TR omits επτα, *seven.* [b](16:4) TR adds αγγελος, *angel.* [c](16:5) TR adds Κυριε, *O Lord.*

*(16:1) θυμός *(thymos).* Noun meaning *wrath.* It is compared with the near synonym ὀργή, *anger, wrath,* which stresses more the various manifestations of anger. θυμός implies the underlying and abiding passion involved in wrath. Both words can be used of the holy and just wrath or anger of God against wickedness which is the basis for judgment of sinners (as here and elsewhere in Revelation). The word is also used for the wrath of Satan (Rev. 12:12) and of men (Heb. 11:27). The plural in 2 Cor. 12:20; Gal. 5:20 probably refers to particular outbursts of wrath. Cf. the cognate verb θυμόω, *make angry* or, in the passive voice, *become angry* (only in Matt. 2:16).

The One who is and who
was and who is to be,
Because You have judged
these things.
6 For they have shed the
blood of saints and
prophets,
And You have given them
blood to drink.
For it is their just due."

7 And I heard another from
the altar saying, "Even so,
Lord God Almighty, true and
righteous *are* Your judgments."
8 Then the fourth angel
poured out his bowl on the sun,
and power was given to him to
scorch men with fire.
9 And men were scorched
with great heat, and they blasphemed the name of God who
has power over these plagues;
and they did not repent and
give Him glory.
10 Then the fifth angel poured
out his bowl on the throne of
the beast, and his kingdom became full of darkness; and they
gnawed their tongues because
of the pain.
11 They blasphemed the God
of heaven because of their pains
and their sores, and did not repent of their deeds.
12 Then the sixth angel
poured out his bowl on the

Ὁ ὢν καὶ ὁ ἦν, ὅσιος,
The *One* being and the *One* was, holy,
who is who

Ὅτι ταῦτα ἔκρινας.
Because these *things* You judged.
have judged.

6 Ὅτι αἷμα ἁγίων καὶ προφητῶν ἐξέχεαν,
Because [4]*the* [5]blood [6]of [7]saints [8]and [9]prophets [1]they [2]poured [3]out,
shed,

Καὶ αἷμα αὐτοῖς ἔδωκας πιεῖν.
And [5]blood [3]to [4]them [1]You [2]gave to drink.

"Ἄξιοί εἰσι."
[3]worthy [1]They [2]are."
They deserve it."

7 Καὶ ἤκουσα[d] τοῦ θυσιαστηρίου λέγοντος,
And I heard the altar saying,

"Ναί, Κύριε ὁ Θεὸς ὁ Παντοκράτωρ,
"Yes, Lord - God the Almighty,

Ἀληθιναὶ καὶ δίκαιαι αἱ κρίσεις σου."
True and righteous *are* - judgments ˜ Your."

Fourth Bowl: Men Are Scorched

8 Καὶ ὁ τέταρτος[e] ἐξέχεε τὴν φιάλην αὐτοῦ ἐπὶ τὸν
And the fourth *one* poured out bowl ˜ his on the

ἥλιον, καὶ ἐδόθη αὐτῷ καυματίσαι ἐν πυρὶ τοὺς
sun, and it was given to him to burn [2]with [3]fire -
granted

ἀνθρώπους. 9 Καὶ ἐκαυματίσθησαν οἱ ἄνθρωποι καῦμα
[1]men. And [2]were [3]burned - [1]men with a burn ˜
humankind. severe

μέγα, καὶ ἐβλασφήμησαν οἱ ἄνθρωποι[f] τὸ ὄνομα τοῦ Θεοῦ
great, and blasphemed ˜ - men the name - of God
burns,

τοῦ ἔχοντος ἐξουσίαν ἐπὶ τὰς πληγὰς ταύτας. Καὶ οὐ
the *One* having power over - plagues ˜ these. And [3]not
who had

μετενόησαν δοῦναι αὐτῷ δόξαν.
[1]they [2]did repent to give [2]to [3]Him [1]glory.

Fifth Bowl: Darkness and Pain

10 Καὶ ὁ πέμπτος[g] ἐξέχεε τὴν φιάλην αὐτοῦ ἐπὶ τὸν
And the fifth *one* poured out - bowl ˜ his on the

θρόνον τοῦ Θηρίου, καὶ ἐγένετο ἡ βασιλεία αὐτοῦ
throne of the Beast, and [3]became - [2]kingdom [1]his

ἐσκοτωμένη· καὶ ἐμασῶντο τὰς γλώσσας αὐτῶν ἐκ τοῦ
[4]darkened; and they gnawed - tongues ˜ their from the

πόνου. 11 Καὶ ἐβλασφήμησαν τὸν Θεὸν τοῦ οὐρανοῦ ἐκ
pain. And they blasphemed the God - of heaven from
because of

τῶν πόνων αὐτῶν καὶ ἐκ τῶν ἑλκῶν αὐτῶν. Καὶ οὐ
- pains ˜ their and from - ulcers ˜ their. And [3]not
because of Yet

μετενόησαν ἐκ τῶν ἔργων αὐτῶν.
[1]they [2]did repent of - works ˜ their.

Sixth Bowl: Euphrates Dried Up

12 Καὶ ὁ ἕκτος[h] ἐξέχεε τὴν φιάλην αὐτοῦ ἐπὶ τὸν
And the sixth *one* poured out - bowl ˜ his on the

---

[d](16:7) TR adds αλλου εκ, *another one from.*
[e](16:8) TR adds αγγελος, *angel.* [f](16:9) TR, NU omit οι ανθρωποι, *men.*
[g](16:10) TR adds αγγελος, *angel.* [h](16:12) TR adds αγγελος, *angel.*

ποταμὸν τὸν μέγαν Εὐφράτην, καὶ ἐξηράνθη τὸ ὕδωρ αὐτοῦ,
river ˜ - great Euphrates, and [3]dried [4]up - [2]water [1]its,

ἵνα ἑτοιμασθῇ ἡ ὁδὸς τῶν βασιλέων τῶν ἀπὸ
so that [12]might [13]be [14]prepared [1]the [2]way [3]of [4]the [5]kings - [6]from
for

ἀνατολῆς ἡλίου. 13 Καὶ εἶδον ἐκ τοῦ στόματος
[7]*the* [8]rising [9]of [10]*the* [11]sun. And I saw *coming* out of the mouth
east.

τοῦ δράκοντος καὶ ἐκ τοῦ στόματος τοῦ Θηρίου καὶ ἐκ
of the dragon and out of the mouth of the Beast and out of

τοῦ στόματος τοῦ Ψευδοπροφήτου πνεύματα ἀκάθαρτα τρία
the mouth of the False Prophet [3]spirits [2]unclean [1]three

ὡς βάτραχοι. 14 Εἰσὶ γὰρ πνεύματα δαιμονίων ποιοῦντα
like frogs. [2]they [3]are [1]For spirits of demons doing
performing

σημεῖα, ἃ ἐκπορεύεται ἐπὶ τοὺς βασιλεῖς[i] τῆς
signs, which come out on the kings of the

οἰκουμένης ὅλης, συναγαγεῖν αὐτοὺς εἰς τὸν πόλεμον τῆς
[2]inhabited [3]earth [1]whole, to gather them to the battle -
war

ἡμέρας ἐκείνης[j] τῆς μεγάλης τοῦ Θεοῦ τοῦ Παντοκράτορος.
of [3]day [1]that - [2]great - of God - Almighty.

15 "Ἰδού, ἔρχομαι ὡς κλέπτης. Μακάριος ὁ γρηγορῶν
"Behold, I am coming like a thief. Blessed *is* the *one* watching
he who watches

καὶ τηρῶν τὰ ἱμάτια αὐτοῦ, ἵνα μὴ γυμνὸς περιπατῇ
and guarding - robes ˜ his, so that [3]not [5]naked [1]he [2]should [4]walk
guards

καὶ βλέπωσι τὴν ἀσχημοσύνην αὐτοῦ."
and they should see - shame ˜ his."

16 Καὶ συνήγαγεν αὐτοὺς εἰς τὸν τόπον τὸν καλούμενον
And he gathered them to the place - being called

Ἑβραϊστὶ Μαγεδών.[k]
in Hebrew Megiddo.

Seventh Bowl: The Earth Utterly Shaken

17 Καὶ ὁ ἕβδομος[l] ἐξέχεε τὴν φιάλην αὐτοῦ ἐπὶ τὸν
And the seventh *one* poured out - bowl ˜ his on the

ἀέρα, καὶ ἐξῆλθε φωνὴ μεγάλη ἀπὸ τοῦ ναοῦ τοῦ
air, and [4]came [5]out [1]a [3]voice [2]great from the shrine -
loud

οὐρανοῦ,[m] ἀπὸ τοῦ θρόνου, λέγουσα, "Γέγονε!" 18 Καὶ
of heaven, from the throne, saying, "It has been done!" And

ἐγένοντο ἀστραπαὶ καὶ βρονταὶ καὶ φωναὶ καὶ σεισμὸς
there occurred lightnings and thunders and sounds and a(n) earthquake ˜
noises

μέγας, οἷος οὐκ ἐγένετο ἀφ' οὗ οἱ ἄνθρωποι ἐγένοντο ἐπὶ
great, such as not ˜ did occur from when - men came on
severe,

τῆς γῆς, τηλικοῦτος σεισμός, οὕτω μέγας. 19 Καὶ
the earth, so great an earthquake, so great. And

ἐγένετο ἡ πόλις ἡ μεγάλη εἰς τρία μέρη, καὶ αἱ πόλεις
[4]came [5]to [6]be [1]the [3]city - [2]great into three parts, and the cities
was divided

τῶν ἐθνῶν ἔπεσον. Καὶ Βαβυλὼν ἡ μεγάλη ἐμνήσθη
of the nations fell. And Babylon the great was remembered
Gentiles

ἐνώπιον τοῦ Θεοῦ, δοῦναι αὐτῇ τὸ ποτήριον τοῦ οἴνου τοῦ
before - God, to give to her the cup of the wine of the

great river Euphrates, and its water was dried up, so that the way of the kings from the east might be prepared.
13 And I saw three unclean spirits like frogs *coming* out of the mouth of the dragon, out of the mouth of the beast, and out of the mouth of the false prophet.
14 For they are spirits of demons, performing signs, *which* go out to the kings of the earth and of the whole world, to gather them to the battle of that great day of God Almighty.
15 "Behold, I am coming as a thief. Blessed *is* he who watches, and keeps his garments, lest he walk naked and they see his shame."
16 And they gathered them together to the place called in Hebrew, Armageddon.
17 Then the seventh angel poured out his bowl into the air, and a loud voice came out of the temple of heaven, from the throne, saying, "It is done!"
18 And there were noises and thunderings and lightnings; and there was a great earthquake, such a mighty and great earthquake as had not occurred since men were on the earth.
19 Now the great city was divided into three parts, and the cities of the nations fell. And great Babylon was remembered before God, to give her the cup of the wine of the

[i]**(16:14)** TR adds *της γης και, of the earth and.*
[j]**(16:14)** NU omits *εκεινης, that.*
[k]**(16:16)** TR (*Αρμαγεδδων*) and NU (*Αρμαγεδων*) read *Armageddon,* which is Mt. Megiddo.
[l]**(16:17)** TR adds *αγγελος, angel.*
[m]**(16:17)** NU omits *του ουρανου, of heaven.*

fierceness of His wrath.
20 Then every island fled away, and the mountains were not found.
21 And great hail from heaven fell upon men, *each hailstone* about the weight of a talent. Men blasphemed God because of the plague of the hail, since that plague was exceedingly great.

17 Then one of the seven angels who had the seven bowls came and talked with me, saying to me, "Come, I will show you the judgment of the great harlot who sits on many waters,
2 "with whom the kings of the earth committed fornication, and the inhabitants of the earth were made drunk with the wine of her fornication."
3 So he carried me away in the Spirit into the wilderness. And I saw a woman sitting on a scarlet beast *which was* full of names of blasphemy, having seven heads and ten horns.
4 The woman was arrayed in purple and scarlet, and adorned with gold and precious stones and pearls, having in her hand a golden cup full of abominations and the filthiness of her fornication.
5 And on her forehead a name *was* written:

MYSTERY,
BABYLON THE GREAT,
THE MOTHER OF
HARLOTS AND OF THE
ABOMINATIONS OF THE
EARTH.

θυμοῦ τῆς ὀργῆς αὐτοῦ. **20** *Καὶ πᾶσα νῆσος ἔφυγε, καὶ*
rage - of wrath ˜ His. And every island fled, and

ὄρη οὐχ εὑρέθησαν. **21** *Καὶ χάλαζα μεγάλη, ὡς*
mountains not ˜ were found. And hail ˜ great, like *hail*
huge,

ταλαντιαία, καταβαίνει ἐκ τοῦ οὐρανοῦ ἐπὶ τοὺς
weighing a talent, comes down out of - heaven on -
came from the sky

ἀνθρώπους. Καὶ ἐβλασφήμησαν οἱ ἄνθρωποι τὸν Θεὸν ἐκ
men. And blasphemed ˜ - men - God from
because of

τῆς πληγῆς τῆς χαλάζης, ὅτι μεγάλη ἐστὶν ἡ πληγὴ αὕτη[n]
the plague - of hail, because [5]great [3]is - [2]plague [1]this
severe was

σφόδρα.
[4]exceedingly.

The Scarlet Woman and the Scarlet Beast

17 **1** *Καὶ ἦλθεν εἷς ἐκ τῶν ἑπτὰ ἀγγέλων τῶν ἐχόντων*
And [10]came [1]one [2]of [3]the [4]seven [5]angels - [6]having

τὰς ἑπτὰ φιάλας καὶ ἐλάλησε μετ' ἐμοῦ, λέγων,[a] *"Δεῦρο,*
[7]the [8]seven [9]bowls and spoke with me, saying, "Come,

δείξω σοι τὸ κρίμα τῆς πόρνης τῆς μεγάλης τῆς
I will show to you the judgment of the harlot ˜ - great the *one*
who

καθημένης ἐπὶ τῶν ὑδάτων τῶν πολλῶν, **2** *μεθ' ἧς*
sitting on - waters ˜ - many, with whom
sits

ἐπόρνευσαν οἱ βασιλεῖς τῆς γῆς, καὶ ἐμεθύσθησαν
[6]committed [7]fornication [1]the [2]kings [3]of [4]the [5]earth, and [7]became [8]drunk

οἱ κατοικοῦντες τὴν γῆν ἐκ τοῦ οἴνου τῆς
[1]the [2]*ones* [3]dwelling [4]on [5]the [6]earth from the wine -

πορνείας αὐτῆς." **3** *Καὶ ἀπήνεγκέ με εἰς ἔρημον ἐν*
of fornication ˜ her." And he led away ˜ me into a deserted *place* in

Πνεύματι. Καὶ εἶδον γυναῖκα καθημένην ἐπὶ Θηρίον τὸ
the Spirit. And I saw a woman sitting on a Beast ˜ -

κόκκινον γέμον ὀνόματα βλασφημίας, ἔχον κεφαλὰς ἑπτὰ
scarlet being filled with names of blasphemy, having heads ˜ seven

καὶ κέρατα δέκα. **4** *Καὶ ἡ γυνὴ ἦν περιβεβλημένη*
and horns ˜ ten. And the woman was clothed in

πορφυροῦν καὶ κόκκινον, κεχρυσωμένη χρυσίῳ καὶ λίθῳ
purple and scarlet, gilded with gold and stone ˜
stones

τιμίῳ καὶ μαργαρίταις, ἔχουσα ποτήριον χρυσοῦν ἐν τῇ χειρὶ
precious and pearls, having a cup ˜ golden in - hand ˜

αὐτῆς γέμον βδελυγμάτων καὶ τὰ ἀκάθαρτα τῆς πορνείας
her being filled of abominations and the impure *things* of the fornication
with impurities

τῆς γῆς.[b] **5** *Καὶ ἐπὶ τὸ μέτωπον αὐτῆς ὄνομα γεγραμμένον·*
of the earth. And on - forehead ˜ her a name *was* written:

ΜΥΣΤΗΡΙΟΝ
MYSTERY

ΒΑΒΥΛΩΝ Η ΜΕΓΑΛΗ
BABYLON THE GREAT

Η ΜΗΤΗΡ ΤΩΝ ΠΟΡΝΩΝ
THE MOTHER OF HARLOTS

ΚΑΙ ΤΩΝ ΒΔΕΛΥΓΜΑΤΩΝ ΤΗΣ ΓΗΣ.
AND OF THE ABOMINATIONS OF THE EARTH.

---

[n]**(16:21)** TR, NU read *αυτης*, *its.* [a]**(17:1)** TR adds *μοι*, *to me.* [b]**(17:4)** TR, NU read *πορνειας αυτης*, *of her fornication.*

6 Καὶ εἶδον τὴν γυναῖκα μεθύουσαν τοῦ αἵματος τῶν
And I saw the woman being drunk of the blood of the

ἁγίων, ἐκ τοῦ αἵματος τῶν μαρτύρων Ἰησοῦ. Καὶ ἐθαύμασα,
saints, from the blood of the witnesses of Jesus. And I marveled,
martyrs

ἰδὼν αὐτήν, θαῦμα* μέγα.
seeing her, with amazement ˜ great.
when I saw

The Meaning of the Woman and the Beast

7 Καὶ εἶπέ μοι ὁ ἄγγελος, "Διὰ τί
And [3]said [4]to [5]me [1]the [2]angel, "On account of what
"Why

ἐθαύμασας? Ἐγὼ ἐρῶ σοι τὸ μυστήριον τῆς γυναικὸς
did you marvel? I will tell to you the mystery of the woman

καὶ τοῦ Θηρίου τοῦ βαστάζοντος αὐτήν, τοῦ ἔχοντος τὰς
and of the Beast - carrying her, the *one* having the
he who has

ἑπτὰ κεφαλὰς καὶ τὰ δέκα κέρατα. 8 Τὸ Θηρίον ὃ εἶδες
seven heads and the ten horns. The Beast which you saw

ἦν, καὶ οὐκ ἔστι, καὶ μέλλει ἀναβαίνειν ἐκ τῆς ἀβύσσου
was, and not ˜ is, and is about to come up out of the abyss
bottomless pit

καὶ εἰς ἀπώλειαν ὑπάγειν. Καὶ θαυμάσονται οἱ
and [3]to [4]perdition [1]to [2]go. And [7]will [8]marvel [1]the [2]*ones*
those

κατοικοῦντες τὴν γῆν, ὧν οὐ γέγραπται τὸ ὄνομα [c] ἐπὶ
[3]dwelling [4]on [5]the [6]earth, whose [3]not [2]is [4]written - [1]name on
who dwell in

τοῦ Βιβλίου τῆς Ζωῆς ἀπὸ καταβολῆς κόσμου, βλεπόντων
the Book - of Life from *the* foundation of *the* world, seeing
when they see

ὅτι ἦν τὸ Θηρίον, καὶ οὐκ ἔστι, καὶ παρέσται.[d]
that [3]was [1]the [2]Beast, and not ˜ is, and shall be present.

9 "Ὧδε ὁ νοῦς ὁ ἔχων σοφίαν· Αἱ ἑπτὰ κεφαλαὶ
"Here *is* the mind the *one* having wisdom: The seven heads
which has

ἑπτὰ ὄρη εἰσὶν ὅπου ἡ γυνὴ κάθηται ἐπ᾽ αὐτῶν.
[2]seven [3]mountains [1]are where the woman sits on them.
on which the woman sits.

10 Καὶ βασιλεῖς εἰσιν ἑπτά. Οἱ πέντε ἔπεσον, ὁ εἷς
And [4]kings [1]*there* [2]are [3]seven. - Five fell, - one
have fallen,

ἔστιν, ὁ ἄλλος οὔπω ἦλθε. Καὶ ὅταν ἔλθῃ,
is, the other not yet came. And whenever he comes,
has not yet come.

ὀλίγον δεῖ αὐτὸν μεῖναι. 11 Καὶ τὸ
[8]a [9]little [10]*while* [1]it [2]is [3]necessary [4]*for* [5]him [6]to [7]remain. And the
he must

Θηρίον ὃ ἦν, καὶ οὐκ ἔστι, καὶ οὗτος ὄγδοός ἐστι, καὶ
Beast which was, and not ˜ is, and this *one* [2]an [3]eighth [1]is, and

ἐκ τῶν ἑπτά ἐστι, καὶ εἰς ἀπώλειαν ὑπάγει. 12 Καὶ τὰ δέκα
[2]of [3]the [4]seven [1]is, and to perdition he is going. And the ten

κέρατα ἃ εἶδες δέκα βασιλεῖς εἰσιν οἵτινες βασιλείαν
horns which you saw [2]ten [3]kings [1]are who [4]a [5]kingdom

οὔπω ἔλαβον, ἀλλ᾽ ἐξουσίαν ὡς βασιλεῖς μίαν ὥραν
[1]not [2]yet [3]received, but [3]authority [4]as [5]kings [6]for [7]one [8]hour
have received,

6 I saw the woman, drunk with the blood of the saints and with the blood of the martyrs of Jesus. And when I saw her, I marveled with great amazement.
7 But the angel said to me, "Why did you marvel? I will tell you the mystery of the woman and of the beast that carries her, which has the seven heads and the ten horns.
8 "The beast that you saw was, and is not, and will ascend out of the bottomless pit and go to perdition. And those who dwell on the earth will marvel, whose names are not written in the Book of Life from the foundation of the world, when they see the beast that was, and is not, and yet is.
9 "Here *is* the mind which has wisdom: The seven heads are seven mountains on which the woman sits.
10 "There are also seven kings. Five have fallen, one is, *and* the other has not yet come. And when he comes, he must continue a short time.
11 "The beast that was, and is not, is himself also the eighth, and is of the seven, and is going to perdition.
12 "The ten horns which you saw are ten kings who have received no kingdom as yet, but they receive authority for one

---

c(17:8) TR reads *τα ονοματα, (whose) names.*
d(17:8) TR reads *καιπερ εστιν, and yet is.*

***(17:6)** *θαυμα (thauma).* Noun meaning *wonder, amazement, marvel.* In 2 Cor. 11:14 it more generally refers to an object or idea that causes wonder; here in Rev. 17:6 it refers to the wonder or amazement itself. The cognate verb *θαυμάζω, wonder, marvel, be amazed,* occurs often, including the emphatic cognate accusative construction here: "I marveled a great marvel" is the equivalent of "I greatly marveled."

hour as kings with the beast.
13 "These are of one mind,
and they will give their power
and authority to the beast.
14 "These will make war with
the Lamb, and the Lamb will
overcome them, for He is Lord
of lords and King of kings; and
those *who are* with Him *are*
called, chosen, and faithful."
15 Then he said to me, "The
waters which you saw, where
the harlot sits, are peoples,
multitudes, nations, and
tongues.
16 "And the ten horns which
you saw on the beast, these will
hate the harlot, make her desolate and naked, eat her flesh
and burn her with fire.
17 "For God has put it into
their hearts to fulfill His purpose, to be of one mind, and to
give their kingdom to the beast,
until the words of God are fulfilled.
18 "And the woman whom
you saw is that great city which
reigns over the kings of the
earth."
18 After these things I
saw another angel
coming down from heaven, having great authority, and the
earth was illuminated with his
glory.
2 And he cried mightily with
a loud voice, saying, "Babylon
the great is fallen, is fallen, and

λαμβάνουσι μετὰ τοῦ Θηρίου. **13** *Οὗτοι μίαν ἔχουσι γνώμην,*
[1]they [2]receive with the Beast. These one ˜ have mind,
purpose,

καὶ τὴν δύναμιν καὶ ἐξουσίαν αὐτῶν τῷ Θηρίῳ διδόασιν.[e]
and - [2]power [3]and [4]authority [1]their [7]to [8]the [9]Beast [5]they [6]give.

14 *Οὗτοι μετὰ τοῦ Ἀρνίου πολεμήσουσι, καὶ τὸ Ἀρνίον*
These [4]with [5]the [6]Lamb [1]will [2]make [3]war, and the Lamb

νικήσει αὐτούς, ὅτι Κύριος κυρίων ἐστὶ καὶ Βασιλεὺς
will conquer them, because [3]Lord [4]of [5]lords [1]He [2]is and King

βασιλέων· καὶ οἱ μετ' αὐτοῦ κλητοὶ καὶ ἐκλεκτοὶ καὶ
of kings; and the *ones* with Him *are* called and chosen and
those who are elect

πιστοί."
faithful."

15 *Καὶ λέγει μοι, "Τὰ ὕδατα ἃ εἶδες, οὗ ἡ*
And he says to me, "The waters which you saw, where the
said

πόρνη κάθηται, λαοὶ καὶ ὄχλοι εἰσί, καὶ ἔθνη καὶ
harlot sits, [2]peoples [3]and [4]multitudes [1]are, and nations and

γλῶσσαι. **16** *Καὶ τὰ δέκα κέρατα ἃ εἶδες, καὶ*[f] *τὸ*
tongues. And the ten horns which you saw, and the
languages.

Θηρίον, οὗτοι μισήσουσι τὴν πόρνην καὶ ἠρημωμένην
Beast, these will hate the harlot and [4]desolated

ποιήσουσιν αὐτὴν καὶ γυμνὴν ποιήσουσιν αὐτὴν[g] *καὶ τὰς*
[1]will [2]make [3]her and [4]naked [1]will [2]make [3]her and -

σάρκας αὐτῆς φάγονται καὶ αὐτὴν κατακαύσουσιν ἐν πυρί.
[4]flesh [3]her [1]will [2]eat and [3]her [1]will [2]burn [4]up with fire.

17 *Ὁ γὰρ Θεὸς ἔδωκεν εἰς τὰς καρδίας αὐτῶν ποιῆσαι τὴν*
- For God gave into - hearts ˜ their to do -

γνώμην αὐτοῦ καὶ ποιῆσαι γνώμην μίαν καὶ δοῦναι τὴν
mind ˜ His and to make mind ˜ one and to give -
purpose be of

βασιλείαν αὐτῶν τῷ Θηρίῳ ἄχρι τελεσθῶσιν οἱ λόγοι τοῦ
kingdom ˜ their to the Beast until [5]are [6]fulfilled [1]the [2]words -

Θεοῦ. **18** *Καὶ ἡ γυνὴ ἣν εἶδες ἐστὶν ἡ πόλις ἡ*
[3]of [4]God. And the woman whom you saw is the city ˜ -

μεγάλη ἡ ἔχουσα βασιλείαν ἐπὶ τῶν βασιλέων ἐπὶ τῆς
great the *one* having kingship over the kings on the
which has royal rule

γῆς."
earth."

Babylon the Great Is Fallen

18 **1** *Μετὰ ταῦτα εἶδον ἄλλον ἄγγελον καταβαίνοντα*
After these *things* I saw another angel coming down

ἐκ τοῦ οὐρανοῦ, ἔχοντα ἐξουσίαν μεγάλην, καὶ ἡ γῆ
out of - heaven, having authority ˜ great, and the earth
from the sky,

ἐφωτίσθη ἐκ τῆς δόξης αὐτοῦ. **2** *Καὶ ἔκραξε ἰσχυρᾷ*
was lit up from - glory ˜ his. And he cried out with a strong
splendor

φωνῇ,[a] *λέγων,*
voice, saying,

"Ἔπεσεν Βαβυλὼν ἡ μεγάλη,
"[4]fell [1]Babylon [2]the [3]great,
"has fallen

---

[e](17:13) TR reads *διαδιδωσουσιν*, *shall give up*. [f](17:16) TR reads *επι*, *on*. [g](17:16) TR, NU omit *ποιησουσιν αυτην*, *and will make her*. [a](18:2) TR reads *εν ισχυι φωνη μεγαλη*, *mightily with a loud voice*.

Καὶ ἐγένετο κατοικητήριον δαιμόνων,
And she became a dwelling place of demons,
has become

Καὶ φυλακὴ παντὸς πνεύματος ἀκαθάρτου,
And a prison of every spirit ˜ unclean,
cage

Καὶ φυλακὴ παντὸς ὀρνέου ἀκαθάρτου καὶ μεμισημένου.
And a prison of every [4]bird [1]unclean [2]and [3]hated.
cage detestable.

3 Ὅτι ἐκ τοῦ οἴνου τοῦ θυμοῦ τῆς πορνείας αὐτῆς
Because of the wine of the wrath - of fornication ˜ her

Πεπώκασι πάντα τὰ ἔθνη,
[4]have [5]drunk [1]All [2]the [3]nations,

Καὶ οἱ βασιλεῖς τῆς γῆς μετ' αὐτῆς
And the kings of the earth [3]with [4]her

ἐπόρνευσαν,
[1]committed [2]fornication,

Καὶ οἱ ἔμποροι τῆς γῆς ἐκ τῆς δυνάμεως τοῦ
And the merchants of the earth from the strength -
wholesalers wealth

στρήνους αὐτῆς ἐπλούτησαν."
of luxury ˜ her became rich."

4 Καὶ ἤκουσα ἄλλην φωνὴν ἐκ τοῦ οὐρανοῦ λέγουσαν,
And I heard another voice out of - heaven saying,
from the sky

"Ἔξελθε ἐξ αὐτῆς, ὁ λαός μου,
"Come out of her, - people ˜ my,

Ἵνα μὴ συγκοινωνήσητε ταῖς ἁμαρτίαις αὐτῆς,
So that not you participate - in sins ˜ her,
Lest

Καὶ ἐκ τῶν πληγῶν αὐτῆς ἵνα μὴ λάβητε.
And [7]of - [9]plagues [8]her [1]so [2]that [5]not [3]you [4]may [6]receive.
lest

5 Ὅτι ἐκολλήθησαν[b] αὐτῆς αἱ ἁμαρτίαι ἄχρι τοῦ
Because [3]reached [1]her - [2]sins to -
have reached the

οὐρανοῦ,
heaven,
sky,

Καὶ ἐμνημόνευσεν αὐτῆς ὁ Θεὸς τὰ ἀδικήματα αὐτῆς.
And [2]remembered [3]her - [1]God - *for* misdeeds ˜ her.
crimes

6 Ἀπόδοτε αὐτῇ ὡς καὶ αὐτὴ ἀπέδωκεν,[c]
Give back to her as also she gave back,

Καὶ διπλώσατε τὰ διπλᾶ ὡς καὶ αὐτή,
And double the doubles as also she *did,*
pay back double

Καὶ κατὰ τὰ ἔργα αὐτῆς·
And according to - works ˜ her;

Ἐν τῷ ποτηρίῳ αὐτῆς ᾧ ἐκέρασε, κεράσατε αὐτῇ
In - cup ˜ her which she mixed, mix for her

διπλοῦν.
a double *portion.*

7 Ὅσα ἐδόξασεν αὐτὴν καὶ ἐστρηνίασε,
In as many *things* as she glorified herself and lived luxuriously,

Τοσοῦτον δότε αὐτῇ βασανισμὸν καὶ πένθος·
By so much give to her torment and sorrow;

Ὅτι ἐν τῇ καρδίᾳ αὐτῆς λέγει ὅτι
Because in - heart ˜ her she says -

has become a dwelling place of demons, a prison for every foul spirit, and a cage for every unclean and hated bird!
3 "For all the nations have drunk of the wine of the wrath of her fornication, the kings of the earth have committed fornication with her, and the merchants of the earth have become rich through the abundance of her luxury."
4 And I heard another voice from heaven saying, "Come out of her, my people, lest you share in her sins, and lest you receive of her plagues.
5 "For her sins have reached to heaven, and God has remembered her iniquities.
6 "Render to her just as she rendered to you, and repay her double according to her works; in the cup which she has mixed, mix double for her.
7 "In the measure that she glorified herself and lived luxuriously, in the same measure give her torment and sorrow; for she says in her heart, 'I sit

[b](**18:5**) TR reads *ηκολουθησαν, followed.*
[c](**18:6**) TR adds *υμιν, to you.*

as queen, and am no widow,
and will not see sorrow.'
8 "Therefore her plagues will
come in one day—death and
mourning and famine. And she
will be utterly burned with fire,
for strong *is* the Lord God who
judges her.
9 "The kings of the earth
who committed fornication and
lived luxuriously with her will
weep and lament for her, when
they see the smoke of her
burning,
10 "standing at a distance for
fear of her torment, saying,
'Alas, alas, that great city Babylon, that mighty city! For in
one hour your judgment has
come.'
11 "And the merchants of the
earth will weep and mourn over
her, for no one buys their merchandise anymore:
12 "merchandise of gold and
silver, precious stones and
pearls, fine linen and purple,
silk and scarlet, every kind of
citron wood, every kind of object of ivory, every kind of object of most precious wood,
bronze, iron, and marble;
13 "and cinnamon and in-
cense, fragrant oil and frankincense, wine and oil, fine flour

d(18:13) NU adds αμωμον και, *spice and*.

'Κάθημαι βασίλισσα, καὶ χήρα οὐκ εἰμί,
'I sit a queen, and [4]a [5]widow [3]not [1]I [2]am,

Καὶ πένθος οὐ μὴ ἴδω.'
And sorrow not not (by no means) I shall see.'

8 Διὰ τοῦτο ἐν μιᾷ ἡμέρᾳ ἥξουσιν αἱ πληγαὶ
On account of this in one day will come - plagues ˜

αὐτῆς —
her —

Θάνατος, πένθος, καὶ λιμός.
Death, sorrow, and famine.

Καὶ ἐν πυρὶ κατακαυθήσεται,
And in (with) fire she will be burned,

Ὅτι ἰσχυρὸς Κύριος ὁ Θεὸς ὁ κρίνας αὐτήν.
Because strong *is the* Lord - God the *One* judging (who has judged) her.

The World Mourns Babylon's Fall

9 "Καὶ κλαύσουσι καὶ κόψονται ἐπ' αὐτὴν οἱ
"And [17]will [18]weep [19]and [20]will [21]mourn [22]over [23]her [1]the

βασιλεῖς τῆς γῆς οἱ μετ' αὐτῆς
[2]kings [3]of [4]the [5]earth [6]the [7]*ones* [15]with [16]her

πορνεύσαντες καὶ στρηνιάσαντες, ὅταν
[8]having [9]committed [10]fornication [11]and [12]having [13]lived [14]luxuriously, when

βλέπωσι τὸν καπνὸν τῆς πυρώσεως αὐτῆς, 10 ἀπὸ μακρόθεν
they see the smoke - of burning ˜ her, [2]from [3]afar

ἑστηκότες διὰ τὸν φόβον τοῦ βασανισμοῦ αὐτῆς,
[1]standing on account of the fear - of torment ˜ her,

λέγοντες,
saying,

'Οὐαί, οὐαί, ἡ πόλις ἡ μεγάλη Βαβυλών,
'Woe, woe, ('Alas, alas,) the city ˜ - great Babylon,

Ἡ πόλις ἡ ἰσχυρά!
The city ˜ - mighty!

Ὅτι μιᾷ ὥρᾳ ἦλθεν ἡ κρίσις σου.'
Because in one hour [3]came - [2]judgment [1]your.'

11 "Καὶ οἱ ἔμποροι τῆς γῆς κλαύσουσι καὶ πενθήσουσιν
"And the merchants (wholesalers) of the earth will weep and will mourn

ἐπ' αὐτῇ, ὅτι τὸν γόμον αὐτῶν οὐδεὶς ἀγοράζει οὐκέτι·
over her, because - [5]cargo [4]their [1]no [2]one [3]buys any more:

12 γόμον χρυσοῦ καὶ ἀργύρου, καὶ λίθου τιμίου καὶ
cargo of gold and of silver, and of stone ˜ precious and

μαργαρίτου, καὶ βυσσίνου καὶ πορφυροῦ, καὶ σηρικοῦ καὶ
of pearls, and of fine linen and of purple, and of silk and

κοκκίνου, καὶ πᾶν ξύλον θύϊνον, καὶ πᾶν σκεῦος ἐλεφάντινον,
of scarlet, and every wood ˜ citron, and every vessel (object) ˜ ivory,

καὶ πᾶν σκεῦος ἐκ ξύλου τιμιωτάτου καὶ χαλκοῦ καὶ
and every vessel (object) of [3]wood [1]most [2]precious and of bronze and

σιδήρου καὶ μαρμάρου, 13 καὶ κινάμωμον καὶ[d] θυμιάματα,
of iron and of marble, and cinnamon and incense,

καὶ μύρον καὶ λίβανον, καὶ οἶνον καὶ ἔλαιον, καὶ σεμίδαλιν
and perfume and frankincense, and wine and olive oil, and fine flour

καὶ σῖτον, καὶ πρόβατα καὶ κτήνη, καὶ ἵππων καὶ ῥαιδῶν,
and wheat, and sheep and cattle, and of horses and of chariots,

καὶ σωμάτων καὶ ψυχὰς ἀνθρώπων. **14** Καὶ ἡ ὀπώρα τῆς
and of bodies and souls of men. And the fruit of the
lives for

ἐπιθυμίας τῆς ψυχῆς σου ἀπῆλθεν ἀπὸ σοῦ, καὶ πάντα τὰ
craving - of soul ˜ your went from you, and all the
which your soul craved has gone

λιπαρὰ καὶ τὰ λαμπρὰ ἀπώλετο[e] ἀπὸ σοῦ, καὶ
sumptuous *things* and the gaudy *things* perished from you, and
have perished

οὐκέτι αὐτὰ οὐ μὴ εὕρῃς. **15** Οἱ ἔμποροι
no more [6]them [3]not [4]not [1]shall [2]you [5]find. The merchants
by any means wholesalers

τούτων, οἱ πλουτήσαντες ἀπ᾽ αὐτῆς, ἀπὸ μακρόθεν
of these *things,* the *ones* becoming rich from her, [3]from [4]afar
who became

στήσονται διὰ τὸν φόβον τοῦ βασανισμοῦ αὐτῆς, καὶ
[1]will [2]stand on account of the fear - of torment ˜ her, both

κλαίοντες καὶ πενθοῦντες **16** καὶ λέγοντες,
weeping and sorrowing and saying,

'Οὐαί, οὐαί, ἡ πόλις ἡ μεγάλη,
'Woe, woe, the city ˜ - great,
'Alas, alas,

Ἡ περιβεβλημένη βύσσον, καὶ πορφυροῦν καὶ
The *one* having been clothed in fine linen, and purple and
She who was

κόκκινον,
scarlet,

Καὶ κεχρυσωμένη χρυσίῳ καὶ λίθῳ τιμίῳ καὶ
And having been gilded with gold and stone ˜ precious and
stones

μαργαρίταις!
pearls!

17 Ὅτι μιᾷ ὥρᾳ ἠρημώθη ὁ τοσοῦτος πλοῦτος.'
Because in one hour [4]was [5]laid [6]waste - [1]such [2]great [3]wealth.'

"Καὶ πᾶς κυβερνήτης καὶ πᾶς ὁ ἐπὶ τόπον πλέων καὶ
"And every steersman and every - *one* [2]along [3]a [4]place [1]sailing and
captain all those the coast

ναῦται καὶ ὅσοι τὴν θάλασσαν ἐργάζονται, ἀπὸ μακρόθεν
sailors and as many as [2]the [3]sea [1]work, [5]from [6]afar

ἔστησαν **18** καὶ ἔκραζον, βλέποντες τὸν καπνὸν τῆς
[4]stood and were crying out, seeing the smoke -

πυρώσεως αὐτῆς, λέγοντες, 'Τίς ὁμοία τῇ πόλει τῇ μεγάλῃ!'
of burning ˜ her, saying, 'Who *is* like the city ˜ - great!'

19 Καὶ ἔβαλον χοῦν ἐπὶ τὰς κεφαλὰς αὐτῶν καὶ
And they threw dust on - heads ˜ their and

ἔκραζον κλαίοντες καὶ πενθοῦντες καὶ λέγοντες,
were crying out, weeping and sorrowing and saying,

'Οὐαί, οὐαί, ἡ πόλις ἡ μεγάλη,
'Woe, woe, the city ˜ - great,
'Alas, alas,

Ἐν ᾗ ἐπλούτησαν πάντες οἱ ἔχοντες τὰ πλοῖα ἐν
By which [9]became [10]rich [1]all [2]the [3]*ones* [4]having - [5]ships [6]in
those who had

τῇ θαλάσσῃ
[7]the [8]sea

and wheat, cattle and sheep,
horses and chariots, and bodies
and souls of men.
14 "The fruit that your soul
longed for has gone from you,
and all the things which are rich
and splendid have gone from
you, and you shall find them no
more at all.
15 "The merchants of these
things, who became rich by
her, will stand at a distance for
fear of her torment, weeping
and wailing,
16 "and saying, 'Alas, alas,
that great city that was clothed
in fine linen, purple, and scarlet, and adorned with gold and
precious stones and pearls!
17 'For in one hour such great
riches came to nothing.' Every
shipmaster, all who travel by
ship, sailors, and as many as
trade on the sea, stood at a distance
18 "and cried out when they
saw the smoke of her burning,
saying, 'What *is* like this great
city?'
19 "They threw dust on their
heads and cried out, weeping
and wailing, and saying, 'Alas,
alas, that great city, in which all
who had ships on the sea be-

[e](**18:14**) TR reads απηλθεν, *have gone.*

came rich by her wealth! For in
one hour she is made desolate.'
20 "Rejoice over her,
O heaven, and *you* holy apostles and prophets, for God has
avenged you on her!"
21 Then a mighty angel took
up a stone like a great millstone
and threw *it* into the sea, saying, "Thus with violence the
great city Babylon shall be
thrown down, and shall not be
found anymore.
22 "The sound of harpists,
musicians, flutists, and trumpeters shall not be heard in you
anymore. No craftsman of any
craft shall be found in you anymore, and the sound of a millstone shall not be heard in you
anymore.
23 "The light of a lamp shall
not shine in you anymore, and
the voice of bridegroom and
bride shall not be heard in you

Ἐκ τῆς τιμιότητος αὐτῆς!
From - costliness ˜ her!
costly abundance

Ὅτι μιᾷ ὥρᾳ ἠρημώθη.'
Because in one hour she was laid waste.'

20 Εὐφραίνου ἐπ' αὐτῇ, οὐρανέ,
Be glad over her, *O* heaven,

Καὶ οἱ ἅγιοι καὶ οἱ[f] ἀπόστολοι καὶ οἱ προφῆται,
And - *you* saints and - apostles and - prophets,

Ὅτι ἔκρινεν ὁ Θεὸς τὸ κρίμα ὑμῶν ἐξ αὐτῆς!"
Because judged ˜ - God - judgment ˜ your against her!"
has pronounced judgment for you

Finality of Babylon's Fall

21 Καὶ ἦρεν εἷς ἄγγελος ἰσχυρὸς λίθον ὡς μύλον μέγαν καὶ ἔβαλεν εἰς τὴν θάλασσαν, λέγων,
And [4]picked [5]up [1]one [3]angel [2]mighty a stone like a millstone ˜ great and threw *it* into the sea, saying,
a huge

"Οὕτως ὁρμήματι βληθήσεται Βαβυλὼν ἡ μεγάλη πόλις,
"Thus with violence [5]will [6]be [7]cast [8]down [1]Babylon [2]the [3]great [4]city,

Καὶ οὐ μὴ εὑρεθῇ ἔτι.
And [3]not [4]not [1]she [2]shall be found *any* more.
by no means

22 Καὶ φωνὴ κιθαρῳδῶν καὶ μουσικῶν καὶ αὐλητῶν καὶ σαλπιστῶν
And *the* sound of harpists and of musicians and of flutists and of trumpeters

Οὐ μὴ ἀκουσθῇ ἐν σοὶ ἔτι.
[2]not [3]not [1]Shall [4]be [5]heard in you *any* more.
by no means

Καὶ πᾶς τεχνίτης πάσης τέχνης
And every craftsman of every craft
no of any

Οὐ μὴ εὑρεθῇ ἐν σοὶ ἔτι.
[2]not [3]not [1]Shall [4]be [5]found in you *any* more.
Shall by any means

Καὶ φωνὴ μύλου
And *the* sound of a mill

Οὐ μὴ ἀκουσθῇ ἐν σοὶ ἔτι.
[2]not [3]not [1]Shall [4]be [5]heard in you *any* more.
by no means

23 Καὶ φῶς λύχνου
And *the* light of a lamp

Οὐ μὴ φανῇ ἐν σοὶ ἔτι.
[2]not [3]not [1]Shall [4]shine in you *any* more.
by no means

Καὶ φωνὴ νυμφίου καὶ νύμφης
And *the* voice of a bridegroom and of a bride

Οὐ μὴ ἀκουσθῇ ἐν σοὶ ἔτι.
[2]not [3]not [1]Shall [4]be [5]heard in you *any* more.
by no means

---

f(18:20) TR omits και οι, *and the*.

Οἱ[g] ἔμποροί σου ἦσαν οἱ μεγιστᾶνες τῆς γῆς,
- merchants ~ Your were the magnates of the earth,
wholesalers great men

Ὅτι ἐν τῇ φαρμακείᾳ σου ἐπλανήθησαν πάντα τὰ
Because by - sorcery ~ your 4were 5deceived 1all 2the

ἔθνη.
3nations.

24 Καὶ ἐν αὐτῇ αἵματα προφητῶν καὶ ἁγίων εὑρέθη,
And in her *the* blood of prophets and of saints was found,

Καὶ πάντων τῶν ἐσφαγμένων ἐπὶ τῆς γῆς."
And of all the *ones* having been slaughtered on the earth."
those who had been slain

Heaven Exults over the Judgment of Babylon

19 1 Μετὰ ταῦτα ἤκουσα ὡς[a] φωνὴν μεγάλην
After these *things* I heard as *it were* a voice ~ great
loud

ὄχλου πολλοῦ ἐν τῷ οὐρανῷ, λεγόντων,
of a multitude ~ large in - heaven, saying,
huge

"Ἀλληλούϊα!*
"Alleluia!
"Hallelujah!

Ἡ σωτηρία καὶ ἡ δύναμις καὶ ἡ δόξα[b] τοῦ Θεοῦ[c]
- Salvation and - power and - glory *are* - of God ~

ἡμῶν!
our!

2 Ὅτι ἀληθιναὶ καὶ δίκαιαι αἱ κρίσεις αὐτοῦ,
Because true and righteous *are* - judgments ~ His,

Ὅτι ἔκρινε τὴν πόρνην τὴν μεγάλην
Because He judged the harlot ~ - great
has judged

Ἥτις διέφθειρε τὴν γῆν ἐν τῇ πορνείᾳ αὐτῆς·
Who corrupted the earth with - fornication ~ her;

Καὶ ἐξεδίκησε τὸ αἷμα τῶν δούλων αὐτοῦ ἐκ
And He avenged the blood - of bondservants ~ His *shed* by
has avenged slaves

χειρὸς αὐτῆς."
hand ~ her."

3 Καὶ δεύτερον εἴρηκεν,[d]
And a second *one* said,

"Ἀλληλούϊα!
"Alleluia!
"Hallelujah!

Καὶ ὁ καπνὸς αὐτῆς ἀναβαίνει εἰς τοὺς αἰῶνας τῶν
And - smoke ~ her goes up to the ages of the
forever and ever!"

αἰώνων!"
ages!"

4 Καὶ ἔπεσον οἱ πρεσβύτεροι οἱ εἴκοσι τέσσαρες καὶ
And 10fell 11down 1the 4elders - 2twenty- 3four 5and

τὰ τέσσαρα ζῷα καὶ προσεκύνησαν τῷ Θεῷ τῷ
6the 7four 8living 9creatures and they worshiped - God the *One*
who

καθημένῳ ἐπὶ τῷ θρόνῳ, λέγοντες,
sitting on the throne, saying,
sits

anymore. For your merchants
were the great men of the
earth, for by your sorcery all
the nations were deceived.
24 "And in her was found the
blood of prophets and saints,
and of all who were slain on the
earth."

19 After these things I
heard a loud voice of a
great multitude in heaven, saying, "Alleluia! Salvation and
glory and honor and power *belong* to the Lord our God!
2 "For true and righteous *are*
His judgments, because He has
judged the great harlot who
corrupted the earth with her
fornication; and He has avenged
on her the blood of His servants
shed by her."
3 Again they said, "Alleluia!
Her smoke rises up forever and
ever!"
4 And the twenty-four elders
and the four living creatures fell
down and worshiped God who
sat on the throne, saying,

[g](18:23) TR, NU add Οτι, *For.* [a](19:1) TR omits ως, *as (it were).*
[b](19:1) TR reads η δοξα και η τιμη και η δυναμις, *the glory and the honor and the power.*
[c](19:1) TR reads Κυριω τω Θεω ημων, *to the Lord our God.* [d](19:3) TR, NU read δευτερον ειρηκαν, *a second (time) they said.*

*(19:1) ἀλληλούϊα (*allēlouia*). A transliteration of the Hebrew *hallû yāh, praise Yah* (Yah being the poetic form for Yahweh). Since Greek manuscripts added rough breathing marks where the initial "h" sound occurs, it is likely that even in Greek ἀλληλούϊα was originally pronounced "hallēlouia," at least by Hebrew Christians. The spelling *alleluia* found in many hymns is the Latin spelling.

"Amen! Alleluia!"
5 Then a voice came from
the throne, saying, "Praise our
God, all you His servants and
those who fear Him, both small
and great!"
6 And I heard, as it were,
the voice of a great multitude,
as the sound of many waters
and as the sound of mighty
thunderings, saying, "Alleluia!
For the Lord God Omnipotent
reigns!
7 "Let us be glad and rejoice
and give Him glory, for the
marriage of the Lamb has
come, and His wife has made
herself ready."
8 And to her it was granted
to be arrayed in fine linen, clean
and bright, for the fine linen is
the righteous acts of the saints.
9 Then he said to me,
"Write: 'Blessed *are* those who
are called to the marriage supper of the Lamb!'" And he said
to me, "These are the true sayings of God."
10 And I fell at his feet to wor-

"Ἀμήν! Ἀλληλούϊα!"
"Amen! Alleluia!"
Hallelujah!"

5 Καὶ φωνὴ ἀπὸ τοῦ θρόνου ἐξῆλθε, λέγουσα,
And a voice [3]from [4]the [5]throne [1]came [2]out, saying,

"Αἰνεῖτε τῷ Θεὸν ἡμῶν,
"Praise - God ˜ our,

Πάντες οἱ δοῦλοι αὐτοῦ καὶ οἱ φοβούμενοι
All - bondservants ˜ His and the *ones* fearing
slaves those who fear

αὐτόν,
Him,

Οἱ μικροὶ καὶ οἱ μεγάλοι!"
The small and the great!"

6 Καὶ ἤκουσα ὡς φωνὴν ὄχλου πολλοῦ καὶ ὡς
And I heard as *it were* a voice of a multitude ˜ large and like
huge

φωνὴν ὑδάτων πολλῶν καὶ ὡς φωνὴν βροντῶν ἰσχυρῶν,
the sound of waters ˜ many and like *the* sound of thunders ˜ mighty,

λέγοντες,
saying,

"Ἀλληλούϊα!
"Alleluia!
"Hallelujah!

Ὅτι ἐβασίλευσε Κύριος ὁ Θεὸς ἡμῶν,[e] ὁ
Because [7]reigned [1]*the* [2]Lord - [4]God [3]our, [5]the
has begun to reign

Παντοκράτωρ!
[6]Almighty!

7 Χαίρωμεν καὶ ἀγαλλιώμεθα καὶ δῶμεν τὴν δόξαν
Let us rejoice and let us exult and let us give the glory

αὐτῷ,
to Him,

Ὅτι ἦλθεν ὁ γάμος τοῦ Ἀρνίου,
Because [6]came [1]the [2]wedding [3]of [4]the [5]Lamb,
has come

Καὶ ἡ γυνὴ αὐτοῦ ἡτοίμασεν ἑαυτήν."
And - wife ˜ His prepared herself."
has prepared

8 Καὶ ἐδόθη αὐτῇ ἵνα περιβάληται βύσσινον
And it was given to her that she should be dressed in fine linen
granted

λαμπρὸν καὶ καθαρόν, τὸ γὰρ βύσσινον τὰ δικαιώματα
bright and pure, the ˜ for fine linen [2]the [3]righteous [4]deeds

τῶν ἁγίων ἐστί.
[5]of [6]the [7]saints [1]is.

9 Καὶ λέγει μοι, "Γράψον· 'Μακάριοι οἱ εἰς τὸν
And he says to me, "Write: 'Blessed *are* the *ones* [4]to [5]the
said those who

δεῖπνον τοῦ γάμου τοῦ Ἀρνίου κεκλημένοι!'" Καὶ
[6]supper [7]of [8]the [9]wedding [10]of [11]the [12]Lamb [1]having [2]been [3]called!'" And
marriage supper are invited!'"

λέγει μοι, "Οὗτοι οἱ λόγοι ἀληθινοὶ τοῦ Θεοῦ εἰσι."
he says to me, "These [2]the [4]words [3]true - [5]of [6]God [1]are."
said

10 Καὶ ἔπεσα ἔμπροσθεν τῶν ποδῶν αὐτοῦ προσκυνῆσαι
And I fell before - feet ˜ his to worship

[e](19:6) TR omits ημων, *our.*

αὐτῷ. Καὶ λέγει μοι, "Ὅρα μή! Σύνδουλός σού
him. And he says to me, "See *that you do* not! [4]fellow [5]bondservant [3]your
said fellow slave

εἰμι καὶ τῶν ἀδελφῶν σου τῶν ἐχόντων τὴν μαρτυρίαν
[1]I [2]am and - of brothers ˜ your the *ones* having the testimony
who have

Ἰησοῦ. Τῷ Θεῷ προσκύνησον! Ἡ γὰρ μαρτυρία τοῦ Ἰησοῦ
of Jesus. - God ˜ Worship! the ˜ For testimony - of Jesus

ἐστι τὸ πνεῦμα τῆς προφητείας."
is the spirit - of prophecy."

Christ Comes on a White Horse

11 Καὶ εἶδον τὸν οὐρανὸν ἀνεῳγμένον, καὶ ἰδού,
And I saw - heaven having been opened, and behold,
the sky opened,

ἵππος λευκός, καὶ ὁ καθήμενος ἐπ' αὐτόν, καλούμενος
a horse ˜ white, and the *One* sitting on it, being called
He who sat

Πιστὸς καὶ Ἀληθινός, καὶ ἐν δικαιοσύνῃ κρίνει καὶ
Faithful and True, and in righteousness He judges and
with

πολεμεῖ. 12 Οἱ δὲ ὀφθαλμοὶ αὐτοῦ φλὸξ πυρός, καὶ ἐπὶ
makes war. - And eyes ˜ His *were* a flame of fire, and on

τὴν κεφαλὴν αὐτοῦ διαδήματα πολλά, ἔχων ὀνόματα
- head ˜ His *were* diadems ˜ many, having names
crowns

γεγραμμένα, καὶ[f] ὄνομα γεγραμμένον ὃ οὐδεὶς οἶδεν εἰ
written, and a name written which no one knows if
except

μὴ αὐτός, 13 καὶ περιβεβλημένος ἱμάτιον βεβαμμένον
not He *Himself,* and having been clothed in a robe having been dipped
He is

αἵματι, καὶ κέκληται τὸ ὄνομα αὐτοῦ, Ὁ Λόγος τοῦ
in blood, and [3]has [4]been [5]called - [2]name [1]His, The Word -
is

Θεοῦ. 14 Καὶ τὰ στρατεύματα τὰ ἐν τῷ οὐρανῷ ἠκολούθει
of God. And the armies - in - heaven were following

αὐτῷ ἐπὶ ἵπποις λευκοῖς, ἐνδεδυμένοι βύσσινον λευκὸν
Him on horses ˜ white, having been dressed in [3]fine [4]linen [2]white

καθαρόν. 15 Καὶ ἐκ τοῦ στόματος αὐτοῦ ἐκπορεύεται
[1]clean. And out of - mouth ˜ His proceeds

ῥομφαία* δίστομος[g] ὀξεῖα, ἵνα ἐν αὐτῇ πατάξῃ τὰ
a [3]sword [2]double-edged [1]sharp, so that with it He might strike the

ἔθνη. Καὶ αὐτὸς ποιμανεῖ αὐτοὺς ἐν ῥάβδῳ σιδηρᾷ. Καὶ
nations. And He will shepherd them with a(n) rod ˜ iron. And

αὐτὸς πατεῖ τὴν ληνὸν τοῦ οἴνου τοῦ θυμοῦ[h] τῆς ὀργῆς
He treads the winepress of the wine of the rage of the wrath

τοῦ Θεοῦ τοῦ Παντοκράτορος. 16 Καὶ ἔχει ἐπὶ τὸ ἱμάτιον
of the God ˜ - Almighty. And He has on the robe
His

καὶ ἐπὶ τὸν μηρὸν αὐτοῦ ὄνομα γεγραμμένον·
and on - thigh ˜ His a name having been written:

ΒΑΣΙΛΕΥΣ ΒΑΣΙΛΕΩΝ
KING OF KINGS

ΚΑΙ ΚΥΡΙΟΣ ΚΥΡΙΩΝ.
AND LORD OF LORDS.

ship him. But he said to me, "See *that you do* not *do that!* I am your fellow servant, and of your brethren who have the testimony of Jesus. Worship God! For the testimony of Jesus is the spirit of prophecy."

11 Now I saw heaven opened, and behold, a white horse. And He who sat on him *was* called Faithful and True, and in righteousness He judges and makes war.

12 His eyes *were* like a flame of fire, and on His head *were* many crowns. He had a name written that no one knew except Himself.

13 He *was* clothed with a robe dipped in blood, and His name is called The Word of God.

14 And the armies in heaven, clothed in fine linen, white and clean, followed Him on white horses.

15 Now out of His mouth goes a sharp sword, that with it He should strike the nations. And He Himself will rule them with a rod of iron. He Himself treads the winepress of the fierceness and wrath of Almighty God.

16 And He has on *His* robe and on His thigh a name written:

KING OF KINGS
AND LORD OF LORDS.

---

f(**19:12**) TR, NU omit *ονοματα γεγραμμενα και, names written and.*

g(**19:15**) TR, NU omit *διστομος, double-edged.*

h(**19:15**) TR adds *και, and (of the wrath).*

***(19:15)** *ῥομφαία (rhomphaia).* Noun meaning a large, broad Thracian *sword* or *spear.* The *ῥομφαία* is generally distinguished from the *μάχαιρα, short sword* or *dagger,* used both literally and symbolically in the NT. In the LXX *ῥομφαία* and *μάχαιρα* are used interchangeably. However, *ῥομφαία* is only used in figurative contexts within the NT. In most instances in Revelation (including here at 19:15), it refers to an act of divine judgment. In Rev. 6:4 it describes deaths resulting from military conflict. The idiom "a sword will pierce through your own soul" in Luke 2:35 signifies deep personal anguish and sorrow.

17 Then I saw an angel standing in the sun; and he cried with a loud voice, saying to all the birds that fly in the midst of heaven, "Come and gather together for the supper of the great God,
18 "that you may eat the flesh of kings, the flesh of captains, the flesh of mighty men, the flesh of horses and of those who sit on them, and the flesh of all *people,* free and slave, both small and great."
19 And I saw the beast, the kings of the earth, and their armies, gathered together to make war against Him who sat on the horse and against His army.
20 Then the beast was captured, and with him the false prophet who worked signs in his presence, by which he deceived those who received the mark of the beast and those who worshiped his image. These two were cast alive into the lake of fire burning with brimstone.
21 And the rest were killed with the sword which proceeded from the mouth of Him who sat on the horse. And all the birds were filled with their flesh.

20 Then I saw an angel coming down from heaven, having the key to the bottomless pit and a great chain

The Beast and His Armies Are Defeated

17 Καὶ εἶδον[i] ἄγγελον ἑστῶτα ἐν τῷ ἡλίῳ· καὶ ἔκραξεν
And I saw an angel standing in the sun; and he cried out

ἐν φωνῇ μεγάλῃ, λέγων πᾶσι τοῖς ὀρνέοις τοῖς πετομένοις
with a voice ˜ great, saying to all the birds - flying
loud,

ἐν μεσουρανήματι, "Δεῦτε συνάχθητε εἰς τὸν δεῖπνον τὸν
in midheaven, "Come gather together for the supper ˜ -

μέγαν τοῦ Θεοῦ,[j] **18** ἵνα φάγητε σάρκας βασιλέων καὶ
great - of God, so that you may eat *the* flesh of kings and

σάρκας χιλιάρχων καὶ σάρκας ἰσχυρῶν καὶ σάρκας ἵππων
the flesh of chiliarchs and *the* flesh of mighty *men* and *the* flesh of horses
captains

καὶ τῶν καθημένων ἐπ' αὐτῶν καὶ σάρκας πάντων,
and of the *ones* sitting on them and *the* flesh of all *people,*
those who ride

ἐλευθέρων τε καὶ δούλων, καὶ μικρῶν τε καὶ μεγάλων."
[2]free [3]*people* [1]both and slaves, and [2]of [3]small [1]both and of great."

19 Καὶ εἶδον τὸ Θηρίον καὶ τοὺς βασιλεῖς τῆς γῆς καὶ τὰ
And I saw the Beast and the kings of the earth and -

στρατεύματα αὐτῶν συνηγμένα ποιῆσαι τὸν
armies ˜ their having been gathered together to make -

πόλεμον μετὰ τοῦ καθημένου ἐπὶ τοῦ ἵππου καὶ μετὰ τοῦ
war with the *One* sitting on the horse and with -
Him who rode

στρατεύματος αὐτοῦ. **20** Καὶ ἐπιάσθη τὸ Θηρίον, καὶ ὁ
army ˜ His. And [3]was [4]captured [1]the [2]Beast, and the

μετ' αὐτοῦ Ψευδοπροφήτης, ὁ ποιήσας τὰ σημεῖα
[3]with [4]him [1]False [2]Prophet, the *one* having done the signs
he who had performed

ἐνώπιον αὐτοῦ, ἐν οἷς ἐπλάνησε τοὺς λαβόντας τὸ
before him, by which he deceived the *ones* receiving the
had deceived those who had received

χάραγμα τοῦ Θηρίου καὶ τοὺς προσκυνοῦντας τῇ εἰκόνι
mark of the Beast and the *ones* worshiping - image ˜
those who worshiped

αὐτοῦ. Ζῶντες ἐβλήθησαν οἱ δύο εἰς τὴν λίμνην τοῦ πυρὸς
his. [5]living [3]were [4]thrown [1]The [2]two into the lake - of fire
alive

τὴν καιομένην ἐν θείῳ. **21** Καὶ οἱ λοιποὶ ἀπεκτάνθησαν
- burning with sulfur. And the rest were killed
brimstone.

ἐν τῇ ῥομφαίᾳ τοῦ καθημένου ἐπὶ τοῦ ἵππου τῇ
with the sword of the *One* sitting on the horse the *one*
Him who rode which

ἐξελθούσῃ ἐκ τοῦ στόματος αὐτοῦ. Καὶ πάντα τὰ ὄρνεα
proceeding out of - mouth ˜ His. And all the birds
proceeds from

ἐχορτάσθησαν ἐκ τῶν σαρκῶν αὐτῶν.
were filled from - flesh ˜ their.
gorged themselves

Satan Is Bound for 1000 Years

20 **1** Καὶ εἶδον ἄγγελον καταβαίνοντα ἐκ τοῦ οὐρανοῦ,
And I saw an angel coming down out of - heaven,
from the sky,

ἔχοντα τὴν κλεῖν τῆς ἀβύσσου καὶ ἅλυσιν μεγάλην ἐπὶ τὴν
having the key of the abyss and a chain ˜ great on -
bottomless pit huge in

[i](19:17) TR, NU add ενα, *one (angel).*
[j](19:17) TR reads το δειπνον του μεγαλου Θεου, *the supper of the great God.*

χεῖρα αὐτοῦ. **2** Καὶ ἐκράτησε τὸν δράκοντα, τὸν ὄφιν τὸν
hand ˜ his. And he seized the dragon, the serpent ˜ -

ἀρχαῖον ὅς ἐστι διάβολος καὶ ὁ Σατανᾶς, ὁ πλανῶν τὴν
ancient who is a devil and - Satan, the *one* deceiving the
slanderer the Adversary, he who deceives

οἰκουμένην ὅλην,[a] καὶ ἔδησεν αὐτὸν χίλια ἔτη·
[2]inhabited [3]earth [1]whole, and he bound him for a thousand years;

3 καὶ ἔβαλεν αὐτὸν εἰς τὴν ἄβυσσον καὶ ἔκλεισε καὶ
and he threw him into the abyss and closed and
bottomless pit locked

ἐσφράγισεν ἐπάνω αὐτοῦ ἵνα μὴ πλανᾷ ἔτι
sealed *it* over him so that [3]not [1]he [2]should [4]deceive [7]*any* [8]more

τὰ ἔθνη ἄχρι τελεσθῇ τὰ χίλια ἔτη. Μετὰ ταῦτα
[5]the [6]nations until [4]were [5]finished [1]the [2]thousand [3]years. After these *things*

δεῖ λυθῆναι αὐτὸν μικρὸν χρόνον.
it is necessary *for* [2]to [3]be [4]loosed [1]him *for* a small time.
released short

in his hand.
2 He laid hold of the dragon,
that serpent of old, who is *the*
Devil and Satan, and bound him
for a thousand years;
3 and he cast him into the
bottomless pit, and shut him
up, and set a seal on him, so
that he should deceive the nations no more till the thousand
years were finished. But after
these things he must be released for a little while.
4 And I saw thrones, and
they sat on them, and judgment
was committed to them. Then *I
saw* the souls of those who had
been beheaded for their witness to Jesus and for the word
of God, who had not worshiped
the beast or his image, and had
not received *his* mark on their
foreheads or on their hands.
And they lived and reigned with
Christ for a thousand years.
5 But the rest of the dead did
not live again until the thousand
years were finished. This *is* the
first resurrection.
6 Blessed and holy *is* he who
has part in the first resurrection. Over such the second
death has no power, but they
shall be priests of God and of
Christ, and shall reign with Him
a thousand years.
7 Now when the thousand
years have expired, Satan will
be released from his prison
8 and will go out to deceive

The Saints Reign with Christ for 1000 Years

4 Καὶ εἶδον θρόνους, καὶ ἐκάθισαν ἐπ᾽ αὐτούς, καὶ κρίμα
And I saw thrones, and they sat on them, and judgment

ἐδόθη αὐτοῖς, καὶ τὰς ψυχὰς τῶν πεπελεκισμένων
was given to them, and the souls of the *ones* having been beheaded
those who had

διὰ τὴν μαρτυρίαν Ἰησοῦ καὶ διὰ τὸν λόγον τοῦ
on account of the testimony of Jesus and on account of the word -

Θεοῦ, καὶ οἵτινες οὐ προσεκύνησαν τὸ Θηρίον οὐδὲ τὴν
of God, and those who not ˜ did worship the Beast nor -
had not worshiped

εἰκόνα αὐτοῦ, καὶ οὐκ ἔλαβον τὸ χάραγμα ἐπὶ τὸ
image ˜ his, and [3]not [1]they [2]did [4]receive the mark on the
their

μέτωπον καὶ ἐπὶ τὴν χεῖρα αὐτῶν. Καὶ ἔζησαν καὶ
forehead and on - hand ˜ their. And they lived and
came to life

ἐβασίλευσαν μετὰ τοῦ Χριστοῦ τὰ[b] χίλια ἔτη. **5** Καὶ οἱ
reigned with - Christ *for* the thousand years. And the

λοιποὶ τῶν νεκρῶν οὐκ ἔζησαν[c] ἄχρι τελεσθῇ τὰ
rest of the dead not ˜ did live until [4]were [5]finished [1]the
come to life

χίλια ἔτη. Αὕτη ἡ ἀνάστασις ἡ πρώτη.
[2]thousand [3]years. This *is* the resurrection ˜ - first.

6 Μακάριος καὶ ἅγιος ὁ ἔχων μέρος ἐν τῇ
Blessed and holy *is* the *one* having a part in the
who has

ἀναστάσει τῇ πρώτῃ. Ἐπὶ τούτων ὁ δεύτερος θάνατος οὐκ
resurrection ˜ - first. On these the second death not ˜

ἔχει ἐξουσίαν, ἀλλ᾽ ἔσονται ἱερεῖς τοῦ Θεοῦ καὶ τοῦ
does have power, but they will be priests - of God and -

Χριστοῦ, καὶ βασιλεύσουσι μετ᾽ αὐτοῦ χίλια ἔτη.
of Christ, and they will reign with Him for a thousand years.

The Last Satanic Rebellion Is Crushed

7 Καὶ μετὰ[d] τὰ χίλια ἔτη, λυθήσεται ὁ Σατανᾶς
And after the thousand years, [2]will [3]be [4]loosed - [1]Satan
released the Adversary

ἐκ τῆς φυλακῆς αὐτοῦ **8** καὶ ἐξελεύσεται πλανῆσαι τὰ
from - prison ˜ his and he will come out to deceive the

[a](20:2) TR, NU omit ο πλανων την οικουμενην ολην, *he who deceives the whole inhabited earth.*
[b](20:4) TR, NU omit τα, *the.*
[c](20:5) TR reads ουκ ανεζησαν, *did not come to life again.*
[d](20:7) TR, NU read οταν τελεσθη, *when (the thousand years) are finished.*

the nations which are in the
four corners of the earth, Gog
and Magog, to gather them together to battle, whose number
is as the sand of the sea.
9 They went up on the
breadth of the earth and surrounded the camp of the saints
and the beloved city. And fire
came down from God out of
heaven and devoured them.
10 The devil, who deceived
them, was cast into the lake of
fire and brimstone where the
beast and the false prophet *are.*
And they will be tormented day
and night forever and ever.
11 Then I saw a great white
throne and Him who sat on it,
from whose face the earth and the
heaven fled away. And there
was found no place for them.
12 And I saw the dead, small
and great, standing before God,
and books were opened. And
another book was opened,
which is *the Book* of Life. And
the dead were judged according
to their works, by the things
which were written in the
books.
13 The sea gave up the dead
who were in it, and Death and
Hades delivered up the dead
who were in them. And they
were judged, each one according to his works.
14 Then Death and Hades
were cast into the lake of fire.
This is the second death.

ἔθνη τὰ ἐν ταῖς τέσσαρσι γωνίαις τῆς γῆς, τὸν Γὼγ
nations the *ones* in the four corners of the earth, - Gog
which are

καὶ τὸν Μαγώγ, συναγαγεῖν αὐτοὺς εἰς τὸν πόλεμον,
and - Magog, to gather together ˜ them to the war,

ὧν ὁ ἀριθμὸς αὐτῶν ὡς ἡ ἄμμος τῆς θαλάσσης.
of whom the number of them *is* like the sand of the sea.
whose number

9 Καὶ ἀνέβησαν ἐπὶ τὸ πλάτος τῆς γῆς καὶ ἐκύκλευσαν
And they went up on the breadth of the earth and surrounded
broad plain land

τὴν παρεμβολὴν τῶν ἁγίων καὶ τὴν πόλιν τὴν ἠγαπημένην.
the camp of the saints and the city ˜ - beloved.

Καὶ κατέβη πῦρ ἐκ τοῦ οὐρανοῦ ἀπὸ τοῦ Θεοῦ[e] καὶ
And [2]came [3]down [1]fire out of - heaven from - God and
the sky

κατέφαγεν αὐτούς. 10 Καὶ ὁ Διάβολος,* ὁ πλανῶν
ate up ˜ them. And the Devil, the *one* deceiving
devoured who deceived

αὐτούς, ἐβλήθη εἰς τὴν λίμνην τοῦ πυρὸς καὶ θείου ὅπου
them, was thrown into the lake - of fire and sulfur where
brimstone

καὶ τὸ Θηρίον καὶ ὁ Ψευδοπροφήτης. Καὶ βασανισθήσονται
also the Beast and the False Prophet *are.* And they will be tormented

ἡμέρας καὶ νυκτὸς εἰς τοὺς αἰῶνας τῶν αἰώνων.
day and night to the ages of the ages.
forever and ever.

The Great White Throne Judgment

11 Καὶ εἶδον θρόνον μέγαν λευκὸν καὶ τὸν καθήμενον
And I saw a [3]throne [1]great [2]white and the *One* sitting
huge He who sat

ἐπ' αὐτόν, οὗ ἀπὸ προσώπου ἔφυγεν ἡ γῆ καὶ ὁ
on it, whose ˜ from face [5]fled [1]the [2]earth [3]and -
the

οὐρανός. Καὶ τόπος οὐχ εὑρέθη αὐτοῖς. 12 Καὶ εἶδον τοὺς
[4]heaven. And a place not ˜ was found for them. And I saw the
sky. no place

νεκρούς, τοὺς μεγάλους καὶ τοὺς μικρούς, ἑστῶτας ἐνώπιον τοῦ
dead, the great and the small, standing before the

θρόνου,[f] καὶ βιβλία ἠνοιξαν.[g] Καὶ ἄλλο Βιβλίον ἠνεῴχθη,
throne, and [3]books [1]they [2]opened. And another Book was opened,

ὅ ἐστι τῆς Ζωῆς. Καὶ ἐκρίθησαν οἱ νεκροὶ ἐκ
which is *the Book* - of Life. And [3]were [4]judged [1]the [2]dead by

τῶν γεγραμμένων ἐν τοῖς βιβλίοις, κατὰ τὰ ἔργα
the *things* having been written in the books, according to - works ˜

αὐτῶν. 13 Καὶ ἔδωκεν ἡ θάλασσα τοὺς νεκροὺς τοὺς ἐν
their. And [3]gave [4]*up* [1]the [2]sea the dead the *ones* in
who were

αὐτῇ, καὶ ὁ Θάνατος καὶ ὁ Ἅιδης ἔδωκαν τοὺς νεκροὺς τοὺς
it, and - Death and - Hades gave *up* the dead the *ones*
who were

ἐν αὐτοῖς. Καὶ ἐκρίθησαν ἕκαστος κατὰ τὰ ἔργα
in them. And they were judged each one according to - works ˜

αὐτοῦ. 14 Καὶ ὁ Θάνατος καὶ ὁ Ἅιδης ἐβλήθησαν εἰς τὴν
their. And - Death and - Hades were thrown into the

λίμνην τοῦ πυρός.[h] Οὗτος ὁ θάνατος ὁ δεύτερός ἐστιν, ἡ
lake - of fire. This [2]the [4]death - [3]second [1]is, the

---

[e](20:9) NU omits απο του Θεου, *from God.*
[f](20:12) TR reads Θεου, *(before) God.*
[g](20:12) Both TR (ηνεωχθησαν) and NU (ηνοιχθησαν) read *were opened.* [h](20:14) TR omits η λιμνη του πυρος, *the lake of fire.*

---

*(20:10) διάβολος (*diabolos*). Adjective meaning *slanderous,* derived from the verb διαβάλλω, *throw across, defame, slander.* This use of the term is applied to both men and women in certain vice lists within the Pastoral Epistles (cf. 1 Tim. 3:11; 2 Tim. 3:3). Most NT examples of διάβολος are substantive and refer to Satan as *the devil.* In the LXX διάβολος is used to translate Hebrew *sāṭān, adversary.* The *Satan* is the adversary and accuser of the brothers (Zech. 3:1; Rev. 12:10–12) who is opposed to God and His plans. The Christian's defense against the devil is "the whole armor

λίμνη τοῦ πυρός. 15 Καὶ εἴ τις οὐχ εὑρέθη ἐν τῷ Βιβλίῳ
lake - of fire. And if anyone not ˜ was found [4]in [5]the [6]Book

τῆς Ζωῆς γεγραμμένος, ἐβλήθη εἰς τὴν λίμνην τοῦ
- [7]of [8]Life [1]having [2]been [3]written, he was thrown into the lake -

πυρός.
of fire.

All Things Are Made New

21 1 Καὶ εἶδον οὐρανὸν καινὸν καὶ γῆν καινήν, ὁ
And I saw a heaven ˜ new and a earth ˜ new, the ˜

γὰρ πρῶτος οὐρανὸς καὶ ἡ πρώτη γῆ ἀπῆλθον. Καὶ ἡ
for first heaven and the first earth went away. And the
were gone.

θάλασσα οὐκ ἔστιν ἔτι. 2 Καὶ[a] τὴν πόλιν τὴν ἁγίαν,
sea not ˜ is *any* longer. And the city ˜ - holy,
did not exist

Ἰερουσαλὴμ Καινήν, εἶδον καταβαίνουσαν ἐκ τοῦ οὐρανοῦ
Jerusalem ˜ New, I saw coming down out of - heaven
the sky

ἀπὸ τοῦ Θεοῦ, ἡτοιμασμένην ὡς νύμφην κεκοσμημένην
from - God, having been prepared like a bride having been adorned

τῷ ἀνδρὶ αὐτῆς.
for husband ˜ her.

3 Καὶ ἤκουσα φωνῆς μεγάλης ἐκ τοῦ οὐρανοῦ[b]
And I heard a voice ˜ great out of - heaven
loud from the sky

λεγούσης, "Ἰδού, ἡ σκηνὴ τοῦ Θεοῦ μετὰ τῶν ἀνθρώπων,
saying, "Behold, the tent - of God *is* with - men,
tabernacle

καὶ σκηνώσει μετ' αὐτῶν, καὶ αὐτοὶ λαὸς αὐτοῦ ἔσονται,
and He will tabernacle with them, and they [4]people [3]His [1]shall [2]be,
dwell

καὶ αὐτὸς ὁ Θεὸς μετ' αὐτῶν ἔσται. 4 Καὶ ἐξαλείψει
and He - [3]God [4]with [5]them [1]shall [2]be. And He will wipe away

ἀπ' αὐτῶν[c] πᾶν δάκρυον ἀπὸ τῶν ὀφθαλμῶν αὐτῶν, καὶ ὁ
from them every tear from - eyes ˜ their, and -

θάνατος οὐκ ἔσται ἔτι, οὔτε πένθος οὔτε κραυγὴ οὔτε
death not ˜ shall be *any* longer, nor sorrow nor crying out nor
exist

πόνος οὐκ ἔσται ἔτι, ὅτι τὰ πρῶτα ἀπῆλθεν."
pain not ˜ shall be *any* longer, because the first *things* went away."
shall exist have gone."

5 Καὶ εἶπεν ὁ καθήμενος ἐπὶ τῷ θρόνῳ, "Ἰδού,
And [7]said [1]the [2]*One* [3]sitting [4]on [5]the [6]throne, "Behold,
He who sat

πάντα καινὰ ποιῶ." Καὶ λέγει,[d] "Γράψον, ὅτι
[4]all [5]*things* [6]new [1]I [2]am [3]making." And He says, "Write, because
said,

οὗτοι οἱ λόγοι πιστοὶ καὶ ἀληθινοὶ τοῦ Θεοῦ[e] εἰσι."
these - words [2]faithful [3]and [4]true - [5]*words* [6]of [7]God [1]are."
trustworthy

6 Καὶ εἶπέ μοι, "Γέγονα τὸ Ἄλφα καὶ τὸ Ὦ καὶ
And He said to me, "I have become the Alpha and the Omega and
"I am

ἡ Ἀρχὴ καὶ τὸ Τέλος. Ἐγὼ τῷ διψῶντι δώσω αὐτῷ
the Beginning and the End. I to the *one* thirsting will give to him
him who is thirsty

15 And anyone not found written in the Book of Life was cast
into the lake of fire.
21 Now I saw a new
heaven and a new
earth, for the first heaven and
the first earth had passed away.
Also there was no more sea.
2 Then I, John, saw the holy
city, New Jerusalem, coming
down out of heaven from God,
prepared as a bride adorned for
her husband.
3 And I heard a loud voice
from heaven saying, "Behold,
the tabernacle of God *is* with
men, and He will dwell with
them, and they shall be His
people. God Himself will be
with them *and be* their God.
4 "And God will wipe away
every tear from their eyes;
there shall be no more death,
nor sorrow, nor crying. There
shall be no more pain, for the
former things have passed
away."
5 Then He who sat on the
throne said, "Behold, I make all
things new." And He said to
me, "Write, for these words
are true and faithful."
6 And He said to me, "It is
done! I am the Alpha and the
Omega, the Beginning and the
End. I will give of the fountain

---

a(21:2) TR adds εγω Ιωαννης ειδον, *I John saw,* and omits ειδον, *I saw,* after Καινην, *New.*
b(21:3) NU reads θρονου, *throne.* c(21:4) TR reads ο Θεος, *God,* for απ αυτων, *from them;* NU omits both.
d(21:5) TR adds μοι, *to me.*
e(21:5) TR, NU omit του Θεου, *of God.*

---

of God" (Eph. 6:10–17). Jesus calls Judas a διάβολος because his betrayal of Jesus was motivated by Satan (cf. John 6:70; cf. John 13:2, 27).

of the water of life freely to him
who thirsts.
7 "He who overcomes shall
inherit all things, and I will be
his God and he shall be My son.
8 "But the cowardly, unbelieving, abominable, murderers, sexually immoral, sorcerers, idolaters, and all liars
shall have their part in the lake
which burns with fire and brimstone, which is the second
death."
9 Then one of the seven angels who had the seven bowls
filled with the seven last
plagues came to me and talked
with me, saying, "Come, I will
show you the bride, the Lamb's
wife."
10 And he carried me away in
the Spirit to a great and high
mountain, and showed me the
great city, the holy Jerusalem,
descending out of heaven from
God,
11 having the glory of God.
Her light *was* like a most precious stone, like a jasper stone,
clear as crystal.
12 Also she had a great and
high wall with twelve gates, and
twelve angels at the gates, and
names written on them, which
are *the names* of the twelve
tribes of the children of Israel:
13 three gates on the east,
three gates on the north, three
gates on the south, and three
gates on the west.
14 Now the wall of the city
had twelve foundations, and on

---

[f](21:7) TR reads κληρονομησει παντα, *and he will inherit all things;* NU reads κληρονομησει ταυτα, *he will inherit these things.* [g](21:8) TR, NU omit αμαρτωλοις και, *sinners and.* [h](21:8) TR reads φαρμακευσιν, *sorcerers.* [i](21:9) TR adds προς με, *to me.* [j](21:10) TR adds την μεγαλην, *the great (city).* [k](21:12) TR omits ονοματα, *names.*

***(21:11)** φωστήρ *(phōstēr).* Noun derived from φῶς, *light,* meaning *light-bearing body, luminary* (see φῶς at John 8:12). In Phil. 2:15, it is used figuratively of Christians as yielding light in the spiritual darkness of the world. Here in Rev. 21:11 it apparently has the sense of *radiance, shining, brightness,* referring to the New Jerusalem as reflecting the glory of God. Cf. the cognate verb φωτίζω, *shine,*

ἐκ τῆς πηγῆς τοῦ ὕδατος τῆς ζωῆς δωρεάν. **7** Ὁ
from the spring of the water - of life as a gift. The *one*
freely. He who

νικῶν δώσω αὐτῷ ταῦτα,[f] καὶ ἔσομαι αὐτῷ Θεός,
overcoming I will give to him these *things,* and I will be 2to 3him 1God,
overcomes

καὶ αὐτὸς ἔσται μοι υἱός. **8** Τοῖς δὲ δειλοῖς καὶ ἀπίστοις
and he will be to Me a son. 2to 3the 1But cowardly and unbelieving

καὶ ἁμαρτωλοῖς[g] καὶ ἐβδελυγμένοις καὶ φονεῦσι καὶ
and sinners and abominable and murderers and

πόρνοις καὶ φαρμάκοις[h] καὶ εἰδωλολάτραις καὶ πᾶσι τοῖς
fornicators and drug users and idolaters and all -
sexually immoral

ψευδέσι, τὸ μέρος αὐτῶν ἐν τῇ λίμνῃ τῇ καιομένῃ
liars, - part ˜ their *will be* in the lake the *one* burning
which burns

πυρὶ καὶ θείῳ, ὅ ἐστιν ὁ θάνατος ὁ δεύτερος."
with fire and sulfur, which is the death ˜ - second."
brimstone,

John Describes the New Jerusalem

9 Καὶ ἦλθεν[i] εἷς ἐκ τῶν ἑπτὰ ἀγγέλων τῶν ἐχόντων τὰς
And 6came 1one 2of 3the 4seven 5angels - having the

ἑπτὰ φιάλας γεμούσας τῶν ἑπτὰ πληγῶν τῶν ἐσχάτων καὶ
seven bowls being full of the seven plagues ˜ - last and

ἐλάλησε μετ' ἐμοῦ, λέγων, "Δεῦρο, δείξω σοι τὴν
he spoke with me, saying, "Come, I will show to you the

γυναῖκα τὴν νύμφην τοῦ Ἀρνίου." **10** Καὶ ἀπήνεγκέ με
wife the bride of the Lamb." And he carried away ˜ me
transported

ἐν Πνεύματι ἐπ' ὄρος μέγα καὶ ὑψηλόν, καὶ ἔδειξέ
in *the* Spirit onto a 4mountain 1great 2and 3high, and he showed

μοι τὴν πόλιν[j] τὴν ἁγίαν Ἱερουσαλήμ, καταβαίνουσαν ἐκ
to me the city ˜ - holy Jerusalem, coming down out of

τοῦ οὐρανοῦ ἐκ τοῦ Θεοῦ, **11** ἔχουσαν τὴν δόξαν τοῦ Θεοῦ.
- heaven from - God, having the glory - of God.
the sky splendor

Ὁ φωστὴρ* αὐτῆς ὅμοιος λίθῳ τιμιωτάτῳ, ὡς λίθῳ
- radiance ˜ Its *was* similar to a 3stone 1most 2precious, like 1a 4stone

ἰάσπιδι κρυσταλλίζοντι, **12** ἔχουσα τεῖχος μέγα καὶ ὑψηλόν,
3jasper 2crystallizing, having a wall great and high,
crystalline,

ἔχουσα πυλῶνας δώδεκα, καὶ ἐπὶ τοῖς πυλῶσιν ἀγγέλους
having gates ˜ twelve, and at the gates angels ˜

δεκαδύο, καὶ ὀνόματα ἐπιγεγραμμένα, ἅ ἐστι ὀνόματα[k]
twelve, and names having been inscribed, which is *the* names
are

τῶν δώδεκα φυλῶν υἱῶν Ἰσραήλ· **13** ἀπὸ ἀνατολῶν
of the twelve tribes of *the* sons of Israel; from *the* east
on

πυλῶνες τρεῖς καὶ ἀπὸ βορρᾶ πυλῶνες τρεῖς, καὶ ἀπὸ νότου
gates ˜ three and from *the* north gates ˜ three, and from *the* south
on on

πυλῶνες τρεῖς καὶ ἀπὸ δυσμῶν πυλῶνες τρεῖς. **14** Καὶ τὸ
gates ˜ three and from *the* west gates ˜ three. And the
on

τεῖχος τῆς πόλεως ἔχον θεμελίους δώδεκα, καὶ ἐπ' αὐτῶν
wall of the city having foundations ˜ twelve, and on them
had

δώδεκα[l] ὀνόματα τῶν δώδεκα ἀποστόλων τοῦ Ἀρνίου.
the twelve names of the twelve apostles of the Lamb.

15 Καὶ ὁ λαλῶν μετ' ἐμοῦ εἶχε μέτρον,[m] κάλαμον
And the *one* speaking with me had a measure, a reed ˜
he who spoke

χρυσοῦν, ἵνα μετρήσῃ τὴν πόλιν καὶ τοὺς πυλῶνας
golden, so that he might measure the city and - gates ˜

αὐτῆς καὶ τὸ τεῖχος αὐτῆς. 16 Καὶ ἡ πόλις τετράγωνος
its and - wall ˜ its. And the city 4*like* 5a 6square

κεῖται, καὶ τὸ μῆκος αὐτῆς ὅσον τὸ πλάτος. Καὶ
1is 2laid 3out, and - length ˜ its *is* as great as the breadth. And
its

ἐμέτρησε τὴν πόλιν τῷ καλάμῳ ἐπὶ σταδίους δεκαδύο
he measured the city with the reed at 4stadia 1twelve
furlongs

χιλιάδων δώδεκα.[n] Τὸ μῆκος καὶ τὸ πλάτος καὶ τὸ ὕψος
2thousands 3twelve. The length and the breadth and the height
thousand and

αὐτῆς ἴσα ἐστί. 17 Καὶ[o] τὸ τεῖχος αὐτῆς ἑκατὸν
of it equal ˜ is. And - wall ˜ its *is* a hundred
are.

τεσσαράκοντα τεσσάρων πηχῶν, μέτρον ἀνθρώπου, ὅ
forty- four cubits, *by the* measure of a man, which

ἐστιν ἀγγέλου. 18 Καὶ ἦν ἡ ἐνδόμησις τοῦ τείχους αὐτῆς
is of an angel. And 6was 1the 2construction - 3of 5wall 4its

ἴασπις· καὶ ἡ πόλις χρυσίον καθαρόν, ὅμοιον ὑέλῳ καθαρῷ.
jasper; and the city *was* gold ˜ pure, like glass ˜ pure.
transparent.

19 Οἱ θεμέλιοι τοῦ τείχους τῆς πόλεως παντὶ λίθῳ
The foundations of the wall of the city 3with 4every 6stone

τιμίῳ κεκοσμημένοι· ὁ θεμέλιος ὁ πρῶτος ἴασπις, ὁ
5precious 1*were* 2adorned: the foundation ˜ - first *was* jasper, the

δεύτερος σάπφειρος, ὁ τρίτος χαλκηδών, ὁ τέταρτος
second sapphire, the third chalcedony, the fourth

σμάραγδος, 20 ὁ πέμπτος σαρδόνυξ, ὁ ἕκτος σάρδιον, ὁ
emerald, the fifth sardonyx, the sixth sardius, the
carnelian,

ἕβδομος χρυσόλιθος, ὁ ὄγδοος βήρυλλος, ὁ ἔνατος τοπάζιον,
seventh chrysolite, the eighth beryl, the ninth topaz,

ὁ δέκατος χρυσόπρασος, ὁ ἑνδέκατος ὑάκινθος, ὁ
the tenth chrysoprase, the eleventh hyacinth, the
jacinth,

δωδέκατος ἀμέθυσος.
twelfth amethyst.

21 Καὶ οἱ δώδεκα πυλῶνες δώδεκα μαργαρῖται, ἀνὰ εἷς
And the twelve gates *are* twelve pearls, - one ˜

ἕκαστος τῶν πυλώνων ἦν ἐξ ἑνὸς μαργαρίτου. Καὶ ἡ
each of the gates was *made* of one pearl. And the

πλατεῖα τῆς πόλεως χρυσίον καθαρόν, ὡς ὕελος διαυγής.
street of the city *was* gold ˜ pure, like glass ˜ transparent.

The Glory of the New Jerusalem

22 Καὶ ναὸν οὐκ εἶδον ἐν αὐτῇ, ὁ γὰρ Κύριος ὁ
And 5a 6shrine 3not 1I 2did 4see in it, the ˜ for Lord -

Θεὸς ὁ Παντοκράτωρ ναὸς αὐτῆς ἐστι, καὶ τὸ Ἀρνίον.
God the Almighty 3shrine 2its 1is, also the Lamb.

23 Καὶ ἡ πόλις οὐ χρείαν ἔχει τοῦ ἡλίου οὐδὲ τῆς
And the city 2not 4need 1does 3have of the sun nor of the

them were the names of the twelve apostles of the Lamb.
15 And he who talked with me had a gold reed to measure the city, its gates, and its wall.
16 The city is laid out as a square; its length is as great as its breadth. And he measured the city with the reed: twelve thousand furlongs. Its length, breadth, and height are equal.
17 Then he measured its wall: one hundred *and* forty-four cubits, *according* to the measure of a man, that is, of an angel.
18 The construction of its wall was *of* jasper; and the city *was* pure gold, like clear glass.
19 The foundations of the wall of the city *were* adorned with all kinds of precious stones: the first foundation *was* jasper, the second sapphire, the third chalcedony, the fourth emerald,
20 the fifth sardonyx, the sixth sardius, the seventh chrysolite, the eighth beryl, the ninth topaz, the tenth chrysoprase, the eleventh jacinth, and the twelfth amethyst.
21 The twelve gates *were* twelve pearls: each individual gate was of one pearl. And the street of the city *was* pure gold, like transparent glass.
22 But I saw no temple in it, for the Lord God Almighty and the Lamb are its temple.
23 The city had no need of the

---

l(**21:14**) TR omits *δωδεκα, twelve.* *m*(**21:15**) TR omits *μετρον, a measure.* *n*(**21:16**) TR, NU read *σταδιων δωδεκα χιλιαδων, twelve thousand stadia.* *o*(**21:17**) TR, NU add *εμετρησεν, he measured.*

give light, illuminate (as Rev. 21:23; 22:5), *enlighten* (John 1:9; Heb. 6:4), *bring to light, reveal* (Eph. 3:9; 1 Cor. 4:5).

sun or of the moon to shine in
it, for the glory of God illuminated it. The Lamb *is* its light.
24 And the nations of those
who are saved shall walk in its
light, and the kings of the earth
bring their glory and honor into
it.
25 Its gates shall not be shut
at all by day (there shall be no
night there).
26 And they shall bring the
glory and the honor of the nations into it.
27 But there shall by no
means enter it anything that defiles, or causes an abomination
or a lie, but only those who are
written in the Lamb's Book of
Life.
22 And he showed me a
pure river of water of
life, clear as crystal, proceeding
from the throne of God and of
the Lamb.
2 In the middle of its street,
and on either side of the river,
was the tree of life, which bore
twelve fruits, each *tree* yielding
its fruit every month. The
leaves of the tree *were* for the
healing of the nations.
3 And there shall be no more
curse, but the throne of God
and of the Lamb shall be in it,
and His servants shall serve
Him.
4 They shall see His face,
and His name *shall be* on their
foreheads.
5 There shall be no night
there: They need no lamp nor

σελήνης ἵνα φαίνωσιν, αὐτῇ[p] γὰρ ἡ δόξα τοῦ Θεοῦ
moon so that they may shine, [3]very [1]for [2]the [4]glory - of God
(to shine,)

ἐφώτισεν αὐτήν, καὶ ὁ λύχνος αὐτῆς τὸ Ἀρνίον. 24 Καὶ
illuminated it, and - lamp ˜ its *is* the Lamb. And

περιπατήσουσι τὰ ἔθνη[q] διὰ τοῦ φωτὸς αὐτῆς, καὶ οἱ
[3]shall [4]walk [1]the [2]nations through - light ˜ its, and the
(in)

βασιλεῖς τῆς γῆς φέρουσιν αὐτῷ δόξαν καὶ τιμὴν τῶν
kings of the earth bring to it *the* glory and honor of the
(shall bring)

ἐθνῶν εἰς αὐτήν.[r]
nations into it.

25 Καὶ οἱ πυλῶνες αὐτῆς οὐ μὴ κλεισθῶσιν ἡμέρας,
And - gates ˜ its [2]not [3]not [1]shall [4]be [5]closed by day,
(by no means)

νὺξ γὰρ οὐκ ἔσται ἐκεῖ. 26 Καὶ οἴσουσι τὴν δόξαν καὶ
night ˜ for not ˜ shall be there. And they shall bring the glory and
(exist)

τὴν τιμὴν τῶν ἐθνῶν εἰς αὐτὴν ἵνα εἰσελθῶσι.[s]
the honor of the nations into it so that they may enter.

27 Καὶ οὐ μὴ εἰσέλθῃ εἰς αὐτὴν πᾶν κοινὸν[t] καὶ
And *there* [2]not [3]not [1]shall [4]enter into it any common *thing* and
(by no means)

ὁ ποιῶν βδέλυγμα καὶ ψεῦδος, εἰ μὴ οἱ
the *one* doing an abomination and a lie, if not the *ones*
(but only those who)

γεγραμμένοι ἐν τῷ Βιβλίῳ τῆς Ζωῆς τοῦ Ἀρνίου.
having been written in the Book - of Life of the Lamb.
(are)

John Is Shown the River of Life

22 1 Καὶ ἔδειξέ μοι[a] ποταμὸν ὕδατος ζωῆς, λαμπρὸν
And he showed to me a river of water of life, bright

ὡς κρύσταλλον, ἐκπορευόμενον ἐκ τοῦ θρόνου τοῦ Θεοῦ καὶ
as crystal, proceeding from the throne - of God and

τοῦ Ἀρνίου. 2 Ἐν μέσῳ τῆς πλατείας αὐτῆς, καὶ τοῦ
of the Lamb. In *the* midst - of street ˜ its, and [6]of [7]the

ποταμοῦ ἐντεῦθεν καὶ ἐκεῖθεν ξύλον ζωῆς, ποιοῦν
[8]river [1]from [2]here [3]and [4]from [5]there *was* a tree of life, producing
(on both sides)

καρποὺς δώδεκα, κατὰ μῆνα ἀποδιδοὺς ἕκαστον τὸν
fruits ˜ twelve, according to a month yielding each -
(monthly)

καρπὸν αὐτοῦ. Καὶ τὰ φύλλα τοῦ ξύλου εἰς θεραπείαν
fruit ˜ its. And the leaves of the tree *are* for healing

τῶν ἐθνῶν. 3 Καὶ πᾶν κατάθεμα οὐκ ἔσται ἔτι, καὶ ὁ
of the nations. And every curse not ˜ shall be *any* longer, and the
(there shall be no more curse,)

θρόνος τοῦ Θεοῦ καὶ τοῦ Ἀρνίου ἐν αὐτῇ ἔσται, καὶ οἱ
throne - of God and of the Lamb [3]in [4]it [1]shall [2]be, and -

δοῦλοι αὐτοῦ λατρεύουσιν[b] αὐτῷ. 4 Καὶ ὄψονται τὸ
bondservants ˜ His serve Him. And they shall see -
(slaves)

πρόσωπον αὐτοῦ, καὶ τὸ ὄνομα αὐτοῦ ἐπὶ τῶν μετώπων
face ˜ His, and - name ˜ His *shall be* on - foreheads ˜

αὐτῶν. 5 Καὶ νὺξ οὐκ ἔσται,[c] καὶ οὐ χρεία
their. And night not ˜ shall be, and *there shall* not *be a* need
(exist,)

[p](21:23) TR reads *εν αυτη, in it.* [q](21:24) TR adds *των σωζομενων, of those who are saved.*
[r](21:24) TR reads *την δοξαν και την τιμην αυτων, their glory and honor;* NU reads *την δοξαν αυτων, their glory.* [s](21:26) TR, NU omit *ινα εισελθωσι, so that they may enter.*
[t](21:27) TR reads *κοινουν, defiling (thing).*
[a](22:1) TR adds *καθαρον, a pure (river).*
[b](22:3) TR, NU read *λατρευσουσιν, shall serve.*
[c](22:5) TR adds *εκει, there;* NU adds *ετι, any longer.*

λύχνου καὶ φωτός,[d] ὅτι Κύριος ὁ Θεὸς φωτιεῖ[e] αὐτούς.
of a lamp and of light, because *the* Lord - God will illuminate them.

Καὶ βασιλεύσουσιν εἰς τοὺς αἰῶνας τῶν αἰώνων.
And they shall reign to the ages of the ages.
forever and ever.

The Time Is Near

6 Καὶ λέγει μοι, "Οὗτοι οἱ λόγοι πιστοὶ καὶ ἀληθινοί.
And he says to me, "These - words *are* faithful and true.
said trustworthy

Καὶ Κύριος ὁ Θεὸς τῶν πνευμάτων[f] τῶν προφητῶν
And *the* Lord the God of the spirits of the prophets

ἀπέστειλε τὸν ἄγγελον αὐτοῦ δεῖξαι τοῖς δούλοις αὐτοῦ
sent - angel ˜ His to show - to bondservants ˜ His
slaves

ἃ δεῖ γενέσθαι ἐν τάχει."
the things which it is necessary to come about with swiftness."
must happen swiftly."

7 "Καὶ ἰδού, ἔρχομαι ταχύ! Μακάριος* ὁ τηρῶν
"And behold, I am coming swiftly! Blessed *is* the *one* keeping
he who keeps

τοὺς λόγους τῆς προφητείας τοῦ βιβλίου τούτου."
the words of the prophecy - of book ˜ this."

8 Κἀγὼ Ἰωάννης ὁ ἀκούων καὶ βλέπων ταῦτα.
And I John *am* the *one* hearing and seeing these *things*.

Καὶ ὅτε ἤκουσα καὶ ὅτε εἶδον, ἔπεσον προσκυνῆσαι
And when I heard and when I saw, I fell down to worship

ἔμπροσθεν τῶν ποδῶν τοῦ ἀγγέλου τοῦ δεικνύντος μοι
before the feet of the angel - showing to me

ταῦτα.
these *things*.

9 Καὶ λέγει μοι, "Ὅρα μή. Σύνδουλός σού
And he says to me, "See *that you do* not. [4]fellow [5]bondservant [3]your
said

εἰμι καὶ τῶν ἀδελφῶν σου τῶν προφητῶν, καὶ τῶν
[1]I [2]am and - of brothers ˜ your the prophets, and of the *ones*
those

τηρούντων τοὺς λόγους τοῦ βιβλίου τούτου. Τῷ Θεῷ
keeping the words - of book ˜ this. - God ˜
who keep

προσκύνησον."
Worship."

10 Καὶ λέγει μοι, "Μὴ σφραγίσῃς τοὺς λόγους τῆς
And he says to me, "not ˜ Do seal the words of the
said

προφητείας τοῦ βιβλίου τούτου, ὁ καιρὸς γὰρ ἐγγύς ἐστιν.
prophecy - of book ˜ this, [2]the [3]time [1]for [5]near [4]is.

11 Ὁ ἀδικῶν ἀδικησάτω ἔτι, καὶ ὁ ῥυπαρὸς
The *one* acting unjustly let him act unjustly still, and the filthy *person*
He who acts unjustly

ῥυπαρευθήτω ἔτι, καὶ ὁ δίκαιος δικαιοσύνην ποιησάτω[g]
let him be filthy still, and the righteous *person* [4]righteousness [1]let [2]him [3]do

ἔτι, καὶ ὁ ἅγιος ἁγιασθήτω ἔτι."
[5]still, and the holy *person* let him be sanctified still."

Jesus Testifies to the Churches

12 "Ἰδού, ἔρχομαι ταχύ, καὶ ὁ μισθός μου μετ' ἐμοῦ,
"Behold, I am coming swiftly, and - reward ˜ My *is* with Me,

light of the sun, for the Lord
God gives them light. And they
shall reign forever and ever.
6 Then he said to me,
"These words *are* faithful and
true." And the Lord God of the
holy prophets sent His angel to
show His servants the things
which must shortly take place.
7 "Behold, I am coming
quickly! Blessed *is* he who
keeps the words of the prophecy of this book."
8 Now I, John, saw and
heard these things. And when I
heard and saw, I fell down to
worship before the feet of the
angel who showed me these
things.
9 Then he said to me, "See
that you do not *do that.* For I am
your fellow servant, and of your
brethren the prophets, and of
those who keep the words of
this book. Worship God."
10 And he said to me, "Do not
seal the words of the prophecy
of this book, for the time is at
hand.
11 "He who is unjust, let him
be unjust still; he who is filthy,
let him be filthy still; he who is
righteous, let him be righteous
still; he who is holy, let him be
holy still."
12 "And behold, I am coming
quickly, and My reward *is* with

d(22:5) TR, NU add ηλιος, *of sun.* e(22:5) TR reads φωτιζει, *illuminates.*
f(22:6) TR reads αγιων, *holy (prophets).*
g(22:11) TR reads δικαιωθητω, *let him be righteous.*

*(22:7) *μακάριος (makarios).* Adjective typically translated *blessed,* as here and in the beatitudes of Matt. 5, expressing the religious nuance of the word in most of its NT occurrences. In contexts where a religious setting is not emphasized, some translators prefer *happy, fortunate,* perhaps *favored* (cf. Paul's considering himself "happy, favored" to defend himself before Agrippa in Acts 26:2). The word can also be pronounced of God (1 Tim. 1:11; 6:15) and of impersonal things, such as the "eyes" of those who receive special favor from God (Matt. 13:16; Luke 10:23). Cf. the cognate verb *μακαρίζω, call blessed* (Luke 1:48); and the noun *μακαρισμός, blessing* (Gal. 4:15).

Me, to give to every one according to his work.
13 "I am the Alpha and the
Omega, *the* Beginning and *the*
End, the First and the Last."
14 Blessed *are* those who do
His commandments, that they
may have the right to the tree
of life, and may enter through
the gates into the city.
15 But outside *are* dogs and
sorcerers and sexually immoral
and murderers and idolaters,
and whoever loves and practices a lie.
16 "I, Jesus, have sent My angel to testify to you these
things in the churches. I am the
Root and the Offspring of David, the Bright and Morning
Star."
17 And the Spirit and the bride
say, "Come!" And let him who
hears say, "Come!" And let him
who thirsts come. Whoever desires, let him take the water of
life freely.
18 For I testify to everyone
who hears the words of the
prophecy of this book: If anyone adds to these things, God
will add to him the plagues that
are written in this book;
19 and if anyone takes away
from the words of the book of
this prophecy, God shall take
away his part from the Book of
Life, from the holy city, and
from the things which are written in this book.
20 He who testifies to these
things says, "Surely I am com-

ἀποδοῦναι ἑκάστῳ ὡς τὸ ἔργον ἔσται αὐτοῦ. **13** Ἐγὼ τὸ
to render to each as - [2]work [3]shall [4]be [1]his. I *am* the

Ἄλφα καὶ τὸ Ὦ, ὁ Πρῶτος καὶ ὁ Ἔσχατος, ἡ Ἀρχὴ
Alpha and the Omega, the First and the Last, the Beginning

καὶ τὸ Τέλος.[h]
and the End.

14 "Μακάριοι οἱ ποιοῦντες τὰς ἐντολὰς αὐτοῦ,[i]
"Blessed *are* the *ones* doing - commands ˜ His,
those who do

ἵνα ἔσται ἡ ἐξουσία αὐτῶν ἐπὶ τὸ ξύλον τῆς ζωῆς, καὶ
so that [3]shall [4]be - [2]right [1]their to the tree - of life, and

τοῖς πυλῶσιν εἰσέλθωσιν εἰς τὴν πόλιν. **15** Ἔξω οἱ
by the gates they may enter into the city. Outside *are* -

κύνες καὶ οἱ φάρμακοι καὶ οἱ πόρνοι καὶ οἱ φονεῖς καὶ οἱ
dogs and - drug users and - fornicators and - murderers and -

εἰδωλολάτραι καὶ πᾶς ὁ φιλῶν καὶ ποιῶν ψεῦδος.
idolaters and every - *one* loving and doing a lie.
everyone who loves practices

16 "Ἐγὼ Ἰησοῦς ἔπεμψα τὸν ἄγγελόν μου μαρτυρῆσαι
"I Jesus sent - angel ˜ My to testify
have sent

ὑμῖν ταῦτα ἐπὶ ταῖς ἐκκλησίαις. Ἐγώ εἰμι ἡ Ῥίζα καὶ
[3]to [4]you [1]these [2]*things* for the churches. I am the Root and

τὸ Γένος Δαβίδ, ὁ Ἀστὴρ ὁ λαμπρὸς ὁ πρωϊνός."[j]
the Offspring of David, the [3]Star - [1]bright - [2]morning."
Stock

17 Καὶ τὸ Πνεῦμα καὶ ἡ νύμφη λέγουσιν, "Ἔρχου!" Καὶ
And the Spirit and the bride say, "Come!" And

ὁ ἀκούων εἰπάτω, "Ἔρχου!" Καὶ ὁ διψῶν
the *one* hearing let him say, "Come!" And the *one* thirsting
let him who hears say, let him who thirsts

ἐρχέσθω. Ὁ θέλων, λαβέτω ὕδωρ ζωῆς δωρεάν.
let him come. The *one* desiring, let him take *the* water of life freely.
come. He who desires, free of charge.

A Warning

18 Μαρτυρῶ ἐγὼ[k] παντὶ τῷ ἀκούοντι τοὺς λόγους τῆς
testify ˜ I to every - *one* hearing the words of the

προφητείας τοῦ βιβλίου τούτου, ἐάν τις ἐπιθῇ ἐπ' αὐτά,
prophecy - of book ˜ this, if anyone adds to them,

ἐπιθήσαι[l] ὁ Θεὸς ἐπ' αὐτὸν τὰς πληγὰς τὰς γεγραμμένας
[1]may [3]add - [2]God to him the plagues - having been written

ἐν τῷ βιβλίῳ τούτῳ. **19** Καὶ ἐάν τις ἀφέλῃ ἀπὸ τῶν
in - book ˜ this. And if anyone takes away from the

λόγων τοῦ βιβλίου τῆς προφητείας ταύτης, ἀφέλοι[m] ὁ
words of the book - of prophecy ˜ this, [1]may [3]take [4]away -

Θεὸς τὸ μέρος αὐτοῦ ἀπὸ τοῦ ξύλου[n] τῆς ζωῆς καὶ ἐκ τῆς
[2]God - part ˜ his from the tree - of life and out of the
share from

Πόλεως τῆς Ἁγίας, τῶν γεγραμμένων ἐν τῷ βιβλίῳ
City ˜ - Holy, the *things* having been written in - book ˜

τούτῳ.
this.

I Am Coming Quickly

20 Λέγει ὁ μαρτυρῶν ταῦτα, "Ναί, ἔρχομαι
[7]says [1]The [2]*One* [3]testifying [4]to [5]these [6]*things*, "Yes, I am coming
He who testifies

---

[h](**22:13**) TR reads Αρχη και Τελος ο Πρωτος και ο Εσχατος, *Beginning and End, the First and the Last.*
[i](**22:14**) NU reads πλυνοντες τας στολας αυτων, *washing their robes.*
[j](**22:16**) TR reads και ορθρινος, *and early morning.*
[k](**22:18**) TR reads συμμαρτυρομαι γαρ, *for I jointly testify.*
[l](**22:18**) TR, NU read επιθησει, *will add.*
[m](**22:19**) TR (αφαιρησει) and NU (αφελει) read *will take away.*
[n](**22:19**) TR reads βιβλου, *book.*

ταχύ." Ἀμήν.* Ναί,[o] ἔρχου, Κύριε Ἰησοῦ.
swiftly." Amen. (So be it.) Yes, come, Lord Jesus.

21 Ἡ χάρις τοῦ Κυρίου Ἰησοῦ Χριστοῦ[p] μετὰ πάντων
The grace of the Lord Jesus Christ *be* with all
τῶν ἁγίων.[q] Ἀμήν.[r]
the saints. Amen. (So be it.)

ing quickly." Amen. Even so, come, Lord Jesus!
21 The grace of our Lord Jesus Christ *be* with you all. Amen.

[o](**22:20**) NU omits ναι, *yes.*
[p](**22:21**) TR reads Κυριου ημων Ιησου Χριστου, *our Lord Jesus Christ;* NU reads Κυριου Ιησου, *Lord Jesus.*
[q](**22:21**) TR reads παντων υμων, *you all;* NU reads παντων, *all.*
[r](**22:21**) NU omits Αμην, *Amen.*

***(22:20)** ἀμήν *(amēn).* A transliteration of the Hebrew adverb *'āmēn, truly,* into Greek. Following OT usage, the Greek ἀμήν also serves as an exclamation of response: to the promise of the coming Christ (as here in Rev. 22:20); to a prayer (Matt. 6:13); to a doxology (Rev. 1:6); to a blessing at the closing of a letter (Gal. 6:18; Jude 25). The response of affirmation in these cases could be translated, "So be it!" Two uses of ἀμήν are unique to the NT. It is a title of Christ in Rev. 3:14. The other NT use is found in the Gospels where Jesus introduces His own sayings with either ἀμήν (Matt. 5:18) or the double ἀμὴν ἀμήν (John 5:24). Both stress the importance of His words and can be translated by "assuredly" or (the double) by "most assuredly."

Index to Word Studies

arranged alphabetically

by Greek Words

and

by English Meanings

Index to Word Studies

by Greek Words

Word studies of the listed Greek words are located at the Scripture references. The English meanings of the index are not intended to be exhaustive (see the "Index to Word Studies by English Meanings"). The word studies discuss the differences in meaning that words carry from one context to another, as well as the changes in meaning that those words underwent during ancient Greek times.

Greek Word	Transliteration	Meaning	Reference
ἀπολογία	*apologia*	defense, reply	1 Pet. 3:15
ἀπολύτρωσις	*apolytrōsis*	redemption	Rom. 3:24
ἀπορέω	*aporeō*	be uncertain	Luke 24:4
ἀποστέλλω	*apostellō*	send	John 20:21
ἀπώλεια	*apōleia*	perdition, destruction	Matt. 7:13
ἀρετή	*aretē*	virtue	1 Pet. 2:9
ἁρπάζω	*harpazō*	snatch, seize	1 Thess. 4:17
ἀρραβών	*arrabōn*	guarantee, pledge	2 Cor. 1:22
ἀρσενοκοίτης	*arsenokoitēs*	homosexual	1 Cor. 6:9
ἀρχηγός	*archēgos*	leader, originator	Acts 3:15
ἀσέβεια	*asebeia*	ungodliness, impiety	Rom. 11:26
ἀσέλγεια	*aselgeia*	debauchery	Jude 4
βαπτίζω	*baptizō*	baptize	Matt. 28:19
βασανιστής	*basanistēs*	torturer	Matt. 18:34
βεβαιόω	*bebaioō*	confirm, establish	Mark 16:20
βίβλος	*biblos*	book	Matt. 1:1
βλασφημέω	*blasphēmeō*	blaspheme	Matt. 9:3
βραβεύω	*brabeuō*	rule, control	Col. 3:15
γέεννα	*geenna*	Gehenna, hell	James 3:6
γεύομαι	*geuomai*	taste	Heb. 6:5
γινώσκω	*ginōskō*	know	John 10:27
γλωσσόκομον	*glōssokomon*	money box	John 12:6
γογγυσμός	*gongysmos*	grumbling, complaint	John 7:12
γρηγορέω	*grēgoreō*	be watchful	Matt. 24:42
γυμνάζω	*gymnazō*	train, exercise	1 Tim. 4:7
δαιμονίζομαι	*daimonizomai*	be demon-possessed	Matt. 15:22
δεσπότης	*despotēs*	lord, master	1 Tim. 6:1
διάβολος	*diabolos*	devil	Rev. 20:10
διαθήκη	*diathēkē*	covenant	Mark 14:24
διάκονος	*diakonos*	servant, deacon	Mark 9:35
διαλογισμός	*dialogismos*	thought, opinion	Luke 6:8
διαπορέω	*diaporeō*	be greatly perplexed	Luke 24:4
διασπορά	*diaspora*	dispersion	John 7:35
δικαιοσύνη	*dikaiosynē*	righteousness, justice	Rom. 1:17
δικαιόω	*dikaioō*	justify	Acts 13:39
δόξα	*doxa*	glory	John 2:11
δουλεύω	*douleuō*	serve	Rom. 14:18
δοῦλος	*doulos*	bondservant	Rev. 11:18
δύναμις	*dynamis*	power	Acts 1:8
δωρεάν	*dōrean*	freely, undeservedly	2 Cor. 11:7
ἐγκόπτω	*enkoptō*	hinder	1 Thess. 2:18
ἐγκράτεια	*enkrateia*	self-control	Gal. 5:23
ἔθνος	*ethnos*	Gentile, nation	Luke 2:32
εἰρήνη	*eirēnē*	peace	Luke 2:14
ἐκθαμβέω	*ekthambeō*	be astounded	Mark 14:33
ἐκκλησία	*ekklēsia*	church	Acts 8:3
ἐκλέγομαι	*eklegomai*	select, choose	Eph. 1:4
ἐκμυκτηρίζω	*ekmyktērizō*	mock, sneer	Luke 23:35
ἔκστασις	*ekstasis*	trance, amazement	Acts 10:10
ἔλεος	*eleos*	mercy	Rom. 9:23
ἐλευθερόω	*eleutheroō*	set free, liberate	Rom. 8:2
ἐμβριμάομαι	*embrimaomai*	be deeply moved	John 11:38
ἐμφανίζω	*emphanizō*	manifest, reveal	John 14:21

Greek Word	Transliteration	Meaning	Reference
ἐνεργέω	*energeō*	be at work	2 Cor. 4:12
ἐξαλείφω	*exaleiphō*	wipe away, erase	Rev. 3:5
ἔξοδος	*exodos*	departure	Luke 9:31
ἐξομολογέω	*exomologeō*	promise, consent	Luke 10:21
ἐπαγγελία	*epangelia*	promise	Acts 7:17
ἐπιγινώσκω	*epiginōskō*	know completely	2 Cor. 6:9
ἐπιεικής	*epieikēs*	gentle	James 3:17
ἐπιθυμία	*epithymia*	lust	1 Pet. 1:14
ἐπίλυσις	*epilysis*	interpretation	2 Pet. 1:20
ἐπισκοπή	*episkopē*	overseer, visitation	Acts 1:20
ἐπίσκοπος	*episkopos*	bishop, overseer	Titus 1:7
ἐπιστρέφω	*epistrephō*	turn, return	Luke 22:32
ἐπιχορηγέω	*epichorēgeō*	provide, support	2 Pet. 1:5
ἐργάζομαι	*ergazomai*	work, perform	John 9:4
ἔρημος	*erēmos*	desert, desolate	Mark 6:35
ἕτερος	*heteros*	different	Gal. 1:6, 7
εὐγενής	*eugenēs*	noble	1 Cor. 1:26
εὐδοκέω	*eudokeō*	be well pleased	Luke 12:32
εὐχαριστέω	*eucharisteō*	give thanks	Luke 17:16
ἐφάπαξ	*ephapax*	once for all	Heb. 10:10
ζέω	*zeō*	be fervent	Acts 18:25
ζῆλος	*zēlos*	zeal, jealousy	Rom. 10:2
ζήτησις	*zētēsis*	dispute, discussion	Acts 15:2
ζωή	*zōē*	life	John 5:24
ζῷον	*zōon*	living creature	Rev. 4:6
ἡλικία	*hēlikia*	height, age	Luke 19:3
θαῦμα	*thauma*	wonder	Rev. 17:6
θεάομαι	*theaomai*	behold, see	John 1:38
θέατρον	*theatron*	theater, spectacle	1 Cor. 4:9
θηρίον	*thērion*	wild beast	Rev. 6:8
θλίψις	*thlipsis*	tribulation, affliction	John 16:33
θρησκεία	*thrēskeia*	religion	Acts 26:5
θριαμβεύω	*thriambeuō*	lead in triumph	2 Cor. 2:14
θυμός	*thymos*	wrath	Rev. 16:1
θυσιαστήριον	*thysiastērion*	altar	Heb. 13:10
ἴασις	*iasis*	healing, cure	Acts 4:22
ἰατρός	*iatros*	physician	Col. 4:14
ἰδού	*idou*	behold	Matt. 26:47
ἱερόν	*hieron*	temple (compound)	Luke 24:53
Ἰησοῦς	*Iēsous*	Jesus	Matt. 27:17
ἱλάσκομαι	*hilaskomai*	propitiate, expiate	Luke 18:13
ἱλασμός	*hilasmos*	propitiation, expiation	1 John 4:10
ἱμάτιον	*himation*	cloak, garment	Matt. 5:40
ἰῶτα	*iōta*	iota, jot	Matt. 5:18
καθεύδω	*katheudō*	sleep	1 Thess. 5:10
καινός	*kainos*	new	John 13:34
κακοῦργος	*kakourgos*	criminal	2 Tim. 2:9
Κανανίτης	*Kananitēs*	Cananite	Mark 3:18
καταλαλέω	*katalaleō*	defame, slander	James 4:11
καταλαμβάνω	*katalambanō*	comprehend, overtake	Eph. 3:18
καταλλάσσω	*katallassō*	reconcile	Rom. 5:10
καταρτίζω	*katartizō*	equip, restore	Heb. 11:3

Greek Word	Transliteration	Meaning	Reference
καταρτισμός	*katartismos*	equipping	Eph. 4:12
κηρύσσω	*kēryssō*	proclaim	Luke 3:3
κλαίω	*klaiō*	weep, cry	Luke 19:41
κοινός	*koinos*	common	Acts 4:32
κοινωνέω	*koinōneō*	share in	Phil. 4:15
κοινωνία	*koinōnia*	fellowship, communion	Acts 2:42
κοινωνός	*koinōnos*	partaker, partner	Luke 5:10
κολωνεία	*kolōneia*	colony	Acts 16:12
κοσμικός	*kosmikos*	worldly, earthly	Titus 2:12
κοσμοκράτωρ	*kosmokratōr*	world-ruler	Eph. 6:12
κόσμος	*kosmos*	world, order	1 John 5:19
κράσπεδον	*kraspedon*	hem, border	Luke 8:44
κρίνω	*krinō*	judge	Matt. 7:1
κρίσις	*krisis*	judgment	John 3:19
κυβέρνησις	*kybernēsis*	governance, guidance	1 Cor. 12:28
κυνάριον	*kynarion*	little dog	Mark 7:27
κυρία	*kyria*	lady	2 John 1
κυριακός	*kyriakos*	belonging to the Lord	Rev. 1:10
κύριος	*kyrios*	Lord, master	Jude 9
λαλέω	*laleō*	speak	1 Cor. 14:2
λειτουργία	*leitourgia*	service	Phil. 2:30
λέπρα	*lepra*	leprosy	Mark 1:42
λεπτόν	*lepton*	lepton, mite	Mark 12:42
λῃστής	*lēstēs*	bandit	Matt. 21:13
λίτρα	*litra*	pound	John 19:39
λόγος	*logos*	word	John 1:1
λούω	*louō*	bathe, wash	John 13:10
λύτρον	*lytron*	ransom	Mark 10:45
μάγος	*magos*	wise man, magician	Acts 13:8
μαθητεύω	*mathēteuō*	teach, disciple	Matt. 27:57
μακάριος	*makarios*	blessed	Rev. 22:7
μαλακός	*malakos*	effeminate	1 Cor. 6:9
μαμωνᾶς	*mamōnas*	wealth	Luke 16:9
Μαρὰνα θά	*Marana tha*	Come, Lord!	1 Cor. 16:22
μαρτύριον	*martyrion*	testimony, proof	Matt. 8:4
μαστιγόω	*mastigoō*	flog, whip	Matt. 20:19
μάταιος	*mataios*	useless, worthless	Acts 14:15
μεγαλεῖος	*megaleios*	magnificent, grand	Acts 2:11
μεγαλειότης	*megaleiotēs*	majesty, magnificence	Luke 9:43
μεγαλύνω	*megalynō*	magnify	Phil. 1:20
μέριμνα	*merimna*	care, anxiety	1 Pet. 5:7
Μεσίας	*Mesias*	Messiah	John 4:25
μεταμέλομαι	*metamelomai*	regret	2 Cor. 7:8
μετανοέω	*metanoeō*	repent	Acts 26:20
μέτοχος	*metochos*	partner, share in	Heb. 3:1
μιμητής	*mimētēs*	imitator	Eph. 5:1
μισθαποδοσία	*misthapodosia*	eternal reward	Heb. 11:26
μισθός	*misthos*	pay, reward	Matt. 10:41
μοιχεία	*moicheia*	adultery	Mark 7:21
μυστήριον	*mystērion*	mystery, secret	Luke 8:10
μωρός	*mōros*	fool, foolish	Matt. 23:17
ναός	*naos*	shrine, temple	1 Cor. 3:16
νομικός	*nomikos*	lawyer	Luke 11:45

Greek Word	Transliteration	Meaning	Reference
ὀθόνιον	*othonion*	linen cloth	John 20:5
οἰκοδομέω	*oikodomeō*	edify, build	Acts 9:31
ὄλεθρος	*olethros*	destruction	2 Thess. 1:9
ὁμοθυμαδόν	*homothymadon*	of one accord	Acts 12:20
ὄνομα	*onoma*	name	Acts 19:13
ὀρθοτομέω	*orthotomeō*	teach correctly	2 Tim. 2:15
ὀφειλέτης	*opheiletēs*	debtor	Luke 13:4
ὀφείλημα	*opheilēma*	debt	Rom. 4:4
παιδεία	*paideia*	discipline	Heb. 12:5
πανοῦργος	*panourgos*	crafty	2 Cor. 12:16
παράβασις	*parabasis*	transgression	Rom. 2:23
παραβολή	*parabolē*	parable	Matt. 13:3
παράδοξος	*paradoxos*	remarkable, strange	Luke 5:26
Παράκλητος	*Paraklētos*	Helper	1 John 2:1
παρακοή	*parakoē*	disobedience	Rom. 5:19
παράπτωμα	*paraptōma*	trespass	Eph. 2:5
παρθένος	*parthenos*	virgin, chaste woman	Matt. 1:23
παρρησία	*parrēsia*	boldness, openness	John 11:14
πατρίς	*patris*	hometown, fatherland	Mark 6:1
πειράζω	*peirazō*	tempt, test	John 6:6
πενθέω	*pentheō*	grieve, mourn	1 Cor. 5:2
πέτρα	*petra*	rock	Matt. 16:18
πιστεύω	*pisteuō*	believe, trust	Acts 10:43
πίστις	*pistis*	faith, trust	Col. 1:4
πιστός	*pistos*	faithful, believing	2 Thess. 3:3
πλανάω	*planaō*	deceive	Rev. 12:9
πλεονεξία	*pleonexia*	greed	Col. 3:5
πνεῦμα	*pneuma*	wind, spirit	John 3:5
πνευματικός	*pneumatikos*	spiritual	1 Cor. 2:13
πολιτεύομαι	*politeuomai*	conduct oneself	Acts 23:1
πονηρός	*ponēros*	evil, bad	Matt. 6:13
πραιτώριον	*praitōrion*	Praetorium	John 18:28
πραότης	*praotēs*	gentleness, meekness	2 Cor. 10:1
πραΰτης	*praytēs*	gentleness, meekness	2 Cor. 10:1
πρεσβεύω	*presbeuō*	be an ambassador	2 Cor. 5:20
πρεσβύτερος	*presbyteros*	elder, older	Mark 14:53
προσήλυτος	*prosēlytos*	convert, proselyte	Acts 6:5
προσκολλάω	*proskollaō*	join	Mark 10:7
προσκυνέω	*proskyneō*	worship	Matt. 9:18
προσωπολήπτης	*prosōpolēptēs*	one who is partial	Acts 10:34
προσωποληψία	*prosōpolēpsia*	partiality	James 2:1
προφητεία	*prophēteia*	prophecy	Rom. 12:6
πωρόω	*pōroō*	harden	Mark 8:17
ῥάβδος	*rhabdos*	rod, staff	Heb. 9:4
ῥακά	*rhaka*	empty-headed	Matt. 5:22
ῥοιζηδόν	*rhoizēdon*	with a roar	2 Pet. 3:10
ῥομφαία	*rhomphaia*	sword	Rev. 19:15
ῥύομαι	*rhyomai*	rescue, deliver	1 Thess. 1:10
σαβαχθανί	*sabachthani*	you have forsaken me	Mark 15:34
Σαβαώθ	*Sabaōth*	Sabaoth, hosts	James 5:4
σαγήνη	*sagēnē*	dragnet	Matt. 13:47
σαπρός	*sapros*	rotten, decayed	Matt. 12:33
σάρξ	*sarx*	flesh	Rom. 13:14

Greek Word	Transliteration	Meaning	Reference
σεληνιάζομαι	*selēniazomai*	be moonstruck	Matt. 17:15
σημεῖον	*sēmeion*	sign, portent	John 6:26
σίκερα	*sikera*	strong drink	Luke 1:15
σιτομέτριον	*sitometrion*	measured allowance (of food)	Luke 12:42
σκεῦος	*skeuos*	vessel, equipment	Heb. 9:21
σκηνοποιός	*skēnopoios*	tentmaker	Acts 18:3
σκῆνος	*skēnos*	tent, dwelling	2 Cor. 5:1
σκηνόω	*skēnoō*	dwell, live	John 1:14
σκόλοψ	*skolops*	thorn	2 Cor. 12:7
σκώληξ	*skōlēx*	worm	Mark 9:44
σοφία	*sophia*	wisdom	1 Cor. 12:8
σπένδω	*spendō*	offer a drink-offering	Phil. 2:17
σπέρμα	*sperma*	seed, offspring	Rom. 1:3
σπερμολόγος	*spermologos*	babbler	Acts 17:18
σπίλος	*spilos*	spot, stain	2 Pet. 2:13
στάδιον	*stadion*	stade, stadium	Rev. 14:20
σταυρός	*stauros*	cross	Mark 8:34
σταυρόω	*stauroō*	crucify	Gal. 6:14
στέφανος	*stephanos*	garland, crown	Mark 15:17
στεφανόω	*stephanoō*	crown (as victor)	Heb. 2:9
στοά	*stoa*	portico	John 5:2
συγχράομαι	*synchraomai*	associate with	John 4:9
συκοφαντέω	*sykophanteō*	accuse falsely	Luke 3:14
συνέδριον	*synedrion*	Sanhedrin, council	Acts 5:21
σύνεσις	*synesis*	understanding, insight	Mark 12:33
σφραγίζω	*sphragizō*	seal	Rev. 7:3
σῴζω	*sōzō*	save	Matt. 10:22
σῶμα	*sōma*	body	Phil. 3:21
σωτηρία	*sōtēria*	salvation	Luke 1:69, 77
σωφρονισμός	*sōphronismos*	soundness, self-discipline	2 Tim. 1:7
τάλαντον	*talanton*	talent	Matt. 25:15
ταμεῖον	*tameion*	inner room	Luke 12:3
ταπεινοφροσύνη	*tapeinophrosynē*	humility	Acts 20:19
ταπεινόω	*tapeinoō*	humble, make low	Luke 14:11
ταράσσω	*tarassō*	trouble, disturb	Luke 24:38
τεκνίον	*teknion*	little child	Mark 2:5
τέκνον	*teknon*	child	Mark 2:5
τέλειος	*teleios*	mature, complete, perfect	1 Cor. 14:20
τελειόω	*teleioō*	make perfect, complete	Heb. 12:23
τέρας	*teras*	wonder	Acts 2:19
τεχνίτης	*technitēs*	craftsman, designer	Heb. 11:10
τηρέω	*tēreō*	keep	1 John 5:3
τιμή	*timē*	honor, value	1 Tim. 5:17
τράπεζα	*trapeza*	table	Luke 19:23
τροπή	*tropē*	turning	James 1:17
τρυφή	*tryphē*	luxury, splendor	Luke 7:25
ὑβρίζω	*hybrizō*	treat spitefully	Matt. 22:6
ὑγιαίνω	*hygiainō*	be healthy, be sound	1 Tim. 1:10
υἱοθεσία	*huiothesia*	adoption	Gal. 4:5
ὑπακούω	*hypakouō*	obey	Rom. 6:17
ὑπερβολή	*hyperbolē*	excess, excellence	Rom. 7:13
ὑπερήφανος	*hyperēphania*	arrogant, proud	Luke 1:51
ὑπογραμμός	*hypogrammos*	example, pattern	1 Pet. 2:21
ὑπόκρισις	*hypokrisis*	hypocrisy	Gal. 2:13
ὑποκριτής	*hypokritēs*	hypocrite	Mark 7:6

Greek Word	Transliteration	Meaning	Reference
ὑπόστασις	*hypostasis*	reality, essence	Heb. 3:14
ὑψόω	*hypsoō*	lift up, exalt	John 8:28
φανερόω	*phaneroō*	reveal, make known	Mark 4:22
φαρμακεία	*pharmakeia*	sorcery, magic	Rev. 9:21
φιλανθρωπία	*philanthrōpia*	kindness	Acts 28:2
φίλος	*philos*	friend	John 15:14
φιλοτιμέομαι	*philotimeomai*	aspire	Rom. 15:20
φλυαρέω	*phlyareō*	talk nonsense	3 John 10
φρουρέω	*phroureō*	keep under guard	Gal. 3:23
φῶς	*phōs*	light	John 8:12
φωστήρ	*phōstēr*	radiance, luminary	Rev. 21:11
χαλκολίβανον	*chalkolibanon*	fine brass	Rev. 1:15
χαρακτήρ	*charaktēr*	representation	Heb. 1:3
χάρις	*charis*	grace, favor	Acts 14:3
χάρισμα	*charisma*	gift of grace	1 Cor. 1:7
χαριτόω	*charitoō*	favor	Luke 1:28
χειρόγραφον	*cheirographon*	handwritten document	Col. 2:14
χρηστός	*chrēstos*	kind, good	Luke 6:35
Χριστιανός	*Christianos*	Christian	Acts 11:26
Χριστός	*Christos*	Messiah, Christ	Matt. 22:42
ψάλλω	*psallō*	sing praise	Eph. 5:19
ψαλμός	*psalmos*	psalm	Eph. 5:19
ψευδόχριστος	*pseudochristos*	false christ	Matt. 24:24
ψηλαφάω	*psēlaphaō*	touch, grope after	Acts 17:27
ψιθυριστής	*psithyristēs*	gossiper	Rom. 1:29
ψυχή	*psychē*	soul, life	Luke 21:19
ψυχικός	*psychikos*	natural, unspiritual	1 Cor. 15:46
ὥρα	*hōra*	hour, time	Luke 22:53
ὡσαννά	*hōsanna*	save now	Mark 11:9

Index to Word Studies
by English Meanings

The Greek words discussed in the word studies are listed by English meanings. The meanings are not intended to be exhaustive. It is common in the language of the Greek New Testament for words to present many shades of meaning in different contexts, far beyond the meanings listed here. Furthermore, the reader should not assume that a word carries any of these meanings in a specific passage. What the context indicates about a word's meaning, as well as how the New Testament uses a particular word, must always be considered.

Meaning	Greek Word	Transliteration	Reference
abstain from	ἀπέχω	*apechō*	Luke 6:24
accursed	ἀνάθεμα	*anathema*	Rom. 9:3
accuse falsely	συκοφαντέω	*sykophanteō*	Luke 3:14
act of sin	ἁμάρτημα	*hamartēma*	Mark 3:28
adoption	υἱοθεσία	*huiothesia*	Gal. 4:5
adultery	μοιχεία	*moicheia*	Mark 7:21
affliction	θλίψις	*thlipsis*	John 16:33
again	ἄνωθεν	*anōthen*	John 19:11
age	ἡλικία	*hēlikia*	Luke 19:3
altar	θυσιαστήριον	*thysiastērion*	Heb. 13:10
amazement	ἔκστασις	*ekstasis*	Acts 10:10
be an ambassador	πρεσβεύω	*presbeuō*	2 Cor. 5:20
another	ἄλλος	*allos*	Gal. 1:6, 7
anxiety	μέριμνα	*merimna*	1 Pet. 5:7
arrogant	ὑπερήφανος	*hyperēphania*	Luke 1:51
aspire	φιλοτιμέομαι	*philotimeomai*	Rom. 15:20
associate with	συγχράομαι	*synchraomai*	John 4:9
assuredly	ἀμήν	*amēn*	Rev. 22:20
be astounded	ἐκθαμβέω	*ekthambeō*	Mark 14:33
babbler	σπερμολόγος	*spermologos*	Acts 17:18
bad	πονηρός	*ponēros*	Matt. 6:13
bandit	λῃστής	*lēstēs*	Matt. 21:13
baptize	βαπτίζω	*baptizō*	Matt. 28:19
bathe	λούω	*louō*	John 13:10
behold	ἰδού	*idou*	Matt. 26:47
behold	θεάομαι	*theaomai*	John 1:38
believe	πιστεύω	*pisteuō*	Acts 10:43
believing	πιστός	*pistos*	2 Thess. 3:3
belonging to the Lord	κυριακός	*kyriakos*	Rev. 1:10
bishop	ἐπίσκοπος	*episkopos*	Titus 1:7
blameless	ἄμεμπτος	*amemptos*	Heb. 8:7
blaspheme	βλασφημέω	*blasphēmeō*	Matt. 9:3
blessed	μακάριος	*makarios*	Rev. 22:7
body	σῶμα	*sōma*	Phil. 3:21
boldness	παρρησία	*parrēsia*	John 11:14
bondservant	δοῦλος	*doulos*	Rev. 11:18
book	βίβλος	*biblos*	Matt. 1:1
border	κράσπεδον	*kraspedon*	Luke 8:44
brother	ἀδελφός	*adelphos*	Mark 10:29
build	οἰκοδομέω	*oikodomeō*	Acts 9:31
buy	ἀγοράζω	*agorazō*	Rev. 5:9
Cananite	Καναvίτης	*Kananitēs*	Mark 3:18
care	μέριμνα	*merimna*	1 Pet. 5:7
cause to recline	ἀνακλίνω	*anaklinō*	Luke 13:29

Meaning	Greek Word	Transliteration	Reference
chaste woman	παρθένος	*parthenos*	Matt. 1:23
child	τέκνον	*teknon*	Mark 2:5
choose	ἐκλέγομαι	*eklegomai*	Eph. 1:4
Christ	Χριστός	*Christos*	Matt. 22:42
Christian	Χριστιανός	*Christianos*	Acts 11:26
church	ἐκκλησία	*ekklēsia*	Acts 8:3
cloak	ἱμάτιον	*himation*	Matt. 5:40
colony	κολωνεία	*kolōneia*	Acts 16:12
Come, Lord!	Μαρὰνα θά	*Marana tha*	1 Cor. 16:22
common	κοινός	*koinos*	Acts 4:32
communion	κοινωνία	*koinōnia*	Acts 2:42
complaint	γογγυσμός	*gongysmos*	John 7:12
complete	τέλειος	*teleios*	1 Cor. 14:20
complete	τελειόω	*teleioō*	Heb. 12:23
comprehend	καταλαμβάνω	*katalambanō*	Eph. 3:18
conduct oneself	πολιτεύομαι	*politeuomai*	Acts 23:1
confirm	βεβαιόω	*bebaioō*	Mark 16:20
consent	ἐξομολογέω	*exomologeō*	Luke 10:21
control	βραβεύω	*brabeuō*	Col. 3:15
convert	προσήλυτος	*prosēlytos*	Acts 6:5
council	συνέδριον	*synedrion*	Acts 5:21
covenant	διαθήκη	*diathēkē*	Mark 14:24
craftsman	τεχνίτης	*technitēs*	Heb. 11:10
crafty	πανοῦργος	*panourgos*	2 Cor. 12:16
criminal	κακοῦργος	*kakourgos*	2 Tim. 2:9
cross	σταυρός	*stauros*	Mark 8:34
crown	στέφανος	*stephanos*	Mark 15:17
crown (as victor)	στεφανόω	*stephanoō*	Heb. 2:9
crucify	σταυρόω	*stauroō*	Gal. 6:14
cry	κλαίω	*klaiō*	Luke 19:41
cure	ἴασις	*iasis*	Acts 4:22
deacon	διάκονος	*diakonos*	Mark 9:35
debauchery	ἀσέλγεια	*aselgeia*	Jude 4
debt	ὀφείλημα	*opheilēma*	Rom. 4:4
debtor	ὀφειλέτης	*opheiletēs*	Luke 13:4
decayed	σαπρός	*sapros*	Matt. 12:33
deceive	πλανάω	*planaō*	Rev. 12:9
be deeply moved	ἐμβριμάομαι	*embrimaomai*	John 11:38
defame	καταλαλέω	*katalaleō*	James 4:11
defense	ἀπολογία	*apologia*	1 Pet. 3:15
deliver	ῥύομαι	*rhyomai*	1 Thess. 1:10
be demon-possessed	δαιμονίζομαι	*daimonizomai*	Matt. 15:22
departure	ἔξοδος	*exodos*	Luke 9:31
desert	ἔρημος	*erēmos*	Mark 6:35
designer	τεχνίτης	*technitēs*	Heb. 11:10
desolate	ἔρημος	*erēmos*	Mark 6:35
destroy	ἀπόλλυμι	*apollymi*	Luke 9:56
destruction	ἀπώλεια	*apōleia*	Matt. 7:13
destruction	ὄλεθρος	*olethros*	2 Thess. 1:9
devil	διάβολος	*diabolos*	Rev. 20:10
different	ἕτερος	*heteros*	Gal. 1:6, 7
disapproved	ἀδόκιμος	*adokimos*	1 Cor. 9:27
disciple	μαθητεύω	*mathēteuō*	Matt. 27:57
discipline	παιδεία	*paideia*	Heb. 12:5
discussion	ζήτησις	*zētēsis*	Acts 15:2
disobedience	παρακοή	*parakoē*	Rom. 5:19
dispersion	διασπορά	*diaspora*	John 7:35

Meaning	Greek Word	Transliteration	Reference
dispute	ζήτησις	*zētēsis*	Acts 15:2
disqualified	ἀδόκιμος	*adokimos*	1 Cor. 9:27
disturb	ταράσσω	*tarassō*	Luke 24:38
divisive	αἱρετικός	*hairetikos*	Titus 3:10
dragnet	σαγήνη	*sagēnē*	Matt. 13:47
dwell	σκηνόω	*skēnoō*	John 1:14
dwelling	σκῆνος	*skēnos*	2 Cor. 5:1
earthly	κοσμικός	*kosmikos*	Titus 2:12
edify	οἰκοδομέω	*oikodomeō*	Acts 9:31
effeminate	μαλακός	*malakos*	1 Cor. 6:9
elder	πρεσβύτερος	*presbyteros*	Mark 14:53
empty-headed	ῥακά	*rhaka*	Matt. 5:22
equip	καταρτίζω	*katartizō*	Heb. 11:3
equipment	σκεῦος	*skeuos*	Heb. 9:21
equipping	καταρτισμός	*katartismos*	Eph. 4:12
erase	ἐξαλείφω	*exaleiphō*	Rev. 3:5
essence	ὑπόστασις	*hypostasis*	Heb. 3:14
establish	βεβαιόω	*bebaioō*	Mark 16:20
eternal reward	μισθαποδοσία	*misthapodosia*	Heb. 11:26
eternal	αἰώνιος	*aiōnios*	Matt. 25:46
everlasting	αἰώνιος	*aiōnios*	Matt. 25:46
evil	πονηρός	*ponēros*	Matt. 6:13
exalt	ὑψόω	*hypsoō*	John 8:28
example	ὑπογραμμός	*hypogrammos*	1 Pet. 2:21
excellence	ὑπερβολή	*hyperbolē*	Rom. 7:13
excess	ὑπερβολή	*hyperbolē*	Rom. 7:13
exercise	γυμνάζω	*gymnazō*	1 Tim. 4:7
expiate	ἱλάσκομαι	*hilaskomai*	Luke 18:13
expiation	ἱλασμός	*hilasmos*	1 John 4:10
faction	αἵρεσις	*hairesis*	1 Cor. 11:19
factious	αἱρετικός	*hairetikos*	Titus 3:10
faith	πίστις	*pistis*	Col. 1:4
faithful	πιστός	*pistos*	2 Thess. 3:3
false christ	ψευδόχριστος	*pseudochristos*	Matt. 24:24
father	Ἀββᾶ	*Abba*	Rom. 8:15
fatherland	πατρίς	*patris*	Mark 6:1
favor	χάρις	*charis*	Acts 14:3
favor	χαριτόω	*charitoō*	Luke 1:28
fellowship	κοινωνία	*koinōnia*	Acts 2:42
be fervent	ζέω	*zeō*	Acts 18:25
fight	ἀγωνίζομαι	*agōnizomai*	2 Tim. 4:7
fine brass	χαλκολίβανον	*chalkolibanon*	Rev. 1:15
firstfruits	ἀπαρχή	*aparchē*	1 Cor. 15:23
flesh	σάρξ	*sarx*	Rom. 13:14
flog	μαστιγόω	*mastigoō*	Matt. 20:19
follow	ἀκολουθέω	*akoloutheō*	John 12:26
fond of dishonest gain	αἰσχροκερδής	*aischrokerdēs*	1 Tim. 3:8
fool	μωρός	*mōros*	Matt. 23:17
foolish	μωρός	*mōros*	Matt. 23:17
freely	δωρεάν	*dōrean*	2 Cor. 11:7
friend	φίλος	*philos*	John 15:14
from above	ἄνωθεν	*anōthen*	John 19:11
garland	στέφανος	*stephanos*	Mark 15:17
garment	ἱμάτιον	*himation*	Matt. 5:40
Gehenna	γέεννα	*geenna*	James 3:6

Meaning	Greek Word	Transliteration	Reference
Gentile	ἔθνος	*ethnos*	Luke 2:32
gentle	ἐπιεικής	*epieikēs*	James 3:17
gentleness	πραΰτης	*praytēs*	2 Cor. 10:1
gift of grace	χάρισμα	*charisma*	1 Cor. 1:7
give thanks	εὐχαριστέω	*eucharisteō*	Luke 17:16
glory	δόξα	*doxa*	John 2:11
good	ἀγαθός	*agathos*	Matt. 19:17
good	χρηστός	*chrēstos*	Luke 6:35
gossiper	ψιθυριστής	*psithyristēs*	Rom. 1:29
governance	κυβέρνησις	*kybernēsis*	1 Cor. 12:28
grace	χάρις	*charis*	Acts 14:3
grand	μεγαλεῖος	*megaleios*	Acts 2:11
be greatly perplexed	διαπορέω	*diaporeō*	Luke 24:4
greed	πλεονεξία	*pleonexia*	Col. 3:5
grieve	πενθέω	*pentheō*	1 Cor. 5:2
grope after	ψηλαφάω	*psēlaphaō*	Acts 17:27
grumbling	γογγυσμός	*gongysmos*	John 7:12
guarantee	ἀρραβών	*arrabōn*	2 Cor. 1:22
guidance	κυβέρνησις	*kybernēsis*	1 Cor. 12:28
Hades	ᾅδης	*hadēs*	Luke 16:23
handwritten document	χειρόγραφον	*cheirographon*	Col. 2:14
harden	πωρόω	*pōroō*	Mark 8:17
healing	ἴασις	*iasis*	Acts 4:22
be healthy	ὑγιαίνω	*hygiainō*	1 Tim. 1:10
height	ἡλικία	*hēlikia*	Luke 19:3
hell	γέεννα	*geenna*	James 3:6
Helper	Παράκλητος	*Paraklētos*	1 John 2:1
hem	κράσπεδον	*kraspedon*	Luke 8:44
heresy	αἵρεσις	*hairesis*	1 Cor. 11:19
hinder	ἐγκόπτω	*enkoptō*	1 Thess. 2:18
holy	ἅγιος	*hagios*	Rev. 11:2
hometown	πατρίς	*patris*	Mark 6:1
homosexual	ἀρσενοκοίτης	*arsenokoitēs*	1 Cor. 6:9
honor	τιμή	*timē*	1 Tim. 5:17
hosts	Σαβαώθ	*Sabaōth*	James 5:4
hour	ὥρα	*hōra*	Luke 22:53
humble	ταπεινόω	*tapeinoō*	Luke 14:11
humility	ταπεινοφροσύνη	*tapeinophrosynē*	Acts 20:19
husband	ἀνήρ	*anēr*	Matt. 14:21
hypocrisy	ὑπόκρισις	*hypokrisis*	Gal. 2:13
hypocrite	ὑποκριτής	*hypokritēs*	Mark 7:6
illiterate	ἀγράμματος	*agrammatos*	Acts 4:13
imitator	μιμητής	*mimētēs*	Eph. 5:1
impiety	ἀσέβεια	*asebeia*	Rom. 11:26
inner room	ταμεῖον	*tameion*	Luke 12:3
insight	σύνεσις	*synesis*	Mark 12:33
interpretation	ἐπίλυσις	*epilysis*	2 Pet. 1:20
iota	ἰῶτα	*iōta*	Matt. 5:18
jealousy	ζῆλος	*zēlos*	Rom. 10:2
Jesus	Ἰησοῦς	*Iēsous*	Matt. 27:17
join	προσκολλάω	*proskollaō*	Mark 10:7
jot	ἰῶτα	*iōta*	Matt. 5:18
journey from home	ἀποδημέω	*apodēmeō*	Mark 12:1
judge	κρίνω	*krinō*	Matt. 7:1
judgment	κρίσις	*krisis*	John 3:19

Meaning	Greek Word	Transliteration	Reference
justice	δικαιοσύνη	*dikaiosynē*	Rom. 1:17
justify	δικαιόω	*dikaioō*	Acts 13:39
keep	τηρέω	*tēreō*	1 John 5:3
keep under guard	φρουρέω	*phroureō*	Gal. 3:23
kind	χρηστός	*chrēstos*	Luke 6:35
kindness	φιλανθρωπία	*philanthrōpia*	Acts 28:2
know	γινώσκω	*ginōskō*	John 10:27
know completely	ἐπιγινώσκω	*epiginōskō*	2 Cor. 6:9
lady	κυρία	*kyria*	2 John 1
lawlessness	ἀνομία	*anomia*	1 John 3:4
lawyer	νομικός	*nomikos*	Luke 11:45
lead in triumph	θριαμβεύω	*thriambeuō*	2 Cor. 2:14
leader	ἀρχηγός	*archēgos*	Acts 3:15
leprosy	λέπρα	*lepra*	Mark 1:42
lepton	λεπτόν	*lepton*	Mark 12:42
liberate	ἐλευθερόω	*eleutheroō*	Rom. 8:2
life	ζωή	*zōē*	John 5:24
life	ψυχή	*psychē*	Luke 21:19
lift up	αἴρω	*airō*	John 15:2
lift up	ὑψόω	*hypsoō*	John 8:28
light	φῶς	*phōs*	John 8:12
linen cloth	ὀθόνιον	*othonion*	John 20:5
little child	τεκνίον	*teknion*	Mark 2:5
little dog	κυνάριον	*kynarion*	Mark 7:27
live	σκηνόω	*skēnoō*	John 1:14
living creature	ζῷον	*zōon*	Rev. 4:6
lord	δεσπότης	*despotēs*	1 Tim. 6:1
Lord	κύριος	*kyrios*	Jude 9
lose	ἀπόλλυμι	*apollymi*	Luke 9:56
love	ἀγάπη	*agapē*	1 John 2:15
luminary	φωστήρ	*phōstēr*	Rev. 21:11
lust	ἐπιθυμία	*epithymia*	1 Pet. 1:14
luxury	τρυφή	*tryphē*	Luke 7:25
magic	φαρμακεία	*pharmakeia*	Rev. 9:21
magician	μάγος	*magos*	Acts 13:8
magnificence	μεγαλειότης	*megaleiotēs*	Luke 9:43
magnificent	μεγαλεῖος	*megaleios*	Acts 2:11
magnify	μεγαλύνω	*megalynō*	Phil. 1:20
majesty	μεγαλειότης	*megaleiotēs*	Luke 9:43
make known	φανερόω	*phaneroō*	Mark 4:22
make low	ταπεινόω	*tapeinoō*	Luke 14:11
make perfect	τελειόω	*teleioō*	Heb. 12:23
man	ἀνήρ	*anēr*	Matt. 14:21
manifest	ἐμφανίζω	*emphanizō*	John 14:21
market	ἀγορά	*agora*	Acts 16:19
marketplace	ἀγορά	*agora*	Acts 16:19
master	δεσπότης	*despotēs*	1 Tim. 6:1
master	κύριος	*kyrios*	Jude 9
mature	τέλειος	*teleios*	1 Cor. 14:20
measured allowance (of food)	σιτομέτριον	*sitometrion*	Luke 12:42
meekness	πραότης	*praotēs*	2 Cor. 10:1
mercy	ἔλεος	*eleos*	Rom. 9:23
Messiah	Μεσίας	*Mesias*	John 4:25
Messiah	Χριστός	*Christos*	Matt. 22:42
mite	λεπτόν	*lepton*	Mark 12:42

Meaning	Greek Word	Transliteration	Reference
mock	ἐκμυκτηρίζω	*ekmyktērizō*	Luke 23:35
money box	γλωσσόκομον	*glōssokomon*	John 12:6
be moonstruck	σεληνιάζομαι	*selēniazomai*	Matt. 17:15
mourn	πενθέω	*pentheō*	1 Cor. 5:2
mystery	μυστήριον	*mystērion*	Luke 8:10
name	ὄνομα	*onoma*	Acts 19:13
nation	ἔθνος	*ethnos*	Luke 2:32
natural	ψυχικός	*psychikos*	1 Cor. 15:46
new	καινός	*kainos*	John 13:34
noble	εὐγενής	*eugenēs*	1 Cor. 1:26
obey	ὑπακούω	*hypakouō*	Rom. 6:17
of one accord	ὁμοθυμαδόν	*homothymadon*	Acts 12:20
offer a drink-offering	σπένδω	*spendō*	Phil. 2:17
offspring	σπέρμα	*sperma*	Rom. 1:3
older	πρεσβύτερος	*presbyteros*	Mark 14:53
once for all	ἐφάπαξ	*ephapax*	Heb. 10:10
one who is partial	προσωπολήπτης	*prosōpolēptēs*	Acts 10:34
openness	παρρησία	*parrēsia*	John 11:14
opinion	διαλογισμός	*dialogismos*	Luke 6:8
order	κόσμος	*kosmos*	1 John 5:19
originator	ἀρχηγός	*archēgos*	Acts 3:15
overseer	ἐπισκοπή	*episkopē*	Acts 1:20
overseer	ἐπίσκοπος	*episkopos*	Titus 1:7
overtake	καταλαμβάνω	*katalambanō*	Eph. 3:18
parable	παραβολή	*parabolē*	Matt. 13:3
partaker	κοινωνός	*koinōnos*	Luke 5:10
partiality	προσωποληψία	*prosōpolēpsia*	James 2:1
partner	κοινωνός	*koinōnos*	Luke 5:10
partner	μέτοχος	*metochos*	Heb. 3:1
pattern	ὑπογραμμός	*hypogrammos*	1 Pet. 2:21
pay	μισθός	*misthos*	Matt. 10:41
peace	εἰρήνη	*eirēnē*	Luke 2:14
perdition	ἀπώλεια	*apōleia*	Matt. 7:13
perfect	τέλειος	*teleios*	1 Cor. 14:20
perform	ἐργάζομαι	*ergazomai*	John 9:4
pertaining to a market	ἀγοραῖος	*agoraios*	Acts 17:5
physician	ἰατρός	*iatros*	Col. 4:14
pledge	ἀρραβών	*arrabōn*	2 Cor. 1:22
portent	σημεῖον	*sēmeion*	John 6:26
portico	στοά	*stoa*	John 5:2
pound	λίτρα	*litra*	John 19:39
power	δύναμις	*dynamis*	Acts 1:8
Praetorium	πραιτώριον	*praitōrion*	John 18:28
praise Yah	ἀλληλούϊα	*allēlouia*	Rev. 19:1
proclaim	κηρύσσω	*kēryssō*	Luke 3:3
promise	ἐξομολογέω	*exomologeō*	Luke 10:21
promise	ἐπαγγελία	*epangelia*	Acts 7:17
proof	μαρτύριον	*martyrion*	Matt. 8:4
prophecy	προφητεία	*prophēteia*	Rom. 12:6
propitiate	ἱλάσκομαι	*hilaskomai*	Luke 18:13
propitiation	ἱλασμός	*hilasmos*	1 John 4:10
proselyte	προσήλυτος	*prosēlytos*	Acts 6:5
proud	ὑπερήφανος	*hyperēphania*	Luke 1:51
provide	ἐπιχορηγέω	*epichorēgeō*	2 Pet. 1:5
psalm	ψαλμός	*psalmos*	Eph. 5:19

Meaning	Greek Word	Transliteration	Reference
purchase	ἀγοράζω	agorazō	Rev. 5:9
radiance	φωστήρ	phōstēr	Rev. 21:11
ransom	λύτρον	lytron	Mark 10:45
read	ἀναγινώσκω	anaginōskō	Acts 8:28
reality	ὑπόστασις	hypostasis	Heb. 3:14
receive	ἀπέχω	apechō	Luke 6:24
reconcile	καταλλάσσω	katallassō	Rom. 5:10
redemption	ἀπολύτρωσις	apolytrōsis	Rom. 3:24
regret	μεταμέλομαι	metamelomai	2 Cor. 7:8
religion	θρησκεία	thrēskeia	Acts 26:5
remarkable	παράδοξος	paradoxos	Luke 5:26
repayment	ἀνταπόδομα	antapodoma	Rom. 11:9
repent	μετανοέω	metanoeō	Acts 26:20
reply	ἀπολογία	apologia	1 Pet. 3:15
representation	χαρακτήρ	charaktēr	Heb. 1:3
rescue	ῥύομαι	rhyomai	1 Thess. 1:10
rest	ἀναπαύω	anapauō	Matt. 11:28
restore	καταρτίζω	katartizō	Heb. 11:3
resurrection	ἀνάστασις	anastasis	Acts 2:31
return	ἐπιστρέφω	epistrephō	Luke 22:32
reveal	ἐμφανίζω	emphanizō	John 14:21
reveal	φανερόω	phaneroō	Mark 4:22
revelation	ἀποκάλυψις	apokalypsis	Rev. 1:1
reward	μισθός	misthos	Matt. 10:41
righteousness	δικαιοσύνη	dikaiosynē	Rom. 1:17
rock	πέτρα	petra	Matt. 16:18
rod	ῥάβδος	rhabdos	Heb. 9:4
rotten	σαπρός	sapros	Matt. 12:33
rule	βραβεύω	brabeuō	Col. 3:15
Sabaoth	Σαβαώθ	Sabaōth	James 5:4
salt	ἅλας	halas	Luke 14:34
salvation	σωτηρία	sōtēria	Luke 1:69, 77
sanctification	ἁγιασμός	hagiasmos	1 Thess. 4:3
Sanhedrin	συνέδριον	synedrion	Acts 5:21
save	σῴζω	sōzō	Matt. 10:22
save now	ὡσαννά	hōsanna	Mark 11:9
seal	σφραγίζω	sphragizō	Rev. 7:3
secret	μυστήριον	mystērion	Luke 8:10
see	θεάομαι	theaomai	John 1:38
seed	σπέρμα	sperma	Rom. 1:3
seize	ἁρπάζω	harpazō	1 Thess. 4:17
select	ἐκλέγομαι	eklegomai	Eph. 1:4
self-control	ἐγκράτεια	enkrateia	Gal. 5:23
self-discipline	σωφρονισμός	sōphronismos	2 Tim. 1:7
self-indulgence	ἀκρασία	akrasia	1 Cor. 7:5
send	ἀποστέλλω	apostellō	John 20:21
servant	διάκονος	diakonos	Mark 9:35
serve	δουλεύω	douleuō	Rom. 14:18
service	λειτουργία	leitourgia	Phil. 2:30
set free	ἐλευθερόω	eleutheroō	Rom. 8:2
share in	κοινωνέω	koinōneō	Phil. 4:15
share in	μέτοχος	metochos	Heb. 3:1
shrine	ναός	naos	1 Cor. 3:16
sign	σημεῖον	sēmeion	John 6:26
simple	ἁπλοῦς	haplous	Luke 11:34
sin	ἁμαρτία	hamartia	John 9:41

Meaning	Greek Word	Transliteration	Reference
sing praise	ψάλλω	psallō	Eph. 5:19
single	ἁπλοῦς	haplous	Luke 11:34
sister	ἀδελφή	adelphē	Mark 10:29
slander	καταλαλέω	katalaleō	James 4:11
sleep	καθεύδω	katheudō	1 Thess. 5:10
snatch	ἁρπάζω	harpazō	1 Thess. 4:17
sneer	ἐκμυκτηρίζω	ekmyktērizō	Luke 23:35
sorcery	φαρμακεία	pharmakeia	Rev. 9:21
soul	ψυχή	psychē	Luke 21:19
be sound	ὑγιαίνω	hygiainō	1 Tim. 1:10
soundness	σωφρονισμός	sōphronismos	2 Tim. 1:7
speak	λαλέω	laleō	1 Cor. 14:2
speak symbolically	ἀλληγορέω	allēgoreō	Gal. 4:24
spectacle	θέατρον	theatron	1 Cor. 4:9
spirit	πνεῦμα	pneuma	John 3:5
spiritual	πνευματικός	pneumatikos	1 Cor. 2:13
splendor	τρυφή	tryphē	Luke 7:25
spot	σπίλος	spilos	2 Pet. 2:13
stade	στάδιον	stadion	Rev. 14:20
stadium	στάδιον	stadion	Rev. 14:20
staff	ῥάβδος	rhabdos	Heb. 9:4
stain	σπίλος	spilos	2 Pet. 2:13
stay awake	ἀγρυπνέω	agrypneō	Mark 13:33
strange	παράδοξος	paradoxos	Luke 5:26
strong drink	σίκερα	sikera	Luke 1:15
struggle	ἀγωνίζομαι	agōnizomai	2 Tim. 4:7
support	ἐπιχορηγέω	epichorēgeō	2 Pet. 1:5
sword	ῥομφαία	rhomphaia	Rev. 19:15
table	τράπεζα	trapeza	Luke 19:23
take up	αἴρω	airō	John 15:2
talent	τάλαντον	talanton	Matt. 25:15
talk nonsense	φλυαρέω	phlyareō	3 John 10
taste	γεύομαι	geuomai	Heb. 6:5
teach	μαθητεύω	mathēteuō	Matt. 27:57
teach correctly	ὀρθοτομέω	orthotomeō	2 Tim. 2:15
temple	ναός	naos	1 Cor. 3:16
temple (compound)	ἱερόν	hieron	Luke 24:53
tempt	πειράζω	peirazō	John 6:6
tent	σκῆνος	skēnos	2 Cor. 5:1
tentmaker	σκηνοποιός	skēnopoios	Acts 18:3
test	πειράζω	peirazō	John 6:6
testimony	μαρτύριον	martyrion	Matt. 8:4
theater	θέατρον	theatron	1 Cor. 4:9
thorn	σκόλοψ	skolops	2 Cor. 12:7
thought	διαλογισμός	dialogismos	Luke 6:8
time	ὥρα	hōra	Luke 22:53
torturer	βασανιστής	basanistēs	Matt. 18:34
touch	ψηλαφάω	psēlaphaō	Acts 17:27
train	γυμνάζω	gymnazō	1 Tim. 4:7
trance	ἔκστασις	ekstasis	Acts 10:10
transgression	παράβασις	parabasis	Rom. 2:23
treat spitefully	ὑβρίζω	hybrizō	Matt. 22:6
trespass	παράπτωμα	paraptōma	Eph. 2:5
tribulation	θλίψις	thlipsis	John 16:33
trouble	ταράσσω	tarassō	Luke 24:38
trust	πιστεύω	pisteuō	Acts 10:43
trust	πίστις	pistis	Col. 1:4

Meaning	Greek Word	Transliteration	Reference
turn	ἐπιστρέφω	*epistrephō*	Luke 22:32
turning	τροπή	*tropē*	James 1:17
unbelieving	ἄπιστος	*apistos*	Mark 9:19
be uncertain	ἀπορέω	*aporeō*	Luke 24:4
understanding	σύνεσις	*synesis*	Mark 12:33
underworld	ἄβυσσος	*abyssos*	Rev. 9:1
undeservedly	δωρεάν	*dōrean*	2 Cor. 11:7
uneducated	ἀγράμματος	*agrammatos*	Acts 4:13
ungodliness	ἀσέβεια	*asebeia*	Rom. 11:26
unspiritual	ψυχικός	*psychikos*	1 Cor. 15:46
useless	μάταιος	*mataios*	Acts 14:15
value	τιμή	*timē*	1 Tim. 5:17
vessel	σκεῦος	*skeuos*	Heb. 9:21
virgin	παρθένος	*parthenos*	Matt. 1:23
virtue	ἀρετή	*aretē*	1 Pet. 2:9
visitation	ἐπισκοπή	*episkopē*	Acts 1:20
wash	λούω	*louō*	John 13:10
be watchful	γρηγορέω	*grēgoreō*	Matt. 24:42
wealth	μαμωνᾶς	*mamōnas*	Luke 16:9
weep	κλαίω	*klaiō*	Luke 19:41
be well pleased	εὐδοκέω	*eudokeō*	Luke 12:32
whip	μαστιγόω	*mastigoō*	Matt. 20:19
wild beast	θηρίον	*thērion*	Rev. 6:8
wind	πνεῦμα	*pneuma*	John 3:5
wipe away	ἐξαλείφω	*exaleiphō*	Rev. 3:5
wisdom	σοφία	*sophia*	1 Cor. 12:8
wise man	μάγος	*magos*	Acts 13:8
with a roar	ῥοιζηδόν	*rhoizēdon*	2 Pet. 3:10
wonder	θαῦμα	*thauma*	Rev. 17:6
wonder	τέρας	*teras*	Acts 2:19
word	λόγος	*logos*	John 1:1
be at work	ἐνεργέω	*energeō*	2 Cor. 4:12
work	ἐργάζομαι	*ergazomai*	John 9:4
world	κόσμος	*kosmos*	1 John 5:19
world-ruler	κοσμοκράτωρ	*kosmokratōr*	Eph. 6:12
worldly	κοσμικός	*kosmikos*	Titus 2:12
worm	σκώληξ	*skōlēx*	Mark 9:44
worship	προσκυνέω	*proskyneō*	Matt. 9:18
worthless	μάταιος	*mataios*	Acts 14:15
wrath	θυμός	*thymos*	Rev. 16:1
you have forsaken me	σαβαχθανί	*sabachthani*	Mark 15:34
zeal	ζῆλος	*zēlos*	Rom. 10:2